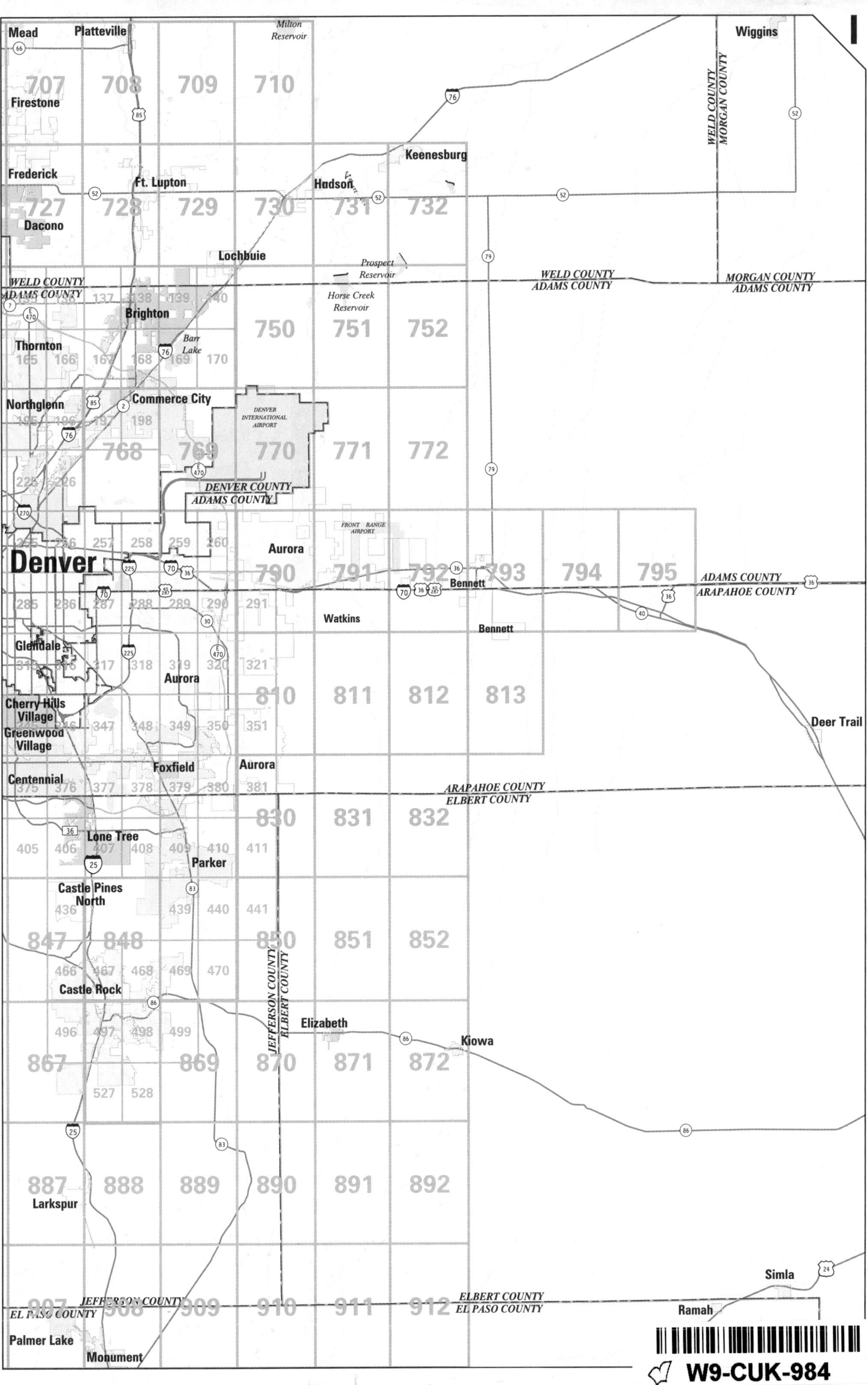
Mead
Platteville
Milton Reservoir
Wiggins
707
708
709
710
Firestone
WELD COUNTY
MORGAN COUNTY
Keenesburg
Frederick
Ft. Lupton
Hudson
727
728
729
730
731
732
Dacono
Lochbuie
Prospect Reservoir
WELD COUNTY
ADAMS COUNTY
MORGAN COUNTY
ADAMS COUNTY
Horse Creek Reservoir
Brighton
Thornton
Barr Lake
750
751
752
Northglenn
Commerce City
DENVER INTERNATIONAL AIRPORT
768
769
770
771
772
DENVER COUNTY
ADAMS COUNTY
FRONT RANGE AIRPORT
Aurora
Denver
790
791
792
793
794
795
Bennett
ADAMS COUNTY
ARAPAHOE COUNTY
Watkins
Glendale
Aurora
810
811
812
813
Cherry Hills Village
Greenwood Village
Deer Trail
Foxfield
Aurora
Centennial
ARAPAHOE COUNTY
ELBERT COUNTY
830
831
832
Lone Tree
Parker
Castle Pines North
847
848
850
851
852
Castle Rock
JEFFERSON COUNTY
ELBERT COUNTY
Elizabeth
Kiowa
867
869
870
871
872
887
888
889
890
891
892
Larkspur
Simla
907
908
909
910
911
912
JEFFERSON COUNTY
EL PASO COUNTY
ELBERT COUNTY
EL PASO COUNTY
Ramah
Palmer Lake
Monument

MOST ACCURATE. MOST CURRENT. MOST TRUSTED.

Table of Contents:

For street information

Call MAPSCO CUSTOMER CONNECTION
Toll Free at 866-277-7264
8 am - 5 pm Monday - Friday

Tell us what you think.

Go to www.mapsco.com/comments and fill out our online survey.
Your comments help us improve maps year after year.

For advertising information, please contact Mapsco at (972) 450-9322.

Although the information in this Mapsco product is based on the most up-to-date information and has been checked for accuracy, Mapsco does not guarantee or warrant the accuracy of any information in this product and shall not be liable in any respect for any errors or omissions.
If you find any errors or omissions, please promptly bring them to our attention so that corrections may be made in future editions.

Published by MAPSCO, Inc. • 4181 CENTURION WAY • ADDISON, TX 75001 • (972) 450-9300

DENVER REGIONAL MAP-30009

PRINTED IN CANADA.

How to use the new MAPSCO index

Denver Regional

Street Atlas

ENGLISH:

If You Know The General Area:

The Key Maps located in the front of your atlas on the inside front cover and page I will help you find the map of the area you are looking for. Use major streets as a guide.

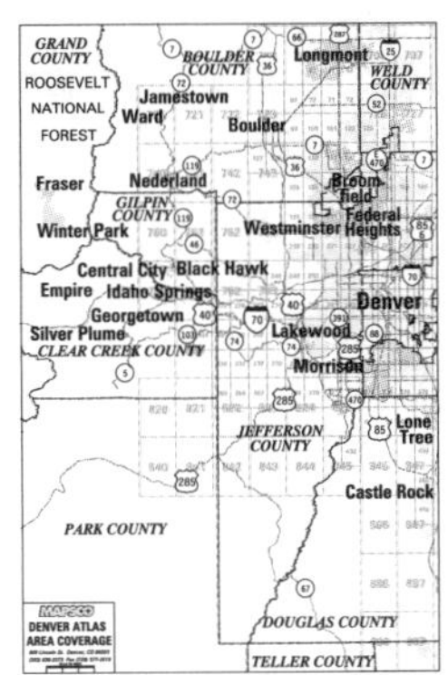

If You Know The Street Name:

To locate a specific street, use the Street Index, which follows the map section (indicated by the black alpha tabs). A sample of the Street Index is shown at the right. The number 284 of the first listing (Lincoln St. in Denver) indicates the map number. The letter "L" indicates a grid on the map. The zip code for the listing is 80203. The numbers 1-1999 indicate the range of blocks of this portion of Lincoln St. To locate Lincoln St., turn to Map 284. A quick glance at the grid lettered L will show you where the name of Lincoln St. appears on the map. To locate a specific street address, use the red hundred block numbers that appear on the map and map borders. To locate 800 Lincoln St., for example, you first would find the name of the street in 284L and then use the hundred block numbers to locate the 800 block of Lincoln St. in 284Q.

Please note: A street or cul-de-sac listed in the index may not appear on the map due to space limitations. Using the page number and grid will help you find the general area where the street is located.

Index Sample

STREET NAME	CITY or COUNTY	MAP GRID	ZIP CODE	BLOCK RANGE O/E
LINCOLN ST	Denver	284L	80203	1-1999 (Odd/Even)
LINCOLN ST	Denver	254Q	80216	4200-5199
LINCOLN ST	Elizabeth	871F	80107	100-299

ESPAÑOL:

Si Conoces La Área General:

Los primeros mapas adentro de esta atlas en página I te ayuda hallar el mapa de la área que buscas, use las mayores calles para guiarte. Algunos números de páginas están omitados. Es para el expansion futuro de la área que vamos a recorrer con tiempo.

Si Conoces El Nombre de la Calle:

Para localizar una calle particular, use el índice de calles que seguín los mapas (indicada con lenguetas negro).Un ejemplo de los indices esta al derecho. El numero 284 de la primer linea (la calle Lincoln) indica el numero de la mapa. La letra "L" indica una cuadricula en la mapa. El codigo de esta lista es 80203. Los numeros 1-1999 indican la gama de cuadras de esta porcion de la calle Lincoln. Para localizar la calle Lincoln en la mapa, regresa al la mapa en pagina 284. Una mirada a la cuadricula L te ensena onde esta la calle Lincoln. Para localizar un espicifico direcion, usen los numeros rojos en la margen de los mapas. Para localizar la direction 800 Lincoln, tienes que hallar la calle en 284L, entonces usando lo numeros en la margen vas a hallar que 800 Lincoln esta en 284Q de la cuadricula.

Por favor nota: Una calle en la lista de índices que no está en el mapa, es por que no tenian lugar. Usando el numero de la página y la reja te ayuda hallar la área general de la calle que buscas.

Illustration of our Easy Index System

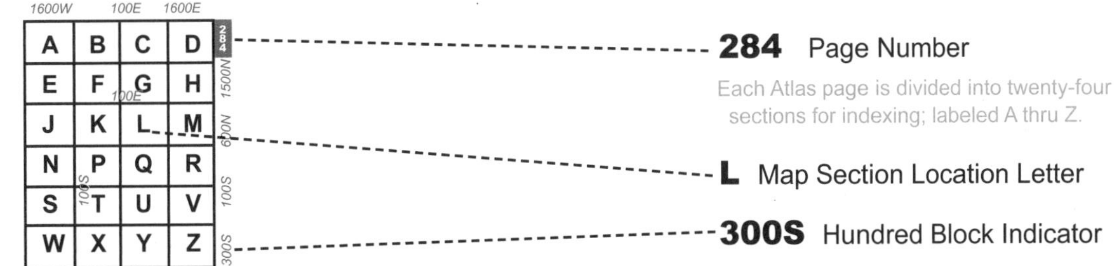

Explanation of Map Symbols

Explicación de Simbología Del Mapa

- The Atlas uses two different scales of maps: large scale in densely populated areas and small scale in rural areas.
- Maps are color-coded for fast location of schools, parks, shopping centers and other points of interest.
- The Index Section contains much more than just street names. You will find a community index listing addresses and/or phone numbers of schools, fire and police departments, city halls, and local transportation. There is also a listing of local points of interest, including parks, golf courses, libraries, shopping centers and malls.
- Numbered streets, county roads, state, U.S. and interstate highways are listed separately at the end of the index.

Large Scale Map Legend/*Escala Grande*

Interstate Highway
Carretera Interestatal
Main Street or Road
Calle Principal
Secondary Street or Road
Calle Secundaria
One-way Street
Calle de Unica Dirección
Railroads
Ferrocarril
25 Interstate Highway Symbol
Símbolo de Carretera Interestatal
87 US Highway Symbol
Símbolo de Carretera E.E.U.U.
61 State Highway Symbol
Símbolo de Carretera Estatal
39 County Road Symbol
Símbolo de Camino de Condado
100 Freeway Exit Number
Número de Salida de Autopista
2401 W Block Range Number
Alcance de la Cuadra
T 8 N Range & Township Number
Municipo Alcance
31 Section Number
Número de Sección
+ Section Corner
Esquina de Sección
0203 Zip Code & Boundary
Codigo Postal Límite
County Boundary
Límite de el Condado
Municipal Boundary
Límite de Municipal
National Park, State Park
Parque Nacional, Parque Estatal
Municipal Park
Parque Municipal
Airport
Aeropuerto
College & Gov't. Reservations
Colegios y Reservas del Gobierno
Military
Militaria
Cemetery
Cementerios
Golf Course
Campo de Golf
Mall or Shopping Center
Multicentro Comercial
Hospital
Hospital
★ City Hall
Ayuntamiento
◇ Fire Station
Cuartel de Bomberos
◆ Police Station
Comisaria
■ Point of Interest
Punto de Interés
■ Post Office or Gov't. Bldg.
Oficina de Correos
● Elementary School
Escuela Primaria
△ Middle & Junior High School
Ensenanza Media
▲ Senior High School
Ensenanza Secundaria
● Libraries
Bibliotecas
RTD Park-n-Rides
RTD Park-n-Ride
Light Rail
Ferrocarril de Ligera

Small Scale Map Legend/*Escala Pequeña*

Interstate Highway
Carretera Interestatal
Main Street or Road
Calle Principal
Secondary Street or Road
Calle Secundaria
One-way Street
Calle de Unica Dirección
Railroads
Ferrocarril
25 Interstate Highway Symbol
Símbolo de Carretera Interestatal
87 US Highway Symbol
Símbolo de Carretera E.E.U.U.
61 State Highway Symbol
Símbolo de Carretera Estatal
39 County Road Symbol
Símbolo de Camino de Condado
125 Freeway Exit Number
Número de Salida de Autopista
2401 W Block Range Number
Alcance de la Cuadra
T 8 N Range & Township Number
Municipo Alcance
31 Section Number
Número de Sección
+ Section Corner
Esquina de Sección
0203 Zip Code & Boundary
Codigo Postal Límite
County Boundary
Límite de el Condado
Municipal Boundary
Límite de Municipal
National Park, State Park
Parque Nacional, Parque Estatal
Municipal Park
Parque Municipal
Airport
Aeropuerto
College & Gov't. Reservations
Colegios y Reservas del Gobierno
Military
Militaria
Cemetery
Cementerios
Golf Course
Campo de Golf
Mall or Shopping Center
Multicentro Comercial
Hospital
Hospital
★ City Hall
Ayuntamiento
■ Government Building
Edificio de Gobierno
● Elementary School (symbol only)
Escuela Primaria (Solamente el Símbolo)
△ Middle & Junior High School (symbol only)
Ensenanza Media (Solamente el Símbolo)
▲ Senior High School
Ensenanza Secundaria
● Libraries (symbol only)
Bibliotecas (Solamente el Símbolo)

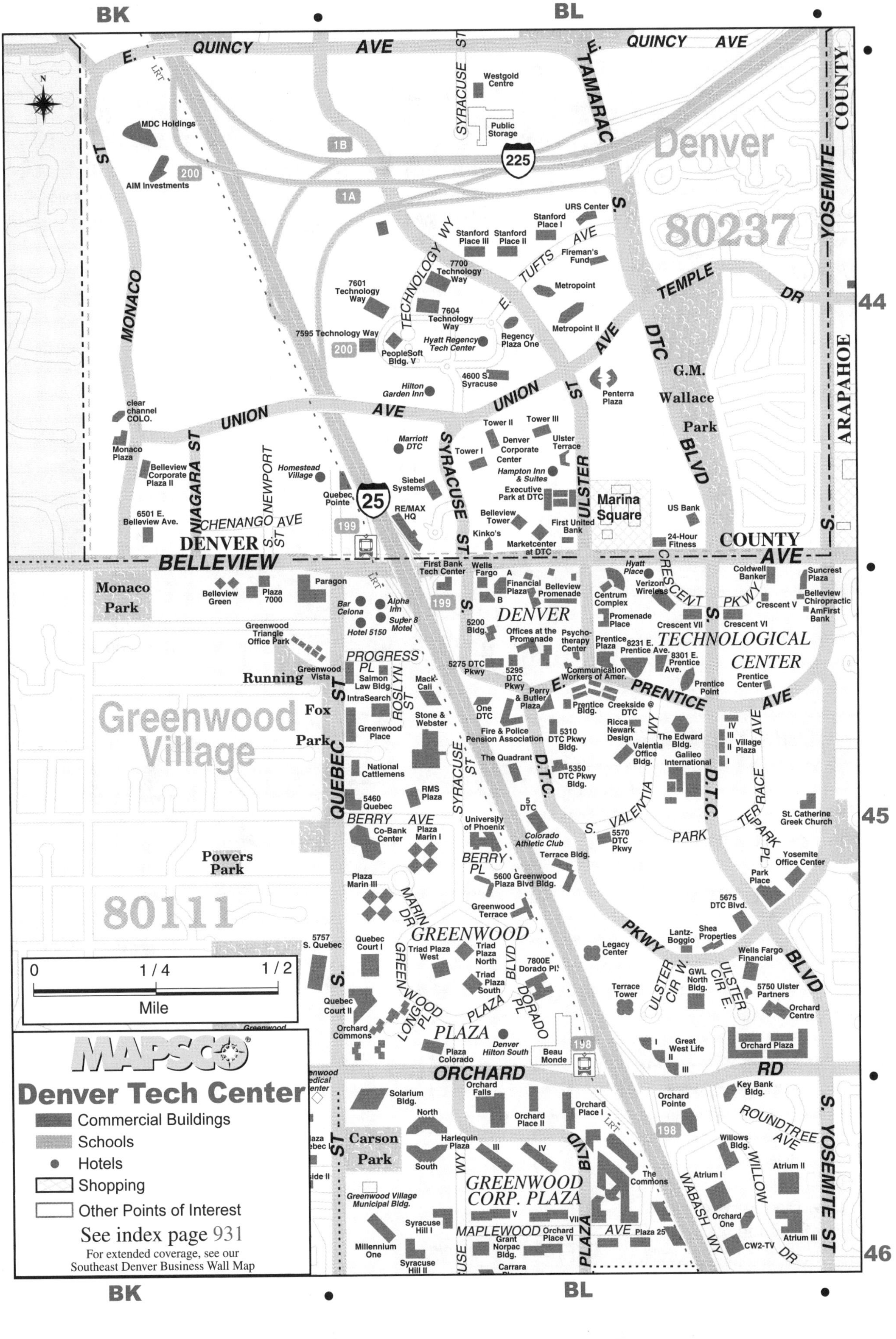

BK
BL
E. QUINCY AVE
QUINCY AVE
S. SYRACUSE ST
Westgold Centre
Public Storage
E. TAMARAC
Denver
COUNTY
MDC Holdings
1B
225
200
AIM Investments
1A
MONACO ST
80237
S. YOSEMITE
URS Center
Stanford Place I
Stanford Place III
Stanford Place II
TECHNOLOGY WY
E. TUFTS AVE
Fireman's Fund
7700 Technology Way
7601 Technology Way
Metropoint
TEMPLE DR
44
7604 Technology Way
Regency Plaza One
Metropoint II
7595 Technology Way
Hyatt Regency Tech Center
PeopleSoft Bldg. V
200
ARAPAHOE
DTC BLVD
4600 S. Syracuse
G.M. Wallace Park
Hilton Garden Inn
Penterra Plaza
clear channel COLO.
UNION AVE
UNION AVE
S. ULSTER ST
Tower II
Tower III
Marriott DTC
Monaco Plaza
Denver Corporate Center
Ulster Terrace
Tower I
Belleview Corporate Plaza II
NIAGARA ST
NEWPORT ST
Homestead Village
Hampton Inn & Suites
Siebel Systems
Executive Park at DTC
Quebec Pointe
25
Marina Square
6501 E. Belleview Ave.
CHENANGO AVE
RE/MAX HQ
Belleview Tower
US Bank
First United Bank
199
Kinko's
24-Hour Fitness
DENVER
COUNTY
Marketcenter at DTC
S.
BELLEVIEW
AVE
First Bank Tech Center
Wells Fargo
Hyatt Place
Coldwell Banker
Suncrest Plaza
Monaco Park
Belleview Green
Plaza 7000
Paragon
A Financial Plaza B
Belleview Promenade
Verizon Wireless
CRESCENT PKWY
Belleview Chiropractic
LRT
Bar Celona
Alpha Inn
199
Centrum Complex
Crescent V
AmFirst Bank
DENVER
Super 8 Motel
5200 Bldg.
Promenade Place
Crescent VII
Crescent VI
Greenwood Triangle Office Park
Hotel 5150
Offices at the Promenade
Psycho-therapy Center
Prentice Plaza
8231 E. Prentice Ave.
TECHNOLOGICAL CENTER
PROGRESS PL
8301 E. Prentice Ave.
Running
Greenwood Vista
5275 DTC Pkwy
5295 DTC Pkwy
Communication Workers of Amer.
Salmon Law Bldg.
Mack-Cali
E. PRENTICE AVE
Prentice Point
Prentice Center
ROSLYN ST
IntraSearch
Perry & Butler Plaza
Greenwood Village
Fox
Stone & Webster
One DTC
Prentice Bldg.
Creekside @ DTC
Park
Greenwood Place
Fire & Police Pension Association
5310 DTC Pkwy Bldg.
Ricca Newark Design
The Edward Bldg.
IV III II I
Village Plaza
TERRACE AVE
QUEBEC ST
Valentia Office Bldg.
Galileo International
SYRACUSE ST
The Quadrant
National Cattlemens
5350 DTC Pkwy Bldg.
D.T.C.
D.T.C.
RMS Plaza
5460 Quebec
5 DTC
S. VALENTIA WY
St. Catherine Greek Church
45
BERRY AVE
University of Phoenix
Co-Bank Center
Plaza Marin I
PARK
TERRACE PARK PL
5570 DTC Pkwy
Colorado Athletic Club
Powers Park
BERRY PL
Terrace Bldg.
Yosemite Office Center
5600 Greenwood Plaza Blvd Bldg.
Park Place
Plaza Marin III
MARIN DR
Greenwood Terrace
5675 DTC Blvd.
80111
GREENWOOD
PKWY
Shea Properties
5757 S. Quebec
Quebec Court I
Lantz-Boggio
Legacy Center
Triad Plaza West
Triad Plaza North
Wells Fargo Financial
BLVD
7800E Dorado Pl.
GWL North Bldg.
S.
Triad Plaza South
ULSTER CIR W.
ULSTER CIR E.
Terrace Tower
5750 Ulster Partners
0
1/4
1/2
Mile
GREENWOOD PLAZA BLVD
DORADO PL
Quebec Court II
LONGWOOD PL
Orchard Centre
Orchard Commons
PLAZA
Denver Hilton South
198
Great West Life
I II III
Orchard Plaza
MAPSCO
Plaza Colorado
Beau Monde
Greenwood Medical Center
ORCHARD
RD
Orchard Falls
Key Bank Bldg.
Solarium Bldg.
Orchard Place I
Orchard Pointe
North
Orchard Place II
S. YOSEMITE ST
ROUNDTREE AVE
Carson Park
Harlequin Plaza
III
IV
198
Willows Bldg.
South
Plaza Quebec I
WILLOW WY
Atrium II
Atrium I
Plaza Quebec II
The Commons
GREENWOOD CORP. PLAZA
WABASH WY
Greenwood Village Municipal Bldg.
V
VII
Syracuse Hill I
Orchard One
MAPLEWOOD
Orchard Place VI
AVE
Plaza 25
Atrium III
Grant Norpac Bldg.
Millennium One
CW2-TV
DR
Syracuse Hill II
Carrara Place
46

Denver Tech Center

Commercial Buildings
Schools
Hotels
Shopping
Other Points of Interest

See index page 931

For extended coverage, see our Southeast Denver Business Wall Map

BK
BL

Inverness (See Map 377)

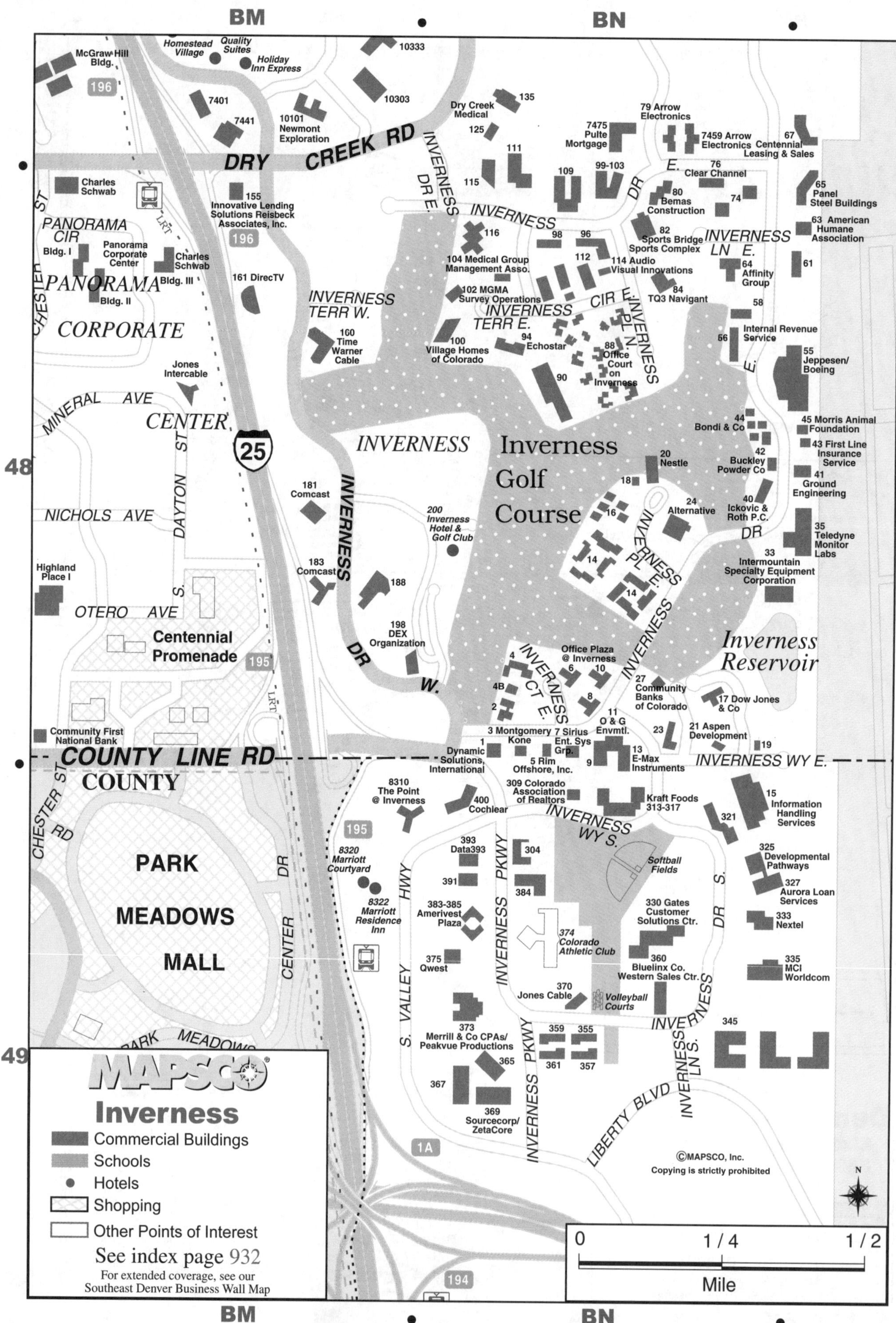

Interchange: I-70/I-225 (See Map 258)

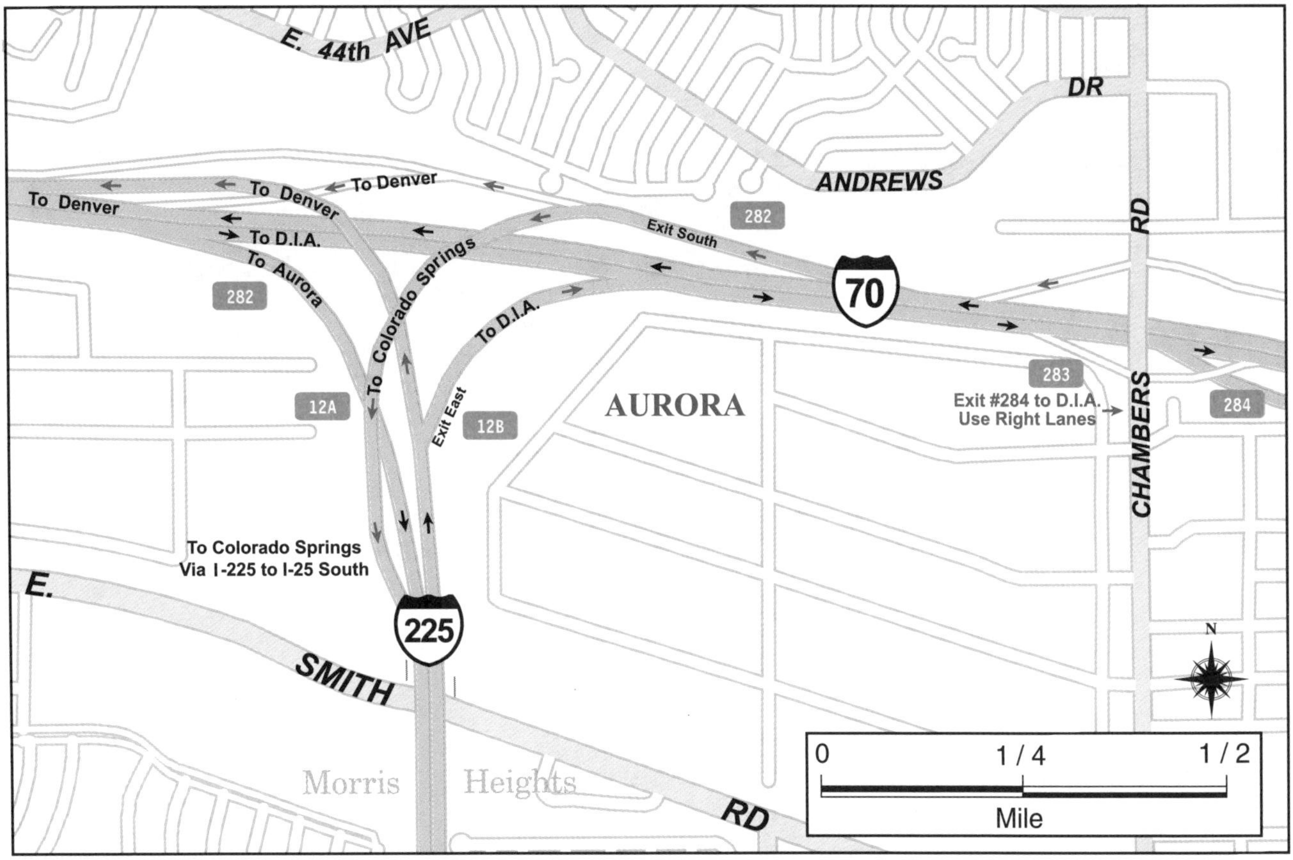

E. 44th AVE
ANDREWS DR
To Denver
To Denver
To Denver
To D.I.A.
To Aurora
To Colorado Springs
Exit South
282
282
70
RD
To D.I.A.
12A
12B
Exit East
AURORA
283
Exit #284 to D.I.A.
Use Right Lanes
284
CHAMBERS
To Colorado Springs
Via I-225 to I-25 South
225
E. SMITH RD
Morris Heights
N
0 1/4 1/2
Mile

Interchange: I-70/Peña Blvd. (See Map 258)

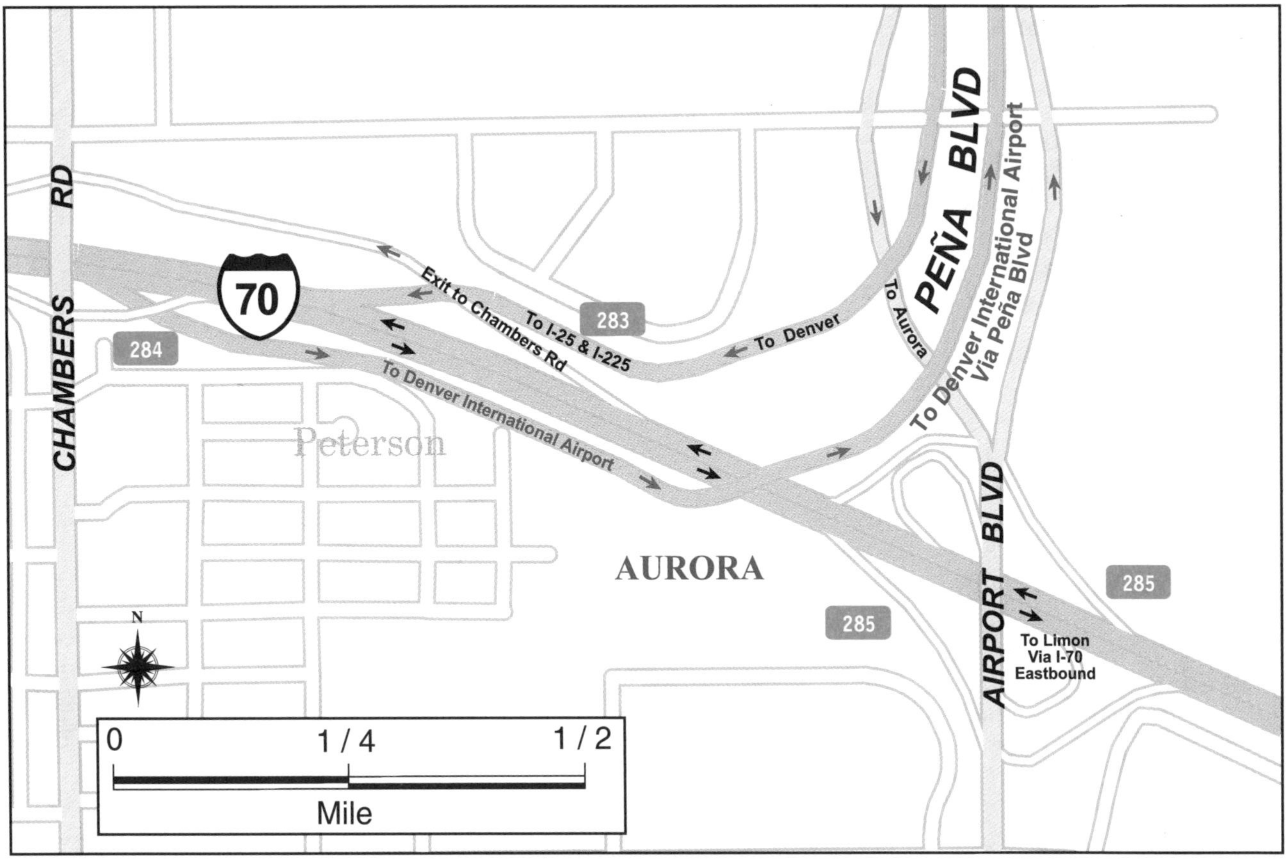

CHAMBERS RD
70
284
Exit to Chambers Rd
To I-25 & I-225
283
To Denver
To Aurora
PEÑA BLVD
To Denver International Airport
Via Peña Blvd
To Denver International Airport
Peterson
AURORA
285
285
AIRPORT BLVD
To Limon
Via I-70
Eastbound
N
0 1/4 1/2
Mile

Interchange: US36/I-25/I-76 (See Map 224)

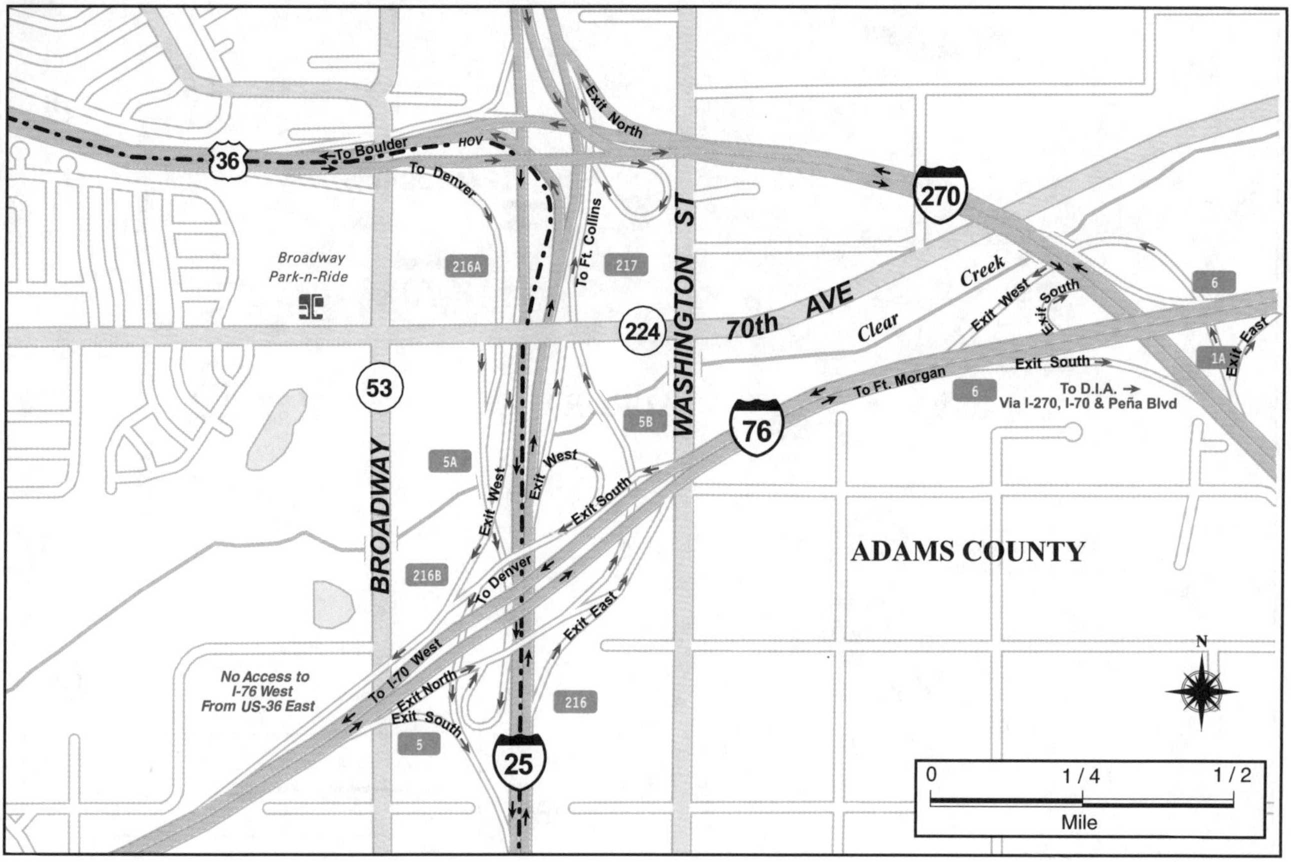

To Boulder
HOV
To Denver
Exit North
To Ft. Collins
36
270
Broadway Park-n-Ride
216A
217
70th AVE
224
WASHINGTON ST
Clear Creek
Exit West
Exit South
6
1A
Exit East
Exit South
To Ft. Morgan
To D.I.A. Via I-270, I-70 & Peña Blvd
53
BROADWAY
5B
76
5A
Exit West
Exit West
Exit South
ADAMS COUNTY
216B
To Denver
Exit East
No Access to I-76 West From US-36 East
To I-70 West
Exit North
Exit South
216
5
25
0 1/4 1/2 Mile

Interchange: I-25/I-70 (See Map 254)

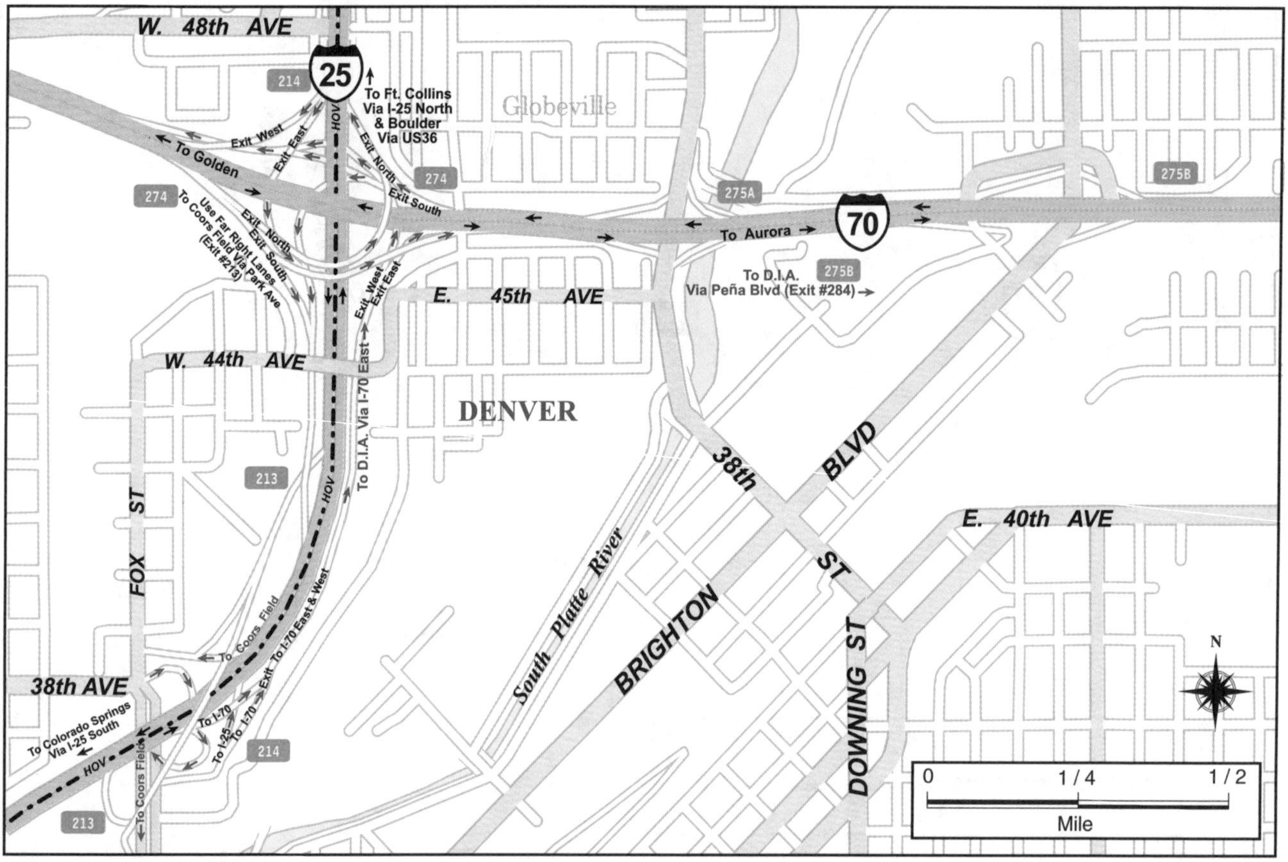

W. 48th AVE
214
25
To Ft. Collins Via I-25 North & Boulder Via US36
Globeville
Exit West
Exit East
To Golden
HOV
Exit North
274
Exit South
274
Use Far Right Lanes To Coors Field Via Park Ave (Exit #213)
Exit North
Exit South
275A
To Aurora
70
275B
To D.I.A. Via Peña Blvd (Exit #284)
275B
Exit West
Exit East
E. 45th AVE
W. 44th AVE
To D.I.A. Via I-70 East
DENVER
213
38th
BLVD
FOX ST
E. 40th AVE
South Platte River
ST
BRIGHTON
To Coors Field
Exit To I-70 East & West
38th AVE
To I-70
To I-25
To I-70
To Colorado Springs Via I-25 South
HOV
To Coors Field
214
DOWNING ST
213
0 1/4 1/2 Mile

Interchange: I-25/I-225 (See Map 346)

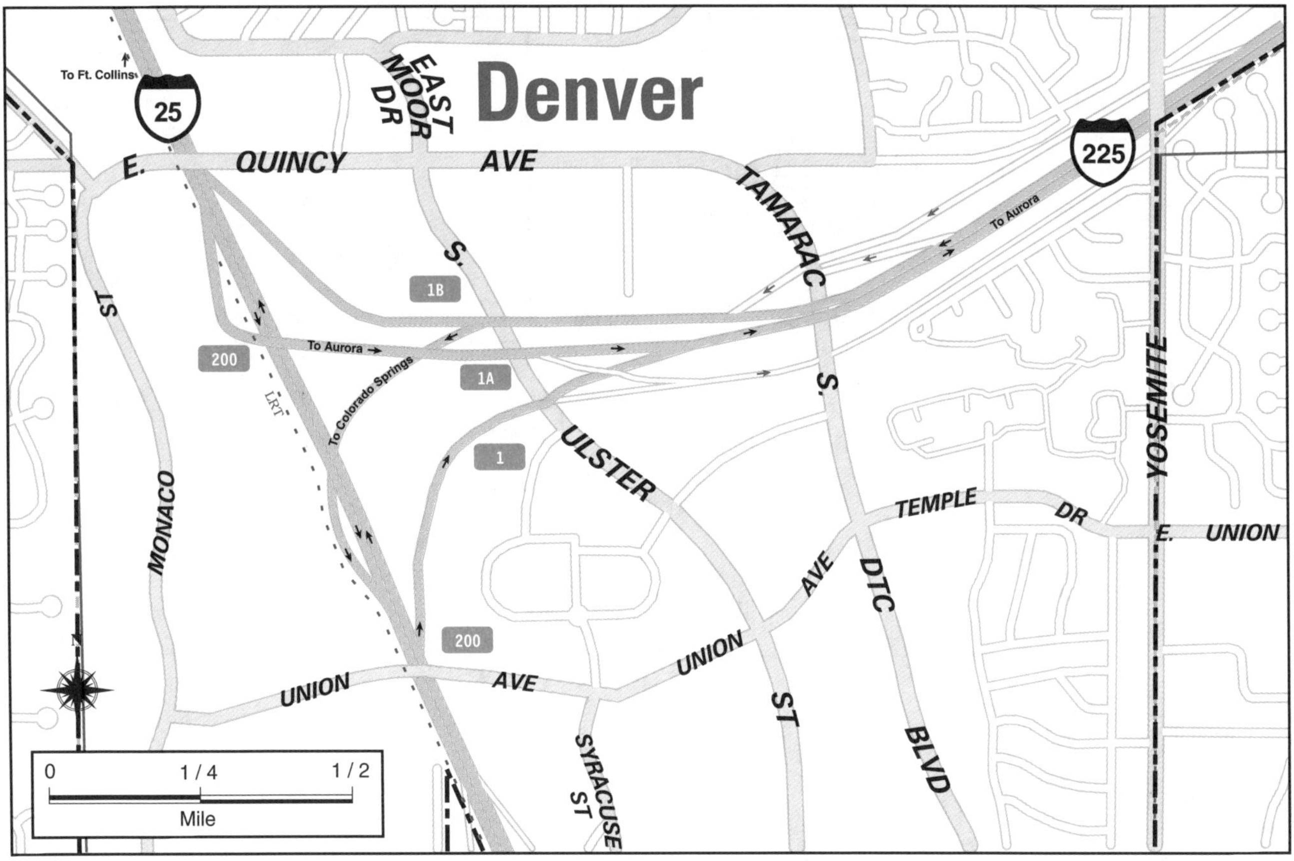

Interchange: I-70/I-76 (See Map 252)

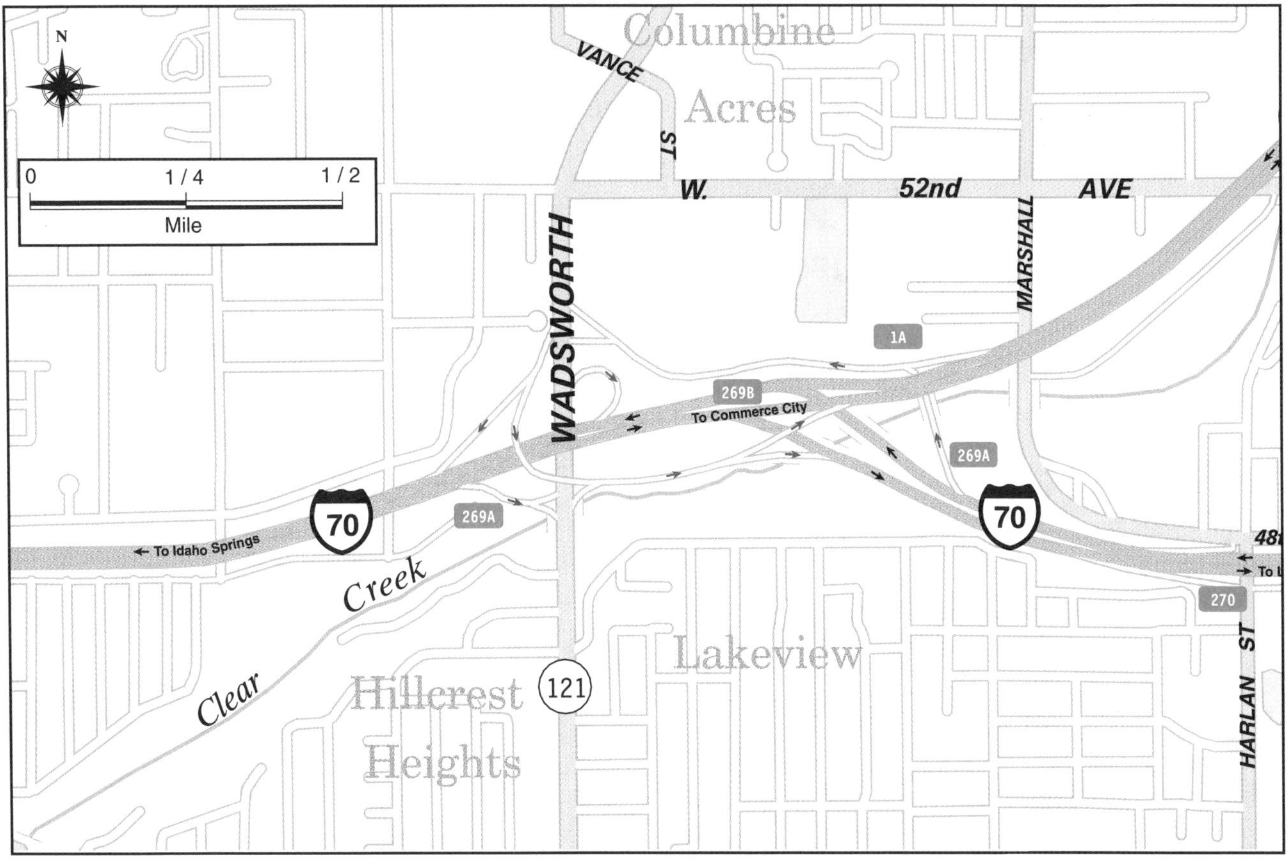

MLS Area Map

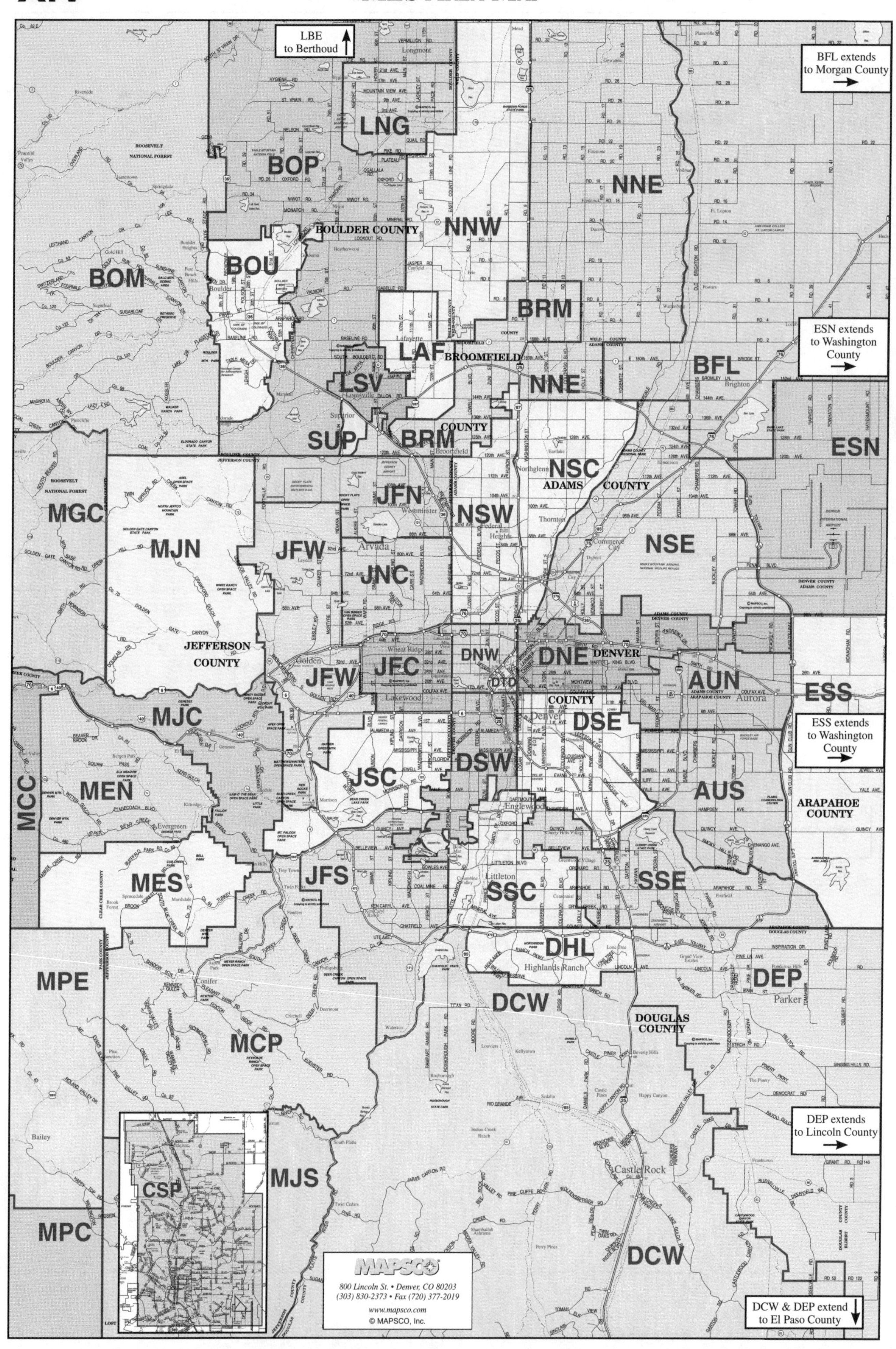

LBE to Berthoud
BFL extends to Morgan County
ESN extends to Washington County
ESS extends to Washington County
DEP extends to Lincoln County
DCW & DEP extend to El Paso County
LNG
BOP
NNE
NNW
BOU
BOM
BRM
LAF
LSV
SUP
BFL
ESN
NSC
MGC
MJN
JFN
NSW
JFW
JNC
NSE
JFC
DNW
DNE
DTD
AUN
ESS
MJC
DSE
MCC
MEN
JSC
DSW
AUS
MES
JFS
SSC
SSE
DHL
MPE
DEP
DCW
MCP
CSP
MJS
MPC
BOULDER COUNTY
BROOMFIELD COUNTY
ADAMS COUNTY
JEFFERSON COUNTY
DENVER COUNTY
ARAPAHOE COUNTY
DOUGLAS COUNTY
ROOSEVELT NATIONAL FOREST
Longmont
Boulder
Lafayette
Louisville
Superior
Broomfield
Northglenn
Thornton
Westminster
Arvada
Commerce City
Wheat Ridge
Golden
Lakewood
Denver
Aurora
Englewood
Littleton
Highlands Ranch
Parker
Castle Rock
Evergreen
Conifer
Brighton
MAPSCO
800 Lincoln St. • Denver, CO 80203
(303) 830-2373 • Fax (720) 377-2019
www.mapsco.com
© MAPSCO, Inc.

DENVER INTERNATIONAL AIRPORT (SEE MAP 770)

Important Numbers

- **DIA Information**.................... 303-342-2000 or 1-800-AIR2DEN
- **DIA Paging**..303-342-2300
- **DIA Parking Info**...................... 303-DIA-PARK (303-342-7275)
- **DIA Ground Transportation Shuttle Service** 303-342-4059
- **RTD Information**...................... 303-299-6000 or 800-366-7433
- **RTD TDD**...303-299-6089
- **RTD Web Site** .... www.rtd-denver.com

For emergency car starts, tire inflations, lock outs, lost vehicles and stays more than 30 days, call 303-342-4645.

For current Road Conditions call 303-639-1111.

www.flydenver.com

- **AGTS Trains - AGTS Level**
  Trains to and from concourses
- **Auto Passenger Drop Off - Level 6**
- **Auto Passenger Pick Up- Level 4**
- **Baggage Claim - Level 5**
- **Commercial Drop Off - Level 5**
  Vans, Limos, Cabs
- **Commercial Pick Up - Level 5**
  Vans, Limos, Cabs
- **RTD Bus - Level 6**
- **Public Parking - Levels 1-5**
- **Ticketing & Check In - Level 6**
  Departures

West Terminal
Ticketing & Baggage

Air Canada
American Trans Air (ATA)
British Airways
Lufthansa
Mexicana
Northwest
Ted
United Express
United

East Terminal
Ticketing & Baggage

AirTran Airways
Alaska Airlines
America West
American Airlines
Big Sky
Charter Airlines
Continental
Delta
Frontier/
Frontier Jet Express
Great Lakes
Horizon
jetBlue
Midwest Express
Southwest Airlines
US Airways

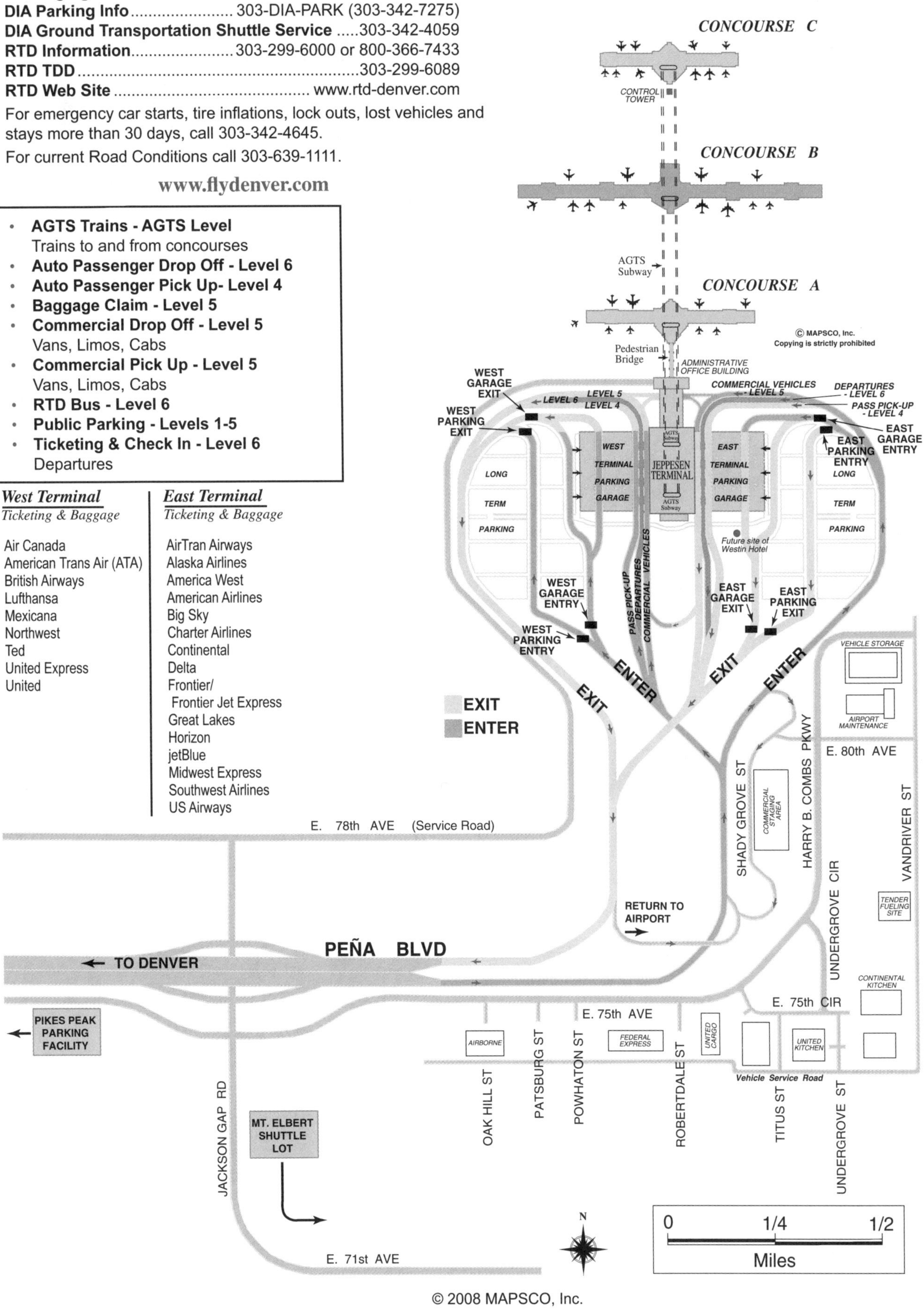

CONCOURSE C
CONTROL TOWER
CONCOURSE B
AGTS Subway
CONCOURSE A
Pedestrian Bridge
ADMINISTRATIVE OFFICE BUILDING

WEST GARAGE EXIT
WEST PARKING EXIT
LEVEL 6
LEVEL 5
LEVEL 4
COMMERCIAL VEHICLES - LEVEL 5
DEPARTURES - LEVEL 6
PASS PICK-UP - LEVEL 4
EAST GARAGE ENTRY
EAST PARKING ENTRY
LONG TERM PARKING
WEST TERMINAL PARKING GARAGE
JEPPESEN TERMINAL
AGTS Subway
EAST TERMINAL PARKING GARAGE
LONG TERM PARKING
Future site of Westin Hotel
WEST GARAGE ENTRY
WEST PARKING ENTRY
PASS PICK-UP DEPARTURES COMMERCIAL VEHICLES
EAST GARAGE EXIT
EAST PARKING EXIT
ENTER
EXIT
EXIT
ENTER
VEHICLE STORAGE
AIRPORT MAINTENANCE
EXIT
ENTER
E. 80th AVE
SHADY GROVE ST
COMMERCIAL STAGING AREA
HARRY B. COMBS PKWY
VANDRIVER ST
UNDERGROVE CIR
TENDER FUELING SITE
E. 78th AVE (Service Road)
RETURN TO AIRPORT
PEÑA BLVD
TO DENVER
CONTINENTAL KITCHEN
E. 75th CIR
E. 75th AVE
PIKES PEAK PARKING FACILITY
AIRBORNE
FEDERAL EXPRESS
UNITED CARGO
UNITED KITCHEN
Vehicle Service Road
OAK HILL ST
PATSBURG ST
POWHATON ST
ROBERTDALE ST
TITUS ST
UNDERGROVE ST
JACKSON GAP RD
MT. ELBERT SHUTTLE LOT
E. 71st AVE
N
0 1/4 1/2
Miles

NORTHWEST DENVER ZIP CODE BOUNDARIES

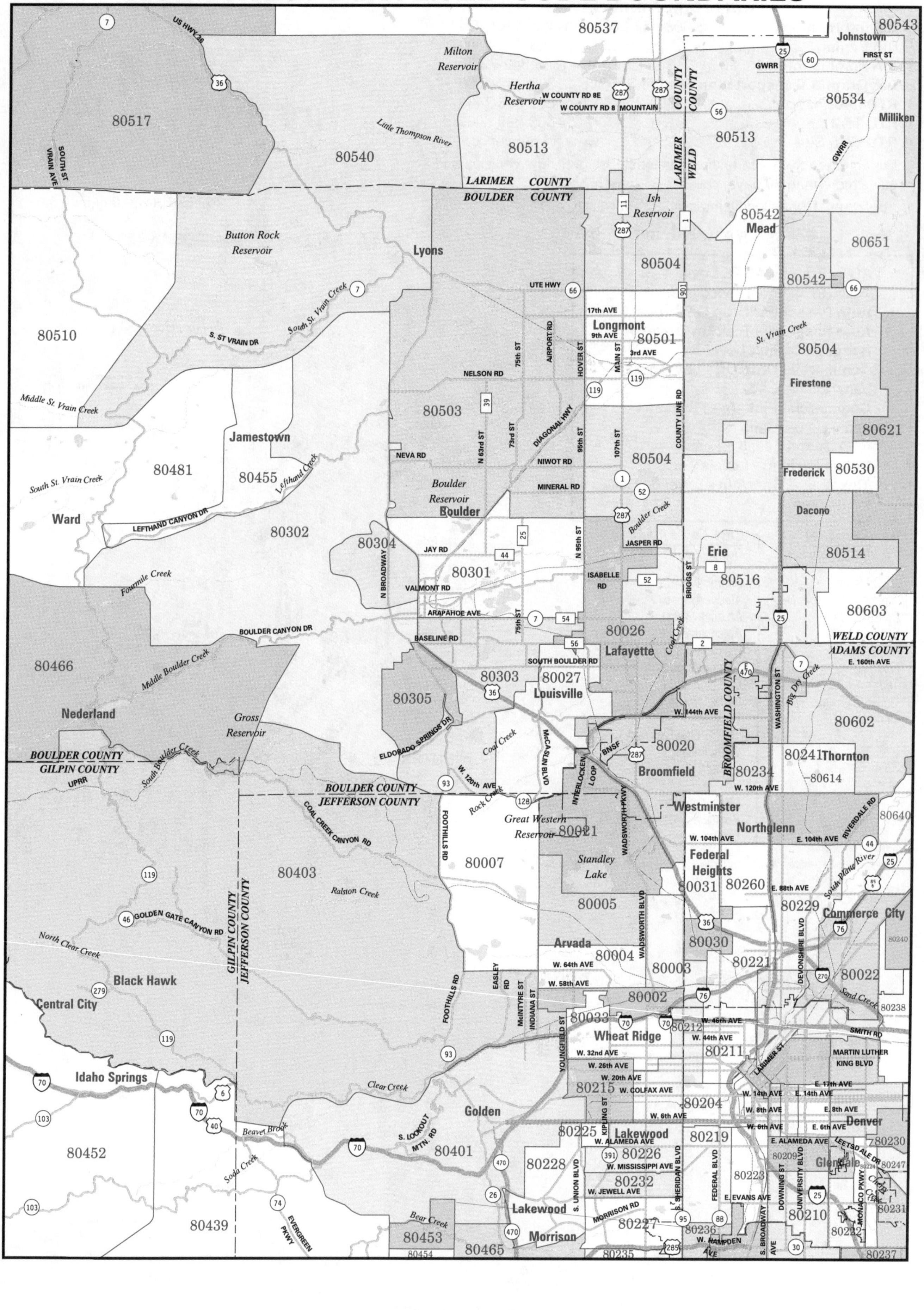

80517
80540
80537
80513
80534
80543
Johnstown
Milliken
Milton Reservoir
Hertha Reservoir
Little Thompson River
LARIMER COUNTY
BOULDER COUNTY
WELD COUNTY
Ish Reservoir
80542
Mead
80651
Button Rock Reservoir
Lyons
80504
80510
Longmont
80501
St. Vrain Creek
Firestone
80503
Jamestown
80481
80455
Ward
80621
Frederick
80530
Dacono
Boulder Reservoir
Boulder
80302
80304
80301
Erie
80516
80514
80603
80466
Nederland
80026
Lafayette
80027
Louisville
80303
80305
Gross Reservoir
BOULDER COUNTY
GILPIN COUNTY
ADAMS COUNTY
80602
80020
Broomfield
80234
80241
Thornton
80614
BROOMFIELD COUNTY
JEFFERSON COUNTY
Westminster
Northglenn
80640
Great Western Reservoir
80021
80007
80403
Standley Lake
Federal Heights
80031
80260
80229
Commerce City
80005
Arvada
80004
80003
80030
80221
80022
Black Hawk
Central City
80002
80033
Wheat Ridge
80212
80211
80216
80238
Idaho Springs
80215
Golden
80204
80225
Lakewood
80219
Denver
80230
80452
80401
80228
80226
80232
80209
Glendale
80223
80247
80439
Lakewood
Morrison
80227
80236
80210
80231
80224
80222
80453
80454
80465
80235
80237
Clear Creek
Bear Creek

NORTHEAST DENVER ZIP CODE BOUNDARIES

SOUTHWEST DENVER ZIP CODE BOUNDARIES

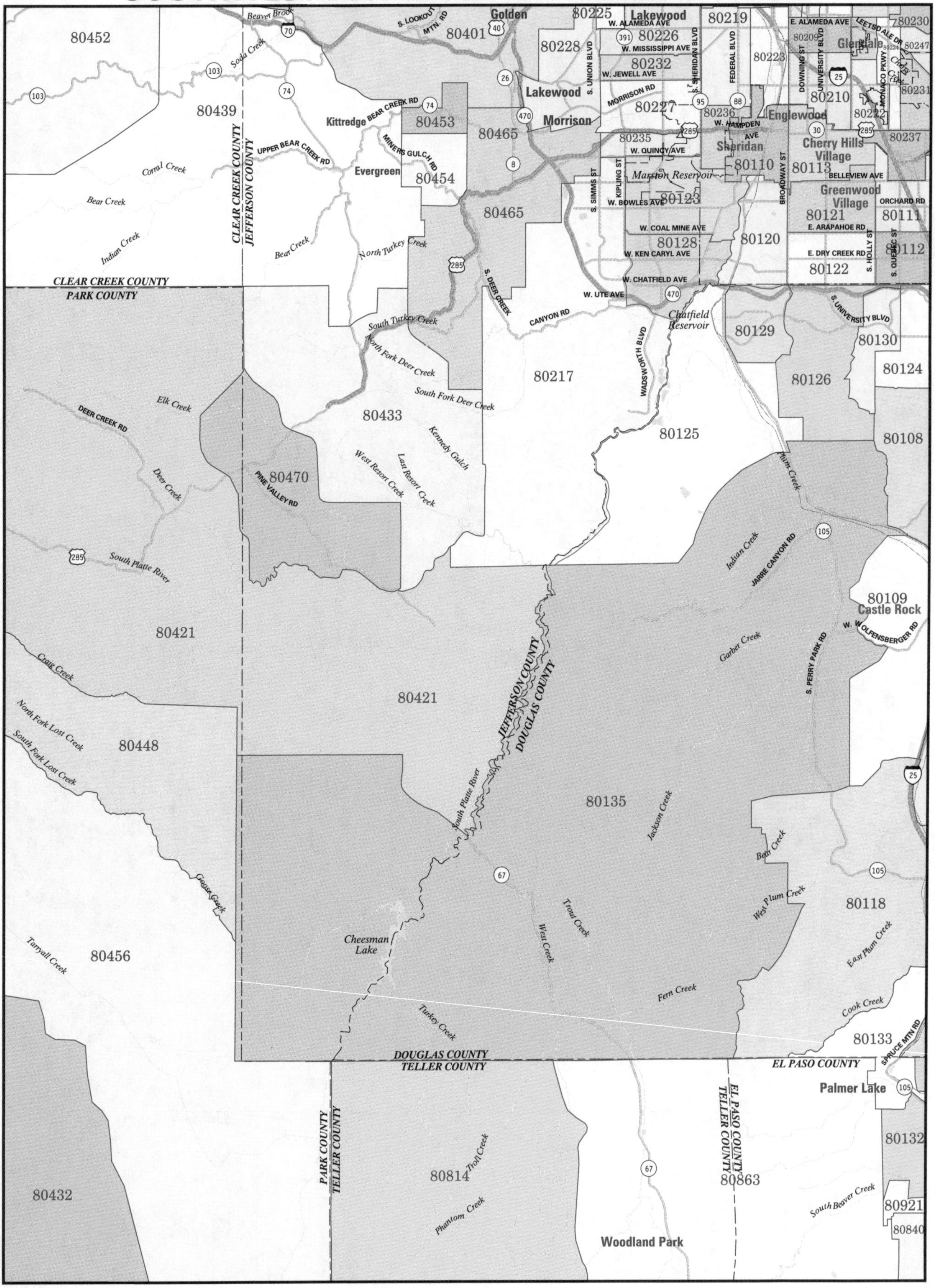

SOUTHEAST DENVER ZIP CODE BOUNDARIES

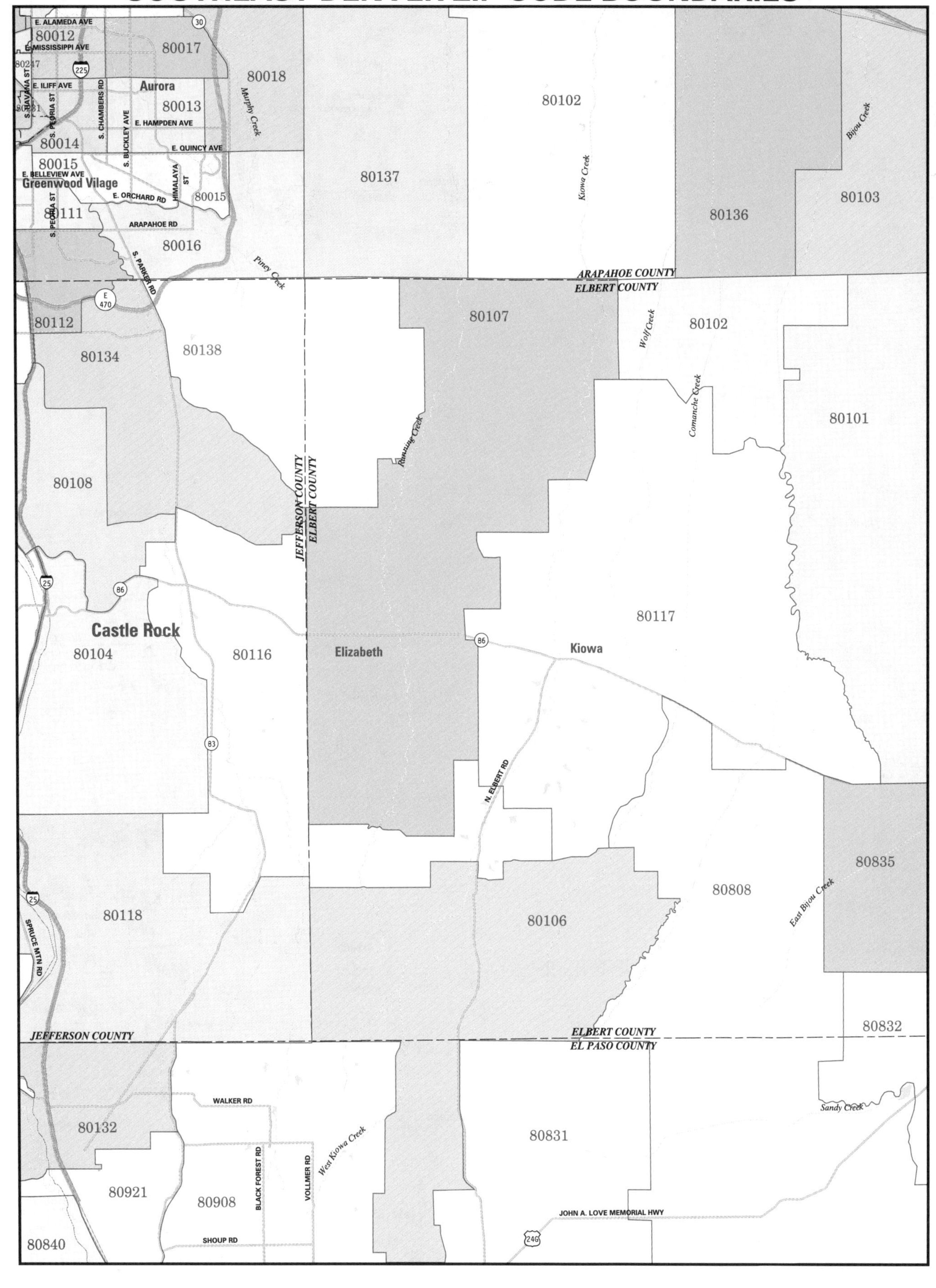

NORTHWEST DENVER SCHOOL DISTRICT BOUNDARIES

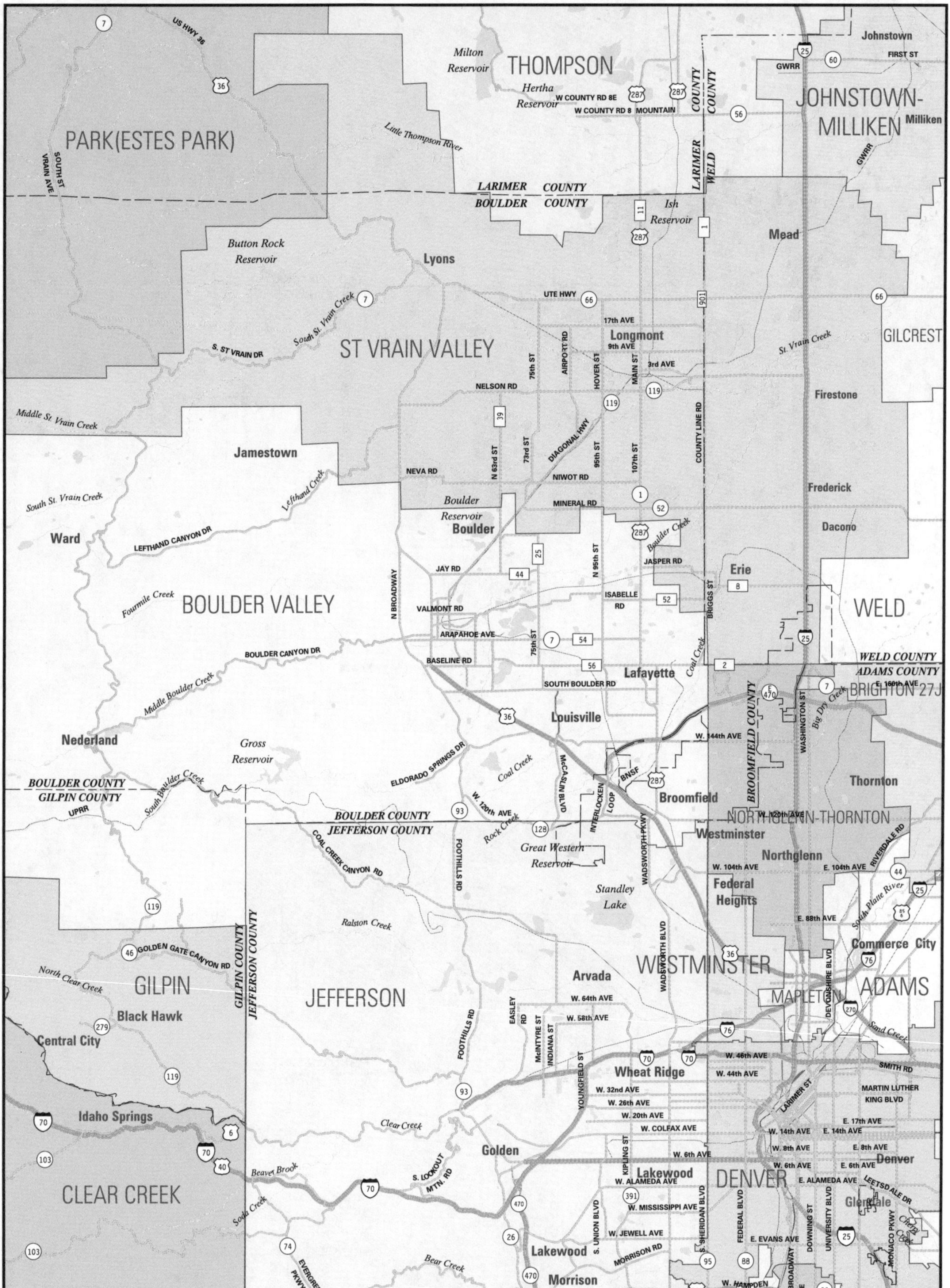

PARK(ESTES PARK)
THOMPSON
JOHNSTOWN-MILLIKEN
ST VRAIN VALLEY
GILCREST
BOULDER VALLEY
WELD
BRIGHTON 27J
NORTHGLENN-THORNTON
WESTMINSTER
MAPLETON
ADAMS
GILPIN
JEFFERSON
CLEAR CREEK
DENVER

NORTHEAST DENVER SCHOOL DISTRICT BOUNDARIES

JOHNSTOWN-MILLIKEN
La Salle
Lower Latham Reservoir
Milliken
COUNTY RD 44
COUNTY RD 42
Gilcrest
PLATTE VALLEY
South Platte River
WIGGINS
GILCREST
Milton Reservoir
South Platte River
Platteville
Beebe Seep Canal
East Neres Canal
Box Elder Creek
Speer Canal
WELD
Fort Lupton
Big Dry Creek
Keenesburg
KEENESBURG
Jack Rabbit Creek
Low Line Canal
Lost Creek
Prospect Reservoir
Lochbuie
BNSF
WELD COUNTY
ADAMS COUNTY
Horse Creek Reservoir
E. BRIDGE ST
E. SOUTHERN ST
E. BROMLEY ST
Brighton
BRIGHTON 27J
SABLE BLVD
BRIGHTON RD
Barr Lake
Commerce City
DENVER INTERNATIONAL AIRPORT
96th AVE
89th AVE
DENVER
PEÑA BLVD
DENVER COUNTY
ADAMS COUNTY
ADAMS
BRIGHTON
STRASBURG
Kiowa Creek
Wolf Creek
Comanche Creek
Lost Sand Creek
PEORIA ST
DENVER
BENNETT
Sand Creek
COOFAX AVE
MONTVIEW BLVD
ADAMS COUNTY
ARAPAHOE COUNTY
N HAVANA ST
E. 6th AVE
Aurora
ALAMEDA PKWY
Watkins
MISSISSIPPI AVE
CHAMBERS RD
AIRPORT BLVD
ADAMS-ARAPAHOE
Bennett
BYERS
ILIFF AVE
PEORIA ST
TOWER RD
GUN CLUB RD
Murphy Creek
HAMPDEN AVE
DENVER
CHERRY CREEK
Bijou Creek

SOUTHWEST DENVER SCHOOL DISTRICT BOUNDARIES

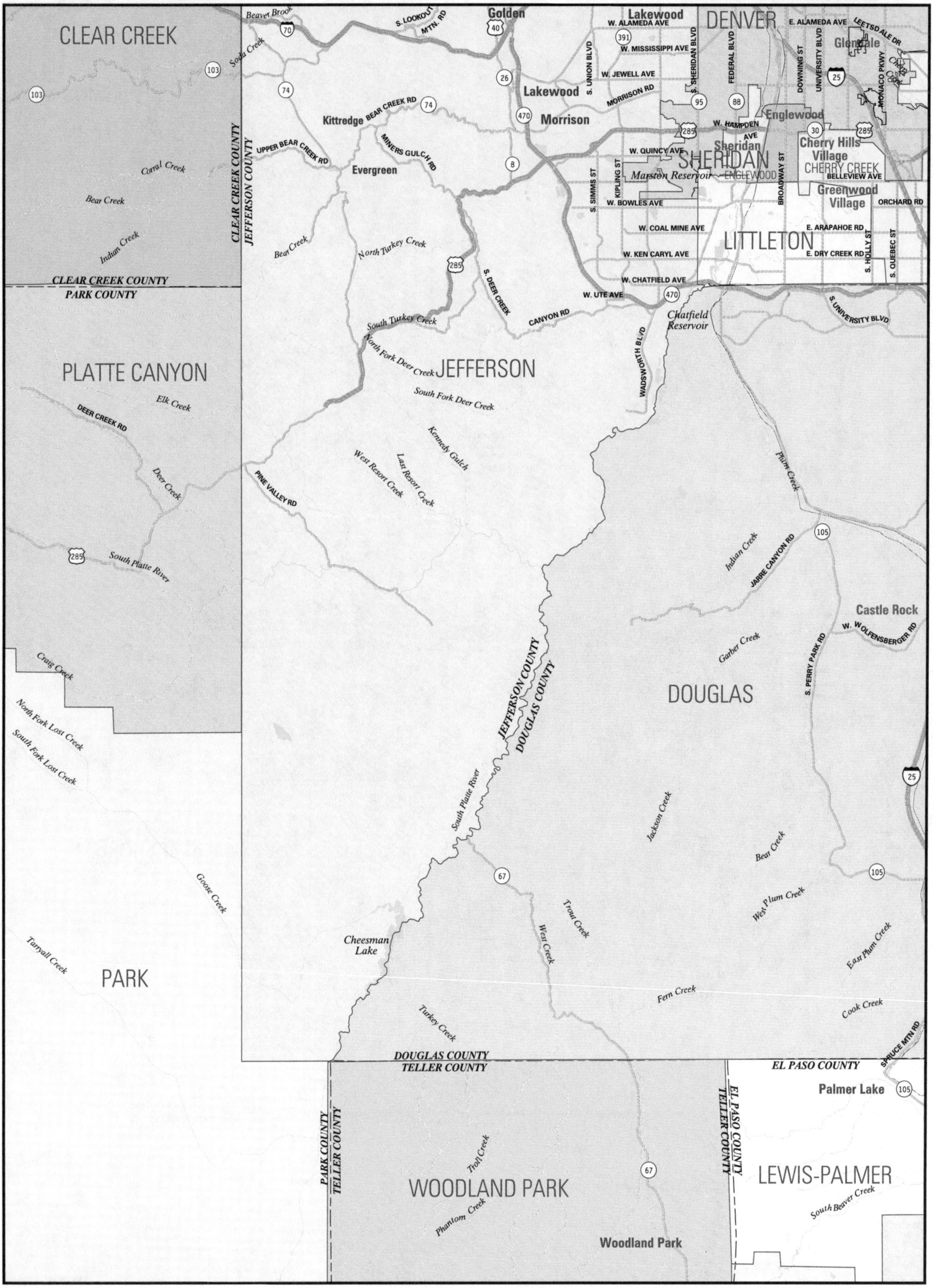

SOUTHEAST DENVER SCHOOL DISTRICT BOUNDARIES

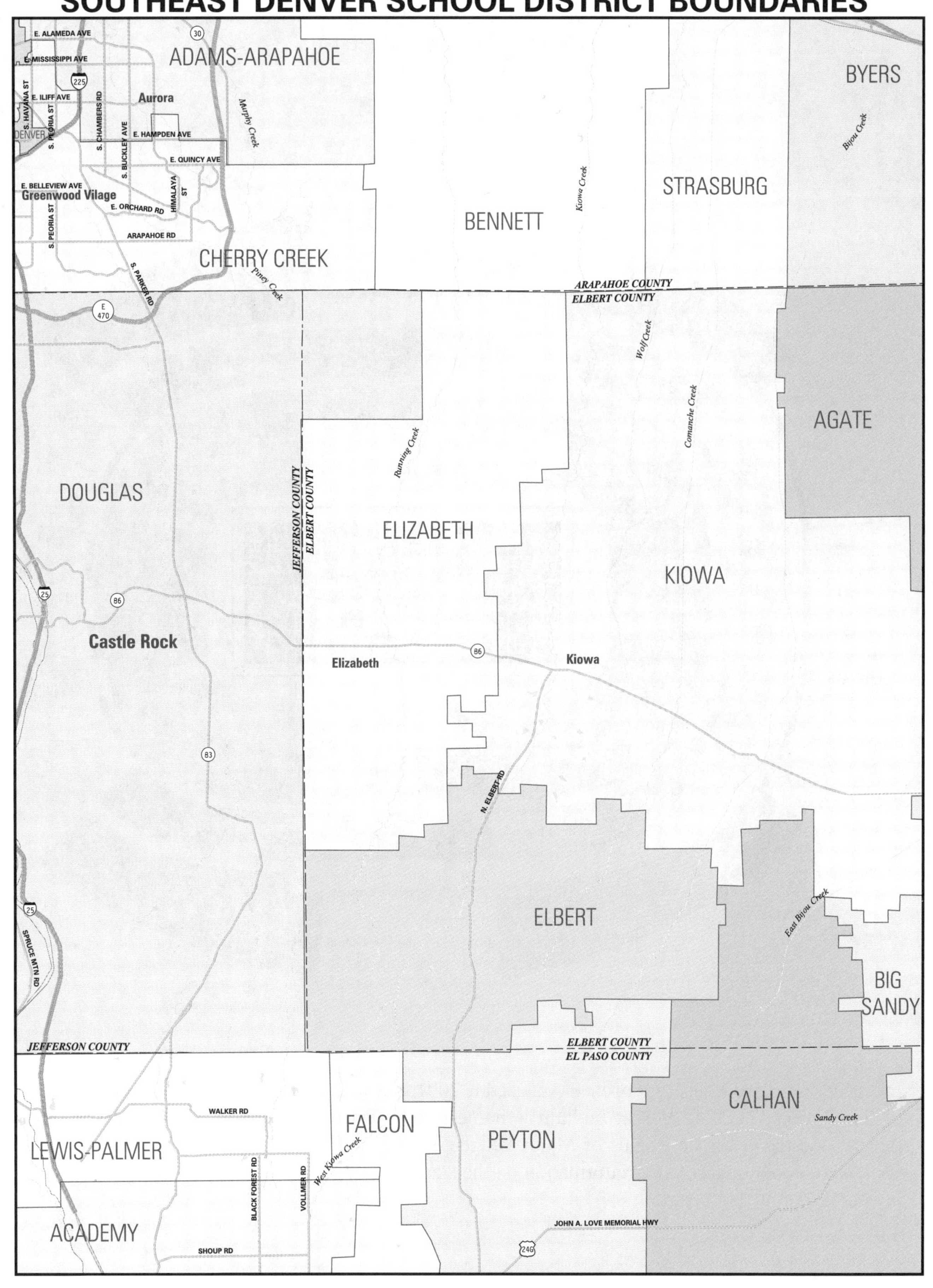

INVESCO FIELD AT MILE HIGH (SEE MAP 283)

1701 Bryant Street
Denver, Colorado 80204
720-258-3333

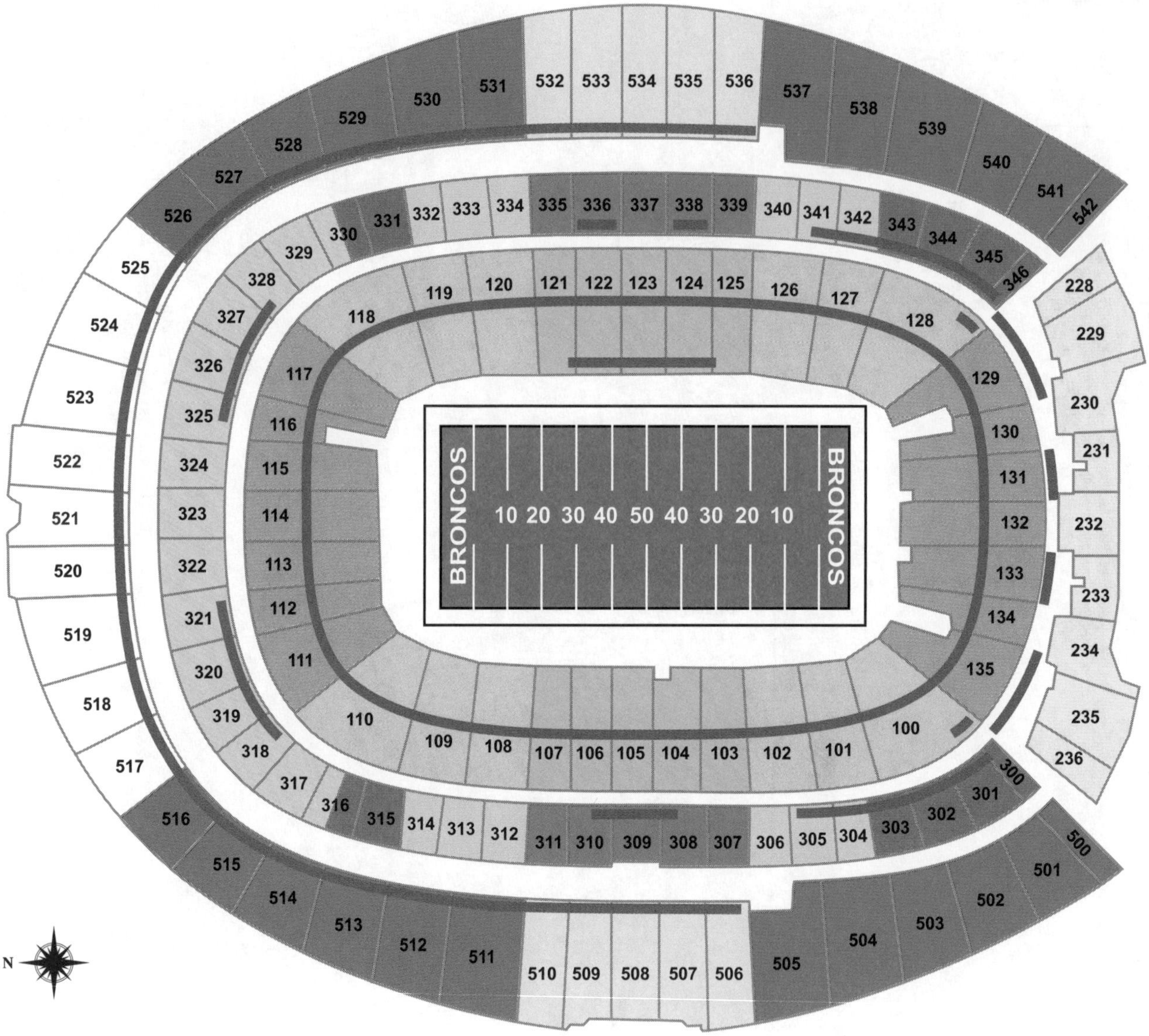

INVESCO Field at Mile High opened August 11, 2001, not with a football game, but with a concert by The Eagles. The 76,125-seat stadium is home to the Denver Broncos of the National Football League and the Colorado Rapids of Major League Soccer, and is the Denver area's primary venue for large outdoor concerts. For information on the stadium and the public events it hosts, visit www.invescofieldatmilehigh.com.

Coors Field (See Map 284)

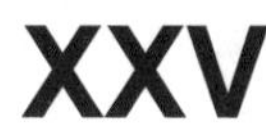

2001 Blake Street
Denver, Colorado 80205
303-762-5437 (Rockies)
1-800-388-ROCK

Coors Field Seating Chart

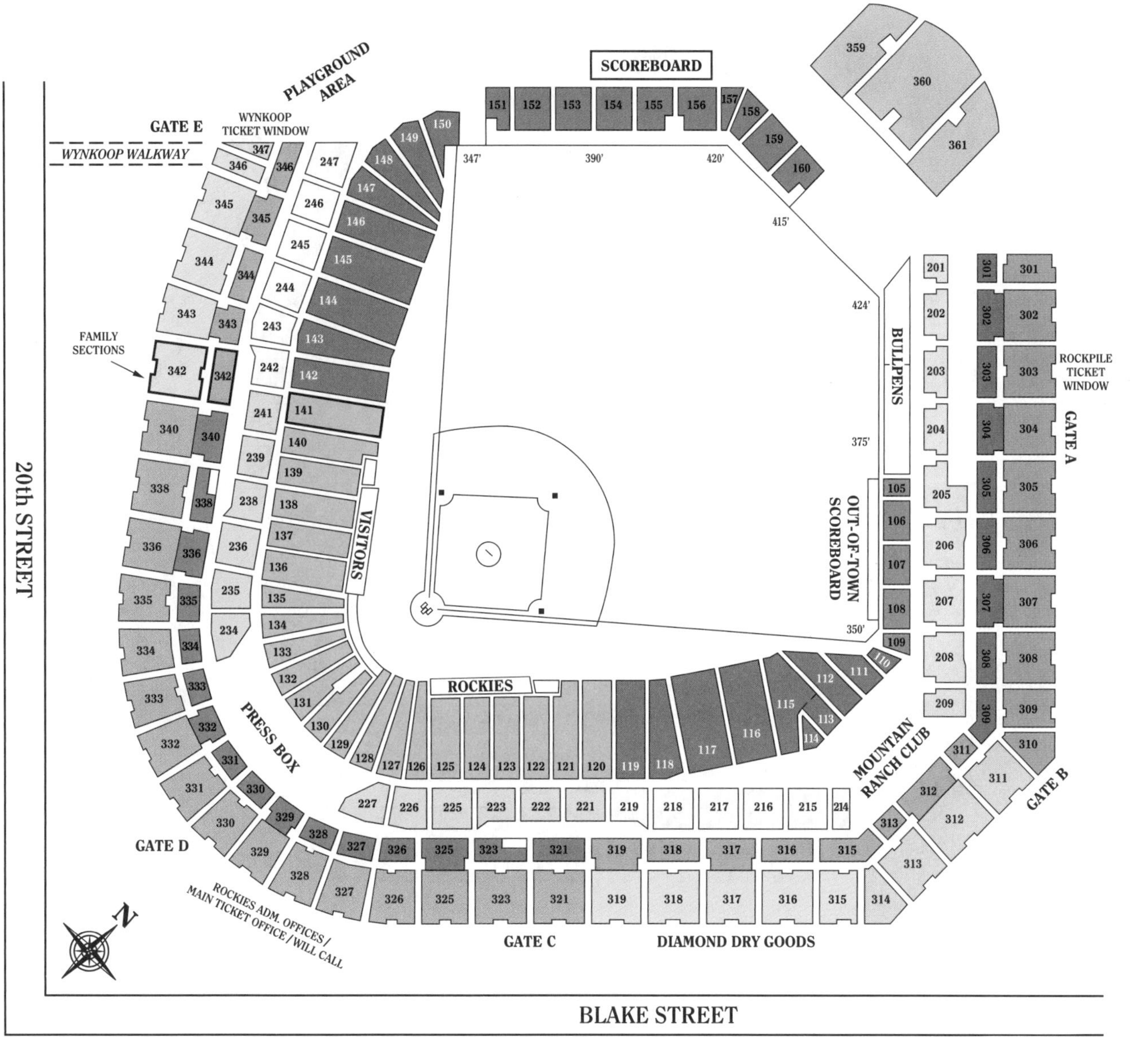

When Coors Field opened in 1995, the ballfield instantly became the standard for all future baseball stadiums built in urban settings. Home to the Colorado Rockies of Major League Baseball, Coors Field successfully blends its distinctive old-fashioned styling with ultramodern technology to provide capacity crowds of 50,249 with full enjoyment of America's favorite pastime. Check out colorado.rockies.mlb.com for more information on the stadium.

Pepsi Center (See Map 284)

1000 Chopper Circle
Denver, Colorado 80204
720-405-1100

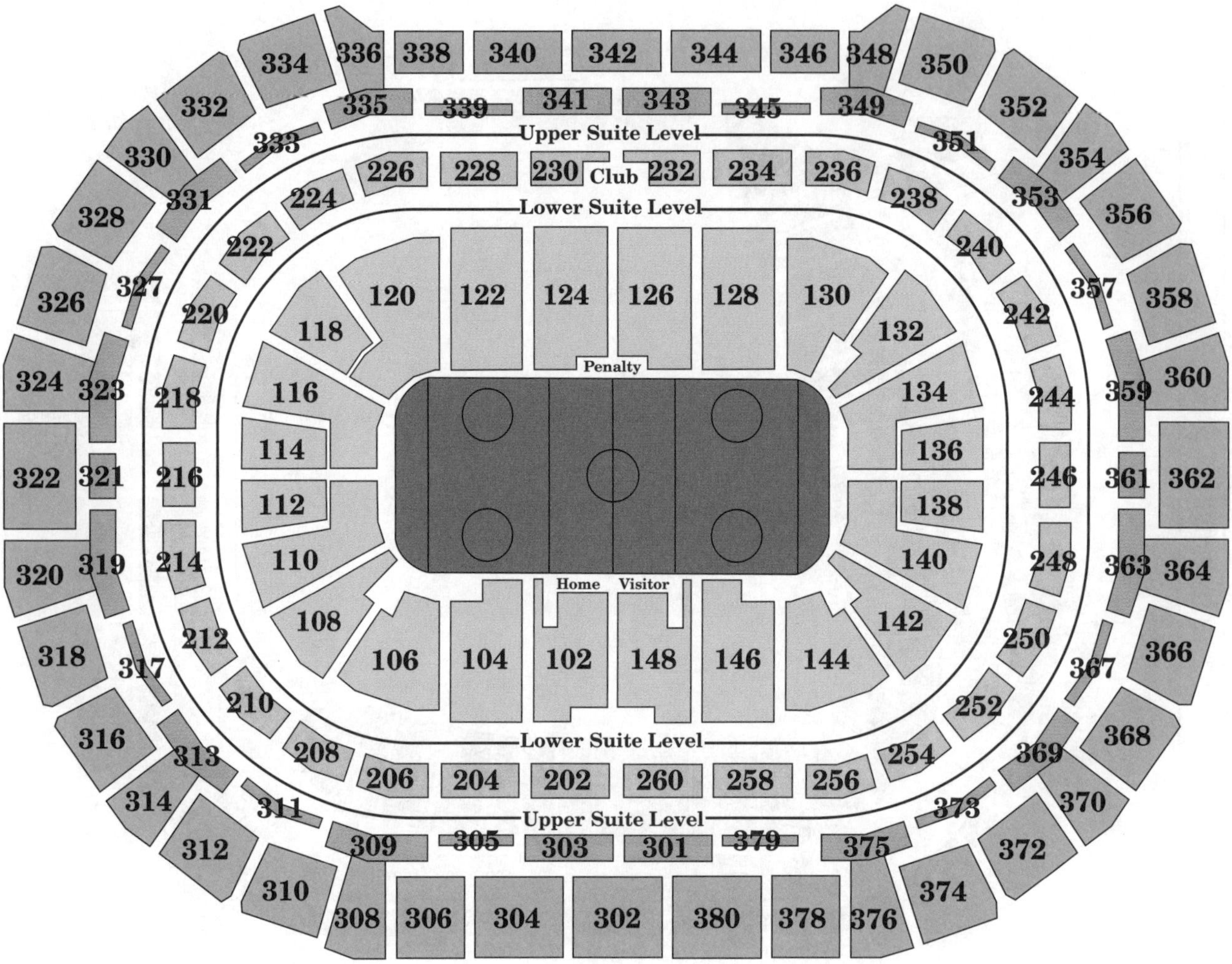

334 336 338 340 342 344 346 348 350
332 335 339 341 343 345 349 352
Upper Suite Level
330 333 226 228 230 Club 232 234 236 351 354
328 331 224 Lower Suite Level 238 353 356
222 240
326 327 220 120 122 124 126 128 130 357 358
118 132 242
324 323 218 116 Penalty 134 244 359 360
114 136
322 321 216 246 361 362
112 138
320 319 214 110 140 248 363 364
Home Visitor
108 142
212 106 104 102 148 146 144 250
318 317 367 366
210 252
316 313 208 Lower Suite Level 254 369 368
206 204 202 260 258 256
314 311 373 370
Upper Suite Level
312 309 305 303 301 379 375 372
310 374
308 306 304 302 380 378 376

Pepsi Center is affectionately, if unofficially, known as "The Can." The Colorado Avalanche of the National Hockey League and the Denver Nuggets of the National Basketball Association have played at Pepsi Center since the building opened in 1999. Newer tenants are the Colorado Mammoth (Major League Lacrosse) and the Colorado Crush (Arena Football League). The arena, which seats a maximum of 19,309, hosts a variety of other sporting events and concerts. Details on Pepsi Center are available at www.pepsicenter.com.

Magness Arena at the Ritchie Center (See Map 315) **XXVII**

2240 E. Buchtel Boulevard
Denver, Colorado 80208
303-871-2336

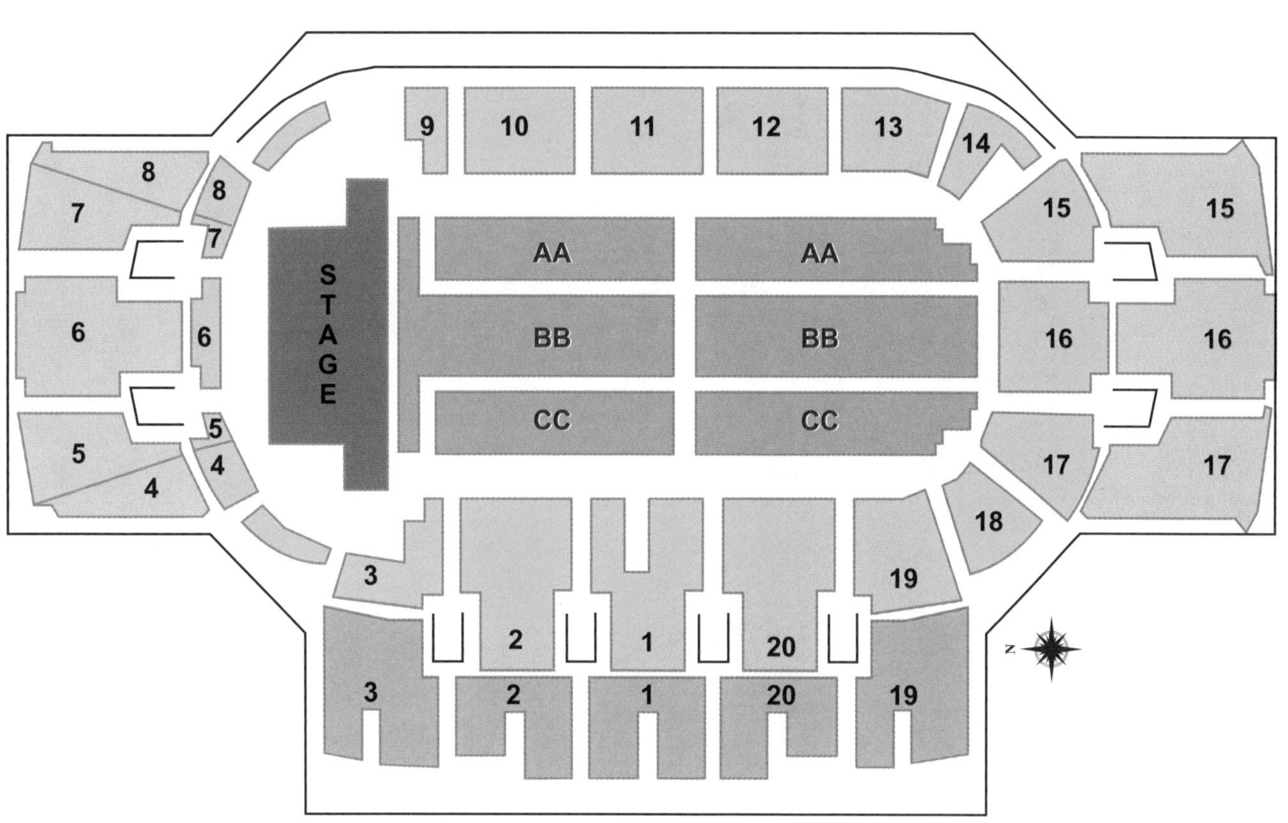

Drivers on I-25 spot the 215-foot-tall Williams Tower long before they see the rest of the Ritchie Center at the University of Denver. While the bell tower distinguishes the Ritchie Center's facade, the building's interior is equally remarkable, housing a natatorium, gymnasium, fieldhouse, fitness center and two arenas. The Magness Arena hosts DU Pioneers hockey and basketball, and seats 8,000 for public concert events. For more information on the Ritchie Center and Magness Arena events, log on to www.du.edu/ritchiecenter.

University of Colorado (See Map 128)

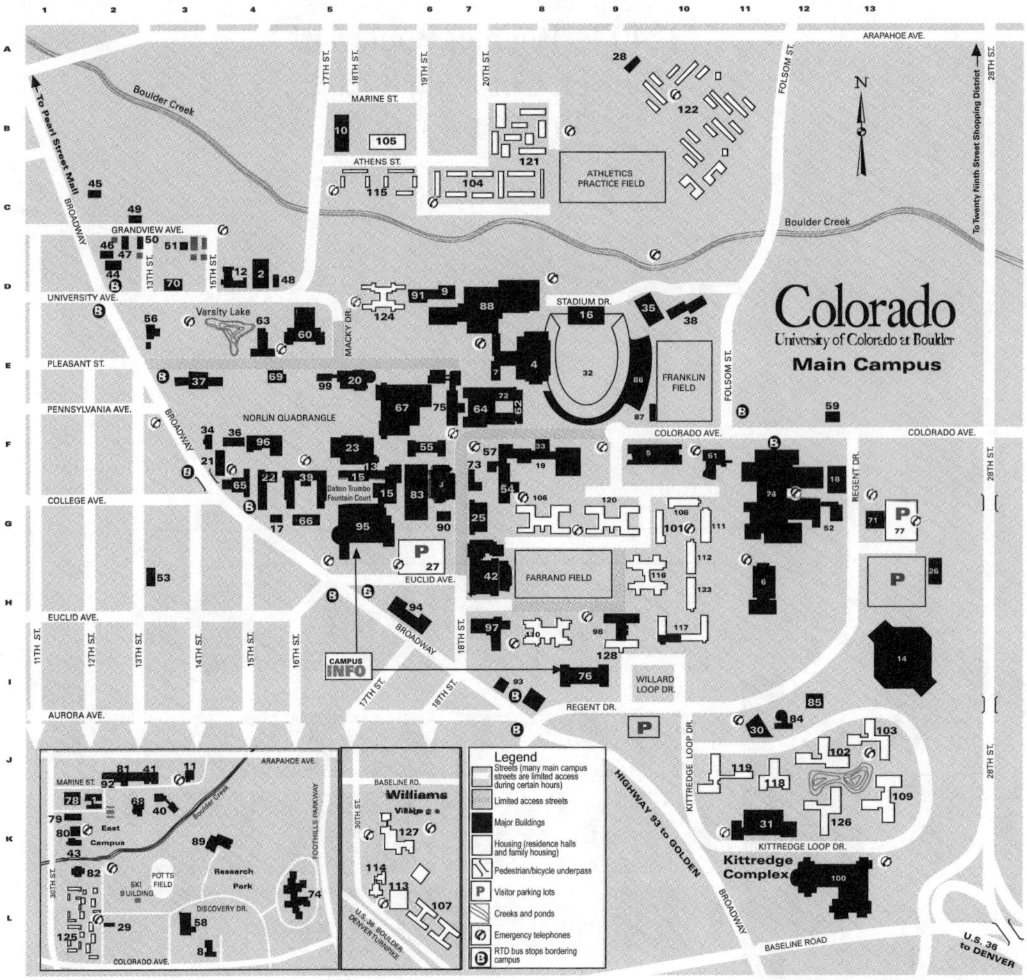

University Buildings

1. Administrative and Research Center-East Campus(J-2)(ARCE)
2. Armory(D-4)(ARMR)
3. ATLAS Building(Alliance for Technology, Learning, and Society)(G-6)(ATLS)
4. Balch Fieldhouse(E-7)(FH)
5. Benson Earth Sciences(F-9)(BESC)

* Bruce Curtis Building. *See Museum Collections.*

6. Business(H-10)(BUS)
7. Carlson Gymnasium(E-7)(CARL)
8. Center for Astrophysics and Space Astronomy(L-3)(CASA)
9. Clare Small Arts and Sciences(D-6)(CLRE)

* Charlotte York Irey Studios(F-4). *See University Theater.*

10. College Inn Conference Center(B-5)(CICC)
11. Computing Center(J-3)(COMP)
12. Continuing Education and Profesional Studies(D-4)(CEDU)
13. Cooperative Institute for Research in Environmental Sciences(F-5)(CIRE)
14. Coors Event/Conference Center(1-12)(EVNT)
15. Cristol Chemistry and Biochemistry(G-5)(CHEM)
16. Dal Ward Athletic Center(D-8)(DALW)
17. Denison Arts and Sciences(G-4)(DEN)
18. Discovery Learning Center(F-11)(DLC)

* Drescher Undergraduate Engineering. *See Integrated Teaching and Learning Laboratory.*

* Duane Physical Laboratories(F-7). *See Duane Physics and Astrophysics, Gamow Tower, Laboratory for Atmospheric and Space Physica, and JILA.*

19. Duane Physics and Astrophysics(F-7)(DUAN)
20. Eaton Humanities Building(E-5)(HUMN)
21. Economics(F-3)(ECON)
22. Education(G-4)(EDUC)
23. Ekeley Sciences(F-5)(EKLC)
24. Engineering Center(F/G-10/11)(EC)
25. Environmental Design(G-7)(ENVD)
26. Environmental Health and Safety Center(H-13)
27. Euclid Avenue AutoPark(G-6)(EPRK)
28. Family Housing Children's Center-Main Offices(A-9)(DACR)
29. Family Housing Children's Center at Smiley Court(L-2)
30. Fiske Planetarium and Science Center(J-10)(FISK)
31. Fleming Law(K-10)(LAW)
32. Folsom Stadium(E-8)(STAD)
33. Gamow Tower (F-7)(DUAN)
34. Gates Woodruff Women'ts Studies Cottage(F-3)(COTT)
35. Groumds and Service Center(D-9)(GRNS)
36. Guggenheim Geography(F-3)(GUGG)
37. Hale Science(E-3)(HALE)
38. Health Physics Laboratory(D-9)(HPHY)
39. Hellems Arts and Sciences/Mary Rippon Theatre(G-4)(HLMS)

* Henderson Building(G-4). *See Museum of Natural History.*

40. Housing System Maintenance Center(K-3)(HSMC)
41. Housing System Service Center(J-2)(HSSC)
42. Imig Music(H-7)(MUS)
43. Institute for Behavioral Genetics(K-1)(IBG)
44. Institute if Behavioral Science No. 1(D-2)(IBS1)
45. IBS No. 2 (C-2)(IBS2)
46. IBS No. 3 (D-2)(IBS3)
47. IBS No. 4 (D-2)(IBS4)
48. IBS No. 5 (D-4)(IBS5)
49. IBS. No. 6 (C-2)(IBS6)
50. IBS No. 7 (C-2)(IBS7)
51. IBS No. 8 (C-3)(IBS8)
52. Integrated Teaching and Learning Laboratory(G-11)(ITLL)
53. International English Center(G-2)(IEC)
54. JILA(G-7)
55. Ketchum Arts and Sciences(F-6)(KTCH)
56. Koenig Alumni Center(E-2)(ALUM)
57. Laboratory for Atmospheric and Space Physics(F-7)(LASP)
58. LASP Space Technology Research Center(L-3)(LSTR)

*Leeds School of Business(H-10). *See Business, Leeds School of.*

59. Lesser House(F-11)(LESS)

*Life Science Laboratories Complex(E-7). *See Muenzinger Psychology, Porter Biosciences, and Ramaley Biology.*

60. Macky Auditorium(D-4)(MCKY)
61. Mathematics Building(F-10)(MATH)
62. MCD Biology(E-7)(MCDB)
63. McKenna Languages(E-4)(MKNA)
64. Muenzinger Psychology(E-7)(MUEN)
65. Museum Collections(Bruce Curtis Building)(G-3)(MCOL)
66. Museum of Natural History, University of Colorado(G-4)(HEND)
67. Norlin LIbrary(E-6)(LIBR)
68. Nuclear Physics Laboratory(K-2)(NPL)
69. Old Main(E-4)(MAIN)
70. Page Foundation Center(D-3)(PFDC)
71. Police and Parking Services(G-12)(PDPS)
72. Porter Biosciences(E-7)(PORT)
73. Power House(F-6)(POWR)
74. Qwest Research Park(L-4)(USW)
75. Ramaley Biology(E-6)(RAMY)
76. Regent Administrative Center(I-8)(RGNT)
77. Regent Drive AutoPark(G-12)(RPRK)
78. Research Laboratory, Litman RL1(J-1)(LITR)
79. Research Laboratory(K-1)(RL2)
80. Research Laboratory, Life Science RL4(K-1)(LSRL)
81. Research Laboratory, RL6 (Marine Street Science Center)(J-2)(MSSC)
82. Research Park Greenhouse(K-1)(GH-3)
83. Sibell Wolle Fine Arts(G-6)(FA)
84. Sommers-Bausch Observatory(I-11)(OBSV)
85. Speech, Language, and Hearing Sciences(I-11)(SLHS)
86. Stadium Building(E-8)(STAD)
87. Stadium Ticket Building (F-9)(STTB)
88. Student Recreation Center (D-6/7)(REC)
89. Sybase (K-3)(SYBS)
90. Telecommunications Building (G-6)(TCOM)
91. Temporary Building No.1 (D-6)(TB01)
92. Transportation Center (J-2)(TRAN)
93. University Administrative Center and Annex (I-7)(UCTR)
94. University Club (H-6)(CLUB)
95. University Memorial Center (G-5)(UMC)
96. University Theater (including Charlotte York Irey Studios)(F-4)(THTR)
97. Wardenburg Health Center (H-7)(WARD)
98. Willard Administrative Center (H-8)(WCTR)
99. Woodbury Arts and Sciences (E-5)(WDBY)
100. Wolf Law Building (L-12)(WLFL)

University Housing

101. Aden Hall-Quadrangle (G-9)(ADEN)
102. Andrews Hall-Kittredge Complex (J-11)(ANDS)
103. Arnett Hall-Kiettredge Complex (J-12)(ARNT)
104. Athens Court (B/C-6/7)(ATCT)
105. Athens North Court (B-6)(ATHN)
106. Baker Hall (G-7)(BKER)
107. Bear Creek Apartments-Williams Village (W-BC)
108. Brackett hall-Quadrangle (G-9)(BRKT)
109. Buckingham Hall-Kittredge Complex (K-12)(BUCK)
110. Cheyenne Arapaho Hall (H-7)(CHEY)
111. Cockerell Hall-Quadrangle (G-10)(CKRL)
112. Crosman Hall-Quadrangle (G-10)(CROS)
113. Darley Commons-Williams Village (L-6))(DYLC)
114. Darley Towers-Williams Village (K-5)(DLYT)
115. Faculty Staff Court (C-5/6)(FACT)
116. Farrand Hall (H-9)(FRND)
117. Hallett Hall (H-9)(HLET)
118. Kittredge Commons-Kittredge Complex (J-10)(KITT)

* Kittredge Complex. *See Kittredge Commons, Andrews, Arnett, Buckingham, Kittredge West, and Smith Halls.*

119. Kittredge West Hall-Kittredge Complex (J-10)(KITW)
120. Libby Hall (G-8)(LIBY)
121. Marine Court (B-7)(MRCT)
122. Newton Court (B/C-9/10)(NTCT)

* Quadrangle (Engineering Quadrangle). *See Aden, Brackett, Cockerell, and Crosman Halls.*

123. Reed Hall (H-10)(REED)
124. Sewall Hall (D-5)(SWLL)
125. Smiley Court (L-1)(SMCT)
126. Smith Hall-Kittredge Complex (K-11)(SMTH)
127. Stearns Tower-Williams Village (K-6)(STRN)
128. Willard Hall-South Wing (H-8)(WLRD)

* Williams Village. *See Bear Creek Apartments, Darley Commons, Darley Towers, and Stearns Towers.*

Folsom Field (See Map 128)

CU Campus, Colorado Avenue
Boulder, Colorado 80302
303-492-8337

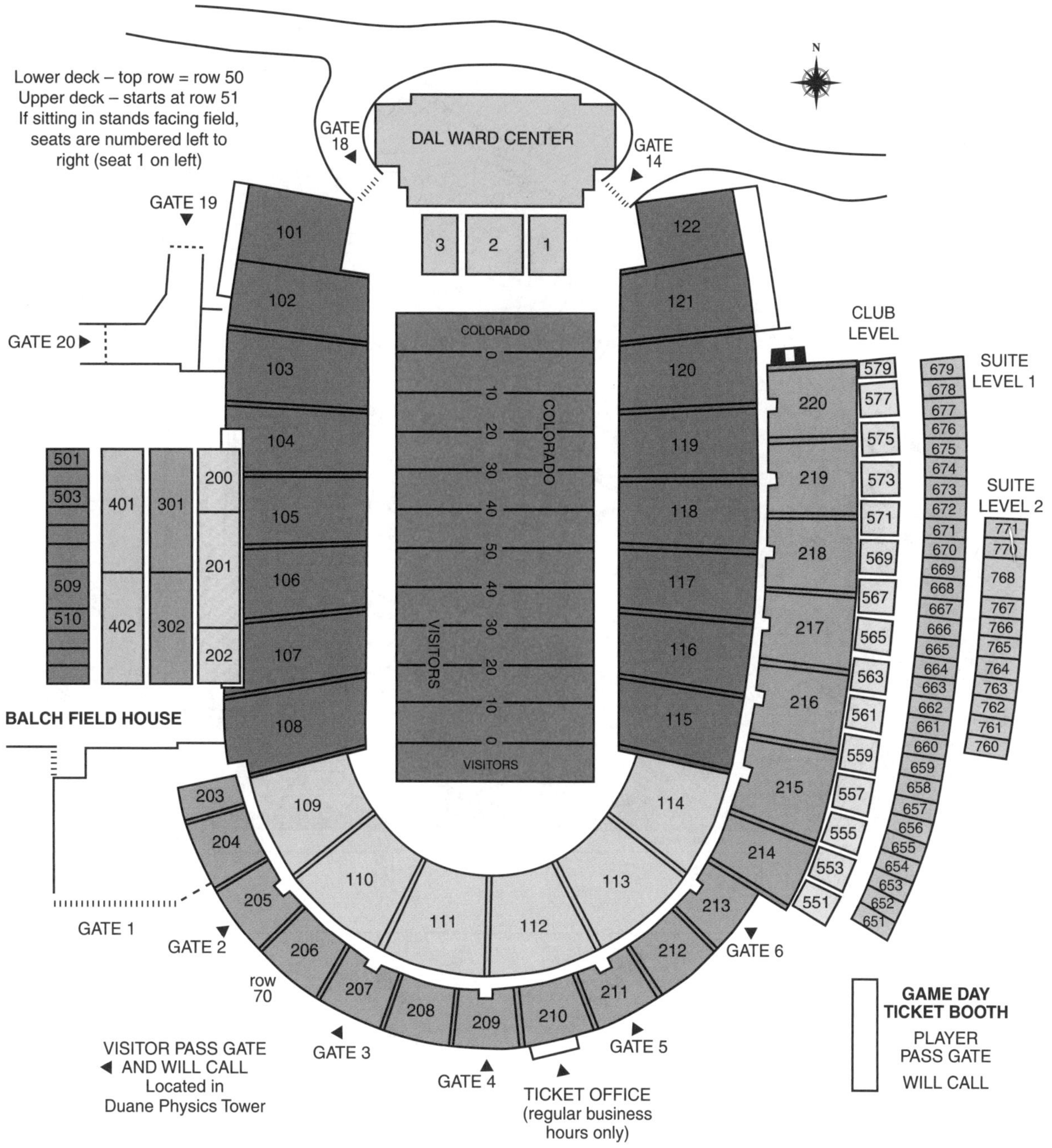

Lower deck – top row = row 50
Upper deck – starts at row 51
If sitting in stands facing field, seats are numbered left to right (seat 1 on left)

DAL WARD CENTER

GATE 18

GATE 14

GATE 19

GATE 20

CLUB LEVEL

SUITE LEVEL 1

SUITE LEVEL 2

COLORADO

VISITORS

BALCH FIELD HOUSE

GATE 1

GATE 2

row 70

GATE 3

GATE 4

GATE 5

GATE 6

VISITOR PASS GATE AND WILL CALL
Located in Duane Physics Tower

TICKET OFFICE
(regular business hours only)

GAME DAY TICKET BOOTH
PLAYER PASS GATE
WILL CALL

Folsom Field is the home of the University of Colorado Buffaloes football team. The venerable stadium seats as many as 52,000 fans for football and other campus athletic events, and is the site of commencement activities every May.

Auraria Campus (See Map 284)

Auraria Higher Education Center
900 Auraria Parkway
Denver, CO 80204

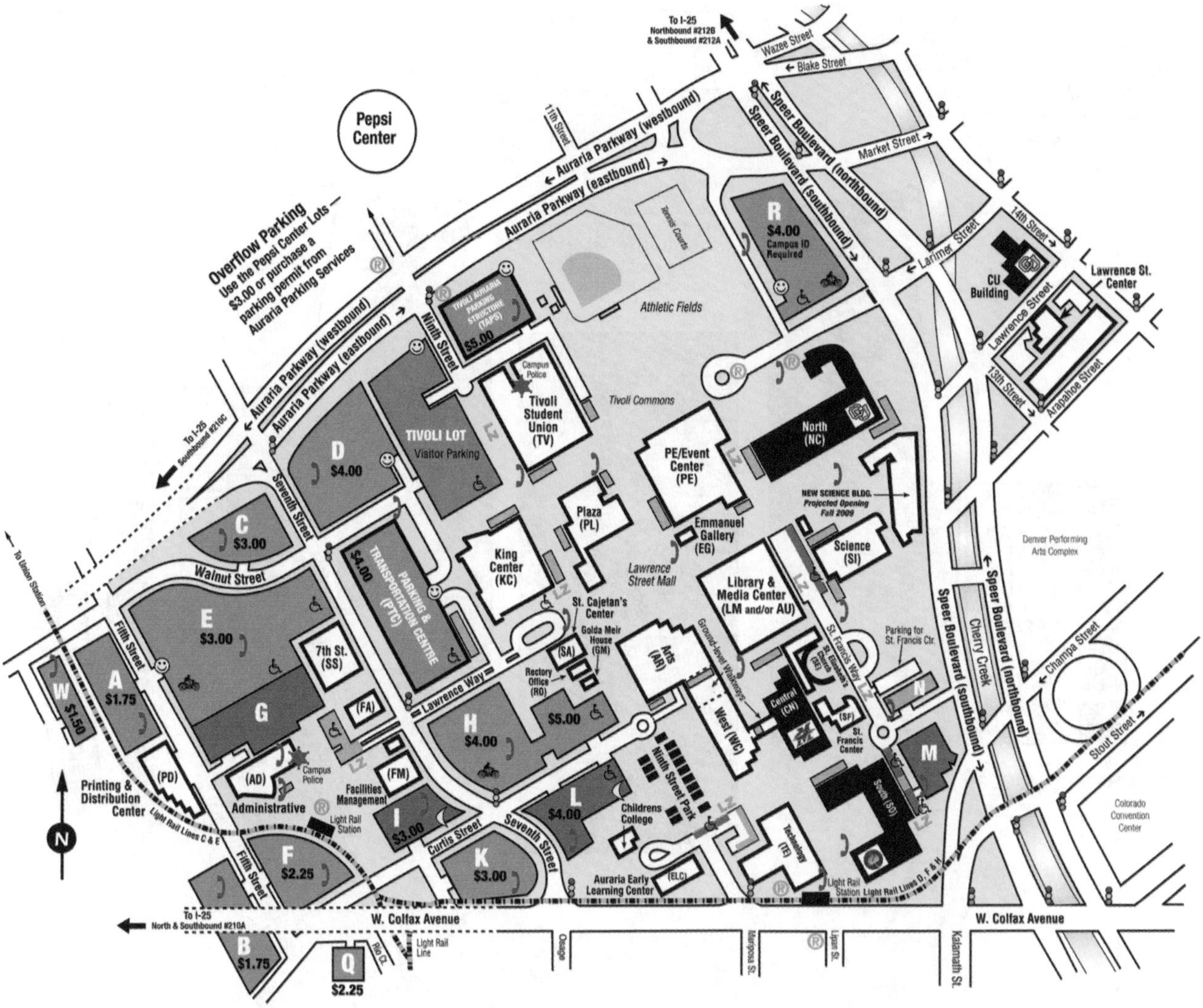

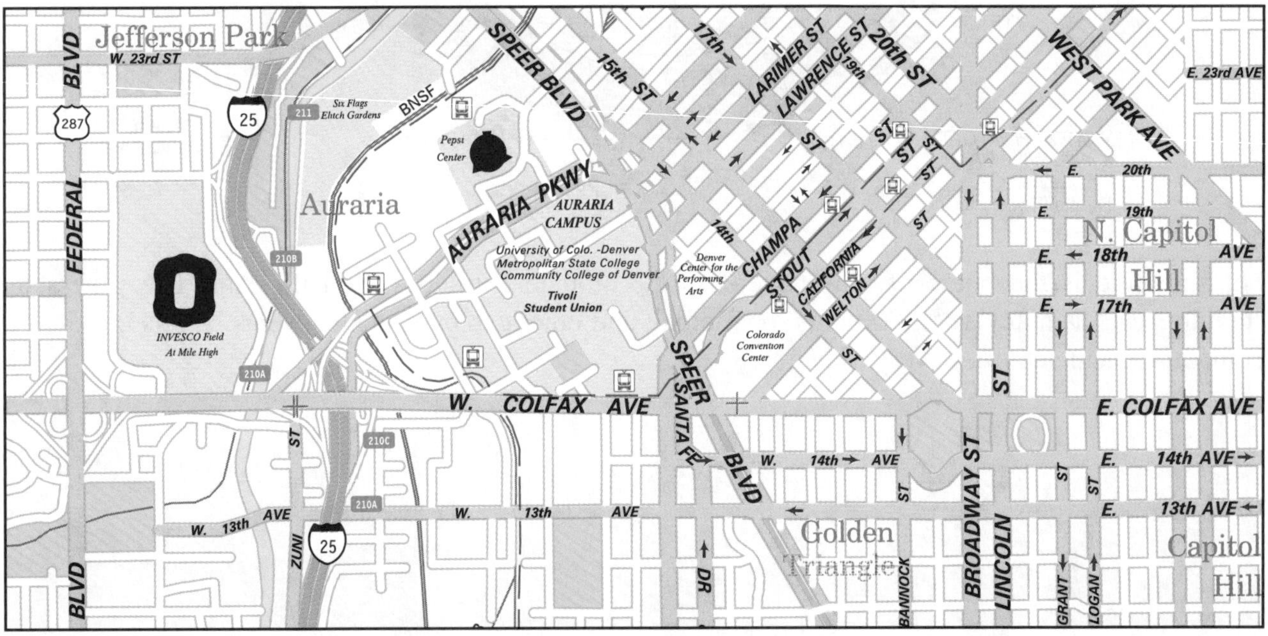

E-470 & Northwest Parkway

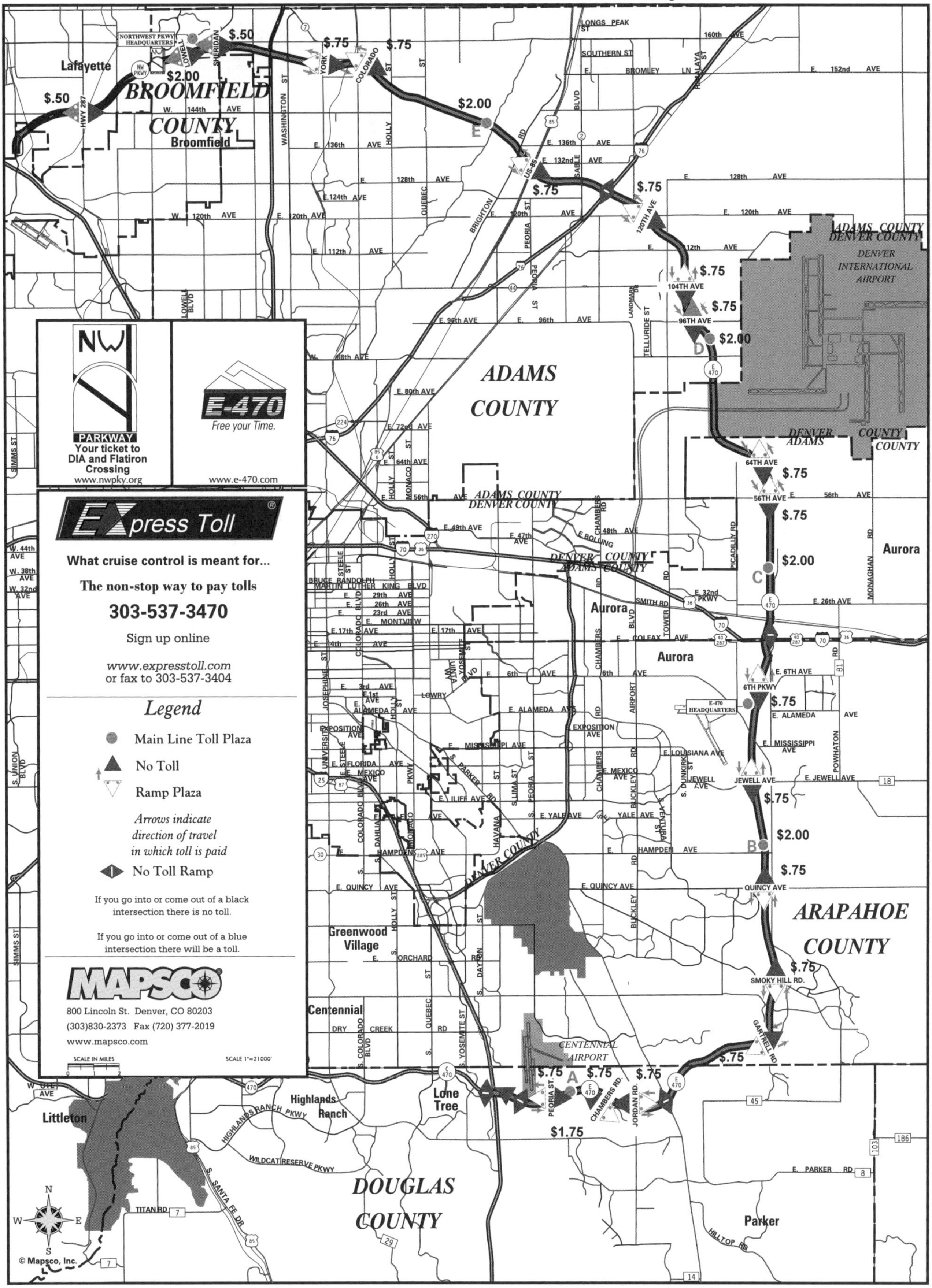
NORTHWEST PKWY HEADQUARTERS
Lafayette
BROOMFIELD COUNTY
Broomfield
ADAMS COUNTY
DENVER COUNTY
DENVER INTERNATIONAL AIRPORT
Aurora
ARAPAHOE COUNTY
DOUGLAS COUNTY
CENTENNIAL AIRPORT
Greenwood Village
Centennial
Highlands Ranch
Lone Tree
Littleton
Parker
E-470 HEADQUARTERS
$.50
$2.00
$.75
$1.75
A
B
C
D
E
NW PARKWAY
Your ticket to DIA and Flatiron Crossing
www.nwpky.org
E-470
Free your Time.
www.e-470.com
Express Toll
What cruise control is meant for...
The non-stop way to pay tolls
303-537-3470
Sign up online
www.expresstoll.com
or fax to 303-537-3404
Legend
Main Line Toll Plaza
No Toll
Ramp Plaza
Arrows indicate direction of travel in which toll is paid
No Toll Ramp
If you go into or come out of a black intersection there is no toll.
If you go into or come out of a blue intersection there will be a toll.
MAPSCO
800 Lincoln St. Denver, CO 80203
(303)830-2373 Fax (720) 377-2019
www.mapsco.com
SCALE IN MILES
SCALE 1"=21000'
N
S
E
W
© Mapsco, Inc.

BROADWAY EAST
0 Broadway
100 E Lincoln St.
200 E Sherman St.
300 E Grant St.
400 E Logan St.
500 E Pennsylvania St.
600 E Pearl St.
700 E Washington St.
800 E Clarkson St.
900 E Emerson St.
1000 E Ogden St.
1100 E Corona St.
1200 E Downing St.
1300 E Marion St.
1400 E Lafayette St.
1500 E Humboldt St.
1600 E Franklin St.
1700 E Gilpin St.
1800 E Williams St.
1900 E High St.
2000 E Race St.
2100 E Vine St.
2200 E Gaylord St.
2300 E York St.
2350 E University Blvd.
2400 E Josephine St.
2500 E Columbine St.
2600 E Elizabeth St.
2700 E Clayton St.
2800 E Detroit St.
2900 E Fillmore St.
3000 E Milwaukee St.
3100 E St. Paul St.
3200 E Steele St.
3300 E Adams St.
3400 E Cook St.
3500 E Madison St.
3600 E Monroe St.
3700 E Garfield St.
3800 E Jackson St.
3900 E Harrison St.
4000 E Colorado Blvd.
4100 E Albion St.
4200 E Ash St.
4300 E Bellaire St.
4400 E Birch St.
4500 E Clermont St.
4600 E Cherry St.
4700 E Dexter St.
4800 E Dahlia St.
4900 E Eudora St.
5000 E Elm St.
5050 E Filbert Ct.
5100 E Fairfax St.
5150 E Flamingo Ct.
5200 E Forest St.
5300 E Glencoe St.
5400 E Grape St.
5500 E Hudson St.
5600 E Holly St.
5700 E Ivanhoe St.
5800 E Ivy St.
5900 E Jersey St.
6000 E Jasmine St.
6100 E Kearney St.
6200 E Krameria St.
6300 E Leyden St.
6350 E Linden Ct.
6400 E Locust St.
6500 E Monaco Pkwy.
6600 E Magnolia St.
6700 E Niagara St.
6800 E Newport St.
6900 E Oneida St.
7000 E Olive St.
7100 E Pontiac St.
7200 E Poplar St.
7300 E Quebec St.
7400 E Quince St.
7500 E Roslyn St.
7600 E Rosemary St.
7700 E Syracuse St.
7800 E Spruce St.
7900 E Trenton St.
8000 E Tamarac St.
8100 E Ulster St.
8200 E Uinta St.
8300 E Valentia St.
8400 E Verbena St.
8500 E Wabash St.
8600 E Willow St.
8700 E Xanthia St.
8800 E Xenia St.
8900 E Yosemite St.
9000 E Akron St.
9100 E Alton St.
9200 E Beeler St.
9300 E Boston St.
9400 E Chester St.
9500 E Clinton St.
9600 E Dallas St.
9700 E Dayton St.
9800 E Emporia St.
9900 E Elmira St.
10000 E Florence St.
10100 E Fulton St.
10200 E Galena St.
10300 E Geneva St.
10400 E Hanover St.
10500 E Havana St.
10600 E Iola St.
10700 E Ironton St.
10800 E Jamaica St.
10900 E Joliet St.
11000 E Kenton St.
11100 E Kingston St.
11200 E Lansing St.
11300 E Lima St.
11400 E Macon St.
11500 E Moline St.
11600 E Newark St.
11700 E Nome St.
11800 E Oakland St.
11900 E Oswego St.
12000 E Paris St.
12100 E Peoria St.
12200 E Quari St.
12300 E Quentin St.
12400 E Racine St.
12500 E Revere St.
12600 E Salem St.
12700 E Scranton St.
12800 E Troy St.
12900 E Tucson St.
13000 E Ursula St.
13100 E Uvalda St.
13200 E Vaughn St.
13300 E Victor St.
13400 E Wheeling St.
13500 E Worchester St.
13600 E Xanadu St.
13700 E Xapary St.
13750 E Potomac St.
13800 E Abilene St.
Yost St.
13900 E Atchison St.
Yuba St.
14000 E Billings St.
Zion St.
14100 E Blackhawk St.
14200 E Carson St.
14300 E Crystal St.
14400 E Dillon St.
14500 E Sable Blvd.
14600 E Dearborn St.
14700 E Eagle St.
14800 E Elkhart St.
14900 E Altura Blvd.
15000 E Fairplay St.
15100 E Fraser St.
15200 E Granby St.
15300 E Chambers Rd.
15400 E Hannibal St.
15500 E Helena St.
15600 E Idalia St.
15700 E Jasper St.
15800 E Joplin St.
15900 E Kalispell St.
16000 E Kittredge St.
16100 E Laredo St.
16200 E Lewiston St.
16300 E Memphis St.
16400 E Mobile St.
16500 E Norfolk St.
16600 E Nucla St.
16700 E Olathe St.
16800 E Ourary St.
16900 E Buckley Rd.
17000 E Pagosa St.
17100 E Pitkin St.
17200 E Quintero St.
17300 E Richfield St.
17400 E Rifle St.
17500 E Salida St.
17600 E Sedalia St.
17700 E Telluride St.
17800 E Truckee St.
17900 E Uravan St.
18000 E Ventura St.
18100 E Waco St.
18200 E Walden St.
18300 E Yampa St.
18400 E Zeno St.
18500 E Tower Rd.
18600 E Andes St.
18700 E Argonne St.
18800 E Bahama
18900 E Biscay St.
19000 E Cathay St.
19100 E Ceylon St.
19200 E Danube St.
19300 E Dunkirk St.
19400 E Ensenada St.
19500 E Espana St.
19600 E Flanders St.
19700 E Fundy St.
19800 E Genoa St.
19900 E Gibraltar St.
20000 E Halifax St.
20100 E Himalaya St.
20200 E Iran St.
20300 E Ireland St.
20400 E Jebel St.
20500 E Jericho St.
20600 E Killarney St.
20700 E Kirk St.
20800 E Lisbon St.
20900 E Liverpool St.
21000 E Malaya St.
21100 E Malta St.
21200 E Nepal St.
21300 E Netherland St.
21400 E Odessa St.
21500 E Orleans St.
21600 E Perth St.
21700 E Picadilly Rd.
21800 E Quatar St.
21900 E Quency St.
22000 E Riviera St.
22100 E Rome St.
22200 E Shawnee St.
22300 E Sicily St.
22400 E Tempe St.
22500 E Tibet St.
22600 E Ukraine St.
22700 E Valdai St.
22800 E Versailles St.
22900 E Wenatchee St.
23000 E Winnipeg St.
23100 E Yakima St.
23200 E Zante St.
23300 E Gun Club Rd.

BROADWAY WEST
0 Broadway
100 W Acoma St.
200 W Bannock St.
300 W Cherokee St.
400 W Delaware St.
500 W Elati St.
600 W Fox St.
700 W Galapago St.
Lakeview St. (Ltln.)
800 W Huron St.
900 W Inca St.
Hickory St. (Ltln.)
1000 W Santa Fe Dr.
Jason St.
Greenwood St. (Ltln.)
1100 W Kalamath St.
Foresthill St. (Ltln.)
1200 W Lipan St.
Gallup St. (Ltln.)
1300 W Mariposa St.
Elmwood St. (Ltln.)
1400 W Navajo St.
Datura St. (Ltln.)
1500 W Osage St.
Cedar St. (Ltln.)
1600 W Pecos St.
Windermere St. (Ltln.)
1700 W Quivas St.
Louthan St. (Ltln.)
1800 W Raritan St.
Crocker St.(Ltln.)
1900 W Shoshone St.
Prescott St. (Ltln.)
2000 W Tejon St.
Spotswood St. (Ltln.)
2100 W Umatilla St.
Bemis St. (Ltln.)
2200 W Vallejo St.
Hill St. (Ltln.)
2300 W Wyandot St.
Sycamore St. (Ltln.)
2350 W Yuma St.
2400 W Zuni St.
Prince St. (Ltln.)
2500 W Alcott St.
Nevada St. (Ltln.)
2550 W Beach Ct.
2600 W Bryant St.
Curtice St. (Ltln.)
2650 W Canosa Ct.
2700 W Clay St.
Rapp St. (Ltln.)
2750 W Dale Ct.
2800 W Decatur St.
2850 W Elm Ct.
2900 W Eliot St.
3000 W Federal Blvd.
3050 W Green Ct.
3100 W Grove St.
3150 W Hazel Ct.
3200 W Hooker St.
3300 W Irving St.
3400 W Julian St.
3450 W Knox Ct.
3500 W King St.
3550 W Linley Ct.
3600 W Lowell Blvd.
3650 W Mabry Ct.
3700 W Mead St.
3800 W Newton St.
3900 W Osceola St.
3950 W Patton Ct.
4000 W Perry St.
4100 W Quitman St.
4200 W Raleigh St.
4300 W Stuart St.
4400 W Tennyson St.
4500 W Utica St.
4600 W Vrain St.
4700 W Winona Ct.
4800 W Wolff St.
4850 W Wolcott Ct.
4900 W Xavier St.
5000 W Yates St.
5100 W Zenobia St.
5150 W Zurich Ct.
5200 W Sheridan Blvd.
5300 W Ames St.
5400 W Benton St.
5500 W Chase St.
5600 W Depew St.
5700 W Eaton St.
5800 W Fenton St.
5900 W Gray St.
6000 W Harlan St.
6100 W Ingalls St.
6200 W Jay St.
6300 W Kendall St.
6400 W Lamar St.
6500 W Marshall St.
6600 W Newland St.
6700 W Otis St.
6800 W Pierce St.
6900 W Quay St.
7000 W Reed St.
7100 W Saulsbury St.
7200 W Teller St.
7300 W Upham St.
7400 W Vance St.
7500 W Webster St.
7600 W Wadsworth Blvd.
7700 W Yukon St.
7800 W Yarrow St.
7900 W Zephyr St.
8000 W Allison St.
8100 W Ammons St.
8200 W Balsam St.
8300 W Brentwood St.
8400 W Carr St.
8500 W Cody St.
8600 W Dover St.
8700 W Dudley St.
8800 W Estes St.
8900 W Everett St.
9000 W Field St.
9100 W Flower St.
9200 W Garrison St.
9300 W Garland St.
9400 W Holland St.
9500 W Hoyt St.
9600 W Independence St.
9700 W Iris St.
9800 W Jellison St.
9900 W Johnson St.
10000 W Kipling St.
10100 W Kline St.
10200 W Lee St.
10300 W Lewis St.
10400 W Miller St.
10500 W Moore St.
10600 W Nelson St.
10700 W Newcombe St.
10800 W Oak St.
10900 W Owens St.
11000 W Parfet St.
11100 W Pierson St.
11200 W Quail St.
11300 W Queen St.
11400 W Robb St.
11500 W Routt St.
11600 W Simms St.
11700 W Swadley St.
11800 W Tabor St.
11900 W Taft St.
12000 W Union Blvd.
12100 W Urban St.
12200 W Van Gordon St.
12300 W Vivian St.
12400 W Ward Rd.
12500 W Welch St.
12500 W Wright St.
12600 W Xenon St.
12700 W Xenophon St.
12800 W Youngfield St.
12900 W Yank St.
13000 W Zang St.
13100 W Zinnia St.
13200 W Alkire St.
13300 W Arbutus St.
13400 W Beech St.
13500 W Braun St.
13600 W Cole St.
13700 W Coors St.
13800 W Deframe St.
13900 W Devinney St.
14000 W Eldridge St.
14100 W Ellis St.
14200 W Fig St.
14300 W Flora St.
14400 W Gardenia St.
14500 W Gladiola St.
14600 W Holman St.
14700 W Howell St.
14800 W Indiana St.
14900 W Isabell St.
15000 W Joyce St.
15100 W Juniper St.
15200 W Kendrick St.
15300 W Kilmer St.
15400 W Loveland St.
15500 W Lupine St.
15600 W McIntyre St.
15700 W Moss St.
15800 W Nile St.
15900 W Norse St.
16000 W Orchard St.
16100 W Orion St.
16200 W Pike St.
16300 W Poppy St.
16400 W Quaker St.
16500 W Quartz St.
16600 W Rogers St.
16700 W Russell St.
16800 W Salvia St.
16900 W Secrest St.
17000 W Terry St.
17100 W Torrey St.
17200 W Ulysses St.
17300 W Utah St.
17400 W Violet St.
17500 W Virgil St.
17600 W Wier St.
17700 W West St.
17800 W Xebec St.
17900 W Xylon St.
18000 W Yankee St.
18100 W Yucca St.
18200 W Zeta St.
18300 W Zircon St.

ELLSWORTH SOUTH
0 Ellsworth Ave
50 S Archer Pl.
100 S Bayaud Ave.
150 S Maple Ave.
200 S Cedar Ave.
250 S Byers Pl.
300 S Alameda Ave.
350 S Nevada Pl.
400 S Dakota Pl.
450 S Alaska Pl.
500 S Virginia Ave.
550 S Custer Pl.
600 S Center Ave.
650 S Gill Pl.
700 S Exposition Ave.
750 S Walsh Pl.
800 S Ohio Ave.
850 S Ada Pl.
900 S Kentucky Ave.
950 S Ford Pl.
1000 S Tennessee Ave.
1100 S Mississippi Ave.
1150 S Mosier Pl.
1200 S Arizona Ave.
1250 S Alabama Pl.
1300 S Louisiana Ave.
1350 S Wyoming Pl.
1400 S Arkansas Ave.
1450 S Idaho Pl.
1500 S Florida Ave.
1550 S Gunnison Pl.
1600 S Iowa Ave.
1650 S Oregon Pl.
1700 S Mexico Ave.
1750 S Montana Pl.
1800 S Colorado Ave.
1850 S Utah Pl.
Bails Pl.
1900 S Jewell Ave.
1950 S Atlantic Pl.
2000 S Asbury Ave.
2050 S Pacific Pl.
2100 S Evans Ave.
2150 S Adriatic Pl.
2200 S Warren Ave.
2250 S Baltic Pl.
2300 S Iliff Ave.
2350 S Caspian Pl.
2400 S Wesley Ave.
2450 S Dickinson Pl.
2500 S Harvard St.
2550 S LaSalle Pl.
Hillside Pl.
2600 S Vassar Ave.
2650 S Villanova Pl.
2700 S Yale Ave.
2750 S Linvale Pl.
2800 S Amherst Ave.
2900 S Bates Ave.
2950 S Bethany Pl.
Bucknell Pl.
3000 S Cornell Ave.
3050 S Colgate Pl.
3100 S Dartmouth Ave.
3150 S Eldorado Pl.
3200 S Eastman Ave.
3300 S Floyd Ave.
3350 S Girton Pl.
3400 S Girard Ave.
3450 S Hamilton Pl.
3500 S Hampden Ave.
3550 S Ithaca Ave.
3600 S Jefferson Ave.
3650 S Jarvis Pl.
3700 S Kenyon Ave.
3750 S Kent Pl.
3800 S Lehigh Ave.
3850 S Milan Pl.
3900 S Mansfield Ave.
4000 S Nassau Ave.
4050 S Navarro Pl.
Napa Pl.
4100 S Oxford Ave.
4150 S Oberlin Pl.
4200 S Princeton Ave.
4250 S Purdue Pl.
4300 S Quincy Ave.
4400 S Radcliff Ave.
4500 S Stanford Ave.
4600 S Tufts Ave.
4700 S Union Ave.
4800 S Layton Ave.
4900 S Chenango Ave.
5000 S Grand Ave.
5100 S Belleview Ave
5200 S Progress Ave.
5300 S Prentice Ave.
5400 S Crestline Ave.
5500 S Berry Ave.
5600 S Powers Ave.
5700 S Dorado Ave.
Littleton Blvd.
Main St. (Ltln.)
5750 S Lilly Ave. (Ltln.)
Lowe Ave. (Ltln.)
5800 S Ida Ave.
5850 S Church Ave. (Ltln.)
Shepherd Ave. (Ltln.)
5900 S Orchard Rd.
Bowles Ave.(Jeffco.)
5950 S Aberdeen Ave. (Ltln.)
6000 S Lake Ave.
6050 S Capri Ave. (Jeffco.)
6100 S Maplewood Ave.
6150 S Park Hill Ave. (Ltln.)
6200 S Fair Ave.
6250 S Arbor Ave. (Ltln.)
6300 S Caley Ave.
6400 S Weaver Ave.
6450 S Longview Ave. (Ltln.)
6500 S Peakview Ave.
6550 S Hoover Ave. (Jeffco.)
6600 S Euclid Ave.
6700 S Arapahoe Rd.
Coal Mine Rd.
(Jeffco.)
6800 S Briarwood Ave.
Ontario Ave. (Jeffco.)
6900 S Costilla Ave.
Plymouth Ave. (Jeffco.)
6950 S Portland Ave. (Jeffco.)
7000 S Davies Ave.
Quarles Ave. (Jeffco.)
7100 S Easter Ave.
Rowland Ave.
7150 S Roxbury Ave.
7200 S Fremont Ave.
7250 S Frost Ave. (Jeffco.)
7300 S Geddes Ave.
7350 S Glasgow Ave. (Jeffco.)
7400 S Hinsdale Ave.
7450 S Indore Ave. (Jeffco.)
7500 S Dry Creek Rd.
Ken Caryl Ave.
7550 S Irish Pl.
7600 S Jamison Ave.
Morraine Ave. (Jeffco.)
7650 S Irwin Pl.
7700 S Kettle Ave.
Fairview Ave. (Jeffco.)
7800 S Long Ave.
Canyon Ave. (Jeffco.)
7900 S Mineral Ave.
Elmhurst Ave. (Jeffco.)
8000 S Nichols Ave.
8100 S Otero Ave.
Clifton Ave. (Jeffco.)
8200 S Phillips Ave.
8300 S County Line Rd.
Chatfield Ave.
(Jeffco.)
8400 S Kingsley Ave.
8500 S San Juan Ave.
Payne Ave. (Jeffco.)
8600 S Teton Ave.
8700 S Ute Ave.
8800 S Vandeventer Ave.
8900 S Weld Ave.
Sabey Ave. (Jeffco.)
9000 S Xapapa Ave.
9100 S Yancey Ave.
9200 S Zebulon Ave.
9300 S Athens Ave.
9350 S Avalon Ave.
9400 S Baden Ave.
9450 S Belfast Ave.
9500 S Cambridge Ave.
9550 S Cannes Ave.
9600 S Danzig Ave.
9650 S Dunklee Ave.
9700 S Eden Ave.
9750 S Edenburg Ave.
9800 S Finland Ave.
9850 S Freiburg Ave.
9900 S Lincoln Ave.
9950 S Greenwich Ave.
10000 S Hamburg Ave.

ELLSWORTH NORTH
0 Ellsworth Ave.
50 Irvington Pl.
100 1st Ave.
200 2nd Ave.
300 3rd Ave.
400 4th Ave.
450 Short Pl.
500 5th Ave.
600 6th Ave.
700 7th Ave.
750 Severn Pl.
800 8th Ave.
850 Barberry Pl.
900 9th Ave.
950 Mulberry Pl.
1000 10th Ave.
1100 11th Ave.
1150 Richthofen Pl.
1200 12th Ave.
1250 Holden Pl.
1300 13th Ave.
1350 Howard Pl.
1400 14th Ave.
1500 Colfax Ave.
1550 Conejos Pl.
1600 16th Ave.
1650 Annie Pl.
Batavia Pl.
1700 17th Ave.
1800 18th Ave.
1900 19th Ave.
2000 20th Ave.
Montview Blvd.
2100 21st Ave.
2200 22nd Ave.
2300 23rd Ave.
2400 24th Ave.
2450 Byron Pl.
2500 25th Ave.
2600 26th Ave.
2700 27th Ave.
2800 28th Ave.
2900 29th Ave.
2950 Hayward Pl.
3000 30th Ave.
3050 Caithness Pl.
3100 31st Ave.
3150 Argyle Pl.
3200 32nd Ave.
Martin Luther King Dr.
3250 Thrill Pl.
Moncrieff Pl.
3300 33rd Ave.
3400 34th Ave.
3500 35th Ave.
Bruce Randolph Ave.
3600 36th Ave.
3700 37th Ave.
3750 Clyde Pl.
3800 38th Ave.
3860 Denver Pl.
3900 39th Ave.
4000 40th Ave.
4100 41st Ave.
4200 42nd Ave.
4250 Mitchell Pl.
4300 43rd Ave.
4350 Kelly Pl.
4400 44th Ave.
4500 45th Ave.
4550 Scott Pl.
Chaffee Pl.
4600 46th Ave.
4650 Alice Pl.
Steavenson Pl.
4700 47th Ave.
4750 Warner Pl.
Elk Pl.
4800 48th Ave.
4850 Elgin Pl.
4900 49th Ave.
4950 Beekman Pl.
5000 50th Ave.
5050 Stoll Pl.
5100 51st Ave.
5150 Burlington Pl.
5200 52nd Ave.
5300 53rd Ave.
5350 Elmendorf Pl.
5400 54th Ave.
5500 55th Ave.
5550 Randolph Pl.
Moffat Pl.
5600 56th Ave.
5700 57th Ave.
5800 58th Ave.
Ralston Rd.
5900 59th Ave.
6000 60th Ave.
6100 61st Ave.
6200 62nd Ave.
6300 63rd Ave.
6400 64th Ave.
6500 65th Ave.
6600 66th Ave.
6700 67th Ave.
6800 68th Ave.
6900 69th Ave.
7000 70th Ave.
7100 71st Ave.
7200 72nd Ave.
7300 73rd Ave.
7400 74th Ave.
7500 75th Ave.
7600 76th Ave.
7700 77th Ave.
7800 78th Ave.
7900 79th Ave.
8000 80th Ave.
8100 81st Ave.
8200 82nd Ave.
8300 83rd Ave.
8400 84th Ave.
8500 85th Ave.
8600 86th Ave.
8700 87th Ave.
8800 88th Ave.
8900 89th Ave.
9000 90th Ave.
9100 91st Ave.
9200 92nd Ave.
9300 93rd Ave.
9400 94th Ave.
9500 95th Ave.
9600 96th Ave.
9700 97th Ave.
9800 98th Ave.
9900 99th Ave.
10000 100th Ave.
10100 101st Ave.
10200 102nd Ave.
10300 103rd Ave.
10400 104th Ave.
10500 105th Ave.
10600 106th Ave.
10700 107th Ave.
10800 108th Ave.
10900 109th Ave.
11000 110th Ave.
11100 111th Ave.
11200 112th Ave.
11300 113th Ave.
11400 114th Ave.
11500 115th Ave.
11600 116th Ave.
11700 117th Ave.
11800 118th Ave.
11900 119th Ave.
12000 120th Ave.
12100 121st Ave.
12200 122nd Ave.
12300 123rd Ave.
12400 124th Ave.
12500 125th Ave.
12600 126th Ave.
12700 127th Ave.
12800 128th Ave.
Henderson Rd.
12900 129th Ave.
13000 130th Ave.
13100 131st Ave.
13200 132nd Ave.
13300 133rd Ave.
13400 134th Ave.
13500 135th Ave.
13600 136th Ave.
13700 137th Ave.
13800 138th Ave.
13900 139th Ave.
14000 140th Ave.
14100 141st Ave.
14200 142nd Ave.
14300 143rd Ave.
14400 144th Ave.
14500 145th Ave.
14600 146th Ave.
14700 147th Ave.
14800 148th Ave.
14900 149th Ave.
15000 150th Ave.
15100 151st Ave.
15200 152nd Ave.
Bromley Ln. (Brn.)
15300 153rd Ave.
15400 154th Ave.
15500 155th Ave.
15600 156th Ave.
15700 157th Ave.
15800 158th Ave.
15900 159th Ave.
16000 160th Ave.
Bridge St. (Brn.)
16100 161st Ave.
16200 162nd Ave.
16300 163rd Ave.
16400 164th Ave.
16500 165th Ave.
16600 166th Ave.
16700 167th Ave.
16800 168th Ave.
County Line Rd.

DOWNTOWN NAMED
From Colfax & Broadway
100 Cheyenne Pl.
200 Cleveland Pl.
300 Court Pl.
400 Tremont Pl.
500 Glenarm Pl.
600 Welton
700 California
800 Stout
900 Champa
1000 Curtis
1100 Arapahoe
1200 Lawrence
1300 Larimer
1400 Market
Walnut
1500 Blake
1600 Wazee
1700 Wynkoop
1800 Wewatta
Brighton Blvd.
1900 Delgany
2000 Chestnut Pl.
2100 Bassett
2300 Water
2400 Platte
2500 Central
2600 Boulder
2700 Erie

DOWNTOWN NUMBERED
500 5th St.
600 6th St.
700 7th St.
800 8th St.
900 9th St.
1100 11th St.
1200 12th St.
1300 13th St.
1400 14th St.
1500 15th St.
1600 16th St. (Bus Mall)
1700 17th St.
1800 18th St.
1900 19th St.
2000 20th St.
2100 21st St.
2200 22nd St.
2300 23rd St.
Park Ave.
2400 24th St.
2500 25th St.
2600 26th St.
2700 27th St.
2800 28th St.
2900 29th St.
3000 30th St.
3100 31st St.
3200 32nd St.
3300 33rd St.
3400 34th St.
3500 35th St.
3600 36th St.
3800 38th St.
3900 39th St.
4000 40th St.
4300 43rd St.
4400 44th St.

Avenues & Places run East - West

METRO DENVER ALPHABETICAL LISTING
Includes Brighton (Brn), Broomfield (Brm) & Golden (Gln)

Aberdeen Ave 5950 S (Lltn)
Abilene St 13800 E
Acoma St 100 W
Ada Pl 850 S
Adams St 3300 E
Adriatic Pl 2150 S
Agate St 200 W (Brm)
Akron St 9000 E
Alabama Pl 1250 S
Alameda Ave 300 S
Alamo Ave 5700 S (Lltn)
Alaska Pl 450 S
Albion St 4100 E
Alcott St 2500 W
Alice Pl 4650
Alkire St 13200 W
Allison St 8000 W
Alton St 9100 E
Altura Blvd 14900 E
Ames St 5300 W
Amherst Ave 2800 S
Ammons St 8100 W
Andes St 18600 E
Annie Pl 1650
Arapahoe 1100 (Dntwn)
Arapahoe Rd 6700 E
Arapahoe St 900 (Gln)
Arbor Ave 6250 S (Lltn)
Arbutus St 13300 W
Archer Pl 50 S
Archer St 400 (Gln)
Argonne St 18700 E
Argyle Pl 3150
Arizona Ave 1200 S
Arkansas Ave 1400 S
Asbury Ave 2000 S
Ash St 4200 E
Ash St 1000 E (Brm)
Aspen St 1100 E (Brm)
Atchison St 13900 E
Athens Ave 9300 S
Atlantic Pl 1950 S
Avalon Ave 9350 S
Baden Ave 9400 S
Bahama St 18800 E
Bails Pl 1850 S
Balsam St 8200 W
Baltic Pl 2250 S
Bannock St 200 W
Barberry Pl 850
Basalt Ct 200 E (Brm)
Bassett 2100
Batavia Pl 1650
Bates Ave 2900 S
Bayaud Ave 100 S
Beach Ct 2550 W
Beech St 13400 W
Beekman Pl 4950
Beeler St 9200 E
Belfast Ave 9450 S
Bellaire St 4300 E
Bellaire St 1200 E (Brm)
Belleview Ave 5100 S
Bemis St 2100 W (Lltn)
Benton St 5400 W
Berry Ave 5500 S
Beryl St 300 W (Brm)
Bethany Pl 2950 S
Billings St 14000 E
Birch St 4400 E
Birch St 1600 (Gln)
Birch St 1300 E (Brm)
Birdie Rd 800 E (Brm)
Biscay St 18900 E
Blackhawk St 14100 E
Blake 1500 (Dntwn)
Boston St 9300 E
Boulder 2600 (Dntwn)
Bowles Ave 5900 S (Jeffco)
Braun St 13500 W
Brentwood St 8300 W
Briarwood Ave 6800 W
Bridge St 0 (Brn)
Brighton Blvd 1800 (Dntwn)
Brighton St 200 N (Brn)
Broadway 0
Bromley Ln 800 S (Brn)
Bruce Randolph Ave 3500
Bryant St 2600 W
Buckley Rd 16900 E
Bucknell Pl 2950 S
Burlington Pl 5150
Bush St 100 S (Brn)
Byers Pl 250 S
Byron Pl 2450
Caithness Pl 3050
Caley Ave 6300 S
California 700 (Dntwn)
Cambridge Ave 9500 S
Campus Rd 1500 (Gln)
Cannes Ave 9550 S
Canosa Ct 2650 W
Canyon Ave 7800 S (Jeffco)
Capri Ave 6050 S (Jeffco)
Carr St 8400 W
Carson St 14200 E
Carter St 200 (Gln)
Caspian Pl 2350 S
Cathay St 19000 E
Cedar Ave 200 S
Cedar St 1400 E (Brm)
Cedar St 1500 W (Lltn)
Center Ave 600 S
Central 2500 (Dntwn)
Ceylon St 19100 E
Chaffee Pl 4550
Chambers Rd 15300 E
Champa 900 (Dntwn)
Chase St 5500 W
Chatfield Ave 8300 S (Jeffco)
Chenango Ave 4900 S
Cherokee St 300 W
Cherry St 4600 E
Chester St 9400 E
Chestnut 2000 (Dntwn)
Cheyenne Pl 100 (Dntwn)
Cheyenne St 1000 (Gln)
Church Ave 5850 S (Lltn)
Clarkson St 800 E
Clay St 2700 W
Clayton St 2700 E
Clermont St 4500 E
Cleveland Pl 200 (Dntwn)
Clifton Ave 8100 S (Jeffco)
Clinton St 9500 E
Clubhurst Dr 500 E (Brm)
Clyde Pl 3750
Coal Mine Rd 6700 S (Jeffco)
Cody St 8500 W
Cole St 13600 W
Colfax Ave 1500
Colgate Pl 3050 S
Colorado Ave 1800 S
Colorado Blvd 4000 E
Columbia Pl 3050 S
Columbine St 2500 E
Conejos Pl 1550
Cook St 3400 E
Coors St 13700 W
Coral St 400 W (Brm)
Cornell Ave 3000 S
Corona St 1100 E
Costilla Ave 6900 S
Cottonwood St 1500 E (Brm)
County Line Rd 8300 S
Court Pl 300 (Dntwn)
Court Pl 50 S (Brn)
Crawford St 100 (Gln)
Crestline Ave 5400 S
Crocker St 1800 W (Lltn)
Crystal St 14300 E
Curtice St 2600 W (Lltn)
Curtis 1000 (Dntwn)
Custer Pl 550 S
Dahlia St 4800 E
Dakota Ave 400 S
Dale Ct 2750 W
Dallas St 9600 E
Danube St 19200 E
Danzig Ave 9600 S
Daphne St 500 W (Brm)
Dartmouth Ave 3100 S
Datura St 1400 W (Lltn)
Davies Ave 7000 S
Dayton St 9700 E
Dearborn St 14600 E
Decatur St 2800 W
Deframe St 13800 W
Delaware St 400 W
Delgany 1900 (Dntwn)
Denver Pl 3850
Denver St 400 N (Brn)
Depew St 5600 W
Detroit St 2800 E
Devinney St 13900 W
Dexter St 4700 E
Dexter St 1600 E (Brm)
Dickinson Pl 2450 S
Dillon St 14400 E
Dorado Ave 5700 S
Dover St 8600 W
Dover St 1700 E (Brm)
Downing St 1200 E
Dry Creek Rd 7500 S
Dudley St 8700 W
Dunkirk St 19300 E
Dunklee Ave 9650 S
Eagle Rd 700 E (Brm)
Eagle St 14700 E
East St 500 (Gln)
Easter Ave 7100 S
Eastman Ave 3200 S
Eaton St 5700 W
Eden Ave 9700 S
Edenburg Ave 9750 S
Egbert St 200 S (Brn)
Elati St 500 W
Eldorado Pl 3150 S
Eldridge St 14000 W
Elgin Pl 4850
Eliot St 2900 W
Elizabeth St 2600 E
Elk Pl 4750
Elkhart St 14800 E
Ellis St 14100 W
Ellsworth Ave 0
Elm Ct 2850 W
Elm St 5000 E
Elm St 1300 (Gln)
Elmendorf Pl 5350
Elmhurst Ave 7900 S (Jeffco)
Elmira St 9900 E
Elmwood St 1800 E (Brm)
Elmwood St 1300 W (Lltn)
Emerald St 600 W (Brm)
Emerson St 900 E
Emporia St 9800 E
Ensenada St 19400 E
Erie 2700 (Dntwn)
Espana St 19500 E
Estes St 8800 W
Euclid Ave 6600 S
Eudora St 4900 E
Evans Ave 2100 S
Everett St 8900 W
Exposition Ave 700 S
Fair Ave 6200 S
Fairfax St 5100 E
Fairplay St 15000 E
Fairview Ave 7700 S (Jeffco)
Federal Blvd 3000 W
Fenton St 5800 W
Field St 9000 W
Fig St 14200 W
Filbert Ct 5050 E
Fillmore St 2900 E
Finland Ave 9800 S
Flamingo Ct 5150 E
Flanders St 19600 E
Flint Way 700 W (Brm)
Flora St 14300 W
Florence St 10000 E
Florida Ave 1500 S
Flower St 9100 W
Floyd Ave 3300 S
Ford Pl 950 S
Ford St 600 (Gln)
Forest St 5200 E
Foresthill St 1100 W (Lltn)
Fox St 600 W
Franklin St 1600 E
Fraser St 15100 E
Freiburg Ave 9850 S
Fremont Ave 7200 S
Frost Ave 7250 S (Jeffco)
Fulton St 10100 E
Fundy St 19700 E
Galapago St 700 W
Galena St 10200 E
Gallup St 1200 W (Lltn)
Gardenia St 14400 W
Garfield St 3700 E
Garland St 9300 W
Garnet St 800 W (Brm)
Garrison St 9200 W
Gaylord St 2200 E
Geddes Ave 7300 S
Geneva St 10300 E
Genoa St 19800 E
Gibralter St 19900 E
Gill Pl 650 S
Gilpin St 1700 E
Girard Ave 3400 S
Girton Pl 3350 S
Givens 0 (Gln)
Gladiola St 14500 W
Glasgow Ave 7350 S (Jeffco)
Glenarm Pl 500 (Dntwn)
Glencoe St 5300 E
Granby St 15200 E
Grand Ave 5000 S
Grant St 300 E
Grape St 5400 E
Gray St 5900 W
Great Western Rd 0 (Brn)
Green Ct 3050 W
Greenwich Ave 9950 S
Greenwood St 1000 W (Lltn)
Grove St 3100 W
Gun Club Rd 23300 E
Gunnison Pl 1550 S
Halifax St 20000 E
Hamburg Ave 10000 S
Hamilton Pl 3450 S
Hampden Ave 3500 S
Hannibal St 15400 E
Hanover St 10400 E
Harlan St 6000 W
Harrison St 3900 E
Harvard St 2500 S
Havana St 10500 E
Hayward Pl 2950
Hazel Ct 3150 W
Helena St 15500 E
Hemlock St 900 W (Brm)
Henderson Rd 12800
Hickory St 900 W (Lltn)
High St 1900 E
Hill St 2200 W (Lltn)
Hillside Pl 2550 S
Himalaya St 20100 E
Hinsdale Ave 7400 S
Holden Pl 1250
Holland St 9400 W
Holly St 5600 E
Holman St 14600 W
Hooker St 3200 W
Hoover Ave 6550 S (Jeffco)
Howard Pl 1350
Howell St 14700 W
Hoyt St 9500 W
Hudson St 5500 E
Humboldt St 1500 E
Huron St 800 W
Ida Ave 5800 W
Idaho Pl 1450 S
Idalia St 15600 E
Iliff Ave 2300 S
Illinois St 1100 (Gln)
Inca St 900 W
Independence St 9600 W
Indiana St 14800 W
Indore Ave 7450 S (Jeffco)
Ingalls St 6100 W
Iola St 10600 E
Iowa Ave 1600 S
Iran St 20200 E
Ireland St 20300 E
Iris St 9700 W
Iris St 1000 W (Brm)
Irish Pl 7550 S
Ironton St 10700 E
Irving St 3300 W
Irvington Pl 50
Irwin Pl 7650 S
Isabell St 14900 W
Ithaca Ave 3550 S
Ivanhoe St 5700 E
Ivy St 5800 E
Jackson St 3800 E
Jackson St 700 (Gln)
Jade St 1100 W (Brm)
Jamaica St 10800 E
Jamison Ave 7600 S
Jarvis Pl 3650 S
Jasmine St 6000 E
Jason St 1000 W
Jasper St 15700 E
Jay St 6200 W
Jebel St 20400 E
Jefferson Ave 3600 S
Jellison St 9800 W
Jericho St 20500 E
Jersey St 5900 E
Jessup St 600 S (Brn)
Jewell Ave 1900 S
Johnson St 9900 W
Joliet St 10900 E
Jones Rd 1400 (Gln)
Joplin St 15800 E
Josephine St 2400 E
Joyce St 15000 W
Julian St 3400 W
Juniper St 15100 W
Kalamath St 1100 W
Kalispell St 15900 E
Kearney St 6100 E
Kelly Pl 4350
Ken Caryl Ave 7500 S (Jeffco)
Kendall St 6300 W
Kendrick St 15200 W
Kent Pl 3750 S
Kenton St 11000 E
Kentucky Ave 900 S
Kenyon Ave 3700 S
Kettle Ave 7700 S
Killarney St 20600 E
Kilmer St 15300 W
King St 3500 W
Kingsley Ave 8400 S
Kingston St 11100 E
Kipling St 10000 W
Kirk St 20700 E
Kittredge St 16000 E
Kline St 10100 W
Knox Ct 3450 W
Kohl St 1200 W (Brm)
Krameria St 6200 E
La Salle Pl 2550 S
Lafayette St 1400 E
Lake Ave 6000 S
Lakeview St 700 W (Lltn)
Lamar St 6400 W
Lansing St 11200 E
Laredo St 16100 E
Larimer 1300 (Dntwn)
Laurel St 1300 W (Brm)
Laurel St 500 S (Brn)
Lawrence 1200 (Dntwn)
Layton Ave 4800 S
Lee St 10200 W
Lehigh Ave 3800 S
Lewis St 10300 W
Lewiston St 16200 E
Leyden St 6300 E
Lilly Ave 5750 S (Lltn)
Lima St 11300 E
Lincoln Ave 9900 S
Lincoln St 100 E
Linden Ct 6350 E
Linley Ct 3550 W
Linvale Pl 2750 S
Lipan St 1200 W
Lisbon St 20800 E
Littleton blvd 5700 S
Liverpool St 20900 E
Locust St 6400 E
Logan St 400 E
Long Ave 7800 S
Longspeak St 300 N (Brm)
Longview Ave 6450 S (Lltn)
Louisiana Ave 1300 S
Louthan St 1700 W (Lltn)
Loveland St 15400 W
Lowe Ave 5750 S (Lltn)
Lowell Blvd 3600 W
Lupine St 15500 W
Mabry Ct 3650 W
Macon St 11400 E
Madison St 3500 E
Magnolia St 6600 E
Main St 100 W; 100 E (Brm)
Main St 150 E (Brn)
Main St 5700 S (Lltn)
Malaya St 21000 E
Malta St 21100 E
Mansfield Ave 3900 S
Maple Ave 150 S
Maple St 1200 (Gln)
Maplewood Ave 6100 S
Marble St 1400 W (Brm)
Marion St 1300 E
Mariposa St 1300 W
Market 1400 (Dntwn)
Marshall St 6500 W
Martin Luther King Blvd 3200
Mather St 400 S (Brn)
McIntyre St 15600 W
Mead St 3700 W
Memphis St 16300 E
Mexico Ave 1700 S
Midland St 500 N (Brn)
Midway Blvd 500 N (Brm)
Milan Pl 3850 S
Miller St 10400 W
Milwaukee St 3000 E
Mineral Ave 7900 S
Miramonte Blvd 1200 N (Brm)
Mississippi Ave 1100 S
Mitchell Pl 4250
Mobile St 16400 E
Moffat Pl 5550
Moline St 11500 E
Monaco Pkwy 6500 E
Moncrieff Pl 3250
Monroe St 3600 E
Montana Pl 1750 S
Montview Blvd 2000
Moore St 10500 W
Morraine Ave 7600 S (Jeffco)
Mosier Pl 1150 S
Moss St 15700 W
Mulberry Pl 950
Myrtle St 150 N (Brn)
Napa Pl 4050 S
Nassau Ave 4000 S
Navajo St 1400 W
Navarro Pl 4050 S
Nelson St 10600 W
Nepal St 21200 E
Netherland St 21300 E
Nevada Pl 350 S
Nevada St 2500 W (Lltn)
Newark St 11600 E
Newcombe St 10700 W
Newland St 6600 W
Newport St 6800 E
Newton St 3800 W
Niagara St 6700 E
Nichols Ave 8000 S
Nickel St 1500 W (Brm)
Nile St 15800 W
Nome St 11700 E
Norfolk St 16500 E
Norse St 15900 W
Nucla St 16600 E
Oak St 10800 W
Oakhurst Dr 400 E (Brm)
Oakland St 11800 E
Oberlin Pl 4150 S
Odessa St 21400 E
Odgen St 1000 E
Ohio Ave 800 S
Olathe St 16700 E
Olive St 7000 E
Oneida St 6900 E
Ontario Ave 6800 S (Jeffco)
Opal Way 1600 W (Brm)
Orchard Rd 5900 S
Orchard St 16000 W
Oregon Pl 1650 S
Orion St 16100 W
Orleans St 21500 E
Osage St 1500 W
Osceola St 3900 W
Oswego St 11900 E
Otero Ave 8100 S
Otis St 6700 W
Ouray St 16800 E
Owens St 10900 W
Oxford Ave 4100 S
Pacific Pl 2050 S
Pagosa St 17000 E
Par Rd 900 E (Brm)
Parfet St 11000 W
Paris St 12000 E
Park Ave 2300 (Dntwn)
Park Hill Ave 6150 S
Patton Ct 3950 W
Payne Ave 8500 S (Jeffco)
Peakview Ave 6500 S
Pearl St 600 E
Pecos St 1600 W
Pennsylvania St 500 E
Peoria St 12100 E
Perry St 4000 W
Perth St 21600 E
Phillips Ave 8200 S
Picadilly Rd 21700 E
Pierce St 6800 W
Pierson St 11100 W
Pike St 16200 W
Pitkin St 17100 E
Platte 2400 (Dntwn)
Plymouth Ave 6900 S (Jeffco)
Pontiac St 7100 E
Poplar St 7200 E
Poppy St 16300 W
Poppy Way 1700 W (Brm)
Portland Ave 6950 S (Jeffco)
Potomac St 13750 E
Powers Ave 5600 S
Prentice Ave 5300 S
Prescott St 1900 W (Lltn)
Prince St 2400 W (Lltn)
Princeton Ave 4200 S
Progress Ave 5200 S
Purdue Pl 4250 S
Quail St 11200 W
Quaker St 16400 W
Quari St 12200 E
Quarles Ave 7000 S (Jeffco)
Quartz St 16500 W
Quartz Way 1800 W (Brm)
Quatar St 21800 E
Quay St 6900 W
Quebec St 7300 E
Queen St 11300 W
Quency St 21900 E
Quentin St 12300 E
Quince St 7400 E
Quincy Ave 4300 S
Quintero St 17200 E
Quitman St 4100 W
Quivas St 1700 W
Race St 2000 E
Racine St 12400 E
Radcliff Ave 4400 S
Raleigh St 4200 W
Ralston Rd 5800
Randolph Pl 5550
Rapp St 2700 W (Lltn)
Raritan St 1800 W
Reed St 7000 W
Revere St 12500 E
Richfield St 17300 E
Richthofen Pl 1150
Rifle St 17400 E
Riviera St 22000 E
Robb St 11400 W
Robin St 600 N (Brn)
Rogers St 16600 W
Rome St 22100 E
Rosemary St 7600 E
Roslyn St 7500 E
Routt St 11500 W
Rowland Ave 7100 S
Roxbury Ave 7150 S
Russell St 16700 W
Sabey Ave 8900 S (Jeffco)
Sable Blvd 14500 E
Salem St 12600 E
Salida St 17500 E
Salvia St 16800 W
San Juan Ave 8500 S
Santa Fe Dr 1000 W
Saulsbury St 7100 W
Scott Pl 4550
Scranton St 12700 E
Secrest St 16900 W
Sedalia St 17600 E
Severn Pl 750
Shawnee St 22200 E
Shepherd Ave 5850 S (Lltn)
Sheridan Blvd 5200 W
Sherman St 200 E
Short Pl 450
Shoshone St 1900 W
Sicily St 22300 E
Simms St 11600 W
Skeel St 300 S (Brn)
Southern St 450 S (Brn)
Spotswood St 2000 W (Lltn)
Spruce St 7800 E
St. Andrews Dr 600 E (Brn)
St. Paul St 3100 E
Stanford Ave 4500 S
Steavenson Pl 4650
Steele St 3200 E
Stoll Pl 5050
Stout 800 (Dntwn)
Strong St 50 N (Brn)
Stuart St 4300 W
Swadley St 11700 W
Sycamore St 2300 W (Lltn)
Syracuse St 7700 E
Table Dr 300 (Gln)
Tabor St 11800 W
Taft St 11900 W
Tamarac St 8000 E
Tejon St 2000 W
Teller St 7200 W
Telluride Ct 300 E (Brm)
Telluride St 17700 E
Tempe St 22400 E
Tennessee Ave 1000 S
Tennyson St 4400 W
Terry St 17000 W
Teton Ave 8600 S
Thrill Pl 3250
Tibet St 22500 E
Torrey St 17100 W
Tower Rd 18500 E
Tremont Pl 400 (Dntwn)
Trenton St 7900 E
Troy St 12800 E
Truckee St 17800 E
Tufts Ave 4600 S
Tucson St 12900 E
U.S. Hwy 6 1700 E (Gln)
U.S. Hwy 287 1900 W (Brm)
Uinta St 8200 E
Ukraine St 22600 E
Ulster St 8100 E
Ulysses St 17200 W
Umatilla St 2100 W
Union Ave 4700 S
Union Blvd 12000 W
University 2350 E
Upham St 7300 W
Uravan St 17900 E
Urban St 12100 W
Ursula St 13000 E
Utah Pl 1850 S
Utah St 17300 W
Ute Ave 8700 S
Utica St 4500 W
Uvalda St 13100 E
Valdai St 22700 E
Valentia St 8300 E
Vallejo St 2200 W
Van Gordon St 12200 W
Vance St 7400 W
Vandeventer Ave 8800 S
Vasquez St 300 (Gln)
Vassar Ave 2600 S
Vaughn St 13200 E
Ventura St 18000 E
Verbena St 8400 E
Vernon St 400 (Gln)
Versailles St 22800 E
Victor St 13300 E
Villanova Pl 2650 S
Vine St 2100 E
Violet St 17400 W
Virgil St 17500 W
Virginia Ave 500 S
Vivian St 12300 W
Voiles St 700 S (Brn)
Vrain St 4600 W
Wabash St 8500 E
Waco St 18100 E
Wadsworth Blvd 7600 W
Walden St 18200 E
Walnut 1400 (Dntwn)
Walnut St 100 N (Brn)
Walsh Pl 750 S
Warner Pl 4750
Warren Ave 2200 S
Washington 800 (Gln)
Washington St 700 E
Water 2300 (Dntwn)
Wazee 1600 (Dntwn)
Weaver Ave 6400 S
Webster St 7500 W
Welch St 12400 W
Weld Ave 8900 S
Welton 600 (Dntwn)
Wenatchee St 22900 E
Wesley Ave 2400 S
West St 17700 W
Wewatta 1800 (Dntwn)
Wheeling St 13400 E
Wier St 17600 W
Williams St 1800 E
Willow St 8600 E
Windermere St 1600 W (Lltn)
Winnipeg St 23000 E
Winona Ct 4700 W
Wolcott Ct 4850 W
Wolff St 4800 W
Worchester St 13500 E
Wright St 12500 W
Wyandot St 2300 W
Wynkoop 1700 (Dntwn)
Wyoming Pl 1350 S
Xanadu St 13600 E
Xanthia St 8700 E
Xapapa Ave 9000 S
Xapary St 13700 E
Xavier St 4900 W
Xenia St 8800 E
Xenon St 12600 W
Xenophon St 12700 W
Xylon St 17900 W
Yakima St 23100 E
Yale Ave 2700 S
Yampa St 18300 E
Yancey Ave 9100 S
Yank St 12900 W
Yankee St 18000 W
Yarrow St 7800 W
Yates St 5000 W
York St 2300 E
Yosemite St 8900 E
Yost St 13800 E
Youngfield St 12800 W
Yuba St 13900 E
Yucca St 18100 W
Yukon St 7700 W
Yuma St 2350 W
Zang St 13000 W
Zante St 23200 E
Zebulon Ave 9200 S
Zeno St 18400 E
Zenobia St 5100 W
Zephyr St 7900 W
Zeta St 18200 W
Zinnia St 13100 W
Zion St 14000 E
Zircon St 18300 W
Zuni St 2400 W
Zurich Ave 9250 S
Zurich Ct 5150 W

BRIGHTON STREETS

BRIDGE ST. NORTH

0 Bridge St
50 Strong St
100 Walnut St
150 Myrtle St
200 Brighton St
300 Longspeak St
400 Denver St
500 Midland St
600 Robin St

BRIDGE ST. SOUTH

0 Bridge St
50 Court Pl
100 Bush St
200 Egbert St
300 Skeel St
400 Mather St
450 Southern St
500 Laurel St
600 Jessup St
700 Voiles St
800 Bromley Ln

GREAT WESTERN RD. EAST

0 Great Western Rd
100 1st Ave
150 Main St
200 2nd Ave
300 3rd Ave
400 4th Ave
500 5th Ave
600 6th Ave
700 7th Ave
800 8th Ave
900 9th Ave
1000 10th Ave
1100 11th Ave
1200 12th Ave
1300 13th Ave
1400 14th Ave
1500 15th Ave
1600 16th Ave
1700 17th Ave
1800 18th Ave
1900 19th Ave
2000 20th Ave
2100 21st Ave
2200 22nd Ave

GOLDEN STREETS

GIVENS ST. WEST

0 Givens
100 Crawford St
200 Carter St
300 Vazquez St - Table Dr
400 Archer St - Vernon St
500 East St
600 Ford St
700 Jackson St
800 Washington St
900 Arapahoe St
1000 Illinois St
1200 Maple St
1300 Elm St
1400 Jones Rd
1500 Campus Rd
1600 Birch St
Hwy 6

IOWA ST. SOUTH

0 Iowa St
100 1st St
200 2nd St
300 3rd St
400 4th St
500 5th St
600 6th St
700 7th St
800 8th St
900 9th St
1000 10th St
1100 11th St
1200 12th St
1300 13th St
1400 14th St
1500 15th St
1600 16th St
1700 17th St
1800 18th St
1900 19th St
2000 20th St
2100 21st St
2200 22nd St
2300 23rd St
2400 24th St

Streets & Courts run North - South

▲ See Northern Colorado Atlas ▲

▲ See Map 704 ▲

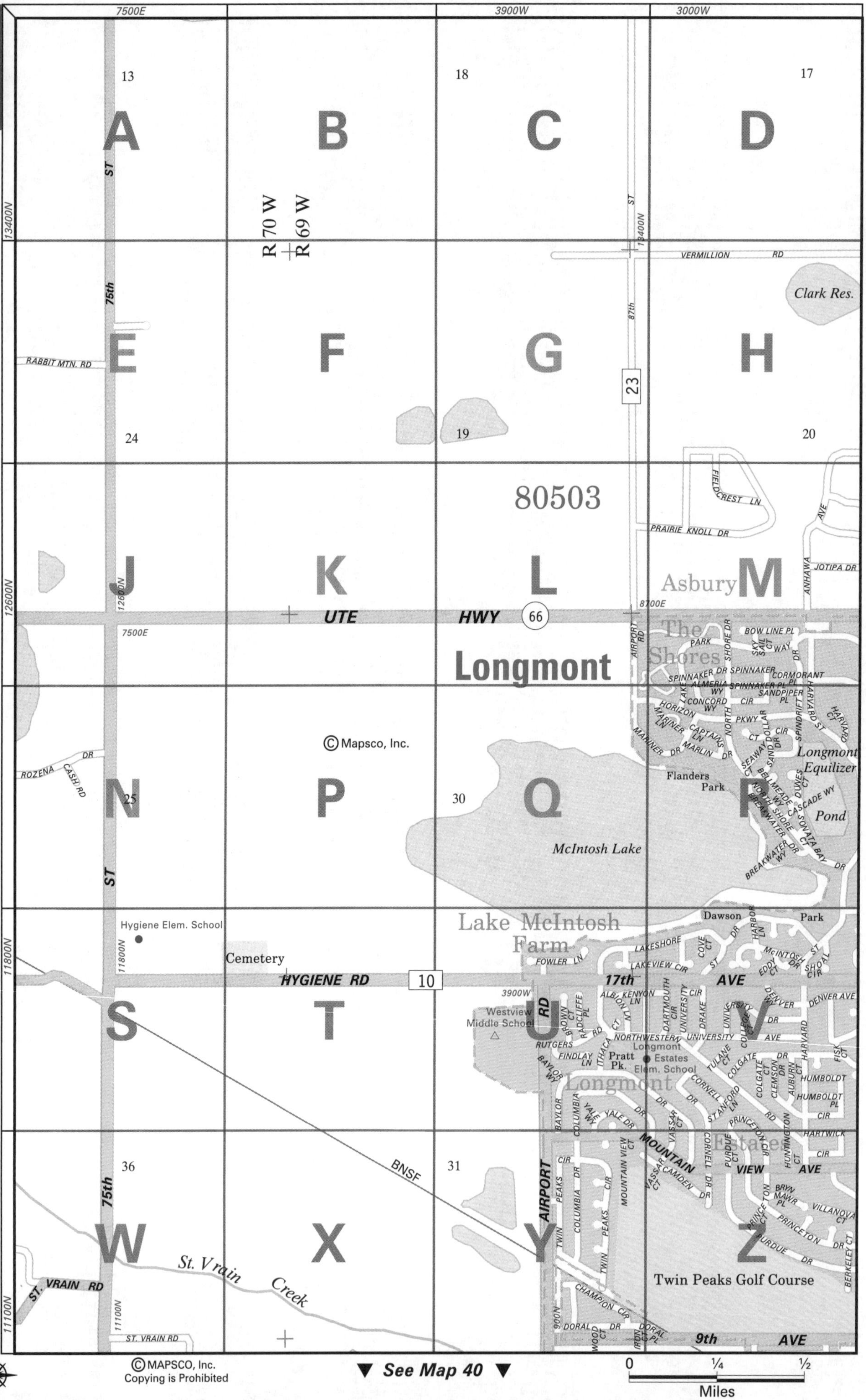

▼ See Map 40 ▼

▲ See Northern Colorado Atlas ▲

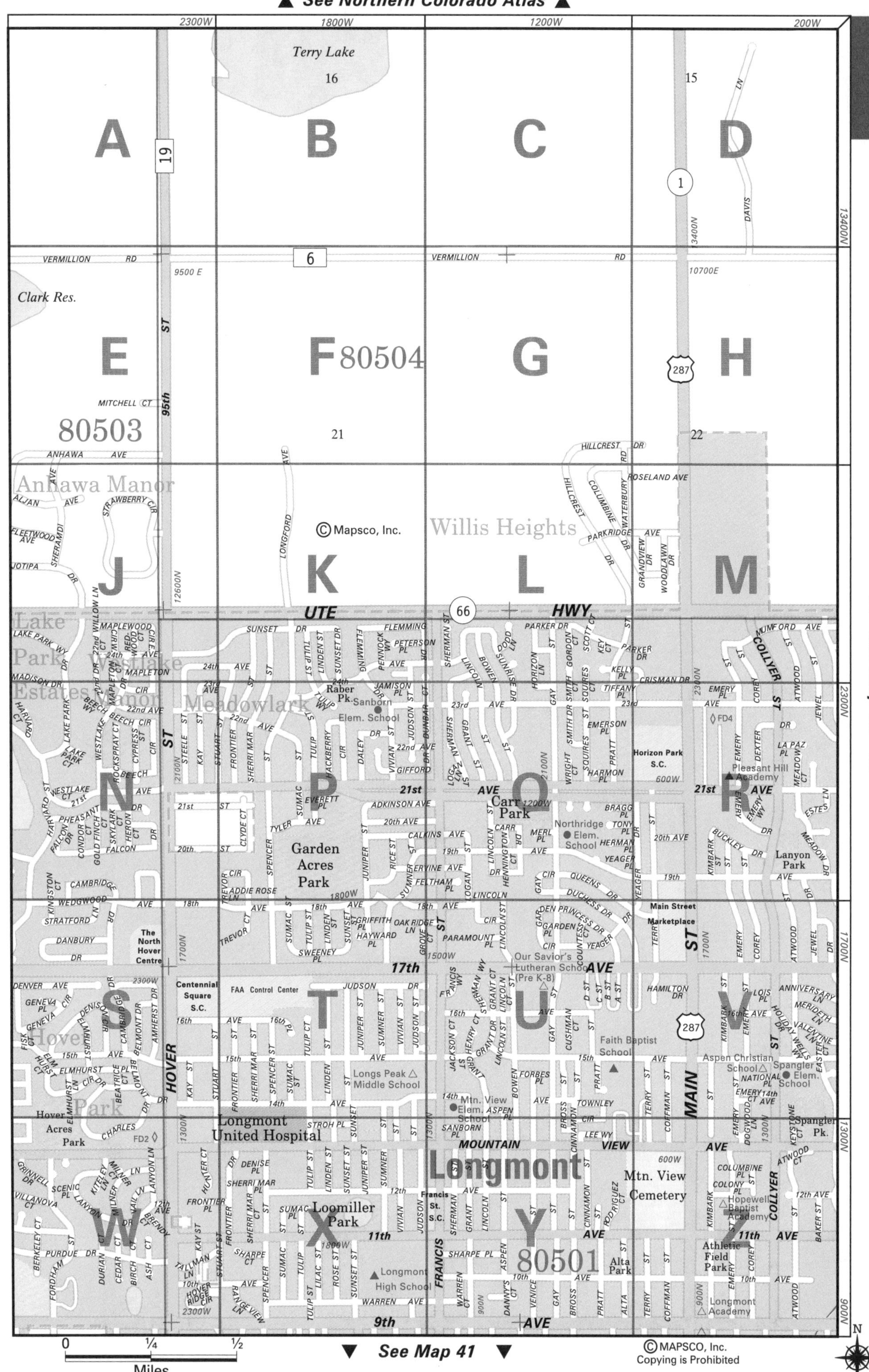

See Map 12

▼ See Map 41 ▼

▲ See Northern Colorado Atlas ▲

◄ See Map 11

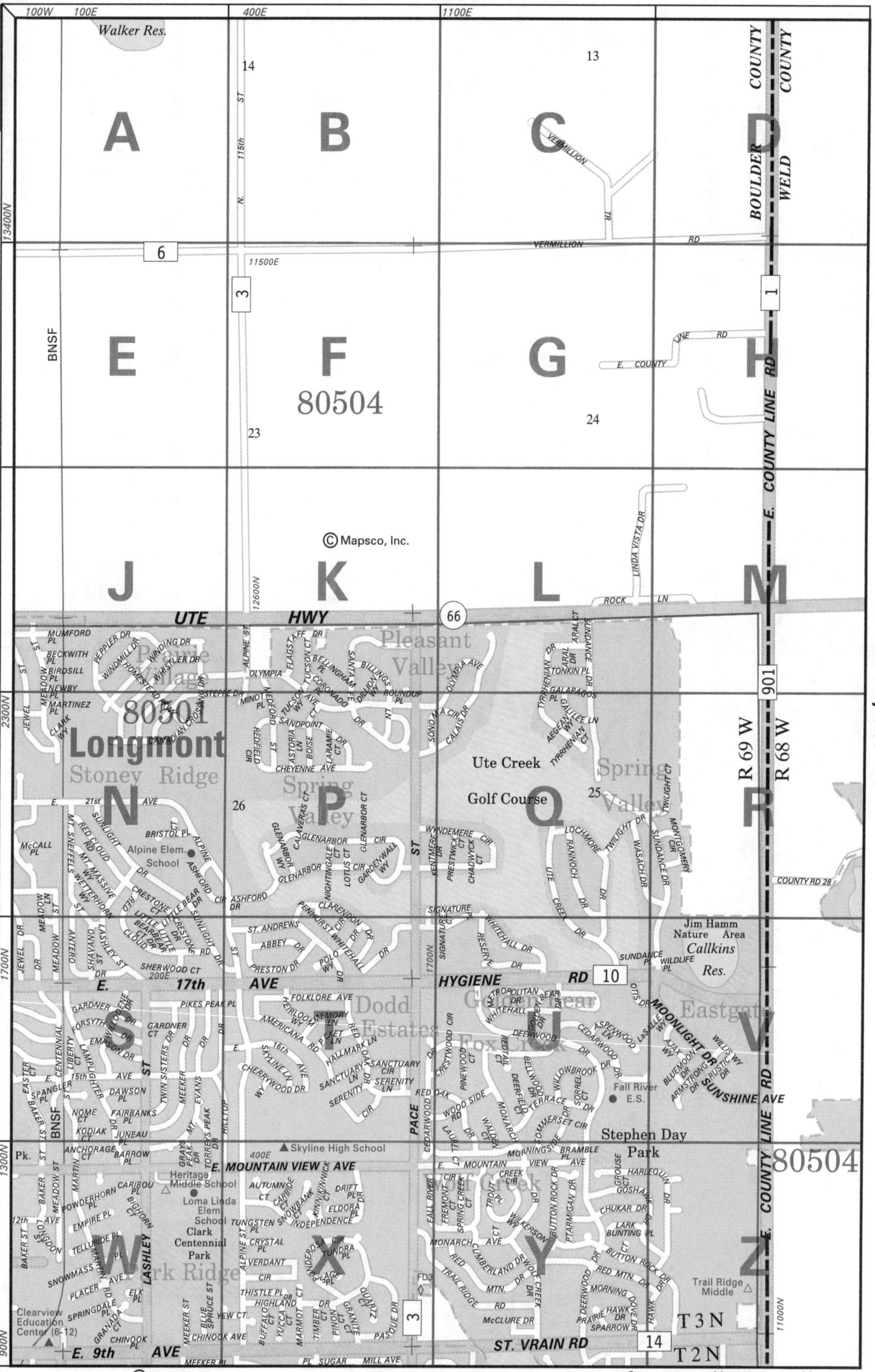

See Map 706 ►

▼ See Map 42 ▼

0 ¼ ½
Miles

See Map 10 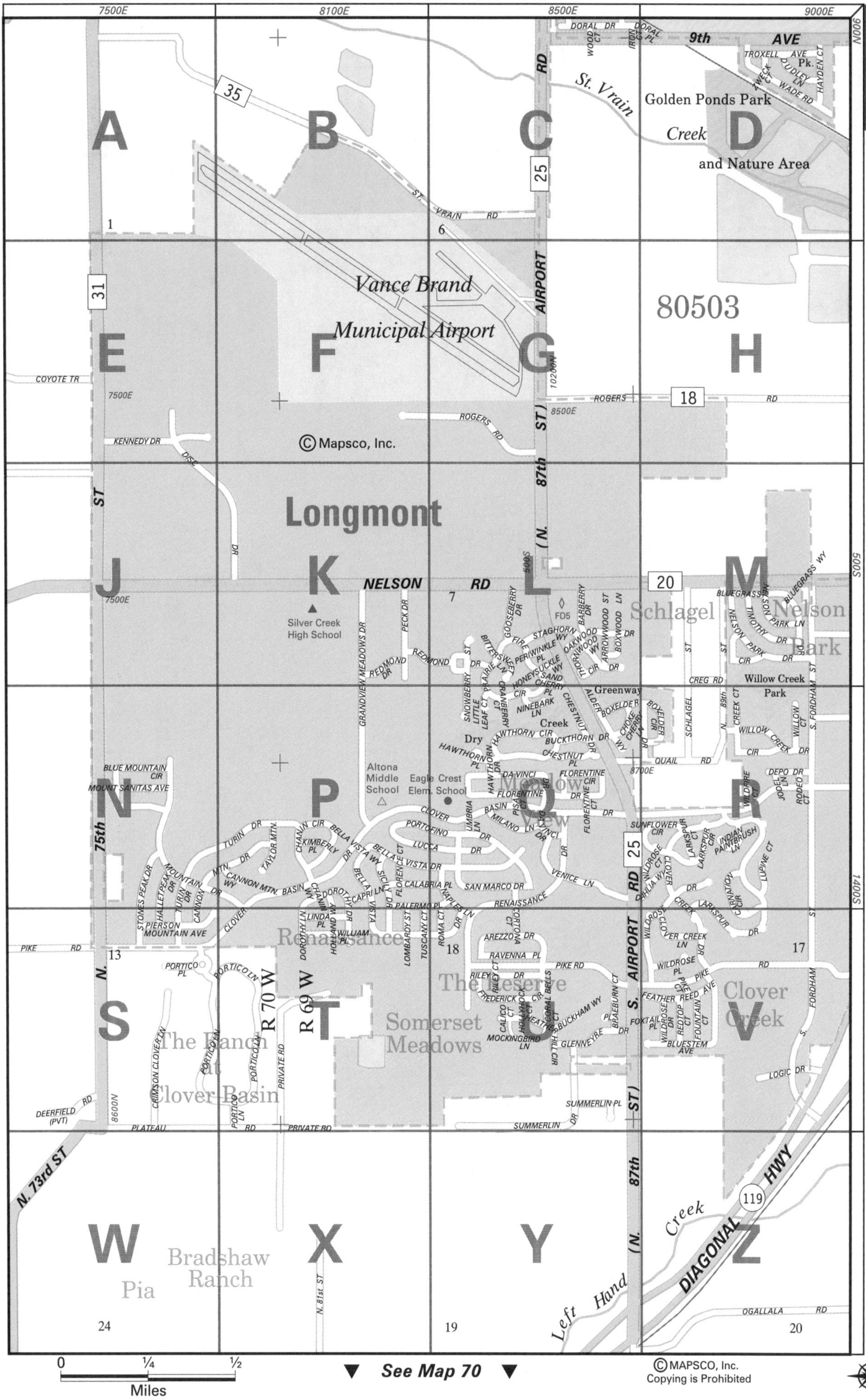
See Map 704
See Map 41
See Map 70

0 ¼ ½ Miles

▲ See Map 11 ▲

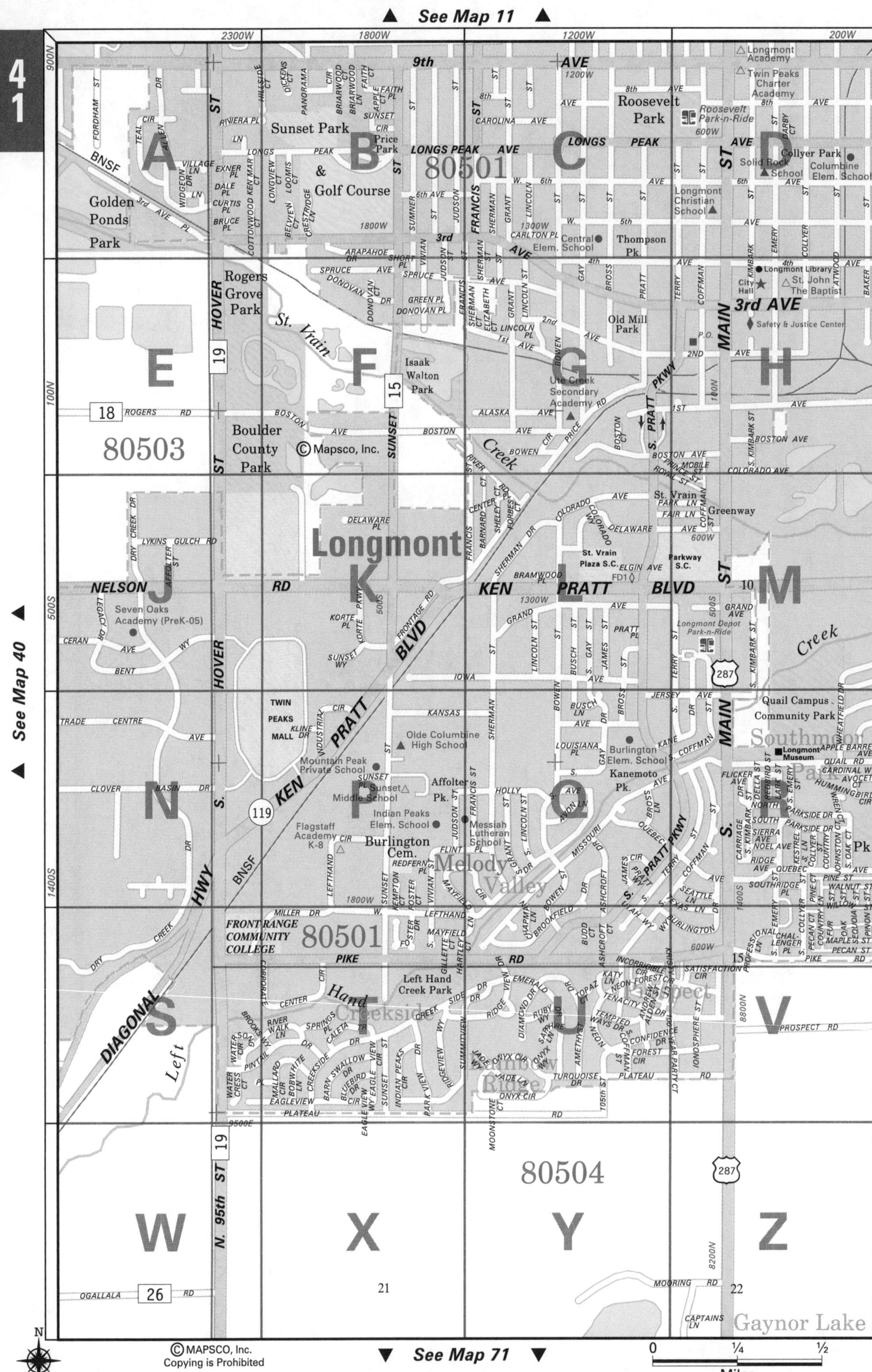

▲ See Map 40 ▲

▼ See Map 71 ▼

0 ¼ ½
Miles

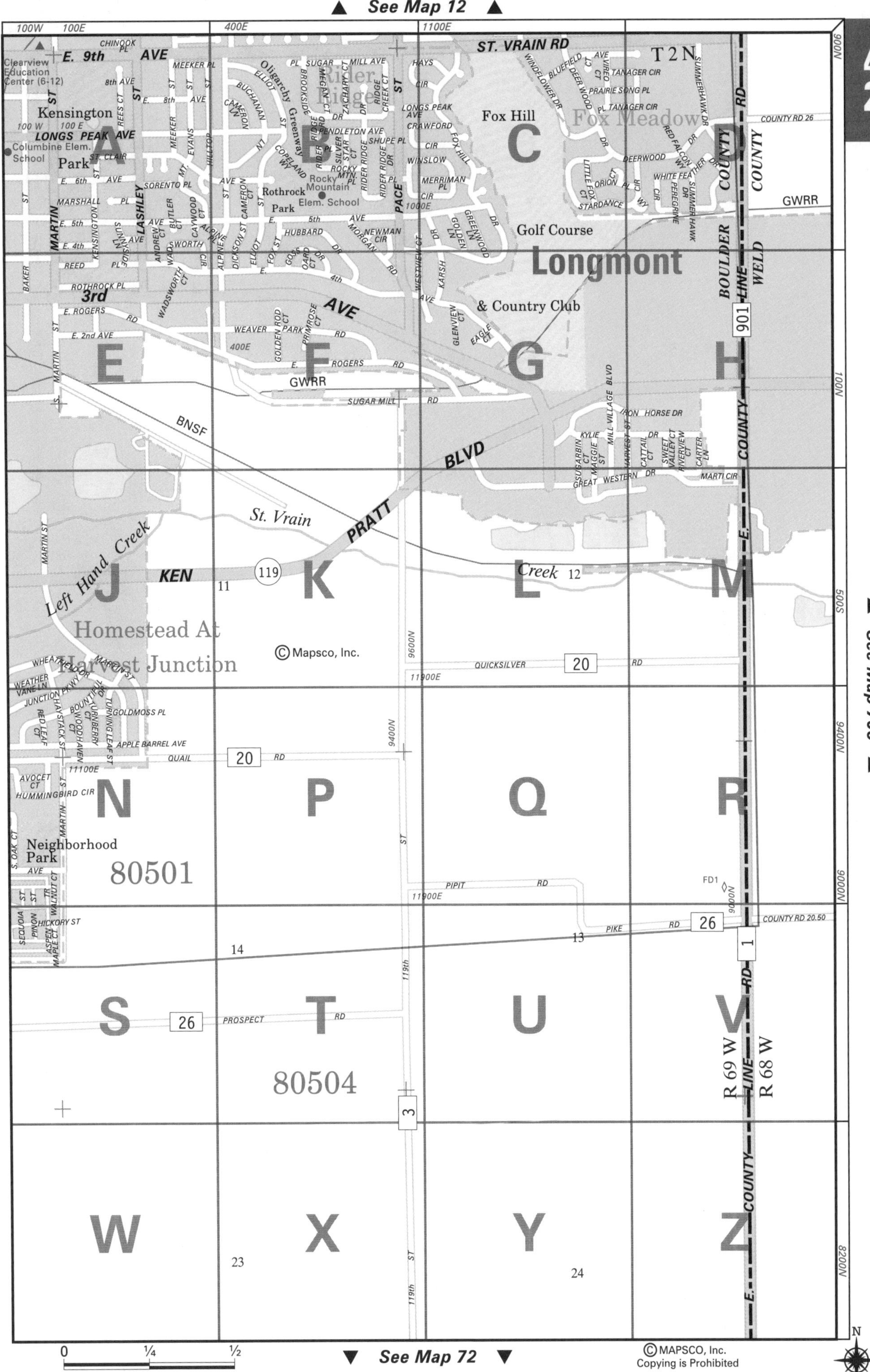

See Map 12
42
See Map 706
See Map 72
100W
100E
400E
1100E
900N
100N
500S
9400N
9000N
8200N
ST. VRAIN RD
T2N
E. 9th AVE
Clearview Education Center (6-12)
Kensington
Columbine Elem. School
Park
LONGS PEAK AVE
Rider Ridge
Oligarchy Greenway
Fox Hill
Fox Meadow
Rothrock Park
Rocky Mountain Elem. School
Golf Course
Longmont
& Country Club
3rd AVE
MARTIN ST
LASHLEY ST
PACE ST
BOULDER COUNTY LINE
WELD COUNTY
COUNTY RD
COUNTY RD 26
GWRR
BNSF
SUGAR MILL RD
E. ROGERS RD
MILL VILLAGE BLVD
PRATT BLVD
KEN PRATT BLVD
119
St. Vrain Creek
Left Hand Creek
901
Homestead At Harvest Junction
© Mapsco, Inc.
QUICKSILVER RD
20
QUAIL RD
11900E
11100E
Neighborhood Park
80501
PIPIT RD
FD1
PIKE RD
26
COUNTY RD 20.50
1
PROSPECT RD
80504
3
119th ST
R 69 W
R 68 W
A
B
C
D
E
F
G
H
J
K
L
M
N
P
Q
R
S
T
U
V
W
X
Y
Z
11
12
13
14
23
24
0
1/4
1/2
Miles
N

▲ See Map 704 ▲

▲ See Map 723 ▲

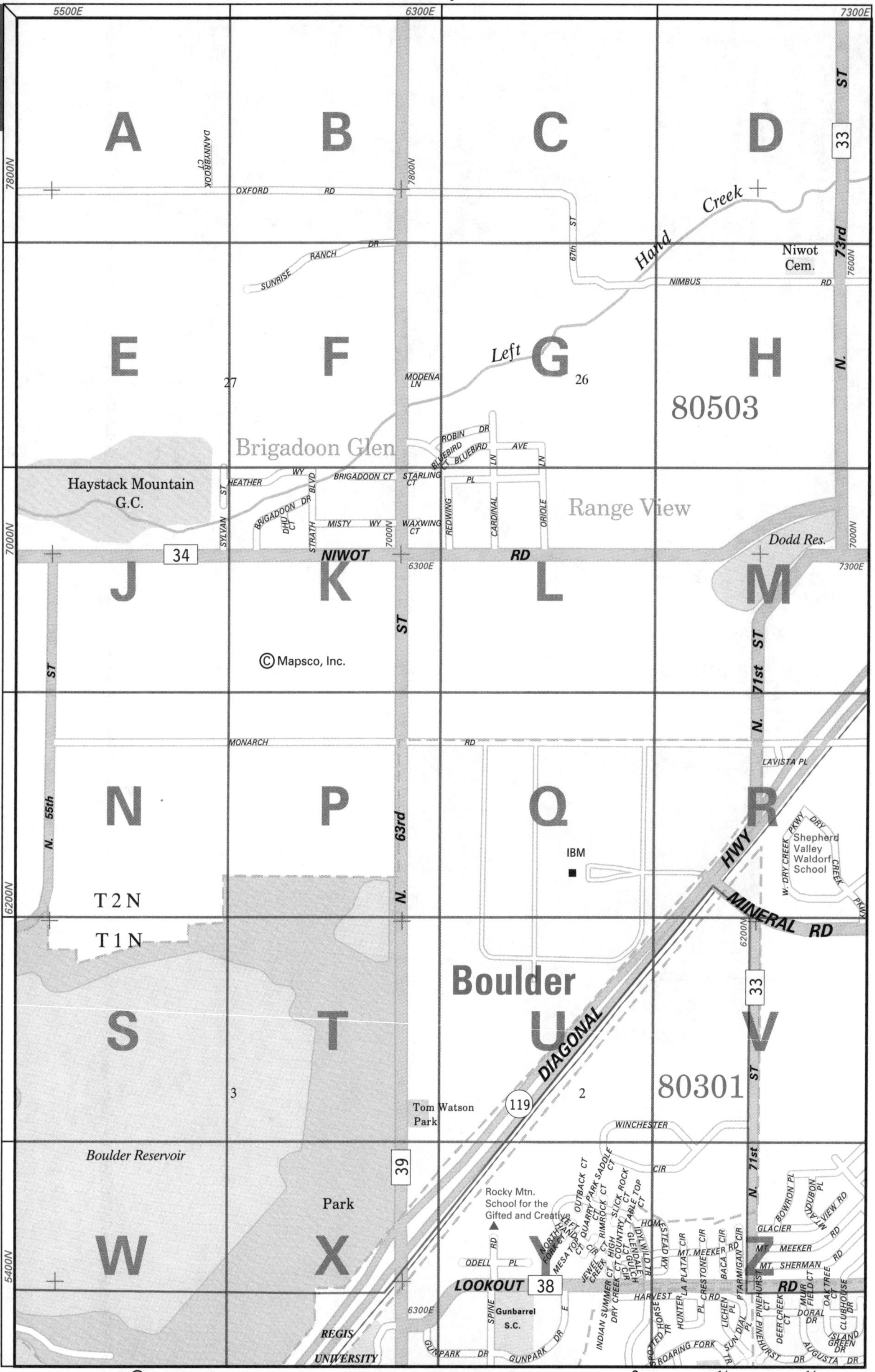

A B C D E F G H J K L M N P Q R S T U V W X Y Z

5500E 6300E 7300E 7800N 7600N 7000N 6200N 5400N 6300E 7300E

OXFORD RD
DANNYBROOK CT
67th ST
Hand Creek
Left Hand Creek
SUNRISE RANCH DR
NIMBUS RD
Niwot Cem.
N. 73rd ST
33
80503
27
26
MODENA LN
Brigadoon Glen
ROBIN DR
BLUEBIRD CT
BLUEBIRD AVE
LN
Haystack Mountain G.C.
HEATHER WY
BRIGADOON CT
STARLING CT
PL
Range View
BRIGADOON DR
DHU CT
STRATH BLVD
MISTY WY
WAXWING CT
REDWING
CARDINAL
ORIOLE
SYLVAN ST
Dodd Res.
34
NIWOT RD
© Mapsco, Inc.
N. 63rd ST
N. 55th ST
N. 71st ST
MONARCH RD
LAVISTA PL
IBM
Shepherd Valley Waldorf School
W. DRY CREEK PKWY
DRY CREEK PKWY
DIAGONAL HWY
MINERAL RD
T 2 N
T 1 N
Boulder
119
80301
3
2
Tom Watson Park
WINCHESTER CIR
39
Boulder Reservoir
Park
Rocky Mtn. School for the Gifted and Creative
OUTBACK CT
SADDLE CT
QUARRY CT
PARK CT
SLICK ROCK CT
TABLE TOP CT
RIMROCK CT
LEFT HAND CT
NORTHFORK
MESA TOP CT
JEWEL CREEK CT
HIGH COUNTRY CT
GLENDALE GULCH CIR
IDYLWILD TR
HOMESTEAD WY
MT. MEEKER CIR
CRESTONE CIR
BACA CIR
PTARMIGAN CIR
GLACIER
MT. MEEKER RD
MT. SHERMAN RD
BOWRON PL
AUDUBON PL
MT. VIEW RD
ODELL PL
RD
LOOKOUT RD
38
HARVEST
INDIAN SUMMER CT
DRY CREEK CT
SPOTTED HORSE TR
HUNTER PL
LA PLATA CIR
CRESTONE RD
LICHEN PL
SUN DIAL PL
PINEHURST CT
PINEHURST
DEER CREEK CT
MUIR FIELD CT
DORAL DR
OAKTREE CT
CLUBHOUSE DR
ISLAND GREEN DR
AUGUSTA DR
ROARING FORK TR
SPINE RD
Gunbarrel S.C.
GUNPARK DR
GUNBARREL
REGIS UNIVERSITY
6300E

▼ See Map 99 ▼

0 ¼ ½
Miles

N

▲ See Map 40 ▲

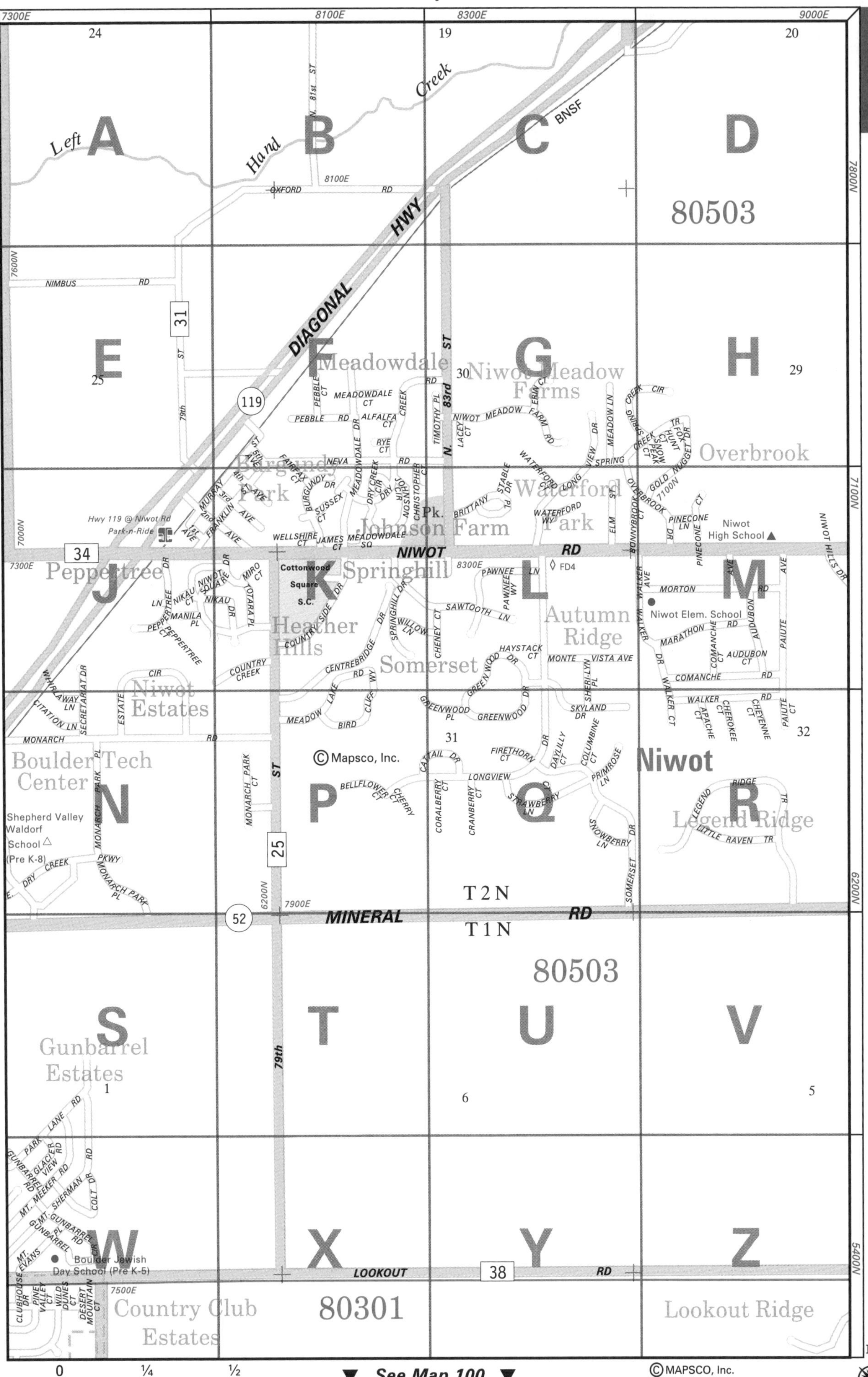

0 ¼ ½
Miles

▼ See Map 100 ▼

▲ See Map 71 ▲

See Map 41

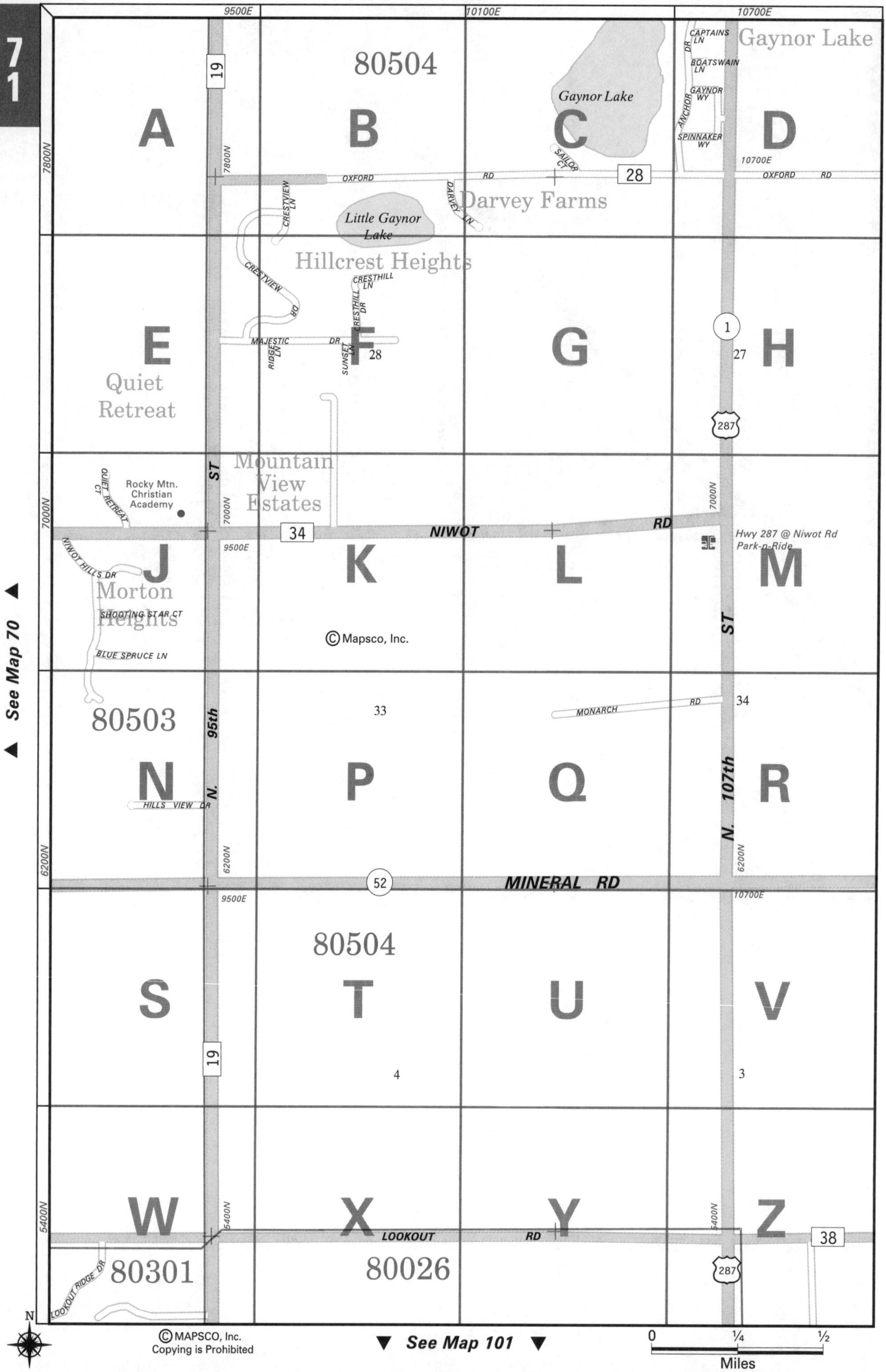

See Map 70

See Map 101

See Map 42

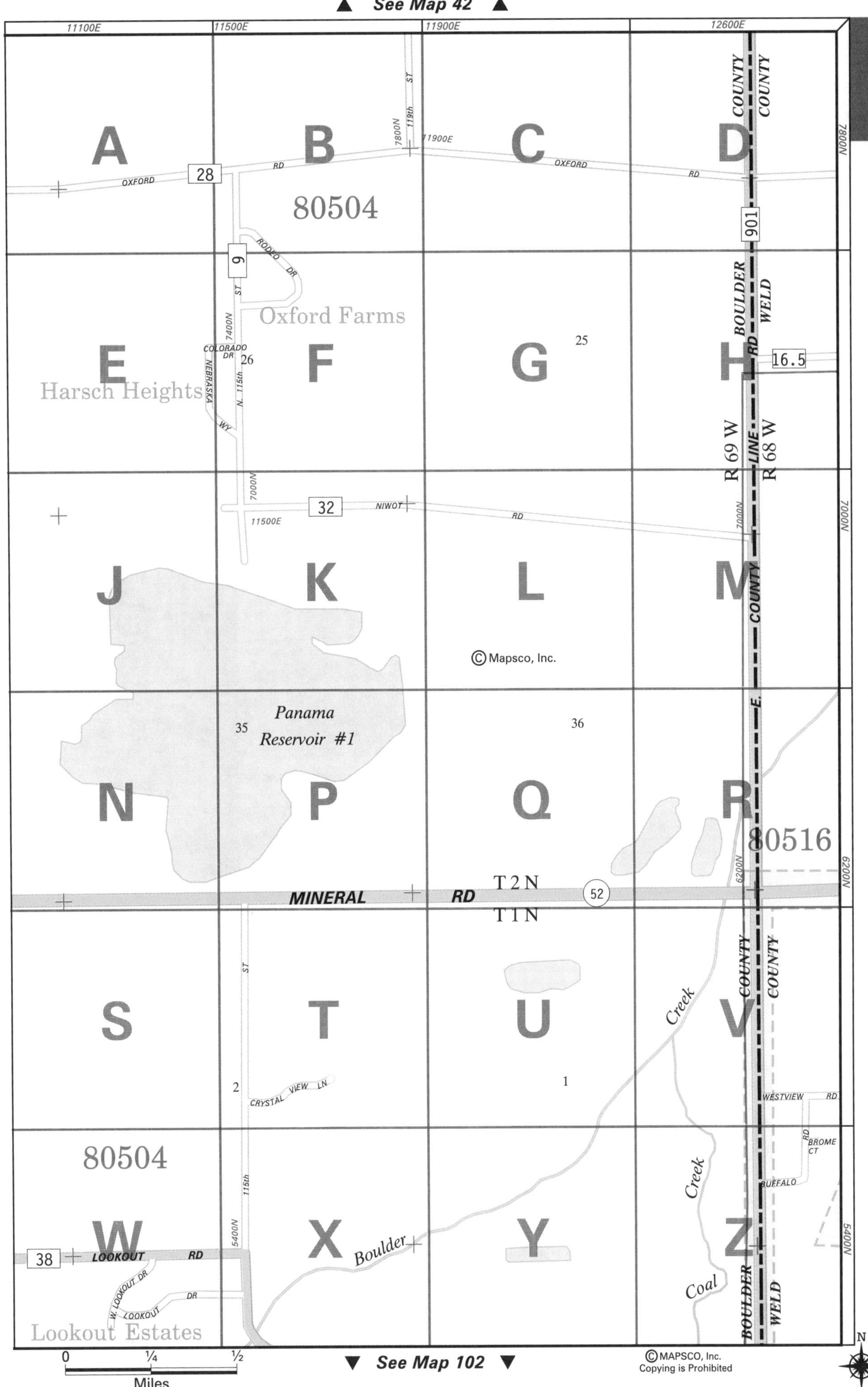

See Map 726

See Map 102

▲ See Map 723 ▲

◄ See Map 722 ◄

100E
500E
1300E
4400N
3900N
3400N
2600N
2100N
4000N
3000N
2800N
2700N

80302
80301
80304
80304
80302

A
B
C
D
E
F
G
H
J
K
L
M
N
P
Q
R
S
T
U
V
W
X
Y
Z

11
12
7
13
14
23
26

LEE HILL DR
OLDE STAGE RD
POINT OF PINES DR
106
WAGON WHEEL GAP RD
36
BROADWAY
Holiday Neighborhood
Palo Park
Vista Terrace
Boulder
Pine Brook Hills
LINDEN DR
7
Foothills Community Park
Shining Mountain Waldorf School
Park
VIOLET AVE
FD5
Crestview Park
Crest View Elem. School
Tara Performing Arts H.S.
Wonderland Lake
Wonderland Lake Park
Park
Jarrow Montessori School
Maxwell Lake Park
KALMIA
Pk
Park
County Health Dept.
IRIS AVE
Foothill Elem. School
People's Clinic
Olmstead Park
Salberg Park
North Boulder Park
Boulder Comm. Hospital
Mount Zion Lutheran School
ALPINE AVE
Casey School Park
Casey Middle School
FD1
Sacred Heart of Jesus School
Carnegie Library
County Courthouse
P.O.
PEARL ST
SUNSHINE CANYON DR
52
Mapleton Center for Rehab
BOULDER MOUNTAIN PARK
Knollwood

▼ See Map 127 ▼

0 ¼ ½
Miles

▲ See Map 723 ▲

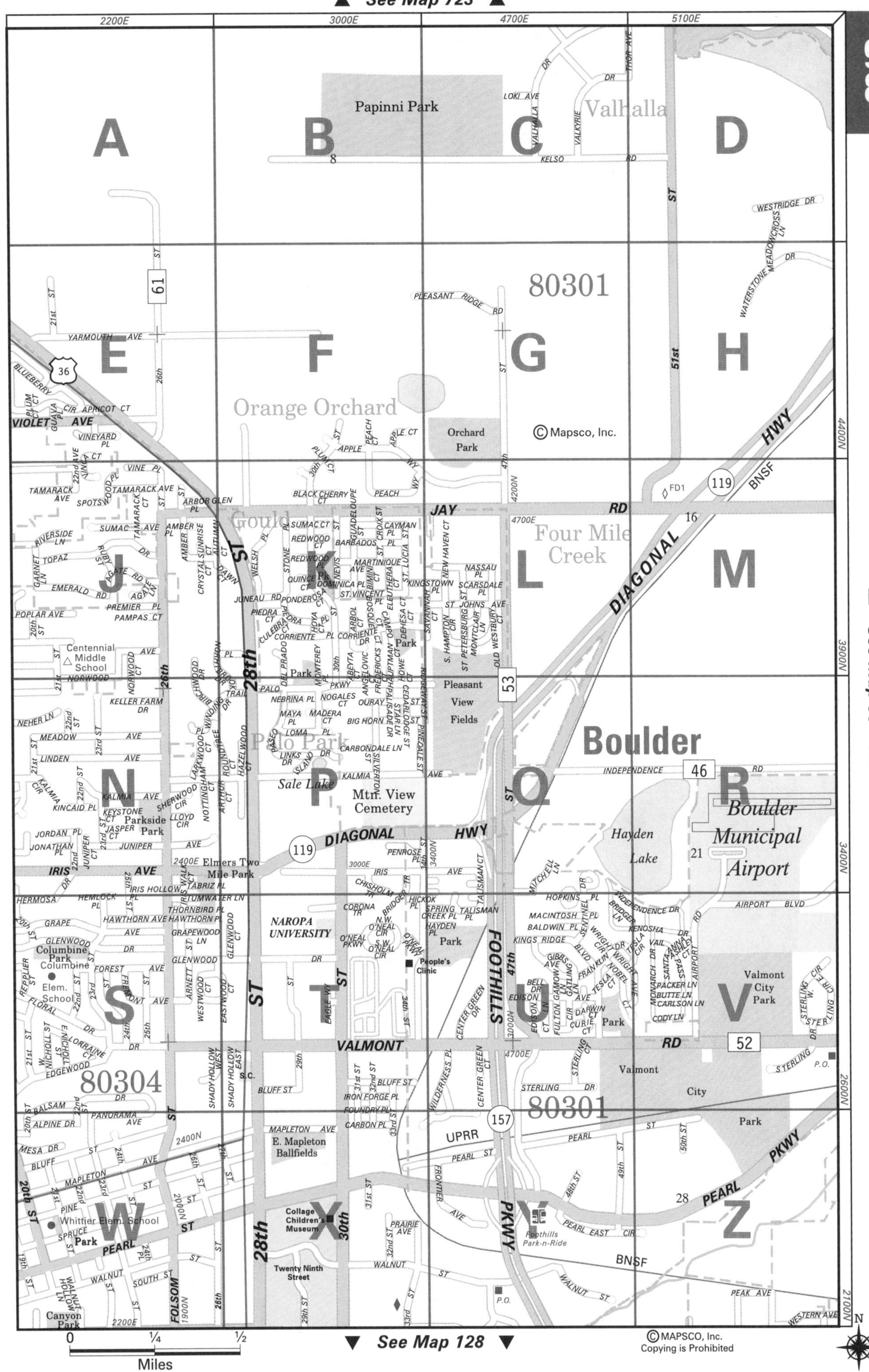

▶ See Map 99 ▶

▼ See Map 128 ▼

See Map 69

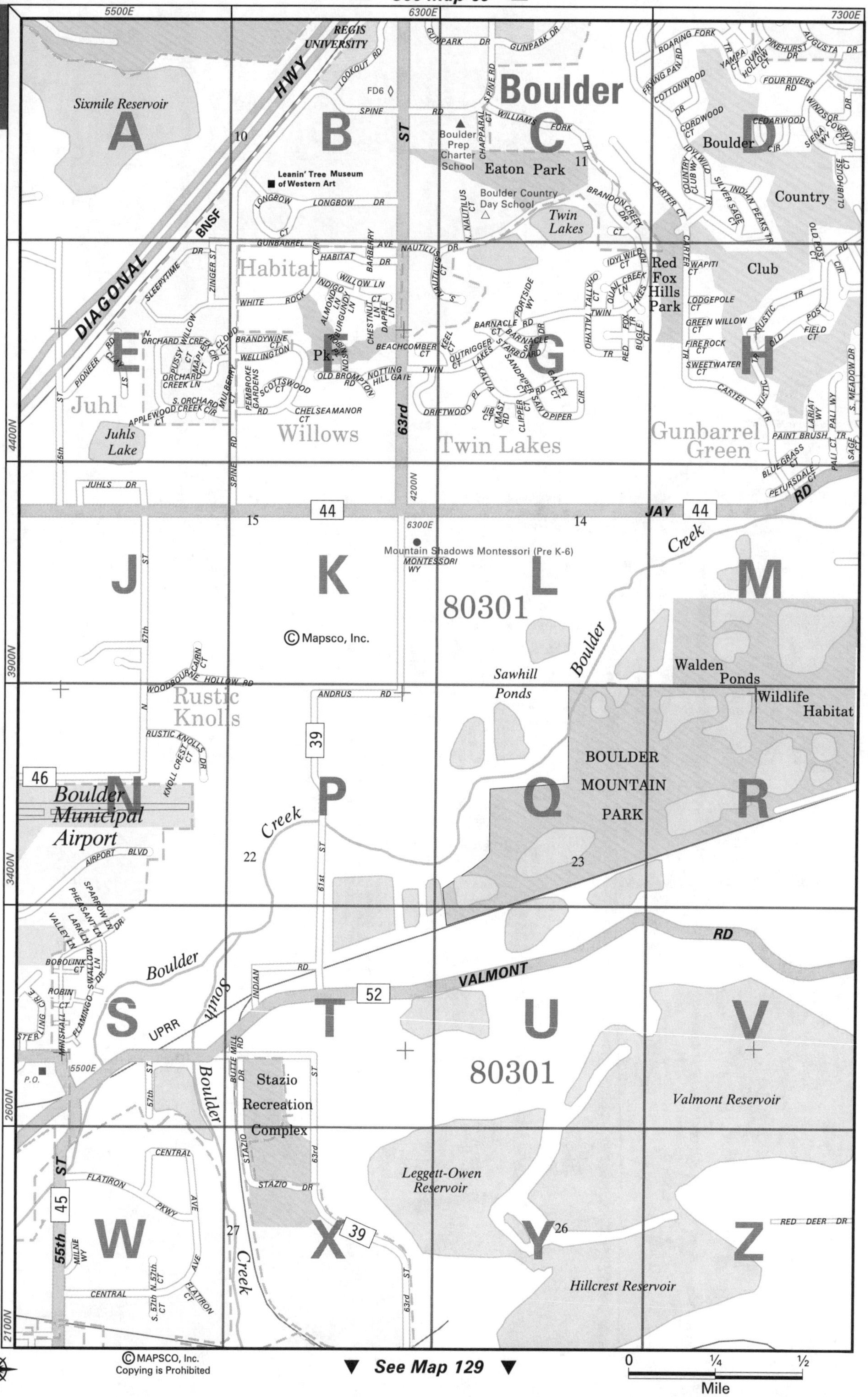

Sixmile Reservoir

Regis University

Leanin' Tree Museum of Western Art

Boulder Prep Charter School

Eaton Park

Boulder Country Day School

Twin Lakes

Boulder

Boulder Country Club

Red Fox Hills Park

Habitat Willows

Juhl

Juhls Lake

Twin Lakes

Gunbarrel Green

Mountain Shadows Montessori (Pre K-6)

80301

Sawhill Ponds

Walden Ponds Wildlife Habitat

Rustic Knolls

Boulder Municipal Airport

Boulder Mountain Park

Stazio Recreation Complex

Valmont Reservoir

Leggett-Owen Reservoir

Hillcrest Reservoir

80301

See Map 98

See Map 129

0 ¼ ½
Mile

▲ See Map 70 ▲

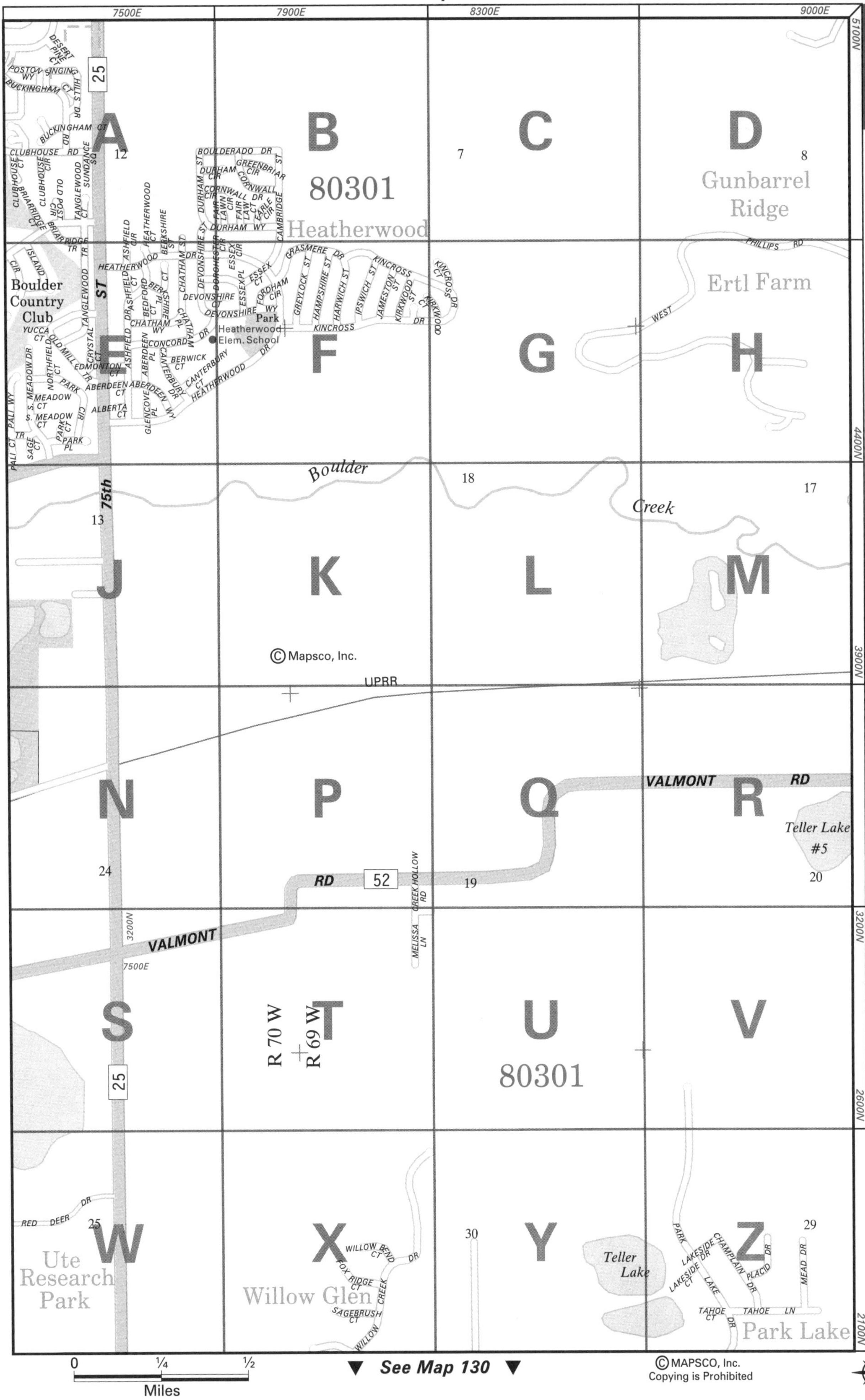

▲ See Map 101 ▲

▼ See Map 130 ▼

See Map 71

See Map 100

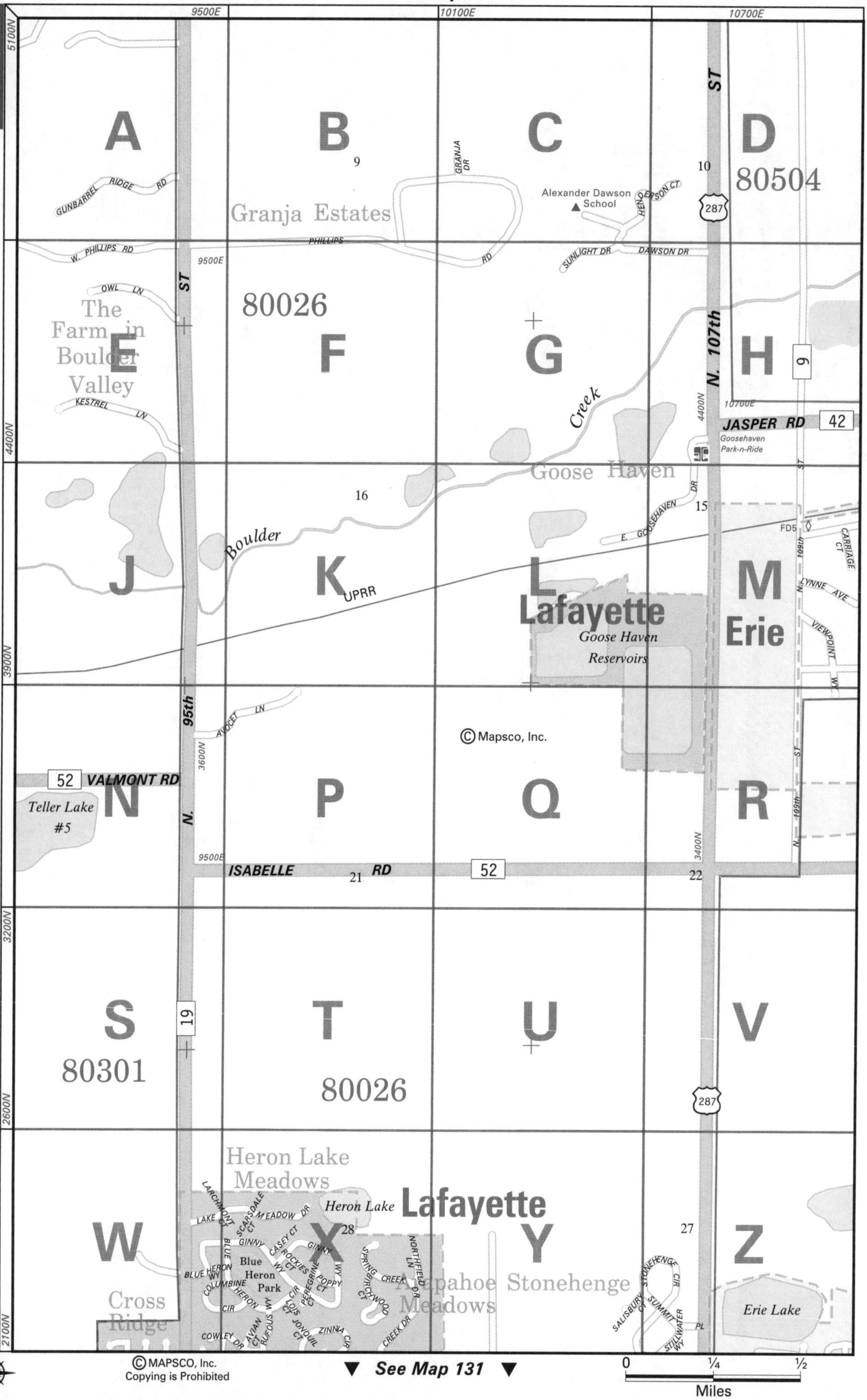

See Map 131

See Map 72

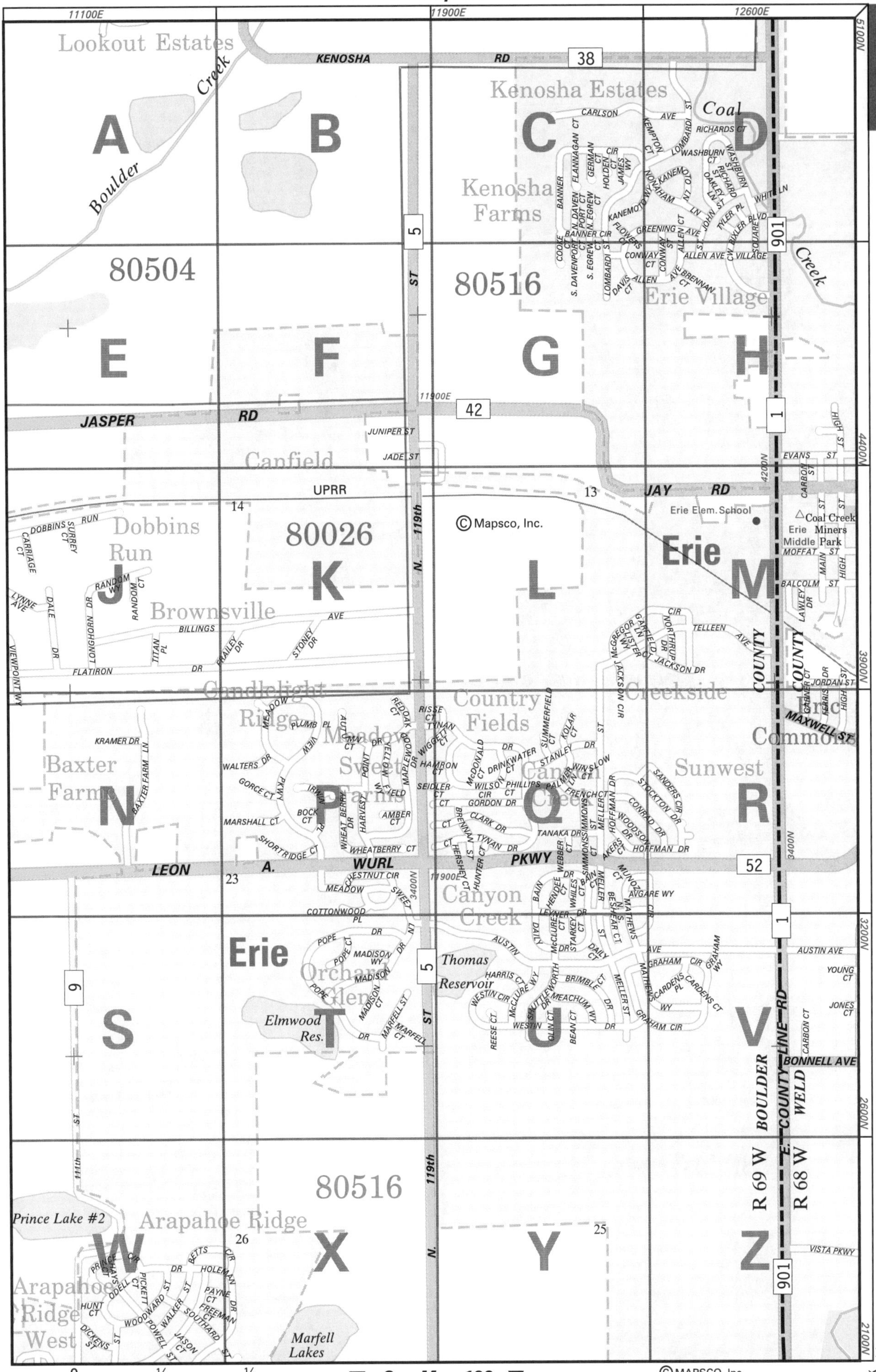

11100E 11900E 12600E

Lookout Estates
Boulder Creek
KENOSHA RD 38
Kenosha Estates
Coal Creek
Kenosha Farms
80504
80516
Erie Village
JASPER RD 42
Canfield
UPRR
JAY RD
Dobbins Run
80026
Brownsville
Erie
Erie Elem. School
Coal Creek Erie Miners Middle Park
Candlelight Ridge
Country Fields
Creekside
Erie Commons
Baxter Farms
Meadow Sweet Farms
Canyon Creek
Sunwest
LEON A. WURL PKWY 52
Erie
Orchard Glen
Thomas Reservoir
Elmwood Res.
80516
Prince Lake #2
Arapahoe Ridge
Arapahoe Ridge West
Marfell Lakes
BOULDER COUNTY
WELD COUNTY
E. COUNTY LINE RD
R 69 W
R 68 W

A B C D E F G H J K L M N P Q R S T U V W X Y Z

See Map 103

0 ¼ ½
Mile

See Map 132

▲ See Map 726 ▲

◄ See Map 102 ◄

See Map 726 ►

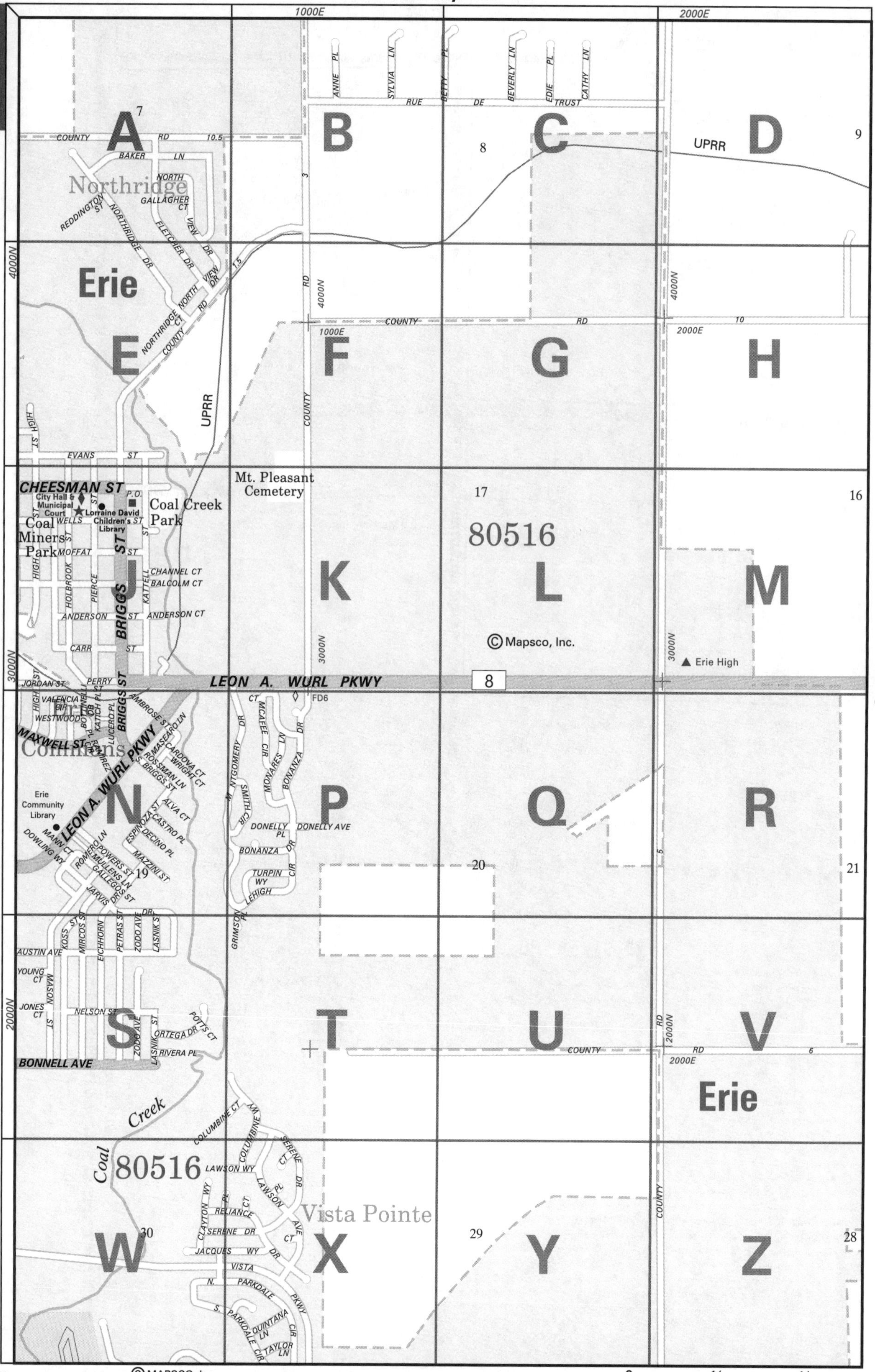

▼ See Map 133 ▼

0 ¼ ½
Miles

▲ See Map 97 ▲

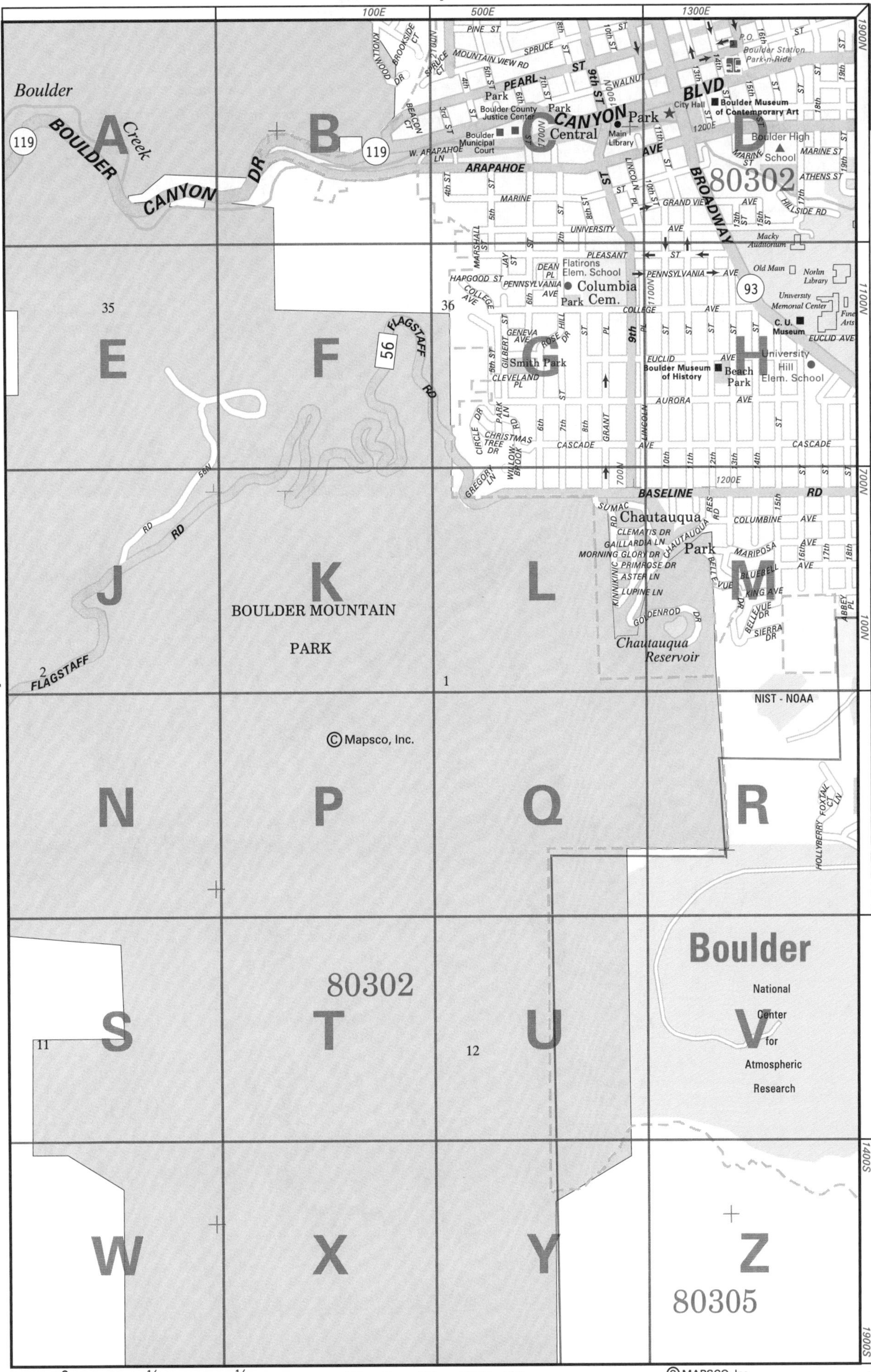

◄ See Map 742 ◄

► See Map 128 ►

▼ See Map 743 ▼

Boulder

BOULDER MOUNTAIN PARK

National Center for Atmospheric Research

0 ¼ ½

Miles

▲ See Map 98 ▲

▲ See Map 127 ▲

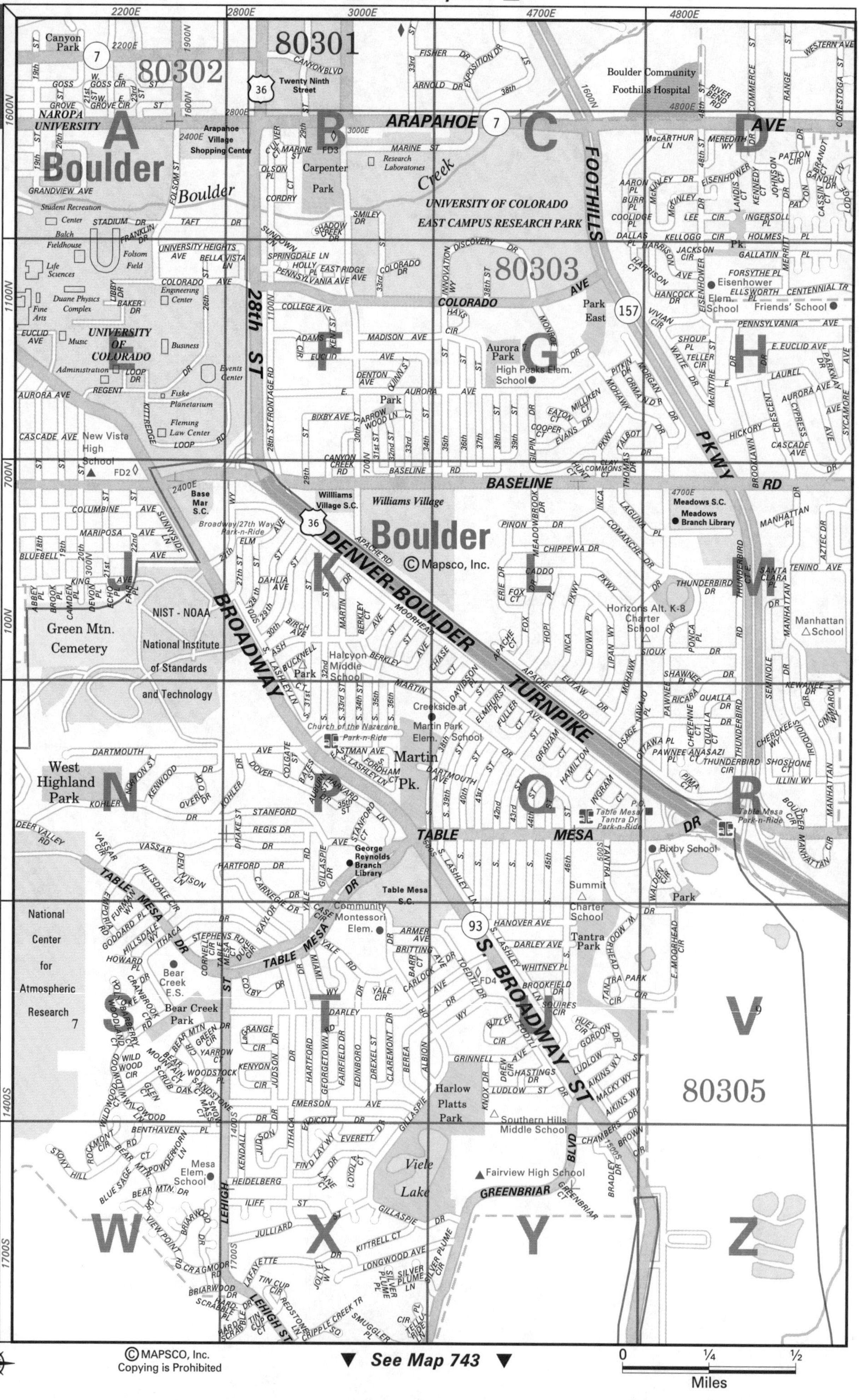

▼ See Map 743 ▼

0 ¼ ½
Miles

▲ See Map 99 ▲

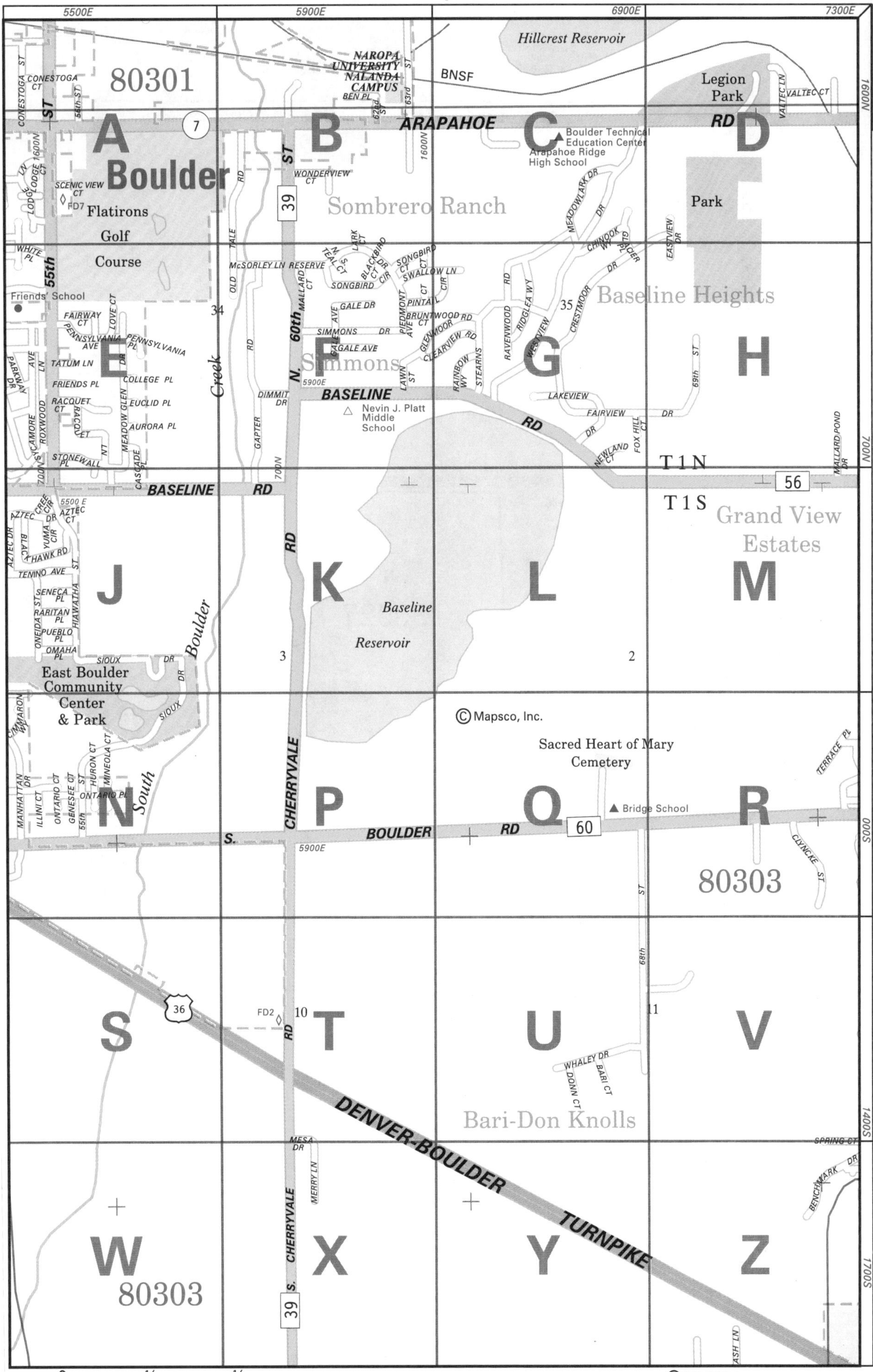

Miles 0 ¼ ½

▼ See Map 159 ▼

▶ See Map 130 ▶

▲ See Map 100 ▲

▲ See Map 129 ▲

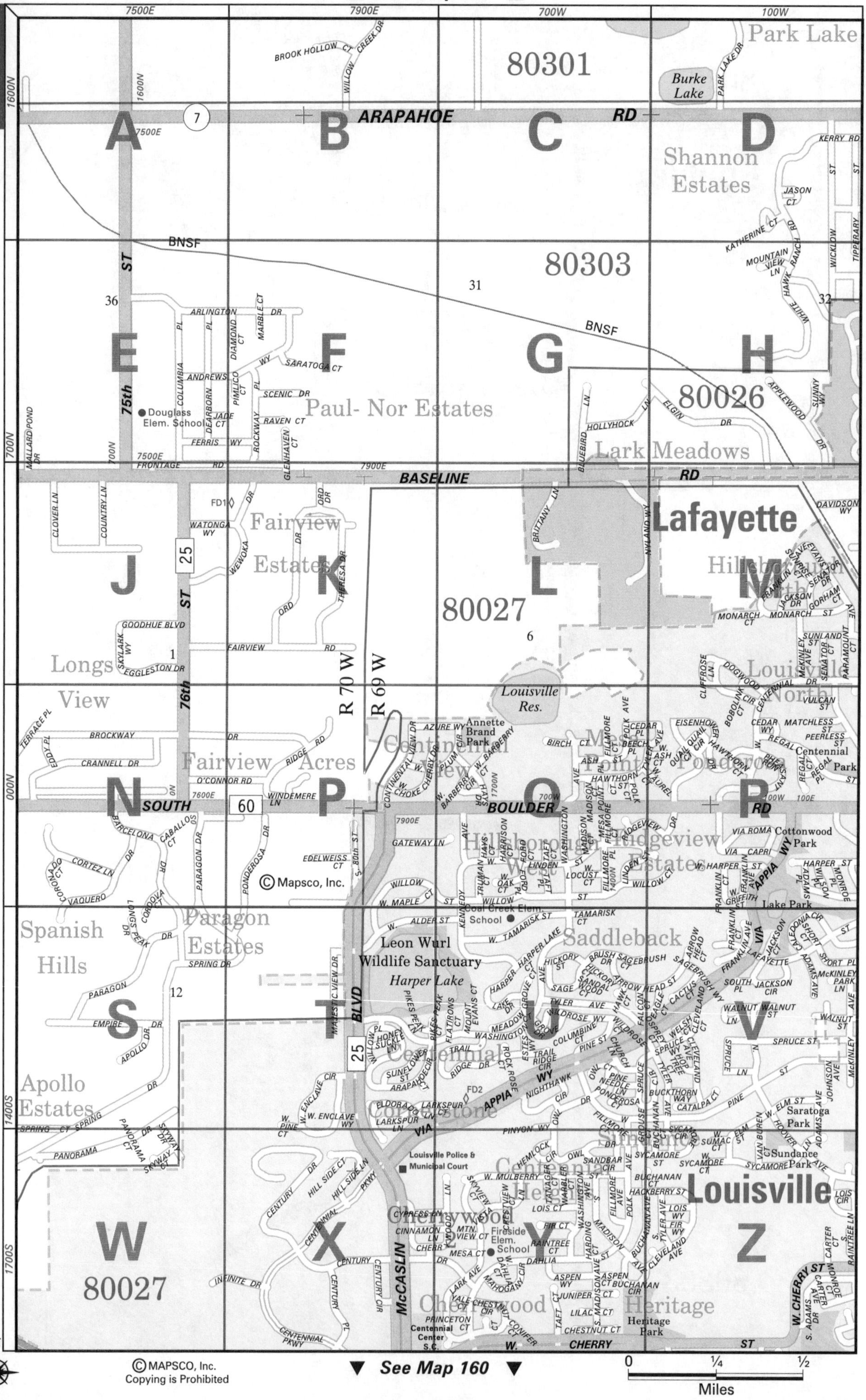

7500E 7900E 700W 100W
1600N 700N 000N 1400S 1700S

A B C D E F G H J K L M N P Q R S T U V W X Y Z

80301 80303 80026 80027

Park Lake
Burke Lake
Shannon Estates
Paul- Nor Estates
Lark Meadows
Lafayette
Fairview Estates
Longs View
Fairview Acres
Centennial View
Mesa Point
Ponderosa
Hillsborough North
Louisville North
Louisville Res.
Annette Brand Park
Centennial Park
Cottonwood Park
Hillsborough West
Ridgeview Estates
Lake Park
Spanish Hills
Paragon Estates
Saddleback
Leon Wurl Wildlife Sanctuary
Harper Lake
Centennial
Apollo Estates
Cornerstone
Saratoga Park
Sundance
Sundance Park
Centennial Heights
Louisville
Cherrywood
Heritage
Heritage Park
Douglass Elem. School
Coal Creek Elem. School
Fireside Elem. School
Louisville Police & Municipal Court
Centennial Center S.C.
FD1 FD2
BNSF
R 70 W
R 69 W
31 32 36 1 6 12

ARAPAHOE RD
BASELINE RD
SOUTH BOULDER RD
McCASLIN BLVD
VIA APPIA WY
W. CHERRY ST
75th ST
76th ST
7 25 60

▼ See Map 160 ▼

0 ¼ ½
Miles

▲ See Map 101 ▲

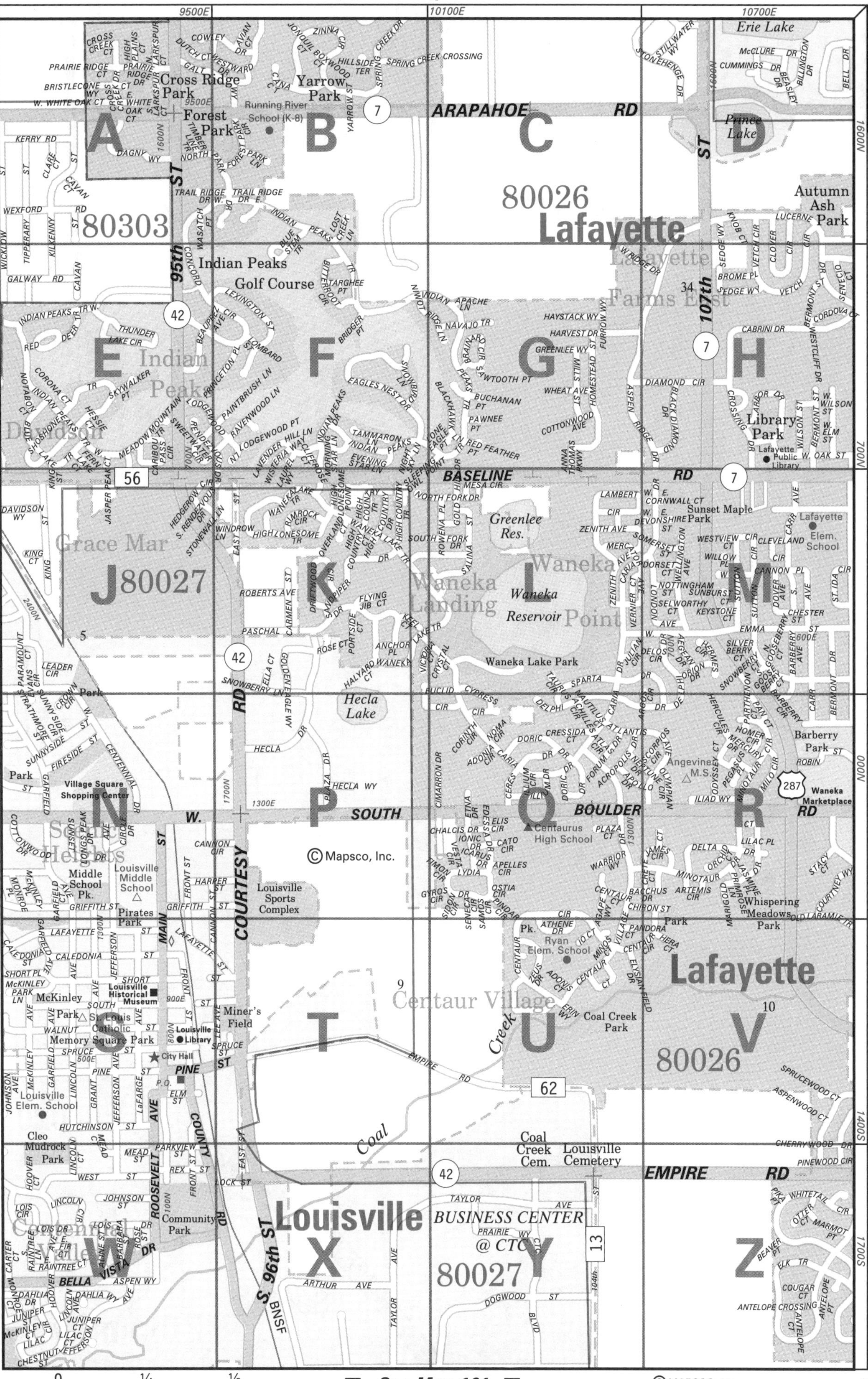

▲ See Map 132 ▲

▼ See Map 161 ▼

▲ See Map 102 ▲

▲ See Map 131 ▲

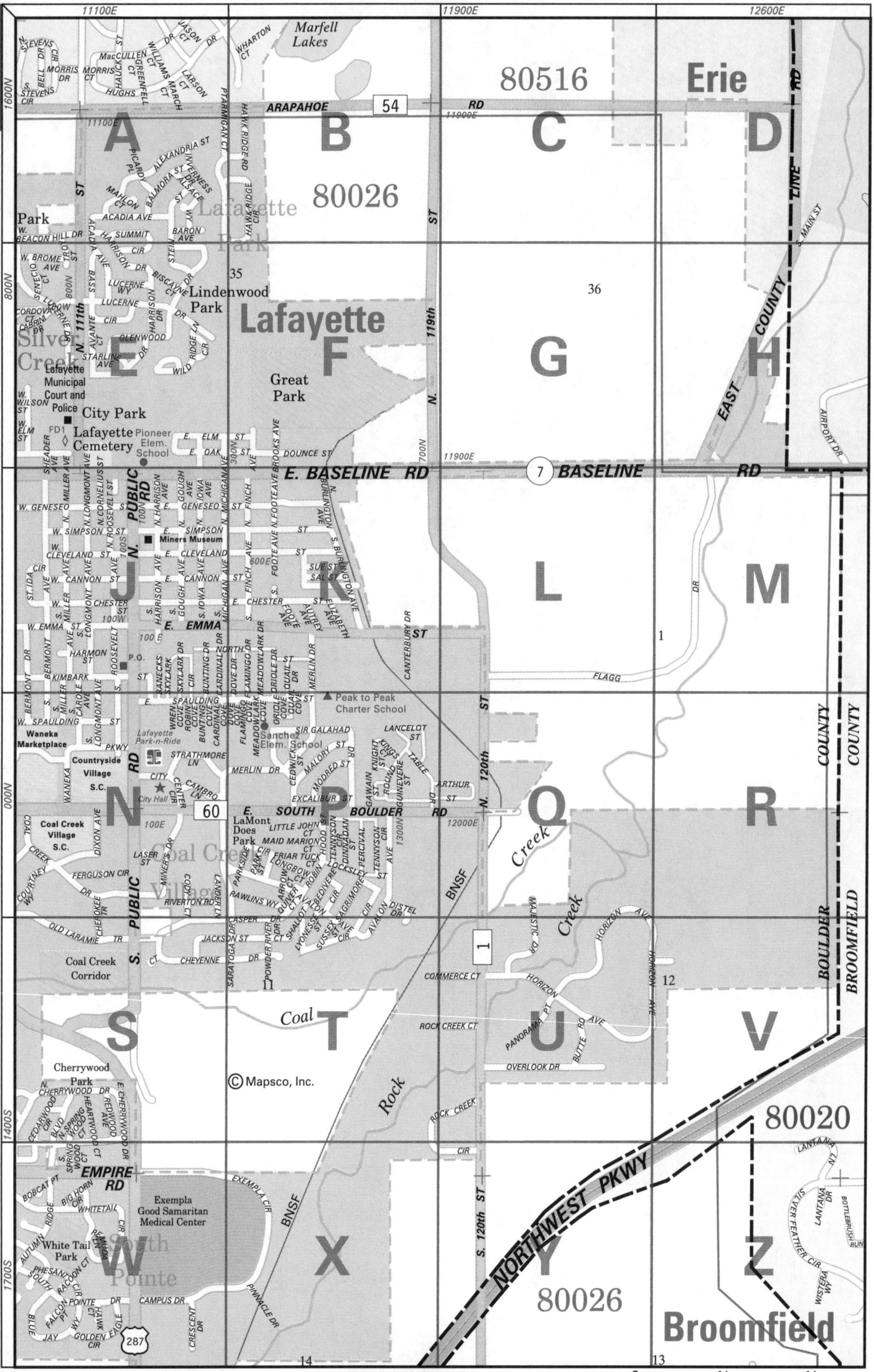

▼ See Map 162 ▼

0 ¼ ½
Miles

▲ See Map 103 ▲

▲ See Map 134 ▲

▼ See Map 163 ▼

0 ¼ ½
Miles

See Map 726

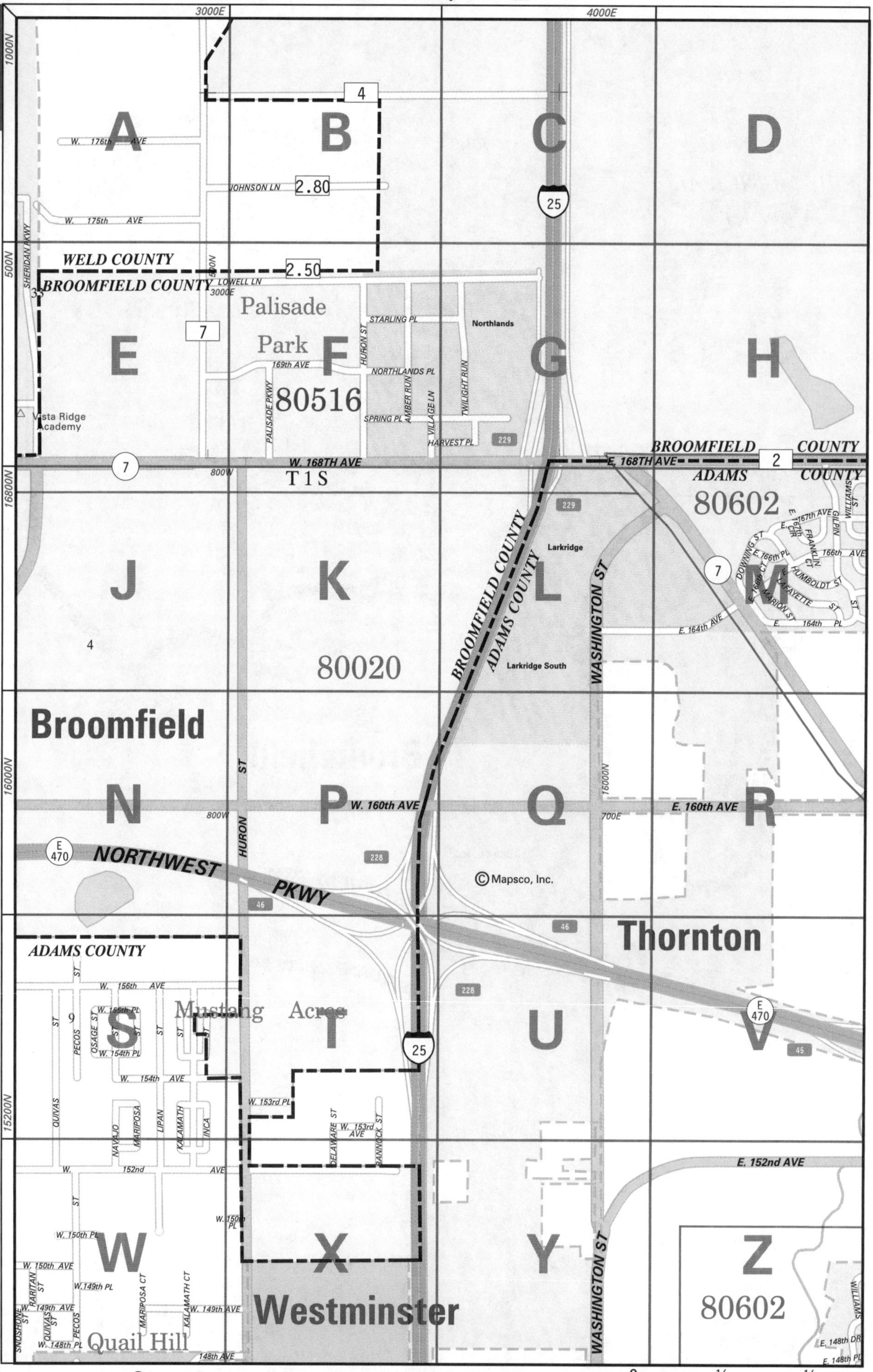

See Map 133

See Map 164

▲ See Map 727 ▲

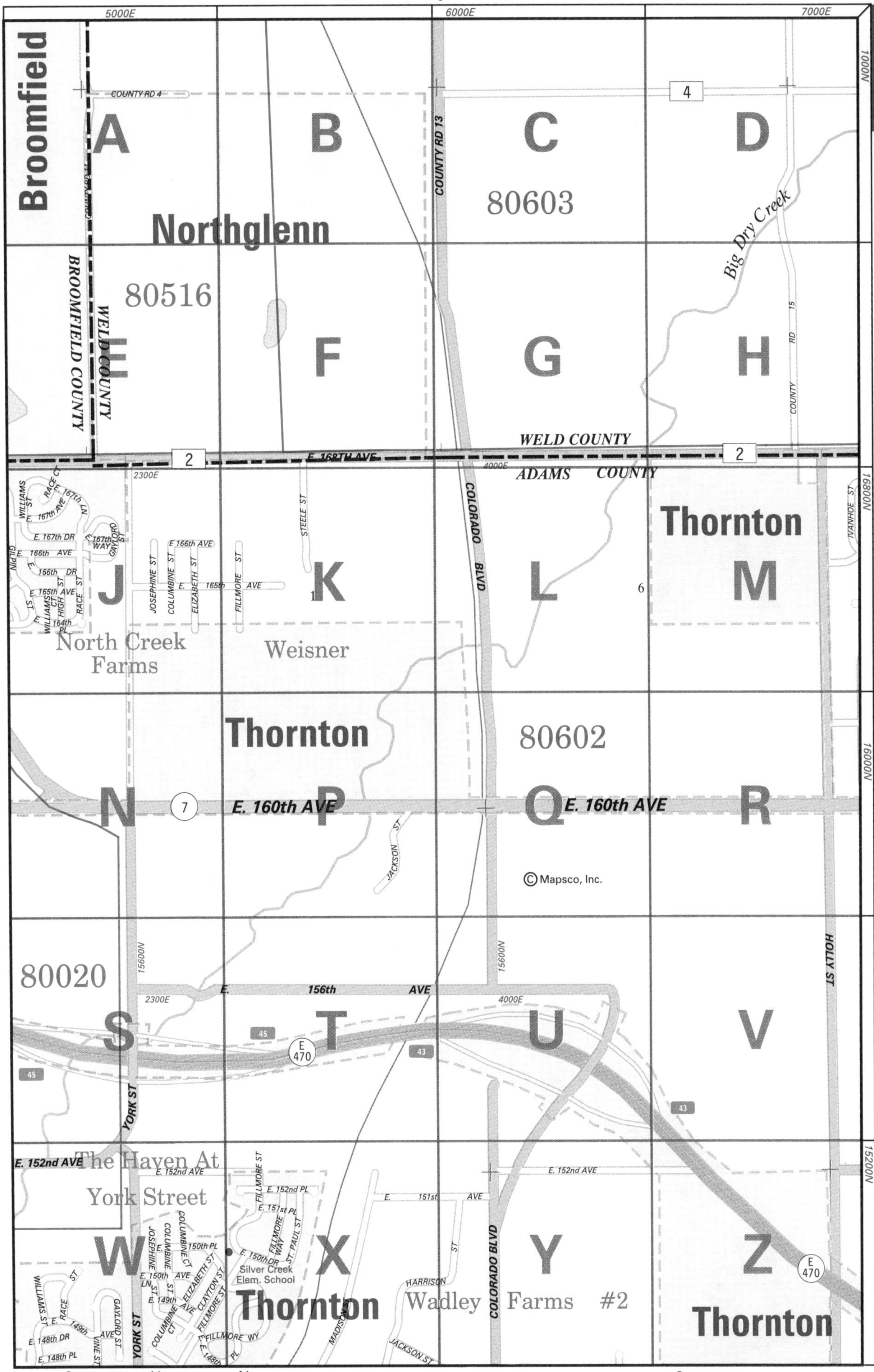

Broomfield

Northglenn

80516

80603

BROOMFIELD COUNTY

WELD COUNTY

ADAMS COUNTY

COUNTY RD 4

COUNTY RD 13

COUNTY RD 15

Big Dry Creek

E. 168TH AVE

Thornton

North Creek Farms

Weisner

80602

E. 160th AVE

COLORADO BLVD

E. 156th AVE

HOLLY ST

YORK ST

80020

The Haven At York Street

E. 152nd AVE

Silver Creek Elem. School

Wadley Farms #2

E. 151st AVE

FILLMORE ST

JACKSON ST

MADISON ST

HARRISON ST

IVANHOE ST

STEELE ST

© Mapsco, Inc.

A B C D E F G H J K L M N P Q R S T U V W X Y Z

See Map 136

▼ See Map 165 ▼

0 ¼ ½ Miles

See Map 727

See Map 135

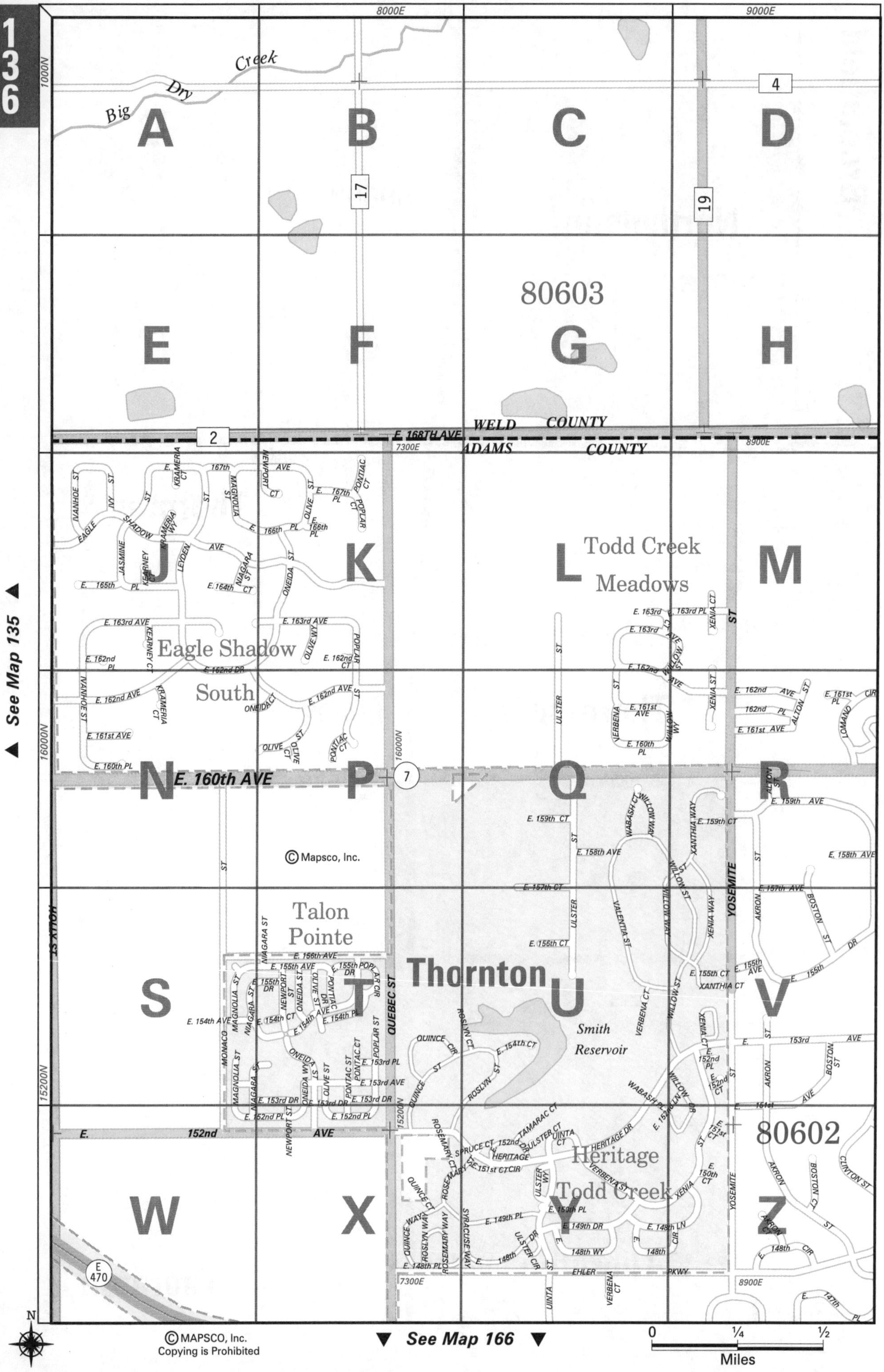

See Map 166

0 ¼ ½
Miles

▲ See Map 728 ▲

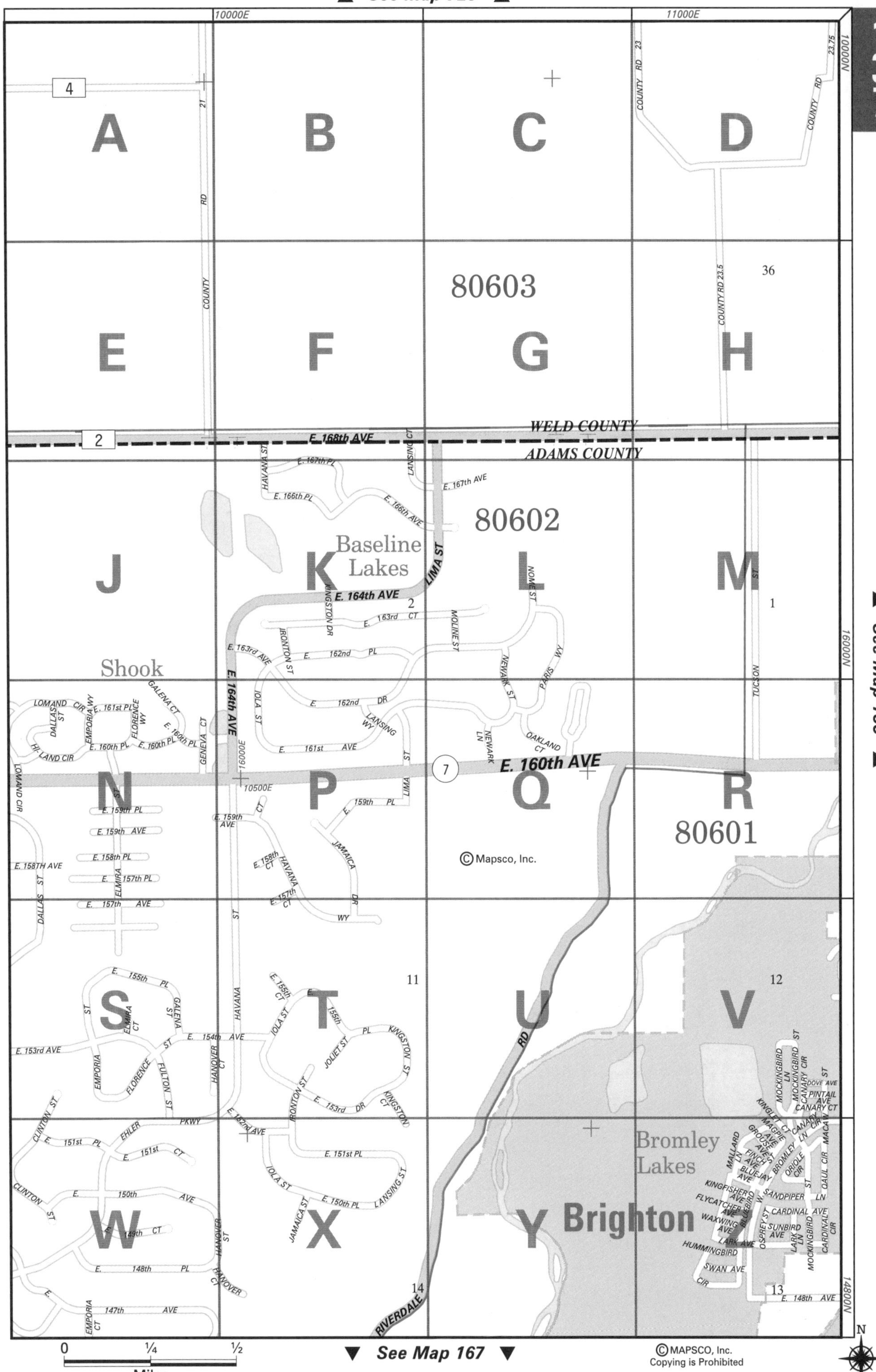

▲ See Map 138 ▲

0 ¼ ½
Miles

▼ See Map 167 ▼

▲ See Map 728 ▲

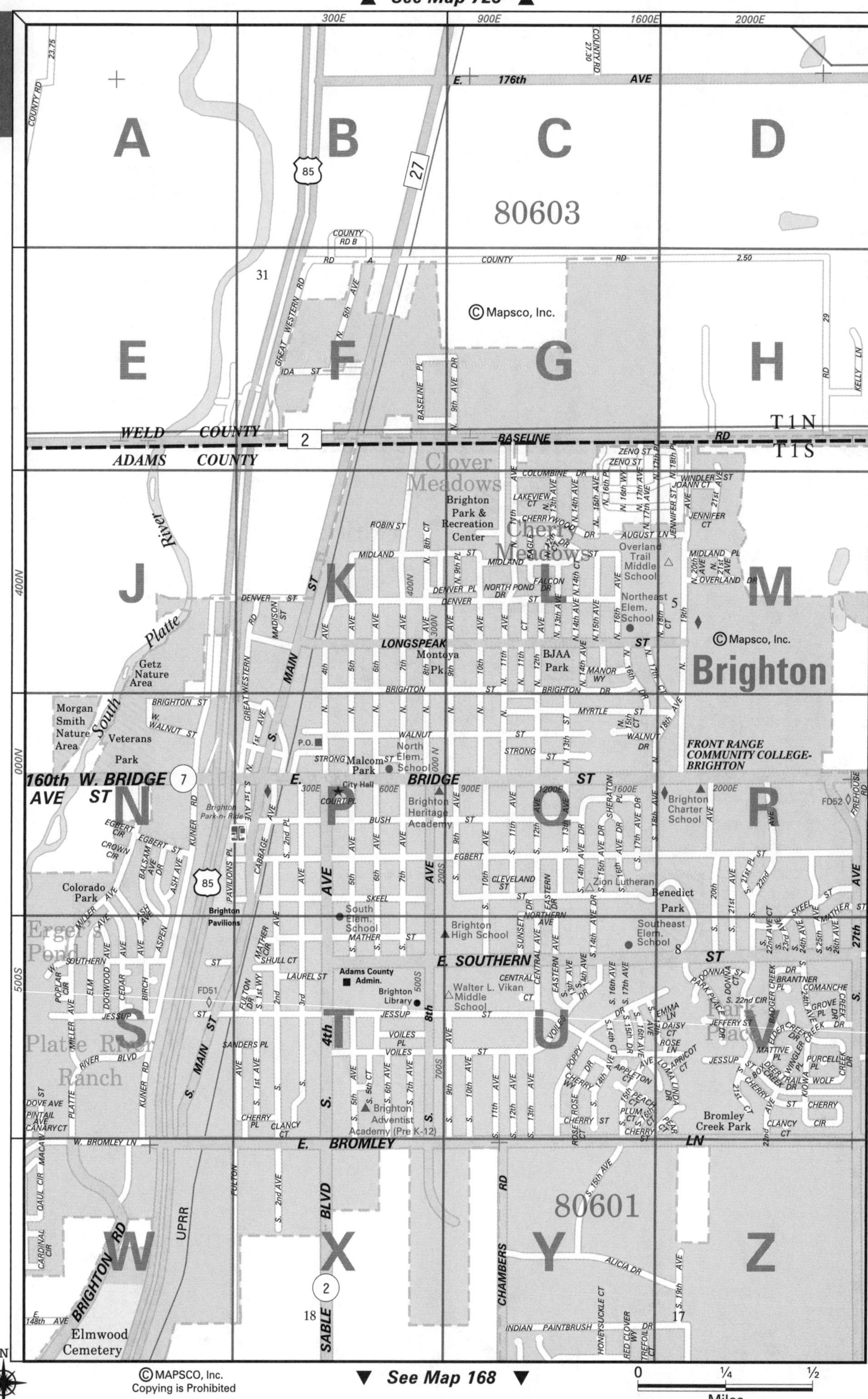

◀ See Map 137 ◀

▼ See Map 168 ▼

0 ¼ ½
Miles

▲ See Map 729 ▲

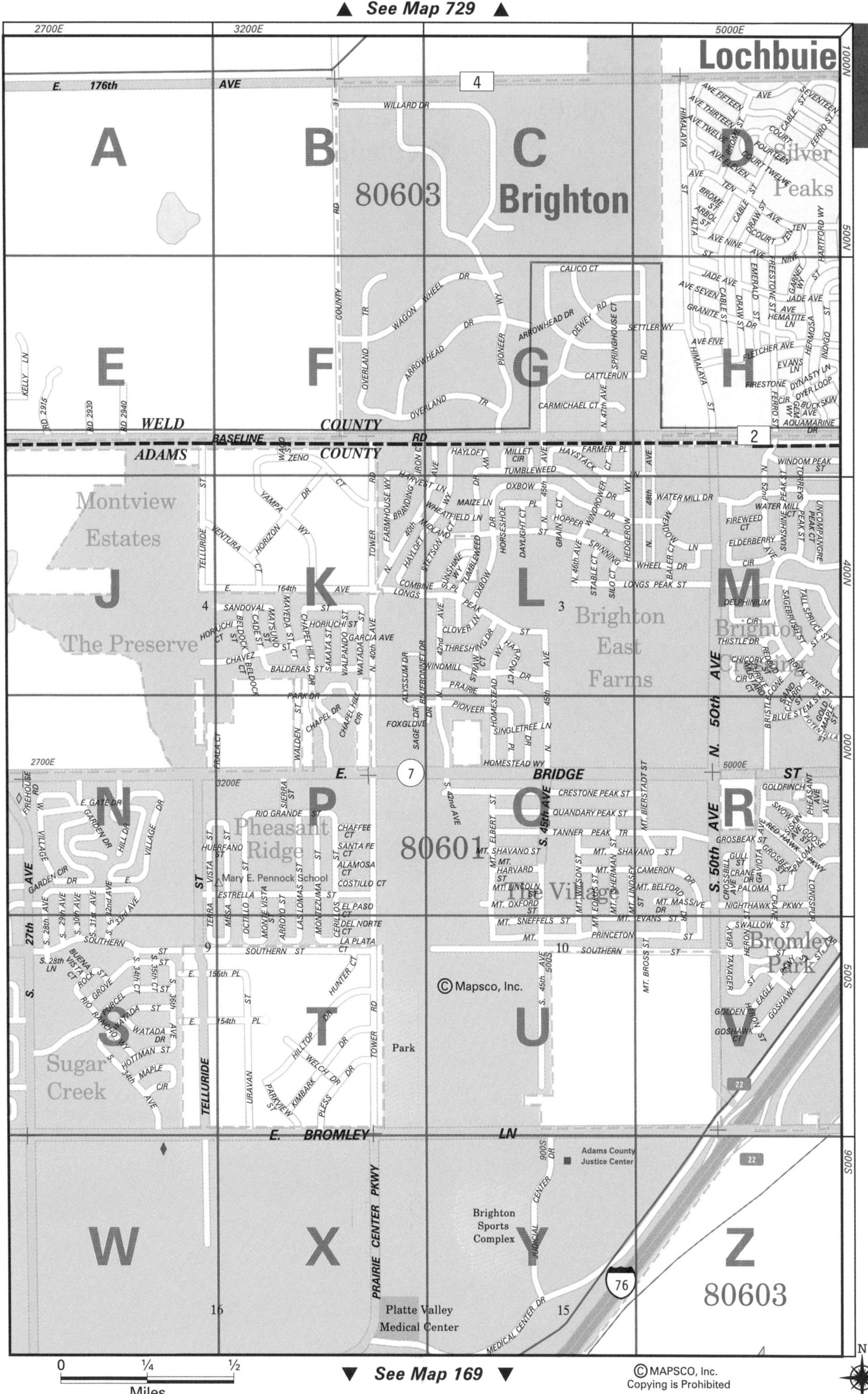

▼ See Map 169 ▼

▶ See Map 140 ▶

▲ See Map 729 ▲

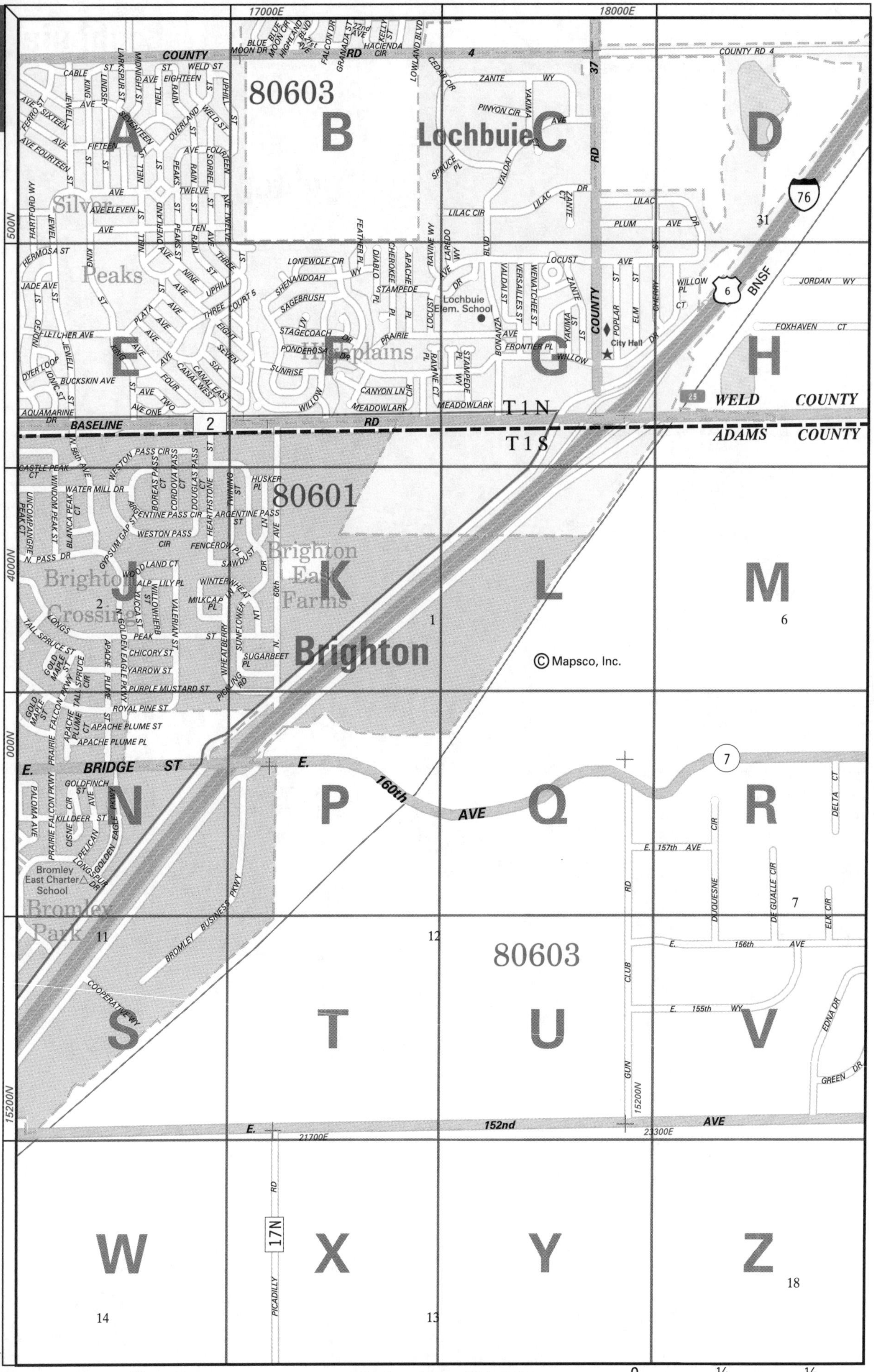

◄ See Map 139 ◄

► See Map 750 ►

80603

Lochbuie

Silver Peaks

Highplains

Lochbuie Elem. School

City Hall

WELD COUNTY

ADAMS COUNTY

BASELINE RD

T1N

T1S

80601

Brighton East Farms

Brighton Crossing

Brighton

© Mapsco, Inc.

E. BRIDGE ST

E. 160th AVE

Bromley East Charter School

Bromley Park

80603

E. 152nd AVE

A B C D E F G H J K L M N P Q R S T U V W X Y Z

▼ See Map 170 ▼

0 ¼ ½
Miles

▲ See Map 129 ▲

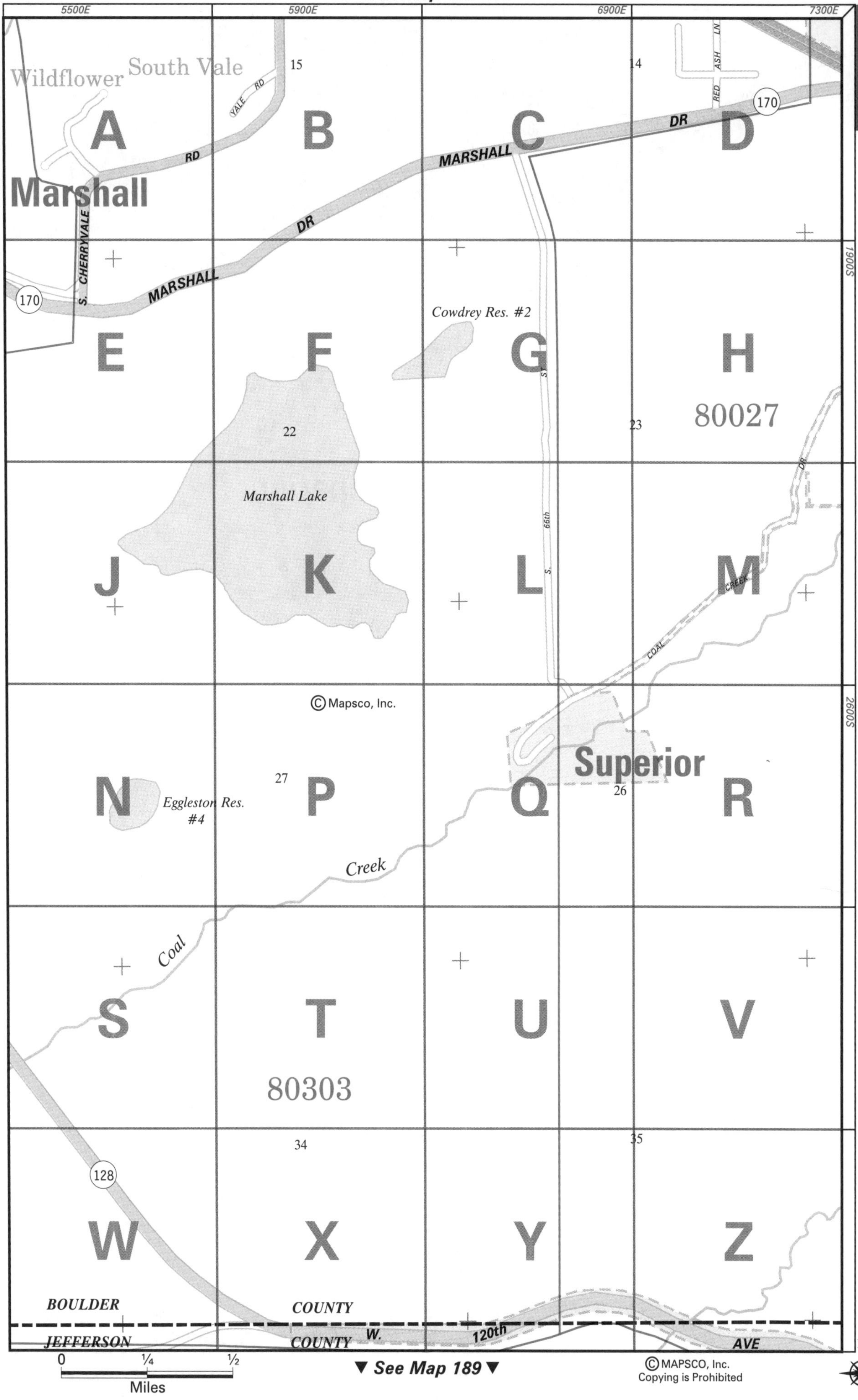

5500E 5900E 6900E 7300E

Wildflower South Vale

Marshall

S. CHERRYVALE

YALE RD

MARSHALL RD

MARSHALL DR

RED ASH LN

170

Cowdrey Res. #2

Marshall Lake

S. 66th ST

80027

COAL CREEK DR

Superior

Eggleston Res. #4

Coal Creek

80303

128

BOULDER COUNTY

JEFFERSON COUNTY

W. 120th AVE

1900S 2600S

15 14 22 23 27 26 34 35

A B C D E F G H J K L M N P Q R S T U V W X Y Z

© Mapsco, Inc.

▲ See Map 743 ▲

▶ See Map 160 ▶

0 ¼ ½ Miles

▼ See Map 189 ▼

N

▲ See Map 130 ▲

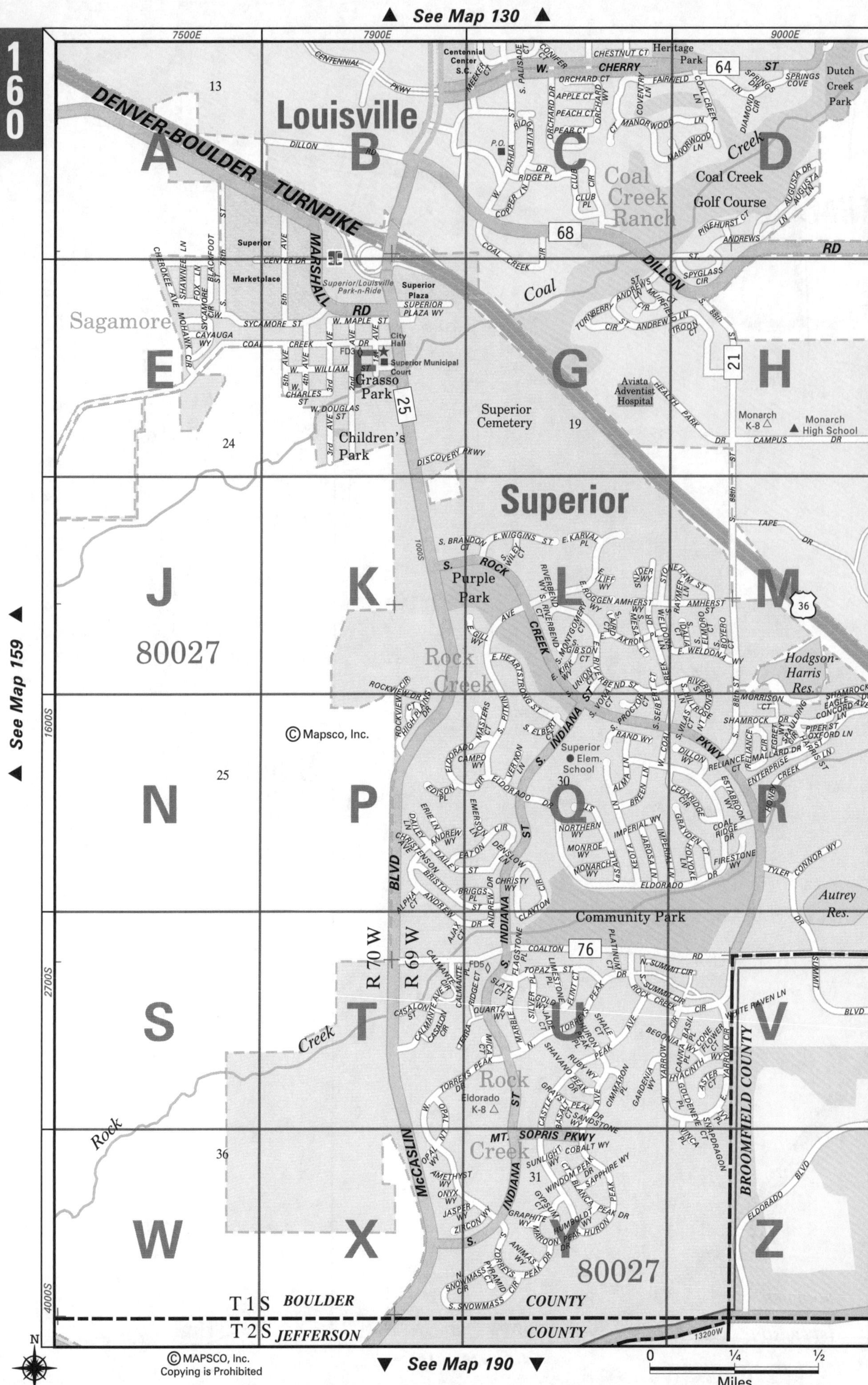

▲ See Map 159 ▲

▼ See Map 190 ▼

0 ¼ ½
Miles

▲ See Map 131 ▲

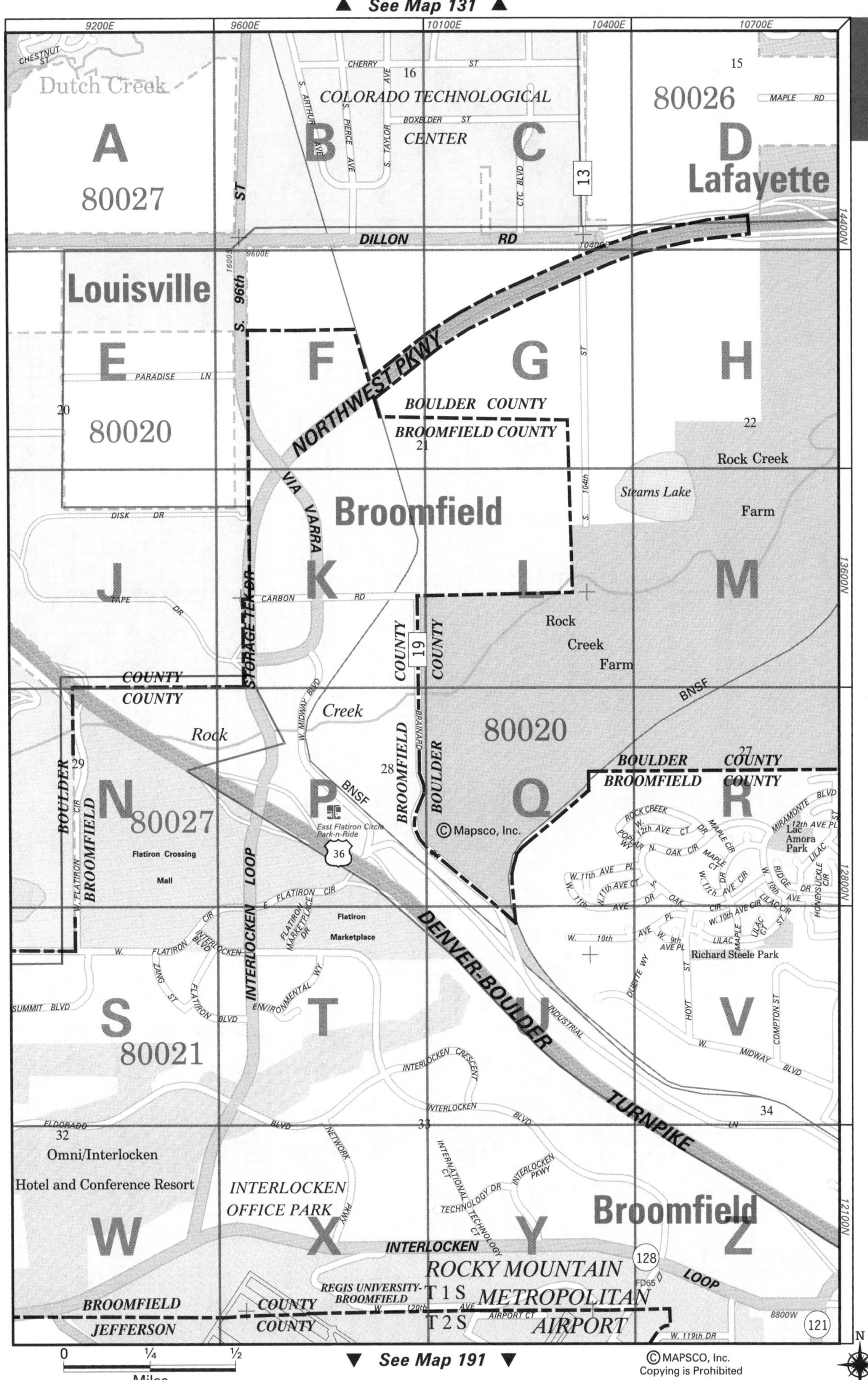

▲ See Map 162 ▶

▼ See Map 191 ▼

0 ¼ ½ Miles

▲ See Map 132 ▲

◄ See Map 161 ◄

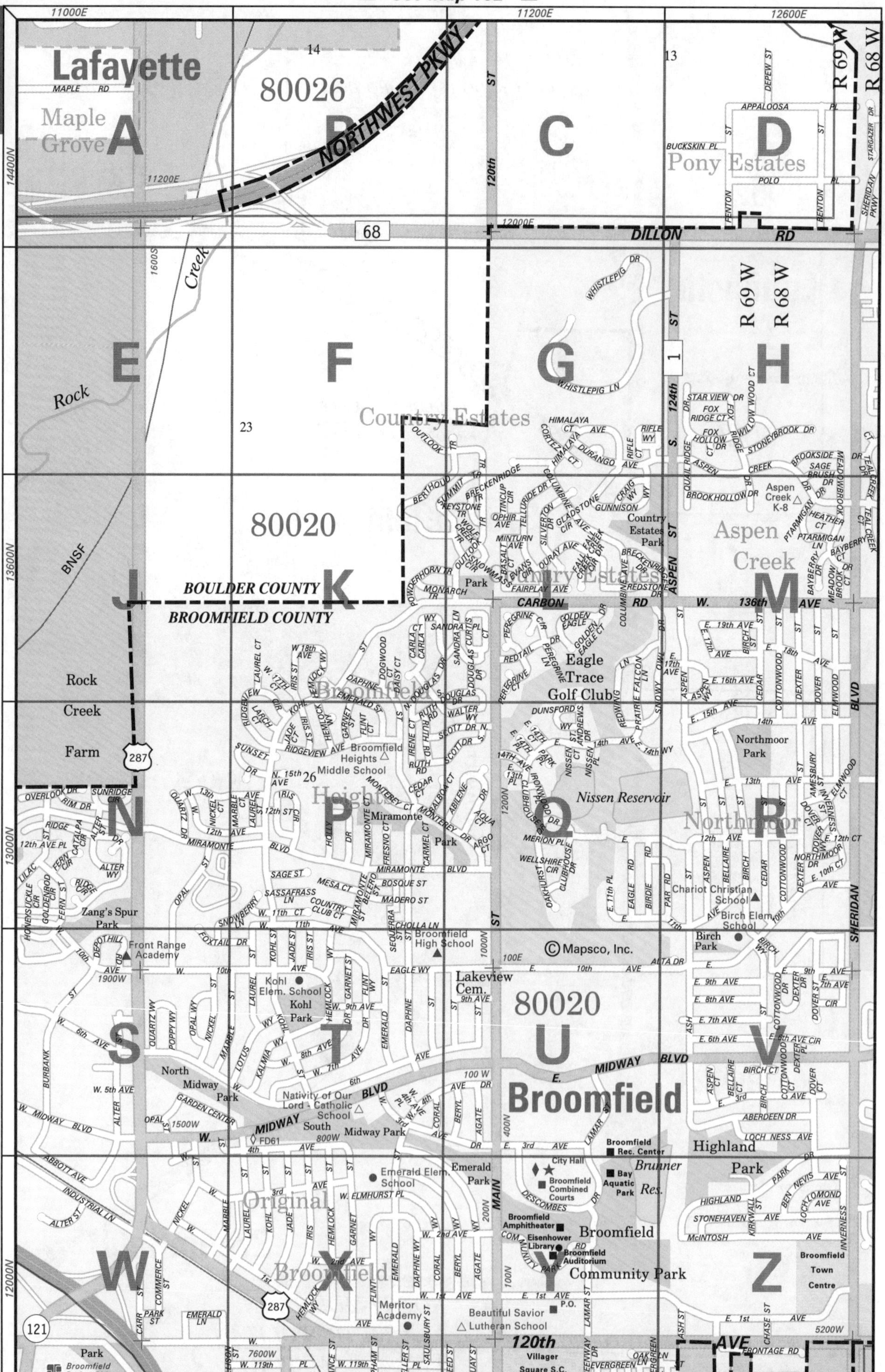

11000E 11200E 12600E 14400N 13600N 13000N 12000N

Lafayette
MAPLE RD
Maple Grove
A
14
80026
NORTHWEST PKWY
B
11200E
120th ST
C
13
APPALOOSA PL
DEPEW ST
BUCKSKIN PL
D
Pony Estates
POLO PL
FENTON
BENTON
R 69 W
R 68 W
STARGAZER DR
SHERIDAN PKWY
68
12000E
DILLON RD

1600S
Creek
Rock
E
F
WHISTLEPIG DR
G
WHISTLEPIG LN
124th S. ST
1
H
R 69 W
R 68 W
23
Country Estates

STAR VIEW DR
FOX RIDGE CT
FOX HOLLOW CT
WILLOW WOOD CT
STONEYBROOK DR
QUAIL RIDGE DR
ASPEN CREEK DR
BROOKHOLLOW DR
BROOKSIDE DR
SAGE BRUSH DR
MEADOWBROOK DR
Aspen Creek K-8
HEATHER CT
PTARMIGAN CT
PTARMIGAN LN
BAYBERRY DR
MEADOW BROOK CT
TEAL CREEK
TEAL CT
Aspen Creek
M

HIMALAYA CT
HIMALAYA AVE
CORTEZ CT
DURANGO AVE
RIFLE WY
RIFLE CT
OUTLOOK TR
BERTHOUD TR
SUMMIT TR
BRECKENRIDGE TR
KEYSTONE TR
WOLF CREEK TR
TINCUP CIR
OPHIR AVE
TELLURIDE DR
COLUMBINE DR
SILVERTON DR
GLADSTONE AVE
GUNNISON
CRAIG WY
Country Estates Park
MINTURN AVE
BASALT CT
EVANS CIR
OURAY AVE
FALL CREEK DR
BRECKENRIDGE DR
REDSTONE DR
POWDERHORN TR
OUTLOOK CIR
SNOWMASS CIR
MONARCH TR
Park
FAIRPLAY AVE
Country Estates
L

80020
BNSF
J
BOULDER COUNTY
K
BROOMFIELD COUNTY
CARBON RD
W. 136th AVE

Rock Creek Farm
287

W 18th AVE
LAUREL CT
W. 17th CIR
IRIS ST
HEMLOCK WY
DOGWOOD CT
DAISY CT
CARLA CT
SANDRA LN
DOUGLAS CIR
DAPHNE
RIDGEVIEW
LARCH CIR
KOHL
EMERALD ST
Broomfield
N. DOUGLAS DR
S. DOUGLAS DR
WALTER WY
RUTH RD
SCOTT DR N.
SCOTT DR S.
JADE CT
GARNET ST
FLINT ST
IRENE CT
SUNSET DR
RIDGEVIEW AVE
Broomfield Heights Middle School
RUTH RD
N. 15th AVE
26
MONTEREY CT
CEDAR CT
BALBOA CT
ABILENE DR
Heights
P
Miramonte Park
MONTEREY DR
ARGO CT
AQUA CT

PEREGRINE CIR
GOLDEN EAGLE DR
GOLDEN EAGLE CT
REDTAIL CT
PEREGRINE LN
PEREGRINE CT
Eagle Trace Golf Club
DUNSFORD WY
E. 14th CT
ST. ANDREWS CT
14th AVE
14th WY
E. 13th PL
CLUBHOUSE DR
IRONWOOD DR
NISSEN ST
NISSEN PL
REDWING LN
PRAIRIE FALCON LN
SNOWY OWL DR
Nissen Reservoir
Q
MERION DR
WELLSHIRE CIR
CLUBHOUSE DR
OAKHURST CIR

E. 19th AVE
17th AVE
BIRCH ST
18th AVE
COTTONWOOD
DEXTER
DOVER
ELMWOOD
E. 16th AVE
E. 15th AVE
14th AVE
Northmoor Park
SHERIDAN BLVD
13th AVE
AMESBURY
ELMWOOD CT
INVERNESS
Northmoor
R
E. 12th CT
NORTHMOOR CT
E. 10th CT
12th AVE
BELLAIRE
BIRCH
CEDAR
COTTONWOOD
Chariot Christian School
Birch Elem. School
Birch Park
EAGLE RD
BIRDIE
PAR RD
E. 11th PL

OVERLOOK DR
SUNRIDGE CIR
RIM DR
W. 13th AVE
NICKEL CT
MARBLE CT
LAUREL CT
IRIS
12th ST
N
RIDGE CIR
CATALPA CIR
ALTER ST
12th AVE PL
FERN CIR
12th AVE
MIRAMONTE BLVD
ALTER WY
LILAC
GOLDENROD CIR
RIDGE CIR
HONEYSUCKLE CIR
FERN ST
Zang's Spur Park
OPAL
SNOWBERRY LN
SAGE ST
SASSAFRASS LN
COUNTRY CLUB CT
MESA CT
MIRAMONTE ST
BELFORD
BOSQUE ST
MADERO ST
HOLLY DR
MIRAMONTE CT
FRESNO CT
CARMEL CT
MIRAMONTE BLVD
SEQUERRA ST
CHOLLA LN
W. 11th CT
11th AVE

DEPOT HILL
Front Range Academy
10th AVE
1900W
FOXTAIL DR
KOHL ST
JADE ST
IRIS ST
Broomfield High School
1000N
100E
Mapsco, Inc.
ALTA DR
EAGLE WY
W. 10th
E. 10th AVE
Kohl Elem. School
Kohl Park
W. 9th AVE
Lakeview Cem.
9th AVE
80020
E. 9th AVE
E. 8th AVE
E. 7th AVE
E. 6th AVE
9th AVE
7th AVE
DOVER ST
CIR
QUARTZ WY
POPPY WY
OPAL WY
NICKEL
MARBLE
LAUREL
W. 6th AVE
S
LOTUS
KALMIA WY
W. 8th AVE
W. 7th AVE
T
U
E. MIDWAY BLVD
V
E. 6th AVE CIR
BIRCH CT
BURBANK
North Midway Park
W. 5th AVE
GARDEN CENTER
6th
Nativity of Our Lord Catholic School
MIDWAY BLVD
W. MIDWAY BLVD
OPAL ST
1500W
W.
South Midway Park
800W
FD61
4th
100 W
CORAL
BERYL
AGATE
400N
Broomfield
LAMAR ST
3rd AVE
Broomfield Rec. Center
BELLAIRE CT
3rd
ABERDEEN DR
LOCH NESS AVE
Highland Park

ABBOTT AVE
INDUSTRIAL LN
ALTER ST
NICKEL
Emerald Elem. School
Emerald Park
City Hall
Broomfield Combined Courts
Bay Aquatic Park
Brunner Res.
W. ELMHURST PL
Original
DESCOMBES
HIGHLAND
KIRKWALL ST
BEN NEVIS AVE
LOCH LOMOND AVE
STONEHAVEN AVE
McINTOSH AVE
INVERNESS
Broomfield Amphitheater
COMMUNITY PARK
Eisenhower Library
Broomfield Auditorium
Broomfield Community Park
Broomfield Town Centre
W
COMMERCE ST
X
Broomfield
W. 2nd AVE
200N
Y
Z
287
HEMLOCK WY
Meritor Academy
W. 1st AVE
E. 1st AVE
P.O.
Beautiful Savior Lutheran School
E. 1st AVE
CHASE ST
5200W
121
CARR ST
PARK ST
EMERALD LN
Park
Broomfield Park-n-Ride
7600W
W. 119th
PL
W. 119th PL
VANCE ST
UPHAM ST
TELLER ST
SAULSBURY ST
REED ST
QUAY ST
120th AVE
Villager Square S.C.
GREENWAY
EVERGREEN
OAK LN
FRONTAGE RD

▼ See Map 192 ▼

0 ¼ ½
Miles

▲ See Map 133 ▲

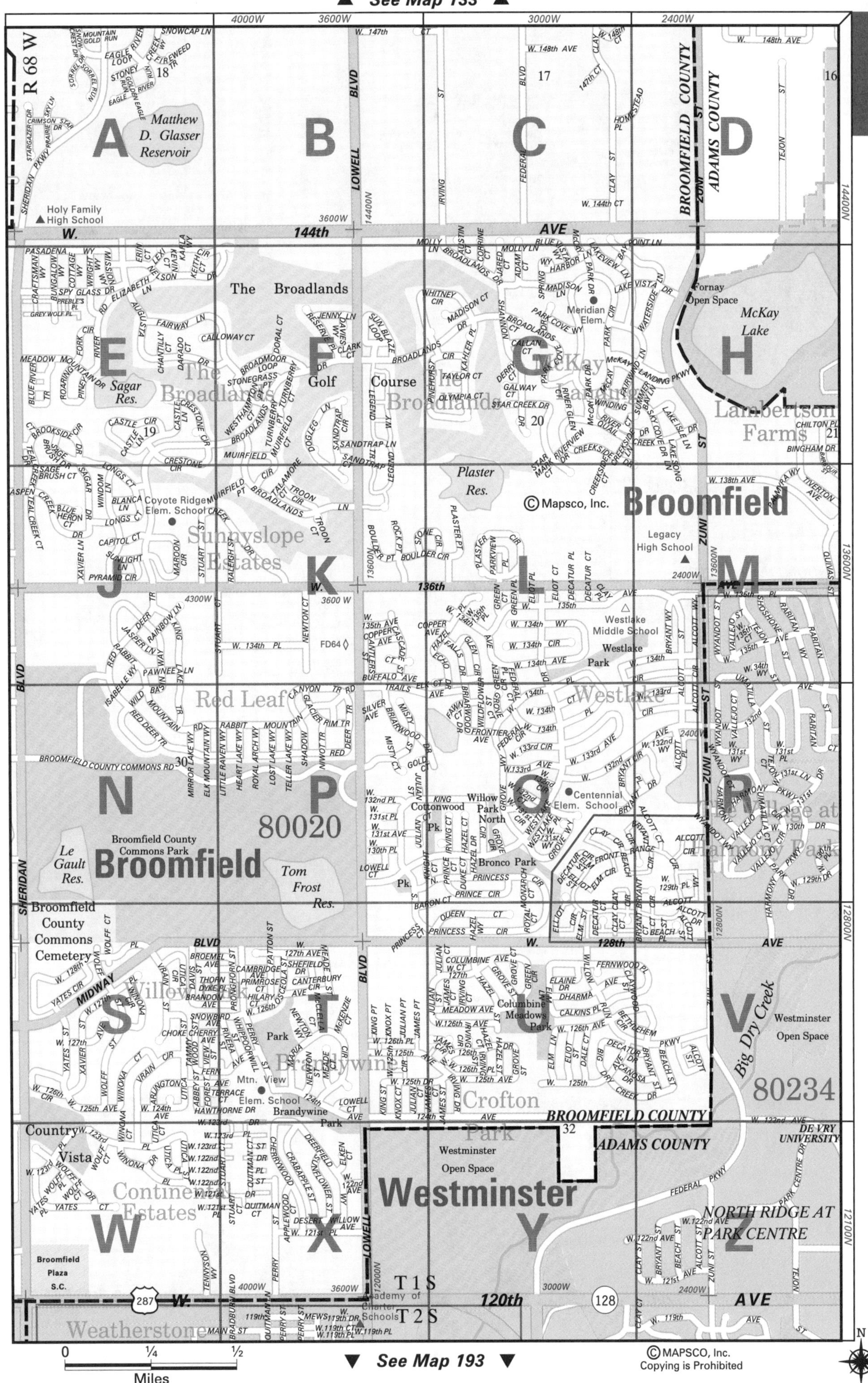

▲ See Map 164 ▲

▼ See Map 193 ▼

▲ See Map 134 ▲

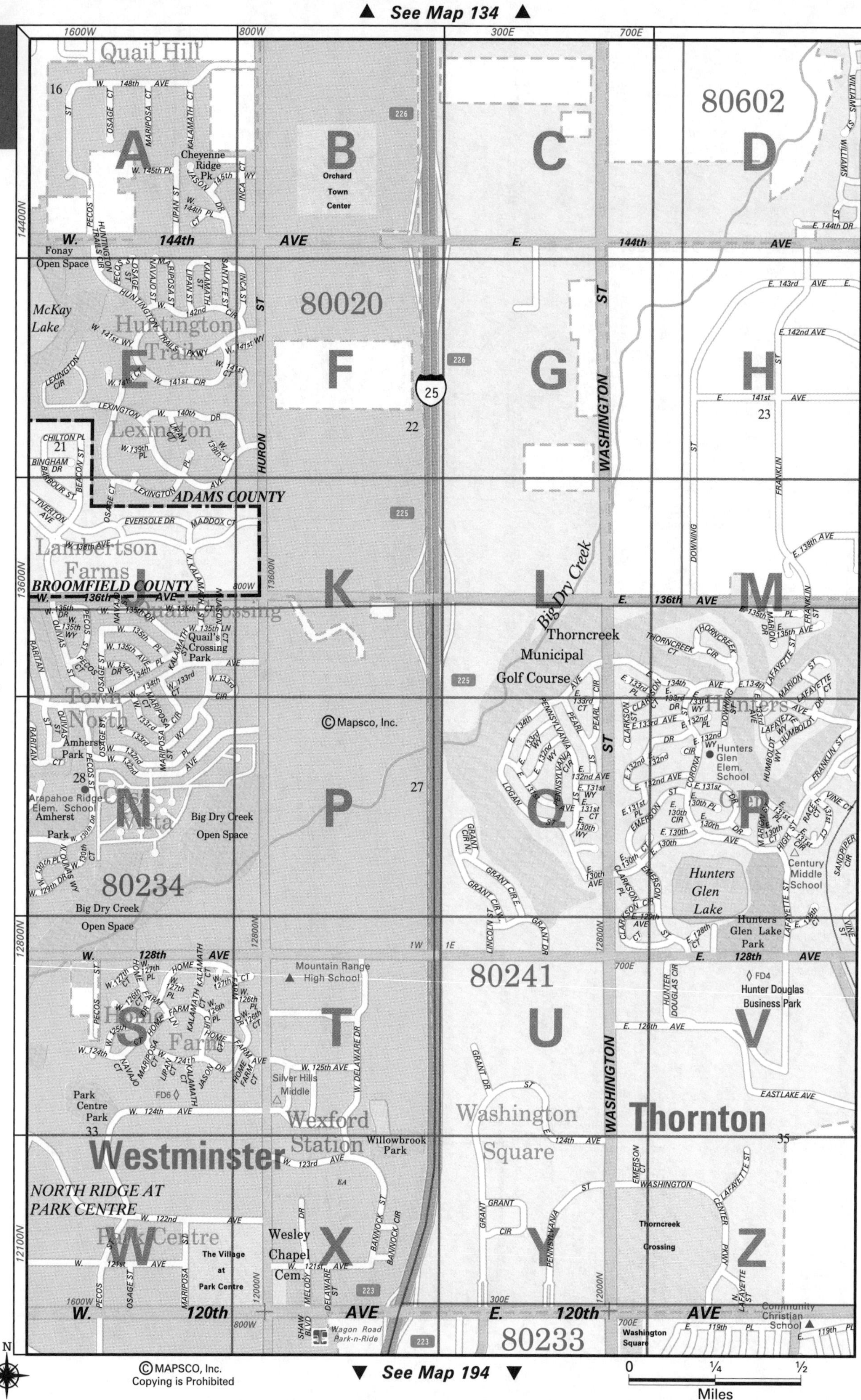

▲ See Map 163 ▲

▼ See Map 194 ▼

0 ¼ ½
Miles

▲ See Map 135 ▲

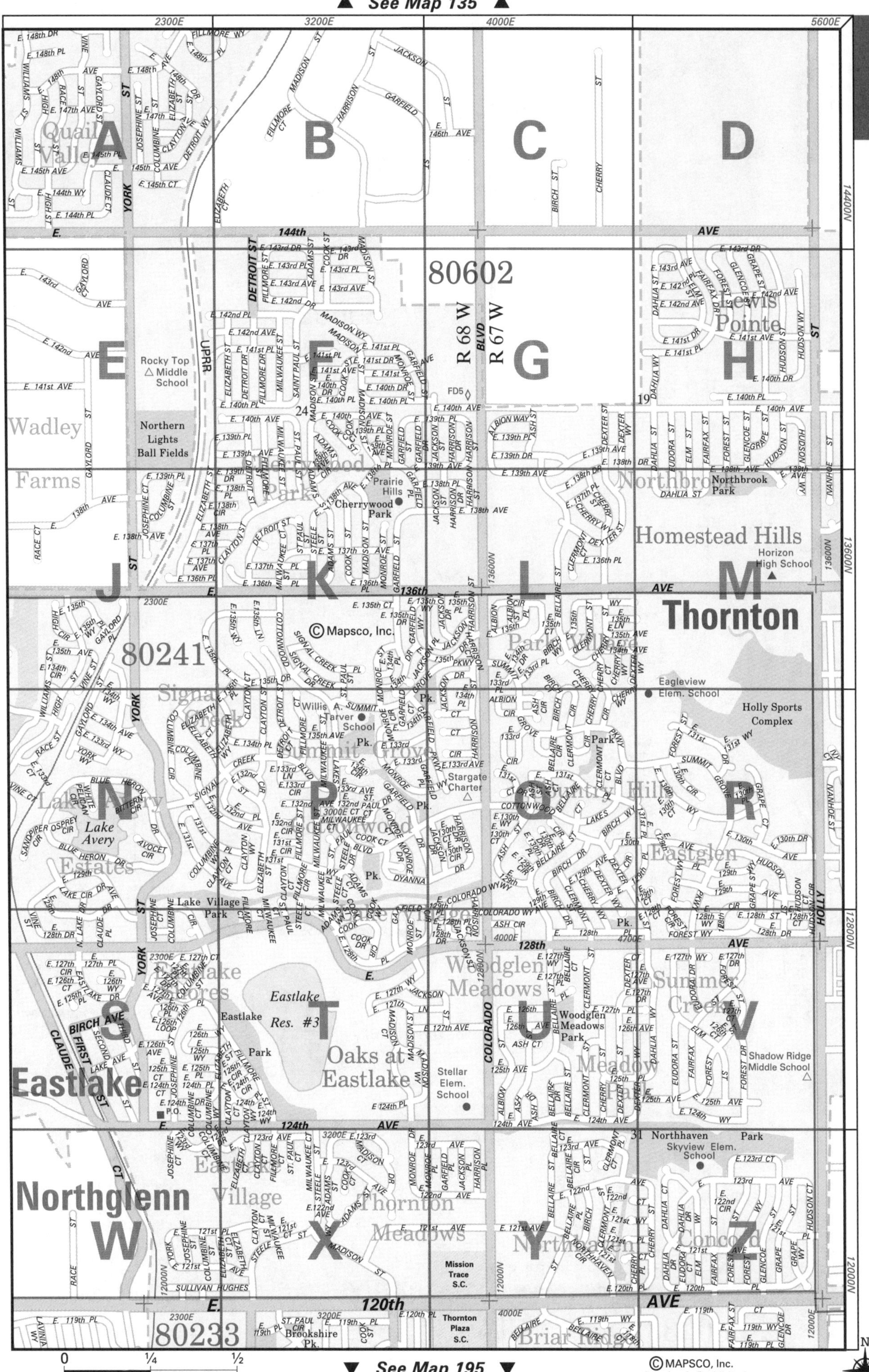

▶ See Map 166 ▶

▼ See Map 195 ▼

▲ See Map 136 ▲

◄ See Map 165 ◄

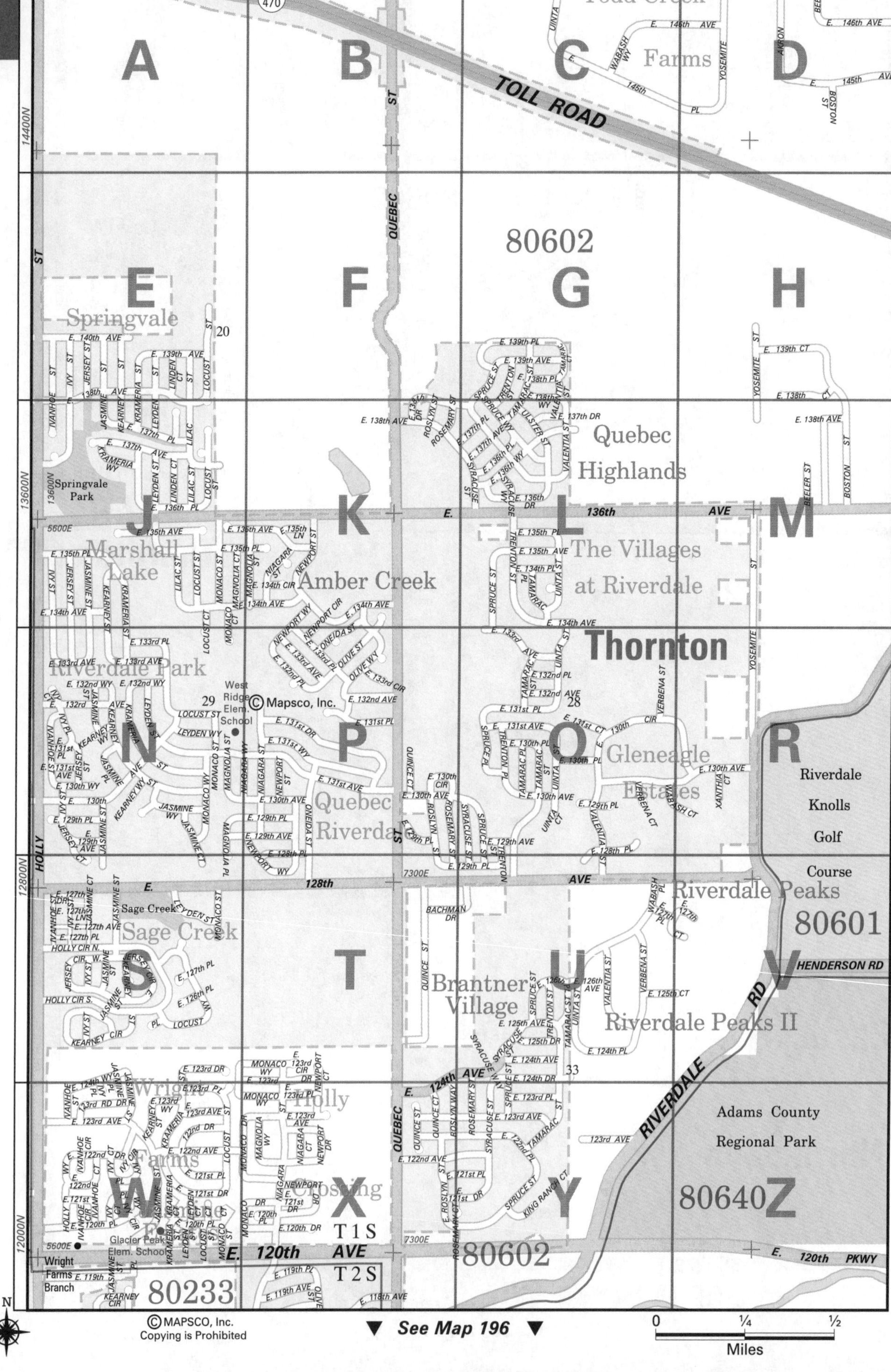

▼ See Map 196 ▼

0 ¼ ½
Miles

▲ See Map 137 ▲

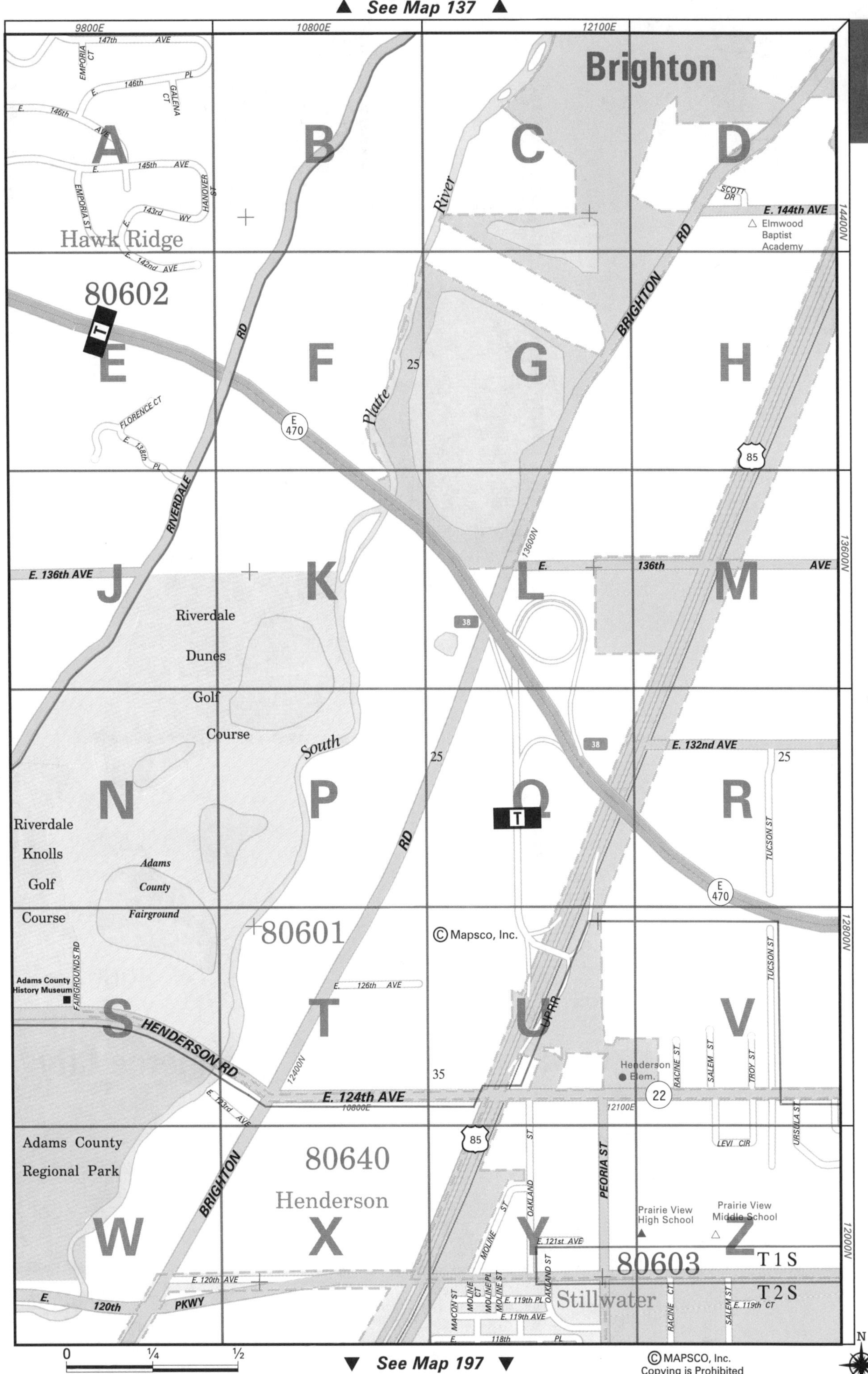

▶ See Map 168 ▶

0 ¼ ½ Miles

▼ See Map 197 ▼

▲ See Map 138 ▲

▲ See Map 167 ▲

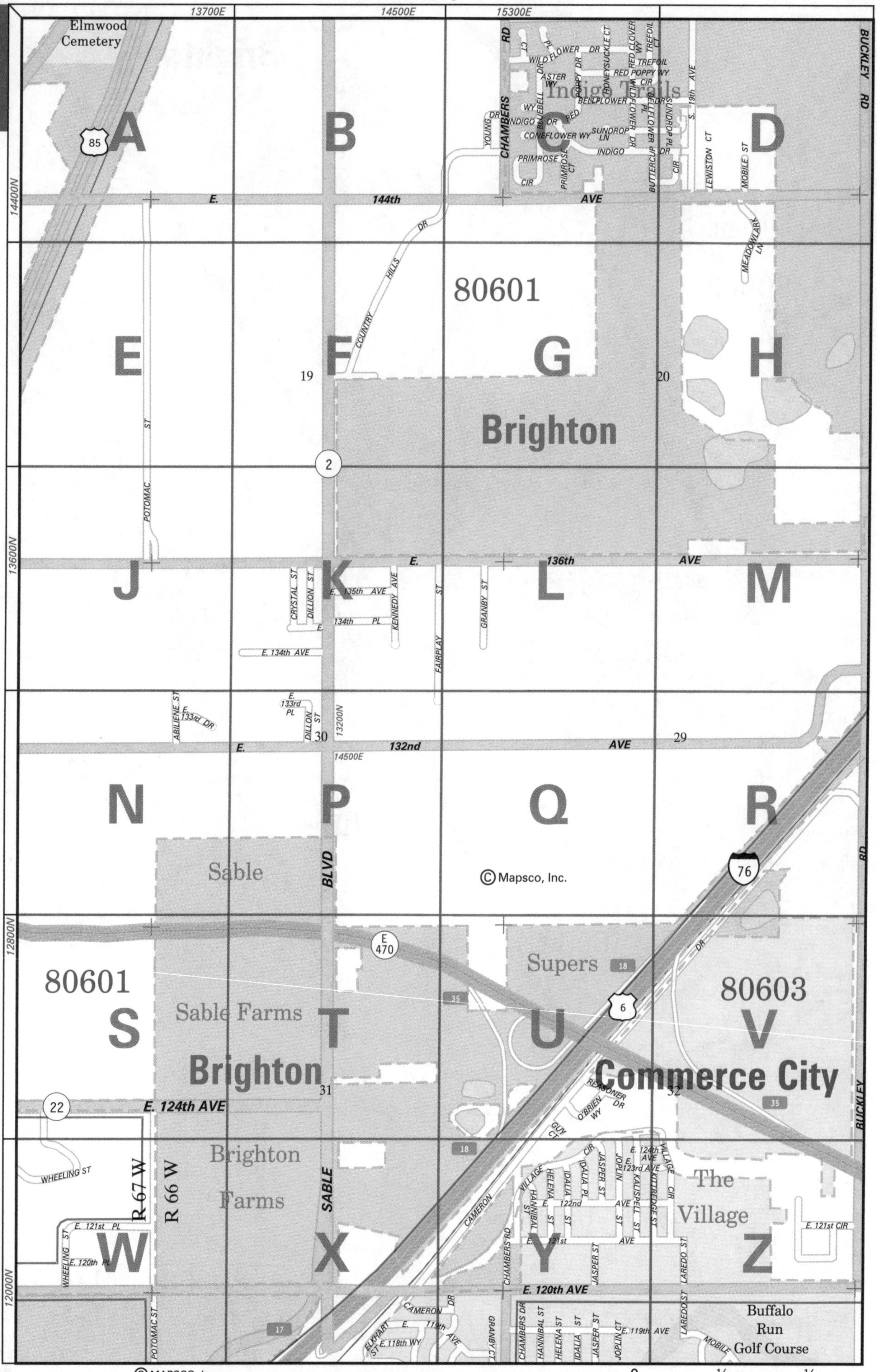

Elmwood Cemetery

Indigo Trails

80601

Brighton

Sable

Sable Farms

Brighton

Brighton Farms

Supers

80603

Commerce City

The Village

Buffalo Run Golf Course

E. 144th AVE

E. 136th AVE

E. 132nd AVE

E. 124th AVE

E. 120th AVE

CHAMBERS RD

BUCKLEY RD

SABLE BLVD

POTOMAC ST

R 67 W

R 66 W

© Mapsco, Inc.

▼ See Map 198 ▼

0 ¼ ½
Miles

▲ See Map 139 ▲

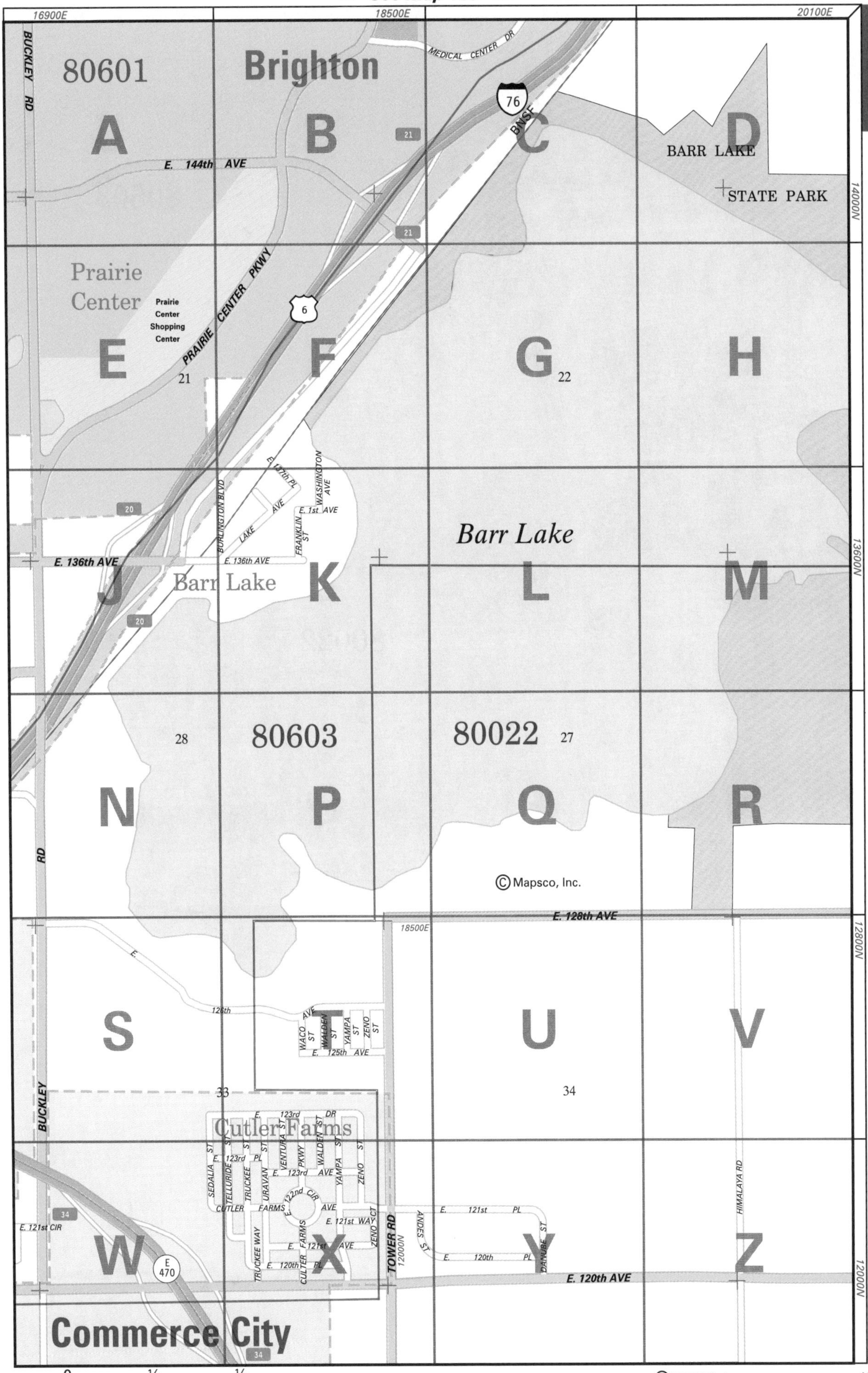

16900E
18500E
20100E

80601
Brighton
BUCKLEY RD
MEDICAL CENTER DR
76
BNSF
E. 144th AVE
BARR LAKE
STATE PARK
14000N
21
Prairie Center
Prairie Center Shopping Center
PRAIRIE CENTER PKWY
6
22
E. 137th PL
WASHINGTON AVE
E. 1st AVE
LAKE AVE
BURLINGTON BLVD
FRANKLIN ST
20
Barr Lake
E. 136th AVE
Barr Lake
13600N

▲ See Map 170 ▲

28
80603
80022
27
RD
© Mapsco, Inc.
E. 128th AVE
18500E
12800N
E. 126th
WACO ST
WALDEN ST
YAMPA ST
ZENO ST
E. 125th AVE
33
34
BUCKLEY
Cutler Farms
E. 123rd DR
E. 123rd PL
E. 123rd AVE
SEDALIA ST
TELLURIDE ST
TRUCKEE ST
URAVAN ST
VENTURA ST
PKWY
WALDEN ST
YAMPA ST
ZENO ST
E. 122nd CIR
CUTLER FARMS AVE
E. 121st WAY
ZENO CT
E. 121st AVE
TRUCKEE WAY
CULTER FARMS
E. 120th PL
E. 121st CIR
E 470
TOWER RD
12000N
ANDES ST
E. 121st PL
E. 120th PL
DANUBE ST
HIMALAYA RD
E. 120th AVE
12000N
Commerce City

A B C D E F G H J K L M N P Q R S T U V W X Y Z

0 ¼ ½
Miles

▼ See Map 769 ▼

N

▲ See Map 140 ▲

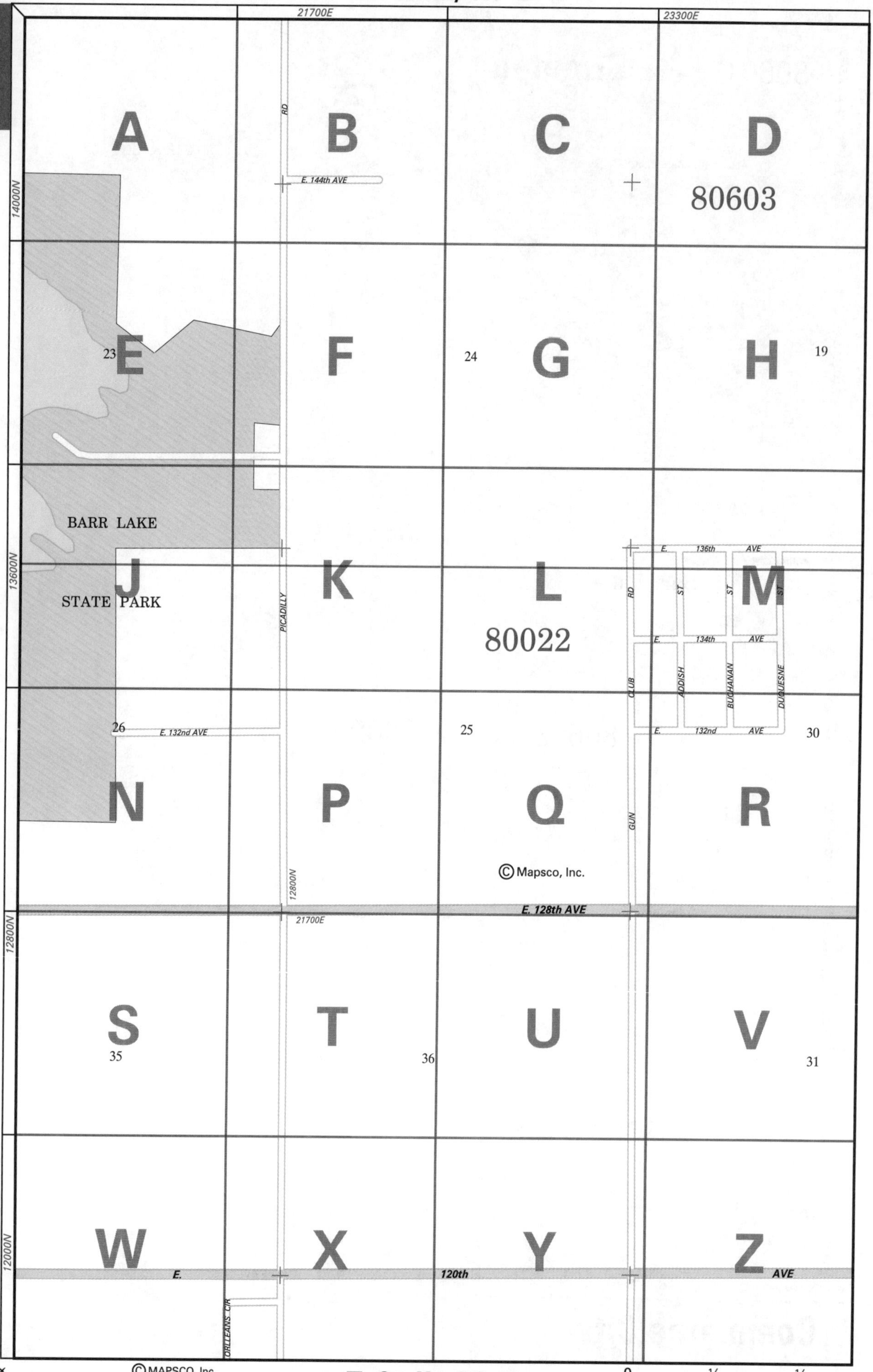

21700E
23300E
14000N
13600N
12800N
12000N
12800N
21700E

A
B
C
D
E
F
G
H
J
K
L
M
N
P
Q
R
S
T
U
V
W
X
Y
Z

80603
80022

BARR LAKE
STATE PARK

E. 144th AVE
E. 136th AVE
E. 134th AVE
E. 132nd AVE
E. 128th AVE
E. 120th AVE
PICADILLY RD
CLUB RD
GUN
ADDISH ST
BUCHANAN ST
DUQUESNE ST
ORLLEANS CIR

23
24
19
26
25
30
35
36
31

© Mapsco, Inc.

▲ See Map 169 ▲

▼ See Map 769 ▼

0 ¼ ½
Miles
N

▲ See Map 159 ▲

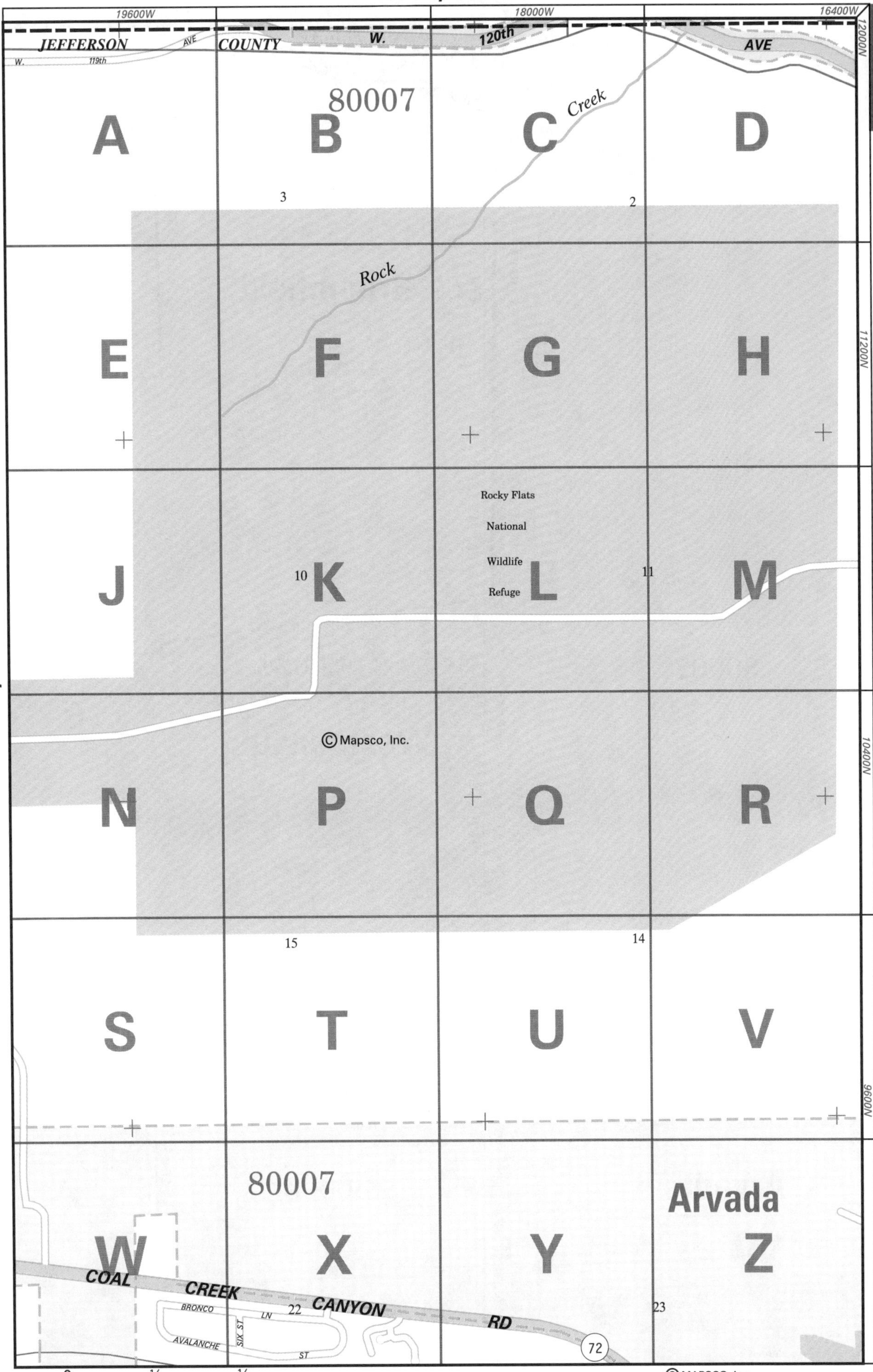

◄ See Map 763 ►

► See Map 190 ►

0 ¼ ½
Miles

▼ See Map 219 ▼

N

See Map 160

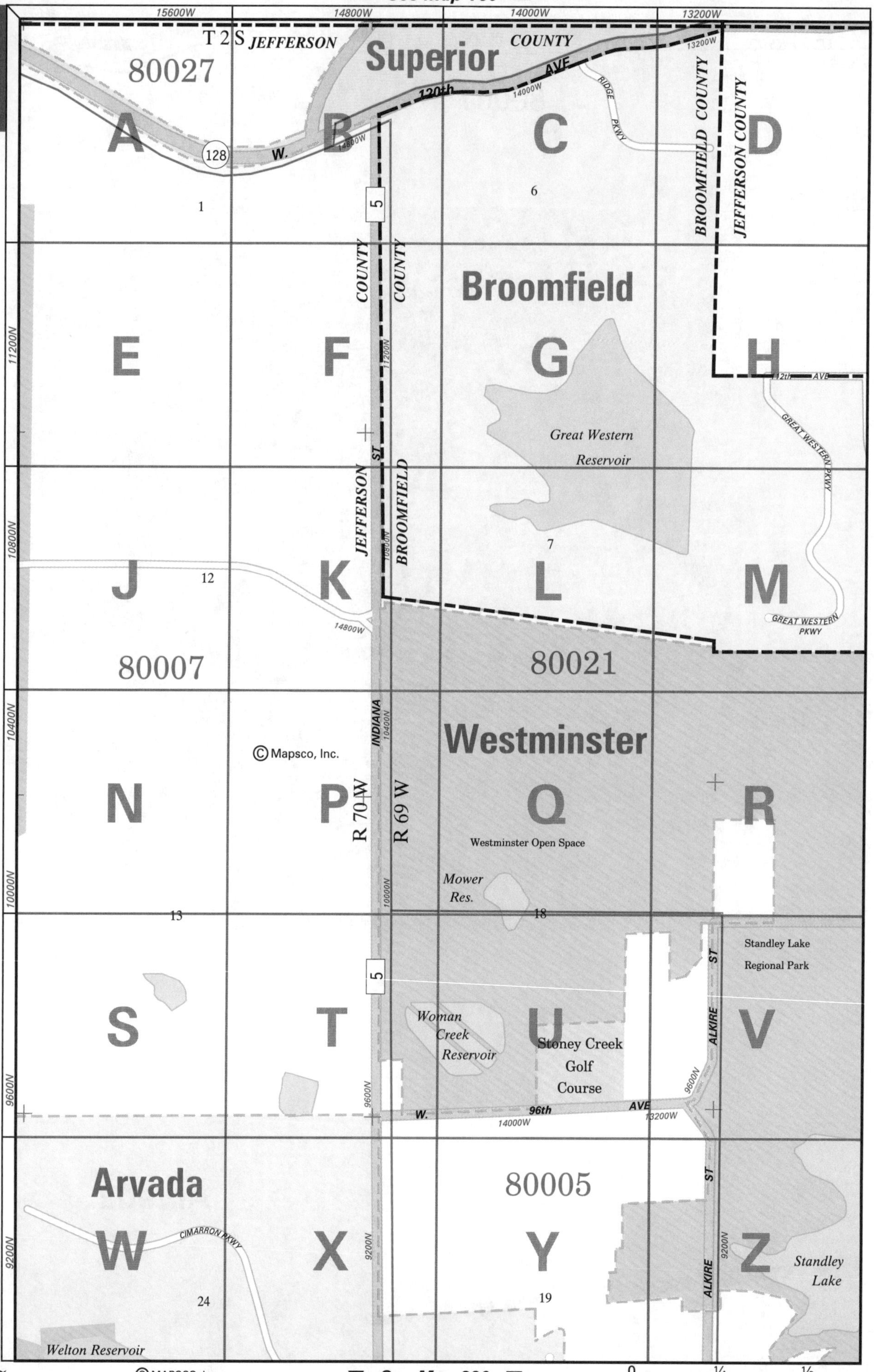

15600W 14800W 14000W 13200W

T 2 S JEFFERSON COUNTY

Superior

80027

W. 120th AVE

128

14800W 14000W 13200W

RIDGE PKWY

BROOMFIELD COUNTY

JEFFERSON COUNTY

A B C D

1 6

5

COUNTY COUNTY

Broomfield

11200N

E F G H

112th AVE

Great Western Reservoir

GREAT WESTERN PKWY

JEFFERSON ST

BROOMFIELD

10800N

J K L M

12 7

14800W

GREAT WESTERN PKWY

80007

80021

INDIANA

10400N

Westminster

© Mapsco, Inc.

R 70 W R 69 W

N P Q R

Westminster Open Space

Mower Res.

10000N

13 18

Standley Lake Regional Park

5

ALKIRE ST

Woman Creek Reservoir

Stoney Creek Golf Course

S T U V

9600N

W. 96th AVE

14000W 13200W

Arvada

80005

CIMARRON PKWY

9200N

ALKIRE ST

W X Y Z

Standley Lake

24 19

Welton Reservoir

See Map 189

N

See Map 220

0 ¼ ½
Miles

▲ See Map 161 ▲

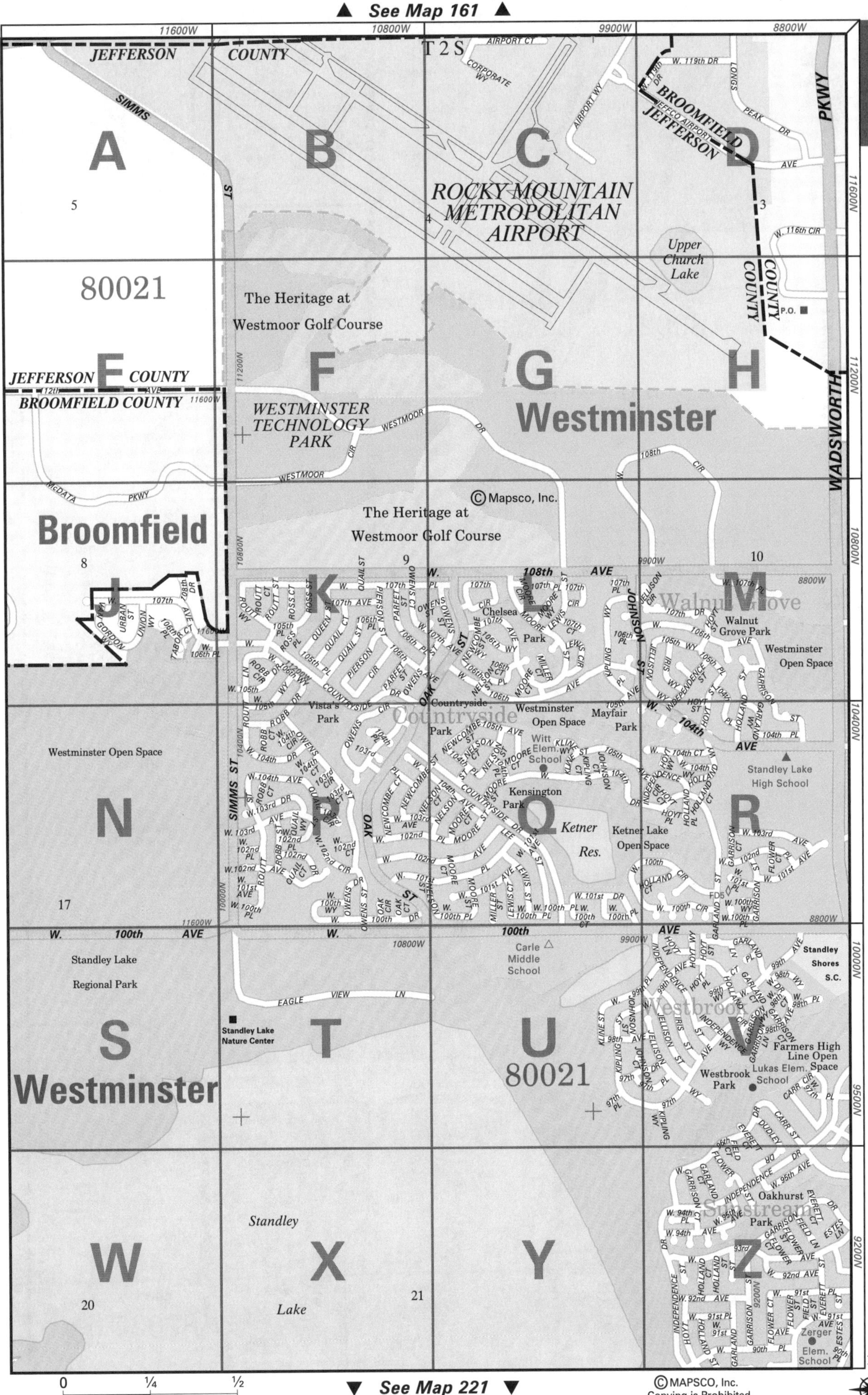

▲ See Map 192 ▶

0 ¼ ½
Miles

▼ See Map 221 ▼

See Map 162

See Map 191

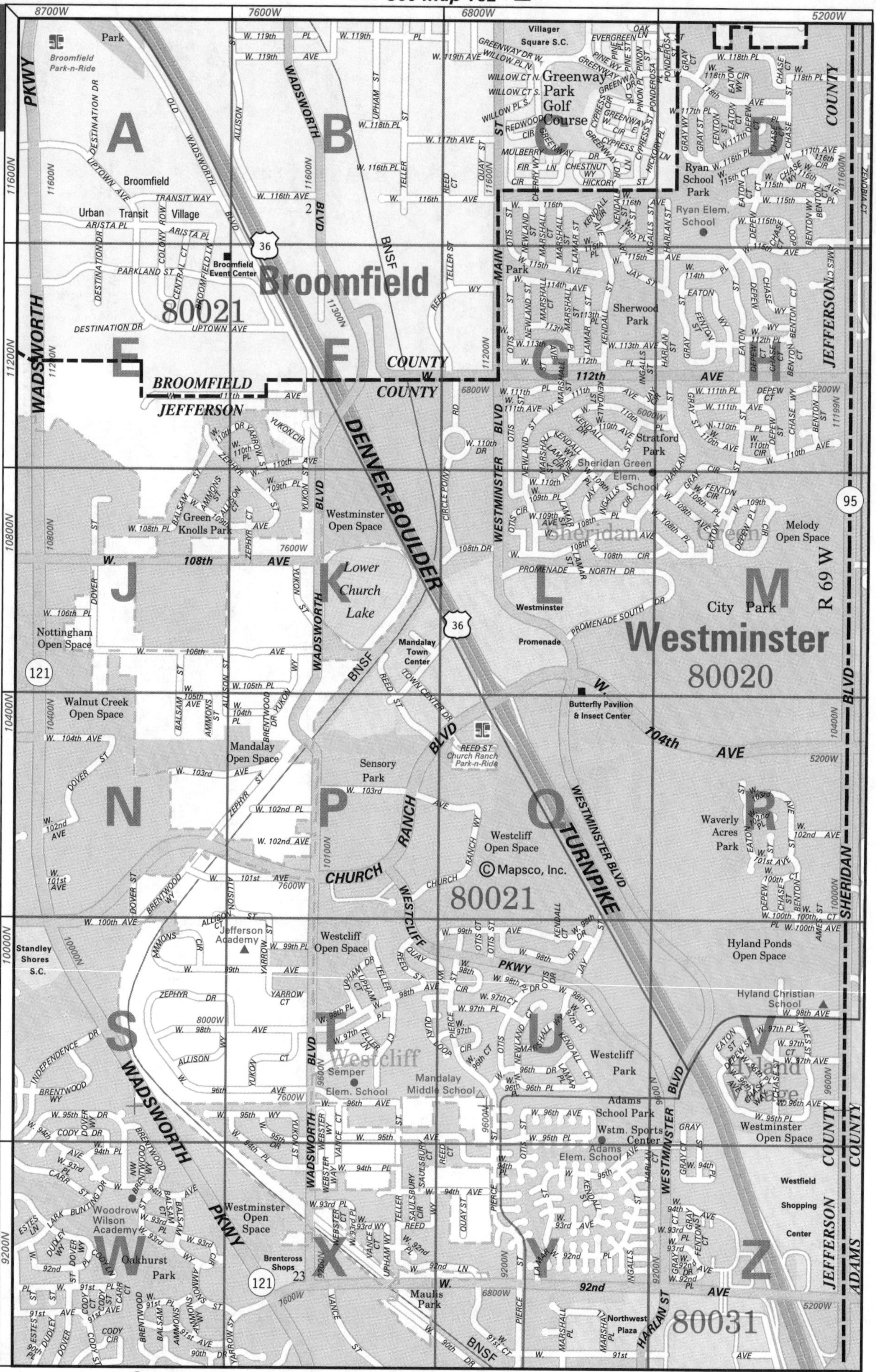

See Map 222

0 ¼ ½
Miles

▲ See Map 163 ▲

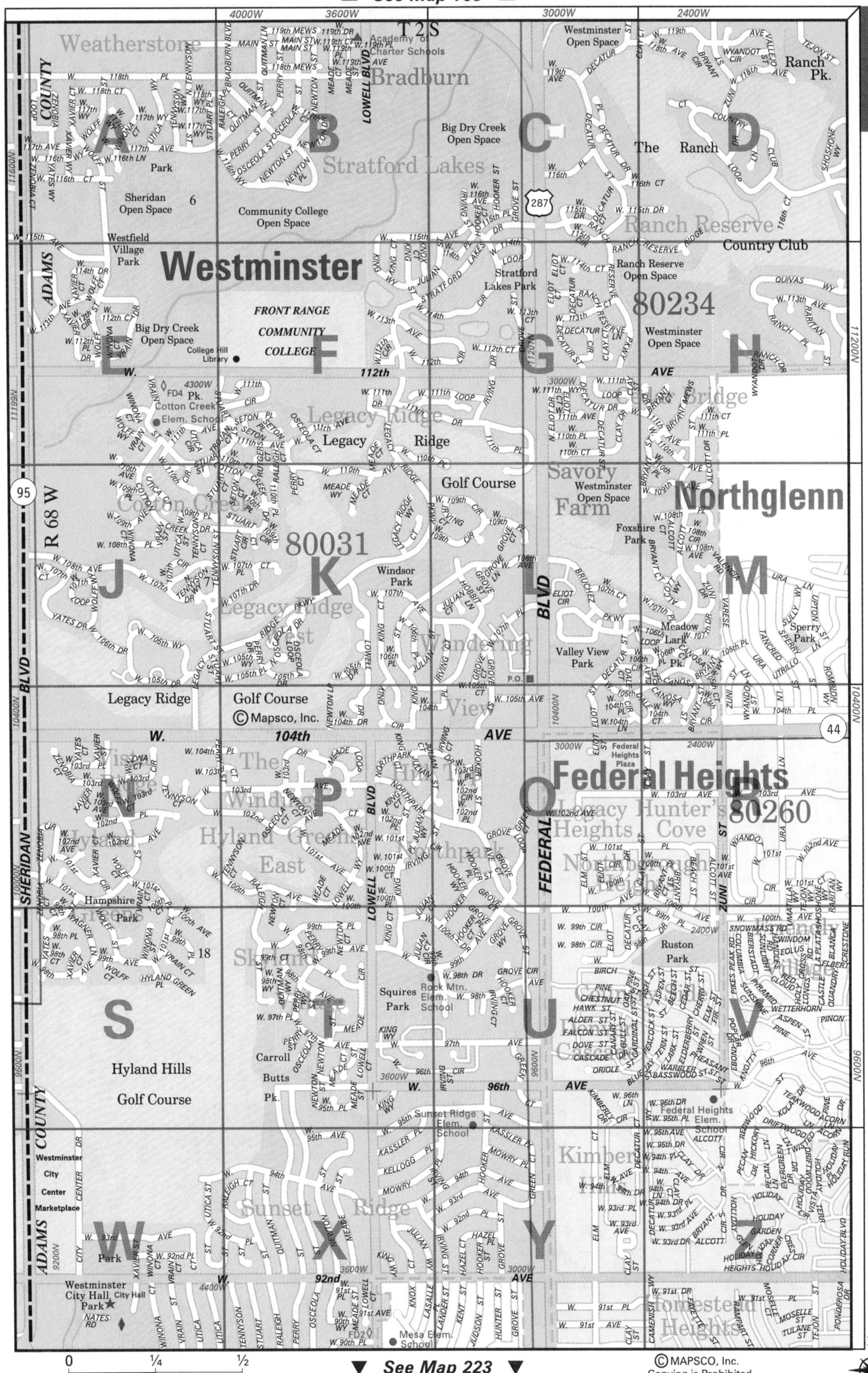

▲ See Map 194 ▲

0 ¼ ½
Miles

▼ See Map 223 ▼

▲ See Map 164 ▲

◀ See Map 193 ▶

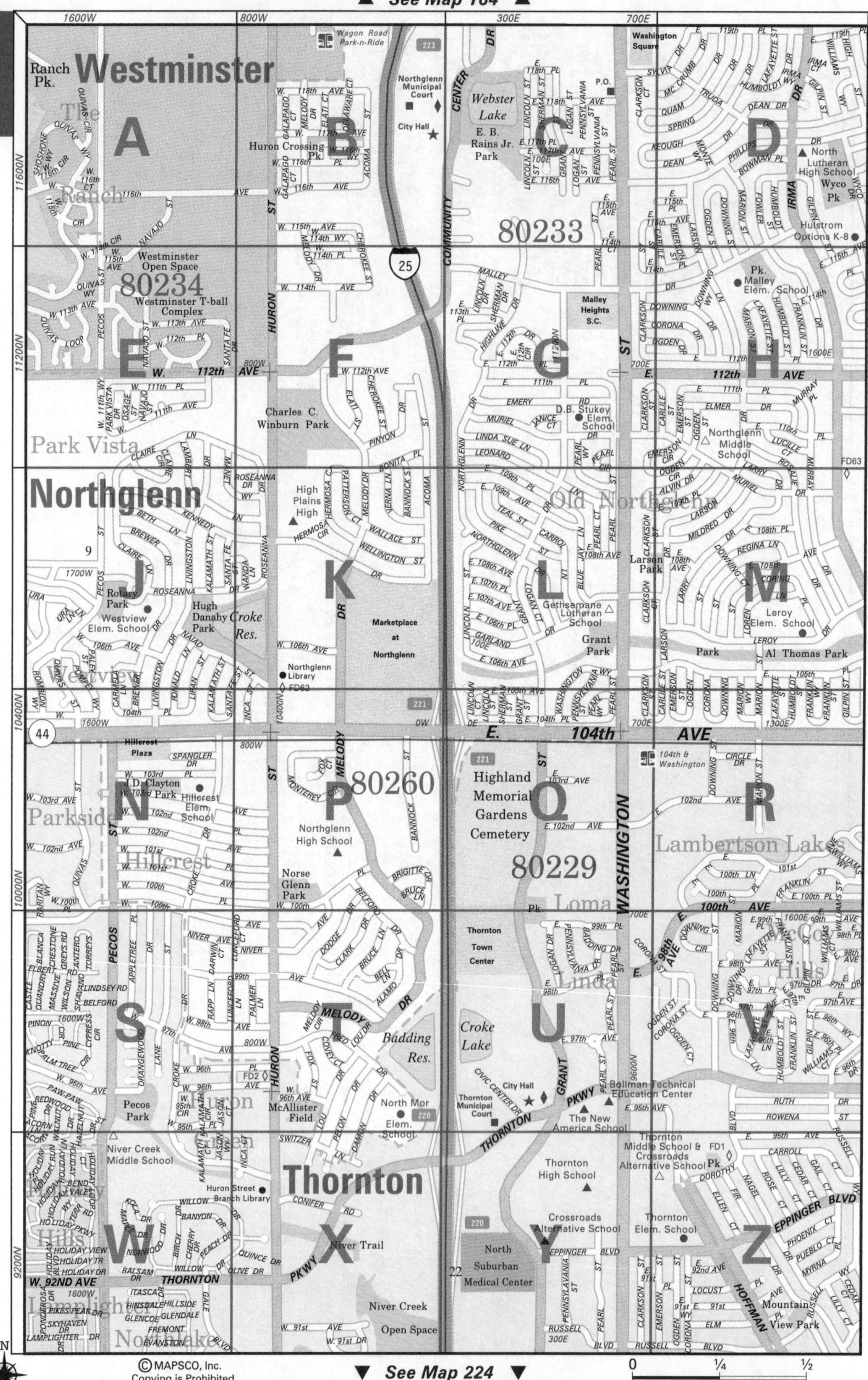

▼ See Map 224 ▼

0 ¼ ½
Miles

▲ See Map 165 ▲

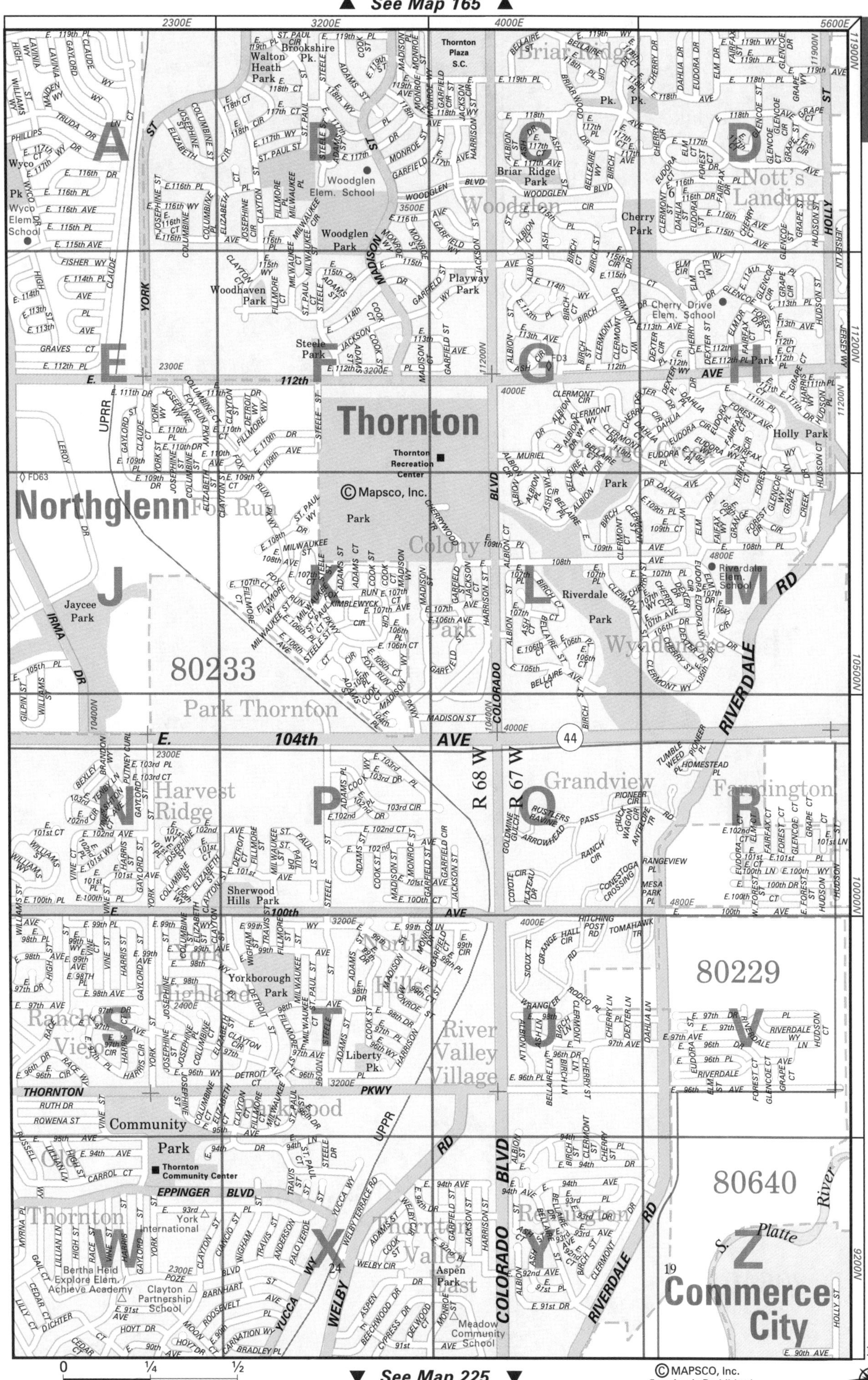

0 ¼ ½
Miles

▼ See Map 225 ▼

▶ See Map 196 ▶

▲ See Map 166 ▲

◄ See Map 195 ◄

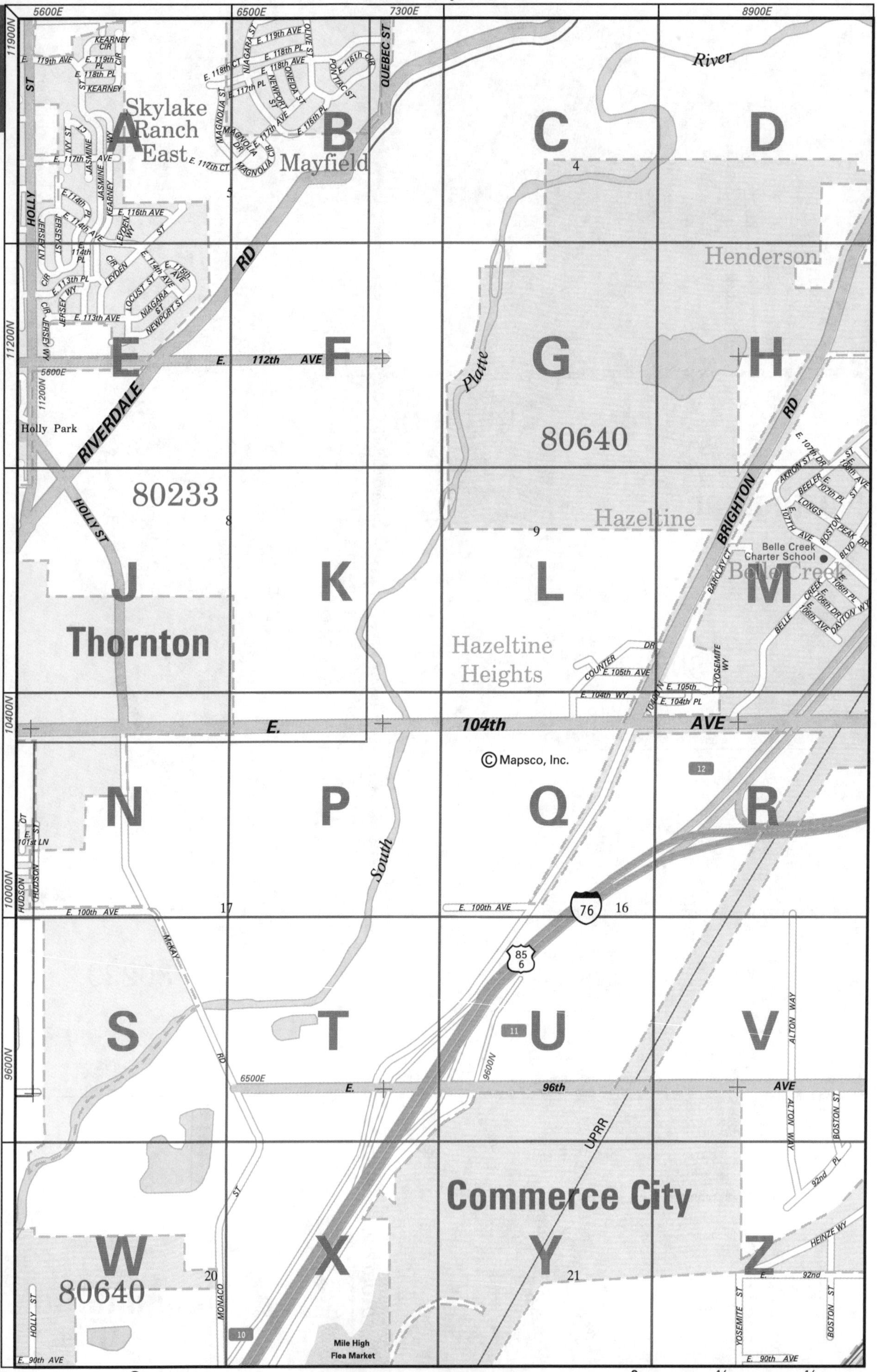
5600E
6500E
7300E
8900E
11900N
11200N
10400N
10000N
9600N
A
B
C
D
E
F
G
H
J
K
L
M
N
P
Q
R
S
T
U
V
W
X
Y
Z
Skylake Ranch East
Mayfield
Henderson
Holly Park
Thornton
Hazeltine
Hazeltine Heights
Belle Creek
Belle Creek Charter School
Commerce City
Mile High Flea Market
80233
80640
80640
River
Platte
South
RIVERDALE RD
BRIGHTON RD
QUEBEC ST
HOLLY ST
E. 112th AVE
E. 104th AVE
E. 100th AVE
E. 96th AVE
E. 92nd
E. 90th AVE
McKAY RD
MONACO ST
UPRR
ALTON WAY
BOSTON ST
YOSEMITE ST
HEINZE WY
HUDSON ST
COUNTER DR
E. 105th AVE
E. 104th WY
E. 104th PL
E. 113th AVE
E. 116th AVE
E. 117th AVE
E. 119th AVE
E. 118th PL
76
85
6
© Mapsco, Inc.

▼ See Map 226 ▼

0 ¼ ½
Miles

▲ See Map 167 ▲

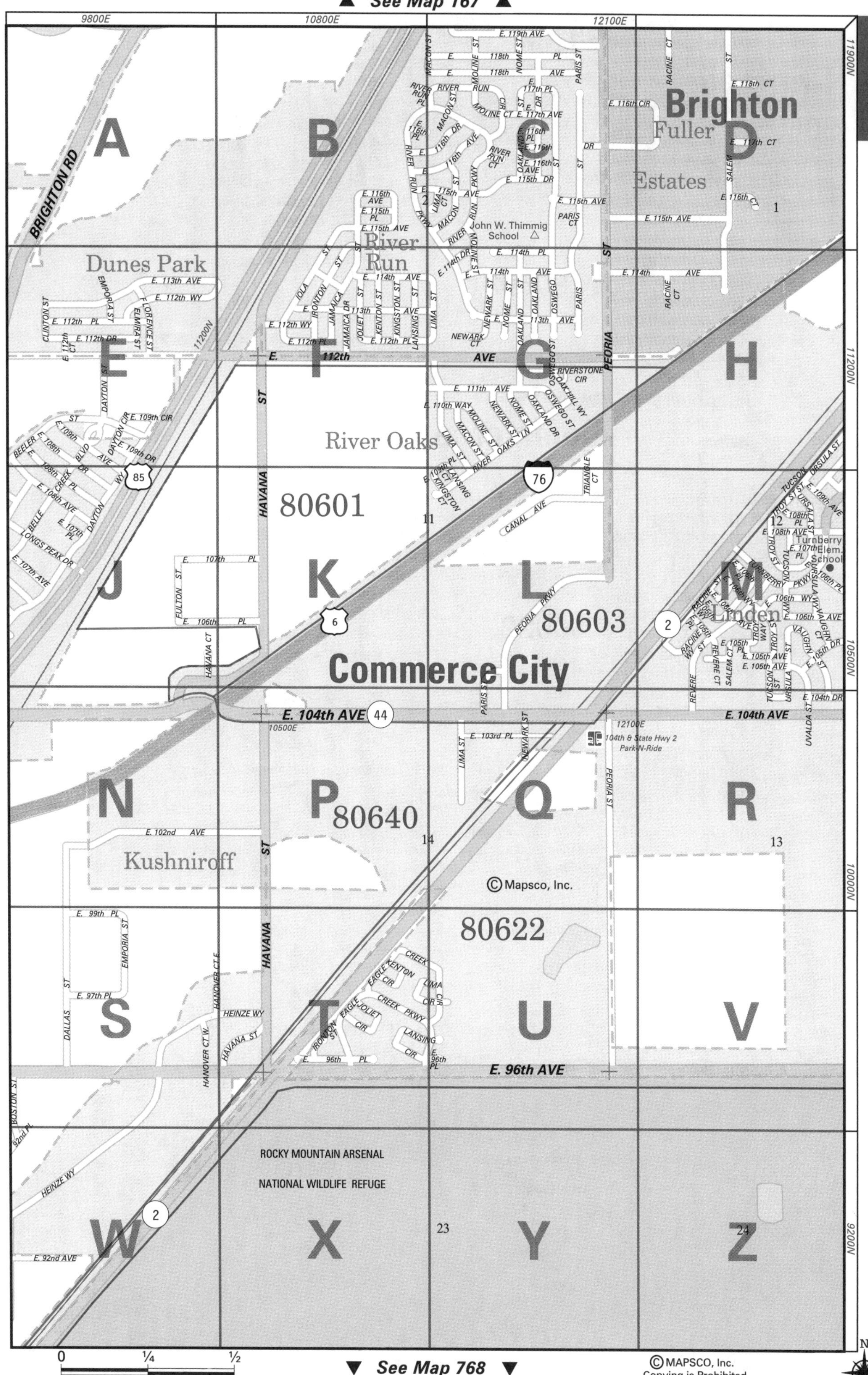

▶ See Map 198 ▶

0 ¼ ½
Miles

▼ See Map 768 ▼

N

See Map 168

See Map 197

See Map 769

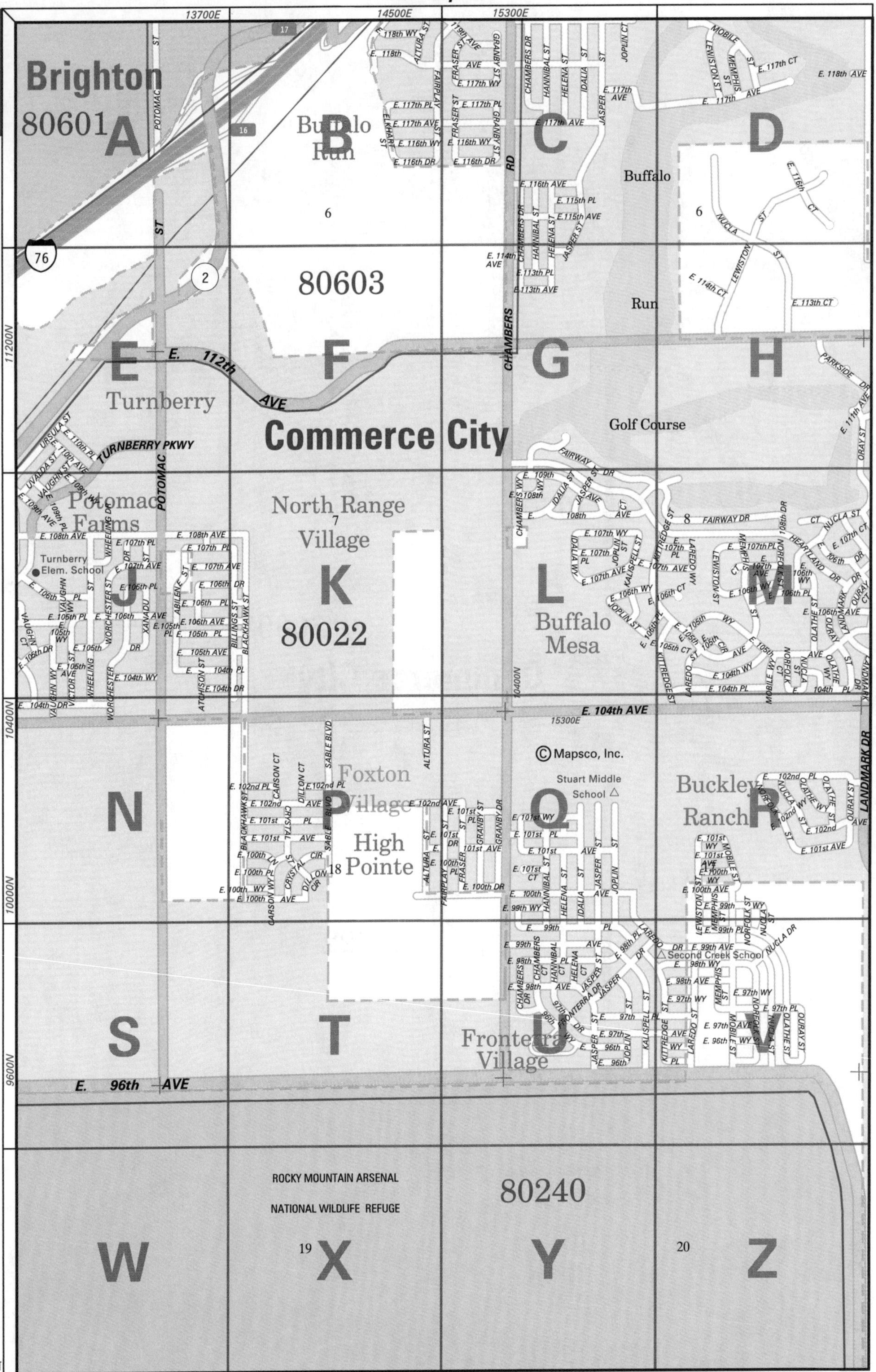

See Map 768

▲ See Map 189 ▲

19600W 18000W 17200W 16400W

8800N 8200N 7600N 7400N 6700N 6400N

AVALANCHE ST
SIX ST
72
UMBER CT
COAL CREEK CANYON RD
UPRR
Arvada

A B C D

E F G H

27 26

W. 82nd AVE
16400W
3rd AVE
2nd AVE
SCOTT ST
1st AVE

J K L M

Eldorado Estates
Spring Mesa
©Mapsco, Inc.
80007
34 35

Quaker Acres Park
Quaker Acres
Tucker Lake
Tucker Lake Open Space Park
West Woods Elem. School
West Woods Park

N P Q R

FOOTHILLS RD
Arvada

S T U V

Lower Long Lake
Arvada/Blunn Reservoir
Ralston Creek
Trail Village
West Woods Ranch Golf Club
3 2

W. 68th AVE
DUNRAVEN ST

W X Y Z

80403
93
Jefferson County North Athletic Complex
Long Lake Regional Park
W. 64th PKWY
W. 64th AVE
EASLEY RD
QUAKER ST
West Woods Ranch
Sunrise Ridge
Fieldstone
FD8

1. TORREY WY
2. W. 63rd DR
3. SALVIA ST
4. SALVIA ST
5. SECREST LN
6. TERRY WY
7. W. 63rd DR
8. W. 61st PL

◀ See Map 763 ▶

▶ See Map 220 ◀

0 ¼ ½
Miles

▼ See Map 249 ▼

N

▲ See Map 190 ▲

▲ See Map 219 ▲

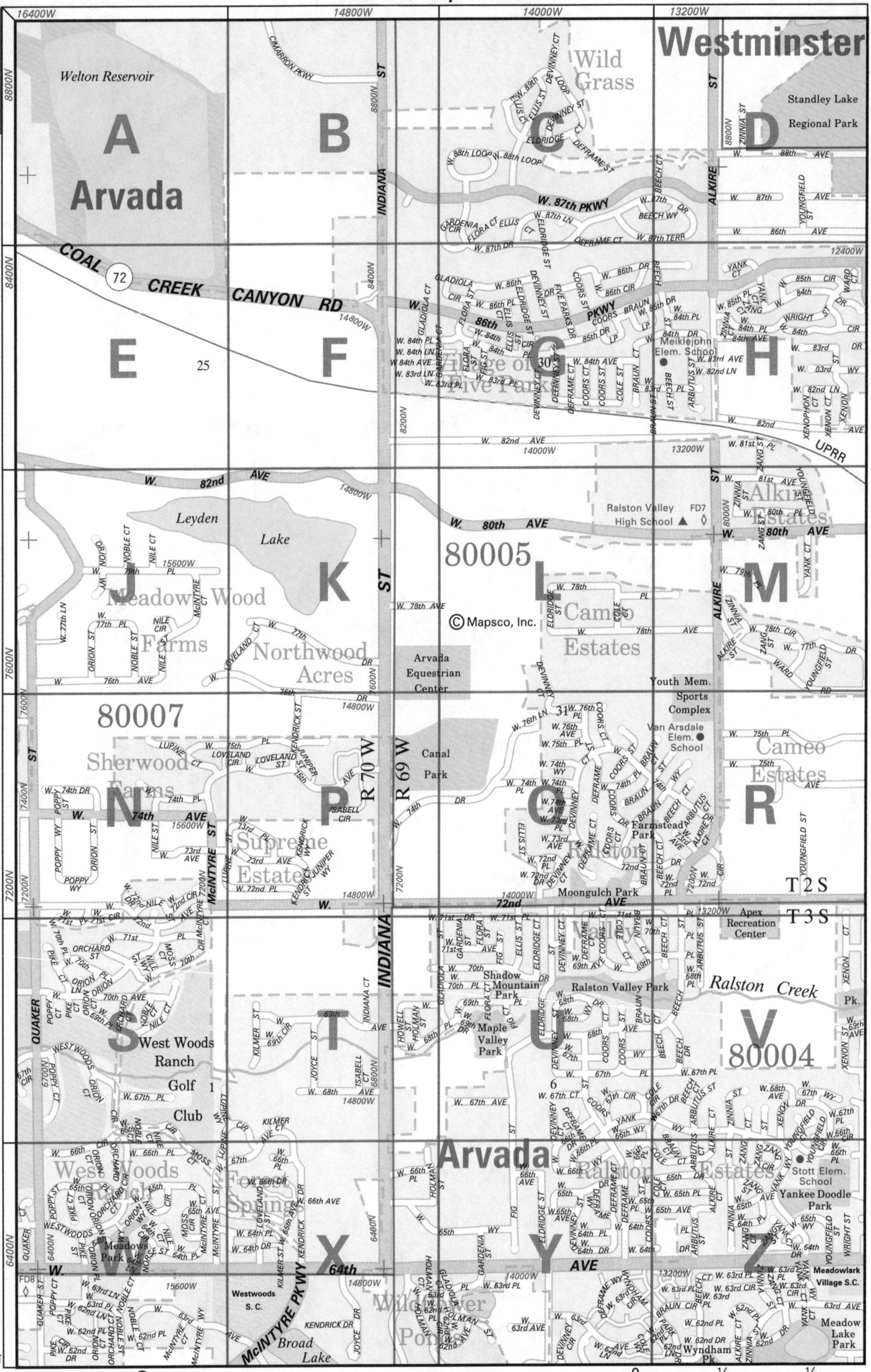
16400W
14800W
14000W
13200W
8800N
8400N
7600N
7200N
6400N
Westminster
Standley Lake Regional Park
Welton Reservoir
Arvada
Wild Grass
COAL CREEK CANYON RD
72
W. 87th PKWY
W. 86th PKWY
Village of Five Parks
Meiklejohn Elem. School
INDIANA ST
ALKIRE ST
UPRR
W. 82nd AVE
W. 80th AVE
Leyden Lake
80005
80007
80004
Meadow Wood Farms
Northwood Acres
Arvada Equestrian Center
Mapsco, Inc.
Cameo Estates
Ralston Valley High School
FD7
Alkire Estates
Youth Mem. Sports Complex
Van Arsdale Elem. School
Canal Park
R 70 W
R 69 W
Sherwood Farms
Supreme Estates
Farmstead Park
Ralston
Moonglulch Park
T 2 S
T 3 S
W. 72nd AVE
W. 74th AVE
Apex Recreation Center
QUAKER ST
McINTYRE ST
Shadow Mountain Park
Ralston Valley Park
Ralston Creek
Maple Valley Park
West Woods Ranch Golf Club
West Woods Ranch
Forest Springs
Meadows Park
Ralston Estates
Stott Elem. School
Yankee Doodle Park
Meadowlark Village S.C.
W. 64th AVE
FD8
Westwoods S.C.
McINTYRE PKWY
Broad Lake
Wildflower Ponds
Wyndham Pk.
Meadow Lake Park
A
B
C
D
E
F
G
H
J
K
L
M
N
P
Q
R
S
T
U
V
W
X
Y
Z

▼ See Map 250 ▼

0 ¼ ½
Miles

▲ See Map 191 ▲

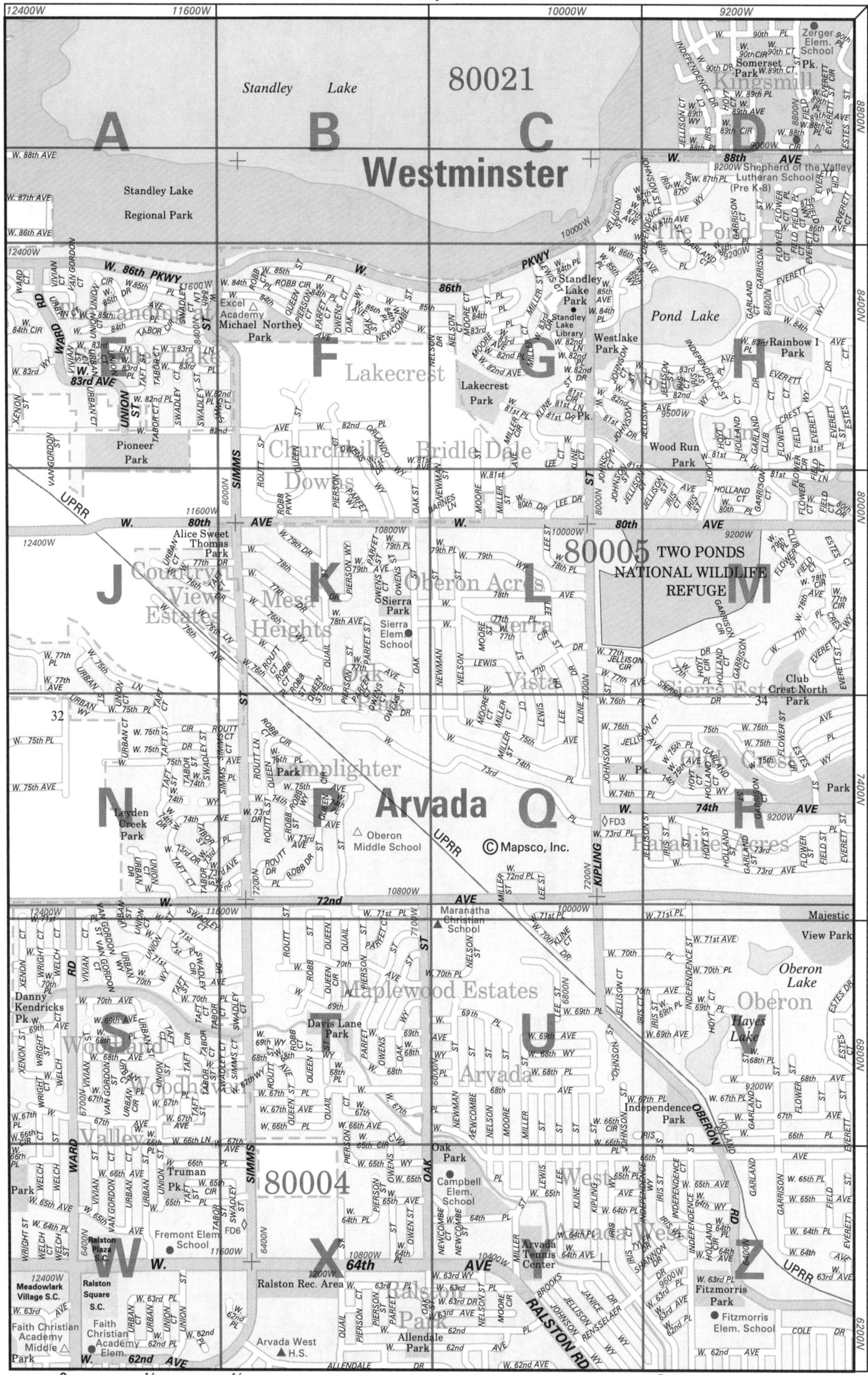

▼ See Map 251 ▼

▲ See Map 222 ▲

▲ See Map 192 ▲

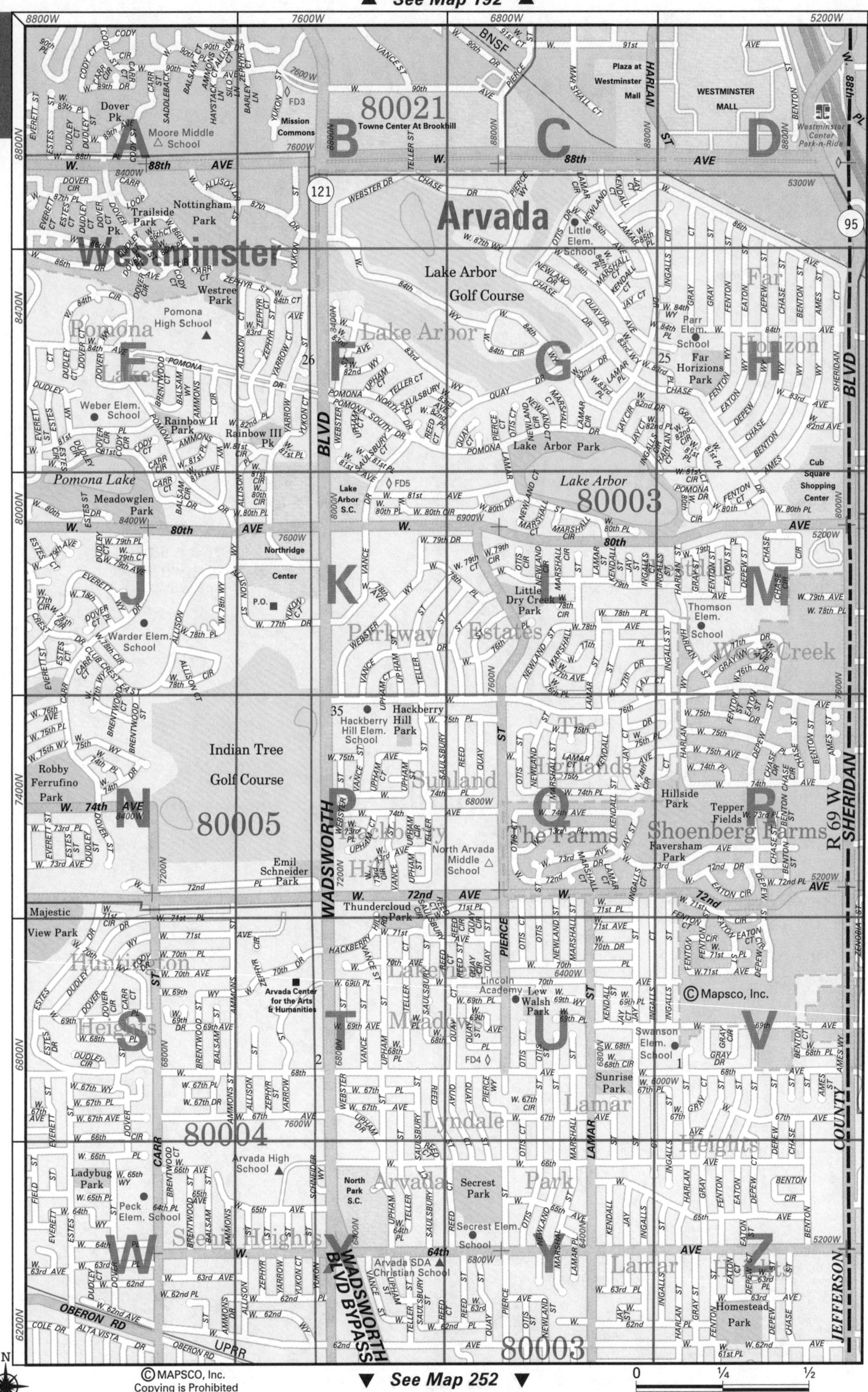

▲ See Map 221 ▲

▼ See Map 252 ▼

0 ¼ ½
Miles

▲ See Map 193 ▲

Westminster

Federal Heights

Arvada

80031

80260

80030

80221

80003

Shaw Heights

Greenbrier

Westminster Hills

Hidden Creek Park

Fairview

Perl Mack Manor

Skyline Vista

Harris Park

Lakeview Estates

Hidden Lake

Pioneer Mobile Gardens

Tennyson Park

▶ See Map 224 ▶

▼ See Map 253 ▼

Miles

▲ See Map 194 ▲

◀ See Map 223 ◀

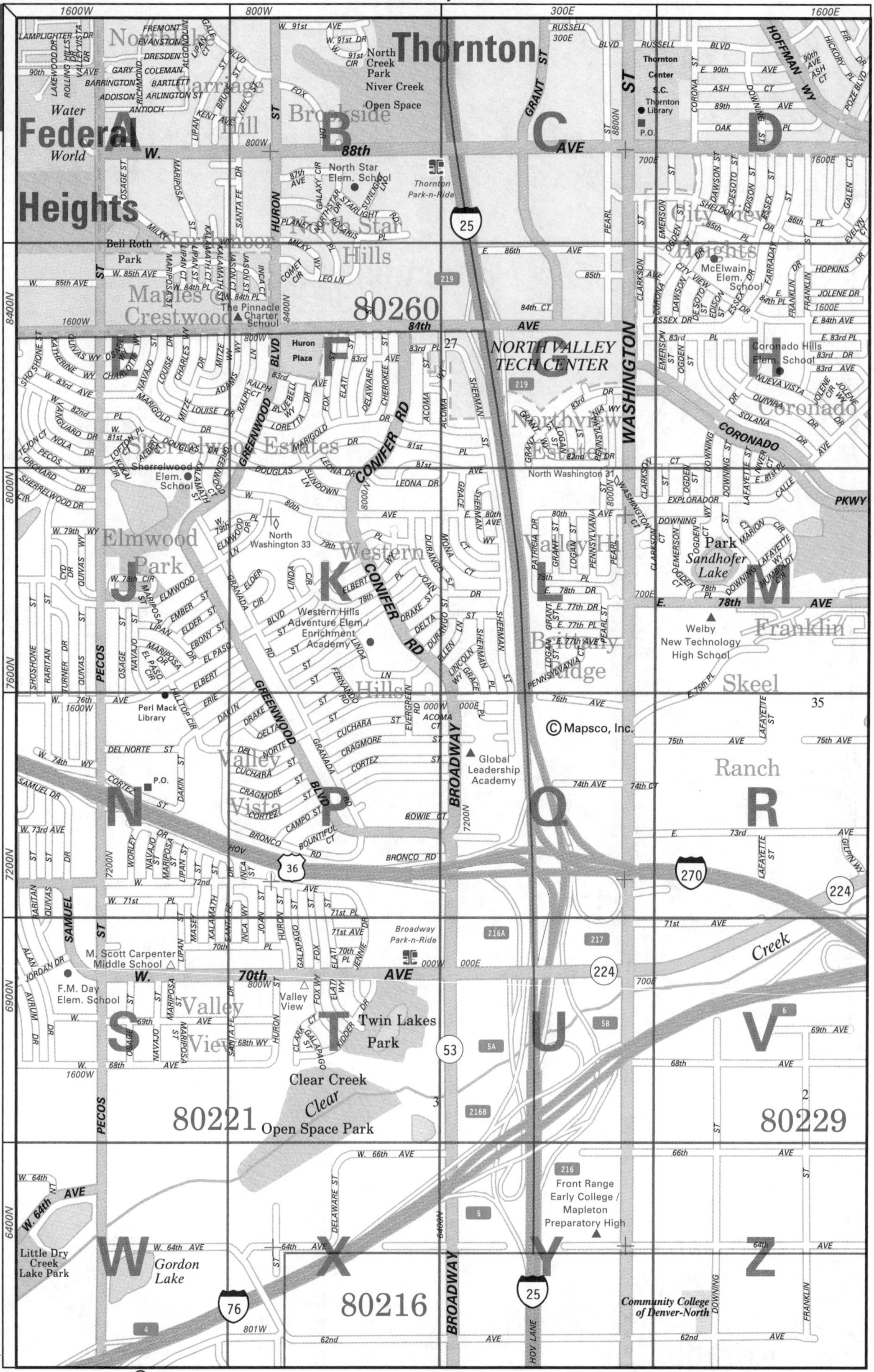
Thornton
Federal Heights
Water World
Northglenn
Carriage Hill
Brookside
North Creek Park
Niver Creek Open Space
Thornton Center S.C.
Thornton Library
P.O.
W. 88th AVE
North Star Elem. School
Thornton Park-n-Ride
North Star Hills
Northmoor
Bell Roth Park
Maples @ Crestwood
The Pinnacle Charter School
80260
W. 84th AVE
Huron Plaza
NORTH VALLEY TECH CENTER
City View Heights
McElwain Elem. School
Coronado Hills Elem. School
Coronado
Sherrelwood Estates
Sherrelwood Elem. School
Northview Estates
North Washington 31
North Washington 33
Elmwood Park
Western Hills
Western Hills Adventure Elem./ Enrichment Academy
Valley Hi
Brittany Ridge
Park Sandhofer Lake
Welby New Technology High School
Franklin
Skeel Ranch
Perl Mack Library
© Mapsco, Inc.
Global Leadership Academy
Valley Vista
CONIFER RD
GREENWOOD BLVD
BROADWAY
WASHINGTON ST
PECOS ST
GRANT ST
HURON ST
CORONADO PKWY
W. 70th AVE
M. Scott Carpenter Middle School
F.M. Day Elem. School
Broadway Park-n-Ride
Valley View
Twin Lakes Park
Clear Creek Open Space Park
Clear Creek
80221
80229
Front Range Early College / Mapleton Preparatory High
Little Dry Creek Lake Park
Gordon Lake
80216
Community College of Denver-North
HOV LANE
W. 64th AVE
62nd AVE
25
36
53
76
224
270
A
B
C
D
E
F
G
H
J
K
L
M
N
P
Q
R
S
T
U
V
W
X
Y
Z

▼ See Map 254 ▼

0 ¼ ½
Miles

▲ See Map 195 ▲

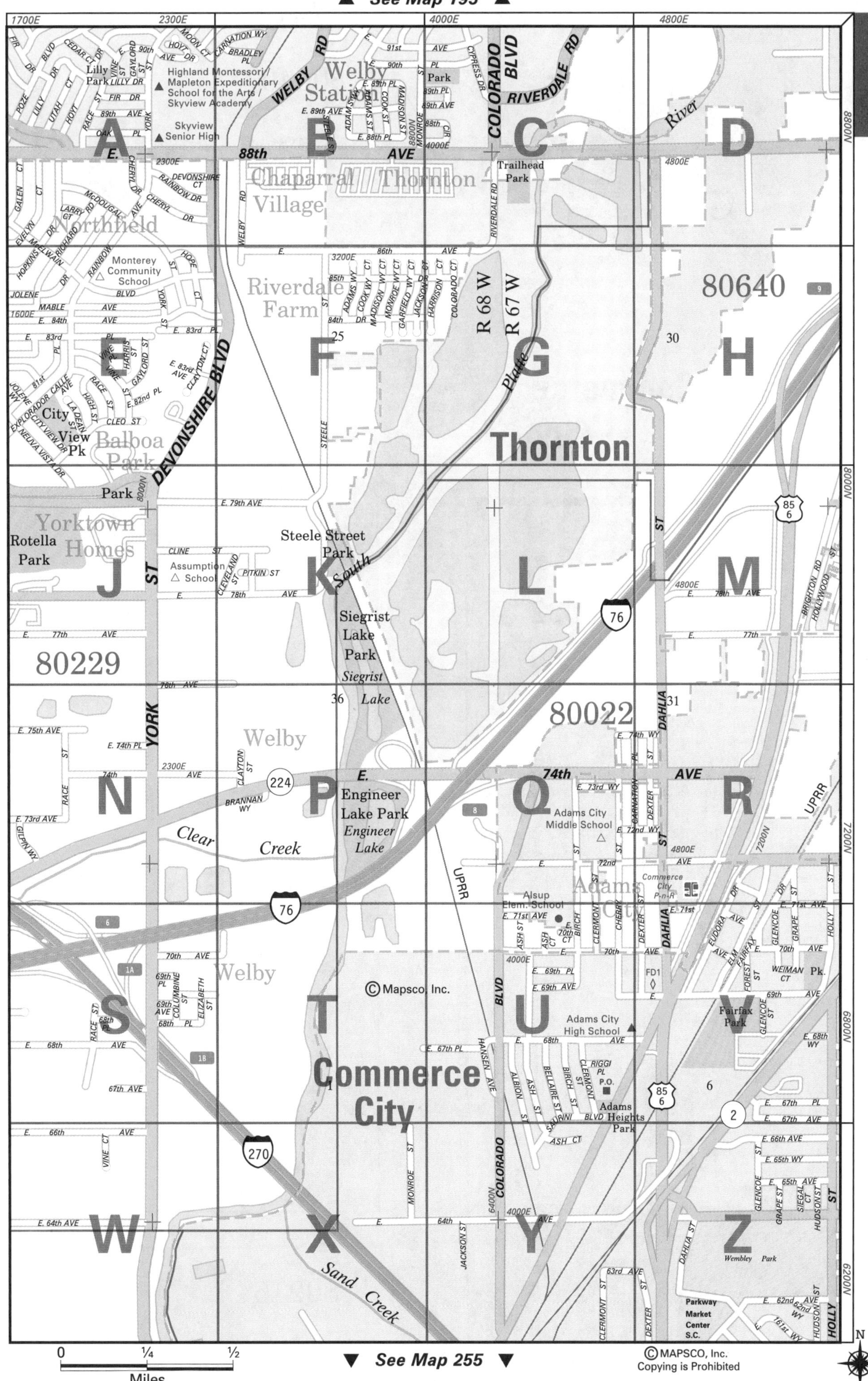

▼ See Map 255 ▼

▶ See Map 226 ▶

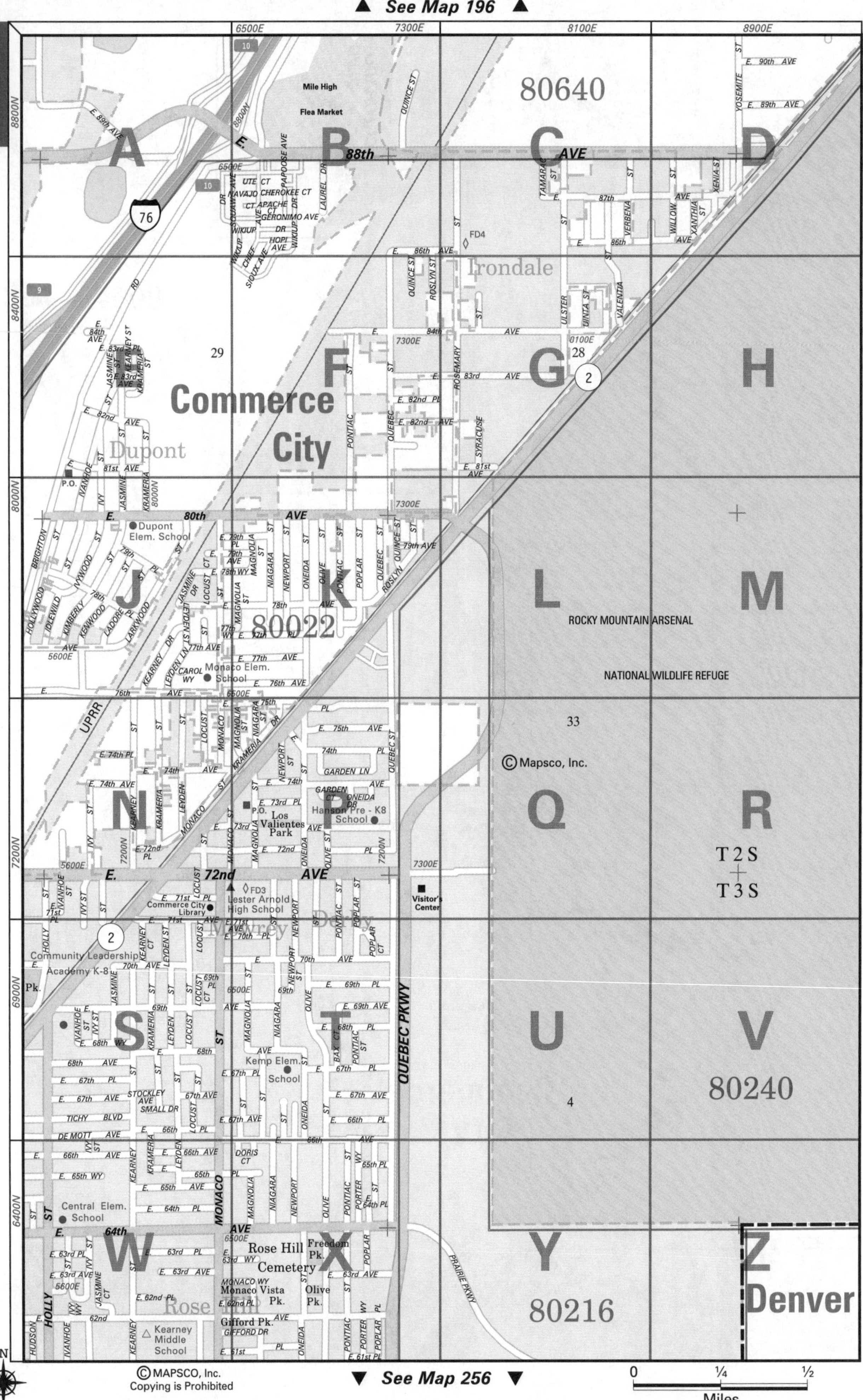
▲ See Map 196 ▲
6500E
7300E
8100E
8900E
8800N
8400N
8000N
7200N
6900N
6400N
80640
Mile High
Flea Market
E. 88th AVE
76
10
9
E. 90th AVE
E. 89th AVE
YOSEMITE ST
E. 87th
E. 86th AVE
Irondale
FD4
QUINCE ST
ROSLYN ST
ROSEMARY ST
SYRACUSE
ULSTER
UINTA ST
VALENTIA
TAMARAC
VERBENA
WILLOW
XANTHIA
XENIA ST
UTE CT
NAVAJO
CHEROKEE CT
APACHE
GERONIMO AVE
WIKIUP DR
HOPI
CHIEF
SIOUX AVE
SQUAW
PAPOOSE AVE
LAUREL DR
E. 84th
E. 83rd AVE
E. 82nd PL
E. 82nd AVE
E. 81st AVE
29
28
2
Commerce
City
Dupont
P.O.
JASMINE
KEARNEY ST
KRAMERIA ST
IVANHOE
IVY
PONTIAC
QUEBEC
E. 80th AVE
Dupont
Elem. School
BRIGHTON
HOLLYWOOD
IDLEWILD
KIMBERLY
IVYWOOD
KENWOOD
LADORE
LARKWOOD
LOCUST
MAGNOLIA
NIAGARA
NEWPORT
ONEIDA
OLIVE
POPLAR
79th AVE
80022
5600E
E. 77th AVE
CAROL WY
Monaco Elem.
School
E. 76th AVE
UPRR
E. 75th AVE
74th
GARDEN LN
QUEBEC ST
E. 74th AVE
E. 73rd PL
P.O.
Los
Valientes
Park
Hanson Pre - K8
School
E. 72nd PL
E. 72nd AVE
7300E
Visitor's
Center
FD3
Lester Arnold
High School
Commerce City
Library
Mowrey
Derby
Community Leadership
Academy K-8
Pk.
MONACO ST
QUEBEC PKWY
E. 70th AVE
E. 69th PL
E. 69th AVE
E. 68th PL
E. 67th PL
E. 67th AVE
E. 66th PL
Kemp Elem.
School
STOCKLEY AVE
SMALL DR
TICHY BLVD
DE MOTT AVE
E. 66th AVE
E. 65th WY
DORIS CT
E. 65th AVE
E. 64th PL
Central Elem.
School
E. 64th AVE
E. 63rd PL
E. 63rd AVE
E. 62nd PL
Rose Hill
Cemetery
Freedom
Pk.
Monaco Vista
Pk.
Olive
Pk.
Gifford Pk.
GIFFORD DR
Rose Hill
Kearney
Middle
School
HUDSON
HOLLY ST
E. 61st PL
PRAIRIE PKWY
ROCKY MOUNTAIN ARSENAL
NATIONAL WILDLIFE REFUGE
33
4
©Mapsco, Inc.
T 2 S
T 3 S
80240
80216
Denver
A
B
C
D
F
G
H
J
K
L
M
N
P
Q
R
S
T
U
V
W
X
Y
Z
◀ See Map 225 ◀
▶ See Map 768 ▶
©MAPSCO, Inc.
Copying is Prohibited
▼ See Map 256 ▼
0
¼
½
Miles
N

▲ See Map 763 ▲

◄ See Map 783 ►

◄ See Map 249 ►

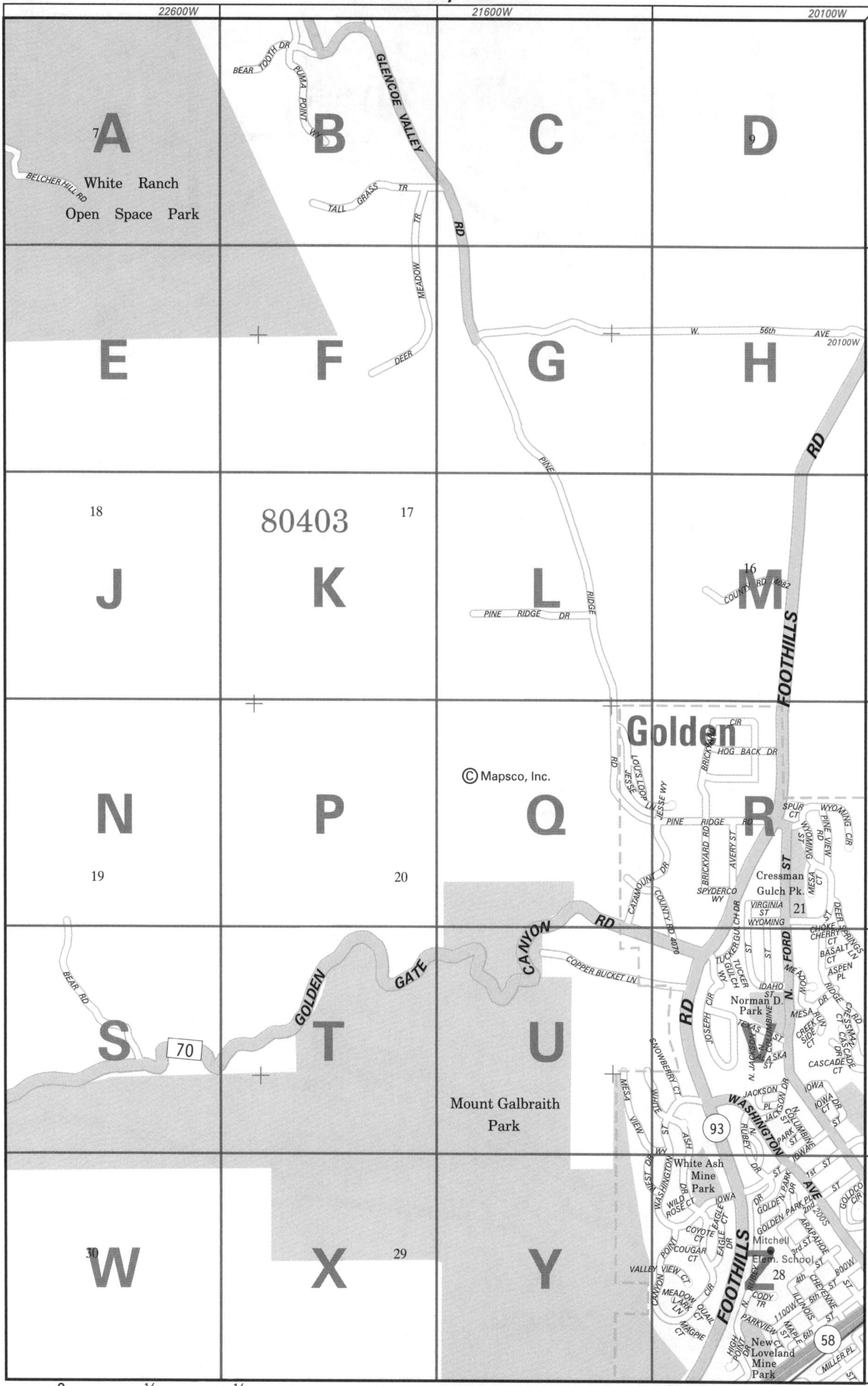

0 ¼ ½
Miles

▼ See Map 278 ▼

N

▲ See Map 219 ▲

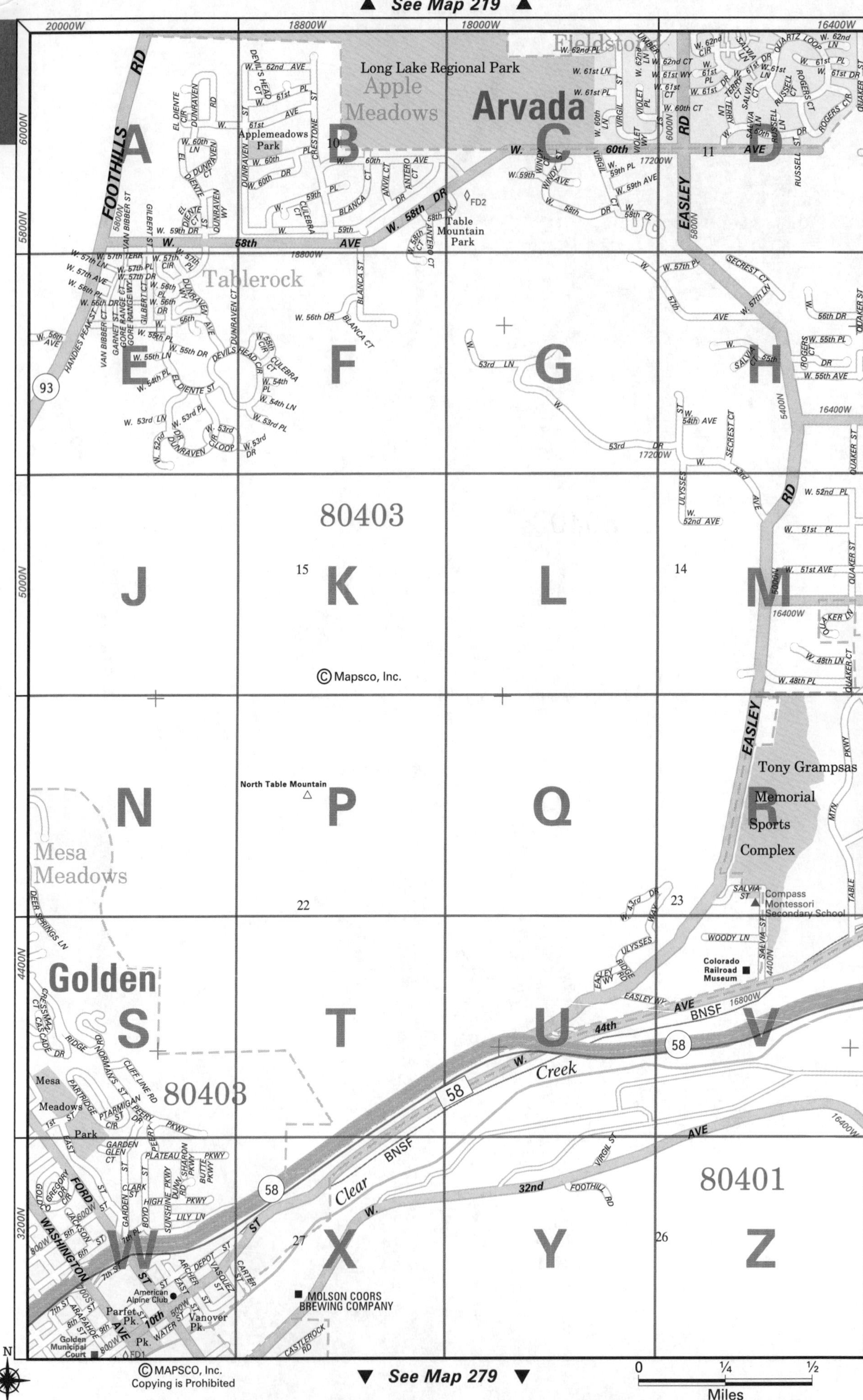

▲ See Map 248 ▲

▼ See Map 279 ▼

▲ See Map 220 ▲

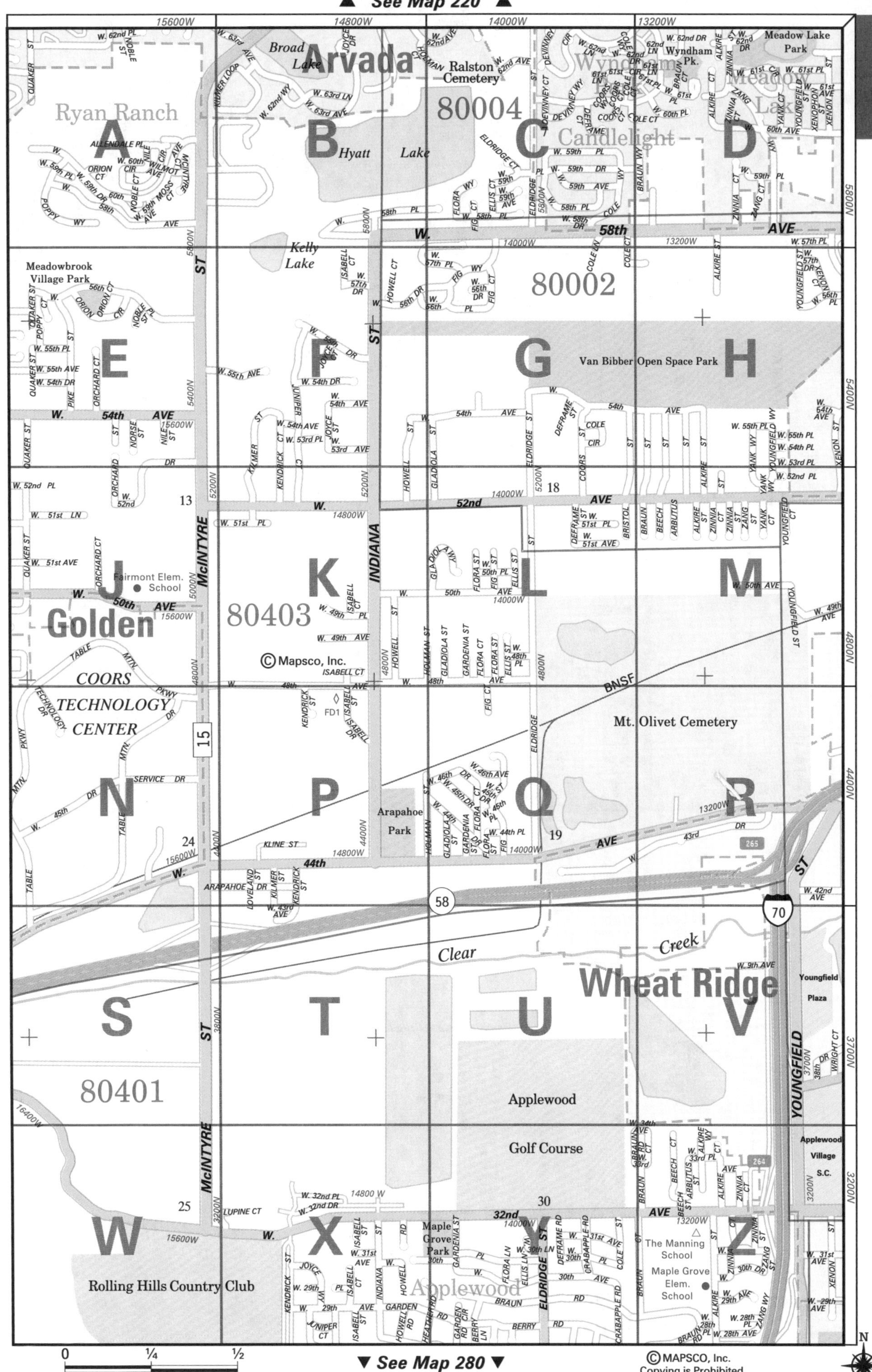

▶ See Map 251 ▶

▼ See Map 280 ▼

▲ See Map 221 ▲

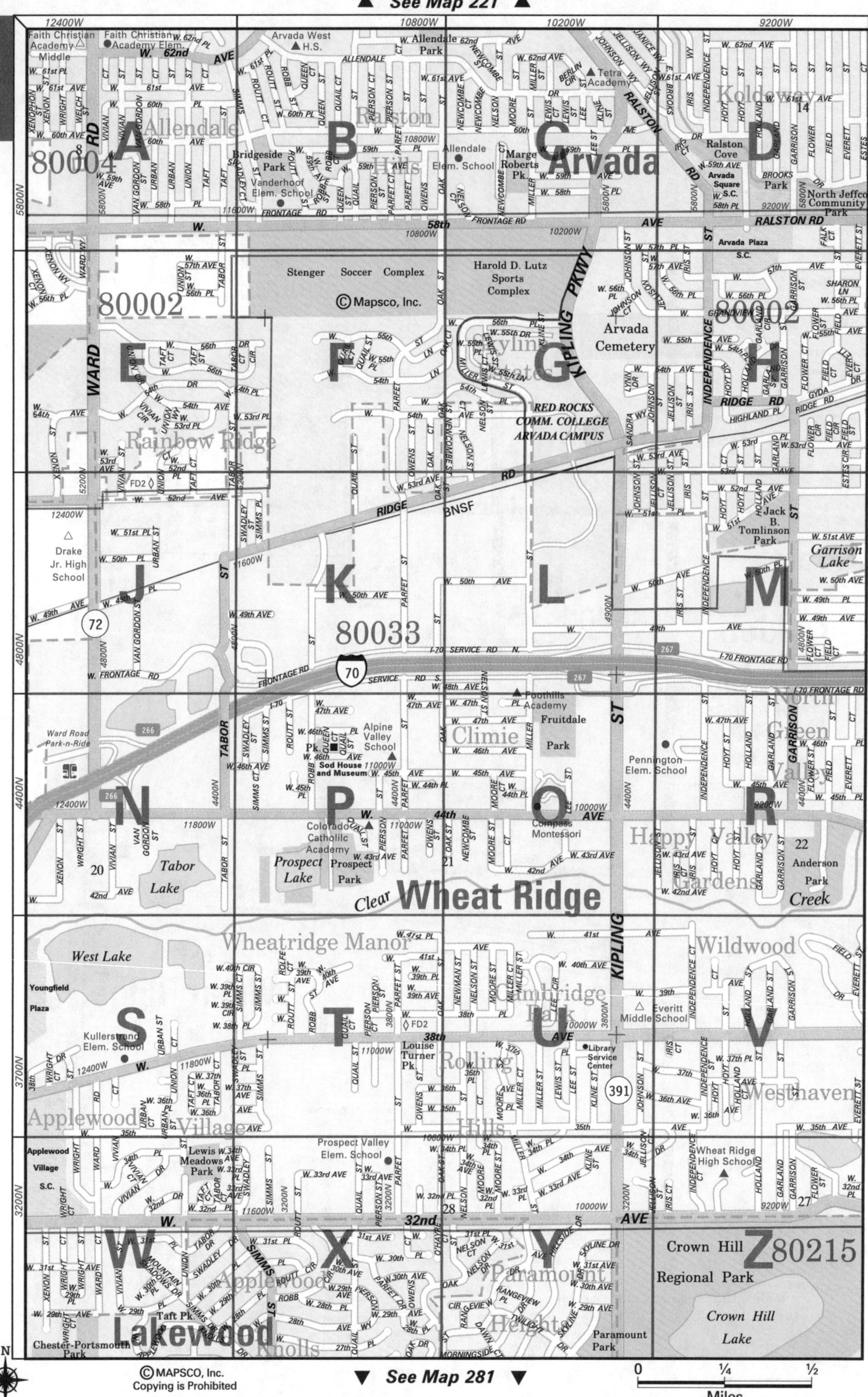

◄ See Map 250 ►

▼ See Map 281 ▼

0 ¼ ½
Miles

▲ See Map 222 ▲

0 ¼ ½ Miles

▼ See Map 282 ▼

▶ See Map 253 ▶

▲ See Map 223 ▲

◀ See Map 252 ◀

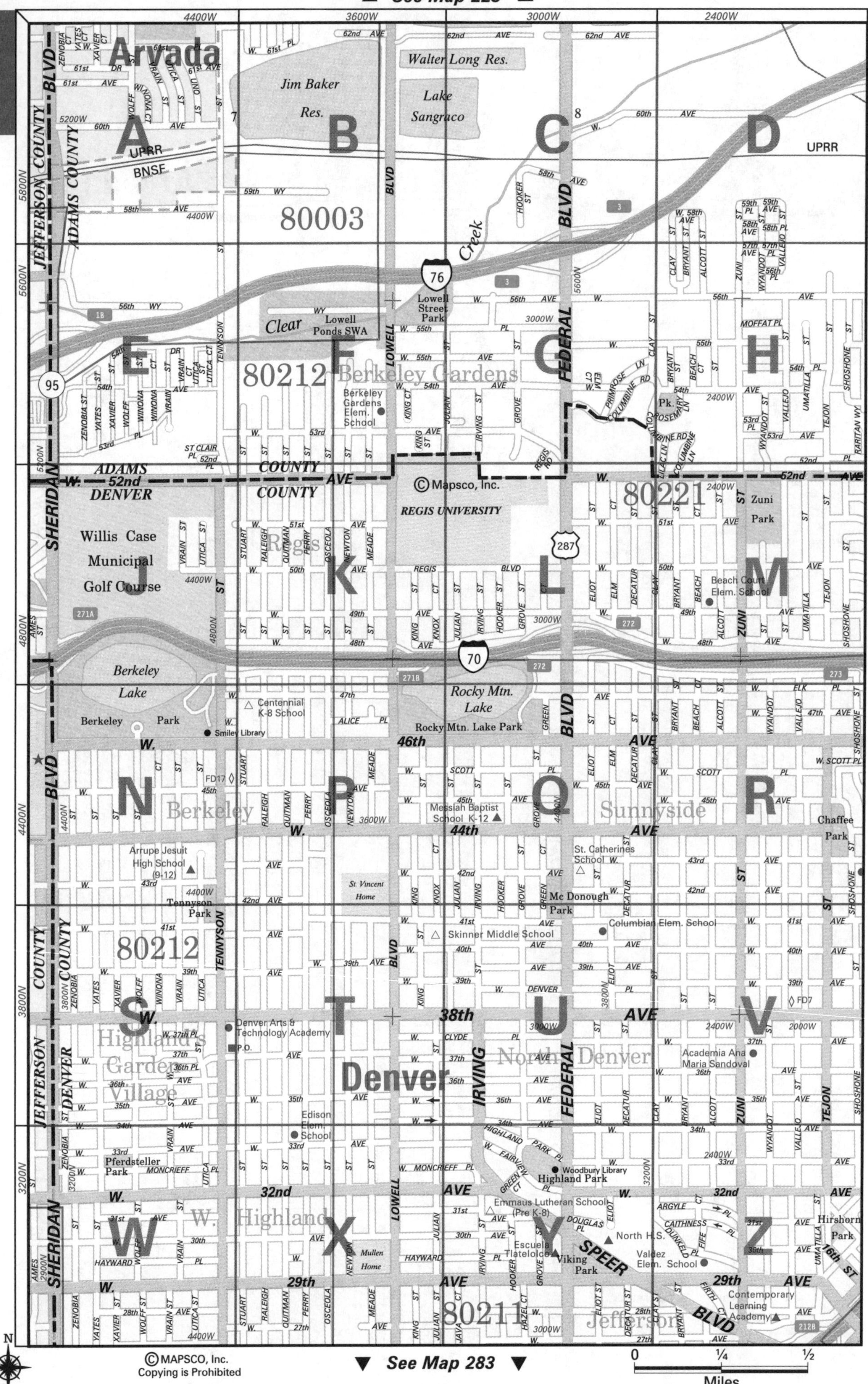

▼ See Map 283 ▼

▲ See Map 224 ▲

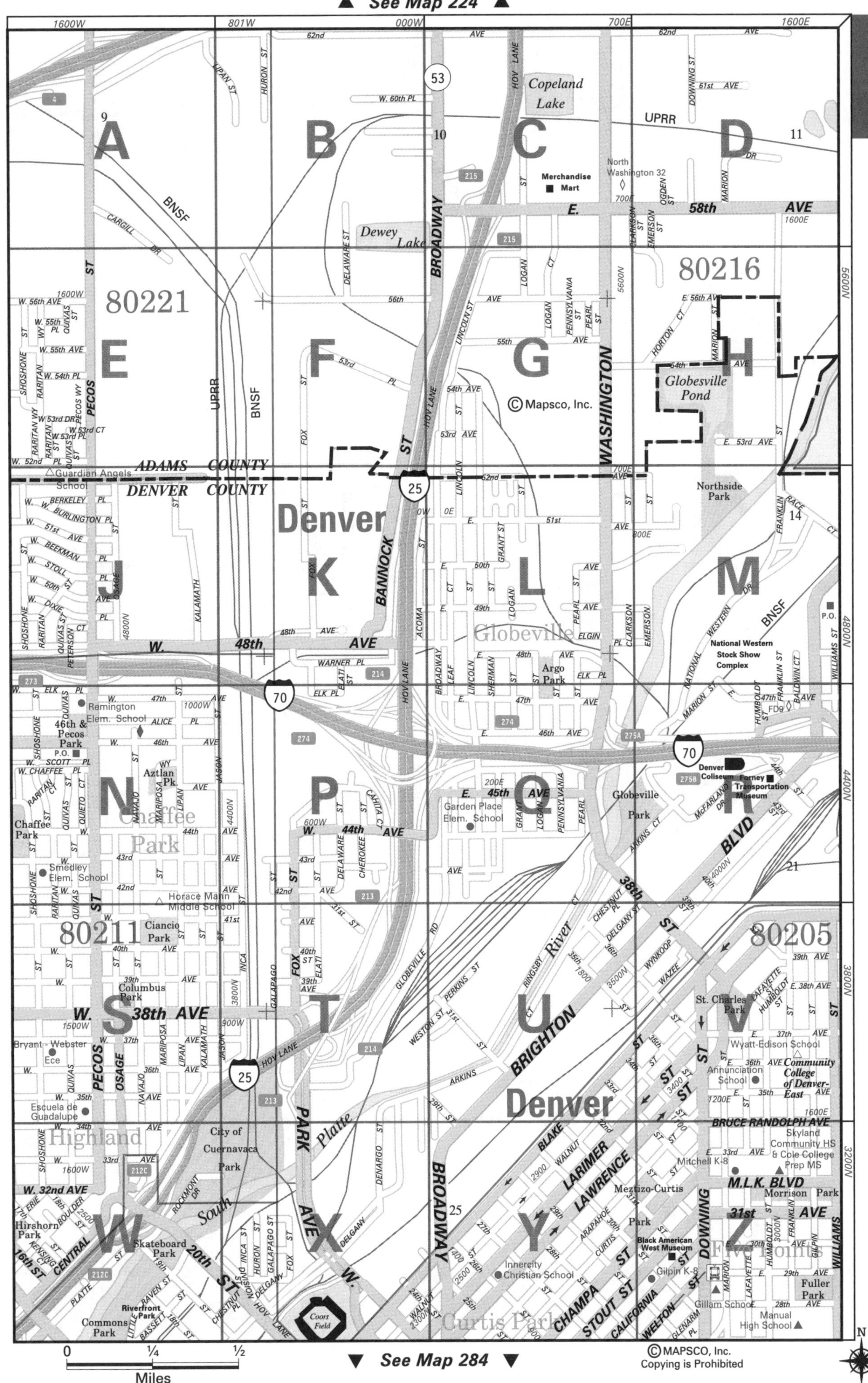

▲ See Map 255 ▲

0 1/4 1/2 Miles

▼ See Map 284 ▼

▲ See Map 225 ▲

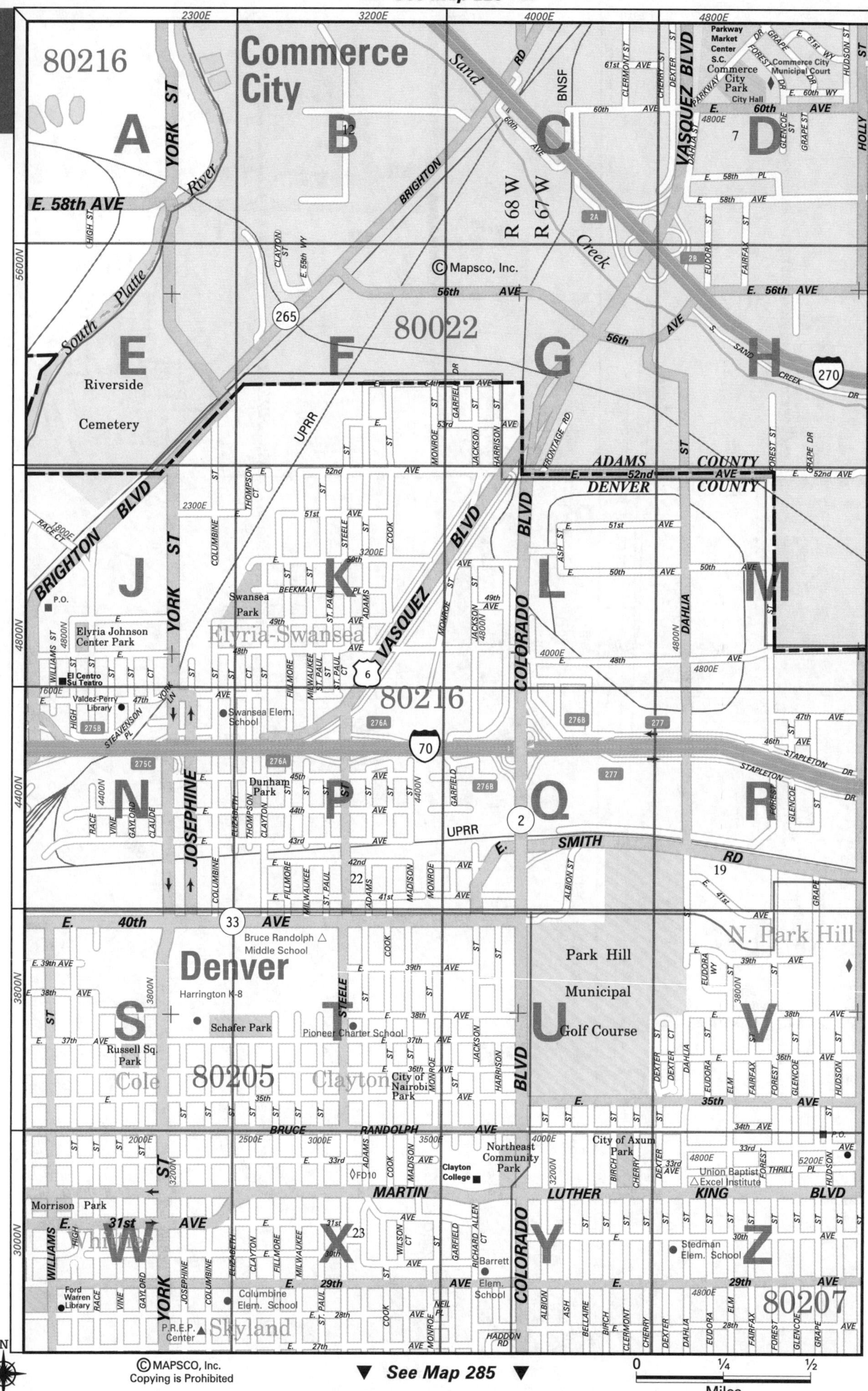

▲ See Map 254 ▲

▼ See Map 285 ▼

0 ¼ ½
Miles

▲ See Map 226 ▲

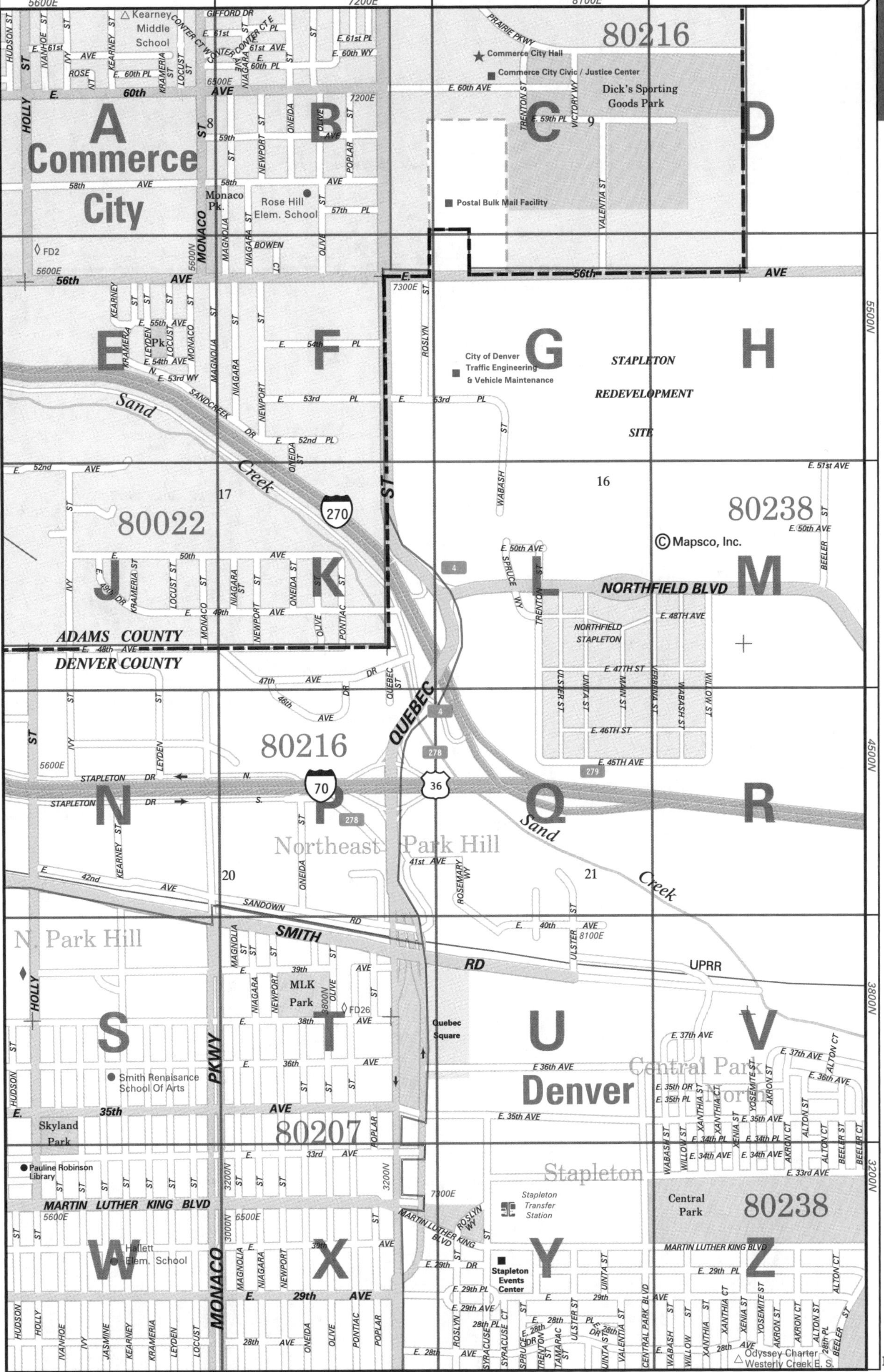

▶ See Map 257 ▶

0 ¼ ½
Miles

▼ See Map 286 ▼

▲ See Map 768 ▲

◄ See Map 256 ◄

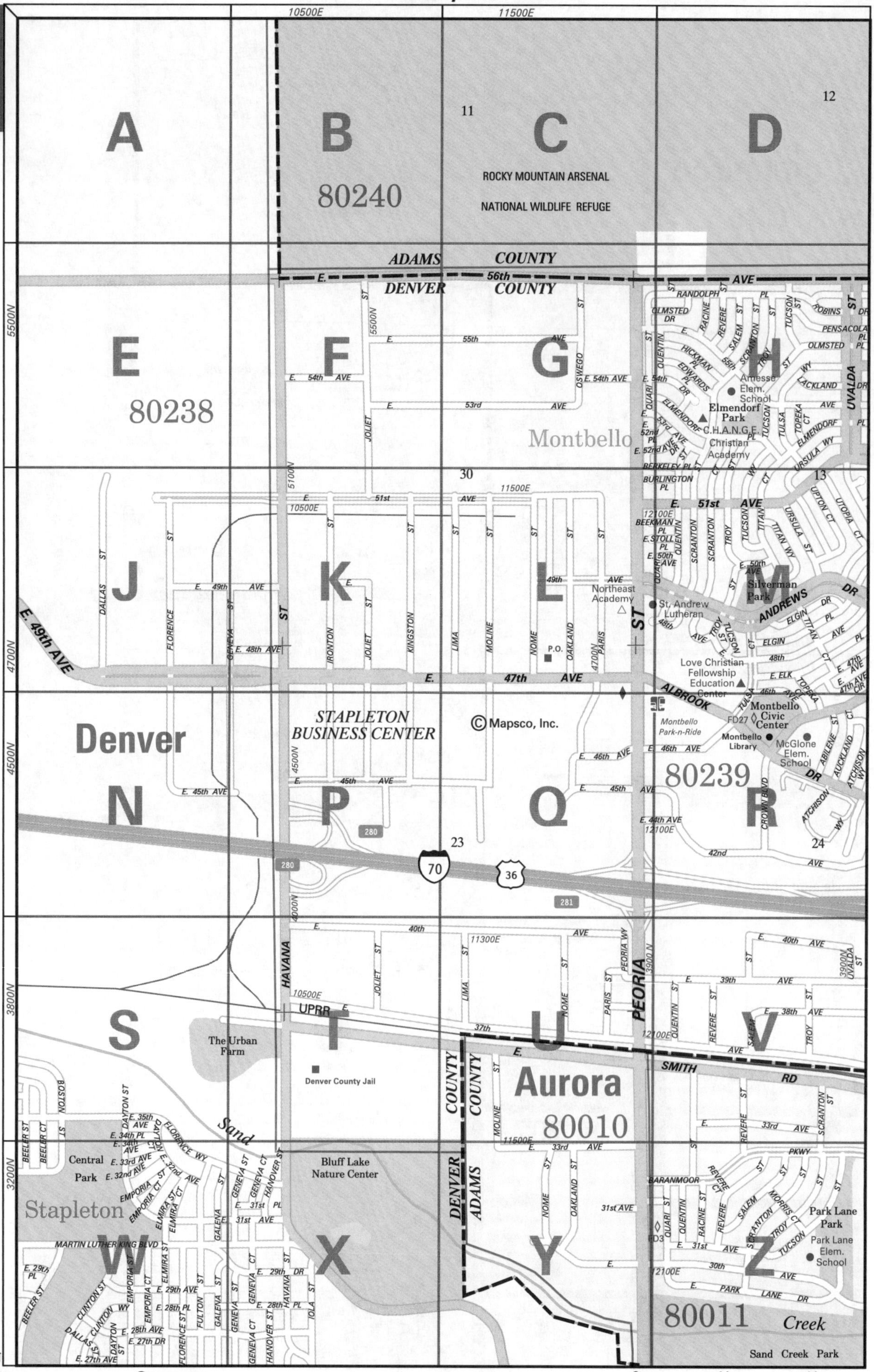

ROCKY MOUNTAIN ARSENAL
NATIONAL WILDLIFE REFUGE

80240

ADAMS COUNTY
DENVER COUNTY

E. 56th AVE

80238

Montbello

STAPLETON BUSINESS CENTER

Denver

80239

Aurora

80010

80011

Stapleton

The Urban Farm

Denver County Jail

Bluff Lake Nature Center

Central Park

Park Lane Park

Sand Creek Park

HAVANA ST

PEORIA ST

E. 47th AVE

E. 49th AVE

UPRR

SMITH RD

MARTIN LUTHER KING BLVD

© Mapsco, Inc.

▼ See Map 287 ▼

0 ¼ ½
Miles

▲ See Map 768 ▲

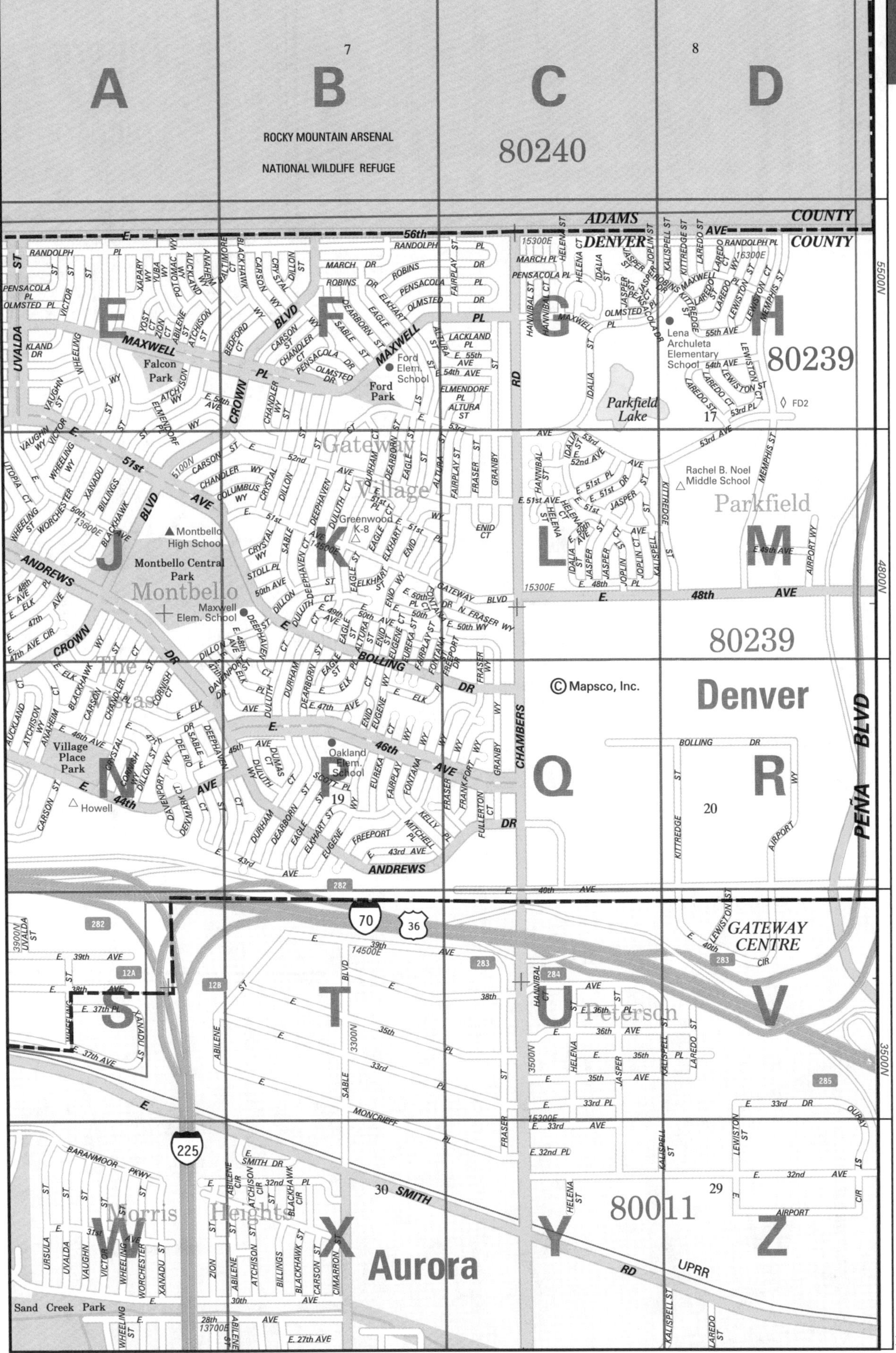

▲ See Map 259 ▲

0 ¼ ½
Miles

▼ See Map 288 ▼

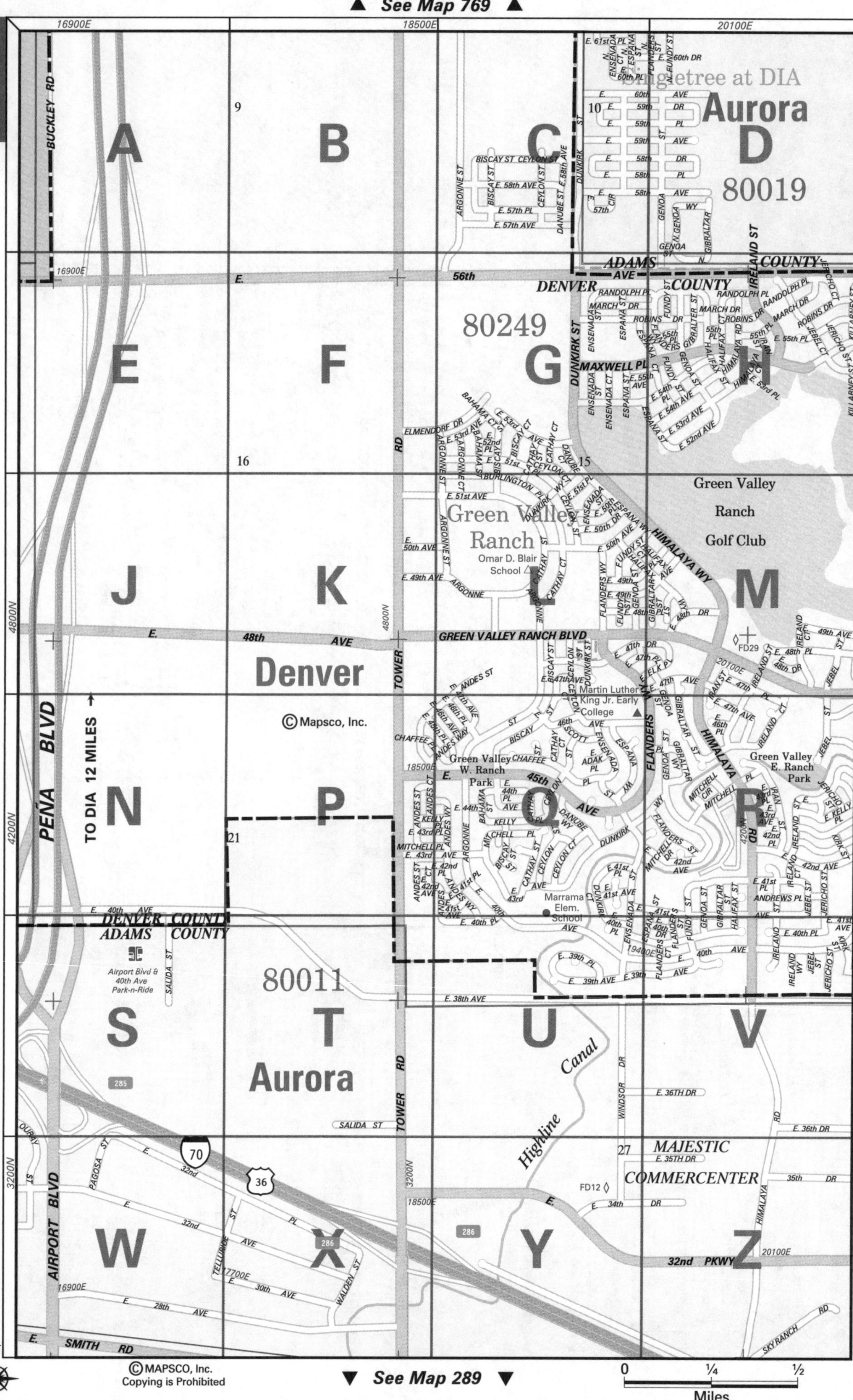

259
See Map 769
See Map 258
See Map 289
16900E
18500E
20100E
4800N
4200N
3200N
A
B
C
D
E
F
G
H
J
K
L
M
N
P
Q
R
S
T
U
V
W
X
Y
Z
Singletree at DIA
Aurora
80019
80249
80011
Denver
Aurora
BUCKLEY RD
ADAMS COUNTY
DENVER COUNTY
E. 56th AVE
E. 48th AVE
GREEN VALLEY RANCH BLVD
TOWER RD
PEÑA BLVD
AIRPORT BLVD
TO DIA 12 MILES
DUNKIRK ST
MAXWELL PL
HIMALAYA WY
HIMALAYA RD
IRELAND ST
FLANDERS ST
Green Valley Ranch
Green Valley Ranch Golf Club
Omar D. Blair School
Martin Luther King Jr. Early College
Green Valley W. Ranch Park
Green Valley E. Ranch Park
Marrama Elem. School
E. 45th AVE
E. 40th AVE
E. 38th AVE
E. 36TH DR
E. 35TH DR
E. 34th DR
32nd PKWY
Highline Canal
MAJESTIC COMMERCENTER
FD12
FD29
Airport Blvd & 40th Ave Park-n-Ride
SALIDA ST
E. 32nd PL
E. 32nd AVE
E. 30th AVE
E. 28th AVE
E. SMITH RD
SKYRANCH RD
70
36
285
286
© Mapsco, Inc.
©MAPSCO, Inc.
Copying is Prohibited
0
¼
½
Miles
N

▲ See Map 769 ▲

▲ See Map 790 ▲

▼ See Map 290 ▼

0 ¼ ½
Miles

▲ See Map 782 ▲

▲ See Map 781 ▲

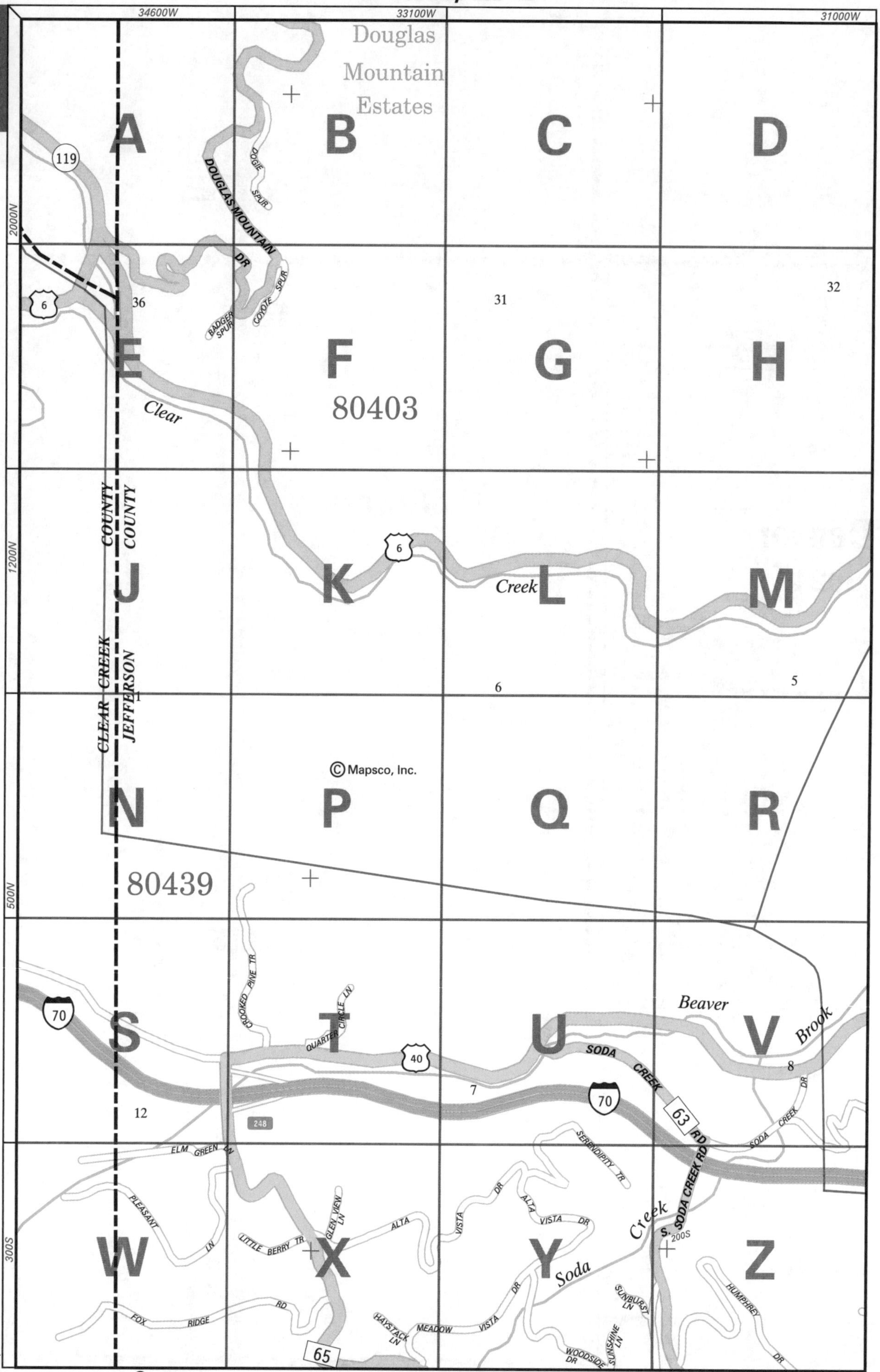

N

▼ See Map 305 ▼

0 ¼ ½
Miles

▲ See Map 782 ▲

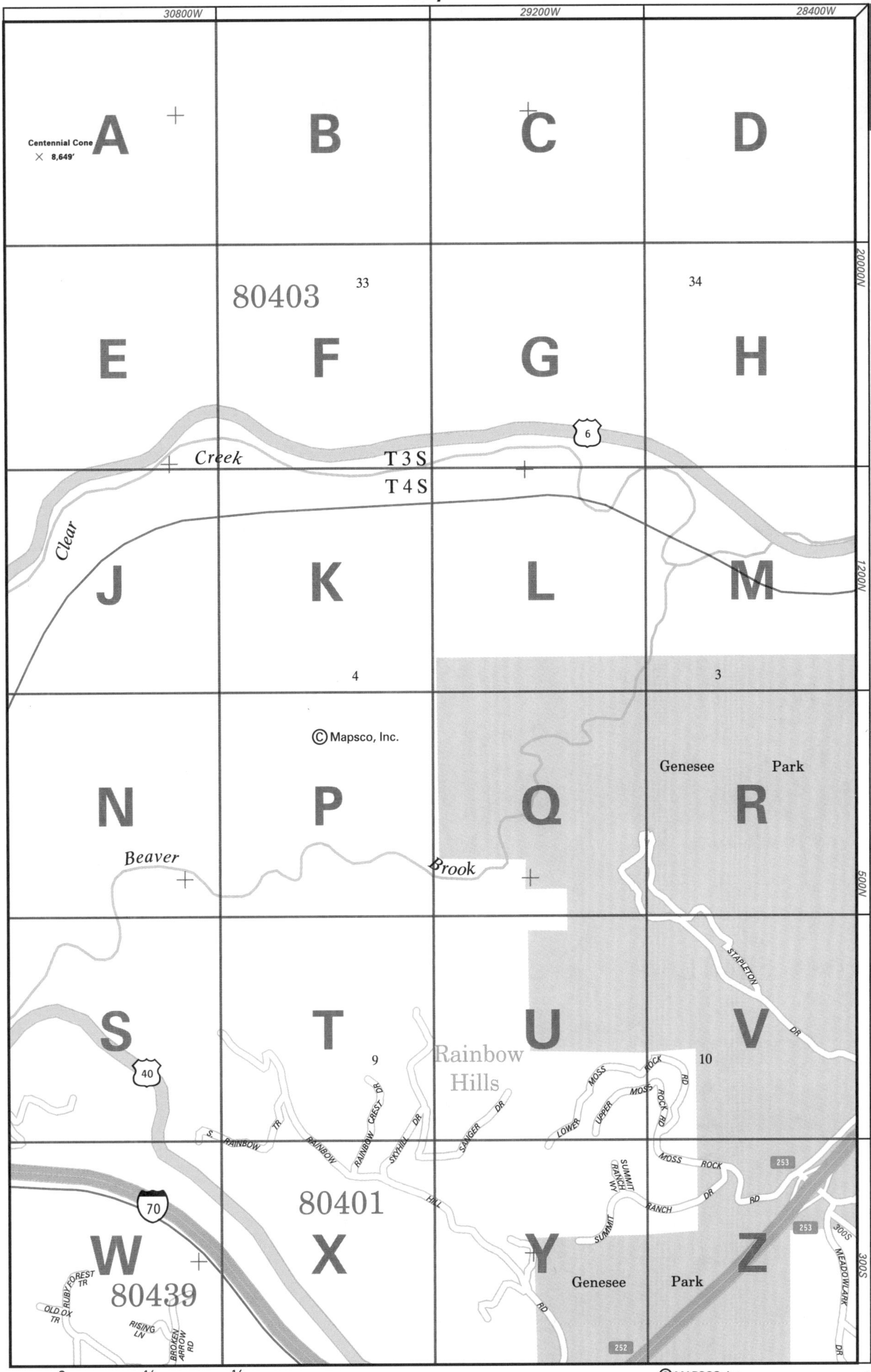

0 ¼ ½
Miles

▶ See Map 277 ▶

▼ See Map 306 ▼

N

See Map 783

See Map 276

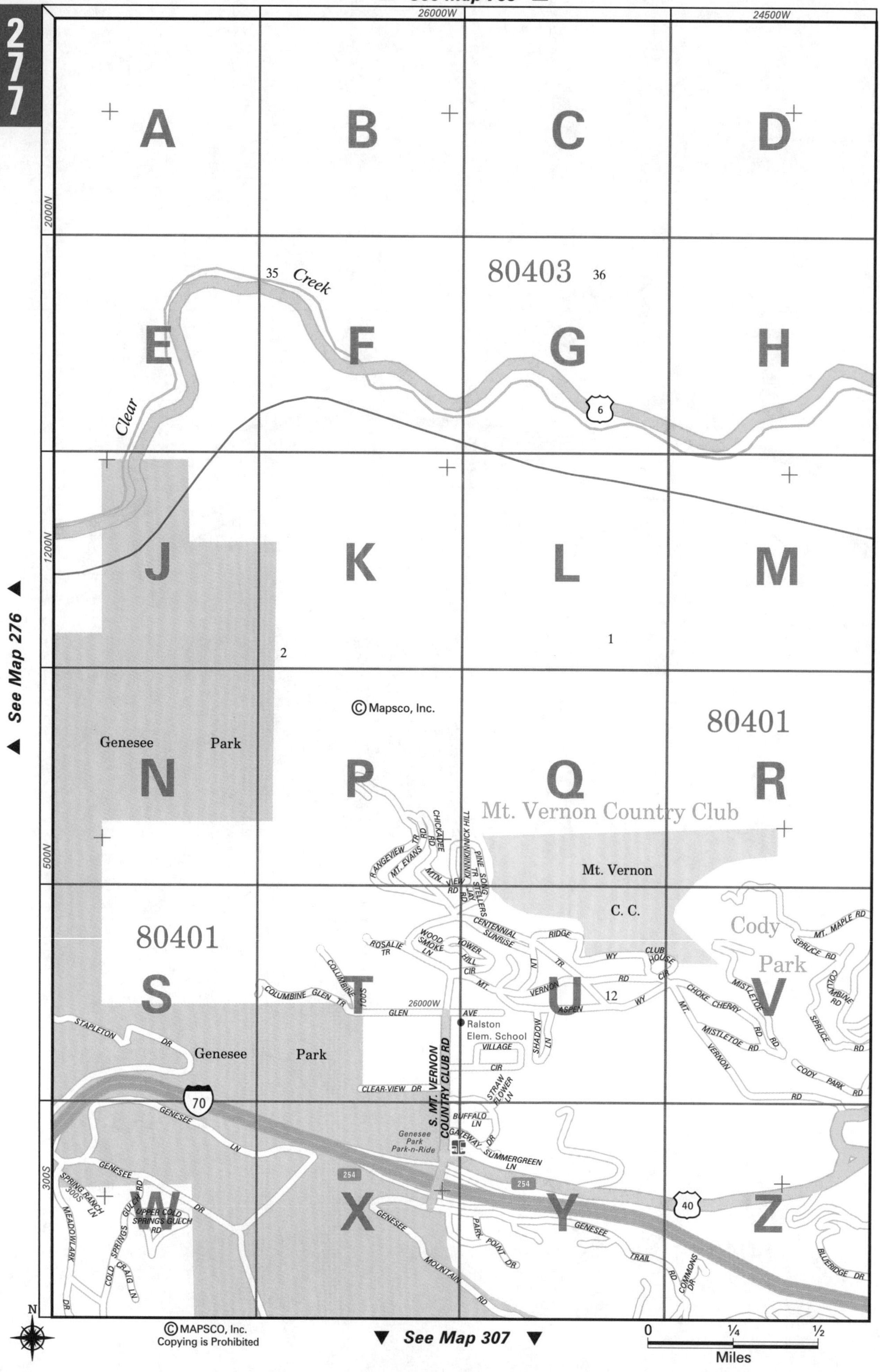

See Map 307

▲ See Map 248 ▲

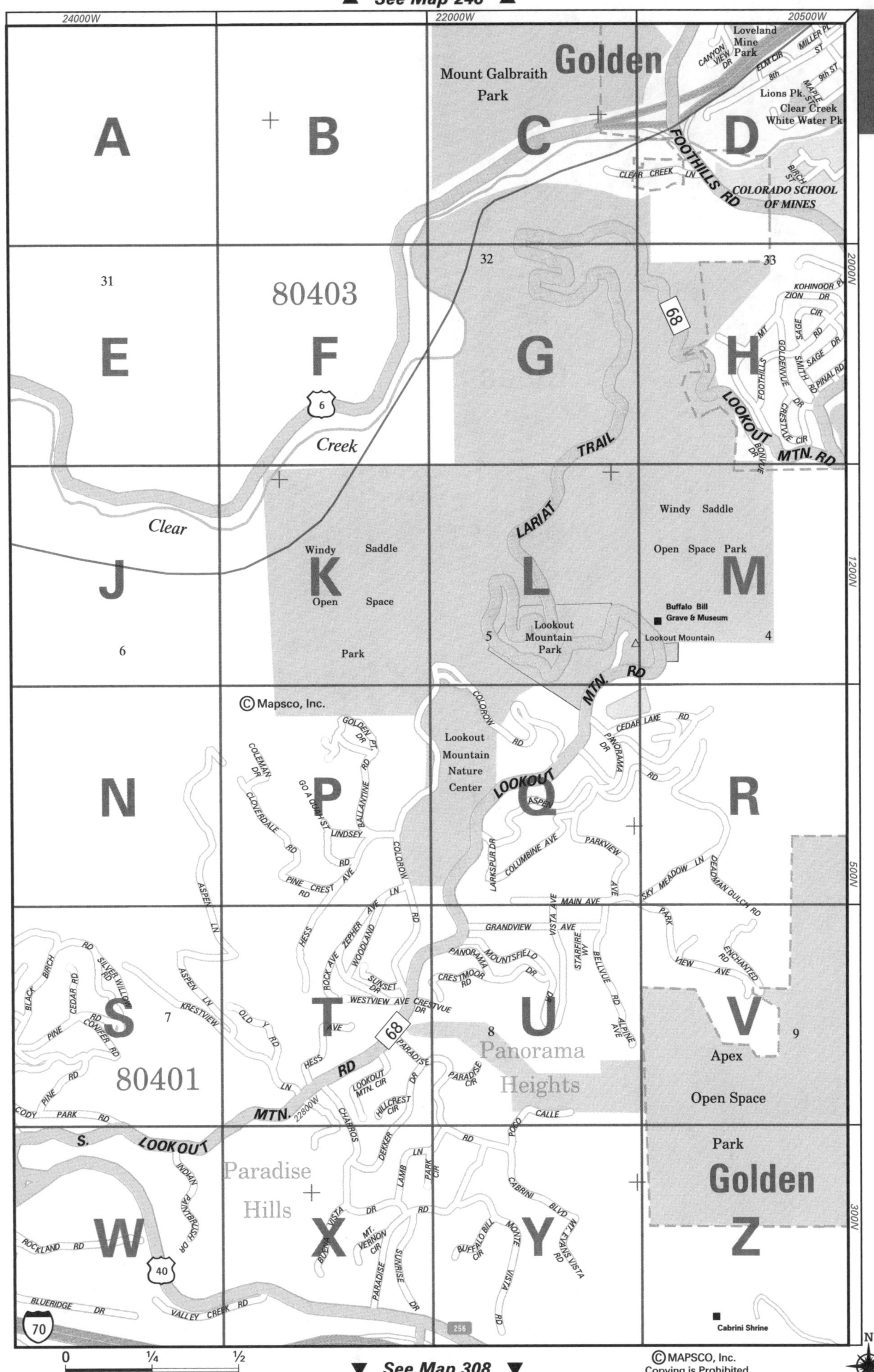

▲ See Map 279 ▶

▼ See Map 308 ▼

▲ See Map 249 ▲

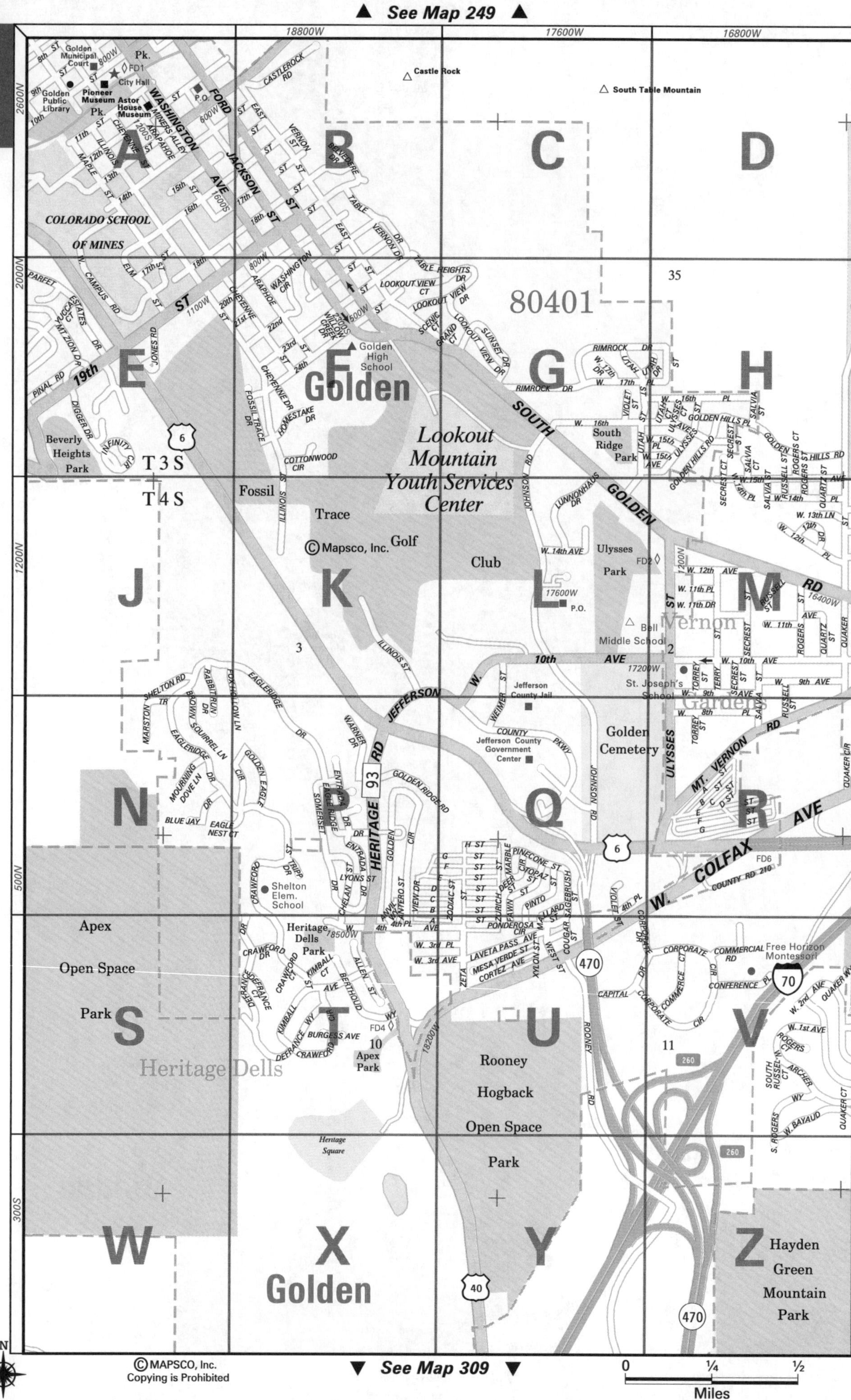

See Map 278

▼ See Map 309 ▼

0 ¼ ½
Miles

▲ See Map 250 ▲

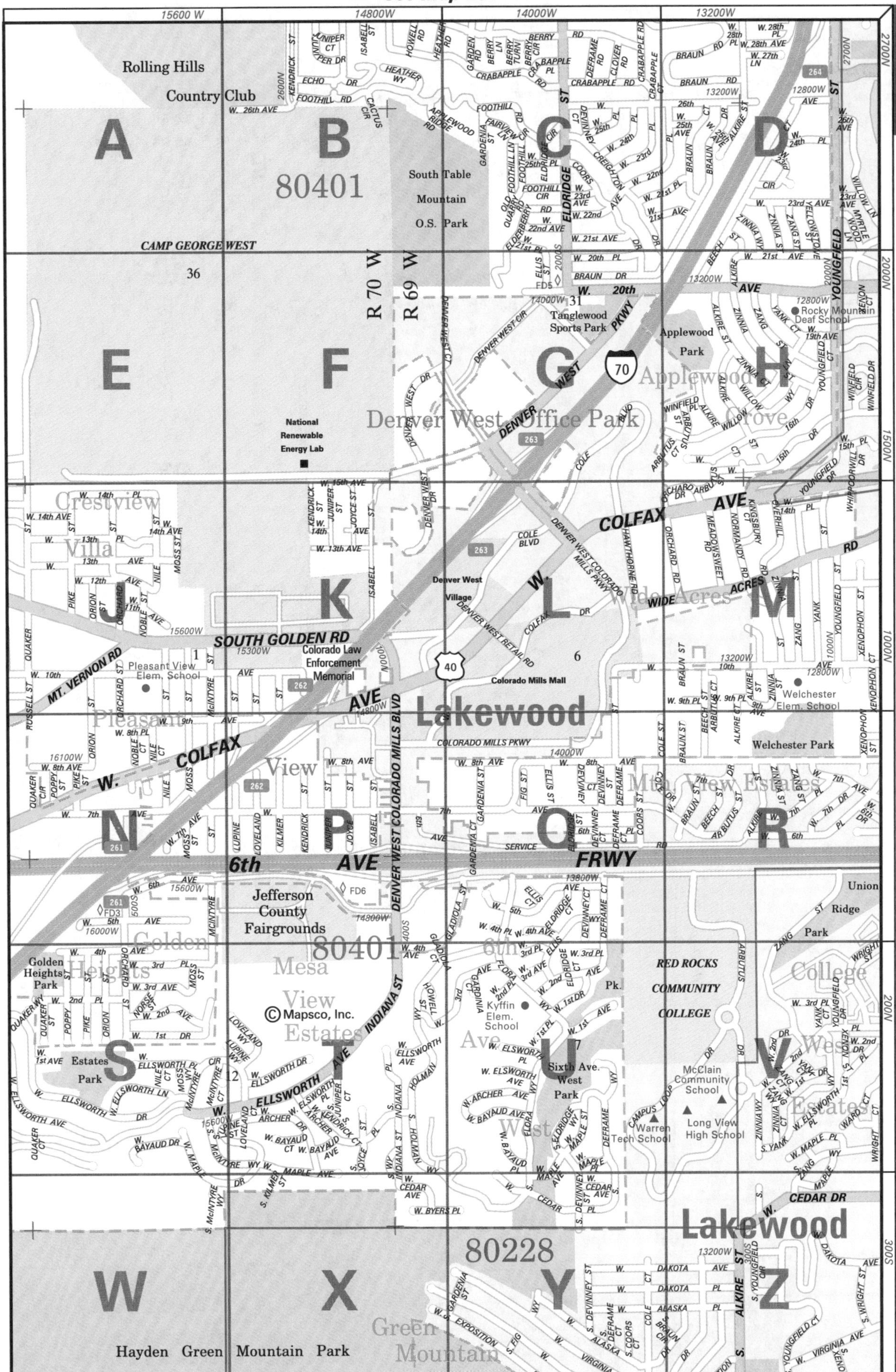

▶ See Map 281 ▶

Rolling Hills Country Club

South Table Mountain O.S. Park

80401

CAMP GEORGE WEST

R 70 W

R 69 W

Tanglewood Sports Park

Applewood Park

Applewood Grove

Rocky Mountain Deaf School

National Renewable Energy Lab

Denver West Office Park

Crestview Villa

Denver West Village

Wide Acres

Colorado Law Enforcement Memorial

Pleasant View Elem. School

Colorado Mills Mall

Lakewood

Welchester Elem. School

Welchester Park

Pleasant View

Mtn. View Estates

Union Ridge Park

Jefferson County Fairgrounds

80401

Golden Heights Park

Mesa View Estates

6th Ave. West

Kyffin Elem. School

RED ROCKS COMMUNITY COLLEGE

College West Estates

Estates Park

Sixth Ave. West Park

McClain Community School

Warren Tech School

Long View High School

Lakewood

80228

Hayden Green Mountain Park

Green Mountain

Foothills Park

W. COLFAX AVE

6th AVE FRWY

SOUTH GOLDEN RD

DENVER WEST PKWY

DENVER WEST COLORADO MILLS BLVD

COLORADO MILLS PKWY

W. ELLSWORTH AVE

YOUNGFIELD ST

W. 20th AVE

CEDAR DR

▼ See Map 310 ▼

0 ¼ ½ Miles

▲ See Map 251 ▲

◀ See Map 280 ◀

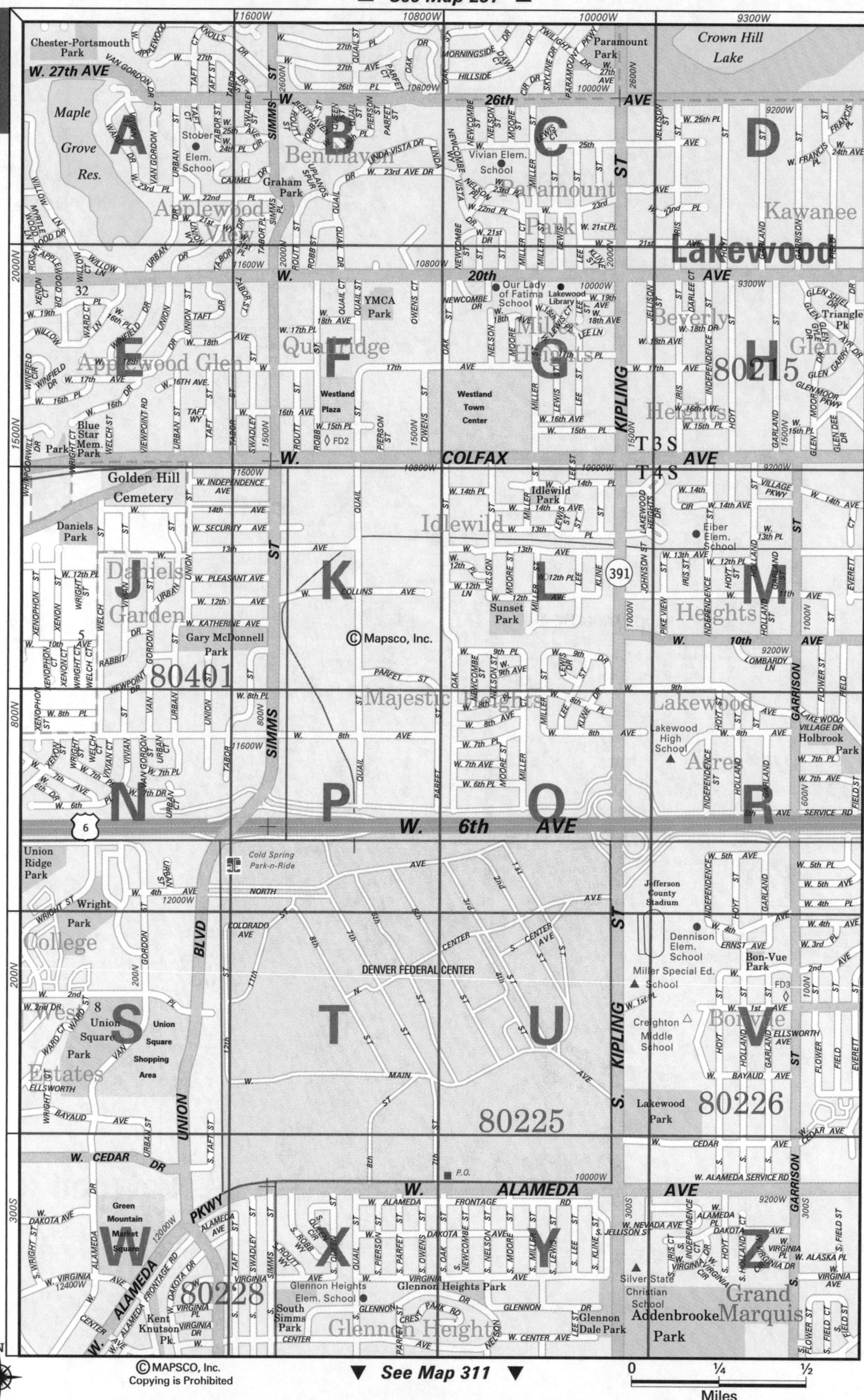

▼ See Map 311 ▼

▲ See Map 252 ▲

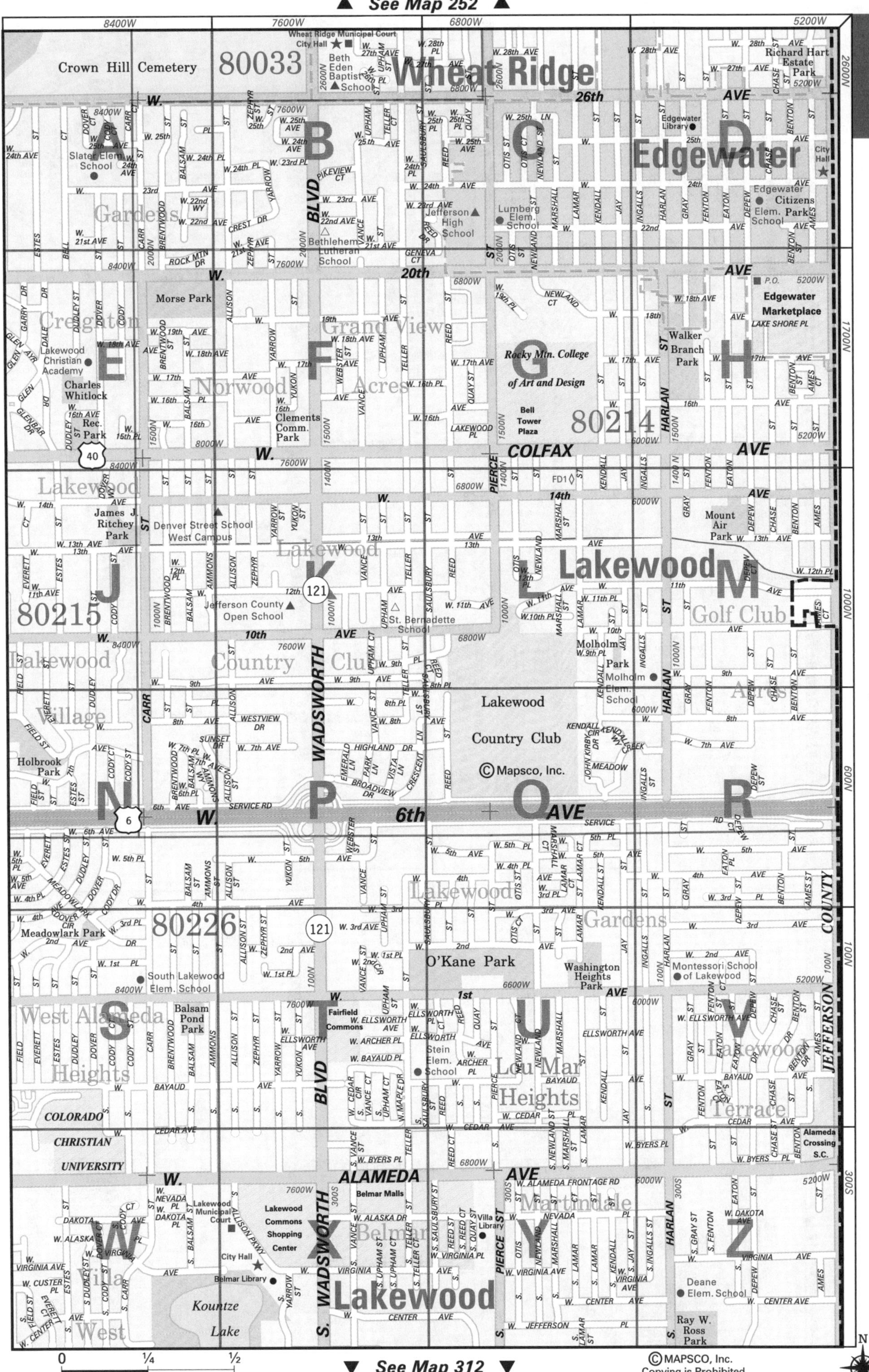

See Map 283 ▶

▼ See Map 312 ▼

▲ See Map 253 ▲

◄ See Map 282 ◄

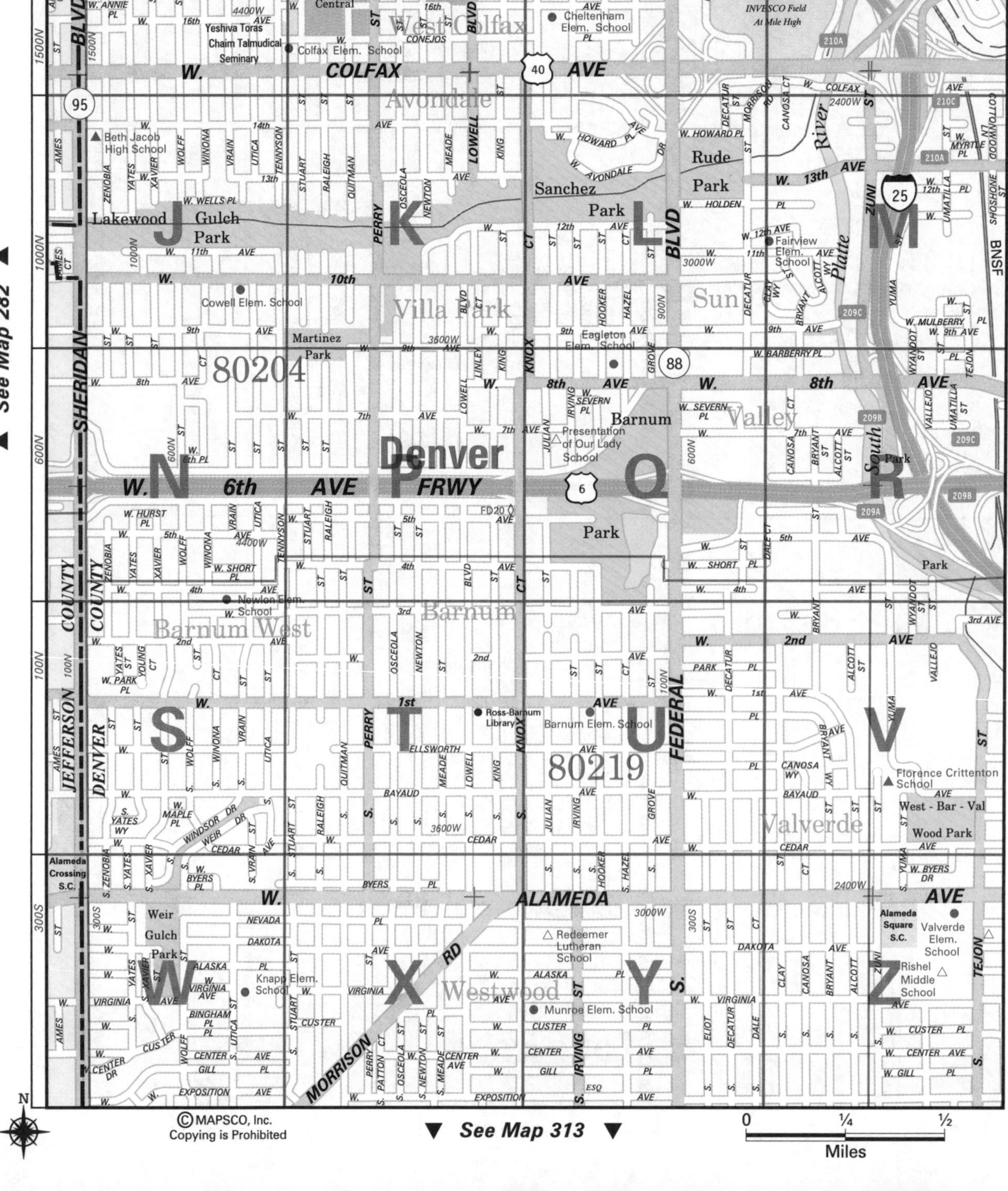

▼ See Map 313 ▼

0 ¼ ½
Miles

▲ See Map 254 ▲

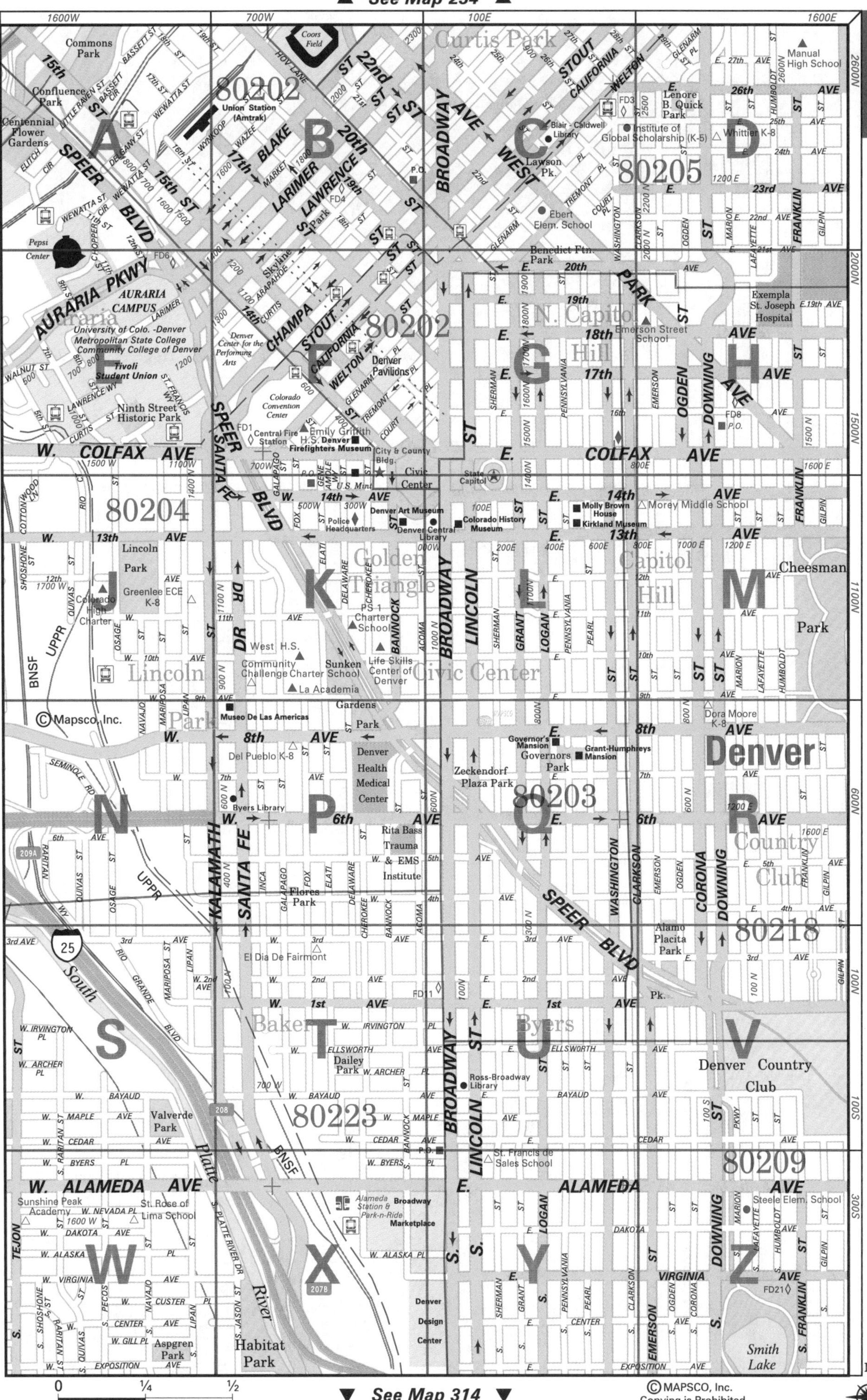

▲ See Map 285 ▲

0 ¼ ½
Miles

▼ See Map 314 ▼

▲ See Map 255 ▲

▲ See Map 284 ▲

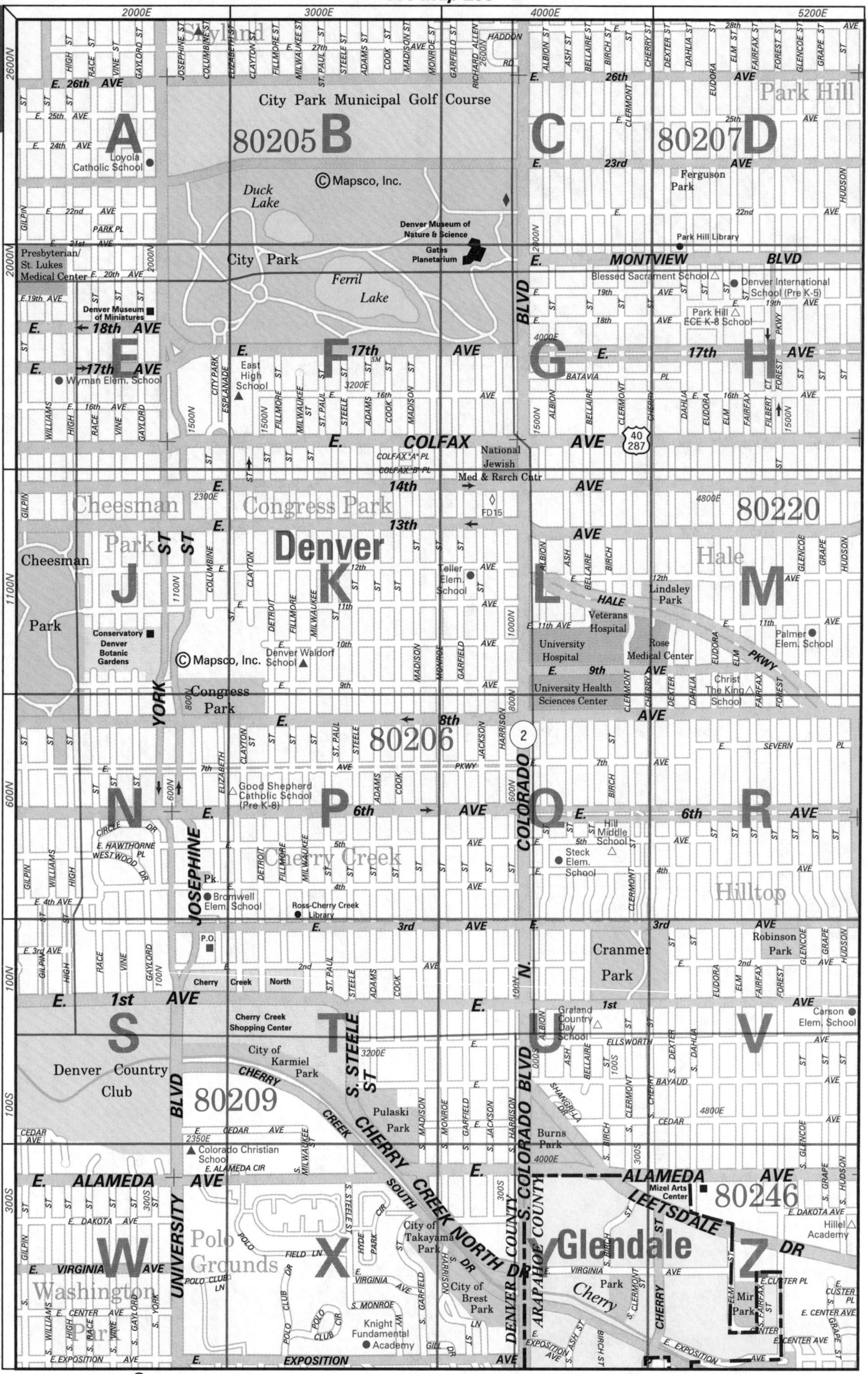

2000E 3000E 4000E 5200E

2600N 2000N 1500N 1100N 600N 100N 100S 300S

A B C D E F G H J K L M N P Q R S T U V W X Y Z

Skyland
Park Hill
City Park Municipal Golf Course
80205
80207
Loyola Catholic School
Ferguson Park
© Mapsco, Inc.
Duck Lake
Denver Museum of Nature & Science
Gates Planetarium
Park Hill Library
Presbyterian/ St. Lukes Medical Center
City Park
Ferril Lake
MONTVIEW BLVD
Blessed Sacrament School
Denver International School (Pre K-5)
Park Hill ECE K-8 School
Denver Museum of Miniatures
E. 18th AVE
E. 17th AVE
Wyman Elem. School
East High School
COLFAX AVE
National Jewish Med & Rsrch Cntr
E. 14th AVE
Cheesman Park
Congress Park
FD15
80220
E. 13th AVE
Denver
Hale
Cheesman Park
Teller Elem. School
Lindsley Park
HALE PKWY
Veterans Hospital
University Hospital
Rose Medical Center
Palmer Elem. School
Conservatory Denver Botanic Gardens
© Mapsco, Inc.
Denver Waldorf School
E. 9th AVE
University Health Sciences Center
Christ The King School
YORK ST
Congress Park
E. 8th AVE
80206
SEVERN PL
7th AVE PKWY
Good Shepherd Catholic School (Pre K-8)
E. 6th AVE
COLORADO BLVD
Hill Middle School
Steck Elem. School
CIRCLE DR
E. HAWTHORNE PL
WESTWOOD DR
Cherry Creek
Hilltop
Bromwell Elem. School
Ross-Cherry Creek Library
JOSEPHINE
E. 3rd AVE
Cranmer Park
Robinson Park
P.O.
Cherry Creek North
E. 1st AVE
Cherry Creek Shopping Center
Graland Country Day School
Carson Elem. School
City of Karmiel Park
ELLSWORTH
Denver Country Club
CHERRY CREEK
STEELE ST
80209
Pulaski Park
BAYAUD
CEDAR AVE
Burns Park
Colorado Christian School
E. ALAMEDA CIR
E. ALAMEDA AVE
Mizel Arts Center
80246
LEETSDALE DR
E. DAKOTA AVE
Hillel Academy
UNIVERSITY BLVD
Polo Grounds
CHERRY CREEK NORTH DR
CHERRY CREEK SOUTH DR
City of Takayama Park
Glendale
DENVER COUNTY
ARAPAHOE COUNTY
E. VIRGINIA AVE
Washington Park
City of Brest Park
Cherry Creek
Park
Mir Park
E. CUSTER PL
E. CENTER AVE
Knight Fundamental Academy
E. EXPOSITION AVE

▼ See Map 315 ▼

0 ¼ ½
Miles

▲ See Map 256 ▲

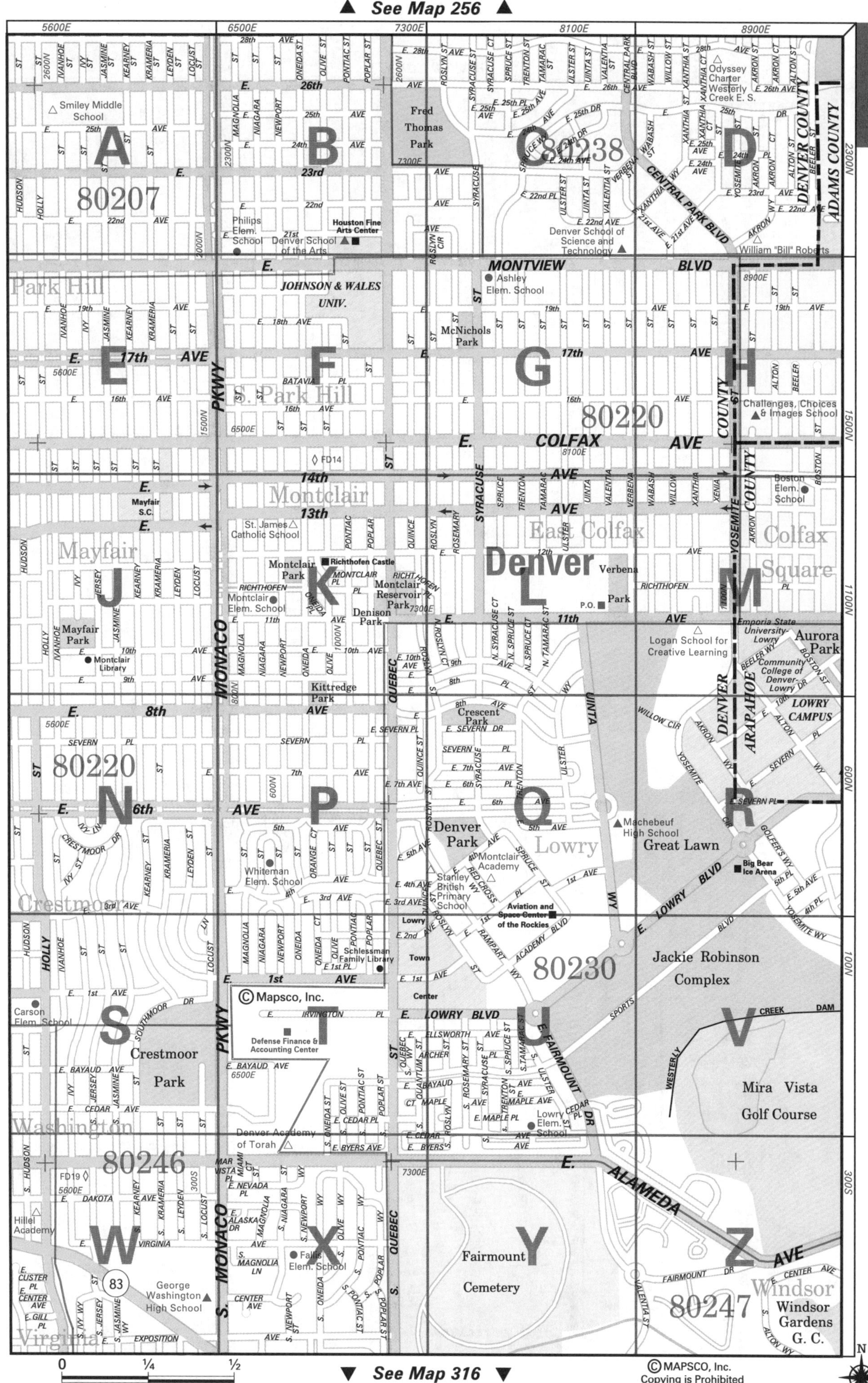

▶ See Map 287 ▶

▼ See Map 316 ▼

▲ See Map 257 ▲

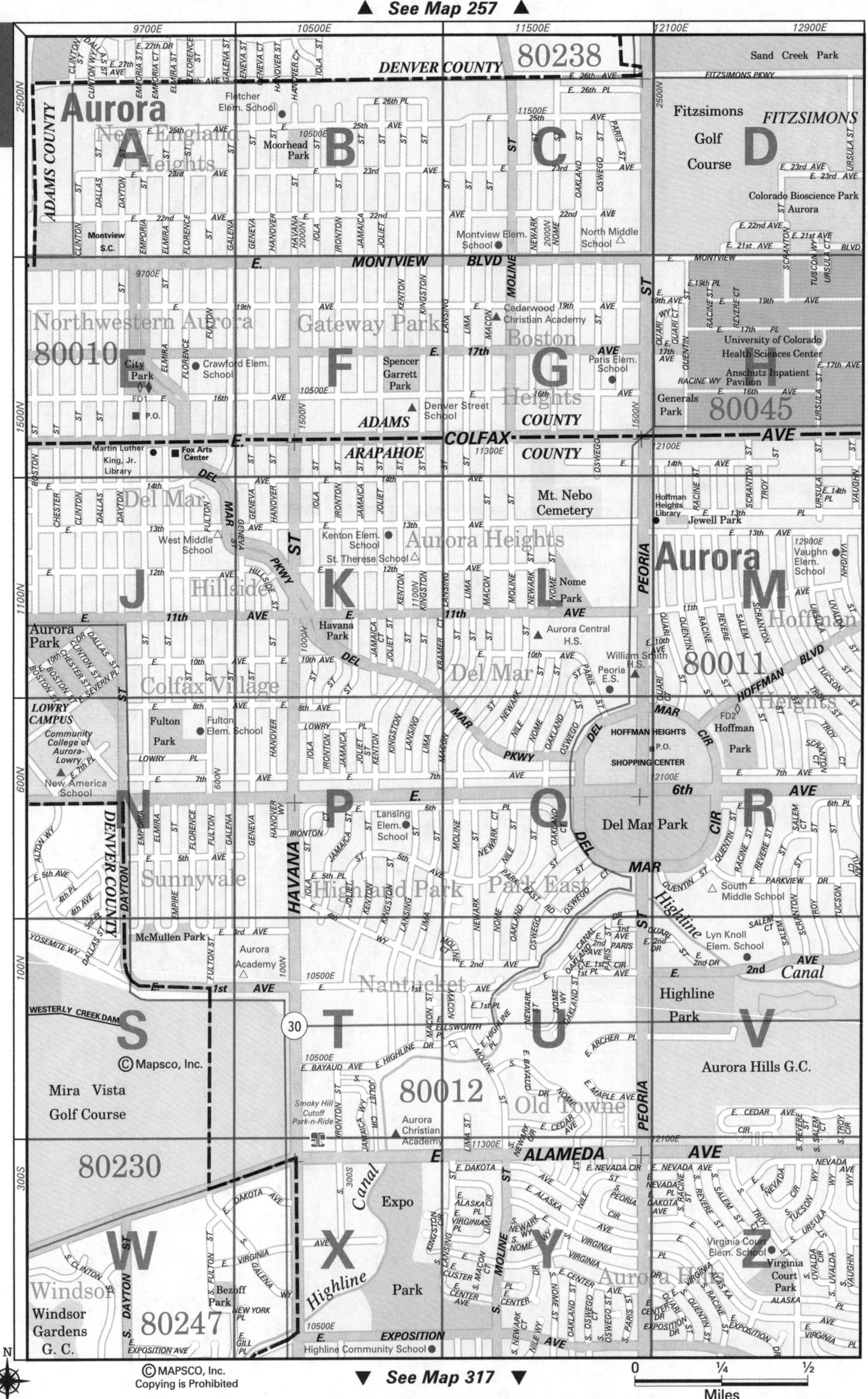

▲ See Map 286 ▲

▼ See Map 317 ▼

0 ¼ ½
Miles

▲ See Map 258 ▲

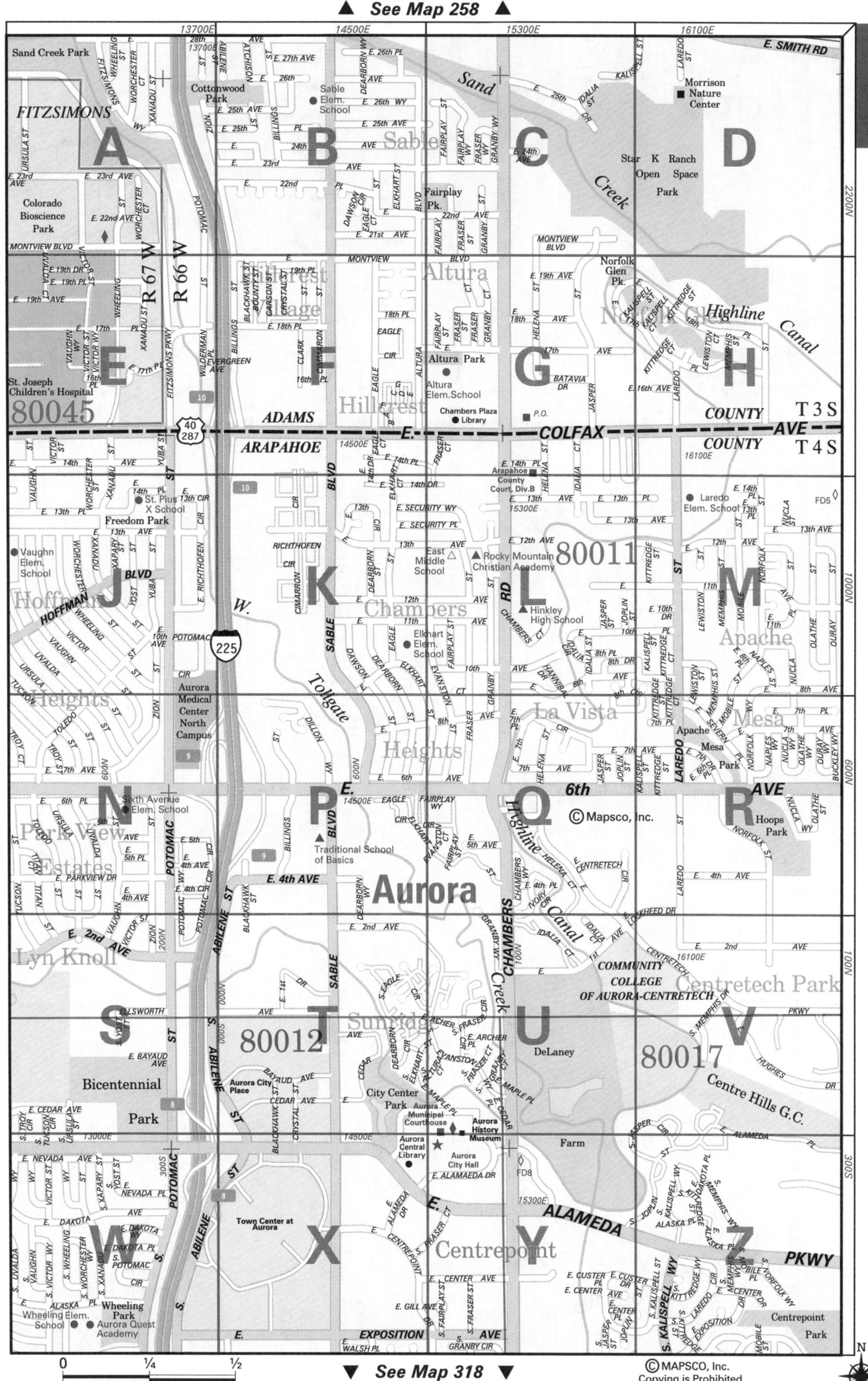

▲ See Map 289 ▲

▼ See Map 318 ▼

▲ See Map 259 ▲

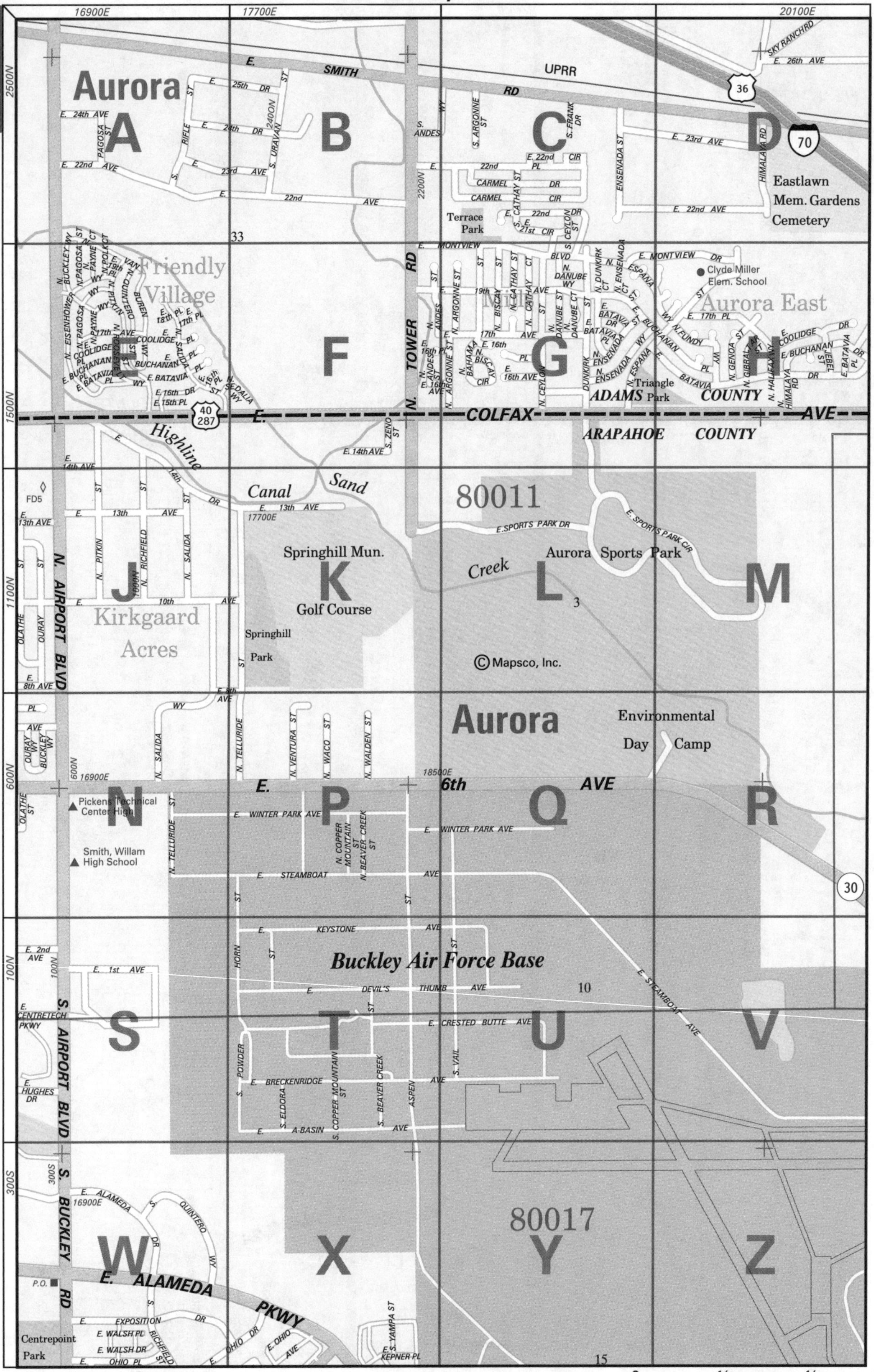

▲ See Map 288 ▲

▼ See Map 319 ▼

0 ¼ ½
Miles

▲ See Map 260 ▲

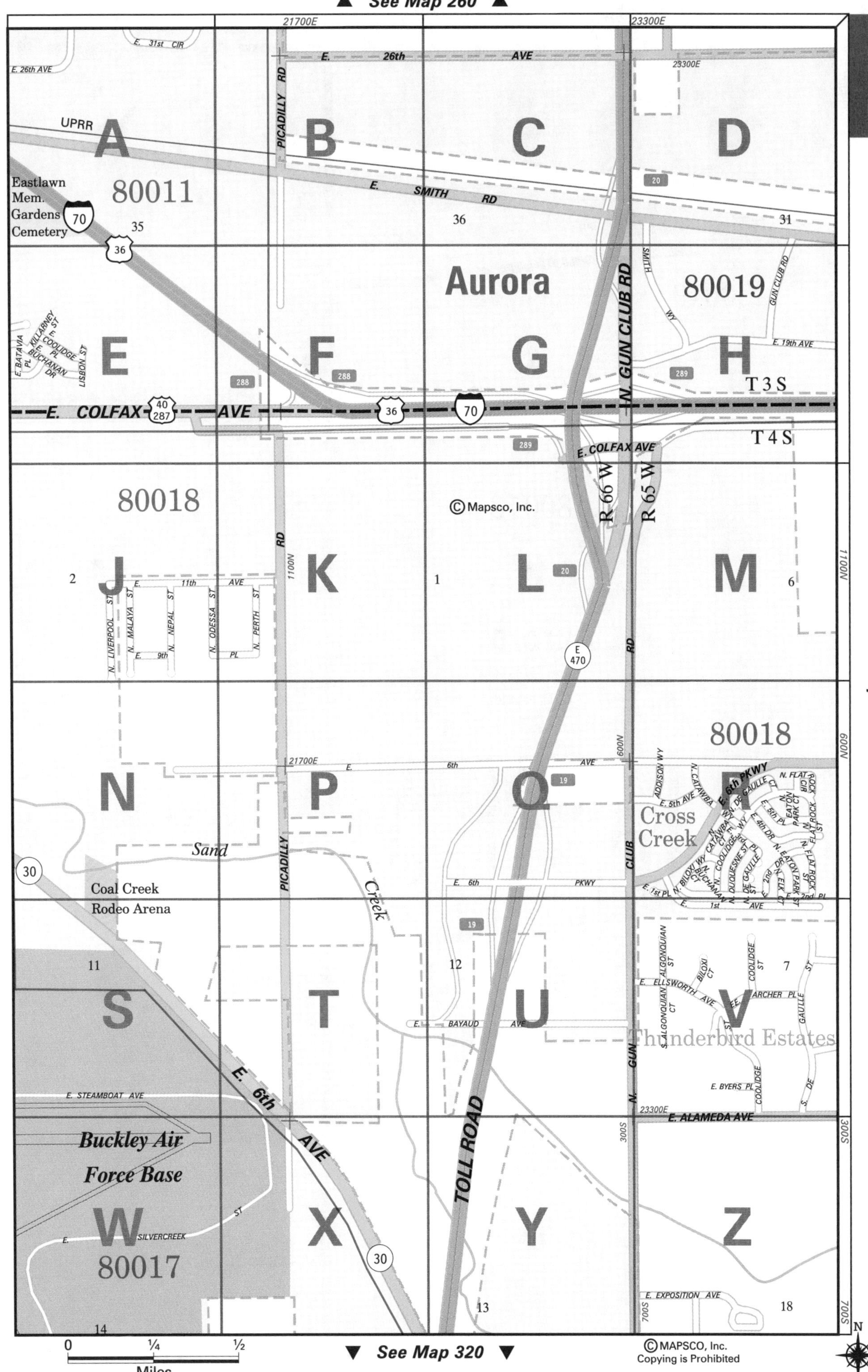

▶ See Map 291 ▶

▼ See Map 320 ▼

0 ¼ ½
Miles

▲ See Map 790 ▲

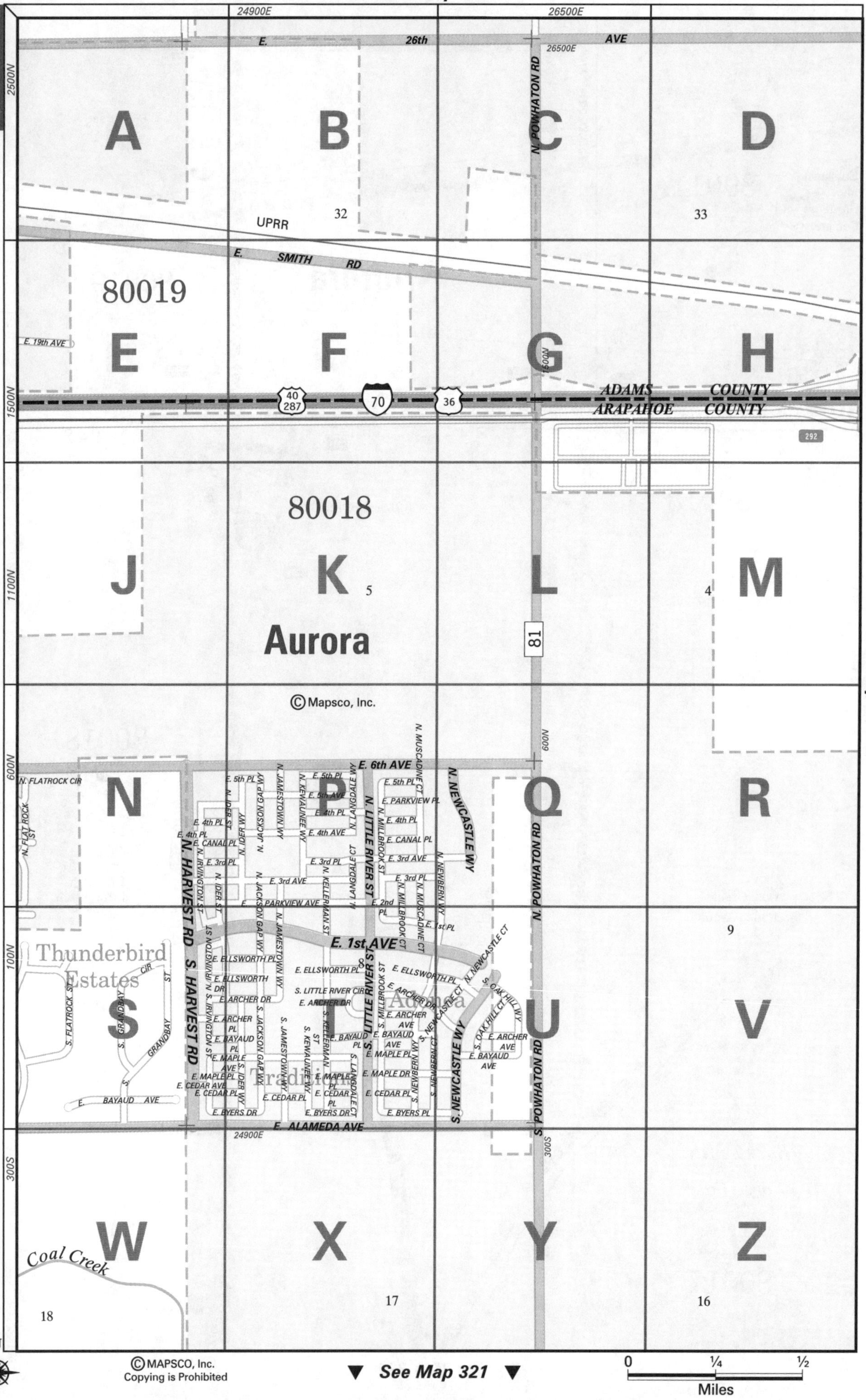

24900E
26500E
2500N
1500N
1100N
600N
100N
300S
E. 26th AVE
26500E
N. POWHATON RD
A
B
C
D
UPRR
32
33
E. SMITH RD
80019
E. 19th AVE
E
F
G
H
1500N
40
287
70
36
ADAMS COUNTY
ARAPAHOE COUNTY
292
80018
J
K
L
M
5
4
81
Aurora
© Mapsco, Inc.
E. 6th AVE
N. FLATROCK CIR
N. FLAT ROCK ST
N
P
Q
R
N. HARVEST RD
N. LITTLE RIVER ST
N. NEWCASTLE WY
N. POWHATON RD
600N
E. 5th PL
E. 5th AVE
E. 4th PL
E. 4th AVE
E. CANAL PL
E. 3rd PL
E. 3rd AVE
E. PARKVIEW PL
E. PARKVIEW AVE
E. 2nd PL
E. 1st PL
N. IDER ST
N. IRVINGTON ST
N. JACKSON GAP WY
N. JAMESTOWN WY
N. KEWAUNEE WY
N. KELLERMAN ST
N. LANGDALE CT
N. LANGDALE WY
N. MILLBROOK ST
N. MILLBROOK CT
N. MUSCADINE CT
N. NEWBERN WY
E. 1st AVE
Thunderbird Estates
S. FLATROCK ST
S. GRANDBAY CIR
S. GRANDBAY ST
E. BAYAUD AVE
S. HARVEST RD
S
T
U
V
9
E. ELLSWORTH PL
E. ELLSWORTH AVE
E. ELLSWORTH DR
E. ARCHER DR
E. ARCHER PL
E. ARCHER AVE
E. BAYAUD PL
E. BAYAUD AVE
E. MAPLE AVE
E. MAPLE PL
E. MAPLE DR
E. CEDAR AVE
E. CEDAR PL
E. BYERS DR
E. BYERS PL
S. LITTLE RIVER CIR
S. LITTLE RIVER ST
S. IRVINGTON ST
S. IDER ST
S. JACKSON GAP WY
S. JAMESTOWN WY
S. KEWAUNEE WY
S. KELLERMAN ST
S. LANGDALE CT
S. MILLBROOK ST
S. NEWBERN WY
S. NEWCASTLE CT
N. NEWCASTLE CT
S. NEWCASTLE WY
S. OAK HILL CT
S. OAK HILL WY
S. POWHATON RD
Adonea
Traditions
E. ALAMEDA AVE
24900E
300S
W
X
Y
Z
Coal Creek
18
17
16
N
0
¼
½
Miles

See Map 290

See Map 790

▼ See Map 321 ▼

▲ See Map 781 ▲

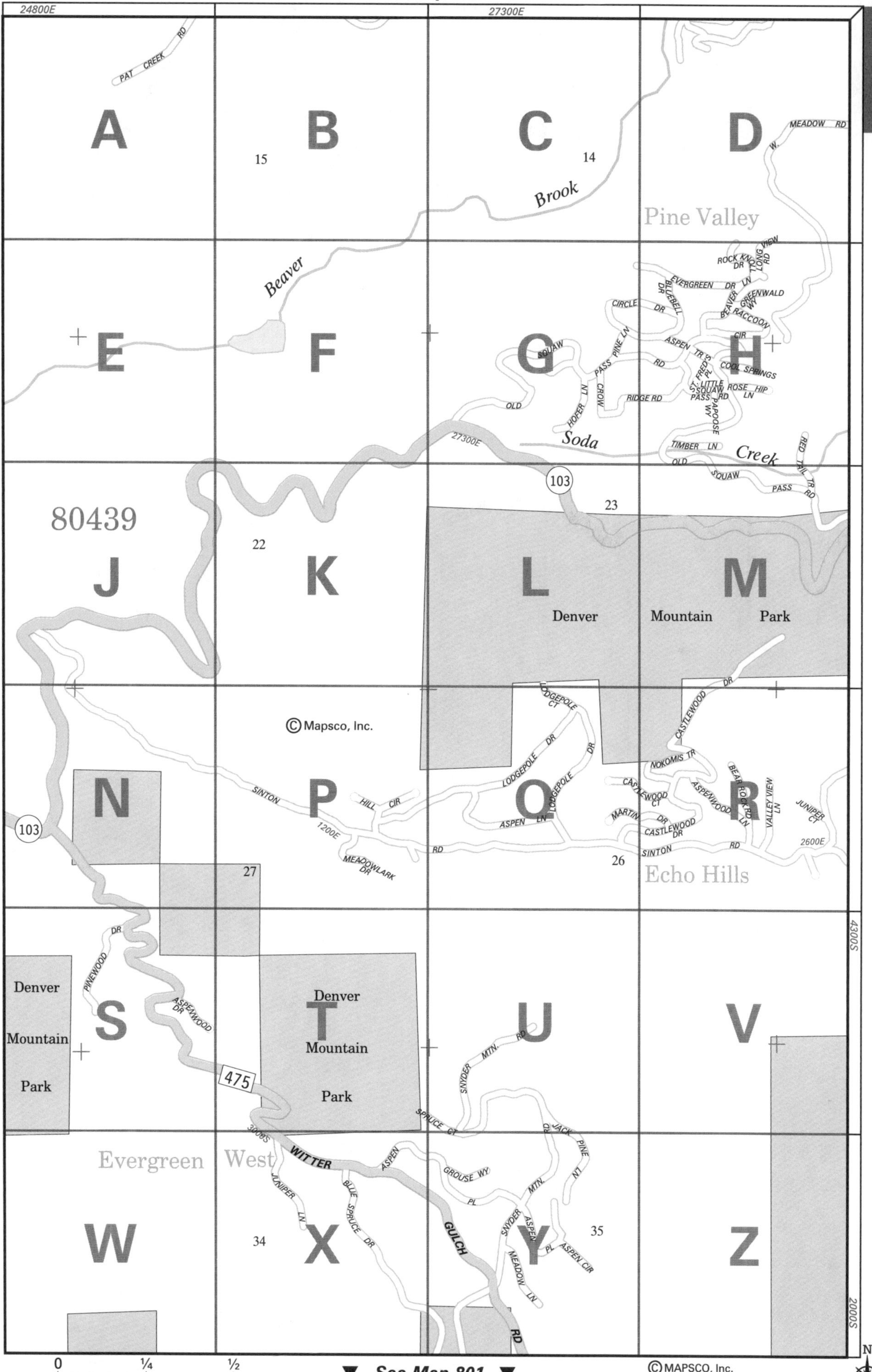

▶ See Map 305 ▶

▼ See Map 801 ▼

▲ See Map 275 ▲

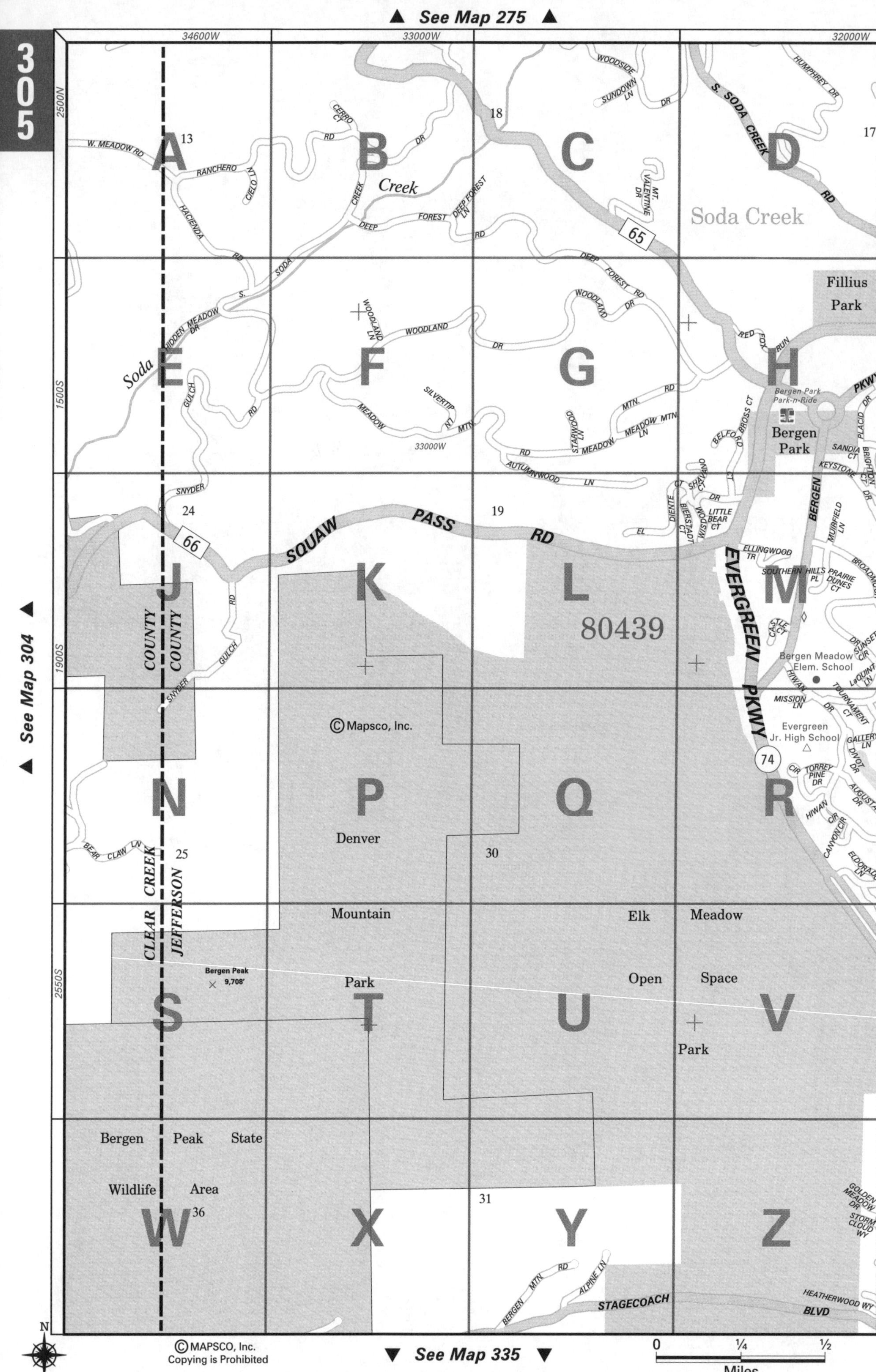

▲ See Map 304 ▲

▼ See Map 335 ▼

0 ¼ ½
Miles

▲ See Map 276 ▲

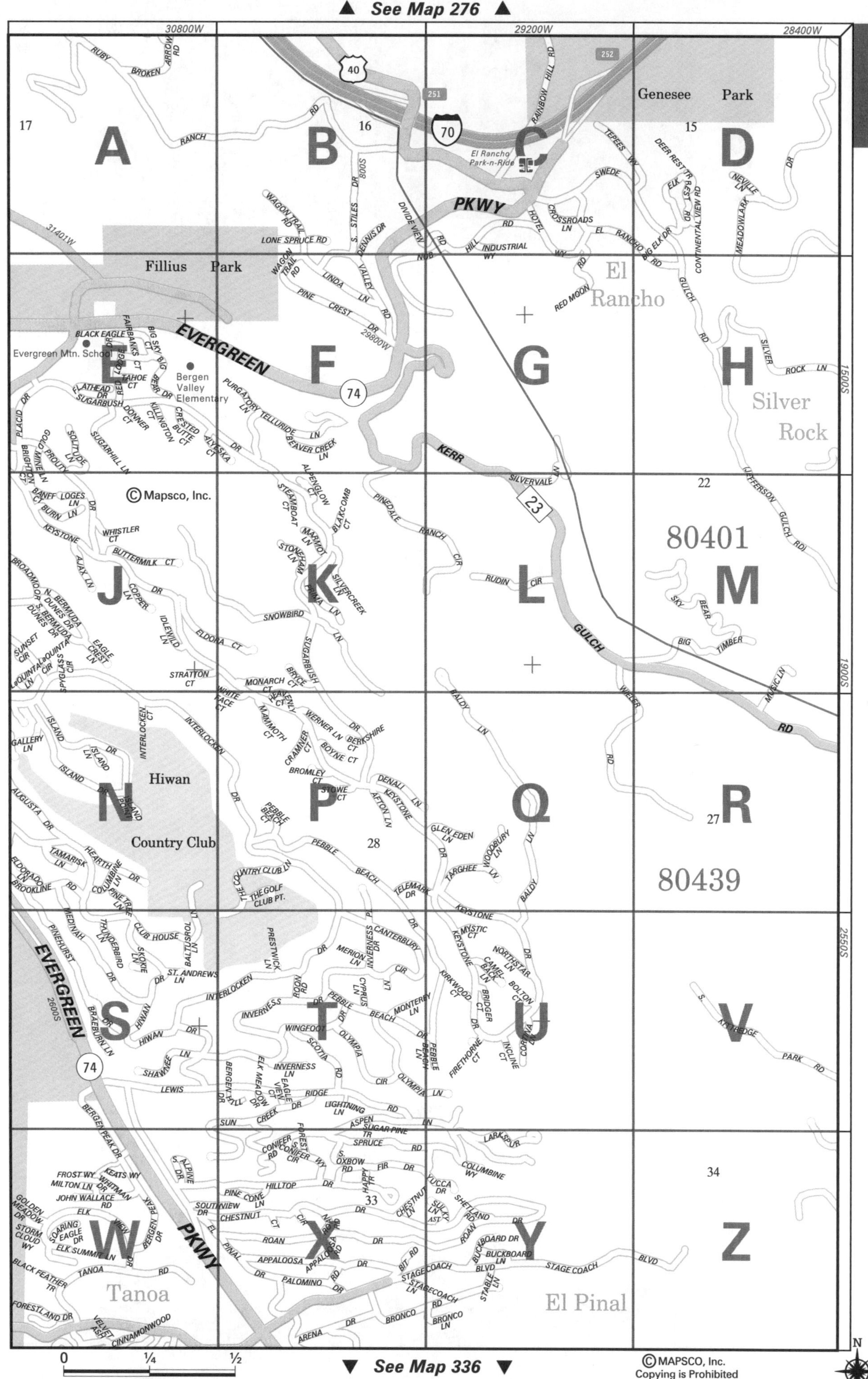

▶ See Map 307 ▶

▼ See Map 336 ▼

0 ¼ ½
Miles

▲ See Map 277 ▲

▲ See Map 306 ▲

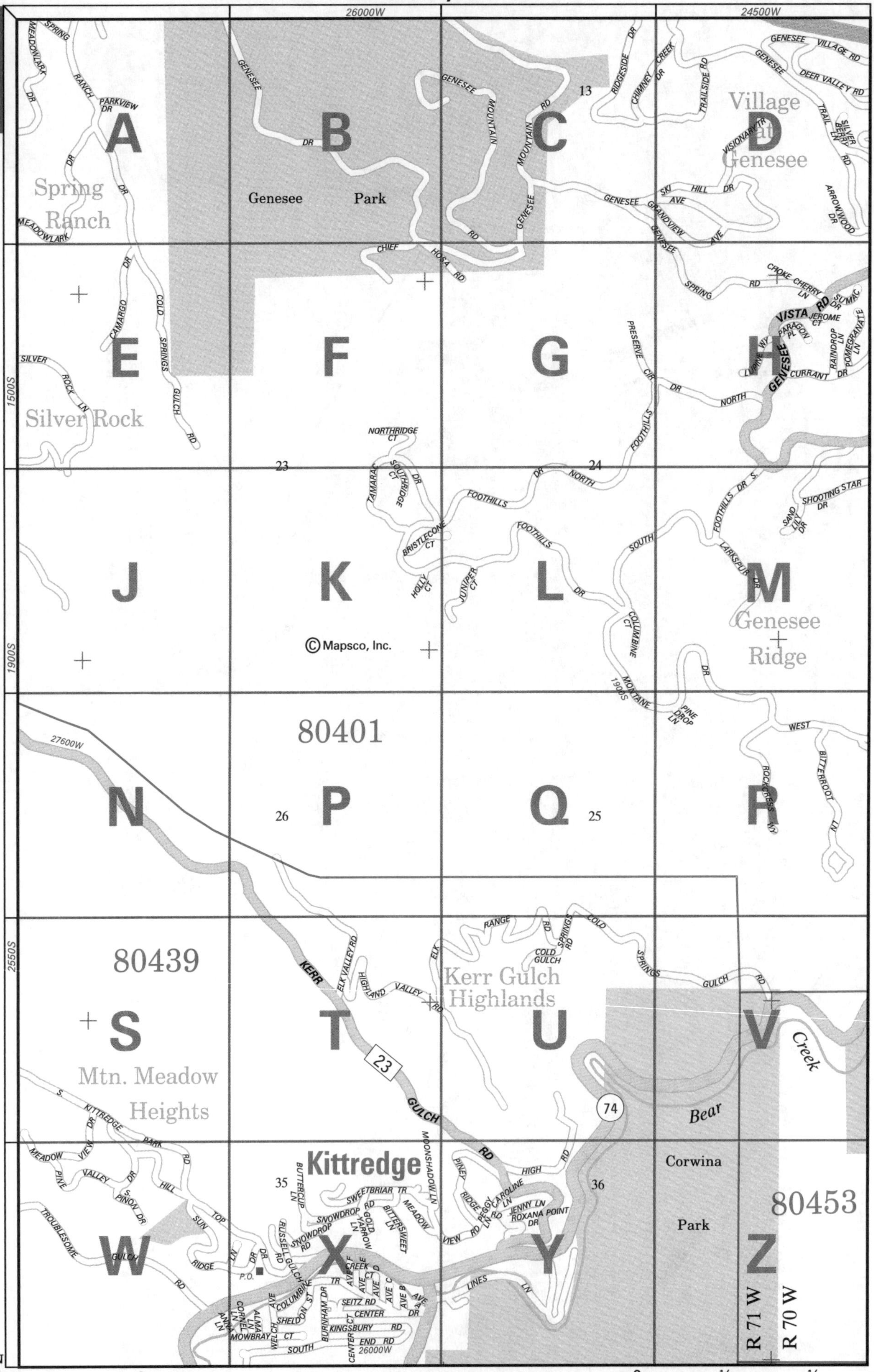
26000W
24500W
1500S
1900S
2550S
27600W
A
B
C
D
E
F
G
H
J
K
L
M
N
P
Q
R
S
T
U
V
W
X
Y
Z
Spring Ranch
Genesee Park
Village at Genesee
Silver Rock
Genesee Ridge
80401
80439
Kerr Gulch Highlands
Mtn. Meadow Heights
Kittredge
Corwina Park
80453
Bear Creek
R 71 W
R 70 W
© Mapsco, Inc.
13
23
24
26
25
35
36
23
74
GENESEE DR
MOUNTAIN RD
GENESEE MOUNTAIN RD
CHIEF HOSA RD
SKI HILL DR
GRANDVIEW AVE
SPRING RD
NORTH DR
FOOTHILLS DR
SOUTH DR
KERR GULCH RD
ELK VALLEY RD
HIGHLAND VALLEY RD
COLD SPRINGS GULCH RD
RANGE RD
MOONSHADOW LN
SWEETBRIAR TR
LINES LN
TROUBLESOME GULCH RD
SUN RIDGE RD
KINGSBURY RD
SEITZ RD
CENTER RD
END RD
P.O.

▼ See Map 337 ▼

0 ¼ ½
Miles

▲ See Map 278 ▲

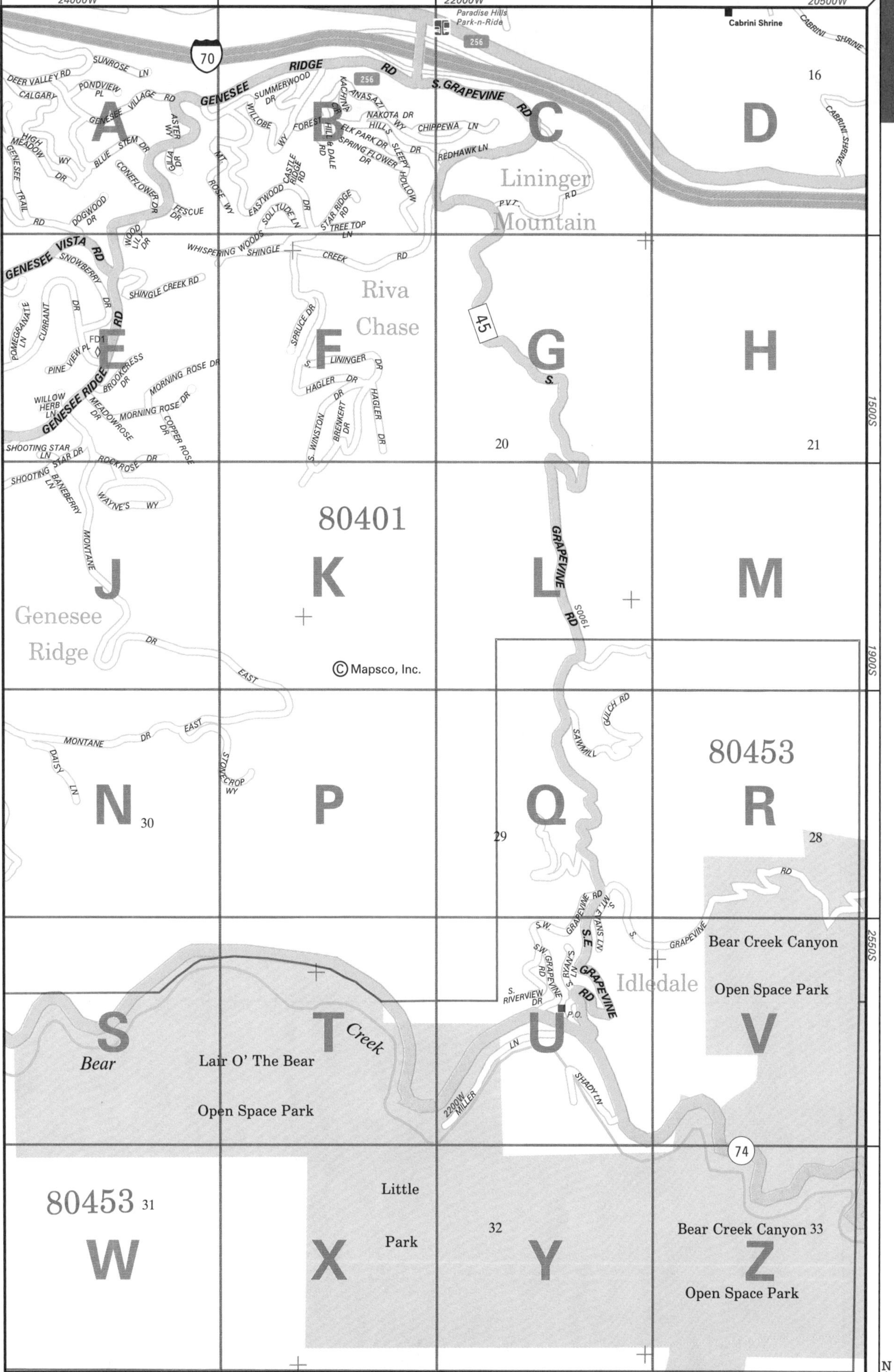

▶ See Map 309 ▶

▼ See Map 338 ▼

0 ¼ ½ Miles

▲ See Map 279 ▲

◀ See Map 308 ◀

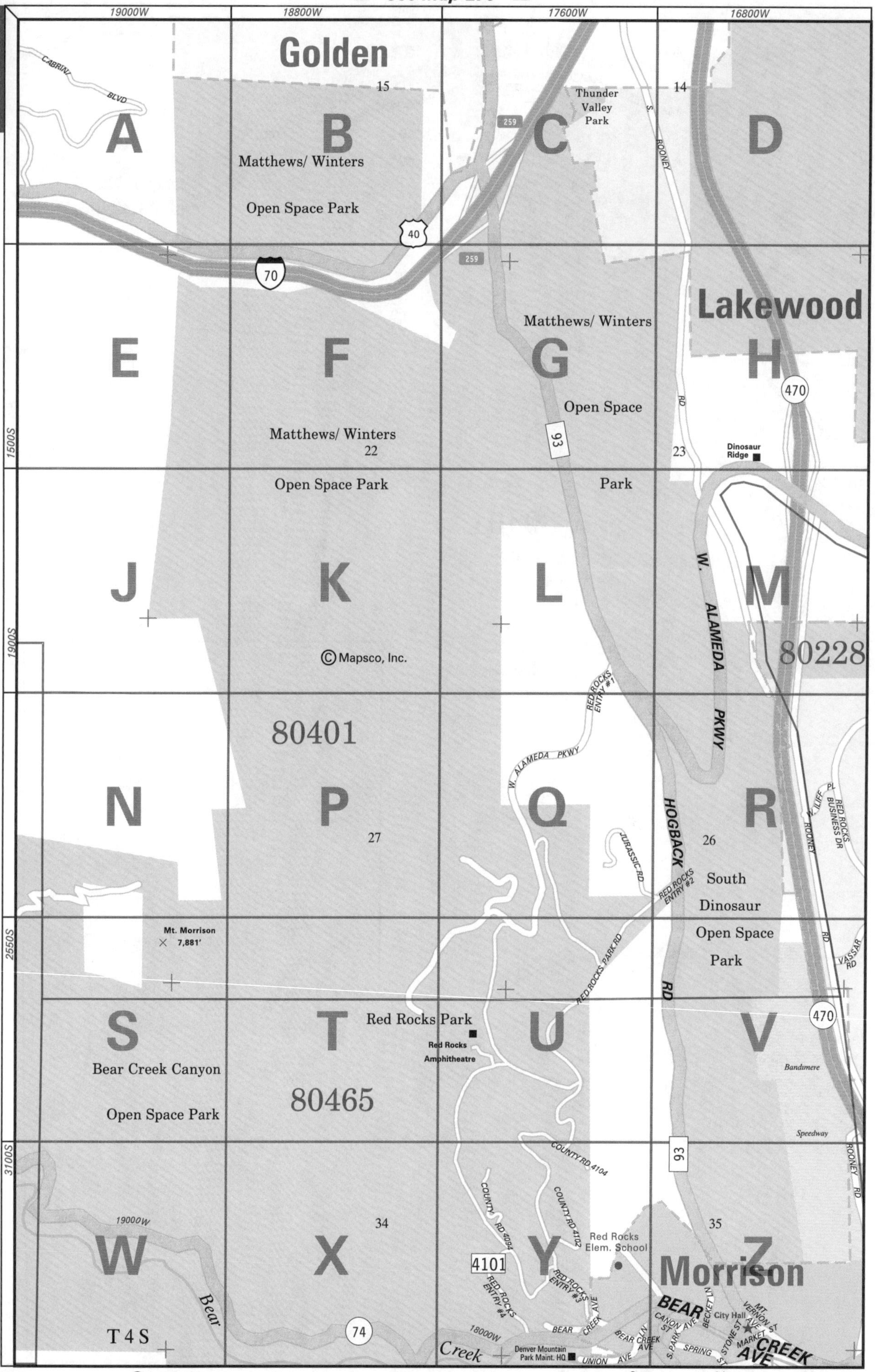

19000W
18800W
17600W
16800W
1500S
1900S
2550S
3100S

Golden

Lakewood

Morrison

A B C D E F G H J K L M N P Q R S T U V W X Y Z

Matthews/ Winters Open Space Park

Thunder Valley Park

Matthews/ Winters Open Space Park

Matthews/ Winters Open Space Park

South Dinosaur Open Space Park

Bear Creek Canyon Open Space Park

Red Rocks Park

Red Rocks Amphitheatre

Dinosaur Ridge

Mt. Morrison 7,881'

Red Rocks Elem. School

City Hall

Denver Mountain Park Maint. HQ

Bandimere Speedway

CABRINI BLVD

S. ROONEY RD

W. ALAMEDA PKWY

HOGBACK RD

JURASSIC RD

RED ROCKS ENTRY #1

RED ROCKS ENTRY #2

RED ROCKS ENTRY #3

RED ROCKS ENTRY #4

RED ROCKS PARK RD

W. ILIFF PL

RED ROCKS BUSINESS DR

ROONEY RD

VASSAR RD

COUNTY RD 4104

COUNTY RD 4102

COUNTY RD 4094

4101

BEAR CREEK AVE

BEAR CREEK LN

CANON ST

S. PARK AVE

BECKET LN

STONE ST

MT. VERNON ST

MARKET ST

SPRING ST

UNION AVE

18000W

19000W

Bear Creek

T4S

15 14 22 23 27 26 34 35

40 70 259 93 470 74

80401 80228 80465

© Mapsco, Inc.

▼ See Map 339 ▼

0 ¼ ½
Miles

N

▲ See Map 280 ▲

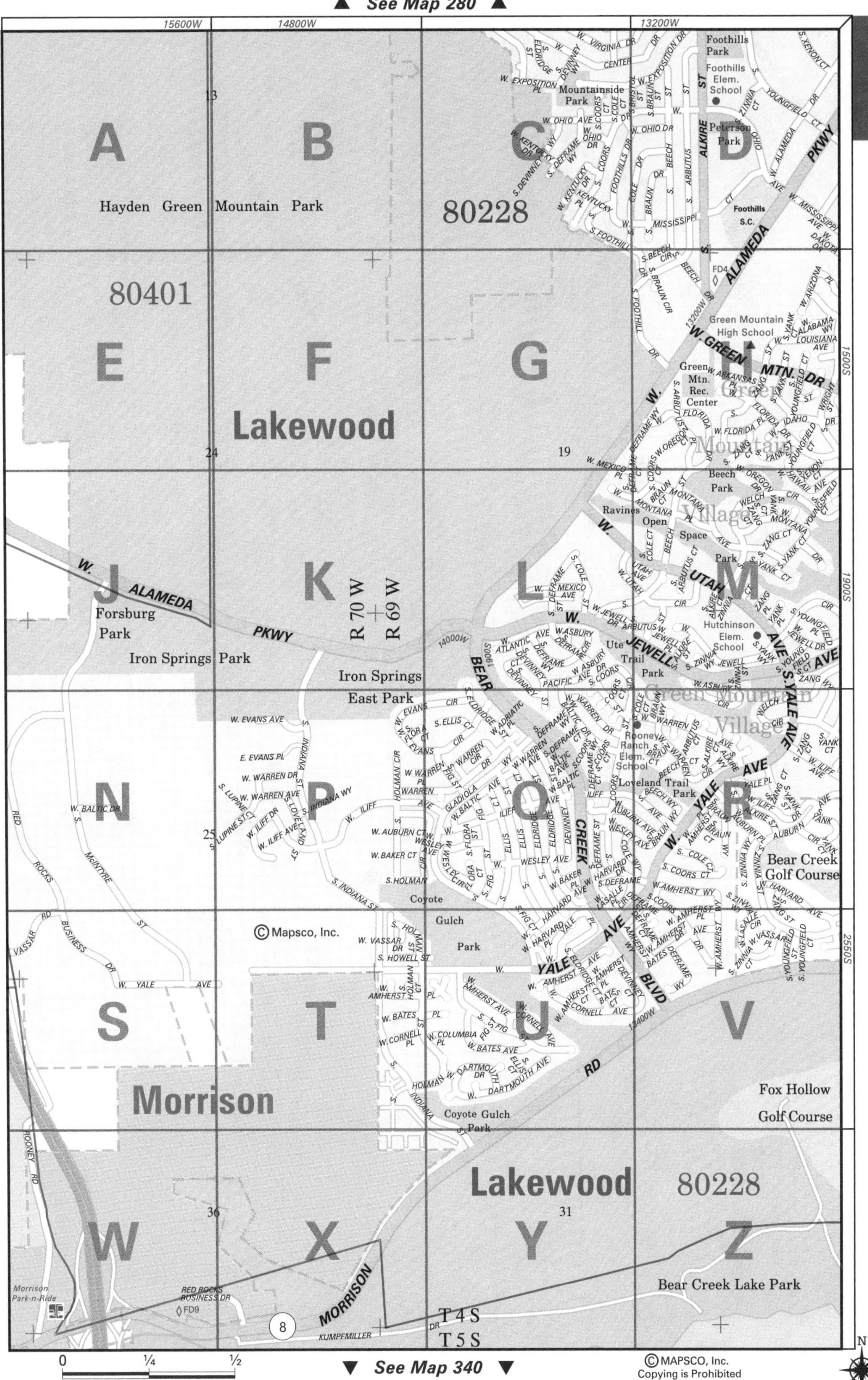

See Map 311 ▶

0 ¼ ½
Miles

▼ See Map 340 ▼

N

▲ See Map 281 ▲

◄ See Map 310 ◄

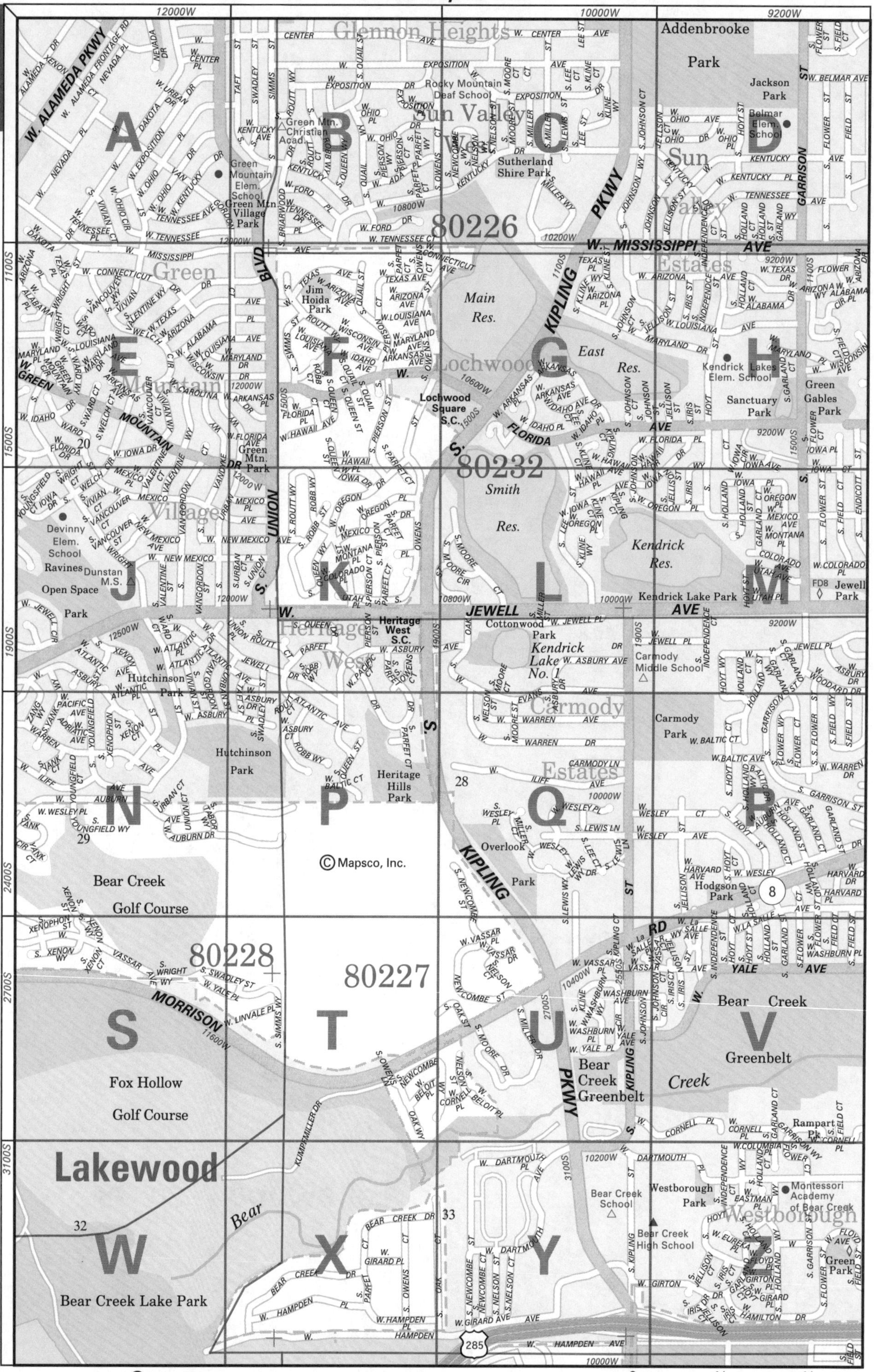

▼ See Map 341 ▼

0 ¼ ½
Miles

▲ See Map 282 ▲

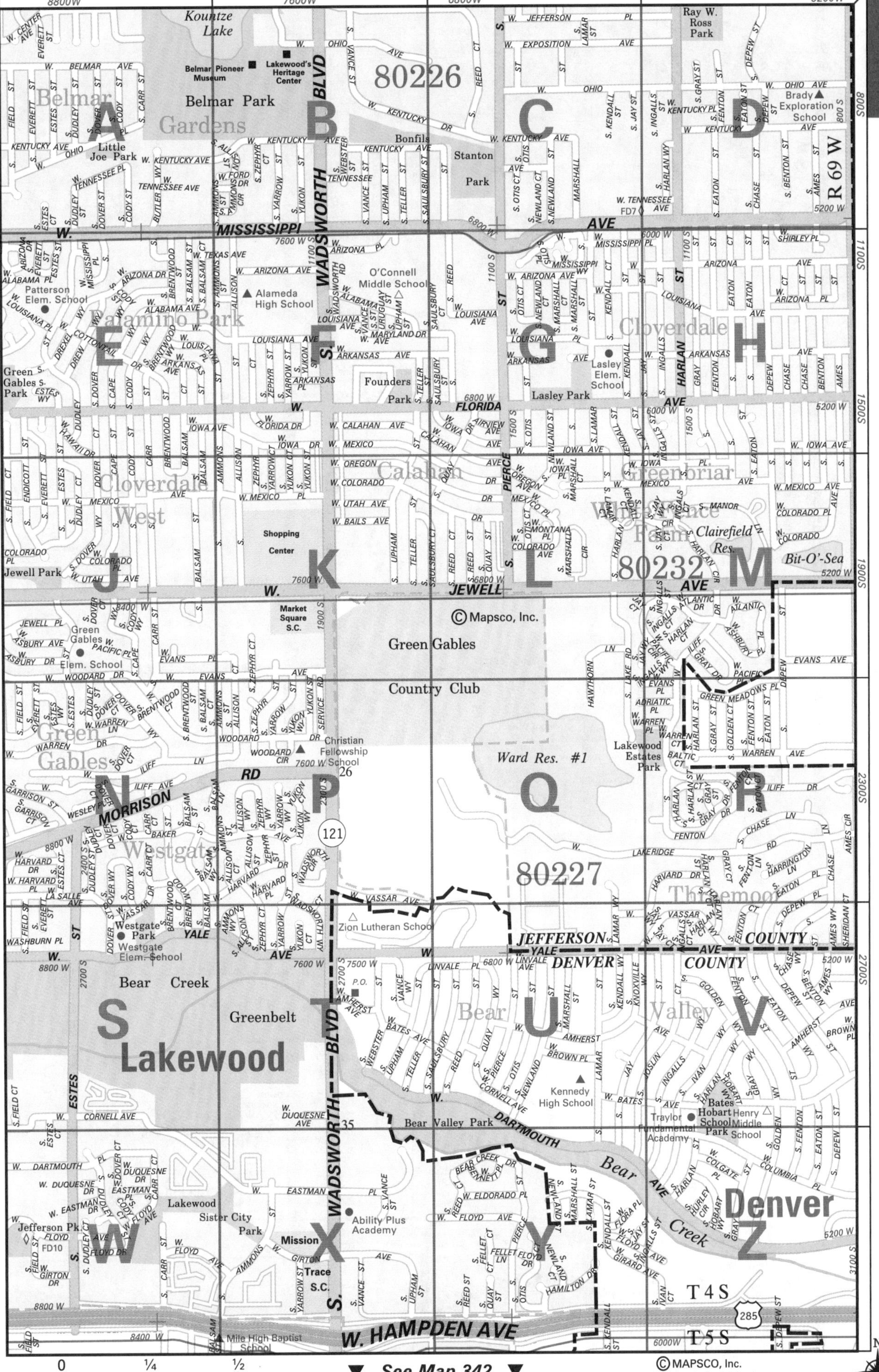

▶ See Map 313 ▶

0 ¼ ½
Miles

▼ See Map 342 ▼

See Map 283

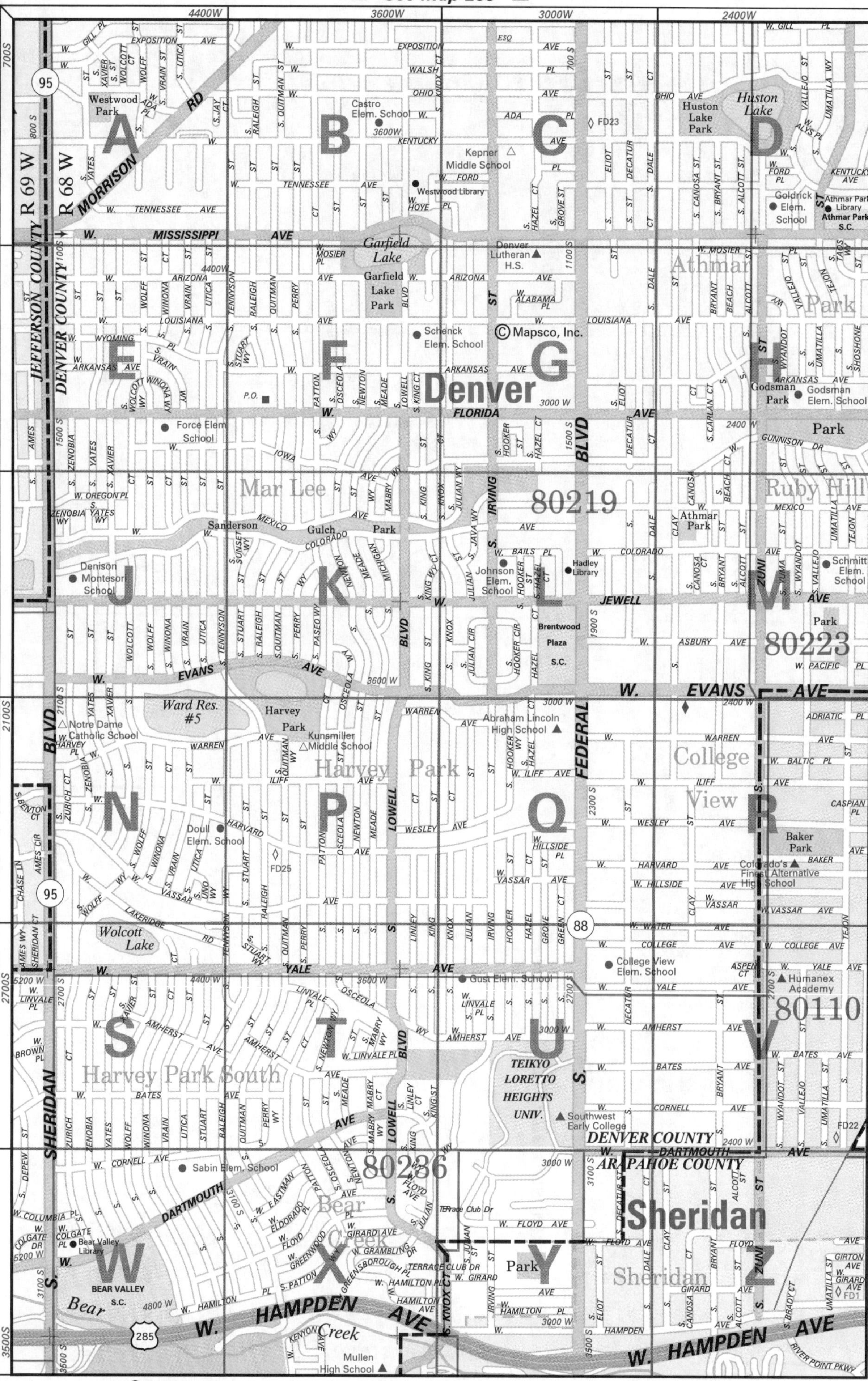

See Map 312

See Map 343

0 1/4 1/2
Miles

▲ See Map 284 ▲

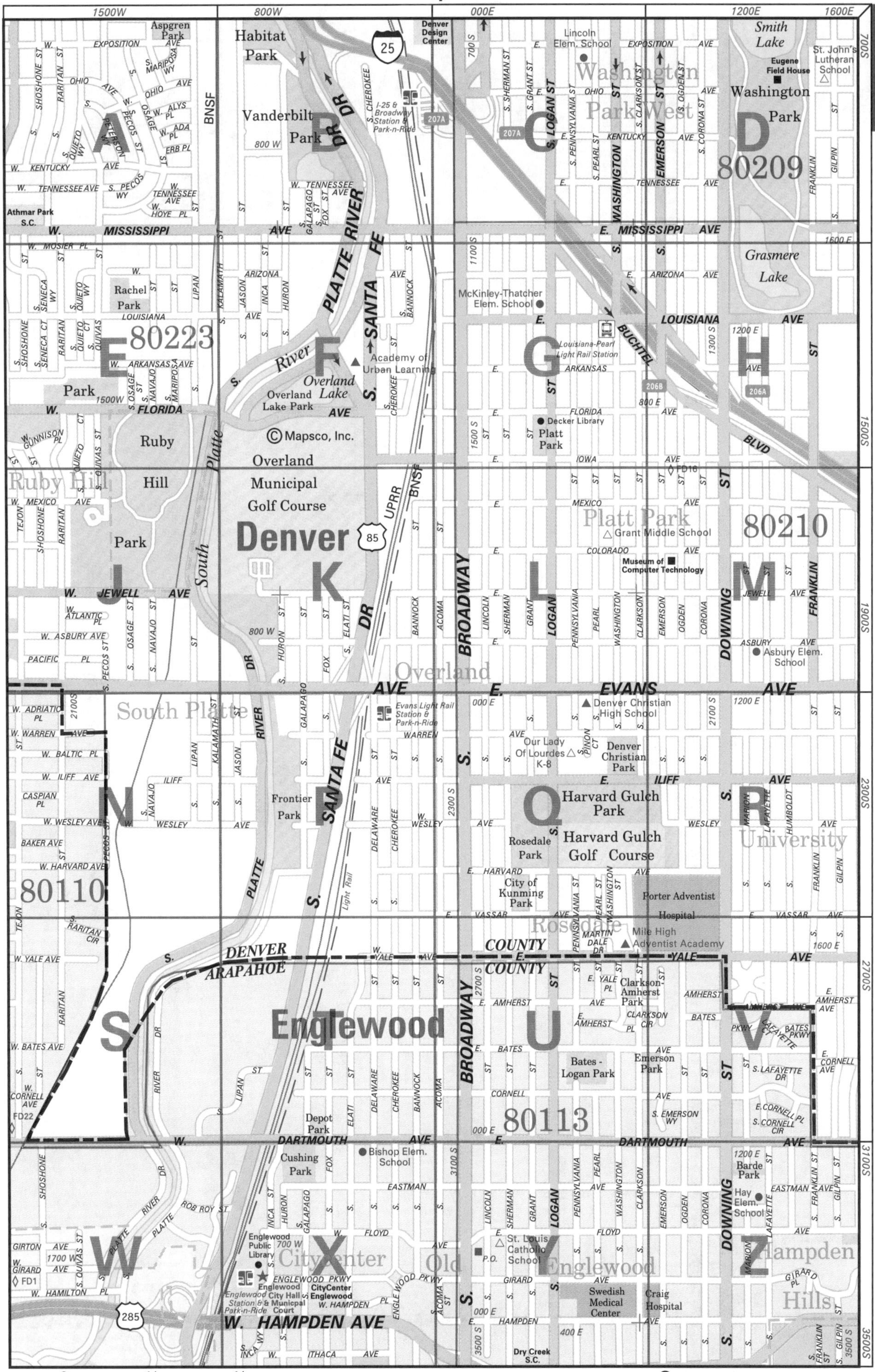

1500W
800W
000E
1200E
1600E
700S
1500S
1900S
2300S
2700S
3100S
3500S
Aspgren Park
Habitat Park
Vanderbilt Park
Denver Design Center
25
I-25 & Broadway Station & Park-n-Ride
207A
BNSF
EXPOSITION
OHIO
MARIPOSA
ALYS PL
ADA PL
ERB PL
KENTUCKY
TENNESSEE AVE
HOYE PL
Athmar Park S.C.
MISSISSIPPI
AVE
Lincoln Elem. School
Washington Park West
Smith Lake
Eugene Field House
St. John's Lutheran School
Washington Park
80209
A
B
C
D
E. MISSISSIPPI AVE
Grasmere Lake
MOSIER PL
Rachel Park
LOUISIANA
ARIZONA
80223
ARKANSAS AVE
Park
FLORIDA
PLATTE RIVER DR
SANTA FE
River
Academy of Urban Learning
Overland Lake
Overland Lake Park
McKinley-Thatcher Elem. School
Louisiana-Pearl Light Rail Station
BUCHTEL
206B
206A
E
F
G
H
Decker Library
Platt Park
BLVD
GUNNISON PL
Ruby Hill
Park
Mapsco, Inc.
Overland Municipal Golf Course
Denver
85
UPRR
IOWA
FD16
MEXICO
Platt Park
Grant Middle School
80210
COLORADO
Museum of Computer Technology
South Platte
J
K
L
M
JEWELL AVE
ATLANTIC PL
ASBURY AVE
PACIFIC PL
BROADWAY
DOWNING
FRANKLIN
Asbury Elem. School
Overland
EVANS AVE
ADRIATIC PL
WARREN
BALTIC PL
ILIFF AVE
CASPIAN PL
WESLEY AVE
BAKER AVE
HARVARD AVE
80110
South Platte
Evans Light Rail Station & Park-n-Ride
Denver Christian High School
Our Lady Of Lourdes K-8
Denver Christian Park
Frontier Park
Harvard Gulch Park
Harvard Gulch Golf Course
Rosedale Park
City of Kunming Park
Porter Adventist Hospital
University
N
P
Q
R
Light Rail
VASSAR
Rosedale
Mile High Adventist Academy
RARITAN CIR
YALE AVE
DENVER COUNTY
ARAPAHOE COUNTY
Englewood
Clarkson-Amherst Park
AMHERST
BATES
S
T
U
V
Bates-Logan Park
Emerson Park
CORNELL
80113
Depot Park
S. EMERSON WY
S. LAFAYETTE DR
E. CORNELL PL
S. CORNELL CIR
FD22
DARTMOUTH AVE
Cushing Park
Bishop Elem. School
EASTMAN
Barde Park
Hay Elem. School
ROB ROY ST
FLOYD
GIRTON AVE
GIRARD AVE
1700 W
FD1
HAMILTON PL
Englewood Public Library
CityCenter
Old Englewood
St. Louis Catholic School
P.O.
Hampden Hills
W
X
Y
Z
ENGLEWOOD PKWY
Englewood City Hall & Municipal Court
Englewood Station & Park-n-Ride
CityCenter Englewood
285
W. HAMPDEN AVE
Swedish Medical Center
Craig Hospital
HAMPDEN
ITHACA AVE
Dry Creek S.C.
N

0 ¼ ½
Miles

▶ See Map 315 ▶

▼ See Map 344 ▼

▲ See Map 285 ▲

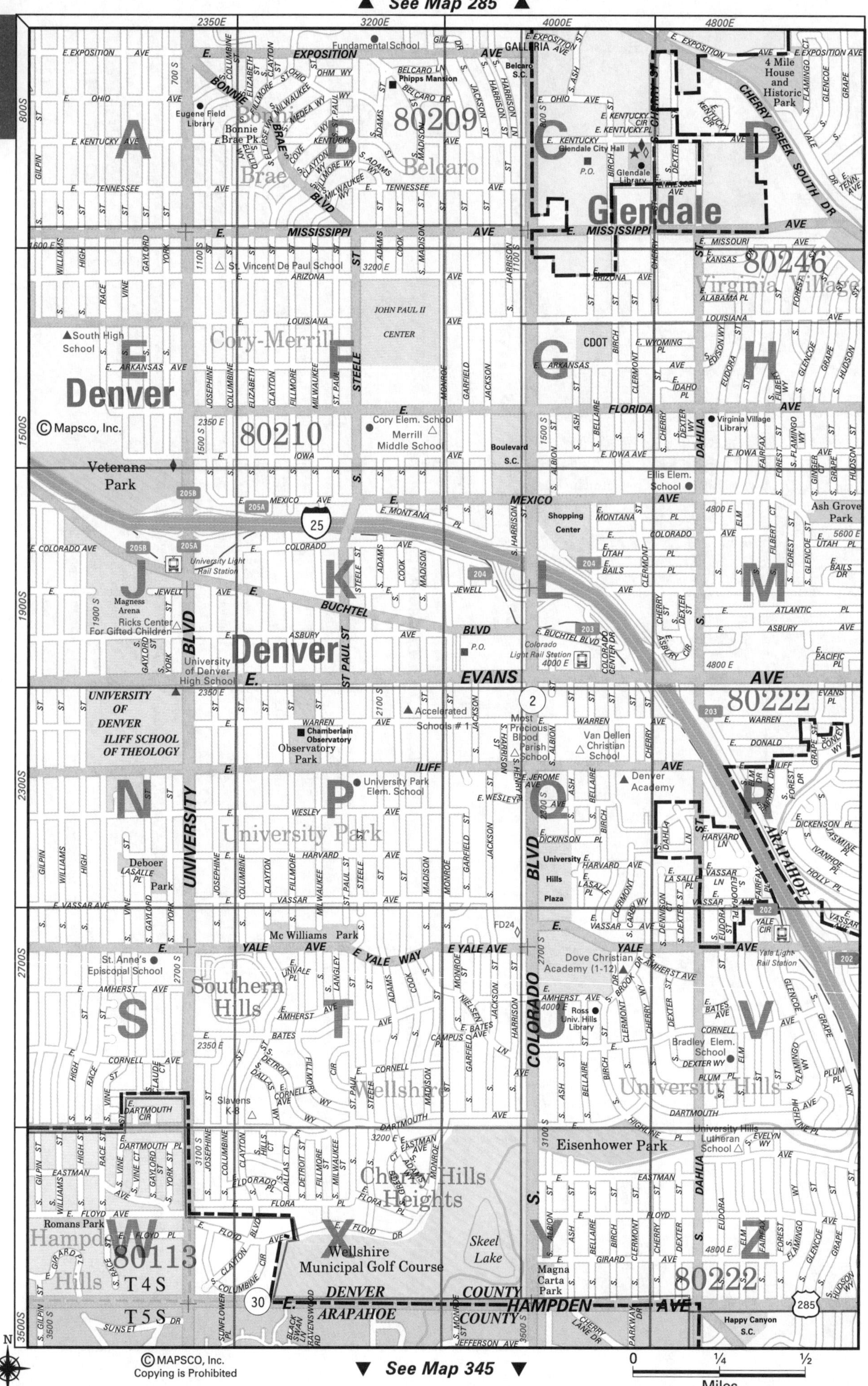

▲ See Map 314 ▲

▼ See Map 345 ▼

0 ¼ ½
Miles

▲ See Map 286 ▲

▶ See Map 317 ▶

▼ See Map 346 ▼

▲ See Map 287 ▲

9700E 10500E 11300E 12800E

Windsor Gardens G. C.

Highline Community School

Havana Village

Challenge Magnet School

Aurora

Queensborough

Wood Advntist Christian School

Aurora Hills Middle School

FD4

Hallcrafts Village East

Canterbury Park

Village East Park

Village East Elem. School

Peoria Hills Park

Fountain Side

Ponderosa Elem. School

Village East

80247

80012

Utah Park

© Mapsco, Inc.

Overland High School

Prairie Middle School

Peora Park

Havana Heights Park

FD11

Iliff Square Library

FD61

Heather Ridge

Eastridge Park

Eastridge Elem. School

Eastridge

80231

80014

Babi Yar Park

Cherry Creek Country Club

The Dam

Denver

Arapahoe County

Crescent View Academy

Marketplace Courtyard S.C.

Polton Elem. School

Regatta Plaza

Denver County

Nine Mile Light Rail Station & Park-n-Ride

Kennedy Softball Complex

Hampden Heights Park

Hampden Library

J. F. Kennedy Municipal Golf Course

Cherry Creek

Cherry Creek Dam - Crest Rd

T4S

T5S

E. Exposition Ave · E. Mississippi Ave · E. Florida Ave · E. Jewell Ave · E. Iliff Ave · E. Yale Ave · E. Dartmouth Ave · S. Havana St · S. Peoria St · S. Parker Rd · S. Dayton St

A B C D E F G H J K L M N P Q R S T U V W X Y Z

700S 1100S 1500S 1900S 2300S 2700S 3100S 3500S

◀ See Map 316 ◀

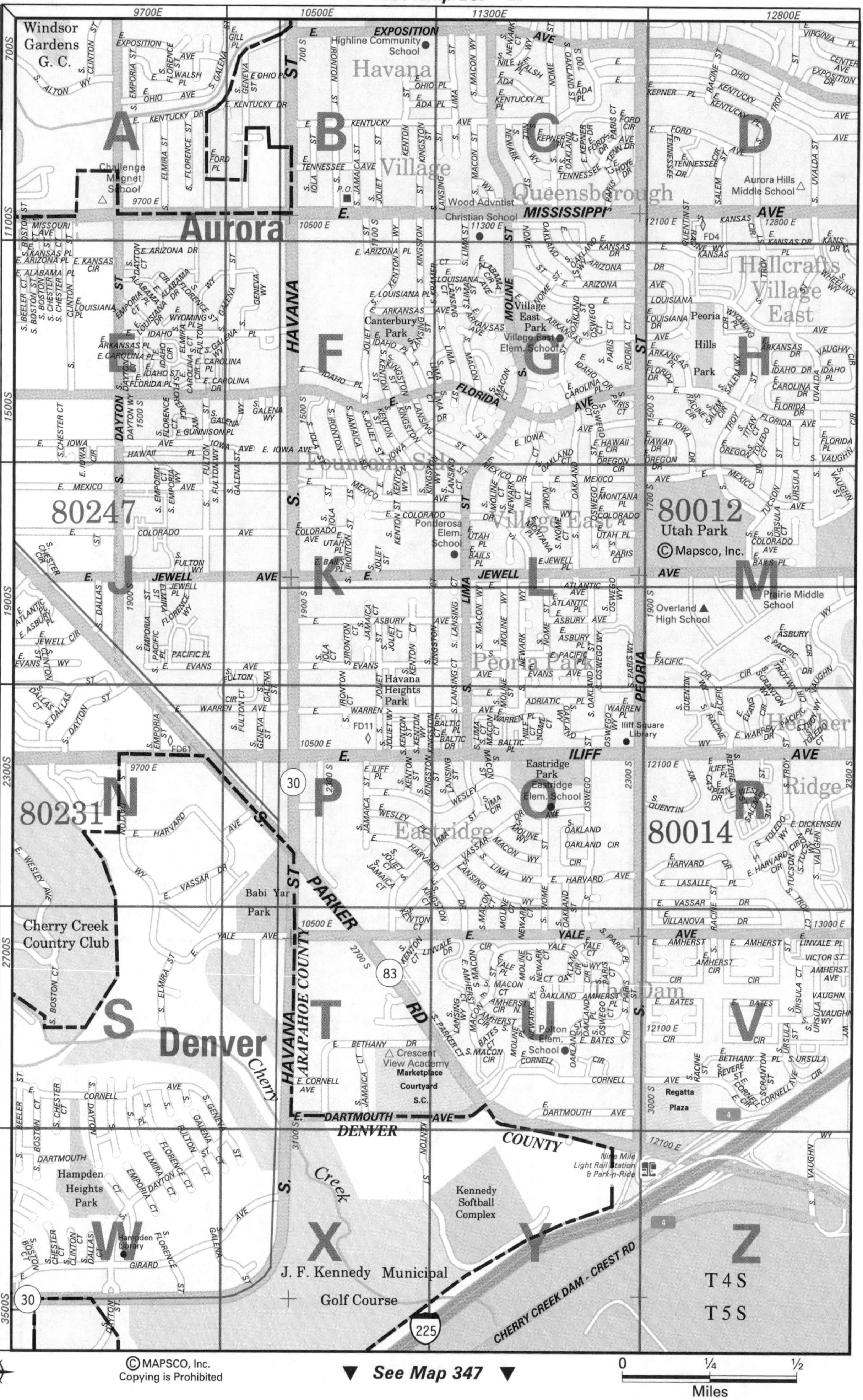

▼ See Map 347 ▼

0 ¼ ½ Miles

▲ See Map 288 ▲

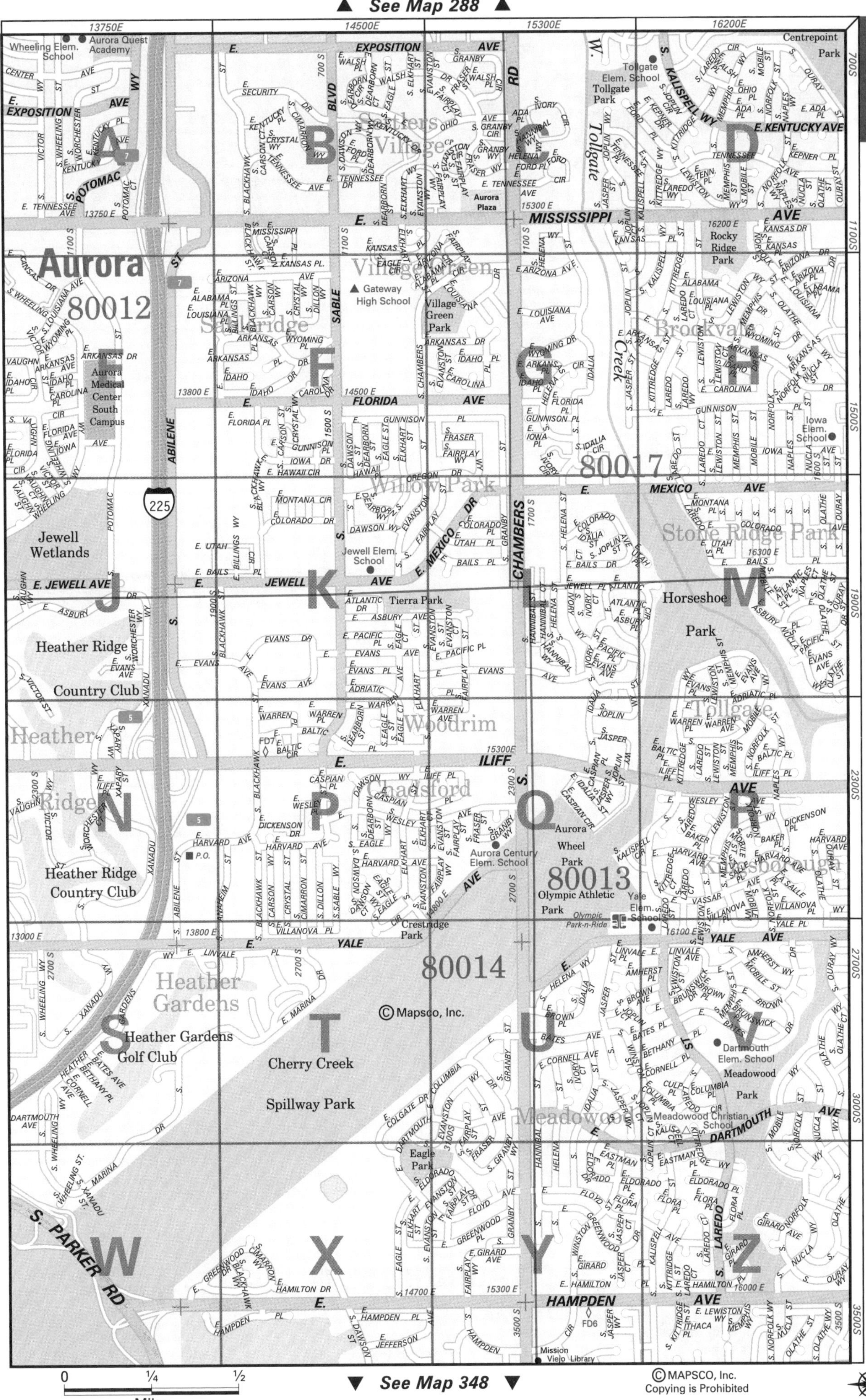

▲ See Map 319 ▲

▼ See Map 348 ▼

▲ See Map 289 ▲

◀ See Map 318 ◀

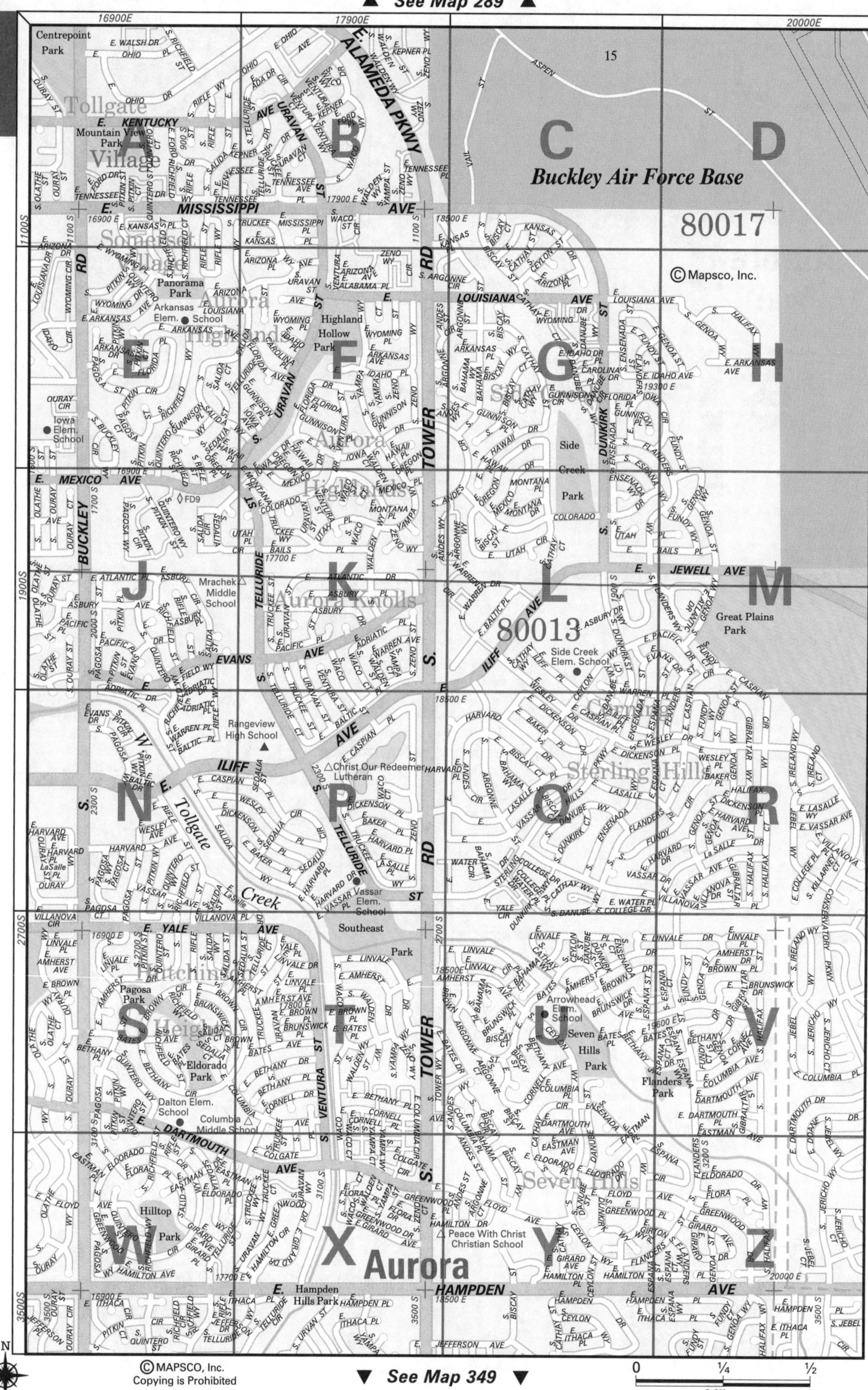

▼ See Map 349 ▼

0 ¼ ½
Miles

▲ See Map 290 ▲

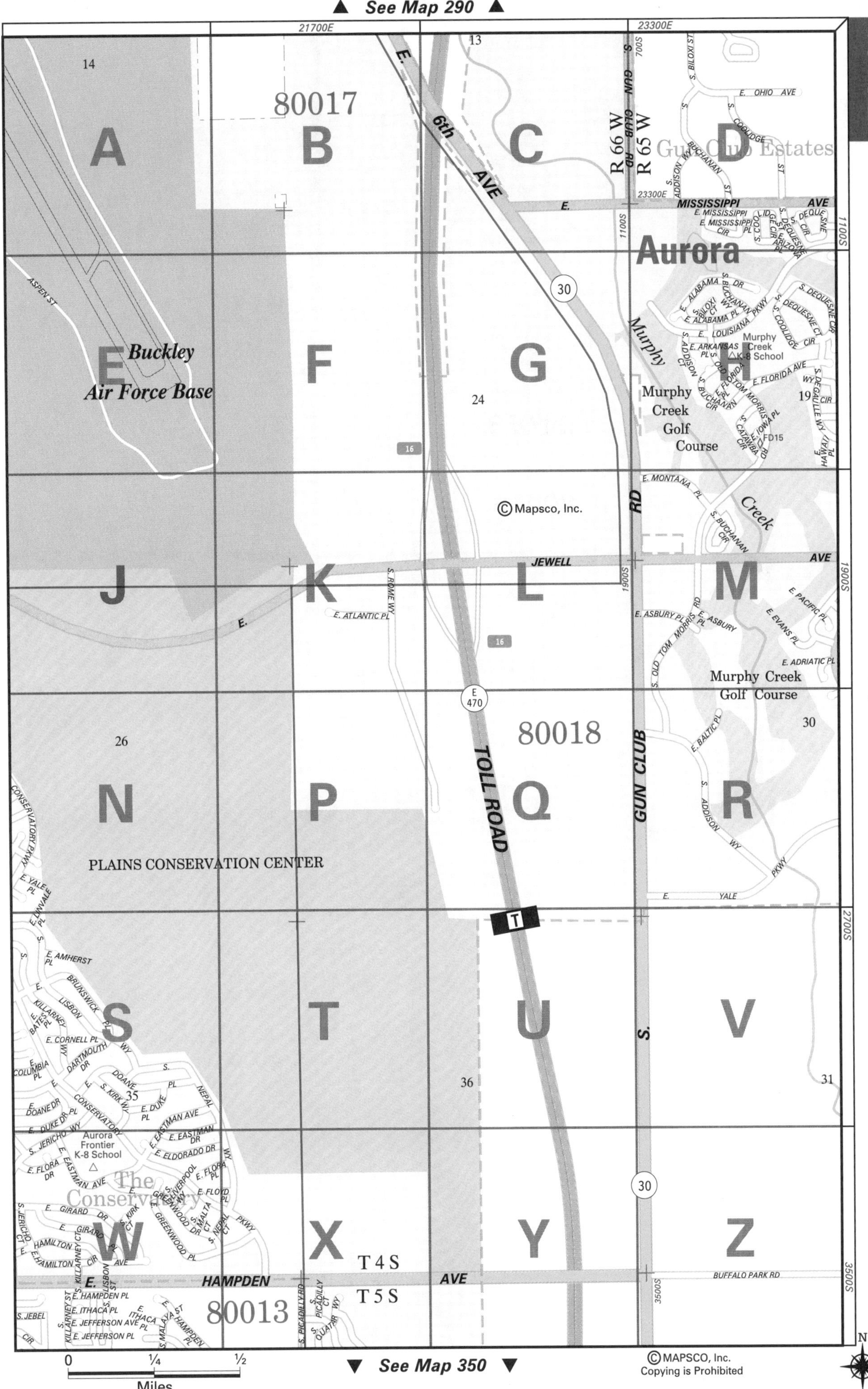

▲ See Map 321 ▶

▼ See Map 350 ▼

0 ¼ ½
Miles

▲ See Map 291 ▲

◄ See Map 320 ◄

► See Map 810 ►

▼ See Map 351 ▼

0 ¼ ½
Miles

▲See Map 305▲

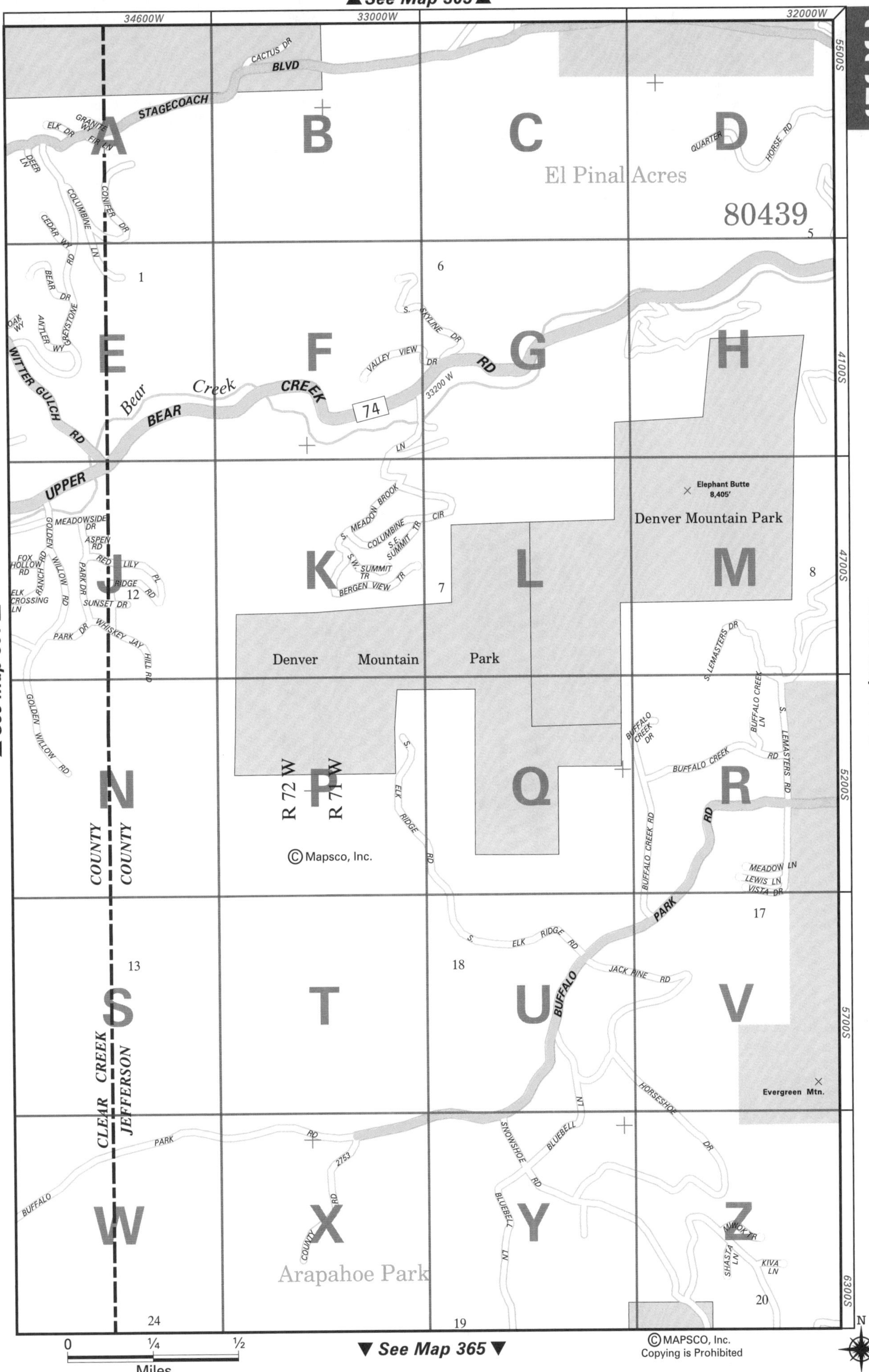

See Map 801

See Map 336

▼See Map 365▼

▲ See Map 306 ▲

▲ See Map 335 ▲

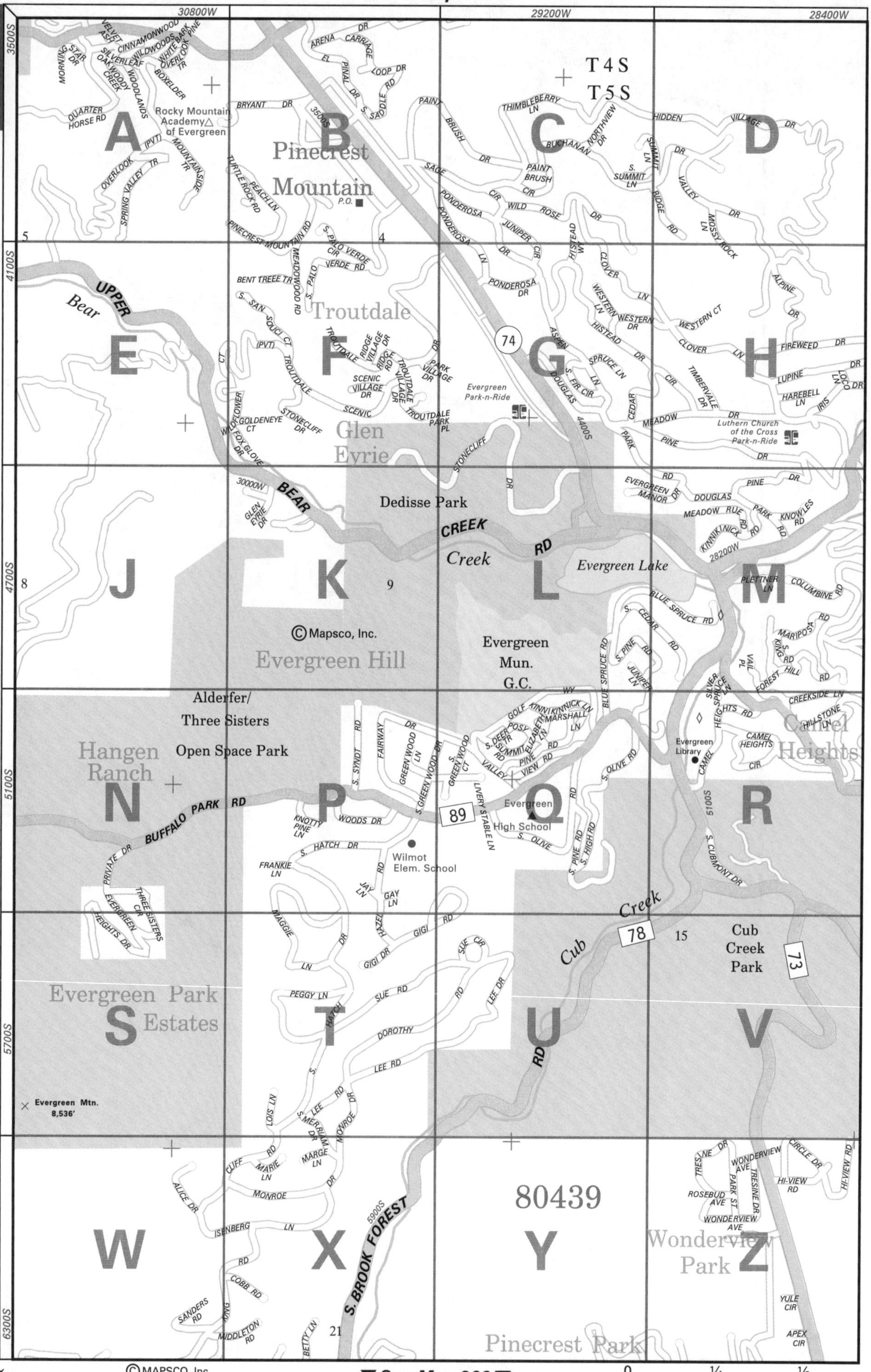
30800W
29200W
28400W
3500S
4100S
4700S
5100S
5700S
6300S
T4S
T5S
A
B
C
D
E
F
G
H
J
K
L
M
N
P
Q
R
S
T
U
V
W
X
Y
Z
Rocky Mountain Academy of Evergreen
Pinecrest Mountain
P.O.
Troutdale
Glen Eyrie
Evergreen Park-n-Ride
Luthern Church of the Cross Park-n-Ride
Dedisse Park
Evergreen Lake
Evergreen Hill
Evergreen Mun. G.C.
Alderfer/ Three Sisters Open Space Park
Hangen Ranch
Evergreen High School
Wilmot Elem. School
Evergreen Library
Camel Heights
Cub Creek Park
Evergreen Park Estates
Evergreen Mtn. 8,536′
80439
Wonderview Park
Pinecrest Park
©Mapsco, Inc.
UPPER Bear
BEAR CREEK RD
Creek
BUFFALO PARK RD
Cub Creek
S. BROOK FOREST RD
74
89
78
73
BRYANT DR
QUARTER HORSE RD
TURTLE ROCK RD
PEACH LN
PINECREST MOUNTAIN RD
MEADOWOOD RD
BENT TREEE TR
THIMBLEBERRY LN
BUCHANAN
NORTHVIEW DR
HIDDEN
VILLAGE DR
PAINT BRUSH DR
PAINT BRUSH CIR
WILD ROSE DR
PONDEROSA DR
JUNIPER CIR
HISTEAD WY
CLOVER LN
WESTERN LN
WESTERN DR
WESTERN CT
FIREWEED DR
LUPINE DR
HAREBELL LN
MEADOW DR
PINE DR
DOUGLAS
KINNIKINICK RD
KNOWLES RD
28200W
30000W
PLETTNER LN
COLUMBINE RD
MARIPOSA RD
BLUE SPRUCE RD
S. CEDAR RD
CREEKSIDE LN
HILLSTONE LN
CAMEL HEIGHTS CIR
S. CUBMONT DR
FAIRWAY DR
GREEN WOOD LN
S. SYNDT RD
LIVERY STABLE LN
S. OLIVE RD
WOODS DR
S. HATCH DR
FRANKIE LN
JAY LN
GAY LN
MAGGIE LN
GIGI DR
SUE RD
PEGGY LN
DOROTHY
LEE RD
LEE DR
LOIS LN
MONROE DR
S. MERRIAM DR
MARGE LN
MARIE LN
CLIFF RD
ALICE DR
ISENBERG LN
COBB RD
SANDERS RD
MIDDLETON RD
BETTY LN
5900S
TRESINE DR
WONDERVIEW AVE
CIRCLE DR
HI-VIEW RD
ROSEBUD AVE
PARK ST
YULE CIR
APEX CIR
PRIVATE DR
EVERGREEN HEIGHTS DR
THREE SISTERS CIR
5
4
8
9
15
21

▼ See Map 366 ▼

0 ¼ ½
Miles

▲ See Map 307 ▲

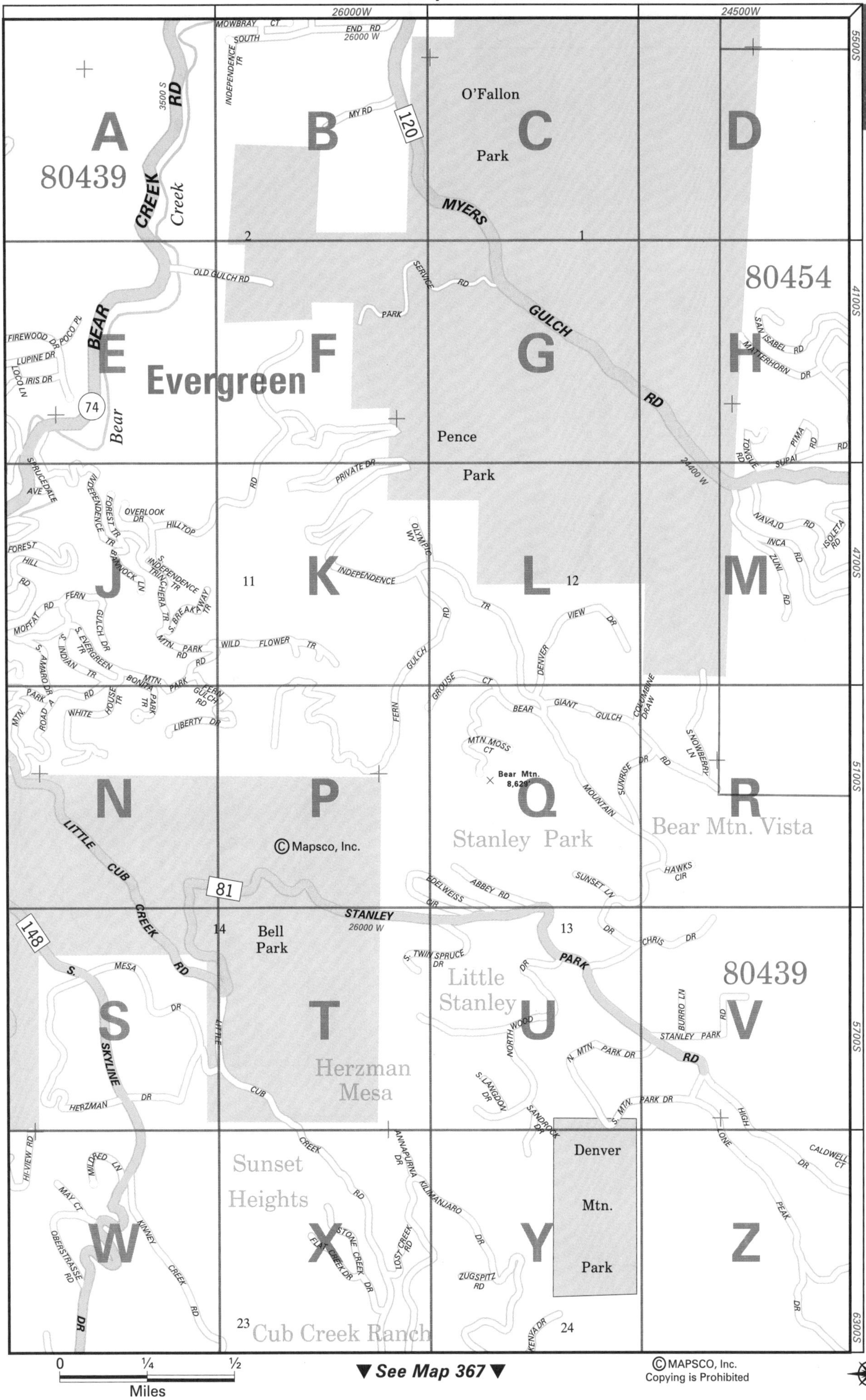

▲ See Map 338 ▲

▼ See Map 367 ▼

▲ See Map 308 ▲

▲ See Map 337 ▲

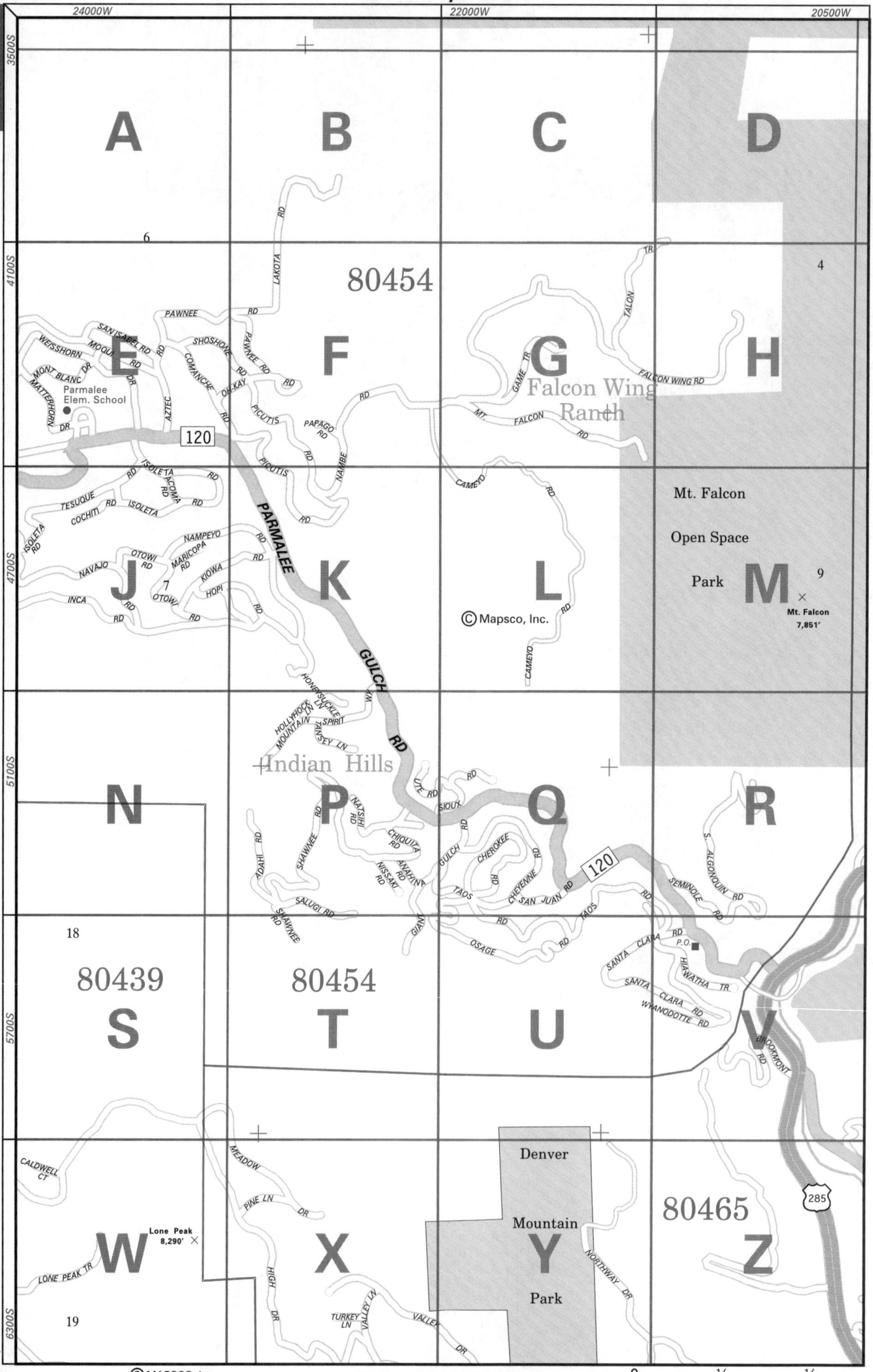

80454

Falcon Wing Ranch

Mt. Falcon Open Space Park

Mt. Falcon 7,851′

Parmalee Elem. School

Indian Hills

80439

80454

80465

Denver Mountain Park

Lone Peak 8,290′

▼ See Map 368 ▼

0 ¼ ½
Miles

▲ See Map 309 ▲

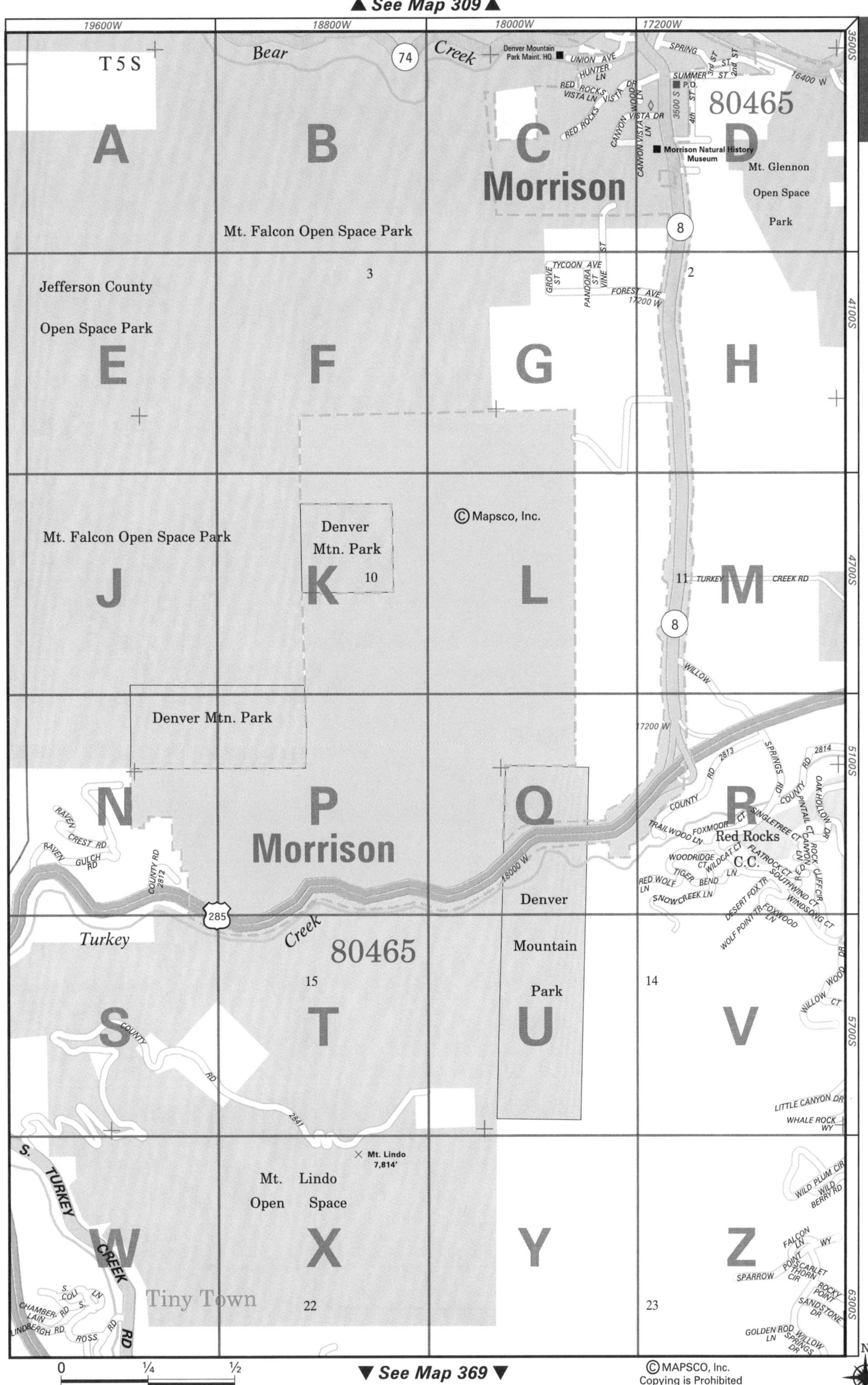

▲ See Map 340 ▲

▼ See Map 369 ▼

▲ See Map 310 ▲

▲ See Map 339 ▲

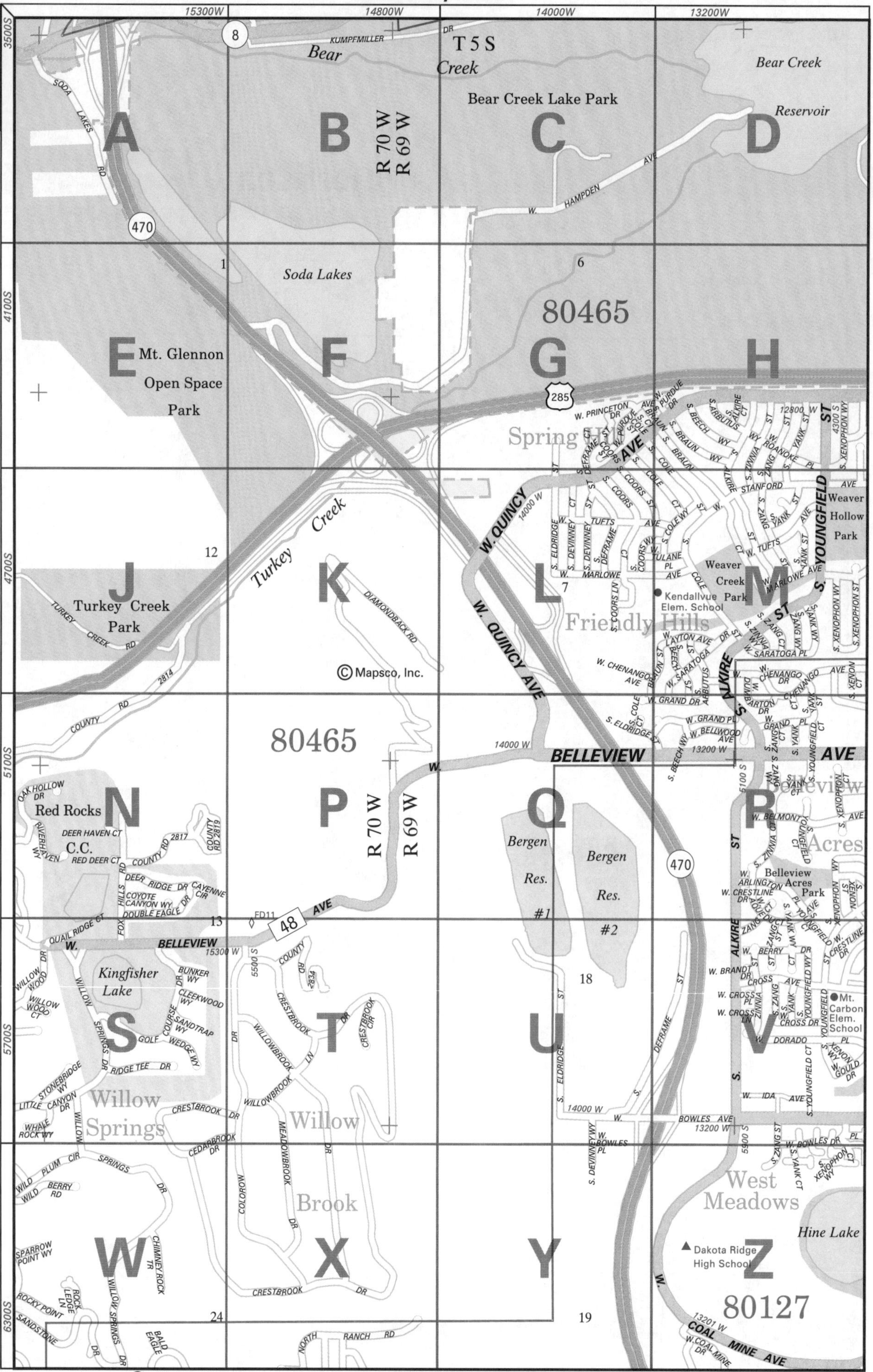

15300W 14800W 14000W 13200W

3500S 4100S 4700S 5100S 5700S 6300S

T 5 S

R 70 W R 69 W

A B C D E F G H J K L M N P Q R S T U V W X Y Z

Bear Creek Lake Park

Bear Creek Reservoir

Soda Lakes

Mt. Glennon Open Space Park

Turkey Creek Park

Weaver Hollow Park

Weaver Creek Park

Kendallvue Elem. School

Spring Hill

Friendly Hills

Red Rocks C.C.

Bergen Res. #1

Bergen Res. #2

Belleview Acres

Belleview Acres Park

Mt. Carbon Elem. School

Kingfisher Lake

Willow Springs

Willow Brook

West Meadows

Hine Lake

Dakota Ridge High School

80465

80127

W. HAMPDEN AVE

W. QUINCY AVE

W. BELLEVIEW AVE

W. BOWLES AVE

W. COAL MINE AVE

S. ALKIRE ST

S. YOUNGFIELD ST

S. DEFRAME ST

S. ELDRIDGE ST

COUNTY RD

KUMPFMILLER DR

SODA LAKES RD

TURKEY CREEK RD

DIAMONDBACK RD

CRESTBROOK DR

WILLOWBROOK DR

MEADOWBROOK DR

WILLOW SPRINGS DR

NORTH RANCH RD

▼ See Map 370 ▼

0 ¼ ½ Miles

▲ See Map 311 ▲

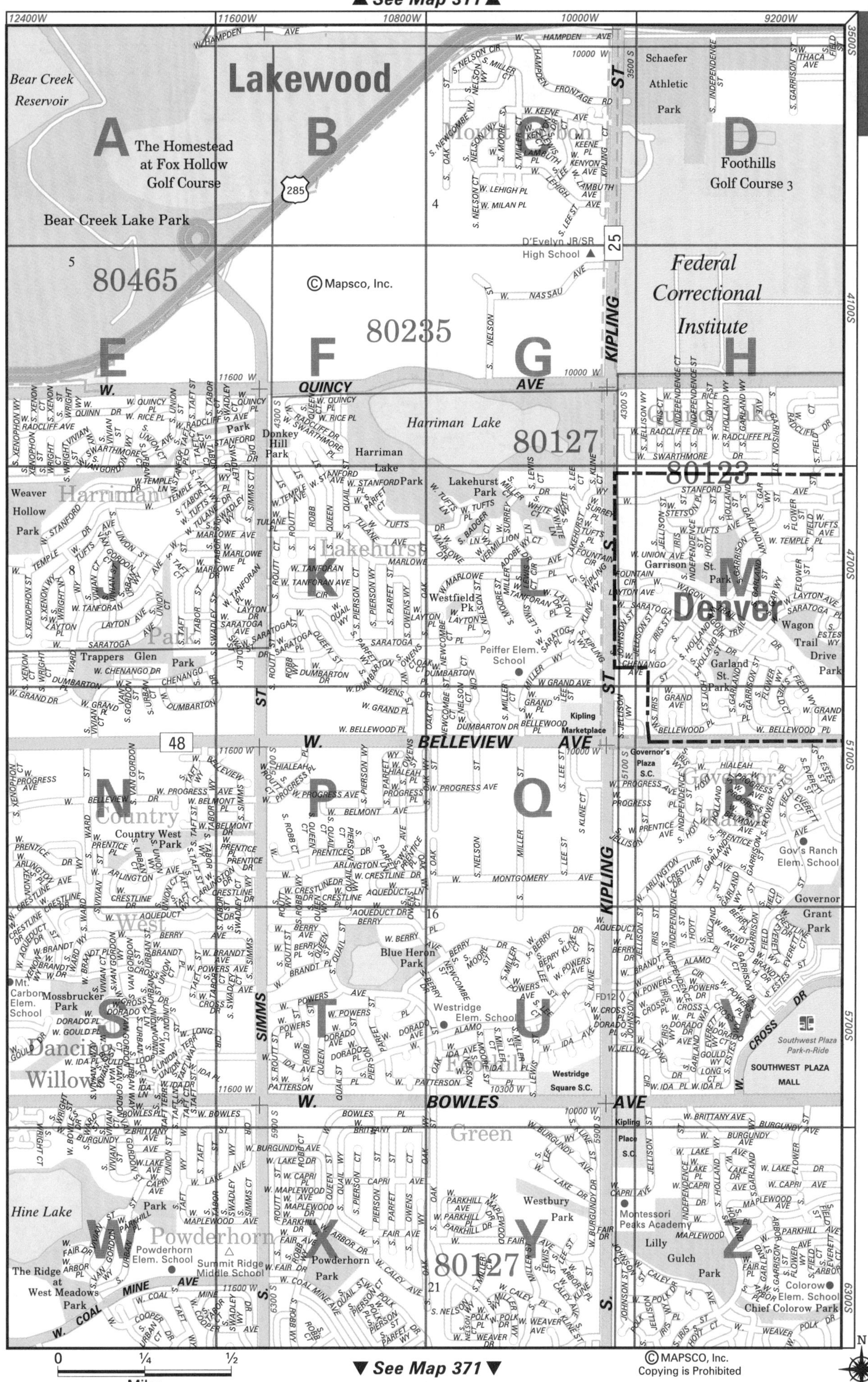

▶ See Map 342 ▶

▼ See Map 371 ▼

▲ See Map 312 ▲

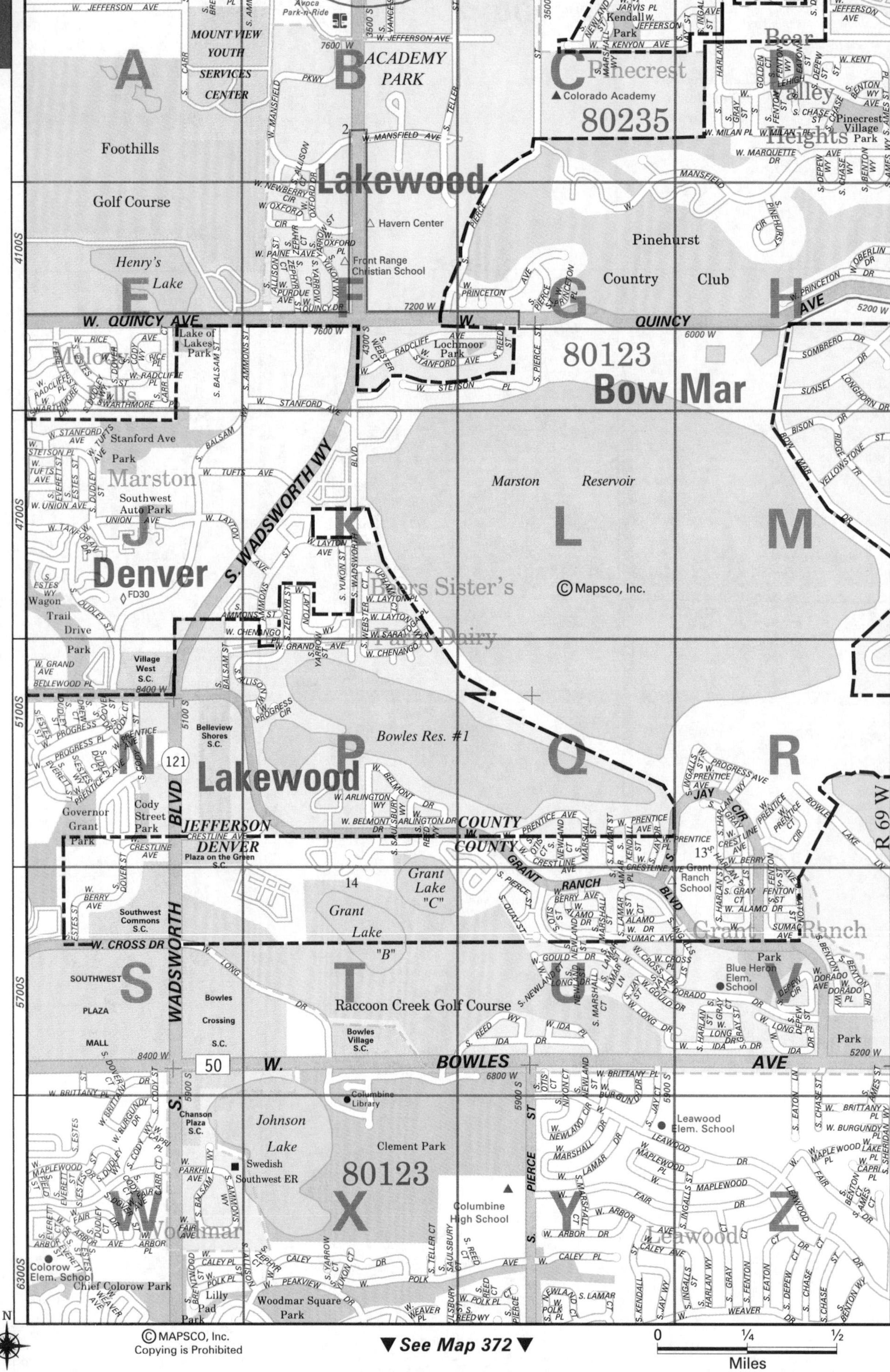

▲ See Map 341 ▲

▼ See Map 372 ▼

▲ See Map 313 ▲

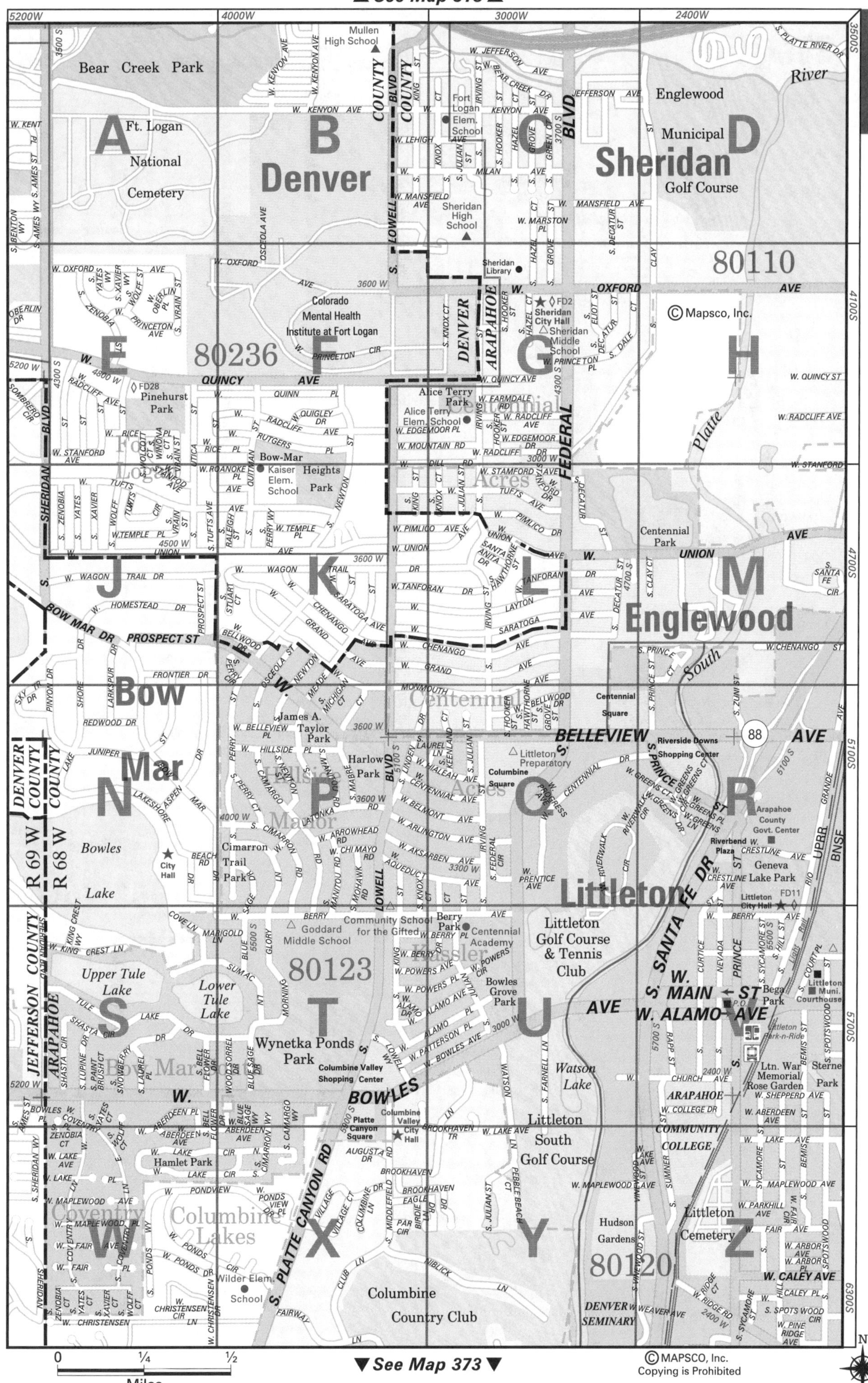

▲ See Map 344 ▶

▼ See Map 373 ▼

0 ¼ ½
Miles

▲See Map 314▲

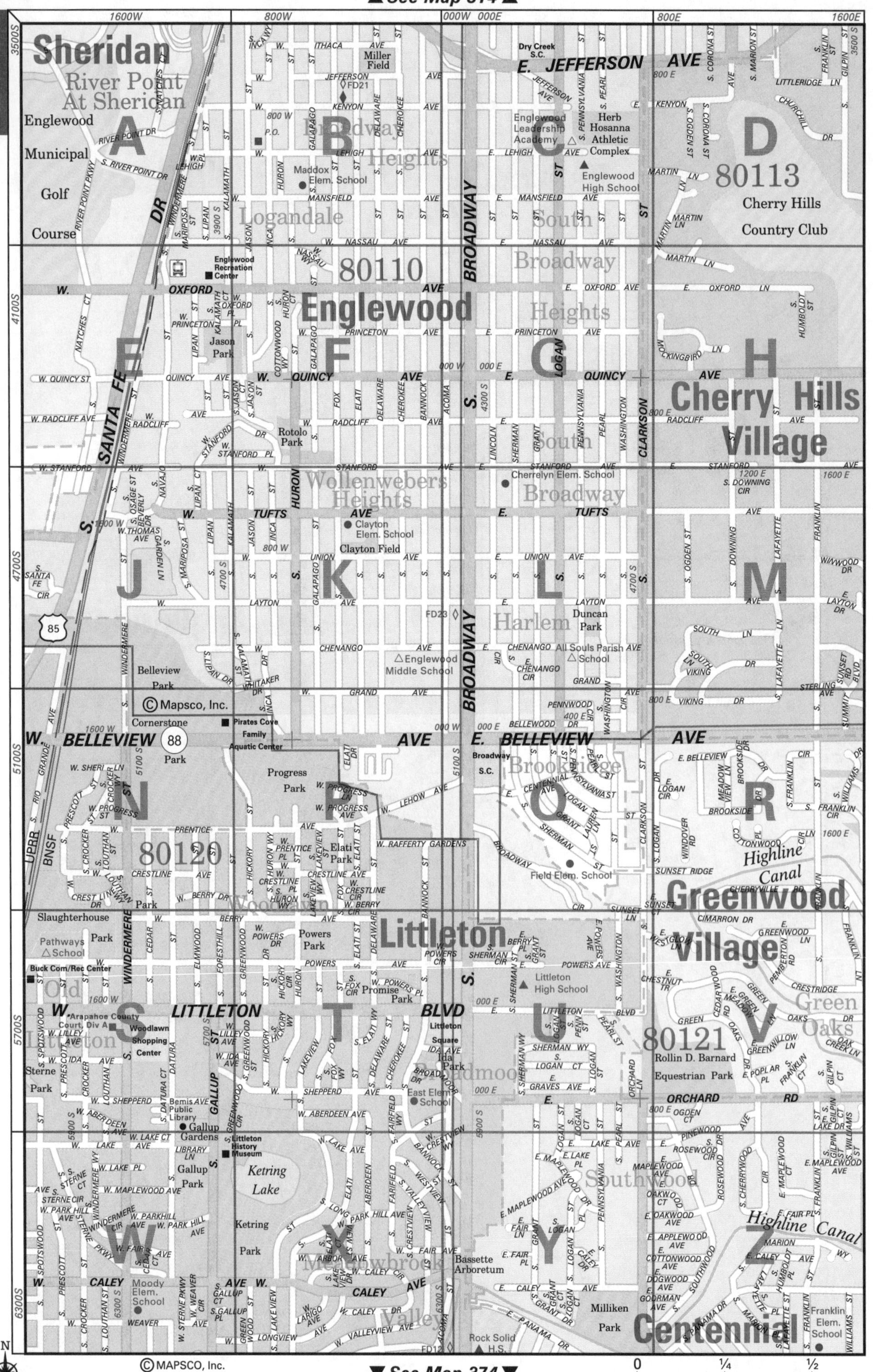

▲See Map 343▲

▼See Map 374▼

0 ¼ ½
Miles

▲ See Map 315 ▲

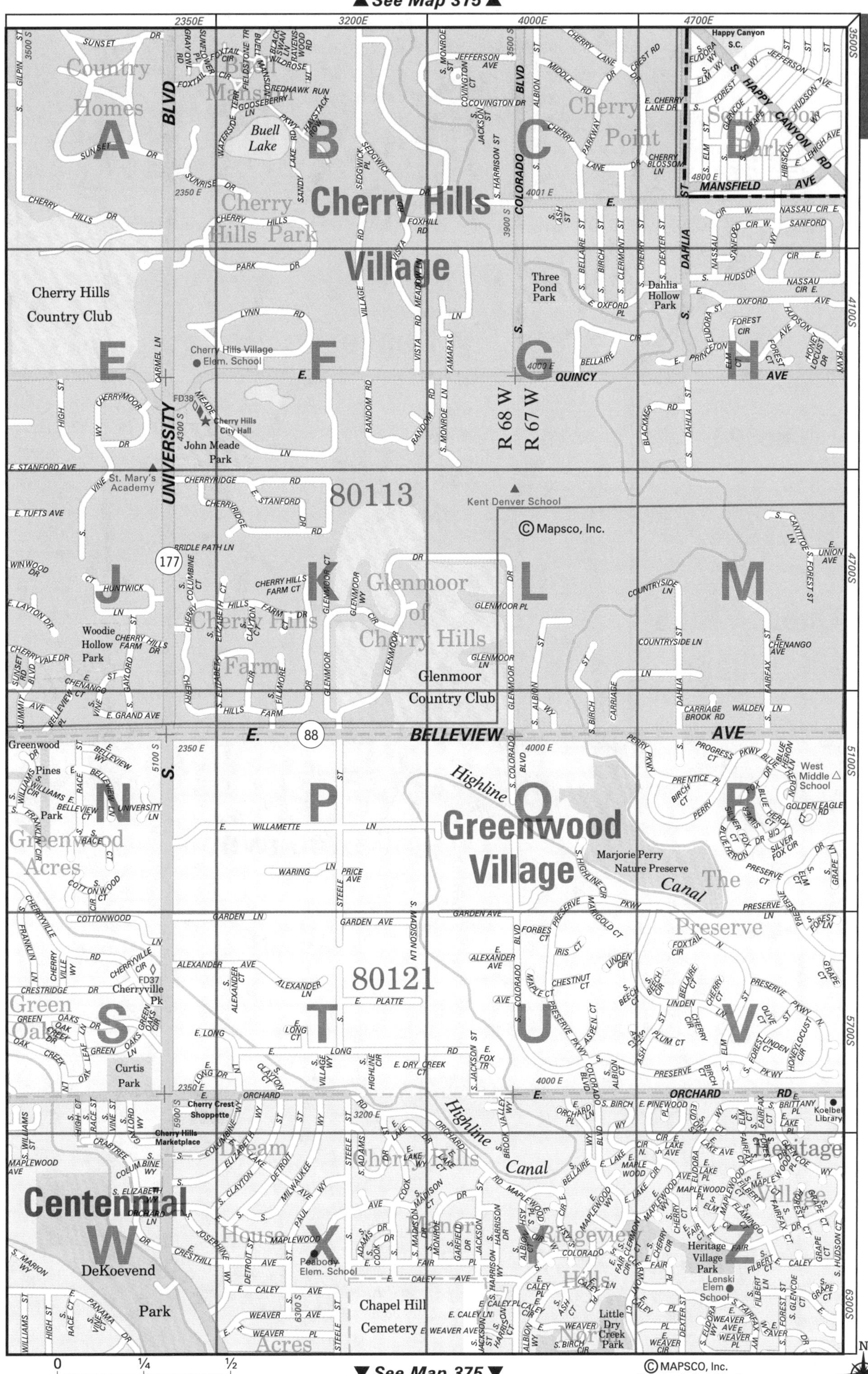

▲ See Map 346 ▶

▼ See Map 375 ▼

0 ¼ ½
Miles

▲ See Map 316 ▲

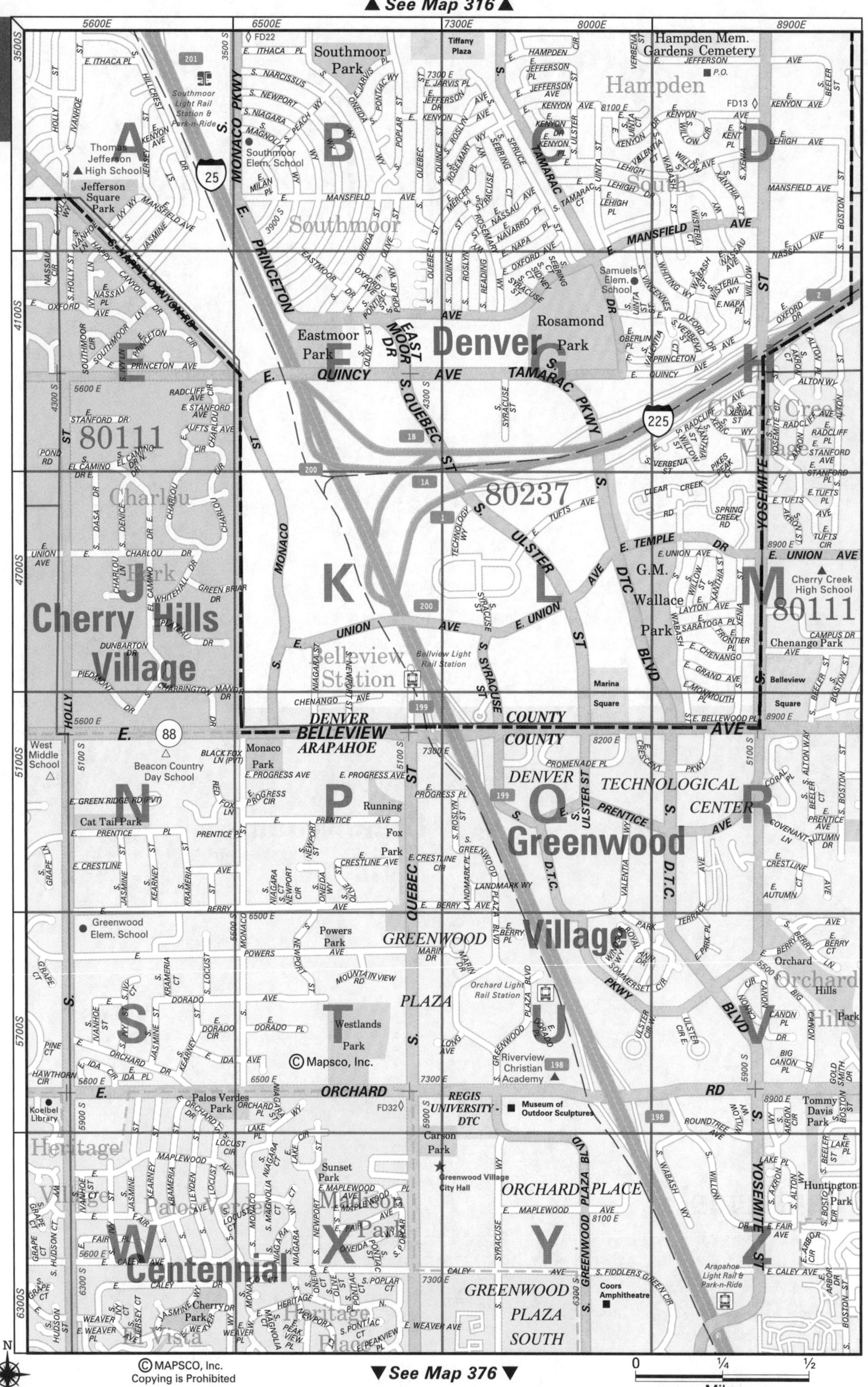

▲ See Map 345 ▲

▼ See Map 376 ▼

0 ¼ ½ Miles

▲ See Map 317 ▲

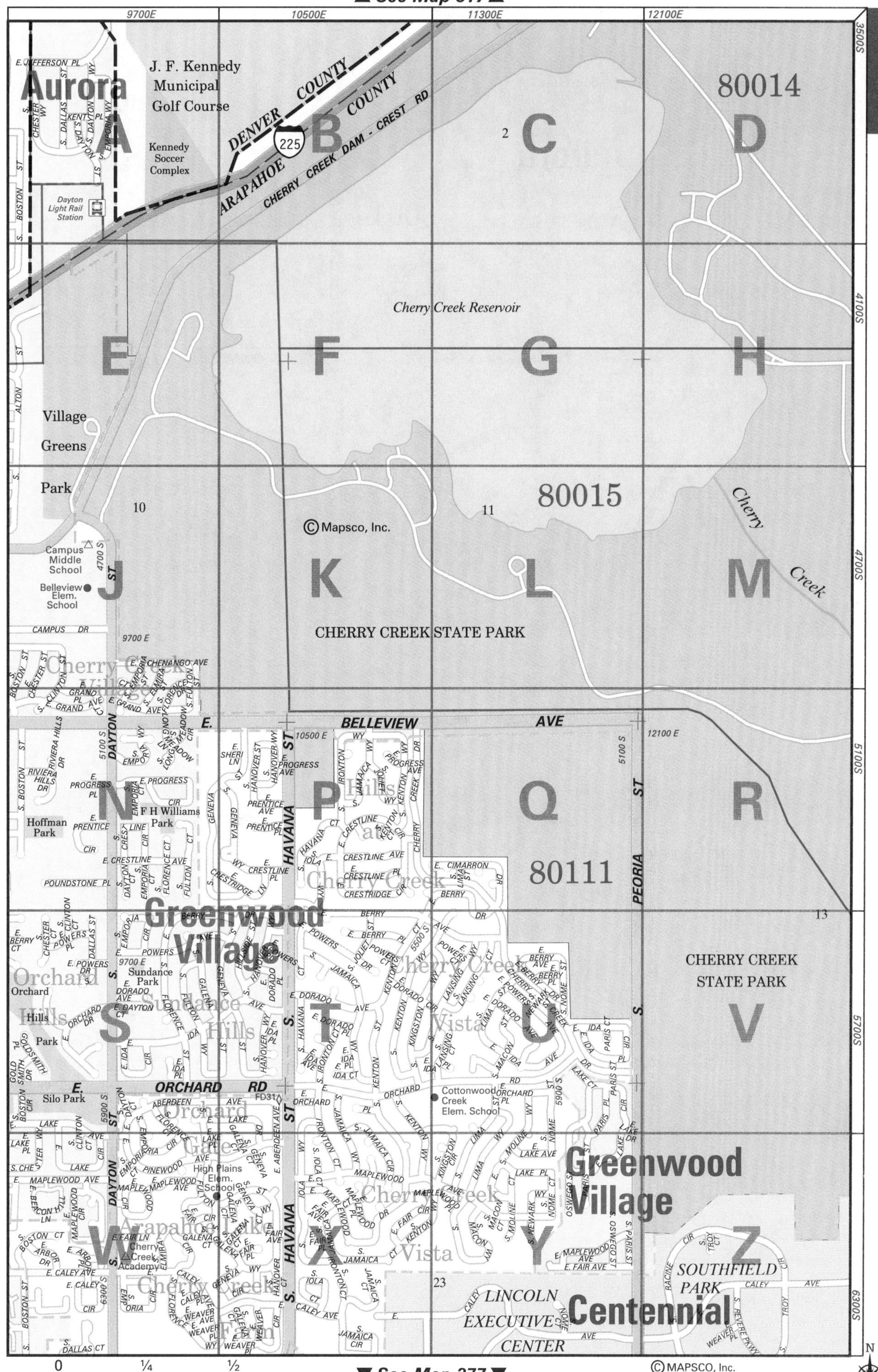

▲ See Map 348 ▲

▼ See Map 377 ▼

▲ See Map 318 ▲

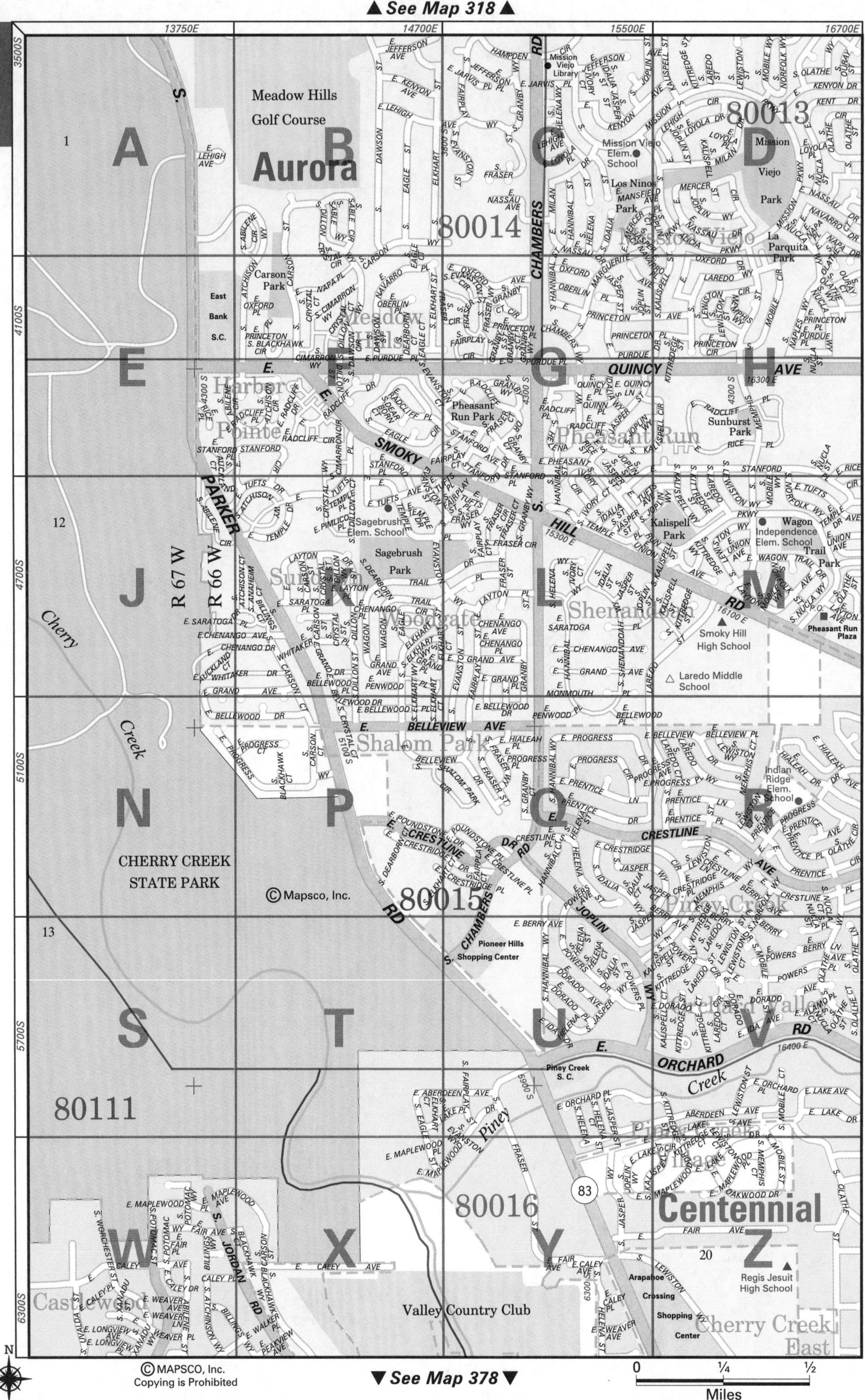

▲ See Map 347 ▲

▼ See Map 378 ▼

0 ¼ ½
Miles

▲ See Map 319 ▲

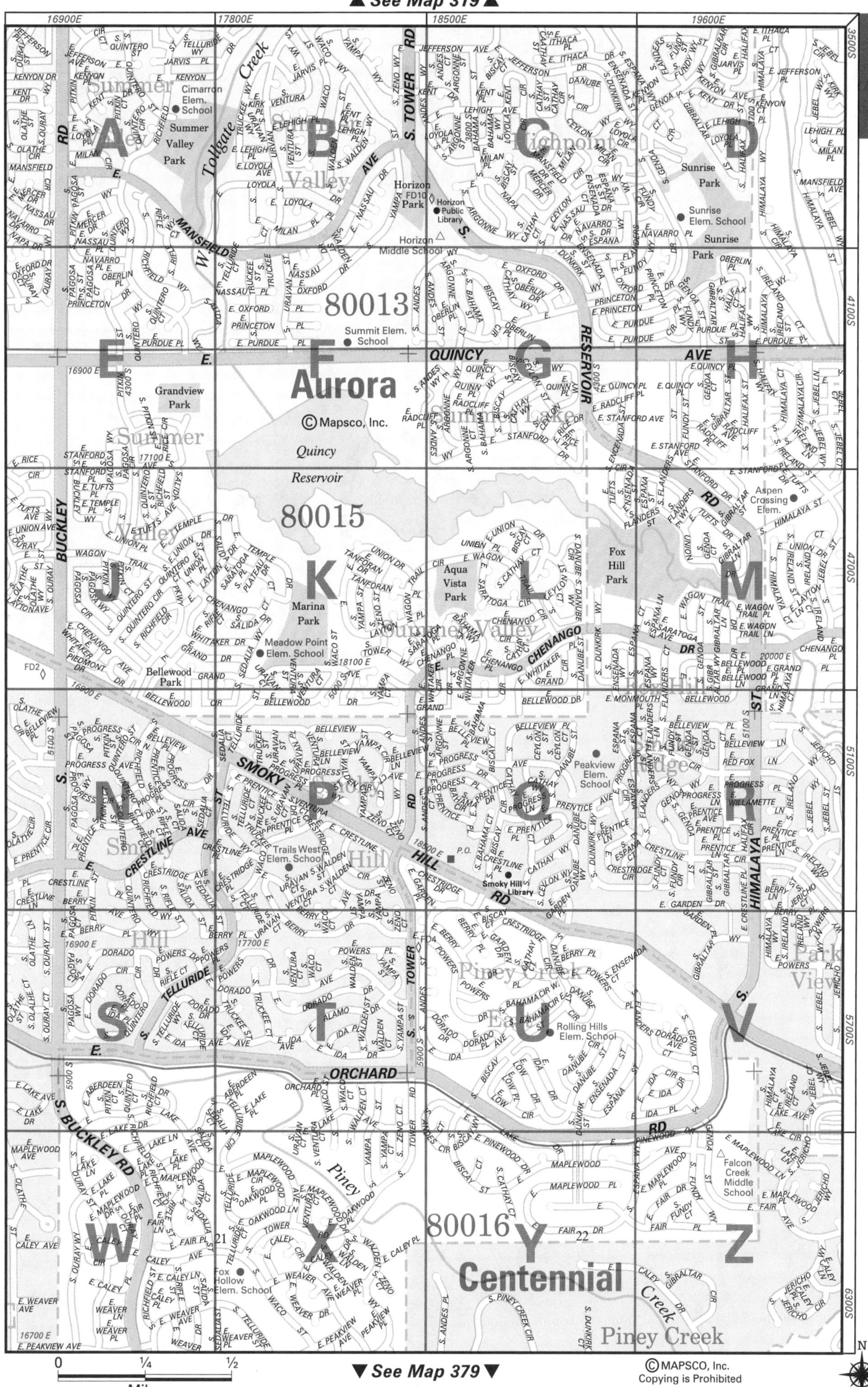

▲ See Map 350 ▲

0 ¼ ½
Miles

▼ See Map 379 ▼

▲ See Map 320 ▲

▲ See Map 349 ▲

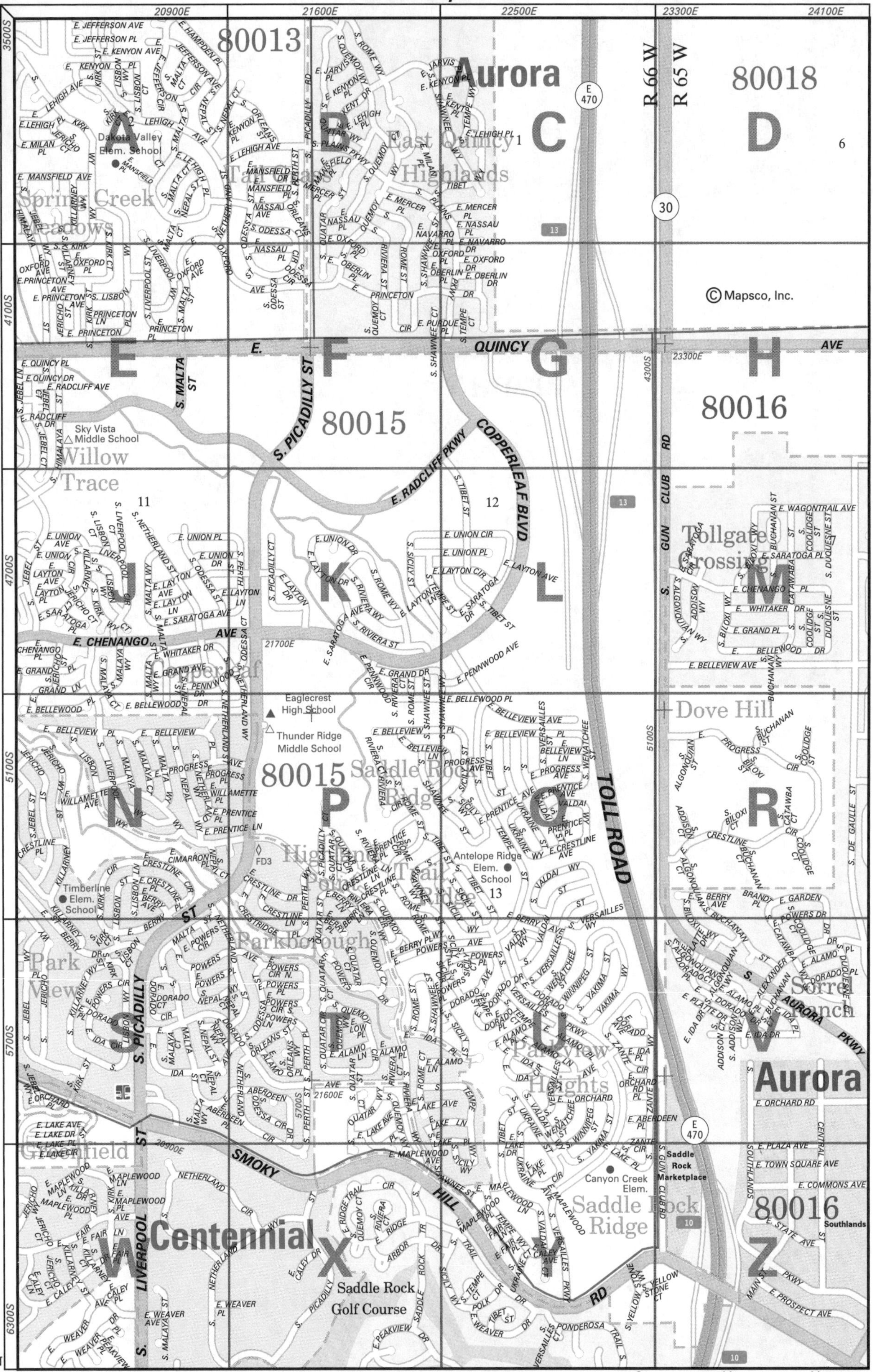

▼ See Map 380 ▼

0 ¼ ½
Miles

▲ See Map 321 ▲

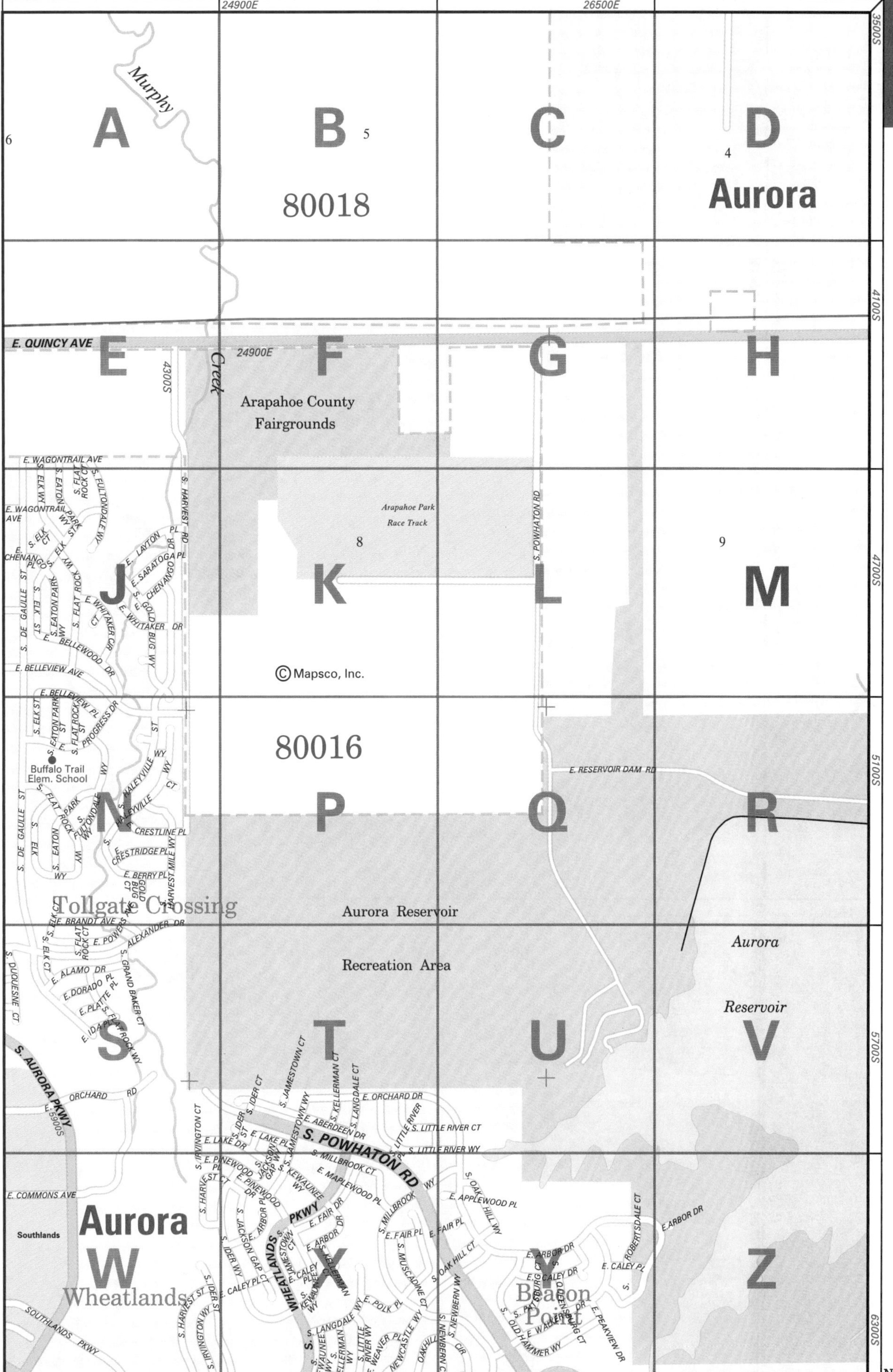

0 ¼ ½
Miles

▼ See Map 381 ▼

▲ See Map 810 ▲

N

▲ See Map 335 ▲

▲ See Map 821 ▲

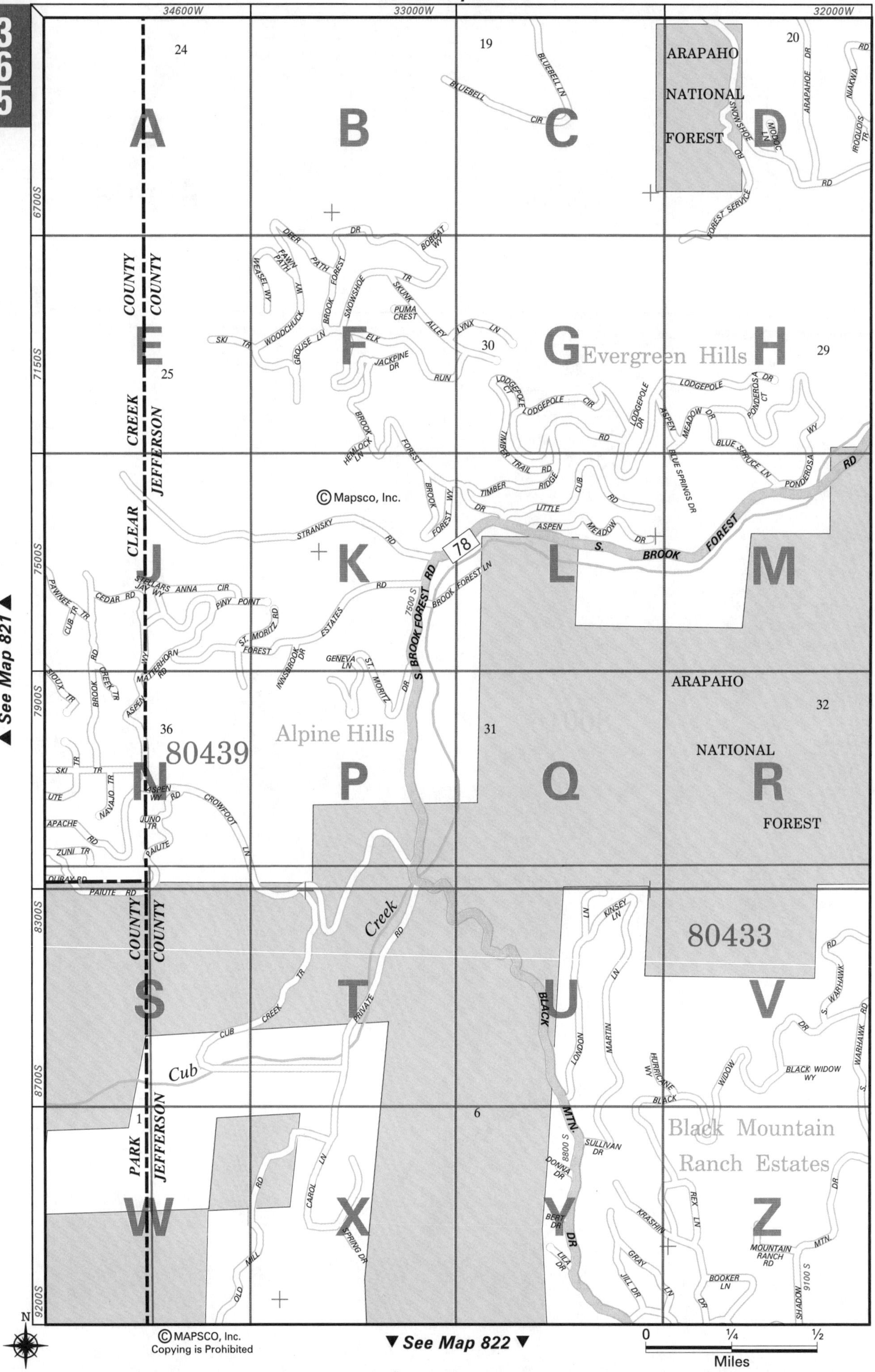

34600W 33000W 32000W

6700S 7150S 7500S 7900S 8300S 8700S 9200S

A B C D E F G H J K L M N P Q R S T U V W X Y Z

ARAPAHO NATIONAL FOREST

Evergreen Hills

Alpine Hills

80439

80433

Black Mountain Ranch Estates

CLEAR CREEK COUNTY

JEFFERSON COUNTY

PARK COUNTY

S. BROOK FOREST RD

78

BLACK MTN. DR

Cub Creek

© Mapsco, Inc.

▼ See Map 822 ▼

0 ¼ ½
Miles

▲ See Map 336 ▲

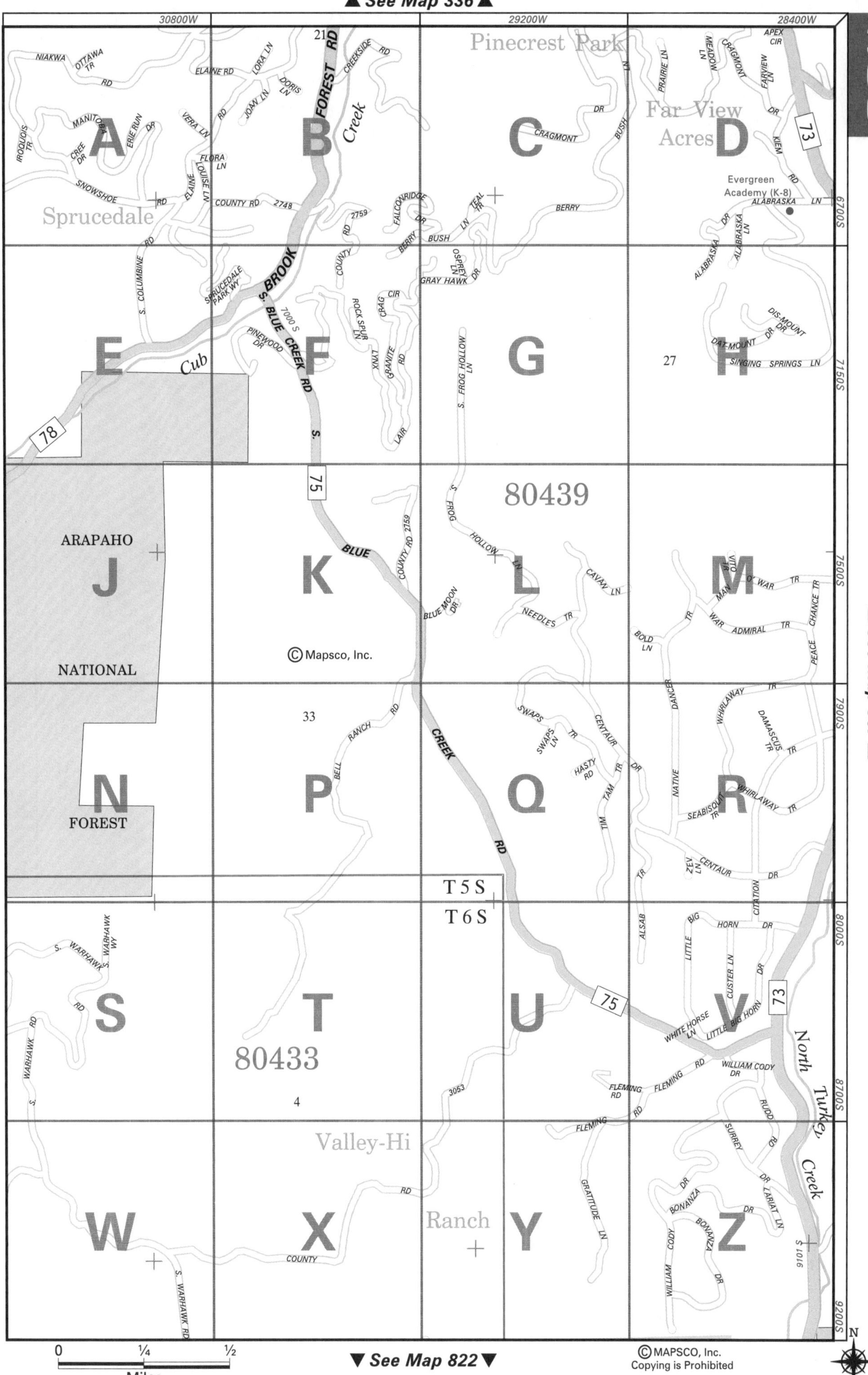

▲ See Map 367 ▶

▼ See Map 822 ▼

0 ¼ ½
Miles

▲ See Map 337 ▲

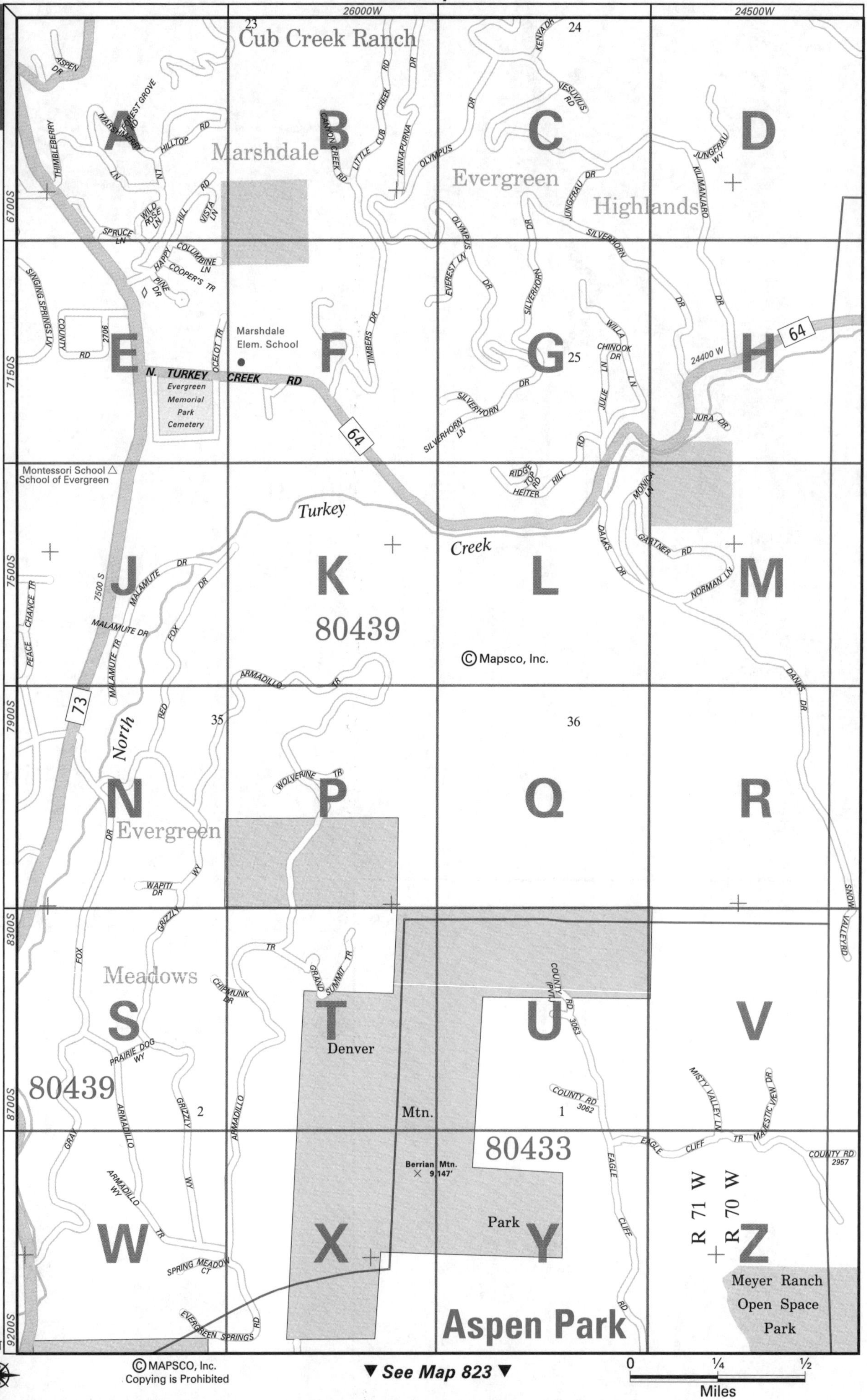

▲ See Map 366 ▲

▼ See Map 823 ▼

▲ See Map 338 ▲

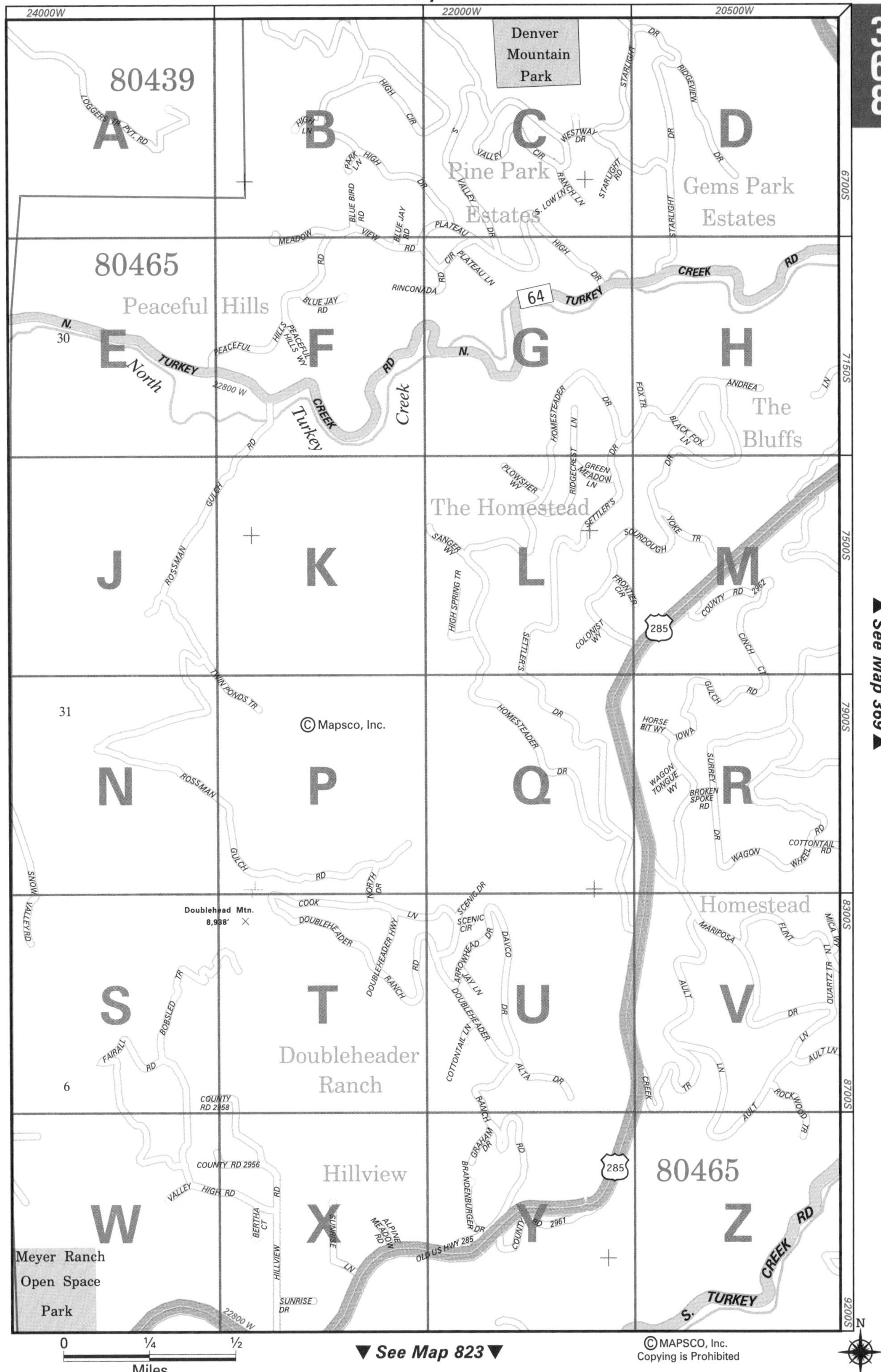

▲ See Map 369 ▶

▼ See Map 823 ▼

▲ See Map 339 ▲

▲ See Map 368 ▲

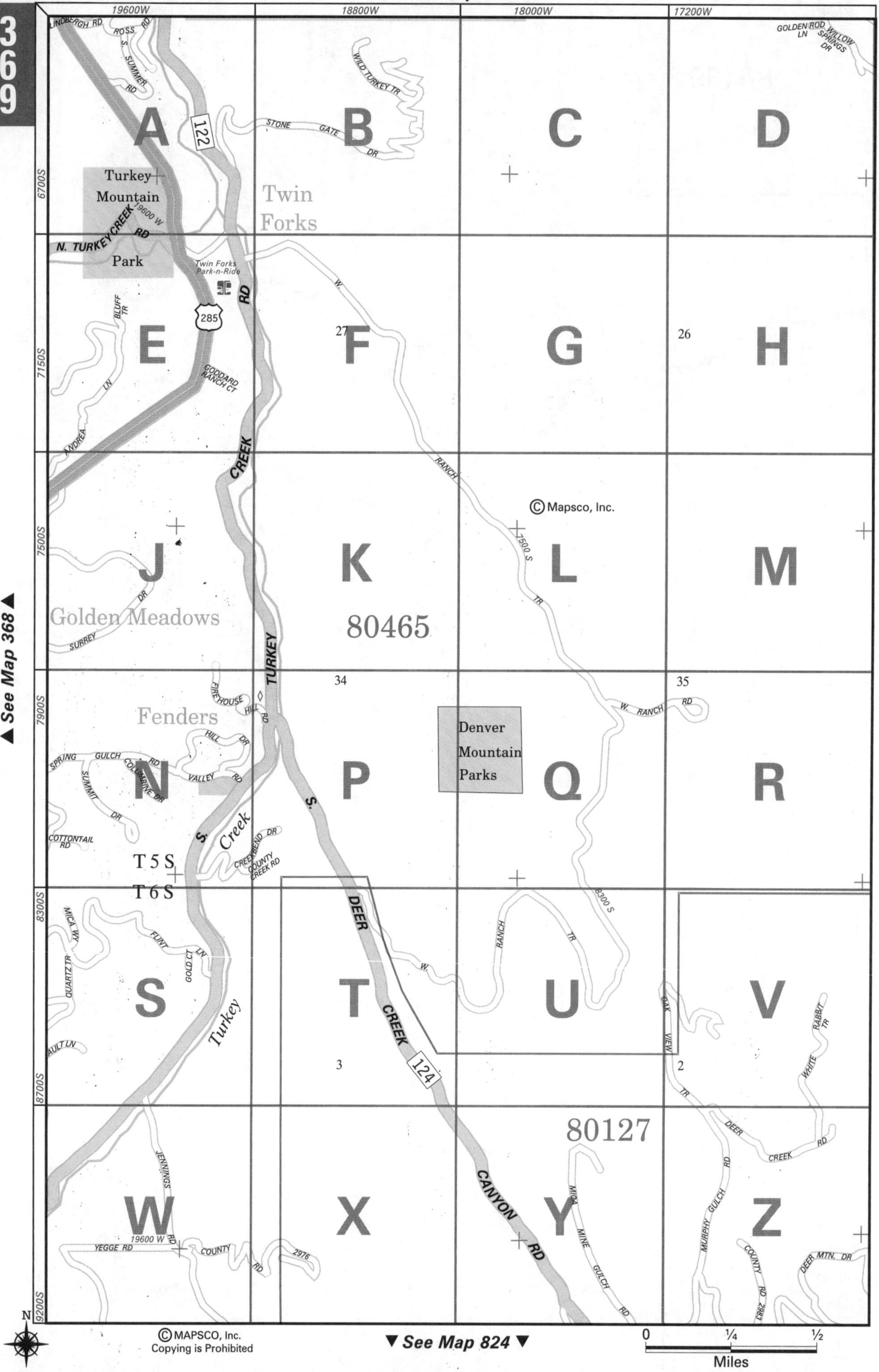

▼ See Map 824 ▼

▲ See Map 340 ▲

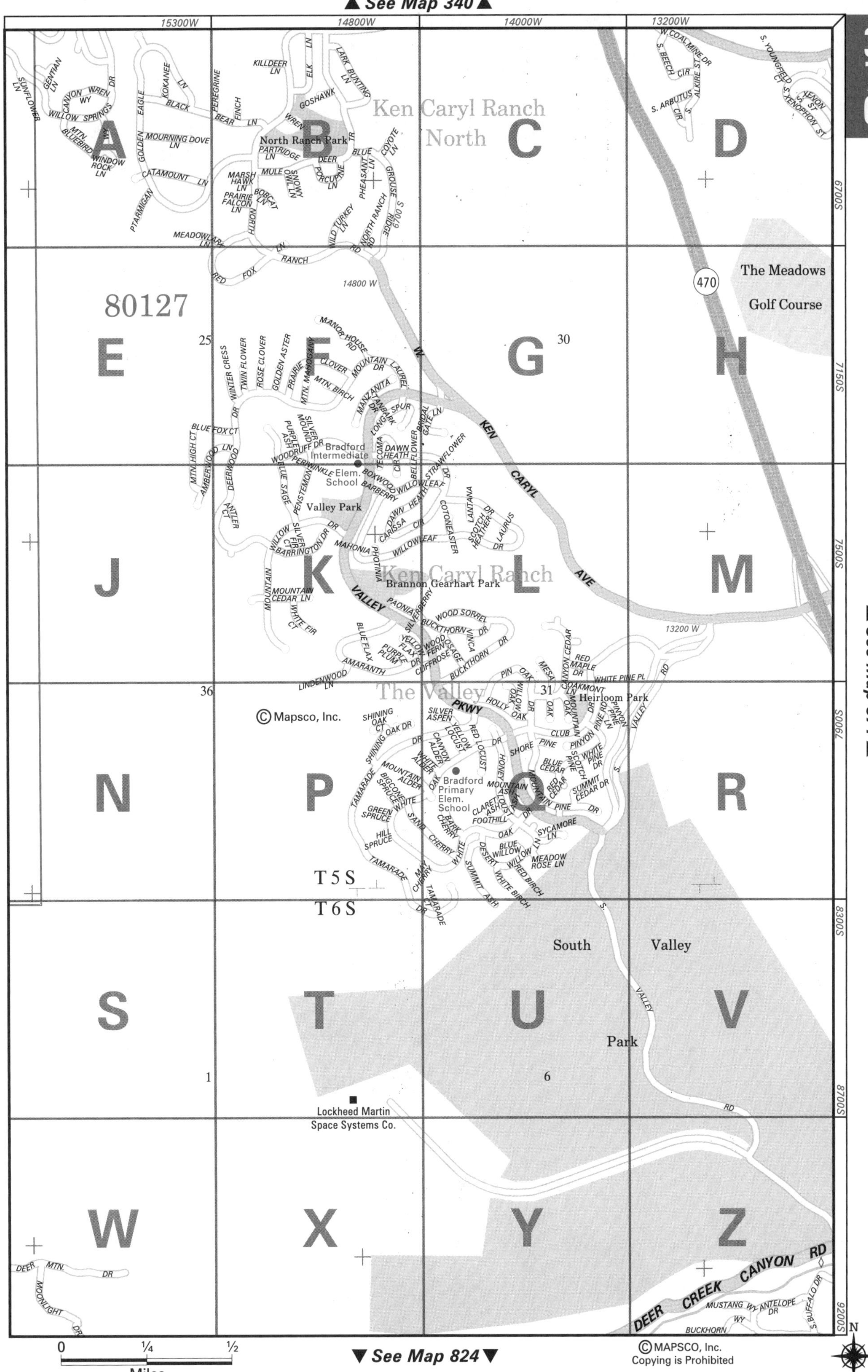

▼ See Map 824 ▼

▲ See Map 371 ▶

▲ See Map 341 ▲

◀ See Map 370 ◀

▼ See Map 825 ▼

▲ See Map 342 ▲

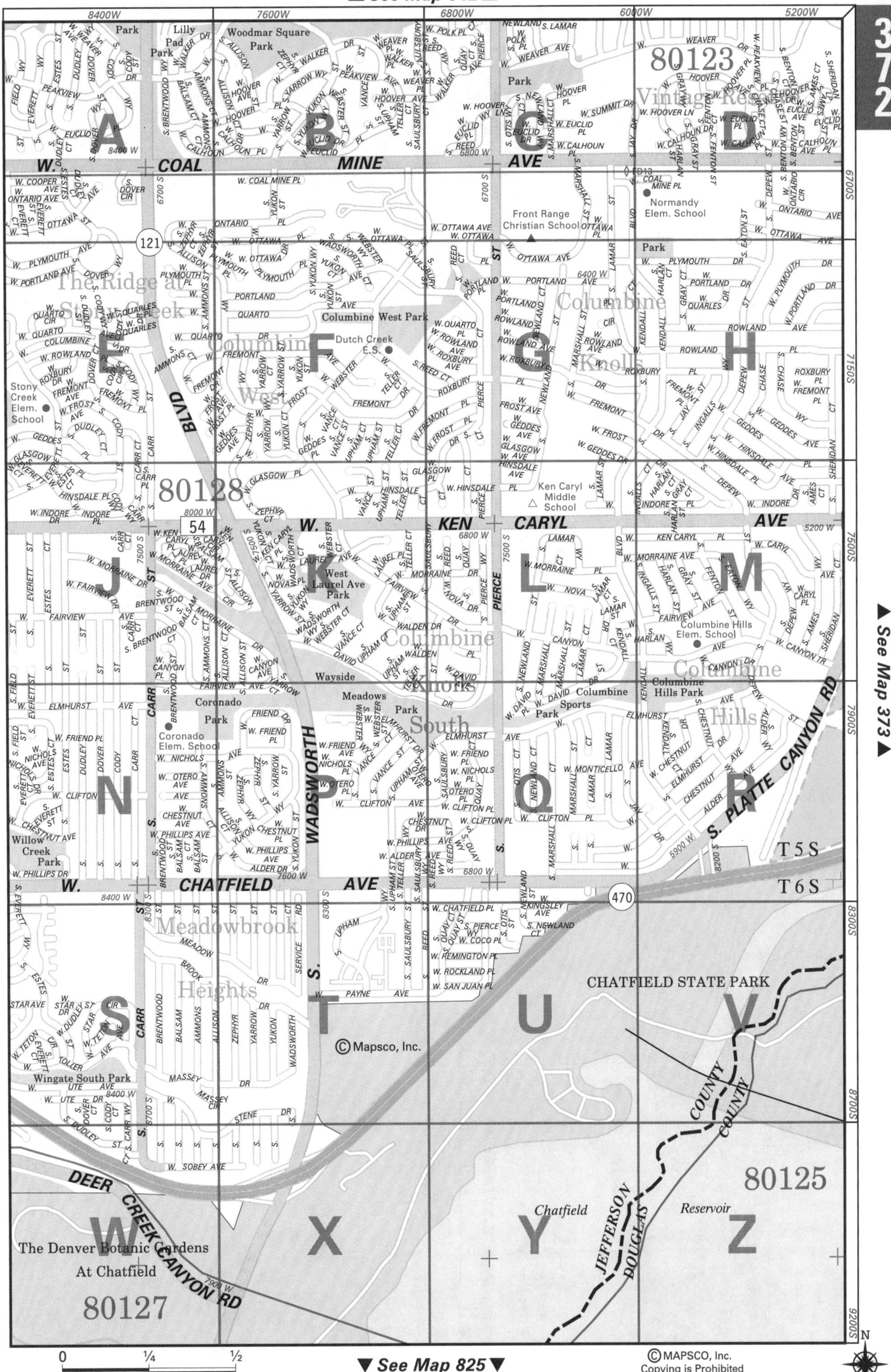

8400W 7600W 6800W 6000W 5200W

W. COAL MINE AVE

W. KEN CARYL AVE

W. CHATFIELD AVE

WADSWORTH BLVD

S. CARR ST

S. PIERCE ST

S. PLATTE CANYON RD

DEER CREEK CANYON RD

80123 80128 80125 80127

Vintage Reserve

The Ridge at Stony Creek

Columbine West

Columbine Knolls

Columbine Knolls South

Columbine Hills

Meadowbrook Heights

Woodmar Square Park

Lilly Pad Park

Columbine West Park

Dutch Creek E.S.

Stony Creek Elem. School

Normandy Elem. School

Front Range Christian School

Ken Caryl Middle School

West Laurel Ave Park

Wayside Meadows Park

Coronado Park

Coronado Elem. School

Columbine Hills Elem. School

Columbine Hills Park

Columbine Sports Park

Willow Creek Park

Wingate South Park

CHATFIELD STATE PARK

Chatfield Reservoir

The Denver Botanic Gardens At Chatfield

JEFFERSON COUNTY

DOUGLAS COUNTY

T5S T6S

6700S 7150S 7500S 7900S 8300S 8700S 9200S

A B C D E F G H J K L M N P Q R S T U V W X Y Z

© Mapsco, Inc.

0 ¼ ½ Miles

▼ See Map 825 ▼

▲ See Map 343 ▲

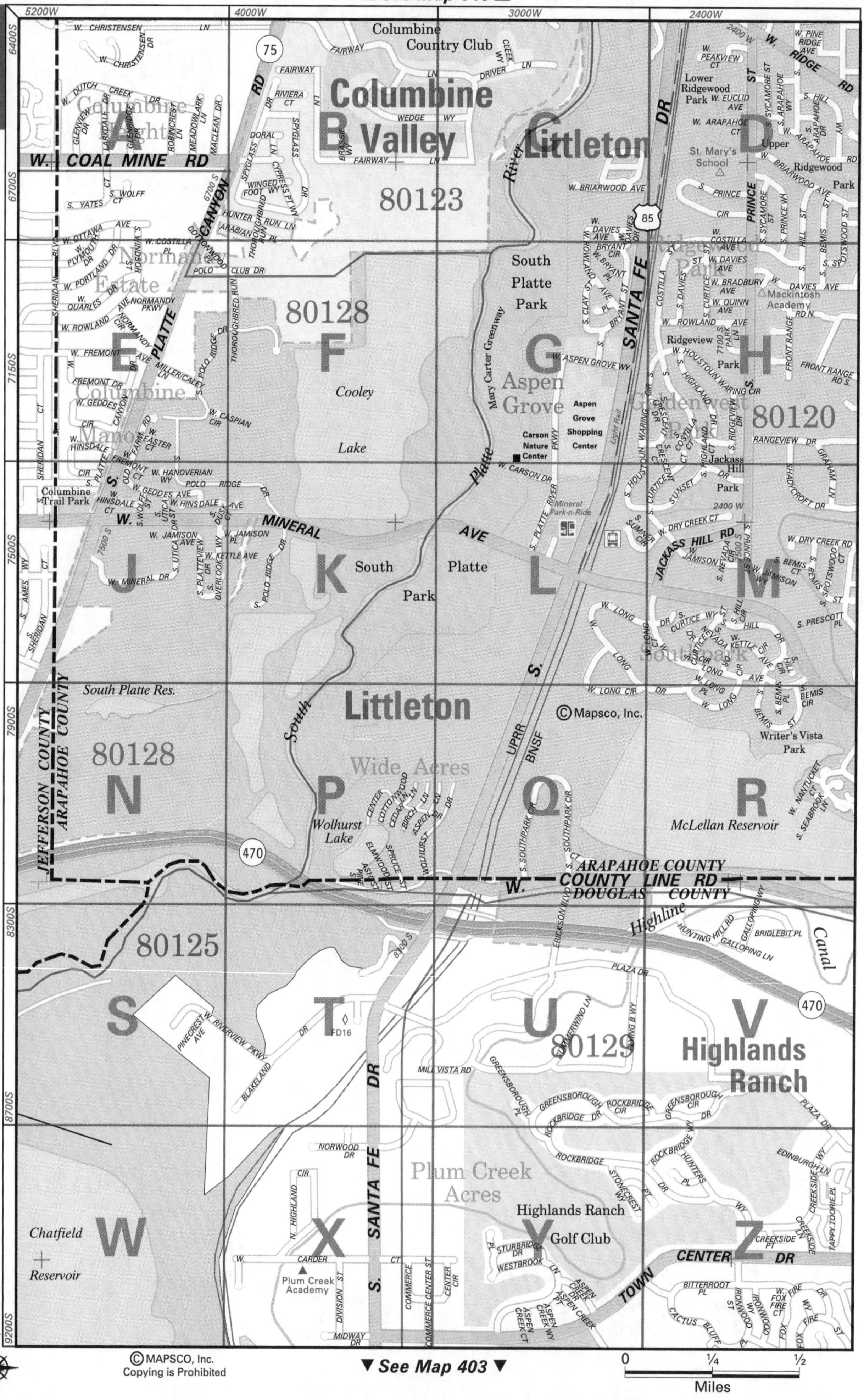
5200W
4000W
3000W
2400W
6400S
6700S
7150S
7500S
7900S
8300S
8700S
9200S
Columbine Country Club
Columbine Valley
Littleton
80123
80128
80120
80125
80129
Columbine Heights
Normandy Estate
Columbine Manor
Lower Ridgewood Park
Upper Ridgewood Park
St. Mary's School
Mackintosh Academy
Ridgeview Park
Jackass Hill Park
Ridgewood Park
Glendenwest Park
Southpark
Writer's Vista Park
South Platte Park
Aspen Grove
Aspen Grove Shopping Center
Carson Nature Center
Mineral Park-n-Ride
Mary Carter Greenway
Cooley Lake
South Platte River
South Platte Res.
Columbine Trail Park
Wide Acres
Wolhurst Lake
McLellan Reservoir
JEFFERSON COUNTY
ARAPAHOE COUNTY
DOUGLAS COUNTY
W. COUNTY LINE RD
W. COAL MINE RD
W. MINERAL AVE
S. SANTA FE DR
S. PLATTE CANYON RD
SHERIDAN BLVD
JACKASS HILL RD
PRINCE ST
W. RIDGE RD
UPRR
BNSF
Highline Canal
Plum Creek Acres
Highlands Ranch
Highlands Ranch Golf Club
TOWN CENTER DR
Plum Creek Academy
Chatfield Reservoir
FD16
© Mapsco, Inc.
75
85
470
A
B
C
D
E
F
G
H
J
K
L
M
N
P
Q
R
S
T
U
V
W
X
Y
Z
N
0
¼
½
Miles

▲ See Map 372 ▲

▼ See Map 403 ▼

▲ See Map 344 ▲

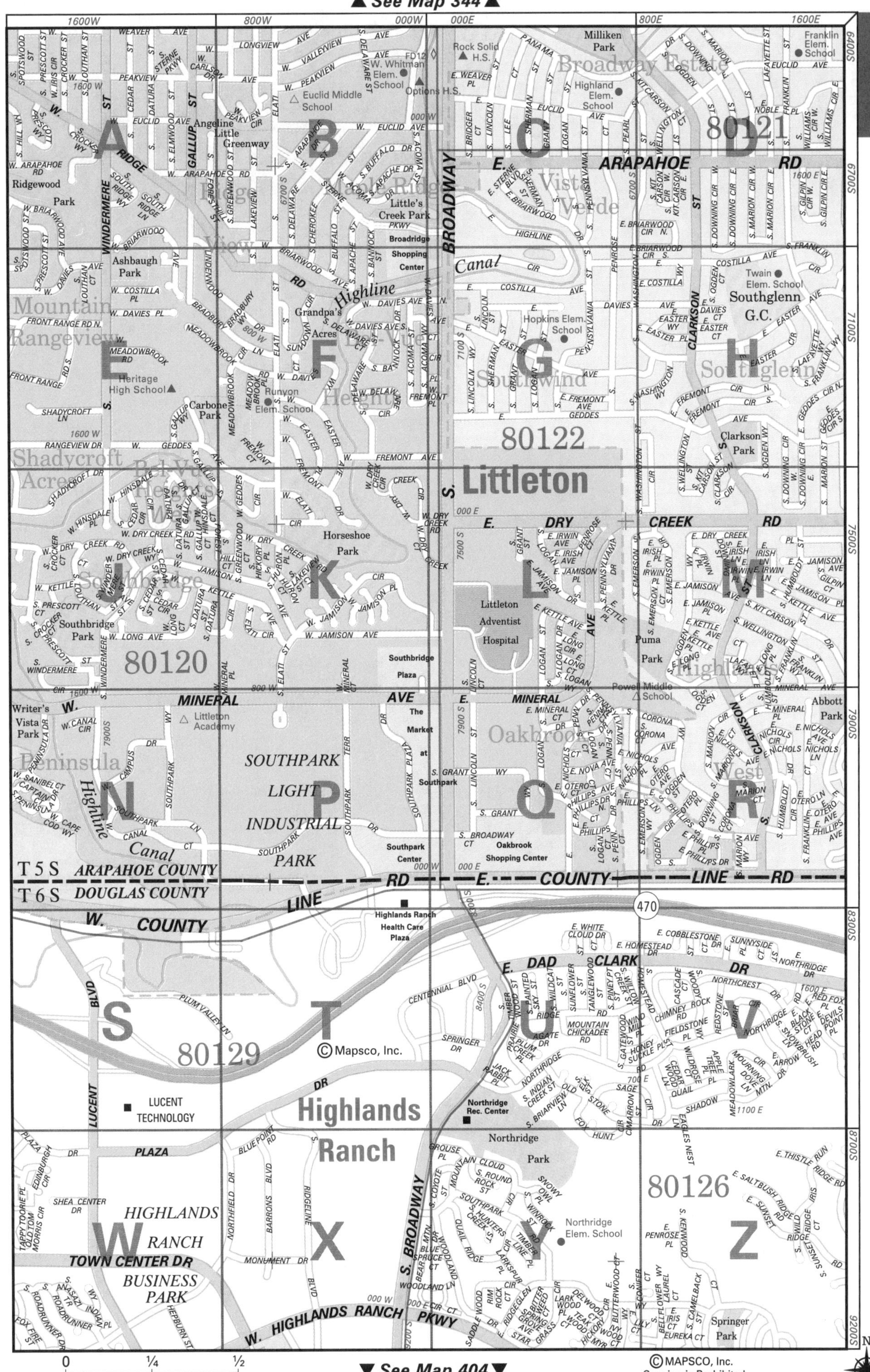

0 ¼ ½
Miles

▶ See Map 375 ▶

▼ See Map 404 ▼

▲ See Map 345 ▲

▲ See Map 374 ▲

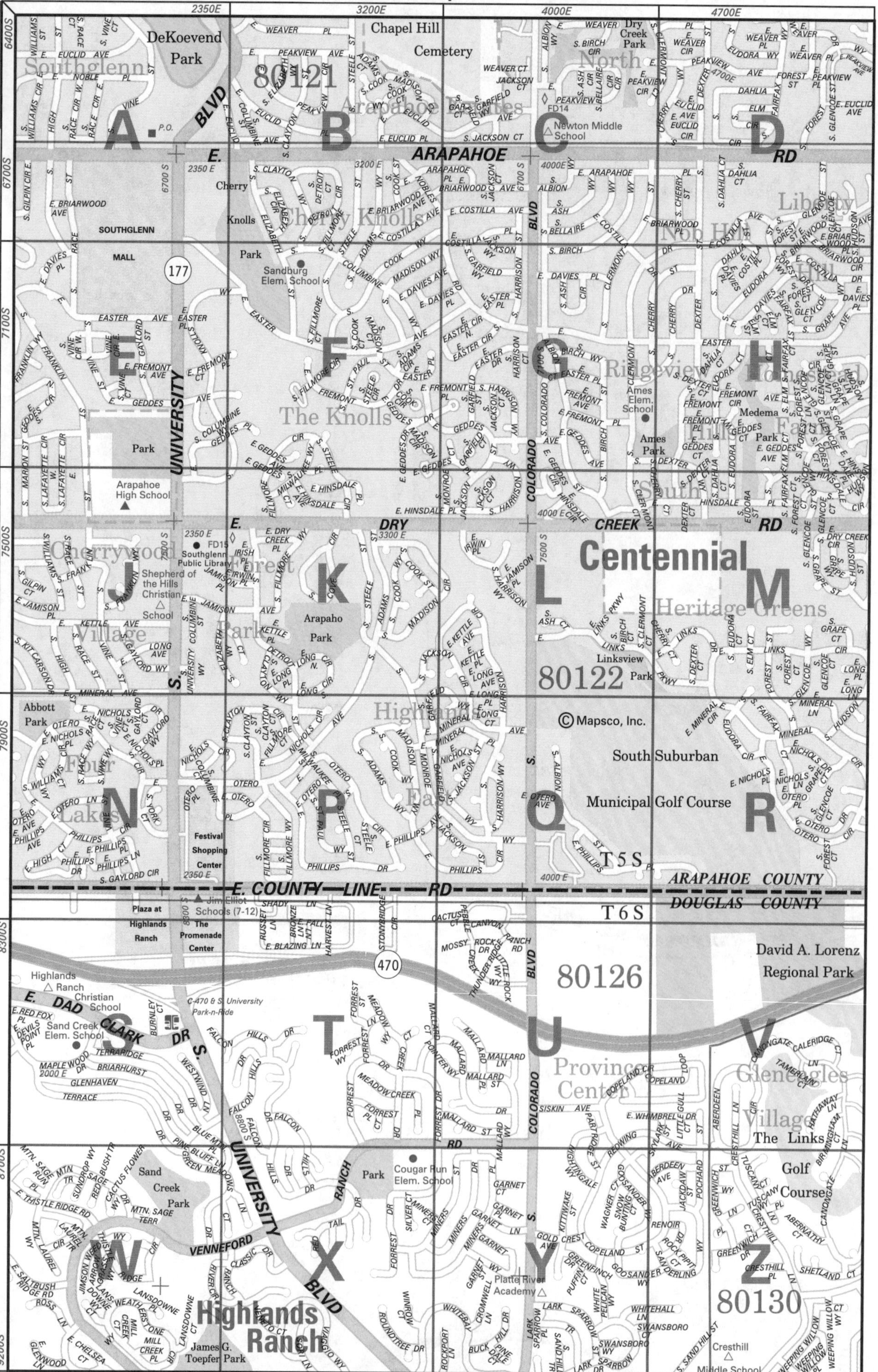

Southglenn
DeKoevend Park
Chapel Hill Cemetery
80121
Arapahoe Estates
Dry Creek Park
North
Newton Middle School
E. ARAPAHOE RD
Cherry Knolls Park
SOUTHGLENN MALL
Sandburg Elem. School
Cherry Knolls
Liberty
Nob Hill
Hill
The Knolls
Ridgeview
Ames Elem. School
Ames Park
Homestead
Medema Park
Farm
Arapahoe High School
Park
South
E. DRY CREEK RD
Cherrywood
Southglenn Public Library
Forest
Shepherd of the Hills Christian School
Arapaho Park
Centennial
Heritage Greens
Village
Park
Linksview Park
80122
Abbott Park
Four Lakes
Highland
East
South Suburban Municipal Golf Course
Festival Shopping Center
T5S
ARAPAHOE COUNTY
E. COUNTY LINE RD
DOUGLAS COUNTY
T6S
Jim Elliot Schools (7-12)
Plaza at Highlands Ranch
The Promenade Center
David A. Lorenz Regional Park
80126
Highlands Ranch Christian School
Sand Creek Elem. School
C-470 & S. University Park-n-Ride
Province Center
Gleneagles Village
The Links Golf Course
Sand Creek Park
Cougar Run Elem. School
Platte River Academy
80130
Highlands Ranch
James G. Toepfer Park
Cresthill Middle School
S. UNIVERSITY BLVD
S. COLORADO BLVD

▼ See Map 405 ▼

0 ¼ ½ Miles

▲ See Map 346 ▲

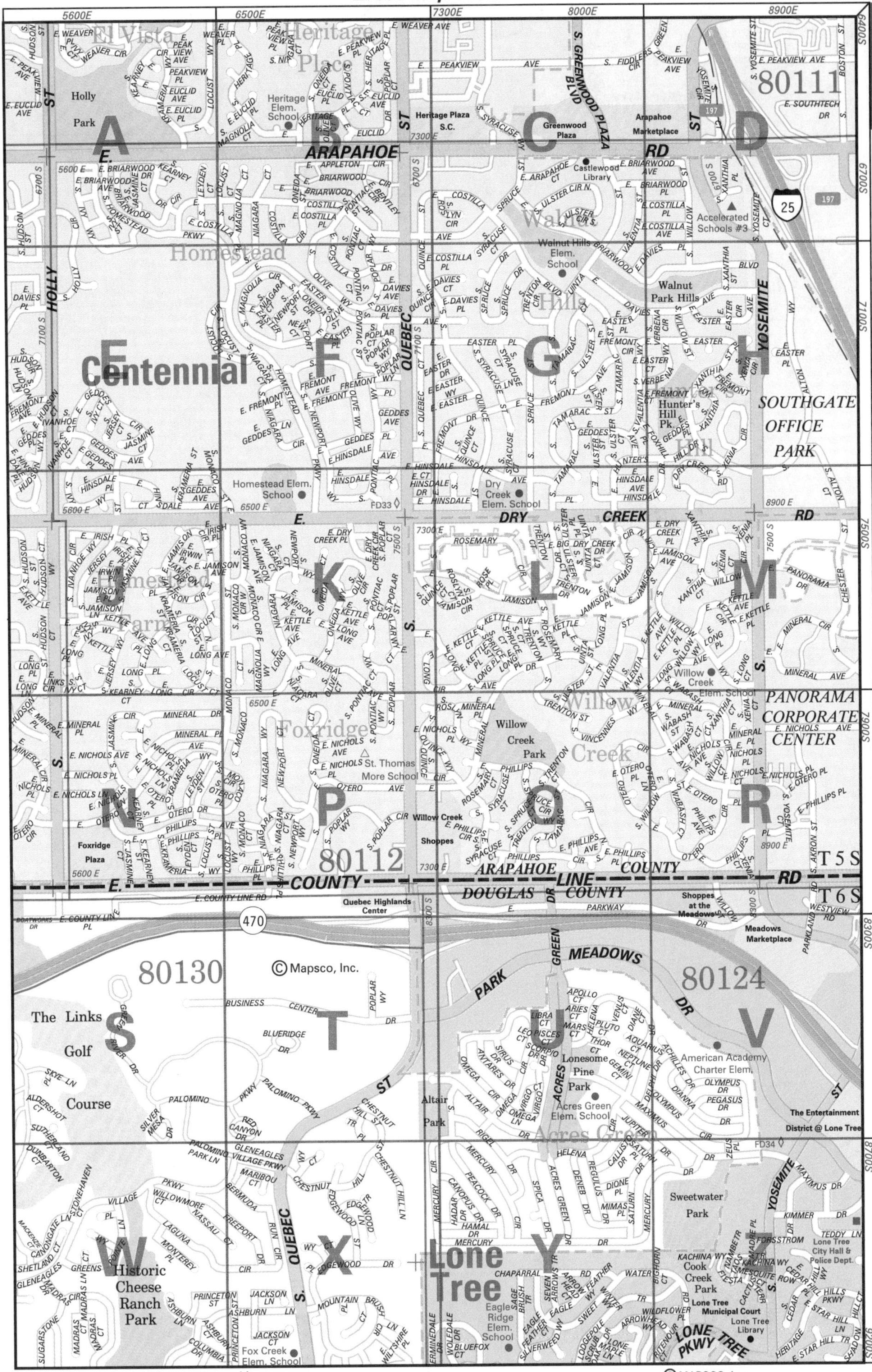

El Vista · Heritage Place · Holly Park · Heritage Elem. School · Heritage Plaza S.C. · Greenwood Plaza · Arapahoe Marketplace · Castlewood Library · Accelerated Schools #3 · Homestead · Walnut Hills · Walnut Hills Elem. School · Walnut Park Hills · Centennial · Hunter's Hill · Hunter's Hill Pk · SOUTHGATE OFFICE PARK · Homestead Elem. School · Dry Creek Elem. School · Homestead Farm · Willow Creek · Willow Creek Elem. School · Willow Creek Park · Foxridge · St. Thomas More School · Foxridge Plaza · Willow Creek Shoppes · PANORAMA CORPORATE CENTER · Quebec Highlands Center · Shoppes at the Meadows · Meadows Marketplace · The Links Golf Course · Altair Park · Lonesome Pine Park · Acres Green Elem. School · Acres Green · American Academy Charter Elem. · The Entertainment District @ Lone Tree · Sweetwater Park · Lone Tree City Hall & Police Dept. · Historic Cheese Ranch Park · Lone Tree · Cook Creek Park · Lone Tree Municipal Court · Lone Tree Library · Eagle Ridge Elem. School · Fox Creek Elem. School

80111 · 80112 · 80130 · 80124

E. ARAPAHOE RD · E. DRY CREEK RD · E. COUNTY LINE RD · ARAPAHOE COUNTY · DOUGLAS COUNTY · 470 · 25 · 197 · S. QUEBEC ST · S. HOLLY ST · S. YOSEMITE ST · S. GREENWOOD PLAZA BLVD · PARK MEADOWS DR · ACRES GREEN DR · LONE TREE PKWY · T 5 S · T 6 S

5600E · 6500E · 7300E · 8000E · 8900E · 6400S · 6700S · 7100S · 7500S · 7900S · 8300S · 8700S · 9200S

A · B · C · D · E · F · G · H · J · K · L · M · N · P · Q · R · S · T · U · V · W · X · Y · Z

© Mapsco, Inc.

0 · 1/4 · 1/2 Miles

▼ See Map 406 ▼

▲ See Map 347 ▲

▲ See Map 376 ▲

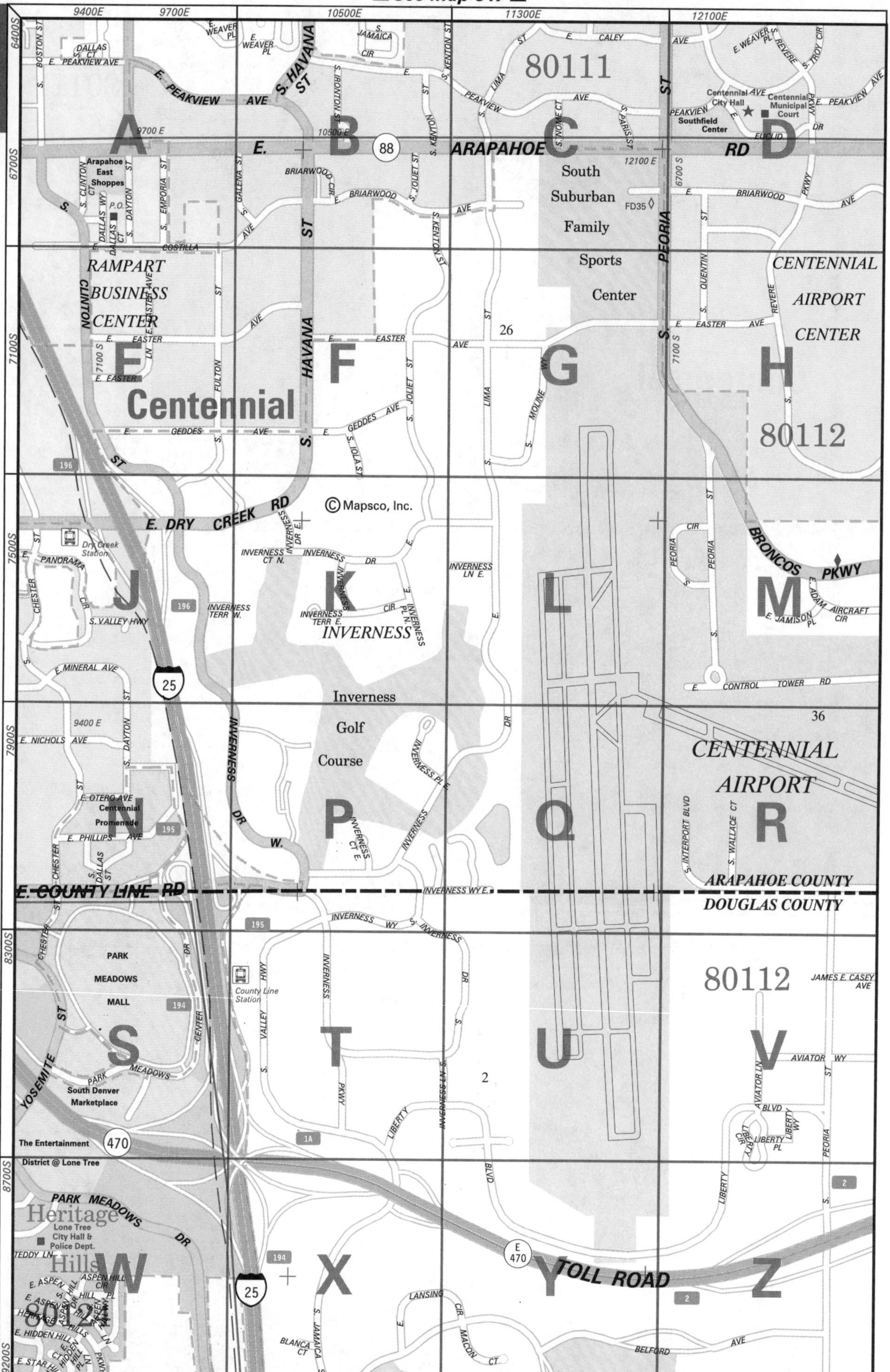

80111

80112

Centennial

RAMPART BUSINESS CENTER

South Suburban Family Sports Center

CENTENNIAL AIRPORT CENTER

INVERNESS

Inverness Golf Course

CENTENNIAL AIRPORT

ARAPAHOE COUNTY

DOUGLAS COUNTY

PARK MEADOWS MALL

South Denver Marketplace

The Entertainment District @ Lone Tree

Heritage Hills

80124

E. ARAPAHOE RD

E. DRY CREEK RD

E. COUNTY LINE RD

BRONCOS PKWY

TOLL ROAD

© Mapsco, Inc.

▼ See Map 407 ▼

0 ¼ ½
Miles

▲ See Map 348 ▲

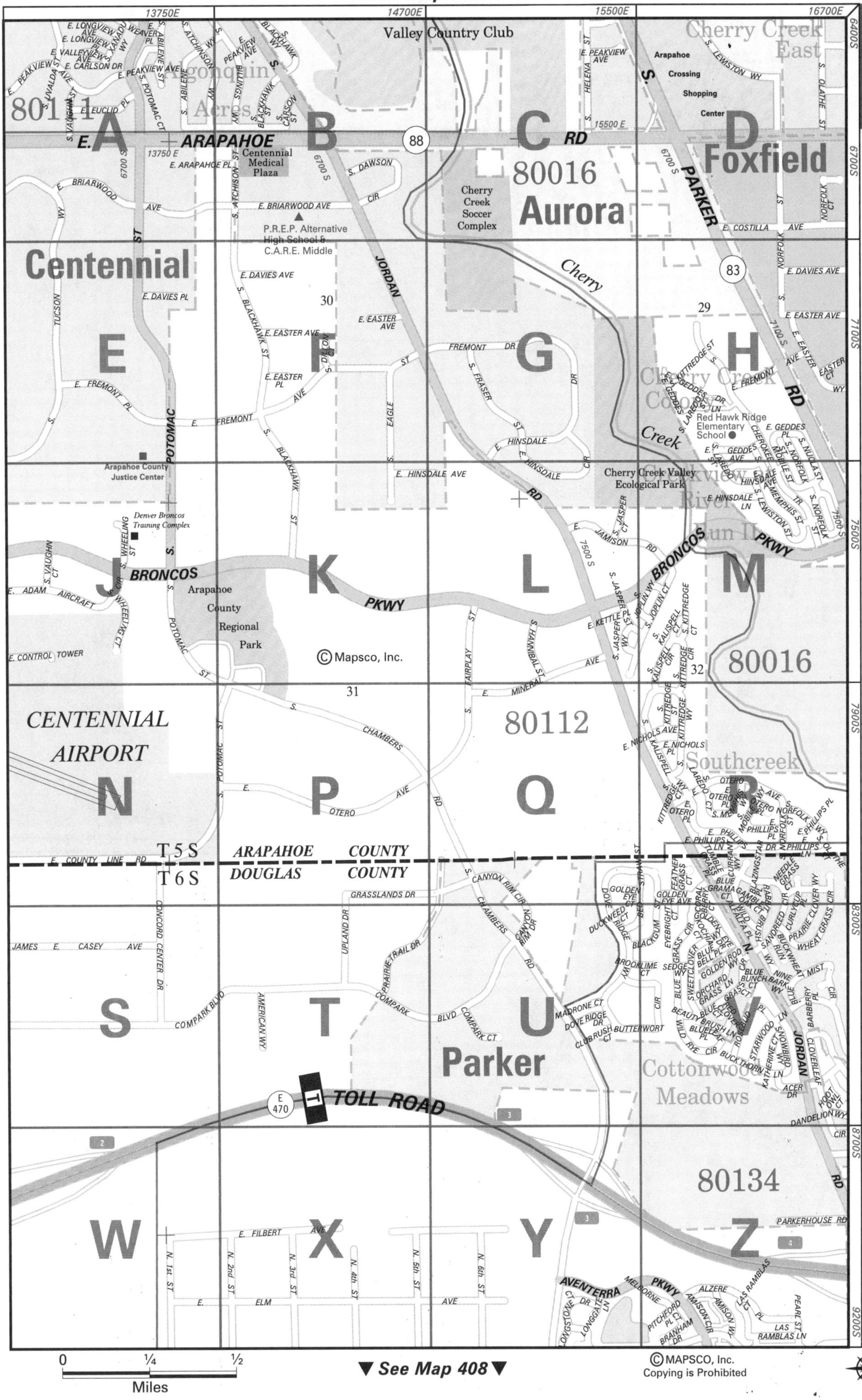

Valley Country Club

Centennial

Aurora

Foxfield

Parker

CENTENNIAL AIRPORT

Arapahoe County Regional Park

Centennial Medical Plaza

Cherry Creek Soccer Complex

Arapahoe Crossing Shopping Center

P.R.E.P. Alternative High School & C.A.R.E. Middle

Arapahoe County Justice Center

Denver Broncos Training Complex

Red Hawk Ridge Elementary School

Cherry Creek Valley Ecological Park

Cherry Creek East

Algonquin Acres

Southcreek

Cottonwood Meadows

80111 80016 80112 80134

ARAPAHOE COUNTY

DOUGLAS COUNTY

T5S T6S

E. ARAPAHOE RD

BRONCOS PKWY

S. PARKER RD

JORDAN RD

TOLL ROAD E 470

© Mapsco, Inc.

▲ See Map 379 ▲

0 ¼ ½ Miles

▼ See Map 408 ▼

▲ See Map 349 ▲

▲ See Map 378 ▲

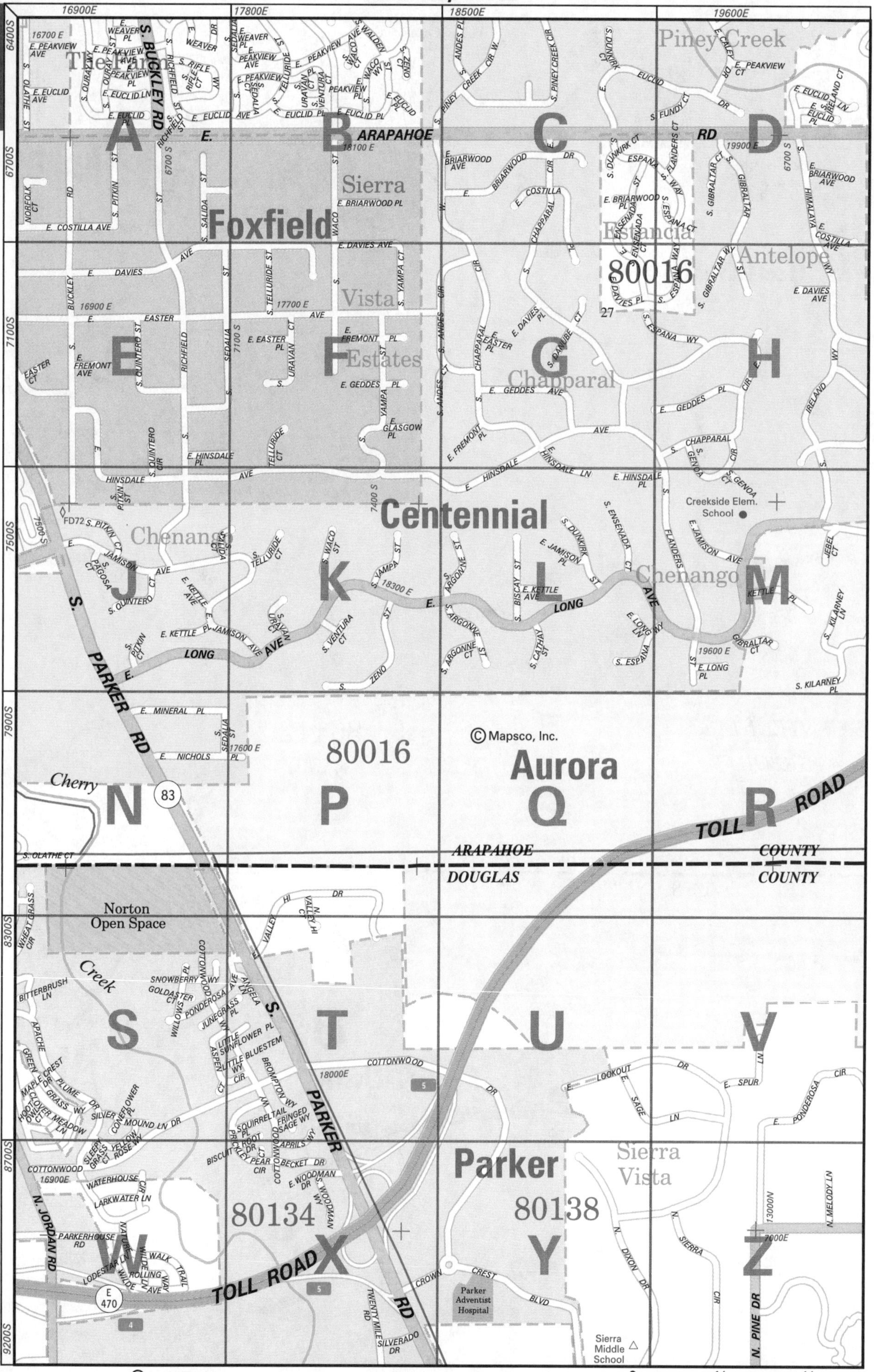

▼ See Map 409 ▼

0 ¼ ½
Miles

▲ See Map 350 ▲

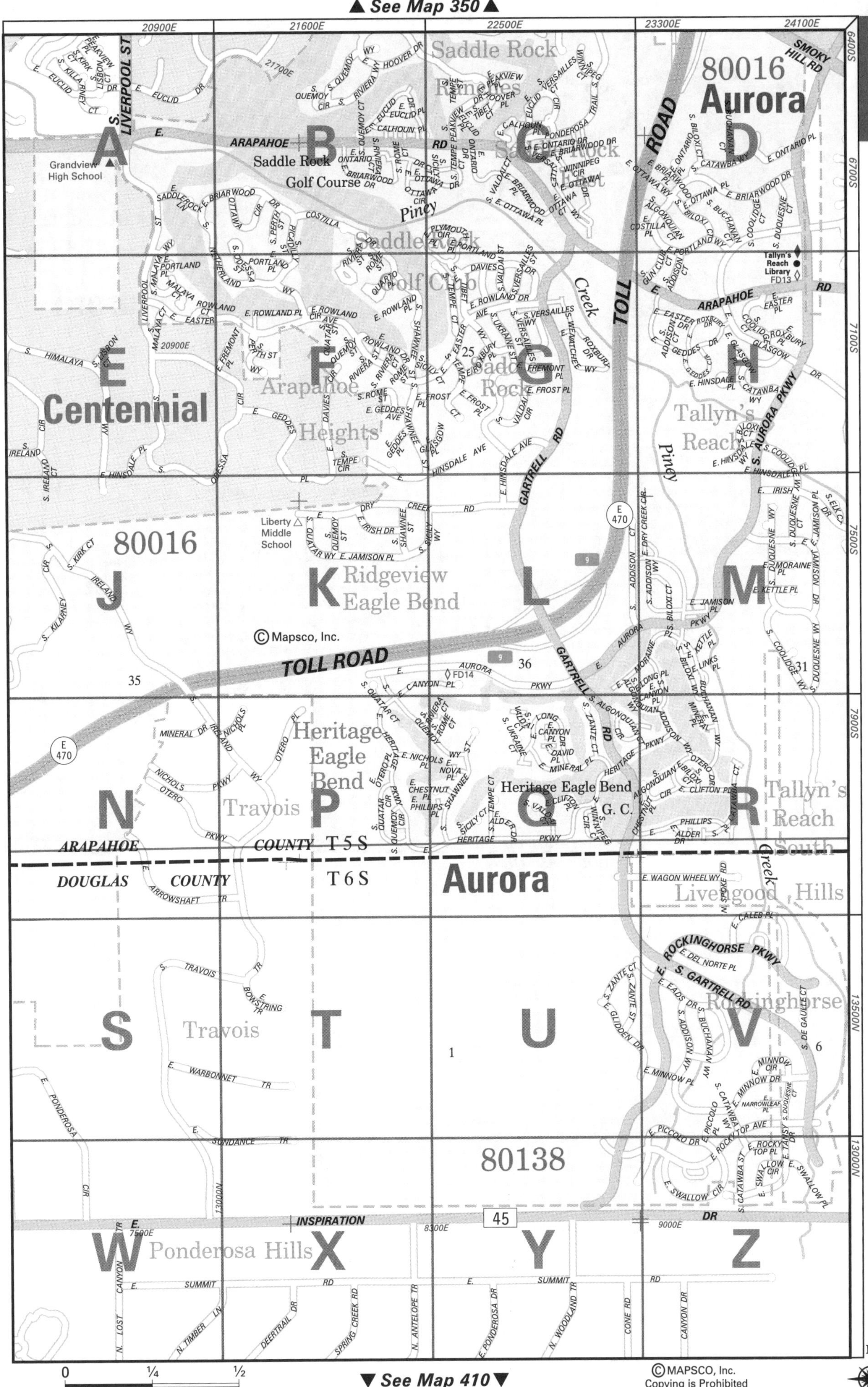

▲ See Map 381 ▶

▼ See Map 410 ▼

▲ See Map 351 ▲

▲ See Map 380 ▲

▲ See Map 830 ▲

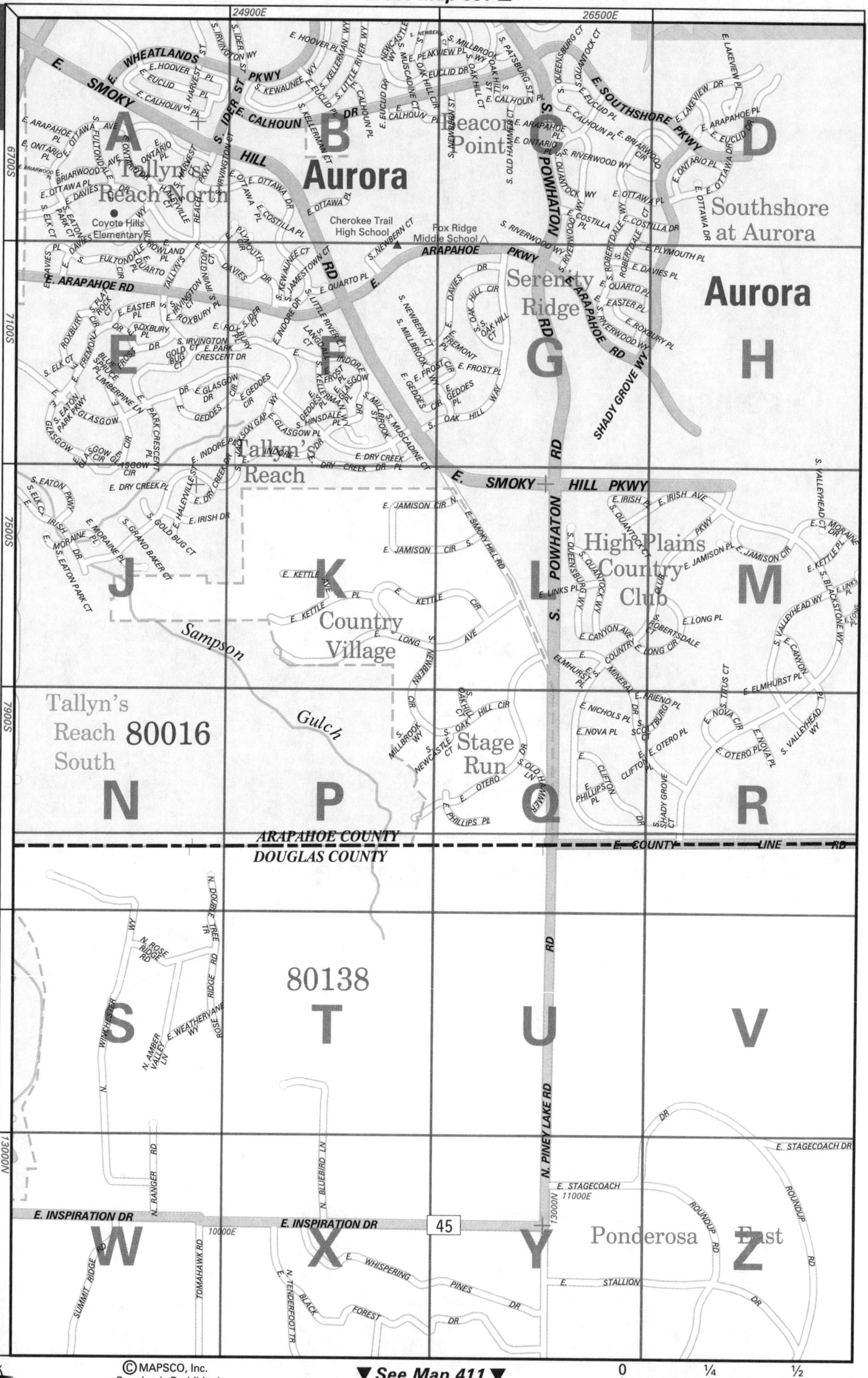

24900E
26500E
6700S
7100S
7500S
7900S
13000N
A
B
C
D
E
F
G
H
J
K
L
M
N
P
Q
R
S
T
U
V
W
X
Y
Z
Aurora
Tallyn's Reach North
Coyote Hills Elementary
Beacon Point
Cherokee Trail High School
Fox Ridge Middle School
Southshore at Aurora
Serenity Ridge
Tallyn's Reach
High Plains Country Club
Country Village
Tallyn's Reach South
80016
Stage Run
80138
Ponderosa East
E. SMOKY HILL RD
E. WHEATLANDS PKWY
S. IDER ST
E. CALHOUN DR
E. ARAPAHOE RD
E. ARAPAHOE PKWY
S. POWHATON RD
E. SOUTHSHORE PKWY
SHADY GROVE WY
E. SMOKY HILL PKWY
Sampson Gulch
ARAPAHOE COUNTY
DOUGLAS COUNTY
E. COUNTY LINE RD
N. PINEY LAKE RD
E. INSPIRATION DR
45
E. STAGECOACH
E. STAGECOACH DR
ROUNDUP RD
E. STALLION
E. WHISPERING PINES DR
BLACK FOREST DR
N. TENDERFOOT TR
TOMAHAWK RD
SUMMIT RIDGE RD
N. RANGER RD
N. WINCHESTER WY
N. BLUEBIRD LN
N. DOUBLE TREE TR
ROSE RIDGE RD
E. WEATHERVANE WY
N. AMBER VALLEY LN
N. ROSE RIDGE
10000E
11000E
13000N

▼ See Map 411 ▼

0 1/4 1/2
Miles

▲ See Map 373 ▲

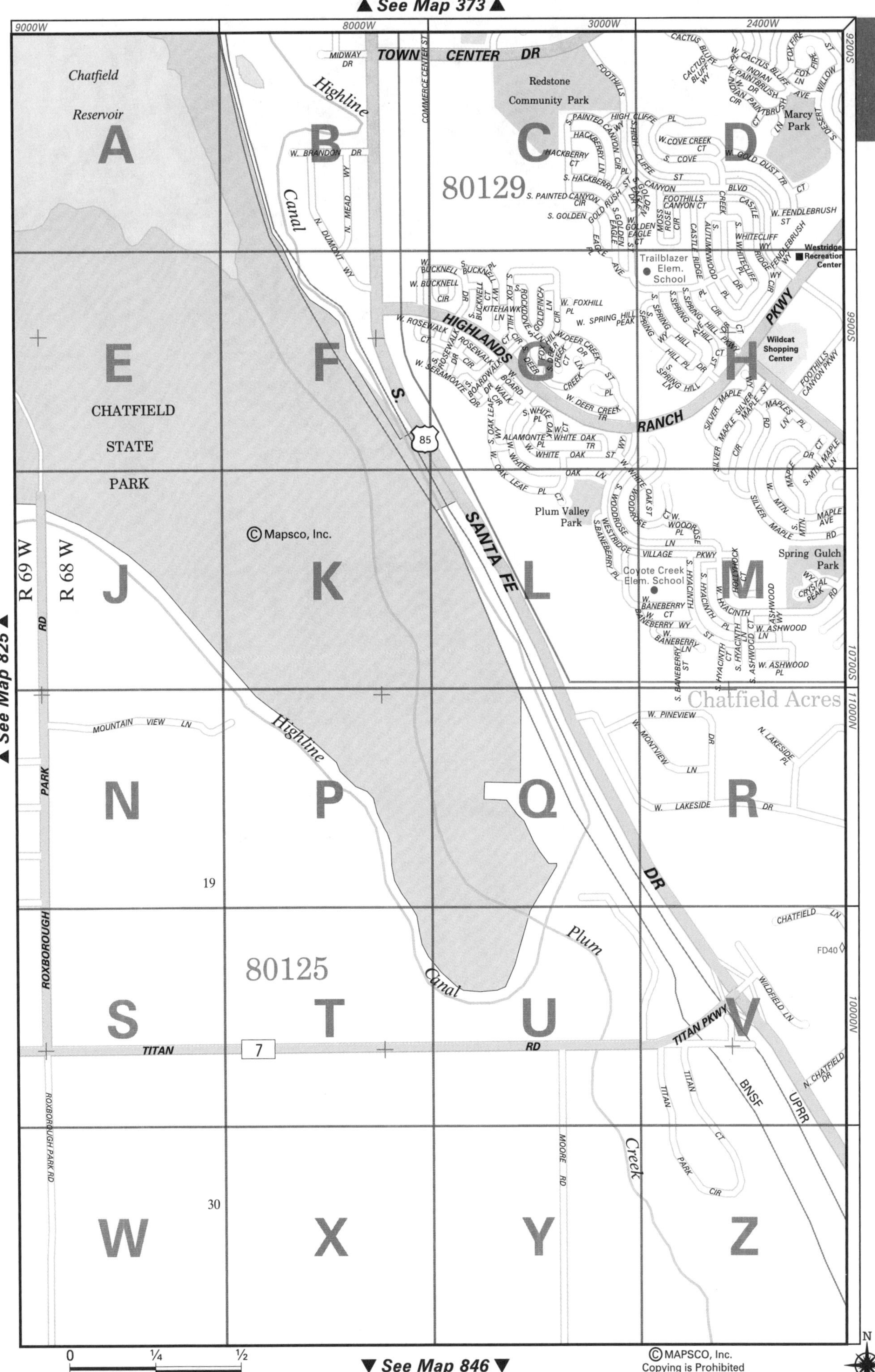

◄ See Map 825 ◄

► See Map 404 ►

▼ See Map 846 ▼

▲See Map 374▲

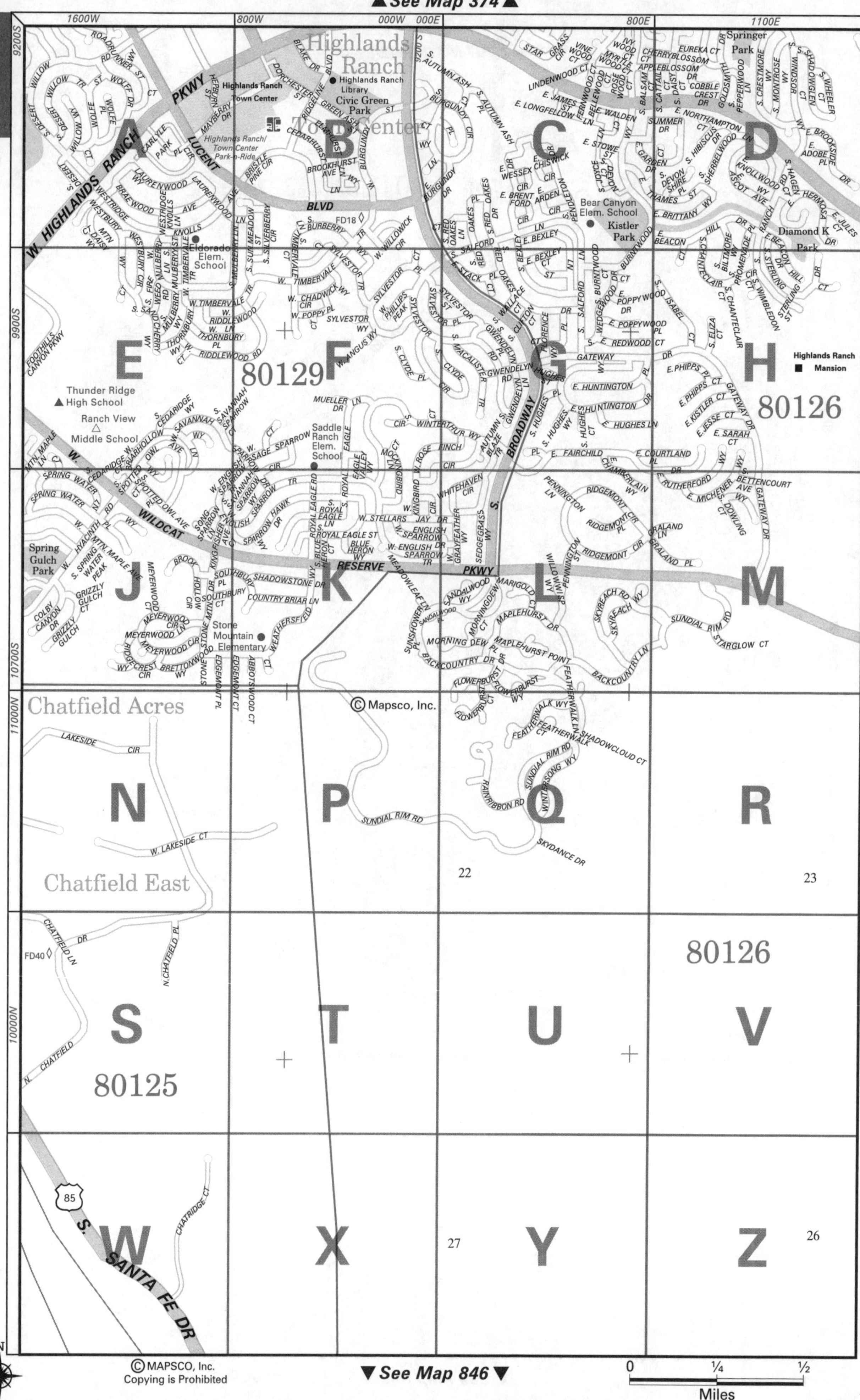

▲See Map 403▲

▼See Map 846▼

0 ¼ ½
Miles

▲ See Map 375 ▲

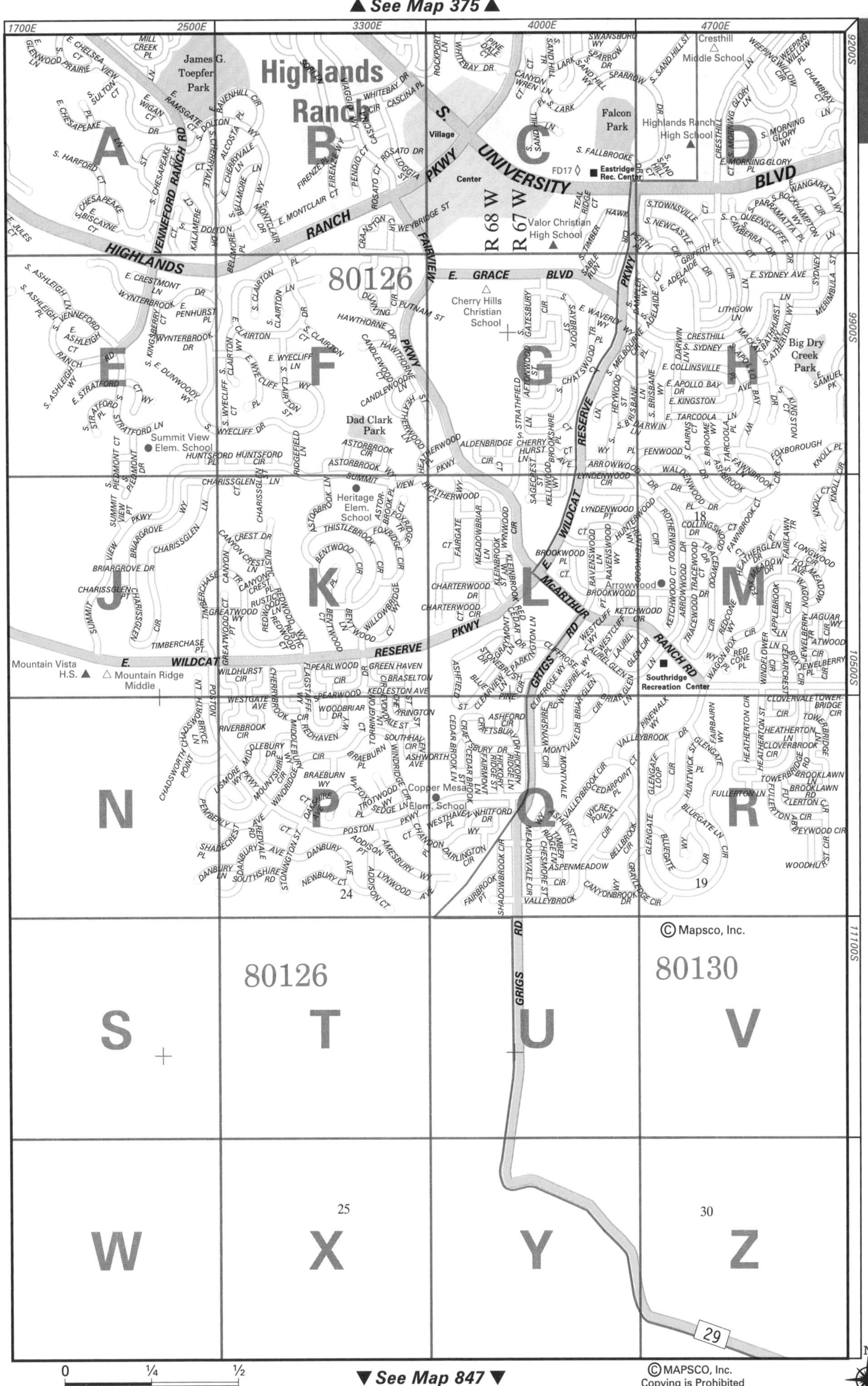

▲ See Map 406 ▶

0 ¼ ½
Miles

▼ See Map 847 ▼

▲See Map 376▲

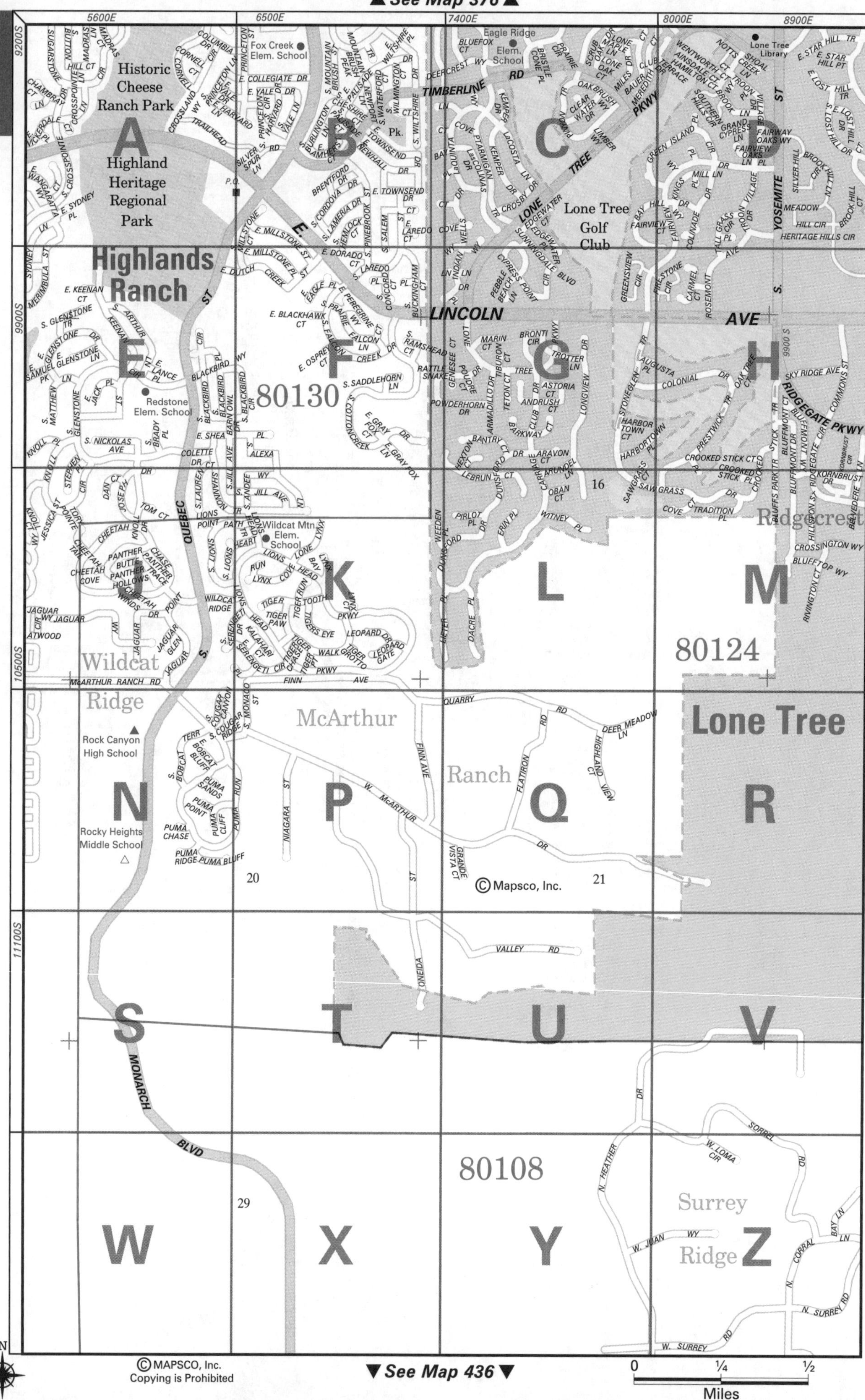

▲See Map 405▲

▼See Map 436▼

▲ See Map 377 ▲

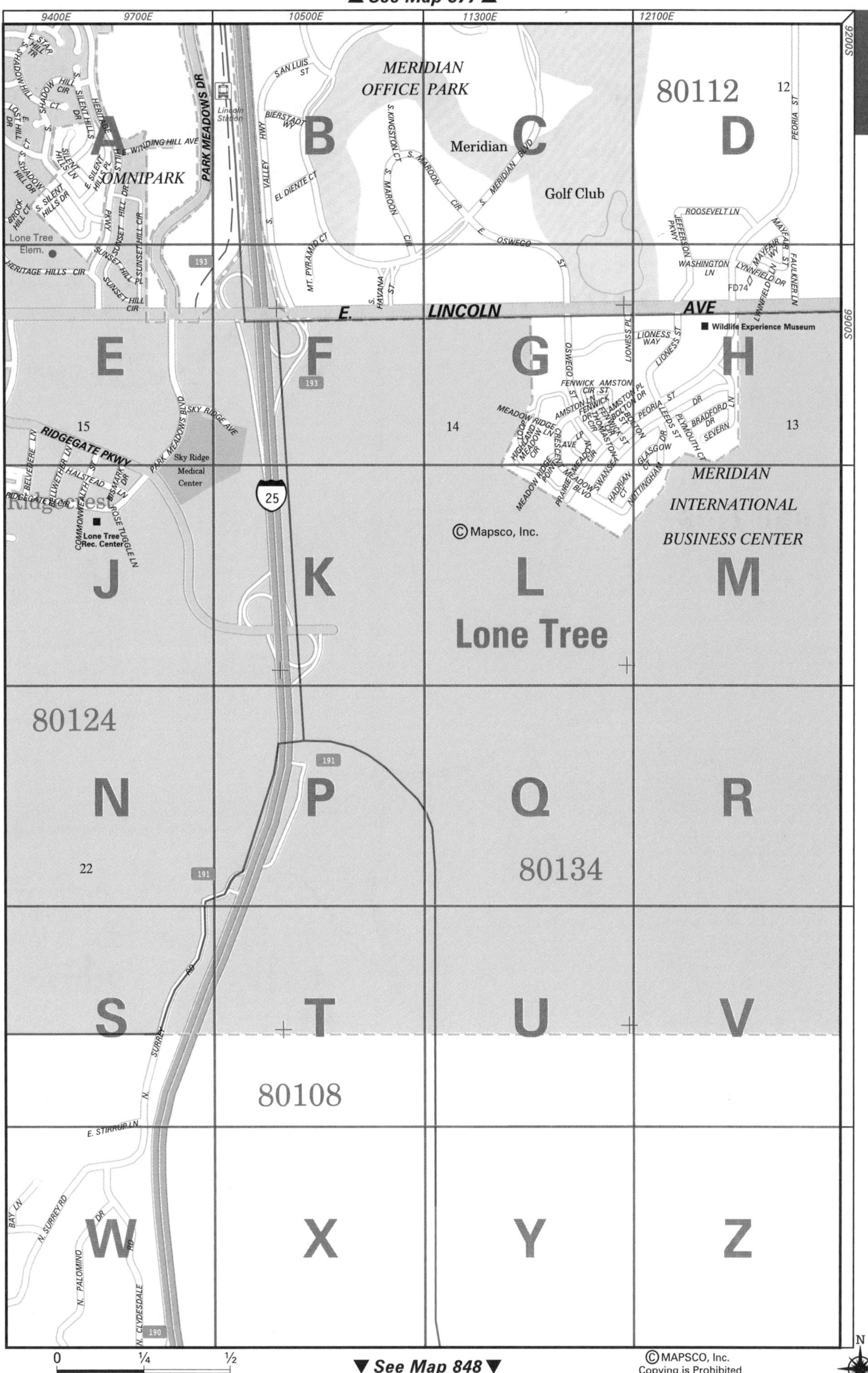

▲ See Map 408 ▲

▼ See Map 848 ▼

▲ See Map 378 ▲

▲ See Map 407 ▲

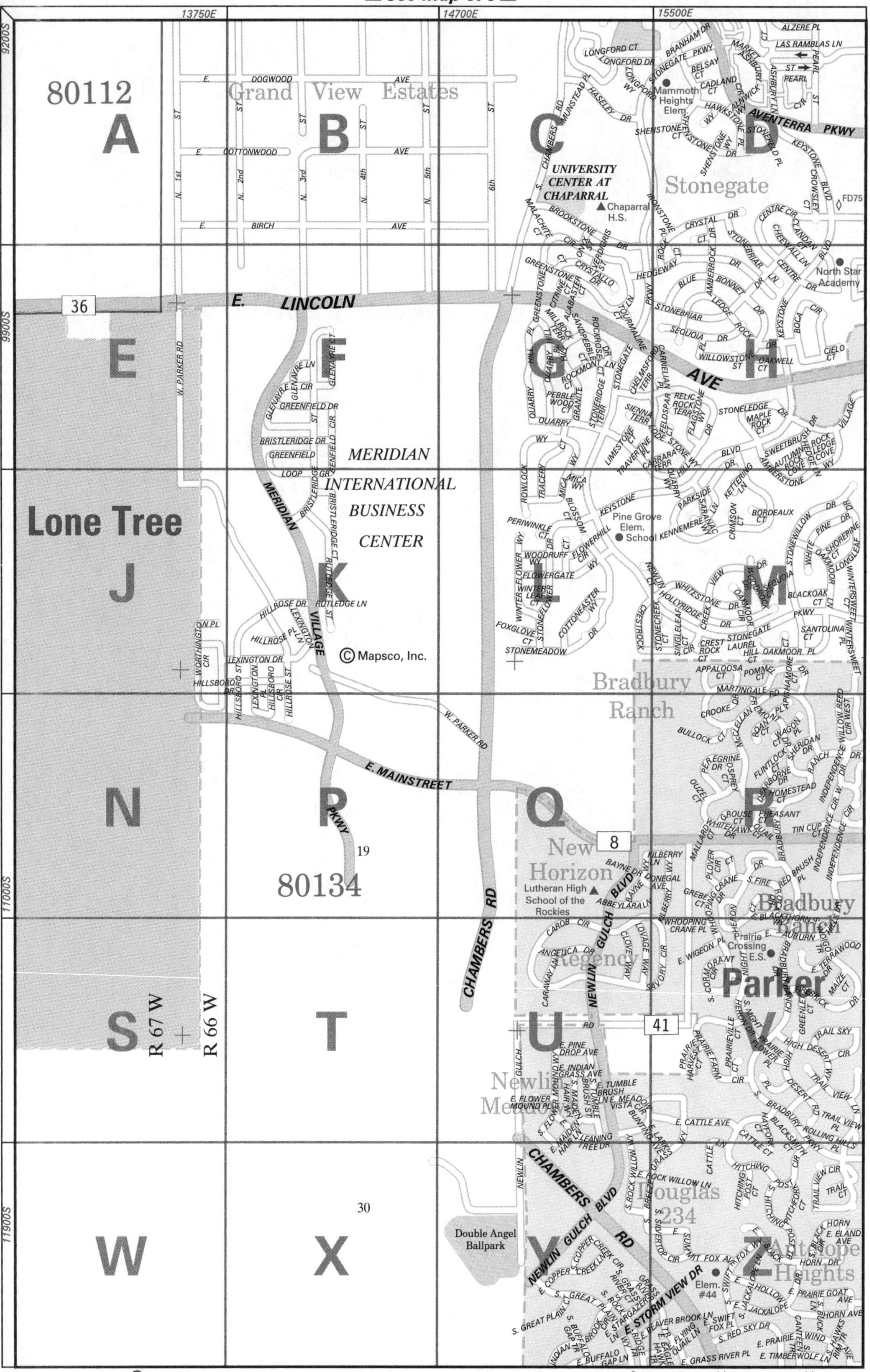

13750E
14700E
15500E
9200S
9900S
11000S
11900S

80112
Grand View Estates
A B C D
E F G H
J K L M
N P Q R
S T U V
W X Y Z

UNIVERSITY CENTER AT CHAPARRAL
Chaparral H.S.
Mammoth Heights Elem.
Stonegate
North Star Academy
FD75
E. LINCOLN AVE
36
MERIDIAN INTERNATIONAL BUSINESS CENTER
Lone Tree
Pine Grove Elem. School
© Mapsco, Inc.
Bradbury Ranch
E. MAINSTREET
MERIDIAN VILLAGE PKWY
8
19
80134
New Horizon
Lutheran High School of the Rockies
Regency
Prairie Crossing E.S.
Parker
41
CHAMBERS RD
NEWLIN GULCH BLVD
R 67 W
R 66 W
Newlin Meadows
30
Double Angel Ballpark
Douglas 234
Antelope Heights
Elem. #44
E. STORM VIEW DR

▼ See Map 848 ▼

0 ¼ ½
Miles

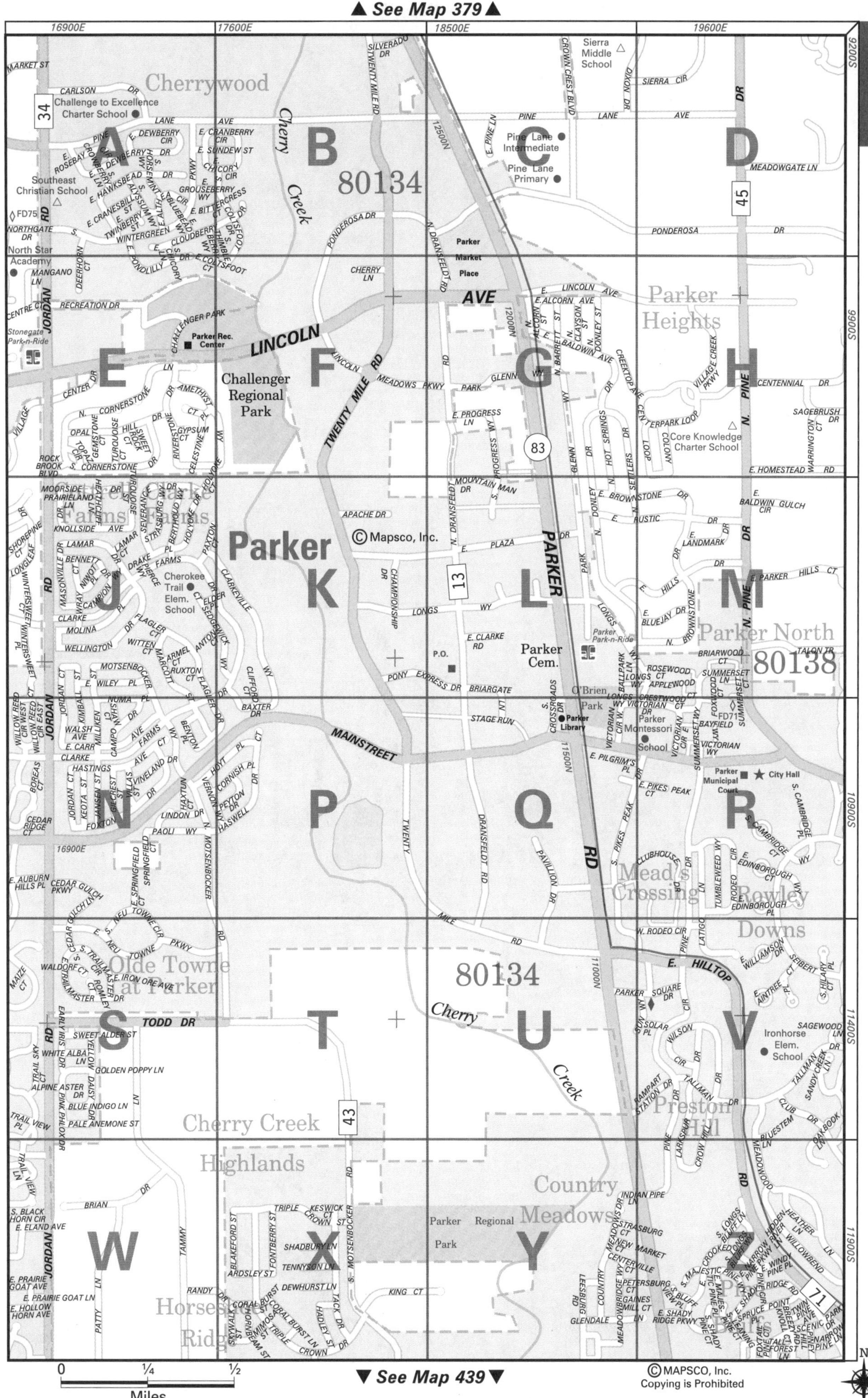

▲ See Map 379 ▲
▼ See Map 439 ▼
▲ See Map 410 ▶
16900E
17600E
18500E
19600E
9200S
9900S
10900S
11400S
11900S
Cherrywood
Challenge to Excellence Charter School
Southeast Christian School
FD75
North Star Academy
Stonegate Park-n-Ride
Parker Rec. Center
Challenger Regional Park
Cherry Creek
80134
Sierra Middle School
Pine Lane Intermediate
Pine Lane Primary
Parker Market Place
Parker Heights
Core Knowledge Charter School
LINCOLN AVE
TWENTY MILE RD
PARKER RD
N. PINE DR
JORDAN RD
MAINSTREET
E. HILLTOP
TODD DR
PINE LANE AVE
PONDEROSA DR
MEADOWGATE LN
SIERRA CIR
RECREATION DR
CENTENNIAL DR
E. HOMESTEAD RD
Parker
© Mapsco, Inc.
Cottrell Clarke Farms
Cherokee Trail Elem. School
Parker Park-n-Ride
Parker Cem.
P.O.
O'Brien Park
Parker Library
Parker Montessori School
Parker North
80138
FD71
Parker Municipal Court
City Hall
Mead's Crossing
Rowley Downs
Olde Towne at Parker
Ironhorse Elem. School
Preston Hill
Cherry Creek Highlands
Country Meadows
Parker Regional Park
Horseshoe Ridge
Pine Bluffs
34
45
83
13
43
71
A B C D E F G H J K L M N P Q R S T U V W X Y Z
0 ¼ ½
Miles
N

▲ See Map 380 ▲

▲ See Map 409 ▲

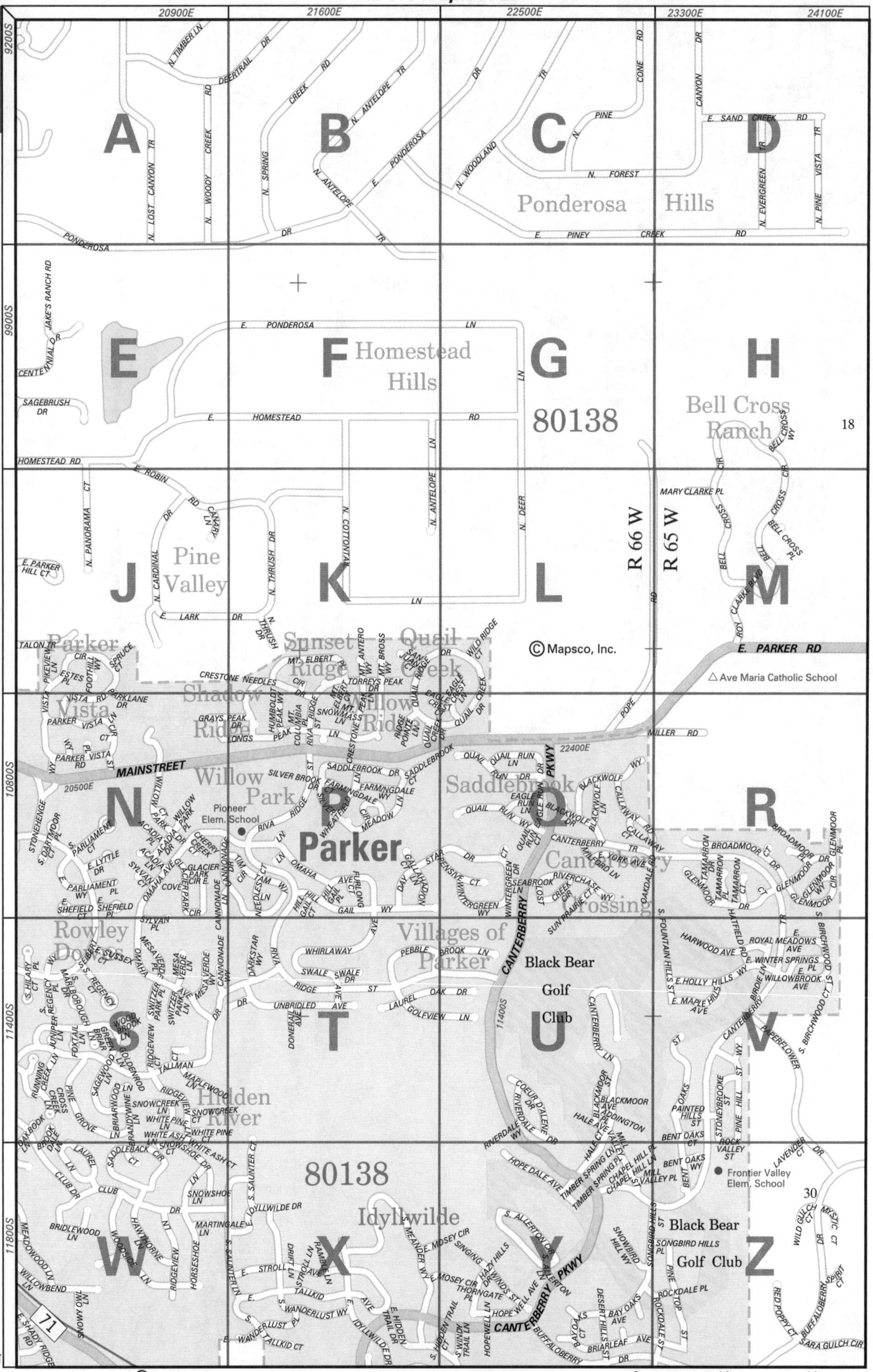

▼ See Map 440 ▼

0 ¼ ½
Miles

▲ See Map 381 ▲

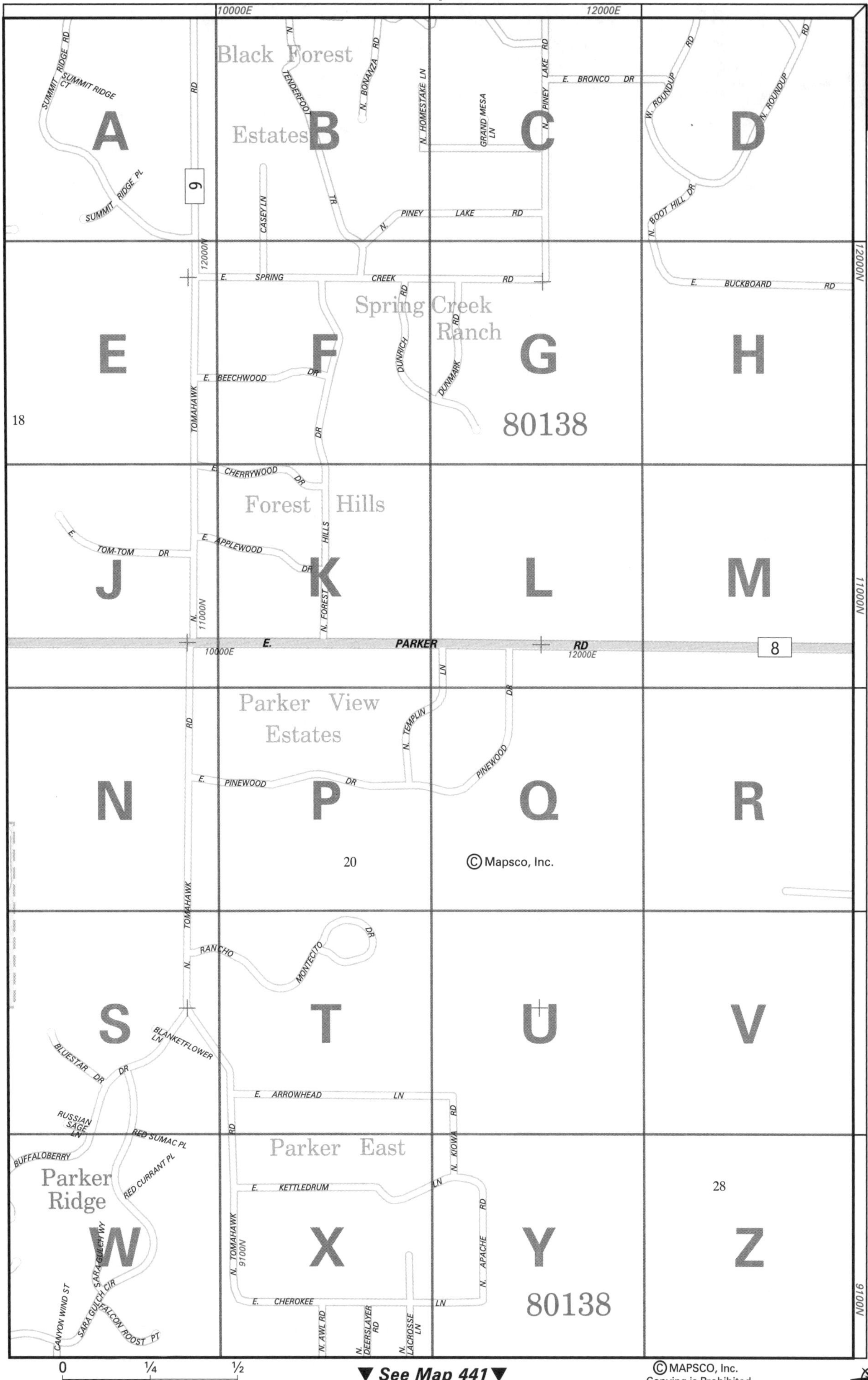

▶ See Map 830 ▶

▼ See Map 441 ▼

▲ See Map 825 ▲

11200W 10000W 9500W

CHATFIELD STATE PARK

Waterton

Platte Canyon Reservoir

Chatfield Farms

Roxborough Library

River Canyon

Roxborough Village

T6S
T7S

Roxborough Elem. School

80125

Roxborough

Foothills Water Treatment Plant

Arrowhead Golf Course

PIKE NATIONAL FOREST

ROXBOROUGH STATE PARK

Southdowns Open Space Park

Aurora Rampart Reservoir

R 69 W

A B C D E F G H J K L M N P Q R S T U V W X Y Z

36 2 1 11 12

8000N 7000N 6300N 5700N

◀ See Map 845 ◀

▶ See Map 846 ▶

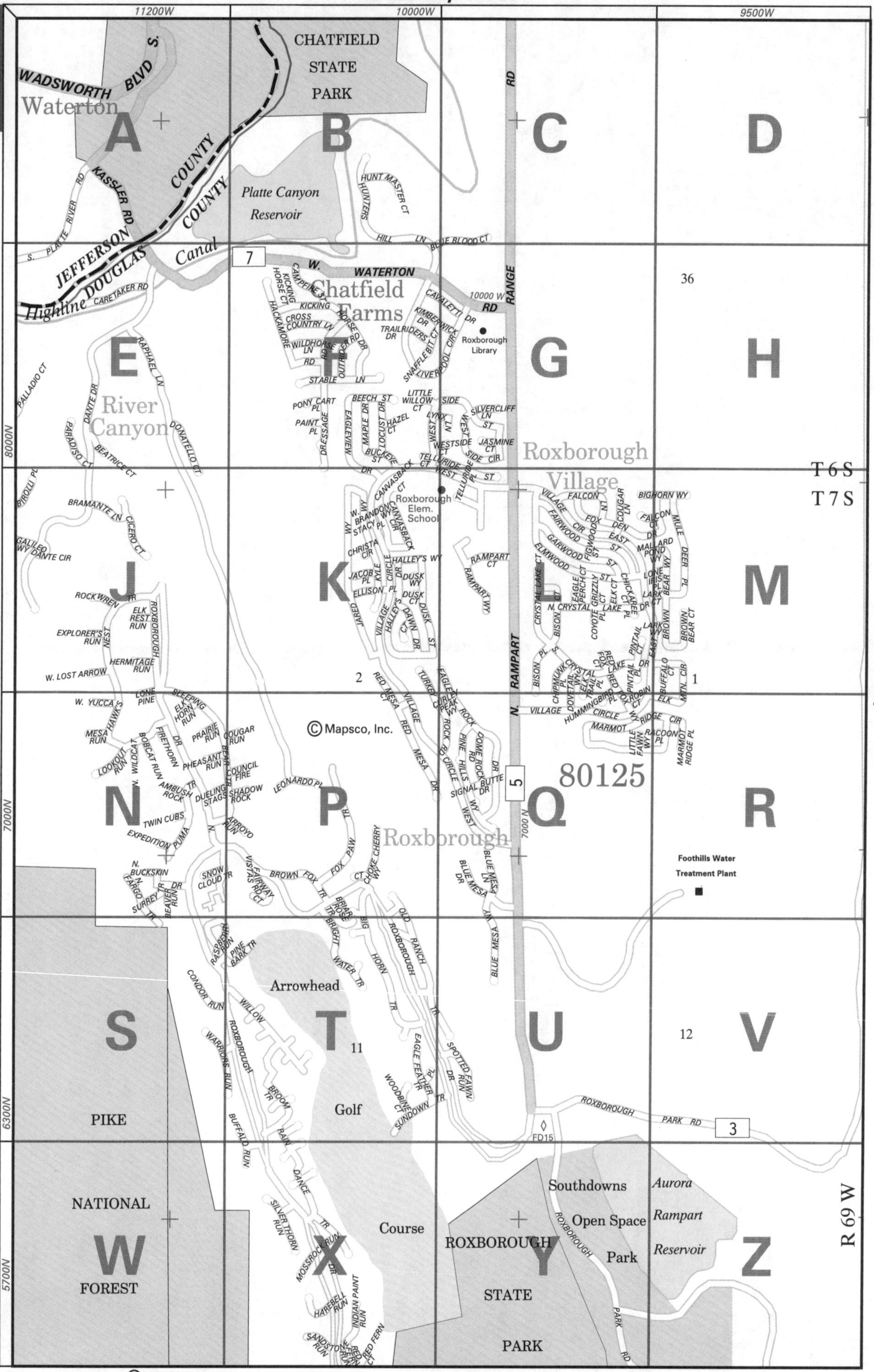

▼ See Map 845 ▼

0 ¼ ½
Miles

▲ See Map 406 ▲

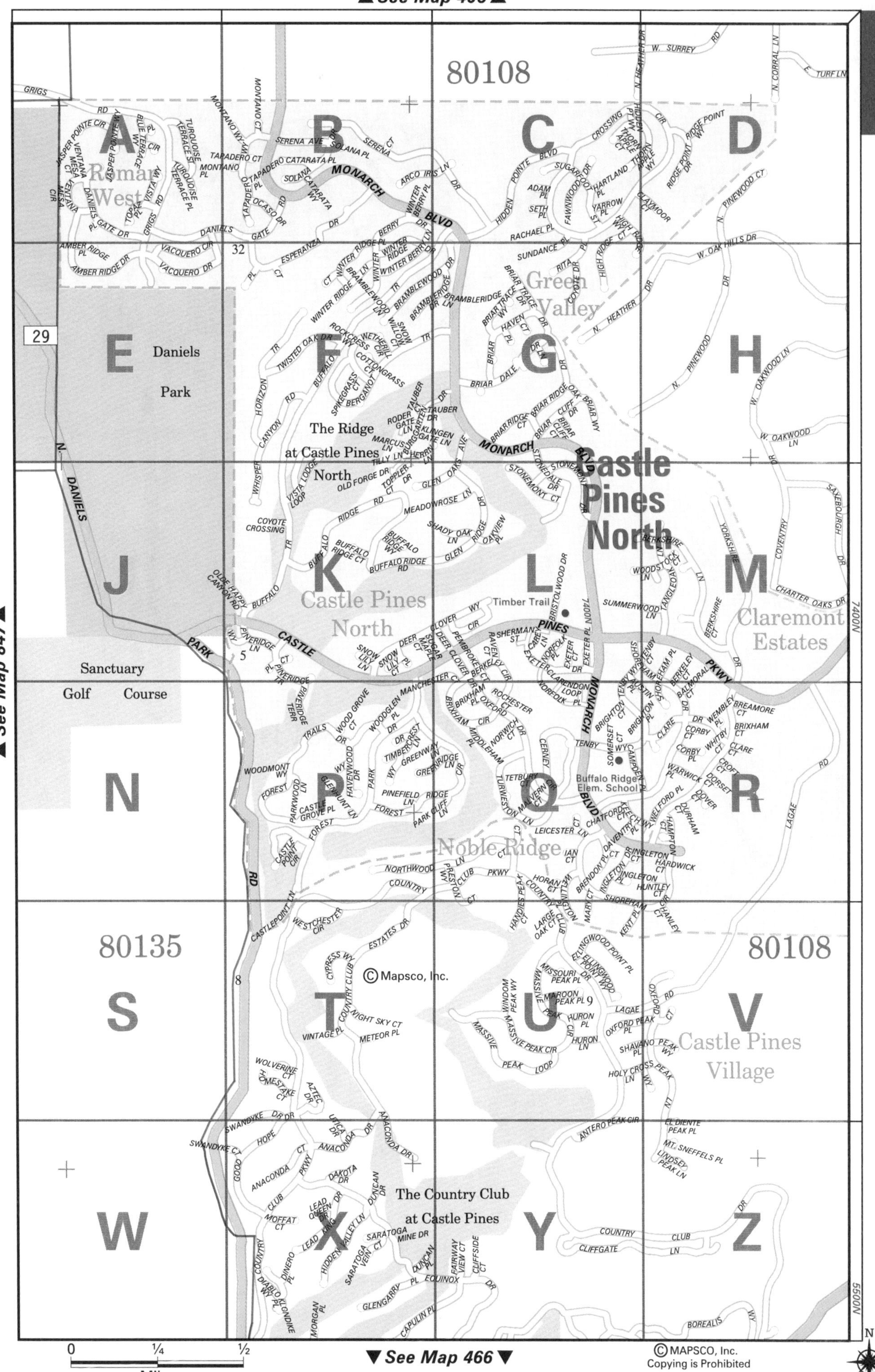

◀ See Map 847 ◀

▶ See Map 848 ▶

0 ¼ ½
Miles

▼ See Map 466 ▼

N

▲See Map 409▲

▲See Map 848▲

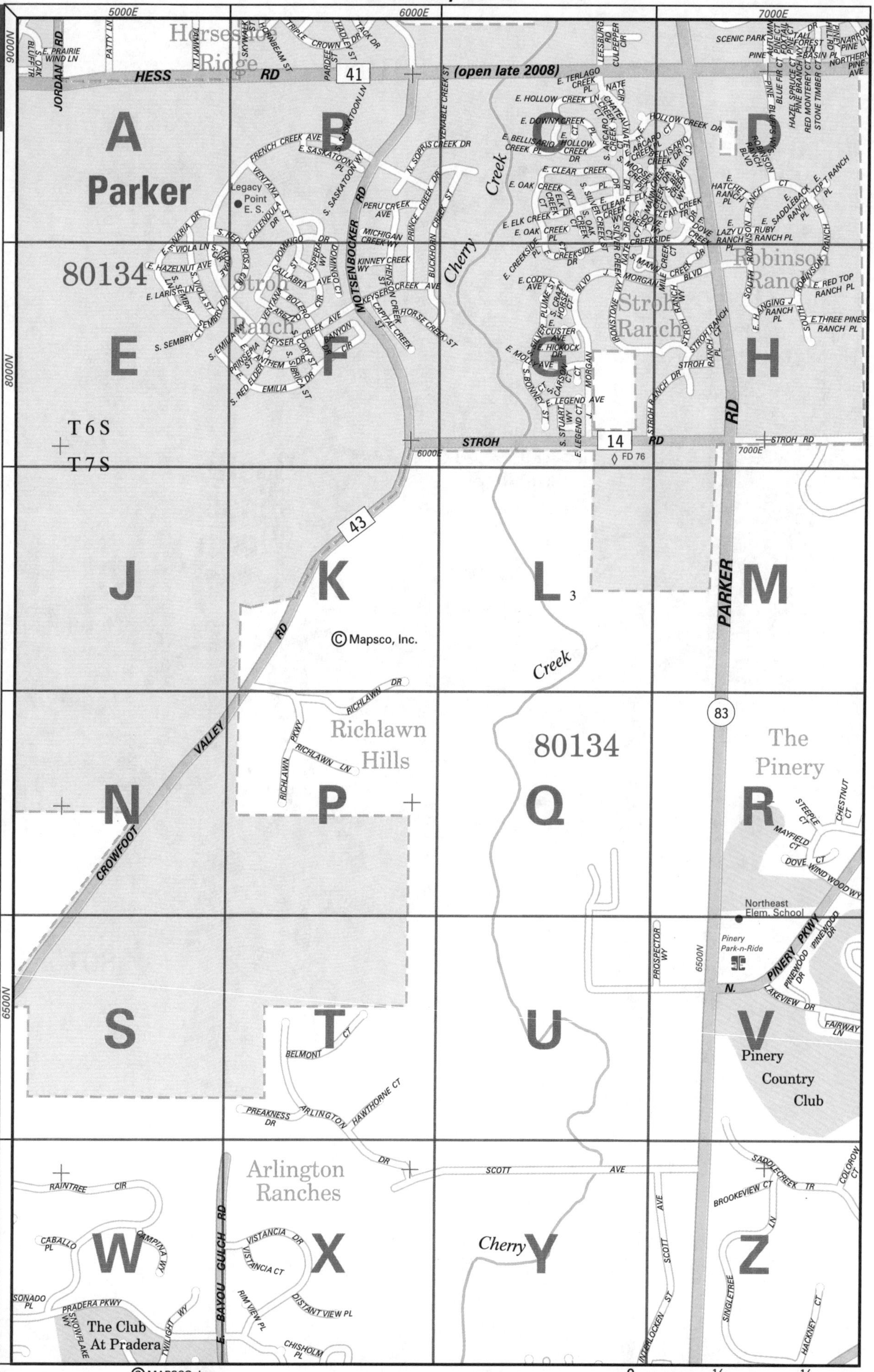
5000E
6000E
7000E
9000N
8000N
6500N
Horseshoe Ridge
HESS RD
41
(open late 2008)
JORDAN RD
Parker
80134
Legacy Point E. S.
Stroh Ranch
Robinson Ranch
MOTSENBOCKER RD
Cherry Creek
T6S
T7S
STROH RD
14
FD 76
43
CROWFOOT VALLEY RD
PARKER RD
83
©Mapsco, Inc.
Richlawn Hills
80134
The Pinery
Northeast Elem. School
Pinery Park-n-Ride
PINERY PKWY
Pinery Country Club
SCOTT AVE
Arlington Ranches
E. BAYOU GULCH RD
Cherry
The Club At Pradera
A
B
C
D
E
F
G
H
J
K
L
M
N
P
Q
R
S
T
U
V
W
X
Y
Z

▼See Map 469▼

0 ¼ ½
Miles

▲ See Map 410 ▲

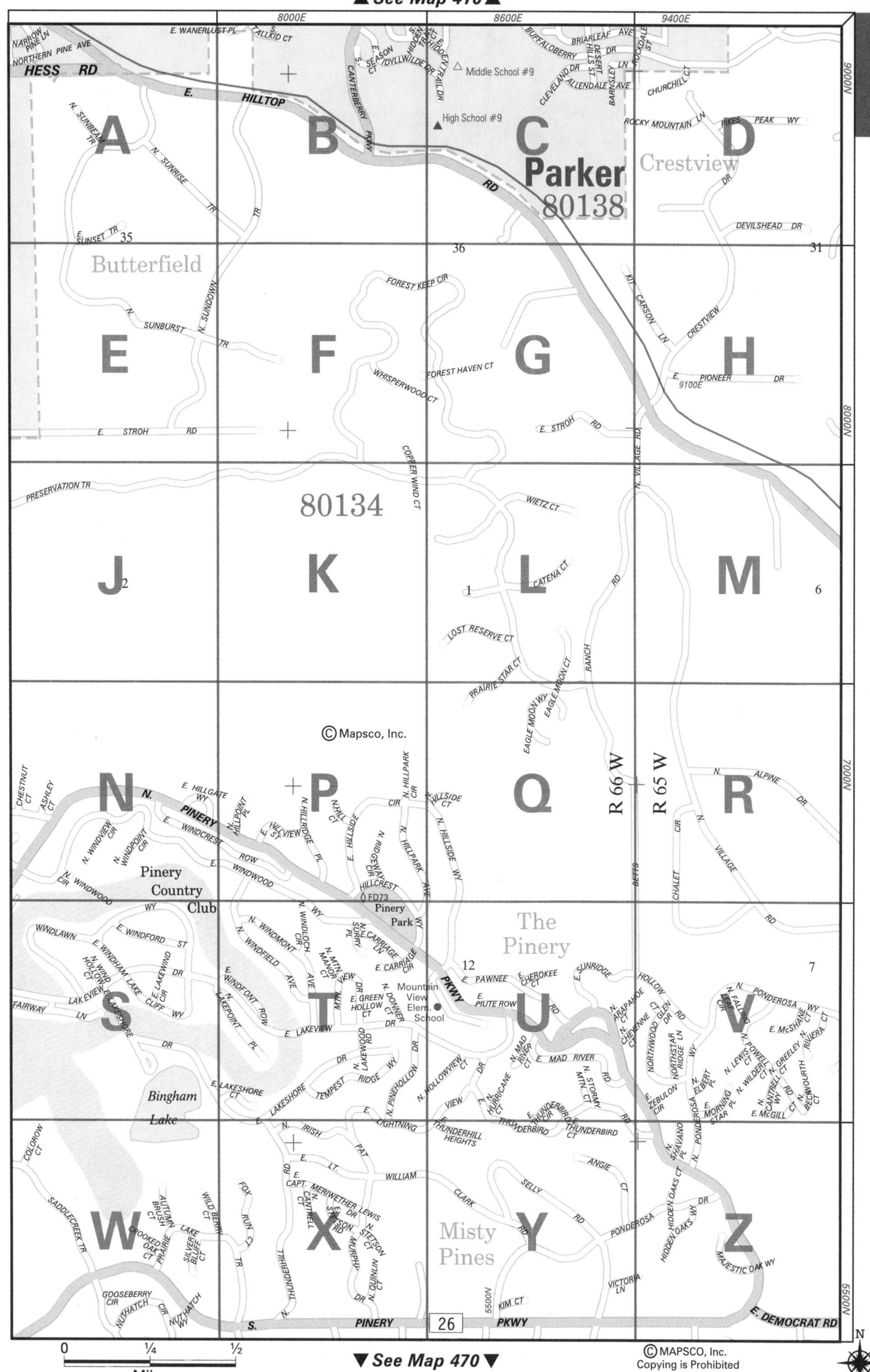

▲ See Map 441 ▲

▼ See Map 470 ▼

0 1/4 1/2
Miles

▲ See Map 411 ▲

▲ See Map 440 ▲

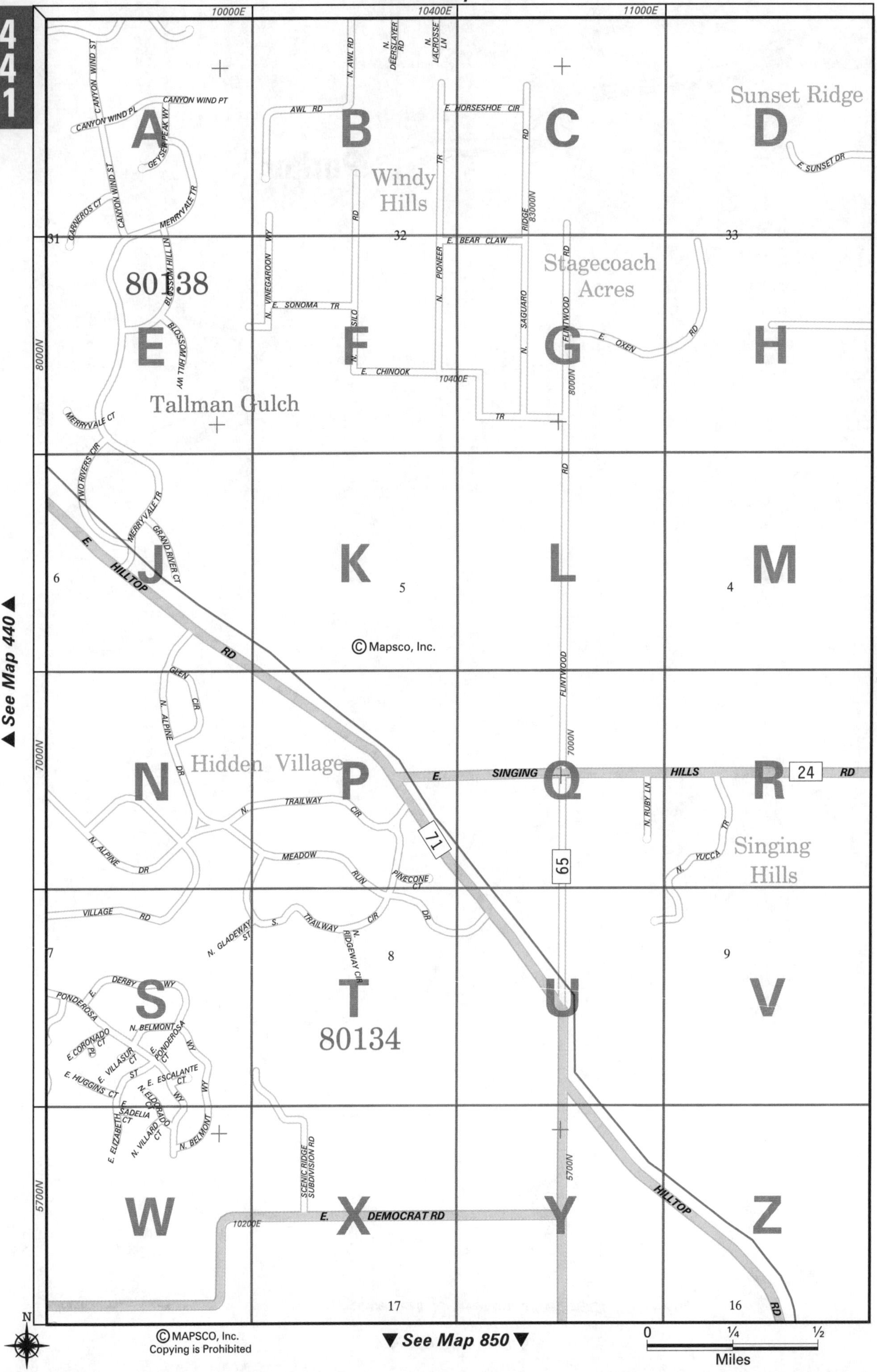

▲ See Map 850 ▲

▼ See Map 850 ▼

▲ See Map 436 ▲

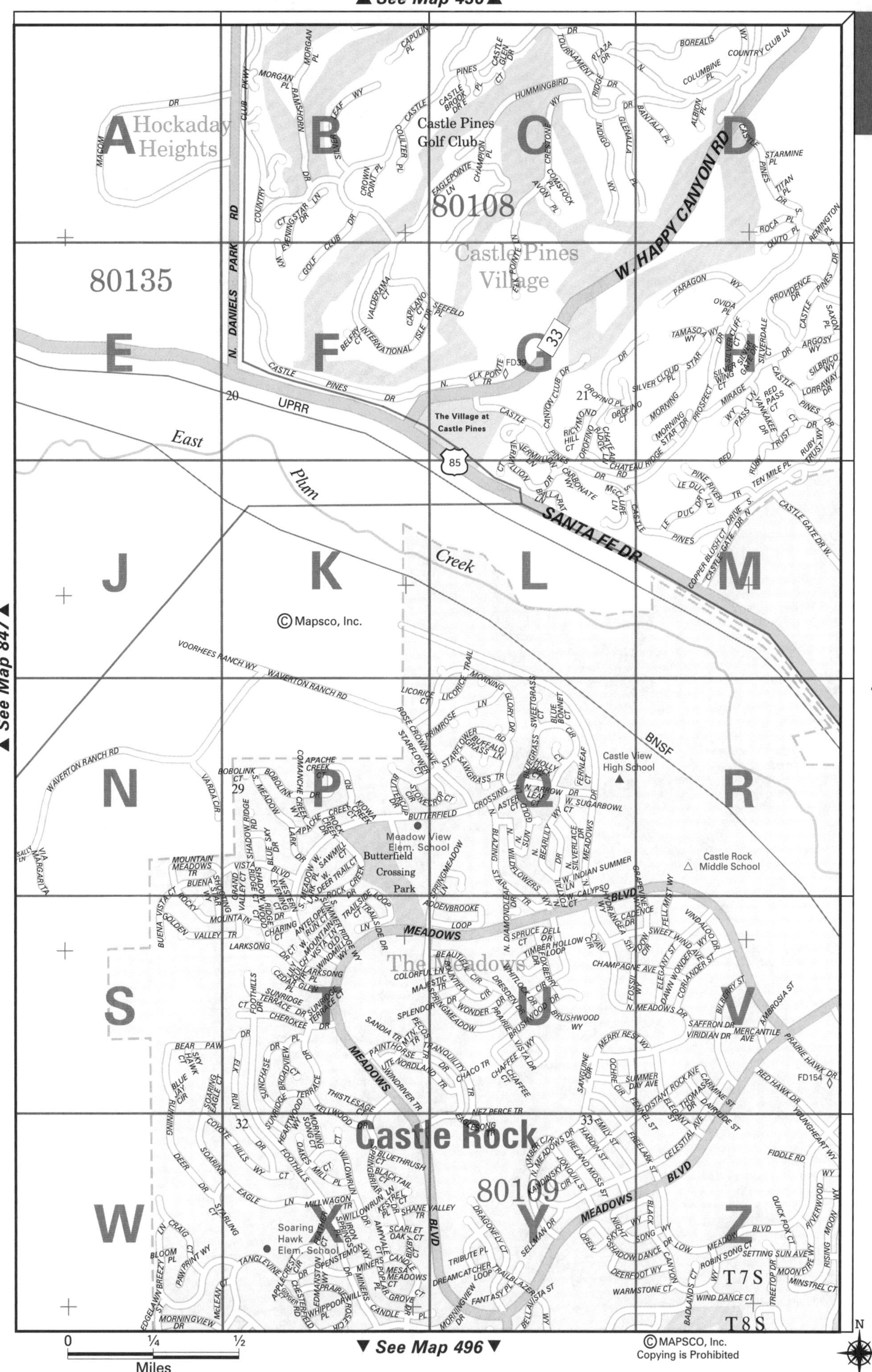

◄ See Map 847 ►

◄ See Map 467 ►

▼ See Map 496 ▼

▲ See Map 848 ▲

▲ See Map 466 ▲

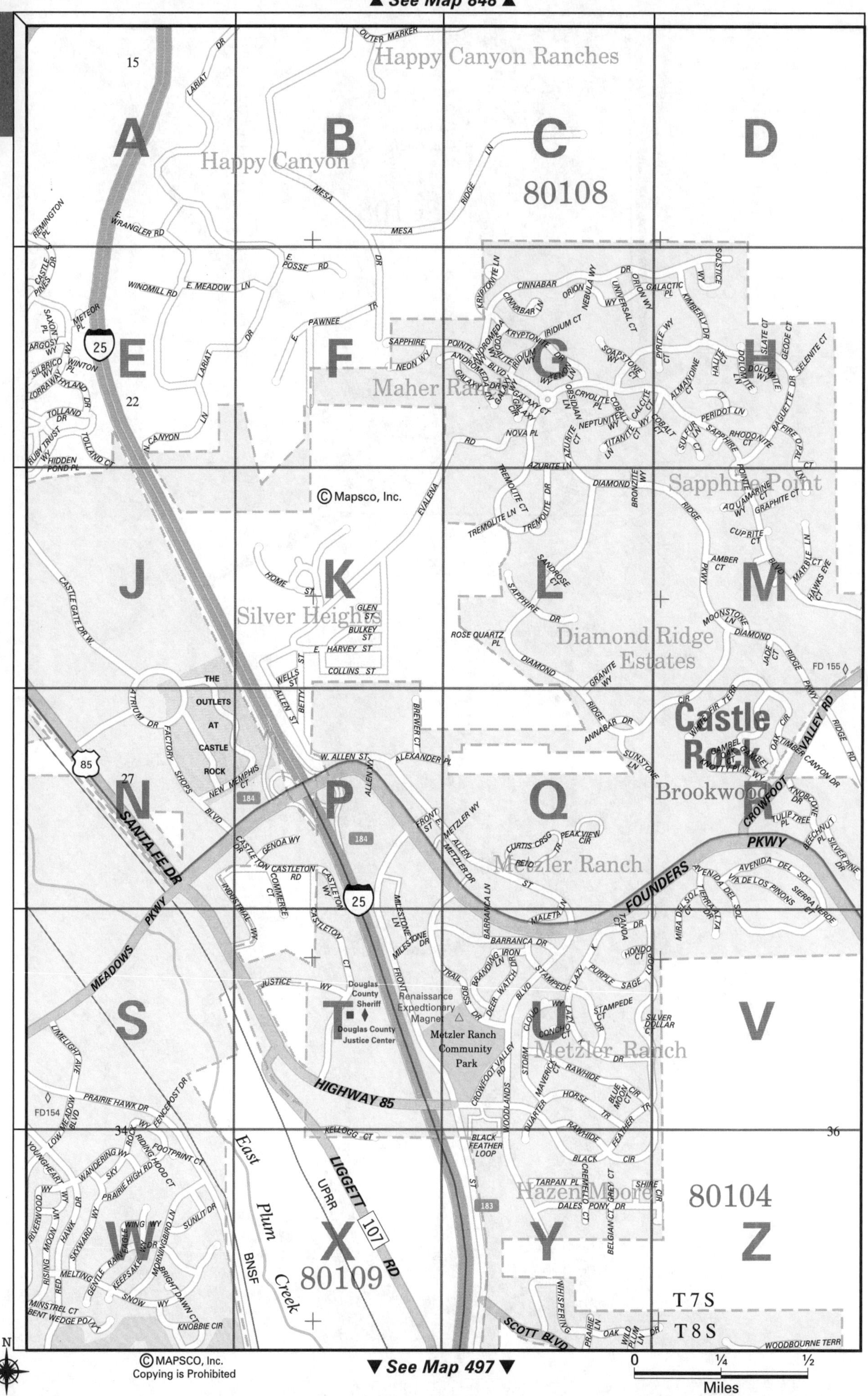

▼ See Map 497 ▼

0 ¼ ½
Miles

▲See Map 848▲

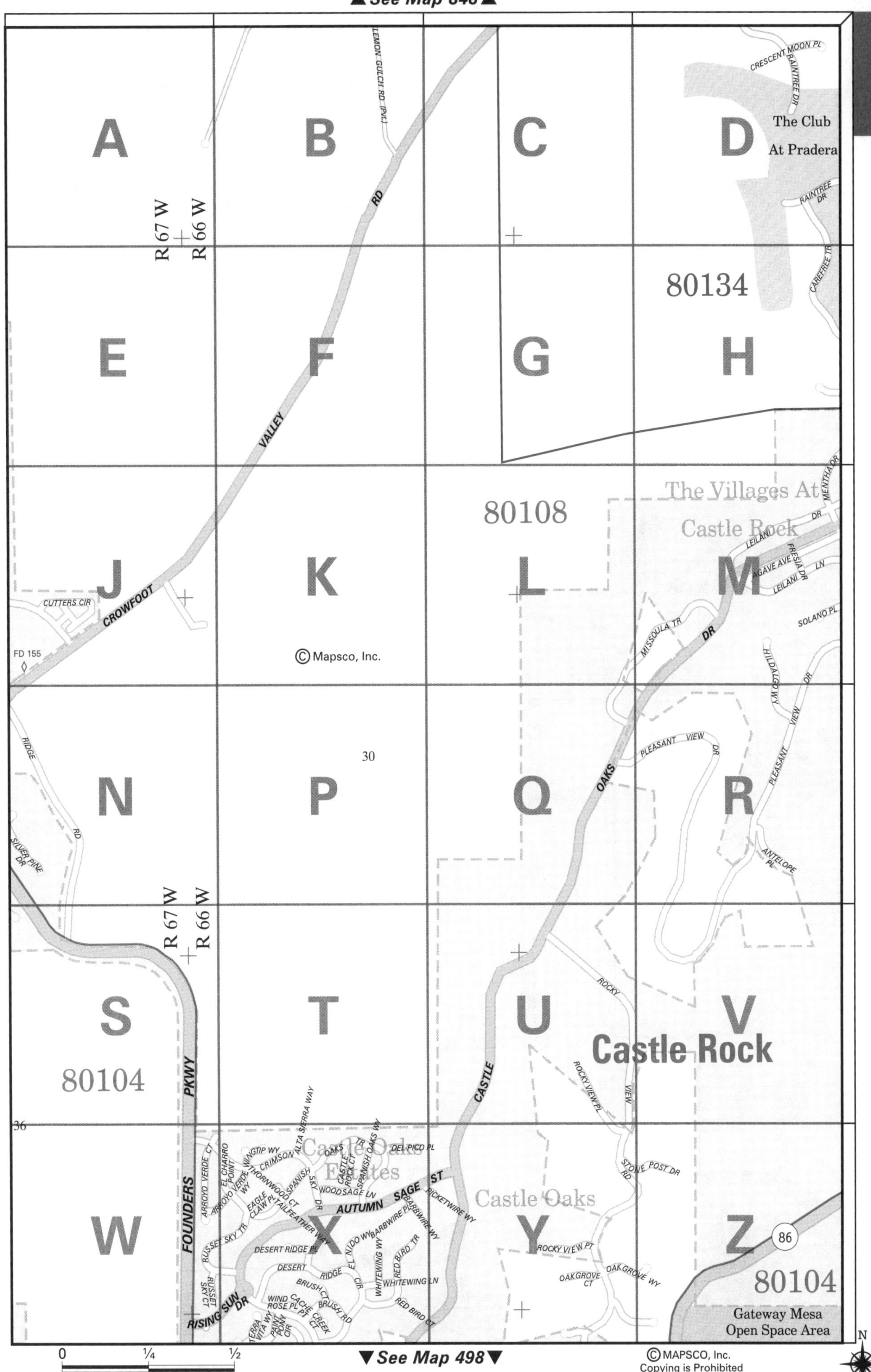

▲See Map 469▲

0 ¼ ½
Miles

▼See Map 498▼

▲ See Map 439 ▲

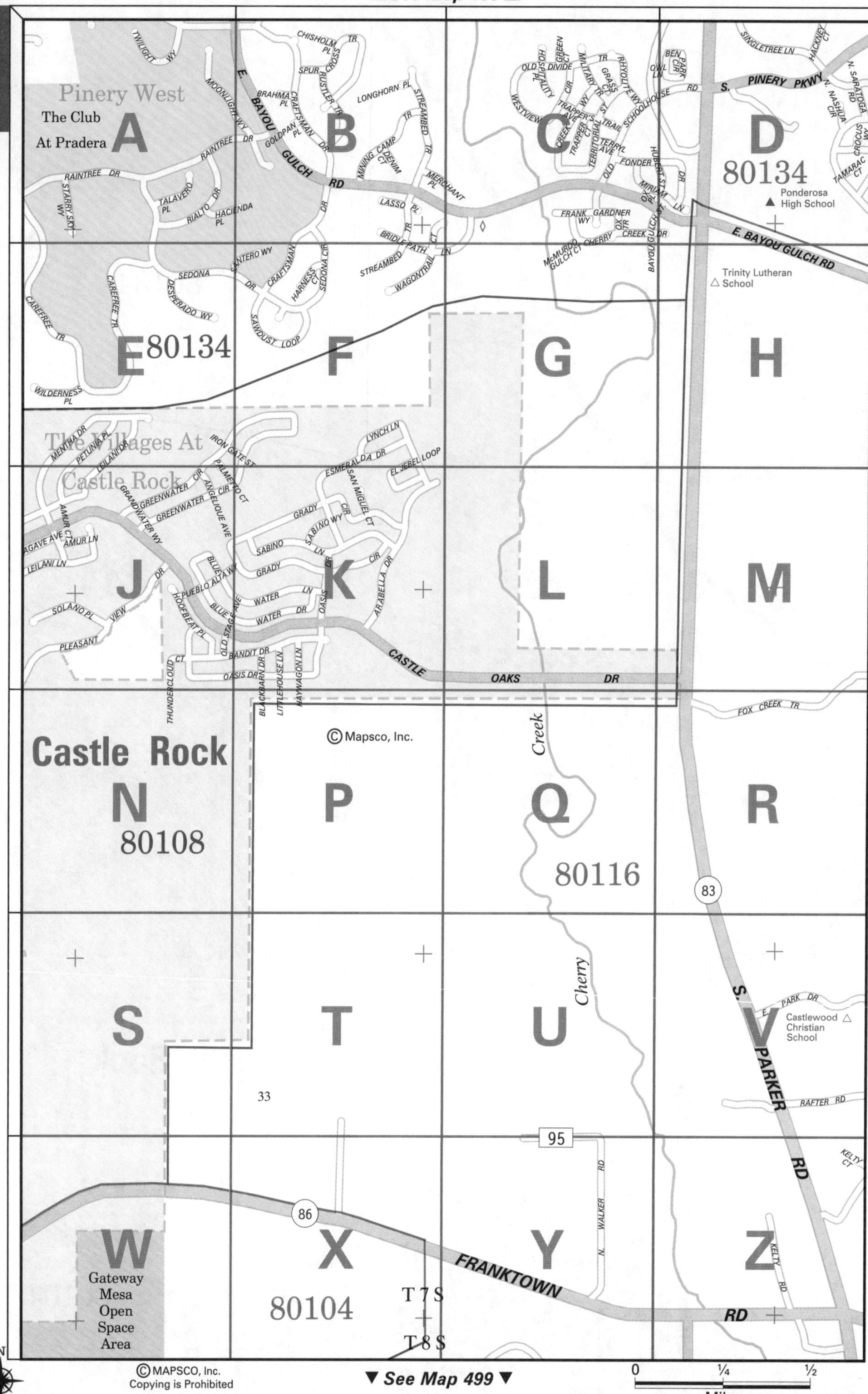

▲ See Map 468 ▲

▼ See Map 499 ▼

0 ¼ ½
Miles

▲ See Map 440 ▲

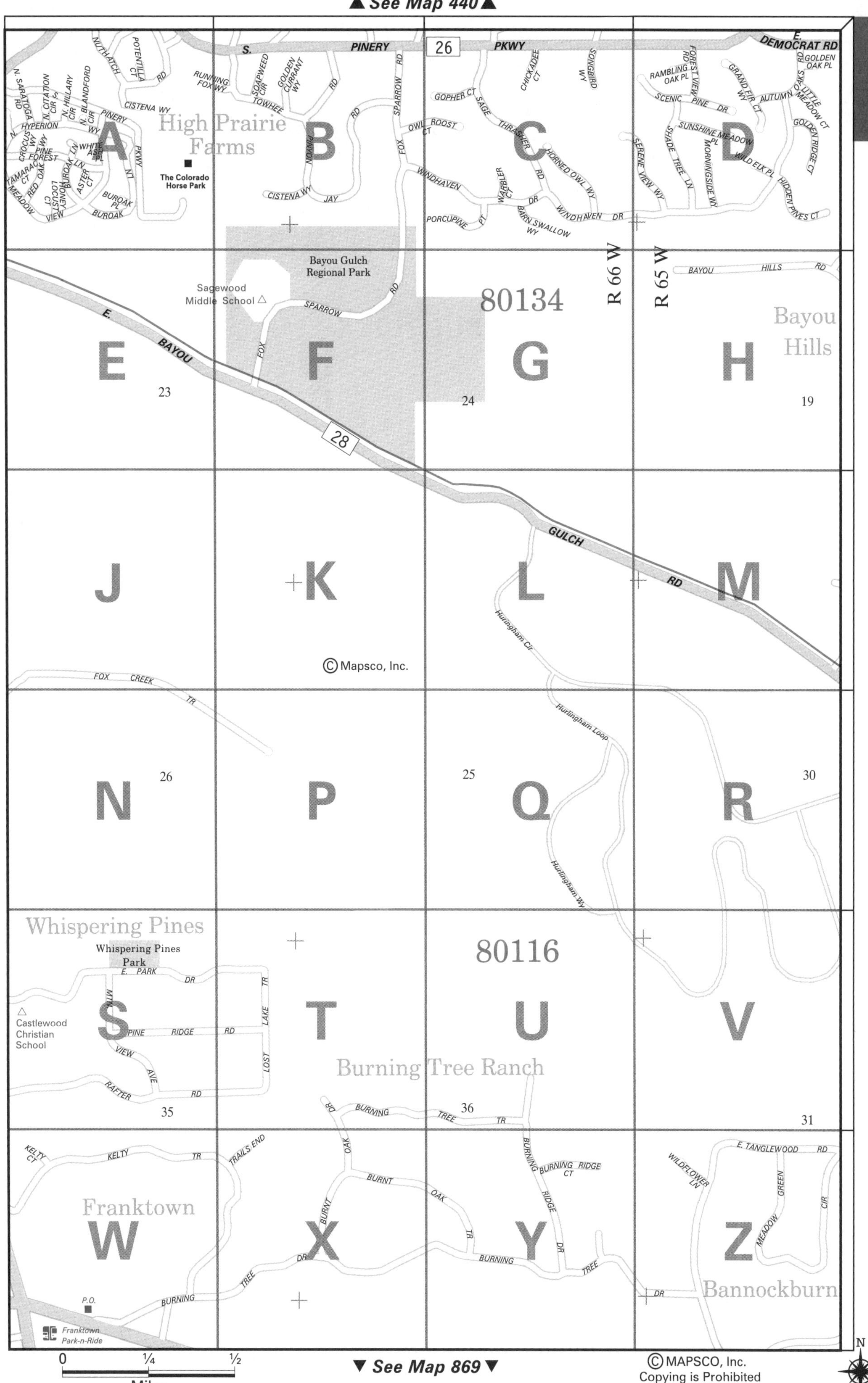

▲ See Map 850 ▲

0 ¼ ½
Miles

▼ See Map 869 ▼

▲ See Map 466 ▲

▲ See Map 867 ▲

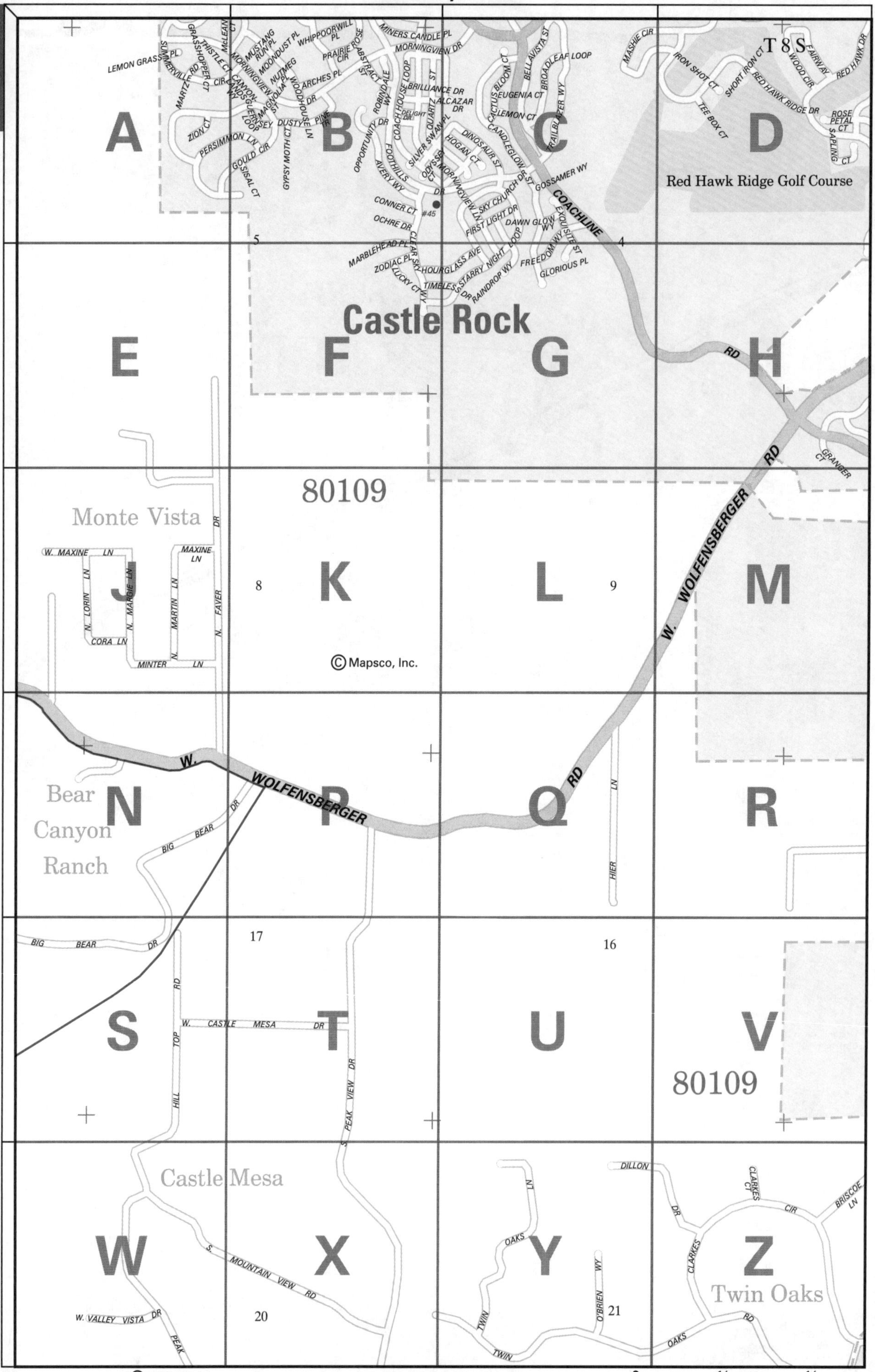

▼ See Map 867 ▼

0 ¼ ½
Miles

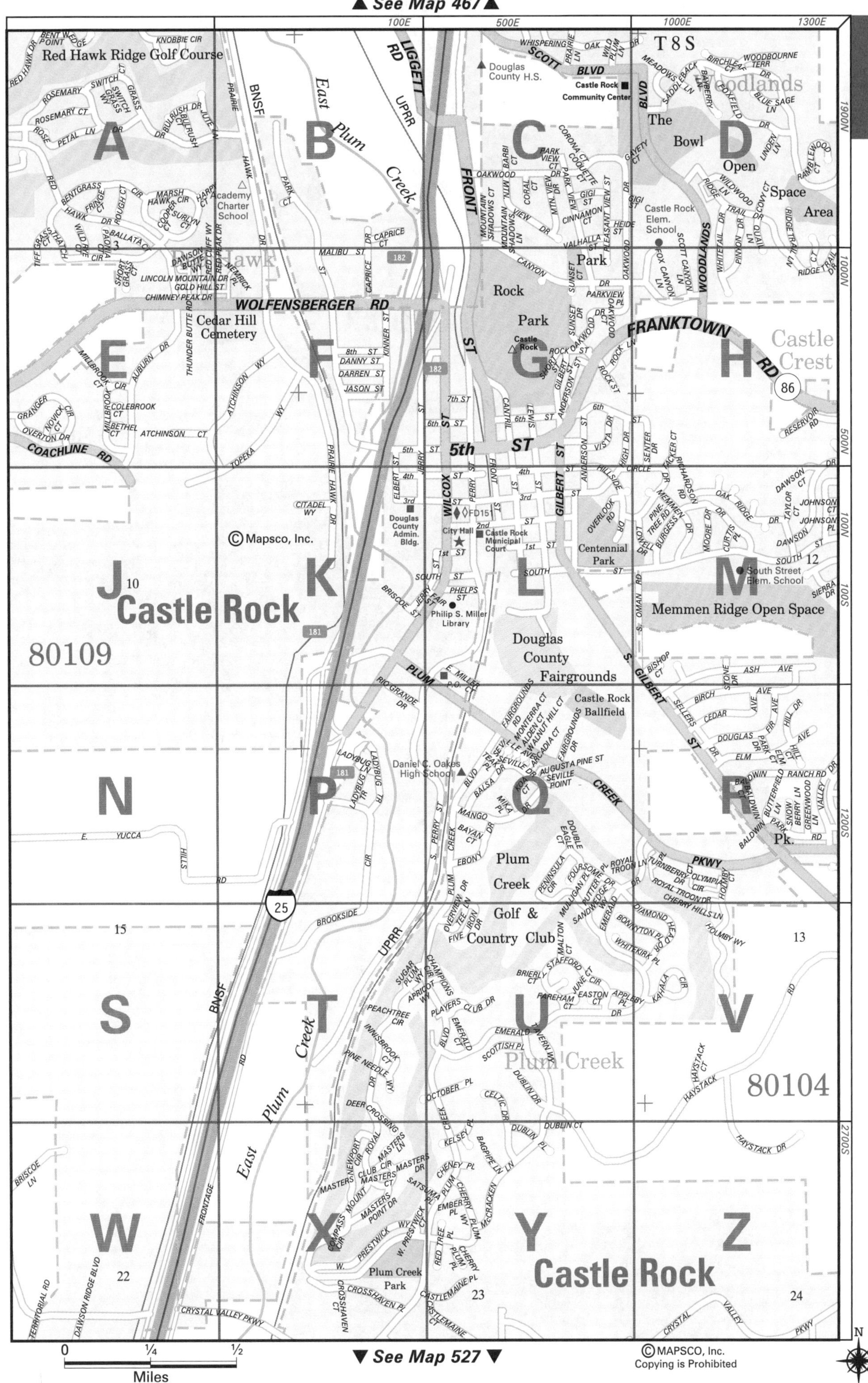
▲ See Map 467 ▲
100E
500E
1000E
1300E
1900N
1000N
500N
100N
100S
1200S
2700S
T8S
Red Hawk Ridge Golf Course
Douglas County H.S.
Castle Rock Community Center
Woodlands
The Bowl
Open Space Area
Academy Charter School
Castle Rock Elem. School
Rock Park
Cedar Hill Cemetery
WOLFENSBERGER RD
FRANKTOWN RD
Castle Crest
5th ST
Douglas County Admin. Bldg.
City Hall
Castle Rock Municipal Court
Philip S. Miller Library
Centennial Park
South Street Elem. School
Memmen Ridge Open Space
© Mapsco, Inc.
Castle Rock
80109
Douglas County Fairgrounds
Castle Rock Ballfield
Daniel C. Oakes High School
Plum Creek Golf & Country Club
Plum Creek
Plum Creek Park
80104
East Plum Creek
A B C D E F G H J K L M N P Q R S T U V W X Y Z
▲ See Map 498 ▲
0 1/4 1/2 Miles
▼ See Map 527 ▼

▲ See Map 468 ▲

◄ See Map 497 ◄

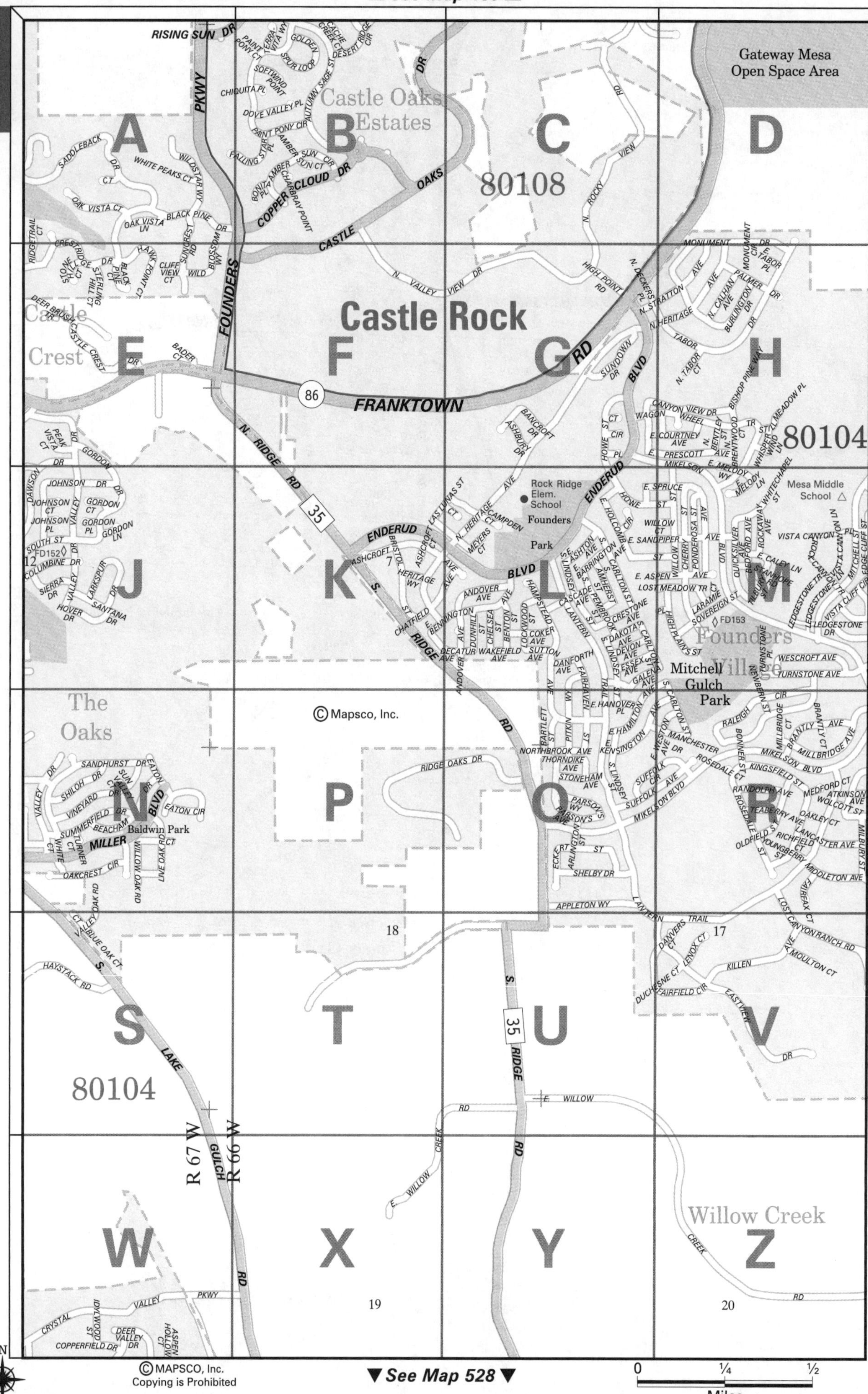

▼ See Map 528 ▼

0 ¼ ½ Miles

▲ See Map 469 ▲

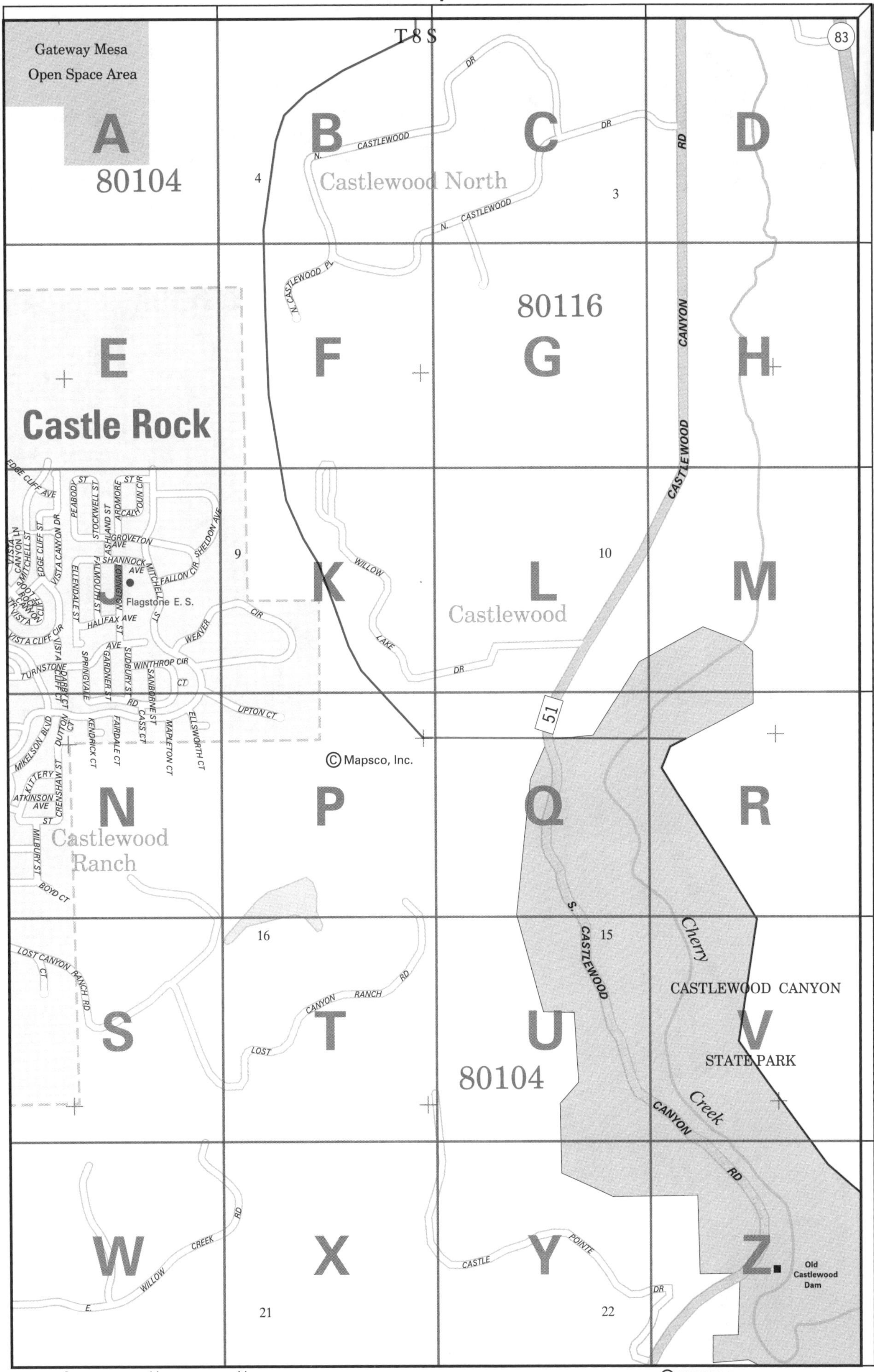
T8S
83
Gateway Mesa
Open Space Area
A
80104
B
N. CASTLEWOOD DR
Castlewood North
C
DR
D
RD
4
3
N. CASTLEWOOD
N. CASTLEWOOD PL
80116
CANYON
E
F
G
H
Castle Rock
CASTLEWOOD
EDGE CLIFF AVE
PEABODY ST
STOCKWELL ST
ASHLAND ST
ARDMORE ST
CALHOUN CIR
GROVETON AVE
SHANNOCK AVE
SHELDON AVE
MITCHELL ST
FALLON CIR
FALMOUTH ST
ELLENDALE ST
VISTA CANYON DR
EDGE CLIFF ST
Flagstone E. S.
HALIFAX AVE
WEAVER
CIR
VISTA CLIFF CIR
TURNSTONE
SPRINGVALE
GARDNER ST
SUDBURY ST
WINTHROP CIR
SANBORNE ST
CT
UPTON CT
CASS CT
MAPLETON CT
ELLSWORTH CT
KENDRICK CT
FAIRDALE CT
MIKELSON BLVD
DUTTON CT
KITTERY
ATKINSON AVE
CRENSHAW ST
MILBURY ST
BOYD CT
9
10
K
WILLOW
LAKE
DR
L
Castlewood
M
51
© Mapsco, Inc.
N
Castlewood
Ranch
P
Q
R
16
15
S. CASTLEWOOD
Cherry
Creek
CASTLEWOOD CANYON
STATE PARK
LOST CANYON RANCH RD
CT
S
CANYON RANCH RD
LOST
T
U
80104
V
CANYON
RD
W
E. WILLOW CREEK RD
X
CASTLE POINTE DR
Y
Z
Old
Castlewood
Dam
21
22
N

0 ¼ ½
Miles

▼ See Map 869 ▼

▲ See Map 869 ▶

▲ See Map 497 ▲

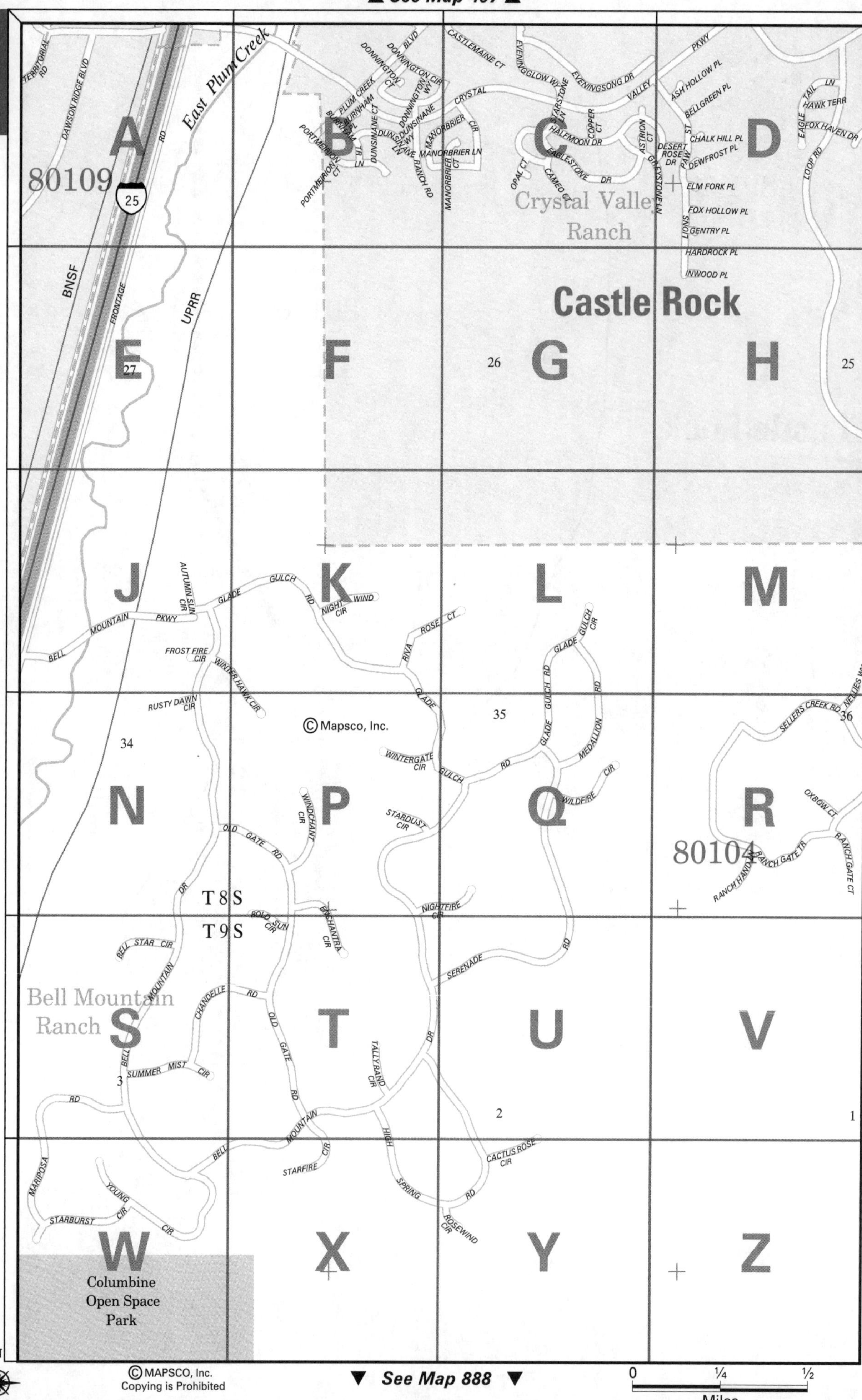

▲ See Map 867 ▲

▼ See Map 888 ▼

▲ See Map 498 ▲

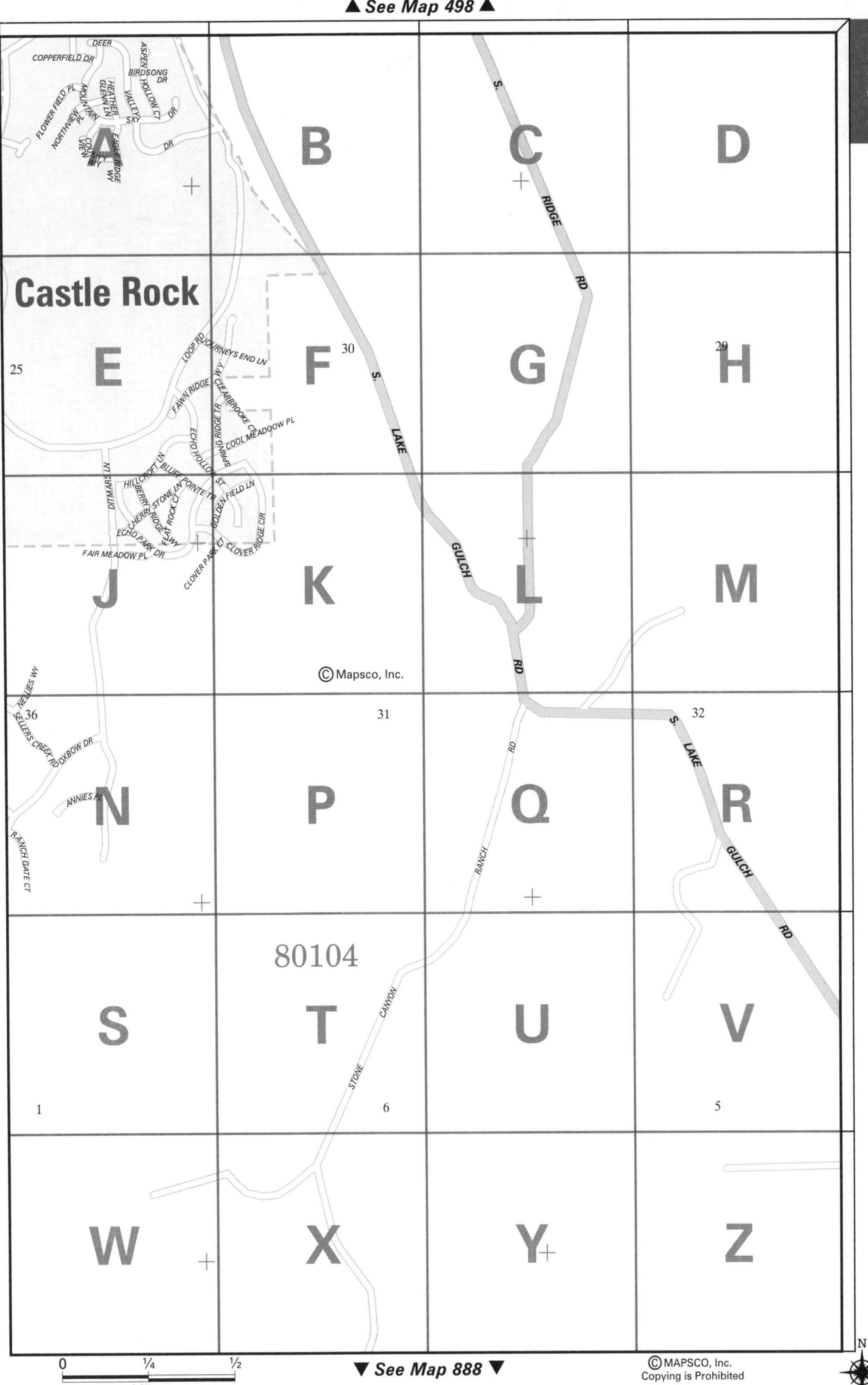

▲ See Map 869 ▲

▼ See Map 888 ▼

See Northern Colorado Atlas

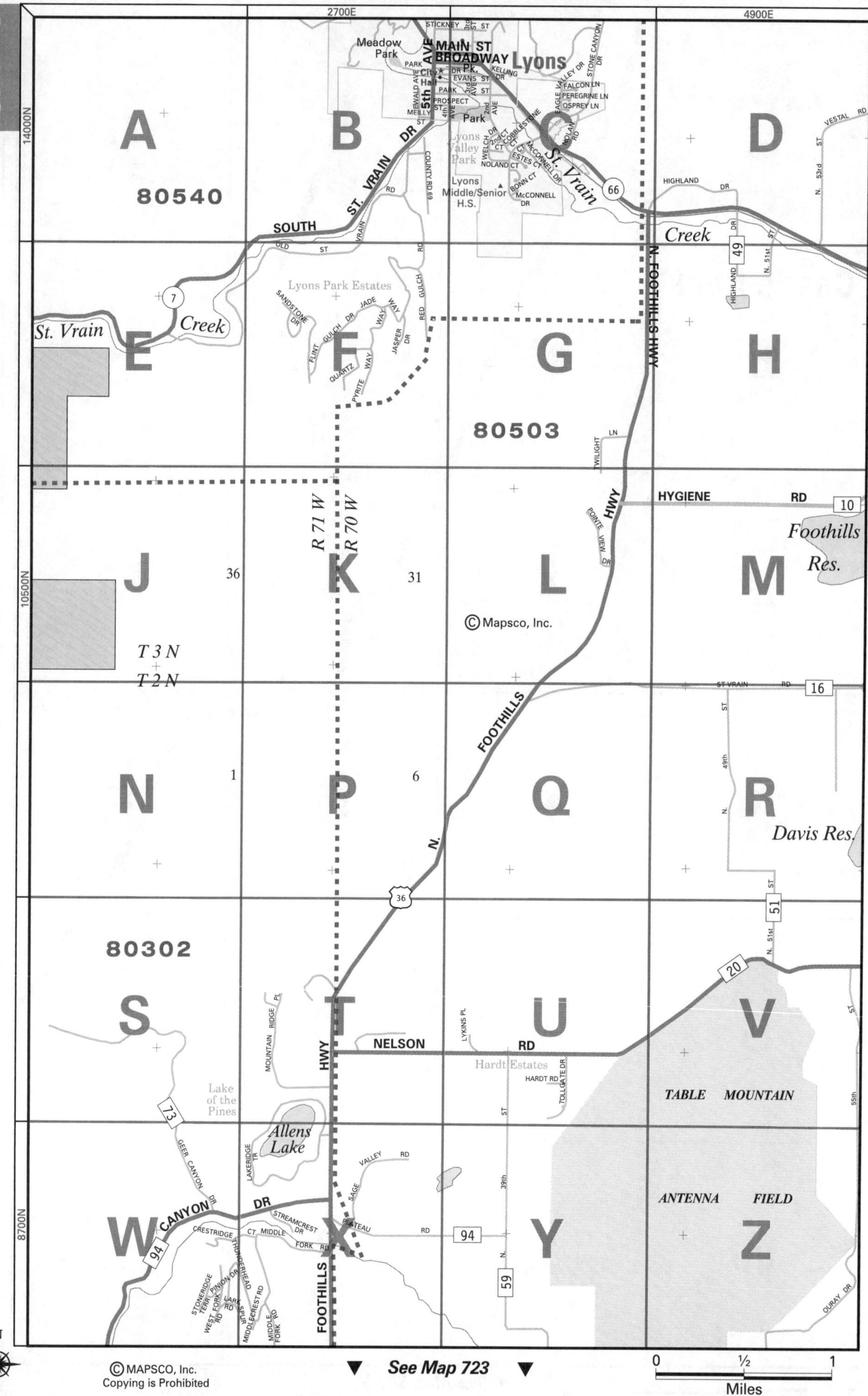

See Map 723

▲ See Northern Colorado Atlas ▲

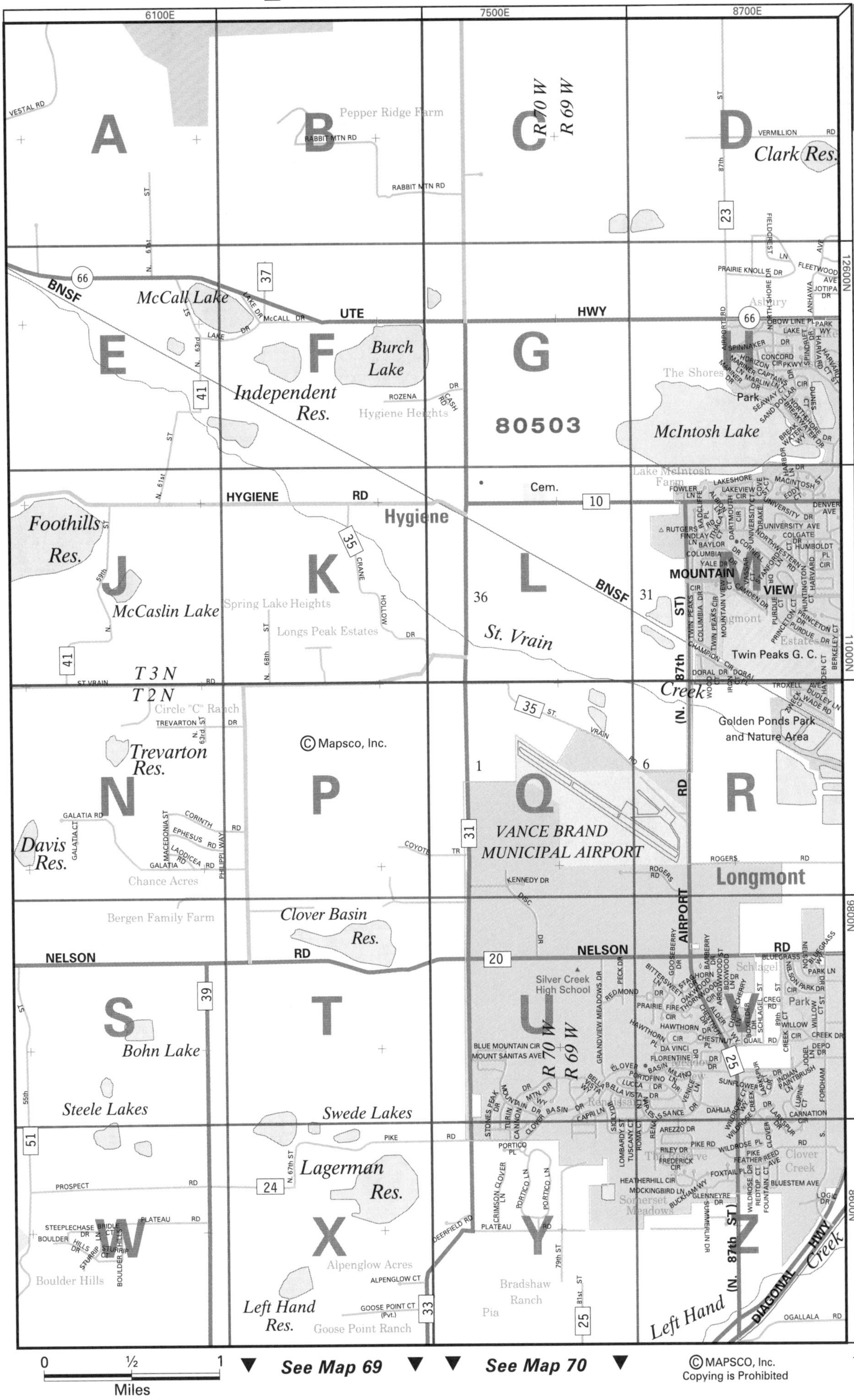

6100E
7500E
8700E

A
VESTAL RD
61st ST

B
Pepper Ridge Farm
RABBIT MTN RD
RABBIT MTN RD

C
R 70 W
R 69 W

D
87th ST
VERMILLION RD
Clark Res.
23

E
66
BNSF
McCall Lake
N. 61st ST
N. 63rd ST
LAKE DR
McCALL DR
41

F
37
Burch Lake
Independent Res.
ROZENA
CASH RD
Hygiene Heights

G
UTE HWY
80503

H
FIELDCREST LN
PRAIRIE KNOLL DR
FLEETWOOD AVE
JOTIPA DR
ANHAWA AVE
Asbury
AIRPORT RD
NORTHSHORE DR
66
OBOW LINE PL
PARK LAKE DR
SPINNAKER DR
HORIZON CIR
CONCORD PKWY
MARINER CAPTAINS LN
MARLIN LN
The Shores
Park
SEAWAY CT
SAND DOLLAR
NORTHSHORE BREAKWATER DR
DUNES
HARVARD
McIntosh Lake
BREAKWATER DR
HARBOR LN
12600N

J
HYGIENE RD
N. 61st ST
Foothills Res.
N. 59th ST
McCaslin Lake
41
ST VRAIN RD
T 3 N
T 2 N

K
Hygiene
35
CRANE HOLLOW DR
Spring Lake Heights
Longs Peak Estates
N. 68th ST

L
Cem.
10
36
BNSF
31
St. Vrain

M
Lake McIntosh Farm
FOWLER
LAKESHORE
LAKEVIEW CIR
MACINTOSH ST
UNIVERSITY DR
DENVER AVE
RUTGERS
FINDLAY
BAYLOR
COLUMBIA
YALE DR
UNIVERSITY AVE
COLGATE
HUMBOLDT PL
NORTHWESTERN RD
MOUNTAIN VIEW
Longmont
TWIN PEAKS CIR
PRINCETON DR
PURDUE DR
Estates
Twin Peaks G. C.
CHAMPION CIR
DORAL DR
BERKELEY CT
11000N

N
Circle "C" Ranch
TREVARTON DR
N. 63rd ST
Trevarton Res.
GALATIA RD
CORINTH
EPHESUS RD
LAODICEA RD
MACEDONIA ST
GALATIA CT
Davis Res.
GALATIA
PHILIPPI WAY
Chance Acres

P
© Mapsco, Inc.
COYOTE TR

Q
35 ST. VRAIN RD
1
6
31
VANCE BRAND MUNICIPAL AIRPORT
KENNEDY DR
DISC DR

R
Creek
(N. 87th ST)
TROXELL AVE
DUDLEY LN
WADE RD
Golden Ponds Park and Nature Area
ROGERS RD
ROGERS RD
Longmont
AIRPORT RD

Bergen Family Farm
Clover Basin Res.
NELSON RD
20
NELSON RD
9800N

S
55th ST
39
Bohn Lake
Steele Lakes

T
Swede Lakes

U
Silver Creek High School
R 70 W
R 69 W
GRANDVIEW MEADOWS DR
PECK DR
REDMOND
BLUE MOUNTAIN CIR
MOUNT SANITAS AVE
GOOSEBERRY
BITTERSWEET LN
PRAIRIE FIRE CIR
HAWTHORN CIR
DA VINCI
FLORENTINE DR
PORTOFINO DR
CLOVER BASIN DR
MILANO LN
BELLA VISTA DR
LUCCA DR
VENICE LN
CAPRI LN
RENAISSANCE
STONES PEAK DR
MOUNTAIN DR
TURIN DR
CANNON WY
CLOVER BASIN DR
Renaissance

V
BARBERRY
STAGHORN
OAKWOOD
THORNWOOD
BOXWOOD
CHERRY
ALDER
CHESTNUT PL
BOXELDER
SCHLAGEL ST
QUAIL RD
Schlagel
BLUEGRASS
PARK LN
PARK DR
CREG RD
Park
WILLOW
CREEK DR
DEPO DR
25
SUNFLOWER
INDIAN PAINTBRUSH
LUPINE CT
FORDHAM
CARNATION
WILDROSE CT
LARKSPUR

W
51
PROSPECT RD
PLATEAU RD
STEEPLECHASE DR
BRIDLE CT
BOULDER HILLS DR
STURRIP CT
BOULDER HILLS
Boulder Hills

X
PIKE RD
N. 67th ST
Lagerman Res.
24
Alpenglow Acres
ALPENGLOW CT
Left Hand Res.
GOOSE POINT CT (Pvt.)
Goose Point Ranch
33
DEERFIELD RD

Y
PORTICO PL
CRIMSON CLOVER LN
PORTICO LN
PLATEAU RD
79th ST
Bradshaw Ranch
81st ST
Pia
25

Z
LOMBARDY ST
TUSCANY CT
ROMA CT
SICILY DR
ARIZZO DR
RILEY DR
FREDERICK CIR
HEATHERHILL CIR
MOCKINGBIRD LN
BUCKHAM WY
GLENNEYRE DR
SUMMERLIN DR
The Preserve
Somerset Meadows
PIKE RD
WILDROSE PL
FEATHER REED AVE
FOXTAIL PL
REDTOP CT
FOUNTAIN CT
BLUESTEM AVE
Clover Creek
LOGIC DR
(N. 87th ST)
DIAGONAL HWY
Left Hand Creek
OGALLALA RD
8600N

See Map 11

See Map 41

0 ½ 1
Miles

▼ See Map 69 ▼ ▼ See Map 70 ▼

N

▲ See Northern Colorado Atlas ▲

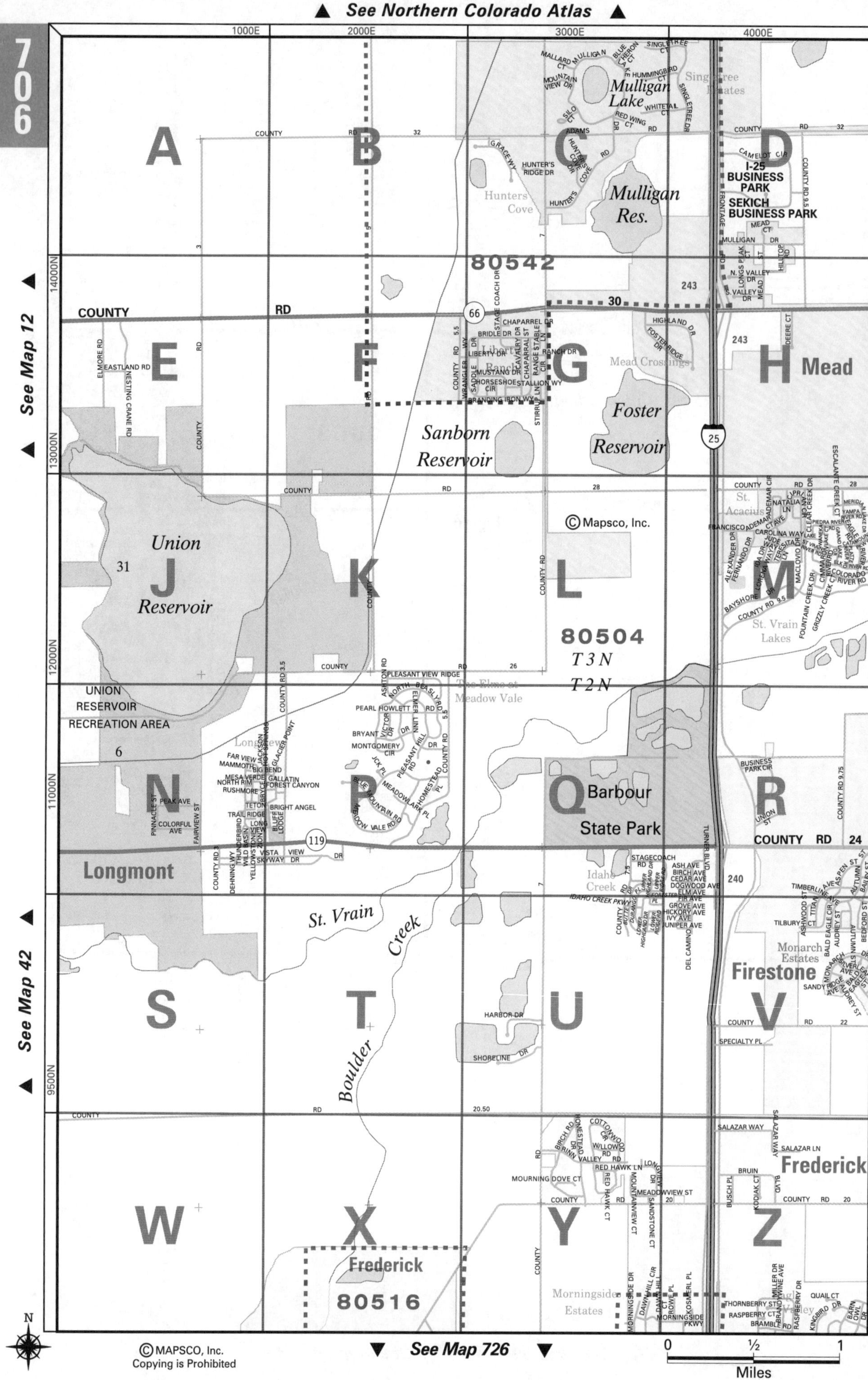

See Map 12

See Map 42

▼ See Map 726 ▼

0 ½ 1
Miles

▲ See Northern Colorado Atlas ▲

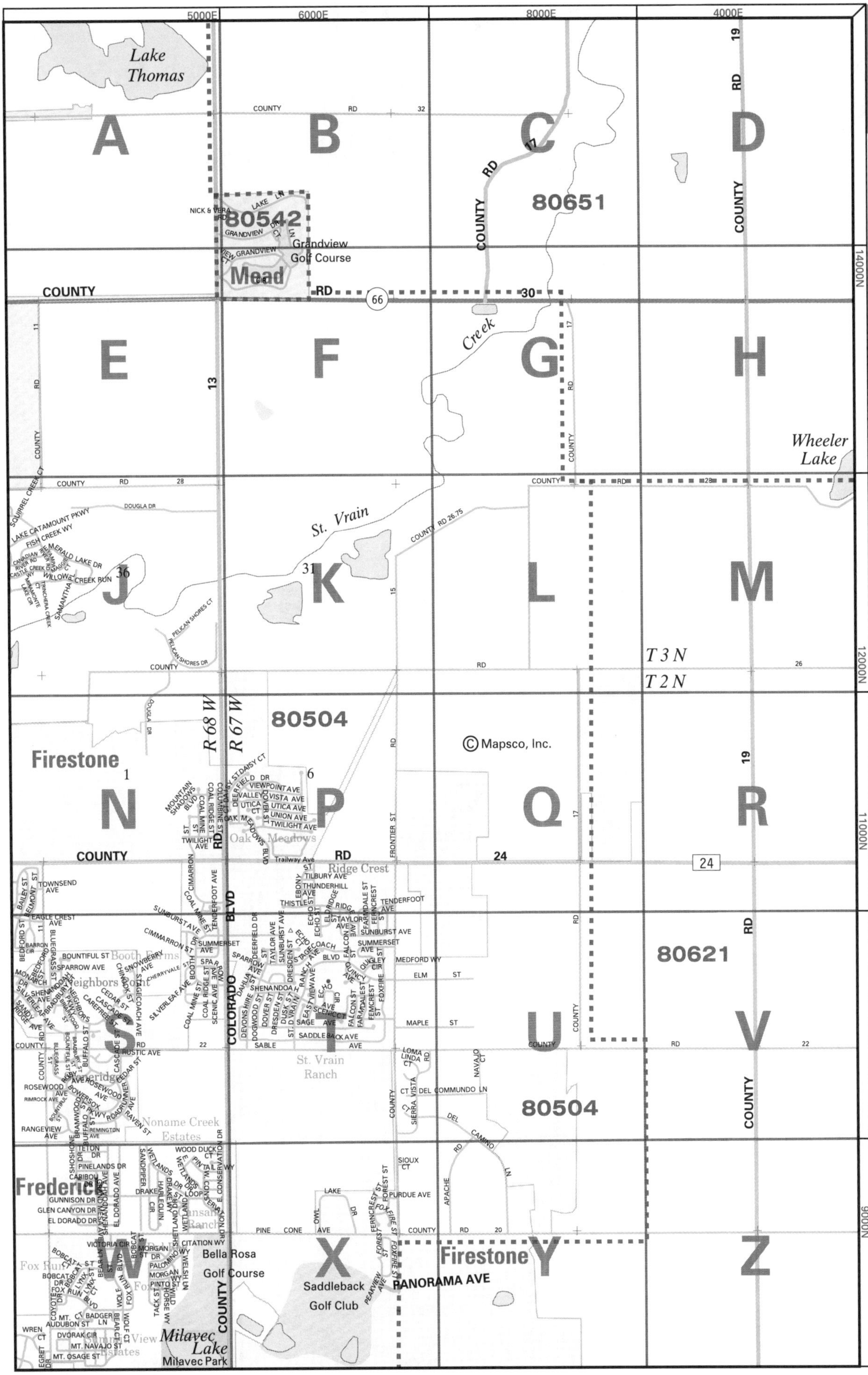

▶ See Map 708 ▶

0 ½ 1
Miles

▼ See Map 727 ▼

N

▲ See Northern Colorado Atlas ▲

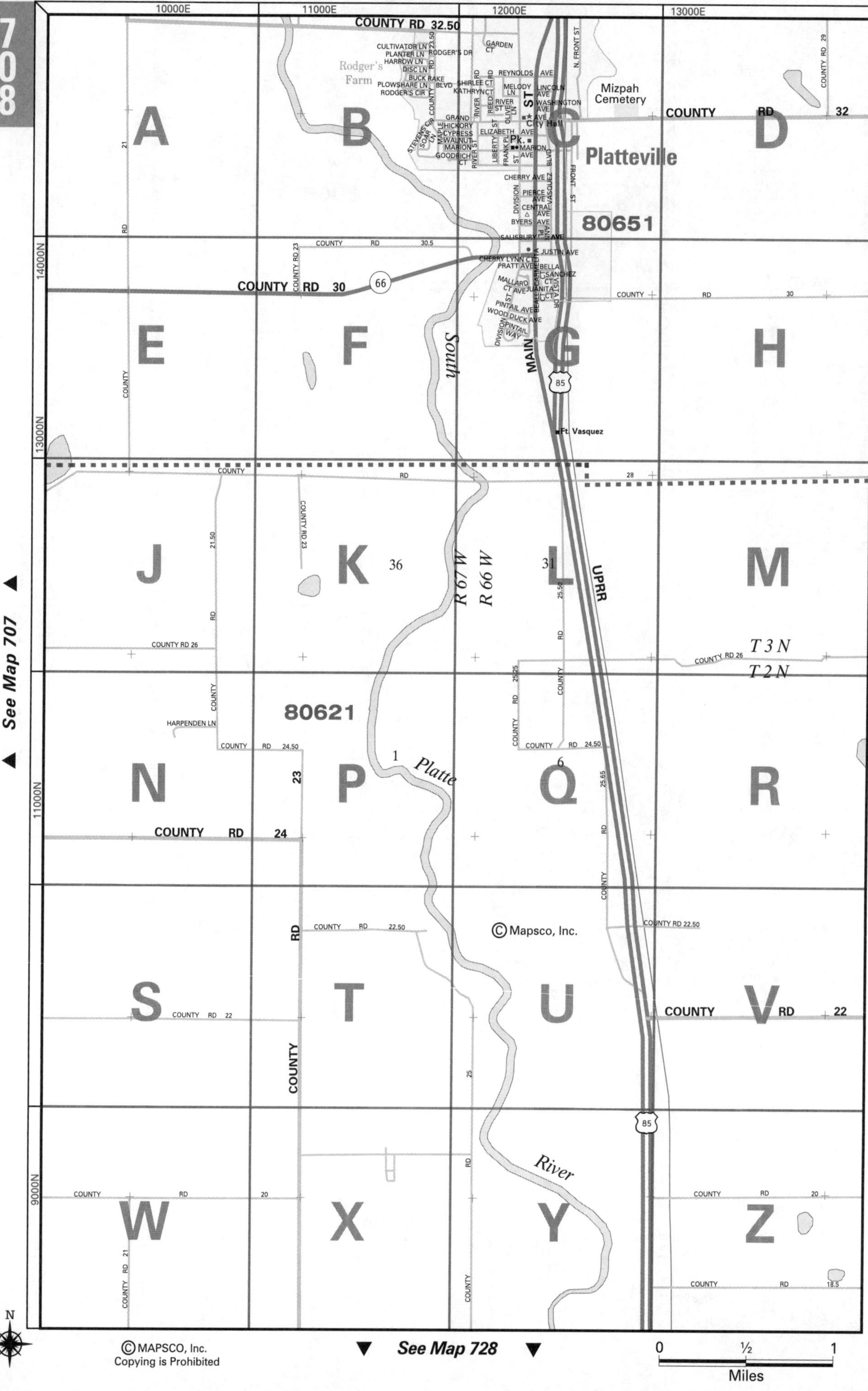

▲ See Map 707 ▲

▼ See Map 728 ▼

0 ½ 1
Miles

▲ See Northern Colorado Atlas ▲

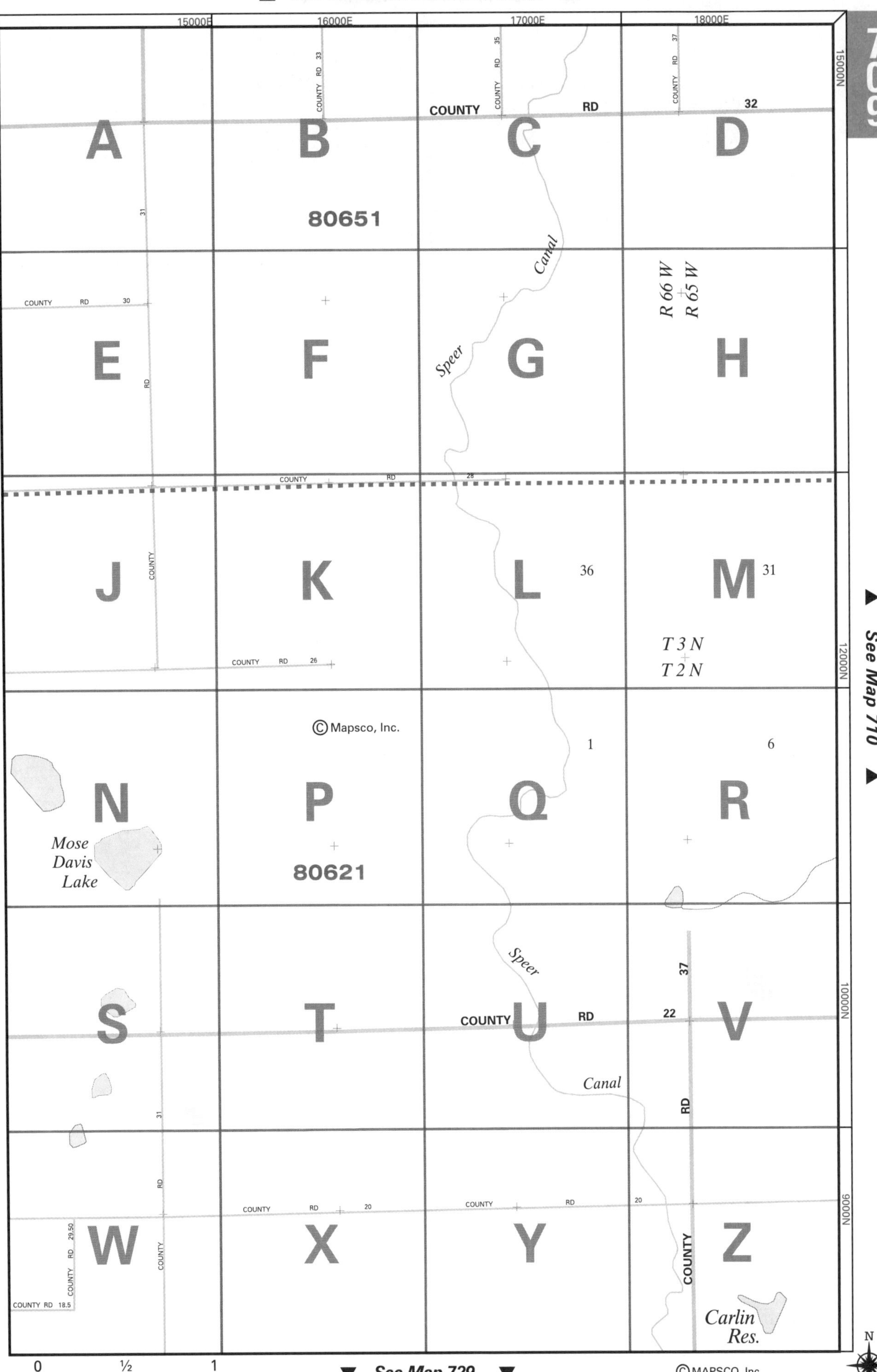

▶ See Map 710 ▶

▼ See Map 729 ▼

▲ See Northern Colorado Atlas ▲

See Map 709

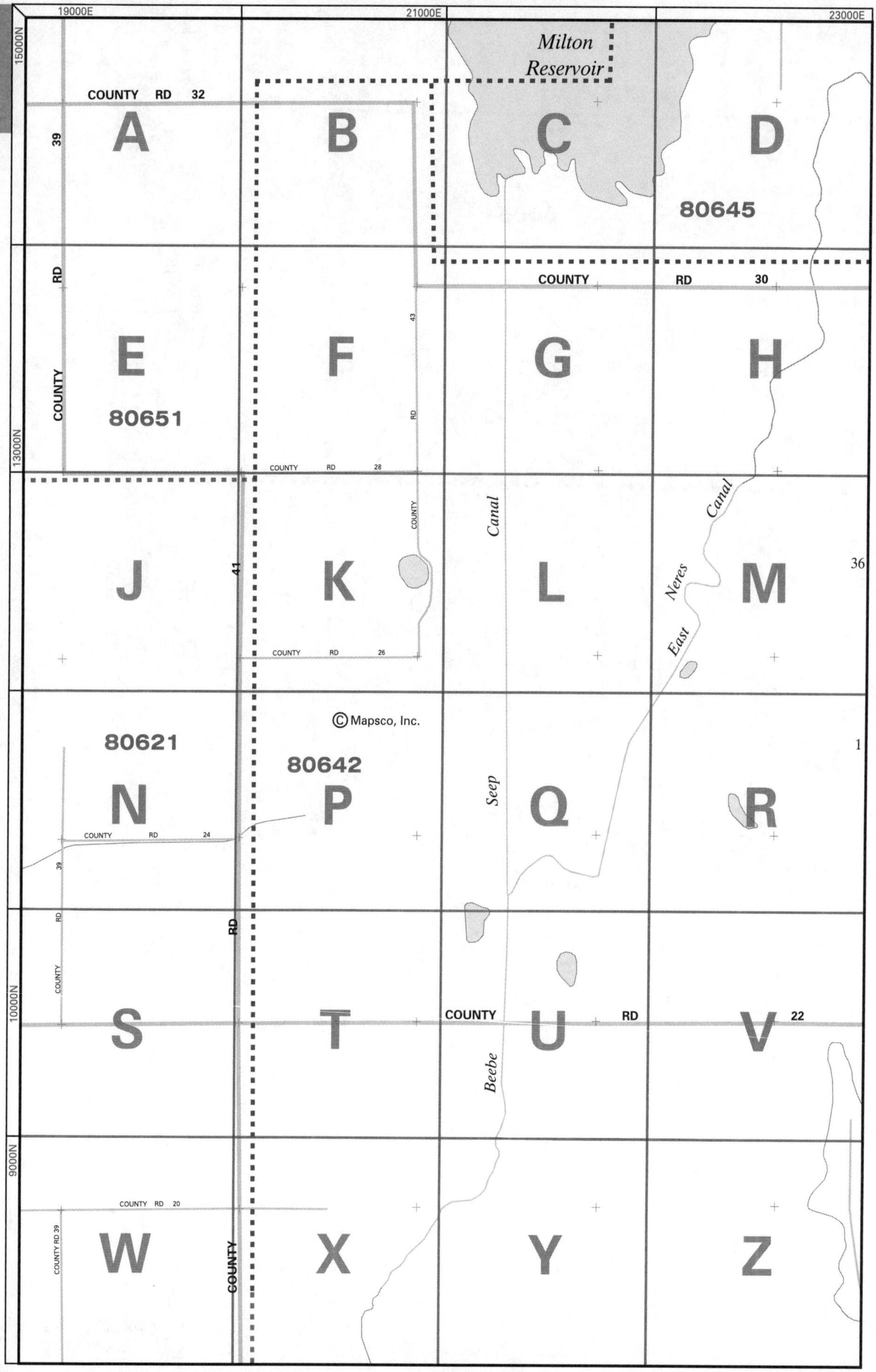

▼ See Map 730 ▼

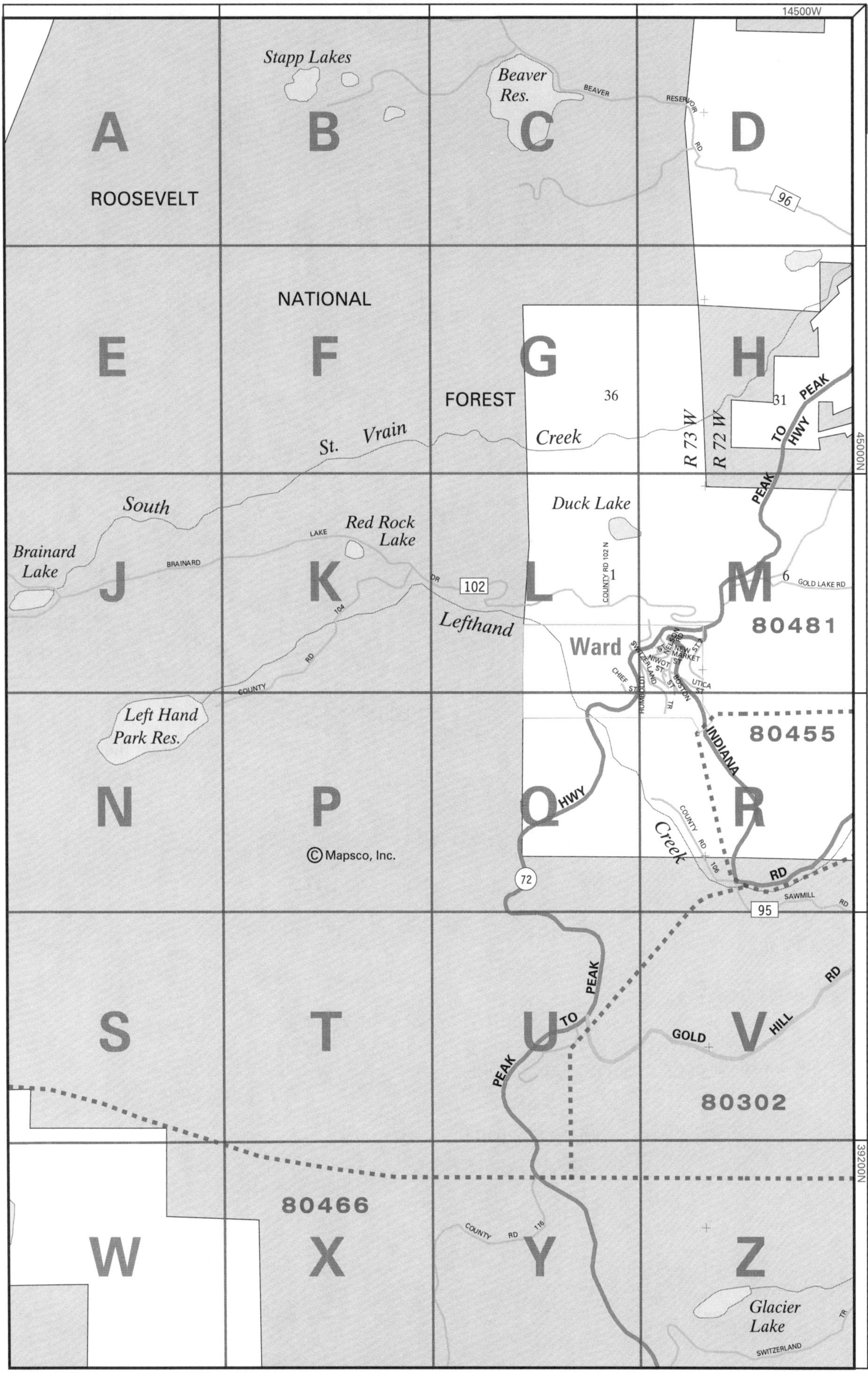

▶ See Map 721 ▶

▼ See Map 740 ▼

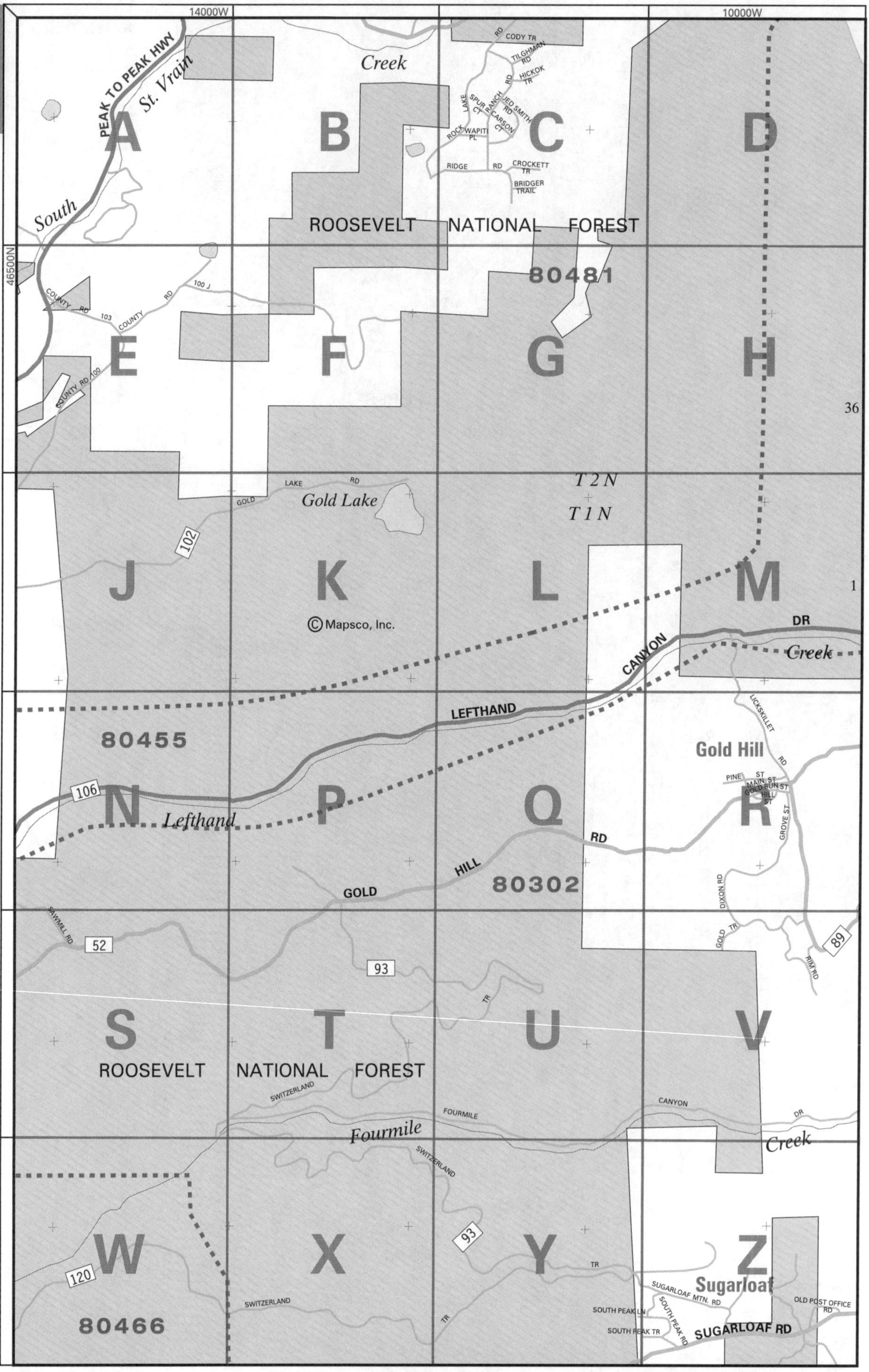

14000W
10000W
46500N

PEAK TO PEAK HWY
St. Vrain
Creek
South
CODY TR
TILGHMAN RD
HICKOK TR
LAKE
SPUR CT
RANCH RD
JED SMITH RD
CARSON CT
ROCK
WAPITI PL
RIDGE RD
CROCKETT TR
BRIDGER TRAIL
ROOSEVELT NATIONAL FOREST
80481
COUNTY RD 103
COUNTY RD 100 J
COUNTY RD 100
36
GOLD LAKE RD
Gold Lake
102
T2N
T1N
1
© Mapsco, Inc.
LEFTHAND CANYON DR
Creek
LICKSKILLET RD
Gold Hill
PINE ST
MAIN ST
GOLD RUN ST
HILL ST
GROVE ST
80455
106
Lefthand
GOLD HILL RD
80302
DIXON RD
GOLD TR
89
RIM RD
SAWMILL RD
52
93
TR
ROOSEVELT NATIONAL FOREST
SWITZERLAND
FOURMILE CANYON DR
Fourmile Creek
SWITZERLAND
93
TR
120
SWITZERLAND
TR
80466
Sugarloaf
SUGARLOAF MTN. RD
SOUTH PEAK LN
SOUTH PEAK RD
SOUTH PEAK TR
SUGARLOAF RD
OLD POST OFFICE RD

A B C D E F G H J K L M N P Q R S T U V W X Y Z

See Map 720
See Map 741

N

0 ½ 1 Miles

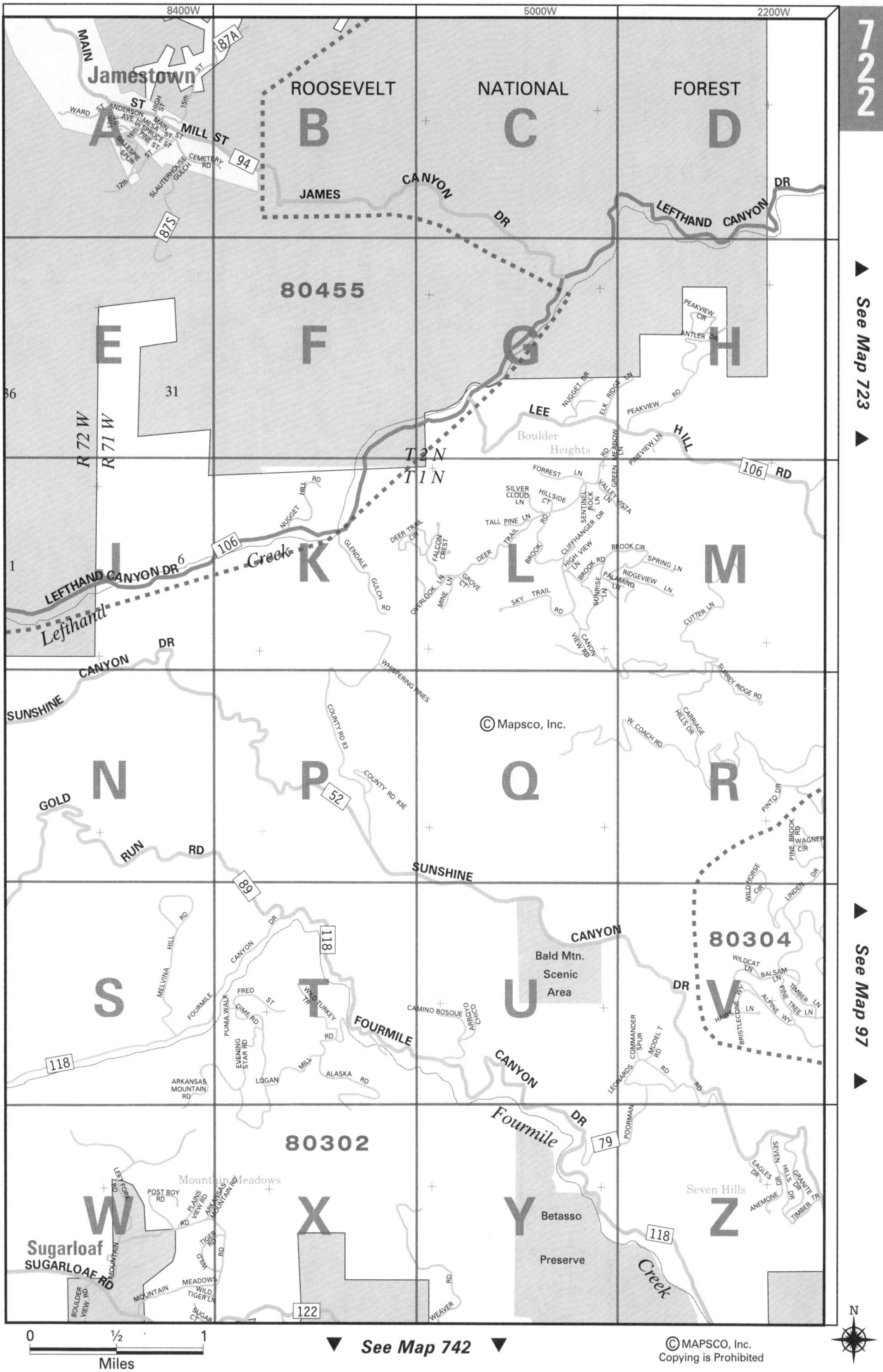

8400W 5000W 2200W

Jamestown

ROOSEVELT NATIONAL FOREST

A B C D E F G H J K L M N P Q R S T U V W X Y Z

MAIN ST, MILL ST, WARD ST, ANDERSON AVE, MESA ST, MAIN ST, SPRUCE ST, PINE ST, GILLESPIE SPUR, HIGH ST, CEMETERY RD, SLAUTERHOUSE GULCH, 15th, 16th, 12th, 87A, 94, 87S

JAMES CANYON DR

LEFTHAND CANYON DR

80455

PEAKVIEW CIR, ANTLER DR, NUGGET DR, ELK RIDGE LN, PEAKVIEW RD, LEE HILL, 106 RD, Boulder Heights, GREEN MEADOW LN, PINEVIEW LN, FORREST LN

R 72 W, R 71 W, 36, 31, 1, 6

T 2 N, T 1 N

NUGGET HILL RD, 106, Lefthand Creek, GLENDALE GULCH RD, DEER TRAIL CIR, FALCON CREST, OVERLOOK LN, MINE LN, GROVE CT, DEER TRAIL RD, SILVER CLOUD LN, HILLSIDE CT, TALL PINE LN, BROOK, SENTINEL ROCK LN, VALLEY VISTA, CLIFFHANGER DR, HIGH VIEW LN, BROOK RD, BROOK CIR, SPRING LN, PALAMINO LN, RIDGEVIEW LN, SUNRISE LN, SKY TRAIL RD, CANYON VIEW RD, CUTTER LN

SUNSHINE CANYON DR, WHISPERING PINES, COUNTY RD 83, COUNTY RD 83E, 52, SURREY RIDGE RD, CARRIAGE HILLS DR, W. COACH RD, PINTO DR, PINE BROOK RD, WAGNER CIR

© Mapsco, Inc.

GOLD RUN RD, 89, SUNSHINE

MELVINA HILL RD, FOURMILE CANYON DR, 118, FRED ST, PUMA WALK, DIME RD, WILD TURKEY TR, FOURMILE CANYON DR, CAMINO BOSQUE, ARROYO CHICO, Bald Mtn. Scenic Area, WILDHORSE CIR, LINDEN DR, 80304, WILDCAT LN, BALSAM LN, TIMBER LN, PINE TREE LN, ALPINE WY, HAWK LN, BRISTLECONE WY, EVENING STAR RD, LOGAN, MILL, ALASKA RD, ARKANSAS MOUNTAIN RD, LEONARDS, COMMANDER SPUR, MODEL T RD, RD

80302

Fourmile Creek, 79, POORMAN, Seven Hills, SEVEN HILLS DR, EAGLES DR, GRANITE TR, ANEMONE, TIMBER TR

Mountain Meadows, LEFT FORK RD, POST BOY RD, PLAINS VIEW RD, ARKANSAS MOUNTAIN RD, TIGER RD, WILD TIGER LN, MEADOWS, MOUNTAIN, SUGAR CT, Sugarloaf, SUGARLOAF RD, BOULDER VIEW RD, Betasso Preserve, 118, 122, WEAVER, RD

0 ½ 1 Miles

N

See Map 723

See Map 97

See Map 742

See Map 703

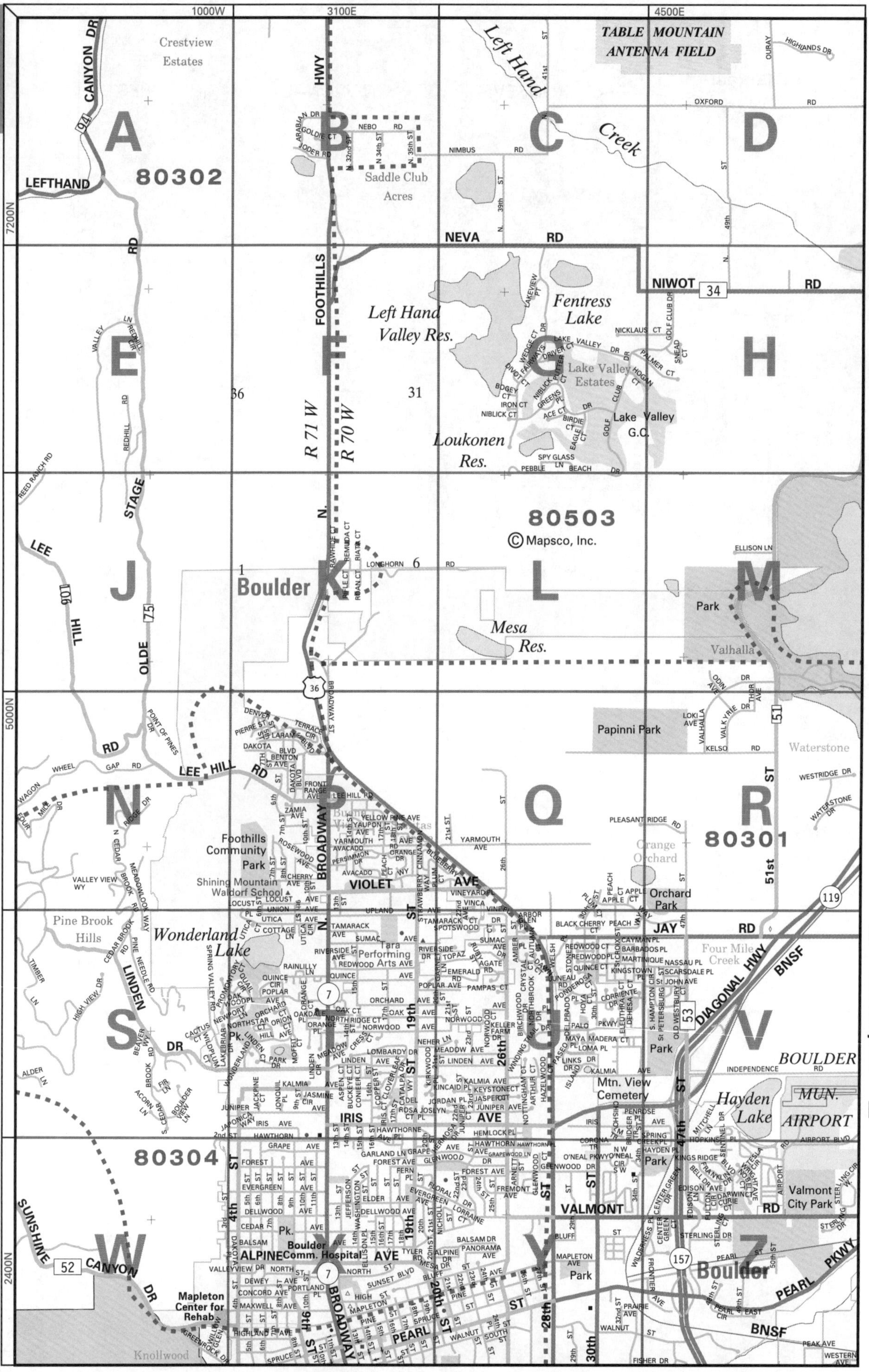

See Map 69

See Map 722

See Map 99

A B C D E F G H J K L M N P Q R S T U V W X Y Z

80302 80503 80301 80304

Crestview Estates
Saddle Club Acres
TABLE MOUNTAIN ANTENNA FIELD
Left Hand Creek
Left Hand Valley Res.
Fentress Lake
Lake Valley Estates
Lake Valley G.C.
Loukonen Res.
Boulder
Mesa Res.
Valhalla Park
Papinni Park
Waterstone
Foothills Community Park
Shining Mountain Waldorf School
Pine Brook Hills
Wonderland Lake
Tara Performing Arts
Orange Orchard
Orchard Park
Four Mile Creek
Mtn. View Cemetery
Hayden Lake
BOULDER MUN. AIRPORT
Valmont City Park
Boulder Comm. Hospital
Mapleton Center for Rehab
Knollwood
Mapleton Park

NEVA RD
NIWOT RD
FOOTHILLS HWY
BROADWAY
LEE HILL RD
OLDE STAGE RD
LEFTHAND CANYON DR
SUNSHINE CANYON DR
VIOLET AVE
JAY RD
IRIS AVE
VALMONT RD
PEARL PKWY
DIAGONAL HWY
ALPINE AVE
28th ST
30th ST
47th ST
51st ST

See Map 127

See Map 128

0 ½ 1
Miles

See Map 706

See Map 72

See Map 727

See Map 102

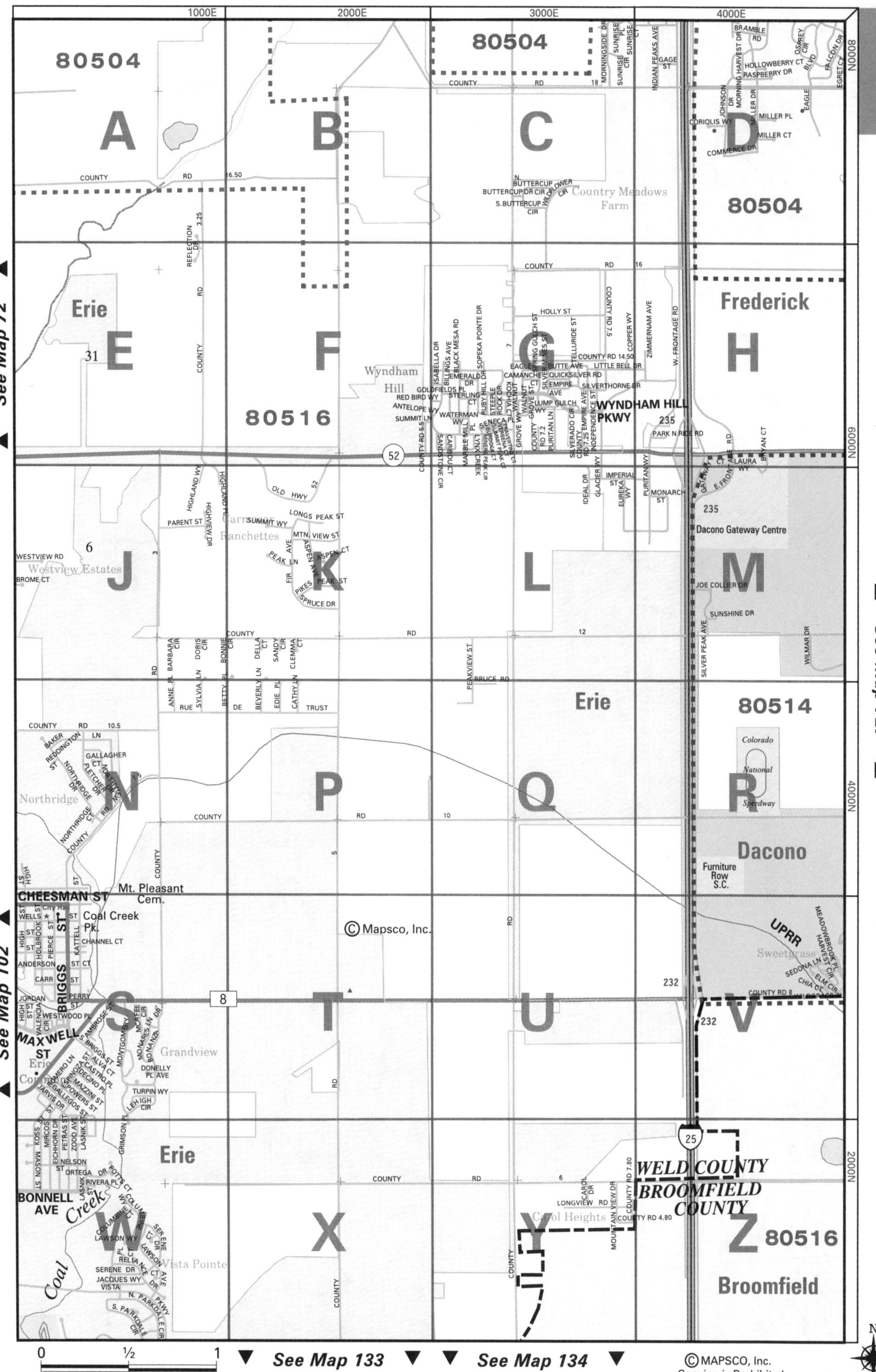

0 ½ 1 Miles

See Map 133 See Map 134

See Map 707

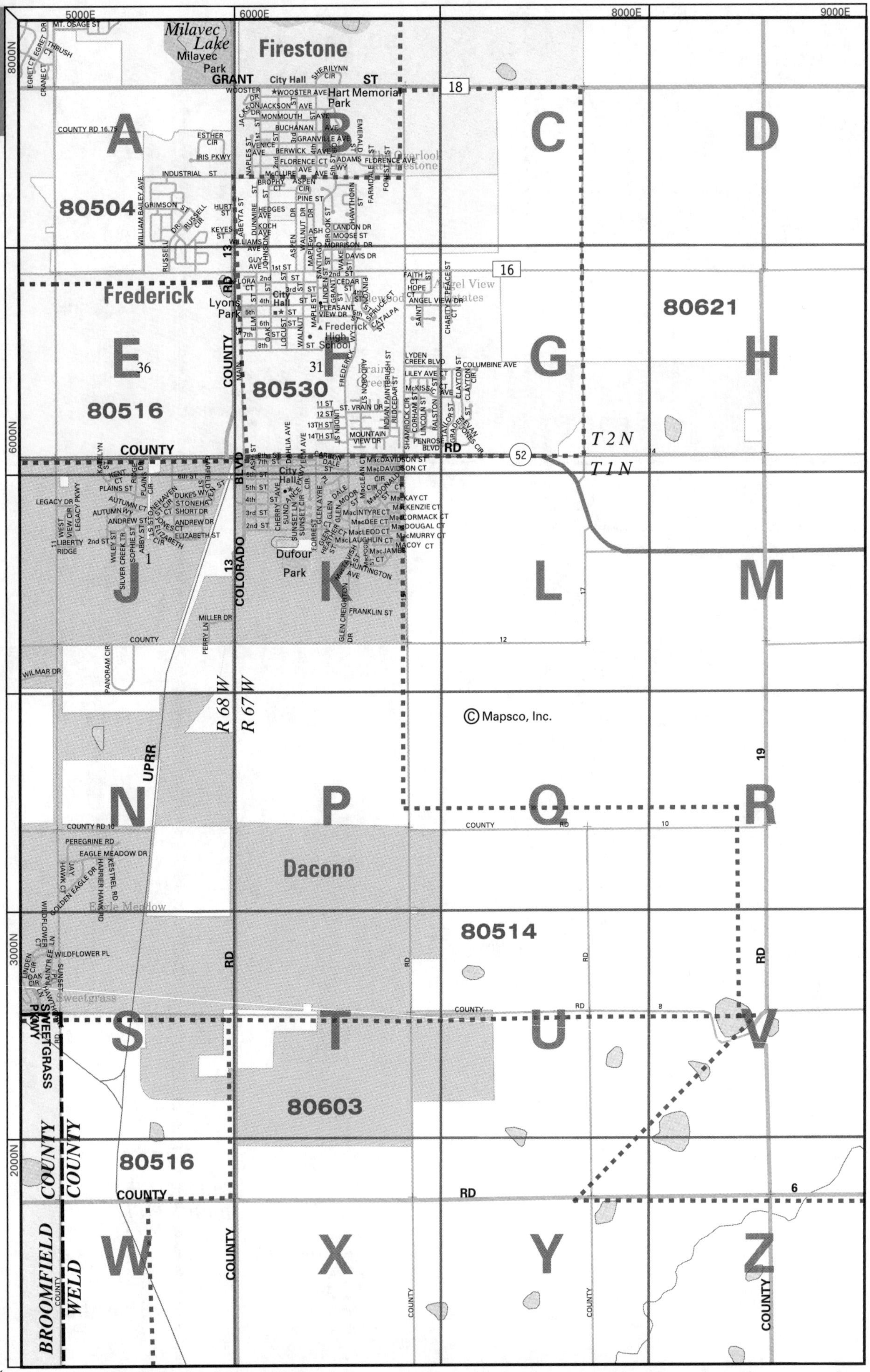

5000E 6000E 8000E 9000E

8000N 6000N 3000N 2000N

Milavec Lake

Milavec Park

Firestone

GRANT ST

City Hall

Hart Memorial Park

COUNTY RD 16.75

INDUSTRIAL ST

18

16

52

A B C D

E F G H

J K L M

N P Q R

S T U V

W X Y Z

80504

80530

80516

80621

80514

80603

80516

Frederick

Lyons Park

City Hall

Frederick High School

Angel View Estates

Overlook at Firestone

COUNTY RD

COUNTY RD 13

COLORADO BLVD

T 2 N

T 1 N

R 68 W

R 67 W

UPRR

Dufour Park

City Hall

MILLER DR

WILMAR DR

PANORAMA CIR

COUNTY RD 10

PEREGRINE RD

EAGLE MEADOW DR

Eagle Meadow

Dacono

WILDFLOWER PL

Sweetgrass

SWEETGRASS PKWY

COUNTY RD 8

COUNTY RD 6

COUNTY RD 19

COUNTY RD 17

COUNTY RD 12

BROOMFIELD COUNTY

WELD COUNTY

© Mapsco, Inc.

See Map 726

See Map 135

See Map 136

0 ½ 1

Miles

See Map 708

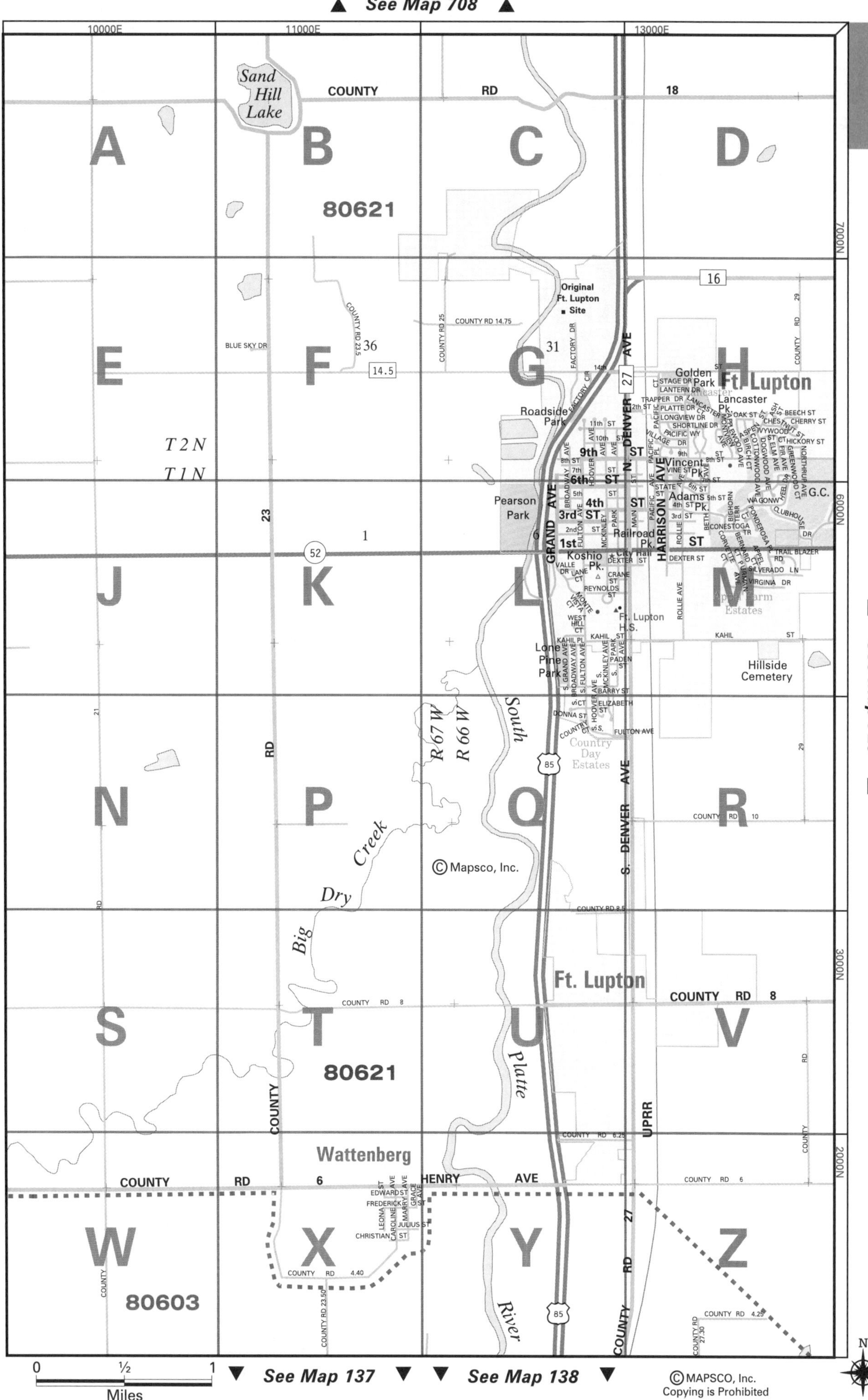

See Map 729

0 ½ 1
Miles

See Map 137 See Map 138

▲ See Map 709 ▲

▼ See Map 139 ▼ ▼ See Map 140 ▼

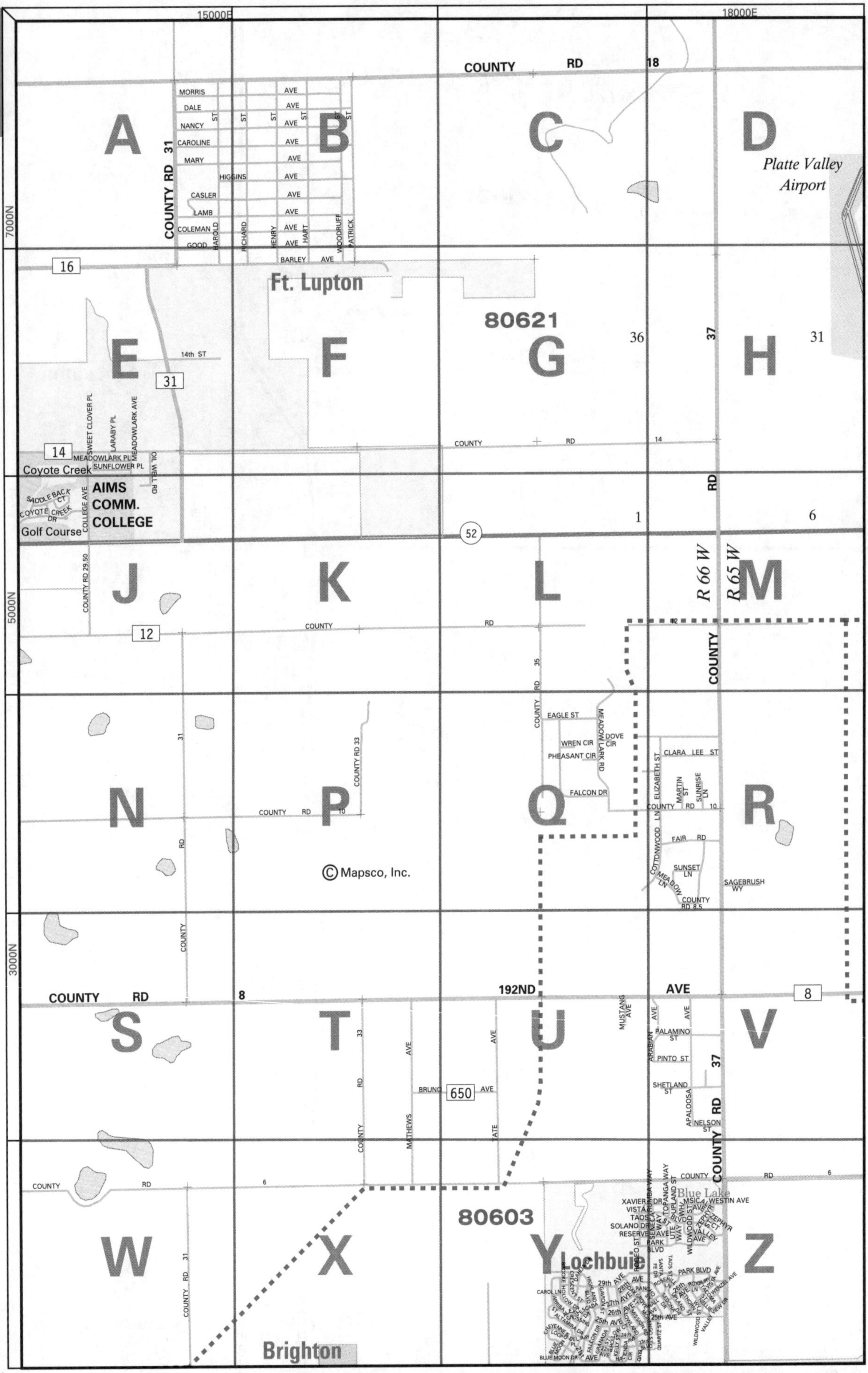

▲ See Map 728 ▲

▲ See Map 710 ▲

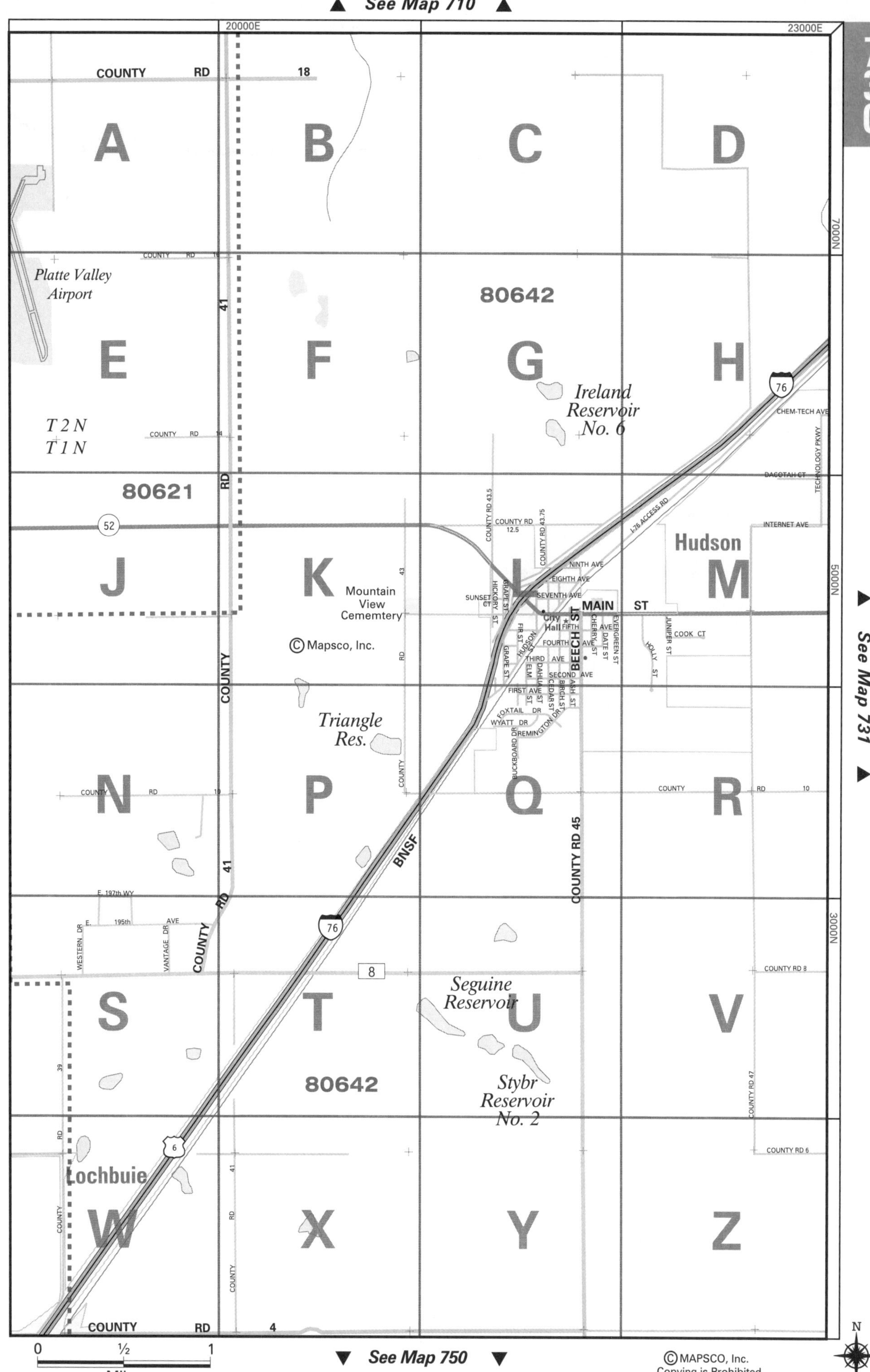

▲ See Map 731 ▲

▼ See Map 750 ▼

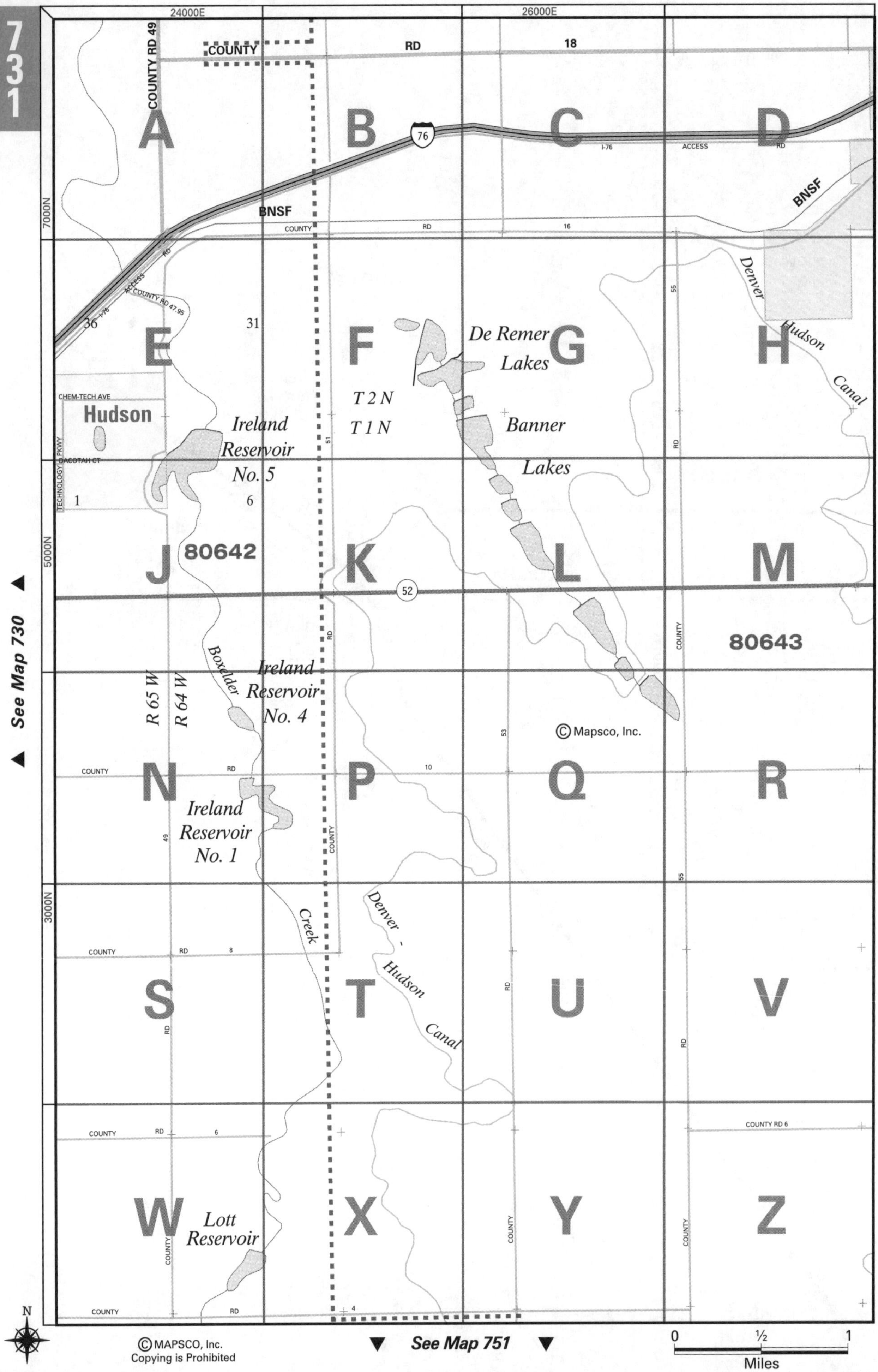

See Map 730

See Map 751

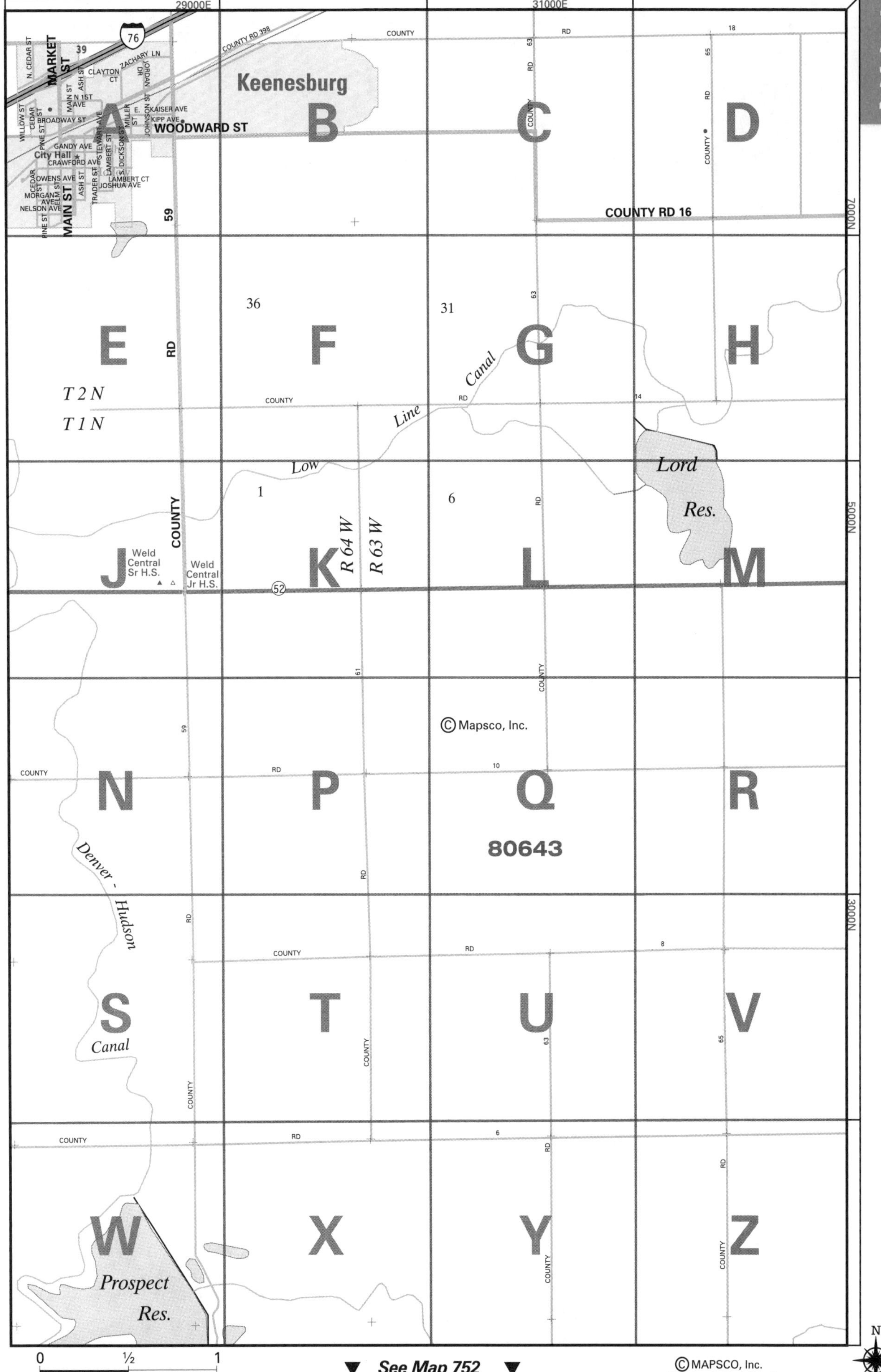

29000E
31000E
Keenesburg
76
39
MARKET ST
MAIN ST
WOODWARD ST
City Hall
COUNTY RD 16
COUNTY RD 398
T 2 N
T 1 N
Low Line Canal
Lord Res.
Weld Central Sr H.S.
Weld Central Jr H.S.
52
R 64 W
R 63 W
© Mapsco, Inc.
80643
Denver - Hudson Canal
Prospect Res.
7000N
5000N
3000N
A
B
C
D
E
F
G
H
J
K
L
M
N
P
Q
R
S
T
U
V
W
X
Y
Z
0
½
1
Miles
N

See Map 752

▲ See Map 720 ▲

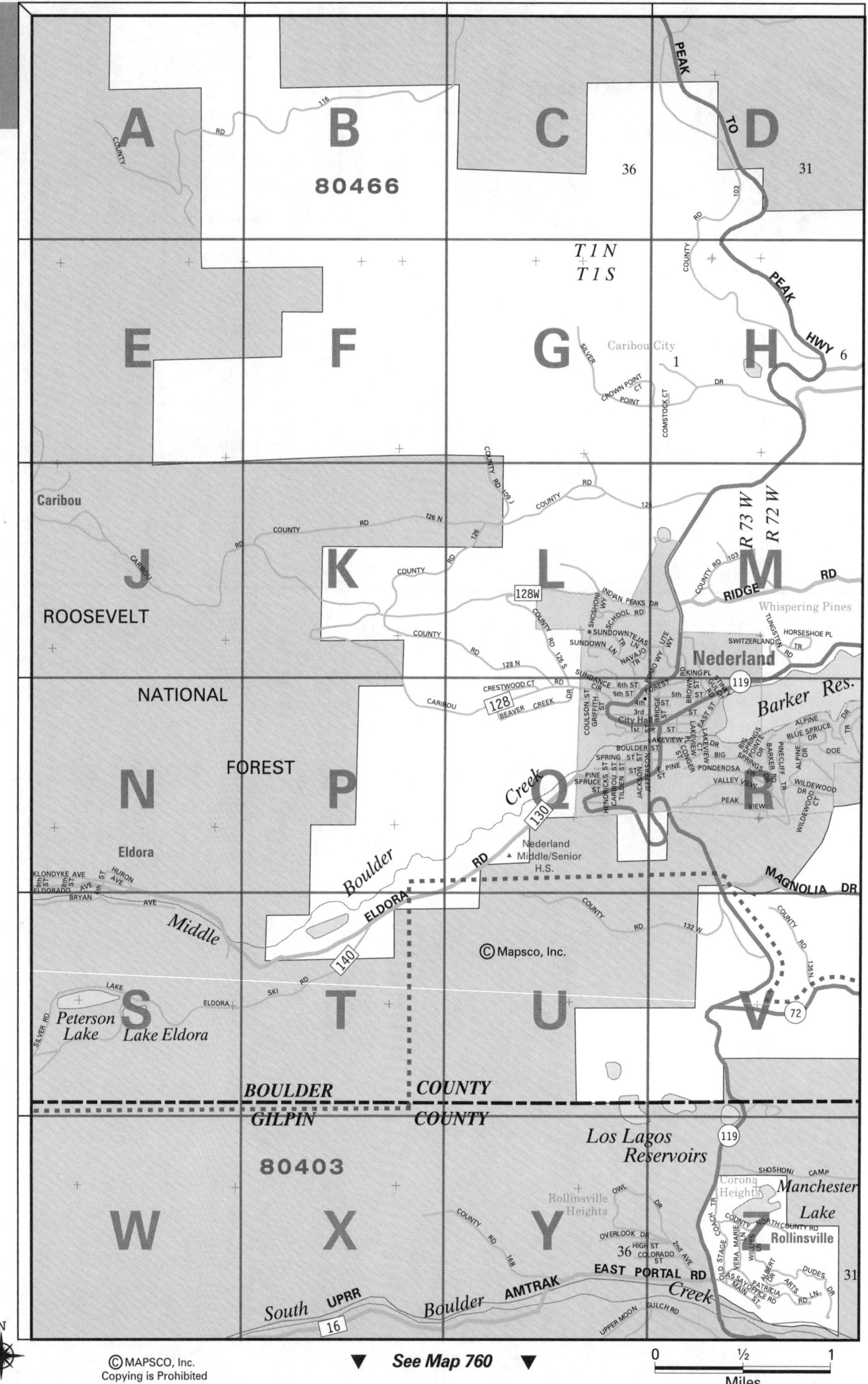

▼ See Map 760 ▼

0 ½ 1
Miles

▲ See Map 721 ▲

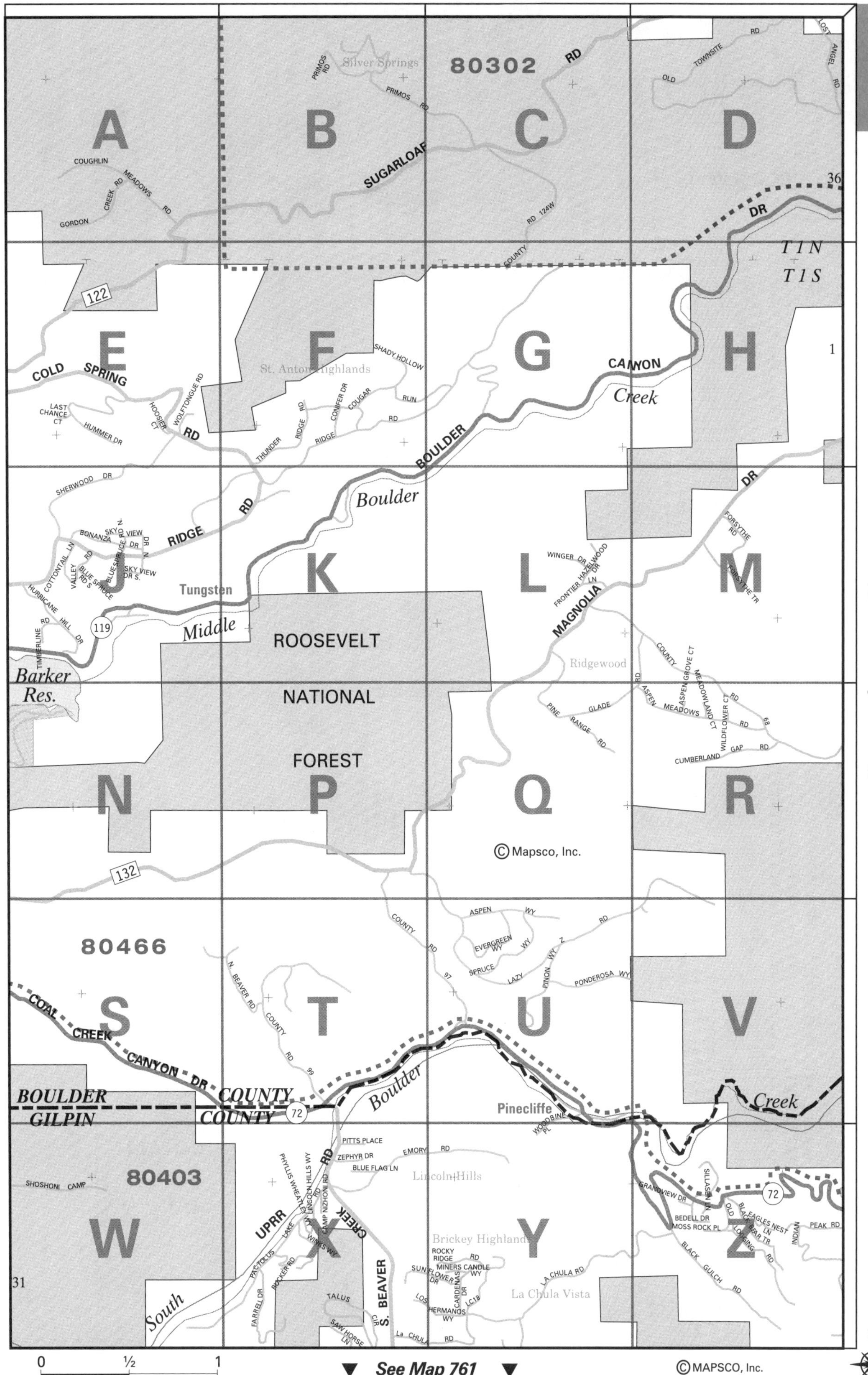

See Map 742 ▶

▼ See Map 761 ▼

See Map 722

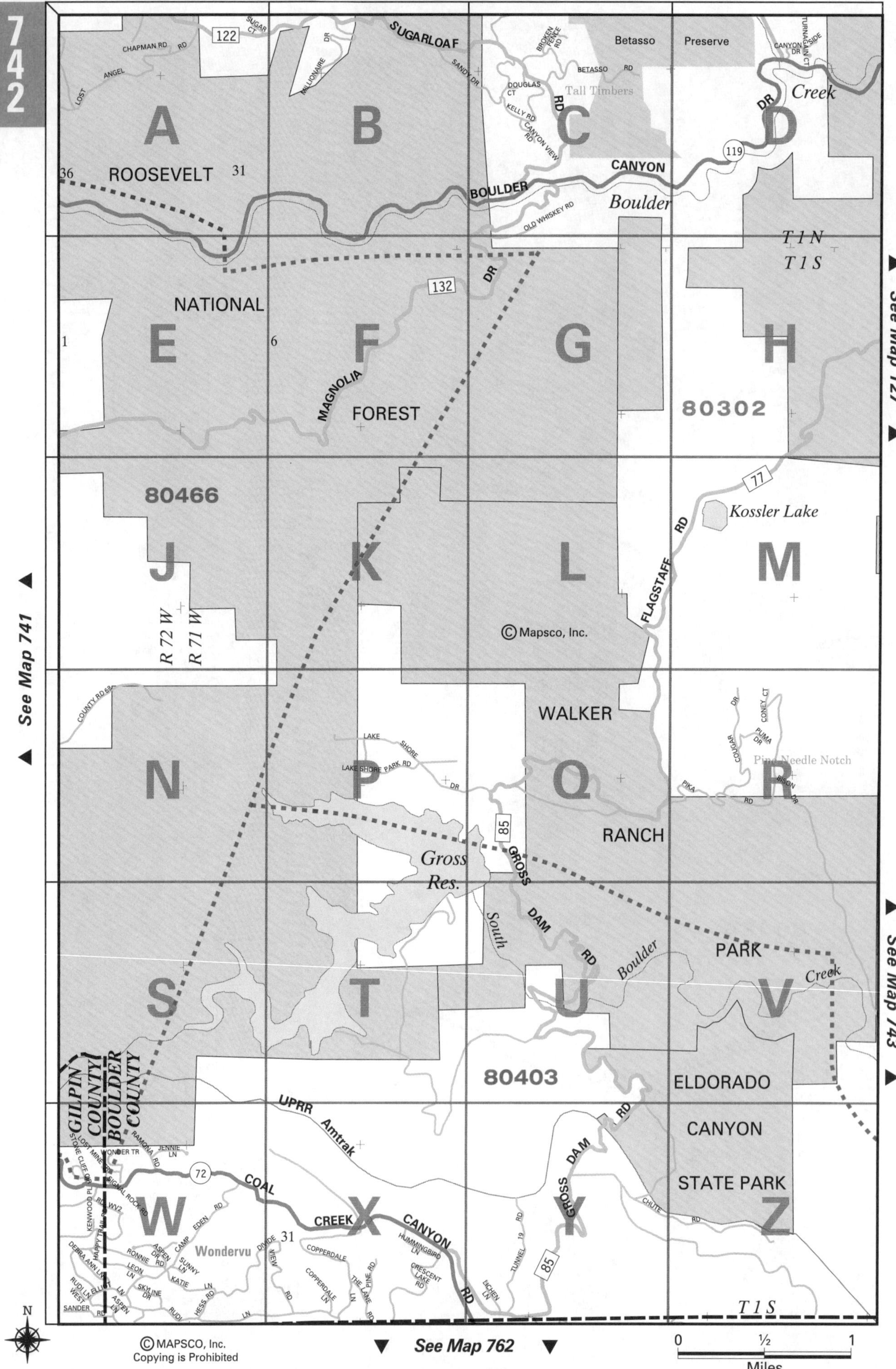

See Map 127

See Map 741

See Map 743

See Map 762

0 ½ 1
Miles

▲ See Map 97 ▲ ▲ See Map 98 ▲

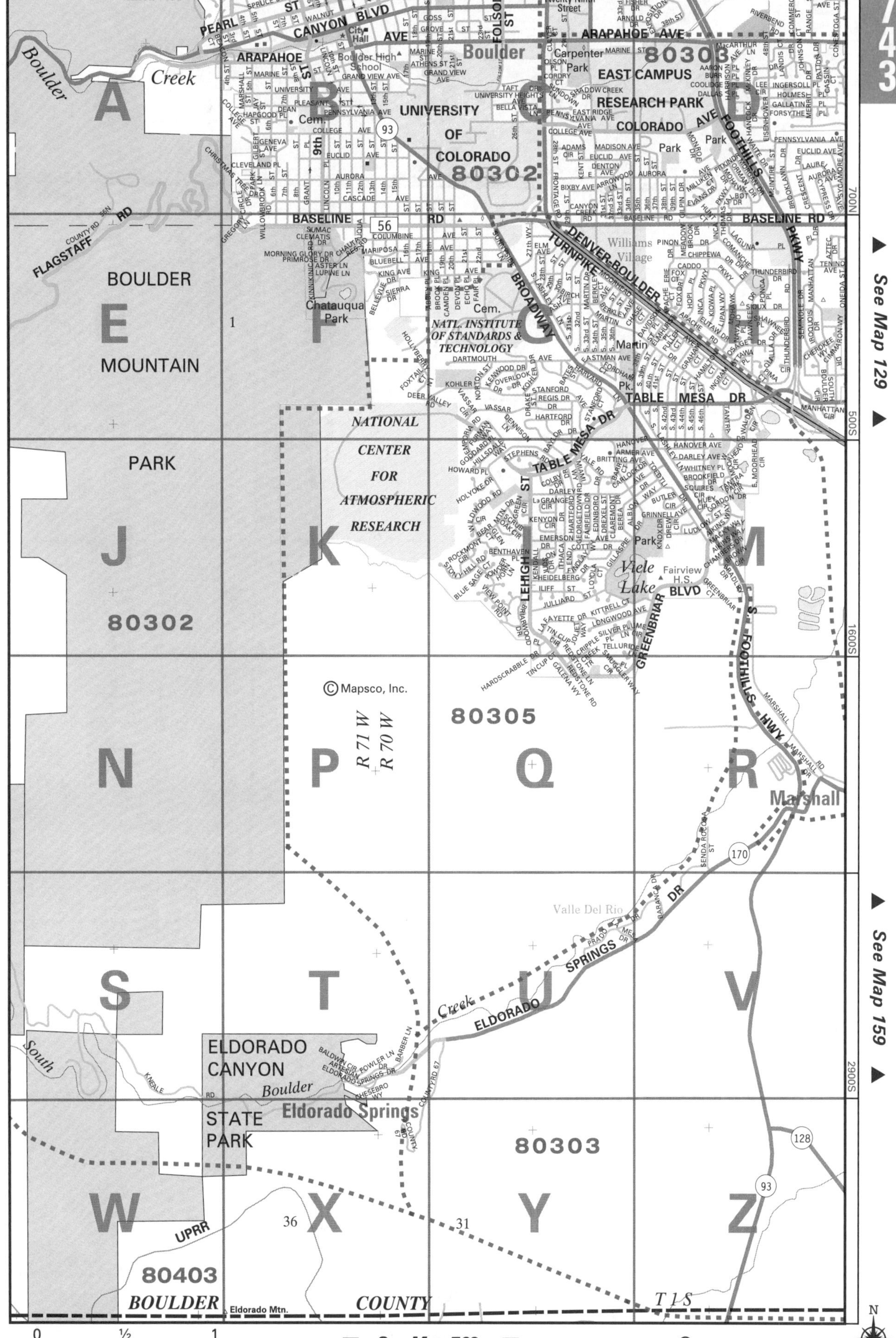

▶ See Map 129 ▶

▶ See Map 159 ▶

0 ½ 1
Miles

▼ See Map 763 ▼

N

See Map 730

See Map 140

See Map 170

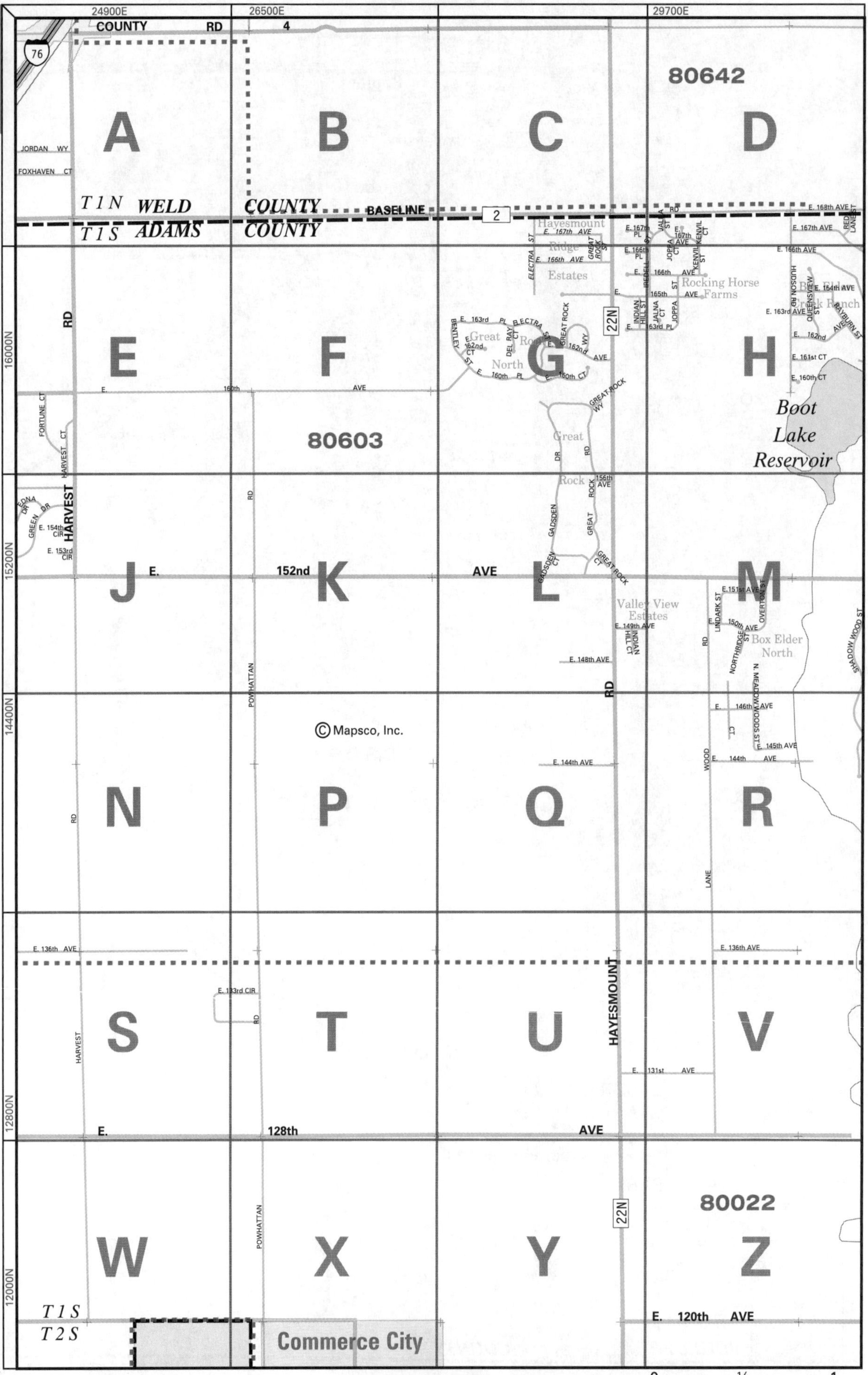

See Map 770

COUNTY RD 4
76
80642
A B C D
JORDAN WY
FOXHAVEN CT
T1N WELD COUNTY
T1S ADAMS COUNTY
BASELINE RD
2
E. 168th AVE
Hayesmount Ridge Estates
E. 167th AVE
E. 166th AVE
Rocking Horse Farms
Box Elder Creek Ranch
Great Rock North
E F G H
E. 160th AVE
80603
Boot Lake Reservoir
Great Rock
22N
HARVEST RD
J K L M
E. 152nd AVE
Valley View Estates
Box Elder North
E. 148th AVE
E. 146th AVE
E. 144th AVE
N P Q R
POWHATTAN RD
WOOD LANE
E. 136th AVE
E. 133rd CIR
S T U V
HAYESMOUNT RD
E. 131st AVE
E. 128th AVE
80022
W X Y Z
E. 120th AVE
T1S
T2S
Commerce City
24900E 26500E 29700E
16000N 15200N 14400N 12800N 12000N
0 ½ 1 Miles

See Map 731

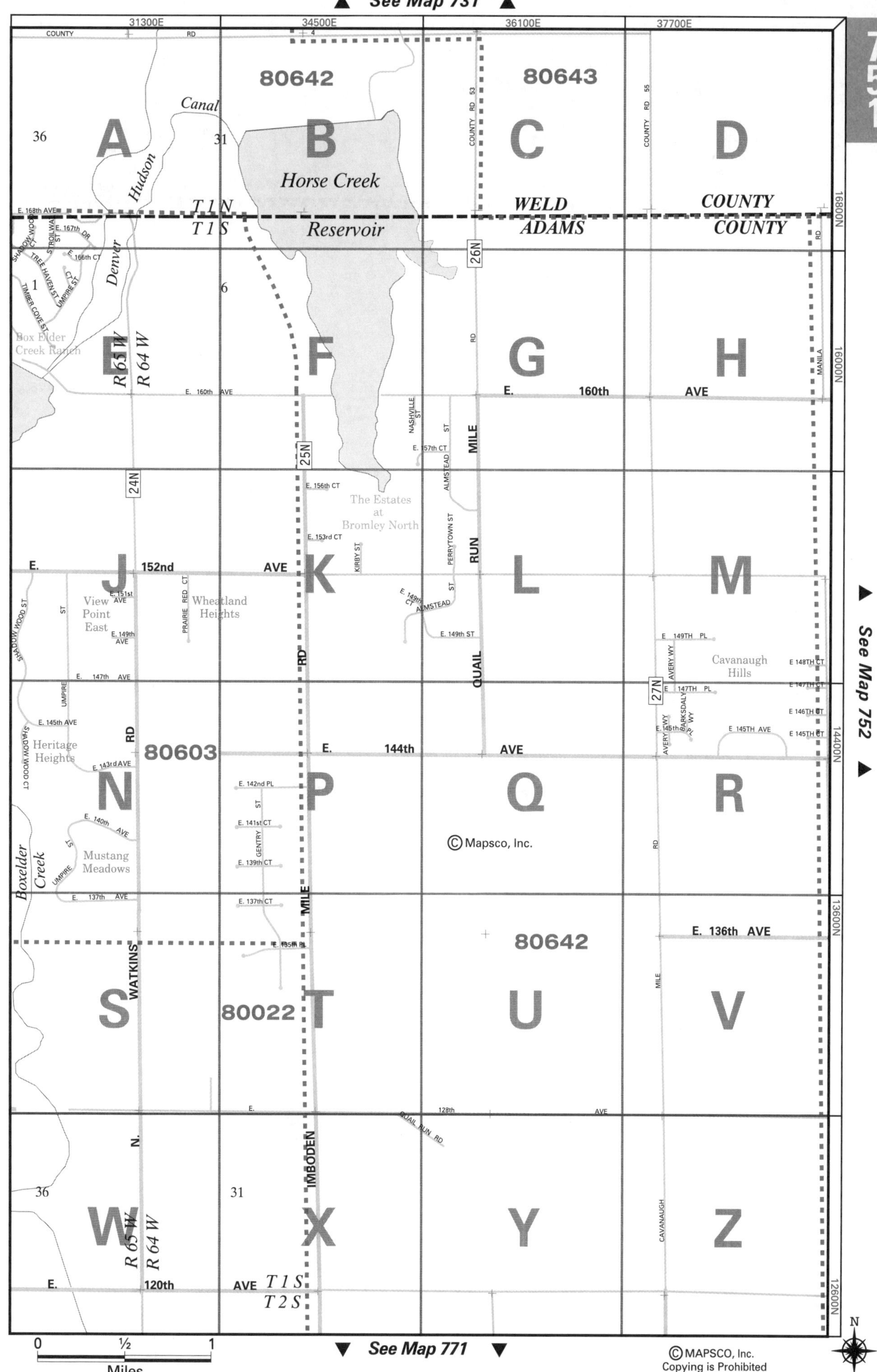

See Map 752

See Map 771

See Map 732

See Map 751

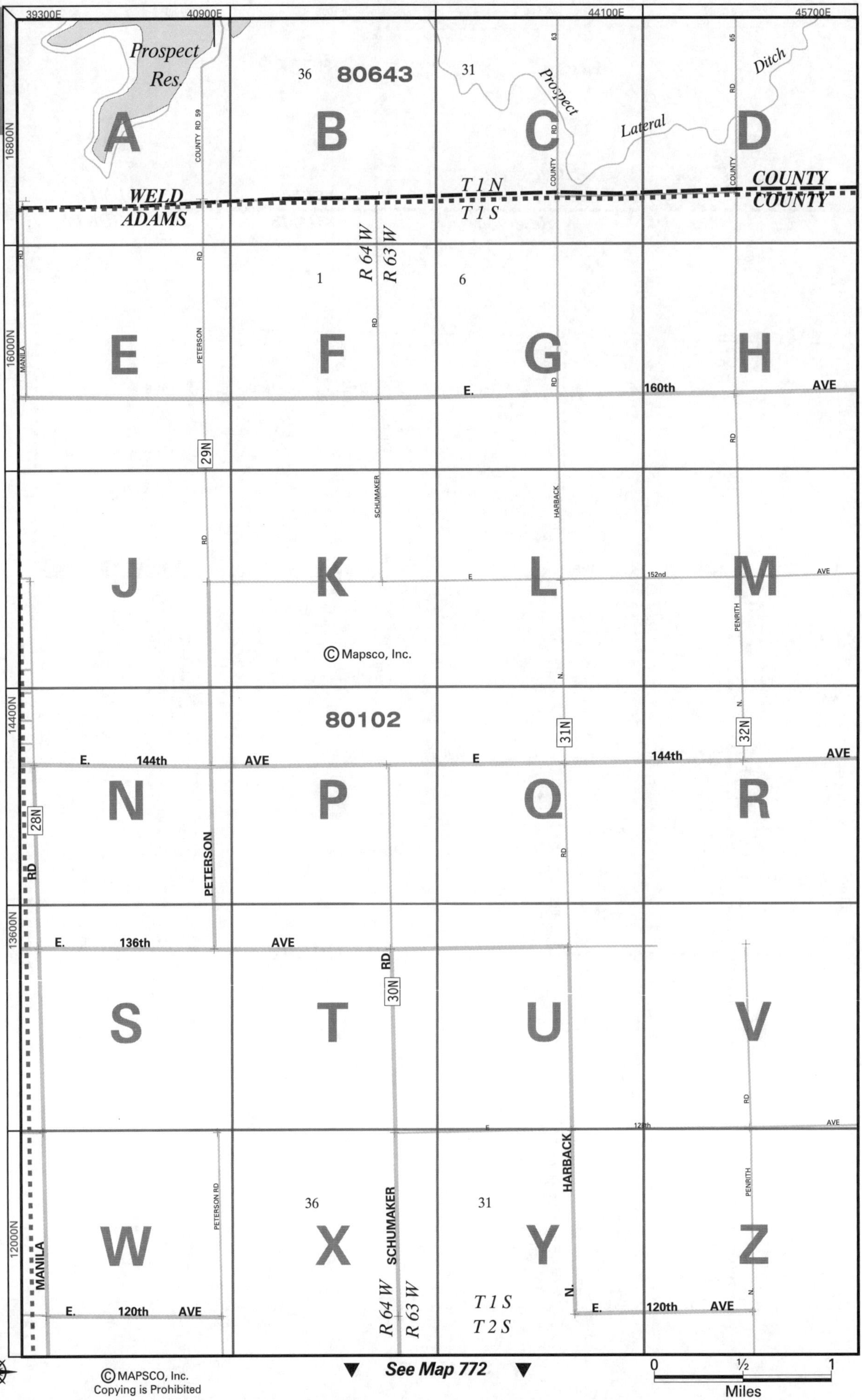

See Map 772

See Map 740

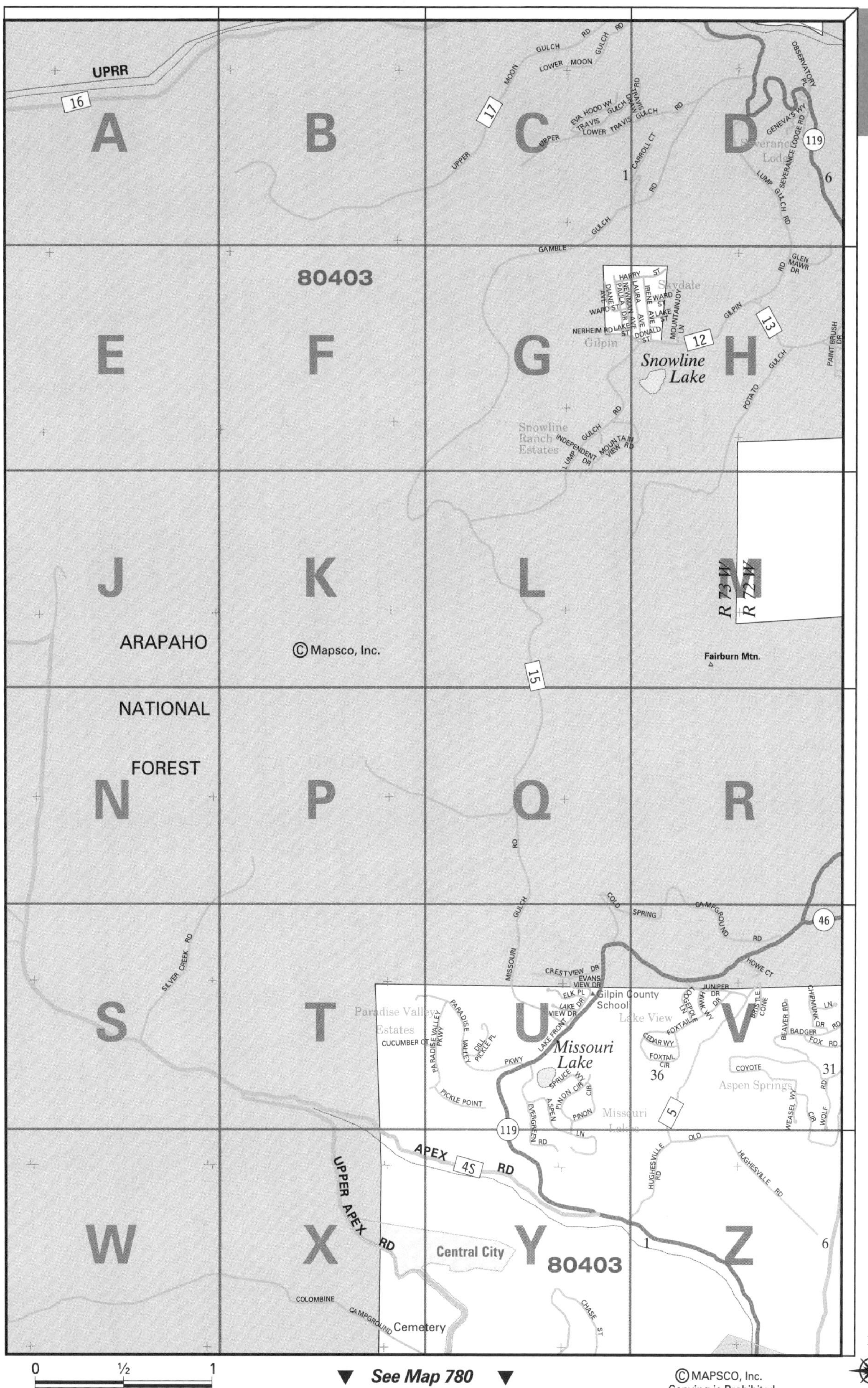

See Map 761

See Map 780

▲ See Map 741 ▲

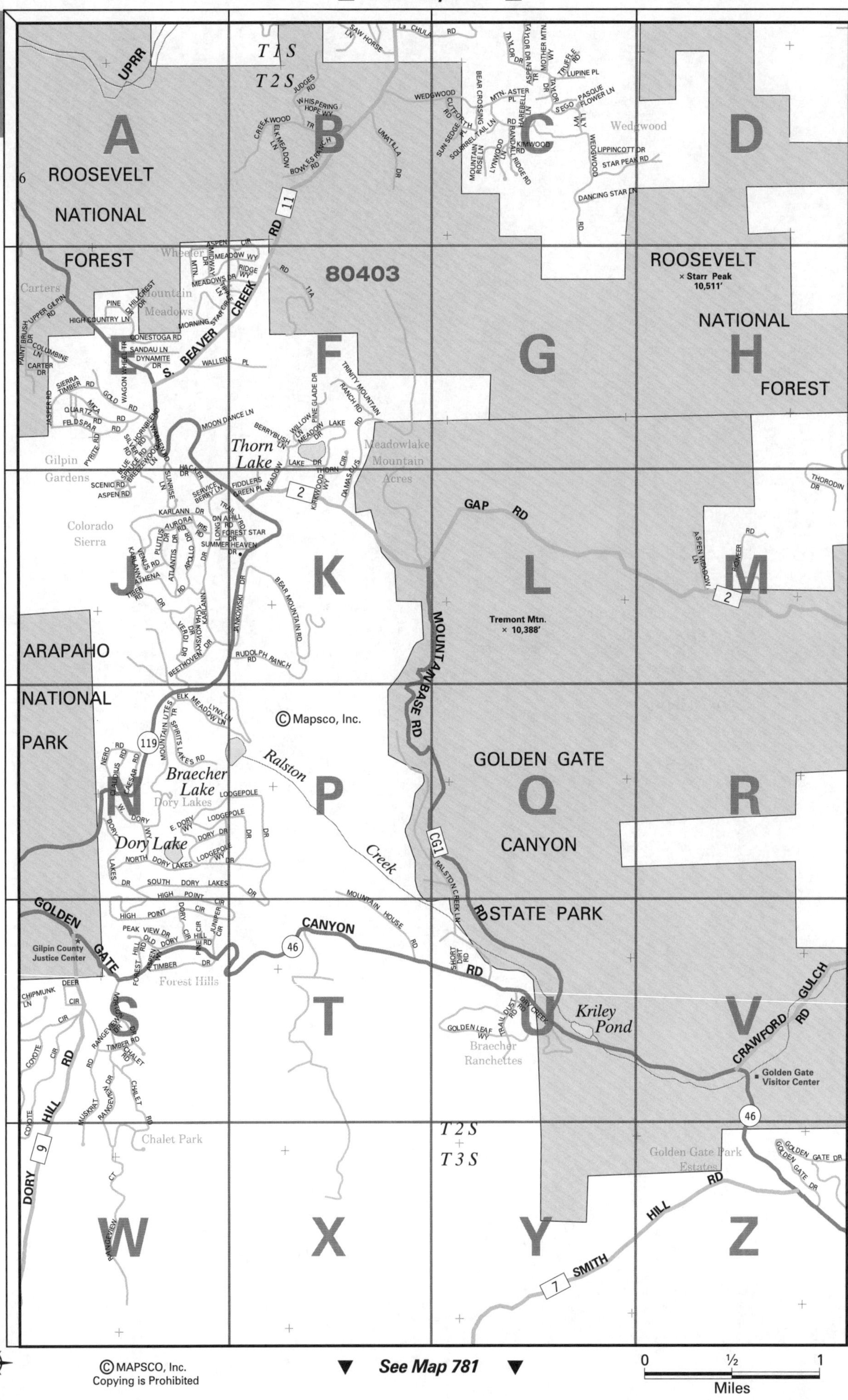

See Map 760

▼ See Map 781 ▼

0 ½ 1
Miles

▲ See Map 742 ▲

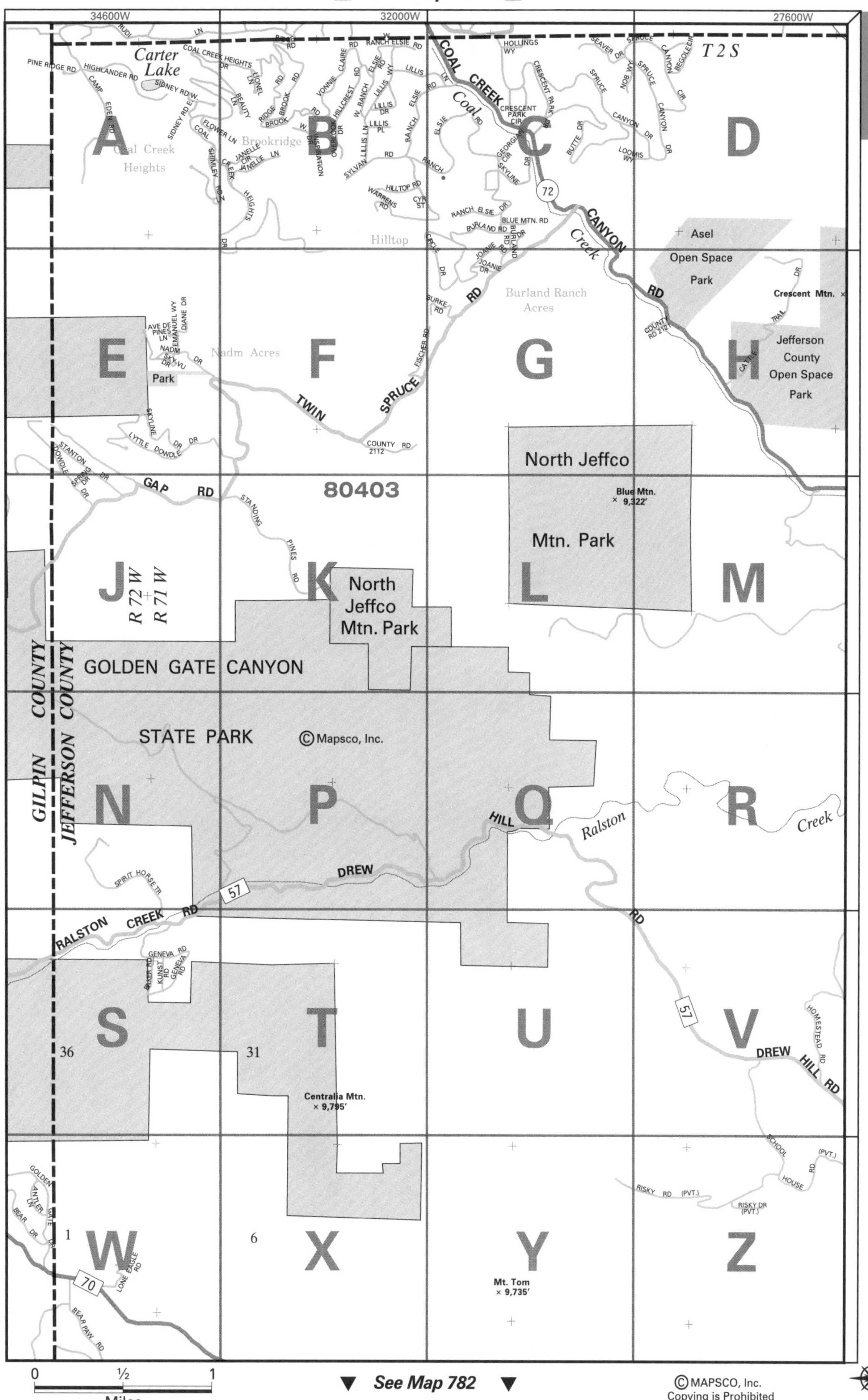

▶ See Map 763 ▶

▼ See Map 782 ▼

See Map 743

See Map 189

See Map 762

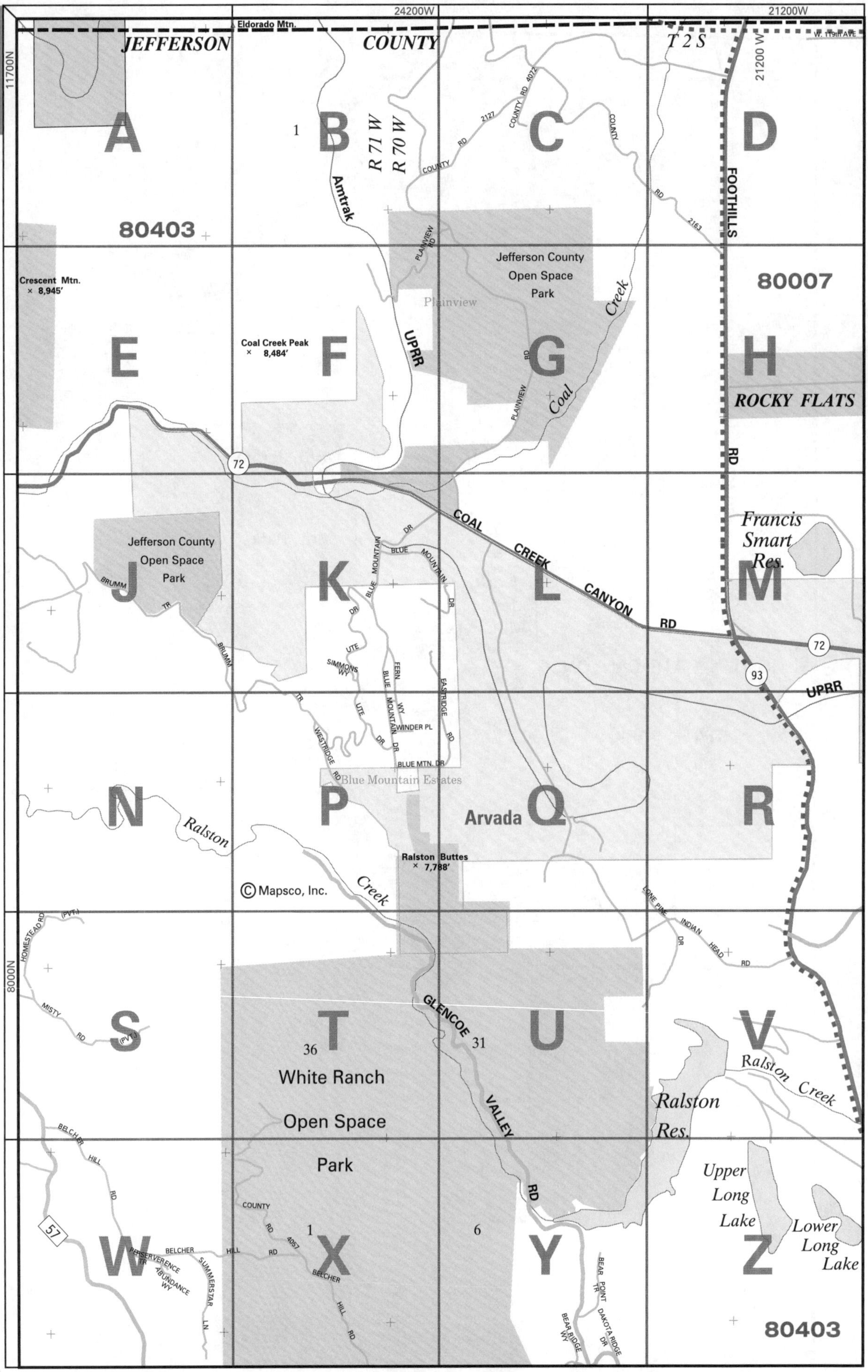

See Map 219

See Map 783

See Map 248

See Map 167
See Map 168

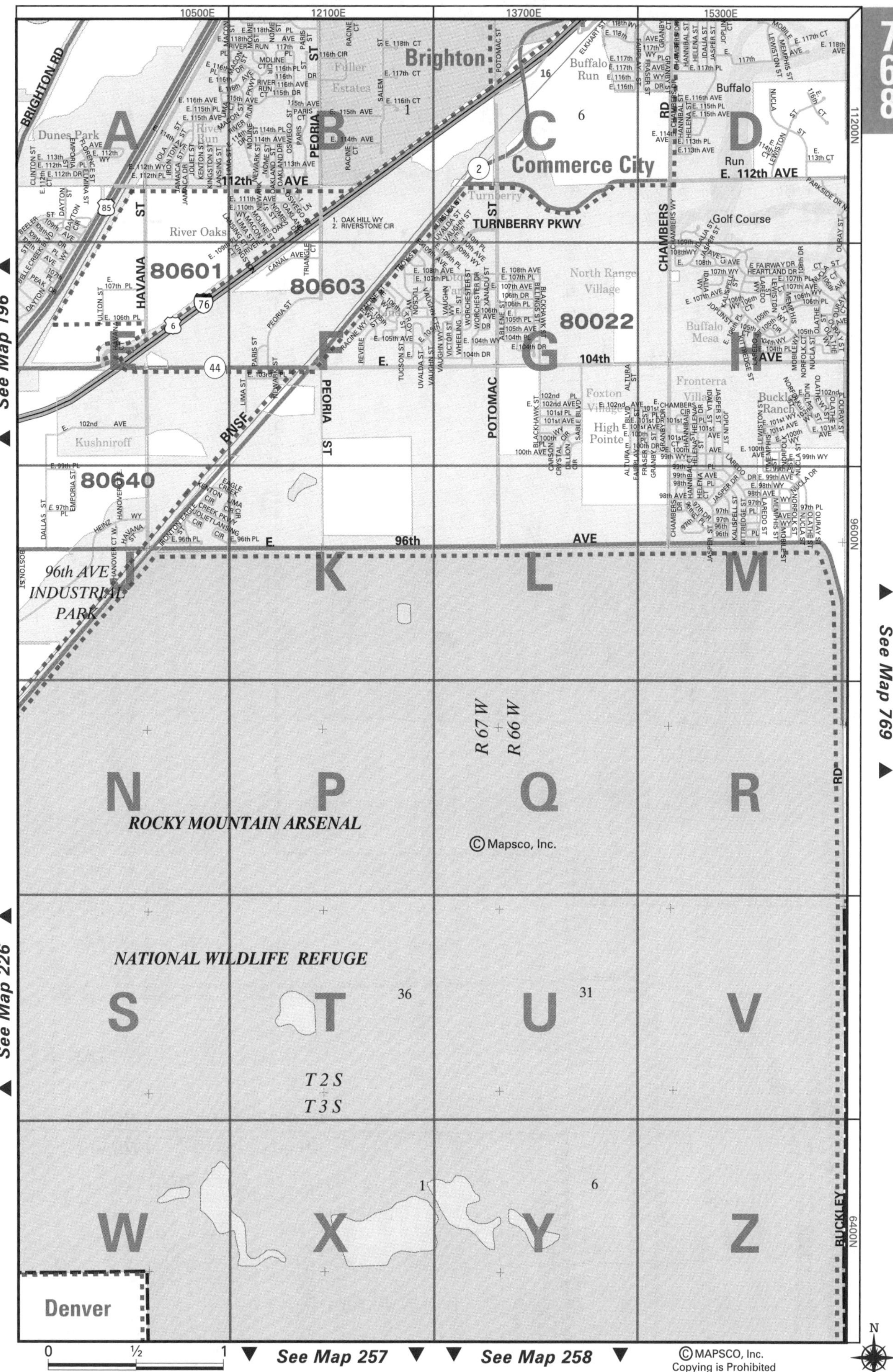

See Map 196
See Map 226
See Map 769
See Map 257
See Map 258

▲ See Map 169 ▲ ▲ See Map 170 ▲

◀ See Map 198 ◀

◀ See Map 768 ◀

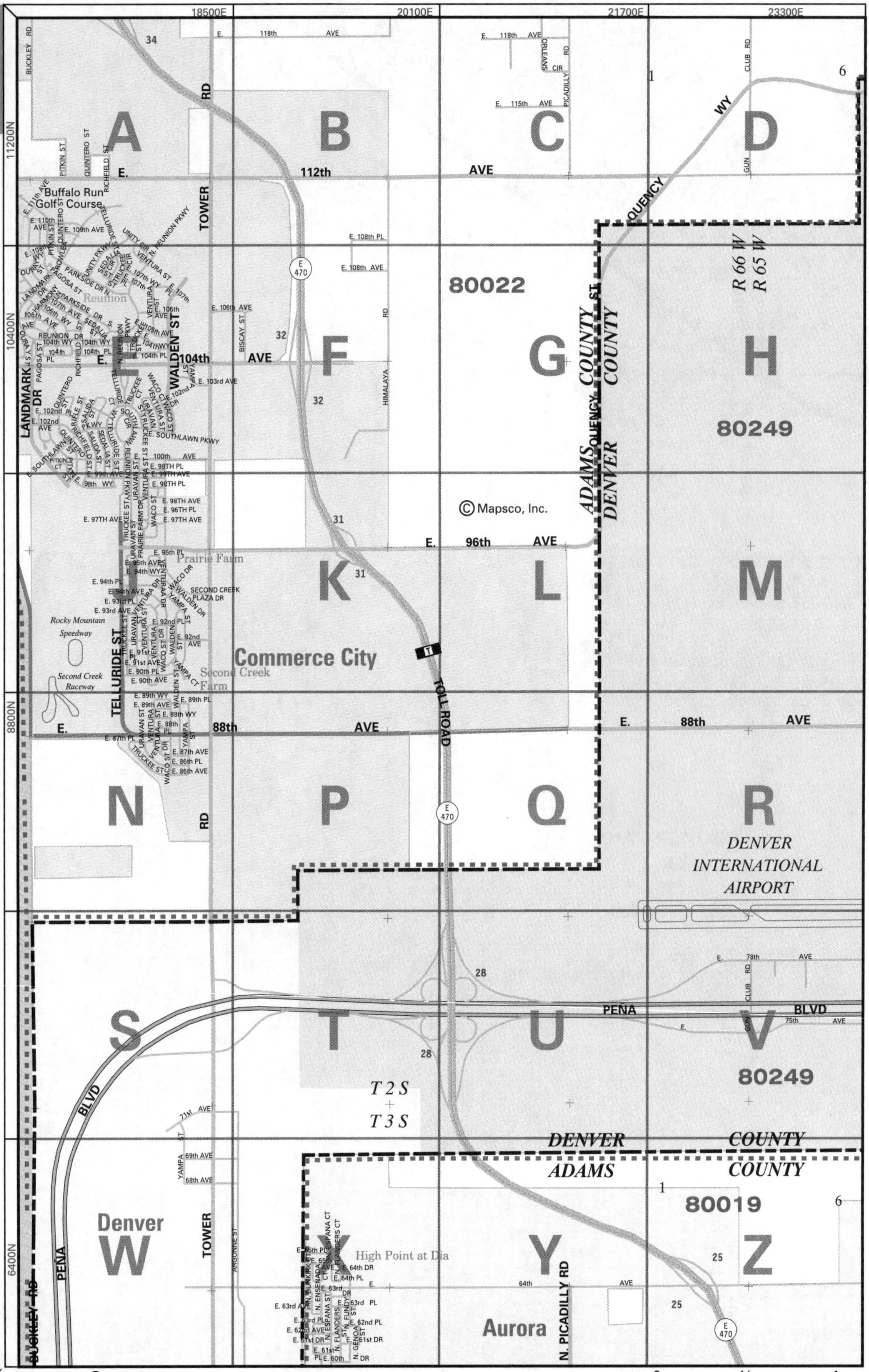

▼ See Map 259 ▼ ▼ See Map 260 ▼

0 ½ 1
Miles

▲ See Map 750 ▲

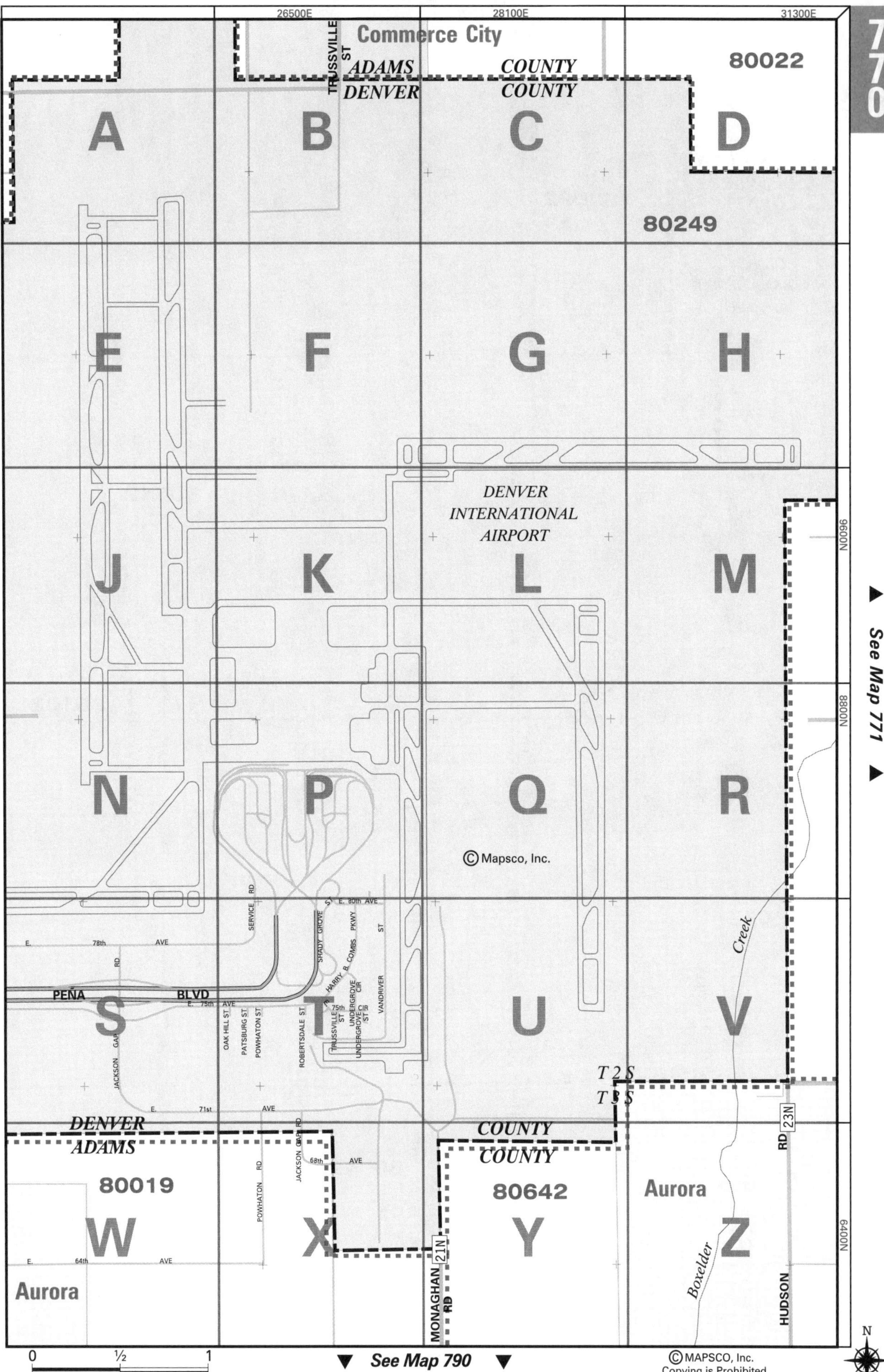

▲ See Map 771 ▲

▼ See Map 790 ▼

▲ See Map 751 ▲

◀ See Map 770 ◀

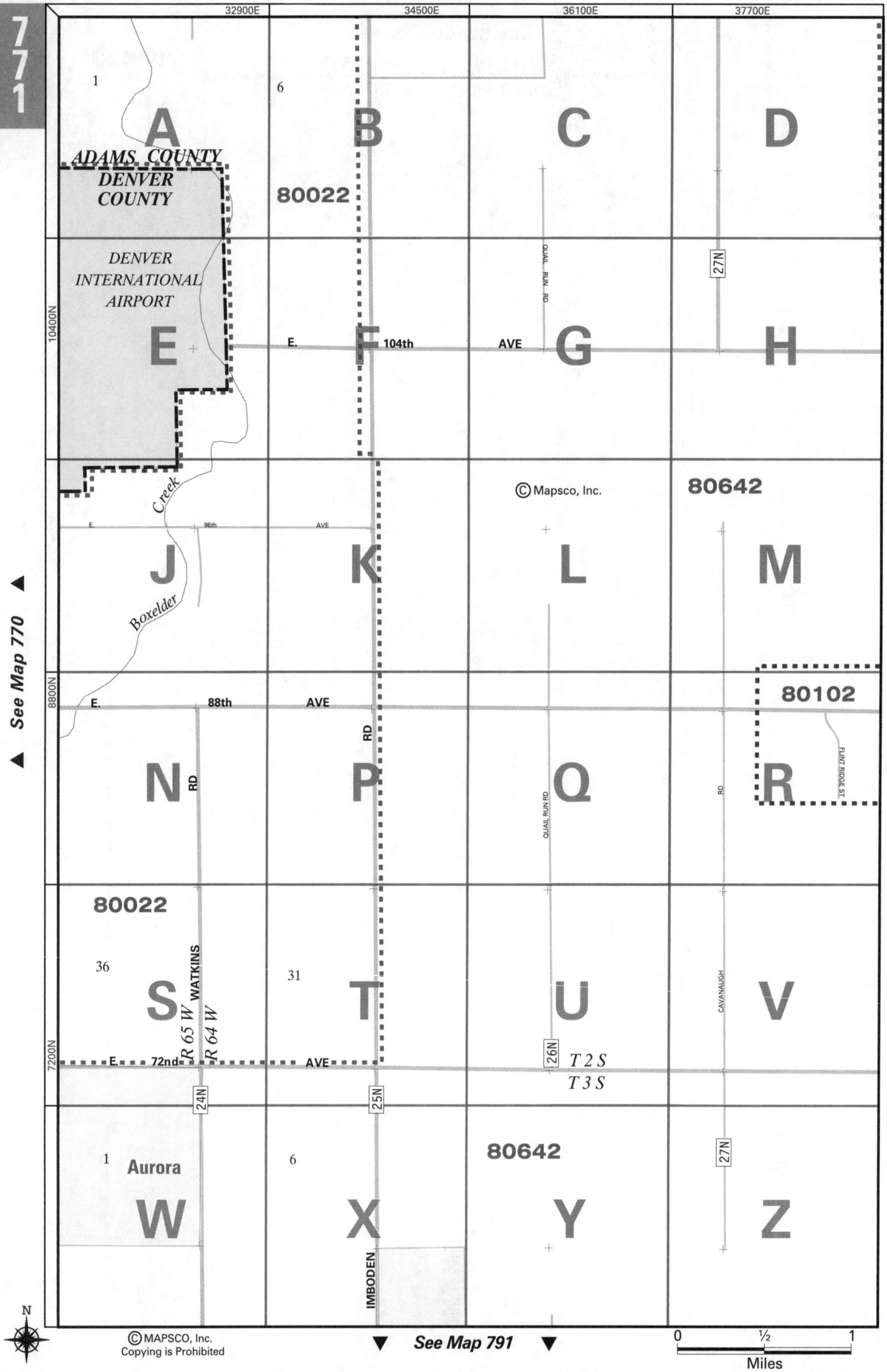

▼ See Map 791 ▼

0 ½ 1
Miles

See Map 752

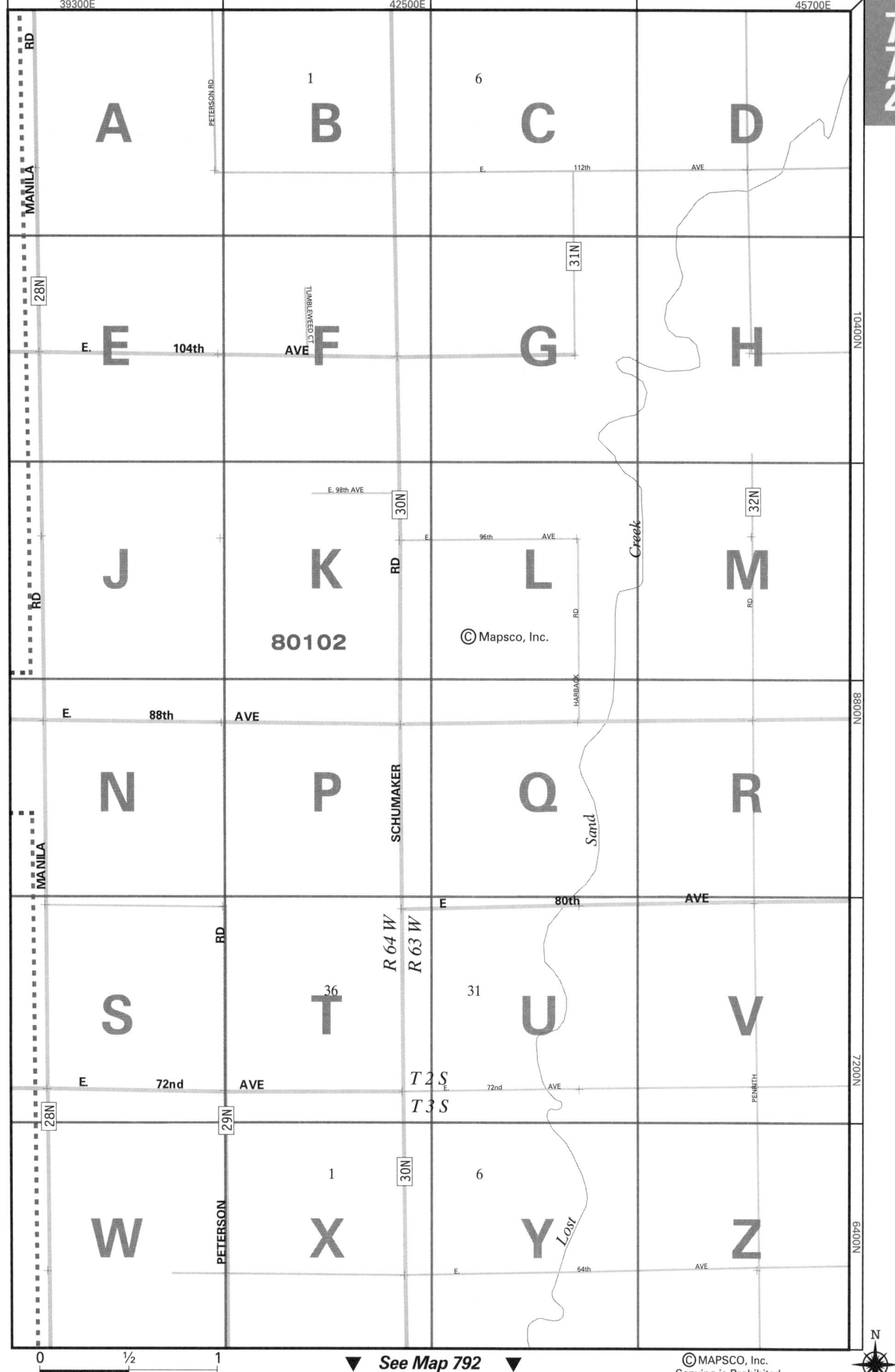

See Map 792

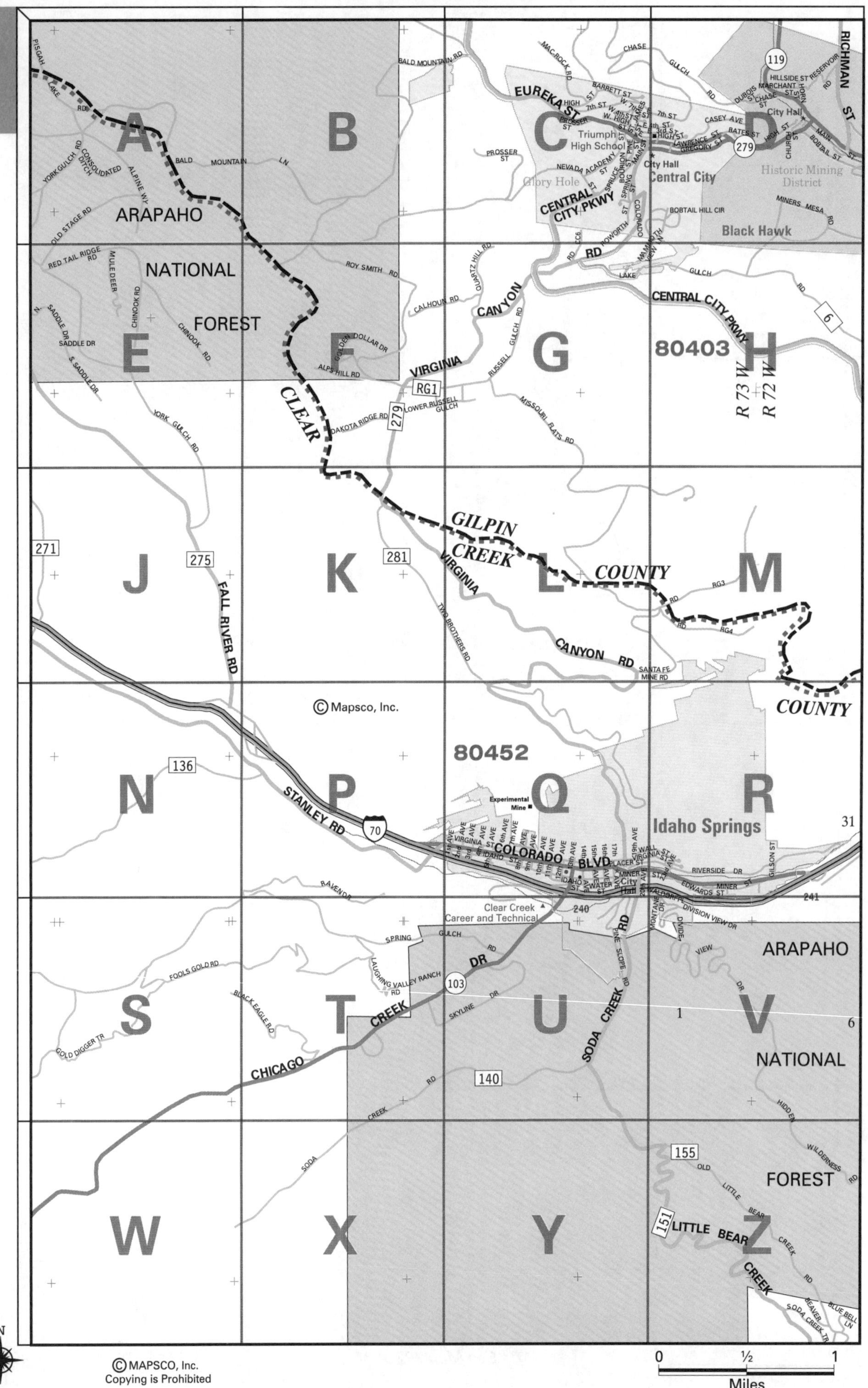
A
B
C
D
E
F
G
H
J
K
L
M
N
P
Q
R
S
T
U
V
W
X
Y
Z
ARAPAHO
NATIONAL
FOREST
CLEAR
CREEK
GILPIN
COUNTY
COUNTY
VIRGINIA
CANYON
RD
VIRGINIA
CANYON RD
80403
80452
Central City
Black Hawk
Historic Mining District
City Hall
Triumph High School
Glory Hole
CENTRAL CITY PKWY
EUREKA ST
RICHMAN ST
Idaho Springs
COLORADO BLVD
STANLEY RD
FALL RIVER RD
CHICAGO CREEK DR
SODA CREEK RD
LITTLE BEAR CREEK
Experimental Mine
Clear Creek Career and Technical
City Hall
R 73 W
R 72 W
119
279
6
70
103
151
RG1
271
275
281
136
140
155
240
241
© Mapsco, Inc.
0
½
1
Miles
N

▲ See Map 761 ▲

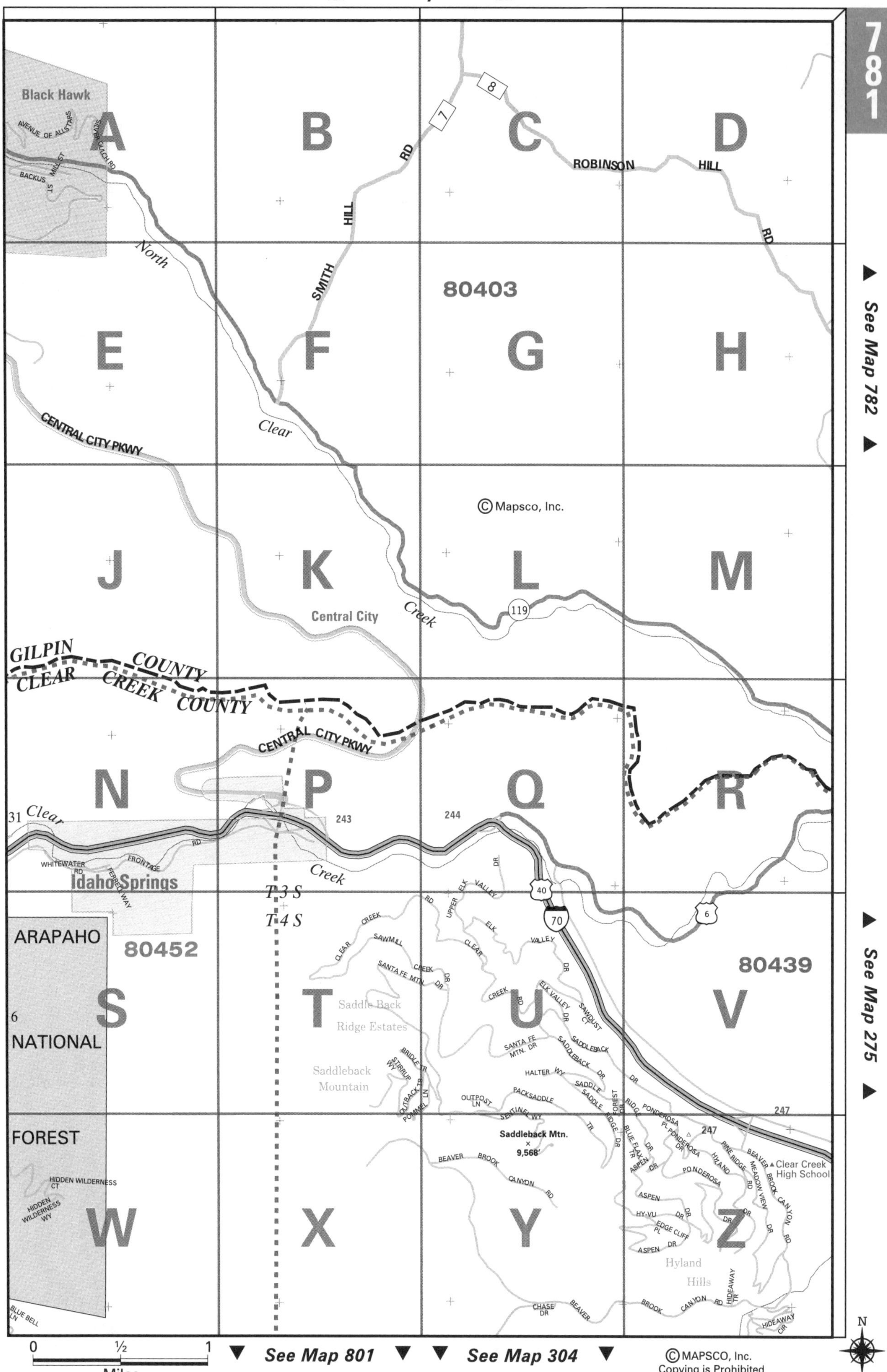

▶ See Map 782 ▶

▶ See Map 275 ▶

0 ½ 1
Miles

▼ See Map 801 ▼ ▼ See Map 304 ▼

See Map 762

See Map 783

See Map 781

See Map 277

See Map 305

See Map 306

▲ See Map 763 ▲

◄ See Map 782 ◄

► See Map 249 ►

◄ See Map 276 ◄

► See Map 279 ►

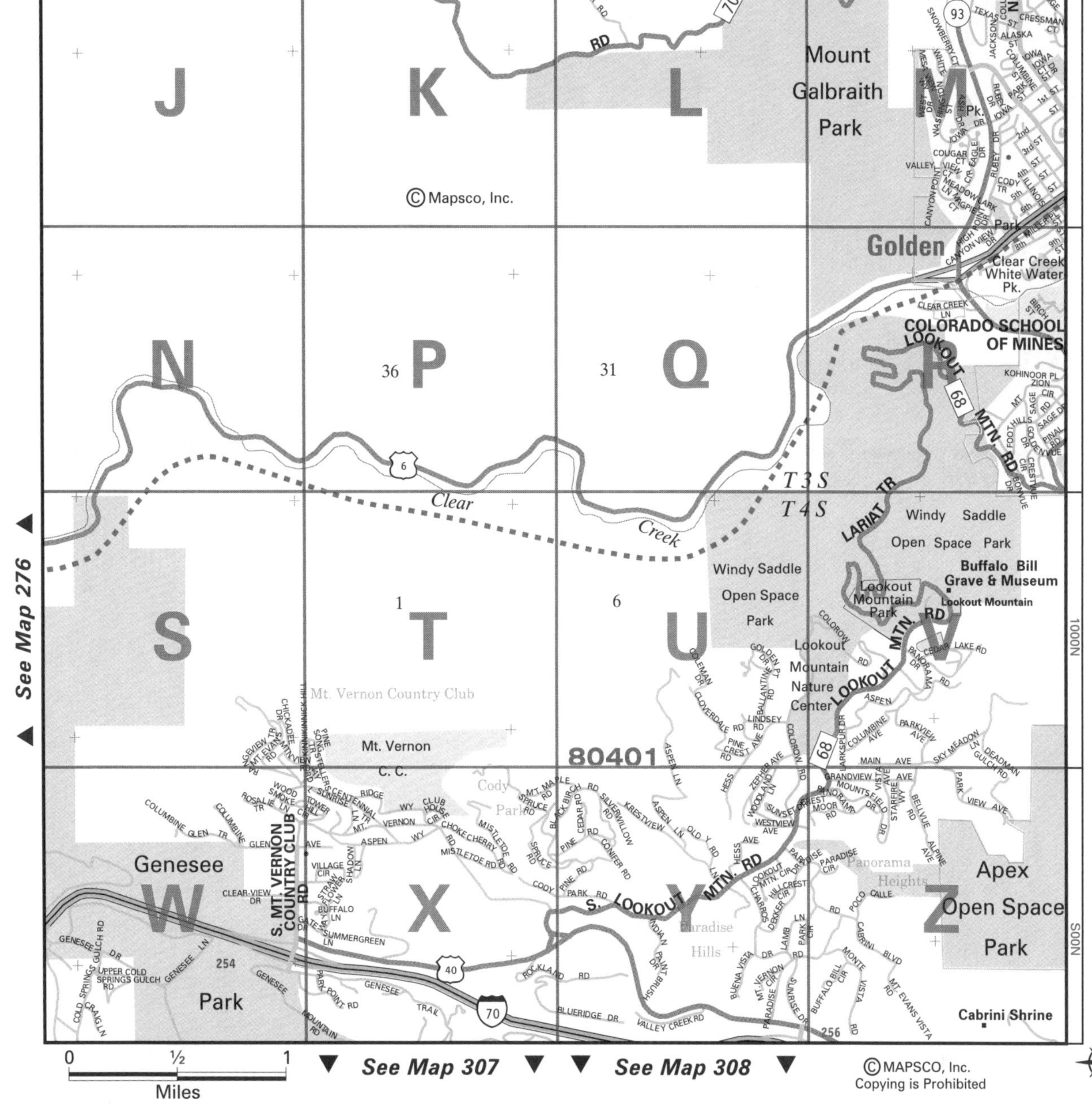

▼ See Map 307 ▼

▼ See Map 308 ▼

▲ See Map 770 ▲

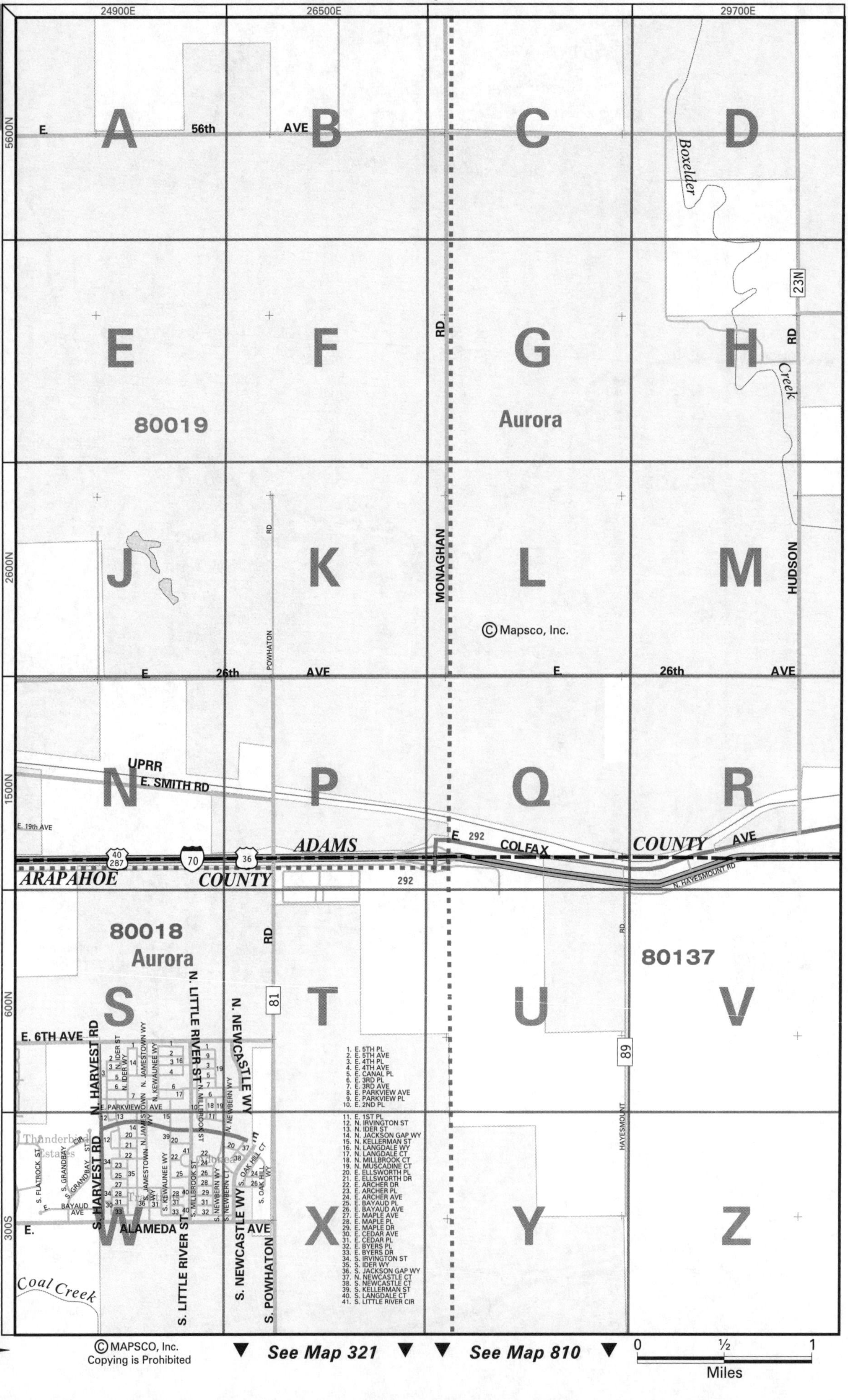

▲ See Map 260 ▲

▲ See Map 290 ▲

24900E 26500E 29700E

5600N 2600N 1500N 600N 300S

A B C D E F G H J K L M N P Q R S T U V W X Y Z

E. 56th AVE

80019

Aurora

Boxelder Creek

23N

MONAGHAN RD

POWHATON RD

HUDSON RD

© Mapsco, Inc.

E. 26th AVE

E. 26th AVE

UPRR

E. SMITH RD

E. 19th AVE

40 287 70 36

ADAMS COUNTY

ARAPAHOE COUNTY

E. 292 COLFAX AVE

292

N. HAYESMOUNT RD

80018

Aurora

80137

81

89

HAYESMOUNT RD

E. 6TH AVE

N. HARVEST RD

N. LITTLE RIVER ST

N. NEWCASTLE WY

N. IDER ST

N. IDER WY

N. JAMESTOWN WY

N. JAMESTOWN WY

N. KEWAUNEE WY

N. MILLBROOK ST

N. NEWBERN WY

E. PARKVIEW AVE

Thunderbird Estates

S. FLATROCK ST

S. GRANDBAY CIR

S. GRANDBAY ST

S. HARVEST RD

S. JAMESTOWN WY

S. KEWAUNEE WY

S. MILLBROOK ST

S. NEWBERN CT

S. NEWBERN WY

S. OAK HILL CT

S. OAK HILL WY

E. BAYAUD AVE

E. ALAMEDA AVE

S. LITTLE RIVER ST

S. NEWCASTLE WY

S. POWHATON RD

Coal Creek

1. E. 5TH PL
2. E. 5TH AVE
3. E. 4TH PL
4. E. 4TH AVE
5. E. CANAL PL
6. E. 3RD PL
7. E. 3RD AVE
8. E. PARKVIEW AVE
9. E. PARKVIEW PL
10. E. 2ND PL
11. E. 1ST PL
12. N. IRVINGTON ST
13. N. IDER ST
14. N. JACKSON GAP WY
15. N. KELLERMAN ST
16. N. LANGDALE WY
17. N. LANGDALE CT
18. N. MILLBROOK CT
19. N. MUSCADINE CT
20. E. ELLSWORTH PL
21. E. ELLSWORTH DR
22. E. ARCHER DR
23. E. ARCHER PL
24. E. ARCHER AVE
25. E. BAYAUD PL
26. E. BAYAUD AVE
27. E. MAPLE AVE
28. E. MAPLE PL
29. E. MAPLE DR
30. E. CEDAR AVE
31. E. CEDAR PL
32. E. BYERS PL
33. E. BYERS DR
34. S. IRVINGTON ST
35. S. IDER WY
36. S. JACKSON GAP WY
37. N. NEWCASTLE CT
38. S. NEWCASTLE CT
39. S. KELLERMAN ST
40. S. LANGDALE CT
41. S. LITTLE RIVER CIR

N

▼ See Map 321 ▼

▼ See Map 810 ▼

0 ½ 1
Miles

See Map 771

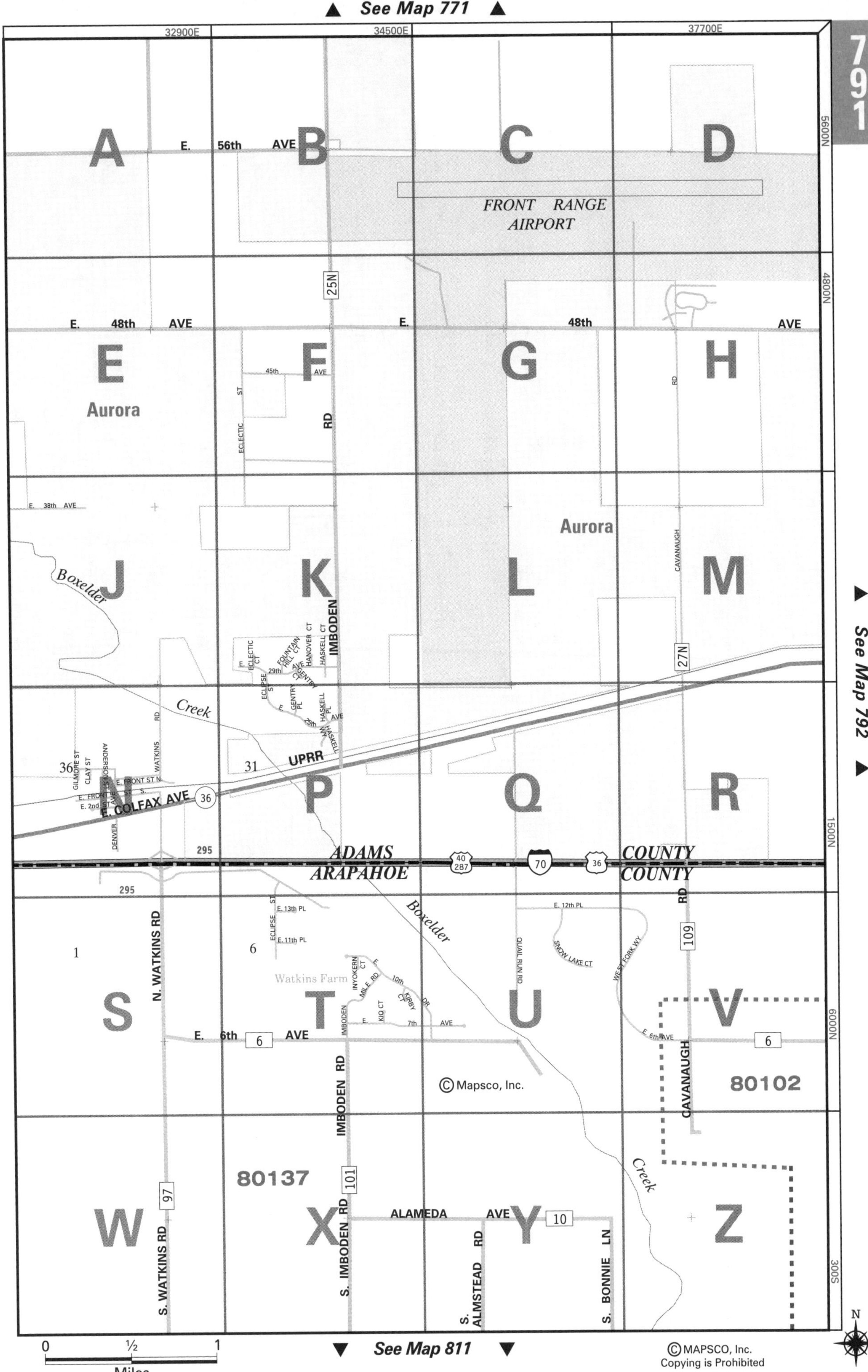

See Map 792

See Map 811

See Map 772

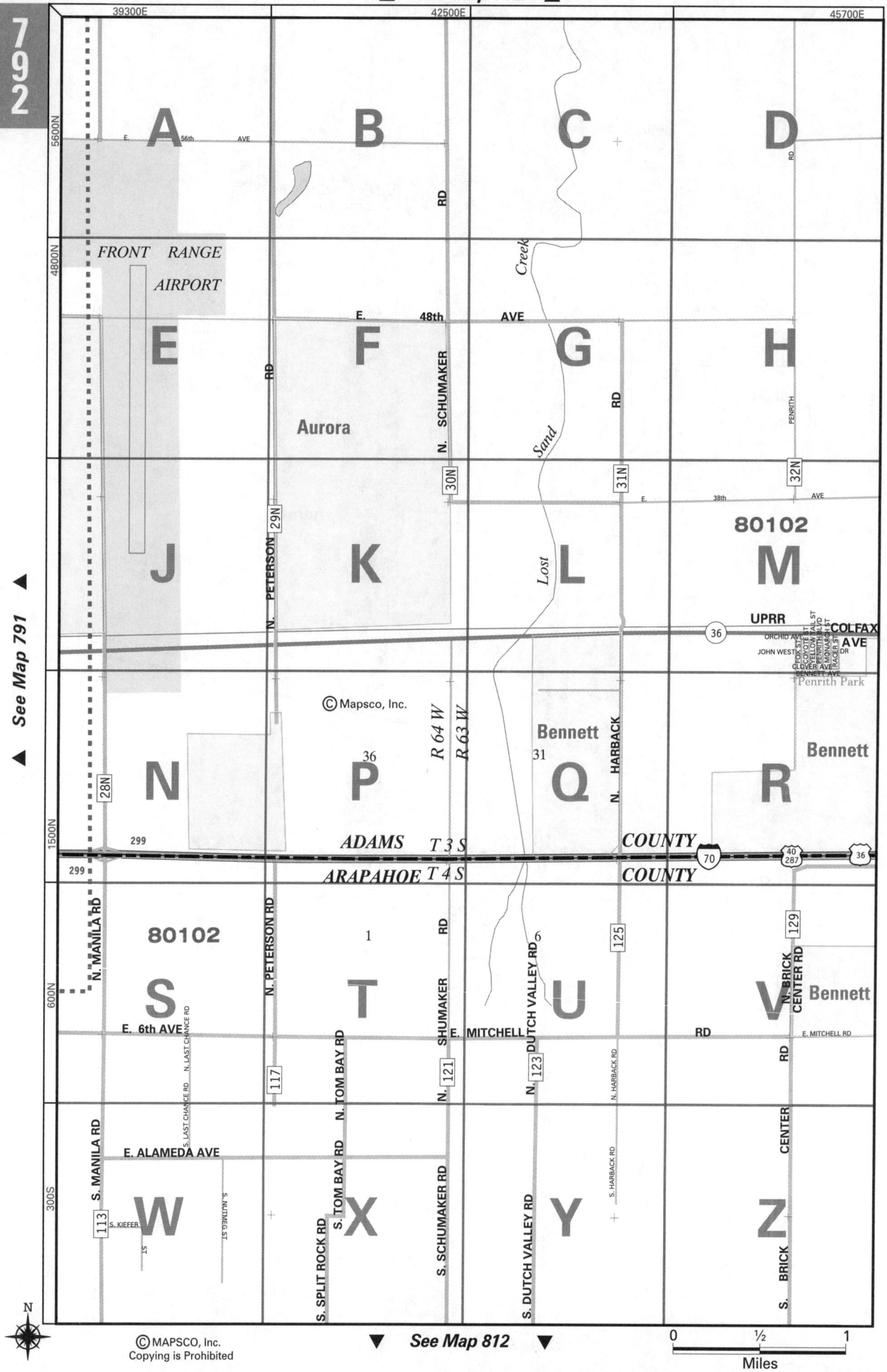

39300E 42500E 45700E

5600N 4800N 1500N 600N 300S

A B C D E F G H J K L M N P Q R S T U V W X Y Z

E. 56th AVE

FRONT RANGE AIRPORT

E. 48th AVE

Aurora

N. SCHUMAKER RD

N. PETERSON RD

Sand Creek

Lost

30N 31N 32N 29N 28N

E. 38th AVE

PENRITH RD

80102

UPRR

36

COLFAX AVE

ORCHID AVE

JOHN WEST

FOX ST

COYOTE ST

YELLOWTAIL ST

PENRITH BLVD

MONARCH ST

RACER ST

CLOVER AVE

BENNETT AVE

DR

Penrith Park

© Mapsco, Inc.

R 64 W

R 63 W

36

31

Bennett

N. HARBACK RD

299

ADAMS T 3 S COUNTY

70

40 287

36

ARAPAHOE T 4 S COUNTY

N. MANILA RD

N. PETERSON RD

80102

1

6

RD

N. DUTCH VALLEY RD

125

129

N. BRICK CENTER RD

Bennett

E. 6th AVE

N. LAST CHANCE RD

E. MITCHELL RD

E. MITCHELL RD

N. TOM BAY RD

N. SHUMAKER RD

N. HARBACK RD

117 121 123

S. LAST CHANCE RD

E. ALAMEDA AVE

S. MANILA RD

S. TOM BAY RD

S. SPLIT ROCK RD

S. SCHUMAKER RD

S. DUTCH VALLEY RD

S. HARBACK RD

S. BRICK CENTER RD

113

S. KIEFER ST

S. NUTMEG ST

See Map 791

N

See Map 812

0 ½ 1
Miles

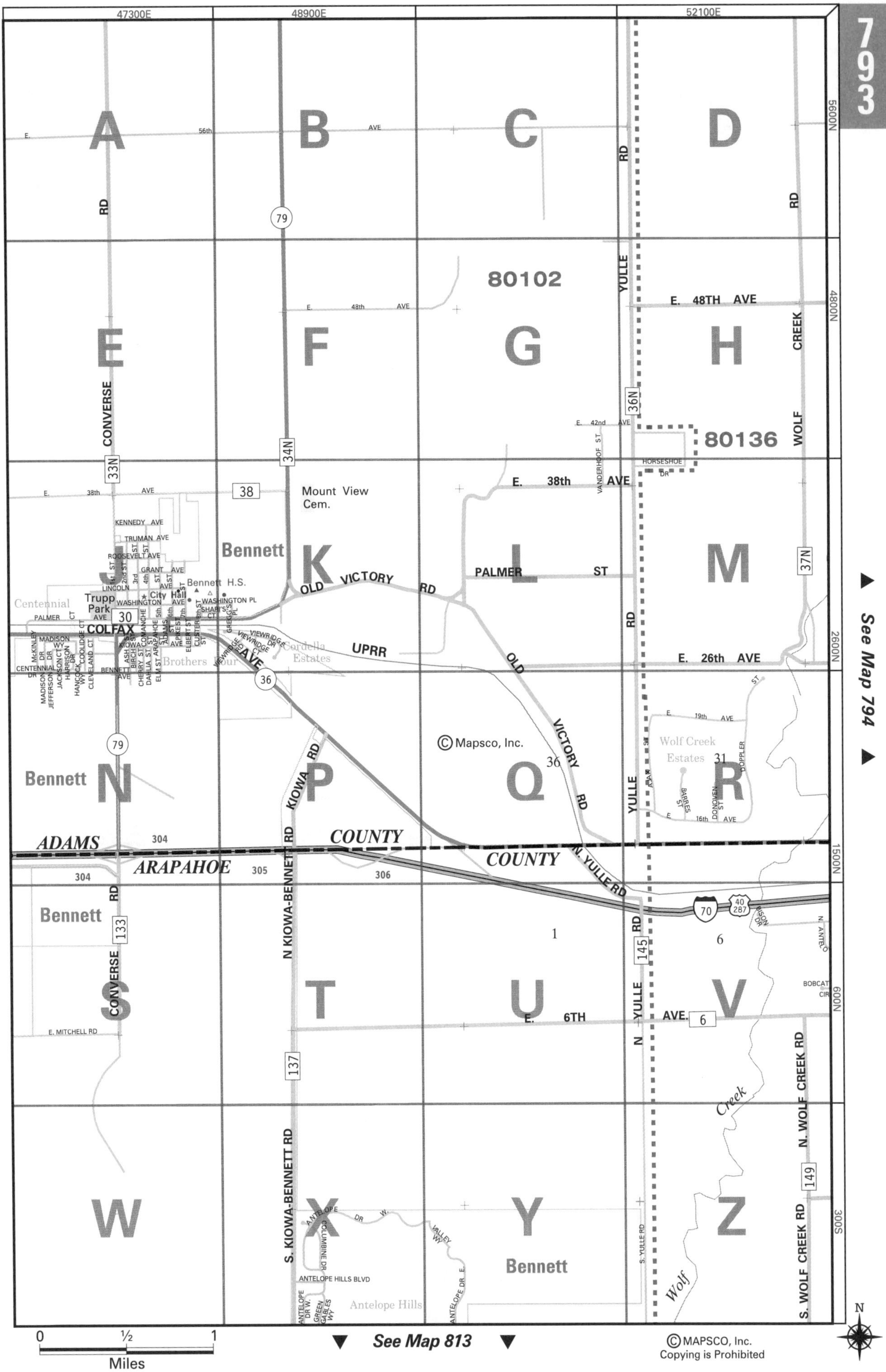

▲ See Map 794 ▲

0 ½ 1
Miles

▼ See Map 813 ▼

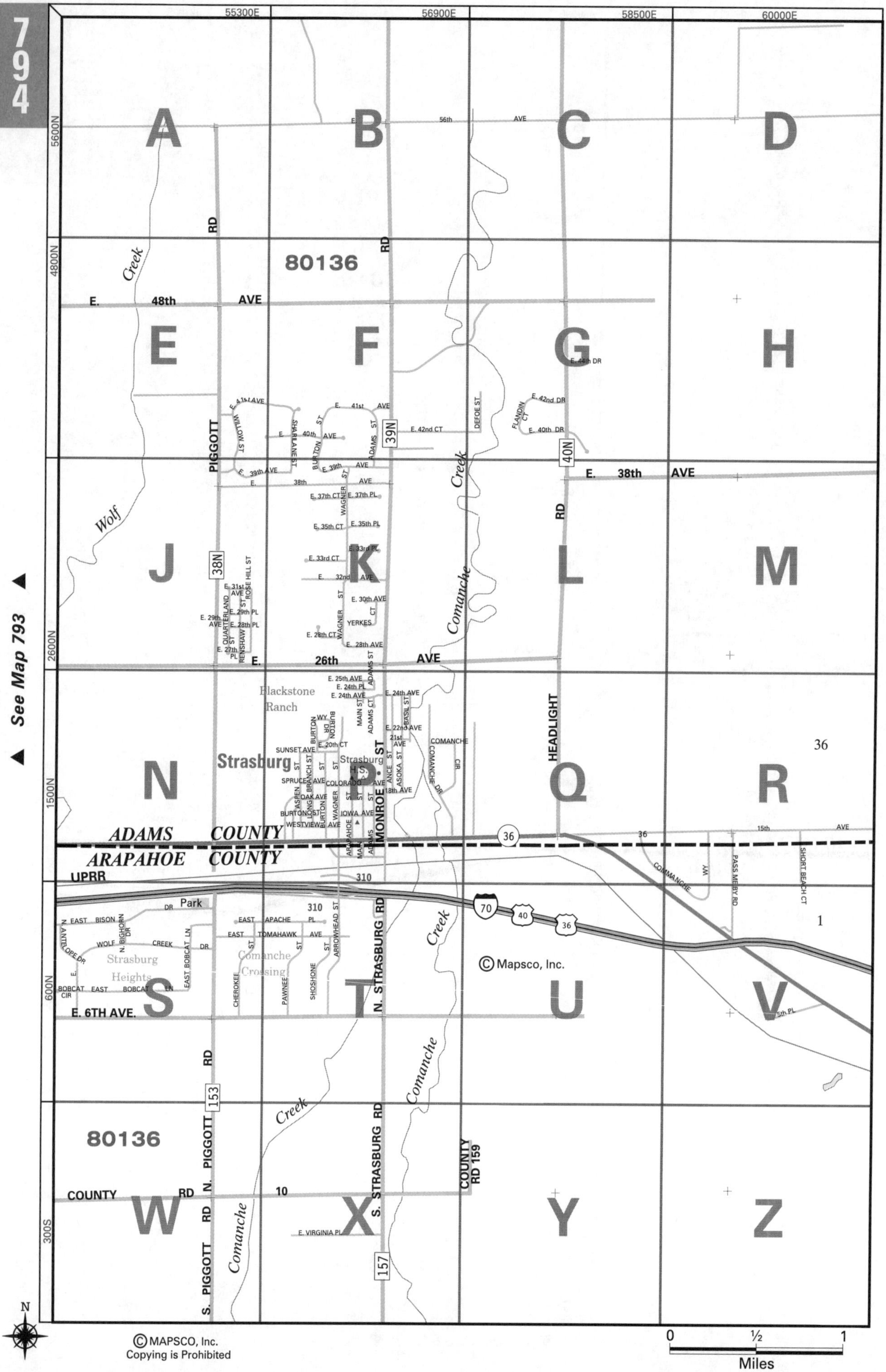
55300E
56900E
58500E
60000E
5600N
4800N
2600N
1500N
600N
300S
A
B
C
D
E
F
G
H
J
K
L
M
N
P
Q
R
S
T
U
V
W
X
Y
Z
80136
E. 56th AVE
E. 48th AVE
Wolf Creek
Comanche Creek
PIGGOTT RD
39N
40N
38N
E. 38th AVE
E. 26th AVE
HEADLIGHT RD
Blackstone Ranch
Strasburg
Strasburg H.S.
MONROE ST
ADAMS COUNTY
ARAPAHOE COUNTY
UPRR
310
36
70
40
E. 15th AVE
Strasburg Heights
Comanche Crossing
E. 6TH AVE.
N. STRASBURG RD
S. STRASBURG RD
N. PIGGOTT RD
S. PIGGOTT RD
153
157
COUNTY RD 10
COUNTY RD 159
E. VIRGINIA PL
1
© Mapsco, Inc.
See Map 793

0 ½ 1
Miles

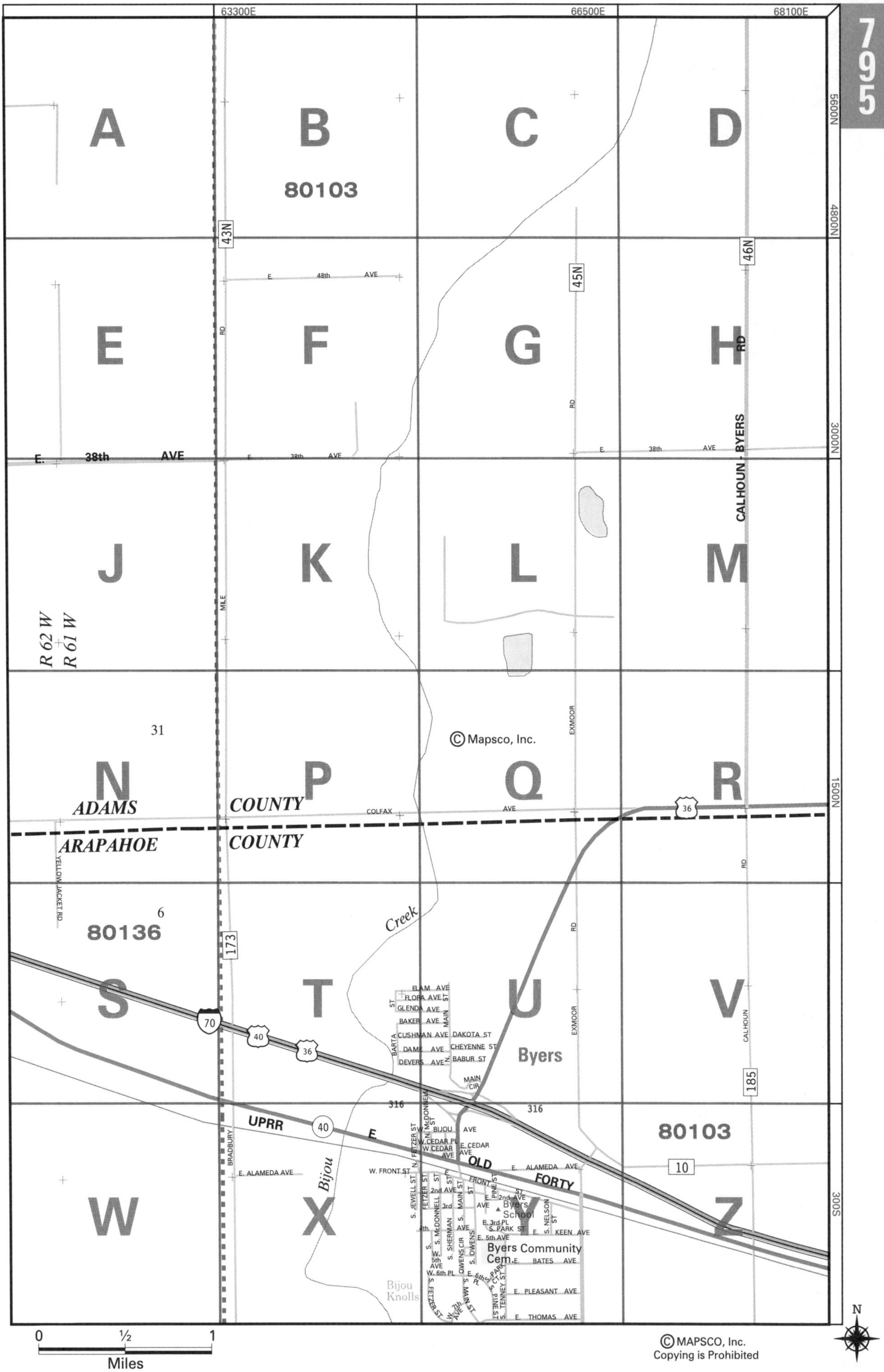

63300E 66500E 68100E

5600N 4800N 3000N 1500N 300S

A B C D

80103

E F G H

E. 48th AVE

43N 45N 46N

E. 38th AVE

CALHOUN - BYERS RD

J K L M

R 62 W
R 61 W

MILE RD

31

© Mapsco, Inc.

EXMOOR RD

N P Q R

ADAMS COUNTY

COLFAX AVE

36

ARAPAHOE COUNTY

YELLOW JACKET RD

6

80136

173

Creek

S T U V

70 40 36

ELAM AVE
FLORA AVE
GLENDA AVE
BAKER AVE
CUSHMAN AVE
DAME AVE
DEVERS AVE
DAKOTA ST
CHEYENNE ST
BABUR ST
BARTA ST
N. MAIN ST
MAIN CIR

Byers

CALHOUN

185

316

UPRR

40

E. OLD FORTY

BIJOU AVE
W. CEDAR PL
W. CEDAR AVE
E. CEDAR AVE
W. FRONT ST
FRONT ST
E. ALAMEDA AVE
N. FETZER ST
N. McDONNELL ST

BRADBURY

E. ALAMEDA AVE

Bijou

80103

10

W X Y Z

S. JEWELL ST
S. FETZER ST
S. McDONNELL ST
S. MAIN ST
S. SHERMAN
S. OWENS
OWENS CIR
2nd AVE
3rd AVE
4th AVE
W. 5th AVE
W. 6th PL
E. 2nd AVE
E. 3rd PL
S. PARK ST
E. 5th AVE
PINE ST
S. NELSON ST
E. KEEN AVE
Byers School
Byers Community Cem.
E. BATES AVE
E. PLEASANT AVE
E. THOMAS AVE
E. 6th PL
S. PARK CT
S. TENNEY ST
S. PINE ST
W. 7th AVE
S. FETZER ST
S. MAIN ST

Bijou Knolls

0 ½ 1
Miles

N

▲ See Map 781 ▲

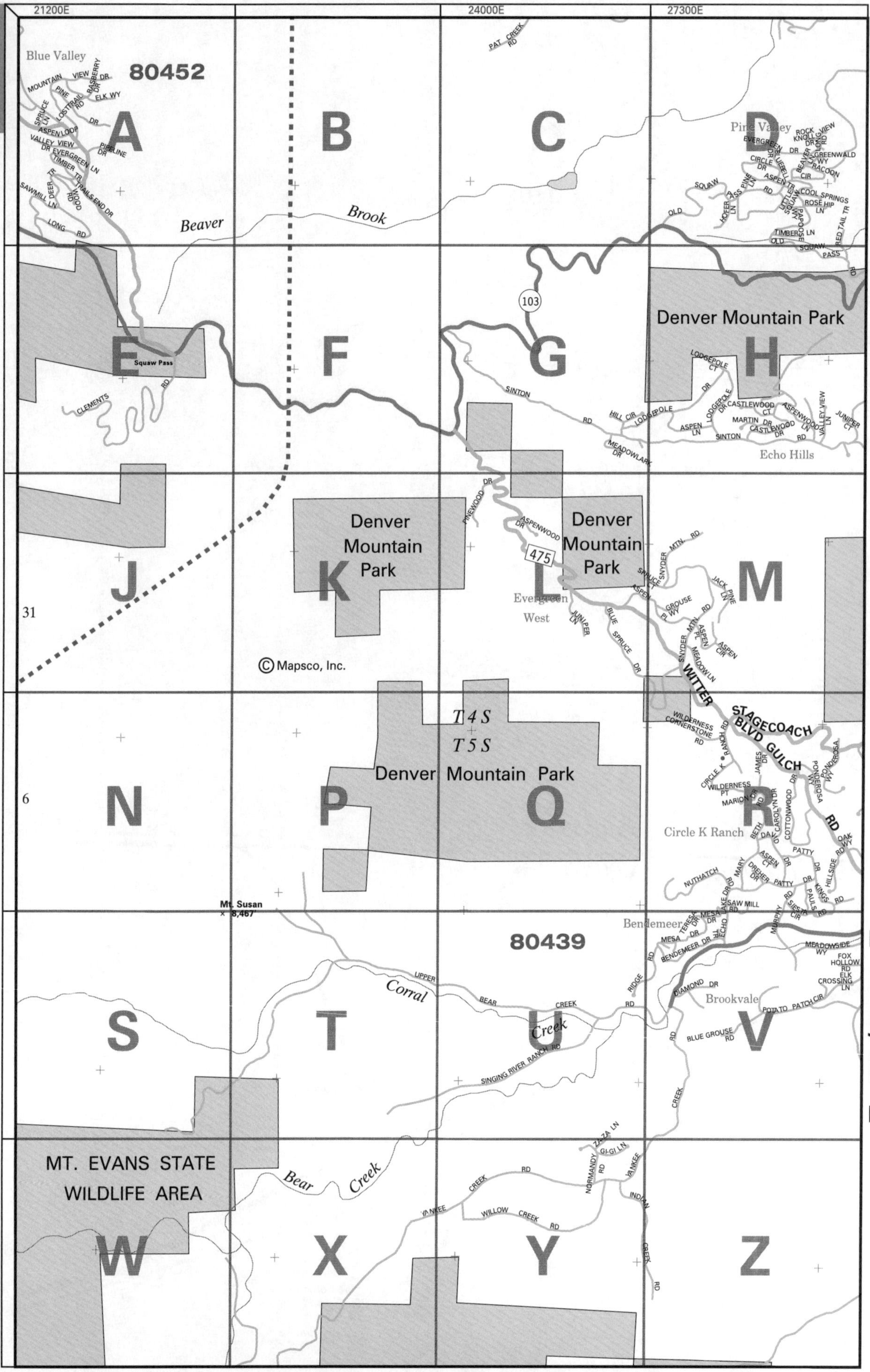

21200E | 24000E | 27300E

80452

A B C D

E F G H

J K L M

N P Q R

S T U V

W X Y Z

80439

Denver Mountain Park

MT. EVANS STATE WILDLIFE AREA

T4S

T5S

See Map 305

See Map 335

▼ See Map 821 ▼

0 ½ 1
Miles

See Map 291
See Map 790
See Map 320
See Map 811
See Map 350
See Map 381
See Map 830

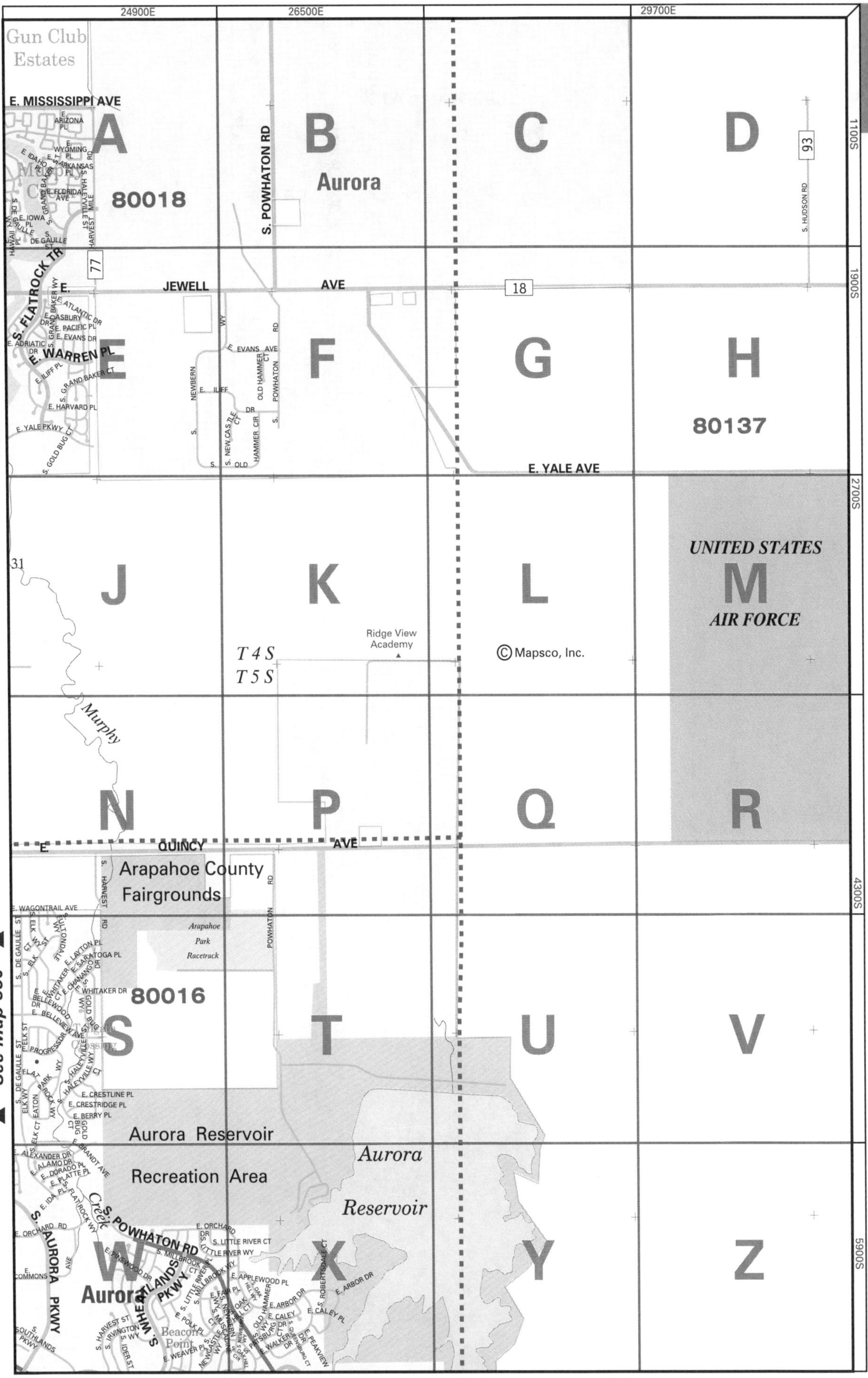

24900E
26500E
29700E
1100S
1900S
2700S
4300S
5900S

Gun Club Estates
E. MISSISSIPPI AVE
A
B
C
D
80018
Aurora
S. POWHATON RD
S. HUDSON RD
93
77
E. JEWELL AVE
18
S. FLATROCK TR
E. WARREN PL
E
F
G
H
80137
E. YALE AVE
J
K
L
M
UNITED STATES AIR FORCE
Ridge View Academy
T 4 S
T 5 S
Murphy
N
P
Q
R
E. QUINCY AVE
Arapahoe County Fairgrounds
Arapahoe Park Racetrack
80016
S
T
U
V
Aurora Reservoir Recreation Area
Aurora Reservoir
Creek
S. POWHATON RD
S. AURORA PKWY
S. WHEATLANDS PKWY
Aurora
Beacon Point
W
X
Y
Z

0 ½ 1
Miles

See Map 791

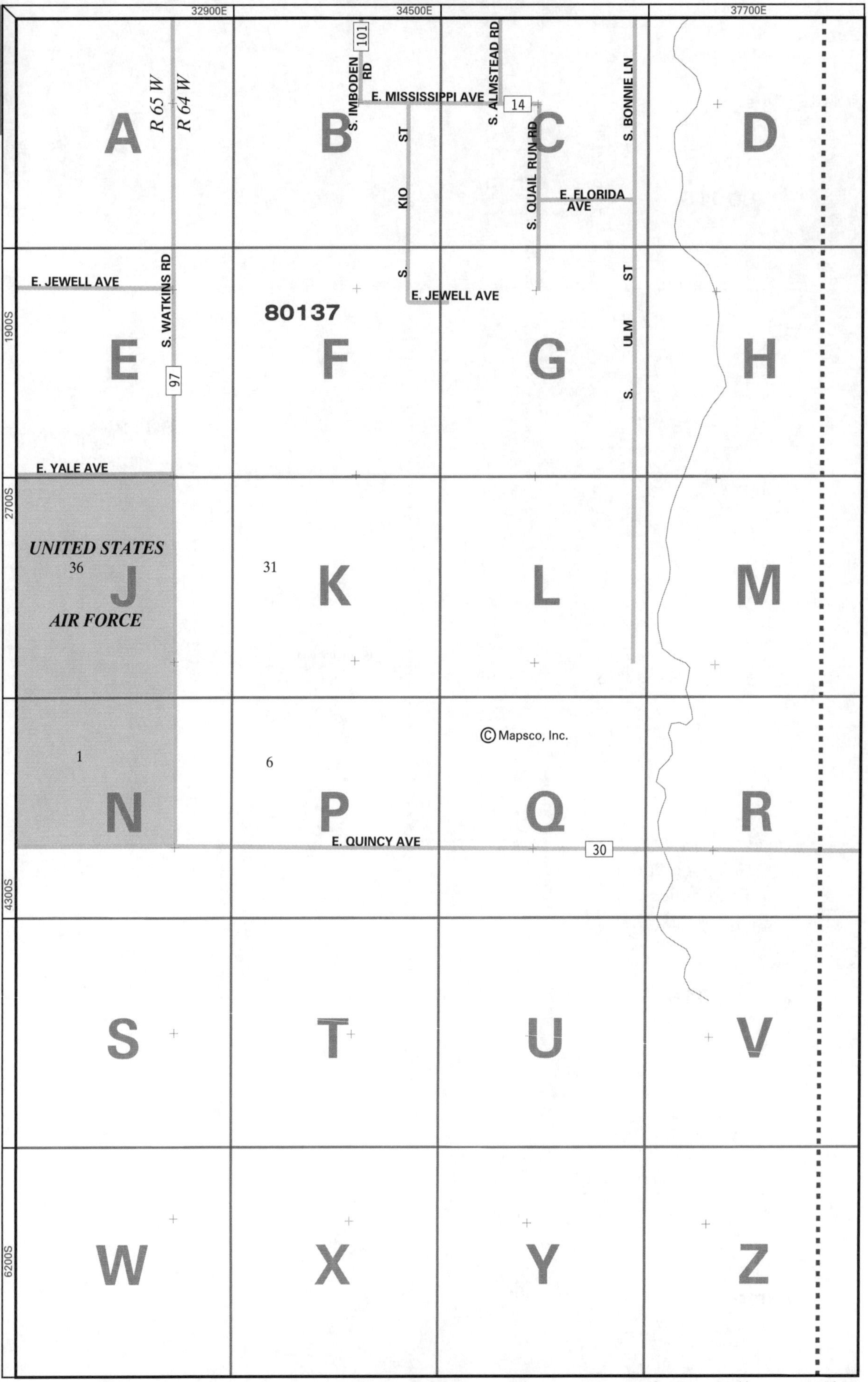

32900E 34500E 37700E

1900S 2700S 4300S 6200S

R 65 W
R 64 W

A B C D E F G H J K L M N P Q R S T U V W X Y Z

S. IMBODEN RD
101
E. MISSISSIPPI AVE
S. ALMSTEAD RD
14
S. BONNIE LN
S. KIO ST
S. QUAIL RUN RD
E. FLORIDA AVE
E. JEWELL AVE
S. WATKINS RD
E. JEWELL AVE
80137
S. ULM ST
97
E. YALE AVE
UNITED STATES AIR FORCE
36
31
1
6
© Mapsco, Inc.
E. QUINCY AVE
30

See Map 810

N

See Map 831

0 ½ 1
Miles

See Map 792

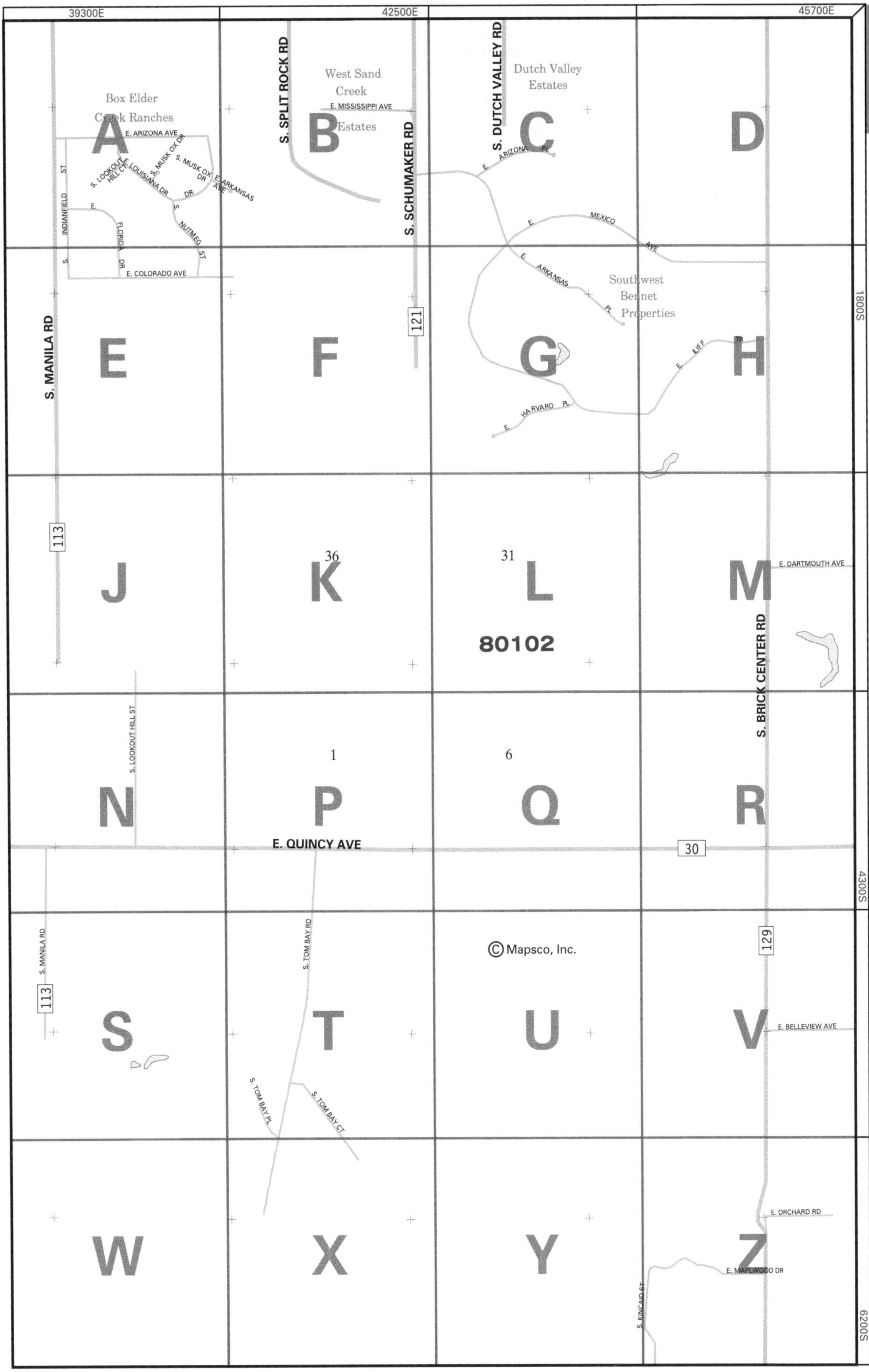

39300E
42500E
45700E

Box Elder Creek Ranches
West Sand Creek Estates
Dutch Valley Estates
Southwest Bennet Properties

A B C D
E F G H
J K L M
N P Q R
S T U V
W X Y Z

S. SPLIT ROCK RD
S. SCHUMAKER RD
S. DUTCH VALLEY RD
S. MANILA RD
S. BRICK CENTER RD
E. QUINCY AVE
E. MISSISSIPPI AVE
E. ARIZONA AVE
E. ARIZONA PL
E. MEXICO AVE
E. ARKANSAS PL
E. ILIFF TR
E. HARVARD PL
E. COLORADO AVE
E. DARTMOUTH AVE
E. BELLEVIEW AVE
E. ORCHARD RD
E. MAPLWOOD DR
S. KINCAID ST
S. TOM BAY RD
S. TOM BAY PL
S. TOM BAY CT
S. LOOKOUT HILL ST
S. INDIANFIELD ST
S. FLORIDA DR
S. NUTMEG ST
S. MUSK OX DR
S. LOOKOUT HILL CT
E. LOUISIANA DR
E. ARKANSAS AVE

121
113
30
129

36
31
1
6

80102

1800S
4300S
6200S

© Mapsco, Inc.

See Map 813

See Map 832

0 ½ 1
Miles

N

See Map 793

See Map 812

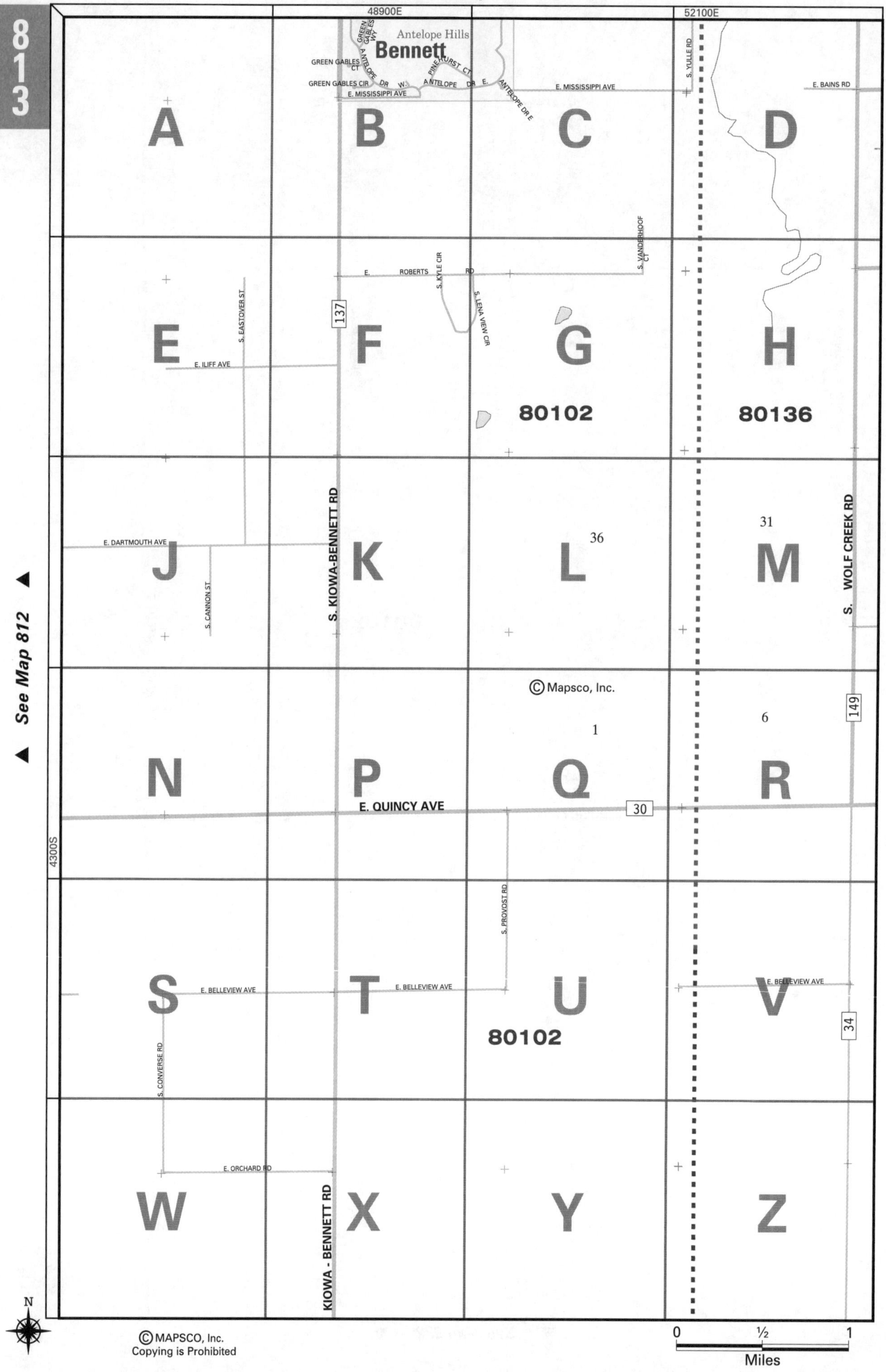

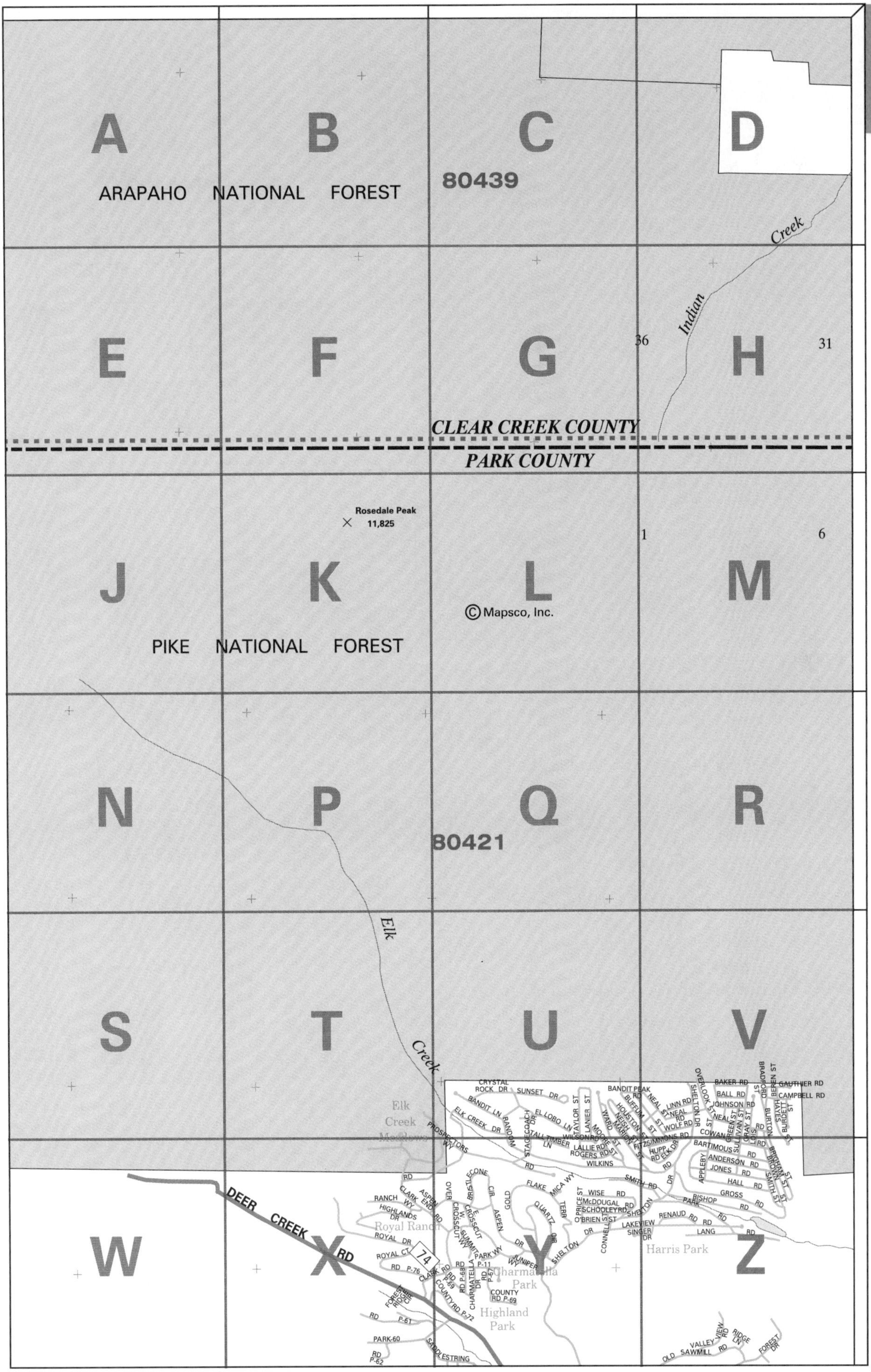

A B C D

ARAPAHO NATIONAL FOREST

80439

Indian Creek

E F G H

36 31

CLEAR CREEK COUNTY

PARK COUNTY

Rosedale Peak 11,825

1 6

J K L M

© Mapsco, Inc.

PIKE NATIONAL FOREST

N P Q R

80421

Elk Creek

S T U V

Elk Creek Meadows

Royal Ranch

Charmatella Park

Highland Park

Harris Park

DEER CREEK RD

74

W X Y Z

0 ½ 1

Miles

See Map 821

See Map 840

N

See Map 801

See Map 365

See Map 820

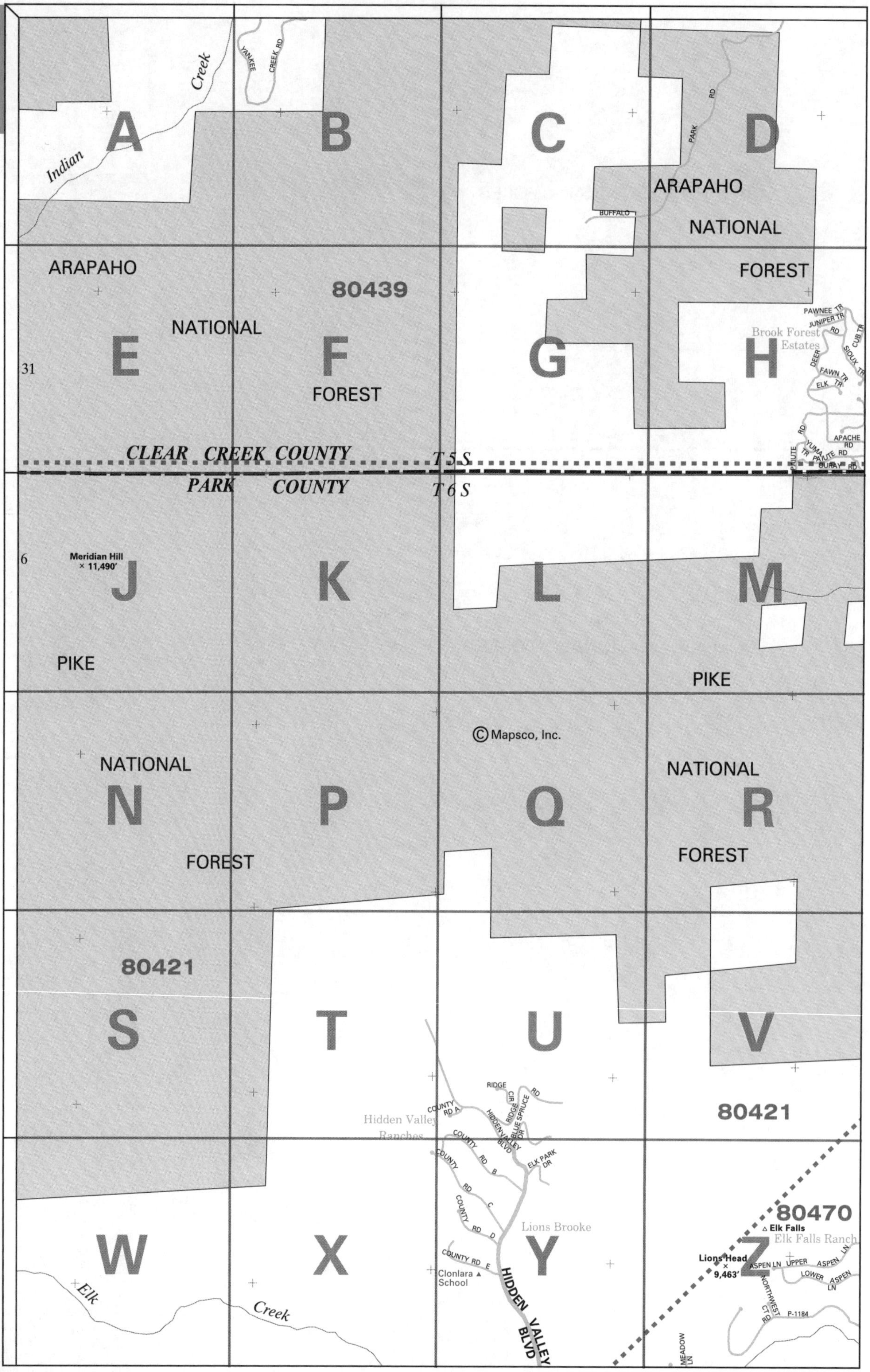

See Map 822

See Map 841

0 ½ 1
Miles

▲ See Map 335 ▲ ▲ See Map 336 ▲

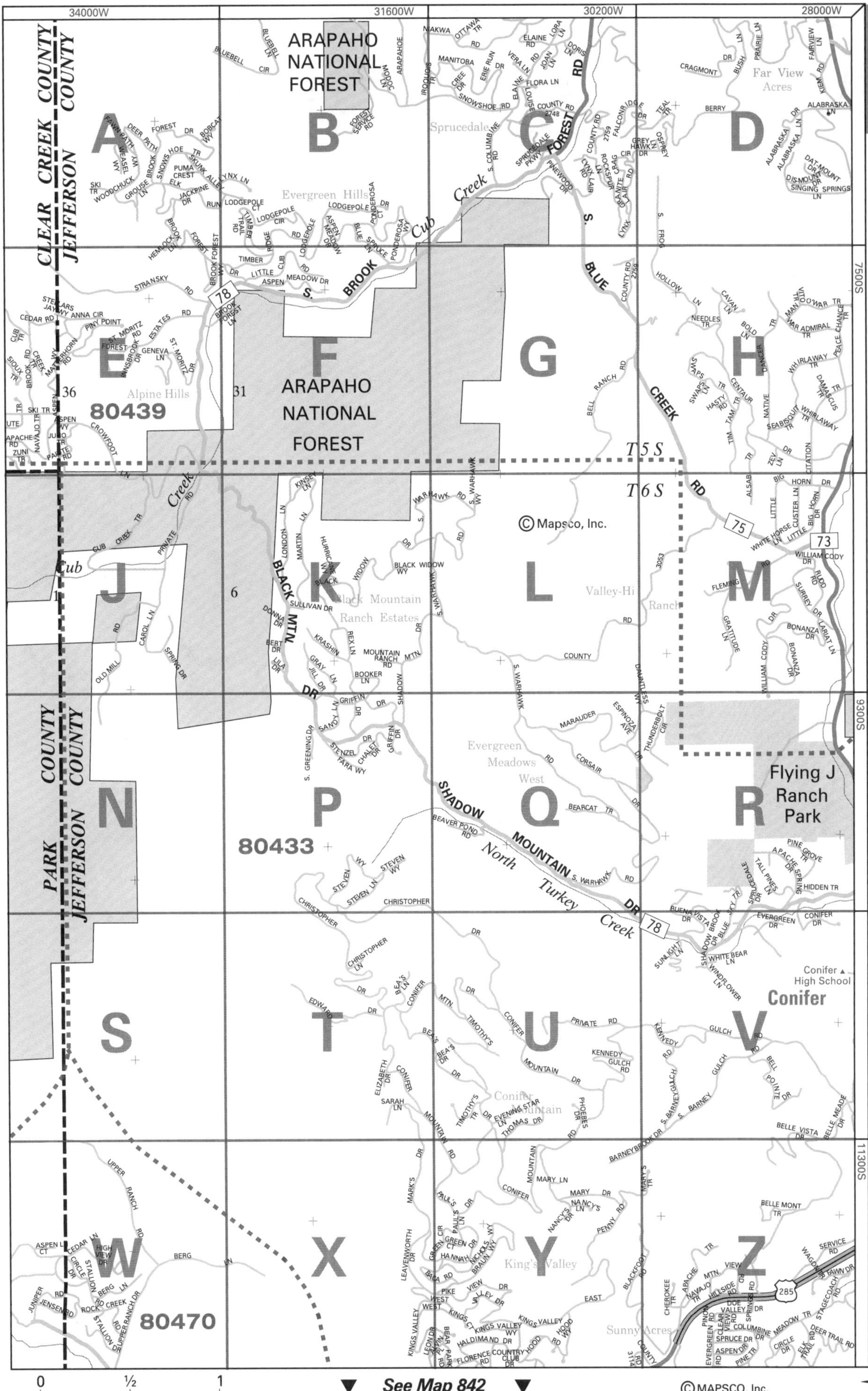

▶ See Map 367 ▶
▶ See Map 823 ▶
▼ See Map 842 ▼

0 ½ 1
Miles

See Map 337
See Map 338
See Map 366
See Map 369
See Map 822
See Map 824
See Map 843

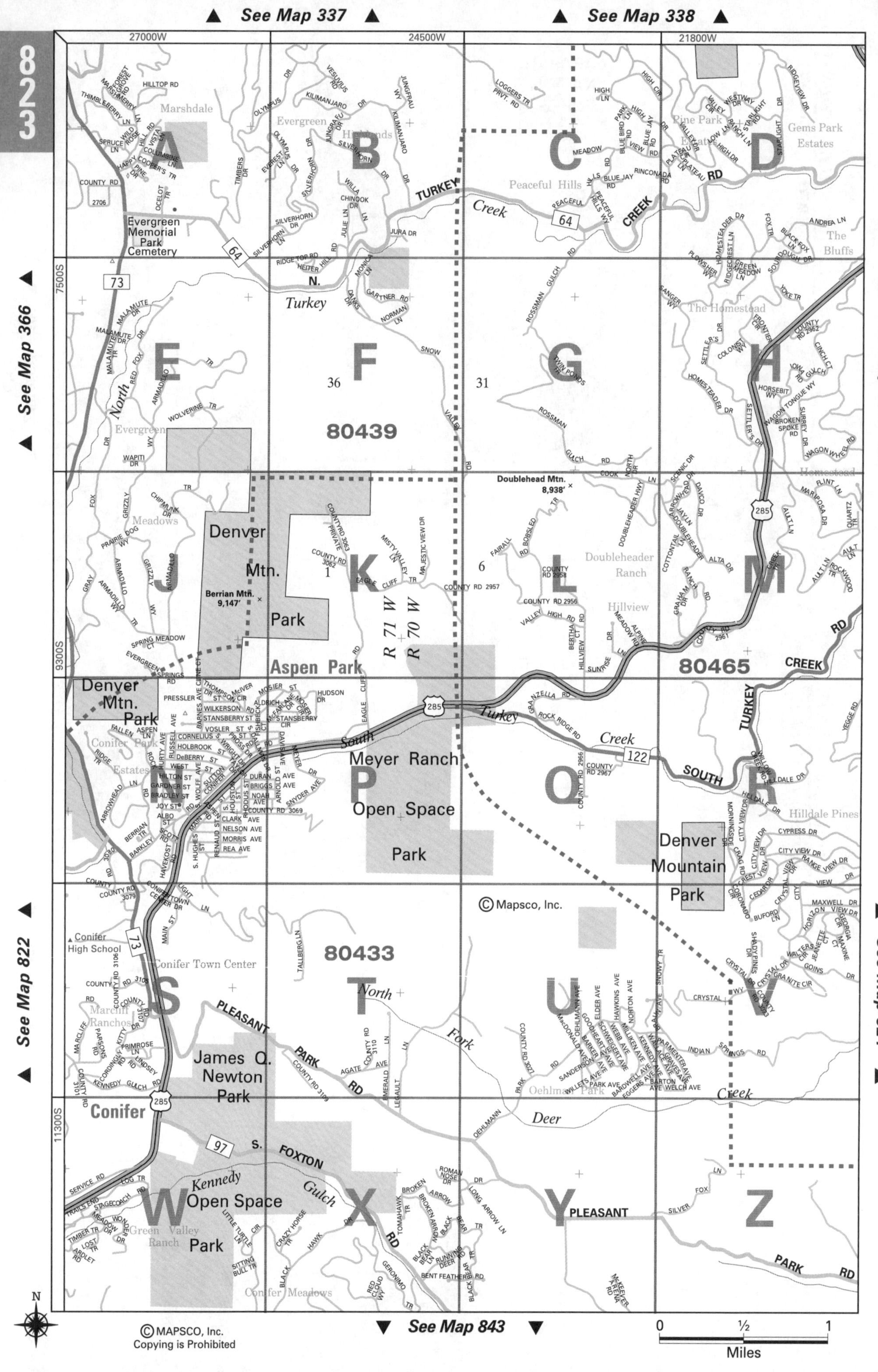

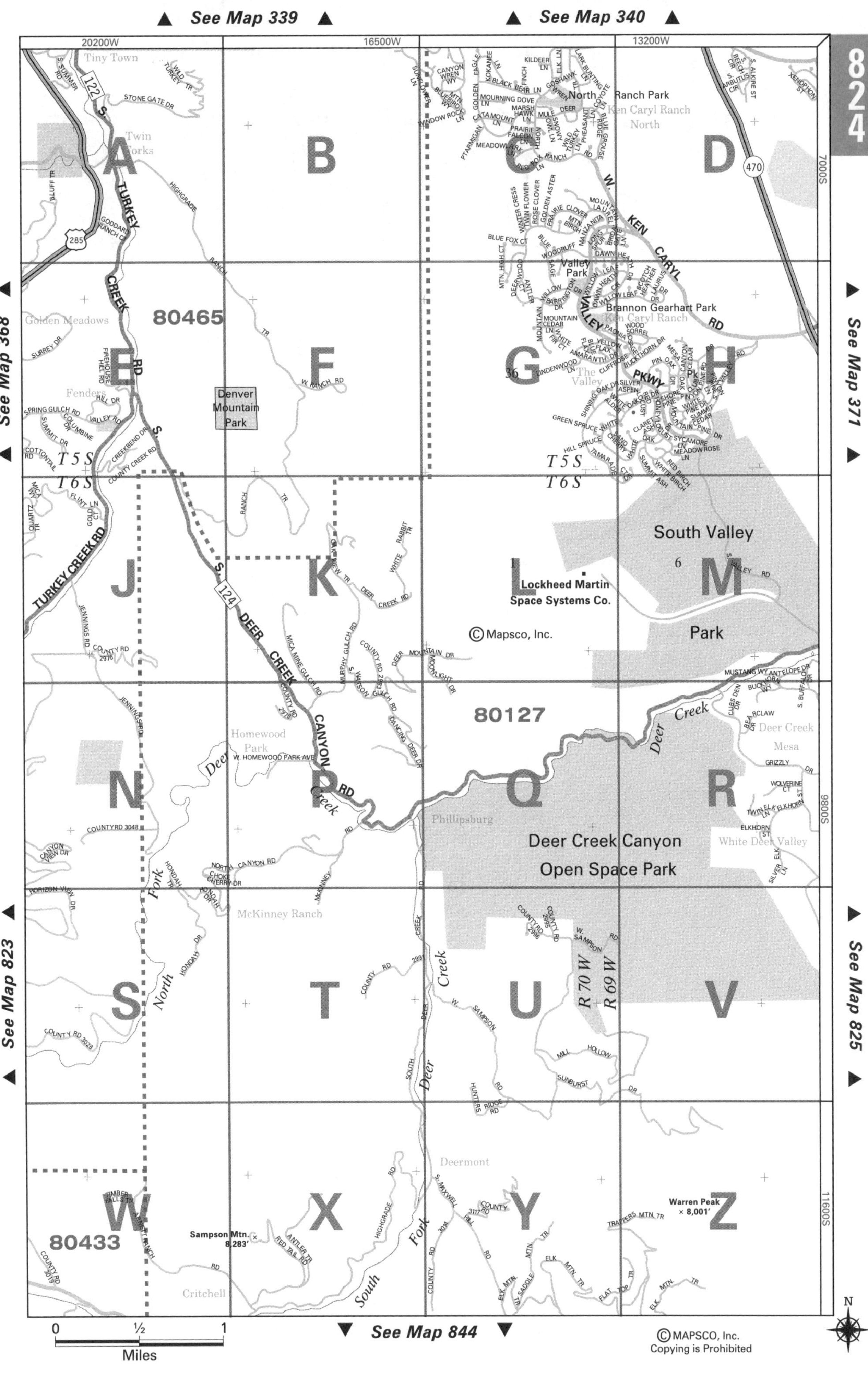

See Map 339
See Map 340
See Map 368
See Map 371
See Map 823
See Map 825
See Map 844
A
B
C
D
E
F
G
H
J
K
L
M
N
P
Q
R
S
T
U
V
W
X
Y
Z
80465
80127
80433
Tiny Town
Twin Forks
Golden Meadows
Fenders
Denver Mountain Park
Ranch Park
Ken Caryl Ranch North
North
Valley Park
Brannon Gearhart Park
Ken Caryl Ranch
The Valley
South Valley Park
Lockheed Martin Space Systems Co.
© Mapsco, Inc.
Homewood Park
Phillipsburg
Deer Creek Canyon Open Space Park
Deer Creek Mesa
White Deer Valley
McKinney Ranch
Deermont
Critchell
Sampson Mtn. 8,283'
Warren Peak × 8,001'
TURKEY CREEK RD
S. DEER CREEK CANYON RD
W. KEN CARYL
VALLEY PKWY
Deer Creek
North Fork
South Fork
South Deer Creek
T5S
T6S
R 70 W
R 69 W
20200W
16500W
13200W
7000S
9800S
11600S
0
½
1
Miles

▲ See Map 341 ▲ ▲ See Map 342 ▲

▲ See Map 370 ▲ ▲ See Map 373 ▲ ▲ See Map 824 ▲ ▲ See Map 403 ▲

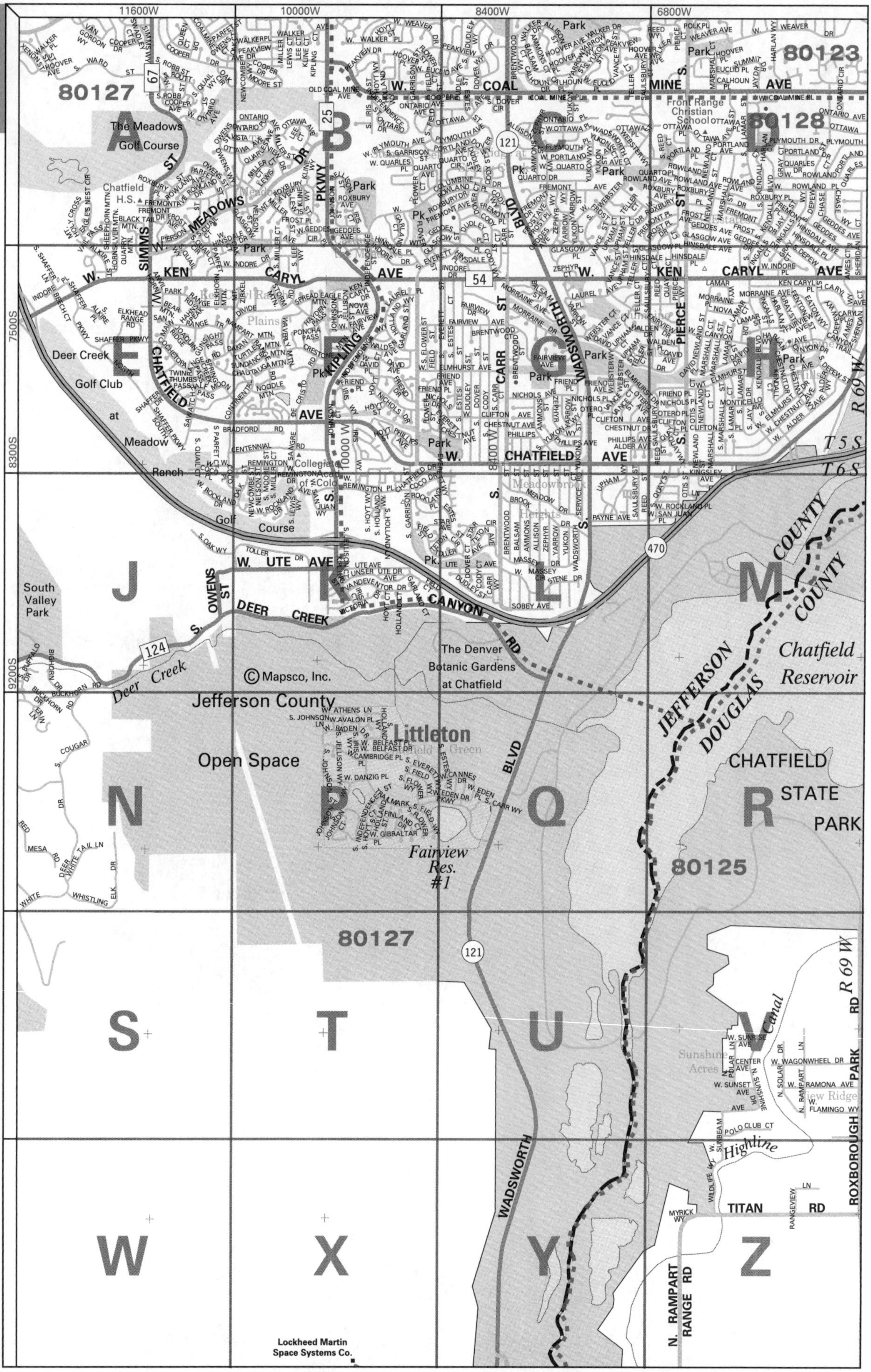

▼ See Map 845 ▼ ▼ See Map 432 ▼

0 ½ 1
Miles

See Map 351
See Map 810

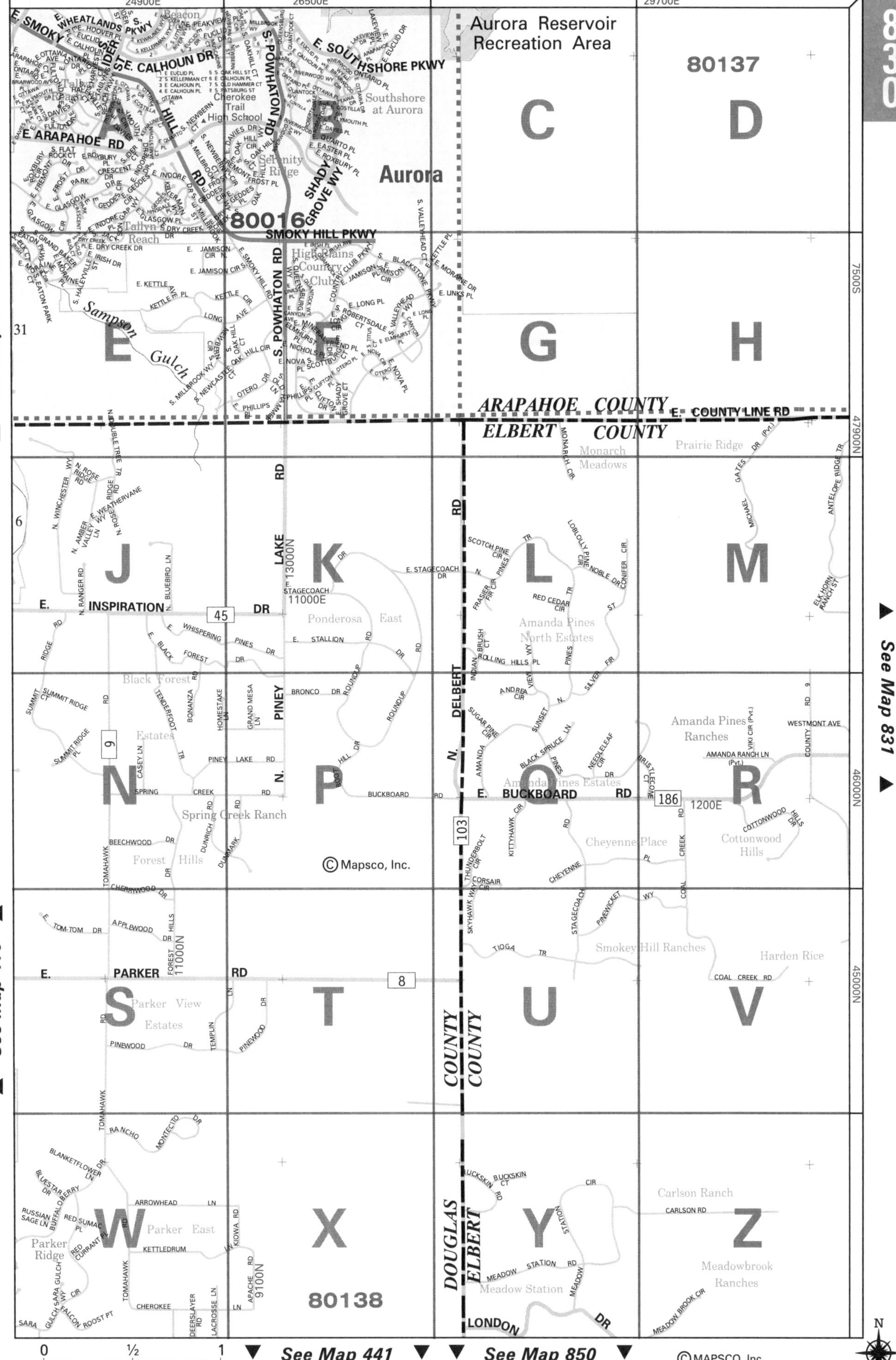

See Map 380
See Map 410
See Map 831
See Map 441
See Map 850

0 ½ 1
Miles

See Map 811

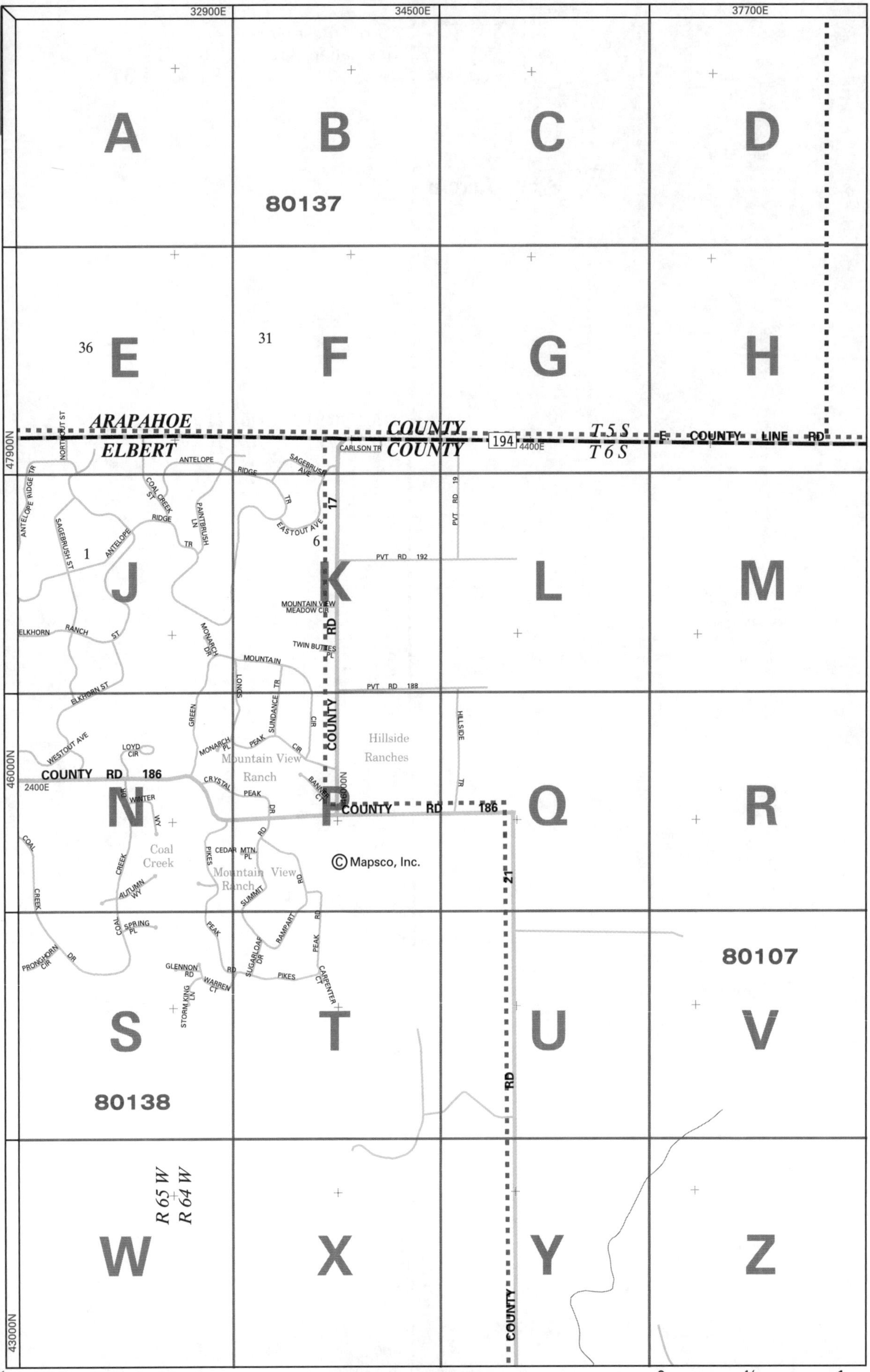

32900E 34500E 37700E

A B C D

80137

36 E 31 F G H

ARAPAHOE COUNTY T5S
ELBERT COUNTY T6S

E. COUNTY LINE RD

194 4400E

47900N

J K L M

N P Q R

Mountain View Ranch

Hillside Ranches

Coal Creek

COUNTY RD 186

46000N 2400E

© Mapsco, Inc.

80107

S T U V

80138

W X Y Z

R 65 W
R 64 W

43000N

See Map 830

See Map 851

0 ½ 1
Miles

▲ See Map 812 ▲

41600E

45700E

A B C D

80137

E. COSTILLA AVE

S. OAKLEAF ST

E. GEDDES AVE

S. KINCAID ST

CENTER RD

E. GEDDES AVE

7300S

E F G H

36

31

E. JAMISON PL

BRICK

ANTELOPE DR

ARAPAHOE COUNTY

194

E. COUNTY LINE RD

10000E

ELBERT COUNTY

J K L M

PVT. RD 192

PVT. RD 39

Elbert Ranch Estates

47900N

1

6

PATRICK TR

BECKY CIR

CHRISTOPHER CT

Foxwood

FOXWOOD DR

◄ See Map 831 ◄

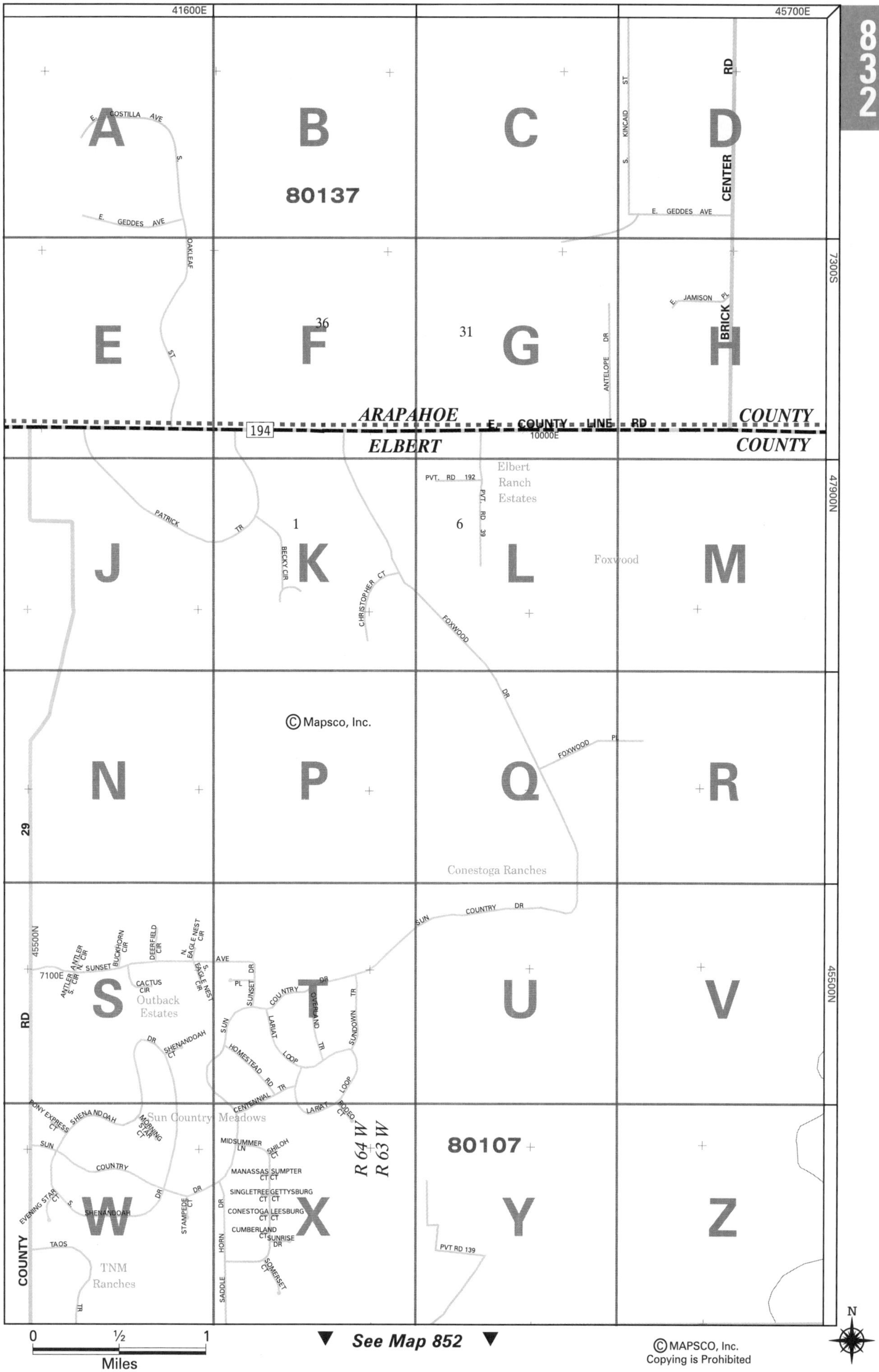

N P Q R

© Mapsco, Inc.

FOXWOOD PL

29

Conestoga Ranches

S T U V

SUN COUNTRY DR

45500N

7100E

ANTLER S. CIR

ANTLER N. CIR

BUCKHORN CIR

DEERFIELD CIR

N. EAGLE NEST CIR

S. EAGLE NEST CIR

SUNSET AVE

CACTUS CIR

Outback Estates

PL

SUNSET DR

COUNTRY DR

OVERLAND TR

SUNDOWN TR

LARIAT LOOP

SUN

HOMESTEAD RD

SHENANDOAH CT

DR

RD

CENTENNIAL TR

LOOP

LARIAT CT

RODEO CT

W X Y Z

PONY EXPRESS CT

SHENANDOAH

MORNING STAR CT

Sun Country Meadows

SUN COUNTRY DR

EVENING STAR CT

S. SHENANDOAH

STAMPEDE CT

TAOS TR

TNM Ranches

COUNTY

MIDSUMMER LN

SHILOH CT

MANASSAS CT

SUMPTER CT

SINGLETREE CT

GETTYSBURG CT

CONESTOGA CT

LEESBURG CT

CUMBERLAND CT

SUNRISE DR

SOMERSET CT

SADDLE HORN DR

R 64 W

R 63 W

80107

PVT RD 139

0 ½ 1

Miles

▼ See Map 852 ▼

N

▲ See Map 820 ▲

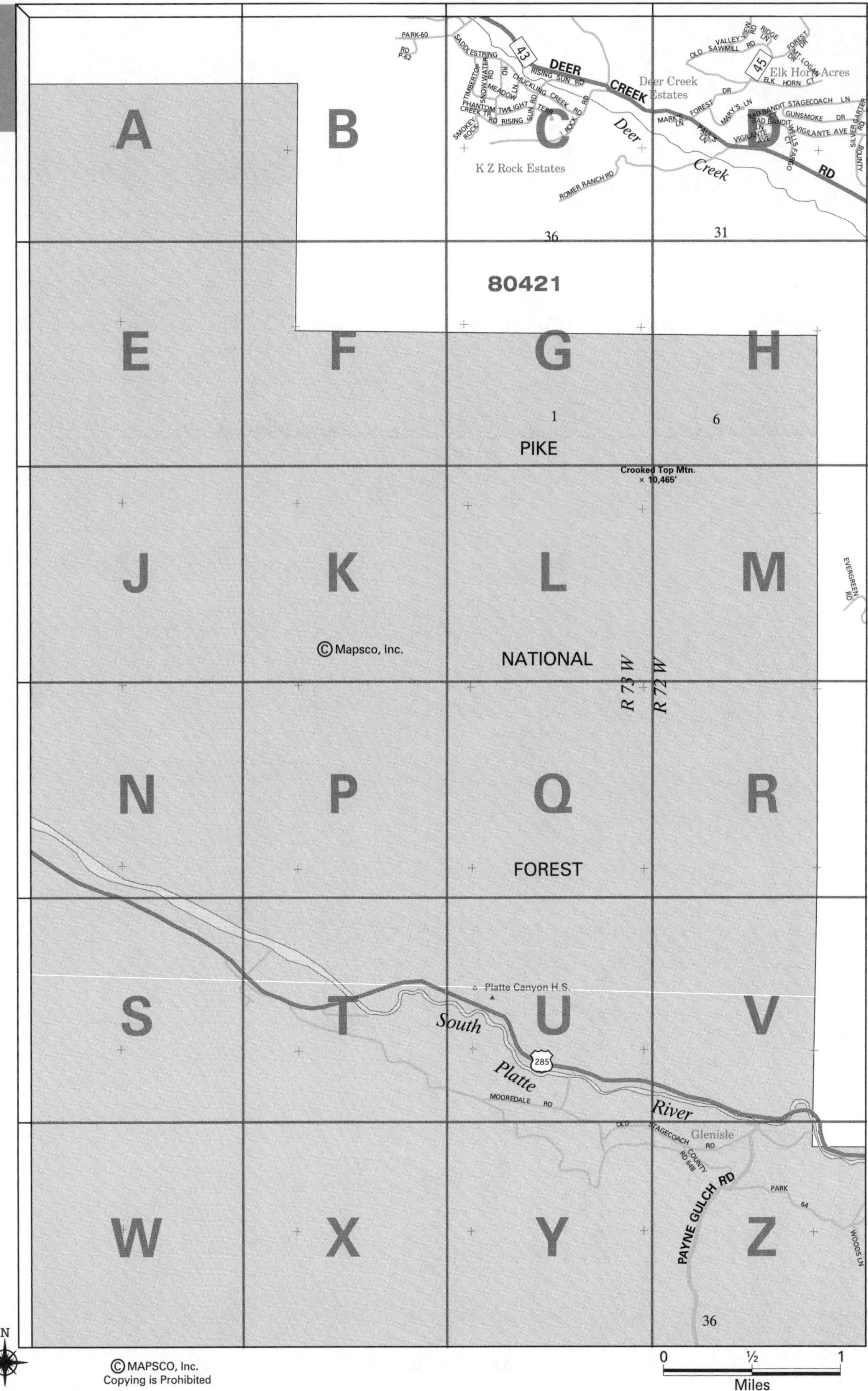

0 ½ 1
Miles

▲ See Map 821 ▲

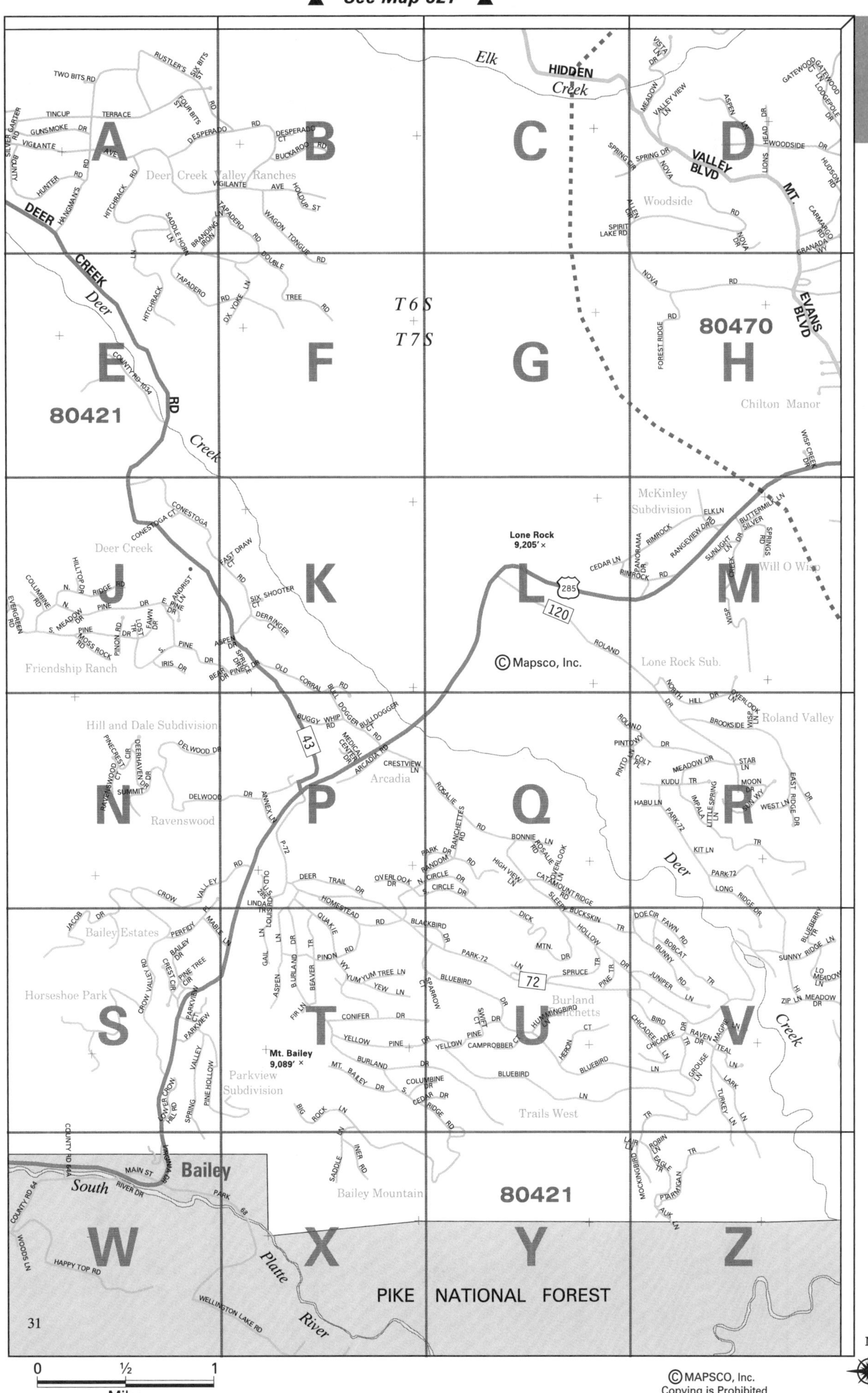

▶ See Map 842 ▶

0 ½ 1
Miles

N

▲ See Map 822 ▲

▲ See Map 841 ▲

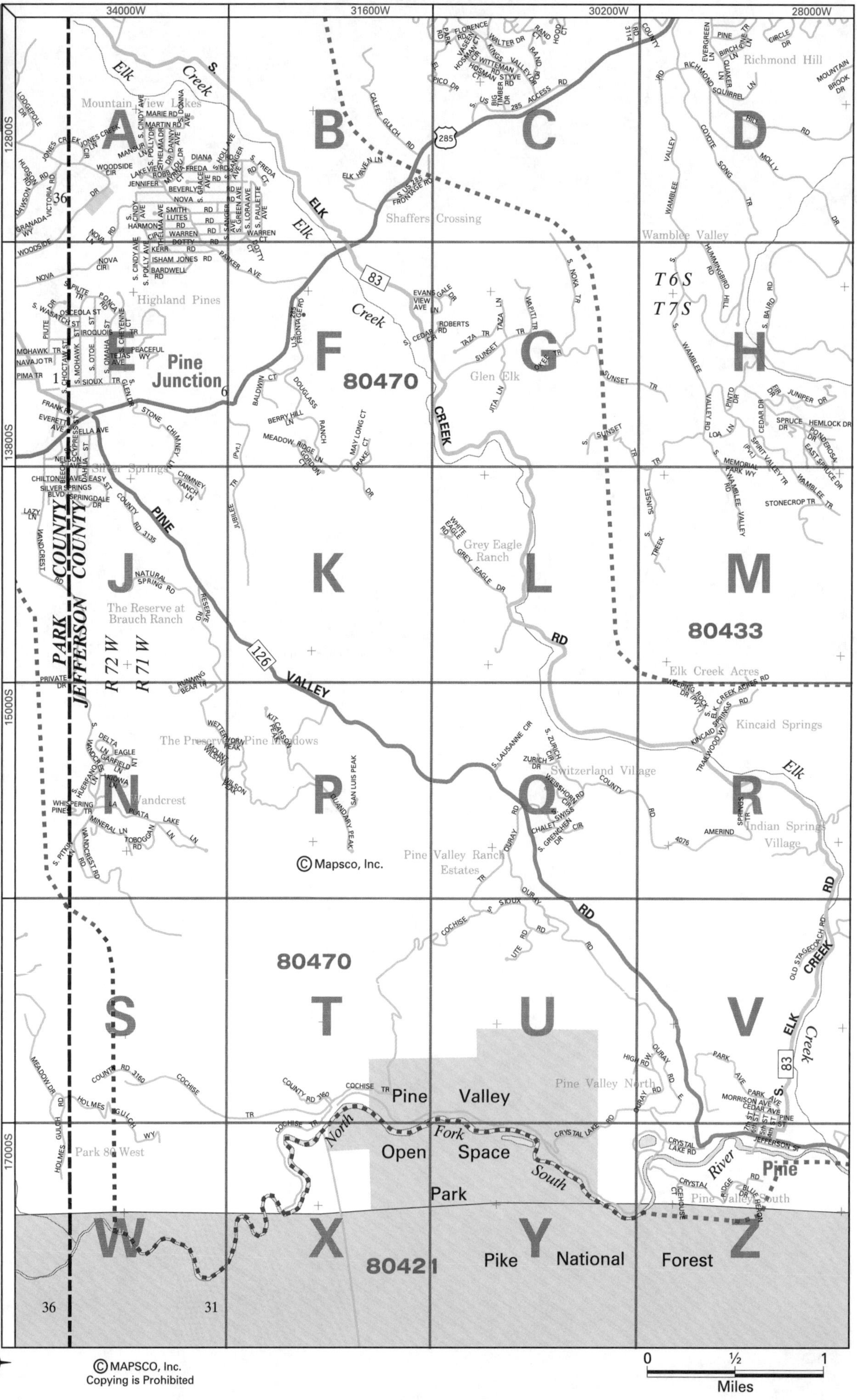

34000W
31600W
30200W
28000W
12800S
13800S
15000S
17000S
A
B
C
D
E
F
G
H
J
K
L
M
N
P
Q
R
S
T
U
V
W
X
Y
Z
Elk Creek
Mountain View Lakes
Shaffers Crossing
Wamblee Valley
Richmond Hill
Highland Pines
Pine Junction
80470
Glen Elk
T 6 S
T 7 S
Silver Springs
PARK COUNTY
JEFFERSON COUNTY
R 72 W
R 71 W
Grey Eagle Ranch
The Reserve at Brauch Ranch
80433
Elk Creek Acres
Kincaid Springs
The Preserve
Pine Meadows
Wandcrest
Switzerland Village
Indian Springs Village
Pine Valley Ranch Estates
© Mapsco, Inc.
PINE VALLEY RD
ELK CREEK RD
285
83
126
Pine Valley Open Space Park
Pine Valley North
North Fork South River
Park 80 West
Pine
Pine Valley South
80421
Pike National Forest
36
31
N
0
½
1
Miles

▲ See Map 823 ▲

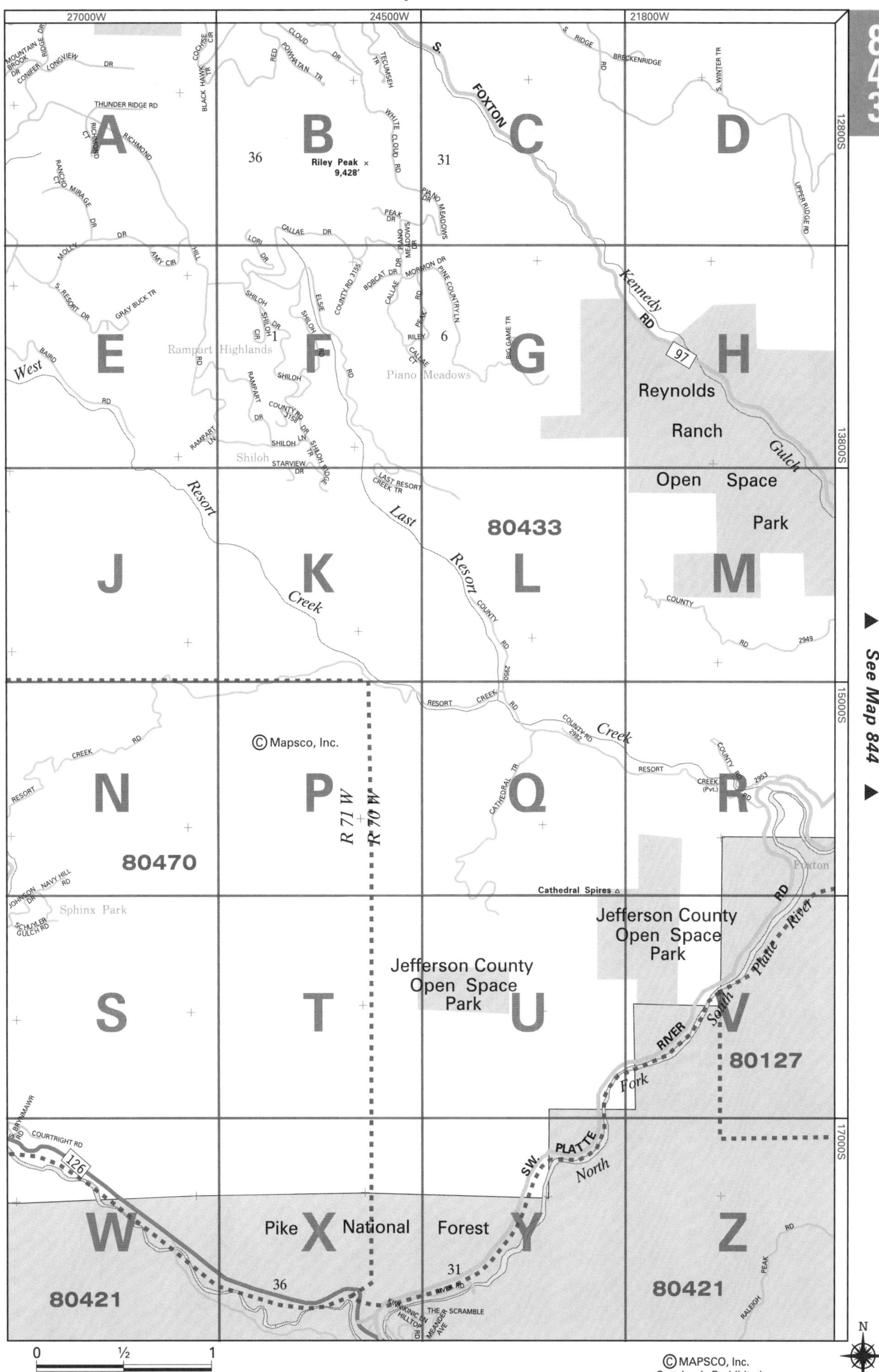

▲ See Map 844 ▲

0 ½ 1
Miles

▲ See Map 824 ▲

▲ See Map 843 ▲

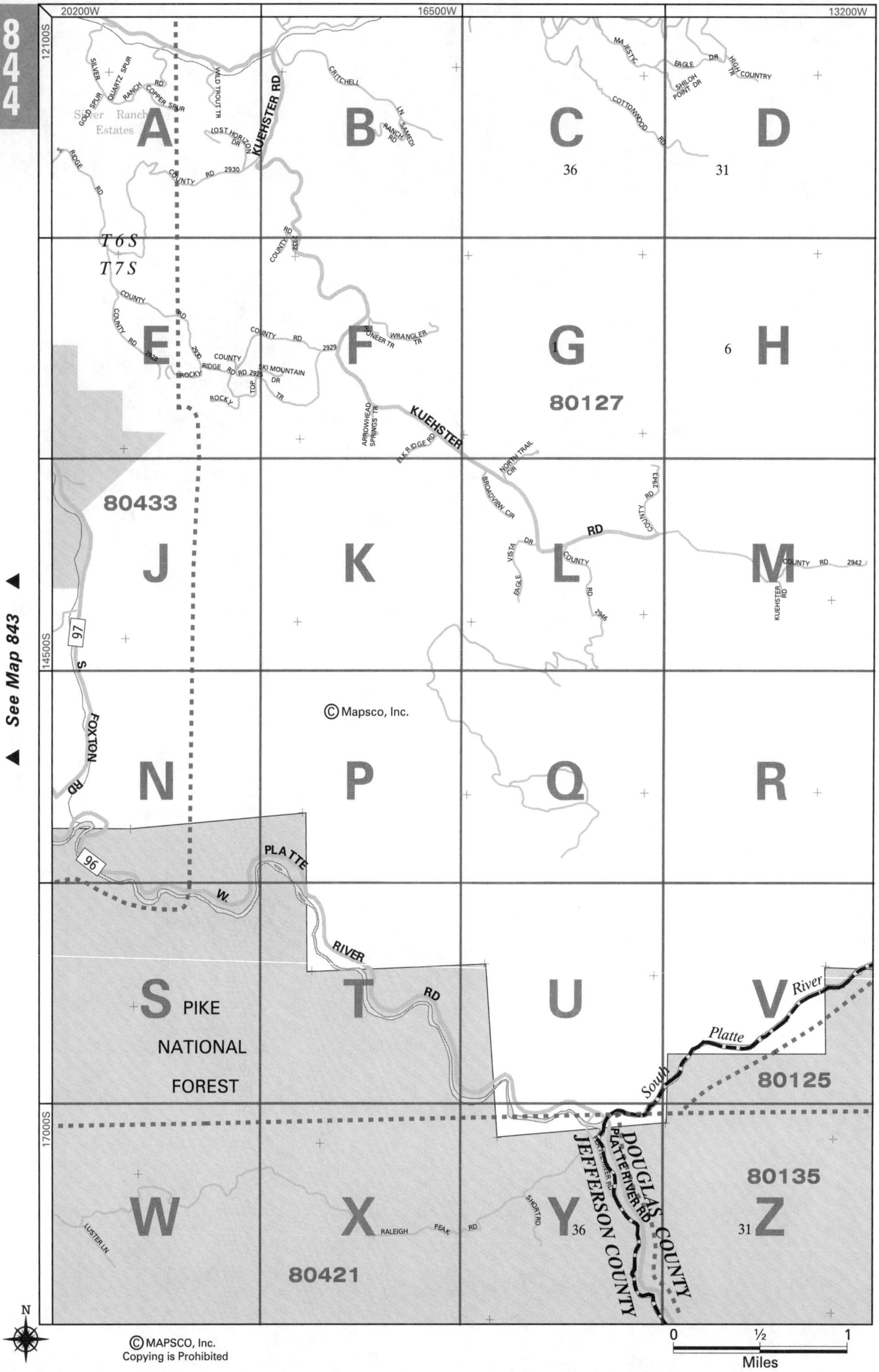

▲ See Map 825 ▲

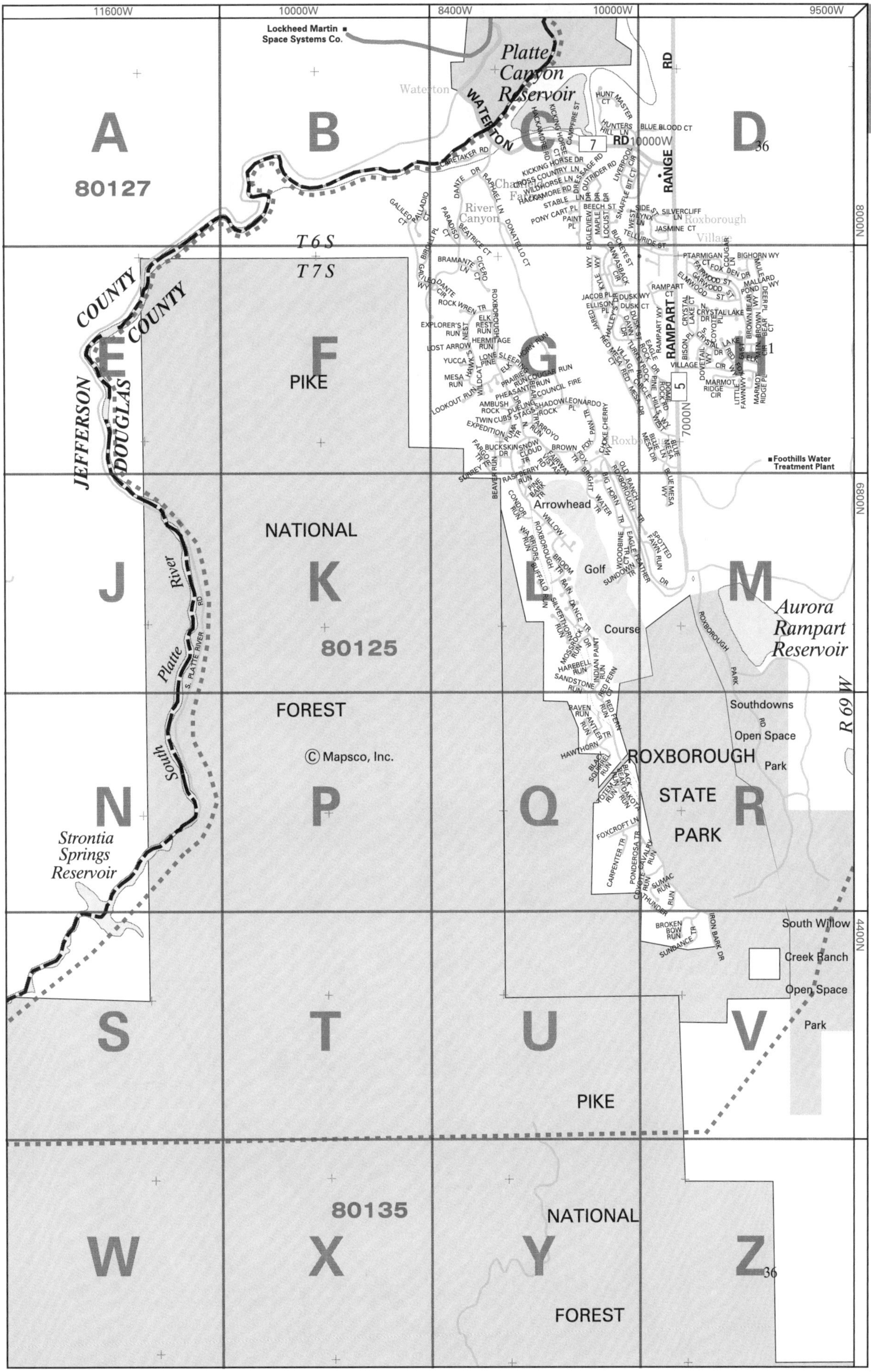

▶ See Map 846 ▶

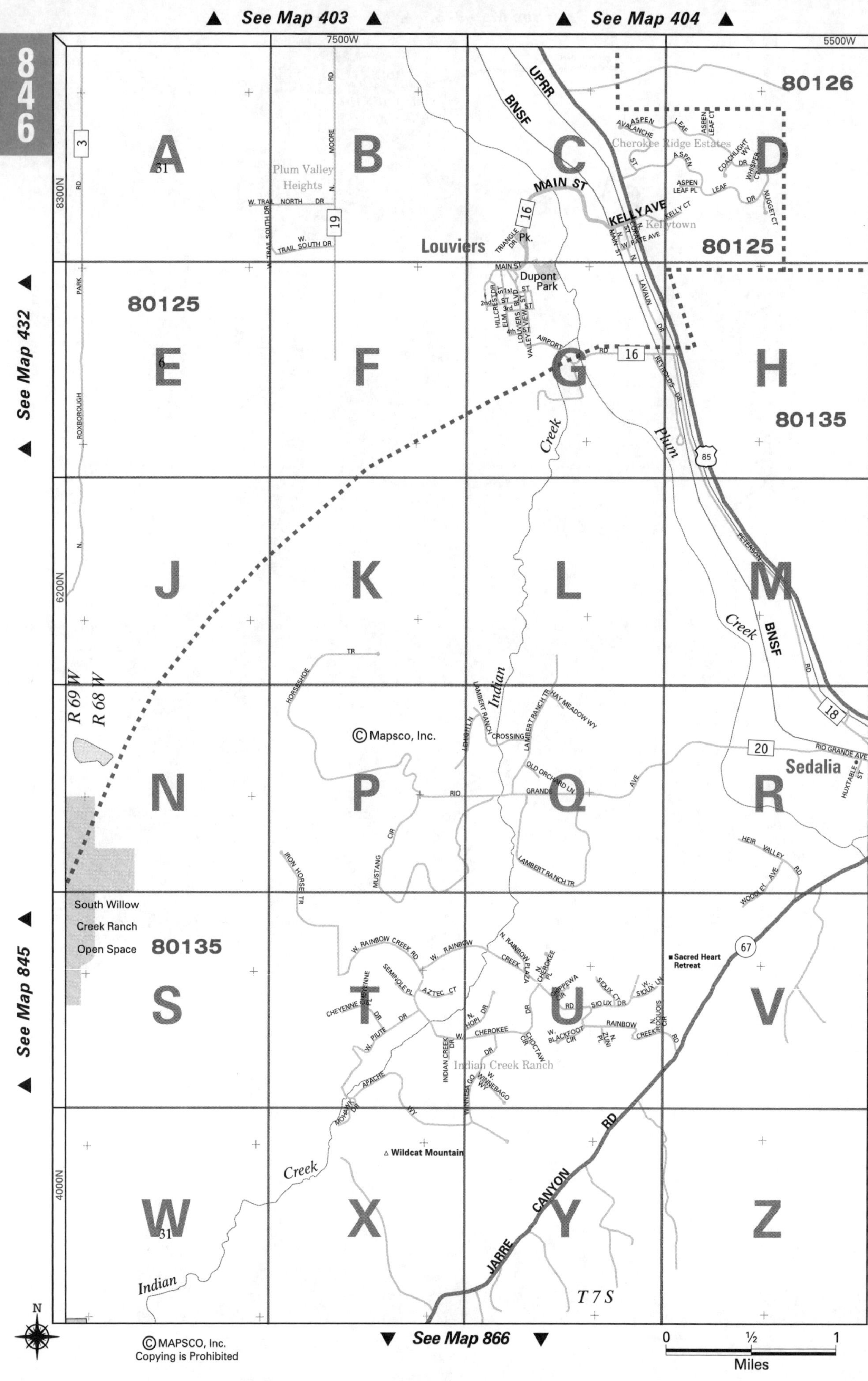
846
See Map 403
See Map 404
See Map 432
See Map 845
See Map 866
7500W
5500W
8300N
6200N
4000N
80126
80125
80135
UPRR
BNSF
A
B
C
D
E
F
G
H
J
K
L
M
N
P
Q
R
S
T
U
V
W
X
Y
Z
Plum Valley
Heights
Cherokee Ridge Estates
ASPEN
AVALANCHE
LEAF
ASPEN LEAF CT
COACHLIGHT WY
WHISPER CT
ASPEN LEAF PL
NUGGET CT
MAIN ST
KELLY AVE
KELLY CT
Kellytown
W. PATE AVE
Louviers
Pk.
TRIANGLE DR
MOORE RD
N.
W. TRAIL NORTH DR
W. TRAIL SOUTH DR
19
16
3
ROXBOROUGH PARK RD
Dupont
Park
HILLCREST DR
ELM ST
LOUVIERS BLVD
VALLEY VIEW ST
AIRPORT RD
LAVAUN DR
REYNOLDS DR
Creek
Plum
Indian
85
PETERSON RD
18
20
Sedalia
RIO GRANDE AVE
HUXTABLE ST
HORSESHOE TR
© Mapsco, Inc.
LAMBERT RANCH
LEHIGH N
CROSSING
LAMBERT RANCH TR
HAY MEADOW WY
OLD ORCHARD LN
RIO GRANDE AVE
MUSTANG CIR
IRON HORSE TR
HEIR VALLEY RD
WOODLEY AVE
R 69 W
R 68 W
South Willow
Creek Ranch
Open Space
W. RAINBOW CREEK RD
W. RAINBOW
N. RAINBOW CREEK PLAZA
N. CHEROKEE PL
SEMINOLE PL
AZTEC CT
CHEYENNE PL
CHEYENNE DR
W. PIUTE DR
N. HOPI DR
CHIPPEWA CIR
SIOUX CT
SIOUX DR
W. SIOUX LN
N. IROQUOIS CIR
RAINBOW CREEK RD
W. BLACKFOOT CIR
N. ZUNI PL
CHOCTAW CIR
W. CHEROKEE DR
INDIAN CREEK DR
Indian Creek Ranch
APACHE WY
MOHAWK DR
W. WINNEBAGO WY
Sacred Heart
Retreat
67
Wildcat Mountain
JARRE CANYON RD
T 7 S
31
6
N
0
½
1
Miles
© MAPSCO, Inc.
Copying is Prohibited

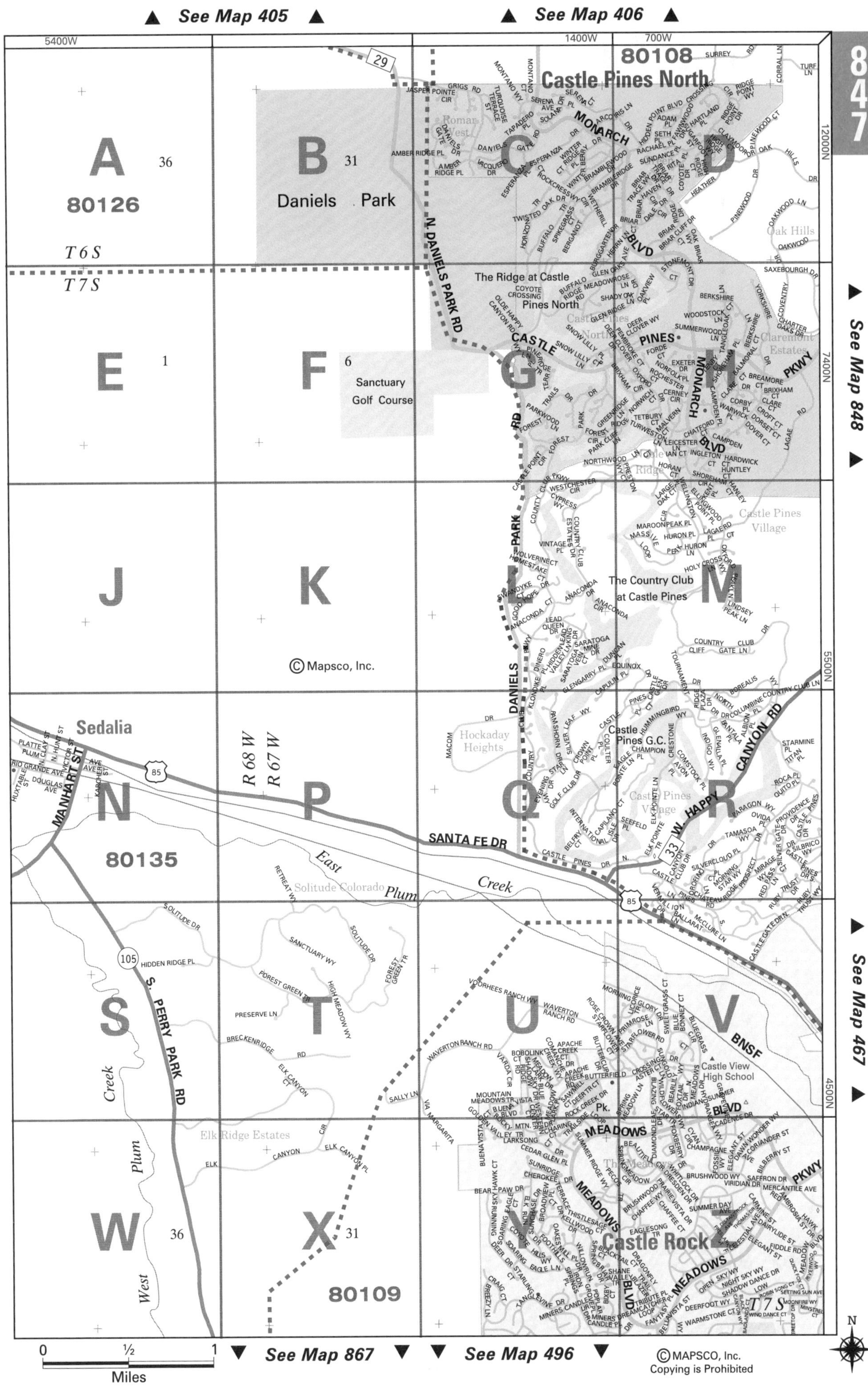
See Map 405
See Map 406
See Map 848
See Map 467
See Map 867
See Map 496
80108
Castle Pines North
80126
Daniels Park
T6S
T7S
N. DANIELS PARK RD
The Ridge at Castle Pines North
CASTLE PINES PKWY
MONARCH BLVD
Sanctuary Golf Course
The Country Club at Castle Pines
Castle Pines Village
Castle Pines G.C.
Hockaday Heights
© Mapsco, Inc.
Sedalia
MANHART ST
R 68 W
R 67 W
SANTA FE DR
80135
East Plum Creek
Solitude Colorado
W. HAPPY CANYON RD
S. PERRY PARK RD
Castle View High School
BNSF
MEADOWS PKWY
Elk Ridge Estates
Castle Rock
80109
West Plum Creek
0 ½ 1 Miles
©MAPSCO, Inc.
Copying is Prohibited

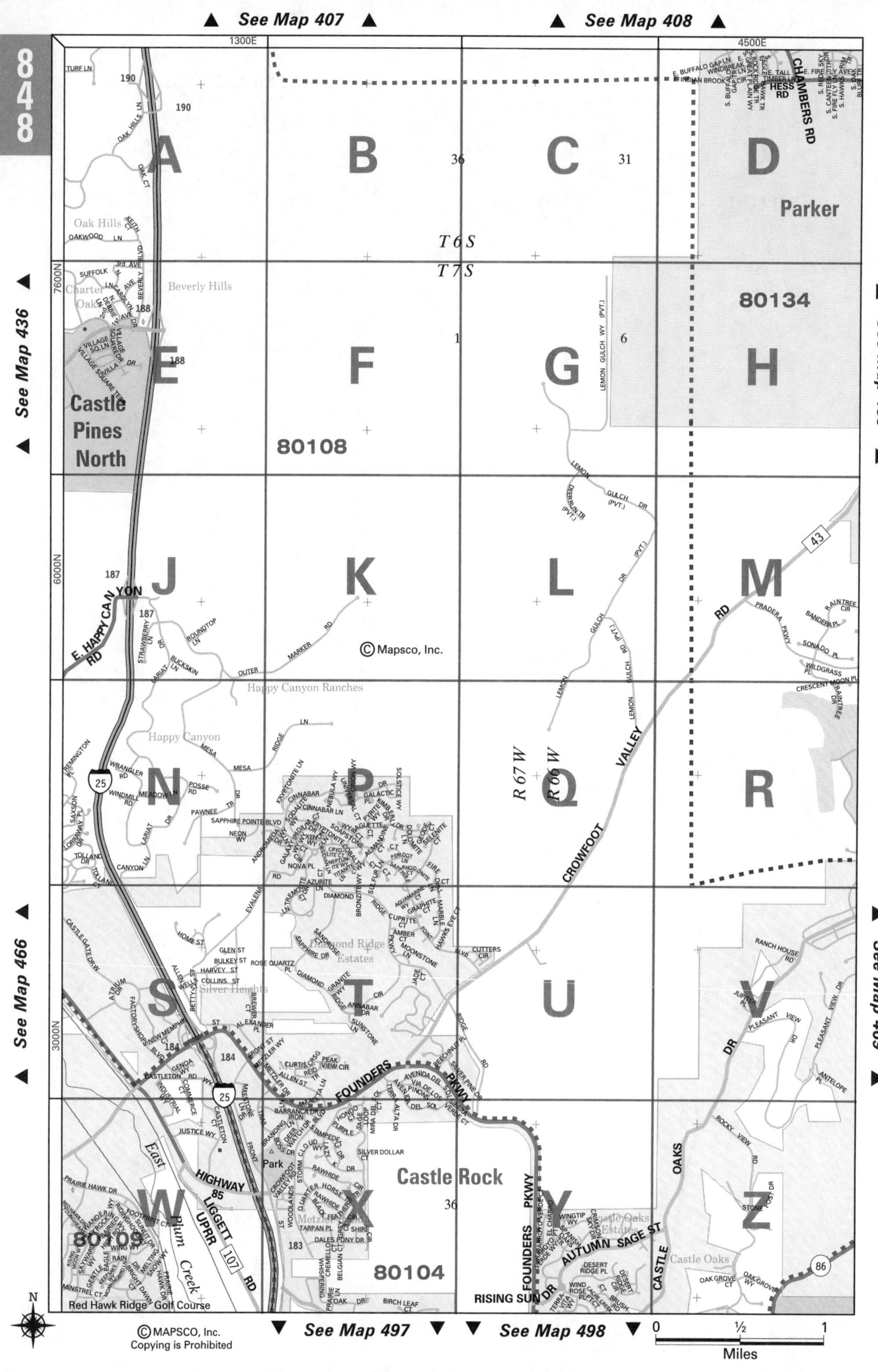
See Map 407
See Map 408
See Map 436
See Map 439
See Map 466
See Map 469
See Map 497
See Map 498
Parker
80134
Castle Pines North
80108
Beverly Hills
Oak Hills
Charter Oaks
Happy Canyon Ranches
Happy Canyon
Diamond Ridge Estates
Silver Heights
Castle Rock
80104
80109
Castle Oaks
Castle Oaks Estates
Red Hawk Ridge Golf Course
East Plum Creek
Park
T 6 S
T 7 S
R 67 W
R 66 W
© Mapsco, Inc.
CROWFOOT VALLEY RD
FOUNDERS PKWY
HIGHWAY 85
LIGGETT RD
UPRR
CHAMBERS RD
HESS RD
E. HAPPY CANYON RD
AUTUMN SAGE ST
RISING SUN DR
CASTLE OAKS DR
LEMON GULCH DR
N

0 ½ 1
Miles

▲ See Map 411 ▲
▲ See Map 830 ▲

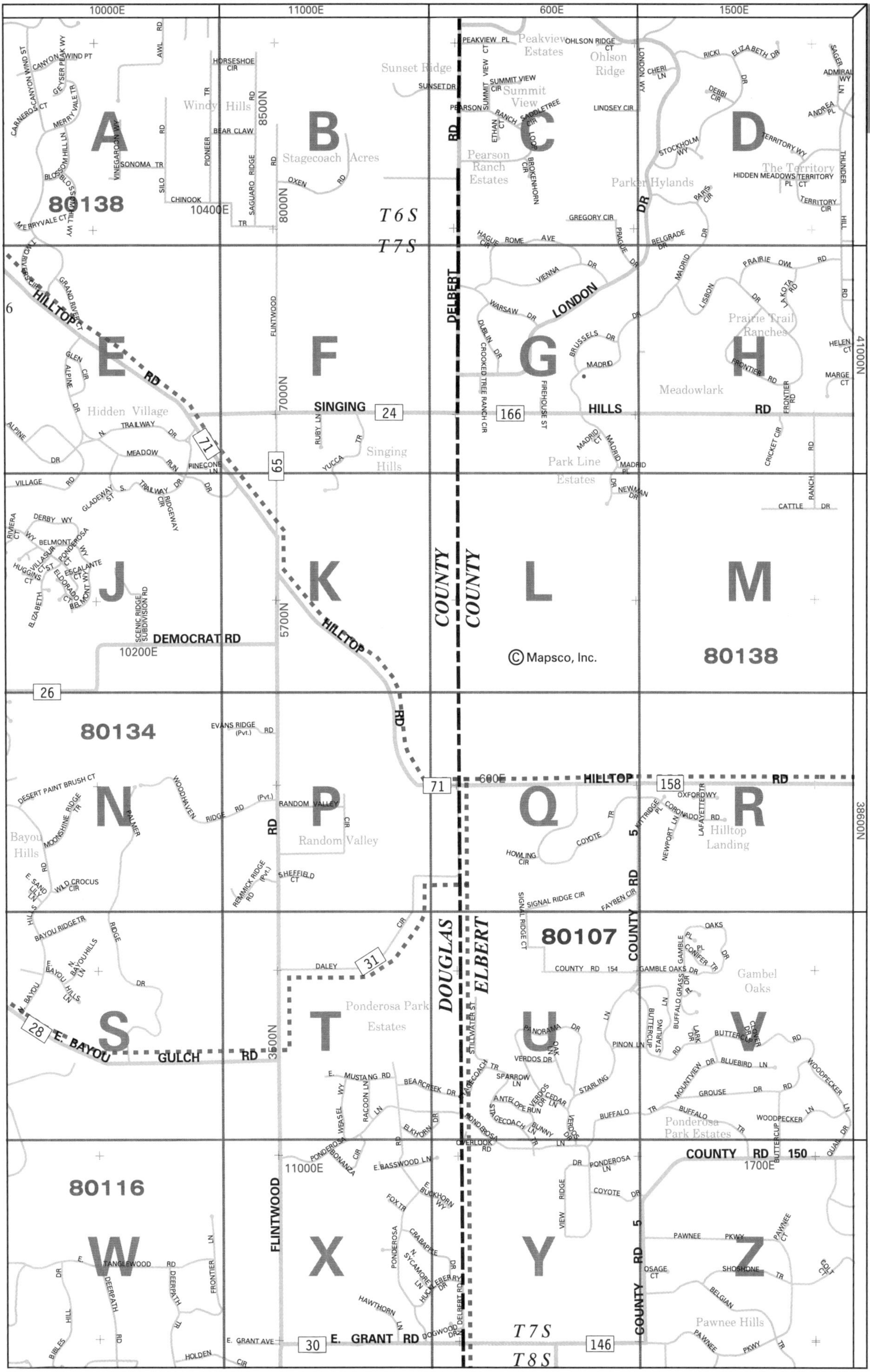

10000E | 11000E | 600E | 1500E

See Map 440
See Map 470

A
CANYON WIND ST
CANYON CT
GEYSER PEAK WY
WIND PT
AWL RD
HORSESHOE CIR
Windy Hills
MERRY VALE TR
CARNEROS CT
VINEGAROON WY
SONOMA TR
BEAR CLAW
PIONEER
SILO
CHINOOK
BLOSSOM HILL LN
80138
MERRYVALE CT
10400E
8500N

B
Sunset Ridge
SUNSET DR
Stagecoach Acres
OXEN RD
SAGUARO RIDGE RD
8000N
T6S
T7S

C
PEAKVIEW PL
Peakview Estates
OHLSON RIDGE CT
Ohlson Ridge
SUMMIT VIEW CIR
Summit View
PEARSON
SADDLETREE CIR
ETHAN CT
RANCH
LOOP
LINDSEY CIR
Pearson Ranch Estates
BROKENHORN CIR
DELBERT RD

D
CHERI LN
RICKI
ELIZABETH DR
DEBBI CIR
SAGER WY
ADMIRAL WY
ANDREA PL
STOCKHOLM WY
TERRITORY WY
THUNDER
The Territory
HIDDEN MEADOWS PL
TERRITORY CT
Parker Hylands
PARIS CIR
TERRITORY CIR
HILL
LONDON WY
DR

E
HILLTOP RD
GRAND RIVER CT
GLEN CIR
ALPINE DR
Hidden Village
TRAILWAY DR
ALPINE
MEADOW RUN
VILLAGE RD
PINECONE LN
71

F
FLINTWOOD
7000N
SINGING
24
RUBY LN
YUCCA
Singing Hills
65

G
HAGUE CIR
ROME AVE
GREGORY CIR
PRAGUE DR
VIENNA DR
LONDON
WARSAW DR
DUBLIN DR
CROOKED TREE RANCH CIR
BRUSSELS DR
MADRID
FIREHOUSE ST
166
HILLS
MADRID CT
MADRID PL
Park Line Estates
NEWMAN DR

H
BELGRADE DR
MADRID
LISBON
PRAIRIE OWL RD
LAKOTA RD
Prairie Trail Ranches
HELEN CT
FRONTIER RD
MARGE CT
Meadowlark
RD
CRICKET CIR
FRONTIER RD
RANCH
CATTLE DR
41000N

J
DERBY WY
RIVIERA CT
BELMONT
VILLASUR
PONDEROSA
HUGGINS CT
ESCALANTE CT
ELDORADO CT
BELMONT WY
ELIZABETH
GLADEWAY ST
TRAILWAY CIR
RIDGEWAY
SCENIC RIDGE SUBDIVISION RD
DEMOCRAT RD
10200E
26

K
HILLTOP RD
5700N

L
DOUGLAS COUNTY
ELBERT COUNTY
© Mapsco, Inc.

M
80138

N
80134
EVANS RIDGE (Pvt.) RD
DESERT PAINT BRUSH CT
WOODHAVEN RIDGE RD
MOONSHINE RIDGE TR
PALMER
Bayou Hills
W. SAND LILY LN
WILD CROCUS CIR

P
RANDOM VALLEY CIR
Random Valley
REMMICK RIDGE (Pvt.) RD
SHEFFIELD CT
71

Q
600E
HILLTOP RD
158
COYOTE TR
HOWLING CIR
SIGNAL RIDGE CIR
SIGNAL RIDGE CT
FAYBEN CIR

R
OXFORD WY
KITTRIDGE PL
CORONADO RD
LAFAYETTE TR
Hilltop Landing
NEWPORT LN
3860N

S
BAYOU RIDGE TR
BAYOU HILLS
E. BAYOU HILLS LN
N. BAYOU
RIDGE DR
28
E. BAYOU GULCH RD

T
DALEY CIR
31
Ponderosa Park Estates
3500N
E. MUSTANG RD
WEASEL WY
RACOON LN
BEARCREEK DR
ELKHORN DR

U
80107
COUNTY RD 154
STILLWATER ST
PANORAMA DR
VERDOS DR
OAK CT
SPARROW LN
STAGECOACH TR
ANTELOPE RUN
CEDAR LN
BUNNY LN
STARLING
BUFFALO
PINON LN
COUNTY RD 5

V
OAKS
GAMBLE PL
CONIFER TR
GAMBLE OAKS DR
Gambel Oaks
BUFFALO GRASS PL
BUTTERCUP
STARLING
LARK DR
BUTTERCUP
CLOVER DR
BLUEBIRD LN
MOUNTVIEW DR
GROUSE DR
WOODPECKER LN
BUFFALO TR
Ponderosa Park Estates
WOODPECKER LN
QUAIL DR

W
80116
E. TANGLEWOOD RD
DEERPATH
FRONTIER
HILL
BIBLES
HOLDEN
CIR

X
FLINTWOOD
11000E
PONDEROSA
BONANZA CIR
E. BASSWOOD LN
E. BUCKHORN WY
FOX TR
CRABAPPLE
N. SYCAMORE LN
HUCKLEBERRY DR
HAWTHORN LN
DOGWOOD DR
E. GRANT AVE
30
E. GRANT RD
OVERLOOK RD

Y
PONDEROSA LN
COYOTE DR
RIDGE
VIEW
T7S
T8S
146

Z
COUNTY RD 150
1700E
PAWNEE PKWY
PAWNEE CT
OSAGE CT
SHOSHONE TR
GOLF CT
BELGIAN
Pawnee Hills
PAWNEE PKWY

0 ½ 1
Miles

▼ See Map 870 ▼

N

See Map 831

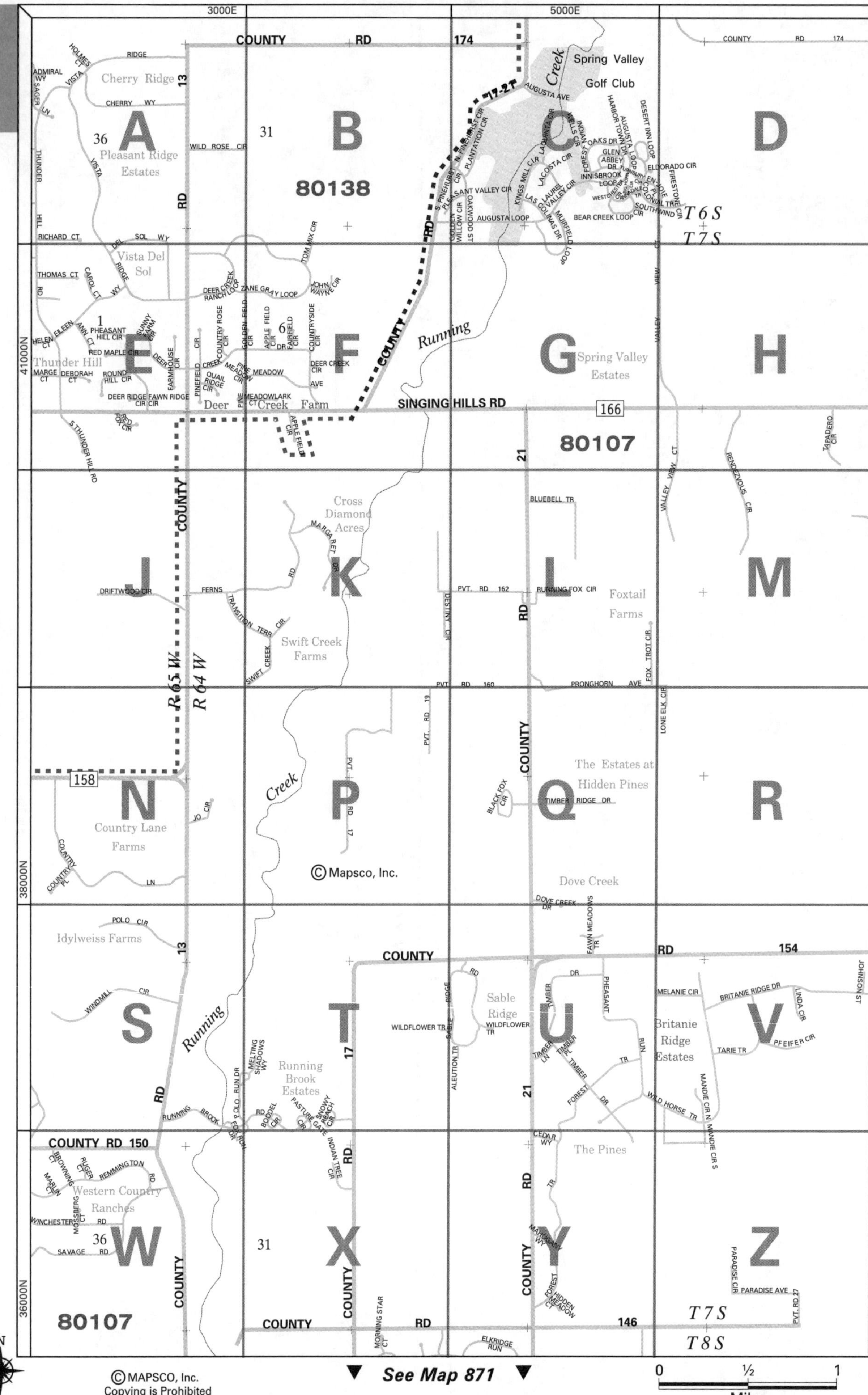

See Map 850

See Map 871

0 ½ 1
Miles

▲ See Map 832 ▲

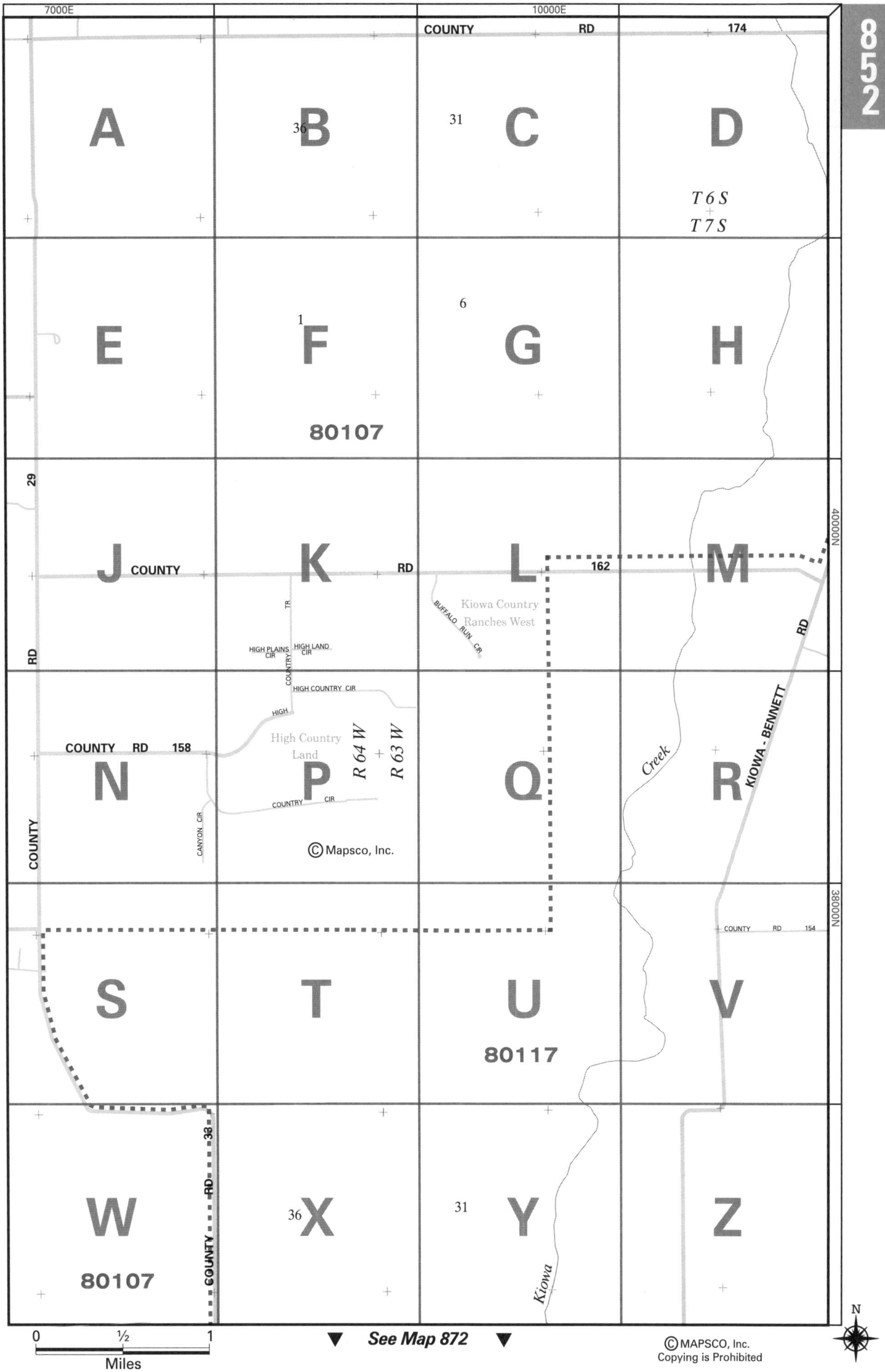

7000E

10000E

COUNTY RD 174

A B C D

36 31

T 6 S

T 7 S

E F G H

1 6

80107

J K L M

COUNTY RD 29

COUNTY RD 162

40000N

TR

HIGH PLAINS CIR

HIGH LAND CIR

COUNTRY

HIGH COUNTRY CIR

HIGH

BUFFALO RUN CIR

Kiowa Country Ranches West

KIOWA - BENNETT RD

COUNTY RD 158

High Country Land

R 64 W

R 63 W

COUNTRY CIR

CANYON CIR

Creek

N P Q R

© Mapsco, Inc.

38000N

COUNTY RD 154

S T U V

80117

COUNTY RD 33

W X Y Z

80107

36 31

Kiowa

0 ½ 1

Miles

▼ See Map 872 ▼

N

▲ See Map 846 ▲

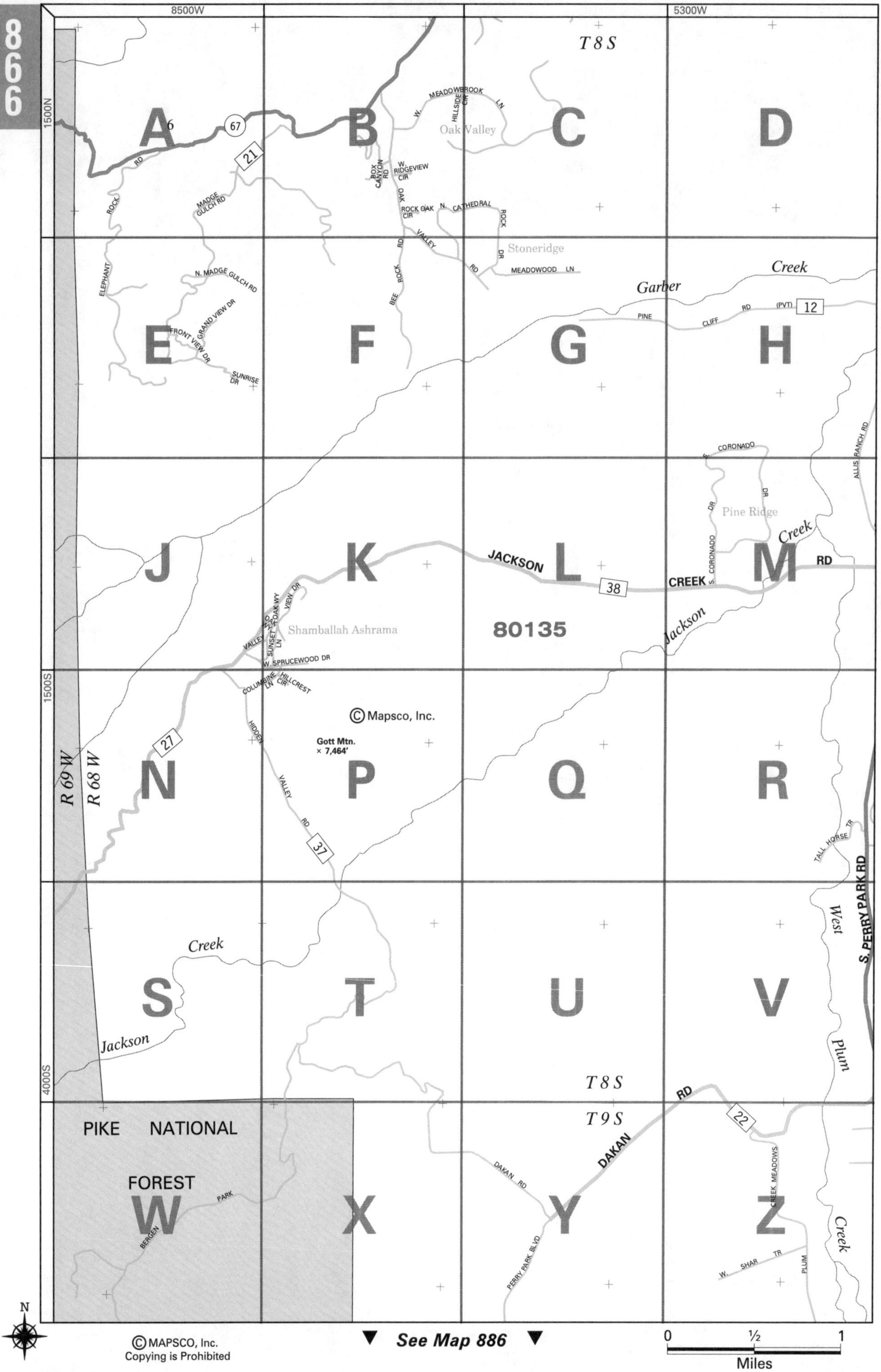

8500W
5300W
1500N
1500S
4000S
T8S
T9S
R 69 W
R 68 W

A B C D
E F G H
J K L M
N P Q R
S T U V
W X Y Z

67
21
12
38
27
37
22

ROCK RD
MADGE GULCH RD
ELEPHANT
N. MADGE GULCH RD
GRAND VIEW DR
FRONT VIEW DR
SUNRISE DR
BOX CANYON RD
W. RIDGEVIEW CIR
OAK
ROCK OAK CIR
N. CATHEDRAL ROCK DR
VALLEY RD
BEE ROCK RD
W. MEADOWBROOK LN
HILLSIDE CIR
Oak Valley
Stoneridge
MEADOWOOD LN
Garber Creek
PINE CLIFF RD (PVT)
S. CORONADO DR
Pine Ridge
ALLIS RANCH RD
Creek
JACKSON CREEK RD
80135
Jackson
OAK WY
VIEW DR
SUNSET LN
VALLEY
Shamballah Ashrama
W. SPRUCEWOOD DR
COLUMBINE LN
HILLCREST CIR
© Mapsco, Inc.
Gott Mtn.
× 7,464'
HIDDEN VALLEY RD
TALL HORSE TR
S. PERRY PARK RD
West Plum Creek
Creek
Jackson
PIKE NATIONAL FOREST
BERGEN PARK
DAKAN RD
PERRY PARK BLVD
CREEK MEADOWS
W. SHAR TR
PLUM

▼ See Map 886 ▼

0 ½ 1
Miles
N

▲ See Map 847 ▲ ▲ See Map 466 ▲

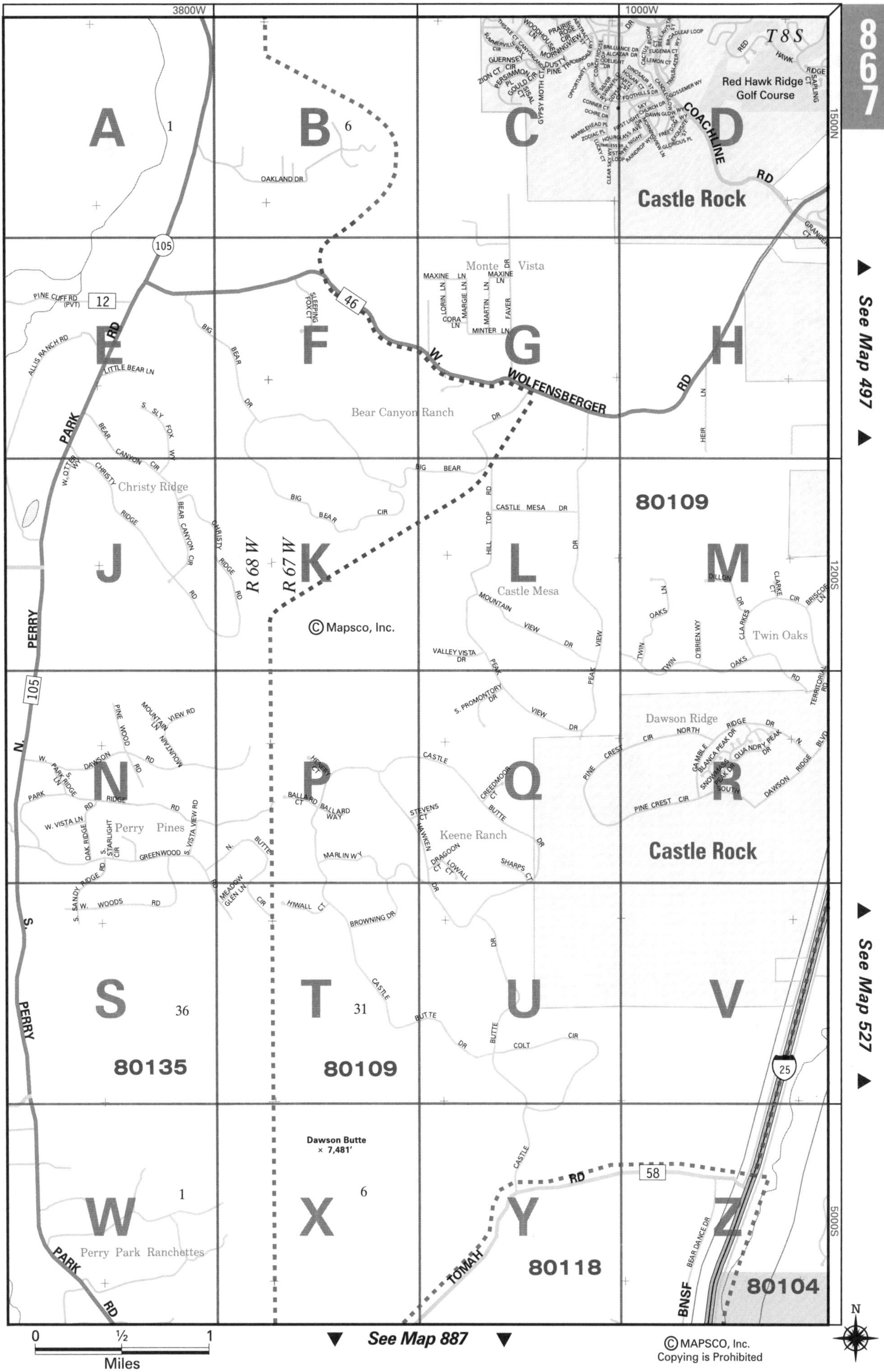
3800W
1000W
1500N
1200S
5000S
T 8 S
Red Hawk Ridge Golf Course
COACHLINE RD
Castle Rock
OAKLAND DR
105
PINE CLIFF RD (PVT)
12
46
Monte Vista
MAXINE LN
LORIN LN
MARGIE LN
MARTIN LN
FAVER DR
CORA LN
MINTER LN
W. WOLFENSBERGER RD
ALLIS RANCH RD
LITTLE BEAR LN
BIG BEAR DR
Bear Canyon Ranch
PARK
Christy Ridge
BEAR CANYON CIR
CHRISTY RIDGE RD
R 68 W
R 67 W
© Mapsco, Inc.
80109
CASTLE MESA DR
HILL TOP RD
Castle Mesa
MOUNTAIN VIEW DR
VALLEY VISTA DR
Twin Oaks
TWIN OAKS
DILLON DR
CLARKE CT
O'BRIEN WY
PERRY
N. PERRY PARK RD
S. PROMONTORY DR
PEAK VIEW DR
Dawson Ridge
PINE CREST CIR
Castle Rock
Perry Pines
W. VISTA LN
GREENWOOD
BALLARD WAY
MARLIN WY
Keene Ranch
STEVENS CT
HAWKEN DR
CREEDMOOR CT
SHARPS CT
W. WOODS RD
HIWALL CT
BROWNING DR
CASTLE BUTTE DR
COLT CIR
S. PERRY
36
31
80135
80109
25
Dawson Butte × 7,481′
CASTLE
RD
58
TOMAH
80118
BEAR DANCE DR
BNSF
80104
Perry Park Ranchettes
PARK RD
1
6
A B C D E F G H J K L M N P Q R S T U V W X Y Z
0 ½ 1
Miles
N

▶ See Map 497 ▶

▶ See Map 527 ▶

▼ See Map 887 ▼

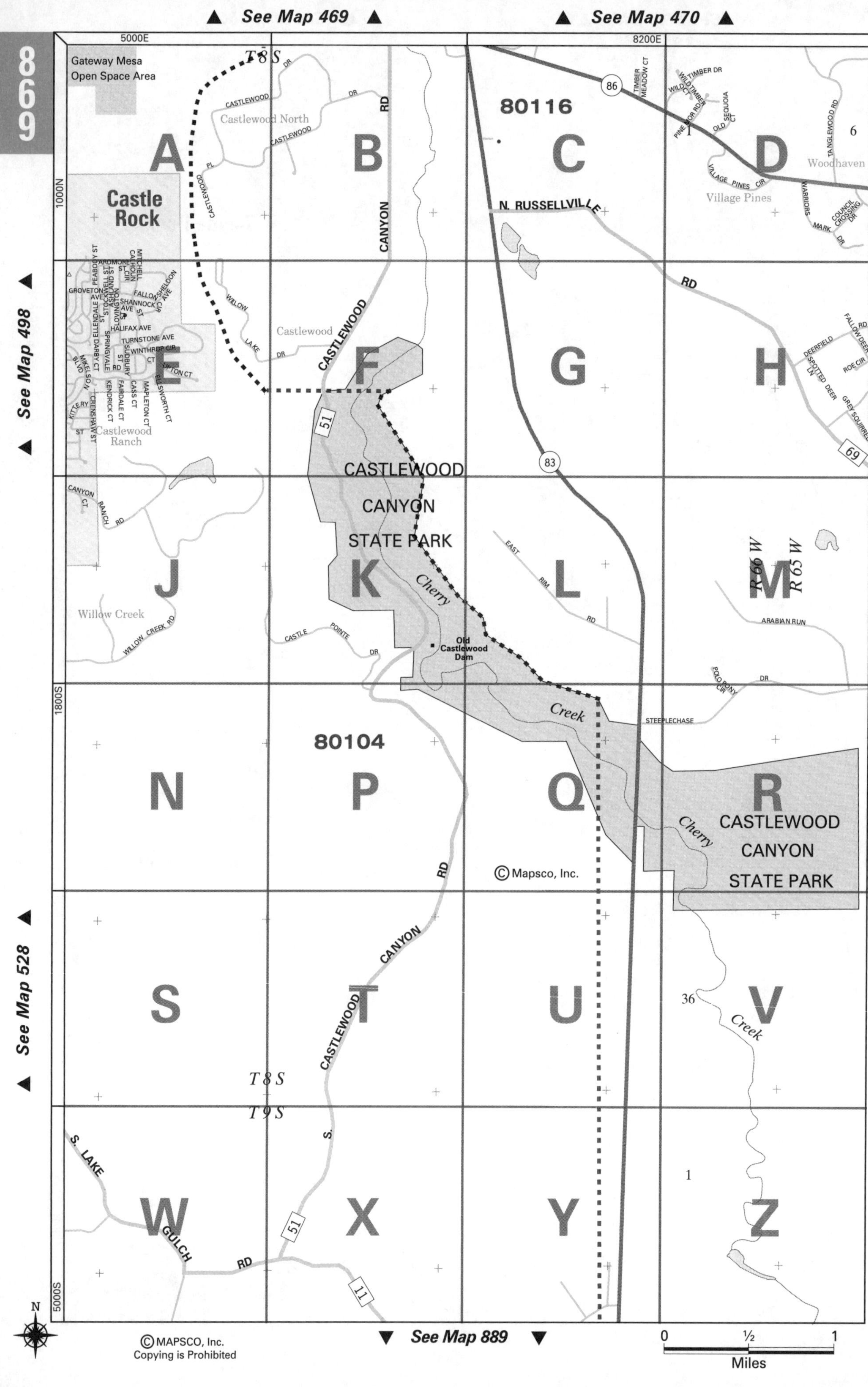

▲ See Map 469 ▲
▲ See Map 470 ▲
◄ See Map 498 ◄
◄ See Map 528 ◄
▼ See Map 889 ▼
5000E
8200E
1000N
1800S
5000S
T8S
T9S
R 66 W
R 65 W
80116
80104
Gateway Mesa
Open Space Area
Castle Rock
Castlewood North
Castlewood
Castlewood Ranch
Willow Creek
Village Pines
Woodhaven
CASTLEWOOD CANYON STATE PARK
CASTLEWOOD CANYON STATE PARK
Old Castlewood Dam
Cherry Creek
Cherry
Creek
CASTLEWOOD CANYON RD
S. CASTLEWOOD CANYON RD
N. RUSSELLVILLE RD
CASTLEWOOD DR
CASTLEWOOD PL
WILLOW LAKE DR
CANYON RANCH RD
CANYON CT
WILLOW CREEK RD
CASTLE POINTE DR
EAST RIM RD
ARABIAN RUN
POLO PONY CIR
STEEPLECHASE DR
S. LAKE GULCH RD
TIMBER MEADOW CT
WILD TIMBER DR
PINE MOR RD
SEQUOIA CT
OLD
VILLAGE PINES CIR
WARRIORS
MARK DR
COUNCIL CROSSING DR
TANGLEWOOD RD
FALLOW DEER RD
DEERFIELD
SPOTTED DEER LN
ROE CIR
GREY SQUIRREL
GROVETON AVE
ARDMORE
MITCHELL
CALHOUN CIR
SHELDON AVE
FALLON CIR
SHANNOCK AVE
HALIFAX AVE
TURNSTONE AVE
WINTHROP CIR
UPTON CT
ELLSWORTH CT
MAPLETON CT
CASS CT
FAIRDALE CT
KENDRICK CT
SPRINGVALE RD
DARBY CT
ELLENDALE ST
PEABODY ST
MIKELSON BLVD
KITTERY ST
CRENSHAW ST
SUDBURY
86
83
51
69
11
1
6
36
A B C D E F G H J K L M N P Q R S T U V W X Y Z
© Mapsco, Inc.
N
0 ½ 1
Miles

See Map 850

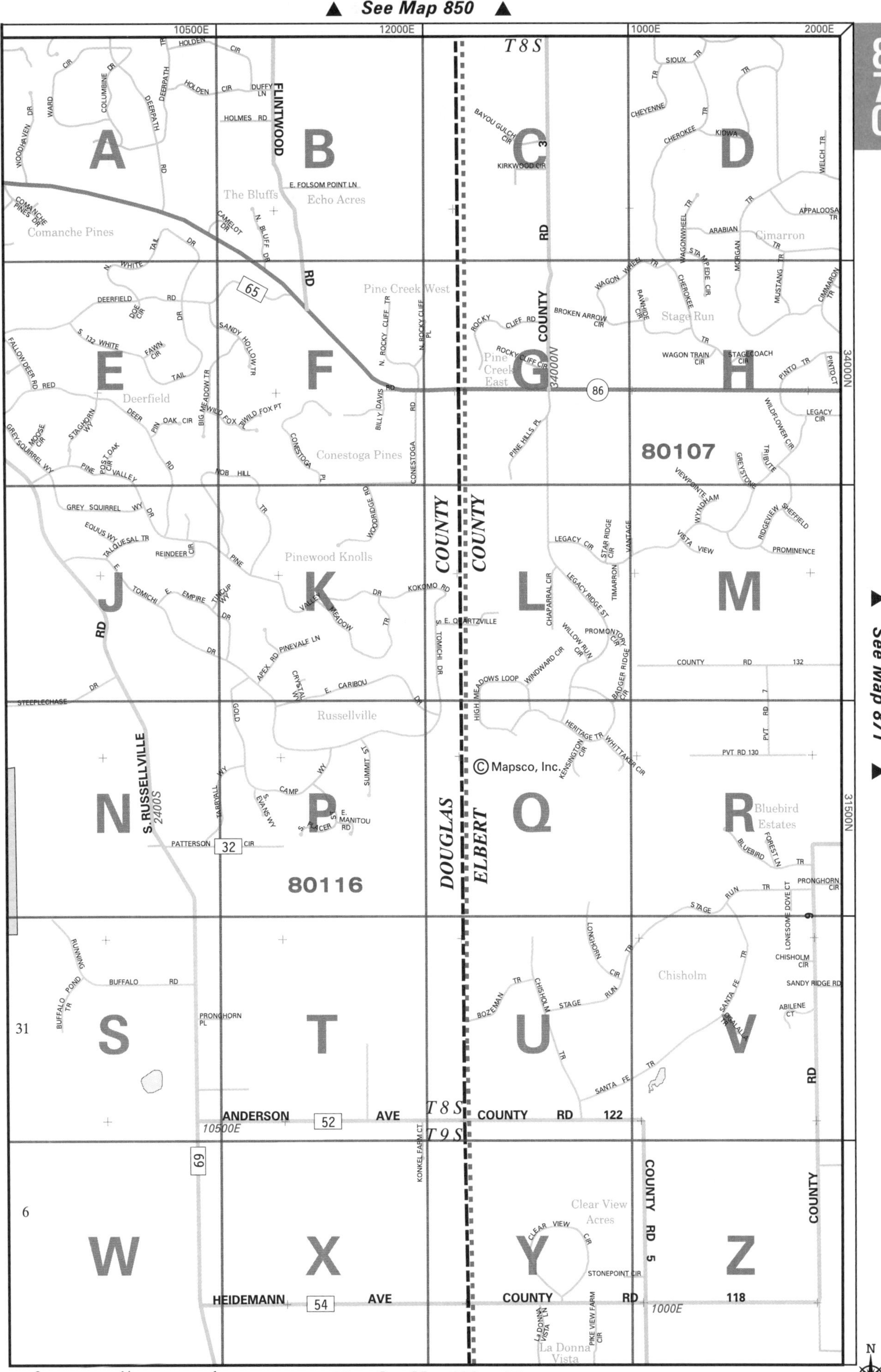

See Map 871

See Map 890

0 ½ 1
Miles

▲ See Map 851 ▲

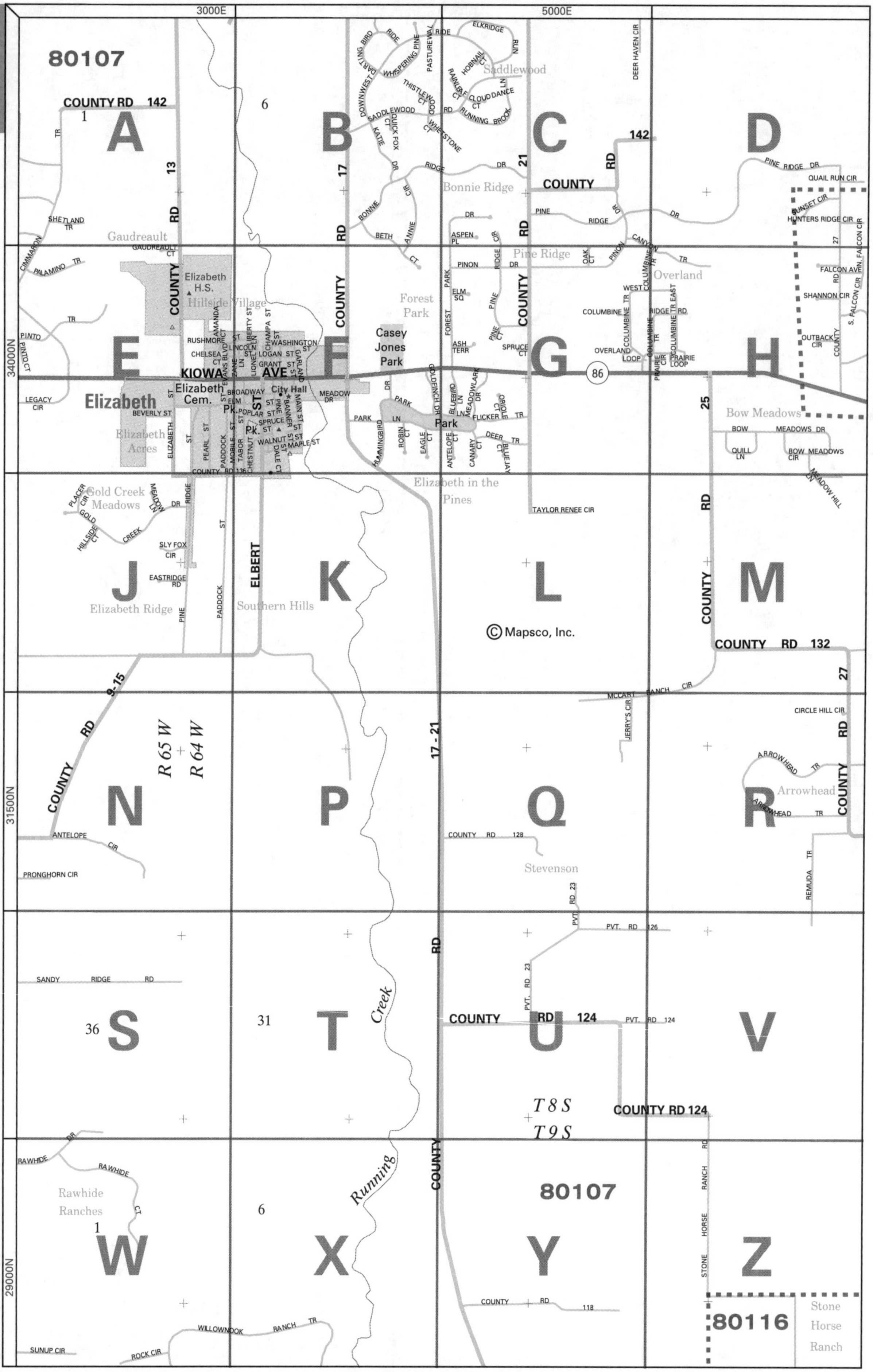
3000E
5000E
34000N
31500N
29000N
80107
A
B
C
D
E
F
G
H
J
K
L
M
N
P
Q
R
S
T
U
V
W
X
Y
Z
COUNTY RD 142
COUNTY RD 13
COUNTY RD 17
COUNTY RD 21
COUNTY RD 25
COUNTY RD 27
COUNTY RD 132
COUNTY RD 124
COUNTY RD 128
COUNTY RD 118
COUNTY RD 9-15
COUNTY RD 17-21
PVT. RD 126
PVT. RD 124
PVT. RD 23
Saddlewood
Bonnie Ridge
Gaudreault
Pine Ridge
Overland
Forest Park
Casey Jones Park
Elizabeth H.S.
Hillside Village
Elizabeth
Elizabeth Cem.
City Hall
Elizabeth Acres
KIOWA AVE
ELBERT ST
86
Park
Bow Meadows
Elizabeth in the Pines
Gold Creek Meadows
Elizabeth Ridge
Southern Hills
© Mapsco, Inc.
R 65 W
R 64 W
Arrowhead
Stevenson
T 8 S
T 9 S
Running Creek
Rawhide Ranches
80116
Stone Horse Ranch
STONE HORSE RANCH RD
TAYLOR RENEE CIR
MCCART RANCH CIR
JERRY'S CIR
CIRCLE HILL CIR
ARROWHEAD TR
REMUDA TR
ANTELOPE CIR
PRONGHORN CIR
SANDY RIDGE RD
RAWHIDE DR
RAWHIDE CT
WILLOWNOOK RANCH TR
SUNUP CIR
ROCK CIR
PINE RIDGE DR
QUAIL RUN CIR
HUNTERS RIDGE CIR
FALCON AVE
SHANNON CIR
OUTBACK CIR
SHETLAND TR
CIMMARON
PALAMINO TR
PINTO CT
LEGACY CIR
BEVERLY ST
SLY FOX CIR
EASTRIDGE RD
1
6
36
31

See Map 870

▼ See Map 891 ▼

N

0 ½ 1
Miles

See Map 852

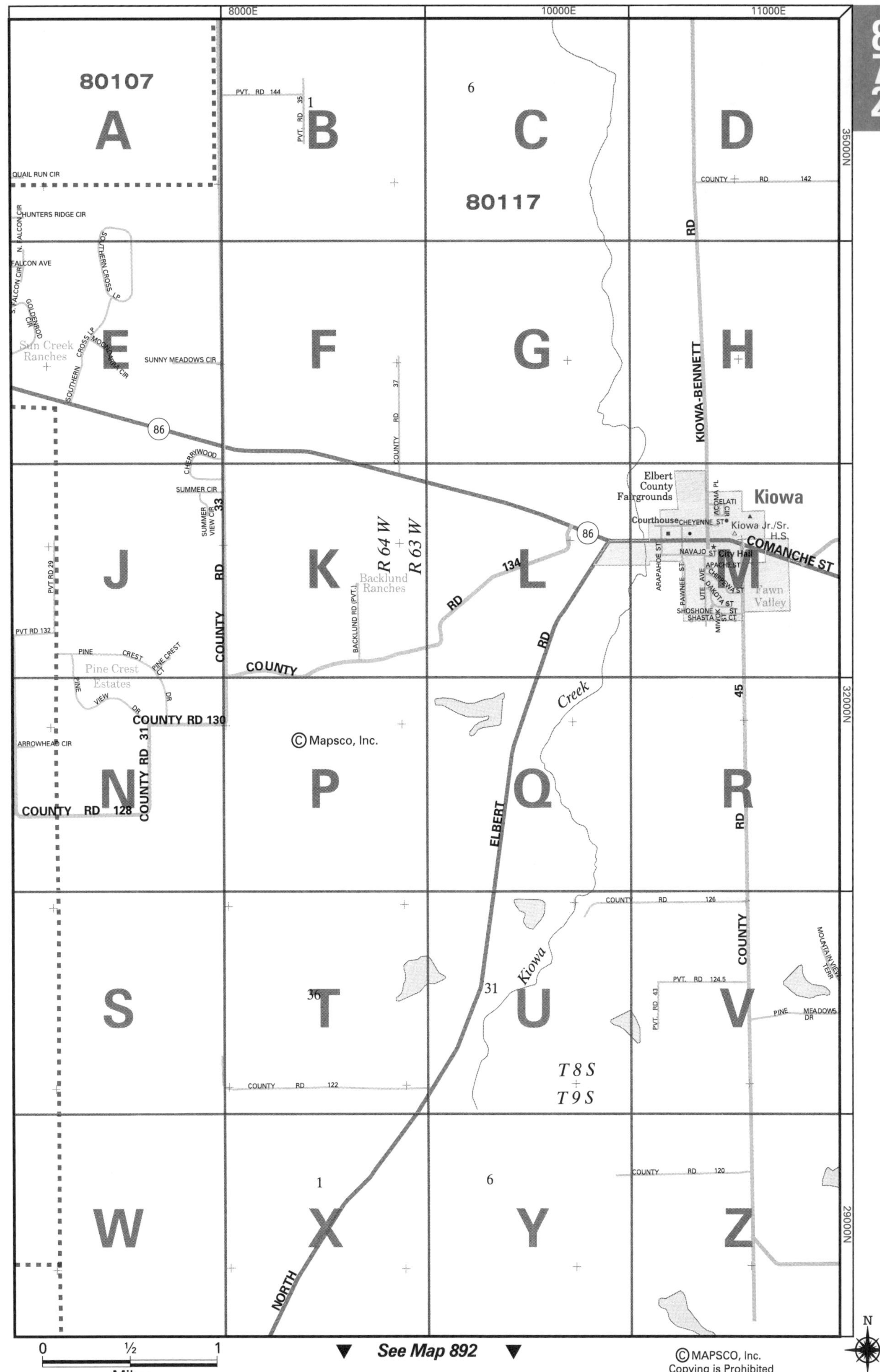

See Map 892

▲ See Map 866 ▲

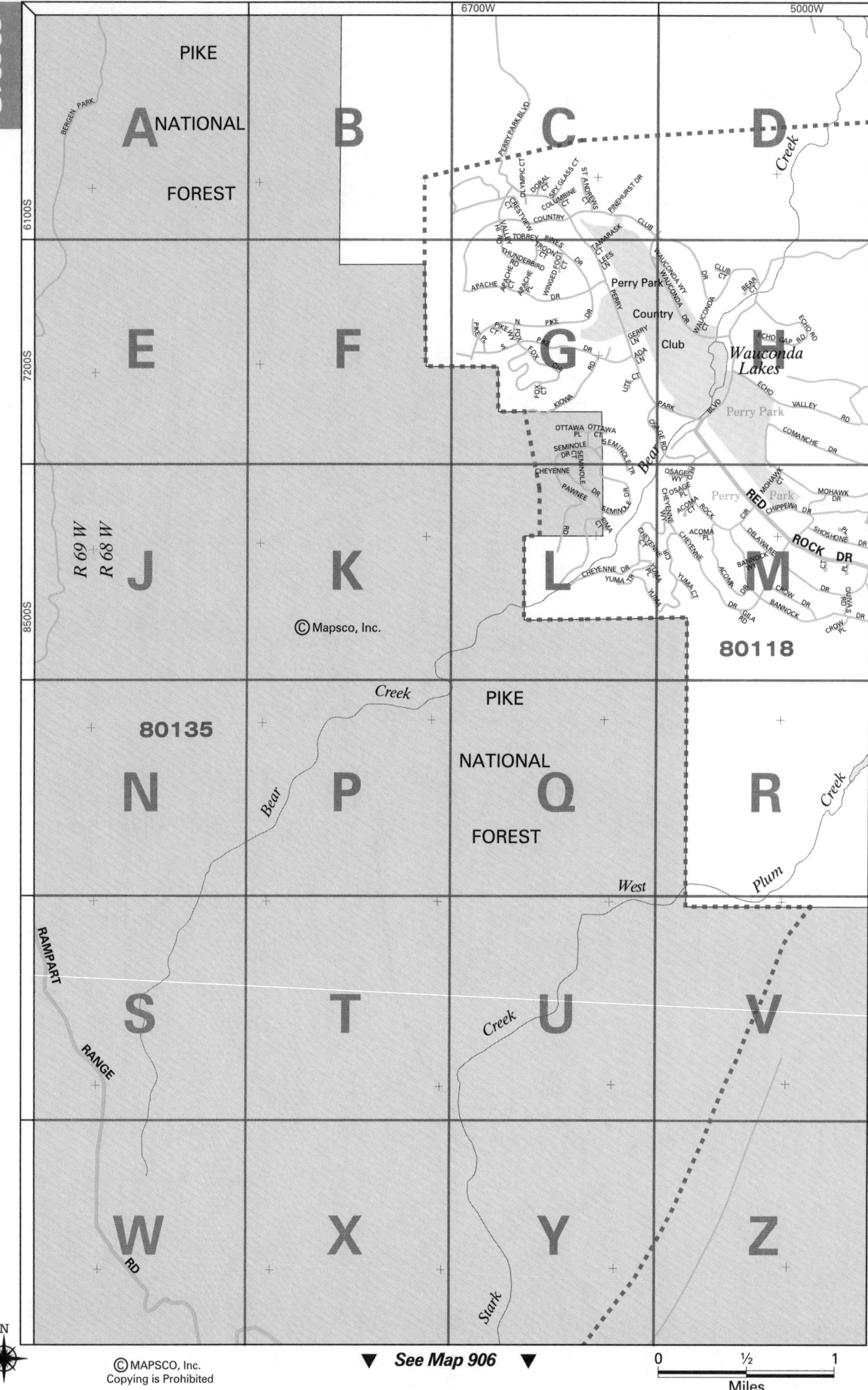

▼ See Map 906 ▼

0 ½ 1
Miles

▲ See Map 867 ▲

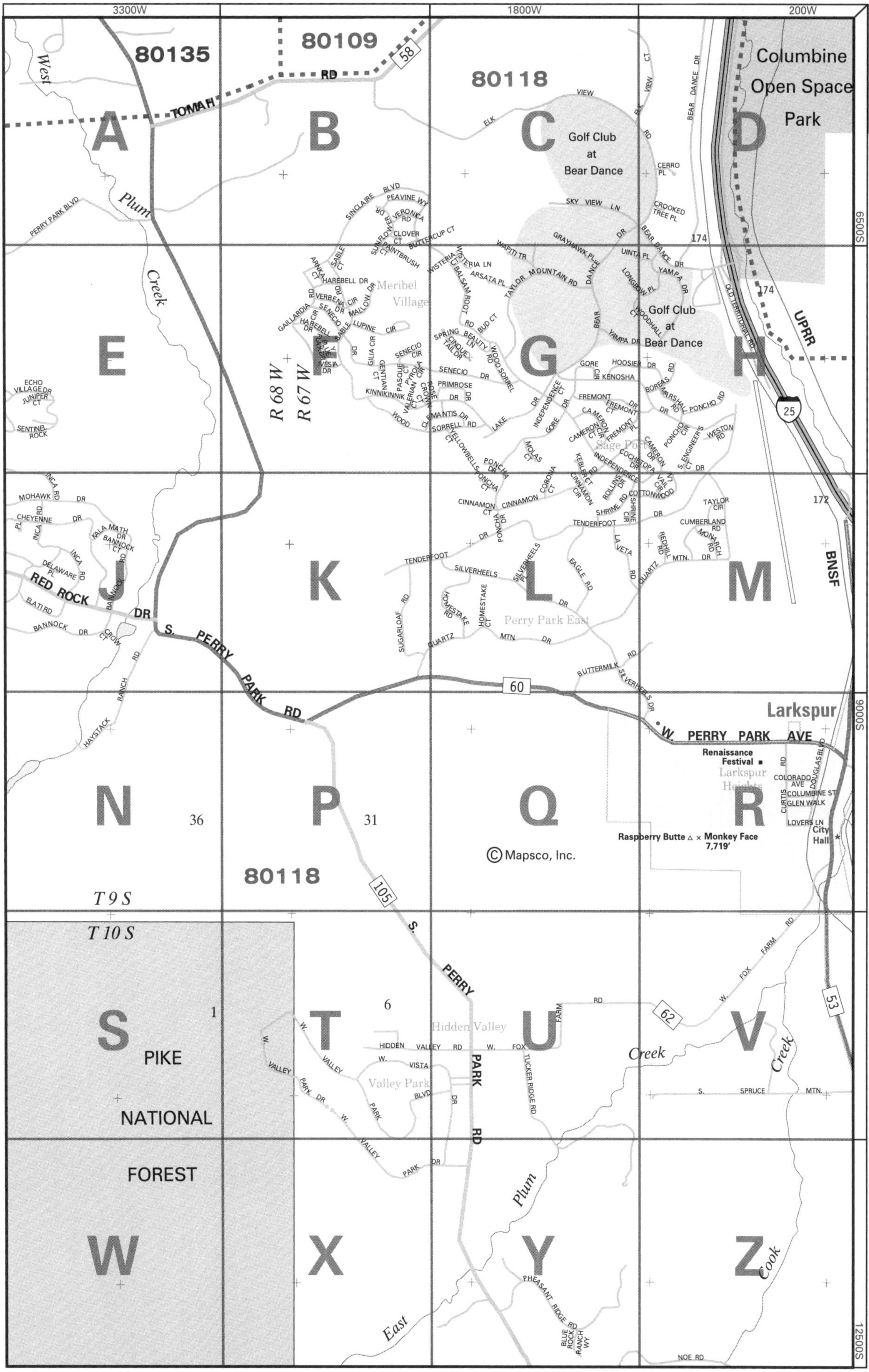

3300W 1800W 200W

80135 80109 80118

Columbine Open Space Park

Golf Club at Bear Dance

Meribel Village

Sage Port

Perry Park East

Larkspur

Larkspur Heights

Renaissance Festival

Raspberry Butte

Monkey Face 7,719'

City Hall

Valley Park

Hidden Valley

PIKE NATIONAL FOREST

R 68 W R 67 W

T 9 S T 10 S

TOMAH RD

PERRY PARK BLVD

S. PERRY PARK RD

W. PERRY PARK AVE

RED ROCK DR

UPRR

BNSF

West Plum Creek

Plum Creek

East Plum Creek

Cook Creek

A B C D E F G H J K L M N P Q R S T U V W X Y Z

36 31 6 1

172 174

© Mapsco, Inc.

6500S 9000S 12500S

See Map 888

0 ½ 1
Miles

▼ See Map 907 ▼

See Map 527
See Map 528

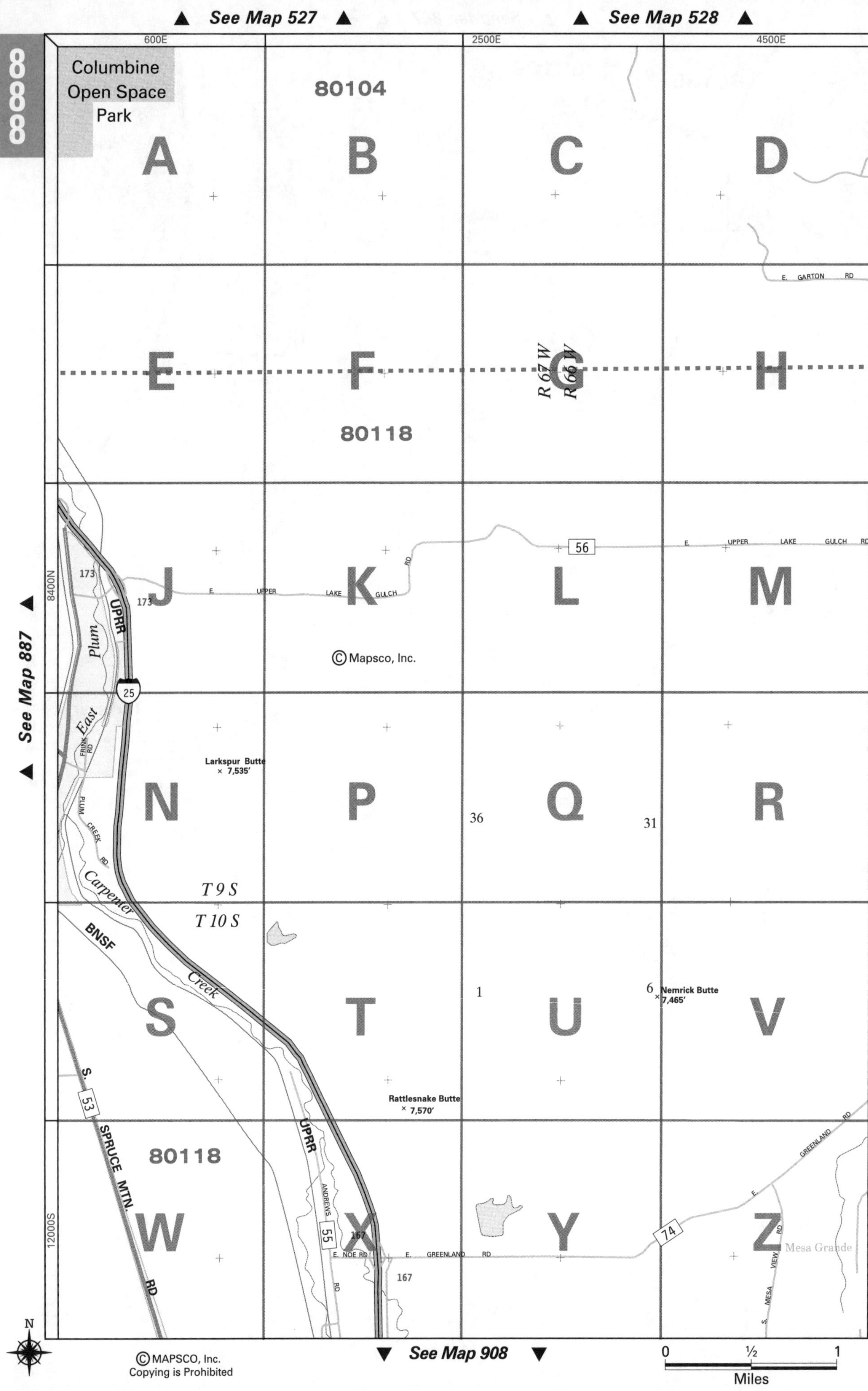

See Map 887

See Map 908

0 ½ 1
Miles

See Map 869

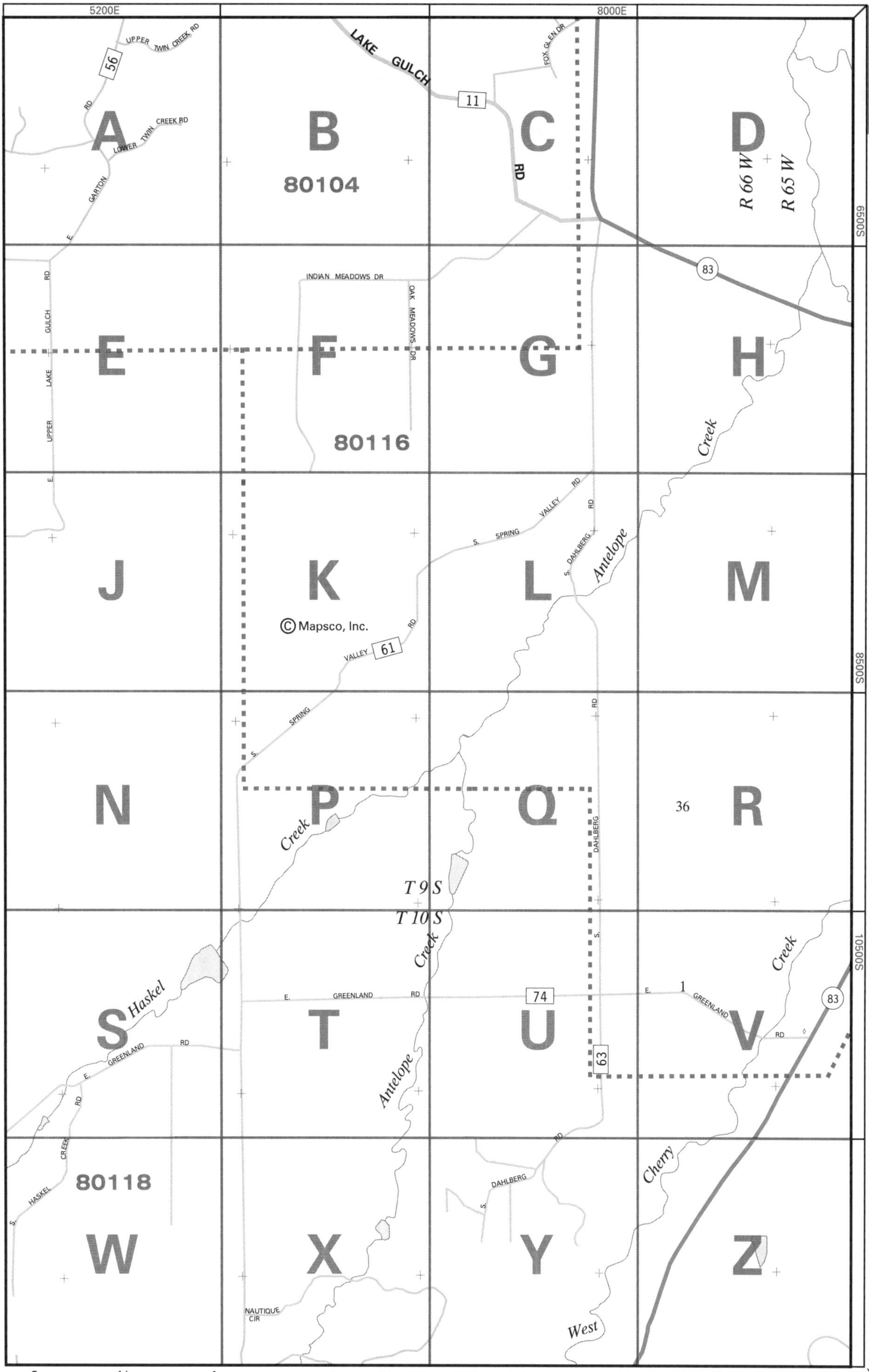

5200E
8000E
6500S
8500S
10500S

A B C D
E F G H
J K L M
N P Q R
S T U V
W X Y Z

80104
80116
80118

UPPER TWIN CREEK RD
56
RD
LOWER TWIN CREEK RD
GARTON
E.
LAKE GULCH RD
11
FOX GLEN DR
R 66 W
R 65 W
83
E. UPPER LAKE GULCH RD
INDIAN MEADOWS DR
OAK MEADOWS DR
Creek
S. SPRING VALLEY RD
61
S. DAHLBERG RD
Antelope
Creek
T 9 S
T 10 S
36
1
E. GREENLAND RD
74
63
Haskel
E. GREENLAND RD
RD
S. HASKEL CREEK RD
Antelope Creek
S. DAHLBERG RD
Cherry
West
NAUTIQUE CIR

See Map 890

See Map 909

0 ½ 1
Miles

N

▲ See Map 870 ▲

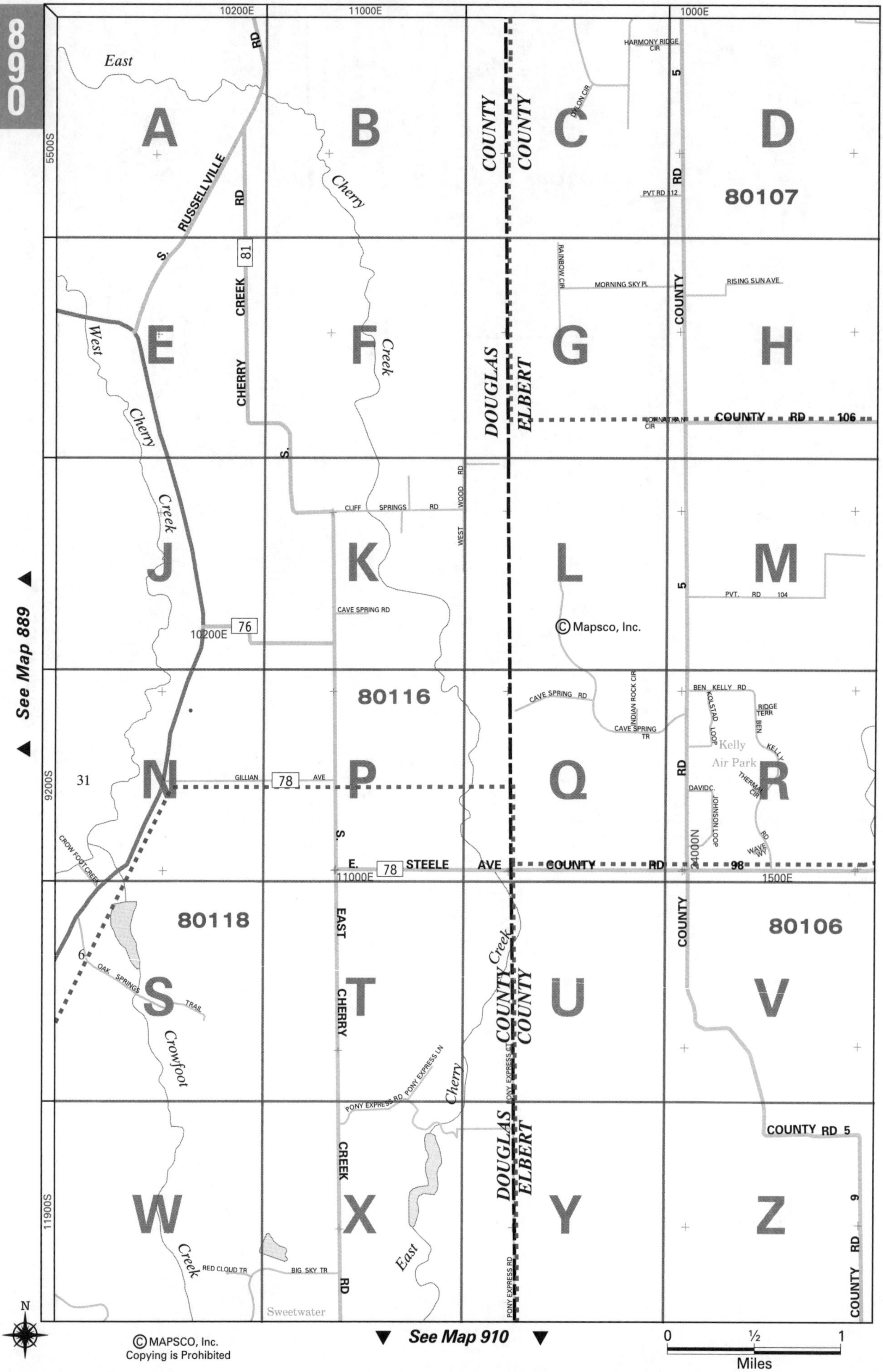

▲ See Map 889 ▲

▼ See Map 910 ▼

0 ½ 1
Miles

See Map 871

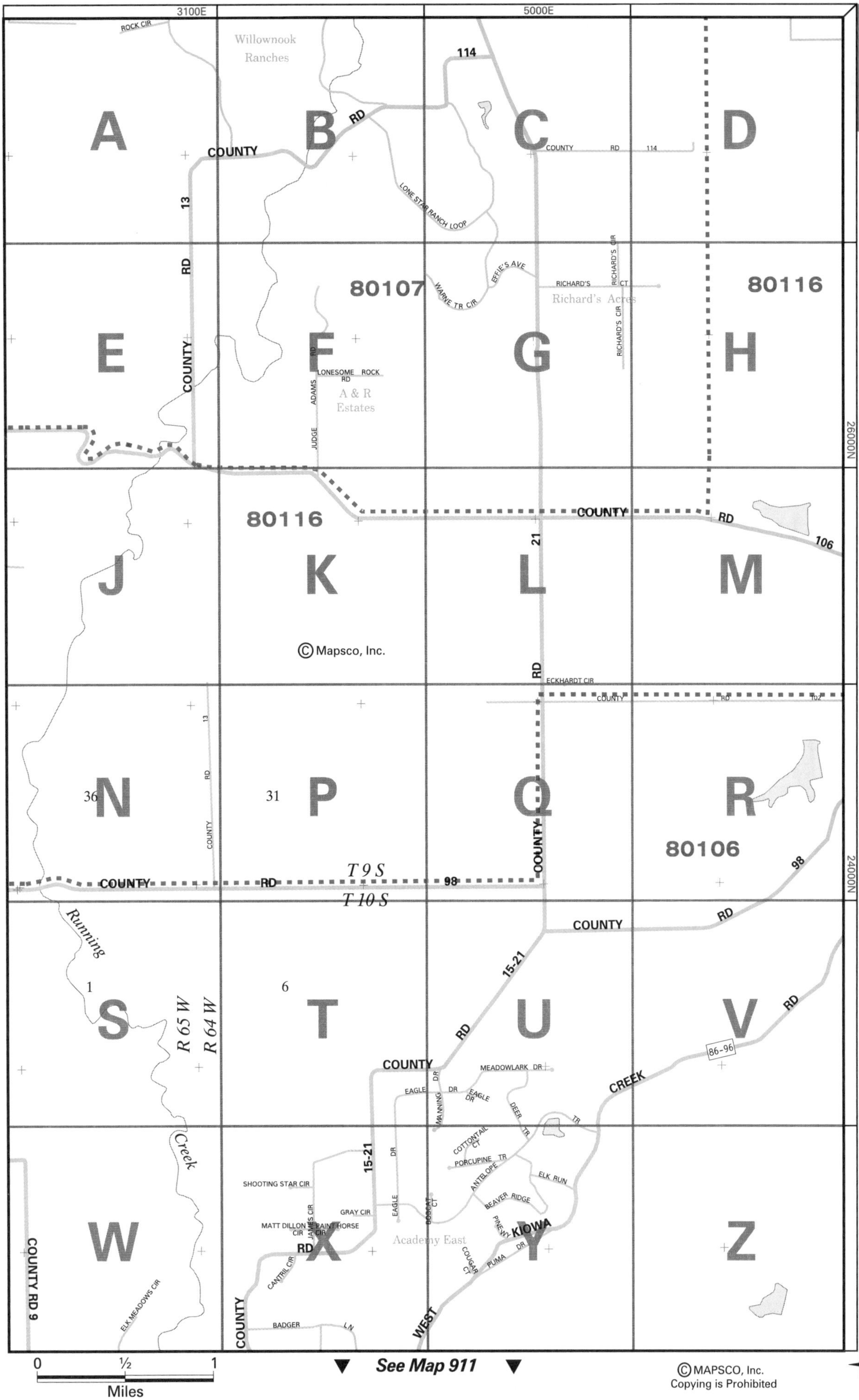

3100E
5000E

A B C D
E F G H
J K L M
N P Q R
S T U V
W X Y Z

ROCK CIR
Willownook Ranches
COUNTY RD 114
COUNTY RD 13
LONE STAR RANCH LOOP
80107
80116
80106
WARNE TR CIR
EFFIE'S AVE
RICHARD'S CT
RICHARD'S CIR
Richard's Acres
LONESOME ROCK RD
ADAMS RD
JUDGE
A & R Estates
COUNTY RD 106
COUNTY RD 21
ECKHARDT CIR
COUNTY RD 102
© Mapsco, Inc.
36
31
COUNTY RD 98
T 9 S
T 10 S
2600N
2400N
Running Creek
1
6
R 65 W
R 64 W
COUNTY RD 15-21
86-96
CREEK RD
MEADOWLARK DR
EAGLE DR
MANNING DR
DEER TR
COTTONTAIL CT
PORCUPINE TR
ANTELOPE
ELK RUN
BEAVER RIDGE
SHOOTING STAR CIR
GRAY CIR
MATT DILLON CIR
JAMES CIR
PAINT HORSE CIR
EAGLE
BOBCAT CT
PINE WY
KIOWA
Academy East
COUGAR CT
PUMA DR
CANTRIL CIR
COUNTY RD 9
ELK MEADOWS CIR
BADGER LN
WEST

See Map 892

See Map 911

0 ½ 1
Miles
N

▲ See Map 872 ▲

▲ See Map 891 ▲

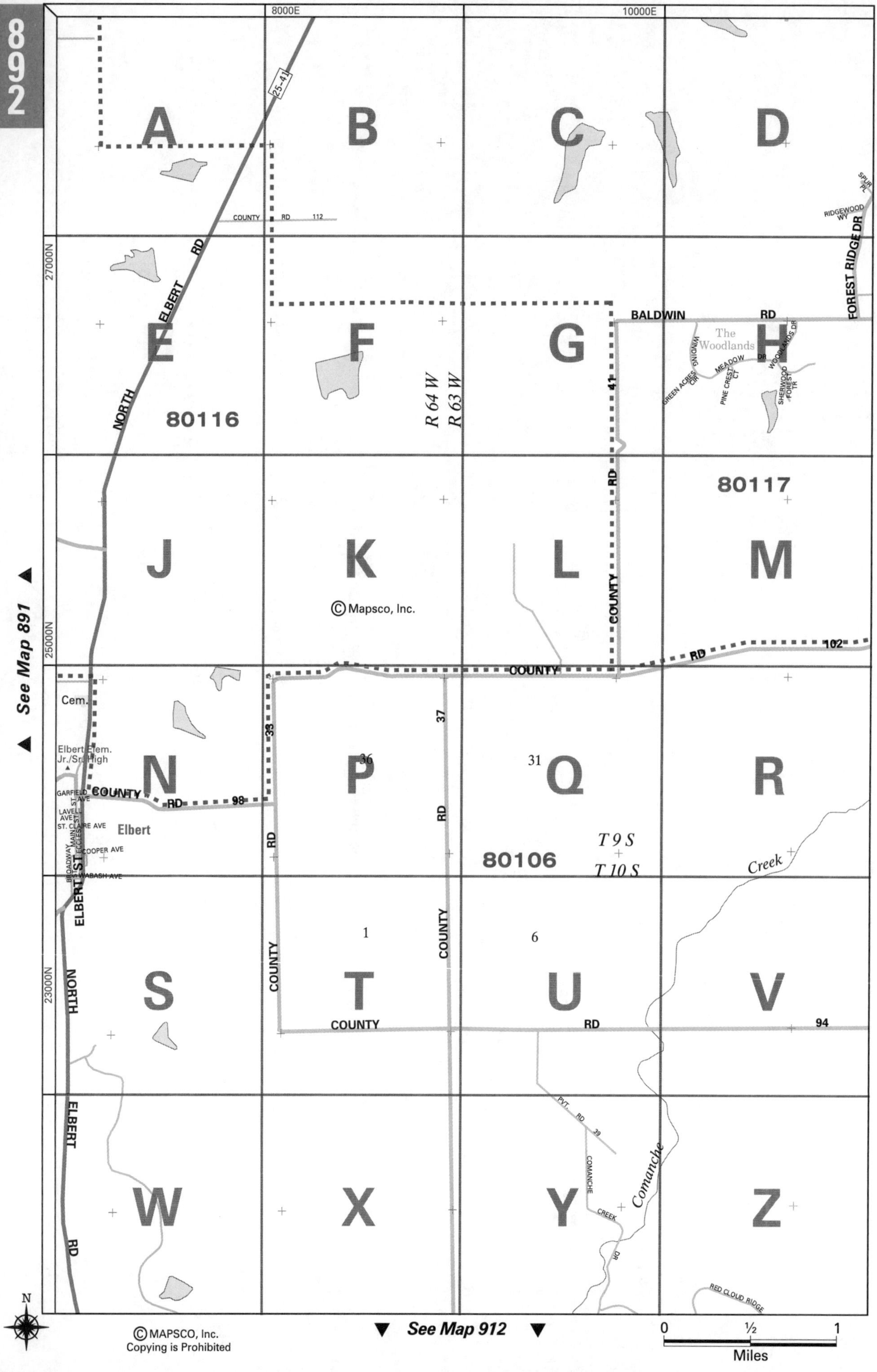

▼ See Map 912 ▼

▲ See Map 886 ▲

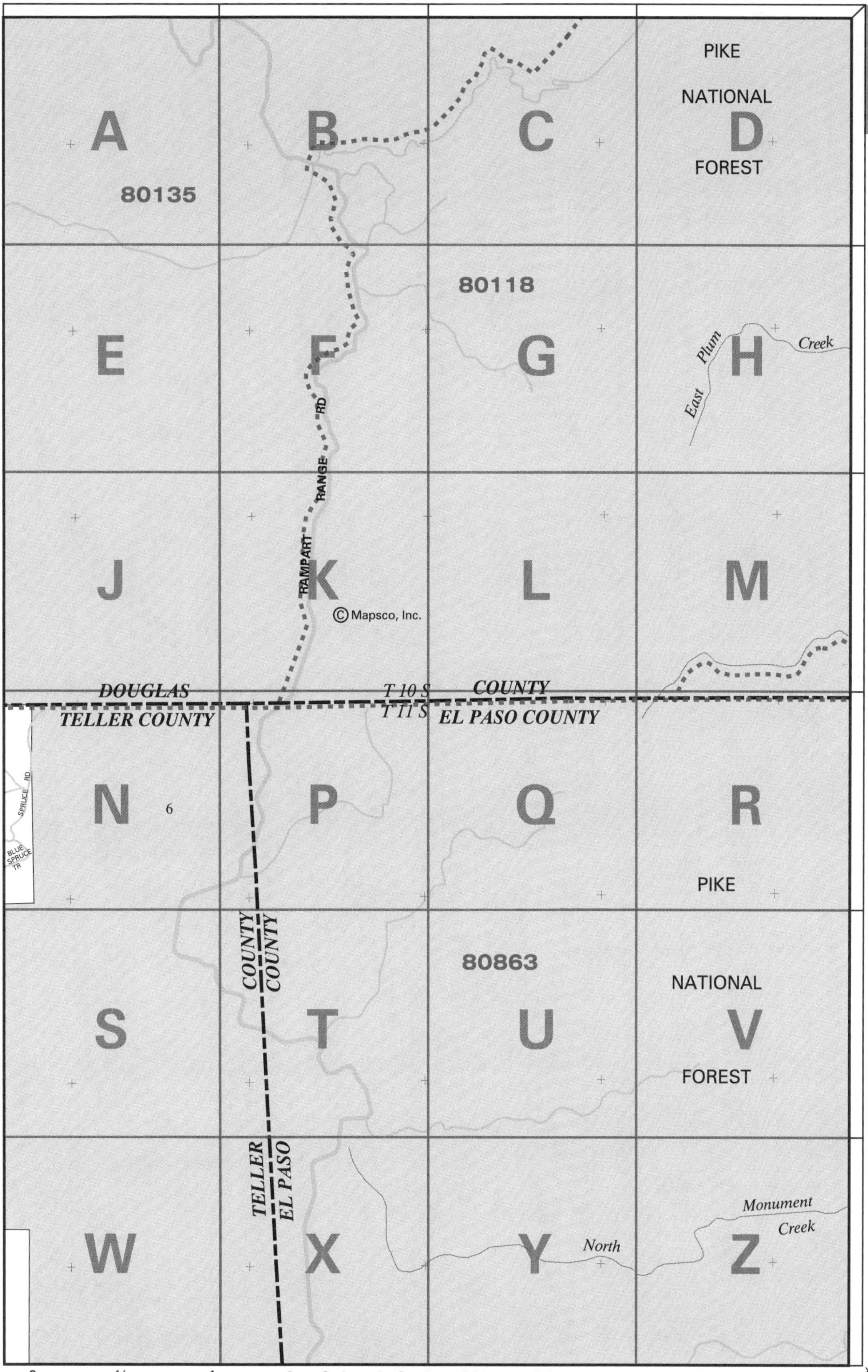

▶ See Map 907 ▶

0 ½ 1
Miles

▼ See Colorado Springs Mapsco Atlas ▼

N

▲ See Map 887 ▲

▲ See Map 906 ▲

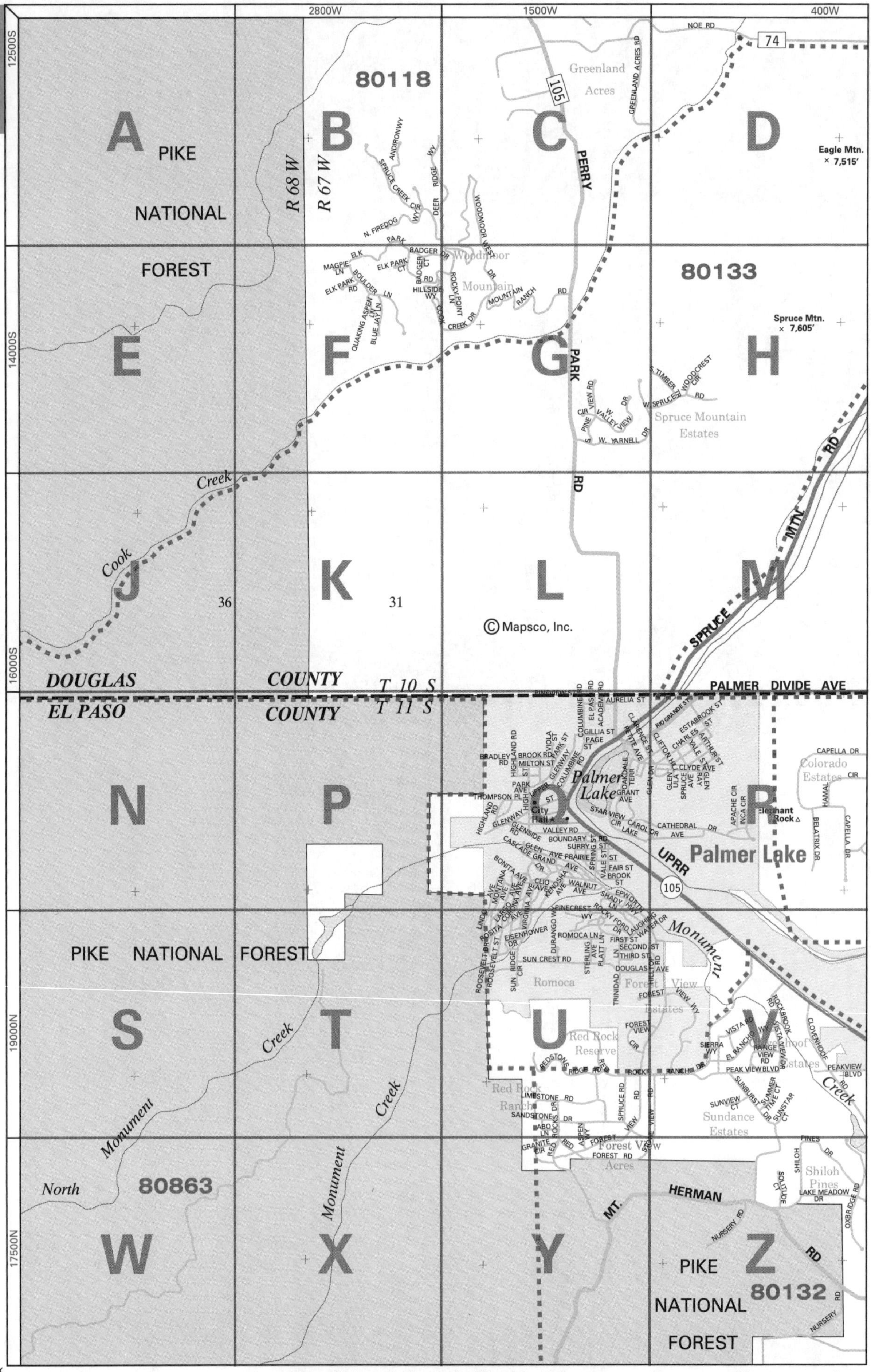

2800W 1500W 400W

12500S 14000S 16000S 19000N 17500N

A B C D E F G H J K L M N P Q R S T U V W X Y Z

PIKE NATIONAL FOREST

80118 80133 80863 80132

Greenland Acres

Woodmoor Mountain

Spruce Mountain Estates

Eagle Mtn. × 7,515′

Spruce Mtn. × 7,605′

PERRY PARK RD

SPRUCE MTN. RD

PALMER DIVIDE AVE

DOUGLAS COUNTY

EL PASO COUNTY

T 10 S

T 11 S

R 68 W

R 67 W

Cook Creek

Monument Creek

North Monument Creek

Palmer Lake

City Hall

Elephant Rock

Colorado Estates

Romoca

Forest View Estates

Red Rock Reserve

Red Rock Ranch

Sundance Estates

Forest View Acres

Shiloh Pines

MT. HERMAN RD

UPRR

© Mapsco, Inc.

▼ See Colorado Springs Mapsco Atlas ▼

0 ½ 1
Miles

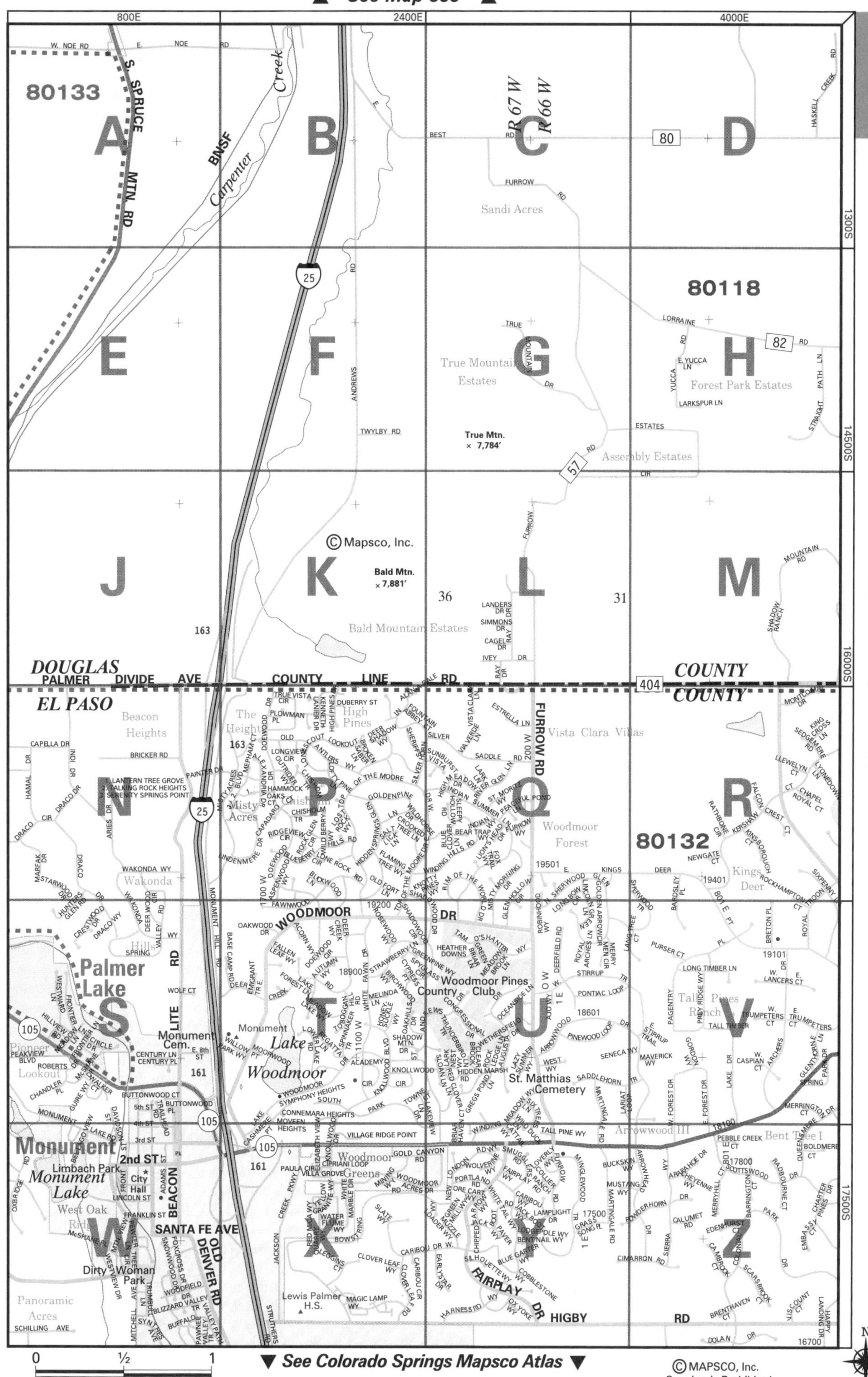

See Map 888
908
800E
2400E
4000E
80133
80118
80132
A
B
C
D
E
F
G
H
J
K
L
M
N
P
Q
R
S
T
U
V
W
X
Y
Z
R 67 W
R 66 W
BNSF
Carpenter Creek
S. SPRUCE MTN RD
W. NOE RD
E. NOE RD
BEST
FURROW RD
Sandi Acres
LORRAINE
True Mountain Estates
Forest Park Estates
Assembly Estates
True Mtn. × 7,784'
Bald Mtn. ×7,881'
Bald Mountain Estates
© Mapsco, Inc.
TWYLBY RD
ANDREWS RD
LARKSPUR LN
DOUGLAS COUNTY
EL PASO COUNTY
PALMER DIVIDE AVE
COUNTY LINE RD
Beacon Heights
The Heights
High Pines
Misty Acres
Vista Clara Villas
Woodmoor Forest
Kings Deer
Wakonda
Palmer Lake
WOODMOOR DR
Woodmoor Pines Country Club
Monument Lake
Woodmoor
St. Matthias Cemetery
Monument Cem.
Pioneer Lookout
Tall Pines Ranch
Arrowwood III
Bent Tree I
Monument
Monument Lake
Limbach Park
City Hall
West Oak Ridge
Dirty Woman Park
Woodmoor Greens
Lewis Palmer H.S.
Panoramic Acres
2nd ST
3rd ST
SANTA FE AVE
OLD DENVER RD
BEACON
HIGBY RD
FAIRPLAY DR
1300S
1450S
1600S
1750S
See Map 909
See Colorado Springs Mapsco Atlas
0
½
1
Miles
N
©MAPSCO, Inc.
Copying is Prohibited

▲ See Map 889 ▲

▲ See Map 908 ▲

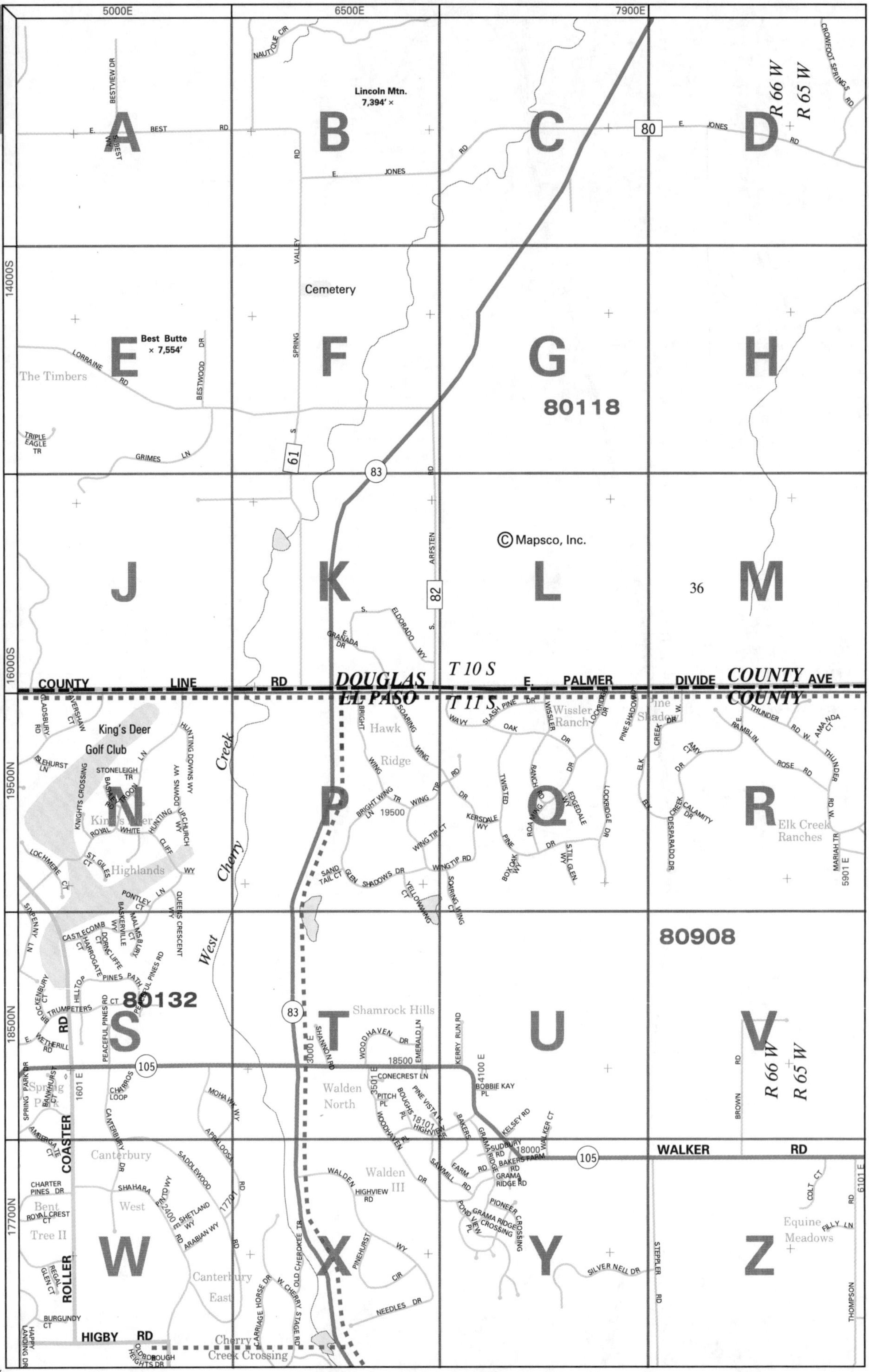

5000E
6500E
7900E
14000S
16000S
19500N
18500N
17700N
A
B
C
D
E
F
G
H
J
K
L
M
N
P
Q
R
S
T
U
V
W
X
Y
Z
Lincoln Mtn.
7,394′ ×
Best Butte
× 7,554′
Cemetery
The Timbers
80118
80908
80132
© Mapsco, Inc.
36
R 66 W
R 65 W
T 10 S
T 11 S
COUNTY LINE RD
E. PALMER DIVIDE AVE
DOUGLAS COUNTY
EL PASO COUNTY
E. BEST RD
E. JONES RD
VALLEY SPRING RD
LORRAINE RD
BESTWOOD DR
BESTVIEW DR
TRIPLE EAGLE TR
GRIMES LN
NAUTIQUE CIR
CROWFOOT SPRINGS RD
ARFSTEN RD
S. ELDORADO WY
E. GRANADA DR
King's Deer Golf Club
King's Deer Highlands
Hawk Ridge
Wissler Ranch
Pine Shadow
Elk Creek Ranches
Shamrock Hills
Walden North
Walden III
Canterbury
Canterbury West
Canterbury East
Bent Tree II
Spring Park
Cherry Creek Crossing
Equine Meadows
West Cherry Creek
COASTER RD
ROLLER RD
HIGBY RD
WALKER RD
BROWN RD
STEPPLER RD
THOMPSON
SILVER NELL DR
NEEDLES DR
PINEHURST WY
OLD CHEROKEE TR
HIGHVIEW RD
WALDEN DR
SAWMILL RD
BAKERS FARM RD
GRAMA RIDGE RD
PIONEER CROSSING
KELSEY RD
WALKER CT
BOBBIE KAY PL
KERRY RUN RD
EMERALD LN
CONECREST LN
WOODHAVEN DR
SHANNON RD
MOHAWK WY
APALOOSA
SADDLEWOOD
SHAHARA
ARABIAN WY
SHETLAND WY
BURGUNDY CT
HAPPY LANDING DR
OLDBOROUGH HEIGHTS DR
CHARTER PINES DR
ROYAL CREST CT
REGAL GLEN CT
TRUMPETERS CT
PEACEFUL PINES RD
HILLTOP
SINKENNY LN
LOCHMERE CT
ST. GILES CT
PONTLEY CT
QUEENS CRESCENT WY
HUNTING DOWNS WY
STONELEIGH TR
KNIGHTS CROSSING
BRIGHT WING TR
SOARING WING
WING TIP RD
SAND TAIL CT
GLEN SHADOWS DR
YELLOWWING CT
KERSDALE WY
TWISTED PINE
ROAMING RANCH DR
EDGEDALE
LOCKRIDGE DR
STILL GLEN WY
BOX OAK WY
WAVY OAK
SLASH PINE DR
WISSLER DR
PINE SHADOW DR
ELK CREEK
AMY CT
ROSE RD
THUNDER RD W.
E. RAMBLIN
CALAMITY DR
DESPARADO DR
MARIAH TR
5901 E
6101 E
COLT CT
FILLY LN
80
83
61
82
105
18500
19500
18000

▼ See Colorado Springs Mapsco Atlas ▼

0 ½ 1
Miles

▲ See Map 890 ▲

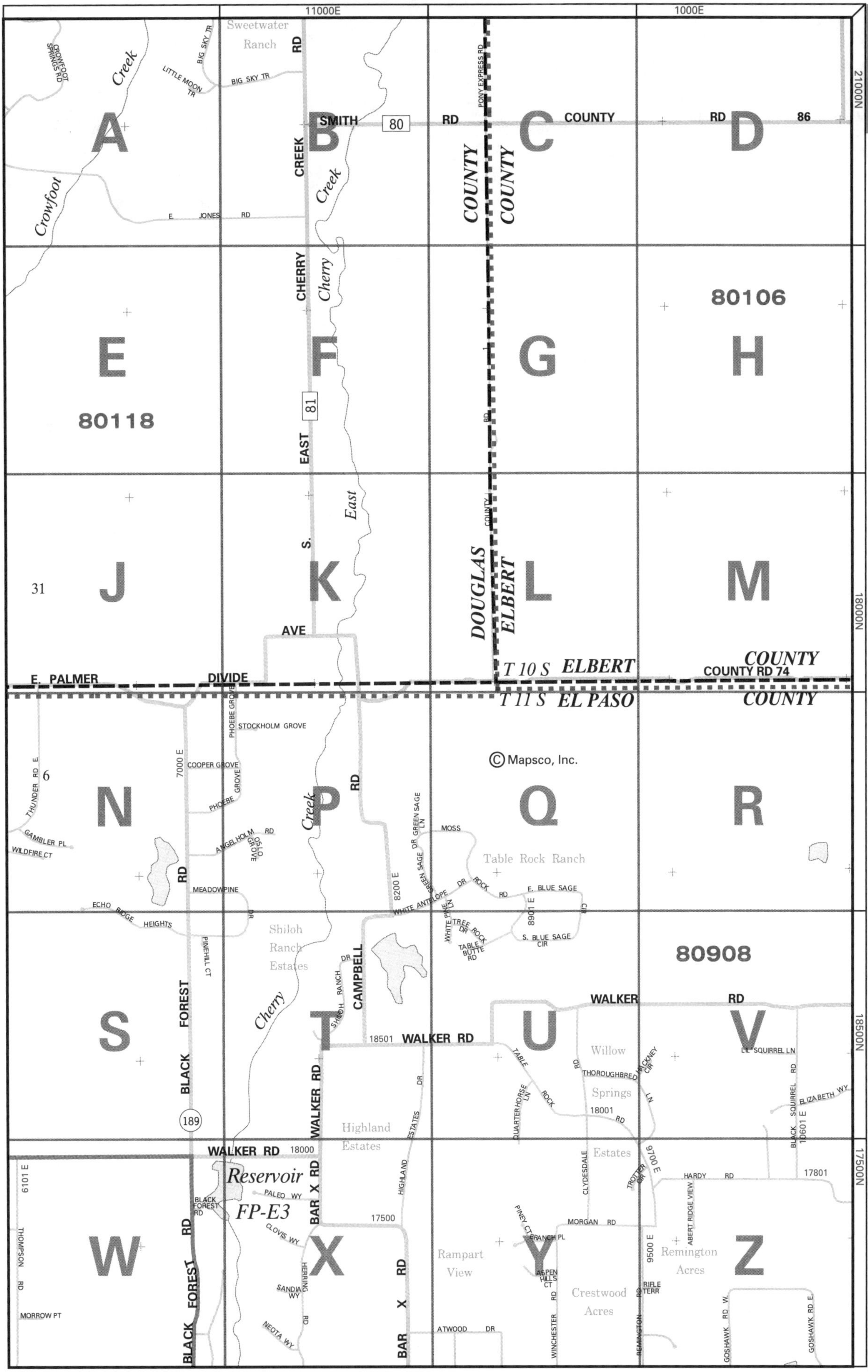

11000E
1000E
21000N

A B C D
E F G H
J K L M
N P Q R
S T U V
W X Y Z

80106
80118
80908

Sweetwater Ranch
Crowfoot Creek
Cherry Creek
East Cherry Creek
SMITH RD
COUNTY RD 86
80
81
189
E. JONES RD
BIG SKY TR
LITTLE MOON TR
CROWFOOT SPRINGS RD
PONY EXPRESS RD
DOUGLAS COUNTY
ELBERT COUNTY
S. CHERRY CREEK RD
EAST AVE
E. PALMER DIVIDE
T 10 S ELBERT COUNTY
COUNTY RD 74
T 11 S EL PASO COUNTY
18000N
18500N
17500N
31
6

© Mapsco, Inc.

Table Rock Ranch
Shiloh Ranch Estates
Willow Springs Estates
Highland Estates
Rampart View
Crestwood Acres
Remington Acres
Reservoir FP-E3
BLACK FOREST RD
WALKER RD
18501 WALKER RD
BAR X RD
CAMPBELL RD
HARDY RD
MORGAN RD
ATWOOD DR
17500
17801
18000
18001

See Map 911

0 ½ 1
Miles

▼ See Colorado Springs Mapsco Atlas ▼

N

▲ See Map 891 ▲

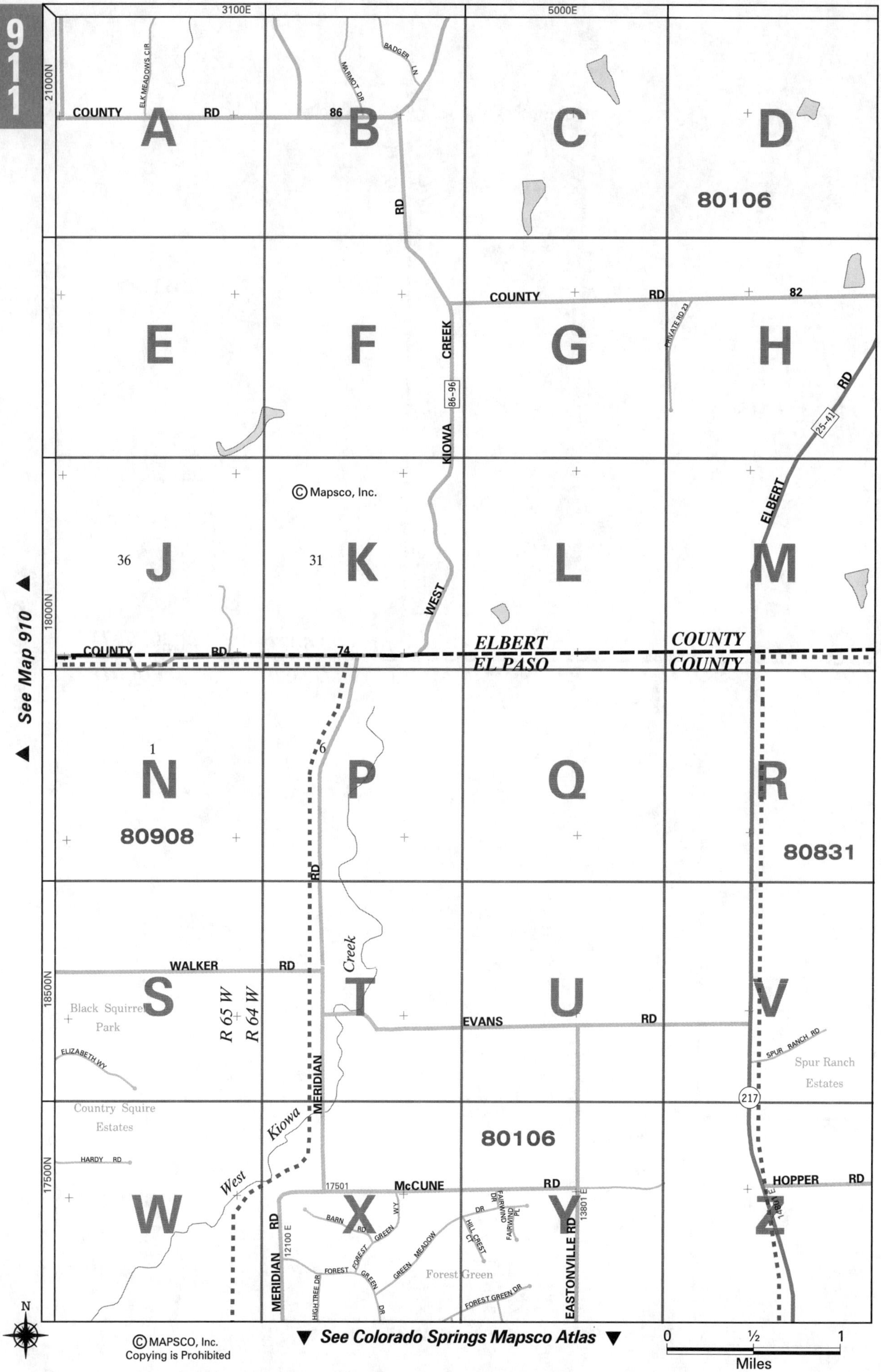

▲ See Map 910 ▲

▼ See Colorado Springs Mapsco Atlas ▼

▲ See Map 892 ▲

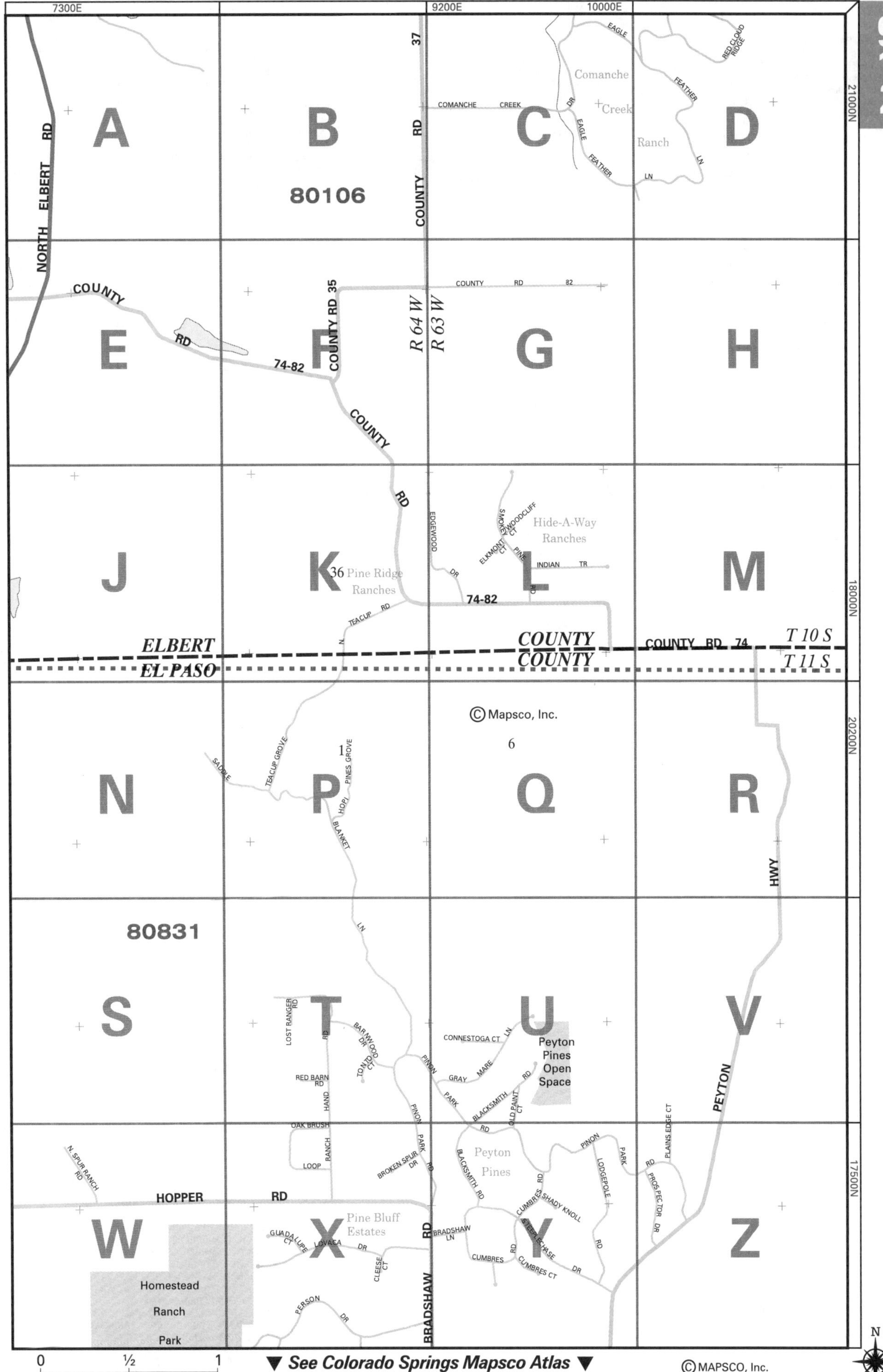

0 ½ 1
Miles

▼ See Colorado Springs Mapsco Atlas ▼

N

Airports

BOULDER MUNICIPAL AIRPORT 98R
CENTENNIAL AIRPORT 377R
DENVER INTERNATIONAL AIRPORT 770L
DENVER INTERNATIONAL AIRPORT 769R
ERIE MUNICIPAL AIRPORT 133A
FRONT RANGE AIRPORT 791C
FRONT RANGE AIRPORT 792E
PLATTE VALLEY AIRPORT 730E
ROCKY MOUNTAIN METROPOLITAN AIRPORT 191B
VANCE BRAND MUNICIPAL AIRPORT 40F

Business Parks

96TH AVENUE INDUSTRIAL PARK 768J
ACADEMY PARK 342B
BUSINESS CENTER @ CTC 131Y
CENTENNIAL AIRPORT CENTER 377H
COLORADO TECHNOLOGICAL CENTER 161B
COORS TECHNOLOGY CENTER 250J
DENVER TECHNOLOGICAL CENTER 346Q
DENVER WEST OFFICE PARK 280G
GATEWAY CENTRE 258V
GREENWOOD PLAZA 316T
GREENWOOD PLAZA SOUTH 346Y
HIGHLANDS RANCH BUSINESS PARK 374W
HIGHLANDS RANCH HEALTHCARE PLAZA 374T
I-25 BUSINESS PARK 706D
INTERLOCKEN OFFICE PARK 161X
INVERNESS 377K
LINCOLN EXECUTIVE CENTER 347Y
LUCENT TECHNOLOGY 374S
MAJESTIC COMMERCENTER 259Z
MERIDIAN INTERNATIONAL BUSINESS CENTER 407M
MERIDIAN INTERNATIONAL BUSINESS CENTER 408K
MERIDIAN OFFICE PARK 407B
NORTH RIDGE @ PARK CENTRE 164W
NORTH VALLEY TECH CENTER 224G
OMNIPARK 407A
ORCHARD PLACE 346Y
PANORAMA CORPORATE CENTER 376R
RAMPART BUSINESS CENTER 377E
SEKICH BUSINESS PARK 706D
SOUTHFIELD PARK 347Z
SOUTHGATE OFFICE PARK 376H
SOUTHPARK LIGHT INDUSTRIAL PARK 374P
STAPLETON BUSINESS CENTER 257P
WESTMINSTER TECHNOLOGY PARK 191F

Cemeteries

ARVADA 251G
BROOMFIELD COUNTY COMMONS CEMETERY 163S
BURLINGTON 41P
BYERS 795Y
CEDAR HILL 497F
CHAPEL HILL MEMORIAL GARDENS 345X
COAL CREEK 131U
COLUMBIA 127G
CROWN HILL 252W
EASTLAWN MEMORIAL GARDENS 289D
ELBERT 892N
ELIZABETH 871E
ELMWOOD 138W
EVERGREEN MEMORIAL PARK 367E
FAIRMOUNT 286Y
FT LOGAN NATIONAL 343A
GOLDEN 279Q
GOLDEN HILL 281J
GREEN MOUNTAIN CEMETERY 128J
HAMPDEN MEMORIAL GARDENS 316Z
HIGHLAND MEMORIAL GARDENS 194Q
HILLSIDE 728M
LAFAYETTE 132E
LAKEVIEW 162U
LITTLETON 343Z
LOUISVILLE 131Y
MIZPAH 708C
MONUMENT 908S
MOUNTAIN VIEW 98P
MOUNTAIN VIEW 11Z
MOUNTAIN VIEW 730K
MT NEBO 287L
MT OLIVET 250R
MT PLEASANT CEMETERY 103F
MT VIEW 793K
NIWOT 69H
PARKER 409L
RALSTON CEMETERY 250C
RIVERSIDE 255E
ROSE HILL 226X
SACRED HEART OF MARY 129Q
ST MATTHIAS 908U
SUPERIOR 160G
WESLEY CHAPEL CEMETERY 164X

City Halls and Courthouses

ADAMS COUNTY ADMN 138T
450 S 4th Ave, Brighton 303-659-2120
ADAMS COUNTY JUSTICE CENTER 139Y
1100 Judicial Center Dr, Brighton 303-659-1161
ARAPAHOE COUNTY ADMN 343R
5334 S Prince St, Littleton 303-795-4400
ARAPAHOE COUNTY COURT, DIV A 344S
1790 W Littleton Blvd, Littleton 303-798-4591
ARAPAHOE COUNTY COURTS, DIV B 288G
15400 E 14th Pl, Aurora 303-363-8004
ARAPAHOE COUNTY JUSTICE CENTER 378J
7325 S Potomac St, Centennial 303-649-6355
ARVADA 252A
8101 Ralston Rd, Arvada 720-898-7000
AURORA 288Y
15151 E Alameda Pkwy 303-739-7000
AURORA MUNICIPAL COURTHOUSE 288T
14999 E Alameda Pkwy 303-739-6440
BENNETT 793J
355 4th St 303-644-3249
BLACK HAWK 780D
201 Selak St 303-582-5221
BOULDER 127D
1777 Broadway 303-441-3388
BOULDER COUNTY COURTHOUSE 97Z
2025 14th St 303-441-3131
BOULDER COUNTY JUSTICE CENTER 127C
1777 6th St, Boulder 303-441-3690
BOULDER MUNICIPAL COURT 127C
1777 6th St 303-441-1842
BOW MAR 343N
5395 Lakeshore Dr 303-794-6065
BRIGHTON 138P
22 S 4th Ave 303-655-2000
BROOMFIELD 162Y
1 Des Combes Dr 303-469-3301
BROOMFIELD COMBINED COURTS 162Y
17 Des Combes Dr 720-887-2100
CASTLE ROCK 497L
100 N Wilcox St 303-660-1015
CASTLE ROCK MUNICIPAL COURT 497L
100 Perry St 303-663-6133
CENTENNIAL 377D
12503 E Euclid Dr, Suite 200 303-734-4567
CENTENNIAL MUNICIPAL COURT 377D
12503 E Euclid Dr, Ste 260 303-754-3380
CENTRAL CITY 780D
141 Nevada St 303-582-5251
CHERRY HILLS VILLAGE 345E
2450 E Quincy Ave 303-789-2541
CLEAR CREEK COUNTY ADMN
405 Argentine, Georgetown 303-679-2300
COLUMBINE VALLEY 343X
2 S Middlefield Rd 303-795-1434
COLUMBINE VALLEY MUNICIPAL COURT 343V
2069 W Littleton Blvd 303-795-1434
COMMERCE CITY CITY HALL 256C
7887 E 60th Ave 303-289-3600
COMMERCE CITY CIVIC/JUSTICE CENTER 256C
7887 E 60th Ave 303-289-3640
DACONO TOWN HALL 727K
512 Cherry 303-833-2317
DENVER CITY & COUNTY 284F
1437 Bannock St 720-913-4900
DOUGLAS COUNTY ADMN 497K
100 Third St, Castle Rock 303-660-7400
DOUGLAS COUNTY COMBINED COURTS 467T
4000 Justice Way 303-663-7200
EDGEWATER 282D
2401 Sheridan Blvd 303-238-7803
ELBERT COUNTY ADMN 872M
215 Comanche 303-621-2341
ELIZABETH 871F
321 Banner St S 303-646-4166
ENGLEWOOD CITY HALL 314X
1000 Englewood Pkwy 303-762-2300
ENGLEWOOD MUNICIPAL COURT 314X
1000 Englewood Pkwy 303-762-2580
ERIE 103J
645 Holbrook St 303-926-2700
ERIE MUNICIPAL COURT 103J
645 Holbrook St 303-926-2851
FEDERAL HEIGHTS CITY HALL 223D
2380 W 90th Ave 303-428-3526
FEDERAL HEIGHTS COURT 223D
2380 W 90th Ave 303-428-3526
FIRESTONE TOWN HALL 727B
151 Grant Ave 303-833-3291
FORT LUPTON CITY HALL 728L
130 S McKinley Ave 303-857-6694
FREDERICK MUNICIPAL COURT 727F
333 5th St 303-833-4733
FREDERICK TOWN HALL 727F
401 Locust St 303-833-2388
GILPIN COUNTY ADMN 780D
203 Eureka St, Central City 303-582-5214
GILPIN COUNTY JUSTICE CENTER 761S
2960 Dory Hill Rd 303-582-5323
GLENDALE 315C
950 S Birch St 303-759-1513
GOLDEN 279A
911 10th St, Golden 303-384-8000
GOLDEN MUNICIPAL COURT 279A
911 10th St 303-384-8006
GREENWOOD VILLAGE 346Y
6060 S Quebec St 303-773-0252
HUDSON TOWN HALL 730L
557 Ash St 303-536-9311
IDAHO SPRINGS 780Q
1711 Miner St 303-567-4421
JEFFERSON COUNTY ADMN 279Q
100 Jefferson County Pkwy, Golden 303-279-6511
KEENESBURG TOWN HALL 732A
140 S Main St 303-732-4281
KIOWA 872M
404 Comanche St 303-621-2366
LAFAYETTE 132N
1290 S Public Rd 303-665-5588
LAFAYETTE MUNICIPAL COURT 132E
451 N 111th Ave 303-604-8000
LAKESIDE 252R
4601 Sheridan Blvd 303-458-1062
LAKEWOOD 282X
480 S Allison Pkwy 303-987-7000
LAKEWOOD MUNICIPAL COURT 282X
445 S Allison Pkwy 303-987-7400
LARKSPUR 887R
9524 S Spruce Mountain Rd 303-681-2324
LITTLETON 343R
2255 W Berry Ave 303-795-3700
LITTLETON MUNICIPAL COURTHOUSE 343V
2069 W Littleton Blvd 303-795-3837
LOCHBUIE 140G
703 Weld County Rd 37 303-655-9308
LONE TREE 377W
9220 KIMMER DR 303-708-1818
LONE TREE MUNICIPAL COURT 376Z
8527 Lone Tree Pkwy 303-339-8177
LONGMONT 41H
350 Kimbark 303-776-6050
LONGMONT MUNICIPAL COURT 41H
225 Kimbark St 303-651-8688
LOUISVILLE 131S
749 Main St 303-666-6565
LOUISVILLE POLICE AND MUNICIPAL COURT 130X
992 W Via Appia Way 303-335-4653
LYONS 703B
432 5th Ave 303-823-6622
MONUMENT 908W
166 2nd St 719-884-8017
MORRISON 309Z
321 State Hwy 8 303-697-8749
MOUNTAIN VIEW 252R
4176 Benton St 303-421-7282
NEDERLAND 740Q
45 W 1st St 303-258-3266
NORTHGLENN 194B
11701 Community Center Dr 303-451-8326
NORTHGLENN MUNICIPAL COURT 194B
11701 Community Center Dr 303-450-8701
PALMER LAKE 907Q
42 Valley Rd S 719-481-2953
PARK COUNTY ADMN
501 Main St, Fairplay 719-836-4201
PARK COUNTY COURT
300 4th St, Fairplay 719-836-2940
PARKER 409R
20120 E Mainstreet 303-841-0353
PARKER MUNICIPAL COURT 409R
20120 E Main St 303-805-3195
PLATTEVILLE MUNICIPAL COURT 708C
400 Grand Ave 970-785-2245
PLATTEVILLE TOWN HALL 708C
400 Grand Ave 970-785-2245
SHERIDAN 343G
4101 S Federal Blvd 303-762-2200
SUPERIOR CITY HALL 160F
124 E Coal Creek Dr 303-499-3675
SUPERIOR MUNICIPAL COURT 160F
124 E Coal Creek Dr 303-499-3675
THORNTON 194U
9500 Civic Center Dr 303-538-7200
THORNTON MUNICIPAL COURT 194U
9551 Civic Center Dr 720-977-5400
WARD 720M
1 Columbia St 303-459-9273
WATKINS 791N
303-513-5500
WESTMINSTER 193W
4800 W 92nd Ave 303-430-2400
WESTMINSTER MUNICIPAL COURT 223L
3030 Turnpike Dr 303-430-2400
WHEAT RIDGE 282B
7500 W 29th Ave 303-234-5900
WHEAT RIDGE MUNICIPAL COURT 282B
7500 W 29th Ave 303-235-2835

Colleges and Universities

AIMS COMMUNITY COLLEGE 729J
ARAPAHOE COMMUNITY COLLEGE 343V
AURARIA CAMPUS 284E
BELLEVIEW COLLEGE 223F
COLORADO CHRISTIAN UNIVERSITY 282S
COLORADO SCHOOL OF MINES 279A
COMMUNITY COLLEGE OF AURORA-CENTRETECH 288U
COMMUNITY COLLEGE OF AURORA-LOWRY 286R
COMMUNITY COLLEGE OF DENVER-AURARIA 284E
COMMUNITY COLLEGE OF DENVER-EAST 254V
COMMUNITY COLLEGE OF DENVER-LOWRY 286M
COMMUNITY COLLEGE OF DENVER-NORTH 224Z
COMMUNITY COLLEGE OF DENVER-SOUTHWEST 283D
DENVER SEMINARY 343Z
EMPORIA STATE UNIVERSITY-LOWRY 286R
FRONT RANGE COMMUNITY COLLEGE-BOULDER 41S
FRONT RANGE COMMUNITY COLLEGE-BRIGHTON 138R
FRONT RANGE COMMUNITY COLLEGE-WESTMINSTER 193F
ILIFF SCHOOL OF THEOLOGY 315N
JOHNSON & WALES UNIVERSITY 286F
LOWRY CAMPUS 286R
METROPOLITAN STATE COLLEGE 284E
NAROPA UNIVERSITY-ARAPAHOE CAMPUS 128A
NAROPA UNIVERSITY-NALANDA CAMPUS 129B
NAROPA UNIVERSITY, PARAMITA CAMPUS 98T
RED ROCKS COMMUNITY COLLEGE, ARVADA CAMPUS 251G
RED ROCKS COMMUNITY COLLEGE-LAKEWOOD 280V
REGIS UNIVERSITY-BOULDER 69X
REGIS UNIVERSITY-BROOMFIELD 161X
REGIS UNIVERSITY-DTC 346U
REGIS UNIVERSITY-MAIN CAMPUS 253K
RITA BASS TRAUMA AND EMS EDUCATION INSTITUTE 284P
ROCKY MOUNTAIN COLLEGE OF ART AND DESIGN 282G
TEIKYO LORETTO HEIGHTS UNIVERSITY 313U
UNIVERSITY CENTER @ CHAPARRAL 408C
UNIVERSITY OF COLORADO-BOULDER 128E
UNIVERSITY OF COLORADO-DENVER 284E

UNIV OF COLORADO EAST CAMPUS RESEARCH PARK 128C
UNIVERSITY OF COLORADO HEALTH SCIENCES CENTER 287H
UNIVERSITY OF COLORADO HEALTH SCIENCES CENTER 285L
UNIVERSITY OF DENVER 315N
YESHIVA TORAS CHAIM TALMUDICAL SEMINARY 283F

Country Clubs and Golf Courses

APPLEWOOD 250U
ARROWHEAD 432T
AURORA HILLS 287V
BEAR CREEK GOLF COURSE 311N
BELLA ROSA GOLF COURSE 707W
BLACK BEAR GOLF CLUB 410U
BOULDER COUNTRY CLUB 99D
BROADLANDS 163F
BUFFALO RUN 198C
CASTLE PINES GOLF COURSE 466C
CENTENNIAL SOUTH 343Y
CENTRE HILLS 288V
CHERRY CREEK COUNTRY CLUB 316R
CHERRY HILLS COUNTRY CLUB 345E
CITY PARK MUNICIPAL GOLF COURSE 285B
CLUB AT PRADERA, THE 469A
COAL CREEK 160D
COLUMBINE COUNTRY CLUB 343X
COUNTRY CLUB @ CASTLE PINES, THE 436X
COYOTE CREEK 729J
COYOTE CREEK 728M
DEER CREEK GOLF CLUB AT MEADOW RANCH 371J
DENVER COUNTRY CLUB 285S
EAGLE TRACE GOLF CLUB 162L
ENGLEWOOD MUNICIPAL GOLF COURSE 343D
EVERGREEN MUNICIPAL 336L
FITZSIMONS 287D
FLATIRONS 129A
FOOTHILLS 342A
FOOTHILLS 341D
FOSSIL TRACE GOLF CLUB 279K
FOX HILL COUNTRY CLUB 42C
FOX HOLLOW 311S
FOX HOLLOW 310V
GLENMOOR COUNTRY CLUB 345L
GOLF CLUB @ BEAR DANCE 887C
GRANDVIEW 707B
GREEN GABLES COUNTRY CLUB 312K
GREEN VALLEY RANCH GOLF CLUB 260J
GREENWAY PARK 192C
HARVARD GULCH 314Q
HAYSTACK MOUNTAIN 69J
HEATHER GARDENS 318S
HEATHER RIDGE COUNTRY CLUB 318J
HERITAGE @ WESTMOOR, THE 191F
HERITAGE EAGLE BEND 380Q
HIGHLANDS RANCH GOLF CLUB 373Y
HIWAN COUNTRY CLUB 306N
HOMESTEAD AT FOX HOLLOW GOLF COURSE, THE 341A
HYLAND HILLS 193S
INDIAN PEAKS 131F
INDIAN TREE 222N
INVERNESS 377K
J F KENNEDY MUNICIPAL 347A
KING'S DEER GOLF CLUB 909N
LAKE ARBOR 222F
LAKE VALLEY 723G
LAKEWOOD COUNTRY CLUB 282Q
LEGACY RIDGE 193F
LINKS, THE 376S
LITTLETON GOLF COURSE AND TENNIS CLUB 343U
LONE TREE 406C
MEADOW HILLS 348B
MEADOWS, THE 371F
MEADOWS, THE 370H
MERIDIAN GOLF CLUB 407C
MIRA VISTA 287S
MT VERNON COUNTRY CLUB 277Q
MURPHY CREEK 320M
OMNI INTERLOCKEN HOTEL AND CONFERENCE RESORT 161W
OVERLAND MUNICIPAL GOLF COURSE 314F
PARK HILL MUNICIPAL GOLF COURSE 255U
PERRY PARK COUNTRY CLUB 886G
PINEHURST COUNTRY CLUB 342G
PINERY COUNTRY CLUB 439V
PLUM CREEK GOLF & COUNTRY CLUB 497Q
RACCOON CREEK 342T
RANCH COUNTRY CLUB, THE 193C
RED HAWK 496D
RED ROCKS COUNTRY CLUB 340N
RIDGE AT CASTLE PINES N, THE 436K
RIVERDALE DUNES 167J
RIVERDALE KNOLLS 166R
ROLLING HILLS COUNTRY CLUB 280A
SADDLEBACK 707X
SADDLE ROCK 350X
SANCTUARY 847F
SANCTUARY 436J
SOUTHGLENN 374H
SOUTH SUBURBAN MUNICIPAL GOLF COURSE 375Q
SPRINGHILL MUNICIPAL 289K
SPRING VALLEY GOLF CLUB 851C
STONEY CREEK GOLF COURSE 190U
SUNSET 41B
THORNCREEK MUNICIPAL GOLF COURSE 164L
TWIN PEAKS 10Z
UTE CREEK 12Q
VALLEY COUNTRY CLUB 378B
VISTA RIDGE GOLF CLUB 133G
WELLSHIRE MUNICIPAL 315X
WEST WOODS RANCH 219V
WILLIS CASE MUNICIPAL GOLF COURSE 253J
WINDSOR GARDENS 287W
WOODMOOR PINES COUNTRY CLUB 908U

Fire Departments

ARVADA-FIRE STATION #1 252B
ARVADA-FIRE STATION #2 251J
ARVADA-FIRE STATION #3 221Q
ARVADA-FIRE STATION #4 222U
ARVADA-FIRE STATION #5 222K
ARVADA-FIRE STATION #6 221X
ARVADA-FIRE STATION #7 220M
ARVADA-FIRE STATION #8 219Z
AURORA-FIRE STATION #1 287E
AURORA-FIRE STATION #2 287R
AURORA-FIRE STATION #3 257Z
AURORA-FIRE STATION #4 317D
AURORA-FIRE STATION #5 289J
AURORA-FIRE STATION #6 318Y
AURORA-FIRE STATION #7 318P
AURORA-FIRE STATION #8 288Y
AURORA-FIRE STATION #9 319J
AURORA-FIRE STATION #10 349B
AURORA-FIRE STATION #11 317P
AURORA-FIRE STATION #12 259Y
AURORA-FIRE STATION #13 380H
AURORA-FIRE STATION #14 380L
AURORA-FIRE STATION #15 320H
BENNETT 793J
BOULDER-FIRE STATION #1 97Z
BOULDER-FIRE STATION #2 128J
BOULDER-FIRE STATION #3 128B
BOULDER-FIRE STATION #4 128U
BOULDER-FIRE STATION #5 97H
BOULDER-FIRE STATION #6 99B
BOULDER-FIRE STATION #7 129A
BOULDER RURAL FIRE DEPARTMENT-FIRE STATION #1 98M
BOULDER RURAL FIRE DEPARTMENT-FIRE STATION #2 723G
BRIGHTON-FIRE STATION #51 138S
BRIGHTON-FIRE STATION #52 138R
BRIGHTON-FIRE STATION #53 168Z
BRIGHTON-FIRE STATION #54 750L
BRIGHTON-FIRE STATION #55 750L
CASTLE ROCK-FIRE STATION #151 497L
CASTLE ROCK-FIRE STATION #152 498J
CASTLE ROCK-FIRE STATION #153 498M
CASTLE ROCK-FIRE STATION #154 466V
CASTLE ROCK-FIRE STATION #155 468J
CHERRYVALE FIRE PROTECTION-FIRE STATION #1 130K
CHERRYVALE FIRE PROTECTION-FIRE STATION #2 129T
CHERRYVALE FIRE PROTECTION-FIRE STATION #3 160F
CHERRYVALE FIRE PROTECTION-FIRE STATION #4 742M
CHERRYVALE FIRE PROTECTION-FIRE STATION #5 160U
CUNNINGHAM FIRE PROTECTION-FIRE STATION #1 317N
CUNNINGHAM FIRE PROTECTION-FIRE STATION #2 349J
CUNNINGHAM FIRE PROTECTION-FIRE STATION #3 350P
CUNNINGHAM FIRE PROTECTION-FIRE STATION #4 349T
DENVER FIRE PROTECTION-DIA STATIONS 1-4 770N
DENVER FIRE PROTECTION-FIRE STATION #1 284F
DENVER FIRE PROTECTION-FIRE STATION #2 258H
DENVER FIRE PROTECTION-FIRE STATION #3 284C
DENVER FIRE PROTECTION-FIRE STATION #4 284B
DENVER FIRE PROTECTION-FIRE STATION #6 284E
DENVER FIRE PROTECTION-FIRE STATION #7 253V
DENVER FIRE PROTECTION-FIRE STATION #8 284H
DENVER FIRE PROTECTION-FIRE STATION #9 254R
DENVER FIRE PROTECTION-FIRE STATION #10 255X
DENVER FIRE PROTECTION-FIRE STATION #11 284T
DENVER FIRE PROTECTION-FIRE STATION #12 283C
DENVER FIRE PROTECTION-FIRE STATION #13 346D
DENVER FIRE PROTECTION-FIRE STATION #14 286F
DENVER FIRE PROTECTION-FIRE STATION #15 285L
DENVER FIRE PROTECTION-FIRE STATION #16 314M
DENVER FIRE PROTECTION-FIRE STATION #17 253N
DENVER FIRE PROTECTION-FIRE STATION #19 286W
DENVER FIRE PROTECTION-FIRE STATION #20 283P
DENVER FIRE PROTECTION-FIRE STATION #21 284Z
DENVER FIRE PROTECTION-FIRE STATION #22 316X
DENVER FIRE PROTECTION-FIRE STATION #23 313C
DENVER FIRE PROTECTION-FIRE STATION #24 315U
DENVER FIRE PROTECTION-FIRE STATION #25 313P
DENVER FIRE PROTECTION-FIRE STATION #26 256T
DENVER FIRE PROTECTION-FIRE STATION #27 257R
DENVER FIRE PROTECTION-FIRE STATION #28 343E
DENVER FIRE PROTECTION-FIRE STATION #29 259M
DENVER FIRE PROTECTION-FIRE STATION #30 342J
ELIZABETH-FIRE STATION #11 871F
ELIZABETH-FIRE STATION #12 850Y
ELIZABETH-FIRE STATION #13 850H
ENGLEWOOD-FIRE STATION #21 344B
ENGLEWOOD-FIRE STATION #22 313V
ENGLEWOOD-FIRE STATION #23 344K
FAIRMOUNT FIRE DISTRICT-FIRE STATION #1 250P
FAIRMOUNT FIRE DISTRICT-FIRE STATION #2 249C
FEDERAL HEIGHTS-FIRE STATION #40 223D
GENESEE FIRE & RESCUE-FIRE STATION #1 308E
GOLDEN-FIRE STATION #1 279A
GOLDEN-FIRE STATION #2 279M
GOLDEN-FIRE STATION #3 280N
GOLDEN-FIRE STATION #4 279T
JACKSON 105 FIRE STATION 2 867E
LAFAYETTE-FIRE STATION #1 132E
LITTLETON FIRE RESCUE-FIRE STATION #11 343R
LITTLETON FIRE RESCUE-FIRE STATION #12 374B
LITTLETON FIRE RESCUE-FIRE STATION #13 372D
LITTLETON FIRE RESCUE-FIRE STATION #14 375C
LITTLETON FIRE RESCUE-FIRE STATION #15 375J
LITTLETON FIRE RESCUE-FIRE STATION #16 373T
LITTLETON FIRE RESCUE-FIRE STATION #17 405C
LITTLETON FIRE RESCUE-FIRE STATION #18 404B
LONGMONT-FIRE STATION #1 41L
LONGMONT-FIRE STATION #2 11W
LONGMONT-FIRE STATION #3 12Y
LONGMONT-FIRE STATION #4 11R
LONGMONT-FIRE STATION #5 40L
MOUNTAIN VIEW-FIRE STATION #1 42R
MOUNTAIN VIEW-FIRE STATION #2 707A
MOUNTAIN VIEW-FIRE STATION #4 70L
MOUNTAIN VIEW-FIRE STATION #5 101M
MOUNTAIN VIEW-FIRE STATION #6 103P
MOUNTAIN VIEW-FIRE STATION #7 727J
NORTH METRO FIRE RESCUE DISTRICT-FIRE STATION #61 162T
NORTH METRO FIRE RESCUE DISTRICT-FIRE STATION #62 194K
NORTH METRO FIRE RESCUE DISTRICT-FIRE STATION #63 195J
NORTH METRO FIRE RESCUE DISTRICT-FIRE STATION #64 163K
NORTH METRO FIRE RESCUE DISTRICT-FIRE STATION #65 161Z
NORTH METRO FIRE RESCUE DISTRICT-FIRE STATION #66 133R
NORTH WASHINGTON-FIRE STATION #31 224L
NORTH WASHINGTON-FIRE STATION #32 254C
NORTH WASHINGTON-FIRE STATION #33 224K
PARKER-FIRE STATION #71 409R
PARKER-FIRE STATION #72 379J
PARKER-FIRE STATION #73 440P
PARKER-FIRE STATION #74 407H
PARKER-FIRE STATION #75 409A
PARKER-FIRE STATION #76 439G
RATTLESNAKE FIRE PROTECTION DISTRICT-FIRE STATION #1 831N
RATTLESNAKE FIRE PROTECTION DISTRICT-FIRE STATION #2 832W
RATTLESNAKE FIRE PROTECTION DISTRICT-FIRE STATION #3 850D
RATTLESNAKE FIRE PROTECTION DISTRICT-FIRE STATION #4 832L
SHERIDAN-FIRE STATION #1 313Z
SHERIDAN-FIRE STATION #2 343G
SKYLINE-FIRE STATION #81 316S
SOUTH ADAMS FIRE DISTRICT-FIRE STATION #1 225V
SOUTH ADAMS FIRE DISTRICT-FIRE STATION #2 256E
SOUTH ADAMS FIRE DISTRICT-FIRE STATION #3 226P
SOUTH ADAMS FIRE DISTRICT-FIRE STATION #4 226C
SOUTH ADAMS FIRE DISTRICT-FIRE STATION #5 769E
SOUTH ADAMS FIRE DISTRICT-FIRE STATION #6 768G
SOUTH METRO FIRE DISTRICT-FIRE STATION #31 347T
SOUTH METRO FIRE DISTRICT-FIRE STATION #32 346T
SOUTH METRO FIRE DISTRICT-FIRE STATION #33 376K
SOUTH METRO FIRE DISTRICT-FIRE STATION #34 376Z
SOUTH METRO FIRE DISTRICT-FIRE STATION #35 377C
SOUTH METRO FIRE DISTRICT-FIRE STATION #36 848E
SOUTH METRO FIRE DISTRICT-FIRE STATION #37 345S
SOUTH METRO FIRE DISTRICT-FIRE STATION #38 345E
SOUTH METRO FIRE DISTRICT-FIRE STATION #39 466G
SOUTH METRO FIRE DISTRICT-FIRE STATION #40 404S
THORNTON-FIRE STATION #1 194Z
THORNTON-FIRE STATION #2 194T
THORNTON-FIRE STATION #3 195G
THORNTON-FIRE STATION #4 164V
THORNTON-FIRE STATION #5 165G
WEST METRO FIRE RESCUE-FIRE STATION #1 282L
WEST METRO FIRE RESCUE-FIRE STATION #2 281F
WEST METRO FIRE RESCUE-FIRE STATION #3 281V
WEST METRO FIRE RESCUE-FIRE STATION #4 310H
WEST METRO FIRE RESCUE-FIRE STATION #5 280G
WEST METRO FIRE RESCUE-FIRE STATION #6 280P
WEST METRO FIRE RESCUE-FIRE STATION #7 312C
WEST METRO FIRE RESCUE-FIRE STATION #8 311M
WEST METRO FIRE RESCUE-FIRE STATION #9 310W
WEST METRO FIRE RESCUE-FIRE STATION #10 312W
WEST METRO FIRE RESCUE-FIRE STATION #11 340P
WEST METRO FIRE RESCUE-FIRE STATION #12 341U
WEST METRO FIRE RESCUE-FIRE STATION #13 371J
WEST METRO FIRE RESCUE-FIRE STATION #14 371Q
WEST METRO FIRE RESCUE-FIRE STATION #15 432U
WESTMINSTER-FIRE STATION #1 223P
WESTMINSTER-FIRE STATION #2 223B
WESTMINSTER-FIRE STATION #3 222B
WESTMINSTER-FIRE STATION #4 193E
WESTMINSTER-FIRE STATION #5 191R
WESTMINSTER-FIRE STATION #6 164S
WHEAT RIDGE-FIRE STATION #1 252T
WHEAT RIDGE-FIRE STATION #2 251T

Hospitals

ANSCHUTZ INPATIENT PAVILION 287H
12605 E 16th Ave 720-848-4251
AURORA MEDICAL CENTER NORTH 288N
700 Potomac St 303-363-7200
AURORA MEDICAL CENTER SOUTH 318E
1501 S Potomac St 303-695-2600
AVISTA ADVENTIST 160G
100 Health Park Dr 303-673-1000
BOULDER COMMUNITY 97Y
1100 Balsam Ave 303-440-2273
BOULDER COMMUNITY FOOTHILLS HOSPITAL 128D
4747 Arapahoe Rd 720-854-7600
CENTENNIAL MEDICAL PLAZA 378B
14200 E Arapahoe Rd 303-699-3000
COLORADO MENTAL HEALTH INSTITUTE AT FT LOGAN 343F
3520 W Oxford Ave 303-866-7066
CRAIG HOSPITAL 314Z
3425 S Clarkson St 303-789-8000
DENVER HEALTH MEDICAL CENTER 284P
777 Bannock St 303-436-6000
EXEMPLA GOOD SAMARITAN MEDICAL CENTER 132W
200 Exempla Cir 303-689-4000
EXEMPLA LUTHERAN MEDICAL CENTER 252S
8300 W 38th Ave 303-425-4500
EXEMPLA ST. JOSEPH/CHILDREN'S HOSPITAL 288E
13123 E Colfax Ave 720-777-1234
EXEMPLA ST JOSEPH HOSPITAL 284H
1835 Franklin St 303-837-7111
LITTLETON ADVENTIST HOSPITAL 374L
7700 Broadway S 303-730-8900
LONGMONT UNITED 11X
1950 W Mtn View Ave 303-651-5111
MAPLETON CTR FOR REHAB 97X
311 Mapleton Ave 303-443-0230
NATIONAL JEWISH MEDICAL & RESEARCH CENTER 285G
1400 Jackson St 303-388-4461

Name	Grid / Phone
NORTH SUBURBAN MEDICAL CENTER	194Y
9191 Grant St	303-451-7800
PARKER ADVENTIST HOSPITAL	379Y
9395 Crown Crest Blvd	303-269-4000
PLATTE VALLEY MEDICAL CTR	139X
1600 Prairie Center Pkwy	303-498-1600
PORTER ADVENTIST HOSPITAL	314R
2525 S Downing St	303-778-1955
PRESBYTERIAN/ST LUKES MEDICAL CENTER	285E
1719 E 19th Ave	303-839-6000
ROSE MEDICAL CENTER	285L
4567 E 9th Ave	303-320-2121
ST ANTHONY HOSPITAL CENTRAL	283F
4231 W 16th Ave	303-629-3511
ST ANTHONY HOSPITAL NORTH	223H
2551 W 84th Ave	303-426-2151
SKY RIDGE MEDICAL CENTER	407E
10101 Ridgegate Pkwy	720-225-1000
SWEDISH MEDICAL CENTER	314Y
501 E Hampden Ave	303-788-5000
SWEDISH SOUTHWEST ER	342W
6196 S Ammons Way	303-932-6911
UNIVERSITY HOSPITAL	285L
4200 E 9th Ave	303-372-0000
VA EASTERN COLORADO HEALTH CARE SYSTEM	285L
1055 Clermont St	303-399-8020

Libraries

Name	Grid
AMERICAN ALPINE CLUB	249W
ARVADA	252B
ATHMAR PARK	313D
AURORA CENTRAL	288X
BEAR VALLEY	313W
BELMAR	282X
BEMIS	344S
BENNETT	793J
BLAIR-CALDWELL AARL	284C
BOULDER MAIN	127C
BRIGHTON	138T
BYERS BRANCH	284P
CARBON VALLEY	727F
CARNEGIE (HISTORICAL)	97Y
CASTLEWOOD	376C
CHAMBERS PLAZA	288G
COLLEGE HILL	193E
COLUMBINE	342X
COMMERCE CITY	226N
DACONO PUBLIC	727K
DECKER	314G
DENVER CENTRAL LIBRARY	284K
EDGEWATER	282D
ELIZABETH PUBLIC	871F
ENGLEWOOD PUBLIC	314X
ERIE COMMUNITY	103N
EUGENE FIELD	315A
EVERGREEN	336R
FORD WARREN	255W
FORT LUPTON PUBLIC	728L
GEORGE REYNOLDS BRANCH	128P
GILPIN COUNTY	761K
GLENDALE	315C
GOLDEN	279A
HADLEY BRANCH	313L
HAMPDEN	317W
HIGHLANDS RANCH	404B
HOFFMAN HEIGHTS	287M
HORIZON PUBLIC	349C
HUDSON	730L
HURON STREET BRANCH	194X
IDAHO SPRINGS PUBLIC	780Q
ILIFF SQUARE	317Q
IRVING STREET	223Q
KIOWA PUBLIC	872M
KOELBEL	345V
LAFAYETTE PUBLIC	131H
LAKEWOOD	281G
LIBRARY SERVICE CENTER	251U
LONE TREE	376Z
LONGMONT PUBLIC	41H
LORRAINE DAVID CHILDREN'S	103J
LOUISVILLE PUBLIC	131S
LYONS DEPOT	703B
MAMIE DOUD EISENHOWER PUBLIC	162Y
MARTIN LUTHER KING, JR	287E
MEADOWS BRANCH	128M
MISSION VIEJO	348C
MONTBELLO BRANCH	257R
MONTCLAIR	286J
MONUMENT HILL LIBRARY	908T
NEDERLAND COMMUNITY	740Q
NORTHGLENN	194K
PARKER	409Q
PARKER & FLORIDA	316G
PARK HILL	285D
PAULINE ROBINSON	256W
PERL-MACK	224N
PHILIP S MILLER	497L
PLATTEVILLE PUBLIC	708C
ROSS-BARNUM	283T
ROSS-BROADWAY	284U
ROSS-CHERRY CREEK	285P
ROSS-UNIVERSITY HILLS	315U
ROXBOROUGH LIBRARY	432G
SCHLESSMAN FAMILY	286T
SHERIDAN	343G
SMILEY	253N
SMOKY HILL	349Q
SOUTHGLENN	375J
STANDLEY LAKE	221G
TALLYN'S REACH	380H
THORNTON	224C
VALDEZ-PERRY	255N
VILLA	282X
VIRGINIA VILLAGE	315H
WESTWOOD	313B
WHEAT RIDGE LIBRARY	252Z
WOODBURY	253Y
WRIGHT FARMS BRANCH	166W

Museums

Name	Grid
ADAMS COUNTY HISTORY MUSEUM	167S
ARGO GOLD MILL & MUSEUM	780R
ASTOR HOUSE MUSEUM	279A
AURORA HISTORY MUSEUM	288U
AVIATION AND SPACE CENTER OF THE ROCKIES	286Q
BELMAR PIONEER MUSEUM	312A
BLACK AMERICAN WEST MUSEUM	254Z
BOULDER MUSEUM OF CONTEMPORARY ART	127D
BOULDER MUSEUM OF HISTORY	127H
BUFFALO BILL'S GRAVE & MUSEUM	278M
CHILDREN'S MUSEUM	283H
COLLAGE CHILDREN'S MUSEUM	98X
COLORADO HISTORY MUSEUM	284L
COLORADO RAILROAD MUSEUM	249V
DENVER ART MUSEUM	284K
DENVER FIREFIGHTERS MUSEUM	284F
DENVER MUSEUM OF NATURE & SCIENCE	285B
DENVER MUSEUM OF MINIATURES	285E
DINOSAUR RIDGE	309H
FORNEY TRANSPORTATION MUSEUM	254R
HERITAGE MUSEUM	780R
LAKEWOOD'S HERITAGE CENTER	312B
LEANIN' TREE MUSEUM OF WESTERN ART	99B
LONGMONT MUSEUM	41R
LOUISVILLE HISTORICAL MUSEUM	131S
MINERS MUSEUM	132J
MORRISON NATURAL HISTORY MUSEUM	339D
MUSEO DE LAS AMERICAS	284P
MUSEUM OF COMPUTER TECHNOLOGY	314L
MUSEUM OF OUTDOOR SCULPTURES	346U
PIONEER MUSEUM	279A
SOD HOUSE AND MUSEUM	251P
UNDERHILL MUSEUM	780Q
UNIVERSITY OF COLORADO MUSEUM	127H
VANCE KIRKLAND MUSEUM	284L
WILDLIFE EXPERIENCE MUSEUM	407H

Neighborhood Names

Name	Grid
6TH AVE WEST	280U
A & R ESTATES	891F
ACADEMY EAST	891X
ACRES GREEN	376U
ADAMS CITY	225Q
ADONEA	291T
ALGONQUIN ACRES	378A
ALKIRE ESTATES	220M
ALLENDALE	251A
ALPENGLOW ACRES	704X
ALPINE HILLS	365P
ALTA VISTA	252A
ALTON PARK	316D
ALTURA	288G
AMANDA PINES ESTATES	830Q
AMANDA PINES NORTH ESTATES	830L
AMANDA PINES RANCHES	830R
AMBER CREEK	166K
ANGEL VIEW ESTATES	727G
ANHAWA MANOR	11J
ANTELOPE	379H
ANTELOPE HEIGHTS	408Z
ANTELOPE HILLS	793X
ANTHEM	133K
APACHE MESA	288M
APOLLO ESTATES	130S
APPEL FARM ESTATES	728M
APPLE MEADOWS	249B
APPLEWOOD	250Y
APPLEWOOD GLEN	281E
APPLEWOOD GROVE	280H
APPLEWOOD KNOLLS	251X
APPLEWOOD VIEW	281A
APPLEWOOD VILLAGE	251S
ARAPAHOE ESTATES	375B
ARAPAHOE HEIGHTS	380F
ARAPAHOE LAKE	347W
ARAPAHOE MEADOWS	101X
ARAPAHOE PARK	335X
ARAPAHOE RIDGE	102W
ARAPAHOE RIDGE WEST	102W
ARCADIA	841P
ARLINGTON RANCHES	439W
ARROWHEAD	871R
ARROWWOOD III	908Z
ARVADA PARK	222X
ARVADA WEST	221U
ASBURY	10M
ASH HOLLOW	732A
ASPEN CREEK	162M
ASPEN GROVE	373G
ASPEN MEADOWS	367Y
ASPEN SPRINGS	760V
ASSEMBLY ESTATES	908G
ATHMAR PARK	313H
AURARIA	284E
AURORA EAST	289H
AURORA HEIGHTS	287K
AURORA HIGHLANDS	319E
AURORA HILLS	287Y
AURORA KNOLLS	319K
AUTUMN RIDGE	70L
AVONDALE	283K
BACKLUND RANCHES	872K
BAILEY ESTATES	841S
BAILEY MOUNTAIN	841X
BAKER	284T
BALBOA PARK	225E
BALD MOUNTAIN ESTATES	908K
BANNOCKBURN	470Z
BARI-DON KNOLLS	129U
BARNUM	283T
BARNUM WEST	283S
BARR LAKE	169J
BASELINE HEIGHTS	129G
BASELINE LAKES	137K
BAXTER FARMS	102N
BAYOU HILLS	470H
BEACON HEIGHTS	908N
BEACON POINT	351Y
BEAR CANYON RANCH	496N
BEAR CREEK	313X
BEAR MOUNTAIN VISTA	337R
BEAR VALLEY	312U
BEAR VALLEY HEIGHTS	342D
BEERS SISTERS FARM DAIRY	342K
BELCARO	315B
BELL CROSS RANCH	410H
BELLE CREEK	196M
BELLEVIEW ACRES	340R
BELLEVIEW STATION	346K
BELL MOUNTAIN RANCH	527S
BELMAR	282X
BELMAR GARDENS	312A
BEL-VUE HEIGHTS	374F
BEL-VUE HEIGHTS WEST	374J
BENDEMEER	801V
BENTHAVEN	281B
BENT TREE I	908Z
BENT TREE II	909W
BERGEN FAMILY FARM	704S
BERKELEY	253N
BERKELEY GARDENS	253F
BEVERLY HEIGHTS	281H
BEVERLY HILLS	848E
BIJOU KNOLLS	795Y
BLACK FOREST ESTATES	411B
BLACK MOUNTAIN RANCH ESTATES	365Z
BLACK SQUIRREL PARK	911S
BLACKSTONE RANCH	794P
BLUEBIRD ESTATES	870R
BLUE LAKE	729Y
BLUE MOUNTAIN ESTATES	763P
BLUE VALLEY	801A
BLUFFS, THE	368H
BLUFFS, THE	870B
BONNIE BRAE	315B
BONNIE RIDGE	871C
BONVUE	281V
BOOTH FARMS	707S
BOSTON HEIGHTS	287G
BOULDER HEIGHTS	722G
BOULDER HILLS	704W
BOULDER TECH CENTER	70N
BOW MAR SOUTH	343S
BOW MEADOWS	871H
BOX ELDER CREEK RANCH	750H
BOX ELDER NORTH	750M
BRADBURN	193B
BRADBURY RANCH	408R
BRADSHAW RANCH	40W
BRAECHER RANCHETTES	761U
BRANDYWINE	163T
BRANTNER VILLAGE	166U
BRIAR RIDGE	195C
BRICKEY HIGHLANDS	741Y
BRIDLE DALE	221G
BRIGADOON GLEN	69F
BRIGHTON CROSSING	139M
BRIGHTON CROSSING	140J
BRIGHTON EAST FARMS	139L
BRIGHTON EAST FARMS	140K
BRIGHTON FARMS	168X
BRITANIE RIDGE ESTATES	851V
BRITTANY RIDGE	224L
BROADLANDS, THE	163E
BROADMOOR	344U
BROADWAY ESTATE	374C
BROADWAY HEIGHTS	344B
BROMLEY LAKES	137Z
BROMLEY PARK	140N
BROMLEY PARK	139V
BROOK FOREST ESTATES	821H
BROOKRIDGE	344Q
BROOKRIDGE	762B
BROOKSIDE	224B
BROOKVALE	801V
BROOKVALE	318H
BROOKWOOD	467R
BROOMFIELD HEIGHTS	162K
BROTHERS FOUR	793J
BROWNSVILLE	102J
BUCKLEY RANCH	198R
BUELL MANSION	345B
BUENA VISTA	97H
BUFFALO MESA	198L
BUFFALO RUN	198B
BURGANDY PARK	70F
BURLAND RANCH ACRES	762G
BURLAND RANCHETTES	841U
BURNING TREE RANCH	470T
BUTTERFIELD	440E
BYERS	284U
CALAHAN	312K
CAMBRIDGE PARK	251U

Parks

Points of Interest

Police Departments

DOUGLAS COUNTY SHERIFF 467T
4000 Justice Way, Castle Rock
EDGEWATER 282D
5901 W 25th Ave
ELBERT COUNTY SHERIFF 872M
751 Ute Ave, Kiowa
ELIZABETH 871F
425 S Main St
ENGLEWOOD 344B
3615 S Elati St
ERIE 103J
645 Holbrook St
FEDERAL HEIGHTS 223D
2380 W 90th Ave
FIRESTONE 727B
151 Grant Ave
FORT LUPTON 728L
130 S McKinley Ave
FREDERICK 727F
333 5th St
GILPIN COUNTY SHERIFF 761S
2960 Dory Hill Rd, Blackhawk
GLENDALE 315C
950 S Birch St
GOLDEN 279A
911 10th St
GREENWOOD VILLAGE 346X
6060 S Quebec St
IDAHO SPRINGS 780Q
1711 Miner St
JEFFERSON COUNTY SHERIFF 279L
200 Jefferson County Pkwy, Golden
JEFFERSON COUNTY SHERIFF-MOUNTAIN PRECINCT 336R
4990 Highway 73
JEFFERSON COUNTY SHERIFF-SOUTH PRECINCT 371P
8100 Shaffer Pkwy
KIOWA 872M
404 Comanche St
LAFAYETTE 132E
451 N 111th St
LAKESIDE 252R
5801 W 44th Ave
LAKEWOOD 282X
445 S Allison Pkwy
LITTLETON 343R
2255 W Berry Ave
LOCHBUIE 140G
152 Poplar St
LONE TREE 377W
9220 Kimmer Dr
LONGMONT 41H
225 Kimbark St
LOUISVILLE 130X
992 W Via Appia Way
LYONS 703B
432 5th Ave
MONUMENT 908W
154 N Washington St
MORRISON 309Z
321 State Hwy 8
MOUNTAIN VIEW 252R
4176 Benton St
NEDERLAND 740R
60 Lakeview Dr
NORTHGLENN 194B
11701 Community Center Dr
PARKER 409V
19600 E Parker Square Dr
PLATTEVILLE 708C
400 Grand Ave
SHERIDAN 343G
4101 S Federal Blvd
THORNTON 194U
9551 Civic Center Dr
WESTMINSTER 193W
9110 Yates St
WHEAT RIDGE 282B
7500 W 29th Ave

Private Schools

ABILITY PLUS ACADEMY OF COLORADO 312X
3286 S Wadsworth Blvd, Lakewood 303-781-8071
ACCELERATED SCHOOLS #1 (K-12) 315P
2160 S Cook St, Denver 303-758-2003
ACCELERATED SCHOOLS #3 (K-12) 376D
6830 S Yosemite St, Centennial 303-771-7772
ALEXANDER DAWSON SCHOOL (K-12) 101C
10455 Dawson Dr, Lafayette 303-665-6679
ALL SOULS PARISH SCHOOL (Pre K-8)) 344L
4951 S Pennsylvania St, Englewood 303-789-2155
ALPINE VALLEY SCHOOL (K-12) 251P
4501 Parfet St, Wheat Ridge 303-271-0525
ANNUNCIATION SCHOOL (K-8) 254V
3536 Lafayette St, Denver 303-295-2515
ARRUPE JESUIT HIGH SCHOOL (9-12) 253N
4343 Utica St, Denver 303-477-4023
ARVADA SDA CHRISTIAN SCHOOL (K-12) 222X
7050 W 64th Ave, Arvada 303-422-4114
ASPEN CHRISTIAN SCHOOL (K-8) 11V
316 15th Ave, Longmont 303-776-5866
ASSUMPTION SCHOOL (Pre K-8) 225J
2341 E 78th Ave, Adams Co 303-288-2159
AURORA CHRISTIAN ACADEMY (K-12) 287T
11001 E Alameda Ave, Aurora 303-344-2530
AVE MARIA CATHOLIC SCHOOL (PRE K-8) 410M
9056 E Parker Rd, Parker 720-842-5400
BEACON COUNTRY DAY SCHOOL (Pre K-8) 346N
6100 E Belleview Ave, Greenwood Village 303-771-3990
BEAUTIFUL SAVIOR LUTHERAN SCHOOL (Pre K-8) 162Y
6995 W 120th Ave, Broomfield 303-469-2049
BELLEVIEW CHRISTIAN SCHOOL (K-12) 223F
3455 W 83rd Ave, Westminster 303-427-5459
BETH EDEN BAPTIST SCHOOL (Pre K-12) 282B
2600 Wadsworth Blvd, Wheat Ridge 303-232-2313
BETH JACOB HIGH SCHOOL (9-12) 283J
5100 W 14th Ave, Denver 303-893-1333
BETHLEHEM LUTHERAN SCHOOL (Pre K-8) 282B
2100 Wadsworth Blvd, Lakewood 303-233-0401
BISHOP MACHEBEUF HIGH SCHOOL (9-12) 286Q
458 Uinta Way, Denver 303-344-0082
BIXBY SCHOOL (K-5) 128R
4760 Table Mesa Dr, Boulder 303-494-7508
BLESSED SACRAMENT SCHOOL (Pre K-8) 285G
1973 Elm St, Denver 303-377-8835
BOULDER COUNTRY DAY SCHOOL (K-8) 99C
4820 Nautilus Ct N, Boulder 303-527-4931
BOULDER JEWISH DAY SCHOOL (PRE K-5) 70W
7415 Lookout Rd 303-449-5569
BRIDGE SCHOOL (6-12) 129Q
6717 S Boulder Rd, Boulder 303-494-7551
BRIGHTON ADVENTIST ACADEMY (PRE K-12) 138T
820 S 5th Ave, Brighton 303-659-1223
CASTLEWOOD CHRISTIAN SCHOOL (PRE K-9) 470S
7086 E Park Dr 303-688-5353
CEDARWOOD CHRISTIAN ACADEMY (K-12) 287G
11430 E 19th Ave, Aurora 303-361-6456
C.H.A.N.G.E. CHRISTIAN ACADEMY (K-12) 257H
12505 Elmendorf Pl, Denver 303-373-5200
CHARIOT CHRISTIAN SCHOOL (K-12) 162R
1080 Birch St, Broomfield 303-439-9522
CHERRY HILLS CHRISTIAN SCHOOL (PRE K-8) 405G
3900 E Grace Blvd, Highlands Ranch 303-791-5500
CHRISTIAN FELLOWSHIP SCHOOL (PRE K-12) 312P
7700 W Woodward Dr 303-980-6622
CHRIST OUR REDEEMER LUTHERAN (K-8) 319P
17700 E Iliff Ave, Aurora 303-337-3108
CHRIST THE KING CATHOLIC SCHOOL (Pre K-8) 285M
860 Elm St, Denver 303-321-2123
CLEARVIEW EDUCATION CENTER (6-12) 42A
24 9th Ave, Longmont 303-776-8184
CLONLARA SCHOOL (K-12) 821Y
112 Road D, Pine 303-816-9335
COLORADO ACADEMY (Pre K-12) 342C
3800 S Pierce St, Denver 303-986-1501
COLORADO CATHOLIC ACADEMY (1-12) 251P
11180 W 44th Ave
COLORADO CHRISTIAN SCHOOL (K-12) 285W
200 S University Blvd, Denver 303-777-7723
COLORADO STATE ACADEMY (3-12) 252G
5255 Marshall St, Arvada 303-996-9606
COMMUNITY CHRISTIAN SCHOOL (K-12) 164Z
11980 Irma Dr, Northglenn 303-452-7514
COMMUNITY SCHOOL FOR THE GIFTED (Pre K-8) 343P
5470 S Lowell Blvd, Littleton 303-730-7288
CORNERSTONE CHRISTIAN ACADEMY (K-12) 223D
2300 W 90th Ave 303-451-1421
CRESCENT VIEW ACADEMY (K-8) 317T
10958 E Bethany Dr, Aurora 303-745-2245
DENVER ACADEMY (K-12) 315Q
4400 E Iliff Ave, Denver 303-777-5870
DENVER ACADEMY OF TORAH 286T
6825 E Alameda Ave, Denver 720-859-6806
DENVER CAMPUS FOR JEWISH EDUCATION (K-12) 316R
2450 S Wabash St, Arapahoe Co 303-369-0663
DENVER CHRISTIAN HIGH SCHOOL (9-12) 314Q
2135 S Pearl St, Denver 303-733-2421
DENVER INTERNATIONAL SCHOOL (PRE K -5) 285H
1958 Elm St 303-756-0381
DENVER LUTHERAN HIGH SCHOOL (9-12) 313C
3201 W Arizona Ave, Denver 303-934-2345
DENVER STREET SCHOOL (7-12) 287F
1585 Kingston St 303-860-1702
DENVER STREET SCHOOL WEST CAMPUS (9-12) 282K
1380 Ammons St
DENVER WALDORF SCHOOL (PRE K-12) 285K
940 Fillmore St 303-777-0531
DOVE CHRISTIAN ACADEMY (1-12) 315U
2750 S Clermont Dr 303-627-0299
ELMWOOD BAPTIST ACADEMY 167D
13100 E 144th Ave, Adams Co 303-659-3818
EMMAUS LUTHERAN SCHOOL (PRE K-8) 253Y
3120 Irving St, Denver 303-433-3303
ESCUELA DE GUADALUPE (K-5) 254S
3401 Pecos St, Commerce City 303-964-8456
EVERGREEN ACADEMY (K-8) 366D
27826 Alabraska Ln
EVERGREEN MOUNTAIN SCHOOL 306E
1240 Bergen Pkwy, Evergreen 303-674-3400
FAITH BAPTIST SCHOOL (Pre K-12) 11U
833 15th Ave, Longmont 303-776-5677
FAITH CHRISTIAN ACADEMY ELEMENTARY 251A
6210 Ward Rd, Arvada 303-424-7310
FAITH CHRISTIAN ACADEMY HIGH 252J
4890 Carr St, Arvada 303-424-7310
FAITH CHRISTIAN ACADEMY MIDDLE 251A
6250 Wright St, El Paso Co 303-424-7310
FOOTHILLS ACADEMY (K-12) 251Q
4725 Miller St, Wheat Ridge 303-431-0920
FRIENDS' SCHOOL (PRE K-5) 128H
5465 Pennsylvania Ave, Boulder 303-499-1999
FRONT RANGE ACADEMY 162S
1008 Depot Hill Rd, Broomfield 303-469-0496
FRONT RANGE CHRISTIAN SCHOOL (9-12) 372C
6637 W Ottawa, Littleton 720-922-3269
FRONT RANGE CHRISTIAN SCHOOL (K-8) 342F
4001 S Wadsworth Blvd, Lakewood 303-929-9025
GETHSEMANE LUTHERAN SCHOOL (Pre K-8) 194L
10675 N Washington St, Northglenn 303-451-6908
GOOD SHEPHERD CATHOLIC SCHOOL (PRE K-8) 285P
620 Elizabeth St, Denver 303-321-6231
GRALAND COUNTRY DAY SCHOOL (K-9) 285U
30 Birch St, Denver 303-399-0390
GREEN MOUNTAIN CHRISTIAN ACADEMY (K-10) 311B
822 S Simms St, Lakewood 303-986-1987
GUARDIAN ANGELS SCHOOL (Pre K-8) 254J
1843 W 52nd Ave, Denver 303-480-9005
HAVERN CENTER (1-7) 342F
4000 S Wadsworth Blvd, Littleton 303-986-4587
HIGHLANDS RANCH CHRISTIAN SCHOOL (K-8) 375S
1733 E Dad Clark Dr, Highlands Ranch 303-791-3243
HILLEL ACADEMY (Pre K-8) 285Z
450 S Hudson St, Denver 303-333-1511
HOLY FAMILY HIGH SCHOOL (9-12) 163A
5195 W 144th Ave, Broomfield 303-410-1411
HOLY TRINITY CATHOLIC SCHOOL (Pre K-8) 223Q
3050 W 76th Ave, Westminster 303-427-5632
HOPEWELL BAPTIST ACADEMY (Pre K-10) 11Z
1146 Kimbark St, Longmont 303-651-1325
HUMANEX ACADEMY (7-12) 313V
2700 S Zuni St, Englewood 303-783-0137
HYLAND CHRISTIAN SCHOOL (K-12) 192V
5255 W 98th Ave, Westminster 303-466-1673
INNERCITY CHRISTIAN SCHOOL (Pre K-5) 254Y
2609 Lawrence St, Denver 303-296-4801
INSTITUTE OF GLOBAL SCHOLARSHIP (K-5) 284C
710 E 25th Ave, Denver 303-832-6393
JARROW MONTESSORI SCHOOL (Pre K-6) 97L
3900 Orange Ct, Boulder 303-443-0511
JIM ELLIOT SCHOOLS (7-12) 375N
2860 E County Line Rd, Highlands Ranch 303-922-0011
KENT DENVER SCHOOL (6-12) 345L
4000 E Quincy Ave, Englewood 303-770-7660
KINDERCARE (PRE K-3) 130P
107 McCaslin Blvd, Louisville 303-666-9999
LA ACADEMIA (6-12) 284K
910 Galapago St, Denver 303-629-0636
LAKEWOOD CHRISTIAN ACADEMY (K-4) 282E
1755 Dover St, Lakewood 303-274-0865
LOGAN SCHOOL FOR CREATIVE LEARNING (K-8) 286M
1005 Yosemite St, Denver 303-340-2444
LONGMONT ACADEMY (K-9) 11Z
911 Kimbark St, Longmont 303-772-1981
LONGMONT CHRISTIAN SCHOOL (Pre K-12) 41D
550 Coffman St, Longmont 303-776-3254
LOVE CHRISTIAN FELLOWSHIP EDUC CENTER (PRE K-12) 257M
4651 Tulsa Ct, Denver 303-576-8408
LOYOLA CATHOLIC SCHOOL (K-6) 285A
2350 Gaylord St, Denver 303-355-9900
LUTHERAN HIGH SCHOOL OF THE ROCKIES (9-12) 408Q
11249 Newlin Gulch Blvd 303-841-5551
MACKINTOSH ACADEMY (K-8) 373H
7018 S Prince St, Littleton 303-794-6222
MARANATHA CHRISTIAN SCHOOL (K-12) 221Q
7180 Oak St, Arvada 303-431-5653
MEADOWOOD CHRISTIAN SCHOOL (Pre K-8) 318V
16051 E Dartmouth Ave, Aurora 303-690-2309
MERITOR ACADEMY (Pre K-6) 162X
7203 W 120th Ave, Broomfield 303-469-6449
MERITOR ACADEMY (K-3) 221D
8851 Field St, Westminster 303-431-1012
MERITOR ACADEMY AT GRANT RANCH (Pre K-3) 342V
6000 W Grant Ranch Blvd, Denver 303-730-2568
MESSIAH BAPTIST SCHOOL (K-12) 253Q
3241 W 44th Ave, Denver 303-455-6120
MESSIAH LUTHERAN SCHOOL (PRE K-4) 41Q
1335 Francis St, Longmont 303-776-3466
MILE HIGH ADVENTIST ACADEMY (K-12) 314U
711 E Yale Ave 303-744-1069
MILE HIGH BAPTIST SCHOOL (K-12) 342B
8100 W Hampden Ave, Jefferson Co 303-986-2183
MONTCLAIR ACADEMY (PRE K-8) 286Q
206 Red Cross Way 303-366-7588
MONTESSORI ACADEMY OF BEAR CREEK (Pre K-4) 311Z
9300 W Dartmouth Pl, Lakewood 303-980-1040
MONTESSORI SCHOOL OF DENVER (K-6) 316E
1460 S Holly St, Denver 303-756-9441
MONTESSORI SCHOOL OF EVERGREEN (Pre K-8) 367J
6979 County Rd 73, Evergreen 303-674-0093
MONTESSORI SCHOOL OF LAKEWOOD (Pre K-6) 282V
5925 W 1st Ave, Lakewood 303-232-7030
MOST PRECIOUS BLOOD PARISH SCHOOL (PRE K-8) 315Q
3959 E Iliff Ave, Denver 303-757-1279
MOUNTAIN PEAK PRIVATE SCHOOL (PRE K-6) 41P
1833 Sunset Pl, Longmont 720-494-1622
MOUNTAIN SHADOWS MONTESSORI (PRE K-6) 99K
4154 N 63rd St, Boulder Co 303-530-5353
MOUNT ZION LUTHERAN SCHOOL (Pre K-8) 97Z
1680 Balsam Ave, Boulder 303-443-8477
MULLEN HIGH SCHOOL (9-12) 343B
3601 S Lowell Blvd, Denver 303-761-1764
NATIVITY OF OUR LORD CATHOLIC SCHOOL (K-8) 162T
900 W Midway Blvd, Broomfield
NORTH LUTHERAN HIGH SCHOOL (9-12) 194D
11700 Irma Dr, Northglenn 720-887-9031
NOTRE DAME CATHOLIC SCHOOL (Pre K-8) 313N
2165 S Zenobia St, Denver 303-935-3549
OUR LADY OF FATIMA (Pre K-8) 281G
10530 W 20th Ave, Lakewood 303-233-2500
OUR LADY OF LOURDES (K-8) 314Q
2256 S Logan St, Denver 303-722-7525
OUR LADY OF THE ROSARY ACADEMY (K-12) 252V
4165 Eaton St, Mountain View 303-424-1531
OUR SAVIOR'S LUTHERAN SCHOOL (PRE K-8) 11U
1219 17th Ave, Longmont 303-776-1688
PARKER MONTESSORI SCHOOL (PRE K-3) 409R
10750 E Victorian Dr 303-841-4325
PEACE WITH CHRIST CHRISTIAN SCHOOL (K-8) 319Y
3290 S Tower Rd, Aurora 303-766-7116
PLEASANT HILL ACADEMY (Pre K-12) 11R
421 21st Ave, Longmont 303-682-5309
PRESENTATION OF OUR LADY SCHOOL (Pre K-8) 283Q
660 Julian St, Denver 303-629-6562
REDEEMER LUTHERAN SCHOOL (K-8) 283Y
3400 W Nevada Pl, Denver 303-934-0422
REGIS JESUIT HIGH SCHOOL (9-12) 348Z
6400 S Lewiston Way, Aurora 303-269-8000

RICKS CENTER FOR GIFTED CHILDREN (Pre K-8) **315J**
2040 S York St, Denver 303-871-2982
RIVERVIEW CHRISTIAN ACADEMY (K-12) **346U**
8081 E Orchard Rd, Greenwood Village 303-771-4042
ROCK SOLID HIGH SCHOOL (9-12) **374C**
6570B Broadway S, Littleton 303-797-1005
ROCKY MOUNTAIN CHRISTIAN ACADEMY (3-12) **288L**
1294 Fraser St, Aurora 303-366-1161
ROCKY MOUNTAIN CHRISTIAN ACADEMY (Pre K-8) **71J**
9447 Niwot Rd 303-652-9162
ROCKY MOUNTAIN SCHOOL FOR THE GIFTED & CREATIVE **69Y**
5490 Spine Rd 303-545-9230
RUNNING RIVER SCHOOL (K-8) **131B**
1370 Forest Park Cir 303-499-2059
SACRED HEART OF JESUS SCHOOL (Pre K-8) **97Z**
1317 Mapleton Ave, Boulder 303-447-2362
ST ANDREW LUTHERAN SCHOOL (Pre K-3) **257M**
12150 E Andrews Dr, Denver 303-371-7014
ST ANNE'S EPISCOPAL SCHOOL (Pre K-8) **315S**
2701 S York St, Denver 303-756-9481
ST BERNADETTE SCHOOL (K-8) **282K**
1100 Upham St, Lakewood 303-237-0401
ST CATHERINE OF SIENA SCHOOL (K-8) **253Q**
4200 Federal Blvd, Denver 303-477-8035
ST FRANCIS DE SALES (Pre K-8) **284Y**
235 S Sherman St, Denver 303-744-7231
ST JAMES CATHOLIC SCHOOL (Pre K-8) **286K**
1250 Newport St, Denver 303-333-8275
ST JOHN'S LUTHERAN SCHOOL (Pre K-8) **314D**
700 S Franklin St, Denver 303-733-3777
ST JOHN THE BAPTIST CATHOLIC SCHOOL (Pre K-8) **41H**
350 Emery St, Longmont 303-776-8760
ST LOUIS CATHOLIC SCHOOL (Pre K-8) **131S**
925 Grant Ave, Louisville 303-666-6220
ST LOUIS CATHOLIC SCHOOL (K-8) **314Y**
3301 S Sherman St 303-762-8307
ST MARY'S ACADEMY (K-12) **345J**
4545 S University Blvd, Englewood 303-762-8300
ST MARY'S OF LITTLETON (K-8) **343V**
5592 S Nevada St 303-794-4757
ST PIUS X SCHOOL **288J**
13680 E 14th Pl, Aurora 303-364-6515
ST ROSE OF LIMA (K-8) **284W**
1345 W Dakota Ave, Denver 303-733-5806
STS PETER & PAUL CATHOLIC SCHOOL (Pre K-8) **252U**
3920 Pierce St, Wheat Ridge 303-424-0402
ST THERESE SCHOOL (K-8) **287K**
1200 Kenton St, Aurora 303-364-7494
ST THOMAS MORE SCHOOL (K-8) **376P**
7071 E Otero Ave 303-770-0441
ST VINCENT DE PAUL SCHOOL (Pre K-8) **315E**
1164 S Josephine St, Denver 303-777-3812
SEVEN OAKS ACADEMY (PRE K-5) **41J**
1011 Dry Creek Dr, Longmont 303-682-0102
SHEPHERD OF THE HILLS CHRISTIAN SCHOOL (PRE K-8) **375J**
7691 S University Blvd 303-798-0711
SHEPHERD OF THE VALLEY LUTHERAN SCHOOL (Pre K-8) **221D**
8820 Field St, Westminster 303-424-1306
SHEPHERD VALLEY WALDORF SCHOOL (PRE K-8) **70N**
6500 W Dry Creek Pkwy, Niwot 303-652-0130
SHINING MOUNTAIN WALDORF SCHOOL (K-12) **97G**
999 Violet Ave 303-444-7697
SHRINE OF ST ANNE CATHOLIC SCHOOL (K-8) **252F**
7320 Grant Pl, Arvada 303-422-1800
SILVER STATE CHRISTIAN SCHOOL (K-12) **281Y**
480 S Kipling St, Lakewood 303-922-8850
SOLID ROCK SCHOOL **41D**
605 Emery St, Longmont 303-772-6820
SOUTHEAST CHRISTIAN SCHOOL (PRE K-8) **409A**
9650 S Jordan Rd, Parker 303-841-5988
STANLEY BRITISH PRIMARY (K-8) **286P**
350 Quebec St, Denver 303-360-0803
TARA PERFORMING ARTS HIGH SCHOOL (9-12) **97M**
4180 19th St 303-440-4510
TETRA ACADEMY (3-7) **251C**
10050 Ralston Rd, Arvada 303-424-8072
TRADITIONAL SCHOOL OF BASICS (Pre K-12) **288P**
485 Sable Blvd, Aurora 303-363-8117
TRI-LAKES MONTESSORI **908Y**
18075 Minglewood Trail, El Paso Co 719-488-8723
TRINITY LUTHERAN SCHOOL (Pre K-8) **469H**
4740 N State Hwy 83, Franktown 303-841-4660
UNION BAPTIST EXCEL INSTITUTE (Pre K-8) **255Z**
3200 Dahlia St, Denver 303-355-0667
UNIVERSITY HILLS LUTHERAN SCHOOL (Pre K-8) **315Z**
4949 E Eastman Ave, Denver 303-759-5363
UNIVERSITY OF DENVER HIGH SCHOOL **315N**
2306 E Evans Ave 303-871-2636
VALOR CHRISTIAN HIGH SCHOOL (9-12) **405C**
9473-A S University Blvd ....
VANDELLEN CHRISTIAN SCHOOL (K-8) **315Q**
4200 E Warren Ave, Denver 303-757-8501
VISTA RIDGE ACADEMY (K-10) **133H**
3100 Ridgeview Dr, Erie 303-828-4944
WOOD ADVENTIST CHRISTIAN SCHOOL (PRE K-6) **317G**
1159 S Moline St ....
YESHIVA TORAS CHAIM (9-12) **283F**
1555 Stuart St 303-629-8200
ZION LUTHERAN SCHOOL (K-8) **312T**
2600 S Wadsworth Blvd, Denver 303-985-2334
ZION LUTHERAN SCHOOL (Pre K-8) **138Q**
1400 Skeel St, Brighton 303-659-3443

Public Schools

ADAMS COUNTY - BENNETT DISTRICT 29

BENNETT ELEMENTARY **793K**
462 8th St, Bennett 303-644-3234
BENNETT HIGH **793J**
610 7th St, Bennett 303-644-3234
BENNETT MIDDLE **793J**
455 8th St, Bennett 303-644-3234
CORRIDOR COMMUNITY ACADEMY **793J**
420 7th St, Bennett 303-644-5180

ADAMS COUNTY - BRIGHTON DISTRICT 27J

BRIGHTON CHARTER HIGH **138R**
1931 E Bridge St, Brighton 303-655-0773
BRIGHTON CHARTER MIDDLE **138R**
1931 E Bridge St, Brighton 303-655-0773
BRIGHTON HERITAGE ACADEMY HIGH **138P**
830 E Bridge St, Brighton 303-655-2850
BRIGHTON HERITAGE ACADEMY MIDDLE **138P**
830 E Bridge St, Brighton 303-655-2850
BRIGHTON HIGH **138U**
360 S 8th Ave, Brighton 303-655-4200
BROMLEY EAST CHARTER ELEMENTARY **140N**
356 Longspur Dr, Brighton 720-685-3297
BROMLEY EAST CHARTER MIDDLE **140N**
356 Longspur Dr, Brighton 720-685-3297
NORTHEAST ELEMENTARY **138L**
1605 Longs Peak St, Brighton 303-655-2550
NORTH ELEMENTARY **138P**
89 N 6th St, Brighton 303-655-2500
OVERLAND TRAIL MIDDLE **138L**
455 N 19th Ave, Brighton 303-655-4000
PENNOCK, MARY E ELEMENTARY **139P**
3707 Estrella St, Brighton 720-685-7500
PENNOCK, MARY E MIDDLE **139P**
3707 Estrella St, Brighton 720-685-7500
PRAIRIE VIEW MIDDLE **167Z**
12915 E 120th Ave, Brighton 720-685-5400
SOUTHEAST ELEMENTARY **138U**
1595 Southern St, Brighton 303-655-2650
SOUTH ELEMENTARY **138P**
305 S 5th Ave, Brighton 303-655-2600
VIKAN, WALTER L MIDDLE **138U**
879 E Jessup St, Brighton 303-655-4050
SECOND CREEK ELEMENTARY **198V**
9950 Laredo Dr, Commerce City 720-685-7550
SECOND CREEK MIDDLE **198V**
9950 Laredo Dr, Commerce City 720-685-7550
STUART MIDDLE **198Q**
Jasper St, Commerce City 720-685-5400
TURNBERRY ELEMENTARY **198J**
13069 E 106th Pl, Commerce City 720-685-5351
BELLE CREEK CHARTER ELEM **196M**
9290 E 107th Ave, Henderson 303-468-0160
BELLE CREEK CHARTER MIDDLE **196M**
9290 E 107th Ave, Henderson 303-468-0160
HENDERSON ELEMENTARY **167V**
12301 E 124th Ave, Henderson 303-655-2700
PRAIRIE VIEW HIGH **167Z**
12909 E 120th Ave, Henderson 303-655-8801
THIMMIG, JOHN W ELEMENTARY **197C**
11453 Oswego St, Henderson 303-655-2750
THIMMIG, JOHN W MIDDLE **197C**
11453 Oswego St, Henderson 303-655-2750
WEST RIDGE ELEMENTARY **166N**
13102 Monaco St, Thornton 720-685-5300

ADAMS COUNTY - DISTRICT 14

ADAMS CITY HIGH **225U**
4625 E 68th Ave, Commerce City 303-289-3111
ADAMS CITY MIDDLE **225Q**
4451 E 72nd Ave, Commerce City 303-289-5881
ALSUP ELEMENTARY **225Q**
7101 Birch St, Commerce City 303-288-6865
ARNOLD, LESTER R HIGH **226P**
6500 E 72nd Ave, Commerce City 303-289-2983
CENTRAL ELEMENTARY **226W**
6450 Holly St, Commerce City 303-287-0327
COMMUNITY LEADERSHIP ACADEMY (K-8) **226S**
6888 Holly St, Commerce City 303-288-2711
DUPONT ELEMENTARY **226J**
7970 Kimberly St, Commerce City 303-287-0189
HANSON PRE K-8 .... **226P**
7133 E 73rd Ave, Commerce City 303-853-5800
KEARNEY MIDDLE **226W**
6160 Kearney St, Commerce City 303-287-0261
KEMP ELEMENTARY **226T**
6775 Oneida St, Commerce City 303-288-6633
MONACO ELEMENTARY **226J**
7631 Monaco St, Commerce City 303-287-0307
ROSE HILL ELEMENTARY **256B**
6900 E 58th Ave, Commerce City 303-287-0163
NEW AMERICA SCHOOL, THE **194U**
550 E Thornton Pkwy, Thornton 303-991-0130

ADAMS COUNTY - MAPLETON DISTRICT 1

FRONT RANGE EARLY COLLEGE **224Y**
601 E 64th Ave, Denver 303-853-1960
GLOBAL LEADERSHIP ACADEMY **224Q**
7480 Conifer Rd, Denver 303-853-1930
MAPLETON PREPARATORY HIGH **224Y**
601 E 64th Ave, Denver 303-853-1980
MONTEREY COMMUNITY SCHOOL **225E**
2201 McElwain Blvd, Denver 303-853-1360
VALLEY VIEW K-8 .... **224T**
660 W 70th Ave, Denver 303-853-1560
WELBY NEW TECHNOLOGY **224M**
1200 E 78th Ave, Denver 303-853-1660
WESTERN HILLS ADVENTURE ELEMENTARY **224K**
7700 Delta St, Denver 303-853-1410
WESTERN HILLS ENRICHMENT ACADEMY **224K**
7700 Delta St, Denver 303-853-1400
CLAYTON PARTNERSHIP SCHOOL **195W**
2410 Poze Blvd, Thornton 303-853-1460
HEID, BERTHA ACHIEVE ACADEMY **195W**
9100 Poze Blvd, Thornton 303-853-1300
HEID, BERTHA EXPLORE ELEMENTARY **195W**
9100 Poze Blvd, Thornton 303-853-1310
HIGHLAND MONTESSORI **225A**
8990 York St, Thornton 303-853-1700
MAPLETON EXPEDITIONARY SCHOOL FOR THE ARTS **225A**
8990 York St, Thornton 303-853-1270
MEADOW COMMUNITY SCHOOL **195Y**
9150 Monroe St, Thornton 303-853-1505
SKYVIEW ACADEMY **225A**
8990 York ST, Thornton 303-853-1900
SKYVIEW SENIOR HIGH **225A**
9000 York St, Thornton 303-853-1200
YORK INTERNATIONAL **195W**
9200 York St, Thornton 303-853-1600

ADAMS COUNTY - NORTHGLENN-THORNTON DISTRICT 12

GLACIER PEAK ELEMENTARY **166W**
12060 Jasmine St, Brighton 720-972-5940
CENTENNIAL ELEMENTARY **163Q**
13200 Westlake Dr, Broomfield 720-972-5280
COYOTE RIDGE ELEMENTARY **163J**
13770 Broadlands Dr, Broomfield 720-972-5780
LEGACY HIGH **163M**
2701 W 136th Ave, Broomfield 720-972-6700
MERIDIAN ELEMENTARY **163G**
14256 McKay Park Cir, Broomfield 720-972-7880
MOUNTAIN VIEW ELEMENTARY **163T**
12401 Perry St, Broomfield 720-972-5520
WESTLAKE MIDDLE **163L**
2800 W 135th Ave, Broomfield 720-972-5200
CORONADO HILLS ELEMENTARY **224H**
8300 Downing Dr, Denver 720-972-5320
McELWAIN ELEMENTARY **224H**
1020 Dawson Dr, Denver 720-972-5500
PINNACLE CHARTER, THE ELEMENTARY **224F**
1001 W 84th Ave, Denver 303-450-3985
PINNACLE CHARTER, THE HIGH **224F**
1001 W 84th Ave, Denver 303-450-3985
PINNACLE CHARTER, THE MIDDLE **224F**
1001 W 84th Ave, Denver 303-450-3985
FEDERAL HEIGHTS ELEMENTARY **193V**
2500 W 96th Ave, Federal Heights 720-972-5360
HILLCREST ELEMENTARY **194N**
10335 Croke Dr, Northglenn 720-972-5380
LEROY DRIVE ELEMENTARY **194M**
1451 E Leroy Dr, Northglenn 720-972-5460
MALLEY DRIVE ELEMENTARY **194H**
1300 E Malley Dr, Northglenn 720-972-5480
NORTHGLENN HIGH **194P**
601 W 100th Pl, Northglenn 720-972-4600
NORTHGLENN MIDDLE **194H**
1123 Muriel Dr, Northglenn 720-972-5080
NORTH MOR ELEMENTARY **194T**
9580 Damon Dr, Northglenn 720-972-5540
STUKEY ELEMENTARY **194G**
11080 Grant Dr, Northglenn 720-972-5420
WESTVIEW ELEMENTARY **194J**
1300 Roseanna Dr, Northglenn 720-972-5680
BOLLMAN TECHNICAL EDUCATION CENTER **194U**
9451 Washington St, Thornton 720-972-5820
CENTURY MIDDLE **164R**
13000 Lafayette St, Thornton 720-972-5240
CHERRY DRIVE ELEMENTARY **195H**
11500 Cherry Dr, Thornton 720-972-5300
CROSSROADS ALTERNATIVE MIDDLE @ NORTHEAST **194Z**
9451 Hoffman Way, Thornton 720-972-5900
CROSSROADS ALTERNATIVE SCHOOL **194Y**
455 E Eppinger Blvd, Thornton 720-972-5800
EAGLEVIEW ELEMENTARY **165M**
4601 Summit Grove Pkwy, Thornton 720-972-5760
HIGH PLAINS HIGH **194K**
10900 Huron St, Thornton 720-972-5000
HORIZON HIGH **165M**
5321 E 136th Ave, Thornton 720-972-4400
HULSTROM OPTIONS K-8 .... **194D**
11551 Wyco Dr, Thornton 720-972-5720
HUNTERS GLEN ELEMENTARY **164R**
13222 Corona St, Thornton 720-972-5440
NIVER CREEK MIDDLE **194W**
9450 Pecos St, Thornton 720-972-5120
NORTH STAR ELEMENTARY **224B**
8740 North Star Dr, Thornton 720-972-5560
PRAIRIE HILLS ELEMENTARY **165K**
13801 Garfield Pl, Thornton 720-972-8780
RIVERDALE ELEMENTARY **195M**
10724 Elm Dr, Thornton 720-972-5580
ROCKY TOP MIDDLE **165E**
14150 York St, Thornton 720-972-2200
SHADOW RIDGE MIDDLE **165V**
12551 Holly St, Thornton 720-972-5040
SILVER CREEK ELEMENTARY **135X**
15101 Fillmore St, Thornton 720-972-3940
SKYVIEW ELEMENTARY **165Z**
5021 E 123rd Ave, Thornton 720-972-5620
STARGATE CHARTER ELEMENTARY **165Q**
3951 Cottonwood Lakes Blvd, Thornton 303-450-3936
STARGATE CHARTER MIDDLE **165Q**
3951 Cottonwood Lakes Blvd, Thornton 303-450-3936
STELLAR ELEMENTARY **165U**
3901 E 124th Ave, Thornton 720-972-2340
TARVER ELEMENTARY **165P**
3500 Summit Grove Pkwy, Thornton 720-972-5640
THORNTON ELEMENTARY **194Z**
991 Eppinger Blvd, Thornton 720-972-5660
THORNTON HIGH **194Y**
9351 Washington St, Thornton 720-972-4800
THORNTON MIDDLE **194Z**
9451 Hoffman Way, Thornton 720-972-5160
WOODGLEN ELEMENTARY **195B**
11717 Madison St, Thornton 720-972-5700
ACADEMY OF CHARTER ELEMENTARY **163X**
11800 Lowell Blvd, Westminster 303-289-8088

ACADEMY OF CHARTER HIGH 163X
11800 Lowell Blvd, Westminster 303-289-8088
ACADEMY OF CHARTER MIDDLE 163X
11800 Lowell Blvd, Westminster 303-289-8088
ARAPAHOE RIDGE ELEMENTARY 164N
13095 Pecos St, Westminster 720-972-5740
COTTON CREEK ELEMENTARY 193E
11100 Vrain St, Westminster 720-972-5340
MOUNTAIN RANGE HIGH 164T
12500 Huron St, Westminster 720-972-6300
ROCKY MOUNTAIN ELEMENTARY 193T
3350 W 99th Ave, Westminster 720-972-5600
SILVER HILLS MIDDLE 164T
12400 Huron St, Westminster 720-972-5000

ADAMS COUNTY - STRASBURG DISTRICT 31J

HEMPHILL MIDDLE 794P
56729 E Colorado Ave, Strasburg 303-622-9211
PRAIRIE CREEKS CHARTER HIGH 794P
56635 Iowa Ave, Strasburg 303-622-6328
STRASBURG ELEMENTARY 794P
56729 E Colorado Ave, Strasburg 303-622-9211
STRASBURG HIGH 794P
56729 E Colorado Ave, Strasburg 303-622-9211

ADAMS COUNTY - WESTMINSTER DISTRICT 50

TENNYSON KNOLLS ELEMENTARY 223W
6330 Tennyson St, Arvada 303-429-4090
BAKER ELEMENTARY 223X
3555 W 64th Ave, Denver 303-428-1121
BERKELEY GARDENS ELEMENTARY 253F
5301 Lowell Blvd, Denver 303-650-3000
CARPENTER, M SCOTT MIDDLE 224S
7001 Lipan St, Denver 303-428-8583
CLEAR LAKE MIDDLE 223M
1941 Elmwood Ln, Denver 303-428-7526
DAY, FRANCIS M ELEMENTARY 224S
1740 Jordan Dr, Denver 303-428-1330
FAIRVIEW ELEMENTARY 223L
7826 Fairview Ave, Denver 303-428-1405
METZ, CLARA E ELEMENTARY 223H
2341 Sherrelwood Dr, Denver 303-428-1884
RANUM, IVER C HIGH 223M
2401 W 80th Ave, Denver 303-428-9577
SHERRELWOOD ELEMENTARY 224J
8095 Kalamath St, Denver 303-428-5353
SKYLINE VISTA ELEMENTARY 223R
7395 Zuni St, Denver 303-428-2300
CROWN POINTE ACADEMY ELEMENTARY 223Q
7281 Irving St, Westminster 303-428-1882
CROWN POINTE ACADEMY MIDDLE 223Q
7281 Irving St, Westminster 303-428-1882
FLYNN ELEMENTARY 223B
8731 Lowell Blvd, Westminster 303-428-2161
HARRIS PARK ELEMENTARY 223N
4300 W 75th Ave, Westminster 303-428-1721
HIDDEN LAKE HIGH 223P
7300 Lowell Blvd, Westminster 303-428-2600
HODGKINS MIDDLE 223T
3475 W 67th Ave, Westminster 303-428-7503
MESA ELEMENTARY 193Y
9100 Lowell Blvd, Westminster 303-428-2891
SHAW HEIGHTS MIDDLE 223B
8780 Circle Dr, Westminster 303-428-9533
SUNSET RIDGE ELEMENTARY 193U
9451 Hooker St, Westminster 303-426-8907
VISTA GRANDE ELEMENTARY 223A
8845 Wagner St, Westminster 303-429-8081
WESTMINSTER ELEMENTARY 223Q
7482 Irving St, Westminster 303-428-2494
WESTMINSTER HIGH 223T
4276 W 68th Ave, Westminster 303-428-9541
WESTMINSTER HILLS ELEMENTARY 223J
4105 W 80th Ave, Westminster 303-428-2511

ARAPAHOE COUNTY - AURORA PUBLIC SCHOOLS ADAMS-ARAPAHOE DISTRICT 28J

ALTURA ELEMENTARY 288G
1650 Altura Blvd, Aurora 303-340-3500
ARKANSAS ELEMENTARY 319E
17301 E Arkansas Ave, Aurora 303-755-0323
AURORA ACADEMY ELEMENTARY 287T
10251 E 1st Ave, Aurora 303-367-5983
AURORA ACADEMY MIDDLE 287T
10251 E 1st Ave, Aurora 303-367-5983
AURORA CENTRAL HIGH 287L
11700 E 11th Ave, Aurora 303-340-1600
AURORA CENTURY ELEMENTARY 318Q
2500 S Granby Way, Aurora 303-745-4424
AURORA FRONTIER K-8 320W
3200 S Jericho Way, Aurora 303-693-1995
AURORA HILLS MIDDLE 317D
1009 S Uvalda St, Aurora 303-341-7450
AURORA QUEST ACADEMY ELEMENTARY 288W
472 S Wheeling St, Aurora 303-343-3664
BOSTON ELEMENTARY 286M
1365 Boston St, Aurora 303-364-6878
COLUMBIA MIDDLE 319S
17600 E Columbia Ave, Aurora 303-690-6570
COURT, VIRGINIA ELEMENTARY 287Z
395 S Troy St, Aurora 303-366-9594
CRAWFORD ELEMENTARY 287E
1600 Florence St, Aurora 303-340-3290
DALTON ELEMENTARY 319S
17401 E Dartmouth Ave, Aurora 303-693-7561
DARTMOUTH ELEMENTARY 318V
3050 S Laredo St, Aurora 303-690-1155
EAST MIDDLE 288L
1275 Fraser St, Aurora 303-340-0660
ELKHART ELEMENTARY 288K
1020 Eagle St, Aurora 303-340-3050
FLETCHER ELEMENTARY 287B
10455 E 25th Ave, Aurora 303-343-1707
FULTON ELEMENTARY 287N
755 Fulton St, Aurora 303-364-8078
GATEWAY HIGH 318F
1300 S Sable Blvd, Aurora 303-755-7160
HINKLEY HIGH 288L
1250 Chambers Rd, Aurora 303-340-1500
IOWA ELEMENTARY 318H
16701 E Iowa Ave, Aurora 303-754-3660
JEWELL ELEMENTARY 318K
14601 E Jewell Ave, Aurora 303-751-8862
KENTON ELEMENTARY 287K
1255 Kenton St, Aurora 303-364-0947
KNOLL, LYN ELEMENTARY 287V
12445 E 2nd Ave, Aurora 303-364-8455
LANSING ELEMENTARY 287P
551 Lansing St, Aurora 303-364-8297
LAREDO ELEMENTARY 288M
1350 Laredo St, Aurora 303-366-0314
MILLER, CLYDE ELEMENTARY 289H
1701 Espana St, Aurora 303-364-7918
MONTVIEW ELEMENTARY 287C
2055 Moline St, Aurora 303-364-8549
MRACHEK MIDDLE 319J
1955 S Telluride St, Aurora 303-750-2836
MURPHY CREEK K-8 320H
1400 S Old Tom Morris Rd, Aurora 303-365-7812
NORTH MIDDLE 287C
12095 Montview Blvd, Aurora 303-364-7411
PARIS ELEMENTARY 287G
1635 Paris St, Aurora 303-341-1702
PARK LANE ELEMENTARY 257Z
13001 E 30th Ave, Aurora 303-343-8313
PEORIA ELEMENTARY 287L
875 Peoria St, Aurora 303-340-0770
PICKENS, T H TECHNICAL CENTER HIGH 289N
500 Airport Blvd, Aurora 303-344-4910
RANGEVIEW HIGH 319P
17599 E Iliff Ave, Aurora 303-695-6848
SABLE ELEMENTARY 288B
2601 Sable Blvd, Aurora 303-340-3140
SIDE CREEK ELEMENTARY 319L
19191 E Iliff Pl, Aurora 303-755-1785
SIXTH AVENUE ELEMENTARY 288N
560 Vaughn St, Aurora 303-366-6019
SMITH, WILLIAM HIGH 289N
400 Airport Blvd, Aurora 303-364-8715
SOUTH MIDDLE 287R
12310 E Parkview Dr, Aurora 303-364-7623
TOLLGATE ELEMENTARY 318D
701 S Kalispell Way, Aurora 303-696-0944
VASSAR ELEMENTARY 319P
18101 E Vassar Pl, Aurora 303-752-3772
VAUGHN ELEMENTARY 287M
1155 Vaughn St, Aurora 303-366-8430
WEST MIDDLE 287J
10100 E 13th Ave, Aurora 303-366-2671
WHEELING ELEMENTARY 288W
472 S Wheeling St, Aurora 303-344-8670
YALE ELEMENTARY 318R
16001 E Yale Ave, Aurora 303-751-7470
NEW AMERICA SCHOOL 287N
9125 E 7th Pl, Denver 303-320-9854

ARAPAHOE COUNTY - BYERS DISTRICT 32J

BYERS SCHOOL (K-12) 795Y
444 E Front St, Byers 303-822-5292

ARAPAHOE COUNTY - CHERRY CREEK DISTRICT 5

ANTELOPE RIDGE ELEMENTARY 350Q
5455 S Tempe St, Aurora 720-886-3300
ARROWHEAD ELEMENTARY 319U
19100 E Bates Ave, Aurora 720-886-2800
ASPEN CROSSING ELEMENTARY 349M
4655 S Himalaya St, Aurora 720-886-3700
BUFFALO TRAIL ELEMENTARY 351N
24300 E Progress Dr, Aurora 720-886-4000
CANYON CREEK ELEMENTARY 350Y
6070 S Versailles Pkwy, Aurora 720-886-3600
CHEROKEE TRAIL HIGH 381B
25901 E Arapahoe Rd, Aurora 720-886-1900
CIMARRON ELEMENTARY 349A
17373 E Lehigh Pl, Aurora 720-886-8100
COYOTE HILLS ELEMENTARY 381A
24605 E Davies Way, Aurora 720-886-3900
DAKOTA VALLEY ELEMENTARY 350A
3950 S Kirk Way, Aurora 720-886-3000
EASTRIDGE ELEMENTARY 317Q
11777 E Wesley Ave, Aurora 720-747-2200
FALCON CREEK MIDDLE 349Z
6100 S Genoa St, Aurora 720-886-7700
FOX HOLLOW ELEMENTARY 349X
6363 S Waco St, Aurora 720-886-8700
FOX RIDGE MIDDLE 381C
26301 E Arapahoe Rd, Aurora 720-886-4400
GRANDVIEW HIGH 380A
20500 E Arapahoe Rd, Aurora 720-886-6500
HIGHLINE COMMUNITY ELEMENTARY 317B
11000 E Exposition Ave, Aurora 720-747-2300
HORIZON MIDDLE 349B
3981 S Reservoir Rd, Aurora 720-886-6100
INDEPENDENCE ELEMENTARY 348M
4700 S Memphis St, Aurora 720-886-8200
INDIAN RIDGE ELEMENTARY 348R
16501 E Progress Dr, Aurora 720-886-8400
LAREDO MIDDLE 348M
5000 S Laredo St, Aurora 720-886-5000
LIBERTY MIDDLE 380K
21500 E Dry Creek Rd, Aurora 720-886-2400
MEADOW POINT ELEMENTARY 349K
17901 E Grand Ave, Aurora 720-886-8600
MISSION VIEJO ELEMENTARY 348C
3855 S Alicia Pkwy, Aurora 720-886-8000
OVERLAND HIGH 317M
12400 E Jewell Ave, Aurora 720-747-3700
PEAKVIEW ELEMENTARY 349Q
19451 E Progress Cir, Aurora 720-886-3100
POLTON ELEMENTARY 317U
2985 S Oakland St, Aurora 720-747-2600
PONDEROSA ELEMENTARY 317K
1885 S Lima St, Aurora 720-747-2800
PRAIRIE MIDDLE 317M
12600 E Jewell Ave, Aurora 720-747-3000
ROLLING HILLS ELEMENTARY 349U
5756 S Biscay St, Aurora 720-886-3400
SAGEBRUSH ELEMENTARY 348K
14700 E Temple Pl, Aurora 720-886-8300
SKY VISTA MIDDLE 350E
4500 S Himalaya St, Aurora 720-886-4710
SMOKY HILL HIGH 348M
16100 E Smoky Hill Rd, Aurora 720-886-5300
SUMMIT ELEMENTARY 349F
18201 E Quincy Ave, Aurora 720-886-6400
SUNRISE ELEMENTARY 349D
4050 S Genoa Way, Aurora 720-886-2900
TIMBERLINE ELEMENTARY 350N
5500 S Killarney St, Aurora 720-886-3200
VILLAGE EAST ELEMENTARY 317G
1433 S Oakland St, Aurora 720-747-2000
C. A. R. E. MIDDLE 378B
14076 E Briarwood Ave, Centennial 720-886-7200
CHERRY CREEK P.R.E.P. ALTERNATIVE HIGH 378B
14076 E Briarwood Ave, Centennial 720-886-7200
CREEKSIDE ELEMENTARY 379M
19993 E Long Ave, Centennial 720-886-3500
DRY CREEK ELEMENTARY 376L
7686 E Hinsdale Ave, Centennial 720-554-3300
EAGLECREST HIGH 350P
5100 S Picadilly Rd, Centennial 720-886-1000
HERITAGE ELEMENTARY 376B
6867 E Heritage Pl S, Centennial 720-554-3500
HOMESTEAD ELEMENTARY 376K
7451 S Homestead Pkwy, Centennial 720-554-3700
RED HAWK RIDGE ELEMENTARY 378H
16251 E Geddes Ave, Centennial 720-886-3800
THUNDER RIDGE MIDDLE 350P
5250 S Picadilly St, Centennial 720-886-1500
TRAILS WEST ELEMENTARY 349P
5400 S Waco St, Centennial 720-886-8500
WALNUT HILLS ELEMENTARY 376G
8195 E Costilla Blvd, Centennial 720-554-3800
WILLOW CREEK ELEMENTARY 376M
7855 S Willow Way, Centennial 720-554-3900
CHALLENGE MAGNET MIDDLE 317A
9659 E Mississippi Ave, Denver 720-747-2100
CHALLENGE MAGNET SCHOOL ELEMENTARY 317A
9659 E Mississippi Ave, Denver 720-747-2100
HOLLY HILLS ELEMENTARY 316S
6161 E Cornell Ave, Denver 720-747-2500
HOLLY RIDGE ELEMENTARY 316W
3301 S Monaco Pkwy, Denver 720-747-2400
CHERRY CREEK ACADEMY ELEMENTARY 347W
6260 S Dayton St, Englewood 303-779-8988
CHERRY CREEK ACADEMY MIDDLE 347W
6260 S Dayton St, Englewood 303-779-8988
CHERRY CREEK HIGH 346M
9300 E Union Ave, Englewood 720-554-2285
CHERRY HILLS VILLAGE ELEMENTARY 345E
2400 E Quincy Ave, Englewood 720-747-2700
COTTONWOOD CREEK ELEMENTARY 347U
11200 E Orchard Ave, Englewood 720-554-3200
HIGH PLAINS ELEMENTARY 347W
6100 S Fulton St, Englewood 720-554-3600
BELLEVIEW ELEMENTARY 347J
4851 S Dayton St, Greenwood Village 720-554-3100
CAMPUS MIDDLE 347J
4785 S Dayton St, Greenwood Village 720-554-2677
GREENWOOD ELEMENTARY 346S
5550 S Holly St, Greenwood Village 720-554-3400
WEST MIDDLE 345R
5151 S Holly St, Greenwood Village 720-554-5180

ARAPAHOE COUNTY - ENGLEWOOD DISTRICT 1

BISHOP, WILLIAM E ELEMENTARY 314X
3100 S Elati St, Englewood 303-761-1496
CHERRELYN ELEMENTARY 344L
4500 S Lincoln St, Englewood 303-761-2102
CLAYTON ELEMENTARY 344K
4600 S Fox St, Englewood 303-781-7831
COLORADO'S FINEST ALTERNATIVE HIGH 313R
2323 W Baker Ave, Englewood 303-934-5786
ENGLEWOOD HIGH 344C
3800 S Logan St, Englewood 303-806-2266
ENGLEWOOD LEADERSHIP ACADEMY MIDDLE 344C
3794 S Logan St, Englewood 303-806-7150
ENGLEWOOD MIDDLE 344K
300 W Chenango Ave, Englewood 303-781-7817
HAY, CHARLES ELEMENTARY 314Z
3195 S Lafayette St, Englewood 303-761-2433
MADDOX ELEMENTARY 344B
700 W Mansfield Ave, Englewood 303-761-2331

ARAPAHOE COUNTY - LITTLETON DISTRICT 6

AMES ELEMENTARY 375G
7300 S Clermont Dr, Centennial 303-347-4400
ARAPAHOE HIGH 375J
2201 E Dry Creek Rd, Centennial 303-347-6000

FRANKLIN ELEMENTARY 344Z
1603 E Euclid Ave, Centennial 303-347-4500
HIGHLAND ELEMENTARY 374C
711 E Euclid Ave, Centennial 303-347-4525
HOPKINS ELEMENTARY 374G
7171 S Pennsylvania St, Centennial 303-347-4550
LENSKI ELEMENTARY 345Z
6350 S Fairfax Way, Centennial 303-347-4575
NEWTON MIDDLE 375C
4001 E Arapahoe Rd, Centennial 303-347-7900
PEABODY ELEMENTARY 345X
3128 E Maplewood Ave, Centennial 303-347-4625
POWELL MIDDLE 374Q
8000 S Corona Way, Centennial 303-347-7950
SANDBURG ELEMENTARY 375F
6900 S Elizabeth St, Centennial 303-347-4675
TWAIN ELEMENTARY 374H
6901 S Franklin St, Centennial 303-347-4700
CENTENNIAL ACADEMY 343U
3306 W Berry Ave, Littleton 303-347-4425
EAST ELEMENTARY 344T
5933 S Fairfield St, Littleton 303-347-4450
EUCLID MIDDLE 374B
777 W Euclid Ave, Littleton 303-347-7800
FIELD ELEMENTARY 344Q
5402 S Sherman Way, Littleton 303-347-4475
GODDARD MIDDLE 343T
3800 W Berry Ave, Littleton 303-347-7850
HERITAGE HIGH 374E
1401 W Geddes Ave, Littleton 303-347-7600
LITTLETON ACADEMY (K-8) 374N
1200 W Mineral Ave, Littleton 303-798-5252
LITTLETON HIGH 344U
199 E Littleton Blvd, Littleton 303-347-7700
LITTLETON PREPARATORY (K-8) 343Q
5151 S Federal Blvd, Littleton 303-734-1995
MOODY ELEMENTARY 344W
6390 S Windermere St, Littleton 303-347-4600
OPTIONS HIGH 374B
6558 S Acoma St, Littleton 303-347-3580
PATHWAYS ALTERNATIVE MIDDLE 344S
1907 W Powers Ave, Littleton 303-347-4980
RUNYON ELEMENTARY 374F
7455 S Elati St, Littleton 303-347-4650
WHITMAN, W ELEMENTARY 374B
6557 S Acoma St, Littleton 303-347-4725
WILDER ELEMENTARY 343X
4300 W Ponds Cir, Littleton 303-347-4750

ARAPAHOE COUNTY - SHERIDAN DISTRICT 2

FORT LOGAN ELEMENTARY 343C
3700 S Knox Ct, Denver 720-833-6989
SHERIDAN HIGH 343C
3201 W Oxford Ave, Englewood 720-833-6987
SHERIDAN MIDDLE 343G
4107 S Federal Blvd, Englewood 720-833-6988
TERRY, ALICE B ELEMENTARY 343F
4485 S Irving St, Englewood 720-833-6990

BOULDER COUNTY - BOULDER VALLEY DISTRICT RE-2

ARAPAHOE RIDGE HIGH 129C
6600 Arapahoe Rd, Boulder 303-447-5284
BEAR CREEK ELEMENTARY 128S
2500 Table Mesa Dr, Boulder 303-499-8555
BOULDER COMMUNITY SCHOOL OF INTEGRATED STUDIES ELEMENTARY 128G
3995 E Aurora Ave, Boulder 303-494-1454
BOULDER HIGH 127D
1604 Arapahoe Ave, Boulder 303-442-2430
BOULDER PREP CHARTER HIGH 99C
5075 Chaparral Ct, Boulder 303-545-6186
BOULDER TECHNICAL EDUCATION CENTER 129C
6600 Arapahoe Rd, Boulder 303-447-5220
CASEY MIDDLE 97Z
2410 13th St, Boulder 303-442-5235
CENTENNIAL MIDDLE 98J
2205 Norwood Ave, Boulder 303-443-3760
COLUMBINE ELEMENTARY 98S
3130 Repplier Dr, Boulder 303-443-0792
COMMUNITY MONTESSORI ELEMENTARY 128T
805 Gillaspie Dr, Boulder 303-444-7479
CREEKSIDE AT MARTIN PARK ELEMENTARY 128P
3740 Martin Dr, Boulder 303-494-1069
CREST VIEW ELEMENTARY 97M
1897 Sumac Ave, Boulder 303-443-6363
DOUGLASS ELEMENTARY 130E
840 75th St, Boulder 303-499-4884
EISENHOWER ELEMENTARY 128H
1220 Eisenhower Dr, Boulder 303-443-4260
FAIRVIEW HIGH 128Y
1515 Greenbriar Blvd, Boulder 303-499-7600
FLATIRONS ELEMENTARY 127G
1150 7th St, Boulder 303-442-7205
FOOTHILL ELEMENTARY 97Q
1001 Hawthorn Ave, Boulder 303-443-1847
HALCYON MIDDLE 128K
3100 Bucknell Ct, Boulder 303-499-1121
HEATHERWOOD ELEMENTARY 100F
7750 Concord Dr, Boulder 303-530-1234
HIGH PEAKS ELEMENTARY 128G
3995 E Aurora Ave, Boulder 303-494-1454
HORIZONS ALTERNATIVE K-8 CHARTER SCHOOL 128L
4545 Sioux Dr, Boulder 303-447-5580
JUSTICE HIGH 127C
1777 6th St, Boulder 303-441-4862
MANHATTAN SCHOOL OF ARTS AND ACADEMICS 128M
290 Manhattan Dr, Boulder 303-494-0335
MESA ELEMENTARY 128W
1575 Lehigh St, Boulder 303-494-4704
NEW VISTA HIGH 128J
700 20th St, Boulder 303-494-8037
PLATT, NEVIN J MIDDLE 129F
6096 Baseline Rd, Boulder 303-499-6800
SOUTHERN HILLS MIDDLE 128U
1500 Knox Dr, Boulder 303-494-2866
SUMMIT CHARTER MIDDLE 128Q
4655 Hanover Ave, Boulder 303-447-5529
UNIVERSITY HILL ELEMENTARY 127H
956 16th St, Boulder 303-442-6735
WHITTIER ELEMENTARY 98W
2008 Pine St, Boulder 303-442-2282
ASPEN CREEK K-8 .... 162M
5500 Aspen Creek Dr, Broomfield 720-887-4537
BIRCH ELEMENTARY 162R
1035 Birch St, Broomfield 303-469-3397
BROOMFIELD HEIGHTS MIDDLE 162P
1555 Daphne St, Broomfield 303-466-2387
BROOMFIELD HIGH 162T
1 Eagle Way, Broomfield 303-466-7344
EMERALD ELEMENTARY 162X
755 W Elmhurst Pl, Broomfield 303-466-2316
KOHL ELEMENTARY 162T
1000 W 10th Ave, Broomfield 303-466-5944
GOLD HILL ELEMENTARY 721R
890 Main St, Gold Hill 303-245-5940
JAMESTOWN ELEMENTARY 722A
111 Mesa St, Jamestown 303-442-6613
ANGEVINE MIDDLE 131R
1150 W South Boulder Rd, Lafayette 303-665-5540
CENTAURUS HIGH 131Q
10300 S Boulder Rd, Lafayette 303-665-9211
LAFAYETTE ELEMENTARY 131M
101 N Bermont Ave, Lafayette 303-665-5046
PEAK TO PEAK CHARTER ELEMENTARY 132P
800 Merlin Dr, Lafayette 303-453-4600
PEAK TO PEAK CHARTER HIGH 132P
800 Merlin Dr, Lafayette 303-453-4600
PEAK TO PEAK CHARTER MIDDLE 132P
800 Merlin Dr, Lafayette 303-453-4600
PIONEER ELEMENTARY 132E
101 Baseline Rd, Lafayette 303-666-4971
RYAN ELEMENTARY 131U
1405 Centaur Village Dr, Lafayette 303-665-3345
SANCHEZ ELEMENTARY 132P
655 Sir Galahad Dr, Lafayette 303-665-2044
COAL CREEK ELEMENTARY 130U
801 W Tamarisk St, Louisville 303-666-4843
FIRESIDE ELEMENTARY 130Y
845 W Dahlia St, Louisville 303-665-0700
LOUISVILLE ELEMENTARY 131S
400 Hutchinson St, Louisville 303-666-6562
LOUISVILLE MIDDLE 131N
1341 Main St, Louisville 303-666-6503
MONARCH HIGH 160H
329 Campus Dr, Louisville 303-665-5888
MONARCH K-8 .... 160H
263 Campus Dr, Louisville 303-665-6424
NEDERLAND ELEMENTARY 740L
1 Sundown Trail, Nederland 303-258-7092
NEDERLAND MIDDLE SENIOR HIGH 740Q
597 County Rd 130, Nederland 303-258-3212
ELDORADO K-8 .... 160U
3351 Indiana St, Superior 720-304-6524
SUPERIOR ELEMENTARY 160Q
1800 S Indiana St, Superior 303-534-9330

BOULDER COUNTY - ST. VRAIN VALLEY DISTRICT RE1J

ERIE ELEMENTARY 102M
4137 E County Line Rd, Erie 303-828-2450
ERIE HIGH 103M
3180 Weld County Rd 5, Erie 303-828-4213
ERIE MIDDLE 102M
650 Main St, Erie 303-828-3391
COAL RIDGE MIDDLE 707T
6201 Booth Dr, Firestone 303-833-4176
PRAIRIE RIDGE ELEMENTARY 707T
6632 St Vrain Ranch Blvd, Firestone 720-494-3641
CARBON VALLEY ACADEMY 726D
4040 Corolis Way, Frederick 303-774-9555
FREDERICK ELEMENTARY 727F
555 8th St, Frederick 303-833-2456
FREDERICK HIGH 727F
600 Fifth St, Frederick 303-833-3533
LEGACY ELEMENTARY 726D
7701 Eagle Blvd, Frederick 720-652-8160
ALPINE ELEMENTARY 12N
2005 Alpine St, Longmont 720-652-8140
ALTONA MIDDLE 40P
4600 Clover Basin Dr, Longmont 720-494-3980
BURLINGTON ELEMENTARY 41Q
1051 S Pratt Pkwy, Longmont 303-776-8861
CENTRAL ELEMENTARY 41C
1020 4th Ave, Longmont 303-776-3236
COLUMBINE ELEMENTARY 42A
111 Longs Peak Ave, Longmont 303-776-2840
EAGLE CREST ELEMENTARY 40Q
4444 Clover Basin Dr, Longmont 303-485-6073
FALL RIVER ELEMENTARY 12U
1400 Deerwood Dr, Longmont 720-652-7920
FLAGSTAFF ACADEMY K-8 .... 41P
1841 Lefthand Cir, Longmont 303-651-7900
HERITAGE MIDDLE 12W
233 E Mountain View Ave, Longmont 303-772-7900
HYGIENE ELEMENTARY 10S
11968 N 75th St, Longmont 720-652-8021
INDIAN PEAKS ELEMENTARY 41P
1335 S Judson St, Longmont 303-772-7240
LOMA LINDA ELEMENTARY 12W
333 E Mountain View Ave, Longmont 303-772-4280
LONGMONT ESTATES ELEMENTARY 10V
1601 Northwestern Rd, Longmont 720-652-8101
LONGMONT HIGH 11X
1040 N Sunset St, Longmont 303-776-6014
LONGS PEAK MIDDLE 11T
1500 14th Ave, Longmont 303-776-5611
MOUNTAIN VIEW ELEMENTARY 11U
1415 14th Ave, Longmont 720-652-8261
NORTHRIDGE ELEMENTARY 11Q
1200 19th Ave, Longmont 303-772-3040
OLDE COLUMBINE HIGH 41P
1200 S Sunset, Longmont 720-494-3961
ROCKY MOUNTAIN ELEMENTARY 42B
800 E 5th Ave, Longmont 303-772-6750
SANBORN ELEMENTARY 11P
2235 Vivian St, Longmont 303-772-3838
SILVER CREEK HIGH 40K
4901 Nelson Rd, Longmont 720-494-3721
SKYLINE HIGH 12X
600 E Mountain View Ave, Longmont 720-494-3741
SPANGLER ELEMENTARY 11V
1440 Collyer St, Longmont 720-494-3761
SUNSET MIDDLE 41P
1300 Sunset St, Longmont 303-776-3963
TRAIL RIDGE MIDDLE 12Z
1000 Button Rock Dr, Longmont 720-494-3820
TWIN PEAKS CHARTER ACADEMY (K-8) 41D
820 Main St, Longmont 720-652-8201
UTE CREEK SECONDARY ACADEMY HIGH 41G
1198 Boston Ave, Longmont 303-774-0066
WESTVIEW MIDDLE 10U
1651 Airport Rd, Longmont 303-772-3134
LYONS ELEMENTARY 703C
338 High St, Lyons 303-823-6915
LYONS MIDDLE/SENIOR HIGH 703C
100 S 2nd Ave, Lyons 303-823-6631
NIWOT ELEMENTARY 70M
8778 Morton Rd, Niwot 303-652-2828
NIWOT HIGH 70M
8989 E Niwot Rd, Niwot 303-652-2550

CLEAR CREEK COUNTY - DISTRICT RE-1

KING-MURPHY ELEMENTARY 801R
425 Circle K Rd, Evergreen 303-670-0005
CARLSON ELEMENTARY 780Q
1300 Miner St, Idaho Springs 303-567-4431
CLEAR CREEK CAREER/TECHNICAL 780U
320 State Hwy 103, Idaho Springs 303-567-3848
CLEAR CREEK HIGH 781Z
185 Beaver Brook Canyon Rd, Idaho Springs 303-679-4600
CLEAR CREEK MIDDLE 780U
320 State Hwy 103, Idaho Springs 303-567-4461

DENVER DISTRICT 1 ELEMENTARY SCHOOLS

ACADEMIA ANA MARIA SANDOVAL 253V
3655 Wyandot St, Denver 303-455-9326
AMESSE 257H
5440 Scranton St, Denver 303-371-0940
ASBURY 314M
1320 E Asbury Ave, Denver 303-722-4695
ASHLEY 286G
1914 Syracuse St, Denver 303-322-1853
BARNUM 283U
85 Hooker St, Denver 303-935-3509
BARRETT 255Y
2900 Richard Allen Ct, Denver 303-388-5841
BEACH COURT 253M
4950 Beach Ct, Denver 303-455-3607
BRADLEY 315V
3051 S Elm St, Denver 303-756-8386
BROMWELL 285N
2500 E 4th Ave, Denver 303-388-5969
BROWN 283B
2550 Lowell Blvd, Denver 303-477-1611
CARSON 285V
5420 E 1st Ave, Denver 303-355-7316
CASTRO 313B
845 S Lowell Blvd, Denver 303-935-2458
CENTENNIAL K-8 SCHOOL 253P
4665 Raleigh St, Denver 303-433-6489
CHALLENGES, CHOICES & IMAGES 286H
1537 Alton St, Denver 303-341-7554
CHELTENHAM 283G
1580 Julian St, Denver 303-825-3323
COLFAX 283F
1526 Tennyson St, Denver 303-623-6148
COLLEGE VIEW 313U
2675 S Decatur St, Denver 303-934-5689
COLUMBIAN 253U
2925 W 40th Ave, Denver 303-433-2539
COLUMBINE 255X
2540 E 29th Ave, Denver 303-388-3617
CORY 315F
1550 S Steele St, Denver 303-744-2726
COWELL 283J
4540 W 10th Ave, Denver 303-571-0617
DENISON MONTESSORI 313J
1821 S Yates St, Denver 303-934-7805
DENVER ARTS & TECHNOLOGY ACADEMY 253S
3752 Tennyson St, Denver 720-855-7504
DOULL 313N
2520 S Utica St, Denver 303-935-2489
EAGLETON 283L
880 Hooker St, Denver 303-623-0181
EBERT 284C
410 Park Ave W, Denver 303-292-4629
EDISON 253T
3350 Quitman St, Denver 303-455-3615
ELLIS 315M
1651 S Dahlia St, Denver 303-756-8363
FAIRVIEW 283M
2715 W 11th Ave, Denver 303-623-7193

FALLIS 286X
6700 E Virginia Ave, Denver 303-388-5981

FORCE 313E
1550 S Wolff St, Denver 303-935-3595

FORD 258F
14500 E Maxwell Pl, Denver 303-371-6990

GARDEN PLACE 254Q
4425 Lincoln St, Denver 303-295-7785

GODSMAN 313H
2120 W Arkansas Ave, Denver 303-936-3466

GOLDRICK 313D
1050 S Zuni St, Denver 303-935-3544

GREEN VALLEY 260N
4100 Jericho St, Denver 303-307-1659

GUST 313U
3440 W Yale Ave, Denver 303-935-4613

HALLETT 256W
2950 Jasmine St, Denver 303-355-7359

HOLM 316Y
3185 S Willow Ct, Denver 303-751-3157

JOHNSON 313L
1850 S Irving St, Denver 303-935-4659

KAISER 343K
4500 S Quitman St, Denver 303-795-6014

KNAPP 283W
500 S Utica St, Denver 303-935-4663

KNIGHT FUNDAMENTAL ACADEMY 285X
3245 E Exposition Ave, Denver 303-722-4681

LENA ARCHULETA 258H
16000 E Maxwell Pl, Denver 303-371-6363

LINCOLN 314C
710 S Pennsylvania St, Denver 303-744-1785

LOWRY 286U
8001 E Cedar Ave, Denver 303-340-0179

MARRAMA 259Q
19100 E 40th Ave, Denver 303-371-3780

MAXWELL 258J
14390 E Bolling Dr, Denver 303-576-6557

McGLONE 257R
4500 Crown Blvd, Denver 303-373-5080

MCKINLEY-THATCHER 314G
1230 S Grant St, Denver 303-777-8816

McMEEN 316A
1000 S Holly St, Denver 303-388-5649

MONTCLAIR 286K
1151 Newport St, Denver 303-333-5497

MUNROE 283Y
3440 W Virginia Ave, Denver 303-934-5547

NEWLON 283N
361 Vrain St, Denver 303-934-2441

OAKLAND 258P
4580 Dearborn St, Denver 303-371-2960

PALMER 285M
995 Grape St, Denver 303-388-5929

PHILIPS 286B
6550 E 21st Ave, Denver 303-388-5313

PIONEER CHARTER 255T
3230 E 38th Ave, Denver 303-329-8412

REMINGTON 254N
4735 Pecos St, Denver 303-433-6461

SABIN 313W
3050 S Vrain St, Denver 303-936-3413

SAMUELS 346G
3985 S Vincennes Ct, Denver 303-770-2215

SCHENCK 313F
1300 S Lowell Blvd, Denver 303-935-4606

SCHMITT 313M
1820 S Vallejo St, Denver 303-935-4651

SMEDLEY 254N
4250 Shoshone St, Denver 303-433-3321

SMITH RENAISSANCE SCHOOL OF THE ARTS 256S
3590 Jasmine St, Denver 303-388-1658

SOUTHMOOR 346B
3755 S Magnolia Way, Denver 303-756-0392

STECK 285Q
425 Ash St, Denver 303-355-7314

STEDMAN 255Z
2940 Dexter St, Denver 303-322-7781

STEELE 284Z
320 S Marion Pkwy, Denver 303-744-1717

SWANSEA 255P
4650 Columbine St, Denver 303-296-8429

TELLER 285L
1150 Garfield St, Denver 303-333-4285

TRAYLOR FUNDAMENTAL ACADEMY 312V
2900 S Ivan Way, Denver 303-985-1535

UNIVERSITY PARK 315P
2300 S St Paul St, Denver 303-756-9407

VALDEZ 253Y
2525 W 29th Ave, Denver 303-433-2581

VALVERDE 283Z
2030 W Alameda Ave, Denver 303-722-4697

WESTERLY CREEK 256Z
8800 E 28th Ave, Denver 303-322-5877

WHITEMAN 286P
451 Newport St, Denver 303-355-7333

WYMAN 285E
1690 Williams St, Denver 303-320-1632

DENVER DISTRICT 1 K-8 SCHOOLS

BLAIR, OMAR D 259L
4905 Cathay St, Denver 303-371-9570

BRYANT-WEBSTER 254S
3635 Quivas St, Denver 303-433-3336

DEL PUEBLO 284P
750 Galapago St, Denver 303-629-1473

EL DIA DE FAIRMONT 284T
520 W 3rd Ave, Denver 303-893-1957

GILPIN 254Z
2949 California St, Denver 303-297-0313

GRANT RANCH 342V
5400 S Jay Cir, Denver 720-424-6880

GREENLEE ECE 284J
1150 Lipan St, Denver 303-629-6364

GREENWOOD 258K
5130 Durham Ct, Denver 303-371-0247

HARRINGTON 255S
2401 E 37th Ave, Denver 303-333-4293

HIGHLINE ACADEMY 316L
7808 Cherry Creek Dr S, Denver 720-449-0317

HOWELL, FARRELL B 258N
14250 E Albrook Dr, Denver 720-424-2740

MITCHELL 254Z
1350 E 33rd Ave, Denver 303-296-8412

MOORE, DORA 284R
846 Corona St, Denver 303-831-7044

NORTHEAST ACADEMY 257L
4895 Peoria St, Denver 303-307-8837

ODYSSEY CHARTER SCHOOL 256Z
8750 E 28th Ave, Denver 303-316-3944

PARK HILL ECE-8 SCHOOL 285H
5050 E 19th Ave, Denver 303-322-1811

ROBERTS, WILLIAM "BILL" 286D
2100 Akron Way, Denver 720-424-2640

SLAVENS 315S
3000 S Clayton St, Denver 303-753-9151

WALLER, FLORIDA PITT 260F
21601 E 51st Pl, Denver 720-424-2840

WHITTIER 284D
2480 Downing St, Denver 303-861-1310

WYATT-EDISON 254V
3620 Franklin St, Denver 303-292-5515

DENVER DISTRICT 1 MIDDLE/JUNIOR HIGH SCHOOLS

BRUCE RANDOLPH 255T
3955 Steele St, Denver 720-424-1080

CHALLENGES, CHOICES & IMAGES SCHOOL 286H
1537 Alton St, Denver 303-341-7554

COLE COLLEGE PREP MIDDLE 254Z
3240 Humboldt St, Denver 303-293-2653

COMMUNITY CHALLENGE CHARTER SCHOOL 284K
948 Santa Fe Dr, Denver 303-436-9588

DENVER SCHOOL OF THE ARTS 286B
7111 Montview Blvd, Denver 720-424-1700

DPS CAREER EDUCATION CENTER 283C
2650 Eliot St, Denver 720-423-6600

EL DIA DE FAIRMONT 284T
520 W 3rd Ave, Denver 303-893-1957

EMERSON STREET 284G
835 E 18th Ave, Denver 720-424-1660

GRANT 314L
1751 S Washington St, Denver 720-423-9360

HAMILTON 316Y
8600 EDartmouth Ave, Denver 720-423-9500

HENRY 312V
3005 S Golden Way, Denver 720-423-9560

HILL 285Q
451 Clermont St, Denver 720-423-9680

HORACE MANN 254N
4130 Navajo St, Denver 720-423-9800

KEPNER 313C
911 S Hazel St, Denver 720-424-0000

KIPP SUNSHINE PEAK ACADEMY 284W
375 S Tejon St, Denver 303-623-5772

KUNSMILLER 313P
2250 S Quitman Way, Denver 720-424-0200

LAKE 283F
1820 Lowell Blvd, Denver 720-424-0260

MARTIN LUTHER KING JR EARLY COLLEGE 259L
19535 E 46th Ave, Denver 720-424-0420

MERRILL 315F
1551 S Monroe St, Denver 720-424-0600

MOREY 284M
840 E 14th Ave, Denver 720-424-0700

PLACE 316F
7125 Cherry Creek Dr N, Denver 720-424-0960

PS 1 CHARTER SCHOOL 284K
1062 Delaware St, Denver 303-575-6690

RACHEL B NOEL 258M
5290 Kittridge St, Denver 720-424-0800

RISHEL 283Z
451 S Tejon St, Denver 720-424-1260

SKINNER 253U
3435 W 40th Ave, Denver 720-424-1420

SMILEY 286A
2540 Holly St, Denver 720-424-1540

DENVER DISTRICT 1 SENIOR HIGH SCHOOLS

ABRAHAM LINCOLN 313Q
2285 S Federal Blvd, Denver 720-423-5000

ACADEMY OF URBAN LEARNING 314F
1380 S Santa Fe Dr, Denver 303-282-0900

CHALLENGES, CHOICES & IMAGES SCHOOL 286H
1537 Alton St, Denver 303-341-7554

COLORADO HIGH CHARTER 284J
1175 Osage St, Denver 303-892-8475

CONTEMPORARY LEARNING ACADEMY 253Z
2211 W 27th Ave, Denver 720-423-6900

DENVER SCHOOL OF SCIENCE & TECHNOLOGY 286C
2000 Valentia St, Denver 303-320-5570

DENVER SCHOOL OF THE ARTS 286B
7111 Montview Blvd, Denver 720-424-1700

DPS CAREER EDUCATION CENTER 283C
2650 Eliot St, Denver 720-423-6600

EAST 285F
1545 Detroit St, Denver 720-423-8300

EMERSON STREET 284G
835 E 18th Ave, Denver 720-424-1660

EMILY GRIFFITH 284F
1250 Welton St, Denver 720-423-4700

ESCUELA TLATELOLCO (Pre K-12) 253Y
2949 Federal Blvd, Denver 303-964-8993

FLORENCE CRITTENTON 283V
96 S Zuni St, Denver 303-733-7686

GEORGE WASHINGTON 286W
655 S Monaco St, Denver 720-423-8600

GILLIAM SCHOOL 254Z
2844 Downing St, Denver 303-291-8930

JOHN F KENNEDY 312U
2855 S Lamar St, Denver 720-423-4300

LIFE SKILLS CENTER OF DENVER 284K
1000 Cherokee St, Denver 720-889-2898

MANUAL 254Z
1700 E 28th Ave, Denver 303-391-6330

MARTIN LUTHER KING JR EARLY COLLEGE 259L
19535 E 46th Ave, Denver 720-424-0420

MONTBELLO 258J
5000 Crown Blvd, Denver 720-423-5700

NORTH 253Y
2960 N Speer Blvd, Denver 720-423-2700

P. R. E. P. CENTER 255W
2727 Columbine St, Denver 720-424-8451

PS 1 CHARTER SCHOOL 284K
1062 Delaware St, Denver 303-575-6690

RIDGE VIEW ACADEMY 321Z
28101 E Quincy Ave, Denver 303-214-1139

ROCKY MOUNTAIN SCHOOL FOR EXPEDITIONARY LEARNING 316J
1700 S Holly St, Denver 303-759-2076

SKYLAND COMMUNITY 254Z
3240 Humboldt St, Denver 303-388-4759

SOUTH 315E
1700 E Louisiana Ave, Denver 720-423-6000

SOUTHWEST EARLY COLLEGE 313U
3001 S Federal Blvd, Denver 303-935-5473

THOMAS JEFFERSON 346A
3950 S Holly St, Denver 720-423-7000

WEST 284K
951 Elati St, Denver 720-423-5300

DOUGLAS COUNTY - DISTRICT RE-1

ACADEMY CHARTER ELEMENTARY 497B
1551 Prairie Hawk Dr, Castle Rock 303-660-4881

ACADEMY CHARTER MIDDLE 497B
1551 Prairie Hawk Dr, Castle Rock 303-660-4881

BUFFALO RIDGE ELEMENTARY 436Q
7075 Shoreham Dr, Castle Rock 303-387-5575

CASTLE ROCK ELEMENTARY 497D
1103 Canyon Dr, Castle Rock 303-387-5000

CASTLE ROCK MIDDLE 466R
2575 Meadows Blvd, Castle Rock 303-387-1300

CASTLE VIEW HIGH 466Q
5254 N Meadows Dr, Castle Rock 303-387-9000

DCS MONTESSORI CHARTER ELEMENTARY 848E
311 E Castle Pines Pkwy, Castle Rock 303-387-5625

DOUGLAS COUNTY HIGH 497C
2842 Front St, Castle Rock 303-387-1000

ELEMENTARY #45 496B
1470 Clear Sky Way, Castle Rock 303-387-5852

FLAGSTONE ELEMENTARY 499J
104 Lovington St, Castle Rock 303-387-5225

MEADOW VIEW ELEMENTARY 466P
3700 Butterfield Crossing Dr, Castle Rock 303-387-5425

MESA MIDDLE 498M
365 Mitchell St, Castle Rock 303-387-1169

OAKES, DANIEL C HIGH 497Q
961 Plum Creek Blvd, Castle Rock 303-387-0650

RENAISSANCE EXPEDITIONARY MAGNET 467U
3960 Trail Boss Ln, Castle Rock 303-387-8000

ROCK RIDGE ELEMENTARY 498L
400 N Heritage Ave, Castle Rock 303-387-5150

SOARING HAWK ELEMENTARY 466X
4665 Tanglevine Dr, Castle Rock 303-387-5825

SOUTH STREET ELEMENTARY 497M
1100 South St, Castle Rock 303-387-5075

TIMBER TRAIL ELEMENTARY 436L
690 W Castle Pines Pkwy, Castle Rock 303-387-5700

CHERRY VALLEY ELEMENTARY 890N
9244 S State Hwy 83, Franktown 303-688-3211

FRANKTOWN ELEMENTARY 869C
1384 N State Hwy 83, Franktown 303-387-5300

ARROWWOOD ELEMENTARY 405L
10345 S Arrowwood Dr, Highlands Ranch 303-387-6875

BEAR CANYON ELEMENTARY 404C
9660 Salford Ln, Highlands Ranch 303-387-6475

COPPER MESA ELEMENTARY 405P
3501 Poston Pkwy, Highlands Ranch 303-387-7375

COUGAR RUN ELEMENTARY 375X
8780 Venneford Ranch Rd, Highlands Ranch 303-387-6675

COYOTE CREEK ELEMENTARY 403M
2861 Baneberry Ct, Highlands Ranch 303-387-6175

CRESTHILL MIDDLE 405D
9195 Cresthill Ln, Highlands Ranch 303-387-2800

EAGLE ACADEMY HIGH @ HIGHLANDS RANCH 405D
9375 Cresthill Ln, Highlands Ranch 303-387-2700

ELDORADO ELEMENTARY 404A
1305 Timbervale Trail, Highlands Ranch 303-387-6325

FOX CREEK ELEMENTARY 406B
6585 Collegiate Dr, Highlands Ranch 303-387-7000

HERITAGE ELEMENTARY 405K
3350 Summit View Pkwy, Highlands Ranch 303-387-6725

HIGHLANDS RANCH HIGH 405D
9375 Cresthill Ln, Highlands Ranch 303-387-2500

MOUNTAIN RIDGE MIDDLE 405J
10590 Mountain Vista Ridge, Highlands Ranch 303-387-1800

MOUNTAIN VISTA HIGH 405J
10585 Mountain Vista Ridge, Highlands Ranch 303-387-1500

NORTHRIDGE ELEMENTARY 374Y
555 Southpark Rd, Highlands Ranch 303-387-6525

PLATTE RIVER ACADEMY ELEMENTARY 375Y
4085 Lark Sparrow St, Highlands Ranch 303-221-1070

PLATTE RIVER ACADEMY MIDDLE 375Y
4085 Lark Sparrow St, Highlands Ranch 303-221-1070

RANCH VIEW MIDDLE 404E
1731 Wildcat Reserve Pkwy, Highlands Ranch 303-387-2300

REDSTONE ELEMENTARY 406E
9970 Glenstone Cir, Highlands Ranch 303-387-7300
ROCK CANYON HIGH 406N
5810 MacArthur Ranch Rd, Highlands Ranch 303-387-3000
ROCKY HEIGHTS MIDDLE SCHOOL 406N
11033 Monarch Blvd, Highlands Ranch 303-387-3300
SADDLE RANCH ELEMENTARY 404F
805 W English Sparrow Trail, Highlands Ranch 303-387-6400
SAND CREEK ELEMENTARY 375S
8898 Maplewood Dr, Highlands Ranch 303-387-6600
STONE MOUNTAIN ELEMENTARY 404K
10635 Weatherfield Way, Highlands Ranch 303-387-2038
SUMMIT VIEW ELEMENTARY 405E
10200 S Piedmont Dr, Highlands Ranch 303-387-6800
THUNDERRIDGE HIGH 404E
1991 Wildcat Reserve Pkwy, Highlands Ranch 303-387-2000
TRAILBLAZER ELEMENTARY 403H
9760 S Hackberrry St, Highlands Ranch 303-387-6250
LARKSPUR ELEMENTARY 887R
1103 W Perry Park Ave, Larkspur 303-387-5375
ACRES GREEN ELEMENTARY 376U
13524 Acres Green Dr, Littleton 303-387-7125
PLUM CREEK ACADEMY ELEMENTARY 373X
8236 Carder Ct, Littleton 303-387-6075
PLUM CREEK ACADEMY HIGH 373X
8236 Carder Ct, Littleton 303-387-6075
PLUM CREEK ACADEMY MIDDLE 373X
8236 Carder Ct, Littleton 303-387-6075
ROXBOROUGH ELEMENTARY 432K
8000 Village Cir W, Littleton 303-387-6000
WILDCAT MOUNTAIN ELEMENTARY 406K
6585 Lionshead Pkwy, Littleton 303-387-6925
AMERICAN ACADEMY CHARTER ELEMENTARY 376V
8600 Park Meadows Dr, Lone Tree 720-873-7395
EAGLE RIDGE ELEMENTARY 376Y
7716 Timberline Rd, Lone Tree 303-387-7075
LONE TREE ELEMENTARY 407E
9375 Heritage Hills Cir, Lone Tree 303-387-0253
CHALLENGE TO EXCELLENCE ELEMENTARY CHARTER 409A
16995 E Carlson Dr, Parker 303-841-9816
CHAPARRAL HIGH 408C
15655 Brookstone Dr, Parker 303-387-3500
CHEROKEE TRAIL ELEMENTARY 409J
17302 Clarke Farms Dr, Parker 303-387-8125
CORE KNOWLEDGE ELEMENTARY 409H
11661 Pine Dr, Parker 303-840-7070
CORE KNOWLEDGE MIDDLE 409H
11661 Pine Dr, Parker 303-840-7070
ELEMENTARY #44 408Z
12021 S Swift Fox Way, Parker 303-387-0708
FRONTIER VALLEY ELEMENTARY 410Z
23919 E Canterberry Trail, Parker 303-387-8475
HIGH SCHOOL #9 440C
22219 Hilltop Rd, Parker 303-387-9798
IRON HORSE ELEMENTARY 409V
20151 Tallman Dr, Parker 303-387-8525
LEGACY POINT ELEMENTARY 439B
12736 S Red Rosa Cir, Parker 303-387-8725
MAMMOTH HEIGHTS ELEMENTARY 408D
9500 Stonegate Pkwy, Parker 303-387-3740
MIDDLE SCHOOL #9 440C
22219 Hilltop Rd, Parker 303-387-0708
MOUNTAIN VIEW ELEMENTARY 440T
8502 E Pinery Pkwy, Parker 303-387-8675
NORTHEAST ELEMENTARY 439R
6598 N State Hwy 83, Parker 303-387-8600
NORTH STAR ACADEMY 408H
16700 Keystone Blvd, Parker 720-851-7827
PINE GROVE ELEMENTARY 408L
10450 Stonegate Pkwy, Parker 303-387-8075
PINE LANE INTERMEDIATE 409C
6485 E Ponderosa Dr, Parker 303-387-8275
PINE LANE PRIMARY 409C
6475 E Ponderosa Dr, Parker 303-387-8325
PIONEER ELEMENTARY 410N
10881 Riva Ridge St, Parker 303-387-8400
PONDEROSA HIGH 469D
7007 E Bayou Gulch Rd, Parker 303-387-4000
PRAIRIE CROSSING ELEMENTARY 408V
11605 S Bradbury Ranch Dr, Parker 303-387-8200
SAGEWOOD MIDDLE 470E
4725 Fox Sparrow Rd, Parker 303-387-4300
SIERRA MIDDLE 379Y
6651 Pine Lane Ave, Parker 303-387-3800
SEDALIA ELEMENTARY 846R
5449 N Huxtable St, Sedalia 303-387-5500

EL PASO COUNTY - LEWIS-PALMER SCHOOL DISTRICT NO. 38

RAY E KILMER ELEMENTARY 909U
4285 Walker Rd, Colorado Springs 719-488-4740
GRACE BEST ELEMENTARY 908W
66 Jefferson St, Monument 719-488-4770
LEWIS-PALMER ELEMENTARY 908T
1315 Lake Woodmoor Dr, Monument 719-488-4750
LEWIS-PALMER HIGH 908X
1300 Higby Rd, Monument 719-488-4720
LEWIS-PALMER MIDDLE 908T
1776 Woodmoor Dr, Monument 719-488-4776
MONUMENT CHARTER ACADEMY ELEMENTARY 908T
1890 Willow Park Way, Monument 719-481-1950
MONUMENT CHARTER ACADEMY JUNIOR/SENIOR HIGH 908T
1808 Woodmoore Dr, Monument 719-481-1950
PRAIRIE WINDS ELEMENTARY 908V
790 E Kings Deer Pt, Monument 719-559-0800
PALMER LAKE ELEMENTARY 907Q
115 Upper Glenway, Palmer Lake 719-488-4760

ELBERT COUNTY - ELBERT 200

ELBERT ELEMENTARY 892N
, Elbert 303-648-3030
ELBERT JUNIOR/SENIOR HIGH 892N
, Elbert 303-648-3030

ELBERT COUNTY - ELIZABETH DISTRICT C-1

ELBERT COUNTY CHARTER ELEMENTARY 871F
823 S Banner St, Elizabeth 303-646-2636
ELBERT COUNTY CHARTER MIDDLE 871F
823 S Banner St, Elizabeth 303-646-2636
ELIZABETH HIGH 871E
34500 County Rd 13, Elizabeth 303-646-4616
ELIZABETH MIDDLE 871E
34427 County Rd 13, Elizabeth 303-646-4520
FRONTIER HIGH 871F
589 S Banner St, Elizabeth 303-646-1798
RUNNING CREEK ELEMENTARY 871F
900 S Elbert St, Elizabeth 303-646-4620
SINGING HILLS ELEMENTARY 850G
41012 Madrid Dr, Parker 303-646-1858

ELBERT COUNTY - KIOWA DISTRICT C-2

KIOWA ELEMENTARY 872M
525 Comanche St, Kiowa 303-621-2042
KIOWA MIDDLE 872M
525 Comanche St, Kiowa 303-621-2785
KIOWA SENIOR 872M
525 Comanche St, Kiowa 303-621-2115

GILPIN COUNTY - DISTRICT RE1

GILPIN COUNTY ELEMENTARY 760U
10595 State Hwy 119, Black Hawk 303-582-3444
GILPIN COUNTY HIGH 760U
10595 State Hwy 119, Black Hawk 303-582-3444
GILPIN COUNTY MIDDLE 760U
10595 State Hwy 119, Black Hawk 303-582-3444
GILPIN COUNTY MONTESSORI ELEMENTARY 760U
10595 State Hwy 119, Black Hawk 303-582-3444
TRIUMPH HIGH 780C
107 Eureka St, Central City 303-582-9975

JEFFERSON COUNTY DISTRICT R-1 ELEMENTARY SCHOOLS

ALLENDALE 251C
5900 Oak St, Arvada 303-982-1165
CAMPBELL 221Y
6500 Oak St, Arvada 303-982-1440
EXCEL ACADEMY 221F
11500 W 84th Ave, Arvada 303-467-2295
FITZMORRIS 221Z
6250 Independence St, Arvada 303-982-1640
FOSTER 252F
5300 Saulsbury Ct, Arvada 303-982-1680
FREMONT 221W
6420 Urban St, Arvada 303-982-1699
HACKBERRY HILL 222P
7300 W 76th Ave, Arvada 303-982-0260
LAWRENCE 252F
5611 Zephyr St, Arvada 303-982-1825
LINCOLN ACADEMY 222U
6980 Pierce St, Arvada 303-467-5363
LITTLE 222C
8448 Otis Dr, Arvada 303-982-0310
MEIKLEJOHN, AL 220H
13405 W 83rd Pl, Arvada 303-982-5695
PARR 222H
5800 W 84th Ave, Arvada 303-982-9890
PECK 222W
6495 Carr St, Arvada 303-982-0590
RUSSELL 252K
5150 Allison St, Arvada 303-982-2145
SECREST 222Y
6875 W 64th Ave, Arvada 303-982-0760
SIERRA 221K
7751 Oak St, Arvada 303-982-0821
STOTT 220Z
6600 Yank Way, Arvada 303-982-2638
SWANSON 222V
6055 W 68th Ave, Arvada 303-982-0891
THOMSON 222M
7750 Harlan St, Arvada 303-982-9935
VAN ARSDALE 220R
7535 Alkire St, Arvada 303-982-1080
VANDERHOOF 251B
5875 Routt Ct, Arvada 303-982-2744
WARDER 222J
7840 Carr Dr, Arvada 303-982-0950
WEBER 222E
8725 W 81st Pl, Arvada 303-982-1012
WEST WOODS 219V
16650 W 72nd Ave, Arvada 303-982-5649
JEFFERSON ACADEMY 192T
9955 Yarrow St, Broomfield 303-438-1011
WEST JEFFERSON 823N
26501 Barkley Rd, Conifer 303-982-2975
EDGEWATER 282D
5570 W 24th Ave, Edgewater 303-982-6050
LUMBERG 282C
6705 W 22nd Ave, Edgewater 303-982-6182
BERGEN MEADOW 305M
1892 Bergen Pkwy, Evergreen 303-982-4890
BERGEN VALLEY 306E
1422 Sugarbush Dr, Evergreen 303-982-4964
MARSHDALE 367F
26663 N Turkey Creek Rd, Evergreen 303-982-5188
ROCKY MOUNTAIN ACADEMY OF EVERGREEN 336A
30616 Bryant Dr, Evergreen 303-670-1070
WILMOT 336P
5124 S Hatch Dr, Evergreen 303-982-5370
COAL CREEK CANYON 762C
11719 Ranch Elsie Rd, Golden 303-982-3409
FAIRMOUNT 250J
15975 W 50th Ave, Golden 303-982-5422
FREE HORIZON MONTESSORI 279V
581 Conference Pl, Golden 303-231-9801
KYFFIN 280U
205 N Flora Way, Golden 303-982-5760
MAPLE GROVE 250Z
3085 Alkire St, Golden 303-982-5808
MITCHELL 248Z
201 Rubey Dr, Golden 303-982-5875
PLEASANT VIEW 280J
15920 W 10th Ave, Golden 303-982-5921
RALSTON 277U
25856 Columbine Glen Rd, Golden 303-982-4386
ROCKY MOUNTAIN DEAF SCHOOL 280H
1921 Youngfield St, Golden 303-984-5749
SHELTON 279P
420 Crawford St, Golden 303-982-5686
WELCHESTER 280M
13000 W 10th Ave, Golden 303-982-7450
PARMALEE 338E
4460 S Parmalee Gulch Rd, Indian Hills 303-982-8014
BEAR CREEK 311Y
3125 S Kipling St, Lakewood 303-982-8714
BELMAR 311D
885 S Garrison St, Lakewood 303-982-8220
BRADY EXPLORATION SCHOOL 312D
5290 W Ohio Ave, Lakewood 303-982-6722
DEANE 282Z
580 S Harlan St, Lakewood 303-982-9655
DENNISON 281V
401 Independence St, Lakewood 303-982-6382
DEVINNY 311J
1725 S Wright St, Lakewood 303-982-9200
EIBER 281M
1385 Independence St, Lakewood 303-982-6406
FOOTHILLS 310D
13165 W Ohio Ave, Lakewood 303-982-9324
GLENNON HEIGHTS 281X
11025 W Glennon Dr, Lakewood 303-982-8240
GREEN GABLES 312J
8701 W Woodard Dr, Lakewood 303-982-8314
GREEN MOUNTAIN 311B
12250 W Kentucky Dr, Lakewood 303-982-9380
HUTCHINSON 310M
12900 W Utah Ave, Lakewood 303-982-9561
JEFFERSON COUNTY OPEN SCHOOL 282K
7655 W 10th Ave, Lakewood 303-982-7045
KENDRICK LAKES 311H
1350 S Hoyt St, Lakewood 303-982-8324
LASLEY 312G
1401 S Kendall St, Lakewood 303-982-9720
MILLER SPECIAL EDUCATION 281U
200 Kipling St, Lakewood 303-982-7200
MOLHOLM 282L
6000 W 9th Ave, Lakewood 303-982-6240
PATTERSON 312E
1263 S Dudley St, Lakewood 303-982-8470
ROONEY RANCH 310R
2200 S Coors St, Lakewood 303-982-9620
SLATER 282A
8605 W 23rd Ave, Lakewood 303-982-7575
SOUTH LAKEWOOD 282S
8425 W 1st Ave, Lakewood 303-982-7325
STEIN 282U
80 S Teller St, Lakewood 303-982-7407
STOBER 281A
2300 Urban St, Lakewood 303-982-7610
VIVIAN 281C
10500 W 25th Ave, Lakewood 303-982-7670
WESTGATE 312S
8550 W Vassar Dr, Lakewood 303-982-9130
BLUE HERON 342V
5987 W Dorado Dr, Littleton 303-982-2770
BRADFORD INTERMEDIATE 370F
2 Woodruff, Littleton 303-982-4882
BRADFORD PRIMARY 370Q
1 White Oak Dr, Littleton 303-982-3480
COLLEGIATE ACADEMY OF COLORADO 371Q
8420 Sangre De Cristo Rd, Littleton 303-972-7433
COLOROW 341Z
6317 S Estes St, Littleton 303-982-5480
COLUMBINE HILLS 372M
6005 W Canyon Ave, Littleton 303-982-5540
CORONADO 372N
7922 S Carr St, Littleton 303-982-3737
DUTCH CREEK 372F
7304 W Roxbury Pl, Littleton 303-982-4565
GOVERNOR'S RANCH 341R
5354 S Field St, Littleton 303-982-4625
LEAWOOD 342Z
6155 W Leawood Dr, Littleton 303-982-7860
MONTESSORI PEAKS ACADEMY 341Y
9904 W Capri Ave, Littleton 303-948-5991
MORTENSEN 371R
8006 S Iris Way, Littleton 303-982-0022
MT CARBON 340V
12776 W Cross Ave, Littleton 303-982-7900
NORMANDY 372D
6750 S Kendall Blvd, Littleton 303-982-4766
PEIFFER 341L
4997 S Miller Way, Littleton 303-982-4800
POWDERHORN 341W
12109 W Coal Mine Ave, Littleton 303-982-0074
SHAFFER 371Q
7961 S Sangre de Cristo Rd, Littleton 303-982-3901

STONY CREEK 372E
7203 S Everett St, Littleton 303-982-4120
UTE MEADOWS 371F
11050 W Meadows Dr, Littleton 303-982-4044
WESTRIDGE 341U
10785 W Alamo Pl, Littleton 303-982-3975
KENDALLVUE 340M
13658 W Marlowe Ave, Morrison 303-982-7990
RED ROCKS 309Y
17199 State Hwy 74, Morrison 303-982-8063
ELK CREEK 842F
13304 S US Hwy 285, Pine 303-982-2900
ADAMS 192Y
6450 W 95th Pl, Westminster 303-982-9790
LUKAS 191V
9650 W 97th Ave, Westminster 303-982-0368
RYAN 192D
5851 W 115th Ave, Westminster 303-982-3105
SEMPER 192T
7575 W 96th Ave, Westminster 303-982-6460
SHERIDAN GREEN 192G
10951 Harlan St, Westminster 303-982-3182
WITT 191Q
10255 W 104th Dr, Westminster 303-982-3380
WOODROW WILSON ACADEMY 192W
8300 W 94th Ave, Westminster 303-431-3694
ZERGER 191Z
9050 Field St, Westminster 303-982-1075
COMPASS MONTESSORI 251Q
10399 W 44th Ave, Wheat Ridge 303-420-8288
KULLERSTRAND 251S
12225 W 38th Ave, Wheat Ridge 303-982-1780
MARTENSEN 252Q
6625 W 45th Pl, Wheat Ridge 303-982-1870
PENNINGTON 251Q
4645 Independence St, Wheat Ridge 303-982-2083
PROSPECT VALLEY 251X
3400 Pierson St, Wheat Ridge 303-982-7535
STEVENS 252T
4001 Reed St, Wheat Ridge 303-982-2198
WILMORE-DAVIS 252N
7975 W 41st Ave, Wheat Ridge 303-982-2890

JEFFERSON COUNTY DISTRICT R-1 MIDDLE/JUNIOR HIGH SCHOOLS

ARVADA 252A
5751 Balsam St, Arvada 303-982-1240
BEAR CREEK 311Y
3125 S Kipling St, Arvada 303-982-8714
DRAKE 251J
12550 W 52nd Ave, Arvada 303-982-1510
EXCEL ACADEMY 221F
11500 W 84th Ave, Arvada 303-467-2295
MOORE 222A
8455 W 88th Ave, Arvada 303-982-0400
NORTH ARVADA 222Q
7285 Pierce St, Arvada 303-982-0528
OBERON 221P
7300 Quail St, Arvada 303-982-2020
JEFFERSON ACADEMY 192T
9955 Yarrow St, Broomfield 720-887-1992
WEST JEFFERSON 823N
9449 S Barnes Ave, Conifer 303-982-3056
D'EVELYN 341C
10359 W Nassau Ave, Denver 303-982-2600
EVERGREEN 305R
2059 Hiwan Dr, Evergreen 303-982-5020
ROCKY MOUNTAIN ACADEMY OF EVERGREEN 336A
30616 Bryant Dr, Evergreen 303-670-1070
BELL 279L
1001 Ulysses St, Golden 303-982-4280
MANNING SCHOOL, THE 250Z
13200 W 32nd Ave, Golden 303-982-6340
ROCKY MOUNTAIN DEAF SCHOOL 280H
1921 Youngfield St, Golden 303-984-5749
BRADY EXPLORATION SCHOOL 312D
5290 W Ohio Ave, Lakewood 303-982-6722
CARMODY 311L
2050 S Kipling St, Lakewood 303-982-8930
CREIGHTON 281V
75 Independence St, Lakewood 303-982-6282
DUNSTAN 311J
1855 S Wright St, Lakewood 303-982-9270
JEFFERSON COUNTY OPEN SCHOOL 282K
7655 W 10th Ave, Lakewood 303-982-7045
MILLER SPECIAL EDUCATION 281U
200 Kipling St, Lakewood 303-982-7200
O'CONNELL 312F
1275 S Teller Pl, Lakewood 303-982-8370
COLLEGIATE ACADEMY OF COLORADO 371Q
8420 Sangre De Cristo Rd, Littleton 303-972-7433
DEER CREEK 371H
9201 W Columbine Dr, Littleton 303-982-3820
FALCON BLUFFS 371V
8449 S Garrison St, Littleton 303-982-9900
KEN CARYL 372L
6509 W Ken Caryl Ave, Littleton 303-982-4710
SUMMIT RIDGE 341X
11809 W Coal Mine Ave, Littleton 303-982-9013
CARLE, WAYNE 191U
10200 W 100th Ave, Westminster 303-982-9070
MANDALAY 192T
9651 Pierce St, Westminster 303-982-9802
EVERITT 251V
3900 Kipling St, Wheat Ridge 303-982-1580
WHEAT RIDGE 252T
7101 W 38th Ave, Wheat Ridge 303-982-2833

JEFFERSON COUNTY DISTRICT R-1 SENIOR HIGH SCHOOLS

ARVADA 222X
7951 W 65th Ave, Arvada 303-982-0162
ARVADA WEST 251B
11325 Allendale Dr, Arvada 303-982-1303
BEAR CREEK 311Z
3490 S Kipling St, Arvada 303-982-8855
POMONA 222E
8101 W Pomona Dr, Arvada 303-982-0710
RALSTON VALLEY 220L
13355 W 80th Ave, Arvada 303-982-5600
JEFFERSON ACADEMY 192T
9955 Yarrow St, Broomfield 720-887-1992
CONIFER 822V
10441 County Rd 73, Conifer 303-982-5255
D'EVELYN 341C
10359 W Nassau Ave, Denver 303-982-2600
JEFFERSON 282C
2305 Pierce St, Edgewater 303-982-6056
EVERGREEN 336Q
29300 Buffalo Park Rd, Evergreen 303-982-5140
COMPASS MONTESSORI 249R
4441 Salvia St, Golden 303-271-1977
GOLDEN 279F
701 24th St, Golden 303-982-4200
MILLER SPECIAL EDUCATION 281U
200 Kipling St, Indian Hills 303-982-7200
ALAMEDA 312F
1255 S Wadsworth Blvd, Lakewood 303-982-8160
BRADY EXPLORATION SCHOOL 312D
5290 W Ohio Ave, Lakewood 303-982-6722
GREEN MOUNTAIN 310H
13175 W Green Mtn Dr, Lakewood 303-982-9500
JEFFERSON COUNTY OPEN SCHOOL 282K
7655 W 10th Ave, Lakewood 303-982-7045
LAKEWOOD 281R
9700 W 8th Ave, Lakewood 303-982-7096
LONG VIEW 280V
13301 W 2nd Pl, Lakewood 303-982-8523
McCLAIN COMMUNITY SCHOOL 280V
13600 W 2nd Pl, Lakewood 303-982-7460
WARREN TECH SCHOOL 280V
13300 W 2nd Pl, Lakewood 303-982-8600
CHATFIELD 371E
7227 S Simms St, Littleton 303-982-3670
COLLEGIATE ACADEMY OF COLORADO 371Q
8420 Sangre De Cristo Rd, Littleton 303-972-7433
COLUMBINE 342Y
6201 S Pierce St, Littleton 303-982-4400
DAKOTA RIDGE 340Z
13399 W Coal Mine Ave, Littleton 303-982-1970
STANDLEY LAKE 191R
9300 W 104th Ave, Westminster 303-982-3311
WHEAT RIDGE 251Z
9505 W 32nd Ave, Wheat Ridge 303-982-7695

PARK COUNTY - PLATTE CANYON DISTRICT 1

DEER CREEK ELEMENTARY 841J
1737 Deer Creek Rd, Fairplay 303-838-7666
FITZSIMMONS MIDDLE 840U
57093 US Hwy 285, Fairplay 303-838-2054
PLATTE CANYON HIGH 840U
57393 US Hwy 285, Fairplay 303-838-4642

WELD COUNTY - FT. LUPTON DISTRICT RE-8

BUTLER, LEO WM ELEMENTARY 728L
411 S McKinley Ave, Ft. Lupton 303-857-7300
FORT LUPTON HIGH 728L
530 Reynolds St, Ft. Lupton 303-857-7100
FORT LUPTON MIDDLE 728L
201 S McKinley Ave, Ft. Lupton 303-857-7200
TWOMBLY PRIMARY ELEMENTARY 728H
1600 9th St, Ft. Lupton 303-857-7400

WELD COUNTY - GILCREST DISTRICT RE-1

PLATTEVILLE ELEMENTARY 708G
1202 Main St, Platteville 970-785-2271
SOUTH VALLEY MIDDLE 708C
1004 Main St, Platteville 970-785-2205

WELD COUNTY - KEENESBURG DISTRICT RE-3(J)

HUDSON ELEMENTARY 730L
300 Beech St, Hudson 303-536-2200
CARDINAL COMMUNITY ACADEMY CHARTER SCHOOL 732D
3101 Weld County Rd 65, Keenesburg 303-732-9312
HOFF ELEMENTARY 732A
7558 Weld County Rd 59, Keenesburg 303-536-2300
WELD CENTRAL JUNIOR HIGH 732J
4977 Weld County Rd 59, Keenesburg 303-536-2100
WELD CENTRAL SENIOR HIGH 732J
4715 Weld County Rd 59, Keenesburg 303-536-2100
WELD COUNTY ALTERNATIVE EDUCATION CENTER 732A
95 W Broadway St, Keenesburg 303-536-2000
LOCHBUIE ELEMENTARY 140G
201 Bonanza Blvd, Lochbuie 303-536-2400

Shopping Centers and Malls

16TH ST MALL 284F
ALAMEDA CROSSING 282Z
ALAMEDA SQUARE 283Z
APPLEWOOD VILLAGE 251W
ARAPAHOE CROSSING 378D
ARAPAHOE EAST SHOPPES 377A
ARAPAHOE MARKETPLACE 376D
ARAPAHOE VILLAGE SHOPPING CENTER 128A
ARLINGTON SHOPPING CENTER 223W
ARVADA MARKETPLACE 252K
ARVADA PLAZA 251D
ARVADA SQUARE 251D
ASPEN GROVE SHOPPING CENTER 373G
ATHMAR PARK 313D
AURORA CITY PLACE 288T
AURORA PLAZA 318C
BASE MAR SHOPPING CENTER 128J
BEAR VALLEY 313W
BELCARO 315C
BELLEVIEW SHORES SHOPPING CENTER 342N
BELLEVIEW SQUARE 346M
BELL TOWER PLAZA 282G
BELMAR 282X
BOULEVARD 315G
BOWLES CROSSING 342S
BOWLES VILLAGE SHOPPING CENTER 342T
BRENTCROSS SHOPS 192X
BRENTWOOD PLAZA 313L
BRIGHTON PAVILIONS 138N
BROADRIDGE 374F
BROADWAY 344Q
BROADWAY MARKETPLACE 284X
BROOMFIELD PLAZA 163W
BROOMFIELD TOWN CENTRE 162Z
CENTENNIAL CENTER SHOPPING CENTER 160B
CENTENNIAL PROMENADE 377N
CENTENNIAL SQUARE 343Q
CENTENNIAL SQUARE 11S
CHANSON PLAZA SHOPPING CENTER 342W
CHERRY CREEK 285T
CHERRY CREEK NORTH 285S
CHERRY CREST SHOPETTE 345S
CHERRY HILLS MARKETPLACE 345W
CITYCENTER ENGLEWOOD 314X
COAL CREEK VILLAGE 132N
COLORADO MILLS MALL 280L
COLUMBINE SQUARE 343Q
COLUMBINE VALLEY 343T
COTTONWOOD SQUARE 70K
COUNTRYSIDE VILLAGE 132N
CUB SQUARE 222H
DACONO GATEWAY CENTRE 726M
DENVER DESIGN CENTER 284X
DENVER PAVILIONS 284F
DENVER WEST VILLAGE 280L
DRY CREEK 344C
EAST BANK 348E
EDGEWATER MARKETPLACE 282H
FAIRFIELD COMMONS 282T
FEDERAL HEIGHTS PLAZA 193Q
FESTIVAL 375N
FLATIRON CROSSING 161N
FLATIRON MARKETPLACE 161T
FOOTHILLS 310D
FOXRIDGE PLAZA 376N
FRANCIS STREET SHOPPING CENTER 11Y
FURNITURE ROW SHOPPING CENTER 726V
GOVERNOR'S PLAZA 341R
GREEN MOUNTAIN MARKET SQUARE 281W
GREENWOOD PLAZA 376C
GUNBARREL 69Y
HAPPY CANYON 315Z
HERITAGE PLAZA 376C
HERITAGE WEST 311K
HIGHLANDS RANCH TOWN CENTER 404B
HILLCREST PLAZA 194N
HOFFMAN HEIGHTS 287Q
HORIZON PARK 11R
HURON PLAZA 224F
KIPLING MARKETPLACE 341Q
KIPLING PLACE 341U
LAKE ARBOR 222K
LAKESIDE MALL 252R
LAKEWOOD COMMONS SHOPPING CENTER 282X
LARKRIDGE 134L
LARKRIDGE SOUTH 134L
LITTLETON SQUARE 344T
LLOYD KING SHOPPING CENTER 223W
LOCHWOOD SQUARE 311F
LOWRY TOWN CENTER 286T
MAIN STREET MARKETPLACE 11V
MALLEY HEIGHTS 194G
MANDALAY TOWN CENTER 192K
MARINA SQUARE 346L
MARKET AT SOUTHPARK, THE 374P
MARKETPLACE @ NORTHGLENN 194K
MARKETPLACE COURTYARD 317T
MARKET SQUARE 312K
MAYFAIR 286J
MEADOWLAKE VILLAGE SHOPPING CENTER 221W
MEADOWS MARKET PLACE 376V
MEADOWS SHOPPING CENTER 371D
MEADOWS SHOPPING CENTER 128M
MISSION COMMONS 222B
MISSION TRACE 165X
MISSION TRACE 312X
MONTVIEW 287A
NORTHFIELD STAPLETON 256L
NORTH HOVER CENTRE 11S
NORTHLANDS 134G
NORTH PARK SHOPPING CENTER 222X
NORTHRIDGE CENTER 222K
NORTHWEST PLAZA 192Y
OAKBROOK SQUARE 374Q
ORCHARD TOWN CENTER 164B
OUTLETS AT CASTLE ROCK, THE 467N
PARKER MARKET PLACE 409C
PARK MEADOWS 377S

Transportation - RTD

This index is for the Denver Tech Center
Front Section Page IX

Commercial

Hotels and Motels

Other

This index is for the Denver Central Area
Front Section Page VIII

Hotels and Motels

Points of Interest

This index is for Inverness
Front Section Page X

Commercial

Hotels and Motels

Other

Retail

Interstate Highways

STREET NAME	CITY or COUNTY	MAP GRID	ZIP CODE	BLOCK RANGE	O/E
IH 25	Adams Co	224Y	80216	None	
	Adams Co	224Y	80221	None	
	Adams Co	224Y	80229	None	
	Broomfield	134C	80516	None	
	Broomfield	134T	80020	None	
	Broomfield	726Z	80516	None	
	Castle Rock	467P	80104	None	
	Castle Rock	467P	80109	None	
	Centennial	377J	80112	None	
	Dacono	726Z	80514	None	
	Denver	254K	80216	None	
	Denver	254T	80211	None	
	Denver	283D	80211	None	
	Denver	283M	80204	None	
	Denver	284S	80223	None	
	Denver	314B	80223	None	
	Denver	315K	80210	None	
	Denver	316S	80222	None	
	Denver	346A	80237	None	
	Douglas Co	407K	80108	None	
	Douglas Co	467E	80108	None	
	Douglas Co	467P	80104	None	
	Douglas Co	467P	80109	None	
	Douglas Co	497T	80104	None	
	Douglas Co	497T	80109	None	
	Douglas Co	527A	80104	None	
	Douglas Co	527A	80109	None	
	Douglas Co	867V	80118	None	
	Douglas Co	867V	80109	3600S-4599S	
See.. US HWY 85 & 87					
	Douglas Co	887H	80118	4600S-7999S	
	Douglas Co	888N	80118	8000S-12499S	
	Douglas Co	908F	80118	14000S-15999S	
	El Paso Co	908N	80132	None	
	Frederick	726Z	80530	None	
	Greenwood Village	346A	80111	None	
	Greenwood Village	376D	80111	None	
	Greenwood Village	376D	80112	None	
	Lone Tree	377X	80112	None	
	Lone Tree	407K	80108	None	
	Lone Tree	407K	80112	None	
	Lone Tree	407K	80134	None	
	Northglenn	194F	80233	None	
	Northglenn	194F	80234	None	
	Thornton	164F	80020	None	
	Thornton	164F	80241	None	
	Thornton	195Q	80229	None	
	Thornton	224C	80229	None	
	Weld Co	726Z	80514	None	
	Weld Co	726Z	80530	None	
	Westminster	164F	80234	None	
IH 70	Adams Co	290G	80011	None	
	Adams Co	291F	80019	None	
	Adams Co	291F	80137	None	
	Arapahoe Co	791Q	80137	None	
	Arapahoe Co	792R	80102	None	
	Arapahoe Co	793V	80102	None	
	Arapahoe Co	793V	80136	None	
	Arapahoe Co	794U	80136	None	
	Arapahoe Co	795S	80103	None	
	Arapahoe Co	795S	80136	None	
	Aurora	258T	80011	None	
	Aurora	259W	80011	None	
	Aurora	290A	80011	None	
	Clear Creek Co	275S	80439	None	
	Clear Creek Co	780P	80452	None	
	Clear Creek Co	781U	80439	None	
	Denver	253L	80221	None	
	Denver	254P	80216	None	
	Denver	254R	80216	None	
	Denver	255P	80216	None	
	Denver	256P	80216	None	
	Denver	257P	80239	None	
	Golden	279V	80401	None	
	Idaho Springs	780P	80452	None	
	Jefferson Co	275U	80439	None	
	Jefferson Co	276W	80439	None	
	Jefferson Co	277S	80401	None	
	Jefferson Co	308A	80439	None	
	Jefferson Co	309F	80401	None	
	Lakewood	280G	80401	None	
	Wheat Ridge	250V	80401	None	
	Wheat Ridge	251K	80033	None	
	Wheat Ridge	252J	80033	None	
	Wheat Ridge	252L	80033	None	
IH 70 FRONTAGE RD	Wheat Ridge	252J	80002	7800N-8999N	
	Wheat Ridge	251M	80002	9000N-9199N	
IH 70 SERVICE RD	Wheat Ridge	251K	80033	10000N-11799N	
	Wheat Ridge	251K	80033	9800S-11799S	
IH 76	Adams Co	196Q	80640	None	
	Adams Co	198E	80603	None	
	Adams Co	224X	80221	None	
	Adams Co	225L	80022	None	
	Adams Co	225T	80229	None	
	Adams Co	226A	80640	None	
	Adams Co	253F	80221	None	
	Brighton	168R	80603	None	
	Brighton	169J	80603	None	
	Commerce City	197L	80601	None	
	Commerce City	197L	80603	None	
See.. US HWY 6					
	Jefferson Co	252H	80002	None	
	Weld Co	140D	80603	None	
	Weld Co	730T	80642	None	
	Weld Co	731B	80642	None	
IH 76 ACCESS RD	Weld Co	730M	80642	22300-23799	
	Weld Co	731C	80643	None	
	Weld Co	731C	80642	None	
IH 225	Arapahoe Co	317X	80014	None	
	Arapahoe Co	347B	80111	None	
	Aurora	258W	80011	None	
	Aurora	288K	80011	None	
	Aurora	318J	80012	None	
	Aurora	318J	80014	None	
	Denver	346H	80237	None	
	Greenwood Village	347B	80111	None	

STREET NAME	CITY or COUNTY	MAP GRID	ZIP CODE	BLOCK RANGE	O/E
IH 270	Adams Co	224R	80229	None	
	Commerce City	225X	80022	None	
	Commerce City	255H	80022	None	
	Commerce City	256K	80022	None	

Toll Roads

STREET NAME	CITY or COUNTY	MAP GRID	ZIP CODE	BLOCK RANGE	O/E
E 470	Adams Co	135T	80602	None	
	Adams Co	166B	80602	None	
	Adams Co	167F	80601	None	
	Adams Co	260Q	80019	None	
	Adams Co	769Q	80022	None	
	Adams Co	769Z	80019	None	
	Arapahoe Co	290L	80018	None	
	Arapahoe Co	320Q	80018	None	
	Arapahoe Co	350V	80015	None	
	Aurora	260Q	80019	None	
	Aurora	290L	80018	None	
	Aurora	290L	80019	None	
	Aurora	320Q	80018	None	
	Aurora	350C	80018	None	
	Aurora	350V	80016	None	
	Aurora	379W	80016	None	
	Aurora	379W	80138	None	
	Aurora	380L	80016	None	
	Brighton	168T	80601	None	
	Commerce City	169W	80603	None	
	Commerce City	769F	80022	None	
	Denver	769Q	80249	None	
	Douglas Co	377Y	80112	None	
	Douglas Co	378T	80134	None	
	Douglas Co	379W	80134	None	
	Parker	379W	80134	None	
	Parker	379W	80138	None	
	Thornton	134V	80020	None	
	Thornton	136W	80602	None	
NORTHWEST PKWY	Boulder Co	162B	80020	None	
	Broomfield	132Y	80026	None	
	Broomfield	133Q	80020	None	
	Broomfield	134N	80020	None	
	Broomfield	161F	80020	None	
	Louisville	161F	80020	None	

U.S. Highways

STREET NAME	CITY or COUNTY	MAP GRID	ZIP CODE	BLOCK RANGE	O/E
US HWY 6	Adams Co	196U	80640	None	
	Adams Co	225M	80022	None	
	Adams Co	226A	80640	None	
	Brighton	168U	80603	None	
	Brighton	169F	80601	None	
	Clear Creek Co	781V	80439	None	
	Commerce City	197K	80601	None	
	Commerce City	197K	80603	None	
	Commerce City	225V	80022	None	
See.. DAHLIA ST					
	Denver	255K	80216	None	
	Denver	283R	80204	None	
	Golden	279E	80401	None	
	Jefferson Co	275K	80403	None	
	Jefferson Co	276G	80403	None	
	Jefferson Co	277G	80403	None	
	Jefferson Co	278F	80403	None	
	Lakewood	281N	80401	None	
	Lakewood	282N	80215	None	
See.. W 6TH AVE					
	Weld Co	140H	80603	None	
	Weld Co	730W	80642	None	
	Adams Co	224P	80221	None	
	Adams Co	290F	80019	None	
	Adams Co	291G	80019	None	
	Adams Co	291G	80137	None	
	Adams Co	795R	80103	None	
	Arapahoe Co	791Q	80137	None	
	Arapahoe Co	792R	80102	None	
	Arapahoe Co	794U	80136	None	
	Arapahoe Co	795T	80103	None	
	Arapahoe Co	795T	80136	None	
	Aurora	258T	80011	None	
	Aurora	259X	80011	None	
See.. IH 70					
	Aurora	289D	80011	None	
	Aurora	290E	80019	None	
	Boulder	128B	80301	None	
	Boulder	128K	80305	None	
	Boulder Co	129S	80303	None	
	Boulder Co	160M	80027	None	
	Boulder Co	703P	80503	None	
See.. N FOOTHILLS HWY					
	Boulder Co	723K	80302	None	
	Boulder Co	97H	80301	None	
	Boulder Co	98E	80301	None	
	Broomfield	161P	80020	None	
	Denver	256P	80238	None	
	Denver	257Q	80239	None	
	Jefferson Co	192B	80020	None	
	Jefferson Co	192L	80020	None	
	Westminster	192L	80020	None	
	Westminster	223E	80031	None	
US HWY 40	Adams Co	290E	80019	None	
	Adams Co	291F	80019	None	
	Adams Co	291F	80137	None	
	Adams Co	792J	80102	None	
	Arapahoe Co	791Q	80137	None	
	Arapahoe Co	792R	80102	None	
	Arapahoe Co	793V	80136	None	
	Arapahoe Co	794U	80136	None	
	Arapahoe Co	795T	80103	None	
	Arapahoe Co	795T	80136	None	
	Aurora	288E	80011	None	
See.. E COLFAX AVE					
	Aurora	290E	80011	None	
	Clear Creek Co	781Q	80439	None	
	Denver	283G	80204	None	
See.. COLFAX AVE					
	Denver	285G	80220	None	
	Jefferson Co	279Y	80401	18200-18299	

Continued on next column

STREET NAME	CITY or COUNTY	MAP GRID	ZIP CODE	BLOCK RANGE	O/E
US HWY 40 (Cont'd)	Jefferson Co	309B	80401	18300-19999	
	Jefferson Co	277Z	80401	22500-25699	
	Jefferson Co	275S	80439	32000-34999	
	Jefferson Co	276S	80401	None	
	Jefferson Co	278W	80401	None	
	Lakewood	280L	80401	None	
See.. COLFAX AVE					
	Lakewood	282E	80215	None	
See.. W COLFAX AVE					
US HWY 85	Adams Co	167H	80601	None	
	Adams Co	196U	80640	None	
	Adams Co	225M	80022	None	
See.. BRIGHTON BLVD					
	Adams Co	226A	80640	None	
	Brighton	138N	80601	12200-12299	
	Brighton	168A	80601	None	
	Castle Rock	467N	80108	None	
	Castle Rock	467N	80109	None	
	Commerce City	197E	80640	None	
	Commerce City	225V	80022	None	
See.. DAHLIA ST					
	Denver	314K	80223	None	
See.. S SANTA FE DR					
	Douglas Co	466L	80109	2800-3299	
	Douglas Co	466L	80108	3600-4399	
	Douglas Co	403G	80125	9900-13499	
See.. S SANTA FE DR					
	Douglas Co	404W	80125	None	
	Douglas Co	527B	80104	None	
	Douglas Co	527B	80109	None	
	Douglas Co	867Z	80109	None	
See.. IH 25					
	Douglas Co	867Z	80118	None	
	Douglas Co	466L	80135	4000N-4799N	
	Douglas Co	847N	80135	5000N-5699N	
	Douglas Co	846H	80135	5800N-8099N	
	Douglas Co	846H	80125	7500N-8299N	
	Douglas Co	846H	80125	8300N-9099N	
	El Paso Co	908N	80132	None	
	Englewood	344J	80110	None	
	Fort Lupton	728Q	80621	None	
	Littleton	373D	80120	6300-8299	
	Littleton	344J	80110	None	
	Platteville	708G	80651	None	
	Sheridan	344J	80110	None	
	Weld Co	138B	80603	1-1499	
	Weld Co	728Y	80603	1500-1999	
	Weld Co	728Q	80621	2000-8399	
	Weld Co	708Y	80621	8400-11999	
	Weld Co	708G	80651	12000-13799	
US HWY 285	Denver	313X	80236	None	
See.. W HAMPDEN AVE					
	Denver	315Z	80222	None	
See.. E HAMPDEN AVE					
	Jefferson Co	368U	80465	5900-6199	
	Jefferson Co	369E	80465	6200-6499	
	Jefferson Co	823W	80433	6500-10399	
	Jefferson Co	822Z	80433	10400-11999	
	Jefferson Co	842C	80433	12000-12999	
	Jefferson Co	842C	80470	13000-34699	
	Jefferson Co	340G	80465	None	
	Jefferson Co	339N	80465	None	
	Lakewood	341B	80227	None	
	Lakewood	311Y	80227	None	
	Park Co	840U	80421	None	
	Park Co	841L	80421	None	
	Sheridan	314W	80110	None	
See.. W HAMPDEN AVE					
US HWY 287	Adams Co	223G	80221	None	
See.. FEDERAL BLVD					
	Adams Co	290E	80019	None	
	Adams Co	291F	80019	None	
	Adams Co	291F	80137	None	
	Arapahoe Co	791Q	80137	None	
	Arapahoe Co	792R	80102	None	
	Arapahoe Co	793V	80136	None	
	Aurora	288E	80011	None	
See.. E COLFAX AVE					
	Aurora	290E	80011	None	
	Boulder Co	101V	80026	1600-5299	
See.. N 107TH ST					
	Boulder Co	71Z	80026	5300-5399	
	Boulder Co	71H	80504	5400-8099	
	Boulder Co	41Z	80501	8200-8999	
	Boulder Co	11H	80504	12600-13999	
	Broomfield	162X	80020	400-999	
	Broomfield	162N	80020	1000-7699	
	Broomfield	163W	80020	None	
See.. W 120TH AVE					
	Denver	253L	80221	None	
See.. FEDERAL BLVD					
	Denver	283C	80211	None	
	Denver	285G	80220	None	
See.. COLFAX AVE					
	Federal Heights	223G	80260	None	
See.. FEDERAL BLVD					
	Lafayette	132W	80026	200-399	
	Lafayette	131R	80026	400-598	E
See.. 107TH ST					
	Longmont	11V	80501	None	
See.. MAIN ST					
	Longmont	41M	80501	None	
	Westminster	193C	80234	9000-11999	
See.. FEDERAL BLVD					
	Westminster	223G	80030	None	
	Westminster	223G	80260	None	

State Highways

STREET NAME	CITY or COUNTY	MAP GRID	ZIP CODE	BLOCK RANGE	O/E
STATE HWY 1	Boulder Co	71H	80026	5300-5399	
See.. N 107TH					
	Boulder Co	71H	80504	5400-8099	
	Boulder Co	11D	80504	None	
See.. US HWY 287					
STATE HWY 2	Adams Co	226G	80022	7700-9399	
	Adams Co	138X	80601	None	
See.. SABLE BLVD					

Continued on next page

STREET NAME	CITY or COUNTY	MAP GRID	ZIP CODE	BLOCK RANGE O/E
STATE HWY 2 (Cont'd)	Adams Co	168F	80601	None
	Brighton	197M	80601	None
	Commerce City	225V	80022	6400-6799
	Commerce City	226S	80022	6800-7699
	Commerce City	197M	80022	9400-10799
	Commerce City	197M	80603	10400-11499
	Commerce City	198E	80603	None
STATE HWY 2	Commerce City	225V	80022	None
	Denver	255Q	80216	None
See.. COLORADO BLVD				
	Denver	285Q	80206	None
	Denver	315Q	80222	None
STATE HWY 7	Adams Co	135N	80602	None
	Adams Co	137Q	80602	None
	Adams Co	138N	80601	None
See.. E 160TH AVE				
	Boulder	128A	80302	None
See.. CANYON BLVD				
	Boulder	128C	80303	None
	Boulder	129A	80303	None
See.. ARAPAHOE RD				
	Boulder	97L	80304	None
	Boulder Co	130A	80303	None
	Boulder Co	703E	80540	None
See.. S ST VRAIN DR				
	Brighton	138N	80601	None
See.. BRIDGE ST				
	Brighton	139P	80601	None
	Erie	133H	80516	1600-1799
	Lafayette	131B	80026	None
See.. ARAPAHOE RD				
	Lafayette	131H	80026	None
See.. 107TH ST				
	Lafayette	131M	80026	None
See.. BASELINE RD				
	Lafayette	132L	80026	None
	Thornton	134M	80602	None
	Thornton	136P	80602	None
	Weld Co	134E	80020	None
STATE HWY 8	Lakewood	310X	80228	None
See.. MORRISON RD				
	Lakewood	311R	80227	None
	Morrison	339D	80465	300-19299
STATE HWY 21	Jefferson Co	306F	80439	None
See.. EVERGREEN PKWY				
STATE HWY 22	Brighton	167U	80640	None
	Brighton	167V	80601	None
	Brighton	168S	80601	None
STATE HWY 30	Arapahoe Co	315X	80110	None
See.. E HAMPDEN AVE				
	Arapahoe Co	320Z	80018	None
	Arapahoe Co	350D	80018	None
See.. S GUN CLUB RD				
	Aurora	290X	80018	19300-20999
See.. E 6TH AVE				
	Aurora	320G	80018	None
	Aurora	287T	80010	None
See.. HAVANA ST				
	Aurora	289R	80018	None
	Aurora	317P	80014	None
	Denver	316Z	80231	None
See.. E HAMPDEN AVE				
	Denver	317W	80231	None
STATE HWY 33	Denver	255S	80205	None
See.. E 40TH AVE				
STATE HWY 35	Adams Co	791P	80137	None
STATE HWY 36	Adams Co	792M	80102	39300-52099
STATE HWY 36	Adams Co	793P	80102	None
	Adams Co	794Q	80136	None
	Arapahoe Co	794Q	80136	None
STATE HWY 40	Arapahoe Co	795S	80136	None
	Arapahoe Co	795Y	80103	None
STATE HWY 42	Lafayette	131E	80026	None
See.. 95TH ST				
	Louisville	131K	80027	None
See.. COURTESY RD				
	Louisville	131Y	80026	None
STATE HWY 44	Commerce City	197P	80603	None
See.. E 104TH AVE				
	Commerce City	197P	80640	None
	Northglenn	194N	80234	None
See.. E 104TH AVE				
	Thornton	195Q	80229	None
See.. E 104TH AVE				
STATE HWY 46	Boulder Co	760V	80403	None
	Gilpin Co	761V	80403	None
	Gilpin Co	761T	80403	None
See.. GOLDEN GATE CANYON RD				
STATE HWY 52	Boulder Co	70T	80503	7400-9099
See.. MINERAL RD				
	Boulder Co	71P	80503	9100-9499
	Boulder Co	71P	80504	9500-10999
	Boulder Co	72Q	80504	11100-12699
	Dacono	727G	80514	None
	Frederick	727G	80516	None
	Frederick	727G	80530	None
	Weld Co	72R	80516	1-199
See.. MINERAL RD				
	Weld Co	726G	80516	None
	Weld Co	727G	80516	None
	Weld Co	727G	80530	None
	Weld Co	727G	80621	None
	Weld Co	728K	80621	None
	Weld Co	730J	80621	None
	Weld Co	730J	80642	None
	Weld Co	731K	80643	None
STATE HWY 53	Adams Co	254C	80221	None
STATE HWY 53	Adams Co	224U	80221	None
STATE HWY 58	Jefferson Co	249V	80403	None
	Jefferson Co	250Q	80403	None
STATE HWY 66	Boulder Co	703C	80540	None
	Boulder Co	704E	80503	None
	Boulder Co	10L	80503	None
See.. UTE HWY				
	Boulder Co	11L	80504	None
	Boulder Co	12L	80504	None
	Mead	706G	80504	2600-4799
See.. COUNTY RD 30				

Continued on next column

STREET NAME	CITY or COUNTY	MAP GRID	ZIP CODE	BLOCK RANGE O/E
STATE HWY 66 (Cont'd)	Weld Co	706G	80504	100-2599
See.. COUNTY RD 30				
	Weld Co	707F	80504	4800-5999
	Weld Co	707F	80651	6000-9499
	Weld Co	708F	80651	9500-11199
STATE HWY 67	Douglas Co	866A	80135	2300N-3599N
	Douglas Co	846V	80135	3600N-5299N
STATE HWY 72	Arvada	220E	80007	14800-16399
	Arvada	219C	80007	16400-17999
	Arvada	763M	80007	20000-21999
See.. COAL CREEK CANYON RD				
	Arvada	763L	80403	22000-24798 E
	Arvada	763F	80403	24800-25399
	Arvada	763E	80403	25400-26598 E
	Boulder Co	720Q	80481	None
See.. PEAK TO PEAK HWY				
	Boulder Co	740V	80403	None
See.. COAL CREEK CANYON RD				
	Boulder Co	742W	80403	None
	Gilpin Co	741T	80403	None
See.. COAL CREEK CANYON DR				
	Gilpin Co	741Z	80403	None
	Jefferson Co	189Y	80007	18000-21999
	Jefferson Co	763L	80403	22001-24799 O
See.. COAL CREEK CANYON RD				
	Jefferson Co	763F	80403	25401-26599 O
	Jefferson Co	763E	80403	26600-27799
	Jefferson Co	762C	80403	27800-31399
	Wheat Ridge	251J	80033	None
See.. WARD RD				
STATE HWY 74	Jefferson Co	309X	80465	17100-20999
	Jefferson Co	337E	80439	25000-27799
See.. BEAR CREEK RD				
	Jefferson Co	305R	80439	None
See.. EVERGREEN PKWY				
	Jefferson Co	305Z	80453	None
	Jefferson Co	307U	80439	None
	Jefferson Co	308Z	80453	None
	Jefferson Co	336G	80439	None
STATE HWY 75	Arapahoe Co	373B	80128	6900-7899
	Columbine Valley	343X	80123	5900-6399
	Columbine Valley	373B	80123	6400-6899
	Littleton	373B	80128	7100-7599
STATE HWY 79	Bennett	793N	80102	1100-16799
STATE HWY 83	Arapahoe Co	378H	80016	7100-7499
See.. S PARKER RD				
	Arapahoe Co	316M	80231	None
	Arapahoe Co	379N	80016	None
	Aurora	348Y	80014	3500-4299
See.. S PARKER RD				
	Aurora	348Y	80015	4300-5899
	Aurora	378H	80016	6200-7099
	Aurora	317T	80014	None
	Centennial	348Y	80016	5900-6199
See.. S PARKER RD				
	Denver	286W	80224	None
See.. LEETSDALE DR				
	Douglas Co	909F	80118	14000-15999
	Douglas Co	439R	80134	None
See.. PARKER RD				
	Douglas Co	469R	80134	None
	Douglas Co	469R	80116	None
	Douglas Co	869G	80116	1N-1999N
	Douglas Co	869G	80116	1S-4999S
	Douglas Co	889H	80116	5000S-6599S
	Douglas Co	889V	80116	10400S-12999S
	Douglas Co	889V	80118	13000S-13999S
	El Paso Co	909T	80132	13000-15999
	Parker	409G	80134	None
	Parker	439R	80134	None
	Parker	379N	80134	None
See.. S PARKER RD				
STATE HWY 83 S	Douglas Co	890S	80116	6600-11199
STATE HWY 85	Littleton	343V	80120	4900-6399
See.. W BELLEVIEW AVE				
STATE HWY 86	Elbert Co	870G	80107	1-1999
	Elbert Co	871G	80107	2000-6899
	Elbert Co	872E	80117	6900-11499
STATE HWY 86 E	Castle Rock	497H	80104	1-2299
	Castle Rock	498F	80104	2300-4699
	Douglas Co	469X	80104	4700-5599
	Douglas Co	469X	80116	5600-7499
	Douglas Co	869C	80116	7700-9199
	Douglas Co	870G	80116	9200-11999
STATE HWY 88	Aurora	378B	80112	14000-15199
See.. E ARAPAHOE RD				
	Aurora	378B	80016	15200-16199
	Centennial	378B	80112	13000-13999
See.. E ARAPAHOE RD				
	Centennial	377B	80112	None
	Cherry Hills Village	345P	80121	1601-4299 O
See.. E BELLEVIEW AVE				
	Cherry Hills Village	346P	80111	None
	Denver	283Q	80204	None
See.. FEDERAL BLVD				
	Denver	313Q	80219	None
	Englewood	344N	80110	None
	Englewood	344N	80120	None
	Foxfield	378B	80016	16200-16799
See.. E ARAPAHOE RD				
	Greenwood Village	345P	80121	1600-4298 E
See.. E BELLEVIW AVE				
	Greenwood Village	344N	80121	None
	Greenwood Village	346P	80111	None
	Littleton	343Q	80120	2600-2699
	Littleton	343Q	80123	2700-4399
	Littleton	344N	80120	None
STATE HWY 93	Arvada	763M	80403	9000-9399
See.. FOOTHILLS RD				
	Boulder	127H	80302	None
See.. BROADWAY				
	Boulder	128U	80305	None
	Boulder Co	743Z	80303	11000-12999
See.. S FOOTHILLS HWY				
	Golden	248V	80403	4100-4899
	Jefferson Co	249E	80403	4900-6299

Continued on next column

STREET NAME	CITY or COUNTY	MAP GRID	ZIP CODE	BLOCK RANGE O/E
STATE HWY 93 (Cont'd)	Jefferson Co	219W	80007	6300-7499
	Jefferson Co	763R	80403	7500-8999
See.. FOOTHILLS RD				
	Jefferson Co	763M	80403	9400-11999
STATE HWY 95	Adams Co	253E	80002	None
	Denver	283J	80214	None
See.. SHERIDAN BLVD				
	Denver	313A	80226	None
See.. S SHERIDAN BLVD				
	Denver	313N	80219	None
	Lakewood	283J	80241	None
	Lakewood	313A	80226	None
See.. S SHERIDAN BLVD				
	Lakewood	313N	80227	None
	Westminster	192M	80031	9100-9799
See.. SHERIDAN BLVD				
	Westminster	192M	80020	9800-11999
	Westminster	222D	80003	None
STATE HWY 103	Clear Creek Co	780U	80452	1-11999
See.. CHICAGO CREEK DR				
	Clear Creek Co	304L	80439	23600-28499
STATE HWY 105	Douglas Co	867E	80135	1N-1999N
See.. PERRY PARK RD				
	Douglas Co	847S	80135	2000N-4799N
	El Paso Co	909S	80132	1300-2999
	El Paso Co	909Z	80908	None
STATE HWY 105 E	El Paso Co	908X	80132	300-1399
STATE HWY 105 S	Monument	908R	80132	1-14399
STATE HWY 105 W	El Paso Co	908X	80132	400-1499
STATE HWY 119	Black Hawk	780D	80422	12800-13199
	Boulder	127A	80302	None
See.. BOULDER CANYON DR				
	Boulder Co	69U	80503	5300-7199
See.. DIAGONAL HWY				
	Boulder Co	70F	80503	7200-8099
	Boulder Co	40Z	80503	None
See.. DIAGONAL HWY				
	Boulder Co	740M	80466	None
	Boulder Co	741J	80466	None
See.. BOULDER CANYON RD				
	Boulder Co	742D	80302	None
	Boulder Co	98M	80301	None
	Gilpin Co	781A	80403	10000-12799
	Gilpin Co	761N	80403	None
	Gilpin Co	740Z	80403	None
	Gilpin Co	760U	80403	None
	Gilpin Co	760D	80403	None
	Longmont	706P	80504	1-999
	Longmont	41P	80501	None
See.. KEN PRATT BLVD				
	Longmont	41M	80501	None
	Weld Co	706P	80504	1000-3999
STATE HWY 121	Arvada	222B	80003	None
See.. WADSWORTH BLVD				
	Broomfield	162W	80020	None
	Jefferson Co	192J	80021	11300-11399
See.. WADSWORTH PKWY				
	Jefferson Co	372A	80128	None
See.. S WADSWORTH BLVD				
	Jefferson Co	825U	80127	None
	Lakewood	282K	80214	None
See.. W 12TH AVE				
	Lakewood	282T	80226	None
See.. WADSWORTH BLVD				
	Lakewood	312P	80227	None
	Lakewood	342N	80123	None
	Westminster	192J	80021	9100-11299
See.. WADSWORTH PKWY				
STATE HWY 128	Boulder Co	159W	80303	None
	Boulder Co	743Z	80303	None
	Broomfield	161Z	80021	None
See.. INTERLOCKEN LOOP				
	Superior	190A	80027	None
	Westminster	163Y	80234	None
See.. W 120TH AVE				
STATE HWY 157	Boulder	98Y	80301	None
	Boulder	128G	80303	None
STATE HWY 170	Boulder Co	159D	80303	None
See.. MARSHALL DR				
	Boulder Co	743R	80303	None
See.. ELDORADO SPRINGS DR				
STATE HWY 177	Centennial	345J	80121	6000-6499
See.. S UNIVERSITY BLVD				
	Centennial	375E	80122	None
	Cherry Hills Village	345J	80110	3500-5099
See.. S UNIVERSITY BLVD				
	Greenwood Village	345J	80121	5100-6099
See.. S UNIVERSITY BLVD				
STATE HWY 189	El Paso Co	910S	80908	None
See.. BLACK FOREST RD				
STATE HWY 217	El Paso Co	911V	80106	None
STATE HWY 224	Adams Co	225P	80229	None
See.. E 74TH AVE				
STATE HWY 224 E	Adams Co	224R	80229	700-3199
STATE HWY 265	Commerce City	255F	80022	None
See.. BRIGHTON BLVD				
STATE HWY 391	Lakewood	281L	80215	None
	Wheat Ridge	251Q	80033	None
See.. KIPLING ST				
STATE HWY 470	Highlands Ranch	374S	80129	None
	Highlands Ranch	374V	80126	None
	Highlands Ranch	375T	80126	None
	Jefferson Co	309H	80401	None
	Jefferson Co	340A	80465	None
	Jefferson Co	340R	80127	None
	Jefferson Co	370H	80127	None
	Jefferson Co	371T	80127	None
	Jefferson Co	372Q	80128	None
	Lone Tree	377S	80124	None
	Morrison	309V	80465	None
	Adams Co	167A	80601	None
	Adams Co	167A	80602	None
	Highlands Ranch	373P	80128	None
	Highlands Ranch	373V	80129	None
	Highlands Ranch	376T	80130	None
	Lone Tree	376T	80124	None

County Roads

STREET NAME	CITY or COUNTY	MAP GRID	ZIP CODE	BLOCK RANGE	O/E
COUNTY RD 1	Boulder Co	132U	80026	None	
	Broomfield	162H	80020	None	
	Erie	102H	80516	1600-5299	
	Lafayette	132U	80026	None	
COUNTY RD 1	Elbert Co	910L	80106	18000-19999	
COUNTY RD 1	Weld Co	42V	80504	8100-10999	
	Weld Co	12H	80504	11000-13999	
COUNTY RD 1.5	Erie	103F	80516	3700-4099	
	Weld Co	103F	80516	4100-4299	
COUNTY RD 2	Adams Co	135H	80602	None	
COUNTY RD 2	Broomfield	134H	80516	4000-4199	
	Erie	133E	80516	None	
	Weld Co	135H	80603	6001-7199	O
	Weld Co	136E	80603	7201-9499	O
	Weld Co	136E	80603	9501-11499	O
	Weld Co	140E	80601	12301-12899	O
	Weld Co	750C	80603	None	
COUNTY RD 2	Brighton	139H	80601	None	
COUNTY RD 2	Gilpin Co	761K	80403	None	
	Gilpin Co	761M	80403	None	
COUNTY RD 2 1/4	Weld Co	138H	80603	12400-12799	
COUNTY RD 2 1/2	Weld Co	138G	80603	12500-14199	
COUNTY RD 2.5	Broomfield	134F	80516	None	
COUNTY RD 2.8	Broomfield	134B	80516	None	
COUNTY RD 3	Boulder Co	12F	80504	13000-13999	
COUNTY RD 3	Central City	760Y	80403	None	
COUNTY RD 3	Douglas Co	846A	80125	6500-9099	
	Douglas Co	432V	80125	None	
COUNTY RD 3	Elbert Co	870C	80107	34000-35999	
COUNTY RD 3	Erie	133F	80516	1-5999	
COUNTY RD 3	Weld Co	103B	80516	3000-4799	
	Weld Co	706E	80504	13000-14999	
	Weld Co	706N	80504	None	
COUNTY RD 3.25	Weld Co	726A	80516	6000-7499	
COUNTY RD 3.5	Weld Co	706P	80504	11000-11999	
COUNTY RD 4	Boulder Co	99K	80301	None	
COUNTY RD 4	Broomfield	134B	80516	3000-3999	
	Thornton	135A	80516	None	
	Weld Co	135C	80603	6000-7199	
	Weld Co	140B	80603	6000-19899	
	Weld Co	136B	80603	7200-9499	
	Weld Co	137A	80603	9500-9999	
	Weld Co	135A	80516	None	
	Weld Co	729W	80603	None	
	Weld Co	730W	80642	None	
	Weld Co	731W	80642	None	
	Weld Co	731W	80643	None	
	Weld Co	750B	80642	None	
COUNTY RD 4.25	Weld Co	728Z	80603	13300-13799	
COUNTY RD 4.40	Weld Co	728X	80621	10900-11499	
COUNTY RD 4.80	Broomfield	726Z	80516	None	
COUNTY RD 4S	Gilpin Co	760Y	80403	None	
COUNTY RD 5	Boulder Co	102T	80516	1600-2699	
	Boulder Co	102B	80516	3900-5299	
COUNTY RD 5	Douglas Co	432Q	80125	None	
COUNTY RD 5	Elbert Co	890M	80106	22500-23999	
	Elbert Co	890M	80116	24000-25999	
	Elbert Co	890D	80107	26000-28799	
	Elbert Co	870Z	80107	28800-29999	
	Elbert Co	850Y	80107	36000-36999	
	Elbert Co	850Q	80107	37500-38999	
COUNTY RD 5	Erie	103R	80516	1200-2999	
	Erie	102T	80516	2700-3899	
COUNTY RD 5	Gilpin Co	760V	80403	None	
COUNTY RD 5	Jefferson Co	190B	80007	None	
COUNTY RD 5	Weld Co	103R	80516	3000-4799	
	Weld Co	706B	80504	12200-15499	
COUNTY RD 5.5	Frederick	726F	80516	None	
COUNTY RD 5.5	Mead	706G	80504	None	
COUNTY RD 5.5	Weld Co	706P	80504	10000-11999	
COUNTY RD 6	Arapahoe Co	792U	80102	37700-47299	
	Arapahoe Co	793V	80136	52100-53699	
	Arapahoe Co	791T	80137	None	
	Arapahoe Co	791V	80102	None	
COUNTY RD 6	Boulder Co	11F	80504	None	
	Boulder Co	12E	80504	None	
COUNTY RD 6	Broomfield	726Y	80516	None	
	Broomfield	727Z	80516	None	
	Broomfield	727Z	80603	None	
COUNTY RD 6	Erie	103V	80516	2000-2499	
COUNTY RD 6	Gilpin Co	780H	80403	100-399	
COUNTY RD 6	Weld Co	103V	80516	1000-1999	
	Weld Co	728W	80621	8700-12499	
	Weld Co	727Z	80621	None	
	Weld Co	729X	80621	None	
	Weld Co	729Z	80603	None	
	Weld Co	731W	80642	None	
COUNTY RD 6.25	Fort Lupton	728Y	80621	12500-12999	
COUNTY RD 7	Broomfield	726G	80516	None	
	Broomfield	134E	80516	None	
COUNTY RD 7	Douglas Co	403T	80125	6900-10099	
	Douglas Co	432F	80125	None	
COUNTY RD 7	Gilpin Co	761Y	80403	None	
	Gilpin Co	781C	80403	None	
COUNTY RD 7	Weld Co	706Y	80504	8600-11499	
	Weld Co	706L	80504	11500-13999	
	Weld Co	706L	80542	14000-14198	E
	Weld Co	706L	80542	14001-14199	O
	Weld Co	706L	80542	14200-14499	
	Weld Co	706L	80542	14500-15599	
COUNTY RD 7.20	Weld Co	726G	80516	None	
COUNTY RD 7.25	Frederick	726G	80516	None	
COUNTY RD 7.5	Frederick	726G	80516	None	
COUNTY RD 7.5	Weld Co	706U	80504	None	
COUNTY RD 7.80	Broomfield	726Y	80516	None	
COUNTY RD 8	Broomfield	727V	80514	None	
	Broomfield	727V	80516	None	
COUNTY RD 8	Dacono	726V	80516	None	
	Dacono	727V	80516	None	
COUNTY RD 8	Douglas Co	408Q	80134	3000-5999	
	Douglas Co	411M	80138	None	
COUNTY RD 8	Gilpin Co	781C	80403	None	
COUNTY RD 8	Lone Tree	408Q	80134	6000-6199	
COUNTY RD 8	Thornton	726V	80516	None	
COUNTY RD 8	Weld Co	103M	80516	500-2499	
	Weld Co	728U	80621	9500-13999	
	Weld Co	727V	80514	None	
	Weld Co	727V	80516	None	
	Weld Co	727V	80621	None	
	Weld Co	729T	80621	None	
	Weld Co	729V	80603	None	
	Weld Co	730T	80642	None	
	Weld Co	731S	80642	None	
COUNTY RD 8.5	Weld Co	728U	80621	12600-12999	
	Weld Co	729R	80603	17800-18999	
COUNTY RD 9	Boulder Co	101H	80026	3400-5299	
	Boulder Co	72F	80504	6900-7799	
COUNTY RD 9	Douglas Co	411A	80138	None	
COUNTY RD 9	Elbert Co	890Z	80106	21000-22499	
	Elbert Co	870V	80107	28800-31599	
	Elbert Co	830R	80138	46200-46999	
COUNTY RD 9	Erie	102S	80026	500-1799	
COUNTY RD 9	Gilpin Co	761W	80403	None	
COUNTY RD 9-15	Elbert Co	871N	80107	31500-32499	
COUNTY RD 9.5	Weld Co	706M	80504	None	
COUNTY RD 10	Arapahoe Co	794X	80136	53700-57699	
	Arapahoe Co	791Y	80137	None	
	Arapahoe Co	795Z	80103	None	
COUNTY RD 10	Boulder Co	10T	80503	7400-8599	
	Boulder Co	703M	80503	None	
COUNTY RD 10	Dacono	727N	80514	None	
COUNTY RD 10	Weld Co	103H	80516	1000-2499	
	Weld Co	728R	80621	7000-12999	
	Weld Co	729R	80603	17600-18999	
	Weld Co	727R	80514	None	
	Weld Co	729P	80621	None	
	Weld Co	730N	80642	None	
	Weld Co	730R	80642	None	
	Weld Co	731N	80642	None	
	Weld Co	731N	80643	None	
COUNTY RD 10.5	Weld Co	103A	80516	1-999	
COUNTY RD 11	Broomfield	135E	80516	None	
	Broomfield	727J	80516	None	
COUNTY RD 11	Douglas Co	869X	80104	3500-4999	
	Douglas Co	889C	80104	5000-6399	
COUNTY RD 11	Firestone	707S	80504	10000-10999	
	Frederick	707S	80504	8300-9499	
	Frederick	727J	80530	None	
COUNTY RD 11	Gilpin Co	761B	80403	None	
COUNTY RD 11	Northglenn	135E	80516	None	
COUNTY RD 11	Weld Co	707S	80504	9500-9999	
	Weld Co	707E	80504	13000-14999	
	Weld Co	727J	80514	None	
	Weld Co	727J	80530	None	
COUNTY RD 12	Dacono	727L	80514	None	
	Dacono	727L	80516	None	
COUNTY RD 12	Douglas Co	867E	80135	4000-9099	
COUNTY RD 12	Gilpin Co	760H	80403	None	
COUNTY RD 12	Weld Co	726L	80516	1000-1999	
	Weld Co	726L	80514	None	
	Weld Co	727L	80514	None	
	Weld Co	727L	80516	None	
	Weld Co	727L	80621	None	
	Weld Co	729J	80603	None	
	Weld Co	729J	80621	None	
COUNTY RD 12.5	Weld Co	730L	80642	21200-22099	
COUNTY RD 13	Broomfield	135C	80603	None	
	Broomfield	727J	80603	None	
COUNTY RD 13	Dacono	727J	80516	None	
COUNTY RD 13	Elbert Co	891N	80116	24000-24999	
	Elbert Co	891A	80107	26200-27999	
	Elbert Co	871A	80107	34000-35999	
	Elbert Co	851S	80107	36000-40999	
	Elbert Co	851A	80138	41000-42999	
COUNTY RD 13	Firestone	707W	80504	8300-8998	E
	Firestone	707W	80504	10000-11399	
	Firestone	727E	80504	None	
	Frederick	707W	80504	8301-9499	O
	Frederick	727E	80516	None	
COUNTY RD 13	Gilpin Co	760H	80403	1-899	
COUNTY RD 13	Louisville	131Y	80026	None	
	Louisville	161C	80026	None	
COUNTY RD 13	Parker	409L	80134	None	
COUNTY RD 13	Weld Co	707W	80504	9000-9498	E
	Weld Co	707W	80504	9500-9999	
	Weld Co	707W	80504	11400-14999	
	Weld Co	707W	80542	15000-15499	
	Weld Co	727J	80516	None	
COUNTY RD 14	Arapahoe Co	811C	80137	None	
COUNTY RD 14	Dacono	727H	80514	None	
	Fort Lupton	729E	80621	None	
	Frederick	727H	80516	None	
	Frederick	727H	80530	None	
COUNTY RD 14	Parker	439G	80134	None	
COUNTY RD 14	Weld Co	727H	80516	None	
	Weld Co	727H	80530	None	
	Weld Co	727H	80621	None	
	Weld Co	729H	80621	None	
	Weld Co	730E	80621	None	
COUNTY RD 14.50	Weld Co	726G	80516	3000-3599	
	Weld Co	728F	80621	10000-12999	
COUNTY RD 14.75	Weld Co	728G	80621	11500-12099	
COUNTY RD 15	Broomfield	727K	80603	None	
COUNTY RD 15	Dacono	727K	80621	None	
	Firestone	707T	80504	10001-10999	O
	Firestone	727K	80621	None	
	Frederick	727K	80621	None	
	Weld Co	135H	80603	1-2999	
COUNTY RD 15	Gilpin Co	760L	80501	None	
COUNTY RD 15	Golden	250N	80403	None	
COUNTY RD 15	Weld Co	707T	80504	9000-9999	
	Weld Co	707T	80504	10000-10998	E
	Weld Co	707T	80504	11000-12999	
	Weld Co	727K	80514	None	
	Weld Co	727K	80603	None	
	Weld Co	727K	80621	None	
COUNTY RD 15-21	Elbert Co	891U	80106	21000-23999	
COUNTY RD 16	Boulder Co	703M	80503	None	
COUNTY RD 16	Douglas Co	846G	80135	5500-6499	
	Douglas Co	846C	80125	7900-7999	
	Douglas Co	846C	80125	8000-8299	
COUNTY RD 16	Gilpin Co	740X	80403	None	
	Gilpin Co	760A	80403	None	
COUNTY RD 16	Fort Lupton	729E	80621	None	
	Frederick	727G	80504	5000-5599	
	Frederick	727G	80530	None	
	Frederick	727G	80516	None	
	Weld Co	726H	80516	3000-3999	
	Weld Co	728H	80621	8000-9999	
	Weld Co	728H	80621	None	
	Weld Co	732C	80643	None	
	Weld Co	730E	80621	None	
	Weld Co	731B	80643	None	
	Weld Co	731B	80642	None	
	Weld Co	727G	80621	None	
COUNTY RD 16.50	Weld Co	72H	80504	1-199	
	Weld Co	726A	80504	200-1999	
COUNTY RD 16.75	Weld Co	727A	80504	5000-5499	
COUNTY RD 16B	Gilpin Co	740Y	80403	None	
COUNTY RD 17	Elbert Co	871B	80107	33700-35999	
	Elbert Co	851T	80107	36000-37999	
	Elbert Co	831K	80138	46000-49999	
COUNTY RD 17	Gilpin Co	760C	80403	None	
COUNTY RD 17	Weld Co	136F	80603	1-2999	
	Weld Co	707U	80504	10000-12999	
	Weld Co	707G	80651	13000-13999	
	Weld Co	707C	80651	14000-15499	
	Weld Co	727L	80514	None	
	Weld Co	727L	80603	None	
	Weld Co	727L	80621	None	
COUNTY RD 17-21	Elbert Co	871P	80107	28000-33699	
	Elbert Co	851B	80138	41000-42999	
COUNTY RD 18	Arapahoe Co	810G	80137	None	
COUNTY RD 18	Boulder Co	40D	80503	None	
	Boulder Co	41E	80503	None	
COUNTY RD 18	Douglas Co	846R	80135	5300-7499	
COUNTY RD 18	Firestone	727C	80504	None	
	Firestone	727C	80621	None	
	Frederick	726C	80504	None	
	Frederick	726C	80530	None	
	Frederick	727C	80504	None	
	Weld Co	728B	80621	7900-12999	
	Weld Co	727C	80504	None	
	Weld Co	727C	80621	None	
	Weld Co	729D	80621	None	
	Weld Co	730A	80621	None	
	Weld Co	731A	80642	None	
	Weld Co	731A	80643	None	
COUNTY RD 18.5	Weld Co	708Z	80621	13000-14999	
COUNTY RD 19	Boulder Co	101S	80026	1600-5299	
	Boulder Co	71S	80026	5300-5399	
	Boulder Co	71A	80504	5400-8099	
	Boulder Co	11A	80504	None	
COUNTY RD 19	Broomfield	161K	80020	None	
COUNTY RD 19	Douglas Co	846B	80125	7500-9999	
COUNTY RD 19	Weld Co	136D	80603	1-1599	
	Weld Co	707V	80621	8300-11999	
	Weld Co	707D	80651	12000-14999	
	Weld Co	727R	80603	None	
	Weld Co	727Z	80621	None	
COUNTY RD 20	Boulder Co	42L	80501	None	
	Boulder Co	42P	80501	None	
	Boulder Co	703V	80503	None	
	Douglas Co	846R	80135	5700-6599	
COUNTY RD 20	Firestone	707X	80504	5900-7099	
	Frederick	707X	80504	4600-5899	
	Frederick	706Y	80504	None	
	Weld Co	706Y	80504	2800-4599	
	Weld Co	707X	80504	7100-7999	
	Weld Co	707X	80621	8000-9699	
	Weld Co	708W	80621	9700-10799	
	Weld Co	708Z	80621	13000-13999	
	Weld Co	709X	80621	14000-18899	
COUNTY RD 20.5	Weld Co	706W	80504	1-3999	
COUNTY RD 21	Adams Co	770Y	80019	None	
COUNTY RD 21	Douglas Co	866A	80135	500-1399	
COUNTY RD 21	Elbert Co	891L	80106	24000-24999	
	Elbert Co	891L	80116	25000-25999	
	Elbert Co	891L	80107	26000-27999	
	Elbert Co	871B	80107	33200-35999	
	Elbert Co	851U	80107	36000-40999	
	Elbert Co	831Q	80107	43000-45999	
COUNTY RD 21	Jefferson Co	306L	80439	None	
COUNTY RD 21	Louisville	160H	80027	None	
COUNTY RD 21	Weld Co	728S	80603	1-999	
	Weld Co	137E	80603	1000-1999	
	Weld Co	728S	80621	2000-9099	
	Weld Co	708E	80651	13000-15999	
COUNTY RD 21.5	Weld Co	708N	80621	10900-12999	
COUNTY RD 22	Douglas Co	866Z	80135	4000-7999	
COUNTY RD 22	Firestone	706V	80504	4300-4799	
	Firestone	707T	80504	6001-6099	O
	Firestone	707U	80504	7700-7998	E
COUNTY RD 22	Jefferson Co	823Q	80465	None	
COUNTY RD 22	Weld Co	706V	80504	4000-4299	
	Weld Co	707S	80504	4800-5999	
	Weld Co	707T	80504	6000-6098	E
	Weld Co	707U	80504	7000-7699	
	Weld Co	707U	80504	7701-7999	O
	Weld Co	707U	80621	8000-10199	
	Weld Co	708V	80621	10200-13999	
	Weld Co	709U	80621	14000-18899	
	Weld Co	710U	80621	18900-19999	
	Weld Co	710U	80642	20000-23999	
COUNTY RD 22.5	Weld Co	708T	80621	11000-11099	
	Weld Co	708V	80621	13000-17999	
COUNTY RD 22N	Adams Co	750G	80603	None	
	Adams Co	750Y	80022	None	
	Adams Co	750Y	80603	None	
COUNTY RD 23	Adams Co	770Z	80642	None	
COUNTY RD 23	Boulder Co	10G	80503	12600-14199	
COUNTY RD 23	Jefferson Co	307T	80439	None	
COUNTY RD 23	Weld Co	728T	80621	1500-8399	
	Weld Co	708T	80621	8400-12999	
	Weld Co	137D	80603	None	
	Weld Co	708F	80651	None	
COUNTY RD 23	Weld Co	708K	80621	12100-12199	
COUNTY RD 23 3/4	Weld Co	137D	80603	700-1299	
	Weld Co	138A	80603	1300-1499	
COUNTY RD 23.5	Platteville	708B	80651	15000-15499	

STREET NAME	CITY or COUNTY	MAP GRID	ZIP CODE	BLOCK RANGE	O/E
COUNTY RD 23.5	Weld Co	728F	80621	6500-7099	
COUNTY RD 23.50	Weld Co	728X	80603	1-1799	
	Weld Co	137H	80603	1800-1998	E
COUNTY RD 23N	Adams Co	790H	80137	None	
COUNTY RD 24	Adams Co	771S	80022	None	
	Adams Co	771S	80642	None	
COUNTY RD 24	Boulder Co	704X	80503	None	
COUNTY RD 24	Douglas Co	441R	80138	None	
COUNTY RD 24	Firestone	706R	80504	4100-4599	
	Firestone	707N	80504	4601-5599	O
	Firestone	707N	80504	5600-7399	
	Weld Co	707N	80504	4600-5598	E
	Weld Co	707N	80504	7400-7999	
	Weld Co	707R	80621	8000-9499	
	Weld Co	708N	80621	9500-10699	
	Weld Co	710N	80621	None	
COUNTY RD 24.5	Weld Co	708N	80621	10500-10699	
	Weld Co	708Q	80621	11000-12999	
COUNTY RD 24N	Adams Co	751J	80603	None	
COUNTY RD 25	Adams Co	771T	80022	None	
	Adams Co	771T	80642	None	
COUNTY RD 25	Boulder Co	70P	80503	5400-6999	
	Boulder Co	40C	80503	None	
	Boulder Co	40X	80503	None	
	Boulder Co	100A	80301	None	
	Boulder Co	130J	80303	None	
COUNTY RD 25	Elbert Co	871M	80107	32500-33999	
COUNTY RD 25	Jefferson Co	371C	80127	6400-8699	
	Lakewood	341G	80235	None	
COUNTY RD 25	Louisville	130T	80027	None	
COUNTY RD 25	Superior	160F	80027	None	
COUNTY RD 25	Weld Co	708Y	80621	8500-12999	
COUNTY RD 25	Weld Co	728G	80621	6500-7099	
COUNTY RD 25.25	Weld Co	708Q	80621	11500-11999	
COUNTY RD 25-41	Elbert Co	892B	80117	None	
	Elbert Co	911H	80106	None	
COUNTY RD 25.5	Weld Co	708Q	80621	10000-12999	
	Weld Co	708Q	80651	13000-13799	
COUNTY RD 25.65	Weld Co	708Q	80621	None	
COUNTY RD 25N	Adams Co	751F	80642	None	
	Adams Co	791F	80137	None	
COUNTY RD 26	Adams Co	771U	80642	None	
COUNTY RD 26	Boulder Co	42S	80504	None	
	Boulder Co	42V	80501	None	
COUNTY RD 26	Douglas Co	440Y	80134	None	
COUNTY RD 26	Weld Co	706K	80504	1-2999	
	Weld Co	707J	80504	5000-7999	
	Weld Co	707J	80621	8000-9499	
	Weld Co	708J	80621	9500-13999	
	Weld Co	709K	80621	14000-15799	
	Weld Co	710K	80642	20000-21999	
	Weld Co	708M	80621	None	
COUNTY RD 26N	Adams Co	751G	80642	None	
COUNTY RD 27	Adams Co	771Z	80642	None	
COUNTY RD 27	Douglas Co	866N	80135	8300-9099	
COUNTY RD 27	Elbert Co	871R	80107	31500-32499	
	Elbert Co	871D	80117	34000-35099	
COUNTY RD 27	Fort Lupton	728G	80621	2000-4999	
	Weld Co	138B	80603	1-1499	
COUNTY RD 27 1/3	Weld Co	138C	80603	None	
COUNTY RD 27.30	Weld Co	728Z	80603	1-1999	
COUNTY RD 27N	Adams Co	751R	80642	None	
	Adams Co	791M	80137	None	
COUNTY RD 28	Adams Co	772E	80102	None	
COUNTY RD 28	Boulder Co	71C	80504	9500-10999	
	Boulder Co	72A	80504	11000-12699	
COUNTY RD 28	Douglas Co	470F	80116	None	
	Douglas Co	850S	80134	None	
COUNTY RD 28	Weld Co	72A	80504	1-199	
	Weld Co	706K	80504	200-4599	
	Weld Co	707J	80504	4600-5999	
	Weld Co	707L	80621	8000-9499	
	Weld Co	708J	80621	9500-12499	
	Weld Co	708J	80651	12500-13999	
	Weld Co	709K	80651	14000-16399	
	Weld Co	710F	80651	19000-19999	
	Weld Co	710F	80642	20000-20999	
	Weld Co	707L	80504	None	
COUNTY RD 28N	Adams Co	752N	80642	19000-20199	
	Adams Co	792N	80102	None	
COUNTY RD 29	Adams Co	772X	80102	None	
COUNTY RD 29	Castle Pines North	436E	80135	5500-8699	
	Douglas Co	405Z	80130	None	
COUNTY RD 29	Elbert Co	852J	80107	37000-42999	
COUNTY RD 29	Weld Co	138H	80603	1-499	
	Weld Co	728Z	80621	1500-3999	
	Weld Co	728R	80621	4000-4799	
	Weld Co	728H	80621	6500-6599	
COUNTY RD 29.5	Fort Lupton	729J	80621	5300-5398	E
	Weld Co	709W	80621	None	
COUNTY RD 29N	Adams Co	752E	80642	None	
	Adams Co	792K	80102	None	
COUNTY RD 30	Adams Co	772K	80102	None	
COUNTY RD 30	Arapahoe Co	812R	80102	37000-45699	
	Arapahoe Co	813Q	80102	45700-52099	
	Arapahoe Co	813Q	80136	52100-53699	
	Arapahoe Co	811Q	80137	None	
COUNTY RD 30	Douglas Co	850X	80116	None	
COUNTY RD 30	Mead	706E	80504	2600-4799	
	Weld Co	706E	80504	100-2599	
	Weld Co	707E	80504	4800-5999	
	Weld Co	707E	80651	6000-9499	
	Weld Co	708G	80651	12500-14099	
	Weld Co	709E	80651	14100-14499	
	Weld Co	710G	80642	21000-23999	
COUNTY RD 30.5	Weld Co	708F	80651	10000-14199	
COUNTY RD 30N	Adams Co	752T	80102	None	
	Adams Co	792K	80102	None	
COUNTY RD 31	Adams Co	772G	80102	None	
COUNTY RD 31	Boulder Co	70E	80503	7200-7699	
	Boulder Co	40E	80503	None	
COUNTY RD 31	Douglas Co	850T	80134	None	
COUNTY RD 31	Elbert Co	872N	80117	31500-31999	
COUNTY RD 31	Fort Lupton	729E	80621	None	
	Weld Co	139B	80603	500-1099	
	Weld Co	709W	80621	8500-10699	
	Weld Co	709J	80621	10700-10999	

Continued on next column

STREET NAME	CITY or COUNTY	MAP GRID	ZIP CODE	BLOCK RANGE	O/E
COUNTY RD 31 (Cont'd)	Weld Co	709J	80651	11000-15599	
	Weld Co	729N	80621	None	
	Weld Co	729A	80621	None	
COUNTY RD 31N	Adams Co	752Q	80102	None	
	Adams Co	792L	80102	None	
COUNTY RD 32	Adams Co	772M	80102	None	
COUNTY RD 32	Boulder Co	72K	80504	11400-12699	
COUNTY RD 32	Douglas Co	870N	80116	None	
COUNTY RD 32	Mead	706A	80542	2700-3999	
	Weld Co	706A	80504	1000-1999	
	Weld Co	706A	80542	2000-2699	
	Weld Co	706D	80504	4000-4599	
	Weld Co	707B	80542	4600-6799	
	Weld Co	708D	80651	12700-14099	
	Weld Co	709C	80651	14100-18199	
COUNTY RD 32.5	Platteville	708B	80651	12200-12299	
	Weld Co	708B	80651	10000-11999	
COUNTY RD 32N	Adams Co	752R	80102	None	
	Adams Co	792M	80102	None	
COUNTY RD 33	Boulder	69V	80503	5400-6199	
	Boulder Co	69D	80503	6500-8099	
	Boulder Co	40W	80503	None	
COUNTY RD 33	Douglas Co	466G	80108	None	
COUNTY RD 33	Elbert Co	892P	80106	23000-24999	
	Elbert Co	872J	80117	32000-35999	
	Elbert Co	852W	80117	36000-36999	
COUNTY RD 33	Weld Co	729P	80621	4000-4099	
COUNTY RD 33	Weld Co	729T	80621	None	
COUNTY RD 33N	Adams Co	793J	80102	None	
COUNTY RD 34	Arapahoe Co	813V	80136	None	
COUNTY RD 34	Boulder Co	70J	80503	7400-9099	
	Boulder Co	71K	80503	9100-9499	
	Boulder Co	71K	80504	9500-10699	
	Boulder Co	723H	80503	None	
COUNTY RD 34	Douglas Co	409A	80134	None	
	Parker	409A	80134	None	
COUNTY RD 34N	Adams Co	793F	80102	None	
COUNTY RD 35	Boulder Co	40B	80503	None	
	Boulder Co	704K	80503	None	
COUNTY RD 35	Castle Rock	498K	80104	None	
	Douglas Co	498U	80104	None	
COUNTY RD 35	Elbert Co	912F	80106	20100-20199	
COUNTY RD 35	Weld Co	709C	80651	15000-15599	
	Weld Co	729L	80621	None	
COUNTY RD 36	Douglas Co	408E	80134	12700-16799	
COUNTY RD 36N	Adams Co	793H	80102	None	
COUNTY RD 37	Boulder Co	704F	80303	None	
COUNTY RD 37	Douglas Co	866P	80135	1500-3999	
COUNTY RD 37	Elbert Co	912B	80106	20000-21499	
	Elbert Co	892P	80106	21500-24999	
	Elbert Co	872F	80117	33501-33599	O
COUNTY RD 37	Weld Co	140C	80603	1-4399	
	Weld Co	709Z	80621	7500-11899	
	Weld Co	709D	80651	15000-15599	
	Weld Co	729H	80621	None	
	Weld Co	729H	80603	None	
COUNTY RD 37N	Adams Co	793M	80136	None	
COUNTY RD 38	Adams Co	793K	80102	None	
COUNTY RD 38	Boulder	69Y	80301	6300-6899	
	Boulder	69Y	80503	7100-7399	
	Boulder	70Y	80503	7400-7499	
	Boulder Co	69Y	80301	6900-7099	
	Boulder Co	70Y	80503	7500-9099	
	Boulder Co	71Z	80503	9100-9499	
	Boulder Co	71Z	80026	9500-10699	
	Boulder Co	71Z	80504	10700-10999	
	Boulder Co	72W	80504	11100-11499	
	Boulder Co	102C	80504	11600-11999	
	Boulder Co	102C	80516	12000-12699	
COUNTY RD 38	Douglas Co	866L	80135	4000-6299	
COUNTY RD 38N	Adams Co	794J	80136	None	
COUNTY RD 39	Boulder	69X	80301	5300-5399	
	Boulder	69X	80503	5400-6699	
	Boulder Co	69X	80503	6700-8099	
	Boulder Co	99P	80301	None	
	Boulder Co	129B	80303	None	
	Boulder Co	704S	80503	None	
COUNTY RD 39	Weld Co	710W	80621	8500-8799	
	Weld Co	710S	80621	10200-11999	
	Weld Co	710E	80651	13000-15599	
	Weld Co	730W	80621	None	
COUNTY RD 39N	Adams Co	794K	80136	None	
COUNTY RD 40N	Adams Co	794G	80136	None	
COUNTY RD 41	Boulder Co	704E	80503	None	
	Boulder Co	704J	80503	None	
COUNTY RD 41	Douglas Co	408V	80134	9000-10499	
	Douglas Co	439B	80134	None	
COUNTY RD 41	Elbert Co	892G	80117	25000-26999	
COUNTY RD 41	Weld Co	730S	80642	1000-4999	
	Weld Co	730K	80621	5000-8499	
	Weld Co	710X	80621	8500-10999	
	Weld Co	710X	80642	11000-12999	
	Weld Co	730X	80642	None	
COUNTY RD 42	Boulder Co	101H	80026	10700-10999	
	Boulder Co	102G	80026	11000-11399	
	Boulder Co	102G	80026	11900-11999	
	Boulder Co	102G	80516	12000-12699	
	Erie	102G	80026	11400-11899	
COUNTY RD 43	Douglas Co	409T	80134	None	
	Douglas Co	439K	80108	None	
	Douglas Co	439K	80134	None	
	Douglas Co	848M	80108	None	
COUNTY RD 43	Park Co	840C	80421	None	
	Park Co	841P	80421	None	
COUNTY RD 43	Parker	439K	80134	None	
COUNTY RD 43	Weld Co	730P	80642	4000-14999	
	Weld Co	710K	80642	12400-14999	
COUNTY RD 43.5	Weld Co	730L	80642	5200-5599	
COUNTY RD 43.75	Weld Co	730L	80642	5200-5299	
COUNTY RD 43N	Adams Co	795F	80103	None	
COUNTY RD 45	Boulder	99W	80301	None	
COUNTY RD 45	Douglas Co	409D	80134	None	
	Douglas Co	381Y	80138	None	
COUNTY RD 45	Elbert Co	872R	80117	28500-32999	
COUNTY RD 45	Jefferson Co	308G	80401	None	
COUNTY RD 45	Park Co	840D	80421	None	
COUNTY RD 45	Weld Co	730Q	80642	1-4499	
COUNTY RD 45N	Adams Co	795G	80103	None	

STREET NAME	CITY or COUNTY	MAP GRID	ZIP CODE	BLOCK RANGE	O/E
COUNTY RD 46	Boulder Co	98R	80301	None	
	Boulder Co	99N	80301	None	
COUNTY RD 46	Douglas Co	867F	80135	2600-3599	
	Douglas Co	867F	80109	None	
COUNTY RD 46N	Adams Co	795H	80103	None	
COUNTY RD 47	Weld Co	730V	80642	None	
COUNTY RD 47.95	Weld Co	731E	80642	6600-6799	
COUNTY RD 48	Jefferson Co	340T	80465	None	
	Jefferson Co	341N	80127	None	
COUNTY RD 49	Boulder Co	703H	80503	None	
COUNTY RD 49	Weld Co	731W	80642	None	
COUNTY RD 50	Jefferson Co	342S	80123	7000-8999	
	Lakewood	342S	80123	5200-6999	
COUNTY RD 51	Boulder Co	703V	80503	None	
	Boulder Co	704W	80503	None	
COUNTY RD 51	Douglas Co	499Q	80104	None	
	Douglas Co	499Q	80116	None	
	Douglas Co	869X	80104	800S-4999S	
COUNTY RD 51	Weld Co	731P	80643	None	
COUNTY RD 52	Boulder Co	101N	80301	9100-9499	
	Boulder Co	101Q	80026	9500-10999	
	Boulder Co	97X	80304	None	
	Boulder Co	98V	80301	None	
	Boulder Co	99T	80301	None	
	Boulder Co	100P	80301	None	
	Boulder Co	721S	80302	None	
	Boulder Co	722P	80302	None	
COUNTY RD 52	Douglas Co	870T	80116	None	
COUNTY RD 52	Erie	102R	80026	11000-11899	
	Erie	102R	80516	11900-12699	
COUNTY RD 53	Boulder	98Q	80301	None	
COUNTY RD 53	Douglas Co	887V	80118	10000-10999	
	Douglas Co	888S	80118	11000-12499	
	Larkspur	887V	80118	8000-9999	
COUNTY RD 53	Weld Co	731Y	80643	None	
	Weld Co	751C	80642	None	
COUNTY RD 54	Boulder Co	132B	80026	None	
	Douglas Co	870X	80116	None	
COUNTY RD 54	Erie	132B	80026	None	
COUNTY RD 54	Jefferson Co	372J	80128	5200-9099	
	Jefferson Co	371K	80127	9100-9699	
	Jefferson Co	371K	80128	9700-12499	
COUNTY RD 54	Lafayette	132B	80026	None	
COUNTY RD 55	Douglas Co	888X	80118	12500-15999	
COUNTY RD 55	Weld Co	731M	80643	None	
	Weld Co	751D	80643	None	
COUNTY RD 56	Boulder	127F	80302	None	
	Boulder Co	129M	80303	None	
COUNTY RD 56	Douglas Co	888L	80118	600-3399	
	Douglas Co	889A	80104	3400-5499	
COUNTY RD 56	Lafayette	131J	80026	None	
COUNTY RD 57	Douglas Co	908G	80118	None	
COUNTY RD 57	Jefferson Co	783F	80403	4500-6299	
	Jefferson Co	762P	80403	None	
	Jefferson Co	762V	80403	None	
	Jefferson Co	763W	80403	None	
COUNTY RD 58	Douglas Co	867Z	80118	1-1799	
	Douglas Co	887B	80118	1800-3299	
COUNTY RD 58	Golden	249U	80401	None	
COUNTY RD 59	Boulder Co	703Y	80503	None	
COUNTY RD 59	Weld Co	732J	80643	None	
	Weld Co	752A	80643	None	
COUNTY RD 60	Boulder Co	129Q	80303	None	
	Boulder Co	130P	80303	None	
COUNTY RD 60	Douglas Co	887L	80118	1-1599	O
	Douglas Co	887L	80118	1600-2699	
COUNTY RD 60	Jefferson Co	782K	80403	2700-4199	
COUNTY RD 60	Lafayette	132N	80026	None	
COUNTY RD 60	Larkspur	887L	80118	2-1598	E
COUNTY RD 60	Louisville	130P	80303	None	
COUNTY RD 61	Boulder Co	98E	80301	None	
COUNTY RD 61	Douglas Co	889K	80116	7600-10499	
	Douglas Co	889K	80118	10500-11999	
	Douglas Co	909F	80118	None	
COUNTY RD 62	Douglas Co	887V	80118	1-1999	
	Larkspur	887V	80118	None	
COUNTY RD 62	Louisville	131U	80026	None	
COUNTY RD 63	Douglas Co	889U	80116	6200-12999	
	Douglas Co	889U	80118	None	
COUNTY RD 63	Jefferson Co	275V	80439	None	
COUNTY RD 63	Weld Co	752C	80643	None	
COUNTY RD 64	Jefferson Co	368G	80465	19400-23699	
	Jefferson Co	367F	80439	24000-27199	
COUNTY RD 64	Louisville	160D	80027	None	
COUNTY RD 64	Park Co	841W	80421	None	
COUNTY RD 64A	Park Co	841W	80421	None	
COUNTY RD 64B	Park Co	840Z	80421	None	
COUNTY RD 65	Douglas Co	441Q	80134	None	
	Douglas Co	441Q	80138	None	
	Douglas Co	870F	80116	None	
COUNTY RD 65	Jefferson Co	275X	80439	1-699	
	Jefferson Co	305C	80439	700-1399	
COUNTY RD 65	Weld Co	752D	80643	None	
COUNTY RD 66	Jefferson Co	305J	80439	None	
COUNTY RD 67	Boulder Co	743X	80303	2800-2999	
COUNTY RD 67	Jefferson Co	371B	80127	6400-7499	
COUNTY RD 68	Boulder Co	741M	80466	1-2099	
	Boulder Co	162B	80026	None	
COUNTY RD 68	Jefferson Co	278H	80401	None	
	Jefferson Co	278L	80401	None	
	Jefferson Co	278T	80401	None	
COUNTY RD 68	Louisville	160C	80027	None	
COUNTY RD 69	Boulder Co	703B	80540	1-499	
COUNTY RD 69	Douglas Co	870W	80116	None	
	Douglas Co	869H	80116	1N-999N	
COUNTY RD 69	Jefferson Co	782G	80403	30200-35299	
COUNTY RD 70	Jefferson Co	248T	80403	24000-27999	
	Jefferson Co	782B	80403	28000-34799	
	Jefferson Co	762W	80403	None	
COUNTY RD 71	Douglas Co	441P	80134	None	
	Parker	409Z	80134	None	
COUNTY RD 72	Park Co	841U	80421	1-5699	
COUNTY RD 73	Boulder Co	703S	80302	None	
COUNTY RD 73	Jefferson Co	366V	80439	6000-9499	
	Jefferson Co	823S	80433	9500-10899	
	Jefferson Co	336V	80439	None	
	Jefferson Co	367N	80439	None	

STREET NAME	CITY or COUNTY	MAP GRID	ZIP CODE	BLOCK RANGE	O/E
COUNTY RD 74	Douglas Co	888Z	80118	4100-4799	
	Douglas Co	889U	80118	6000-7999	
	Douglas Co	889V	80116	8000-9099	
	Douglas Co	907D	80118	None	
COUNTY RD 74	Elbert Co	910M	80106	1-1999	
	Elbert Co	911K	80106	2000-3999	
	Elbert Co	912M	80106	10000-10999	
COUNTY RD 74	Jefferson Co	335F	80439	None	
COUNTY RD 74	Park Co	820Y	80421	None	
COUNTY RD 74-82	Elbert Co	912F	80106	7300-9899	
COUNTY RD 75	Boulder Co	723J	80302	None	
COUNTY RD 75	Jefferson Co	366K	80439	6900-8999	
COUNTY RD 76	Douglas Co	890J	80116	None	
COUNTY RD 76	Superior	160U	80027	None	
COUNTY RD 77	Arapahoe Co	321A	80018	None	
COUNTY RD 77	Boulder Co	742M	80302	None	
COUNTY RD 78	Douglas Co	890P	80116	None	
COUNTY RD 78	Jefferson Co	365L	80439	None	
	Jefferson Co	366E	80439	None	
	Jefferson Co	822V	80433	None	
COUNTY RD 79	Boulder Co	722Y	80302	None	
COUNTY RD 79	Jefferson Co	336U	80439	None	
COUNTY RD 80	Douglas Co	908D	80118	None	
	Douglas Co	909D	80118	None	
	Douglas Co	910B	80118	None	
COUNTY RD 81	Arapahoe Co	291L	80018	None	
COUNTY RD 81	Douglas Co	890E	80116	None	
	Douglas Co	910F	80118	None	
COUNTY RD 81	Jefferson Co	337P	80439	None	
COUNTY RD 82	Douglas Co	908H	80118	None	
	Douglas Co	909K	80118	None	
COUNTY RD 82	Elbert Co	911H	80106	4200-7299	
	Elbert Co	912G	80106	8500-9999	
COUNTY RD 83	Boulder Co	722P	80302	1-1699	
COUNTY RD 83	Jefferson Co	842F	80470	11900-16299	
COUNTY RD 83E	Boulder Co	722P	80302	None	
COUNTY RD 85	Boulder Co	742Q	80302	None	
	Boulder Co	742Y	80403	None	
COUNTY RD 86	Elbert Co	910D	80106	1-1999	
	Elbert Co	911B	80106	2000-3999	
COUNTY RD 86-96	Elbert Co	891V	80106	None	
	Elbert Co	911F	80106	None	
COUNTY RD 87A	Boulder Co	722B	80455	None	
COUNTY RD 87S	Boulder Co	722A	80302	None	
COUNTY RD 89	Arapahoe Co	790U	80137	None	
COUNTY RD 89	Boulder Co	721V	80302	None	
	Boulder Co	722T	80302	None	
COUNTY RD 89	Jefferson Co	336Q	80439	None	
COUNTY RD 93	Arapahoe Co	810D	80137	None	
COUNTY RD 93	Boulder Co	721T	80302	None	
	Boulder Co	721Y	80302	None	
COUNTY RD 93	Golden	279P	80401	None	
COUNTY RD 93	Jefferson Co	309Z	80401	101-299	O
COUNTY RD 94	Boulder Co	703W	80302	None	
	Boulder Co	703Y	80503	None	
	Boulder Co	723A	80302	None	
COUNTY RD 94	Elbert Co	892V	80106	8000-12999	
COUNTY RD 94	Jamestown	722B	80481	None	
COUNTY RD 95	Boulder Co	720R	80302	None	
COUNTY RD 95	Douglas Co	469Y	80116	None	
COUNTY RD 96	Boulder Co	720D	80481	100-3399	
COUNTY RD 96	Jefferson Co	844N	80441	None	
COUNTY RD 97	Arapahoe Co	791W	80137	None	
	Arapahoe Co	811E	80137	None	
COUNTY RD 97	Boulder Co	741U	80466	1-399	
COUNTY RD 97	Jefferson Co	843H	80433	12000-14199	
	Jefferson Co	823W	80433	None	
	Jefferson Co	844J	80433	None	
COUNTY RD 98	Elbert Co	890R	80106	1-1999	
	Elbert Co	891Q	80106	2000-4999	
	Elbert Co	891R	80106	5000-6499	
	Elbert Co	892N	80106	6500-7999	
COUNTY RD 99	Boulder Co	741T	80403	1000-1399	
COUNTY RD 100	Boulder Co	721E	80481	200-2899	
COUNTY RD 100J	Boulder Co	721E	80481	800-1899	
COUNTY RD 101	Arapahoe Co	791X	80137	None	
	Arapahoe Co	811B	80137	None	
COUNTY RD 102	Boulder Co	720L	80481	None	
	Boulder Co	721J	80481	None	
COUNTY RD 102	Elbert Co	891R	80106	4000-6499	
	Elbert Co	892M	80106	9000-12999	
COUNTY RD 102 N	Boulder Co	720L	80481	None	
COUNTY RD 103	Boulder Co	721E	80481	100-199	
	Boulder Co	740H	80466	1500-2099	
	Boulder Co	740M	80466	None	
COUNTY RD 103	Douglas Co	830Q	80138	None	
COUNTY RD 104	Boulder Co	720K	80481	1900-1999	
COUNTY RD 105	Douglas Co	887P	80118	8300-12499	
	Douglas Co	907C	80133	14000-15999	
	Douglas Co	867N	80135	None	
COUNTY RD 106	Boulder Co	720R	80455	None	
	Boulder Co	721N	80455	None	
	Boulder Co	722K	80455	None	
	Boulder Co	722M	80302	None	
	Boulder Co	723J	80302	None	
	Boulder Co	97B	80302	None	
COUNTY RD 106	Elbert Co	890H	80107	1000-1999	
	Elbert Co	891M	80116	2000-6499	
COUNTY RD 107	Douglas Co	467X	80109	1900-2799	
COUNTY RD 109J	Boulder Co	740G	80466	None	
COUNTY RD 112	Elbert Co	892B	80117	7500-8999	
COUNTY RD 113	Arapahoe Co	792W	80102	None	
	Arapahoe Co	812J	80102	None	
	Arapahoe Co	812S	80102	None	
COUNTY RD 114	Elbert Co	891C	80107	3000-4999	
	Elbert Co	891D	80107	5000-5999	
COUNTY RD 116	Boulder Co	740A	80466	800-899	
	Boulder Co	720Y	80466	None	
COUNTY RD 117	Arapahoe Co	792T	80102	None	
COUNTY RD 118	Boulder Co	722S	80302	None	
	Boulder Co	722T	80302	None	
	Boulder Co	722Z	80302	None	
COUNTY RD 118	Elbert Co	870Z	80107	1-1999	
	Elbert Co	871Y	80107	4000-4999	
COUNTY RD 120	Boulder Co	721W	80466	None	
COUNTY RD 120	Elbert Co	872Z	80117	10000-10999	
COUNTY RD 120	Jefferson Co	337B	80439	None	
	Jefferson Co	338E	80454	None	
COUNTY RD 120	Park Co	841L	80421	1-2399	
COUNTY RD 121	Arapahoe Co	792G	80102	None	
	Arapahoe Co	812F	80102	None	
COUNTY RD 122	Boulder Co	741E	80466	None	
	Boulder Co	742A	80302	None	
COUNTY RD 122	Elbert Co	870U	80107	1-999	
	Elbert Co	872T	80117	8000-9599	
COUNTY RD 122	Jefferson Co	369A	80465	6200-9199	
COUNTY RD 123	Arapahoe Co	792Y	80102	None	
COUNTY RD 124	Elbert Co	871U	80107	4500-5999	
COUNTY RD 124	Jefferson Co	369T	80465	8000-8299	
	Jefferson Co	369T	80127	8300-9299	
	Jefferson Co	371X	80127	9100-12499	
COUNTY RD 124W	Boulder Co	741G	80302	None	
COUNTY RD 125	Arapahoe Co	792U	80102	None	
COUNTY RD 126	Boulder Co	740K	80466	1-599	
COUNTY RD 126	Elbert Co	872V	80117	10000-10999	
COUNTY RD 126	Jefferson Co	842K	80470	12500-29999	
	Jefferson Co	843W	80470	16000-22499	
COUNTY RD 126N	Boulder Co	740K	80466	1-999	
COUNTY RD 126S	Boulder Co	740L	80466	None	
COUNTY RD 128	Boulder Co	740Q	80466	1-599	
COUNTY RD 128	Elbert Co	871Q	80107	5000-6499	
	Elbert Co	872N	80117	6500-7499	
COUNTY RD 128N	Boulder Co	740K	80466	1-599	
COUNTY RD 128W	Boulder Co	740L	80466	None	
COUNTY RD 129	Arapahoe Co	792V	80102	1-1499	
COUNTY RD 129 S	Arapahoe Co	812V	80102	1-799	
	Arapahoe Co	812V	80102	800-6199	
COUNTY RD 130	Boulder Co	740Q	80466	None	
COUNTY RD 130	Clear Creek Co	780T	80452	1-399	
COUNTY RD 130	Elbert Co	872N	80117	7500-7999	
COUNTY RD 132	Boulder Co	741N	80466	None	
	Boulder Co	742F	80466	None	
COUNTY RD 132	Elbert Co	870M	80107	1000-1999	
	Elbert Co	871M	80107	6000-6499	
COUNTY RD 132W	Boulder Co	740U	80403	None	
COUNTY RD 133	Arapahoe Co	793S	80102	1-1499	
COUNTY RD 134	Elbert Co	872L	80117	8000-9799	
COUNTY RD 136	Clear Creek Co	780N	80452	800-2099	
COUNTY RD 136	Elbert Co	871F	80107	3000-3499	
COUNTY RD 136N	Boulder Co	740V	80403	None	
COUNTY RD 137	Arapahoe Co	793T	80102	1-1499	
COUNTY RD 137 S	Arapahoe Co	813F	80102	800-6699	
COUNTY RD 140	Boulder Co	740T	80466	None	
COUNTY RD 140	Clear Creek Co	780U	80452	1-3199	
COUNTY RD 142	Elbert Co	871A	80107	2800-2999	
	Elbert Co	871B	80107	5000-5599	
	Elbert Co	872D	80117	10700-11499	
COUNTY RD 145	Arapahoe Co	793V	80102	1-1499	
COUNTY RD 146	Elbert Co	850Z	80107	1-999	
	Elbert Co	851Y	80107	3300-6999	
COUNTY RD 148	Jefferson Co	337S	80439	None	
COUNTY RD 149	Arapahoe Co	793Z	80136	1-799	
COUNTY RD 149	Arapahoe Co	793Z	80136	1N-1099N	
COUNTY RD 149 S	Arapahoe Co	813R	80136	800-6699	
COUNTY RD 150	Elbert Co	850Z	80107	1000-1999	
	Elbert Co	851W	80107	2000-2999	
COUNTY RD 151	Clear Creek Co	780Z	80452	1300-5999	
COUNTY RD 153	Arapahoe Co	794S	80136	1-1499	
COUNTY RD 154	Elbert Co	850U	80107	300-999	
	Elbert Co	851V	80107	4000-6999	
	Elbert Co	852V	80117	10500-11999	
COUNTY RD 155	Clear Creek Co	780Z	80452	1-5799	
COUNTY RD 157	Arapahoe Co	794X	80136	300-1499	
COUNTY RD 158	Elbert Co	850R	80107	1-1999	
	Elbert Co	851N	80107	2000-2999	
	Elbert Co	852N	80107	7000-9999	
COUNTY RD 159	Arapahoe Co	794Y	80136	1-299	
COUNTY RD 162	Elbert Co	852L	80107	7000-9999	
	Elbert Co	852L	80117	10000-11999	
COUNTY RD 166	Elbert Co	851G	80138	5000-6999	
	Elbert Co	850H	80138	None	
COUNTY RD 173	Arapahoe Co	795T	80103	1-1499	
COUNTY RD 174	Elbert Co	831X	80138	2000-2999	
	Elbert Co	851B	80138	3000-4999	
	Elbert Co	851D	80107	5000-6999	
	Elbert Co	852C	80107	7000-11999	
COUNTY RD 185	Arapahoe Co	795V	80103	1-1499	
COUNTY RD 186	Elbert Co	830R	80138	1-1999	
	Elbert Co	831N	80138	2000-2999	
	Elbert Co	831N	80107	3000-4999	
COUNTY RD 194	Elbert Co	831E	80107	2000-6999	
COUNTY RD 210	Jefferson Co	279R	80401	None	
COUNTY RD 271	Clear Creek Co	780J	80452	1-999	
COUNTY RD 275	Clear Creek Co	780J	80452	1000-2099	
COUNTY RD 281	Clear Creek Co	780K	80452	1300-2199	
COUNTY RD 398	Keenesburg	732B	80643	29000-30999	
COUNTY RD 475	Clear Creek Co	304S	80439	None	
COUNTY RD 650	Weld Co	729U	80621	None	
COUNTY RD 901	Boulder Co	72D	80504	5301-8099	O
	Boulder Co	12M	80504	None	
	Boulder Co	42H	80504	None	
	Erie	102Z	80516	1600-5299	
COUNTY RD 1034	Park Co	841E	80421	200-799	
COUNTY RD 2112	Jefferson Co	762E	80403	None	
COUNTY RD 2121	Jefferson Co	762H	80403	None	
COUNTY RD 2127	Jefferson Co	763C	80403	None	
COUNTY RD 2163	Jefferson Co	763C	80403	None	
COUNTY RD 2482	Jefferson Co	305N	80439	None	
COUNTY RD 2706	Jefferson Co	367E	80439	None	
COUNTY RD 2748	Jefferson Co	366B	80439	None	
COUNTY RD 2753	Jefferson Co	335X	80439	None	
COUNTY RD 2759	Jefferson Co	366B	80439	None	
	Jefferson Co	366K	80439	None	
COUNTY RD 2812	Jefferson Co	339N	80465	None	
COUNTY RD 2813	Jefferson Co	339R	80465	None	
COUNTY RD 2814	Jefferson Co	339R	80465	None	
	Jefferson Co	340N	80465	None	
COUNTY RD 2817	Jefferson Co	340N	80465	None	
COUNTY RD 2819	Jefferson Co	340N	80465	None	
COUNTY RD 2834	Jefferson Co	340T	80465	None	
COUNTY RD 2841	Jefferson Co	339S	80465	None	
COUNTY RD 2925	Jefferson Co	844E	80127	None	
COUNTY RD 2928	Jefferson Co	844E	80433	None	
COUNTY RD 2929	Jefferson Co	844F	80127	None	
COUNTY RD 2930	Jefferson Co	844A	80127	None	
	Jefferson Co	844E	80433	None	
COUNTY RD 2932	Jefferson Co	844F	80127	None	
COUNTY RD 2942	Jefferson Co	844M	80127	None	
COUNTY RD 2943	Jefferson Co	844L	80127	None	
COUNTY RD 2946	Jefferson Co	844L	80127	None	
COUNTY RD 2949	Jefferson Co	843M	80441	None	
COUNTY RD 2950	Jefferson Co	843L	80433	None	
COUNTY RD 2953	Jefferson Co	843R	80433	None	
COUNTY RD 2956	Jefferson Co	368X	80465	None	
COUNTY RD 2957	Jefferson Co	367Z	80433	None	
COUNTY RD 2958	Jefferson Co	368S	80465	None	
COUNTY RD 2961	Jefferson Co	368Y	80465	None	
COUNTY RD 2962	Jefferson Co	368M	80465	None	
COUNTY RD 2966	Jefferson Co	823Q	80465	None	
COUNTY RD 2967	Jefferson Co	823Q	80465	None	
COUNTY RD 2976	Jefferson Co	369X	80465	None	
COUNTY RD 2978	Jefferson Co	824P	80127	None	
COUNTY RD 2982	Jefferson Co	843Q	80441	None	
COUNTY RD 2983	Jefferson Co	369Z	80127	None	
COUNTY RD 2991	Jefferson Co	824T	80127	None	
COUNTY RD 2995	Jefferson Co	824U	80127	None	
COUNTY RD 2996	Jefferson Co	824U	80127	None	
COUNTY RD 3014	Jefferson Co	824Y	80127	None	
COUNTY RD 3019	Jefferson Co	824W	80433	None	
COUNTY RD 3023	Jefferson Co	823V	80465	None	
COUNTY RD 3027	Jefferson Co	823U	80433	None	
COUNTY RD 3028	Jefferson Co	824S	80465	None	
COUNTY RD 3048	Jefferson Co	824N	80465	None	
COUNTY RD 3053	Jefferson Co	366U	80433	None	
COUNTY RD 3062	Jefferson Co	367U	80433	None	
COUNTY RD 3063	Jefferson Co	367U	80433	None	
COUNTY RD 3069	Jefferson Co	823N	80433	None	
COUNTY RD 3079	Jefferson Co	823S	80433	None	
COUNTY RD 3080	Jefferson Co	823N	80433	None	
COUNTY RD 3083	Jefferson Co	823S	80433	None	
COUNTY RD 3101	Jefferson Co	823S	80433	None	
COUNTY RD 3105	Jefferson Co	823S	80433	None	
COUNTY RD 3106	Jefferson Co	823S	80433	None	
COUNTY RD 3107	Jefferson Co	823S	80433	None	
COUNTY RD 3109	Jefferson Co	823T	80433	None	
COUNTY RD 3110	Jefferson Co	823T	80433	None	
COUNTY RD 3114	Jefferson Co	842C	80433	None	
COUNTY RD 3117	Jefferson Co	824Y	80127	None	
COUNTY RD 3135	Jefferson Co	842J	80470	None	
COUNTY RD 3155	Jefferson Co	843F	80433	None	
COUNTY RD 3158	Jefferson Co	843F	80433	None	
COUNTY RD 3160	Jefferson Co	842S	80421	None	
	Jefferson Co	842T	80470	None	
COUNTY RD 4057	Jefferson Co	763X	80403	None	
COUNTY RD 4070	Golden	248Q	80403	None	
COUNTY RD 4072	Jefferson Co	763C	80403	None	
COUNTY RD 4076	Jefferson Co	842R	80470	None	
COUNTY RD 4082	Jefferson Co	248M	80403	None	
COUNTY RD 4094	Jefferson Co	309Y	80401	None	
COUNTY RD 4101	Jefferson Co	309Y	80401	None	
COUNTY RD 4102	Jefferson Co	309Y	80401	None	
COUNTY RD 4104	Jefferson Co	309Y	80401	None	
COUNTY RD A	Park Co	821U	80421	1-99	
COUNTY RD A	Weld Co	138F	80603	None	
COUNTY RD B	Park Co	821Y	80421	1-599	
COUNTY RD B	Weld Co	138B	80603	None	
COUNTY RD C	Park Co	821Y	80421	1-699	
COUNTY RD CG 1	Gilpin Co	761Q	80403	None	
COUNTY RD D	Park Co	821Y	80421	1-499	
COUNTY RD E	Park Co	821Y	80421	None	
COUNTY RD P-72	Park Co	820Y	80421	1-399	

Numbered Streets

STREET NAME	CITY or COUNTY	MAP GRID	ZIP CODE	BLOCK RANGE	O/E
1ST AVE	Boulder Co	70J	80503	100-199	
1ST AVE	Douglas Co	848E	80108	500-699	
1ST AVE	Idaho Springs	780Q	80452	100-499	
1ST AVE	Jefferson Co	219M	80007	8000-8199	
1ST AVE	Longmont	41H	80501	1-899	
	Longmont	41G	80501	1200-1299	
1ST AVE	Superior	160F	80027	100-499	
1ST AVE E	Adams Co	169K	80603	None	
1ST AVE E	Aurora	287S	80010	9700-11599	
	Aurora	287U	80012	12000-12098	E
	Aurora	288U	80011	15300-15799	
	Aurora	289S	80011	16900-17299	
	Aurora	291T	80018	25702-25999	E
	Aurora	290V	80018	None	
1ST AVE E	Broomfield	162Z	80020	100-1299	
1ST AVE E	Denver	284U	80203	1-799	
	Denver	284V	80218	800-1699	
	Denver	285S	80218	1700-1899	
	Denver	285S	80206	1900-3999	
	Denver	285U	80220	4000-5499	
	Denver	286T	80220	5500-7299	
	Denver	286T	80230	7401-7699	O
1ST AVE N	Brighton	138P	80601	1-199	
1ST AVE N	Keenesburg	732A	80643	None	
1ST AVE S	Brighton	138P	80601	1-299	
	Brighton	138T	80601	600-899	
1ST AVE W	Broomfield	162Y	80020	100-599	
	Broomfield	162X	80020	600-1699	
1ST AVE W	Denver	284T	80223	1-1199	
	Denver	283T	80219	2600-5199	
1ST AVE W	Jefferson Co	280U	80401	13900-14299	
	Jefferson Co	279V	80401	16400-16799	
	Lakewood	282U	80226	5200-8899	
	Lakewood	281V	80226	8900-9599	
1ST DR E	Aurora	288T	80011	14200-14499	
1ST DR W	Golden	280S	80401	15600-15999	
	Jefferson Co	280U	80401	13900-14299	
	Lakewood	280V	80228	12900-13099	
1ST PL E	Aurora	287U	80010	11500-11599	
	Aurora	287U	80012	11800-11999	
	Aurora	291T	80018	25700-25999	
	Aurora	290R	80018	None	
1ST PL E	Denver	286T	80220	6900-7199	
	Denver	286U	80230	7500-7799	
1ST PL W	Jefferson Co	280U	80401	14300-14499	
	Lakewood	282T	80226	7200-7999	
	Lakewood	282S	80226	8400-8699	
	Lakewood	281U	80226	9900-9999	
	Lakewood	280V	80228	12500-12699	

STREET NAME	CITY or COUNTY	MAP GRID	ZIP CODE	BLOCK RANGE	O/E
1ST ST	Bennett	793J	80102	300-799	
1ST ST	Castle Rock	497L	80104	200-799	
1ST ST	Denver Federal Center	281Q	80225	None	
1ST ST	Douglas Co	846G	80125	6400-6499	
	Douglas Co	408A	80134	12000-12699	
1ST ST	Firestone	727B	80504	None	
1ST ST	Fort Lupton	728L	80621	1-1199	
1ST ST	Frederick	727F	80530	400-599	
1ST ST	Golden	249S	80403	400-499	
	Golden	248Z	80403	500-799	
1ST ST	Monument	908W	80132	1-199	
1ST ST	Nederland	740Q	80466	None	
1ST ST	Thornton	165S	80241	12400-12599	
1ST ST N	Douglas Co	378W	80134	12700-12999	
1ST ST N	Keenesburg	732A	80643	None	
1ST WAY S	Brighton	138T	80601	500-599	
2ND AVE	Boulder Co	70J	80503	1-299	
2ND AVE	Douglas Co	848E	80108	300-699	
2ND AVE	Gilpin Co	740Z	80403	None	
2ND AVE	Idaho Springs	780Q	80452	100-399	
2ND AVE	Jefferson Co	219M	80007	8100-8199	
2ND AVE	Longmont	41H	80501	300-1299	
2ND AVE	Lyons	703C	80540	None	
2ND AVE	Superior	160F	80027	100-499	
2ND AVE E	Arapahoe Co	795Y	80103	100-399	
2ND AVE E	Aurora	287U	80010	11500-11899	
	Aurora	287U	80012	11901-11999	O
	Aurora	288S	80011	12000-13799	
	Aurora	287V	80011	12100-12899	
	Aurora	288T	80011	14700-14899	
	Aurora	288V	80011	16200-16899	
2ND AVE E	Denver	284U	80203	1-799	
	Denver	285T	80206	2300-3999	
	Denver	285U	80220	4000-4299	
	Denver	285V	80220	4700-5499	
	Denver	286S	80220	5500-5599	
	Denver	286T	80220	6900-7199	
	Denver	286T	80230	None	
2ND AVE S	Brighton	138T	80601	200-899	
2ND AVE W	Broomfield	162X	80020	200-999	
2ND AVE W	Denver	284T	80223	1-1099	
	Denver	283V	80223	2000-2499	
	Denver	283U	80219	2500-3599	
	Denver	283S	80219	4000-5199	
	Denver	284S	80223	None	
	Golden	280S	80401	15700-15999	
	Jefferson Co	280U	80401	13800-14299	
	Jefferson Co	279V	80401	16600-16799	
	Lakewood	282V	80226	5600-5999	
	Lakewood	282U	80226	6400-7199	
	Lakewood	282T	80226	7600-7999	
	Lakewood	282S	80226	8500-8899	
	Lakewood	281V	80226	8900-9599	
2ND CIR W	Lakewood	282T	80226	7300-7399	
2ND CT	Lyons	703C	80540	None	
2ND CT E	Adams Co	791N	80137	31700-31899	
2ND DR E	Aurora	287V	80011	12100-12399	
	Aurora	290R	80018	None	
2ND DR W	Lakewood	280V	80228	12400-12599	
	Lakewood	280V	80228	13000-13099	
2ND PL E	Aurora	291P	80018	None	
2ND PL E	Longmont	42E	80501	1-199	
2ND PL S	Brighton	138P	80601	100-199	
2ND PL W	Golden	280S	80401	16000-16299	
	Jefferson Co	280U	80401	14300-14399	
	Lakewood	281S	80228	11800-12499	
	Lakewood	280V	80228	12500-13699	
2ND ST	Bennett	793J	80102	400-799	
2ND ST	Boulder	97C	80304	5000-5099	
2ND ST	Castle Rock	497L	80104	300-799	
2ND ST	Dacono	727K	80514	100-799	
	Dacono	727J	80514	700-799	
2ND ST	Denver Federal Center	281Q	80225	None	
2ND ST	Douglas Co	846G	80125	6400-6599	
	Douglas Co	408B	80134	12000-12699	
2ND ST	Firestone	727B	80504	None	
2ND ST	Fort Lupton	728L	80621	100-1299	
2ND ST	Frederick	727F	80530	600-899	
2ND ST	Golden	248Z	80403	600-999	
2ND ST	Monument	908W	80132	301-399	O
2ND ST	Morrison	339D	80465	3500-3599	
2ND ST	Thornton	165S	80241	12400-12599	
2ND ST N	Douglas Co	378X	80134	12700-12999	
2ND STREET CT	Dacono	727K	80514	800-899	
3 ACRES LN	Wheat Ridge	252T	80033	1-7799	
3RD AVE	Boulder Co	70K	80503	100-299	
3RD AVE	Douglas Co	848E	80108	300-699	
3RD AVE	Idaho Springs	780Q	80452	100-399	
3RD AVE	Jefferson Co	219M	80007	8100-8199	
3RD AVE	Longmont	41H	80501	1-599	
	Longmont	41B	80503	600-2299	
3RD AVE	Longmont	42G	80501	None	
3RD AVE	Lyons	703C	80540	None	
3RD AVE	Superior	160F	80027	100-499	
3RD AVE E	Arapahoe Co	795Y	80103	1-399	
3RD AVE E	Aurora	287S	80010	10001-10299	O
	Aurora	287U	80011	12000-12099	
	Aurora	291P	80018	25400-25999	
3RD AVE E	Broomfield	162V	80020	900-1399	
	Broomfield	162U	80020	None	
3RD AVE E	Denver	284U	80203	1-599	
	Denver	284V	80218	800-1699	
	Denver	285S	80218	1700-1899	
	Denver	285T	80206	1900-3999	
	Denver	285V	80220	4000-5499	
	Denver	286N	80220	5500-6199	
	Denver	286P	80220	6900-7299	
	Denver	286P	80230	None	
	Longmont	42E	80501	None	
	See.. STATE HWY 119				
3RD AVE S	Brighton	138T	80601	1-899	
3RD AVE W	Broomfield	162X	80020	800-1599	
3RD AVE W	Denver	284T	80223	1-1699	
	Denver	283V	80223	2000-2099	
	Denver	283T	80219	2600-4799	
	Golden	280S	80401	15700-15999	
	Golden	279T	80401	18200-18299	
Continued on next column					
3RD AVE W (Cont'd)	Jefferson Co	280U	80401	14100-14699	
	Lakewood	282V	80226	5200-5999	
	Lakewood	282U	80226	6400-6799	
	Lakewood	282T	80226	7200-7399	
3RD PL	Denver	287N	80230	None	
3RD PL E	Arapahoe Co	795Y	80103	200-299	
3RD PL E	Aurora	291N	80018	25000-25199	
	Aurora	290R	80018	None	
	Aurora	291P	80018	None	
3RD PL E	Denver	285N	80206	None	
3RD PL W	Golden	280S	80401	15600-15999	
	Golden	279T	80401	18200-18299	
	Jefferson Co	280U	80401	13800-14199	
	Lakewood	282R	80226	5300-5899	
	Lakewood	282Q	80226	6400-7099	
	Lakewood	282T	80226	7200-7399	
	Lakewood	282S	80226	8400-8599	
	Lakewood	281V	80226	8900-9199	
	Lakewood	280V	80228	12800-12999	
3RD ST	Bennett	793J	80102	200-999	
3RD ST	Boulder	127C	80302	1900-1999	
	Boulder	97T	80304	2601-3299	O
3RD ST	Castle Rock	497L	80104	100-899	
3RD ST	Dacono	727K	80514	100-399	
3RD ST	Denver Federal Center	281Q	80225	None	
3RD ST	Douglas Co	846G	80125	6400-6499	
	Douglas Co	408B	80134	12000-12699	
3RD ST	Firestone	727B	80504	None	
3RD ST	Fort Lupton	728L	80621	100-1199	
	Fort Lupton	728M	80621	1200-1499	
3RD ST	Frederick	727F	80530	600-699	
3RD ST	Golden	248Z	80403	900-999	
3RD ST	Jefferson Co	339D	80465	3500-3599	
3RD ST	Monument	908W	80132	100-499	
3RD ST	Nederland	740Q	80466	None	
3RD ST	Thornton	165S	80241	12400-12599	
3RD ST N	Douglas Co	378X	80134	12700-12999	
3RD AVENUE DR W	Broomfield	162T	80020	100-599	
3RD AVENUE PL	Longmont	41A	80503	2400-2499	
4TH AVE	Arapahoe Co	795Y	80103	1-399	
4TH AVE	Boulder Co	70K	80503	100-299	
4TH AVE	Denver	287N	80230	None	
4TH AVE	Idaho Springs	780Q	80452	200-399	
4TH AVE	Longmont	41G	80501	1-1199	
4TH AVE	Lyons	703B	80540	None	
4TH AVE	Superior	160F	80027	100-299	
4TH AVE E	Aurora	288N	80011	13200-13799	
	Aurora	288P	80011	14200-14799	
	Aurora	288R	80011	16100-16299	
	Aurora	291P	80018	25401-25699	O
	Denver	284R	80218	800-1699	
	Denver	285N	80218	1700-1899	
	Denver	285P	80206	1900-3999	
	Denver	285R	80220	4000-5499	
	Denver	286N	80220	5500-6199	
	Denver	286P	80220	6200-7299	
	Denver	286P	80230	7300-7399	
	Denver	286Q	80230	7400-7799	
4TH AVE E	Denver	284Q	80203	1-799	
4TH AVE E	Longmont	42A	80501	1-199	
	Longmont	42B	80501	None	
4TH AVE N	Brighton	138K	80601	1-299	
4TH AVE S	Brighton	138T	80601	1-1099	
4TH AVE W	Broomfield	162T	80020	800-1399	
4TH AVE W	Denver	284Q	80223	1-1399	
	Denver	283U	80219	2500-2999	
	Denver	283P	80219	3200-5199	
	Golden	280S	80401	16000-16099	
	Golden	279T	80401	18200-18799	
	Golden	280T	80401	None	
	Jefferson Co	280Q	80401	14100-14199	
	Lakewood	282R	80226	5200-6199	
	Lakewood	282Q	80226	6400-7199	
	Lakewood	282N	80226	7600-8499	
	Lakewood	281V	80226	8900-9599	
	Lakewood	281N	80228	12000-12199	
4TH CIR E	Aurora	288N	80011	13700-13799	
4TH DR E	Aurora	290R	80018	None	
4TH PL	Denver	287N	80230	None	
4TH PL E	Aurora	288Q	80011	15300-15399	
	Aurora	291N	80018	25000-25599	
	Aurora	291P	80018	25700-25999	
	Lakewood	282Q	80226	6600-6799	
4TH PL W	Golden	279T	80401	18500-18599	
	Golden	279Q	80401	None	
	Jefferson Co	280Q	80401	14300-14399	
	Lakewood	281R	80226	8900-9199	
4TH ST	Bennett	793J	80102	300-799	
4TH ST	Boulder	127C	80302	1600-2099	
	Boulder	97U	80304	2400-4899	
	Boulder	97C	80304	None	
4TH ST	Castle Rock	497L	80104	100-799	
4TH ST	Dacono	727K	80514	100-499	
	Dacono	727J	80514	None	
4TH ST	Denver Federal Center	281U	80225	None	
4TH ST	Douglas Co	846G	80125	6400-6499	
	Douglas Co	408B	80134	12000-12699	
4TH ST	Firestone	727B	80504	None	
4TH ST	Fort Lupton	728L	80621	100-1599	
4TH ST	Frederick	727F	80530	600-799	
4TH ST	Golden	248Z	80403	900-1099	
4TH ST	Jefferson Co	339D	80465	3600-3699	
	Jefferson Co	842V	80470	16800-16898	E
4TH ST	Monument	908S	80132	1-399	
4TH ST	Nederland	740Q	80466	None	
4TH ST E	Central City	780D	80427	1-99	
4TH ST N	Douglas Co	378X	80134	12700-12999	
4TH ST W	Central City	780C	80427	1-99	
4TH WAY E	Aurora	287P	80010	10500-11499	
4TH AVENUE DR W	Broomfield	162T	80020	100-499	
4TH AVENUE PL W	Broomfield	162T	80020	400-499	
5TH AVE	Boulder Co	70F	80503	100-199	
5TH AVE	Idaho Springs	780Q	80452	100-399	
5TH AVE	Longmont	41C	80501	1-1199	
5TH AVE	Lyons	703B	80540	None	
5TH AVE	Superior	160F	80027	None	
5TH AVE E	Arapahoe Co	795Y	80103	100-299	
5TH AVE E	Aurora	287N	80010	9700-10299	
	Aurora	287P	80010	10900-11599	
	Aurora	288N	80011	13100-13699	
	Aurora	288Q	80011	14900-15299	
	Aurora	291P	80018	25000-25599	
	Aurora	290R	80018	None	
5TH AVE E	Denver	284Q	80203	1-799	
	Denver	284R	80218	800-1699	
	Denver	285N	80218	1700-1899	
	Denver	285N	80206	1900-1999	
	Denver	285P	80206	2300-3999	
	Denver	285Q	80220	4000-4899	
	Denver	286N	80220	6100-6399	
	Denver	286P	80220	6600-7199	
	Denver	286P	80230	7300-7499	
	Denver	286Q	80230	7900-8299	
5TH AVE E	Longmont	42B	80501	1-1299	
5TH AVE N	Brighton	138K	80601	1-499	
5TH AVE S	Brighton	138P	80601	1-499	
	Brighton	138T	80601	600-899	
5TH AVE W	Arapahoe Co	795Y	80103	None	
5TH AVE W	Broomfield	162S	80020	1900-1999	
5TH AVE W	Denver	284Q	80204	1-1199	
	Denver	283R	80204	2300-2999	
	Denver	283P	80204	3300-5199	
	Golden	280N	80401	15800-16199	
	Jefferson Co	280Q	80401	13800-14399	
	Lakewood	282R	80226	5200-5999	
	Lakewood	282Q	80226	6000-7099	
	Lakewood	282P	80226	7400-8199	
	Lakewood	281R	80226	8900-9599	
5TH CIR E	Aurora	288N	80011	13700-13799	
	Aurora	288Q	80011	14800-14899	
5TH CT S	Brighton	138T	80601	700-799	
5TH PL	Arapahoe Co	795S	80136	60600-61099	
5TH PL	Denver	286R	80230	None	
5TH PL E	Aurora	287P	80010	10600-10799	
	Aurora	288N	80011	13300-13699	
	Aurora	291P	80018	25100-25999	
	Aurora	290R	80018	None	
5TH PL W	Denver	283R	80204	None	
5TH PL W	Lakewood	282Q	80226	6200-6799	
	Lakewood	282N	80226	8400-8499	
	Lakewood	281R	80226	8900-9199	
5TH ST	Bennett	793J	80102	300-699	
5TH ST	Boulder	127G	80302	800-1399	
	Boulder	127C	80302	1500-2099	
	Boulder	97U	80304	2400-3299	
	Boulder	97C	80304	4800-5199	
	Boulder Co	132Q	80026	None	
5TH ST	Castle Rock	497G	80104	100-899	
5TH ST	Dacono	727K	80514	100-399	
5TH ST	Denver	284E	80204	1100-1399	
	Denver	283H	80204	1400-1599	
5TH ST	Denver Federal Center	281T	80225	None	
5TH ST	Douglas Co	408B	80134	12000-12699	
5TH ST	Firestone	727B	80504	None	
5TH ST	Fort Lupton	728L	80621	100-699	
	Fort Lupton	728M	80621	700-1499	
5TH ST	Frederick	727F	80530	600-899	
5TH ST	Golden	249W	80403	500-699	
	Golden	248Z	80403	700-1399	
5TH ST	Jefferson Co	842V	80470	16700-16999	
5TH ST	Monument	908S	80132	None	
5TH ST	Nederland	740R	80466	None	
5TH ST N	Brighton	138F	80603	800-999	
5TH ST N	Douglas Co	378X	80134	12700-12999	
5TH HIGH ST	Central City	780C	80427	None	
6TH AVE	Arapahoe Co	792S	80102	37700-42499	
	Arapahoe Co	794S	80136	53700-58999	
6TH AVE	Idaho Springs	780Q	80452	100-399	
6TH AVE	Longmont	41C	80501	1-1399	
	Longmont	41B	80501	1400-1798	E
6TH AVE E	Arapahoe Co	791S	80137	32900-35799	
	Arapahoe Co	791V	80102	37200-37699	
	Arapahoe Co	793V	80136	52100-53699	
	Aurora	287P	80010	9300-11999	
	Aurora	287R	80011	12000-12799	
	Aurora	288N	80011	12800-13699	
	Aurora	288Q	80011	12900-14599	
	Aurora	288P	80011	14600-14999	
	Aurora	289Q	80011	16800-19299	
	Aurora	290T	80018	17600-19299	
	Aurora	320C	80015	17600-20899	
	Aurora	290Q	80018	20900-24099	
	Aurora	291P	80018	None	
6TH AVE E	Broomfield	162V	80020	900-999	
6TH AVE E	Denver	284R	80203	1-799	
	Denver	284R	80218	800-1699	
	Denver	285N	80218	1700-1899	
	Denver	285P	80206	1900-3999	
	Denver	285R	80220	4000-5499	
	Denver	286N	80220	5500-7299	
	Denver	286Q	80230	7300-8299	
6TH AVE E	Longmont	42A	80501	1-199	
6TH AVE N	Brighton	138K	80601	1-699	
6TH AVE S	Brighton	138P	80601	1-499	
	Brighton	138T	80601	200-899	
6TH AVE W	Broomfield	162T	80020	200-1999	
	Broomfield	162S	80020	2000-2199	
6TH AVE W	Denver	284P	80204	1-1899	
	Denver	283N	80204	2100-5199	
	Golden	280P	80401	None	
	Lakewood	280P	80401	None	
	Lakewood	281N	80401	None	
	Lakewood	281R	80215	None	
	Lakewood	282P	80215	None	
	Lakewood	282P	80214	None	
6TH DR W	Lakewood	281N	80401	12600-12699	
6TH PKWY E	Aurora	290Q	80018	22400-22499	
6TH PL E	Aurora	287P	80010	10500-11799	
	Aurora	287R	80011	12200-12299	
	Aurora	288R	80011	16200-16299	
6TH PL E	Denver	286Q	80230	7500-8199	
6TH PL W	Arapahoe Co	795Y	80103	None	
6TH PL W	Denver	283N	80204	4700-4799	

STREET NAME	CITY or COUNTY	MAP GRID	ZIP CODE	BLOCK RANGE	O/E
6TH PL W	Jefferson Co	280Q	80401	13700-13999	
	Lakewood	282N	80214	8100-8299	
	Lakewood	281Q	80215	10300-10799	
	Lakewood	281N	80401	12300-12499	
	Lakewood	280R	80401	12500-13999	
6TH ST	Bennett	793J	80102	300-699	
6TH ST	Boulder	127G	80302	700-1399	
	Boulder	127C	80302	1900-1999	
	Boulder	97U	80304	2400-3299	
	Boulder	97G	80304	4300-4899	
	Boulder Co	740N	80466	100-199	
6TH ST	Castle Rock	497G	80104	200-999	
6TH ST	Dacono	727K	80514	100-399	
6TH ST	Denver	284E	80204	1400-1599	
6TH ST	Denver Federal Center	281T	80225	None	
6TH ST	Douglas Co	408C	80134	12000-12699	
6TH ST	Fort Lupton	728G	80621	100-699	
	Fort Lupton	728M	80621	700-1499	
6TH ST	Frederick	727F	80530	200-399	
6TH ST	Golden	249W	80403	600-699	
	Golden	248Z	80403	700-1299	
6TH ST	Jefferson Co	842V	80470	16900-16999	
6TH ST	Nederland	740Q	80466	None	
6TH ST E	Central City	780C	80427	None	
6TH ST N	Douglas Co	378Y	80134	12700-12999	
6TH AVENUE CIR E	Broomfield	162V	80020	None	
6TH AVENUE PKWY E	Denver	286Q	80230	8000-8098	E
6TH AVENUE FRONTAGE RD W					
	Jefferson Co	280N	80401	14700-15999	
6TH AVENUE SERVICE RD W					
	Lakewood	280P	80401	None	
	Lakewood	281R	80215	None	
	Lakewood	282N	80215	None	
6TH HIGH ST	Central City	780C	80427	1-99	
7TH AVE	Idaho Springs	780Q	80452	300-499	
7TH AVE E	Arapahoe Co	791T	80137	None	
	Aurora	287P	80010	9700-11999	
	Aurora	287R	80011	12500-13099	
	Aurora	288N	80011	13100-13699	
	Aurora	288Q	80011	15300-16099	
7TH AVE E	Broomfield	162V	80020	900-999	
7TH AVE E	Denver	284Q	80203	1-799	
	Denver	284R	80218	800-1699	
	Denver	285N	80218	1700-1899	
	Denver	285Q	80220	4000-4799	
	Denver	286P	80220	6400-7299	
	Denver	286P	80230	7300-7399	
	Denver	286Q	80230	7500-7899	
7TH AVE N	Brighton	138K	80601	1-799	
7TH AVE S	Brighton	138P	80601	1-499	
	Brighton	138T	80601	700-899	
7TH AVE W	Arapahoe Co	795Y	80103	None	
7TH AVE W	Denver	284P	80204	100-1399	
	Denver	283R	80204	2000-2999	
	Denver	283P	80204	3300-4799	
	Jefferson Co	280P	80401	13400-15499	
	Jefferson Co	280N	80401	15500-16399	
	Lakewood	282R	80214	5600-5999	
	Lakewood	282P	80214	7700-7999	
	Lakewood	282N	80215	8000-8899	
	Lakewood	281R	80215	8900-9199	
	Lakewood	281Q	80215	10500-10799	
	Lakewood	280R	80401	12500-12899	
7TH CIR E	Aurora	288Q	80011	15300-15699	
7TH DR E	Aurora	288R	80011	15900-16399	
7TH DR W	Lakewood	281N	80401	12000-12199	
	Lakewood	280R	80401	12900-13599	
7TH PL	Golden	249W	80403	None	
7TH PL E	Aurora	288Q	80011	15900-16099	
	Aurora	288R	80011	16500-16899	
	Aurora	287N	80230	None	
7TH PL W	Lakewood	282N	80214	8200-8299	
	Lakewood	281R	80215	9000-9199	
	Lakewood	281Q	80215	10400-10799	
	Lakewood	281N	80401	12000-12299	
	Lakewood	280R	80401	12800-13199	
7TH ST	Bennett	793J	80102	300-799	
7TH ST	Boulder	127G	80302	700-1699	
	Boulder	127C	80302	1700-1999	
	Boulder	97U	80304	2400-2499	
	Boulder	97U	80304	2500-2999	
	Boulder	97C	80304	4500-4899	
7TH ST	Castle Rock	497G	80104	301-399	O
7TH ST	Central City	780C	80427	1-299	
7TH ST	Dacono	727F	80514	100-599	
7TH ST	Denver	284E	80204	1200-1999	
	Denver	283D	80211	2200-2399	
7TH ST	Denver Federal Center	281T	80225	None	
	Denver Federal Center	281X	80225	None	
7TH ST	Fort Lupton	728G	80621	100-699	
	Fort Lupton	728M	80621	700-1499	
7TH ST	Frederick	727F	80530	100-399	
7TH ST	Golden	249W	80401	700-1099	
7TH ST	Jefferson Co	842V	80470	16700-16999	
7TH ST E	Aurora	288R	80011	16400-16899	
7TH ST E	Central City	780C	80427	None	
7TH ST W	Central City	780C	80427	1-199	
7TH AVENUE CIR E	Broomfield	162V	80020	1100-1199	
7TH AVENUE DR W	Broomfield	162T	80020	700-1299	
7TH AVENUE PKWY E	Denver	285N	80206	1900-3999	
8TH AVE	Idaho Springs	780Q	80452	200-699	
8TH AVE	Longmont	41D	80501	1-699	
	Longmont	41C	80501	700-1399	
8TH AVE E	Aurora	287N	80010	9700-10799	
	Aurora	288Q	80011	14600-15299	
	Aurora	288L	80011	15300-16099	
	Aurora	288M	80011	16500-16899	
	Aurora	289J	80011	17600-17699	
8TH AVE E	Broomfield	162V	80020	900-999	
8TH AVE E	Denver	284Q	80203	1-799	
	Denver	284R	80218	800-1699	
	Denver	285N	80218	1700-1899	
	Denver	285Q	80206	1900-3999	
	Denver	285R	80220	4000-5499	
	Denver	286N	80220	5500-7299	
	Denver	286Q	80230	7301-7899	O
8TH AVE E	Longmont	42A	80501	100-399	
8TH AVE N	Brighton	138K	80601	1-699	
8TH AVE S	Brighton	138T	80601	1-899	
8TH AVE W	Arapahoe Co	795Y	80103	None	
8TH AVE W	Denver	284P	80204	1-1899	
	Denver	283R	80204	1900-3699	
	Denver	283N	80204	4500-5199	
	Golden	280N	80401	16200-16399	
	Jefferson Co	280Q	80401	13700-14799	
	Lakewood	282R	80214	5200-6299	
	Lakewood	282P	80214	7000-7999	
	Lakewood	282N	80214	8000-8399	
	Lakewood	282N	80215	8400-8899	
	Lakewood	281R	80215	9200-9899	
	Lakewood	281Q	80215	9900-10799	
	Lakewood	281P	80215	10900-11599	
	Lakewood	281P	80401	11600-12699	
	Lakewood	280Q	80401	12700-13699	
	Lakewood	280P	80401	15000-15099	
8TH CIR E	Aurora	288L	80011	15800-15899	
8TH CT N	Brighton	138K	80601	500-599	
8TH DR E	Aurora	288L	80011	15700-15899	
8TH PL E	Aurora	288L	80011	15700-15799	
	Aurora	288M	80011	16300-16399	
	Denver	286L	80247	7300-8099	
8TH PL W	Golden	280N	80401	15900-15999	
	Golden	279R	80401	16800-17199	
8TH PL W	Jefferson Co	281N	80401	12400-12699	
	Lakewood	282L	80214	7000-7099	
	Lakewood	282P	80214	7100-8199	
	Lakewood	281Q	80215	10000-10799	
	Lakewood	281P	80401	11600-11699	
8TH ST	Bennett	793J	80102	300-499	
8TH ST	Boulder	127G	80302	700-1399	
	Boulder	127C	80302	1500-2099	
	Boulder	97U	80304	2700-2799	
	Boulder	97U	80304	3000-3299	
	Boulder	97G	80304	4500-4899	
8TH ST	Boulder Co	740N	80466	100-199	
8TH ST	Castle Rock	497F	80109	2-198	E
8TH ST	Dacono	727F	80514	100-898	E
8TH ST	Denver	284E	80204	900-1499	
8TH ST	Denver Federal Center	281T	80225	None	
	Denver Federal Center	281X	80225	None	
8TH ST	Fort Lupton	728H	80621	100-299	
	Fort Lupton	728G	80621	1200-1499	
8TH ST	Frederick	727F	80530	501-599	O
8TH ST	Golden	249W	80401	700-999	
	Golden	278D	80401	1100-1699	
8TH ST E	Monument	908S	80132	200-1499	
8TH AVENUE DR W	Broomfield	162T	80020	800-1299	
9TH AVE	Boulder Co	40D	80503	8900-9099	
9TH AVE	Idaho Springs	780Q	80452	100-499	
9TH AVE	Jefferson Co	250V	80401	None	
9TH AVE	Longmont	41B	80503	100-2799	
	Longmont	40D	80503	2800-3899	
9TH AVE E	Broomfield	162V	80020	900-1199	
9TH AVE E	Denver	284L	80203	1-799	
	Denver	284M	80218	800-1599	
	Denver	285J	80206	1900-2399	
	Denver	285J	80206	2401-2699	O
	Denver	285K	80206	2800-3999	
	Denver	285L	80220	4000-5499	
	Denver	286J	80220	5500-7299	
	Denver	286L	80247	7300-8099	
9TH AVE E	Longmont	42A	80501	1-999	
9TH AVE N	Brighton	138L	80601	1-699	
9TH AVE S	Brighton	138Q	80601	1-299	
	Brighton	138U	80601	700-899	
9TH AVE W	Broomfield	162T	80020	100-299	
	Broomfield	162T	80020	300-899	
9TH AVE W	Denver	284K	80204	1-299	
	Denver	284J	80204	400-1399	
	Denver	283L	80204	2400-4099	
	Denver	283J	80204	4400-5199	
	Golden	280N	80401	15400-15899	
	Jefferson Co	280M	80401	13100-13199	
	Jefferson Co	279M	80401	16400-17199	
	Lakewood	282M	80214	5200-6099	
	Lakewood	282J	80214	7100-8399	
	Lakewood	281M	80215	9200-9999	
	Lakewood	281L	80215	10400-10599	
9TH DR W	Lakewood	281L	80215	10000-10399	
9TH PL E	Arapahoe Co	290J	80018	21000-21499	
9TH PL N	Brighton	138L	80601	400-499	
9TH PL W	Jefferson Co	280M	80401	13200-13499	
	Lakewood	282L	80214	6300-6399	
	Lakewood	282K	80214	6900-7399	
	Lakewood	281L	80215	10400-10799	
9TH ST	Boulder	127C	80302	1200-2099	
	Boulder	97U	80304	2500-3599	
	Boulder	97Q	80304	3300-3599	
	Boulder	97L	80304	4200-4899	
	Boulder Co	740N	80466	None	
9TH ST	Denver	284E	80204	1200-1399	
	Denver	284E	80204	None	
9TH ST	Fort Lupton	728G	80621	100-1999	
9TH ST	Golden	249W	80401	200-1099	
	Golden	279A	80401	1100-1299	
9TH AVENUE DR N	Brighton	138G	80603	700-899	
9TH AVENUE PL W	Broomfield	161V	80020	3100-3199	
10TH AVE	Idaho Springs	780Q	80452	200-399	
10TH AVE	Longmont	11W	80501	2100-2299	
10TH AVE E	Aurora	287J	80010	9700-10599	
	Aurora	287L	80010	11300-11799	
	Aurora	287M	80011	12100-12199	
	Aurora	288J	80011	13500-13699	
	Aurora	288L	80011	14500-15699	
	Aurora	289J	80011	16800-17699	
10TH AVE E	Broomfield	162U	80020	100-899	
	Broomfield	162V	80020	900-1199	
10TH AVE E	Denver	284L	80203	1-799	
	Denver	284M	80218	800-1599	
	Denver	285K	80206	2700-3999	
	Denver	286K	80220	5700-7299	
10TH AVE N	Brighton	138L	80601	1-699	
10TH AVE S	Brighton	138Q	80601	1-299	
	Brighton	138U	80601	700-899	
10TH AVE W	Broomfield	162S	80020	100-1999	
	Broomfield	161R	80020	2000-2399	
10TH AVE W	Denver	284K	80204	1-299	
	Denver	284J	80204	700-1499	
	Denver	283K	80204	2600-5199	
	Golden	279L	80401	16400-17999	
	Jefferson Co	280M	80401	12700-13799	
	Jefferson Co	280J	80401	15200-16399	
	Lakewood	282L	80214	5200-6399	
	Lakewood	282K	80214	6800-8399	
	Lakewood	282K	80215	8400-8899	
	Lakewood	281M	80215	8900-9999	
10TH CT E	Broomfield	162R	80020	1100-1199	
10TH DR E	Arapahoe Co	791T	80137	None	
10TH DR E	Aurora	288L	80011	16000-16099	
	Aurora	286R	80230	None	
10TH PL E	Aurora	288L	80011	15600-15999	
10TH PL W	Lakewood	282L	80214	6400-6699	
10TH ST	Boulder	127H	80302	700-1099	
	Boulder	127D	80302	1100-1499	
	Boulder	127C	80302	2000-2099	
	Boulder	97U	80304	2400-2599	
	Boulder	97U	80304	2800-3299	
	Boulder	97C	80304	4600-4999	
10TH ST	Fort Lupton	728G	80621	300-699	
10TH ST	Golden	249W	80401	200-999	
	Golden	279A	80401	1000-1499	
10TH ST	Longmont	11Y	80501	100-1499	
10TH AVENUE CIR W	Broomfield	161V	80020	2900-3099	
10TH AVENUE PL W	Broomfield	161U	80020	3100-3399	
11TH AVE	Idaho Springs	780Q	80452	100-399	
11TH AVE	Longmont	11X	80501	100-2299	
11TH AVE E	Arapahoe Co	290J	80018	20900-21699	
	Aurora	286M	80010	8900-9299	
	Aurora	287L	80010	9300-12099	
	Aurora	287M	80011	12100-13199	
	Aurora	288K	80011	14400-15199	
	Aurora	288M	80011	15700-16799	
	Denver	284L	80203	1-799	
	Denver	284M	80218	800-1599	
	Denver	285K	80206	1900-3999	
	Denver	285L	80220	4000-4299	
	Denver	285M	80220	4800-5499	
	Denver	286L	80220	5500-8899	
11TH AVE N	Brighton	138L	80601	1-699	
11TH AVE S	Brighton	138Q	80601	1-299	
	Brighton	138U	80601	700-899	
11TH AVE W	Broomfield	162P	80020	800-999	
11TH AVE W	Denver	284K	80204	1-1599	
	Denver	283L	80204	2500-2999	
	Denver	283J	80204	4400-4999	
	Jefferson Co	280J	80401	15700-16099	
	Jefferson Co	279M	80401	16500-16999	
	Lakewood	282M	80214	5200-6199	
	Lakewood	282L	80214	6200-6999	
	Lakewood	282J	80215	8800-8899	
	Lakewood	281M	80215	8900-9999	
11TH CT N	Brighton	138L	80601	200-399	
11TH CT W	Broomfield	162P	80020	900-1299	
11TH DR W	Jefferson Co	279M	80401	17000-17099	
11TH PL E	Arapahoe Co	791T	80137	None	
11TH PL E	Aurora	288M	80011	16500-16699	
11TH PL E	Broomfield	162Q	80020	100-199	
11TH PL W	Jefferson Co	279M	80401	17000-17099	
	Lakewood	282L	80214	6200-6399	
11TH ST	Boulder	127H	80302	700-1499	
	Boulder	97Y	80302	1900-2199	
	Boulder	97U	80304	2800-3299	
11TH ST	Denver	284A	80204	None	
	Denver	284E	80204	None	
11TH ST	Denver Federal Center	281T	80225	None	
11TH ST	Fort Lupton	728G	80621	200-699	
11TH ST	Frederick	727F	80530	None	
11TH ST	Golden	279A	80401	600-799	
11TH ST E	Aurora	288K	80011	14500-15199	
11TH AVENUE CIR W	Broomfield	161R	80020	2900-3099	
11TH AVENUE CT W	Broomfield	161Q	80020	3100-3299	
11TH AVENUE DR W	Broomfield	161Q	80020	3100-3399	
11TH AVENUE PL W	Broomfield	161Q	80020	3200-3399	
12TH AVE	Idaho Springs	780Q	80452	100-399	
12TH AVE	Longmont	12W	80501	1-99	
	Longmont	11Z	80501	100-499	
	Longmont	11X	80501	1100-1999	
	Longmont	11W	80503	2300-2399	
12TH AVE E	Aurora	286M	80010	8900-9299	
	Aurora	287J	80010	9300-10299	
	Aurora	287K	80010	10500-12099	
	Aurora	288K	80011	14500-15299	
	Aurora	288L	80011	15300-15399	
	Aurora	288M	80011	15700-16499	
12TH AVE E	Broomfield	162R	80020	200-1199	
12TH AVE E	Denver	284L	80203	1-799	
	Denver	284M	80218	800-1599	
	Denver	285K	80206	1900-3999	
	Denver	285M	80220	4000-5499	
	Denver	286L	80220	5500-8899	
12TH AVE N	Brighton	138L	80601	1-399	
12TH AVE S	Brighton	138Q	80601	1-299	
	Brighton	138U	80601	700-899	
12TH AVE W	Broomfield	162N	80020	1200-1499	
12TH AVE W	Denver	284K	80204	1-1199	
	Denver	284J	80204	1400-1899	
	Denver	283L	80204	2600-3999	
	Jefferson Co	280J	80401	15800-16199	
	Jefferson Co	279M	80401	16900-17299	
	Lakewood	282K	80214	6900-8399	
	Lakewood	281L	80215	10100-10599	
	Lakewood	281J	80401	11600-11999	
12TH CT E	Broomfield	162R	80020	1100-1199	
12TH CT N	Brighton	138L	80601	500-599	
12TH DR W	Jefferson Co	279M	80401	16400-16699	
12TH LN W	Lakewood	281L	80215	10600-10799	
12TH PL E	Arapahoe Co	791U	80137	36300-36999	
12TH PL W	Denver	283M	80204	1800-1999	
	Jefferson Co	279M	80401	16400-16699	
	Lakewood	282M	80214	5200-5399	
	Lakewood	282L	80214	6600-6699	

Continued on next page

STREET NAME	CITY or COUNTY	MAP GRID	ZIP CODE	BLOCK RANGE	O/E
12TH PL W (Cont'd)	Lakewood	282J	80214	8200-8299	
	Lakewood	281M	80215	9400-9599	
	Lakewood	281L	80215	10300-10799	
	Lakewood	281J	80401	12400-12599	
12TH ST	Boulder	127H	80302	800-1099	
12TH ST	Broomfield	162P	80020	None	
12TH ST	Denver	284F	80204	500-599	
	Denver	284A	80204	None	
12TH ST	Denver Federal Center	281S	80225	None	
12TH ST	Fort Lupton	728G	80621	700-899	
12TH ST	Frederick	727F	80530	None	
12TH ST	Golden	279A	80401	500-1299	
12TH ST	Jamestown	722A	80455	None	
12TH AVENUE CT W	Broomfield	161R	80020	3000-3299	
12TH AVENUE PL W	Broomfield	162N	80020	2600-2799	
13TH AVE	Idaho Springs	780Q	80452	1-499	
13TH AVE E	Aurora	286M	80010	8900-9299	
	Aurora	287K	80010	9300-12099	
	Aurora	287M	80011	12100-13199	
	Aurora	288J	80011	13200-13799	
	Aurora	288K	80011	14400-15299	
	Aurora	288L	80011	15300-16099	
	Aurora	288M	80011	16300-16899	
	Aurora	289J	80011	16900-17499	
	Aurora	289K	80011	18200-18299	
13TH AVE E	Broomfield	162R	80020	1000-1199	
13TH AVE E	Denver	284L	80203	1-799	
	Denver	284M	80218	800-1699	
	Denver	285J	80218	1700-1899	
	Denver	285K	80206	1900-3999	
	Denver	285L	80220	4000-5499	
	Denver	286K	80220	5500-8899	
13TH AVE N	Brighton	138Q	80601	1-199	
	Brighton	138L	80601	300-699	
13TH AVE S	Brighton	138Q	80601	1-299	
	Brighton	138U	80601	400-899	
13TH AVE W	Broomfield	162N	80020	1200-1399	
13TH AVE W	Denver	284J	80204	1-1899	
	Denver	283M	80204	1900-2799	
	Denver	283J	80204	3400-5199	
	Jefferson Co	280K	80401	14900-15199	
	Jefferson Co	280J	80401	15700-16399	
	Lakewood	282M	80214	5200-5699	
	Lakewood	282J	80215	6000-8899	
	Lakewood	281M	80215	8900-9899	
	Lakewood	281L	80215	9900-10799	
	Lakewood	281J	80215	11200-11599	
	Lakewood	281J	80401	11600-12399	
13TH CIR E	Aurora	288J	80011	13700-13899	
	Aurora	288K	80011	14600-14699	
13TH LN W	Jefferson Co	279M	80401	16400-16599	
13TH PL E	Arapahoe Co	791T	80137	None	
13TH PL E	Aurora	287M	80011	12300-13199	
	Aurora	288J	80011	13200-13699	
	Aurora	288L	80011	15700-15999	
	Aurora	288M	80011	16300-16499	
13TH PL E	Broomfield	162Q	80020	1-99	
13TH PL W	Jefferson Co	280J	80401	15800-16399	
	Lakewood	281M	80215	9300-9399	
	Lakewood	281L	80215	10000-10599	
13TH ST	Boulder	127H	80302	400-1099	
	Boulder	127D	80302	1400-2099	
	Boulder	97Z	80302	2100-2299	
	Boulder	97Z	80304	2300-2699	
	Boulder	97V	80304	2700-3099	
	Boulder	97R	80304	3300-3399	
	Boulder	97H	80304	None	
13TH ST	Denver	284F	80204	300-1699	
13TH ST	Frederick	727F	80530	None	
13TH ST	Golden	279A	80401	100-1199	
14TH AVE	Idaho Springs	780Q	80452	1-499	
14TH AVE	Longmont	11V	80501	300-399	
	Longmont	11U	80501	1300-1499	
	Longmont	11T	80501	1500-2299	
14TH AVE E	Aurora	286H	80010	8900-9299	
	Aurora	287J	80010	9300-9999	
	Aurora	287K	80010	10200-11299	
	Aurora	287G	80010	11700-12099	
	Aurora	287H	80011	12100-13199	
	Aurora	288E	80011	13200-13699	
	Aurora	289J	80011	16900-17099	
14TH AVE E	Broomfield	162Q	80020	200-499	
	Broomfield	162R	80020	1000-1099	
14TH AVE E	Denver	284L	80203	1-799	
	Denver	284M	80218	800-1699	
	Denver	285J	80218	1700-1899	
	Denver	285K	80206	1900-3999	
	Denver	285L	80220	4000-5499	
	Denver	286K	80220	5500-8899	
14TH AVE N	Brighton	138L	80601	200-499	
14TH AVE S	Brighton	138Q	80601	200-299	
	Brighton	138U	80601	300-899	
14TH AVE W	Denver	284K	80204	1-1299	
	Denver	283J	80204	3000-5199	
	Golden	279L	80401	17600-17899	
	Jefferson Co	281J	80401	12000-12399	
	Jefferson Co	280K	80401	14900-15199	
	Jefferson Co	280J	80401	15700-16399	
	Lakewood	282L	80214	5200-8399	
	Lakewood	282J	80215	8400-8899	
	Lakewood	281M	80215	8900-9599	
	Lakewood	281L	80215	10200-10599	
	Lakewood	281J	80401	11600-11999	
14TH CIR W	Lakewood	281M	80215	9600-9699	
14TH CT E	Broomfield	162Q	80020	100-199	
14TH CT N	Brighton	138L	80601	400-499	
14TH CT S	Brighton	138U	80601	500-599	
14TH DR E	Aurora	288F	80011	14500-15299	
	Aurora	289J	80011	17100-17699	
14TH PL E	Aurora	287M	80011	13100-13199	
	Aurora	288J	80011	13600-13699	
	Aurora	288F	80011	14500-15299	
	Aurora	288G	80011	15300-15499	
	Aurora	288M	80011	16400-16499	
14TH PL E	Broomfield	162Q	80020	1-99	
14TH PL W	Golden	279M	80401	16400-16899	
	Jefferson Co	280M	80401	12800-12999	
	Jefferson Co	280J	80401	15800-16399	
	Lakewood	281L	80215	10000-10599	

STREET NAME	CITY or COUNTY	MAP GRID	ZIP CODE	BLOCK RANGE	O/E
14TH ST	Boulder	127H	80302	500-1099	
	Boulder	97Z	80302	2000-2299	
	Boulder	97Z	80304	2300-2399	
	Boulder	97V	80304	2700-2899	
	Boulder	97R	80304	3300-3399	
	Boulder	97R	80304	3801-3899	O
	Boulder	97H	80304	4600-4698	E
14TH ST	Denver	284F	80202	200-1699	
14TH ST	Fort Lupton	728G	80621	100-1999	
14TH ST	Frederick	727F	80530	None	
14TH ST	Golden	279A	80401	500-1199	
14TH ST	Weld Co	729E	80621	None	
14TH ST E	Aurora	289F	80011	18300-18499	
14TH WAY E	Broomfield	162Q	80020	900-999	
14TH AVENUE DR S	Brighton	138Q	80601	1-199	
15TH AVE	Idaho Springs	780Q	80452	1-499	
15TH AVE	Longmont	11U	80501	100-1399	
	Longmont	11T	80501	1900-2299	
	Longmont	11S	80503	2300-2899	
15TH AVE E	Broomfield	162R	80020	1000-1199	
15TH AVE E	Longmont	12S	80501	1-399	
15TH AVE N	Brighton	138L	80601	200-699	
15TH AVE S	Brighton	138Q	80601	200-299	
	Brighton	138U	80601	600-899	
15TH AVE W	Broomfield	162P	80020	1000-1099	
15TH AVE W	Golden	279H	80401	15100-17299	
15TH AVE W	Jefferson Co	280K	80401	15000-15099	
15TH CT N	Brighton	138Q	80601	100-199	
15TH DR S	Brighton	138U	80601	500-599	
15TH DR W	Jefferson Co	280H	80401	12800-13399	
15TH PL E	Aurora	289E	80011	17400-17499	
15TH PL W	Golden	279H	80401	17200-17299	
	Lakewood	282E	80215	8400-8499	
	Lakewood	281H	80215	8900-9699	
	Lakewood	281G	80215	10000-10399	
	Lakewood	280H	80215	12600-12799	
	Lakewood	281F	80215	None	
15TH ST	Boulder	127M	80302	300-1099	
	Boulder	127D	80302	1400-2099	
	Boulder	97Z	80302	2100-2299	
	Boulder	97V	80304	2700-3399	
	Boulder	97M	80304	4000-4699	
	Boulder	97H	80301	None	
15TH ST	Denver	284A	80202	100-1899	
	Denver	284A	80202	2100-2499	
15TH ST	Golden	279A	80401	500-899	
15TH ST	Jamestown	722A	80455	None	
15TH AVENUE DR S	Brighton	138Q	80601	100-199	
16TH AVE	Idaho Springs	780Q	80452	1-499	
16TH AVE	Longmont	11V	80501	300-399	
	Longmont	11U	80501	1000-1499	
	Longmont	11S	80501	1700-2299	
16TH AVE E	Adams Co	793R	80136	52000-53699	
16TH AVE E	Aurora	286H	80010	8900-9299	
	Aurora	287G	80010	9300-12099	
	Aurora	288H	80011	16000-16099	
	Aurora	289F	80011	18500-19299	
16TH AVE E	Aurora	287H	80010	None	
16TH AVE E	Broomfield	162M	80020	1000-1199	
16TH AVE E	Denver	284G	80202	1-99	
	Denver	284G	80203	100-799	
	Denver	284H	80218	800-1699	
	Denver	285E	80218	1700-1899	
	Denver	285E	80206	1900-2399	
	Denver	285F	80206	2800-3999	
	Denver	285H	80220	4000-5499	
	Denver	286G	80220	5500-8899	
16TH AVE E	Longmont	12T	80501	400-599	
16TH AVE N	Brighton	138L	80601	100-699	
16TH AVE S	Brighton	138Q	80601	200-299	
	Brighton	138U	80601	400-799	
16TH AVE W	Denver	283E	80204	3000-5199	
	Golden	279G	80401	17000-17799	
	Lakewood	282H	80214	5200-6199	
	Lakewood	282G	80214	6200-7199	
	Lakewood	282F	80214	7200-7999	
	Lakewood	282E	80215	8100-8799	
	Lakewood	281H	80215	9600-9699	
	Lakewood	281G	80215	10200-10399	
	Lakewood	281F	80215	11400-11699	
	Lakewood	281E	80215	None	
16TH CIR	Boulder	97R	80304	3400-3499	
16TH CT S	Brighton	138U	80601	800-899	
16TH DR E	Aurora	289E	80011	17300-17499	
16TH DR W	Jefferson Co	280H	80401	12800-13499	
	Lakewood	281E	80215	12200-12599	
16TH PL	Longmont	11T	80501	1500-1699	
16TH PL E	Aurora	288E	80045	13300-13399	
	Aurora	288F	80011	14400-14499	
	Aurora	289E	80011	17500-17599	
	Aurora	289F	80011	18500-19099	
16TH PL N	Brighton	138L	80601	None	
16TH PL W	Golden	279H	80401	16800-17299	
	Lakewood	282F	80214	7000-7199	
	Lakewood	282E	80214	8000-8399	
	Lakewood	281E	80215	12400-12799	
16TH ST	Boulder	127M	80302	300-1099	
	Boulder	97Z	80302	2100-2299	
	Boulder	97V	80304	2800-2999	
	Boulder	97R	80304	3300-3399	
	Boulder	97R	80304	3400-3799	
	Boulder	97H	80304	None	
16TH ST	Denver	284F	80202	1-1699	
	Denver	284A	80202	2100-2198	E
	Denver	254W	80211	2500-2699	
16TH ST	Golden	279A	80401	400-1299	
16TH ST	Jamestown	722A	80455	None	
16TH WAY N	Brighton	138L	80601	None	
16TH AVENUE DR S	Brighton	138Q	80601	100-199	
17TH AVE	Idaho Springs	780Q	80452	100-399	
17TH AVE	Longmont	11T	80501	100-2799	
	Longmont	10U	80503	2800-3999	
17TH AVE E	Aurora	286H	80010	8900-9299	
	Aurora	287G	80010	9300-12099	
	Aurora	287H	80010	12100-12299	
	Aurora	288G	80011	14900-15699	
	Aurora	289E	80011	17000-17299	

Continued on next column

STREET NAME	CITY or COUNTY	MAP GRID	ZIP CODE	BLOCK RANGE	O/E
17TH AVE E (Cont'd)	Aurora	289G	80011	18500-19299	
	Aurora	287H	80045	None	
	Aurora	288E	80011	None	
	Aurora	288E	80045	None	
17TH AVE E	Broomfield	162M	80020	1000-1199	
17TH AVE E	Denver	284G	80202	1-99	
	Denver	284G	80203	100-799	
	Denver	284H	80218	800-1699	
	Denver	285E	80218	1700-1899	
	Denver	285E	80206	1900-2299	
	Denver	285F	80206	2800-3999	
	Denver	285H	80220	4000-5499	
	Denver	286E	80220	5500-8899	
17TH AVE E	Longmont	12S	80501	1-11199	
17TH AVE N	Brighton	138L	80601	500-599	
17TH AVE S	Brighton	138U	80601	400-899	
17TH AVE W	Denver	283F	80204	2900-5199	
	Lakewood	282H	80214	5200-6099	
	Lakewood	282G	80214	6100-6999	
	Lakewood	282F	80214	7400-7799	
	Lakewood	282E	80214	7800-8399	
	Lakewood	281G	80215	9600-9999	
	Lakewood	281F	80215	10400-11999	
	Lakewood	281E	80215	12200-12499	
17TH CT N	Brighton	138L	80601	100-299	
17TH CT W	Broomfield	162K	80020	1000-1099	
17TH DR W	Golden	279G	80401	1700-1799	
17TH PL E	Aurora	287H	80010	12300-13199	
	Aurora	288E	80045	13200-13599	
	Aurora	288G	80011	15800-16099	
	Aurora	289E	80011	17500-17599	
	Aurora	289H	80011	19500-19799	
17TH PL N	Brighton	138L	80601	None	
17TH PL W	Golden	279G	80401	17200-17599	
	Lakewood	281G	80215	10000-10399	
	Lakewood	281F	80215	11401-11499	O
17TH ST	Boulder	127M	80302	300-999	
	Boulder	127D	80302	1600-2099	
	Boulder	97Z	80302	2100-2229	
	Boulder	97V	80304	2700-2999	
	Boulder	97R	80304	3000-3499	
	Boulder	97M	80304	3800-4699	
	Boulder	97H	80304	4600-4699	
17TH ST	Denver	284B	80202	300-1699	
	Denver	254W	80211	2500-2799	
17TH ST	Golden	279A	80401	400-899	
	Golden	279E	80401	1100-1299	
17TH ST	Jamestown	722A	80455	None	
17TH AVENUE DR S	Brighton	138Q	80601	100-299	
18TH AVE	Adams Co	794P	80136	None	
18TH AVE	Longmont	11T	80501	1500-1899	
18TH AVE E	Aurora	288G	80011	15300-15699	
18TH AVE E	Broomfield	162M	80020	None	
18TH AVE E	Denver	284G	80202	1-99	
	Denver	284G	80203	100-799	
	Denver	284H	80218	800-1699	
	Denver	285E	80218	1700-1899	
	Denver	285E	80206	1900-2299	
	Denver	285G	80220	4000-4999	
	Denver	285H	80220	5100-5199	
	Denver	286F	80220	6500-7099	
18TH AVE N	Brighton	138R	80601	1-199	
18TH AVE S	Brighton	138Q	80601	1-199	
18TH AVE W	Broomfield	162K	80020	901-999	O
18TH AVE W	Denver	283G	80204	2900-3799	
	Lakewood	282H	80214	5600-6299	
	Lakewood	282F	80214	7400-7499	
	Lakewood	282E	80215	8000-8599	
	Lakewood	281H	80215	9600-9899	
	Lakewood	281G	80215	10000-10599	
	Lakewood	281F	80215	11200-11399	
	Lakewood	281E	80215	11700-11999	
18TH CT N	Brighton	138M	80601	300-399	
18TH DR W	Lakewood	281H	80215	9600-9699	
	Lakewood	281E	80215	11900-12499	
18TH PL E	Aurora	288F	80011	14200-15199	
	Aurora	288H	80011	15800-16499	
	Aurora	289E	80011	17400-17599	
18TH PL N	Brighton	138H	80601	None	
18TH PL W	Lakewood	281G	80215	10200-10399	
18TH ST	Boulder	128J	80302	300-999	
	Boulder	127D	80302	1200-2099	
	Boulder	97Z	80302	2100-2299	
	Boulder	97V	80304	2800-3199	
	Boulder	97H	80304	4600-4699	
18TH ST	Denver	284B	80202	500-1599	
	Denver	254W	80202	1600-1799	
	Denver	254W	80211	2500-2699	
18TH ST	Golden	279B	80401	300-699	
19TH AVE	Idaho Springs	780Q	80452	500-599	
19TH AVE	Longmont	11Q	80501	100-1699	
19TH AVE E	Aurora	286H	80010	8900-9299	
	Aurora	287G	80010	9300-12099	
	Aurora	287H	80010	12400-13199	
	Aurora	288G	80011	15400-15699	
	Aurora	289G	80011	18500-19299	
	Aurora	290H	80019	None	
19TH AVE E	Broomfield	162M	80020	1000-1199	
19TH AVE E	Denver	284G	80202	1-99	
	Denver	284G	80203	100-799	
	Denver	284G	80218	800-1099	
	Denver	284H	80218	1600-1699	
	Denver	285E	80218	1700-1899	
	Denver	285G	80220	4000-5499	
	Denver	286G	80220	5500-8899	
19TH AVE N	Brighton	138M	80601	1-699	
19TH AVE S	Adams Co	168D	80601	None	
19TH AVE S	Brighton	138Z	80601	None	
19TH AVE W	Denver	283G	80204	2900-3799	
	Jefferson Co	280H	80401	None	
	Lakewood	282F	80214	7200-7999	
	Lakewood	282E	80214	8000-8399	
	Lakewood	281G	80215	10000-10199	
19TH DR E	Aurora	288E	80045	13100-13299	
19TH PL E	Aurora	288E	80045	13000-13599	
	Aurora	289E	80011	17000-17099	
	Aurora	287H	80010	None	

STREET NAME	CITY or COUNTY	MAP GRID	ZIP CODE	BLOCK RANGE	O/E
19TH PL W	Lakewood	282G	80214	6500-6799	
	Lakewood	281E	80215	12300-12799	
19TH ST	Boulder	128J	80302	300-899	
	Boulder	127D	80302	1200-1999	
	Boulder	97Z	80302	2100-2299	
	Boulder	97M	80304	2300-4599	
19TH ST	Denver	284B	80202	600-1999	
	Denver	254W	80202	2000-2299	
19TH ST	Golden	279E	80401	300-2099	
19TH ST E	Adams Co	793R	80136	52300-52999	
20TH AVE	Idaho Springs	780Q	80452	200-399	
20TH AVE	Longmont	11Q	80501	601-699	O
20TH AVE E	Denver	284G	80202	1-99	
	Denver	284C	80205	100-1499	
	Denver	285E	80205	1900-2299	
20TH AVE S	Brighton	138R	80601	1-399	
20TH AVE W	Denver	283C	80211	2600-3899	
	Denver	283B	80212	3901-4299	O
	Jefferson Co	280G	80401	12800-14199	
	Lakewood	282F	80214	5200-8399	
	Lakewood	282F	80215	8400-8899	
	Lakewood	281G	80215	8900-12799	
20TH CT E	Adams Co	794P	80136	56200-56299	
20TH PL W	Denver	283B	80211	3400-3599	
	Jefferson Co	280G	80401	13600-13999	
20TH ST	Boulder	128J	80302	200-899	
	Boulder	128A	80302	1300-1799	
	Boulder	98W	80302	1900-2299	
	Boulder	97V	80304	2800-3299	
	Boulder	97M	80304	3900-3999	
20TH ST	Denver	284B	80202	500-1699	
	Denver	254W	80202	1700-2499	
20TH ST	Golden	279F	80401	400-1099	
20TH ST	Longmont	11P	80501	1600-1899	
	Longmont	11N	80501	2000-2299	
21ST AVE	Adams Co	794P	80136	None	
21ST AVE	Lochbuie	140B	80603	None	
21ST AVE	Longmont	11R	80501	400-599	
	Longmont	11P	80501	600-2299	
	Longmont	11N	80503	None	
21ST AVE E	Aurora	287D	80010	12400-13199	
21ST AVE E	Longmont	12N	80501	100-199	
	Aurora	288B	80011	14500-14899	
	Denver	284D	80205	1200-1699	
	Denver	285A	80205	1700-2299	
	Denver	286B	80207	6500-7599	
	Denver	286D	80238	None	
21ST AVE N	Brighton	138M	80601	400-799	
21ST AVE S	Brighton	138R	80601	200-399	
21ST AVE W	Denver	283C	80211	2700-3899	
	Denver	283B	80212	3900-4299	
	Jefferson Co	280H	80401	12800-13199	
	Jefferson Co	280C	80401	13400-13999	
	Lakewood	282B	80214	7200-7399	
	Lakewood	282F	80214	7800-7999	
	Lakewood	282A	80215	8600-8699	
	Lakewood	281C	80215	9600-10599	
21ST CIR E	Aurora	289C	80011	19000-19199	
21ST CT S	Brighton	138V	80601	700-799	
21ST PL S	Brighton	138R	80601	200-399	
21ST PL W	Jefferson Co	280C	80401	13400-14299	
	Lakewood	281C	80215	10000-10199	
	Lakewood	281F	80215	11700-11799	
21ST ST	Boulder	128J	80302	300-699	
	Boulder	128A	80302	1500-1799	
	Boulder	98W	80302	1900-2299	
	Boulder	97V	80304	2800-2999	
	Boulder	98N	80304	3800-3899	
	Boulder Co	98E	80301	None	
21ST ST	Denver	284B	80205	300-1599	
21ST ST	Golden	279F	80401	300-1099	
21ST ST	Longmont	11N	80501	2000-2299	
21ST WAY W	Lakewood	281A	80215	11700-12099	
22ND AVE	Boulder	98J	80304	None	
22ND AVE	Lochbuie	140B	80603	None	
22ND AVE	Longmont	11P	80501	1500-1598	E
	Longmont	11P	80501	2200-2299	
	Longmont	11N	80503	2300-2599	
22ND AVE E	Adams Co	794P	80136	None	
22ND AVE E	Aurora	287B	80010	9500-11999	
	Aurora	288A	80045	13400-13499	
	Aurora	288C	80011	14700-15299	
	Aurora	289B	80011	17400-18099	
	Aurora	289A	80011	None	
	Aurora	289C	80011	None	
	Aurora	287D	80010	None	
	Denver	284D	80205	700-1699	
	Denver	285A	80205	1700-2299	
	Denver	285D	80207	4000-5499	
	Denver	286B	80207	5500-7699	
	Denver	286C	80238	None	
	Denver	286D	80238	None	
22ND AVE S	Brighton	138R	80601	1-399	
	Brighton	138R	80601	600-799	
	Brighton	138V	80601	None	
22ND AVE W	Denver	283B	80211	2700-3899	
	Denver	283B	80212	4100-4298	E
	Edgewater	282D	80214	5200-6799	
	Jefferson Co	280C	80401	13700-13999	
	Jefferson Co	280C	80401	14000-14199	
	Lakewood	282B	80214	7400-7599	
	Lakewood	282A	80215	8000-8199	
22ND CIR E	Aurora	289C	80011	19100-19299	
22ND CIR S	Brighton	138V	80601	None	
22ND CT	Longmont	11J	80503	2500-2599	
22ND DR	Longmont	11N	80503	2500-2599	
22ND DR E	Aurora	289C	80011	18800-19299	
22ND PL E	Aurora	288B	80011	14000-14699	
	Aurora	289C	80011	18800-19299	
	Denver	286C	80238	None	
22ND PL W	Jefferson Co	280C	80401	13300-13599	
	Lakewood	281D	80215	9600-9899	
	Lakewood	281C	80215	10400-10599	
	Lakewood	281A	80215	11600-12099	
22ND ST	Boulder	128J	80302	300-699	
	Boulder	98W	80302	1900-2299	
	Boulder	98N	80304	3500-3799	
22ND ST	Denver	284B	80205	300-1499	
	Denver	254X	80205	1500-1599	
22ND ST	Golden	279F	80401	300-899	
22ND WAY W	Lakewood	282A	80215	8100-8199	
22ND AVENUE CT S	Brighton	138V	80601	300-399	
23RD BLVD	Lochbuie	729Y	80603	None	
23RD AVE	Idaho Springs	780R	80452	200-599	
23RD AVE	Longmont	11Q	80501	201-1699	O
	Longmont	11N	80501	2100-2299	
23RD AVE E	Aurora	287B	80010	9500-12099	
	Aurora	287D	80010	12700-13199	
	Aurora	288B	80011	13700-15299	
	Aurora	289B	80011	17400-17899	
	Aurora	289D	80011	None	
	Aurora	288A	80010	None	
	Denver	284D	80205	700-1699	
	Denver	285A	80205	1700-3199	
	Denver	285C	80205	3201-3999	O
	Denver	285C	80207	4000-5499	
	Denver	286B	80207	5500-7699	
	Denver	286B	80238	7700-8399	
	Denver	286D	80238	None	
23RD AVE S	Brighton	138V	80601	300-399	
23RD AVE W	Denver	283C	80211	2500-3899	
	Denver	283B	80212	3900-4299	
	Jefferson Co	280D	80401	12800-13199	
	Jefferson Co	280C	80401	13800-13999	
	Lakewood	282B	80214	7000-8399	
	Lakewood	282A	80215	8400-8699	
	Lakewood	281C	80215	9600-10499	
	Lakewood	280D	80215	12700-12799	
23RD CIR W	Jefferson Co	280D	80401	2300-2399	
23RD PL W	Jefferson Co	280C	80401	13300-13599	
	Lakewood	282B	80214	7600-7799	
	Lakewood	281C	80215	10400-10599	
	Lakewood	281A	80215	12000-12199	
23RD ST	Boulder	128A	80302	1500-1599	
	Boulder	98W	80302	1600-2299	
	Boulder	98W	80304	2300-2599	
	Boulder	98S	80304	2900-3399	
	Boulder	98N	80304	3400-3699	
23RD ST	Denver	254X	80216	1800-2199	
23RD ST	Golden	279F	80401	300-1099	
23RD AVENUE DR W	Lakewood	281B	80215	10700-11199	
24TH AVE	Longmont	11K	80501	1400-1999	
	Longmont	11J	80501	2100-2299	
	Longmont	11J	80503	2300-2599	
24TH AVE E	Adams Co	794P	80136	56800-57099	
24TH AVE E	Aurora	288B	80011	13700-14999	
	Aurora	288C	80011	15300-15399	
	Aurora	289A	80011	None	
	Denver	284D	80205	700-1699	
	Denver	285A	80205	1700-2299	
	Denver	286B	80207	6500-7299	
	Denver	286C	80238	7701-8099	O
	Denver	286D	80238	None	
24TH AVE S	Brighton	138V	80601	300-699	
24TH AVE W	Denver	283C	80211	2500-3899	
	Denver	283B	80212	3900-4299	
	Edgewater	282C	80214	5200-6999	
	Lakewood	282C	80214	7000-7199	
	Lakewood	282B	80214	7600-7699	
	Lakewood	282A	80215	8400-9099	
24TH DR E	Aurora	289B	80011	17400-17999	
	Denver	286C	80238	8001-8299	O
24TH PL	Boulder	98W	80304	1900-1999	
24TH PL E	Adams Co	794P	80136	None	
	Denver	286D	80238	None	
24TH PL W	Jefferson Co	280D	80401	12800-12999	
	Jefferson Co	280C	80401	13300-13599	
	Lakewood	282B	80214	7100-7999	
	Lakewood	282A	80215	8000-8199	
24TH ST	Boulder	98W	80302	2100-2299	
	Boulder	98W	80304	2300-2399	
	Boulder	98S	80304	2900-3199	
24TH ST	Denver	284C	80205	300-1299	
	Denver	254X	80205	1300-1599	
24TH ST	Golden	279F	80401	400-1099	
24TH PLACE CIR W	Lakewood	281A	80215	11600-11899	
25TH AVE	Lochbuie	729Y	80603	None	
25TH AVE E	Adams Co	791P	80137	33900-34299	
	Adams Co	794P	80136	None	
25TH AVE E	Aurora	287B	80010	9600-12099	
	Aurora	288B	80011	13700-14999	
	Denver	284D	80205	700-1699	
	Denver	285A	80205	1700-2299	
	Denver	285D	80207	4000-5499	
	Denver	286B	80207	5500-7299	
	Denver	286C	80238	7700-8099	
	Denver	286D	80238	None	
25TH AVE S	Brighton	138V	80601	200-399	
25TH AVE W	Denver	283B	80211	2600-3899	
	Denver	283B	80212	3900-4299	
	Denver	283A	80212	4600-4699	
	Edgewater	282D	80214	5200-6499	
	Jefferson Co	280D	80401	13200-13599	
	Lakewood	282C	80214	6800-6999	
	Lakewood	282B	80214	7200-7899	
	Lakewood	282A	80215	8400-8599	
	Lakewood	281D	80215	9600-10799	
	Lakewood	281A	80215	11600-11899	
25TH DR E	Aurora	289B	80011	2400-2699	
	Aurora	288C	80011	15300-15599	
25TH DR E	Denver	286D	80238	7800-9199	
25TH LN W	Edgewater	282C	80214	6500-6699	
25TH PL E	Aurora	288B	80011	13700-14299	
	Denver	286C	80238	None	
25TH PL W	Jefferson Co	280C	80401	13300-13599	
	Jefferson Co	280C	80401	14000-14099	
	Lakewood	282C	80214	6900-7099	
	Lakewood	282A	80215	8000-8399	
	Lakewood	281D	80215	9600-9699	
	Lakewood	281B	80215	11100-11499	
25TH ST	Boulder	98S	80304	2900-3399	
25TH ST	Denver	284C	80205	300-1099	
	Denver	254Y	80205	1100-1499	
26TH AVE	Lochbuie	729Y	80603	None	
26TH AVE	Lochbuie	729Z	80603	None	
26TH AVE E	Adams Co	793M	80136	52100-53899	
	Adams Co	794K	80136	53900-58499	
26TH AVE E	Aurora	287C	80010	11700-12099	
	Aurora	288B	80011	14000-14899	
	Aurora	289D	80011	20100-20799	
	Aurora	290B	80019	21700-24099	
	Aurora	291B	80019	24100-24399	
	Aurora	790M	80019	28100-34499	
	Denver	284D	80205	700-1699	
	Denver	285A	80205	1700-3999	
	Denver	285C	80207	4000-5499	
	Denver	286B	80207	5500-7299	
	Denver	286C	80238	7300-8799	
	Denver	286D	80238	9001-9099	O
	Denver	287A	80238	None	
26TH AVE S	Brighton	138V	80601	300-399	
26TH AVE W	Denver	283B	80211	2400-3899	
	Denver	283B	80212	3900-5199	
	Edgewater	282C	80214	5200-6299	
	Jefferson Co	280D	80401	12800-13999	
	Jefferson Co	280B	80401	15200-15799	
	Lakewood	281C	80215	8900-12299	
	Lakewood	280D	80215	None	
	Wheat Ridge	282A	80214	6300-6799	
	Wheat Ridge	282A	80215	6800-8899	
26TH PL E	Aurora	287B	80010	10800-11099	
	Aurora	287C	80010	11700-12099	
26TH PL E	Aurora	288B	80011	14500-14799	
26TH PL W	Lakewood	281B	80215	11000-11599	
	Wheat Ridge	282B	80214	7200-7399	
26TH ST	Boulder	98W	80302	1900-2299	
	Boulder	128E	80302	None	
	Boulder Co	98E	80301	None	
26TH ST	Denver	284C	80205	400-899	
	Denver	254Y	80205	900-1499	
26TH WAY E	Aurora	288B	80011	14500-14899	
27TH AVE	Idaho Springs	780R	80452	100-199	
27TH AVE	Lochbuie	729Y	80603	None	
27TH AVE E	Denver	284D	80205	1200-1499	
	Denver	285B	80205	1800-3799	
	Denver	287A	80238	None	
27TH AVE S	Brighton	138V	80601	1-899	
27TH AVE W	Denver	283C	80211	2200-3899	
	Denver	283A	80212	3900-4899	
	Lakewood	281B	80215	11000-11599	
	Lakewood	281A	80215	12300-12599	
	Wheat Ridge	282D	80214	5300-5799	
	Wheat Ridge	282C	80214	6900-7199	
	Wheat Ridge	282B	80214	7200-7399	
	Wheat Ridge	281C	80215	10000-10199	
27TH DR E	Denver	287A	80238	None	
27TH DR W	Lakewood	281A	80215	11700-12199	
27TH LN W	Jefferson Co	280D	80401	None	
27TH PL E	Adams Co	794J	80136	None	
27TH PL E	Aurora	288B	80011	14000-14299	
27TH PL W	Lakewood	251X	80215	11000-11599	
27TH ST	Boulder	128K	80305	300-499	
	Boulder	98W	80302	2100-2299	
27TH ST	Denver	284C	80205	600-799	
	Denver	254Y	80205	800-1499	
27TH WAY	Boulder	128K	80305	400-699	
28TH AVE	Lochbuie	729Y	80603	None	
28TH AVE E	Adams Co	794K	80136	55000-56999	
28TH AVE E	Aurora	258W	80011	14000-14398	E
	Aurora	259W	80011	16900-18499	
	Denver	254Z	80205	1200-1799	
	Denver	255X	80205	1800-3999	
	Denver	255Z	80207	4000-5599	
	Denver	256W	80207	5600-6999	
	Denver	286B	80238	7300-9199	
	Denver	257W	80238	None	
28TH AVE S	Brighton	139S	80601	300-399	
28TH AVE W	Denver	253Y	80211	2000-3299	
	Denver	253W	80212	4400-4999	
	Lakewood	251X	80215	11200-11799	
	Wheat Ridge	282D	80214	5200-6599	
	Wheat Ridge	282C	80214	6600-6799	
	Wheat Ridge	252X	80033	7200-7399	
28TH CT E	Adams Co	794K	80136	56100-56499	
28TH DR E	Denver	256Y	80238	7800-8098	E
28TH LN S	Brighton	139S	80601	400-499	
28TH PL E	Adams Co	794J	80136	None	
28TH PL E	Denver	256Y	80238	7801-8099	O
	Denver	256E	80238	None	
	Denver	257W	80238	None	
28TH PL W	Jefferson Co	250Z	80401	13000-13299	
	Jefferson Co	280D	80401	13100-13299	
	Lakewood	251X	80215	10700-11899	
	Wheat Ridge	282C	80214	7000-7099	
28TH ST	Boulder	128K	80305	200-399	
	Boulder	128F	80303	700-1598	E
	Boulder	98X	80301	1600-4999	
28TH ST	Denver	284D	80205	400-699	
	Denver	254Y	80205	700-1299	
28TH ST FRONTAGE RD	Boulder	128F	80303	700-1599	
29TH AVE	Lochbuie	729Y	80603	None	
29TH AVE E	Adams Co	791K	80137	33700-34499	
	Adams Co	794J	80136	None	
29TH AVE E	Denver	254Z	80205	1200-1799	
	Denver	255X	80205	1800-3999	
	Denver	255Z	80207	4000-5599	
	Denver	256X	80207	5600-7699	
	Denver	256Y	80238	7700-9198	E
	Denver	257W	80238	None	
29TH AVE S	Brighton	139S	80601	300-399	
29TH AVE W	Denver	254X	80216	600-699	
	Denver	254X	80202	700-999	
	Denver	253Z	80211	2100-3899	
	Denver	253X	80212	3900-5199	
	Jefferson Co	250Z	80401	13000-13199	
	Jefferson Co	250X	80401	14800-15199	
	Lakewood	251X	80215	10800-11399	
	Lakewood	251W	80215	None	
	Wheat Ridge	252Y	80214	5200-6799	
	Wheat Ridge	252Y	80033	6800-7599	
	Wheat Ridge	251Y	80215	10000-10199	
	Wheat Ridge	251W	80215	12400-12699	

STREET NAME	CITY or COUNTY	MAP GRID	ZIP CODE	BLOCK RANGE	O/E
29TH DR E	Denver	256Y	80238	7300-7399	
	Denver	257X	80238	None	
29TH PL E	Adams Co	794J	80136	None	
	Denver	256Y	80207	None	
29TH PL E	Denver	256Z	80238	None	
29TH PL W	Jefferson Co	250X	80401	14900-15099	
	Lakewood	251W	80215	11400-11899	
	Wheat Ridge	252Z	80214	6100-6199	
	Wheat Ridge	252X	80033	7000-7199	
	Wheat Ridge	251W	80215	12000-12599	
29TH ST	Boulder	128K	80305	200-399	
	Boulder	128K	80303	700-899	
	Boulder	98T	80301	2600-3199	
29TH ST	Denver	284D	80205	400-599	
	Denver	254Y	80205	600-1399	
	Denver	254U	80216	1800-1999	
30TH AVE E	Adams Co	794K	80136	56600-56899	
30TH AVE E	Aurora	257Y	80010	11400-12099	
	Aurora	257Z	80011	12100-13099	
	Aurora	258X	80011	13100-13298	E
	Aurora	259X	80011	17700-18199	
	Denver	254Z	80205	1200-1799	
	Denver	255X	80205	1800-3799	
	Denver	255Z	80207	4000-5599	
	Denver	256X	80207	5600-7299	
30TH AVE S	Brighton	139S	80601	300-399	
30TH AVE W	Denver	254X	80216	600-699	
	Denver	253Z	80211	2000-2399	
	Denver	253Y	80211	3200-3899	
	Denver	253W	80212	3900-5199	
	Jefferson Co	250Y	80401	13600-14399	
	Lakewood	251X	80215	10800-11299	
	Wheat Ridge	252Z	80214	5200-6199	
	Wheat Ridge	252Y	80214	6200-6799	
	Wheat Ridge	252X	80033	7000-7399	
	Wheat Ridge	251Y	80215	10000-10099	
30TH DR W	Jefferson Co	250Z	80401	13000-13199	
30TH LN W	Jefferson Co	250Y	80401	14000-14099	
30TH PL W	Jefferson Co	250Y	80401	13600-14599	
	Lakewood	251X	80215	10800-11299	
	Lakewood	251W	80215	11700-11999	
	Wheat Ridge	251W	80215	12100-12199	
30TH ST	Boulder	128K	80305	100-399	
	Boulder	128F	80303	501-1599	O
	Boulder	98X	80301	1600-3499	
	Boulder Co	98K	80301	3800-4499	
30TH ST	Denver	254Y	80205	500-1299	
31ST AVE E	Adams Co	794J	80136	None	
31ST AVE E	Aurora	257Z	80011	12200-12899	
	Aurora	258W	80011	13100-13499	
	Aurora	257Y	80010	None	
	Denver	254Z	80205	1200-1799	
	Denver	255W	80205	1800-3199	
	Denver	255X	80205	3300-3799	
	Denver	257W	80238	9800-10099	
31ST AVE S	Brighton	139S	80601	300-399	
31ST AVE W	Denver	254X	80216	600-699	
	Denver	253Z	80211	2000-2399	
	Denver	253Y	80211	3100-3599	
	Denver	253W	80212	4400-4999	
	Jefferson Co	250Z	80401	13000-13199	
	Jefferson Co	250Y	80401	13600-13999	
	Jefferson Co	250X	80401	14800-14999	
	Lakewood	251Y	80215	10400-10599	
	Lakewood	251X	80215	10800-11299	
	Wheat Ridge	252Y	80214	6400-6799	
	Wheat Ridge	252Y	80033	6900-6999	
	Wheat Ridge	251Y	80215	10000-10399	
	Wheat Ridge	251W	80215	12300-12799	
31ST CIR E	Aurora	260W	80011	None	
31ST PL E	Denver	257X	80238	None	
31ST PL W	Lakewood	251Y	80215	10500-10999	
	Lakewood	251X	80215	11500-11699	
	Wheat Ridge	252X	80033	7200-7399	
	Wheat Ridge	251W	80215	12000-12299	
31ST ST	Boulder	128F	80303	700-899	
	Boulder	98X	80301	1900-1999	
	Boulder	98T	80301	2500-2699	
31ST ST	Denver	254Y	80205	700-1399	
	Denver	254U	80216	1800-2199	
	Denver	254T	80216	2600-2799	
32ND AVE E	Adams Co	794K	80136	56600-56999	
32ND AVE E	Aurora	258Z	80011	15300-16899	
	Denver	257W	80238	None	
	Aurora	259W	80011	16900-18199	
32ND AVE S	Brighton	139N	80601	300-399	
32ND AVE W	Denver	254W	80211	1500-1899	
	Denver	253Z	80211	1900-3899	
	Denver	253W	80212	3900-5199	
	Jefferson Co	250Y	80401	12800-16399	
	Jefferson Co	249Y	80401	16400-17799	
	Wheat Ridge	252Y	80212	5200-5999	
	Wheat Ridge	252Y	80033	6000-8899	
	Wheat Ridge	251X	80033	8900-12799	
32ND DR W	Jefferson Co	250X	80401	14900-15199	
	Wheat Ridge	251W	80033	12000-12199	
32ND PKWY E	Aurora	259Z	80011	18500-20799	
	Aurora	260W	80011	20800-21699	
32ND PL E	Aurora	258X	80011	13700-14299	
	Aurora	259W	80011	17000-18199	
	Aurora	258Y	80011	None	
32ND PL W	Jefferson Co	250X	80401	14900-15199	
	Wheat Ridge	252Y	80033	6800-7299	
	Wheat Ridge	252W	80033	8500-8999	
	Wheat Ridge	251Y	80033	10500-10699	
	Wheat Ridge	251W	80033	11700-11999	
32ND ST	Boulder	128F	80303	700-899	
	Boulder	98X	80301	1900-2199	
	Boulder	98T	80301	None	
32ND ST	Denver	254Y	80205	800-1499	
32ND ST N	Boulder Co	723B	80302	7600-7699	
32ND ST S	Boulder	128K	80305	1-199	
33RD AVE E	Aurora	257Y	80010	11400-12099	
	Aurora	257V	80011	12500-12699	
	Aurora	258Y	80011	15300-15699	
	Denver	254Z	80205	1200-1799	
	Denver	255X	80205	1800-3599	

Continued on next column

STREET NAME	CITY or COUNTY	MAP GRID	ZIP CODE	BLOCK RANGE	O/E
33RD AVE E (Cont'd)	Denver	255Z	80207	4600-5599	
	Denver	256X	80207	5600-7299	
	Denver	256Z	80238	None	
	Denver	257W	80238	None	
33RD AVE S	Brighton	139S	80601	300-399	
33RD AVE W	Denver	254W	80211	1400-1899	
	Denver	253Z	80211	1900-2999	
	Denver	253X	80211	3300-3899	
	Denver	253W	80212	3900-5199	
	Jefferson Co	250Z	80401	13100-13599	
	Wheat Ridge	252Z	80212	5200-5999	
	Wheat Ridge	252Y	80033	6000-7199	
	Wheat Ridge	252X	80033	7200-7599	
	Wheat Ridge	252X	80033	7700-8199	
	Wheat Ridge	251Y	80033	10100-10399	
	Wheat Ridge	251X	80033	11100-11799	
33RD CT	Adams Co	794K	80136	56100-56599	
33RD DR E	Aurora	258V	80011	16200-16699	
	Aurora	260W	80011	None	
33RD PL E	Adams Co	794K	80136	56600-56999	
33RD PL E	Aurora	258T	80011	13800-15699	
33RD PL W	Jefferson Co	250Z	80401	13200-13399	
	Wheat Ridge	251Y	80033	10400-10499	
	Wheat Ridge	251Y	80033	11700-11799	
33RD ST	Boulder	128F	80303	700-899	
	Boulder	128B	80303	1600-1799	
	Boulder	98X	80301	1800-1999	
	Boulder	98X	80301	None	
	Boulder	128F	80303	None	
33RD ST	Denver	254U	80205	900-1199	
33RD ST S	Boulder	128P	80305	1-199	
34TH AVE E	Denver	255V	80207	5000-5199	
34TH AVE E	Denver	256V	80238	None	
	Denver	257S	80238	None	
34TH AVE S	Brighton	139S	80601	600-899	
34TH AVE W	Denver	254W	80211	1400-1899	
	Denver	253U	80211	1900-3699	
	Denver	253S	80212	4400-5199	
	Jefferson Co	250Z	80401	13500-13599	
	Wheat Ridge	252Z	80212	5800-5999	
	Wheat Ridge	252Y	80033	6500-6599	
	Wheat Ridge	252X	80033	7200-7599	
	Wheat Ridge	252W	80033	8700-8799	
	Wheat Ridge	251Y	80033	10000-10599	
	Wheat Ridge	251X	80033	11700-11799	
34TH CT S	Brighton	139S	80601	None	
34TH DR E	Aurora	259Y	80011	19100-19699	
34TH DR W	Wheat Ridge	252X	80033	7800-7999	
	Wheat Ridge	251Y	80033	9700-9999	
34TH PL E	Denver	256V	80238	None	
34TH PL E	Denver	257S	80238	None	
34TH PL W	Wheat Ridge	252X	80033	7000-7299	
	Wheat Ridge	251Y	80033	10200-10799	
	Wheat Ridge	251W	80033	12000-12399	
34TH ST	Boulder	128F	80303	700-999	
	Boulder	98T	80301	3000-3299	
	Boulder	98P	80301	3300-3499	
34TH ST	Denver	254U	80205	1000-1499	
34TH ST N	Boulder Co	723B	80302	7600-7699	
34TH ST S	Boulder	128P	80305	1-199	
35TH AVE E	Aurora	258U	80011	15800-15899	
	Denver	254V	80205	1200-1799	
	Denver	255T	80205	1800-3999	
	Denver	255V	80207	4000-5599	
	Denver	256S	80207	5600-7299	
	Denver	256U	80238	None	
	Denver	256V	80238	None	
	Denver	257S	80238	None	
35TH AVE W	Denver	254S	80211	1300-1899	
	Denver	253U	80211	1900-3899	
	Denver	253S	80212	3900-5199	
	Wheat Ridge	252U	80212	5200-5999	
	Wheat Ridge	252U	80033	6000-7199	
	Wheat Ridge	252T	80033	7300-7999	
	Wheat Ridge	252S	80033	8700-8899	
	Wheat Ridge	251V	80033	8900-9899	
	Wheat Ridge	251U	80033	9900-10799	
	Wheat Ridge	251S	80033	11600-12599	
35TH CT E	Adams Co	794K	80136	56100-56599	
35TH CT S	Brighton	139S	80601	None	
35TH DR E	Aurora	259Z	80011	20100-20799	
35TH DR E	Denver	256V	80238	8500-8799	
35TH PL E	Adams Co	794K	80136	56600-56899	
35TH PL E	Aurora	258T	80011	13800-16099	
35TH PL E	Denver	256V	80238	None	
35TH PL W	Wheat Ridge	252U	80033	6100-6199	
	Wheat Ridge	252T	80033	7200-7299	
	Wheat Ridge	251U	80033	10400-10799	
35TH ST	Boulder	128G	80303	700-1199	
35TH ST	Denver	254V	80205	1200-1499	
	Denver	254U	80216	1600-1999	
35TH ST N	Boulder Co	723B	80302	7600-7699	
35TH ST S	Boulder	128P	80305	1-199	
36TH AVE E	Aurora	258U	80011	15600-16099	
	Denver	254V	80205	1200-1799	
	Denver	255T	80205	1800-3999	
	Denver	255V	80207	4800-5599	
	Denver	256T	80207	5600-7699	
	Denver	256V	80238	None	
36TH AVE S	Brighton	139S	80601	600-798	E
36TH AVE W	Denver	254S	80211	1100-1899	
	Denver	253U	80211	1900-3499	
	Denver	253S	80212	4400-5199	
	Wheat Ridge	252U	80033	6700-7199	
	Wheat Ridge	252T	80033	7300-7599	
	Wheat Ridge	251V	80033	9400-9899	
	Wheat Ridge	251U	80033	10400-10799	
	Wheat Ridge	251S	80033	11600-11899	
36TH DR E	Aurora	259V	80011	20100-20799	
	Aurora	260S	80011	None	
36TH PL E	Aurora	258U	80011	None	
36TH PL W	Denver	253S	80212	4400-4799	
	Wheat Ridge	252V	80212	5600-5699	
	Wheat Ridge	252U	80033	6700-6899	
	Wheat Ridge	251U	80033	10500-10599	
	Wheat Ridge	251S	80033	11800-12199	
36TH ST	Boulder	128G	80303	700-1099	
36TH ST	Denver	254V	80205	1300-1599	
	Denver	254U	80216	1600-2099	
36TH ST S	Boulder	128P	80305	1-399	
37TH AVE E	Aurora	258S	80239	13400-13599	
	Denver	254V	80205	1200-1799	
	Denver	255T	80205	1800-3999	
	Denver	257U	80239	10500-13099	
	Denver	258S	80239	13100-13399	
	Denver	256V	80238	None	
37TH AVE W	Denver	254S	80211	1000-1899	
	Denver	253U	80211	1900-3899	
	Denver	253S	80212	3900-5199	
	Wheat Ridge	252V	80212	5700-5999	
	Wheat Ridge	252U	80033	7000-7199	
	Wheat Ridge	251V	80033	9200-9899	
	Wheat Ridge	251T	80033	11600-11699	
37TH CT E	Adams Co	794K	80136	56200-56599	
37TH PL E	Adams Co	794K	80136	56600-56899	
	Aurora	258S	80239	13400-13599	
37TH PL W	Denver	253S	80212	None	
	Wheat Ridge	252V	80212	5800-5999	
	Wheat Ridge	252U	80033	6700-6799	
	Wheat Ridge	252S	80033	8800-8899	
	Wheat Ridge	251V	80033	9400-9599	
	Wheat Ridge	251U	80033	10100-10299	
	Wheat Ridge	251S	80033	11600-12199	
37TH ST	Boulder	128G	80303	700-999	
38TH AVE E	Adams Co	792M	80102	42500-45499	
	Adams Co	793J	80102	45500-48499	
	Adams Co	793L	80102	48500-52099	
	Adams Co	794K	80136	58500-61699	
	Adams Co	794L	80136	61700-64899	
	Adams Co	795H	80103	64900-72899	
	Adams Co	795H	80136	None	
38TH AVE E	Aurora	258U	80011	14500-15299	
	Aurora	259U	80011	None	
	Aurora	260S	80011	None	
	Denver	254V	80205	1200-1799	
	Denver	255S	80205	1800-2299	
	Denver	255T	80205	3200-3999	
	Denver	255V	80207	4800-5599	
	Denver	256T	80207	5600-7299	
	Denver	257U	80239	12000-12099	
	Denver	257V	80239	12600-13099	
	Denver	258S	80239	13100-13599	
38TH AVE E	Aurora	791J	80137	33700-33799	
38TH AVE W	Denver	254S	80211	900-1899	
	Denver	253U	80211	1900-3899	
	Denver	253S	80212	3900-5199	
	Wheat Ridge	252V	80212	5200-5999	
	Wheat Ridge	252U	80033	6000-8899	
	Wheat Ridge	251T	80033	8900-12799	
38TH DR W	Wheat Ridge	251S	80033	12400-12699	
38TH PL E	Denver	260S	80249	20600-21799	
38TH PL W	Wheat Ridge	252S	80033	8200-8299	
	Wheat Ridge	251U	80033	10400-11199	
	Wheat Ridge	251S	80033	11500-11699	
38TH ST	Boulder	128G	80303	700-1299	
38TH ST	Denver	254V	80205	1400-1599	
	Denver	254U	80216	1600-2199	
38TH ST S	Boulder	128Q	80305	1-499	
	Boulder	128C	80301	1600-1899	
39TH AVE E	Adams Co	794K	80136	55400-55899	
	Adams Co	794J	80136	56300-56899	
39TH AVE E	Aurora	258T	80011	13800-15099	
	Denver	254V	80205	1600-1799	
	Denver	255S	80205	1800-1999	
	Denver	255T	80205	3200-3899	
	Denver	255V	80207	4800-5399	
	Denver	256T	80207	5600-7299	
	Denver	257V	80239	12000-13099	
	Denver	258S	80239	13100-13599	
	Denver	259U	80249	19100-19899	
	Denver	260S	80249	20700-21599	
39TH AVE W	Denver	254T	80216	600-899	
	Denver	254S	80211	1000-1899	
	Denver	253U	80211	1900-3899	
	Denver	253S	80212	3900-5199	
	Wheat Ridge	252V	80212	5800-5999	
	Wheat Ridge	252V	80033	6000-6099	
	Wheat Ridge	252U	80033	6200-6399	
	Wheat Ridge	252T	80033	7000-8199	
	Wheat Ridge	252S	80033	8600-8699	
	Wheat Ridge	251V	80033	9400-9999	
	Wheat Ridge	251T	80033	10800-10999	
39TH CIR W	Wheat Ridge	251S	80033	11600-11699	
39TH PL E	Denver	259U	80249	19100-19399	
39TH PL W	Wheat Ridge	252V	80212	5900-5999	
	Wheat Ridge	252V	80033	6000-6099	
	Wheat Ridge	251T	80033	10800-11599	
	Wheat Ridge	251S	80033	11600-11699	
39TH ST	Boulder	128G	80303	700-899	
39TH ST	Denver	254V	80216	1700-1799	
39TH ST N	Boulder Co	723C	80503	7200-7599	
	Boulder Co	703Y	80503	8200-9399	
39TH ST S	Boulder	128Q	80305	200-499	
40TH AVE E	Adams Co	794F	80136	None	
40TH AVE E	Aurora	258V	80011	15900-16299	
	Denver	254V	80205	1600-1799	
	Denver	255S	80205	1800-3999	
	Denver	256U	80238	4000-7999	
	Denver	257T	80239	10500-12099	
	Denver	257V	80239	12600-13099	
	Denver	258Q	80239	14700-15599	
	Denver	259V	80249	19100-20499	
	Denver	260S	80249	20200-21599	
	Denver	259N	80249	None	
40TH AVE N	Brighton	139K	80601	None	
40TH AVE W	Denver	254T	80216	501-599	O
	Denver	254S	80211	900-1899	
	Denver	253U	80211	1900-3599	
	Wheat Ridge	252V	80212	5300-5399	
	Wheat Ridge	252V	80033	6000-6199	
	Wheat Ridge	252U	80033	6200-6299	
	Wheat Ridge	252S	80033	8200-8399	
	Wheat Ridge	251U	80033	10000-10199	
	Wheat Ridge	251T	80033	11000-11399	

STREET NAME	CITY or COUNTY	MAP GRID	ZIP CODE	BLOCK RANGE	O/E
40TH CIR E	Aurora	258V	80011	16400-16499	
40TH CIR W	Wheat Ridge	251S	80033	11600-11699	
40TH DR E	Adams Co	794G	80136	58100-58899	
	Denver	259V	80249	19500-19599	
40TH PL E	Denver	259U	80249	19300-20099	
	Denver	259V	80249	20100-20499	
	Denver	260S	80249	20700-21599	
40TH ST	Denver	254V	80205	1300-1499	
	Denver	254R	80216	1700-1799	
40TH ST S	Boulder	128Q	80305	200-699	
41ST AVE E	Adams Co	794E	80136	55300-56899	
41ST AVE E	Denver	255P	80216	2700-3999	
	Denver	255R	80216	4800-5199	
	Denver	256P	80216	7400-7599	
	Denver	259Q	80249	18600-18699	
	Denver	259R	80249	19300-20399	
	Denver	260S	80249	21000-21099	
	Denver	260N	80249	21100-21399	
41ST AVE W	Denver	254T	80216	601-699	O
	Denver	254S	80211	900-1899	
	Denver	253U	80211	1900-3899	
	Denver	253S	80212	3900-5199	
	Mountain View	252U	80212	5201-5999	O
	Wheat Ridge	252U	80212	5200-5998	E
	Wheat Ridge	252U	80033	6000-6999	
	Wheat Ridge	252N	80033	7600-8899	
	Wheat Ridge	251T	80033	10000-11199	
41ST PL E	Denver	259Q	80249	18600-19399	
	Denver	259R	80249	19700-20499	
	Denver	260N	80249	20900-21599	
41ST PL W	Wheat Ridge	251T	80033	10800-11099	
41ST ST N	Boulder Co	723C	80503	7600-8199	
41ST ST S	Boulder	128Q	80305	200-799	
42ND AVE E	Adams Co	793G	80102	None	
42ND AVE E	Denver	255P	80216	2701-3599	O
	Denver	256N	80216	5701-6299	O
	Denver	257R	80239	12400-14199	
	Denver	259P	80249	18600-18699	
	Denver	259R	80249	19400-20799	
	Denver	260P	80249	20200-21699	
42ND AVE N	Brighton	139L	80601	None	
42ND AVE S	Brighton	139Q	80601	None	
42ND AVE W	Denver	254P	80216	400-798	E
	Denver	254N	80211	900-1899	
	Denver	253Q	80211	1900-3599	
	Denver	253P	80212	4000-4399	
	Wheat Ridge	252Q	80033	6100-6299	
	Wheat Ridge	252T	80033	7000-7199	
	Wheat Ridge	252P	80033	7600-7999	
	Wheat Ridge	251N	80033	12200-12799	
	Wheat Ridge	251Q	80033	None	
	Wheat Ridge	251R	80033	None	
42ND CT E	Adams Co	794F	80136	56900-57699	
42ND DR E	Adams Co	794G	80136	58100-58899	
42ND PL E	Denver	259P	80249	18500-18699	
	Denver	259R	80249	20100-20199	
42ND ST S	Boulder	128Q	80305	100-799	
43RD AVE E	Aurora	260R	80019	23300-23999	
	Denver	254Q	80216	1-299	
	Denver	255P	80216	1900-3499	
	Denver	255R	80216	5300-5399	
	Denver	258P	80239	14400-15099	
	Denver	259P	80249	18500-19299	
	Denver	259R	80249	20100-20699	
	Denver	260N	80249	20200-21199	
	Denver	260P	80249	None	
43RD AVE W	Denver	254P	80216	400-799	
	Denver	254N	80211	1000-1899	
	Denver	253R	80211	1900-2999	
	Denver	253N	80212	3900-5199	
	Jefferson Co	250T	80403	15200-15499	
	Mountain View	252R	80212	5200-5799	
	Wheat Ridge	252Q	80033	6200-6299	
	Wheat Ridge	252P	80033	7000-7199	
	Wheat Ridge	251R	80033	9700-9799	
	Wheat Ridge	251Q	80033	10000-10299	
	Wheat Ridge	251P	80033	11000-11099	
43RD DR W	Jefferson Co	249Q	80403	17200-17499	
	Wheat Ridge	250R	80033	12800-13699	
43RD PL E	Denver	259R	80249	20100-20199	
	Denver	259P	80249	None	
	Denver	260P	80249	None	
43RD PL W	Wheat Ridge	252P	80033	7000-7199	
43RD ST	Denver	254R	80216	1700-1799	
43RD ST S	Boulder	128Q	80305	300-799	
44TH AVE E	Denver	254Q	80216	1-599	
	Denver	255P	80216	1900-3799	
	Denver	258N	80239	14400-14599	
	Denver	259Q	80249	18700-18999	
	Denver	259R	80249	20200-20799	
	Denver	260N	80249	20800-21599	
44TH AVE E	Denver	257R	80239	None	
44TH AVE W	Denver	254P	80216	1-599	
	Denver	254N	80211	900-1899	
	Denver	253Q	80211	2000-3899	
	Denver	253P	80212	3900-5199	
	Golden	249U	80403	16400-16999	
	Golden	249U	80403	17001-17799	O
	Golden	249U	80401	17901-18199	O
	Jefferson Co	250N	80403	12600-16399	
	Lakeside	252Q	80212	5200-5999	
	Wheat Ridge	252Q	80033	6000-8899	
	Wheat Ridge	251P	80033	8900-12599	
44TH DR E	Adams Co	794G	80136	58600-58799	
44TH DR W	Jefferson Co	250Q	80403	14201-14399	O
44TH PL E	Denver	259Q	80249	18800-18999	
44TH PL W	Jefferson Co	250Q	80403	14100-14299	
	Wheat Ridge	252Q	80033	6300-6799	
	Wheat Ridge	252P	80033	7300-7399	
	Wheat Ridge	252N	80033	8000-8699	
	Wheat Ridge	251Q	80033	10300-10499	
	Wheat Ridge	251P	80033	10800-10999	
44TH ST	Denver	254R	80216	1700-1999	
44TH ST S	Boulder	128Q	80305	300-799	
45TH AVE	Adams Co	791F	80137	None	
45TH AVE E	Denver	254Q	80216	1-699	
	Denver	255P	80216	2400-3999	
	Denver	257P	80239	10500-11299	
	Denver	257Q	80239	11700-12099	
	Denver	258P	80239	14400-14999	
	Denver	259Q	80249	18500-19499	
	Denver	260N	80249	20400-21199	
	Denver	260P	80249	21500-21599	
	Denver	256Q	80238	None	
	Denver	257N	80238	None	
45TH AVE N	Brighton	139L	80601	None	
45TH AVE S	Brighton	139Q	80601	None	
45TH AVE W	Denver	254P	80216	301-599	O
	Denver	254N	80211	900-1299	
	Denver	253Q	80211	1900-3899	
	Denver	253N	80212	3900-5199	
	Wheat Ridge	252Q	80033	6000-7599	
	Wheat Ridge	252P	80033	8000-8599	
	Wheat Ridge	251R	80033	9200-9499	
	Wheat Ridge	251P	80033	10300-11299	
45TH DR W	Golden	250N	80403	16100-16199	
	Jefferson Co	250Q	80403	14200-14599	
45TH PL E	Denver	259Q	80249	18600-18699	
45TH PL W	Jefferson Co	250Q	80403	14200-14299	
	Wheat Ridge	252Q	80033	6200-6799	
	Wheat Ridge	252P	80033	7400-7599	
	Wheat Ridge	252N	80033	8000-8099	
	Wheat Ridge	251P	80033	11400-11499	
45TH ST S	Boulder	128Q	80305	300-499	
46TH AVE E	Denver	254Q	80216	1-699	
	Denver	254R	80216	800-2099	
	Denver	255N	80216	2100-2299	
	Denver	255Q	80216	4100-4499	
	Denver	255R	80216	4600-5399	
	Denver	257Q	80239	12000-12399	
	Denver	257M	80239	12900-12999	
	Denver	258N	80239	14000-14299	
	Denver	258P	80239	14500-15299	
	Denver	259Q	80249	18600-19599	
	Denver	259R	80249	20100-20399	
	Denver	260N	80249	21000-21199	
	Denver	260P	80249	21400-21599	
	Denver	256Q	80238	None	
46TH AVE N	Brighton	139L	80601	None	
46TH AVE W	Denver	254N	80211	1000-1899	
	Denver	253P	80211	1900-3899	
	Denver	253N	80212	3900-5199	
	Jefferson Co	250Q	80403	14100-14299	
	Wheat Ridge	252Q	80033	6000-6599	
	Wheat Ridge	252P	80033	7400-8299	
	Wheat Ridge	252N	80033	8300-8899	
	Wheat Ridge	251Q	80033	10300-10799	
	Wheat Ridge	251P	80033	11200-11799	
46TH CIR W	Wheat Ridge	252N	80033	8000-8099	
46TH DR W	Jefferson Co	250Q	80403	14400-14599	
46TH PL E	Denver	259Q	80249	18600-19199	
	Denver	259R	80249	20100-20299	
46TH PL W	Wheat Ridge	252Q	80033	6200-6899	
	Wheat Ridge	252P	80033	7200-7399	
	Wheat Ridge	251R	80033	8800-9199	
	Wheat Ridge	251P	80033	10800-11399	
46TH ST S	Boulder	128Q	80305	500-1099	
46TH AVENUE DR E	Denver	256P	80216	6700-7099	
47TH AVE E	Denver	254Q	80216	1-699	
	Denver	254R	80216	1400-1699	
	Denver	255N	80216	1700-3199	
	Denver	255R	80216	5200-5599	
	Denver	257J	80238	9900-10299	
	Denver	257L	80239	10500-12099	
	Denver	257M	80239	12900-12999	
	Denver	258J	80239	13000-13199	
	Denver	258P	80239	14400-14899	
	Denver	259Q	80249	18600-18699	
	Denver	259L	80249	18900-19199	
	Denver	259R	80249	19600-20699	
	Denver	260N	80249	20400-21199	
	Denver	260K	80249	21400-21599	
	Denver	256L	80238	None	
47TH AVE N	Brighton	139G	80601	None	
47TH AVE W	Denver	254N	80211	1000-1899	
	Denver	253R	80211	1900-3099	
	Denver	253P	80211	3600-3899	
	Denver	253P	80212	3900-4399	
	Wheat Ridge	252Q	80033	6000-6799	
	Wheat Ridge	252P	80033	7300-8099	
	Wheat Ridge	251R	80033	9400-9599	
	Wheat Ridge	251Q	80033	10300-10799	
	Wheat Ridge	251P	80033	10800-11399	
	Denver	258N	80239	14300-14599	
47TH DR E	Denver	259L	80249	None	
47TH PL E	Denver	259M	80249	20200-20399	
	Denver	259L	80249	None	
47TH PL W	Wheat Ridge	252Q	80033	6100-6999	
	Wheat Ridge	251Q	80033	10300-10799	
47TH ST	Boulder	98U	80301	2500-4899	
47TH ST	Boulder Co	98G	80301	None	
47TH AVENUE CIR E	Denver	258J	80239	12900-13099	
47TH AVENUE DR E	Denver	256K	80216	6600-7299	
47TH AVE E	Adams Co	792K	80102	39300-48899	
	Adams Co	793F	80102	48900-50199	
	Adams Co	793H	80136	52100-53899	
	Adams Co	794E	80136	53900-57199	
	Adams Co	795H	80103	65000-67999	
	Aurora	791E	80137	34100-37799	
48TH AVE E	Commerce City	255M	80216	5201-5599	O
	Commerce City	256J	80216	5600-6898	E
	Denver	254L	80216	1-699	
	Denver	255K	80216	1700-5199	
	Denver	256J	80216	5601-6899	O
	Denver	257M	80239	12100-13199	
	Denver	258K	80239	14400-14599	
	Denver	258M	80239	15300-16899	
	Denver	256L	80238	None	
	Denver	257K	80238	None	
48TH AVE N	Brighton	139M	80601	None	
48TH AVE W	Denver	254L	80216	1-799	
	Denver	254J	80221	800-1899	
	Denver	253M	80221	1900-2899	
	Denver	253K	80221	3100-3899	
	Denver	253K	80212	3900-4399	
	Denver	252M	80212	5200-5999	
	Jefferson Co	250L	80403	14000-14799	
	Jefferson Co	250K	80403	14800-15599	
	Wheat Ridge	252M	80033	6000-6499	
	Wheat Ridge	252K	80033	6500-7499	
	Wheat Ridge	252P	80033	7600-7799	
	Wheat Ridge	252J	80033	7800-8399	
	Wheat Ridge	251L	80033	10600-10899	
48TH CIR W	Wheat Ridge	252P	80033	7300-7499	
48TH DR E	Denver	259M	80249	20300-20399	
	Denver	260J	80249	None	
48TH LN W	Jefferson Co	249M	80403	None	
48TH PL E	Denver	258L	80239	15600-15899	
	Denver	259L	80249	19601-20299	O
	Denver	260J	80249	20200-21199	
	Denver	259M	80249	20401-20899	O
	Denver	260K	80249	None	
48TH PL W	Golden	249M	80403	16900-16999	
	Jefferson Co	252J	80002	8500-8599	
	Jefferson Co	250L	80403	14000-14099	
	Jefferson Co	249M	80403	None	
	Wheat Ridge	252L	80033	6200-6499	
48TH ST	Boulder	128D	80303	1500-1599	
	Boulder	128D	80301	1600-1699	
	Boulder	98Y	80301	None	
48TH AVENUE DR W	Denver	253R	80211	2200S-2298S	E
49TH AVE E	Commerce City	256K	80022	6000-7299	
	Denver	254L	80216	1-899	
	Denver	255K	80216	1900-3399	
	Denver	257J	80238	10300-10499	
	Denver	257K	80239	10700-10899	
	Denver	257L	80239	11700-12099	
	Denver	259L	80249	19600-20099	
	Denver	260J	80249	20200-21199	
	Denver	259M	80249	20300-20999	
	Denver	258K	80239	None	
	Denver	258M	80239	None	
	Denver	259K	80249	None	
	Denver	260J	80249	None	
49TH AVE W	Denver	254L	80216	2-98	E
	Denver	254J	80221	1800-1899	
	Denver	253M	80221	1900-3899	
	Denver	253K	80212	3900-4399	
	Denver	252M	80212	5200-5999	
	Jefferson Co	251M	80002	8800-9199	
	Jefferson Co	250K	80403	14800-14899	
	Wheat Ridge	251M	80033	9200-10299	
	Wheat Ridge	251K	80033	11700-11899	
	Wheat Ridge	251J	80033	12400-12799	
49TH CIR W	Jefferson Co	252J	80002	None	
49TH DR E	Commerce City	256J	80022	None	
49TH DR W	Wheat Ridge	252L	80002	6300-6399	
49TH PL E	Denver	259L	80249	19600-20099	
	Denver	260J	80249	None	
49TH PL W	Jefferson Co	251M	80002	8800-9199	
	Jefferson Co	250K	80403	14800-15099	
	Wheat Ridge	252M	80033	6000-6199	
	Wheat Ridge	251J	80033	12300-12399	
49TH ST	Boulder	98Y	80301	2400-2599	
49TH ST N	Boulder Co	723D	80503	7000-7999	
	Boulder Co	703R	80503	10200-10999	
50TH AVE E	Commerce City	256J	80022	5900-6999	
	Denver	254L	80216	1-1599	
	Denver	255K	80216	2700-5099	
	Denver	257M	80239	12200-12999	
	Denver	258J	80239	13500-14199	
	Denver	258K	80239	14400-15199	
	Denver	258L	80239	15600-15699	
	Denver	259L	80249	19600-19798	E
	Denver	259K	80249	None	
	Denver	260K	80249	None	
	Denver	260J	80249	None	
	Denver	256L	80238	None	
	Denver	256M	80238	None	
50TH AVE W	Arvada	252L	80002	6500-6799	
	Denver	254L	80216	1-99	
	Denver	254K	80216	601-699	O
	Denver	254J	80221	1500-1899	
	Denver	253M	80221	1900-2999	
	Denver	253K	80221	3600-3899	
	Denver	253K	80212	3900-4699	
	Denver	252M	80212	5400-5999	
	Golden	250J	80403	15600-16399	
	Golden	249M	80403	16400-16799	
	Jefferson Co	252J	80002	8400-8999	
	Jefferson Co	250M	80033	12800-12899	
	Jefferson Co	250L	80403	14000-14799	
	Wheat Ridge	251M	80002	9600-9999	
	Wheat Ridge	251L	80033	10400-10799	
	Wheat Ridge	251K	80033	11000-11399	
50TH DR E	Denver	258K	80239	14900-15099	
	Denver	259L	80249	None	
50TH PL E	Denver	260J	80249	None	
	Denver	259L	80249	None	
50TH PL W	Jefferson Co	250L	80403	14100-14299	
	Wheat Ridge	251J	80033	12000-12399	
	Wheat Ridge	251M	80033	None	
50TH ST	Boulder	98Y	80301	None	
50TH WAY E	Denver	258L	80239	15000-15299	
51ST AVE E	Denver	254L	80216	1-899	
	Denver	255K	80216	2400-3199	
	Denver	255L	80216	4300-4799	
	Denver	257K	80239	10500-11999	
	Denver	257M	80239	12100-13099	
	Denver	258J	80239	13100-14799	
	Denver	258L	80239	15400-15999	
	Denver	259L	80249	None	
	Denver	260K	80249	None	
	Denver	259L	80249	None	
51ST AVE W	Arvada	252L	80002	6500-6799	
	Arvada	252K	80002	7600-7999	
	Arvada	252J	80002	8400-8899	
	Arvada	251M	80002	8900-9599	

Continued on next page

STREET NAME	CITY or COUNTY	MAP GRID	ZIP CODE	BLOCK RANGE	O/E
51ST AVE W (Cont'd)	Denver	**254L**	80216	1-99	
	Denver	**254J**	80221	1500-1899	
	Denver	**253M**	80221	1900-1999	
	Denver	**253M**	80221	2400-2999	
	Denver	**253K**	80221	3600-3899	
	Denver	**253K**	80212	3900-4399	
	Denver	**252M**	80212	5200-5999	
	Jefferson Co	**252J**	80002	8000-8399	
	Jefferson Co	**250L**	80002	13600-13799	
	Jefferson Co	**249M**	80403	16400-16699	
	Jefferson Co	**250J**	80403	None	
51ST DR E	Denver	**258L**	80239	15600-15699	
	Denver	**260J**	80249	None	
51ST LN W	Jefferson Co	**250J**	80403	16100-16399	
51ST PL E	Denver	**258K**	80239	14500-14999	
	Denver	**258L**	80239	15600-15699	
	Denver	**260K**	80249	None	
	Denver	**259G**	80249	None	
	Denver	**260E**	80249	None	
51ST PL W	Arvada	**251M**	80002	9600-9999	
	Denver	**252M**	80212	5500-5599	
	Jefferson Co	**250L**	80002	13600-13799	
	Jefferson Co	**250K**	80403	15200-15599	
	Jefferson Co	**249M**	80403	16400-16699	
	Wheat Ridge	**251J**	80033	None	
51ST ST	Boulder Co	**98H**	80301	4200-5599	
51ST ST N	Boulder Co	**723M**	80301	5600-6099	
	Boulder Co	**703V**	80503	10000-10199	
	Boulder Co	**703H**	80503	None	
52ND AVE E	Adams Co	**254L**	80216	1-499	O
	Adams Co	**254M**	80216	801-899	O
	Commerce City	**255L**	80022	4201-5299	O
	Commerce City	**255M**	80022	5300-5599	
	Commerce City	**256J**	80022	5600-6199	
	Denver	**254L**	80216	2-498	E
	Denver	**255K**	80216	2500-3899	
	Denver	**255L**	80022	4200-4598	E
	Denver	**258K**	80239	14100-14999	
	Denver	**258L**	80239	15500-15999	
	Denver	**259H**	80249	None	
	Denver	**260J**	80249	None	
	Denver	**260E**	80249	None	
52ND AVE N	Brighton	**139M**	80601	None	
52ND AVE W	Adams Co	**254J**	80221	901-1899	O
	Adams Co	**253M**	80221	1901-2599	O
	Adams Co	**253K**	80221	3601-3899	O
	Adams Co	**253J**	80212	3901-5199	O
	Arvada	**252L**	80212	5200-5999	
	Arvada	**252L**	80002	6000-8899	
	Arvada	**251M**	80002	8900-9599	
	Arvada	**250L**	80002	12600-13199	
	Denver	**254J**	80221	900-1898	E
	Denver	**253M**	80221	1900-2598	E
	Denver	**253L**	80221	2600-2999	
	Denver	**253K**	80221	3600-3898	E
	Denver	**253J**	80212	3900-5198	E
	Jefferson Co	**251J**	80002	12400-12599	
	Jefferson Co	**250L**	80002	13200-14799	
	Jefferson Co	**250L**	80403	14800-15599	
	Jefferson Co	**249M**	80403	None	
	Wheat Ridge	**251J**	80033	11600-12399	
52ND DR W	Jefferson Co	**250J**	80403	15600-16499	
	Jefferson Co	**249E**	80403	None	
52ND PL E	Commerce City	**256F**	80022	6800-7099	
	Denver	**257G**	80239	12200-12299	
	Denver	**260F**	80249	None	
	Denver	**259G**	80249	None	
52ND PL W	Adams Co	**254E**	80221	1600-1899	
	Adams Co	**253H**	80221	1900-2199	
	Adams Co	**253E**	80212	4400-4599	
	Arvada	**252G**	80002	6800-6999	
	Arvada	**252E**	80002	8400-8499	
	Arvada	**251E**	80002	11900-12099	
	Jefferson Co	**250M**	80002	12800-12899	
	Jefferson Co	**249M**	80403	16400-16499	
52ND AVENUE DR E	Denver	**257H**	80239	12200-12299	
53RD AVE E	Adams Co	**254G**	80216	100-198	E
	Adams Co	**254H**	80216	None	
	Denver	**255G**	80216	3200-3999	
	Denver	**257G**	80239	10900-11899	
	Denver	**257H**	80239	12100-12699	
	Denver	**258M**	80239	14500-15699	
	Denver	**260F**	80249	None	
	Denver	**259G**	80249	None	
	Denver	**259H**	80249	None	
	Denver	**260E**	80249	None	
53RD AVE W	Adams Co	**253H**	80221	2000-2399	
	Adams Co	**253F**	80221	3000-3899	
	Adams Co	**253F**	80212	3900-4399	
	Arvada	**252G**	80002	6100-6899	
	Arvada	**252E**	80002	8400-8699	
	Arvada	**251H**	80002	8900-9999	
	Arvada	**251E**	80002	12300-12399	
	Arvada	**251K**	80033	None	
	Jefferson Co	**252H**	80002	5200-5299	
	Jefferson Co	**250F**	80403	14800-14999	
	Jefferson Co	**249H**	80403	17000-17199	
	Wheat Ridge	**251G**	80033	None	
53RD CT W	Adams Co	**254E**	80221	None	
53RD DR W	Adams Co	**254E**	80221	1700-1798	E
	Jefferson Co	**249G**	80403	17100-17899	
	Jefferson Co	**249E**	80403	None	
53RD LN W	Arvada	**252E**	80002	None	
53RD LN W	Jefferson Co	**249G**	80403	18000-18098	E
	Jefferson Co	**249E**	80403	None	
53RD LOOP W	Jefferson Co	**249E**	80403	None	
53RD PL	Denver	**258H**	80239	None	
53RD PL E	Adams Co	**254F**	80216	300-699	
	Commerce City	**256F**	80022	6800-7299	
	Denver	**256G**	80238	7300-7599	
	Denver	**260F**	80249	None	
	Denver	**259H**	80249	None	
	Denver	**260E**	80249	None	
53RD PL W	Adams Co	**254E**	80221	1700-1799	
	Adams Co	**253H**	80221	2300-2399	
	Adams Co	**253E**	80212	None	
	Arvada	**252G**	80002	6800-6999	

Continued on next column

STREET NAME	CITY or COUNTY	MAP GRID	ZIP CODE	BLOCK RANGE	O/E
53RD PL W (Cont'd)	Arvada	**252E**	80002	8300-8399	
	Arvada	**251H**	80002	9200-9999	
	Arvada	**251F**	80002	11700-11799	
	Arvada	**251E**	80002	12000-12099	
	Jefferson Co	**250H**	80002	12800-12899	
	Jefferson Co	**250F**	80403	15000-15199	
	Jefferson Co	**249E**	80403	None	
53RD ST N	Boulder Co	**703D**	80503	13000-13399	
53RD WAY E	Commerce City	**256E**	80022	6400-6499	
54TH AVE	Denver	**258H**	80239	None	
54TH AVE E	Adams Co	**254G**	80216	200-298	E
	Adams Co	**254H**	80216	801-999	O
	Commerce City	**256E**	80022	6300-6499	
	Denver	**254H**	80216	1001-1299	O
	Denver	**255F**	80216	3300-3398	E
	Denver	**257F**	80239	10500-10899	
	Denver	**257G**	80239	11900-12099	
	Denver	**258E**	80239	14000-14099	
	Denver	**258G**	80239	14800-15499	
	Denver	**260F**	80249	None	
	Denver	**259H**	80249	None	
	Denver	**260E**	80249	None	
54TH AVE W	Adams Co	**253F**	80221	1900-3799	
	Adams Co	**253E**	80212	None	
	Arvada	**252G**	80002	6000-6999	
	Arvada	**252F**	80002	7600-7999	
	Arvada	**252E**	80002	8200-8599	
	Arvada	**251H**	80002	9600-9999	
	Arvada	**251F**	80033	10800-10999	
	Arvada	**251F**	80033	11200-11299	
	Arvada	**251E**	80002	12000-12199	
	Jefferson Co	**250G**	80002	13200-14699	
	Jefferson Co	**250F**	80403	14800-15199	
	Jefferson Co	**250E**	80403	15600-16399	
	Jefferson Co	**249H**	80403	16400-17199	
	Wheat Ridge	**251F**	80033	10600-10799	
	Wheat Ridge	**251F**	80033	11000-11199	
54TH DR W	Adams Co	**253E**	80212	None	
	Arvada	**251E**	80002	12000-12399	
	Jefferson Co	**250E**	80403	16200-16398	E
	Jefferson Co	**250F**	80403	None	
54TH LN W	Arvada	**251F**	80033	10700-11399	
	Jefferson Co	**249E**	80403	None	
54TH PL E	Commerce City	**256F**	80022	6800-7299	
	Denver	**260F**	80249	None	
	Denver	**259G**	80249	None	
54TH PL W	Adams Co	**254E**	80221	1600-1799	
	Adams Co	**253H**	80221	2000-2399	
	Arvada	**252G**	80002	6500-6799	
	Arvada	**252E**	80002	8000-8999	
	Arvada	**251H**	80002	9400-9599	
	Arvada	**251G**	80033	10400-10999	
	Arvada	**251F**	80002	11700-11799	
	Jefferson Co	**250H**	80002	12800-12899	
	Jefferson Co	**249E**	80403	None	
54TH AVENUE CT W	Wheat Ridge	**251G**	80033	None	
54TH AVENUE DR E	Denver	**257H**	80239	12200-12399	
55TH AVE	Denver	**258H**	80239	None	
55TH AVE E	Adams Co	**254G**	80216	1-399	
	Commerce City	**256E**	80022	6100-6499	
	Denver	**257G**	80239	10900-11899	
	Denver	**257H**	80239	12100-13099	
	Denver	**258E**	80239	13100-13399	
	Denver	**258G**	80239	14900-15499	
	Denver	**259G**	80249	None	
	Denver	**260E**	80249	None	
	Denver	**260E**	80249	None	
55TH AVE W	Adams Co	**254E**	80221	1600-1899	
	Adams Co	**253H**	80221	1900-3599	
	Arvada	**252F**	80002	6000-7599	
	Arvada	**252E**	80002	7600-7999	
	Arvada	**251H**	80002	8800-9099	
	Jefferson Co	**250F**	80403	15300-15599	
	Jefferson Co	**250E**	80403	16400-16498	E
	Jefferson Co	**249H**	80403	None	
55TH CIR W	Jefferson Co	**249E**	80403	None	
55TH DR W	Arvada	**252E**	80002	8500-8699	
55TH DR W	Arvada	**251G**	80002	10000-10299	
	Jefferson Co	**249H**	80403	16400-17099	
	Jefferson Co	**249E**	80403	None	
	Jefferson Co	**250F**	80403	None	
55TH LN W	Arvada	**251G**	80002	10200-10298	E
55TH LN W	Arvada	**251F**	80033	10700-11499	
	Jefferson Co	**249E**	80403	None	
55TH PL	Denver	**259H**	80249	None	
55TH PL E	Denver	**259H**	80249	None	
55TH PL E	Denver	**260E**	80249	None	
55TH PL E	Denver	**260E**	80249	None	
55TH PL W	Adams Co	**254E**	80221	1700-1799	
	Adams Co	**253F**	80221	3000-3599	
	Arvada	**252H**	80002	6000-6199	
	Arvada	**252G**	80002	6800-6999	
55TH PL W	Arvada	**251G**	80002	10300-10999	
	Arvada	**251F**	80033	11000-11199	
	Jefferson Co	**250H**	80002	12800-12999	
	Jefferson Co	**250E**	80403	16200-16399	
	Jefferson Co	**249H**	80403	16400-16699	
	Jefferson Co	**249E**	80403	None	
55TH ST	Boulder	**129N**	80303	1-199	
55TH ST	Boulder	**129E**	80303	700-1599	
	Boulder	**129A**	80301	1600-1699	
	Boulder	**99W**	80301	1700-2999	
	Boulder Co	**99E**	80301	4200-4799	
	Boulder Co	**69N**	80503	6500-6999	
55TH ST N	Boulder Co	**704S**	80503	8500-9399	
	Boulder Co	**704A**	80503	None	
55TH WAY E	Commerce City	**255F**	80022	None	
56TH AVE E	Adams Co	**254G**	80216	1-799	
	Adams Co	**254H**	80216	1201-1299	O
	Adams Co	**791B**	80137	5600-34799	
	Adams Co	**256G**	80022	7301-8899	O
	Adams Co	**260F**	80019	22400-23299	
	Adams Co	**793A**	80102	45700-52099	
	Aurora	**259H**	80249	18901-19299	O
	Aurora	**790L**	80019	19900-19999	
	Aurora	**260F**	80019	21700-24099	
	Aurora	**791A**	80642	None	

Continued on next column

STREET NAME	CITY or COUNTY	MAP GRID	ZIP CODE	BLOCK RANGE	O/E
56TH AVE E (Cont'd)	Commerce City	**255G**	80022	3100-5599	
	Commerce City	**256F**	80022	5600-7299	
	Denver	**256G**	80238	7300-8898	E
	Denver	**256H**	80238	8900-9199	
	Denver	**257G**	80239	10500-13099	
	Denver	**258F**	80239	13100-16899	
	Denver	**259G**	80249	16900-18899	
	Denver	**259H**	80249	18900-19298	E
	Denver	**260F**	80125	20200-21699	
56TH AVE N	Brighton	**140E**	80601	None	
56TH AVE W	Adams Co	**254F**	80216	101-899	O
	Adams Co	**254E**	80221	1600-1899	
	Adams Co	**253G**	80221	1900-3199	
	Arvada	**252G**	80002	5200-7199	
	Jefferson Co	**248H**	80403	20000-21599	
	Jefferson Co	**249E**	80403	None	
56TH CIR W	Arvada	**251E**	80002	11700-12099	
56TH DR W	Arvada	**251E**	80002	11700-12099	
	Jefferson Co	**250G**	80002	14500-14599	
	Jefferson Co	**250F**	80002	14600-14699	
	Jefferson Co	**249H**	80403	16400-16699	
	Jefferson Co	**249E**	80403	None	
	Jefferson Co	**249F**	80403	None	
56TH LN W	Jefferson Co	**249E**	80403	None	
56TH PL W	Adams Co	**253H**	80221	2200-2299	
	Arvada	**252G**	80002	6400-6499	
	Arvada	**252F**	80002	7300-7399	
	Arvada	**251H**	80002	8900-9699	
	Arvada	**251G**	80002	9900-9999	
	Arvada	**251G**	80033	None	
	Jefferson Co	**251E**	80002	11800-11999	
	Jefferson Co	**251E**	80002	12500-12899	
	Jefferson Co	**250G**	80002	14300-14699	
	Jefferson Co	**250E**	80403	15600-16399	
	Jefferson Co	**249E**	80403	None	
56TH WAY W	Adams Co	**253E**	80003	None	
57TH AVE E	Adams Co	**254G**	80216	300-399	
	Denver	**259C**	80249	18700-19299	
57TH AVE W	Adams Co	**253H**	80221	2300-2399	
	Arvada	**252E**	80002	7300-8799	
	Arvada	**251H**	80002	8800-9599	
	Arvada	**251G**	80002	9600-9799	
	Jefferson Co	**251E**	80002	11800-11999	
	Jefferson Co	**249H**	80403	16800-17499	
	Jefferson Co	**249E**	80403	None	
57TH CIR E	Aurora	**259C**	80019	None	
57TH CIR W	Jefferson Co	**249E**	80403	None	
57TH CT N	Boulder	**99W**	80301	1900-1999	
57TH CT S	Boulder	**99W**	80301	1800-1899	
57TH DR W	Jefferson Co	**250D**	80002	12700-12799	
	Jefferson Co	**250F**	80403	14800-14999	
	Jefferson Co	**249E**	80403	None	
57TH LN W	Jefferson Co	**249H**	80403	16800-16899	
	Jefferson Co	**249E**	80403	None	
57TH PL E	Commerce City	**256B**	80022	7000-7299	
	Denver	**259C**	80249	18700-19299	
57TH PL W	Adams Co	**253H**	80221	2200-2299	
	Arvada	**251G**	80002	9600-9999	
	Jefferson Co	**250D**	80002	12600-12799	
	Jefferson Co	**250G**	80002	14400-14599	
	Jefferson Co	**249H**	80403	17100-17299	
	Jefferson Co	**249E**	80403	None	
57TH ST	Boulder Co	**99S**	80301	None	
57TH ST N	Boulder Co	**99J**	80301	3600-4299	
57TH TERRACE W	Jefferson Co	**249E**	80403	None	
58TH AVE E	Adams Co	**254D**	80216	1-1799	
	Adams Co	**255A**	80216	1800-2199	
	Adams Co	**794B**	80136	None	
	Aurora	**259C**	80019	None	
	Commerce City	**255D**	80022	4800-5599	
	Commerce City	**256A**	80022	5600-7299	
	Denver	**259C**	80249	18700-19299	
58TH AVE W	Adams Co	**253D**	80221	2300-2699	
	Adams Co	**253C**	80221	3000-3099	
	Adams Co	**253A**	80003	None	
	Arvada	**251B**	80002	9000-12599	
	Jefferson Co	**250G**	80002	12600-14799	
	Jefferson Co	**250A**	80403	15600-16299	
	Jefferson Co	**249B**	80403	17900-19699	
58TH CT W	Jefferson Co	**249B**	80403	18400-18499	
58TH DR E	Aurora	**259C**	80019	None	
58TH DR W	Arvada	**250C**	80004	13700-13899	
	Jefferson Co	**249C**	80403	17500-17799	
	Jefferson Co	**249B**	80403	17800-18699	
58TH PL E	Aurora	**259C**	80019	None	
	Commerce City	**255D**	80022	4800-5199	
58TH PL W	Adams Co	**253D**	80221	2200-2299	
	Arvada	**252C**	80003	6600-6799	
	Arvada	**251C**	80004	10100-10399	
	Arvada	**251A**	80004	11900-12199	
	Arvada	**250C**	80004	13700-13999	
58TH PL W	Arvada	**251D**	80004	None	
	Jefferson Co	**250C**	80004	14000-14799	
	Jefferson Co	**250C**	80403	14800-15099	
	Jefferson Co	**249C**	80403	17400-17599	
	Jefferson Co	**249B**	80403	18200-18399	
59TH AVE E	Aurora	**259C**	80019	None	
	Commerce City	**256B**	80022	6500-7299	
59TH AVE W	Adams Co	**253A**	80003	None	
	Adams Co	**253D**	80221	None	
	Arvada	**252D**	80003	5400-6199	
	Arvada	**252B**	80003	7300-7599	
	Arvada	**252A**	80004	7600-8799	
	Arvada	**251D**	80004	9400-9699	
	Arvada	**251C**	80004	10100-10399	
	Arvada	**251B**	80004	10900-11499	
	Arvada	**251A**	80004	12300-12399	
	Arvada	**250C**	80004	13600-13999	
	Jefferson Co	**250C**	80004	14000-14199	
	Jefferson Co	**249C**	80403	17500-17999	
	Jefferson Co	**250A**	80403	None	
59TH DR E	Aurora	**259C**	80019	None	
59TH DR W	Arvada	**250C**	80004	13400-13999	
	Jefferson Co	**249B**	80403	18300-19099	
	Jefferson Co	**249A**	80403	19200-19299	
	Jefferson Co	**250A**	80403	None	
59TH PL E	Aurora	**259C**	80019	None	
59TH PL E	Commerce City	**256C**	80216	None	

STREET NAME	CITY or COUNTY	MAP GRID	ZIP CODE	BLOCK RANGE	O/E
59TH PL W	Adams Co	253D	80221	2200-2399	
	Arvada	251C	80004	9800-10399	
	Arvada	251B	80004	10800-11599	
	Arvada	250D	80004	13000-13299	
	Arvada	250C	80004	13600-13999	
	Jefferson Co	250C	80004	14000-14099	
	Jefferson Co	249C	80403	17500-17799	
	Jefferson Co	249B	80403	18700-19099	
	Jefferson Co	250A	80403	None	
59TH ST N	Boulder Co	704J	80503	11100-11799	
60TH PL W	Adams Co	254B	80216	None	
60TH AVE E	Aurora	259C	80019	None	
	Commerce City	255C	80022	2900-5599	
	Commerce City	256A	80022	5600-7299	
60TH AVE N	Brighton	140K	80601	None	
60TH AVE W	Adams Co	253C	80221	1800-2999	
	Arvada	253A	80003	4400-5199	
	Arvada	252D	80003	5200-6799	
	Arvada	252B	80003	7300-7599	
	Arvada	252B	80004	7600-7899	
	Arvada	252A	80004	8600-8899	
	Arvada	251C	80004	10000-11599	
	Arvada	251A	80004	11600-12599	
	Arvada	250D	80004	12600-13299	
	Jefferson Co	249C	80403	17100-17999	
	Jefferson Co	249B	80403	18100-18799	
	Jefferson Co	250A	80403	None	
	Jefferson Co	250A	80403	None	
60TH CIR W	Jefferson Co	250A	80403	None	
60TH CT W	Arvada	249D	80403	17200-17299	
60TH DR E	Aurora	259D	80019	None	
60TH DR W	Arvada	249D	80403	16600-16999	
	Jefferson Co	249B	80403	18900-19099	
60TH LN W	Arvada	249C	80403	17500-17599	
	Jefferson Co	249A	80403	19100-19199	
60TH PL E	Adams Co	254B	80216	100-399	
	Commerce City	256A	80022	6100-6299	
	Commerce City	256B	80022	6600-7099	
60TH PL E	Aurora	259C	80019	None	
60TH PL W	Arvada	252D	80003	5500-5799	
	Arvada	252C	80003	6400-6499	
	Arvada	251B	80004	11300-11499	
	Arvada	251A	80004	11600-12399	
	Arvada	250D	80004	13300-13499	
	Jefferson Co	249B	80403	18800-19099	
60TH ST N	Boulder Co	129F	80303	None	
60TH WAY E	Commerce City	255D	80022	5200-5499	
	Commerce City	256B	80022	7100-7299	
61ST AVE E	Adams Co	254D	80216	1400-1499	
	Commerce City	255C	80022	4400-4499	
	Commerce City	256A	80022	5600-6299	
	Commerce City	256B	80022	6700-6899	
61ST AVE W	Arvada	253A	80003	4400-5199	
	Arvada	252C	80003	6000-7599	
	Arvada	252B	80004	7600-7899	
	Arvada	252A	80004	8200-8599	
	Arvada	251D	80004	8900-9799	
	Arvada	251B	80004	10700-10899	
	Arvada	251A	80004	11600-12399	
	Arvada	250D	80004	12600-12899	
	Jefferson Co	249B	80403	18800-19199	
61ST CIR W	Arvada	250D	80004	12900-13099	
	Arvada	250C	80004	13600-13899	
61ST CT W	Arvada	249D	80403	17200-17299	
61ST DR E	Aurora	769X	80019	None	
61ST DR W	Arvada	253A	80003	4800-5199	
	Arvada	252D	80003	5700-5799	
	Arvada	249D	80403	16400-17199	
61ST LN W	Arvada	250D	80004	13500-13599	
	Arvada	250C	80004	13700-13799	
	Arvada	249D	80403	16700-16799	
	Arvada	249C	80403	17500-17599	
61ST PL E	Aurora	259C	80019	None	
61ST PL E	Commerce City	256B	80022	6500-7299	
61ST PL W	Arvada	223W	80003	4400-5099	
	Arvada	252D	80003	5700-5899	
	Arvada	252C	80003	6000-6399	
	Arvada	251B	80004	11400-11599	
	Arvada	250D	80004	12600-12899	
	Arvada	250D	80004	13300-13499	
	Arvada	249D	80403	16400-17199	
	Arvada	249C	80403	17500-17599	
	Jefferson Co	249B	80403	18800-19099	
61ST ST	Boulder Co	99P	80301	3100-3799	
61ST ST N	Boulder Co	704J	80503	11800-12199	
	Boulder Co	704A	80503	12700-13299	
61ST WAY E	Commerce City	255D	80022	5300-5499	
61ST WAY W	Arvada	249D	80403	17200-17299	
62ND AVE E	Adams Co	224Y	80216	1-1499	
62ND AVE E	Aurora	769X	80019	None	
	Commerce City	225Z	80022	4800-5599	
	Commerce City	226W	80022	5600-7299	
62ND AVE W	Adams Co	224X	80216	100-799	
	Adams Co	224X	80221	800-1499	
	Adams Co	254A	80221	1500-1699	
	Adams Co	223Y	80221	2800-3599	
	Adams Co	223X	80003	3600-3899	
	Arvada	223W	80003	4900-5199	
	Arvada	222X	80003	5200-7599	
	Arvada	222X	80004	7600-7999	
	Arvada	222W	80004	8000-8799	
	Arvada	221Z	80004	9200-9599	
	Arvada	221Y	80004	10300-11199	
	Arvada	221W	80004	11400-12699	
	Arvada	220Y	80004	14600-14699	
	Jefferson Co	250C	80004	14000-14099	
	Jefferson Co	249B	80403	18800-19099	
62ND CIR W	Arvada	220Y	80004	14600-14699	
	Arvada	219Z	80403	16900-17199	
62ND CT W	Adams Co	223Z	80221	2400-2599	
	Arvada	219Z	80403	17200-17299	
62ND CT W	Arvada	249D	80403	None	
62ND DR W	Arvada	220Z	80004	13000-13399	
	Arvada	220Y	80004	13400-13799	
62ND DR W	Arvada	220W	80007	None	
62ND LN W	Arvada	220Z	80004	13500-13699	
	Arvada	220Y	80004	13602-13798	E
	Arvada	219Z	80403	16400-16899	
	Arvada	219Y	80403	17300-17399	
62ND PL E	Aurora	769X	80019	None	
62ND PL E	Commerce City	226W	80022	6100-6699	
62ND PL W	Adams Co	223X	80003	3900-4399	
	Arvada	223W	80003	4400-4899	
	Arvada	222Y	80003	5800-7099	
	Arvada	222X	80004	7600-7999	
	Arvada	222W	80004	8200-8699	
	Arvada	221Z	80004	9600-9699	
	Arvada	221Y	80004	10300-11199	
	Arvada	221W	80004	11900-12199	
	Arvada	220Z	80004	13100-13699	
	Arvada	220X	80004	14600-14699	
	Arvada	220X	80403	15800-15899	
	Arvada	219Z	80403	16700-16899	
	Arvada	219Y	80403	17500-17599	
62ND PL W	Arvada	220W	80007	None	
62ND ST	Boulder	129B	80301	1600-1699	
62ND WAY E	Commerce City	225Z	80022	5300-5499	
62ND WAY W	Arvada	222X	80004	7700-7999	
	Arvada	250B	80403	None	
63RD N	Boulder	69P	80301	5300-5399	
	Boulder	69P	80503	5400-6699	
63RD AVE E	Aurora	769X	80019	None	
63RD AVE E	Commerce City	225Y	80022	4500-4699	
	Commerce City	226W	80022	5600-6499	
	Commerce City	226X	80022	7000-7299	
63RD AVE W	Adams Co	223Y	80221	2800-3399	
	Adams Co	223X	80003	3800-3899	
	Arvada	223W	80003	4300-4899	
	Arvada	222Y	80003	6100-6999	
	Arvada	222W	80004	8000-9199	
	Arvada	221Z	80004	9600-9699	
	Arvada	221Y	80004	10400-10899	
	Arvada	220Z	80004	12700-13099	
	Arvada	220Y	80004	13500-13999	
	Arvada	250B	80403	15200-15499	
	Arvada	220X	80403	15600-15999	
	Jefferson Co	220Y	80004	14000-14199	
63RD CIR W	Arvada	220S	80004	12900-13299	
	Arvada	220Z	80004	13300-13599	
	Arvada	220Y	80004	13600-13698	E
63RD CT W	Adams Co	223Z	80221	2400-2599	
63RD DR E	Aurora	769X	80019	None	
63RD DR W	Arvada	223W	80003	4400-4698	E
	Arvada	221Y	80004	10600-10698	E
	Arvada	219Z	80403	16900-17099	
	Arvada	219Y	80403	17300-17799	
63RD LN W	Arvada	220Y	80004	13700-13799	
	Arvada	219Z	80403	16800-16999	
63RD LN W	Arvada	220W	80007	None	
	Arvada	250B	80403	None	
63RD PL E	Aurora	769X	80019	None	
63RD PL E	Commerce City	226W	80022	5600-6499	
63RD PL W	Adams Co	223X	80003	3800-3999	
	Arvada	223W	80003	4400-4999	
	Arvada	222Z	80003	5600-5699	
	Arvada	222Y	80003	6100-6399	
	Arvada	222W	80004	8400-8799	
	Arvada	221Z	80004	9600-9699	
	Arvada	221Y	80004	10500-10799	
	Arvada	221X	80004	10800-11199	
	Arvada	221W	80004	12000-12199	
	Arvada	220Z	80004	12900-13499	
	Arvada	220Z	80004	13500-13599	
	Arvada	220X	80004	14000-14799	
	Arvada	219Z	80403	16800-16999	
	Arvada	219Y	80403	17300-17799	
63RD PL W	Arvada	220W	80007	None	
	Jefferson Co	219Z	80403	16400-16799	
63RD ST	Boulder	129B	80301	1600-3099	
	Boulder	99X	80301	3100-5699	
	Boulder	99F	80301	4400-5699	
	Boulder Co	129B	80303	1500-1599	
	Boulder Co	99F	80301	3700-4399	
63RD ST N	Boulder Co	69P	80503	6700-8099	
	Boulder Co	704W	80503	8300-9699	
	Boulder Co	704E	80503	12200-12699	
	Boulder Co	704N	80503	None	
63RD WAY E	Commerce City	226W	80022	6500-6599	
63RD WAY W	Arvada	221Y	80004	10601-10699	O
	Arvada	220Z	80004	13500-13599	
64TH AVE E	Adams Co	224Z	80229	300-1799	
	Adams Co	225W	80229	1800-2299	
	Adams Co	769Y	80019	19000-22099	
	Adams Co	770W	80019	None	
	Adams Co	772Y	80102	None	
	Commerce City	225Y	80022	3200-4699	
	Commerce City	225Z	80022	4800-5599	
	Commerce City	226W	80022	5600-7299	
	Denver	769Y	80249	17700-18499	
	Denver	769Y	80239	None	
64TH AVE W	Adams Co	224X	80221	1-1599	
	Adams Co	223X	80221	1700-3599	
	Adams Co	223X	80003	3600-5199	
	Arvada	222X	80003	5200-7599	
	Arvada	222X	80004	7600-8399	
	Arvada	221Z	80004	8900-9599	
	Arvada	221Y	80004	10000-10199	
	Arvada	221X	80004	10300-12699	
	Arvada	220X	80004	12700-14799	
	Arvada	220X	80007	14800-16399	
	Arvada	219Y	80007	16400-17599	
64TH CIR W	Arvada	223W	80003	4500-4599	
	Arvada	220W	80007	15900-15999	
	Arvada	219Z	80007	17000-17199	
64TH DR E	Aurora	769X	80019	None	
64TH DR W	Arvada	220Z	80004	12900-13399	
	Arvada	220Y	80004	13600-13899	
	Arvada	219Z	80007	16700-17199	
	Arvada	220X	80007	None	
64TH LN W	Adams Co	224W	80221	1700-2099	
	Arvada	220W	80007	15900-15999	
64TH PKWY W	Arvada	219X	80007	17700-19699	
64TH PL E	Aurora	769X	80019	None	
	Commerce City	226W	80022	6100-6499	
	Commerce City	226X	80022	7100-7299	
64TH PL W	Arvada	222X	80003	7200-7399	
	Arvada	222W	80004	8300-8799	
	Arvada	221Z	80004	8900-9799	
	Arvada	221Y	80004	9800-10699	
	Arvada	221X	80004	10900-11199	
	Arvada	221W	80004	12400-12499	
	Arvada	220Z	80004	13000-13399	
	Arvada	220Y	80004	13700-13899	
	Arvada	220W	80007	15600-15999	
	Arvada	220X	80007	None	
64TH WAY E	Commerce City	225Z	80022	4600-4799	
64TH WAY W	Arvada	222W	80004	8600-8899	
	Arvada	221Z	80004	9400-9599	
	Arvada	220W	80007	16000-16199	
65TH AVE E	Aurora	769X	80019	None	
	Commerce City	225Z	80022	5300-5599	
	Commerce City	226W	80022	6100-6499	
65TH AVE W	Adams Co	223Z	80221	2400-2699	
	Adams Co	223X	80221	2700-3599	
	Adams Co	223X	80003	4400-4499	
	Arvada	223W	80003	4500-5199	
	Arvada	222Z	80003	5400-6099	
	Arvada	222Y	80003	6100-6799	
	Arvada	222X	80004	7600-8199	
	Arvada	222W	80004	8200-8299	
	Arvada	221Z	80004	8800-9899	
	Arvada	221Y	80004	9800-10499	
	Arvada	221X	80004	10800-11099	
	Arvada	221W	80004	12100-12499	
	Arvada	220Z	80004	13000-13799	
	Arvada	220Y	80004	13900-13999	
	Arvada	220W	80007	None	
	Arvada	220X	80007	None	
65TH CIR W	Arvada	221X	80004	10900-10999	
	Arvada	221W	80004	11700-11899	
	Arvada	219Z	80007	16700-17199	
65TH CT W	Adams Co	223X	80003	4200-4299	
65TH DR W	Arvada	220Y	80004	13200-13999	
	Arvada	220Y	80004	14600-14799	
65TH PL E	Aurora	769X	80019	None	
	Commerce City	226W	80022	6100-6699	
	Commerce City	226X	80022	7100-7299	
65TH PL W	Adams Co	223Z	80221	2400-2699	
	Adams Co	223Y	80221	2700-2999	
	Arvada	223W	80003	4900-5099	
	Arvada	222W	80004	8600-8699	
	Arvada	221Z	80004	9000-9199	
	Arvada	221Y	80004	9800-9899	
	Arvada	221X	80004	10500-10899	
	Arvada	221W	80004	11600-12099	
	Arvada	220Z	80004	13200-13499	
	Arvada	220Y	80004	13500-13799	
	Arvada	220W	80007	15600-16299	
65TH ST N	Boulder Co	704T	80503	9800-10999	
65TH WAY E	Commerce City	225Z	80022	5300-5599	
	Commerce City	226W	80022	5600-5899	
65TH WAY W	Arvada	222W	80004	8500-8599	
	Arvada	221X	80004	10800-11099	
	Arvada	220Z	80004	12800-12899	
	Arvada	220Y	80004	14200-14799	
66TH AVE E	Adams Co	224Z	80229	300-1799	
	Adams Co	225W	80229	1800-2299	
	Commerce City	226W	80022	5600-7299	
66TH AVE W	Adams Co	223X	80221	3000-3599	
	Adams Co	223W	80003	3600-4499	
	Adams Co	224X	80221	None	
	Arvada	223W	80003	4500-5099	
	Arvada	222Y	80003	5300-7599	
	Arvada	222W	80004	8200-8399	
	Arvada	221Z	80004	8800-10799	
	Arvada	221T	80004	10900-10999	
	Arvada	221W	80004	12100-12499	
	Arvada	220Y	80004	14000-14199	
	Arvada	220X	80007	None	
66TH CIR W	Arvada	222S	80004	8400-8799	
	Arvada	221U	80004	9900-9999	
	Arvada	220V	80004	12600-12699	
	Arvada	220S	80007	15700-16399	
66TH DR W	Arvada	220U	80004	13800-13899	
	Arvada	220X	80007	None	
66TH LN W	Arvada	221S	80004	11600-11799	
	Arvada	219Z	80007	16800-17099	
66TH PL E	Commerce City	226S	80022	6100-6499	
	Commerce City	226T	80022	7000-7299	
66TH PL W	Adams Co	223U	80221	2400-2999	
	Arvada	222W	80004	8400-8799	
	Arvada	221V	80004	8900-9399	
	Arvada	221U	80004	9900-9999	
	Arvada	221T	80004	11200-11599	
	Arvada	221W	80004	11600-11999	
	Arvada	221S	80004	12000-12099	
	Arvada	220Z	80004	12600-12699	
	Arvada	220Y	80004	13600-13899	
	Arvada	220X	80004	14700-14799	
	Arvada	220X	80007	15200-15399	
	Arvada	220W	80007	15700-15999	
	Arvada	219Z	80007	16800-16899	
66TH ST	Boulder Co	159L	80303	1600-2499	
66TH ST N	Boulder Co	704F	80503	12400-12699	
66TH WAY E	Commerce City	225Z	80022	5200-5599	
66TH WAY W	Arvada	220U	80004	13600-13799	
	Arvada	220Y	80004	13800-13899	
67TH AVE E	Adams Co	225S	80229	2000-2299	
	Commerce City	225V	80022	5200-5599	
	Commerce City	226S	80022	5600-6499	
	Commerce City	226T	80022	7000-7299	
67TH AVE W	Adams Co	223T	80221	3000-3599	
	Arvada	222V	80003	5200-5999	
	Arvada	222U	80003	6000-6799	
	Arvada	222T	80003	7100-7599	
	Arvada	222T	80004	7600-7899	
	Arvada	222S	80004	7900-8799	
	Arvada	221V	80004	8900-9499	
	Arvada	221S	80004	11200-11699	
	Arvada	221S	80004	11700-12599	
	Arvada	220U	80004	14200-14499	
	Arvada	220X	80007	15300-15599	
	Arvada	219Y	80007	None	

STREET NAME	CITY or COUNTY	MAP GRID	ZIP CODE	BLOCK RANGE	O/E
67TH CIR W	Arvada	**222U**	80003	6700-6799	
	Arvada	**220U**	80004	13600-13799	
	Arvada	**219V**	80007	16400-17099	
67TH CT W	Arvada	**220U**	80004	13800-13899	
67TH DR W	Arvada	**220V**	80004	13300-13499	
	Arvada	**222S**	80004	None	
67TH LN W	Arvada	**219V**	80007	17000-17099	
67TH PL E	Commerce City	**225V**	80022	5200-5599	
	Commerce City	**226S**	80022	5600-6399	
	Commerce City	**226T**	80022	6500-7299	
	Commerce City	**225U**	80022	None	
67TH PL W	Adams Co	**223U**	80221	2700-2999	
	Arvada	**222U**	80003	6100-7199	
	Arvada	**222T**	80003	7200-7499	
	Arvada	**222S**	80004	8500-8699	
	Arvada	**221V**	80004	9300-9699	
	Arvada	**221U**	80004	9600-9899	
	Arvada	**221T**	80004	10700-11599	
	Arvada	**221S**	80004	12000-12099	
	Arvada	**220V**	80004	12600-12699	
	Arvada	**220U**	80004	13200-13999	
	Arvada	**220S**	80007	15600-15999	
	Arvada	**219V**	80007	16800-17099	
	Arvada	**219T**	80007	None	
	Arvada	**222S**	80004	None	
67TH ST N	Boulder Co	**69G**	80503	7600-7799	
	Boulder Co	**704X**	80503	None	
67TH WAY W	Arvada	**221T**	80004	10900-11599	
	Arvada	**220V**	80004	12600-12999	
	Arvada	**220U**	80004	13400-13899	
	Arvada	**222S**	80004	None	
68TH AVE E	Adams Co	**224V**	80229	700-1799	
	Adams Co	**225S**	80229	1800-2599	
	Adams Co	**770X**	80019	None	
	Commerce City	**225U**	80022	4000-4799	
	Commerce City	**226S**	80022	5600-6999	
	Denver	**769W**	80249	None	
	Denver	**769W**	80239	None	
	Denver	**770X**	80019	None	
68TH AVE W	Adams Co	**224S**	80221	800-1799	
	Adams Co	**223V**	80221	1800-2399	
	Adams Co	**223U**	80221	3000-3599	
	Arvada	**223S**	80003	4500-5199	
	Arvada	**222V**	80003	5200-6099	
	Arvada	**222T**	80003	6100-7599	
	Arvada	**222T**	80004	7600-8699	
	Arvada	**221V**	80004	8800-9499	
	Arvada	**221U**	80004	10000-11199	
	Arvada	**221S**	80004	11400-12599	
	Arvada	**220V**	80004	12800-12999	
	Arvada	**220U**	80004	13400-14199	
	Arvada	**220T**	80007	None	
	Jefferson Co	**219S**	80007	19200-19699	
	Westminster	**223S**	80030	3600-4499	
68TH CIR W	Arvada	**222U**	80003	6200-6399	
68TH DR W	Arvada	**220U**	80004	13700-13899	
68TH PL E	Adams Co	**225S**	80229	2000-2599	
	Commerce City	**226T**	80022	6900-7299	
68TH PL W	Adams Co	**223U**	80221	3400-3499	
	Arvada	**222V**	80003	5200-6199	
	Arvada	**222U**	80003	6200-6999	
	Arvada	**222T**	80003	7000-7299	
	Arvada	**222S**	80004	8400-8799	
	Arvada	**221V**	80004	9200-9299	
	Arvada	**221U**	80004	10000-10399	
	Arvada	**221T**	80004	10700-11199	
	Arvada	**221S**	80004	12100-12299	
	Arvada	**220V**	80004	13300-13399	
	Arvada	**220T**	80004	14400-14699	
	Arvada	**219V**	80007	16900-17099	
68TH ST	Boulder Co	**129U**	80303	1-899	
68TH ST N	Boulder Co	**704K**	80503	None	
68TH WAY E	Commerce City	**226S**	80022	5700-6099	
68TH WAY W	Adams Co	**224T**	80221	800-999	
	Arvada	**221U**	80004	10000-10399	
	Arvada	**221T**	80004	10700-11499	
	Arvada	**220U**	80004	13800-13899	
69TH AVE E	Adams Co	**224V**	80229	1400-1899	
	Adams Co	**225S**	80229	2300-2499	
	Commerce City	**225U**	80022	4200-4399	
	Commerce City	**225V**	80022	4600-5599	
	Commerce City	**226S**	80022	5600-6699	
	Commerce City	**226T**	80022	7000-7299	
	Denver	**769W**	80249	None	
	Denver	**769W**	80239	None	
69TH AVE W	Adams Co	**224S**	80221	800-1799	
	Adams Co	**223T**	80221	3300-3599	
	Arvada	**222V**	80003	5200-6399	
	Arvada	**222U**	80003	6800-7299	
	Arvada	**222T**	80003	7300-7499	
	Arvada	**222S**	80004	8100-8399	
	Arvada	**221V**	80004	9600-9799	
	Arvada	**221U**	80004	10000-10399	
	Arvada	**221T**	80004	10700-10999	
	Arvada	**221S**	80004	12000-12699	
	Arvada	**220U**	80004	13700-13899	
	Arvada	**220T**	80007	14900-16399	
	Arvada	**219Y**	80007	None	
	Westminster	**223S**	80030	4500-5199	
69TH CIR W	Arvada	**219V**	80007	16500-16999	
	Arvada	**220T**	80007	None	
69TH CT W	Westminster	**223S**	80030	4900-4999	
69TH DR W	Arvada	**222S**	80004	8300-8399	
	Arvada	**220U**	80004	14300-14399	
	Westminster	**223S**	80030	4500-4899	
69TH LOOP W	Westminster	**223S**	80030	5000-5199	
69TH PL E	Adams Co	**225S**	80229	2300-2799	
	Commerce City	**225U**	80022	4200-4399	
	Commerce City	**226S**	80022	6400-6499	
	Commerce City	**226T**	80022	6700-7299	
69TH PL W	Arvada	**222U**	80003	6200-7399	
	Arvada	**222T**	80003	7400-7599	
	Arvada	**222S**	80004	8400-8799	
	Arvada	**221V**	80004	9600-9699	
	Arvada	**221U**	80004	10000-10799	
	Arvada	**221T**	80004	11000-11499	
	Arvada	**220U**	80004	13300-14699	
	Arvada	**220S**	80007	16000-16199	
	Westminster	**223T**	80030	3600-3799	
	Westminster	**223S**	80030	5000-5199	
69TH ST	Boulder Co	**129H**	80303	900-1099	
69TH WAY W	Arvada	**222U**	80003	6400-6699	
	Arvada	**222S**	80004	8100-8399	
	Arvada	**221T**	80004	11400-11599	
70TH AVE E	Adams Co	**224U**	80221	1-199	
	Adams Co	**224U**	80229	300-699	
	Adams Co	**225S**	80229	2300-2799	
	Adams Co	**225U**	80022	4001-4899	O
	Commerce City	**225U**	80022	4000-4898	E
	Commerce City	**225V**	80022	4900-5599	
	Commerce City	**226S**	80022	6000-6399	
	Commerce City	**226T**	80022	6500-7299	
70TH AVE W	Adams Co	**224T**	80221	1-1599	
	Adams Co	**223U**	80030	2801-2899	O
	Arvada	**222U**	80003	6000-6999	
	Arvada	**222T**	80003	7000-7399	
	Arvada	**222S**	80004	8200-8399	
	Arvada	**221U**	80004	9400-9999	
	Arvada	**221T**	80004	10800-11599	
	Arvada	**221S**	80004	12100-12399	
	Arvada	**220S**	80007	15800-16399	
	Arvada	**219V**	80007	16600-16799	
	Arvada	**219U**	80007	17100-17599	
	Westminster	**223S**	80030	4200-5199	
70TH CT E	Adams Co	**225U**	80022	4300-4399	
70TH CT W	Westminster	**223S**	80030	5000-5099	
70TH DR W	Arvada	**222U**	80003	6200-6399	
	Arvada	**222T**	80004	7600-8099	
	Arvada	**221Q**	80005	10100-10299	
	Arvada	**220U**	80004	14000-14599	
	Arvada	**220S**	80007	15700-15999	
70TH PL E	Commerce City	**226T**	80022	6400-6699	
70TH PL W	Adams Co	**224T**	80221	400-599	
	Adams Co	**224S**	80221	800-1199	
	Arvada	**222U**	80003	6200-6799	
	Arvada	**222S**	80004	8200-8399	
	Arvada	**221V**	80004	9400-9999	
	Arvada	**221U**	80004	10500-10799	
	Arvada	**221S**	80004	11500-11999	
	Arvada	**220V**	80004	13300-13399	
	Arvada	**220U**	80004	14200-14599	
	Arvada	**220S**	80007	16100-16299	
	Westminster	**223T**	80030	4200-4299	
	Westminster	**223S**	80030	4900-5199	
70TH WAY W	Arvada	**222S**	80004	8500-8899	
	Arvada	**221S**	80004	11900-11999	
71ST AVE E	Adams Co	**224V**	80229	700-1399	
	Adams Co	**225U**	80022	4000-4099	
	Commerce City	**225U**	80022	4100-4199	
	Commerce City	**225V**	80022	4800-5599	
	Commerce City	**226S**	80022	6100-6699	
	Denver	**769S**	80239	None	
	Denver	**769S**	80249	None	
	Denver	**770S**	80249	None	
71ST AVE W	Adams Co	**224T**	80221	400-599	
	Arvada	**222U**	80003	6200-6899	
	Arvada	**222T**	80003	6900-7399	
	Arvada	**222S**	80004	7600-8399	
	Arvada	**221V**	80004	9200-9599	
	Arvada	**221S**	80004	11600-12599	
	Arvada	**220U**	80004	14200-14499	
	Arvada	**219V**	80007	16700-16999	
	Westminster	**223U**	80030	2600-3399	
	Westminster	**222V**	80003	5600-5799	
71ST CIR W	Arvada	**222N**	80004	8500-8699	
	Jefferson Co	**220S**	80007	16100-16199	
	Westminster	**222R**	80003	5600-5799	
71ST CT W	Westminster	**223N**	80030	5000-5099	
71ST DR W	Arvada	**221S**	80004	11600-12099	
	Arvada	**220U**	80004	14200-14599	
71ST PL E	Commerce City	**226N**	80022	5600-6499	
71ST PL W	Adams Co	**224P**	80221	400-599	
	Adams Co	**224N**	80221	1200-1599	
	Arvada	**222Q**	80003	6200-7099	
	Arvada	**222N**	80004	8300-8399	
	Arvada	**221Q**	80004	10100-10299	
	Arvada	**221P**	80004	10800-11399	
	Arvada	**221S**	80004	11700-11999	
	Arvada	**221N**	80004	12000-12499	
	Arvada	**220Q**	80004	13300-13799	
	Arvada	**220U**	80004	14000-14299	
	Arvada	**220S**	80007	15700-16199	
	Arvada	**219V**	80007	16900-17099	
	Arvada	**221R**	80004	None	
	Jefferson Co	**220S**	80007	16200-16299	
	Westminster	**223T**	80030	3300-3599	
	Westminster	**223N**	80030	4900-5099	
	Westminster	**222V**	80003	5600-5799	
71ST ST N	Boulder	**69Z**	80503	5400-6199	
	Boulder	**69R**	80503	6500-6899	
71ST WAY W	Westminster	**223Q**	80030	3000-3199	
72ND AVE E	Adams Co	**225Q**	80022	4600-4699	
	Adams Co	**771S**	80642	None	
	Adams Co	**772S**	80102	None	
	Aurora	**771S**	80642	None	
	Commerce City	**225Q**	80022	4000-4599	
	Commerce City	**225R**	80022	4700-5599	
	Commerce City	**226N**	80022	5600-7299	
72ND AVE W	Adams Co	**224N**	80221	200-1799	
	Adams Co	**223P**	80221	1800-2399	
	Arvada	**222P**	80003	6200-7599	
	Arvada	**222N**	80005	7600-8799	
	Arvada	**221N**	80005	8800-12599	
	Arvada	**220Q**	80005	12600-14799	
	Arvada	**220S**	80007	15600-16399	
	Arvada	**219R**	80007	16400-17499	
	Jefferson Co	**220S**	80007	14800-15599	
	Westminster	**223P**	80030	2400-5199	
	Westminster	**222R**	80003	5200-6199	
72ND CIR W	Arvada	**220R**	80005	13200-13399	
	Arvada	**220N**	80007	15600-15899	
72ND DR W	Arvada	**220Q**	80005	13400-13999	
	Arvada	**220N**	80007	15900-15999	
	Westminster	**222R**	80003	5500-6299	
	Westminster	**222Q**	80003	6300-6699	
72ND PL E	Commerce City	**226P**	80022	6300-7299	
72ND PL W	Arvada	**222N**	80005	7600-8499	
	Arvada	**221Q**	80005	10200-10399	
	Arvada	**221N**	80005	11300-11899	
	Arvada	**220R**	80005	13400-13499	
	Arvada	**220Q**	80005	13900-13999	
	Jefferson Co	**220P**	80007	15200-15499	
	Westminster	**223N**	80030	4900-4999	
	Westminster	**222R**	80003	5400-5599	
72ND WAY E	Adams Co	**225Q**	80022	4600-4799	
72ND WAY W	Westminster	**223P**	80030	3800-3999	
73RD AVE E	Adams Co	**224R**	80229	700-1799	
	Adams Co	**225N**	80229	1800-1999	
	Commerce City	**226P**	80022	6400-7299	
73RD AVE W	Adams Co	**224N**	80221	1700-1799	
	Adams Co	**223R**	80221	1800-2399	
	Arvada	**222P**	80003	7200-7399	
	Arvada	**222N**	80005	8700-8999	
	Arvada	**221R**	80005	9000-9999	
	Arvada	**221N**	80005	11300-11399	
	Arvada	**221N**	80005	11600-11799	
	Arvada	**220R**	80005	13400-13599	
	Arvada	**220Q**	80005	13900-14099	
	Jefferson Co	**220P**	80007	15100-15599	
	Jefferson Co	**220N**	80007	15600-15999	
	Jefferson Co	**219R**	80007	16500-17099	
	Westminster	**223Q**	80030	2700-2999	
	Westminster	**223P**	80030	3300-3599	
	Westminster	**223P**	80030	3600-3999	
	Westminster	**223N**	80030	4800-5199	
	Westminster	**222Q**	80003	5500-6699	
73RD CIR W	Arvada	**222P**	80003	7400-7499	
73RD DR W	Arvada	**221N**	80005	11800-11999	
	Arvada	**221P**	80005	None	
	Jefferson Co	**219R**	80007	16500-16899	
73RD PL E	Commerce City	**226P**	80022	6600-6899	
73RD PL W	Adams Co	**223R**	80221	1900-2399	
	Arvada	**222P**	80003	7400-7499	
	Arvada	**222N**	80005	8700-8999	
	Arvada	**221R**	80005	9000-9799	
	Arvada	**221Q**	80005	9800-11299	
	Arvada	**221N**	80005	11600-11899	
	Arvada	**220Q**	80005	13900-13999	
	Jefferson Co	**220P**	80007	15300-15499	
	Jefferson Co	**219R**	80007	16800-16999	
	Westminster	**222Q**	80003	6400-6699	
	Westminster	**222R**	80003	None	
73RD ST N	Boulder Co	**69H**	80503	7000-7999	
	Boulder Co	**40W**	80503	8000-8599	
73RD WAY E	Adams Co	**225Q**	80022	4400-4599	
74TH AVE E	Adams Co	**225N**	80229	2000-2799	
	Adams Co	**225Q**	80022	3800-3999	
	Adams Co	**225R**	80022	4600-4799	
	Adams Co	**226N**	80022	5800-6099	
	Adams Co	**224Q**	80229	None	
	Commerce City	**225Q**	80022	4000-4599	
	Commerce City	**225R**	80022	4800-5299	
	Commerce City	**226P**	80022	6600-7299	
74TH AVE W	Adams Co	**223Q**	80221	2000-2399	
	Arvada	**222Q**	80003	6200-6699	
	Arvada	**222P**	80003	6800-7599	
	Arvada	**222N**	80005	8400-8999	
	Arvada	**221R**	80005	9000-9999	
	Arvada	**221N**	80005	11200-11599	
	Arvada	**221N**	80005	11600-11999	
	Arvada	**220Q**	80005	13900-13999	
	Jefferson Co	**220N**	80007	15600-16399	
	Jefferson Co	**219R**	80007	16400-16999	
	Westminster	**223Q**	80030	2400-3299	
	Westminster	**223P**	80030	3900-4099	
	Westminster	**223N**	80030	4100-4899	
	Westminster	**222R**	80003	5300-5799	
74TH CIR W	Arvada	**222Q**	80003	6200-6299	
74TH CT E	Adams Co	**224Q**	80229	None	
74TH DR W	Arvada	**222N**	80005	8400-8499	
	Arvada	**221N**	80005	11900-11999	
	Arvada	**220R**	80005	13200-13799	
	Jefferson Co	**220P**	80005	13800-14799	
	Jefferson Co	**220N**	80007	16100-16399	
74TH PL E	Adams Co	**225N**	80229	2100-2299	
74TH PL E	Commerce City	**226N**	80022	5900-6099	
	Commerce City	**226P**	80022	6900-7299	
74TH PL W	Arvada	**222Q**	80003	5600-5999	
	Arvada	**222P**	80003	6900-7599	
	Arvada	**222N**	80005	8400-8499	
	Arvada	**221Q**	80005	9600-9899	
	Arvada	**221Q**	80005	10000-10699	
	Arvada	**221N**	80005	11200-11399	
	Arvada	**221N**	80005	11600-11899	
	Arvada	**220Q**	80005	13500-14099	
	Arvada	**220N**	80007	None	
	Jefferson Co	**220Q**	80005	14100-14299	
	Jefferson Co	**219R**	80007	16500-17199	
	Westminster	**222R**	80003	5600-5999	
74TH WAY E	Adams Co	**225R**	80022	4700-4798	E
74TH WAY W	Adams Co	**224N**	80221	1600-1899	
	Arvada	**221R**	80005	9300-9899	
	Arvada	**221N**	80005	11600-11899	
	Arvada	**220Q**	80005	13900-13999	
75TH AVE E	Adams Co	**224R**	80229	700-1799	
	Adams Co	**225N**	80229	1800-2099	
	Commerce City	**226P**	80022	6900-7299	
	Denver	**769V**	80249	25600-26599	
75TH AVE W	Arvada	**222Q**	80003	6200-6299	
	Arvada	**222P**	80003	7200-7599	
	Arvada	**221R**	80005	9500-9699	
	Arvada	**221Q**	80005	10100-10599	
	Arvada	**221N**	80005	11000-11499	
	Arvada	**221N**	80005	11600-12399	
	Arvada	**220P**	80007	None	
	Jefferson Co	**221N**	80005	12400-12499	
	Jefferson Co	**220R**	80005	12500-13199	
	Westminster	**223P**	80030	3400-4099	
	Westminster	**223N**	80030	4100-5199	
	Westminster	**222R**	80003	5900-6199	
75TH CIR E	Denver	**770T**	80249	None	
75TH CIR W	Arvada	**221N**	80005	11600-11999	

STREET NAME	CITY or COUNTY	MAP GRID	ZIP CODE	BLOCK RANGE	O/E
75TH DR W	Arvada	222Q	80003	5800-6599	
	Arvada	221N	80005	11700-11999	
	Westminster	222R	80003	5500-5799	
75TH LN W	Arvada	221J	80005	11900-12199	
75TH PL E	Adams Co	226P	80022	6500-6899	
	Commerce City	226P	80022	6900-7299	
75TH PL W	Arvada	222Q	80003	5800-6299	
	Arvada	222P	80003	6800-7199	
	Arvada	221R	80005	8500-9699	
	Arvada	221N	80005	11300-11499	
	Arvada	221N	80005	11900-12499	
	Arvada	220Q	80005	13800-13899	
	Arvada	220P	80007	None	
	Jefferson Co	221N	80005	12400-12499	
	Jefferson Co	220R	80005	12500-13199	
	Jefferson Co	219R	80007	13500-16899	
	Westminster	223Q	80030	3300-3399	
	Westminster	223P	80030	3500-3599	
	Westminster	223N	80030	4600-4699	
	Westminster	222R	80003	5500-5799	
75TH ST	Boulder Co	130E	80303	700-1599	
	Boulder Co	100J	80301	1600-5399	
	Boulder Co	10W	80503	11100-14199	
75TH ST N	Boulder Co	40N	80503	8600-10999	
75TH WAY W	Arvada	222N	80005	8300-8399	
	Arvada	221R	80005	8400-9999	
76TH AVE E	Adams Co	224Q	80229	300-699	
	Adams Co	225J	80229	2300-2599	
	Adams Co	226J	80022	5400-6499	
76TH AVE W	Adams Co	224N	80221	1600-1799	
	Adams Co	223R	80221	1800-2399	
	Arvada	222Q	80003	6000-7599	
	Arvada	221R	80005	8500-9699	
	Arvada	221Q	80005	9700-9899	
	Arvada	221J	80005	11600-12299	
	Arvada	220Q	80005	13800-13899	
	Jefferson Co	220J	80007	15800-16499	
	Westminster	223P	80030	3000-5199	
	Westminster	222Q	80003	5200-5999	
76TH DR W	Arvada	221K	80005	10800-11599	
	Arvada	221J	80005	11600-12199	
	Arvada	219R	80007	16400-16599	
	Jefferson Co	220K	80007	14800-16399	
	Westminster	222M	80003	5600-5799	
76TH LN W	Arvada	221J	80005	11600-11899	
	Jefferson Co	220Q	80005	None	
76TH PL E	Adams Co	226K	80022	6500-6899	
76TH PL W	Arvada	222L	80003	6400-6799	
	Arvada	221Q	80005	9700-9999	
	Arvada	221K	80005	11000-11599	
	Jefferson Co	220Q	80005	None	
76TH ST	Boulder Co	130J	80303	1-699	
76TH ST S	Superior	160E	80027	1401-1799	O
76TH WAY W	Arvada	221K	80005	11200-11599	
77TH AVE E	Adams Co	225J	80229	1800-2299	
	Adams Co	225M	80022	4800-5499	
	Adams Co	226J	80022	5500-5899	
	Adams Co	226K	80022	6300-7099	
	Adams Co	224L	80229	None	
77TH AVE W	Arvada	222L	80003	6400-6599	
	Arvada	221L	80005	9700-9999	
	Arvada	221K	80005	10800-11099	
	Westminster	223K	80030	3600-3999	
	Westminster	223J	80030	5000-5199	
	Westminster	222M	80003	5600-5699	
77TH CIR W	Arvada	222J	80005	8800-8899	
	Arvada	221L	80005	10200-10399	
77TH DR E	Adams Co	224L	80229	400-599	
77TH DR W	Arvada	222L	80003	6100-6299	
	Arvada	222K	80005	7600-7999	
	Arvada	221M	80005	9200-9799	
	Arvada	221L	80005	9800-10599	
	Arvada	221K	80005	11200-11499	
	Arvada	221J	80005	11600-11699	
	Arvada	220M	80005	12100-12999	
	Arvada	219M	80007	16500-16799	
	Jefferson Co	220K	80007	14800-15499	
	Westminster	223J	80030	5000-5099	
	Westminster	222M	80003	5700-6099	
77TH LN W	Arvada	219L	80007	None	
	Jefferson Co	220J	80007	16200-16399	
77TH PL E	Adams Co	224L	80229	400-599	
	Adams Co	226K	80022	6500-6899	
77TH PL W	Arvada	222L	80003	6100-6499	
	Arvada	221M	80005	8900-9799	
	Arvada	221L	80005	10200-10799	
	Arvada	219L	80007	None	
	Jefferson Co	220J	80007	15900-16199	
	Westminster	223K	80030	3500-3599	
	Westminster	223K	80030	4000-4099	
77TH WAY E	Adams Co	226J	80022	5600-5699	
77TH WAY W	Arvada	222J	80005	8200-8499	
78TH AVE E	Adams Co	224M	80229	600-1799	
	Adams Co	225J	80229	1800-3199	
	Adams Co	225M	80022	4800-5399	
	Adams Co	226K	80022	6500-7199	
	Commerce City	226J	80022	6200-6499	
	Denver	769V	80249	23000-24599	
	Denver	770S	80249	24600-25599	
78TH AVE W	Arvada	222L	80003	6100-6399	
	Arvada	222K	80003	7400-7498	E
	Arvada	221M	80005	8900-8999	
	Arvada	221L	80005	10000-10699	
	Arvada	221K	80005	11000-11199	
	Arvada	220L	80005	13200-14099	
	Jefferson Co	220K	80005	14500-14799	
	Jefferson Co	219M	80007	16600-16799	
	Westminster	223J	80030	3600-5199	
78TH CIR W	Adams Co	224J	80221	1200-1599	
	Arvada	222L	80003	6500-6599	
	Arvada	222J	80005	8000-8899	
	Arvada	221M	80005	8900-8999	
	Arvada	220M	80005	12800-13199	
78TH DR E	Adams Co	224L	80229	400-599	
78TH DR W	Arvada	221K	80005	11100-11599	
	Arvada	219M	80007	None	
78TH PL E	Adams Co	224L	80229	400-498	E
	Adams Co	224M	80229	900-1199	
	Adams Co	225K	80229	2800-2999	
	Adams Co	226J	80022	5600-6199	
78TH PL W	Adams Co	224K	80221	100-599	
	Arvada	222L	80003	6000-7499	
	Arvada	222J	80005	8000-8899	
	Arvada	221L	80005	10000-10199	
	Arvada	220L	80005	13300-13399	
	Jefferson Co	219M	80007	16500-16599	
	Westminster	222M	80003	5200-5499	
78TH WAY E	Adams Co	226J	80022	6500-6699	
	Commerce City	226J	80022	6300-6499	
78TH WAY W	Arvada	222J	80005	8000-8099	
	Westminster	223K	80030	3900-3999	
79TH AVE E	Adams Co	225J	80229	2400-2799	
	Adams Co	226K	80022	6500-6699	
79TH AVE W	Arvada	222L	80003	5600-6799	
	Arvada	222J	80005	8400-8899	
	Arvada	221K	80005	10800-11099	
	Westminster	223K	80030	3200-3699	
	Westminster	222M	80003	5200-5599	
79TH CIR W	Arvada	222L	80003	6700-6799	
79TH CT E	Commerce City	226J	80022	6300-6499	
79TH CT W	Arvada	222L	80003	6800-6899	
	Arvada	222J	80005	8400-8599	
79TH DR W	Arvada	222K	80003	6800-7399	
	Arvada	221K	80005	11200-11499	
	Jefferson Co	219M	80007	16400-16599	
79TH PL E	Adams Co	226J	80022	6100-6299	
	Adams Co	226K	80022	6500-6699	
79TH PL W	Adams Co	224K	80221	200-699	
	Adams Co	224J	80221	900-1099	
	Arvada	222M	80003	5600-5999	
	Arvada	222J	80005	8400-8699	
	Arvada	221M	80005	9100-9199	
	Arvada	221L	80005	10600-10699	
	Arvada	221K	80005	10800-11099	
	Jefferson Co	220M	80005	12900-13199	
	Jefferson Co	220J	80007	15600-16399	
79TH ST N	Boulder Co	70T	80503	5400-6999	
	Boulder Co	70E	80503	7200-7699	
79TH WAY W	Adams Co	224J	80221	1600-1999	
	Arvada	221L	80005	10200-10599	
80TH AVE E	Adams Co	224L	80221	1-199	
	Adams Co	224L	80229	300-699	
	Adams Co	225M	80022	5100-5599	
	Adams Co	226J	80022	5600-6299	
	Adams Co	226K	80022	6700-7299	
	Adams Co	772U	80102	None	
	Commerce City	226J	80022	6300-6699	
	Commerce City	226K	80022	7300-7599	
	Denver	770T	80249	27500-27598	E
80TH AVE W	Adams Co	224K	80221	1-999	
	Adams Co	223M	80221	2000-2999	
	Arvada	222L	80003	5200-7599	
	Arvada	222J	80005	7600-8899	
	Arvada	221L	80005	8900-12599	
	Arvada	220M	80005	12600-13799	
	Jefferson Co	220L	80005	13800-14799	
	Westminster	223K	80030	3000-5199	
80TH CIR W	Arvada	222M	80003	5700-5899	
	Arvada	222K	80005	6600-7099	
	Arvada	222K	80005	7800-7899	
80TH DR W	Arvada	222K	80003	6400-6699	
	Arvada	222J	80005	8700-8999	
	Arvada	221M	80005	9000-9199	
	Arvada	221L	80005	10200-10399	
	Westminster	223K	80031	3700-3799	
80TH PL W	Adams Co	223M	80221	2000-2299	
	Arvada	222M	80003	5500-5999	
	Arvada	222L	80003	6200-6399	
	Arvada	222K	80003	6400-7199	
	Arvada	222K	80005	7800-7999	
	Arvada	221M	80005	9200-9399	
	Arvada	220M	80005	12800-13199	
	Westminster	223H	80030	2600-2699	
	Westminster	223J	80031	4100-4299	
80TH ST S	Louisville	130P	80303	1-199	
80TH WAY W	Westminster	223G	80030	2600-2699	
81ST AVE E	Adams Co	224L	80221	1-199	
	Adams Co	226E	80022	5800-6299	
	Commerce City	226G	80022	7600-7799	
81ST AVE W	Adams Co	224F	80221	1-299	
	Arvada	222K	80003	6400-7399	
	Arvada	222F	80003	7400-7499	
	Arvada	222J	80005	8100-8199	
	Arvada	221G	80005	9400-10399	
	Arvada	221L	80005	10000-10499	
	Arvada	220M	80005	12800-13199	
	Jefferson Co	221F	80005	10600-10799	
	Westminster	223G	80030	2600-2999	
	Westminster	223K	80031	3000-3699	
	Westminster	223K	80031	3700-3899	
81ST CIR W	Arvada	222M	80003	5700-5899	
	Arvada	222K	80005	7800-7899	
	Arvada	222F	80005	8000-8099	
	Arvada	221G	80005	10000-10099	
81ST DR W	Arvada	222E	80005	8100-8899	
	Arvada	221G	80005	9800-10099	
	Jefferson Co	221F	80005	None	
81ST LN W	Arvada	221M	80005	8900-9199	
	Arvada	221G	80005	10000-10099	
81ST PL E	Adams Co	224G	80221	1-199	
	Adams Co	224M	80229	1300-1499	
	Adams Co	224H	80229	1700-1799	
	Adams Co	225E	80229	1800-1999	
81ST PL W	Adams Co	224F	80221	1-299	
	Adams Co	224E	80221	1400-1599	
	Arvada	222H	80003	5700-5899	
	Arvada	222F	80003	7400-7499	
	Arvada	222F	80005	7700-7799	
	Arvada	222E	80005	8100-8999	
	Arvada	221H	80005	9000-9399	
	Arvada	221G	80005	10300-10499	
	Arvada	220H	80005	12900-13099	
	Westminster	223K	80031	3700-3799	
	Westminster	223J	80031	4800-5199	
81ST ST N	Boulder Co	70B	80503	7700-8099	
	Boulder Co	40X	80503	8000-8599	
82ND AVE E	Adams Co	226E	80022	6001-6299	O
	Commerce City	226F	80022	7300-7699	
82ND AVE W	Arvada	222H	80003	5200-5399	
	Arvada	221G	80005	9200-10499	
	Arvada	220G	80005	13200-14799	
	Jefferson Co	221F	80005	11400-12599	
	Jefferson Co	220H	80005	12600-13199	
	Jefferson Co	220J	80007	14800-16399	
	Jefferson Co	219F	80007	16400-19999	
	Westminster	223F	80031	3000-3599	
	Westminster	223E	80031	4200-4399	
82ND CIR W	Arvada	222H	80003	5700-5899	
82ND DR E	Adams Co	224G	80229	300-699	
82ND DR W	Arvada	222G	80003	6000-6199	
	Arvada	221G	80005	10000-10099	
82ND LN W	Arvada	221G	80005	10000-10099	
	Arvada	220H	80005	12600-13299	
	Arvada	220H	80005	12601-12699	O
82ND PL E	Adams Co	225E	80229	2200-2299	
	Adams Co	226F	80022	7300-7499	
82ND PL W	Adams Co	224E	80221	1600-1799	
	Adams Co	223H	80221	1800-2399	
	Arvada	222H	80003	6000-6099	
	Arvada	222F	80003	6900-7099	
	Arvada	222F	80005	7800-7999	
	Arvada	221H	80005	9500-9999	
	Arvada	221G	80005	10000-10499	
	Arvada	221E	80005	11600-11899	
	Jefferson Co	221F	80005	10800-11199	
	Westminster	223H	80030	2400-2699	
	Westminster	223E	80031	None	
82ND WAY W	Arvada	222F	80003	7300-7499	
	Westminster	223H	80030	2500-2699	
83RD AVE E	Adams Co	224H	80229	1600-1899	
	Adams Co	225E	80229	None	
	Adams Co	226E	80022	None	
	Commerce City	226G	80022	7300-8399	
83RD AVE W	Adams Co	224F	80221	200-799	
	Adams Co	224E	80221	1600-1899	
	Arvada	222H	80003	5200-5499	
	Arvada	222F	80003	6900-7599	
	Arvada	222F	80005	7900-7999	
	Arvada	221H	80005	8900-9999	
	Arvada	221G	80005	10400-10499	
	Arvada	221E	80005	11900-12199	
	Arvada	220H	80005	13200-13299	
	Arvada	220G	80005	13500-13899	
	Westminster	223G	80221	2900-2999	
	Westminster	223G	80031	3000-3299	
83RD DR E	Adams Co	224G	80229	300-699	
	Adams Co	224H	80229	1600-1899	
83RD DR W	Arvada	221G	80005	10400-10499	
	Arvada	220H	80005	12600-12799	
83RD LN W	Arvada	221E	80005	11600-12299	
83RD LN W	Arvada	220F	80005	14200-14299	
83RD PL E	Adams Co	224H	80229	700-1799	
	Adams Co	225E	80229	1800-2299	
	Adams Co	226E	80022	5900-6199	
83RD PL W	Arvada	222G	80003	6000-6499	
	Arvada	221H	80005	9200-9299	
	Arvada	221G	80005	10400-10599	
	Arvada	221E	80005	11600-11999	
	Arvada	220H	80005	13200-13599	
	Arvada	220G	80005	14202-14298	E
	Arvada	220G	80005	None	
	Thornton	224F	80260	1-99	
83RD ST N	Boulder Co	70G	80503	7000-7699	
83RD WAY W	Arvada	222G	80003	6100-6199	
	Arvada	222F	80003	6900-7599	
	Arvada	220H	80005	12400-12799	
	Westminster	223H	80030	2500-2599	
84TH AVE E	Adams Co	224H	80229	1400-1699	
	Adams Co	225E	80229	1700-2699	
	Adams Co	226E	80022	5801-5899	O
	Commerce City	226F	80022	7000-8499	
	Thornton	224G	80602	100-699	
84TH AVE W	Adams Co	224F	80260	800-1899	
	Adams Co	223G	80260	1900-2399	
	Arvada	222H	80003	5200-5999	
	Arvada	222G	80003	6000-6799	
	Arvada	222E	80005	8500-8999	
	Arvada	221H	80005	9000-9199	
	Arvada	221F	80005	10700-11199	
	Arvada	220H	80005	12800-13199	
	Arvada	220G	80005	13500-13899	
	Arvada	220G	80005	14200-14299	
84TH AVE W	Thornton	224F	80260	1-799	
	Westminster	223G	80030	2400-3199	
	Westminster	223G	80031	3200-3599	
	Westminster	223F	80031	3600-4099	
	Westminster	223E	80031	5000-5199	
84TH CIR W	Arvada	222G	80003	6500-6899	
	Arvada	222E	80005	8500-8699	
	Arvada	220H	80005	12400-12799	
	Arvada	220G	80005	None	
84TH CT E	Thornton	224G	80229	None	
84TH CT W	Arvada	222F	80005	7800-7899	
84TH DR E	Adams Co	225F	80229	3200-3899	
84TH DR W	Arvada	220H	80005	12400-12999	
	Arvada	220H	80005	12500-13599	
84TH LN W	Arvada	221E	80005	11600-11699	
84TH LN W	Arvada	220G	80005	14200-14299	
84TH PL E	Adams Co	224H	80229	1400-1599	
84TH PL W	Arvada	222H	80003	6000-6499	
	Arvada	222G	80003	6500-6599	
	Arvada	221G	80005	9900-10699	
	Arvada	221F	80005	10700-11599	
	Arvada	221E	80005	11600-12299	
	Arvada	220H	80005	12600-13399	
	Arvada	220H	80005	12800-13199	
	Arvada	220F	80005	None	
	Federal Heights	224E	80260	1100-1198	E
84TH WAY W	Arvada	222H	80003	6000-6599	
	Arvada	222G	80003	6600-7299	
	Arvada	222F	80003	7300-7599	

STREET NAME	CITY or COUNTY	MAP GRID	ZIP CODE	BLOCK RANGE	O/E
85TH AVE E	Adams Co	224G	80229	700-899	
	Commerce City	226G	80022	8201-8499	O
	Thornton	224G	80229	600-699	
85TH AVE W	Arvada	222C	80003	6100-6699	
	Arvada	221G	80005	9900-9999	
	Arvada	221F	80005	10800-10899	
	Arvada	221E	80005	11700-12499	
	Federal Heights	224E	80260	1001-1899	O
	Federal Heights	223H	80260	2100-2299	
	Westminster	223G	80260	2600-2699	
	Westminster	223F	80031	3600-3799	
85TH CIR W	Arvada	220H	80005	12500-12899	
85TH DR E	Adams Co	225F	80229	3200-3999	
85TH DR W	Arvada	221E	80005	12000-12099	
	Arvada	220G	80005	13400-13999	
85TH PL E	Adams Co	224D	80229	1000-1399	
85TH PL W	Arvada	222C	80003	6000-6199	
	Arvada	221G	80005	9900-9999	
	Arvada	221G	80005	10400-10799	
	Arvada	221F	80005	10800-11499	
	Arvada	221E	80005	11700-11999	
	Arvada	220H	80005	12900-13199	
85TH WAY W	Arvada	221G	80005	9900-9999	
86TH AVE E	Adams Co	225F	80229	2700-3999	
	Commerce City	226B	80022	7300-7599	
	Commerce City	226C	80022	8100-8799	
	Commerce City	769N	80022	None	
	Thornton	224G	80229	200-699	
86TH AVE W	Arvada	222D	80003	5200-6399	
	Arvada	221G	80005	9800-9999	
	Federal Heights	223H	80260	1900-2099	
	Jefferson Co	220D	80005	12500-13199	
	Westminster	223G	80260	2700-2999	
	Westminster	222A	80005	8600-8899	
	Westminster	221D	80021	8900-9199	
86TH CIR W	Arvada	220G	80005	13400-13599	
	Westminster	222A	80005	8500-8699	
86TH CT W	Westminster	222E	80005	8600-8699	
86TH DR W	Arvada	220G	80005	13200-14299	
	Westminster	222E	80005	8700-8899	
86TH PKWY W	Arvada	221G	80005	9900-12499	
	Arvada	220G	80005	12500-14799	
86TH PL E	Adams Co	224D	80229	1500-1699	
	Commerce City	769N	80022	None	
86TH PL W	Arvada	221H	80005	9200-9999	
	Arvada	220G	80005	14000-14299	
	Westminster	222E	80005	8600-8699	
87TH AVE E	Commerce City	226C	80022	8000-8799	
	Commerce City	769N	80022	None	
	Thornton	224C	80229	600-699	
87TH AVE W	Adams Co	223A	80031	4500-4799	
	Arvada	221D	80005	9700-9799	
	Arvada	221C	80005	9900-9999	
	Jefferson Co	220D	80005	12500-13199	
	Thornton	224B	80260	None	
	Westminster	223C	80031	3400-3499	
87TH CIR W	Arvada	221D	80005	9600-9699	
87TH DR W	Arvada	220G	80005	None	
	Westminster	222B	80005	7600-8399	
87TH LN W	Arvada	220C	80005	None	
87TH PKWY W	Arvada	220C	80005	None	
87TH PL E	Commerce City	769N	80022	None	
87TH PL W	Adams Co	223A	80031	4500-4799	
	Arvada	221D	80005	9200-9999	
	Westminster	223C	80260	2600-2799	
	Westminster	222A	80005	8600-8899	
	Westminster	221D	80021	9000-9199	
87TH ST N	Boulder Co	40L	80503	8100-9899	
	See.. AIRPORT RD				
	Boulder Co	10G	80503	12600-14199	
87TH WAY W	Arvada	222C	80003	6900-6999	
87TH TERRACE W	Arvada	220D	80005	None	
88TH AVE E	Adams Co	225C	80229	4000-4399	
	Adams Co	226B	80640	5600-7299	
	Adams Co	226C	80640	7601-8999	O
	Adams Co	771N	80022	32900-33699	
	Adams Co	771N	80642	33700-39499	
	Adams Co	772N	80102	39500-52099	
	Commerce City	225C	80229	4400-4799	
	Commerce City	225D	80640	4800-5599	
	Commerce City	226B	80640	7300-7599	
	Commerce City	226C	80640	7600-8998	E
	Commerce City	769N	80022	16900-21899	
	Denver	769R	80249	21900-23599	
	Thornton	224C	80229	100-1599	
	Thornton	225B	80229	1700-3999	
88TH AVE W	Adams Co	223B	80031	3000-4899	
	Arvada	221D	80005	9100-9999	
	Federal Heights	223C	80260	2401-2999	O
	Jefferson Co	220D	80005	12500-13199	
	Thornton	224B	80229	1-1599	
	Westminster	223C	80260	2400-2998	E
	Westminster	222C	80031	5200-6799	
	Westminster	222C	80021	6800-7599	
	Westminster	222A	80005	7600-8899	
	Westminster	221D	80005	8900-9099	
88TH CIR E	Thornton	225C	80229	3600N-3799N	
88TH CIR W	Westminster	221D	80021	9100-9199	
88TH LOOP W	Arvada	220C	80005	None	
88TH PL E	Commerce City	769N	80022	None	
88TH PL E	Thornton	225B	80229	None	
88TH PL W	Adams Co	223A	80031	4700-5199	
	Adams Co	223B	80031	None	
	Westminster	222A	80021	8500-8799	
	Westminster	221D	80005	8900-9799	
88TH ST S	Louisville	160H	80027	1000-2399	
	Superior	160R	80027	None	
88TH WAY E	Commerce City	769N	80022	None	
88TH WAY W	Adams Co	223B	80031	3600-3999	
89TH AVE E	Adams Co	226A	80640	5500-5999	
	Adams Co	226D	80640	8900-9199	
	Commerce City	769N	80022	None	
	Thornton	224D	80229	900-1599	
	Thornton	225A	80229	2000-2299	
	Thornton	225C	80229	3500-3799	
	Thornton	225B	80229	None	
89TH AVE W	Adams Co	223B	80031	3500-3599	
	Federal Heights	223C	80260	None	
	Westminster	222A	80021	8400-8699	
	Westminster	221D	80021	8900-9199	
89TH CIR W	Westminster	221D	80021	9400-9799	
89TH CT W	Westminster	221D	80021	9100-9199	
89TH DR W	Westminster	222A	80021	8500-8699	
89TH LOOP W	Arvada	220C	80005	None	
89TH PL E	Commerce City	769N	80022	None	
	Thornton	225C	80229	3600-3799	
	Thornton	225B	80229	None	
89TH PL W	Adams Co	223B	80031	3400-4099	
	Westminster	222A	80021	8700-8799	
	Westminster	221D	80021	8900-9599	
89TH ST N	Boulder Co	40M	80503	9400-9899	
89TH WAY E	Commerce City	769N	80022	None	
89TH WAY W	Adams Co	223A	80031	3600-4799	
	Westminster	221D	80021	9600-9799	
90TH AVE E	Commerce City	769J	80022	None	
90TH AVE W	Federal Heights	224A	80260	1600-1999	
	Federal Heights	223D	80260	2000-2299	
	Federal Heights	223C	80260	2300-2999	
	Westminster	223B	80031	3600-3699	
	Westminster	223A	80031	4200-4799	
	Westminster	222B	80021	6800-7799	
	Westminster	222A	80021	7800-8499	
90TH CIR W	Westminster	221D	80021	9200-9299	
90TH CT W	Westminster	221D	80021	9100-9199	
90TH DR W	Westminster	222C	80021	6800-6999	
	Westminster	192Y	80021	7000-7199	
	Westminster	222B	80021	7700-8099	
	Westminster	221D	80021	9200-9399	
90TH PL E	Commerce City	769J	80022	None	
	Thornton	195X	80229	2400-2899	
	Thornton	225B	80229	3500-3699	
90TH PL W	Adams Co	223C	80260	2600-2999	
	Adams Co	223C	80031	3100-3199	
	Westminster	223B	80031	3600-3699	
	Westminster	222A	80021	7900-8399	
	Westminster	191Z	80021	8700-8799	
	Westminster	191Z	80021	9100-9599	
90TH WAY W	Westminster	193X	80031	3700-3799	
90TH AVE E	Adams Co	226D	80640	8900-9199	
	Thornton	224D	80229	900-1599	
	Thornton	225A	80229	2100-2599	
91ST AVE E	Commerce City	769J	80022	None	
	Thornton	194Z	80229	900-1299	
	Thornton	195W	80229	2100-2399	
	Thornton	195X	80229	3500-3799	
91ST AVE W	Federal Heights	193Y	80260	2700-2999	
	Thornton	194W	80260	500-799	
	Westminster	192Z	80031	5300-5399	
	Westminster	192Y	80031	6000-6799	
	Westminster	192W	80021	7800-8899	
	Westminster	191Z	80021	8900-9299	
91ST CIR W	Thornton	224B	80260	400-699	
91ST CT W	Westminster	192Y	80021	6800-6999	
91ST DR E	Thornton	195Y	80229	4100-4299	
91ST DR W	Federal Heights	193Z	80260	2400-2599	
	Thornton	224B	80260	500-799	
91ST PL E	Commerce City	769J	80022	None	
	Thornton	195Y	80229	4200-4299	
	Thornton	194Z	80221	None	
91ST PL W	Federal Heights	193Z	80260	2000-2299	
	Federal Heights	193Y	80260	2700-2999	
	Westminster	193X	80031	3700-3799	
	Westminster	192W	80021	8400-8899	
	Westminster	191Z	80021	8900-9399	
92ND AVE E	Adams Co	196Z	80640	None	
	Commerce City	197W	80640	None	
	Commerce City	769J	80022	None	
	Thornton	194Z	80229	900-1099	
	Thornton	195Y	80229	4000-4299	
92ND AVE W	Federal Heights	194W	80260	1600-1999	
	Federal Heights	193X	80260	2000-2999	
	Westminster	193X	80031	3000-5199	
	Westminster	192Y	80031	5200-6799	
	Westminster	192Y	80021	6800-7899	
	Westminster	191Z	80021	8900-9399	
92ND CT E	Thornton	195Y	80229	4300-4399	
92ND DR W	Westminster	192Z	80031	5800-5999	
92ND LN W	Westminster	192X	80021	6900-7299	
92ND PL E	Adams Co	196Z	80640	None	
	Commerce City	769J	80022	None	
	Thornton	195Y	80229	3600-3899	
92ND PL W	Westminster	193Y	80031	3200-3399	
	Westminster	193W	80031	4200-4899	
	Westminster	192Z	80031	5800-5899	
	Westminster	192Y	80031	6100-6399	
	Westminster	192X	80021	7100-7299	
	Westminster	192W	80021	8500-8799	
93RD AVE E	Commerce City	769J	80022	None	
	Thornton	195Y	80229	3700-4499	
93RD AVE W	Federal Heights	193Z	80260	2500-2699	
	Federal Heights	193Y	80260	2700-2899	
	Westminster	193Y	80031	3100-3399	
	Westminster	193W	80031	4800-4999	
	Westminster	192Z	80031	5800-6099	
	Westminster	192Y	80031	6300-6599	
	Westminster	191Z	80021	8700-9599	
93RD CIR W	Westminster	192W	80021	8100-8199	
93RD DR E	Thornton	195Y	80229	4300-4499	
93RD DR W	Federal Heights	193Z	80260	2600-2699	
93RD PL E	Commerce City	769J	80022	None	
	Thornton	195W	80229	2300-2499	
	Thornton	195X	80229	2500-2999	
	Thornton	195Y	80229	4300-4499	
93RD PL W	Federal Heights	193Z	80260	2500-2699	
	Federal Heights	193Y	80260	2700-2799	
	Westminster	192Z	80031	5800-5999	
	Westminster	192X	80021	7400-7599	
	Westminster	192W	80021	8200-8299	
	Westminster	192W	80021	8600-8699	
93RD WAY W	Westminster	192X	80021	7300-7499	
	Westminster	192W	80021	8000-8299	
94TH AVE E	Commerce City	769J	80022	None	
	Thornton	195W	80229	1900-2199	
	Thornton	195X	80229	3500-3599	
	Thornton	195Y	80229	3600-4599	
94TH AVE W	Federal Heights	193Y	80260	2400-2899	
	Westminster	193X	80031	3000-4599	
	Westminster	192Z	80031	5800-5999	
	Westminster	192X	80021	6800-7399	
	Westminster	192S	80021	8100-8699	
	Westminster	191Z	80021	9000-9399	
94TH DR E	Thornton	195X	80229	2500-3299	
	Thornton	195X	80229	3500-3699	
	Thornton	195Y	80229	4300-4599	
94TH DR W	Federal Heights	193Z	80260	2600-2699	
	Federal Heights	193Y	80260	2700-2799	
94TH LN E	Thornton	195X	80229	3000-3199	
94TH LN W	Federal Heights	193Z	80260	2600-2799	
94TH PL E	Commerce City	769J	80022	None	
	Thornton	195Y	80229	4100-4599	
94TH PL W	Federal Heights	193Z	80260	2600-2799	
	Westminster	192Y	80031	6700-6799	
	Westminster	192X	80021	7200-7999	
	Westminster	192W	80021	8400-8599	
	Westminster	191Z	80021	9200-9299	
	Westminster	192Z	80031	None	
94TH WAY E	Commerce City	769J	80022	None	
	Commerce City	769J	80022	None	
95TH AVE E	Commerce City	769J	80022	None	
	Thornton	194Z	80229	700-799	
	Thornton	194Z	80229	1100-1599	
	Thornton	195S	80229	1600-2199	
	Thornton	195T	80229	2400-2999	
95TH AVE W	Federal Heights	193Z	80260	2600-2799	
	Jefferson Co	192T	80021	7200-7399	
	Westminster	193T	80031	3000-3599	
	Westminster	193X	80031	3700-3799	
	Westminster	192Y	80031	6000-6499	
	Westminster	192T	80021	6800-7199	
	Westminster	191Z	80021	8700-9199	
95TH CIR W	Thornton	194S	80260	1100-1199	
95TH DR E	Thornton	195T	80229	3100-3199	
95TH DR W	Federal Heights	193Z	80260	2600-2799	
	Westminster	192S	80021	8400-8699	
95TH PL E	Commerce City	769J	80022	None	
95TH PL W	Federal Heights	193V	80260	2600-2799	
	Westminster	193T	80031	3700-3799	
	Westminster	192U	80031	6400-6799	
	Westminster	192V	80031	None	
95TH ST	Boulder Co	71N	80026	5300-5399	
	Boulder Co	71N	80504	5400-8099	
95TH ST	Lafayette	131E	80026	700-1599	
95TH ST N	Boulder Co	101N	80026	1600-5299	
95TH ST N	Boulder Co	11E	80504	12600-13999	
95TH WAY W	Westminster	192T	80021	7700-8199	
96TH AVE E	Adams Co	196U	80640	6500-9399	
	Adams Co	771J	80022	32900-33399	
	Adams Co	772L	80102	None	
	Commerce City	197U	80640	9900-10499	
	Commerce City	197U	80022	10500-13199	
	Commerce City	198S	80022	13200-16899	
	Commerce City	769L	80022	18500-21899	
	Thornton	195V	80229	4800-5599	
96TH AVE W	Federal Heights	193U	80260	2400-2999	
	Jefferson Co	192S	80021	7600-8299	
	Thornton	194T	80260	500-799	
	Thornton	194S	80260	800-1299	
	Thornton	194S	80260	1500-1899	
	Thornton	193V	80260	1900-2399	
	Westminster	193U	80031	3000-3999	
	Westminster	192U	80031	6500-6699	
	Westminster	192S	80021	7200-7599	
	Westminster	190U	80005	13200-14799	
	Westminster	192V	80031	None	
96TH CIR E	Commerce City	198U	80022	None	
96TH CIR E	Thornton	195S	80229	1800-1999	
	Thornton	195T	80229	3500-3599	
96TH CIR W	Westminster	193T	80031	3200-3599	
96TH CT W	Westminster	192U	80021	6700-6799	
96TH DR E	Thornton	194V	80229	1400-1699	
	Thornton	195S	80229	1700-1899	
	Thornton	195V	80229	4800-4899	
	Thornton	195U	80229	None	
96TH DR W	Federal Heights	193V	80260	2600-2799	
	Westminster	192U	80021	6300-6799	
	Westminster	191V	80021	8700-8799	
96TH LN E	Thornton	194V	80229	1400-1499	
96TH LN W	Federal Heights	193U	80260	2800-2899	
96TH PL E	Commerce City	197T	80022	10600-10999	
	Commerce City	197T	80022	11200-11299	
	Commerce City	198U	80022	15700-16099	
	Commerce City	198V	80022	16400-16799	
96TH PL E	Commerce City	769J	80022	None	
	Thornton	194V	80229	1200-1599	
	Thornton	194V	80229	1600-1799	
	Thornton	195T	80229	2900-3599	
	Thornton	195V	80229	4800-4899	
	Thornton	194V	80229	None	
	Thornton	195U	80229	None	
96TH PL W	Thornton	194S	80260	800-1299	
	Westminster	192U	80021	6300-6699	
	Westminster	192R	80031	None	
96TH ST S	Louisville	161F	80027	800-1499	
	Louisville	131X	80027	None	
96TH WAY E	Commerce City	198U	80022	15500-16099	
	Commerce City	198V	80022	16400-16499	
	Thornton	194V	80229	1600-1799	
	Thornton	195S	80229	2400-2799	
	Thornton	195T	80229	3400-3599	
97TH AVE E	Commerce City	198U	80022	15500-16099	
	Commerce City	198V	80022	16400-16499	
	Commerce City	769J	80022	None	
	Thornton	194V	80229	1200-1599	
	Thornton	194V	80229	1600-1999	
	Thornton	195S	80229	2000-2599	
	Thornton	195T	80229	2600-3199	
	Thornton	194U	80229	None	
	Thornton	195U	80229	None	
	Thornton	195V	80229	None	
97TH AVE W	Northglenn	194S	80260	800-1299	
	Thornton	194S	80260	1300-1599	
	Westminster	193U	80031	3000-3399	

Continued on next page

STREET NAME	CITY or COUNTY	MAP GRID	ZIP CODE	BLOCK RANGE	O/E
97TH AVE W (Cont'd)	Westminster	193T	80031	3400-3899	
	Westminster	191V	80021	9500-9899	
	Westminster	192V	80031	None	
97TH CIR E	Commerce City	769J	80022	None	
	Thornton	195S	80229	2100-2299	
97TH CIR W	Westminster	192U	80021	6700-6799	
97TH CT E	Thornton	194V	80229	1500-1599	
97TH CT W	Westminster	192U	80021	6600-6799	
	Westminster	192V	80031	None	
97TH DR E	Thornton	194V	80229	1700-1799	
	Thornton	195S	80229	1800-2299	
	Thornton	195V	80229	4800-4999	
97TH DR W	Westminster	191U	80021	9700-9799	
97TH PL E	Commerce City	197S	80640	9600-9799	
	Commerce City	198U	80022	15300-16099	
	Commerce City	198V	80022	16400-16799	
	Thornton	194V	80229	1200-1499	
	Thornton	195S	80229	2000-2299	
	Thornton	195T	80229	3400-3699	
	Thornton	195V	80229	4800-5499	
97TH PL W	Westminster	193T	80031	3900-3999	
	Westminster	192U	80021	6400-6799	
	Westminster	192T	80021	7200-7399	
	Westminster	191V	80021	8400-8499	
	Westminster	191U	80021	None	
	Westminster	192R	80031	None	
97TH WAY E	Commerce City	198V	80022	16000-16499	
98TH AVE E	Adams Co	772K	80102	42201-43299	O
98TH AVE E	Commerce City	198V	80022	16000-16299	
	Commerce City	198U	80022	None	
	Commerce City	769J	80022	None	
	Thornton	194V	80229	1200-1599	
	Thornton	195S	80229	1800-2699	
	Thornton	195T	80229	2700-3699	
	Thornton	194V	80229	None	
98TH AVE W	Jefferson Co	192S	80021	7600-8299	
	Northglenn	194S	80260	800-1299	
	Westminster	193U	80031	3000-3199	
	Westminster	193T	80031	3800-3999	
	Westminster	193S	80031	4800-5199	
	Westminster	192V	80020	5200-5999	
	Westminster	192T	80021	6800-7599	
	Westminster	191V	80021	9200-9499	
	Westminster	191U	80021	9800-10099	
98TH CIR W	Federal Heights	193U	80260	2800-2899	
	Westminster	192U	80021	6700-6799	
98TH CT W	Westminster	193S	80031	5000-5099	
	Westminster	192U	80021	6400-6499	
	Westminster	191V	80021	9300-9399	
98TH DR E	Thornton	195T	80229	3300-3499	
98TH DR W	Federal Heights	193U	80260	2600-2899	
	Westminster	192U	80021	6200-6699	
98TH PL E	Commerce City	198U	80022	15300-15899	
	Commerce City	769J	80022	None	
	Thornton	194U	80229	300-699	
	Thornton	194V	80229	1800-1899	
	Thornton	195S	80229	2000-2799	
	Thornton	195U	80229	None	
98TH PL W	Westminster	193U	80031	3300-3498	E
	Westminster	193T	80031	3700-4099	
	Westminster	193S	80031	5000-5099	
	Westminster	192U	80021	6600-6799	
	Westminster	192T	80021	7300-7399	
	Westminster	191V	80021	9200-9299	
98TH WAY E	Commerce City	198V	80022	15900-16499	
	Commerce City	769J	80022	None	
	Thornton	195S	80229	2400-2699	
98TH WAY W	Westminster	193T	80031	4100-4199	
	Westminster	191V	80021	9200-9299	
99TH AVE E	Commerce City	198U	80022	15300-15799	
	Commerce City	198V	80022	16100-16699	
	Commerce City	769J	80022	None	
	Thornton	194V	80229	1700-1799	
	Thornton	195S	80229	1800-2699	
	Thornton	195T	80229	2800-3199	
99TH AVE W	Jefferson Co	192T	80021	7600-8399	
	Northglenn	194T	80260	300-1299	
	Westminster	193U	80031	3100-3299	
	Westminster	193T	80031	3300-3999	
	Westminster	193S	80031	4600-4899	
	Westminster	192U	80021	6200-6899	
	Westminster	191V	80021	9100-10099	
99TH CIR E	Thornton	195U	80229	3800-3899	
99TH CIR W	Federal Heights	193U	80260	2800-2899	
	Westminster	193T	80031	3400-3499	
99TH CT E	Thornton	195T	80229	3600-3799	
99TH CT W	Westminster	193T	80031	4100-4199	
	Westminster	193N	80031	5100-5199	
99TH DR E	Thornton	195T	80229	3400-3599	
99TH LN E	Thornton	195T	80229	3500-3999	
99TH PL E	Commerce City	197S	80640	9600-9799	
	Commerce City	198U	80022	15300-15899	
	Commerce City	198V	80022	16100-16699	
	Commerce City	769E	80022	None	
	Thornton	194U	80229	300-699	
	Thornton	194V	80229	1500-1599	
	Thornton	195S	80229	2000-2299	
	Thornton	195U	80229	3600-3799	
99TH PL W	Federal Heights	193V	80260	2400-2699	
	Jefferson Co	192T	80021	7600-7799	
	Westminster	193T	80031	3700-4199	
	Westminster	193S	80031	4600-4699	
	Westminster	191U	80021	9600-9899	
99TH WAY E	Commerce City	198Q	80022	15300-15399	
	Commerce City	198R	80022	16200-16599	
	Thornton	195S	80229	2000-2099	
	Thornton	195S	80229	2300-2699	
	Thornton	195T	80229	2700-3799	
99TH WAY W	Westminster	191V	80021	9400-9499	
100TH AVE E	Adams Co	196Q	80640	7500-8099	
	Thornton	196N	80640	5500-6299	
	Adams Co	198P	80022	None	
	Commerce City	198Q	80022	None	
	Commerce City	769E	80022	None	
	Thornton	194R	80229	700-1799	
	Thornton	195N	80229	1800-5499	
100TH AVE W	Federal Heights	193U	80260	2400-2699	
	Federal Heights	193U	80260	2700-2999	
	Northglenn	194S	80260	600-1199	
	Northglenn	194N	80260	1201-1599	O
	Thornton	194N	80260	1200-1598	E
	Thornton	194N	80260	1600-1899	
	Thornton	193V	80260	1900-2399	
	Westminster	193P	80031	3600-4599	
	Westminster	193S	80031	4600-4699	
	Westminster	192V	80020	5200-5399	
	Westminster	192S	80021	8400-8599	
	Westminster	191U	80021	8800-11599	
	Westminster	191S	80021	11600-13499	
100TH CIR W	Westminster	192H	80020	5600-5699	
	Westminster	191R	80021	9200-9399	
100TH CT E	Thornton	195R	80229	4900-5199	
100TH CT W	Westminster	193N	80031	4700-4799	
	Westminster	192R	80020	5200-5699	
	Westminster	191Q	80021	10100-10199	
	Westminster	193P	80031	None	
100TH DR E	Commerce City	198Q	80022	15201-15299	O
	Thornton	195R	80229	4800-5599	
100TH DR W	Federal Heights	193Q	80260	2700-2899	
	Westminster	193U	80031	3100-3499	
	Westminster	191P	80021	10800-10999	
100TH LN E	Commerce City	198P	80022	14100-14199	
	Thornton	195R	80229	4800-5199	
	Thornton	194R	80229	None	
100TH PL E	Commerce City	198P	80022	14100-14199	
	Commerce City	198Q	80022	None	
	Commerce City	768H	80022	None	
	Thornton	195N	80229	2000-2299	
	Thornton	195R	80229	5200-5399	
	Thornton	194R	80229	None	
100TH PL W	Federal Heights	193R	80260	2600-2699	
	Northglenn	194N	80260	400-1599	
	Westminster	193P	80031	3500-3599	
	Westminster	192R	80020	5400-5699	
	Westminster	191R	80021	9200-9299	
	Westminster	191Q	80021	10000-10599	
	Westminster	191P	80021	11500-11599	
100TH WAY E	Commerce City	198N	80022	14100-14199	
	Commerce City	198R	80022	None	
	Thornton	195N	80229	2500-2599	
	Thornton	195R	80229	5200-5599	
100TH WAY W	Westminster	191R	80021	9200-9299	
	Westminster	191P	80021	10900-10999	
100 YEAR PARTY CT	Longmont	41V	80504	2001-2099	O
101ST AVE E	Commerce City	198P	80022	14100-14499	
	Commerce City	198Q	80022	15300-15599	
	Commerce City	198R	80022	16600-16899	
	Commerce City	198Q	80022	None	
	Thornton	195N	80229	2100-2399	
	Thornton	195N	80229	2700-3099	
	Thornton	195P	80229	3400-3699	
	Thornton	195Q	80229	3700-3799	
	Thornton	194R	80229	None	
101ST AVE W	Jefferson Co	192P	80021	7700-8099	
	Northglenn	194N	80260	800-1599	
	Thornton	193R	80260	2300-2399	
	Westminster	193P	80031	3600-3799	
	Westminster	193N	80031	5100-5199	
	Westminster	192R	80020	5400-5699	
	Westminster	192N	80021	8700-8799	
	Westminster	191R	80021	9100-9299	
	Westminster	193P	80031	10000-10099	
	Westminster	191Q	80021	10300-10599	
	Westminster	191P	80021	11500-11599	
101ST CIR W	Thornton	193R	80260	2100-2299	
	Westminster	193P	80031	3200-3599	
	Westminster	193N	80031	4800-5199	
101ST CT E	Commerce City	198Q	80022	None	
	Thornton	195N	80229	2400-3099	
	Thornton	195R	80229	4800-4999	
	Thornton	195P	80229	None	
101ST CT W	Thornton	193R	80260	1900-1999	
101ST DR E	Commerce City	198Q	80022	None	
101ST DR W	Westminster	191Q	80021	10000-10199	
101ST LN E	Thornton	195R	80229	5300-5599	
101ST PL E	Commerce City	198P	80022	14100-14499	
	Commerce City	198Q	80022	15300-15599	
	Commerce City	198Q	80022	None	
	Thornton	195N	80229	2000-2199	
	Thornton	195N	80229	2300-2399	
	Thornton	195R	80229	5400-5598	E
101ST PL W	Federal Heights	193Q	80260	2600-2799	
	Northglenn	194N	80260	800-1599	
	Westminster	193P	80031	3400-3599	
	Westminster	193S	80031	4500-4799	
	Westminster	191R	80021	9200-9299	
	Westminster	191P	80021	10200-10799	
101ST ST W	Thornton	194N	80260	1700-1899	
101ST WAY	Commerce City	198Q	80022	None	
101ST WAY E	Commerce City	198R	80022	None	
	Thornton	195N	80229	2000-2199	
	Thornton	195N	80229	2300-2499	
102ND AVE E	Commerce City	197N	80640	9600-9699	
	Commerce City	198P	80022	14100-14499	
	Commerce City	198R	80022	16600-16899	
	Commerce City	198P	80022	None	
	Commerce City	769E	80022	None	
	Thornton	194Q	80229	300-699	
	Thornton	194R	80229	1200-1299	
	Thornton	195N	80229	2000-2899	
	Thornton	195P	80229	3200-3799	
102ND AVE W	Jefferson Co	192P	80021	7600-8099	
	Northglenn	194N	80260	800-1599	
	Thornton	193R	80260	1700-2099	
	Westminster	193P	80031	3600-4099	
	Westminster	193N	80031	4700-5099	
	Westminster	192R	80020	5200-5499	
	Westminster	192N	80021	8400-8799	
	Westminster	191P	80021	10200-10799	
	Westminster	191P	80021	11100-11599	
102ND CIR E	Thornton	195N	80229	1900-2099	
102ND CIR W	Westminster	193Q	80031	3200-3299	
	Westminster	191P	80021	10900-10999	
102ND CT E	Thornton	195P	80229	3200-3699	
	Thornton	195R	80229	4900-4999	
102ND CT W	Westminster	191P	80021	10900-10999	
102ND DR E	Commerce City	769E	80022	None	
102ND DR E	Thornton	195P	80229	3200-3299	
102ND DR W	Westminster	191P	80021	11200-11299	
102ND LN E	Thornton	195R	80229	5200-5499	
102ND PL E	Commerce City	198P	80022	14100-14498	E
	Commerce City	198R	80022	None	
	Commerce City	769E	80022	None	
	Thornton	195N	80229	2000-2099	
	Thornton	195P	80229	3200-3299	
102ND PL W	Jefferson Co	192P	80021	7600-7999	
	Northglenn	194N	80260	800-1599	
	Westminster	193Q	80031	3200-3599	
	Westminster	193N	80031	4600-4899	
	Westminster	192R	80020	5400-5699	
	Westminster	191R	80021	9100-9299	
	Westminster	191P	80021	10500-11599	
102ND WAY E	Commerce City	198R	80022	None	
103RD AVE E	Commerce City	769E	80022	None	
103RD AVE E	Thornton	194X	80229	300-399	
	Thornton	195N	80229	1900-2299	
103RD AVE W	Federal Heights	193R	80260	2400-2699	
	Jefferson Co	192N	80021	7700-7999	
	Northglenn	194N	80260	800-1599	
	Thornton	193R	80260	1700-2399	
	Westminster	193P	80031	3600-4099	
	Westminster	193N	80031	4800-4899	
	Westminster	192R	80020	5400-5699	
	Westminster	192P	80021	7100-7599	
	Westminster	191R	80021	9000-9299	
	Westminster	191P	80021	10600-11599	
103RD CIR E	Thornton	195P	80229	None	
103RD CIR W	Westminster	193N	80031	4600-4899	
	Westminster	191P	80021	10900-11199	
103RD CT E	Thornton	195N	80229	2200-2299	
103RD CT W	Westminster	193N	80031	3900-4099	
103RD CT W	Westminster	193N	80031	4700-4799	
	Westminster	191P	80021	10900-10999	
103RD DR E	Thornton	195P	80229	3200-3299	
103RD DR W	Westminster	193P	80031	3600-3899	
	Westminster	191P	80021	11200-11599	
103RD PL E	Commerce City	197Q	80640	None	
	Thornton	195N	80229	2100-2299	
	Thornton	195P	80229	3200-3299	
103RD PL W	Northglenn	194N	80260	800-1599	
	Westminster	193Q	80031	3200-3299	
	Westminster	193N	80031	4800-5099	
	Westminster	191P	80021	10700-10999	
104TH AVE E	Adams Co	196Q	80233	5500-7299	
	Adams Co	196Q	80640	7600-10499	
	Adams Co	772E	80102	None	
	Commerce City	197Q	80603	10500-12099	
	Commerce City	768G	80603	10500-12099	
	Commerce City	197Q	80022	12100-13199	
	Commerce City	198Q	80022	13200-16899	
	Commerce City	769E	80022	16500-16899	
	Commerce City	769E	80022	None	
	Thornton	194Q	80233	1-1799	
	Thornton	195N	80233	1800-5499	
	Thornton	196Q	80640	7300-7599	
104TH AVE W	Federal Heights	193P	80234	2400-2998	E
	Northglenn	194Q	80234	1-1899	
	Northglenn	193P	80234	1900-2399	
	Westminster	193P	80234	2401-2999	O
	Westminster	193P	80031	3000-5199	
	Westminster	192R	80020	5200-6799	
	Westminster	192N	80021	8400-8799	
	Westminster	191R	80021	8800-9799	
	Westminster	191Q	80021	10500-10799	
	Westminster	191P	80021	11200-11499	
104TH CIR W	Westminster	193M	80234	2500-2599	
	Westminster	191P	80021	10900-10999	
104TH CT W	Westminster	193M	80234	2600-2699	
	Westminster	191R	80021	9400-9599	
	Westminster	191P	80021	10900-10999	
104TH DR E	Commerce City	197R	80022	12900-13199	
	Commerce City	198N	80022	13200-13499	
	Commerce City	198J	80022	13900-14099	
104TH DR W	Westminster	193P	80031	3600-3799	
	Westminster	191Q	80021	9200-10299	
	Westminster	191P	80021	10900-11499	
104TH LN W	Westminster	193Q	80234	2700-2799	
104TH PL E	Adams Co	196R	80640	None	
	Commerce City	198J	80022	13800-14099	
	Commerce City	198M	80022	16000-16799	
	Commerce City	769E	80022	None	
	Commerce City	769E	80022	None	
	Northglenn	194Q	80233	100-699	
104TH PL W	Jefferson Co	192P	80021	7800-7999	
	Northglenn	194N	80234	1200-1699	
	Northglenn	193R	80234	1700-2399	
	Westminster	193Q	80234	2700-2799	
	Westminster	193P	80031	3400-3499	
	Westminster	193N	80031	3900-4099	
	Westminster	191R	80021	9200-9299	
	Westminster	191M	80021	9400-9499	
	Westminster	191Q	80021	10500-10699	
	Westminster	191P	80021	10900-10999	
104TH ST	Louisville	131Y	80026	600-799	
104TH ST S	Louisville	161L	80020	600-2399	
104TH WAY E	Adams Co	196Q	80640	8100-8499	
	Commerce City	198M	80022	16100-16399	
	Commerce City	198J	80022	None	
	Commerce City	768H	80022	None	
104TH WAY W	Westminster	191R	80021	9400-9499	
	Northglenn	195P	80233	3500-3599	
105TH AVE E	Adams Co	196L	80640	8200-8599	
	Commerce City	198J	80022	13800-14099	
	Commerce City	769E	80022	16900-17099	
	Commerce City	198M	80022	16000-16899	
	Commerce City	769E	80022	None	
	Commerce City	197M	80022	None	
	Northglenn	194Q	80233	1-399	
	Thornton	195L	80233	4100-4399	

STREET NAME	CITY or COUNTY	MAP GRID	ZIP CODE	BLOCK RANGE	O/E
105TH AVE W	Jefferson Co	192N	80021	8000-8199	
	Westminster	193Q	80031	3001-3099	O
	Westminster	191Q	80021	9600-10699	
105TH CIR E	Commerce City	198M	80022	16100-16299	
105TH CT E	Adams Co	196M	80640	8500-8899	
	Commerce City	198M	80022	16000-16099	
	Northglenn	195K	80233	3300-3499	
105TH CT W	Westminster	193M	80234	2500-2599	
	Westminster	193L	80234	3100-3199	
	Commerce City	197M	80022	None	
	Commerce City	198J	80022	13500-13598	E
	Thornton	195M	80233	4600-5299	
105TH DR W	Westminster	193Q	80234	2500-2899	
	Westminster	193K	80031	3600-3999	
	Westminster	193J	80031	4300-4799	
	Westminster	191K	80021	11400-11599	
105TH PL E	Commerce City	198J	80022	13800-14099	
	Commerce City	197M	80022	None	
	Northglenn	194M	80233	700-1699	
	Northglenn	195J	80233	1700-1899	
	Northglenn	195K	80233	3100-3299	
105TH PL W	Jefferson Co	192K	80021	7600-7999	
	Northglenn	193M	80234	2200-2399	
	Westminster	193M	80234	2500-2599	
	Westminster	193K	80031	4000-4299	
	Westminster	191M	80021	9500-9699	
	Westminster	191K	80021	11300-11499	
105TH ST N	Boulder Co	41U	80504	None	
105TH WAY E	Commerce City	197M	80022	None	
	Commerce City	198J	80022	13201-13299	O
	Commerce City	198M	80022	16100-16299	
105TH WAY W	Westminster	193K	80031	4000-4299	
	Westminster	193J	80031	4300-4799	
	Westminster	191M	80021	9600-9799	
	Westminster	191P	80021	11400-11499	
106TH AVE E	Commerce City	198M	80022	16700-16899	
106TH AVE E	Commerce City	196M	80640	9400-9599	
	Commerce City	769E	80022	16900-17099	
	Commerce City	197M	80022	12400-13199	
	Commerce City	198J	80022	13200-14099	
	Commerce City	769E	80022	None	
	Northglenn	194L	80233	1-399	
	Northglenn	195K	80233	3000-3199	
	Thornton	195L	80233	3500-4099	
106TH AVE W	Northglenn	194K	80234	500-799	
	Northglenn	194J	80234	1400-1699	
	Westminster	192J	80021	7600-8599	
	Westminster	191M	80021	9200-9899	
	Westminster	191L	80021	9900-10799	
	Westminster	191K	80021	10800-11199	
106TH CIR E	Thornton	195M	80233	4500-5099	
106TH CIR W	Westminster	193L	80234	2700-2799	
106TH CT E	Commerce City	198M	80022	16600-16699	
	Northglenn	195K	80233	3300-3499	
	Thornton	195L	80233	4100-4299	
106TH CT W	Westminster	191L	80021	10500-10599	
106TH DR E	Commerce City	196M	80640	9400-9499	
	Commerce City	198J	80022	13900-14099	
	Commerce City	198M	80022	None	
	Thornton	195M	80233	4400-4799	
106TH DR W	Westminster	193J	80031	4800-4899	
106TH LOOP W	Westminster	193M	80234	2600-2799	
106TH PL E	Adams Co	197J	80601	10100-10499	
	Commerce City	196M	80640	9400-9499	
	Commerce City	198J	80022	13800-14099	
	Commerce City	197M	80022	None	
	Commerce City	198L	80022	15800-15999	
	Commerce City	198M	80022	16300-16799	
	Northglenn	194L	80233	1-299	
	Northglenn	195K	80233	3000-3499	
	Thornton	195L	80233	4200-4299	
106TH PL W	Jefferson Co	191J	80021	11800-11999	
	Westminster	193M	80234	2700-2799	
	Westminster	193K	80031	3400-3499	
	Westminster	191L	80021	9900-10699	
	Westminster	191K	80021	10900-11299	
	Westminster	192J	80021	None	
	Westminster	191J	80021	None	
106TH WAY E	Commerce City	198L	80022	15700-15999	
	Commerce City	198M	80022	16600-16699	
	Commerce City	769E	80022	16900-17099	
	Commerce City	197M	80022	None	
	Commerce City	197M	80022	None	
106TH WAY W	Westminster	191L	80021	10500-10599	
	Westminster	191K	80021	11400-11599	
107TH AVE E	Commerce City	196M	80640	9100-9399	
	Commerce City	197J	80640	9400-9599	
	Commerce City	198J	80022	13800-13999	
	Commerce City	198L	80022	15600-16099	
	Commerce City	198M	80022	16300-16499	
	Commerce City	769E	80022	16900-17299	
	Commerce City	197M	80022	None	
	Northglenn	194L	80233	1-299	
	Northglenn	195K	80233	3400-3499	
	Thornton	195L	80233	3500-3899	
	Thornton	195M	80233	4500-4699	
107TH AVE W	Jefferson Co	191J	80021	11600-12299	
	Westminster	193K	80031	3100-3599	
	Westminster	191L	80021	10400-10899	
	Westminster	191K	80021	10900-11399	
107TH CIR W	Westminster	193J	80031	4401-4599	O
	Westminster	191L	80021	10300-10799	
107TH CT E	Commerce City	198M	80022	16600-16698	
	Northglenn	195K	80233	2700-3499	
	Thornton	195L	80233	4100-4399	
107TH CT W	Westminster	193L	80234	2700-2799	
	Westminster	193K	80031	4000-4199	
	Westminster	193J	80031	5000-5099	
	Westminster	191L	80021	10300-10399	
107TH DR E	Commerce City	196H	80640	9150-9198	E
107TH DR E	Thornton	195M	80233	4800-4999	
107TH DR W	Westminster	193M	80234	2400-2499	
	Westminster	193K	80031	4000-4399	
	Westminster	193J	80031	4400-4799	
	Westminster	191M	80021	9400-9899	
107TH LOOP W	Westminster	193J	80031	4900-4999	
107TH PL E	Adams Co	197J	80601	9400-10499	
	Commerce City	196M	80640	9200-9599	
	Commerce City	198J	80022	13800-13999	
	Commerce City	198L	80022	15600-15799	
	Commerce City	198M	80022	16000-16499	
	Commerce City	197J	80640	None	
	Commerce City	197M	80022	None	
	Commerce City	769E	80022	None	
	Commerce City	769E	80022	None	
	Northglenn	194M	80233	1-299	
	Thornton	195L	80233	4100-4199	
	Thornton	195L	80233	4400-4799	
107TH PL W	Westminster	193M	80234	2500-2699	
	Westminster	193L	80031	3000-3099	
	Westminster	193K	80031	4100-4299	
	Westminster	191M	80021	9100-9499	
	Westminster	191L	80021	9900-10499	
	Westminster	191K	80021	10800-11599	
107TH ST	Boulder Co	71R	80026	5300-5399	
	Boulder Co	71R	80504	5400-8099	
	Boulder Co	131H	80026	None	
107TH ST N	Boulder Co	101H	80026	1600-5299	
107TH WAY E	Commerce City	198L	80022	15600-15899	
	Commerce City	769E	80022	None	
	Thornton	195M	80233	None	
108TH AVE E	Adams Co	769F	80022	19300-20099	
	Commerce City	196M	80640	9200-9298	E
	Commerce City	197M	80022	12800-12999	
	Commerce City	198L	80022	15300-15999	
	Commerce City	197J	80640	None	
	Commerce City	198J	80022	None	
	Northglenn	194L	80233	1-699	
	Northglenn	194M	80233	900-1599	
	Northglenn	195K	80233	3300-3499	
	Thornton	195L	80233	3700-4699	
108TH AVE W	Jefferson Co	192J	80021	7700-7899	
	Westminster	193M	80234	2500-2599	
	Westminster	193L	80031	2700-3099	
	Westminster	192L	80020	5700-6899	
	Westminster	192J	80021	7900-8799	
	Westminster	191L	80021	8800-11599	
108TH CIR W	Westminster	192L	80020	5900-6399	
	Westminster	191H	80021	9000-9999	
	Westminster	193M	80234	None	
108TH CT E	Commerce City	198L	80022	15801-15899	O
108TH DR	Westminster	192L	80020	None	
108TH DR E	Commerce City	197E	80640	None	
	Northglenn	195K	80233	2900-3199	
108TH DR W	Jefferson Co	191J	80021	11800-11899	
108TH PL E	Adams Co	769B	80022	19300-20099	
	Commerce City	197J	80640	None	
	Commerce City	197M	80022	None	
	Northglenn	194M	80233	1200-1499	
	Thornton	195M	80233	4700-5499	
108TH PL W	Westminster	193M	80234	2500-2599	
	Westminster	193J	80031	4600-4799	
	Westminster	192M	80020	5700-5999	
	Westminster	192L	80020	6000-6599	
	Westminster	192J	80021	8200-8399	
108TH ST N	Westminster	193J	80031	4800-5199	
108TH WAY E	Commerce City	198L	80022	15300-15498	E
	Commerce City	769E	80022	None	
	Commerce City	198L	80022	15300-15799	
109TH AVE E	Commerce City	197E	80640	None	
	Commerce City	197M	80022	None	
	Commerce City	769A	80022	None	
	Northglenn	194L	80233	1-499	
	Northglenn	195F	80233	2400-3199	
	Thornton	195L	80233	4300-4599	
	Thornton	195M	80233	4600-4699	
109TH AVE W	Westminster	193M	80234	2500-2599	
	Westminster	193J	80031	4600-4799	
	Westminster	192M	80020	5700-5999	
	Westminster	192L	80020	6400-6699	
	Westminster	192J	80021	7800-8199	
109TH CIR E	Commerce City	197E	80640	9400-9599	
109TH CIR W	Westminster	193L	80031	3300-3499	
	Westminster	193K	80031	4200-4299	
	Westminster	192M	80020	5600-5799	
109TH CT E	Northglenn	195K	80233	2600-2799	
	Thornton	195M	80233	4600-4999	
109TH DR E	Commerce City	197E	80640	9400-9599	
	Northglenn	195J	80233	2200-2499	
109TH PL E	Commerce City	198J	80022	None	
	Commerce City	197L	80601	None	
	Northglenn	194L	80233	1-399	
	Northglenn	195E	80233	2200-2299	
	Northglenn	194M	80233	10900-10999	
	Thornton	195L	80233	4000-4199	
	Thornton	195M	80233	4400-4699	
109TH PL W	Westminster	193L	80031	3000-3299	
	Westminster	193J	80031	4400-4699	
	Westminster	192M	80020	5700-5899	
	Westminster	192L	80020	6200-6699	
	Westminster	192K	80021	7700-7899	
109TH ST N	Boulder Co	101M	80026	3400-4399	
	Boulder Co	101M	80026	4400-5299	
109TH WAY E	Commerce City	198J	80022	None	
110TH AVE E	Commerce City	769A	80022	None	
	Commerce City	198E	80022	None	
	Northglenn	195E	80233	2500-2699	
	Thornton	195G	80233	3200-4899	
	Thornton	195M	80233	4900-5599	
110TH AVE W	Westminster	193H	80234	2500-2699	
	Westminster	193K	80031	3700-3999	
	Westminster	193J	80031	4600-4699	
	Westminster	192H	80020	5300-5799	
	Westminster	192G	80020	6200-6299	
	Westminster	192L	80020	6300-6599	
	Westminster	192F	80021	7600-7899	
110TH CIR W	Westminster	193J	80031	4400-4599	
110TH CT E	Northglenn	195F	80233	2600-2699	
110TH CT W	Westminster	193G	80234	2700-2999	
	Westminster	193F	80031	4300-4399	
110TH DR E	Northglenn	195E	80233	2301-2699	O
	Northglenn	195F	80233	2600-3199	
110TH DR W	Westminster	192E	80021	7800-7899	
	Westminster	192G	80020	None	
110TH PL E	Commerce City	198E	80022	None	
	Northglenn	194H	80233	1200-1599	
	Northglenn	195E	80233	2300-2599	
	Thornton	195H	80229	4800-4899	
110TH PL W	Westminster	193M	80234	2500-2599	
	Westminster	193G	80234	2800-2999	
	Westminster	193F	80031	3500-3599	
	Westminster	193K	80031	4200-4399	
	Westminster	192H	80020	5600-5899	
	Westminster	192G	80020	6000-6699	
	Westminster	192F	80021	7800-7899	
110TH WAY E	Commerce City	197G	80601	None	
111TH AVE E	Commerce City	769A	80022	None	
	Commerce City	197G	80601	None	
111TH AVE W	Broomfield	192E	80021	7600-8399	
	Northglenn	194E	80234	1100-1599	
	Westminster	193H	80234	2500-2899	
	Westminster	193G	80234	2900-2999	
	Westminster	193F	80031	3700-4399	
	Westminster	193E	80031	4400-4599	
	Westminster	192H	80020	5600-5899	
	Westminster	192G	80020	6000-6799	
111TH CIR W	Westminster	193F	80031	4100-4299	
111TH CT W	Westminster	193H	80234	2400-2499	
111TH DR E	Northglenn	195E	80233	2200-2699	
	Thornton	195H	80229	5200-5499	
	Thornton	195H	80233	5500-5599	
111TH DR W	Westminster	193F	80031	3000-3699	
111TH LOOP W	Westminster	193G	80234	2700-2899	
	Westminster	193G	80031	3200-3499	
111TH PL E	Northglenn	194G	80233	100-699	
	Northglenn	194H	80233	900-1599	
	Thornton	195H	80229	4800-5399	
	Thornton	195H	80233	5500-5599	
111TH PL W	Northglenn	194E	80234	1100-1599	
	Westminster	193H	80234	2400-2799	
	Westminster	193G	80031	3000-3299	
	Westminster	192H	80020	5700-5899	
	Westminster	192G	80020	6500-6799	
111TH ST	Erie	102W	80026	500-1799	
	Erie	132E	80026	1800-1999	
	Lafayette	132E	80026	300-1599	
111TH WAY W	Northglenn	194E	80234	None	
	Westminster	193G	80234	2800-2999	
112TH AVE E	Adams Co	196F	80233	5600-5999	
	Commerce City	768B	80640	9200-12598	E
	Adams Co	769B	80022	20900-23299	
	Adams Co	772C	80102	None	
	Commerce City	768B	80640	9201-12599	O
	Commerce City	198E	80603	13000-15299	
	Commerce City	198E	80022	15300-16899	
	Commerce City	769B	80022	16900-20899	
	Northglenn	194H	80233	600-1799	
	Northglenn	195F	80233	1800-2299	
	Thornton	195E	80233	2300-5599	
112TH AVE W	Broomfield	192G	80020	6800-7599	
	Broomfield	191E	80021	11600-11899	
	Broomfield	190H	80021	11900-12099	
	Northglenn	194F	80234	400-799	
	Northglenn	194E	80234	800-1798	E
	Northglenn	193F	80234	1800-2398	E
	Westminster	194E	80234	801-1799	O
	Westminster	193F	80234	1801-2399	O
	Westminster	193F	80234	2400-2999	
	Westminster	193F	80031	3600-5199	
	Westminster	192G	80020	5200-6799	
112TH CIR E	Northglenn	194G	80233	300-399	
112TH CIR W	Westminster	193F	80031	3200-3599	
	Westminster	193E	80031	4800-4899	
112TH CT E	Commerce City	197E	80640	None	
	Thornton	195H	80229	5000-5399	
112TH CT W	Westminster	193E	80031	4600-4799	
	Westminster	193G	80031	None	
112TH DR E	Commerce City	197E	80640	9500-9999	
	Northglenn	194G	80233	200-399	
112TH PL E	Commerce City	197E	80640	9500-9999	
	Commerce City	197F	80640	10600-11299	
	Northglenn	194G	80233	100-499	
	Northglenn	194H	80233	700-1699	
	Northglenn	195E	80233	1700-2099	
	Thornton	195F	80233	3100-3899	
	Thornton	195G	80233	4300-4699	
	Thornton	195H	80229	4700-4999	
	Thornton	195H	80229	5000-5399	
112TH PL W	Westminster	193E	80031	4800-4899	
	Westminster	192H	80020	5400-5899	
	Westminster	192G	80020	6000-6799	
	Westminster	194E	80234	None	
112TH WAY E	Commerce City	197E	80640	9800-10399	
	Commerce City	197F	80640	10500-10699	
	Thornton	195H	80229	None	
113TH AVE E	Commerce City	197F	80640	10600-10698	E
	Westminster	193G	80234	None	
	Commerce City	197E	80640	9500-10399	
	Commerce City	198G	80022	15301-15499	O
	Commerce City	197G	80640	None	
	Northglenn	195E	80233	1800-2099	
	Thornton	195G	80233	3700-4399	
	Thornton	195H	80233	4700-5499	
	Thornton	196E	80233	None	
113TH AVE W	Westminster	194E	80234	1000-1399	
	Westminster	194E	80234	1600-1699	
	Westminster	193H	80234	1700-1799	
	Westminster	193F	80031	3200-3599	
	Westminster	193E	80031	4600-5199	
	Westminster	192G	80020	6000-6699	
113TH CIR E	Thornton	196E	80233	None	
113TH CT E	Adams Co	198H	80022	16700-16899	
113TH CT W	Westminster	193G	80234	2700-2899	
113TH PL E	Commerce City	198G	80022	15300-15499	
113TH PL E	Northglenn	194G	80233	100-199	
	Northglenn	195E	80233	1700-2199	
	Thornton	195G	80233	4000-4399	
	Thornton	195H	80229	5300-5399	
	Thornton	196E	80233	5600-5899	
113TH PL W	Westminster	192G	80020	6300-6799	

STREET NAME	CITY or COUNTY	MAP GRID	ZIP CODE	BLOCK RANGE	O/E
114TH AVE E	Brighton	197D	80640	12100-12699	
	Commerce City	197F	80640	10901-11299	O
	Commerce City	197G	80640	11400-11899	
	Commerce City	198G	80022	None	
	Northglenn	195E	80233	1700-2199	
	Thornton	196E	80233	None	
114TH AVE W	Northglenn	194F	80234	300-799	
	Westminster	192G	80020	6400-6799	
114TH CIR W	Westminster	193G	80031	3200-3499	
	Westminster	194E	80234	11400-11499	
114TH CT E	Adams Co	198H	80022	16100-16199	
	Northglenn	194C	80233	600-699	
114TH CT W	Westminster	193G	80234	2700-2799	
114TH DR E	Commerce City	197G	80640	11400-11499	
	Thornton	195F	80233	3200-3899	
114TH DR W	Westminster	193E	80031	4800-4899	
114TH LOOP W	Westminster	193G	80031	None	
114TH PL E	Commerce City	197G	80640	11700-11899	
	Northglenn	194H	80233	700-1099	
	Northglenn	195E	80233	1700-2199	
	Thornton	195H	80229	5100-5499	
	Thornton	196A	80233	None	
	Thornton	196E	80233	None	
114TH PL W	Northglenn	194F	80234	300-699	
	Westminster	193G	80031	3300-3399	
	Westminster	192H	80020	5700-5899	
114TH WAY E	Thornton	195G	80233	4200-4399	
114TH WAY W	Northglenn	194B	80234	300-699	
115TH AVE E	Adams Co	769C	80022	21000-21299	
	Brighton	197D	80640	12100-12599	
	Commerce City	197B	80640	10900-11299	
	Commerce City	197C	80640	11300-11399	
	Commerce City	198C	80022	None	
	Northglenn	194C	80233	600-699	
	Northglenn	194D	80233	700-999	
	Northglenn	195A	80233	1600-2199	
	Thornton	195F	80233	2700-4499	
	Thornton	195D	80233	4500-5499	
	Thornton	196E	80233	None	
115TH AVE W	Northglenn	194B	80234	100-799	
	Westminster	194E	80234	1500-1599	
	Westminster	193B	80031	3300-3599	
	Westminster	193A	80031	4800-5199	
	Westminster	192D	80020	5300-5699	
	Westminster	192G	80020	5700-6599	
115TH CIR E	Thornton	195G	80233	4600-4699	
115TH CIR W	Westminster	194A	80234	1600-1799	
	Westminster	193C	80234	2700-2999	
115TH CT E	Thornton	195H	80233	4700-4999	
115TH CT W	Westminster	192D	80020	5600-5799	
115TH DR E	Commerce City	197C	80640	11800-11899	
	Thornton	195F	80233	3200-3499	
115TH DR W	Westminster	193C	80234	2400-2999	
	Westminster	192D	80021	5400-5599	
115TH PL E	Commerce City	197B	80640	10900-11099	
	Commerce City	198C	80022	None	
	Northglenn	194D	80233	800-999	
	Northglenn	195A	80233	1800-2199	
	Thornton	195C	80233	4000-4499	
115TH PL W	Westminster	193C	80031	3100-3299	
	Westminster	192D	80021	5200-5799	
	Westminster	192C	80020	6100-6199	
	Westminster	192G	80020	6300-6399	
115TH ST	Boulder Co	72X	80504	5300-6199	
	Boulder Co	72F	80504	6900-7799	
115TH ST N	Boulder Co	12B	80504	12600-13999	
115TH WAY E	Thornton	195F	80233	2200-2899	
116TH AVE E	Commerce City	197B	80640	10900-11099	
	Commerce City	197C	80640	11300-11899	
	Commerce City	198C	80022	None	
	Northglenn	194C	80233	300-699	
	Northglenn	195A	80233	1800-2199	
	Thornton	195A	80233	2400-2799	
	Thornton	195B	80233	3600-3899	
	Thornton	195D	80233	4900-5399	
	Thornton	196A	80233	None	
116TH AVE W	Broomfield	192B	80020	6800-7299	
	Jefferson Co	192B	80020	7600-7999	
	Northglenn	194B	80234	100-799	
	Westminster	194A	80234	800-1799	
	Westminster	193D	80234	1800-2299	
	Westminster	193C	80031	3200-3299	
	Westminster	192D	80021	5200-5499	
	Westminster	192C	80020	6000-6799	
116TH CIR E	Brighton	197C	80640	12100-12399	
	Thornton	195B	80233	2600-2899	
	Thornton	196B	80233	None	
116TH CIR W	Broomfield	191D	80021	8800-8899	
	Westminster	194A	80234	1700-1799	
	Westminster	192D	80021	5200-5499	
116TH CT E	Adams Co	198D	80022	16500-16899	
	Brighton	197D	80640	12600-12899	
	Thornton	195A	80233	2300-2399	
116TH CT W	Westminster	194A	80234	1600-1699	
	Westminster	193C	80234	2700-2799	
	Westminster	193A	80031	4800-5199	
	Westminster	193D	80234	None	
116TH DR E	Commerce City	197C	80640	11300-11899	
	Commerce City	198B	80603	14800-15199	
	Commerce City	198C	80603	15100-15199	
	Northglenn	195A	80233	1900-2299	
	Thornton	195D	80233	4800-5099	
116TH LN W	Westminster	193A	80031	4700-4899	
116TH PL E	Commerce City	197B	80640	11300-11399	
	Commerce City	197C	80640	11800-11899	
	Northglenn	195A	80233	1800-2299	
	Thornton	195A	80233	2500-2599	
	Thornton	195B	80233	2800-2999	
	Thornton	195D	80233	4500-5299	
	Thornton	196B	80233	None	
116TH PL W	Northglenn	194B	80234	100-799	
	Westminster	193C	80234	2800-2999	
	Westminster	192D	80020	5600-5899	
116TH WAY E	Commerce City	198B	80603	14800-15199	
	Commerce City	198C	80603	15100-15199	
	Thornton	195A	80233	2300-2499	
116TH WAY W	Northglenn	194B	80234	100-699	
	Westminster	193B	80031	3700-4099	
	Westminster	193A	80031	4800-5199	
117TH AVE E	Commerce City	197C	80640	11800-11898	E
	Commerce City	198B	80603	14800-15199	
	Commerce City	198C	80022	15300-15699	
	Commerce City	198D	80022	15700-16499	
	Northglenn	194C	80233	300-699	
	Thornton	195C	80233	3700-5599	
	Thornton	196A	80233	None	
	Thornton	196B	80233	None	
117TH AVE W	Broomfield	192B	80020	6800-7199	
	Northglenn	194B	80234	100-799	
	Westminster	193A	80031	4400-5199	
	Westminster	192D	80021	5200-5499	
117TH CIR E	Thornton	195D	80233	5500-5599	
117TH CT E	Brighton	197D	80640	12600-12899	
	Commerce City	198D	80022	16400-16499	
	Northglenn	195A	80233	2800-2899	
	Thornton	195C	80233	4100-4499	
	Thornton	195D	80233	5100-5299	
	Thornton	195B	80233	None	
	Thornton	196A	80233	None	
117TH CT W	Westminster	193B	80031	3800-3899	
	Westminster	193A	80031	4200-4299	
117TH DR E	Thornton	195B	80233	3400-3599	
	Thornton	195D	80233	4800-5199	
117TH PL E	Commerce City	197C	80640	11800-11899	
	Commerce City	198B	80603	14800-15199	
	Commerce City	198C	80603	15100-15199	
	Northglenn	194C	80233	2-498	E
	Thornton	195B	80233	3000-3599	
	Thornton	195C	80233	4300-4399	
	Thornton	196B	80233	None	
117TH PL W	Westminster	192D	80020	5500-5999	
117TH WAY E	Commerce City	198C	80603	None	
	Northglenn	195A	80233	2600-2899	
	Thornton	195B	80233	None	
117TH WAY W	Westminster	193A	80031	4400-4999	
118TH AVE E	Adams Co	769B	80022	17800-20099	
	Adams Co	769C	80022	20900-21699	
	Commerce City	197C	80640	11400-11899	
	Commerce City	198B	80603	14800-15199	
	Commerce City	198D	80022	None	
	Northglenn	194C	80233	1-699	
	Thornton	195B	80233	3500-3899	
	Thornton	195C	80233	4000-5599	
	Thornton	196B	80233	None	
118TH AVE W	Broomfield	192D	80020	None	
	Northglenn	194B	80234	100-799	
	Westminster	193D	80234	2200-2399	
	Westminster	192D	80020	5500-5999	
118TH CIR W	Westminster	192D	80020	4500-5899	
118TH CT E	Brighton	197D	80640	12600-12899	
	Thornton	195B	80233	2800-2899	
	Thornton	195C	80233	4300-4499	
	Thornton	196B	80233	None	
118TH CT W	Westminster	193A	80031	4600-4999	
118TH PL E	Commerce City	197C	80640	11400-11899	
	Northglenn	194C	80233	300-499	
	Thornton	195C	80233	4300-5399	
	Thornton	196A	80233	5800-5899	
	Thornton	196B	80233	None	
118TH PL W	Broomfield	192B	80020	7200-7399	
	Westminster	193A	80031	3700-5199	
	Westminster	192D	80020	5200-5899	
118TH WAY E	Commerce City	168X	80603	None	
	Thornton	195B	80233	3200-3899	
118TH WAY W	Westminster	193B	80031	None	
118TH MEWS	Westminster	193B	80031	3801-4099	O
119TH AVE E	Adams Co	167Y	80640	11400-11799	
	Commerce City	168X	80603	14800-15199	
	Commerce City	168Y	80022	None	
	Thornton	195B	80233	3400-3499	
	Thornton	195B	80233	3500-3599	
	Thornton	196A	80233	5300-5999	
	Thornton	166X	80233	None	
119TH AVE W	Broomfield	192C	80020	6900-6999	
	Broomfield	192B	80020	7400-7999	
	Jefferson Co	189A	80007	None	
	Westminster	193D	80234	2300-2599	
	Westminster	193C	80234	2600-2999	
	Westminster	193B	80031	None	
119TH CT E	Brighton	167Z	80640	12600-12899	
	Thornton	165Z	80233	4800-5299	
119TH CT W	Westminster	193B	80031	None	
119TH DR W	Broomfield	191D	80021	9700-9799	
	Westminster	193B	80031	None	
119TH PL E	Adams Co	167Y	80640	11400-11799	
	Northglenn	194D	80233	1000-1599	
	Northglenn	194D	80233	1600-1899	
	Northglenn	195A	80233	1900-2199	
	Thornton	195B	80233	2300-4299	
	Thornton	195D	80233	5100-5299	
	Thornton	166W	80233	5600-6099	
	Thornton	196A	80233	5800-5899	
	Thornton	166X	80233	None	
119TH PL W	Broomfield	192B	80020	7000-7999	
	Westminster	193B	80031	None	
119TH ST	Erie	102X	80516	2700-3899	
119TH ST N	Boulder Co	132F	80026	400-1599	
	Boulder Co	102X	80516	1600-2699	
	Boulder Co	102K	80516	3900-4399	
	Boulder Co	102K	80516	4400-5299	
	Boulder Co	72B	80504	7800-8099	
	Boulder Co	42X	80504	8100-8999	
	Boulder Co	42T	80501	9000-10999	
119TH WAY E	Thornton	195C	80233	4300-4499	
	Thornton	195D	80233	5001-5299	O
119TH MEWS	Westminster	193B	80031	3800-4099	
120TH AVE E	Adams Co	169Y	80022	18800-20399	
	Adams Co	170Y	80022	20400-24899	
	Adams Co	751W	80642	32000-39299	
	Adams Co	752Z	80102	39300-50099	
	Adams Co	751W	80022	None	
	Adams Co	752W	80642	None	
	Brighton	167X	80601	11800-13399	

Continued on next column

STREET NAME	CITY or COUNTY	MAP GRID	ZIP CODE	BLOCK RANGE	O/E
120TH AVE E (Cont'd)	Brighton	168Y	80601	13400-14599	
	Commerce City	167X	80640	10100-11799	
	Commerce City	168Y	80603	14800-16899	
	Commerce City	169Y	80603	16900-17699	
	Northglenn	164Y	80233	2-1698	E
	Northglenn	165X	80233	1700-2299	
	Thornton	164Y	80233	1-1599	O
	Thornton	165X	80233	2300-5599	
	Thornton	166X	80602	5600-7399	
120TH AVE W	Broomfield	162Y	80020	5200-8399	
	Broomfield	161X	80021	8800-11199	
	Superior	190B	80021	12000-14799	
	Superior	159Y	80027	None	
	Superior	159Y	80303	None	
	Westminster	164W	80234	1-1699	
	Westminster	163Y	80234	1700-3599	
	Westminster	163Y	80020	3600-5199	
120TH DR E	Thornton	166X	80602	6700-6899	
120TH PKWY E	Adams Co	167W	80640	None	
120TH PL E	Adams Co	169Y	80022	18600-18699	
	Adams Co	168W	80601	None	
	Commerce City	169X	80603	None	
	Thornton	165X	80233	3500-3599	
	Thornton	165Y	80241	4500-4599	
	Thornton	165Z	80241	4800-5499	
	Thornton	166W	80602	5600-6399	
	Thornton	166X	80602	6500-6699	
120TH ST	Boulder Co	162C	80020	None	
120TH ST N	Lafayette	132Q	80026	100-399	
120TH ST S	Lafayette	132Y	80026	100-2499	
121ST AVE E	Adams Co	167Y	80640	11800-12099	
	Commerce City	169X	80603	15800-15898	E
	Commerce City	168Y	80603	None	
	Thornton	165W	80241	2300-2599	
	Thornton	165X	80241	2600-2699	
	Thornton	165X	80241	3500-3999	
	Thornton	165Y	80241	4000-4299	
	Thornton	165Z	80241	4900-5399	
121ST AVE W	Westminster	164X	80234	200-799	
	Westminster	164W	80234	1300-1699	
	Westminster	163Z	80234	2501-2699	O
121ST CIR E	Adams Co	168Z	80603	16500-16899	
121ST CT E	Thornton	165Y	80241	4400-4499	
121ST DR E	Thornton	166W	80602	6100-6399	
	Thornton	166X	80602	6700-6899	
121ST DR W	Broomfield	163W	80020	None	
121ST PL E	Adams Co	168W	80601	13400-13699	
	Adams Co	169Y	80022	18600-19199	
	Thornton	165W	80241	2300-2599	
	Thornton	165X	80241	2600-2799	
	Thornton	165Y	80241	4400-4499	
	Thornton	165Z	80241	4500-4599	
	Thornton	165Z	80241	5400-5599	
	Thornton	166W	80602	5600-5999	
	Thornton	166W	80602	6100-6399	
	Thornton	166Y	80602	None	
121ST PL W	Broomfield	163X	80020	None	
	Broomfield	163W	80020	None	
121ST WAY E	Commerce City	169X	80603	None	
	Thornton	165Y	80241	4400-4499	
122ND AVE E	Commerce City	168Y	80603	None	
	Thornton	165X	80241	3200-3299	
	Thornton	165Y	80241	3500-4599	
	Thornton	166W	80602	6100-6399	
	Thornton	166X	80602	None	
	Thornton	165Y	80241	None	
122ND AVE W	Broomfield	163X	80020	None	
	Westminster	164W	80234	800-1899	
	Westminster	163Y	80234	2401-12299	O
	Westminster	163Z	80234	None	
122ND CIR E	Commerce City	169X	80603	None	
	Thornton	165Z	80241	5100-5199	
122ND CT E	Thornton	165Y	80241	4400-4499	
	Thornton	165Z	80241	4500-4599	
122ND DR E	Thornton	166W	80602	5600-5899	
	Thornton	166W	80602	6200-6299	
122ND DR W	Broomfield	163W	80020	None	
122ND PL E	Thornton	166W	80602	5600-5999	
	Thornton	166Y	80602	None	
122ND PL W	Broomfield	163W	80020	None	
122ND ST W	Broomfield	163W	80020	None	
122ND WAY E	Thornton	165Z	80241	4500-4599	
123RD AVE E	Adams Co	166Y	80602	8100-8199	
	Adams Co	167T	80640	None	
	Commerce City	168Y	80603	None	
	Commerce City	169X	80603	None	
	Thornton	165X	80241	2500-3599	
	Thornton	165Y	80241	3600-4499	
	Thornton	165Z	80241	5000-5599	
	Thornton	166W	80602	5600-5899	
	Thornton	166W	80602	6200-6299	
	Thornton	166X	80602	6700-6899	
	Thornton	166Y	80602	None	
123RD AVE W	Westminster	164X	80234	200-799	
123RD CIR E	Thornton	165Z	80241	5100-5299	
	Thornton	166X	80602	6600-6799	
123RD DR E	Commerce City	169T	80603	15901-16099	O
	Thornton	165W	80241	2500-2599	
	Thornton	165X	80241	3200-3499	
	Thornton	166W	80602	5700-12399	
	Thornton	166S	80602	6200-6299	
	Thornton	166X	80602	6600-6799	
123RD DR W	Broomfield	163W	80020	None	
123RD PL E	Commerce City	169W	80603	None	
	Thornton	166W	80602	6200-6299	
	Thornton	166X	80602	6700-6799	
	Thornton	166Y	80602	None	
123RD PL W	Broomfield	163W	80020	4400-5199	
	Broomfield	163W	80020	None	
123RD ST W	Broomfield	163W	80020	None	
123RD WAY E	Thornton	165W	80241	2400-2599	
	Thornton	166W	80602	6100-6199	
124TH AVE E	Adams Co	167T	80601	10700-13399	
	Adams Co	167T	80640	11600-13199	
	Brighton	168S	80601	13400-14499	
	Commerce City	168Y	80603	None	
	Thornton	164U	80241	400-499	
	Thornton	165T	80241	2800-4699	
	Thornton	166X	80602	None	

STREET NAME	CITY or COUNTY	MAP GRID	ZIP CODE	BLOCK RANGE	O/E
124TH AVE W	Broomfield	163T	80020	3600-3999	
	Broomfield	163S	80020	4602-4698	E
	Broomfield	163T	80020	2900-3599	
	Westminster	164S	80234	200-1599	
124TH CIR E	Thornton	165T	80241	2700-2799	
124TH CT E	Thornton	165S	80241	2300-2399	
124TH CT W	Westminster	164S	80234	1100-1199	
124TH DR E	Thornton	165S	80241	2400-2599	
	Thornton	166U	80602	None	
124TH DR W	Westminster	164S	80234	800-1099	
124TH PL E	Adams Co	166U	80602	8200-8399	
	Thornton	165S	80241	2500-2599	
	Thornton	165T	80241	2600-2899	
	Thornton	165T	80241	None	
124TH ST S	Broomfield	162H	80020	1600-13699	
124TH WAY E	Thornton	165V	80241	4900-5099	
	Thornton	166W	80602	5600-5999	
125TH AVE E	Adams Co	169T	80022	None	
	Thornton	165U	80241	4000-4299	
	Thornton	165V	80241	4700-5099	
	Thornton	166U	80602	None	
125TH AVE W	Broomfield	163U	80020	2701-2799	O
	Broomfield	163S	80020	4700-4999	
	Broomfield	163T	80020	None	
	Broomfield	163U	80020	None	
125TH AVE W	Westminster	164T	80020	200-799	
125TH CIR E	Thornton	165T	80241	2700-2799	
125TH CIR W	Broomfield	163T	80020	3400-3599	
125TH CT E	Adams Co	166U	80602	8400-8799	
	Thornton	165S	80241	2300-2399	
	Thornton	166U	80602	None	
125TH DR W	Broomfield	163T	80020	3400-3598	E
	Westminster	164S	80234	1000-1199	
125TH PL E	Thornton	165S	80241	1900-2599	
	Thornton	165U	80241	3500-4699	
	Thornton	165V	80241	4700-4799	
125TH WAY E	Thornton	165S	80241	2500-2599	
126TH AVE E	Adams Co	167T	80601	10800-11299	
	Adams Co	169T	80022	18400-18499	
	Adams Co	166U	80602	None	
	Adams Co	169T	80603	None	
	Thornton	164U	80241	700-999	
	Thornton	164V	80241	1000-1099	
	Thornton	165U	80241	4000-4699	
	Thornton	165V	80241	4700-4799	
	Thornton	165S	80241	None	
126TH AVE W	Broomfield	163U	80020	2600-2899	
	Broomfield	163U	80020	3200-3399	
	Broomfield	163T	80020	3700-3999	
126TH CIR W	Broomfield	163S	80020	5000-5199	
126TH CT E	Thornton	165S	80241	1900-2099	
	Thornton	165V	80241	5100-5199	
126TH CT W	Westminster	164T	80234	800-899	
	Westminster	164S	80234	1100-1199	
126TH DR W	Broomfield	163U	80020	3300-3599	
126TH LOOP E	Thornton	165S	80241	2300-2499	
126TH PL E	Thornton	165S	80241	2500-2699	
	Thornton	165U	80241	4000-4399	
	Thornton	166S	80602	None	
	Thornton	166U	80602	None	
126TH PL W	Broomfield	163U	80020	3300-3599	
	Broomfield	163T	80020	3400-3599	
	Westminster	164T	80234	800-899	
	Westminster	164S	80234	900-999	
126TH WAY E	Thornton	165S	80241	2000-2599	
127TH AVE E	Thornton	165U	80241	3800-3999	
	Thornton	165V	80241	4700-4799	
	Thornton	166S	80602	None	
127TH AVE W	Broomfield	163U	80020	3000-3399	
	Broomfield	163T	80020	3700-3999	
	Broomfield	163S	80020	4800-4899	
127TH CIR E	Thornton	165S	80241	1900-2099	
127TH CT E	Adams Co	166V	80602	8500-8599	
	Thornton	165S	80241	2400-2599	
	Thornton	165V	80241	5100-5199	
127TH CT W	Westminster	164S	80234	800-1199	
127TH DR E	Thornton	165S	80241	2300-2499	
	Thornton	165V	80241	4700-5299	
	Thornton	166S	80602	None	
127TH LN E	Thornton	165T	80241	3700-3899	
	Thornton	166S	80602	None	
127TH PL E	Adams Co	166U	80602	8700-8799	
	Thornton	165S	80241	2000-2599	
	Thornton	165U	80241	4300-4799	
	Thornton	166S	80602	None	
	Thornton	166S	80602	None	
127TH PL W	Broomfield	163S	80020	4700-4899	
	Westminster	164S	80234	1000-1099	
127TH WAY E	Thornton	165T	80241	3700-3899	
	Thornton	165U	80241	4300-4399	
	Thornton	165V	80241	5000-5099	
128TH AVE E	Adams Co	170Q	80022	18400-20399	
	Adams Co	750T	80022	21300-31599	
	Adams Co	751U	80642	31600-39299	
	Adams Co	752U	80102	44000-48999	
	Thornton	164V	80241	1-1699	
	Thornton	165U	80241	1700-5599	
	Thornton	166T	80602	5600-9599	
128TH AVE W	Broomfield	163U	80234	2400-2999	
	Westminster	164S	80234	1-1699	
	Westminster	163V	80234	1700-2399	
128TH CIR E	Thornton	165V	80241	5200-5399	
128TH CT E	Thornton	164V	80241	900-999	
	Thornton	164R	80241	1400-1499	
	Thornton	165V	80241	4700-5599	
	Thornton	165R	80241	5200-5299	
128TH DR E	Thornton	165S	80241	1900-2099	
	Thornton	165V	80241	5200-5399	
	Thornton	165U	80241	None	
128TH PL E	Thornton	165T	80241	3200-3699	
	Thornton	165U	80241	4300-4799	
	Thornton	166Q	80602	8100-8299	
	Thornton	166P	80602	None	
128TH PL W	Broomfield	163S	80020	4600-5199	
128TH WAY E	Thornton	165V	80241	5200-5299	
129TH AVE E	Thornton	164Q	80241	800-899	
	Thornton	165N	80241	1900-2299	
	Thornton	165Q	80241	4300-4799	
	Thornton	165R	80241	5200-5499	
	Thornton	166Q	80602	7700-7899	
	Thornton	166P	80602	None	
	Thornton	166N	80602	None	
129TH CIR E	Thornton	165Q	80241	4100-4799	
129TH CT E	Thornton	165R	80241	4700-4799	
129TH DR E	Thornton	165N	80241	1900-2099	
129TH DR W	Westminster	164N	80234	None	
129TH PL E	Thornton	165Q	80241	4600-4699	
	Thornton	165R	80241	4700-5299	
	Thornton	166U	80602	7300-7899	
	Thornton	166P	80602	None	
	Thornton	166Q	80602	None	
	Thornton	166N	80602	None	
129TH PL W	Broomfield	163R	80234	None	
129TH WAY E	Thornton	165Q	80241	4000-4099	
	Thornton	165R	80241	5200-5399	
130TH AVE E	Thornton	164Q	80241	600-799	
	Thornton	164R	80241	800-1599	
	Thornton	165Q	80241	4700-4799	
	Thornton	165R	80241	4800-5599	
	Thornton	166N	80602	5600-6299	
	Thornton	166Q	80602	7300-8899	
	Thornton	166P	80602	None	
130TH CIR E	Thornton	164R	80241	900-999	
	Thornton	165Q	80241	3800-4299	
	Thornton	165R	80241	5200-5299	
	Thornton	166P	80602	7400-7599	
	Thornton	166Q	80602	8200-8499	
130TH CT E	Thornton	164Q	80241	500-899	
	Thornton	164R	80241	900-1599	
	Thornton	165Q	80241	3800-3899	
	Thornton	165Q	80241	4000-4099	
	Thornton	165R	80241	None	
130TH CT W	Westminster	164N	80234	None	
130TH DR E	Thornton	164R	80241	900-1499	
	Thornton	165Q	80241	4200-4299	
	Thornton	165R	80241	5500-5599	
130TH DR W	Westminster	164N	80234	1600-1998	E
130TH PL E	Thornton	164R	80241	1000-1299	
	Thornton	165Q	80241	4100-4199	
	Thornton	165R	80241	5300-5399	
	Thornton	166Q	80602	7800-8199	
130TH PL W	Broomfield	163P	80020	3400-3599	
	Westminster	163R	80234	1700-1899	
	Westminster	164N	80234	None	
130TH WAY E	Thornton	164Q	80241	500-699	
	Thornton	165Q	80241	4000-4099	
	Thornton	165R	80241	5200-5399	
	Thornton	166N	80602	5600-5899	
131ST AVE E	Adams Co	750V	80022	29700-30499	
	Thornton	164Q	80241	400-499	
	Thornton	165N	80241	2500-2699	
	Thornton	166N	80602	5600-5799	
	Thornton	166Q	80602	7700-8099	
	Thornton	166P	80602	None	
131ST AVE W	Broomfield	163P	80020	3400-3599	
131ST CIR E	Thornton	164R	80241	1600-1699	
	Thornton	165P	80241	2800-2899	
131ST CIR W	Broomfield	163Q	80020	3100-3199	
131ST CT E	Thornton	164Q	80241	500-699	
	Thornton	165Q	80241	4000-4099	
	Thornton	166Q	80602	8100-8199	
131ST DR E	Thornton	164R	80241	1000-1399	
	Thornton	165Q	80241	4000-4199	
	Thornton	165R	80241	5200-5299	
	Thornton	166P	80602	None	
131ST DR W	Westminster	163R	80234	1800-1999	
131ST LN W	Westminster	163R	80234	1800-1999	
131ST PL E	Thornton	164Q	80241	800-899	
	Thornton	164R	80241	1500-1599	
	Thornton	165P	80241	2600-2699	
	Thornton	165Q	80241	4200-4799	
	Thornton	165R	80241	4800-4899	
	Thornton	166N	80602	5700-5799	
	Thornton	166Q	80602	7700-8199	
	Thornton	166P	80602	None	
131ST PL W	Broomfield	163P	80020	3400-3599	
	Westminster	163R	80234	1900-2199	
131ST WAY E	Thornton	164Q	80241	500-699	
	Thornton	165P	80241	2700-3199	
	Thornton	165R	80241	5300-5399	
	Thornton	166P	80602	None	
131ST WAY W	Broomfield	163Q	80020	2900-2999	
	Westminster	163R	80234	2100-2299	
132ND AVE E	Adams Co	167R	80601	11700-13399	
	Adams Co	168P	80601	13400-16899	
	Adams Co	170N	80022	21000-21699	
	Adams Co	170R	80022	21000-23999	
	Thornton	164Q	80241	500-999	
	Thornton	165P	80241	2600-3099	
	Thornton	166N	80602	5600-6199	
	Thornton	166Q	80602	8100-8199	
	Thornton	166P	80602	None	
132ND AVE W	Broomfield	163Q	80020	2400-2999	
	Westminster	164N	80234	800-1599	
	Westminster	163R	80234	1700-2399	
132ND CIR E	Thornton	164R	80241	900-999	
	Thornton	165P	80241	2700-2899	
132ND CIR W	Broomfield	163Q	80020	3100-3199	
132ND CT W	Broomfield	163Q	80020	3100-3199	
132ND DR E	Thornton	164Q	80241	800-899	
132ND PL E	Thornton	164R	80241	1000-1199	
	Thornton	165P	80241	2600-2799	
	Thornton	166Q	80602	8000-8199	
	Thornton	166P	80602	None	
132ND PL W	Broomfield	163P	80020	3400-3599	
	Westminster	164N	80234	1100-1499	
132ND WAY E	Thornton	164Q	80241	400-499	
	Thornton	164R	80241	1000-1199	
	Thornton	166N	80602	5700-6199	
132ND WAY W	Broomfield	163R	80020	2500-2599	
133RD AVE E	Thornton	164R	80241	800-1599	
	Thornton	165P	80241	3100-3199	
	Thornton	165Q	80241	3700-3999	
	Thornton	166Q	80602	7700-8199	
	Thornton	166N	80602	None	
	Thornton	166P	80602	None	
133RD AVE W	Broomfield	163Q	80020	2800-3299	
133RD CIR E	Adams Co	750S	80022	None	
133RD CIR E	Thornton	165P	80241	2900-3099	
	Thornton	165P	80241	3600-3699	
	Thornton	165Q	80241	3700-3899	
	Thornton	165Q	80241	4000-4099	
	Thornton	166P	80602	None	
133RD CIR W	Broomfield	163R	80020	2500-2699	
	Broomfield	163Q	80020	3100-3299	
133RD CIR W	Westminster	164J	80234	900-999	
	Westminster	164N	80234	1200-1399	
133RD CT E	Thornton	164Q	80241	500-599	
	Thornton	165N	80241	2000-2099	
	Thornton	165P	80241	3600-3699	
	Thornton	165Q	80241	3700-3999	
133RD CT W	Westminster	164J	80234	1100-1199	
133RD DR E	Adams Co	168N	80601	13800-13899	
	Thornton	164R	80241	900-999	
133RD LN E	Thornton	165P	80241	2900-2999	
133RD PL E	Adams Co	168P	80601	14200-14399	
	Thornton	164L	80241	800-899	
	Thornton	165L	80241	4000-4299	
	Thornton	166P	80602	None	
133RD WAY E	Thornton	164Q	80241	400-499	
	Thornton	164R	80241	1000-1099	
	Thornton	165N	80241	2000-3099	
133RD WAY W	Westminster	164N	80234	1000-1399	
134TH AVE E	Adams Co	168K	80601	14100-14499	
	Adams Co	170M	80022	23300-23999	
	Thornton	164Q	80241	400-799	
	Thornton	164M	80241	800-1399	
	Thornton	164R	80241	1400-1799	
	Thornton	165N	80241	1800-2099	
	Thornton	165L	80241	4600-4699	
	Thornton	166L	80602	7900-7999	
	Thornton	166J	80602	None	
	Thornton	166K	80602	None	
134TH AVE W	Broomfield	163L	80020	2800-3499	
	Westminster	164J	80234	800-1799	
134TH CIR E	Thornton	165J	80241	1800-1899	
	Thornton	165P	80241	3100-3199	
	Thornton	166K	80602	None	
134TH CIR W	Broomfield	163L	80020	2500-3299	
134TH CT E	Thornton	165Q	80241	3700-3999	
134TH CT W	Broomfield	163Q	80020	2800-3199	
134TH DR E	Thornton	165K	80241	3500-3699	
	Thornton	165L	80241	4100-4199	
134TH DR W	Westminster	164J	80234	1300-1499	
134TH PL E	Adams Co	168K	80601	14500-14799	
	Thornton	165P	80241	2700-2799	
	Thornton	165K	80241	3500-3599	
	Thornton	165Q	80241	3900-3999	
	Thornton	166L	80602	7800-8199	
	Thornton	166N	80602	None	
134TH PL W	Broomfield	163Q	80020	2800-3299	
	Broomfield	163K	80020	3800-4299	
	Westminster	164J	80234	1100-1499	
134TH WAY E	Thornton	165N	80241	1800-2099	
	Thornton	165P	80241	3600-3699	
134TH WAY W	Broomfield	163L	80020	3000-3299	
	Westminster	163M	80234	2000-2099	
135TH AVE E	Adams Co	168K	80601	14500-14799	
	Thornton	164M	80241	1300-1399	
	Thornton	165J	80241	1800-1899	
	Thornton	165K	80241	2600-2699	
	Thornton	165P	80241	3000-3099	
	Thornton	165L	80241	4600-4699	
	Thornton	166L	80602	7700-8199	
	Thornton	166J	80602	None	
	Thornton	166J	80602	None	
135TH AVE W	Broomfield	163L	80020	2500-3299	
	Broomfield	163K	80020	3500-3599	
	Westminster	164J	80234	1200-1499	
	Westminster	163M	80234	1800-2299	
135TH CT E	Thornton	165K	80241	2600-2699	
	Thornton	165K	80241	3500-3599	
	Thornton	165L	80241	4200-4299	
135TH CT W	Westminster	164J	80234	1000-1299	
	Westminster	163M	80234	2000-2099	
135TH DR E	Thornton	165K	80241	2700-2899	
	Thornton	165K	80241	3600-3699	
	Thornton	165K	80241	3700-3799	
	Thornton	165L	80241	3800-3999	
135TH DR W	Westminster	164J	80234	1100-1699	
135TH LN E	Thornton	165K	80241	2900-2999	
	Thornton	165L	80241	4600-4699	
	Thornton	166K	80602	None	
135TH LN W	Westminster	164J	80234	1000-1199	
135TH PL E	Adams Co	751T	80603	None	
135TH PL E	Thornton	164M	80241	1200-1399	
	Thornton	165J	80241	1900-1999	
	Thornton	165K	80241	2500-2999	
	Thornton	165L	80241	3900-3999	
	Thornton	165L	80241	4000-4199	
	Thornton	166L	80602	7900-8199	
	Thornton	166J	80602	None	
135TH PL W	Broomfield	163L	80020	13400-13499	
	Westminster	164J	80234	1100-1499	
	Westminster	163M	80020	1800-2299	
135TH WAY E	Thornton	165J	80241	1900-1999	
	Thornton	165K	80241	2900-2999	
	Thornton	165K	80241	3800-3899	
	Thornton	165L	80241	4300-4699	
135TH WAY W	Westminster	164J	80234	1600-1699	
136TH AVE	Adams Co	169K	80603	17300-18499	
136TH AVE E	Adams Co	167J	80601	9400-9899	
	Adams Co	168L	80601	13400-16899	
	Adams Co	170M	80603	17300-18499	
	Adams Co	752S	80642	39300-43999	
	Adams Co	752S	80102	40900-44099	
	Adams Co	750V	80603	None	
	Brighton	167M	80601	11800-13399	

Continued on next page

STREET NAME	CITY or COUNTY	MAP GRID	ZIP CODE	BLOCK RANGE	O/E
136TH AVE E (Cont'd)	Brighton	169J	80601	16900-17299	
	Thornton	164M	80020	1-699	
	Thornton	164M	80602	700-1699	
	Thornton	165K	80602	1700-5599	
	Thornton	166L	80602	5600-9399	
136TH AVE W	Broomfield	163L	80020	2400-5199	
	Broomfield	162M	80020	5200-5999	
	Westminster	164J	80020	1-1699	
	Westminster	163L	80020	1700-2399	
136TH DR E	Thornton	166L	80602	None	
136TH PL E	Thornton	165J	80602	2500-2699	
	Thornton	165K	80602	2700-3599	
	Thornton	166J	80602	6300-6499	
	Thornton	165L	80602	None	
	Thornton	166L	80602	None	
136TH WAY E	Thornton	166L	80602	None	
137TH AVE E	Adams Co	751N	80603	18200-18299	
	Thornton	165J	80602	2600-2699	
	Thornton	165K	80602	3000-3699	
	Thornton	166J	80602	6000-6499	
	Thornton	166L	80602	None	
137TH CT E	Adams Co	751P	80603	None	
137TH DR E	Thornton	166L	80602	None	
137TH PL E	Adams Co	169F	80603	18000-18299	
	Thornton	165J	80602	2600-2699	
	Thornton	165K	80602	2800-3199	
	Thornton	166J	80602	6000-6399	
	Thornton	165L	80602	None	
	Thornton	166L	80602	None	
138TH AVE E	Adams Co	164H	80602	1700-1999	
	Adams Co	165J	80602	2000-2299	
	Adams Co	166M	80602	9200-9299	
	Thornton	165J	80602	2300-2499	
	Thornton	165K	80602	2600-13799	
	Thornton	165L	80602	3700-3999	
	Thornton	165H	80602	5100-5599	
	Thornton	166E	80602	5600-6399	
	Thornton	165J	80602	None	
	Thornton	166K	80602	None	
138TH AVE W	Broomfield	163M	80020	None	
	Broomfield	164J	80020	None	
138TH CIR E	Thornton	165K	80602	2600-2699	
138TH CT E	Adams Co	166H	80602	9000-9199	
138TH DR E	Thornton	165L	80602	None	
	Thornton	166K	80602	None	
138TH PL E	Adams Co	167E	80602	9800-10199	
	Thornton	165K	80602	2700-2799	
	Thornton	165K	80602	3400-3599	
	Thornton	165L	80602	3700-3899	
	Thornton	166G	80602	None	
138TH WAY E	Thornton	166G	80602	None	
139TH AVE E	Thornton	165F	80602	2700-3599	
	Thornton	165F	80602	3700-3799	
	Thornton	165G	80602	3800-3899	
	Thornton	166G	80602	None	
	Thornton	165G	80602	None	
139TH CT E	Adams Co	166H	80602	9000-9199	
139TH CT E	Adams Co	751P	80603	None	
139TH CT W	Westminster	164E	80020	900-999	
139TH DR E	Thornton	165K	80602	2700-2799	
	Thornton	165G	80602	None	
139TH PL E	Thornton	165J	80602	2400-2599	
	Thornton	165F	80602	2700-3599	
	Thornton	165G	80602	3601-3899	O
	Thornton	166G	80602	None	
	Thornton	165G	80602	None	
139TH PL W	Westminster	164E	80020	1200-1399	
140TH AVE E	Adams Co	751N	80603	None	
	Thornton	165F	80602	2700-3599	
	Thornton	165H	80602	4800-5599	
	Thornton	166E	80602	5600-6099	
140TH DR E	Thornton	165F	80602	None	
	Thornton	165H	80602	None	
140TH DR W	Westminster	164E	80020	800-1299	
140TH PL E	Thornton	165F	80602	None	
	Thornton	165H	80602	None	
141ST AVE E	Adams Co	164H	80602	1200-1999	
	Adams Co	165E	80602	2000-2299	
	Thornton	165F	80602	None	
	Thornton	165H	80602	None	
141ST CIR W	Westminster	164E	80020	None	
141ST CT E	Adams Co	751P	80603	None	
	Westminster	164E	80020	None	
141ST CT W	Westminster	164E	80020	None	
141ST DR E	Thornton	165F	80602	None	
	Thornton	165H	80602	None	
141ST PL E	Thornton	165F	80602	None	
	Thornton	165H	80602	None	
141ST WAY W	Westminster	164E	80020	None	
	Westminster	164F	80020	None	
142ND AVE E	Adams Co	164H	80602	1600-1999	
	Adams Co	165E	80602	2000-2299	
	Adams Co	167E	80602	None	
	Thornton	165F	80602	None	
	Thornton	165H	80602	None	
	Thornton	165H	80602	None	
142ND CIR W	Westminster	164E	80020	None	
142ND PL E	Adams Co	751P	80603	None	
	Thornton	165F	80602	None	
	Thornton	165H	00602	None	
143RD AVE E	Adams Co	164H	80602	1400-1999	
	Adams Co	165E	80602	2000-2299	
	Adams Co	751N	80603	32400-32899	
	Thornton	165F	80602	None	
	Thornton	165H	80602	None	
143RD DR E	Thornton	165F	80602	None	
	Thornton	165H	80602	None	
143RD PL E	Thornton	165F	80602	None	
143RD WAY E	Adams Co	167A	80602	None	
144TH AVE E	Adams Co	167D	80601	12500-13399	
	Adams Co	168B	80601	13400-16899	
	Adams Co	170B	80603	21801-21899	O
	Adams Co	751P	80642	34500-42799	
	Adams Co	752R	80102	42800-55299	
	Adams Co	750Q	80603	None	
	Adams Co	750R	80603	None	

Continued on next column

STREET NAME	CITY or COUNTY	MAP GRID	ZIP CODE	BLOCK RANGE	O/E
144TH AVE E (Cont'd)	Adams Co	752N	80642	None	
	Brighton	169A	80601	16900-18899	
	Thornton	164C	80020	1-699	
	Thornton	164C	80602	700-1699	
	Thornton	165B	80602	1700-5599	
144TH AVE W	Adams Co	163B	80020	1800-2399	
	Broomfield	163B	80020	2400-5199	
	Thornton	164B	80020	1-399	
	Westminster	164A	80020	400-1799	
144TH CT W	Broomfield	163C	80020	2700-2899	
	Westminster	164A	80020	1000-1199	
144TH DR E	Thornton	164D	80602	None	
144TH PL E	Thornton	165A	80602	None	
144TH PL W	Westminster	164A	80020	1000-1199	
144TH WAY E	Thornton	165A	80602	None	
145TH AVE E	Adams Co	166D	80602	9100-9599	
	Adams Co	167A	80602	9600-10399	
	Adams Co	751N	80603	30800-31299	
	Adams Co	751R	80642	None	
	Adams Co	750R	80603	None	
	Thornton	165A	80602	2300-2699	
145TH CT E	Adams Co	751R	80642	None	
	Thornton	165A	80602	2300-2699	
145TH DR E	Thornton	165A	80602	2400-2799	
145TH PL E	Adams Co	166C	80602	8200-8899	
	Adams Co	751R	80642	None	
	Thornton	165A	80602	None	
145TH PL W	Westminster	164A	80020	1300-1399	
145TH WAY W	Westminster	164A	80020	800-999	
146TH AVE E	Adams Co	165C	80602	3800-3999	
	Adams Co	166C	80602	8500-8799	
	Adams Co	166D	80602	9200-9599	
	Adams Co	167A	80602	9600-9999	
	Adams Co	750R	80603	None	
146TH CT E	Adams Co	751R	80642	None	
146TH PL E	Adams Co	167A	80602	9600-10499	
	Thornton	165A	80602	2500-2699	
147TH AVE E	Adams Co	137W	80602	9400-10499	
	Adams Co	751J	80603	32400-32999	
	Thornton	165A	80602	2400-2799	
147TH CT E	Adams Co	751M	80642	None	
147TH CT W	Broomfield	163C	80020	2800-3299	
	Broomfield	133X	80020	3300-3599	
147TH PL E	Adams Co	166D	80602	9200-9599	
	Adams Co	751R	80642	None	
148TH AVE E	Adams Co	138W	80601	13100-13198	E
	Adams Co	750L	80603	29000-29499	
	Brighton	137Z	80601	13100-13199	
	Thornton	165A	80602	2300-2599	
148TH AVE W	Broomfield	133Y	80020	2800-2899	
	Westminster	164A	80020	800-1599	
148TH CIR E	Adams Co	136Z	80602	8900-9299	
	Thornton	136Y	80602	8600-8799	
	Adams Co	751M	80642	None	
148TH CT W	Broomfield	133Y	80020	2500-2599	
148TH DR E	Thornton	136Y	80602	None	
	Thornton	165A	80602	None	
148TH LN E	Thornton	136Y	80602	8600-8899	
148TH PL E	Adams Co	137W	80602	9700-10399	
	Thornton	136X	80602	None	
	Thornton	165A	80602	None	
148TH PL W	Adams Co	133Z	80020	2200-2399	
	Adams Co	134W	80020	None	
148TH WAY E	Thornton	136Y	80602	8200-8499	
149TH AVE E	Adams Co	751J	80603	32000-32999	
	Thornton	135W	80602	2100-2699	
149TH AVE W	Adams Co	134W	80020	800-2199	
	Adams Co	133Z	80020	2200-2399	
	Broomfield	133Y	80020	2700-2999	
149TH CT E	Adams Co	137W	80602	9800-10299	
	Adams Co	750L	80603	None	
149TH CT W	Broomfield	133X	80020	3200-3599	
149TH DR E	Thornton	136Y	80602	8200-8599	
149TH PL E	Adams Co	751M	80642	None	
	Thornton	136Y	80602	None	
149TH PL W	Adams Co	134W	80020	1400-1599	
149TH ST E	Adams Co	751L	80642	None	
150TH AVE E	Adams Co	137W	80602	9500-10399	
	Adams Co	750M	80603	30500-30699	
	Thornton	135W	80602	2400-2599	
150TH AVE W	Adams Co	133Z	80020	2200-2399	
150TH CT E	Thornton	136Z	80602	8700-8899	
150TH CT W	Broomfield	133X	80020	3200-3599	
150TH DR E	Thornton	135X	80602	2900-3199	
150TH PL E	Adams Co	137X	80602	10800-11199	
	Thornton	136Y	80602	None	
	Thornton	135W	80602	2400-2699	
150TH PL W	Adams Co	134X	80020	800-1199	
	Adams Co	134W	80020	1400-1799	
151ST AVE E	Adams Co	135X	80602	3400-3999	
	Adams Co	136V	80602	9000-9299	
	Adams Co	750M	80603	30600-31799	
	Adams Co	751J	80603	31800-32999	
151ST CT E	Adams Co	137W	80602	9900-10399	
	Thornton	136Z	80602	8800-8899	
151ST CT W	Broomfield	133Y	80020	3000-3399	
151ST PL E	Adams Co	137W	80602	9500-9899	
	Adams Co	137X	80602	10600-11199	
	Thornton	135X	80602	2900-2999	
152ND AVE E	Adams Co	136W	80602	5600-8399	
	Adams Co	137X	80602	10500-10699	
	Adams Co	140U	80603	20000-24999	
	Adams Co	751J	80603	25000-34499	
	Adams Co	751J	80642	34500-36099	
	Adams Co	752M	80102	44100-47299	
	Adams Co	134Z	80020	None	
	Adams Co	135W	80602	None	
	Adams Co	750K	80603	None	
152ND AVE W	Adams Co	134W	80020	300-2199	
	Adams Co	133Z	80020	2200-2399	
152ND CT E	Thornton	136V	80602	8700-8899	
152ND DR E	Thornton	136Y	80602	None	
152ND LN E	Thornton	136Y	80602	None	
152ND PL E	Thornton	135X	80602	2900-3199	
	Thornton	136X	80602	6600-7199	
	Thornton	136V	80602	8700-8899	
152ND PL W	Adams Co	133Z	80020	2200-2399	

STREET NAME	CITY or COUNTY	MAP GRID	ZIP CODE	BLOCK RANGE	O/E
153RD AVE E	Adams Co	136V	80602	8900-9599	
	Adams Co	137S	80602	9600-9999	
	Thornton	136T	80602	6600-7199	
153RD CIR E	Adams Co	750J	80603	None	
153RD CT E	Adams Co	751K	80642	None	
153RD DR E	Adams Co	137T	80602	10500-11199	
	Thornton	136T	80602	6700-7199	
153RD PL E	Thornton	136T	80602	7100-7199	
153RD PL W	Adams Co	133V	80020	2200-2399	
	Broomfield	134T	80020	None	
154TH AVE E	Adams Co	137S	80602	10100-10199	
	Thornton	136T	80602	6500-7199	
154TH AVE W	Adams Co	134S	80020	800-1399	
154TH CIR E	Adams Co	750J	80603	None	
	Thornton	136T	80602	6700-6799	
154TH CT E	Thornton	136U	80602	None	
154TH PL E	Brighton	139T	80601	None	
154TH PL E	Thornton	136T	80602	7000-7099	
154TH PL W	Adams Co	133V	80020	2200-2399	
155TH AVE E	Adams Co	136V	80602	8900-9099	
	Thornton	136T	80602	6700-7099	
155TH CT E	Adams Co	137T	80602	10500-10699	
	Thornton	136V	80602	None	
155TH DR E	Adams Co	136V	80602	9100-9499	
	Thornton	136T	80602	6700-6799	
	Thornton	136T	80602	7100-7199	
155TH PL E	Adams Co	137S	80602	9800-10299	
	Adams Co	137T	80602	10700-11199	
	Brighton	139T	80601	17800-17999	
155TH PL W	Adams Co	133V	80020	2200-2399	
	Adams Co	134S	80020	None	
155TH WAY E	Adams Co	140V	80603	23000-24999	
156TH AVE E	Adams Co	135T	80602	3200-3799	
	Adams Co	140V	80603	23000-24999	
	Adams Co	750L	80603	25000-29999	
	Thornton	136T	80602	6500-7299	
156TH AVE W	Adams Co	134S	80020	800-2199	
	Adams Co	133V	80020	2200-2399	
156TH CT E	Adams Co	751K	80642	None	
	Thornton	136U	80602	8100-8299	
157TH AVE E	Adams Co	136V	80602	9200-9299	
	Adams Co	137S	80602	9700-10099	
	Adams Co	140R	80603	23000-23999	
157TH CT E	Adams Co	137P	80602	10600-10799	
	Adams Co	751G	80642	None	
	Thornton	136U	80602	8100-8299	
157TH PL E	Adams Co	137N	80602	9700-10099	
158TH AVE E	Adams Co	136R	80602	9300-9599	
	Thornton	136Q	80602	None	
158TH CT E	Adams Co	137P	80602	10500-10599	
158TH PL E	Adams Co	137N	80602	9700-10099	
159TH AVE E	Adams Co	136R	80602	9000-9699	
	Adams Co	137N	80602	9700-10099	
	Adams Co	137P	80602	10400-10499	
159TH CT E	Thornton	136Q	80602	8100-8299	
	Thornton	136R	80602	None	
159TH PL E	Adams Co	137N	80602	9700-10099	
	Adams Co	137P	80602	10800-11299	
160TH AVE E	Adams Co	136N	80602	8500-9499	
	Adams Co	137Q	80602	9600-12899	
	Adams Co	138N	80601	13100-13299	
	Adams Co	751G	80642	32900-37699	
	Adams Co	752G	80102	40900-52099	
	Adams Co	750E	80603	None	
	Adams Co	751E	80603	None	
	Adams Co	752G	80642	None	
	Brighton	140N	80601	21700-29999	
	Thornton	134R	80020	1-2099	
	Thornton	135P	80602	2100-5599	
160TH AVE W	Broomfield	134P	80020	1-2199	
	Broomfield	133Q	80020	2200-4299	
160TH CT E	Adams Co	750G	80603	29000-29599	
	Adams Co	750H	80603	None	
160TH PL E	Adams Co	136Q	80602	8400-8599	
	Adams Co	750G	80603	28500-29099	
	Adams Co	136N	80602	None	
	Adams Co	137N	80602	None	
161ST AVE E	Adams Co	136Q	80602	8400-8599	
	Adams Co	136R	80602	8900-9099	
	Adams Co	136N	80602	None	
	Adams Co	137P	80602	None	
161ST CT E	Adams Co	750H	80603	None	
161ST PL E	Adams Co	136R	80602	8900-8999	
	Adams Co	137N	80602	None	
162ND AVE E	Adams Co	136P	80602	6600-7299	
	Adams Co	136L	80602	8400-8899	
	Adams Co	136R	80602	8900-8999	
	Adams Co	750G	80603	29200-29599	
	Adams Co	136N	80602	None	
	Adams Co	750H	80603	None	
162ND CT E	Adams Co	136K	80602	7100-7199	
	Adams Co	750G	80603	28400-28599	
162ND DR E	Adams Co	137P	80602	None	
	Adams Co	136J	80602	None	
	Adams Co	137K	80602	None	
163RD AVE E	Adams Co	136K	80602	6600-7199	
	Adams Co	136L	80602	8400-8599	
	Adams Co	136J	80602	None	
	Adams Co	137K	80602	None	
	Adams Co	750H	80603	None	
163RD CT E	Adams Co	136L	80602	8400-8599	
	Adams Co	137K	80602	None	
163RD PL E	Adams Co	136M	80602	8600-8799	
	Adams Co	750G	80603	None	
	Adams Co	750H	80603	None	
	Adams Co	137K	80602	None	
	Adams Co	750H	80603	None	
	Thornton	134L	80602	None	
164TH AVE E	Weld Co	139K	80601	17700-18499	
164TH CT E	Adams Co	136J	80602	6400-6799	
164TH PL E	Adams Co	134M	80602	1600-1699	
	Thornton	135J	80602	1700-1999	
165TH AVE E	Adams Co	135J	80602	2300-3299	
	Adams Co	750H	80603	29100-30499	
	Thornton	135J	80602	None	
165TH PL E	Adams Co	136J	80602	5600-6299	

A

STREET NAME	CITY or COUNTY	MAP GRID	ZIP CODE	BLOCK RANGE	O/E
166TH AVE E	Adams Co	135J	80602	2300-3299	
	Adams Co	750H	80603	29700-30499	
	Adams Co	137K	80602	None	
	Adams Co	750G	80603	None	
	Adams Co	750H	80603	None	
	Thornton	135J	80602	1700-1999	
	Thornton	134M	80602	None	
166TH CT E	Adams Co	751E	80603	None	
	Thornton	134M	80602	1500-1599	
166TH DR E	Thornton	135J	80602	1900-1999	
166TH PL E	Adams Co	136K	80602	6600-7099	
	Adams Co	750H	80603	29700-29999	
	Adams Co	137K	80602	None	
	Thornton	134M	80602	1500-1599	
167TH AVE E	Adams Co	136J	80602	6100-6899	
	Adams Co	750D	80603	30200-30399	
	Adams Co	137L	80602	None	
	Adams Co	750C	80603	None	
	Adams Co	750D	80603	None	
	Thornton	134M	80602	1600-1699	
	Thornton	135J	80602	None	
167TH CIR E	Thornton	134M	80602	1600-1799	
167TH DR E	Adams Co	751A	80603	None	
	Thornton	135J	80602	None	
167TH LN E	Thornton	135J	80602	None	
167TH PL E	Adams Co	136K	80602	7000-7199	
	Adams Co	750C	80603	29700-29999	
	Adams Co	137K	80602	None	
167TH WAY E	Thornton	135J	80602	None	
168TH AVE E	Adams Co	136F	80602	9600-12998	E
	Adams Co	750D	80603	None	
	Broomfield	134G	80020	1-699	
	Broomfield	134G	80602	1000-1698	E
	Weld Co	135F	80516	1700-5598	E
	Weld Co	136F	80602	5600-9598	E
168TH AVE W	Broomfield	134F	80020	1-799	O
169TH AVE	Broomfield	134F	80516	None	
175TH AVE W	Broomfield	134A	80516	2300-2999	
176TH AVE E	Weld Co	138C	80603	None	
	Weld Co	139A	80603	None	
176TH AVE W	Broomfield	134A	80516	None	
192ND AVE E	Weld Co	729U	80603	None	
	Weld Co	729U	80621	None	
195TH AVE E	Weld Co	730S	80642	19000-19999	
197TH WAY E	Weld Co	730N	80642	18000-19499	
A					
A	Aurora	288F	80011	None	
A ST	Golden	279T	80401	100-1199	
	Jefferson Co	279R	80401	None	
A ST	Longmont	11U	80501	None	
AARON PL	Boulder	128C	80303	4400-4499	
A-BASIN AVE E	Buckley Air Force Base	289T	80017	None	
ABBEY DR	Longmont	12T	80501	500-599	
ABBEY PL	Boulder	128J	80302	200-299	
ABBEY RD	Jefferson Co	337Q	80439	5300-5399	
ABBEY ST	Broomfield	163S	80020	12400-12499	
ABBEYLARA LN	Parker	408Q	80134	None	
ABBEYWOOD CIR	Highlands Ranch	405R	80130	None	
ABBOTSWOOD CT	Highlands Ranch	404K	80129	10600-10699	
ABBOTT AVE	Broomfield	162W	80020	2100-2299	
ABBY ST	Dacono	727J	80514	None	
ABERDEEN AVE	Highlands Ranch	375Z	80126	4600-4799	
ABERDEEN AVE E	Arapahoe Co	347S	80111	9700-10499	
	Centennial	348T	80016	14700-15099	
	Centennial	348V	80016	15700-16499	
ABERDEEN AVE W	Littleton	344T	80120	400-699	
	Littleton	344S	80120	1600-1799	
	Littleton	343V	80120	2100-2199	
	Littleton	343X	80123	4200-4599	
ABERDEEN CIR	Highlands Ranch	375V	80126	8600-8799	
ABERDEEN CT	Boulder Co	100E	80301	4400-4499	
ABERDEEN DR	Broomfield	162V	80020	900-1399	
ABERDEEN DR E	Arapahoe Co	349S	80016	17000-17499	
	Aurora	351T	80016	None	
	Centennial	350T	80013	21200-21699	
ABERDEEN PL	Boulder Co	100E	80301	4400-4599	
ABERDEEN PL E	Arapahoe Co	349T	80016	17700-17799	
	Arapahoe Co	350U	80015	23200-23299	
	Centennial	350T	80015	21200-21399	
ABERDEEN PL W	Littleton	343W	80123	4400-4799	
ABERDEEN ST S	Littleton	344X	80120	5900-6299	
ABERDEEN WAY	Boulder Co	100E	80301	7500-7699	
ABERNANTHY CT	Highlands Ranch	375Z	80126	1-99	
ABERT RIDGE VIEW	El Paso Co	910Z	80908	17500-17599	
ABEYTA CT	Boulder Co	98K	80301	3800-3899	
ABEYTA ST	Weld Co	727B	80530	200-299	
ABILENE CIR	Aurora	258X	80011	3200-3299	
ABILENE CIR S	Aurora	348B	80014	4000-4099	
	Aurora	348E	80015	4300-4499	
	Aurora	348J	80015	4500-4699	
ABILENE CT	Elbert Co	870V	80107	1700-1999	
ABILENE DR	Broomfield	162Q	80020	1300-1699	
ABILENE ST	Adams Co	168N	80601	13200-13399	
	Aurora	288S	80011	1-399	
	Aurora	288B	80011	2600-2799	
	Aurora	258X	80011	3000-3299	
	Commerce City	198J	80022	10400-10799	
	Denver	257R	80239	4400-4599	
	Denver	258E	80239	5500-5599	
ABILENE ST S	Aurora	288S	80012	1-299	
	Aurora	288W	80012	300-699	
	Aurora	318E	80014	700-1899	
	Aurora	318E	80012	1900-2299	
	Aurora	318N	80014	2500-2799	
	Centennial	348W	80111	None	
	Centennial	378A	80111	None	
ABILENE WAY S	Centennial	378A	80111	6500-6699	
ABO LN	El Paso Co	907U	80132	4800-4899	
ABSTRACT ST	Castle Rock	496B	80109	4200-4399	
ABUNDANCE WAY	Jefferson Co	763W	80403	6700-6799	
ACADEMY BLVD	Denver	286U	80230	7700-8499	
ACADEMY CIR	El Paso Co	908T	80132	18300-18499	
ACADEMY RD	Palmer Lake	907Q	80133	None	
ACADEMY ST	Central City	780C	80427	1-199	
ACADIA AVE	Lafayette	132A	80026	200-1099	
ACADIA DR	Parker	410N	80138	21000-21099	
ACADIA LN	Parker	410N	80138	10900-10999	
ACADIA PL	Parker	410N	80138	10800-10899	
ACE CT	Boulder Co	723G	80503	6400-6499	
ACER DR	Douglas Co	378V	80134	None	
ACHILLES CIR	Lafayette	131Q	80026	1100-1199	
ACHILLES DR	Highlands Ranch	376V	80124	13400-13699	
ACOMA CIR S	Littleton	374F	80120	7100-7199	
ACOMA CT	Adams Co	224P	80221	7600-7699	
ACOMA CT	Douglas Co	886M	80118	7800-7899	
ACOMA CT S	Littleton	374F	80120	7100-7199	
ACOMA DR	Douglas Co	886M	80118	7900-8399	
ACOMA DR W	Littleton	374B	80120	100-499	
ACOMA PL	Douglas Co	886M	80118	5300-5399	
	Kiowa	872M	80117	None	
ACOMA RD	Jefferson Co	338J	80454	4400-4499	
ACOMA ST	Adams Co	224F	80221	8100-8399	
	Denver	284P	80223	1-399	
	Denver	284K	80204	400-1399	
	Denver	254K	80216	4900-5098	E
	Northglenn	194K	80234	10700-11199	
	Northglenn	194B	80234	11600-11899	
ACOMA ST S	Denver	314L	80223	1200-2699	
	Englewood	314U	80110	2700-3499	
	Englewood	344F	80110	3600-5099	
	Littleton	344X	80120	6300-6599	
	Littleton	374B	80120	6600-6699	
	Littleton	374F	80120	7100-7299	
	Littleton	374F	80120	7200-7299	
ACOMA WAY	Adams Co	224G	80221	8100-8399	
ACOMA WAY S	Littleton	374F	80120	7100-7299	
ACORN DR	Thornton	193Z	80260	None	
ACORN LN	Boulder Co	97P	80304	1-299	
ACORN LN	Thornton	193V	80260	None	
ACORN WAY	El Paso Co	908T	80132	1500-1599	
ACRES GREEN DR	Highlands Ranch	376Y	80124	13000-13299	
	Lone Tree	376U	80124	None	
ACROPOLIS DR	Lafayette	131Q	80026	1200-1399	
ADA DR E	Aurora	319B	80017	17700-17899	
ADA LN	Douglas Co	886G	80118	5700-5799	
ADA PL E	Aurora	317B	80012	11000-11299	
	Aurora	317C	80012	11500-11899	
	Aurora	318D	80017	16300-16799	
ADA PL W	Denver	314A	80223	1200-1499	
	Denver	313C	80219	3000-3599	
	Denver	313A	80219	4200-4799	
	Lakewood	311B	80226	10900-11299	
ADAHI RD	Jefferson Co	338P	80454	5200-5399	
ADAK PL E	Denver	259Q	80249	19300-19399	
ADAM CT	Broomfield	163G	80020	14100-14399	
ADAM PL	Castle Pines North	436C	80108	500-599	
ADAM AIRCRAFT CIR E	Arapahoe Co	377M	80112	12800-12999	
	Arapahoe Co	378J	80112	13000-13098	E
ADAMS AVE	Louisville	130V	80027	500-599	
	Louisville	130V	80027	1000-1199	
ADAMS CIR	Boulder	128F	80303	1000-1099	
ADAMS CIR	Northglenn	195K	80233	10500-10599	
	Thornton	165F	80602	13800-13999	
ADAMS CIR S	Centennial	375F	80122	7100-7199	
ADAMS CT	Adams Co	225F	80229	8500-8599	
	Adams Co	794P	80136	None	
	Northglenn	195K	80233	10500-10799	
	Thornton	165P	80241	13000-13099	
ADAMS CT S	Centennial	375B	80121	6500-6599	
ADAMS DR S	Centennial	345X	80121	6200-6299	
ADAMS DR S	Louisville	130Z	80027	200-399	
ADAMS PL	Louisville	130R	80027	1400-1499	
	Thornton	195P	80229	10300-10399	
ADAMS RD	Mead	706C	80542	2700-3999	
ADAMS ST	Adams Co	794P	80136	1500-1899	
	Adams Co	794F	80136	3800-4099	
ADAMS ST	Bennett	793J	80102	None	
ADAMS ST	Denver	285P	80206	1-1699	
	Denver	285B	80205	2600-2699	
	Denver	255X	80205	2700-3999	
	Denver	255P	80216	4000-4599	
	Denver	255K	80216	4800-5399	
	Monument	908W	80132	100-199	
	Northglenn	195K	80233	10400-10799	
	Thornton	195X	80229	9200-9299	
	Thornton	195T	80229	9600-9999	
	Thornton	195P	80229	10000-10199	
	Thornton	195F	80233	11200-11599	
	Thornton	195B	80233	11600-11899	
	Thornton	165X	80241	12100-12299	
	Thornton	165K	80602	13600-13899	
	Thornton	165F	80602	13900-13999	
	Thornton	165F	80602	None	
	Thornton	225B	80229	None	
ADAMS ST S	Centennial	345X	80121	5900-6299	
	Centennial	375K	80122	7500-7799	
	Denver	285T	80209	1-199	
	Denver	315B	80209	700-1099	
	Denver	315B	80210	1100-1199	
	Denver	315T	80210	1600-3099	
ADAMS WAY	Adams Co	224E	80221	8200-8399	
	Adams Co	225F	80229	8400-8499	
ADAMS WAY	Firestone	727B	80504	None	
ADAMS WAY	Thornton	225B	80229	8400-8499	
	Thornton	165X	80241	12100-12199	
	Thornton	165T	80241	12800-12899	
ADAMS WAY S	Centennial	375F	80122	6900-7899	
	Centennial	375P	80122	7900-8199	
	Denver	315B	80209	900-999	
	Denver	315X	80210	3100-3299	
ADDENBROOKE LOOP	Castle Rock	466U	80109	4400-4599	
ADDIE ROSE LN	Longmont	11P	80501	None	
ADDINGTON PL	Parker	410U	80138	None	
ADDISH ST	Adams Co	170M	80022	13200-13599	
ADDISON	Thornton	224A	80260	None	
ADDISON CT	Highlands Ranch	405P	80126	10600-10799	
ADDISON CT S	Arapahoe Co	350R	80016	5300-5399	
	Aurora	320H	80018	1300-1499	
	Aurora	380H	80016	7200-7299	
	Aurora	350V	80016	None	
	Aurora	380H	80016	None	
	Aurora	380M	80016	None	
ADDISON PT	Highlands Ranch	405P	80126	3000-3099	
ADDISON WAY N	Aurora	290R	80018	None	
ADDISON WAY S	Arapahoe Co	320D	80018	1000-1099	
	Aurora	380R	80016	7700-8099	
	Aurora	380V	80138	8600-8799	
	Aurora	320M	80018	None	
	Aurora	350M	80016	None	
	Aurora	350V	80016	None	
	Aurora	380M	80016	None	
ADELAIDE CIR S	Highlands Ranch	405H	80130	9600-9799	
ADELAIDE CT S	Highlands Ranch	405H	80130	9700-9799	
ADELAIDE PL E	Highlands Ranch	405H	80130	4700-4799	
ADEMAR CIR	Mead	706M	80504	None	
ADEMAR CT	Mead	706M	80504	None	
ADKINSON AVE	Longmont	11P	80501	1600-1799	
ADLER AVE W	Jefferson Co	372P	80128	7000-7299	
ADLER DR W	Jefferson Co	372P	80128	7700-7899	
ADMIRAL WAY	Elbert Co	850D	80138	2000-2199	
ADOBE CT S	Jefferson Co	341L	80127	4600-4699	
ADOBE LN S	Jefferson Co	341L	80127	4600-4699	
ADOBE PL E	Highlands Ranch	404D	80126	1600-1699	
ADOBE WAY S	Jefferson Co	341L	80127	4600-4699	
ADONIA CIR	Lafayette	131Q	80026	1500-1599	
ADONIS CT	Lafayette	131U	80026	1400-1499	
ADRIATIC AVE W	Lakewood	311N	80228	12800-12899	
ADRIATIC DR E	Aurora	319N	80013	17100-17399	
ADRIATIC DR E	Aurora	321J	80018	None	
ADRIATIC PL E	Aurora	317Q	80014	11400-11799	
	Aurora	318K	80014	14500-14999	
	Aurora	318M	80013	16000-16499	
	Aurora	319N	80013	17100-17399	
	Aurora	319K	80013	18100-18299	
	Aurora	321J	80018	None	
ADRIATIC PL W	Englewood	314N	80110	1800-1998	E
	Englewood	313R	80110	2000-2199	
	Lakewood	312R	80227	6000-6099	
	Lakewood	310Q	80228	14000-14099	
AEGEAN DR	Lafayette	131M	80026	700-899	
AEGEAN WAY	Longmont	12Q	80501	None	
AFFOLTER ST	Longmont	41J	80503	500-599	
AFTON LN	Jefferson Co	306P	80439	2200-2299	
AFTONWOOD ST	Highlands Ranch	405G	80126	9700-9999	
AGAPE WAY	Lafayette	131Q	80026	1300-1599	
AGATE AVE	Jefferson Co	823T	80433	24500-25199	
AGATE DR	Highlands Ranch	374U	80126	100-299	
AGATE LN	Boulder	98J	80304	2400-2599	
AGATE RD	Boulder Co	98J	80304	2400-4499	
AGATE ST	Broomfield	162U	80020	300-899	
AGATE WAY	Broomfield	162Y	80020	100-299	
AGAVE AVE	Castle Rock	468M	80108	6200-6599	
AIKINS WAY	Boulder	128U	80305	1200-1299	
AINSDALE CT	Lone Tree	406D	80124	8600-8699	
AINTREE CT E	Parker	409V	80138	20100-20199	
AINTREE PL E	Parker	409V	80138	20100-20199	
AIRPORT BLVD	Aurora	259W	80011	3001-3299	O
AIRPORT BLVD	Boulder	98V	80301	5100-5499	
	Boulder	99N	80301	5500-5699	
AIRPORT BLVD S	Aurora	289W	80017	401-499	O
AIRPORT CIR	Aurora	258Z	80011	16300-16498	E
AIRPORT CT	Broomfield	161Y	80021	10100-10899	
AIRPORT DR	Erie	132H	80516	300-2899	
	Erie	133E	80516	2900-3099	
AIRPORT RD	Boulder	98V	80301	3000-3399	
	Boulder Co	40G	80503	200-298	E
AIRPORT RD	Douglas Co	846G	80135	5500-6499	
	Douglas Co	846G	80125	None	
AIRPORT RD	Longmont	40G	80503	201-399	O
	Longmont	10Y	80503	900-1799	
	Longmont	10L	80503	2200-2399	
AIRPORT RD N	Aurora	289J	80011	1-2499	
AIRPORT RD S	Aurora	289N	80017	1-399	
AIRPORT RD S	Longmont	40U	80503	600-699	
AIRPORT WAY	Denver	258R	80239	4501-4599	O
	Denver	258M	80239	None	
AIRPORT WAY	Jefferson Co	191C	80021	11600-12399	
AIRVIEW AVE W	Lakewood	312G	80232	6800-6999	
AJAX CT	Superior	160T	80027	2400-2499	
AJAX LN	Jefferson Co	306J	80439	1600-1699	
AJAX ST	Adams Co	793R	80136	1500-1899	
AJAX WAY	Longmont	12V	80501	None	
AJO WAY	El Paso Co	908U	80132	1-299	
AKERS CT	Erie	102Q	80516	1400-1499	
AKRON CIR S	Greenwood Village	346V	80111	5900-5999	
AKRON CT	Adams Co	136Z	80602	14800-14999	
	Denver	256Z	80238	2600-2999	
	Denver	256Z	80238	3300-3699	
	Denver	286D	80238	None	
AKRON CT S	Arapahoe Co	316H	80247	1200-1399	
	Denver	316V	80231	2900-3199	
	Greenwood Village	346H	80111	4200-4399	
AKRON PL E	Superior	160L	80027	1000-1199	
AKRON ST	Adams Co	166D	80602	14500-14799	
	Adams Co	136V	80602	14800-15899	
	Aurora	286M	80010	1100-1499	
	Aurora	286H	80010	1600-1999	
	Commerce City	196M	80640	10700-10799	
	Denver	286D	80238	2300-2899	
	Denver	256V	80238	3300-3699	
AKRON ST S	Arapahoe Co	316H	80247	1301-1399	O
	Centennial	376R	80112	8000-8299	
	Denver	316Z	80231	2900-3499	
	Greenwood Village	346H	80111	4200-4599	
	Greenwood Village	346M	80111	4600-4699	
AKRON WAY	Denver	286R	80230	700-1099	
	Denver	286D	80220	None	
AKRON WAY S	Arapahoe Co	316H	80247	1200-1399	
	Greenwood Village	346Z	80111	5900-6199	
AKSARBEN AVE W	Littleton	343P	80123	3300-3399	
ALABAMA AVE W	Lakewood	312E	80232	8200-8399	
ALABAMA CIR E	Aurora	317E	80247	9901-9999	O
	Aurora	317G	80112	11301-11399	O
ALABAMA DR E	Aurora	317E	80247	9800-9999	
	Aurora	318H	80017	16000-16399	
	Aurora	320H	80018	23500-23999	
ALABAMA DR W	Lakewood	312F	80232	7000-7599	
	Lakewood	311H	80232	9200-9499	

A

STREET NAME	CITY or COUNTY	MAP GRID	ZIP CODE	BLOCK RANGE	O/E
ALABAMA PL E	Arapahoe Co	316H	80247	9101-9299	O
	Arapahoe Co	317E	80247	9301-9499	O
	Aurora	317E	80247	9500-9899	
	Aurora	318E	80012	13900-13999	
	Aurora	318F	80012	14700-14899	
	Aurora	318H	80017	16700-16799	
	Aurora	319F	80017	18100-18399	
	Aurora	320H	80018	23600-23999	
	Denver	315H	80246	4800-4899	
ALABAMA PL W	Denver	313G	80219	3100-3299	
	Lakewood	311H	80232	9000-9099	
	Lakewood	311E	80228	12000-12399	
	Lakewood	311E	80228	12500-12799	
ALABAMA WAY W	Lakewood	310H	80228	12500-12699	
ALABASTER CT	Douglas Co	408G	80134	9800-9899	
ALABRASKA DR	Jefferson Co	366H	80439	None	
ALABRASKA LN	Jefferson Co	366H	80439	27800-28399	
ALAMEDA AVE	Palmer Lake	907Q	80133	None	
ALAMEDA AVE E	Arapahoe Co	290Z	80018	23300-24599	
	Arapahoe Co	791X	80137	32900-36299	
	Arapahoe Co	792W	80102	39300-42499	
	Arapahoe Co	795X	80103	63300-64099	
	Arapahoe Co	795Y	80103	65700-72899	
	Aurora	287Y	80012	10600-13099	
	Aurora	291T	80018	None	
	Denver	284Y	80209	1-1699	
	Denver	285W	80209	1700-3999	
	Denver	285Z	80246	4002-4798	E
	Denver	285Z	80246	4800-5499	
	Denver	286T	80246	5500-5599	
	Denver	286W	80224	5600-7299	
	Denver	286Y	80230	7301-9499	O
	Denver	286Y	80247	7400-9498	E
	Denver	287W	80231	9500-10499	
	Glendale	285Z	80246	4000-4799	
ALAMEDA AVE W	Denver	284X	80223	1-199	
	Denver	284W	80223	1300-1599	
	Denver	283Z	80223	2000-2499	
	Denver	283Y	80219	2500-5199	
	Lakewood	282X	80226	5200-8899	
	Lakewood	281Y	80226	8900-11499	
	Lakewood	281Y	80228	11500-11899	
ALAMEDA CIR E	Denver	285X	80209	2500-2599	
ALAMEDA DR E	Aurora	288X	80012	14600-14899	
	Aurora	289W	80017	16500-17299	
	Aurora	288U	80012	None	
ALAMEDA DR W	Lakewood	281W	80228	12200-12499	
	Lakewood	310D	80228	12800-13099	
ALAMEDA PKWY E	Aurora	288Y	80017	13100-16899	
	Aurora	289W	80017	16900-18099	
	Aurora	319B	80017	18100-18499	
ALAMEDA PKWY W	Jefferson Co	309Q	80401	16500-18299	
	Jefferson Co	309M	80401	None	
	Lakewood	281W	80228	11900-12299	
	Lakewood	310H	80228	12300-14499	
	Lakewood	310J	80228	14500-14799	
	Lakewood	310J	80465	14800-16499	
ALAMEDA PL E	Aurora	288Z	80017	16200-16999	
ALAMEDA PL W	Lakewood	281Z	80226	9500-9599	
ALAMEDA FRONTAGE RD W					
	Lakewood	282Y	80226	6400-6799	
	Lakewood	281X	80226	10100-11199	
	Lakewood	281W	80228	11500-12299	
ALAMEDA SERVICE RD W	Lakewood	281Z	80226	9200-9599	
ALAMO AVE W	Littleton	343V	80120	2100-2699	
	Littleton	343U	80123	3400-3599	
ALAMO CT S	Denver	342U	80123	5600-5699	
ALAMO DR	Northglenn	194T	80260	9700-9999	
ALAMO DR E	Aurora	351S	80016	None	
	Centennial	349T	80015	18000-18299	
ALAMO DR W	Denver	342V	80123	5700-5999	
	Denver	342U	80123	6100-6699	
	Littleton	343T	80123	3500-3599	
ALAMO LN E	Arapahoe Co	350U	80015	22700-22899	
	Centennial	350T	80015	21700-22299	
ALAMO PL E	Arapahoe Co	350U	80015	22400-23199	
	Aurora	350V	80016	None	
	Aurora	350V	80016	None	
	Centennial	348V	80015	16500-16599	
	Centennial	350T	80015	21500-21699	
	Centennial	350T	80015	22000-22099	
ALAMO PL W	Jefferson Co	341V	80123	8900-9999	
	Jefferson Co	341U	80127	10100-11199	
	Littleton	343U	80123	3100-3599	
ALAMONTE PL	Highlands Ranch	403G	80129	None	
ALAMOSA AVE	Palmer Lake	907Q	80133	None	
ALAMOSA CT	Brighton	139P	80601	None	
ALAN DR	Adams Co	223V	80221	6800-7399	
ALAN-A-DALE	El Paso Co	908P	80132	20300-20499	
ALASKA AVE	Longmont	41G	80501	1200-1299	
ALASKA AVE E	Aurora	287Y	80012	11500-13099	
ALASKA DR E	Denver	286X	80224	6500-6599	
ALASKA DR W	Lakewood	282X	80226	6900-7599	
	Lakewood	280Y	80228	13700-14199	
ALASKA PL E	Aurora	287Y	80012	11200-11299	
	Aurora	287Z	80012	12100-13099	
	Aurora	288Z	80017	15900-16299	
ALASKA PL W	Denver	284W	80223	1200-1599	
	Denver	283Y	80219	3000-3599	
	Denver	283W	80219	4300-5199	
	Denver	284X	80223	None	
	Lakewood	282W	80226	8400-8799	
	Lakewood	281Z	80226	9000-9099	
	Lakewood	280Z	80228	13200-13899	
ALASKA RD	Boulder Co	722T	80302	1-1099	
ALASKA ST	Golden	248V	80403	600-699	
ALBERT CT	Adams Co	224E	80221	8100-8199	
ALBERT DR	Gilpin Co	740Z	80474	None	
ALBERTA CT	Boulder Co	100E	80301	4400-4499	
ALBION CIR	Thornton	195L	80233	10900-10999	
	Thornton	165Q	80241	13300-13399	
	Thornton	165L	80241	13500-13599	
ALBION CT	Thornton	195L	80233	10800-10999	
	Thornton	195G	80233	11100-11199	
	Thornton	195C	80233	11500-11599	
ALBION CT S	Centennial	345Y	80121	6200-6299	
	Greenwood Village	345U	80121	5800-5899	
ALBION DR	Thornton	195L	80233	10800-11099	
	Thornton	195G	80229	11000-11099	
ALBION LN	Longmont	10U	80503	1600-1699	
ALBION LN	Thornton	195U	80229	9600-9799	
ALBION PL	Douglas Co	466D	80108	1-99	
	Thornton	195L	80233	10800-10899	
ALBION ST	Commerce City	225U	80022	6500-6799	
	Denver	285U	80220	1-799	
	Denver	285L	80220	1100-1999	
	Denver	285C	80207	2000-2799	
	Denver	255Y	80207	2800-3499	
	Denver	255Q	80216	4000-4098	E
	Thornton	195Y	80229	9100-9599	
	Thornton	195L	80233	10500-10799	
	Thornton	195G	80233	11200-11599	
	Thornton	195C	80233	11700-11799	
	Thornton	165U	80241	12400-12699	
	Thornton	165L	80241	13500-13599	
ALBION ST S	Centennial	375G	80122	6700-7499	
	Centennial	375Q	80122	8000-8299	
	Cherry Hills Village	345C	80113	3500-3899	
	Cherry Hills Village	345Q	80121	4800-5099	
	Denver	285U	80246	1-99	
	Denver	315G	80222	1500-1699	
	Denver	315Q	80222	2000-2399	
	Denver	315Y	80222	3100-3399	
	Denver	315L	80222	None	
ALBION WAY	Boulder	128T	80305	1000-1299	
ALBION WAY	Thornton	195G	80233	11100-11199	
	Thornton	165G	80602	None	
ALBION WAY S	Centennial	375C	80121	6400-6599	
	Centennial	375C	80122	6700-6799	
	Cherry Hills Village	345Q	80121	5000-5099	
ALBO ST	Jefferson Co	823N	80433	26600-26799	
ALBROOK DR	Denver	257M	80239	12100-13899	
	Denver	258N	80239	13900-14499	
ALBY TRAIL	Jefferson Co	782G	80403	5000-5399	
ALCAZAR DR	Castle Rock	496C	80109	None	
ALCORN AVE E	Douglas Co	409G	80138	6400-6599	
ALCORN ST N	Douglas Co	409G	80138	11800-11999	
ALCOSTA PL S	Highlands Ranch	405B	80126	9300-9499	
ALCOTT CIR	Broomfield	163R	80234	13200-13499	
	Federal Heights	193Z	80260	9300N-9499N	
	Federal Heights	193Z	80260	9200S-9299S	
ALCOTT CT	Broomfield	163R	80234	None	
	Westminster	193M	80234	10800-10899	
ALCOTT DR	Broomfield	163V	80234	None	
	Westminster	193M	80234	10900-11099	
ALCOTT PL	Broomfield	163R	80020	13000-13199	
ALCOTT ST	Adams Co	253H	80221	5400-5799	
	Broomfield	163V	80020	12500-12599	
	Broomfield	163M	80020	13200-13398	E
	Broomfield	163V	80234	None	
	Denver	283V	80219	1-99	
	Denver	283R	80204	500-799	
	Denver	283D	80211	2300-2799	
	Denver	253Z	80211	2700-3199	
	Denver	253R	80211	3200-4799	
	Denver	253M	80221	4800-5199	
	Federal Heights	193R	80260	9900-10099	
	Westminster	223V	80030	7000-7199	
	Westminster	223R	80030	7400-7499	
	Westminster	223H	80260	8300-8599	
	Westminster	193M	80234	10700-11199	
	Westminster	163Z	80234	12100-12299	
ALCOTT ST S	Denver	283Z	80219	1-699	
	Denver	313H	80219	700-2199	
	Sheridan	313Z	80110	3100-3499	
ALCOTT WAY	Broomfield	163M	80020	13400-13599	
	Broomfield	163R	80234	None	
	Denver	283M	80204	900-1099	
	Westminster	223H	80030	8300-8399	
	Westminster	193M	80234	10700-10799	
ALDEN CT	Castle Rock	497Q	80104	None	
ALDENBRIDGE CIR	Highlands Ranch	405G	80126	3700-3999	
ALDENRIDGE CT	Highlands Ranch	405G	80126	10200-10299	
ALDER AVE W	Jefferson Co	372R	80128	5400-6599	
	Aurora	380Q	80016	22400-22599	
ALDER DR E	Aurora	380R	80016	23500-23699	
ALDER ST	Federal Heights	193U	80260	2900-2999	
ALDER ST W	Louisville	130T	80027	900-1099	
ALDER WAY	Longmont	40Q	80503	900-1199	
ALDER WAY W	Jefferson Co	372R	80128	5600-5699	
ALDERSHOT CT	Highlands Ranch	376S	80130	1-99	
ALDRICH RD	Jefferson Co	823N	80433	9400-9499	
ALEUTION TRAIL	Elbert Co	851U	80107	37400-37499	
ALEX CT	Douglas Co	848E	80108	400-499	
ALEXA LN S	Highlands Ranch	406F	80130	10100-10299	
ALEXANDER AVE	Greenwood Village	345S	80121	2400-2799	
ALEXANDER AVE E	Greenwood Village	345U	80121	3700-3999	
ALEXANDER CT S	Greenwood Village	345T	80121	5600-5699	
ALEXANDER DR	Mead	706M	80504	None	
ALEXANDER DR E	Aurora	350V	80016	None	
	Aurora	351S	80016	None	
ALEXANDER LN	Greenwood Village	345T	80121	1-99	
ALEXANDER PL	Castle Rock	467Q	80108	300-499	
ALEXANDER WAY	Broomfield	133L	80020	None	
ALEXANDRIA DR	El Paso Co	908P	80132	None	
ALEXANDRIA ST	Lafayette	132A	80026	1100-1399	
ALEXIS CROSSING	Lochbuie	729Y	80603	None	
ALFALFA CT	Boulder Co	70F	80503	8100-8199	
ALGONQUIAN CIR S	Aurora	380Q	80016	7900-8099	
	Aurora	380R	80016	8100-8199	
ALGONQUIAN CT S	Arapahoe Co	290V	80018	1-99	
ALGONQUIAN CT S	Arapahoe Co	350R	80016	5400-5499	
	Aurora	350V	80016	None	
ALGONQUIAN CT S	Aurora	380Q	80016	7900-7999	
	Aurora	380D	80016	None	
ALGONQUIAN ST N	Arapahoe Co	290V	80018	1-199	
ALGONQUIAN ST S	Arapahoe Co	350R	80016	5200-5299	
ALGONQUIAN WAY S	Aurora	380L	80016	7600-7999	
	Aurora	350M	80016	None	
	Aurora	350V	80016	None	
ALGONQUIN	Thornton	224A	80260	None	
ALGONQUIN RD S	Jefferson Co	338R	80454	5200-5499	
ALIANTE DR	Broomfield	133K	80020	None	
ALICE DR	Jefferson Co	336W	80439	30600-30899	
ALICE PL W	Denver	253P	80211	3600-3899	
	Denver	254N	80211	None	
ALICIA DR	Brighton	138Y	80601	None	
ALICIA PKWY S	Aurora	348D	80013	3800-4099	
ALINE ST	Louisville	131W	80027	100-199	
ALJAN AVE	Boulder Co	11J	80503	9100-9299	
ALKIRE CT	Arvada	250D	80004	6000-6199	
	Arvada	220Z	80004	6200-6299	
	Arvada	220V	80004	6400-6699	
	Arvada	220Z	80004	6500-6599	
	Arvada	220R	80005	7300-7399	
	Jefferson Co	280R	80401	900-999	
	Jefferson Co	280H	80401	1500-1899	
	Jefferson Co	250Z	80401	3200-3399	
ALKIRE CT S	Jefferson Co	340H	80465	4300-4399	
	Lakewood	310M	80228	1800-1899	
	Lakewood	310R	80228	2200-2299	
ALKIRE PL S	Jefferson Co	371J	80127	7600-7699	
ALKIRE ST	Arvada	220M	80005	7200-8199	
	Arvada	220D	80005	8200-8599	
	Jefferson Co	280M	80401	900-1099	
	Jefferson Co	280H	80401	1500-2299	
	Jefferson Co	280D	80401	2400-2799	
	Jefferson Co	250Z	80401	2800-3199	
	Jefferson Co	250M	80002	5100-5399	
	Jefferson Co	250H	80002	5600-5799	
	Jefferson Co	220D	80005	8600-8799	
	Lakewood	280R	80401	600-799	
	Westminster	190V	80005	8800-9799	
ALKIRE ST S	Jefferson Co	340M	80465	4300-5099	
	Jefferson Co	340V	80127	5100-5899	
	Jefferson Co	370D	80127	6400-7499	
	Jefferson Co	371J	80127	7500-7599	
	Lakewood	280Z	80228	400-599	
	Lakewood	310D	80228	600-1199	
	Lakewood	310M	80228	1800-1899	
	Lakewood	310R	80228	None	
ALKIRE WAY	Jefferson Co	250Z	80401	3200-3499	
ALKIRE WAY S	Lakewood	310R	80228	2200-2299	
ALLEN AVE	Erie	102H	80516	1100-1499	
ALLEN CIR	Park Co	841D	80470	1-199	
ALLEN CT	Erie	102D	80516	1100-1199	
ALLEN DR	Longmont	41A	80503	300-899	
	Douglas Co	467P	80108	3500-3799	
ALLEN ST	Golden	279T	80401	200-399	
ALLEN ST E	Castle Rock	467Q	80108	301-399	O
ALLEN ST W	Castle Rock	467P	80108	1-399	
ALLEN WAY	Castle Rock	467P	80108	None	
ALLENDALE AVE	Parker	440C	80138	None	
ALLENDALE DR	Arvada	251B	80004	10000-11599	
ALLENDALE LN	Jefferson Co	250A	80403	None	
ALLENDALE PL	Jefferson Co	250A	80403	None	
ALLERTON CIR S	Parker	410Y	80138	None	
ALLERTON LN S	Parker	410Y	80138	None	
ALLISON CIR	Wheat Ridge	252T	80033	3800-3899	
ALLISON CIR S	Jefferson Co	372K	80128	7600-7699	
ALLISON CT	Arvada	222J	80005	7800-7899	
	Arvada	222F	80005	8200-8499	
	Jefferson Co	192S	80021	10000-10099	
	Westminster	222A	80021	9000-9099	
	Westminster	192J	80021	10900-10999	
	Wheat Ridge	252T	80033	3500-3799	
ALLISON CT S	Jefferson Co	372B	80123	6500-6699	
	Jefferson Co	372K	80128	7600-7699	
	Jefferson Co	372P	80128	8100-8199	
	Lakewood	312P	80227	2000-2599	
	Lakewood	342B	80235	3900-3999	
ALLISON DR	Westminster	222A	80005	8700-8799	
ALLISON PKWY S	Lakewood	282X	80226	300-499	
ALLISON PL	Arvada	222K	80005	8000-8199	
ALLISON ST	Arvada	252K	80002	4900-5599	
	Arvada	252F	80002	5600-5799	
	Arvada	252B	80004	5800-6199	
	Arvada	222X	80004	6200-6499	
	Arvada	222T	80004	6700-6899	
	Arvada	222K	80005	7700-7899	
	Broomfield	192B	80020	11600-11999	
	Jefferson Co	192P	80021	10000-10099	
	Jefferson Co	192N	80021	10400-10599	
	Lakewood	282T	80226	1-399	
	Lakewood	282P	80226	400-499	
	Lakewood	282P	80214	600-899	
	Lakewood	282K	80214	900-1499	
	Lakewood	282F	80214	1500-2599	
	Westminster	222A	80005	8700-8799	
	Wheat Ridge	252X	80033	3200-3299	
	Wheat Ridge	252T	80033	3500-4099	
	Wheat Ridge	252P	80033	4400-4699	
ALLISON ST S	Jefferson Co	342X	80123	6300-6399	
	Jefferson Co	372B	80123	6400-6599	
	Jefferson Co	372K	80128	7600-7699	
	Jefferson Co	372S	80128	8300-8999	
	Lakewood	282T	80226	1-299	
	Lakewood	312B	80226	900-1099	
	Lakewood	312F	80232	1100-1899	
	Lakewood	312P	80227	2400-2599	
	Lakewood	312T	80227	2600-2699	
	Lakewood	342F	80235	4000-4299	
ALLISON WAY	Arvada	222J	80005	7600-7799	
	Jefferson Co	192S	80021	9600-9799	
ALLISON WAY S	Jefferson Co	372E	80128	6800-7299	
	Lakewood	312P	80227	2300-2499	
	Lakewood	342P	80123	5000-5299	
ALMA LN	Jefferson Co	307X	80439	3400-3499	
ALMA LN	Superior	160Q	80027	1700-1899	
ALMANDINE CT	Castle Rock	467H	80108	7200-7399	
ALMERIA WAY	Longmont	10M	80503	3100-3199	
ALMOND LN	Boulder Co	99F	80301	4600-4699	
ALMSTEAD RD S	Arapahoe Co	791Y	80137	300-799	
	Watkins	811C	80137	800-1099	
ALMSTEAD ST	Adams Co	751L	80642	15100-15999	
ALNWICK WAY	Douglas Co	408D	80134	None	
ALPENGLOW CT	Boulder Co	704X	80503	7100-7299	
ALPENGLOW CT	Jefferson Co	306K	80439	1500-1599	
ALPHA CT	Superior	160P	80027	2300-2399	
ALPINE AVE	Boulder	97Y	80304	200-1999	
ALPINE AVE	Jefferson Co	278U	80401	100-399	

STREET NAME	CITY or COUNTY	MAP GRID	ZIP CODE	BLOCK RANGE	O/E
ALPINE CT	Erie	133C	80516	None	
ALPINE DR	Boulder	98W	80304	2000-2299	
ALPINE DR	Erie	133C	80516	None	
ALPINE DR	Jefferson Co	336D	80439	3800-4199	
ALPINE DR	Nederland	740R	80466	None	
ALPINE DR N	Douglas Co	440R	80134	6300-7299	
	Douglas Co	441N	80134	7300-7399	
ALPINE DR S	Jefferson Co	306W	80439	3000-3099	
ALPINE LN	Jefferson Co	305Y	80439	32900-33299	
ALPINE PL	Longmont	42B	80501	1-99	
ALPINE ST	Longmont	42B	80501	200-899	
	Longmont	12X	80501	900-1699	
	Longmont	12N	80501	1700-2099	
	Longmont	12K	80501	2300-2499	
ALPINE WAY	Boulder Co	722V	80304	1-499	
ALPINE WAY	Clear Creek Co	780A	80452	1-999	
ALPINE ASTER DR	Parker	409S	80134	None	
ALPINE MEADOW RD	Jefferson Co	368X	80465	22200-22299	
ALP LILY PL	Brighton	140J	80601	None	
ALPS HILL RD	Gilpin Co	780F	80403	None	
ALSAB TRAIL	Jefferson Co	366V	80439	8000-8399	
ALSACE WAY	Lafayette	132A	80026	1000-1299	
ALTA DR	Broomfield	162V	80020	800-898	E
ALTA DR	Jefferson Co	368U	80465	21200-21699	
ALTA ST	Lochbuie	139D	80603	None	
ALTA ST	Longmont	11Y	80501	900-1099	
ALTAIR DR	Highlands Ranch	376U	80124	600-899	
ALTAMIRA DR	Lochbuie	729Y	80603	None	
ALTA SIERRA WAY	Castle Rock	468X	80104	None	
ALTA VISTA DR	Arvada	222W	80004	8400-8799	
ALTA VISTA DR	Jefferson Co	275X	80439	32700-33999	
ALTER ST	Broomfield	162W	80020	100-199	
	Broomfield	162S	80020	200-599	
	Broomfield	162N	80020	600-699	
ALTER WAY	Broomfield	162N	80020	1100-1199	
ALTHEA CIR E	Parker	409A	80134	17400-17599	
ALTON CT	Denver	256Z	80238	2900-2999	
ALTON CT	Denver	256Z	80238	None	
ALTON CT S	Arapahoe Co	316H	80247	1100-1399	
	Arapahoe Co	316M	80231	2000-2099	
	Centennial	376M	80112	7400-7499	
	Denver	316V	80231	3000-3199	
ALTON PL S	Greenwood Village	346H	80111	4200-4399	
ALTON ST	Adams Co	136R	80602	15901-15999	O
	Aurora	286R	80010	1100-1399	
	Aurora	286H	80010	1500-1999	
	Denver	256Z	80238	2600-2899	
	Denver	256V	80238	None	
	Denver	286D	80220	None	
ALTON ST S	Arapahoe Co	316H	80247	1101-1199	O
	Denver	316Z	80231	3300-3399	
	Greenwood Village	346H	80111	4200-4599	
ALTON WAY	Adams Co	196V	80640	9700-9898	E
	Aurora	286R	80230	500-1099	
	Denver	287N	80230	None	
	Greenwood Village	346H	80111	4300-4399	
ALTON WAY S	Arapahoe Co	316R	80231	2000-2299	
	Centennial	376H	80112	7000-7399	
	Denver	286Z	80247	600-699	
	Denver	316D	80247	700-799	
	Greenwood Village	346R	80111	5100-5199	
	Greenwood Village	346Z	80111	6000-6199	
ALTURA BLVD	Aurora	288F	80011	1500-2599	
ALTURA CT S	Aurora	288T	80012	1-199	
ALTURA ST	Commerce City	198B	80603	11800-11899	
	Commerce City	198P	80022	None	
	Denver	258K	80239	4700-4999	
	Denver	258G	80239	5200-5599	
ALVA CT	Erie	103N	80516	None	
ALVIN DR	Northglenn	194M	80233	10900-10999	
ALVIN PL	Jefferson Co	822Y	80433	12000-12099	
ALYESKA CT	Jefferson Co	306E	80439	1400-1499	
ALYS PL W	Denver	314A	80223	1200-1499	
	Denver	313D	80223	2100-2199	
ALYSSUM DR	Brighton	139K	80601	100-299	
ALYSSUM WAY S	Parker	409R	80134	9400-9599	
ALZERE PL	Douglas Co	378Z	80134	None	
AMANDA CT	El Paso Co	909R	80908	20000-20499	
AMANDA CT	Elizabeth	871E	80107	300-499	
AMANDA PINES DR	Elbert Co	830Q	80138	1-1199	
AMANDA RANCH LN	Elbert Co	830R	80138	1200-1299	
AMARANTH	Jefferson Co	370K	80127	1-99	
AMARO DR S	Jefferson Co	337J	80439	4800-4999	
AMBER CT	Castle Rock	467M	80108	1500-1599	
	Erie	102P	80516	2000-2199	
AMBER PL	Boulder	98J	80304	4100-4199	
AMBER ST	Boulder	98J	80304	4100-4299	
AMBERGATE CT	El Paso Co	909S	80132	1300-1399	
AMBER RIDGE DR	Castle Pines North	436E	80108	5600-5999	
AMBER RIDGE PL	Castle Pines North	436E	80108	5700-5799	
AMBER ROCK CT	Douglas Co	408D	80134	16000-16199	
AMBER ROCK DR	Douglas Co	408H	80134	9800-9899	
AMBER RUN	Broomfield	134F	80516	None	
AMBERSTONE WAY	Douglas Co	408H	80134	16400-16999	
AMBER SUN CIR	Castle Rock	498B	80108	3400-3899	
AMBER SUN CT	Castle Rock	498B	80108	1900-1999	
AMBER VALLEY LN N	Douglas Co	381S	80138	13400-13699	
AMBERWOOD LN	Jefferson Co	370J	80127	1-99	
AMBROSE ST	Erie	103N	80516	None	
AMBROSIA ST	Castle Rock	466V	80109	None	
AMBUSH ROCK	Douglas Co	432N	80125	10900-10999	
AMERICAN WAY	Douglas Co	378T	80112	8800-8898	E
AMERICANA RD	Longmont	12T	80501	500-799	
AMERIND SPRINGS TRAIL					
	Jefferson Co	842R	80470	28500-29199	
AMES CIR S	Lakewood	312R	80227	2400-2599	
AMES CT	Denver	282M	80214	1000-1099	
	Lakewood	282H	80214	1600-1699	
	Westminster	192D	80020	None	
AMES CT S	Jefferson Co	342Z	80123	6100-6299	
	Jefferson Co	372M	80128	7400-7499	
	Jefferson Co	372D	80123	None	
AMES ST	Arvada	252D	80003	6000-6199	
	Arvada	222V	80003	6700-6799	
	Arvada	222H	80003	8400-8599	
	Denver	252M	80212	4800-4899	
	Edgewater	282D	80214	2000-2599	
	Lakewood	282V	80226	1-99	

Continued on next column

STREET NAME	CITY or COUNTY	MAP GRID	ZIP CODE	BLOCK RANGE	O/E
AMES ST (Cont'd)	Lakewood	282R	80226	300-599	
	Lakewood	282M	80214	1100-1599	
	Mountain View	252V	80212	4100-4399	
	Westminster	222R	80003	7400-7599	
	Westminster	192V	80031	None	
	Wheat Ridge	282D	80214	2600-2799	
	Wheat Ridge	252Z	80212	2800-3199	
	Wheat Ridge	252Z	80212	3200-3799	
	Wheat Ridge	252V	80212	4000-4099	
AMES ST S	Denver	342D	80235	3700-3899	
	Jefferson Co	342V	80123	5900-5999	
	Jefferson Co	372D	80123	None	
	Lakewood	282V	80226	1-199	
	Lakewood	282Z	80226	300-599	
	Lakewood	312D	80226	900-1099	
	Lakewood	312H	80232	1200-1699	
AMES WAY	Arvada	222V	80003	6800-6899	
	Arvada	222H	80003	8100-8399	
	Denver	252M	80212	5000-5099	
AMES WAY S	Denver	312V	80227	2700-2799	
	Denver	342D	80235	3900-3999	
	Jefferson Co	372M	80128	7500-7799	
	Lakewood	312V	80227	2600-2699	
AMESBURY ST	Broomfield	162R	80020	1-99	
AMESBURY WAY	Highlands Ranch	405P	80126	10600-10799	
AMETHYST DR	Longmont	41U	80504	1900-2199	
AMETHYST WAY	Douglas Co	409E	80134	10100-10299	
AMETHYST WAY	Superior	160X	80027	300-399	
AMHERST AVE E	Arapahoe Co	316S	80222	5600-5699	
	Aurora	317V	80014	13000-13299	
	Aurora	319S	80013	16800-16899	
	Aurora	319T	80013	17800-17999	
	Aurora	319U	80013	18400-18999	
	Denver	314V	80210	1201-1599	O
	Denver	314V	80210	1600-1699	
	Denver	315S	80210	1700-2399	
	Denver	315T	80210	2700-3099	
	Denver	315U	80210	3700-3999	
	Denver	315U	80222	4000-4399	
	Denver	315V	80222	4600-4799	
	Denver	316S	80222	5500-5599	
	Denver	316T	80224	6500-6799	
	Denver	316U	80231	7500-8099	
	Englewood	314U	80113	100-1199	
	Englewood	314V	80113	1200-1598	E
AMHERST AVE W	Denver	313S	80236	2400-5199	
	Denver	312V	80227	5200-5599	
	Denver	312U	80227	6400-6899	
	Denver	312T	80227	7500-7599	
	Englewood	314T	80110	1-499	
	Englewood	313V	80110	2001-2199	O
	Lakewood	310U	80228	14000-14099	
	Lakewood	310U	80228	14100-14199	
AMHERST CIR E	Arapahoe Co	316V	80231	8300-8599	
	Aurora	317V	80014	12100-12599	
	Aurora	317U	80014	11400N-11599N	
	Denver	314V	80210	1301-1399	O
AMHERST CT E	Aurora	317U	80014	11300-11399	
	Highlands Ranch	406B	80130	6700-6899	
AMHERST CT W	Lakewood	310U	80228	14000-14099	
AMHERST DR	Longmont	11S	80503	1500-1699	
AMHERST DR E	Aurora	319S	80013	16900-17199	
	Aurora	319T	80013	18100-18499	
	Aurora	319U	80013	19100-19199	
	Aurora	319V	80013	19200-19999	
	Denver	316V	80231	8600-9199	
AMHERST DR W	Lakewood	310V	80228	13800-13899	
AMHERST PKWY E	Englewood	314V	80110	None	
AMHERST PL E	Aurora	317U	80014	12000-12099	
	Aurora	318U	80013	15700-15799	
	Aurora	319T	80013	17600-17699	
	Aurora	320S	80013	None	
	Englewood	314U	80113	500-799	
AMHERST PL W	Lakewood	310R	80228	13500-13599	
	Lakewood	310V	80228	13600-13699	
	Lakewood	310U	80228	14000-14099	
	Lakewood	310T	80228	14500-14699	
AMHERST ST	Superior	160M	80027	1200-1599	
AMHERST ST S	Castle Rock	498L	80104	1-299	
AMHERST WAY	Superior	160L	80027	1100-1299	
AMHERST WAY W	Lakewood	310R	80228	13700-13899	
AMHURST WAY E	Aurora	318V	80013	16200-16599	
AMISON CIR	Douglas Co	378Z	80134	9300-9399	
AMISON WAY	Douglas Co	378Z	80134	None	
AMMONS CIR	Arvada	222E	80005	8200-8299	
	Jefferson Co	192S	80021	9900-9999	
AMMONS CIR S	Lakewood	312B	80226	None	
AMMONS CT	Wheat Ridge	252W	80033	3200-3299	
AMMONS CT S	Jefferson Co	372A	80123	6500-6699	
	Jefferson Co	372E	80128	7100-7199	
	Jefferson Co	372J	80128	7600-7699	
	Jefferson Co	372N	80128	8000-8299	
AMMONS DR	Arvada	222W	80004	6200-6299	
AMMONS ST	Arvada	252E	80002	5600-5799	
	Arvada	252A	80004	6000-6199	
	Arvada	222W	80004	6400-6499	
	Arvada	222S	80004	6700-7199	
	Jefferson Co	192N	80021	10400-10499	
	Lakewood	282S	80226	1-399	
	Lakewood	282N	80226	400-499	
	Lakewood	282N	80214	600-699	
	Lakewood	282J	80214	1000-1499	
	Westminster	192W	80021	9100-9199	
	Westminster	192J	80021	10900-10999	
	Wheat Ridge	252S	80033	3800-4099	
	Wheat Ridge	252N	80033	4100-4399	
AMMONS ST S	Denver	342F	80123	4300-4499	
	Denver	342J	80123	4800-4999	
	Jefferson Co	342B	80235	3500-3599	
	Jefferson Co	372E	80128	6900-7099	
	Jefferson Co	372P	80128	8000-8099	
	Jefferson Co	372S	80128	8300-8999	
	Lakewood	282S	80226	1-299	
	Lakewood	312F	80232	1100-1299	
	Lakewood	312K	80232	1300-1899	
	Lakewood	312P	80227	2100-2499	
	Lakewood	312X	80227	3100-3499	
	Lakewood	312B	80226	None	

STREET NAME	CITY or COUNTY	MAP GRID	ZIP CODE	BLOCK RANGE	O/E
AMMONS WAY	Arvada	222E	80005	8000-8199	
	Lakewood	282N	80214	600-699	
	Westminster	192W	80021	9100-9199	
AMMONS WAY S	Lakewood	312T	80227	2600-2699	
	Lakewood	342W	80123	6100-6199	
AMSTON LN	Douglas Co	407G	80134	11800-11899	
AMSTON PL	Douglas Co	407G	80134	11700-11999	
AMSTON ST	Douglas Co	407G	80134	10000-10199	
AMUR CT	Castle Rock	469J	80108	6400-6499	
AMUR LN	Castle Rock	469J	80108	6500-6698	E
AMY CIR	Jefferson Co	843E	80433	26000-26199	
AMY CT	El Paso Co	909R	80908	20100-20199	
AMYVALE CT	Castle Rock	466X	80109	2800-2899	
ANACONDA CT	Douglas Co	436X	80108	800-999	
ANACONDA DR	Douglas Co	436X	80108	900-1099	
ANAHEIM CT	Denver	258N	80239	4400-4699	
ANAHEIM CT S	Aurora	348K	80015	4700-4899	
ANAHEIM ST S	Aurora	318P	80014	2500-2699	
ANAHEIM WAY	Denver	258E	80239	5500-5599	
ANAHINA RD	Jefferson Co	338P	80454	5300-5399	
ANASAZI CT	Boulder	128R	80303	4600-4699	
ANASAZI WAY	Jefferson Co	308B	80401	21900-22699	
ANASAZI INDIAN PL S					
	Highlands Ranch	374W	80129	1600-1699	
ANASAZI INDIAN WAY S					
	Highlands Ranch	374W	80129	9100-9199	
ANASAZI INDIAN TRAIL S					
	Highlands Ranch	374W	80129	9100-9299	
ANCE ST	Adams Co	794P	80136	1800-2099	
ANCHOR DR	Boulder Co	71D	80504	7800-8199	
ANCHOR PL	Lafayette	131K	80026	1600-1699	
ANCHORAGE CT	Longmont	12W	80501	1-99	
ANDEE WAY S	Highlands Ranch	406K	80130	10200-10299	
ANDERSON AVE	Douglas Co	870T	80116	10500-11999	
ANDERSON AVE	Jamestown	722A	80455	None	
ANDERSON CT	Erie	103J	80516	200-399	
ANDERSON RD	Park Co	820Z	80421	1-399	
ANDERSON ST	Adams Co	791N	80137	1900-1999	
ANDERSON ST	Castle Rock	497L	80104	300-599	
	Castle Rock	497G	80104	600-799	
ANDERSON ST	Erie	103J	80516	100-399	
ANDERSON ST	Thornton	195X	80229	9200-9399	
ANDES CIR S	Arapahoe Co	349Y	80016	6000-6099	
	Aurora	319L	80017	1500-1799	
	Aurora	319Q	80013	2400-2599	
	Centennial	379G	80016	6900-7199	
ANDES CT	Denver	259Q	80249	4000-4199	
	Denver	259P	80249	4200-4499	
ANDES CT	Denver	259L	80249	None	
ANDES CT S	Arapahoe Co	349Y	80016	6000-6099	
	Aurora	349C	80013	3600-3699	
	Centennial	349P	80015	5200-5299	
	Centennial	379F	80016	7200-7299	
ANDES PL S	Centennial	379C	80016	6300-6599	
ANDES ST	Adams Co	169X	80022	12000-12099	
	Aurora	289F	80011	1600-1999	
	Denver	259L	80249	4200-4799	
ANDES ST S	Arapahoe Co	349U	80015	5600-5799	
	Aurora	319F	80017	1300-1399	
	Aurora	319Y	80013	3000-3299	
	Aurora	319Y	80013	3300-3399	
	Aurora	349G	80013	4100-4299	
	Centennial	349P	80015	5100-5199	
ANDES WAY	Aurora	289B	80011	None	
	Denver	259Q	80249	4000-4699	
ANDES WAY S	Aurora	319G	80017	1400-1499	
	Aurora	319K	80017	1700-1899	
	Aurora	319U	80013	2900-3099	
	Aurora	349C	80013	3600-3899	
	Aurora	349F	80013	4100-4299	
	Aurora	349G	80015	4300-4499	
ANDIRON WAY	Douglas Co	907B	80118	13000-13299	
ANDOVER AVE	Castle Rock	498L	80104	4300-4699	
ANDREA CIR	Elbert Co	830Q	80138	200-499	
ANDREA LN	Jefferson Co	368H	80465	7000-7399	
ANDREA PL	Elbert Co	850D	80138	1700-2199	
ANDREW CT	Longmont	42A	80501	200-299	
ANDREW DR	Dacono	727J	80514	100-199	
ANDREW DR	Superior	160P	80027	2100-2599	
ANDREW ST	Dacono	727J	80514	700-799	
ANDREW WAY	Superior	160P	80027	300-499	
ANDREW ALDEN ST	Longmont	41U	80504	1900-2199	
ANDREWS DR	Denver	257M	80239	12100-13099	
	Denver	258J	80239	13100-15599	
ANDREWS PL	Denver	259R	80249	20100-20399	
ANDREWS RD	Douglas Co	888X	80118	12500-12999	
	Douglas Co	908F	80118	13000-15999	
ANDREWS WAY	Boulder Co	130E	80303	7600-7899	
ANDRIST LN	Park Co	841J	80421	1-99	
ANDROMEDA LN	Castle Rock	467G	80108	None	
ANDROMEDA WAY	Castle Rock	467G	80108	None	
ANDRUS RD	Boulder Co	99P	80301	6100-6299	
ANDRUSH CT	Lone Tree	406G	80124	10000-10099	
ANEMONE DR	Boulder Co	722Z	80302	1-299	
ANGELA LN	Parker	379T	80134	8500-8599	
ANGELHOLM RD	El Paso Co	910P	80908	7000-7799	
ANGELICA DR	Parker	408U	80134	15400-15699	
ANGELIQUE AVE	Castle Rock	469J	80108	6600-6798	E
ANGELOVIC CT	Boulder Co	98K	80301	3800-3899	
ANGEL VIEW DR	Frederick	727F	80530	7900-7999	
ANGIE CT	Douglas Co	440Y	80134	5700-5999	
ANGUS WAY W	Highlands Ranch	404F	80129	400-499	
ANHAWA AVE	Boulder Co	11E	80503	9200-9499	
	Boulder Co	10M	80503	12600-12999	
ANIMAS WAY	Superior	160Y	80027	3800-3899	
ANN CT	Elbert Co	851E	80138	41200-41399	
ANN PL	Platteville	708C	80651	None	
ANNA CIR	Jefferson Co	365J	80439	34800-35099	
ANNA LN	Jefferson Co	307W	80439	3400-3499	
ANNABAR DR	Castle Rock	467Q	80108	1000-1199	
ANNADALE TRAIL	Elbert Co	851C	80107	None	
ANNAPURNA DR	Jefferson Co	337X	80439	5900-6399	
	Jefferson Co	367B	80439	6400-6699	
ANNA THOMAS PKWY	Lafayette	131G	80026	None	
ANNE PL	Weld Co	103B	80516	4600-4799	
ANNEX LN	Park Co	841P	80421	None	
ANNIE CIR	Elbert Co	871B	80107	34700-34999	

STREET NAME	CITY or COUNTY	MAP GRID	ZIP CODE	BLOCK RANGE	O/E
ANNIE PL W	Denver	283E	80204	5000-5199	
ANNIES PL	Douglas Co	528N	80104	2500-2699	
ANNIVERSARY LN	Longmont	11V	80501	1-199	
ANTARES DR	Highlands Ranch	376U	80124	13400-13599	
ANTELOPE CIR	Elbert Co	871N	80107	2200-3499	
ANTELOPE CT	Elbert Co	871G	80107	33500-33599	
ANTELOPE CT	Lafayette	131Z	80026	2800-2899	
ANTELOPE DR	Arapahoe Co	832G	80137	44500-44599	
ANTELOPE DR	Bennett	793Y	80102	500E-599E	
	Bennett	793X	80102	300W-49699W	
ANTELOPE DR	Jefferson Co	370Z	80127	12800-12999	
ANTELOPE DR N	Arapahoe Co	794S	80136	800-1099	
ANTELOPE LN N	Douglas Co	410K	80138	11300-11599	
ANTELOPE PL	Douglas Co	468R	80108	4500-4699	
ANTELOPE WAY	Frederick	726F	80516	None	
ANTELOPE CROSSING	Lafayette	131Z	80026	400-499	
ANTELOPE HILLS BLVD	Bennett	793X	80102	600-698	E
ANTELOPE PT	Lafayette	131Z	80026	200-299	
ANTELOPE RIDGE TRAIL	Elbert Co	831J	80138	2300-2599	
ANTELOPE RUN	Elbert Co	850U	80107	200-499	
ANTELOPE RUN CT	Castle Rock	466T	80109	4300-4599	
ANTELOPE TRAIL	Elbert Co	891Y	80106	4000-5299	
ANTELOPE TRAIL	Thornton	195Q	80229	None	
ANTELOPE TRAIL N	Douglas Co	410B	80138	12000-12999	
ANTERO CIR	Broomfield	133J	80020	None	
ANTERO CT	Jefferson Co	249B	80403	5800-5999	
ANTERO DR	Longmont	12S	80501	1700-1899	
ANTERO RD	Thornton	194S	80260	None	
ANTERO ST	Broomfield	133J	80020	None	
ANTERO ST	Golden	279P	80401	400-499	
ANTERO PEAK CIR	Douglas Co	436Y	80108	None	
ANTHEM DR E	Parker	439F	80134	17700-17799	
ANTHEM RANCH RD	Broomfield	133N	80020	None	
ANTIOCH	Thornton	224A	80260	None	
ANTLER CT	Jefferson Co	370K	80127	1-99	
ANTLER DR	Boulder Co	722H	80302	1-699	
ANTLER LN	Gilpin Co	762W	80403	1-399	
ANTLER WAY	Clear Creek Co	335E	80439	1-199	
ANTLER NORTH CIR	Elbert Co	832S	80107	45000-45099	
ANTLER RUN	Douglas Co	845Q	80125	5400-5499	
ANTLERS ST	Broomfield	163K	80020	13400-13499	
ANTLER SOUTH CIR	Elbert Co	832S	80107	45000-45099	
ANTLER TRAIL	Jefferson Co	824X	80127	11600-12099	
ANTON CT	Parker	409J	80134	17600-17699	
ANVIL CT	Jefferson Co	249B	80403	5900-5999	
ANVIL WAY	Golden	279P	80401	400-499	
ANVIL HORN	Jefferson Co	371K	80127	7500-7599	
APACHE CIR	Palmer Lake	907R	80133	None	
APACHE CT	Adams Co	226B	80022	None	
APACHE CT	Boulder	128L	80303	3900E-3999E	
	Boulder	128L	80303	3800W-3899W	
	Boulder Co	70R	80503	6600-6699	
APACHE CT	Douglas Co	886G	80118	6500-6699	
APACHE DR	Douglas Co	886G	80118	5900-6599	
	Parker	409K	80134	18200-18399	
APACHE DR S	Littleton	374B	80120	6600-6699	
APACHE LN	Lafayette	131G	80026	2000-2098	E
APACHE PL	Douglas Co	886G	80118	6600-6699	
APACHE PL	Lochbuie	140F	80603	200-399	
APACHE PL E	Arapahoe Co	794T	80136	55300-56299	
APACHE RD	Boulder	128K	80303	4000-4699	
APACHE RD	Clear Creek Co	365N	80439	1-599	
APACHE RD	Weld Co	707Y	80504	9000-9499	
APACHE RD N	Douglas Co	411Y	80138	9200-9499	
APACHE ST	Kiowa	872M	80117	400-499	
APACHE ST S	Littleton	374F	80120	6700-7199	
APACHE WAY	Douglas Co	846T	80135	6600-7499	
APACHE CREEK CT	Castle Rock	466P	80109	5200-5299	
APACHE CREEK RD	Castle Rock	466P	80109	4900-5299	
APACHE PLUME CT	Brighton	140N	80601	None	
APACHE PLUME DR	Parker	379S	80134	8500-9099	
APACHE PLUME PL	Brighton	140N	80601	5500-5599	
APACHE PLUME ST	Brighton	140J	80601	1-199	
APACHE SPRING DR	Jefferson Co	822R	80433	9900-10199	
APACHE TRAIL	Jefferson Co	822Z	80433	11500-11999	
APALOOSA TRAIL	Elbert Co	870D	80107	1700-2299	
APELLES CIR	Lafayette	131Q	80026	1700-1799	
APEX CIR	Jefferson Co	336Z	80439	27800-27899	
APEX LN	Westminster	223E	80031	4300-4399	
APEX RD	Douglas Co	870K	80116	10500-11999	
APEX RD	Gilpin Co	760X	80452	None	
	Gilpin Co	760Y	80403	None	
APISHAMORE CT	Parker	408R	80134	10600-10699	
APOLLO CT	Highlands Ranch	376U	80124	500-599	
APOLLO DR	Boulder Co	130S	80303	400-599	
APOLLO DR	Gilpin Co	761J	80403	1-299	
APOLLO DR	Lafayette	131Q	80026	1200-1299	
APOLLO BAY DR E	Highlands Ranch	405H	80130	4800-4999	
APOLLO BAY WAY S	Highlands Ranch	405H	80130	9900-10099	
APPALOOSA AVE	Weld Co	729V	80603	2200-3099	
APPALOOSA CT	Parker	408M	80134	10700-10799	
APPALOOSA DR	Jefferson Co	306X	80439	29900-30599	
APPALOOSA PL	Broomfield	162D	80020	12400-12799	
APPALOOSA RD	El Paso Co	909S	80132	17700-18499	
APPALOOSA RD	Jefferson Co	306X	80439	3100-3299	
APPLE CT	Boulder Co	98F	80301	4300-4399	
APPLE CT	Longmont	41B	80501	800-899	
APPLE CT	Louisville	160C	80027	700-799	
APPLE WAY	Boulder Co	98F	80301	4300-4699	
APPLE BARREL AVE	Longmont	42N	80501	None	
APPLEBLOSSOM DR E					
	Highlands Ranch	404C	80126	900-1199	
APPLEBLOSSOM LN	Westminster	223K	80030	3100-7999	
APPLEBROOK CIR	Highlands Ranch	405M	80130	None	
APPLEBROOK LN	Highlands Ranch	405M	80130	None	
APPLEBY PL	Castle Rock	497U	80104	700-899	
APPLEBY ST	Park Co	820Z	80421	1-599	
APPLECREST CIR	Castle Rock	466X	80109	4300-4699	
APPLEFIELD CIR	Elbert Co	851F	80107	40900-40999	
APPLE FIELD CIR	Elbert Co	851F	80138	41400-41499	
APPLETON CIR E	Centennial	376B	80112	6800-7299	
APPLETON CT	Brighton	138U	80601	1500-1599	
APPLETON WAY	Castle Rock	498Q	80104	5100-5299	
APPLE TREE CT	Boulder	97H	80304	None	
APPLETREE PL	Highlands Ranch	374V	80126	8700-8799	
APPLETREE PL	Thornton	194S	80260	9700-9999	
APPLEWOOD AVE	Fort Lupton	728H	80621	1000-1199	
APPLEWOOD AVE E	Centennial	344Z	80121	800-999	

STREET NAME	CITY or COUNTY	MAP GRID	ZIP CODE	BLOCK RANGE	O/E
APPLEWOOD CT	Boulder	99E	80301	4400-4499	
APPLEWOOD CT	Broomfield	163X	80020	12100-12199	
APPLEWOOD CT	Parker	409M	80138	19600-19899	
APPLEWOOD DR	Boulder Co	130H	80026	700-999	
APPLEWOOD DR	Lakewood	280H	80215	1800-2199	
APPLEWOOD DR E	Douglas Co	411K	80138	10000-10399	
APPLEWOOD LN	Adams Co	223M	80221	7700-7899	
	Thornton	194S	80260	None	
APPLEWOOD PL E	Aurora	351Y	80016	26100-26199	
APPLEWOOD KNOLLS DR W					
	Lakewood	251W	80215	11200-11699	
APPLEWOOD RIDGE RD	Jefferson Co	280C	80401	14400-14599	
APRICOT CT	Boulder	98E	80304	None	
APRICOT PL	Erie	133F	80516	None	
APRICOT WAY	Castle Rock	497T	80104	100-199	
APRILS WAY	Parker	379X	80134	17900-18199	
APSEN DR	Bow Mar	343N	80123	5000-5299	
AQUA CT	Broomfield	162Q	80020	1-99	
AQUAMARINE CT	Castle Rock	467M	80108	1800-1999	
AQUAMARINE DR	Lochbuie	140E	80603	1600-1699	
	Lochbuie	139H	80603	1700-1799	
AQUAMARINE WAY	Castle Rock	467M	80108	1600-1899	
AQUARIUS CT	Highlands Ranch	376U	80124	300-399	
AQUEDUCT AVE W	Jefferson Co	340R	80127	12800-13099	
	Littleton	343P	80123	3300-3399	
AQUEDUCT DR W	Jefferson Co	341T	80127	10900-12799	
AQUEDUCT LN W	Jefferson Co	341P	80127	10900-11199	
AQUEDUCT PL W	Jefferson Co	341U	80123	9800-9899	
ARABELLA DR	Castle Rock	469K	80108	6100-6598	E
ARABIAN AVE	Weld Co	729V	80603	2600-3099	
ARABIAN DR	Boulder Co	723B	80302	None	
ARABIAN PL	Columbine Valley	373B	80123	1-99	
ARABIAN WAY	El Paso Co	909W	80132	2400-2499	
ARABIAN TRAIL	Elbert Co	870D	80107	1400-2399	
ARAL CT	Longmont	12L	80501	None	
ARAL DR	Longmont	12L	80501	None	
ARAPAHO RD E	Aurora	830A	80016	24700-24899	
ARAPAHO ST	Adams Co	794P	80136	1600-1799	
ARAPAHOE AVE	Boulder	127C	80302	1-1699	
	Boulder	128C	80302	1700-2799	
	Boulder	128B	80303	2800-5299	
ARAPAHOE CIR	Louisville	130T	80027	900-1099	
ARAPAHOE CT	Louisville	130T	80027	900-999	
ARAPAHOE CT E	Centennial	376C	80112	7800-8099	
ARAPAHOE CT N	Douglas Co	440U	80134	6300-6399	
ARAPAHOE CT W	Littleton	373D	80120	2400-2499	
ARAPAHOE DR	Douglas Co	846A	80125	None	
ARAPAHOE DR	El Paso Co	908Z	80132	600-799	
ARAPAHOE DR	Jefferson Co	365D	80439	6300-6699	
	Jefferson Co	250N	80403	15200-15599	
ARAPAHOE DR	Longmont	41B	80501	1800-1999	
ARAPAHOE DR S	Littleton	373D	80120	6600-6699	
	Littleton	374B	80120	6700-6799	
ARAPAHOE LN W	Boulder	127C	80302	300-399	
ARAPAHOE PKWY E	Aurora	381F	80016	25901-25999	O
ARAPAHOE PL E	Aurora	381A	80016	24200-24399	
	Aurora	381C	80016	26500-26599	
	Centennial	375B	80122	3400-3599	
	Centennial	375C	80122	4200-4699	
ARAPAHOE RD	Boulder Co	129C	80303	6000-7299	
	Boulder Co	130B	80303	7300-9499	
	Boulder Co	131C	80026	9500-10699	
	Boulder Co	132B	80026	11500-12299	
	Erie	132B	80026	12300-12599	
	Lafayette	132B	80026	10900-11499	
ARAPAHOE RD E	Arapahoe Co	374C	80122	1-1799	
	Arapahoe Co	376B	80112	7800-9299	
	Arapahoe Co	379B	80016	16901-18499	O
	Aurora	378A	80112	14000-15199	
	Aurora	378A	80016	15200-16199	
	Aurora	380B	80016	19400-24899	
	Aurora	381E	80016	24900-25799	
	Aurora	381G	80016	None	
	Centennial	375B	80122	1700-5599	
	Centennial	376B	80112	5600-7799	
	Centennial	377B	80112	9800-12499	
	Centennial	378A	80112	13000-13999	
	Centennial	379B	80016	16700-20499	
	Foxfield	378A	80016	16200-16699	
	Foxfield	379B	80016	16900-18498	E
	Greenwood Village	377B	80112	9200-9799	
ARAPAHOE RD W	Littleton	374A	80120	800-1399	
	Littleton	373D	80120	1900-2299	
ARAPAHOE ST	Bennett	793J	80102	None	
ARAPAHOE ST	Denver	284E	80204	1200-1399	
	Denver	284F	80202	1400-1999	
	Denver	284B	80205	2000-2499	
	Denver	254Y	80205	2500-3499	
ARAPAHOE ST	Golden	248Z	80403	100-699	
	Golden	249W	80401	700-999	
	Golden	279A	80401	1100-1799	
	Golden	279F	80401	1800-2399	
ARAPAHOE ST	Kiowa	872M	80117	400-499	
ARAPAHOE WAY S	Littleton	373D	80120	6400-6799	
ARAVON CT	Lone Tree	406G	80124	7800-7899	
ARBOL CT	Boulder Co	98K	80301	3800-3999	
ARBOL ST	Lochbuie	139D	80603	None	
ARBOR AVE W	Jefferson Co	342Y	80123	6100-6599	
	Jefferson Co	342W	80123	8600-8999	
	Jefferson Co	341Z	80123	9000-9299	
	Littleton	344X	80123	500-799	
	Littleton	343Z	80120	2000-2199	
ARBOR CIR E	Greenwood Village	346Z	80111	9100-9299	
ARBOR DR	Lafayette	131H	80026	400-599	
ARBOR DR E	Arapahoe Co	347W	80111	9300-9499	
	Aurora	350X	80016	22000-22099	
	Aurora	351Y	80016	26400-26899	
	Aurora	351X	80016	None	
	Greenwood Village	346Z	80111	None	
ARBOR DR W	Jefferson Co	342Y	80123	6400-6799	
	Jefferson Co	342W	80123	8800-9099	
	Jefferson Co	341X	80127	11100-11299	
ARBOR PL E	Arapahoe Co	347W	80111	9500-9699	
	Aurora	351X	80016	None	
ARBOR PL W	Jefferson Co	342W	80123	8500-8599	
	Jefferson Co	341Z	80123	9200-9399	
	Jefferson Co	341Y	80127	10000-10199	
	Jefferson Co	341W	80127	12400-12499	
	Littleton	343Z	80120	2000-2199	

STREET NAME	CITY or COUNTY	MAP GRID	ZIP CODE	BLOCK RANGE	O/E
ARBOR GLEN PL	Boulder	98J	80304	2700-2799	
ARBUTUS CIR S	Jefferson Co	370D	80127	6500-6699	
ARBUTUS CT	Arvada	220Z	80004	6500-6699	
	Arvada	220R	80005	7300-7499	
	Jefferson Co	280R	80401	800-999	
	Jefferson Co	280G	80401	1500-1599	
ARBUTUS CT S	Lakewood	310M	80228	1800-1899	
	Lakewood	310R	80228	2200-2299	
ARBUTUS DR	Lakewood	280V	80401	None	
ARBUTUS PL S	Lakewood	310H	80228	1400-1699	
ARBUTUS ST	Arvada	220Z	80004	6400-6499	
	Arvada	220V	80004	6600-7199	
	Arvada	220H	80005	8300-8499	
	Jefferson Co	280M	80401	1500-1599	
	Jefferson Co	280H	80401	1700-1799	
	Jefferson Co	250Z	80401	3200-3299	
	Jefferson Co	250M	80002	5100-5399	
	Lakewood	280R	80401	600-799	
ARBUTUS ST S	Jefferson Co	340M	80465	4800-5099	
	Lakewood	310D	80228	600-1199	
	Lakewood	310M	80228	1800-1899	
ARBUTUS WAY S	Jefferson Co	340H	80465	4300-4499	
ARCADIA CT	Castle Rock	497Q	80104	None	
ARCADIA RD	Park Co	841P	80421	1-299	
ARCARO CREEK CT S	Parker	439C	80134	12400-12499	
ARCARO CREEK PL E	Parker	439C	80134	19400-19499	
ARCHER AVE E	Aurora	291T	80018	None	
	Aurora	291U	80018	None	
ARCHER AVE W	Jefferson Co	280U	80401	14300-14599	
	Jefferson Co	279V	80401	16500-16799	
ARCHER CIR E	Aurora	288U	80012	14900-15099	
	Aurora	291T	80018	None	
ARCHER DR W	Jefferson Co	280T	80401	15100-15499	
ARCHER PL E	Arapahoe Co	290V	80018	23700-23999	
	Aurora	287U	80012	11800-12099	
	Aurora	288U	80012	15100-15199	
ARCHER PL E	Aurora	291T	80018	None	
	Denver	286U	80230	7300-7899	
ARCHER PL W	Denver	284T	80223	1-499	
	Denver	283U	80219	2500-2999	
	Jefferson Co	280T	80401	15100-15299	
	Lakewood	282U	80226	6800-6999	
	Lakewood	282T	80226	7200-7399	
ARCHER ST	Golden	249W	80401	1000-1099	
ARCHERS DR	El Paso Co	908V	80132	18000-19099	
ARCHES PL	Castle Rock	496B	80109	4400-4599	
ARCO IRIS LN	Castle Pines North	436B	80108	7200-7499	
ARDEN CIR E	Highlands Ranch	404C	80126	400-599	
ARDLET RD	Jefferson Co	823W	80433	11800-11899	
ARDMORE ST	Castle Rock	499J	80104	1-599	
ARDSLEY ST	Douglas Co	409X	80134	None	
ARENA DR	Jefferson Co	336B	80439	30000-30399	
AREZZO CIR	Parker	439F	80134	12800-12999	
AREZZO DR	Longmont	40U	80503	None	
ARFSTEN RD S	Douglas Co	909K	80118	2100-15999	
ARGENTINE PASS CIR	Brighton	140J	80601	None	
ARGENTINE PASS ST	Brighton	140K	80601	None	
ARGO CT	Broomfield	162Q	80020	1-99	
ARGONNE CIR S	Aurora	319G	80017	1200-1299	
	Aurora	319F	80017	1300-1499	
ARGONNE CT	Denver	259G	80249	None	
ARGONNE CT S	Aurora	319U	80013	2900-2999	
	Aurora	319Y	80013	3300-3399	
	Aurora	349G	80015	4400-4499	
	Centennial	379L	80016	7800-7899	
ARGONNE ST	Aurora	289G	80011	1600-1999	
	Aurora	289C	80011	None	
	Denver	259Q	80249	4000-4799	
	Denver	259C	80249	5600-7099	
	Denver	259G	80249	None	
	Denver	259L	80249	None	
	Denver	769X	80249	None	
ARGONNE ST S	Aurora	319G	80017	1300-1399	
	Aurora	319Q	80013	2300-2699	
	Aurora	319U	80013	2700-2999	
	Aurora	349C	80013	3600-3899	
	Aurora	349C	80013	3900-3999	
	Aurora	349G	80013	4100-4299	
	Aurora	349L	80015	4800-4899	
	Centennial	349Q	80015	5100-5299	
	Centennial	379L	80016	7500-7899	
ARGONNE WAY	Denver	259L	80249	4800-4898	E
ARGONNE WAY S	Aurora	319L	80017	1600-1899	
	Aurora	349G	80015	4300-4499	
ARGOS CIR	Lafayette	131Q	80026	800-899	
ARGOSY WAY	Douglas Co	466H	80108	400-499	
ARGYLE PL W	Denver	253Z	80211	2400-2699	
ARIES CT	Highlands Ranch	376U	80124	500-599	
ARIES DR	El Paso Co	908N	80132	19500-19999	
ARISTA PL	Broomfield	192A	80021	8000-8799	
ARIZONA AVE E	Arapahoe Co	812A	80102	39300-40799	
	Aurora	317G	80112	11900-12299	
	Aurora	318F	80012	13900-14499	
	Aurora	319E	80017	17400-18399	
	Denver	314G	80210	1-599	
	Denver	314B	80210	700-1199	
	Denver	314H	80210	1600-1699	
	Denver	315F	80210	1700-3999	
	Denver	315H	80246	4800-4999	
	Denver	316F	80224	6500-6899	
ARIZONA AVE W	Denver	314G	80223	1-399	
	Denver	314F	80223	800-1599	
	Denver	313E	80219	3000-5199	
	Jefferson Co	311F	80232	10900-11999	
	Lakewood	312H	80232	5200-6299	
	Lakewood	312G	80232	6400-6799	
	Lakewood	312F	80232	7600-7799	
	Lakewood	311H	80232	9200-9899	
	Lakewood	311E	80228	12000-12399	
ARIZONA CIR E	Aurora	321A	80018	24600-24799	
ARIZONA DR E	Arapahoe Co	316G	80231	7600-7799	
	Aurora	317E	80247	1000-9799	
	Aurora	317G	80112	11900-12399	
	Aurora	318G	80017	15200-15599	
	Aurora	318H	80017	16500-16799	
ARIZONA DR W	Lakewood	312E	80232	8300-8799	
	Lakewood	311H	80232	9000-9099	

STREET NAME	CITY or COUNTY	MAP GRID	ZIP CODE	BLOCK RANGE	O/E
ARIZONA PL E	Arapahoe Co	316H	80247	9100-9299	
	Arapahoe Co	317E	80247	9300-9499	
	Arapahoe Co	812C	80102	42900-43699	
	Aurora	318F	80012	14800-14999	
	Aurora	318H	80017	16500-16799	
	Aurora	319F	80017	17700-17799	
	Aurora	319G	80017	18900-19299	
ARIZONA PL E	Aurora	320D	80018	23900-23999	
	Aurora	321A	80018	24000-24799	
	Aurora	317F	80112	None	
ARIZONA PL W	Lakewood	312H	80232	5300-5599	
	Lakewood	312F	80232	7200-7599	
	Lakewood	311G	80232	10100-10199	
	Lakewood	310H	80228	12500-12899	
ARIZONA WAY W	Lakewood	311H	80232	9000-9099	
ARKANSAS AVE E	Arapahoe Co	316F	80231	7300-7599	
	Arapahoe Co	812B	80102	40800-40899	
	Aurora	317G	80112	10900-12399	
	Aurora	318E	80012	13300-13399	
	Aurora	318H	80017	16500-16699	
	Aurora	319E	80017	16800-17099	
	Aurora	319E	80017	17300-17499	
	Aurora	319F	80017	18300-18399	
ARKANSAS AVE E	Aurora	319H	80017	None	
	Denver	314G	80210	1-899	
	Denver	314H	80210	1100-1599	
	Denver	315F	80210	2000-3199	
	Denver	315G	80222	4000-4799	
	Denver	316F	80224	6900-7199	
ARKANSAS AVE W	Denver	314G	80223	1-399	
	Denver	314E	80223	1200-1999	
	Denver	313H	80223	2000-2499	
	Denver	313G	80219	2500-4399	
	Denver	313E	80219	4800-5199	
	Jefferson Co	311F	80232	10900-10999	
	Lakewood	312H	80232	5200-6299	
	Lakewood	312G	80232	6400-6799	
	Lakewood	312F	80232	7000-7599	
	Lakewood	312E	80232	8200-8399	
	Lakewood	311G	80232	10200-10299	
	Lakewood	311E	80228	12400-12499	
ARKANSAS DR E	Aurora	317H	80112	12800-13099	
	Aurora	318E	80012	13200-13499	
	Aurora	318F	80012	13900-14499	
	Aurora	318G	80012	14800-15199	
	Aurora	318H	80017	15800-16899	
	Aurora	319E	80017	17000-17099	
	Aurora	319G	80017	19100-19299	
ARKANSAS DR W	Lakewood	311G	80232	10000-10499	
ARKANSAS PL E	Arapahoe Co	812G	80102	42600-44299	
	Aurora	317E	80247	9600-9899	
	Aurora	317H	80112	12100-12399	
	Aurora	318F	80012	13900-14099	
	Aurora	318G	80017	15300-15399	
	Aurora	318H	80017	15800-15999	
	Aurora	319G	80017	18700-19399	
	Aurora	320H	80018	23500-23599	
	Aurora	321E	80018	24400-24799	
ARKANSAS PL W	Lakewood	312F	80232	7600-7799	
	Lakewood	311G	80232	10400-10499	
	Lakewood	311F	80228	12000-12099	
	Lakewood	310H	80228	13000-13099	
ARKANSAS MOUNTAIN RD	Boulder Co	722W	80302	1-1599	
ARKINS CT	Denver	254U	80216	2900-3798	E
ARLINGTON AVE	Broomfield	163S	80020	4200-12499	
ARLINGTON AVE W	Jefferson Co	341R	80123	9500-9999	
	Jefferson Co	341N	80127	11600-12299	
	Littleton	343P	80123	3300-3399	
ARLINGTON DR	Boulder Co	130E	80303	7500-7899	
ARLINGTON DR	Douglas Co	439T	80134	None	
ARLINGTON DR W	Jefferson Co	341N	80127	11800-11899	
	Lakewood	342P	80123	7000-7099	
ARLINGTON PL W	Jefferson Co	341N	80127	12500-12699	
	Jefferson Co	340R	80127	12800-13099	
ARLINGTON ST	Castle Rock	498Q	80104	None	
ARLINGTON ST	Thornton	224A	80260	None	
ARLINGTON WAY W	Lakewood	342P	80123	7100-7199	
ARMADILLO DR	Lone Tree	406G	80124	10000-10099	
ARMADILLO WAY	Jefferson Co	367W	80439	27200-27299	
ARMADILLO TRAIL	Jefferson Co	367K	80439	7700-9199	
ARMEL CT	Parker	409J	80134	17400-17499	
ARMER AVE	Boulder	128T	80305	3700-3899	
ARMSTRONG DR	Longmont	12V	80501	None	
ARNETT ST	Boulder	98S	80304	3000-3299	
ARNETT RANCH RD	Jefferson Co	824W	80433	11500-12199	
ARNKA CT	Douglas Co	887F	80118	6500-6599	
ARNOLD DR	Boulder	128B	80301	3300-3599	
ARNOLD ST	Jefferson Co	823P	80433	9700-9899	
ARRIBA ST	Lochbuie	729Y	80603	None	
ARROW CT	Lafayette	132P	80026	700-799	
ARROW GRASS WAY	Highlands Ranch	375W	80126	9000-9099	
ARROWHEAD CIR	Elbert Co	872N	80107	6700-6799	
ARROWHEAD CT	Lone Tree	376Y	80124	7900-8099	
ARROW HEAD CT	Louisville	130V	80027	500-599	
ARROWHEAD DR	Brighton	139G	80603	15100-15499	
ARROWHEAD DR	El Paso Co	908Z	80132	None	
ARROWHEAD DR	Jefferson Co	368U	80465	8300-8499	
ARROWHEAD LN	Jefferson Co	823N	80433	26800-27599	
ARROWHEAD LN E	Douglas Co	411T	80138	10100-10799	
ARROWHEAD RD E	Highlands Ranch	374V	80126	1400-1599	
ARROWHEAD RD W	Littleton	343P	80123	3600-4099	
ARROWHEAD ST	Arapahoe Co	794T	80136	None	
ARROW HEAD ST	Louisville	130U	80027	500-599	
ARROWHEAD WAY	Lone Tree	376Y	80124	8100-8299	
ARROWHEAD PASS RD	Thornton	195Q	80229	None	
ARROWHEAD SPRINGS TRAIL	Jefferson Co	844F	80127	17200-17299	
ARROWHEAD TRAIL	Elbert Co	871R	80107	6000-6799	
ARROW LEAF CT	Boulder Co	97P	80304	1-299	
ARROWLEAF CT W	Castle Rock	466Q	80109	3200-3399	
ARROWSHAFT TRAIL E	Arapahoe Co	380N	80016	20900-20999	
	Douglas Co	380N	80138	7500-7799	
ARROWWOOD DR	El Paso Co	908U	80132	17400-18799	
ARROWWOOD DR	Highlands Ranch	405M	80130	10300-10399	
ARROW WOOD DR	Jefferson Co	307D	80401	900-1099	
ARROWWOOD LN	Boulder	128F	80303	3100-3299	
ARROWWOOD ST	Longmont	40L	80503	700-899	
ARROYA AVE	Palmer Lake	907Q	80133	None	
ARROYO ST	Brighton	139P	80601	None	
ARROYO CHICO	Boulder Co	722U	80302	1-1299	
ARROYO RUN	Douglas Co	432P	80125	7000-7099	
ARROYO VERDE CT	Castle Rock	468W	80108	3000-3499	
ARROYO VERDE WAY	Castle Rock	468X	80108	3100-3399	
ARSATA PL	Douglas Co	887G	80118	1800-1899	
ARTEMIS CIR	Lafayette	131R	80026	1000-1099	
ARTESIAN DR	Boulder Co	743T	80025	None	
ARTHUR AVE	Louisville	131X	80027	1400-1498	E
ARTHUR AVE S	Louisville	161B	80027	400-699	
ARTHUR CT	Boulder	98P	80304	3500-3599	
ARTHUR LN S	Highlands Ranch	406E	80130	9800-9999	
ARTHUR ST	Lafayette	132Q	80026	1-299	
ARTHUR ST	Palmer Lake	907R	80133	None	
ARTS LN	Gilpin Co	740Z	80474	None	
ARUNDEL LN	Lone Tree	406L	80124	7800-7899	
ASBURY AVE E	Aurora	317K	80014	10500-11199	
	Aurora	317L	80014	11700-11799	
	Aurora	318K	80014	14500-14999	
	Aurora	319J	80013	16800-17299	
	Denver	314M	80210	1-1699	
	Denver	315K	80210	1700-3699	
	Denver	315M	80222	4600-5599	
	Denver	316J	80224	6300-6699	
	Denver	316K	80224	6900-7299	
ASBURY AVE W	Denver	314K	80223	1-799	
	Denver	314J	80223	1600-1999	
	Denver	313M	80223	2000-2399	
	Denver	313M	80219	2400-2999	
	Lakewood	312J	80227	8800-9099	
	Lakewood	311L	80227	10000-10299	
	Lakewood	311K	80227	10800-11299	
ASBURY CIR E	Aurora	317M	80014	12700-12799	
	Aurora	319J	80013	17300-17499	
	Denver	315M	80222	4600-4699	
ASBURY CIR W	Lakewood	310M	80228	13100-13199	
	Lakewood	310L	80228	13700-13799	
ASBURY CT W	Lakewood	311P	80227	11400-11499	
ASBURY DR E	Aurora	319K	80013	17700-18199	
	Aurora	319L	80013	19300-19499	
ASBURY DR E	Aurora	321J	80018	None	
ASBURY DR S	Lakewood	311L	80227	2000-2099	
ASBURY DR W	Lakewood	312J	80227	8800-9199	
	Lakewood	311P	80228	11700-11899	
	Lakewood	310L	80228	13700-13799	
ASBURY PL E	Arapahoe Co	317J	80231	9300-9399	
	Aurora	317L	80014	11500-11799	
	Aurora	318L	80013	15600-15699	
	Aurora	319J	80013	17200-17499	
	Aurora	320M	80018	None	
	Aurora	321J	80018	None	
ASBURY PL W	Lakewood	312M	80227	5700-5899	
	Lakewood	311N	80228	11600-12499	
	Lakewood	311J	80228	12500-13099	
ASBURY ST E	Aurora	319K	80013	18000-18299	
ASCOT AVE E	Highlands Ranch	404D	80126	1200-1399	
ASH AVE	Boulder	128K	80305	3000-3499	
ASH AVE	Brighton	138S	80601	200-399	
ASH AVE	Castle Rock	497M	80104	100-299	
ASH AVE	Weld Co	706R	80504	None	
ASH CIR	Thornton	195G	80233	11200-11299	
	Thornton	195C	80233	11500-11599	
	Thornton	165U	80241	12800-12899	
	Thornton	165Q	80241	13300-13399	
	Thornton	195L	80233	None	
ASH CIR S	Centennial	375C	80121	6500-6599	
	Centennial	375G	80122	6900-7099	
	Centennial	345Y	80121	6100E-6299E	
ASH CT	Adams Co	225U	80022	7000-7099	
ASH CT	Commerce City	225Y	80022	6500-6599	
ASH CT	Longmont	11W	80503	1-99	
ASH CT	Thornton	224D	80229	900-1599	
	Thornton	195Y	80229	9200-9399	
	Thornton	195L	80233	10600-10799	
	Thornton	165U	80241	12500-12599	
	Thornton	165Q	80241	13100-13199	
ASH CT S	Centennial	345Y	80121	6300-6399	
	Centennial	375L	80122	7700-7799	
	Greenwood Village	345U	80121	5700-5799	
ASH CT W	Louisville	130R	80027	500-599	
ASH DR	Thornton	165U	80241	12400-12499	
ASH LN	Thornton	195U	80229	None	
ASH PL	Thornton	195L	80233	10900-11099	
ASH ST	Adams Co	225U	80022	None	
ASH ST	Arapahoe Co	373P	80128	None	
ASH ST	Bennett	793J	80102	200-299	
ASH ST	Broomfield	162V	80020	300-1199	
	Broomfield	162Z	80020	None	
ASH ST	Commerce City	225U	80022	6600-6699	
ASH ST	Dacono	727F	80514	200-799	
ASH ST	Denver	285U	80220	1-799	
	Denver	285L	80220	1100-1499	
	Denver	285C	80207	2000-2799	
	Denver	255Y	80207	2800-3499	
	Denver	255L	80216	5000-5098	E
	Federal Heights	193V	80260	9800-9899	
ASH ST	Fort Lupton	728H	80621	1100-1199	
ASH ST	Frederick	727B	80530	201-299	O
ASH ST	Greenwood Village	345V	80121	5700-5899	
ASH ST	Hudson	730Q	80642	None	
ASH ST	Keenesburg	732A	80643	None	
ASH ST	Louisville	130Q	80027	500-699	
ASH ST	Thornton	195Y	80229	9100-9399	
	Thornton	195C	80233	11600-11799	
	Thornton	165U	80241	12400-12599	
	Thornton	165Q	80241	12900-13199	
	Thornton	165G	80602	None	
ASH ST S	Cherry Hills Village	345C	80110	3900-3999	
	Denver	285U	80246	1-199	
	Denver	315G	80222	1400-1599	
	Denver	315Q	80222	2100-2499	
	Denver	315Y	80222	3000-3499	
	Glendale	285Y	80246	600-699	
	Glendale	315C	80246	700-799	
ASH WAY	Thornton	195L	80233	10900-10999	
ASH WAY S	Centennial	375C	80122	6700-6799	
ASHBROOK CIR	Highlands Ranch	405H	80130	4800-5299	
ASHBURN CT	Highlands Ranch	376W	80130	9200-9299	
ASHBURN LN	Highlands Ranch	376W	80130	6300-6599	
ASHBURY CIR	Douglas Co	408D	80134	9300-9499	
ASHBURY DR	Castle Rock	498G	80104	4600-4699	
ASHBURY DR E	Aurora	318J	80014	13200-13599	
ASHBURY LN	Douglas Co	408D	80134	None	
ASHBURY PL E	Aurora	318L	80013	15600-15699	
	Aurora	318M	80013	16500-16699	
ASHCROFT AVE	Castle Rock	498K	80104	3900-4499	
ASHCROFT CT	Castle Rock	498K	80104	4000-4299	
ASHCROFT CT	Longmont	41U	80501	1600-1699	
ASHCROFT DR	Longmont	41Q	80501	1300-1599	
ASHFIELD CIR	Boulder Co	100E	80301	4700-4799	
ASHFIELD CT	Boulder Co	100E	80301	4600-4799	
ASHFIELD DR	Boulder Co	100E	80301	4400-4799	
ASHFIELD ST	Highlands Ranch	405L	80126	None	
ASHFORD CIR	Highlands Ranch	405Q	80126	10700-10799	
ASHFORD CIR	Longmont	12N	80501	1800-1999	
ASHFORD DR	Longmont	12P	80501	500-599	
ASH HOLLOW PL	Castle Rock	527D	80104	1200-1399	
ASHLAND ST	Castle Rock	499J	80104	None	
ASHLEIGH CT E	Highlands Ranch	405E	80126	1900-2099	
ASHLEIGH LN S	Highlands Ranch	405E	80126	9700-9799	
ASHLEIGH PL S	Highlands Ranch	405E	80126	9700-9799	
ASHLEIGH WAY S	Highlands Ranch	405E	80126	9900-9999	
ASHLEY CT	Boulder	98V	80301	None	
ASHLEY CT	Douglas Co	440N	80134	6900-6999	
ASH TERRACE	Elbert Co	871G	80107	4600-4799	
ASHTON AVE E	Castle Rock	498L	80104	4800-4999	
ASHTON CT	Thornton	195N	80229	10300-10399	
ASHTON RD	Weld Co	706P	80504	None	
ASHURST LN	Highlands Ranch	405Q	80130	10900-10999	
ASHURST WAY	Highlands Ranch	405Q	80130	10900-10999	
ASHWOOD CT S	Highlands Ranch	403M	80129	10500-10699	
ASHWOOD LN W	Highlands Ranch	403M	80129	2200-2299	
ASHWOOD PL W	Highlands Ranch	403M	80129	2000-2299	
ASHWOOD ST	Firestone	706V	80504	4600-10699	
ASHWOOD WAY	Highlands Ranch	403M	80129	None	
ASHWORTH AVE	Highlands Ranch	405P	80126	3200-3399	
ASOKA ST	Adams Co	794P	80136	1800-2099	
ASPEN AVE	Weld Co	726K	80516	5300-5699	
ASPEN AVE E	Castle Rock	498M	80104	5200-5599	
ASPEN CIR	Clear Creek Co	304Y	80439	1-199	
ASPEN CIR	Frederick	727B	80530	400-699	
ASPEN CIR	Gilpin Co	761S	80403	1-99	
	Gilpin Co	761A	80403	100-399	
ASPEN CIR	Parker	379S	80134	8600-8799	
ASPEN CT	Boulder	97R	80304	3600-3699	
ASPEN CT	Broomfield	162V	80020	300-499	
ASPEN CT	Clear Creek Co	801R	80439	1-99	
ASPEN CT	Greenwood Village	345U	80121	5700-5799	
ASPEN CT	Louisville	130Y	80027	600-699	
ASPEN CT	Parker	379S	80134	8700-8799	
ASPEN CT	Weld Co	726K	80516	4800-5399	
ASPEN CT W	Denver	313V	80219	2400-2599	
ASPEN DR	Boulder Co	742W	80403	1-299	
ASPEN DR	Bow Mar	343N	80123	5000-5299	
ASPEN DR	Brighton	138N	80601	200-399	
ASPEN DR	Clear Creek Co	781Z	80439	1-27699	
ASPEN DR	Frederick	727F	80530	100-398	E
ASPEN DR	Jefferson Co	367A	80439	27500-27699	
	Jefferson Co	822Z	80433	28400-28799	
ASPEN DR	Park Co	820Y	80421	1-999	
ASPEN DR	Park Co	841K	80421	None	
ASPEN DR	Thornton	195X	80229	9000-9299	
ASPEN LN	Boulder Co	742W	80403	1-99	
ASPEN LN	Clear Creek Co	304Q	80439	1-299	
	Gilpin Co	760U	80403	300-799	
ASPEN LN	Jefferson Co	278N	80401	200-799	
	Jefferson Co	823N	80433	9500-9699	
	Jefferson Co	336G	80439	29800-30299	
	Jefferson Co	306T	80439	None	
	Littleton	373P	80120	None	
ASPEN LN	Park Co	841D	80470	1-499	
	Park Co	841T	80421	500-699	
	Park Co	821Z	80470	None	
ASPEN LOOP	Clear Creek Co	801A	80452	1-299	
ASPEN PL	Clear Creek Co	304X	80439	1-1199	
ASPEN PL	Elbert Co	871B	80107	4600-4799	
ASPEN PL	Golden	248V	80403	400-499	
ASPEN PL	Longmont	11U	80501	1300-1399	
ASPEN RD	Gilpin Co	761J	80403	1-99	
ASPEN RD	Jefferson Co	278Q	80401	500-899	
	Jefferson Co	823N	80433	None	
ASPEN ST	Adams Co	794P	80136	1500-1999	
ASPEN ST	Broomfield	162R	80020	1100-1499	
	Broomfield	162M	80020	1500-1999	
ASPEN ST	Buckley Air Force Base	319C	80017	None	
ASPEN ST	Federal Heights	193V	80260	9700-9799	
ASPEN ST	Firestone	706R	80504	4800-10799	
ASPEN ST	Fort Lupton	728H	80621	1100-1999	
ASPEN ST	Longmont	11Y	80501	1000-1399	
ASPEN ST	Thornton	193V	80260	None	
ASPEN ST N	Buckley Air Force Base	289T	80011	None	
ASPEN ST S	Buckley Air Force Base	289T	80017	None	
ASPEN WAY	Boulder Co	741U	80466	1-699	
ASPEN WAY	Broomfield	162M	80020	1000-1099	
ASPEN WAY	Clear Creek Co	365N	80439	1-799	
ASPEN WAY	El Paso Co	907Y	80132	1-18299	
ASPEN WAY	Gilpin Co	761S	80403	1-99	
ASPEN WAY	Jefferson Co	277U	80401	24900-25999	
	Jefferson Co	365N	80439	None	
ASPEN WAY	Louisville	131W	80027	600-799	
	Louisville	130Y	80027	None	
ASPEN CREEK CT	Highlands Ranch	373Y	80129	9200-9299	
ASPEN CREEK DR	Broomfield	163J	80020	4800-5199	
	Broomfield	162H	80020	5500-5998	E
ASPEN CREEK DR	Highlands Ranch	373Y	80129	3000-3199	
ASPEN CREEK PT	Highlands Ranch	373Y	80129	9100-9299	
ASPEN CREEK WAY	Highlands Ranch	373Y	80129	9200-9299	
ASPEN END	Park Co	820Y	80421	1-99	
ASPEN GROVE CT	Boulder Co	741R	80466	1-99	
ASPEN GROVE WAY W	Littleton	373G	80120	None	
ASPEN HILL CIR	Lone Tree	377W	80124	9400-9699	
ASPEN HILL DR S	Lone Tree	377W	80124	None	
ASPEN HILL LN E	Lone Tree	377W	80124	9300-9699	
ASPEN HILL PL E	Lone Tree	377W	80124	9200-9699	
ASPEN HILL WAY S	Lone Tree	377W	80124	9400-9499	

STREET NAME	CITY or COUNTY	MAP GRID	ZIP CODE	BLOCK RANGE	O/E
ASPEN HILLS CT	El Paso Co	910Y	80908	8800-8899	
ASPEN HOLLOW CT	Castle Rock	528A	80104	3600-3998	E
ASPEN LANE CT	Park Co	822W	80470	34800-34899	
ASPEN LEAF CT	Douglas Co	846D	80125	8800-8999	
ASPEN LEAF DR	Douglas Co	846C	80125	5100-5999	
ASPEN LEAF PL	Douglas Co	846D	80125	5500-5599	
ASPEN LODGE DR	Broomfield	133J	80020	None	
ASPENMEADOW CIR	Highlands Ranch	405Q	80130	4100-4299	
ASPEN MEADOW DR	Jefferson Co	365H	80439	7100-7299	
	Jefferson Co	365L	80439	32200-32999	
ASPEN MEADOW LN	Gilpin Co	761M	80403	1-399	
ASPEN MEADOWS RD	Boulder Co	741R	80466	1-799	
ASPEN RIDGE DR	Lafayette	131G	80026	500-799	
ASPEN TRAIL	Clear Creek Co	304H	80439	1-99	
ASPEN TRAIL	Gilpin Co	761C	80403	1-99	
ASPEN TRAIL	Longmont	42N	80501	None	
ASPENWOOD CT	Lafayette	131V	80026	300-399	
ASPENWOOD DR	Clear Creek Co	304S	80439	1-99	
ASPENWOOD DR	El Paso Co	908P	80132	19300-19499	
ASPENWOOD DR	Longmont	12U	80501	1500-1599	
ASPENWOOD LN	Clear Creek Co	304R	80439	1-399	
ASSAY OFFICE RD	Gilpin Co	740Z	80403	None	
ASTER CT	Douglas Co	470A	80134	5100-5199	
ASTER CT	Superior	160U	80027	1400-1599	
ASTER CT W	Castle Rock	466Q	80109	3400-3499	
ASTER LN	Boulder	127L	80302	None	
ASTER WAY	Brighton	168C	80601	1200-1299	
ASTER WAY	Jefferson Co	308A	80401	800-899	
ASTORBROOK CIR	Highlands Ranch	405F	80126	3200-3399	
ASTORBROOK LN	Highlands Ranch	405K	80126	10000-10199	
ASTORBROOK PL	Highlands Ranch	405K	80126	None	
ASTORBROOK WAY	Highlands Ranch	405F	80126	3100-3499	
ASTORIA CT	Lone Tree	406G	80124	10000-10099	
ASTORIA LN	Longmont	12P	80501	2100-2199	
ASTRION CT	Castle Rock	527C	80104	4100-4199	
ATCHINSON CT	Castle Rock	497E	80109	1000-1099	
ATCHINSON WAY	Castle Rock	497F	80109	500-699	
ATCHINSON WAY S	Arapahoe Co	348W	80111	6500-6599	
ATCHISON CIR	Aurora	258X	80011	3200-3299	
ATCHISON CIR S	Aurora	348F	80015	4300-4499	
ATCHISON CT S	Aurora	348K	80015	4700-4899	
ATCHISON ST	Aurora	288B	80011	2300-2799	
	Aurora	258X	80011	3000-3199	
	Commerce City	198N	80022	10401-10699	O
	Denver	258E	80239	5400-5599	
ATCHISON ST S	Arapahoe Co	378F	80112	6700-6999	
ATCHISON WAY	Denver	258N	80239	4400-4699	
	Denver	258E	80239	5300-5399	
	Denver	257R	80239	None	
ATCHISON WAY S	Aurora	348F	80014	3800-4299	
	Aurora	348K	80015	4500-4599	
	Centennial	378A	80111	6500-6699	
ATHENA RD	Gilpin Co	761J	80403	1-499	
ATHENE DR	Lafayette	131U	80026	1400-1499	
ATHENS LN W	Littleton	825P	80127	9400-9999	
ATHENS ST	Boulder	127D	80302	1700-2099	
ATHERTON WAY S	Highlands Ranch	405H	80130	9800-9899	
ATKINSON AVE	Castle Rock	499N	80104	1100-1299	
ATLANTIC AVE E	Aurora	317L	80014	11700-11899	
ATLANTIC AVE W	Lakewood	311P	80227	11400-11599	
	Lakewood	311J	80228	11700-12799	
	Lakewood	310L	80228	13800-14099	
ATLANTIC CIR E	Aurora	318L	80013	15600-15699	
ATLANTIC DR E	Aurora	318K	80014	14500-14699	
	Aurora	319K	80017	17900-18499	
	Aurora	319M	80013	19600-19799	
	Aurora	321J	80018	None	
	Aurora	321J	80018	None	
ATLANTIC DR W	Lakewood	312M	80227	5800-5999	
	Lakewood	311J	80228	12100-12499	
ATLANTIC PL E	Arapahoe Co	316M	80231	9300-9399	
	Aurora	317L	80014	11700-11799	
	Aurora	318L	80013	15600-15699	
	Aurora	318M	80013	16600-16699	
	Aurora	319J	80013	17000-17299	
	Aurora	320K	80018	None	
	Denver	315M	80222	4800-5699	
	Denver	316K	80224	7000-7199	
	Denver	316K	80231	9300-9399	
ATLANTIC PL W	Denver	314J	80223	1600-1799	
	Lakewood	312M	80227	5700-5899	
	Lakewood	311J	80228	12200-12499	
	Lakewood	311N	80228	12600-12699	
ATLANTIS AVE	Lafayette	131Q	80026	1000-1399	
ATLANTIS DR	Gilpin Co	761J	80403	1-399	
ATLAS CIR	Lafayette	131Q	80026	1000-1199	
ATRIUM DR	Castle Rock	467N	80108	None	
ATWOOD CIR	Highlands Ranch	405M	80130	None	
ATWOOD CT	Longmont	11Z	80501	1200-1299	
ATWOOD DR	El Paso Co	910Y	80908	None	
ATWOOD ST	Longmont	41H	80501	300-899	
	Longmont	11Z	80501	900-1299	
	Longmont	11V	80501	1500-1899	
	Longmont	11R	80501	2300-2499	
AUBURN AVE S	Lakewood	311R	80227	9300-9499	
AUBURN AVE W	Jefferson Co	310R	80228	12800-12999	
	Lakewood	311N	80228	11700-12799	
	Lakewood	310Q	80228	13400-13899	
AUBURN CT	Longmont	10V	80503	1400-1499	
AUBURN CT W	Lakewood	310P	80228	14600-14699	
AUBRUN DR	Castle Rock	497E	80109	500-1199	
AUBURN DR W	Jefferson Co	311N	80228	11600-12499	
AUBURN LN	Westminster	223F	80031	8100-8399	
AUBURN PL W	Jefferson Co	310R	80228	13000-13199	
AUBURN ST	Boulder	128P	80305	300-399	
AUBURN HILLS DR E	Parker	408V	80134	None	
AUBURN HILLS PL E	Parker	409N	80134	None	
AUCKLAND CT	Denver	257R	80239	4400-4699	
AUCKLAND CT S	Aurora	348E	80015	4400-4599	
	Aurora	348J	80015	5000-5099	
AUCKLAND WAY	Denver	258E	80239	5500-5599	
AUDOBON ST	Frederick	727F	80530	None	
AUDREY ST	Firestone	706V	80504	4900-10999	
AUDUBON AVE	Boulder Co	70M	80503	6700-6998	E
AUDUBON CT	Boulder Co	70M	80503	8800-8999	
AUGUST LN	Brighton	138L	80601	1500-1899	
AUGUSTA AVE	Elbert Co	851C	80107	None	
AUGUSTA DR	Boulder	99D	80301	7200-7499	

STREET NAME	CITY or COUNTY	MAP GRID	ZIP CODE	BLOCK RANGE	O/E
AUGUSTA DR	Broomfield	163E	80020	4300-14299	
AUGUSTA DR	Columbine Valley	343X	80123	1-99	
AUGUSTA DR	El Paso Co	908U	80132	18100-18999	
AUGUSTA DR	Jefferson Co	306N	80439	2100-2399	
AUGUSTA DR	Louisville	160D	80027	501-699	O
AUGUSTA LN	Louisville	160D	80027	501-599	O
AUGUSTA LOOP	Elbert Co	851C	80107	None	
AUGUSTA PL	Lone Tree	406G	80124	8300-8399	
AUGUSTA PINE ST	Castle Rock	497Q	80108	None	
AUK LN	Park Co	841Z	80421	1-99	
AULT LN	Jefferson Co	368V	80465	8100-8799	
AURARIA PKWY	Denver	284E	80204	900-1299	
AURELIA ST	Palmer Lake	907Q	80133	None	
AURORA AVE	Boulder	127H	80302	500-1699	
	Boulder	128E	80302	1700-1999	
	Boulder	128H	80303	5000-5499	
AURORA AVE E	Boulder	128F	80303	2800-3899	
AURORA PKWY E	Aurora	380L	80016	22500-23599	
AURORA PKWY S	Aurora	350V	80016	6100-6399	
	Aurora	351W	80016	None	
	Aurora	380H	80016	None	
AURORA PL	Boulder	129E	80303	5600-5699	
AURORA RD	Gilpin Co	761J	80403	1-399	
AUSTIN AVE	Erie	103S	80516	100-798	E
	Erie	102U	80516	None	
AUSTIN CT	Broomfield	163C	80020	14100-14399	
AUSTIN PL	Douglas Co	436Q	80108	300-399	
AUTREY AVE	Lafayette	132K	80026	400-499	
AUTUMN CT	Boulder	98J	80304	4100-4999	
AUTUMN CT	Dacono	727J	80514	None	
AUTUMN CT	Erie	102P	80516	1-199	
AUTUMN CT	Longmont	12X	80501	1200-1299	
AUTUMN CT E	Greenwood Village	346R	80111	5400-5499	
AUTUMN DR	Greenwood Village	346R	80111	5300-5499	
AUTUMN ST	Firestone	706R	80504	4900-10999	
	Firestone	706V	80504	None	
AUTUMN WAY	Dacono	727J	80514	None	
AUTUMN WAY	El Paso Co	908T	80132	18700-18999	
AUTUMN WAY	Elbert Co	831N	80138	2600-2899	
AUTUMN ASH CT S	Highlands Ranch	404B	80126	9300-9399	
AUTUMN ASH PL S	Highlands Ranch	404C	80126	9300-9499	
AUTUMN BLAZE TRAIL					
	Highlands Ranch	404G	80129	10100-10199	
AUTUMN BRUSH CT	Douglas Co	440W	80134	5700-5799	
AUTUMN OAKS RD	Douglas Co	470D	80134	None	
AUTUMN PINE CT	Parker	439D	80134	12200-12299	
AUTUMN RIDGE BLVD	Lafayette	132W	80026	2200-2699	
AUTUMN ROCK COVE	Douglas Co	408H	80134	16600-16699	
	Castle Rock	468X	80108	None	
AUTUMN SUN CIR	Douglas Co	527J	80104	3200-3299	
AUTUMNWOOD LN	Jefferson Co	305G	80439	1400-1499	
AUTUMNWOOD PL S	Highlands Ranch	403D	80129	9600-9799	
AVALANCHE ST	Douglas Co	846C	80125	None	
AVALANCHE ST	Jefferson Co	189W	80007	None	
AVALANCHE RUN	Broomfield	133L	80020	None	
AVALON AVE	Lafayette	132P	80026	700-1799	
AVALON DR W	Littleton	825P	80127	9500-9599	
AVALON PL W	Littleton	825P	80127	9700-9799	
AVANTE CT	Lafayette	132E	80026	600-699	
AVE DE PINES LN	Jefferson Co	762E	80403	33800-33899	
AVE EIGHTEEN	Lochbuie	140A	80603	None	
AVE ELEVEN	Lochbuie	139D	80603	None	
	Lochbuie	140A	80603	None	
AVE FIFTEEN	Lochbuie	139D	80603	None	
	Lochbuie	140A	80603	None	
AVE FIVE	Lochbuie	139H	80603	None	
AVE FOURTEEN	Lochbuie	140A	80603	None	
AVENIDA DEL SOL	Castle Rock	467R	80104	1400-2199	
AVE NINE	Lochbuie	139D	80603	None	
	Lochbuie	140E	80603	None	
AVENTERRA PKWY	Douglas Co	378Y	80134	None	
	Douglas Co	408D	80134	None	
AVENUE A	Jefferson Co	307X	80439	3400-3499	
AVENUE B	Jefferson Co	307X	80439	3400-3499	
AVENUE C	Jefferson Co	307X	80439	3400-3499	
AVENUE D	Jefferson Co	307X	80439	3300-3499	
AVENUE E	Jefferson Co	307X	80439	3300-3499	
AVENUE F	Jefferson Co	307X	80439	3300-3399	
AVENUE OF ALLSTARS	Black Hawk	781A	80403	None	
AVERY ST	Golden	248R	80403	1200-1399	
AVERY WAY	Adams Co	751R	80642	None	
AVERY WAY	Castle Rock	496B	80109	None	
AVE SEVEN	Lochbuie	140E	80603	None	
AVE SEVENTEEN	Lochbuie	139D	80603	None	
	Lochbuie	140A	80603	None	
	Lochbuie	140E	80603	None	
AVE SIXTEEN	Lochbuie	140A	80603	None	
AVE TEN	Lochbuie	139D	80603	None	
	Lochbuie	140A	80603	None	
AVE THIRTEEN	Lochbuie	139D	80603	None	
	Weld Co	140E	80603	None	
AVE TWELVE	Lochbuie	139D	80603	None	
	Lochbuie	140A	80603	None	
AVGARE WAY	Erie	102Q	80516	1300-1499	
AVIAN CT	Lafayette	131B	80026	1600-1699	
AVIATOR LN	Douglas Co	377V	80112	8501-8799	O
AVIATOR WAY	Douglas Co	377V	80112	13000-13098	E
AVOCADO RD	Boulder	97H	80304	None	
AVOCADO WAY	Boulder	97H	80304	None	
AVOCET CIR	Thornton	165N	80241	1-99	
AVOCET CT	Longmont	42R	80501	None	
AVOCET LN	Boulder Co	101P	80026	9600-9799	
AVON LN	Longmont	41Q	80501	1100-1199	
AVON PL	Douglas Co	466C	80104	1-99	
AVONDALE DR W	Denver	283L	80204	3000-3299	
AVRUM DR	Adams Co	223V	80221	6800-7299	
AWL RD N	Douglas Co	411X	80138	8500-9199	
AZALEA	Erie	133H	80516	None	
AZTEC CT	Boulder	129J	80303	5500-5599	
AZTEC CT	Douglas Co	846T	80135	6700-6999	
AZTEC DR	Boulder	129J	80303	500-5499	
AZTEC DR	Douglas Co	436T	80108	900-999	
AZTEC RD	Jefferson Co	338E	80454	4000-4399	
AZURE WAY	Louisville	130Q	80027	900-1099	
AZURITE CT	Castle Rock	467G	80108	6800-7099	
AZURITE LN	Castle Rock	467G	80108	None	

B

STREET NAME	CITY or COUNTY	MAP GRID	ZIP CODE	BLOCK RANGE	O/E
B	Aurora	288F	80011	None	
B ST	Golden	279P	80401	200-1299	
B ST	Jefferson Co	279R	80401	None	
B ST	Longmont	11U	80501	None	
BABUR ST	Arapahoe Co	795U	80103	None	
BABY DOE RD	Jefferson Co	783E	80403	5000-5299	
BACA CIR	Boulder Co	69Z	80301	5400-5599	
BACA RD	Jefferson Co	822Y	80433	11600-11899	
BACCHUS DR	Lafayette	131R	80026	1100-1199	
BACHMAN DR	Adams Co	166T	80602	7500-7599	
BACKBARN DR	Castle Rock	469K	80108	5700-5898	E
BACKCOUNTRY DR	Highlands Ranch	404K	80126	10600-10899	
BACKCOUNTRY LN	Highlands Ranch	404L	80126	401-599	O
BACKLUND RD	Elbert Co	872K	80117	8700-8799	
BACKUS ST	Black Hawk	781A	80403	None	
BAD BANDIT CT	Park Co	840D	80421	1-199	
BAD BANDIT LN	Park Co	840D	80421	1-199	
BADDING DR	Thornton	194U	80229	600-9999	
BADEN DR W	Littleton	825P	80127	9700-9999	
BADER CT	Douglas Co	498E	80104	1000-1199	
BADGER CT	Douglas Co	907F	80118	13600-13799	
BADGER CT	Frederick	707W	80504	5300-5399	
BADGER CT S	Jefferson Co	341L	80127	4600-4699	
BADGER DR	Douglas Co	907F	80118	2100-2499	
BADGER LN	Elbert Co	891X	80106	3300-4199	
BADGER LN	Frederick	707W	80504	5300-5399	
BADGER LN S	Jefferson Co	341L	80127	4600-4699	
BADGER RD	Gilpin Co	760V	80403	1-599	
BADGER WAY S	Jefferson Co	341L	80127	4600-4699	
BADGER CREEK DR	Brighton	138V	80601	400-599	
BADGER RIDGE CIR	Elbert Co	870L	80107	33300-33398	E
BADGER SPUR	Jefferson Co	275E	80403	1800-1999	
BADLANDS CT	Castle Rock	466Z	80109	None	
BAGPIPE LN	Castle Rock	497Y	80104	None	
BAGUETTE DR	Castle Rock	467H	80108	1100-2199	
BAHAMA CIR S	Arapahoe Co	349U	80015	5700E-5799E	
	Aurora	319Q	80013	None	
	Centennial	349Q	80015	5200-5299	
BAHAMA CT	Denver	259G	80249	None	
BAHAMA CT S	Aurora	319U	80013	2700-2799	
	Aurora	349L	80015	4900-4999	
	Centennial	349Q	80015	5100-5499	
BAHAMA ST	Aurora	289G	80011	1600-1999	
	Denver	259Q	80249	4300-4499	
	Denver	259G	80249	None	
BAHAMA ST S	Aurora	319G	80017	1100-1599	
	Aurora	319U	80013	2800-2899	
	Aurora	319Y	80013	2900-3299	
	Aurora	349C	80013	3600-3999	
	Aurora	349G	80013	4100-4299	
BAHAMA WAY S	Aurora	319G	80017	1400-1499	
	Aurora	319Q	80013	2400-2599	
	Aurora	349C	80013	3800-3899	
	Aurora	349G	80015	4300-4499	
	Aurora	349L	80015	4800-4899	
BAILEY DR	Park Co	841S	80421	1-399	
BAILEY ST	Firestone	707N	80504	10600-10999	
BAILS AVE W	Lakewood	312K	80232	7300-7599	
BAILS DR E	Aurora	318L	80017	15500-15899	
	Denver	315M	80222	5300-5599	
BAILS PL E	Aurora	317K	80112	10600-10699	
	Aurora	317L	80112	11300-11399	
	Aurora	317M	80112	12900-12999	
	Aurora	318K	80012	13900-14099	
	Aurora	318L	80012	15000-15199	
	Aurora	318M	80017	16100-16899	
	Aurora	319K	80017	17700-18199	
	Aurora	319M	80017	19400-19799	
	Denver	315L	80222	4300-4799	
BAILS PL W	Denver	313L	80219	3100-3299	
BAILY ST	Firestone	707S	80504	10300-10399	
BAIN CT	Erie	102Q	80516	1500-1599	
BAIN DR	Erie	102Q	80516	1500-1799	
BAINS RD E	Arapahoe Co	813D	80136	1-99	
BAIRD RD S	Jefferson Co	843E	80433	13000-13299	
	Jefferson Co	842H	80433	13300-13699	
BAKER AVE	Arapahoe Co	795T	80103	1-299	
BAKER AVE W	Englewood	314N	80110	1800-1999	
	Englewood	313R	80110	2000-2399	
	Lakewood	312N	80227	7800-8699	
BAKER CT W	Lakewood	310P	80228	14600-14699	
BAKER DR	Boulder	128E	80302	None	
BAKER LN	Erie	103A	80516	1-499	
BAKER PL E	Aurora	318R	80013	16100-16199	
	Aurora	318R	80013	16500-16599	
	Aurora	319P	80013	17400-18399	
	Aurora	319Q	80013	18900-19299	
	Aurora	319R	80013	19700-19799	
	Aurora	321N	80018	None	
	Denver	316N	80222	6400-6499	
	Denver	316P	80224	6500-6699	
BAKER PL W	Lakewood	310Q	80228	13900-13999	
BAKER RD	Jefferson Co	762S	80403	7800-7999	
BAKER RD	Park Co	820V	80421	1-299	
BAKER ST	Longmont	41H	80501	200-899	
	Longmont	12W	80501	1000-1499	
BAKERS FARM RD	El Paso Co	909Y	80908	17700-18199	
	El Paso Co	909U	80908	18200-18399	
BALBOA CT	Broomfield	162P	80020	1400-1599	
BALCOLM CT	Erie	103J	80516	300-499	
BALCOLM ST	Erie	103J	80516	100-299	
	Erie	102M	80516	300-499	
BALD EAGLE	Jefferson Co	340W	80127	1-99	
BALD EAGLE CIR	Firestone	706V	80504	4700-10699	
BALD EAGLE ST	Firestone	707V	80504	10200-10399	
BALDERAS ST	Brighton	139K	80601	None	
BALD MOUNTAIN LN	Gilpin Co	780A	80403	100-199	
BALD MOUNTAIN RD	Gilpin Co	780A	80403	1-199	
BALD MOUNTAIN RD	Gilpin Co	780B	80403	800-3399	
BALDWIN AVE E	Douglas Co	409G	80138	6400-19099	
BALDWIN CIR	Boulder Co	743T	80025	None	
BALDWIN CT	Castle Rock	497R	80104	100-199	
BALDWIN CT	Denver	254R	80216	4600-4799	
	Jefferson Co	842F	80470	12300-13599	

B

STREET NAME	CITY or COUNTY	MAP GRID	ZIP CODE	BLOCK RANGE	O/E
BALDWIN PL	Boulder	**98U**	80301	4800-4899	
BALDWIN RD	Elbert Co	**892G**	80117	10300-11099	
BALDWIN GULCH CIR E	Douglas Co	**409M**	80138	7000-7199	
BALDWIN PARK RD	Castle Rock	**497R**	80104	800-1999	
BALDWIN RANCH RD	Castle Rock	**497R**	80104	100-199	
BALDY LN	Jefferson Co	**306Q**	80439	1900-2499	
BALER CT	Brighton	**139M**	80601	None	
BALL RD	Park Co	**820V**	80421	1-199	
BALLANTINE RD	Jefferson Co	**278P**	80401	700-999	
BALLARAT LN	Douglas Co	**466L**	80108	5000-5099	
BALLARD CT	Douglas Co	**867P**	80109	2800-2999	
BALLARD WAY	Douglas Co	**867P**	80109	2600-2799	
BALLATA CT	Castle Rock	**497A**	80109	1200-1399	
BALMORA ST	Lafayette	**132A**	80026	1100-1399	
BALMORAL CT	Castle Pines North	**436R**	80108	7300-7399	
BALSA DR	Castle Rock	**497Q**	80104	300-799	
BALSAM AVE	Boulder	**97U**	80304	400-1899	
BALSAM AVE	Brighton	**138N**	80601	200-399	
BALSAM CIR	Arvada	**222J**	80005	8100-8199	
BALSAM CT	Arvada	**252E**	80002	5400-5499	
	Westminster	**192W**	80021	9300-9399	
BALSAM CT S	Highlands Ranch	**404C**	80126	9300-9399	
	Jefferson Co	**372A**	80123	6500-6599	
	Jefferson Co	**372J**	80128	7600-7699	
	Jefferson Co	**372N**	80128	8200-8299	
	Lakewood	**312E**	80232	1400-1699	
	Lakewood	**312N**	80227	2100-2199	
	Lakewood	**312E**	80226	None	
BALSAM DR	Boulder	**98S**	80304	1900-2599	
BALSAM DR	Thornton	**194W**	80260	None	
BALSAM LN	Boulder Co	**722V**	80304	1-399	
BALSAM LN S	Lakewood	**312N**	80227	2300-2399	
BALSAM PL	Arvada	**252A**	80004	5800-5999	
BALSAM ST	Arvada	**252E**	80002	5200-5799	
	Arvada	**252A**	80004	6000-6199	
	Arvada	**222W**	80004	6200-6699	
	Arvada	**222S**	80004	6800-6999	
	Jefferson Co	**192N**	80021	10400-10599	
	Lakewood	**282S**	80226	1-399	
	Lakewood	**282N**	80226	400-499	
	Lakewood	**282N**	80214	600-899	
	Lakewood	**282J**	80214	1000-1499	
	Lakewood	**282E**	80214	1500-1899	
	Lakewood	**282B**	80215	2100-2599	
	Westminster	**192J**	80021	10800-11099	
	Wheat Ridge	**252W**	80033	3200-3299	
	Wheat Ridge	**252S**	80033	3800-4099	
	Wheat Ridge	**252N**	80033	4100-4699	
BALSAM ST S	Denver	**342E**	80123	4301-4399	O
	Jefferson Co	**342A**	80235	3500-3599	
	Jefferson Co	**372J**	80128	7500-7699	
	Jefferson Co	**372N**	80128	8200-8299	
	Jefferson Co	**372S**	80128	8300-8999	
	Lakewood	**282S**	80226	1-299	
	Lakewood	**282W**	80226	300-499	
	Lakewood	**312J**	80232	1400-1899	
	Lakewood	**312J**	80227	1900-2099	
	Lakewood	**312N**	80227	2300-2399	
	Lakewood	**312S**	80227	2400-2699	
	Lakewood	**342N**	80123	8300-8399	
	Lakewood	**312E**	80226	None	
BALSAM WAY	Arvada	**222E**	80005	8200-8299	
	Westminster	**192W**	80021	9100-9199	
	Westminster	**192W**	80021	9300-9399	
BALSAM WAY S	Denver	**342J**	80123	4600-4899	
	Lakewood	**312N**	80227	2400-2599	
	Lakewood	**342W**	80123	6100-6199	
BALSAMROOT RD	Douglas Co	**887G**	80118	6000-6999	
BALTIC AVE W	Lakewood	**311R**	80227	9300-9499	
	Lakewood	**310Q**	80228	13800-13899	
	Lakewood	**310Q**	80228	14000-14299	
BALTIC CIR E	Aurora	**318P**	80014	14200-14399	
BALTIC CT W	Lakewood	**312R**	80227	6000-6099	
	Lakewood	**311R**	80227	9400-9499	
	Lakewood	**311P**	80227	11300-11399	
BALTIC DR E	Aurora	**317Q**	80014	11100-11299	
	Aurora	**319N**	80013	17000-17199	
BALTIC DR W	Lakewood	**311R**	80227	9200-9399	
	Lakewood	**310Q**	80228	13700-14099	
	Lakewood	**310N**	80228	16200-16299	
BALTIC PL E	Aurora	**317Q**	80014	10900-11699	
	Aurora	**318P**	80014	14100-14799	
	Aurora	**318R**	80013	15900-16599	
	Aurora	**319N**	80013	17200-17299	
	Aurora	**319P**	80013	17700-18399	
	Aurora	**319L**	80013	18600-18999	
	Aurora	**320R**	80018	None	
BALTIC PL W	Englewood	**314N**	80110	1700-1999	
	Englewood	**313R**	80110	2000-2399	
	Lakewood	**310Q**	80228	13800-13899	
BALTIMORE CT	Denver	**258F**	80239	5500-5599	
BALTUSROL LN	Jefferson Co	**306S**	80439	2500-2599	
BAMBOO ST	Thornton	**194S**	80260	None	
BANCROFT DR	Castle Rock	**498G**	80104	4600-4699	
BANDERA PL	Douglas Co	**848M**	80134	4600-4899	
BANDIT DR	Castle Rock	**469K**	80108	7100-7899	
BANDIT LN	Park Co	**820U**	80421	1-399	
BANDIT PEAK RD	Park Co	**820U**	80421	1-199	
BANEBERRY CT W	Highlands Ranch	**403M**	80129	2600-2899	
BANEBERRY LN	Jefferson Co	**308J**	80401	1500-1799	
BANEBERRY LN W	Highlands Ranch	**403M**	80129	2500-2699	
BANEBERRY PL S	Highlands Ranch	**403L**	80129	10200-10399	
BANEBERRY ST S	Highlands Ranch	**403M**	80129	10600-10699	
BANEBERRY WAY W					
	Highlands Ranch	**403M**	80129	2500-2699	
BANECKS	Lafayette	**132J**	80026	None	
BANFF CT	Jefferson Co	**306J**	80439	31400-31499	
BANNER CIR	Erie	**102C**	80516	1200-1499	
BANNER CT	Elbert Co	**831P**	80138	3700-3999	
BANNER ST N	Elizabeth	**871F**	80107	100-499	
BANNER ST S	Elizabeth	**871F**	80107	100-899	
BANNOCK CIR	Westminster	**164X**	80234	12100-12299	
BANNOCK CT	Douglas Co	**887J**	80118	3900-3999	
BANNOCK DR	Douglas Co	**886M**	80118	7900-8199	
BANNOCK DR S	Littleton	**374F**	80120	7200-7399	
BANNOCK LN	Jefferson Co	**337J**	80439	4400-4699	
BANNOCK RD	Douglas Co	**887J**	80118	8200-8399	
BANNOCK ST	Adams Co	**254C**	80216	5200-6199	
	Adams Co	**224P**	80221	7500-7699	
	Adams Co	**134X**	80020	15200-15399	
	Denver	**284P**	80223	1-399	
	Denver	**284K**	80204	400-1499	
	Denver	**254K**	80216	4801-5199	O
	Northglenn	**194P**	80260	10100-10399	
	Northglenn	**194K**	80234	10800-10999	
	Westminster	**164X**	80234	12100-12399	
BANNOCK ST S	Denver	**284T**	80223	1-299	
	Denver	**314F**	80223	1100-1499	
	Denver	**314K**	80223	1700-2699	
	Englewood	**314T**	80110	2700-3399	
	Englewood	**314X**	80110	3500-3599	
	Englewood	**344F**	80110	3600-4899	
	Littleton	**344P**	80120	5300-6099	
	Littleton	**374F**	80120	6800-7199	
BANNOCK WAY	Douglas Co	**886M**	80118	5100-5199	
BANTALA PL	Douglas Co	**466D**	80108	1-99	
BANTRY CT	Lone Tree	**406G**	80124	7500-7699	
BANYON CIR	Parker	**439F**	80134	12900-13099	
BANYON DR	Thornton	**194W**	80260	None	
BARANCA DR	Boulder Co	**743V**	80303	None	
BARANMOR PKWY	Aurora	**257Z**	80011	12400-12998	E
	Aurora	**258W**	80011	None	
BARBADOS PL	Boulder	**98K**	80301	3300-3799	
BARBARA CIR	Weld Co	**726J**	80516	1100-1199	
BARBARA ST	Louisville	**131W**	80027	100-199	
BARBARA ANN DR	Arvada	**252B**	80004	7600-7999	
BARBER LN	Boulder Co	**743T**	80025	None	
BARBERRY	Boulder Co	**99F**	80301	None	
BARBERRY	Jefferson Co	**370K**	80127	1-99	
BARBERRY AVE	Lafayette	**131M**	80026	500-799	
BARBERRY CIR	Lafayette	**131R**	80026	700-799	
BARBERRY CIR W	Louisville	**130Q**	80027	800-1799	
BARBERRY CT	Boulder	**128S**	80305	1100-1199	
BARBERRY CT W	Louisville	**130Q**	80027	1800-1899	
BARBERRY DR	Longmont	**40L**	80503	600-698	E
BARBERRY PL	Parker	**378V**	80134	8600-8699	
BARBERRY PL W	Denver	**283R**	80204	2500-2999	
BARBI CT	Castle Rock	**497C**	80104	1000-1099	
BARBOUR ST	Broomfield	**164J**	80020	13800-13999	
BARBWIRE PL	Castle Rock	**468X**	80104	None	
BARBWIRE WAY	Castle Rock	**468X**	80104	None	
BARCELONA DR	Boulder Co	**130N**	80303	1-299	
BARCLAY CT	Adams Co	**196M**	80640	None	
BARDSLEY PL	El Paso Co	**908R**	80132	19300-19599	
BARDWELL AVE	Jefferson Co	**823U**	80433	22000-22099	
BARDWELL RD	Jefferson Co	**842E**	80470	33600-33899	
BARI CT	Boulder Co	**129U**	80303	500-599	
BARK CHERRY	Jefferson Co	**370Q**	80127	1-99	
BARKER AVE	Jefferson Co	**823U**	80433	10900-11099	
BARKER RD	Nederland	**740R**	80466	None	
BARKLEY RD	Jefferson Co	**823N**	80433	26500-27099	
BARKSDALY WAY	Adams Co	**751R**	80642	None	
BARKWAY CT	Lone Tree	**406G**	80124	7700-7899	
BARLEY AVE	Fort Lupton	**729F**	80621	15000-16899	
BARLEY LN	Westminster	**222B**	80021	None	
BARN OWL DR	Frederick	**706Z**	80504	4800-4899	
BARN RD	El Paso Co	**911X**	80106	None	
BARNACLE CT	Boulder Co	**99G**	80301	4500-6599	
BARNACLE ST	Boulder Co	**99G**	80301	6500-6599	
BARNARD CT	Longmont	**41L**	80501	300-499	
BARNES AVE	Jefferson Co	**823N**	80433	9300-9499	
BARNES LN	Arvada	**221L**	80005	None	
BARNETT PL	Denver	**283B**	80212	4200-4299	
BARNEY BROOK DR	Jefferson Co	**822Y**	80433	29300-29799	
BARNEY GULCH RD S	Jefferson Co	**822V**	80433	10900-11499	
BARNHART ST	Thornton	**195X**	80229	2500-2999	
BARN OWL DR	Highlands Ranch	**406E**	80130	None	
BARNSLEY LN	Parker	**440C**	80138	None	
BARN SWALLOW DR	Longmont	**41T**	80504	2200-2399	
BARN SWALLOW WAY	Douglas Co	**470C**	80134	5000-5199	
BARNWOOD DR	El Paso Co	**912T**	80831	16800-18999	
BARON AVE	Lafayette	**132A**	80026	300-499	
BARON CT	Broomfield	**163T**	80020	3400-3499	
BARON CT	Erie	**133E**	80516	300-399	
BARR CT	Boulder	**128T**	80305	3800-3899	
BARR LN	Westminster	**223E**	80031	4200-4299	
BARRANCA DR	Castle Rock	**467U**	80104	501-899	O
BARRANCA LN	Castle Rock	**467U**	80104	501-899	O
BARRES ST	Adams Co	**793R**	80136	1500-1899	
BARRETT ST	Central City	**780C**	80427	100-299	
BARRETT ST N	Douglas Co	**409G**	80138	11800-11999	
BARRINGTON	Thornton	**224A**	80260	None	
BARRINGTON AVE E	Castle Rock	**498L**	80104	4900-5099	
BARRINGTON CT	El Paso Co	**908Z**	80132	17700-17899	
BARRINGTON DR	Jefferson Co	**370K**	80127	1-99	
BARRON CIR	Firestone	**707S**	80504	4800-10699	
BARRON ST	Firestone	**707S**	80504	10200-10299	
BARRONS BLVD	Highlands Ranch	**374X**	80129	8800-8999	
BARROW PL	Longmont	**12W**	80501	1-99	
BARRY ST	Fort Lupton	**728L**	80621	400-499	
BARTA ST	Arapahoe Co	**795U**	80103	None	
BARTIMOUS RD	Park Co	**820Z**	80421	1-399	
BARTLETT	Thornton	**224A**	80260	None	
BARTLETT ST	Castle Rock	**498Q**	80104	1200-1299	
BARTON AVE	Jefferson Co	**823V**	80433	22000-22099	
BAR X RD	El Paso Co	**910X**	80908	16500-19999	
BASALT CT	Broomfield	**162L**	80020	13600-13799	
BASALT CT	Golden	**248V**	80403	400-499	
BASALT CT	Superior	**160U**	80027	3200-3399	
BASE CAMP RD	El Paso Co	**908T**	80132	18900-18999	
BASELINE PL	Brighton	**138F**	80603	700-899	
BASELINE RD	Adams Co	**138G**	80601	500-898	E
	Boulder	**127M**	80302	400-1799	
	Boulder	**128L**	80302	1800-2299	
	Boulder	**128L**	80305	2400-2799	
	Boulder	**128K**	80303	2800-5299	
	Boulder Co	**129J**	80303	5300-5999	
	Boulder Co	**129F**	80303	6000-7199	
	Boulder Co	**130K**	80303	7200-8499	
	Brighton	**139F**	80601	None	
	Lafayette	**131L**	80026	100-999	
	Lafayette	**130L**	80026	8500-9199	
	Lafayette	**132L**	80026	11700-12699	
	Weld Co	**140E**	80601	None	
	Weld Co	**750B**	80603	None	
BASELINE RD E	Lafayette	**132K**	80026	100-999	
BASELINE RD W	Lafayette	**132J**	80026	100-599	
BASHLEY RD	El Paso Co	**909N**	80132	None	
BASIL PL	Superior	**160U**	80027	2900-2999	
BASIL ST	Adams Co	**794P**	80136	None	
BASKERVILLE WAY	El Paso Co	**909S**	80132	None	
BASS CIR	Lafayette	**132E**	80026	100-999	
BASSETT CIR	Denver	**284A**	80202	None	
BASSETT ST	Denver	**254W**	80202	1700-1899	
BASSWOOD LN E	Douglas Co	**850X**	80116	11500-11899	
BASSWOOD ST	Federal Heights	**193V**	80260	2500-2799	
BATAVIA DR	Aurora	**288G**	80011	15400-15699	
	Aurora	**289G**	80011	19300-19399	
BATAVIA DR E	Aurora	**289H**	80011	19500-20699	
BATAVIA PL	Aurora	**289G**	80011	19300-19399	
	Denver	**285G**	80220	4000-4799	
	Denver	**286F**	80220	6500-7499	
BATAVIA PL E	Aurora	**289E**	80011	17000-17599	
	Aurora	**289H**	80011	20100-20199	
BATES AVE E	Arapahoe Co	**795Y**	80103	300-799	
	Aurora	**318S**	80014	13600-13699	
	Aurora	**318U**	80014	15100-15299	
	Aurora	**318U**	80013	15300-15799	
	Aurora	**319S**	80013	16800-17399	
	Aurora	**319T**	80013	17700-17999	
	Aurora	**319U**	80013	18800-19999	
	Denver	**315T**	80210	2700-3699	
	Denver	**315V**	80222	4800-4999	
	Denver	**316S**	80222	5500-5599	
	Denver	**316S**	80222	6400-6499	
	Denver	**316T**	80224	6500-6799	
	Englewood	**314U**	80113	1-1599	
BATES AVE W	Denver	**313V**	80236	2400-2999	
	Denver	**313S**	80236	3900-5199	
	Denver	**312U**	80227	5200-6399	
	Denver	**312T**	80227	6900-7499	
	Englewood	**314T**	80110	200-699	
	Englewood	**314S**	80110	1900-1999	
	Englewood	**313V**	80110	2000-2399	
	Lakewood	**310V**	80228	13600-13999	
	Lakewood	**310U**	80228	14100-14199	
BATES CIR E	Aurora	**317U**	80014	11800-11999	
	Aurora	**317V**	80014	12200-12699	
	Aurora	**319S**	80013	17100-17299	
BATES CT E	Aurora	**317U**	80014	11400-11499	
BATES CT W	Lakewood	**310U**	80228	14000-14099	
BATES DR E	Aurora	**318V**	80013	16100-16499	
	Aurora	**319U**	80013	18500-18599	
	Aurora	**319V**	80013	19400-19799	
	Denver	**316U**	80231	7300-7699	
BATES PKWY E	Englewood	**314V**	80113	1000-1599	
BATES PL E	Aurora	**318V**	80013	15900-15999	
	Aurora	**319S**	80013	17300-17399	
	Aurora	**319T**	80013	18100-18199	
	Aurora	**319U**	80013	19300-19399	
	Aurora	**320S**	80013	None	
BATES PL W	Lakewood	**310T**	80228	14500-14699	
BATES ST	Boulder	**128P**	80305	300-399	
BATES ST	Central City	**780D**	80427	300-399	
BATHHURST WAY S	Highlands Ranch	**405H**	80130	9800-9899	
BAUER CT	Lone Tree	**406C**	80124	9200-9399	
BAUM CT	Dacono	**727J**	80514	300-399	
BAX CT	Commerce City	**226T**	80022	6700-6899	
BAXTER DR	Parker	**409P**	80134	10900-17799	
BAXTER FARM LN	Erie	**102N**	80516	1-499	
BAY LN	Douglas Co	**406Z**	80108	9400-9799	
BAYAN CT	Castle Rock	**497Q**	80104	300-499	
BAYAUD AVE E	Arapahoe Co	**291S**	80018	24300-24899	
	Aurora	**287T**	80012	10500-11099	
	Aurora	**288S**	80012	13600-13699	
	Aurora	**288U**	80012	15100-15199	
	Aurora	**290U**	80018	22100-23299	
	Aurora	**288T**	80012	None	
	Aurora	**291T**	80018	None	
	Aurora	**291U**	80018	None	
	Denver	**284U**	80209	1-1599	
	Denver	**285U**	80209	3100-3999	
	Denver	**285V**	80246	4000-5499	
	Denver	**286S**	80246	5500-5599	
	Denver	**286S**	80224	5600-6099	
	Denver	**286T**	80224	6500-6699	
	Denver	**286U**	80230	6900-8199	
BAYAUD AVE W	Denver	**284T**	80223	1-1099	
	Denver	**284S**	80223	1200-1999	
	Denver	**283V**	80223	2000-2299	
	Denver	**283T**	80219	2500-5199	
	Jefferson Co	**280U**	80401	14300-14599	
	Jefferson Co	**280T**	80401	15100-15199	
	Lakewood	**282V**	80226	5200-5999	
	Lakewood	**282U**	80226	6100-7199	
	Lakewood	**282S**	80226	7400-8899	
	Lakewood	**281V**	80226	8900-9399	
	Lakewood	**281S**	80228	12100-12699	
BAYAUD CT W	Jefferson Co	**280T**	80401	15200-15399	
BAYAUD DR E	Aurora	**287U**	80012	11500-11698	E
BAYAUD DR W	Jefferson Co	**280S**	80401	15800-15999	
	Jefferson Co	**280S**	80401	16100-16399	
	Jefferson Co	**279V**	80401	16400-16999	
BAYAUD PL E	Aurora	**291T**	80016	None	
BAYAUD PL W	Jefferson Co	**280U**	80401	14300-14399	
	Lakewood	**282T**	80226	7100-7399	
BAYBERRY CT	Broomfield	**162M**	80020	5300-5399	
BAYBERRY DR	Broomfield	**162M**	80020	13700-13799	
BAYBERRY LN	Castle Rock	**497D**	80104	2300-2399	
BAYBERRY WAY	Erie	**133D**	80516	None	
BAYFIELD WAY	Parker	**409R**	80138	10800-10999	
BAY HILL DR	Lone Tree	**406C**	80124	9600-9799	
BAY HILL WAY	Lone Tree	**406D**	80124	9700-9799	
BAYLOR DR	Boulder	**128T**	80305	2900-3199	
BAYLOR DR	Longmont	**10U**	80503	1-199	
BAYLOR LN	Westminster	**223F**	80031	8100-8399	
BAYLOR WAY	Longmont	**10U**	80503	100-199	
BAYNE DR	Parker	**408Q**	80134	None	
BAYNE WAY	Parker	**408Q**	80134	None	
BAY OAKS AVE	Parker	**410Y**	80138	22900-23299	
BAY OAKS CT	Parker	**410Y**	80138	12000-12199	
BAYOU GULCH CIR	Elbert Co	**870C**	80107	None	

STREET NAME	CITY or COUNTY	MAP GRID	ZIP CODE	BLOCK RANGE	O/E
BAYOU GULCH RD E	Douglas Co	469D	80134	6900-7199	
	Douglas Co	470E	80116	7200-9599	
	Douglas Co	850S	80134	9600-10999	
	Douglas Co	439W	80134	None	
	Douglas Co	469B	80134	None	
BAYOU GULCH ST	Douglas Co	469G	80134	4900-5099	
BAYOU HILLS LN E	Douglas Co	850S	80134	9700-9999	
BAYOU HILLS LN N	Douglas Co	850S	80134	3900-4099	
BAYOU HILLS RD N	Douglas Co	850S	80134	3600-4799	
	Douglas Co	470H	80134	4800-4999	
BAYOU RIDGE TRAIL	Douglas Co	850S	80134	9600-9999	
BAY POINT LN	Broomfield	163G	80020	None	
BAYSHORE DR	Weld Co	706M	80504	None	
BEACH CIR	Broomfield	163Q	80234	None	
BEACH CT	Adams Co	253H	80221	5400-5499	
	Broomfield	163V	80020	None	
	Denver	253R	80211	4400-4799	
	Denver	253M	80221	4800-5199	
	Westminster	223R	80030	7400-7599	
BEACH CT S	Denver	313H	80219	1100-1699	
BEACH PL	Broomfield	163V	80234	None	
BEACH RD	Bow Mar	343N	80123	5400-5499	
BEACH ST	Adams Co	223Z	80221	6200-6399	
	Broomfield	163V	80020	12400-12599	
	Broomfield	163V	80234	None	
	Federal Heights	193R	80260	10000-10099	
	Westminster	223V	80030	7000-7199	
	Westminster	163Z	80234	12100-12199	
BEACHAM DR	Castle Rock	498N	80104	2100-2399	
BEACHCOMBER CT	Boulder Co	99F	80301	4500-4599	
BEACON CT	Boulder	127B	80302	1900-1999	
BEACON ST	Broomfield	164J	80020	13800-13999	
BEACON WAY	Westminster	223V	80030	7000-7099	
BEACON HILL CT S	Highlands Ranch	404H	80126	9600-9699	
BEACON HILL DR E	Highlands Ranch	404D	80126	900-1399	
BEACON HILL DR W	Lafayette	132A	80026	100-399	
BEACON HILL LN E	Greenwood Village	347W	80111	1-99	
BEACON LITE RD	El Paso Co	908W	80132	19000-20499	
BEACON LITE RD	Monument	908W	80132	200-899	
BEALL CT	Platteville	708G	80651	1700-1799	
BEAN CT	Erie	102U	80516	900-999	
BEAR CT	Douglas Co	886H	80118	6500-6699	
BEAR CT	Frederick	707W	80504	5300-5399	
BEAR DR	Clear Creek Co	335E	80439	1-299	
BEAR DR	Gilpin Co	762W	80403	1-699	
BEAR DR	Park Co	841K	80421	1-99	
BEAR LN	Frederick	707W	80504	5400-5499	
BEAR RD	Jefferson Co	248S	80403	3800-4299	
BEAR CANYON CIR	Douglas Co	867E	80135	3400-4099	
BEARCAT TRAIL	Jefferson Co	822Q	80433	29600-30699	
BEAR CLAW AVE E	Douglas Co	441G	80138	10400-10899	
BEAR CLAW DR	Jefferson Co	824R	80127	9500-9599	
BEAR CLAW LN	Clear Creek Co	305N	80439	1-299	
BEAR CREED DR	Lakewood	312Y	80227	6800-6999	
BEAR CREEK AVE	Morrison	309Y	80465	100-999	
BEAR CREEK BLVD	Lakewood	310Q	80228	2000-2999	
BEARCREEK DR	Douglas Co	850T	80116	11600-11999	
BEAR CREEK DR	Jefferson Co	311X	80227	10900-11899	
BEAR CREEK DR W	Sheridan	343C	80123	3000-3299	
BEAR CREEK LN	Morrison	309Y	80465	100-299	
BEAR CREEK LOOP	Elbert Co	851C	80107	None	
BEAR CREEK RD	Jefferson Co	307U	80439	None	
	Jefferson Co	337E	80439	None	
BEAR CROSSING	Gilpin Co	761C	80403	100-299	
BEAR DANCE DR	Douglas Co	887G	80118	6600-6699	
BEAR DANCE DR	Douglas Co	887D	80118	None	
BEARLILY WAY N	Castle Rock	466Q	80109	4600-5099	
BEAR MOUNTAIN	Jefferson Co	371K	80127	7600-7699	
BEAR MOUNTAIN CT	Boulder	128S	80305	1200-1399	
BEAR MOUNTAIN DR	Boulder	128S	80305	1100-1799	
BEAR MOUNTAIN DR	Jefferson Co	337Q	80439	4800-5699	
BEAR MOUNTAIN DR S	Highlands Ranch	374X	80126	9000-9199	
BEAR MOUNTAIN RD	Gilpin Co	761K	80403	400-999	
BEAR PARK RD	Jefferson Co	822Y	80433	11900-12199	
BEAR PAW DR	Castle Rock	466S	80109	4900-5299	
BEAR PAW RD	Jefferson Co	761Z	80403	5300-6399	
	Jefferson Co	782A	80403	5300-6399	
BEAR POINT TRAIL	Jefferson Co	763Y	80403	6700-6799	
BEAR RIDGE WAY	Jefferson Co	763Y	80403	6500-6599	
BEAR ROCK RD	Clear Creek Co	304R	80439	1-499	
BEAR TRAP WAY	El Paso Co	908Q	80132	600-699	
BEA'S DR	Jefferson Co	822T	80433	10600-10999	
BEA'S LN	Jefferson Co	822T	80433	10300-10699	
BEASLEY DR	Erie	131D	80026	None	
BEATRICE CT	Douglas Co	432E	80125	None	
BEATRICE CT	Longmont	11S	80503	1400-1499	
BEAUPREZ AVE	Lafayette	131E	80026	500-899	
BEAUTIFUL CIR	Castle Rock	466U	80109	None	
BEAUTY LN	Jefferson Co	762B	80403	11600-11799	
BEAUTY BUSH PL	Parker	378V	80134	16200-16399	
BEAVER LN	Clear Creek Co	304H	80439	1-399	
BEAVER PT	Lafayette	131Z	80026	400-499	
BEAVER RD	Gilpin Co	760V	80403	1-299	
BEAVER RD N	Boulder Co	741T	80403	1-1199	
BEAVER WAY	Boulder Co	97P	80304	1-299	
BEAVER BROOK LN E	Parker	408Z	80134	None	
BEAVER BROOK CANYON RD	Clear Creek Co	781Y	80439	1-4999	
BEAVER CREEK CT S	Parker	439D	80134	12600-12699	
BEAVER CREEK DR	Boulder Co	740Q	80466	1-1399	
BEAVER CREEK LN	Jefferson Co	306F	80439	30200-30399	
BEAVER CREEK RD S	Gilpin Co	741X	80403	1-499	
	Gilpin Co	761E	80403	500-4999	
BEAVER CREEK ST N	Buckley Air Force Base	289P	80011	None	
BEAVER CREEK ST S	Buckley Air Force Base	289T	80017	None	
BEAVER CREEK WAY S	Parker	439D	80134	12500-12599	
BEAVER POND RD	Jefferson Co	822Q	80433	9700-9799	
BEAVER RESERVOIR RD	Boulder Co	720C	80481	None	
BEAVER RIDGE	Elbert Co	891Y	80106	4600-4999	
BEAVER RUN	Douglas Co	432N	80125	6800-6999	
BEAVER TRAIL	Clear Creek Co	780Z	80452	1-199	
BEAVER TRAIL	Park Co	841T	80421	1-599	
BECKET DR	Parker	379X	80134	17900-18199	
BECKETT LN	Morrison	309Z	80465	100-299	
BECKWITH PL	Longmont	12J	80501	1-99	
BECKWOURTH CT N	Douglas Co	440V	80134	6100-6199	
BECKY CIR	Elbert Co	832K	80107	46000-49999	
BEDELL DR	Gilpin Co	741Z	80403	1-199	
BEDFORD AVE N	Castle Rock	498M	80104	1-199	
BEDFORD AVE S	Castle Rock	498M	80104	1-199	
BEDFORD CT	Boulder Co	100E	80301	4600-4699	
BEDFORD CT	Denver	258F	80239	5500-5599	
BEDFORD ST	Firestone	707S	80504	10300-10699	
BEDIVERE CIR	Lafayette	132P	80026	700-1699	
BED STRAW ST	Douglas Co	378U	80134	8300-8499	
BEECH CIR	Longmont	11N	80503	2600-2699	
BEECH CIR S	Greenwood Village	345V	80121	5600-5699	
	Jefferson Co	370D	80127	6400-6499	
	Lakewood	310H	80228	1000-1099	
BEECH CT	Arvada	220Z	80004	6300-6399	
	Arvada	220V	80004	6700-7199	
	Arvada	220R	80005	7200-7599	
	Arvada	220D	80005	None	
BEECH CT	Erie	133A	80516	100-199	
BEECH CT	Jefferson Co	280H	80401	2000-2599	
	Jefferson Co	250Z	80401	3200-3399	
	Jefferson Co	371J	80127	7400-7499	
BEECH CT S	Greenwood Village	345U	80121	5700-5799	
	Lakewood	310R	80228	2200-2299	
BEECH DR	Arvada	220V	80004	6700-6799	
BEECH DR S	Lakewood	310D	80228	1000-1199	
BEECH PL	Louisville	130Q	80027	500-599	
BEECH ST	Arvada	220V	80004	6800-7199	
	Arvada	220H	80005	8300-8599	
	Douglas Co	432F	80125	10300-10499	
	Federal Heights	193V	80260	9700-9799	
	Fort Lupton	728H	80621	1100-1199	
	Jefferson Co	280R	80401	800-999	
	Jefferson Co	250M	80002	5100-5399	
	Jefferson Co	250Z	80401	None	
	Lakewood	280R	80401	600-799	
BEECH ST S	Jefferson Co	340M	80465	4800-5099	
	Jefferson Co	842J	80470	13800-13899	
	Lakewood	310D	80228	700-999	
	Lakewood	310M	80228	1500-1999	
BEECH WAY	Arvada	220D	80005	None	
BEECH WAY	Longmont	11N	80503	2700-2799	
BEECH WAY S	Jefferson Co	340H	80465	4300-4499	
	Jefferson Co	340R	80465	None	
	Lakewood	310R	80228	2100-2299	
BEECHNUT PL	Castle Rock	467R	80108	2000-2299	
BEECHWOOD DR	Thornton	195X	80229	9000-9199	
BEECHWOOD DR E	Douglas Co	411F	80138	10000-10399	
BEEKMAN PL	Denver	257L	80239	12100-12299	
	Denver	260J	80249	None	
BEEKMAN PL E	Denver	255K	80216	2600-3399	
BEEKMAN PL W	Denver	254J	80221	1500-1899	
BEELER CT	Denver	257S	80238	None	
BEELER CT S	Arapahoe Co	316D	80247	1100-1399	
	Greenwood Village	346R	80111	5200-5299	
BEELER ST	Adams Co	166M	80602	13600-13799	
	Adams Co	166D	80602	14600-14699	
	Aurora	286H	80010	1100-1999	
	Commerce City	197E	80640	10800-10999	
	Commerce City	196M	80640	None	
	Denver	256Z	80238	2600-2999	
	Denver	256M	80238	None	
	Denver	256Z	80238	None	
	Denver	286D	80220	None	
BEELER ST S	Arapahoe Co	316H	80247	1200-1399	
	Arapahoe Co	316M	80247	1600-1698	E
	Denver	316V	80231	3000-3299	
	Denver	346D	80237	3600-3699	
	Greenwood Village	346M	80111	4900-5099	
	Greenwood Village	346Z	80111	6000-6099	
BEELER WAY	Aurora	286M	80230	None	
BEELER WAY S	Arapahoe Co	316R	80231	2100-2299	
BEE ROCK RD	Douglas Co	866F	80135	500-1499	
BEETHOVEN DR	Gilpin Co	761J	80403	1-499	
BEGOLE CIR	Jefferson Co	762D	80403	11800-11999	
BEGONIA WAY	Superior	160U	80027	1400-1599	
BELATRIX DR	El Paso Co	907R	80132	19400-19999	
BELCARO DR	Denver	315B	80209	3200-3599	
BELCARO LN	Denver	315B	80209	3300-3599	
BELCHER HILL RD	Jefferson Co	783B	80403	24400-24899	
	Jefferson Co	763S	80403	25300-27499	
BELDOCK CT	Brighton	139K	80601	None	
BELDOCK ST	Brighton	139K	80601	None	
BELERO ST	Broomfield	162P	80020	1500-1699	
BELFAST DR W	Littleton	825P	80127	9600-9699	
BELFAST PL W	Littleton	825P	80127	9400-9599	
BELFORD AVE	Douglas Co	377Y	80112	12100-12599	
BELFORD CIR	Broomfield	133N	80020	4600-4899	
BELFORD CT	Jefferson Co	305H	80439	1400-1599	
BELFORD DR	Northglenn	194P	80260	100-499	
BELFORD RD	Thornton	194S	80260	None	
BELFRY CT	Douglas Co	466F	80108	700-799	
	Castle Rock	467Y	80104	3300-3399	
BELGIAN TRAIL	Elbert Co	850Z	80107	1000-1999	
BELGRADE DR	Elbert Co	850D	80138	1100-1299	
BELL CT	Lakewood	282A	80215	2000-2599	
BELL DR	Boulder	98U	80301	3100-3199	
BELL DR	Erie	132A	80026	1800-1999	
	Erie	131D	80026	None	
BELL LN	Northglenn	194T	80260	300-399	
BEL LAGO VIEW	Monument	908W	80132	None	
BELLAIRE CIR	Thornton	195G	80233	10900-11099	
	Thornton	195C	80233	11800-11999	
	Thornton	165Y	80241	12200-12299	
	Thornton	165Q	80241	13200-13299	
BELLAIRE CIR S	Centennial	375C	80121	6500-6599	
	Cherry Hills Village	345G	80113	4200-4299	
BELLAIRE CT	Broomfield	162V	80020	300-499	
	Thornton	195L	80233	10400-10499	
	Thornton	165Y	80241	12300-12399	
	Thornton	165U	80241	12700-12799	
	Thornton	165Q	80241	13100-13199	
BELLAIRE CT S	Greenwood Village	345V	80121	5600-5699	
BELLAIRE DR	Thornton	195Y	80229	9300-9399	
	Thornton	165U	80241	12400-12499	
	Thornton	165Q	80241	13100-13199	
BELLAIRE LN	Thornton	195U	80229	None	
BELLAIRE PL	Thornton	195L	80233	10800-10899	
	Thornton	165Y	80241	12100-12199	
BELLAIRE ST	Broomfield	162R	80020	1100-1399	
	Commerce City	225U	80022	6600-6799	
	Denver	285U	80220	1-799	
	Denver	285L	80220	1100-1999	
	Denver	285C	80207	2000-2799	
	Denver	255Y	80207	2800-3499	
	Thornton	195Y	80229	9100-9499	
	Thornton	195L	80233	10500-10699	
	Thornton	195C	80233	11900-11999	
	Thornton	165Y	80241	12000-12299	
	Thornton	165U	80241	12400-12899	
	Thornton	165Q	80241	12800-13199	
	Thornton	165L	80241	13400-13699	
BELLAIRE ST S	Cherry Hills Village	345G	80113	3900-4199	
	Denver	285U	80246	1-199	
	Denver	315G	80246	1200-1299	
	Denver	315G	80222	1400-2199	
	Denver	315Q	80222	2300-3499	
	Glendale	315G	80246	1100-1199	
BELLAIRE WAY	Thornton	195L	80233	10900-11099	
	Thornton	195C	80233	11600-11699	
BELLAIRE WAY S	Centennial	345Y	80121	5900-6099	
	Centennial	375C	80122	6700-6899	
BELLANCA CT	Erie	133B	80516	2400-2499	
BELLA VISTA DR	Longmont	40P	80503	4400-5299	
	Longmont	40Q	80503	None	
BELLA VISTA DR	Louisville	131W	80027	500-799	
BELLA VISTA DR	Platteville	708G	80651	1400-1799	
BELLA VISTA LN	Boulder	128E	80302	2600-2799	
BELLAVISTA ST	Castle Rock	496C	80109	1800-2699	
BELLA VISTA WAY	Longmont	40P	80503	None	
BELLBROOK CIR	Highlands Ranch	405Q	80130	10900-11099	
BELL CROSS CIR	Douglas Co	410M	80138	11200-11999	
BELL CROSS PL	Douglas Co	410M	80138	11800-19999	
BELL CROSS WAY	Douglas Co	410H	80138	11800-11999	
BELLE CREEK BLVD	Commerce City	196M	80640	10600-10699	
	Commerce City	197J	80640	10700-10799	
BELLE MEADE DR	Jefferson Co	822V	80433	11200-11599	
BELLE MONT TRAIL	Jefferson Co	822Z	80433	28000-28499	
BELLEVIEW AVE E	Arapahoe Co	350Q	80015	22400-22899	
	Arapahoe Co	812V	80102	45700-46499	
	Arapahoe Co	813T	80102	47300-50499	
	Arapahoe Co	813V	80136	52100-53699	
	Aurora	348P	80015	14200-15299	
	Aurora	350M	80016	None	
	Aurora	351J	80016	None	
	Cherry Hills Village	345Q	80121	1601-4299	O
	Cherry Hills Village	346P	80111	4300-6499	
	Englewood	344Q	80113	1-799	
	Greenwood Village	344Q	80121	800-1599	
	Greenwood Village	345Q	80121	1600-4298	E
	Greenwood Village	346P	80111	6500-9699	
	Greenwood Village	347P	80111	9200-12599	
BELLEVIEW AVE W	Denver	341R	80123	9001-9899	O
	Englewood	344N	80110	1-1099	
	Englewood	344N	80120	1100-1599	
	Jefferson Co	341Q	80127	10000-12699	
	Jefferson Co	340R	80465	12700-13199	
	Jefferson Co	340Q	80465	13200-16499	
	Lakewood	342N	80123	8100-8899	
	Lakewood	341R	80123	9000-9898	E
	Lakewood	341R	80123	9900-9999	
	Littleton	344N	80120	1600-2199	
	Littleton	343Q	80120	2200-2699	
	Littleton	343Q	80123	2700-4399	
BELLEVIEW CT E	Greenwood Village	345N	80121	1-1999	
BELLEVIEW DR E	Aurora	348P	80015	14800-15299	
	Centennial	348R	80015	16100-16299	
BELLEVIEW DR W	Jefferson Co	341N	80127	11600-12399	
BELLEVIEW LN E	Arapahoe Co	350P	80015	22100-22499	
	Arapahoe Co	350Q	80015	22800-22899	
	Centennial	349P	80015	18100-18199	
	Centennial	349R	80015	19900-20299	
	Greenwood Village	345N	80121	1-1999	
BELLEVIEW PL E	Arapahoe Co	350P	80015	22000-22299	
	Arapahoe Co	350Q	80015	22500-22899	
	Aurora	351J	80016	24200-24599	
	Centennial	348R	80015	16200-16299	
	Centennial	349N	80015	16700-16799	
	Centennial	349N	80015	17200-17499	
	Centennial	349P	80015	17400-18499	
	Centennial	349Q	80015	18600-19199	
	Centennial	349R	80015	19500-20299	
	Centennial	350N	80015	20600-21399	
	Cherry Hills Village	345N	80110	1-99	
BELLEVIEW WAY E	Greenwood Village	345N	80121	1-99	
BELLE VISTA DR	Jefferson Co	822V	80433	27800-28299	
BELLEWOOD CIR E	Aurora	349N	80015	17400-17599	
BELLEWOOD CT	Highlands Ranch	404C	80126	9300-9399	
BELLEWOOD DR E	Aurora	348N	80015	13800-14199	
	Aurora	348K	80015	14300-14399	
	Aurora	348Q	80015	15000-15199	
	Aurora	349K	80015	17700-18399	
	Aurora	349Q	80015	19000-19199	
	Aurora	350M	80016	23500-24199	
	Aurora	351J	80016	24200-24599	
	Centennial	349R	80015	19700-20099	
BELLEWOOD DR E	Englewood	344Q	80113	200-499	
BELLEWOOD LN E	Centennial	349M	80015	20000-20099	
BELLEWOOD PL E	Arapahoe Co	350N	80015	20300-20899	
	Arapahoe Co	350Q	80015	None	
	Aurora	348K	80015	14300-14399	
	Aurora	348P	80015	14600-14799	
	Aurora	348Q	80015	15700-15799	
	Centennial	349M	80015	20000-20099	
	Denver	346M	80237	8500-8799	
BELLEWOOD PL W	Denver	341R	80123	8900-9699	
	Jefferson Co	341Q	80127	10200-10399	
BELLFLOWER	Jefferson Co	370K	80127	1-99	
BELLFLOWER CT	Boulder Co	70P	80503	8000-8399	
BELLFLOWER DR	Brighton	168C	80601	None	
BELL FLOWER DR	Littleton	343S	80123	4900-5999	
BELLFLOWER PL	Brighton	168C	80601	None	
BELLFLOWER WAY S	Highlands Ranch	374Z	80126	9100-9299	
BELLGREEN PL	Castle Rock	527D	80104	1300-1499	

STREET NAME	CITY or COUNTY	MAP GRID	ZIP CODE	BLOCK RANGE	O/E
BELLINGHAM PL	Longmont	12K	80501	600-699	
BELLISARIO CREEK CT S	Parker	439D	80134	12400-12499	
BELLISARIO CREEK DR E	Parker	439D	80134	19400-19699	
BELLISARIO CREEK PL E	Parker	439C	80134	18900-19099	
BELLMEADE WAY	Longmont	10R	80503	2900-2999	
BELLMORE LN S	Highlands Ranch	405B	80126	9400-9699	
BELLMORE PL	Highlands Ranch	405B	80126	9600-9699	
BELL MOUNTAIN DR	Douglas Co	527S	80104	3400-4599	
BELL MOUNTAIN PKWY	Douglas Co	527J	80104	2-498	E
BELL POINTE DR	Jefferson Co	822V	80433	None	
BELL RANCH RD	Jefferson Co	366P	80439	8200-8499	
BELL STAR CIR	Douglas Co	527S	80104	400-499	
BELLVIEW DR E	Greenwood Village	344R	80121	1-99	
BELLVIEW PL W	Littleton	343P	80123	4100-4399	
BELLVUE DR	Boulder	127M	80302	1-1499	
BELLVUE RD	Jefferson Co	278U	80401	100-398	E
BELLWETHER LN	Lone Tree	407J	80124	None	
BELLWOOD AVE W	Jefferson Co	340R	80465	None	
BELLWOOD DR	Longmont	12U	80501	1400-1599	
BELLWOOD DR E	Arapahoe Co	350N	80015	None	
BELLWOOD DR W	Denver	343K	80123	4300-4399	
BELMAR AVE W	Lakewood	312A	80226	8400-8899	
	Lakewood	311D	80226	8900-8999	
BELMONT AVE W	Jefferson Co	341R	80123	9000-9199	
	Jefferson Co	341P	80127	10800-11499	
	Jefferson Co	341N	80127	12400-12699	
	Jefferson Co	340R	80127	12700-12999	
	Littleton	343P	80123	3300-3399	
BELMONT CT	Douglas Co	439T	80134	None	
BELMONT DR	Longmont	11S	80503	1400-1599	
BELMONT DR W	Jefferson Co	341P	80127	11600-11899	
	Lakewood	342P	80123	7000-7199	
BELMONT PL W	Jefferson Co	341N	80127	11700-11799	
BELMONT ST	Firestone	707N	80504	10000-10999	
BELMONT WAY N	Douglas Co	441S	80134	5900-6299	
BELOIT PL W	Jefferson Co	311U	80227	10500-10599	
	Jefferson Co	311T	80227	10800-10899	
BELSAY CT	Douglas Co	408D	80134	16100-16299	
BELVEDERE LN	Lone Tree	406H	80124	None	
BELVEDERE TERRACE DR	Golden	279B	80401	1700-1999	
BELVIEW CT	Longmont	41B	80501	300-399	
BEMIS CIR S	Littleton	373M	80120	7900-7999	
BEMIS CT S	Littleton	373M	80120	7500-7599	
BEMIS PL S	Littleton	373R	80120	7900-7999	
BEMIS ST S	Littleton	343Z	80120	5700-6199	
	Littleton	373H	80120	6800-6999	
	Littleton	373R	80120	7500-7999	
BEN PL	Boulder	129B	80301	6100-6199	
BENCHMARK DR	Boulder Co	129Z	80303	1-99	
BENDEMEER DR	Clear Creek Co	801V	80439	1-799	
BEND IN THE TRAIL RD	El Paso Co	908P	80132	800-999	
BEN KELLY RD	Elbert Co	890R	80116	24000-24999	
BENNETT AVE	Bennett	792M	80102	None	
	Bennett	793J	80102	None	
BENNETT DR	Parker	409J	80134	17000-17099	
BENNETT PL W	Lakewood	312Y	80227	6800-6999	
BEN NEVIS AVE	Broomfield	162Z	80020	1300-1499	
BENNINGTON AVE E	Castle Rock	498L	80104	4200-4699	
BEN PARK CIR	Douglas Co	469D	80134	5300-5499	
BENT WAY	Longmont	41J	80503	2300-2399	
BENT FEATHER RD	Jefferson Co	823X	80433	23300-24999	
BENTGRASS CIR	Castle Rock	497A	80109	1200-1699	
BENTHAVEN DR	Lakewood	281B	80215	11200-11599	
BENTHAVEN PL	Boulder	128W	80305	1-199	
BENTLEY CIR E	Centennial	376B	80112	7100-7299	
BENTLEY ST	Adams Co	750G	80603	16100-16299	
BENTLEY ST N	Castle Rock	498H	80104	600-699	
BENT NAIL WAY	El Paso Co	908Y	80132	200-299	
BENT OAK LN	El Paso Co	908U	80132	18200-18399	
BENT OAKS CT	Parker	410V	80138	23400-23599	
BENT OAKS ST	Parker	410Z	80138	11500-11999	
BENT OAKS WAY	Parker	410Z	80138	23400-23599	
BENTON AVE	Boulder	97C	80304	None	
BENTON CIR	Arvada	222Z	80003	6500-6599	
BENTON CIR S	Lakewood	342V	80123	5700-5799	
BENTON CT	Arvada	222V	80003	6800-6999	
	Westminster	192H	80020	11200-11499	
	Westminster	192D	80020	11500-11599	
BENTON CT S	Jefferson Co	342Z	80123	6100-6299	
	Jefferson Co	372D	80123	None	
	Lakewood	312R	80227	2300-2399	
BENTON DR S	Lakewood	282V	80226	1-99	
BENTON PL	Parker	409N	80134	10900-10999	
BENTON ST	Arvada	252D	80003	6000-6199	
	Arvada	222Z	80003	6400-6799	
	Arvada	222H	80003	8400-8599	
BENTON ST	Boulder Co	162D	80020	14400-14799	
BENTON ST	Castle Rock	498L	80104	200-499	
	Denver	252M	80212	4800-5199	
	Edgewater	282D	80214	2400-2599	
	Lakewood	282V	80226	1-99	
	Lakewood	282R	80226	300-499	
	Lakewood	282R	80214	800-899	
	Lakewood	282M	80214	900-1499	
	Lakewood	282H	80214	1500-2199	
	Mountain View	252V	80212	4100-4399	
	Westminster	222R	80003	7200-7599	
	Westminster	222D	80031	8800-9199	
	Westminster	192R	80020	10000-10299	
	Westminster	192H	80020	11000-11199	
	Wheat Ridge	282D	80214	2600-2699	
	Wheat Ridge	252Z	80214	2800-3199	
	Wheat Ridge	252Z	80212	3200-3799	
	Wheat Ridge	252V	80212	4000-4099	
BENTON ST S	Denver	312V	80227	2700-2799	
	Jefferson Co	372D	80123	None	
	Lakewood	282V	80226	100-199	
	Lakewood	282Z	80226	200-299	
	Lakewood	312D	80226	900-1099	
	Lakewood	312H	80232	1200-1699	
	Lakewood	312V	80227	2600-2699	
BENTON WAY	Arvada	222H	80003	8200-8399	
	Denver	252M	80212	5000-5099	
	Westminster	192D	80020	None	
BENTON WAY S	Denver	342D	80235	3700-3999	
	Jefferson Co	342Z	80123	6200-6399	
	Jefferson Co	372D	80123	None	
	Lakewood	342V	80123	5600-5799	

STREET NAME	CITY or COUNTY	MAP GRID	ZIP CODE	BLOCK RANGE	O/E
BENT TREE TRAIL	Jefferson Co	336F	80439	None	
BENT TWIG LN	El Paso Co	908P	80132	1200-1299	
BENT WEDGE PT	Castle Rock	467W	80109	None	
BENTWOOD CIR	Highlands Ranch	405K	80126	10100-10299	
BENTWOOD CT	Highlands Ranch	405K	80126	10200-10399	
BENTWOOD LN	Highlands Ranch	405K	80126	10200-10399	
BENTWOOD PL	Highlands Ranch	405K	80126	3100-3299	
BEREA DR	Boulder	128T	80305	1000-1299	
BEREN ST	Park Co	820V	80421	1-99	
BERG LN	Jefferson Co	822W	80470	33400-35599	
BERGANOT TRAIL					
	Castle Pines North	436F	80108	900-1299	
BERGEN PKWY	Jefferson Co	305M	80439	1100-2099	
BERGEN HILL DR	Jefferson Co	306T	80439	2800-2999	
BERGEN MTN RD	Jefferson Co	305Y	80439	33000-33599	
BERGEN PARK	Douglas Co	866W	80135	None	
	Douglas Co	886A	80135	None	
BERGEN PEAK DR	Jefferson Co	306W	80439	2800-3199	
	Jefferson Co	306W	80439	31200-31299	
BERGEN VIEW TRAIL	Jefferson Co	335K	80439	33800-33999	
BERKELEY CIR	Castle Pines North	436L	80108	7400-7499	
BERKELEY CT	Douglas Co	436M	80108	7400-7499	
BERKELEY CT	Longmont	11W	80503	1000-1199	
BERKELEY PL	Denver	257G	80239	12200-12299	
BERKELEY PL W	Denver	254J	80221	1500-1899	
BERKLEY AVE	Boulder	128K	80305	3400-3699	
BERKLEY CT	Boulder	128K	80305	3300-3399	
BERKSHIRE CT	Boulder Co	100E	80301	4700-4799	
BERKSHIRE CT	Castle Pines North	436M	80108	7500-7599	
	Jefferson Co	306P	80439	30000-30099	
BERKSHIRE LN	Castle Pines North	436M	80108	7400-7999	
BERKSHIRE PL	Boulder Co	100E	80301	4600-4799	
BERKSHIRE ST	Boulder Co	100E	80301	4700-4799	
BERLIN CIR	Arvada	251C	80004	6100-6199	
BERMONT AVE N	Lafayette	132J	80026	100-899	
BERMONT AVE S	Lafayette	132J	80026	100-899	
BERMONT DR	Lafayette	131M	80026	500-899	
BERMONT ST	Lafayette	131H	80026	400-899	
BERMUDA DUNES DR N	Jefferson Co	306J	80439	31300-31599	
BERMUDA DUNES DR S	Jefferson Co	306J	80439	31300-31499	
BERMUDA RUN CIR	Highlands Ranch	376X	80130	8900-9099	
BERRIAN TRAIL	Jefferson Co	823N	80433	26900-26999	
BERRY AVE E	Arapahoe Co	347T	80111	10500-11199	
	Arapahoe Co	347U	80111	11600-11699	
	Arapahoe Co	350U	80015	20900-20999	
	Aurora	350R	80016	None	
	Centennial	348R	80015	16300-16499	
	Centennial	349N	80015	16900-17199	
	Centennial	349T	80015	17800-18199	
	Centennial	350N	80015	20900-20999	
	Centennial	348R	80015	None	
	Centennial	348U	80015	None	
	Greenwood Village	346N	80111	5600-7299	
	Greenwood Village	346P	80111	7300-7699	
	Greenwood Village	346V	80111	8900-9299	
BERRY AVE W	Denver	342V	80123	5701-5999	O
	Denver	342U	80123	6100-6699	
	Denver	342S	80123	8600-8799	
	Jefferson Co	341S	80127	10700-12499	
	Littleton	344S	80120	400-1599	
	Littleton	343V	80120	2100-2599	
	Littleton	343T	80123	2700-4499	
BERRY CIR	Jefferson Co	280C	80401	2700-2799	
BERRY CIR W	Littleton	344P	80120	500-599	
BERRY CT E	Greenwood Village	346V	80111	9100-9399	
BERRY DR E	Arapahoe Co	347Q	80111	11100-11499	
	Arapahoe Co	347U	80111	11600-11699	
	Arapahoe Co	349U	80015	18500-19199	
	Centennial	348V	80015	16000-16299	
	Centennial	350S	80015	17100-20999	
	Centennial	349T	80015	17800-18599	
	Greenwood Village	347S	80111	9900-10499	
BERRY DR W	Jefferson Co	341U	80123	9800-9899	
	Jefferson Co	341U	80127	10100-10799	
	Jefferson Co	340V	80127	12800-13199	
	Littleton	344N	80120	900-1399	
	Littleton	343T	80123	3400-3599	
BERRY LN	Jefferson Co	280C	80401	2700-2899	
BERRY LN E	Centennial	348V	80015	16500-16799	
	Centennial	349R	80015	20100-20299	
	Centennial	350P	80015	21800-21899	
BERRY LN S	Greenwood Village	346V	80111	5400-5699	
BERRY PL E	Arapahoe Co	347T	80111	10800-10999	
	Arapahoe Co	347U	80111	11600-11699	
	Arapahoe Co	349U	80015	18700-19399	
	Arapahoe Co	350T	80015	22100-22199	
	Aurora	351N	80016	24500-24899	
	Centennial	348V	80015	16300-16499	
	Centennial	349S	80015	16900-17299	
	Centennial	349T	80015	17500-17799	
	Centennial	349V	80015	20100-20399	
	Centennial	350S	80015	20800-20999	
	Centennial	350T	80015	21800-21899	
	Greenwood Village	346U	80111	7700-7899	
	Littleton	344U	80121	None	
BERRY PL W	Jefferson Co	341V	80123	9200-9299	
	Jefferson Co	341T	80127	10100-11599	
	Littleton	343T	80123	3400-3599	
BERRY RD	Jefferson Co	250Y	80401	13600-14399	
BERRY WAY W	Denver	342U	80123	None	
BERRYBUSH LN	Gilpin Co	761F	80403	1-99	
BERRY BUSH LN	Jefferson Co	366C	80439	6300-6899	
BERRY HILL LN	Jefferson Co	842F	80470	None	
BERRY RIDGE WAY	Castle Rock	528E	80104	None	
BERRY TURN	Jefferson Co	280C	80401	2700-2799	
BERT DR	Jefferson Co	365Y	80433	32600-32699	
BERTHA CT	Jefferson Co	368X	80465	9000-9099	
BERTHOUD ST	Westminster	223R	80030	7100-7199	
BERTHOUD WAY	Golden	279T	80401	200-399	
BERTHOUD WAY	Parker	409J	80134	10500-10599	
BERTHOUD TRAIL	Broomfield	162K	80020	200-299	
BERWICK AVE	Firestone	727B	80504	None	
BERWICK CT	Boulder Co	100E	80301	7600-7699	
BERYL RD	Gilpin Co	761E	80403	100-199	
BERYL ST	Broomfield	162U	80020	300-999	
BERYL WAY	Broomfield	162Y	80020	100-299	
BESHEAR CT N	Erie	102Q	80516	600-699	
BESHEAR CT S	Erie	102Q	80516	600-799	

STREET NAME	CITY or COUNTY	MAP GRID	ZIP CODE	BLOCK RANGE	O/E
BEST RD E	Douglas Co	908C	80118	2000-4699	
	Douglas Co	909A	80118	4700-5999	
BEST WAY S	Douglas Co	909A	80118	None	
BESTVIEW DR	Douglas Co	909A	80118	12400-12799	
BESTWOOD DR	Douglas Co	909E	80118	5400-5699	
BETASSO RD	Boulder Co	742C	80302	1-1099	
BETH AVE	Fort Lupton	728M	80621	200-899	
BETH CT	Elbert Co	871B	80107	4000-4299	
BETH LN	Northglenn	194J	80234	1200-1499	
BETHANY CIR E	Aurora	319S	80013	17100-17699	
BETHANY DR E	Aurora	317T	80014	10600-11199	
	Aurora	319T	80013	17600-17999	
	Aurora	319U	80013	19400-19599	
	Aurora	319V	80013	19600-19899	
BETHANY PL E	Aurora	317V	80014	12700-13299	
	Aurora	318S	80014	13600-13699	
	Aurora	318V	80013	15900-16199	
	Aurora	319S	80013	16900-16999	
	Aurora	319T	80013	17600-17999	
	Aurora	319T	80013	18000-18499	
	Aurora	319U	80013	19000-19099	
	Denver	316S	80222	6400-6499	
	Denver	316T	80224	6500-6799	
	Denver	316U	80231	7800-8199	
BETHEL CT	Castle Rock	497E	80109	1300-1499	
BETHLEHEM CIR	Broomfield	163U	80020	2700-2799	
BETTENCOURT AVE	Highlands Ranch	404M	80126	1100-1199	
BETTS CIR	Erie	102W	80516	2500-2699	
BETTS RANCH RD	Douglas Co	440Q	80134	None	
BETTY LN	Jefferson Co	336X	80439	6300-6399	
BETTY PL	Weld Co	103C	80516	4600-4799	
BETTY ST	Douglas Co	467P	80108	3600-3899	
BEVERLY BLVD	Douglas Co	848E	80108	7600-7999	
BEVERLY DR S	Englewood	344J	80110	4600-4699	
BEVERLY LN	Weld Co	103C	80516	4600-4799	
BEVERLY RD	Jefferson Co	842A	80470	33300-33999	
BEVERLY ST	Elbert Co	871E	80107	600-699	
BEXLEY	Thornton	195N	80229	None	
BEXLEY CT E	Highlands Ranch	404G	80126	400-499	
BEXLEY DR S	Highlands Ranch	404G	80126	9400-9799	
BEXLEY LN E	Highlands Ranch	404C	80126	400-599	
BEXLEY ST E	Highlands Ranch	404G	80126	400-499	
BIBLES HILL DR	Douglas Co	850W	80116	1900-2399	
BIERSTADT	Douglas Co	407B	80112	10400-10599	
BIERSTADT CT	Jefferson Co	305M	80439	1500-1599	
BIERSTADT LOOP	Broomfield	133J	80020	None	
BIERSTADT RD	Thornton	193V	80260	None	
BIG BEAR CIR	Douglas Co	867K	80109	2200-3399	
BIG BEAR DR	Douglas Co	496S	80109	1600-3499	
BIG BEAR DR	Douglas Co	867E	80135	2200-3499	
	Douglas Co	867E	80109	None	
	Jefferson Co	306E	80439	31000-31199	
BIG BEND	Weld Co	706P	80504	3300-11499	
BIG CANON DR	Greenwood Village	346V	80111	5600-5899	
BIG CANON PL	Greenwood Village	346V	80111	8900-9099	
BIGCONE SPRUCE	Jefferson Co	370P	80127	1-99	
BIG DRY CREEK DR	Broomfield	163U	80020	2600-12599	
BIG DRY CREEK DR E	Centennial	376L	80112	7900-8299	
BIG ELK DR	Jefferson Co	306D	80401	None	
BIG GAME TRAIL	Jefferson Co	843G	80433	23000-23099	
BIG HORN CIR	Elbert Co	851C	80107	None	
BIG HORN CIR	Lafayette	132W	80026	2600-2799	
BIGHORN CT	Lone Tree	376Z	80124	8200-8299	
BIGHORN CT	Longmont	12W	80501	1100-1199	
BIG HORN DR	Jefferson Co	371W	80127	9100-9299	
BIGHORN DR N	Arapahoe Co	794S	80136	900-999	
BIG HORN ST	Boulder	98P	80301	None	
BIGHORN WAY	Douglas Co	432L	80125	9500-9699	
BIGHORN TERRACE	Fort Lupton	728M	80621	200-399	
BIG HORN TRAIL	Douglas Co	432T	80125	6400-6999	
BIG MEADOW TRAIL	Douglas Co	870E	80116	None	
BIG ROCK LN	Park Co	841T	80421	1-299	
BIG SKY CT	Jefferson Co	306E	80439	1100-1299	
BIG SKY TRAIL	Douglas Co	890X	80118	None	
BIG SPRINGS DR	Nederland	740R	80466	None	
BIG SPRINGS POINTE DR	Nederland	740R	80466	None	
BIG TIMBER	Jefferson Co	306M	80401	None	
BIG TIMBER DR	Jefferson Co	842C	80433	12400-12499	
BIJOU AVE	Palmer Lake	907U	80133	None	
BIJOU AVE W	Arapahoe Co	795Y	80103	1-299	
BILBERRY ST	Castle Rock	466V	80109	None	
BILLINGS AVE	Boulder Co	102J	80026	11200-11899	
BILLINGS AVE	Frederick	726G	80516	None	
BILLINGS CIR S	Aurora	348F	80015	4300-4399	
BILLINGS CT S	Aurora	348K	80015	4800-4899	
BILLINGS LN	Longmont	12K	80501	2200-2399	
BILLINGS ST	Aurora	288P	80011	400-799	
	Aurora	288F	80011	1500-2199	
	Aurora	288B	80011	2300-2799	
	Aurora	258X	80011	3000-3299	
	Commerce City	198K	80022	10400-10798	E
	Denver	258J	80239	4900-5599	
BILLINGS ST S	Aurora	318F	80012	1200-1399	
BILLINGS WAY	Centennial	348W	80111	6200-6599	
BILLINGS WAY S	Aurora	318K	80012	1800-1899	
	Centennial	378B	80111	6200-6699	
BILLINGTON DR	Erie	131D	80026	None	
BILLY DAVIS RD	Douglas Co	870F	80116	1-1199	
BILOXI CT E	Aurora	380R	80016	8100-8199	
BILOXI CT N	Arapahoe Co	290V	80018	1-99	
BILOXI CT S	Arapahoe Co	350R	80016	5300-5399	
BILOXI CT S	Aurora	380D	80016	6800-7499	
	Aurora	380M	80016	8100-8199	
	Aurora	320H	80018	None	
BILOXI ST S	Arapahoe Co	320D	80018	700-799	
	Arapahoe Co	350R	80016	5200-5299	
BILOXI WAY N	Aurora	290R	80018	None	
BILOXI WAY S	Aurora	380M	80016	7600-7899	
	Aurora	350R	80016	None	
	Aurora	350M	80016	None	
BILTMORE WAY S	Highlands Ranch	404H	80126	9600-9699	
BIMINI CT	Boulder	98K	80301	4000-4099	
BINGHAM DR	Broomfield	164E	80020	1700-1799	
BINGHAM PL W	Denver	283W	80219	4300-5199	
BIRCH AVE	Boulder	128K	80305	3000-3099	
	Brighton	138S	80601	200-499	
	Castle Rock	497R	80104	100-299	
	Thornton	165S	80241	2200-2399	
	Weld Co	706R	80504	None	

B

STREET NAME	CITY or COUNTY	MAP GRID	ZIP CODE	BLOCK RANGE	O/E
BIRCH AVE E	Douglas Co	408B	80134	3000-3999	
BIRCH CIR	Thornton	165Q	80241	13300-13399	
BIRCH CIR E	Centennial	345Y	80121	6400-6499	
BIRCH CIR S	Centennial	375C	80121	6400-6499	
BIRCH CT	Broomfield	162V	80020	None	
BIRCH CT	Fort Lupton	728H	80621	900-999	
BIRCH CT	Greenwood Village	345R	80121	5300-5399	
	Greenwood Village	345V	80121	5800-5899	
BIRCH CT	Longmont	11W	80503	1-99	
BIRCH CT	Louisville	130Q	80027	600-799	
BIRCH CT	Thornton	195L	80233	10700-10799	
	Thornton	195G	80233	11300-11599	
	Thornton	165L	80241	13300-13399	
BIRCH CT S	Centennial	375L	80122	7700-7799	
BIRCH DR	Thornton	195L	80233	10800-10999	
	Thornton	195C	80233	11200-11899	
	Thornton	165Q	80241	12800-13099	
	Thornton	194W	80260	None	
BIRCH LN	Jefferson Co	842D	80433	28500-28599	
BIRCH LN	Littleton	373P	80120	None	
BIRCH LN	Thornton	195U	80229	None	
BIRCH RD	Frederick	706Y	80504	3300-9399	
BIRCH ST	Adams Co	225U	80022	7000-7199	
	Adams Co	165C	80602	14400-14499	
BIRCH ST	Bennett	793J	80102	None	
BIRCH ST	Broomfield	162V	80020	300-999	
	Broomfield	162R	80020	1000-1799	
	Broomfield	162M	80020	1800-1899	
BIRCH ST	Commerce City	225U	80022	6600-6999	
	Commerce City	225Q	80022	7200-7399	
	Denver	285U	80220	1-99	
	Denver	285Q	80220	300-899	
	Denver	285L	80220	1100-1499	
	Denver	285C	80207	2000-2799	
	Denver	255Y	80207	2800-3499	
	Federal Heights	193U	80260	2700-2799	
	Federal Heights	193U	80260	9700-9899	
BIRCH ST	Golden	278D	80401	None	
BIRCH ST	Hudson	730Q	80642	None	
BIRCH ST	Thornton	195Y	80229	9100-9499	
	Thornton	195L	80233	10400-10699	
	Thornton	195G	80233	11200-11599	
	Thornton	165Y	80241	12100-12299	
BIRCH ST S	Centennial	375G	80122	7200-7499	
	Cherry Hills Village	345G	80113	3900-4199	
	Cherry Hills Village	345Q	80121	4900-5099	
	Denver	285Y	80246	1-299	
	Denver	315G	80246	1200-1299	
	Denver	315G	80222	1300-1699	
	Denver	315U	80222	2100-3499	
	Glendale	285Y	80246	300-499	
	Glendale	315C	80246	800-1199	
BIRCH WAY	Broomfield	162V	80020	None	
	Thornton	165Q	80241	13100-13199	
	Thornton	165L	80241	13400-13499	
BIRCH WAY S	Centennial	345U	80121	5900-5999	
	Centennial	375G	80122	6700-7199	
BIRCHLEAF CT	Castle Rock	497D	80104	1600-1899	
BIRCHWOOD CT	Lafayette	101X	80026	1501-1699	O
BIRCHWOOD CT S	Parker	410V	80138	11300-11499	
BIRCHWOOD DR	Boulder	98N	80304	3700-3899	
BIRCHWOOD ST S	Parker	410V	80138	11300-11399	
BIRCHWOOD WAY	El Paso Co	908T	80132	18900-18999	
BIRD CLIFF WAY	Boulder Co	70P	80503	6600-6799	
BIRDIE CT	Boulder Co	723G	80503	4200-4299	
BIRDIE LN	Columbine Valley	343X	80123	1-99	
BIRDIE LN	Parker	410V	80138	11300-11399	
BIRDIE RD	Broomfield	162Q	80020	1100-1199	
BIRDSILL PL	Longmont	12J	80501	1-99	
BIRD SONG DR	Castle Rock	528A	80104	None	
BIRD TRAIL	Park Co	841V	80421	None	
BIRMINGHAM CT	Highlands Ranch	375Z	80126	1-99	
BIROLLI PL	Douglas Co	432J	80125	None	
BISCAY CIR	Aurora	289G	80011	1600-1699	
BISCAY CIR S	Aurora	319U	80013	3000-3099	
	Aurora	349G	80013	4100-4299	
	Centennial	349Q	80015	5100-5499	
BISCAY CT	Denver	259L	80249	None	
BISCAY CT S	Arapahoe Co	349U	80015	5600-5699	
	Arapahoe Co	349Y	80016	6000-6099	
	Aurora	319C	80017	1100-1199	
	Aurora	319G	80017	1400-1599	
	Aurora	319L	80017	1800-1899	
	Aurora	319Q	80013	2400-2599	
	Aurora	319U	80013	2800-2899	
	Aurora	349C	80013	3600-3699	
	Aurora	349L	80015	4700-4799	
	Centennial	349Q	80015	5100-5199	
BISCAY ST	Aurora	289G	80011	1700-1999	
	Commerce City	769F	80022	None	
	Denver	259Q	80249	4300-4699	
	Denver	259C	80249	5700-5899	
	Denver	259G	80249	None	
	Denver	259L	80249	None	
BISCAY ST S	Arapahoe Co	349U	80015	5700-5899	
	Arapahoe Co	349Y	80016	5900-6099	
	Aurora	319G	80017	1100-1299	
	Aurora	319G	80017	1300-1399	
	Aurora	319U	80013	2900-3099	
	Aurora	319Y	80013	3300-3599	
	Aurora	349C	80013	3800-3899	
	Centennial	379L	80016	7500-7799	
BISCAY WAY S	Arapahoe Co	349Y	80016	5900-6099	
	Aurora	319G	80017	1400-1499	
	Aurora	319Y	80013	3200-3299	
	Aurora	349G	80015	4300-4499	
BISCAYNE CT	Lafayette	132E	80026	300-399	
BISCAYNE CT E	Highlands Ranch	405A	80126	2100-2199	
BISCUIT ROOT DR	Parker	379W	80134	17700-17799	
BISHOP CT	Castle Rock	497M	80104	900-999	
BISHOP RD	Park Co	820Z	80421	1-599	
BISHOP PINE WAY	Castle Rock	498H	80104	600-899	
BISMARK DR	Lone Tree	407J	80124	None	
BISON CT	Douglas Co	432L	80125	7500-7799	
BISON DR	Arapahoe Co	793V	80136	53300-53899	
BISON DR	Boulder Co	742R	80302	1-3999	
BISON DR	Bow Mar	342M	80123	5300-5599	
BISON DR E	Arapahoe Co	794S	80136	53300-55299	
BISON PL	Douglas Co	432L	80125	7400-7599	
BIT RD	Jefferson Co	306X	80439	3200-3299	
BITTERBRUSH LN	Parker	379S	80134	16800-16899	
BITTERCRESS CT E	Parker	409A	80134	17600-17799	
BITTERN CIR	Thornton	165N	80241	None	
BITTERROOT CIR	Lafayette	131F	80026	2400-2499	
BITTERROOT LN	Jefferson Co	307R	80401	2100-2499	
BITTERROOT PL	Highlands Ranch	373Z	80129	2200-2799	
BITTERSWEET LN	Jefferson Co	307X	80439	3100-3299	
BITTERSWEET LN	Longmont	40L	80503	700-899	
BITTERWEED CT	Highlands Ranch	374Y	80126	9100-9199	
BIXBY AVE	Boulder	128F	80303	2900-2999	
BIXBY CT	Castle Rock	466X	80109	2800-2999	
BLACK BEAR LN	Jefferson Co	370A	80127	1-99	
	Jefferson Co	823X	80433	22900-24199	
BLACK BEAR RUN	Douglas Co	845Q	80125	5100-5199	
BLACK BEAR TRAIL	Gilpin Co	741Z	80403	1-499	
BLACK BEAR TRAIL	Jefferson Co	823X	80433	22800-23999	
BLACK BIRCH RD	Jefferson Co	278S	80401	1-399	
BLACKBIRD CIR S	Highlands Ranch	406E	80130	9900-10099	
BLACKBIRD CT	Boulder Co	129F	80303	1200-1299	
BLACKBIRD DR	Park Co	841T	80421	1-399	
BLACKBIRD PL S	Highlands Ranch	406E	80130	9900-10099	
BLACKBIRD WAY	Highlands Ranch	406E	80130	None	
BLACK CANYON WAY	Castle Rock	466Z	80109	None	
BLACK CHERRY CT	Boulder Co	98K	80301	4200-4399	
BLACK DIAMOND DR	Lafayette	131H	80026	None	
BLACK EAGLE	Jefferson Co	306E	80439	None	
BLACK EAGLE RD	Clear Creek Co	780T	80452	1-399	
BLACK FEATHER LOOP	Castle Rock	467Y	80104	400-499	
BLACK FEATHER TRAIL	Castle Rock	467Y	80104	3700-4299	
BLACK FEATHER TRAIL	Jefferson Co	306W	80439	31400-31499	
BLACKFOOT CIR	Douglas Co	846U	80135	6000-6299	
BLACKFOOT RD	Jefferson Co	822Y	80433	11400-12099	
BLACKFOOT ST	Superior	160E	80027	300-499	
BLACK FOREST DR E	Douglas Co	381X	80138	10200-10999	
BLACK FOREST RD	El Paso Co	910S	80908	16500-21999	
BLACK FOX CIR	Elbert Co	851Q	80107	4900-4999	
BLACK FOX LN	Greenwood Village	346N	80111	1-99	
BLACK FOX LN	Jefferson Co	368H	80465	20600-20699	
BLACK GULCH RD	Gilpin Co	741Z	80403	None	
BLACK GUM ST	Douglas Co	378V	80134	8300-8599	
BLACKHAWK CIR	Aurora	258X	80011	3200-3299	
BLACKHAWK CIR S	Aurora	348F	80014	4200-4299	
BLACKHAWK CT E	Highlands Ranch	406F	80130	6700-6799	
BLACKHAWK CT S	Arapahoe Co	348P	80015	5100-5199	
	Centennial	348X	80016	6200-6299	
BLACK HAWK DR	Jefferson Co	823X	80433	11700-12299	
BLACKHAWK LN	Lafayette	131G	80026	300-399	
BLACKHAWK RD	Boulder	129J	80303	500-5499	
	Aurora	288P	80011	300-399	
	Aurora	288F	80011	1900-1999	
	Aurora	258X	80011	3000-3199	
	Commerce City	198K	80022	None	
BLACKHAWK ST S	Arapahoe Co	378F	80112	7000-7699	
	Aurora	318B	80012	600-1299	
	Aurora	318P	80014	1800-2699	
	Aurora	288T	80012	None	
	Centennial	378B	80111	6600-6699	
BLACKHAWK WAY	Denver	258J	80239	4600-5399	
	Denver	258F	80239	5500-5599	
BLACKHAWK WAY S	Aurora	318F	80012	1200-1399	
	Aurora	318K	80012	1600-1799	
	Aurora	318X	80014	3400-3499	
	Aurora	348F	80015	4300-4399	
	Aurora	348X	80016	6200-6399	
	Aurora	378B	80016	None	
BLACKHAWK TRAIL	Jefferson Co	843A	80433	12200-12299	
BLACK HORN CIR S	Parker	408Z	80134	None	
BLACK HORN DR E	Parker	408Z	80134	None	
BLACKMER RD	Cherry Hills Village	345H	80113	1-99	
BLACK MESA RD	Frederick	726G	80516	6300-6599	
BLACKMOOR AVE	Parker	410Q	80138	None	
BLACKMOOR ST	Parker	410U	80138	None	
BLACK MOUNTAIN DR	Jefferson Co	365U	80439	7700-8399	
	Jefferson Co	365U	80433	8400-9099	
BLACK OAK CT	Douglas Co	408M	80134	16600-16699	
BLACK PINE CT	Castle Rock	498E	80104	1300-1499	
BLACK PINE DR	Castle Rock	498A	80104	2500-2699	
BLACKSMITH CT	Parker	408V	80134	11800-11899	
BLACKSMITH RD	El Paso Co	912U	80831	17500-18399	
BLACK SPRUCE LN	Elbert Co	830Q	80138	46000-46499	
BLACK SQUIRREL RD	El Paso Co	910V	80908	17800-18799	
BLACK SQUIRREL RUN	Douglas Co	845Q	80125	5100-5399	
BLACKSTONE CT E	Highlands Ranch	374V	80126	1500-1599	
BLACKSTONE PKWY S	Aurora	381R	80016	7900-8199	
BLACK SWAN LN	Cherry Hills Village	345B	80113	1-99	
BLACKTAIL CT	Castle Rock	466X	80109	4000-4199	
BLACKTAIL MOUNTAIN	Jefferson Co	371F	80127	11600-12099	
BLACKTHORN CT E	Parker	408R	80134	11300-11499	
BLACKTHORN WAY E	Parker	408R	80134	16200-16599	
BLACK WIDOW DR	Jefferson Co	365V	80433	31400-32399	
BLACK WIDOW WAY	Jefferson Co	365V	80433	31500-31699	
BLACKWOLF DR	Parker	410Q	80138	11000-11199	
BLACKWOLF LN	Parker	410Q	80138	11000-11199	
BLACKWOLF WAY	Parker	410Q	80138	22900-23299	
BLAIR DR	Idaho Springs	780R	80452	1600-1699	
BLAKCOMB CT	Jefferson Co	306K	80439	1500-1599	
BLAKE DR	Highlands Ranch	404B	80129	None	
BLAKE ST	Denver	284A	80204	1300-1399	
	Denver	284B	80202	1400-1999	
	Denver	284B	80205	2000-2299	
	Denver	254Y	80205	2300-4099	
BLAKEFORD ST	Douglas Co	409X	80134	None	
BLAKELAND DR	Highlands Ranch	373T	80125	8000-8599	
BLANCA CT	Douglas Co	377X	80112	None	
BLANCA CT	Jefferson Co	249B	80403	5900-6099	
	Jefferson Co	249F	80403	None	
BLANCA LN	Broomfield	163J	80020	4600-4699	
BLANCA RD	Thornton	193V	80260	None	
BLANCA ST	Jefferson Co	249F	80403	5600-5799	
BLANCA PEAK CT	Brighton	140J	80601	None	
BLANCA PEAK CT	Superior	160Y	80027	3400-3599	
BLANCA PEAK DR	Superior	160Y	80027	3500-3699	
BLANDFORD CIR N	Douglas Co	470A	80134	5200-5399	
BLANKETFLOWER LN	Douglas Co	411S	80138	9600-9699	
BLAZING LN E	Highlands Ranch	375T	80126	2800-3099	
BLAZING STAR PL	Parker	378R	80134	8400-8499	
BLAZING STAR TRAIL N	Castle Rock	466Q	80109	4500-5099	
BLIZZARD VALLEY TRAIL	Monument	908W	80132	2100-2299	
BLOOM PL	Castle Rock	466W	80109	5100-5199	
BLOSSOM CT	Douglas Co	408L	80134	10300-10399	
BLOSSOM HILL LN	Douglas Co	441E	80138	8300-8599	
BLOSSOM HILL WAY	Douglas Co	441E	80138	8100-8299	
BLUEBEAD WAY E	Parker	409A	80134	9500-9599	
BLUEBELL AVE	Boulder	127M	80302	1300-1599	
	Boulder	128J	80302	1600-2299	
BLUEBELL CIR	Jefferson Co	365C	80439	32900-33599	
BLUEBELL DR	Brighton	168C	80601	1600-1899	
BLUEBELL DR	Clear Creek Co	304H	80439	1-99	
BLUEBELL LN	Clear Creek Co	781W	80452	1-199	
BLUEBELL LN	Jefferson Co	335Y	80439	5800-5999	
	Jefferson Co	365C	80439	6000-6699	
BLUEBELL PL	Douglas Co	378V	80134	16200-16399	
BLUEBELL WAY	Adams Co	224F	80221	8200-8299	
BLUEBELL WAY	Brighton	168C	80601	1100-1199	
BLUE BELL TRAIL	Elbert Co	851L	80107	5100-40599	
BLUEBERRY CIR	Boulder	98E	80304	None	
BLUEBERRY HILLS RD	El Paso Co	908P	80132	1200-1699	
BLUEBERRY TRAIL	Park Co	841V	80421	1-299	
BLUEBIRD AVE	Boulder Co	69G	80503	6300-6699	
BLUEBIRD CT	Boulder Co	69G	80503	6300-6399	
BLUEBIRD DR	Longmont	41T	80504	2200-2399	
BLUEBIRD DR	Park Co	841U	80421	1-799	
BLUEBIRD LN	Elbert Co	871G	80107	33800-33999	
	Elbert Co	850V	80107	37500-37599	
BLUEBIRD LN	Lafayette	130G	80026	700-899	
BLUEBIRD LN	Park Co	841U	80421	1-1299	
BLUE BIRD LN N	Douglas Co	830J	80138	10200-13699	
BLUE BIRD RD	Jefferson Co	368B	80465	6700-6799	
BLUEBIRD ST	Brighton	137Z	80601	1100-1399	
BLUEBIRD TRAIL	Elbert Co	870R	80107	1500-1599	
BLUE BLOOD CT	Douglas Co	432C	80125	None	
BLUE BONNET CT	Castle Rock	466Q	80109	5300-5399	
BLUEBONNET DR	Brighton	139K	80601	100-299	
BLUE BONNET DR	Douglas Co	408H	80134	15900-16599	
BLUE BUNCH CT	Parker	378V	80134	8600-8699	
BLUE CEDAR	Jefferson Co	370Q	80127	1-99	
BLUE CLOVER LN	El Paso Co	908Q	80132	19600-19699	
BLUE CREEK RD S	Jefferson Co	366F	80439	6900-8999	
BLUEFIELD AVE	Longmont	42C	80501	1400-1699	
BLUEFIELD CT	Longmont	42C	80501	800-899	
BLUE FIR CT	Parker	439D	80134	12200-12299	
BLUE FLAG LN	Gilpin Co	741X	80403	1-199	
BLUE FLAX	Jefferson Co	370K	80127	1-99	
BLUE FLAX DR	Douglas Co	887F	80118	6900-7099	
BLUE FLAX TRAIL	Clear Creek Co	781Z	80439	1-299	
BLUE FOX CT	Jefferson Co	370E	80127	1-99	
BLUEFOX CT	Lone Tree	376Y	80124	7400-7499	
BLUE GARTER WAY	El Paso Co	908Y	80132	200-299	
BLUEGATE DR	Highlands Ranch	405R	80130	4700-4999	
BLUEGATE LN	Highlands Ranch	405R	80130	4800-4999	
BLUEGATE WAY	Highlands Ranch	405R	80130	10900-11099	
BLUE GRAMA CT	Parker	378R	80134	8400-8499	
BLUE GRASS CIR	Castle Rock	466Q	80109	3200-3399	
BLUEGRASS CIR	Douglas Co	378V	80134	8300-8599	
BLUEGRASS CIR	Parker	378V	80134	8600-8699	
BLUEGRASS CT S	Boulder Co	99H	80301	7100-7299	
BLUE GRASS CT	Castle Rock	466Q	80109	3200-3299	
BLUEGRASS CT	Parker	378V	80134	8600-8699	
BLUEGRASS DR	Longmont	40M	80503	600-899	
BLUEGRASS ST	Firestone	707S	80504	None	
BLUEGRASS WAY	Longmont	40M	80503	700-799	
BLUE GROUSE RD	Clear Creek Co	801V	80439	1-399	
BLUE GROUSE RIDGE	Jefferson Co	370B	80127	1-99	
BLUE HERON CIR	Greenwood Village	345R	80121	1-199	
BLUE HERON CIR	Lafayette	101X	80026	2400W-3599W	
BLUE HERON CT	Broomfield	163J	80020	4800-4999	
BLUE HERON CT	Greenwood Village	345R	80121	1-199	
BLUE HERON CT	Mead	706C	80542	100-199	
BLUE HERON CT S	Highlands Ranch	404K	80129	10300-10399	
BLUE HERON DR	Greenwood Village	345R	80121	1-199	
BLUE HERON DR	Jefferson Co	842Z	80421	None	
BLUE HERON DR	Thornton	165N	80241	1-99	
BLUE HERON LN	Greenwood Village	345R	80121	1-99	
BLUE HERON WAY	Highlands Ranch	404K	80129	600-699	
BLUE HERON WAY	Lafayette	101W	80026	2600-3699	
BLUE INDIGO LN	Parker	409S	80134	None	
BLUEJAY AVE	Brighton	137Z	80601	1200-1299	
BLUE JAY CIR	Castle Rock	466S	80109	5100-5299	
BLUEJAY CT	Elbert Co	871G	80107	33500-33599	
BLUE JAY DR	Golden	279N	80401	500-699	
BLUEJAY DR E	Douglas Co	409M	80138	6700-6899	
BLUE JAY LN	Douglas Co	907F	80118	13900-14099	
BLUE JAY LN	Northglenn	194L	80233	10600-10999	
BLUE JAY RD	Jefferson Co	368B	80465	6700-6799	
	Jefferson Co	368F	80465	22500-22599	
BLUE JAY ST	Federal Heights	193U	80260	2800-2899	
BLUE JAY WAY	Lafayette	132W	80026	2800-2999	
BLUE LAKE TRAIL	Lafayette	131E	80026	400-598	E
BLUELEAF PL	Douglas Co	378V	80134	16200-16299	
BLUE MESA DR	Douglas Co	432Q	80125	10001-10099	O
BLUE MESA LN	Douglas Co	432Q	80125	6900-6999	
BLUE MESA WAY	Douglas Co	432U	80125	6800-6999	
BLUE MIST CIR	Parker	378V	80134	16600-16999	
BLUE MOON CIR	Lochbuie	140B	80603	None	
BLUE MOON CT	Castle Rock	467U	80104	3700-3899	
BLUE MOON DR	Jefferson Co	366L	80439	None	
BLUE MOON DR	Lochbuie	140B	80603	None	
BLUEMOON DR	Longmont	12V	80501	None	
BLUE MOUNTAIN CIR	Longmont	40N	80503	None	
BLUE MOUNTAIN DR	Arvada	763K	80403	9500-9899	
	Jefferson Co	763K	80403	8700-9499	
BLUE MOUNTAIN PL	Highlands Ranch	375S	80126	8800-8899	
BLUE MOUNTAIN RD	Jefferson Co	762C	80403	30500-30699	
BLUE MOUNTAIN RD	Weld Co	706P	80504	1800-2199	
BLUE OAK CT	Castle Rock	498S	80104	None	
BLUE PINE CIR	Highlands Ranch	405L	80126	None	
BLUEPOINT RD	Highlands Ranch	374X	80129	None	
BLUERIDGE DR	Highlands Ranch	376T	80130	6000-6199	
BLUERIDGE DR	Jefferson Co	278W	80401	400-599	
BLUE RIVER TRAIL	Broomfield	163E	80020	14000-14199	
BLUE SAGE	Jefferson Co	370K	80127	1-99	
BLUE SAGE CIR E	El Paso Co	910Q	80908	8900-9299	
BLUE SAGE CIR S	El Paso Co	910U	80908	8900-9299	
BLUE SAGE CT	Boulder	128W	80305	1400-1699	

STREET NAME	CITY or COUNTY	MAP GRID	ZIP CODE	BLOCK RANGE	O/E
BLUE SAGE DR	Littleton	343T	80123	5400-5999	
BLUE SAGE LN	Castle Rock	497D	80104	1800-2099	
BLUE SAGE WAY	Littleton	343U	80123	5900-5999	
BLUE SKY DR	Castle Rock	466P	80109	4800-4999	
BLUE SKY DR	Weld Co	728F	80621	10900-10999	
BLUESKY TRAIL	Jefferson Co	822V	80433	None	
BLUE SPRINGS DR	Jefferson Co	365M	80439	32200-32299	
BLUE SPRUCE CT E	Highlands Ranch	374Y	80126	100-199	
BLUE SPRUCE DR	Clear Creek Co	304X	80439	1-399	
BLUE SPRUCE DR	Nederland	740R	80466	None	
BLUE SPRUCE DR	Park Co	821U	80421	1-499	
BLUE SPRUCE LN	Boulder Co	71J	80503	None	
BLUE SPRUCE LN	Jefferson Co	365H	80439	7200-7699	
BLUE SPRUCE PL	Aurora	381E	80016	None	
BLUE SPRUCE RD	Boulder Co	741J	80466	1N-99N	
	Boulder Co	741J	80466	1S-299S	
BLUE SPRUCE RD	Gilpin Co	761E	80403	1-499	
BLUE SPRUCE RD	Jefferson Co	336Q	80439	4400-4999	
BLUE SPRUCE ST	Longmont	12W	80501	900-999	
BLUE SPRUCE TRAIL	Teller Co	906N	80863	1-299	
BLUESTAR DR	Douglas Co	411S	80138	9700-9999	
BLUESTEM AVE	Longmont	40U	80503	3300-3599	
BLUESTEM DR	Jefferson Co	308A	80401	23400-23799	
BLUESTEM LN	Parker	409V	80138	20200-20299	
BLUESTEM ST	Brighton	139R	80601	None	
BLUE STEM TRAIL	Lafayette	131F	80026	1100-1199	
BLUE TERRACE CIR					
	Castle Pines North	436A	80108	6000-6099	
BLUE TERRACE PL	Castle Pines North	436A	80108	6000-6099	
BLUE TERRACE WAY					
	Castle Pines North	436A	80108	12300-12499	
BLUETHRUSH CT	Castle Rock	466X	80109	4000-4199	
BLUE VISTA WAY	Broomfield	163C	80020	None	
BLUE WATER CIR	Castle Rock	469J	80108	6200-6399	
BLUE WATER DR	Castle Rock	469J	80108	7300-7899	
BLUE WATER LN	Castle Rock	469K	80108	7400-7899	
BLUE WILLOW	Jefferson Co	370Q	80127	1-99	
BLUFF DR N	Douglas Co	870B	80116	700-999	
BLUFF ST	Boulder	98W	80304	1700-2599	
	Boulder	98T	80301	2800-3399	
BLUFF LODGE	Weld Co	706P	80504	11100-11199	
BLUFFMONT CT	Lone Tree	406H	80124	10000-10099	
BLUFFMONT DR	Lone Tree	406M	80124	10100-10499	
BLUFFMONT WAY	Lone Tree	406H	80124	None	
BLUFF POINTE TRAIL	Castle Rock	528E	80104	None	
BLUFFS PARK TRAIL	Lone Tree	406M	80124	None	
BLUFFTOP WAY	Lone Tree	406M	80124	9000-9099	
BLUFF TRAIL	Jefferson Co	369E	80465	7000-7099	
BLUFF VIEW PL S	Parker	409Z	80134	None	
BOARDWALK CIR W	Highlands Ranch	403G	80129	3500-3599	
BOARDWALK DR S	Highlands Ranch	403G	80129	9900-9999	
BOATSWAIN LN	Boulder Co	71D	80504	8000-8099	
BOATWORKS DR	Highlands Ranch	376S	80126	5400-5599	
BOBBIE KAY PL	El Paso Co	909U	80908	4100-4299	
BOBCAT CIR	Arapahoe Co	794S	80136	53700-53899	
BOBCAT CT	Elbert Co	891X	80106	22200-22399	
BOBCAT CT	Frederick	707W	80504	5400-5499	
BOBCAT DR	Frederick	707W	80504	5400-5499	
BOBCAT DR	Jefferson Co	843F	80433	24100-24299	
BOBCAT LN	Jefferson Co	370B	80127	1-99	
BOBCAT LN E	Arapahoe Co	794S	80136	13700-15199	
BOBCAT PT	Lafayette	132W	80026	300-399	
BOBCAT ST	Frederick	707W	80504	5300-5499	
BOBCAT WAY	Jefferson Co	365F	80439	6700-6799	
BOBCAT BLUFF E	Douglas Co	406N	80124	6100-6199	
BOBCAT RUN	Douglas Co	432N	80125	7200-7399	
BOBCAT TERRACE S	Douglas Co	406N	80124	10800-10899	
BOB CAT TRAIL	Park Co	841V	80421	1-599	
BOBLINK CT	Boulder Co	99S	80301	None	
	Louisville	130R	80027	300-399	
BOBOLINK CT	Castle Rock	466P	80109	4700-4899	
BOBOLINK DR	Castle Rock	466P	80109	4300-4799	
BOBSLED TRAIL	Jefferson Co	368S	80465	8500-8599	
BOBTAIL ST	Black Hawk	780D	80422	12900-12999	
	Black Hawk	781A	80422	None	
BOBWHITE LN	Longmont	41T	80504	2300-2399	
BOCA CIR	Douglas Co	408H	80134	9900-10099	
BOCK CT	Erie	102P	80516	None	
BOGEY CT	Boulder Co	723G	80503	3900-3999	
BOISE CT	Longmont	12P	80501	2100-2299	
BOLD LN	Jefferson Co	366M	80439	28400-28599	
BOLDMERE CT	El Paso Co	908Z	80132	1301-1399	O
BOLD SUN CIR	Douglas Co	527T	80104	700-799	
BOLERO DR	Parker	439F	80134	17900-18199	
BOLLER ST	Palmer Lake	907R	80133	None	
BOLLING DR	Denver	258K	80239	14300-15299	
	Denver	258R	80239	None	
BOLTON CIR	Douglas Co	407G	80134	11800-11999	
BOLTON DR	Douglas Co	407G	80134	11800-11999	
BOLTON ST	Douglas Co	407G	80134	None	
BONANZA BLVD	Lochbuie	140G	80603	201-299	O
BONANZA CIR	Douglas Co	850X	80116	11200-11499	
BONANZA DR	Boulder Co	741J	80466	1-399	
BONANZA DR	Erie	103P	80516	1-499	
	Erie	133F	80516	2400-3099	
BONANZA DR	Jefferson Co	366Z	80439	27800-28499	
BONANZA RD N	Douglas Co	411B	80138	12400-12799	
BONITA AVE	Palmer Lake	907Q	80133	None	
BONITA PL	Castle Rock	498B	80108	3300-3499	
BONITA PL	Northglenn	194F	80234	100-399	
BONITA PARK TRAIL	Jefferson Co	337J	80439	4900-4999	
BONN CT	Lyons	703C	80540	None	
BONNELL AVE	Erie	102V	80516	400-499	
	Erie	103S	80516	None	
BONNER ST	Castle Rock	498R	80104	None	
BONNEY CT E	Parker	439G	80134	19000-19099	
BONNEY ST S	Parker	439G	80134	12900-13099	
BONNIE CIR	Weld Co	726J	80516	1500-1599	
BONNIE LN	Park Co	841Q	80421	1000-1099	
BONNIE LN S	Arapahoe Co	791Y	80137	300-799	
	Watkins	811C	80137	800-1499	
BONNIE BRAE BLVD	Denver	315A	80209	700-1099	
BONNIE RIDGE DR	Elbert Co	871B	80107	3900-4999	
BONNY BROOK CT	Boulder Co	70L	80503	7100-7199	
BONNYTON PL	Castle Rock	497V	80104	None	
BONVUE DR	Golden	278H	80401	2100-2199	
BOODEL CIR	Elbert Co	851T	80107	3500-3599	
BOOKER LN	Jefferson Co	365Z	80433	9100-9299	
BOOTH DR	Firestone	707S	80504	5800-10599	
	Firestone	707T	80504	None	
BOOT HILL DR N	Douglas Co	411H	80138	12000-12399	
BORDEAUX CT	Douglas Co	408M	80134	16300-16399	
BOREALIS WAY	Douglas Co	466D	80108	1-99	
BOREAS CT	Parker	409N	80134	16800-16899	
BOREAS RD	Douglas Co	887H	80118	7000-7299	
BOREAS PASS CT	Brighton	140J	80601	None	
BOSQUE CT	Boulder Co	98K	80301	3800-3999	
BOSQUE ST	Broomfield	162P	80020	1100-1399	
BOSTON AVE	Longmont	41G	80501	400-1099	
	Longmont	41F	80501	1100-1899	
BOSTON CIR S	Greenwood Village	346Z	80111	None	
BOSTON CT	Adams Co	136Z	80602	14900-15199	
BOSTON CT	Longmont	41G	80501	1-99	
BOSTON CT S	Arapahoe Co	317E	80247	1100-1299	
	Arapahoe Co	347W	80111	6200-6299	
	Arapahoe Co	317J	80231	None	
	Arapahoe Co	317S	80231	None	
	Denver	317W	80231	3000-3299	
BOSTON ST	Adams Co	196Z	80640	9100-9199	
	Adams Co	166M	80602	13600-13799	
	Adams Co	166D	80602	14400-14499	
	Adams Co	136V	80602	15200-15799	
	Adams Co	196V	80640	None	
	Aurora	287J	80230	700-1099	
	Aurora	286H	80010	1100-1899	
	Aurora	287J	80230	None	
	Denver	257S	80238	None	
	Ward	720M	80481	None	
BOSTON ST S	Arapahoe Co	316H	80247	1100-1299	
	Denver	346D	80237	3900-4099	
	Denver	347A	80237	None	
	Greenwood Village	346M	80111	4900-5099	
	Greenwood Village	346R	80111	5100-5399	
	Greenwood Village	347S	80111	5900-5999	
BOSTON ST S	Greenwood Village	346V	80111	5901-5999	O
	Greenwood Village	346Z	80111	6300-6499	
	Greenwood Village	376D	80111	6500-6699	
BOTTINELLI DR	Erie	103N	80516	None	
BOTTLEBRUSH RUN	Broomfield	133W	80026	5100-15099	
BOUGHS PL	El Paso Co	909T	80908	18000-18399	
BOULDER CIR	Broomfield	163K	80020	3200-13699	
BOULDER CIR S	Boulder	128R	80303	1-99	
BOULDER LN	Douglas Co	907F	80118	13800-14099	
BOULDER PT	Broomfield	163K	80020	13600-13799	
BOULDER RD S	Boulder Co	129P	80303	5000-7599	
	Boulder Co	130Q	80303	7600-8299	
BOULDER RD S	Gilpin Co	741X	80403	None	
BOULDER RD S	Lafayette	131Q	80026	None	
BOULDER RD S	Louisville	130Q	80027	None	
BOULDER ST	Boulder Co	721R	80302	1-1599	
BOULDER ST	Denver	254W	80211	1500-1899	
BOULDER ST	Nederland	740Q	80466	None	
BOULDERADO DR	Boulder Co	100B	80301	7700-7899	
BOULDER CANYON DR	Boulder Co	741G	80466	26900-26999	
	Boulder Co	742A	80466	27000-27899	
	Boulder Co	742C	80302	28000-38999	
	Boulder Co	127A	80302	39000-40599	
BOULDER HILLS DR	Boulder Co	704W	80503	5500-8599	
BOULDER VIEW LN	Boulder Co	97P	80304	1-299	
BOULDER VIEW RD	Boulder Co	722W	80302	1-399	
BOUNDARY RD	Palmer Lake	907Q	80133	None	
BOUNTIFUL CIR	Castle Rock	466U	80109	4000-4299	
BOUNTIFUL CT	Adams Co	224P	80221	500-699	
BOUNTIFUL DR	Longmont	42N	80501	None	
BOUNTIFUL ST	Firestone	707S	80504	None	
BOUNTY ST	Aurora	288F	80011	1800-1999	
BOUNTY HUNTER RD	Park Co	841A	80421	1-599	
BOWEN CIR	Longmont	41G	80501	1100-1299	
BOWEN CT	Commerce City	256F	80022	5600-5699	
BOWEN ST	Longmont	41G	80501	1-899	
	Longmont	11U	80501	1300-1699	
	Longmont	11L	80501	2100-2499	
BOWEN ST S	Longmont	41Q	80501	1-1299	
	Longmont	41Q	80501	1300-1499	
BOWERSOX PKWY	Firestone	707S	80504	None	
BOWIE CT	Adams Co	224P	80221	1-199	
BOWLES AVE	Palmer Lake	907R	80133	None	
BOWLES AVE W	Jefferson Co	342U	80123	7000-8999	
	Jefferson Co	341V	80123	9000-9999	
	Jefferson Co	341U	80127	10000-12699	
	Jefferson Co	340V	80127	12700-13999	
	Lakewood	342U	80123	5200-6999	
	Littleton	343T	80120	2700-2799	
	Littleton	343T	80123	2800-5199	
BOWLES CIR W	Jefferson Co	341S	80127	11600-11999	
BOWLES DR W	Jefferson Co	341W	80127	12400-12499	
	Jefferson Co	340V	80127	None	
BOWLES PL W	Jefferson Co	341T	80127	10800-11499	
	Jefferson Co	340V	80127	12000-12199	
	Jefferson Co	340U	80127	13700-13799	
BOWLES LAKE LN	Bow Mar	342R	80123	5400-5699	
BOWLES RANCH RD	Gilpin Co	761B	80403	1-399	
BOW LINE PL	Longmont	10M	80503	2800-2999	
BOWMAN PL	Northglenn	194D	80233	1200-1599	
BOW MAR DR	Bow Mar	342M	80123	4200-4799	
	Bow Mar	343N	80123	4800-5599	
BOW MEADOWS CIR	Elbert Co	871H	80107	33500-33699	
BOW MEADOWS DR	Elbert Co	871H	80107	6000-6999	
BOW MOUNTAIN RD	Boulder Co	97E	80304	500-799	
BOWRON PL	Boulder Co	69Z	80503	5500-5699	
BOWSTRING RD	El Paso Co	908X	80132	700-1699	
BOWSTRING WAY	El Paso Co	908Y	80132	700-799	
BOWSTRING TRAIL E	Douglas Co	380T	80138	7800-7999	
BOX CANYON RD	Douglas Co	866B	80135	7200-7299	
BOXELDER	Jefferson Co	336A	80439	3400-3499	
BOXELDER CIR	Longmont	40R	80503	900-1099	
BOXELDER DR	Longmont	40Q	80503	3400-3799	
BOXELDER ST	Louisville	161B	80027	1600-1899	
BOX ELDER CREEK DR	Brighton	138V	80601	600-699	
BOX OAK WAY	El Paso Co	909Q	80908	19500-19699	
BOXWOOD	Jefferson Co	370K	80127	1-99	
BOXWOOD CT	Lafayette	131B	80026	2400-2499	
BOXWOOD LN	Longmont	40L	80503	700-799	
BOYD CT	Castle Rock	499N	80104	6400-6499	
BOYD ST	Golden	249W	80403	200-699	
BOYERO CT S	Superior	160M	80027	1200-1399	
BOYNE CT	Jefferson Co	306P	80439	30100-30199	
BOZEMAN TRAIL	Elbert Co	870U	80107	1-399	
BRADBURN BLVD	Westminster	223P	80030	7200-7999	
	Westminster	193B	80031	11600-11799	
BRADBURN DR	Westminster	223F	80031	3600-3999	
	Westminster	223F	80031	8100-8299	
BRADBURY AVE W	Littleton	373H	80120	2400-2499	
BRADBURY LN	Littleton	374E	80120	1-99	
BRADBURY PKWY S	Parker	408V	80134	None	
BRADBURY RD	Arapahoe Co	795X	80103	300-5099	
BRADBURY ST	Firestone	707S	80504	None	
BRADBURY WAY	Littleton	374F	80120	900-1099	
BRADBURY RANCH DR	Parker	408V	80134	11300-11699	
BRADFORD DR	Douglas Co	407H	80134	12300-12599	
BRADFORD DR S	Jefferson Co	371Q	80127	8100-8199	
BRADFORD RD	Jefferson Co	371Q	80127	10300-10799	
	Jefferson Co	371P	80127	11100-11199	
BRADFORD ST	Park Co	820V	80421	1-199	
BRADLEY DR	Boulder	128Y	80305	1400-1599	
BRADLEY PL	Thornton	225B	80229	2600-2899	
BRADLEY RD	Palmer Lake	907Q	80133	None	
BRADLEY ST	Jefferson Co	823N	80433	26600-26799	
BRADSHAW LN	El Paso Co	912Y	80831	17000-17999	
BRADY CT S	Sheridan	313Z	80110	3300-3498	E
BRADY PL S	Highlands Ranch	406E	80130	10100-10199	
BRAEBURN CT	Longmont	40U	80503	None	
BRAEBURN LN	Jefferson Co	306S	80439	2600-2899	
BRAEBURN PL	Highlands Ranch	405P	80126	3000-3199	
BRAEBURN PL	Longmont	40U	80503	None	
BRAEBURN WAY	Highlands Ranch	405P	80126	2900-3099	
BRAEWOOD AVE W	Highlands Ranch	404A	80129	1200-1599	
BRAGG PL	Longmont	11Q	80501	900-1099	
BRAHMA PL	Douglas Co	469B	80134	5600-5699	
BRAINARD CIR	Lafayette	131G	80026	500-699	
BRAINARD DR	Broomfield	161P	80020	2800-2899	
BRAINARD LAKE DR	Boulder Co	720J	80481	None	
BRAMANTE LN	Douglas Co	432J	80125	None	
BRAMBLE PL	Longmont	12Y	80501	1300-1399	
BRAMBLE RD	Frederick	706Z	80504	None	
BRAMBLERIDGE DR					
	Castle Pines North	436F	80108	8400-8599	
BRAMBLERIDGE LN					
	Castle Pines North	436G	80108	800-899	
BRAMBLEWOOD DR					
	Castle Pines North	436F	80108	800-1099	
BRAMBLEWOOD LN					
	Castle Pines North	436F	80108	None	
BRAMWOOD PL	Longmont	41L	80501	1200-1299	
BRAMWOOD ST	Firestone	707S	80504	9600-9699	
BRANCH PL	El Paso Co	910Y	80908	8800-8899	
BRANDENBURGER DR	Jefferson Co	368Y	80465	8900-9099	
BRANDING IRON CT	Brighton	139K	80601	None	
BRANDING IRON LN	Castle Rock	467U	80104	500-799	
BRANDING IRON LN	Park Co	841A	80421	1-499	
BRANDING IRON WAY	Mead	706G	80542	None	
BRANDON AVE	Broomfield	163S	80020	4100-4399	
BRANDON CT S	Superior	160K	80027	500-599	
BRANDON DR W	Douglas Co	403B	80125	8000-8199	
BRANDON WAY	Thornton	195N	80229	10300-10399	
BRANDON WAY W	Douglas Co	432K	80125	8000-8199	
BRANDON CREEK CT	Boulder	99C	80301	None	
BRANDON CREEK DR	Boulder	99C	80301	4800-4999	
BRANDT AVE E	Aurora	351N	80016	None	
BRANDT AVE W	Jefferson Co	341V	80123	9200-9299	
	Jefferson Co	341T	80127	11600-11899	
BRANDT CT	Boulder	128D	80303	1500-1599	
BRANDT DR W	Jefferson Co	341V	80123	8900-8999	
	Jefferson Co	341S	80127	12500-12699	
	Jefferson Co	340V	80127	13100-13199	
BRANDT PL	Aurora	350R	80016	None	
BRANDT PL W	Jefferson Co	341V	80123	8900-9999	
	Jefferson Co	341T	80127	11200-12699	
BRANDYWINE AVE	Frederick	706Z	80504	None	
BRANDYWINE CT	Boulder	99F	80301	5900-6099	
BRANDYWINE LN	Parker	410S	80138	11600-11699	
BRANHAM DR	Douglas Co	408D	80134	9300-9399	
BRANNAN WAY	Adams Co	225P	80229	2500-2598	E
BRANTLY AVE	Castle Rock	498R	80104	6000-6399	
BRANTLY CT	Castle Rock	498R	80104	6100-6298	E
BRANTNER PL	Brighton	138V	80601	2200-2299	
BRASELTON ST	Highlands Ranch	405K	80126	10600-10799	
BRASSIE WAY	Columbine Valley	373B	80123	1-99	
BRAUN AVE	Jefferson Co	823V	80433	None	
BRAUN CIR	Arvada	220Z	80007	6200-6399	
BRAUN CIR S	Lakewood	280Z	80228	500-599	
	Lakewood	310H	80228	1100-1199	
BRAUN CT	Arvada	250D	80004	6100-6299	
	Arvada	220Z	80004	6500-6699	
	Arvada	220U	80004	6800-7199	
	Arvada	220Q	80005	7200-7599	
	Arvada	220G	80005	8300-8499	
	Jefferson Co	280R	80401	800-899	
	Jefferson Co	280D	80401	2100-2599	
	Jefferson Co	250Z	80401	2800-3499	
BRAUN CT S	Jefferson Co	340H	80465	4200-4699	
	Lakewood	310R	80228	2200-2799	
BRAUN DR	Jefferson Co	280D	80401	2000-2599	
	Jefferson Co	280G	80401	13600-13999	
BRAUN DR S	Lakewood	310D	80228	900-1099	
BRAUN LN	Arvada	220Z	80004	6301-6399	O
BRAUN LOOP	Arvada	220G	80005	8400-8599	
BRAUN RD	Jefferson Co	250Y	80401	3300-3399	
	Jefferson Co	280D	80401	13300-13399	
	Jefferson Co	250Y	80401	13400-14399	
BRAUN ST	Arvada	220Q	80005	7300-7599	
	Arvada	220G	80005	8300-8399	
	Jefferson Co	250M	80002	5100-5399	
	Jefferson Co	280M	80401	None	
	Lakewood	280R	80401	600-799	
BRAUN ST S	Jefferson Co	340M	80465	4800-5099	
	Lakewood	310D	80228	700-799	
BRAUN WAY	Arvada	250D	80004	5900-5999	
	Arvada	220Z	80004	6300-6399	
	Arvada	220Q	80005	7200-7599	
	Jefferson Co	822Y	80433	11500-11799	
BRAUN WAY S	Jefferson Co	340H	80465	4300-4499	
	Lakewood	310R	80228	2100-2799	
BREAKAWAY TRAIL S	Jefferson Co	337J	80439	4600-4799	

B

STREET NAME	CITY or COUNTY	MAP GRID	ZIP CODE	BLOCK RANGE	O/E
BREAKWATER DR	Longmont	10R	80503	2901-2999	O
BREAKWATER WAY	Longmont	10R	80503	2901-2999	O
BREAMORE CT	Castle Pines North	436R	80108	1-99	
BRECKENRIDGE	Jefferson Co	843C	80433	None	
BRECKENRIDGE AVE E					
	Buckley Air Force Base	289T	80017	None	
BRECKENRIDGE DR	Broomfield	162L	80020	500-699	
BRECKENRIDGE RD	Douglas Co	847T	80109	None	
BRECKENRIDGE TRAIL	Broomfield	162L	80020	100-299	
BREEN LN	Superior	160Q	80027	1800-1999	
BREEZE GRASS WAY S	Parker	408Y	80134	None	
BREEZEWOOD LN	Gilpin Co	761E	80403	100-299	
BREEZY LN	Castle Rock	466W	80109	2500-3099	
BREEZY KNOLL ST	Parker	409Z	80134	12101-12199	O
BRENDON CT	Douglas Co	436Q	80108	400-499	
BRENDON PL	Castle Pines North	436Q	80108	6800-6999	
BRENDY CT	Longmont	11W	80503	2300-2399	
BRENKERT DR	Jefferson Co	308F	80401	1500-1599	
BRENNAN CT	Erie	102H	80516	1200-1299	
BRENNAN ST	Erie	102Q	80516	None	
BRENTFORD CIR E	Highlands Ranch	404C	80126	300-399	
BRENTFORD DR S	Highlands Ranch	406B	80130	9500-9599	
BRENTHAVEN CT	El Paso Co	908Z	80132	1100-1199	
BRENTON PL	El Paso Co	908V	80132	19100-19199	
BRENTWOOD	Westminster	192W	80021	None	
BRENTWOOD CT	Arvada	222W	80004	6400-6599	
	Arvada	222N	80005	7700-7899	
	Arvada	222E	80005	8200-8299	
BRENTWOOD CT N	Castle Rock	498H	80104	600-699	
BRENTWOOD CT S	Jefferson Co	372J	80128	7600-7699	
	Lakewood	312N	80227	2100-2199	
	Lakewood	312S	80227	2500-2699	
BRENTWOOD DR	Jefferson Co	192P	80021	10400-10499	
BRENTWOOD ST	Arvada	252E	80002	5500-5699	
	Arvada	252A	80004	5800-6199	
	Arvada	222W	80004	6300-6599	
	Arvada	222S	80004	6800-6999	
	Arvada	222N	80005	7700-7799	
	Lakewood	282S	80226	1-399	
	Lakewood	282N	80214	600-999	
	Lakewood	282J	80214	1000-1499	
	Lakewood	282E	80214	1500-1899	
	Lakewood	282B	80215	2000-2599	
	Westminster	192S	80021	8200-9499	
	Wheat Ridge	252S	80033	3800-4399	
	Wheat Ridge	252N	80033	4400-4599	
BRENTWOOD ST S	Jefferson Co	342A	80235	3500-3599	
	Jefferson Co	342W	80123	6300-6399	
	Jefferson Co	372J	80128	7600-7899	
	Jefferson Co	372N	80128	8200-8299	
	Jefferson Co	372S	80128	8300-8999	
	Lakewood	282S	80226	1-299	
	Lakewood	312E	80232	1100-1699	
	Lakewood	312N	80227	2100-2199	
	Lakewood	312S	80227	2300-2699	
BRENTWOOD WAY	Jefferson Co	192N	80021	10000-10099	
	Westminster	192S	80021	9500-9699	
BRENTWOOD WAY NW	Westminster	192W	80021	9400-9499	
BRENTWOOD WAY S	Jefferson Co	372A	80123	6400-6599	
	Lakewood	312E	80232	1200-1599	
BRETTONWOOD WAY					
	Highlands Ranch	404J	80129	1200-1599	
BREWER CT	Castle Rock	467Q	80108	None	
BREWER DR	Northglenn	194J	80234	10400-10899	
BRIAN DR	Douglas Co	409W	80134	5000-5399	
BRIAR CIR	Highlands Ranch	374V	80126	1300-1499	
BRIAR CLIFF CT	Castle Pines North	436G	80108	8100-8199	
BRIAR CLIFF DR	Castle Pines North	436G	80108	8100-8199	
BRIAR DALE DR	Castle Pines North	436G	80108	500-799	
BRIAR DALE LN	Castle Pines North	436G	80108	8200-8399	
BRIARGATE LN	Parker	409L	80134	18900-18999	
BRIAR GLEN CIR	Highlands Ranch	405Q	80126	10600-10799	
BRIAR GLEN LN	Highlands Ranch	405Q	80126	4600-4799	
BRIARGROVE DR	Highlands Ranch	405J	80126	2200-2399	
BRIARGROVE WAY	Highlands Ranch	405J	80126	100-10299	
BRIAR HAVEN CT	Castle Pines North	436G	80108	8300-8399	
BRIARHAVEN CT	El Paso Co	908Y	80132	18000-18199	
BRIAR HAVEN DR	Castle Pines North	436G	80108	500-699	
BRIAR HAVEN PL	Castle Pines North	436G	80108	8300-8399	
BRIARHOLLOW LN W					
	Highlands Ranch	404E	80129	1200-1599	
BRIARHOLLOW WAY W					
	Highlands Ranch	404E	80129	1100-1299	
BRIARHURST DR	Highlands Ranch	375S	80126	2100-2499	
BRIARLEAF AVE	Parker	410Y	80138	22900-23499	
BRIARLEAF CT	Parker	410Y	80138	12100-12199	
BRIARRIDGE CT	Boulder Co	100A	80301	4800-4899	
BRIAR RIDGE CT	Castle Pines North	436G	80108	700-799	
BRIAR RIDGE DR	Castle Pines North	436G	80108	8100-8399	
BRIARRIDGE TRAIL	Boulder Co	100A	80301	4700-4799	
BRIAR ROSE TRAIL	Douglas Co	432P	80125	6800-6899	
BRIAR TRACE DR	Castle Pines North	436G	80108	8300-8499	
BRIAR TRACE WAY					
	Castle Pines North	436G	80108	8300-8399	
BRIARVIEW LN S	Highlands Ranch	374U	80126	8800-8899	
BRIARWOOD AVE E	Arapahoe Co	377B	80112	11300-11399	
	Aurora	381A	80016	24300-24399	
	Centennial	375E	80121	1900-1999	
	Centennial	375B	80122	3300-3499	
	Centennial	375C	80122	3600-3999	
	Centennial	375D	80122	5200-5599	
	Centennial	376A	80112	5800-5899	
	Centennial	376D	80112	8200-8499	
	Centennial	377B	80112	10500-11299	
	Centennial	377H	80112	12100-13199	
	Centennial	378A	80112	13100-13699	
	Centennial	378B	80112	13800-14299	
	Centennial	379C	80016	18600-18799	
	Centennial	379D	80016	20200-20499	
BRIARWOOD AVE W	Littleton	374F	80120	500-899	
	Littleton	373C	80120	900-2099	
	Littleton	374A	80120	1300-1599	
	Littleton	374A	80120	1800-2099	
	Littleton	373D	80120	2100-2399	
BRIARWOOD BLVD E	Centennial	376G	80112	7800-8899	
BRIARWOOD CIR	Centennial	377B	80112	10501-10699	O
BRIARWOOD CIR E	Arapahoe Co	374D	80122	800N-1099N	
	Arapahoe Co	374H	80122	800S-1099S	
	Aurora	381C	80016	26800-26999	
	Centennial	375H	80122	5200-5599	
	Centennial	376A	80112	5900-6199	
	Centennial	376B	80112	6800-7299	
BRIARWOOD CT	Longmont	41B	80501	800-899	
BRIARWOOD CT	Parker	409M	80138	19900-20099	
BRIARWOOD DR	Boulder	128W	80305	2400-2699	
BRIARWOOD DR	Broomfield	163P	80020	3300-3399	
	Broomfield	163Q	80020	13300-13399	
	Thornton	195C	80233	4300-11999	
BRIARWOOD DR E	Arapahoe Co	374C	80122	200-599	
	Aurora	380B	80016	21300-21699	
	Aurora	380B	80016	21700-22099	
	Aurora	380C	80016	None	
	Aurora	380D	80016	None	
	Centennial	376A	80112	5900-6199	
	Centennial	376B	80112	6700-7199	
	Centennial	379C	80016	18600-19299	
BRIARWOOD DR S	Lakewood	311B	80226	700-1099	
BRIARWOOD LN	Longmont	41B	80501	800-8998	E
BRIARWOOD LN	Parker	410S	80138	11500-11599	
BRIARWOOD PL E	Arapahoe Co	379C	80016	None	
	Aurora	380C	80016	22700-22899	
	Aurora	380D	80016	24200-24299	
	Aurora	381A	80016	24200-24299	
	Centennial	375D	80122	4500-4699	
	Centennial	375D	80122	5400-5499	
	Centennial	376D	80112	8200-8599	
	Foxfield	379B	80016	None	
BRIARWOOD ST	Firestone	707S	80504	None	
	Arapahoe Co	832H	80137	None	
BRICK CENTER RD N	Arapahoe Co	792V	80102	1-1499	
BRICK CENTER RD S	Arapahoe Co	792Z	80102	1-799	
	Arapahoe Co	812R	80102	None	
BRICKER RD	El Paso Co	908N	80132	2200-2699	
BRICKYARD CIR	Golden	248R	80403	800-999	
BRICKYARD RD	Golden	248R	80403	1200-1499	
BRIDAL GATE LN	Jefferson Co	370G	80127	1-99	
BRIDGE ST	Central City	780C	80427	1-99	
BRIDGE ST	Nederland	740R	80466	None	
BRIDGE ST E	Brighton	138Q	80601	100-2699	
BRIDGE ST W	Brighton	138N	80601	1-199	
BRIDGER CT	Jefferson Co	306U	80439	2600-2699	
BRIDGER CT S	Arapahoe Co	374C	80121	6600-6699	
BRIDGER LN	Boulder	98U	80301	None	
BRIDGER PT	Lafayette	131F	80026	700-798	E
BRIDGER TRAIL	Boulder	98T	80301	3300-3399	
	Boulder Co	721C	80481	1-199	
BRIDLE CT	Boulder Co	704W	80503	8500-8599	
BRIDLE DR	Mead	706G	80542	2500-2599	
BRIDLEBIT PL	Douglas Co	373V	80129	None	
BRIDLE PATH LN	Cherry Hills Village	345J	80113	1-199	
BRIDLE PATH LN	Douglas Co	469B	80134	5800-6199	
BRIDLE TRAIL	Clear Creek Co	781T	80439	None	
BRIDLEWOOD LN	Parker	410W	80138	11500-11599	
BRIERLY CT	Castle Rock	497U	80104	2100-2199	
BRIGADOON CT	Boulder Co	69K	80503	6100-6299	
BRIGADOON DR	Boulder Co	69K	80503	6000-7099	
BRIGGS AVE	Jefferson Co	823N	80433	25600-25899	
BRIGGS PL	Superior	160Q	80027	400-699	
BRIGGS ST	Erie	103J	80516	100-999	
	Erie	103N	80516	None	
BRIGGS ST S	Erie	103N	80516	None	
BRIGHAM ST	Park Co	820Z	80421	1-399	
BRIGHT ANGEL	Weld Co	706P	80504	3400-3499	
BRIGHT DAWN CT	Castle Rock	467W	80109	None	
BRIGHTON BLVD	Adams Co	225V	80022	7000-7199	
	Commerce City	255E	80022	5400-6199	
	Commerce City	225Y	80022	6200-6999	
	Commerce City	225R	80022	7200-7799	
	Denver	254U	80216	2900-4499	
	Denver	255J	80216	4500-5399	
BRIGHTON CT	Castle Pines North	436Q	80108	7200-7299	
BRIGHTON CT	Jefferson Co	306E	80439	1300-1499	
BRIGHTON DR	Brighton	138L	80601	1100-1599	
BRIGHTON PL	Douglas Co	436Q	80108	7200-7299	
BRIGHTON RD	Adams Co	225M	80022	7800-7999	
	Adams Co	226J	80022	8000-8899	
	Adams Co	196M	80640	9000-11299	
	Adams Co	167W	80640	12000-12399	
	Adams Co	167G	80601	12400-13999	
	Adams Co	138W	80601	14800-15199	
	Brighton	138W	80601	1000-1199	
	Brighton	167W	80601	14000-14799	
	Commerce City	225R	80022	7200-7799	
	Commerce City	196M	80640	10000-11399	
	Commerce City	197A	80640	11300-11999	
BRIGHTON ST	Brighton	138K	80601	500-1199	
BRIGHTON ST W	Brighton	138N	80601	1-299	
BRIGHT WATER TRAIL	Douglas Co	432T	80125	6600-6799	
BRIGHT WING LN	El Paso Co	909P	80908	None	
BRIGHT WING TRAIL	El Paso Co	909P	80908	19400-20399	
BRIGITTE DR	Northglenn	194P	80260	200-10099	
BRILLIANCE DR	Castle Rock	496B	80109	None	
BRIMBLE CT	Erie	102U	80516	800-899	
BRIMBLE DR	Erie	102U	80516	1400-1699	
BRISBANE LN S	Highlands Ranch	405G	80130	10000-10099	
BRISBANE WAY S	Highlands Ranch	405H	80130	10000-10099	
BRISCOE LN	Douglas Co	496Z	80109	100-299	
BRISCOE ST	Castle Rock	497K	80104	None	
BRISTLECONE CIR	Park Co	820Y	80421	1-499	
BRISTLECONE CT	Elbert Co	830R	80138	46000-46199	
BRISTLECONE CT	Jefferson Co	307K	80401	25600-25899	
BRISTLECONE CT	Lafayette	131A	80026	None	
BRISTLE CONE PL	Lone Tree	406C	80124	7800-7899	
BRISTLECONE ST	Brighton	139R	80601	None	
BRISTLECONE WAY	Boulder Co	722V	80304	1-399	
BRISTLECONE WAY	Gilpin Co	760W	80403	1-299	
BRISTLECONE WAY	Lafayette	131A	80026	None	
BRISTLE PINE CIR	Highlands Ranch	404B	80129	600-799	
BRISTLERIDGE CT	Douglas Co	408K	80134	None	
BRISTLERIDGE DR	Douglas Co	408F	80134	None	
BRISTLERIDGE ST	Douglas Co	408K	80134	None	
BRISTOL CT	Longmont	12N	80501	2000-2099	
BRISTOL PL	Longmont	12N	80501	300-399	
BRISTOL ST	Castle Rock	498K	80104	1-299	
BRISTOL ST	Jefferson Co	250L	80002	5100-5399	
BRISTOL ST	Superior	160P	80027	2100-2499	
BRISTOL ST S	Lakewood	310D	80228	700-799	
BRISTOLWOOD DR	Castle Pines North	436L	80108	None	
BRITANIE RIDGE DR	Elbert Co	851V	80107	None	
BRITTANY AVE W	Jefferson Co	341V	80123	9300-9699	
	Jefferson Co	341W	80127	12000-12199	
BRITTANY CT	Dacono	727J	80514	100-199	
BRITTANY DR W	Jefferson Co	342W	80123	8500-8799	
	Jefferson Co	341X	80127	10900-11299	
BRITTANY LN	Lafayette	130L	80027	None	
BRITTANY PL	Boulder Co	70L	80503	8400-8499	
BRITTANY PL E	Centennial	345V	80121	5300-5399	
BRITTANY PL W	Jefferson Co	342Z	80123	5200-5399	
	Jefferson Co	342U	80123	6200-6599	
	Jefferson Co	342S	80123	8600-8699	
	Jefferson Co	342Z	80123	None	
BRITTANY WAY E	Highlands Ranch	404D	80126	900-1199	
BRITTING AVE	Boulder	128T	80305	3700-3999	
BRIXHAM CIR	Castle Pines North	436Q	80108	7200-7399	
BRIXHAM CT	Castle Pines North	436R	80108	1-99	
BRIXHAM PL	Castle Pines North	436Q	80108	1-99	
BROADLANDS CT	Broomfield	163G	80020	2900-2999	
BROADLANDS DR	Broomfield	163F	80020	13700-13898	E
	Broomfield	163G	80020	None	
BROADLANDS LN	Broomfield	163K	80020	3500-13899	
BROADLEAF LOOP	Castle Rock	496C	80109	2000-2499	
BROADMOOR CT	Parker	410R	80138	11100-11199	
BROADMOOR DR	Jefferson Co	305M	80439	31500-31899	
BROADMOOR DR	Parker	410R	80138	23400-23899	
BROADMOOR DR W	Littleton	344T	80120	1-199	
BROADMOOR LOOP	Broomfield	163F	80020	3800-4199	
BROADMOOR PL	Parker	410R	80138	23900-23999	
BROADVIEW CIR	Jefferson Co	844L	80127	14100-14799	
BROADVIEW CT	Castle Rock	466T	80109	4500-4599	
BROADVIEW DR	Lakewood	282P	80214	7200-7599	
BROADVIEW PL	Castle Rock	466T	80109	3600-3999	
BROADWAY	Adams Co	254G	80216	5200-5699	
	Adams Co	224Q	80216	6200-6399	
	Adams Co	224Q	80221	6400-7599	
	Denver	284L	80203	1-1499	
	Denver	284G	80202	1500-1999	
	Denver	284C	80205	2000-2399	
	Denver	254Y	80216	2400-2999	
	Denver	254Q	80216	4300-4599	
	Denver	254L	80216	4700-5199	
BROADWAY	Lyons	703C	80540	None	
BROADWAY S	Denver	284U	80209	1-699	
	Denver	314C	80209	700-1099	
	Denver	314L	80210	1100-2699	
	Englewood	314U	80113	2700-3599	
	Englewood	344L	80110	3600-5299	
	Highlands Ranch	374X	80129	8300-9199	
	Highlands Ranch	404G	80129	9200-10399	
	Littleton	344L	80110	5300-6399	
	Littleton	374C	80121	6500-6699	
	Littleton	374C	80122	6700-8299	
BROADWAY AVE	Fort Lupton	728L	80621	400-999	
BROADWAY AVE S	Fort Lupton	728L	80621	600-899	
BROADWAY CIR S	Englewood	344Q	80110	5300-5399	
BROADWAY CT S	Littleton	374Q	80122	8200-8299	
BROADWAY ST	Boulder	128K	80305	1-699	
	Boulder	128G	80302	700-899	
	Boulder	127D	80302	900-1999	
	Boulder	97Y	80302	2000-2299	
	Boulder	97G	80304	2300-4999	
	Boulder Co	97C	80301	None	
BROADWAY ST	Elbert Co	892N	80106	23700-23999	
BROADWAY ST	Keenesburg	732A	80643	None	
BROADWAY ST	Palmer Lake	907R	80133	None	
BROADWAY ST E	Elizabeth	871F	80107	100-399	
BROADWAY ST S	Boulder	128U	80305	100-1599	
BROADWAY ST W	Elizabeth	871F	80107	100-199	
BROCKENBURY CT	El Paso Co	909S	80132	18600-18799	
BROCKWAY DR	Boulder Co	130N	80303	7000-7899	
BROEMEL AVE	Broomfield	163S	80020	4100-4399	
BROKEN ARROW CIR	Elbert Co	870G	80107	1000-1199	
BROKEN ARROW DR	Jefferson Co	823X	80433	11500-12199	
BROKEN ARROW RD	Jefferson Co	306A	80401	300-599	
BROKEN BOW RUN	Douglas Co	845V	80125	4300-4399	
BROKEN FENCE RD	Boulder Co	742C	80302	1-499	
BROKEN FENCE WAY	El Paso Co	908P	80132	19300-19599	
BROKENHORN CIR	Elbert Co	850C	80138	42100-42499	
BROKEN SABRE LN	El Paso Co	908P	80132	20000-20199	
BROKEN SPOKE RD	Jefferson Co	368R	80465	20700-20799	
BROKEN SPUR DR	El Paso Co	912X	80831	17000-17999	
BROME AVE W	Lafayette	132E	80026	200-399	
BROME CT	Weld Co	72Z	80516	5200-5399	
BROME PL	Lafayette	131H	80026	700-799	
BROME ST	Lochbuie	139D	80603	None	
BROMLEY CT	Jefferson Co	306P	80439	30200-30299	
BROMLEY LN	Brighton	139X	80601	2700-18899	
BROMLEY LN E	Brighton	138X	80601	100-2399	
BROMLEY LN W	Brighton	138W	80601	1-699	
BROMLEY BUSINESS PKWY					
	Brighton	140S	80603	100-298	E
BROMPTON WAY	Parker	379T	80134	8800-8999	
BRONCO DR E	Douglas Co	411C	80138	11000-11399	
BRONCO LN	Jefferson Co	189W	80007	None	
	Jefferson Co	306Y	80439	None	
BRONCO RD	Adams Co	224P	80221	1-7499	
BRONCO RD	Jefferson Co	306X	80439	29500-31399	
BRONCOS PKWY	Arapahoe Co	377H	80112	12400-12999	
	Arapahoe Co	378J	80112	13000-16799	
BRONTI CIR	Lone Tree	406G	80124	9900-9999	
BRONZE LN	Highlands Ranch	375T	80126	8300-8499	
BROOK CIR	Boulder Co	722M	80302	1-1099	
BROOK DR S	Denver	315U	80222	2700-2799	
BROOK DR W	Jefferson Co	372S	80128	7600-8399	
BROOK LN	Lone Tree	406D	80124	9400-9499	
BROOK PL	Boulder	128J	80302	200-299	
BROOK RD	Boulder Co	722L	80302	1-1099	
BROOK RD	Clear Creek Co	365N	80439	1-499	
BROOK RD	Jefferson Co	762B	80403	11500-11999	
BROOK RD	Palmer Lake	907Q	80133	None	
BROOK ST	Frederick	727B	80530	None	
BROOKCRESS DR	Jefferson Co	308E	80401	1300-1399	
BROOKDALE LN	Parker	410S	80138	20400-20499	

STREET NAME	CITY or COUNTY	MAP GRID	ZIP CODE	BLOCK RANGE	O/E
BROOKE HOLLOW DR	Lochbuie	**729Y**	80603	None	
BROOKEVIEW CT	Douglas Co	**439Z**	80134	6900-6999	
BROOKFIELD DR	Boulder	**128U**	80305	4300-4599	
BROOKFIELD DR	Longmont	**41U**	80501	1200-1499	
BROOK FOREST DR	Jefferson Co	**365F**	80439	6700-7599	
BROOK FOREST LN	Jefferson Co	**365K**	80439	7500-7699	
BROOK FOREST RD S	Jefferson Co	**365K**	80439	5400-7699	
	Jefferson Co	**366F**	80439	6200-6699	
	Jefferson Co	**336X**	80439	7700-8299	
BROOK FOREST WAY	Jefferson Co	**365K**	80439	7300-7499	
BROOKHAVEN DR	Columbine Valley	**343X**	80123	1-99	
BROOKHAVEN LN	Columbine Valley	**343X**	80123	5800-6999	
BROOKHAVEN TRAIL					
	Columbine Valley	**343Y**	80123	3400-3799	
BROOK HILL AVE	Lone Tree	**406D**	80124	9600-9799	
BROOK HILL CT	Lone Tree	**406D**	80124	9600-9799	
BROOK HILL DR	Lone Tree	**406D**	80124	9500-9599	
BROOK HILL LN	Lone Tree	**406D**	80124	9500-9699	
BROOKHOLLOW CIR	Highlands Ranch	**404J**	80129	10300-10499	
BROOK HOLLOW CT	Boulder Co	**130B**	80301	7900-8099	
BROOK HOLLOW DR	Broomfield	**162M**	80020	5600-5999	
BROOKHURST AVE	Highlands Ranch	**404B**	80129	500-699	
BROOKLAWN DR	Boulder	**128M**	80303	700-999	
BROOKLAWN LN	Highlands Ranch	**405R**	80130	None	
BROOKLAWN RD	Highlands Ranch	**405R**	80130	None	
BROOKLIME CT	Douglas Co	**378U**	80134	15900-16099	
BROOKLINE RD	Jefferson Co	**306N**	80439	31300-31599	
BROOKMONT RD	Jefferson Co	**338V**	80465	20300-20499	
BROOKRIDGE AVE	Palmer Lake	**907U**	80133	None	
BROOKS AVE	Lafayette	**132F**	80026	300-599	
BROOKS DR	Arvada	**251D**	80004	5900-6199	
	Arvada	**221Y**	80004	6200-6399	
	Arvada	**252A**	80004	8000-8999	
	Arvada	**251D**	80004	9000-9599	
BROOKS WAY	Longmont	**41S**	80504	2101-2199	O
BROOKSHIRE PL	Highlands Ranch	**405G**	80126	None	
BROOKSIDE CIR	Broomfield	**163E**	80020	13900-13999	
BROOKSIDE CIR	Castle Rock	**497T**	80104	1000-1099	
BROOKSIDE CT	Boulder Co	**97X**	80302	200-299	
BROOKSIDE CT	Broomfield	**163E**	80020	13900-13999	
BROOKSIDE DR	Broomfield	**163E**	80020	4800-5199	
	Broomfield	**162H**	80020	5300-5499	
BROOKSIDE DR	Greenwood Village	**344R**	80121	1-99	
BROOKSIDE DR	Longmont	**42B**	80501	500-899	
BROOKSIDE DR	Park Co	**841R**	80421	1-899	
BROOKSIDE DR E	Highlands Ranch	**404D**	80126	1600-1799	
BROOKSTONE DR	Douglas Co	**408C**	80134	15600-16599	
BROOK VALLEY WAY S	Centennial	**345Y**	80121	5900-6099	
BROOKWOOD CT	Highlands Ranch	**405L**	80130	4100-4299	
BROOKWOOD DR	Highlands Ranch	**405L**	80130	4300-4699	
BROOKWOOD PL	Highlands Ranch	**405L**	80130	4200-4399	
BROOKWOOD PT	Highlands Ranch	**405L**	80130	10400-10499	
BROOME WAY S	Highlands Ranch	**405H**	80130	10000-10099	
BROOMFIELD LN	Broomfield	**192E**	80021	11200-11599	
BROOMFIELD COUNTY COMMONS DR					
	Broomfield	**163N**	80020	None	
BROPHY CT	Weld Co	**727B**	80530	None	
BROSS CT	Jefferson Co	**305H**	80439	1300-1399	
BROSS LN	Longmont	**41Q**	80501	1200-1399	
BROSS PL	Broomfield	**133J**	80020	None	
BROSS ST	Longmont	**41G**	80501	100-899	
	Longmont	**11Y**	80501	900-1299	
	Longmont	**11U**	80501	1300-1499	
BROSS ST S	Longmont	**41Q**	80501	800-1099	
BROWN AVE E	Aurora	**318U**	80013	15700-15899	
BROWN CIR	Boulder	**128Y**	80305	1300-1499	
BROWN CIR E	Aurora	**319S**	80013	17400-17699	
BROWN CT	Longmont	**10U**	80503	1600-1699	
BROWN DR E	Aurora	**318V**	80013	16300-16699	
	Aurora	**319U**	80013	19200-19599	
BROWN PL E	Aurora	**318U**	80013	15300-15599	
	Aurora	**318V**	80013	16200-16299	
	Aurora	**319S**	80013	16800-16899	
	Aurora	**319S**	80013	17600-17699	
	Aurora	**319T**	80013	17900-17999	
	Aurora	**319T**	80013	18100-18199	
	Aurora	**319U**	80013	18600-18799	
	Aurora	**319V**	80013	19800-19999	
	Denver	**316T**	80224	6500-6799	
BROWN PL W	Denver	**312V**	80227	5200-5299	
	Denver	**312U**	80227	6400-6599	
BROWN RD	El Paso Co	**909V**	80908	18000-18899	
BROWN ST	Nederland	**740R**	80466	None	
BROWN ST	Park Co	**820Z**	80421	1-499	
BROWN BEAR CT	Douglas Co	**432M**	80125	7500-7699	
BROWN BEAR WAY	Douglas Co	**432M**	80125	7500-7899	
BROWN FOX TRAIL	Douglas Co	**432P**	80125	6900-10699	
BROWNING CT	Elbert Co	**851W**	80107	36800-36999	
BROWNING DR	Douglas Co	**867T**	80109	2200-2699	
BROWN SQUIRREL LN	Golden	**279N**	80401	800-899	
BROWNSTONE DR N	Douglas Co	**409L**	80138	11000-11499	
BRUCE LN	Northglenn	**194P**	80260	200-399	
	Northglenn	**194T**	80260	9800-9999	
BRUCE PL	Longmont	**41A**	80501	1-99	
BRUCE RD	Weld Co	**726Q**	80516	2800-2899	
BRUCE ST	Thornton	**224A**	80260	8800-8999	
BRUCE RANDOLPH AVE	Denver	**254Z**	80205	1200-1799	
	Denver	**255T**	80205	1800-3999	
	Denver	**255Y**	80207	4000-4799	
BRUCHEZ PKWY	Westminster	**193L**	80234	2500-10799	
BRUIN BLVD	Frederick	**706Z**	80504	9000-9299	
BRUMM TRAIL	Jefferson Co	**763J**	80403	9000-9299	
BRUNO AVE	Weld Co	**729T**	80621	16000-16799	
BRUNSWICK DR E	Aurora	**318V**	80013	15800-16299	
	Aurora	**319U**	80013	19300-19599	
	Aurora	**319V**	80013	19800-19999	
BRUNSWICK PL E	Aurora	**318V**	80013	16300-16399	
	Aurora	**319S**	80013	17400-17699	
	Aurora	**319T**	80013	17900-17999	
	Aurora	**319U**	80013	18900-18999	
	Aurora	**320S**	80013	None	
BRUNTWOOD CT	Boulder Co	**129F**	80303	6300-6399	
BRUSH CT	Castle Rock	**468X**	80108	2700-2899	
BRUSH RD	Castle Rock	**468X**	80108	3800-3999	
BRUSHWOOD WAY	Castle Rock	**466U**	80109	3900-4099	
BRUSSELS DR	Elbert Co	**850G**	80138	600-799	
BRYAN AVE	Boulder Co	**740S**	80466	1-1099	
BRYAN CT	Weld Co	**726H**	80514	None	
BRYANT CIR	Broomfield	**163Q**	80020	13100-13299	
	Broomfield	**163R**	80234	None	
	Westminster	**193D**	80234	11800-11899	
BRYANT CT	Broomfield	**163V**	80234	None	
	Federal Heights	**193R**	80260	10000-10099	
	Westminster	**193M**	80234	10700-10799	
	Westminster	**193H**	80234	11100-11199	
BRYANT DR	Broomfield	**163Q**	80020	2600-2799	
	Federal Heights	**193Z**	80260	9200-9599	
	Jefferson Co	**336B**	80439	30400-30799	
BRYANT DR	Weld Co	**706P**	80504	2000-2199	
BRYANT DR	Westminster	**193H**	80234	11100-11199	
BRYANT PL	Broomfield	**163Q**	80020	13100-13199	
BRYANT PL W	Littleton	**373G**	80120	2800-2999	
BRYANT ST	Adams Co	**253H**	80221	5400-6299	
	Broomfield	**163V**	80020	12400-12599	
	Denver	**283V**	80219	100-399	
	Denver	**283M**	80204	400-1199	
	Denver	**283D**	80211	2000-2699	
	Denver	**253Z**	80211	2700-2899	
	Denver	**253R**	80211	3200-4799	
	Denver	**253M**	80221	4800-5199	
	Federal Heights	**193R**	80260	9900-10099	
	Westminster	**223R**	80030	7100-7599	
	Westminster	**223M**	80030	8000-8099	
	Westminster	**223H**	80260	8400-8599	
	Westminster	**193M**	80234	10400-10499	
	Westminster	**193M**	80234	10800-11099	
	Westminster	**163Z**	80234	12100-12299	
BRYANT ST S	Denver	**283Z**	80219	1-699	
	Denver	**313M**	80219	700-2299	
	Denver	**313V**	80236	2700-3099	
	Littleton	**373G**	80120	6900-7199	
	Sheridan	**313Z**	80110	3100-3499	
BRYANT WAY	Broomfield	**163M**	80020	13400-13499	
	Denver	**283V**	80219	1-99	
	Westminster	**223V**	80030	7000-7099	
	Westminster	**193M**	80234	10500-10599	
BRYANT MEWS	Westminster	**193H**	80234	11100-11199	
BRYCE	Weld Co	**706N**	80504	11200-11399	
BRYCE CT	Jefferson Co	**306K**	80439	1900-1999	
BRYCE LN	Highlands Ranch	**405N**	80126	10600-10799	
BRYN MAWR PL	Longmont	**10Z**	80503	2900-2999	
BRYNMAWR RD S	Jefferson Co	**843W**	80470	16700-16999	
BUCHANAN AVE	Firestone	**727B**	80504	None	
BUCHANAN AVE	Louisville	**130Z**	80027	100-299	
BUCHANAN CIR	Louisville	**130Y**	80027	200-299	
BUCHANAN CIR S	Aurora	**320H**	80018	1300-1699	
	Aurora	**320M**	80018	None	
BUCHANAN CT	Louisville	**130Z**	80027	300-399	
BUCHANAN CT N	Aurora	**290R**	80018	None	
BUCHANAN CT S	Arapahoe Co	**350R**	80016	5400-5499	
	Aurora	**350V**	80016	5400-5799	
	Aurora	**380D**	80016	None	
BUCHANAN CT S	Louisville	**130Z**	80027	100-199	
BUCHANAN DR	Jefferson Co	**336C**	80439	28500-29599	
BUCHANAN DR E	Aurora	**289H**	80011	20100-20199	
BUCHANAN LN	Longmont	**42B**	80501	600-899	
BUCHANAN PL E	Aurora	**289E**	80011	17000-17599	
	Aurora	**289G**	80011	19300-19699	
BUCHANAN PT	Lafayette	**131G**	80026	2000-2099	
BUCHANAN ST	Adams Co	**170R**	80022	13200-13599	
BUCHANAN ST E	Aurora	**289G**	80011	None	
BUCHANAN ST S	Arapahoe Co	**320D**	80018	800-1099	
	Arapahoe Co	**350R**	80016	5100-5199	
	Aurora	**350M**	80016	None	
	Aurora	**350V**	80016	None	
BUCHANAN WAY S	Aurora	**380R**	80016	7600-8099	
	Aurora	**380V**	80138	8600-8799	
	Aurora	**320H**	80018	None	
	Aurora	**350M**	80016	None	
BUCHTEL BLVD	Denver	**314G**	80210	400-1699	
	Denver	**315K**	80210	1700-3999	
	Denver	**315L**	80222	4000-4299	
BUCKAROO RD	Park Co	**841B**	80421	1-299	
BUCKBOARD DR	Hudson	**730Q**	80642	None	
BUCKBOARD DR	Jefferson Co	**306Y**	80439	3100-3299	
BUCKBOARD LN	Jefferson Co	**306Y**	80439	29400-29599	
BUCKBOARD RD E	Douglas Co	**411H**	80138	11400-11999	
BUCKBOARD RD E	Elbert Co	**830Q**	80138	None	
BUCKEYE CT	Boulder	**97R**	80304	3600-3699	
BUCKEYE ST	Douglas Co	**432F**	80125	10400-10499	
BUCKHAM WAY	Longmont	**40U**	80503	None	
BUCK HILL DR	Highlands Ranch	**375Y**	80126	9100-9199	
BUCKHORN CIR	Elbert Co	**832S**	80107	45300-45399	
BUCKHORN DR	Jefferson Co	**371W**	80127	9200-9299	
BUCKHORN RD	Jefferson Co	**371W**	80127	12300-13099	
BUCKHORN WAY	Jefferson Co	**370Z**	80127	13000-13199	
BUCKHORN WAY E	Douglas Co	**850X**	80116	11800-11999	
BUCKHORN CREEK ST	Parker	**439G**	80134	12600-12899	
BUCKINGHAM CT	Boulder Co	**100A**	80301	7300-7399	
BUCKINGHAM CT S	Highlands Ranch	**406F**	80130	9700-9899	
BUCKINGHAM PL E	Highlands Ranch	**406F**	80130	7200-7299	
BUCKINGHAM RD	Boulder	**100A**	80301	7300-7499	
BUCKLEY CIR S	Aurora	**319E**	80017	1500-1699	
BUCKLEY DR	Longmont	**11R**	80501	300-499	
BUCKLEY RD	Adams Co	**769W**	80022	8000-9599	
	Adams Co	**169S**	80603	12500-13199	
	Brighton	**169A**	80601	13200-14299	
	Brighton	**139E**	80601	None	
	Commerce City	**169S**	80603	12000-12499	
	Denver	**259A**	80249	5600-6099	
	Denver	**769W**	80239	7000-7999	
BUCKLEY RD S	Arapahoe Co	**349W**	80016	5900-6499	
	Arapahoe Co	**379A**	80016	6500-6699	
	Aurora	**289W**	80017	400-899	
	Aurora	**319J**	80017	700-1999	
	Aurora	**319J**	80013	2000-3599	
	Aurora	**349J**	80013	3600-4299	
	Aurora	**349J**	80015	4300-5899	
	Foxfield	**379E**	80016	6700-7499	
BUCKLEY WAY	Aurora	**288R**	80011	600-699	
	Aurora	**289E**	80011	1900-1999	
BUCKLEY WAY S	Aurora	**319E**	80017	1500-1699	
	Aurora	**349J**	80015	4500-4699	
BUCKNELL CIR W	Highlands Ranch	**403G**	80129	3600-3799	
BUCKNELL CT	Boulder	**128K**	80305	1-3199	
BUCKNELL CT S	Highlands Ranch	**403G**	80129	9700-9899	
BUCKNELL DR W	Highlands Ranch	**403G**	80129	3600-3799	
BUCKNELL PL E	Denver	**316T**	80224	6800-7199	
	Denver	**316U**	80231	7800-8199	
BUCKNELL PL W	Highlands Ranch	**403G**	80129	3400-3499	
BUCKNELL WAY S	Highlands Ranch	**403G**	80129	9700-9899	
BUCK RAKE BLVD	Platteville	**708B**	80651	200-299	
BUCKSKIN AVE	Lochbuie	**140E**	80603	1600-1699	
	Lochbuie	**139H**	80603	1700-1899	
BUCKSKIN CT	Elbert Co	**830Y**	80138	200-499	
BUCKSKIN DR N	Douglas Co	**432N**	80125	6900-7099	
BUCKSKIN LN	Douglas Co	**848J**	80108	800-999	
BUCKSKIN PL	Broomfield	**162D**	80020	None	
BUCKSKIN RD	Elbert Co	**830Y**	80138	43700-43999	
BUCKSKIN WAY	Broomfield	**133K**	80020	16600-16799	
BUCKSKIN WAY	El Paso Co	**908Y**	80132	300-399	
BUCKSKIN TRAIL	Park Co	**841Q**	80421	1-399	
BUCKTHORN DR	Jefferson Co	**370L**	80127	1-99	
BUCKTHORN DR	Longmont	**40Q**	80503	3801-3999	O
BUCKTHORN LN	Douglas Co	**378V**	80134	16300-16599	
BUCKTHORN WAY	Louisville	**130V**	80027	500-599	
BUCKWHEAT RUN	Parker	**378V**	80134	8500-8599	
BUCKWOOD LN	El Paso Co	**908P**	80132	1300-1399	
BUD CT	Douglas Co	**887G**	80118	1900-1999	
BUDD CT	Longmont	**41U**	80501	1600-1699	
BUELL MANSION PKWY					
	Cherry Hills Village	**345B**	80113	1-99	
BUENA VISTA AVE	Palmer Lake	**907Q**	80133	None	
BUENA VISTA BLVD	Castle Rock	**466N**	80109	4400-5199	
BUENA VISTA CT	Brighton	**139S**	80601	None	
BUENA VISTA CT	Castle Rock	**466S**	80109	4400-4699	
BUENA VISTA DR	Jefferson Co	**822V**	80433	10000-10399	
BUENA VISTA RD	Jefferson Co	**278X**	80401	300-599	
BUFFALO AVE	Broomfield	**163K**	80020	3500-3599	
BUFFALO CT	Douglas Co	**432M**	80125	7400-7499	
BUFFALO CT	Longmont	**12X**	80501	900-999	
BUFFALO DR S	Jefferson Co	**370Z**	80127	9100-9299	
	Littleton	**374B**	80120	6600-6699	
BUFFALO LN	Jefferson Co	**277Y**	80401	25800-25899	
BUFFALO RD	Weld Co	**72Z**	80516	5100-5499	
BUFFALO ST	Firestone	**707S**	80504	None	
BUFFALO ST S	Littleton	**374B**	80120	6800-7099	
BUFFALOBERRY DR	Douglas Co	**411W**	80138	9500-9999	
	Douglas Co	**410Z**	80138	None	
	Parker	**410Y**	80138	22900-23499	
BUFFALO BILL CIR	Jefferson Co	**278Y**	80401	300-699	
BUFFALO CREEK DR	Jefferson Co	**335R**	80439	4800-5099	
BUFFALO CREEK LN	Jefferson Co	**335R**	80439	4900-5099	
BUFFALO CREEK RD	Jefferson Co	**335R**	80439	31700-32999	
BUFFALO GAP LN E	Parker	**848D**	80134	None	
BUFFALO GAP TRAIL S	Parker	**408Y**	80134	None	
BUFFALO GRASS DR	Elbert Co	**850V**	80107	37700-37999	
BUFFALO GRASS LN	Castle Rock	**466Q**	80109	3500-3699	
BUFFALO GRASS LOOP	Broomfield	**133W**	80026	4900-5099	
BUFFALO GRASS PL	Elbert Co	**850V**	80107	1200-1399	
BUFFALO PARK RD	Clear Creek Co	**821C**	80439	100-1999	
	Clear Creek Co	**335W**	80439	None	
	Jefferson Co	**335W**	80439	30200-34799	
	Jefferson Co	**336N**	80439	None	
BUFFALO POND TRAIL	Douglas Co	**870S**	80116	3500-3598	E
BUFFALO RIDGE CT					
	Castle Pines North	**436K**	80108	1100-1199	
BUFFALO RIDGE RD					
	Castle Pines North	**436K**	80108	900-1399	
BUFFALO RIDGE WAY					
	Castle Pines North	**436K**	80108	1000-1199	
BUFFALO RUN	Douglas Co	**432T**	80125	6100-6299	
BUFFALO RUN CIR	Elbert Co	**852L**	80107	39400-39799	
BUFFALO TRAIL	Castle Pines North	**436F**	80108	7400-8199	
BUFFALO TRAIL	Elbert Co	**850U**	80107	500-1699	
BUFFALO VALLEY PATH	Monument	**908W**	80132	16900-17299	
BUFFUM ST	Park Co	**820V**	80421	1-499	
BUFORD LN	Jefferson Co	**823V**	80465	20600-20799	
BUGGY WHIP RD	Park Co	**841P**	80421	1-299	
BUGLE CT	Boulder Co	**99G**	80301	6700-6899	
BULKEY ST	Douglas Co	**467K**	80108	1000-1199	
BULL DOGGER CT	Park Co	**841P**	80421	1-199	
BULL DOGGER RD	Park Co	**841P**	80421	1-399	
BULLOCK CT	Parker	**408R**	80134	10800-10899	
BULRUSH CT	Castle Rock	**497A**	80109	2100-2299	
BULRUSH DR	Castle Rock	**497A**	80109	1000-1299	
BUNGALOW WAY	Broomfield	**163E**	80020	14300-14399	
BUNKER WAY	Jefferson Co	**340S**	80465	15700-15799	
BUNNY LN	Elbert Co	**850U**	80107	300-499	
BUNNY RD	Park Co	**841V**	80421	1-399	
BUNTING COVE	Lafayette	**132N**	80026	800-899	
BUNTING DR	Lafayette	**132J**	80026	700-799	
BURBANK ST	Broomfield	**162S**	80020	400-899	
BURBERRY LN S	Highlands Ranch	**404B**	80129	9600-9699	
BURBERRY WAY S	Highlands Ranch	**404B**	80129	9600-9899	
BURDETT ST	Park Co	**820Z**	80421	1-199	
BURDOCK CT	Frederick	**726G**	80516	None	
BURGESS AVE	Golden	**279T**	80401	100-199	
BURGESS DR	Castle Rock	**497M**	80104	1-499	
BURGGARTEN DR	Castle Pines North	**436F**	80108	None	
BURGUNDY AVE W	Jefferson Co	**341Z**	80123	9300-9699	
	Jefferson Co	**341Y**	80127	10100-10399	
	Jefferson Co	**341X**	80127	11400-11699	
	Jefferson Co	**341W**	80127	12000-12399	
BURGUNDY CIR S	Highlands Ranch	**404C**	80126	9300-9599	
BURGUNDY CT	El Paso Co	**909W**	80132	None	
BURGUNDY CT E	Highlands Ranch	**404B**	80126	1-99	
BURGUNDY DR	Boulder Co	**70K**	80503	7000-7199	
BURGUNDY DR E	Highlands Ranch	**404B**	80126	1-199	
BURGUNDY DR W	Jefferson Co	**342U**	80123	6300-6599	
	Jefferson Co	**342W**	80123	8500-8799	
	Jefferson Co	**341Y**	80127	10000-10299	
BURGUNDY LN	Boulder Co	**99F**	80301	4600-4699	
BURGUNDY LN E	Highlands Ranch	**404B**	80126	1-99	
BURGUNDY PL S	Highlands Ranch	**404C**	80126	9400-9499	
BURGUNDY PL W	Jefferson Co	**342Z**	80123	5200-5399	
BURGUNDY ST E	Highlands Ranch	**404B**	80126	1-99	
BURGUNDY ST W	Highlands Ranch	**404B**	80129	1-599	
BURGUNDY WAY E	Highlands Ranch	**404B**	80126	1-99	
BURION ST	Central City	**780C**	80427	100-199	
BURKE RD	Jefferson Co	**762G**	80403	31200-31499	
BURLAND DR	Jefferson Co	**762C**	80403	11000-11199	
BURLAND DR	Park Co	**841T**	80421	1-2099	
BURLAND RD	Jefferson Co	**762C**	80403	30700-31299	

STREET NAME	CITY or COUNTY	MAP GRID	ZIP CODE	BLOCK RANGE	O/E
BURLINGTON AVE N	Lafayette	132K	80026	100-199	
BURLINGTON AVE S	Lafayette	132K	80026	100-499	
BURLINGTON BLVD	Brighton	169K	80601	13600-13899	
BURLINGTON DR	Castle Rock	498H	80104	1100-5599	
BURLINGTON DR	Longmont	41V	80501	1-1499	
BURLINGTON LN S	Highlands Ranch	406B	80130	9300-9599	
BURLINGTON PL	Denver	257M	80239	12100-12299	
	Denver	259L	80249	None	
BURLINGTON PL W	Denver	254J	80221	1500-1899	
BURLINGTON WAY	Longmont	41U	80501	1-99	
BURN LN	Jefferson Co	306J	80439	31300-31399	
BURNHAM DR	Jefferson Co	307X	80439	3400-3499	
BURNHAM PL	Castle Rock	527B	80104	4000-4199	
BURNHAM TRAIL	Castle Rock	527B	80104	4100-4199	
BURNING OAK WAY	El Paso Co	908T	80132	1500-1699	
BURNING RIDGE CT	Douglas Co	470Y	80116	8700-8999	
BURNING RIDGE DR	Douglas Co	470Y	80116	2100-2499	
BURNING TREE DR	Douglas Co	470W	80116	7600-9099	
BURNING TREE TRAIL	Douglas Co	470T	80116	8100-8699	
BURNLEY CT	Highlands Ranch	375S	80126	8300-8399	
BURNT LEAF WAY	El Paso Co	908T	80132	18900-19099	
BURNT OAK DR	Douglas Co	470X	80116	2100-2599	
BURNT OAK TRAIL	Douglas Co	470X	80116	8100-8499	
BURNTWOOD CT S	Highlands Ranch	404G	80126	9700-9799	
BURNTWOOD WAY	Highlands Ranch	404G	80126	9200-9799	
BUROAK LN	Douglas Co	470A	80134	4900-5299	
BUROAK PL	Douglas Co	470A	80134	7400-7499	
BURR PL	Boulder	128C	80303	4400-4499	
BURRO LN	Jefferson Co	337V	80439	5600-5699	
BURT ST	Central City	780C	80427	100-199	
BURTON DR	Adams Co	794P	80136	None	
BURTON ST	Adams Co	794P	80136	1500-1999	
	Adams Co	794F	80136	3900-4099	
BURTON ST	Park Co	820Z	80421	1-699	
BURTON WAY	Adams Co	794P	80136	None	
BUSCH LN S	Longmont	41L	80501	1-99	
BUSCH PL	Frederick	706Z	80504	None	
BUSCH ST	Longmont	41L	80501	700-899	
BUSH ST	Brighton	138P	80601	1-1399	
BUSINESS CENTER DR					
	Highlands Ranch	376T	80130	6100-7199	
BUSINESS PARK CIR	Firestone	706R	80504	11200-11499	
BUTLER CIR	Boulder	128U	80305	4300-4399	
BUTLER CT	Longmont	42A	80501	200-299	
BUTLER WAY S	Lakewood	312A	80226	900-1099	
	Lakewood	312A	80232	1100-1199	
BUTTE CIR	Douglas Co	867N	80135	2500-2999	
BUTTE DR	Jefferson Co	762C	80403	29600-30299	
BUTTE DR	Weld Co	706U	80504	10400-10799	
BUTTE LN	Boulder	98V	80301	None	
BUTTE PKWY	Golden	249W	80403	400-499	
BUTTE RD	Lafayette	132U	80026	None	
BUTTEMILL RD	Boulder Co	99T	80301	5800-6299	
BUTTERCUP CIR	Brighton	168C	80601	None	
BUTTERCUP CIR N	Frederick	726C	80516	3100-3299	
BUTTERCUP CIR S	Frederick	726C	80516	3000-3199	
BUTTERCUP DR	Castle Rock	466P	80109	4900-5099	
BUTTERCUP DR	Frederick	726C	80516	None	
BUTTERCUP LN	Jefferson Co	307X	80401	3100-3199	
BUTTERCUP RD	Elbert Co	850V	80107	1000-1999	
BUTTERCUP ST	Erie	133D	80516	None	
BUTTERFIELD LN	Castle Rock	497R	80104	1200-1299	
BUTTERFIELD CROSSING DR					
	Castle Rock	466P	80109	3700-3999	
BUTTERMILK CT	Jefferson Co	306J	80439	30900-31099	
BUTTERMILK LN	Park Co	841M	80421	1-199	
BUTTERMILK RD	Douglas Co	887M	80118	1000-1599	
BUTTERWOOD CT	Highlands Ranch	374Y	80126	9100-9299	
BUTTERWORT CIR	Douglas Co	378U	80134	15800-16099	
BUTTESFIELD ST	Firestone	707S	80504	None	
BUTTON HILL CT	Highlands Ranch	376W	80130	9200-9899	
BUTTON HILL CT S	Highlands Ranch	406A	80130	9200-9299	
BUTTON ROCK CT	Longmont	12Y	80501	1100-1199	
BUTTON ROCK DR	Longmont	12Y	80501	900-1299	
BUTTONWOOD CT	Monument	908S	80132	300-399	
BUTTONWOOD PL	Monument	908S	80132	300-399	
BYERS AVE	Platteville	708C	80651	300-499	
BYERS AVE E	Denver	286X	80230	7001-7299	O
	Denver	286Y	80230	7701-8099	O
BYERS DR E	Aurora	291T	80018	None	
BYERS DR W	Denver	283Z	80223	2100-2399	
BYERS PL E	Arapahoe Co	290V	80018	23700-23799	
BYERS PL E	Aurora	291T	80018	None	
BYERS PL W	Denver	284X	80223	1-199	
	Denver	284W	80223	900-1599	
	Denver	283X	80219	3700-4299	
	Denver	283W	80219	4700-4799	
	Jefferson Co	280X	80401	14500-14799	
	Lakewood	282Z	80226	5400-6199	
	Lakewood	282Y	80226	6300-6599	
	Lakewood	282X	80226	7200-7599	
BYRON PL W	Denver	283D	80211	2400-2599	
	Denver	283B	80211	3600-3899	
	Denver	283B	80212	3900-4299	
	Denver	283A	80212	4600-5199	

C

STREET NAME	CITY or COUNTY	MAP GRID	ZIP CODE	BLOCK RANGE	O/E
C	Aurora	288F	80011	None	
C ST	Golden	279P	80401	300-1399	
C ST	Jefferson Co	279R	80401	None	
C ST	Longmont	11U	80501	None	
CABALLO CT	Boulder Co	130N	80303	1-99	
CABALLO PL	Douglas Co	439W	80134	4900-5099	
CABBAGE AVE S	Brighton	138P	80601	1-299	
CABLE ST	Lochbuie	139D	80603	None	
	Lochbuie	140A	80603	None	
CABRINI BLVD	Jefferson Co	278Y	80401	19600-21899	
CABRINI DR	Lafayette	131H	80026	700-799	
CACHE CREEK CT	Castle Rock	468X	80108	2500-2699	
CACHE CREEK PT	Castle Rock	468X	80108	2700-2799	
CACTUS CIR	Elbert Co	832S	80107	45100-45199	
CACTUS CIR	Jefferson Co	280B	80401	2600-2699	
CACTUS CT	Boulder Co	97P	80304	200-299	
CACTUS CT	Highlands Ranch	375Q	80126	3700-3799	
CACTUS CT	Lone Tree	376Z	80124	9100-9199	
CACTUS CT	Louisville	130V	80027	500-599	
CACTUS DR	Jefferson Co	335B	80439	34000-34299	
CACTUS BLOOM CT	Castle Rock	496C	80109	2000-2599	
CACTUS BLUFF AVE W					
	Highlands Ranch	403D	80129	2000-2399	
CACTUS FLOWER WAY					
	Highlands Ranch	375W	80126	8800-8999	
CACTUS ROSE CIR	Douglas Co	527Y	80104	1400-1499	
CADDO PKWY	Boulder	128L	80303	3600-4499	
CADE ST	Brighton	139K	80601	None	
CADENCE DR	Castle Rock	466U	80109	None	
CADLAND CT	Douglas Co	408D	80134	16100-16299	
CAESAR RD	Gilpin Co	761N	80403	1-599	
CAGEL DR	Douglas Co	908L	80118	2500-2899	
CAHITA CT	Denver	254P	80216	4401-4499	O
CAIRN CT	Boulder Co	99J	80301	None	
CAIRNS CT S	Highlands Ranch	405H	80130	10000-10099	
CAITHNESS PL W	Denver	253Z	80211	2400-2699	
CALABRIA PL	Longmont	40P	80503	4500-4598	E
CALAHAN AVE W	Lakewood	312F	80232	6800-7599	
CALAIS DR	Longmont	12Q	80501	2100-2499	
CALAMITY DR	El Paso Co	909R	80908	None	
CALAVERAS CT	Longmont	12P	80501	2000-2099	
CALCITE CT	Castle Rock	467G	80108	7100-7299	
CALDWELL CT	Jefferson Co	338W	80439	23700-23999	
CALEB PL E	Aurora	380V	80138	None	
CALEDONIA CIR	Louisville	130V	80027	1300-1399	
CALEDONIA ST	Louisville	131S	80027	200-999	
CALENDULA DR E	Parker	439B	80134	None	
CALERIDGE CT	Highlands Ranch	375V	80126	None	
CALETA TRAIL	Longmont	41T	80501	None	
CALEY AVE	Greenwood Village	346Y	80111	6500-8099	
	Arapahoe Co	347W	80111	9300-10699	
	Arapahoe Co	349W	80016	17200-17499	
	Aurora	348X	80111	14200-14699	
	Centennial	344Y	80121	200-799	
	Centennial	344Z	80121	1200-1599	
	Centennial	345X	80121	2700-3199	
	Centennial	345Y	80121	3200-3999	
	Centennial	345Z	80121	5100-6099	
	Centennial	348Y	80016	15300-15599	
	Centennial	349W	80016	16800-16899	
	Denver	347Y	80111	10900-12899	
	Greenwood Village	346Z	80111	8700-9299	
CALEY AVE W	Jefferson Co	342Y	80123	6100-6299	
	Jefferson Co	341Z	80123	9500-9999	
	Jefferson Co	341Y	80127	10100-10199	
	Jefferson Co	341X	80127	10800-11299	
	Littleton	344X	80120	1-2099	
CALEY CIR E	Arapahoe Co	347W	80111	9500-9699	
	Arapahoe Co	349W	80016	16800-16899	
	Arapahoe Co	349X	80016	18100-18199	
	Centennial	345Y	80121	4000-4099	
CALEY CIR W	Littleton	344X	80120	300-699	
CALEY DR E	Arapahoe Co	349X	80016	18100-18299	
CALEY DR E	Aurora	351Y	80016	26300-26699	
	Centennial	344Y	80121	500-599	
	Centennial	346W	80111	5700-6299	
	Centennial	349Z	80016	19300-19899	
	Centennial	350W	80016	20500-20699	
	Centennial	350X	80016	21600-21699	
	Centennial	348W	80111	None	
CALEY DR W	Jefferson Co	342X	80123	7300-7999	
	Littleton	344X	80120	300-599	
CALEY LN E	Arapahoe Co	349W	80016	17300-17499	
CALEY LN E	Castle Rock	498M	80104	5700-5899	
CALEY LN E	Centennial	345Y	80121	3800-4499	
	Centennial	349Z	80016	20500-20599	
CALEY PL E	Arapahoe Co	347W	80111	10000-10099	
	Arapahoe Co	349W	80016	16800-17399	
	Arapahoe Co	349X	80016	18200-18299	
	Arapahoe Co	350W	80016	20700-20799	
CALEY PL E	Aurora	351Y	80016	26700-26898	E
	Aurora	351X	80016	None	
	Aurora	351X	80016	None	
	Centennial	345Y	80121	4000-4799	
	Centennial	348W	80111	14000-14199	
	Centennial	348Y	80016	15600-15699	
	Centennial	349Z	80016	20500-20599	
	Centennial	348W	80111	None	
CALEY PL W	Jefferson Co	342Y	80123	6300-6799	
	Jefferson Co	342W	80123	8000-8299	
	Jefferson Co	341Y	80127	10300-10499	
	Littleton	343Z	80120	2000-2399	
CALFEE GULCH RD	Jefferson Co	842B	80433	12200-12499	
CALGARY WAY	Jefferson Co	308A	80401	700-999	
CALHAN AVE N	Castle Rock	498H	80104	1100-1399	
CALHOUN AVE W	Jefferson Co	372D	80123	None	
CALHOUN CIR	Castle Rock	499J	80104	100-499	
CALHOUN DR E	Aurora	381B	80016	None	
CALHOUN DR W	Jefferson Co	372A	80123	8000-8399	
	Jefferson Co	372D	80123	None	
CALHOUN PL E	Aurora	380B	80016	22000-22299	
	Aurora	380C	80016	22600-22899	
	Aurora	381A	80016	24500-24999	
	Aurora	381B	80016	25700-26099	
	Aurora	381C	80016	26200-26399	
	Aurora	381C	80016	26500-26699	
CALHOUN PL S	Jefferson Co	371D	80123	9100-9199	
CALHOUN PL W	Jefferson Co	372C	80123	6500-6599	
	Jefferson Co	372B	80123	7900-8099	
	Jefferson Co	372D	80123	None	
CALHOUN RD	Arapahoe Co	795V	80103	1-1899	
CALHOUN RD	Gilpin Co	780F	80403	None	
CALHOUN BYERS RD	Adams Co	795M	80103	1-8799	
CALICO CT	Brighton	139G	80601	None	
CALICO CT	Longmont	40U	80503	None	
CALIFORNIA ST	Denver	284F	80202	1400-1999	
	Denver	284C	80205	2000-2799	
	Denver	254Y	80205	2800-3199	
CALKINS AVE	Longmont	11P	80501	1500-1899	
CALKINS PL	Broomfield	163U	80020	2600-2999	
CALLABRA AVE	Parker	439F	80134	18000-18099	
CALLAE CT	Jefferson Co	843F	80433	13400-13599	
CALLAE DR	Jefferson Co	843B	80433	12400-13599	
CALLAN CT	Broomfield	163G	80020	2800-2899	
CALLAWAY CT	Parker	410Q	80138	11000-11199	
CALLAWAY RD	Parker	410Q	80138	11000-11199	
CALLE LOUISA RD	Jefferson Co	782F	80403	4500-4999	
CALLISTO DR	Highlands Ranch	376X	80124	13200-13399	
CALLOWAY CT	Broomfield	163E	80020	4300-4499	
CALMANTE AVE	Superior	160T	80027	None	
CALMANTE CIR	Superior	160T	80027	1-199	
CALMANTE PL	Superior	160T	80027	None	
CALUMET RD	El Paso Co	908Z	80132	600-799	
CALVIN DR	Arvada	252E	80002	8600-8699	
CALYPSO CT W	Castle Rock	466Q	80109	3100-3199	
CAMANCHE CT	Frederick	726G	80516	3100-3199	
CAMARGO DR	Jefferson Co	307E	80401	27400-27799	
CAMARGO DR	Park Co	841D	80470	1-199	
CAMARGO RD S	Littleton	343P	80123	3200-5499	
CAMARGO WAY S	Littleton	343X	80123	5900-5999	
CAMBRIDGE AVE	Broomfield	163T	80020	3900-4399	
CAMBRIDGE CT S	Parker	409R	80138	11100-11199	
CAMBRIDGE DR	Longmont	11S	80503	1500-1899	
	Longmont	11N	80503	1900-2599	
CAMBRIDGE PL S	Parker	409R	80138	11000-11099	
CAMBRIDGE PL W	Littleton	825P	80127	9600-9899	
CAMBRIDGE ST	Boulder Co	100B	80301	4700-4999	
CAMBRIDGE WAY E	Parker	409R	80138	20200-20299	
CAMBRO LN	Lafayette	132N	80026	None	
CAMBROOK CT	El Paso Co	908Z	80132	1100-1199	
CAMDEN DR	Longmont	10Z	80503	3300-3599	
CAMDEN PL	Boulder	128J	80302	200-299	
CAMELBACK LN	Jefferson Co	306U	80439	29300-29499	
CAMELBACK ST S	Highlands Ranch	374Z	80126	9200-9399	
CAMEL HEIGHTS CIR	Jefferson Co	336R	80439	27900-28399	
CAMEL HEIGHTS RD	Jefferson Co	336R	80439	4900-5099	
CAMELITA CT	Platteville	708G	80651	1500-1599	
CAMELOT CIR	Weld Co	706D	80504	4000-4099	
CAMELOT DR	Douglas Co	870B	80116	10600-10799	
CAMENISH WAY	Federal Heights	223D	80260	8900-9099	
	Federal Heights	193Z	80260	9100-9199	
CAMEO CT	Castle Rock	527C	80104	4200-4399	
CAMERON CIR	Douglas Co	887G	80118	7200-7499	
CAMERON CT	Douglas Co	887G	80118	1300-1399	
CAMERON CT	Longmont	42B	80501	500-599	
CAMERON DR	Adams Co	168Y	80603	12000-12599	
	Commerce City	168Y	80603	12600-13299	
CAMERON DR	Douglas Co	887H	80118	7400-7599	
CAMERON LN	Longmont	42B	80501	700-899	
CAMERON WAY	Broomfield	133N	80020	16000-16199	
CAMEYO RD	Jefferson Co	338L	80454	3900-5099	
CAMINO BOSQUE	Boulder Co	722U	80302	1-499	
CAMINO PERDIDO	Jefferson Co	782G	80403	4200-4899	
CAMPBELL RD	El Paso Co	910T	80908	18000-20499	
CAMPBELL RD	Park Co	820V	80421	1-199	
CAMPDEN CT	Castle Rock	498L	80104	4500-4699	
CAMPDEN PL	Douglas Co	436Q	80108	7000-7299	
CAMP EDEN RD	Boulder Co	742W	80403	1-11299	
	Jefferson Co	762A	80403	11300-11999	
CAMPFIRE ST	Douglas Co	432F	80125	None	
CAMPINA WAY	Douglas Co	439W	80134	5600-5899	
CAMPION WAY	Parker	409J	80134	17100-17199	
CAMP NIZHONI RD	Gilpin Co	741X	80403	None	
CAMPO CT	Boulder Co	98K	80301	3800-3999	
CAMPO DR	Parker	409N	80134	17000-17099	
CAMPO ST	Adams Co	224P	80221	1-899	
CAMPO WAY	Superior	160Q	80027	400-599	
CAMPROBBER CT	Park Co	841U	80421	1-199	
CAMPUS DR	Greenwood Village	347J	80111	None	
CAMPUS DR	Lafayette	132W	80026	2600-2698	E
	Louisville	160H	80027	1-399	O
CAMPUS DR W	Littleton	374N	80120	1200-1599	
CAMPUS PL	Denver	315U	80210	3500-3699	
CAMPUS RD W	Golden	279E	80401	1600-1899	
CAMPUS LOOP DR	Lakewood	280V	80401	None	
CANA CT	Lafayette	131B	80026	2400-2499	
CANADIAN CROSSING DR	Longmont	12N	80501	None	
CANADIAN RIVER RD	Weld Co	706M	80504	None	
CANAL AVE	Commerce City	197L	80603	None	
CANAL CIR W	Littleton	374N	80120	1600-1699	
CANAL CT W	Littleton	374N	80120	1100-1699	
CANAL DR E	Aurora	287U	80012	11700-12099	
CANAL PL E	Aurora	291N	80018	25000-25199	
	Aurora	291P	80018	25700-25999	
CANAL EAST	Lochbuie	140E	80603	None	
CANALWEST	Lochbuie	140E	80603	None	
CANARY CIR	Brighton	137V	80601	None	
CANARY CT	Brighton	138S	80601	900-999	
CANARY CT	Elbert Co	871G	80107	33500-33599	
CANARY LN N	Douglas Co	410J	80138	11200-11399	
CANARY ST	Federal Heights	193U	80260	2900-9799	
CANBERRA CT S	Highlands Ranch	405D	80130	9700-9799	
CANBERRA DR S	Highlands Ranch	405D	80130	9500-9799	
CANBY WAY	Broomfield	133K	80020	16600-16799	
CANDLEGLOW ST	Castle Rock	496C	80109	1000-2499	
CANDLEWOOD CT	Highlands Ranch	405F	80126	9900-9999	
CANDLEWOOD LN	Highlands Ranch	405F	80126	9900-9999	
CANNA PL	Superior	160U	80027	3000-3999	
CANNES DR W	Littleton	825Q	80127	8500-8899	
CANNON CIR	Louisville	131N	80027	1300-1699	
CANNON PL W	Lafayette	131M	80026	600-1099	
CANNON ST	Louisville	131S	80027	1300-1499	
CANNON ST E	Lafayette	132J	80026	100-599	
CANNON ST S	Arapahoe Co	813J	80102	3200-3499	
CANNON ST W	Lafayette	132J	80026	100-499	
CANNONADE DR	Parker	410N	80138	10900-11099	
CANNONADE LN	Parker	410N	80138	11000-11099	
CANNONADE WAY	Parker	410S	80138	11400-11499	
CANNON MOUNTAIN DR	Longmont	40P	80503	None	
CANNON MOUNTAIN WAY	Longmont	40P	80503	None	
CANON CIR	Greenwood Village	346V	80111	1-99	
CANON DR	Greenwood Village	346V	80111	1-99	
CANON PL	Greenwood Village	346V	80111	1-99	
CANON ST	Morrison	309Z	80465	100-199	
CANON CITY CREST	Palmer Lake	907U	80133	None	
CANONGATE LN	Highlands Ranch	375V	80126	1-8699	
	Highlands Ranch	376W	80130	None	
CANON VIEW RD	Boulder Co	722L	80302	1-2999	
CANOPUS DR	Highlands Ranch	376X	80124	13100-13299	
CANOSA CT	Denver	283R	80204	600-799	
	Denver	283M	80204	1400-1499	
	Westminster	223V	80030	7000-7199	
	Westminster	223R	80030	7200-7599	
	Westminster	193M	80234	10500-10599	
CANOSA CT S	Denver	283Z	80219	100-699	
	Denver	313M	80219	700-1899	
	Sheridan	313Z	80110	3300-3499	

STREET NAME	CITY or COUNTY	MAP GRID	ZIP CODE	BLOCK RANGE	O/E
CANOSA DR	Broomfield	163U	80020	2600-2799	
CANOSA ST	Westminster	193M	80234	10400-10499	
CANOSA WAY	Westminster	193M	80234	10400-10499	
CANOSA WAY S	Denver	283V	80219	1-99	
CANTEEN TRAIL S	Parker	408Z	80134	None	
CANTERBERRY LN	Parker	410U	80138	11300-11599	
CANTERBERRY PKWY	Parker	410U	80138	10800-11699	
CANTERBERRY TRAIL	Parker	410V	80138	11700-22499	
CANTERBURY CIR	Broomfield	163T	80020	3700-3799	
	Jefferson Co	306T	80439	29400-30199	
CANTERBURY CT	Boulder Co	100E	80301	7600-7799	
CANTERBURY DR	Boulder Co	100E	80301	4400-4599	
CANTERBURY DR	El Paso Co	909S	80132	17600-18499	
CANTERBURY DR	Lafayette	132K	80026	600-699	
CANTERBURY LN	Jefferson Co	306T	80439	2600-2699	
CANTITOE LN	Cherry Hills Village	345M	80110	1-99	
CANTRELL CT N	Douglas Co	440X	80134	5700-5899	
CANTRELL WAY N	Douglas Co	440V	80134	6000-6199	
CANTRIL CIR	Elbert Co	891X	80106	None	
CANTRIL ST	Castle Rock	497G	80104	1-799	
CANTRIL ST S	Castle Rock	497G	80104	1-99	
CANVASBACK CIR	Douglas Co	432K	80125	7800-7899	
CANVASBACK CT	Douglas Co	432K	80125	7900-7999	
CANYON AVE	Frederick	727E	80516	None	
CANYON AVE E	Aurora	381L	80016	None	
CANYON AVE W	Jefferson Co	372L	80128	5600-6799	
	Jefferson Co	372K	80128	7900-7999	
	Jefferson Co	371L	80127	9900-9999	
CANYON BLVD	Boulder	127C	80302	100-1999	
	Boulder	128A	80302	2000-2799	
	Boulder	128B	80301	None	
CANYON CIR	Elbert Co	852N	80107	6100-6199	
CANYON CIR	Frederick	727E	80516	None	
	Jefferson Co	305R	80439	31600-31699	
CANYON DR	Castle Rock	497G	80104	600-1599	
CANYON DR W	Jefferson Co	372M	80128	5600-6099	
CANYON LN	Lochbuie	140F	80603	700-799	
CANYON LN N	Douglas Co	467E	80108	4300-4599	
CANYON PL E	Aurora	380M	80016	23400-23499	
	Aurora	381M	80016	27500-27599	
	Aurora	380K	80016	None	
	Aurora	380Q	80016	None	
CANYON PL W	Jefferson Co	372J	80128	8300-8399	
	Jefferson Co	371M	80128	9200-9399	
CANYON RD N	Jefferson Co	824N	80127	17300-18299	
CANYON WAY	Frederick	727A	80516	None	
CANYON ALDER	Jefferson Co	370Q	80127	1-99	
CANYONBROOK DR	Highlands Ranch	405Q	80130	4300-4699	
CANYONBROOK WAY					
	Highlands Ranch	405Q	80130	11000-11099	
CANYON CEDAR	Jefferson Co	370L	80127	1-99	
CANYON CLUB DR	Douglas Co	466G	80108	4500-4599	
CANYON CREEK RD	Boulder	128K	80303	2900-2999	
CANYON CREEK RD	Jefferson Co	367B	80439	None	
CANYON CREST DR	Highlands Ranch	405K	80126	2700-2899	
CANYON CREST LN	Highlands Ranch	405K	80126	2800-2999	
CANYON CREST PL	Highlands Ranch	405K	80126	2800-2999	
CANYONLANDS WAY	Castle Rock	496B	80109	None	
CANYON POINT CIR	Golden	248Z	80403	100-699	
CANYON RANCH RD	Highlands Ranch	375U	80126	3800-3999	
CANYON RIM CIR	Douglas Co	378Q	80112	8401-8499	O
CANYON RIM DR	Douglas Co	378U	80012	15400-15499	
CANYONSIDE DR	Boulder Co	742D	80302	1-599	
CANYON TRAIL	Elbert Co	871B	80107	5600-5999	
CANYON TRAIL W	Jefferson Co	372M	80128	5200-5599	
CANYON VIEW DR	Castle Rock	498H	80104	5200-5699	
CANYON VIEW DR	Golden	278D	80403	500-599	
	Jefferson Co	824N	80465	19800-19999	
CANYON VIEW RD	Boulder Co	742C	80302	1-99	
CANYON VISTA DR	Morrison	339C	80465	1-199	
CANYON VISTA LN	Morrison	339D	80465	100-199	
CANYON WIND PL	Douglas Co	441A	80138	9500-9699	
CANYON WIND PT	Douglas Co	441A	80138	9700-9999	
CANYON WIND ST	Douglas Co	441A	80138	None	
CANYON WREN CT S	Highlands Ranch	405C	80126	9200-9399	
CANYON WREN LN	Highlands Ranch	405C	80126	None	
CANYON WREN WAY	Jefferson Co	370A	80127	16100-16199	
CAPADARO CT	El Paso Co	908P	80132	1500-1699	
CAPE ST S	Lakewood	312J	80232	1500-1799	
CAPE WAY S	Lakewood	312E	80232	1200-1399	
	Lakewood	312J	80227	1900-2099	
CAPE COD WAY W	Littleton	374N	80120	1800-1899	
CAPELLA DR	El Paso Co	907R	80132	19500-20999	
	El Paso Co	908N	80132	21000-21099	
CAPILANO CT	Douglas Co	466F	80108	700-799	
CAPITAL DR	Golden	279U	80401	100-199	
CAPITAL CREEK ST	Parker	439F	80134	12800-12899	
CAPITOL CT	Broomfield	163J	80020	4600-4799	
CAPRI AVE W	Jefferson Co	341Z	80123	8800-9599	
	Jefferson Co	341Y	80123	9600-9999	
	Jefferson Co	341X	80127	10800-11299	
	Jefferson Co	341W	80127	12000-12199	
CAPRI DR W	Jefferson Co	341Z	80123	9500-9599	
CAPRI LN	Longmont	40P	80503	None	
CAPRI PL W	Jefferson Co	342Z	80123	5200-5399	
	Jefferson Co	342W	80123	8400-8499	
	Jefferson Co	341X	80127	11300-11499	
CAPRICE CT	Castle Rock	497B	80109	100-199	
CAPRICE DR	Castle Rock	497F	80109	1000-1399	
CAPTAIN CT	Littleton	374N	80120	None	
CAPTAIN MERIWETHER LEWIS DR E					
	Douglas Co	440X	80134	8000-8199	
CAPTAINS LN	Boulder Co	41Z	80504	8100-8199	
	Longmont	10R	80503	3100-3199	
CAPULIN PL	Douglas Co	436X	80108	100-199	
CARAWAY LN	Parker	408U	80134	11300-11399	
CARBIDE CT	Longmont	12X	80501	1200-1299	
CARBON CT	Erie	102V	80516	1000-1099	
CARBON PL	Boulder	98X	80301	3000-3299	
CARBON RD	Broomfield	161K	80020	9500-9999	
	Broomfield	162L	80020	None	
CARBON ST	Erie	102M	80516	700-799	
CARBONATE WAY	Douglas Co	466L	80108	5000-5099	
CARBONDALE LN	Boulder	98P	80301	None	
CARBONDALE ST	Dacono	727F	80514	700-999	
CARDENAS DR	Gilpin Co	741Y	80403	None	
CARDENS CT	Erie	102V	80516	None	
CARDENS PL	Erie	102V	80516	None	
CARDER CT W	Highlands Ranch	373X	80125	8000-8399	
CARDINAL CIR	Brighton	138W	80601	1100-1199	
CARDINAL COVE	Lafayette	132N	80026	800-899	
CARDINAL DR	Lafayette	132J	80026	700-799	
CARDINAL DR N	Douglas Co	410J	80138	11000-11399	
CARDINAL LN	Boulder Co	69L	80503	7000-7499	
CARDINAL ST	Federal Heights	193U	80260	9600-9699	
CARDINAL WAY	Longmont	41R	80501	None	
CARDOVA CT	Erie	103N	80516	None	
CAREFREE ST	Firestone	707S	80504	None	
CAREFREE TRAIL	Douglas Co	469E	80134	4500-5199	
CARETAKER RD	Douglas Co	432E	80125	11200-11299	
CAREY LN	Castle Pines North	436L	80108	7400-7599	
CAREY WAY S	Denver	315U	80222	2500-2599	
CARGILL DR	Adams Co	254A	80221	1400-1499	
CARIA DR	Lafayette	131L	80026	1200-1599	
CARIBOU CIR	El Paso Co	908X	80132	800-899	
CARIBOU CT	Frederick	726G	80516	None	
CARIBOU DR	El Paso Co	908Y	80132	17300E-17799E	
	El Paso Co	908X	80132	600W-1099W	
CARIBOU DR	Frederick	707W	80504	None	
CARIBOU DR E	Douglas Co	870K	80116	10900-11899	
CARIBOU PL	Longmont	12W	80501	100-199	
CARIBOU RD	Boulder Co	740J	80466	1-4899	
CARIBOU ST	Nederland	740Q	80466	None	
CARIBOU WAY	El Paso Co	908Y	80132	200-299	
CARIBOU PASS CIR	Lafayette	131E	80026	300-399	
CARISSA	Jefferson Co	370K	80127	1-99	
CARLA CT	Broomfield	162K	80020	None	
CARLA WAY	Broomfield	162K	80020	1-99	
CARLAN CT S	Denver	313H	80219	1400-1599	
CARLILE ST	Northglenn	194R	80233	10400-10599	
	Northglenn	194H	80233	11000-11199	
	Northglenn	194D	80233	11400-11599	
CARLOCK DR	Boulder	128T	80305	3800-4099	
CARLSON AVE	Erie	102C	80516	1300-1799	
CARLSON DR	Parker	409A	80134	16900-17199	
CARLSON DR E	Centennial	378A	80111	None	
CARLSON DR W	Littleton	374A	80120	1000-1199	
CARLSON LN	Boulder	99A	80301	None	
CARLSON RD	Elbert Co	830Z	80138	1-1999	
CARLSON TRAIL	Elbert Co	831F	80138	None	
CARLTON PL	Longmont	41C	80501	1200-1299	
CARLTON ST S	Castle Rock	498L	80104	1-599	
	Castle Rock	498R	80104	600-899	
CARLYLE PARK CIR	Highlands Ranch	404A	80129	1200-1499	
CARLYLE PARK PL	Highlands Ranch	404A	80129	9400-9499	
CARMEL CIR E	Aurora	289C	80011	18700-19299	
CARMEL CT	Broomfield	162P	80020	1300-1399	
CARMEL CT	Lone Tree	406H	80124	9800-9899	
CARMEL DR	Lakewood	281B	80215	11600-11899	
CARMEL DR E	Aurora	289C	80011	18800-19199	
CARMEL LN	Cherry Hills Village	345E	80113	None	
CARMELA LN	Northglenn	194N	80234	10400-10599	
CARMEN ST	Boulder Co	131K	80027	300-499	
CARMICHAEL CT	Brighton	139G	80601	None	
CARMINE ST	Castle Rock	466V	80109	None	
CARMODY LN	Lakewood	311Q	80227	10000-10299	
CARNATION CIR	Longmont	40R	80503	1300-1399	
CARNATION PL	Adams Co	225Q	80022	7200-7499	
CARNATION WAY	Thornton	225B	80229	2400-2899	
CARNEGIE DR	Boulder	128P	80305	2700-3099	
CARNELIAN PL	Douglas Co	408H	80134	10000-10099	
CARNEROS CT	Douglas Co	441A	80138	8400-8699	
CAROB CIR	Parker	408U	80134	15400-15799	
CAROL CT	Elbert Co	851E	80138	41500-41699	
CAROL DR	Broomfield	726Y	80516	1800-1999	
CAROL DR	Palmer Lake	907Q	80133	None	
CAROL LN	Jefferson Co	365X	80433	8700-8999	
CAROL LN	Lochbuie	729Y	80603	None	
CAROL WAY	Adams Co	226J	80022	6200-6299	
CAROLE AVE S	Lafayette	132N	80026	700-899	
CAROLINA AVE	Longmont	41C	80501	1200-1399	
CAROLINA CIR E	Aurora	317E	80247	9900-9999	
CAROLINA DR E	Aurora	317H	80112	12800-13099	
	Aurora	318F	80012	14300-14499	
	Aurora	318H	80017	16300-16499	
	Aurora	319G	80017	19200-19299	
	Aurora	317E	80247	None	
CAROLINA DR W	Lakewood	311E	80228	12000-12399	
CAROLINA PL E	Aurora	317E	80247	9700-9899	
	Aurora	317G	80112	11800-11899	
	Aurora	318E	80012	13300-13399	
	Aurora	318G	80012	14800-15099	
	Aurora	319F	80017	17800-17899	
	Aurora	319G	80017	19200-19299	
	Aurora	317E	80247	None	
CAROLINA WAY	Mead	706M	80504	None	
CAROLINE AVE	Weld Co	728X	80621	1500-1999	
	Weld Co	729A	80621	2000-16499	
CAROLINE LN	Jefferson Co	307Y	80439	3100-3199	
CAROLYN DR	Clear Creek Co	801R	80439	1-199	
CAROLYN DR	Douglas Co	848E	80108	7600-7999	
CARPENTER CT	Elbert Co	831T	80138	45100-45199	
CARPENTER TRAIL	Douglas Co	845Q	80125	None	
CARR AVE E	Parker	409N	80134	17000-17099	
CARR AVE S	Lafayette	131M	80026	200-899	
CARR CIR	Arvada	222E	80005	8100-8199	
	Westminster	222A	80021	8900-8999	
	Westminster	191V	80021	9700-9899	
CARR CT	Arvada	222S	80004	6900-7099	
	Arvada	222J	80005	7700-7799	
	Arvada	222J	80005	8100-8199	
	Lakewood	282A	80215	2500-2599	
	Longmont	11Q	80501	1900-1999	
	Westminster	222E	80005	8500-8599	
	Westminster	222A	80021	8900-8999	
	Westminster	192W	80021	9000-9199	
CARR CT S	Jefferson Co	342E	80123	4300-4499	
	Jefferson Co	342W	80123	6100-6299	
	Jefferson Co	372J	80128	7300-7799	
	Jefferson Co	372N	80128	7800-8299	
	Jefferson Co	372W	80128	8800-8899	
	Lakewood	312N	80227	2300-2599	
	Lakewood	312W	80227	3100-3299	
CARR DR	Arvada	222J	80005	7400-7999	
CARR DR	Longmont	11Q	80501	1900-1999	
CARR LOOP	Westminster	222A	80005	8600-8799	
CARR PL S	Jefferson Co	372J	80128	8500-8599	
CARR ST	Arvada	252J	80002	5100-5699	
	Arvada	252A	80004	5800-6099	
	Arvada	222W	80004	6100-7199	
	Arvada	222W	80005	7200-7399	
	Broomfield	162W	80020	None	
	Erie	103J	80516	None	
	Jefferson Co	252J	80002	4800-5099	
	Lakewood	282S	80226	1-599	
	Lakewood	282N	80214	600-1999	
	Lakewood	282A	80214	2000-2599	
	Westminster	222A	80021	8900-8999	
	Westminster	192W	80021	9300-9499	
	Westminster	191V	80021	9500-9699	
	Wheat Ridge	252S	80033	3800-4399	
	Wheat Ridge	252N	80033	4400-4799	
CARR ST S	Jefferson Co	342A	80235	3500-4199	
	Jefferson Co	372N	80128	7100-9299	
	Lakewood	282S	80226	1-199	
	Lakewood	282W	80226	200-699	
	Lakewood	312A	80226	700-899	
	Lakewood	312E	80232	1400-1899	
	Lakewood	312J	80227	1900-2199	
	Lakewood	312N	80227	2300-2399	
	Lakewood	312W	80227	3100-3499	
CARR WAY S	Jefferson Co	372J	80128	7400-7499	
	Jefferson Co	372W	80128	8700-8899	
	Littleton	825Q	80127	9700-9799	
CARRARA TERRACE	Douglas Co	408H	80134	10200-10299	
CARRIAGE CIR E	Douglas Co	440T	80134	8200-8399	
CARRIAGE CT	Boulder Co	101M	80026	4000-4199	
CARRIAGE DR	Longmont	41R	80501	1200-1398	E
CARRIAGE LN	Cherry Hills Village	345Q	80121	1-99	
	Douglas Co	440T	80134	8100-8299	
CARRIAGE BROOK RD					
	Cherry Hills Village	345R	80121	1-99	
CARRIAGE CLUB DR	Lone Tree	406L	80124	10200-10499	
CARRIAGE HILLS DR	Boulder Co	722R	80302	1-3099	
CARRIAGE HORSE DR	El Paso Co	909X	80132	16800-17299	
CARRIAGE LOOP DR	Jefferson Co	336B	80439	29800-30299	
CARROL CT	Thornton	194Z	80229	1100-1699	
	Thornton	195W	80229	1700-2199	
CARROL LN	Northglenn	194L	80233	10600-10899	
CARROLL CT	Gilpin Co	760D	80403	None	
CARSON CT	Boulder Co	721C	80481	1-99	
CARSON CT	Commerce City	198P	80022	None	
CARSON CT S	Arapahoe Co	348P	80015	4900-5199	
	Aurora	318B	80012	900-1199	
	Parker	439G	80134	12900-12999	
CARSON DR W	Littleton	373L	80120	None	
CARSON ST	Aurora	288F	80011	1800-1999	
	Aurora	258X	80011	3000-3299	
	Denver	258N	80239	4200-4899	
	Denver	258J	80239	5100-5199	
	Denver	258F	80239	5500-5599	
CARSON ST S	Aurora	318F	80012	1500-1599	
	Aurora	348F	80014	3800-4299	
	Aurora	348K	80015	4800-4999	
	Centennial	378B	80111	6100-6699	
CARSON WAY	Broomfield	133L	80020	16600-16799	
CARSON WAY	Commerce City	198P	80022	10000-10099	
	Denver	258F	80239	5500-5599	
CARSON WAY S	Aurora	318F	80012	1200-1399	
	Aurora	318P	80014	2500-2699	
	Aurora	348B	80014	4000-4099	
	Aurora	348F	80015	4400-4499	
CARTER AVE	Louisville	130Z	80027	200-299	
CARTER CIR	Arapahoe Co	316S	80222	3000-3099	
CARTER CT	Boulder Co	99D	80301	4900-5099	
	Louisville	130Z	80027	100-199	
CARTER DR	Gilpin Co	761E	80403	1-199	
CARTER LN	Longmont	42H	80501	200-399	
CARTER ST	Golden	249X	80401	None	
CARTER TRAIL	Boulder Co	99H	80301	4200-7199	
CARYL AVE W	Jefferson Co	372M	80128	5200-5699	
CARYL PL W	Jefferson Co	372M	80128	5300-5499	
CASALON CIR	Superior	160T	80027	None	
CASALON ST	Superior	160T	80027	None	
CASCADE AVE	Boulder	127G	80302	500-1699	
	Boulder	128E	80302	1700-1999	
	Boulder	128H	80303	5000-5099	
CASCADE AVE	Castle Rock	498L	80104	None	
CASCADE CT	Broomfield	163K	80020	3500-3599	
CASCADE CT	Golden	248V	80403	600-699	
CASCADE CT	Highlands Ranch	374V	80126	8400-8499	
CASCADE DR	Federal Heights	193U	80260	2600-2999	
CASCADE DR	Golden	248V	80403	500-799	
CASCADE DR	Palmer Lake	907Q	80133	None	
CASCADE PL	Boulder	129E	80303	5600-5699	
CASCADE ST	Broomfield	163K	80020	13400-13599	
CASCADE ST	Firestone	707S	80504	None	
CASCADE WAY	Longmont	10R	80503	1900-1999	
CASCINA CIR	Highlands Ranch	405B	80126	3200-3499	
CASCINA PL	Highlands Ranch	405B	80126	3400-3599	
CASCO PL	Broomfield	133N	80020	4700-4799	
CASE CIR	Boulder	128T	80305	3300-3499	
CASEY AVE	Central City	780D	80427	1-399	
CASEY CT	Lafayette	101X	80026	1700-1799	
CASEY LN	Douglas Co	411B	80138	12000-12299	
CASH RD	Boulder Co	10N	80503	12200-12299	
CASHMERE PT	El Paso Co	908T	80132	1600-1699	
CASLER AVE	Weld Co	729A	80621	15000-16599	
CASPER DR	Lafayette	132S	80026	None	
CASPIAN CIR E	Aurora	318Q	80013	15600-15799	
	Aurora	319M	80013	19600-20099	
CASPIAN CIR W	Littleton	373E	80128	4400-4499	
CASPIAN CT E	El Paso Co	908V	80132	700-899	
CASPIAN CT W	El Paso Co	908V	80132	700-799	
CASPIAN DR E	Aurora	317R	80014	12300-12499	
	Aurora	321N	80018	None	
CASPIAN PL E	Aurora	318P	80014	14300-14499	
	Aurora	318P	80014	14600-15099	
	Aurora	318Q	80013	15500-15799	
	Aurora	319N	80013	17300-17599	
	Aurora	319P	80013	17800-18399	
	Aurora	319Q	80013	None	
CASPIAN PL W	Englewood	314N	80110	1801-1999	O
CASS CT	Castle Rock	499N	80104	800-899	

C

STREET NAME	CITY or COUNTY	MAP GRID	ZIP CODE	BLOCK RANGE	O/E
CASSIN CT	Boulder	128D	80303	1400-1499	
CASTLE CIR	Broomfield	163E	80020	4500-4799	
CASTLE CT	Jefferson Co	305M	80439	31900-32199	
CASTLE LN	Broomfield	163E	80020	4400-4599	
CASTLE RD	Thornton	193V	80260	None	
CASTLE BROOK DR	Douglas Co	466C	80108	2700E-2799E	
CASTLE BUTTE DR	Douglas Co	867Y	80109	2900-4499	
CASTLECOMBE LN	El Paso Co	909S	80132	1200-1299	
CASTLE CREEK WAY	Weld Co	706M	80504	None	
CASTLE CREST DR	Douglas Co	498E	80104	2600-2799	
CASTLE GATE DR	Castle Rock	467J	80108	6000W-6299W	
	Douglas Co	466M	80108	2200N-2399N	
CASTLE GLENN CT	Douglas Co	466C	80108	2700-2799	
CASTLE GLENN DR	Douglas Co	466C	80108	2700-2799	
CASTLE GLENN PL	Douglas Co	466C	80108	2700-2799	
CASTLE GROVE PL	Castle Pines North	436P	80108	1200-1399	
CASTLEMAINE CT	Castle Rock	497Y	80104	None	
CASTLEMAINE PL	Castle Rock	497Y	80104	None	
CASTLE MESA DR W	Douglas Co	496S	80109	1300-1699	
CASTLE OAKS DR	Castle Rock	498B	80108	1400-1999	
	Castle Rock	468U	80108	2000-4299	
	Castle Rock	469K	80116	6600-6699	
CASTLE OAKS RD	Castle Rock	469K	80108	3900-6599	
CASTLE PEAK AVE	Superior	160U	80027	2800-3799	
CASTLE PEAK CT	Brighton	140J	80601	None	
CASTLE PEAK LN	Castle Rock	867R	80109	None	
CASTLE PINES DR	Douglas Co	466B	80108	1N-199N	
CASTLE PINES DR	Douglas Co	466D	80108	1S-5099S	
CASTLE PINES PKWY	Castle Pines North	436K	80108	300-1499	
CASTLEPOINT CIR	Castle Pines North	436P	80108	1200-1499	
CASTLEPOINT LN	Castle Pines North	436T	80108	6700-6899	
CASTLE POINTE DR	Douglas Co	499Y	80104	1100-1699	
CASTLE RIDGE CIR S	Highlands Ranch	403D	80129	9500-9899	
CASTLE RIDGE CT S	Highlands Ranch	403H	80129	9800-9899	
CASTLE RIDGE DR	Highlands Ranch	403H	80129	None	
CASTLE RIDGE PL W	Highlands Ranch	403H	80129	2500-2599	
CASTLE RIDGE RD	Jefferson Co	308B	80401	900-999	
CASTLE RIDGE WAY W	Highlands Ranch	403H	80129	2100-2199	
CASTLE ROCK CT	Castle Rock	468X	80104	None	
CASTLEROCK RD	Golden	279B	80401	None	
CASTLETON CT	Castle Rock	467T	80109	3000-4699	
CASTLETON DR	Castle Rock	467P	80109	900-4999	
CASTLETON RD	Castle Rock	467P	80109	600-899	
CASTLETON WAY	Castle Rock	467P	80109	4500-4899	
CASTLEWOOD CT	Clear Creek Co	304Q	80439	1-199	
CASTLEWOOD DR	Clear Creek Co	304R	80439	1-799	
CASTLEWOOD DR N	Douglas Co	499B	80116	900-1899	
CASTLEWOOD PL N	Douglas Co	499F	80104	1100-1299	
CASTLEWOOD CANYON RD	Douglas Co	499M	80116	1-1999	
	Douglas Co	869T	80104	800-4999	
CASTLEWOOD CANYON RD S	Douglas Co	499M	80116	1-999	
	Douglas Co	499U	80104	1000-1699	
CASTRO PL	Erie	103N	80516	200-299	
CATALPA CIR	Broomfield	162N	80020	1200-1299	
CATALPA CT	Louisville	130V	80027	400-599	
CATALPA PL	Erie	133B	80516	None	
CATALPA ST	Frederick	727F	80530	800-898	E
CATALPA WAY	Boulder	97R	80304	3400-3699	
CATAMARAN LN	El Paso Co	908T	80132	1300-1499	
CATAMOUNT DR	Golden	248Q	80403	None	
CATAMOUNT LN	Jefferson Co	370A	80127	1-99	
CATAMOUNT RIDGE RD	Park Co	841Q	80421	1-399	
CATARATA PL	Castle Pines North	436B	80108	6600-6899	
CATARATA WAY	Castle Pines North	436B	80108	None	
CATAWBA CIR S	Aurora	320H	80018	1500-1699	
CATAWBA CT N	Aurora	290R	80018	None	
CATAWBA CT S	Arapahoe Co	350R	80016	5300-5399	
	Aurora	380R	80016	8000-8299	
CATAWBA ST S	Aurora	350M	80016	None	
	Aurora	380Z	80138	None	
CATAWBA WAY N	Aurora	290R	80018	None	
CATAWBA WAY S	Aurora	350R	80016	5500-5799	
CATAWBA WAY S	Aurora	380D	80016	None	
	Aurora	380H	80016	7300-7499	
	Aurora	380V	80138	None	
CATENA CT	Douglas Co	440L	80134	8400-8799	
CATHAY CIR S	Aurora	319U	80013	3000-3299	
	Aurora	349C	80013	3600-3799	
CATHAY CT	Aurora	289G	80011	1700-1999	
	Denver	259Q	80249	4500-4599	
	Denver	259G	80249	None	
	Denver	259L	80249	None	
CATHAY CT S	Arapahoe Co	349U	80015	5600-5699	
	Aurora	319G	80017	1300-1399	
	Aurora	319L	80017	1800-1899	
	Aurora	319U	80013	2700-2799	
	Aurora	349L	80015	4700-4999	
	Aurora	349C	80013	19100-19199	
	Centennial	349Q	80015	5200-5499	
CATHAY ST	Aurora	289G	80011	1700-1999	
	Aurora	289C	80011	None	
	Denver	259Q	80249	4300-4599	
	Denver	259L	80249	4901-5099	O
	Denver	259G	80249	None	
CATHAY ST S	Aurora	319G	80017	1100-1199	
	Aurora	319G	80017	1300-1499	
	Aurora	319Y	80013	3300-3499	
	Aurora	319Y	80013	3500-3599	
	Aurora	349C	80013	3600-3799	
	Centennial	379L	80016	7500-7799	
CATHAY WAY S	Aurora	319L	80013	2000-2199	
	Aurora	319U	80013	2700-2899	
	Aurora	349G	80013	4100-4299	
	Aurora	349G	80015	4300-4499	
	Aurora	319Q	80013	None	
	Centennial	349Q	80015	5200-5499	
CATHEDRAL DR	Palmer Lake	907R	80133	None	
CATHEDRAL WAY	Broomfield	133L	80020	16600-16799	
CATHEDRAL PEAK	Jefferson Co	371P	80127	7800-7899	
CATHEDRAL ROCK DR	Douglas Co	866C	80135	1000-1499	
CATHEDRAL TRAIL	Jefferson Co	843Q	80433	15300-15899	
CATHY LN	Weld Co	103C	80516	4600-4799	
CATO CIR	Lafayette	131Q	80026	1700-1799	
CATTAIL CT	Longmont	42H	80501	200-399	
CATTAIL CT S	Highlands Ranch	404D	80126	9300-9399	
CATTAIL DR	Boulder Co	70P	80503	8200-8299	
CATTAIL WAY	El Paso Co	908Y	80132	300-399	
CATTLE AVE	Parker	408V	80134	16100-16399	
CATTLE CT	Parker	408V	80134	11800-11899	
CATTLE DR	Elbert Co	850M	80138	1700-2199	
CATTLE LN	Parker	408Z	80134	11800-11899	
CATTLE TRAIL DR	Jefferson Co	762H	80403	10500-11099	
CAVALETTI DR	Douglas Co	432F	80125	10100-10299	
CAVALRY DR	Mead	706G	80542	None	
CAVALRY RUN	Douglas Co	845R	80125	10100-10199	
CAVAN CT	Boulder Co	131A	80303	1400-1499	
CAVAN LN	Jefferson Co	366L	80439	28500-28799	
CAVAN ST	Boulder Co	131E	80303	1200-1399	
CAVANAUGH RD	Adams Co	751Z	80642	12000-16799	
	Adams Co	771V	80642	None	
	Adams Co	791M	80137	None	
	Arapahoe Co	791V	80102	1-599	
CAVE SPRING RD	Douglas Co	890K	80116	11000-11099	
CAVE SPRING RD	Elbert Co	890Q	80107	11000-11099	
CAVE SPRING TRAIL	Elbert Co	890Q	80107	24900-25999	
CAYAUGA WAY	Superior	160E	80027	100-199	
CAYENNE CIR	Jefferson Co	340N	80465	15700-15799	
CAYMAN PL	Boulder	98K	80301	3200-3899	
CAYWOOD CT	Longmont	42A	80501	200-299	
CEDAR AVE	Aurora	288T	80012	None	
CEDAR AVE	Boulder	97U	80304	300-1899	
CEDAR AVE	Brighton	138S	80601	300-499	
CEDAR AVE	Castle Rock	497R	80104	100-299	
CEDAR AVE	Jefferson Co	842V	80470	28200-28499	
CEDAR AVE	Weld Co	706R	80504	None	
CEDAR AVE E	Arapahoe Co	795Y	80103	1-99	
CEDAR AVE E	Aurora	287U	80012	11500-11799	
	Aurora	287V	80012	12500-12899	
	Aurora	288S	80012	12900-13099	
	Aurora	288T	80012	None	
	Aurora	291S	80018	None	
	Denver	284V	80209	1-1699	
	Denver	285S	80209	1700-1899	
	Denver	285T	80209	2400-3099	
	Denver	285U	80209	3500-3999	
	Denver	285V	80246	4200-5499	
	Denver	286S	80246	5500-5599	
	Denver	286S	80224	5600-6799	
	Denver	286X	80230	7100-8099	
CEDAR AVE W	Arapahoe Co	795Y	80103	1-199	
	Denver	284T	80223	1-599	
	Denver	284S	80223	1200-1599	
	Denver	283Z	80223	2000-2499	
	Denver	283T	80219	2500-5199	
	Jefferson Co	280Y	80401	13800-13899	
	Jefferson Co	280X	80401	14600-14799	
	Lakewood	282V	80226	5300-5899	
	Lakewood	282U	80226	6500-7199	
	Lakewood	282W	80226	8200-8599	
	Lakewood	281Z	80226	9200-9999	
CEDAR CIR	Jefferson Co	336G	80439	28700-28999	
CEDAR CIR	Lochbuie	140C	80603	900-999	
CEDAR CIR E	Aurora	287V	80012	12300-12499	
CEDAR CIR S	Jefferson Co	842F	80470	13200-13399	
	Littleton	374J	80120	7900-7999	
	Littleton	374J	80120	7600E-7699E	
CEDAR CIR W	Lakewood	282T	80226	7100-7499	
CEDAR CT	Broomfield	162P	80020	1-99	
CEDAR CT	Longmont	11W	80503	1-99	
CEDAR CT	Thornton	225A	80229	1900-2099	
	Thornton	194Z	80229	9000-9499	
CEDAR CT S	Littleton	344W	80120	6200-6299	
CEDAR DR	Jefferson Co	842H	80433	13500-13699	
	Jefferson Co	823V	80465	20400-20999	
CEDAR DR	Park Co	841T	80421	1-299	
CEDAR DR W	Lakewood	281Z	80226	9100-9199	
	Lakewood	281W	80228	11800-12199	
	Lakewood	280Z	80228	12200-12899	
CEDAR LN	Elbert Co	850U	80107	400-599	
CEDAR LN	Jefferson Co	822W	80470	34500-34599	
	Littleton	373P	80120	None	
CEDAR LN	Park Co	841L	80421	1-199	
CEDAR LN	Westminster	223F	80031	8500-8699	
CEDAR PL	Louisville	130Q	80027	500-599	
CEDAR PL E	Aurora	288U	80012	15200-15299	
	Aurora	291T	80018	None	
	Denver	286T	80230	6900-8199	
CEDAR PL W	Arapahoe Co	795Y	80103	1-299	
CEDAR PL W	Jefferson Co	280Y	80401	13900-14499	
	Lakewood	282U	80226	6400-6799	
CEDAR RD	Clear Creek Co	365J	80439	1-699	
CEDAR RD	Jefferson Co	278S	80401	100-299	
CEDAR RD S	Jefferson Co	336L	80439	4700-4899	
CEDAR ST	Broomfield	162R	80020	1000-1299	
	Broomfield	162M	80020	1400-1999	
	Federal Heights	193V	80260	9700-9799	
CEDAR ST	Firestone	707S	80504	None	
CEDAR ST	Frederick	727F	80530	700-799	
CEDAR ST	Hudson	730Q	80642	700-799	
CEDAR ST	Keenesburg	732A	80643	None	
CEDAR ST N	Keenesburg	732A	80643	300-399	
CEDAR ST S	Littleton	344S	80120	5300-5699	
	Littleton	374A	80120	6400-6699	
	Littleton	374J	80120	7700-8099	
CEDAR WAY	Clear Creek Co	335A	80439	1-199	
CEDAR WAY	Elbert Co	851Y	80107	5000-5099	
CEDAR WAY	Gilpin Co	760V	80403	1-299	
CEDAR WAY	Louisville	130R	80027	100-299	
CEDARBROOK DR	Jefferson Co	340W	80465	15600-15699	
CEDAR BROOK LN	Highlands Ranch	405Q	80126	10700-10899	
CEDAR BROOK RD	Boulder Co	97E	80304	1N-1399N	
CEDAR BROOK RD	Boulder Co	97P	80304	1S-499S	
CEDAR BROOK ST	Highlands Ranch	405Q	80126	10700-10899	
CEDARCREST CIR	Highlands Ranch	405M	80130	None	
CEDAR GLEN PL	Castle Rock	466T	80109	4400-4799	
CEDAR GULCH LN S	Parker	409S	80134	None	
CEDAR GULCH PKWY	Parker	409N	80134	None	
CEDAR HILL PL E	Lone Tree	376Z	80124	9000-9299	
CEDAR HILL WAY S	Lone Tree	376Z	80124	8900-8999	
CEDARHURST LN	Highlands Ranch	404B	80129	9400-9599	
CEDARIDGE CIR	Superior	160R	80027	1800-2099	
CEDARIDGE CT S	Highlands Ranch	404J	80129	10200-10299	
CEDARIDGE WAY S	Highlands Ranch	404E	80129	10000-10099	
CEDAR LAKE RD	Jefferson Co	278Q	80401	20900-21399	
CEDARLODGE ST	Boulder	98P	80301	None	
CEDAR MOUNTAIN PL	Elbert Co	831P	80138	3300-3499	
CEDARPOINT PL	Highlands Ranch	405Q	80130	4300-4499	
CEDAR RIDGE CT	Parker	409N	80134	16800-16899	
CEDARWOOD CIR	Boulder Co	99D	80301	7100-7299	
	Lafayette	132S	80026	2300-2399	
CEDARWOOD DR	Longmont	12T	80501	1200-1599	
	Longmont	12U	80501	1600-1699	
CEDARWOOD LN	Highlands Ranch	374V	80126	8700-8799	
CEDARWOOD RD	Greenwood Village	344V	80121	5600-5799	
CEDWICK ST	Lafayette	132P	80026	900-999	
CELESTIAL AVE	Castle Rock	466Z	80109	None	
CELESTINE CT	Douglas Co	409E	80134	17500-17599	
CELESTINE PL	Douglas Co	409E	80134	10200-10299	
CELTIC DR	Castle Rock	497U	80104	None	
CEMETERY RD	Jamestown	722A	80455	None	
CENTAUR CIR	Lafayette	131U	80026	1100-1999	
CENTAUR CT	Lafayette	131Q	80026	1-1599	
CENTAUR DR	Jefferson Co	366Q	80439	7500-8299	
CENTAUR VILLAGE CT	Lafayette	131U	80026	1200-1499	
CENTAUR VILLAGE DR	Lafayette	131U	80026	1100-1999	
CENTENNIAL AVE E	Arapahoe Co	344Q	80121	200-599	
	Englewood	344Q	80110	1-199	
CENTENNIAL AVE W	Littleton	343P	80123	3300-3399	
CENTENNIAL BLVD	Highlands Ranch	374T	80129	100-199	
CENTENNIAL DR	Bennett	793J	80102	100-199	
CENTENNIAL DR	Broomfield	133K	80020	None	
CENTENNIAL DR	Douglas Co	409H	80138	7000-7299	
CENTENNIAL DR	Longmont	12S	80501	1400-1799	
CENTENNIAL DR	Louisville	131N	80027	100-2299	
CENTENNIAL DR W	Littleton	343Q	80123	2700-3099	
CENTENNIAL DR W	Louisville	130R	80027	1800-2199	
CENTENNIAL PKWY	Louisville	130X	80027	100-499	
CENTENNIAL RD W	Jefferson Co	371Q	80127	10000-10799	
CENTENNIAL WAY	El Paso Co	908S	80132	2300-2399	
CENTENNIAL TRAIL	Boulder	128H	80303	5200-5499	
CENTENNIAL TRAIL	Elbert Co	832T	80107	8100-8599	
CENTENNIAL TRAIL	Jefferson Co	277U	80401	25200-26499	
CENTER	Littleton	373P	80120	None	
CENTER AVE	Douglas Co	825V	80125	None	
CENTER AVE E	Aurora	287Y	80012	11200-11499	
	Aurora	287Y	80012	11700-12199	
	Aurora	317D	80012	12800-13299	
	Aurora	288X	80012	14800-15299	
	Aurora	288X	80017	15300-15499	
	Aurora	288Y	80017	15700-15799	
	Denver	284Y	80209	1-1199	
	Denver	284Z	80209	1600-1699	
	Denver	285W	80209	1700-2399	
	Denver	286W	80246	5400-5599	
	Denver	286X	80224	6500-6899	
	Denver	286Z	80247	9100-9399	
	Denver	287W	80247	9601-9699	O
	Glendale	285Z	80246	5000-5199	
CENTER AVE N	Denver Federal Center	281U	80225	None	
CENTER AVE S	Denver Federal Center	281U	80225	None	
CENTER AVE W	Denver	284W	80223	1000-1999	
	Denver	283Z	80223	2000-2499	
	Denver	283Y	80219	2500-3999	
	Denver	283W	80219	4300-4799	
	Lakewood	282Z	80226	5200-5799	
	Lakewood	282Y	80226	6000-6499	
	Lakewood	282X	80226	7100-7599	
	Lakewood	282W	80226	8400-8999	
	Lakewood	281Z	80226	9000-9199	
	Lakewood	311C	80226	10000-10599	
	Lakewood	311B	80226	10600-11599	
	Lakewood	311B	80228	11600-12099	
	Lakewood	281W	80228	12200-12499	
CENTER CT	Jefferson Co	307X	80439	3400-3499	
CENTER DR	Jefferson Co	307X	80439	26100-26299	
CENTER DR	Superior	160E	80027	300-699	
CENTER DR E	Aurora	287Y	80012	11500-11599	
	Aurora	287Z	80012	12100-12199	
	Aurora	288Z	80017	16200-16499	
CENTER DR W	Denver	283W	80219	5000-5199	
	Lakewood	280Y	80228	13200-14199	
CENTER PL	Longmont	41L	80501	None	
CENTER PL E	Aurora	288Y	80017	15700-15799	
CENTER PL W	Lakewood	311A	80228	12000-12099	
CENTER ALLEY	Idaho Springs	780Q	80452	800-1699	
CENTER GREEN CT	Boulder	98U	80301	2900-2999	
CENTER GREEN DR	Boulder	98U	80301	3000-3099	
CENTERPARK LOOP	Douglas Co	409H	80138	None	
CENTERPOINT DR E	Aurora	288X	80012	14500-14899	
CENTERVILLE CT	Parker	409Y	80134	19700-19899	
CENTRAL AVE	Boulder	99W	80301	1800-5799	
CENTRAL AVE	Brighton	138U	80601	300-599	
CENTRAL AVE	Platteville	708C	80651	300-399	
CENTRAL CT	Brighton	138U	80601	None	
CENTRAL CT	Broomfield	192E	80021	11200-11499	
CENTRAL ST	Aurora	350Z	80016	None	
CENTRAL ST	Denver	254W	80211	1400-1799	
CENTRAL CITY PKWY	Central City	780G	80403	None	
	Clear Creek Co	781P	80439	None	
	Clear Creek Co	781P	80452	None	
	Gilpin Co	780H	80403	None	
CENTRAL PARK BLVD	Denver	286D	80238	2400-2799	
	Denver	256Z	80238	2800-2999	
CENTRE CIR	Douglas Co	408D	80134	9700-9899	
CENTRE CT	Douglas Co	409E	80134	16700-16799	
CENTRE DR	Douglas Co	408H	80134	16700-16799	
CENTREBRIDGE DR	Boulder Co	70K	80503	7900-8199	
CENTRETECH CIR	Aurora	288Q	80011	15700-15799	
CENTRETECH PKWY E	Aurora	288V	80011	15500-16699	
CENTURY CIR	Louisville	130X	80027	200-299	
CENTURY DR	Louisville	130X	80027	1000-1399	
	Monument	908S	80132	700-799	
CENTURY PL	Louisville	130X	80027	None	
CENTURY PL	Monument	908S	80132	700-799	
CERAN AVE	Longmont	41J	80503	2801-2899	O
CERES DR	Lafayette	131Q	80026	1200-1399	
CERILLOS ST	Brighton	139P	80601	None	
CERNEY CIR	Castle Pines North	436Q	80108	7000-7299	
CERRO CT	Jefferson Co	305B	80439	500-699	

STREET NAME	CITY or COUNTY	MAP GRID	ZIP CODE	BLOCK RANGE	O/E
CERRO PL	Douglas Co	887D	80118	800-999	
CESSNA CT	Erie	133F	80516	None	
CESSNA DR	Erie	133A	80516	1-2599	
CEYLON CT	Denver	259Q	80249	4300-4399	
	Denver	259L	80249	4600-4699	
CEYLON CT S	Aurora	349L	80015	4800-4899	
	Centennial	349Q	80015	5100-5199	
	Aurora	289G	80011	1500-1999	
	Aurora	289C	80011	None	
CEYLON ST	Denver	259Q	80249	4300-4599	
	Denver	259C	80249	5700-5899	
	Denver	259L	80249	None	
CEYLON ST S	Aurora	319G	80017	1100-1199	
	Aurora	319U	80013	2700-2899	
	Aurora	319Y	80013	3400-3599	
	Aurora	349G	80015	4300-4399	
	Aurora	349L	80015	4800-4899	
	Centennial	349Q	80015	5100-5199	
CEYLON WAY S	Aurora	319L	80013	2000-2499	
	Aurora	319U	80013	2800-3499	
	Aurora	319Y	80013	3500-3599	
	Aurora	349C	80013	3600-4099	
	Aurora	349G	80015	4300-4499	
	Centennial	349Q	80015	5400-5599	
CHACO TRAIL	Castle Rock	466U	80109	None	
CHADSWORTH LN	Highlands Ranch	405N	80126	10500-10799	
CHADSWORTH PT	Highlands Ranch	405N	80126	10700-10899	
CHADWICK CIR W	Highlands Ranch	404F	80129	500-799	
CHADWICK CT	Longmont	12Q	80501	2000-2099	
CHADWICK WAY S	Highlands Ranch	404F	80129	9800-9899	
CHAFFEE CT	Brighton	139P	80601	None	
CHAFFEE CT	Castle Rock	466U	80109	3700-3899	
CHAFFEE PL	Denver	259P	80249	18600-18699	
	Denver	259Q	80249	18900-19399	
CHAFFEE PL W	Denver	254N	80211	1700-1999	
CHAFFEE WAY	Castle Rock	466U	80109	3300-3599	
CHALCIS DR	Lafayette	131Q	80026	1800-1999	
CHALET CIR	Douglas Co	440R	80134	6500-6999	
	Jefferson Co	842Q	80470	30000-30399	
CHALET DR	Gilpin Co	761S	80403	1-699	
CHALET DR	Jefferson Co	822P	80433	31700-31799	
CHALK HILL PL	Castle Rock	527D	80104	1300-1599	
CHALLENGER PL	Longmont	41V	80501	300-399	
CHALLENGER PARK	Douglas Co	409E	80134	None	
CHAMBERLAIN RD	Jefferson Co	339W	80465	19800-19999	
CHAMBERLAIN WAY E	Highlands Ranch	404G	80126	600-899	
CHAMBERS CIR S	Aurora	318F	80012	1100-1499	
CHAMBERS CT	Aurora	288L	80011	1000-1099	
	Commerce City	198U	80022	9600-9899	
CHAMBERS DR	Boulder	128Y	80305	1200-1599	
CHAMBERS DR	Commerce City	198U	80022	9700-9999	
	Commerce City	198G	80022	11300-11599	
	Commerce City	198C	80022	11700-11899	
CHAMBERS RD	Adams Co	138Y	80601	14700-15299	
	Aurora	288U	80011	1-2999	
	Aurora	258Y	80011	2800-3899	
	Brighton	168C	80601	14400-14699	
	Commerce City	198G	80022	9600-11199	
	Commerce City	198G	80603	11300-11899	
	Commerce City	168Y	80603	11900-12099	
	Denver	258Q	80239	4000-5599	
	Douglas Co	378U	80112	None	
	Douglas Co	408U	80134	None	
	Douglas Co	469C	80116	None	
	Parker	408Y	80134	None	
CHAMBERS RD S	Aurora	288U	80017	1-699	
	Aurora	318L	80017	700-2099	
	Aurora	318L	80014	2100-3499	
	Aurora	348C	80014	3500-4299	
	Aurora	348Q	80015	4300-5799	
	Douglas Co	408C	80134	9200-9899	
CHAMBERS WAY	Aurora	288Q	80011	300-499	
	Commerce City	198L	80022	10801-10899	O
CHAMBERS WAY S	Aurora	348G	80014	4200-4299	
CHAMBRAY CT	Highlands Ranch	405D	80130	5400-5599	
CHAMBRAY LN	Highlands Ranch	405D	80130	9300-9399	
CHAMPA ST	Denver	284F	80204	1100-1399	
	Denver	284F	80202	1400-1999	
	Denver	284C	80205	2000-2699	
	Denver	254Y	80205	2700-3299	
CHAMPA ST	Elizabeth	871F	80107	None	
CHAMPAGNE AVE	Castle Rock	466U	80109	None	
CHAMPION CIR	Longmont	10Y	80503	900-1099	
CHAMPION PL	Douglas Co	466C	80108	1000-1099	
CHAMPIONS CIR	Castle Rock	497U	80104	1900-2099	
CHAMPIONSHIP DR	Parker	409K	80134	None	
CHAMPLAIN DR	Boulder Co	100Z	80301	2000-2299	
CHANDELLE RD	Douglas Co	527S	80104	500-799	
CHANDLER CT	Denver	258N	80239	4600-4899	
	Denver	258F	80239	5500-5599	
CHANDLER PL	El Paso Co	908S	80132	18100-18499	
CHANDLER WAY	Denver	258J	80239	5100-5499	
CHANDON CT	Highlands Ranch	405P	80126	3200-3299	
CHANDON PL	Highlands Ranch	405P	80126	10600-10699	
CHANDON WAY	Highlands Ranch	405P	80126	3200-3599	
CHANIN CIR	Longmont	40P	80503	None	
CHANIN WAY	Longmont	40P	80503	None	
CHANNEL CT	Erie	103J	80516	400-499	
CHANTECLAIR CIR S	Highlands Ranch	404H	80126	9600-9799	
CHANTECLAIR CT S	Highlands Ranch	404H	80126	9700-9799	
CHANTILLY CT	Broomfield	163E	80020	14100-14199	
CHAPARRAL CIR	Elbert Co	870L	80107	32600-32698	E
CHAPARRAL RD	Lone Tree	376Y	80124	7700-8199	
CHAPARRAL ST	Mead	706G	80542	None	
CHAPARREL DR	Mead	706G	80542	None	
CHAPEL DR	Brighton	139P	80601	None	
CHAPEL HILL CIR	Brighton	139P	80601	None	
CHAPEL HILL DR	Brighton	139K	80601	200-299	
CHAPEL HILL LN	Parker	410Y	80138	None	
CHAPEL HILL PL	Parker	410Y	80138	None	
CHAPEL ROYAL CT	El Paso Co	908R	80132	1300-1399	
CHAPIN PL	Broomfield	133L	80020	None	
CHAPMAN LN	Longmont	41U	80501	1500-1599	
CHAPMAN RD	Boulder Co	742A	80302	1-199	
CHAPPARAL CIR S	Centennial	379C	80016	6700E-7499E	
	Centennial	379G	80016	6700W-7399W	
CHAPPARAL CT	Boulder	99C	80301	5000-5199	
CHARBRAY PT	Castle Rock	498B	80108	1900-1999	
CHARING CT	Castle Rock	466T	80109	4600-4799	
CHARING DR	Castle Rock	466T	80109	4400-4499	
CHARISSGLEN CIR	Highlands Ranch	405J	80126	10200-10399	
CHARISSGLEN CT	Highlands Ranch	405J	80126	10000-10099	
CHARISSGLEN LN	Highlands Ranch	405J	80126	10000-10299	
CHARISSGLEN ST	Highlands Ranch	405K	80126	None	
CHARISSGLEN POINTE	Highlands Ranch	405J	80126	2200-2299	
CHARITY CT	Frederick	727G	80530	6900-6999	
CHARLES CT	El Paso Co	908P	80132	None	
CHARLES DR	Longmont	11W	80503	1300-1399	
CHARLES ST	Palmer Lake	907R	80133	None	
CHARLES ST W	Superior	160F	80027	300-499	
CHARLES WAY	Adams Co	224E	80221	8200-8399	
CHARLOTTE WAY	Adams Co	224E	80221	8200-8399	
CHARLOU CIR	Cherry Hills Village	346E	80111	100-4699	
CHARLOU DR E	Cherry Hills Village	346J	80111	5600-6299	
CHARLOU LN	Cherry Hills Village	346J	80111	5700-5799	
CHARMATELLA DR	Park Co	820Y	80421	1-199	
CHARRINGTON DR	Cherry Hills Village	346J	80111	6200-6499	
CHARROS DR	Jefferson Co	278T	80401	1-399	
CHARROS LOOP	El Paso Co	909S	80132	2000-2199	
CHARTER OAKS DR	Douglas Co	436M	80108	1-499	
CHARTER PINES DR	El Paso Co	908Z	80132	17300-17799	
CHARTERWOOD CIR	Highlands Ranch	405L	80126	3600-3899	
CHARTERWOOD CT	Highlands Ranch	405L	80126	10200-10299	
CHARTERWOOD DR	Highlands Ranch	405L	80126	3600-3899	
	Arvada	222M	80003	7900-7999	
CHASE CIR	Westminster	222R	80003	7300-7599	
CHASE CT	Boulder	128L	80305	3600-3699	
	Westminster	192H	80020	11200-11299	
	Westminster	192D	80020	11500-11899	
CHASE CT S	Jefferson Co	342Z	80123	6200-6399	
	Jefferson Co	372H	80128	6900-7299	
	Jefferson Co	372D	80123	None	
	Lakewood	312H	80232	1200-1699	
CHASE DR	Arvada	222H	80003	8000-8299	
	Arvada	222G	80003	8300-8699	
	Arvada	222B	80003	8700-8799	
CHASE DR	Clear Creek Co	781Y	80439	1-299	
CHASE DR	Westminster	222R	80003	7400-7499	
CHASE DR S	Lakewood	282V	80226	1-99	
CHASE LN S	Lakewood	312R	80227	2400-2699	
CHASE ST	Arvada	252D	80003	6000-6199	
	Arvada	222Z	80003	6200-6799	
	Arvada	222H	80003	8400-8599	
CHASE ST	Black Hawk	780D	80422	100-299	
CHASE ST	Broomfield	162Z	80020	10000-10999	
	Denver	252M	80212	4800-5199	
	Edgewater	282D	80214	2400-2599	
CHASE ST	Gilpin Co	760Y	80403	None	
CHASE ST	Lakewood	282V	80226	1-99	
	Lakewood	282M	80214	800-1699	
	Mountain View	252V	80212	4100-4399	
	Westminster	222R	80003	7400-7599	
	Westminster	192R	80020	10000-10099	
	Westminster	192D	80020	11700-11899	
	Westminster	192V	80031	None	
	Wheat Ridge	282D	80214	2600-2799	
	Wheat Ridge	252Z	80214	2800-3199	
	Wheat Ridge	252Z	80212	3200-4099	
CHASE ST S	Denver	342D	80235	3700-3899	
	Jefferson Co	342Z	80123	6200-6399	
	Jefferson Co	372D	80123	None	
	Lakewood	282V	80226	100-199	
	Lakewood	282Z	80226	200-299	
	Lakewood	312D	80226	900-1099	
	Lakewood	312H	80232	1200-1699	
CHASE WAY	Arvada	222H	80003	8200-8399	
	Westminster	192H	80020	11000-11499	
	Westminster	192D	80020	11500-11599	
CHASE WAY S	Denver	312V	80227	2700-2799	
	Denver	342D	80235	3900-3999	
	Jefferson Co	372H	80128	7100-7299	
CHASE GULCH RD	Central City	780C	80427	400-599	
CHATAUQUA ST	Palmer Lake	907Q	80133	None	
CHATEAU CREEK CT S	Parker	439C	80134	12300-12399	
CHATEAU RIDGE LN	Douglas Co	466G	80108	4300-4399	
CHATEAU RIDGE RD	Douglas Co	466L	80108	4300-4399	
CHATFIELD AVE	Castle Rock	498K	80104	1-299	
CHATFIELD AVE W	Jefferson Co	372N	80128	6100-9099	
	Jefferson Co	371P	80127	9100-9999	
	Jefferson Co	371P	80128	10000-11599	
CHATFIELD DR N	Douglas Co	404S	80125	10000-10999	
CHATFIELD DR W	Jefferson Co	371V	80128	9000-9199	
CHATFIELD LN W	Douglas Co	403V	80125	6600-6699	
CHATFIELD PL N	Douglas Co	404S	80125	10100-10399	
CHATFIELD PL W	Douglas Co	372U	80128	6800-6999	
	Jefferson Co	371R	80128	9200-9399	
CHATFORD CT	Castle Pines North	436Q	80108	6900-7099	
CHATHAM PL	Boulder Co	100E	80301	4600-4699	
CHATHAM ST	Boulder Co	100E	80301	4600-4799	
CHATHAM WAY	Boulder Co	100E	80301	7500-7699	
CHATRIDGE CT	Douglas Co	404W	80125	None	
CHATSWOOD CT E	Highlands Ranch	405G	80126	4300-4399	
CHATSWOOD PL E	Highlands Ranch	405G	80126	4300-4399	
CHATSWOOD TRAIL S	Highlands Ranch	405G	80126	9800-9999	
CHAUTAUGA MOUNTAIN	Jefferson Co	371Q	80127	10500-10799	
CHAUTAUQUA RES RD	Boulder	127M	80302	None	
CHAVEZ ST	Brighton	139K	80601	None	
CHEESMAN ST	Erie	103J	80516	100-799	
CHEETAH COVE	Douglas Co	406J	80124	5800-5899	
CHEETAH CHASE	Douglas Co	406J	80124	5600-6199	
CHEETAH TAIL	Douglas Co	406J	80124	10300-10399	
CHEETAH WINDS	Douglas Co	406J	80124	10400-10499	
CHEEWALL LN	Douglas Co	408D	80134	9700-9899	
CHELAN ST	Golden	279P	80401	400-599	
CHELMSFORD TERRACE	Douglas Co	408G	80134	10000-10099	
CHELSEA CT	Elizabeth	871E	80107	400-499	
CHELSEA CT E	Highlands Ranch	405A	80126	2000-2099	
CHELSEA ST	Castle Rock	498L	80104	200-499	
CHELSEA MANOR CT	Boulder Co	99F	80301	6000-6199	
CHEM-TECH AVE	Weld Co	731E	80642	23000-23999	
CHENANGO AVE	Denver	346P	80237	6500-7099	
CHENANGO AVE E	Arapahoe Co	350J	80015	20100-21999	
	Aurora	348J	80015	13800-14199	
	Aurora	348L	80015	15000-15799	
	Aurora	349J	80015	16900-17199	
	Cherry Hills Village	345M	80121	5100-5299	
	Denver	346M	80237	8500-8899	
	Englewood	344L	80113	1-799	
	Greenwood Village	346M	80111	8900-9999	
	Greenwood Village	347J	80111	9400-9899	
CHENANGO AVE W	Denver	343K	80123	3600-3799	
	Denver	341L	80123	9500-9899	
	Englewood	344K	80110	1-1299	
	Englewood	343L	80110	2800-3599	
	Jefferson Co	341J	80465	12400-12699	
	Jefferson Co	340M	80465	12700-13199	
	Jefferson Co	340L	80465	13500-13599	
CHENANGO CIR E	Aurora	349L	80015	19000-19099	
	Englewood	344L	80113	200-299	
CHENANGO CIR S	Englewood	344L	80110	4900-4999	
CHENANGO CT E	Cherry Hills Village	345J	80110	1900-2099	
CHENANGO DR E	Arapahoe Co	349L	80015	20000-21499	
	Aurora	348J	80015	13800-14099	
	Aurora	349K	80015	17500-17599	
	Aurora	349L	80015	18500-19299	
	Aurora	351J	80016	24600-24799	
	Centennial	349L	80015	19300-19999	
CHENANGO DR W	Jefferson Co	341J	80465	11600-12399	
	Jefferson Co	340M	80465	12800-13099	
CHENANGO PL E	Arapahoe Co	350J	80015	20300-20499	
	Aurora	348K	80015	14100-14399	
	Aurora	348L	80015	15000-15199	
	Aurora	349L	80015	18600-18899	
	Aurora	350M	80016	None	
	Aurora	351J	80016	None	
CHENANGO PL W	Denver	342K	80123	8000-8099	
	Jefferson Co	340M	80465	13200-13299	
	Lakewood	342P	80123	7400-7499	
CHENANGO ST W	Englewood	343M	80120	2100-2199	
	Littleton	343M	80120	1900-2099	
CHENEY CT	Boulder Co	70L	80503	6800-6899	
CHENEY PL	Castle Rock	497Y	80104	100-299	
CHERI LN	Elbert Co	850D	80138	1000-1299	
CHEROKEE AVE	Superior	160E	80027	300-399	
CHEROKEE CT	Adams Co	226B	80022	None	
CHEROKEE CT	Boulder Co	70R	80503	6600-6699	
CHEROKEE CT	Erie	133F	80516	2900-3099	
CHEROKEE CT E	Douglas Co	440U	80134	8500-8799	
CHEROKEE DR	Castle Rock	466T	80109	None	
CHEROKEE DR W	Douglas Co	846U	80135	6300-7399	
CHEROKEE LN E	Douglas Co	411X	80138	10100-10999	
CHEROKEE PL	Douglas Co	846U	80135	3900-4199	
	Lochbuie	140F	80603	200-399	
CHEROKEE RD	Jefferson Co	338Q	80454	5200-5499	
CHEROKEE ST	Adams Co	224F	80221	8200-8399	
	Arapahoe Co	794S	80136	1000-1199	
	Denver	284T	80223	1-399	
	Denver	284P	80204	400-599	
	Denver	284K	80204	1000-1499	
	Denver	254P	80216	4300-4499	
	Northglenn	194F	80234	11000-11499	
CHEROKEE ST S	Denver	284T	80223	1-399	
	Denver	314F	80223	1100-1699	
	Denver	314P	80223	1900-2699	
	Englewood	314T	80110	2700-3299	
	Englewood	314X	80110	3500-3599	
	Englewood	344F	80110	3600-4899	
	Littleton	344T	80120	5700-5899	
	Littleton	374B	80120	6600-7099	
CHEROKEE WAY	Boulder	128R	80303	100-199	
CHEROKEE TRAIL	Elbert Co	870D	80107	34200-35799	
	Jefferson Co	822Z	80433	11700-11899	
CHEROKEE TRAIL	Lafayette	132S	80026	None	
CHEROKEE TRAIL S	Arapahoe Co	378H	80016	7100-7199	
CHERRINGTON ST	Highlands Ranch	405P	80126	10600-10799	
CHERRY AVE	Boulder	97G	80304	701-799	O
CHERRY AVE	Dacono	727K	80514	200-799	
CHERRY AVE	Platteville	708C	80651	300-499	
CHERRY CIR	Brighton	138V	80601	2400-2699	
CHERRY CIR	Greenwood Village	345V	80121	5700-5799	
	Thornton	195G	80233	11100-11299	
	Thornton	165Q	80241	13300-13399	
CHERRY CIR S	Centennial	345Z	80121	6200-6299	
CHERRY CT	Boulder Co	70P	80503	6400-6499	
CHERRY CT	Greenwood Village	345V	80121	5600-5699	
	Thornton	195M	80233	10700-10799	
	Thornton	195D	80233	11500-11599	
	Thornton	165L	80241	13300-13399	
	Thornton	165L	80241	13400-13499	
CHERRY CT S	Centennial	345Z	80121	6100-6199	
	Centennial	375L	80122	7400-7499	
	Centennial	375M	80122	7700-7799	
CHERRY DR	Thornton	195H	80233	11200-11599	
	Thornton	195D	80233	11700-11899	
	Thornton	194W	80260	None	
CHERRY DR S	Centennial	375H	80122	7000-7299	
CHERRY LN	Parker	409F	80134	None	
CHERRY LN	Thornton	195U	80229	None	
CHERRY LN	Westminster	223F	80031	8500-8699	
CHERRY PL	Brighton	138T	80601	1-199	
CHERRY PL	Erie	133C	80516	None	
CHERRY PL	Thornton	165Z	80241	12000-12099	
CHERRY ST	Adams Co	225U	80022	7000-7199	
	Adams Co	165C	80602	14400-14799	
CHERRY ST	Bennett	793N	80102	200-299	
CHERRY ST	Brighton	138U	80601	1300-1899	
	Brighton	138V	80601	2100-2399	
CHERRY ST	Castle Rock	498M	80104	1-399	
CHERRY ST	Commerce City	255D	80022	6000-6099	
	Commerce City	225U	80022	6800-6999	
	Commerce City	225Q	80022	7200-7499	
	Denver	285Q	80220	1-899	
	Denver	285G	80220	1100-1999	
	Denver	285C	80207	2000-2799	
	Denver	255Y	80207	2800-3499	
	Federal Heights	193V	80260	9700-9799	
CHERRY ST	Fort Lupton	728H	80621	1100-1199	
CHERRY ST	Hudson	730L	80642	None	
CHERRY ST	Lochbuie	140G	80603	300-499	

C

STREET NAME	CITY or COUNTY	MAP GRID	ZIP CODE	BLOCK RANGE	O/E
CHERRY ST	Louisville	161B	80027	1400-8399	
CHERRY ST	Thornton	195Y	80229	9400-9499	
	Thornton	195M	80233	10500-10699	
	Thornton	195L	80233	10700-10799	
	Thornton	165Z	80241	12000-12299	
	Thornton	165U	80241	12400-12699	
	Thornton	165L	80241	13400-13599	
	Thornton	165L	80602	None	
	Thornton	195U	80229	None	
CHERRY ST S	Centennial	375G	80122	6700-7199	
	Cherry Hills Village	345H	80113	3900-4199	
	Denver	285V	80246	1-299	
	Denver	315G	80246	1000-1299	
	Denver	315H	80222	1400-1599	
	Denver	315Q	80222	1900-2699	
	Denver	315Z	80222	3100-3499	
	Glendale	285Z	80246	400-699	
	Glendale	315C	80246	700-999	
CHERRY ST W	Louisville	130Z	80027	100-999	
CHERRY WAY	Brighton	138U	80601	1300-1499	
CHERRY WAY	Elbert Co	851A	80138	2400-2999	
CHERRY WAY	Thornton	165Q	80241	12800-13399	
	Thornton	165L	80241	13400-13499	
	Thornton	165L	80602	None	
CHERRY WAY S	Centennial	375D	80121	6500-6699	
	Denver	315U	80222	2800-3099	
CHERRY BLOSSOM CT E	Highlands Ranch	404D	80126	900-1199	
CHERRY BLOSSOM LN	Cherry Hills Village	345D	80113	1-99	
CHERRYBROOK CIR	Highlands Ranch	405K	80126	10500-10799	
CHERRY CREEK CT	Parker	410N	80138	10900-10999	
CHERRY CREEK DR	Arapahoe Co	347U	80111	5100-5999	
CHERRY CREEK DR	Douglas Co	469C	80134	6400-6799	
CHERRY CREEK DR	Glendale	285Y	80246	4000S-4799S	
CHERRY CREEK DAM RD					
	Arapahoe Co	347B	80111	9500-9699	
	Arapahoe Co	347B	80014	9700-9799	
	Arapahoe Co	317Z	80014	None	
	Denver	316E	80224	5600N-7199N	
	Denver	285T	80209	2400S-3698S	E
	Arapahoe Co	316Q	80231	7700S-7998S	E
	Denver	285T	80209	3501N-3899N	O
	Denver	315D	80246	4700S-5599S	
	Denver	316F	80224	6500S-7299S	
	Denver	316L	80231	7301S-7699S	O
	Denver	316V	80231	9000S-9298S	E
CHERRY HILLS DR	Cherry Hills Village	345A	80113	1-99	
CHERRY HILLS LN	Castle Rock	497V	80104	1500-1699	
CHERRY HILLS FARM CT	Cherry Hills Village	345K	80113	1-99	
CHERRY HILLS FARM DR	Cherry Hills Village	345J	80113	1-99	
	Cherry Hills Village	345J	80113	2200-2299	
CHERRY HILLS PARK DR	Cherry Hills Village	345B	80113	1-99	
CHERRYHURST AVE	Highlands Ranch	405G	80126	None	
CHERRYHURST CT E	Highlands Ranch	405G	80126	4100-4299	
CHERRYHURST LN S	Highlands Ranch	405G	80126	10100-10399	
CHERRY LANE DR	Cherry Hills Village	345C	80113	1-99	
CHERRY LANE DR E	Cherry Hills Village	345D	80113	4700-4799	
CHERRY LYNN CT	Platteville	708G	80651	None	
CHERRYMOOR DR	Cherry Hills Village	345E	80113	1-99	
CHERRY PLUM PL	Castle Rock	497Y	80104	3200-3399	
CHERRY PLUM WAY	Castle Rock	497Y	80104	3000-3299	
CHERRYRIDGE RD	Cherry Hills Village	345J	80113	2400-3299	
CHERRY STAGE RD W	El Paso Co	909X	80132	16900-17899	
CHERRY STONE LN	Castle Rock	528J	80104	None	
CHERRYVALE CT E	Highlands Ranch	405A	80126	2500-2599	
CHERRYVALE DR	Cherry Hills Village	344M	80113	1-99	
CHERRYVALE DR S	Highlands Ranch	405A	80126	9400-9699	
CHERRYVALE LN S	Highlands Ranch	405B	80126	9400-9599	
CHERRYVALE RD	Boulder Co	129P	80303	1-1599	
	Boulder Co	159E	80303	None	
CHERRYVALE RD S	Boulder Co	129X	80303	1-1599	
	Boulder Co	159E	80303	1600-1899	
CHERRYVALE ST	Firestone	707S	80504	10300-10499	
CHERRYVILLE CIR	Greenwood Village	345S	80121	2200-2299	
CHERRYVILLE RD	Greenwood Village	344R	80121	1200-1599	
	Greenwood Village	345S	80121	1600-2399	
CHERRYVILLE WAY	Greenwood Village	345S	80121	5500-5599	
CHERRYWOOD	Elbert Co	872J	80017	None	
CHERRYWOOD AVE	Thornton	194S	80260	None	
CHERRYWOOD CIR S	Centennial	344Z	80121	5900-6199	
CHERRYWOOD DR	Brighton	138L	80601	1100-1499	
CHERRYWOOD DR	Longmont	12T	80501	500-599	
CHERRYWOOD DR E	Douglas Co	411K	80138	10000-10399	
CHERRYWOOD DR E	Lafayette	132S	80026	2200-2499	
CHERRYWOOD DR N	Lafayette	132S	80026	200-399	
CHERRYWOOD DR S	Lafayette	131V	80026	300-499	
CHERRYWOOD DR W	Lafayette	132S	80026	300-499	
CHERRYWOOD LN	Louisville	130Y	80027	100-199	
CHERRYWOOD ST	Broomfield	163X	80020	12100-12399	
CHERRYWOOD WAY	Longmont	12T	80501	1400-1499	
CHERRYWOOD TRAIL	Thornton	195L	80233	None	
CHERYL DR	Adams Co	225A	80229	2300-8799	
CHESAPEAKE CT S	Highlands Ranch	405A	80126	9400-9499	
CHESAPEAKE DR	Broomfield	133K	80020	None	
CHESAPEAKE LN E	Highlands Ranch	405A	80126	1900-2399	
CHESAPEAKE PL E	Highlands Ranch	405A	80126	2000-2099	
CHESAPEAKE ST S	Highlands Ranch	405A	80126	9400-9699	
CHESEBRO WAY	Boulder Co	743T	80025	None	
CHESHIRE CT S	Highlands Ranch	406B	80130	9300-9499	
CHESMORE ST	Highlands Ranch	405U	80130	10900-11099	
CHESTER CIR S	Arapahoe Co	317E	80247	1800-1899	
CHESTER CT S	Arapahoe Co	317E	80247	1100-1299	
	Arapahoe Co	317E	80247	None	
	Denver	317S	80231	3000-3199	
	Denver	317W	80231	3300-3499	
	Greenwood Village	347S	80111	5400-5599	
CHESTER ST	Aurora	287J	80010	1100-1999	
	Aurora	287J	80230	None	
CHESTER ST	Lafayette	131M	80026	702-798	E
CHESTER ST	Lone Tree	376V	80124	None	
CHESTER ST E	Lafayette	132K	80026	100-899	
CHESTER ST S	Arapahoe Co	317E	80247	1100-1299	
	Centennial	376M	80112	7500-7899	
	Centennial	377J	80112	7900-8299	
	Greenwood Village	347N	80111	4900-5099	
	Lone Tree	377S	80124	None	

STREET NAME	CITY or COUNTY	MAP GRID	ZIP CODE	BLOCK RANGE	O/E
CHESTER ST W	Lafayette	132J	80026	100-499	
CHESTER WAY S	Aurora	347A	80014	3600-3799	
	Greenwood Village	347W	80111	6000-6099	
CHESTERFIELD RD	Castle Rock	466X	80109	2400-2699	
CHESTNUT AVE W	Jefferson Co	372R	80128	5600-6399	
	Jefferson Co	372N	80128	8100-8299	
	Jefferson Co	372N	80128	8800-9199	
CHESTNUT CIR	Erie	102P	80516	2000-2299	
CHESTNUT CIR	Jefferson Co	306X	80439	3100-3199	
CHESTNUT CIR	Louisville	130Y	80027	800-999	
CHESTNUT CT	Douglas Co	440N	80134	6900-6999	
	Greenwood Village	345U	80121	4000-4099	
	Jefferson Co	306X	80439	3100-3199	
CHESTNUT CT	Louisville	130Y	80027	600-699	
CHESTNUT DR	Jefferson Co	306X	80439	29500-30899	
CHESTNUT DR	Longmont	40Q	80503	1000-1199	
CHESTNUT DR S	Jefferson Co	372R	80128	7900-8099	
CHESTNUT DR W	Jefferson Co	372P	80128	7000-7299	
CHESTNUT LN	Boulder Co	99F	80301	4600-4699	
CHESTNUT LN	Jefferson Co	306X	80439	3100-3199	
	Westminster	223B	80031	3600-8799	
CHESTNUT PL	Boulder	97V	80304	1400-1499	
CHESTNUT PL	Denver	254W	80202	1900-1999	
	Denver	254U	80216	3500-3799	
CHESTNUT PL	Longmont	40Q	80503	3700-3799	
CHESTNUT PL E	Aurora	380P	80016	22000-22199	
	Aurora	380R	80016	23300-23399	
CHESTNUT PL W	Jefferson Co	372P	80128	7700-7799	
CHESTNUT ST	Denver	284A	80202	None	
	Federal Heights	193U	80260	2600-2899	
CHESTNUT ST	Fort Lupton	728H	80621	1800-1999	
CHESTNUT ST	Louisville	131W	80027	100-399	
CHESTNUT ST S	Elizabeth	871F	80107	800-999	
CHESTNUT WAY	Broomfield	192C	80020	400-499	
CHESTNUT WAY S	Jefferson Co	372R	80128	7900-8099	
CHESTNUT HILL CT	Highlands Ranch	376X	80130	8800-8899	
CHESTNUT HILL LN	Highlands Ranch	376X	80130	8800-8999	
CHESTNUT HILL PL	Highlands Ranch	376T	80130	8800-8899	
CHESTNUT HILL ST	Highlands Ranch	376T	80130	6800-7199	
CHESTNUT HILL WAY	Highlands Ranch	376X	80130	8800-8899	
CHESTNUT TRAIL E	Greenwood Village	344V	80121	800-999	
CHESTNUT HILL TRAIL	Highlands Ranch	376T	80130	7000-7099	
CHEYENNE AVE	Longmont	12P	80501	600-698	E
CHEYENNE CT	Boulder	128R	80303	4700-4799	
	Boulder Co	70R	80503	6600-6699	
	Douglas Co	886L	80118	7900-8099	
CHEYENNE CT	Lafayette	132S	80026	None	
CHEYENNE CT N	Douglas Co	440U	80134	6200-6399	
CHEYENNE DR	Douglas Co	887J	80118	4000-4499	
	Douglas Co	886M	80118	4500-4999	
	Douglas Co	846T	80135	7200-7499	
CHEYENNE DR	Golden	279F	80401	2400-2499	
CHEYENNE DR	Lafayette	132S	80026	None	
CHEYENNE LOOP	Lochbuie	729Y	80603	None	
CHEYENNE PL	Denver	284G	80202	1500-1599	
	Douglas Co	846T	80135	3800-3899	
	Elbert Co	830Q	80138	500-1199	
CHEYENNE RD	Jefferson Co	338Q	80454	5200-5499	
CHEYENNE ST	Arapahoe Co	795U	80103	None	
CHEYENNE ST	Golden	248Z	80403	100-699	
	Golden	279A	80401	1900-2399	
CHEYENNE ST	Kiowa	872M	80117	200-499	
CHEYENNE ST S	Jefferson Co	842E	80470	13200-13499	
CHEYENNE WAY	Douglas Co	886M	80118	7800-7899	
CHEYENNE WAY	El Paso Co	908Z	80132	700-799	
CHEYENNE TRAIL	Elbert Co	870D	80107	33500-35799	
CHIA CT	Dacono	726V	80514	None	
CHICADEE DR	Park Co	841V	80421	1-299	
CHICADEE LN	Park Co	841V	80421	1-599	
CHICAGO CREEK DR	Clear Creek Co	780T	80452	1-11999	
CHICKADEE RD	Jefferson Co	277P	80401	400-699	
CHICKAREE CT	Douglas Co	432L	80125	7600-7699	
CHICKAREE PL	Douglas Co	432L	80125	7600-7699	
CHICORY CIR	Brighton	139M	80601	None	
CHICORY CIR E	Parker	409B	80134	17600-17899	
CHICORY LN S	Parker	409E	80134	9500-9599	
CHICORY ST	Brighton	140J	80601	None	
CHIEF AVE	Adams Co	226F	80022	None	
CHIEF ST	Ward	720L	80481	None	
CHIEF HOSA RD	Jefferson Co	307F	80401	26000-26199	
CHILDREN'S MUSEUM DR	Denver	283H	80211	None	
CHILTON AVE	Jefferson Co	842J	80470	34100-34699	
CHILTON PL	Broomfield	164E	80020	1700-1899	
CHIMAYO RD W	Littleton	343P	80123	3600-3899	
CHIMNEY CREEK DR	Jefferson Co	307C	80401	600-799	
CHIMNEY PEAK DR	Castle Rock	497E	80109	1500-1599	
CHIMNEY RANCH LN	Jefferson Co	842J	80470	33400-33499	
CHIMNEY ROCK RD	Highlands Ranch	374V	80126	900-1199	
CHIMNEY ROCK TRAIL	Jefferson Co	340W	80465	6200-6299	
CHINLE AVE	Boulder	97C	80304	None	
CHINOOK AVE	Longmont	12W	80501	300-399	
CHINOOK DR	Jefferson Co	367G	80439	7000-7099	
CHINOOK PL	Longmont	12W	80501	100-199	
CHINOOK RD	Clear Creek Co	780E	80452	700-799	
CHINOOK ST	Firestone	707S	80504	None	
CHINOOK WAY	Boulder Co	129G	80303	1100-1299	
CHINOOK TRAIL E	Douglas Co	441F	80138	10300-10899	
CHIPMUNK DR	Gilpin Co	760V	80403	None	
CHIPMUNK DR	Jefferson Co	367S	80439	26700-26899	
CHIPMUNK LN	Gilpin Co	761V	80403	None	
CHIPMUNK PL	Douglas Co	432Q	80125	7400-7599	
CHIPPED ARROW WAY	El Paso Co	908Y	80132	17400-17599	
CHIPPEWA CIR	Douglas Co	846U	80135	3700-3999	
CHIPPEWA DR	Boulder	128L	80303	3800-4499	
CHIPPEWA DR	Douglas Co	886M	80118	4800-5999	
CHIPPEWA LN	Jefferson Co	308B	80401	22000-22299	
CHIPPEWA ST	Kiowa	872M	80117	400-699	
CHIQUITA PL	Castle Rock	498B	80108	3300-3399	
CHIQUITA RD	Jefferson Co	338P	80454	5200-5299	
CHIRON ST	Lafayette	131R	80026	1100-1199	
CHISHOLM CIR	Elbert Co	870V	80107	1900-1999	
CHISHOLM PL	Douglas Co	469B	80134	5700-5799	
CHISHOLM TRAIL	Boulder	98P	80301	3300-3399	

STREET NAME	CITY or COUNTY	MAP GRID	ZIP CODE	BLOCK RANGE	O/E
CHISHOLM TRAIL	El Paso Co	908P	80132	1300-20099	
CHISHOLM TRAIL	Elbert Co	870U	80107	30000-30999	
CHISWICK CIR E	Highlands Ranch	404C	80126	400-599	
CHOCTAW CIR	Douglas Co	846U	80135	3500-3699	
CHOCTAW ST S	Jefferson Co	842E	80470	13300-13699	
CHOKE CHERRY AVE	Broomfield	163S	80020	4200-4399	
CHOKE CHERRY CT	Douglas Co	432P	80125	10400-10499	
CHOKE CHERRY CT	Golden	248V	80403	400-499	
CHOKE CHERRY DR	Jefferson Co	824N	80127	18000-18199	
CHOKE CHERRY DR W	Louisville	130P	80027	1000-1899	
CHOKE CHERRY LN	Jefferson Co	307H	80401	24100-24499	
CHOKECHERRY LN	Longmont	40Q	80503	1000-1199	
CHOKE CHERRY RD	Jefferson Co	277V	80401	1-199	
CHOKE CHERRY WAY	Douglas Co	432P	80125	6900-7099	
CHOLLA CT	Boulder Co	97P	80304	3600-3699	
CHOLLA LN	Broomfield	162P	80020	1100-1199	
CHOPPER CIR	Denver	284A	80204	1000-1098	E
CHRIS DR	Jefferson Co	337V	80439	24500-24899	
CHRISTA CIR	Douglas Co	432K	80125	10400-10499	
CHRISTENSEN CIR W	Arapahoe Co	343W	80123	4400-4599	
	Jefferson Co	343W	80123	None	
CHRISTENSEN DR W	Arapahoe Co	373A	80123	4800-5099	
	Arapahoe Co	343W	80123	None	
	Jefferson Co	343W	80123	None	
CHRISTENSEN LN W	Arapahoe Co	343W	80123	4200-5199	
CHRISTENSON AVE	Superior	160P	80027	None	
CHRISTIAN ST	Weld Co	728X	80621	11500-11699	
CHRISTMAS TREE DR	Boulder	127G	80302	400-499	
CHRISTOPER CT	Boulder Co	70K	80503	7100-7199	
CHRISTOPHER CT	Elbert Co	832K	80107	9200-9499	
CHRISTOPHER DR	Jefferson Co	822P	80433	10100-10699	
CHRISTOPHER LN	Jefferson Co	822T	80433	32000-32199	
CHRISTY WAY	Superior	160Q	80027	None	
CHRISTY RIDGE RD	Douglas Co	867J	80135	3200-4299	
CHUCKLING CREEK RD	Park Co	840C	80421	100-499	
CHUCKWAGON CIR	Thornton	195Q	80229	None	
CHUKAR DR	Longmont	12Y	80501	1500-1599	
CHURCH AVE W	Littleton	343V	80120	2400-2899	
CHURCH LN	Louisville	130U	80027	701-799	O
CHURCH ST	Black Hawk	780D	80422	100-199	
CHURCHILL CT	Douglas Co	440D	80138	None	
CHURCHILL DR	Cherry Hills Village	344D	80113	1-99	
CHURCH RANCH BLVD	Westminster	192P	80021	6800-8799	
CHURCH RANCH WAY	Westminster	192P	80021	10100-10299	
CHUTE RD	Boulder Co	742Y	80403	200-1199	
CIANCO ST	Thornton	195X	80229	9200-9399	
CICERO CT	Douglas Co	432J	80125	None	
CIELO CT	Douglas Co	408H	80134	16600-16799	
CIELO LN	Jefferson Co	305A	80439	700-799	
CIMARRON CIR	Aurora	288K	80011	1000-1099	
CIMARRON CIR S	Aurora	348F	80015	4500-4599	
CIMARRON DR	Greenwood Village	344V	80121	1-99	
CIMARRON DR	Lafayette	131Q	80026	None	
CIMARRON DR E	Arapahoe Co	347Q	80111	11200-11499	
CIMARRON PKWY	Arvada	190X	80007	None	
CIMARRON PL E	Centennial	350N	80015	21200-21299	
CIMARRON RD	El Paso Co	908Z	80132	300-699	
CIMARRON RD S	Littleton	343P	80123	5300-5499	
CIMARRON ST	Aurora	258X	80011	3000-3199	
	Firestone	707N	80504	None	
CIMARRON ST	Highlands Ranch	374U	80126	8700-8799	
CIMARRON ST S	Aurora	318P	80014	2500-2699	
CIMARRON WAY S	Aurora	318B	80012	800-998	E
	Aurora	318X	80014	3400-3499	
	Aurora	348F	80014	None	
	Littleton	343X	80123	5900-6099	
CIMARRONA PEAK	Jefferson Co	371K	80127	11400-11499	
CIMMARON PL	Superior	160U	80027	3100-3299	
CIMMARON ST	Aurora	288F	80011	1600-1999	
CIMMARON WAY	Boulder	128R	80303	200-299	
CIMMARON RIVER RD	Weld Co	706M	80504	None	
CIMMARON TRAIL	Elbert Co	871E	80107	34000-35599	
CIMMARRON ST	Firestone	707S	80504	10400-10599	
CINCH CT	Jefferson Co	368M	80465	7600-7899	
CINDY AVE S	Jefferson Co	842A	80470	12300-12899	
	Jefferson Co	842E	80470	12900-12999	
CINNABAR DR	Castle Rock	467G	80108	None	
CINNABAR LN	Castle Rock	467G	80108	500-899	
CINNAMON CIR	Boulder	97H	80304	None	
CINNAMON CT	Castle Rock	497C	80104	800-899	
CINNAMON ST	Douglas Co	887L	80118	1900-1999	
CINNAMON LN	Louisville	130X	80027	900-999	
CINNAMON RD	Douglas Co	887L	80118	1800-1899	
CINNAMON ST	Longmont	11Y	80501	1300-1499	
CINNAMONWOOD	Jefferson Co	336A	80439	31100-31199	
CINQUE TAIL DR	Douglas Co	887G	80118	6800-7099	
CIPRIAN CIR	Mead	706M	80504	None	
CIPRIANI LOOP	Monument	908X	80132	None	
CIRCLE DR	Boulder	127G	80302	700-899	
CIRCLE DR	Castle Rock	497M	80104	1-99	
CIRCLE DR	Clear Creek Co	304G	80439	1-399	
CIRCLE DR	Denver	285N	80206	400-599	
	Jefferson Co	762C	80403	11000-11199	
	Jefferson Co	822T	80433	12000-12299	
	Jefferson Co	336Z	80439	27600-27899	
	Jefferson Co	822W	80470	34400-35699	
CIRCLE DR	Louisville	131N	80027	1600-1699	
CIRCLE DR	Palmer Lake	908S	80133	800-899	
CIRCLE DR	Thornton	194R	80229	1200-1299	
	Westminster	223F	80031	8200-8599	
	Westminster	223B	80031	8600-8999	
CIRCLE DR	Wheat Ridge	281C	80215	1-99	
CIRCLE DR N	Park Co	841Q	80421	1-399	
CIRCLE DR S	Park Co	841Q	80421	1-299	
CIRCLE HILL CIR	Elbert Co	871R	80107	None	
CIRCLE K RANCH	Clear Creek Co	801R	80439	200-899	
CIRCLE POINT RD	Westminster	192L	80020	11000-11099	
CISNE CIR	Brighton	140N	80601	None	
CISNE ST	Brighton	140N	80601	None	
CISTENA WAY	Douglas Co	470A	80134	7500-7599	
	Douglas Co	470B	80134	7900-8099	
CITADEL WAY	Castle Rock	497K	80109	None	
CITATION CIR N	Douglas Co	470A	80134	5300-5399	
CITATION LN	Boulder Co	70N	80503	None	
CITATION WAY	Frederick	707W	80504	None	
CITATION TRAIL	Jefferson Co	366V	80439	7900-8399	
CITRINE CT	Douglas Co	408G	80134	9800-9899	
CITY CENTER CIR	Lafayette	132N	80026	None	

STREET NAME	CITY or COUNTY	MAP GRID	ZIP CODE	BLOCK RANGE	O/E
CITY CENTER DR	*Westminster*	**193W**	80031	9200-9799	
CITY PARK ESPLANADE	*Denver*	**285E**	80206	None	
CITY VIEW DR	*Adams Co*	**224H**	80229	700-8199	
	Adams Co	**225E**	80229	8100-8199	
CITY VIEW DR	*Jefferson Co*	**823R**	80465	9600-10399	
CIVIC CENTER DR	*Thornton*	**194U**	80234	9500-9599	
CLAIRE CIR	*Northglenn*	**194E**	80234	11000-11099	
CLAIRE LN	*Northglenn*	**194E**	80234	800-11099	
CLAIRTON CT S	*Highlands Ranch*	**405F**	80126	9800-9899	
CLAIRTON DR E	*Highlands Ranch*	**405F**	80126	2800-3099	
CLAIRTON LN S	*Highlands Ranch*	**405F**	80126	9700-9899	
CLAIRTON PL S	*Highlands Ranch*	**405F**	80126	9700-9899	
CLAIRTON ST S	*Highlands Ranch*	**405F**	80126	9900-9999	
CLAIRTON WAY S	*Highlands Ranch*	**405F**	80126	9800-9999	
CLANCY CT	*Brighton*	**138T**	80601	200-299	
	Brighton	**138V**	80601	2200-2299	
CLANDAN CT	*Douglas Co*	**408D**	80138	9700-9899	
CLARA BELLE DR	*Arvada*	**252E**	80002	8400-8699	
CLARA LEE ST	*Weld Co*	**729R**	80603	17000-17999	
CLARE CT	*Boulder Co*	**131A**	80303	9200-9299	
CLARE CT	*Castle Pines North*	**436R**	80108	1-99	
CLARE DR	*Castle Pines North*	**436R**	80108	100-399	
CLAREMONT DR	*Boulder*	**128T**	80305	1100-1399	
CLARENCE ST	*Palmer Lake*	**907Q**	80133	None	
CLARENDON DR	*Longmont*	**12P**	80501	600-799	
CLARENDON LOOP	*Douglas Co*	**436Q**	80108	400-699	
CLARET ASH	*Jefferson Co*	**370Q**	80127	1-99	
CLARK AVE	*Jefferson Co*	**823N**	80433	26000-26399	
CLARK CT	*Adams Co*	**224T**	80221	6800-6899	
CLARK CT	*Broomfield*	**163F**	80020	None	
CLARK CT	*Erie*	**102Q**	80516	1800-1999	
CLARK DR	*Erie*	**102Q**	80516	1700-1899	
CLARK DR	*Northglenn*	**194T**	80260	9900-9999	
CLARK RD	*Park Co*	**820X**	80421	1-1999	
CLARK ST	*Aurora*	**288F**	80011	1600-1799	
CLARK ST	*Golden*	**249W**	80403	500-599	
CLARK WAY	*Longmont*	**12N**	80501	1-99	
CLARKE RD E	*Parker*	**409L**	80134	18800-19199	
CLARKE FARMS DR	*Parker*	**409N**	80134	10600-17399	
CLARKES CIR	*Douglas Co*	**496Z**	80109	1100-1599	
CLARKES CT	*Douglas Co*	**496Z**	80109	1000-1499	
CLARKEVILLE WAY	*Parker*	**409K**	80134	10600-10699	
CLARKSON CIR	*Thornton*	**164U**	80241	12800-12999	
CLARKSON CIR S	*Arapahoe Co*	**374M**	80122	7400-7499	
	Englewood	**314U**	80113	2800-2898	E
CLARKSON CT	*Adams Co*	**224L**	80229	8000-8099	
	Northglenn	**194L**	80233	10600-10799	
	Northglenn	**194C**	80233	11800-11899	
	Thornton	**164U**	80241	12802-12898	E
	Thornton	**164Q**	80241	13300-13399	
CLARKSON DR	*Adams Co*	**224G**	80229	8300-8499	
CLARKSON PL	*Thornton*	**164Q**	80241	12900-12999	
CLARKSON ST	*Adams Co*	**254D**	80216	5700-5798	E
	Denver	**284Q**	80218	1-1999	
	Denver	**284D**	80205	2000-2599	
	Denver	**254L**	80216	4800-5199	
	Northglenn	**194Q**	80233	10400-10599	
	Northglenn	**194L**	80233	10800-10999	
	Northglenn	**194G**	80233	11000-11599	
	Thornton	**194Y**	80229	9000-9199	
	Thornton	**164Q**	80241	13200-13399	
	Thornton	**224D**	80229	None	
CLARKSON ST S	*Arapahoe Co*	**374H**	80121	6400-6699	
	Arapahoe Co	**374R**	80122	6700-8299	
	Cherry Hills Village	**344H**	80110	3500-5098	E
	Denver	**284Y**	80209	1-699	
	Denver	**314C**	80209	700-1099	
	Denver	**314L**	80210	1100-2299	
	Denver	**314U**	80210	2500-2699	
	Englewood	**314Y**	80113	2700-3599	
	Englewood	**344H**	80110	3501-5099	O
	Greenwood Village	**344Q**	80121	5100-5899	
CLASSIC DR	*Highlands Ranch*	**375X**	80126	2700-2899	
CLAUDE CT	*Denver*	**255N**	80216	4300-4799	
	Northglenn	**195E**	80233	11000-11199	
	Northglenn	**195E**	80233	11200-11999	
	Northglenn	**165S**	80241	12000-12399	
	Thornton	**165S**	80241	12400-12799	
	Thornton	**165A**	80602	None	
CLAUDE CT S	*Denver*	**315S**	80210	3000-3099	
CLAUDE PL	*Thornton*	**165S**	80241	12800-12899	
CLAUDE WAY	*Northglenn*	**195A**	80233	11800-11999	
CLAUDIUS RD	*Gilpin Co*	**761N**	80403	1-299	
CLAY CIR	*Broomfield*	**163Q**	80234	None	
CLAY CT	*Broomfield*	**163U**	80234	None	
	Federal Heights	**193V**	80260	2600-2699	
	Federal Heights	**193Z**	80260	9300-9399	
	Westminster	**223Q**	80030	7300-7599	
	Westminster	**193M**	80234	10600-10699	
	Westminster	**193G**	80234	11200-11299	
	Westminster	**163Z**	80234	11900-11999	
CLAY DR	*Federal Heights*	**193Z**	80260	9400-9499	
	Westminster	**223L**	80030	8000-8099	
	Westminster	**193G**	80234	11000-11099	
CLAY PL	*Broomfield*	**163L**	80020	13500-13599	
	Adams Co	**791N**	80137	1900-1999	
CLAY ST	*Adams Co*	**253G**	80221	5400-5799	
	Adams Co	**223Y**	80221	6300-6599	
	Boulder Co	**99E**	80301	4400-4499	
	Broomfield	**163C**	80020	14400-14699	
	Broomfield	**133T**	80020	14700-14899	
	Denver	**283V**	80219	1-199	
	Denver	**283D**	80211	2000-2699	
	Denver	**253Z**	80211	2700-2899	
	Denver	**253Q**	80211	3100-4799	
	Denver	**253L**	80221	4800-5199	
	Douglas Co	**847N**	80135	5400-5699	
	Federal Heights	**223C**	80260	8600-9099	
	Federal Heights	**193Y**	80260	9200-9299	
	Federal Heights	**193Q**	80260	10000-10199	
	Federal Heights	**193R**	80260	10300-10399	
	Westminster	**223U**	80030	6900-7199	
	Westminster	**223G**	80030	8000-8099	
	Westminster	**223H**	80030	8200-8299	
	Westminster	**223G**	80260	8400-8499	
	Westminster	**193G**	80234	11000-11199	
	Westminster	**163Y**	80234	12100-12199	
	Westminster	**223L**	80030	None	

STREET NAME	CITY or COUNTY	MAP GRID	ZIP CODE	BLOCK RANGE	O/E
CLAY ST S	*Denver*	**283Z**	80219	1-699	
	Denver	**313M**	80219	700-2699	
	Denver	**313M**	80219	None	
	Englewood	**343M**	80110	4700-4799	
	Littleton	**373G**	80120	7000-7199	
	Sheridan	**313Z**	80110	3100-3499	
	Sheridan	**343H**	80110	3500-4499	
CLAY WAY	*Denver*	**283M**	80204	900-999	
CLAY COMMONS CT	*Boulder*	**128L**	80303	4300-4399	
CLAYMOOR CT	*Douglas Co*	**436D**	80108	200-299	
CLAYSON ST N	*Douglas Co*	**409G**	80138	11800-11999	
CLAYTON AVE	*Adams Co*	**225P**	80229	7300-7499	
CLAYTON BLVD S	*Arapahoe Co*	**315W**	80113	3300-3499	
CLAYTON CIR	*Frederick*	**727G**	80530	6200-7999	
CLAYTON CIR	*Superior*	**160Q**	80027	2200-2699	
CLAYTON CIR	*Thornton*	**195T**	80229	9700-9799	
CLAYTON CIR S	*Centennial*	**375P**	80122	7900-8099	
CLAYTON CT	*Adams Co*	**225E**	80229	8200-8399	
CLAYTON CT	*Keenesburg*	**732A**	80643	None	
	Thornton	**195T**	80229	9500-9599	
	Thornton	**195F**	80233	11500-11599	
	Thornton	**165X**	80241	12100-12399	
	Thornton	**165T**	80241	12400-12499	
	Thornton	**165P**	80241	13000-13099	
	Thornton	**165K**	80241	13100-13199	
CLAYTON CT S	*Centennial*	**375P**	80122	7900-7999	
	Cherry Hills Village	**345K**	80113	4700-4799	
	Greenwood Village	**345T**	80121	5800-5899	
	Commerce City	**255F**	80022	None	
	Denver	**285P**	80206	200-799	
	Denver	**285K**	80206	1000-1499	
	Denver	**285B**	80205	2600-2699	
	Denver	**255X**	80205	2700-3699	
	Denver	**255P**	80216	4000-4999	
CLAYTON ST	*Frederick*	**727G**	80530	6100-6399	
	Northglenn	**195K**	80233	10900-10999	
	Northglenn	**195F**	80233	11000-11199	
	Thornton	**195W**	80229	9000-9399	
	Thornton	**195S**	80229	9900-9999	
	Thornton	**195N**	80229	10000-10099	
	Thornton	**195B**	80233	11400-11899	
	Thornton	**165P**	80241	13300-13499	
	Thornton	**165K**	80241	13500-13599	
	Thornton	**165A**	80602	14500-14799	
	Thornton	**135W**	80602	14800-15099	
CLAYTON ST S	*Centennial*	**345X**	80121	5900-6099	
	Centennial	**375B**	80121	6500-6699	
	Centennial	**375P**	80122	7900-7999	
	Denver	**315B**	80209	700-799	
	Denver	**315P**	80210	1100-3299	
CLAYTON WAY	*Erie*	**103W**	80516	None	
CLAYTON WAY	*Thornton*	**165T**	80241	12400-12499	
	Thornton	**165P**	80241	13100-13199	
CLAYTON WAY S	*Centennial*	**375B**	80122	6700-6899	
	Centennial	**375K**	80122	7800-7899	
	Denver	**315B**	80209	900-1099	
CLAYTONS ST	*Thornton*	**165K**	80602	13600-13799	
CLAYWOOD ST	*Broomfield*	**163U**	80020	12700-12798	E
CLEARBROOK LN	*El Paso Co*	**908U**	80132	500-599	
CLEARBROOKE CT	*Castle Rock*	**528F**	80104	5200-5499	
CLEAR CREEK DR	*Denver*	**252M**	80212	5400-5999	
CLEAR CREEK DR	*Weld Co*	**706M**	80504	None	
CLEAR CREEK DR E	*Parker*	**439C**	80134	18900-19399	
CLEAR CREEK LN	*Golden*	**278C**	80401	1-599	
CLEAR CREEK PL E	*Parker*	**439C**	80134	19100-19299	
CLEAR CREEK RD	*Clear Creek Co*	**781T**	80439	1-1699	
CLEAR CREEK RD	*Denver*	**346M**	80237	None	
CLEAR CREEK WAY E	*Parker*	**439C**	80134	19200-19399	
CLEAR CREEK TRAIL E	*Parker*	**439D**	80134	19400-19699	
CLEAR SKY WAY	*Castle Rock*	**496B**	80109	800-1599	
CLEAR-VIEW DR	*Jefferson Co*	**277T**	80401	26000-26399	
CLEARVIEW LN	*Highlands Ranch*	**405L**	80126	None	
CLEARVIEW RD	*Boulder Co*	**129G**	80303	6300-6499	
CLEAR VIEW RD	*Elbert Co*	**870Y**	80107	29000-29499	
CLEAR VIEW RD	*Jefferson Co*	**822Z**	80433	11900-11999	
CLEAR WATER DR	*Lone Tree*	**406C**	80124	7900-8099	
CLEEK WAY	*Columbine Valley*	**343Y**	80123	1-99	
CLEEKWOOD WAY	*Jefferson Co*	**340S**	80465	15700-15799	
CLEESE CT	*El Paso Co*	**912X**	80831	16800-17799	
CLEMANTIS DR	*Douglas Co*	**887F**	80118	2000-2299	
CLEMATIS DR	*Boulder*	**127L**	80302	None	
CLEMENTS RD	*Clear Creek Co*	**801E**	80452	1-2199	
CLEMMA CT	*Weld Co*	**726K**	80516	1900-1999	
CLEMSON DR	*Longmont*	**10V**	80503	1300-1499	
CLEMSON LN	*Westminster*	**223F**	80031	8200-8399	
CLEO ST	*Adams Co*	**225E**	80229	2000-2299	
CLERMONT	*Thornton*	**195D**	80233	11500-11699	
CLERMONT CIR	*Thornton*	**195G**	80233	11100-11199	
	Thornton	**165Q**	80241	13200-13299	
CLERMONT CT	*Thornton*	**195L**	80233	10900-10999	
	Thornton	**195G**	80233	11200-11299	
	Thornton	**165Y**	80241	12200-12299	
	Thornton	**165Q**	80241	13100-13199	
	Thornton	**165L**	80602	None	
	Thornton	**195M**	80233	None	
CLERMONT CT S	*Centennial*	**345Y**	80121	6200-6299	
	Centennial	**375C**	80121	6400-6599	
	Centennial	**375L**	80122	7400-7499	
	Centennial	**375Q**	80122	7700-7799	
CLERMONT DR	*Thornton*	**195Y**	80229	9100-9499	
	Thornton	**195G**	80233	11000-11199	
	Thornton	**195G**	80233	11200-11399	
CLERMONT DR S	*Centennial*	**375G**	80122	6800-7499	
	Denver	**315U**	80222	2700-3099	
CLERMONT LN	*Thornton*	**195U**	80229	None	
CLERMONT PKWY	*Denver*	**285Q**	80220	300-1999	
CLERMONT PL	*Thornton*	**165Y**	80241	12300-12399	
CLERMONT ST	*Commerce City*	**255C**	80022	6000-6199	
	Commerce City	**225Y**	80022	6200-6399	
	Commerce City	**225U**	80022	6600-7199	
	Denver	**285U**	80220	1-99	
	Denver	**285C**	80207	2000-2799	
	Denver	**255Y**	80207	2800-3199	
	Thornton	**195Y**	80229	9400-9499	
	Thornton	**195L**	80233	10600-10799	
	Thornton	**195L**	80233	10900-10999	
	Thornton	**165Y**	80241	12100-12299	
	Thornton	**165U**	80241	12400-12799	
	Thornton	**165Q**	80241	12800-12899	
	Thornton	**165L**	80241	13400-13599	

STREET NAME	CITY or COUNTY	MAP GRID	ZIP CODE	BLOCK RANGE	O/E
CLERMONT ST S	*Centennial*	**375G**	80122	6700-7099	
	Cherry Hills Village	**345G**	80113	3900-4199	
	Denver	**285U**	80246	1-299	
	Denver	**315G**	80246	1100-1299	
	Denver	**315G**	80222	1300-1899	
	Denver	**315Q**	80222	2100-2599	
	Denver	**315Y**	80222	3200-3499	
	Glendale	**285Y**	80246	None	
CLERMONT WAY	*Thornton*	**195L**	80233	10500-10699	
	Thornton	**195G**	80233	11000-11199	
	Thornton	**195G**	80233	11200-11399	
CLEVELAND AVE	*Louisville*	**130Z**	80027	100-299	
	Louisville	**130V**	80027	500-799	
CLEVELAND CIR	*Lafayette*	**131M**	80026	700-799	
CLEVELAND CT	*Bennett*	**793N**	80102	100-299	
CLEVELAND CT	*Louisville*	**130V**	80027	800-999	
CLEVELAND DR	*Parker*	**440C**	80138	None	
CLEVELAND PL	*Boulder*	**127G**	80302	400-499	
CLEVELAND PL	*Denver*	**284G**	80202	1400-1599	
CLEVELAND ST	*Adams Co*	**225K**	80229	7800-7899	
CLEVELAND ST E	*Lafayette*	**132J**	80026	100-899	
CLEVELAND ST S	*Brighton*	**138Q**	80601	1000-1099	
CLEVELAND ST W	*Lafayette*	**132J**	80026	100-499	
CLIFF RD	*Jefferson Co*	**336X**	80439	5900-6099	
CLIFFGATE LN	*Douglas Co*	**436Y**	80108	600-699	
CLIFFHANGER DR	*Boulder Co*	**722L**	80302	1-99	
CLIFF LINE RD	*Golden*	**249S**	80403	300-399	
CLIFFORD CT	*Parker*	**409K**	80134	10900-10999	
CLIFFROSE	*Jefferson Co*	**370L**	80127	1-99	
CLIFFROSE CT	*Lafayette*	**131F**	80026	300-399	
CLIFFROSE LN	*Highlands Ranch*	**405L**	80126	None	
CLIFFROSE LN	*Louisville*	**130M**	80027	2100-2399	
CLIFFROSE WAY	*Highlands Ranch*	**405Q**	80126	10500-10799	
CLIFFSIDE CT	*Douglas Co*	**436Y**	80108	2900-2999	
CLIFF SPRINGS RD	*Douglas Co*	**890K**	80116	None	
CLIFF VIEW CT	*Castle Rock*	**498E**	80104	2800-3099	
CLIFTON AVE W	*Jefferson Co*	**372P**	80128	6900-7499	
	Jefferson Co	**372N**	80128	8400-8999	
	Jefferson Co	**371R**	80128	9100-9199	
CLIFTON CT S	*Highlands Ranch*	**404G**	80126	9800-9899	
CLIFTON DR E	*Aurora*	**381Q**	80016	26600-26799	
CLIFTON PL E	*Aurora*	**380Q**	80016	22800-22999	
	Aurora	**380R**	80016	23500-23799	
	Aurora	**381Q**	80016	26800-26899	
CLIFTON PL W	*Jefferson Co*	**372Q**	80128	6300-6799	
CLIFTON HILL	*Palmer Lake*	**907R**	80133	None	
CLINE CT	*Jefferson Co*	**823N**	80433	9300-9399	
CLINE ST	*Adams Co*	**225J**	80229	None	
CLINTON CT S	*Denver*	**317W**	80231	3300-3499	
	Greenwood Village	**347S**	80111	5400-5499	
	Greenwood Village	**347W**	80111	6000-6099	
	Greenwood Village	**377A**	80112	6700-6799	
CLINTON ST	*Adams Co*	**137W**	80602	14900-15399	
	Aurora	**287J**	80010	1100-2299	
	Aurora	**287J**	80230	None	
	Commerce City	**198E**	80640	None	
	Denver	**257W**	80238	None	
CLINTON ST S	*Arapahoe Co*	**317E**	80247	1100-1499	
	Arapahoe Co	**317J**	80231	2000-2199	
	Arapahoe Co	**377E**	80112	7200-7499	
	Centennial	**377E**	80112	7100-7199	
	Denver	**287W**	80231	300-699	
	Denver	**317A**	80247	700-799	
	Greenwood Village	**347N**	80111	4900-5099	
	Greenwood Village	**377E**	80112	6800-7099	
CLINTON WAY	*Denver*	**257W**	80238	None	
CLIO AVE	*Palmer Lake*	**907Q**	80133	None	
CLIPPER CT	*Boulder Co*	**99G**	80301	4400-4499	
CLOUD CT	*Boulder*	**99E**	80301	4600-4699	
CLOUDBERRY DR E	*Parker*	**409A**	80134	17300-17899	
CLOUD DANCE CT	*Elbert Co*	**871B**	80107	35400-35599	
CLOVE WAY	*Parker*	**408U**	80134	11300-11499	
CLOVEN HOOF RD	*El Paso Co*	**907V**	80133	18700-18999	
CLOVER AVE	*Adams Co*	**792M**	80102	None	
CLOVER CIR	*Boulder*	**97R**	80304	3500-3599	
CLOVER CIR	*Lafayette*	**131H**	80026	900-999	
CLOVER CT	*Douglas Co*	**887B**	80118	2300-2499	
CLOVER DR	*Elbert Co*	**850V**	80107	37600-37999	
CLOVER LN	*Boulder Co*	**130J**	80303	400-699	
CLOVER LN	*Brighton*	**139L**	80601	None	
CLOVER LN	*Jefferson Co*	**336G**	80439	28300-29299	
CLOVER RD	*Jefferson Co*	**280C**	80401	2700-2799	
CLOVER BASIN DR	*Longmont*	**41N**	80503	2300-2699	
	Longmont	**40P**	80503	2900-4499	
CLOVERBROOK CIR	*Highlands Ranch*	**405R**	80130	None	
CLOVER CREEK DR	*Longmont*	**40R**	80503	1400-1999	
CLOVER CREEK LN	*Longmont*	**40V**	80503	3600-3699	
CLOVERDALE RD	*Jefferson Co*	**278P**	80401	500-799	
CLOVERLEAF CIR	*Parker*	**378V**	80134	8600-8999	
CLOVERLEAF DR	*Boulder*	**97R**	80304	3500-3899	
CLOVERLEAF RD	*El Paso Co*	**908X**	80132	17200-17399	
CLOVERLEAF WAY	*El Paso Co*	**908X**	80132	None	
CLOVER MEADOW LN	*Douglas Co*	**379S**	80134	8800-8999	
CLOVERVALE CIR	*Highlands Ranch*	**405R**	80130	None	
CLOVIS WAY	*El Paso Co*	**910X**	80908	7300-7799	
CLUB CIR	*Louisville*	**160C**	80027	600-799	
CLUB CT	*Douglas Co*	**886H**	80118	5200-5399	
CLUB DR	*Jefferson Co*	**370Q**	80127	1-99	
CLUB DR	*Parker*	**409V**	80138	11500-11699	
	Parker	**410W**	80138	11700-20499	
CLUB LN	*Columbine Valley*	**343X**	80123	1-99	
CLUB PL	*Louisville*	**160C**	80027	700-799	
CLUB CREST DR	*Arvada*	**222J**	80005	7700-7999	
	Arvada	**221M**	80005	8000-8099	
	Arvada	**221H**	80005	8100-8399	
CLUB CREST EAST	*Arvada*	**222J**	80005	None	
CLUBHOUSE CIR	*Boulder Co*	**100A**	80301	4900-4999	
CLUB HOUSE CIR	*Jefferson Co*	**277U**	80401	24900-25399	
CLUBHOUSE CT	*Boulder Co*	**99D**	80301	4900-4999	
CLUBHOUSE DR	*Boulder*	**69Z**	80301	None	
CLUBHOUSE DR	*Broomfield*	**162Q**	80020	1100-1299	
CLUBHOUSE DR	*Fort Lupton*	**728M**	80621	200-298	E
CLUBHOUSE DR	*Parker*	**409R**	80138	19600-19799	
CLUB HOUSE LN	*Jefferson Co*	**306S**	80439	30400-30899	
CLUBHOUSE RD	*Boulder Co*	**100A**	80301	5100-7499	
CLUB RUSH CT	*Douglas Co*	**378U**	80134	15700-16099	
CLUB TERRACE DR	*Lone Tree*	**406C**	80124	None	
CLYDE AVE	*Palmer Lake*	**907R**	80133	None	

C

C

STREET NAME	CITY or COUNTY	MAP GRID	ZIP CODE	BLOCK RANGE	O/E
CLYDE CIR S	Highlands Ranch	404G	80129	9000-10099	
CLYDE CT	Longmont	11P	80501	2000-2199	
CLYDE PL S	Highlands Ranch	404F	80129	9900-9999	
CLYDE PL W	Denver	253U	80211	3000-3599	
CLYDESDALE RD	El Paso Co	910Y	80908	17500-18799	
CLYDESDALE RD N	Douglas Co	407W	80108	9000-9899	
CLYNCKE ST	Boulder Co	129R	80303	None	
COACH RD W	Boulder Co	722R	80302	1-2099	
COACH HOUSE LOOP	Castle Rock	496B	80109	1700-2699	
COACHLIGHT WAY	Douglas Co	846D	80125	8600-8699	
COACHLINE RD	Castle Rock	496C	80109	None	
	Castle Rock	497E	80109	None	
COAL CREEK CIR	Louisville	160C	80027	800-899	
COAL CREEK DR	Elbert Co	831N	80138	45000-46299	
COAL CREEK DR	Lafayette	132N	80026	1300-1699	
COAL CREEK DR	Superior	160E	80027	100-7799	
	Superior	159M	80027	None	
COAL CREEK RD	Elbert Co	830V	80138	45200-46199	
COAL CREEK ST	Elbert Co	831J	80138	None	
COAL CREEK CANYON DR					
	Boulder Co	741S	80403	None	
COAL CREEK CANYON RD	Arvada	189W	80007	None	
See.. STATE HWY 72					
	Arvada	219C	80007	None	
	Arvada	220E	80007	None	
	Arvada	763M	80007	None	
	Boulder Co	742W	80403	None	
	Jefferson Co	762C	80403	None	
	Jefferson Co	763L	80403	None	
COAL CREEK HEIGHTS DR					
	Jefferson Co	762A	80403	11300-12099	
COAL MINE AVE W	Jefferson Co	372A	80123	5200-9099	
	Jefferson Co	371D	80123	9100-9999	
	Jefferson Co	371B	80127	10000-11599	
	Jefferson Co	341W	80127	11600-12699	
	Jefferson Co	340Z	80127	12700-13399	
COAL MINE DR W	Jefferson Co	371B	80127	11200-11499	
	Jefferson Co	341W	80127	11500-12299	
	Jefferson Co	340Z	80127	13200-13398	E
COAL MINE PL W	Jefferson Co	372D	80128	6100-6299	
	Jefferson Co	372B	80128	7600-7899	
	Jefferson Co	371C	80127	10400-10599	
COAL MINE ST	Firestone	707S	80504	10300-10399	
	Firestone	707N	80504	None	
	Firestone	707N	80504	None	
COAL RIDGE DR	Superior	160R	80027	None	
COAL RIDGE ST	Firestone	707S	80504	10300-10499	
	Firestone	707N	80504	None	
COALTON RD	Superior	160U	80027	1500-1999	
COBALT LN	Castle Rock	467H	80108	7000-7199	
COBALT WAY	Castle Rock	467G	80108	1400-1499	
COBALT WAY	Superior	160Y	80027	900-999	
COBB RD	Jefferson Co	336X	80439	30400-30999	
COBBLECREST DR S	Highlands Ranch	404D	80126	9300-9499	
COBBLESTONE CT	Lyons	703C	80540	None	
COBBLESTONE CT S	Highlands Ranch	374V	80126	8300-8399	
COBBLESTONE DR E					
	Highlands Ranch	374V	80126	900-1199	
COBBLESTONE ST S	Highlands Ranch	374V	80126	8300-8399	
COBBLESTONE WAY	El Paso Co	908Y	80132	200-299	
COCHETOPA PASS	Jefferson Co	371K	80127	8000-8199	
COCHISE CIR	Jefferson Co	823X	80433	11800-12099	
	Jefferson Co	843A	80433	12100-12299	
COCHISE TRAIL	Jefferson Co	842U	80470	15500-17299	
COCHITI RD	Jefferson Co	338J	80454	4400-4499	
COCKER ST S	Littleton	344S	80120	5500-5999	
COCO CIR W	Jefferson Co	371V	80128	9600-9699	
COCO DR W	Jefferson Co	371V	80128	9000-9199	
COCO PL W	Jefferson Co	372U	80128	6800-6899	
	Jefferson Co	371V	80128	9200-9299	
	Jefferson Co	371T	80127	10800-11199	
CODY AVE E	Parker	439G	80134	19000-19199	
CODY CIR	Arvada	222E	80005	8100-8199	
	Westminster	192W	80021	9000-9099	
CODY CIR S	Jefferson Co	372E	80128	7100-7199	
CODY CT	Arvada	252E	80002	5500-5599	
	Arvada	252A	80004	5800-5899	
	Arvada	222E	80005	8100-8199	
CODY CT	Lafayette	132S	80026	None	
	Lakewood	282S	80226	1-99	
	Lakewood	282N	80215	600-699	
	Lakewood	282A	80215	2500-2599	
	Westminster	222E	80005	8500-8599	
	Westminster	222A	80021	8900-9099	
	Westminster	192W	80021	9100-9199	
	Wheat Ridge	252W	80033	3200-3299	
CODY CT S	Jefferson Co	342N	80123	5100-5199	
	Jefferson Co	342W	80123	6100-6199	
	Jefferson Co	372S	80128	8700-8799	
	Lakewood	282S	80226	1-299	
	Lakewood	282W	80226	300-499	
	Lakewood	312E	80232	1200-1299	
	Lakewood	312N	80227	2400-2499	
	Lakewood	312W	80227	3200-3299	
CODY DR	Arvada	222S	80004	7000-7099	
	Lakewood	282N	80226	400-599	
	Westminster	192S	80021	9300-9499	
CODY LN	Boulder	98V	80301	None	
CODY LN	Westminster	192W	80021	9200-9299	
CODY ST	Arvada	252E	80002	5200-5699	
	Arvada	252A	80004	6000-6199	
	Jefferson Co	252J	80002	5000-5099	
	Lakewood	282S	80226	1-199	
	Lakewood	282N	80215	600-699	
	Lakewood	282J	80215	1000-1299	
	Lakewood	282E	80215	1600-2299	
	Westminster	222A	80021	8800-9099	
	Westminster	192W	80021	9100-9199	
	Wheat Ridge	252S	80033	3800-4199	
	Wheat Ridge	252N	80033	4400-4799	
CODY ST S	Jefferson Co	342N	80123	5100-5399	
	Jefferson Co	342W	80123	5900-5999	
	Jefferson Co	372A	80123	6400-6499	
	Jefferson Co	372E	80128	7200-7499	
	Jefferson Co	372N	80128	7700-8299	
	Lakewood	282S	80226	1-299	
	Lakewood	282W	80226	500-699	
	Lakewood	312A	80226	700-1099	
	Lakewood	312J	80232	1500-1899	
CODY WAY S	Jefferson Co	342E	80123	4300-4499	
	Jefferson Co	342W	80123	5900-6199	
	Jefferson Co	372A	80123	6400-6599	
	Jefferson Co	372E	80128	7100-7299	
	Jefferson Co	372J	80128	7300-7499	
	Jefferson Co	372E	80128	None	
	Lakewood	312E	80232	1200-1399	
	Lakewood	312J	80227	1900-1999	
	Lakewood	312N	80227	2400-2599	
CODY PARK RD	Jefferson Co	278S	80401	23700-23999	
	Jefferson Co	277V	80401	24000-24399	
CODY TRAIL	Boulder Co	721C	80481	1-99	
CODY TRAIL	Golden	248Z	80403	1300-1399	
COEUR D'ALENE LN	Parker	410U	80138	11500-11799	
COFFMAN ST	Longmont	41H	80501	100-899	
	Longmont	11Z	80501	900-1099	
	Longmont	11V	80501	1300-1499	
COFFMAN ST S	Longmont	41M	80501	101-199	O
	Longmont	41R	80501	800-1099	
	Longmont	41R	80501	1200-1699	
	Longmont	41U	80504	1800-2199	
COKER AVE	Castle Rock	498L	80104	4700-4899	
COLBY DR	Boulder	128T	80305	2800-2999	
COLBY CANYON DR S					
	Highlands Ranch	404J	80129	10400-10599	
COLD SPRING RD	Boulder Co	741E	80466	700-2399	
COLD SPRING CAMPGROUND RD					
	Gilpin Co	760Q	80403	None	
COLD SPRINGS GULCH RD					
	Jefferson Co	277W	80401	300-1098	E
	Jefferson Co	307E	80401	1100-1699	
	Jefferson Co	307U	80439	2500-2899	
COLE BLVD	Lakewood	280G	80401	1500-1799	
COLE CIR	Arvada	220V	80004	6700-6799	
	Jefferson Co	250G	80002	5300-5399	
COLE CT	Arvada	250D	80004	6000-6099	
	Arvada	250C	80004	6100-6199	
	Arvada	220Z	80004	6300-6399	
	Arvada	220Z	80004	6500-6799	
	Arvada	220U	80004	6900-7199	
	Arvada	220L	80005	7800-7899	
	Jefferson Co	250G	80002	5700-5799	
COLE CT S	Jefferson Co	340M	80465	4200-4599	
	Lakewood	280S	80228	300-699	
	Lakewood	310C	80228	700-799	
	Lakewood	310M	80228	1800-1899	
	Lakewood	310R	80228	2100-2799	
COLE DR	Arvada	221Z	80004	8800-9199	
	Lakewood	280Q	80401	700-799	
COLE DR S	Lakewood	310D	80228	800-1099	
COLE LN	Arvada	220Z	80004	6300-6399	
	Jefferson Co	250G	80002	5700-5799	
COLE ST	Arvada	220G	80005	8300-8399	
	Jefferson Co	280Q	80401	800-999	
	Jefferson Co	250Y	80401	3000-3199	
COLE ST S	Jefferson Co	340H	80465	4200-4899	
	Jefferson Co	340Q	80465	None	
	Lakewood	310L	80228	1600-1899	
COLE WAY	Arvada	250C	80004	5800-5899	
	Arvada	220Y	80004	6200-6299	
COLE WAY S	Jefferson Co	340M	80465	4400-4699	
	Lakewood	310Q	80228	2400-2599	
COLEBROOK CT	Castle Rock	497E	80109	1300-1499	
COLEMAN	Thornton	224A	80260	None	
COLEMAN AVE	Weld Co	729A	80621	15000-16599	
COLEMAN DR	Jefferson Co	278P	80401	600-799	
COLETTE DR	Highlands Ranch	406E	80130	None	
COLFAX AVE E	Adams Co	791N	80137	34000-36899	
	Adams Co	795P	80136	60000-69999	
	Adams Co	790Q	80137	None	
	Adams Co	792M	80102	None	
	Adams Co	793J	80102	None	
	Adams Co	795P	80103	None	
	Arapahoe Co	790Q	80137	33000-33999	
	Aurora	286H	80010	8900-9299	
	Aurora	287G	80010	9300-12099	
	Aurora	287H	80011	12100-13198	E
	Aurora	288G	80011	13200-16899	
	Aurora	289G	80011	16900-20199	
	Aurora	290E	80011	20200-21799	
	Aurora	290G	80018	None	
	Denver	284G	80202	1-99	
	Denver	284G	80203	100-799	
	Denver	284H	80218	800-1699	
	Denver	285E	80218	1700-1899	
	Denver	285F	80206	1900-3999	
	Denver	285G	80220	4000-5499	
	Denver	286E	80220	5500-8899	
COLFAX AVE W	Denver	284F	80202	1-299	
	Denver	284E	80204	300-1899	
	Denver	283F	80204	1900-5199	
	Golden	279R	80401	16400-18399	
	Jefferson Co	280N	80401	14700-16399	
	Lakewood	282G	80214	5200-8399	
	Lakewood	282G	80215	8400-8899	
	Lakewood	281G	80215	8900-13399	
	Lakewood	280L	80401	13400-14699	
COLFAX DR W	Lakewood	280L	80401	None	
COLFAX "A" PL	Denver	285F	80206	3400-3499	
COLFAX "B" PL	Denver	285K	80206	3400-3499	
COLGATE CIR E	Aurora	319X	80013	18400-18499	
COLGATE CT	Longmont	10V	80503	1-99	
COLGATE DR	Longmont	10V	80503	2900-3199	
COLGATE DR E	Aurora	318T	80014	14700-14899	
COLGATE DR W	Denver	313W	80227	5200-5599	
COLGATE PL E	Aurora	319X	80013	17700-17999	
	Denver	316U	80231	7400-7899	
COLGATE PL W	Denver	313W	80236	5100-5199	
	Denver	312Z	80227	5900-5999	
COLGATE ST	Boulder	128P	80305	300-399	
COLI LN S	Jefferson Co	339W	80465	6200-6399	
COLINADE DR	Lone Tree	406D	80124	9600-9799	
COLLEGE AVE	Boulder	127G	80302	400-1399	
	Boulder	128F	80303	2800-2999	
COLLEGE AVE	Fort Lupton	729J	80621	200-298	E
COLLEGE AVE W	Denver	313V	80219	2400-2999	
	Englewood	313V	80110	2000-2399	
COLLEGE CT	Longmont	10V	80503	1-99	
COLLEGE DR E	Aurora	319Q	80013	None	
COLLEGE DR W	Littleton	343V	80120	2400-2699	
COLLEGE PL	Boulder	129E	80303	5600-5699	
COLLEGE PL E	Aurora	319Q	80013	None	
	Aurora	319R	80013	None	
COLLEGIATE DR E	Highlands Ranch	406B	80130	6200-6599	
COOLIDGE PL E	Aurora	290E	80011	20500-20799	
COLLIER RANCH RD	El Paso Co	908Y	80132	101-199	O
COLLINGSWOOD CT	Highlands Ranch	405M	80130	4900-5099	
COLLINGSWOOD DR	Highlands Ranch	405M	80130	4800-4999	
COLLINS AVE W	Lakewood	281K	80215	10800-11399	
COLLINS ST	Douglas Co	467K	80108	3500-3999	
COLLINSVILLE PL E	Highlands Ranch	405H	80130	4800-4999	
COLLYER ST	Longmont	41D	80501	200-899	
	Longmont	11Z	80501	900-2499	
COLLYER ST S	Longmont	41V	80501	1300-1699	
COLOMBINE CAMPGROUND	Gilpin Co	760X	80403	None	
COLONIAL DR	Lone Tree	406H	80124	8300-8699	
COLONIAL PARK DR	El Paso Co	908Z	80132	17000-17599	
COLONIAL TRAIL	Elbert Co	851C	80107	None	
COLONIST WAY	Jefferson Co	368L	80465	21200-21399	
COLONY PL	Longmont	11Z	80501	300-399	
COLONY LOOP	Douglas Co	409H	80138	None	
COLONY ROW	Broomfield	192E	80021	11200-11699	
COLORADO AVE	Adams Co	794P	80136	56400-56899	
	Boulder	128E	80302	2400-2799	
	Boulder	128G	80303	2800-4499	
COLORADO AVE	Larkspur	887R	80118	100-299	
COLORADO AVE	Longmont	41L	80501	900-1199	
	Longmont	41H	80501	None	
COLORADO AVE E	Arapahoe Co	317J	80247	9200-9699	
COLORADO AVE E	Arapahoe Co	812E	80102	39500-40999	
	Aurora	317J	80247	9700-13999	
	Aurora	317K	80112	10700-10799	
	Aurora	317M	80112	12900-13099	
	Aurora	318L	80017	15500-15899	
	Aurora	318M	80017	16100-16699	
	Denver	314L	80210	1-1699	
	Denver	315J	80210	1700-1999	
	Denver	315K	80210	2400-3799	
	Denver	315M	80222	4300-5599	
	Denver	316J	80224	5600-5799	
	Denver	316K	80224	6900-7299	
	Denver	316L	80231	7800-8199	
COLORADO AVE S	Denver	315Q	80222	1300-3499	
COLORADO AVE W	Denver	314K	80223	1-199	
	Denver	314J	80223	1800-1999	
	Denver	313M	80223	2000-2399	
	Denver	313K	80219	2400-5199	
	Lakewood	312M	80232	5300-5699	
	Lakewood	312L	80232	6600-6799	
	Lakewood	311M	80232	9200-9399	
COLORADO BLVD	Adams Co	225U	80022	7000-7199	
	Adams Co	165U	80602	13900-14799	
	Adams Co	135L	80602	14800-16799	
	Commerce City	225Y	80022	6200-6999	
	Commerce City	225Q	80022	7200-7399	
	Dacono	727K	80516	None	
	Denver	285Q	80206	1-1499	
	Denver	285G	80207	2000-2598	E
	Denver	285C	80207	2600-2799	
	Denver	255Y	80207	2801-3299	O
	Denver	255U	80205	3300-3999	
	Denver	255L	80216	4000-5199	
	Firestone	707T	80504	None	
	Highlands Ranch	375U	80126	None	
	Idaho Springs	780Q	80452	1-2999	
	Thornton	225C	80229	8600-9099	
	Thornton	195Q	80229	9100-10399	
	Thornton	195C	80233	10400-11899	
	Thornton	165U	80241	12000-13899	
COLORADO BLVD S	Centennial	345Y	80121	5900-6299	
	Centennial	375C	80121	6300-6699	
	Centennial	375L	80122	6700-8299	
	Cherry Hills Village	345C	80113	3500-4299	
	Denver	285U	80246	1-299	
	Denver	315C	80246	701-1199	O
	Denver	315G	80246	1200-1299	
	Glendale	315C	80246	700-1198	E
	Greenwood Village	345Q	80121	5300-5399	
	Greenwood Village	345U	80121	5400-5899	
COLORADO CIR E	Arapahoe Co	316M	80231	9000-9099	
COLORADO CT	Adams Co	225G	80229	8500-8599	
COLORADO CT S	Centennial	375G	80122	7100-7299	
COLORADO DR	Boulder	128F	80303	None	
	Boulder Co	72F	80504	11400-11499	
COLORADO DR E	Arapahoe Co	316M	80231	8900-9099	
	Aurora	317K	80112	10800-11699	
	Aurora	318K	80012	13900-14499	
	Aurora	319K	80017	17700-17999	
	Aurora	319L	80017	18600-19499	
	Denver	316K	80224	6500-6699	
COLORADO DR W	Lakewood	312K	80232	6800-7599	
COLORADO PL E	Aurora	317L	80112	11800-12099	
	Aurora	318L	80012	15000-15199	
COLORADO PL W	Jefferson Co	311K	80232	11200-11299	
	Lakewood	312M	80232	5300-5599	
	Lakewood	312J	80232	8500-8699	
	Lakewood	312J	80232	8700-8999	
	Lakewood	311M	80232	9000-9199	
COLORADO ST	Central City	780C	80427	100-299	
COLORADO ST	Gilpin Co	740Z	80403	None	
COLORADO WAY	Longmont	41L	80501	None	
COLORADO WAY	Thornton	165U	80241	None	
COLORADO CENTER DR	Denver	315L	80222	None	
COLORADO MILLS PKWY	Lakewood	280Q	80401	None	
COLORADO RIVER RD	Weld Co	706M	80504	None	
COLORADO SPRINGS CIR					
	Palmer Lake	907U	80133	None	
COLORFUL AVE	Longmont	706N	80504	2900-2999	
COLORFUL LN	Castle Rock	466T	80109	3700-3899	
COLOROW CT	Douglas Co	440W	80134	5900-5999	
COLOROW DR	Jefferson Co	340X	80465	5500-6299	
COLOROW RD	Jefferson Co	278Q	80401	200-1199	
COLT CIR	Douglas Co	867U	80109	1000-1599	
COLT CT	El Paso Co	909Z	80908	17700-17999	
COLT CT	Elbert Co	850Z	80107	1900-2099	
COLT DR	Boulder Co	70W	80503	5500-5599	

STREET NAME	CITY or COUNTY	MAP GRID	ZIP CODE	BLOCK RANGE	O/E
COLT PL	Park Co	841R	80421	1-199	
COLTSFOOT CT E	Parker	409E	80134	17600-17699	
COLTSFOOT DR S	Parker	409B	80134	9500-9699	
COLUMBIA AVE E	Aurora	319S	80013	17600-17999	
	Aurora	319V	80013	19600-19999	
COLUMBIA CIR E	Aurora	319T	80013	18400-18499	
COLUMBIA DR	Highlands Ranch	376W	80130	6200-6399	
COLUMBIA DR	Longmont	10Y	80503	1100-1299	
	Longmont	10U	80503	3500-3899	
COLUMBIA DR E	Aurora	318U	80014	14800-15299	
COLUMBIA DR E	Highlands Ranch	406A	80130	6200-6399	
COLUMBIA PL	Boulder Co	130E	80303	700-1099	
COLUMBIA PL E	Aurora	318V	80013	15800-16099	
	Aurora	319U	80013	18600-19099	
	Aurora	319V	80013	None	
	Denver	315S	80210	2100-2399	
	Denver	316T	80224	6500-6699	
	Denver	316U	80231	7400-7699	
COLUMBIA PL W	Denver	313W	80236	5100-5199	
	Denver	312Z	80227	5200-6099	
	Lakewood	311Z	80227	9300-9499	
	Lakewood	310U	80228	14500-14599	
COLUMBIA RD	Thornton	193V	80260	None	
COLUMBINE AVE	Boulder	127M	80302	1200-1599	
	Boulder	128J	80302	1600-2299	
COLUMBINE AVE	Broomfield	162L	80020	200-699	
COLUMBINE AVE	Frederick	727G	80530	7900-7999	
COLUMBINE AVE	Jefferson Co	278Q	80401	400-699	
COLUMBINE CIR	Jefferson Co	335K	80439	33600-34199	
COLUMBINE CIR	Lafayette	101W	80026	2500-3599	
COLUMBINE CIR	Thornton	165S	80241	12800-12999	
	Thornton	165N	80241	13400-13599	
COLUMBINE CIR S	Arapahoe Co	315W	80113	3300-3499	
COLUMBINE CT	Boulder Co	70Q	80503	6500-6599	
COLUMBINE CT	Broomfield	163U	80020	3200-3399	
COLUMBINE CT	Douglas Co	886C	80118	6100-6199	
COLUMBINE CT	Erie	103S	80516	None	
COLUMBINE CT	Jefferson Co	307L	80401	1800-1999	
COLUMBINE CT	Louisville	130U	80027	600-699	
COLUMBINE CT	Northglenn	195E	80233	11100-11199	
	Thornton	195S	80229	9500-9799	
	Thornton	195N	80229	10000-10099	
	Thornton	165W	80241	12300-12399	
	Thornton	165S	80241	12400-12499	
	Thornton	165N	80241	13200-13299	
	Thornton	135W	80602	14800-15099	
COLUMBINE CT S	Centennial	375N	80122	8000-8199	
	Cherry Hills Village	345J	80113	4600-4699	
	Arvada	252G	80002	5400-5499	
COLUMBINE DR	Bennett	793X	80102	300-599	
COLUMBINE DR	Boulder Co	11L	80504	12600-12999	
COLUMBINE DR	Brighton	138L	80601	1100-1298	E
COLUMBINE DR	Castle Rock	498J	80104	1200-1499	
COLUMBINE DR	Douglas Co	870A	80116	1200-1999	
COLUMBINE DR	Jefferson Co	369N	80465	8000-8199	
	Jefferson Co	822Z	80433	28300-28799	
COLUMBINE DR	Park Co	841T	80421	1-199	
COLUMBINE DR W	Jefferson Co	372E	80128	8900-9099	
	Jefferson Co	371H	80128	9200-9699	
COLUMBINE LN	Adams Co	253M	80221	5200-5499	
COLUMBINE LN	Clear Creek Co	335A	80439	1-399	
COLUMBINE LN	Columbine Valley	343X	80123	1-99	
	Douglas Co	866N	80135	7700-7899	
	Gilpin Co	761E	80403	100-399	
COLUMBINE LN	Jefferson Co	306N	80439	2300-2399	
	Jefferson Co	367E	80439	26800-26999	
COLUMBINE PL	Douglas Co	466D	80108	1-99	
COLUMBINE PL	Longmont	11Z	80501	300-399	
COLUMBINE PL	Thornton	195A	80233	11600-11699	
COLUMBINE RD	Adams Co	253G	80221	2800-5499	
	Jefferson Co	277V	80401	100-299	
	Jefferson Co	336M	80439	27800-28099	
COLUMBINE RD	Palmer Lake	907Q	80133	None	
COLUMBINE RD	Park Co	841J	80421	1-199	
COLUMBINE RD S	Jefferson Co	366E	80439	6600-7099	
COLUMBINE ST	Adams Co	225S	80229	6800-6899	
	Adams Co	135J	80602	16500-16599	
	Denver	285N	80206	200-799	
	Denver	285J	80206	900-1499	
	Denver	285A	80205	2600-2699	
	Denver	255W	80205	2700-3799	
	Denver	255N	80216	4200-4799	
	Denver	255J	80216	5100-5299	
COLUMBINE ST	Firestone	707N	80504	None	
COLUMBINE ST	Larkspur	887R	80118	100-299	
COLUMBINE ST	Northglenn	195J	80233	10900-11099	
	Thornton	195S	80229	9900-9999	
	Thornton	195A	80233	11600-11699	
	Thornton	195A	80233	11800-11899	
	Thornton	165W	80241	12100-12199	
	Thornton	165S	80241	12700-12799	
	Thornton	165J	80602	13700-13899	
	Thornton	165A	80602	14500-14799	
	Thornton	135W	80602	14900-15099	
COLUMBINE ST N	Golden	248V	80403	300-1099	
COLUMBINE ST S	Centennial	375B	80121	6600-6699	
	Centennial	375J	80122	7700-7799	
	Denver	315A	80209	700-1099	
	Denver	315E	80210	1100-1699	
	Denver	315P	80210	1800-2699	
	Denver	315W	80210	2900-3299	
COLUMBINE WAY	Erie	103X	80516	None	
COLUMBINE WAY	Jefferson Co	306Y	80439	29500-29599	
	Thornton	165S	80241	12400-12499	
	Thornton	165N	80241	13000-13099	
COLUMBINE WAY S	Centennial	375F	80122	6900-7099	
	Centennial	375E	80122	7300-7399	
	Greenwood Village	345W	80121	6100-6199	
COLUMBINE DRAW	Jefferson Co	337R	80439	4900-5099	
COLUMBINE GLEN AVE	Jefferson Co	277T	80401	25800-26999	
COLUMBINE GLEN TRAIL					
	Jefferson Co	277T	80401	26300-26499	
COLUMBINE RIDGE RD	Elbert Co	871G	80107	5600-5699	
COLUMBINE TRAIL	Elbert Co	871G	80107	34300-34699	
	Elbert Co	871H	80107	34000E-34599E	
	Elbert Co	871G	80107	34000W-34599W	
COLUMBINE TRAIL	Jefferson Co	307X	80439	26000-26399	
COLUMBUS WAY	Denver	258K	80239	5100-5199	

STREET NAME	CITY or COUNTY	MAP GRID	ZIP CODE	BLOCK RANGE	O/E
COLUMINE WAY S	Centennial	345X	80121	5900-6099	
COMANCHE CIR	Adams Co	794P	80136	1800-2299	
COMANCHE CT	Boulder Co	70M	80503	6700-6799	
COMANCHE CT	Frederick	726G	80516	None	
COMANCHE DR	Boulder	128L	80303	4300-4599	
COMANCHE DR	Douglas Co	886H	80118	4700-4999	
COMANCHE RD	Boulder Co	70M	80503	8700-9099	
COMANCHE RD	Jefferson Co	338E	80454	4100-4399	
COMANCHE ST	Adams Co	794P	80136	1900-2299	
COMANCHE ST	Bennett	793J	80102	None	
COMANCHE ST	Kiowa	872M	80117	200-799	
COMANCHE CREEK DR	Brighton	138V	80601	2400-2699	
COMANCHE CREEK DR	Elbert Co	912C	80106	9000-22099	
	Elbert Co	892Y	80106	22102-22198	E
COMANCHE CREEK WAY	Castle Rock	466P	80109	4900-5199	
COMANCHE PINES DR	Douglas Co	870A	80116	9300-9399	
COMBINE PL	Brighton	139K	80601	None	
COMET CIR	Thornton	224F	80260	700-799	
COMMANCHE WAY	Arapahoe Co	794R	80136	59200-59999	
COMMANDER CIR	Erie	133A	80516	None	
COMMANDER DR	Erie	133A	80516	100-299	
COMMANDER SPUR	Boulder Co	722V	80302	1-199	
COMMERCE CT	Castle Rock	467P	80109	3100-3299	
COMMERCE CT	Golden	279V	80401	200-299	
COMMERCE CT	Lafayette	132U	80026	1200-1299	
COMMERCE DR	Frederick	726D	80504	4200-4299	
COMMERCE ST	Boulder	128D	80301	1600-1899	
COMMERCE ST	Broomfield	162W	80020	100-299	
COMMERCE CENTER CIR					
	Highlands Ranch	373X	80129	9100-9199	
COMMERCE CENTER ST	Douglas Co	403B	80129	9300-9398	E
	Douglas Co	373X	80129	None	
COMMERCIAL RD	Golden	279V	80401	300-399	
COMMONS AVE E	Aurora	350Z	80016	23800-24199	
COMMONS DR	Jefferson Co	277Z	80401	500-599	
COMMONS ST	Lone Tree	406H	80124	None	
COMMONWEALTH ST	Lone Tree	407J	80124	None	
COMMUNITY CENTER DR	Northglenn	194C	80233	11200-11999	
COMMUNITY PARK RD	Broomfield	162U	80020	1-99	
COMPARK BLVD	Douglas Co	378T	80112	13100-15599	
COMPARK CT	Douglas Co	378U	80112	None	
COMPASS CIR	Castle Rock	497X	80104	3200-3399	
COMPTON ST	Broomfield	161V	80020	400-899	
COMSTOCK CT	Boulder Co	740H	80466	None	
COMSTOCK PL	Douglas Co	466C	80108	1-99	
CONCHO CT	Castle Rock	467U	80104	800-899	
CONCORD AVE	Boulder	97Y	80304	400-899	
CONCORD CIR	Lafayette	131E	80026	2400-2598	E
CONCORD CT S	Highlands Ranch	406F	80130	9800-9899	
CONCORD DR	Boulder Co	100E	80301	4600-7799	
CONCORD LN	Superior	160R	80027	2000-2199	
CONCORD LN	Westminster	223B	80031	8500-8699	
CONCORD PL E	Highlands Ranch	406F	80130	7100-7199	
CONCORD WAY	Longmont	10R	80503	3100-3199	
CONCORD CENTER DR	Douglas Co	378S	80112	8400-8598	E
CONDOR CT	Longmont	11N	80503	2000-2099	
CONDOR RUN	Douglas Co	432S	80125	6600-6799	
CONECREST LN	El Paso Co	909T	80908	3500-3599	
CONEFLOWER CT	Superior	160U	80027	2900-2999	
CONEFLOWER DR	Jefferson Co	308A	80401	None	
CONEFLOWER PL	Parker	379S	80134	8800-8899	
CONEFLOWER WAY	Brighton	168C	80601	1100-1199	
CONEJOS PL W	Denver	283F	80204	3100-4399	
CONESTOGA CT	Boulder	129A	80301	5400-5499	
CONESTOGA CT	Elbert Co	832X	80107	8200-8299	
CONESTOGA CT	Park Co	841J	80421	1-499	
CONESTOGA PL	Douglas Co	870F	80116	1-499	
CONESTOGA RD	Douglas Co	870F	80116	1-599	
CONESTOGA RD	Gilpin Co	761E	80403	1-299	
CONESTOGA RD	Park Co	841J	80421	1-1299	
CONESTOGA ST	Boulder	128D	80301	1600-1899	
CONESTOGA CROSSING	Thornton	195Q	80229	None	
CONESTOGA TRAIL	Fort Lupton	728M	80621	1500-1699	
CONEY CT	Boulder Co	742R	80302	1-99	
CONFERENCE PL	Golden	279V	80401	500-599	
CONGER ST	Nederland	740R	80466	None	
CONGRESSIONAL DR	El Paso Co	908U	80132	400-699	
CONIFER CIR	Elbert Co	830L	80138	47000-47499	
CONIFER CIR S	Jefferson Co	306X	80439	2900-3099	
CONIFER CT	Boulder	97R	80304	3600-3699	
CONIFER CT	Louisville	130Y	80027	800-899	
CONIFER CT E	Highlands Ranch	374Y	80126	900-1199	
CONIFER DR	Boulder Co	741F	80466	1-299	
CONIFER DR	Clear Creek Co	335A	80439	1-699	
CONIFER DR	Jefferson Co	822V	80433	10200-10499	
CONIFER DR	Park Co	841T	80421	1-699	
CONIFER PL	Elbert Co	850V	80107	1200-1399	
CONIFER RD	Adams Co	224F	80221	7400-8399	
CONIFER RD	Jefferson Co	278S	80401	1-199	
	Jefferson Co	823N	80433	25601-26599	O
	Jefferson Co	306X	80439	None	
CONIFER RD	Thornton	194X	80260	600-799	
CONIFER MOUNTAIN DR	Jefferson Co	822T	80433	29900-31699	
CONIFER MOUNTAIN RD	Jefferson Co	822T	80433	10600-11399	
CONIFER RIDGE DR	Jefferson Co	843A	80433	11500-12299	
CONIFER TOWN CENTER DR					
	Jefferson Co	823S	80433	26700-26798	E
CONIFER TRAIL	Elbert Co	850V	80107	1200-1499	
CONLEY WAY S	Arapahoe Co	315R	80222	2200-2299	
CONNECTICUT AVE W	Jefferson Co	311F	80232	10800-10899	
CONNECTICUT DR W	Lakewood	311E	80228	12200-12499	
CONNELL ST	Park Co	820Y	80421	None	
CONNEMARA HEIGHTS	El Paso Co	908T	80132	18900-18999	
CONNER CT	Castle Rock	496B	80109	4000-4099	
CONNESTOGA CT	El Paso Co	912U	80831	17900-18199	
CONNOR WAY	Superior	160R	80027	None	
CONRAD DR	Erie	102Q	80516	200-499	
CONSERVATION DR E	Frederick	707W	80504	5800-5999	
CONSERVATION DR W	Frederick	707W	80504	5700-5899	
CONSERVATORY PKWY	Aurora	319R	80013	None	
	Aurora	320S	80013	None	
CONSOLIDATED DITCH					
	Clear Creek Co	780A	80452	None	
CONTER AVE	Commerce City	256B	80022	None	
CONTER CT	Commerce City	256B	80022	None	
	Commerce City	256A	80022	None	
CONTINENTAL DIVIDE RD S					
	Jefferson Co	371P	80127	7500-8499	

STREET NAME	CITY or COUNTY	MAP GRID	ZIP CODE	BLOCK RANGE	O/E
CONTINENTAL VIEW DR	Louisville	130P	80027	1000-1999	
CONTINENTAL VIEW RD	Jefferson Co	306D	80401	None	
CONTROL TOWER RD E	Arapahoe Co	377M	80112	12000-13099	
CONVERSE RD	Adams Co	793E	80102	None	
	Arapahoe Co	793S	80102	1-1499	
CONVERSE RD	Bennett	793E	80102	None	
CONVERSE RD S	Arapahoe Co	813W	80102	5100-5899	
CONWAY CT	Erie	102G	80516	1300-1499	
CONWAY ST	Erie	102H	80516	1000-1299	
COOK CIR	Thornton	165T	80241	12800-12899	
COOK CIR S	Centennial	375F	80122	7200-7299	
COOK CT	Adams Co	225F	80229	8500-8599	
COOK CT	Hudson	730M	80642	1-99	
COOK CT	Northglenn	195K	80233	10400-10799	
	Thornton	195F	80233	11300-11499	
	Thornton	165X	80241	12200-12299	
	Thornton	165P	80241	13100-13199	
	Thornton	165F	80602	13900-13999	
	Thornton	165T	80241	None	
COOK CT S	Centennial	375B	80121	6500-6699	
	Centennial	375F	80122	7000-7099	
COOK DR S	Centennial	345X	80121	6200-6299	
COOK LN	Jefferson Co	368T	80465	21800-22799	
COOK ST	Denver	285P	80206	1-1699	
	Denver	285B	80205	2600-2699	
	Denver	255X	80205	2700-3999	
	Denver	255P	80216	4000-4599	
	Denver	255K	80216	4800-5399	
	Northglenn	195K	80233	10700-10799	
	Thornton	195X	80229	9200-9299	
	Thornton	195T	80229	9700-9899	
	Thornton	195P	80229	10000-10199	
	Thornton	195F	80233	11200-11299	
	Thornton	195B	80233	11800-11899	
	Thornton	165T	80241	12800-12899	
	Thornton	165K	80602	13600-13899	
	Thornton	165F	80602	13800-13999	
	Thornton	225B	80229	None	
COOK ST S	Centennial	345X	80121	5900-6299	
	Centennial	375B	80122	6700-6799	
	Centennial	375K	80122	7500-7699	
	Denver	315B	80209	1000-1099	
	Denver	315B	80210	1100-1199	
	Denver	315T	80210	1600-3099	
COOK WAY	Adams Co	225F	80229	8400-8499	
	Thornton	165T	80241	None	
	Thornton	195P	80229	None	
COOK WAY S	Centennial	375B	80121	6500-6599	
	Centennial	375F	80122	6800-7099	
	Centennial	375K	80122	7500-7699	
	Centennial	375P	80122	7900-8099	
COOK CREEK DR	Douglas Co	907G	80118	2200-14099	
COOKE CT	Erie	102G	80516	1000-1199	
COOLIDGE CIR S	Aurora	320D	80018	1100-1299	
	Aurora	320H	80018	None	
COOLIDGE CT	Bennett	793J	80102	100-299	
COOLIDGE CT S	Arapahoe Co	350R	80016	5400-5499	
	Aurora	350V	80016	5500-5699	
	Aurora	380H	80016	7000-7199	
	Aurora	380D	80016	None	
COOLIDGE DR E	Aurora	289H	80011	20000-20199	
COOLIDGE PL	Boulder	128C	80303	4400-4499	
COOLIDGE PL E	Aurora	289E	80011	17000-17599	
COOLIDGE ST N	Arapahoe Co	290V	80018	1-99	
COOLIDGE ST S	Arapahoe Co	290V	80018	1-299	
	Arapahoe Co	320D	80018	800-1099	
	Arapahoe Co	350R	80016	5100-5199	
	Aurora	350M	80016	None	
COOLIDGE WAY N	Aurora	290R	80018	None	
COOLIDGE WAY S	Aurora	380M	80016	None	
	Aurora	380R	80016	None	
COOL MEADOW PL	Castle Rock	528F	80104	3001-3199	O
COOL SPRINGS	Clear Creek Co	304H	80439	1-199	
COOPER AVE	Elbert Co	892N	80106	6701-6799	O
COOPER AVE W	Jefferson Co	372A	80128	8800-8999	
	Jefferson Co	371B	80127	11000-11599	
	Jefferson Co	341W	80127	11700-11899	
COOPER CT	Boulder	128G	80303	4100-4199	
COOPER CT	Castle Rock	497A	80109	1700-1899	
COOPER DR W	Jefferson Co	371C	80127	10500-10799	
	Jefferson Co	371B	80127	10900-11599	
	Jefferson Co	371A	80127	11600-11899	
	Jefferson Co	341W	80127	11900-12199	
COOPER LN W	Jefferson Co	371C	80127	10700-10799	
COOPER PL W	Jefferson Co	371C	80127	10400-10699	
	Jefferson Co	371B	80127	11000-11599	
COOPERATIVE WAY	Brighton	140S	80603	500-598	E
COOPER GROVE	El Paso Co	910N	80908	7000-7299	
COOPER'S TRAIL	Jefferson Co	367E	80439	26900-27099	
COORS CIR S	Lakewood	310L	80228	2000-2199	
COORS CT	Arvada	250C	80004	6000-6099	
	Arvada	220U	80004	6700-7199	
	Arvada	220Q	80005	7200-7699	
	Arvada	220G	80005	8300-8399	
COORS CT S	Jefferson Co	340L	80465	4200-4699	
	Lakewood	280S	80228	500-599	
	Lakewood	310C	80228	700-799	
	Lakewood	310M	80228	1700-1799	
	Lakewood	310Q	80228	2000-2099	
	Lakewood	310Q	80228	2200-2299	
	Lakewood	310R	80228	2700-2799	
COORS DR	Arvada	220Q	80005	7300-7499	
	Jefferson Co	280C	80401	2000-2499	
COORS DR S	Lakewood	310C	80228	800-999	
	Lakewood	310R	80228	2800-2999	
COORS LN	Arvada	220Y	80004	6300-6399	
COORS LN S	Jefferson Co	340L	80465	None	
COORS LOOP	Arvada	220G	80005	8400-8599	
COORS ST	Arvada	220Y	80004	6400-6599	
	Arvada	220U	80004	6700-6899	
	Arvada	220Q	80005	7400-7599	
	Arvada	220G	80005	8300-8699	
	Jefferson Co	250L	80002	5200-5399	
	Lakewood	280Q	80401	600-799	
COORS ST S	Jefferson Co	340L	80465	4200-4599	
	Lakewood	310Q	80228	2100-2499	
COORS WAY	Arvada	250C	80004	6100-6199	
COORS WAY S	Jefferson Co	340L	80465	4600-4699	
	Lakewood	310Q	80228	2200-2299	

C

STREET NAME	CITY or COUNTY	MAP GRID	ZIP CODE	BLOCK RANGE	O/E
COPELAND CIR	Highlands Ranch	375U	80126	4400-4899	
COPELAND ST	Highlands Ranch	375Y	80126	8800-9099	
COPELAND WAY	Longmont	42B	80501	500-599	
COPELAND LOOP	Highlands Ranch	375V	80126	4400-4699	
COPPER AVE	Broomfield	163L	80020	3300-3399	
	Broomfield	163K	80020	3500-3599	
COPPER CT	Castle Rock	527C	80104	4000-4199	
COPPER LN	Jefferson Co	306J	80439	1700-1799	
COPPER LN	Louisville	160C	80027	700-799	
COPPER ST	Boulder	97R	80304	3500-3599	
COPPER WAY	Frederick	726G	80516	None	
	Frederick	726H	80516	None	
COPPER BLUSH CT	Douglas Co	466M	80108	None	
COPPER BUCKET LN	Jefferson Co	248U	80403	20900-21399	
COPPER CLOUD DR	Castle Rock	498B	80108	None	
COPPER CREEK CIR S	Parker	408Y	80134	None	
COPPER CREEK LN E	Parker	408Y	80134	None	
COPPERDALE LN	Boulder Co	742X	80403	1-1399	
COPPERFIELD DR	Castle Rock	528A	80104	None	
COPPERLEAF BLVD	Arapahoe Co	350G	80015	None	
COPPER MOUNTAIN ST N					
	Buckley Air Force Base	289P	80011	None	
COPPER MOUNTAIN ST S					
	Buckley Air Force Base	289T	80017	None	
COPPER ROSE DR	Jefferson Co	308E	80401	1500-1599	
COPPER SPUR	Jefferson Co	844A	80433	19000-19299	
COPPER WIND CT	Douglas Co	440F	80134	7800-7999	
COQUETTE CT	Castle Rock	497C	80104	900-999	
CORA LN	Douglas Co	496J	80109	1900-1999	
CORA ST	Douglas Co	846C	80125	8100-8299	
CORAL CT	Castle Rock	497C	80104	900-999	
CORAL PL	Greenwood Village	346R	80111	1-99	
CORAL ST	Broomfield	162T	80020	300-999	
CORAL WAY	Broomfield	162X	80020	100-299	
CORALBELLS CT	Longmont	40U	80503	None	
CORALBERRY CT	Boulder Co	70Q	80503	6400-6499	
CORALBERRY CT	Douglas Co	378R	80134	8400-8499	
CORAL BURST LN	Douglas Co	409X	80134	None	
CORAL BURST ST	Douglas Co	409X	80134	None	
CORBY CT	Castle Pines North	436R	80108	200-299	
CORBY PL	Castle Pines North	436R	80108	200-299	
CORDINGLY RD	Jefferson Co	823S	80433	11000-11099	
CORDOVA CT	Boulder Co	130N	80303	100-199	
CORDOVA CT	Lafayette	131H	80026	500-599	
CORDOVA DR S	Highlands Ranch	406B	80130	9500-9699	
CORDOVA PASS CT	Brighton	140J	80601	None	
CORDRY CT	Boulder	128B	80303	2800-2899	
CORDWOOD CT	Boulder Co	99D	80301	6900-6999	
COREY ST	Longmont	11Z	80501	900-1099	
	Longmont	11V	80501	1700-1999	
	Longmont	11R	80501	2300-2499	
CORHAM ST	Frederick	727F	80530	None	
CORIANDER ST	Castle Rock	466V	80109	None	
CORING PL	Northglenn	194M	80233	1200-1599	
CORINTH CIR	Lafayette	131Q	80026	1500-1599	
CORINTH RD	Boulder Co	704N	80503	6200-6399	
CORIOLIS WAY	Frederick	726D	80504	4000-4099	
CORMORANT CIR S	Parker	408V	80134	11600-11799	
CORMORANT PL	Longmont	10M	80503	2900-2999	
CORNEL LN	Jefferson Co	307X	80439	3400-3499	
CORNELIUS ST	Jefferson Co	823N	80433	25900-26699	
CORNELIUS ST	Lafayette	132J	80026	100-298	E
CORNELL AVE E	Arapahoe Co	316S	80222	5600-5799	
	Arapahoe Co	316S	80222	6100-6499	
	Aurora	317U	80014	11900-12999	
	Aurora	318S	80014	13500-13699	
	Aurora	318U	80013	15400-15599	
	Aurora	319T	80013	18100-18599	
	Aurora	319U	80013	18800-19099	
	Aurora	319V	80013	19600-19999	
	Aurora	317T	80014	None	
	Denver	314V	80210	1600-1699	
	Denver	315S	80210	1700-2399	
	Denver	315T	80210	2700-3599	
	Denver	315U	80210	3900-3999	
	Denver	315V	80222	4000-4799	
	Denver	316T	80224	6500-7299	
	Denver	316U	80231	7300-7899	
	Denver	316Z	80231	8901-9199	O
	Denver	317S	80231	9201-10099	O
	Englewood	314U	80113	1-1599	
CORNELL AVE W	Denver	313V	80236	2400-2999	
	Denver	313W	80236	4200-5199	
	Denver	312U	80227	6600-6899	
	Englewood	314T	80110	100-599	
	Englewood	314S	80110	1900-1999	
	Englewood	313V	80110	2000-2399	
	Lakewood	312S	80227	8400-8799	
	Lakewood	310U	80228	13900-14199	
	Lakewood	310U	80228	14100-14199	
CORNELL CIR	Boulder	128S	80305	2600-2699	
CORNELL CIR E	Aurora	317U	80014	11500-11999	
	Aurora	317V	80014	12500-12599	
CORNELL CIR S	Englewood	314V	80113	3000-3099	
CORNELL CIR S	Highlands Ranch	406A	80130	9200-9399	
CORNELL CT	Highlands Ranch	376W	80130	6200-6299	
CORNELL CT E	Highlands Ranch	406A	80130	6200-6299	
CORNELL DR	Longmont	10V	80503	1-99	
	Longmont	10Z	80503	1200-1299	
CORNELL DR E	Aurora	319S	80013	17700-17999	
	Denver	316U	80231	8400-8799	
CORNELL PL E	Aurora	318V	80013	16000-16099	
	Aurora	319T	80013	18400-18499	
	Aurora	320S	80013	None	
	Englewood	314V	80113	1400-1499	
CORNELL PL W	Jefferson Co	311U	80227	10600-10699	
	Lakewood	312S	80227	8800-8999	
	Lakewood	311V	80227	9000-9999	
	Lakewood	310T	80228	14600-14699	
CORNERSTONE DR S	Douglas Co	409E	80134	16900-17399	
CORNERSTONE LN N	Douglas Co	409E	80134	16900-17599	
CORNISH CT	Denver	258N	80239	4700-4899	
CORNISH PL	Parker	409P	80134	17600-17699	
CORNISH WAY	Denver	258N	80239	4400-4699	
CORNWALL CIR	Boulder Co	100B	80301	7700-7799	
CORNWALL CT E	Lafayette	131M	80026	200-299	
CORNWALL CT W	Lafayette	131M	80026	200-299	
CORNWALL DR	Boulder Co	100B	80301	4900-4999	
CORONA AVE	Palmer Lake	907U	80133	None	
CORONA CT	Castle Rock	497C	80104	1000-1099	
CORONA CT	Douglas Co	887L	80118	7700-7799	
CORONA CT	Lafayette	131E	80026	601-699	O
CORONA CT S	Arapahoe Co	374R	80122	7900-8199	
CORONA DR	Northglenn	194R	80233	11200-11399	
CORONA ST	Adams Co	224H	80229	8400-8799	
	Denver	284R	80218	1-1499	
	Northglenn	194R	80233	10400-10799	
	Thornton	224D	80229	8000-8999	
	Thornton	194Z	80229	9000-9199	
	Thornton	164R	80241	13000-13399	
	Thornton	194V	80229	None	
CORONA ST S	Cherry Hills Village	344D	80113	3700-3899	
	Denver	284Z	80209	100-699	
	Denver	314D	80209	700-1099	
	Denver	314H	80210	1100-1399	
	Denver	314M	80210	1500-2499	
	Englewood	314Z	80110	2800-3599	
CORONA WAY S	Arapahoe Co	374R	80122	7900-8199	
CORONADO CIR	Jefferson Co	823V	80465	10000-10199	
CORONADO CT	Boulder Co	130N	80303	7300-7399	
CORONADO CT E	Douglas Co	441S	80134	9500-9699	
CORONADO DR	Douglas Co	866M	80135	200-999	
CORONADO PKWY	Adams Co	224H	80229	801N-1799N	O
	Adams Co	225J	80229	1800N-2299N	
	Adams Co	224H	80229	700S-1698S	E
	Adams Co	225J	80229	1800S-2298S	E
CORONADO PL	Longmont	12K	80501	600-699	
CORONADO PL N	Douglas Co	441S	80134	6100-6299	
CORONADO RD	Elbert Co	850R	80107	1-1499	
CORONA TRAIL	Boulder	98T	80301	3000-3199	
CORPORATE CIR	Golden	279V	80401	200-799	
CORPORATE DR	Golden	279U	80401	300-399	
CORPORATE WAY	Jefferson Co	191C	80021	11800-11999	
CORPORATE CENTER CIR	Longmont	41T	80504	2100-2299	
CORRAL LN N	Douglas Co	436D	80108	8900-9199	
	Douglas Co	406Z	80108	9200-9499	
CORRIENTE DR	Boulder Co	98K	80301	3000-3999	
CORRIENTE PL	Boulder Co	98K	80301	4100-4299	
CORRINE CT	Broomfield	163G	80020	14100-14399	
CORSAIR CIR	Elbert Co	830Q	80138	None	
CORSAIR DR	Jefferson Co	822Q	80433	9400-9899	
CORTE BELLA DR	Broomfield	133J	80020	None	
CORTEZ AVE	Golden	279U	80401	100-199	
CORTEZ CT	Broomfield	162G	80020	13900-14099	
CORTEZ LN	Boulder Co	130N	80303	7300-7399	
CORTEZ ST	Adams Co	224P	80221	1-1099	
	Adams Co	224N	80221	1200-1599	
CORTINA LN	Jefferson Co	306U	80439	2600-2899	
CORTONA CT	Longmont	40U	80503	None	
CORY ST S	Parker	439F	80134	None	
COSMOS WAY	Broomfield	133W	80026	15000-15099	
COSTILLA AVE E	Arapahoe Co	374G	80122	1-599	
	Arapahoe Co	374H	80122	600-1599	
	Arapahoe Co	832A	80137	39800-39999	
	Centennial	375B	80122	3300-3399	
	Centennial	375D	80122	4700-4899	
	Centennial	376B	80112	6200-7699	
	Centennial	376D	80112	8300-8599	
	Centennial	377E	80112	10100-10499	
	Centennial	379D	80016	20300-20499	
	Foxfield	378D	80016	16600-17099	
	Foxfield	379A	80016	17100-17199	
	Greenwood Village	377E	80112	9200-10099	
COSTILLA AVE W	Littleton	373D	80120	2200-2499	
COSTILLA BLVD E	Centennial	376C	80112	7400-8199	
COSTILLA CIR E	Centennial	376B	80112	6700-6799	
COSTILLA CT S	Littleton	373H	80120	7300-7399	
COSTILLA DR E	Aurora	380B	80016	21600-22199	
	Aurora	381C	80016	26800-27099	
	Centennial	375C	80122	4300-4599	
	Centennial	375H	80122	5200-5399	
	Centennial	376F	80112	7000-7299	
COSTILLA PL E	Aurora	381B	80016	25300-25399	
	Aurora	381C	80016	26500-26699	
	Aurora	380D	80016	None	
	Centennial	375C	80122	3600-3999	
	Centennial	375H	80122	4800-4899	
	Centennial	376A	80112	6300-6999	
	Centennial	376F	80112	7200-7299	
	Centennial	376G	80112	7400-7599	
	Centennial	376D	80112	8300-8599	
	Centennial	379C	80016	18900-19299	
COSTILLA PL W	Arapahoe Co	373E	80218	None	
	Littleton	374E	80120	1300-1599	
COSTILLA ST S	Littleton	373H	80120	7000-7399	
COSTILLA WAY E	Arapahoe Co	374H	80122	800-1099	
COSTILLO CT	Brighton	139P	80601	None	
COTONEASTER	Jefferson Co	370L	80127	1-99	
COTTONWOOD WAY	Parker	379X	80134	8500-8999	
COTTAGE LN	Boulder	97L	80304	700-799	
COTTAGE WAY	Broomfield	163E	80020	14300-14399	
COTTON CREEK DR	Westminster	193K	80031	4300-4499	
	Westminster	193J	80031	4500-4899	
	Westminster	193K	80031	10900-11199	
COTTON CREEK DR S					
	Highlands Ranch	406F	80130	9900-10199	
COTTONEASTER WAY	Douglas Co	408L	80134	10500-10699	
COTTONGRASS CT	Castle Pines North	436F	80108	8100-8299	
COTTONTAIL CT	Elbert Co	891Y	80106	22500-22699	
COTTONTAIL DR W	Lakewood	312E	80232	8300-8899	
COTTONTAIL LN	Boulder Co	741J	80466	1-199	
COTTONTAIL LN	Jefferson Co	368U	80465	8600-8699	
COTTONTAIL LN N	Douglas Co	410K	80138	11000-11599	
COTTONTAIL RD	Jefferson Co	369N	80465	20000-20099	
COTTONWOOD LN	Frederick	706Y	80504	None	
COTTONWOOD AVE	Fort Lupton	728H	80621	1000-1199	
COTTONWOOD AVE	Lafayette	131G	80026	None	
COTTONWOOD AVE E	Centennial	344Z	80121	800-999	
	Douglas Co	408B	80134	3000-3999	
COTTONWOOD CIR	Frederick	706Y	80504	3400-9499	
COTTONWOOD CIR	Golden	279F	80401	900-1099	
COTTONWOOD CIR	Greenwood Village	344R	80121	None	
	Greenwood Village	345N	80121	None	
COTTONWOOD CT	Broomfield	162V	80020	300-499	
COTTONWOOD CT	Longmont	41A	80501	300-399	
COTTONWOOD CT S					
	Greenwood Village	345N	80121	5400-5499	
COTTONWOOD DR	Adams Co	223M	80221	2400-2799	
	Adams Co	223L	80221	2800-2999	
COTTONWOOD DR	Boulder Co	99D	80301	5000-5099	
COTTONWOOD DR	Broomfield	162V	80020	700-899	
COTTONWOOD DR	Clear Creek Co	801R	80439	1-899	
COTTONWOOD DR	Louisville	131N	80027	1600-1699	
COTTONWOOD DR	Parker	379W	80134	16000-17999	
	Parker	379T	80138	18000-19399	
COTTONWOOD DR	Thornton	194S	80260	None	
COTTONWOOD LN	Denver	284J	80204	1400-1499	
COTTONWOOD LN	Douglas Co	887M	80118	800-1099	
COTTONWOOD LN	Greenwood Village	345S	80121	1-99	
	Greenwood Village	344R	80121	1500-1599	
	Littleton	373P	80120	None	
COTTONWOOD LN	Weld Co	729R	80603	3500-4099	
COTTONWOOD PL	Columbine Valley	373A	80123	4400-4499	
COTTONWOOD PL	Erie	102P	80516	2100-2299	
COTTONWOOD PL	Greenwood Village	344R	80121	None	
COTTONWOOD RD	Jefferson Co	844C	80127	12300-12799	
COTTONWOOD ST	Broomfield	162R	80020	1000-1299	
	Broomfield	162M	80020	1400-1999	
COTTONWOOD WAY	Englewood	344F	80110	1-99	
COTTONWOOD HILLS DR	Elbert Co	830R	80138	45500-45999	
COTTONWOOD LAKES BLVD	Thornton	165P	80241	3700-13499	
	Thornton	165K	80241	13500-13599	
COTTONWOOD MOUNTAIN					
	Jefferson Co	371L	80127	7500-7799	
COTTONWOOD PEAK	Jefferson Co	371L	80127	7500-7599	
COUGAR CT	Elbert Co	891Y	80106	21800-28299	
COUGAR CT	Golden	248V	80403	1500-1599	
COUGAR CT	Lafayette	131Z	80026	400-499	
COUGAR DR	Boulder Co	742R	80302	1-799	
COUGAR LN	Douglas Co	432L	80125	7900-7999	
COUGAR RD S	Jefferson Co	825N	80127	9300-9799	
COUGAR ST	Golden	279U	80401	1-99	
COUGAR CANYON S	Douglas Co	406N	80124	10700-10799	
COUGAR RIDGE S	Douglas Co	406N	80124	10700-10799	
COUGAR RUN	Boulder Co	741F	80466	1-899	
COUGAR RUN	Douglas Co	432P	80125	10700-10799	
COUGHLIN MEADOWS RD	Boulder Co	741A	80466	None	
COULSON ST	Nederland	740Q	80466	None	
COULTER PL	Douglas Co	466B	80108	1-199	
COUNCIL CROSSING DR	Douglas Co	869D	80116	9100-9199	
COUNCIL FIRE	Douglas Co	432P	80125	10700-10799	
COUNTER DR	Adams Co	196L	80640	8100-10499	
COUNTESS CT	Longmont	11U	80501	1700-1799	
COUNTRY CIR	Elbert Co	852P	80107	8300-9399	
COUNTRY CT	Fort Lupton	728Q	80621	200-299	
COUNTRY CT	Longmont	41R	80501	1300-1399	
COUNTRY DR	El Paso Co	908U	80132	600-799	
COUNTRY LN	Boulder Co	130J	80303	400-699	
COUNTRY LN	Elbert Co	851N	80107	38801-38899	O
COUNTRY LN	Longmont	41V	80501	None	
COUNTRY PL	Elbert Co	851N	80107	None	
COUNTRYBRIAR LN	Highlands Ranch	404K	80129	700-999	
COUNTRY CLUB CT	Broomfield	162P	80020	800-999	
	Westminster	193D	80234	2500-2599	
COUNTRY CLUB DR	Douglas Co	436Q	80108	100-6499	
	Douglas Co	436X	80108	800-999	
COUNTRY CLUB DR	Douglas Co	886C	80118	5200-5799	
COUNTRY CLUB DR	Jefferson Co	822Y	80433	12000-12099	
COUNTRY CLUB DR	Westminster	193D	80234	11600-11699	
COUNTRY CLUB LN	Douglas Co	466D	80108	600-699	
COUNTRY CLUB LN	Westminster	193D	80234	11600-11699	
COUNTRY CLUB LOOP	Westminster	193D	80234	2200-2599	
	Douglas Co	466B	80108	200-3399	
COUNTRY CLUB PKWY S	Aurora	381L	80016	7500-8299	
COUNTRY CLUB WAY	Boulder Co	99D	80301	4800-4999	
COUNTRY CLUB ESTATES DR					
	Douglas Co	436T	80108	1000-1099	
COUNTRY CREEK	Boulder Co	70K	80503	7700-7899	
COUNTRY HILLS DR	Adams Co	168F	80601	14000-14599	
COUNTRY MEADOWS DR	Parker	409Y	80134	12300-12699	
COUNTRY ROSE CIR	Elbert Co	851E	80138	41300-41499	
COUNTRYSIDE CIR	Elbert Co	851F	80138	41400-41499	
COUNTRY SIDE DR	Boulder Co	70K	80503	7900-7999	
COUNTRYSIDE DR	Westminster	191Q	80021	10000-10799	
	Westminster	191K	80021	10800-11699	
COUNTRYSIDE LN	Cherry Hills Village	345M	80121	1-99	
COUNTY RD	Central City	780C	80427	1-99	
COUNTY RD	Louisville	131S	80027	100-599	
COUNTY CREEK RD	Jefferson Co	369P	80465	8200-8299	
COUNTY LINE PL E	Highlands Ranch	376N	80126	5600-5899	
COUNTY LINE RD	Douglas Co	908K	80118	4801-4899	O
	Douglas Co	909J	80132	5500-8299	
COUNTY LINE RD E	Arapahoe Co	378N	80112	13100-13899	
	Arapahoe Co	831H	80137	48900-50999	
	Arapahoe Co	832G	80137	51000-53699	
	Arapahoe Co	830H	80138	None	
	Aurora	381R	80138	26501-27899	O
COUNTY LINE RD E	Boulder Co	72M	80504	5301-8099	O
	Boulder Co	42Z	80504	8101-8699	O
	Boulder Co	42H	80501	9001-10199	O
	Boulder Co	12Z	80501	10201-12599	O
	Boulder Co	12M	80504	12601-13999	O
COUNTY LINE RD E	Centennial	375P	80122	1601-5599	O
	Centennial	376N	80112	5600-9399	
	Centennial	377N	80112	9401-9799	O
	Douglas Co	374P	80122	2-1598	E
	Douglas Co	830H	80138	27901-28099	O
	Douglas Co	381R	80138	None	
COUNTY LINE RD E	Elbert Co	830H	80138	None	
COUNTY LINE RD E	Erie	132H	80516	300-999	
	Erie	102V	80516	1600-5299	
COUNTY LINE RD E	Highlands Ranch	375P	80126	1600-5598	E
	Littleton	374Q	80122	1-1599	O
COUNTY LINE RD E	Weld Co	72M	80516	None	
COUNTY LINE RD W	Highlands Ranch	373U	80120	3100-3699	
	Littleton	374P	80120	1-3099	
	Littleton	373U	80120	None	
COUNTY VIEW WAY	Castle Rock	528A	80104	4000-4199	
COURT 5	Weld Co	140F	80603	None	
COURT PL	Brighton	138P	80601	400-499	
COURT PL	Denver	284F	80204	1300-1399	
	Denver	284F	80202	1400-1699	
	Denver	284C	80205	2200-2499	
COURT PL S	Littleton	343V	80120	5600-5699	
COURTESY RD	Louisville	131P	80027	400-1699	

STREET NAME	CITY or COUNTY	MAP GRID	ZIP CODE	BLOCK RANGE	O/E
COURT FOURTEEN	Lochbuie	139D	80603	None	
COURTLAND PL E	Highlands Ranch	404H	80126	800-999	
COURTNEY AVE E	Castle Rock	498H	80104	5300-5599	
COURTNEY WAY	Lafayette	132N	80026	300-599	
COURT RIGHT RD	Jefferson Co	843W	80470	27400-27799	
COURT TEN	Lochbuie	139D	80603	None	
COURT TWELVE	Lochbuie	139D	80603	None	
COVE CIR S	Centennial	375K	80122	7500-7799	
COVE CT	Lone Tree	406M	80124	8500-8599	
COVE CT	Longmont	10V	80503	1700-1799	
COVE LN	Littleton	343S	80123	1-99	
COVE WAY S	Denver	315B	80209	700-1099	
COVE CREEK CT W	Highlands Ranch	403D	80129	2400-2699	
COVE CREEK DR S	Highlands Ranch	403D	80129	9300-9799	
COVENANT LN	Greenwood Village	346R	80111	5300-5399	
COVENTRY CT	Boulder Co	99D	80301	5000-5099	
COVENTRY DR	Douglas Co	436M	80108	7600-8099	
COVENTRY LN	Louisville	160C	80027	500-699	
COVENTRY LN S	Littleton	343W	80123	5900E-6399E	
	Littleton	343W	80123	5900W-6499W	
COVENTRY PL W	Littleton	343W	80123	5000-5099	
COVEY CT	Northglenn	194T	80260	9600-9799	
COVINGTON CT	Cherry Hills Village	345C	80113	1-99	
COVINGTON DR	Cherry Hills Village	345C	80113	1-99	
COVY CT	Castle Rock	497D	80104	1700-1899	
COWAN RD	Park Co	820Z	80421	1-399	
COWLEY DR	Lafayette	131B	80026	2500-2599	
COYOTE CIR	Gilpin Co	760V	80403	1-2999	
COYOTE CIR	Thornton	195Q	80229	None	
COYOTE CT	Golden	248Z	80403	1500-1599	
COYOTE DR	Castle Pines North	436G	80108	8300-8499	
COYOTE DR	Elbert Co	850Y	80107	700-799	
COYOTE DR	Frederick	707W	80504	5300-5399	
COYOTE LN	Jefferson Co	370B	80127	1-99	
COYOTE PL	Douglas Co	432L	80125	7600-7699	
COYOTE ST	Adams Co	792M	80102	None	
COYOTE ST S	Highlands Ranch	374Y	80126	8900-8999	
COYOTE CANYON WAY	Jefferson Co	340N	80465	5400-5499	
COYOTE CREEK DR	Fort Lupton	729J	80621	None	
COYOTE CROSSING	Castle Pines North	436K	80108	6600-6699	
COYOTE HILLS CT	Castle Rock	466X	80109	3200-3299	
COYOTE HILLS WAY	Castle Rock	466W	80109	3200-3599	
COYOTE RUN	Douglas Co	845R	80125	4500-4699	
COYOTE SONG TRAIL	Jefferson Co	842D	80433	12300-13499	
COYOTE SPUR	Jefferson Co	275F	80403	2000-2199	
COYOTE TRAIL	Boulder Co	40E	80503	None	
COYOTE TRAIL	Elbert Co	850Q	80107	600-799	
CRABAPPLE CT	Jefferson Co	280C	80401	2600-2799	
CRABAPPLE LN	Douglas Co	850X	80116	11700-12099	
CRABAPPLE PL	Jefferson Co	280C	80401	14000-14099	
CRABAPPLE RD	Jefferson Co	280C	80401	2700-2799	
	Jefferson Co	250Y	80401	2800-3199	
	Jefferson Co	280C	80401	14000-14799	
CRABAPPLE ST	Broomfield	163X	80020	12100-12299	
CRABTREE DR	Centennial	345W	80121	2200-2399	
	Greenwood Village	345W	80121	2000-2199	
CRAFT WAY	Westminster	223U	80030	3000-3199	
CRAFTSBURY DR	Highlands Ranch	405Q	80126	3400-3699	
CRAFTSMAN DR	Douglas Co	469B	80134	4800-5499	
CRAFTSMAN WAY	Broomfield	163E	80020	14200-14399	
CRAG RD	Jefferson Co	823R	80465	9600-10099	
CRAGMONT DR	Jefferson Co	366C	80439	27800-28999	
CRAGMOOR RD	Boulder	128W	80305	2300-2599	
CRAGMORE ST	Adams Co	224P	80221	1-1099	
CRAIG CT	Castle Rock	466W	80109	2800-3199	
CRAIG LN	Jefferson Co	277W	80401	26400-27599	
CRAIG WAY	Broomfield	162L	80020	13900-13999	
CRAINSBILL ST E	Parker	409A	80134	17200-17399	
CRAMNER CT	Jefferson Co	306P	80439	2000-2199	
CRANBERRY CIR E	Parker	409B	80134	17600-17899	
CRANBERRY CT	Boulder Co	70Q	80503	6400-6499	
	Longmont	40Q	80503	900-999	
CRANBROOK CT	Boulder	128S	80305	1100-1199	
CRANE CT	Frederick	727A	80504	4800-4898	E
CRANE DR	Brighton	139R	80601	5000-5199	
CRANE ST	Brighton	139R	80601	400-499	
CRANE ST	Fort Lupton	728L	80621	None	
CRANE HOLLOW DR	Boulder Co	704K	80503	11100-11799	
CRANNELL DR	Boulder Co	130N	80303	7200-7599	
CRANSTON CIR	Highlands Ranch	405B	80126	3300-3499	
CRAWFORD AVE	Keenesburg	732A	80643	None	
CRAWFORD CIR	Golden	279T	80401	100-299	
CRAWFORD CIR	Longmont	42C	80501	600-699	
CRAWFORD CT	Golden	279T	80401	200-399	
CRAWFORD DR	Golden	279T	80401	200-499	
CRAWFORD ST	Golden	279P	80401	300-599	
CRAWFORD GULCH RD	Gilpin Co	761V	80403	1-7199	
CRAWFORD GULCH RD	Jefferson Co	783A	80403	4500-6299	
CRAZY HORSE CT S	Parker	439G	80134	12800-12899	
CRAZY HORSE TRAIL	Jefferson Co	823X	80433	11700-11899	
CREDIGHTON DR	Jefferson Co	280C	80401	2000-2599	
CREE CIR	Boulder	129J	80303	600-699	
CREE DR	Jefferson Co	366A	80439	31100-31299	
CREEDMOOR CT	Douglas Co	867Q	80109	1600-1799	
CREEK CT	Jefferson Co	307X	80439	26100-26299	
CREEK CT	Longmont	40R	80503	1000-1099	
CREEK DR	Broomfield	163K	80020	3900-4299	
CREEK WAY	Douglas Co	469C	80134	5100-5399	
CREEKBEND DR	Jefferson Co	369N	80465	19200-19299	
CREEK HOLLOW RD	Boulder Co	100P	80301	8200-8299	
CREEKSIDE CT	Broomfield	163L	80020	2600-2699	
CREEKSIDE CT	Broomfield	163G	80020	None	
CREEKSIDE CT	Golden	248V	80403	500-599	
CREEKSIDE CT S	Parker	439G	80134	12600-12699	
CREEKSIDE DR	Broomfield	163L	80020	2400-2699	
CREEKSIDE DR	Longmont	41T	80504	1900-2399	
CREEKSIDE DR E	Parker	439G	80134	18900-19699	
CREEKSIDE LN	Highlands Ranch	373Z	80129	None	
CREEKSIDE LN	Jefferson Co	336R	80439	27900-27999	
CREEKSIDE PL E	Parker	439G	80134	18900-18999	
CREEKSIDE PT	Highlands Ranch	373Z	80129	2100-2299	
CREEKSIDE RD	Jefferson Co	366B	80439	6400-6499	
CREEKSIDE WAY	Highlands Ranch	373Z	80129	8700-9099	
CREEKTOP AVE	Douglas Co	409H	80138	None	
CREEK TRAIL	Clear Creek Co	365N	80439	1-99	
CREEK TRAIL	Jefferson Co	368V	80465	8600-8799	
CREEK VIEW DR	Douglas Co	408M	80134	16200-16499	
CREEKWOOD TRAIL	Gilpin Co	761B	80403	1-599	
CREG RD	Boulder Co	40M	80503	8700-8899	
CREIGHTON DR	Jefferson Co	280C	80401	2000-2599	
CREMELLO CT	Castle Rock	467Y	80104	3300-3399	
CRENSHAW ST	Castle Rock	499N	80104	800-1299	
CRESCENT	Palmer Lake	907Q	80133	None	
CRESCENT CT S	Littleton	373H	80120	7400-7499	
CRESCENT DR	Boulder	128H	80303	700-999	
CRESCENT DR	Lafayette	132W	80026	2600-2699	
CRESCENT DR	Westminster	223F	80031	8500-8799	
CRESCENT DR S	Littleton	373H	80120	7200-7399	
CRESCENT LN	Lakewood	282P	80214	600-899	
CRESCENT PKWY E	Greenwood Village	346Q	80111	8300-8499	
CRESCENT ST	Lochbuie	729Y	80603	None	
CRESCENT LAKE RD	Boulder Co	742X	80403	1-999	
CRESCENT MEADOW AVE	Douglas Co	407G	80134	11800-11899	
CRESCENT MEADOW BLVD	Douglas Co	407G	80134	10100-10299	
CRESCENT MEADOW LOOP	Douglas Co	407G	80134	None	
CRESCENT MOON PL	Douglas Co	468D	80134	4800-4999	
CRESCENT PARK CIR	Jefferson Co	762C	80403	11600-11798	E
CRESCENT PARK DR	Jefferson Co	762C	80403	11600-11999	
CRESS CT	Boulder	97R	80304	1500-1599	
CRESSIDA CT	Lafayette	131Q	80026	1200-1299	
CRESSMAN CT	Golden	248V	80403	600-799	
CREST CIR	Park Co	841S	80421	1-199	
CREST DR	Lakewood	282B	80214	2200-7999	
CREST RD	Cherry Hills Village	345D	80113	1-99	
CRESTBROOK CIR	Jefferson Co	340T	80465	5700-5899	
CRESTBROOK DR	Jefferson Co	340T	80465	5500-6699	
CRESTED BUTTE AVE E	Buckley Air Force Base	289T	80017	None	
CRESTED BUTTE CT	Jefferson Co	306E	80439	1300-1399	
CRESTHILL AVE E	Centennial	345W	80121	2400-3099	
CRESTHILL DR	Boulder Co	71F	80504	7400-7999	
CRESTHILL LN	Boulder Co	71F	80504	None	
CRESTHILL LN	Highlands Ranch	405H	80130	9200-9899	
	Highlands Ranch	375Z	80126	None	
CRESTHILL PL	Highlands Ranch	375Z	80126	None	
CRESTLINE AVE E	Arapahoe Co	347P	80111	10600-10999	
	Arapahoe Co	350Q	80015	22600-22699	
	Centennial	348R	80015	15300-16899	
	Centennial	349N	80015	16900-17699	
	Greenwood Village	346N	80111	5600-6398	E
	Greenwood Village	346P	80111	6800-7299	
	Greenwood Village	346R	80111	8900-9299	
	Greenwood Village	347N	80111	9700-10099	
CRESTLINE AVE W	Denver	342V	80123	5800-5999	
	Denver	342Q	80123	6200-6799	
	Denver	342N	80123	8100-8599	
	Jefferson Co	341N	80127	12400-12799	
	Littleton	344P	80120	400-899	
	Littleton	344N	80120	1200-1999	
	Littleton	343R	80120	2000-2599	
CRESTLINE CIR E	Arapahoe Co	347P	80111	10600-11099	
	Arapahoe Co	350R	80016	23300-24099	
	Centennial	349P	80015	18100-18499	
	Centennial	349R	80015	19400-20199	
	Centennial	350N	80015	20900-21199	
	Greenwood Village	346P	80111	5100-5199	
	Greenwood Village	347N	80111	9700-9899	
CRESTLINE CIR W	Littleton	344P	80120	500-599	
CRESTLINE DR E	Centennial	350P	80015	21400-21699	
CRESTLINE DR E	Centennial	348P	80015	None	
CRESTLINE DR W	Jefferson Co	341V	80123	8800-8899	
	Jefferson Co	341R	80123	9500-9599	
	Jefferson Co	341P	80127	10900-11799	
	Jefferson Co	341N	80127	12100-12699	
	Jefferson Co	340R	80127	13100-13199	
	Littleton	344N	80120	1600-1899	
CRESTLINE LN E	Arapahoe Co	350P	80015	21900-21999	
	Centennial	348R	80015	16100-16299	
	Centennial	349N	80015	16700-16899	
	Centennial	350P	80015	21400-21699	
CRESTLINE PL E	Arapahoe Co	347P	80111	10400-10499	
	Arapahoe Co	347P	80111	10700-10999	
	Arapahoe Co	350P	80015	21900-21999	
	Aurora	351N	80016	24600-24799	
	Aurora	348Q	80015	None	
	Centennial	348Q	80015	15400-15499	
	Centennial	348R	80015	16100-16899	
	Centennial	349N	80015	16900-17199	
	Centennial	349P	80015	17700-17899	
	Centennial	349Q	80015	18800-18899	
	Centennial	349R	80015	19900-19999	
	Centennial	350N	80015	20300-20499	
	Centennial	350N	80015	20900-21099	
CRESTLINE PL W	Jefferson Co	341P	80127	11200-11399	
	Littleton	344P	80120	800-899	
CRESTMONT LN E	Highlands Ranch	405E	80126	2300-2399	
CRESTMOOR DR	Boulder Co	129G	80303	900-1299	
CRESTMOOR DR	Denver	286N	80220	1-99	
CRESTMOOR RD	Jefferson Co	278U	80401	21800-22199	
CRESTMORE WAY S	Highlands Ranch	404D	80126	9200-9499	
CRESTONE AVE	Castle Rock	498L	80104	5000-5299	
CRESTONE CIR	Boulder Co	69Z	80301	5400-5599	
CRESTONE CIR	Broomfield	163E	80020	4300-14099	
CRESTONE CT	Longmont	12N	80501	1800-1899	
CRESTONE DR	Longmont	12S	80501	1700-1799	
CRESTONE RD	Thornton	194S	80260	None	
CRESTONE ST	Jefferson Co	249B	80403	5800-6299	
CRESTONE WAY	Douglas Co	466C	80108	1-99	
CRESTONE MOUNTAIN	Jefferson Co	371L	80127	10200-10499	
CRESTONE NEEDLES CIR	Parker	410K	80138	10400-10499	
CRESTONE NEEDLES DR	Parker	410J	80138	10700-21699	
CRESTONE PEAK LN	Parker	410P	80138	10400-10599	
CRESTONE PEAK ST	Brighton	139Q	80601	None	
CREST PARK RD	Lakewood	281X	80226	10600-10999	
CRESTRIDGE AVE E	Centennial	349N	80015	17300-17699	
CRESTRIDGE CIR E	Arapahoe Co	347P	80111	10700-11099	
	Arapahoe Co	349U	80015	18700-19199	
	Centennial	348Q	80015	15700-15999	
	Centennial	349Q	80015	19400-19599	
CRESTRIDGE CT	Boulder Co	703W	80302	2500-2799	
CRESTRIDGE DR	Castle Rock	498E	80104	2300-2599	
CRESTRIDGE DR	Greenwood Village	344V	80121	1100-2299	
CRESTRIDGE DR E	Arapahoe Co	349Q	80015	18500-18799	
	Aurora	348P	80015	None	
	Centennial	349P	80015	18000-18499	
CRESTRIDGE LN	Longmont	41B	80501	300-399	
CRESTRIDGE LN E	Arapahoe Co	347P	80111	10100-10399	
CRESTRIDGE PL E	Aurora	351N	80016	24500-24799	
	Aurora	348Q	80015	None	
	Centennial	348R	80015	15900-15999	
	Centennial	349P	80015	17700-17799	
	Centennial	350P	80015	21400-21699	
CREST ROCK CIR	Douglas Co	408M	80134	10600-15899	
CREST ROCK CT	Douglas Co	408M	80134	16100-16199	
CREST STONE PEAK	Jefferson Co	371L	80127	7700-7799	
CRESTVIEW CT	Douglas Co	886C	80118	6400-6499	
CRESTVIEW CT	Louisville	130Y	80027	100-199	
CRESTVIEW DR	Boulder Co	71F	80504	7500-7799	
CRESTVIEW DR	Douglas Co	440H	80138	8000-8999	
CREST VIEW DR	Gilpin Co	760U	80403	1-499	
CREST VIEW DR	Jefferson Co	823R	80465	10000-10299	
CRESTVIEW DR	Monument	908W	80132	None	
CRESTVIEW LN	Adams Co	223L	80221	7800-7999	
CRESTVIEW LN	Boulder Co	71B	80504	7500-7799	
CRESTVIEW LN	Erie	133C	80516	1600-1899	
CRESTVIEW LN	Park Co	841P	80421	1-199	
CRESTVIEW ST S	Littleton	344X	80120	5900-6199	
CRESTVIEW WAY W	Littleton	344X	80120	6000-6099	
CRESTVUE CIR	Golden	278H	80401	2000-2099	
CRESTVUE DR	Jefferson Co	278T	80401	22100-22199	
CRESTWOOD CIR	Longmont	12U	80501	1400-1599	
CRESTWOOD CT	Boulder Co	740Q	80466	100-299	
CRESTWOOD CT	Parker	409M	80138	19600-19799	
CRESTWOOD DR	El Paso Co	908S	80132	2600-2799	
CRETE CT	Lafayette	131R	80026	1400-1499	
CRICKET CIR	Elbert Co	850H	80138	40500-40999	
CRIMSON CT	Douglas Co	408M	80134	10300-10399	
CRIMSON CLOVER LN	Boulder Co	40S	80503	8600-8999	
CRIMSON SKY DR	Castle Rock	468X	80108	None	
CRIMSON STAR DR	Broomfield	163A	80020	4900-4999	
CRIPPLE CREEK	Boulder	128X	80305	3400-3499	
CRIPPLE CREEK TRAIL	Boulder	128X	80305	3100-3399	
CRISMAN DR	Longmont	11M	80501	800-899	
CRITCHELL LN	Jefferson Co	844B	80127	12100-12599	
CROCKER CT S	Littleton	374J	80120	7500-7699	
CROCKER ST S	Littleton	344N	80120	5200-5399	
	Littleton	344W	80120	6200-6499	
CROCKER WAY S	Littleton	344N	80120	5200-5299	
	Littleton	374A	80120	6600-6799	
CROCKETT TRAIL	Boulder Co	721C	80481	1-199	
CROCUS WAY	Douglas Co	470A	80134	5200-5299	
CROFT CT	Castle Pines North	436R	80108	1-199	
CROKE DR	Northglenn	194N	80260	10000-10399	
	Thornton	194S	80260	1200-9999	
CROMWELL LN	Highlands Ranch	375Y	80126	9100-9199	
CROOKE DR	Parker	408R	80134	10800-10899	
CROOKED OAK CT	Douglas Co	440W	80134	7500-7599	
CROOKED PINE CIR E	Parker	409Z	80134	None	
CROOKED PINE TRAIL	Jefferson Co	275T	80439	300-599	
CROOKED STICK CT	Lone Tree	406H	80124	8700-8799	
CROOKED STICK PL	Lone Tree	406H	80124	8600-8799	
CROOKED STICK TRAIL	Lone Tree	406M	80124	10200-10299	
CROOKED TREE LN	El Paso Co	908P	80132	800-899	
CROOKED TREE PL	Douglas Co	887D	80118	900-999	
CROOKED TREE RANCH CIR	Elbert Co	850G	80138	None	
CROSBY DR	Broomfield	133K	80020	None	
CROSBY DR	Lone Tree	406C	80124	7600-7799	
CROSS AVE W	Jefferson Co	341S	80127	11600-12699	
	Jefferson Co	340V	80127	12700-13199	
CROSS DR W	Jefferson Co	342S	80123	8400-9199	
	Jefferson Co	341V	80123	9200-9399	
	Jefferson Co	341S	80127	11700-12399	
	Jefferson Co	340V	80127	12700-13099	
	Lakewood	342U	80123	6100-6399	
CROSS LN W	Jefferson Co	340V	80127	13100-13199	
CROSS PL W	Jefferson Co	341V	80123	8800-9999	
	Jefferson Co	340V	80127	13100-13199	
	Lakewood	342V	80123	6100-6299	
CROSSBILL AVE	Brighton	139R	80601	None	
CROSS COUNTRY LN	Douglas Co	432F	80125	10500-10699	
CROSS CREEK CT	Lafayette	131A	80026	1400-1599	
CROSS CREEK DR	Lafayette	131A	80026	1400-1499	
CROSS CREEK LN	Parker	410S	80138	11500-11699	
CROSSCUT E	Park Co	820Y	80421	1-199	
CROSSCUT W	Park Co	820Y	80421	1-99	
CROSSHAVEN CT	Castle Rock	497X	80104	3600-3699	
CROSSHAVEN PL	Castle Rock	497X	80104	1-499	
CROSSING CIR	Castle Pines North	436C	80108	300-599	
CROSSING DR	Lafayette	131H	80026	301-599	O
CROSSINGTON WAY	Lone Tree	406M	80124	None	
CROSSLAND WAY S	Highlands Ranch	406A	80130	9400-9499	
CROSSPOINTE DR S	Highlands Ranch	406A	80130	9300-9799	
CROSSPOINTE LN	Highlands Ranch	406A	80130	None	
CROSSROADS DR S	Parker	409Q	80134	10800-10899	
CROSSROADS LN	Jefferson Co	306C	80401	29000-29099	
CROW CT	Douglas Co	887J	80118	8400-8499	
CROW DR	Douglas Co	886M	80118	4800-5099	
CROW PL	Douglas Co	886M	80118	8400-8499	
CROWBERRY LN S	Parker	409A	80134	9400-9499	
CROWFOOT LN	Jefferson Co	365N	80439	8100-8299	
CROWFOOT SPRINGS RD	Douglas Co	910A	80118	12400-13199	
CROWFOOT VALLEY RD	Castle Rock	467R	80108	3000-3499	
	Castle Rock	467U	80104	None	
CROWFOOT VALLEY RD	Douglas Co	439N	80108	3000-3499	
	Douglas Co	468J	80108	3500-5399	
	Douglas Co	439N	80134	5400-7199	
CROWFOOT VALLEY RD	Douglas Co	848M	80108	None	
	Parker	439N	80134	7200-7999	
CROW HILL DR	Parker	409Z	80134	11500-11899	
CROWN BLVD	Denver	257R	80239	4200-4599	
	Denver	258J	80239	4600-5599	
CROWN CIR	Brighton	138N	80601	400-499	
CROWN CIR	Louisville	131N	80027	2200-2299	
CROWN CREST BLVD	Parker	379Y	80138	9100-9399	
CROWN POINT CT	Boulder Co	740G	80466	None	
CROWN POINT DR	Westminster	223G	80031	8201-8299	O
CROWN POINT PL	Douglas Co	466B	80108	1-99	
CROW RIDGE RD	Clear Creek Co	304G	80439	1-199	
CROWSLEY CT	Douglas Co	408D	80134	9600-9799	
CROWS NEST WAY	El Paso Co	908Q	80132	19500-19599	

C
D

STREET NAME	CITY or COUNTY	MAP GRID	ZIP CODE	BLOCK RANGE	O/E
CROW VALLEY RD	Park Co	841N	80421	100-1899	
CRYOLITE PL	Castle Rock	467G	80108	900-1099	
CRYSTAL CIR	Commerce City	198P	80022	10000-10099	
CRYSTAL CIR S	Aurora	348B	80014	4000-4099	
CRYSTAL CT	Aurora	348F	80014	4100-4299	
CRYSTAL CT	Boulder	98J	80304	4000-4099	
	Boulder Co	100E	80301	None	
CRYSTAL CT	Lafayette	113L	80026	700-799	
CRYSTAL CT S	Aurora	348P	80015	5000-5099	
CRYSTAL DR	Broomfield	133N	80020	4200-4599	
CRYSTAL DR	Jefferson Co	823V	80433	10100-10699	
CRYSTAL PL	Longmont	12X	80501	400-499	
CRYSTAL ST	Adams Co	168K	80601	13400-13599	
	Aurora	288F	80011	1800-1999	
	Aurora	288T	80012	None	
	Commerce City	198P	80022	10000-10099	
	Denver	258N	80239	4400-4899	
	Denver	258K	80239	5100-5499	
CRYSTAL ST S	Aurora	318P	80014	2500-2699	
	Aurora	348K	80015	4800-4999	
CRYSTAL WAY	Denver	258K	80239	5000-5099	
	Denver	258F	80239	5500-5599	
	Douglas Co	870K	80116	1500-1699	
	Jefferson Co	823V	80433	10600-10799	
CRYSTAL WAY S	Aurora	318B	80012	900-999	
	Aurora	318F	80012	1200-1399	
	Aurora	318F	80012	1500-1599	
	Aurora	348K	80015	4500-4699	
CRYSTAL LAKE CT	Douglas Co	432L	80125	7500-7799	
CRYSTAL LAKE DR N	Douglas Co	432L	80125	9600-9899	
CRYSTAL LAKE DR S	Douglas Co	432L	80125	9600-9899	
CRYSTAL LAKE RD	Jefferson Co	842Z	80470	29200-30499	
CRYSTALLO CT	Douglas Co	408G	80134	9800-9899	
CRYSTALLO DR	Douglas Co	408G	80134	15500-15799	
CRYSTAL PEAK	Jefferson Co	371K	80127	7700-7799	
CRYSTAL PEAK W	Highlands Ranch	403M	80129	10300-10399	
CRYSTAL PEAK DR	Elbert Co	831N	80138	3100-3599	
CRYSTAL PEAK WAY S	Highlands Ranch	403M	80129	1900-2099	
CRYSTAL RIDGE RD	Jefferson Co	842Z	80421	None	
CRYSTAL ROCK DR	Park Co	820U	80421	1-299	
CRYSTAL VALLEY PKWY	Castle Rock	527C	80104	1100-1199	
CRYSTAL VIEW DR	Jefferson Co	823V	80465	10000-10099	
CRYSTAL VIEW LN	Boulder Co	72T	80504	11700-11799	
CTC BLVD	Louisville	131Y	80027	100-399	
	Louisville	161C	80027	None	
CUBMONT DR S	Jefferson Co	336R	80439	5200-5399	
CUBS DEN DR	Jefferson Co	824R	80127	9400-9499	
CUB TRAIL	Clear Creek Co	365J	80439	1-99	
CUB CREEK TRAIL	Jefferson Co	365S	80433	8200-8699	
CUCHARA AVE	Palmer Lake	907Q	80133	None	
CUCHARA ST	Adams Co	224P	80221	200-1099	
CUCUMBER CT	Gilpin Co	760T	80403	1-99	
CULEBRA	Thornton	193V	80260	None	
CULEBRA CT	Boulder Co	98K	80301	4100-4199	
CULEBRA CT	Jefferson Co	249B	80403	5900-5999	
	Jefferson Co	249E	80403	None	
CULEBRA WAY	Broomfield	133J	80020	None	
CULEBRA PEAK	Jefferson Co	371Q	80127	8000-8099	
CULEBRA RANGE RD	Jefferson Co	371Q	80127	10400-10899	
CULP PL E	Aurora	318V	80013	None	
CULPEPPER CIR	Parker	439C	80134	19500-19699	
CULTIVATOR LN	Platteville	708B	80651	600-699	
CULVER CT	Boulder	128B	80303	1500-1599	
CUMBERLAND CT	Elbert Co	832X	80107	8200-8299	
CUMBERLAND DR	Longmont	12Y	80501	1200-1399	
CUMBERLAND RD	Douglas Co	887M	80118	500-799	
CUMBERLAND GAP RD	Boulder Co	741R	80466	1-299	
CUMBRES CT	El Paso Co	912Y	80831	18200-18299	
CUMBRES RD	El Paso Co	912Y	80831	17800-18499	
CUMMINGS DR	Erie	131D	80026	None	
CUPRITE CT	Castle Rock	467M	80108	1700-1899	
CURIE CT	Boulder	98U	80301	4800-4899	
CURLEY PEAK WAY	Douglas Co	432Q	80125	None	
CURLYCUP PL	Parker	378V	80134	8300-8499	
CURRANT DR	Jefferson Co	308E	80401	23400-24499	
CURRANT WAY	Parker	378R	80134	8300-8399	
CURTICE CIR S	Littleton	373M	80120	7700-7799	
CURTICE CT S	Littleton	373M	80120	7400-7499	
CURTICE DR S	Littleton	373M	80120	7700-7799	
CURTICE ST S	Littleton	343V	80120	5400-5899	
	Littleton	373H	80120	6900-7199	
	Littleton	373M	80120	7600-7899	
CURTICE WAY S	Littleton	373M	80120	7700-7799	
CURTIS CT	Broomfield	162L	80020	1-99	
CURTIS PL	Castle Rock	497M	80104	1-99	
CURTIS PL	Longmont	41A	80501	1-99	
CURTIS RD	Larkspur	887R	80118	9000-9399	
CURTIS ST	Denver	284E	80204	600-1399	
	Denver	284F	80202	1400-1999	
	Denver	284C	80205	2000-2599	
	Denver	254Y	80205	2600-3399	
CURTIS CROSSING	Castle Rock	467Q	80108	None	
CUSHMAN AVE	Arapahoe Co	795T	80103	1-299	
CUSHMAN CT	Longmont	11U	80501	1500-1599	
CUSTER AVE E	Parker	439G	80134	19100-19199	
CUSTER DR E	Aurora	288Y	80017	15700-15899	
CUSTER LN	Jefferson Co	366V	80439	8300-8599	
CUSTER PL E	Aurora	287Y	80012	11200-11599	
	Aurora	288Y	80017	15600-15699	
	Denver	286W	80246	5300-5599	
	Glendale	285Z	80246	None	
CUSTER PL W	Denver	284W	80223	1100-1399	
	Denver	283Z	80223	2000-2299	
	Denver	283Y	80219	3000-3899	
	Denver	283W	80219	4100-5199	
	Lakewood	282W	80226	8800-8899	
CUSTER ST	Bennett	793J	80102	None	
CUTFORTH RD	Gilpin Co	761C	80403	1-299	
CUTLER FARMS AVE	Commerce City	169X	80603	None	
CUTLER FARMS PKWY	Commerce City	169X	80603	None	
CUTTER LN	Boulder Co	722M	80302	1-1599	
CUTTERS CIR	Castle Rock	468J	80108	2300-2699	
C W BIXLER BLVD	Erie	102D	80516	None	
CYAN CIR	Castle Rock	466U	80109	None	
CYD DR	Adams Co	224J	80221	7800-7999	
CYPRESS	Platteville	708B	80651	None	
CYPRESS CIR	Broomfield	192C	80020	200-299	
CYPRESS CIR	Lafayette	131Q	80026	1400-1499	
CYPRESS CIR	Thornton	194S	80260	None	
CYPRESS DR	Boulder	128H	80303	700-5499	
CYPRESS DR	Jefferson Co	823R	80465	19500-20799	
CYPRESS DR	Thornton	225C	80229	8900-8999	
	Thornton	195X	80229	9000-9299	
CYPRESS LN	Broomfield	192C	80020	200-299	
CYPRESS LN	Louisville	130X	80027	900-999	
CYPRESS PT	El Paso Co	908T	80132	18900-18999	
CYPRESS ST	Broomfield	192C	80020	300-499	
CYPRESS ST	Longmont	11N	80503	2100-2199	
CYPRESS ST S	Jefferson Co	842E	80470	13700-13899	
CYPRESS WAY	Douglas Co	436T	80108	1000-1099	
CYPRESS POINT CIR	Lone Tree	406G	80124	9700-9899	
CYPRESS POINT WAY	Columbine Valley	373B	80123	1-99	
CYPRUS LN	Jefferson Co	306T	80439	2600-2699	
CYR ST	Jefferson Co	762B	80403	None	

D

STREET NAME	CITY or COUNTY	MAP GRID	ZIP CODE	BLOCK RANGE	O/E
D	Aurora	288F	80011	None	
D ST	Golden	279P	80401	400-1499	
	Jefferson Co	279R	80401	None	
D ST	Longmont	11U	80501	None	
DACOTAH CT	Hudson	730M	80642	23100-23199	
DACRE PL	Lone Tree	406L	80124	10500-10699	
DAD CLARK DR	Highlands Ranch	375S	80126	1700-2199	
DAD CLARK DR E	Highlands Ranch	374U	80126	300-1699	
DAGNY WAY	Lafayette	131A	80026	None	
DAHLBERG RD	Douglas Co	889L	80116	6200-12999	
	Douglas Co	889Y	80118	None	
DAHLIA AVE	Boulder	128K	80305	2800-2999	
DAHLIA AVE	Dacono	727F	80514	700-799	
DAHLIA CIR S	Centennial	375D	80121	6500-6699	
DAHLIA CT	Thornton	195H	80229	11000-11099	
	Thornton	165Z	80241	12100-12299	
DAHLIA CT S	Centennial	375D	80122	6700-6799	
	Centennial	375H	80122	7100-7199	
	Centennial	375M	80122	7400-7499	
DAHLIA CT W	Louisville	130Y	80027	800-899	
DAHLIA DR	Lochbuie	729Y	80603	None	
DAHLIA DR	Louisville	131W	80027	100-299	
DAHLIA DR	Thornton	195H	80229	11000-11199	
	Thornton	195D	80233	11800-11999	
	Thornton	165Z	80241	12000-12299	
DAHLIA LN	Thornton	195U	80229	None	
DAHLIA LN S	Arapahoe Co	315R	80222	2400-2599	
DAHLIA PL	Thornton	195H	80229	11100-11199	
DAHLIA ST	Adams Co	225V	80022	7000-7099	
	Adams Co	225M	80022	7500-7899	
	Adams Co	225H	80640	7900-8799	
DAHLIA ST	Bennett	793N	80102	100-299	
DAHLIA ST	Commerce City	255H	80022	5200-5599	
	Commerce City	255D	80022	5800-6199	
	Commerce City	225V	80022	6200-6999	
	Commerce City	225R	80022	7100-7499	
	Denver	285M	80220	1-1999	
	Denver	285D	80207	2000-2799	
	Denver	255Z	80207	2800-3999	
	Denver	255M	80216	4000-5099	
DAHLIA ST	Firestone	707T	80504	10300-10399	
DAHLIA ST	Hudson	730L	80642	400-599	
DAHLIA ST	Louisville	130Y	80027	400-799	
DAHLIA ST	Thornton	195D	80233	11500-11699	
	Thornton	165H	80602	13800-13999	
	Thornton	165H	80602	None	
	Thornton	165M	80602	None	
DAHLIA ST S	Arapahoe Co	315R	80222	2400-2499	
	Arapahoe Co	315R	80222	2500-2698	E
	Centennial	375H	80122	6900-7099	
	Cherry Hills Village	345H	80113	3500-4499	
	Cherry Hills Village	345M	80121	4600-5099	
	Denver	285V	80246	1-399	
	Denver	315D	80246	900-999	
	Denver	315H	80246	1100-1299	
	Denver	315H	80222	1300-2399	
	Denver	315R	80222	2501-2699	O
	Denver	315Z	80222	2700-3499	
	Glendale	315D	80246	1000-1099	
	Jefferson Co	842E	80470	13700-13899	
DAHLIA ST W	Louisville	160C	80027	900-999	
DAHLIA WAY	Longmont	40Q	80503	3600-3699	
DAHLIA WAY	Louisville	131W	80027	400-799	
DAHLIA WAY	Thornton	195M	80233	10800-10999	
	Thornton	165V	80241	12500-12799	
DAILEY LN	Superior	160P	80027	1900-2099	
DAILEY ST	Superior	160P	80027	2100-2399	
DAILY CT	Erie	102U	80516	1500-1598	E
DAILY DR	Erie	102U	80516	1500-1799	
DAIRYLIDE ST	Castle Rock	466V	80109	None	
DAISY CT	Brighton	138V	80601	1700-1799	
DAISY CT	Broomfield	162K	80020	1700-1799	
DAISY CT	Firestone	707P	80504	11200-11499	
DAISY CT S	Highlands Ranch	404D	80126	9200-9399	
DAISY LN	Jefferson Co	308N	80401	2100-2499	
DAISY ST	Firestone	707P	80504	11300-11499	
DAKAN RD	Douglas Co	866Y	80135	4000-7999	
DAKAN MOUNTAIN	Jefferson Co	371L	80127	10400-10799	
DAKIN ST	Adams Co	224N	80221	100-7499	
DAKOTA AVE	Castle Rock	498L	80104	5000-5299	
DAKOTA AVE E	Aurora	287Y	80012	11200-11799	
	Aurora	287Z	80012	12100-12399	
	Aurora	288W	80012	13000-13699	
	Denver	284Y	80209	1-1699	
	Denver	285W	80209	1700-2399	
	Denver	285Y	80209	3702-3998	E
	Denver	285Z	80246	5100-5499	
	Denver	286W	80246	5500-5599	
	Denver	286W	80224	5600-6699	
	Denver	287X	80231	10200-10499	
DAKOTA AVE W	Denver	284X	80223	100-198	E
	Denver	284W	80223	1300-1599	
	Denver	283W	80219	2500-5199	
	Lakewood	282Z	80226	5600-5699	
	Lakewood	282W	80226	8400-8799	

Continued on next column

STREET NAME	CITY or COUNTY	MAP GRID	ZIP CODE	BLOCK RANGE	O/E
DAKOTA AVE W (Cont'd)	Lakewood	281Z	80226	9200-9899	
	Lakewood	281Y	80226	10400-11199	
	Lakewood	281W	80228	12400-12499	
	Lakewood	280Z	80228	12500-12799	
	Lakewood	280Z	80228	13200-13899	
DAKOTA BLVD	Boulder	97C	80304	4800-4999	
DAKOTA DR	Douglas Co	436X	80108	900-999	
DAKOTA DR W	Lakewood	281W	80228	11800-12199	
	Lakewood	311A	80228	12200-12699	
DAKOTA PL	Boulder	97Y	80304	2600-2699	
DAKOTA PL E	Aurora	288W	80012	13600-13699	
	Aurora	288Z	80017	15900-16299	
DAKOTA PL W	Lakewood	282W	80226	8200-8399	
	Lakewood	280Z	80228	13200-13899	
DAKOTA ST	Arapahoe Co	795U	80103	None	
DAKOTA ST	Kiowa	872M	80117	400-699	
DAKOTA WAY E	Aurora	288W	80012	13600-13699	
DAKOTA RIDGE DR	Jefferson Co	763Y	80403	6400-6499	
DAKOTA RIDGE RD	Gilpin Co	780F	80403	6400-6499	
DAKOTA RUN	Douglas Co	845Q	80125	5000-5099	
DALE AVE	Weld Co	729A	80621	15000-15999	
DALE CIR	Westminster	193M	80234	10400-10499	
DALE CT	Broomfield	163U	80020	12500-12599	
DALE CT	Denver	283R	80204	400-699	
DALE CT	Douglas Co	847E	80108	500-599	
DALE CT	Elizabeth	871F	80107	500-699	
DALE CT	Westminster	223Q	80030	7300-7599	
	Westminster	193L	80234	10600-10699	
DALE CT S	Denver	283Y	80219	100-699	
	Denver	313L	80219	700-1899	
	Sheridan	343G	80110	4100-4299	
DALE DR	Boulder Co	102J	80026	3900-4099	
DALE PL	Longmont	41A	80501	1-99	
DALE ST S	Sheridan	313Y	80110	3100-3499	
DALES PONY DR	Castle Rock	467Y	80104	800-999	
DALEY CIR E	Douglas Co	850T	80134	11000-11999	
DALEY DR	Longmont	11P	80501	2100-2299	
DALLAS CT S	Arapahoe Co	317N	80231	2200-2299	
	Arapahoe Co	377A	80111	6400-6499	
	Denver	315X	80210	3100-3299	
	Denver	317W	80231	3300-3499	
	Greenwood Village	377E	80112	6800-6899	
DALLAS PL	Boulder	128C	80303	4400-4499	
DALLAS ST	Adams Co	137S	80602	15600-15899	
	Adams Co	137N	80602	16100-16199	
DALLAS ST	Aurora	287J	80010	1100-2599	
	Aurora	287J	80230	None	
	Commerce City	197S	80640	9600-10099	
	Denver	257J	80238	None	
	Denver	287A	80238	None	
	Denver	287S	80230	None	
DALLAS ST S	Arapahoe Co	317J	80247	1701-1799	O
	Arapahoe Co	317N	80231	2100-2299	
	Aurora	347A	80014	3600-3699	
	Centennial	377N	80112	None	
	Greenwood Village	347S	80111	5400-5599	
DALLAS WAY S	Denver	315T	80210	2900-3099	
	Greenwood Village	377A	80112	6800-6899	
DALLMAN DR S	Jefferson Co	823N	80433	9500-9599	
DAMASCUS RD	Gilpin Co	761K	80403	1-2799	
DAMASCUS TRAIL	Jefferson Co	366R	80439	7800-7999	
DAME AVE	Arapahoe Co	795T	80103	1-299	
DAMON DR	Northglenn	194T	80260	9400-9699	
DAMPLER WAY S	Highlands Ranch	405H	80130	9700-9799	
DAN CT	Highlands Ranch	406J	80130	10200-10299	
DANBURY AVE	Highlands Ranch	405P	80126	2600-3199	
DANBURY DR	Longmont	11S	80503	1700-2699	
DANBURY LN	Highlands Ranch	405N	80126	2500-2799	
DANCING DEER DR	Jefferson Co	824P	80127	16700-16899	
DANCING STAR LN	Gilpin Co	761C	80403	1-199	
DANDELION WAY	Parker	378V	80134	16800-16999	
DANFORTH AVE	Castle Rock	498L	80104	400-499	
DANIELS GATE DR	Castle Pines North	436A	80108	12400-12699	
DANIELS GATE PL	Castle Pines North	436A	80108	5700-5799	
DANIELS PARK RD N	Douglas Co	466F	80135	5000-5499	
	Douglas Co	436J	80135	5500-8699	
DANKS DR	Jefferson Co	367L	80439	7400-8299	
DANNY AVE S	Jefferson Co	842A	80470	12300-12499	
DANNY ST	Castle Rock	497F	80109	1-99	
DANNY BROOK CT	Boulder Co	69A	80503	7800-7899	
DANNY'S CT	Longmont	11Y	80501	900-999	
DANTE CIR	Douglas Co	432J	80125	11300-11398	E
DANTE DR	Douglas Co	432E	80125	7600-8299	
DANUBE CIR S	Arapahoe Co	349U	80015	5700-5899	
	Aurora	349L	80015	4700-4799	
	Aurora	319G	80017	19200-19299	
DANUBE CT	Aurora	289G	80011	1700-1899	
	Denver	259G	80249	None	
DANUBE CT S	Aurora	319G	80017	1300-1399	
	Aurora	319Q	80013	None	
	Centennial	349Q	80015	5300-5399	
	Centennial	379G	80016	7100-7199	
DANUBE ST	Adams Co	169Y	80022	12000-12099	
	Aurora	289G	80011	1700-1899	
	Denver	259C	80249	5700-5799	
DANUBE ST S	Arapahoe Co	349U	80015	5800-5899	
	Aurora	319U	80013	2700-2899	
	Aurora	319Y	80013	3000-3399	
	Aurora	349L	80015	4900-5099	
	Centennial	349Q	80015	5100-5299	
	Centennial	349U	80015	5400-5799	
DANUBE WAY	Aurora	289G	80011	1900-1999	
	Denver	259Q	80249	4300-4499	
DANUBE WAY S	Aurora	319G	80017	1300-1699	
	Aurora	319Q	80013	2600-2699	
	Aurora	349L	80015	4800-4899	
	Aurora	319Q	80013	None	
	Centennial	349Q	80015	5400-5599	
DANVERS CT	Castle Rock	498V	80104	5300-5399	
DANZIG PL W	Littleton	825P	80127	9600-9899	
DAPHNE ST	Broomfield	162K	80020	500-1799	
DAPHNE WAY	Broomfield	162X	80020	100-299	
DAPPLE LN	Boulder Co	99F	80301	4600-4699	
DARADO CT	Broomfield	163E	80020	14100-14199	
DARBY CT	Castle Rock	499J	80104	500-799	
DARBY CT	Longmont	41D	80501	700-799	
DARKSTAR WAY	Parker	410T	80138	11400-11499	
DARLEE CT	Lakewood	281H	80215	1800-1999	

D

STREET NAME	CITY or COUNTY	MAP GRID	ZIP CODE	BLOCK RANGE	O/E
DARLEY AVE	Boulder	128T	80305	2600-4099	
	Boulder	128U	80305	4100-4599	
DARLINGTON CIR	Highlands Ranch	405Q	80126	3300-3499	
DARMOUTH AVE W	Lakewood	311Y	80227	10000-10999	
DARMOUTH PL W	Lakewood	311Z	80227	9000-9899	
DARREN ST	Castle Rock	497F	80109	1-99	
DARTING BIRD RIDE	Elbert Co	871B	80107	35200-35899	
DARTMOOR CT S	Parker	410N	80138	11100-11199	
DARTMOOR PL S	Parker	410N	80138	11000-11099	
DARTMOUTH AVE	Boulder	128N	80305	1900-3699	
	Boulder	128Q	80305	3700-3899	
DARTMOUTH AVE E	Arapahoe Co	316S	80222	6000-6099	
	Arapahoe Co	812M	80102	45700-46499	
	Arapahoe Co	813J	80102	46500-48899	
	Aurora	317T	80014	10501-11299	O
	Aurora	318V	80013	14700-16799	
	Aurora	319W	80013	16800-17999	
	Aurora	319X	80013	18100-18499	
	Aurora	319U	80013	19000-19099	
	Aurora	319V	80013	19600-19999	
	Aurora	317U	80014	None	
	Denver	314V	80210	1601-1699	O
	Denver	315S	80210	1701-2199	O
	Denver	315T	80210	2300-3999	
	Denver	315V	80222	4000-5299	
	Denver	316S	80222	5900-5999	
	Denver	316X	80224	6600-7099	
	Denver	316U	80231	7300-8899	
	Denver	317T	80014	10500-11298	E
	Englewood	314U	80113	1-1599	
	Englewood	314Z	80110	1600-1698	E
	Englewood	315W	80110	1700-2298	E
	Englewood	315S	80110	2300-2399	
DARTMOUTH AVE W	Denver	313V	80236	2401-2799	O
	Denver	313Y	80236	2800-2999	
	Denver	313W	80236	3400-5199	
	Denver	312U	80227	5200-7499	
	Englewood	314S	80110	100-1999	
	Englewood	313V	80110	2000-2399	
	Lakewood	311Y	80227	10000-10899	
	Lakewood	310U	80228	14000-14199	
	Sheridan	313Z	80110	2500-2798	E
DARTMOUTH CIR	Longmont	10V	80503	1-99	
DARTMOUTH CIR E	Englewood	315S	80113	2100-2299	
DARTMOUTH DR E	Aurora	319V	80013	None	
	Aurora	320S	80013	None	
DARTMOUTH DR W	Lakewood	310U	80228	14200-14599	
DARTMOUTH PL E	Aurora	319V	80013	19600-19999	
	Denver	316Z	80231	9000-9399	
	Denver	317W	80231	9700-9999	
	Englewood	315W	80113	2101-2399	O
DARTMOUTH PL W	Lakewood	312W	80227	8400-8999	
	Lakewood	311Y	80227	10100-10199	
DARVEY LN	Boulder Co	71B	80504	7700-7799	
DARWIN CT	Boulder	98U	80301	4800-4899	
DARWIN CT	Northglenn	194S	80260	1000-1099	
DARWIN LN	Highlands Ranch	405H	80130	9900-10099	
DASA DR S	Cherry Hills Village	346J	80111	4500-4799	
DATE ST	Hudson	730L	80642	None	
DAT-MOUNT DR	Jefferson Co	366H	80439	None	
DATURA CIR S	Littleton	374J	80120	7600E-7699E	
	Littleton	374J	80120	7900E-7999E	
DATURA CT S	Littleton	344S	80120	5900-5999	
DATURA ST S	Littleton	344S	80120	5300-6299	
	Littleton	374A	80120	6400-6699	
	Littleton	374J	80120	7700-7799	
DAUNTLESS WAY	Jefferson Co	366Y	80433	9200-9399	
DAVCO DR	Jefferson Co	368U	80465	8300-8699	
DAVENPORT CT N	Erie	102C	80516	1200-1299	
DAVENPORT CT S	Erie	102G	80516	1100-1199	
DAVENPORT ST	Denver	258N	80239	4700-4799	
DAVENPORT WAY	Denver	258N	80239	4300-4599	
DAVENTRY PL	Castle Pines North	436Q	80108	6900-7099	
DAVID AVE W	Jefferson Co	372L	80128	6800-6999	
	Jefferson Co	371R	80128	9200-9699	
DAVID CT	Platteville	708C	80651	500-599	
DAVID DR	Clear Creek Co	801R	80439	1-499	
DAVID DR W	Jefferson Co	372Q	80128	6300-6599	
	Jefferson Co	372K	80128	7000-7899	
DAVID PL E	Aurora	380Q	80016	None	
DAVID PL W	Jefferson Co	372Q	80128	6600-6799	
	Jefferson Co	371R	80128	9500-9699	
DAVID C JOHNSON LOOP	Elbert Co	890R	80116	24100-24599	
DAVIDSON PL	Boulder	128Q	80305	3700-3799	
DAVIDSON ST	El Paso Co	908S	80132	None	
DAVIDSON WAY	Boulder Co	131J	80026	9000-9199	
DAVIES AVE E	Arapahoe Co	374G	80122	100-499	
	Arapahoe Co	374H	80122	600-1099	
	Arapahoe Co	378F	80112	13900-14299	
	Centennial	375F	80122	3300-3599	
	Centennial	376F	80112	7200-7299	
	Centennial	376G	80112	8100-8899	
	Centennial	379H	80016	20100-20299	
	Foxfield	379E	80016	16900-18099	
	Foxfield	379F	80016	18200-18399	
DAVIES AVE W	Littleton	374F	80120	1-299	
	Littleton	374E	80120	1600-2099	
	Littleton	373H	80120	2100-2499	
	Littleton	373C	80120	2800-2999	
	Littleton	374F	80120	200N-399N	
DAVIES CIR E	Centennial	380F	80016	21700-21899	
DAVIES CT E	Arapahoe Co	374H	80122	1100-1199	
	Centennial	376G	80112	7400-7599	
DAVIES CT W	Littleton	374F	80120	600-799	
DAVIES DR E	Aurora	380G	80016	22500-22899	
	Aurora	381A	80016	22900-25299	
	Aurora	381F	80016	24900-25299	
	Aurora	381G	80016	25900-26299	
	Centennial	375H	80122	4900-5399	
DAVIES DR W	Littleton	373C	80120	2800-2899	
DAVIES PL E	Aurora	381E	80016	24200-24399	
	Aurora	381G	80016	26800-26999	
DAVIES PL E	Arapahoe Co	379G	80016	None	
	Centennial	375E	80122	1900-1999	
	Centennial	375F	80122	3400-3699	
	Centennial	375G	80122	4000-4299	
	Centennial	375H	80122	5500-5599	
	Centennial	376F	80112	7200-7299	

Continued on next column

STREET NAME	CITY or COUNTY	MAP GRID	ZIP CODE	BLOCK RANGE	O/E
DAVIES PL E (Cont'd)	Centennial	376G	80112	7400-7599	
	Centennial	376H	80112	8300-8599	
	Centennial	378E	80112	13600-13699	
	Centennial	379G	80016	19000-19099	
DAVIES PL W	Littleton	374E	80120	1300-1599	
DAVIES ST E	Centennial	375H	80122	4800-4899	
DAVIES ST S	Littleton	373H	80120	7000-7199	
DAVIES WAY	Broomfield	163F	80020	None	
DAVIES WAY E	Aurora	381A	80016	24300-24699	
DAVIES WAY W	Littleton	374F	80120	500-799	
DA VINCI DR	Longmont	40Q	80503	3900-4299	
DAVIS AVE	Jefferson Co	823P	80433	9500-9599	
DAVIS CT	Erie	102G	80516	1400-1499	
DAVIS DR	Frederick	727F	80530	None	
DAVIS LN	Boulder Co	11D	80504	13400-13899	
DAVIS ST	Broomfield	163S	80020	12600-12799	
DAVISPEAK	Jefferson Co	371K	80127	7600-7699	
DAWN CT	Boulder	98K	80304	4000-4099	
DAWN CT	Douglas Co	432K	80125	7500-7599	
DAWN CT	Wheat Ridge	251Y	80215	2700-2899	
DAWN DR	Douglas Co	432K	80125	7500-7699	
DAWN GLOW WAY	Castle Rock	496C	80109	3200-3399	
DAWN HEATH CIR	Jefferson Co	370K	80127	1-99	
DAWN HEATH DR	Jefferson Co	370F	80127	1-99	
DAWN HILL CIR	Frederick	706Y	80530	8000-8099	
DAWN HILL CT	Frederick	706Y	80530	8000-8099	
DAWN WONDER WAY	Castle Rock	466V	80109	None	
DAWSON CIR	Aurora	288B	80011	2200-2299	
DAWSON CIR S	Aurora	348F	80014	None	
	Centennial	378B	80112	6700-6899	
DAWSON CT	Castle Rock	497M	80104	300-499	
DAWSON CT S	Aurora	318P	80014	2500-2599	
DAWSON DR	Adams Co	224H	80229	900-8599	
DAWSON DR	Boulder Co	101H	80026	10400-10599	
DAWSON DR	Castle Rock	497M	80104	100-499	
DAWSON PL	Longmont	12S	80501	100-199	
DAWSON RD	Douglas Co	867N	80135	3200-4499	
DAWSON RD	Park Co	842A	80470	1-599	
DAWSON ST	Adams Co	224D	80229	8600-8799	
	Aurora	288K	80011	600-1099	
DAWSON ST S	Aurora	318F	80012	1500-1599	
	Aurora	348B	80014	3500-3999	
	Aurora	348F	80014	4100-4299	
DAWSON WAY S	Aurora	318B	80012	900-999	
	Aurora	318K	80012	1600-1799	
	Aurora	318P	80014	2300-2599	
DAWSON BUTTE WAY	Castle Rock	497E	80109	1500-1599	
DAWSON RIDGE BLVD	Castle Rock	527A	80109	None	
	Castle Rock	867R	80109	None	
DAYDREAM RD	Jefferson Co	782H	80403	4300-4799	
DAYLIGHT CT	Brighton	139L	80601	None	
DAYLILLY CT	Boulder Co	70Q	80503	6500-6599	
DAY STAR CT	Parker	410P	80138	11200-11299	
DAY STAR DR	Parker	410P	80138	22000-22099	
DAYTON CIR	Commerce City	197E	80640	None	
DAYTON CIR S	Aurora	317E	80247	1400-1499	
DAYTON CT	Denver	257S	80238	None	
DAYTON CT S	Arapahoe Co	347S	80111	5900-5999	
	Aurora	317E	80247	1201-1499	O
	Denver	317S	80231	3000-3399	
	Greenwood Village	347N	80111	5400-5499	
	Greenwood Village	347S	80111	5800-5899	
	Aurora	287N	80010	2-1098	E
	Aurora	287J	80010	1100-2499	
	Commerce City	197E	80640	None	
	Denver	257W	80238	None	
	Denver	287A	80238	None	
DAYTON ST S	Arapahoe Co	317E	80247	1101-2099	O
	Arapahoe Co	317N	80231	2100-2299	
	Arapahoe Co	347W	80111	6100-6499	
	Aurora	317E	80247	1100-2098	E
	Aurora	347A	80014	3500-3899	
	Centennial	377N	80112	7800-8099	
	Denver	287W	80231	300-699	
	Denver	317A	80247	700-1098	E
	Denver	317W	80231	3200-3499	
	Greenwood Village	347N	80111	4600-6099	
	Greenwood Village	377A	80112	6500-6899	
DAYTON WAY	Commerce City	196M	80640	10600-10699	
	Commerce City	196M	80640	10700-10899	
DAYTON WAY S	Aurora	347A	80014	3600-3799	
	Aurora	317E	80247	None	
	Denver	317N	80231	2500-2699	
DEADMAN GULCH RD	Jefferson Co	278R	80401	400-499	
DEAN DR	Northglenn	194D	80233	700-1599	
DEAN PL	Boulder	127G	80302	1200-1299	
DEARBORN CIR S	Aurora	288T	80012	1-299	
	Aurora	318B	80012	700-799	
DEARBORN CT S	Aurora	318B	80012	700-799	
	Aurora	348F	80014	4200-4299	
	Aurora	348F	80015	4300-4399	
	Aurora	348K	80015	None	
	Aurora	348P	80015	None	
DEARBORN PL	Boulder Co	130E	80303	800-1099	
DEARBORN ST	Aurora	288K	80011	600-1299	
	Denver	258P	80239	4300-4899	
	Denver	258K	80239	5200-5299	
	Denver	258F	80239	5500-5599	
DEARBORN ST S	Aurora	318B	80012	1000-1099	
	Aurora	318F	80012	1500-1599	
	Aurora	318P	80014	2200-2499	
	Aurora	318P	80014	2400-2499	
DEARBORN WAY	Aurora	288P	80011	200-399	
	Aurora	288B	80011	None	
DEARBORN WAY S	Aurora	318B	80012	900-999	
	Aurora	318K	80012	1600-1799	
DEARBORNE DR	Parker	408R	80134	10900-10999	
DEBBI CIR	Elbert Co	850D	80138	1400-1599	
DEBBIE LN	Douglas Co	848E	80108	7600-7799	
DE BERRY ST	Jefferson Co	823N	80433	26100-26799	
DEBORAH CT	Elbert Co	851E	80138	2300-2499	
DEBRA ANN LN	Gilpin Co	742W	80403	1-299	
DECATUR AVE	Castle Rock	498L	80104	4200-4499	
	Broomfield	163Q	80234	None	
	Westminster	193G	80234	None	
DECATUR CT	Broomfield	163L	80020	13500-13599	
	Broomfield	163U	80234	None	
	Federal Heights	193Y	80260	9300-9599	

Continued on next column

STREET NAME	CITY or COUNTY	MAP GRID	ZIP CODE	BLOCK RANGE	O/E
DECATUR CT (Cont'd)	Westminster	223L	80030	8000-8099	
	Westminster	193G	80234	11300-11499	
	Westminster	193C	80234	11500-11599	
DECATUR DR	Broomfield	163U	80020	2700-2899	
	Westminster	193G	80234	11100-11199	
	Westminster	193C	80234	11600-11799	
DECATUR PL	Broomfield	163L	80020	13500-13599	
	Westminster	193C	80234	11800-11899	
DECATUR ST	Adams Co	223U	80221	6600-6799	
	Denver	283U	80219	1-399	
	Denver	283L	80204	400-1499	
	Denver	283C	80211	2100-2599	
	Denver	253Y	80211	2700-2899	
	Denver	253U	80211	3300-3799	
	Denver	253Q	80211	4100-4799	
	Denver	253L	80221	4800-5199	
	Federal Heights	193U	80260	2600-2699	
	Federal Heights	223C	80260	8900-8999	
	Federal Heights	193U	80260	9800-9899	
	Westminster	193C	80234	2800-2999	
	Westminster	223Q	80030	7300-7599	
	Westminster	223L	80030	8000-8099	
	Westminster	223G	80260	8400-8699	
	Westminster	193L	80234	10400-10599	
	Westminster	193G	80234	11000-11099	
	Westminster	193C	80234	11500-11899	
DECATUR ST S	Denver	283Y	80219	1-699	
	Denver	313G	80219	700-1999	
	Denver	313U	80219	2200-2699	
	Denver	313U	80236	2700-3299	
	Englewood	343L	80110	4500-4999	
	Sheridan	343D	80110	3900-3999	
	Sheridan	343G	80110	4100-4299	
DECATUR WAY	Federal Heights	193Z	80260	9200-9599	
DECINO PL	Erie	103N	80516	300-399	
DECKERS PL N	Castle Rock	498G	80104	1100-1399	
DEEP FOREST LN	Jefferson Co	305B	80439	700-899	
DEEP FOREST RD	Jefferson Co	305B	80439	32600-33999	
DEEPHAVEN CT	Denver	258N	80239	4300-4699	
	Denver	258K	80239	4800-5399	
DEER CIR	Gilpin Co	761S	80403	1-299	
DEER LN	Clear Creek Co	335A	80439	1-299	
DEER LN N	Douglas Co	410L	80138	11100-11899	
DEER RD	Clear Creek Co	821H	80439	1-599	
DEER ST	Golden	279Q	80401	1-99	
DEER BRUSH TRAIL	Douglas Co	498E	80104	None	
DEER CLOVER CIR	Castle Pines North	436L	80108	700-899	
DEER CLOVER DR	Castle Pines North	436L	80108	800-899	
DEER CLOVER WAY	Castle Pines North	436K	80108	700-1099	
DEER CREEK CIR	El Paso Co	908T	80132	1200-1499	
DEER CREEK CIR	Elbert Co	851F	80138	41300-41499	
DEER CREEK CT	Boulder	69Z	80301	5200-5399	
DEER CREEK CT S	Highlands Ranch	403G	80129	9900-9999	
DEER CREEK DR	Elbert Co	851E	80138	3300-3799	
DEER CREEK DR W	Highlands Ranch	403G	80129	3000-3199	
DEER CREEK LN S	Highlands Ranch	403G	80129	9900-9999	
DEER CREEK PL W	Highlands Ranch	403G	80129	2800-2999	
DEERCREEK RD	El Paso Co	908T	80132	1100-1899	
DEER CREEK RD	Jefferson Co	369Z	80127	9800-11599	
DEER CREEK RD	Park Co	840C	80421	None	
	Park Co	841A	80421	None	
DEER CREEK RD S	Jefferson Co	824T	80127	9800-11599	
DEER CREEK ST S	Highlands Ranch	403G	80129	9900-10099	
DEER CREEK CANYON RD					
	Jefferson Co	372W	80127	7700-9099	
	Jefferson Co	371Y	80127	9100-12499	
	Jefferson Co	370Z	80127	12500-14099	
DEER CREEK CANYON RD S					
	Jefferson Co	369T	80465	8000-8299	
	Jefferson Co	369T	80127	8300-9299	
	Jefferson Co	824P	80127	9300-9999	
DEER CREEK RANCH LOOP	Elbert Co	851E	80138	3000-3599	
DEER CREEK TRAIL W					
	Highlands Ranch	403G	80129	2800-3099	
DEERCREST WAY	Lone Tree	406B	80124	7300-7499	
DEER CROSSING	Castle Rock	497T	80104	300-399	
DEERE CT	Mead	706H	80504	13700-13999	
DEERFIELD CIR	Elbert Co	832S	80107	45100-45599	
DEERFIELD CT	Longmont	12U	80501	1400-1499	
DEERFIELD DR	Firestone	707P	80504	11200-11499	
DEERFIELD RD	Douglas Co	869H	80116	9100-9299	
	Douglas Co	870E	80116	9300-10999	
DEERFIELD RD	El Paso Co	908U	80132	18600-19199	
DEERFIELD ST	Firestone	707T	80504	10400-10599	
DEERFIELD WAY	Broomfield	163X	80020	12100-12399	
DEERFOOT WAY	Castle Rock	466Y	80109	None	
DEER HAVEN CIR	Elbert Co	871C	80107	35500-35599	
DEER HAVEN CT	Jefferson Co	340N	80465	16200-16299	
DEERHAVEN DR	Park Co	841N	80421	1-299	
DEERHORN CT	Parker	409E	80134	9500-9699	
DEER MEADOW LN	Douglas Co	406Q	80124	300-599	
DEER MOUNTAIN DR	Jefferson Co	369Z	80127	16200-16699	
DEER PATH	Jefferson Co	365F	80439	6700-6899	
DEERPATH RD	Douglas Co	870A	80116	1000-2099	
	Douglas Co	850W	80116	2100-2399	
DEERPATH TRAIL	Douglas Co	870A	80116	1200-1999	
	Douglas Co	850W	80116	2000-2699	
DEER REST TRAIL	Jefferson Co	306D	80401	None	
DEER RIDGE CIR	Elbert Co	851E	80138	2800-2899	
DEER RIDGE DR	Jefferson Co	340N	80465	15800-16099	
DEER RIDGE WAY	Douglas Co	907B	80118	13000-13499	
DEER RUN TRAIL	Douglas Co	848L	80108	6500-6799	
DEER SHADOW WAY	El Paso Co	908P	80132	20100-20299	
DEERSLAYER RD N	Douglas Co	411X	80138	8900-9199	
DEER SPRINGS LN	Golden	248R	80403	1000-1199	
DEER TRAIL	Clear Creek Co	801A	80452	1-99	
	Elbert Co	871G	80107	4600-4999	
	Elbert Co	891U	80106	22600-22999	
DEER TRAIL S	Jefferson Co	336Q	80439	4900-5099	
DEER TRAIL CIR	Boulder Co	722K	80302	1-899	
DEERTRAIL CT W	Castle Rock	466P	80109	4200-4399	
DEER TRAIL DR	Park Co	841P	80421	1-399	
DEERTRAIL DR E	Douglas Co	410A	80138	7500-7999	
DEER TRAIL RD	Boulder Co	722L	80302	1-2099	
DEER TRAIL RD	Jefferson Co	822Z	80433	11900-12099	
DEER TRAIL CREEK DR	Brighton	138V	80601	2200-2399	
DEER VALLEY DR	Castle Rock	528A	80104	None	
DEER VALLEY RD	Boulder	128N	80305	1700-1899	

D

STREET NAME	CITY or COUNTY	MAP GRID	ZIP CODE	BLOCK RANGE	O/E
DEER VALLEY RD	Jefferson Co	307D	80401	23900-24399	
DEER WATCH DR	Castle Rock	467U	80104	4100-4399	
DEERWOOD CIR	El Paso Co	908S	80132	19200-19499	
DEERWOOD DR	Jefferson Co	370K	80127	1-99	
DEERWOOD DR	Longmont	12Y	80501	900-1299	
	Longmont	12U	80501	1300-1399	
	Longmont	42C	80501	1400-1699	
	Longmont	42D	80501	None	
DEFOE ST	Adams Co	794G	80136	4000-4298	E
DEFRAME CIR S	Lakewood	310Q	80228	2600-2799	
DEFRAME CT	Arvada	250C	80004	6000-6099	
	Arvada	220Y	80004	6400-6599	
	Arvada	220U	80004	6600-7199	
	Arvada	220Q	80005	7200-7399	
	Arvada	220G	80005	8300-8399	
	Arvada	220C	80005	None	
	Jefferson Co	280Q	80401	300-699	
DEFRAME CT S	Jefferson Co	340G	80465	4100-4199	
	Lakewood	280Y	80228	500-599	
	Lakewood	310M	80228	1600-1799	
	Lakewood	310Q	80228	2100-2299	
	Lakewood	310V	80228	2800-2899	
DEFRAME RD	Jefferson Co	280C	80401	2700-2799	
	Jefferson Co	250Y	80401	3000-3199	
DEFRAME ST	Arvada	220Y	80004	6400-6799	
	Arvada	220Q	80005	7400-7599	
	Arvada	220C	80005	None	
	Jefferson Co	280Q	80401	700-999	
	Jefferson Co	250L	80002	5100-5199	
	Jefferson Co	250G	80002	5300-5399	
DEFRAME ST S	Jefferson Co	340L	80465	4100-4699	
	Jefferson Co	340V	80127	5501-5899	O
	Lakewood	310L	80228	1600-2199	
	Lakewood	310Q	80228	2400-2599	
	Lakewood	310R	80228	2700-2899	
DEFRAME WAY	Arvada	220Y	80004	6300-6599	
DEFRAME WAY	Lakewood	310H	80228	None	
DEFRAME WAY S	Jefferson Co	280U	80401	1-299	
	Lakewood	310L	80228	1900-2099	
	Lakewood	310Q	80228	2100-2299	
	Lakewood	310V	80228	2900-2999	
DEFRAME WAY W	Lakewood	310C	80228	700-1099	
DEFRANCE CT	Golden	279T	80401	300-399	
DEFRANCE DR	Golden	279T	80401	300-499	
DEFRANCE WAY	Golden	279T	80401	1-299	
DEGAULLE CIR	Adams Co	140R	80603	15600-15899	
DE GAULLE CIR S	Aurora	321E	80018	1500-1599	
DE GAULLE CT E	Aurora	321E	80018	1400-1499	
DE GAULLE CT N	Aurora	290R	80018	None	
DE GAULLE CT S	Aurora	380V	80138	None	
DE GAULLE ST N	Aurora	290R	80018	None	
DE GAULLE ST S	Arapahoe Co	290V	80018	1-299	
	Aurora	350R	80016	None	
	Aurora	351N	80016	None	
DE GAULLE WAY S	Aurora	320H	80018	1500-1699	
DEHESA CT	Boulder Co	98K	80301	3900-3999	
DEHNING WAY	Weld Co	706N	80504	None	
DEKKER DR	Jefferson Co	278X	80401	1-299	
DELAWARE CIR W	Littleton	374F	80120	200N-299N	
DELAWARE CT	Northglenn	194B	80234	11700-11899	
DELAWARE CT S	Littleton	374F	80120	7300-7399	
DELAWARE DR	Douglas Co	886M	80118	4300-5099	
DELAWARE DR W	Westminster	164T	80234	12300-12799	
DELAWARE PL	Douglas Co	887J	80118	8100-8199	
DELAWARE PL	Longmont	41K	80501	1800-1899	
DELAWARE ST	Adams Co	254F	80221	5600-5899	
	Adams Co	224X	80221	6400-6599	
	Adams Co	224F	80221	8200-8399	
	Adams Co	134X	80020	15200-15399	
	Denver	284P	80223	100-399	
	Denver	284P	80204	400-899	
	Denver	284K	80204	1000-1499	
	Denver	254P	80216	4200-4499	
	Thornton	224F	80260	8400-8499	
	Westminster	164X	80234	12001-12099	O
DELAWARE ST S	Denver	314P	80223	2000-2699	
	Englewood	314T	80110	2700-3299	
	Englewood	314X	80110	3500-3599	
	Englewood	344F	80110	3600-5099	
	Littleton	344T	80120	5000-5699	
	Littleton	344T	80120	5700-5899	
	Littleton	374B	80120	6300-6499	
	Littleton	374B	80120	6600-6999	
	Littleton	374F	80120	7200-7499	
DELBERT RD N	Douglas Co	850Y	80116	2000-2499	
	Douglas Co	850G	80138	7100-9099	
	Douglas Co	830Q	80138	9100-13999	
DEL CAMINO	Weld Co	706V	80504	None	
DEL CAMINO LN	Weld Co	707U	80504	9000-9899	
DEL COMMUNDO CT	Weld Co	707T	80504	7000-7099	
DEL COMMUNDO LN	Weld Co	707T	80504	7200-7399	
DELEWARE AVE	Longmont	41L	80501	700-1199	
DELGANY ST	Denver	284A	80202	1400-1599	
	Denver	254X	80202	2000-2099	
	Denver	254X	80216	2300-2499	
	Denver	254U	80216	3400-3799	
DELIGHT DR	Castle Rock	496B	80109	None	
DELLA CT	Weld Co	726K	80516	1600-1699	
DELLA ST	Longmont	41R	80501	1200-1299	
DELLWOOD AVE	Boulder	97U	80304	300-1199	
	Boulder	97V	80304	1300-1799	
DEL MAR CIR	Aurora	287Q	80011	1-199	
DEL MAR PKWY	Aurora	287E	80010	1000-1999	
	Aurora	287K	80010	10800-11999	
DEL NORTE CT	Brighton	139T	80601	None	
DEL NORTE PL E	Aurora	380V	80138	None	
DEL NORTE ST	Adams Co	224P	80221	1-1099	
	Adams Co	224N	80221	1400-1599	
DEL NORTE ST E	Adams Co	224Q	80221	1-299	
DELOS CIR	Lafayette	131M	80026	900-999	
DELPHI DR	Highlands Ranch	376U	80124	13400-13599	
DELPHI DR	Lafayette	131Q	80026	700-1299	
DELPHINIUM CIR	Brighton	139M	80601	None	
DEL PICO PL	Castle Rock	468X	80104	None	
DEL RAY CT	Adams Co	750G	80603	16100-16299	
DEL RAY PL	Lochbuie	729Y	80603	None	
DEL RIO CT	Denver	258N	80239	4300-4699	
DEL ROSA CT	Boulder	97R	80304	1800-1899	
DEL SOL WAY	Elbert Co	851A	80138	2500-2899	
DELTA CT	Adams Co	140R	80603	15800-15999	
DELTA DR	Lafayette	131R	80026	900-1099	
DELTA LN	Jefferson Co	842N	80470	14900-15299	
DELTA ST	Adams Co	224K	80221	1-199	
	Adams Co	224P	80221	500-7799	
DELTA ST E	Adams Co	224L	80221	1-199	
DELWOOD CT	Highlands Ranch	374Y	80126	600-699	
DELWOOD CT	Thornton	195X	80229	9100-9199	
DELWOOD DR	Park Co	841N	80421	1-1499	
DEMOCRAT DR	Broomfield	133J	80020	None	
DEMOCRAT RD E	Douglas Co	440Z	80134	7200-9599	
	Douglas Co	441X	80134	9600-10999	
DEMOTT AVE	Commerce City	226S	80022	5600-6099	
DENALI LN	Jefferson Co	306P	80439	29700-29999	
DENARGO ST	Denver	254X	80216	3200-3399	
DENEB DR	Highlands Ranch	376X	80124	13000-13299	
DENICE DR S	Cherry Hills Village	346J	80111	4600-4799	
DENIM CT	Douglas Co	469B	80134	5100-5299	
DENISE PL	Longmont	11X	80501	1-99	
DENISON CIR	Longmont	11S	80503	1500-1699	
DENMARK CT	Denver	258N	80239	4300-4399	
DENNIS DR	Jefferson Co	306B	80439	900-999	
DENNISON CT S	Denver	315V	80222	2500-2699	
DENNISON LN	Boulder	128N	80305	2300-2399	
DENSLOW LN	Superior	160Q	80027	None	
DENTON AVE	Boulder	128F	80303	3000-3199	
DENVER AVE	Adams Co	791N	80137	1600-1699	E
DENVER AVE	Fort Lupton	728L	80621	100-1899	
DENVER AVE	Longmont	11S	80503	2600-2899	
DENVER AVE S	Fort Lupton	728Q	80621	500-1199	
	Weld Co	728Q	80621	100-499	
	Weld Co	728Q	80603	None	
DENVER PL	Brighton	138K	80601	800-999	
DENVER PL W	Denver	253U	80211	2700-3299	
DENVER ST	Boulder	97C	80304	None	
DENVER ST	Brighton	138K	80601	100-299	
	Brighton	138L	80601	500-1699	
DENVER WAY	Longmont	10V	80503	1-99	O
DENVER-BOULDER TURNPIKE					
	Boulder	128K	80305	None	
	Boulder Co	129T	80303	None	
	Boulder Co	160A	80027	None	
	Broomfield	161U	80020	None	
	Broomfield	161U	80027	None	
	Jefferson Co	192F	80020	None	
	Westminster	192F	80020	None	
DENVER VIEW DR	Jefferson Co	337L	80439	4700-4999	
DENVER WEST CIR	Lakewood	280G	80401	13900-14599	
DENVER WEST CT	Lakewood	280G	80401	1800-1999	
DENVER WEST DR	Jefferson Co	280F	80401	1800-1999	
DENVER WEST PKWY	Lakewood	280G	80401	13700-15599	
DENVER WEST COLORADO MILLS BLVD					
	Lakewood	280P	80401	None	
DENVER WEST COLORADO MILLS PKWY					
	Lakewood	280L	80401	1600-1699	
DENVER WEST MARRIOTT BLVD					
	Lakewood	280F	80401	1700-1999	
DENVER WEST RETAIL RD	Lakewood	280L	80401	None	
DEPEW CIR	Westminster	222V	80003	7100-7199	
DEPEW CIR S	Lakewood	342V	80123	5600-5799	
DEPEW CT	Arvada	222Z	80003	6300-6699	
	Denver	252M	80212	5100-5199	
	Lakewood	282R	80226	500-599	
	Lakewood	282M	80214	1100-1199	
	Westminster	192H	80020	11000-11299	
	Westminster	192D	80020	11500-11799	
DEPEW CT S	Jefferson Co	342Z	80123	6100-6399	
DEPEW DR S	Lakewood	282V	80226	1-99	
DEPEW PL	Westminster	192M	80020	10800-10999	
DEPEW PL S	Lakewood	312V	80227	2600-2699	
DEPEW ST	Arvada	252D	80003	6000-6199	
	Arvada	222Z	80003	6200-6799	
	Arvada	222M	80003	7900-7999	
	Arvada	222H	80003	8400-8599	
DEPEW ST	Boulder Co	162D	80020	None	
DEPEW ST	Denver	252M	80212	4800-4899	
	Edgewater	282D	80214	1700-2599	
	Lakewood	282V	80226	1-499	
	Lakewood	282R	80214	600-899	
	Lakewood	282M	80214	900-1699	
	Mountain View	252V	80212	4100-4399	
	Westminster	222R	80003	7100-7799	
	Westminster	192R	80020	10000-10199	
	Westminster	192H	80020	11000-11099	
	Westminster	192V	80031	None	
	Wheat Ridge	282D	80214	2600-2799	
	Wheat Ridge	252Z	80214	2800-3199	
	Wheat Ridge	252V	80212	3200-4099	
DEPEW ST S	Denver	312M	80227	1900-2199	
	Denver	312V	80227	2700-2899	
	Denver	312Z	80227	2900-3099	
	Denver	342D	80235	3700-3799	
	Jefferson Co	342D	80235	3500-3699	
	Jefferson Co	372M	80128	6700-7799	
	Jefferson Co	372D	80123	None	
	Lakewood	282Z	80226	1-699	
	Lakewood	312D	80226	700-899	
	Lakewood	312H	80232	1100-1899	
	Lakewood	312M	80227	2200-2299	
	Lakewood	342V	80123	5700-5899	
DEPEW WAY	Arvada	222H	80003	8200-8399	
	Westminster	192H	80020	11300-11599	
DEPEW WAY S	Denver	342D	80235	3900-3999	
	Jefferson Co	372M	80128	7500-7799	
DEPO DR	Longmont	40R	80503	3000-3199	
DEPOT ST	Golden	249W	80401	200-399	
DEPOT HILL RD	Broomfield	162S	80020	1000-1098	E
DEQUESNE CIR S	Aurora	320D	80018	None	
	Aurora	320H	80015	None	
DEQUESNE CT S	Aurora	320H	80015	None	
DEQUESNE ST S	Aurora	320D	80018	None	
DERBY WAY E	Douglas Co	441S	80134	9600-9999	
DERRINGER CT	Park Co	841K	80421	1-299	
DERRY CT	Broomfield	163G	80020	14000-14099	
DESCOMBES DR	Broomfield	162U	80020	1-99	
DESERT FOX TRAIL	Jefferson Co	339R	80465	5400-5499	
DESERT HILLS ST	Parker	410Y	80138	12000-12199	
DESERT INN LOOP	Elbert Co	851C	80107	None	
DESERT MOUNTAIN CT	Boulder	70W	80301	5300-5399	
DESERT PAINT BRUSH CT	Douglas Co	850N	80134	9600-9699	
DESERT PINE CT	Boulder	100A	80301	5200-5299	
DESERT RIDGE CIR	Castle Rock	468X	80108	3400-4199	
DESERT RIDGE PL	Castle Rock	468X	80108	3500-3799	
DESERT ROSE DR	Castle Rock	527D	80104	None	
DESERT WILLOW AVE	Broomfield	163X	80020	3700-3899	
DESERT WILLOW LN	Jefferson Co	370Q	80127	1-99	
DESERT WILLOW RD S					
	Highlands Ranch	404A	80129	9200-9499	
DESERT WILLOW WAY S					
	Highlands Ranch	404A	80129	9300-9599	
DESERT WILLOW TRAIL S					
	Highlands Ranch	404A	80129	9300-9499	
DE SOTO ST	Adams Co	224H	80229	8400-8499	
	Adams Co	224D	80229	8600-8799	
DESPARADO DR	El Paso Co	909R	80908	19500-19699	
DESPERADO CT	Park Co	841B	80421	1-99	O
DESPERADO RD	Park Co	841A	80421	100-999	
DESPERADO WAY	Douglas Co	469B	80134	4700-4799	
DESTINATION DR	Broomfield	192E	80021	11200-11599	
	Broomfield	192A	80021	11700-11999	
DESTINY CIR	Elbert Co	851K	80107	39700-39799	
DETROIT CIR S	Centennial	375B	80122	6700-6899	
DETROIT CT	Thornton	195T	80229	9600-9699	
	Thornton	195N	80229	10100-10199	
	Thornton	165P	80241	13300-13499	
DETROIT CT S	Centennial	375B	80122	6700-6799	
DETROIT DR	Thornton	165F	80602	None	
DETROIT ST	Denver	285K	80206	100-1699	
	Thornton	195T	80229	9700-9999	
	Thornton	165P	80241	13500-13599	
	Thornton	165K	80602	13600-13999	
	Thornton	165F	80602	None	
DETROIT ST S	Centennial	345X	80121	5900-6099	
	Centennial	345X	80121	6200-6299	
	Centennial	375K	80122	7500-8099	
	Denver	315X	80210	3100-3299	
DETROIT WAY	Northglenn	195F	80233	11000-11199	
	Thornton	165A	80602	14500-14799	
DETROIT WAY S	Denver	315T	80210	2900-3099	
DEVERS AVE	Arapahoe Co	795T	80103	None	
DEVILS HEAD	Jefferson Co	371L	80127	10600-10799	
DEVILS HEAD CIR	Jefferson Co	249E	80403	None	
DEVILS HEAD CT	Jefferson Co	249B	80403	6100-6199	
DEVILSHEAD DR	Douglas Co	440D	80138	9200-9499	
DEVILS POINT PL E	Highlands Ranch	374V	80126	1600-1699	
DEVIL'S THUMB AVE E					
	Buckley Air Force Base	289T	80011	None	
DEVINNEY CIR	Arvada	220Y	80004	6200-6299	
DEVINNEY CT	Arvada	250C	80004	6000-6199	
	Arvada	220U	80004	6600-7199	
	Arvada	220Q	80005	7200-7599	
	Arvada	220C	80005	None	
	Arvada	220G	80005	None	
	Jefferson Co	280Q	80401	400-799	
	Jefferson Co	280C	80401	2500-2599	
	Jefferson Co	220L	80005	None	
DEVINNEY CT S	Jefferson Co	340L	80465	4300-4699	
	Lakewood	310L	80228	1900-2099	
	Lakewood	310U	80228	2800-2999	
DEVINNEY ST	Arvada	220Y	80004	6400-6599	
	Arvada	220U	80004	6700-6899	
	Arvada	220G	80005	8300-8699	
	Arvada	220C	80005	None	
	Jefferson Co	280Q	80401	700-799	
DEVINNEY ST S	Jefferson Co	280Y	80401	1-299	
	Jefferson Co	340L	80465	4300-4699	
	Lakewood	280Y	80228	400-599	
	Lakewood	310L	80228	1900-2199	
	Lakewood	310Q	80228	2200-2399	
DEVINNEY WAY	Arvada	250C	80004	6000-6199	
DEVINNEY WAY S	Jefferson Co	340Y	80127	6000-6199	
	Lakewood	280Y	80228	600-699	
	Lakewood	310C	80228	800-1099	
DEVON AVE	Castle Rock	498L	80104	5100-5299	
DEVON CT S	Highlands Ranch	404C	80126	9400-9599	
DEVON PL	Boulder	128J	80302	200-299	
DEVONSHIRE BLVD	Adams Co	225F	80229	8400-8799	
DEVONSHIRE CT	Adams Co	225A	80229	2200-2699	
DEVONSHIRE CT	Boulder Co	100E	80301	7700-7799	
DEVONSHIRE PL S	Highlands Ranch	404D	80126	9400-9599	
DEVONSHIRE ST	Boulder Co	100E	80301	4600-4899	
DEVONSHIRE ST	Firestone	707T	80504	10300-10599	
DEVONSHIRE ST E	Lafayette	131M	80026	1100-1199	
DEVONSHIRE ST W	Lafayette	131M	80026	1200-1299	
DEVONSHIRE WAY	Boulder Co	100F	80301	7700-7899	
DEWBERRY CIR E	Parker	409A	80134	17200-17599	
DEWBERRY DR E	Parker	409A	80134	17000-17599	
DEWEY AVE	Boulder	97Y	80304	400-899	
DEWEY RD	Brighton	139G	80601	None	
DEWFROST PL	Castle Rock	527D	80104	1300-1599	
DEWHURST LN	Douglas Co	409X	80134	None	
DEXTER CIR	Thornton	195H	80233	11200-11299	
DEXTER CT	Denver	255V	80207	3500-3799	
	Thornton	165U	80241	12600-12799	
DEXTER CT S	Centennial	375M	80122	7400-7499	
	Centennial	375M	80122	7700-7799	
DEXTER DR	Broomfield	162V	80020	700-899	
DEXTER DR	Longmont	11R	80501	2100-2299	
DEXTER DR	Thornton	195M	80233	10500-10799	
	Thornton	195H	80229	11100-11199	
DEXTER LN	Thornton	195U	80229	None	
DEXTER PL	Broomfield	162V	80020	None	
DEXTER PL	Thornton	195H	80229	11100-11199	
	Thornton	165Q	80241	None	
DEXTER ST	Adams Co	225V	80022	7000-7499	
DEXTER ST	Broomfield	162M	80020	1000-1999	
DEXTER ST	Commerce City	255D	80022	5600-6199	
	Commerce City	225Z	80022	6200-6399	
	Commerce City	225V	80022	6900-6999	
	Denver	285M	80220	1-1099	
	Denver	285H	80220	1200-1499	
	Denver	285D	80207	2000-2799	
	Denver	255Z	80207	2800-3799	
DEXTER ST	Fort Lupton	728L	80621	300-899	
	Fort Lupton	728M	80621	1300-1398	E

D

STREET NAME	CITY or COUNTY	MAP GRID	ZIP CODE	BLOCK RANGE	O/E
DEXTER ST	Thornton	195H	80229	11200-11299	
	Thornton	165U	80241	12400-12699	
	Thornton	165V	80241	12800-12999	
	Thornton	165Q	80241	12900-13099	
	Thornton	165G	80602	None	
DEXTER ST S	Centennial	345Z	80121	6300-6399	
	Centennial	375D	80121	6400-6699	
	Centennial	375H	80122	6700-7499	
	Cherry Hills Village	345H	80113	3900-4099	
	Denver	285V	80246	1-299	
	Denver	315D	80246	701-799	O
	Denver	315D	80246	800-1099	
	Denver	315U	80222	1900-2699	
	Denver	315Z	80222	3100-3499	
	Glendale	315D	80246	700-798	E
DEXTER WAY	Thornton	165V	80241	12400-12699	
	Thornton	165Q	80241	12800-12999	
	Thornton	165L	80241	13400-13499	
	Thornton	165G	80602	None	
DEXTER WAY S	Centennial	375H	80122	7300-7499	
	Denver	315H	80222	1500-1599	
	Denver	315V	80222	2800-3099	
DHARMA AVE	Broomfield	163U	80020	2700-2899	
DHU CT	Boulder Co	69K	80503	6000-6099	
DIABLO PL	Lochbuie	140F	80603	None	
DIABLO WAY	Douglas Co	436X	80108	3300-3399	
DIAGONAL HWY	Boulder	98P	80301	2800-3599	
	Boulder Co	69U	80503	7000-7299	
	Boulder Co	70F	80503	7300-8599	
	Boulder Co	40Z	80503	8600-9199	
	Boulder Co	41S	80503	9200-9499	
	Boulder Co	98M	80301	None	
	Boulder Co	99E	80301	None	
DIAMOND CIR	Lafayette	131H	80026	900-1299	
DIAMOND CIR	Louisville	160D	80027	300-399	
DIAMOND CT	Boulder Co	130E	80303	1000-1099	
DIAMOND DR	Clear Creek Co	801V	80439	1-399	
DIAMOND DR	Longmont	41U	80504	1900-2199	
DIAMONDBACK RD	Jefferson Co	340K	80465	4600-5099	
DIAMOND HEAD DR	Castle Rock	497V	80104	1800-1999	
DIAMOND LEAF DR N	Castle Rock	466U	80109	4400-4699	
DIAMOND RIDGE CIR	Castle Rock	467L	80108	800-1699	
DIAMOND RIDGE PKWY	Castle Rock	467L	80108	5700-6899	
DIANA RD	Jefferson Co	842A	80470	33100-33599	
DIANE AVE	Gilpin Co	760G	80403	1-299	
DIANE CT	Highlands Ranch	376U	80124	300-399	
DIANE DR	Jefferson Co	762E	80403	10800-10899	
DIANNA DR	Highlands Ranch	376V	80124	1-299	
DICHTER CT	Thornton	195W	80229	1800-2099	
DICKENS CT	Longmont	41B	80501	800-899	
DICKENS ST	Erie	102W	80516	2800-2999	
DICKENSON PL E	Aurora	317R	80014	12500-12899	
DICKENSON DR E	Aurora	318P	80014	14100-14299	
	Aurora	319Q	80013	18800-19299	
DICKENSON PL E	Arapahoe Co	315R	80222	5200-5599	
	Aurora	318R	80013	16500-16599	
	Aurora	319N	80013	17500-17599	
	Aurora	319P	80013	17800-18499	
	Aurora	319Q	80013	19300-19599	
	Aurora	319R	80013	19800-20099	
	Denver	315Q	80222	4000-4399	
	Denver	316N	80222	6300-6499	
	Denver	316P	80224	6500-6999	
DICK MOUNTAIN DR	Park Co	841U	80421	1-1299	
DICKSON ST	Longmont	42F	80501	400-499	
DICKSON ST S	Keenesburg	732A	80643	1-99	
DIGGER DR	Golden	279E	80401	1901-1999	O
DILL RD W	Sheridan	343G	80110	3300-3599	
DILLARD PL E	Denver	316Y	80231	8600-8699	
DILLION CT S	Aurora	348K	80015	4600-4699	
DILLION WAY	Longmont	12P	80501	2300-2399	
DILLON CIR	Commerce City	198P	80022	10000-10099	
DILLON CT	Commerce City	198P	80603	10201-10299	O
DILLON CT S	Arapahoe Co	378F	80112	7100-7199	
DILLON DR	Douglas Co	496Y	80109	300-599	
DILLON RD	Broomfield	162G	80020	11100-12799	
	Louisville	160B	80027	701-1299	O
	Louisville	161B	80027	9100-9298	E
	Louisville	161B	80020	9600-10499	
DILLON ST	Adams Co	168P	80601	13200-13399	
	Adams Co	168K	80601	13400-13599	
	Denver	258K	80239	4400-5499	
	Denver	258F	80239	5500-5599	
DILLON ST S	Aurora	318P	80014	2300-2699	
	Aurora	348F	80014	4300-4399	
	Aurora	348K	80015	4800-5099	
DILLON WAY	Aurora	288P	80011	600-799	
DILLON WAY	Superior	160R	80027	1300-1599	
DILLON WAY S	Aurora	318F	80012	1200-1399	
	Aurora	348F	80014	3900-4299	
	Aurora	348K	80015	4800-4899	
DIME RD	Boulder Co	722T	80302	1-399	
DIMMIT DR	Boulder Co	129F	80303	5800-5999	
DINERO PL	Douglas Co	436X	80108	3300-3399	
DINNADAN ST	Lafayette	132P	80026	None	
DINOSAUR ST	Castle Rock	496C	80109	3400-3899	
DIONE PL	Highlands Ranch	376X	80124	400-499	
DISC DR	Longmont	40E	80503	301-399	O
DISC LN	Platteville	708B	80651	300-399	
DISCOVERY CT	Broomfield	133L	80020	None	
DISCOVERY DR	Boulder	128G	80303	3100-4099	
DISCOVERY DR	Broomfield	133L	80020	None	
DISCOVERY PKWY	Superior	160F	80027	500-598	E
DISK DR	Louisville	161J	80027	None	
DIS-MOUNT DR	Jefferson Co	366H	80439	None	
DISTANT ROCK AVE	Castle Rock	466V	80109	None	
DISTANT VIEW PL	Douglas Co	439X	80134	5600-5799	
DISTEL DR	Lafayette	132P	80026	1100-1399	
DITMARS LN	Castle Rock	528J	80104	None	
	Douglas Co	528J	80104	3100-3899	
DIVIDE VIEW DR	Clear Creek Co	780V	80452	None	
DIVIDE VIEW RD	Boulder Co	742W	80403	1-1099	
DIVIDE VIEW RD	Jefferson Co	306B	80439	29600-29699	
DIVISION ST	Denver	254X	80202	1900-1999	
DIVISION ST	Highlands Ranch	373X	80125	12900-12999	
DIVISION ST	Platteville	708C	80651	100-1299	
DIVISION VIEW DR	Idaho Springs	780V	80452	100-399	
DIVOT CT	Boulder Co	723G	80503	3900-3999	
DIVOT DR	Jefferson Co	306N	80439	31200-31299	
DIXIE PL W	Denver	254J	80221	1500-1899	
DIXIE ST	Palmer Lake	907Q	80133	None	
DIXON AVE	Lafayette	132N	80026	1300-1599	
DIXON DR	Adams Co	223E	80031	4200-4799	
DIXON DR	Douglas Co	409C	80138	12500-13199	
DIXON DR N	Douglas Co	379Y	80138	12500-13199	
DIXON RD	Boulder Co	721R	80302	1-1999	
DOANE DR E	Aurora	319V	80013	None	
DOANE PL E	Aurora	320S	80013	None	
	Denver	316Z	80231	8600-8799	
DOBBINS RUN	Boulder Co	102J	80026	10900-11299	
DODD LN	Longmont	11L	80501	2400-2499	
DODGE DR	Northglenn	194T	80260	9900-10099	
DOE CIR	Douglas Co	870E	80116	300-499	
DOE CIR	Park Co	841V	80421	1-499	
DOENING ST	Thornton	224D	80229	8800-9099	
DOE TRAIL	Nederland	740R	80466	None	
DOE VALLEY DR	Jefferson Co	822Z	80433	28400-28799	
DOEWOOD CIR	El Paso Co	908T	80132	19000-19199	
DOEWOOD DR	El Paso Co	908P	80132	19000-20399	
DOGIE SPUR	Jefferson Co	275B	80403	2200-2599	
DOGLEG LN	Broomfield	163F	80020	13800-14099	
DOGWOOD AVE	Brighton	138S	80601	300-499	
DOGWOOD AVE	Fort Lupton	728H	80621	900-1099	
DOGWOOD AVE	Weld Co	706Q	80504	None	
DOGWOOD AVE E	Centennial	344Z	80121	800-999	
DOGWOOD AVE E	Douglas Co	408B	80134	3000-3999	
DOGWOOD CIR	Erie	133H	80516	None	
DOGWOOD CIR	Louisville	130M	80027	2100-2399	
DOGWOOD CT	Broomfield	162K	80020	1700-1799	
DOGWOOD DR	Douglas Co	850Y	80116	11900-11999	
DOGWOOD DR	Jefferson Co	308A	80401	900-1099	
DOGWOOD LN	Boulder	97R	80304	1600-1799	
DOGWOOD LN	Longmont	11Z	80501	1300-1399	
DOGWOOD ST	Firestone	707T	80504	None	
DOGWOOD ST	Louisville	131Y	80027	1700-2099	
DOLAN DR	El Paso Co	908Z	80132	800-1299	
DOLOMITE LN	Castle Rock	467H	80108	7100-7399	
DOLOMITE WAY	Castle Rock	467H	80108	1800-2099	
DOLTON CT S	Highlands Ranch	405A	80126	9600-9699	
DOLTON WAY S	Highlands Ranch	405A	80126	9400-9699	
DOME PEAK	Jefferson Co	371K	80127	7500-7599	
DOME ROCK RD	Douglas Co	432Q	80125	7100-7299	
DOMINGO CT	Parker	439F	80134	12700-12899	
DOMINGO DR	Parker	439F	80134	17800-18199	
DOMINICA PL	Boulder	98K	80301	3100-3299	
DONALD AVE E	Denver	315R	80222	4800-5299	
DONALD ST	Gilpin Co	760H	80403	None	
DONATELLO CT	Douglas Co	432E	80125	8000-8199	
DONAVAN DR	Longmont	41F	80501	1800-1999	
DONEGAL AVE	Parker	408R	80134	None	
DONELLY AVE	Erie	103P	80516	None	
DONELLY PL	Erie	103P	80516	800-899	
DONERAIL AVE	Parker	410T	80138	None	
DONLEY DR N	Douglas Co	409L	80138	11100-11699	
DONLEY ST N	Douglas Co	409G	80138	11800-11999	
DONN CT	Boulder Co	129U	80303	500-599	
DONNA AVE S	Jefferson Co	842A	80470	12300-12499	
DONNA CT	Brighton	138V	80601	None	
DONNA DR	Jefferson Co	365Y	80433	32600-32699	
DONNA ST	Brighton	138V	80601	None	
DONNA ST	Fort Lupton	728Q	80621	200-299	
DONNER CT	Jefferson Co	306E	80439	1300-1399	
DONNER CT N	Douglas Co	440T	80134	6200-6399	
DONNINGTON CIR	Castle Rock	527B	80104	3800-4099	
DONNINGTON CT	Castle Rock	527B	80104	1-99	
DONNINGTON WAY	Castle Rock	527B	80104	3900-3999	
DONOVAN CT	Longmont	41F	80501	100-199	
DONOVAN PL	Longmont	41F	80501	1500-1699	
DONOVEN ST	Adams Co	793R	80136	1600-1699	
DOPPLER ST	Adams Co	793R	80136	1600-2199	
DORADO AVE E	Arapahoe Co	347T	80111	10500-10899	
	Arapahoe Co	347U	80111	11300-11699	
	Arapahoe Co	350U	80015	22200-23299	
	Centennial	348U	80015	15400-15699	
	Centennial	348V	80015	16300-16699	
	Centennial	349T	80015	17500-18499	
	Centennial	350T	80015	19700-22199	
	Greenwood Village	346S	80111	5700-6899	
	Greenwood Village	347S	80111	9700-9899	
DORADO AVE W	Jefferson Co	341T	80127	10800-11299	
	Lakewood	342V	80123	5400-5499	
DORADO CIR E	Arapahoe Co	347T	80111	10900-11199	
	Centennial	348V	80015	16000-16199	
	Centennial	349S	80015	17000-17299	
	Centennial	350S	80015	20900-21099	
DORADO CIR S	Greenwood Village	346S	80111	6300-6399	
DORADO CT E	Centennial	350S	80015	20900-20999	
DORADO CT E	Highlands Ranch	406F	80130	6900-6999	
DORADO CT W	Jefferson Co	341V	80123	8800-8899	
DORADO DR E	Arapahoe Co	349U	80015	18600-18799	
	Arapahoe Co	350U	80015	22300-22999	
	Aurora	350V	80016	None	
	Centennial	349S	80015	16900-17799	
	Centennial	349T	80015	17900-18299	
DORADO DR W	Denver	342V	80123	6400-6599	
	Jefferson Co	341V	80123	9500-9699	
	Lakewood	342V	80123	5400-6399	
DORADO PL E	Arapahoe Co	347T	80111	10600-10799	
	Arapahoe Co	349U	80015	18800-18999	
	Arapahoe Co	350U	80015	22300-22499	
	Aurora	350V	80016	None	
	Aurora	350V	80016	None	
	Aurora	351S	80016	None	
	Centennial	348U	80015	15400-15699	
	Centennial	348V	80015	16100-16299	
	Centennial	350S	80015	20600-20799	
	Greenwood Village	346T	80111	6500-6899	
	Greenwood Village	346U	80111	7700-7899	
	Greenwood Village	347T	80111	10400-10499	
DORADO PL S	Centennial	349S	80015	17100-17299	
DORADO PL W	Jefferson Co	341U	80123	9900-9999	
	Jefferson Co	341T	80127	11100-11199	
	Jefferson Co	341S	80127	12100-12399	
	Jefferson Co	340V	80127	12600-13199	
	Jefferson Co	341S	80127	None	
	Lakewood	342V	80123	5300-5399	
DORAL CT	Broomfield	163F	80020	14100-14199	
DORAL CT	Douglas Co	886C	80118	6000-6099	
DORAL DR	Boulder	69Z	80301	7100-7399	
DORAL DR	Longmont	10Y	80503	3700-3899	
DORAL LN	Columbine Valley	373B	80123	1-99	
DORAL PL	Longmont	10Z	80503	None	
DORAN DR	Boulder	70W	80301	7300-7499	
DORCHESTER CIR	Boulder Co	100F	80301	4700-4799	
DORCHESTER ST	Highlands Ranch	404B	80129	None	
DORIC DR	Lafayette	131Q	80026	1200-1399	
DORIS CIR	Weld Co	726J	80516	1200-1299	
DORIS CT	Commerce City	226X	80022	6500-6699	
DORIS LN	Jefferson Co	366B	80439	6400-6499	
DORIS PL	Palmer Lake	907Q	80133	None	
DORNCLIFFE CT	El Paso Co	909S	80132	None	
DOROTHY BLVD	Thornton	194V	80229	900-9599	
DOROTHY LN	Longmont	40T	80503	None	
DOROTHY RD	Jefferson Co	336T	80439	29400-29999	
DORSET CT	Castle Pines North	436R	80108	1-199	
DORSET CT	Lafayette	131M	80026	1100-1199	
DORY CIR	Gilpin Co	761S	80403	1-199	
DORY DR E	Gilpin Co	761N	80403	1-299	
DORY WAY E	Gilpin Co	761N	80403	1-199	
DORY WAY W	Gilpin Co	761N	80403	1-599	
DORY HILL RD	Gilpin Co	761W	80403	1100-2999	
DORY LAKES DR	Gilpin Co	761N	80403	1-399	
DORY LAKES DR N	Gilpin Co	761N	80403	1-999	
DORY LAKES DR S	Gilpin Co	761N	80403	1-1199	
DOS LOBOS DR	Gilpin Co	761E	80403	1-199	
DOTTY CT	Jefferson Co	842F	80470	33100-33299	
DOTTY RD	Jefferson Co	842A	80470	33300-33899	
DOUBLE EAGLE CT	Castle Rock	497Q	80104	1200-1399	
DOUBLE EAGLE DR	Jefferson Co	340N	80465	15700-16099	
DOUBLEHEADER HWY	Jefferson Co	368T	80465	8300-8599	
DOUBLEHEADER RANCH RD					
	Jefferson Co	368T	80465	8300-8899	
DOUBLE TREE RD	Park Co	841F	80421	1-599	
DOUBLE TREE TRAIL N	Douglas Co	830E	80138	13500-13999	
DOUGLA DR	Weld Co	707J	80504	12600-12698	E
DOUGLAS AVE	Douglas Co	847N	80135	4000-5499	
DOUGLAS AVE	Palmer Lake	907U	80133	None	
DOUGLAS BLVD	Larkspur	887R	80118	9100-9399	
DOUGLAS CT	Boulder Co	742C	80302	1-99	
DOUGLAS DR	Adams Co	224E	80221	300-1599	
DOUGLAS DR	Broomfield	162L	80020	None	
DOUGLAS DR N	Broomfield	162K	80020	1-99	
DOUGLAS DR S	Broomfield	162L	80020	1-99	
DOUGLAS PL W	Denver	253Y	80211	2200-2299	
DOUGLAS ST W	Superior	160F	80027	100-299	
DOUGLAS FIR AVE	Castle Rock	497R	80104	100-299	
DOUGLAS MOUNTAIN DR	Jefferson Co	275B	80403	100-2699	
	Jefferson Co	782J	80403	2700-4199	
DOUGLAS PARK RD	Jefferson Co	336G	80439	28000-29099	
DOUGLAS PASS CT	Brighton	140J	80601	None	
DOUGLASS RANCH DR	Jefferson Co	842F	80470	13300-14199	
DOUNCE ST	Lafayette	132F	80026	600-899	
DOVE AVE	Brighton	138S	80601	800-899	
DOVE COVE	Lafayette	132P	80026	800-899	
DOVE CT	Douglas Co	439R	80134	7100-7299	
DOVE DR	Lafayette	132K	80026	700-799	
DOVE ST	Federal Heights	193U	80260	2900-2999	
DOVE CREEK CT S	Parker	439C	80134	12600-12699	
DOVE CREEK DR	Elbert Co	851Q	80107	38100-38399	
DOVE CREEK PL E	Parker	439D	80134	19600-19699	
DOVE CREEK WAY S	Parker	439C	80134	12500-12699	
DOVER AVE	Lafayette	131M	80026	300-599	
DOVER CIR	Arvada	222S	80004	6900-6999	
	Arvada	222E	80005	8100-8199	
	Lakewood	282S	80226	8700-8899	
	Westminster	222E	80005	8500-8599	
	Westminster	222A	80005	8700-8799	
DOVER CIR S	Jefferson Co	372A	80128	6700-6899	
DOVER CT	Arvada	252E	80002	5400-5499	
	Arvada	252A	80004	5800-5899	
	Arvada	222J	80005	7800-7899	
	Arvada	222E	80005	8300-8499	
	Broomfield	162V	80020	200-499	
	Broomfield	162R	80020	1200-1299	
	Castle Pines North	436R	80108	100-199	
	Lakewood	282A	80215	2500-2599	
	Westminster	222E	80005	8500-8699	
	Westminster	222A	80005	8700-8799	
DOVER CT S	Jefferson Co	342E	80123	4300-4499	
	Jefferson Co	342S	80123	5900-5999	
	Jefferson Co	372E	80128	7100-7299	
	Jefferson Co	372S	80128	8700-8799	
	Lakewood	282W	80226	400-499	
	Lakewood	312J	80232	1500-1699	
	Lakewood	312J	80227	1900-1999	
	Lakewood	312N	80227	2100-2499	
	Lakewood	312W	80227	3100-3299	
DOVER DR	Boulder	128P	80305	2800-3399	
DOVER ST	Arvada	252J	80002	5100-5299	
	Arvada	252E	80002	5400-5799	
	Arvada	252A	80004	5900-6199	
	Arvada	222W	80004	6200-6599	
	Arvada	222S	80004	6600-6899	
	Arvada	222N	80005	7300-7399	
	Broomfield	162V	80020	700-899	
	Broomfield	162M	80020	1300-1999	
	Firestone	707P	80504	11200-11499	
	Firestone	707T	80504	None	
	Jefferson Co	252J	80002	4800-5099	
	Lakewood	282S	80226	1-199	
	Lakewood	282N	80226	400-599	
	Lakewood	282E	80215	1500-2299	
	Westminster	222A	80005	8600-8899	
	Westminster	192W	80021	9000-9199	
	Westminster	192N	80021	10100-10399	
	Westminster	192J	80021	10600-10999	
	Wheat Ridge	252S	80033	3800-4399	
	Wheat Ridge	252N	80033	4400-4799	
DOVER ST S	Denver	342S	80123	5400-5499	
	Jefferson Co	342N	80123	5100-5199	
	Jefferson Co	342W	80123	6100-6299	
	Jefferson Co	372A	80123	6400-6599	
	Jefferson Co	372N	80128	7700-8299	

Continued on next page

STREET NAME	CITY or COUNTY	MAP GRID	ZIP CODE	BLOCK RANGE	O/E
DOVER ST S (Cont'd)	Lakewood	282S	80226	1-99	
	Lakewood	312A	80226	700-1099	
	Lakewood	312E	80232	1100-1199	
	Lakewood	312S	80227	2500-2699	
DOVER WAY	Arvada	222S	80004	6800-7099	
	Arvada	222E	80005	8200-8599	
	Broomfield	162R	80020	1100-1199	
	Lakewood	282J	80215	1400-1499	
	Westminster	192W	80021	9200-9299	
	Westminster	192S	80021	9400-9499	
DOVER WAY S	Jefferson Co	372A	80123	6500-6699	
	Jefferson Co	372E	80128	6800-6999	
	Lakewood	312E	80232	1200-1499	
	Lakewood	312J	80232	1700-1899	
	Lakewood	312N	80227	2100-2599	
	Littleton	825Q	80127	9600-9699	
DOVE RIDGE DR	Douglas Co	378U	80134	None	
DOVE RIDGE WAY	Douglas Co	378Q	80134	8200-8699	
DOVETAIL WAY	Douglas Co	432Q	80125	7400-7499	
DOVE VALLEY PL	Castle Rock	498B	80108	3300-3599	
DOWDLE DR	Gilpin Co	761M	80403	10200-10499	
DOWDLE DR	Jefferson Co	762E	80403	10000-10199	
DOWLING CT S	Highlands Ranch	404M	80126	10200-10299	
DOWLING WAY	Erie	103N	80516	None	
DOWLING WAY S	Highlands Ranch	404M	80126	10200-10299	
DOWNING CIR	Thornton	194V	80229	None	
DOWNING CIR S	Arapahoe Co	374D	80122	6700E-6899E	
	Arapahoe Co	374M	80122	7300E-7499E	
	Cherry Hills Village	344M	80113	4500-4599	
	Denver	314V	80210	2700-2798	E
DOWNING CT	Northglenn	194M	80233	None	
DOWNING DR	Adams Co	224H	80229	8000-8399	
	Northglenn	194H	80233	11200-11399	
DOWNING DR E	Thornton	194V	80229	9700-9799	
	Adams Co	254D	80216	5800-6199	
	Adams Co	224Z	80216	6200-6399	
	Adams Co	224Z	80229	6400-6899	
	Adams Co	224M	80229	7800-8199	
	Adams Co	164M	80602	13600-14299	
	Denver	284H	80218	1-1999	
	Denver	284D	80205	2000-2799	
	Denver	254Z	80205	2800-3799	
	Northglenn	194R	80233	10400-10799	
	Northglenn	194D	80233	11400-11699	
	Thornton	194V	80229	9600-9999	
	Thornton	194R	80229	10200-10399	
	Thornton	164R	80241	13200-13399	
	Thornton	134M	80602	16600-16699	
DOWNING ST S	Arapahoe Co	374D	80121	6400-6699	
	Arapahoe Co	374M	80122	7500-7599	
	Arapahoe Co	374R	80122	8100-8299	
	Cherry Hills Village	344M	80113	4300-4799	
	Denver	284Z	80209	1-699	
	Denver	314D	80209	700-1099	
	Denver	314M	80210	1100-2699	
	Denver	314V	80210	2700-2798	E
	Englewood	314V	80110	2701-2899	O
	Englewood	314Z	80113	2900-3599	
DOWNING WAY	Adams Co	224M	80229	700-1099	
	Northglenn	194H	80233	None	
DOWNWEST RIDE	Elbert Co	871B	80107	4100-4899	
DOWNY CREEK CT S	Parker	439C	80134	12400-12499	
DOWNY CREEK PL E	Parker	439C	80134	19000-19299	
DRACO CIR	El Paso Co	908N	80132	2900-3199	
DRACO DR	El Paso Co	908N	80132	19200-19899	
DRACO WAY	El Paso Co	908S	80132	2500-2799	
DRAGONFLY CT	Castle Rock	466Y	80109	2600-2899	
DRAGOON CT	Douglas Co	867Q	80109	2000-2199	
DRAKE CT	Jefferson Co	842F	80470	13600-13899	
DRAKE PL	Parker	409J	80134	10400-10499	
DRAKE ST	Adams Co	224K	80221	100-299	
	Adams Co	224P	80221	400-1099	
DRAKE ST	Boulder	128P	80305	400-599	
DRAKE ST	Frederick	707W	80504	5500-5599	
DRAKE ST	Longmont	10V	80503	1400-1799	
DRAKE WAY	Frederick	707W	80504	5500-9099	
DRANSFELDT RD	Parker	409C	80134	9800-10899	
DRAW ST	Lochbuie	139H	80603	None	
	Castle Rock	466Y	80109	None	
DREHER DR	Clear Creek Co	801R	80439	1-199	
DRESDEN	Thornton	224A	80260	None	
DRESDEN DR	Castle Rock	466U	80109	None	
DRESDEN ST	Firestone	707T	80504	10100-10599	
DRESSAGE RD	Douglas Co	432F	80125	8000-8499	
DREW CIR	Boulder	128U	80305	4300-4399	
DREW CT S	Jefferson Co	342N	80123	5100-5199	
DREW WAY S	Lakewood	312E	80232	1200-1499	
DREW HILL RD	Jefferson Co	763W	80403	7200-7299	
	Jefferson Co	762P	80403	7300-9999	
DREXEL ST	Boulder	128T	80305	1100-1399	
DREXEL WAY S	Lakewood	312E	80232	1200-1499	
DRIFT LN	Parker	410X	80138	None	
DRIFT PL	Longmont	12X	80501	700-799	
DRIFTWOOD CIR	Elbert Co	851J	80138	None	
DRIFTWOOD CIR	Lafayette	131K	80026	300-399	
DRIFTWOOD DR	Thornton	193Z	80260	None	
DRIFTWOOD LN	Thornton	193V	80260	None	
DRIFTWOOD PL	Boulder Co	99G	80301	4400-4599	
DRINKWATER CT	Erie	102Q	80516	1700-1799	
DRIVER CT	Boulder Co	723G	80503	4000-4099	
DRIVER LN	Columbine Valley	373B	80123	1-99	
DRIVER LN	Erie	133B	80516	None	
DRY CREEK CIR	Boulder Co	70K	80503	8000-8199	
DRY CREEK CIR E	Aurora	380M	80016	None	
DRY CREEK RD	Boulder Co	70K	80503	7200-7399	
DRY CREEK CIR E	Centennial	375M	80122	5400-5499	
	Centennial	376K	80112	7000-7199	
DRY CREEK CIR W	Littleton	374K	80120	1-99	
DRY CREEK CT	Boulder	69Y	80301	5400-5499	
DRY CREEK CT S	Greenwood Village	345T	80121	5800-5899	
DRY CREEK CT W	Littleton	374K	80120	1-99	
	Littleton	373M	80120	2400-2599	
DRY CREEK DR	Longmont	41N	80503	900-1299	
	Longmont	41S	80503	1300-1899	
DRY CREEK DR E	Aurora	381K	80016	25400-25899	
	Aurora	381J	80016	None	
DRY CREEK PKWY	Boulder Co	69R	80503	6200-6599	
DRY CREEK PKWY E	Boulder Co	70N	80503	7400-7499	

STREET NAME	CITY or COUNTY	MAP GRID	ZIP CODE	BLOCK RANGE	O/E
DRY CREEK PKWY W	Boulder Co	69R	80503	6300-6599	
DRY CREEK PL E	Arapahoe Co	374M	80122	1100-1399	
	Arapahoe Co	374M	80122	1500-1799	
DRY CREEK PL E	Aurora	381J	80016	24700-24799	
	Aurora	381F	80016	25800-25999	
DRY CREEK PL E	Centennial	375K	80122	2800-2999	
	Centennial	376K	80112	7000-7099	
	Centennial	376M	80112	8500-8599	
DRY CREEK RD	Gilpin Co	761U	80403	100-199	
DRY CREEK RD E	Arapahoe Co	374L	80122	800-1699	
	Arapahoe Co	377J	80112	9700-10399	
	Aurora	380K	80016	None	
	Centennial	375K	80122	1700-5399	
	Centennial	376L	80112	5600-9299	
	Centennial	376M	80112	8600-8799	
	Centennial	377J	80112	8900-9699	
	Littleton	374L	80122	1-799	
DRY CREEK RD W	Littleton	374L	80120	1-199	
	Littleton	374K	80120	800-1499	
	Littleton	374J	80120	1500-1999	
	Littleton	373M	80120	2000-2299	
DRY CREEK WAY W	Littleton	374J	80120	1400-1499	
DTC BLVD S	Denver	346L	80237	4600-5099	
DTC BLVD S	Greenwood Village	346R	80111	5100-5899	
D T C PKWY S	Greenwood Village	346Q	80111	5100-5799	
DUBERRY ST	El Paso Co	908P	80132	None	
DUBLIN CT	Castle Rock	497U	80104	None	
DUBLIN DR	Castle Rock	497U	80104	None	
DUBLIN DR	Elbert Co	850G	80138	41200-41599	
DUBLIN PL	Castle Rock	497U	80104	None	
DUBOIS ST	Black Hawk	780D	80422	None	
DUCHESNE CT	Castle Rock	498V	80104	5300-5399	
DUCHESS DR	Longmont	11Q	80501	1700-1899	
DUCKWEED CT	Douglas Co	378U	80134	15800-15999	
DUDES DR	Gilpin Co	740Z	80474	None	
DUDLEY CIR	Arvada	222S	80004	6800-6899	
	Arvada	222E	80005	8100-8199	
DUDLEY CT	Arvada	252E	80002	5400-5599	
	Arvada	252A	80004	5900-6199	
	Arvada	222J	80005	7900-7999	
	Arvada	222E	80005	8300-8399	
	Arvada	222W	80004	None	
	Westminster	222A	80005	8600-8799	
	Westminster	222A	80021	8800-8899	
DUDLEY CT S	Jefferson Co	342N	80123	5200-5299	
	Jefferson Co	342W	80123	6200-6299	
	Jefferson Co	372A	80123	6600-6699	
	Jefferson Co	372A	80128	6700-6899	
	Jefferson Co	372E	80128	7200-7399	
	Lakewood	312J	80232	1600-1799	
	Lakewood	312N	80227	2400-2499	
	Lakewood	312W	80227	3200-3499	
DUDLEY DR	Arvada	222S	80004	6900-7199	
	Westminster	191V	80021	9500-9599	
DUDLEY LN	Longmont	40D	80503	601-799	O
DUDLEY ST	Arvada	252J	80002	5100-5299	
	Arvada	252E	80002	5600-5799	
	Arvada	252A	80004	5900-6199	
	Arvada	222N	80005	7300-7399	
	Lakewood	282S	80226	1-199	
	Lakewood	282N	80226	400-599	
	Lakewood	282N	80215	600-1299	
	Lakewood	282E	80215	1500-1999	
	Westminster	222A	80021	8800-8999	
	Westminster	192W	80021	9000-9199	
	Wheat Ridge	252S	80033	3200-4399	
	Wheat Ridge	252N	80033	4600-4799	
DUDLEY ST S	Denver	342J	80123	4500-5099	
	Jefferson Co	342N	80123	5100-5199	
	Jefferson Co	372E	80128	7000-7099	
	Jefferson Co	372N	80128	7700-8299	
	Jefferson Co	372S	80128	8300-8699	
	Jefferson Co	372W	80128	8700-8899	
	Lakewood	282S	80226	1-99	
	Lakewood	282W	80226	400-699	
	Lakewood	312A	80226	700-1099	
	Lakewood	312E	80232	1100-1599	
	Lakewood	312N	80227	2100-2599	
	Lakewood	312W	80227	3000-3399	
DUDLEY WAY	Arvada	222E	80005	8100-8399	
	Westminster	192W	80021	9200-9299	
DUDLEY WAY S	Jefferson Co	342E	80123	4400-4499	
	Jefferson Co	342W	80123	6000-6099	
	Jefferson Co	372A	80123	6300-6599	
	Littleton	825Q	80127	9600-9699	
DUELING STAGS	Douglas Co	432N	80125	10800-10899	
DUETTE WAY	Broomfield	161V	80020	1-99	
DUFFER CIR	Erie	133G	80516	None	
DUFFY LN	Douglas Co	870B	80116	10900-10999	
DUKE CIR	Boulder	128T	80305	2800-2899	
DUKE CT	Broomfield	163Q	80020	12900-12999	
DUKE DR E	Aurora	320S	80013	None	
DUKE PL E	Aurora	320S	80013	None	
	Denver	316Z	80231	8600-8699	
DUKES WAY	Dacono	727J	80514	100-399	
DULUTH CT	Denver	258P	80239	4600-5199	
DULUTH WAY	Denver	258P	80239	4400-4499	
DUMAS CT	Denver	258P	80239	4400-4499	
DUMBARTON CIR W	Jefferson Co	341L	80127	10600-11099	
DUMBARTON DR W	Jefferson Co	341Q	80127	10800-10899	
	Jefferson Co	341K	80127	11300-11399	
	Jefferson Co	341N	80465	11800-12099	
	Jefferson Co	340M	80465	13000-13199	
DUMBARTON PL W	Jefferson Co	341L	80127	10800-10899	
	Jefferson Co	341J	80465	12400-12499	
DUMBARTON WAY W	Jefferson Co	341K	80127	11100-11199	
DUMONT WAY N	Douglas Co	403B	80125	12100-12499	
DUNBAR CT	Longmont	11P	80501	2200-2399	
DUNBARTON CT	Highlands Ranch	376S	80130	1-99	
DUNBARTON DR	Cherry Hills Village	346J	80111	5700-5799	
DUNCAN DR	Douglas Co	436X	80108	None	
DUNCAN PL	Douglas Co	436X	80108	100-198	E
DUNDEE PL	Erie	133G	80516	None	
DUNES CT	Longmont	10R	80503	2900-2999	
DUNHILL ST	Castle Rock	498L	80104	200-499	
DUNKELD PL W	Denver	253Z	80211	2400-2699	
DUNKIRK AVE S	Centennial	349Q	80015	5300-5499	
DUNKIRK CT	Aurora	289G	80011	1600-1999	
	Denver	259Q	80249	4000-4199	

STREET NAME	CITY or COUNTY	MAP GRID	ZIP CODE	BLOCK RANGE	O/E
DUNKIRK CT N	Aurora	769X	80019	None	
DUNKIRK CT S	Arapahoe Co	379C	80016	None	
	Aurora	319Q	80013	2500-2699	
	Aurora	319U	80013	2700-2799	
	Centennial	379C	80016	6400-6599	
DUNKIRK ST	Aurora	289G	80011	1500-1999	
	Aurora	259C	80019	None	
	Denver	259G	80249	None	
	Denver	259L	80249	None	
DUNKIRK ST S	Arapahoe Co	349U	80015	5900-6199	
	Aurora	319G	80017	1300-1899	
	Aurora	319L	80013	1900-2299	
	Centennial	379L	80016	7500-7799	
DUNKIRK WAY	Denver	259Q	80249	4300-4499	
	Denver	259L	80249	None	
DUNKIRK WAY E	Aurora	349C	80013	3600-3899	
DUNKIRK WAY S	Aurora	319Y	80013	3300-3399	
	Aurora	349G	80013	4000-4199	
	Aurora	319Q	80013	None	
	Centennial	349L	80015	4800-5099	
	Centennial	349Q	80015	5300-5499	
DUNMARK RD	Douglas Co	411G	80138	11900-11999	
DUNMIRE ST	Weld Co	727B	80530	200-599	
DUNN RD	Golden	249W	80403	200-499	
DUNNING CIR	Highlands Ranch	405F	80126	9600-9899	
DUNRAVEN CIR	Jefferson Co	249E	80403	None	
DUNRAVEN CT	Jefferson Co	249A	80403	5900-5999	
	Jefferson Co	249E	80403	None	
DUNRAVEN LN	Jefferson Co	249E	80403	None	
DUNRAVEN RD	Jefferson Co	249A	80403	6000-6199	
DUNRAVEN ST	Jefferson Co	249B	80403	5900-6199	
	Jefferson Co	219S	80007	6400-6799	
DUNRAVEN WAY	Jefferson Co	249A	80403	5900-5999	
	Jefferson Co	249E	80403	None	
DUNRICH RD	Douglas Co	411F	80138	11600-11999	
DUNSFORD DR	Lone Tree	406L	80124	10200-10499	
DUNSFORD WAY	Broomfield	162Q	80020	1400-1499	
DUNSINANE CT	Castle Rock	527B	80104	4100-4299	
DUNSINANE LN	Castle Rock	527B	80104	1-299	
DUNSINANE WAY	Castle Rock	527B	80104	4200-4299	
DUNWOODY WAY E	Highlands Ranch	405E	80126	2500-2599	
DUQUESNE AVE W	Lakewood	312T	80227	7600-7899	
DUQUESNE CIR	Adams Co	140R	80603	15600-15999	
DUQUESNE CT S	Aurora	380M	80016	7500-7599	
	Aurora	350V	80016	None	
	Aurora	380D	80016	None	
	Aurora	380V	80138	None	
DUQUESNE DR W	Lakewood	312W	80227	8400-8799	
DUQUESNE ST	Adams Co	170M	80022	13200-13599	
DUQUESNE ST N	Aurora	290R	80018	None	
DUQUESNE ST S	Aurora	350M	80016	None	
DUQUESNE WAY S	Aurora	380M	80016	None	
DURAN AVE	Jefferson Co	823N	80433	25600-25999	
DURANGO AVE	Broomfield	162G	80020	400-498	E
DURANGO PL	Weld Co	706U	80504	10400-10799	
DURANGO ST	Adams Co	224K	80221	7700-7999	
DURANGO WAY	Palmer Lake	907U	80133	None	
DURHAM CIR	Boulder Co	100B	80301	7700-7799	
DURHAM CIR	Denver	258K	80239	4900-4999	
DURHAM CT	Castle Pines North	436R	80108	200-299	
DURHAM CT	Denver	258K	80239	4200-5299	
DURHAM ST	Boulder Co	100A	80301	4800-4999	
DURHAM WAY	Boulder Co	100B	80301	7700-7899	
DURIAN CT	Longmont	11W	80503	1-99	
DUSK CT	Douglas Co	432K	80125	10200-10299	
DUSK CT S	Littleton	373J	80128	7400-7599	
DUSK ST	Douglas Co	432K	80125	7500-7799	
DUSK ST	Firestone	707T	80504	10100-10299	
DUSK WAY	Douglas Co	432K	80125	10200-10299	
DUSTY PINE TRAIL	Castle Rock	496B	80109	4400-4799	
DUTCH CT	Lafayette	131A	80026	2500-2599	
DUTCH CREEK DR W	Arapahoe Co	373A	80123	1-99	
DUTCH CREEK ST E	Highlands Ranch	406F	80130	6300-6799	
DUTCH VALLEY RD N	Arapahoe Co	792Y	80102	1-599	
DUTCH VALLEY RD S	Arapahoe Co	792Y	80102	1-799	
	Arapahoe Co	812C	80102	800-1099	
DUTTON CT	Castle Rock	499N	80104	700-899	
DYANNA DR	Thornton	165P	80241	3500-13099	
DYER LOOP	Lochbuie	140E	80603	1600-1799	
DYER WAY	Broomfield	133L	80020	16500-16699	
DYLON CIR	Elbert Co	890C	80107	None	
DYNAMITE DR	Gilpin Co	761E	80403	1-299	
DYNASTY LN	Lochbuie	139H	80603	1801-1899	O

E

STREET NAME	CITY or COUNTY	MAP GRID	ZIP CODE	BLOCK RANGE	O/E
E	Aurora	288F	80011	None	
E ST	Golden	279Q	80401	500-1599	
	Jefferson Co	279R	80401	None	
EADS DR E	Aurora	380V	80138	23400-23899	
EAGLE AVE	Superior	160R	80027	2000-2199	
EAGLE BLVD	Frederick	726D	80504	4800-7799	
EAGLE CIR	Aurora	288P	80011	500-599	
	Aurora	288F	80011	2100-2199	
EAGLE CIR	Erie	133G	80516	None	
EAGLE CIR S	Aurora	288P	80011	1-299	
	Aurora	318F	80012	1100-1199	
	Aurora	318P	80014	2500-2599	
	Aurora	348F	80015	4300-4499	
	Aurora	348K	80015	4800-4999	
EAGLE CT	Aurora	288F	80011	1300-1499	
	Aurora	288B	80011	2100-2199	
EAGLE CT	Boulder Co	723G	80503	6300-6499	
EAGLE CT	Denver	258K	80239	5100-5198	E
EAGLE CT	Elbert Co	871F	80107	33500-33599	
EAGLE CT	Golden	248Z	80403	100-199	
EAGLE CT	Longmont	42G	80501	300-399	
EAGLE CT	Louisville	130V	80027	1000-1099	
EAGLE CT S	Aurora	318P	80014	2000-2299	
	Aurora	348F	80014	4100-4299	
EAGLE DR	Brighton	138L	80601	1100-1499	
EAGLE DR	Columbine Valley	343X	80123	1-99	
EAGLE DR	Elbert Co	891X	80106	22300-22999	
EAGLE DR	Erie	133G	80516	None	
EAGLE DR	Golden	248Z	80403	100-299	
EAGLE LN	Jefferson Co	842N	80470	34000-34199	
EAGLE PL E	Highlands Ranch	406F	80130	6700-6899	
EAGLE RD	Broomfield	162Q	80020	1100-1199	

STREET NAME	CITY or COUNTY	MAP GRID	ZIP CODE	BLOCK RANGE	O/E
EAGLE RD	Douglas Co	887L	80118	7900-8299	
EAGLE ST	Aurora	288K	80011	1000-1399	
	Aurora	288F	80011	1500-2299	
	Denver	258P	80239	4300-4599	
	Denver	258K	80239	4700-5099	
	Denver	258F	80239	5200-5299	
EAGLE ST	Weld Co	729Q	80621	17000-17199	
EAGLE ST S	Aurora	318B	80012	700-799	
	Aurora	318F	80012	1500-1599	
	Aurora	318P	80014	2200-2299	
	Aurora	318P	80014	2500-2599	
	Aurora	318X	80014	3300-3499	
	Aurora	348B	80014	3800-3999	
	Centennial	348T	80016	5900-6099	
	Centennial	378F	80112	7200-7499	
EAGLE WAY	Boulder	98T	80301	2900-2999	
EAGLE WAY	Broomfield	162T	80020	1-99	
EAGLE WAY	Erie	133G	80516	None	
EAGLE WAY S	Aurora	318P	80014	2400-2499	
EAGLE BUTTE AVE	Frederick	726G	80516	3000-3299	
EAGLE CLAW PL	Castle Rock	468X	80104	None	
EAGLE CLIFF RD	Jefferson Co	367Y	80433	8500-9299	
	Jefferson Co	823P	80433	9300-9599	
EAGLE CLIFF TRAIL	Jefferson Co	367Z	80433	24000-24499	
EAGLE CREEK CIR	Commerce City	197T	80022	9700-11299	
EAGLE CREEK PKWY	Commerce City	197T	80022	9700-11299	
EAGLE CREST AVE	Firestone	707S	80504	None	
EAGLE CREST CT	Parker	410P	80138	10700-10899	
EAGLE CREST LN	Jefferson Co	306J	80439	31100-31399	
EAGLE CREST LN	Parker	410L	80138	10700-10899	
EAGLE FEATHER CT	Lone Tree	376Y	80124	7900-7999	
EAGLE FEATHER LN	Elbert Co	912C	80106	20500-21299	
EAGLE FEATHER PL	Douglas Co	432T	80125	10200-10299	
EAGLE FEATHER WAY	Lone Tree	376Y	80124	7900-8099	
EAGLE FEATHER TRAIL	Douglas Co	432T	80125	6300-6499	
EAGLE HAWK TRAIL S	Parker	408Z	80134	None	
EAGLE MEADOW DR	Dacono	727N	80514	None	
EAGLE MOON CT	Douglas Co	440Q	80134	7201-7499	O
EAGLE MOON WAY	Douglas Co	440Q	80134	8600-8899	
EAGLE NEST CIR N	Elbert Co	832S	80107	44500-44999	
EAGLE NEST CIR S	Elbert Co	832S	80107	44500-44999	
EAGLE NEST CT	Golden	279N	80401	500-599	
EAGLE PERCH CT	Douglas Co	432L	80125	7600-7699	
EAGLE POINTE LN	Douglas Co	466B	80108	1-99	
EAGLE RIDGE DR	Golden	279K	80401	700-19199	
EAGLE RIDGE WAY	Castle Rock	528A	80104	4000-4299	
EAGLE RIVER LOOP	Broomfield	163A	80020	14700-14799	
EAGLE RIVER RD	Weld Co	706M	80504	None	
EAGLE RIVER RUN	Broomfield	163A	80020	4400-14699	
EAGLE ROCK DR	Douglas Co	432L	80125	7000-7499	
EAGLE RUN DR	Parker	410Q	80138	10900-10999	
EAGLE RUN LN	Parker	410Q	80138	22300-22399	
EAGLES DR	Boulder Co	722Z	80302	1-199	
EAGLE SHADOW AVE	Adams Co	136J	80602	5600-7299	
EAGLE'S NEST CIR	Jefferson Co	371E	80127	7100-7399	
EAGLES NEST DR	Lafayette	131F	80026	2200-2399	
EAGLES NEST LN	Gilpin Co	741Z	80403	1-299	
EAGLES NEST LN	Highlands Ranch	374V	80129	8800-8899	
EAGLESONG TRAIL	Castle Rock	466Y	80109	3600-3798	E
EAGLESTONE DR	Castle Rock	527C	80104	300-1199	
EAGLE TRAIL	Park Co	841Z	80421	1-699	
EAGLE TRAIL LN	Castle Rock	527D	80104	None	
EAGLE VALLEY DR	Lyons	703C	80540	None	
EAGLE VALLEY WAY S					
	Highlands Ranch	404F	80129	10000-10099	
EAGLEVIEW CIR	Longmont	41T	80504	2200-2599	
EAGLEVIEW CT	Erie	133G	80516	None	
EAGLE VIEW CT	Jefferson Co	306T	80439	2800-2899	
EAGLEVIEW DR	Douglas Co	432F	80125	8000-8299	
EAGLEVIEW DR	Erie	133G	80516	None	
EAGLE VIEW LN	Westminster	191T	80021	None	
EAGLEVIEW PL	Erie	133G	80516	None	
EAGLEVIEW WAY	Longmont	41T	80504	2201-2399	O
EAGLE VISTA DR	Jefferson Co	844L	80127	14400-14499	
EAGLE WING WAY	Castle Rock	467W	80109	None	
EARLE CIR	Boulder Co	100B	80301	4800-4899	
EARLY IRIS DR	Parker	409S	80134	None	
EARLY STAR DR	El Paso Co	908Y	80132	17100-17399	
EASLEY RD	Arvada	249D	80403	6000-6199	
	Arvada	219Z	80403	6200-6399	
	Arvada	219Z	80007	None	
	Golden	249R	80403	3800-4399	
	Jefferson Co	249D	80403	4400-5999	
EASLEY WAY	Jefferson Co	249U	80403	3900-4099	
EAST ST	Golden	249W	80403	100-599	
	Golden	249W	80401	800-999	
	Golden	279B	80401	1300-2399	
EAST ST	Lafayette	131K	80026	300-699	
EAST ST	Louisville	131X	80027	301-599	O
EAST ST	Nederland	740R	80466	None	
EAST CHERRY CREEK RD S					
	Douglas Co	890E	80116	6000-9499	
	Douglas Co	890T	80118	9500-13199	
	Douglas Co	910F	80118	13200-15999	
EASTER AVE E	Arapahoe Co	374G	80122	1-899	
	Arapahoe Co	374H	80122	1100-1899	
	Arapahoe Co	377F	80112	10500-12099	
	Arapahoe Co	378F	80112	14100-14299	
	Aurora	380G	80016	None	
	Centennial	375E	80122	1700-2399	
	Centennial	375F	80122	2400-3699	
	Centennial	375H	80122	4000-5599	
	Centennial	376F	80112	6500-7499	
	Centennial	376H	80112	8600-8899	
	Centennial	377E	80112	9600-10499	
	Centennial	377H	80112	12100-12499	
	Centennial	378F	80112	14500-14799	
	Foxfield	379E	80016	16900-18599	
EASTER AVE W	Littleton	374F	80120	400-799	
EASTER CIR E	Arapahoe Co	374H	80122	1300-1599	
	Centennial	376H	80112	8700-8899	
	Centennial	375G	80122	3600N-3799N	
EASTER CT	Longmont	11V	80501	1500-1599	
EASTER CT E	Arapahoe Co	374H	80122	1100-1199	
	Centennial	376G	80112	8300-8399	
	Foxfield	378H	80016	16500-16799	
EASTER CT W	Littleton	373E	80128	4700-4799	
EASTER DR E	Aurora	380H	80016	None	
	Centennial	375G	80122	3700-3999	
	Centennial	376F	80112	7400-7499	
EASTER LN E	Centennial	376G	80112	7500-7799	
	Centennial	377E	80112	9600-9799	
EASTER PL E	Arapahoe Co	374H	80122	800-1099	
	Arapahoe Co	378F	80112	14100-14299	
	Aurora	381E	80016	24500-24599	
	Aurora	381G	80016	26800-26999	
	Aurora	380H	80016	None	
	Centennial	375E	80122	2400-2499	
	Centennial	375F	80122	3200-3499	
	Centennial	375G	80122	3800-4299	
	Centennial	376F	80112	6500-6999	
	Centennial	376G	80112	7300-9099	
	Centennial	379G	80016	18800-18899	
	Foxfield	379F	80016	17800-17899	
EASTER PL W	Littleton	374F	80120	500-799	
EASTER WAY E	Arapahoe Co	374H	80122	900-1099	
	Centennial	376G	80112	7400-7499	
	Foxfield	378H	80016	16300-16899	
EASTERN AVE	Brighton	138U	80601	1-599	
EASTERN DR	Brighton	138Q	80601	None	
EASTLAKE AVE	Thornton	164V	80241	None	
EASTLAKE DR	Thornton	165S	80241	12500-12799	
EASTLAND RD	Weld Co	706E	80504	400-499	
EASTMAN AVE	Boulder	128P	80305	3200-3599	
EASTMAN AVE E	Arapahoe Co	316W	80222	6100-6499	
	Aurora	319Y	80013	19000-19099	
	Aurora	319V	80013	19600-19999	
	Aurora	320W	80013	None	
	Denver	315X	80210	2700-2799	
	Denver	315X	80210	3300-3599	
	Denver	315Y	80222	4000-5599	
	Denver	316X	80224	6500-7099	
	Denver	316Y	80231	7300-8099	
	Denver	316Z	80231	8600-9199	
	Englewood	314Y	80113	1-1699	
	Englewood	315W	80110	2000-2298	E
EASTMAN AVE W	Denver	313T	80236	3600-3799	
	Denver	313X	80236	3900-4199	
	Englewood	314X	80110	100-599	
EASTMAN DR E	Aurora	319W	80013	17400-17599	
	Aurora	320W	80013	None	
EASTMAN DR W	Lakewood	312W	80227	8700-8799	
EASTMAN PL E	Aurora	318Y	80013	15600-15799	
	Aurora	319W	80013	16900-17699	
	Aurora	319Y	80013	19300-19499	
	Denver	316Z	80231	8700-9399	
EASTMAN PL W	Lakewood	312X	80227	7100-8399	
	Lakewood	312W	80227	8400-8599	
	Lakewood	311Z	80227	9300-9499	
EASTMOOR DR	Denver	346F	80237	6700-7299	
EASTON CT	Castle Rock	497U	80104	600-799	
EASTONVILLE RD	El Paso Co	911Y	80106	None	
EASTOUT AVE	Elbert Co	831K	80138	None	
EASTOVER ST S	Arapahoe Co	813E	80102	1900-3199	
EAST RIDGE AVE	Boulder	128F	80303	None	
EAST RIDGE DR	Park Co	841R	80421	1-299	
EASTRIDGE PL E	Aurora	318Z	80013	16000-16099	
EAST RIDGE RD	Elbert Co	871J	80107	2800-2999	
EASTRIDGE RD	Jefferson Co	763L	80403	8800-9399	
EAST RIM RD	Douglas Co	869L	80116	700-1499	
	Douglas Co	869L	80116	None	
EASTVIEW AVE	Firestone	707T	80504	6500-10399	
EASTVIEW DR	Boulder Co	129D	80303	None	
EASTVIEW DR	Castle Rock	498V	80104	1701-2399	O
	Castle Rock	498V	80104	2400-2599	
EASTWOOD CT	Boulder	98T	80304	3100-3199	
EASTWOOD DR	Jefferson Co	308B	80401	1-1099	
EASY ST S	Jefferson Co	842J	80470	13800-13899	
EASY RIDER LN	Boulder	97H	80304	None	
EATON CIR	Castle Rock	498N	80104	1100-1199	
EATON CIR	Superior	160Q	80027	400-799	
EATON CIR	Westminster	222R	80003	7200-7299	
EATON CT	Arvada	222Z	80003	6300-6399	
EATON CT	Boulder	128G	80303	4200-4299	
EATON CT	Lakewood	282V	80226	1-199	
	Westminster	222V	80003	7100-7199	
	Westminster	192D	80020	11500-11899	
EATON CT S	Jefferson Co	342Z	80123	6100-6399	
	Lakewood	282V	80226	1-199	
	Lakewood	312H	80232	1100-1499	
	Lakewood	312R	80227	2300-2399	
EATON LN S	Jefferson Co	342Z	80123	5900-6099	
EATON PKWY S	Aurora	321J	80018	None	
	Aurora	321N	80018	None	
	Aurora	381J	80016	None	
EATON PL	Lakewood	282R	80226	400-499	
EATON PL S	Lakewood	312R	80227	2500-2699	
EATON ST	Arvada	252D	80003	6000-6199	
	Arvada	222Z	80003	6400-6899	
	Arvada	222M	80003	7900-7999	
	Arvada	222H	80003	8400-8599	
EATON ST	Castle Rock	498N	80104	900-1099	
EATON ST	Denver	252M	80212	4800-5199	
	Edgewater	282D	80214	2000-2699	
	Lakewood	282V	80226	1-99	
	Lakewood	282M	80214	1400-1999	
	Mountain View	252V	80212	4100-4399	
EATON ST	Palmer Lake	907U	80133	None	
EATON ST	Westminster	222V	80003	7100-7199	
	Westminster	222R	80003	7500-7599	
	Westminster	192R	80020	10000-10399	
	Westminster	192H	80020	10800-11499	
	Westminster	192V	80031	None	
	Wheat Ridge	252Z	80214	2800-3199	
	Wheat Ridge	252V	80212	3600-4099	
EATON ST S	Denver	312R	80227	2100-2199	
	Denver	312Z	80227	2900-3099	
	Denver	342D	80235	3700-3899	
	Denver	342V	80123	5500-5699	
	Jefferson Co	372D	80128	None	
	Lakewood	282V	80226	1-199	
	Lakewood	282Z	80226	200-599	
	Lakewood	312D	80226	800-1099	
	Lakewood	312H	80232	1100-1699	
EATON WAY	Arvada	222H	80003	8200-8399	
	Westminster	192H	80020	11200-11399	
	Westminster	192D	80020	11800-11899	
EATON WAY S	Denver	312V	80227	2700-2899	
	Jefferson Co	372M	80128	7600-7799	
EATON PARK CT N	Aurora	290R	80018	None	
EATON PARK CT S	Aurora	381A	80016	6900-6999	
	Aurora	830A	80016	7200-7298	E
	Aurora	380M	80016	None	
	Aurora	381J	80016	None	
EATON PARK PKWY S	Aurora	381E	80016	7200-7299	
EATON PARK ST N	Aurora	790S	80018	None	
EATON PARK ST S	Aurora	351N	80016	None	
EATON PARK WAY S	Aurora	351J	80016	None	
EBONY CIR	Thornton	193V	80260	None	
EBONY DR	Castle Rock	497Q	80104	1300-1599	
EBONY ST	Adams Co	224J	80221	1100-1299	
EBONY ST	Firestone	707P	80504	None	
ECCLES ST	Elbert Co	892N	80106	23001-24199	O
ECHO CIR	Firestone	707T	80504	6500-10399	
ECHO CT	Firestone	707T	80504	10500-10599	
ECHO DR	Broomfield	163L	80020	13400-13499	
ECHO DR	Jefferson Co	280B	80401	14800-15199	
ECHO PL	Boulder	128J	80302	200-299	
ECHO RD	Douglas Co	886H	80118	None	
ECHO ST	Firestone	707T	80504	None	
ECHO GAP RD	Douglas Co	886H	80118	4800-4899	
ECHO HOLLOW ST	Castle Rock	528E	80104	5300-5699	
ECHO LAKE DR	Clear Creek Co	801R	80439	1-299	
ECHO PARK DR	Castle Rock	528J	80104	None	
ECHO RIDGE HEIGHTS	El Paso Co	910N	80908	6000-6999	
ECHO TRAIL	Clear Creek Co	801V	80439	1-99	
ECHO VALLEY RD	Douglas Co	886H	80118	5100-5199	
ECHO VILLAGE DR	Douglas Co	887E	80118	7000-7999	
ECKERT ST	Castle Rock	498Q	80104	4800-5199	
ECKHARDT CIR	Elbert Co	891L	80116	None	
ECLECTIC ST	Aurora	791F	80137	4100-4199	
ECLIPSE CT	Adams Co	791K	80137	None	
ECLIPSE ST	Adams Co	791P	80137	None	
ECLIPSE ST	Arapahoe Co	791T	80137	1200-2899	
EDDY CT	Longmont	10V	80503	1700-1799	
EDDY PL	Boulder Co	130N	80303	100-299	
EDELWEISS CIR	Jefferson Co	337Q	80439	25800-26199	
EDELWEISS CT	Boulder Co	130P	80303	7800-7999	
EDEN DR W	Littleton	825Q	80127	8500-8899	
EDEN PL W	Littleton	825Q	80127	8400-8499	
EDENBURG PL W	Littleton	825P	80127	9500-9999	
EDENHURST CT	El Paso Co	908Z	80132	1100-1199	
EDESSA DR	Lafayette	131Q	80026	1700-1799	
EDGE CLIFF AVE	Castle Rock	499J	80104	6400-6499	
EDGE CLIFF PL	Clear Creek Co	781Z	80439	1-299	
EDGE CLIFF ST	Castle Rock	499J	80104	100-499	
EDGEDALE WAY	El Paso Co	909Q	80908	4400-4699	
EDGELAWN ST	Castle Rock	466W	80109	None	
EDGEMONT CT	Highlands Ranch	404K	80129	10600-10699	
EDGEMONT PL	Highlands Ranch	404J	80129	10600-10699	
EDGEMOOR DR W	Sheridan	343G	80110	3000-3199	
EDGEMOOR PL W	Sheridan	343F	80110	3400-3599	
EDGEWATER CT	Lone Tree	406C	80124	7700-7799	
EDGEWATER PL	Lone Tree	406C	80124	9700-9799	
EDGEWOOD CT	Highlands Ranch	376X	80130	6900-6999	
EDGEWOOD DR	Boulder	98S	80304	1900-2299	
EDGEWOOD DR	Elbert Co	912L	80106	18200-18999	
EDGEWOOD LN	Highlands Ranch	376X	80130	8900-9099	
EDGEWOOD PL	Highlands Ranch	376X	80130	6800-6899	
EDGEWOOD ST	Highlands Ranch	376X	80130	8800-9099	
EDGEWOOD WAY	Highlands Ranch	376X	80130	6800-6899	
EDGEWOOD TRAIL	Highlands Ranch	376X	80130	6900-6999	
EDIE PL	Weld Co	103C	80516	4600-4799	
EDINBORO DR	Boulder	128T	80305	1000-1399	
EDINBOROUGH CT E	Parker	409R	80138	20100-20199	
EDINBOROUGH PL E	Parker	409R	80138	20100-20199	
EDINBOROUGH WAY S	Parker	409R	80138	11200-11299	
EDINBURGH CIR	Highlands Ranch	374W	80129	8800-8899	
EDINBURGH LN	Highlands Ranch	373Z	80129	None	
EDISON AVE	Boulder	98U	80301	4700-4899	
EDISON CT	Boulder	98U	80301	3000-3099	
EDISON LN	Boulder	98U	80301	4700-4799	
EDISON PL	Superior	160P	80027	200-499	
EDISON ST	Adams Co	224D	80229	8600-8799	
	Adams Co	224H	80229	None	
EDISON WAY S	Denver	315H	80222	1300-1399	
EDMANSTON WAY	Castle Rock	466X	80109	2700-2799	
EDMONTON CT	Boulder Co	100E	80301	4500-4599	
EDNA DR	Adams Co	140V	80603	None	
EDWARD DR	Jefferson Co	822T	80433	31900-32999	
EDWARD ST	Weld Co	728X	80621	11500-11699	
EDWARDS PL	Denver	257H	80239	12300-12699	
EDWARDS ST	Idaho Springs	780R	80452	2300-2699	
EDWARDS WAY	Broomfield	133L	80020	16500-16699	
EFFIE'S AVE	Elbert Co	891G	80107	None	
EGBERT CIR W	Brighton	138N	80601	400-499	
EGBERT ST E	Brighton	138Q	80601	1-2699	
EGBERT ST W	Brighton	138N	80601	100-399	
EGGERS AVE	Jefferson Co	823U	80433	22000-22099	
EGGLESTON DR	Boulder Co	130J	80303	7400-7599	
EGRET CT	Frederick	726D	80504	None	
EGRET DR	Frederick	727A	80504	4800-4899	
EGRET WAY	Superior	160R	80027	1600-1699	
EGREW CT N	Erie	102C	80516	1200-1299	
EGREW CT S	Erie	102G	80516	1100-1199	
EHLER PKWY	Adams Co	137W	80602	None	
	Thornton	136Y	80602	8500-8798	
EICHHORN DR	Erie	103S	80516	800-1199	
EIGHTH AVE	Hudson	730L	80642	None	
EILEEN WAY	Elbert Co	851E	80138	2200-2699	
EISENHOWER DR	Boulder	128D	80303	1200-4999	
EISENHOWER DR	Louisville	130R	80027	300-2099	
EISENHOWER DR	Palmer Lake	907U	80133	None	
EISENHOWER WAY	Aurora	289E	80011	1600-1899	
ELAINE DR	Broomfield	163U	80020	2800-2899	
ELAINE RD	Jefferson Co	366A	80439	6300-6699	
ELAM AVE	Arapahoe Co	795T	80103	1-299	
ELAND AVE E	Parker	409W	80134	None	
ELATI CIR	Kiowa	872M	80117	None	
ELATI CIR S	Littleton	374K	80120	7900-7999	
ELATI CIR W	Littleton	374K	80120	700-799	
ELATI CT	Northglenn	194B	80234	11700-11799	

STREET NAME	CITY or COUNTY	MAP GRID	ZIP CODE	BLOCK RANGE	O/E
ELATI CT S	Littleton	344X	80120	6100-6199	
ELATI DR S	Littleton	344P	80120	5100-5199	
ELATI RD	Douglas Co	887J	80118	4200-4299	
ELATI ST	Adams Co	224T	80221	7000-7199	
	Adams Co	224F	80221	8200-8399	
	Denver	284P	80223	1-399	
	Denver	284P	80204	400-1399	
	Denver	254T	80216	3900-4399	
	Denver	254K	80216	4701-4799	O
	Northglenn	194F	80234	11000-11199	
ELATI ST S	Denver	284T	80223	1-199	
	Denver	314K	80223	1900-2099	
	Englewood	314T	80110	2700-3599	
	Englewood	344F	80110	3600-5099	
	Littleton	344P	80120	5300-5399	
	Littleton	344T	80120	5500-5599	
	Littleton	344X	80120	5700-6499	
	Littleton	374B	80120	6400-7599	
	Littleton	374K	80120	7700-7899	
ELATI WAY	Adams Co	224T	80221	6800-6999	
ELATI WAY W	Littleton	344T	80120	5700-5799	
ELBERT CT	Broomfield	133J	80020	None	
ELBERT CT S	Superior	160Q	80027	1600-1699	
ELBERT PL N	Douglas Co	440V	80134	6100-6299	
ELBERT RD	Elbert Co	911M	80106	17500-20499	
ELBERT RD	Thornton	193V	80260	None	
ELBERT RD N	Elbert Co	912A	80106	20500-21499	
	Elbert Co	892W	80106	21500-24999	
	Elbert Co	892E	80116	25000-28499	
	Elbert Co	872Q	80117	28500-32999	
ELBERT ST	Adams Co	224J	80221	500-1299	
ELBERT ST	Bennett	793J	80102	None	
ELBERT ST	Castle Rock	497K	80104	300-499	
ELBERT ST	Elbert Co	871K	80107	1000-1799	
	Elbert Co	892S	80106	23800-24099	
ELBERT ST N	Elizabeth	871K	80107	100-499	
ELBERT ST S	Elizabeth	871K	80107	100-999	
ELBERT WAY	Adams Co	224K	80221	200-599	
EL CAMINO DR S	Cherry Hills Village	346E	80111	4500E-5799E	
	Cherry Hills Village	346E	80111	5700N-5899N	
EL CHARRO PT	Castle Rock	468X	80108	3200-3399	
ELDER AVE	Boulder	97V	80304	1200-1899	
ELDER AVE	Jefferson Co	823U	80433	10800-10899	
ELDER CIR	Adams Co	224K	80221	7800-7899	
ELDER PL	Parker	409J	80134	17600-17699	
ELDER ST	Adams Co	224J	80221	1100-1399	
ELDERBERRY CIR	Brighton	139M	80601	None	
ELDERBERRY RD	Jefferson Co	280C	80401	2000-14199	
ELDERBERRY ST	Federal Heights	193V	80260	9700-9799	
EL DIENTE	Douglas Co	407B	80112	10500-10599	
EL DIENTE CIR	Jefferson Co	249A	80403	6000-6199	
EL DIENTE CT	Jefferson Co	305L	80439	1-32799	
	Jefferson Co	249A	80403	5900-5999	
EL DIENTE DR	Broomfield	133J	80020	None	
EL DIENTE ST	Jefferson Co	249A	80403	5800-5999	
	Jefferson Co	249E	80403	None	
EL DIENTE PEAK PL	Douglas Co	436Z	80108	6200-6299	
ELDORA CT	Jefferson Co	306J	80439	30600-30899	
ELDORA PL	Longmont	12X	80501	700-799	
ELDORA RD	Boulder Co	740T	80466	1-2599	
ELDORA ST N	Buckley Air Force Base	289T	80017	None	
	Buckley Air Force Base	289T	80011	None	
ELDORA ST S	Buckley Air Force Base	289T	80017	None	
ELDORADO AVE	Boulder Co	740N	80466	1-1299	
EL DORADO AVE	Frederick	707W	80504	None	
ELDORADO BLVD	Broomfield	161S	80021	400-1099	
	Broomfield	160Z	80021	None	
ELDORADO CIR	Elbert Co	851C	80107	None	
ELDORADO CIR	Superior	160P	80027	1600-1999	
ELDORADO CIR E	Aurora	319W	80013	16900-17599	
ELDORADO CT N	Douglas Co	441S	80134	6000-6199	
EL DORADO DR	Frederick	707W	80504	None	
ELDORADO DR	Superior	160Q	80027	1300-2299	
ELDORADO DR E	Aurora	318X	80014	14700-15099	
	Aurora	319Y	80013	19100-19399	
	Aurora	319Z	80013	19600-19999	
	Aurora	320W	80013	None	
ELDORADO LN	Jefferson Co	306N	80439	2300-2399	
ELDORADO LN	Louisville	130T	80027	900-999	
ELDORADO PL E	Aurora	318Y	80013	15700-15799	
	Aurora	318Z	80013	16000-16299	
	Aurora	319W	80013	17600-17799	
	Aurora	319Y	80013	19000-19099	
	Denver	315X	80210	2500-2799	
	Denver	316W	80222	5600-5799	
ELDORADO PL W	Denver	313X	80236	3900-4199	
	Denver	312Y	80227	6300-6699	
	Lakewood	312Y	80227	6800-6999	
ELDORADO ST E	Aurora	318Y	80013	15600-15699	
EL DORADO WAY	El Paso Co	908U	80132	700-799	
ELDORADO WAY S	Douglas Co	909K	80118	15000-15999	
ELDORADO SPRINGS DR	Boulder Co	743U	80303	3300-5199	
	Boulder Co	743R	80305	5200-5599	
	Boulder Co	743T	80025	None	
ELDRIDGE CIR	Jefferson Co	280C	80401	2500-2599	
ELDRIDGE CT	Arvada	220U	80004	7000-7199	
	Arvada	220C	80005	None	
	Jefferson Co	280U	80401	200-299	
	Jefferson Co	280Q	80401	400-499	
	Jefferson Co	250C	80004	5900-5999	
ELDRIDGE CT S	Lakewood	310Q	80228	2200-2599	
	Lakewood	310U	80228	2800-2899	
ELDRIDGE ST	Arvada	220U	80004	6200-6599	
	Arvada	220L	80005	7800-7899	
	Arvada	220G	80005	8600-8699	
	Arvada	220C	80005	None	
ELDRIDGE ST	Firestone	707T	80504	None	
	Jefferson Co	280Q	80401	600-699	
	Jefferson Co	280C	80401	2000-2799	
	Jefferson Co	250Y	80401	2800-3199	
	Jefferson Co	250Q	80403	4400-5199	
	Jefferson Co	250G	80002	5200-5499	
	Jefferson Co	250C	80004	5800-6199	
ELDRIDGE ST S	Jefferson Co	340L	80465	4200-4699	
	Jefferson Co	340Q	80465	5000-5099	
	Jefferson Co	340U	80127	5500-5599	
	Lakewood	280Y	80228	600-699	
	Lakewood	310Q	80228	2100-2599	
ELDRIDGE WAY S	Jefferson Co	280U	80401	1-199	
ELECTRA ST	Adams Co	750G	80603	16100-16399	
	Adams Co	750G	80603	None	
ELEGANT ST	Castle Rock	466Z	80109	None	
	Castle Rock	466V	80109	None	
ELEPHANT ROCK RD	Douglas Co	866E	80135	None	
ELEUTHERA CT	Boulder	98K	80301	4000-4099	
ELGIN AVE	Longmont	41L	80501	900-999	
ELGIN DR	Boulder Co	130H	80026	8500-8999	
ELGIN DR	Denver	257M	80239	12900-13099	
ELGIN PL	Denver	257M	80239	12900-13199	
ELGIN PL E	Denver	254L	80216	600-899	
ELIOT CIR	Federal Heights	193Q	80260	10000-10099	
	Westminster	223Q	80030	2700-2999	
	Westminster	193L	80234	10700-10799	
ELIOT CT	Broomfield	163L	80020	13500-13599	
ELIOT CT	Westminster	193G	80234	11100-11199	
	Westminster	193G	80234	11200-11499	
ELIOT DR	Westminster	193G	80234	11000-11199	
ELIOT PL	Broomfield	163L	80020	13500-13599	
ELIOT ST	Broomfield	163U	80020	12500-12599	
ELIOT ST	Denver	283C	80211	2000-2699	
	Denver	253Y	80211	2700-2899	
	Denver	253Q	80211	3100-4799	
	Denver	253L	80221	4800-5199	
ELIOT ST	Federal Heights	193U	80260	9800-9999	
	Federal Heights	193Q	80260	None	
ELIOT ST	Westminster	223Q	80030	7300-7599	
	Westminster	223L	80030	8000-8099	
	Westminster	193Q	80234	10400-10499	
ELIOT ST S	Denver	283Y	80219	100-699	
	Denver	313C	80219	700-1499	
	Denver	313L	80219	1800-1899	
	Sheridan	313Y	80110	3300-3499	
	Sheridan	343G	80110	4100-4199	
ELIS CIR	Lafayette	131Q	80026	1700-1799	
ELISABETH CT	Fort Lupton	728Q	80621	200-299	
ELISABETH ST	Fort Lupton	728Q	80621	400-499	
ELITCH CIR	Denver	284A	80204	None	
ELIZA CT S	Highlands Ranch	404H	80126	9800-9899	
ELIZABETH AVE	Lafayette	132K	80026	400-499	
ELIZABETH AVE	Platteville	708C	80651	300-699	
ELIZABETH CIR	Thornton	195B	80233	11600-11699	
	Thornton	195A	80233	11700-11899	
ELIZABETH CIR S	Centennial	375B	80122	6800-6899	
	Cherry Hills Village	345K	80113	4800-4999	
ELIZABETH CT	Adams Co	165B	80602	14400-14499	
ELIZABETH CT	Longmont	41G	80501	1-99	
ELIZABETH CT	Thornton	195S	80229	9500-9599	
	Thornton	195B	80233	11700-11799	
	Thornton	165X	80241	12100-12399	
	Thornton	165N	80241	13300-13399	
ELIZABETH CT S	Centennial	375K	80122	7700-7799	
	Cherry Hills Village	345K	80113	4600-4799	
ELIZABETH DR	Elbert Co	850D	80138	1100-1999	
ELIZABETH DR	Jefferson Co	822T	80433	10900-10999	
ELIZABETH LN	Broomfield	163E	80020	4500-4599	
	Jefferson Co	336Q	80439	4900-5099	
ELIZABETH PL	Thornton	195B	80233	11600-11799	
ELIZABETH ST	Adams Co	225S	80229	6800-7099	
	Adams Co	135J	80602	16400-16599	
	Dacono	727J	80514	100-699	
	Denver	285N	80206	600-799	
	Denver	285K	80206	1000-1499	
	Denver	285B	80205	2600-2699	
	Denver	255W	80205	2700-3699	
	Denver	255P	80216	4200-4799	
ELIZABETH ST	Elizabeth	871E	80107	100-298	E
ELIZABETH ST	Northglenn	195J	80233	10900-10999	
	Thornton	195T	80229	9700-9799	
	Thornton	195S	80229	9900-9999	
	Thornton	195N	80229	10000-10199	
	Thornton	165W	80241	12100-12199	
	Thornton	165S	80241	12500-12599	
	Thornton	165P	80241	13100-13299	
	Thornton	165N	80241	13300-13499	
	Thornton	165E	80602	13800-13999	
	Thornton	165A	80602	14500-14799	
	Thornton	135W	80602	14900-15099	
	Thornton	165F	80602	None	
ELIZABETH ST	Weld Co	729R	80603	4100-4399	
ELIZABETH ST E	Douglas Co	441W	80134	9700-9899	
ELIZABETH ST S	Centennial	375B	80122	6600-7099	
	Denver	315B	80209	700-1099	
	Denver	315F	80210	1100-1699	
ELIZABETH WAY	El Paso Co	910V	80908	10600-11099	
ELIZABETH WAY	Thornton	165P	80241	13300-13599	
ELIZABETH WAY S	Centennial	345X	80121	5900-6099	
	Centennial	375B	80121	6500-6599	
	Centennial	375J	80122	7700-7899	
	Greenwood Village	345W	80121	6100-6199	
ELIZABETH ST CIR	Dacono	727J	80514	100-699	
ELIZABETH VIEW	Monument	908X	80132	None	
EL JEBEL LOOP	Castle Rock	469K	80108	8100-8399	
ELK CIR	Adams Co	140V	80603	15500-15799	
ELK CT	Broomfield	163P	80020	3400-3499	
ELK CT	Douglas Co	432L	80125	7600-7699	
ELK CT N	Aurora	290R	80018	None	
ELK CT S	Aurora	351J	80016	4800-4899	
	Aurora	381A	80016	6900-6999	
	Aurora	381E	80016	7100-7199	
	Aurora	351S	80016	None	
	Aurora	351S	80016	None	
	Aurora	380M	80016	None	
	Aurora	380R	80016	None	
ELK DR	Clear Creek Co	335A	80439	1-199	
ELK DR	Park Co	820Z	80421	1-199	
ELK DR	Westminster	223P	80030	3800-3999	
ELK DR E	Denver	258N	80239	14300-14599	
ELK LN	Jefferson Co	370B	80127	1-99	
ELK LN	Park Co	841M	80421	1-199	
	Denver	258N	80239	13900-15099	
ELK PL	Gilpin Co	760U	80403	1-299	
ELK PL	Longmont	12W	80501	100-199	
ELK PL E	Denver	254L	80216	600-699	
	Denver	257M	80239	12900-13199	
	Denver	259M	80249	19700-19999	
ELK PL W	Denver	254P	80216	500-598	E
	Denver	254N	80211	1700-1899	
	Denver	253R	80211	1900-2399	
ELK ST S	Aurora	351J	80016	4800-5099	
	Aurora	351N	80016	None	
ELK ST S	Highlands Ranch	374U	80126	8700-8799	
ELK WAY	Clear Creek Co	801A	80452	1-199	
ELK WAY S	Aurora	351J	80016	4700-4899	
	Aurora	380R	80016	None	
ELK CANYON CIR	Douglas Co	847W	80135	2500-3499	
ELK CANYON CT	Douglas Co	847T	80109	3400-3599	
ELK CANYON PL	Douglas Co	847X	80109	2500-2699	
ELK CREEK CT S	Parker	439C	80134	12500-12599	
ELK CREEK DR	El Paso Co	909R	80908	19000E-20499E	
	El Paso Co	909Q	80908	5000W-20999W	
ELK CREEK DR	Park Co	820Y	80421	1-699	
ELK CREEK DR E	Parker	439C	80134	18900-19699	
ELK CREEK RD S	Jefferson Co	842B	80470	11900-16299	
ELK CREEK WAY S	Parker	439D	80134	12500-12599	
ELK CREEK ACRES RD S	Jefferson Co	842R	80470	15100-15299	
ELK CROSSING LN	Clear Creek Co	335J	80439	1-199	
ELKEN CT	Broomfield	163X	80020	12200-12299	
ELKHART CT	Aurora	288K	80011	1400-1499	
ELKHART CT S	Aurora	318P	80014	2400-2499	
	Aurora	348K	80015	4800-4999	
	Aurora	348P	80015	5000-5099	
	Aurora	348P	80015	None	
	Centennial	348T	80016	5900-5999	
ELKHART ST	Aurora	288P	80011	400-599	
	Aurora	288K	80011	600-999	
	Aurora	288B	80011	2200-2299	
	Commerce City	198B	80603	11600-11799	
	Commerce City	168X	80603	11800-11999	
	Denver	258P	80239	4300-4599	
	Denver	258F	80239	5000-5599	
ELKHART ST S	Aurora	288T	80012	1-199	
	Aurora	318B	80012	700-1299	
	Aurora	318F	80012	1500-1799	
	Aurora	318P	80014	2000-2299	
	Aurora	318P	80014	2300-2699	
	Aurora	318X	80014	3300-3399	
	Aurora	348B	80014	3500-3999	
	Aurora	348F	80014	4100-4299	
	Aurora	348K	80015	4800-5099	
ELKHART WAY S	Aurora	318B	80012	1000-1099	
	Aurora	348K	80015	4900-4999	
	Aurora	348P	80015	5000-5099	
ELK HAVEN LN	Jefferson Co	842B	80433	12500-12699	
ELK HEAD RANGE RD	Jefferson Co	371J	80127	11600-11999	
ELK HORN CT	Park Co	840D	80421	None	
ELKHORN DR	Douglas Co	850T	80116	11700-11899	
ELKHORN ST	Elbert Co	831N	80138	2300-2499	
ELKHORN ST	Jefferson Co	824R	80127	9600-9999	
ELKHORN MOUNTAIN	Jefferson Co	371K	80127	7500-7599	
ELKHORN RANCH ST	Elbert Co	831J	80138	2300-2499	
ELK HORN RUN	Douglas Co	432N	80125	10900-10999	
ELK MEADOW DR	Jefferson Co	306T	80439	2800-2899	
ELK MEADOW LN	Gilpin Co	761B	80403	1-299	
ELK MEADOW LN	Gilpin Co	761N	80403	1-299	
ELK MEADOWS CIR	Elbert Co	911A	80106	None	
ELKMONT CT	Elbert Co	912L	80106	9200-9399	
ELK MOUNTAIN CIR	Douglas Co	432R	80125	9500-9699	
ELK MOUNTAIN WAY	Broomfield	163N	80020	13200-13299	
ELK MOUNTAIN TRAIL	Jefferson Co	824Y	80127	13700-15699	
ELK PARK CT	Douglas Co	907F	80118	2400-2499	
ELK PARK DR	Jefferson Co	308B	80401	800-899	
ELK PARK DR	Park Co	821Y	80421	1-299	
ELK PARK RD	Douglas Co	907F	80118	2100-4099	
ELK POINTE LN	Douglas Co	466G	80108	1-99	
ELK POINTE TRAIL	Douglas Co	466G	80108	1-99	
ELK RANGE RD	Jefferson Co	307U	80439	None	
ELK REST RD	Jefferson Co	306D	80401	None	
ELK REST RUN	Douglas Co	432J	80125	11000-11099	
ELK RIDGE LN	Boulder Co	722G	80302	1-299	
ELK RIDGE RD	Jefferson Co	844F	80127	16700-17099	
ELK RIDGE RD S	Jefferson Co	335P	80439	4800-5399	
ELKRIDGE RUN	Elbert Co	871B	80107	35600-35999	
ELK RIVER RD	Weld Co	706M	80504	None	
ELK RUN	Elbert Co	891Y	80106	4800-5199	
ELK RUN	Jefferson Co	365F	80439	33300-33799	
ELK RUN DR	Castle Rock	466T	80109	3200-3999	
ELK SONG TRAIL	Jefferson Co	782B	80403	5900-6099	
ELK SUMMIT LN	Jefferson Co	306W	80439	2900-2999	
ELK TRAIL	Clear Creek Co	821H	80439	1-199	
ELK TRAIL	Lafayette	131Z	80026	300-499	
ELK TRAIL PL	Douglas Co	432L	80125	7400-7499	
ELK TRAIL RD	Jefferson Co	822Z	80433	11900-12099	
ELK VALLEY DR	Clear Creek Co	781U	80439	1-2099	
ELK VALLEY RD	Jefferson Co	307T	80439	1-2099	
ELK VIEW CT	Douglas Co	887D	80118	5500-5799	
ELK VIEW DR	Jefferson Co	306W	80439	2900-3399	
ELK VIEW RD	Douglas Co	887C	80118	1300-2399	
ELLA AVE	Jefferson Co	842E	80470	34300-34499	
ELLA CT	Louisville	131K	80027	None	
ELLEN CT	Thornton	194Z	80229	9200-9399	
ELLEN LN	Adams Co	224L	80221	7600-7799	
ELLENDALE ST	Castle Rock	499J	80104	1-499	
ELLINGWOOD WAY	Broomfield	133J	80020	None	
ELLINGWOOD POINT PL	Douglas Co	436U	80108	6200-6399	
ELLINGWOOD POINT WAY	Douglas Co	436U	80108	6200-6299	
ELLINGWOOD TRAIL	Jefferson Co	305M	80439	32000-32299	
ELLIOT CIR	Broomfield	163U	80234	None	
ELLIOT LN	Boulder Co	742W	80403	1-99	
ELLIOT LN	Gilpin Co	742W	80403	101-199	O
	Broomfield	163Q	80234	None	
ELLIOT ST	Longmont	42B	80501	400-899	
ELLIPSE WAY S	Denver	315B	80209	800-999	
ELLIS CT	Arvada	220G	80005	8600-8699	
	Arvada	220C	80005	None	
	Jefferson Co	280Q	80401	500-599	
	Jefferson Co	250C	80004	5800-5999	
ELLIS CT S	Lakewood	310Q	80228	2100-2199	
	Lakewood	310Q	80228	2200-2499	
ELLIS LN	Jefferson Co	250Y	80401	3000-3099	
ELLIS ST	Arvada	220U	80004	7000-7199	
	Arvada	220C	80005	None	
	Arvada	220G	80005	None	

Continued on next page

STREET NAME	CITY or COUNTY	MAP GRID	ZIP CODE	BLOCK RANGE	O/E
ELLIS ST (Cont'd)	Arvada	220Q	80005	None	
	Jefferson Co	280Q	80401	700-799	
	Jefferson Co	280G	80401	2000-2199	
	Jefferson Co	250L	80403	4800-5199	
ELLIS ST S	Lakewood	310Q	80228	2200-2499	
ELLIS WAY	Jefferson Co	280U	80401	200-599	
ELLISON LN	Boulder Co	723M	80503	None	
ELLISON PL	Boulder	97V	80304	2800-2899	
ELLISON PL	Douglas Co	432K	80125	10400-10499	
ELLISON ST	Boulder	97V	80304	None	
EL LOBO LN	Park Co	820Y	80421	1-199	
ELLSWORTH AVE E	Arapahoe Co	290V	80018	23300-23799	
	Aurora	288S	80011	13600-14499	
	Denver	284U	80209	1-1199	
	Denver	285T	80209	3200-3999	
	Denver	285V	80246	4000-5499	
	Denver	286S	80246	5500-5599	
	Denver	286U	80230	7300-8099	
ELLSWORTH AVE W	Denver	284T	80223	1-1099	
	Denver	283T	80219	2500-5199	
	Jefferson Co	280U	80401	14300-14499	
	Jefferson Co	280T	80401	14600-16099	
	Jefferson Co	280S	80401	16100-16699	
	Lakewood	282V	80226	5600-5899	
	Lakewood	282U	80226	6200-6799	
	Lakewood	282T	80226	6800-7799	
	Lakewood	281V	80226	9200-9299	
ELLSWORTH CT	Castle Rock	499N	80104	700-899	
ELLSWORTH DR E	Aurora	291T	80018	None	
ELLSWORTH DR W	Jefferson Co	280T	80401	15100-15399	
	Jefferson Co	280S	80401	15400-16599	
ELLSWORTH LN W	Jefferson Co	280S	80401	15800-16199	
ELLSWORTH PL	Boulder	128H	80303	5000-5199	
ELLSWORTH PL E	Aurora	287U	80010	11400-11599	
ELLSWORTH PL E	Aurora	291T	80018	None	
ELLSWORTH PL W	Jefferson Co	280U	80401	14300-14499	
	Jefferson Co	280T	80401	15200-15299	
	Jefferson Co	280S	80401	15600-15999	
	Lakewood	282T	80226	7000-7199	
	Lakewood	281S	80228	12400-12499	
	Lakewood	280V	80228	12800-12899	
ELM AVE	Boulder	128K	80305	2700-2899	
ELM AVE	Brighton	138S	80601	300-499	
ELM AVE	Castle Rock	497R	80104	100-299	
ELM AVE	Dacono	727F	80514	None	
ELM AVE	Fort Lupton	728H	80621	900-999	
ELM AVE	Weld Co	706R	80504	None	
ELM AVE E	Douglas Co	378X	80134	3000-3999	
ELM CIR	Broomfield	163Q	80234	None	
ELM CIR	Dacono	726V	80514	None	
ELM CIR	Federal Heights	193Y	80260	9300-9599	
ELM CIR	Golden	278D	80401	700-799	
ELM CIR	Thornton	195H	80233	11500-11599	
ELM CIR S	Centennial	375D	80121	6500-6699	
ELM CT	Adams Co	253G	80003	5400-5499	
ELM CT	Castle Rock	497R	80104	200-299	
ELM CT	Denver	253Q	80211	4400-4799	
	Denver	253L	80221	4800-5199	
	Federal Heights	223C	80260	8800-8999	
	Federal Heights	193Y	80260	9000-9599	
	Thornton	195R	80229	10100-10199	
	Thornton	195H	80233	11500-11599	
	Thornton	195D	80233	11700-11799	
ELM CT S	Centennial	345V	80121	5900-6099	
	Centennial	345Z	80121	6100-6199	
	Centennial	375H	80122	7000-7499	
	Centennial	375M	80122	7700-7799	
	Cherry Hills Village	345M	80113	4200-4299	
	Greenwood Village	345R	80121	5400-5499	
ELM DR	Thornton	195M	80233	10500-10999	
	Thornton	195H	80229	11200-11399	
	Thornton	195D	80233	11800-11899	
ELM DR S	Arapahoe Co	315R	80222	2300-2399	
ELM LN	Broomfield	163U	80020	12500-12799	
ELM PL	Thornton	194Z	80229	900-1499	
ELM ST	Bennett	793N	80102	200-299	
ELM ST	Boulder Co	70L	80503	7000-7399	
	Broomfield	163Q	80234	None	
	Broomfield	163U	80234	None	
ELM ST	Commerce City	225V	80022	6900-7199	
	Denver	285M	80220	1-1999	
	Denver	285D	80207	2000-2799	
	Denver	255V	80207	2800-3899	
ELM ST	Douglas Co	846G	80125	7500-7999	
ELM ST	Elizabeth	871F	80107	100-199	
ELM ST	Federal Heights	193V	80260	9700-9799	
	Federal Heights	193Q	80260	10000-10099	
ELM ST	Frederick	727F	80530	None	
ELM ST	Golden	279E	80401	1800-1899	
ELM ST	Hudson	730L	80642	None	
ELM ST	Keenesburg	732A	80643	None	
ELM ST	Lafayette	132E	80026	300-599	
ELM ST	Lochbuie	140G	80603	200-399	
ELM ST	Louisville	131S	80027	None	
ELM ST	Thornton	165V	80241	12500-12799	
	Thornton	165H	80602	13800-13999	
	Thornton	165H	80602	None	
ELM ST	Weld Co	707T	80504	7000-7499	
ELM ST E	Elizabeth	871F	80107	100-498	E
ELM ST S	Centennial	375H	80122	7000-7099	
	Denver	285V	80246	1-299	
	Denver	285Z	80246	400-699	
	Denver	315H	80246	1100-1299	
	Denver	315M	80222	1300-1899	
	Denver	315V	80222	2700-3499	
	Denver	345D	80237	3700-3899	
	Greenwood Village	345V	80121	5600-5899	
ELM ST W	Elizabeth	871F	80107	100-499	
ELM ST W	Lafayette	131H	80026	500-599	
ELM ST W	Louisville	130V	80027	100-399	
ELM WAY	Thornton	195H	80233	11400-11599	
	Thornton	165Z	80241	12000-12399	
ELM WAY S	Denver	345D	80237	3600-3699	
ELMENDORF DR	Denver	259F	80249	None	
ELMENDORF PL	Denver	257H	80239	12200-13099	
	Denver	258E	80239	13100-13399	
	Denver	258G	80239	14800-15599	
ELMER DR	Northglenn	194H	80233	900-1499	
ELMER LINN DR	Weld Co	706P	80504	2600-11799	
ELM FORK PL	Castle Rock	527D	80104	1300-1499	
ELMGREEN LN	Jefferson Co	275W	80439	1-99	
ELMHURST AVE W	Jefferson Co	372Q	80128	5600-7199	
	Jefferson Co	372N	80128	8400-9199	
ELMHURST CIR	Longmont	11S	80503	2600-2699	
ELMHURST CT	Longmont	11S	80503	1400-1499	
ELMHURST DR	Longmont	11S	80503	1400-1599	
ELMHURST DR W	Jefferson Co	372R	80128	6100-6399	
	Jefferson Co	372P	80128	7300-7699	
	Jefferson Co	371R	80128	9200-9499	
ELMHURST LN	Highlands Ranch	404B	80129	9400-9599	
ELMHURST LN	Longmont	11S	80503	1400-1499	
ELMHURST PL	Boulder	128Q	80305	3800-3899	
ELMHURST PL	Longmont	11S	80503	2400-2599	
ELMHURST PL E	Aurora	380R	80016	23300-23399	
	Aurora	381L	80016	26000-26099	
	Aurora	381M	80016	27500-27599	
ELMHURST PL W	Broomfield	162X	80020	600-799	
ELMHURST PL W	Jefferson Co	371R	80128	9400-9899	
ELMHURST WAY	Highlands Ranch	404B	80129	400-599	
ELMIRA CIR S	Arapahoe Co	347W	80111	6200E-6299E	
ELMIRA CT	Adams Co	137S	80602	15400-15499	
	Denver	257W	80238	None	
ELMIRA CT S	Aurora	317E	80247	None	
	Denver	317W	80231	3000-3399	
ELMIRA ST	Adams Co	137N	80602	15700-15999	
	Aurora	287N	80010	300-599	
	Aurora	287E	80010	800-2599	
	Commerce City	197E	80640	11200-11298	E
	Denver	257W	80238	None	
ELMIRA ST S	Aurora	317J	80247	None	
	Denver	317A	80247	900-1099	
	Denver	317S	80231	2700-2799	
	Greenwood Village	347J	80111	4900-5099	
ELMORE RD	Weld Co	706E	80504	13500-13999	
ELMORO CT S	Superior	160M	80027	1200-1399	
ELM SQUARE	Elbert Co	871G	80107	4600-4799	
ELMWOOD CT	Broomfield	162R	80020	1200-1299	
ELMWOOD DR	Adams Co	224J	80221	7900-7999	
ELMWOOD LN	Adams Co	223M	80221	800-7499	
	Adams Co	224J	80221	7500-7999	
ELMWOOD PL	Adams Co	223M	80221	7700-7899	
ELMWOOD ST	Arapahoe Co	373P	80128	None	
ELMWOOD ST	Broomfield	162M	80020	1300-1999	
ELMWOOD ST	Douglas Co	432L	80125	7500-7999	
ELMWOOD ST S	Littleton	344S	80120	5300-5699	
	Littleton	374A	80120	6500-6699	
EL NIDO WAY	Castle Rock	468X	80104	None	
EL PASO BLVD	Adams Co	224J	80221	400-1599	
EL PASO BLVD	Palmer Lake	907Q	80133	None	
EL PASO CIR	Adams Co	224J	80221	7600-7699	
EL PASO CT	Brighton	139P	80601	None	
EL PASO RD	Palmer Lake	907Q	80133	None	
EL PICO RD	Jefferson Co	842C	80433	12300-12399	
EL PINAL DR	Jefferson Co	306X	80439	3100-3599	
	Jefferson Co	336B	80439	3300-3599	
EL RANCHO RD	Jefferson Co	306C	80401	1000-1099	
EL RANCHO WAY	El Paso Co	907V	80132	3500-3899	
ELSIE PL	Palmer Lake	907Q	80133	None	
ELSIE RD	Jefferson Co	843F	80433	13100-24199	
ELYSIAN FIELD DR	Lafayette	131U	80026	1100-1199	
EMANUEL WAY	Jefferson Co	762E	80403	10700-10799	
EMBASSY CT	El Paso Co	908Z	80132	1300-1399	
EMBER PL	Castle Rock	497Y	80104	200-299	
EMBER ST	Adams Co	224J	80221	1200-1499	
EMERALD CT	Castle Rock	497U	80104	200-299	
EMERALD DR	Castle Rock	497U	80104	2200-2399	
EMERALD DR	Frederick	726G	80516	2600-2699	
EMERALD DR	Longmont	41U	80504	1100-2199	
EMERALD LN	Broomfield	162W	80020	7900-8199	
EMERALD LN	El Paso Co	909T	80908	18500-18799	
EMERALD LN	Jefferson Co	823T	80433	10700-11299	
EMERALD LN	Lakewood	282P	80214	700-799	
EMERALD RD	Boulder Co	98J	80304	2000-2399	
EMERALD ST	Broomfield	162X	80020	1-299	
	Broomfield	162T	80020	600-1099	
	Broomfield	162K	80020	1600-1799	
EMERALD ST	Firestone	727B	80504	None	
EMERALD ST	Lochbuie	139H	80603	300-398	E
EMERALD LAKE DR	Weld Co	707J	80504	None	
EMERALD PEAK	Jefferson Co	371K	80127	7700-7799	
EMERSON AVE	Boulder	128T	80305	2600-3799	
EMERSON AVE	Frederick	727F	80530	7900-7999	
EMERSON CIR	Northglenn	194H	80233	700-999	
EMERSON CIR S	Arapahoe Co	374M	80122	7500-7699	
EMERSON CT	Adams Co	224D	80229	8600-8699	
	Thornton	224D	80229	8700-8799	
	Thornton	164Z	80241	None	
EMERSON CT S	Arapahoe Co	374M	80122	7600-7699	
EMERSON LN	Superior	160Q	80027	2000-2099	
EMERSON PL	Longmont	11Q	80501	1000-1099	
EMERSON ST	Adams Co	254D	80216	5600-5799	
	Adams Co	224M	80229	7900-8099	
	Adams Co	224H	80229	8300-8399	
	Denver	284R	80218	1-1999	
	Denver	284D	80205	2000-2599	
	Denver	254M	80216	4800-5199	
	Northglenn	194R	80233	10400-10599	
	Northglenn	194H	80233	11000-11199	
	Northglenn	194D	80233	11400-11499	
	Thornton	194Z	80229	9000-9199	
	Thornton	164V	80241	12800-12899	
	Thornton	164R	80241	12900-12999	
	Thornton	164Q	80241	13000-13199	
EMERSON ST S	Arapahoe Co	374L	80122	7500-7699	
	Denver	284Z	80209	1-699	
	Denver	314D	80209	700-1099	
	Denver	314M	80210	1100-2399	
	Englewood	314Z	80113	2700-3599	
EMERSON WAY S	Arapahoe Co	374R	80122	8100-8299	
	Englewood	314V	80113	3000-3099	
EMERY CT	Longmont	11V	80501	1400-1498	E
EMERY DR	Longmont	11R	80501	300-499	
EMERY PL	Longmont	11R	80501	2300-2399	
EMERY RD	Northglenn	194G	80233	100-699	
EMERY ST	Longmont	41D	80501	100-899	
	Longmont	11Z	80501	900-1499	
	Longmont	11V	80501	1500-1999	
	Longmont	11R	80501	2000-2499	
EMERY ST S	Longmont	41R	80501	1200-1399	
	Longmont	41V	80501	1500-1698	E
EMERY WAY	Longmont	11R	80501	1-99	
EMIGRANT TRAIL	El Paso Co	908T	80132	18900E-18999E	
EMILIA DR E	Parker	439F	80134	17600-17899	
EMILIA WAY S	Parker	439E	80134	12901-12999	O
EMILY ST	Castle Rock	466Y	80109	None	
EMMA LN	Brighton	138V	80601	1700-1799	
EMMA ST E	Lafayette	132J	80026	100-999	
EMMA ST W	Lafayette	132J	80026	100-599	
	Lafayette	131M	80026	600-799	
EMORY RD	Gilpin Co	741X	80403	1-999	
EMPIRE AVE	Frederick	726G	80516	3300-3399	
EMPIRE DR	Boulder Co	130S	80303	7200-7599	
EMPIRE DR E	Douglas Co	870J	80116	10400-10899	
EMPIRE PL	Longmont	12W	80501	1-99	
EMPIRE RD	Boulder Co	131Z	80026	9700-11199	
	Lafayette	132W	80026	300-398	E
EMPIRE ST	Aurora	287N	80010	300-599	
EMPORIA CIR S	Arapahoe Co	347W	80111	5900-6099	
	Arapahoe Co	347W	80111	6300-6399	
	Greenwood Village	347S	80111	5500-5599	
EMPORIA CT	Adams Co	167A	80602	14600-14699	
EMPORIA CT	Denver	257W	80238	None	
	Denver	257W	80238	None	
	Denver	287A	80238	None	
EMPORIA CT S	Arapahoe Co	347W	80111	6000-6099	
	Aurora	317E	80247	1200-1699	
	Denver	317W	80231	3000-3399	
	Greenwood Village	347J	80111	4900-4999	
	Greenwood Village	347N	80111	5200-5499	
EMPORIA RD	Boulder	128S	80305	600-699	
EMPORIA ST	Adams Co	137S	80602	15200-15599	
	Adams Co	167A	80602	None	
	Aurora	287N	80010	301-1599	O
	Aurora	287A	80010	2000-2499	
	Commerce City	197S	80640	9700-9999	
	Commerce City	197E	80640	11200-11399	
	Denver	257W	80238	None	
	Denver	257W	80238	None	
EMPORIA ST S	Arapahoe Co	317N	80231	2200-2298	E
	Aurora	317J	80247	None	
	Denver	317A	80247	700-999	
	Greenwood Village	347J	80111	4900-5099	
	Greenwood Village	377A	80112	6700-6899	
EMPORIA WAY	Adams Co	137N	80602	None	
EMPORIA WAY S	Aurora	317J	80247	1600-1699	
	Aurora	347A	80014	3600-3799	
	Greenwood Village	347N	80111	5100-5299	
EMPSON DR	Longmont	12S	80501	1-199	
ENCHANTED RD	Jefferson Co	278V	80401	100-199	
ENCHANTRA CIR	Douglas Co	527T	80104	4000-4199	
ENCLAVE CIR W	Louisville	130T	80027	1100-1199	
ENCLAVE WAY W	Louisville	130T	80027	None	
ENDERUD BLVD	Castle Rock	498K	80104	None	
ENDICOTT CT S	Denver	341M	80123	4500-4599	
ENDICOTT DR	Boulder	128T	80305	3100-3699	
ENDICOTT ST S	Lakewood	312J	80232	1500-1899	
ENGINEER'S CT S	Douglas Co	887H	80118	7400-7599	
ENGLEWOOD PKWY	Englewood	314X	80110	1-1099	
ENGLISH SPARROW DR W	Highlands Ranch	404K	80129	300-499	
ENGLISH SPARROW TRAIL W	Highlands Ranch	404J	80129	300-1199	
ENID CT	Denver	258L	80239	5100-5199	
ENID WAY	Denver	258P	80239	4600-5199	
EN-JOIE PL	Elbert Co	851C	80107	None	
ENSENADA CT	Aurora	289G	80011	1900-1999	
ENSENADA CT	Denver	259G	80249	None	
ENSENADA CT N	Aurora	259C	80019	None	
ENSENADA CT S	Arapahoe Co	349U	80015	5600-5699	
	Arapahoe Co	379G	80016	None	
	Aurora	319U	80013	2700-2899	
	Aurora	349C	80013	3900-3999	
	Centennial	379L	80016	7500-7799	
ENSENADA ST	Aurora	289G	80011	1600-1999	
	Aurora	289C	80011	None	
	Denver	259Q	80249	3900-4599	
	Denver	259G	80249	None	
	Denver	259L	80249	None	
ENSENADA ST S	Arapahoe Co	349U	80015	5800-5899	
	Arapahoe Co	379C	80016	None	
	Aurora	319G	80017	1200-1899	
	Aurora	319Q	80013	2100-2399	
	Aurora	349C	80013	3700-3799	
	Aurora	349G	80013	4100-4199	
	Aurora	349G	80013	None	
	Centennial	349M	80015	4600-4699	
ENSENADA WAY	Aurora	289G	80011	1600-1699	
ENSENADA WAY S	Aurora	319L	80017	1700-1799	
	Aurora	319L	80013	2000-2099	
	Aurora	319Q	80013	2400-2699	
	Aurora	319U	80013	3100-3499	
	Centennial	349L	80015	4900-5099	
ENTERPRISE ST	Superior	160R	80027	1800-2199	
ENTRADA DR	Golden	279P	80401	400-799	
ENVIRONMENTAL WAY	Broomfield	161T	80021	1-99	
EOLUS PL	Broomfield	133J	80020	None	
EOLUS RD	Thornton	193V	80260	None	
EOLUS WAY	Broomfield	133J	80020	None	
EPHESUS RD	Boulder Co	704N	80503	6200-6399	
EPPINGER BLVD	Thornton	194Y	80229	300-1699	
	Thornton	195W	80229	1700-3099	
EPWORTH HWY	Palmer Lake	907Q	80133	None	
EQUINOX DR	Douglas Co	436Y	80108	1-499	
EQUUS WAY	Douglas Co	870J	80116	None	
ERB PL	Denver	314A	80223	1200-1499	
ERICA CT	Dacono	727J	80514	100-199	
ERICKSON BLVD	Littleton	373Q	80129	None	
ERIE DR	Boulder	128L	80303	300-599	
ERIE LN	Superior	160P	80027	2000-2099	
ERIE ST	Adams Co	224N	80221	400-1199	
	Denver	254W	80211	1600-1799	
ERIE RUN	Jefferson Co	366A	80439	6400-6599	
ERIN CT	Boulder Co	70G	80503	7300-7398	E
ERIN CT	Broomfield	163E	80020	14300-14399	
ERIN PL	Lone Tree	406L	80124	10300-10399	
ERIN WAY	Lafayette	131U	80026	1600-1699	

STREET NAME	CITY or COUNTY	MAP GRID	ZIP CODE	BLOCK RANGE	O/E
ERMINEDALE DR	Lone Tree	376Y	80124	9200-9399	
ERNST AVE	Lakewood	281V	80226	300-9599	
ERVINE AVE	Longmont	11Q	80501	1500-1699	
ESCADA DR	Lochbuie	729Y	80603	None	
ESCALANTE CT E	Douglas Co	441S	80134	9800-9999	
ESCALANTE CREEK CT	Weld Co	706M	80504	None	
ESMERELDA DR	Castle Rock	469K	80108	6300-6899	
ESPANA CIR S	Aurora	319Z	80013	3200-3299	
	Centennial	349Q	80015	5200-5299	
ESPANA CT	Denver	259G	80249	None	
ESPANA CT N	Aurora	769X	80019	None	
ESPANA CT S	Arapahoe Co	379D	80016	None	
	Aurora	319L	80013	1900-2099	
	Aurora	319Q	80013	2400-2599	
	Aurora	319V	80013	2800-2999	
	Aurora	319Z	80013	3400-3499	
	Centennial	349L	80015	4800-5099	
	Centennial	349Q	80015	5100-5299	
ESPANA LN S	Centennial	349M	80015	4800-4899	
ESPANA ST	Aurora	289G	80011	1700-2099	
	Denver	259V	80249	4001-4099	O
	Denver	259G	80249	None	
ESPANA ST N	Aurora	259C	80019	None	
ESPANA ST S	Arapahoe Co	349U	80015	5800-5899	
	Aurora	319Q	80013	2100-2399	
	Aurora	319U	80013	2800-2899	
	Aurora	319Y	80013	3400-3499	
	Aurora	349C	80013	3900-3999	
	Centennial	349M	80015	4600-4699	
	Centennial	349Q	80015	5100-5499	
ESPANA WAY	Aurora	289G	80011	1700-2099	
	Denver	259Q	80249	4500-4599	
	Denver	259L	80249	None	
ESPANA WAY S	Arapahoe Co	349Z	80016	6000-6199	
	Arapahoe Co	379H	80016	None	
	Aurora	319V	80013	3000-3099	
	Aurora	349C	80013	3600-4199	
	Aurora	319G	80017	None	
	Centennial	349M	80015	4900-5099	
	Centennial	379H	80016	7100-7199	
	Centennial	379L	80016	7800-7899	
ESPERA WAY	Parker	439F	80134	12700-12799	
ESPERANZA CT	Castle Pines North	436F	80108	12600-12699	
ESPERANZA DR	Castle Pines North	436F	80108	6500-7099	
ESPERANZA PL	Castle Pines North	436F	80108	12600-12799	
ESPINOZA AVE	Jefferson Co	822Q	80433	None	
ESPINOZA ST	Erie	103N	80516	1-99	O
ESSEX AVE	Castle Rock	498L	80104	5100-5299	
ESSEX CIR	Boulder Co	100F	80301	4700-4799	
ESSEX CT	Boulder Co	100F	80301	4700-4799	
ESSEX DR	Adams Co	224H	80229	700-8699	
ESSEX PL	Boulder Co	100F	80301	7700-7799	
ESSEX ST	Adams Co	224D	80229	8600-8799	
ESTABROOK ST	Palmer Lake	907R	80133	None	
ESTABROOK WAY	Superior	160R	80027	1800-2099	
ESTACK CT S	Highlands Ranch	404G	80126	9700-9799	
ESTACK PL E	Highlands Ranch	404G	80126	1-199	
ESTATE CIR	Boulder Co	70N	80503	7500-7699	
ESTATES CIR	Douglas Co	908H	80118	2000-4099	
ESTES CIR	Arvada	252J	80002	5200-5299	
	Arvada	222E	80005	8100-8199	
ESTES CT	Arvada	252E	80002	5400-5499	
	Arvada	252A	80004	5900-6199	
	Arvada	222J	80005	7700-7999	
	Arvada	222E	80005	8100-8399	
	Arvada	222S	80004	None	
	Jefferson Co	252J	80002	4900-4999	
ESTES CT	Lyons	703C	80540	None	
ESTES CT	Westminster	222A	80005	8700-8799	
ESTES CT S	Jefferson Co	372J	80128	7300-7499	
	Jefferson Co	372J	80128	7500-7799	
	Jefferson Co	372N	80128	7800-8099	
	Lakewood	312A	80226	1000-1099	
	Lakewood	312N	80227	2400-2599	
	Lakewood	312W	80227	3000-3099	
ESTES DR	Arvada	222S	80004	6800-7199	
ESTES LN	Longmont	11R	80501	2000-2099	
ESTES LN	Westminster	192W	80021	9300-9399	
ESTES PL	Parker	410J	80138	20300-20399	
ESTES ST	Arvada	252E	80002	5300-5799	
	Arvada	252A	80004	5900-6199	
	Arvada	222W	80004	6200-6799	
	Arvada	222N	80005	7300-7399	
	Arvada	221R	80005	7400-7699	
	Arvada	222J	80005	8000-8099	
	Jefferson Co	252J	80002	4800-4899	
	Lakewood	282S	80226	1-199	
	Lakewood	282N	80226	400-599	
	Lakewood	282J	80215	1000-1499	
	Lakewood	282A	80215	2000-2599	
	Westminster	222A	80021	8800-8999	
	Westminster	191Z	80021	9000-9199	
	Wheat Ridge	252S	80033	3200-4099	
	Wheat Ridge	252N	80033	4600-4799	
ESTES ST S	Denver	342J	80123	4500-4699	
	Denver	342S	80123	5400-5499	
	Jefferson Co	342E	80123	4300-4499	
	Jefferson Co	342N	80123	5100-5199	
	Jefferson Co	341V	80123	5400-5499	
	Jefferson Co	342W	80123	5900-6199	
	Jefferson Co	372A	80123	6200-6699	
	Jefferson Co	372A	80128	6700-6999	
	Jefferson Co	372N	80128	7500-8299	
	Jefferson Co	372S	80128	8400-8699	
	Lakewood	282S	80226	1-99	
	Lakewood	282W	80226	300-699	
	Lakewood	312A	80226	700-999	
	Lakewood	312E	80232	1100-1199	
	Lakewood	312J	80232	1500-1799	
	Lakewood	312N	80227	1900-2299	
	Lakewood	312S	80227	2400-8399	
ESTES WAY	Louisville	130U	80027	900-999	
ESTES WAY S	Denver	342J	80123	4800-4899	
	Jefferson Co	342N	80123	5200-5299	
	Jefferson Co	341V	80123	5600-5799	
	Lakewood	312E	80232	1400-1499	
	Lakewood	312N	80227	2100-2199	
	Littleton	825Q	80127	9500-9699	

STREET NAME	CITY or COUNTY	MAP GRID	ZIP CODE	BLOCK RANGE	O/E
ESTESS ST	Lakewood	282N	80215	600-999	
ESTHER CIR	Frederick	727A	80504	None	
ESTRELLA LN	El Paso Co	908Q	80132	200-399	
ESTRELLA ST	Brighton	139P	80601	None	
ETHAN CT	Elbert Co	850C	80138	42700-42899	
ETNA DR	Lafayette	131Q	80026	1300-1498	E
EUCLID AVE	Boulder	127H	80302	800-1599	
	Boulder	128F	80303	2800-3399	
EUCLID AVE E	Arapahoe Co	374C	80121	1-799	
	Arapahoe Co	374D	80121	1000-1799	
	Arapahoe Co	379B	80016	17300-17699	
EUCLID AVE E	Boulder	128H	80303	4900-5499	
EUCLID AVE E	Centennial	375A	80121	1800-2199	
	Centennial	375B	80121	2700-3999	
	Centennial	375D	80121	4600-4699	
	Centennial	375D	80121	5200-5598	E
	Centennial	376A	80111	6000-6299	
	Centennial	376B	80111	7200-7299	
	Centennial	379A	80016	16700-16799	
EUCLID AVE W	Jefferson Co	371D	80123	9200-9299	
	Jefferson Co	372D	80123	None	
	Littleton	374B	80120	100-799	
	Littleton	374A	80120	1200-1599	
	Littleton	373D	80120	2400-2499	
EUCLID CIR	Lafayette	131Q	80026	1500-1599	
EUCLID CIR E	Aurora	380C	80016	22700-22999	
	Centennial	375D	80121	4600-4699	
EUCLID DR E	Arapahoe Co	380A	80016	20400-20899	
	Aurora	380B	80016	21900-22399	
	Aurora	381B	80016	25700-26199	
	Aurora	381D	80016	None	
	Centennial	376B	80111	7000-7299	
	Centennial	377D	80111	12300-12699	
	Centennial	379C	80016	19100-19999	
	Centennial	380A	80016	20900-21499	
EUCLID DR W	Jefferson Co	372C	80123	6600-6699	
	Jefferson Co	372B	80123	7500-7699	
	Jefferson Co	371D	80123	9600-9799	
EUCLID LN E	Arapahoe Co	379A	80016	16800-16899	
	Arapahoe Co	379D	80016	20200-20499	
EUCLID PL	Boulder	129E	80303	5600-5699	
EUCLID PL E	Arapahoe Co	379A	80016	16800-16899	
	Arapahoe Co	379B	80016	17700-18299	
	Arapahoe Co	379D	80016	20200-20399	
	Aurora	380B	80016	22100-22299	
	Aurora	380C	80016	22500-22699	
	Aurora	381A	80016	24500-24999	
	Aurora	381C	80016	26500-26699	
	Centennial	375B	80121	2700-3499	
	Centennial	376A	80111	6200-6299	
	Centennial	376B	80111	6500-6999	
	Centennial	378A	80111	None	
EUCLID PL W	Jefferson Co	372D	80123	5200-5799	
	Jefferson Co	372C	80123	6500-6999	
	Jefferson Co	372B	80123	7300-7699	
	Jefferson Co	372A	80123	8600-8799	
EUCLID WAY S	Denver	315B	80209	900-999	
EUDORA CIR	Thornton	195M	80233	10700-10799	
	Thornton	195H	80229	11000-11199	
EUDORA CIR S	Centennial	375R	80122	7800-7999	
EUDORA CT	Thornton	195R	80229	10100-10199	
	Thornton	195D	80233	11700-11799	
EUDORA CT S	Centennial	345V	80121	5900-5999	
	Centennial	375H	80122	7100-7399	
	Centennial	375M	80122	7700-7799	
EUDORA DR	Commerce City	225V	80022	6800-7199	
	Thornton	195D	80233	11800-11999	
	Thornton	165V	80241	12700-12799	
EUDORA LN	Thornton	195R	80229	10000-10099	
EUDORA PL	Thornton	195H	80229	11000-11199	
EUDORA PL S	Arapahoe Co	315R	80222	2600-2699	
EUDORA ST	Commerce City	255H	80022	5600-5799	
	Denver	285M	80220	1-1699	
	Denver	285H	80220	1900-1999	
	Denver	285D	80207	2000-2799	
	Denver	255Z	80207	2800-3199	
	Denver	255V	80207	3500-3799	
	Thornton	195D	80233	11500-11699	
	Thornton	165V	80241	12400-12699	
	Thornton	165H	80602	13800-13999	
EUDORA ST S	Arapahoe Co	315V	80222	2600-2699	
	Centennial	345V	80121	5900-5999	
	Centennial	375H	80122	6900-7099	
	Centennial	375M	80122	7400-7499	
	Cherry Hills Village	345H	80113	4100-4299	
	Denver	285Z	80246	1-299	
	Denver	315H	80246	1200-1299	
	Denver	315H	80222	1300-1899	
	Denver	315R	80222	2300-2399	
	Denver	315Z	80222	3000-3499	
EUDORA WAY	Denver	255V	80207	3800-3899	
	Thornton	195M	80233	10500-10699	
	Thornton	195H	80229	11000-11099	
EUDORA WAY S	Centennial	345Z	80121	5900-6199	
	Centennial	375D	80121	6300-6499	
	Centennial	375H	80122	7300-7499	
	Denver	345D	80237	3500-3599	
EUGENE CT	Denver	258K	80239	4900-4999	
EUGENE WAY	Denver	258P	80239	4300-4899	
EUGENIA CT	Castle Rock	496C	80109	3500-3599	
EUREKA CT	Denver	258P	80239	4500-4699	
	Denver	258K	80239	4900-4999	
EUREKA CT E	Highlands Ranch	404D	80126	1200-1299	
EUREKA PL W	Lakewood	311Z	80227	9400-9699	
EUREKA ST	Central City	780C	80427	100-299	
EUREKA WAY	Frederick	726L	80516	3700-3799	
EUTAW DR	Boulder	128Q	80303	4100-4299	
EVA HOOD WAY	Gilpin Co	760C	80403	1-399	
EVALENA RD	Douglas Co	467K	80108	1000-1799	
EVAN JONES CIR	Frederick	727G	80530	None	
EVANS AVE	Louisville	130M	80027	2300-2599	
EVANS AVE E	Arapahoe Co	316K	80224	7001-7299	O
	Arapahoe Co	316M	80231	8500-8899	
	Aurora	317J	80247	9900-10499	
	Aurora	317K	80014	10500-11799	
	Aurora	318J	80014	13500-14099	
	Aurora	318K	80014	14100-14899	

Continued on next column

STREET NAME	CITY or COUNTY	MAP GRID	ZIP CODE	BLOCK RANGE	O/E
EVANS AVE E (Cont'd)	Aurora	318L	80014	14900-14999	
	Aurora	318L	80013	15000-15599	
	Aurora	318M	80013	16400-16699	
	Aurora	319J	80013	16900-18499	
	Aurora	321L	80018	26100-26499	
	Denver	314L	80210	1-1699	
	Denver	315L	80210	1700-3999	
	Denver	315L	80222	4000-5499	
	Denver	316J	80222	5500-6499	
	Denver	316K	80224	6500-6999	
	Denver	316K	80224	7000-7298	E
EVANS AVE W	Denver	314J	80223	1-1599	
	Denver	314N	80110	1600-1798	E
	Denver	314N	80223	1601-1999	O
	Denver	313M	80223	2000-2398	E
	Denver	313M	80223	2001-2399	O
	Denver	313J	80219	2400-5199	
	Denver	312M	80227	5200-5599	
	Englewood	314N	80110	1801-1999	O
	Lakewood	312J	80227	7600-8399	
	Lakewood	311Q	80227	10000-10899	
	Lakewood	310P	80228	14800-14899	
EVANS BLVD	Elizabeth	871E	80107	200-399	
EVANS CIR	Broomfield	162L	80020	100-199	
EVANS CIR	Louisville	131N	80027	2100-2299	
EVANS CIR E	Aurora	317R	80014	12500-12699	
EVANS CIR W	Lakewood	310P	80228	14000-14299	
EVANS CT E	Arapahoe Co	316M	80231	9000-9099	
EVANS DR	Boulder	128G	80303	4000-4299	
EVANS DR E	Aurora	318K	80014	14200-14399	
	Aurora	319J	80013	17100-17299	
	Aurora	319M	80013	19400-19599	
EVANS DR E	Aurora	321J	80018	None	
EVANS LN	Lochbuie	139H	80603	1700-1899	
EVANS PL E	Arapahoe Co	316M	80231	9100-9299	
	Arapahoe Co	317J	80231	9300-9499	
	Aurora	318K	80014	14500-14799	
	Aurora	318M	80013	16000-16099	
	Aurora	319L	80013	19200-19299	
	Aurora	321M	80018	None	
	Denver	315R	80222	5400-5499	
EVANS PL W	Lakewood	312R	80227	6000-6199	
	Lakewood	312J	80227	8000-8399	
	Lakewood	310P	80228	None	
EVANS RD	El Paso Co	911U	80106	12000-14799	
EVANS ST	Erie	103E	80516	200-499	
	Erie	102H	80516	500-799	
EVANS ST	Lyons	703C	80540	None	
EVANS WAY E	Arapahoe Co	316M	80231	9100-9299	
	Arapahoe Co	317J	80231	9300-9499	
EVANS WAY S	Douglas Co	870P	80116	2200-2399	
EVANS RIDGE RD	Douglas Co	850P	80134	10600-10899	
EVANSTON	Thornton	194W	80260	None	
EVANSTON CIR S	Aurora	318C	80012	800-1099	
	Aurora	348G	80014	4100-4199	
EVANSTON CT	Aurora	288Q	80011	500-599	
EVANSTON CT S	Aurora	318L	80014	2000-2099	
	Aurora	348F	80015	4300-4399	
EVANSTON ST	Aurora	288L	80011	600-1199	
EVANSTON ST S	Aurora	318C	80012	700-799	
	Aurora	318G	80012	1400-1499	
	Aurora	318K	80012	1500-1899	
	Aurora	318L	80014	2000-2099	
	Aurora	318Q	80014	2400-2499	
	Aurora	318X	80014	3200-3399	
	Aurora	348C	80014	3800-3899	
	Aurora	348K	80015	4400-4599	
	Aurora	348L	80015	4800-5099	
EVANSTON WAY S	Aurora	288U	80011	1-99	
	Aurora	288U	80012	100-299	
	Aurora	318B	80012	1000-1099	
	Aurora	318U	80014	3000-3199	
	Aurora	348K	80015	4600-4799	
	Centennial	348U	80016	6000-6099	
EVANS VIEW AVE	Jefferson Co	842F	80470	31200-31599	
EVANS VIEW DR	Gilpin Co	760U	80403	1-199	
EVELYN CIR	Adams Co	225A	80229	8600-8799	
EVELYN WAY S	Denver	315Z	80222	3100-3199	
EVENINGGLOW WAY	Castle Rock	527C	80104	3600-3999	
EVENINGSONG DR	Castle Rock	527C	80104	500-1099	
EVENING STAR CT	Douglas Co	466B	80108	700-799	
EVENING STAR CT	Elbert Co	832W	80107	43500-43799	
EVENING STAR DR	Douglas Co	466B	80108	700-799	
EVENING STAR LN	Douglas Co	466B	80108	700-799	
EVENING STAR LN	Jefferson Co	822U	80433	30700-30999	
EVENING STAR LN	Lafayette	131F	80026	2200-2499	
EVENING STAR RD	Boulder Co	722T	80302	1-299	
EVENING STAR WAY	Douglas Co	466F	80108	700-799	
EVEREST LN	Jefferson Co	367G	80439	6800-7099	
EVERETT AVE	Park Co	842E	80470	1-99	
EVERETT CIR	Westminster	221D	80021	8700-8799	
	Westminster	221D	80021	8900-8999	
EVERETT CT	Arvada	251H	80002	5400-5499	
	Lakewood	281M	80215	1000-1399	
	Westminster	221H	80021	8500-8599	
	Westminster	221D	80021	8700-8799	
	Westminster	191Z	80021	9300-9399	
	Westminster	191V	80021	9500-9599	
	Wheat Ridge	251R	80033	4500-4799	
EVERETT CT S	Jefferson Co	342E	80123	4400-4499	
	Jefferson Co	341R	80123	5200-5299	
	Jefferson Co	341V	80123	5400-5499	
	Jefferson Co	342W	80123	6200-6299	
	Jefferson Co	372A	80128	6800-6899	
	Jefferson Co	372J	80128	7300-7499	
	Jefferson Co	372N	80128	8000-8099	
	Jefferson Co	372S	80128	8600-8699	
	Lakewood	282W	80226	500-599	
EVERETT DR	Boulder	128X	80305	3300-3599	
EVERETT DR	Wheat Ridge	252W	80033	3600-3699	
	Wheat Ridge	252S	80033	4100-4199	
	Wheat Ridge	252N	80033	4400-4599	
EVERETT PL	Longmont	11P	80501	1800-1899	
EVERETT ST	Arvada	251H	80002	5300-5799	
	Arvada	251D	80004	5900-6199	
	Arvada	222W	80004	6300-6599	
	Arvada	222S	80004	6600-6799	

Continued on next page

STREET NAME	CITY or COUNTY	MAP GRID	ZIP CODE	BLOCK RANGE	O/E
EVERETT ST (Cont'd)	Arvada	222N	80005	7300-7399	
	Arvada	222J	80005	7700-7799	
	Arvada	221H	80005	8100-8299	
	Lakewood	282S	80226	1-199	
	Lakewood	282N	80226	500-599	
	Lakewood	282N	80215	600-999	
	Westminster	221D	80021	8800-8899	
	Westminster	191Z	80021	9100-9299	
	Wheat Ridge	252S	80033	3400-4099	
	Wheat Ridge	252N	80033	4200-4799	
EVERETT ST S	Denver	342J	80123	4500-4699	
	Jefferson Co	342E	80123	4300-4499	
	Jefferson Co	341R	80123	5100-5199	
	Jefferson Co	342N	80123	5200-5299	
	Jefferson Co	342W	80123	6100-6299	
	Jefferson Co	372A	80128	6800-6899	
	Jefferson Co	372J	80128	7000-7499	
	Jefferson Co	372J	80128	7500-7999	
	Jefferson Co	372N	80128	8000-8199	
	Jefferson Co	371V	80128	8500-8699	
	Lakewood	282S	80226	1-99	
	Lakewood	312A	80226	600-899	
	Lakewood	312E	80232	1100-1199	
	Lakewood	312J	80232	1500-1799	
	Lakewood	312M	80227	2100-2299	
	Lakewood	312S	80227	2600-2699	
EVERETT WAY	Arvada	222J	80005	7600-7899	
	Arvada	221H	80005	8100-8499	
EVERETT WAY S	Jefferson Co	341V	80123	5400-5799	
	Jefferson Co	372A	80123	6400-6699	
	Jefferson Co	371V	80128	8300-8599	
	Littleton	825P	80127	9500-9699	
EVERGREEN AVE	Boulder	97U	80304	300-1199	
	Boulder	97V	80304	1900-2099	
EVERGREEN AVE E	Aurora	288E	80011	13800-14099	
EVERGREEN DR	Clear Creek Co	304H	80439	1-399	
EVERGREEN DR	Jefferson Co	822V	80433	28200-28499	
EVERGREEN DR	Thornton	193Z	80260	None	
EVERGREEN LN	Clear Creek Co	801A	80452	1-299	
EVERGREEN PKWY	Jefferson Co	305M	80439	1200-2899	
	Jefferson Co	306S	80439	2900-3599	
	Jefferson Co	306E	80401	None	
	Jefferson Co	306E	80439	None	
	Jefferson Co	306M	80439	None	
	Jefferson Co	306S	80439	None	
EVERGREEN PL	Broomfield	162Y	80020	1-99	
EVERGREEN RD	Adams Co	224P	80221	7400-7499	
EVERGREEN RD	Gilpin Co	760U	80403	1-699	
EVERGREEN RD	Jefferson Co	822Z	80433	11900-12099	
EVERGREEN RD	Park Co	841J	80421	1-99	
EVERGREEN ST	Broomfield	192C	80020	1-499	
EVERGREEN ST	Hudson	730L	80642	None	
EVERGREEN WAY	Boulder Co	741U	80466	1-1899	
EVERGREEN HEIGHTS DR	Jefferson Co	336N	80439	5300-5499	
EVERGREEN MANOR DR	Jefferson Co	336L	80439	28500-28799	
EVERGREEN SPRINGS RD	Jefferson Co	367W	80439	26800-26899	
EVERGREEN TRAIL E	Douglas Co	410D	80138	12100-12499	
EVERGREEN TRAIL S	Jefferson Co	337J	80439	4700-4999	
EVERSOLE DR	Broomfield	164J	80020	1200-1499	
EVONDALE ST	Highlands Ranch	404G	80126	10600-10799	
EWALD AVE	Lyons	703B	80540	None	
EXCALIBUR ST	Lafayette	132P	80026	500-1099	
EXEMPLA CIR	Lafayette	132W	80026	2-98	E
EXETER CT	Castle Pines North	436L	80108	7400-7499	
EXETER DR	Castle Pines North	436L	80108	7401-7499	O
EXETER PL	Castle Pines North	436L	80108	7400-7499	
EXMOOR RD	Adams Co	795Q	80103	None	
	Arapahoe Co	795U	80103	1-1499	
EXNER PL	Longmont	41A	80501	1-99	
EXPEDITION	Douglas Co	432N	80125	10900-10999	
EXPLORADOR CALLE	Adams Co	225E	80229	8100-8399	
EXPLORADOR CALLE AVE	Adams Co	224M	80229	700-1499	
EXPLORER'S RUN	Douglas Co	432J	80125	11100-11299	
EXPOSITION AVE E	Arapahoe Co	290Z	80018	23300-23599	
	Aurora	317B	80012	10600-13299	
	Denver	314C	80209	1-1199	
	Denver	314D	80209	1600-1699	
	Denver	315B	80209	1700-3999	
	Denver	315D	80246	5000-5499	
	Denver	316A	80246	5500-5599	
	Denver	316A	80224	5600-7299	
	Denver	317A	80247	9700-10499	
	Glendale	315C	80246	4000-4199	
	Glendale	315D	80246	4600-4999	
EXPOSITION AVE W	Denver	314A	80223	1100-1999	
	Denver	313D	80223	2000-2499	
	Denver	313B	80219	2500-4099	
	Denver	313A	80219	4300-5199	
	Lakewood	312C	80226	6000-6799	
	Lakewood	311B	80226	10000-11599	
EXPOSITION DR	Boulder	128C	80301	1600-1799	
EXPOSITION DR E	Aurora	287Z	80012	12100-12799	
	Aurora	317D	80012	12800-13299	
	Aurora	288Y	80017	15700-15899	
	Aurora	288Z	80017	15900-16399	
	Aurora	289W	80017	16900-17699	
EXPOSITION DR W	Lakewood	311C	80226	10000-10799	
	Lakewood	311B	80226	10900-11499	
	Lakewood	311A	80228	12000-12299	
	Lakewood	280Y	80228	13200-14199	
	Lakewood	310D	80228	13400-13699	
EXPOSITION PL W	Lakewood	311B	80226	10900-10999	
	Lakewood	310C	80228	13900-13999	
EXQUISITE ST	Castle Rock	496C	80109	1200-1699	
EYE BRIGHT CT	Douglas Co	378V	80134	8400-8499	
F					
F	Aurora	288F	80011	None	
F ST	Golden	279Q	80401	600-1699	
F ST	Jefferson Co	279R	80401	None	
FACTORY CIR	Fort Lupton	728G	80621	1200-1599	
FACTORY DR	Fort Lupton	728G	80621	1200-1399	
FACTORY SHOPS BLVD	Castle Rock	467N	80108	4900-5099	
FAIR AVE E	Arapahoe Co	347X	80111	10400-10499	
	Arapahoe Co	347X	80111	10600-10699	
	Arapahoe Co	348Z	80016	15700-16599	
	Centennial	346W	80111	5600-6499	
	Centennial	346X	80111	6900-7199	
	Centennial	348W	80111	14000-14099	
	Centennial	348Y	80016	15500-15599	
	Centennial	350W	80016	17100-20899	
	Centennial	349Z	80016	20100-20499	
	Greenwood Village	346Z	80111	8900-9199	
	Greenwood Village	347Y	80111	11800-12099	
FAIR AVE W	Jefferson Co	342W	80123	8400-8599	
	Jefferson Co	341Y	80127	10000-11599	
	Lakewood	342W	80123	8300-8399	
	Littleton	344X	80120	1-399	
	Littleton	344W	80120	1400-1599	
	Littleton	343Z	80120	2000-2399	
	Littleton	343W	80123	4800-5199	
FAIR CIR E	Arapahoe Co	347W	80111	10100-10199	
	Arapahoe Co	347X	80111	11000-11199	
	Centennial	345Y	80121	4400-4499	
FAIR CIR W	Littleton	343Z	80120	2100-2199	
FAIR CT E	Centennial	345Z	80121	4800-4899	
FAIR DR E	Arapahoe Co	349Y	80016	19100-19499	
	Arapahoe Co	349Z	80016	19600-19799	
	Aurora	351X	80016	None	
	Centennial	345Z	80121	4900-5499	
FAIR DR W	Jefferson Co	342Y	80123	5200-6799	
	Jefferson Co	342W	80123	8600-8899	
	Jefferson Co	341X	80127	11400-11599	
	Jefferson Co	341W	80127	12400-12499	
FAIR LN	Longmont	41M	80501	700-899	
FAIR LN E	Arapahoe Co	347W	80111	9700-9899	
	Arapahoe Co	349W	80016	17300-17399	
	Arapahoe Co	350Y	80015	22400-22499	
	Centennial	344Y	80121	200-299	
	Centennial	350W	80016	20600-20799	
FAIR PL	Boulder	128J	80302	200-299	
FAIR PL E	Arapahoe Co	347X	80111	10200-10399	
	Arapahoe Co	347X	80111	10600-10699	
	Arapahoe Co	349W	80016	16800-17499	
	Arapahoe Co	349Z	80016	19200-19899	
	Arapahoe Co	350Y	80015	22400-22499	
	Aurora	351X	80016	25801-25899	O
	Aurora	351Y	80016	26000-26199	
	Centennial	345X	80121	3200-3999	
	Centennial	345Z	80121	4600-4699	
	Centennial	346W	80111	5600-5899	
	Centennial	348W	80111	13900-14099	
	Centennial	350W	80016	20700-20799	
	Centennial	344Z	80121	None	
	Littleton	344Y	80121	200-299	
FAIR PL W	Jefferson Co	341Z	80123	9300-9399	
	Littleton	343W	80123	4800-5199	
FAIR RD	Weld Co	729R	80603	17500-17999	
FAIR ST	Castle Rock	497L	80104	None	
FAIR ST	Palmer Lake	907Q	80133	None	
FAIRALL RD	Jefferson Co	368S	80465	8500-8999	
FAIRBAIRN WAY	Highlands Ranch	405R	80130	10700-10799	
FAIRBANKS CT	Jefferson Co	306E	80439	1200-1299	
FAIRBANKS PL	Longmont	12S	80501	100-199	
FAIRBROOK PT	Highlands Ranch	405U	80130	3700-3899	
FAIRCHILD DR E	Highlands Ranch	404G	80126	100-1099	
FAIRCHILD PL E	Highlands Ranch	404G	80126	100-199	
FAIRDALE CT	Castle Rock	499N	80104	700-899	
FAIRFAX CIR	Thornton	195H	80233	11000-11099	
FAIRFAX CT	Boulder Co	70F	80503	7900-7999	
FAIRFAX CT	Castle Rock	498R	80104	1400-1699	
FAIRFAX CT	Thornton	195R	80229	10100-10199	
	Thornton	195H	80233	10900-10999	
	Thornton	195H	80229	11100-11199	
	Thornton	195H	80229	11200-11299	
FAIRFAX CT S	Centennial	345V	80121	5900-5999	
	Centennial	345Z	80121	6000-6299	
	Centennial	375H	80122	7100-7199	
	Centennial	375M	80122	7400-7499	
	Centennial	375R	80122	7800-8099	
FAIRFAX DR	Commerce City	225V	80022	6900-7199	
	Thornton	195D	80233	11600-11699	
	Thornton	165H	80602	None	
FAIRFAX DR S	Arapahoe Co	315R	80222	2300-2499	
FAIRFAX PL S	Arapahoe Co	315R	80222	2500-2599	
FAIRFAX ST	Commerce City	255H	80022	5600-5799	
	Denver	285R	80220	1-1999	
	Denver	285D	80207	2000-2799	
	Denver	255Z	80207	2800-3199	
	Denver	255V	80207	3500-3799	
	Thornton	165Z	80233	11900-11999	
	Thornton	165Z	80241	12000-12399	
	Thornton	165V	80241	12500-12799	
	Thornton	165H	80602	13800-13999	
FAIRFAX ST S	Centennial	375H	80122	7000-7099	
	Cherry Hills Village	345M	80121	4800-5099	
	Denver	285V	80246	1-399	
	Denver	285Z	80246	500-699	
	Denver	315H	80246	1100-1299	
	Denver	315H	80222	1300-1999	
	Denver	315Z	80222	2700-3499	
FAIRFAX WAY	Thornton	195M	80233	10800-10899	
	Thornton	195H	80233	11000-11099	
FAIRFAX WAY S	Centennial	375D	80121	6300-6699	
FAIRFIELD CIR	Castle Rock	498U	80104	5100-5499	
FAIRFIELD CIR	Elbert Co	851F	80138	41400-41499	
FAIRFIELD DR	Boulder	128T	80305	1100-1399	
FAIRFIELD LN	Louisville	160C	80027	100-699	
FAIRFIELD ST S	Littleton	344X	80120	5900-6199	
FAIRFIELD WAY S	Littleton	344T	80120	5900-5999	
FAIRGATE CT	Highlands Ranch	405L	80126	3600-3799	
FAIRGATE WAY	Highlands Ranch	405L	80126	10000-10399	
FAIRGROUNDS DR	Castle Rock	497Q	80104	None	
FAIRGROUNDS RD	Brighton	167S	80601	None	
FAIRGROUNDS RD	Castle Rock	497Q	80104	400-599	
FAIRHAVEN ST	Castle Rock	498L	80104	400-999	
FAIR LAWN CIR	Boulder Co	100B	80301	4800-4899	
FAIR LAWN CT	Boulder Co	100B	80301	4800-4899	
FAIRLAWN TRAIL	Highlands Ranch	405M	80130	None	
FAIR MEADOW PL	Castle Rock	528J	80104	None	
FAIRMONT LN	Highlands Ranch	405Q	80126	10700-10899	
FAIRMOUNT DR	Denver	286Z	80247	8200-8599	
FAIRMOUNT DR E	Denver	286U	80230	8000-8199	
FAIRPLAY AVE	Broomfield	162L	80020	1-399	
FAIRPLAY CIR S	Aurora	318C	80012	1100-1199	
	Aurora	348G	80014	4200-4299	
FAIRPLAY CT S	Aurora	318C	80012	700-799	
	Aurora	348F	80015	4500-4599	
	Aurora	348L	80015	4700-4799	
	Aurora	348Q	80015	None	
FAIRPLAY DR	El Paso Co	908Y	80132	17200-17399	
FAIRPLAY ST	Adams Co	168K	80601	13300-13599	
	Aurora	288Q	80011	400-599	
	Aurora	288L	80011	1000-1099	
	Aurora	288G	80011	1700-1799	
	Aurora	288C	80011	2000-2599	
	Commerce City	198B	80603	11600-11999	
	Commerce City	198Q	80022	None	
	Denver	258K	80239	4900-4999	
	Denver	258L	80239	5200-5299	
	Denver	258G	80239	5500-5599	
FAIRPLAY ST S	Arapahoe Co	378L	80112	None	
	Aurora	288Y	80012	600-699	
	Aurora	318C	80012	800-999	
	Aurora	318K	80012	1600-1899	
	Aurora	318L	80014	2000-2199	
	Aurora	318Q	80014	2400-2499	
	Aurora	318U	80014	3000-3299	
	Aurora	318Y	80014	3300-3399	
	Aurora	348L	80015	4500-4599	
	Aurora	348L	80015	4900-5199	
	Centennial	348U	80016	5900-5999	
FAIRPLAY WAY	Aurora	288Q	80011	500-599	
	Aurora	288C	80011	2300-2599	
	Denver	258P	80239	4400-4699	
FAIRPLAY WAY	El Paso Co	908Y	80132	17800-17899	
FAIRPLAY WAY S	Aurora	318C	80012	1000-1199	
	Aurora	318G	80012	1500-1599	
	Aurora	318Q	80014	2500-2599	
	Aurora	318Y	80014	3400-3499	
	Aurora	348C	80014	3600-3799	
FAIRVIEW AVE	Adams Co	223M	80221	7700-7999	
FAIRVIEW AVE	Jefferson Co	371L	80127	9700-9999	
FAIRVIEW AVE W	Jefferson Co	372M	80128	5900-6399	
	Jefferson Co	372J	80128	7800-9199	
	Jefferson Co	371M	80128	9500-9599	
FAIRVIEW CT	Lone Tree	406C	80124	8400-8499	
FAIRVIEW DR	Boulder Co	129G	80303	6600-6999	
FAIRVIEW DR	Lone Tree	406D	80124	9500-9899	
FAIRVIEW DR W	Jefferson Co	372K	80128	6800-7499	
	Jefferson Co	372J	80128	8500-8799	
FAIRVIEW LN	Jefferson Co	280C	80401	14300-14399	
FAIRVIEW PKWY	Highlands Ranch	405B	80126	9500-10299	
FAIRVIEW PL	Lone Tree	406D	80124	9500-9599	
FAIRVIEW PL W	Denver	253Y	80211	3200-3299	
FAIRVIEW RD	Boulder Co	130K	80303	7600-7999	
FAIRVIEW ST	Longmont	706N	80504	None	
FAIRVIEW WAY	Lone Tree	406D	80124	8400-8499	
FAIRVIEW OAKS LN	Lone Tree	406D	80124	8700-8799	
FAIRVIEW OAKS PL	Lone Tree	406D	80124	8800-8899	
FAIRVIEW OAKS WAY	Lone Tree	406D	80124	8800-8899	
FAIRWAY CT	Boulder	129E	80303	1000-1099	
FAIRWAY DR	Commerce City	198G	80022	15400-15499	
	Commerce City	198M	80022	None	
FAIRWAY DR	Jefferson Co	336P	80439	29400-29899	
FAIRWAY LN	Broomfield	163E	80020	4300-14299	
FAIRWAY LN	Columbine Valley	373B	80123	1-99	
	Columbine Valley	343X	80123	None	
FAIRWAY LN	Douglas Co	440S	80134	7200-7499	
FAIRWAY POINTE DR	Erie	133G	80516	None	
FAIRWAYS DR	Boulder Co	723G	80503	6300-7199	
FAIRWAY VIEW CT	Douglas Co	436Y	80108	2900-2999	
FAIRWAY VISTAS CT	Douglas Co	432P	80125	10700-10799	
FAIRWAY VISTAS RD	Douglas Co	432P	80125	6900-6999	
FAIRWAY WOOD CIR	Castle Rock	496D	80109	None	
FAIRWIND DR	El Paso Co	911Y	80106	17300-17499	
FAIRWIND LN	Broomfield	163G	80020	14000-14099	
FAIRWIND PL	El Paso Co	911Y	80106	17100-17199	
FAIRWOOD ST	Douglas Co	432L	80125	9600-9999	
FAITH CT	Frederick	727F	80530	7900-7999	
FAITH CT	Longmont	41B	80501	800-899	
FAITH PL	Longmont	41B	80501	1800-1899	
FALCON AVE	Elbert Co	871H	80117	None	
FALCON CIR N	Elbert Co	872E	80117	34600-34899	
FALCON CIR S	Elbert Co	872E	80117	34400-34499	
FALCON CT	Douglas Co	432M	80125	9600-9699	
FALCON CT	Louisville	130U	80027	1000-1099	
FALCON DR	Brighton	138L	80601	1100-1299	
FALCON DR	Broomfield	133W	80026	None	
FALCON DR	Frederick	726D	80504	4700-4899	
FALCON DR	Lochbuie	140B	80603	None	
	Lochbuie	729Y	80603	None	
FALCON DR	Longmont	11N	80503	2000-2799	
FALCON DR	Weld Co	729Q	80621	4300-17299	
FALCON LN	Douglas Co	432L	80125	9700-9899	
FALCON LN	Jefferson Co	339Z	80465	6100-6199	
	Lyons	703C	80540	None	
FALCON PL	Erie	133G	80516	None	
FALCON PT	Lafayette	132W	80026	2800-2899	
FALCON ST	Federal Heights	193U	80260	2900-2999	
FALCON ST	Firestone	707T	80504	10100-10599	
FALCON CREEK DR S	Highlands Ranch	406F	80130	9800-10099	
FALCON CREST	Boulder Co	722L	80302	1-2099	
FALCON CREST CT	El Paso Co	908R	80132	19600-19799	
FALCON HILLS DR	Highlands Ranch	375T	80126	1-199	
FALCON RIDGE DR	Jefferson Co	366B	80439	29400-29599	
FALCON ROOST PT	Douglas Co	411W	80138	None	
FALCON WING RD	Jefferson Co	338H	80454	20600-21799	
FALK CT	Arvada	251H	80002	5700-5799	
FALL LN E	Highlands Ranch	375T	80126	2900-3199	
FALLBROOKE DR S	Highlands Ranch	405C	80126	9500-9599	
FALL CREEK CIR	Broomfield	162L	80020	13600-13699	
FALL CREEK RD	Broomfield	162L	80020	None	
FALLEN LEAF WAY	El Paso Co	908T	80132	1600-1699	
FALLEN ROCK RD	Jefferson Co	823N	80433	9100-10099	
FALLEN TREE RD	El Paso Co	908P	80132	1200-1299	
FALLING LEAF CIR N	Douglas Co	440V	80134	6200-6499	
FALLING STAR PL	Castle Rock	498B	80108	3100-3499	

STREET NAME	CITY or COUNTY	MAP GRID	ZIP CODE	BLOCK RANGE	O/E
FALLON CIR	Castle Rock	499J	80104	6900-7299	
FALLOW DEER RD	Douglas Co	870E	80116	1-399	
FALL RIVER CIR	Longmont	12Y	80501	1100-1299	
FALL RIVER RD	Clear Creek Co	780P	80452	1000-2099	
FALLS DR	Broomfield	163L	80020	13400-13499	
FALMOUTH ST	Castle Rock	499J	80104	1-299	
FANTASY PL	Castle Rock	466Y	80109	3300-3499	
FARA WAY	Jefferson Co	822P	80433	9400-9499	
FARADAY ST	Adams Co	224H	80229	1300-8799	
FAREHAM CT	Castle Rock	497U	80104	500-699	
FARGO TRAIL N	Douglas Co	432N	80125	6800-6999	
FARMDALE RD W	Sheridan	343G	80110	3100-3299	
FARMDALE ST	Firestone	707T	80504	10100-10399	
	Firestone	707T	80504	None	
	Firestone	727B	80504	None	
FARMER PL	Brighton	139G	80601	None	
FARMHOUSE CIR	Elbert Co	851E	80138	41200-41499	
FARMHOUSE WAY	Brighton	139K	80601	None	
FARMINGDALE CT	Parker	410P	80138	21700-21799	
FARMINGDALE WAY	Parker	410P	80138	21700-21899	
FARNELL LN S	Littleton	343U	80123	None	
FARRELL DR	Gilpin Co	741X	80403	None	
FAR VIEW	Weld Co	706N	80504	3200-11499	
FARVIEW LN	Jefferson Co	366D	80439	6300-6499	
FAST DRAW CT	Park Co	841K	80421	1-99	
FAULKNER LN	Douglas Co	407H	80134	None	
FAVER DR N	Douglas Co	496J	80109	1-1299	
FAWN CIR	Douglas Co	870E	80116	10200-10399	
FAWN CT	Broomfield	163Q	80020	13300-13399	
FAWN DR	Jefferson Co	822Z	80433	27500-27899	
FAWN DR	Park Co	841J	80421	1-199	
FAWN RD	Park Co	841V	80421	1-299	
FAWN ST	Golden	279Q	80401	1-299	
FAWNBROOK CT	Highlands Ranch	405M	80130	10200-10299	
FAWNBROOK LN	Highlands Ranch	405H	80130	10100-10199	
FAWN MEADOWS TRAIL	Elbert Co	851U	80107	38000-38199	
FAWNPATH	Jefferson Co	365F	80439	6800-6899	
FAWN RIDGE CIR	Elbert Co	851E	80138	2600-2899	
FAWN RIDGE WAY	Castle Rock	528E	80104	4900-5599	
FAWN TRAIL	Clear Creek Co	821H	80439	1-299	
FAWNWOOD DR	Castle Pines North	436C	80108	8600-8799	
FAWNWOOD RD	El Paso Co	908T	80132	1100-1799	
FAYBEN CIR	Elbert Co	850Q	80107	900-999	
FAYETTE ST	Federal Heights	223D	80260	9000-9099	
	Federal Heights	193Z	80260	9100-9199	
FEATHER CT	Castle Rock	466X	80109	2800-2999	
FEATHER PL	Lochbuie	140F	80603	None	
FEATHER GRASS CT	Douglas Co	378R	80134	8300-8399	
FEATHER GRASS RD	Broomfield	133W	80026	None	
FEATHER REED AVE	Longmont	40V	80503	3300-3599	
FEATHERWALK CT	Highlands Ranch	404Q	80126	200-399	
FEATHERWALK LN	Highlands Ranch	404L	80126	10601-10799	O
FEATHERWALK WAY	Highlands Ranch	404Q	80126	10600-10799	
FEDERAL BLVD	Adams Co	253G	80221	5201-5299	O
	Adams Co	253G	80221	5300-6199	
	Adams Co	223L	80221	6200-6999	
	Broomfield	163C	80020	14400-14799	
	Broomfield	133Y	80020	14700-15199	
	Denver	283U	80219	1-399	
	Denver	283G	80204	400-1999	
	Denver	283C	80211	2000-2699	
	Denver	253U	80211	2700-4799	
	Denver	253L	80221	4800-5199	
	Denver	253G	80221	5200-5298	E
	Federal Heights	223L	80260	8800-9198	E
	Federal Heights	193Q	80260	9000-10398	E
	Westminster	223L	80030	7000-8399	
	Westminster	223L	80260	8400-8799	
	Westminster	223L	80260	8801-8999	O
	Westminster	193Q	80260	9001-10399	O
	Westminster	193Q	80234	10400-11999	
FEDERAL BLVD S	Arapahoe Co	313Y	80110	3301-3499	O
	Denver	283U	80219	1-699	
	Denver	313Q	80219	700-2699	
	Denver	313U	80236	2700-3199	
	Denver	313Y	80236	3200-3298	E
	Englewood	343L	80110	4500-5099	
	Littleton	343L	80123	5100-5799	
	Sheridan	313Y	80110	3300-3498	E
	Sheridan	343L	80110	3500-4499	
FEDERAL CIR	Broomfield	163Q	80020	3200-3299	
FEDERAL CIR S	Littleton	343Q	80123	5300-5499	
FEDERAL CT	Broomfield	163Q	80020	13300-13399	
FEDERAL PKWY	Westminster	163Y	80234	None	
FEDERAL PL	Broomfield	163L	80020	13400-13499	
FELDSPAR CT	Douglas Co	408H	80134	10100-10299	
FELDSPAR RD	Gilpin Co	761E	80403	1-499	
FELLET CT S	Lakewood	312Y	80227	3200-3399	
FELLET LN W	Lakewood	312Y	80227	6800-6899	
FELL MIST WAY	Castle Rock	466V	80109	None	
FELTHAM PL	Longmont	11Q	80501	1500-1699	
FENCEPOST DR	Castle Rock	467S	80109	None	
FENCEROW PL	Brighton	140J	80601	None	
FENDLEBRUSH ST W					
	Highlands Ranch	403D	80129	2000-2199	
FENDLEBRUSH WAY	Highlands Ranch	403H	80129	None	
FENNEL ST	Castle Rock	466U	80109	None	
FENTON CIR	Westminster	222V	80003	7100-7199	
	Westminster	192M	80020	10900-10999	
FENTON CT	Arvada	222M	80003	8000-8099	
	Westminster	222V	80003	7100-7199	
	Westminster	192Z	80031	9300-9399	
	Wheat Ridge	252V	80212	4000-4099	
FENTON CT S	Jefferson Co	342Z	80123	6100-6399	
	Jefferson Co	372D	80123	None	
	Lakewood	312V	80227	2600-2699	
	Lakewood	312R	80227	None	
FENTON DR S	Lakewood	312R	80227	2300-2499	
FENTON LN S	Lakewood	312R	80227	2500-2599	
FENTON ST	Arvada	252D	80003	6000-6199	
	Arvada	222Z	80003	6200-6799	
	Arvada	222M	80003	7900-7999	
	Arvada	222H	80003	8400-8599	
	Boulder Co	162D	80020	14400-14799	
	Denver	252M	80212	4800-4999	
	Edgewater	282D	80214	1700-2599	
	Jefferson Co	252H	80002	5400-5599	
Continued on next column					
FENTON ST (Cont'd)	Lakewood	282V	80226	1-99	
	Lakewood	282R	80214	800-999	
	Lakewood	282M	80214	1400-1699	
	Mountain View	252V	80212	4100-4198	E
	Westminster	222V	80003	7100-7199	
	Westminster	222R	80003	7500-7599	
	Westminster	192H	80020	11200-11399	
	Westminster	192D	80020	11700-11799	
	Wheat Ridge	252Z	80214	2800-3199	
	Wheat Ridge	252Z	80212	3200-3799	
	Wheat Ridge	252V	80212	4101-4399	O
FENTON ST S	Denver	312R	80227	2100-2199	
	Denver	312V	80227	2700-3099	
	Denver	342D	80235	3800-3899	
	Denver	342V	80123	5500-5699	
	Jefferson Co	372M	80128	7500-7799	
	Jefferson Co	372D	80123	None	
	Lakewood	282V	80226	1-199	
	Lakewood	282Z	80226	200-499	
	Lakewood	312D	80226	700-899	
	Lakewood	312H	80232	1100-1699	
FENTON WAY	Arvada	222H	80003	8200-8399	
FENTON WAY S	Denver	342D	80235	3700-3799	
FENWICK CIR	Douglas Co	407G	80134	11500-11799	
FENWICK DR	Douglas Co	407G	80134	None	
FENWICK ST	Douglas Co	407G	80134	10000-10199	
FENWOOD DR	Highlands Ranch	405H	80130	4500-5099	
FENWOOD PL	Highlands Ranch	405H	80130	4500-4599	
FERGUSON CIR	Lafayette	132N	80026	100-499	
FERN AVE	Broomfield	163S	80020	4000-4399	
FERN CIR	Broomfield	162N	80020	1200-1299	
FERN DR	Adams Co	223V	80030	6800-6999	
	Westminster	223V	80030	2300-2699	
FERN PL	Boulder	97V	80304	3100-3199	
FERN ST	Broomfield	162N	80020	1100-1199	
FERN WAY	Jefferson Co	763K	80403	8900-9399	
FERNANDO DR	Mead	706M	80504	None	
FERNANDO RD	Adams Co	224K	80221	7600-7699	
FERNCREST ST	Firestone	707T	80504	10100-10399	
	Firestone	707T	80504	None	
	Firestone	707X	80504	None	
FERN GULCH DR	Jefferson Co	337J	80439	27600-27699	
FERN GULCH RD	Jefferson Co	337P	80439	25900-26999	
FERN LAKE CT	Lafayette	131E	80026	300-398	E
FERNLEAF CT	Castle Rock	466Q	80109	3200-3299	
FERNS RD	Elbert Co	851J	80107	3500-40499	
FERNWOOD CT	Highlands Ranch	404C	80126	9300-9399	
FERNWOOD PL	Broomfield	163U	80020	2600-2899	
FERRELL WAY	Idaho Springs	781N	80452	None	
FERRIS DR	Erie	102R	80516	None	
FERRIS WAY	Boulder Co	130E	80303	7600-7799	
FESQUE DR	Jefferson Co	308A	80401	23300-23499	
FETZER ST N	Arapahoe Co	795X	80103	1-299	
FETZER ST S	Arapahoe Co	795Y	80103	100-599	
FIDDLE RD	Castle Rock	466Z	80109	None	
FIDDLERS GREEN CIR S					
	Greenwood Village	376C	80111	6400-6599	
FIDDLERS GREEN PL	Gilpin Co	761K	80403	1-299	
FIELD CIR	Arvada	251H	80002	5300-5399	
FIELD CT	Arvada	251H	80002	5400-5499	
	Arvada	221M	80005	7900-8199	
	Arvada	221H	80005	8200-8399	
FIELD CT	Boulder Co	99H	80301	4600-4699	
FIELD CT	Jefferson Co	251M	80002	4800-4899	
	Westminster	221D	80021	8500-8799	
	Westminster	191Z	80021	9500-9599	
FIELD CT S	Denver	341R	80123	4900-5099	
	Jefferson Co	341H	80123	4300-4499	
	Jefferson Co	341R	80123	5300-5399	
	Jefferson Co	371D	80123	6600-6699	
	Jefferson Co	371M	80128	7300-7499	
	Jefferson Co	371V	80128	8800-8999	
	Lakewood	281Z	80226	500-599	
	Lakewood	311H	80232	1300-1399	
	Lakewood	311M	80232	1500-1799	
	Lakewood	311V	80227	2500-2699	
	Lakewood	311V	80227	2900-2999	
FIELD DR	Wheat Ridge	251V	80033	3800-4099	
FIELD LN	Westminster	191Z	80021	9300-9399	
FIELD PL	Westminster	221D	80021	8700-8799	
FIELD ST	Arvada	251H	80002	5300-5799	
	Arvada	251D	80004	5900-6199	
	Arvada	221Z	80004	6400-6799	
	Arvada	221R	80005	7300-7399	
	Lakewood	281V	80226	1-199	
	Lakewood	282N	80215	600-799	
	Lakewood	281M	80215	800-1099	
	Lakewood	281D	80215	2000-2599	
	Westminster	221D	80021	8800-9099	
	Westminster	191Z	80021	9100-9199	
	Wheat Ridge	251R	80033	4300-4799	
FIELD ST S	Denver	341M	80123	4500-4799	
	Jefferson Co	341D	80235	3500-3599	
	Jefferson Co	341V	80123	5100-5599	
	Jefferson Co	342W	80123	6100-6199	
	Jefferson Co	371D	80123	6600-6699	
	Jefferson Co	371D	80128	6700-6899	
	Jefferson Co	372N	80128	7500-8099	
	Jefferson Co	371V	80128	8500-8699	
	Lakewood	281Z	80226	400-499	
	Lakewood	281Z	80226	500-599	
	Lakewood	311D	80226	700-1099	
	Lakewood	311R	80227	2100-2199	
	Lakewood	312S	80227	2500-2699	
	Lakewood	312W	80227	3300-3399	
FIELD WAY	Westminster	221D	80021	8700-8799	
FIELD WAY S	Denver	341M	80123	4800-5099	
	Jefferson Co	371D	80123	6300-6599	
	Lakewood	311R	80227	2100-2299	
	Littleton	825P	80127	9500-9899	
FIELDCREST LN	Boulder Co	10M	80503	8900-9099	
FIELDSTONE PL	Highlands Ranch	374V	80126	900-1199	
FIELDSTONE TRAIL					
	Cherry Hills Village	345B	80113	1-99	
FIESTA TERRACE	Lone Tree	376Z	80124	8600-8899	
FIFE CT	Denver	253Z	80211	2900-3199	
FIFTH AVE	Hudson	730L	80642	400-499	
FIG CT	Arvada	220U	80004	6900-6999	
	Jefferson Co	250Q	80403	4700-4799	
	Jefferson Co	250G	80002	5600-5799	
	Jefferson Co	250C	80004	5800-5899	
FIG CT S	Lakewood	310U	80228	2400-2499	
FIG ST	Arvada	220Y	80004	6400-6799	
	Arvada	220U	80004	7000-7199	
	Arvada	220G	80005	None	
	Jefferson Co	280Q	80401	700-799	
	Jefferson Co	250Q	80403	4400-4699	
	Jefferson Co	250L	80403	5000-5199	
FIG ST S	Lakewood	310Q	80228	2200-2499	
	Lakewood	310U	80228	2800-2899	
FIG WAY	Jefferson Co	250G	80002	5600-5799	
FIG WAY S	Lakewood	280Y	80228	400-699	
FIGWOOD ST	Douglas Co	432L	80125	None	
FILBERT AVE E	Douglas Co	378X	80134	3000-3999	
FILBERT CT	Denver	285H	80220	1500-1699	
FILBERT CT S	Centennial	345Z	80121	6000-6299	
	Denver	315M	80222	1700-1899	
FILBERT LN S	Centennial	345Z	80121	6300-6499	
FILBERT WAY S	Denver	315H	80222	1400-1499	
FILLMORE AVE	Louisville	130Y	80027	100-299	
FILLMORE CIR	Thornton	165P	80241	13000-13099	
FILLMORE CIR S	Centennial	375F	80122	7100-7499	
	Centennial	375P	80122	8100-8299	
FILLMORE CT	Adams Co	165B	80602	14600-14699	
FILLMORE CT	Louisville	130U	80027	400-499	
	Louisville	130Q	80027	1500-1899	
FILLMORE CT	Northglenn	195K	80233	10700-10799	
	Thornton	195T	80229	9500-9599	
	Thornton	195F	80233	11500-11599	
	Thornton	165X	80241	12300-12399	
	Thornton	165T	80241	12800-12999	
	Thornton	165P	80241	13300-13599	
FILLMORE CT S	Centennial	375B	80122	6800-6899	
	Centennial	375F	80122	7000-7099	
	Centennial	375P	80122	7900-7999	
	Cherry Hills Village	345P	80113	4700-4999	
FILLMORE DR	Thornton	165F	80602	None	
FILLMORE PL	Louisville	130Q	80027	1400-1499	
FILLMORE PL	Thornton	195A	80233	11600-11799	
FILLMORE ST	Adams Co	225K	80229	7800-7999	
	Adams Co	135K	80602	16400-16599	
	Denver	285K	80206	100-1699	
	Denver	285B	80205	2600-2699	
	Denver	255X	80205	2700-3799	
	Denver	255P	80216	4000-5199	
	Thornton	195T	80229	9600-9799	
	Thornton	195T	80229	9900-9999	
	Thornton	195N	80229	10100-10199	
	Thornton	165T	80241	11200-12599	
	Thornton	165S	80241	12600-12799	
	Thornton	165P	80241	13100-13199	
	Thornton	165K	80602	13800-13899	
	Thornton	165F	80602	13900-13999	
	Thornton	135X	80602	15100-15199	
	Thornton	165F	80602	None	
FILLMORE ST S	Denver	315B	80209	700-899	
	Denver	315P	80210	1100-2899	
	Denver	315X	80210	3100-3299	
FILLMORE WAY	Northglenn	195K	80233	10600-10799	
	Northglenn	195F	80233	11000-11199	
	Thornton	135X	80602	14800-15199	
	Thornton	165A	80602	None	
FILLMORE WAY S	Centennial	375K	80122	7500-7699	
	Centennial	375P	80122	8000-8299	
	Denver	315B	80209	900-1099	
	Denver	315T	80210	2900-3099	
FILLY LN	El Paso Co	909Z	80908	5800-6099	
FINCH	Jefferson Co	370B	80127	1-99	
FINCH AVE	Brighton	137Z	80601	1200-1299	
FINCH AVE N	Lafayette	132K	80026	100-499	
FINCH AVE S	Lafayette	132K	80026	100-499	
FINDLAY LN	Longmont	10U	80503	3700-3899	
FINDLAY WAY	Boulder	128X	80305	1400-1599	
FINLAND DR W	Littleton	825P	80127	9100-9499	
FINN AVE	Douglas Co	406P	80124	900-1499	
FIR AVE	Fort Lupton	728H	80621	900-999	
	Weld Co	726K	80516	5300-5699	
	Weld Co	706V	80504	None	
FIR CIR S	Jefferson Co	336G	80439	4100-4299	
FIR CT	Louisville	130Y	80027	700-799	
FIR CT E	Louisville	131W	80027	400-499	
FIR DR	Jefferson Co	842H	80433	13600-13699	
	Jefferson Co	306X	80439	29700-30199	
	Thornton	225A	80229	2000-2299	
	Thornton	194Z	80229	8900-9499	
FIR LN	Broomfield	192C	80020	300-399	
FIR LN	Park Co	841T	80421	1-99	
FIR ST	Federal Heights	193V	80260	9700-9799	
FIR ST	Hudson	730L	80642	500-599	
FIR WAY	Louisville	130Z	80027	500-599	
FIRE BRICK DR	Parker	408V	80134	16500-16799	
FIREDOG WAY N	Douglas Co	907B	80118	13100-13399	
FIRE FLY AVE E	Parker	848D	80134	None	
FIRE FLY LN S	Parker	848D	80134	None	
FIREHOUSE RD	Brighton	138R	80601	1-99	
FIREHOUSE ST	Elbert Co	850G	80138	None	
FIREHOUSE HILL RD	Jefferson Co	369N	80465	7600-7999	
FIRENZE PL	Highlands Ranch	405B	80126	3100-3199	
FIRENZE WAY	Highlands Ranch	405B	80126	9500-9699	
FIRE OPAL CT	Castle Rock	467H	80108	2000-2199	
FIRE OPAL LN	Castle Rock	467H	80108	6600-6999	
FIREROCK CT	Boulder Co	99H	80301	6900-6999	
FIRE ROCK DR S	Parker	408R	80134	11300-11399	
FIRESIDE ST	Louisville	131N	80027	400-699	
FIRESTONE CIR	Elbert Co	851D	80107	None	
FIRESTONE CIR	Lochbuie	139H	80603	100-299	
FIRESTONE CIR	Lone Tree	406H	80124	9800-9899	
FIRESTONE WAY	Superior	160R	80027	2000-2299	
FIRETHORN	Douglas Co	432N	80125	7200-7399	
FIRETHORN CT	Boulder Co	70Q	80503	8400-8499	
FIRETHORNE CT	Jefferson Co	306U	80439	29400-29499	
FIREWEED CT	Brighton	139M	80601	None	
FIREWEED DR	Jefferson Co	336H	80439	27500-28599	
FIREWEED RD S	Highlands Ranch	404E	80129	9800-9899	
FIREWEED TRAIL	Broomfield	163A	80020	4400-4499	

STREET NAME	CITY or COUNTY	MAP GRID	ZIP CODE	BLOCK RANGE	O/E
FIRST AVE	Hudson	730Q	80642	None	
FIRST ST	Palmer Lake	907U	80133	None	
FIRST LIGHT DR	Castle Rock	496C	80109	3400-3699	
FIRTH CT	Denver	253Z	80211	2800-2899	
FISCHER RD	Jefferson Co	762F	80403	None	
FISHBECK CT	Jefferson Co	823N	80433	25800-25899	
FISH CREEK WAY	Weld Co	707J	80504	None	
FISHER DR	Boulder	128B	80301	3300-3599	
FISHER WAY	Northglenn	195E	80233	1900-2199	
FISK CT	Longmont	11S	80503	1500-1599	
FITZSIMMONS RD	Park Co	820Z	80421	1-399	
FITZSIMMONS WAY	Aurora	288A	80011	13300-13699	
FITZSIMONS PKWY	Aurora	288E	80011	1500-1598	E
	Aurora	287D	80011	None	
FIVE IRON DR	Castle Rock	497U	80104	1800-1999	
FIVE PARKS DR	Arvada	220G	80005	8500-8699	
FLAGG DR	Boulder Co	132L	80026	12000-12699	
FLAGLER CT	Parker	409J	80134	10600-10699	
FLAGLER DR	Parker	409J	80134	10700-10999	
FLAGSTAFF DR	Longmont	12K	80501	2300-2499	
FLAGSTAFF RD	Boulder Co	127F	80302	4000-4999	
	Boulder Co	742L	80302	5000-8999	
FLAGSTAFF WAY	Highlands Ranch	405K	80126	10500-10699	
FLAGSTONE PL	Superior	160U	80027	600-799	
FLAGSTONE WAY	Douglas Co	408H	80134	10100-10199	
FLAMINGO COVE	Lafayette	132P	80026	800-899	
FLAMINGO CT S	Centennial	345Z	80121	6100-6199	
	Denver	315D	80246	700-899	
FLAMINGO DR	Boulder Co	99S	80301	None	
FLAMINGO DR	Lafayette	132K	80026	700-799	
FLAMINGO WAY S	Denver	315H	80222	1500-1599	
	Denver	315Z	80222	3000-3399	
FLAMINGO WAY W	Douglas Co	825V	80125	9000-9299	
FLAMING TREE WAY	El Paso Co	908P	80132	800-999	
FLANDERS CT	Denver	259V	80249	None	
FLANDERS CT N	Aurora	769X	80019	None	
FLANDERS CT S	Arapahoe Co	349V	80015	5600-5799	
	Arapahoe Co	379D	80016	None	
	Aurora	319Q	80013	2300-2699	
	Centennial	349R	80015	5000-5199	
FLANDERS LN S	Centennial	349R	80015	5100-5199	
FLANDERS ST	Denver	259V	80249	4000-4099	
	Denver	259R	80249	4200-4499	
	Denver	259H	80249	None	
FLANDERS ST N	Aurora	259D	80019	None	
FLANDERS ST S	Aurora	319Z	80013	2600-3499	
	Aurora	349D	80013	3600-3699	
	Aurora	319G	80017	None	
	Centennial	349H	80015	4200-4599	
	Centennial	349M	80015	4600-4799	
	Centennial	349R	80015	5200-5299	
	Centennial	379M	80016	7100-7999	
FLANDERS WAY	Denver	259R	80249	4500-4999	
	Denver	259H	80249	None	
FLANDERS WAY S	Aurora	319G	80017	1500-1999	
	Aurora	319L	80013	1900-2099	
	Aurora	319Z	80013	3400-3499	
	Aurora	349G	80013	3900-4199	
	Centennial	349M	80015	4600-4699	
	Centennial	349R	80015	5300-5399	
FLANDIN CT	Adams Co	794G	80136	4000-4299	
FLANNAGAN CT	Erie	102C	80516	1300-1499	
FLASH CT	Broomfield	133N	80020	4800-4899	
FLAT CREEK DR	Jefferson Co	337X	80439	None	
FLATHEAD DR	Jefferson Co	306E	80439	None	
FLATIRON BLVD	Broomfield	161S	80021	400-599	
FLATIRON CIR E	Broomfield	161P	80021	100-399	
FLATIRON CIR W	Broomfield	161S	80021	1-99	O
	Broomfield	161N	80021	None	
FLATIRON CT	Boulder	99W	80301	1800-1899	
FLATIRON DR	Boulder Co	102J	80026	11000-11899	
FLATIRON PKWY	Boulder	99W	80301	5500-5799	
FLATIRON RD	Douglas Co	406Q	80124	10600-10899	
FLATIRON MARKETPLACE DR					
	Broomfield	161P	80021	601-699	O
FLATIRONS CT	Louisville	130U	80027	800-899	
FLAT ROCK CIR N	Aurora	290R	80018	None	
FLATROCK CIR S	Aurora	321A	80018	1100-1299	
FLAT ROCK CT	Castle Rock	528J	80104	None	
FLATROCK CT	Jefferson Co	339R	80465	5300-5499	
FLAT ROCK CT S	Aurora	351J	80016	4700-4899	
	Aurora	381E	80016	7100-7199	
	Aurora	351S	80016	None	
FLAT ROCK ST N	Aurora	290R	80018	None	
FLAT ROCK ST S	Arapahoe Co	291S	80018	1-299	
FLAT ROCK ST S	Aurora	351N	80016	None	
FLAT ROCK WAY S	Aurora	351J	80016	4900-5099	
	Aurora	351S	80016	None	
	Aurora	380R	80016	None	
FLATROCK TRAIL S	Aurora	321N	80018	1-299	
FLAT TOP TRAIL	Jefferson Co	824Y	80127	11700-11999	
FLEETWOOD AVE	Boulder Co	11J	80503	9100-9299	
FLEMING RD	Jefferson Co	366V	80439	28000-29199	
FLEMMING DR	Longmont	11K	80501	1500-1799	
FLETCHER AVE	Lochbuie	140E	80603	1600-1699	
	Lochbuie	139H	80603	1700-1899	
FLETCHER DR	Erie	103A	80516	1100-1499	
FLICKER AVE	Longmont	41R	80501	400-598	E
FLICKER TRAIL	Elbert Co	871G	80107	4400-4999	
FLINT CT	Broomfield	162P	80020	1600-1699	
	Superior	160U	80027	2700-2899	
FLINT LN	Jefferson Co	369S	80465	19600-19999	
	Jefferson Co	368V	80465	20000-20599	
FLINT ST	Longmont	41P	80501	1401-1599	O
FLINT WAY	Broomfield	162X	80020	100-299	
	Broomfield	162T	80020	900-1099	
FLINT GULCH DR	Boulder Co	703F	80540	1-699	
FLINTLOCK CT	Parker	408R	80134	16300-16399	
FLINT RIDGE ST	Adams Co	771R	80102	8000-8499	
FLINTWOOD N	Douglas Co	441Q	80134	3500-6499	
	Douglas Co	441G	80138	6500-8499	
FLINTWOOD RD	Douglas Co	870B	80116	500-1899	
	Douglas Co	850X	80116	1900-3499	
	Douglas Co	850X	80134	3500-6399	
FLORA AVE	Arapahoe Co	795T	80103	1-299	
FLORA CT	Arvada	220U	80004	6900-6999	
	Arvada	220C	80005	None	
FLORA CT	Frederick	727F	80530	None	
FLORA CT	Jefferson Co	250Q	80403	4400-4599	
	Jefferson Co	250L	80403	4800-4899	
FLORA CT S	Lakewood	310P	80228	2100-2199	
	Lakewood	310Q	80228	2400-2499	
FLORA DR E	Aurora	319X	80013	None	
	Aurora	320W	80013	None	
FLORA LN	Jefferson Co	250Y	80401	3000-3099	
	Jefferson Co	366A	80439	30500-30699	
FLORA PL E	Aurora	318Y	80013	15700-15799	
	Aurora	318Z	80013	15800-16199	
	Aurora	319W	80013	17000-17499	
	Aurora	319Z	80013	19600-19999	
	Aurora	319X	80013	None	
	Aurora	320W	80013	None	
	Denver	315X	80210	2300-3599	
	Denver	316W	80222	5600-5799	
FLORA PL W	Denver	312Y	80227	6200-6299	
FLORA ST	Arvada	220U	80004	7100-7199	
	Arvada	220G	80005	8600-8699	
	Jefferson Co	250Q	80403	4400-4499	
	Jefferson Co	250L	80403	4800-5199	
	Jefferson Co	280Q	80401	None	
FLORA ST S	Lakewood	310Q	80228	2300-2399	
FLORA WAY	Jefferson Co	280U	80401	1-599	
	Jefferson Co	250C	80004	5800-5999	
FLORA WAY S	Jefferson Co	280U	80401	1-299	
FLORADO ST	Adams Co	223M	80221	7700-8099	
FLORAL DR	Boulder	98S	80304	1900-2299	
FLORENCE AVE	Firestone	727B	80504	None	
FLORENCE CT	Adams Co	167E	80602	13900-14099	
FLORENCE CT	Firestone	727B	80504	None	
FLORENCE CT	Longmont	40P	80503	1501-1599	O
FLORENCE CT E	Highlands Ranch	404G	80126	300-399	
FLORENCE CT S	Arapahoe Co	347S	80111	5900-6099	
	Aurora	317E	80247	1500-1599	
	Denver	317W	80231	3000-3399	
	Greenwood Village	347N	80111	5300-5499	
FLORENCE DR S	Greenwood Village	347N	80111	5000-5099	
FLORENCE PL S	Highlands Ranch	404G	80126	9800-9899	
FLORENCE RD	Jefferson Co	822Y	80433	31200-31299	
FLORENCE ST	Adams Co	137S	80602	15200-15399	
	Aurora	287N	80010	300-599	
	Aurora	287E	80010	800-2499	
	Commerce City	197E	80640	11200-11298	E
	Denver	257J	80238	4400-5099	
	Denver	257W	80238	None	
FLORENCE ST S	Aurora	317E	80247	1301-1399	O
	Denver	317A	80247	600-1099	
	Denver	317W	80231	3400-3499	
	Greenwood Village	347S	80111	5600-5899	
FLORENCE WAY	Adams Co	137N	80602	None	
	Denver	257W	80238	3300-3499	
FLORENCE WAY	Highlands Ranch	404G	80126	None	
FLORENCE WAY S	Arapahoe Co	347W	80111	6300-6499	
	Aurora	317E	80247	1501-1599	O
	Aurora	317J	80247	None	
FLORENTINE CIR	Longmont	40Q	80503	3700-3899	
FLORENTINE CT	Longmont	40Q	80503	None	
FLORENTINE DR	Longmont	40Q	80503	3700-4299	
FLORIDA AVE E	Arapahoe Co	316G	80231	8101-8399	O
	Arapahoe Co	316H	80247	8700-9199	
	Arapahoe Co	317E	80247	9200-9699	
	Aurora	317E	80247	9700-10499	
	Aurora	317G	80112	11400-13199	
	Aurora	318E	80012	13300-13399	
	Aurora	318F	80012	13700-15399	
	Aurora	320H	80018	13800-24199	
	Aurora	319F	80017	17600-17899	
	Aurora	321E	80018	24500-24799	
	Denver	314G	80210	1-1099	
	Denver	314H	80210	1400-1599	
	Denver	315F	80210	2000-3999	
	Denver	315G	80222	4000-5599	
	Denver	316E	80224	5600-6499	
	Denver	316G	80231	7300-8098	E
FLORIDA AVE E	Watkins	811C	80137	36100-36899	
FLORIDA AVE W	Denver	314E	80223	1-1999	
	Denver	313H	80223	2000-2499	
	Denver	313G	80219	2500-5199	
	Lakewood	312G	80232	5200-8999	
	Lakewood	311G	80232	9200-10899	
	Lakewood	311G	80232	10900-11999	
	Lakewood	311F	80228	12000-12099	
FLORIDA DR E	Arapahoe Co	812A	80102	39600-40199	
	Aurora	317H	80112	12100-13099	
	Aurora	319F	80017	17900-18099	
FLORIDA DR W	Lakewood	312F	80232	7700-7899	
	Lakewood	311E	80228	12400-12499	
	Lakewood	310H	80228	12500-13199	
	Lakewood	310H	80228	13400-13499	
FLORIDA PL E	Aurora	317E	80247	9700-9899	
	Aurora	317H	80112	13100-13199	
	Aurora	318F	80012	14100-14199	
	Aurora	318G	80017	15500-15599	
	Aurora	319E	80017	17000-17299	
	Aurora	319F	80017	17900-17999	
	Aurora	319G	80017	19300-19499	
FLORIDA PL E	Aurora	320H	80018	23700-23799	
FLORIDA PL W	Jefferson Co	311F	80232	11400-11499	
	Lakewood	311H	80232	9500-9999	
	Lakewood	310H	80228	13000-13099	
FLOWER CIR	Arvada	251H	80002	5300-5399	
	Arvada	221M	80005	8100-8199	
FLOWER CIR S	Lakewood	311H	80232	1100-1299	
FLOWER CT	Arvada	251H	80002	5400-5499	
	Arvada	221M	80005	8000-8099	
	Arvada	221H	80005	8100-8399	
	Jefferson Co	251M	80002	4800-4899	
	Westminster	221H	80021	8500-8599	
	Westminster	221D	80021	8700-8799	
	Westminster	191Z	80021	9000-9399	
	Westminster	191R	80021	10100-10199	
FLOWER CT S	Jefferson Co	371H	80128	7000-7099	
	Jefferson Co	371R	80128	7800-7999	
	Jefferson Co	371V	80128	8500-8599	
	Lakewood	311H	80232	1500-1599	
	Lakewood	311R	80227	2100-2299	
	Lakewood	311V	80227	2500-2699	
	Lakewood	311Z	80227	2900-3199	
	Littleton	825P	80127	9700-9899	
FLOWER LN	Jefferson Co	762A	80403	11600-11699	
FLOWER PL	Westminster	221D	80021	8700-8799	
FLOWER ST	Arvada	251H	80002	5500-5599	
	Arvada	251D	80004	5900-6199	
	Arvada	221V	80004	6700-6899	
	Arvada	221R	80005	7300-7599	
	Arvada	221M	80005	7900-7999	
	Lakewood	281V	80226	1-199	
	Lakewood	281M	80215	800-999	
	Westminster	191Z	80021	9100-9599	
	Wheat Ridge	251Z	80033	3200-3499	
	Wheat Ridge	251R	80033	4500-4599	
FLOWER ST S	Denver	341M	80123	4500-4599	
	Jefferson Co	341R	80123	5100-5299	
	Jefferson Co	341Z	80123	6000-6199	
	Jefferson Co	371D	80123	6500-6599	
	Jefferson Co	371H	80128	7000-7099	
	Jefferson Co	371M	80128	7100-7399	
	Jefferson Co	371R	80128	7700-8099	
	Jefferson Co	371V	80128	8500-8599	
	Lakewood	281V	80226	1-99	
	Lakewood	281Z	80226	500-699	
	Lakewood	311D	80226	700-1099	
	Lakewood	311M	80232	1600-1899	
	Lakewood	311R	80227	2100-2299	
	Lakewood	311V	80227	2500-2699	
	Lakewood	311Z	80227	3300-3499	
FLOWER WAY S	Denver	341R	80123	4800-4999	
	Jefferson Co	341Z	80123	6200-6299	
	Lakewood	311R	80227	2100-2299	
	Littleton	825P	80127	9500-9799	
FLOWERBURST CT	Highlands Ranch	404Q	80126	10600-10799	
FLOWERBURST DR	Highlands Ranch	404Q	80126	1-2099	
FLOWERBURST WAY	Highlands Ranch	404Q	80126	1-199	
FLOWERED MEADOW LN	El Paso Co	908U	80132	18100-18199	
FLOWER FIELD PL	Castle Rock	528A	80104	2300-2499	
FLOWERGATE WAY	Douglas Co	408L	80134	15300-15399	
FLOWERHILL CIR	Douglas Co	408L	80134	15500-15599	
FLOWERHILL CT	Douglas Co	408L	80134	10400-10499	
FLOWER MOUND PL E	Parker	408U	80134	None	
FLOWER MOUND WAY S	Parker	408U	80134	None	
FLOWERS CT	Erie	102C	80516	1400-1499	
FLOYD AVE E	Arapahoe Co	315W	80110	2400-2799	
	Arapahoe Co	316W	80222	6400-6499	
	Aurora	318Y	80014	14600-15299	
	Aurora	318Y	80013	15300-16199	
	Aurora	319W	80013	16800-17099	
	Aurora	319Y	80013	18500-19599	
	Denver	315Z	80222	4100-5599	
	Denver	316W	80222	5600-5799	
	Denver	316X	80224	6500-6899	
	Denver	316Z	80231	9000-9299	
	Englewood	314Y	80113	200-1699	
	Englewood	315W	80110	2000-2399	
FLOYD AVE W	Denver	313Y	80236	2801-2999	O
	Denver	313X	80236	3400-4699	
	Denver	312Y	80227	6000-6299	
	Englewood	314X	80110	1-199	O
	Lakewood	312Y	80227	6800-7199	
	Lakewood	312W	80227	8100-9099	
	Sheridan	313Y	80110	2500-3299	
FLOYD CIR E	Denver	316Z	80231	8700-8799	
FLOYD DR E	Denver	315X	80210	2800-3599	
	Denver	316W	80222	6300-6399	
FLOYD DR W	Lakewood	312Y	80227	6700-6799	
	Lakewood	312W	80227	8600-8799	
FLOYD PL E	Aurora	320W	80013	21200-21399	
	Denver	316Z	80231	9000-9199	
	Englewood	315W	80113	2000-2399	
FLOYD PL W	Lakewood	311Z	80227	9300-9399	
FLYCATCHER AVE	Brighton	137Z	80601	1300-1399	
FLYING B WAY	Douglas Co	373V	80129	None	
FLYING CIRCLE BLVD	Dacono	727J	80514	100-799	
FLYING JIB CT	Lafayette	131K	80026	500-599	
FLYING QUAIL LN E	Parker	408Z	80134	None	
FOLKLORE AVE	Longmont	12T	80501	500-799	
FOLSOM ST	Boulder	128A	80302	1200-1899	
	Boulder	98W	80302	1900-2299	
	Boulder	98W	80304	2300-3399	
FOLSOM POINT LN E	Douglas Co	870B	80116	11000-11599	
FONDER DR	Douglas Co	469C	80134	6500-6799	
FONTAINE ST	Federal Heights	223D	80260	9000-9099	
	Federal Heights	193Z	80260	9100-9199	
FONTANA CT	Denver	258K	80239	4700-5199	
FONTANA WAY	Denver	258P	80239	4500-4699	
FONTBERRY ST	Douglas Co	409X	80134	None	
FOOLS GOLD RD	Clear Creek Co	780T	80452	None	
FOOTE AVE N	Lafayette	132K	80026	100-299	
FOOTE AVE S	Lafayette	132K	80026	100-499	
FOOTHILL CIR	Jefferson Co	280C	80401	2500-14299	
FOOTHILL DR S	Lakewood	310C	80228	800-1199	
	Lakewood	310H	80228	1200-1399	
FOOTHILL LN	Jefferson Co	280C	80401	14100-14299	
FOOTHILL RD	Jefferson Co	280B	80401	14000-15199	
	Jefferson Co	249Y	80401	17400-17598	E
FOOTHILL WAY	Parker	410J	80138	10700-10799	
FOOTHILL ASH	Jefferson Co	370Q	80127	1-99	
FOOTHILLS CT	Castle Rock	466T	80109	4800-4899	
FOOTHILLS DR	Castle Rock	466T	80109	4000-4198	E
	Castle Rock	466X	80109	None	
	Castle Rock	496B	80109	None	
FOOTHILLS DR	Jefferson Co	307L	80401	24500N-25899N	
	Jefferson Co	307L	80401	1600S-2399S	
FOOTHILLS HWY N	Boulder Co	723F	80302	5000-8299	
	Boulder Co	703X	80302	8300-9699	
	Boulder Co	703Q	80503	9700-13999	
FOOTHILLS HWY S	Boulder Co	743R	80303	1600-3399	
FOOTHILLS PKWY	Boulder	128C	80303	1600-3399	
	Boulder	98U	80301	None	
FOOTHILLS RD	Golden	278H	80401	1900-2099	
	Golden	248Z	80403	None	
See.. STATE HWY 93					
	Jefferson Co	219N	80007	None	
See.. STATE HWY 93					
	Jefferson Co	248M	80403	None	
	Jefferson Co	763D	80403	None	
FOOTHILLS ST	Frederick	727A	80516	None	
FOOTHILLS CANYON BLVD S					
	Highlands Ranch	403C	80129	9600-9799	

F

STREET NAME	CITY or COUNTY	MAP GRID	ZIP CODE	BLOCK RANGE	O/E
FOOTHILLS CANYON CT W	Highlands Ranch	403H	80129	2500-2699	
FOOTHILLS CANYON PKWY	Highlands Ranch	403D	80129	None	
FOOTPRINT CT	Castle Rock	467W	80109	None	
FORBES CT	Greenwood Village	345U	80121	4000-4099	
FORBES CT	Longmont	41L	80501	400-499	
FORBES PL	Longmont	11U	80501	1200-1399	
FORD AVE E	Aurora	317D	80012	12101-12799	O
FORD CIR E	Aurora	317C	80012	12000-12099	
	Aurora	318C	80017	15400-15599	
FORD CT	Louisville	130Q	80027	1500-1599	
FORD DR E	Aurora	317C	80012	11901-11999	O
	Aurora	319A	80017	16900-17499	
FORD DR W	Lakewood	312B	80226	7900-8099	
	Lakewood	311B	80226	11200-11299	
FORD PL	Louisville	130Q	80027	1400-1499	
FORD PL E	Aurora	317A	80247	10100-10199	
	Aurora	318B	80012	14500-14599	
	Aurora	318C	80017	15300-15999	
	Aurora	319B	80017	18000-18099	
FORD PL W	Denver	313D	80223	2200-2399	
	Denver	313C	80219	3000-3499	
	Lakewood	311B	80226	11300-11599	
FORD ST	Golden	249W	80403	100-699	
	Golden	249W	80401	1000-1099	
	Golden	279A	80401	1100-2999	
FORD ST N	Golden	248V	80403	100-1399	
FORDHAM CIR	Boulder Co	100F	80301	4600-4699	
FORDHAM CT S	Boulder	128P	80305	3400-3599	
FORDHAM ST	Longmont	41A	80503	600-899	
	Longmont	11W	80503	1000-1299	
FORDHAM ST S	Longmont	40R	80503	1200-1999	
FOREST	Thornton	165R	80241	12800-12999	
FOREST AVE	Boulder	97U	80304	300-1199	
	Boulder	97V	80304	1700-1899	
	Boulder	98S	80304	2200-2599	
FOREST AVE	Jefferson Co	339G	80465	17300-17999	
FOREST AVE	Thornton	195H	80229	11000-11199	
FOREST CIR	Thornton	195M	80233	10900-10999	
FOREST CIR E	Thornton	195R	80229	5100-10199	
	Thornton	165V	80241	12800-12899	
FOREST CIR S	Cherry Hills Village	345H	80113	4200-4299	
FOREST CIR W	Thornton	195R	80229	10000-10099	
FOREST CT	Highlands Ranch	375T	80126	8700-8799	
FOREST CT	Thornton	195R	80229	10100-10199	
	Thornton	195D	80233	11700-11799	
FOREST CT E	Thornton	195V	80229	9600-9699	
FOREST CT S	Centennial	345Z	80121	6000-6299	
	Centennial	375H	80122	7000-7099	
	Centennial	375H	80122	7300-7499	
	Centennial	375M	80122	7700-7799	
	Centennial	375R	80122	8200-8299	
	Cherry Hills Village	345H	80113	4200-4299	
FOREST DR	Clear Creek Co	781U	80439	1-299	
FOREST DR	Commerce City	255D	80022	6000-6099	
FOREST DR	Frederick	727A	80516	None	
FOREST DR	Highlands Ranch	375X	80126	8600-9099	
FOREST DR	Park Co	840D	80421	1-1099	
FOREST DR	Thornton	195H	80229	11200-11399	
	Thornton	165V	80241	12400-12699	
FOREST DR E	El Paso Co	908V	80132	18000-18599	
FOREST DR S	Arapahoe Co	315R	80222	2300-2399	
FOREST DR W	El Paso Co	908V	80132	18000-18499	
FOREST LN	Elbert Co	870R	80107	31500-31599	
FOREST LN S	Centennial	375H	80122	7100-7199	
	Greenwood Village	345R	80121	5500-5599	
FOREST PKWY	Denver	285H	80220	1700-1999	
FOREST ST	Commerce City	255M	80022	4800-4998	E
	Commerce City	255H	80022	5200-5498	E
	Commerce City	225V	80022	6900-6999	
	Denver	285M	80220	1-1699	
	Denver	285D	80207	2000-2799	
	Denver	255V	80207	2800-3999	
	Denver	255R	80216	4000-4799	
	Denver	255M	80022	4801-4899	O
FOREST ST	Firestone	707X	80504	None	
	Firestone	707X	80504	None	
FOREST ST	Firestone	727B	80504	None	
FOREST ST	Thornton	165Z	80241	12000-12299	
	Thornton	165V	80241	12500-12799	
	Thornton	165R	80241	13100-13199	
	Thornton	165H	80602	13800-13999	
	Thornton	165H	80602	None	
FOREST ST S	Centennial	345Z	80121	6400-6599	
	Centennial	375D	80122	6800-6899	
	Centennial	375M	80122	7700-7899	
	Cherry Hills Village	345M	80110	4700-4799	
	Denver	285V	80246	1-499	
	Denver	285Z	80246	500-798	E
	Denver	315H	80246	1100-1299	
	Denver	315M	80222	1300-1899	
	Denver	315Z	80222	2700-3499	
	Glendale	285Z	80246	501-799	O
	Greenwood Village	345V	80121	5700-5899	
FOREST WAY	Jefferson Co	306X	80439	2900-3099	
FOREST WAY	Thornton	195H	80233	10900-11099	
	Thornton	165Z	80241	12000-12299	
	Thornton	165R	80241	12800-12899	
FOREST WAY S	Centennial	375D	80121	6400-6699	
	Centennial	375H	80122	6900-6999	
	Denver	345D	80237	3600-3799	
FOREST CANYON	Weld Co	706P	80504	3400-3499	
FOREST CANYON DR N	Douglas Co	410C	80138	12300-12899	
FORESTER PL	Weld Co	706U	80504	10400-10699	
FOREST ESTATES RD	Jefferson Co	365K	80439	33300-35099	
FOREST GREEN DR	El Paso Co	911X	80106	12100-16699	
FOREST GREEN WAY	El Paso Co	911X	80106	17000-17499	
FOREST GREEN TRAIL	Douglas Co	847T	80109	2000-2999	
FOREST GROVE RD	Jefferson Co	367A	80439	27100-27299	
FOREST HAVEN CT	Douglas Co	440G	80134	8300-8499	
FOREST HILL CT S	Littleton	374K	80120	7700-7799	
FOREST HILL RD	Gilpin Co	761S	80403	1-199	
FOREST HILL RD	Jefferson Co	337J	80439	4500-4999	
FORESTHILL ST S	Littleton	344S	80120	5300-5699	
	Littleton	374A	80120	6500-6899	
FOREST HILLS DR	Jefferson Co	308B	80401	22100-22699	
FOREST HILLS DR N	Douglas Co	411K	80138	11000-11999	
FOREST KEEP CIR	Douglas Co	440F	80134	7800-8099	
FORESTLAND DR	Jefferson Co	306W	80439	31400-31499	
FOREST OAKS DR	Elbert Co	851C	80107	None	
FOREST PARK CIR	Lafayette	131B	80026	1300-1399	
FOREST PARK DR	Castle Pines North	436P	80108	None	
FOREST PARK DR	Elbert Co	871G	80107	34000-34999	
FOREST RIDGE CIR	Castle Pines North	436P	80108	6900-7299	
FOREST RIDGE CIR	Park Co	820X	80421	1-99	
FOREST RIDGE DR	Elbert Co	892H	80117	27000-27999	
FOREST RIDGE RD	Park Co	841H	80470	1-499	
FOREST SERVICE RD	Jefferson Co	365D	80439	6500-6799	
FOREST STAR DR	Gilpin Co	761K	80403	1-199	
FOREST TRAIL	Elbert Co	851Y	80107	36000-37399	
FOREST TRAIL	Jefferson Co	337J	80439	4400-4599	
FOREST TRAILS DR	Castle Pines North	436P	80108	1100-1499	
FOREST VIEW CIR	Palmer Lake	907U	80133	700-899	
FOREST VIEW CT	Palmer Lake	907V	80133	601-699	O
FOREST VIEW RD	Douglas Co	470D	80134	5400-5499	
FOREST VIEW RD	El Paso Co	907Y	80132	700-19299	
FOREST VIEW ST	Broomfield	163S	80020	12400-12599	
FOREST VIEW WAY	Palmer Lake	907V	80133	500-699	
FORK DR N	Lafayette	131L	80026	1900-2199	
FORK DR S	Lafayette	131L	80026	1900-2099	
FORK RD W	Boulder Co	703W	80302	8300-8599	
FORREST DR	Highlands Ranch	375T	80126	8600-9099	
FORREST LN	Boulder Co	722L	80302	1-299	
FORREST LN	Highlands Ranch	375T	80126	8500-8599	
FORREST PL	Highlands Ranch	375T	80126	3200-3399	
FORREST ST	Dacono	727K	80514	100-198	E
FORREST ST	Highlands Ranch	375T	80126	8500-8599	
FORREST WAY	Highlands Ranch	375T	80126	8600-8699	
FORSSTROM DR	Lone Tree	376Z	80124	9001-9099	O
FORSYTH DR	Longmont	12S	80501	1-199	
FORSYTHE PL	Boulder	128H	80303	5000-5199	
FORSYTHE RD	Boulder Co	741M	80466	1-599	
FORSYTHE TRAIL	Boulder Co	741M	80466	1-199	
FORSYTHIA CT	Erie	133H	80516	None	
FORSYTHIA PL	Erie	133H	80516	None	
FORSYTHIA ST	Erie	133H	80516	None	
FORT COLLINS DR	Palmer Lake	907U	80133	None	
FORTUNE CT	Adams Co	750E	80603	15700-15999	
FORUM DR	Lafayette	131Q	80026	1200-1299	
FOSSIL WAY	Castle Rock	466U	80109	None	
FOSSIL TRACE DR	Golden	279F	80401	2300-2499	
FOSTER CT	Longmont	41P	80501	1500-1599	
FOSTER DR	Longmont	41T	80501	1600-1799	
FOSTER RIDGE DR	Mead	706G	80504	None	
FOUNDERS PKWY	Castle Rock	498E	80104	1000-1999	
	Castle Rock	468W	80104	2000-2299	
	Castle Rock	467Q	80104	2300-5899	
FOUNDRY PL	Boulder	98X	80301	3100-3299	
FOUNTAIN CIR S	Jefferson Co	341L	80127	4600-4799	
FOUNTAIN CT	Longmont	40V	80503	1800-1999	
FOUNTAIN ST	Boulder	97C	80304	4800-4999	
FOUNTAIN ABBEY CT	El Paso Co	908P	80132	20300-20399	
FOUNTAIN CREEK DR	Weld Co	706M	80504	None	
FOUNTAIN HILL CT	Adams Co	791K	80137	2900-2999	
FOUNTAIN HILLS ST S	Parker	410V	80138	11300-11499	
FOUR BITS ST	Park Co	841A	80421	1-199	
FOURMILE CANYON DR	Boulder Co	722T	80302	1-8999	
	Boulder Co	721U	80302	9000-11999	
FOUR RIVERS RD	Boulder Co	99D	80301	7100-7299	
FOURSOME DR	Castle Rock	497Q	80104	800-1299	
FOURTH AVE	Hudson	730L	80642	None	
FOUR WINDS WAY	El Paso Co	908P	80132	19500-19799	
FOWLER DR	Northglenn	194D	80233	11200-11699	
FOWLER LN	Boulder Co	743T	80025	None	
FOWLER LN	Longmont	10U	80503	3700-4099	
FOWLER BRANCH	Palmer Lake	907U	80133	None	
FOX CIR	Douglas Co	886G	80118	6800-7199	
FOX CIR S	Littleton	344T	80120	5600-5699	
FOX CT	Boulder	128L	80303	300-399	
FOX CT	Douglas Co	886G	80118	7100-7199	
FOX CT	Northglenn	194P	80260	10300-10399	
FOX DR	Boulder	128L	80303	200-399	
FOX DR	Thornton	224B	80260	8800-8999	
FOX LN	Superior	160E	80027	300-399	
FOX RD	Gilpin Co	760V	80403	1-299	
FOX ST	Adams Co	254F	80216	5200-5799	
	Adams Co	224T	80221	7000-7199	
	Adams Co	224F	80221	8200-8399	
	Adams Co	792M	80102	None	
	Denver	284P	80223	1-399	
	Denver	284P	80204	400-899	
	Denver	284K	80204	1200-1499	
	Denver	254T	80216	2900-4399	
	Denver	254K	80216	4700-5199	
FOX ST	Longmont	42F	80501	400-499	
FOX ST	Northglenn	194T	80260	9600-9799	
FOX ST S	Denver	284T	80223	1-99	
	Denver	314B	80223	1000-1099	
	Denver	314K	80223	1900-2299	
	Englewood	314T	80110	2900-3299	
	Englewood	314X	80110	3500-3599	
	Englewood	344F	80110	3600-5099	
	Littleton	344P	80120	5200-5499	
	Littleton	344T	80120	5600-5899	
FOX WAY	Adams Co	224T	80221	6800-6999	
FOX WAY	Douglas Co	886G	80118	6800-6899	
FOX WAY S	Littleton	344T	80120	5800-5899	
FOX RUN BLVD	Frederick	707W	80504	5300-5499	
FOX RUN CIR	Northglenn	195K	80233	None	
FOX RUN CT	Douglas Co	440X	80134	5700-5899	
FOX RUN DR	Elbert Co	851S	80107	37000-37499	
FOX RUN PKWY	Northglenn	195F	80233	10900-10998	E
	Northglenn	195E	80233	None	
	Northglenn	195B	80233	None	
FOXBERRY DR	Castle Rock	466U	80109	4200-4399	
FOXBOROUGH CT	Highlands Ranch	405H	80130	5200-5399	
FOX CANYON LN	Castle Rock	497H	80104	1300-1499	
FOX CREEK TRAIL	Douglas Co	469R	80016	6700-7999	
FOXCROFT LN	Douglas Co	845Q	80125	10300-10399	
FOXCROSS DR	Monument	908W	80132	17000-17199	
FOX DEN DR	Douglas Co	432L	80125	9500-9899	
FOX FARM RD W	Douglas Co	887U	80118	1-1999	
	Larkspur	887V	80118	None	
FOXFIELD DR	Castle Rock	497D	80104	1700-2099	
FOX FIRE CT W	Highlands Ranch	373Z	80129	2200-2299	
FOXFIRE ST	Firestone	707T	80504	10100-10599	
	Firestone	707X	80504	None	
	Firestone	707X	80504	None	
FOX FIRE WAY S	Highlands Ranch	373Z	80129	9100-9199	
FOX GLEN DR	Douglas Co	889C	80116	7500-7999	
FOXGLOVE CT	Douglas Co	408L	80134	15300-15399	
FOXGLOVE DR	Brighton	139P	80601	100-199	
FOX GLOVE DR	Jefferson Co	336F	80439	30500-30599	
FOXGLOVE TRAIL	Broomfield	133W	80026	5000-5199	
FOXHAVEN CT	Weld Co	750A	80603	18500-18999	
FOX HAVEN DR	Castle Rock	527D	80104	1800-2099	
FOXHILL CIR S	Highlands Ranch	403G	80129	9700-9999	
FOX HILL CT	Boulder Co	129G	80303	700-899	
FOXHILL CT W	Highlands Ranch	403G	80129	3400-3499	
FOX HILL DR	Longmont	42C	80501	1100-8099	
FOXHILL PL E	Centennial	376H	80112	8300-8499	
FOXHILL PL W	Highlands Ranch	403G	80129	3100-3199	
FOXHILL RD	Cherry Hills Village	345B	80113	1-99	
FOX HILLS RD	Jefferson Co	340S	80465	5300-5499	
FOX HOLLOW CT	Broomfield	162H	80020	13900-13999	
FOX HOLLOW DR	Broomfield	162H	80020	5800-5999	
FOX HOLLOW LN	Golden	279J	80401	800-899	
FOX HOLLOW PL	Castle Rock	527D	80104	1300-1499	
FOX HOLLOW RD	Clear Creek Co	335J	80439	1-299	
FOX HUNT CIR	Highlands Ranch	374U	80126	400-599	
FOX HUNT CT	Boulder Co	70H	80503	7200-7299	
FOX MEADOW AVE	Highlands Ranch	405M	80130	None	
FOX MEADOW DR	Highlands Ranch	405M	80130	None	
FOXMOOR CT	Jefferson Co	339R	80465	None	
FOX PAW TRAIL	Douglas Co	432P	80125	6900-7299	
FOXRIDGE CIR	Highlands Ranch	405K	80126	10100-10299	
FOX RIDGE CT	Boulder Co	100X	80301	8000-8099	
FOX RIDGE CT	Broomfield	162H	80020	5800-5999	
FOXRIDGE CT	Highlands Ranch	405K	80126	10000-10199	
FOX RIDGE DR	Broomfield	162H	80020	13800-14099	
FOX RIDGE RD	Jefferson Co	275W	80439	34300-34799	
FOXRIDGE TRAIL	Highlands Ranch	405K	80126	3400-3599	
FOX RUN LN	Jefferson Co	305H	80439	None	
FOX SEDGE LN	Highlands Ranch	405P	80126	2900-3299	
FOX SEDGE PL	Highlands Ranch	405P	80126	3000-3199	
FOX SEDGE WAY	Highlands Ranch	405P	80126	10800-10899	
FOX SPARROW RD	Douglas Co	470F	80134	4700-5499	
FOXTAIL CIR	Cherry Hills Village	345A	80113	1-99	
FOXTAIL CIR	Gilpin Co	760V	80403	1-699	
FOXTAIL CIR	Greenwood Village	345V	80121	4500-4599	
FOXTAIL CT	Boulder	127R	80305	300-399	
FOXTAIL CT	Jefferson Co	339R	80465	16700-16799	
FOXTAIL DR	Broomfield	162S	80020	1300-1499	
FOXTAIL DR	Gilpin Co	760V	80403	1-299	
FOXTAIL DR	Hudson	730Q	80642	None	
FOXTAIL DR N	Castle Rock	466Q	80109	4500-4999	
FOXTAIL LN	Parker	410S	80138	11500-11599	
FOXTAIL PL	Longmont	40V	80503	3500-3599	
FOX TAIL WAY	El Paso Co	908Q	80132	19500-19599	
FOXTAIL PINE CT	Parker	439D	80134	12200-12299	
FOXTON DR	Parker	409N	80134	17000-17099	
FOXTON RD S	Jefferson Co	823X	80433	11200-11999	
	Jefferson Co	843C	80433	12000-14199	
	Jefferson Co	844N	80433	14200-15399	
FOX TRAIL	Douglas Co	850X	80116	None	
FOX TRAIL	Jefferson Co	368H	80465	7100-7299	
FOX TRAIL E	Greenwood Village	345U	80121	3800-3899	
FOX TROT CIR	Elbert Co	851L	80107	39600-39799	
FOXWOOD CT	Parker	409R	80138	10700-10799	
FOXWOOD DR	Elbert Co	832L	80107	46100-47799	
FOXWOOD LN	Jefferson Co	339R	80465	16600-16799	
FOXWOOD PL	Elbert Co	832Q	80107	10200-10699	
FRAILEY DR	Boulder Co	102K	80026	3900-3999	
FRANCIS PL W	Lakewood	281D	80215	8800-8999	
FRANCIS ST	Longmont	41F	80501	100-299	
	Longmont	41C	80501	300-899	
	Longmont	11Y	80501	900-2399	
FRANCIS ST S	Longmont	41L	80501	1-599	
	Longmont	41Q	80501	1300-1399	
FRANCIS WAY	Longmont	11U	80501	1600-1699	
FRANCISCO AVE	Mead	706M	80504	None	
FRANK DR N	Aurora	289C	80011	None	
FRANK PL	Platteville	708C	80651	None	
FRANK RD	Park Co	842E	80470	1-99	
FRANKFORT WAY	Denver	258Q	80239	4500-4799	
FRANK GARDNER WAY	Douglas Co	469C	80134	6400-6599	
FRANKIE LN	Jefferson Co	336P	80439	30200-30299	
FRANKLIN AVE	Louisville	130R	80027	1100-1499	
	Louisville	130V	80027	2400-2599	
	Louisville	130M	80027	None	
FRANKLIN CIR S	Arapahoe Co	374H	80122	6800-6899	
	Greenwood Village	344R	80121	1-5399	
FRANKLIN CT	Louisville	130R	80027	1300-1499	
	Louisville	130V	80027	None	
FRANKLIN CT	Thornton	134M	80602	16500-16599	
FRANKLIN CT S	Arapahoe Co	374R	80122	7900-8299	
	Greenwood Village	344V	80121	5800-5899	
FRANKLIN DR	Adams Co	224H	80229	8400-8599	
FRANKLIN DR	Boulder	98U	80301	4700-4999	
	Boulder	128A	80302	None	
FRANKLIN LN S	Greenwood Village	345S	80121	5400-5599	
FRANKLIN ST	Adams Co	254H	80216	5400-5598	E
	Adams Co	254H	80216	5600-5799	
	Adams Co	224Z	80216	6200-6399	
	Adams Co	224Z	80229	6400-6899	
	Adams Co	224H	80229	8200-8799	
	Adams Co	164M	80241	13300-13599	
	Adams Co	164M	80602	13600-14399	
FRANKLIN ST	Adams Co	169K	80603	None	
FRANKLIN ST	Boulder Co	70K	80503	1-499	
FRANKLIN ST	Dacono	727K	80514	None	
FRANKLIN ST	Denver	284R	80218	100-799	
	Denver	284M	80218	1300-1999	
	Denver	284D	80205	2000-2599	
	Denver	254Z	80205	2800-3999	
	Denver	254M	80216	4600-5399	
	Denver	254H	80216	5401-5599	O
	Northglenn	194R	80233	10400-10599	
	Northglenn	194H	80233	11200-11399	
	Thornton	194V	80229	9600-9999	
	Thornton	164R	80241	13300-13399	

F

STREET NAME	CITY or COUNTY	MAP GRID	ZIP CODE	BLOCK RANGE	O/E
FRANKLIN ST S	Arapahoe Co	**374D**	80121	6500-6699	
	Arapahoe Co	**374H**	80122	6700-7099	
	Arapahoe Co	**374M**	80122	7700-7899	
	Centennial	**344Z**	80121	5900-6499	
	Centennial	**375E**	80122	7000-7199	
	Centennial	**375J**	80122	7200-7699	
	Cherry Hills Village	**344D**	80113	3500-3699	
	Cherry Hills Village	**344M**	80113	4300-5099	
	Denver	**284Z**	80209	100-699	
	Denver	**314D**	80209	700-1099	
	Denver	**314M**	80210	1100-2799	
	Denver	**314V**	80210	2800-3098	E
	Englewood	**314V**	80110	2901-3099	O
	Englewood	**314Z**	80113	3100-3299	
	Greenwood Village	**344R**	80121	5100-5599	
FRANKLIN WAY	Northglenn	**194R**	80233	10400-10599	
FRANKLIN WAY S	Arapahoe Co	**374H**	80122	7100-7199	
	Arapahoe Co	**374M**	80122	7800-7899	
	Centennial	**375J**	80122	7500-7699	
FRANKLYN ST	Monument	**908W**	80132	100-198	E
FRANKTOWN RD	Castle Rock	**469Y**	80104	None	
See.. STATE HWY 86					
	Castle Rock	**498F**	80104	None	
	Douglas Co	**469Y**	80104	None	
	Douglas Co	**498F**	80104	None	
FRASER CIR S	Aurora	**288U**	80012	100-199	
	Aurora	**348G**	80014	4100-4199	
	Aurora	**348L**	80015	4600-4699	
FRASER CT	Aurora	**288L**	80011	800-999	
	Aurora	**288G**	80011	1300-1499	
	Aurora	**288G**	80011	1700-1999	
FRASER CT S	Aurora	**288U**	80012	100-199	
	Aurora	**348G**	80015	4400-4499	
	Aurora	**348L**	80015	4600-4699	
	Aurora	**288Y**	80012	None	
FRASER ST	Aurora	**288Q**	80011	600-1299	
	Aurora	**288G**	80011	1700-1799	
	Aurora	**288C**	80011	2000-2199	
	Aurora	**258Y**	80011	3200-3799	
	Commerce City	**198Q**	80022	10000-10198	E
	Commerce City	**198C**	80603	11600-11899	
	Denver	**258L**	80239	5100-5299	
FRASER ST S	Aurora	**318Q**	80014	2400-2499	
	Aurora	**318Y**	80014	3000-3199	
	Aurora	**348C**	80014	3800-3899	
	Aurora	**348G**	80014	4100-4199	
	Aurora	**348L**	80015	4700-5099	
	Aurora	**348Q**	80015	5100-5299	
	Aurora	**288Y**	80012	None	
	Centennial	**348Y**	80016	5900-6099	
	Centennial	**378G**	80112	7100-7399	
FRASER WAY	Aurora	**288C**	80011	2300-2499	
	Denver	**258Q**	80239	4500-5099	
FRASER WAY S	Aurora	**318C**	80012	800-1099	
	Aurora	**318G**	80012	1500-1599	
	Aurora	**348G**	80014	4100-4199	
	Aurora	**348L**	80015	4500-4599	
	Aurora	**348Q**	80015	5100-5299	
FRASIER FIR CIR	Elbert Co	**830L**	80138	47000-47199	
FRED DR	Northglenn	**194T**	80260	9500-9799	
FRED ST	Boulder Co	**722T**	80302	1-999	
FREDA CT S	Jefferson Co	**842B**	80470	12300-12599	
FREDA RD	Jefferson Co	**842A**	80470	33100-33799	
FREDERICK CIR	Longmont	**40U**	80503	4000-4299	
FREDERICK ST	Weld Co	**728X**	80621	11500-11699	
FREDERICK WAY	Frederick	**727F**	80530	6201-6299	O
FREDERICKS CT	Boulder Co	**98P**	80301	3800-3899	
FREEDOM WAY	Castle Rock	**496G**	80109	1100-1499	
FREELARK ST	Castle Rock	**466Z**	80109	None	
FREEMAN CT	Erie	**102W**	80516	2500-2699	
FREEMONT AVE E	Centennial	**376E**	80122	5400-5599	
	Centennial	**376F**	80112	6900-6999	
	Centennial	**376G**	80112	7300-8199	
FREEMONT AVE W	Arapahoe Co	**373E**	80128	5000-5199	
FREEMONT CIR E	Centennial	**376G**	80112	8200-8399	
	Centennial	**376H**	80112	8700-8899	
FREEMONT CT E	Centennial	**376H**	80112	8300-8399	
FREEMONT CT W	Littleton	**374F**	80120	800-899	
	Littleton	**373J**	80128	4700-4799	
FREEMONT DR W	Arapahoe Co	**373E**	80128	5000-5199	
FREEMONT PL E	Centennial	**376F**	80112	6700-7299	
FREEMONT WAY E	Centennial	**376F**	80112	7000-7299	
FREEPORT DR	Highlands Ranch	**376X**	80130	6300-6599	
	Highlands Ranch	**376X**	80130	6800-7199	
FREEPORT WAY	Denver	**258P**	80239	4200-4799	
	Denver	**258Q**	80239	4900-4999	
FREESTONE ST	Lochbuie	**139H**	80603	400-498	E
FREIBURG DR W	Littleton	**825P**	80127	9700-9899	
FREIBURG PL W	Littleton	**825P**	80127	9000-9499	
FREMONT	Thornton	**194W**	80260	None	
FREMONT AVE	Boulder	**98S**	80304	2400-3199	
FREMONT AVE E	Arapahoe Co	**374G**	80122	600-699	
	Arapahoe Co	**378F**	80112	13800-14699	
	Arapahoe Co	**378H**	80016	None	
	Centennial	**375E**	80122	2300-2399	
	Centennial	**375G**	80122	4200-4299	
	Foxfield	**379E**	80016	16900-17099	
FREMONT AVE W	Jefferson Co	**372F**	80128	7400-8199	
	Jefferson Co	**372E**	80128	8700-8899	
	Jefferson Co	**371G**	80127	10000-10299	
	Jefferson Co	**371F**	80127	11100-11399	
	Littleton	**374F**	80120	1-399	
FREMONT CIR E	Arapahoe Co	**374H**	80122	1000N-1499N	
FREMONT CIR E	Arapahoe Co	**374H**	80122	1000S-1599S	
FREMONT CIR E	Centennial	**375H**	80122	4800-4899	
FREMONT CT	Douglas Co	**887G**	80118	7200-7299	
FREMONT CT	Longmont	**12Y**	80501	1200-1299	
FREMONT CT E	Centennial	**375E**	80122	2400-2599	
FREMONT DR	Douglas Co	**887G**	80118	1000-1299	
	Parker	**408R**	80134	10700-10899	
FREMONT DR E	Aurora	**381E**	80016	24200-24599	
	Centennial	**375F**	80122	2900-3299	
	Centennial	**378G**	80112	15000-15599	
FREMONT DR W	Jefferson Co	**372G**	80128	5600-6299	
	Jefferson Co	**372F**	80128	6300-6499	
	Jefferson Co	**372E**	80128	7200-8199	
	Jefferson Co	**371F**	80127	11400-11499	
	Littleton	**374K**	80120	400-799	
FREMONT PL	Centennial	**378E**	80112	None	
FREMONT PL	Douglas Co	**887G**	80118	7200-7399	
FREMONT PL E	Adams Co	**381G**	80016	26000-26199	
	Aurora	**380G**	80016	22600-22799	
	Centennial	**375E**	80122	2600-2799	
	Centennial	**375G**	80122	3500-3699	
	Centennial	**375G**	80122	4200-4499	
	Centennial	**375H**	80122	4600-4799	
	Centennial	**378E**	80112	13200-13799	
	Centennial	**379G**	80016	18700-18799	
	Centennial	**380F**	80016	21300-21399	
	Foxfield	**379F**	80016	18100-18499	
	Jefferson Co	**372H**	80128	5300-6299	
FREMONT PL W	Jefferson Co	**372G**	80128	6800-7299	
	Jefferson Co	**372E**	80128	8400-8699	
	Jefferson Co	**371H**	80128	9700-9799	
	Jefferson Co	**371G**	80127	10000-10499	
	Littleton	**374F**	80120	1-99	
FRENCH CT	Erie	**102Q**	80516	1500-1699	
FRENCH CREEK AVE	Parker	**439B**	80134	None	
FRESIA DR	Castle Rock	**468M**	80108	None	
FRESNO CT	Broomfield	**162P**	80020	1300-1399	
FRIAR TUCK CT	Lafayette	**132P**	80026	1500-1599	
FRIEND AVE W	Jefferson Co	**372P**	80128	7500-7699	
	Jefferson Co	**372N**	80128	8800-9099	
FRIEND DR W	Jefferson Co	**372P**	80128	7700-7999	
	Jefferson Co	**371R**	80128	9200-9399	
FRIEND PL E	Aurora	**381R**	80016	26900-27099	
FRIEND PL W	Jefferson Co	**372Q**	80128	6800-6999	
	Jefferson Co	**372P**	80128	7700-7899	
	Jefferson Co	**372N**	80128	9100-9199	
	Jefferson Co	**371R**	80128	9600-9899	
FRIENDS PL	Boulder	**129E**	80303	5500-5599	
FRINGE CT	Castle Rock	**497A**	80109	1800-1999	
FRINGED SAGE WAY	Parker	**379T**	80134	17800-17899	
FRINK RD	Larkspur	**888N**	80118	9000-9199	
FROG HOLLOW LN S	Jefferson Co	**366L**	80439	7000-7699	
FRONT VIEW CRESCENT	Denver	**283D**	80211	2600-2699	
FRONT ST	Castle Rock	**467T**	80104	2000-2499	
	Castle Rock	**467P**	80108	2500-2599	
FRONT ST	Louisville	**131S**	80027	100-1299	
	Louisville	**131N**	80027	1400-1499	
FRONT ST	Monument	**908W**	80132	1-299	
FRONT ST	Platteville	**708C**	80651	100-15299	
FRONT ST E	Adams Co	**791N**	80137	32500N-32599N	
	Adams Co	**791N**	80137	32800S-32898S	E
FRONT ST W	Arapahoe Co	**795X**	80103	400-799	
FRONT RANGE AVE	Boulder	**97C**	80304	900-1099	
FRONT RANGE CIR	Broomfield	**163Q**	80234	None	
FRONT RANGE RD	Littleton	**374E**	80120	500N-799N	
	Littleton	**373H**	80128	800N-999N	
	Wheat Ridge	**251J**	80033	11900-12399	
FRONTAGE RD	Arvada	**251C**	80004	None	
	Arvada	**251B**	80004	None	
FRONTAGE RD	Boulder Co	**130J**	80303	None	
FRONTAGE RD	Broomfield	**162Z**	80020	None	
FRONTAGE RD	Clear Creek Co	**781N**	80452	None	
FRONTAGE RD	Commerce City	**255G**	80022	None	
FRONTAGE RD	Denver	**253K**	80212	None	
FRONTAGE RD	Longmont	**41K**	80501	600-699	
FRONTAGE RD E	Weld Co	**726M**	80516	2-7998	E
	Weld Co	**726M**	80514	None	
FRONTAGE RD W	Frederick	**726H**	80516	None	
FRONTERRA DR	Commerce City	**198U**	80022	None	
FRONTIER AVE	Boulder	**98Y**	80301	2500-3999	
FRONTIER AVE	Broomfield	**163Q**	80020	3100-3199	
FRONTIER CIR	Jefferson Co	**368L**	80465	7600-7699	
FRONTIER DR	Bow Mar	**343J**	80123	4400-4999	
FRONTIER DR	Longmont	**11X**	80501	1100-1299	
FRONTIER LN	Boulder Co	**741L**	80466	1-299	
FRONTIER LN	Douglas Co	**850W**	80116	2100-2699	
FRONTIER LN	Palmer Lake	**908S**	80133	700-18699	
FRONTIER PL	Lochbuie	**140G**	80603	500-599	
FRONTIER PL	Longmont	**11X**	80501	1-99	
FRONTIER PL E	Denver	**346M**	80237	8700-8799	
FRONTIER RD	Elbert Co	**850H**	80138	41000-41599	
FRONTIER ST	Firestone	**707T**	80504	None	
FRONTIER ST	Longmont	**11T**	80501	1400-1599	
	Longmont	**11P**	80501	2100-2499	
FRONT VIEW DR	Douglas Co	**866E**	80135	None	
FROST AVE W	Jefferson Co	**372G**	80128	6600-6799	
	Jefferson Co	**372F**	80128	8000-8199	
	Jefferson Co	**372E**	80128	8600-8899	
	Jefferson Co	**371F**	80127	11100-11399	
FROST CIR E	Aurora	**381F**	80016	25900-26099	
FROST DR E	Aurora	**381E**	80016	24300-24599	
FROST DR W	Jefferson Co	**372G**	80128	5700-6499	
	Jefferson Co	**372F**	80128	7100-7899	
FROST PL E	Aurora	**380G**	80016	22200-22799	
FROST PL E	Aurora	**381F**	80016	25500-25599	
	Aurora	**381G**	80016	26100-26299	
FROST PL W	Jefferson Co	**372G**	80128	6800-7199	
	Jefferson Co	**372F**	80128	8000-8199	
	Jefferson Co	**371H**	80128	9700-9799	
	Jefferson Co	**371G**	80127	10200-10499	
	Jefferson Co	**371F**	80127	11400-11499	
FROST WAY	Jefferson Co	**306W**	80439	31200-31399	
FROST FIRE CIR	Douglas Co	**527J**	80104	500-599	
FRYING PAN RD	Boulder Co	**99D**	80301	6800-6999	
FULLER CT	Boulder	**128Q**	80305	3900-3999	
FULLERTON CIR	Highlands Ranch	**405R**	80130	5300-5599	
FULLERTON CT	Denver	**258Q**	80239	4500-4599	
FULLERTON LN	Highlands Ranch	**405R**	80130	None	
FULTON AVE	Brighton	**138X**	80601	600-899	
FULTON AVE	Fort Lupton	**728L**	80621	100-1199	
FULTON AVE S	Fort Lupton	**728L**	80621	100-1099	
FULTON CIR	Boulder	**98U**	80301	3000-3099	
FULTON CIR S	Aurora	**317K**	80247	2100-2199	
FULTON CT S	Aurora	**317P**	80247	None	
FULTON CT S	Denver	**317W**	80231	3000-3399	
FULTON CT S	Greenwood Village	**347N**	80111	5300-5499	
FULTON DR	Brighton	**138T**	80601	500-599	
FULTON ST	Adams Co	**137S**	80602	15200-15399	
	Aurora	**287N**	80010	100-1199	
	Aurora	**287J**	80010	1300-1399	
	Aurora	**287E**	80010	1500-2499	
	Commerce City	**197J**	80601	10600-10799	
	Denver	**257W**	80238	None	
FULTON ST S	Arapahoe Co	**347W**	80111	5900-6199	
	Arapahoe Co	**377E**	80112	7300-7399	
	Aurora	**317J**	80247	1601-1699	O
	Centennial	**377E**	80112	6900-7299	
	Denver	**287W**	80231	400-699	
	Denver	**317A**	80247	700-1099	
	Greenwood Village	**347N**	80111	4900-5099	
FULTON WAY S	Aurora	**317E**	80247	1300-1698	E
	Aurora	**317J**	80247	1800-1899	
	Greenwood Village	**347S**	80111	5600-5899	
FULTONDALE CIR S	Aurora	**381E**	80016	6900-7099	
	Aurora	**381A**	80016	6700-6899	
	Aurora	**321A**	80018	None	
	Aurora	**321J**	80018	None	
FULTONDALE WAY S	Aurora	**351J**	80016	4700-4999	
	Aurora	**321J**	80018	None	
FUNDY CIR S	Aurora	**319R**	80013	2400-2699	
	Aurora	**349D**	80013	3900-3999	
	Centennial	**349R**	80015	5400-5499	
FUNDY CT S	Arapahoe Co	**349Z**	80016	6100-6199	
	Aurora	**319M**	80013	2000-2099	
	Aurora	**319V**	80013	2900-2999	
	Aurora	**319Z**	80013	3500-3599	
	Centennial	**349R**	80015	5400-5499	
	Centennial	**379D**	80016	6600-6699	
FUNDY ST	Denver	**259V**	80249	4000-4199	
	Denver	**259L**	80249	4800-4999	
	Denver	**259H**	80249	None	
FUNDY ST E	Aurora	**319G**	80017	None	
FUNDY ST N	Aurora	**259D**	80019	None	
FUNDY ST S	Aurora	**319H**	80017	1600-1699	
	Aurora	**319V**	80013	2800-2899	
	Aurora	**349D**	80013	3600-3699	
	Aurora	**349H**	80013	19600-19799	
	Centennial	**349H**	80015	4300-4499	
	Centennial	**349R**	80015	5100-5199	
FUNDY WAY	Aurora	**289H**	80011	1600-1799	
FUNDY WAY S	Arapahoe Co	**349Z**	80016	6100-6199	
	Aurora	**319M**	80017	1800-1899	
	Aurora	**319R**	80013	2200-2399	
	Aurora	**349D**	80013	3600-3699	
	Aurora	**349G**	80013	4000-4099	
	Aurora	**349H**	80013	4200-4299	
FUR ST	Longmont	**41V**	80501	None	
FURBUR ST	Palmer Lake	**907R**	80133	None	
FURLONG CT	Parker	**410P**	80138	10900-10999	
FURMAN WAY	Boulder	**128S**	80305	600-699	
FURROW RD	Douglas Co	**908C**	80118	13000-15999	
FURROW RD	El Paso Co	**908Y**	80132	17000-20099	
FURROW WAY	El Paso Co	**908Q**	80132	200-299	
FURROW WAY	Lafayette	**131G**	80026	None	

G

STREET NAME	CITY or COUNTY	MAP GRID	ZIP CODE	BLOCK RANGE	O/E
G	Aurora	**288F**	80011	None	
G ST	Golden	**279Q**	80401	700-1799	
	Jefferson Co	**279R**	80401	None	
GADSDEN CT	Adams Co	**750L**	80603	15200-15399	
GADSDEN DR	Adams Co	**750L**	80603	15200-29499	
GAGE ST	Frederick	**726D**	80516	8100-8199	
GAIL CT	Thornton	**195W**	80229	1800-9499	
GAIL LN	Park Co	**841T**	80421	1-199	
GAILLARDIA LN	Boulder	**127L**	80302	None	
GAILLARDIA RD	Douglas Co	**887F**	80118	6500-7099	
GAINES MILL CT	Parker	**409Z**	80134	19700-19899	
GALACTIC PL	Castle Rock	**467H**	80108	1200-1399	
GALAPAGO CT	Northglenn	**194B**	80234	11600-11699	
	Northglenn	**194B**	80234	11700-11799	
GALAPAGO ST	Adams Co	**224T**	80221	6800-7199	
	Denver	**284P**	80223	1-399	
	Denver	**284P**	80204	400-1499	
	Denver	**254X**	80216	2900-2999	
	Denver	**254T**	80216	3700-4399	
GALAPAGO ST S	Denver	**284T**	80223	1-99	
	Denver	**314B**	80223	1000-1099	
	Denver	**314P**	80223	1900-2499	
	Englewood	**314T**	80110	2900-3099	
	Englewood	**314X**	80110	3200-3299	
	Englewood	**344B**	80110	3600-3999	
	Englewood	**344K**	80110	4000-5099	
GALAPAGOS PL	Longmont	**12L**	80501	None	
GALATIA CT	Boulder Co	**704N**	80503	10300-10399	
GALATIA RD	Boulder Co	**704N**	80503	5600-6399	
GALAXY CIR	Castle Rock	**467G**	80108	None	
GALAXY CIR	Thornton	**224B**	80260	500-699	
GALAXY CT	Castle Rock	**467G**	80108	None	
GALAXY DR	Castle Rock	**467G**	80108	None	
GALAXY WAY	Castle Rock	**467G**	80108	None	
GALE AVE	Boulder Co	**129F**	80303	1000-1299	
GALE BLVD	Thornton	**224B**	80260	800-1199	
	Thornton	**194W**	80260	9000-9199	
GALE DR	Boulder Co	**129F**	80303	6100-6299	
GALE DR	Jefferson Co	**842G**	80470	31200-31299	
GALEN CT	Adams Co	**224D**	80229	8600-8799	
GALENA AVE	Castle Rock	**498L**	80104	5100-5399	
GALENA CT	Adams Co	**167A**	80602	14500-14599	
	Adams Co	**137N**	80602	None	
GALENA CT S	Arapahoe Co	**347X**	80111	6000-6499	
	Arapahoe Co	**347W**	80111	6100-6199	
	Denver	**317S**	80231	3000-3399	
GALENA ST	Adams Co	**137S**	80602	15400-15599	
	Aurora	**287N**	80010	300-1199	
	Aurora	**287A**	80010	1400-2599	
	Denver	**257W**	80238	None	
GALENA ST S	Aurora	**317B**	80247	900-999	
	Aurora	**317F**	80247	1300-1699	
	Aurora	**317P**	80247	None	
	Centennial	**377B**	80112	6700-6899	
	Denver	**317A**	80247	700-899	
	Denver	**317W**	80231	3400-3499	
	Greenwood Village	**347S**	80111	5500-5899	
GALENA WAY	Boulder	**743Q**	80305	3000-3199	
GALENA WAY S	Arapahoe Co	**347X**	80111	6100-6299	
	Aurora	**317E**	80247	1500-1599	
	Aurora	**317E**	80247	None	
	Denver	**287X**	80231	300-599	
GALENA PEAK	Jefferson Co	**371L**	80127	7600-7699	
GALILEE LN	Longmont	**12Q**	80501	None	

F

G

STREET NAME	CITY or COUNTY	MAP GRID	ZIP CODE	BLOCK RANGE	O/E
GALILEO CT	Douglas Co	845B	80125	8100-8299	
GALILEO WAY	Douglas Co	432J	80125	7800-8199	
GALLAGHER CT	Erie	103A	80516	200-299	
GALLAHADION CT	Parker	410P	80138	11200-11299	
GALLAHADION LN	Parker	410P	80138	11200-11299	
GALLATIN	Weld Co	706P	80504	3400-3499	
GALLATIN PL	Boulder	128H	80303	5000-5399	
GALLEGOS ST	Erie	103N	80516	600-699	
GALLERY LN	Jefferson Co	306N	80439	31600-31699	
	Jefferson Co	306N	80439	None	
GALLEY CT	Boulder Co	99G	80301	4400-4499	
GALLOPING LN	Douglas Co	373V	80129	None	
GALLOPING WAY	Douglas Co	373V	80129	None	
GALLUP CT S	Littleton	344W	80120	6300-6399	
	Littleton	374A	80120	7600-7799	
GALLUP PL S	Littleton	344W	80120	6300-6399	
GALLUP ST S	Littleton	344S	80120	5700-6499	
	Littleton	374A	80120	6500-7699	
GALLUP WAY S	Littleton	374E	80120	7400-7499	
GALT WAY	Lafayette	131A	80026	2500-2599	
GALWAY CT	Broomfield	163G	80020	2800-2999	
GALWAY RD	Boulder Co	131E	80303	9100-9299	
GAMBEL OAK CIR	Castle Rock	467R	80108	None	
GAMBEL OAK CT	Castle Rock	467R	80108	None	
GAMBLE GULCH RD	Gilpin Co	760G	80403	2500-4799	
GAMBLE OAK CT	Parker	378R	80134	8400-8499	
GAMBLE OAKS DR	Elbert Co	850V	80107	900-1499	
GAMBLE OAKS PL	Elbert Co	850V	80107	1200-1399	
GAMBLER PL	El Paso Co	910N	80908	6000-6299	
GAMBLE RIDGE DR	Castle Rock	867R	80109	None	
GAME TRAIL	Jefferson Co	338G	80454	None	
GAMMA RIDGE	El Paso Co	909Y	80908	None	
GAMOW LN	Boulder	98U	80301	3100-3199	
GANDHI DR	Boulder	128D	80303	5300-5399	
GANDY AVE	Keenesburg	732A	80643	None	
GAP RD	Gilpin Co	761L	80403	1-599	
GAP RD	Jefferson Co	762J	80403	33500-34799	
GAPTER RD	Boulder Co	129F	80303	700-1299	
GAR WAY S	Denver	341M	80123	4500-4799	
GARCIA AVE	Brighton	139K	80601	None	
GARDEN AVE	Greenwood Village	345U	80121	3600-3999	
	Greenwood Village	345T	80121	None	
GARDEN AVE E	Centennial	349R	80015	19600-19999	
GARDEN CIR	Brighton	139N	80601	None	
GARDEN CIR	Jefferson Co	250Y	80401	14300-14499	
GARDEN CIR	Longmont	11U	80501	1300-1399	
GARDEN CT	Commerce City	226P	80022	6900-7099	
GARDEN CT	Platteville	708C	80651	400-499	
GARDEN CT S	Highlands Ranch	404D	80126	9400-9499	
GARDEN DR	Brighton	139N	80601	None	
GARDEN DR E	Arapahoe Co	349Q	80015	18800-18999	
	Aurora	350R	80016	None	
GARDEN DR E	Highlands Ranch	404C	80126	800-999	
GARDEN LN	Commerce City	226P	80022	6900-7499	
GARDEN LN	Greenwood Village	345T	80121	2400-3199	
GARDEN LN S	Englewood	344J	80110	4600-4699	
GARDEN PL	Longmont	11U	80501	1300-1399	
GARDEN PL E	Arapahoe Co	349P	80015	18500-18699	
	Centennial	349Q	80015	19100-19199	
	Centennial	349V	80015	19800-19899	
GARDEN RD	Jefferson Co	280C	80401	2700-2899	
	Jefferson Co	250X	80401	14400-14799	
GARDEN ST	Golden	249W	80403	300-699	
GARDEN CENTER	Broomfield	162S	80020	1-99	
GARDEN GLEN CT	Golden	249W	80403	400-499	
GARDENIA CIR	Arvada	220C	80005	None	
GARDENIA CT	Arvada	220G	80005	None	
GARDENIA CT	Jefferson Co	280U	80401	200-299	
	Jefferson Co	280Q	80401	600-699	
GARDENIA ST	Arvada	220Y	80004	6300-6499	
	Arvada	220U	80004	7100-7199	
GARDENIA ST	Jefferson Co	280Q	80401	700-799	
	Jefferson Co	250Y	80401	3000-3199	
	Jefferson Co	250P	80403	4400-4499	
	Jefferson Co	250L	80403	None	
	Jefferson Co	280C	80401	None	
GARDENIA ST S	Lakewood	280Y	80228	500-699	
GARDENIA WAY	Superior	160U	80027	3000-3199	
GARDENWALL WAY	Longmont	12P	80501	1900-1999	
GARDNER CT	Longmont	12S	80501	1-99	
GARDNER DR	Longmont	12S	80501	1-199	
GARDNER ST	Castle Rock	499J	80104	400-699	
GARDNER ST	Jefferson Co	823N	80433	26600-26799	
GARFIELD AVE	Elbert Co	892N	80106	6700-6799	
GARFIELD AVE	Louisville	131S	80027	600-999	
	Louisville	131N	80027	1100-2299	
GARFIELD CIR	Adams Co	225F	80229	8300-8399	
	Thornton	165T	80241	12800-12899	
GARFIELD CIR S	Denver	315U	80210	2600-2699	
GARFIELD CT	Adams Co	225F	80229	8500-8599	
GARFIELD CT	Louisville	131N	80027	1400-1499	
GARFIELD CT	Thornton	195T	80229	9900-9999	
	Thornton	165P	80241	13400-13499	
GARFIELD CT S	Centennial	375C	80121	6500-6599	
	Centennial	375G	80122	7300-7399	
GARFIELD DR	Thornton	195Q	80229	10100-10199	
	Thornton	165T	80241	13000-13299	
	Thornton	165F	80602	13900-13999	
GARFIELD DR S	Centennial	345Y	80121	6100-6299	
GARFIELD LN	Erie	102L	80516	100-299	
GARFIELD LN	Jefferson Co	842N	80470	34000-34399	
GARFIELD PKWY	Thornton	165Q	80241	13100-13499	
GARFIELD PL	Thornton	165Y	80241	12200-12299	
	Thornton	165K	80602	13800-13898	E
GARFIELD ST	Adams Co	165B	80602	14400-14799	
GARFIELD ST	Dacono	727E	80514	100-599	
	Denver	285L	80206	1-1699	
	Denver	285C	80205	2600-2699	
	Denver	255Y	80205	2700-3099	
	Denver	255U	80205	3300-3799	
	Denver	255Q	80216	4100-4599	
	Denver	255G	80216	5300-5399	
	Thornton	195Y	80229	9200-9399	
	Thornton	195P	80229	10000-10199	
	Thornton	195L	80233	10500-10799	
	Thornton	195G	80233	11200-11299	
	Thornton	195F	80233	11400-11499	

Continued on next column

STREET NAME	CITY or COUNTY	MAP GRID	ZIP CODE	BLOCK RANGE	O/E
GARFIELD ST (Cont'd)	Thornton	195B	80233	11600-11899	
	Thornton	165K	80602	13400-13799	
	Thornton	165F	80602	13900-13999	
	Thornton	165G	80602	None	
GARFIELD ST S	Centennial	375G	80122	7200-7299	
	Denver	285X	80209	1-699	
	Denver	315C	80209	700-1099	
	Denver	315G	80210	1100-1899	
	Denver	315Q	80210	2300-2599	
	Denver	315U	80210	2700-3099	
GARFIELD WAY	Adams Co	225F	80229	8400-8499	
	Centennial	375G	80122	6900-6999	
	Thornton	195C	80233	11500-11599	
	Thornton	165K	80241	13500-13599	
GARFIELD WAY S	Centennial	375C	80121	6500-6599	
	Centennial	375P	80122	7700-8199	
	Denver	315Q	80210	2600-2699	
GARLAND CIR	Arvada	251H	80002	None	
GARLAND CIR S	Jefferson Co	371V	80128	8300-8399	
GARLAND CT	Arvada	221H	80005	8400-8699	
	Arvada	221V	80004	None	
	Westminster	221D	80021	8900-9099	
	Westminster	191Z	80021	9500-9599	
	Westminster	191V	80021	9800-9999	
GARLAND CT S	Jefferson Co	341Z	80123	6100-6199	
	Jefferson Co	371D	80123	6300-6499	
	Jefferson Co	371H	80128	7200-7299	
	Jefferson Co	371M	80128	7500-7599	
	Jefferson Co	371R	80128	7800-8099	
	Jefferson Co	371Z	80128	8700-8799	
	Lakewood	311H	80232	1300-1399	
	Lakewood	311M	80232	1600-1799	
	Lakewood	311M	80227	1900-1999	
	Lakewood	311R	80227	2300-2499	
	Lakewood	311V	80227	2900-3099	
	Littleton	825P	80127	9700-9899	
GARLAND DR	Arvada	221H	80005	8100-8399	
	Northglenn	194L	80233	1-699	
	Westminster	191V	80021	9800-9999	
GARLAND LN	Boulder	97V	80304	1700-1899	
GARLAND LN	Westminster	191V	80021	9900-9999	
GARLAND PL	Westminster	191V	80021	9900-9999	
GARLAND ST	Arvada	251H	80002	5300-5699	
	Arvada	251D	80004	5900-6199	
	Arvada	221Z	80004	6500-6599	
	Arvada	221V	80004	6700-6899	
	Arvada	221R	80005	7300-7599	
GARLAND ST	Elizabeth	871F	80107	100-399	
GARLAND ST	Lakewood	281V	80226	1-399	
	Lakewood	281R	80226	400-599	
	Lakewood	281R	80215	600-899	
	Lakewood	281M	80215	1100-1199	
	Lakewood	281H	80215	1500-2099	
	Lakewood	281D	80215	2100-2599	
	Westminster	191Z	80021	9000-9299	
	Westminster	191R	80021	10000-10199	
	Wheat Ridge	251Z	80033	3200-3799	
	Wheat Ridge	251V	80033	3800-3999	
	Wheat Ridge	251R	80033	4100-4799	
GARLAND ST S	Denver	341M	80123	4700-5099	
	Jefferson Co	341Z	80123	6100-6299	
	Jefferson Co	371M	80128	7500-7799	
	Jefferson Co	371R	80128	7802-8098	E
	Lakewood	281V	80226	1-299	
	Lakewood	311M	80232	1600-1799	
	Lakewood	311R	80227	2300-2399	
	Lakewood	311V	80227	2500-2699	
GARLAND WAY	Westminster	191R	80021	10400-10499	
GARLAND WAY S	Denver	341M	80123	4500-4699	
	Jefferson Co	341V	80123	5300-6099	
	Jefferson Co	371D	80123	6500-6699	
	Jefferson Co	371V	80128	8300-8399	
	Jefferson Co	341H	80123	None	
	Lakewood	311D	80226	900-1099	
	Lakewood	311D	80232	1100-1199	
	Lakewood	311M	80227	1900-1999	
	Lakewood	311Z	80227	3100-3399	
GARNER CT	Erie	102R	80516	None	
GARNET CT	Highlands Ranch	375Y	80126	3900-3999	
GARNET LN	Boulder Co	98J	80304	4000-4599	
GARNET LN	Highlands Ranch	375Y	80126	3900-3999	
GARNET PL	Highlands Ranch	375Y	80126	3900-3999	
GARNET RD	Gilpin Co	761E	80403	100-199	
GARNET ST	Broomfield	162X	80020	100-399	
	Broomfield	162T	80020	900-999	
	Broomfield	162P	80020	1600-1699	
GARNET ST	Highlands Ranch	375Y	80126	9000-9099	
GARNET ST	Jefferson Co	249E	80403	None	
GARNET WAY	Highlands Ranch	375Y	80126	3800-3899	
GARNET WAY	Lochbuie	139H	80603	None	
GARRISON CIR	Arvada	221M	80005	7800-7899	
GARRISON CT	Arvada	221R	80005	7400-7499	
	Arvada	221M	80005	7600-8099	
	Arvada	221D	80005	8600-8799	
	Westminster	191Z	80021	9500-9599	
	Westminster	191V	80021	9800-9899	
	Westminster	191R	80021	10200-10299	
GARRISON CT S	Jefferson Co	341V	80123	5300-5599	
	Jefferson Co	371D	80123	6400-6499	
	Jefferson Co	371H	80128	7200-7299	
	Jefferson Co	371R	80128	7700-7999	
	Lakewood	312N	80227	2300-2499	
GARRISON DR	Westminster	192W	80021	9200-9299	
	Westminster	191Z	80021	9300-9399	
GARRISON LN	Westminster	191V	80021	9700-9799	
GARRISON ST	Arvada	251R	80002	4800-5098	E
	Arvada	251R	80033	4801-5099	O
	Arvada	251H	80002	5300-5699	
	Arvada	251D	80004	5800-6299	
	Arvada	221Z	80004	6400-7099	
	Arvada	221H	80005	8400-8799	
	Lakewood	281R	80215	1-1699	
	Lakewood	281D	80215	2000-2599	
	Westminster	191Z	80021	9000-9399	
	Westminster	191R	80021	10000-10299	
	Westminster	191M	80021	10400-10599	
	Wheat Ridge	251Z	80033	3200-3799	
	Wheat Ridge	251V	80033	3800-3999	
	Wheat Ridge	251R	80033	4200-4799	
	Wheat Ridge	251R	80002	5100-5299	

STREET NAME	CITY or COUNTY	MAP GRID	ZIP CODE	BLOCK RANGE	O/E
GARRISON ST S	Denver	341M	80123	4400-5099	
	Jefferson Co	341D	80235	3500-3799	
	Jefferson Co	341H	80123	4300-4399	
	Jefferson Co	341V	80123	5300-5599	
	Jefferson Co	341Z	80123	6100-6299	
	Jefferson Co	371D	80128	6400-6699	
	Jefferson Co	371H	80128	6900-7099	
	Jefferson Co	371R	80128	7500-8599	
	Jefferson Co	371V	80128	8700-8799	
	Lakewood	281Z	80226	1-599	
	Lakewood	311D	80226	600-1099	
	Lakewood	311D	80232	1100-1899	
	Lakewood	311R	80227	1900-2299	
	Lakewood	312N	80227	2300-2499	
	Lakewood	311Z	80227	3100-3399	
GARRISON WAY	Westminster	191V	80021	9800-9899	
GARRISON WAY S	Jefferson Co	371R	80128	7900-8199	
	Lakewood	311V	80227	2900-3099	
GARTNER RD	Jefferson Co	367M	80439	7500-7699	
GARTON RD	Douglas Co	888H	80104	4500-4899	
	Douglas Co	889A	80104	4900-5499	
GARTRELL RD S	Aurora	380L	80016	6900-8299	
	Aurora	380L	80016	None	
	Aurora	380V	80138	None	
GARWOOD ST	Douglas Co	432L	80125	9700-9999	
GARY	Thornton	224A	80260	None	
GATE DR E	Brighton	139N	80601	None	
GATESBURY CIR S	Highlands Ranch	405G	80126	9700-9899	
GATEWAY BLVD	Denver	258L	80239	None	
GATEWAY CT	Dacono	726M	80516	None	
GATEWAY DR	Highlands Ranch	404H	80126	9900-9999	
GATEWAY DR	Jefferson Co	277Y	80401	25800-25999	
GATEWAY LN	Louisville	130P	80027	None	
GATEWOOD CT	Park Co	841D	80470	1-599	
GATEWOOD LN	Park Co	841D	80470	1-599	
GATEWOOD ST S	Highlands Ranch	374U	80126	8500-8699	
GATLING LN	Boulder	98U	80301	3100-3199	
GAUDREAULT CT	Elbert Co	872E	80117	34600-34699	
GAUTHIER RD	Park Co	820V	80421	1-199	
GAVION ST	Lochbuie	729Y	80603	None	
GAVIOTA AVE	Brighton	139R	80601	1-199	
GAWAIN ST	Lafayette	132P	80026	1-299	
GAY CIR	Longmont	11Q	80501	1300-1399	
GAY DR S	Longmont	41Q	80501	1-1199	
GAY LN	Jefferson Co	336P	80439	29700-29799	
GAY ST	Longmont	41G	80501	1-899	
	Longmont	11U	80501	900-2499	
GAY ST S	Longmont	41L	80501	700-899	
GAYETY CT	Castle Rock	497C	80104	800-899	
GAYLORD CIR S	Centennial	375N	80122	8200-8299	
GAYLORD CT	Adams Co	165E	80602	14100-14399	
GAYLORD CT S	Centennial	375N	80122	7900-7999	
GAYLORD PL	Thornton	165J	80241	2000-2299	
GAYLORD ST	Adams Co	225E	80229	8200-8399	
	Adams Co	165E	80602	13800-14199	
	Denver	285E	80206	100-399	
	Denver	285E	80206	600-1999	
	Denver	285A	80205	2000-2699	
	Denver	255W	80205	2700-3799	
	Denver	255N	80216	4200-4899	
	Northglenn	195E	80233	10900-11199	
	Thornton	225A	80229	8900-8999	
	Thornton	195W	80229	9100-9499	
	Thornton	195S	80229	9800-9999	
	Thornton	195N	80229	10000-10399	
	Thornton	165N	80241	13300-13499	
	Thornton	135W	80602	14800-14999	
	Thornton	135J	80602	None	
	Thornton	165A	80602	None	
GAYLORD ST S	Centennial	375E	80122	7100-7299	
	Cherry Hills Village	345J	80113	4800-4999	
	Denver	285W	80209	300-699	
	Denver	315A	80209	700-1099	
	Denver	315E	80210	1100-1599	
	Denver	315J	80210	2000-2099	
	Denver	315S	80210	2300-3099	
	Englewood	315W	80113	3100-3199	
GAYLORD WAY	Northglenn	195A	80233	11700-11999	
GAYLORD WAY S	Centennial	375J	80122	7700-7899	
	Centennial	375N	80122	7900-7999	
	Greenwood Village	345S	80121	5900-5999	
GAYNOR WAY	Boulder Co	71D	80504	7900-7999	
GEDDES AVE E	Arapahoe Co	374G	80122	1-1799	
	Arapahoe Co	377E	80112	9600-10899	
	Arapahoe Co	832D	80137	44400-45199	
	Arapahoe Co	378H	80016	None	
	Arapahoe Co	832E	80137	None	
	Aurora	380F	80016	22100-22199	
	Centennial	375E	80122	2100-2799	
	Centennial	375F	80122	2900-2999	
	Centennial	375G	80122	3500-4299	
	Centennial	375H	80122	5100-5199	
	Centennial	376E	80112	5600-6499	
	Centennial	376F	80112	7200-7299	
	Centennial	376G	80112	8000-8299	
	Centennial	379G	80016	18800-19199	
GEDDES AVE W	Jefferson Co	372H	80128	5200-5499	
	Jefferson Co	372G	80128	6600-6799	
	Jefferson Co	372F	80128	8000-8199	
	Jefferson Co	371H	80128	9600-9999	
	Jefferson Co	371F	80127	11100-11199	
	Littleton	374E	80120	800-1599	
	Littleton	373J	80128	4400-4699	
GEDDES CIR E	Arapahoe Co	374H	80122	1600N-1899N	
	Arapahoe Co	374H	80122	1700S-1899S	
	Aurora	381E	80016	24800-25199	
	Aurora	381F	80016	25900-26099	
	Aurora	380H	80016	None	
	Centennial	375L	80122	4000-4099	
	Centennial	376E	80112	5700-6099	
	Centennial	375E	80122	1600S-1899S	
GEDDES CIR W	Arapahoe Co	373E	80128	5000-5199	
	Jefferson Co	371G	80127	10000-10299	
	Littleton	374K	80120	800-899	
GEDDES CT E	Centennial	375H	80122	4600-4999	
GEDDES DR E	Arapahoe Co	378H	80016	16000-16199	
	Aurora	380H	80016	None	
	Centennial	375F	80122	3300-3699	

STREET NAME	CITY or COUNTY	MAP GRID	ZIP CODE	BLOCK RANGE	O/E
GEDDES DR W	Jefferson Co	372G	80128	6300-6499	
	Arapahoe Co	378H	80016	None	
GEDDES LN E	Centennial	376F	80112	6700-6799	
GEDDES PL E	Arapahoe Co	378H	80016	None	
	Aurora	380F	80016	22100-22199	
	Aurora	381F	80016	25300-25399	
	Aurora	381G	80016	26000-26099	
	Centennial	375E	80122	2500-2899	
	Centennial	375K	80122	2900-3099	
	Centennial	375F	80122	3600-3799	
	Centennial	376E	80122	5400-5499	
	Centennial	376E	80112	5800-5899	
	Centennial	376F	80112	6900-7299	
	Centennial	376H	80112	8400-8599	
	Centennial	379H	80016	19500-19899	
	Centennial	380F	80016	21400-21899	
	Foxfield	379F	80016	18100-18499	
GEDDES PL S	Jefferson Co	372E	80128	8500-9099	
GEDDES PL W	Jefferson Co	372H	80128	5200-5799	
	Jefferson Co	372F	80128	7700-7999	
	Jefferson Co	371H	80128	9100-9499	
	Jefferson Co	371L	80127	10000-10099	
GEER CANYON DR	Boulder Co	703W	80302	1-3299	
GELANA ST	Central City	780C	80427	100-199	
GEM WAY	Lochbuie	139H	80603	100-198	E
GEMINI CT	Highlands Ranch	376U	80124	400-499	
GEMINI LOOP	Broomfield	133L	80020	2800-3099	
GEMSTONE CT	Douglas Co	409E	80134	10200-10299	
GENE AMOLE WAY	Denver	284K	80204	1400-1499	
GENESEE AVE	Jefferson Co	307C	80401	24200-25599	
GENESEE CT	Boulder	129N	80303	1-199	
GENESEE CT	Lone Tree	406G	80124	10000-10099	
GENESEE DR	Jefferson Co	307B	80401	25700-26999	
	Jefferson Co	277W	80401	27000-27699	
GENESEE LN	Jefferson Co	277W	80401	26300-27299	
GENESEE MOUNTAIN RD	Jefferson Co	307C	80401	600-1099	
GENESEE RIDGE RD	Jefferson Co	308B	80401	None	
GENESEE SPRING RD	Jefferson Co	307H	80401	24900-25199	
GENESEE TRAIL RD	Jefferson Co	307D	80401	23700-24999	
	Jefferson Co	277Y	80401	25000-25999	
GENESEE VILLAGE RD	Jefferson Co	308A	80439	23400-23999	
	Jefferson Co	307D	80401	24000-24499	
GENESEO ST E	Lafayette	132J	80026	100-899	
GENESEO ST W	Lafayette	132J	80026	100-499	
GENESSEE MOUNTAIN RD	Jefferson Co	277X	80401	400-599	
GENEVA AVE	Boulder	127G	80302	500-599	
GENEVA CIR	Longmont	11S	80503	1600-1699	
GENEVA CIR S	Arapahoe Co	347X	80111	6300-6399	
GENEVA CT	Adams Co	137N	80602	16000-16199	
	Lakewood	282F	80214	7000-7199	
GENEVA CT	Denver	257X	80238	None	
GENEVA CT S	Arapahoe Co	347X	80111	6000-6199	
GENEVA LN	Jefferson Co	365K	80439	32800-32999	
GENEVA PL	Longmont	11S	80503	2700-2799	
GENEVA RD	Jefferson Co	762S	80403	7800-8199	
GENEVA ST	Aurora	287P	80010	300-1299	
	Aurora	287K	80010	1300-2599	
	Denver	257K	80238	4501-4899	O
	Denver	257X	80238	2600-2999	
GENEVA ST S	Arapahoe Co	347N	80111	5100-5499	
	Aurora	317B	80247	800-999	
	Aurora	317P	80247	2201-2299	O
	Denver	317B	80247	1000-1099	
	Denver	317S	80231	3000-3399	
	Greenwood Village	347T	80111	5500-5899	
GENEVA WAY S	Arapahoe Co	347P	80111	5200-5499	
	Arapahoe Co	347X	80111	6100-6199	
	Aurora	317F	80247	1301-1399	O
GENEVA'S WAY	Gilpin Co	760D	80403	None	
GENOA CIR S	Aurora	349D	80013	3700-3899	
GENOA CIR S	Centennial	379H	80016	7300-7499	
GENOA CT S	Arapahoe Co	349V	80015	5700-5899	
	Aurora	319R	80013	2500-2599	
	Aurora	349D	80013	3700-3899	
	Centennial	349H	80015	4300-4399	
	Centennial	349M	80015	4700-4799	
	Centennial	349R	80015	5100-5199	
	Centennial	379M	80016	7400-7499	
GENOA ST	Aurora	289H	80011	1600-1699	
	Aurora	259C	80019	None	
	Denver	259R	80249	4000-4699	
	Denver	259L	80249	4800-4999	
	Denver	259H	80249	None	
GENOA ST N	Aurora	769X	80019	None	
GENOA ST S	Arapahoe Co	349Z	80016	5900-6199	
	Aurora	319M	80017	1700-1899	
	Aurora	319R	80013	2100-2599	
	Aurora	319V	80013	2800-2999	
	Aurora	319Z	80013	3400-3599	
	Aurora	349H	80013	4000-4299	
	Centennial	349M	80015	4800-5099	
	Centennial	349R	80015	5100-5199	
	Centennial	349R	80015	5300-5499	
GENOA WAY	Castle Rock	467P	80109	500-799	
GENOA WAY N	Aurora	259D	80019	None	
GENOA WAY S	Aurora	319H	80017	1200-1499	
	Aurora	319M	80017	1700-2199	
	Aurora	319R	80013	2200-2499	
	Aurora	349D	80013	3400-4099	
	Centennial	349R	80015	5200-5399	
GENTIAN CT	Douglas Co	887F	80118	7000-7099	
GENTIAN LN	Jefferson Co	370A	80127	16300-16499	
GENTLE RAIN DR	Castle Rock	467W	80109	None	
GENTRY CT	Adams Co	791K	80137	2700-2899	
GENTRY PL	Adams Co	791P	80137	2500-2599	
GENTRY PL	Castle Rock	527D	80104	1300-1499	
GENTRY ST	Adams Co	751T	80603	None	
GEODE CT	Castle Rock	467H	80108	7300-7499	
GEORGETOWN RD	Boulder	128T	80305	1100-1399	
GEORGIA CIR	Jefferson Co	823V	80465	10300-10399	
GEORGIAN CIR	Jefferson Co	762C	80403	11400-11599	
GERANIUM WAY	Gilpin Co	761C	80403	1-99	
GERMAIN ST	Federal Heights	223D	80260	2000-2099	
GERMAN CT	Erie	102C	80516	1300-1499	
GERONIMO AVE	Adams Co	226B	80022	None	
GERONIMO TRAIL	Jefferson Co	823X	80433	11700-12299	
GERRY LN	Douglas Co	886G	80118	5700-5799	
GETTYSBURG CT	Elbert Co	832X	80107	8300-8399	
GEYSER PEAK WAY	Douglas Co	441A	80138	8700-8899	
GIANT GULCH RD	Jefferson Co	337Q	80439	25000-25399	
	Jefferson Co	338T	80454	None	
GIBBS AVE	Boulder	98U	80301	4700-4899	
GIBRALTAR CIR S	Aurora	349D	80013	3500-3699	
	Centennial	349Z	80016	6300-6499	
GIBRALTAR CT	Aurora	379M	80016	None	
GIBRALTAR CT S	Centennial	349R	80015	5100-5499	
	Centennial	379D	80016	6700-6899	
GIBRALTAR LN S	Centennial	349M	80015	4700-4899	
GIBRALTAR PL W	Littleton	825P	80127	9300-9599	
GIBRALTAR ST	Aurora	289H	80011	1600-1699	
	Denver	259R	80249	4100-4199	
	Denver	259R	80249	4500-4699	
	Denver	259M	80249	4800-4899	
GIBRALTAR ST S	Aurora	319R	80013	2600-2699	
	Aurora	319V	80013	2700-3199	
	Aurora	349D	80013	3700-3899	
	Aurora	349H	80013	4200-4299	
	Centennial	349H	80015	4300-4499	
	Centennial	349M	80015	4500-4799	
	Centennial	349R	80015	5400-5499	
	Centennial	379D	80016	6700-7099	
GIBRALTAR WAY	Denver	259R	80249	4500-4599	
GIBRALTAR WAY N	Aurora	259D	80019	None	
GIBRALTAR WAY S	Aurora	319R	80013	2100-2499	
	Centennial	349M	80015	4900-5099	
	Centennial	349V	80015	5500-5799	
	Centennial	379H	80016	6900-7099	
GIBRALTER ST	Denver	259H	80249	None	
GIBSON AVE	Idaho Springs	780R	80452	200-299	
GIBSON CT S	Superior	160L	80027	1300-1399	
GIFFORD DR	Commerce City	226X	80022	6500-6699	
GIFFORD DR	Longmont	11P	80501	1600-1799	
GIGI DR	Jefferson Co	336T	80439	29700-29999	
GIGI LN	Clear Creek Co	801Y	80439	1-99	
GIGI RD	Jefferson Co	336T	80439	29400-29899	
GIGI ST	Castle Rock	497C	80104	800-999	
GILA CIR	Douglas Co	887F	80118	7000-7099	
GILA RD	Douglas Co	886M	80118	8400-8499	
GILBERT CT	Jefferson Co	249E	80403	None	
GILBERT ST	Boulder	127G	80302	900-1099	
GILBERT ST	Castle Rock	497G	80104	1-799	
GILBERT ST	Jefferson Co	249E	80403	5700-5799	
GILBERT ST S	Castle Rock	497M	80104	1-1099	
GILCREST ST	Parker	409N	80134	11200-11299	
GILIA DR	Jefferson Co	308A	80401	900-999	
GILL AVE E	Aurora	288X	80012	14900-14999	
GILL DR	Denver	285X	80209	3700-3799	
GILL PL E	Denver	286W	80246	5400-5599	
	Denver	317B	80247	10200-10299	
GILL PL W	Denver	284W	80223	1100-1399	
	Denver	283Z	80223	2000-2299	
	Denver	283Y	80219	3000-3599	
	Denver	283W	80219	4300-5199	
GILL WAY E	Superior	160L	80027	500-599	
GILLASPIE DR	Boulder	128P	80305	500-799	
	Boulder	128T	80305	800-1799	
GILLESPIE SPUR	Jamestown	722A	80455	None	
GILLETTE CT	Longmont	41T	80501	1600-1699	
GILLIA ST	Palmer Lake	907Q	80133	None	
GILLIAN AVE	Douglas Co	890N	80116	10000-10999	
GILMORE ST	Adams Co	791N	80137	1900-1999	
GILPIN CIR S	Arapahoe Co	374D	80122	6700E-6899E	
GILPIN CT S	Arapahoe Co	374M	80122	7600-7699	
	Centennial	344Z	80121	5900-5999	
	Greenwood Village	344V	80121	5800-5899	
GILPIN DR	Boulder	128G	80303	700-4299	
GILPIN RD	Gilpin Co	760H	80403	200-899	
GILPIN ST	Denver	284R	80218	100-799	
	Denver	284M	80218	1200-1999	
	Denver	284D	80205	2100-2599	
	Denver	254Z	80205	2900-3899	
	Northglenn	195N	80233	10400-10599	
	Northglenn	194D	80233	11400-11899	
	Thornton	194V	80229	9600-9699	
	Thornton	194V	80229	9700-9899	
	Thornton	134M	80602	16400-16599	
GILPIN ST S	Centennial	344Z	80121	6100-6199	
	Cherry Hills Village	314Z	80110	3500-3599	
	Cherry Hills Village	344D	80113	3600-3999	
	Denver	284Z	80209	200-699	
	Denver	314D	80209	700-1099	
	Denver	314H	80210	1100-1299	
	Denver	314R	80210	1600-3099	
	Englewood	314Z	80113	3100-3299	
GILPIN WAY	Adams Co	225N	80229	None	
GILSON ST	Idaho Springs	780R	80452	None	
GINGER CT	Castle Rock	466X	80109	4400-4699	
GINGER CT S	Denver	315M	80222	1600-1699	
GINNY WAY	Lafayette	101X	80026	2300-2599	
GIRARD AVE E	Aurora	318Y	80014	15000-15299	
	Aurora	318Z	80013	16400-16599	
	Aurora	319W	80013	17600-17699	
	Aurora	319X	80013	18100-18499	
	Aurora	319Y	80013	19000-19099	
	Aurora	319Z	80013	19600-19899	
	Denver	315Y	80222	4000-5199	
	Denver	316W	80222	5600-5799	
	Denver	316X	80224	6500-7299	
	Denver	316Y	80231	8000-8799	
	Denver	317W	80231	9000-10299	
	Englewood	314Y	80113	1-1399	
GIRARD AVE W	Arapahoe Co	313Y	80110	3000-3299	
	Denver	313X	80236	3600-3999	
	Denver	312Y	80227	6000-6199	
	Lakewood	311Y	80227	10600-10699	
	Sheridan	314W	80110	1600-1999	
	Sheridan	313Z	80110	None	
GIRARD DR E	Aurora	319X	80013	17800-17999	
	Aurora	319Z	80013	19600-19899	
	Aurora	320W	80013	None	
GIRARD PL E	Aurora	318Y	80013	15600-15899	
	Aurora	318Z	80013	16200-16299	
	Aurora	319W	80013	17600-17699	
	Aurora	320W	80013	None	
	Englewood	314Z	80110	1400-1699	
	Englewood	315W	80110	1700-1999	
GIRARD PL W	Jefferson Co	311X	80227	11000-11099	
	Lakewood	311Z	80227	9300-9399	
GIRTON AVE W	Lakewood	312X	80227	7100-7899	
	Sheridan	314W	80110	1700-1999	
GIRTON DR W	Lakewood	312W	80227	8800-8999	
	Lakewood	311Z	80227	9600-9999	
GIRTON PL E	Aurora	319Y	80013	19500-19599	
GIRTON PL W	Lakewood	311Z	80227	9300-9399	
GIRTON WAY E	Aurora	319Y	80013	19400-19599	
GLACIER CT	Boulder Co	129G	80303	1200-1299	
GLACIER PT	Weld Co	706P	80504	11400-11499	
GLACIER WAY	Frederick	726L	80516	None	
GLACIER PARK CIR	Parker	410N	80138	10900-11199	
	Parker	410N	80138	11000E-11199E	
GLACIER PARK COVE	Parker	410N	80138	21000-21099	
GLACIER RIM TRAIL	Broomfield	163P	80020	13300-13399	
GLACIER VIEW RD	Boulder Co	69Z	80503	7100-7299	
	Boulder Co	70W	80503	7300-7399	
GLADE GULCH CIR	Douglas Co	527L	80104	3100-3299	
GLADE GULCH RD	Douglas Co	527J	80104	700-3299	
GLADEWAY ST N	Douglas Co	441S	80134	6500-6599	
GLADIOLA CIR	Arvada	220G	80005	8600-8699	
GLADIOLA CT	Arvada	220Y	80004	6300-6399	
GLADIOLA CT	Arvada	220F	80005	None	
	Jefferson Co	280T	80401	None	
GLADIOLA ST	Arvada	220U	80004	6800-7199	
	Golden	280Q	80401	300-599	
	Jefferson Co	250P	80403	4400-4499	
	Jefferson Co	250L	80002	5200-5399	
	Jefferson Co	250L	80403	None	
	Jefferson Co	280Q	80401	None	
GLADIOLA WAY	Jefferson Co	250L	80403	None	
GLADIOLA WAY S	Lakewood	310Q	80228	2200-2799	
GLADSBURY RD	El Paso Co	909N	80132	20300-20399	
GLADSTONE CIR	Broomfield	162L	80020	300-399	
GLASGOW AVE	Jefferson Co	371G	80127	10200-10899	
GLASGOW AVE W	Jefferson Co	372G	80128	6600-6799	
	Jefferson Co	371F	80127	11100-11199	
GLASGOW CIR E	Aurora	381E	80016	24200-24599	
GLASGOW CT	Douglas Co	407H	80134	12100-12299	
GLASGOW DR E	Aurora	381E	80016	24000-25899	
	Aurora	380H	80016	None	
GLASGOW PL E	Aurora	380G	80016	22200-22299	
	Aurora	381F	80016	25200-25499	
	Aurora	381F	80016	25500-25699	
	Foxfield	379F	80016	18300-18499	
GLASGOW PL W	Jefferson Co	372L	80128	7000-7199	
	Jefferson Co	372K	80128	7500-7999	
	Jefferson Co	372E	80128	8500-9099	
GLEN AVE	Palmer Lake	907Q	80133	None	
GLEN CIR	Broomfield	163L	80020	13400-13499	
GLEN CIR	Douglas Co	441N	80134	7100-7399	
GLEN CT	Boulder	128S	80305	1300-1399	
GLEN DR	Palmer Lake	907R	80133	None	
GLEN DR S	Jefferson Co	842E	80470	13500-13699	
GLEN ST	Douglas Co	467K	80108	1100-1199	
GLEN WAY	Palmer Lake	907Q	80133	None	
GLEN ABBEY DR	Elbert Co	851C	80107	None	
GLENALLA PL	Douglas Co	466C	80108	1-99	
GLENARBOR CIR	Longmont	12P	80501	500-999	
GLENARBOR CT	Longmont	12P	80501	2000-2099	
GLENARBOR WAY	Longmont	12P	80501	1900-1999	
GLENARM PL	Denver	284F	80204	1200-1399	
	Denver	284F	80202	1400-1899	
	Denver	284C	80205	2000-3099	
GLENARM ST	Palmer Lake	907Q	80133	None	
GLEN AYR DR	Lakewood	282E	80215	1500-1799	
	Lakewood	281H	80215	1800-1999	
GLENAYRE CIR	Douglas Co	408F	80134	None	
GLENAYRE CT	Douglas Co	408F	80134	None	
GLENAYRE LN	Douglas Co	408F	80134	None	
GLEN AYRE PL	Dacono	727K	80514	700-799	
GLEN AYRE ST	Dacono	727K	80514	100-999	
GLEN BAR DR	Lakewood	282E	80215	1500-1799	
GLEN CANNON WAY	El Paso Co	908Q	80132	19300-19499	
GLEN CANYON DR	Frederick	707W	80504	None	
GLENCO CT S	Centennial	345Z	80121	6300-6499	
GLENCO ST S	Denver	345D	80237	3500-3899	
GLENCOE	Thornton	194W	80260	None	
GLENCOE CIR	Thornton	195H	80229	11300-11399	
	Thornton	195D	80233	11700-11799	
GLENCOE CIR S	Centennial	375H	80122	7100-7199	
GLENCOE CT	Commerce City	255D	80022	5800-5899	
	Thornton	195V	80229	9600-9699	
	Thornton	195R	80229	10100-10199	
	Thornton	195D	80233	11700-11799	
GLENCOE CT S	Centennial	375D	80122	6800-6899	
	Centennial	375H	80122	7000-7199	
	Centennial	375H	80122	7300-7399	
	Centennial	375M	80122	7400-7499	
	Centennial	375M	80122	7700-7799	
	Centennial	375R	80122	8100-8199	
GLENCOE DR	Thornton	195H	80229	11200-11499	
	Thornton	165Z	80233	11900-11999	
GLENCOE LN S	Centennial	375H	80122	7100-7199	
GLENCOE PL	Thornton	195M	80233	10900-10999	
GLENCOE ST	Commerce City	255D	80022	5900-5999	
	Commerce City	225Z	80022	6400-6699	
	Commerce City	225V	80022	7000-7099	
	Denver	285M	80220	100-1999	
	Denver	285D	80207	2000-2799	
	Denver	255V	80207	2800-3799	
	Denver	255R	80216	4300-4699	
	Thornton	195D	80233	11500-11899	
	Thornton	165Z	80241	12000-12399	
	Thornton	165H	80602	13800-13999	
	Thornton	165H	80602	None	
	Centennial	375D	80121	6501-6599	O
GLENCOE ST S	Centennial	375D	80122	6700-6899	
	Centennial	375M	80122	7400-7599	
	Denver	285Z	80246	1-399	
	Denver	285Z	80246	600-699	
	Denver	315D	80246	700-899	
	Denver	315H	80246	1100-1299	
	Denver	315M	80222	1300-2099	
	Denver	315Z	80222	2700-3499	
GLENCOE WAY S	Centennial	345Z	80121	5900-6199	
	Centennial	375M	80122	7300-7499	
	Centennial	375M	80122	7700-7899	

STREET NAME	CITY or COUNTY	MAP GRID	ZIP CODE	BLOCK RANGE	O/E
GLENCOE VALLEY RD	Jefferson Co	248B	80403	5600-6999	
	Jefferson Co	763U	80403	6601-6699	O
GLENCOVE PL	Boulder Co	100E	80301	4400-4499	
GLEN CREIGHTON DR	Dacono	727K	80514	100-1099	
GLENDA AVE	Arapahoe Co	795T	80103	1-299	
GLENDALE	Thornton	194W	80260	None	
GLEN DALE CIR	Dacono	727K	80514	1000-1199	
GLEN DALE DR	Lakewood	282E	80215	1700-1999	
GLENDALE LN	Parker	409Y	80134	19500-19899	
GLENDALE GULCH CIR	Boulder	69Y	80301	5400-5599	
GLENDALE GULCH RD	Boulder Co	722K	80455	1-399	
GLEN DEE DR	Lakewood	281H	80215	1500-1799	
GLENEAGLES VILLAGE PKWY					
	Highlands Ranch	376X	80130	5800-6099	
GLEN EDEN LN	Jefferson Co	306Q	80439	29500-29699	
GLEN ELLEN DR	Arvada	252E	80002	8500-8599	
GLEN EYRIE DR	Jefferson Co	336K	80439	30100-30199	
GLEN GARRY DR	Lakewood	281H	80215	1700-1999	
GLENGARRY PL	Douglas Co	436X	80108	100-199	
GLENGATE CIR	Highlands Ranch	405R	80130	10700-11099	
GLENGATE LOOP	Highlands Ranch	405R	80130	10700-10899	
GLEN GYLE DR	Lakewood	281H	80215	1800-1899	
GLENHAVEN CT	Boulder Co	130F	80303	700-799	
GLENHAVEN DR	Highlands Ranch	375S	80126	2000-2499	
GLEN HEATHER CT	Dacono	727K	80514	900-999	
GLEN HEATHER ST	Dacono	727K	80514	100-199	
GLEN HOLLOW CIR	El Paso Co	908U	80132	19200-19399	
GLENHUNT LN	Castle Pines North	436P	80108	6900-6999	
GLEN MAWR DR	Gilpin Co	760H	80403	1-599	
GLENMOOR CIR	Cherry Hills Village	345K	80113	1-99	
GLENMOOR CIR	Parker	410R	80138	11100-23999	
GLENMOOR CT	Cherry Hills Village	345K	80113	1-99	
GLENMOOR CT	Parker	410R	80138	11100-11299	
GLENMOOR DR	Cherry Hills Village	345K	80113	1-199	
GLEN MOOR DR	Lakewood	281H	80215	1600-1899	
GLENMOOR DR	Parker	410R	80138	23400-24099	
GLENMOOR LN	Cherry Hills Village	345L	80113	1-199	
GLEN MOOR PKWY	Lakewood	281H	80215	1600-1799	
GLENMOOR PL	Cherry Hills Village	345L	80113	1-99	
GLENMOOR PL	Parker	410R	80138	11100-11199	
GLENMOOR RD	Boulder Co	129F	80303	6300-6499	
GLEN MOOR ST	Dacono	727K	80514	600-999	
GLENMOOR WAY	Cherry Hills Village	345K	80110	1-99	
GLENMOOR WAY	Parker	410R	80138	23900-23999	
GLENNEYRE DR	Longmont	40U	80503	None	
GLENNON DR	Lakewood	281Y	80226	10100-10699	
	Lakewood	281X	80226	10700-11399	
GLENNON RD	Elbert Co	831S	80138	3000-3399	
GLEN OAKS AVE	Castle Pines North	436L	80108	800-999	
GLEN RAY	Palmer Lake	907R	80133	None	
GLENRIDGE DR	Arapahoe Co	373A	80123	1-99	
GLEN RIDGE DR	Castle Pines North	436L	80108	7400-7999	
GLEN SHADOWS DR	El Paso Co	909P	80908	19600-19699	
GLEN SHEILD DR	Lakewood	281H	80215	1900-1999	
GLENSIDE RD	Palmer Lake	907Q	80133	None	
GLENSTONE CIR S	Highlands Ranch	406E	80130	10000-10199	
GLENSTONE DR E	Highlands Ranch	406E	80130	5600-5799	
GLENSTONE LN E	Highlands Ranch	406E	80130	5700-5799	
GLENSTONE TRAIL S					
	Highlands Ranch	406E	80130	9800-9899	
GLENTHORNE LN	El Paso Co	908V	80132	18400-18598	E
GLEN ULA	Palmer Lake	907R	80133	None	
GLENVIEW CT	Longmont	42G	80501	300-399	
GLENVIEW DR	Arapahoe Co	373A	80123	1-99	
GLEN VIEW LN	Jefferson Co	275X	80439	100-299	
GLEN WALK	Larkspur	887R	80118	100-299	
GLENWOOD CT	Boulder	98T	80304	2700-2799	
GLENWOOD DR	Boulder	98S	80304	1900-2799	
	Boulder	98S	80301	2800-2999	
GLENWOOD DR	Lafayette	132E	80026	600-1099	
GLENWOOD LN E	Highlands Ranch	405A	80126	1700-1899	
GLIDDEN DR E	Aurora	380U	80138	23201-23399	O
GLOBEVILLE RD	Denver	254T	80216	3700-4299	
GLORIOUS PL	Castle Rock	496G	80109	3200-3399	
GO A QUAH ST	Jefferson Co	278P	80401	601-699	O
GODDARD PL	Boulder	128S	80305	2100-2199	
GODDARD RANCH CT	Jefferson Co	369E	80465	19300-19399	
GOINS DR	Jefferson Co	823V	80465	20100-20399	
	Jefferson Co	824S	80465	20400-20799	
GOLD CT	Broomfield	163P	80020	3300-3399	
GOLD CT	Jefferson Co	369S	80465	8300-8399	
GOLD RD	Gilpin Co	761E	80403	1-399	
GOLD WAY	Superior	40U	80027	700-799	
GOLDASTER CT	Parker	379S	80134	8500-8599	
GOLD BUG CIR S	Aurora	321E	80018	1500-1599	
GOLD BUG CT	Aurora	351N	80016	None	
GOLD BUG CT S	Aurora	381E	80016	7200-7299	
	Aurora	321N	80018	None	
	Aurora	381J	80016	None	
GOLD BUG WAY S	Aurora	351J	80016	4800-5199	
	Aurora	321J	80018	None	
GOLD CAMP WAY	Douglas Co	870P	80116	1500-2299	
GOLD CANYON RD	Monument	908X	80132	None	
GOLDCO CIR	Golden	248Z	80403	300-399	
GOLD CREEK DR	Elbert Co	871J	80107	2500-2999	
GOLD CREST AVE	Highlands Ranch	375Y	80126	None	
GOLD DIGGER TRAIL	Clear Creek Co	780S	80452	None	
GOLD DUST CT W	Highlands Ranch	403D	80129	2000-2099	
GOLD DUST LN W	Highlands Ranch	403D	80129	2100-2399	
GOLD DUST PEAK	Jefferson Co	371K	80127	7700-7799	
GOLD DUST TRAIL W					
	Highlands Ranch	403D	80129	2100-2499	
GOLDEN CIR	Golden	279P	80401	400-1499	
GOLDEN CT	Denver	252M	80212	4800-4899	
GOLDEN CT S	Denver	312R	80227	2100-2199	
	Denver	342D	80235	3700-3899	
GOLDEN LN	Longmont	42C	80501	400-499	
GOLDEN RD S	Golden	279L	80401	16400-17899	
	Jefferson Co	280J	80401	15000-16399	
GOLDEN WAY S	Denver	312V	80227	2700-3099	
GOLDEN ARROW CIR	El Paso Co	908U	80132	19100-19199	
GOLDEN ASTER	Jefferson Co	370F	80127	1-99	
GOLDEN BEAR DR	Longmont	12U	80501	1600-1699	
GOLDEN CURRANT WAY	Douglas Co	470B	80134	5400-5499	
GOLDEN DOLLAR DR	Gilpin Co	780F	80403	None	
GOLDEN EAGLE AVE S					
	Highlands Ranch	403C	80129	9600-9799	
GOLDEN EAGLE CIR	Golden	279P	80401	600-699	
GOLDEN EAGLE CIR	Lafayette	132W	80026	2800-2999	
GOLDEN EAGLE CT	Broomfield	162L	80020	1800-1999	
GOLDEN EAGLE CT	Greenwood Village	345R	80121	1-99	
GOLDEN EAGLE CT W					
	Highlands Ranch	403D	80129	2700-2799	
GOLDEN EAGLE DR	Broomfield	162L	80020	300-599	
GOLDEN EAGLE DR	Dacono	727N	80514	None	
GOLDEN EAGLE DR S					
	Highlands Ranch	403D	80129	9600-9699	
GOLDEN EAGLE LN	Jefferson Co	370A	80127	1-99	
GOLDEN EAGLE PKWY	Brighton	139V	80601	4900-5399	
	Brighton	140N	80601	None	
GOLDEN EAGLE PKWY N	Brighton	140J	80601	None	
GOLDEN EAGLE PL S					
	Highlands Ranch	403C	80129	9500-9699	
GOLDEN EAGLE RD					
	Greenwood Village	345R	80121	1-99	
GOLDEN EAGLE WAY	Louisville	131K	80027	None	
GOLDEN EAGLE RUN	Broomfield	163A	80020	14601-14699	O
GOLDEN EYE AVE	Douglas Co	378R	80134	None	
GOLDEN EYE CT	Douglas Co	378Q	80134	15800-15999	
GOLDENEYE CT	Jefferson Co	336F	80439	30500-30599	
GOLDEN EYE DR	Douglas Co	378V	80134	8400-8599	
GOLDENEYE PL	Superior	160U	80027	3100-3299	
GOLDEN FIELD CIR	Elbert Co	851E	80138	41400-41499	
GOLDEN GATE DR	Gilpin Co	761Z	80403	1-1799	
GOLDEN GATE CANYON RD	Gilpin Co	761S	80403	None	
	Jefferson Co	248U	80403	20000-23999	
	Jefferson Co	783E	80403	24000-27999	
	Jefferson Co	782B	80403	28000-34799	
GOLDEN HILLS PL	Golden	279H	80401	17100-17199	
GOLDEN HILLS RD	Golden	279H	80401	1400-17099	
GOLDEN LEAF WAY	Gilpin Co	761U	80403	1-799	
GOLDEN MEADOW DR	Jefferson Co	306W	80439	31500-31599	
GOLDEN OAK PL	Douglas Co	470D	80134	9400-9499	
GOLDEN PARK DR	Golden	248Z	80403	900-1099	
GOLDEN PARK PL	Golden	248Z	80403	900-1099	
GOLDEN PINE LN	El Paso Co	908P	80132	1000-1099	
GOLDEN POINT DR	Jefferson Co	278P	80401	800-899	
GOLDEN POPPY LN	Parker	409S	80134	None	
GOLDEN RIDGE CT	Douglas Co	470D	80134	5100-5399	
GOLDEN RIDGE RD	Golden	279P	80401	500-799	E
GOLDENROD CIR	Broomfield	162N	80020	1100-1199	
GOLDENROD CIR	Elbert Co	872E	80117	34000-34499	
GOLDEN ROD CT	Longmont	42F	80501	200-299	
GOLDENROD DR	Boulder	127M	80302	None	
GOLDEN ROD LN	Jefferson Co	339Z	80465	16600-16699	
GOLDENROD LN	Parker	410S	80138	20400-20499	
GOLDEN ROD WAY	Parker	378V	80134	16200-16499	
GOLDEN SPUR LOOP	Castle Rock	498B	80108	3400-3699	
GOLDEN VALLEY TRAIL	Castle Rock	466S	80109	4800-5299	
GOLDENVUE DR	Golden	278H	80401	1900-2099	
GOLDEN WILLOW CIR	Elbert Co	851G	80107	None	
GOLDEN WILLOW RD	Clear Creek Co	335E	80439	200-1399	
GOLDFIELDS PL	Frederick	726G	80516	None	
GOLD FINCH CT	Longmont	11N	80503	2000-2099	
GOLDFINCH DR	Elbert Co	871F	80107	33800-33999	
GOLDFINCH LN S	Highlands Ranch	403G	80129	9700-9899	
GOLDFINCH ST	Brighton	139R	80601	5200-5598	E
GOLDFINCH ST	Brighton	140N	80601	5500-5598	E
GOLD FLAKE TERRACE	Park Co	820Y	80421	1-999	
GOLD HILL DR	Lafayette	131L	80026	100-199	
GOLD HILL RD	Boulder Co	721P	80302	9900-13999	
	Boulder Co	720V	80302	14000-16999	
GOLD RUN ST	Boulder Co	721R	80302	None	
GOLD HILL ST	Castle Rock	497E	80109	1500-1599	
GOLDIE CT	Boulder Co	723B	80302	None	
GOLD LAKE RD	Boulder Co	721K	80481	1-3499	
	Boulder Co	720M	80481	None	
GOLD MAPLE ST	Brighton	140J	80601	None	
GOLD MINE LN	Jefferson Co	306E	80439	1300-1399	
GOLD MINE GULCH	Thornton	195Q	80229	None	
GOLDMOSS PL	Longmont	42N	80501	None	
GOLD NUGGET DR	Boulder Co	70M	80503	7100-7299	
GOLDPAN PL	Douglas Co	469B	80134	5600-5699	
GOLD RUN RD	Boulder Co	722N	80302	1-4999	
GOLD RUSH CT	Highlands Ranch	403C	80129	None	
GOLDSMITH DR	Greenwood Village	346V	80111	5800-5899	
GOLDSMITH DR E	Highlands Ranch	404D	80126	1200-1599	
GOLDSMITH PL	Greenwood Village	347S	80111	5700-5899	
GOLD SPUR	Jefferson Co	844A	80433	12400-12499	
GOLD TRAIL	Boulder Co	721V	80302	1-299	
GOLD YARROW LN	Jefferson Co	307X	80439	3100-3199	
GOLF WAY	Jefferson Co	336Q	80439	28900-29399	
GOLF CLUB DR	Boulder Co	723H	80503	6600-6999	
GOLF CULB DR	Douglas Co	466F	80108	700-799	
GOLF COURSE DR	Jefferson Co	340S	80465	5200-5699	
GOLFER'S WAY	Denver	286R	80230	400-498	E
GOLFVIEW LN	Parker	410T	80138	22100-22499	
GOOD AVE	Weld Co	729A	80621	15000-16599	
GOODHEART AVE	Jefferson Co	823U	80433	10800-11099	
GOOD HOPE DR	Douglas Co	436X	80108	800-899	
GOODHUE BLVD	Boulder Co	130J	80303	7300-7599	
GOODRICH CT	Platteville	708B	80651	700-799	
GOORMAN AVE E	Centennial	344Z	80121	800-899	
GOOSANDER WAY	Highlands Ranch	375Y	80126	8700-9099	
GOOSEBERRY CIR	Douglas Co	440W	80134	7400-7499	
GOOSEBERRY CT N	Lafayette	131M	80026	600-699	
GOOSEBERRY CT S	Lafayette	131M	80026	700-799	
GOOSEBERRY DR	Longmont	40L	80503	600-699	
GOOSEBERRY LN	Cherry Hills Village	345B	80113	1-99	
GOOSEHAVEN DR E	Boulder Co	101M	80026	10300-10699	
GOOSE POINT CT	Boulder Co	704X	80503	6900-7099	
GOPHER CT	Douglas Co	470C	80134	8300-8499	
GORCE CT	Erie	102P	80516	2400-2499	
GORDON CT	Castle Rock	498J	80104	1-299	
GORDON CT	Erie	102Q	80516	1900-1999	
GORDON CT	Jefferson Co	842F	80470	13400-13899	
GORDON CT	Longmont	11L	80501	2400-2499	
GORDON DR	Boulder	128U	80305	4600-4699	
GORDON DR	Castle Rock	498E	80104	1-499	
GORDON DR	Erie	102Q	80516	1700-1999	
GORDON LN	Castle Rock	498J	80104	1-199	
GORDON PL	Castle Rock	498J	80104	1-199	
GORDON WAY	El Paso Co	908V	80132	18000-18999	
GORDON CREEK RD	Boulder Co	741A	80466	None	
GORE CIR	Douglas Co	887G	80118	1300-1499	
GORE DR	Douglas Co	887G	80118	1600-1899	
GORE RANGE CT	Jefferson Co	249E	80403	None	
GORE RANGE RD	Jefferson Co	371F	80127	7200-7499	
GORE RANGE WAY	Jefferson Co	249E	80403	None	
GORHAM CT	Frederick	727F	80530	7900-7999	
GORHAM CT	Louisville	130M	80027	300-399	
GOSHAWK	Jefferson Co	370B	80127	1-99	
GOSHAWK CT	Brighton	139V	80601	5000-5099	
GOSHAWK DR	Longmont	12Y	80501	1500-1699	
GOSHAWK RD	El Paso Co	910Z	80908	16500E-17499E	
GOSHAWK ST	Brighton	139V	80601	5100-5399	
GOSS CIR	Boulder	128A	80302	2200E-2299E	
	Boulder	128A	80302	2100W-2199W	
GOSS DR	Longmont	42F	80504	600-799	
GOSS ST	Boulder	128A	80302	1800-1899	
GOSSAMER WAY	Castle Rock	496C	80109	3300-3399	
GOUCH AVE N	Lafayette	132J	80026	100-599	
GOUCH AVE S	Lafayette	132J	80026	100-499	
GOULD AVE W	Jefferson Co	341V	80123	9600-9999	
GOULD CIR	Castle Rock	496B	80109	4700-5399	
GOULD DR W	Jefferson Co	341S	80127	12500-12799	
	Lakewood	342U	80123	6100-6799	
GOULD LOOP W	Jefferson Co	341S	80127	None	
GOULD PL W	Jefferson Co	341S	80127	None	
GOULD WAY W	Jefferson Co	341V	80123	8800-8999	
GRACE AVE	Weld Co	728X	80621	1800-1999	
GRACE AVE S	Jefferson Co	842A	80470	12500-12699	
GRACE BLVD E	Highlands Ranch	405G	80126	3900-3999	
GRACE CT	Adams Co	224L	80221	7800-8099	
GRACE PL	Adams Co	224L	80221	7600-7699	
GRACE WAY	Weld Co	706C	80542	2600-2799	
GRADEN ST	Frederick	727G	80530	6100-6199	
GRADY CIR	Castle Rock	469K	80108	7200-8199	
GRAHAM CIR	Erie	102U	80516	None	
GRAHAM CT	Boulder	128Q	80305	3900-3999	
GRAHAM DR	Jefferson Co	368Y	80465	8800-8899	
GRAHAM LN	Littleton	373H	80120	1700-1799	
GRAHAM WAY	Erie	102V	80516	None	
GRAIN CT	Brighton	139L	80601	None	
GRALAND LN	Highlands Ranch	404M	80126	800-999	
GRALAND PL	Highlands Ranch	404M	80126	800-1099	
GRAMA RIDGE	El Paso Co	909Y	80908	17600-17999	
GRAMA RIDGE CROSSING	El Paso Co	909Y	80908	None	
GRAMBLING DR W	Denver	313X	80236	3600-3999	
GRANADA CT	Longmont	12W	80501	100-199	
GRANADA DR E	Douglas Co	909K	80118	6400-6499	
GRANADA RD	Adams Co	224K	80221	7300-7999	
GRANADA ST	Lochbuie	140B	80603	None	
	Lochbuie	729Y	80603	None	
GRANADA WAY	Park Co	841D	80470	1-299	
GRANBY CIR S	Aurora	318C	80012	700-899	
	Aurora	348G	80014	4100-4199	
GRANBY CT S	Aurora	348G	80014	4100-4299	
	Aurora	348G	80015	4400-4499	
	Aurora	348Q	80015	5200-5299	
GRANBY DR	Commerce City	198Q	80022	10000-10199	
GRANBY ST	Adams Co	168L	80601	13400-13699	
	Aurora	288L	80011	800-1399	
	Commerce City	198Q	80022	10000-10199	
	Commerce City	198C	80603	11600-11799	
	Commerce City	198C	80603	11800-11899	
	Denver	258Q	80239	4900-4999	
	Denver	258L	80239	5100-5599	
GRANBY ST S	Aurora	318L	80012	1500-1899	
	Aurora	318U	80014	2900-3099	
	Aurora	318Y	80014	3200-3399	
	Aurora	348G	80014	4200-4299	
	Aurora	348L	80015	4800-5099	
GRANBY WAY	Aurora	288U	80011	100-399	
	Denver	258Q	80239	4500-4899	
GRANBY WAY S	Aurora	318C	80012	900-999	
	Aurora	318Q	80014	2400-2599	
	Aurora	318Y	80014	3100-3299	
	Aurora	348C	80014	3600-3799	
	Aurora	348G	80014	4200-4299	
	Aurora	348G	80015	4300-4399	
	Aurora	348L	80015	4600-4699	
GRAND AVE	Fort Lupton	728L	80621	100-999	
GRAND AVE	Longmont	41M	80501	600-699	
	Longmont	41L	80501	800-1399	
GRAND AVE	Palmer Lake	907Q	80133	None	
GRAND AVE	Platteville	708B	80651	300-899	
GRAND AVE E	Aurora	348J	80015	13800-14199	
	Aurora	348K	80015	14600-14799	
	Aurora	348L	80015	14900-15799	
	Aurora	349J	80015	17400-18499	
	Cherry Hills Village	345N	80110	2100-2299	
	Denver	346M	80237	8500-8799	
	Englewood	344L	80113	500-799	
	Greenwood Village	347N	80111	9200-10099	
GRAND AVE S	Fort Lupton	728L	80621	1-999	
GRAND AVE W	Denver	341R	80123	8900-9699	
	Denver	343K	80123	None	
	Englewood	344P	80110	100-799	
	Englewood	343L	80110	3000-3599	
	Jefferson Co	341L	80127	10000-10399	
	Lakewood	342P	80123	7800-8199	
	Littleton	343L	80110	3600-3799	
GRAND CIR E	Aurora	349Q	80015	18500-19099	
GRAND CT	Golden	279G	80401	400-499	
GRAND CT E	Greenwood Village	347N	80111	9500-9699	
GRAND DR E	Arapahoe Co	350J	80015	None	
	Arapahoe Co	350K	80015	None	
	Aurora	348K	80015	14200-14399	
	Aurora	349J	80015	17400-17599	
GRAND DR W	Jefferson Co	341N	80465	12400-12799	
	Jefferson Co	340R	80465	13300-13599	
GRAND LN E	Arapahoe Co	349M	80015	20000-20099	
	Arapahoe Co	350J	80015	20400-20899	
GRAND PL E	Arapahoe Co	349M	80015	20000-20099	
	Arapahoe Co	350J	80015	20400-20899	
	Aurora	348K	80015	14800-14899	
	Aurora	348L	80015	15000-15199	
	Aurora	350M	80015	None	
	Greenwood Village	347N	80111	9500-9599	
GRAND PL W	Jefferson Co	341Q	80127	10200-11099	
	Jefferson Co	341N	80465	12300-12399	
	Jefferson Co	340R	80465	12800-13199	
	Jefferson Co	340R	80465	None	

STREET NAME	CITY or COUNTY	MAP GRID	ZIP CODE	BLOCK RANGE	O/E
GRAND BAKER CIR S	Aurora	321E	80018	1400-1499	
GRAND BAKER CT S	Aurora	321N	80018	None	
	Aurora	351S	80016	None	
	Aurora	381J	80016	None	
GRAND BAKER ST S	Aurora	321A	80018	None	
GRAND BAKER WAY S	Aurora	321J	80018	None	
GRANDBAY CIR S	Arapahoe Co	291S	80018	1-199	
GRANDBAY ST S	Arapahoe Co	291S	80018	1-299	
GRANDBY CT	Aurora	288G	80011	1700-1999	
GRANDBY CT S	Aurora	288U	80012	100-199	
GRANDBY ST	Aurora	288C	80011	2000-2299	
GRANDBY WAY	Aurora	288C	80011	2300-2499	
GRAND CYPRESS COVE	Lone Tree	406D	80124	9500-9599	
GRAND CYPRESS LN	Lone Tree	406D	80124	8600-8799	
GRANDE RIVER CT	Douglas Co	441J	80138	7500-7799	
GRANDE VISTA CT	Douglas Co	406Q	80124	10300-10399	
GRAND FIR CT	Douglas Co	470D	80134	5300-5399	
GRAND FIR WAY	Douglas Co	470D	80134	None	
GRAND LAKE DR	Weld Co	706M	80504	None	
GRAND MESA AVE	Frederick	707W	80504	None	
GRAND MESA LN	Douglas Co	411C	80138	12300-12399	
GRAND SUMMIT TRAIL	Jefferson Co	367T	80439	26200-26499	
GRAND VALLEY CT	Castle Rock	466P	80109	4600-4799	
GRANDVIEW AVE	Arvada	252E	80002	6300-8799	
GRANDVIEW AVE	Boulder	127D	80302	900-1499	
	Boulder	128A	80302	1900-2099	
	Jefferson Co	278U	80401	21401-21999	O
	Jefferson Co	307D	80401	24801-24999	O
GRANDVIEW AVE W	Arvada	251H	80002	8800-9899	
GRANDVIEW CIR	Mead	707B	80542	100-299	
GRANDVIEW CT	Mead	707B	80542	100-299	
GRANDVIEW DR	Boulder Co	11M	80504	12600-12799	
GRAND VIEW DR	Douglas Co	866E	80135	None	
GRANDVIEW DR	Gilpin Co	741Z	80403	1-99	
GRANDVIEW DR	Mead	707B	80542	100-199	
GRANDVIEW MEADOWS DR					
	Longmont	40P	80503	600-899	
GRANDWATER WAY	Castle Rock	469J	80108	6401-6599	O
GRANGE CREEK DR	Thornton	195M	80233	10800-11099	
GRANGE HALL CIR	Thornton	195U	80229	None	
GRANGER CIR	Castle Rock	497E	80109	1600-2099	
GRANGER CT	Castle Rock	496H	80109	500-699	
GRANITE AVE	Boulder	97C	80304	None	
GRANITE CIR	El Paso Co	907Y	80132	17000-18099	
GRANITE CIR	Jefferson Co	823V	80465	20200-20699	
GRANITE CT	Longmont	12X	80501	900-999	
GRANITE DR	Boulder Co	722Z	80302	1-599	
GRANITE DR	Lochbuie	139H	80603	1701-1899	O
GRANITE WAY	Castle Rock	467L	80108	5800-5899	
GRANITE WAY	Clear Creek Co	335A	80439	1-199	
GRANITE CRAG CIR	Jefferson Co	366F	80439	6900-7199	
GRANITE HILL DR	Douglas Co	408G	80134	10000-10199	
GRANJA DR	Boulder Co	101C	80026	None	
GRANT AVE	Bennett	793J	80102	300-699	
GRANT AVE	Louisville	131S	80027	400-1399	
GRANT AVE	Palmer Lake	907Q	80133	None	
GRANT AVE E	Douglas Co	850X	80116	10700-10999	
GRANT CIR	Thornton	164Y	80241	None	
	Thornton	164Q	80241	None	
	Thornton	164Q	80241	None	
	Thornton	164Q	80241	None	
GRANT CT	Longmont	11U	80501	1600-1699	
GRANT CT S	Centennial	344Y	80121	6300-6399	
GRANT DR	Longmont	11U	80501	None	
GRANT DR	Northglenn	194L	80233	10400-11399	
	Thornton	164U	80241	12500-12599	
	Thornton	164U	80241	None	
GRANT DR S	Centennial	344Y	80121	6300-6399	
GRANT PL	Arvada	252B	80002	7300-7599	
GRANT PL	Boulder	127G	80302	700-1099	
GRANT RD E	Douglas Co	850X	80116	11000-11999	
GRANT ST	Adams Co	224L	80229	7700-7999	
	Adams Co	224G	80229	8200-8399	
	Denver	284L	80203	1-1999	
	Denver	254Q	80216	4400-5199	
GRANT ST	Elizabeth	871F	80107	100-399	
GRANT ST	Firestone	727A	80504	None	
	Firestone	727A	80621	None	
GRANT ST	Frederick	727F	80530	200-399	
	Frederick	727A	80504	None	
GRANT ST	Longmont	41G	80501	100-299	
	Longmont	41C	80501	300-899	
	Longmont	11Y	80501	900-1399	
	Longmont	11Q	80501	2100-2399	
GRANT ST	Northglenn	194Q	80233	10400-10499	
	Northglenn	194C	80233	11500-11999	
	Northglenn	194C	80233	11800-11999	
	Thornton	224C	80229	8400-8999	
	Thornton	194U	80229	9000-10399	
	Thornton	164Y	80241	12000-12199	
	Thornton	164U	80241	12200-12399	
	Weld Co	727A	80621	None	
GRANT ST	Weld Co	727A	80504	None	
GRANT ST S	Arapahoe Co	344Q	80121	5100-5399	
	Arapahoe Co	374C	80121	6500-6899	
	Arapahoe Co	374G	80122	7100-7299	
	Centennial	344Y	80121	5900-6299	
	Denver	284Y	80209	1-699	
	Denver	314C	80209	700-899	
	Denver	314L	80210	1100-2299	
	Denver	314U	80210	2500-2699	
	Englewood	314Y	80113	2700-3499	
	Englewood	344G	80110	3600-5099	
	Littleton	344U	80121	5500-5599	
	Littleton	374L	80122	7500-7699	
GRANT ST S	Longmont	41Q	80501	1300-1499	
GRANT WAY	Adams Co	224G	80229	100-299	
GRANT WAY S	Littleton	374Q	80122	7900-8199	
GRANT RANCH BLVD W	Denver	342U	80123	6000-6799	
	Lakewood	342Q	80123	6800-7399	
GRANVIEW LN	Mead	707B	80542	300-399	
GRANVILLE AVE	Firestone	727B	80504	None	
GRANVILLE CIR	Firestone	727B	80504	None	
GRANZELLA RD	Jefferson Co	823Q	80465	9300-9499	
GRAPE AVE	Boulder	97U	80304	400-1199	
	Boulder	97V	80304	1700-1899	
	Boulder	98S	80304	1900-2599	
GRAPE CIR	Thornton	195H	80229	11300-11399	
GRAPE CT	Thornton	195V	80229	9600-9699	
	Thornton	195R	80229	10100-10199	
	Thornton	195H	80233	11100-11199	
	Thornton	195D	80640	11800-11899	
	Thornton	165R	80241	13000-13199	
GRAPE CT S	Centennial	345Z	80121	6100-6399	
	Centennial	375M	80122	7700-7799	
	Centennial	375R	80122	8000-8099	
	Greenwood Village	346S	80121	5600-5699	
GRAPE DR	Commerce City	255H	80022	5201-5299	O
	Commerce City	255D	80022	6000-6199	
GRAPE LN	Boulder	97U	80304	300-399	
GRAPE LN S	Greenwood Village	345R	80121	5300-5499	
GRAPE ST	Commerce City	255D	80022	5900-5999	
	Commerce City	225Z	80022	6400-6499	
	Commerce City	225V	80022	6900-7399	
	Denver	285M	80220	1-1999	
	Denver	285D	80207	2000-2799	
	Denver	255Z	80207	2800-3199	
	Denver	255R	80207	3300-3999	
	Denver	255R	80216	4000-4699	
GRAPE ST	Hudson	730L	80642	200-799	
GRAPE ST	Thornton	195D	80233	11500-11799	
	Thornton	165Z	80241	12000-12299	
	Thornton	165R	80241	12800-12899	
	Thornton	165H	80602	13900-13999	
	Thornton	165H	80602	None	
GRAPE ST S	Arapahoe Co	315R	80222	2200-2299	
	Centennial	375H	80122	7100-7299	
	Centennial	375M	80122	7600-7699	
	Denver	285Z	80246	1-699	
	Denver	315D	80246	700-899	
	Denver	315H	80246	1100-1299	
	Denver	315H	80222	1300-1699	
	Denver	315M	80222	2100-2299	
	Denver	315Z	80222	3200-3499	
	Denver	345D	80237	3500-3899	
GRAPE WAY	Thornton	195M	80233	10900-11099	
	Thornton	195D	80233	11800-11999	
	Thornton	165Z	80241	12000-12199	
GRAPE WAY S	Centennial	375H	80122	7000-7099	
	Centennial	375M	80122	7600-7699	
	Denver	315V	80222	2800-3199	
GRAPEVINE RD S	Jefferson Co	308C	80401	800-2499	
GRAPEVINE RD SE	Jefferson Co	308U	80453	2300-2899	
GRAPEVINE RD SW	Jefferson Co	308U	80453	2500-2799	
GRAPEVINE WAY	Castle Rock	466R	80109	None	
GRAPEWOOD LN	Boulder	98S	80304	2600-2699	
GRAPHITE CT	Castle Rock	467M	80108	1800-1999	
GRAPHITE WAY	Superior	160Y	80027	700-799	
GRASMERE DR	Boulder Co	100F	80301	7800-8099	
GRASS CT	Douglas Co	469C	80134	6400-6599	
GRASSHOPPER CT	Castle Rock	496A	80109	None	
GRASSLANDS DR	Douglas Co	378P	80112	14401-14499	O
GRASS RIVER CT S	Parker	408Y	80134	None	
GRASS RIVER PL E	Parker	848D	80134	None	
GRASS RIVER TRAIL S	Parker	408Y	80134	None	
GRASS SONG PL	El Paso Co	908Y	80132	1-99	
GRATITUDE LN	Jefferson Co	366Y	80439	8700-9199	
GRAVES AVE	Jefferson Co	823V	80433	None	
GRAVES AVE E	Centennial	344U	80121	200-299	
GRAVES CT	Northglenn	195E	80233	1700-2099	
GRAY CIR	Arvada	222V	80003	6800-6899	
	Westminster	192M	80020	10800-10999	
	Westminster	192D	80020	11700-11799	
GRAY CIR	Elbert Co	891X	80106	3500-3599	
GRAY CT	Arvada	252H	80002	5300-5398	E
	Arvada	222V	80003	6700-6799	
	Arvada	222H	80003	8100-8299	
	Arvada	222H	80003	8400-8599	
	Westminster	192Z	80031	9200-9399	
	Westminster	192D	80020	11800-11899	
GRAY CT S	Denver	342V	80123	None	
	Jefferson Co	342Z	80123	6200-6499	
	Jefferson Co	372H	80128	7000-7299	
	Jefferson Co	372M	80128	7300-7499	
	Lakewood	312R	80227	2500-2599	
	Lakewood	342V	80123	5700-5799	
GRAY DR	Arvada	222V	80003	6800-6899	
GRAY DR S	Lakewood	312M	80227	2000-2099	
	Lakewood	312R	80227	2300-2499	
GRAY LN	Jefferson Co	365Y	80433	9000-9299	
GRAY ST	Arvada	252D	80003	6000-6199	
	Arvada	222Z	80003	6200-6799	
	Arvada	222M	80003	7900-7999	
	Arvada	222H	80003	8400-8599	
	Denver	252M	80212	4800-5199	
	Edgewater	282D	80214	1700-2599	
	Jefferson Co	252H	80002	5500-5799	
	Lakewood	282V	80226	1-99	
	Lakewood	282R	80226	300-599	
	Lakewood	282R	80214	800-899	
	Lakewood	282M	80214	900-1499	
GRAY ST	Westminster	192Z	80031	9300-9399	
	Westminster	192H	80020	11000-11499	
	Wheat Ridge	282D	80214	2600-2799	
	Wheat Ridge	252Z	80214	2800-3199	
	Wheat Ridge	252Z	80212	3200-3699	
	Wheat Ridge	252V	80212	4100-4399	
GRAY ST S	Denver	312R	80227	2100-2199	
	Denver	312Z	80227	3000-3099	
	Denver	342D	80235	3800-3899	
	Denver	342R	80123	5300-5899	
	Jefferson Co	372M	80128	7600-7799	
	Jefferson Co	372D	80123	None	
	Lakewood	282V	80226	1-99	
	Lakewood	312D	80226	700-799	
	Lakewood	312H	80232	1100-1599	
	Lakewood	312R	80227	2300-2499	
	Lakewood	342V	80123	5700-5899	
	Lakewood	282Z	80226	None	
GRAY WAY	Westminster	222M	80003	7600-7799	
	Westminster	192D	80020	11700-11799	
GRAY WAY S	Denver	312V	80227	2800-2899	
	Jefferson Co	372D	80123	None	
GRAY BUCK TRAIL	Jefferson Co	843E	80433	26500-26799	
GRAYDEN CT	Superior	160R	80027	1900-2299	
GRAYFEATHER WAY W					
	Highlands Ranch	404L	80129	10200-10299	
GRAY FOX CT E	Highlands Ranch	406F	80130	7100-7199	
GRAY FOX DR	Jefferson Co	367W	80439	7800-9199	
GRAY FOX LN E	Highlands Ranch	406F	80130	7000-7099	
GRAY HAWK DR	Jefferson Co	366G	80439	29300-29499	
GRAYHAWK PL	Douglas Co	887C	80118	1300-1399	
GRAYLEDGE CIR	Highlands Ranch	405Q	80130	11000-11199	
GRAYLOCK RUN	Broomfield	133J	80020	None	
GRAY MARE LN	El Paso Co	912U	80831	17000-18399	
GRAYMONT LN	Highlands Ranch	405L	80126	None	
GRAY OWL RD	Cherry Hills Village	345A	80113	1-99	
GRAYS WAY	Broomfield	133J	80020	None	
GRAYS PEAK DR	Longmont	12W	80501	1300-1399	
GRAYS PEAK DR	Parker	410N	80138	21400-21599	
GRAYS PEAK DR	Superior	160U	80027	800-999	
GRAYSTONE CT	Broomfield	133J	80020	None	
GRAY SWALLOW ST	Brighton	139V	80601	None	
GRAY WOLF LOOP	Broomfield	133L	80020	2600-2799	
GREAT PLAIN CT S	Parker	408Y	80134	None	
GREAT PLAIN WAY S	Parker	408Y	80134	None	
GREAT ROCK CT	Adams Co	750L	80603	15300-15398	E
GREAT ROCK RD	Adams Co	750L	80603	15000-29699	
GREAT ROCK ST	Adams Co	750G	80603	None	
GREAT ROCK WAY	Adams Co	750G	80603	15900-16399	
GREAT WESTERN DR	Longmont	42L	80501	1600-1899	
GREAT WESTERN PKWY	Broomfield	190H	80021	10600-11199	
GREAT WESTERN RD	Brighton	138P	80601	2-398	E
	Weld Co	138F	80603	800-998	E
GREATWOOD CT	Highlands Ranch	405K	80126	10200-10299	
GREATWOOD WAY	Highlands Ranch	405K	80126	2600-2799	
GREATWOOD POINTE					
	Highlands Ranch	405K	80126	10200-10399	
GREBE CT	Parker	408R	80134	16100-16199	
GREELEY BLVD	Palmer Lake	907Q	80133	None	
GREELEY CT N	Douglas Co	440V	80134	6200-6299	
GREEN AVE S	Jefferson Co	842B	80470	12600-12799	
GREEN CIR	Boulder	128S	80305	1100-1199	
GREEN CIR	Broomfield	163U	80020	12600-12699	
	Broomfield	163L	80020	13400-13499	
	Jefferson Co	822Y	80433	11500-11699	
GREEN CT	Adams Co	223U	80221	6600-6799	
	Broomfield	163L	80020	13500-13599	
	Denver	253Q	80211	4100-4399	
	Denver	253L	80221	4900-4999	
	Denver	253Q	80211	None	
	Denver	253Y	80211	None	
	Douglas Co	469C	80134	5400-5499	
	Jefferson Co	822Y	80433	11500-11599	
	Westminster	223L	80031	8000-8099	
	Westminster	223L	80030	8200-8399	
	Westminster	223G	80031	8300-8399	
	Westminster	193Y	80260	9300-9499	
	Westminster	193U	80031	9500-9699	
	Westminster	193Q	80031	10100-10199	
GREEN CT S	Denver	313U	80219	2600-2699	
	Denver	313U	80236	2700-2799	
	Sheridan	343C	80110	3700-3899	
GREEN DR	Adams Co	750J	80603	None	
GREEN PL	Broomfield	163L	80020	13500-13599	
GREEN PL	Longmont	41F	80501	1500-1699	
GREEN ST	Park Co	820Z	80421	1-199	
GREEN ACRES CIR	Elbert Co	892H	80117	26600-26799	
GREEN ASH ST	Highlands Ranch	404B	80129	500-699	
GREENBRIAR BLVD	Boulder	128Y	80305	1300-4599	
GREENBRIAR CIR	Boulder Co	100B	80301	7800-7899	
GREENBRIAR CT	Boulder	128Y	80305	4600-4699	
GREENBRIAR DR	Cherry Hills Village	346J	80111	6300-6499	
GREENBRIAR LN	El Paso Co	908U	80132	19000-19199	
GREENBRIAR LN	Parker	410S	80138	11500-11599	
GREENFELL CT	Erie	132A	80026	1800-1899	
GREENFIELD CIR	Douglas Co	408F	80134	None	
GREENFIELD DR	Douglas Co	408F	80134	None	
GREENFIELD LN	Broomfield	133Z	80020	2400-2599	
GREENFIELD LOOP	Douglas Co	408F	80134	None	
GREENFINCH DR	Highlands Ranch	375Y	80126	4200-4299	
GREEN GABLES CIR	Bennett	813B	80102	900-1099	
GREEN GABLES CT	Bennett	813B	80102	800-999	
GREEN GABLES WAY	Bennett	793X	80102	600-899	
GREENGRASS WAY	Parker	379S	80134	8600-8999	
GREEN HAVEN CIR	Highlands Ranch	405K	80126	3100-3299	
GREEN HOLLOW CT E	Douglas Co	440T	80134	8100-8299	
GREENING AVE	Erie	102D	80516	1200-1499	
GREENING DR S	Jefferson Co	822P	80433	9300-9499	
GREEN ISLAND CIR	Lone Tree	406D	80124	8300-8599	
GREEN ISLAND PL	Lone Tree	406D	80124	9400-9499	
GREENLAND RD E	Douglas Co	888Y	80118	4100-4799	
	Douglas Co	889T	80118	6000-7999	
	Douglas Co	889V	80116	8000-9099	
GREENLAND ACRES RD	Douglas Co	907C	80118	11000-12999	
GREENLEAF LN	Adams Co	223M	80221	7700-7899	
GREENLEE WAY	Lafayette	131G	80026	None	
GREENLET CT	Parker	408V	80134	None	
GREEN MEADOW DR	El Paso Co	911X	80106	12500-13599	
GREEN MEADOW LN	Boulder Co	722L	80302	1-299	
GREEN MEADOW LN	Jefferson Co	368L	80465	21200-21299	
GREENMEADOW LN E					
	Greenwood Village	344V	80121	1100-1399	
GREEN MEADOWS CT					
	Highlands Ranch	375W	80126	8900-8999	
GREEN MEADOWS DR					
	Highlands Ranch	375W	80126	8800-8999	
GREEN MEADOWS LN					
	Highlands Ranch	375W	80126	8900-8999	
GREEN MEADOWS PL W	Denver	312R	80227	5600-5999	
GREEN MOUNTAIN CIR	Douglas Co	831N	80138	3000-3899	
GREEN MOUNTAIN CIR W	Lakewood	311E	80228	12400-12499	
GREEN MOUNTAIN DR W	Lakewood	311E	80228	11600-12499	
	Lakewood	310H	80228	12500-13299	
GREEN OAKS CIR	Greenwood Village	345S	80121	2200-2399	
GREEN OAKS DR	Greenwood Village	344V	80121	900-5899	
GREEN OAKS LN	Greenwood Village	345S	80121	2000-2299	
GREENPINE WAY	El Paso Co	908T	80132	19100-19199	
GREENRIDGE LN	Castle Pines North	436P	80108	800-999	
GREENRIDGE RD E	Greenwood Village	346N	80111	1-99	
GREEN RIVER DR	Highlands Ranch	376S	80130	6600-6799	
GREENROCK DR	Boulder Co	97X	80302	100-299	
GREENS CIR S	Littleton	343R	80123	2700-2799	
GREENS CIR W	Littleton	343R	80123	5200-5299	
GREENS CT W	Littleton	343R	80123	2700-2799	

G

STREET NAME	CITY or COUNTY	MAP GRID	ZIP CODE	BLOCK RANGE	O/E
GREENS DR W	Littleton	343R	80123	2700-2799	
GREENS LN W	Littleton	343R	80123	2700-2799	
GREENS PL	Boulder Co	723G	80503	4000-4199	
GREENS PL	Erie	133B	80516	None	
GREENS PL W	Littleton	343R	80123	2700-2799	
GREEN SAGE DR	El Paso Co	910P	80908	19300-19799	
GREEN SAGE LN	El Paso Co	910P	80908	None	
GREENSBOROUGH CIR	Highlands Ranch	373U	80129	2400-2699	
GREENSBOROUGH DR	Highlands Ranch	373U	80129	2300-3399	
GREENSBOROUGH PL	Highlands Ranch	373U	80129	8700-8899	
GREENSBOROUGH PL W	Denver	313X	80236	3600-3899	
GREENS POINTE CT	Highlands Ranch	376W	80130	9000-9099	
GREENS POINTE LN	Highlands Ranch	376W	80130	8900-9099	
GREENS POINTE PL	Highlands Ranch	376W	80130	5700-5799	
GREENS POINTE WAY	Highlands Ranch	376W	80130	5700-5799	
GREEN SPRUCE	Jefferson Co	370P	80127	1-99	
GREENSTONE CIR	Douglas Co	408G	80134	15300-15899	
GREENSTONE LN	Douglas Co	408G	80134	15500-15899	
	Denver	259L	80249	18500-20199	
	Denver	260J	80249	20200-21699	
GREENSVIEW CIR	Lone Tree	406G	80124	9800-9899	
GREENWALD WAY	Clear Creek Co	304H	80439	1-199	
GREENWATER CIR	Castle Rock	469J	80108	6800-7799	
GREENWAY CIR	Broomfield	192C	80020	200E-299E	
GREENWAY DR	Broomfield	192C	80020	2-498	E
GREENWAY LN	Broomfield	192C	80020	400-499	
GREENWAY LN	Castle Pines North	436P	80108	900-999	
GREENWICH CT	Highlands Ranch	375Z	80126	8900-8999	
GREENWICH DR	Highlands Ranch	375Z	80126	4800-5099	
GREENWICH LN	Highlands Ranch	375Z	80126	4900-4999	
GREENWICH PL	Highlands Ranch	375Z	80126	4800-4899	
GREENWICH ST	Highlands Ranch	375Z	80126	8800-9099	
GREENWICH WAY	Highlands Ranch	375Z	80126	4900-4999	
GREEN WILLOW CT	Boulder Co	99H	80301	6900-6999	
GREENWILLOW LN E	Greenwood Village	344V	80121	1300-1499	
GREENWOOD BLVD	Adams Co	224F	80221	1-7599	
	Adams Co	224F	80221	7600-8399	
GREENWOOD CIR E	Aurora	319W	80013	16900-17599	
GREENWOOD CIR S	Littleton	344T	80120	5900-5999	
GREENWOOD CT	Adams Co	224E	80221	8000-8199	
GREENWOOD CT	Fort Lupton	728H	80621	900-999	
GREEN WOOD CT S	Jefferson Co	336Q	80439	5000-5299	
GREENWOOD CT S	Littleton	374K	80120	7700-7799	
GREENWOOD DR	Boulder Co	70L	80503	8300-8499	
GREENWOOD DR	El Paso Co	908P	80132	19200-19499	
GREENWOOD DR E	Aurora	318W	80014	13800-14099	
	Aurora	318Y	80013	15400-15799	
	Aurora	319X	80013	17700-18299	
	Aurora	319Z	80013	19600-19999	
	Aurora	320W	80013	None	
GREEN WOOD DR S	Jefferson Co	336P	80439	5000-5199	
GREENWOOD LN	Castle Rock	497R	80104	1200-1299	
GREEN WOOD LN	Jefferson Co	336P	80439	29300-29599	
GREENWOOD LN	Longmont	42C	80501	400-499	
GREENWOOD LN E	Greenwood Village	344V	80121	1300-1599	
GREENWOOD PL	Boulder Co	70Q	80503	8200-8299	
GREENWOOD PL E	Aurora	318Y	80014	14800-15199	
	Aurora	319X	80013	18500-18599	
	Aurora	319X	80013	19300-19599	
	Aurora	320W	80013	None	
	Denver	316W	80222	5600-5799	
GREENWOOD PL W	Denver	313X	80236	3400-4199	
GREENWOOD RD	Douglas Co	867N	80135	3000-4499	
GREENWOOD ST S	Littleton	344T	80120	5300-5899	
	Littleton	374B	80120	6600-6899	
GREENWOOD PLAZA BLVD S	Greenwood Village	346Q	80111	5400-5499	
	Greenwood Village	346U	80111	5500-5899	
	Greenwood Village	346Y	80111	5900-7299	
	Greenwood Village	376C	80111	6500-6699	
GREGG CT S	Denver	315X	80210	3200-3299	
GREGG'S PL	Bennett	793K	80102	300-399	
GREGORY CIR	Elbert Co	850C	80138	601-899	O
GREGORY DR	Golden	248Z	80403	300-399	
GREGORY LN	Boulder	127L	80302	400-599	
GREGORY ST	Central City	780D	80427	100-199	
GREGS POND LN	El Paso Co	908U	80132	18400-18499	
GRENCHEN DR S	Jefferson Co	842Q	80470	15300-15399	
GREY CT	Castle Rock	467Y	80104	3400-3599	
GREY EAGLE DR	Jefferson Co	842L	80470	None	
GREYLOCK ST	Boulder Co	100F	80301	4600-4799	
GREYS RD	Thornton	194S	80260	None	
GREY SQUIRREL WAY	Douglas Co	870E	80116	1-699	
GREYSTONE	Elbert Co	870H	80107	None	
GREYSTONE LN	Castle Rock	527D	80104	4100-4399	
GREYSTONE RD	Clear Creek Co	335E	80439	1-1799	
GREY WOLF PL	Broomfield	163E	80020	4900-5199	
GRIFFIN DR	Jefferson Co	822P	80433	31500-32299	
GRIFFITH PL	Highlands Ranch	405H	80130	None	
GRIFFITH PL	Longmont	11T	80501	1900-1999	
GRIFFITH ST	Louisville	131N	80027	400-1199	
GRIFFITH ST	Nederland	740Q	80466	None	
GRIFFITH ST W	Louisville	130R	80027	300-498	E
GRIG'S RD	Castle Pines North	436A	80108	None	
GRIGS RD	Highlands Ranch	405L	80126	10500-10899	
	Highlands Ranch	405U	80130	None	
GRIMES LN	Douglas Co	909E	80118	5200-5799	
GRIMSON PL	Erie	103T	80516	600-699	
GRIMSON ST	Frederick	727A	80504	None	
GRINNELL AVE	Boulder	128U	80305	4200-4499	
GRINNELL DR	Longmont	11W	80503	2700-2799	
GRIST MILL WAY	El Paso Co	908Y	80132	17600-17699	
GRIZZLY CT	Douglas Co	432L	80125	7600-7699	
GRIZZLY DR	Jefferson Co	824R	80127	12500-13899	
GRIZZLY WAY	Jefferson Co	367S	80439	7800-9099	
GRIZZLY CREEK CT	Weld Co	706M	80504	None	
GRIZZLY GULCH S	Highlands Ranch	404J	80129	10400-10599	
GRIZZLY GULCH CT W	Highlands Ranch	404J	80129	1700-1799	
GROSBEAK ST	Brighton	139R	80601	5000-5299	
GROSS RD	Park Co	820Z	80421	1-699	
GROSS DAM RD	Boulder Co	742Q	80403	1-3999	

STREET NAME	CITY or COUNTY	MAP GRID	ZIP CODE	BLOCK RANGE	O/E
GROUSE AVE	Adams Co	137Z	80601	1200-1299	
GROUSE CT	Jefferson Co	337Q	80439	4900-4999	
GROUSE CT	Longmont	12Y	80501	1200-1299	
GROUSE CT	Louisville	130Z	80027	300-499	
GROUSE CT	Parker	408R	80134	11000-11099	
GROUSE DR	Elbert Co	850V	80107	1400-1799	
GROUSE LN	Jefferson Co	365F	80439	34000-34599	
GROUSE LN	Park Co	841V	80421	1-99	
GROUSE PL	Highlands Ranch	374Y	80126	100-299	
GROUSE WAY	Clear Creek Co	304Y	80439	1-199	
GROUSEBERRY WAY E	Parker	409A	80134	17600-17699	
GROVE AVE	Weld Co	706V	80504	None	
GROVE CIR	Boulder	128A	80302	2200E-2299E	
	Boulder	128A	80302	2100W-2199W	
GROVE CIR	Broomfield	163Q	80020	13000-13099	
	Westminster	193Q	80031	9800-9899	
GROVE CT	Boulder Co	722L	80302	1-499	
GROVE CT	Broomfield	163U	80020	12600-12699	
	Broomfield	163Q	80020	13300-13399	
	Longmont	11T	80501	1700-1799	
	Louisville	130U	80027	1100-1199	
	Westminster	193Q	80031	9900-10099	
	Westminster	193L	80031	10500-10699	
	Westminster	193L	80031	10800-10899	
GROVE DR	Louisville	130U	80027	900-999	
GROVE LN	Westminster	193L	80031	10700-10799	
GROVE LOOP	Westminster	193Q	80031	10000-10199	
GROVE PL	Brighton	138V	80601	2400-2499	
GROVE PL	Westminster	193U	80031	9900-9999	
GROVE ST	Adams Co	253G	80221	5200-5599	
	Adams Co	223U	80221	6600-6799	
	Adams Co	223C	80031	8800-9099	
GROVE ST	Boulder	128A	80302	1800-2399	
GROVE ST	Boulder Co	721R	80302	1-2399	
GROVE ST	Brighton	139S	80601	None	
GROVE ST	Broomfield	163U	80020	12500-12699	
	Denver	283U	80219	1-399	
	Denver	283Q	80204	800-1299	
	Denver	283G	80204	1400-1999	
	Denver	283C	80211	2000-2699	
	Denver	253Q	80211	2700-4699	
	Denver	253L	80221	4800-4999	
	Jefferson Co	339G	80465	3900-4099	
	Westminster	223U	80030	7100-7198	E
	Westminster	223L	80030	7600-7999	
	Westminster	223L	80031	8000-8099	
	Westminster	223G	80031	8300-8399	
	Westminster	193Y	80031	9100-9399	
	Westminster	193U	80031	9700-9999	
	Westminster	193L	80031	10500-10799	
	Westminster	193G	80031	11200-11298	E
	Westminster	193G	80234	11201-11299	O
	Westminster	193G	80031	11300-11399	
	Westminster	193C	80031	11500-11699	
GROVE ST S	Denver	283U	80219	1-399	
	Denver	313C	80219	1000-1299	
	Denver	313L	80219	1800-1899	
	Denver	313U	80219	2500-2699	
	Denver	313U	80236	2700-2799	
	Littleton	343Q	80110	5000-5099	
	Sheridan	343C	80110	3600-4099	
GROVE WAY	Broomfield	163Q	80020	12900-13499	
	Westminster	193U	80031	9900-9999	
GROVETON AVE	Castle Rock	499J	80104	6600-6999	
GUADALOUPE ST	Boulder	98K	80301	4000-4199	
GUADALUPE CT	El Paso Co	912X	80831	16800-16899	
GUAVA PL	Boulder	98E	80304	None	
GUERNSEY LOOP	Castle Rock	496B	80109	4700-4899	
GUINEVERE ST	Lafayette	132P	80026	1-299	
GUIRE WAY	El Paso Co	908S	80132	18300-18399	
GULL ST	Brighton	139R	80601	5000-5099	
GULL ST	Federal Heights	193U	80260	9600-9799	
GUN CLUB CT S	Aurora	380H	80016	None	
GUN CLUB RD	Adams Co	170Q	80022	10700-13599	
	Adams Co	140U	80603	15200-15999	
	Adams Co	260Z	80019	None	
	Adams Co	769D	80022	None	
	Aurora	290H	80019	None	
	Denver	769V	80249	8800-10399	
GUN CLUB RD N	Aurora	290G	80018	1-1499	
GUN CLUB RD S	Arapahoe Co	290U	80018	1-899	
	Arapahoe Co	320D	80018	700-1099	
	Arapahoe Co	320R	80018	2900-3499	
	Arapahoe Co	350H	80018	3500-4299	
	Arapahoe Co	350M	80016	4300-5499	
	Aurora	320R	80018	1100-2899	
GUNBARREL AVE	Boulder Co	99F	80301	5800-6299	
GUNBARREL CIR	Boulder Co	70W	80503	5300-5499	
GUNBARREL RD	Boulder Co	70W	80503	5400-5799	
GUNBARREL RIDGE RD	Boulder Co	101A	80301	9100-9499	
GUNNISON CIR E	Aurora	319G	80017	19200-19299	
GUNNISON DR	Frederick	707W	80504	None	
GUNNISON DR E	Aurora	319E	80017	16800-16898	E
	Aurora	321E	80018	24700-24799	
GUNNISON DR W	Denver	313H	80219	2400-2699	
GUNNISON PL E	Aurora	317E	80247	10000-10098	E
	Aurora	318F	80012	14100-15199	
	Aurora	318G	80017	15300-15599	
	Aurora	318H	80017	15700-16699	
	Aurora	319E	80017	17400-17499	
	Aurora	319F	80017	17800-18399	
	Aurora	319G	80017	18800-18999	
	Aurora	319G	80017	19200-19499	
	Denver	316E	80224	5600-5799	
	Denver	316G	80231	7500-7899	
GUNNISON PL W	Denver	314E	80223	1800-1999	
	Denver	313H	80219	2000-2399	
GUNNISON WAY	Broomfield	162L	80020	13800-13999	
GUNPARK DR	Boulder	99C	80301	6300-6599	
GUNSIGHT PASS	Jefferson Co	371K	80127	7700-7799	
GUNSMOKE DR	Park Co	841A	80421	1-999	
	Park Co	840D	80421	None	
GUY AVE	Weld Co	727F	80530	None	
GUY CT	Adams Co	168U	80603	15500-15699	
GUY HILL RD	Jefferson Co	782H	80403	4300-4799	
GWENDELYN LN S	Highlands Ranch	404G	80129	10000-10099	
GWENDELYN PL S	Highlands Ranch	404G	80129	9900-9999	
GWENDELYN RD	Highlands Ranch	404G	80129	None	

STREET NAME	CITY or COUNTY	MAP GRID	ZIP CODE	BLOCK RANGE	O/E
GYDA DR	Arvada	251H	80002	8900-9099	
GYPSUM CT	Douglas Co	409E	80134	17500-17599	
GYPSUM CT	Superior	160Y	80027	3700-3899	
GYPSUM GAP ST	Brighton	140J	80601	None	
GYPSY MOTH CT	Castle Rock	496B	80109	2000-2099	
GYROS CIR	Lafayette	131Q	80026	2000-2099	

H

STREET NAME	CITY or COUNTY	MAP GRID	ZIP CODE	BLOCK RANGE	O/E
H ST	Golden	279Q	80401	800-899	
HABITAT DR	Boulder Co	99F	80301	6100-6299	
HABU LN	Park Co	841R	80421	1-99	
HACIENDA CIR	Lochbuie	140B	80603	None	
HACIENDA PL	Douglas Co	469A	80134	5300-5499	
HACIENDA RD	Jefferson Co	305A	80439	700-999	
HACKAMORE RD	Douglas Co	432F	80125	8300-8599	
HACKBERRY CIR	Longmont	11P	80501	2100-2199	
HACKBERRY CT	Highlands Ranch	403C	80129	2900-2999	
HACKBERRY LN	Highlands Ranch	403C	80129	9400-9499	
HACKBERRY ST	Louisville	130Z	80027	500-599	
HACKBERRY ST S	Highlands Ranch	403C	80129	9500-9799	
HACKBERRY HILL RD	Arvada	222T	80003	None	
HACKNEY CIR	El Paso Co	910U	80908	18300-18499	
HACKNEY CT	Douglas Co	439Z	80134	5400-5699	
HADAR DR	Highlands Ranch	376X	80124	13100-13199	
HADDON RD	Denver	285C	80205	3900-3999	
HADLEY ST	Douglas Co	409X	80134	None	
HADRIAN CT	Douglas Co	407L	80134	10200-10399	
HAGEN CT S	Highlands Ranch	404D	80126	9500-9599	
HAGLER DR	Jefferson Co	308F	80401	22600-22999	
HAGUE CIR	Elbert Co	850C	80138	100-199	
HAHNSPEAK	Jefferson Co	371K	80127	7600-7699	
HALDIMAND DR	Jefferson Co	822Y	80433	31000-31199	
HALE AVE	Parker	410U	80138	None	
HALE CT	Parker	410Y	80138	None	
HALE PKWY	Denver	285L	80220	4100-5399	
HALEYVILLE CIR S	Aurora	321E	80018	1400-1499	
HALEYVILLE CT S	Aurora	381A	80016	6800-6999	
	Aurora	321N	80018	None	
	Aurora	351N	80016	None	
HALEYVILLE ST S	Aurora	321E	80018	None	
	Aurora	351N	80016	None	
	Aurora	381J	80016	None	
HALEYVILLE WAY S	Aurora	351J	80016	5100-5399	
	Aurora	321J	80018	None	
HALFMOON DR	Castle Rock	527C	80104	700-1299	
HALF MOON PASS	Jefferson Co	371P	80127	10800-11099	
HALIFAX AVE	Castle Rock	499J	80104	None	
HALIFAX CIR S	Centennial	349R	80015	5300-5399	
HALIFAX CT	Denver	259M	80249	4900-4999	
	Denver	259H	80249	None	
HALIFAX CT S	Aurora	319R	80013	2500-2699	
	Aurora	349H	80013	4200-4299	
HALIFAX ST	Denver	259V	80249	4100-4199	
	Denver	259M	80249	4800-4899	
	Denver	259H	80249	None	
HALIFAX ST S	Aurora	319R	80013	2500-2699	
	Aurora	319V	80013	2700-3199	
	Aurora	349D	80013	3700-3999	
	Centennial	349H	80015	4300-4499	
HALIFAX WAY	Aurora	289H	80011	1600-1699	
	Denver	259M	80249	4800-4999	
HALIFAX WAY S	Arapahoe Co	349H	80015	None	
	Aurora	319R	80013	2400-2499	
	Aurora	319Z	80013	3300-3499	
	Aurora	319Z	80013	3500-3699	
	Aurora	349H	80013	4200-4299	
	Aurora	319H	80017	None	
HALITE CT	Castle Rock	467H	80108	7200-7499	
HALL RD	Park Co	820Z	80421	1-699	
HALLET PEAK DR	Longmont	40N	80503	None	
HALLEY'S DR	Douglas Co	432K	80125	7500-7799	
HALLEY'S WAY	Douglas Co	432K	80125	10200-10399	
HALLMARK LN	Longmont	12T	80501	700-799	
HALSTEAD LN	Lone Tree	407J	80124	None	
HALTER WAY	Clear Creek Co	781U	80439	200-299	
HALYARD CT	Lafayette	131K	80026	1600-1699	
HAMAL CIR	El Paso Co	907R	80132	3000-3299	
HAMAL DR	El Paso Co	908N	80132	19800-20099	
HAMAL DR	Highlands Ranch	376X	80124	700-999	
HAMILTON AVE E	Aurora	319W	80013	17200-17399	
	Aurora	320W	80013	None	
HAMILTON AVE E	Castle Rock	498Q	80104	5100-5399	
HAMILTON AVE W	Denver	313X	80236	3600-3899	
HAMILTON CIR E	Aurora	319X	80013	17700-17799	
	Aurora	320W	80013	None	
HAMILTON CT	Boulder	128Q	80305	4400-4499	
HAMILTON CT	Lone Tree	406D	80124	8600-8699	
HAMILTON DR	Longmont	11V	80501	1-99	
HAMILTON DR E	Aurora	318X	80014	13700-14199	
	Aurora	319Y	80013	18500-18799	
HAMILTON DR W	Lakewood	312Y	80227	6600-6699	
	Lakewood	311Z	80227	9100-9599	
HAMILTON PL E	Aurora	318Y	80013	15600-15899	
	Aurora	318Z	80013	15900-16299	
	Aurora	319Y	80013	19000-19899	
	Denver	316X	80224	7100-7199	
HAMILTON PL W	Arapahoe Co	313Y	80110	3001-3299	O
	Denver	313X	80236	3500-3599	
	Denver	313W	80236	4200-4898	E
	Sheridan	314W	80110	1600-1999	
HAMMOCK OAKS CT	El Paso Co	908P	80132	None	
HAMPDEN AVE E	Aurora	318Y	80014	13600-15299	
	Aurora	318Y	80013	15300-16799	
	Aurora	319Y	80013	16800-20199	
	Aurora	320X	80015	20200-24899	
	Cherry Hills Village	314Z	80110	1400-1698	E
	Cherry Hills Village	315Y	80110	3800-4598	E
	Denver	315Y	80222	4001-4799	O
	Denver	315Z	80222	4800-5499	
	Denver	316W	80222	5500-6499	
	Denver	316X	80224	6500-7299	
	Denver	316Y	80231	7300-9199	
	Denver	317W	80231	9501-10199	O
	Englewood	314Y	80113	100-1399	
	Englewood	314Z	80110	1401-1699	O
	Englewood	315W	80110	1701-1799	O

STREET NAME	CITY or COUNTY	MAP GRID	ZIP CODE	BLOCK RANGE	O/E
HAMPDEN AVE W	Arapahoe Co	313Y	80110	3400-3498	E
	Denver	312X	80227	6001-6399	O
	Denver	342D	80235	None	
	Englewood	314X	80110	200-1099	
	Jefferson Co	340C	80465	14500-14999	
	Lakewood	342B	80227	6400-7598	E
	Lakewood	312X	80227	6401-7599	O
	Lakewood	312W	80227	7601-8799	O
	Lakewood	342A	80227	7900-8898	E
	Lakewood	311Y	80227	9000-9998	E
	Lakewood	311X	80227	10000-11699	
	Sheridan	314W	80110	1500-1998	E
	Sheridan	313Y	80110	2100-3399	
HAMPDEN CIR E	Aurora	318Y	80014	14900-15299	
	Aurora	318Y	80013	15300-15599	
	Denver	316Y	80237	7700-8099	
HAMPDEN DR E	Aurora	319Y	80013	19000-19199	
HAMPDEN PL E	Aurora	318X	80014	13800-14199	
	Aurora	318X	80014	14600-14899	
	Aurora	319X	80013	18200-18399	
	Aurora	319Y	80013	19300-19699	
	Aurora	319Z	80013	20100-20499	
	Aurora	320W	80013	20600-20799	
HAMPDEN PL W	Englewood	314X	80110	None	
	Jefferson Co	311X	80227	10800-10999	
	Jefferson Co	311X	80227	11000-11699	
HAMPDEN FRONTAGE RD W	Jefferson Co	341C	80235	None	
HAMPSHIRE ST	Boulder Co	100F	80301	4600-4799	
HAMPSTEAD AVE	Castle Rock	498L	80104	1-799	
HAMPTON CIR S	Boulder	98L	80301	4100-4699	
HAMPTON CT	Castle Pines North	436R	80108	6900-6999	
HAMRON CT	Erie	102Q	80516	1900-1999	
HANCOCK CT	Bennett	793J	80102	100-199	
HANCOCK DR	Boulder	128H	80303	1100-4799	
HANCOCK WAY	Bennett	793N	80102	200-299	
HANDIES WAY	Broomfield	133N	80020	None	
HANDIES PEAK CT	Douglas Co	436U	80108	6200-6299	
HANDIES PEAK ST	Jefferson Co	249E	80403	None	
HANDLES RD	Thornton	193V	80260	None	
HANGING J RANCH PL E	Douglas Co	439H	80134	20000-20299	
HANGMAN'S RD	Park Co	841A	80421	100-1199	
HANLEY CT	Castle Pines North	436V	80108	6700-6799	
HANNAH DR	Jefferson Co	822Y	80433	11500-11699	
HANNIBAL CT	Aurora	258U	80011	None	
	Commerce City	198U	80022	9700-9899	
	Denver	258G	80239	5500-5599	
HANNIBAL CT S	Aurora	318L	80013	1900-1999	
	Centennial	348Q	80015	5400-5499	
HANNIBAL DR	Aurora	288L	80011	800-899	
HANNIBAL ST	Commerce City	198Q	80022	9900-10199	
	Commerce City	198C	80022	11700-11899	
	Commerce City	168Y	80603	None	
	Commerce City	198G	80022	None	
	Denver	258L	80239	5000-5299	
	Denver	258G	80239	5500-5599	
HANNIBAL ST S	Arapahoe Co	378L	80112	None	
	Aurora	318L	80013	1900-2099	
	Aurora	318Y	80013	2900-3399	
	Aurora	348C	80013	3800-3999	
	Aurora	348G	80013	4100-4199	
	Aurora	348L	80015	4500-4599	
HANNIBAL WAY	Denver	258G	80239	5400-5599	
HANNIBAL WAY S	Aurora	318C	80017	900-999	
	Aurora	318L	80013	2000-2099	
	Aurora	348L	80015	4700-5099	
	Centennial	348Q	80015	5100-5299	
	Centennial	348U	80015	5400-5799	
HANOVER AVE	Boulder	128U	80305	4000-4699	
HANOVER CT	Adams Co	791K	80137	2900-2999	
	Adams Co	137X	80602	14700-14799	
	Adams Co	137S	80602	15200-15399	
	Commerce City	197S	80640	9700E-9799E	
	Commerce City	197S	80640	9600W-9699W	
HANOVER CT	Denver	287B	80238	None	
HANOVER CT S	Arapahoe Co	347X	80111	6300-6399	
HANOVER PL E	Castle Rock	498Q	80104	5100-5199	
HANOVER ST	Adams Co	167A	80602	14300-14499	
	Adams Co	137W	80602	14800-14999	
	Aurora	287K	80010	700-2499	
	Denver	257X	80238	2600-2799	
HANOVER ST S	Arapahoe Co	347P	80111	5100-5299	
HANOVER WAY	Aurora	287P	80010	500-599	
HANOVER WAY S	Arapahoe Co	347P	80111	5100-5299	
	Greenwood Village	347T	80111	5500-5699	
	Greenwood Village	347T	80111	5700-5899	
HANOVERIAN WAY W	Littleton	373J	80128	4600-4699	
HANSEN AVE	Commerce City	225U	80022	None	
HAPGOOD ST	Boulder	127G	80302	400-599	
HAPPY CANYON DR	Cherry Hills Village	346E	80111	5700-6099	
HAPPY CANYON RD	Denver	345D	80237	4800-5599	
	Denver	345A	80237	5600-6499	
HAPPY CANYON RD E	Douglas Co	848J	80108	100-699	
HAPPY CANYON RD W	Douglas Co	466G	80108	100-599	
HAPPY HILL RD	Jefferson Co	367E	80439	6700-6899	
HAPPY TOP RD	Park Co	841W	80421	None	
HAPPY TRAIL	Jefferson Co	306X	80439	3000-3099	
HAPPY TRAIL RD	Gilpin Co	742W	80403	None	
HARBACK RD	Adams Co	752Y	80102	None	
	Adams Co	792Q	80102	None	
	Bennett	792Q	80102	None	
HARBACK RD N	Adams Co	752Y	80102	None	
	Arapahoe Co	792U	80102	1-1499	
HARBACK RD S	Arapahoe Co	792Y	80102	1-299	
HARBOR DR	Weld Co	706U	80504	9800-9999	
HARBOR LN	Longmont	10V	80503	1700-1799	
HARBOR TOWN CT	Lone Tree	406G	80124	None	
HARBOR TOWN DR	Elbert Co	851C	80107	None	
HARBOR TOWN PL	Lone Tree	406G	80124	8200-8399	
HARDIN ST	Castle Rock	466Y	80109	None	
HARDING CT	Louisville	130Y	80027	200-299	
HARDROCK PL	Castle Rock	527H	80104	1300-1499	
HARDSCRABBLE DR	Boulder	128X	80305	1900-2099	
HARDSCRABBLE PL	Boulder	128X	80305	1900-1999	
HARDT RD	Boulder Co	703U	80503	None	
HARDWICK CT	Castle Pines North	436R	80108	200-299	
HARDY RD	El Paso Co	910Z	80908	9700-10599	
	El Paso Co	911W	80908	10600-11299	
HAREBELL DR	Douglas Co	887F	80118	2700-2999	
HAREBELL LN	Gilpin Co	761C	80403	1-199	
HAREBELL LN	Jefferson Co	336H	80439	28000-28299	
HAREBELL RUN	Douglas Co	432X	80125	10500-10699	
HARFORD CT S	Highlands Ranch	405A	80126	9500-9599	
HARKWOOD RUN TRAIL	Jefferson Co	782K	80403	30500-33599	
HARLAN CIR S	Lakewood	312L	80232	None	
HARLAN CT	Arvada	222H	80003	8200-8299	
	Westminster	192Y	80031	9400-9499	
	Wheat Ridge	252R	80033	4400-4499	
HARLAN CT S	Denver	342R	80123	5500-5599	
	Jefferson Co	372H	80128	6900-6999	
	Jefferson Co	372M	80128	7300-7499	
	Lakewood	312M	80227	1900-1999	
	Lakewood	312R	80227	2300-2499	
	Lakewood	312R	80227	2500-2599	
	Lakewood	312V	80227	2600-2699	
HARLAN ST	Arvada	252D	80003	6000-6199	
	Arvada	222Z	80003	6200-6899	
	Arvada	222M	80003	7800-7999	
	Edgewater	282D	80214	1700-2599	
	Jefferson Co	252H	80002	5300-5599	
	Lakewood	282V	80226	1-599	
	Lakewood	282R	80214	600-1499	
	Lakewood	282G	80214	1500-1699	
	Westminster	222M	80003	7500-7799	
	Westminster	222C	80031	8800-9099	
	Westminster	192Z	80031	9100-9199	
	Westminster	192H	80020	10800-11399	
	Westminster	192D	80020	11300-11599	
	Wheat Ridge	282D	80214	2600-2899	
	Wheat Ridge	252V	80214	3000-3199	
	Wheat Ridge	252V	80033	3200-4399	
	Wheat Ridge	252V	80212	4400-4998	E
	Wheat Ridge	252V	80033	4401-4999	O
HARLAN ST S	Denver	312R	80227	2100-2299	
	Denver	312Z	80227	3000-3099	
	Denver	342D	80235	3500-3899	
	Denver	342V	80123	5500-5699	
	Jefferson Co	372M	80128	7400-7799	
	Jefferson Co	372D	80123	None	
	Lakewood	282V	80226	1-199	
	Lakewood	282Z	80226	200-699	
	Lakewood	312H	80226	700-1099	
	Lakewood	312H	80232	1100-1799	
	Lakewood	312R	80227	2300-2599	
	Lakewood	342V	80123	5700-5899	
HARLAN WAY	Westminster	222R	80003	7400-7699	
HARLAN WAY S	Denver	312V	80227	2800-2899	
	Denver	342R	80123	5200-5499	
	Jefferson Co	342Z	80123	6200-6499	
	Jefferson Co	372M	80128	7700-7799	
	Lakewood	312D	80226	900-1099	
HARLEQUIN CIR	Frederick	707W	80504	9000-9199	
HARLEQUIN DR	Longmont	12Y	80501	1500-1699	
HARMON PL	Longmont	11Q	80501	1000-1099	
HARMON RD	Jefferson Co	842A	80470	33600-33999	
HARMON ST	Lafayette	132J	80026	300-399	
HARMONY LN	Commerce City	769E	80022	10500-10799	
HARMONY PKWY	Westminster	163R	80234	12800-13099	
HARMONY PARK DR	Westminster	163R	80234	1900-2399	
HARMONY RIDGE CIR	Elbert Co	890C	80107	900-999	
HARNESS CT	Douglas Co	469F	80134	4800-4999	
HARNESS RD	El Paso Co	908Y	80132	500-699	
HARNESS WAY	El Paso Co	908Y	80132	400-499	
HAROLD ST	Weld Co	729A	80621	7000-7999	
HARPENDEN LN	Weld Co	708N	80621	None	
HARPER DR	Louisville	130R	80027	None	
HARPER ST	Louisville	131N	80027	1000-1199	
HARPER ST W	Louisville	130R	80027	300-499	
HARPER LAKE CT	Louisville	130U	80027	1200-1299	
HARPER LAKE DR	Louisville	130U	80027	1100-1199	
HARPY CT	Castle Rock	497A	80109	900-999	
HARRIER HAWK RD	Dacono	727N	80514	None	
HARRINGTON LN S	Lakewood	312R	80227	2500-2699	
HARRIS CIR	Thornton	195S	80229	9600-9699	
HARRIS CT	Erie	102U	80516	None	
HARRIS CT	Thornton	195S	80229	9600-9799	
HARRIS ST	Adams Co	225E	80229	8300-8399	
HARRIS ST	Superior	160R	80027	1600-1699	
HARRIS ST	Thornton	195W	80229	9100-9399	
	Thornton	195S	80229	9800-9999	
	Thornton	195N	80229	10100-10199	
HARRIS WAY	Thornton	195H	80233	11100-11199	
HARRISON AVE	Boulder	128H	80303	1200-4799	
HARRISON AVE	Fort Lupton	728M	80621	100-899	
HARRISON AVE N	Lafayette	132J	80026	100-299	
HARRISON AVE S	Lafayette	132J	80026	100-699	
HARRISON CIR	Adams Co	225G	80229	8300-8399	
HARRISON CIR S	Centennial	375Q	80122	7700-8199	
HARRISON CT	Adams Co	225G	80229	8500-8599	
HARRISON CT	Boulder	128H	80303	1200-1299	
HARRISON CT	Louisville	130Q	80027	1500-1599	
HARRISON CT	Thornton	165L	80241	13400-13499	
	Thornton	165U	80241	None	
HARRISON CT S	Centennial	345Y	80121	6300-6499	
	Centennial	375G	80122	7100-7199	
HARRISON DR	Bennett	793J	80102	200-299	
HARRISON DR	Lafayette	132E	80026	700-1099	
HARRISON DR	Thornton	165Q	80241	13000-13099	
	Thornton	165L	80602	13800-13899	
	Thornton	165G	80602	13900-13999	
HARRISON DR S	Centennial	345Y	80121	6100-6299	
HARRISON LN S	Denver	285Y	80209	500-699	
	Denver	315C	80209	700-899	
HARRISON PL	Thornton	165Y	80241	12200-12299	
HARRISON ST	Adams Co	165B	80602	14500-14899	
	Adams Co	135X	80602	14900-15099	
	Denver	285Q	80206	1-1399	
	Denver	285G	80206	1500-1699	
	Denver	255Y	80205	2800-2899	
	Denver	255U	80205	3300-3999	
	Denver	255G	80216	5200-5399	
	Thornton	195Y	80229	9100-9399	
	Thornton	195T	80229	9600-9999	
	Thornton	195L	80233	10600-10799	
	Thornton	195C	80233	11700-11899	
	Thornton	165Q	80241	13300-13499	
	Thornton	165L	80241	13500-13599	
	Thornton	165L	80602	13800-13899	
	Thornton	165G	80602	13900-13999	
HARRISON ST S	Centennial	375G	80122	6800-7099	
	Cherry Hills Village	345C	80113	3800-3899	
	Denver	285U	80209	1-399	
	Denver	285Y	80209	600-699	
	Denver	315C	80209	700-1099	
	Denver	315G	80210	1100-1299	
	Denver	315L	80210	1700-1799	
	Denver	315Q	80210	2200-2299	
	Denver	315U	80210	2700-3099	
HARRISON WAY	Adams Co	225G	80229	8400-8499	
HARRISON WAY S	Centennial	345Y	80121	6300-6399	
	Centennial	375G	80122	7100-7399	
	Centennial	375L	80122	7400-7699	
	Centennial	375Q	80122	7700-8199	
HARRISS ST	Thornton	195N	80229	10100-10199	
HARROGATE CT	El Paso Co	909S	80132	19000-19099	
HARROW CT	Brighton	139L	80601	None	
HARROW LN	Platteville	708B	80651	400-499	
HARRY ST	Gilpin Co	760G	80403	None	
HARRY B COMBS PKWY	Denver	770T	80249	7800-7898	E
HART ST	Weld Co	729B	80621	7000-7999	
HARTFORD DR	Boulder	128T	80305	500-1399	
HARTFORD WAY	Lochbuie	139D	80603	None	
HARTLAND LN	Castle Pines North	436C	80108	400-499	
HARTLEY CT	Longmont	41T	80501	1600-1699	
HARTWICK CIR	Longmont	10Z	80503	2800-2899	
HARVARD AVE E	Arapahoe Co	316Q	80231	7300-8199	
	Arapahoe Co	316R	80231	None	
	Aurora	317Q	80014	11700-12099	
	Aurora	318N	80014	13800-14099	
	Aurora	318P	80014	14100-14399	
	Aurora	318P	80014	14500-14999	
	Aurora	318R	80013	16000-16599	
	Aurora	319N	80013	16800-17399	
	Aurora	319R	80013	19800-19999	
	Denver	314Q	80210	1-1699	
	Denver	315P	80210	1700-3699	
	Denver	315Q	80222	4200-4599	
	Denver	316N	80222	6400-6499	
	Denver	316P	80224	6500-6999	
	Denver	317N	80231	9700-10399	
HARVARD AVE W	Denver	314P	80223	1-799	
	Denver	313P	80219	2400-5199	
	Englewood	314N	80110	1600-1999	
	Englewood	313R	80110	2000-2399	
	Lakewood	311R	80227	9700-9799	
	Lakewood	310R	80228	12600-12799	
	Lakewood	310U	80228	13900-14199	
HARVARD CIR E	Arapahoe Co	316Q	80231	7900-8199	
	Arapahoe Co	316U	80231	None	
	Aurora	317R	80014	12500-12799	
HARVARD CT	Longmont	10R	80503	2200-2299	
HARVARD DR E	Aurora	317P	80014	10800-11299	
	Aurora	317R	80014	12100-12599	
	Aurora	319P	80013	18100-18199	
	Aurora	319Q	80013	18500-19199	
	Aurora	319R	80013	19600-19799	
HARVARD DR S	Highlands Ranch	406B	80130	9300-9499	
HARVARD DR W	Lakewood	312R	80227	6000-6399	
	Lakewood	312P	80227	7700-8199	
	Lakewood	312N	80227	8800-9099	
	Lakewood	310Q	80228	13700-13899	
HARVARD LN	Boulder	128P	80305	300-599	
HARVARD LN E	Arapahoe Co	315R	80222	4800-4899	
	Highlands Ranch	406A	80130	6200-6499	
HARVARD PL	Aurora	317Q	80014	None	
HARVARD PL E	Arapahoe Co	812G	80102	43000-43899	
HARVARD PL E	Aurora	319N	80013	16800-16899	
	Aurora	319P	80013	18100-18399	
	Aurora	319Q	80013	18600-18699	
	Aurora	321N	80018	None	
HARVARD PL W	Lakewood	312P	80227	7900-7999	
	Lakewood	312N	80227	8800-9099	
	Lakewood	310U	80228	14100-14199	
HARVARD ST	Longmont	10V	80503	1300-1899	
	Longmont	11N	80503	1900-2199	
	Longmont	10R	80503	2200-2299	
HARVEST CIR	Dacono	726V	80514	None	
HARVEST CT	Adams Co	750E	80603	None	
HARVEST CT S	Aurora	381A	80016	6800-6899	
	Aurora	351W	80016	None	
HARVEST DR	Lafayette	131G	80026	1400-1599	
HARVEST LN	Brighton	139K	80601	None	
HARVEST LN	Highlands Ranch	375T	80126	8300-8499	
HARVEST PL	Broomfield	134G	80516	None	
HARVEST RD	Adams Co	750S	80022	12800-13599	
	Adams Co	750J	80603	None	
	Aurora	810E	80018	1100-1899	
HARVEST RD	Boulder Co	69Y	80301	6700-7099	
HARVEST RD N	Aurora	291N	80018	None	
HARVEST RD S	Arapahoe Co	351J	80016	None	
	Aurora	291S	80018	None	
	Aurora	351J	80016	None	
HARVEST ST	Longmont	42G	80501	200-399	
HARVEST ST S	Aurora	830A	80016	None	
HARVEST MILE WAY S	Aurora	351N	80016	None	
HARVEST POINT DR	Erie	102P	80516	100-499	
HARVEY PL W	Denver	313N	80219	5100-5199	
HARVEY ST E	Douglas Co	467K	80108	800-1199	
HARWICH ST	Boulder Co	100F	80301	4600-4799	
HARWOOD AVE	Parker	410V	80138	23600-23899	
HASELEY DR	Douglas Co	408C	80134	15700-15799	
HASKEL CREEK RD	Douglas Co	889W	80118	11100-11999	
	Douglas Co	908D	80118	12300-12599	
HASKELL CT	Adams Co	791K	80137	2700-2999	
HASKELL PL	Adams Co	791P	80137	2500-2599	
HASKELL WAY	Adams Co	791P	80137	2200-2399	
HASS CT	Dacono	727J	80514	400-499	
HASTINGS AVE	Parker	409N	80134	17000-17099	
HASTINGS CT	Parker	409N	80134	17000-17099	
HASTINGS DR	Boulder	128U	80305	4400-4499	
HASTINGS WAY	Adams Co	223C	80031	8800-8999	
HASTY RD	Jefferson Co	366Q	80439	28700-28899	
HASWELL CT	Parker	409P	80134	11300-11399	
HASWELL DR	Parker	409P	80134	11300-11399	
HATCH DR S	Jefferson Co	336T	80439	5100-5699	
HATCHET RANCH PL E	Douglas Co	439D	80134	20000-20999	
HATFIELD RD	Parker	410V	80138	11300-11399	

H

STREET NAME	CITY or COUNTY	MAP GRID	ZIP CODE	BLOCK RANGE	O/E
HATHAWAY LN	Highlands Ranch	375V	80126	1-99	
HAUCK ST	Erie	132A	80516	1700-1999	
HAUPTMAN CT	Boulder Co	98P	80301	3800-3899	
HAVANA CT	Adams Co	137P	80602	15900-15999	
	Commerce City	197J	80601	10400-10599	
HAVANA CT S	Arapahoe Co	347P	80111	5300-5499	
	Arapahoe Co	347T	80111	5500-5899	
HAVANA ST	Adams Co	137P	80602	15000-15999	
	Adams Co	137K	80602	None	
	Aurora	287P	80010	1-2499	
	Commerce City	197T	80640	9600-10399	
	Commerce City	197K	80601	10400-11199	
	Commerce City	197K	80640	11200-11999	
	Denver	257T	80239	3600-5599	
HAVANA ST S	Arapahoe Co	347P	80111	5100-6399	
	Arapahoe Co	377F	80112	7300-7399	
	Aurora	287X	80012	2-698	E
	Aurora	317B	80112	700-999	
	Aurora	317B	80012	1000-1098	E
	Aurora	317F	80012	1100-1899	
	Aurora	317P	80014	1900-2499	
	Aurora	317T	80014	2500-3098	E
	Centennial	377F	80112	6700-7299	
	Denver	317B	80012	1001-1099	O
	Denver	317T	80014	2701-2799	O
	Denver	317X	80014	3100-3499	
	Douglas Co	407E	80112	None	
HAVANA WAY	Adams Co	137P	80602	15600-15999	
	Denver	257X	80238	None	
	Denver	257X	80239	None	
HAVEKOST RD	Jefferson Co	823N	80433	9900-9999	
HAVENWOOD DR	Castle Pines North	436P	80108	7100-7299	
HAVENWOOD WAY	Castle Pines North	436P	80108	1200-1299	
HAVILAH ST	Central City	780D	80427	300-399	
HAWAII AVE W	Jefferson Co	311F	80232	11400-11499	
	Lakewood	311G	80232	10000-10099	
	Lakewood	310M	80228	12500-12699	
HAWAII CIR E	Aurora	317G	80112	11900-12099	
	Aurora	318F	80012	14200-14499	
HAWAII DR E	Arapahoe Co	316M	80231	8600-8699	
	Aurora	317H	80112	12100-12199	
	Aurora	319E	80017	16801-16899	O
	Aurora	319G	80017	18700-18999	
HAWAII DR W	Lakewood	312E	80232	8600-8799	
	Lakewood	311G	80232	9800-9999	
HAWAII LN E	Arapahoe Co	316M	80231	8400-8499	
	Arapahoe Co	316H	80247	None	
HAWAII PL E	Aurora	317E	80247	9700-10099	
	Aurora	318F	80012	14500-14799	
	Aurora	319E	80017	17600-17699	
	Aurora	319F	80017	17800-18399	
	Aurora	319G	80017	18800-18999	
	Aurora	320H	80018	None	
HAWAII PL W	Jefferson Co	311F	80232	11100-11299	
	Lakewood	311L	80232	10100-10199	
HAWK CT	Lafayette	132W	80026	2900-2999	
HAWK CT	Louisville	130U	80027	1000-1099	
HAWK LN	Boulder Co	722V	80304	1-399	
HAWK ST	Federal Heights	193U	80260	2400-2999	
HAWK WAY	Gilpin Co	760V	80403	1-199	
HAWKEN DR	Douglas Co	867Q	80109	2200-2799	
HAWKINS AVE	Jefferson Co	823U	80433	10800-11999	
HAWK POINT CT	Castle Rock	498E	80104	2600-2899	
HAWK RIDGE CIR	Lafayette	132B	80026	None	
HAWK RIDGE RD	Lafayette	132B	80026	1200-1299	
HAWKS CIR	Jefferson Co	337R	80439	24400-24699	
HAWKSBEAD DR E	Parker	409A	80134	17100-17599	
HAWKS EYE CT	Castle Rock	467M	80108	6100-6299	
HAWK'S NEST TRAIL W	Douglas Co	432N	80125	6300-7799	
HAWKS RIM TRAIL S	Parker	408Z	80134	None	
HAWKSTONE PL	Douglas Co	408D	80134	16200-16399	
HAWKSTONE WAY	Douglas Co	408D	80134	9500-9599	
HAWK TERRACE	Castle Rock	527D	80104	None	
HAWTHORN AVE	Boulder	97U	80304	200-1899	
	Boulder	98S	80304	2300-2599	
HAWTHORN CIR	Greenwood Village	346S	80121	5400-5599	
HAWTHORN CT	Louisville	130R	80027	300-399	
HAWTHORN LN	Douglas Co	850X	80116	2000-2199	
HAWTHORN LN	Lakewood	312Q	80227	6300-6399	
HAWTHORN PL	Boulder	97R	80304	1700-1899	
	Boulder	98S	80304	2600-2699	
HAWTHORN ST	Frederick	727B	80530	100-799	
HAWTHORN ST	Louisville	130Q	80027	500-699	
HAWTHORNE CIR	Longmont	40Q	80503	3900-4099	
HAWTHORNE CT	Douglas Co	439T	80134	None	
HAWTHORNE DR	Broomfield	163S	80020	4200-4399	
HAWTHORNE DR	Highlands Ranch	405F	80126	3300-3599	
HAWTHORNE DR	Longmont	40Q	80503	None	
HAWTHORNE LN	Dacono	727S	80514	None	
HAWTHORNE LN	Parker	410W	80138	21000-21199	
HAWTHORNE PL	Longmont	40Q	80503	4100-4199	
HAWTHORNE PL E	Denver	285N	80206	2100-2199	
HAWTHORNE PL W	Adams Co	223Y	80221	3000-3299	
HAWTHORNE RD	Lakewood	280L	80401	1000-1399	
HAWTHORNE ST	Highlands Ranch	405F	80126	9800-9999	
HAWTHORNE ST S	Denver	343L	80110	4700-4799	
	Littleton	343Q	80110	5000-5099	
HAWTHORN HOLLOW	Boulder	97V	80304	3200-3299	
HAWTHORN TRAIL	Douglas Co	845Q	80125	5300-5499	
HAXTUN CT	Parker	409N	80134	11200-11299	
HAYDEN CT	Longmont	40D	80503	700-899	
HAYDEN PL	Boulder	98U	80301	3400-3799	
HAYDEN PASS	Jefferson Co	371L	80127	10300-10399	
HAYES ST	Park Co	820V	80421	1-399	
HAYESMOUNT RD	Adams Co	750U	80022	12800-13598	E
	Adams Co	750U	80603	14000-16799	
HAYESMOUNT RD	Arapahoe Co	790Y	80137	600-1499	
HAYESMOUNT RD N	Arapahoe Co	790V	80137	300-598	E
HAYFORK CT	Parker	408V	80134	11800-11899	
HAYLOFT WAY	Brighton	139K	80601	None	
HAYS CIR	Boulder	128G	80303	None	
HAYS CIR	Longmont	42C	80501	700-899	
HAYS CT	Erie	102W	80516	1500-1599	
HAYS CT	Louisville	130Q	80027	1500-1599	
HAYS DR	Louisville	130Q	80027	1700-1799	
HAYSTACK CT	Boulder Co	70L	80503	8400-8499	
HAYSTACK CT	Douglas Co	497V	80104	800-999	
HAYSTACK DR	Castle Rock	497Z	80104	1000-1599	
HAYSTACK LN	Brighton	139G	80601	None	
HAYSTACK LN	Jefferson Co	275X	80439	33600-33799	
HAYSTACK LN	Westminster	222A	80021	None	
HAYSTACK RD	Douglas Co	497V	80104	1000-3599	
HAYSTACK ST	Longmont	42J	80501	None	
HAYSTACK WAY	Lafayette	131G	80026	None	
HAYSTACK RANCH RD	Douglas Co	887J	80118	None	
HAYSTACK ROW	Cherry Hills Village	345B	80113	1-99	
HAYWAGON LN	Castle Rock	469K	80108	5700-5999	
HAYWARD PL	Longmont	11T	80501	1800-1999	
HAYWARD PL W	Denver	253Y	80211	3200-3499	
	Denver	253X	80212	4001-4099	O
	Denver	253W	80212	4400-4999	
HAZEL AVE S	Jefferson Co	842J	80470	13900-14099	
HAZEL CT	Broomfield	163U	80020	12600-12699	
	Broomfield	163Q	80020	13000-13199	
	Denver	283U	80219	1-299	
	Denver	283L	80204	700-1199	
	Denver	283C	80211	2600-2699	
	Denver	253Y	80211	2700-2899	
HAZEL CT	Douglas Co	432F	80125	10300-10399	
	Westminster	193Y	80031	9200-9299	
HAZEL CT S	Denver	283Y	80219	1-699	
	Denver	313C	80219	900-1099	
	Denver	313L	80219	1500-2699	
	Denver	313U	80236	2700-2799	
	Sheridan	343C	80110	3600-3899	
	Sheridan	343G	80110	3900-4199	
HAZEL DR	Broomfield	163Q	80020	12900-12999	
HAZEL PL	Broomfield	163L	80020	13400-13599	
	Westminster	193Y	80031	3200-3399	
HAZEL RD	Jefferson Co	336T	80439	5100-5499	
HAZEL ST	Broomfield	163U	80020	12500-12799	
HAZEL WAY	Broomfield	163U	80020	None	
HAZEL WAY S	Denver	313Q	80219	None	
HAZELNUT AVE E	Parker	439E	80134	None	
HAZEL SPRUCE CT	Parker	439D	80134	12200-12299	
HAZELWOOD CT	Boulder	98P	80304	3600-3699	
HAZELWOOD DR	Boulder Co	741L	80466	1-299	
HAZY HILLS DR	Parker	410Y	80138	None	
HEADLIGHT RD	Adams Co	794Q	80136	1500-15999	
HEALTH PARK DR	Louisville	160G	80027	2-198	E
HEARTH DR	Jefferson Co	306N	80439	2300-2499	
HEARTHSTONE ST	Brighton	140J	80601	None	
HEART LAKE WAY	Broomfield	163P	80020	13201-13299	O
HEARTLAND DR	Commerce City	198M	80022	None	
HEARTSTRONG ST E	Superior	160L	80027	600-899	
HEARTWOOD CT	Lafayette	132S	80026	2300-2399	
HEARTWOOD WAY	Castle Rock	466X	80109	4500-4699	
HEATHCLIFF LN	Parker	409J	80134	10300-10399	
HEATHER CT	Broomfield	162M	80020	5300-5399	
	Castle Pines North	436C	80108	9000-9199	
HEATHER DR N	Douglas Co	436G	80108	8300-8599	
	Douglas Co	406Y	80108	9200-10099	
HEATHER LN	Parker	409Z	80138	20300-20499	
HEATHER PL	Adams Co	223R	80221	7500-7699	
HEATHER RD	Jefferson Co	250X	80401	2800-2899	
HEATHER WAY	Boulder Co	69K	80503	5900-6099	
HEATHER WAY	Jefferson Co	280B	80401	1-2699	
HEATHERDOWNS	El Paso Co	908U	80132	500-699	
HEATHER GARDENS WAY S	Aurora	318S	80014	2700-3199	
HEATHERGLEN CT	Highlands Ranch	405M	80130	None	
HEATHERGLEN DR	Highlands Ranch	405M	80130	None	
HEATHERGLEN PT	Highlands Ranch	405M	80130	None	
HEATHERGLENN LN	Castle Rock	528A	80104	None	
HEATHERHILL CIR	Longmont	40U	80503	None	
HEATHERTON CIR	Highlands Ranch	405R	80130	None	
HEATHERTON LN	Highlands Ranch	405R	80130	None	
HEATHERTON ST	Highlands Ranch	405R	80130	None	
HEATHERWOOD CT	Boulder Co	100E	80301	4700-4799	
HEATHERWOOD CT	Highlands Ranch	405L	80126	10000-10098	E
HEATHERWOOD DR	Boulder Co	100E	80301	7500-7999	
HEATHERWOOD LN	Highlands Ranch	405F	80126	9900-10099	
HEATHERWOOD PL	Highlands Ranch	405F	80126	10000-10099	
HEATHERWOOD WAY	Jefferson Co	305Z	80439	3600-3699	
HEAVENLY CT	Jefferson Co	306P	80439	30400-30499	
HECLA DR	Louisville	131P	80027	1300-1399	
HECLA WAY	Louisville	131P	80027	1400-1499	
HEDGE LN	Douglas Co	408H	80134	10200-10299	
HEDGEROW CIR	Lafayette	131J	80027	2600-2799	
HEDGEROW WAY	Brighton	139L	80601	None	
HEDGES AVE	Weld Co	727B	80530	100-199	
HEDGEWAY CT	Douglas Co	408H	80134	9800-9899	
HEDGEWAY DR	Douglas Co	408G	80134	15900-16399	
HEIDE ST	Castle Rock	497C	80104	None	
HEIDELBERG DR	Boulder	128X	80305	2600-3499	
HEIDEMANN AVE	Douglas Co	870X	80116	11000-11599	
HEINZE WAY	Commerce City	196Z	80640	9200-9299	
HEINZE WAY	Commerce City	197W	80640	10400-10499	
HEIRLOOM WAY	Longmont	12T	80501	1600-1699	
HEIR VALLEY RD	Douglas Co	846R	80135	None	
HEITER HILL RD	Jefferson Co	367L	80439	7200-7399	
HELEHA ST	Aurora	288G	80011	1700-2099	
HELEN CT	Elbert Co	851E	80138	2000-2199	
HELENA CIR	Highlands Ranch	376Y	80124	1-599	
HELENA CIR S	Aurora	318G	80017	1400-1599	
HELENA CT	Aurora	288Q	80011	400-599	
	Commerce City	198U	80022	9800-9899	
	Denver	258L	80239	5000-5099	
	Denver	258G	80239	5500-5599	
HELENA CT S	Centennial	348U	80015	5600-5699	
	Centennial	348U	80016	5900-5999	
HELENA DR	Highlands Ranch	376U	80124	None	
HELENA ST	Aurora	288Q	80011	600-799	
	Aurora	288L	80011	1300-1499	
	Aurora	288G	80011	1700-2098	E
	Aurora	258U	80011	3300-3698	E
	Commerce City	198Q	80022	9900-10199	
	Commerce City	198C	80022	11700-11899	
	Commerce City	168Y	80603	None	
	Commerce City	198G	80022	None	
	Denver	258L	80239	5000-5299	
	Denver	258G	80239	5500-5599	
HELENA ST S	Aurora	318L	80017	1700-1899	
	Aurora	318L	80013	1900-2099	
	Aurora	318Y	80013	2900-3399	
	Aurora	348C	80013	3800-3999	
	Centennial	348Q	80015	5400-5599	
	Centennial	348U	80015	5600-5699	
	Centennial	348U	80016	5900-5999	
	Centennial	378C	80016	6300-6699	
HELENA WAY S	Aurora	318C	80017	900-1199	
	Aurora	318U	80013	2700-2899	
	Aurora	348C	80013	3600-3899	
	Aurora	348G	80015	4300-4499	
	Aurora	348L	80015	4700-4799	
HEMATITE LN	Lochbuie	139H	80603	1700-1899	
HEMLOCK CIR	Louisville	130Y	80027	700-799	
HEMLOCK CT S	Highlands Ranch	406B	80130	9600-9699	
HEMLOCK DR	Jefferson Co	842H	80433	27600-27799	
HEMLOCK DR S	Jefferson Co	842H	80433	27600-27699	
HEMLOCK LN	Jefferson Co	365F	80439	33800-33899	
HEMLOCK PL	Boulder	98S	80304	3300-3399	
HEMLOCK ST	Broomfield	162X	80020	100-399	
HEMLOCK WAY	Broomfield	162X	80020	1-199	
	Broomfield	162T	80020	800-1099	
	Broomfield	162P	80020	1600-1799	
HENDEE CT	Erie	102Q	80516	500-699	
HENDERSON CT	Boulder Co	101C	80026	4800-4899	
HENDERSON RD	Adams Co	166V	80640	9600-9799	
	Brighton	167S	80601	8900-10499	
HENDRICKS ST	Nederland	740Q	80466	None	
HENERY CT	Douglas Co	867P	80109	2000-2199	
HENNINGTON CT	Longmont	11Q	80501	1800-1899	
HENRY AVE	Weld Co	728Y	80621	7000-7999	
HENRY CT	Longmont	11U	80501	None	
HENRY PL S	Denver	315Q	80210	2300-2399	
HENRY ST	Weld Co	729B	80621	7000-7999	
HENSON CREEK ST	Parker	439F	80134	12700-12799	
HEPBURN ST	Highlands Ranch	404A	80129	None	
	Highlands Ranch	374W	80129	None	
HERA CT	Lafayette	131V	80026	1100-1199	
HERCULES CIR	Lafayette	131R	80026	900-999	
HERITAGE AVE N	Castle Rock	498H	80104	1-1499	
HERITAGE AVE S	Castle Rock	498L	80104	1-199	
HERITAGE CIR	Thornton	136Y	80602	15300-15399	
HERITAGE DR	Thornton	136Y	80602	None	
HERITAGE PKWY E	Aurora	380Q	80016	22900-23499	
HERITAGE PL E	Centennial	346X	80111	6500N-7199N	
	Centennial	376B	80111	6600S-7199S	
HERITAGE PL S	Centennial	376B	80111	6400E-6599E	
	Centennial	376B	80111	6400W-6699W	
HERITAGE RD	Golden	279P	80401	600-799	
HERITAGE WAY	Castle Rock	498K	80104	4100-4199	
HERITAGE HILLS CIR	Lone Tree	406D	80124	8900-9199	
	Lone Tree	407E	80124	9200-9599	
HERITAGE HILLS PKWY	Lone Tree	407A	80124	9200-9899	
HERITAGE HILLS PKWY S	Lone Tree	376Z	80124	9200-9299	
	Lone Tree	377W	80124	None	
HERITAGE TRAIL	Elbert Co	870Q	80107	400-599	
HERMAN PL	Longmont	11Q	80501	900-1099	
HERMES CIR	Lafayette	131M	80026	700-999	
HERMITAGE RUN	Douglas Co	432J	80125	11000-11099	
HERMOSA CIR	Northglenn	194K	80234	None	
HERMOSA CT	Northglenn	194K	80234	10800-10999	
HERMOSA DR	Boulder	98S	80304	2000-2199	
HERMOSA DR E	Highlands Ranch	404D	80126	1400-1799	
HERMOSA ST	Lochbuie	139H	80603	100-499	
HERON CT	Longmont	11N	80503	2000-2099	
HERON CT	Park Co	841U	80421	1-399	
HERON ST	Brighton	139V	80601	101-599	O
HERRING RD	El Paso Co	910X	80908	16500-17499	
HERRN LN	Castle Pines North	436F	80108	1-99	
HERSHEY CT	Erie	102Q	80516	400-499	
HERZMAN DR	Jefferson Co	337S	80439	5500-6199	
HESS AVE	Jefferson Co	278T	80401	1-599	
HESS RD	Boulder Co	742W	80403	1201-1299	O
HESS RD	Douglas Co	439A	80134	5100-5999	
HESS RD	Parker	439C	80134	19000-20099	
	Parker	439D	80134	None	
	Parker	440A	80134	None	
	Parker	848D	80134	None	
HESSIE CT	Lafayette	131E	80026	501-599	O
HEXTON CT	Lone Tree	406G	80124	10200-10299	
HEYWOOD LN S	Highlands Ranch	405G	80130	10000-10099	
HEYWOOD ST S	Highlands Ranch	405G	80130	9900-10199	
HEYWOOD WAY	Highlands Ranch	405G	80130	4300-4499	
HIALEAH AVE E	Centennial	348R	80015	16600-16699	
HIALEAH AVE W	Littleton	343Q	80123	3300-3399	
HIALEAH DR E	Centennial	348R	80015	16300-16899	
HIALEAH PL S	Aurora	348Q	80015	15200-15299	
HIALEAH PL W	Jefferson Co	341R	80123	9100-9599	
	Jefferson Co	341P	80127	10800-11699	
HIAWATHA ST	Boulder	129J	80303	200-599	
HIAWATHA TRAIL	Jefferson Co	338V	80454	5500-5699	
HIBISCUS DR S	Highlands Ranch	404D	80126	9400-9499	
HIBISCUS WAY S	Denver	345D	80237	3600-3899	
HICKMAN PL	Denver	257H	80239	12300-12699	
HICKOCK DR E	Parker	439G	80134	19000-19299	
HICKOK PL	Boulder	98T	80301	3300-3399	
HICKOK TRAIL	Boulder Co	721C	80481	1-199	
HICKORY	Platteville	708B	80651	None	
HICKORY AVE	Boulder	128H	80303	100-5399	
HICKORY AVE	Weld Co	706U	80504	None	
HICKORY CIR	Frederick	727A	80516	None	
HICKORY CIR	Highlands Ranch	374Y	80126	9100-9399	
HICKORY CIR S	Littleton	344T	80120	5600-5699	
HICKORY CT	Erie	133C	80516	None	
HICKORY CT	Louisville	130U	80027	600-699	
HICKORY DR	Erie	133B	80516	1200-1599	
HICKORY DR S	Littleton	344T	80120	5500-5599	
HICKORY LN	Thornton	193Z	80260	None	
HICKORY PL	Broomfield	192C	80020	400-499	
HICKORY PL	Erie	133G	80516	None	
HICKORY PL	Thornton	224D	80229	8900-9099	
HICKORY PL S	Littleton	374K	80120	7700-7799	
HICKORY ST	Broomfield	192C	80020	400-499	
HICKORY ST	Fort Lupton	728H	80621	2000-2099	
HICKORY ST	Hudson	730L	80642	None	
HICKORY ST	Longmont	42N	80501	None	
HICKORY ST	Louisville	130U	80027	600-699	
HICKORY ST S	Littleton	344P	80120	5100-5499	
	Littleton	344T	80120	5600-5899	
HICKORY WAY S	Littleton	344T	80120	5700-5799	
HICKORY RIDGE LN	Highlands Ranch	405Q	80126	10700-10899	
HICKORY RIDGE ST	Highlands Ranch	405Q	80126	10700-10899	
HIDALGO WAY	Castle Rock	468M	80108	5500-6099	
HIDDEN HILL CT E	Lone Tree	377W	80124	9200-9399	
HIDDEN HILL LN E	Lone Tree	377W	80124	9300-9599	

STREET NAME	CITY or COUNTY	MAP GRID	ZIP CODE	BLOCK RANGE	O/E
HIDDEN HILL PL	Lone Tree	377W	80124	None	
HIDDENMARSH RD	El Paso Co	908U	80132	500-699	
HIDDEN MEADOW CT	Elbert Co	851Y	80107	5000-5199	
HIDDEN MEADOW DR	Jefferson Co	305E	80439	34600-34799	
HIDDEN MEADOWS PL	Elbert Co	850D	80138	None	
HIDDEN OAKS CT	Douglas Co	440Z	80134	None	
HIDDEN OAKS WAY	Douglas Co	440Z	80134	None	
HIDDEN PINES CT	Douglas Co	470D	80134	9300-9499	
HIDDEN POINT WAY	Castle Pines North	436C	80108	None	
HIDDEN POINTE BLVD					
	Castle Pines North	436C	80108	500-599	
HIDDEN POND PL	Douglas Co	467E	80108	5000-5099	
HIDDEN RIDGE PL	Douglas Co	847S	80109	3100-3399	
HIDDEN RIVER LN	Parker	409Z	80138	None	
HIDDEN SPRINGS GLEN	El Paso Co	908P	80132	19500-19899	
HIDDEN TRAIL	Jefferson Co	822R	80433	27700-27999	
HIDDEN TRAIL CT S	Parker	410Y	80138	None	
HIDDEN TRAIL DR E	Parker	410X	80138	22100-22499	
HIDDEN VALLEY BLVD	Park Co	821U	80421	1-2499	
	Park Co	841C	80470	2500-3199	
HIDDEN VALLEY LN	Douglas Co	436X	80108	200-299	
HIDDEN VALLEY RD	Douglas Co	866N	80135	1500-3999	
	Douglas Co	887T	80118	None	
HIDDEN VILLAGE DR	Jefferson Co	336D	80439	27600-29299	
HIDDEN WILDERNESS CT					
	Clear Creek Co	781W	80452	None	
HIDDEN WILDERNESS WAY					
	Clear Creek Co	781W	80452	None	
HIDEAWAY CIR	Clear Creek Co	781Z	80439	1-3699	
HIDEAWAY TRAIL	Clear Creek Co	781Z	80439	1-99	
HIDEOUT CIR	Elbert Co	851M	80107	6800-6999	
HIER LN	Douglas Co	496Q	80109	1-599	
HIGBY RD	El Paso Co	908Z	80132	1-1399	
	El Paso Co	909W	80132	1400-2099	
HIGGINS AVE	Weld Co	729A	80621	15000-16599	
HIGH CIR	Jefferson Co	368B	80465	6300-6599	
HIGH CIR	Thornton	165J	80241	13500-13599	
HIGH CT	Wheat Ridge	252T	80033	3500-3899	
HIGH CT E	Centennial	375N	80122	8200-8299	
HIGH CT S	Greenwood Village	345S	80121	5900-5999	
HIGH DR	Castle Rock	497G	80104	300-599	
HIGH DR	Jefferson Co	337V	80439	5700-5899	
	Jefferson Co	338X	80465	5900-6199	
	Jefferson Co	368B	80465	6200-6999	
HIGH LN	Jefferson Co	368B	80465	22400-22599	
HIGH PKWY	Golden	249W	80403	100-599	
HIGH RD	Jefferson Co	307Y	80439	25000-25099	
HIGH RD S	Jefferson Co	336Q	80439	5200-5399	
HIGH ST	Adams Co	255A	80216	5500-5598	E
	Adams Co	225E	80229	8200-8299	
HIGH ST	Black Hawk	780D	80422	1-99	
HIGH ST	Boulder	97Z	80304	1200-1699	
HIGH ST	Central City	780C	80427	400-499	
HIGH ST	Denver	285N	80218	100-799	
	Denver	285E	80218	1200-1999	
	Denver	285A	80205	2000-2699	
	Denver	255W	80205	2700-3999	
	Denver	255N	80216	4600-4799	
HIGH ST	Erie	102H	80516	100-898	E
	Erie	102R	80516	None	
HIGH ST	Frederick	727A	80516	None	
HIGH ST	Gilpin Co	740Y	80403	None	
HIGH ST	Idaho Springs	780Q	80452	700-899	
HIGH ST	Jamestown	722A	80455	None	
HIGH ST	Northglenn	195E	80233	11200-11499	
	Northglenn	194D	80233	11700-11999	
HIGH ST	Palmer Lake	907Q	80133	None	
HIGH ST	Thornton	195W	80229	9100-9499	
	Thornton	195N	80229	9700-9899	
	Thornton	164R	80241	13000-13299	
	Thornton	165N	80241	13300-13499	
	Thornton	165J	80241	13500-13599	
	Thornton	135J	80602	16500-16599	
	Thornton	165A	80602	None	
HIGH ST E	Central City	780D	80427	1-299	
HIGH ST S	Centennial	375A	80121	6300-6799	
	Centennial	375J	80122	7700-7999	
	Cherry Hills Village	345E	80113	4300-4599	
	Denver	285W	80209	200-699	
	Denver	315A	80209	700-1099	
	Denver	315E	80210	1100-1299	
	Denver	315N	80210	1700-3099	
	Englewood	315W	80113	3100-3299	
HIGH ST W	Central City	780C	80427	1-99	
	Gilpin Co	761E	80403	1-199	
HIGH CANAL CT	Broomfield	133L	80020	None	
HIGH CLIFFE PL W	Highlands Ranch	403C	80129	2700-2899	
HIGH CLIFFE ST S	Highlands Ranch	403C	80129	9400-9599	
HIGH COUNTRY CT	Boulder	69Y	80301	5500-5599	
HIGH COUNTRY CT	Lafayette	131K	80026	100-199	
HIGH COUNTRY DR	Lafayette	131K	80026	100-199	
HIGH COUNTRY TRAIL	Elbert Co	852P	80107	7900-8899	
HIGH COUNTRY TRAIL	Lafayette	131K	80026	100-199	
HIGH COUNTY TRAIL	Jefferson Co	844D	80127	12200-12499	
HIGH DESERT PL	Parker	408V	80134	16500-16599	
HIGH DESERT RD	Parker	408V	80134	11800-11899	
HIGH DESERT WAY	Parker	408V	80134	16500-16599	
HIGHGRADE RD	Jefferson Co	824X	80127	16300-18099	
HIGHLAND AVE	Boulder	97Y	80302	400-799	
HIGHLAND BLVD	Lochbuie	140B	80603	None	
	Lochbuie	729Y	80603	None	
HIGH LAND CIR	Elbert Co	852K	80107	8600-8899	
HIGHLAND CIR N	Highlands Ranch	373X	80125	13000-13299	
HIGHLAND CT S	Littleton	373M	80120	7400-7499	
HIGHLAND DR	Boulder Co	703D	80503	4500-5099	
HIGHLAND DR	Lakewood	282P	80214	7000-7599	
HIGHLAND DR	Longmont	12X	80501	400-699	
HIGHLAND DR	Mead	706G	80504	None	
HIGHLAND DR S	Littleton	373H	80120	7200-7399	
HIGHLAND PL	Adams Co	223C	80031	3100-3599	
HIGHLAND PL	Arvada	251H	80002	9200-9499	
HIGHLAND PL	Weld Co	726J	80516	None	
HIGHLAND RD	Palmer Lake	907Q	80133	None	
HIGHLAND WAY	Weld Co	726J	80516	None	
HIGHLANDER RD	Jefferson Co	762A	80403	11900-11999	
HIGHLAND ESTATES DR	El Paso Co	910X	80908	17500-18499	
HIGHLAND MEADOW CIR	Douglas Co	407G	80134	10100-10399	
HIGHLAND MEADOW LOOP					
	Douglas Co	407G	80134	10100-10199	
HIGHLAND PARK DR	Broomfield	162Z	80020	900-1499	
HIGHLAND PARK PL W	Denver	253Y	80211	3000-3299	
HIGHLANDS DR	Boulder Co	723D	80503	5300-5399	
HIGHLANDS DR	Park Co	820X	80421	1-499	
HIGHLANDS RANCH PKWY E					
	Highlands Ranch	404D	80126	1-2199	
	Highlands Ranch	405A	80126	2200-3799	
HIGHLANDS RANCH PKWY W					
	Highlands Ranch	404A	80129	1-1899	
	Highlands Ranch	403G	80129	1900-3699	
HIGHLANDS VIEW CT	Douglas Co	406Q	80124	10700-10899	
HIGHLANDS VIEW RD	Jefferson Co	307T	80439	None	
HIGHLINE CIR E	Arapahoe Co	374C	80122	1-599	
HIGHLINE CIR S	Greenwood Village	345Q	80121	5400-5499	
	Greenwood Village	345T	80121	5800-5899	
HIGHLINE DR	Northglenn	194G	80233	11200-11399	
HIGHLINE DR E	Aurora	287T	80010	11100-11499	
HIGHLINE PL	Denver	315U	80222	4400-4799	
	Denver	315V	80222	5200-5399	
HIGHLINE PL E	Aurora	287U	80010	11500-11599	
HIGH LONESOME PT	Lafayette	131K	80026	100-299	
HIGH LONESOME TRAIL	Lafayette	131K	80026	2300-2499	
HIGH MEADOW DR	El Paso Co	908Q	80132	19900-19999	
HIGH MEADOW DR	Jefferson Co	308A	80401	23800-24099	
HIGH MEADOW WAY	Douglas Co	847T	80109	3800-4099	
HIGH MEADOWS LOOP	Elbert Co	870Q	80107	200-299	
HIGH PINES DR	El Paso Co	908P	80132	None	
HIGH PLAINS CIR	Elbert Co	852K	80107	8000-8299	
HIGH PLAINS CT	Lafayette	131A	80026	1400-1499	
HIGHPLAINS CT	Superior	160P	80027	1601-1799	O
HIGHPLAINS DR	Superior	160P	80027	1600-2098	E
HIGH PLAINS PL	Castle Rock	498M	80104	None	
HIGH PLAINS ST	Castle Rock	498M	80104	None	
HIGHPOINT CIR	Gilpin Co	761N	80403	1-1899	
HIGH POINT DR	Golden	248Z	80403	500-599	
HIGH POINT RD	Castle Rock	498G	80108	4100-4199	
HIGH PRAIRIE WAY	Broomfield	133Y	80020	2600-2999	
HIGH RIDGE CT	Castle Pines North	436G	80108	8400-8599	
HIGH RIDGE WAY	Castle Pines North	436C	80108	300-399	
HIGH SPRING RD	Douglas Co	527X	80104	4500-4699	
HIGH SPRING TRAIL	Jefferson Co	368L	80465	7600-7799	
HIGHTREE DR	El Paso Co	911X	80106	16600-16999	
HIGH VIEW DR	Boulder Co	97J	80304	1-299	
HIGHVIEW DR	El Paso Co	909T	80908	3500-4199	
HIGHVIEW DR	Jefferson Co	822W	80470	11700-35599	
HIGHVIEW DR	Weld Co	726J	80516	None	
HIGH VIEW LN	Boulder Co	722L	80302	1-599	
HIGH VIEW LN	Park Co	841Q	80421	1-99	
HIGHVIEW RD	El Paso Co	909X	80908	3500-3999	
HIGHWAY 85	Castle Rock	467T	80109	None	
HI-LAND CIR	Adams Co	137N	80602	16000-16199	
	Adams Co	137N	80602	None	
HILARY CT	Broomfield	163T	80020	3900-3999	
HILARY CT S	Parker	409V	80138	11400-11499	
HILARY PL S	Parker	409V	80138	11300-11399	
HILL CIR	Clear Creek Co	304P	80439	1-99	
HILL CIR S	Littleton	373M	80120	7700-7899	
HILL CT	Castle Rock	497R	80104	200-299	
HILL CT N	Douglas Co	440P	80134	6900-6999	
HILL DR	Brighton	139N	80601	None	
HILL DR	Castle Rock	497R	80104	100-199	
HILL DR	Jefferson Co	369N	80465	19300-19699	
HILL DR N	Park Co	841M	80421	1-599	
HILL DR S	Littleton	373M	80120	7600-7899	
HILL ST	Boulder Co	721R	80302	1-899	
HILL ST S	Littleton	343V	80120	5500-5599	
	Littleton	343Z	80120	5900-6399	
	Littleton	373D	80120	6400-6799	
	Littleton	373H	80120	6800-7099	
HILL WAY S	Littleton	373D	80120	6500-6699	
HILL AND DALE RD	Jefferson Co	308B	80401	800-899	
HILLARY CIR N	Douglas Co	470A	80134	5300-5399	
HILLCREST CIR	Douglas Co	866P	80135	7700-7799	
HILLCREST CIR	Jefferson Co	278T	80401	22300-22499	
HILL CREST CT	El Paso Co	911Y	80106	17000-17199	
HILLCREST DR	Boulder Co	11G	80504	10500-10599	
	Boulder Co	11L	80504	12600-12999	
HILLCREST DR	Douglas Co	846G	80135	7800-7999	
HILLCREST DR	Federal Heights	224A	80260	None	
HILLCREST DR S	Denver	346A	80237	3500-3999	
HILLCREST RD	Jefferson Co	762B	80403	11600-11999	
HILLCREST WAY E	Douglas Co	440P	80134	8100-8399	
HILLCROFT LN	Castle Rock	528J	80104	2800-2999	
HILLDALE DR	Jefferson Co	823R	80465	9700-9899	
HILL GAIL CT	Parker	410P	80138	11000-11099	
HILL GAIL PL	Parker	410P	80138	21600-21699	
HILL GAIL WAY	Parker	410P	80138	21500-22099	
HILLGATE WAY E	Douglas Co	440N	80134	7600-7799	
HILLPARK AVE N	Douglas Co	440P	80134	6600-6999	
HILL PARK CIR N	Douglas Co	440P	80134	6900-6999	
HILLPOINT PL N	Douglas Co	440P	80134	6800-6999	
HILLRIDGE PL N	Douglas Co	440P	80134	6700-6999	
HILLROSE DR	Douglas Co	408K	80134	None	
HILLROSE LN S	Superior	160R	80027	1500-1599	
HILLROSE PL	Douglas Co	408K	80134	None	
HILLROSE ST	Douglas Co	408K	80134	None	
HILLS CT S	Denver	315X	80210	3100-3199	
HILLS DR E	Douglas Co	409M	80138	6600-6999	
HILLSBORO CIR	Douglas Co	408P	80134	None	
HILLSBORO DR	Douglas Co	408L	80134	None	
HILLSBORO ST	Douglas Co	408P	80134	None	
HILLSDALE CIR	Boulder	128N	80305	2000-2299	
HILLSDALE WAY	Boulder	128S	80305	2300-2399	
HILLSIDE	Thornton	194W	80260	None	
HILLSIDE AVE W	Denver	313R	80219	2400-2799	
	Englewood	313R	80110	2000-2399	
HILLSIDE CIR	Douglas Co	866P	80135	1500-1699	
HILLSIDE CIR E	Douglas Co	440P	80134	8400-8499	
HILLSIDE CT	Boulder Co	722L	80302	1-299	
HILLSIDE CT	Broomfield	133U	80020	15300-15399	
HILLSIDE CT	Douglas Co	440Q	80134	None	
HILLSIDE CT	Elbert Co	871J	80107	33000-33199	
HILLSIDE CT	Longmont	41A	80501	800-899	
HILL SIDE CT	Louisville	130X	80027	1100-1199	
HILLSIDE DR	Castle Rock	497L	80104	100-399	
	Wheat Ridge	251Y	80215	1-99	
HILLSIDE DR	Wheat Ridge	281C	80215	1-99	
HILL SIDE LN	Louisville	130X	80027	1100-1199	
HILLSIDE PL E	Denver	316T	80224	6900-6999	
HILLSIDE PL W	Denver	313Q	80219	3000-3199	
	Littleton	343P	80123	3800-4399	
HILLSIDE RD	Boulder	127D	80302	1500-1899	
HILLSIDE RD	Clear Creek Co	801R	80439	1-299	
HILLSIDE RD	Jefferson Co	822Z	80433	11800-11999	
HILLSIDE RD	Palmer Lake	907Q	80133	None	
HILLSIDE ST	Aurora	287K	80010	1100-1299	
HILLSIDE ST	Black Hawk	780D	80422	100-199	
HILLSIDE ST S	Greenwood Village	347T	80111	5500-5799	
HILLSIDE WAY	Douglas Co	907F	80118	None	
HILLSIDE WAY N	Douglas Co	440Q	80134	6500-6999	
HILLSIDE TERRACE	Lafayette	131B	80026	2300-2399	
HILLSIDE TRAIL	Elbert Co	831Q	80138	46000-46799	
HILL SPRUCE	Jefferson Co	370P	80127	1-99	
HILLSTON ST	Lone Tree	406M	80124	None	
HILLSTONE LN	Jefferson Co	336R	80439	5000-5099	
HILLS VIEW DR	Boulder Co	71N	80503	9200-9499	
HILLTOP CIR	Adams Co	224N	80221	7500-7699	
HILLTOP CT	Broomfield	133L	80020	None	
HILLTOP DR	Brighton	139T	80601	15300-15699	
HILL TOP DR	Jefferson Co	307W	80439	26200-27399	
HILLTOP DR	Jefferson Co	306X	80439	29900-30999	
HILLTOP DR	Longmont	12T	80501	1300-1699	
HILLTOP DR	Park Co	841J	80421	1-199	
HILL TOP RD	Douglas Co	496S	80109	None	
HILLTOP RD	Elbert Co	850Q	80107	None	
HILLTOP RD	Jefferson Co	337J	80439	4100-4699	
	Jefferson Co	843X	80470	23500-24199	
	Jefferson Co	367A	80439	26700-27099	
	Jefferson Co	762B	80403	31400-31799	
HILLTOP RD	Mead	706H	80504	4300-14399	
HILLTOP RD	Palmer Lake	907V	80133	None	
HILLTOP RD E	Douglas Co	440B	80134	7200-9599	
	Douglas Co	441J	80134	9400-11199	
	Parker	409V	80134	18500-20199	
HILLTOP ST	Longmont	42A	80501	500-899	
HILLTOP PINES PATH	El Paso Co	909S	80132	None	
HILLVIEW RD	Jefferson Co	368X	80465	8800-9299	
HILLVIEW RD	Palmer Lake	908S	80133	700-799	
HILLVIEW ST E	Douglas Co	440P	80134	7800-7999	
HILTON ST	Jefferson Co	823N	80433	26600-26799	
HIMALAYA AVE	Broomfield	162G	80020	200-599	
HIMALAYA CIR S	Arapahoe Co	349D	80013	4000-4099	
	Arapahoe Co	349H	80015	None	
HIMALAYA CT	Broomfield	162G	80020	300-499	
HIMALAYA CT	Denver	259H	80249	None	
HIMALAYA CT S	Arapahoe Co	349D	80013	3600-3699	
	Arapahoe Co	349M	80015	4700-4899	
	Arapahoe Co	349R	80015	4900-5099	
	Arapahoe Co	349H	80015	None	
	Centennial	349V	80016	5900-5999	
HIMALAYA RD	Adams Co	769F	80022	10800-11099	
	Adams Co	169Z	80022	None	
HIMALAYA RD	Aurora	259Z	80011	2500-3599	
	Aurora	289D	80011	None	
	Aurora	289H	80011	None	
	Denver	259R	80249	4200-4999	
	Denver	259H	80249	None	
	Lochbuie	139D	80603	None	
HIMALAYA ST S	Arapahoe Co	349D	80013	3500-4299	
	Arapahoe Co	349M	80015	None	
	Arapahoe Co	350E	80015	None	
	Centennial	349R	80015	4600-5799	
HIMALAYA WAY	Denver	259L	80249	None	
HIMALAYA WAY S	Arapahoe Co	349D	80013	3700-4299	
	Centennial	349V	80015	5500-5699	
	Centennial	379D	80016	6000-7199	
	Centennial	380E	80016	6800-7499	
HI MEADOW DR	Park Co	841V	80421	1-1499	
HINDSALE CIR E	Centennial	375L	80122	4000-4299	
HINSDALE	Thornton	194W	80260	None	
HINSDALE AVE E	Arapahoe Co	378M	80016	16100-16299	
	Aurora	380F	80016	22000-22299	
	Aurora	380G	80016	22500-22699	
	Centennial	375K	80122	3000-3199	
	Centennial	376J	80112	6000-6499	
	Centennial	376F	80112	6900-7299	
	Centennial	376G	80112	7300-7999	
	Centennial	376L	80112	8200-8399	
	Centennial	378K	80112	14700-14899	
	Centennial	379L	80016	18500-19399	
	Foxfield	379J	80016	16900-18499	
HINSDALE AVE W	Jefferson Co	372H	80128	5300-5599	
	Jefferson Co	372L	80128	6600-6799	
	Littleton	373J	80128	4300-4599	
HINSDALE CIR E	Centennial	375L	80122	4000-4299	
	Centennial	375M	80122	5300-5599	
	Centennial	378L	80112	7300-15699	
HINSDALE CIR W	Arapahoe Co	373E	80128	4900-5199	
HINSDALE CT E	Centennial	376J	80112	6000-6299	
	Centennial	376K	80112	7300-7399	
HINSDALE CT W	Littleton	374J	80120	1000-1199	
	Littleton	373J	80128	4700-4799	
HINSDALE DR E	Centennial	376K	80112	7300-7399	
	Centennial	376L	80112	8100-8499	
	Centennial	378G	80112	15300-15699	
HINSDALE DR W	Jefferson Co	372K	80128	6900-7499	
HINSDALE DR W	Jefferson Co	371F	80127	10700-11099	
	Littleton	374J	80120	1100-1199	
HINSDALE LN E	Arapahoe Co	378M	80016	None	
	Centennial	379G	80016	18900-19299	
HINSDALE LN W	Jefferson Co	371H	80128	None	
HINSDALE PKWY E	Centennial	376K	80112	7300-7599	
HINSDALE PL E	Aurora	380H	80016	23700-23799	
	Aurora	381F	80016	25400-25599	
	Centennial	375K	80122	3100-3799	
	Centennial	375M	80122	4300-5199	
	Centennial	376E	80122	5400-5499	
	Centennial	376J	80112	5700-5899	
	Centennial	376F	80112	7100-7599	
	Centennial	379L	80016	19300-19599	
	Centennial	380E	80016	20800-20999	
	Foxfield	379E	80016	17500-17699	
HINSDALE PL W	Jefferson Co	372H	80128	5400-5599	
	Jefferson Co	372L	80128	6600-6999	
	Jefferson Co	372J	80128	8500-8899	
	Jefferson Co	371M	80128	9100-9599	
	Littleton	374J	80120	None	

STREET NAME	CITY or COUNTY	MAP GRID	ZIP CODE	BLOCK RANGE	O/E
HINSDALE WAY E	Aurora	**380M**	80016	None	
HISTEAD DR	Jefferson Co	**336G**	80439	28800-29299	
HISTEAD WAY	Jefferson Co	**336G**	80439	3900-4099	
HITCHING POST CIR	Parker	**408Z**	80134	16500-16699	
HITCHING POST CT	Parker	**408Z**	80134	11800-11899	
HITCHING POST RD	Thornton	**195U**	80229	None	
HITCHING POST TRAIL	Parker	**408Z**	80134	11800-11899	
HITCHRACK LN	Park Co	**841E**	80421	None	
HITCHRACK RD	Park Co	**841A**	80421	1-1699	
HI-VIEW RD	Jefferson Co	**336Z**	80439	27600-27899	
HIWALL CT	Douglas Co	**867T**	80109	2700-2999	
HIWAN CIR	Jefferson Co	**305R**	80439	2200-2299	
HIWAN DR	Jefferson Co	**305M**	80439	1000-2499	
	Jefferson Co	**306S**	80439	2600-3299	
HOBART WAY S	Denver	**312V**	80227	2800-2899	
	Denver	**312Z**	80227	3000-3099	
HOBBIT LN	Westminster	**193L**	80031	10400-10899	
HOBNAIL CT	Elbert Co	**871B**	80107	35600-35799	
HOFER LN	Clear Creek Co	**304G**	80439	1-199	
HOFFMAN BLVD	Aurora	**287M**	80011	12400-12698	E
	Aurora	**288J**	80011	13000-13799	
HOFFMAN DR	Erie	**102Q**	80516	1200-1499	
HOFFMAN WAY	Thornton	**225A**	80229	1600-1899	
	Thornton	**224D**	80229	8800-8999	
	Thornton	**194Z**	80229	9000-9499	
HOGAN CT	Boulder Co	**723G**	80503	4400-4499	
HOGAN CT	Castle Rock	**496C**	80109	1700-1999	
HOG BACK DR	Golden	**248L**	80403	700-899	
HOGBACK RD	Jefferson Co	**309R**	80401	None	
HOLBROOK ST	Erie	**103J**	80516	100-799	
HOLBROOK ST	Jefferson Co	**823N**	80433	26100-26699	
HOLCOMB CIR N	Castle Rock	**498L**	80104	200-399	
HOLCOMB ST E	Castle Rock	**498L**	80104	5200-5399	
HOLCOMB ST N	Castle Rock	**498M**	80104	1-399	
HOLDEN CIR	Douglas Co	**870A**	80116	10300-10999	
HOLDEN CT	Erie	**102C**	80516	1300-1499	
HOLDEN PL W	Denver	**283L**	80204	2500-2999	
HOLDUP ST	Park Co	**841B**	80421	1-99	
HOLEMAN DR	Erie	**102W**	80516	1500-1799	
HOLIDAY BLVD	Federal Heights	**194W**	80260	None	
HOLIDAY CIR	Federal Heights	**193Z**	80260	None	
HOLIDAY CT	Federal Heights	**194W**	80260	None	
HOLIDAY DR	Boulder	**97H**	80304	None	
HOLIDAY DR	Federal Heights	**193Z**	80260	None	
	Federal Heights	**194W**	80260	None	
HOLIDAY DR	Longmont	**11V**	80501	1500-1599	
HOLIDAY LN	Federal Heights	**194W**	80260	None	
HOLIDAY LOOP	Federal Heights	**194W**	80260	None	
HOLIDAY PKWY	Federal Heights	**194W**	80260	None	
HOLIDAY PL	Federal Heights	**193Z**	80260	None	
HOLIDAY RD	Federal Heights	**194W**	80260	None	
HOLIDAY WAY	Federal Heights	**194W**	80260	None	
HOLIDAY BEND	Federal Heights	**194W**	80260	None	
HOLIDAY CORNER	Federal Heights	**193Z**	80260	None	
HOLIDAY CRESCENT	Federal Heights	**193Z**	80260	None	
HOLIDAY GARDEN	Federal Heights	**193Z**	80260	None	
HOLIDAY GLEN	Federal Heights	**193Z**	80260	None	
HOLIDAY HEIGHTS	Federal Heights	**193Z**	80260	None	
HOLIDAY PASS	Federal Heights	**194W**	80260	None	
HOLIDAY RUN	Federal Heights	**193Z**	80260	None	
HOLIDAY TERRACE	Federal Heights	**193Z**	80260	None	
	Federal Heights	**194W**	80260	None	
HOLIDAY TRAIL	Federal Heights	**193Z**	80260	None	
	Federal Heights	**194W**	80260	None	
HOLIDAY VALE	Federal Heights	**194W**	80260	None	
HOLIDAY VIEW	Federal Heights	**193Z**	80260	None	
	Federal Heights	**194W**	80260	None	
HOLIDAY VISTA	Federal Heights	**193Z**	80260	None	
HOLL AVE S	Jefferson Co	**842A**	80470	12400-12599	
HOLLAND CIR	Arvada	**221Z**	80004	6400-6499	
	Westminster	**191V**	80021	9700-9999	
HOLLAND CT	Arvada	**221V**	80004	6600-6699	
	Arvada	**221R**	80005	7400-7499	
	Arvada	**221M**	80005	7700-8099	
	Arvada	**221H**	80005	8100-8299	
	Westminster	**191Z**	80021	9200-9299	
	Westminster	**191V**	80021	9900-9999	
	Westminster	**191R**	80021	10000-10499	
	Wheat Ridge	**251V**	80033	3500-3699	
HOLLAND CT S	Denver	**341M**	80123	4800-4899	
	Jefferson Co	**371D**	80123	6400-6499	
	Jefferson Co	**371M**	80128	7500-7599	
	Jefferson Co	**371R**	80128	7700-8098	E
	Jefferson Co	**371V**	80128	8400-8499	
	Jefferson Co	**371Z**	80128	8800-8899	
	Lakewood	**281Z**	80226	300-499	
	Lakewood	**311D**	80226	900-1099	
	Lakewood	**311H**	80232	1100-1299	
	Lakewood	**311M**	80232	1500-1699	
	Lakewood	**311R**	80227	2300-2499	
	Lakewood	**311R**	80227	2500-2599	
	Lakewood	**311Z**	80227	3000-3299	
HOLLAND DR	Arvada	**251H**	80002	5400-5599	
HOLLAND PL	Westminster	**191R**	80021	10400-10499	
HOLLAND ST	Arvada	**251M**	80002	5100-5399	
	Arvada	**251D**	80004	5900-6199	
	Arvada	**221R**	80005	7300-7399	
	Lakewood	**281V**	80226	1-399	
	Lakewood	**281R**	80215	600-899	
	Lakewood	**281M**	80215	1000-1499	
	Westminster	**191Z**	80021	9000-9299	
	Westminster	**191R**	80021	10400-10699	
	Wheat Ridge	**251Z**	80033	3200-3799	
	Wheat Ridge	**251V**	80033	3800-4099	
	Wheat Ridge	**251R**	80033	4400-4799	
HOLLAND ST S	Denver	**341M**	80123	4500-4899	
	Jefferson Co	**341R**	80123	5100-5499	
	Jefferson Co	**341Z**	80123	6100-6199	
	Jefferson Co	**371M**	80128	7500-7599	
	Lakewood	**281V**	80226	1-299	
	Lakewood	**311D**	80226	900-1099	
	Lakewood	**311D**	80232	1100-1199	
	Lakewood	**311M**	80232	1600-1799	
	Lakewood	**311R**	80227	1900-2499	
	Lakewood	**311V**	80227	2500-2699	
	Littleton	**825P**	80127	9700-9899	
HOLLAND WAY	Longmont	**40T**	80503	None	
HOLLAND WAY	Westminster	**191R**	80021	10400-10499	
HOLLAND WAY S	Denver	**341M**	80123	4800-4899	
	Jefferson Co	**341Z**	80123	6101-6199	O
	Jefferson Co	**371D**	80128	6700-6799	
	Jefferson Co	**371M**	80128	7500-7799	
	Jefferson Co	**371R**	80128	7800-7999	
	Jefferson Co	**371V**	80128	8300-8499	
	Jefferson Co	**341H**	80123	None	
	Lakewood	**311R**	80227	2200-2299	
	Lakewood	**311R**	80227	2500-2599	
	Lakewood	**311Z**	80227	3200-3499	
	Littleton	**825P**	80127	9300-9499	
HOLLINGS WAY	Jefferson Co	**762C**	80403	30400-30699	
HOLLOW CT	Lochbuie	**729Y**	80603	None	
HOLLOWBERRY CT	Frederick	**726D**	80504	None	
HOLLOW CREEK CT S	Parker	**439C**	80134	12400-12599	
HOLLOW CREEK DR E	Parker	**439C**	80134	18900-19699	
HOLLOW CREEK LN E	Parker	**439C**	80134	18900-19299	
HOLLOW HORN AVE E	Parker	**408Z**	80134	None	
HOLLOWVIEW CT N	Douglas Co	**440U**	80134	6100-6299	
HOLLY AVE	Longmont	**41Q**	80501	1100-1499	
HOLLY CIR	Thornton	**166S**	80602	None	
	Thornton	**166S**	80602	None	
HOLLY CIR S	Centennial	**376E**	80112	6800-6999	
HOLLY CT	Jefferson Co	**307K**	80401	2200-2399	
HOLLY DR	Broomfield	**162P**	80020	1300-1499	
HOLLY DR	Erie	**133D**	80516	None	
HOLLY PL	Boulder	**128F**	80303	1200-1299	
HOLLY PL S	Arapahoe Co	**315R**	80222	2300-2599	
	Arapahoe Co	**316S**	80222	2700-3099	
	Denver	**316W**	80222	3100-3399	
HOLLY ST	Adams Co	**165R**	80602	14400-14799	
	Adams Co	**135V**	80602	14800-16799	
	Commerce City	**256A**	80022	5400-6099	
	Commerce City	**226W**	80022	6200-6899	
	Commerce City	**225V**	80022	6900-7199	
	Denver	**286S**	80220	1-1999	
	Denver	**286A**	80207	2000-2799	
	Denver	**256S**	80207	2800-3999	
	Denver	**256N**	80216	4000-4799	
HOLLY ST	Hudson	**730M**	80642	300-799	
HOLLY ST	Thornton	**196A**	80233	10800-11999	
	Thornton	**165A**	80602	12000-14399	
HOLLY ST	Weld Co	**726G**	80516	3000-3999	
HOLLY ST S	Arapahoe Co	**316N**	80222	2300-2699	
	Centennial	**376E**	80111	6400-6698	E
	Centennial	**376E**	80121	6401-6699	O
	Centennial	**376E**	80112	6700-7498	E
	Centennial	**376E**	80112	6701-7499	O
	Centennial	**376E**	80122	7500-8299	
	Cherry Hills Village	**346E**	80111	4000-4299	
	Cherry Hills Village	**346N**	80111	4300-5099	
	Denver	**286W**	80246	1-699	
	Denver	**316A**	80246	700-1299	
	Denver	**316J**	80222	1300-2299	
	Denver	**316W**	80222	3100-3499	
	Denver	**346A**	80237	3500-3999	
	Greenwood Village	**346N**	80111	5100-6398	E
	Greenwood Village	**346N**	80121	5101-6398	O
HOLLY WAY	Cherry Hills Village	**346A**	80111	3900-3999	
HOLLY WAY	Thornton	**166W**	80602	12000-12299	
HOLLYBERRY LN	Boulder	**127R**	80305	300-399	
HOLLY HILLS WAY E	Parker	**410V**	80138	23600-23699	
HOLLY HOCK CT	Castle Rock	**466Q**	80109	3300-3399	
HOLLYHOCK CT	Longmont	**40U**	80503	None	
HOLLYHOCK CT S	Highlands Ranch	**403M**	80129	10400-10499	
HOLLYHOCK LN	Boulder Co	**130G**	80026	8500-8699	
HOLLYHOCK LN	Jefferson Co	**338P**	80454	4900-4999	
HOLLY OAK	Jefferson Co	**370Q**	80127	1-99	
HOLLYRIDGE DR	Douglas Co	**408M**	80134	16000-16499	
HOLLYWOOD ST	Adams Co	**226J**	80022	7700-7999	
HOLMAN CIR S	Lakewood	**310P**	80228	2200-2499	
HOLMAN CT	Arvada	**220X**	80004	6100-6399	
HOLMAN CT S	Lakewood	**310T**	80228	2700-2799	
HOLMAN ST	Arvada	**220Y**	80004	6200-6399	
	Arvada	**220X**	80004	6500-6699	
	Arvada	**220T**	80004	6800-6999	
	Jefferson Co	**250P**	80403	4400-4699	
	Jefferson Co	**250K**	80403	4800-4899	
HOLMAN ST S	Lakewood	**310T**	80228	2600-3099	
HOLMAN WAY	Jefferson Co	**280T**	80401	1-599	
HOLMAN WAY S	Jefferson Co	**280T**	80401	1-299	
HOLMBY CT	Castle Rock	**497R**	80104	None	
HOLMBY WAY	Castle Rock	**497V**	80104	None	
HOLMES CT	Elbert Co	**851A**	80138	2300-2499	
HOLMES PL	Boulder	**128D**	80303	5000-5399	
HOLMES RD	Douglas Co	**870B**	80116	1400-1499	
HOLMES GULCH RD	Park Co	**842S**	80421	1-1099	
HOLMES GULCH WAY	Jefferson Co	**842S**	80421	1-1099	
HOLY CROSS LN	Douglas Co	**436U**	80108	6300-6399	
HOLY CROSS RD	Thornton	**193V**	80260	None	
HOLY CROSS WAY	Douglas Co	**436V**	80108	6200-6299	
HOLYOKE CT	Parker	**409J**	80134	17500-17599	
HOLYOKE DR	Boulder	**128S**	80305	2200-2299	
HOLYOKE DR	Parker	**409J**	80134	10500-10599	
HOLYOKE LN	Superior	**160R**	80027	2100-2299	
HOME ST	Douglas Co	**467K**	80108	3900-4399	
HOME FARM AVE	Westminster	**164S**	80234	800-899	
HOME FARM CIR	Westminster	**164S**	80234	900-1199	
HOME FARM CT	Westminster	**164T**	80234	12400-12499	
HOME FARM DR	Westminster	**164T**	80234	12500-12799	
HOME FARM LN	Westminster	**164S**	80234	12600-12799	
HOMER CIR	Lafayette	**131R**	80026	900-999	
HOMESTAKE CT	Douglas Co	**436T**	80108	800-899	
	Douglas Co	**887L**	80118	8400-8499	
HOMESTAKE DR	Golden	**279F**	80401	800-1099	
HOMESTAKE LN N	Douglas Co	**411B**	80138	12300-12699	
HOMESTAKE RD	Douglas Co	**887L**	80118	8200-8399	
HOMESTAKE PEAK	Jefferson Co	**371K**	80127	11500-11599	
HOMESTEAD CT	Parker	**408R**	80134	16400-16499	
HOMESTEAD DR	Frederick	**706Y**	80504	9300-9499	
HOMESTEAD DR E	Highlands Ranch	**374U**	80126	700-899	
HOMESTEAD DR W	Bow Mar	**343J**	80123	None	
HOMESTEAD PKWY	Longmont	**12N**	80501	None	
HOMESTEAD PKWY S	Centennial	**376F**	80112	6700-7499	
HOMESTEAD PL	Broomfield	**163C**	80020	None	
HOMESTEAD PL	Thornton	**195R**	80229	None	
HOMESTEAD RD	Elbert Co	**832T**	80107	44200-44599	
HOMESTEAD RD	Jefferson Co	**762V**	80403	7800-7999	
HOMESTEAD RD	Park Co	**841P**	80421	1-599	
HOMESTEAD RD E	Douglas Co	**409H**	80138	7000-7299	
	Douglas Co	**410F**	80138	7500-8599	
HOMESTEAD ST	Lafayette	**131G**	80026	None	
HOMESTEAD ST S	Highlands Ranch	**374V**	80126	None	
HOMESTEAD WAY	Boulder Co	**69Z**	80301	5400-5599	
HOMESTEAD WAY	Brighton	**139L**	80601	None	
	Brighton	**139Q**	80601	None	
HOMESTEADER DR	Jefferson Co	**368Q**	80465	7200-8299	
HOMEWOOD PARK AVE W					
	Jefferson Co	**824P**	80127	17400-17799	
HONDAH DR	Jefferson Co	**824S**	80127	10100-10799	
HONDAH TRAIL	Jefferson Co	**824N**	80127	10300-10399	
HONDO CT	Castle Rock	**467U**	80104	1100-1199	
HONEY WAY S	Denver	**316E**	80224	1100-1399	
HONEY CREEK LN	Superior	**160R**	80027	2100-2199	
HONEY LOCUST	Jefferson Co	**370Q**	80127	1-99	
HONEYLOCUST CIR					
	Greenwood Village	**345V**	80121	5700-5899	
HONEY LOCUST CT	Douglas Co	**470A**	80134	5000-5099	
HONEY LOCUST DR					
	Cherry Hills Village	**345H**	80113	4200-4299	
HONEYSUCKLE CIR	Broomfield	**161R**	80020	1100-1199	
HONEYSUCKLE CT	Brighton	**138Y**	80601	None	
HONEYSUCKLE LN	Jefferson Co	**338K**	80454	4900-4999	
HONEY SUCKLE LN	Louisville	**130T**	80027	1000-1099	
HONEYSUCKLE PL	Highlands Ranch	**374V**	80126	700-899	
HONEYSUCKLE WAY	El Paso Co	**908T**	80132	18500-18699	
HONEYSUCKLE WAY	Longmont	**40L**	80503	4000-4099	
HOOD CT	Jefferson Co	**842C**	80433	12000-12099	
HOOD RD	Jefferson Co	**822Y**	80433	30200-30899	
HOOD WAY	Jefferson Co	**822Y**	80433	30200-30399	
HOOFBEAT PL	Castle Rock	**469J**	80108	5800-6299	
HOOKER CIR S	Denver	**313L**	80219	1900-2099	
HOOKER CT	Westminster	**193U**	80031	9700-10099	
	Westminster	**193C**	80031	11500-11599	
HOOKER PL	Westminster	**193Q**	80031	10000-10099	
HOOKER ST	Adams Co	**253C**	80221	5500-5799	
	Adams Co	**223U**	80221	6600-6799	
	Denver	**283U**	80219	1-399	
	Denver	**283L**	80204	600-1199	
	Denver	**283G**	80204	1500-1999	
	Denver	**283C**	80211	2000-2599	
	Denver	**253Y**	80211	2700-3099	
	Denver	**253Q**	80211	4100-4599	
	Denver	**253L**	80221	4800-4999	
	Westminster	**223U**	80030	7000-7199	
	Westminster	**223L**	80030	7600-7999	
	Westminster	**223G**	80031	8100-8199	
	Westminster	**193Y**	80031	9200-9599	
	Westminster	**193U**	80031	10000-10099	
	Westminster	**193Q**	80031	10200-10399	
	Westminster	**193C**	80031	11500-11599	
HOOKER ST S	Denver	**283Y**	80219	1-299	
	Denver	**313L**	80219	1200-1899	
	Denver	**313U**	80219	2500-2699	
	Denver	**313U**	80236	2700-2799	
	Englewood	**343Q**	80110	5000-5099	
	Sheridan	**343C**	80110	3600-3799	
	Sheridan	**343G**	80236	4100-4299	
	Sheridan	**343G**	80110	4400-4499	
HOOKER WAY	Adams Co	**223C**	80031	8800-8899	
	Westminster	**193Q**	80031	10000-10099	
HOOKER WAY S	Denver	**313Q**	80219	2100-2399	
HOOPER ST	Central City	**780C**	80427	100-199	
HOOSIER CT	Boulder Co	**741E**	80466	1-99	
HOOSIER DR	Douglas Co	**887G**	80118	900-1299	
HOOT OWL CT	Douglas Co	**379S**	80134	16800-16899	
HOOVER AVE	Fort Lupton	**728G**	80621	600-1199	
HOOVER AVE	Louisville	**131W**	80027	100-399	
HOOVER AVE N	Louisville	**130Z**	80027	100-899	
HOOVER AVE S	Fort Lupton	**728Q**	80621	800-999	
HOOVER AVE W	Jefferson Co	**372B**	80123	7000-8199	
	Jefferson Co	**371A**	80127	12400-12599	
	Jefferson Co	**372D**	80123	None	
HOOVER CT	Louisville	**130Z**	80027	200-299	
HOOVER DR E	Aurora	**380B**	80016	22000-22199	
HOOVER DR W	Jefferson Co	**372D**	80123	None	
HOOVER LN	Palmer Lake	**907U**	80133	None	
HOOVER LN W	Jefferson Co	**372C**	80123	6700-6799	
	Jefferson Co	**372D**	80123	None	
HOOVER PL E	Aurora	**380C**	80016	22500-22599	
	Aurora	**381A**	80016	24500-24999	
	Aurora	**830A**	80016	None	
HOOVER PL S	Jefferson Co	**371D**	80123	6500-6599	
HOOVER PL W	Jefferson Co	**372C**	80123	6500-6599	
	Jefferson Co	**372B**	80123	7800-8299	
	Jefferson Co	**372D**	80123	None	
HOPE CIR	Broomfield	**133N**	80020	4500-4699	
HOPE CT	Adams Co	**225E**	80229	8400-8699	
HOPE CT	Frederick	**727F**	80530	7900-7999	
HOPE DALE AVE	Parker	**410Y**	80138	22500-23199	
HOPEWELL AVE	Parker	**410Y**	80138	None	
HOPEWELL LN	Parker	**410Y**	80138	None	
HOPI AVE	Adams Co	**226B**	80022	None	
HOPI DR	Douglas Co	**846U**	80135	3500-3899	
HOPI PL	Boulder	**128L**	80303	200-399	
HOPI RD	Jefferson Co	**338J**	80454	None	
HOPI PINES GROVE	El Paso Co	**912P**	80831	19600-20199	
HOPKINS DR	Adams Co	**224H**	80229	1600-1799	
	Adams Co	**225A**	80229	8600-8799	
HOPKINS PL	Boulder	**98U**	80301	4800-4899	
HOPPER PL	Brighton	**139L**	80601	None	
HOPPER RD	El Paso Co	**911Z**	80831	14900-15999	
	El Paso Co	**912W**	80831	16000-17799	
HOPTREE CT	Louisville	**130V**	80027	500-599	
HORAN CT	Castle Pines North	**436Q**	80108	600-699	
HORIUCHI CT	Brighton	**139K**	80601	None	
HORIUCHI ST	Brighton	**139K**	80601	None	
HORIZON AVE	Lafayette	**132U**	80026	1301-1499	O
HORIZON DR	Weld Co	**139K**	80601	16600-16699	
HORIZON LN	Longmont	**11L**	80501	1300-1399	
HORIZON PKWY	Longmont	**10R**	80503	2900-3299	
HORIZON TRAIL	Castle Pines North	**436F**	80108	12700-13099	
HORIZON VIEW DR	Jefferson Co	**824S**	80465	10100-10399	
	Jefferson Co	**823V**	80465	10400-19999	
HORN ST	Black Hawk	**780D**	80422	100-399	
HORNBEAM ST	Douglas Co	**409X**	80134	None	

STREET NAME	CITY or COUNTY	MAP GRID	ZIP CODE	BLOCK RANGE	O/E
HORNBLEND RD	Gilpin Co	761E	80403	1-199	
HORNED OWL WAY	Douglas Co	470C	80134	5000-5299	
HORNSILVER MOUNTAIN	Jefferson Co	371E	80127	11600-12099	
HORSE BIT WAY	Jefferson Co	368R	80465	20900-21099	
HORSE CREEK ST	Parker	439F	80134	18600-18799	
HORSEMINT WAY S	Parker	409A	80134	9400-9499	
HORSERADISH GULCH RD	Jefferson Co	782D	80403	4800-5899	
HORSESHOE CIR	Mead	706G	80542	None	
HORSESHOE CIR E	Douglas Co	441C	80138	10400-10899	
HORSESHOE DR	Adams Co	793M	80102	None	
HORSESHOE DR	Jefferson Co	335V	80439	31400-32499	
HORSESHOE LN	Parker	410W	80138	11800-12099	
HORSESHOE PL	Boulder Co	740M	80466	1-599	
HORSESHOE PL	Brighton	139L	80601	None	
HORSESHOE TRAIL	Douglas Co	846P	80135	5400-5799	
HOSMAN CIR	Jefferson Co	842C	80433	12100-12199	
HOSMAN CT	Jefferson Co	842C	80433	12200-12299	
HOSPITALITY PL	Douglas Co	469C	80134	5300-5499	
HOTEL WAY	Jefferson Co	306C	80401	28900-29199	
HOT SPRINGS	Weld Co	706P	80504	11400-11499	
HOT SPRINGS DR N	Douglas Co	409G	80138	11400-11699	
HOTTMAN ST	Brighton	139S	80601	3400-3599	
HOURGLASS AVE	Castle Rock	496F	80109	3700-4099	
HOURGLASS PL	Broomfield	133L	80020	None	
HOUSTON ST	Park Co	820Z	80421	1-499	
HOUSTON ST S	Jefferson Co	823N	80433	9700-9999	
HOUSTOUN WARING CIR S	Littleton	373L	80120	7200-7499	
HOUSTOUN WARING CIR W	Littleton	373H	80120	2400-2599	
HOVER DR	Castle Rock	498J	80104	2300-2599	
HOVER RD	Longmont	11S	80501	900-2499	
HOVER ST	Boulder Co	41E	80501	9901-10199	O
HOVER ST	Longmont	41E	80501	100-899	
HOVER ST S	Longmont	41J	80503	1-1699	
HOVER RIDGE CIR	Longmont	11W	80501	900-999	
HOWARD PL	Boulder	128S	80305	2200-2299	
HOWARD PL W	Denver	283L	80204	2800-2999	
HOWE CIR	Castle Rock	498G	80104	600-699	
HOWE CT	Boulder Co	98K	80301	3800-3899	
HOWE CT	Castle Rock	498G	80104	600-799	
HOWE CT	Gilpin Co	760V	80403	1-299	
HOWE PL	Castle Rock	498G	80104	500-599	
HOWE ST	Castle Rock	498G	80104	500-5299	
HOWELL CT	Jefferson Co	250F	80002	5600-5799	
HOWELL RD	Jefferson Co	250X	80401	2700-3199	
HOWELL ST	Arvada	220T	80004	6800-6999	
	Jefferson Co	280T	80401	300-399	
	Jefferson Co	250K	80403	4800-4999	
	Jefferson Co	250K	80002	5200-5399	
HOWELL ST S	Lakewood	310T	80228	2600-2699	
HOWLING CIR	Elbert Co	850Q	80107	500-599	
HOYA CT	Boulder Co	98K	80301	3900-4099	
HOYE DR E	Aurora	317C	80012	12000-12099	
HOYE PL W	Denver	314A	80223	1200-1699	
	Denver	313B	80219	3400-3599	
HOYT CIR	Arvada	221M	80005	7700-7799	
HOYT CT	Arvada	251M	80002	5100-5199	
	Arvada	251D	80004	6000-6199	
	Arvada	221V	80004	6900-6999	
	Arvada	221R	80005	7400-7499	
	Arvada	221H	80005	8100-8299	
	Westminster	221D	80021	9000-9099	
	Westminster	191R	80021	10400-10499	
	Wheat Ridge	251V	80033	3600-4099	
	Wheat Ridge	251R	80033	4200-4399	
HOYT CT S	Jefferson Co	371D	80123	6400-6499	
	Jefferson Co	371R	80128	7800-7999	
	Jefferson Co	371Z	80128	8800-8899	
	Lakewood	311R	80227	2100-2499	
	Lakewood	311V	80227	2500-2699	
	Lakewood	311Z	80227	3300-3399	
	Littleton	825P	80127	9300-9399	
	Littleton	825P	80127	9800-9899	
HOYT DR	Arvada	251H	80002	5400-5499	
HOYT DR	Thornton	225A	80229	2000-8999	
HOYT LN	Westminster	191V	80021	9900-9999	
HOYT PL	Parker	409P	80134	17600-17699	
HOYT PL	Westminster	191V	80021	9900-9999	
	Westminster	191R	80021	10400-10499	
HOYT ST	Arvada	251M	80002	5100-5399	
	Arvada	251D	80004	6000-6199	
	Arvada	221R	80005	7300-7399	
	Broomfield	161V	80020	400-899	
	Lakewood	281V	80226	1-399	
	Lakewood	281R	80226	400-499	
	Lakewood	281R	80215	600-899	
	Lakewood	281M	80215	1200-1499	
	Lakewood	281H	80215	1500-2099	
	Lakewood	281D	80215	2100-2599	
	Westminster	191Z	80021	9000-9299	
	Westminster	191V	80021	9900-9999	
	Westminster	191M	80021	10400-10699	
	Wheat Ridge	251V	80033	3500-3999	
	Wheat Ridge	251R	80033	4200-4699	
HOYT ST S	Denver	341M	80123	4500-5099	
	Jefferson Co	341R	80123	5100-5599	
	Jefferson Co	371D	80123	6400-6499	
	Jefferson Co	371M	80128	7500-7799	
	Jefferson Co	371R	80128	7800-8099	
	Jefferson Co	341H	80123	None	
	Lakewood	281V	80226	1-199	
	Lakewood	281Z	80226	200-499	
	Lakewood	311D	80226	700-999	
	Lakewood	311H	80232	1100-1799	
	Lakewood	311M	80232	1800-1899	
	Lakewood	311R	80227	2200-2499	
	Lakewood	311V	80227	2500-2699	
HOYT WAY	Arvada	221H	80005	8000-8399	
	Westminster	191V	80021	9900-9999	
	Westminster	191R	80021	10400-10499	
HOYT WAY S	Jefferson Co	371D	80123	6400-6599	
	Jefferson Co	371V	80128	8400-8499	
	Lakewood	311R	80227	1900-2199	
	Lakewood	311Z	80227	3000-3299	
HUBBARD DR	Longmont	42B	80501	600-899	
HUBERT ST	Douglas Co	469C	80134	5100-5199	
HUCKLEBERRY DR	Douglas Co	850X	80116	11700-11999	
HUDSON S	Centennial	375D	80121	6300-6499	

STREET NAME	CITY or COUNTY	MAP GRID	ZIP CODE	BLOCK RANGE	O/E
HUDSON CIR	Thornton	165V	80241	5500-5699	
HUDSON CIR S	Centennial	376E	80122	7000-7199	
HUDSON CT	Adams Co	195V	80229	9600-9699	
	Thornton	196N	80640	10000-10199	
	Thornton	165Z	80241	12000-12299	
	Thornton	165R	80241	12900-12999	
HUDSON CT S	Centennial	346W	80121	6200-6299	
	Centennial	376E	80122	7200-7299	
	Centennial	375M	80122	7500-7599	
	Centennial	376J	80122	7600-7799	
HUDSON DR	Jefferson Co	823P	80433	None	
HUDSON LN S	Centennial	376E	80122	7100-7199	
HUDSON PKWY S	Cherry Hills Village	345H	80113	4100-4299	
HUDSON RD	Adams Co	750H	80603	None	
	Aurora	790M	80137	3900-3999	
	Aurora	770Z	80642	None	
HUDSON RD	Park Co	842A	80470	1-199	
HUDSON RD S	Arapahoe Co	810D	80137	1100-1899	
HUDSON ST	Commerce City	255D	80022	6000-6199	
	Commerce City	225Z	80022	6400-6499	
	Denver	285M	80220	1-1999	
	Denver	285D	80207	2000-2799	
	Denver	255V	80207	2800-3799	
HUDSON ST	Hudson	730L	80642	None	
HUDSON ST	Thornton	196N	80640	10000-10199	
	Thornton	195H	80640	11200-11499	
	Thornton	195D	80640	11500-11599	
	Thornton	165V	80241	12800-12899	
	Thornton	165R	80241	12900-13099	
	Thornton	165H	80602	13800-13999	
	Thornton	165H	80602	None	
HUDSON ST S	Centennial	346W	80121	6300-6499	
	Centennial	376E	80122	6800-6899	
	Centennial	376J	80122	7600-7699	
	Centennial	375R	80122	7800-7999	
	Denver	285Z	80246	1-499	
	Denver	316A	80246	700-1299	
	Denver	316E	80222	1300-1699	
	Denver	316S	80222	2700-2999	
	Denver	345D	80237	3500-3999	
HUDSON WAY	Thornton	165H	80602	13800-13999	
	Thornton	165H	80602	None	
HUDSON WAY S	Centennial	376J	80122	7200-7499	
	Centennial	376J	80122	7600-7699	
	Cherry Hills Village	345H	80113	3900-4099	
	Denver	316W	80222	3400-3499	
HUERFANO LN S	Jefferson Co	842N	80470	15100-15299	
HUERFANO ST	Brighton	139P	80601	None	
HUEY CIR	Boulder	128U	80305	4600-4699	
HUGGINS CT E	Douglas Co	441S	80134	9500-9699	
HUGHES CT S	Highlands Ranch	404G	80126	10000-10099	
HUGHES DR E	Aurora	288V	80017	16500-16799	
HUGHES LN E	Highlands Ranch	404G	80126	700-899	
HUGHES PL S	Highlands Ranch	404G	80126	10000-10099	
HUGHES ST E	Highlands Ranch	404G	80126	400-499	
HUGHES ST S	Jefferson Co	823N	80433	10000-10099	
HUGHES WAY S	Highlands Ranch	404G	80126	10000-10099	
HUGHESVILLE RD	Gilpin Co	760Z	80403	1100-1699	
HUGHS DR	Erie	132A	80026	2600-2999	
HUKILL GULCH	Clear Creek Co	780P	80452	None	
HULL'S WAY	Monument	908W	80132	17200-17299	
HUMBOLDT CIR	Adams Co	224M	80229	7800-7999	
HUMBOLDT CIR	Longmont	10V	80503	2800-2899	
HUMBOLDT CIR S	Arapahoe Co	374R	80122	8100-8199	
HUMBOLDT DR	Northglenn	194D	80233	11800-11999	
	Thornton	164R	80241	13300-13499	
HUMBOLDT PL	Longmont	10V	80503	2800-2899	
HUMBOLDT PL S	Centennial	344Z	80121	6200-6299	
HUMBOLDT ST	Denver	284M	80218	100-1999	
	Denver	284D	80205	2000-2799	
	Denver	254Z	80205	2800-3999	
	Denver	254R	80216	4600-4699	
	Northglenn	194R	80233	10400-10599	
	Northglenn	194H	80233	11200-11399	
	Northglenn	194D	80233	11400-11699	
	Thornton	194V	80229	9600-9699	
	Thornton	134M	80602	16400-16699	
HUMBOLDT ST	Ward	720M	80481	None	
HUMBOLDT ST S	Arapahoe Co	374M	80122	7500-7699	
	Arapahoe Co	374R	80122	7900-7999	
HUMBOLDT ST S	Cherry Hills Village	344H	80113	4100-4199	
	Denver	284Z	80209	100-499	
	Denver	314R	80210	1300-2799	
	Englewood	314Z	80113	3100-3299	
HUMBOLDT WAY	Superior	160Y	80027	900-999	
HUMBOLDT WAY	Thornton	164R	80241	13200-13299	
HUMBOLDT PEAK WAY	Parker	410P	80138	10500-10599	
HUMMER DR	Boulder Co	741E	80466	1-999	
HUMMINGBIRD CIR	Brighton	137Z	80601	1300-1499	
HUMMINGBIRD CIR	Longmont	42N	80501	None	
HUMMINGBIRD CT	Mead	706C	80542	3700-3899	
HUMMINGBIRD DR	Douglas Co	466C	80108	1-1099	
HUMMINGBIRD DR	Elbert Co	871F	80107	33500-33999	
HUMMINGBIRD LN	Boulder Co	742X	80403	1-299	
HUMMINGBIRD LN	Broomfield	133W	80026	4600-4699	
HUMMINGBIRD LN	Park Co	841U	80421	1-299	
HUMMINGBIRD PL	Douglas Co	432Q	80125	9700-9799	
HUMMINGBIRD HILL RD	Jefferson Co	842H	80433	27000-29099	
HUMPHREY DR	Jefferson Co	275Z	80439	300-799	
HUNT CT	Boulder	128L	80303	4100-4199	
HUNT CT	Erie	102W	80516	2900-2999	
HUNT ST	Douglas Co	847N	80135	4100-5699	
HUNTER CT	Brighton	139T	80601	None	
HUNTER CT	Erie	102Q	80516	400-499	
HUNTER CT	Longmont	11X	80501	1200-1299	
HUNTER LN	Morrison	339C	80465	100-199	
HUNTER PL	Boulder Co	69Z	80301	6900-6999	
HUNTER ST	Westminster	193Y	80031	9000-9199	
HUNTER WAY	Adams Co	223C	80031	8800-9099	
HUNTER DOUGLAS CIR	Thornton	164V	80241	1-99	
HUNTER RUN LN	Columbine Valley	373B	80123	1-99	
HUNTERS PL	Highlands Ranch	373Z	80129	2500-2699	
HUNTERS WAY	Highlands Ranch	373Z	80129	8800-9099	
HUNTER'S COVE DR	Mead	706C	80542	200-299	
HUNTER'S COVE RD	Mead	706C	80542	100-199	
HUNTERS CREEK ST S	Highlands Ranch	374Y	80126	9000-9099	
HUNTERS GLEN RD	El Paso Co	908S	80132	2700-2999	

STREET NAME	CITY or COUNTY	MAP GRID	ZIP CODE	BLOCK RANGE	O/E
HUNTER'S HILL DR E	Centennial	376L	80112	8100-8599	
HUNTERS HILL LN	Douglas Co	432B	80125	8600-8899	
HUNTERS RIDGE CIR	Elbert Co	871D	80117	6800-6899	
HUNTERS RIDGE DR	Mead	706C	80542	300-399	
HUNTERS RIDGE RD	Jefferson Co	824U	80127	10000-11299	
HUNTERWOOD DR	Highlands Ranch	405L	80130	4300-4899	
HUNTERWOOD WAY	Highlands Ranch	405M	80130	10200-10399	
HUNTING DOWNS WAY	El Paso Co	909N	80132	19700-20499	
HUNTING HILL RD	Douglas Co	373V	80129	None	
HUNTINGTON AVE	Dacono	727K	80514	None	
HUNTINGTON CT	Longmont	10Z	80503	1-99	
HUNTINGTON DR E	Highlands Ranch	404G	80126	600-899	
HUNTINGTON PL E	Highlands Ranch	404G	80126	600-899	
HUNTINGTON WAY	Highlands Ranch	404G	80126	None	
HUNTINGTON TRAILS CIR	Westminster	164A	80020	None	
HUNTINGTON TRAILS PKWY	Westminster	164E	80020	None	
HUNTLEY CT	Castle Pines North	436R	80108	200-299	
HUNT MASTER CT	Douglas Co	432B	80125	None	
HUNTSFORD CIR	Highlands Ranch	405F	80126	2700-2999	
HUNTSFORD PL	Highlands Ranch	405E	80126	2500-2799	
HUNTWICK CT	Cherry Hills Village	345J	80110	1-99	
HUNTWICK LN	Cherry Hills Village	345J	80113	1-99	
HUNTWICK PL	Highlands Ranch	405R	80130	4900-4999	
HUNTWICK ST	Highlands Ranch	405R	80130	10700-10999	
HUPP RD	Park Co	820Z	80421	1-199	
HURLEY CIR S	Denver	312Z	80227	3000-3099	
HURLINGHAM CIR	Douglas Co	470L	80116	None	
HURLINGHAM WAY	Douglas Co	470Q	80116	3001-3499	O
HURLINGHAM LOOP	Douglas Co	470Q	80116	8700-9799	
HURON AVE	Boulder Co	740N	80466	300-699	
HURON CT	Boulder	129N	80303	1-199	
HURON CT S	Englewood	344F	80110	4100-4199	
	Littleton	374K	80120	7700-7799	
HURON LN	Douglas Co	436U	80108	6100-6199	
HURON PL	Douglas Co	436U	80108	6100-6199	
HURON PL S	Littleton	374K	80120	7600-7799	
HURON ST	Adams Co	254B	80221	6000-6199	
	Adams Co	224X	80221	6300-6499	
	Adams Co	224T	80221	6800-7299	
	Broomfield	134P	80020	14800-16799	
	Broomfield	134F	80516	None	
	Denver	254X	80202	2900-3099	
	Northglenn	194T	80260	9700-10399	
	Northglenn	194F	80234	10400-11199	
	Thornton	224B	80260	8400-9099	
	Thornton	194X	80260	9100-9699	
	Westminster	194F	80234	11200-11999	
	Westminster	164F	80234	12000-13599	
	Westminster	164F	80020	13600-14799	
HURON ST S	Denver	314F	80223	700-1399	
	Denver	314K	80223	1800-2099	
	Englewood	314X	80110	3200-3299	
	Englewood	314X	80110	3501-3599	O
	Englewood	344B	80110	3600-4099	
	Englewood	344K	80110	4100-5099	
	Littleton	344T	80120	5200-5899	
HURON WAY S	Littleton	344P	80120	5300-5499	
HURON PEAK AVE	Superior	160Y	80027	900-3699	
HURON PEAK PL	Superior	160U	80027	3000-3099	
HURRICANE CT N	Douglas Co	440U	80134	6100-6199	
HURRICANE WAY	Jefferson Co	365U	80433	8600-8699	
HURRICANE HILL DR	Boulder Co	741J	80466	1-699	
HURST PL W	Denver	283N	80204	4900-4999	
HURT ST	Frederick	727A	80504	None	
HURTY AVE	Jefferson Co	823N	80433	9500-9999	
HUSKER PL	Brighton	140K	80601	None	
HUTCHINSON ST	Louisville	131S	80027	400-799	
HUXTABLE ST	Douglas Co	846R	80135	5400-6499	
HYACINTH CT S	Highlands Ranch	403M	80129	10600-10699	
HYACINTH LN S	Highlands Ranch	403M	80129	10500-10699	
HYACINTH PL S	Highlands Ranch	403M	80129	10400-10599	
HYACINTH RD W	Highlands Ranch	404J	80129	1700-1899	
	Highlands Ranch	403M	80129	1900-2399	
HYACINTH ST S	Highlands Ranch	403M	80129	10300-10699	
HYACINTH WAY	Superior	160U	80027	1300-1599	
HYDE ST	Palmer Lake	907Q	80133	None	
HYDE PARK CIR	Denver	285X	80209	1-99	
HYDRANGEA WAY	Castle Rock	466U	80109	None	
HYGIENE RD	Boulder Co	703M	80503	4300-5499	
	Boulder Co	704K	80503	5500-7199	
	Boulder Co	10T	80503	7400-8599	
HYGIENE RD	Longmont	12U	80501	11200-12799	
HYLAND DR	Clear Creek Co	781Z	80439	1-1699	
HYLAND DR	Douglas Co	467E	80108	400-499	
HYLAND GREEN PL	Westminster	193S	80031	4600-4699	
HYPERION WAY N	Douglas Co	470A	80134	7100-7499	
HY-VU DR	Clear Creek Co	781Z	80439	1-1399	

I

STREET NAME	CITY or COUNTY	MAP GRID	ZIP CODE	BLOCK RANGE	O/E
IAN CT	Castle Pines North	436Q	80108	500-699	
ICARUS DR	Lafayette	131Q	80026	1800-1899	
ICEHOUSE CT	Jefferson Co	842Z	80421	None	
IDA AVE E	Arapahoe Co	347T	80111	10600-10699	
	Arapahoe Co	347U	80111	11300-11699	
	Arapahoe Co	349U	80015	18600-18899	
	Arapahoe Co	350U	80015	22500-23199	
	Centennial	348V	80015	16300-16499	
	Centennial	349S	80015	17700-17799	
	Centennial	349T	80015	17800-17899	
	Centennial	350S	80015	20900-21399	
	Greenwood Village	346S	80111	6400-6599	
	Greenwood Village	347S	80111	9700-10499	
IDA AVE W	Jefferson Co	341U	80127	10100-10699	
	Jefferson Co	341T	80127	11400-11499	
	Jefferson Co	340V	80127	None	
	Jefferson Co	341T	80127	None	
	Littleton	344T	80120	1-199	
	Littleton	344T	80120	1100-1199	
	Littleton	344S	80120	1600-1999	
IDA CIR E	Arapahoe Co	347U	80111	11800-12099	
	Arapahoe Co	349V	80015	19600-19899	
	Arapahoe Co	350U	80015	22600-22799	
	Centennial	350S	80015	20600-20799	
	Greenwood Village	346S	80111	5600-5799	
	Greenwood Village	347S	80111	9700-9899	

STREET NAME	CITY or COUNTY	MAP GRID	ZIP CODE	BLOCK RANGE	O/E
IDA CT E	Arapahoe Co	347T	80111	10700-10799	
IDA DR	Mead	706M	80504	None	
IDA DR E	Arapahoe Co	349U	80015	18900-19299	
	Arapahoe Co	349V	80015	19600-19799	
	Aurora	350V	80016	None	
	Centennial	349T	80015	18000-18299	
	Centennial	348U	80015	None	
IDA DR W	Jefferson Co	341S	80127	None	
	Lakewood	342V	80123	5500-6199	
	Lakewood	342U	80123	6600-6699	
IDA LN W	Jefferson Co	341S	80127	None	
IDA PL E	Arapahoe Co	347T	80111	10700-10799	
	Arapahoe Co	347U	80111	11100-11299	
	Arapahoe Co	347U	80111	11800-11999	
	Arapahoe Co	349V	80015	19500-19799	
	Arapahoe Co	350U	80015	23200-23299	
	Aurora	350V	80016	None	
	Aurora	351S	80016	None	
	Centennial	349S	80015	17100-17299	
	Centennial	349T	80015	18100-18199	
	Centennial	350T	80015	22100-22399	
	Greenwood Village	346S	80111	5800-5899	
	Greenwood Village	347S	80111	9900-9999	
	Greenwood Village	347T	80111	10400-10499	
IDA PL W	Jefferson Co	341V	80123	8800-9799	
	Jefferson Co	341U	80127	10400-10699	
	Jefferson Co	341S	80127	None	
	Lakewood	342U	80123	6600-6999	
IDA ST	Brighton	138F	80603	400-12699	
IDAHO AVE E	Aurora	319G	80017	None	
IDAHO AVE W	Jefferson Co	311F	80232	11100-11299	
	Lakewood	311G	80232	10200-10299	
IDAHO CIR E	Aurora	317E	80247	9900-9999	
	Aurora	319E	80017	16800-16899	
IDAHO DR E	Aurora	317G	80112	11800-11999	
	Aurora	317H	80112	12800-13099	
	Aurora	318F	80012	13900-14299	
	Aurora	319G	80017	19200-19299	
IDAHO DR W	Lakewood	311E	80228	12300-12399	
	Lakewood	310H	80228	12400-12899	
IDAHO PL E	Aurora	317E	80247	10101-10499	O
	Aurora	317F	80112	11000-11098	E
	Aurora	317H	80112	13100-13399	
	Aurora	318E	80012	13300-13399	
	Aurora	318F	80012	13900-14299	
	Aurora	318G	80012	15000-15099	
	Aurora	318G	80017	15300-15399	
	Aurora	318H	80017	16200-16399	
	Aurora	319F	80017	17800-17899	
	Aurora	319F	80017	17900-18399	
	Aurora	321E	80018	24500-24599	
	Denver	315H	80222	4600-4799	
IDAHO PL W	Denver	313H	80219	2600-2699	
	Lakewood	311G	80232	10100-10499	
IDAHO ST	Golden	248V	80403	600-699	
IDAHO ST	Idaho Springs	780Q	80452	100-799	
IDAHO ST E	Aurora	317E	80247	9800-9899	
IDAHO CREEK PKWY	Weld Co	706U	80504	None	
IDALIA CIR	Aurora	288L	80011	800-999	
IDALIA CIR S	Aurora	318G	80017	15500-15699	
IDALIA CT	Aurora	288U	80011	1-299	
	Aurora	288L	80011	1200-1499	
IDALIA CT S	Centennial	348Q	80015	5400-5499	
IDALIA CT S	Superior	160M	80027	1200-1399	
IDALIA PL	Commerce City	168Y	80603	None	
IDALIA ST	Aurora	288L	80011	700-999	
	Aurora	288C	80011	None	
	Commerce City	198Q	80022	9900-10199	
	Commerce City	198L	80022	10800-10899	
	Commerce City	198C	80022	11700-11899	
	Commerce City	168Y	80603	None	
	Denver	258L	80239	4800-5299	
	Denver	258G	80239	5500-5599	
IDALIA ST S	Aurora	318G	80017	1100-1699	
	Aurora	318L	80017	1800-1899	
	Aurora	318Q	80013	2000-2399	
	Aurora	318U	80013	2700-3299	
	Aurora	348C	80013	3600-3999	
	Aurora	348L	80015	4600-4799	
	Centennial	348U	80015	5600-5699	
	Commerce City	198L	80022	10700-10799	
IDALIA WAY S	Aurora	348G	80015	4300-4399	
	Centennial	348Q	80015	5400-5499	
	Frederick	726L	80516	None	
IDER CT S	Aurora	381F	80016	7100-7199	
	Aurora	351T	80016	None	
IDER ST N	Aurora	291N	80018	100-499	
IDER ST S	Aurora	351T	80016	None	
	Aurora	381B	80016	None	
IDER WAY N	Aurora	291P	80018	400-598	E
IDER WAY S	Aurora	291T	80018	None	
	Aurora	351X	80016	None	
IDLEWILD LN	Jefferson Co	306J	80439	1700-1799	
IDLEWILD ST	Adams Co	226J	80022	7700-7999	
IDYLLWILDE DR E	Parker	440B	80138	21900-22299	
	Parker	410X	80138	None	
IDYLWILD CT	Boulder Co	99G	80301	6700-6899	
IDYLWILD TRAIL	Boulder Co	99D	80301	4800-5299	
	Boulder Co	69Y	80301	5300-5599	
IDYLWOOD ST	Castle Rock	498W	80104	None	
ILIAD WAY	Lafayette	131R	80026	1000-1099	
ILIFF AVE E	Arapahoe Co	315R	80222	5100-5599	
	Arapahoe Co	316R	80231	7300-9299	
	Arapahoe Co	317N	80231	9300-9698	E
	Arapahoe Co	813E	80102	47300-48899	
	Aurora	317P	80247	10001-10399	O
	Aurora	317Q	80014	10500-13299	
	Aurora	319L	80017	11900-19299	
	Aurora	318Q	80014	12700-15299	
	Aurora	318Q	80013	15300-16899	
	Aurora	319N	80013	16800-18999	
	Denver	314R	80210	1-1699	
	Denver	315P	80210	1700-3999	
	Denver	315R	80222	4000-5099	
	Denver	316N	80222	5600-6499	
	Denver	316N	80224	6500-7199	
	Denver	317N	80231	9700-9798	E
ILIFF AVE W	Denver	314P	80223	1-799	
	Denver	314N	80223	900-1499	
	Denver	313R	80219	2400-3199	
	Denver	313P	80219	3600-4599	
	Englewood	314N	80110	1700-1999	
	Englewood	313R	80110	2000-2399	
	Lakewood	312N	80227	8300-8999	
	Lakewood	311Q	80227	10000-10899	
	Lakewood	311N	80228	12500-13099	
	Lakewood	310Q	80228	13400-14499	
	Lakewood	310P	80228	14500-14799	
	Lakewood	310P	80228	None	
ILIFF DR E	Arapahoe Co	316R	80231	None	
	Aurora	321Q	80018	26000-26499	
ILIFF DR W	Jefferson Co	310R	80228	12800-13199	
	Lakewood	312R	80227	5200-5799	
	Lakewood	312M	80227	5800-6799	
	Lakewood	310P	80228	None	
ILIFF LN W	Lakewood	312N	80227	8000-8999	
ILIFF PL E	Aurora	317P	80014	10800-10999	
	Aurora	317R	80014	12300-12499	
	Aurora	318N	80014	13600-13699	
	Aurora	318Q	80014	14800-15099	
	Aurora	318R	80013	15900-16599	
	Aurora	319L	80013	19100-19199	
	Aurora	319Q	80013	None	
	Aurora	321N	80018	None	
	Denver	316P	80224	6800-6999	
ILIFF PL W	Lakewood	309R	80228	16600-16799	
ILIFF ST	Boulder	128X	80305	2600-2899	
ILIFF WAY E	Superior	160L	80027	1000-1199	
ILIFF TRAIL E	Arapahoe Co	8112H	80102	43200-45299	
ILLINI CT	Boulder	129N	80303	1-99	
ILLINI WAY	Boulder	128R	80303	5100-5499	
ILLINOIS ST	Golden	248Z	80403	400-699	
	Golden	279A	80401	700-2099	
	Golden	279K	80401	2100-3199	
ILLINOIS ST	Idaho Springs	780Q	80452	400-499	
ILLIUM CIR	Lafayette	131Q	80026	1200-1299	
ILLIUM DR	Lafayette	131Q	80026	1200-1399	
IMBODEN RD	Adams Co	751X	80642	10700-15999	
	Adams Co	771X	80022	None	
	Adams Co	771X	80642	None	
	Arapahoe Co	791X	80137	1-1099	
	Aurora	791K	80137	None	
IMBODEN RD S	Arapahoe Co	791X	80137	1-799	
	Arapahoe Co	811B	80137	800-1099	
IMPALA TRAIL	Park Co	841R	80421	1-1299	
IMPERIAL LN	Superior	160Q	80027	2000-2299	
IMPERIAL ST	Frederick	726L	80516	None	
IMPERIAL WAY	Superior	160Q	80027	1101-1399	O
INCA CIR	Palmer Lake	907R	80133	None	
INCA CT	Federal Heights	224F	80260	8400-8499	
	Thornton	194X	80260	9400-9499	
	Westminster	164A	80020	14400-14599	
INCA DR S	Englewood	344P	80110	4900-5099	
INCA RD	Douglas Co	887J	80118	7800-8399	
INCA RD	Jefferson Co	337M	80439	22200-24399	
INCA ST	Adams Co	224P	80221	7200-7299	
	Adams Co	134S	80020	None	
	Denver	284P	80223	1-399	
	Denver	284P	80204	400-1199	
	Denver	254X	80202	2900-2999	
	Denver	254T	80211	3600-4499	
	Northglenn	194P	80260	10400-10599	
	Westminster	164F	80020	None	
INCA ST S	Denver	314F	80223	1100-1399	
	Englewood	314X	80110	3401-3499	O
	Englewood	344B	80110	3600-4299	
	Englewood	344K	80110	4500-4899	
INCA WAY	Adams Co	224T	80221	7000-7199	
INCA WAY S	Englewood	314X	80110	3500-3598	E
INCA PKWY	Boulder	128L	80303	100-899	
INCLINE CT	Jefferson Co	306U	80439	2700-2799	
INCORRIGIBLE CIR	Longmont	41U	80504	801-899	O
INDEPENDENCE AVE W	Lakewood	281J	80401	11600-11999	
INDEPENDENCE CIR	Parker	408R	80134	10900E-11099E	
INDEPENDENCE CIR	Westminster	191R	80021	10400-10499	
INDEPENDENCE CIR S	Jefferson Co	371V	80128	8300-8399	
INDEPENDENCE CT	Arvada	221Z	80004	6400-6599	
	Wheat Ridge	251Z	80033	3200-3499	
	Wheat Ridge	251V	80033	3800-4199	
INDEPENDENCE CT S	Denver	341R	80123	5000-5099	
	Jefferson Co	341V	80123	5600-5699	
	Jefferson Co	371Z	80128	8800-8899	
	Jefferson Co	341H	80123	None	
	Jefferson Co	371M	80128	None	
	Lakewood	281Z	80226	400-499	
	Lakewood	311H	80226	1000-1099	
	Lakewood	311H	80232	1100-1199	
	Lakewood	311M	80227	1900-1999	
	Lakewood	311V	80227	2500-2699	
	Lakewood	311Z	80227	3100-3199	
INDEPENDENCE DR	Boulder	98V	80301	4800-5699	
INDEPENDENCE DR	Douglas Co	887G	80118	700-1799	
INDEPENDENCE DR	Longmont	12X	80501	400-899	
INDEPENDENCE DR	Parker	408R	80134	10900-10999	
INDEPENDENCE DR	Westminster	221D	80021	8800-8999	
	Westminster	191Z	80021	9000-9399	
	Westminster	192S	80021	9600-9799	
INDEPENDENCE RD	Boulder Co	98Q	80301	4800-5699	
INDEPENDENCE ST	Arvada	251M	80002	5000-5299	
	Arvada	251G	80002	5300-5799	
	Arvada	251D	80004	5800-6199	
	Arvada	221Z	80004	6200-6699	
	Arvada	221V	80004	6900-7199	
	Arvada	221V	80005	7300-7399	
	Arvada	221H	80005	8200-8299	
	Frederick	726G	80516	6300-6399	
	Jefferson Co	371D	80128	6700-6899	
	Lakewood	281R	80226	400-499	
	Lakewood	281R	80215	600-799	
	Lakewood	281M	80215	900-1499	
	Lakewood	281H	80215	1500-1999	
	Westminster	191V	80021	9700-9999	
	Westminster	191M	80021	10400-10499	
	Wheat Ridge	251V	80033	3500-3799	
	Wheat Ridge	251R	80033	4400-4799	
	Wheat Ridge	251M	80033	4800-4999	
INDEPENDENCE ST S	Denver	341M	80123	4500-4699	
	Jefferson Co	341D	80235	3500-3699	
	Jefferson Co	341R	80123	5100-5499	
	Jefferson Co	341Z	80123	5900-6399	
	Jefferson Co	371M	80128	7100-7399	
	Jefferson Co	341H	80123	None	
	Lakewood	311V	80227	2500-2599	
	Littleton	825P	80127	9700-9999	
INDEPENDENCE WAY	Arvada	221Y	80004	6300-6599	
	Arvada	221D	80005	8400-8799	
	Westminster	191V	80021	9700-9799	
INDEPENDENCE WAY S	Denver	341R	80123	4900-5099	
	Jefferson Co	371R	80128	7600-7899	
INDEPENDENCE TRAIL	Jefferson Co	337J	80439	25500-26999	
	Jefferson Co	337B	80439	None	
INDEPENDENCE TRAIL S	Jefferson Co	337J	80439	4300-4699	
INDEPENDENT DR	Gilpin Co	760G	80403	1-199	
INDI DR	El Paso Co	908N	80132	19700-20499	
INDIAN RD	Boulder Co	99T	80301	3100-6099	
INDIAN WAY	El Paso Co	908Q	80132	400-499	
INDIAN PEAKS TRAIL	Boulder Co	99D	80301	6900-7099	
INDIAN PEAKS TRAIL	Lafayette	131F	80026	2300-2399	
	Lafayette	131B	80026	None	
	Lafayette	131E	80026	300W-699W	
INDIANA CT	Arvada	220T	80007	6900-6999	
INDIANA PL S	Jefferson Co	280T	80401	1-99	
INDIANA RD	Boulder Co	720R	80455	None	
INDIANA ST	Arapahoe Co	190P	80007	9000-9599	
	Arvada	220P	80007	6400-6999	
	Arvada	220B	80007	8200-8999	
	Golden	280P	80401	300-499	
	Jefferson Co	250X	80401	2700-3199	
	Jefferson Co	250K	80403	4400-5899	
	Jefferson Co	220P	80007	7000-8199	
	Jefferson Co	190P	80007	9600-11999	
	Lakewood	280T	80401	500-1099	
INDIANA ST S	Jefferson Co	280T	80401	1-299	
	Lakewood	310P	80228	2000-2699	
	Lakewood	310T	80228	2700-3299	
	Superior	160Q	80027	1700-3399	
INDIANA WAY S	Jefferson Co	280T	80401	100-199	
	Lakewood	310P	80228	None	
INDIAN BROOK CIR E	Parker	408Y	80134	None	
INDIAN BRUSH CT	Elbert Co	830L	80138	46400-46699	
INDIAN CREEK DR	Douglas Co	846T	80135	3500-3599	
INDIAN CREEK RD	Clear Creek Co	801Y	80439	None	
INDIAN CREEK ST S	Highlands Ranch	374U	80126	8800-8899	
INDIANFIELD ST S	Arapahoe Co	812A	80102	1200-1799	
INDIAN GRASS AVE E	Parker	408U	80134	None	
INDIAN HEAD RD	Jefferson Co	763V	80403	21000-22999	
INDIAN HILL CT	Adams Co	750L	80603	None	
INDIAN HILLS ST	Adams Co	750H	80603	16300-16499	
INDIAN PAINTBRUSH CIR W	Highlands Ranch	403D	80129	2200-2399	
INDIAN PAINTBRUSH CT S	Highlands Ranch	403D	80129	9400-9499	
INDIAN PAINTBRUSH DR	Brighton	138Y	80601	1100-1999	
INDIAN PAINTBRUSH DR	Jefferson Co	278W	80401	1-399	
INDIAN PAINTBRUSH DR W	Highlands Ranch	403D	80129	2100-2399	
INDIAN PAINTBRUSH LN	Longmont	40R	80503	1300-1399	
INDIAN PAINTBRUSH LN S	Highlands Ranch	403D	80129	9400-9499	
INDIAN PAINTBRUSH ST	Frederick	727F	80530	None	
INDIAN PAINTBRUSH WAY	Erie	133D	80516	None	
INDIAN PAINT RUN	Douglas Co	432X	80125	5600-5799	
INDIAN PEAK RD	Gilpin Co	741Z	80403	1-1599	
INDIAN PEAKS AVE	Frederick	726D	80530	8100-8199	
INDIAN PEAKS CIR	Longmont	41T	80504	2100-2299	
INDIAN PEAKS DR	Boulder Co	740L	80466	None	
INDIAN PEAKS DR	Lafayette	131F	80026	None	
INDIAN PEAKS DR	Nederland	740L	80466	None	
INDIAN PEAKS PKWY	Broomfield	133L	80020	None	
INDIAN PIPE LN	Parker	409Y	80134	19700-19799	
INDIAN ROCK CIR	Elbert Co	890Q	80107	None	
INDIAN SPRINGS RD	Jefferson Co	823V	80433	10700-21799	
INDIAN SUMMER CT	Boulder	69Y	80301	5400-5499	
INDIAN SUMMER LN	El Paso Co	908Q	80132	19200-19999	
INDIAN SUMMER LN W	Castle Rock	466Q	80109	3100-3199	
INDIAN TRAIL	Elbert Co	912L	80106	9600-9999	
INDIAN TRAIL S	Jefferson Co	337J	80439	4800-4999	
INDIAN TREE CIR	Elbert Co	851X	80107	None	
INDIAN WELLS CIR	Elbert Co	851C	80107	None	
INDIAN WELLS COVE	Lone Tree	406C	80124	7400-7499	
INDIAN WELLS CT	Lone Tree	406C	80124	7400-7499	
INDIAN WELLS DR	Lone Tree	406G	80124	9600-9899	
INDIAN WELLS LN	Lone Tree	406G	80124	7400-7599	
INDIAN WELLS PL	Lone Tree	406G	80124	700-7599	
INDIAN WELLS WAY	Lone Tree	406G	80124	7400-7599	
INDIGO CT	Boulder Co	99F	80301	6100-6299	
INDIGO DR	Brighton	168C	80601	1300-1398	E
INDIGO ST	Lochbuie	140E	80603	200-499	
INDIGO WAY	Douglas Co	466C	80108	1-99	
INDIGO TRAIL S	Parker	408V	80134	None	
INDORE DR E	Aurora	381F	80016	25200-25699	
INDORE DR W	Jefferson Co	372M	80128	5400-5599	
	Jefferson Co	372J	80128	8700-8799	
	Jefferson Co	371M	80128	9200-9599	
	Jefferson Co	371L	80128	10300-10999	
INDORE PL	Jefferson Co	371J	80127	12600-12699	
INDORE PL E	Aurora	381E	80016	25000-25099	
INDORE PL W	Jefferson Co	372M	80128	5900-6499	
	Jefferson Co	372J	80128	8500-8799	
INDORE ST E	Aurora	830A	80016	25300-25599	
INDUSTRIAL CIR	Longmont	41P	80501	1800-1999	
INDUSTRIAL LN	Broomfield	161U	80020	2000-3899	
INDUSTRIAL ST	Frederick	727A	80504	None	
INDUSTRIAL WAY	Castle Rock	467N	80109	3100-4999	
INDUSTRIAL WAY	Jefferson Co	306C	80401	29300-29399	
INER RD	Park Co	841X	80421	None	
INFINITE DR	Louisville	130X	80027	1400-1499	
INFINITY CIR	Golden	279E	80401	2001-2099	O
INGALLS CIR	Arvada	252D	80003	6000-6099	
	Arvada	222G	80003	8200-8299	
	Arvada	222H	80003	8400-8699	
	Westminster	192L	80020	10800-10899	

STREET NAME	CITY or COUNTY	MAP GRID	ZIP CODE	BLOCK RANGE	O/E
INGALLS CT	Arvada	222Y	80003	6200-6799	
	Arvada	222U	80003	6900-7199	
	Arvada	222L	80003	7900-7999	
	Westminster	222Q	80003	7200-7299	
	Westminster	222R	80003	7400-7499	
	Wheat Ridge	252Y	80214	3000-3199	
	Wheat Ridge	252U	80033	4100-4199	
INGALLS CT S	Jefferson Co	372M	80128	7200-7499	
	Lakewood	312M	80227	1900-1999	
	Lakewood	312V	80227	2600-2699	
	Lakewood	312M	80232	None	
INGALLS PL	Wheat Ridge	252U	80033	3800-3999	
INGALLS ST	Arvada	252D	80003	5900-5999	
	Arvada	222Z	80003	6200-6799	
	Arvada	222V	80003	6900-7299	
	Arvada	222M	80003	7600-7999	
	Edgewater	282D	80214	2000-2799	
	Jefferson Co	252G	80002	5200-5299	
	Lakewood	282V	80226	1-599	
	Lakewood	282R	80214	600-699	
	Lakewood	282M	80214	900-1999	
	Westminster	192Y	80031	9200-9499	
	Westminster	192G	80020	11200-11299	
	Westminster	192C	80020	11500-11699	
	Wheat Ridge	252Z	80214	2900-3199	
	Wheat Ridge	252Z	80033	3200-3799	
	Wheat Ridge	252V	80033	4100-4399	
	Wheat Ridge	252Q	80033	4400-4799	
	Wheat Ridge	252M	80033	4800-4999	
INGALLS ST S	Denver	312Y	80227	3200-3399	
	Denver	342D	80235	3600-3699	
	Denver	342R	80123	5200-5299	
	Jefferson Co	342Z	80123	6000-6499	
	Jefferson Co	372M	80128	7600-7699	
	Lakewood	282V	80226	1-299	
	Lakewood	282Z	80226	300-599	
	Lakewood	312D	80226	800-899	
	Lakewood	312H	80232	1100-1499	
	Lakewood	312M	80227	1900-1999	
	Lakewood	342U	80123	5600-5699	
INGALLS WAY S	Denver	312V	80227	2700-3099	
	Jefferson Co	372H	80128	7100-7399	
	Lakewood	312M	80227	2000-2099	
INGERSOLL PL	Boulder	128D	80303	5000-5199	
INGLETON CT	Douglas Co	436Q	80108	300-399	
INGLETON DR	Castle Pines North	436Q	80108	6700-6899	
INGLETON PL	Castle Pines North	436Q	80108	300-399	
INGRAM CT	Boulder	128Q	80305	4600-4699	
INNISBROOK CT	Castle Rock	497T	80104	2500-2599	
INNISBROOK LOOP	Elbert Co	851C	80107	None	
INNOVATION WAY	Boulder	128G	80303	None	
INNSBROOK DR	Jefferson Co	365P	80439	7700-7799	
INSPIRATION DR E	Douglas Co	380X	80138	7000-9799	
	Douglas Co	381X	80138	9000-10999	
INSPIRATION RD	Jefferson Co	762B	80403	11400-11699	
INSPIRATION RD W	Jefferson Co	762B	80403	32400-32699	
INSPIRATION POINT DR	Denver	252M	80212	None	
INTERLOCKEN BLVD	Broomfield	161U	80021	200-599	
	Broomfield	161S	80021	600-699	
INTERLOCKEN CT	Jefferson Co	306N	80439	2000-2099	
INTERLOCKEN DR	Jefferson Co	306N	80439	1800-30099	
	Jefferson Co	306N	80439	None	
INTERLOCKEN LOOP	Broomfield	161T	80021	None	
	Broomfield	161X	80021	None	
INTERLOCKEN PKWY	Broomfield	161Y	80021	100-399	
INTERLOCKEN ST	Douglas Co	469C	80134	5400-5499	
INTERLOCKEN CRESCENT	Broomfield	161T	80021	300-398	E
INTERNATIONAL CT	Broomfield	161Y	80021	1-99	
INTERNATIONAL ISLE DR	Douglas Co	466F	80108	700-799	
INTERNET AVE	Weld Co	731M	80642	None	
INTERPORT BLVD S	Arapahoe Co	377R	80112	8000-8299	
INVERNESS CIR	Arapahoe Co	377K	80112	2E-198E	E
INVERNESS CT	Arapahoe Co	377P	80112	1E-99E	
	Arapahoe Co	377K	80112	None	
INVERNESS DR	Arapahoe Co	377P	80112	1E-99E	
	Arapahoe Co	377K	80112	100E-199E	
	Arapahoe Co	377P	80112	100W-299W	
INVERNESS DR	Jefferson Co	306T	80439	32100-33799	
INVERNESS DR	Lafayette	132A	80026	1300-1399	
INVERNESS LN	Arapahoe Co	377L	80112	1E-99E	
INVERNESS LN	Douglas Co	377T	80112	None	
INVERNESS LN	Jefferson Co	306T	80439	30200-30499	
INVERNESS PKWY	Douglas Co	377T	80112	300-499	
INVERNESS PL	Arapahoe Co	377P	80112	1E-99E	
	Arapahoe Co	377K	80112	None	
INVERNESS PL	Jefferson Co	306T	80439	2400-2499	
INVERNESS ST	Broomfield	162Z	80020	200-299	
	Broomfield	162R	80020	1100-1299	
INVERNESS WAY	Douglas Co	377P	80112	1E-99E	
	Douglas Co	377P	80112	1S-399S	
INVERNESS TERRACE	Arapahoe Co	377K	80112	100E-199E	
	Arapahoe Co	377J	80112	100W-199W	
INWOOD PL	Castle Rock	527H	80104	1300-1499	
INYOKERN CT	Arapahoe Co	791T	80137	None	
IO CT	Lafayette	131U	80026	1600-1699	
IOLA CT S	Arapahoe Co	347X	80111	6000-6299	
	Aurora	317K	80014	2000-2099	
IOLA ST	Adams Co	137X	80602	15000-15199	
	Adams Co	137T	80602	15400-15499	
	Adams Co	137P	80602	None	
	Aurora	287P	80010	400-999	
	Aurora	287K	80010	1100-1499	
	Aurora	287B	80010	1600-2499	
	Commerce City	197F	80640	11200-11499	
	Denver	257X	80238	None	
IOLA ST S	Arapahoe Co	377F	80112	7300-7399	
	Aurora	317B	80112	900-998	E
	Aurora	317F	80112	1500-1799	
	Aurora	317P	80014	2200-2299	
IOLA WAY S	Arapahoe Co	347P	80111	5400-5499	
	Arapahoe Co	347X	80111	5900-6299	
IONIC DR	Lafayette	131Q	80026	1800-1899	
IONIC ST	Lochbuie	140E	80603	200-299	
IONOSPHERE ST	Longmont	41V	80504	1900-2099	
IOWA AVE	Adams Co	794P	80136	None	
IOWA AVE	Longmont	41L	80501	900-1399	

STREET NAME	CITY or COUNTY	MAP GRID	ZIP CODE	BLOCK RANGE	O/E
IOWA AVE E	Arapahoe Co	317E	80247	9200-9599	
	Arapahoe Co	317E	80247	10100-10299	
	Aurora	317F	80112	10500-10598	E
	Aurora	317G	80112	11600-12099	
	Aurora	318E	80012	13300-13499	
	Aurora	318H	80017	16100-16799	
	Aurora	319F	80017	17800-17899	
	Denver	314G	80210	1-1499	
	Denver	315F	80210	2100-3999	
	Denver	315H	80222	4000-5599	
	Denver	316E	80224	5600-6499	
	Denver	316F	80231	7300-7999	
IOWA AVE N	Lafayette	132J	80026	100-599	
IOWA AVE S	Lafayette	132J	80026	100-499	
IOWA AVE W	Denver	314F	80223	1-399	
	Denver	313F	80219	2700-4899	
	Lakewood	312H	80232	5200-5599	
	Lakewood	312G	80232	6400-7199	
	Lakewood	312E	80232	8000-8299	
	Lakewood	311H	80232	9200-9499	
	Lakewood	311L	80232	10000-10199	
IOWA CIR E	Arapahoe Co	317E	80247	9500-9599	
	Aurora	319G	80017	19400-19599	
IOWA CIR W	Lakewood	311H	80232	9300-9499	
IOWA CT	Golden	248V	80403	300-399	
IOWA CT W	Lakewood	311M	80232	8900-9199	
IOWA DR	Golden	248V	80403	200-399	
IOWA DR E	Arapahoe Co	316G	80231	8300-8499	
	Aurora	317F	80112	10800-11299	
	Aurora	317H	80112	12100-12399	
	Aurora	318F	80012	14100-14499	
	Aurora	319F	80017	17700-18399	
IOWA DR W	Jefferson Co	311K	80232	11100-11299	
	Lakewood	312F	80232	7600-7999	
	Lakewood	311M	80232	9700-9999	
	Lakewood	311E	80228	12300-12499	
	Lakewood	311J	80228	12600-12699	
IOWA PL E	Arapahoe Co	316H	80231	8500-8599	
	Aurora	318G	80017	15300-15399	
	Aurora	320H	80018	23800-23899	
	Aurora	321E	80018	24100-24299	
IOWA PL W	Lakewood	312M	80232	5800-6399	
	Lakewood	312L	80232	6500-6599	
	Lakewood	311H	80232	9000-9199	
	Lakewood	311M	80232	9300-9499	
	Lakewood	312M	80232	None	
IOWA ST	Golden	248V	80403	600-799	
IOWA GULCH RD	Jefferson Co	368R	80465	7600-8299	
IPSWICH ST	Boulder Co	100F	80301	4600-4799	
IRAN ST	Denver	259R	80249	4200-4599	
	Denver	259M	80249	4700-4799	
	Denver	259H	80249	None	
IREDELL ST	Adams Co	750H	80603	16600-16799	
IRELAND CIR S	Centennial	380E	80016	7200-7499	
IRELAND CT	Denver	259R	80249	3800-4199	
	Denver	259M	80249	4600-4899	
IRELAND CT S	Arapahoe Co	349H	80013	4100-4299	
	Arapahoe Co	349M	80015	4700-4899	
	Arapahoe Co	379D	80016	6600-6699	
	Aurora	319R	80013	None	
	Centennial	349V	80016	5900-5999	
	Centennial	380E	80016	7300-7499	
IRELAND LN S	Arapahoe Co	349H	80015	None	
IRELAND ST	Denver	259V	80249	3800-4799	
	Denver	259H	80249	None	
IRELAND ST S	Arapahoe Co	349H	80013	4200-4299	
	Arapahoe Co	349M	80015	4700-4899	
	Arapahoe Co	349H	80015	None	
	Centennial	349V	80015	5400-5699	
	Denver	259V	80249	None	
IRELAND WAY S	Arapahoe Co	380P	80016	7700-8299	
	Aurora	380J	80016	7500-7699	
	Aurora	319R	80013	None	
	Aurora	319V	80013	None	
	Centennial	349R	80015	5100-5499	
	Centennial	349V	80015	5500-5699	
	Centennial	379H	80016	7100-7499	
IRELAND MOSS ST	Castle Rock	466Y	80109	None	
IRENE AVE	Gilpin Co	760H	80403	1-399	
IRENE CT	Broomfield	162P	80020	1-99	
IRIDIUM CT	Castle Rock	467G	80108	None	
IRIDIUM WAY	Castle Rock	467G	80108	None	
IRIS AVE	Boulder	97Q	80304	400-899	
	Boulder	97R	80304	1200-1899	
	Boulder	98N	80304	1900-2799	
	Boulder	98P	80301	2800-4699	
IRIS CIR	Broomfield	162P	80020	1300-1399	
IRIS CIR W	Littleton	374A	80120	1800-1899	
IRIS CT	Arvada	221Y	80004	6300-6499	
	Arvada	221U	80005	6900-6999	
	Arvada	221M	80005	8000-8099	
	Arvada	221H	80005	8200-8299	
	Arvada	251D	80004	None	
IRIS CT	Boulder	97R	80304	3400-3499	
IRIS CT	Greenwood Village	345U	80121	4000-4099	
	Westminster	221D	80005	8800-9099	
	Wheat Ridge	251Z	80033	3200-3299	
	Wheat Ridge	251V	80033	3700-3799	
	Wheat Ridge	251R	80033	4200-4299	
IRIS CT E	Highlands Ranch	374Z	80126	1200-1299	
IRIS CT S	Jefferson Co	371D	80123	6400-6499	
	Jefferson Co	371H	80128	7100-7299	
	Jefferson Co	371Z	80128	8800-8899	
	Jefferson Co	341H	80123	None	
	Lakewood	281Z	80226	400-499	
	Lakewood	311V	80227	2500-2699	
	Lakewood	311Z	80227	3300-3499	
	Littleton	825P	80127	9700-9899	
IRIS DR	Jefferson Co	336H	80439	27700-28099	
IRIS DR	Park Co	841J	80421	1-299	
IRIS DR S	Lakewood	311Z	80227	3300-3499	
IRIS PKWY	Frederick	727A	80504	None	
IRIS RD	Gilpin Co	761J	80403	1-199	
IRIS ST	Arvada	251M	80002	5000-5299	
	Arvada	251G	80002	5300-5799	
	Arvada	221V	80004	6400-6999	
	Arvada	221R	80005	7300-7399	
	Arvada	221M	80005	8000-8099	
	Arvada	221H	80005	8200-8299	

Continued on next column

STREET NAME	CITY or COUNTY	MAP GRID	ZIP CODE	BLOCK RANGE	O/E
IRIS ST (Cont'd)	Arvada	221D	80005	8600-8799	
	Broomfield	162X	80020	100-399	
	Broomfield	162T	80020	1000-1099	
	Broomfield	162K	80020	1600-1699	
	Lakewood	281M	80215	1200-1299	
	Lakewood	281H	80215	1500-2099	
	Lakewood	281D	80215	2100-2599	
	Westminster	191V	80021	9700-9899	
	Wheat Ridge	251R	80033	4200-4399	
	Wheat Ridge	251M	80033	4900-4999	
IRIS ST S	Denver	341M	80123	4500-5099	
	Jefferson Co	341V	80123	5400-5599	
	Jefferson Co	371D	80123	6400-6699	
	Jefferson Co	371D	80128	6700-6899	
	Lakewood	311D	80226	900-1099	
	Lakewood	311H	80232	1100-1499	
	Lakewood	311V	80227	2500-2699	
IRIS WAY	Arvada	251D	80004	6000-6199	
	Arvada	221Y	80004	6200-6599	
IRIS WAY	Westminster	191M	80021	10400-10499	
IRIS WAY S	Jefferson Co	341R	80123	5100-5199	
	Jefferson Co	341V	80123	5600-5799	
	Jefferson Co	341Z	80123	6300-6499	
	Jefferson Co	371R	80128	7900-8399	
	Lakewood	311M	80232	1600-1699	
	Littleton	825P	80127	9300-9398	E
IRIS WAY W	Jefferson Co	341V	80123	5700-5799	
IRISH AVE E	Aurora	381M	80016	None	
	Littleton	374L	80122	400-699	
IRISH DR E	Aurora	381J	80016	24800-24999	
	Aurora	380K	80016	None	
	Aurora	380M	80016	None	
IRISH LN E	Arapahoe Co	374M	80122	1300-1499	
IRISH PL E	Arapahoe Co	374M	80122	900-999	
	Aurora	381L	80016	None	
	Centennial	375K	80122	2700-2799	
	Centennial	376J	80112	5700-6499	
IRIS HOLLOW PL	Boulder	98N	80304	2600-2699	
IRISH PAT MURPHY DR N	Douglas Co	440X	80134	5500-6099	
IRIS WALK CT	Boulder	98S	80304	3300-3398	E
IRMA CT	Northglenn	194D	80233	None	
IRMA DR	Northglenn	195J	80233	10400-11199	
	Northglenn	194D	80233	11200-11999	
IRMA WAY	Northglenn	194D	80233	None	
IRON CT	Boulder Co	723G	80503	3900-3999	
IRON CT	Longmont	40C	80503	900-999	
IRON BARK DR	Douglas Co	845V	80125	None	
IRON FORGE PL	Boulder	98T	80301	3100-3399	
IRON GATE ST	Castle Rock	469E	80108	6701-6799	O
IRON HORSE DR	Longmont	42H	80501	1600-1899	
IRON HORSE TRAIL	Douglas Co	846P	80135	None	
IRON ORE AVE E	Parker	409S	80134	None	
IRON SHOT CT	Castle Rock	496D	80109	None	
IRON SPRINGS PL	Castle Rock	466X	80109	2900-3099	
IRONSTONE PL	Douglas Co	408D	80134	9700-9799	
IRONSTONE WAY	Parker	439G	80134	12700-12999	
IRONTON CT	Aurora	287P	80010	500-599	
IRONTON CT S	Arapahoe Co	347T	80111	5700-6199	
	Arapahoe Co	347X	80111	6300-6399	
	Aurora	317P	80014	2000-2299	
IRONTON ST	Adams Co	137T	80602	15200-15399	
	Adams Co	137K	80602	None	
	Aurora	287K	80010	700-2499	
IRONTON ST	Commerce City	197T	80022	9600-9799	
	Commerce City	197F	80640	11200-11499	
	Denver	257K	80239	4500-5099	
IRONTON ST S	Aurora	287T	80012	100-499	
	Aurora	317B	80112	700-1099	
	Aurora	317F	80112	1500-1899	
	Centennial	377B	80111	None	
IRONTON WAY S	Arapahoe Co	347P	80111	5100-5399	
IRONWOOD PL	Broomfield	162Q	80020	1200-1299	
IRONWOOD PL	Erie	133G	80516	None	
IRONWOOD ST	Highlands Ranch	373Z	80129	9100-9299	
IRONWOOD WAY	Erie	133G	80516	None	
IRONWOOD WAY	Highlands Ranch	373Z	80129	9100-9299	
IROQUOIS CIR	Douglas Co	846U	80135	3600-3799	
IROQUOIS DR	Boulder	128R	80303	100-299	
IROQUOIS TRAIL	Jefferson Co	366A	80439	6500-6599	
	Jefferson Co	842E	80470	33400-34799	
IRVING CIR	Broomfield	163U	80020	12600-12699	
IRVING CT	Broomfield	163U	80020	12600-12699	
	Broomfield	163Q	80020	13000-13199	
	Broomfield	133Y	80020	None	
	Westminster	193U	80031	9700-9799	
	Westminster	193P	80031	10300-10399	
	Westminster	193L	80031	10500-10699	
	Westminster	193L	80031	10800-10899	
IRVING DR	Broomfield	163U	80020	12400-12499	
	Westminster	193G	80031	11100-11299	
IRVING ST	Adams Co	253G	80221	5200-5399	
	Adams Co	223Y	80221	6400-6899	
	Broomfield	163U	80020	12501-12599	O
	Broomfield	163C	80020	14400-14699	
	Broomfield	133Y	80020	14700-15199	
	Denver	283U	80219	1-399	
	Denver	283Q	80204	600-1199	
	Denver	283G	80204	1300-1999	
	Denver	283C	80211	2000-2699	
	Denver	253U	80211	2700-4599	
	Denver	253L	80221	4800-4999	
	Westminster	223Q	80030	7100-7599	
	Westminster	223L	80030	7600-7999	
	Westminster	223G	80031	8000-8699	
	Westminster	223C	80031	8700-8799	
	Westminster	193Y	80031	9200-9499	
	Westminster	193P	80031	10000-10199	
	Westminster	193C	80031	11500-11599	
IRVING ST S	Arapahoe Co	313Y	80110	3200-3499	
	Denver	283U	80219	1-699	
	Denver	313L	80219	700-2699	
	Denver	313U	80236	2700-3099	
	Denver	343L	80110	4700-4799	
	Englewood	343G	80110	4500-4699	
	Englewood	343L	80110	4800-5099	
	Littleton	343Q	80123	5100-5499	
	Sheridan	343C	80110	3500-3699	
	Sheridan	343C	80236	3700-3799	
	Sheridan	343G	80110	4100-4499	

STREET NAME	CITY or COUNTY	MAP GRID	ZIP CODE	BLOCK RANGE	O/E
IRVINGTON CT S	Aurora	381A	80016	6800-6899	
	Aurora	381E	80016	7000-7299	
	Aurora	351S	80016	None	
IRVINGTON PL E	Denver	286T	80230	7201-7299	O
IRVINGTON PL W	Denver	284T	80223	1-499	
	Denver	284S	80223	1801-1899	O
	Denver	283U	80219	2700-2999	
IRVINGTON ST N	Aurora	291N	80018	100-499	
	Aurora	291S	80018	None	
IRVINGTON ST S	Aurora	291S	80018	None	
IRVINGTON WAY S	Aurora	830A	80016	None	
IRWIN AVE E	Littleton	374L	80122	400-599	
IRWIN LN E	Arapahoe Co	374M	80122	1400-1499	
IRWIN PL	Erie	102P	80516	200-499	
IRWIN PL E	Arapahoe Co	374M	80122	900-999	
	Arapahoe Co	374M	80122	1100-1199	
	Arapahoe Co	374M	80122	1300-1399	
	Centennial	375K	80122	2700-2799	
	Centennial	375L	80122	3800-3899	
	Centennial	376J	80112	5900-6399	
ISABEL CT S	Highlands Ranch	404H	80126	9700-9899	
ISABELL CIR	Arvada	220P	80007	None	
ISABELL CT	Arvada	220T	80007	None	
	Jefferson Co	250X	80401	2900-3099	
	Jefferson Co	250K	80403	4900-4999	
ISABELL CT	Jefferson Co	250K	80403	5700-5899	
ISABELL DR	Jefferson Co	250N	80403	None	
ISABELL ST	Jefferson Co	280P	80401	600-799	
	Jefferson Co	280K	80401	1100-1499	
	Jefferson Co	250X	80401	2800-3199	
	Jefferson Co	250N	80403	4700-4799	
ISABELLA DR	Frederick	726G	80516	None	
ISABELLE RD	Boulder Co	101P	80026	9500-10999	
	Erie	102R	80516	11900-12699	
ISABELLE WAY	Broomfield	163N	80020	13300-13499	
ISENBERG LN	Jefferson Co	336X	80439	30000-30999	
ISHAM JONES RD	Jefferson Co	842E	80470	33700-33899	
ISLAND CIR	Boulder Co	100E	80301	7300-7399	
ISLAND DR	Boulder Co	98P	80301	2800-2999	
ISLAND DR	Jefferson Co	306N	80439	1-31599	
ISLAND LN	Jefferson Co	306N	80439	1-2199	
ISLAND PT	Jefferson Co	306N	80439	1-2299	
ISLAND GREEN DR	Boulder	69Z	80301	7200-7399	
ISLEHURST LN	El Paso Co	909N	80132	1700-1799	
ISOLETA RD	Jefferson Co	338J	80454	23000-23999	
ITASCA	Thornton	194W	80260	None	
ITHACA AVE W	Englewood	344B	80110	300-899	
	Jefferson Co	341D	80235	9000-9199	
ITHACA CIR E	Aurora	319W	80013	16900-17199	
ITHACA CT	Longmont	10U	80503	1500-1699	
ITHACA DR E	Aurora	349C	80013	18900-19199	
ITHACA PL E	Aurora	318Z	80013	16000-16099	
	Aurora	319X	80013	17600-18399	
	Aurora	319Y	80013	19000-19699	
	Aurora	319Z	80013	20100-20199	
	Aurora	320W	80013	20600-20699	
	Denver	346A	80237	5700-5899	
	Denver	346B	80237	6500-6899	
ITHACA PL W	Denver	342C	80235	6300-6399	
	Jefferson Co	342A	80235	8200-8299	
ITHACA WAY	Adams Co	223C	80031	8800-9099	
ITHICA DR	Boulder	128S	80305	500-699	
	Boulder	128X	80305	700-1799	
IVAN CT S	Denver	312Z	80227	3400-3499	
IVAN WAY S	Denver	312V	80227	2700-3099	
IVANHOE CIR	Centennial	376J	80112	7500-7599	
	Thornton	166W	80602	12000-12299	
IVANHOE CT	Thornton	166W	80602	12000-12299	
IVANHOE CT S	Centennial	346W	80111	6100-6199	
	Centennial	376E	80112	7200-7399	
IVANHOE LN S	Cherry Hills Village	346A	80111	4000-4099	
IVANHOE PL S	Arapahoe Co	315R	80222	2400-2599	
IVANHOE ST	Adams Co	226N	80022	7200-7399	
	Adams Co	226J	80022	8000-8299	
	Adams Co	136N	80602	16000-16299	
	Adams Co	136J	80602	16600-16799	
	Commerce City	256A	80022	6000-6099	
	Commerce City	226W	80022	6300-6599	
	Commerce City	226S	80022	6800-6899	
	Commerce City	226N	80022	7100-7199	
	Denver	286S	80220	1-499	
	Denver	286J	80220	600-1999	
	Denver	286A	80207	2000-2799	
	Denver	256W	80207	2800-3799	
	Greenwood Village	346S	80111	5700-5799	
	Thornton	166S	80602	12300-12599	
	Thornton	166N	80602	13000-13199	
	Thornton	166J	80602	13700-13999	
	Thornton	166S	80602	None	
IVANHOE ST S	Arapahoe Co	316S	80222	2800-3099	
	Centennial	346W	80111	6100-6199	
	Denver	316J	80224	1600-1899	
	Denver	316N	80222	2100-2199	
	Denver	346A	80237	3500-3699	
IVANHOE WAY S	Centennial	376J	80112	7500-7699	
	Denver	316E	80224	1100-1399	
	Denver	316W	80222	3400-3499	
IVESIA DR	Douglas Co	887F	80118	2700-2899	
IVEY DR	Douglas Co	908L	80118	2700-2999	
IVORY CIR	Aurora	288Q	80011	300-499	
IVORY CIR S	Aurora	318C	80017	900-1099	
	Aurora	318G	80017	1600-1699	
	Aurora	348L	80015	4600-4699	
IVORY CT S	Aurora	318L	80017	1800-1899	
	Aurora	318L	80013	1900-1999	
	Aurora	318U	80013	2900-3099	
	Aurora	348C	80013	3600-3699	
	Aurora	348L	80015	4600-4799	
IVORY ST S	Aurora	318L	80013	2000-2199	
IVORY WAY S	Aurora	318L	80013	1900-2099	
IVY AVE	Weld Co	706V	80504	None	
IVY CIR	Boulder	97R	80304	3500-3599	
IVY CIR	Thornton	166W	80602	12000-12299	
IVY CT	Greenwood Village	346S	80111	5600-5699	
	Thornton	166W	80602	12000-12299	
	Thornton	166N	80602	13200-13299	
IVY CT S	Centennial	346W	80111	6300-6399	
	Centennial	376A	80111	6400-6499	
	Centennial	376E	80112	7200-7299	
	Centennial	376J	80112	7800-7899	
IVY LN	Denver	286N	80220	1-99	
IVY LN S	Cherry Hills Village	346E	80111	4000-4299	
IVY PL	Superior	160U	80027	1500-1599	
IVY PL	Thornton	166S	80602	12300-12399	
	Thornton	166N	80602	13100-13199	
IVY ST	Adams Co	226N	80022	7200-7399	
	Adams Co	226J	80022	8000-8199	
	Adams Co	136J	80602	16600-16799	
	Commerce City	256J	80022	5000-5199	
	Commerce City	256A	80022	6000-6099	
	Commerce City	226W	80022	6200-6799	
	Commerce City	226S	80022	6800-6899	
	Commerce City	226N	80022	7100-7199	
	Denver	286N	80220	1-399	
	Denver	286J	80220	600-1999	
	Denver	286A	80207	2000-2799	
	Denver	256W	80207	2800-3799	
	Denver	256N	80216	4500-4799	
	Greenwood Village	346S	80111	5700-5799	
	Thornton	196A	80233	11600-11899	
	Thornton	166N	80602	12900-12999	
	Thornton	166E	80602	13700-13999	
IVY ST	Thornton	166J	80602	16600-16799	
	Thornton	166S	80602	None	
IVY ST S	Arapahoe Co	316N	80222	2500-2699	
	Centennial	346W	80111	6000-6299	
	Centennial	376A	80112	6700-6799	
	Denver	286S	80224	1-499	
	Denver	316A	80224	700-999	
	Denver	316J	80224	1500-1899	
IVY WAY	Commerce City	226W	80022	6200-6299	
IVY WAY	Erie	133H	80516	None	
IVY WAY	Thornton	166W	80602	12000-12299	
IVY WAY S	Centennial	376A	80112	6700-6899	
	Centennial	376J	80112	7300-7899	
	Denver	286W	80224	600-699	
	Denver	316E	80224	1200-1699	
	Denver	316W	80222	3200-3499	
	Denver	346A	80237	3900-3999	
IVYCREST PT	Highlands Ranch	405Q	80130	4300-4499	
IVYWOOD CT	Fort Lupton	728H	80621	2000-2099	
IVYWOOD CT	Highlands Ranch	374Y	80126	700-799	
IVYWOOD CT E	Highlands Ranch	404C	80126	700-799	
IVYWOOD ST	Adams Co	226J	80022	7800-7999	
IVYWOOD ST	Fort Lupton	728H	80621	1800-1999	

J

STREET NAME	CITY or COUNTY	MAP GRID	ZIP CODE	BLOCK RANGE	O/E
JACK PL E	Highlands Ranch	406E	80130	5700-5799	
JACKALOPE DR E	Parker	408Z	80134	None	
JACKALOPE LN S	Parker	408Z	80134	None	
JACKASS HILL RD	Littleton	373M	80120	7500-7699	
JACK BOOT RD	El Paso Co	908Y	80132	300-599	
JACKBOOT WAY	El Paso Co	908Y	80132	200-299	
JACKDAW ST	Highlands Ranch	375Z	80126	8800-8899	
JACKPINE CT	Boulder	97Q	80304	500-599	
JACK PINE DR	Jefferson Co	365F	80439	33600-33699	
JACK PINE LN	Clear Creek Co	304Y	80439	1-199	
JACK PINE RD	Jefferson Co	335U	80439	5500-5999	
JACK RABBIT PL	Highlands Ranch	374U	80126	1-99	
JACKSON	Weld Co	706N	80504	11400-11499	
JACKSON AVE	Firestone	727B	80504	None	
JACKSON CIR	Adams Co	225F	80229	8300-8399	
JACKSON CIR	Boulder	128H	80303	4700-4799	
JACKSON CIR	Erie	102L	80516	None	
JACKSON CIR	Louisville	130V	80027	100-399	
JACKSON CIR	Thornton	195C	80233	11800-11899	
JACKSON CIR S	Centennial	375K	80122	7700-7999	
JACKSON CT	Adams Co	225F	80229	8500-8599	
JACKSON CT	Bennett	793N	80102	200-299	
JACKSON CT	Erie	102M	80516	None	
JACKSON CT	Highlands Ranch	376X	80130	6500-6699	
JACKSON CT	Lafayette	132T	80026	None	
JACKSON CT	Longmont	11U	80501	None	
JACKSON CT	Louisville	130V	80027	1300-1399	
JACKSON CT	Thornton	195L	80233	10700-10799	
JACKSON CT S	Centennial	375C	80121	6600-6699	
	Centennial	375C	80122	6700-6799	
	Centennial	375G	80122	7200-7299	
	Centennial	375L	80122	7400-7499	
	Centennial	375C	80121	None	
JACKSON DR	Erie	102M	80516	1200-1498	E
	Erie	102M	80516	None	
JACKSON DR	Firestone	727B	80504	None	
JACKSON DR	Golden	248V	80403	300-399	
JACKSON DR	Louisville	130M	80027	100-199	
JACKSON DR	Thornton	165Q	80241	13000-13099	
	Thornton	165L	80241	13400-13499	
	Thornton	165L	80241	13500-13599	
JACKSON LN	Highlands Ranch	376X	80130	6500-6699	
JACKSON PL	Golden	248V	80403	300-399	
JACKSON PL	Thornton	165Y	80241	12200-12299	
	Thornton	165K	80241	13400-13499	
JACKSON ST	Adams Co	165B	80602	14500-14899	
	Adams Co	135P	80602	15800-15999	
	Commerce City	225Y	80022	6200-6399	
	Denver	285Q	80206	1-1699	
	Denver	285C	80205	2600-2699	
	Denver	255Y	80205	2700-2899	
	Denver	255U	80205	3300-3999	
	Denver	255Q	80216	4000-4499	
	Denver	255L	80216	4500-4999	
	Denver	255G	80216	5200-5399	
JACKSON ST	Golden	249W	80403	400-699	
	Golden	249W	80401	900-998	E
	Golden	279B	80401	1300-2399	
JACKSON ST	Lafayette	132S	80026	None	
JACKSON ST	Nederland	740Q	80466	None	
JACKSON ST	Thornton	195Y	80229	9200-9399	
	Thornton	195Q	80229	10000-10099	
	Thornton	195C	80233	11400-11799	
	Thornton	165U	80241	12700-12799	
	Thornton	165L	80241	13500-13599	
	Thornton	165L	80602	13800-13899	
	Thornton	165G	80602	13900-13999	
	Thornton	165G	80602	None	
	Thornton	165U	80241	None	
JACKSON ST N	Golden	248V	80403	500-1199	
JACKSON ST S	Centennial	345Y	80121	6000-6599	
	Centennial	375L	80122	7300-7599	
	Centennial	375Q	80122	7900-8299	
	Cherry Hills Village	345C	80113	3700-3799	
	Denver	285U	80209	1-399	
	Denver	315C	80209	700-1099	
	Denver	315G	80210	1100-1899	
	Denver	315U	80210	2100-3099	
	Greenwood Village	345U	80121	5800-5899	
JACKSON WAY	Adams Co	225F	80229	8400-8499	
	Thornton	195F	80233	3200-3999	
JACKSON WAY S	Centennial	375G	80122	6900-6999	
JACKSON GAP RD	Adams Co	770X	80019	None	
	Denver	770S	80249	None	
	Denver	770X	80019	None	
JACKSON GAP WAY S	Aurora	381J	80016	7300-7699	
JACKSON CREEK PKWY	Monument	908X	80132	None	
JACKSON CREEK RD	Douglas Co	866L	80135	4000-9099	
JACKSON GAP CT S	Aurora	351X	80016	None	
JACKSON GAP WAY N	Aurora	291P	80018	100-599	
JACKSON GAP WAY S	Aurora	291T	80018	None	
	Aurora	351X	80016	None	
JACOB DR	Park Co	841S	80421	1-699	
JACOB PL	Douglas Co	432K	80125	10400-10499	
JACQUES WAY	Erie	103W	80516	None	
JADE AVE	Lochbuie	140E	80603	1600-1698	E
	Lochbuie	139H	80603	1700-1898	E
JADE CT	Boulder Co	130E	80303	7700-7799	
JADE CT	Broomfield	162P	80020	1600-1699	
JADE CT	Castle Rock	467M	80108	5900-5999	
JADE CT	Superior	160U	80027	2900-2999	
JADE LN	Longmont	41U	80504	None	
JADE ST	Boulder Co	102F	80026	11800-11899	
JADE ST	Broomfield	162X	80020	100-399	
	Broomfield	162T	80020	1000-1099	
JADE WAY	Boulder Co	703F	80540	100-298	E
JADE WAY	Longmont	41U	80504	None	
JAGUAR DR	Douglas Co	406J	80124	10500-10599	
JAGUAR PT	Douglas Co	406J	80124	10500-10799	
JAGUAR WAY	Douglas Co	406J	80124	5600-6099	
	Highlands Ranch	405M	80130	None	
JAGUAR GLEN	Douglas Co	406J	80124	10500-10599	
JAKE'S RANCH RD	Douglas Co	410E	80138	11900-11999	
JALNA CT	Adams Co	750H	80603	16300-16399	
JALNA ST	Adams Co	750D	80603	16700-16799	
JAMAICA CIR S	Arapahoe Co	347X	80111	5900-6199	
	Arapahoe Co	377B	80111	6400-6499	
JAMAICA CT	Aurora	287K	80010	900-1099	
JAMAICA CT S	Arapahoe Co	347X	80111	6000-6299	
	Arapahoe Co	347X	80111	6300-6399	
	Aurora	317K	80014	1900-2099	
	Aurora	317P	80014	2600-2699	
	Aurora	317T	80014	2900-3099	
JAMAICA DR	Adams Co	137P	80602	15700-15999	
	Commerce City	197F	80640	None	
JAMAICA ST	Adams Co	137X	80602	None	
	Aurora	287P	80010	300-599	
	Aurora	287K	80010	700-1499	
	Aurora	287B	80010	1600-2599	
	Commerce City	197F	80640	11200-11499	
JAMAICA ST S	Aurora	317B	80112	900-1099	
	Aurora	317F	80112	1500-1599	
	Aurora	317P	80014	2300-2599	
	Douglas Co	377X	80112	9100-9199	
JAMAICA WAY	Aurora	287X	80012	200-299	
JAMAICA WAY S	Arapahoe Co	347P	80111	5100-5299	
	Arapahoe Co	347T	80111	5500-5899	
	Arapahoe Co	347T	80111	5900-6099	
JAMES CIR	Broomfield	163U	80020	12600-12699	
JAMES CIR	Elbert Co	891X	80106	None	
JAMES CIR	Lafayette	131R	80026	1100-1299	
JAMES CIR	Longmont	41Q	80501	1-99	
JAMES CT	Boulder Co	70K	80503	7900-8099	
JAMES CT	Broomfield	163U	80020	12400-12699	
JAMES CT	Lafayette	131R	80026	1100-1299	
JAMES DR	Clear Creek Co	801R	80439	1-199	
JAMES PT	Broomfield	163T	80020	12500-12699	
JAMES ST	Broomfield	163U	80020	12400-12499	
JAMES ST	Longmont	41L	80501	700-899	
JAMES ST E	Highlands Ranch	404C	80126	500-699	
JAMES WAY	Erie	102C	80516	1300-1499	
JAMES WAY	Westminster	223L	80030	7600-7799	
JAMES CANYON DR	Boulder Co	722B	80302	1-2999	
JAMES E CASEY AVE	Douglas Co	378S	80112	13101-13299	O
JAMESTON ST	Boulder Co	100F	80301	4600-4799	
JAMESTOWN CT S	Aurora	381F	80016	7000-7099	
	Aurora	351X	80016	None	
JAMESTOWN WAY N	Aurora	291P	80018	None	
	Aurora	291T	80018	None	
JAMESTOWN WAY S	Aurora	291T	80018	None	
	Aurora	351T	80016	None	
JAMISON AVE E	Arapahoe Co	374M	80122	1000-1399	
	Arapahoe Co	374M	80122	1500-1799	
	Centennial	375J	80122	1800-2799	
	Centennial	376J	80112	6400-6499	
	Centennial	376K	80112	6600-6699	
	Centennial	376M	80112	8500-8699	
	Centennial	379J	80016	16800-17799	
	Centennial	379M	80016	19700-19899	
	Littleton	374L	80122	400-499	
JAMISON AVE W	Littleton	374K	80120	1-1299	
	Littleton	373J	80128	4500-4599	
	Arapahoe Co	830E	80016	26000N-26199N	
	Arapahoe Co	381K	80016	26000S-26199S	
	Aurora	381M	80016	27300-27599	
	Centennial	376L	80112	7300-7599	
	Centennial	376J	80112	6200N-6499N	
	Centennial	376L	80112	8300N-8499N	
	Centennial	376J	80112	6100S-6499S	
JAMISON CIR W	Littleton	374K	80120	200-799	
JAMISON DR E	Aurora	380M	80016	None	
	Centennial	376J	80112	6200-6299	
	Centennial	376L	80112	7300-8099	
JAMISON LN E	Centennial	376J	80112	5900-5999	
JAMISON PL	Longmont	11P	80501	1600-1699	
JAMISON PL E	Arapahoe Co	374M	80122	1100-1299	
	Arapahoe Co	374M	80122	1500-1799	
	Arapahoe Co	832H	80137	45100-45599	

Continued on next page

STREET NAME	CITY or COUNTY	MAP GRID	ZIP CODE	BLOCK RANGE	O/E
JAMISON PL E (Cont'd)	Arapahoe Co	377M	80112	None	
	Aurora	381M	80016	27200-27299	
	Aurora	380K	80016	None	
	Aurora	380M	80016	None	
	Centennial	375J	80122	1500-2799	
	Centennial	375L	80122	3900-3999	
	Centennial	376J	80112	5900-5999	
	Centennial	376K	80112	6700-6799	
	Centennial	376L	80112	8200-8299	
	Centennial	379L	80016	19200-19299	
	Littleton	374L	80122	500-599	
JAMISON PL W	Littleton	374K	80120	300-599	
	Littleton	373K	80128	4400-4499	
JAMISON RD E	Arapahoe Co	378L	80112	15600-15899	
JAMISON WAY W	Littleton	373M	80120	2100-2499	
JANELLE CIR	Jefferson Co	762B	80403	33000-33199	
JANELLE LN	Jefferson Co	762B	80403	32600-32899	
JANICE CT	Northglenn	194G	80233	300-499	
JANICE WAY	Arvada	251C	80004	6100-6199	
	Arvada	221Y	80004	6200-6399	
JANKOWSKI DR	Gilpin Co	761K	80403	2-398	E
JANSEN ST	Parker	409N	80134	11200-11299	
JAPONICA WAY	Boulder	97Q	80304	400-499	
JARED CT	Broomfield	163G	80020	14100-14399	
JARED WAY	Douglas Co	432K	80125	7500-8099	
JAROSA LN	Superior	160Q	80027	2000-2299	
JARRE CANYON RD	Douglas Co	846Y	80135	3600-5299	
See.. STATE HWY 67					
JARVIS DR	Erie	103N	80516	700-999	
JARVIS PL E	Aurora	348C	80014	15000-15099	
	Aurora	348C	80013	15300-15499	
	Aurora	349A	80013	17100-17599	
	Aurora	349B	80013	17900-18099	
	Aurora	349D	80013	19900-19999	
	Aurora	350B	80018	21700-21799	
	Aurora	350C	80018	None	
	Denver	346B	80237	6900-7799	
JARVIS PL W	Denver	342C	80235	6300-6399	
JASMINE CIR	Boulder	97Q	80304	900-1099	
JASMINE CIR E	Centennial	376N	80112	7900-8099	
JASMINE CT	Commerce City	226W	80022	5900-6299	
JASMINE CT	Douglas Co	432G	80125	10000-10099	
JASMINE CT	Thornton	196A	80233	11600-11899	
	Thornton	166N	80602	12900-12999	
	Thornton	166S	80602	None	
JASMINE CT S	Centennial	376A	80112	6800-6899	
	Centennial	376E	80112	7200-7299	
	Centennial	376J	80112	7500-7599	
	Centennial	376N	80112	8200-8299	
JASMINE DR	Commerce City	226J	80022	7800-7899	
JASMINE PL	Lafayette	131R	80026	900-999	
JASMINE PL	Thornton	166W	80602	12300-12399	
	Thornton	166N	80602	13000-13199	
JASMINE PL S	Arapahoe Co	315R	80222	2300-2599	
JASMINE ST	Adams Co	226J	80022	8000-8399	
	Adams Co	136J	80602	16500-16699	
	Commerce City	226S	80022	6800-7199	
	Denver	286S	80220	1-499	
	Denver	286J	80220	600-1999	
	Denver	286A	80207	2000-2799	
	Denver	256W	80207	2800-3799	
	Greenwood Village	346S	80111	5700-5799	
	Thornton	166W	80233	11900-11999	
	Thornton	166S	80602	12000-12399	
	Thornton	166N	80602	13100-13299	
	Thornton	166J	80602	13700-13999	
	Thornton	166J	80602	16500-16699	
	Thornton	196A	80233	None	
JASMINE ST S	Arapahoe Co	316S	80222	2400-2699	
	Arapahoe Co	316W	80222	3000-3099	
	Centennial	346W	80111	5900-6199	
	Denver	286S	80224	1-499	
	Denver	316A	80224	700-999	
	Denver	316J	80224	1500-1899	
	Denver	316N	80222	2100-2299	
	Denver	346A	80237	3700-3999	
	Greenwood Village	346N	80111	5300-5499	
	Thornton	166N	80602	12800-12999	
JASMINE WAY S	Centennial	346W	80111	6300-6399	
	Centennial	376J	80112	7500-7699	
	Denver	286W	80224	600-699	
	Denver	316E	80224	1300-1499	
	Denver	316W	80222	3100-3199	
JASON CT	Boulder Co	130D	80303	9000-9099	
JASON CT	Erie	102W	80516	2600-2699	
JASON CT	Federal Heights	224F	80260	8400-8499	
	Thornton	194S	80260	9500-9599	
	Westminster	164S	80234	12400-12599	
	Westminster	164J	80234	13400-13599	
JASON CT S	Englewood	344F	80110	4300-4399	
JASON DR	Westminster	164A	80020	14400-14599	
JASON ST	Castle Rock	497F	80109	1-99	
JASON ST	Denver	254T	80211	3600-4799	
	Federal Heights	224F	80260	8400-8499	
JASON ST S	Denver	284W	80223	500-699	
	Denver	314F	80223	700-1499	
	Denver	314P	80223	2100-2399	
	Englewood	314X	80110	3500-3599	
	Englewood	344B	80110	3600-4399	
	Englewood	344K	80110	4500-4899	
JASON WAY	Thornton	194S	80260	9400-9499	
JASPER CIR S	Aurora	288Z	80017	200-299	
JASPER CT	Boulder	98N	80304	2300-2499	
JASPER CT	Denver	258L	80239	4800-5199	
	Denver	258G	80239	5500-5599	
JASPER CT S	Arapahoe Co	378L	80112	7500-7599	
JASPER CT S	Aurora	318Y	80013	3300-3499	
	Aurora	348C	80014	3900-3999	
JASPER DR	Boulder Co	703F	80540	1-699	
JASPER DR	Commerce City	198U	80022	9700-9999	
JASPER LN	Broomfield	163J	80020	4600-4699	
JASPER RD	Boulder Co	101H	80026	10700-10999	
	Boulder Co	102E	80026	11000-11399	
	Boulder Co	102E	80026	11900-11999	
	Boulder Co	102E	80516	12000-12699	
	Erie	102E	80026	11400-11899	
JASPER RD	Gilpin Co	761E	80403	100-199	
JASPER ST	Aurora	288Q	80011	600-699	
	Aurora	288L	80011	1000-1099	
	Aurora	288G	80011	1500-19999	
	Aurora	258U	80011	3500-3798	E
	Commerce City	198U	80022	9700-10199	
	Commerce City	198L	80022	10800-10899	
	Commerce City	198C	80022	11700-11899	
	Commerce City	168Y	80603	None	
	Commerce City	768Z	80022	None	
	Denver	258L	80239	4800-5299	
	Denver	258G	80239	5500-5599	
	Denver	258G	80239	None	
JASPER ST S	Arapahoe Co	378L	80016	None	
	Aurora	288Y	80017	600-699	
	Aurora	318C	80017	1000-1099	
	Aurora	318G	80017	1400-1499	
	Aurora	318U	80013	2700-2999	
	Aurora	348C	80013	3600-3699	
	Aurora	348G	80014	4100-4199	
	Aurora	348G	80015	4300-4499	
	Aurora	348G	80015	4500-4599	
	Aurora	348L	80015	4600-4799	
	Centennial	348U	80016	5900-5999	
JASPER WAY	Superior	160X	80027	400-499	
JASPER WAY S	Arapahoe Co	348Y	80016	5900-6299	
	Arapahoe Co	378L	80016	None	
	Aurora	318Q	80013	2200-2299	
	Aurora	318Q	80013	2300-2399	
	Aurora	318U	80013	3000-3199	
	Aurora	318Y	80013	3500-3599	
	Centennial	348Q	80015	5400-5599	
	Centennial	348U	80015	5600-5799	
JASPER PEAK CT	Lafayette	131J	80026	300-399	
JASPER POINTE CIR					
	Castle Pines North	436A	80108	5600-12499	
JASPER POINTE WAY					
	Castle Pines North	436A	80108	12300-12499	
JAVA CT	Denver	283C	80211	2600-2699	
	Denver	253Y	80211	2700-2899	
JAVA WAY S	Denver	313L	80219	1600-1899	
JAY CIR	Arvada	222G	80003	8200-8299	
	Westminster	192G	80020	11100-11199	
JAY CIR S	Denver	342R	80123	5300-5498	E
JAY CT	Arvada	222U	80003	6900-6999	
	Arvada	222Q	80003	7400-7599	
	Arvada	222L	80003	7600-7699	
	Arvada	222G	80003	8200-8299	
	Arvada	222G	80003	8400-8599	
	Arvada	222C	80003	8600-8799	
JAY CT S	Denver	313A	80219	800-899	
	Jefferson Co	342Y	80123	5900-6099	
	Lakewood	312L	80227	1900-1999	
	Lakewood	312V	80227	2600-2699	
	Lakewood	312M	80232	None	
JAY DR S	Denver	342Q	80123	5300-5499	
	Jefferson Co	372C	80123	6500-6699	
	Jefferson Co	372Q	80128	7900-8199	
JAY LN	Jefferson Co	336P	80439	5300-5399	
	Jefferson Co	368U	80465	8400-8599	
JAY RD	Boulder	98L	80301	2800-5399	
	Boulder Co	99M	80301	5400-7499	
	Boulder Co	102M	80516	12000-12699	
JAY ST	Arvada	252C	80003	5900-6099	
	Arvada	222Y	80003	6200-6599	
	Arvada	222U	80003	6600-7199	
	Arvada	222L	80003	7900-7999	
JAY ST	Boulder	127G	80302	1100-1299	
JAY ST	Edgewater	282C	80214	2000-2599	
	Jefferson Co	252L	80002	None	
	Lakewood	282U	80226	1-599	
	Lakewood	282L	80214	900-1999	
	Westminster	222Q	80003	7300-7399	
	Westminster	192U	80021	9800-9999	
	Westminster	192L	80020	10800-11099	
	Westminster	192G	80020	11300-11699	
	Wheat Ridge	252Y	80214	2900-3199	
	Wheat Ridge	252Y	80033	3200-3799	
	Wheat Ridge	252U	80033	3900-4399	
	Wheat Ridge	252Q	80033	4400-4699	
JAY ST S	Denver	312U	80227	2700-3099	
	Denver	312Y	80227	3200-3299	
	Denver	342D	80235	3600-3699	
	Jefferson Co	372H	80128	7200-7399	
	Lakewood	282U	80226	1-199	
	Lakewood	282Y	80226	200-499	
	Lakewood	312C	80226	800-899	
	Lakewood	312H	80232	1100-1499	
	Lakewood	312G	80232	1500-1699	
	Lakewood	342U	80123	5700-5799	
JAY WAY S	Jefferson Co	342Y	80123	6300-6499	
	Lakewood	312L	80227	2000-2099	
	Lakewood	312V	80227	2500-2699	
	Lakewood	312M	80232	None	
JAY HAWK CT	Dacono	727N	80514	None	
JEANETTE CT	Jefferson Co	823V	80465	10400-10499	
JEBEL CIR S	Aurora	319Z	80013	3500-3699	
JEBEL CT	Aurora	379M	80016	None	
JEBEL CT	Denver	259H	80249	None	
JEBEL CT S	Arapahoe Co	350E	80015	None	
	Aurora	319Z	80013	None	
	Centennial	349V	80016	5900-5999	
JEBEL LN S	Arapahoe Co	349H	80015	None	
JEBEL ST	Aurora	289H	80011	1600-1699	
	Denver	259V	80249	3800-4099	
	Denver	259R	80249	4100-4199	
	Denver	259R	80249	4300-4899	
JEBEL ST S	Arapahoe Co	350J	80015	4600-4899	
	Centennial	348R	80015	5100-5399	
JEBEL WAY S	Arapahoe Co	350A	80013	3700-4199	
	Arapahoe Co	350S	80016	5900-5999	
	Arapahoe Co	349H	80015	None	
	Aurora	319R	80013	None	
	Aurora	319V	80013	None	
	Aurora	319Z	80013	None	
	Centennial	349R	80015	5200-5399	
	Centennial	350S	80015	5500-5899	
JED SMITH RD	Boulder Co	721C	80481	1-299	
JEFFCO AIRPORT AVE	Jefferson Co	191D	80021	8600-9899	
JEFFERSON AVE	Cherry Hills Village	345C	80113	3900-3999	
	Denver	345D	80237	5500-5599	
JEFFERSON AVE	Louisville	131W	80027	200-399	
	Louisville	131S	80027	400-1699	
JEFFERSON AVE	Sheridan	343C	80110	None	
JEFFERSON AVE E	Arapahoe Co	350A	80013	20600-20699	
	Aurora	318X	80014	14600-14899	
	Aurora	348C	80013	15500-15699	
	Aurora	349A	80013	16900-17199	
	Aurora	349C	80013	18400-18899	
	Denver	346C	80237	7800-8099	
	Denver	346D	80237	8400-9199	
	Englewood	344C	80113	200-1499	
JEFFERSON AVE W	Denver	342D	80235	5200-5499	
	Denver	342C	80235	6000-7099	
	Jefferson Co	342A	80235	8400-9199	
	Lakewood	342B	80235	7100-7599	
	Sheridan	343C	80123	3000-3199	
JEFFERSON CIR E	Arapahoe Co	350A	80013	None	
JEFFERSON DR	Bennett	793N	80102	100-299	
JEFFERSON DR E	Aurora	319W	80013	17300-17799	
	Aurora	349C	80013	18700-19199	
	Denver	346B	80237	7300-7699	
JEFFERSON PKWY	Douglas Co	407D	80112	9700-9899	
	Douglas Co	407D	80134	9900-9999	
JEFFERSON PL E	Arapahoe Co	349D	80013	20100-20199	
	Arapahoe Co	350A	80013	20600-20699	
	Aurora	347A	80014	3500-3699	
	Aurora	348C	80014	15100-15199	
	Denver	346C	80237	7700-8099	
JEFFERSON PL W	Lakewood	282Y	80226	6000-6799	
JEFFERSON ST	Boulder	97V	80304	2900-3199	
JEFFERSON ST	Jefferson Co	842Z	80470	16600-16799	
JEFFERSON ST	Monument	908W	80132	1-599	
JEFFERSON ST	Nederland	740Q	80466	None	
JEFFERSON ST S	Monument	908W	80132	1-199	
JEFFERSON ST W	Englewood	344B	80110	1-999	
JEFFERSON COUNTY PKWY	Golden	279P	80401	100-999	
JEFFERSON GULCH RD	Jefferson Co	306M	80401	None	
JEFFREY ST	Brighton	138V	80601	None	
JELLISON CIR	Arvada	221L	80005	7600-7699	
	Westminster	191M	80021	10700-10799	
JELLISON CT	Arvada	251L	80002	5100-5299	
	Arvada	221U	80004	6900-6999	
	Arvada	221Q	80005	7500-7699	
	Arvada	221L	80005	8000-8099	
	Arvada	221H	80005	8100-8299	
	Westminster	221D	80005	8800-9099	
	Wheat Ridge	251Y	80033	3400-3499	
JELLISON CT S	Jefferson Co	371H	80128	7200-7299	
	Jefferson Co	371V	80128	8700-8799	
	Lakewood	311D	80226	700-899	
	Lakewood	311Z	80227	3300-3499	
JELLISON ST	Arvada	251M	80002	5100-5299	
	Arvada	251H	80002	5300-5799	
	Arvada	251C	80004	6000-6099	
	Arvada	221R	80005	7300-7399	
	Arvada	221M	80005	8000-8099	
	Arvada	221H	80005	8200-8299	
	Arvada	221C	80005	8600-8799	
	Lakewood	281G	80215	1800-1999	
	Lakewood	281D	80215	2500-2599	
	Westminster	191V	80021	9700-9999	
	Wheat Ridge	251Y	80033	3200-3299	
	Wheat Ridge	251R	80033	4200-4399	
JELLISON ST S	Denver	341M	80123	4500-5099	
	Jefferson Co	341Q	80123	5200-5399	
	Jefferson Co	341Z	80123	5400-6399	
	Jefferson Co	371H	80128	7000-7199	
	Jefferson Co	371M	80127	7500-7799	
	Lakewood	311D	80226	900-1099	
	Lakewood	311H	80232	1100-1499	
	Lakewood	311M	80232	1600-1699	
	Lakewood	311R	80227	2200-2599	
	Lakewood	281Y	80226	None	
JELLISON WAY	Arvada	251C	80004	6100-6199	
	Arvada	221Y	80004	6200-6399	
	Westminster	191V	80021	9600-9899	
	Westminster	191M	80021	10400-10499	
JELLISON WAY S	Jefferson Co	341Q	80123	5000-5099	
	Jefferson Co	341H	80123	None	
	Jefferson Co	371M	80128	None	
	Littleton	825P	80127	9300-9399	
	Littleton	825P	80127	9600-9699	
JENNIE DR	Adams Co	224T	80221	6900-7199	
JENNIE LN	Boulder Co	742W	80403	1-299	
JENNIFER CT	Brighton	138M	80601	1902-1998	E
JENNIFER RD	Jefferson Co	842A	80470	33000-33999	
JENNIFER ST	Brighton	138M	80601	None	
JENNINE PL	Boulder	97R	80304	1500-1599	
JENNINGS RD	Jefferson Co	369W	80465	8800-9299	
	Jefferson Co	824N	80465	9300-9699	
JENNY LN	Broomfield	163F	80020	None	
JENNY LN	Jefferson Co	307Y	80439	25600-25699	
JENSEN RD	Park Co	822W	80470	34400-34999	
JERICHO CIR S	Centennial	349Z	80016	6400-6499	
JERICHO CT	Denver	259H	80249	None	
JERICHO CT N	Denver	260J	80249	4800-4899	
JERICHO CT S	Arapahoe Co	350A	80013	3800-4099	
	Arapahoe Co	350J	80015	None	
	Aurora	319V	80013	None	
	Aurora	320W	80013	None	
	Centennial	349R	80015	5400-5599	
	Centennial	350W	80016	6200-6399	
JERICHO ST	Denver	259H	80249	None	
JERICHO ST N	Denver	260J	80249	4800-4899	
JERICHO ST S	Arapahoe Co	350E	80015	4200-4299	
	Arapahoe Co	350J	80015	4900-4999	
	Centennial	349R	80015	5100-5499	
	Centennial	349Z	80016	5900-6199	
JERICHO WAY S	Aurora	319V	80013	None	
	Aurora	319Z	80013	None	
	Centennial	350N	80015	5200-5299	
	Centennial	350S	80015	5400-5899	
	Centennial	349Z	80016	6000-6499	
JEROME AVE E	Denver	315Q	80210	3900-3999	
JEROME CT	Jefferson Co	307H	80401	24000-24199	
JERRY ST	Castle Rock	497F	80104	1-799	

J

STREET NAME	CITY or COUNTY	MAP GRID	ZIP CODE	BLOCK RANGE	O/E
JERRY ST S	Castle Rock	497K	80104	1-199	
JERRY'S CIR	Elbert Co	871Q	80107	32000-32499	
JERSEY AVE	Longmont	41Q	80501	600-899	
JERSEY CIR	Thornton	196E	80233	None	
	Thornton	166S	80602	None	
	Thornton	166S	80602	None	
JERSEY CT	Thornton	166N	80602	None	
JERSEY CT S	Centennial	346W	80111	6300-6399	
	Centennial	376E	80112	7200-7299	
JERSEY LN	Thornton	196A	80233	None	
JERSEY ST	Denver	286J	80220	1-1499	
	Thornton	166N	80602	13000-13199	
	Thornton	166E	80602	13800-13999	
	Thornton	166J	80602	None	
	Thornton	196A	80233	None	
JERSEY ST S	Arapahoe Co	316S	80222	2400-2699	
	Denver	286S	80224	1-699	
	Denver	316A	80224	700-999	
	Denver	316E	80224	1500-1599	
	Denver	346A	80237	3600-3999	
JERSEY WAY	Thornton	196E	80233	None	
JERSEY WAY S	Arapahoe Co	316S	80222	None	
	Denver	316E	80224	1300-1899	
JERSY ST S	Centennial	376J	80112	7300-7799	
JESSE CT E	Highlands Ranch	404H	80126	1100-1299	
JESSE LN	Golden	248Q	80403	None	
JESSE WAY	Golden	248R	80403	None	
JESSICA ST	Highlands Ranch	406J	80130	None	
JESSUP ST	Brighton	138T	80601	1-1399	
	Brighton	138V	80601	2001-2099	O
JESSUP ST W	Brighton	138S	80601	1-599	
JEWEL DR	Longmont	12N	80501	1700-1899	
JEWEL ST	Lochbuie	140A	80603	101-499	O
JEWEL ST	Longmont	12N	80501	2200-2499	
JEWELBERRY CIR	Highlands Ranch	405M	80130	None	
JEWELBERRY PL	Highlands Ranch	405M	80130	None	
JEWELBERRY TRAIL	Highlands Ranch	405M	80130	None	
JEWEL CREEK CT	Boulder	69Y	80301	5400-5599	
JEWELL AVE E	Arapahoe Co	316K	80224	6700-6898	E
	Arapahoe Co	317J	80247	9400-9699	
	Arapahoe Co	811E	80137	31300-32899	
	Aurora	317J	80247	9700-10399	
	Aurora	317L	80112	10500-13299	
	Aurora	318K	80012	13700-14899	
	Aurora	319M	80017	19300-20199	
	Aurora	320L	80018	23300-24199	
	Aurora	321L	80018	24200-27299	
	Aurora	810E	80137	27300-31299	
	Denver	314M	80210	1-1699	
	Denver	315J	80210	1700-1999	
	Denver	315K	80210	2200-2499	
	Denver	315L	80210	3000-3899	
	Denver	315L	80222	4100-5599	
	Denver	316J	80224	5600-6699	
	Denver	316K	80224	6701-6899	O
	Denver	316K	80224	6900-7299	
	Denver	316L	80231	7300-8199	
	Watkins	811F	80137	34900-35399	
JEWELL AVE W	Denver	314K	80223	1-899	
	Denver	314J	80223	1100-1999	
	Denver	313M	80223	2000-2399	
	Denver	313L	80219	2400-5199	
	Lakewood	312L	80232	5200-8999	
	Lakewood	311L	80227	9000-11999	
	Lakewood	311L	80228	12000-12799	
	Lakewood	310M	80228	12800-14099	
JEWELL CIR E	Arapahoe Co	316M	80231	8900-9399	
	Arapahoe Co	317J	80231	9400-9499	
JEWELL CIR W	Lakewood	311J	80228	12700-12799	
	Lakewood	310M	80228	12800-13299	
JEWELL DR	Longmont	11V	80501	1700-1899	
JEWELL DR S	Lakewood	311K	80227	11000-11599	
	Lakewood	311K	80228	11600-12199	
JEWELL DR W	Lakewood	310M	80228	12700-12899	
	Lakewood	310L	80228	13300-13399	
JEWELL PL E	Aurora	317L	80112	11700-11799	
	Aurora	318L	80013	15500-15599	
	Aurora	317J	80247	None	
JEWELL PL W	Lakewood	312J	80227	8800-8999	
	Lakewood	311M	80227	9000-9999	
	Lakewood	311L	80227	10100-10499	
	Lakewood	310M	80228	13200-13299	
JEWELL ST S	Arapahoe Co	795X	80103	1-299	
JIB CT	Boulder Co	99G	80301	6400-6499	
JILL AVE S	Highlands Ranch	406K	80130	10100-10299	
JILL DR	Jefferson Co	365Y	80433	9000-9299	
JIMSON CT	Boulder	97R	80304	1600-1699	
JIMSON WEED WAY	Highlands Ranch	375W	80126	8900-9099	
JITA LN	Jefferson Co	842G	80470	13500-13599	
J MORGAN BLVD	Parker	439G	80134	12400-13099	
JO CIR	Elbert Co	851N	80107	3000-3399	
JOAN DR	Adams Co	224K	80221	1-7999	
JOAN LN	Jefferson Co	366B	80439	6400-6599	
JOAN ST	Adams Co	224T	80221	7000-7199	
JOANIE DR	Jefferson Co	762G	80403	30800-30899	
JOANIE RD	Jefferson Co	762G	80403	30800-31199	
JOANN CT	Brighton	138M	80601	1900-1998	E
JODEL LN	Longmont	40R	80503	1200-1299	
JODER RD	Boulder Co	723B	80302	None	
JOE COLLIER DR	Dacono	726M	80514	None	
JOHNATHAN CIR	Elbert Co	890G	80107	900-999	
JOHN F KIRBY DR	Lakewood	282Q	80214	700-899	
JOHNSON AVE	Louisville	130V	80027	600-699	
JOHNSON CIR	Boulder Co	70K	80503	7000-7199	
JOHNSON CIR S	Lakewood	311U	80227	2600-2699	
JOHNSON CT	Arvada	251G	80002	5600-5699	
	Arvada	221G	80005	8000-8299	
JOHNSON CT	Boulder	128D	80303	1400-1499	
JOHNSON CT	Castle Rock	498J	80104	200-299	
JOHNSON CT	Westminster	191V	80021	9700-9799	
	Westminster	191Q	80021	10400-10499	
JOHNSON CT S	Jefferson Co	341Y	80123	6200-6299	
	Jefferson Co	371Q	80127	7800-7899	
	Jefferson Co	371Q	80128	7900-8099	
	Lakewood	311C	80226	800-999	
	Lakewood	311G	80232	1300-1499	
	Lakewood	311L	80232	1500-1699	
	Lakewood	311V	80227	2500-2699	
	Littleton	825P	80127	9400-9899	
JOHNSON DR	Castle Rock	498J	80104	1-99	O
	Castle Rock	498J	80104	100-499	
JOHNSON DR	Frederick	726D	80504	7200-7699	
JOHNSON DR S	Jefferson Co	843S	80470	15700-15899	
JOHNSON LN	Weld Co	134B	80516	3000-3499	
JOHNSON LN S	Littleton	825P	80127	9300-9399	
JOHNSON PL	Castle Rock	498J	80104	100-199	
JOHNSON RD	Golden	279L	80401	600-1299	
JOHNSON RD	Park Co	820V	80421	100-299	
JOHNSON ST	Arvada	251L	80002	5100-5299	
	Arvada	251G	80002	5300-5799	
	Arvada	221U	80004	6600-6899	
	Arvada	221Q	80005	7400-7699	
	Arvada	221L	80005	8000-8099	
	Arvada	221G	80005	8100-8299	
	Arvada	221D	80005	8700-8799	
JOHNSON ST	Elbert Co	851V	80107	None	
JOHNSON ST	Keenesburg	732A	80643	None	
JOHNSON ST	Lakewood	281L	80215	1100-1199	
JOHNSON ST	Louisville	131W	80027	600-799	
JOHNSON ST	Weld Co	727F	80530	None	
JOHNSON ST	Westminster	191U	80021	9800-9899	
	Westminster	191L	80021	10600-10699	
	Wheat Ridge	251U	80033	3500-3799	
JOHNSON ST S	Denver	341L	80123	4700-4899	
	Jefferson Co	341U	80123	5600-5798	E
	Jefferson Co	341Y	80123	6300-6399	
	Jefferson Co	371H	80128	7000-7299	
	Jefferson Co	371L	80127	7600-7899	
	Lakewood	311C	80226	900-1099	
	Lakewood	311G	80232	1100-1499	
	Littleton	825P	80127	9400-9899	
JOHNSON WAY	Arvada	251C	80004	6000-6199	
	Arvada	221Y	80004	6200-6399	
JOHNSON WAY S	Jefferson Co	371C	80123	6300-6399	
JOHNSON WAY S	Lakewood	311C	80226	900-1099	
	Lakewood	311C	80232	1100-1299	
	Littleton	825P	80127	9600-9999	
JOHNSTON CT	Longmont	41R	80501	1300-1399	
JOHN WAYNE CIR	Elbert Co	851F	80138	3700-3799	
JOHN WEST DR	Adams Co	792M	80102	None	
JOLENE CIR	Adams Co	224H	80229	8200-8299	
JOLENE DR	Adams Co	224H	80229	1600-1799	
	Adams Co	225E	80229	1800-8799	
JOLENE WAY	Adams Co	224H	80229	8200-8299	
JOLIET CIR	Aurora	287T	80012	100-299	
	Commerce City	197T	80022	9700-9899	
JOLIET CT S	Aurora	317K	80014	2000-2199	
	Aurora	317P	80014	2500-2599	
JOLIET ST	Adams Co	137T	80602	None	
	Aurora	287P	80010	300-499	
	Aurora	287P	80010	700-799	
	Aurora	287K	80010	900-2599	
	Commerce City	197F	80640	11200-11399	
	Denver	257T	80239	3700-3999	
	Denver	257K	80239	4500-4899	
	Denver	257F	80239	5100-5599	
JOLIET ST S	Arapahoe Co	347T	80111	5500-5599	
	Arapahoe Co	377F	80112	7100-7499	
	Aurora	317F	80112	900-1899	
	Aurora	317P	80014	2000-2199	
JOLIET WAY	Boulder	128X	80305	1800-1899	
JOLIET WAY S	Arapahoe Co	347P	80111	5200-5299	
	Aurora	317P	80014	2200-2299	
JONATHAN PL	Boulder	98N	80304	2100-2199	
JONES CT	Dacono	727J	80514	600-799	
JONES CT	Erie	103S	80516	400-499	
JONES RD	Golden	279E	80401	1900-2099	
JONES RD	Park Co	820Z	80421	1-499	
JONES RD E	Douglas Co	909D	80118	6400-6599	
	Douglas Co	910A	80118	9600-10999	
JONES CREEK CIR	Park Co	842A	80470	1-199	
JONES CREEK LN	Jefferson Co	842A	80470	1-199	
JONQUIL CT	Lafayette	131B	80026	2400-2499	
JONQUIL PL	Boulder	97Q	80304	700-799	
JONQUIL ST	Castle Rock	466Y	80109	None	
JOPLIN CIR S	Aurora	318D	80017	800-899	
JOPLIN CT	Commerce City	198C	80022	11800-11899	
	Denver	258L	80239	4800-5099	
JOPLIN CT S	Arapahoe Co	378M	80016	None	
	Aurora	318C	80017	1100-1199	
	Aurora	318U	80013	2800-2899	
	Aurora	318V	80013	3000-3099	
	Aurora	318Z	80013	3100-3199	
	Aurora	348D	80014	3900-3999	
JOPLIN ST	Aurora	288Q	80011	600-699	
	Aurora	288L	80011	1000-1099	
	Commerce City	198U	80022	9600-9899	
	Commerce City	198Q	80022	9900-10199	
	Commerce City	198L	80022	10500-10699	
	Commerce City	198L	80022	10700-10799	
	Commerce City	168Y	80603	None	
	Denver	258L	80239	4800-5099	
	Denver	258G	80239	None	
JOPLIN ST S	Aurora	288Z	80017	200-499	
	Aurora	288Y	80017	500-699	
	Aurora	318G	80017	1100-1499	
	Aurora	318L	80017	1800-1899	
	Aurora	318Q	80013	2300-2399	
	Aurora	348C	80013	3500-3699	
	Aurora	348D	80013	3800-3899	
	Aurora	348G	80014	4100-4199	
	Aurora	348G	80015	4500-4599	
	Aurora	348L	80015	4700-4899	
JOPLIN WAY S	Arapahoe Co	348Y	80016	6000-6199	
	Arapahoe Co	378M	80016	None	
	Aurora	318C	80017	900-1099	
	Aurora	318Q	80013	2100-2199	
	Aurora	348D	80013	3900-3999	
	Aurora	348G	80015	4300-4499	
	Aurora	348M	80015	4600-4699	
	Centennial	348U	80015	5700-5898	E
JOPPA CT	Adams Co	750H	80603	16600-16699	
JOPPA ST	Adams Co	750H	80603	16300-16499	
JORDAN CT	Parker	409N	80134	10700-11299	
JORDAN DR	Adams Co	223V	80221	1800-6899	
JORDAN DR	Keenesburg	732A	80643	None	
JORDAN PL	Boulder	98N	80304	2100-2199	
JORDAN RD	Douglas Co	409E	80134	8700-13999	
	Parker	409N	80134	9600-11699	
	Parker	439A	80134	None	
JORDAN RD N	Parker	378V	80134	8300-9199	
JORDAN RD S	Arapahoe Co	348S	80111	6100-6299	
	Arapahoe Co	378B	80112	7500-8299	
	Centennial	378B	80111	6300-6699	
	Centennial	378B	80112	6700-7499	
JORDAN ST	Erie	102R	80516	None	
JORDAN WAY	Weld Co	750A	80603	501-599	O
JOSEPH CIR	Golden	248V	80403	None	
JOSEPH DR	Highlands Ranch	406J	80130	10100-10299	
JOSEPHINE CIR	Thornton	195A	80233	11600-11699	
JOSEPHINE CT	Thornton	165W	80241	12300-12399	
	Thornton	165S	80241	12800-12999	
	Thornton	165J	80602	13600-13699	
JOSEPHINE PL	Thornton	195S	80229	9600-9799	
JOSEPHINE ST	Adams Co	135J	80602	16400-16599	
	Denver	285N	80206	200-1699	
	Denver	285A	80205	2600-2699	
	Denver	255W	80205	2700-3799	
	Denver	255N	80216	4200-4799	
	Northglenn	195J	80233	10900-11099	
	Thornton	195S	80229	9500-9999	
	Thornton	195N	80229	10100-10199	
	Thornton	165W	80241	12100-12199	
	Thornton	165S	80241	12400-12699	
	Thornton	165J	80602	13600-13899	
	Thornton	165A	80602	14500-14799	
	Thornton	135W	80602	14900-15099	
JOSEPHINE ST S	Denver	315A	80209	800-1099	
	Denver	315E	80210	1100-1699	
	Denver	315N	80210	1800-2699	
	Denver	315W	80210	2900-3299	
JOSEPHINE WAY	Northglenn	195E	80233	11000-11199	
JOSEPHINE WAY S	Centennial	345W	80121	6100-6399	
JOSHUA AVE	Keenesburg	732A	80643	None	
JOSLIN CT S	Denver	312V	80227	2700-3099	
JOSLYN CT	Boulder	97R	80304	1900-1999	
JOSLYN PL	Boulder	97R	80304	1900-2099	
JOTIPA DR	Boulder Co	11J	80503	9100-10999	
JOURNEYS END LN	Castle Rock	528F	80104	None	
JOY ST	Jefferson Co	823N	80433	26600-26799	
JOYCE CT	Jefferson Co	250F	80403	None	
JOYCE DR	Arvada	220X	80403	6200-6399	
JOYCE LN S	Highlands Ranch	404C	80126	9400-9599	
JOYCE ST	Arvada	220T	80007	6600-6999	
	Jefferson Co	280P	80401	600-899	
	Jefferson Co	280K	80401	1300-1499	
	Jefferson Co	250F	80403	5300-5399	
JOYCE ST S	Jefferson Co	280T	80401	1-199	
JOYCE WAY	Jefferson Co	250X	80401	2900-3099	
JUAN WAY W	Douglas Co	406Y	80108	1-399	
JUANITA CT	Platteville	708G	80651	1700-1799	
JUBILEE TRAIL (PVT)	Jefferson Co	842K	80470	13700-14299	
JUDE WAY	Mead	706M	80504	None	
JUDGE ADAMS RD	Elbert Co	891F	80107	3600-3699	
JUDGES RD	Gilpin Co	761B	80403	1-699	
JUDICIAL CENTER DR	Brighton	139Y	80601	1100-1198	E
JUDSON DR	Boulder	128X	80305	1100-1399	
	Boulder	128T	80305	1400-1599	
JUDSON DR	Longmont	11T	80501	1602-1798	E
JUDSON ST	Adams Co	223C	80031	8800-9099	
JUDSON ST	Longmont	41F	80501	100-299	
	Longmont	41B	80501	300-899	
	Longmont	11X	80501	1100-1399	
	Longmont	11T	80501	1500-1699	
	Longmont	11P	80501	2100-2399	
JUDSON ST	Westminster	193Y	80031	9100-9199	
JUDSON ST S	Longmont	41P	80501	1300-1399	
JUHLS DR	Boulder Co	99E	80301	5500-5699	
JULES CT E	Highlands Ranch	404D	80126	1700-1799	
JULIAN CIR	Lafayette	131L	80026	700-799	
JULIAN CIR S	Denver	313L	80219	1900-2099	
JULIAN CT	Broomfield	163T	80020	12400-12499	
	Broomfield	163U	80020	12700-12799	
	Broomfield	163P	80020	13000-13199	
	Westminster	193T	80031	9900-10099	
	Westminster	193P	80031	10300-10399	
	Westminster	193L	80031	10700-10799	
JULIAN PT	Broomfield	163T	80020	12600-12699	
JULIAN ST	Adams Co	253G	80221	5200-5599	
	Adams Co	223X	80221	6300-6399	
	Adams Co	223U	80221	6600-6899	
	Broomfield	163U	80020	12600-12699	
	Broomfield	163P	80020	13200-13299	
	Denver	283U	80219	1-399	
	Denver	283Q	80204	400-1199	
	Denver	283G	80204	1300-1999	
	Denver	283C	80211	2000-2699	
	Denver	253X	80211	2700-4599	
	Denver	253L	80221	4800-4999	
	Westminster	223U	80030	7100-7199	
	Westminster	223Q	80030	7200-7599	
	Westminster	223L	80030	7600-7999	
	Westminster	223L	80031	8000-8199	
	Westminster	193P	80031	10200-10399	
	Westminster	193K	80031	10500-10699	
	Westminster	193G	80031	11400-11499	
JULIAN ST S	Arapahoe Co	313Y	80110	3300-3398	E
	Columbine Valley	343Y	80123	6000-6098	E
	Denver	283U	80219	1-299	
	Denver	313G	80219	1100-1299	
	Denver	313U	80219	1600-2699	
	Denver	313U	80236	2700-2799	
	Englewood	343L	80110	4500-4699	
	Englewood	343Q	80110	5000-5099	
	Littleton	343Q	80123	5100-5199	
	Littleton	343U	80123	5400-5899	
	Sheridan	343C	80236	3600-3899	
JULIAN WAY	Denver	283F	80204	1900-1999	
	Denver	283B	80211	2000-2099	
	Westminster	223Q	80030	7100-7199	
	Westminster	193X	80031	9200-9399	
	Westminster	193P	80031	10100-10199	
	Westminster	193G	80031	11400-11499	
JULIAN WAY S	Denver	313L	80219	1600-1699	
	Denver	313X	80236	3000-3399	
JULIE LN	Jefferson Co	367G	80439	7000-7299	
JULIUS ST	Weld Co	728X	80621	11500-11799	

STREET NAME	CITY or COUNTY	MAP GRID	ZIP CODE	BLOCK RANGE	O/E
JULLIARD ST	Boulder	128X	80305	2600-2999	
JUNCTION PKWY	Longmont	42J	80501	None	
JUNE CT	Castle Rock	497U	80104	2000-2099	
JUNEAU PL	Longmont	12S	80501	1-99	
JUNEAU RD	Boulder Co	98K	80301	None	
JUNEGRASS PL	Parker	379S	80134	17600-17799	
JUNGFRAU DR	Jefferson Co	367C	80439	6000-6899	
JUNGFRAU WAY	Jefferson Co	367D	80439	6200-6699	
JUNIPER AVE	Boulder	97Q	80304	400-1199	
	Boulder	98N	80304	2200-2799	
JUNIPER AVE	Frederick	727E	80516	None	
JUNIPER AVE	Weld Co	706U	80504	None	
JUNIPER CIR	Gilpin Co	761S	80403	1-99	
JUNIPER CIR	Jefferson Co	336C	80439	3800-4099	
JUNIPER CT	Boulder	98N	80304	2100-2299	
JUNIPER CT	Clear Creek Co	304R	80439	1-99	
JUNIPER CT	Douglas Co	887E	80118	4000-4599	
JUNIPER CT	Jefferson Co	307L	80401	2200-2599	
	Jefferson Co	250F	80403	5200-5499	
	Jefferson Co	280B	80401	15000-15199	
JUNIPER CT	Louisville	131W	80027	500-599	
	Louisville	130Y	80027	600-699	
JUNIPER CT S	Jefferson Co	280T	80401	1-99	
JUNIPER DR	Gilpin Co	760V	80403	1-199	
	Gilpin Co	761S	80403	200-399	
JUNIPER DR	Jefferson Co	280B	80401	2700-15199	
	Jefferson Co	842H	80433	28000-28399	
JUNIPER LN	Boulder Co	97K	80304	None	
JUNIPER LN	Clear Creek Co	304X	80439	1-299	
JUNIPER LN	Jefferson Co	336L	80439	4800-4899	
JUNIPER LN	Park Co	841V	80421	1-599	
JUNIPER LN	Parker	410S	80138	11500-11599	
JUNIPER RD	Gilpin Co	760V	80403	1-499	
JUNIPER ST	Arvada	220P	80007	None	
JUNIPER ST	Boulder Co	102F	80026	11800-11999	
JUNIPER ST	Bow Mar	343N	80123	500-5199	
JUNIPER ST	Hudson	730M	80642	None	
JUNIPER ST	Jefferson Co	280P	80401	600-999	
	Jefferson Co	280K	80401	1300-1499	
JUNIPER ST	Longmont	11X	80501	1200-1299	
	Longmont	11T	80501	1500-1699	
	Longmont	11P	80501	1700-2099	
JUNIPER ST	Louisville	131W	80027	100-399	
JUNIPER WAY	Erie	133D	80516	None	
JUNIPER WAY	Jefferson Co	220P	80007	7200-7299	
JUNIPER WAY	Park Co	820Y	80421	1-99	
JUNIPER TRAIL	Clear Creek Co	821H	80439	1-199	
JUNO TRAIL	Jefferson Co	365N	80439	None	
JUPITER DR	Highlands Ranch	376U	80124	200-499	
JUPITER WAY	Broomfield	133L	80020	16500-16599	
JURA DR	Jefferson Co	367H	80439	24700-24799	
JURASSIC RD	Jefferson Co	309Q	80401	17300-17499	
JUSTICE WAY	Castle Rock	467T	80109	400-499	
JUSTIN AVE	Platteville	708G	80651	300-399	
JUTE LN	Castle Rock	497A	80109	2100-2399	
K					
KACHINA CIR	Jefferson Co	308B	80401	700-899	
KACHINA WAY	Lone Tree	376Z	80124	8600-8899	
KAHALA CIR	Castle Rock	497V	80104	2000-2199	
KAHIL PL	Fort Lupton	728L	80621	1-399	
KAHIL ST	Fort Lupton	728M	80621	300-699	
KAHLER PL	Broomfield	163G	80020	None	
KAISER AVE E	Keenesburg	732A	80643	500-599	
KALAHARI CT S	Douglas Co	406K	80124	10500-10599	
KALAMATH CIR	Thornton	194S	80260	9500-9599	
KALAMATH CT	Adams Co	134W	80020	14800-14899	
	Federal Heights	224E	80260	8400-8499	
	Thornton	194W	80260	9400-9499	
	Westminster	164S	80234	12400-12799	
	Westminster	164A	80020	14600-14799	
KALAMATH CT S	Englewood	344E	80110	4100-4199	
KALAMATH DR	Douglas Co	887J	80118	3900-4099	
KALAMATH PL W	Thornton	194S	80260	1000-1199	
KALAMATH ST	Adams Co	224S	80221	7000-7299	
	Adams Co	224J	80221	8000-8199	
	Adams Co	134S	80020	None	
	Broomfield	164J	80020	None	
	Denver	284N	80223	1-399	
	Denver	284N	80204	400-1499	
	Denver	254S	80211	3500-4599	
	Denver	254J	80221	4800-5199	
	Federal Heights	224E	80260	8400-8499	
	Northglenn	194N	80234	10400-10599	
	Northglenn	194J	80234	10700-10899	
	Westminster	164J	80234	13400-13599	
	Westminster	164E	80020	None	
KALAMATH ST S	Denver	284X	80223	1-399	
	Denver	314F	80223	1100-1299	
	Denver	314N	80223	2100-2399	
	Englewood	344A	80110	3700-4099	
	Englewood	344J	80110	4300-4999	
KALAMERE CT	Highlands Ranch	405A	80126	9500-9699	
KALISPELL CIR S	Arapahoe Co	378M	80112	7800-7899	
	Aurora	318Q	80013	2400-2599	
	Aurora	348H	80015	4300-4499	
KALISPELL CT	Aurora	288H	80011	1700-1799	
KALISPELL CT S	Arapahoe Co	378M	80112	7700-7899	
	Aurora	318V	80013	3100-3199	
	Centennial	348V	80015	5700-5799	
KALISPELL ST	Aurora	288M	80011	600-699	
	Aurora	288M	80011	800-999	
	Aurora	288H	80011	1800-1899	
	Aurora	258V	80011	3500-3699	
	Aurora	288C	80011	None	
	Commerce City	198U	80022	9600-9899	
	Commerce City	198L	80022	10600-10799	
	Commerce City	168Y	80603	None	
	Denver	258L	80239	4800-5299	
	Denver	258H	80239	None	
KALISPELL ST S	Arapahoe Co	348Y	80016	6000-6199	
	Aurora	288Z	80017	500-699	
	Aurora	318D	80017	1000-1199	
	Aurora	318Z	80013	3100-3499	
	Aurora	348D	80013	3500-3699	
	Aurora	348H	80014	4000-4199	
	Aurora	348M	80015	4700-4899	
	Centennial	348V	80015	5600-5699	
KALISPELL WAY S	Arapahoe Co	378R	80112	7900-8099	
	Aurora	288Z	80017	300-599	
	Aurora	318D	80017	600-899	
	Aurora	318H	80017	1100-1299	
	Aurora	348M	80015	4500-4699	
KALMIA AVE	Boulder	97Q	80304	400-1599	
	Boulder	97R	80304	1600-2199	
	Boulder	98N	80304	2200-2699	
	Boulder Co	98P	80301	2800-4799	
KALMIA CIR	Boulder	98N	80304	2100-2199	
KALMIA WAY	Broomfield	162T	80020	600-899	
KALUA RD	Boulder Co	99G	80301	6400-6699	
KANDINSKY CIR	Castle Rock	466Y	80109	None	
KANE ST	Longmont	41R	80501	800-1099	
KANEMOTO LN	Erie	102D	80516	1200-1399	
KANEMOTO WAY	Erie	102C	80516	1200-1399	
KANSAS AVE	Longmont	41Q	80501	800-1199	
	Longmont	41P	80501	1300-1699	
KANSAS CIR E	Arapahoe Co	317E	80247	9500-9699	
	Aurora	321A	80018	24300-24799	
	Aurora	317D	80112	None	
KANSAS DR E	Aurora	317G	80112	11900-12099	
	Aurora	317D	80112	12500-13298	E
	Aurora	318E	80012	13100-13299	
	Aurora	318D	80017	16500-16699	
	Aurora	319C	80017	18900-19299	
	Denver	315H	80246	4800-4999	
KANSAS PL E	Arapahoe Co	316H	80247	9100-9299	
	Arapahoe Co	317E	80247	9300-9499	
	Aurora	317H	80112	12400-13099	
	Aurora	318F	80012	14100-14899	
	Aurora	318C	80017	15700-16099	
	Aurora	318D	80017	16500-16599	
	Aurora	319B	80017	17700-17899	
	Aurora	319C	80017	18500-18599	
	Aurora	319A	80017	None	
KARHER ST	Douglas Co	847N	80135	5500-5599	
KARLANN DR	Gilpin Co	761J	80403	1-1899	
KARSH DR	Longmont	42G	80501	400-499	
KARVAL PL E	Superior	160L	80027	900-1099	
KASSLER PL	Westminster	193Y	80031	3100-3299	
	Westminster	193X	80031	3300-3599	
KASSLER RD	Jefferson Co	432A	80127	None	
KATELYN ST	Dacono	727E	80514	None	
KATHERINE AVE W	Lakewood	281J	80401	11600-12199	
KATHERINE CT	Boulder Co	130D	80303	8900-8999	
KATHERINE CT	Douglas Co	378V	80134	8700-8799	
KATHERINE WAY	Adams Co	224E	80221	8300-8399	
KATHRYN CT	Platteville	708C	80651	500-599	
KATICH PL	Erie	103N	80516	None	
KATIE DR	Elbert Co	871B	80107	4000-4199	
KATIE LN	Boulder Co	742W	80403	1-299	
KATTELL ST	Erie	103J	80516	100-799	
KATY LN	Longmont	41U	80504	1000-1099	
KAY ST	Longmont	11W	80501	1000-1099	
	Longmont	11S	80501	1400-1499	
	Longmont	11N	80501	2100-2299	
KEARNEY CIR	Thornton	196A	80233	11700-11999	
	Thornton	166S	80602	None	
KEARNEY CIR S	Centennial	376A	80111	6400-6599	
KEARNEY CT	Adams Co	136J	80602	16200-16599	
	Commerce City	226S	80022	7000-7099	
KEARNEY CT S	Centennial	376A	80112	6700-6799	
	Centennial	376J	80112	7700-7899	
	Centennial	376N	80112	8100-8299	
KEARNEY DR	Adams Co	226J	80022	7600-7799	
KEARNEY ST	Adams Co	226N	80022	7300-7599	
	Adams Co	226E	80022	8300-8399	
	Commerce City	256E	80022	5500-5599	
	Commerce City	256A	80022	6000-6099	
	Commerce City	226W	80022	6200-6999	
	Commerce City	226N	80022	7200-7299	
	Denver	286J	80220	1-1999	
	Denver	286A	80207	2000-2799	
	Denver	256W	80207	2800-3999	
	Denver	256N	80216	4200-4399	
	Thornton	166W	80602	12200-12399	
	Thornton	166N	80602	13000-13299	
	Thornton	166J	80602	13700-13999	
	Thornton	166J	80602	None	
	Thornton	166S	80602	None	
KEARNEY ST S	Arapahoe Co	316N	80222	2400-2599	
	Arapahoe Co	316N	80222	2601-2699	O
	Arapahoe Co	316S	80222	2700-3099	
	Centennial	346W	80111	5900-6299	
	Denver	286W	80224	1-499	
	Denver	316A	80224	700-1099	
	Denver	316J	80224	1300-1899	
	Denver	316N	80222	2300-2399	
	Denver	316N	80222	2600-2698	E
	Greenwood Village	346N	80111	5300-5499	
	Greenwood Village	346S	80111	5700-5899	
KEARNEY WAY	Thornton	166N	80602	13100-13199	
	Thornton	196A	80233	None	
KEARNEY WAY S	Denver	316J	80224	1900-1999	
KEATS WAY	Jefferson Co	306W	80439	31200-31299	
KEBLER CT	Douglas Co	887G	80118	7600-7699	
KEDLESTON AVE	Highlands Ranch	405K	80126	3100-3299	
KEECH WAY	Castle Pines North	436Q	80108	6900-7099	
KEEL CT	Boulder Co	99G	80301	4500-4599	
KEEL CT	Lafayette	131K	80026	1800-1899	
KEEN AVE E	Arapahoe Co	795Y	80103	300-799	
KEENAN CT E	Highlands Ranch	406E	80130	5700-5799	
KEENAN ST	Highlands Ranch	406E	80130	9700-10099	
KEENE AVE W	Jefferson Co	341C	80235	10000-10499	
KEENE PL W	Jefferson Co	341C	80235	10000-10199	
KEENLAND CT S	Englewood	343Q	80110	5000-5099	
	Littleton	343Q	80123	5100-5199	
KEEPSAKE WAY	Castle Rock	467W	80109	None	
KEITH CT	Broomfield	163E	80020	14300-14399	
KEITH CT	Douglas Co	848A	80108	8000-8299	
KELLER FARM DR	Boulder	98N	80304	2300-2599	
KELLERMAN CT S	Aurora	351X	80016	None	
	Aurora	381B	80016	None	
KELLERMAN ST N	Aurora	291P	80018	100-199	
KELLERMAN ST S	Aurora	291T	80018	None	
KELLERMAN WAY S	Aurora	381F	80016	7200-7499	
	Aurora	381F	80016	7400-7499	
	Aurora	381B	80016	None	
KELLING DR	Lyons	703C	80540	None	
KELLIWOOD WAY	Highlands Ranch	405L	80126	10100-10399	
KELLOGG CIR	Boulder	128D	80303	4700-4899	
KELLOGG CT	Castle Rock	467X	80109	1-199	
KELLOGG PL	Westminster	193X	80031	3300-3599	
KELLWOOD DR	Castle Rock	466T	80109	4200-4499	
KELLY CT	Douglas Co	846D	80125	5400-5499	
KELLY LN	Weld Co	138H	80603	1-399	
KELLY PL	Denver	258P	80239	15000-15199	
	Denver	259Q	80249	18800-19099	
	Denver	259R	80249	20300-20799	
	Denver	259P	80249	None	
KELLY PL	Longmont	11L	80501	900-1099	
KELLY PL E	Denver	260N	80249	20300-20999	
KELLY RD	Boulder Co	742C	80302	1-1199	
KELLY ST	Lochbuie	140B	80603	None	
	Lochbuie	729Y	80603	None	
KELSEY PL	Castle Rock	497Y	80104	100-299	
KELSEY RD	El Paso Co	909U	80908	2700-4299	
KELSO RD	Boulder Co	98C	80301	4100-5099	
KELTY CT	Douglas Co	470W	80116	2300-2399	
KELTY RD	Douglas Co	469Z	80116	1800-2399	
KELTY TRAIL	Douglas Co	470W	80116	7100-7999	
KEMPER DR	Lone Tree	406C	80124	9400-9699	
KEMPTON CT	Erie	102D	80516	1400-1499	
KEMPTON CT	Longmont	41P	80501	1500-1599	
KEN CARYL AVE W	Jefferson Co	372L	80128	5200-9099	
	Jefferson Co	371K	80127	9100-9699	
	Jefferson Co	371K	80128	9700-12499	
	Jefferson Co	370G	80127	12500-14799	
KEN CARYL CIR W	Jefferson Co	372K	80128	8000-8199	
KEN CARYL DR W	Jefferson Co	371M	80127	9700-9799	
KEN CARYL PL W	Jefferson Co	372M	80128	5600-6299	
	Jefferson Co	372K	80128	7700-7799	
	Jefferson Co	372J	80128	8200-8299	
KENDALL BLVD S	Jefferson Co	372R	80128	6700-8199	
KENDALL CIR	Lakewood	282Q	80214	None	
	Westminster	192C	80020	11600-11699	
KENDALL CT	Arvada	222G	80002	5600-5699	
	Arvada	222G	80003	8400-8599	
	Arvada	222C	80003	8600-8799	
KENDALL CT	Douglas Co	847E	80108	300-499	
KENDALL CT	Westminster	192U	80021	9600-9999	
KENDALL CT S	Jefferson Co	372H	80128	6900-7299	
	Jefferson Co	372L	80128	7700-7799	
	Jefferson Co	372R	80128	7900-8099	
	Lakewood	312G	80232	1100-1399	
	Lakewood	312L	80232	None	
KENDALL DR	Boulder	128X	80305	1400-1599	
KENDALL DR	Westminster	192G	80020	10900-11099	
KENDALL ST	Arvada	222Y	80003	6300-6799	
	Arvada	222U	80003	6900-6999	
	Arvada	222Q	80003	7400-7799	
	Arvada	222L	80003	7900-7999	
	Edgewater	282C	80214	2000-2899	
	Lakewood	282U	80226	1-99	
	Lakewood	282Q	80226	300-499	
	Lakewood	282L	80214	800-1999	
	Westminster	222Q	80003	7300-7399	
	Westminster	192Y	80031	9300-9599	
	Westminster	192G	80020	11000-11299	
	Westminster	192C	80020	11500-11699	
	Wheat Ridge	252Y	80214	2900-3199	
	Wheat Ridge	252Y	80033	3200-3499	
	Wheat Ridge	252U	80033	3800-4399	
KENDALL ST S	Denver	312Y	80227	3200-3399	
	Denver	342C	80235	3500-3599	
	Denver	342Q	80123	5300-5499	
	Jefferson Co	342Y	80123	6200-6499	
	Lakewood	282U	80226	1-299	
	Lakewood	282Y	80226	300-599	
	Lakewood	312C	80226	800-899	
	Lakewood	312G	80232	1100-1799	
KENDALL WAY	Lakewood	282Q	80214	None	
	Westminster	192G	80020	10900-11099	
KENDALL WAY S	Denver	312U	80227	2700-2799	
KENDRICK CT	Castle Rock	499N	80104	700-899	
KENDRICK CT	Jefferson Co	250K	80403	5200-5499	
KENDRICK CT S	Jefferson Co	280T	80401	1-99	
KENDRICK DR	Arvada	220X	80007	6600-6699	
	Arvada	220X	80403	None	
KENDRICK ST	Arvada	220P	80007	None	
	Jefferson Co	280P	80401	600-1099	
	Jefferson Co	280K	80401	1400-1499	
	Jefferson Co	280B	80401	2600-2899	
	Jefferson Co	250X	80401	2900-3199	
	Jefferson Co	250P	80403	4200-4799	
	Jefferson Co	220P	80007	7200-7299	
	Jefferson Co	220P	80007	None	
KENDRICK WAY	Jefferson Co	220P	80007	7300-7399	
KEN MAR CT	Longmont	41A	80501	500-699	
KENNEDY AVE	Adams Co	168K	80601	13400-13699	
KENNEDY AVE	Bennett	793J	80102	None	
KENNEDY AVE	Jefferson Co	823U	80433	11000-11199	
KENNEDY AVE	Louisville	130Q	80027	1200-1599	
KENNEDY CT	Boulder	128D	80303	1400-1499	
KENNEDY DR	Longmont	40E	80503	None	
KENNEDY DR	Northglenn	194J	80234	100-1599	
KENNEDY GULCH RD	Jefferson Co	822U	80433	10800-30199	
KENNEMERE LN	Douglas Co	408M	80134	10300-10499	
KENNETH LANIER DR	El Paso Co	908P	80132	None	
KENOSHA AVE	Palmer Lake	907Q	80133	None	
KENOSHA DR	Boulder	98V	80301	None	
KENOSHA DR	Douglas Co	887G	80118	700-1299	
KENOSHA RD	Boulder Co	102B	80504	11600-11999	
	Boulder Co	102B	80516	12000-12699	
KEN PRATT BLVD	Longmont	41P	80501	700-2299	
KENSING CT	Denver	254W	80211	2500-2599	
KENSINGTON AVE E	Castle Rock	498Q	80104	5100-5399	
KENSINGTON CIR	Elbert Co	870Q	80107	31800-31899	
KENSINGTON ST	Longmont	42A	80501	400-699	
KENT AVE W	Thornton	224A	80260	900-1099	
KENT CIR E	Aurora	349C	80013	18900-18999	
KENT CT	Dacono	727E	80514	None	
KENT DR E	Aurora	348D	80013	16600-16899	
	Aurora	349A	80013	16900-17199	
	Aurora	349C	80013	18600-18699	
	Aurora	349D	80013	19900-19999	
	Aurora	350B	80018	21700-21799	

STREET NAME	CITY or COUNTY	MAP GRID	ZIP CODE	BLOCK RANGE	O/E
KENT PL	Aurora	347A	80014	9500-9599	
	Castle Pines North	436U	80108	6700-6799	
KENT PL E	Aurora	349B	80013	18200-18299	
	Aurora	349C	80013	18800-18899	
	Aurora	350C	80018	None	
	Denver	346D	80237	8700-8799	
KENT PL S	Aurora	349B	80013	17800-17899	
KENT PL W	Denver	342D	80235	5300-5599	
KENT ST	Adams Co	223B	80031	8800-9099	
KENT ST	Boulder	128F	80303	1000-1099	
KENT ST	Palmer Lake	907Q	80133	None	
KENT ST	Westminster	193Y	80031	9100-9199	
KENTMERE DR	Longmont	12Q	80501	2000-2099	
KENTON CIR	Commerce City	197T	80022	9800-9899	
KENTON CT E	Arapahoe Co	347T	80111	5500-5699	
KENTON CT S	Arapahoe Co	347P	80111	5300-5399	
	Aurora	317K	80014	1900-2199	
	Aurora	317T	80014	2600-2899	
KENTON ST	Aurora	287K	80010	100-1499	
	Aurora	287F	80010	1700-2599	
	Commerce City	197F	80640	11200-11499	
KENTON ST S	Arapahoe Co	347T	80111	5700-6099	
	Aurora	317B	80112	700-999	
	Aurora	317F	80112	1400-1799	
	Aurora	317P	80014	2200-2399	
	Centennial	377B	80111	6300-6699	
	Denver	317X	80014	None	
KENTON WAY S	Arapahoe Co	347P	80111	5100-5299	
	Arapahoe Co	347T	80111	5500-6099	
	Arapahoe Co	347X	80111	6100-6299	
	Aurora	317F	80112	1201-1399	O
	Aurora	317K	80112	1600-1699	
	Aurora	317P	80014	2200-2299	
KENTUCKY AVE E	Aurora	317D	80012	10700-13299	
	Aurora	318A	80012	13400-13699	
	Aurora	318D	80017	16000-16799	
	Aurora	319A	80017	16800-18199	
	Denver	314C	80209	200-1199	
	Denver	314D	80209	1600-1699	
	Denver	315A	80209	1700-3899	
	Denver	316A	80246	5400-5599	
	Denver	316A	80224	5600-6699	
	Glendale	315C	80246	4000-4599	
	Glendale	315D	80246	4600-5098	E
	Glendale	315D	80246	4601-5099	O
KENTUCKY AVE W	Denver	314A	80223	1200-1999	
	Denver	313D	80223	2200-2499	
	Denver	313B	80219	2500-5199	
	Lakewood	312D	80226	5200-5999	
	Lakewood	312C	80226	6500-6999	
	Lakewood	312B	80226	7000-7999	
	Lakewood	312A	80226	8000-8399	
	Lakewood	311D	80226	9000-9699	
	Lakewood	311B	80228	11700-11799	
KENTUCKY CIR E	Denver	315D	80246	4800-4999	
	Glendale	315C	80246	4500-4599	
KENTUCKY DR E	Aurora	317B	80247	10200-10399	
	Aurora	318B	80012	14500-14899	
	Denver	317A	80247	9700-10198	E
KENTUCKY DR W	Lakewood	312B	80226	6800-7399	
	Lakewood	311D	80226	9500-9999	
	Lakewood	311C	80226	10000-11299	
	Lakewood	311B	80226	11200-11599	
	Lakewood	311A	80228	12000-12299	
	Lakewood	310C	80228	13700-13899	
KENTUCKY LN E	Denver	316C	80247	7300-7499	
KENTUCKY PL E	Aurora	317C	80012	11500-11699	
	Aurora	317D	80012	12400-12799	
	Aurora	318A	80012	13500-13699	
	Aurora	318B	80012	14100-14399	
	Glendale	315C	80246	4500-4599	
KENTUCKY PL W	Lakewood	312D	80226	5800-5899	
	Lakewood	311D	80226	9200-9699	
	Lakewood	310C	80228	13700-13799	
KENVIL CT	Adams Co	750D	80603	16700-16799	
KENVIL ST	Adams Co	750H	80603	16600-16699	
KENWOOD CT S	Highlands Ranch	374Z	80126	8900-9199	
KENWOOD DR	Boulder	128N	80305	2300-2599	
KENWOOD PL	Gilpin Co	742W	80403	None	
KENWOOD ST	Adams Co	226J	80022	7600-7999	
KENYA DR	Jefferson Co	367C	80439	6300-6499	
KENYON AVE E	Arapahoe Co	350A	80013	20600-20699	
	Aurora	348B	80014	14600-14799	
	Aurora	348C	80013	15500-15899	
	Aurora	349D	80013	19700-20199	
	Cherry Hills Village	344D	80113	1-1199	
	Denver	346A	80237	5900-5999	
	Denver	346B	80237	7300-7799	
	Denver	346C	80237	7800-8499	
	Denver	346C	80237	8500-8899	
	Denver	346D	80237	8900-9299	
KENYON AVE W	Denver	343A	80236	3600-5199	
	Denver	343B	80236	3800-4499	
	Denver	342C	80235	6200-6699	
	Englewood	344B	80110	1-1199	
	Jefferson Co	341C	80235	10000-10199	
	Sheridan	343C	80110	3000-3399	
	Sheridan	343C	80123	3400-3599	
KENYON CIR	Boulder	128T	80305	2800-2899	
KENYON CT E	Arapahoe Co	349D	80013	20100-20199	
KENYON DR E	Aurora	348D	80013	16600-16899	
	Aurora	349A	80013	17200-17799	
	Denver	346C	80237	7800-7999	
	Denver	346C	80237	8000-8399	
KENYON DR W	Jefferson Co	341C	80235	10300-10399	
KENYON LN	Longmont	10U	80503	3600-3699	
KENYON PL E	Arapahoe Co	350A	80013	20500-20899	
	Arapahoe Co	350B	80013	None	
	Aurora	349A	80013	17100-17199	
	Aurora	350B	80018	21700-21799	
	Aurora	350C	80018	None	
	Denver	346C	80237	7900-8099	
KEOTA LN	Superior	160Q	80027	1700-2299	
KEOTA ST	Parker	409N	80134	11200-11299	
KEOUGH DR	Northglenn	194D	80233	11700-11999	
KEPNER DR E	Aurora	317C	80012	11800-11899	
	Aurora	318D	80017	15800-15999	
	Aurora	319B	80017	17700-17899	
	Aurora	319B	80017	17900-18199	

STREET NAME	CITY or COUNTY	MAP GRID	ZIP CODE	BLOCK RANGE	O/E
KEPNER PL E	Aurora	317C	80012	11701-11799	O
	Aurora	317D	80012	12100-12398	E
	Aurora	318D	80017	16500-16599	
	Aurora	319B	80017	18200-18499	
KERR RD	Jefferson Co	842E	80470	33600-33999	
KERR GULCH RD	Jefferson Co	306G	80439	1000-2699	
	Jefferson Co	307T	80439	2700-3299	
	Jefferson Co	307T	80439	None	
KERRY RD	Boulder Co	131A	80303	9100-9299	
KERRY RUN RD	El Paso Co	909U	80908	18500-18799	
KERSDALE WAY	El Paso Co	909Q	80908	4100-4199	
KERSHAW CT	El Paso Co	908R	80132	19400-19899	
KESTRAL CT	Castle Rock	466X	80109	3900-4099	
KESTRAL PL	Castle Rock	466X	80109	4000-4299	
KESTREL LN	Boulder Co	101E	80301	9100-9499	
KESTREL LN	Longmont	41R	80501	1300-1399	
KESTREL RD	Dacono	727N	80514	None	
KESWICK CT	Douglas Co	409X	80134	None	
KETCHWOOD CIR	Highlands Ranch	405L	80130	4400-4799	
KETCHWOOD CT	Highlands Ranch	405M	80130	10400-10599	
KETTERING LN	Douglas Co	408M	80134	10300-10399	
KETTLE AVE E	Arapahoe Co	374L	80122	400-699	
	Arapahoe Co	374M	80122	1100-1299	
	Arapahoe Co	374M	80122	1400-1899	
	Arapahoe Co	381K	80016	25100-25599	
	Centennial	375J	80122	1900-2399	
	Centennial	375L	80122	3700-3899	
	Centennial	376J	80122	5400-5599	
	Centennial	376J	80112	5600-6199	
	Centennial	376K	80112	6700-6999	
	Centennial	376L	80112	7800-7999	
	Centennial	376M	80112	8500-8699	
	Centennial	379J	80016	17600-17699	
	Centennial	379L	80016	18900-18999	
KETTLE AVE W	Littleton	374K	80120	800-1399	
	Littleton	374J	80120	1500-1899	
	Littleton	373M	80120	2300-2499	
	Littleton	373J	80128	4400-4499	
KETTLE CIR E	Arapahoe Co	381K	80016	25600-26299	
KETTLE CIR E	Centennial	376M	80112	8600-8799	
KETTLE CIR W	Littleton	373M	80120	2400-2499	
KETTLE CT E	Centennial	376L	80112	7700-7799	
KETTLE PL	Arapahoe Co	830E	80016	25300-25799	
KETTLE PL E	Arapahoe Co	374M	80122	1100-1299	
	Arapahoe Co	378L	80016	None	
	Aurora	381M	80016	27700-27899	
	Aurora	379M	80016	None	
	Aurora	380M	80016	None	
	Centennial	375K	80122	2800-2899	
	Centennial	375L	80122	3800-3899	
	Centennial	376J	80112	5800-6099	
	Centennial	376L	80112	7700-8199	
	Centennial	376M	80112	8500-8799	
	Centennial	379J	80016	17500-17699	
	Littleton	374L	80122	700-799	
KETTLEDRUM LN E	Douglas Co	411X	80138	10100-10799	
KEVIN CT	Broomfield	163E	80020	14300-14399	
KEWANEE DR	Boulder	128R	80303	5300-5399	
KEWAUNEE CT S	Aurora	381F	80016	7000-7099	
KEWAUNEE WAY N	Aurora	291P	80018	None	
KEWAUNEE WAY S	Aurora	291T	80018	None	
	Aurora	351X	80016	None	
	Aurora	381B	80016	None	
KEY CT	Longmont	11L	80501	2400-2499	
KEYES ST	Frederick	727A	80504	None	
KEYSER CREEK AVE	Parker	439F	80134	18200-18499	
KEYSTONE AVE E					
	Buckley Air Force Base	289T	80011	None	
KEYSTONE BLVD	Douglas Co	408H	80134	16500-16799	
KEYSTONE CT	Boulder	98N	80304	2300-2499	
KEYSTONE CT	Lafayette	131M	80026	1000-1099	
KEYSTONE CT	Longmont	11Z	80501	1300-1399	
KEYSTONE DR	Jefferson Co	305H	80439	None	
	Jefferson Co	306J	80439	None	
KEYSTONE TRAIL	Broomfield	162L	80020	100-199	
KICKING HORSE CT	Douglas Co	432F	80125	8501-8599	O
KICKING HORSE DR	Douglas Co	432F	80125	10400-10699	
KIDDER DR	Adams Co	224T	80221	6800-6999	
KIEFER ST S	Arapahoe Co	792W	80102	800-999	
KIEM RD	Jefferson Co	366D	80439	6500-6699	
KILBERRY LN	Parker	408R	80134	None	
KILBERRY WAY	Parker	408R	80134	None	
KILIMANJARO DR	Jefferson Co	367D	80439	6000-7099	
	Jefferson Co	337X	80439	None	
KILKENNY ST	Boulder Co	131A	80303	1300-1599	
KILLARNEY CIR S	Aurora	380J	80016	None	
KILLARNEY CT	Denver	260E	80249	None	
KILLARNEY CT S	Arapahoe Co	350A	80013	3700-3899	
	Arapahoe Co	380A	80016	6400-6699	
	Arapahoe Co	350J	80015	None	
	Aurora	319R	80013	None	
	Centennial	350W	80016	6200-6299	
KILLARNEY DR S	Centennial	350W	80016	6100-6199	
KILLARNEY LN S	Aurora	379M	80016	None	
KILLARNEY PL S	Aurora	379M	80016	None	
KILLARNEY ST	Aurora	290E	80011	1600-1699	
	Denver	260E	80249	None	
KILLARNEY ST S	Arapahoe Co	350E	80015	4100-4299	
	Aurora	320W	80013	3500-3699	
	Centennial	350N	80015	5300-5599	
	Centennial	350W	80016	6200-6399	
KILLARNEY WAY S	Arapahoe Co	350A	80013	3900-4199	
	Aurora	320S	80013	None	
	Centennial	350S	80015	5600-5899	
KILLDEER LN	Jefferson Co	370B	80127	1-99	
KILLDEER ST	Brighton	140N	80601	None	
KILLEN AVE	Castle Rock	498V	80104	5400-5699	
KILLINGTON CT	Jefferson Co	306E	80439	1300-1399	
KILMER CT	Arvada	220T	80007	6700-6799	
KILMER LOOP	Arvada	250B	80403	6100-6299	
KILMER ST	Arvada	220T	80007	6800-6899	
	Arvada	220X	80007	None	
	Jefferson Co	280P	80401	600-1299	
	Jefferson Co	250N	80403	4300-4399	
	Jefferson Co	250F	80403	5200-5499	
KILMER ST S	Jefferson Co	280X	80401	100-199	
KIM CT	Douglas Co	440Y	80134	8600-8699	
KIMBALL AVE	Golden	279T	80401	100-299	

STREET NAME	CITY or COUNTY	MAP GRID	ZIP CODE	BLOCK RANGE	O/E
KIMBALL CT	Golden	279T	80401	300-399	
KIMBALL ST	Parker	409N	80134	10700-10799	
KIMBARK DR	Brighton	139T	80601	15200-15599	
KIMBARK ST	Lafayette	132J	80026	100-899	
KIMBARK ST	Longmont	41H	80501	100-899	
	Longmont	11Z	80501	900-1299	
	Longmont	11V	80501	1300-1699	
	Longmont	11R	80501	1900-1999	
KIMBARK ST S	Longmont	41R	80501	1200-1399	
	Longmont	41H	80501	None	
KIMBERLY DR	Castle Rock	467H	80108	7400-7699	
KIMBERLY DR	Federal Heights	193U	80260	9500-9699	
KIMBERLY PL	Longmont	40P	80503	None	
KIMBERLY ST	Adams Co	226J	80022	7700-7999	
KIMBERWICK DR	Douglas Co	432F	80125	10100-10299	
KIMBLEWYCK CIR	Northglenn	195K	80233	10700-10798	E
KIMMER DR	Lone Tree	376Z	80124	9200-9299	
KIMWOOD RD	Gilpin Co	761C	80403	None	
KINCAID PL	Boulder	98N	80304	2100-2299	
KINCAID ST S	Arapahoe Co	812Z	80102	6100-6299	
	Arapahoe Co	832D	80137	6300-7199	
KINCAID SPRINGS RD	Jefferson Co	842R	80470	28700-28899	
KINCROSS CT	Boulder Co	100G	80301	4700-4799	
KINCROSS DR	Boulder Co	100F	80301	7900-8299	
KING AVE	Boulder	127M	80302	1300-1599	
	Boulder	128J	80302	1600-2199	
KING CIR	Broomfield	163Q	80020	13000-13099	
KING CIR	Westminster	193P	80031	10400-10499	
KING CT	Adams Co	253F	80221	5300-5399	
KING CT	Boulder Co	131J	80026	9100-9199	
KING CT	Broomfield	133X	80020	15100-15199	
KING CT	Douglas Co	409X	80134	5800-6299	
KING CT	Westminster	193T	80031	9900-9999	
	Westminster	193P	80031	10200-10399	
	Westminster	193K	80031	10500-10699	
	Westminster	193F	80031	11400-11499	
KING CT S	Denver	313F	80219	1400-1499	
KING PL	Nederland	740M	80466	None	
KING PT	Broomfield	163T	80020	12600-12699	
KING RD	Jefferson Co	336X	80439	6300-6399	
KING RD S	Jefferson Co	336M	80439	4700-4899	
KING ST	Adams Co	253F	80221	5200-5399	
	Adams Co	223T	80221	6600-6799	
	Broomfield	163T	80020	12400-12498	E
	Denver	283T	80219	1-399	
	Denver	283P	80204	400-1999	
	Denver	283B	80211	2000-2699	
	Denver	253X	80211	2700-2899	
	Denver	253T	80211	3800-4599	
	Denver	253K	80221	4800-4999	
KING ST	Lafayette	131J	80026	400-599	
KING ST	Lochbuie	140A	80603	None	
KING ST	Westminster	223P	80030	7500-7599	
	Westminster	223K	80030	7600-7899	
	Westminster	223K	80031	8000-8199	
	Westminster	223F	80031	8201-8399	O
	Westminster	193P	80031	9900-10299	
	Westminster	193F	80031	11400-11499	
KING ST S	Denver	283T	80219	1-299	
	Denver	313K	80219	1000-1699	
	Denver	313T	80219	1900-2699	
	Denver	313T	80236	2700-3099	
	Englewood	343K	80110	4500-4699	
	Littleton	343T	80123	5400-5799	
	Sheridan	343B	80236	3500-3899	
KING WAY	Denver	283F	80204	1900-1999	
	Denver	283B	80211	2000-2099	
	Westminster	193X	80031	9200-9299	
	Westminster	193T	80031	9500-9799	
	Westminster	193F	80031	11400-11499	
KING WAY S	Denver	313K	80219	1800-1899	
	Denver	313T	80236	3100-3299	
KING ARTHURS KNOLL	El Paso Co	908U	80132	100-199	
KINGBIRD CIR W	Highlands Ranch	404K	80129	300-399	
KINGBIRD DR	Frederick	706Z	80504	4800-4899	
KINGBURY CT	Jefferson Co	280M	80401	1400-1499	
KING CREST LN W	Bow Mar	343S	80123	5000-5199	
KING CREST WAY	Bow Mar	343S	80123	5000-5599	
KING CROSS LN	El Paso Co	908R	80132	None	
KINGFISHER AVE	Brighton	137Z	80601	1300-1399	
KINGFISHER AVE	Highlands Ranch	404J	80129	10200-10299	
KING LAKE TRAIL	Broomfield	163J	80020	13300-13599	
KING RANCH CT	Thornton	166Y	80602	None	
KINGS CT	Jefferson Co	822Y	80433	11900-11999	
KINGS CT	Lafayette	132P	80026	9100-9199	
KINGS RD	Clear Creek Co	801R	80439	1-399	
KINGSBERRY CT S	Highlands Ranch	405E	80126	9700-9799	
KINGSBURY RD	Jefferson Co	307X	80439	26000-26299	
KINGS DEER LN	El Paso Co	908Q	80132	19400-19499	
KINGS DEER PT E	El Paso Co	908Q	80132	1-999	
KINGSFIELD ST	Castle Rock	498R	80104	1001-1299	O
	Castle Rock	498R	80104	1300-6099	
KINGSLEY AVE W	Jefferson Co	372U	80128	6400-6699	
KINGS MILL CIR	Elbert Co	851C	80107	42000-42999	
KINGS MILL LN	Lone Tree	406D	80124	9600-9699	
KINGS MILL PL	Lone Tree	406D	80124	9600-9699	
KINGS RIDGE BLVD	Boulder	98U	80301	None	
KINGSTON AVE E	Highlands Ranch	405H	80130	4800-4999	
KINGSTON CIR	Aurora	287X	80012	400-499	
KINGSTON CIR S	Arapahoe Co	347Y	80111	6000-6099	
KINGSTON CT	Adams Co	137T	80602	15200-15299	
	Commerce City	197L	80601	None	
KINGSTON CT	Longmont	11S	80503	1900-1999	
KINGSTON CT S	Aurora	317K	80014	1900-2299	
	Aurora	317P	80014	2600-2699	
	Douglas Co	407B	80112	9500-9599	
	Highlands Ranch	405H	80130	10000-10099	
KINGSTON DR	Adams Co	137K	80602	None	
KINGSTON ST	Adams Co	137T	80602	15300-15499	
	Aurora	287P	80010	300-499	
	Aurora	287K	80010	700-2599	
	Commerce City	197F	80640	11200-11599	
	Denver	257K	80239	4500-5099	
KINGSTON ST S	Aurora	317F	80112	900-1699	
	Aurora	317P	80014	2300-2399	
KINGSTON WAY S	Arapahoe Co	347T	80111	5600-5899	
	Aurora	317K	80112	1600-1699	
KINGSTOWN PL	Boulder	98K	80301	3900-4199	

STREET NAME	CITY or COUNTY	MAP GRID	ZIP CODE	BLOCK RANGE	O/E
KINGS VALLEY	Jefferson Co	822Y	80433	29700E-30699E	
	Jefferson Co	822X	80433	31200W-31599W	
KINGS VALLEY DR	Jefferson Co	842C	80433	30300-30899	
	Jefferson Co	822Y	80433	30900-31599	
KINGS VALLEY WAY	Jefferson Co	822Y	80433	30800-30999	
KINGWOOD PL	Boulder	97R	80304	1300-1599	
KINNER ST	Castle Rock	497F	80109	800-899	
KINNEY CREEK RD	Jefferson Co	337W	80439	5900-6499	
KINNEY CREEK WAY	Parker	439F	80134	18200-18299	
KINNIKINIC LN	Jefferson Co	843X	80470	17600-17899	
KINNIKIKIC RD	Boulder	127L	80302	None	
KINNIKINICK CT	Longmont	12X	80501	1200-1299	
KINNIKINICK LN	Jefferson Co	336Q	80439	29000-29199	
KINNIKINICK RD	Jefferson Co	336M	80439	28000-28599	
KINNIKINNIK DR	Douglas Co	887F	80118	2000-2599	
KINNIKINNIK WAY	Erie	133C	80516	None	
KINNIKINNIK HILL	Jefferson Co	277Q	80401	500-799	
KINSBOROUGH CT	El Paso Co	908R	80132	None	
KINSEY LN	Jefferson Co	365U	80433	32500-32699	
KIO CT	Arapahoe Co	791T	80137	None	
KIOWA AVE	Bennett	793J	80102	400-699	
KIOWA AVE E	Elizabeth	871E	80107	100-799	
KIOWA AVE W	Elizabeth	871E	80107	100-799	
KIOWA LN	Jefferson Co	842N	80470	34000-34299	
KIOWA PL	Boulder	128L	80303	200-499	
KIOWA RD	Bennett	793P	80102	None	
KIOWA RD	Douglas Co	886G	80118	7000-7299	
KIOWA RD	Jefferson Co	338J	80454	22800-23399	
KIOWA RD N	Douglas Co	411Y	80138	9500-9899	
	Elbert Co	872H	80117	30000-35999	
	Elbert Co	852R	80117	36000-39999	
KIOWA-BENNETT RD N	Arapahoe Co	793T	80102	1-1499	
KIOWA-BENNETT RD S	Arapahoe Co	793X	80102	1-799	
	Arapahoe Co	813K	80102	None	
KIOWA CREEK DR	Brighton	138V	80601	2400-2699	
KIOWA CREEK DR	Castle Rock	466P	80109	4900-5099	
KIOWA CREEK RD W	Elbert Co	891Y	80106	4000-6499	
	Elbert Co	911F	80106	18000-21499	
KIOWA TRAIL	Elbert Co	870D	80107	700-1999	
KIPLING CT	Westminster	191Q	80021	10400-10499	
KIPLING CT S	Jefferson Co	341C	80235	3600-3799	
	Jefferson Co	371C	80127	6400-6499	
	Jefferson Co	371U	80128	None	
	Lakewood	311G	80232	1500-1599	
	Lakewood	311L	80232	1600-1699	
KIPLING PKWY	Arvada	251G	80002	5700-5799	
KIPLING PKWY S	Jefferson Co	311P	80227	1900-2399	
	Jefferson Co	371R	80127	6400-8699	
	Lakewood	311G	80226	700-1099	
	Lakewood	311G	80232	1100-1899	
	Lakewood	311Q	80227	2400-3499	
KIPLING ST	Arvada	221Y	80004	6400-6899	
	Arvada	221U	80004	6900-7199	
	Arvada	221Q	80005	7200-8799	
	Jefferson Co	281U	80226	1-599	
	Lakewood	281G	80215	600-2799	
	Westminster	191U	80021	9700-9799	
	Wheat Ridge	251Y	80215	2800-3199	
	Wheat Ridge	251U	80033	3200-5399	
KIPLING ST S	Denver	341L	80127	4600-4898	E
	Jefferson Co	341G	80127	4300-4599	
	Jefferson Co	341L	80127	4601-4899	O
	Jefferson Co	341Q	80127	4900-6399	
	Jefferson Co	371V	80128	8700-8799	
	Lakewood	281V	80226	1-699	
	Lakewood	311U	80227	1900-3499	
	Lakewood	341G	80235	3500-4299	
	Lakewood	311Y	80227	None	
KIPLING WAY	Westminster	191L	80021	10500-10799	
	Westminster	191V	80021	None	
KIPLING WAY S	Jefferson Co	341L	80127	4700-4899	
	Jefferson Co	371Y	80128	None	
KIPP AVE	Keenesburg	732A	80643	500-599	
KIRBY CT	Arapahoe Co	791T	80137	None	
KIRBY ST	Adams Co	751K	80642	None	
KIRK CIR S	Centennial	350N	80015	5400-5599	
KIRK CT	Denver	260E	80249	None	
KIRK CT S	Arapahoe Co	350A	80013	3800-3899	
	Arapahoe Co	350E	80013	4000-4199	
	Arapahoe Co	380A	80016	6400-6499	
	Aurora	320W	80013	None	
	Aurora	380J	80016	None	
	Centennial	350S	80015	5500-5599	
KIRK ST	Denver	260E	80249	None	
KIRK ST N	Denver	260N	80249	4100-4399	
	Denver	260J	80249	4700-4899	
KIRK ST S	Arapahoe Co	350A	80013	3500-3799	
	Arapahoe Co	350E	80013	4100-4299	
	Arapahoe Co	350S	80016	5500-5599	
	Centennial	350S	80015	5100-5499	
	Centennial	350W	80016	5600-6199	
KIRK WAY E	Superior	160L	80027	900-999	
KIRK WAY S	Arapahoe Co	350A	80013	3600-3899	
	Arapahoe Co	350E	80013	3900-4099	
	Arapahoe Co	350J	80015	None	
	Aurora	320S	80013	None	
KIRKWALL ST	Broomfield	162Z	80020	200-299	
KIRKWOOD CIR	Elbert Co	870C	80107	35800-35999	
KIRKWOOD CT	Boulder Co	100G	80301	4600-4699	
KIRKWOOD CT	Jefferson Co	306U	80439	29500-29599	
KIRKWOOD CT S	Denver	316N	80222	2300-2499	
KIRKWOOD PL	Boulder	97R	80304	3500-3599	
KIRKWOOD ST	Boulder Co	100F	80301	4600-4799	
KIRKWOOD WAY	Gilpin Co	761K	80403	1-199	
KISMET PL	Broomfield	133N	80020	4700-4799	
KISTLER CT E	Highlands Ranch	404H	80126	1100-1299	
KIT LN	Park Co	841R	80421	1-99	
KIT CARSON CIR S	Arapahoe Co	374D	80122	6700E-6799E	
KIT CARSON DR	Broomfield	133N	80020	None	
KIT CARSON DR S	Arapahoe Co	374M	80122	7600-7899	
KIT CARSON LN	Douglas Co	440G	80138	8900-9099	
KIT CARSON ST S	Arapahoe Co	374D	80121	6500-6699	
	Arapahoe Co	374M	80122	7300-7499	
KIT CARSON PEAK	Jefferson Co	842P	80421	None	
KITE HAWK LN	Highlands Ranch	403G	80129	None	
KITELEY LN	Longmont	11W	80503	1200-1299	
KITTERY ST	Castle Rock	499N	80104	900-1399	
KITTIWAKE ST	Highlands Ranch	375Y	80126	8900-9099	

STREET NAME	CITY or COUNTY	MAP GRID	ZIP CODE	BLOCK RANGE	O/E
KITTREDGE CIR S	Arapahoe Co	378M	80112	7800-7899	
KITTREDGE CT	Aurora	288M	80011	700-799	
	Aurora	288H	80011	1700-1799	
KITTREDGE CT S	Arapahoe Co	348Z	80016	6000-6099	
	Arapahoe Co	378M	80112	7700-8099	
	Aurora	318R	80013	2500-2599	
	Centennial	348V	80015	5700-5799	
KITTREDGE LN S	Centennial	348V	80015	5600-5699	
KITTREDGE ST	Aurora	288M	80011	600-1199	
	Aurora	288H	80011	1800-1899	
	Commerce City	198V	80022	9600-9899	
	Commerce City	198M	80022	10400-10799	
	Commerce City	168Z	80603	None	
	Denver	258M	80239	4200-5599	
	Denver	258H	80239	None	
KITTREDGE ST S	Arapahoe Co	348V	80016	5900-5999	
	Arapahoe Co	378R	80112	7900-7999	
	Arapahoe Co	378H	80016	None	
	Aurora	288Z	80017	400-499	
	Aurora	288Z	80017	600-799	
	Aurora	318H	80017	1100-1499	
	Aurora	318Z	80013	3300-3599	
	Aurora	348D	80013	3600-3699	
	Aurora	348H	80014	4200-4299	
	Aurora	348M	80015	4500-4699	
	Aurora	348M	80015	4800-4899	
	Centennial	348V	80015	5500-5799	
KITTREDGE WAY S	Arapahoe Co	378R	80112	7900-8099	
	Aurora	288Z	80017	500-599	
	Aurora	318D	80017	800-1099	
	Aurora	318R	80013	2100-2599	
	Aurora	318V	80013	3100-3299	
	Aurora	348M	80015	4600-4699	
KITTREDGE LOOP RD	Boulder	128E	80302	None	
KITTREDGE PARK RD S	Jefferson Co	307S	80439	2500-2899	
	Jefferson Co	306V	80439	2900-3099	
KITTRELL CT	Boulder	128X	80305	3100-3199	
KITTRIDGE PL	Elbert Co	850R	80107	38800-38999	
KITTY DR	Jefferson Co	823S	80433	10700-11099	
KITTYHAWK CIR	Elbert Co	830Q	80138	45600-45999	
KIVA LN	Jefferson Co	335Z	80439	31600-31799	
KLEINBROOK ST	Highlands Ranch	405L	80126	10100-10199	
KLEINBROOK WAY	Highlands Ranch	405L	80126	10100-10299	
KLINE CIR S	Lakewood	311U	80227	2600-2799	
KLINE CT	Arvada	221U	80004	7100-7199	
	Arvada	221G	80005	8000-8099	
KLINE CT S	Jefferson Co	341L	80127	4500-4599	
KLINE CT S	Jefferson Co	341Q	80127	5200-5299	
	Jefferson Co	341U	80127	5500-5599	
	Jefferson Co	371C	80127	6400-6499	
	Lakewood	311C	80226	700-799	
	Lakewood	311G	80232	1500-1599	
	Lakewood	311L	80232	1600-1699	
KLINE DR	Arvada	221Q	80005	7400-7799	
	Lakewood	281Q	80215	800-899	
KLINE DR	Longmont	41P	80501	None	
KLINE DR W	Lakewood	281Q	80215	10000-10099	
KLINE ST	Arvada	251C	80004	6000-6099	
	Arvada	221Y	80004	6400-6799	
	Arvada	221G	80005	8100-8299	
	Arvada	251G	80002	None	
	Jefferson Co	250N	80403	None	
	Lakewood	281L	80215	1100-1399	
	Lakewood	281G	80215	2000-2099	
	Westminster	191U	80021	9800-9999	
	Westminster	191Q	80021	10400-10499	
	Wheat Ridge	251Y	80033	3300-3399	
	Wheat Ridge	251U	80033	3500-3799	
KLINE ST S	Jefferson Co	341L	80127	4700-4999	
	Jefferson Co	341U	80127	5500-5899	
	Jefferson Co	371C	80127	6400-6599	
	Jefferson Co	371G	80127	7000-7399	
	Jefferson Co	371Y	80128	None	
	Lakewood	281Y	80226	300-499	
	Lakewood	311G	80232	1100-1399	
KLINE WAY	Westminster	191Q	80021	10500-10599	
KLINE WAY S	Jefferson Co	371G	80127	7000-7299	
	Lakewood	311C	80226	700-899	
	Lakewood	311G	80232	1100-1399	
	Lakewood	311L	80232	1600-1799	
KLINGEN GATE CT	Castle Pines North	436F	80108	1-99	
KLINGEN GATE LN	Castle Pines North	436F	80108	1-99	
KLONDIKE PL	Douglas Co	436X	80108	3300-3399	
KLONDYKE AVE	Boulder Co	740N	80466	None	
KNEALE RD	Boulder Co	743S	80025	None	
KNIGHT CT	Broomfield	163P	80020	12900-12999	
KNIGHT ST	Lafayette	132P	80026	1-299	
KNIGHTS CROSSING	El Paso Co	909N	80132	19700-19799	
KNOB CT	Lafayette	131D	80026	700-799	
KNOBBIE CIR	Castle Rock	467W	80109	None	
KNOBCONE DR	Castle Rock	467R	80108	5000-5299	
KNOLL CIR S	Highlands Ranch	406J	80130	10100-10299	
KNOLL CT S	Highlands Ranch	406J	80130	10200-10299	
KNOLL DR	Douglas Co	406J	80124	None	
	Highlands Ranch	406J	80130	None	
KNOLL PL E	Highlands Ranch	406E	80130	5400-5499	
KNOLL WAY S	Centennial	375E	80122	7100-7499	
KNOLL CREST CT	Boulder Co	99N	80301	5700-5899	
KNOLLSIDE AVE	Parker	409J	80134	10700-17199	
KNOLLSIDE DR	Parker	409J	80134	10300-10399	
KNOLLWOOD BLVD	El Paso Co	908T	80132	17700-18699	
KNOLLWOOD CIR	El Paso Co	908T	80132	900-17799	
KNOLLWOOD DR	Boulder Co	127B	80302	2100-2299	
KNOLLWOOD DR	Monument	908X	80132	18100-18199	
KNOLLWOOD WAY E	Highlands Ranch	404D	80126	1300-1399	
KNOTTY PINE AVE	Thornton	193V	80260	None	
KNOTTY PINE LN	Jefferson Co	336P	80439	5100-5199	
KNOTTY PINE WAY	Castle Rock	467R	80108	None	
KNOTTY PINES WAY	El Paso Co	908Q	80132	19300-19399	
KNOWLES RD	Jefferson Co	336M	80439	27900-28199	
KNOX CIR	Westminster	223P	80030	3500-3599	
KNOX CT	Adams Co	223X	80221	6300-6399	
	Adams Co	223T	80221	6600-6899	
	Broomfield	163T	80020	12400-12499	
	Denver	283T	80219	1-399	
	Denver	283Q	80204	400-1499	
	Denver	253P	80211	4100-4399	
	Denver	253K	80221	4800-4999	

Continued on next column

STREET NAME	CITY or COUNTY	MAP GRID	ZIP CODE	BLOCK RANGE	O/E
KNOX CT (Cont'd)	Westminster	223Q	80030	7400-7599	
	Westminster	223K	80030	7600-7999	
	Westminster	223K	80031	8000-8199	
	Westminster	193X	80031	9100-9399	
	Westminster	193F	80031	11400-11499	
KNOX CT S	Arapahoe Co	313Y	80110	3300-3498	E
	Denver	283T	80219	1-699	
	Denver	313B	80219	700-899	
	Denver	313L	80219	1000-2699	
	Denver	313U	80236	2700-2799	
	Denver	313Y	80236	3301-3499	O
	Denver	343G	80236	3900-4299	
	Englewood	343L	80110	4500-4699	
	Littleton	343P	80123	5400-5499	
	Sheridan	343C	80236	3600-3899	
KNOX DR	Boulder	128U	80305	1300-1599	
KNOX PL	Westminster	223P	80030	7400-7499	
KNOX PT	Broomfield	163T	80020	12600-12699	
KNOXVILLE WAY S	Denver	312U	80227	2700-2899	
KOA CT	Castle Rock	497Q	80104	1100-1199	
KOCH AVE	Weld Co	727B	80530	301-399	O
KOCHIA CT	Douglas Co	378V	80134	8400-8499	
KOCHIA CT	Frederick	726G	80516	None	
KODIAK CT	Frederick	706Z	80504	4100-4199	
KODIAK CT	Longmont	12S	80501	1-99	
KOHINOOR PL	Golden	278H	80401	1800-1999	
KOHL ST	Broomfield	162X	80020	100-399	
	Broomfield	162T	80020	500-1699	
KOHLER DR	Boulder	128N	80305	1800-2699	
KOKAI CIR	Adams Co	224J	80221	1400-1599	
KOKANEE	Jefferson Co	370A	80127	1-99	
KOKOMO RD	Douglas Co	870K	80116	11800-11899	
KOLA DR	Thornton	193V	80260	None	
	Thornton	194W	80260	None	
KOLAR CT	Erie	102Q	80516	1-199	
KOLSTAD LOOP	Elbert Co	890R	80116	24600-24999	
KONKEL FARM CT	Douglas Co	870X	80116	None	
KORNBRUST CIR	Lone Tree	406M	80124	9000-9399	
KORNBRUST DR	Lone Tree	406M	80124	None	
KORTE PKWY	Longmont	41K	80501	600-799	
KORTE PL	Longmont	41K	80501	1801-1899	O
KOSMERL PL	Frederick	706Z	80530	8400-8499	
KOSS ST	Erie	103S	80516	800-1199	
KRAMER CT	Aurora	287K	80010	900-1099	
KRAMER DR	Erie	102N	80516	None	
KRAMERIA CT	Adams Co	136J	80602	16600-16699	
	Adams Co	136N	80602	None	
	Greenwood Village	346S	80111	5600-5699	
	Thornton	166W	80602	12000-12099	
KRAMERIA CT S	Centennial	376J	80112	7700-7799	
KRAMERIA DR	Commerce City	226P	80022	7200-7599	
KRAMERIA ST	Adams Co	226N	80022	7200-7599	
KRAMERIA ST	Adams Co	226J	80022	8001-8199	O
	Adams Co	226E	80022	8100-8399	
	Commerce City	256J	80022	4901-4999	O
	Commerce City	256E	80022	5400-5599	
	Commerce City	256A	80022	6000-6099	
	Commerce City	226S	80022	6500-7099	
	Denver	286J	80220	100-1999	
	Denver	286A	80207	2000-2799	
	Denver	256W	80207	2800-3799	
	Greenwood Village	346N	80111	5300-5599	
	Thornton	166W	80602	12000-12399	
	Thornton	166N	80602	13000-13299	
	Thornton	166J	80602	13600-13899	
	Thornton	166J	80602	None	
KRAMERIA ST S	Arapahoe Co	316N	80222	2300-2499	
	Arapahoe Co	316S	80222	3000-3199	
	Centennial	346W	80111	5900-6299	
	Centennial	376J	80112	7300-7699	
	Denver	286W	80224	200-499	
	Denver	316A	80224	700-1099	
	Denver	316E	80224	1300-1599	
	Denver	316N	80222	2500-2599	
	Denver	316W	80222	3200-3299	
KRAMERIA WAY	Adams Co	136J	80602	16600-16699	
	Thornton	166J	80602	13600-13699	
KRAMERIA WAY S	Centennial	376A	80111	6400-6699	
	Centennial	376N	80112	8000-8299	
	Denver	316J	80224	1700-1799	
KRASHIN DR	Jefferson Co	365Y	80433	8900-9399	
KRESTVIEW LN	Jefferson Co	278S	80401	1-299	
KRISTAL WAY	Adams Co	223R	80221	2000-2399	
KRISTY CT	Longmont	41U	80504	1800-1999	
KRYPTONITE DR	Castle Rock	467G	80108	None	
KRYPTONITE LN	Castle Rock	467G	80108	None	
KUDU TRAIL	Park Co	841R	80421	1-499	
KUEHSTER RD	Jefferson Co	844B	80127	12200-14499	
	Jefferson Co	844M	80127	None	
KUMPFMILLER DR	Lakewood	311T	80227	None	
	Lakewood	310X	80228	None	
KUNER RD N	Brighton	138N	80601	1-499	
KUNER RD S	Brighton	138S	80601	1-899	
KUNST RD	Jefferson Co	762S	80403	7900-7998	E
KYLE CIR S	Arapahoe Co	813F	80102	1900-2299	
KYLE WAY	Douglas Co	432K	80125	7600-7999	
KYLIE DR	Longmont	42G	80501	1500-1799	

L

STREET NAME	CITY or COUNTY	MAP GRID	ZIP CODE	BLOCK RANGE	O/E
LACEY CT	Boulder Co	70G	80503	7200-7299	
LA CHULA RD	Gilpin Co	741X	80403	1-999	
LACKLAND DR	Denver	257H	80239	12900-13099	
	Denver	258E	80239	13100-13299	
LACKLAND PL	Denver	258G	80239	14900-15499	
	Denver	260E	80249	None	
LACOSTA CIR	Elbert Co	851C	80107	5200-5299	
LaCOSTA DR	Lone Tree	406C	80124	9400-9599	
LACROSSE LN N	Douglas Co	411X	80138	9100-9499	
LADEAN ST	Adams Co	225E	80229	8200-8299	
La DONNA VISTA LN	Elbert Co	870Y	80107	28000-29999	
LADORE ST	Adams Co	226J	80022	7700-7899	
LADYBUG LN	Castle Rock	497P	80104	None	
LADYBUG TRAIL	Castle Rock	497P	80104	None	
LaFARGE AVE	Louisville	131S	80027	500-1299	
LAFAYETTE CIR S	Centennial	375J	80122	7300E-7499E	
	Denver	314V	80210	2701-2799	O
LAFAYETTE CT	Thornton	164M	80241	13400-13499	

K L

STREET NAME	CITY or COUNTY	MAP GRID	ZIP CODE	BLOCK RANGE	O/E
LAFAYETTE CT S	Englewood	314V	80113	2800-2899	
LAFAYETTE DR	Boulder	128X	80305	2600-3099	
LAFAYETTE DR S	Englewood	314V	80113	2900-2999	
LAFAYETTE LN S	Cherry Hills Village	344M	80110	4800-5099	
LAFAYETTE PL S	Centennial	344Z	80121	6200-6398	E
LAFAYETTE ST	Adams Co	224R	80229	7100-7699	
	Adams Co	224M	80229	8000-8199	
	Denver	284M	80218	100-1999	
	Denver	284H	80205	2000-2799	
	Denver	254Z	80205	2800-3899	
LAFAYETTE ST	Louisville	130V	80027	100-599	
	Louisville	131S	80027	600-1099	
LAFAYETTE ST	Northglenn	194R	80233	10400-10599	
	Northglenn	194H	80233	11200-11399	
	Northglenn	194D	80233	11800-11999	
	Thornton	194V	80229	9600-9699	
	Thornton	164Z	80241	12000-12099	
	Thornton	164Z	80241	12300-12599	
	Thornton	164R	80241	12800-12999	
	Thornton	164M	80241	13400-13499	
	Thornton	134M	80602	16400-16599	
LAFAYETTE ST E	Thornton	194V	80229	9800-9999	
LAFAYETTE ST S	Arapahoe Co	374D	80121	6400-6699	
	Cherry Hills Village	344M	80113	4300-4799	
	Denver	284Z	80209	100-499	
	Denver	314R	80210	1300-2799	
	Englewood	314Z	80113	2800-3599	
LAFAYETTE WAY	Adams Co	224M	80229	7800-7999	
	Thornton	164R	80241	13300-13399	
LAFAYETTE WAY S	Arapahoe Co	374H	80122	7000-7199	
LAFAYETTE TRAIL	Elbert Co	850R	80107	38800-38999	
LAGAE RD	Castle Pines North	436R	80108	7200-7299	
	Douglas Co	436U	80108	None	
LA GARITA PASS	Jefferson Co	371P	80127	11400-11499	
LaGRANGE CIR	Boulder	128T	80305	2800-2899	
LAGUNA CIR	Highlands Ranch	376W	80130	6100-6699	
LAGUNA PL	Boulder	128L	80303	4300-4599	
LAIR LN	Park Co	841Z	80421	1-899	
LAIRD CT S	Superior	160L	80027	1200-1299	
LAKE AVE	Adams Co	169K	80603	13600-13899	
LAKE AVE	Palmer Lake	907Q	80133	None	
LAKE AVE	Thornton	165S	80241	2200-2399	
LAKE AVE E	Arapahoe Co	347Y	80111	11500-11699	
	Arapahoe Co	349S	80016	16900-17699	
	Arapahoe Co	349T	80016	17900-18499	
	Arapahoe Co	350S	80016	20500-20699	
	Centennial	344Y	80121	400-799	
	Centennial	345Z	80121	4600-4699	
	Centennial	345Z	80121	4900-4999	
	Centennial	349V	80016	20200-20299	
	Centennial	350T	80015	22100-22399	
	Centennial	345X	80121	None	
	Centennial	348V	80016	None	
	Greenwood Village	347S	80111	9300-9799	
LAKE AVE W	Columbine Valley	343Y	80123	3200-3299	
	Jefferson Co	341Z	80123	9400-9699	
	Jefferson Co	341W	80127	11600-12199	
	Littleton	344X	80120	500-599	
	Littleton	344W	80120	1400-2099	
	Littleton	343Z	80120	2100-2799	
	Littleton	343W	80123	5000-5199	
LAKE CIR E	Arapahoe Co	348Y	80016	15700-16099	
	Arapahoe Co	350W	80016	20500-20699	
	Centennial	346X	80111	6700-6899	
	Centennial	349Z	80016	20100-20499	
	Centennial	345Y	80121	4400N-4599N	
	Centennial	345Z	80121	4400S-4599S	
	Greenwood Village	347W	80111	9400-9699	
	Greenwood Village	347Y	80111	None	
LAKE CIR W	Littleton	343W	80123	4100N-4799N	
	Littleton	343W	80123	4200S-4799S	
LAKE CT	Greenwood Village	347U	80111	None	
LAKE CT E	Centennial	345Y	80121	3600-3799	
LAKE CT W	Littleton	344W	80121	1400-1499	
LAKE DR	Boulder Co	704F	80503	6300-6599	
LAKE DR	Douglas Co	887G	80118	1600-1999	
LAKE DR	El Paso Co	908V	80132	18100-18699	
LAKE DR E	Arapahoe Co	347T	80111	10000-10399	
	Arapahoe Co	348Z	80016	16100-16499	
	Arapahoe Co	349S	80016	17100-17399	
	Arapahoe Co	349T	80016	18800-19299	
	Arapahoe Co	350S	80016	20500-20699	
	Arapahoe Co	350Y	80015	22500-22599	
	Aurora	351T	80016	None	
	Centennial	344Z	80121	1600-1899	
	Centennial	345X	80121	3400-3699	
	Centennial	348V	80016	16400-16599	
	Greenwood Village	347U	80111	None	
LAKE DR N	Thornton	165S	80241	12800-12899	
LAKE DR W	Jefferson Co	341Z	80123	8900-9399	
	Jefferson Co	341Y	80127	10000-10299	
	Jefferson Co	341X	80127	11300-11599	
LAKE LN	Jefferson Co	842N	80470	33100-33799	
LAKE LN E	Arapahoe Co	349W	80016	16800-17399	
	Centennial	349Z	80016	20200-20299	
	Centennial	350U	80015	22200-22399	
LAKE PL E	Arapahoe Co	347W	80111	10100-10199	
	Arapahoe Co	347Y	80111	11500-11699	
	Arapahoe Co	349W	80016	16800-17399	
	Arapahoe Co	349T	80016	17700-17799	
	Arapahoe Co	350W	80016	20500-20699	
	Arapahoe Co	350Y	80015	22600-23299	
	Arapahoe Co	350T	80015	None	
	Aurora	351T	80016	None	
	Centennial	344Y	80121	400-499	
	Centennial	345Z	80121	4900-4999	
	Centennial	345V	80121	5300-5399	
	Centennial	346T	80111	6500-6599	
	Centennial	348T	80016	14700-14899	
	Centennial	350U	80015	22200-22399	
	Greenwood Village	346Z	80111	8900-9199	
	Greenwood Village	347W	80111	9200-9299	
LAKE PL W	Jefferson Co	342Z	80123	5200-5399	
	Jefferson Co	341Z	80123	9500-9599	
	Littleton	344W	80120	1600-1699	
	Littleton	343W	80123	4900-5199	
LAKE RD S	Lakewood	312L	80227	1900-1999	
LAKE ST	Gilpin Co	760G	80403	100-299	
LAKE WAY E	Centennial	345X	80121	3400-3699	
LAKEBRIAR DR	Boulder	97P	80304	3700-3899	
LAKE CATAMOUNT PKWY	Weld Co	706M	80504	None	
LAKE CIRCLE DR	Thornton	165N	80241	2000-12999	
LAKECLIFF WAY E	Douglas Co	440T	80134	7500-7699	
LAKE ELDORA SKI RD	Boulder Co	740S	80466	1-2599	
LAKE FOREST LN	El Paso Co	908T	80132	18800-18899	
LAKE GULCH RD	Gilpin Co	780G	80403	100-399	
LAKE GULCH RD S	Douglas Co	498S	80104	1-1899	
	Douglas Co	528F	80104	1900-3499	
	Douglas Co	869W	80104	3500-4999	
	Douglas Co	889B	80104	5000-6399	
LAKEHURST WAY S	Jefferson Co	341L	80127	4500-4799	
LAKE ISLE LN	Broomfield	163H	80020	2400-13999	
LAKE MEADOW DR	El Paso Co	908Z	80132	2400-2999	
LAKE MEADOW DR	Lafayette	101W	80026	2500-2599	
LAKE PARK CT	Longmont	11N	80503	2100-2199	
LAKE PARK DR	Longmont	11N	80503	2100-2599	
LAKE PARK WAY	Longmont	11J	80503	2700-2799	
	Longmont	10M	80503	2800-3199	
LAKEPOINT PL N	Douglas Co	440T	80134	6200-6499	
LAKERIDGE RD W	Denver	313N	80219	4400-5199	
	Lakewood	312Q	80227	5200-6999	
LAKERIDGE TRAIL N	Boulder Co	703T	80302	2700-3099	
LAKERIDGE TRAIL S	Boulder Co	703X	80302	2700-3099	
LAKESHORE CT E	Douglas Co	440T	80134	7800-7899	
LAKESHORE DR	Boulder Co	742P	80302	1-1599	
LAKESHORE DR	Bow Mar	343N	80123	4900-5599	
LAKESHORE DR	Longmont	10V	80503	2901-3599	O
LAKESHORE DR E	Douglas Co	440T	80134	8300-8499	
LAKE SHORE PL	Edgewater	282H	80214	1700-1799	
LAKESHORE PARK RD	Boulder Co	742P	80302	1-1299	
LAKESIDE CIR	Douglas Co	404N	80125	6300-6899	
LAKESIDE CT	Boulder Co	100Z	80301	8800-8899	
LAKESIDE CT W	Douglas Co	404N	80125	6000-6699	
LAKESIDE DR	Boulder Co	100Z	80301	8800-8899	
LAKESIDE DR W	Douglas Co	403R	80125	6600-7499	
LAKESIDE LN	Lakeside	252R	80212	2-98	E
LAKESIDE PL N	Douglas Co	403R	80125	10700-10899	
LAKE SONG LN	Broomfield	163H	80020	13900-13998	E
LAKE VALLEY DR	Boulder Co	723G	80503	4400-4899	
LAKEVIEW CIR	Longmont	10U	80503	3100-3599	
LAKEVIEW CT	Brighton	138L	80601	1100-1299	
LAKEVIEW CT	Nederland	740R	80466	None	
LAKEVIEW CT S	Littleton	374K	80120	7700-7799	
LAKEVIEW DR	Aurora	381D	80016	None	
LAKEVIEW DR	Boulder Co	129G	80303	6500-6799	
LAKEVIEW DR	Douglas Co	439V	80134	7100-8699	
LAKE VIEW DR	Gilpin Co	760U	80403	1-199	
LAKE VIEW DR	Jefferson Co	842A	80470	33800-33999	
LAKEVIEW DR	Nederland	740R	80466	None	
LAKEVIEW DR E	Douglas Co	440T	80134	7000-8699	
LAKEVIEW DR S	Littleton	344X	80120	6200-6299	
LAKEVIEW LN	Broomfield	163G	80020	None	
LAKEVIEW LN	El Paso Co	908U	80132	18100-18299	
LAKEVIEW PL	Nederland	740R	80466	None	
LAKEVIEW PL E	Aurora	381D	80016	None	
LAKEVIEW PT	Boulder Co	723G	80503	None	
LAKEVIEW RD	Park Co	820Z	80421	1-799	
LAKEVIEW ST S	Littleton	344P	80120	5300-5499	
	Littleton	344T	80120	5600-5899	
	Littleton	344X	80120	5900-6499	
	Littleton	374B	80120	6600-7099	
	Littleton	374K	80120	7700-7799	
LAKEVIEW WAY S	Littleton	344P	80120	5400-5499	
LAKE VISTA DR	Broomfield	163G	80020	None	
LAKEWIND CIR E	Douglas Co	440S	80134	6400-6499	
LAKEWOOD DR	Federal Heights	224A	80260	None	
LAKEWOOD PL	Lakewood	282G	80214	6800-6999	
LAKEWOOD RD N	Douglas Co	440T	80134	6200-6399	
LAKEWOOD HEIGHTS DR	Lakewood	281L	80215	1-99	
LAKE WOODMOOR DR	El Paso Co	908T	80132	600-1799	
LAKEWOOD VILLAGE DR	Lakewood	281R	80215	700-899	
LAKOTA RD	Elbert Co	850H	80138	41500-41899	
LAKOTA RD	Jefferson Co	338F	80454	3800-4299	
LALLIE RD	Park Co	820Y	80421	1-199	
LAMAR CIR	Arvada	222G	80003	8200-8299	
	Arvada	222C	80003	8700-8799	
	Westminster	192G	80020	11000-11099	
LAMAR CT	Arvada	222Q	80003	7500-7599	
	Lakewood	282Q	80226	300-599	
LAMAR CT	Parker	409J	80134	17500-17599	
LAMAR CT	Westminster	222Q	80003	7200-7299	
LAMAR CT S	Jefferson Co	372C	80123	6300-6399	
	Jefferson Co	372L	80128	7600-7899	
	Jefferson Co	372Q	80128	7900-8299	
	Lakewood	282Y	80226	300-599	
	Lakewood	312L	80232	None	
LAMAR DR	Arvada	222C	80003	8200-8799	
LAMAR DR	Parker	409J	80134	17000-17099	
LAMAR DR S	Jefferson Co	342Y	80123	6000-6099	
LAMAR LN S	Lakewood	342U	80123	5700-5799	
LAMAR PL	Arvada	222Y	80003	6300-6499	
	Arvada	222G	80003	8200-8299	
	Westminster	192U	80021	9600-9699	
LAMAR PL S	Denver	342U	80123	None	
LAMAR ST	Arvada	252C	80002	5600-5799	
	Arvada	252C	80003	5800-6199	
	Arvada	222U	80003	6200-7199	
	Arvada	222L	80003	7600-7999	
	Arvada	222G	80003	8000-8199	
LAMAR ST	Broomfield	162U	80020	1-399	
LAMAR ST	Edgewater	282C	80214	2000-2599	
	Lakewood	282Y	80226	1-99	
	Lakewood	282Q	80226	100-499	
	Lakewood	282L	80214	900-1499	
	Westminster	192Y	80031	9200-9499	
	Westminster	192L	80020	10700-10899	
	Westminster	192G	80020	11200-11599	
	Wheat Ridge	252Y	80214	2800-3199	
	Wheat Ridge	252Y	80033	3200-3299	
	Wheat Ridge	252U	80033	3900-4399	
	Wheat Ridge	252Q	80033	4500-4799	
LAMAR ST S	Denver	312U	80227	2700-3099	
	Denver	312Y	80227	3200-3299	
	Denver	342Q	80123	5300-5499	
	Denver	342U	80123	5500-5699	
	Jefferson Co	372G	80128	6700-7099	

Continued on next column

STREET NAME	CITY or COUNTY	MAP GRID	ZIP CODE	BLOCK RANGE	O/E
LAMAR ST S (Cont'd)	Jefferson Co	372L	80128	7400-7499	
	Jefferson Co	372L	80128	7600-7899	
	Jefferson Co	372Q	80128	7900-8199	
	Lakewood	282Y	80226	1-599	
	Lakewood	312C	80226	600-699	
	Lakewood	312G	80232	1100-1599	
	Lakewood	342U	80123	5700-5799	
LAMAR WAY S	Jefferson Co	372L	80128	7500-7699	
	Lakewood	312U	80227	2500-2699	
LAMB AVE	Weld Co	729A	80621	15000-16599	
LAMB LN	Jefferson Co	278X	80401	100-399	
LAMBERT CIR	Lafayette	131L	80026	1200-1399	
LAMBERT CT	Keenesburg	732A	80643	None	
LAMBERT LN	Northglenn	194E	80234	900-11099	
LAMBERT ST	Keenesburg	732A	80643	None	
LAMBERT RANCH TRAIL	Douglas Co	846Q	80135	4500-5799	
LAMBUTH AVE W	Jefferson Co	341C	80235	10000-10199	
LAMBUTH PL W	Jefferson Co	341C	80235	10300-10599	
LAMERIA DR S	Highlands Ranch	406B	80130	9600-9699	
LA MESA DR	Boulder Co	743U	80303	2200-2399	
LAMPLIGHT DR	El Paso Co	908Y	80132	None	
LAMPLIGHTER DR	Federal Heights	224A	80260	None	
LAMPLIGHTER DR	Longmont	12S	80501	1300-1699	
LANCASTER AVE	Castle Rock	498R	80104	6200-6399	
LANCASTER CT	Fort Lupton	728H	80621	1200-1299	
LANCE PL E	Highlands Ranch	406E	80130	5900-5999	
LANCELOT ST	Lafayette	132P	80026	1-299	
LANCERS CT	El Paso Co	908V	80132	800E-899E	
	El Paso Co	908V	80132	700W-799W	
LANDER LN	Lafayette	132N	80026	None	
LANDER ST	Adams Co	223B	80031	8800-9099	
	Westminster	193Y	80031	9100-9199	
LANDERS DR	Douglas Co	908L	80118	2700-2999	
LANDIS CT	Boulder	128D	80303	1400-1499	
LANDMARK DR	Commerce City	198M	80022	None	
	Commerce City	769E	80022	None	
LANDMARK DR E	Douglas Co	409M	80138	6800-6999	
LANDMARK PL	Greenwood Village	346Q	80111	None	
LANDMARK WAY	Greenwood Village	346Q	80111	None	
LANDON ST	Frederick	727B	80530	None	
LANE CT	Boulder	128X	80305	3100-3199	
LANE CT	Fort Lupton	728L	80621	100-199	
LANE ST	Thornton	194S	80260	9600-9699	
LANE A	Idaho Springs	780R	80452	None	
LANE B	Idaho Springs	780R	80452	None	
LANE C	Idaho Springs	780R	80452	None	
LANE WOOD RD	Adams Co	750R	80603	13600-15999	
LANG RD	Park Co	820Z	80421	1-299	
LANGDALE CT N	Aurora	291P	80018	300-398	E
LANGDALE CT S	Aurora	291T	80018	None	
	Aurora	351T	80016	None	
LANGDALE WAY N	Aurora	291P	80018	400-598	E
LANGDALE WAY S	Aurora	351X	80016	None	
LANGDALL CT S	Aurora	381F	80016	7100-7199	
LANGDON DR S	Jefferson Co	337U	80439	5700-5999	
LANGLEY CT S	Denver	315T	80210	2700-2799	
LANGTREE CT	El Paso Co	908U	80132	19100-19299	
LANIER ST	Park Co	820Y	80421	1-199	
LANSDOWNE CT	Highlands Ranch	375W	80126	2400-2499	
LANSDOWNE PL	Highlands Ranch	375W	80126	2300-2399	
LANSDOWNE WAY	Highlands Ranch	375W	80126	9100-9199	
LANSING CIR	Commerce City	197T	80022	9600-11299	
LANSING CIR E	Douglas Co	377X	80112	11001-11099	O
LANSING CT	Adams Co	137K	80602	None	
	Commerce City	197L	80601	None	
LANSING CT S	Arapahoe Co	347U	80111	5500-5899	
	Aurora	317G	80112	1300-1399	
	Aurora	317L	80112	1600-1699	
	Aurora	317L	80014	1900-2199	
	Aurora	317Q	80014	None	
LANSING ST	Adams Co	137X	80602	15000-15099	
	Aurora	287T	80010	1-599	
	Aurora	287L	80010	700-2499	
	Commerce City	197F	80640	11200-11399	
LANSING ST S	Aurora	317C	80112	900-999	
	Aurora	317F	80112	1400-1699	
	Aurora	317Q	80014	2300-2399	
LANSING WAY	Adams Co	137P	80602	None	
LANSING WAY S	Arapahoe Co	347U	80111	5500-5799	
	Aurora	317Q	80014	2400-2599	
	Aurora	317U	80014	2700-2999	
LANTANA	Jefferson Co	370L	80127	1-99	
LANTANA DR	Broomfield	132Z	80026	15000-15199	
LANTANA LN	Broomfield	132Z	80026	5200-5499	
LANTERN DR	Fort Lupton	728H	80621	900-1299	
LANTERN TRAIL	Castle Rock	498Q	80104	1-1799	
LANTERN TREE GROVE	El Paso Co	908P	80132	None	
LANYON DR	Longmont	11W	80503	2300-2599	
LANYON LN	Longmont	11W	80503	1200-1298	E
LAODICEA RD	Boulder Co	704N	80503	6200-6399	
LA PAZ PL	Longmont	11R	80501	200-299	
LaPLACE CT	Westminster	223F	80031	8000-8199	
LA PLATA CIR	Boulder Co	69Z	80301	5400-5599	
LA PLATA CT	Brighton	139T	80601	None	
LA PLATA LN	Jefferson Co	842N	80470	33300-33999	
LA PLATA RD	Thornton	193V	80260	None	
LA PLATA WAY	Broomfield	133N	80020	None	
LaQUINTA CIR	Elbert Co	851C	80107	5200-5299	
LaQUINTA CIR	Jefferson Co	306J	80439	1800-1999	
LaQUINTA COVE	Lone Tree	406C	80124	7500-7599	
LaQUINTA CT	Lone Tree	406C	80124	7400-7499	
LaQUINTA DR	Lone Tree	406C	80124	9400-9599	
LaQUINTA LN	Jefferson Co	306J	80439	1900-1999	
LaQUINTA LN	Lone Tree	406C	80124	7400-7499	
LaQUINTA PL	Lone Tree	406C	80124	7400-7499	
LaQUINTA WAY	Lone Tree	406C	80124	9400-9499	
LaQUINTA BAY	Lone Tree	406C	80124	7400-7499	
LARABY PL	Fort Lupton	729E	80621	None	
LARAMIE BLVD	Boulder	97C	80304	None	
LARAMIE CT	Castle Rock	498M	80104	None	
LARAMIE CT	Longmont	12P	80501	2100-2199	
LARCH CT	Broomfield	162P	80020	1100-1199	
LARCHMONT CT	Lafayette	101W	80026	1800-1899	
LAREDO CIR S	Aurora	288Z	80017	500-699	
	Aurora	318D	80017	700-799	
	Aurora	318V	80013	2900-3099	
LAREDO CT	Denver	258H	80239	5500-5599	
	Denver	258H	80239	None	

L

STREET NAME	CITY or COUNTY	MAP GRID	ZIP CODE	BLOCK RANGE	O/E
LAREDO CT E	Highlands Ranch	406B	80130	7200-7299	
LAREDO CT S	Arapahoe Co	378R	80112	8000-8199	
	Aurora	318H	80017	1300-1699	
	Aurora	318R	80013	2500-2699	
	Aurora	318Z	80013	3300-3499	
	Centennial	348R	80015	5100-5199	
	Centennial	348V	80015	5700-5799	
LAREDO DR	Commerce City	198U	80022	9800-9999	
LAREDO LN	El Paso Co	908P	80132	20000-20099	
LAREDO ST	Aurora	288R	80017	200-1799	
	Aurora	258V	80011	None	
	Commerce City	198V	80022	9700-9798	E
	Commerce City	198M	80022	10400-10599	
	Commerce City	168Z	80022	None	
	Commerce City	168Z	80603	None	
	Denver	258H	80239	5500-5599	
	Denver	258H	80239	None	
LAREDO ST S	Arapahoe Co	378H	80016	None	
	Arapahoe Co	378M	80016	None	
	Aurora	318H	80017	1400-1499	
	Aurora	318M	80017	1500-1899	
	Aurora	318R	80013	2200-2499	
	Aurora	318Z	80013	2600-3499	
	Aurora	348D	80013	3600-3699	
	Aurora	348M	80015	4500-4699	
	Aurora	348L	80015	4800-5099	
	Centennial	348L	80015	5100-5399	
	Centennial	348V	80015	5400-5599	
	Highlands Ranch	406F	80130	9600-9799	
LAREDO WAY	Commerce City	198M	80022	10700-10798	E
LAREDO WAY	Denver	258H	80239	None	
LAREDO WAY	Lochbuie	140G	80603	None	
LAREDO WAY S	Aurora	318D	80017	1000-1099	
	Aurora	318H	80017	1400-1499	
	Aurora	348H	80014	4100-4299	
	Centennial	348R	80015	5100-5299	
LARGE OAK CT	Douglas Co	436U	80108	6100-6199	
LARGO AVE	Palmer Lake	907U	80133	None	
LARIAT DR	Douglas Co	467E	80108	4500-5999	
LARIAT LN	Jefferson Co	366Z	80439	9000-9099	
LARIAT LN	El Paso Co	908U	80132	300-499	
LARIAT LOOP	Elbert Co	832T	80107	8500-8999	
LARIAT WAY	Boulder Co	99H	80301	4300-4499	
LARIAT TRAIL	Jefferson Co	278L	80401	None	
LARIGO AVE W	Littleton	344X	80120	700-799	
LARIMER ST	Denver	284E	80204	700-1399	
	Denver	284B	80202	1400-1999	
	Denver	284B	80205	2000-2399	
	Denver	254Y	80205	2400-3599	
LARIS LN E	Parker	439E	80134	None	
LARK AVE	Brighton	137Z	80601	1200-1399	
LARK AVE	Louisville	130Y	80027	200-399	
LARK CT	Boulder Co	129F	80303	1300-1399	
LARK CT	Douglas Co	432M	80125	9500-9699	
LARK DR	Elbert Co	850V	80107	37600-37799	
LARK DR E	Douglas Co	410J	80138	7600-7899	
LARK LN	Boulder Co	99S	80301	None	
LARK LN	Brighton	137Z	80601	1100-1198	E
LARK LN	El Paso Co	908Q	80132	19800-19999	
LARK LN	Park Co	841V	80421	1-499	
LARK ST	Federal Heights	193V	80260	9700-9799	
LARK WAY	Douglas Co	432M	80125	None	
LARK BUNTING AVE E	Parker	408V	80134	None	
LARK BUNTING DR	Westminster	192W	80021	9300-9399	
LARK BUNTING LN	Jefferson Co	370B	80127	1-99	
LARK BUNTING PL	Longmont	12Y	80501	1500-1599	
LARKDALE DR	Arapahoe Co	373A	80123	1-99	
LARK NEST WAY	El Paso Co	908U	80132	600-699	
LARKSONG CT	Castle Rock	466T	80109	4300-4399	
LARKSONG DR	Castle Rock	466T	80109	4500-4999	
LARKSONG PL	Castle Rock	466T	80109	4400-4599	
LARK SPARROW DR S					
	Highlands Ranch	405C	80126	9200-9499	
LARK SPARROW PL	Highlands Ranch	375Y	80126	9100-9199	
LARK SPARROW ST	Highlands Ranch	375Y	80126	4100-4299	
LARK SPARROW TRAIL					
	Highlands Ranch	375Y	80126	9100-9399	
LARKSPUR	Jefferson Co	306Y	80439	29500-29699	
LARKSPUR CIR	Frederick	727F	80530	None	
LARKSPUR CIR	Longmont	40R	80503	3500-3599	
LARKSPUR CT	Longmont	40R	80503	3500-3599	
LARKSPUR CT	Louisville	130T	80027	800-899	
LARKSPUR CT N	Lafayette	131A	80026	1400-1499	
LARKSPUR CT S	Lafayette	131A	80026	1400-1499	
LARKSPUR DR	Bow Mar	343N	80123	4900-5199	
LARKSPUR DR	Castle Rock	498J	80104	1-499	
	Jefferson Co	278Q	80401	500-598	E
	Jefferson Co	307M	80401	1700-1999	
LARKSPUR DR	Longmont	40R	80503	3300-3599	
LARKSPUR DR	Parker	409Z	80134	11500-11899	
LARKSPUR LN	Douglas Co	908H	80118	4000-4199	
LARKSPUR LN	Louisville	130T	80027	900-999	
LARKSPUR PL	Highlands Ranch	374Y	80126	400-599	
LARKSPUR RD	Boulder Co	703W	80302	8300-8399	
LARKSPUR ST	Lochbuie	140A	80603	None	
LARKSPUR ST	Palmer Lake	907Q	80133	None	
LARKWATER LN	Parker	379W	80134	17100-17299	
LARKWOOD CT	Boulder	98N	80304	3600-3699	
LARKWOOD PL	Highlands Ranch	374Y	80126	600-699	
LARKWOOD ST	Adams Co	226J	80022	7700-7799	
LARRY CT	Adams Co	225A	80229	1900-2099	
LARRY DR	Northglenn	194M	80233	10600-11099	
LARSH DR	Adams Co	223V	80221	6800-7299	
	Adams Co	223R	80221	7400-7499	
LARSON CT	Erie	132A	80026	1800-1899	
LARSON DR	Northglenn	194M	80233	10500-11199	
LARSON LN	Northglenn	194D	80233	11200-11599	
LA SALLE AVE W	Lakewood	312N	80227	8800-8999	
LASALLE CIR W	Jefferson Co	310V	80228	13000-13099	
LASALLE DR E	Aurora	319N	80013	17400-17699	
	Aurora	319R	80013	19600-20099	
	Aurora	321N	80018	None	
LASALLE PL	Adams Co	223B	80031	9000-9099	
LA SALLE PL	Denver	315N	80210	2100-2199	
LASALLE PL	Westminster	193X	80031	9100-9199	
LASALLE PL E	Aurora	317R	80014	12100-12699	
	Aurora	318R	80013	16300-16599	
	Aurora	319N	80013	16800-16899	
	Aurora	319P	80013	18000-18399	
	Aurora	319Q	80013	18500-19599	

STREET NAME	CITY or COUNTY	MAP GRID	ZIP CODE	BLOCK RANGE	O/E
LA SALLE PL E	Denver	315Q	80222	4300-4799	
	Denver	316P	80224	6500-6999	
LA SALLE PL W	Lakewood	311V	80227	9000-9699	
	Lakewood	311U	80227	9800-9899	
LASALLE PL W	Lakewood	310Q	80228	13800-13899	
LASALLE ST	Superior	160Q	80027	900-2299	
LASALLE WAY	Longmont	12U	80501	None	
LASALLE WAY E	Aurora	319R	80013	None	
LAS BRISAS DR	Broomfield	133J	80020	None	
LAS COLINAS DR	Elbert Co	851C	80107	None	
LAS COLINAS DR	Lone Tree	406C	80124	9500-9799	
LASER ST	Lafayette	132N	80026	100-198	E
LASHLEY LN S	Boulder	128K	80305	1-399	
	Boulder	128P	80305	400-499	
	Boulder	128Q	80305	500-1299	
LASHLEY ST	Longmont	42A	80501	200-899	
	Longmont	12S	80501	1700-1899	
LAS LOMAS ST	Brighton	139P	80601	100-399	
LAS LUNAS CT	Castle Rock	498L	80104	4300-4499	
LAS LUNAS ST	Castle Rock	498K	80104	100-299	
LASNIK ST	Erie	103S	80516	800-1199	
LAS RAMBLAS CT	Douglas Co	378Y	80134	9300-9399	
LAS RAMBLAS LN	Douglas Co	378Y	80134	16600-16799	
LASSO PL	Douglas Co	469B	80134	5800-5999	
LAST CHANCE CT	Boulder Co	741E	80466	None	
LAST CHANCE RD N	Arapahoe Co	792S	80102	1-599	
LAST CHANCE RD S	Arapahoe Co	792W	80102	1-300	
LAST DOLLAR PASS	Jefferson Co	371P	80127	11300-11499	
LAST RESORT CREEK TRAIL					
	Jefferson Co	843K	80433	24000-24199	
LATIGO LN	Parker	409R	80138	11100-19999	
LATIGO PL	Erie	133B	80516	None	
LATONKA RD W	Littleton	343P	80123	3600-4199	
LAUGHING VALLEY RANCH RD					
	Clear Creek Co	780T	80452	None	
LAUGHING WATER DR	Palmer Lake	907U	80133	None	
LAUGHLIN BLVD	Frederick	727F	80530	None	
LAURA AVE	Gilpin Co	760H	80403	1-299	
LAURA CT	Dacono	726H	80516	None	
LAURA WAY	Dacono	726H	80516	None	
	Weld Co	726H	80514	None	
LAUREL AVE E	Boulder	128H	80303	800-5299	
LAUREL AVE W	Jefferson Co	372K	80128	7400-7699	
LAUREL CT	Broomfield	162K	80020	1700-1799	
LAUREL CT	Longmont	12U	80501	1300-1399	
LAUREL CT S	Highlands Ranch	374Z	80126	9000-9099	
LAUREL CT W	Louisville	130R	80027	500-599	
LAUREL DR	Adams Co	226B	80022	8600-8799	
LAUREL DR W	Jefferson Co	372J	80128	8100-8199	
LAUREL LN	Parker	410W	80138	11600-11699	
LAUREL LN W	Littleton	343P	80123	3300-3399	
LAUREL PL S	Littleton	343S	80123	5800-5899	
LAUREL PL W	Jefferson Co	372K	80128	7200-7399	
	Jefferson Co	372J	80128	8200-8299	
	Jefferson Co	371M	80128	9300-9499	
	Jefferson Co	371L	80127	9800-9999	
LAUREL ST	Brighton	138T	80601	200-399	
LAUREL ST	Broomfield	162X	80020	100-499	
	Broomfield	162T	80020	900-1099	
	Broomfield	162P	80020	1300-1399	
LAUREL WAY	Lafayette	131F	80026	300-399	
LAUREL GLEN CIR	Highlands Ranch	405L	80126	10500-10599	
LAUREL GLEN LN	Highlands Ranch	405L	80126	4500-5099	
LAURELHILL CT	Douglas Co	408M	80134	16200-16299	
LAUREL OAK DR	Parker	410T	80138	22000-22499	
LAUREL VALLEY CIR	Elbert Co	851C	80107	None	
LAUREN CT S	Highlands Ranch	406J	80130	10100-10299	
LAUREN LN	Arapahoe Co	344Q	80121	5300-5399	
LAURENWOOD LN W	Highlands Ranch	404A	80129	1000-1099	
LAURENWOOD WAY W					
	Highlands Ranch	404A	80129	1100-1599	
LAURUS	Jefferson Co	370L	80127	1-99	
LAUSANNE CIR S	Jefferson Co	842Q	80470	15100-15199	
LAVAUNN DR	Douglas Co	846G	80125	7500-7999	
LAVELL AVE	Elbert Co	892N	80106	6700-6799	
LAVENDER CT	Douglas Co	410Z	80138	9300-9399	
LAVENDER HILL LN	Lafayette	131F	80026	2300-2399	
LaVETA AVE	Palmer Lake	907Q	80133	None	
LA VETA RD	Douglas Co	887L	80118	7900-8299	
LAVETA PASS AVE	Golden	279U	80401	300-399	
LAVINIA LN	Northglenn	195A	80233	11700-11999	
LAVINIA WAY	Northglenn	195A	80233	11800-11999	
LAVISTA PL	Boulder	69R	80301	7100-7199	
LAWLEY DR	Erie	102M	80516	100-399	
LAWN ST	Boulder Co	129F	80303	900-1099	
LAWRENCE ST	Central City	780D	80427	100-499	
LAWRENCE ST	Denver	284E	80204	300-1399	
	Denver	284B	80202	1400-1999	
	Denver	284B	80205	2000-2399	
	Denver	254Y	80205	2400-3599	
LAWRENCE WAY	Denver	284E	80204	None	
LAWSON AVE	Erie	103X	80516	None	
LAWSON CT	Erie	103X	80516	None	
LAWSON PL	Erie	103X	80516	None	
LAWSON WAY	Erie	103W	80516	None	
LAYTON AVE E	Arapahoe Co	350J	80015	20400-20499	
	Arapahoe Co	350L	80015	None	
	Aurora	349J	80015	16700-16799	
	Cherry Hills Village	344L	80113	800-1599	
	Denver	346M	80237	8500-8799	
	Englewood	344L	80113	1-799	
LAYTON AVE S	Aurora	348M	80015	16300-16599	
LAYTON AVE W	Denver	343L	80110	3000-3399	
	Denver	342K	80123	7600-7899	
	Denver	342J	80123	7900-8399	
	Denver	341M	80123	8800-9999	
	Englewood	344K	80110	1-1599	
	Englewood	343L	80110	2900-2999	
	Jefferson Co	341J	80465	12000-12399	
	Jefferson Co	340M	80465	13200-13499	
LAYTON CIR E	Arapahoe Co	350L	80015	None	
	Arapahoe Co	350K	80015	None	
LAYTON DR E	Arapahoe Co	350K	80015	None	
	Aurora	348K	80015	14100-14399	
	Aurora	349J	80015	17400-17599	
	Cherry Hills Village	344M	80110	1600-1899	
LAYTON DR W	Denver	341L	80127	10100-10299	
	Jefferson Co	341K	80465	11600-11899	

STREET NAME	CITY or COUNTY	MAP GRID	ZIP CODE	BLOCK RANGE	O/E
LAYTON LN E	Arapahoe Co	349M	80015	20200-20399	
	Arapahoe Co	350J	80015	None	
	Arapahoe Co	350K	80015	None	
LAYTON PL E	Arapahoe Co	350J	80015	20400-20499	
	Aurora	348L	80015	15000-15299	
	Aurora	351J	80016	24500-24799	
	Aurora	348K	80015	None	
LAYTON PL W	Jefferson Co	341L	80127	10100-10799	
	Jefferson Co	341J	80465	12400-12699	
	Lakewood	342K	80123	7400-7499	
LAYTON WAY W	Jefferson Co	342K	80123	None	
	Lakewood	342K	80123	7400-7499	
LAZY LN	Park Co	842J	80470	1-599	
LAZY K DR	Castle Rock	467U	80104	3900-4599	
LAZY SUMMER WAY	El Paso Co	908U	80132	18300-18599	
LAZY U RANCH PL E	Douglas Co	439D	80134	20000-20999	
LAZY Z RD	Boulder Co	741U	80466	1-2199	
LEADER CIR	Louisville	131J	80027	500-599	
LEAD KING DR	Douglas Co	436X	80108	200-299	
LEAD QUEEN DR	Douglas Co	436X	80108	200-299	
LEAF CT	Denver	254L	80216	4400-4999	
LEANING PINE CT S	Parker	409Z	80134	None	
LEANING TREE DR E	Parker	408U	80134	None	
LEAVENWORTH DR	Jefferson Co	822X	80433	11600-11799	
LEAWOOD DR W	Jefferson Co	342Y	80123	5200-6799	
LEBRUN CT	Lone Tree	406L	80124	7500-7799	
LEDGE ROCK DR	Douglas Co	408H	80134	15900-16499	
LEDGESTONE DR	Castle Rock	498M	80104	None	
LEDGESTONE LN	Castle Rock	498M	80104	None	
LEDGESTONE TRAIL	Castle Rock	498M	80104	None	
LE DUC DR	Douglas Co	466M	80108	5100-5199	
LE DUC LN	Douglas Co	466M	80108	5100-5199	
LEE AVE	Louisville	131T	80027	800-899	
LEE CIR	Boulder	128D	80303	4700-4899	
LEE CIR	Wheat Ridge	251U	80033	3800-4099	
LEE CT	Arvada	221G	80005	8000-8099	
LEE CT S	Arapahoe Co	374C	80121	6500-6699	
	Jefferson Co	341C	80235	3600-3799	
	Jefferson Co	341L	80127	4500-4599	
	Jefferson Co	341U	80127	5700-5799	
	Jefferson Co	371C	80127	6400-6499	
	Jefferson Co	371C	80127	6800-6999	
	Lakewood	311C	80226	700-799	
	Lakewood	311G	80232	1400-1499	
	Lakewood	311Q	80227	2400-2498	E
LEE DR	Arvada	221Q	80005	7500-7799	
	Arvada	221L	80005	8000-8099	
	Jefferson Co	336U	80439	5400-5699	
LEE LN	Lakewood	281G	80215	1800-9998	E
LEE RD	Jefferson Co	336T	80439	29200-30999	
LEE ST	Arvada	251C	80004	5800-6199	
	Arvada	221Y	80004	6400-6899	
	Arvada	221U	80004	6900-7099	
	Arvada	221Q	80005	7200-7299	
	Arvada	221L	80005	7700-7999	
	Lakewood	281Q	80215	800-999	
	Lakewood	281L	80215	1000-1499	
	Lakewood	281G	80215	1600-2499	
	Westminster	191Q	80021	10000-10199	
	Wheat Ridge	251U	80033	3500-3799	
	Wheat Ridge	251Q	80033	4400-4498	E
LEE ST S	Jefferson Co	341C	80235	3800-3899	
	Jefferson Co	341Q	80127	5100-5399	
	Jefferson Co	341U	80127	5500-5799	
	Jefferson Co	341Y	80127	6100-6299	
	Lakewood	281Y	80226	300-599	
	Lakewood	311C	80226	700-899	
	Lakewood	311L	80232	1500-1899	
LEE WAY	Longmont	11Y	80501	1000-1099	
LEE WAY S	Jefferson Co	341Y	80127	5900-5999	
	Jefferson Co	371G	80127	6800-7099	
	Jefferson Co	371L	80127	7400-7499	
LEEDS ST	Douglas Co	407H	80134	None	
LEE HILL DR	Boulder Co	723J	80302	1600-1999	
LEE HILL RD	Boulder Co	97A	80304	1-1599	
	Boulder Co	722G	80302	2000-5699	
LEES LN	Douglas Co	886G	80118	5900-5999	
LEESBURG CT	Elbert Co	832X	80107	8200-8399	
LEESBURG RD	Parker	409Y	80134	12500-12999	
LEETSDALE DR	Denver	285U	80246	1-299	
	Denver	285Z	80246	4801-4999	O
	Denver	285Z	80246	5000-5499	
	Glendale	285Z	80246	4400-4799	
	Glendale	285Z	80246	4800-4998	E
LEETSDALE DR S	Denver	316B	80224	6400-7299	
LEFT FORK RD	Boulder Co	722W	80302	1-799	
LEFT HAND CIR	Boulder	69Y	80301	6700-6899	
LEFTHAND CIR	Longmont	41P	80501	1800-1899	
LEFTHAND DR	Longmont	41T	80501	1100-1799	
LEFTHAND CANYON DR	Boulder Co	723A	80302	1-1999	
	Boulder Co	722D	80302	2000-5999	
	Boulder Co	722J	80455	5000-8999	
	Boulder Co	721Q	80455	9000-14999	
LEGACY CIR	Elbert Co	870H	80107	1900-1999	
	Elbert Co	871E	80107	2001-2099	O
LEGACY DR	Dacono	727J	80514	100-199	
LEGACY DR	Longmont	41J	80503	None	
LEGACY PKWY	Dacono	727J	80514	100-399	
LEGACY RIDGE CT	Westminster	193K	80031	10800-10999	
LEGACY RIDGE PKWY	Westminster	193F	80031	10400-11199	
LEGACY RIDGE ST	Elbert Co	870L	80107	32000-33099	
LEGACY RIDGE WAY	Westminster	193K	80031	10800-10999	
LEGACY TRAIL	Elbert Co	870L	80107	500-1999	
LEGAULT LN	Jefferson Co	823T	80433	10500-11199	
LEGEND AVE E	Parker	439G	80134	19100-19299	
LEGEND CT E	Parker	439G	80134	19200-19299	
LEGEND WAY	Broomfield	163F	80020	13700-13999	
LEGEND RIDGE TRAIL	Boulder Co	70R	80503	6400-6699	
LEGEND TRAIL	Broomfield	163F	80020	13700-13999	
LEGGINS CT	El Paso Co	908X	80132	None	
LEGGINS WAY	El Paso Co	908X	80132	17200-17499	
LEHIGH AVE E	Arapahoe Co	350A	80013	20400-20999	
	Aurora	348A	80014	13700-13899	
	Aurora	348B	80014	14600-14999	
	Aurora	348C	80013	15300-15399	
	Aurora	349C	80013	18600-18899	
	Denver	345D	80237	5500-5699	
	Englewood	344C	80113	1-799	

L

STREET NAME	CITY or COUNTY	MAP GRID	ZIP CODE	BLOCK RANGE	O/E
LEHIGH AVE W	Denver	342D	80235	5200-5999	
	Englewood	344B	80110	1-1299	
	Jefferson Co	341C	80235	10000-10599	
	Sheridan	343B	80110	3300-3399	
	Sheridan	343B	80236	3400-3599	
LEHIGH CIR	Erie	103P	80516	500-999	
LEHIGH CIR E	Aurora	348D	80013	15900-16099	
LEHIGH DR E	Denver	346C	80237	8000-8499	
LEHIGH PL E	Arapahoe Co	349D	80013	19900-19999	
	Arapahoe Co	350A	80013	20400-20599	
	Aurora	349B	80013	17800-18299	
	Aurora	349D	80013	20100-20199	
	Aurora	350B	80018	21700-21799	
	Aurora	350C	80018	None	
	Denver	346C	80237	8200-8299	
LEHIGH PL W	Englewood	344A	80110	1200-1299	
	Jefferson Co	341C	80235	10600-10699	
LEHIGH ST	Boulder	128X	80305	1000-2099	
LEHIGH ST E	Denver	346C	80237	7900-8899	
	Denver	346D	80237	8900-9299	
LEHOW AVE W	Littleton	344P	80120	1-399	
LEICESTER CT	Douglas Co	436Q	80108	6900-7099	
LEICESTER LN	Castle Pines North	436Q	80108	500-599	
LEILANI DR	Castle Rock	468M	80108	5900-6299	
	Castle Rock	469E	80108	6300-7099	
LEILANI LN	Castle Rock	468M	80108	6000-6499	
	Castle Rock	469J	80108	6500-6899	
LEMASTERS DR S	Jefferson Co	335M	80439	4700-4999	
LEMASTERS RD S	Jefferson Co	335R	80439	4900-5199	
LEMON CT	Castle Rock	496C	80109	None	
LEMON PL	Boulder	97H	80304	None	
LEMON GRASS PL	Castle Rock	496A	80109	None	
LEMON GULCH CT	Douglas Co	848L	80108	None	
LEMON GULCH DR	Douglas Co	848G	80108	5600-7399	
LEMON GULCH WAY	Douglas Co	848G	80108	7100-7999	
LENAVIEW CIR S	Arapahoe Co	813F	80102	1900-2199	
LENOX CT	Castle Rock	498V	80104	5300-5499	
LEO CT	Highlands Ranch	376U	80124	13600-13699	
LEO LN	Thornton	224F	80260	400-799	
LEON DR	Jefferson Co	822X	80433	11900-12199	
LEON LN	Boulder Co	742W	80403	1-199	
LEONA DR	Adams Co	224K	80221	1-399	
	Adams Co	224F	80221	400-599	
LEONA ST	Weld Co	728X	80621	1700-1999	
LEONARD LN	Northglenn	194G	80233	1-699	
LEONARDO PL	Douglas Co	432P	80125	10500-10699	
LEONARDS RD	Boulder Co	722U	80302	1-499	
LEON A WURL PKWY	Erie	102N	80516	11000-12699	
	Erie	103J	80516	None	
LEOPARD DR	Douglas Co	406K	80124	7000-7199	
LEOPARD GATE	Douglas Co	406K	80124	7000-7199	
LEROY DR	Northglenn	194M	80233	800-1799	
	Northglenn	195E	80233	1800-11099	
LEVI CIR	Adams Co	167Z	80640	12200-12399	
LEWIS CIR	Westminster	191L	80021	10700-10799	
LEWIS CIR S	Jefferson Co	341L	80127	4700-4799	
LEWIS CT	Arvada	251G	80002	5500-5599	
	Arvada	251C	80004	6000-6199	
	Arvada	221L	80005	7500-7999	
	Arvada	221G	80005	8400-8499	
	Lakewood	281G	80215	1800-1999	
	Lakewood	281C	80215	2500-2599	
	Westminster	191Q	80021	10000-10099	
LEWIS CT N	Douglas Co	440V	80134	6200-6299	
LEWIS CT S	Jefferson Co	341C	80235	3700-3799	
	Jefferson Co	341L	80127	4500-4899	
	Jefferson Co	371G	80127	6800-7199	
	Jefferson Co	371L	80127	7400-7499	
	Jefferson Co	371Q	80127	8400-8499	
LEWIS DR	Lakewood	281L	80215	800-899	
LEWIS LN	Jefferson Co	335R	80439	30900-31899	
LEWIS LN S	Lakewood	311Q	80227	2400-2499	
LEWIS ST	Arvada	251G	80002	5500-5599	
	Arvada	251C	80004	6000-6099	
	Arvada	221Y	80004	6500-6799	
	Arvada	221Q	80005	7500-7799	
LEWIS ST	Castle Rock	497G	80104	1-799	
LEWIS ST	Lakewood	281L	80215	1300-1499	
	Lakewood	281G	80215	1600-2099	
	Lakewood	281C	80215	2100-2499	
	Westminster	191Q	80021	10000-10199	
	Westminster	191L	80021	10700-10799	
	Wheat Ridge	251U	80033	3500-3799	
LEWIS ST S	Castle Rock	497G	80104	1-99	
	Jefferson Co	341U	80127	5700-5899	
	Jefferson Co	341Y	80127	6200-6299	
	Jefferson Co	371C	80127	6400-6499	
	Jefferson Co	371G	80127	7100-7299	
	Lakewood	281Y	80226	300-499	
	Lakewood	311C	80226	800-999	
LEWIS WAY S	Jefferson Co	371G	80127	7100-7199	
	Jefferson Co	371U	80127	8500-8699	
	Lakewood	311Q	80227	2500-2699	
LEWIS WAY W	Lakewood	311Q	80227	None	
LEWIS RIDGE RD	Jefferson Co	306S	80439	29800-31299	
LEWISTON CIR S	Aurora	348H	80014	4100-4199	
LEWISTON CT	Adams Co	168D	80601	14400-14599	
	Aurora	288H	80011	1800-1899	
LEWISTON CT	Denver	258H	80239	5500-5599	
	Denver	258H	80239	None	
LEWISTON CT S	Arapahoe Co	348V	80016	6000-6099	
	Aurora	318H	80017	1400-1499	
	Centennial	348R	80015	5300-5399	
	Centennial	348V	80015	5600-5699	
LEWISTON ST	Adams Co	198H	80022	11200-11699	
	Aurora	288M	80011	700-899	
	Aurora	288M	80011	1000-1199	
	Aurora	258Z	80011	3201-3299	O
	Aurora	258V	80011	3902-3998	E
	Commerce City	198V	80022	9900-9999	
	Commerce City	198D	80022	11700-11899	
	Commerce City	198M	80022	None	
	Denver	258H	80239	5500-5599	
	Denver	258H	80239	None	
LEWISTON ST S	Arapahoe Co	378M	80016	None	
	Aurora	318H	80017	1100-1799	
	Aurora	318M	80013	2100-2199	

Continued on next column

STREET NAME	CITY or COUNTY	MAP GRID	ZIP CODE	BLOCK RANGE	O/E
LEWISTON ST S (Cont'd)	Aurora	318R	80013	2200-2599	
	Aurora	318V	80013	2600-2699	
	Aurora	318V	80013	2700-2899	
	Aurora	348D	80013	3500-3799	
	Aurora	348H	80014	4100-4199	
	Centennial	348R	80015	5200-5399	
	Centennial	348V	80015	5500-5599	
	Centennial	348V	80016	5900-5999	
LEWISTON WAY E	Aurora	318Z	80013	3500-3599	
LEWISTON WAY S	Aurora	318D	80017	1000-1099	
	Aurora	318H	80017	1100-1399	
	Aurora	348M	80015	4500-4799	
	Aurora	348Z	80016	None	
	Aurora	378D	80016	None	
	Centennial	348R	80015	5100-5199	
LEXI CIR	Broomfield	163E	80020	4200-4599	
LEXINGTON AVE	Westminster	164E	80020	800-1599	
LEXINGTON CIR	Westminster	164E	80020	14000-14199	
LEXINGTON DR	Douglas Co	408K	80134	None	
LEXINGTON LN	Douglas Co	408L	80134	None	
LEXINGTON PL	Douglas Co	408K	80134	None	
LEXINGTON PL	Westminster	164J	80020	13800-13999	
LEXINGTON ST	Lafayette	131F	80026	2400-2599	
LEYDEN CIR	Thornton	196E	80233	None	
LEYDEN CT	Thornton	166W	80602	12000-12099	
LEYDEN CT S	Centennial	376A	80112	6700-6899	
	Centennial	376N	80112	8200-8299	
LEYDEN LN	Adams Co	226N	80022	7600-7799	
LEYDEN ST	Adams Co	226J	80022	7700-7799	
	Adams Co	136J	80602	16200-16699	
	Commerce City	256E	80022	5400-5799	
	Commerce City	226S	80022	6500-7099	
	Commerce City	226N	80022	7300-7599	
	Denver	286N	80220	100-499	
	Denver	286J	80220	600-1999	
	Denver	286A	80207	2000-2799	
	Denver	256W	80207	2800-3799	
	Denver	256N	80216	4600-4799	
	Thornton	166W	80602	12000-12099	
	Thornton	166S	80602	12700-12799	
	Thornton	166N	80602	12900-13199	
	Thornton	166J	80602	13500-16999	
	Thornton	196E	80233	None	
LEYDEN ST E	Arapahoe Co	316N	80222	2300-2499	
LEYDEN ST S	Arapahoe Co	316S	80222	3000-3199	
	Centennial	346W	80111	5900-6299	
	Centennial	376N	80112	8000-8199	
	Denver	286W	80224	200-499	
	Denver	316A	80224	700-1099	
	Denver	316J	80224	1400-1999	
	Denver	316N	80222	2100-2299	
	Denver	316S	80222	2500-2699	
	Denver	316W	80222	3200-3399	
LEYDEN WAY	Thornton	166N	80602	12900-12999	
LEYDEN WAY	Thornton	196A	80233	None	
LEYNER DR	Erie	102Q	80516	1300-1699	
LIBBY DR	Boulder	128E	80302	None	
LIBERTY BLVD	Douglas Co	377T	80112	12300-13098	E
LIBERTY CIR	Douglas Co	377V	80112	8900-8998	E
LIBERTY CT	Longmont	12S	80501	1500-1599	
LIBERTY DR	Jefferson Co	337N	80439	5000-5099	
LIBERTY DR	Mead	706G	80542	2500-2599	
LIBERTY PL	Douglas Co	377V	80112	None	
LIBERTY ST	Elizabeth	871F	80107	300-499	
LIBERTY ST	Platteville	708C	80651	400-699	
LIBERTY WAY	Douglas Co	377V	80112	None	
LIBERTY RIDGE	Dacono	727J	80514	100-199	
LIBRA CT	Highlands Ranch	376U	80124	13600-13699	
LIBRARY LN	Littleton	344W	80120	None	
LICHEN LN	Boulder Co	742Y	80302	1-199	
LICHEN PL	Boulder Co	69Z	80301	5200-5399	
LICKSKILLET RD	Boulder Co	721R	80302	1-699	
LICORICE CT	Castle Rock	466P	80109	3800-3999	
LICORICE TRAIL	Castle Rock	466Q	80109	3700-3899	
LIETER PL	Lone Tree	406L	80124	10500-10699	
LT WILLIAM CLARK RD E	Douglas Co	440X	80134	8500-8699	
LIGGETT RD	Douglas Co	467X	80109	1900-2799	
LIGHT LN	Jefferson Co	823S	80433	26600-26799	
LIGHTNING LN	Jefferson Co	306T	80439	30000-30299	
LIGHTNING VIEW DR E	Douglas Co	440X	80134	8100-8599	
LILA DR	Jefferson Co	365Y	80433	31800-32699	
LILAC CIR	Broomfield	161R	80020	1000-1199	
LILAC CIR	Erie	133H	80516	None	
LILAC CIR	Lochbuie	140C	80603	300-399	
LILAC CIR	Louisville	131W	80027	200-399	
LILAC CT	Broomfield	161V	80020	1000-1099	
LILAC CT	Louisville	131W	80027	400-499	
	Louisville	130Y	80027	600-699	
LILAC DR	Lochbuie	140C	80603	400-1299	
LILAC LN	Adams Co	253M	80221	5200-5299	
LILAC PL	Lafayette	131R	80026	800-899	
LILAC ST	Broomfield	161V	80020	800-1099	
	Broomfield	161R	80020	1100-1299	
LILAC ST	Longmont	11X	80501	900-1099	
LILAC ST	Thornton	166J	80602	13600-13899	
LILAC ST	Thornton	166J	80602	None	
LILEY AVE	Frederick	727F	80530	7900-7999	
LILEY CT	Frederick	727G	80530	7900-7999	
LILLEY AVE W	Littleton	344T	80120	900-1199	
	Littleton	344S	80120	1800-1999	
LILLIAN LN	Thornton	195W	80229	9100-9499	
LILLIS DR	Jefferson Co	762B	80403	11700-11799	
LILLIS LN	Jefferson Co	762B	80403	11500-11899	
LILLIS PL	Jefferson Co	762B	80403	31700-31999	
LILLIS WAY	Jefferson Co	762B	80403	31200-31399	
LILLY CT	Thornton	194Z	80229	9100-9499	
LILLY DR	Thornton	225A	80229	1900-9099	
LIL' SQUIRREL LN	El Paso Co	910V	80908	None	
LILY CT E	Highlands Ranch	374Y	80126	900-1199	
LILY LN	Golden	249W	80403	200-499	
LILY GULCH TRAIL	Castle Rock	466T	80109	4200-4399	
LIMA CIR	Commerce City	197T	80022	9700-9899	
LIMA CIR S	Aurora	287Y	80012	400-499	
	Aurora	317Q	80014	2300-2399	
LIMA CT	Commerce City	197C	80640	11400-11499	
LIMA CT S	Aurora	317G	80112	1400-1599	
	Aurora	317Q	80014	2200-2299	

STREET NAME	CITY or COUNTY	MAP GRID	ZIP CODE	BLOCK RANGE	O/E
LIMA ST	Adams Co	137L	80602	None	
	Aurora	287T	80010	1-599	
	Aurora	287L	80010	700-2499	
	Commerce City	197G	80640	11200-11399	
	Commerce City	197G	80601	None	
	Commerce City	197Q	80640	None	
	Denver	257U	80239	3700-3999	
	Denver	257L	80239	4700-5099	
LIMA ST S	Arapahoe Co	347Q	80111	5400-5499	
	Arapahoe Co	347U	80111	5600-5799	
	Arapahoe Co	347Y	80111	5900-6099	
	Arapahoe Co	377G	80112	6400-7499	
	Aurora	287Y	80012	200-299	
	Aurora	317C	80112	700-999	
	Aurora	317G	80112	1100-1899	
	Aurora	317L	80014	2300-2699	
	Centennial	377C	80111	6400-6699	
LIMA WAY S	Arapahoe Co	347Y	80111	6000-6299	
	Aurora	317Q	80014	2400-2599	
LIMBER WAY	Lone Tree	406C	80124	None	
LIMBERPINE LN	Aurora	381E	80016	None	
LIMELIGHT AVE	Castle Rock	467S	80109	3900-3999	
LIMESTONE CT	Douglas Co	408G	80134	10200-10299	
LIMESTONE PL	Superior	160U	80027	2700-2799	
LIMESTONE RD	El Paso Co	907U	80132	4600-4899	
LINCOLN AVE	Bennett	793J	80102	None	
LINCOLN AVE	Douglas Co	407G	80134	9800-12699	
	Douglas Co	409F	80134	16800-17399	
	Lone Tree	407G	80124	9200-9799	
LINCOLN AVE	Louisville	131W	80027	200-299	
	Louisville	131S	80027	500-1299	
LINCOLN AVE	Parker	409F	80134	17400-19099	
LINCOLN AVE	Platteville	708C	80651	300-399	
LINCOLN AVE E	Douglas Co	406G	80124	7300-8698	E
	Douglas Co	408F	80134	12700-16799	
	Douglas Co	409H	80138	19101-19199	O
	Highlands Ranch	406G	80130	6500-7299	
	Lone Tree	406G	80124	7300-9199	
LINCOLN CIR	Longmont	11Q	80501	1400-1499	
LINCOLN CIR	Louisville	131W	80027	100-499	
LINCOLN CT	Longmont	11U	80501	1600-1699	
LINCOLN CT	Louisville	131W	80027	300-499	
LINCOLN CT	Northglenn	194Q	80233	10400-10499	
LINCOLN CT S	Littleton	374L	80122	7800-7899	
LINCOLN DR	Longmont	11Q	80501	1800-1999	
LINCOLN DR	Northglenn	194G	80233	11300-11399	
LINCOLN PL	Boulder	127G	80302	700-1199	
	Boulder	127C	80302	1400-1699	
LINCOLN PL	Longmont	41G	80501	1-99	
LINCOLN ST	Adams Co	254G	80216	5200-5399	
	Denver	284L	80203	1-1999	
	Denver	254Q	80216	4200-5199	
LINCOLN ST	Elizabeth	871F	80107	100-299	
LINCOLN ST	Frederick	727F	80530	6100-6199	
LINCOLN ST	Longmont	41G	80501	100-299	
	Longmont	41C	80501	300-899	
	Longmont	11Y	80501	1100-1399	
	Longmont	11U	80501	1700-1799	
	Longmont	11Q	80501	1800-2099	
	Longmont	11L	80501	2100-2499	
	Longmont	11U	80501	None	
LINCOLN ST	Monument	908W	80132	2-98	E
LINCOLN ST	Northglenn	194Q	80233	10400-10499	
	Northglenn	194L	80233	10600-10899	
	Northglenn	194C	80233	11600-11899	
	Thornton	164Q	80241	None	
LINCOLN ST S	Arapahoe Co	374C	80121	6500-6699	
	Arapahoe Co	374G	80122	7000-7199	
	Denver	284Y	80209	1-699	
	Denver	314C	80209	700-899	
	Denver	314L	80210	1100-2699	
	Englewood	314Y	80113	2700-3599	
	Englewood	344G	80110	3600-4799	
	Littleton	374Q	80122	7900-8199	
LINCOLN ST S	Longmont	41L	80501	700-899	
	Longmont	41Q	80501	1300-1399	
LINCOLN WAY	Adams Co	224L	80221	7600-7799	
LINCOLN WAY S	Arapahoe Co	374G	80122	7100-7299	
LINCOLN GREEN LN	El Paso Co	908Q	80132	19200-19499	
LINCOLN HILLS WAY	Gilpin Co	741X	80403	1-299	
LINCOLN MEADOWS PKWY	Parker	409F	80134	None	
LINCOLN MOUNTAIN DR	Castle Rock	497E	80109	None	
LINDA CIR	Adams Co	224K	80221	7800-7999	
LINDA CIR	Elbert Co	851V	80107	None	
LINDA LN	Adams Co	224K	80221	100-7999	
LINDA LN	Jefferson Co	306F	80439	900-1099	
LINDA PL	Longmont	40T	80503	None	
LINDARK ST	Adams Co	750M	80603	15000-15099	
LINDA SUE LN	Northglenn	194G	80233	1-499	
LINDA TRAIL	Park Co	841P	80421	1-199	
LINDA VISTA DR	Lakewood	281B	80215	2100-11299	
LINDA VISTA DR	Longmont	12L	80504	12600-12999	
LINDBERGH RD	Jefferson Co	339W	80465	19800-20099	
LINDEN AVE	Boulder	97Q	80304	400-1799	
	Boulder	98N	80304	2100-2599	
LINDEN CIR	Boulder	97Q	80304	1100-1199	
LINDEN CIR	Dacono	727S	80514	None	
LINDEN CIR	Greenwood Village	345U	80121	4100-4299	
LINDEN CT	Greenwood Village	345V	80121	5200-5299	
	Thornton	166J	80602	13600-13799	
	Thornton	166E	80602	13800-13899	
LINDEN CT S	Denver	316J	80224	1900-1999	
	Denver	316N	80222	2300-2399	
	Denver	316S	80222	2600-2699	
LINDEN DR	Boulder Co	97K	80304	1-1999	
	Boulder Co	722V	80304	2000-3199	
LINDEN DR S	Englewood	343P	80110	5000-5099	
	Littleton	343P	80123	5100-5299	
LINDEN LN	Castle Rock	497D	80104	None	
LINDEN LN	Greenwood Village	345V	80121	4000-4999	
LINDEN PL	Erie	133C	80516	None	
LINDEN ST	Frederick	727F	80530	200-399	
	Frederick	727F	80530	None	
LINDEN ST	Longmont	11X	80501	1200-1299	
	Longmont	11T	80501	1300-1699	
	Longmont	11T	80501	1700-1799	
	Longmont	11K	80501	2400-2499	
LINDEN ST W	Louisville	130Q	80027	500-899	
LINDEN WAY	Erie	133C	80516	None	
LINDEN WAY S	Denver	316J	80224	1800-1899	

L

STREET NAME	CITY or COUNTY	MAP GRID	ZIP CODE	BLOCK RANGE	O/E
LINDENMERE DR	El Paso Co	908P	80132	None	
LINDEN PARK CT	Boulder	97Q	80304	500-599	
LINDEN PARK DR	Boulder	97Q	80304	500-699	
LINDENWOOD CT	Highlands Ranch	404C	80126	500-599	
LINDENWOOD DR	Littleton	374E	80120	1-99	
LINDENWOOD LN	Jefferson Co	370P	80127	1-99	
LINDO AVE	Palmer Lake	907Q	80133	None	
LINDON DR	Parker	409N	80134	17300-17399	
LINDSEY CIR	Elbert Co	850C	80138	900-999	
LINDSEY DR	Broomfield	133N	80020	None	
LINDSEY RD	Jefferson Co	278P	80401	400-699	
	Jefferson Co	823S	80433	11000-11099	
LINDSEY RD	Thornton	194S	80260	None	
LINDSEY ST	Lochbuie	140A	80603	None	
LINDSEY ST S	Castle Rock	498L	80104	1-699	
	Castle Rock	498Q	80104	800-1099	
LINDSEY PEAK LN	Douglas Co	436Z	80108	None	
LINES LN	Jefferson Co	307Y	80439	25300-25999	
LININGER DR S	Jefferson Co	308F	80401	1100-1699	
LINKS CIR E	Centennial	375M	80122	4800-5499	
	Centennial	376J	80122	5500-5599	
LINKS CT	Erie	133F	80516	None	
LINKS DR	Boulder Co	98P	80301	2800-2899	
LINKS DR E	Centennial	375M	80122	4500-4899	
LINKS PKWY E	Centennial	375L	80122	4000-4699	
LINKS PL	Erie	133F	80516	None	
LINKS PL E	Aurora	380M	80016	23600-23699	
	Aurora	381U	80016	27700-27799	
	Aurora	381L	80016	None	
LINLEY CT	Denver	283P	80204	800-999	
LINLEY CT S	Denver	313T	80219	2200-2699	
	Denver	313T	80236	2700-3099	
LINN RD	Park Co	820V	80421	1-199	
LINN ST	Jefferson Co	823N	80433	9700-9799	
LINVALE AVE E	Aurora	318V	80013	15800-16299	
LINVALE AVE W	Denver	312U	80227	None	
LINVALE CIR E	Aurora	319U	80013	18700-18899	
LINVALE DR E	Aurora	317B	80014	11000-11299	
	Aurora	319T	80013	17900-18499	
	Aurora	319V	80013	19500-19899	
LINVALE PL E	Aurora	317V	80014	13000-13299	
	Aurora	318S	80014	13700-14299	
	Aurora	318U	80013	15700-15799	
	Aurora	319S	80013	16800-17099	
	Aurora	319T	80013	17900-17999	
	Aurora	319U	80013	18500-19399	
	Aurora	319V	80013	19800-19999	
	Aurora	320N	80013	None	
	Denver	315T	80210	2700-2899	
	Denver	316U	80231	7900-8199	
LINVALE PL W	Denver	313U	80236	3300-3399	
	Denver	313T	80236	3600-4099	
	Denver	312V	80227	5200-5299	
	Denver	312U	80227	6800-7299	
	Jefferson Co	311T	80228	None	
LIONEL LN	Elizabeth	871F	80107	300-499	
LIONEL LN	Jefferson Co	762B	80403	11800-11899	
LIONESS PL	Douglas Co	407G	80134	None	
LIONESS ST	Douglas Co	407H	80134	None	
LIONESS WAY	Douglas Co	407G	80134	11901-12299	
LIONS PT E	Douglas Co	406J	80124	6200-6299	
LION'S HEAD DR	El Paso Co	908Q	80132	300-399	
LIONS HEAD DR	Park Co	841D	80470	1-399	
LIONSHEAD PKWY	Douglas Co	406K	80124	6500-7199	
LIONSHEAD TRAIL	Douglas Co	406K	80124	None	
LIONS HEART S	Douglas Co	406J	80124	10300-10499	
LIONS PATH S	Douglas Co	406J	80124	10300-10499	
LIONS PAW ST	Castle Rock	527D	80104	3900-4899	
LIPAN CT	Federal Heights	224E	80260	8400-8499	
	Thornton	194W	80260	8900-9099	
	Westminster	164S	80234	12400-12499	
	Westminster	164E	80020	13900-13999	
LIPAN CT S	Englewood	344J	80110	4500-4599	
LIPAN DR	Adams Co	224J	80221	1100-1499	
LIPAN DR S	Englewood	344J	80110	4900-4999	
LIPAN ST	Adams Co	254A	80221	6000-6199	
	Adams Co	224S	80221	7000-7199	
	Adams Co	224N	80221	7200-7299	
	Adams Co	134S	80020	15000-15599	
	Denver	284S	80223	1-399	
	Denver	284N	80204	400-1499	
	Denver	254S	80211	3400-4799	
	Federal Heights	224E	80260	8400-8499	
	Northglenn	194J	80234	10400-10599	
	Thornton	224A	80260	8800-8999	
	Westminster	164A	80020	14500-14599	
	Westminster	164E	80020	None	
LIPAN ST S	Denver	284W	80223	200-699	
	Denver	314E	80223	700-1499	
	Denver	314N	80223	1900-2399	
	Englewood	314T	80110	2900-3098	E
	Englewood	344A	80110	3700-3999	
	Englewood	344E	80110	4100-4299	
	Englewood	344J	80110	4300-4899	
LIPAN WAY	Boulder	128L	80303	100-499	
LIPPINCOTT DR	Gilpin Co	761C	80403	1400-1499	
LISBON CT N	Denver	260S	80249	3800-3899	
	Denver	260N	80249	4300-4399	
LISBON CT S	Arapahoe Co	350A	80013	3700-3799	
	Arapahoe Co	380A	80016	6500-6599	
	Arapahoe Co	350J	80015	None	
	Centennial	350S	80015	5600-5699	
	Centennial	380E	80016	7100-7199	
LISBON DR	Elbert Co	850H	80138	1200-1999	
LISBON LN S	Centennial	350N	80015	5400-5599	
LISBON ST	Denver	260E	80249	None	
LISBON ST N	Aurora	260W	80011	None	
	Aurora	290E	80011	None	
	Denver	260S	80249	3800-3999	
	Denver	260N	80249	4000-4499	
	Denver	260J	80249	4800-4899	
LISBON ST S	Centennial	350N	80015	5400-5599	
LISBON WAY	Denver	260E	80249	None	
LISBON WAY S	Arapahoe Co	350A	80013	3700-3799	
	Arapahoe Co	350E	80013	3900-4199	
	Arapahoe Co	350J	80015	None	
	Aurora	320W	80013	3500-3699	
	Aurora	320S	80013	None	
	Centennial	350N	80015	5100-5399	
	Centennial	350S	80015	5600-5899	
LISMORE WAY	Highlands Ranch	405P	80126	10700-10799	
LISTER WAY	Erie	102L	80516	100-299	
	Erie	102L	80516	None	
LITHGOW LN	Highlands Ranch	405H	80130	None	
LITTLE BEAR	Thornton	193V	80260	None	
LITTLE BEAR CT	Jefferson Co	305M	80439	32300-32399	
LITTLE BEAR CT	Longmont	12S	80501	1800-1899	
LITTLE BEAR DR	Longmont	12S	80501	1700-1799	
LITTLE BEAR PL	Broomfield	133N	80020	4800-4899	
LITTLE BEAR CREEK RD					
	Clear Creek Co	801A	80452	1300-2099	
LITTLE BEAR CREEK RD					
	Clear Creek Co	780Z	80452	2100-5999	
LITTLE BELL DR	Frederick	726G	80516	None	
LITTLE BERRY TRAIL	Jefferson Co	275X	80439	34100-34199	
LITTLE BIG HORN DR	Jefferson Co	366V	80439	27700-29199	
LITTLE BLUESTEM WAY	Parker	379T	80134	8600-8799	
LITTLE CANYON DR	Jefferson Co	340S	80465	16300-16699	
LITTLE CUB RD	Jefferson Co	365L	80439	32400-33099	
LITTLE CUB CREEK RD	Jefferson Co	337N	80439	4800-6299	
	Jefferson Co	367B	80439	None	
LITTLE FAWN WAY	Douglas Co	432Q	80125	7200-7399	
LITTLE FOX CT	Longmont	42C	80501	None	
LITTLE GULL CT	Highlands Ranch	375V	80126	8700-8799	
LITTLE HAYSTACK MOUNTAIN					
	Jefferson Co	371E	80127	12100-12199	
LITTLEHOUSE LN	Castle Rock	469K	80108	5700-5999	
LITTLE JOHN CT	Lafayette	132P	80026	1300-1399	
LITTLE LEAF CT	Longmont	40Q	80503	900-999	
LITTLE MEADOW CT	Douglas Co	470D	80134	5300-5399	
LITTLE MOON TRAIL	Douglas Co	910A	80118	10300-10399	
LITTLE RAVEN ST	Denver	284A	80202	1400-1698	E
	Denver	254W	80202	1700-2099	
LITTLE RAVEN WAY	Broomfield	163P	80020	13200-13299	
LITTLE RAVEN TRAIL	Boulder Co	70R	80503	8900-8999	
LITTLERIDGE LN	Cherry Hills Village	344D	80113	1-99	
LITTLE RIVER CIR S	Aurora	291T	80018	None	
LITTLE RIVER CT S	Aurora	381F	80016	7100-7199	
	Aurora	351T	80016	None	
LITTLE RIVER PL S	Aurora	351X	80016	None	
LITTLE RIVER ST N	Aurora	291P	80018	None	
LITTLE RIVER ST S	Aurora	291T	80018	None	
LITTLE RIVER WAY S	Aurora	351T	80016	None	
	Aurora	381B	80016	None	
LITTLE ROCK WAY	Highlands Ranch	375U	80126	8400-8499	
LITTLE SPRING LN	Park Co	841R	80421	1-199	
LITTLE SQUAW RD	Clear Creek Co	304H	80439	1-199	
LITTLE SUNFLOWER PL	Parker	379T	80134	8600-8699	
LITTLETON BLVD E	Centennial	344U	80121	1-799	
LITTLETON BLVD W	Littleton	344S	80120	1-2099	
LITTLE TURTLE LN	Jefferson Co	823W	80433	11700-11899	
LITTLE WILLOW CT	Douglas Co	432F	80125	10200-10299	
LIVE OAK CT	Castle Rock	498N	80104	2600-2799	
LIVE OAK RD	Castle Rock	498N	80104	1300-1599	
LIVERPOOL CIR	Douglas Co	432F	80125	8200-8599	
LIVERPOOL CIR S	Arapahoe Co	350J	80015	None	
LIVERPOOL CT N	Denver	260S	80249	4000-4099	
	Denver	260N	80249	4300-4399	
LIVERPOOL CT S	Arapahoe Co	350J	80015	None	
LIVERPOOL ST	Denver	260E	80249	None	
LIVERPOOL ST N	Aurora	290J	80018	800-1099	
	Denver	260N	80249	4300-4399	
	Denver	260J	80249	4800-4899	
LIVERPOOL ST S	Arapahoe Co	350A	80013	3700-3799	
	Arapahoe Co	350E	80013	None	
	Aurora	380E	80016	6700-7099	
	Centennial	350W	80016	5900-6699	
	Centennial	380E	80016	7100-7399	
LIVERPOOL WAY	Denver	260E	80249	None	
LIVERPOOL WAY S	Arapahoe Co	350N	80015	4900-5599	
	Arapahoe Co	350E	80013	None	
	Aurora	320W	80013	None	
	Centennial	350N	80015	5100-5399	
LIVERY STABLE LN	Jefferson Co	336Q	80439	None	
LIVINGSTON DR	Northglenn	194J	80234	10400-11199	
LLEWELYN CT	El Paso Co	908R	80132	1200-1299	
LLOYD CIR	Boulder	98N	80304	2600-2699	
LOA LN	Jefferson Co	842H	80433	28700-28899	
LOBLOLLY PINE CIR	Elbert Co	830L	80138	47200-47499	
LOCH LOMOND AVE	Broomfield	162Z	80020	1300-1499	
LOCHMERE CT	El Paso Co	909N	80132	19100-19299	
LOCHMORE DR	Longmont	12Q	80501	1800-1999	
LOCH NESS AVE	Broomfield	162V	80020	1100-1399	
LOCK ST	Louisville	131X	80027	1200-1299	
LOCKHEED DR E	Aurora	288R	80017	15900-16099	
LOCKRIDGE DR	El Paso Co	909Q	80908	19500-20499	
LOCKSLEY ST	Lafayette	132P	80026	None	
LOCKWOOD ST	Castle Rock	498L	80104	1-499	
LOCO LN	Jefferson Co	336H	80439	4200-4399	
LOCUST AVE	Boulder	97G	80304	600-1199	
LOCUST AVE	Lochbuie	140G	80603	100-799	
	Lochbuie	140F	80603	None	
LOCUST CIR S	Centennial	346W	80111	6000-6099	
	Centennial	376E	80112	7000-7199	
LOCUST CT	Commerce City	226S	80022	6900-7099	
	Commerce City	226J	80022	7800-7899	
LOCUST CT	Thornton	166N	80602	12000-12099	
	Thornton	166W	80602	12000-12099	
LOCUST CT S	Centennial	346W	80111	6100-6199	
	Centennial	376B	80112	6700-6899	
	Centennial	376J	80112	7800-7899	
LOCUST CT W	Louisville	130Q	80027	600-699	
LOCUST DR	Douglas Co	432F	80125	8100-8199	
LOCUST LN	Denver	286S	80220	200-299	
LOCUST PL	Boulder	97L	80304	400-599	
LOCUST PL	Thornton	194Z	80229	900-1499	
	Thornton	166S	80602	None	
LOCUST PL S	Centennial	376F	80112	7000-7199	
LOCUST ST	Adams Co	226N	80022	7400-7799	
	Commerce City	256J	80022	4900-4999	
	Commerce City	256E	80022	5400-5599	
	Commerce City	256A	80022	6000-6099	
	Commerce City	226S	80022	6600-7299	
	Denver	286J	80220	1-1999	
	Denver	286A	80207	2000-2799	
	Denver	256W	80207	2800-3699	
LOCUST ST	Frederick	727F	80530	None	
LOCUST ST	Thornton	166W	80602	12000-12399	
	Thornton	166N	80602	12901-13299	O
	Thornton	166J	80602	13600-13799	
	Thornton	166E	80602	13800-14099	
	Thornton	196E	80233	None	
LOCUST ST	Thornton	166J	80602	None	
LOCUST ST S	Arapahoe Co	316W	80222	3200-3399	
	Centennial	346W	80111	6000-6299	
	Centennial	376J	80112	7600-7799	
	Centennial	376N	80112	8200-8299	
	Denver	286W	80224	100-499	
	Denver	316A	80224	700-1099	
	Denver	316J	80224	1400-1999	
	Denver	316N	80222	2300-2399	
	Denver	316S	80222	2600-2999	
	Denver	316W	80222	3400-3499	
	Greenwood Village	346S	80111	5400-5699	
LOCUST WAY	Thornton	166S	80602	None	
LOCUST WAY S	Centennial	376A	80111	6400-6699	
	Centennial	376P	80112	8200-8299	
LODESTAR LN	Parker	379W	80134	9100-9199	
LODESTONE WAY	Douglas Co	408H	80134	10100-10299	
LODGE CT	Boulder	129A	80303	1400-1599	
LODGE LN	Boulder	129A	80303	1300-1599	
LODGEPOLE CIR	Jefferson Co	365G	80439	32500-32799	
LODGEPOLE CT	Boulder Co	99H	80301	6900-6999	
LODGEPOLE CT	Clear Creek Co	304Q	80439	1-199	
LODGEPOLE CT	Jefferson Co	365G	80439	7100-7199	
LODGEPOLE DR	Clear Creek Co	304Q	80439	1-1299	
LODGEPOLE DR	Erie	133C	80516	1800-2099	
LODGE POLE DR	Gilpin Co	761N	80403	1-1499	
LODGEPOLE DR	Jefferson Co	365H	80439	31700-32699	
LODGEPOLE DR	Park Co	842A	80470	1-699	
LODGE POLE LN	Gilpin Co	760V	80403	1-299	
LODGEPOLE RD	El Paso Co	912Y	80831	17000-17799	
LODGEPOLE WAY	El Paso Co	908Y	80132	200-299	
LODGE POLE WAY	Gilpin Co	761N	80403	1-299	
LODGEPOLE TRAIL	Lone Tree	376Y	80124	7900-8399	
LODGEWOOD LN	Lafayette	131E	80026	200-399	
LODGEWOOD PT	Lafayette	131F	80026	300-399	
LOFTON CT	Adams Co	224E	80221	1400-1499	
LOFTYPINE LN	El Paso Co	908P	80132	20000-20099	
LOGAN CIR E	Greenwood Village	344R	80121	900-999	
LOGAN CT	Adams Co	254G	80216	5500-5799	
	Northglenn	194L	80233	10600-10799	
LOGAN CT S	Centennial	344U	80121	5800-5899	
	Centennial	344U	80121	5900-5999	
	Centennial	344Y	80121	6300-6399	
LOGAN CT S	Littleton	374Q	80122	8000-8299	
LOGAN DR	Thornton	194U	80229	9800-9999	
LOGAN DR S	Greenwood Village	344R	80121	5100-5399	
	Littleton	374L	80122	7500-7799	
	Littleton	374L	80122	7800-7899	
	Littleton	374Q	80122	7900-8199	
LOGAN LN	Longmont	11Q	80501	2100-2199	
LOGAN PL S	Centennial	344Y	80121	6100-6299	
LOGAN ST	Adams Co	254G	80216	5600-5899	
	Adams Co	224L	80229	7800-7999	
	Adams Co	224G	80229	8200-8399	
	Denver	284L	80203	1-1999	
	Denver	254Q	80216	4400-5199	
LOGAN ST	Elizabeth	871F	80107	100-399	
LOGAN ST	Longmont	11Q	80501	1800-1999	
LOGAN ST	Northglenn	194C	80233	11600-11799	
	Thornton	164Q	80241	13000-13199	
LOGAN ST S	Arapahoe Co	344Q	80121	5100-5299	
	Arapahoe Co	374C	80121	6500-6899	
	Arapahoe Co	374G	80122	7100-7299	
	Centennial	344U	80121	5700-5899	
	Centennial	344Y	80121	5900-6099	
	Centennial	344Y	80121	6100-6299	
	Denver	284Y	80209	1-699	
	Denver	314C	80209	700-1099	
	Denver	314L	80210	1100-2699	
	Englewood	314Y	80113	2700-3599	
	Englewood	344G	80110	3600-5099	
	Littleton	374L	80122	7800-7999	
LOGAN WAY S	Littleton	374L	80122	7800-7899	
LOGAN MILL RD	Boulder Co	722T	80302	1-1399	
LOGES LN	Jefferson Co	306J	80439	31300-31399	
LOGGERS TRAIL	Jefferson Co	368A	80439	23100-23399	
LOGGIA ST	Highlands Ranch	405B	80126	9300-9599	
LOGIC DR	Longmont	40V	80503	3000-3199	
LOG TRAIL	Jefferson Co	823W	80433	26800-27399	
LOIS CIR	Louisville	130Z	80027	100-299	
LOIS CT	Lafayette	101X	80026	1700-1799	
LOIS CT	Louisville	130Y	80027	700-799	
LOIS DR	Louisville	131W	80027	100-799	
LOIS LN	Jefferson Co	336T	80439	5700-5799	
LOIS PL	Longmont	11V	80501	1-99	
LOIS WAY	Louisville	130Z	80027	500-599	
LOKI AVE	Boulder Co	98C	80301	4700-4799	
LOMA CIR W	Douglas Co	406Z	80108	1-199	
LOMA PL	Boulder Co	98P	80301	2800-2999	
LOMA LINDA CT	Weld Co	707T	80504	7000-7199	
LOMA LINDA DR	Brighton	138V	80601	700-799	
LOMAND CIR	Adams Co	136R	80602	16000-16199	
LOMBARD ST	Lafayette	131F	80026	2500-2599	
LOMBARDI ST	Erie	102G	80516	1100-1499	
LOMBARDY DR	Boulder	97R	80304	1600-1799	
LOMBARDY LN	Lakewood	281M	80215	900-9499	
LOMBARDY ST	Longmont	40T	80503	1700-1799	
LO MEADOW LN	Park Co	841V	80421	1-499	
LONDON AVE	Lafayette	131M	80026	200-599	
LONDON DR	Elbert Co	850G	80138	41000-42999	
	Elbert Co	830Y	80138	43000-43399	
LONDON LN	Jefferson Co	365U	80433	8300-8999	
LONDON WAY	Elbert Co	850D	80138	42500-42999	
LONE EAGLE CT	Boulder	69Y	80301	5400-5599	
LONE EAGLE PT	Lafayette	131G	80026	300-499	
LONE EAGLE RD	Jefferson Co	762W	80403	6400-6498	E
LONE ELK CIR	Elbert Co	851R	80107	39700-39799	
LONE ELK TRAIL	Jefferson Co	336R	80439	None	
LONE IRIS PL	Douglas Co	432M	80125	9500-9699	
LONE LYNX	Highlands Ranch	406K	80124	10300-10499	
LONE MAPLE LN	Lone Tree	406C	80124	8100-8199	
LONE OAK CT	Lone Tree	406C	80124	8100-8199	
LONE PEAK DR	Jefferson Co	337Z	80439	5700-6599	

STREET NAME	CITY or COUNTY	MAP GRID	ZIP CODE	BLOCK RANGE	O/E
LONE PEAK TRAIL	Jefferson Co	338W	80439	23500-23999	
LONE PINE	Douglas Co	432N	80125	11000-11099	
LONE PINE DR	Jefferson Co	763R	80403	7600-8299	
LONE PONDEROSA DR	Gilpin Co	761E	80403	1-299	
LONE ROCK CIR	El Paso Co	908P	80132	1400-1499	
LONESCOUT LOOKOUT	El Paso Co	908P	80132	1100-1499	
LONESOME DOVE CT	Elbert Co	870V	80107	31000-31999	
LONESOME ROCK RD	Elbert Co	891F	80107	3600-3699	
LONE STAR RANCH LOOP	Elbert Co	891C	80107	None	
LONE TREE PKWY	Lone Tree	406C	80124	7700-9899	
	Lone Tree	406G	80124	9900-10099	
LONEWOLF CIR	Lochbuie	140F	80603	None	
	Greenwood Village	346U	80111	1-99	
LONG AVE E	Arapahoe Co	381K	80016	25300-26399	
	Centennial	375J	80122	2200-2399	
	Centennial	375L	80122	3800-3899	
	Centennial	376J	80112	6400-7699	
	Centennial	376M	80112	8400-8599	
	Centennial	379J	80016	16900-20199	
LONG AVE W	Jefferson Co	341V	80123	9600-9699	
	Littleton	374J	80120	1200-1599	
	Littleton	373M	80120	2100-3299	
LONG CIR E	Aurora	381M	80016	27000-27099	
	Centennial	376K	80112	7400-7599	
	Centennial	375K	80122	3000N-3199N	
	Centennial	376J	80112	6100N-6599N	
	Centennial	376J	80112	6100S-6499S	
	Littleton	374L	80122	500-699	
LONG CIR W	Jefferson Co	341S	80127	None	
	Littleton	373R	80120	2400-2799	
	Littleton	373Q	80120	2800-2999	
LONG CT E	Centennial	375Q	80122	3800-3899	
	Centennial	376M	80112	8800-8899	
	Greenwood Village	345T	80121	2800-2999	
	Littleton	374L	80122	500-699	
LONG CT W	Jefferson Co	341V	80123	8800-8999	
	Littleton	374J	80120	1200-1299	
	Littleton	373M	80120	2900-3099	
LONG DR E	Aurora	380Q	80016	None	
	Greenwood Village	345S	80121	2400-2699	
LONG DR W	Jefferson Co	342S	80123	7000-8399	
	Jefferson Co	341V	80123	9600-9799	
	Lakewood	342V	80123	5900-5999	
	Lakewood	342U	80123	6100-6799	
	Littleton	373L	80120	2600-3099	
LONG LN E	Centennial	376J	80122	5200-5299	
	Centennial	379L	80016	19500-19599	
	Greenwood Village	345S	80121	2400-2899	
LONG PKWY E	Centennial	379M	80016	19700-19899	
LONG PL E	Arapahoe Co	374M	80122	1100-1199	
	Arapahoe Co	374M	80122	1400-1499	
LONG PL E	Aurora	380M	80016	23400-23499	
	Aurora	381M	80016	27100-27199	
	Aurora	381M	80016	27700-27899	
	Centennial	375K	80122	2700-2799	
	Centennial	375L	80122	3800-3899	
	Centennial	376J	80122	5400-6199	
	Centennial	376L	80112	7700-8299	
	Centennial	376M	80112	8600-8699	
LONG PL W	Lakewood	342V	80123	5600-5799	
	Littleton	373M	80120	2600-2799	
LONG RD	Clear Creek Co	801A	80452	200-999	
LONG RD E	Greenwood Village	345T	80121	2400-3999	
LONG ARROW LN	Jefferson Co	823Y	80433	23500-23799	
LONG BOW CIR	El Paso Co	908P	80132	1-99	
LONGBOW CT	Boulder	99B	80301	4800-4899	
LONGBOW CT	Lafayette	132P	80026	1600-1699	
LONGBOW DR	Boulder	99B	80301	5900-6299	
LONGBOW PL	Douglas Co	887G	80118	900-1099	
LONG BRANCH ST	Adams Co	794P	80136	1500-1999	
LONGDON ST	Longmont	12W	80501	1100-1199	
LONGFELLOW LN E	Highlands Ranch	404C	80126	400-699	
LONGFELLOW PL W	Adams Co	223Y	80221	3000-3299	
LONGFORD AVE	Boulder Co	11K	80504	None	
LONGFORD CT	Douglas Co	408C	80134	15600-15699	
LONGFORD DR	Douglas Co	408C	80134	15600-16099	
LONGFORD WAY	Douglas Co	408C	80134	9400-9599	
LONGGATE LN	Douglas Co	378Y	80134	9200-9399	
LONGHORN CIR	Elbert Co	870U	80107	30500-31299	
LONGHORN DR	Boulder Co	102J	80026	3900-4099	
LONGHORN DR	Bow Mar	342H	80123	4400-5299	
LONGHORN PL	Douglas Co	469B	80134	5900-5999	
LONGHORN RD	Boulder	723K	80302	3100-3999	
LONGHURST PL	Brighton	138V	80601	500-599	
LONGLEAF DR	Douglas Co	408M	80134	10300-10499	
LONG MEADOW CIR S					
	Greenwood Village	347N	80111	5100-5199	
LONG MEADOW LN S					
	Greenwood Village	347N	80111	5100-5199	
LONGMONT AVE N	Lafayette	132J	80026	100-199	
LONGMONT AVE S	Lafayette	132J	80026	100-899	
LONG RIDGE DR	Park Co	841R	80421	1-499	
LONGS CT	Broomfield	163J	80020	4500-4899	
LONGS RD	Thornton	193V	80260	None	
LONGS WAY	Parker	409L	80134	10600-19299	
LONGS BLUFF LN S	Parker	409Z	80134	None	
LONGS BLUFF WAY S	Parker	409Z	80134	None	
LONGS PEAK DR	Commerce City	197J	80640	9400-9599	
LONGS PEAK AVE	Longmont	41C	80501	1-2299	
LONGS PEAK AVE E	Longmont	42A	80501	1-699	
	Longmont	42B	80501	1000-1099	
LONGS PEAK CIR	Elbert Co	831K	80138	3300-3999	
LONGS PEAK CT	Mead	706H	80504	14200-14499	
LONGS PEAK DR	Boulder Co	130S	80303	600-699	
LONGS PEAK DR	Broomfield	191D	80021	1-99	
LONGS PEAK DR	Commerce City	196M	80640	9200-9399	
LONGS PEAK DR	Louisville	131N	80027	1600-1699	
LONGS PEAK LN	Longmont	41A	80501	2100-2199	
LONGS PEAK LN	Parker	410P	80138	10400-21899	
LONGS PEAK ST	Brighton	139K	80601	None	
	Brighton	140J	80601	None	
LONGS PEAK ST	Weld Co	726K	80516	1700-1999	
LONGS PEAK ST E	Brighton	138K	80601	100-1899	
LONGS PEAK ST W	Brighton	138K	80601	1-199	
LONG SPRINGS BUTTE	Jefferson Co	371E	80127	7200-7299	
LONG SPRUCE RD	Jefferson Co	306B	80439	30300-30399	
LONG SPUR	Jefferson Co	370F	80127	1-99	
LONGSPUR DR	Brighton	139R	80601	201-499	O

STREET NAME	CITY or COUNTY	MAP GRID	ZIP CODE	BLOCK RANGE	O/E
LONGSTONE CT	Douglas Co	378Y	80134	9200-9299	
LONGSTONE DR	Douglas Co	378Y	80134	9200-9599	
LONGTIMBER LN	El Paso Co	908V	80132	800-899	
LONG TRAIL RD	Gilpin Co	761J	80403	1-599	
LONG VIEW	Weld Co	706N	80504	3200-11299	
LONGVIEW AVE E	Centennial	348W	80111	None	
LONGVIEW AVE W	Littleton	344X	80120	600-1199	
LONGVIEW CIR	El Paso Co	908P	80132	1500-1599	
LONGVIEW CT	Longmont	41B	80501	400-499	
LONGVIEW DR	Boulder Co	70Q	80503	6600-6999	
	Boulder Co	70L	80503	7000-7299	
LONGVIEW DR	Fort Lupton	728H	80621	900-1299	
LONGVIEW DR	Frederick	706Y	80504	None	
LONGVIEW DR	Jefferson Co	843A	80433	26400-26799	
LONGVIEW DR	Lone Tree	406G	80124	9900-10299	
LONGVIEW PL E	Centennial	378A	80111	None	
LONGVIEW RD	Broomfield	726Y	80516	1800-3699	
LONG VIEW RD	Clear Creek Co	304H	80439	1-199	
LONGVIEW ST S	Littleton	344X	80120	6000-6199	
LONGWOOD AVE	Boulder	128X	80305	3200-3999	
LONGWOOD CIR	Highlands Ranch	405M	80130	None	
LONGWOOD WAY	Highlands Ranch	405M	80130	None	
LOOKOUT DR	Boulder Co	72W	80504	None	
LOOKOUT DR E	Douglas Co	379U	80138	6400-6999	
LOOKOUT DR W	Boulder Co	72W	80504	None	
LOOKOUT RD	Boulder	99B	80301	6100-6299	
	Boulder	69Y	80301	6300-6899	
	Boulder	69Y	80503	7100-7399	
	Boulder	70X	80503	7400-7499	
	Boulder Co	69Y	80301	6900-7099	
	Boulder Co	70X	80503	7500-9099	
	Boulder Co	71X	80503	9100-9499	
	Boulder Co	71X	80026	9500-10699	
	Boulder Co	71X	80504	10700-10999	
	Boulder Co	72W	80504	11100-11499	
LOOKOUT HILL CT S	Arapahoe Co	812A	80102	1300-1399	
LOOKOUT HILL ST S	Arapahoe Co	812N	80102	3500-4299	
LOOKOUT MOUNTAIN CIR					
	Jefferson Co	278T	80401	1-199	
LOOKOUT MOUNTAIN RD	Golden	278H	80401	2100-2299	
	Jefferson Co	278Q	80401	1-999	
LOOKOUT MOUNTAIN RD S					
	Jefferson Co	278W	80401	1-399	
LOOKOUT RIDGE DR	Boulder Co	71W	80301	5300-5399	
LOOKOUT RUN	Douglas Co	432N	80125	11100-11299	
LOOKOUT VIEW CT	Golden	279F	80401	200-399	
LOOKOUT VIEW DR	Golden	279F	80401	200-499	
	Golden	279G	80401	2700-3099	
LOOMIS CT	Longmont	41B	80501	600-699	
LOOMIS WAY	Jefferson Co	762C	80403	29300-29699	
LOOP DR	Boulder	128E	80302	None	
LOOP RD	Castle Rock	528E	80104	None	
LORA AVE S	Jefferson Co	842B	80470	12500-12799	
LORA LN	Jefferson Co	366B	80439	6300-6399	
LOREN LN	Northglenn	194M	80233	10600-10799	
LORENA WAY	Mead	706M	80504	None	
LORETTA DR	Adams Co	224F	80221	8100-8299	
LORI DR	Jefferson Co	843B	80433	12900-13099	
LORIN LN N	Douglas Co	496J	80109	200-599	
LORRAINE CT	Boulder	98S	80304	2900-2999	
LORRAINE RD	Douglas Co	908H	80118	3000-5199	
	Douglas Co	909E	80118	5200-6999	
LORRAWAY DR	Douglas Co	466H	80108	400-499	
LOS HERMANOS WAY	Gilpin Co	741Y	80403	1-299	
LOST ANGEL RD	Boulder Co	742A	80302	1-1699	
LOST ARROW W	Douglas Co	432J	80125	11100-11299	
LOST ARROWHEAD DR	El Paso Co	908P	80132	20000-20299	
LOST CANYON RANCH CT					
	Castle Rock	498R	80104	1900-2299	
LOST CANYON RANCH RD					
	Castle Rock	498R	80104	6100-6499	
	Castle Rock	499T	80104	6501-6599	O
LOST CANYON TRAIL N	Douglas Co	410A	80138	12100-12599	
	Douglas Co	380W	80138	12600-12999	
LOST CREEK CIR	Parker	410Q	80138	11200-11399	
LOST CREEK LN	Lafayette	131B	80026	1200-1299	
LOST CREEK RD	Jefferson Co	337X	80439	None	
LOST CREEK WAY	El Paso Co	908U	80132	200-299	
LOST HILL DR E	Lone Tree	406D	80124	9100-9299	
LOST HILL DR S	Lone Tree	406D	80124	9100-9299	
LOST HILL TRAIL E	Lone Tree	406D	80124	9000-9299	
LOST HORIZON DR	Jefferson Co	844A	80127	18401-18699	O
LOST LAKE WAY	Broomfield	163P	80020	13200-13299	
LOST LAKE TRAIL	Douglas Co	470T	80116	2500-3099	
LOST MEADOW TRAIL	Castle Rock	498L	80104	None	
LOST MINE TRAIL	Gilpin Co	742W	80403	None	
LOST RANGER RD	El Paso Co	912T	80831	18400-18599	
LOST RANGER PEAK	Jefferson Co	371L	80127	7500-7699	
LOST RESERVE CT	Douglas Co	440L	80134	8400-8699	
LOST ROCK LN	El Paso Co	908P	80132	1200-1299	
LOST TRAIL	Jefferson Co	823W	80433	11800-11899	
LOST TRAIL	Park Co	841J	80421	1-99	
LOST TRAIL RD	Clear Creek Co	801A	80452	1-99	
LOTUS CT	Longmont	12P	80501	1900-1999	
LOTUS WAY	Broomfield	162T	80020	600-899	
LOU DR	Northglenn	194T	80260	9400-9799	
LOUIS RD	Park Co	841T	80421	1-299	
LOUISE DR	Adams Co	224E	80221	8200-8399	
LOUISE LN	Jefferson Co	366A	80439	6600-6699	
LOUISIANA AVE E	Arapahoe Co	316H	80247	8901-9099	O
	Arapahoe Co	317E	80247	9300-9498	E
	Aurora	317G	80112	11100-13299	
	Aurora	318G	80017	15300-15599	
	Aurora	319E	80017	17400-17899	
	Aurora	319G	80017	17900-19699	
	Denver	314H	80210	1-1699	
	Denver	315F	80210	1700-3199	
	Denver	315G	80210	3600-3999	
	Denver	315H	80246	4000-5599	
	Denver	316F	80224	6600-7299	
LOUISIANA AVE W	Denver	314G	80223	1-399	
	Denver	314E	80223	800-1999	
	Denver	313H	80223	2000-2499	
	Denver	313E	80219	2500-5199	
	Jefferson Co	311F	80232	10900-11499	
	Lakewood	312H	80232	5200-6399	
	Lakewood	312G	80232	6800-6999	
	Lakewood	312F	80232	7400-8399	

Continued on next column

STREET NAME	CITY or COUNTY	MAP GRID	ZIP CODE	BLOCK RANGE	O/E
LOUISIANA AVE W (Cont'd)	Lakewood	311H	80232	9200-9799	
	Lakewood	311E	80228	12000-12299	
	Lakewood	311E	80228	12300-12499	
	Lakewood	310H	80228	12500-12999	
LOUISIANA CIR E	Aurora	321E	80018	24400-24799	
LOUISIANA DR E	Arapahoe Co	812A	80102	39900-40799	
	Aurora	317E	80247	9800-9999	
	Aurora	317H	80112	12100-12299	
	Aurora	318G	80012	15000-15199	
	Aurora	318H	80017	16500-16799	
	Aurora	319E	80017	17000-17199	
LOUISIANA PKWY E	Aurora	320H	80018	None	
LOUISIANA PL	Longmont	41Q	80501	1000-11999	
LOUISIANA PL E	Arapahoe Co	316H	80247	8900-9299	
	Arapahoe Co	317E	80247	9500-9599	
	Aurora	317F	80012	11000-11099	
	Aurora	318E	80012	13900-13999	
	Aurora	318H	80017	16200-16299	
	Aurora	321E	80018	24100-24298	E
LOUISIANA PL W	Lakewood	312G	80232	6300-6799	
	Lakewood	312E	80232	8100-8399	
	Lakewood	312E	80232	8800-8899	
LOU'S LOOP	Golden	248Q	80403	None	
LOUTHAN CT S	Littleton	374E	80120	7000-7099	
	Littleton	374J	80120	7700-7799	
LOUTHAN ST S	Littleton	344N	80120	5300-5399	
	Littleton	344S	80120	5600-5999	
	Littleton	344W	80120	6300-6499	
	Littleton	374J	80120	7700-7799	
LOUTHAN WAY S	Littleton	344N	80120	5400-5499	
LOUVIERS AVE	Douglas Co	846C	80125	5700-5899	
LOUVIERS BLVD	Douglas Co	846G	80125	7800-7899	
LOVACA DR	El Paso Co	912X	80831	16500-17299	
LOVAGE WAY	Parker	408U	80134	11200-11499	
LOVE CT	Boulder	129E	80303	1000-1099	
LOVELAND CIR	Arvada	220P	80007	None	
LOVELAND CT	Jefferson Co	220K	80007	7600-7799	
	Jefferson Co	280T	80401	None	
LOVELAND ST	Arvada	220P	80007	None	
	Arvada	220X	80007	None	
	Jefferson Co	280P	80401	600-999	
	Jefferson Co	250N	80403	4300-4399	
LOVELAND ST S	Lakewood	310P	80228	None	
LOVELAND WAY	Jefferson Co	280T	80401	1-199	
LOVELAND SLOPE	Palmer Lake	907Q	80133	None	
LOVERLY WAY	El Paso Co	908Y	80132	17800-17899	
LOVERS LN	Larkspur	887R	80118	100-299	
LOVINGTON ST	Castle Rock	499J	80104	1-299	
LOW CIR E	Arapahoe Co	349U	80015	18900-19099	
LOW DR E	Arapahoe Co	349U	80015	18900-19299	
LOW LN S	Jefferson Co	368C	80465	6700-6799	
LOW PL E	Arapahoe Co	349U	80015	18900-19099	
	Centennial	350T	80015	21900-21999	
LOWALL CT	Douglas Co	867Q	80109	2500-2699	
LOWELL BLVD	Adams Co	253F	80221	5200-6199	
	Adams Co	223K	80221	6200-6999	
	Broomfield	163B	80020	12400-14699	
	Broomfield	133X	80020	14700-15999	
	Denver	283T	80219	1-1999	
	Denver	283K	80204	400-1999	
	Denver	253X	80211	2700-4799	
	Denver	253K	80221	4800-5199	
	Westminster	223K	80030	7000-7999	
	Westminster	223K	80031	8000-9099	
	Westminster	193P	80031	9100-10399	
	Westminster	193B	80031	11800-11898	E
	Westminster	163X	80020	12000-12399	
LOWELL BLVD S	Denver	283T	80219	1-699	
	Denver	313T	80236	2700-3299	
	Denver	343P	80110	4600-4899	
	Englewood	343P	80110	4500-4599	
	Littleton	343P	80110	4900-5099	
	Littleton	343P	80123	5100-5999	
	Sheridan	343B	80236	3500-4099	
	Sheridan	343P	80110	4300-4499	
LOWELL CT	Adams Co	223B	80031	None	
	Broomfield	163T	80020	12400-12499	
	Broomfield	163P	80020	13000-13099	
	Westminster	193X	80031	9000-9199	
	Westminster	193T	80031	9600-9699	
LOWELL DR	Castle Rock	497M	80104	1-99	
	Westminster	193K	80031	10400-10799	
LOWELL LN	Broomfield	134F	80516	3000-3499	
LOWELL ST	Denver	283B	80211	2000-2699	
LOWELL ST S	Denver	313P	80219	700-2699	
LOWELL WAY	Adams Co	223B	80031	None	
	Westminster	193P	80031	10000-10199	
LOWELL WAY S	Littleton	343T	80123	5700-5899	
LOWER ASPEN LN	Park Co	821Z	80470	34900-35199	
LOWER CROW HILL RD	Park Co	841S	80421	None	
LOWER GLEN WAY	Palmer Lake	907Q	80133	None	
LOWER HIGHLAND DR	Weld Co	706U	80504	None	
LOWER LAKE RD	El Paso Co	908T	80132	18300-18699	
LOWER MOON GULCH RD	Gilpin Co	760C	80403	None	
LOWER MOSS ROCK RD	Jefferson Co	276U	80401	28700-29399	
LOWER RIDGE RD	Weld Co	706U	80504	10400-10499	
LOWER RUSSELL GULCH	Gilpin Co	780F	80403	1-199	
LOWER RUSSELL GULCH RD					
	Gilpin Co	780G	80403	1-99	
LOWER TWIN CREEK RD	Douglas Co	889A	80104	5200-5799	
LOWLAND BLVD	Lochbuie	140B	80603	None	
	Lochbuie	729Y	80603	None	
LOW MEADOW BLVD	Castle Rock	466Z	80109	None	
LOWRY BLVD E	Denver	286T	80230	7300-8599	
	Denver	286V	80230	9000-9199	
LOWRY PL	Aurora	287N	80010	9700-10099	
	Aurora	287P	80010	10500-10999	
LOYD CIR	Elbert Co	831N	80138	None	
LOYOLA AVE E	Aurora	349B	80013	17800-17899	
LOYOLA CIR E	Aurora	349C	80013	18900-19799	
LOYOLA CT	Boulder	128X	80305	3300-3399	
LOYOLA DR E	Aurora	348D	80013	15900-16099	
	Aurora	349B	80013	17600-18299	
LOYOLA PL E	Aurora	348C	80013	15300-15499	
	Aurora	348D	80013	16000-16099	
	Aurora	349A	80013	16900-17099	
	Aurora	349B	80013	17800-18299	
	Aurora	349C	80013	18600-18699	
	Aurora	349D	80013	19900-19999	

L

STREET NAME	CITY or COUNTY	MAP GRID	ZIP CODE	BLOCK RANGE	O/E
LUCAS AVE E	Douglas Co	890K	80116	10200-11999	
LUCCA DR	Longmont	40Q	80503	None	
LUCENT BLVD	Highlands Ranch	374S	80129	8700-8799	
	Highlands Ranch	404A	80129	9200-9699	
LUCERNE DR	Lafayette	132E	80026	100-399	
	Lafayette	131D	80026	400-899	
LUCERNE WAY	Lafayette	132E	80026	100-299	
LUCERO PL	Erie	103N	80516	None	
LUCILLE CT	Northglenn	194H	80233	1300-1599	
LUCKY CT	Castle Rock	496F	80109	1000-1199	
LUDLOW ST	Boulder	128U	80305	4300-4799	
LUMP GULCH RD	Gilpin Co	760G	80403	1-699	
	Gilpin Co	760D	80403	700-2999	
LUMP GULCH WAY	Frederick	726G	80516	3100-3399	
LUNCEFORD CT	Northglenn	194T	80260	9900-9999	
LUNCEFORD LN	Northglenn	194S	80260	9800-9899	
LUNNONHAUS DR	Golden	279L	80401	1400-17899	
LUPINE CIR	Arvada	220W	80007	6700-6799	
LUPINE CIR	Douglas Co	887F	80118	2200-2699	
LUPINE CT	Arvada	220N	80007	None	
	Jefferson Co	250X	80401	3200-3299	
LUPINE CT	Longmont	40R	80503	1300-1399	
LUPINE CT S	Lakewood	310P	80228	None	
LUPINE DR	Jefferson Co	336H	80439	27600-28499	
LUPINE DR S	Littleton	343S	80123	5700-5999	
LUPINE LN	Boulder	127L	80302	None	
LUPINE PL	Erie	133D	80516	None	
LUPINE PL	Gilpin Co	761C	80403	1-399	
LUPINE ST	Jefferson Co	280P	80401	600-999	
	Jefferson Co	220N	80007	7200-7399	
LUPINE ST S	Jefferson Co	280S	80401	1-199	
	Lakewood	310P	80228	None	
LUPINE WAY	Arvada	220S	80007	6700-6899	
	Jefferson Co	280T	80401	1-99	
	Jefferson Co	307H	80401	1200-1399	
LUSTER LN	Jefferson Co	844W	80421	17800-17899	
LUTES RD	Jefferson Co	842A	80470	33400-33999	
LUTHERAN PKWY	Wheat Ridge	252W	80033	3200-3799	
	Wheat Ridge	252S	80033	None	
LYDEN CREEK BLVD	Frederick	727F	80530	None	
LYDIA DR	Lafayette	131Q	80026	1400-1999	
LYKINS AVE	Boulder	97C	80304	None	
LYKINS GULCH RD	Longmont	41J	80503	None	
LYNCH LN	Castle Rock	469F	80108	6500-6999	
LYNDENWOOD CIR	Highlands Ranch	405L	80130	4300-4699	
LYNDENWOOD PT	Highlands Ranch	405L	80130	4300-4599	
LYNKS PL	Boulder Co	703U	80503	None	
LYNN DR	Arvada	251G	80002	5300-5399	
LYNN RD	Cherry Hills Village	345F	80113	1-99	
LYNNE AVE	Boulder Co	101M	80026	10900-10999	
LYNNFIELD DR	Douglas Co	407H	80112	12700-12798	E
LYNNFIELD LN	Douglas Co	407H	80112	None	
LYNNWOOD LN	Gilpin Co	761C	80403	1-299	
LYNWOOD AVE	Highlands Ranch	405P	80126	3100-3399	
LYNX COVE	Douglas Co	406K	80124	6500-6699	
LYNX CT	Douglas Co	406K	80124	10500-10599	
LYNX CT	Frederick	707W	80504	5401-5499	O
LYNX LN	Douglas Co	432F	80125	10100-10199	
LYNX LN	Gilpin Co	761N	80403	None	
LYNX LN	Jefferson Co	365G	80439	33000-33399	
LYNX ST	Frederick	707W	80504	5400-5499	
LYNX BAY	Douglas Co	406K	80124	10400-10499	
LYNX CREEK	Frederick	726G	80516	None	
LYNX LAIR RD	Jefferson Co	366F	80439	6900-7599	
LYNX RUN	Douglas Co	406K	80124	10400-10499	
LYONEDOWN LN	El Paso Co	908R	80132	None	
LYONESSE ST	Lafayette	132T	80026	1700-1899	
LYONS ST	Golden	279P	80401	18600-18699	
LYTLE DR E	Parker	410N	80138	20800-20899	
LYTTLE DOWDLE DR	Jefferson Co	762E	80403	33200-34699	

M

STREET NAME	CITY or COUNTY	MAP GRID	ZIP CODE	BLOCK RANGE	O/E
MABLE AVE	Adams Co	224H	80229	1600-1799	
	Adams Co	225E	80229	1800-2399	
MABRE CT S	Littleton	343P	80123	5000-5299	
MABRY CT S	Denver	313T	80236	2800-3099	
MABRY WAY S	Denver	313K	80219	1500-1899	
	Denver	313T	80236	2700-3299	
MacALISTER TRAIL S					
	Highlands Ranch	404G	80129	9900-10099	
MacARTHUR LN	Boulder	128D	80303	4600-4699	
MACAW ST	Brighton	138W	80601	800-899	
MacCORMACK CT	Dacono	727K	80514	1200-1299	
MacCULLEN DR	Erie	132A	80026	1500-1899	
MacDAVIDSON CIR	Dacono	727K	80514	1000-1199	
MacDAVIDSON CT	Dacono	727K	80514	1200-1299	
MacDAVIDSON ST	Dacono	727K	80514	1100-1199	
MacDEE CT	Dacono	727K	80514	1200-1299	
MacDONALD AVE	Jefferson Co	823U	80433	10800-11099	
MacDONALD CT	Dacono	727K	80514	1200-1299	
MacDONALD ST	Dacono	727K	80514	1100-1199	
MacDOUGAL CT	Dacono	727K	80514	1200-1299	
MACEDONIA ST	Boulder Co	704N	80503	10200-10399	
MacINTOSH PL	Boulder	98U	80301	4800-4899	
MacINTYRE CT	Dacono	727K	80514	1200-1299	
MacJAMES CT	Dacono	727K	80514	1200-1299	
MACKAY CT	Dacono	727K	80514	1200-1299	
MACKAY DR	Highlands Ranch	405H	80130	9900-10099	
MacKENZIE CT	Dacono	727K	80514	1200-1299	
MacKENZIE CT	Highlands Ranch	376W	80130	1-99	
MACKY WAY	Boulder	128U	80305	4600-4699	
MacLAUGHLIN CT	Dacono	727K	80514	1200-1299	
MACLEAN CT	Dacono	727K	80514	1100-1199	
MACLEAN DR	Arapahoe Co	373A	80123	1-99	
MACLEAN ST	Dacono	727K	80514	1100-1199	
MacLEOD CT	Dacono	727K	80514	1200-1299	
MACLOVIO DR	Mead	706M	80504	None	
MacMURRY CT	Dacono	727K	80514	1200-1299	
MACOM DR	Douglas Co	466A	80135	1500-1999	
MACON CIR S	Aurora	317U	80014	2700-3099	
MACON CT	Aurora	287U	80010	1-99	
	Douglas Co	377Y	80112	None	
MACON CT S	Arapahoe Co	347Y	80111	6100-6199	
	Aurora	287Y	80012	500-599	
	Aurora	317G	80112	1400-1499	
	Aurora	317Q	80014	2200-2299	
	Aurora	317U	80014	2600-2899	
MACON ST	Adams Co	167Y	80640	11801-11999	O
	Aurora	287T	80010	1-99	
	Aurora	287L	80010	700-1999	
	Aurora	287C	80010	2200-2499	
	Commerce City	197C	80640	11400-11999	
	Commerce City	197G	80601	None	
MACON ST S	Arapahoe Co	347U	80111	5700-5899	
	Aurora	317C	80112	900-1099	
	Aurora	317G	80112	1300-1699	
	Aurora	317Q	80014	2300-2399	
	Aurora	317U	80014	2701-2999	O
MACON WAY S	Arapahoe Co	347Y	80111	6100-6299	
	Aurora	317C	80112	700-1099	
	Aurora	317L	80014	1900-2099	
	Aurora	317Q	80014	2400-2599	
MACOY CT	Dacono	727K	80514	1200-1299	
MacPOOL ST	Dacono	727K	80514	1400-1499	
MacTAVISH CT	Dacono	727K	80514	1400-1499	
MacTAVISH ST	Dacono	727K	80514	1200-1299	
MADDOX CT	Broomfield	164J	80020	900-1199	
MADELINE ST	Federal Heights	223D	80260	9000-9099	
	Federal Heights	193Z	80260	9100-9199	
MADERA CT	Boulder Co	98P	80301	2800-2999	
MADERO ST	Broomfield	162P	80020	1200-1499	
MADGE RIDGE RD	Douglas Co	866A	80135	500-1399	
MADISON AVE	Boulder	128F	80303	3000-3699	
MADISON AVE S	Louisville	130Y	80027	100-299	
MADISON CIR S	Centennial	375F	80122	7300-7399	
	Centennial	375K	80122	7500-7799	
MADISON CT	Adams Co	225F	80229	8500-8599	
MADISON CT	Broomfield	163G	80020	None	
MADISON CT	Erie	102T	80516	800-999	
MADISON CT	Louisville	130Q	80027	1500-1799	
MADISON CT	Thornton	195F	80233	11200-11299	
	Thornton	165X	80241	12300-12399	
	Thornton	165T	80241	None	
MADISON CT S	Centennial	345X	80121	6100-6199	
	Centennial	375B	80121	6500-6599	
	Centennial	375F	80122	7000-7199	
MADISON DR	Bennett	793N	80102	100-299	
MADISON DR	Erie	102T	80516	2000-2299	
MADISON DR	Longmont	11J	80503	2700-2899	
MADISON DR S	Centennial	345X	80121	6100-6299	
MADISON LN	Broomfield	163G	80020	3000-3099	
MADISON LN S	Greenwood Village	345T	80121	5500-5599	
MADISON PL	Thornton	195B	80233	11800-11999	
MADISON ST	Adams Co	165B	80602	14400-14899	
	Adams Co	135X	80602	14900-15199	
MADISON ST	Brighton	138K	80601	300-399	
	Denver	285K	80206	1-1699	
	Denver	285B	80205	2600-2699	
	Denver	255X	80205	2700-2899	
	Denver	255T	80205	3100-3999	
	Denver	255P	80216	4000-4599	
	Thornton	195T	80229	9800-9999	
	Thornton	195P	80229	10000-10199	
	Thornton	195K	80233	10500-10799	
	Thornton	195B	80233	11200-11999	
	Thornton	165X	80241	12000-12099	
	Thornton	165T	80241	12600-12799	
	Thornton	165K	80602	13600-13899	
	Thornton	165F	80602	13900-13999	
	Thornton	165F	80602	None	
	Thornton	195L	80233	None	
	Thornton	225B	80229	None	
MADISON ST S	Denver	285T	80209	1-399	
	Denver	315B	80209	800-1099	
	Denver	315B	80210	1100-1199	
	Denver	315T	80210	1600-3099	
MADISON WAY	Adams Co	225F	80229	8400-8499	
MADISON WAY	Bennett	793J	80102	600-999	
MADISON WAY	Erie	102T	80516	2000-2199	
MADISON WAY	Northglenn	195P	80233	10400-10699	
	Northglenn	195K	80233	10700-10799	
	Thornton	165F	80602	None	
MADISON WAY	Thornton	165T	80241	None	
MADISON WAY S	Centennial	375F	80122	6900-7099	
	Centennial	375P	80122	7900-8199	
MADRAS CT	Highlands Ranch	376W	80130	9100-9299	
MADRAS DR	Highlands Ranch	376W	80130	None	
MADRAS LN	Highlands Ranch	376W	80130	None	
MADRE PL	Lone Tree	376Z	80124	9100-9199	
MADRID CT	Elbert Co	850G	80138	600-799	
MADRID DR	Elbert Co	850G	80138	41000-42199	
MADRID PL	Elbert Co	850G	80138	800-999	
MAD RIVER CT N	Douglas Co	440U	80134	6100-6299	
MAD RIVER RD E	Douglas Co	440U	80134	8600-8999	
MADRONE CT	Douglas Co	378U	80134	15700-15799	
MAGGIE CT	Weld Co	707J	80504	None	
MAGGIE LN	Jefferson Co	336T	80439	5300-5599	
MAGGIE ST	Longmont	42G	80501	200-399	
MAGIC LAMP WAY	El Paso Co	908X	80132	1000-1299	
MAGNOLIA CIR	Thornton	196B	80233	None	
MAGNOLIA CIR S	Centennial	376F	80112	7000-7199	
MAGNOLIA CT	Thornton	166K	80602	None	
MAGNOLIA CT S	Centennial	346X	80111	6100-6199	
	Centennial	346X	80111	6400-6499	
	Centennial	376B	80112	6400-6899	
MAGNOLIA DR	Boulder Co	740R	80466	1-499	
	Boulder Co	741L	80466	500-8999	
	Boulder Co	742F	80466	9000-10199	
MAGNOLIA DR	Thornton	196B	80233	None	
MAGNOLIA LN S	Denver	286X	80224	500-599	
MAGNOLIA PL	Thornton	166N	80602	None	
MAGNOLIA ST	Adams Co	226K	80022	7400-7899	
	Adams Co	136J	80602	16600-16699	
MAGNOLIA ST	Castle Rock	496B	80109	None	
	Commerce City	256E	80022	5300-5999	
	Commerce City	226T	80022	6400-7399	
	Denver	286K	80220	100-1999	
	Denver	286B	80207	2000-2799	
	Denver	256X	80207	2800-3999	
MAGNOLIA ST	Thornton	136S	80602	15200-15399	
	Thornton	136S	80602	15400-15599	
	Thornton	166J	80602	None	
	Thornton	166N	80602	None	
	Thornton	196A	80233	None	
MAGNOLIA ST S	Denver	286X	80224	300-699	
	Denver	316F	80224	1200-1399	
	Denver	316K	80224	1700-1999	
	Denver	316P	80224	2500-2699	
	Denver	316X	80224	3100-3399	
MAGNOLIA WAY	Thornton	166X	80602	12100-12299	
MAGNOLIA WAY S	Centennial	376K	80112	7800-7899	
	Denver	316F	80224	1400-1499	
	Denver	316T	80224	2900-2999	
	Denver	346B	80237	3700-4099	
MAGPIE AVE	Brighton	137Z	80601	1200-1299	
MAGPIE CT	Golden	248Z	80403	1400-1599	
MAGPIE LN	Douglas Co	907F	80118	2700-2799	
MAGPIE LN	Park Co	841V	80421	1-199	
MAHLON CT	Lafayette	132A	80026	1000-1099	
MAHOGANY CIR	Louisville	130Y	80027	800-899	
MAHOGANY WAY	Elbert Co	851Y	80107	5000-5099	
MAHONIA	Jefferson Co	370K	80127	1-99	
MAIDEN WAY	Northglenn	195A	80233	11800-11899	
MAIDEN HAIR LN E	Parker	408U	80134	None	
MAIDEN HAIR WAY S	Parker	408U	80134	None	
MAID MARION CT	Lafayette	132P	80026	1400-1499	
MAIN AVE	Jefferson Co	278Q	80401	21400-21799	
MAIN AVE W	Denver Federal Center	281T	80225	None	
MAIN CIR N	Arapahoe Co	795U	80103	1-99	O
MAIN ST	Adams Co	794P	80136	1500-1799	
MAIN ST	Black Hawk	780D	80422	12900-12999	
MAIN ST	Boulder Co	721R	80302	1-1299	
MAIN ST	Broomfield	162Y	80020	1-13599	
	Broomfield	192G	80020	11201-11699	O
MAIN ST	Central City	780C	80427	1-199	
MAIN ST	Denver	256Q	80238	None	
MAIN ST	Douglas Co	846C	80125	7900-7999	
	Douglas Co	846C	80125	8000-8299	
MAIN ST	Elbert Co	892N	80106	24000-24099	
MAIN ST	Elizabeth	871F	80107	100-499	
MAIN ST	Erie	102M	80516	100-799	
MAIN ST	Fort Lupton	728L	80621	100-1399	
MAIN ST	Frederick	727F	80530	700-798	E
MAIN ST	Gilpin Co	740Z	80474	1-199	
MAIN ST	Hudson	730L	80642	800-1199	
MAIN ST	Jamestown	722A	80455	101-199	O
MAIN ST	Jefferson Co	823N	80433	26000-26899	
	Jefferson Co	823S	80433	26000-27199	
MAIN ST	Keenesburg	732A	80643	1-99	
MAIN ST	Longmont	41H	80501	100-899	
	Longmont	11V	80501	900-2499	
MAIN ST	Louisville	131S	80027	100-1699	
MAIN ST	Lyons	703C	80540	None	
MAIN ST	Platteville	708G	80651	1000-1999	
MAIN ST	Westminster	193B	80031	3800-4199	
	Westminster	192G	80020	11200-11698	E
MAIN ST N	Arapahoe Co	795U	80103	100-499	
MAIN ST N	Brighton	138K	80601	1-799	
MAIN ST S	Arapahoe Co	795Y	80103	100-399	
MAIN ST S	Aurora	350Z	80016	6100-6399	
MAIN ST S	Brighton	138S	80601	1-899	
MAIN ST S	Erie	132D	80516	2500-2799	
MAIN ST S	Longmont	41R	80501	1-1499	
MAIN ST W	Littleton	343V	80120	2100-2799	
MAIN RANGE TRAIL	Jefferson Co	371K	80127	10900-11499	
MAINSTREET	Parker	410N	80138	7100-8399	
	Parker	408R	80134	16200-16799	
	Parker	409P	80134	16800-19299	
	Parker	409P	80138	19300-20199	
MAINSTREET E	Douglas Co	408P	80134	None	
MAIZE CT	Parker	408V	80134	None	
MAIZE LN	Brighton	139L	80601	None	
MAJESTIC DR	Boulder Co	71F	80504	9500-9899	
MAJESTIC DR	Lafayette	132Q	80026	None	
MAJESTIC EAGLE DR	Jefferson Co	844C	80127	14200-14599	
MAJESTIC OAK WAY	Douglas Co	440Z	80134	None	
MAJESTIC PINE PL E	Parker	409Z	80134	None	
MAJESTIC PINE WAY S	Parker	409Z	80134	None	
MAJESTIC TRAIL	Castle Rock	466U	80109	None	
MAJESTIC VIEW DR	Boulder Co	130T	80303	201-499	O
MAJESTIC VIEW DR	Jefferson Co	367Z	80433	8600-8799	
MALACHITE CT	Douglas Co	408C	80134	9700-9799	
MALAMUTE DR	Jefferson Co	367J	80439	7500-7799	
MALAMUTE TRAIL	Jefferson Co	367J	80439	7600-7899	
MALAYA CT N	Denver	260S	80249	3900-3999	
MALAYA CT S	Arapahoe Co	350J	80015	4900-5099	
	Aurora	380E	80016	6900-7099	
	Centennial	350N	80015	5100-5299	
	Centennial	350S	80015	5800-5899	
MALAYA ST	Denver	260E	80249	None	
MALAYA ST N	Arapahoe Co	290J	80018	800-1099	
	Denver	260N	80249	3900-4199	
	Denver	260P	80249	4200-4799	
	Denver	260J	80249	4800-4899	
MALAYA ST S	Arapahoe Co	320W	80013	None	
	Centennial	350W	80016	6300-6499	
MALAYA WAY S	Arapahoe Co	350J	80015	4900-5999	
	Aurora	380E	80016	6900-7099	
	Centennial	350N	80015	5100-5399	
MALETA LN	Castle Rock	467U	80108	700-798	E
MALIBU ST	Castle Rock	497F	80109	200-399	
MALLARD AVE	Platteville	708G	80651	None	
MALLARD CIR	Longmont	41T	80504	2400-2499	
MALLARD CT	Boulder Co	129F	80303	1200-1299	
MALLARD CT	Highlands Ranch	375U	80126	8500-8599	
MALLARD CT	Mead	706C	80542	100-199	
MALLARD CT	Parker	408R	80134	11000-11099	
MALLARD CT	Platteville	708G	80651	None	
MALLARD DR	Highlands Ranch	375U	80126	3500-3999	
MALLARD DR	Superior	160R	80027	1800-1899	
MALLARD LN	Highlands Ranch	375U	80126	3800-3999	
MALLARD PL	Highlands Ranch	375U	80126	8500-8799	
MALLARD PL	Longmont	41T	80504	2100-2199	
MALLARD ST	Golden	279Q	80401	100-199	
MALLARD ST	Highlands Ranch	375U	80126	3600-3999	
MALLARD WAY	Highlands Ranch	375U	80126	None	
MALLARD POND DR	Boulder Co	129H	80303	700-899	
MALLARD POND WAY	Douglas Co	432L	80125	9500-9699	
MALLEY DR	Northglenn	194G	80233	100-1599	
MALLOW DR	Douglas Co	887F	80118	2500-2699	
MALMSBURY CT	El Paso Co	909S	80132	19000-19098	E
MALORY ST	Lafayette	132P	80026	900-1199	

L

M

STREET NAME	CITY or COUNTY	MAP GRID	ZIP CODE	BLOCK RANGE	O/E
MALTA CT S	*Arapahoe Co*	**350A**	80013	None	
	Aurora	**320W**	80013	None	
MALTA ST	*Denver*	**260E**	80249	None	
MALTA ST N	*Denver*	**260S**	80249	3800-3999	
	Denver	**260N**	80249	4000-4599	
MALTA ST S	*Arapahoe Co*	**350A**	80013	None	
	Arapahoe Co	**350E**	80013	None	
	Arapahoe Co	**350E**	80015	None	
	Arapahoe Co	**350J**	80015	None	
	Centennial	**350S**	80015	5500-5999	
MALTA WAY S	*Arapahoe Co*	**350J**	80015	4900-5099	
	Arapahoe Co	**350J**	80015	None	
	Centennial	**350N**	80015	5100-5399	
	Centennial	**350S**	80015	5900-5999	
MALTON CT	*Castle Rock*	**497U**	80104	1700-1999	
MALVERN CT	*Castle Pines North*	**436P**	80108	600-699	
MAMMOTH	*Weld Co*	**706N**	80504	3200-3399	
MAMMOTH CT	*Jefferson Co*	**306P**	80439	2000-2099	
MAMMOTH VIEW LN	*Central City*	**780D**	80403	None	
	Gilpin Co	**780D**	80403	1-99	
	Gilpin Co	**760X**	80452	None	
MANASSAS CT	*Elbert Co*	**832X**	80107	8300-8399	
MANCHESTER CT	*Castle Pines North*	**436P**	80108	7400-7499	
MANCHESTER DR E	*Castle Rock*	**498R**	80104	5300-5499	
MANDEL ST	*Federal Heights*	**223D**	80260	9000-9099	
	Federal Heights	**193Z**	80260	9100-9199	
MANDIE CIR	*Elbert Co*	**851V**	80107	None	
	Elbert Co	**851V**	80107	None	
MANET WAY	*Northglenn*	**194J**	80234	10900-11099	
MANGANO LN	*Douglas Co*	**409E**	80134	9800-9899	
MANGO DR	*Castle Rock*	**497Q**	80104	400-799	
MANHART ST	*Douglas Co*	**847N**	80135	4000-5499	
MANHATTAN CIR	*Boulder*	**128R**	80303	5200-5399	
MANHATTAN DR	*Boulder*	**128R**	80303	1-499	
	Boulder	**128M**	80303	500-699	
MANHATTAN PL	*Boulder*	**128M**	80303	600-699	
MANILA PL	*Boulder Co*	**70J**	80503	7700-7799	
MANILA RD	*Adams Co*	**752W**	80642	12000-15199	
	Adams Co	**772N**	80102	None	
	Adams Co	**792J**	80102	None	
MANILA RD	*Arapahoe Co*	**792W**	80102	1-799	
MANILA RD N	*Arapahoe Co*	**792S**	80102	1-1499	
MANILA RD S	*Arapahoe Co*	**812E**	80102	800-3399	
	Arapahoe Co	**812S**	80102	4300-5099	
MANITOBA DR	*Jefferson Co*	**366A**	80439	30800-31499	
MANITOU AVE	*Palmer Lake*	**907Q**	80133	None	
MANITOU RD E	*Douglas Co*	**870P**	80116	11200-11399	
MANITOU RD S	*Littleton*	**343P**	80123	5200-5499	
MANN CT	*Erie*	**103N**	80516	None	
MANN CREEK CT S	*Parker*	**439D**	80134	12500-12599	
MANN CREEK DR S	*Parker*	**439G**	80134	12500-12599	
MANNING DR	*Elbert Co*	**891T**	80106	22600-22999	
MANOR DR	*Cherry Hills Village*	**346J**	80111	6400-6499	
MANOR LN S	*Lakewood*	**312M**	80232	1800-1899	
MANOR WAY	*Brighton*	**138L**	80601	1400-1599	
MANORBRIER CIR	*Castle Rock*	**527B**	80104	3900-4399	
MANORBRIER CT	*Castle Rock*	**527C**	80104	4200-4399	
MANORBRIER LN	*Castle Rock*	**527B**	80104	None	
MANOR HOUSE RD	*Jefferson Co*	**370F**	80127	1-99	
MANORWOOD CT	*Louisville*	**160C**	80027	600-699	
MANORWOOD LN	*Louisville*	**160C**	80027	500-699	
MAN O' WAR TRAIL	*Jefferson Co*	**366M**	80439	27600-28199	
MANSFIELD AVE E	*Arapahoe Co*	**350A**	80013	20400-20699	
	Aurora	**348C**	80013	15800-15899	
	Aurora	**349A**	80013	16900-18599	
	Denver	**346A**	80237	5900-5999	
	Denver	**346B**	80237	6500-7599	
	Denver	**346C**	80237	8000-9299	
	Englewood	**344C**	80113	1-799	
MANSFIELD AVE W	*Denver*	**342D**	80235	5200-6799	
	Englewood	**344B**	80110	1-1399	
	Lakewood	**342B**	80235	7200-7599	
	Sheridan	**343D**	80110	2700-3099	
	Sheridan	**343B**	80236	3400-3599	
MANSFIELD CIR E	*Aurora*	**349A**	80013	16600-16899	
MANSFIELD DR E	*Arapahoe Co*	**350B**	80013	None	
	Aurora	**349C**	80013	19000-19199	
	Cherry Hills Village	**345D**	80110	3800-4799	
	Denver	**345D**	80222	4800-5599	
MANSFIELD PKWY W	*Lakewood*	**342B**	80235	7600-8099	
MANSFIELD PL E	*Arapahoe Co*	**350A**	80013	None	
	Arapahoe Co	**350B**	80013	None	
	Aurora	**350B**	80018	21700-21799	
MANSUR LN	*Jefferson Co*	**842A**	80470	33800-33999	
MANZANITA	*Jefferson Co*	**370F**	80127	1-99	
MAPLE	*Platteville*	**708B**	80651	None	
MAPLE AVE E	*Aurora*	**287U**	80012	11900-12099	
	Aurora	**291T**	80018	None	
	Denver	**284U**	80209	1-399	
	Denver	**286U**	80230	7300-7999	
MAPLE AVE W	*Denver*	**284U**	80223	1-199	
	Denver	**284S**	80223	1300-1599	
	Jefferson Co	**280Y**	80401	14000-14199	
	Jefferson Co	**280T**	80401	15000-15599	
MAPLE CIR	*Brighton*	**139S**	80601	3400-3599	
MAPLE CIR	*Broomfield*	**161R**	80020	1100-1199	
MAPLE CT	*Boulder*	**99E**	80301	4500-4599	
MAPLE CT	*Broomfield*	**161R**	80020	1100-1199	
MAPLE CT	*Greenwood Village*	**345U**	80121	5700-5799	
MAPLE CT	*Longmont*	**42N**	80501	None	
MAPLE CT W	*Louisville*	**130P**	80027	900-999	
MAPLE DR	*Broomfield*	**161V**	80020	1000-1199	
MAPLE DR	*Douglas Co*	**432F**	80125	8100-8199	
MAPLE DR	*Frederick*	**727F**	80530	1-399	
MAPLE DR	*Thornton*	**194W**	80260	None	
MAPLE DR E	*Aurora*	**291T**	80018	None	
MAPLE DR W	*Jefferson Co*	**280S**	80401	15500-15799	
	Lakewood	**282T**	80226	7200-7499	
MAPLE PL E	*Aurora*	**288T**	80012	14800-14999	
	Aurora	**288U**	80012	15200-15299	
	Aurora	**291S**	80018	None	
	Aurora	**291T**	80018	None	
	Denver	**286U**	80230	7200-7799	
MAPLE PL W	*Denver*	**283S**	80219	4800-4899	
	Jefferson Co	**280U**	80401	13800-13999	
	Lakewood	**280V**	80228	12900-12999	
MAPLE RD	*Boulder Co*	**162A**	80020	None	
MAPLE ST	*Frederick*	**727F**	80530	100-499	
MAPLE ST	*Golden*	**248Z**	80403	500-599	
	Golden	**278D**	80401	900-999	
	Golden	**279A**	80401	1100-1799	
	Jefferson Co	**280U**	80401	None	
MAPLE ST	*Longmont*	**41V**	80501	None	
MAPLE ST	*Weld Co*	**707T**	80504	7000-7499	
MAPLE ST E	*Elizabeth*	**871F**	80107	100-299	
MAPLE ST W	*Superior*	**160F**	80027	100-399	
MAPLE CREST DR	*Douglas Co*	**379S**	80134	16800-16899	
MAPLE HILLS AVE E	*Parker*	**410V**	80138	23400-23699	
MAPLEHURST DR	*Highlands Ranch*	**404L**	80126	400-599	
MAPLEHURST PT	*Highlands Ranch*	**404L**	80126	200-399	
MAPLE ROCK CT	*Douglas Co*	**408H**	80134	16300-16399	
MAPLES LN S	*Highlands Ranch*	**403H**	80129	10000-10099	
MAPLES PL W	*Highlands Ranch*	**403H**	80129	2000-2199	
MAPLETON AVE	*Boulder*	**97Y**	80304	302-1198	E
	Boulder	**98W**	80304	2000-2799	
	Boulder	**98X**	80301	2800-2999	
MAPLETON CIR	*Longmont*	**11J**	80503	2400-2499	
MAPLETON CT	*Castle Rock*	**499N**	80104	800-899	
MAPLETON CT	*Longmont*	**11N**	80503	2500-2599	
MAPLEWOOD AVE E	*Arapahoe Co*	**347W**	80111	9700-10099	
	Arapahoe Co	**347X**	80111	10500-11699	
	Arapahoe Co	**349X**	80016	17500-18499	
	Arapahoe Co	**349Y**	80016	19000-19799	
	Arapahoe Co	**350Y**	80015	22600-22699	
	Centennial	**344Y**	80121	300-499	
	Centennial	**344Z**	80121	800-899	
	Centennial	**344Z**	80121	1600-1799	
	Centennial	**345X**	80121	2400-3399	
	Centennial	**345Y**	80121	4400-4499	
	Centennial	**346W**	80111	5600-6499	
	Centennial	**346X**	80111	6900-7199	
	Centennial	**348X**	80111	14100-14199	
	Centennial	**349W**	80016	16700-16899	
	Centennial	**350X**	80015	None	
	Greenwood Village	**346Y**	80111	7900-8399	
	Greenwood Village	**347W**	80111	9100-9699	
	Greenwood Village	**347Y**	80111	11800-11899	
MAPLEWOOD AVE W	*Centennial*	**344W**	80121	1400-1699	
	Jefferson Co	**341Z**	80123	9100-9599	
	Jefferson Co	**341X**	80127	11300-11999	
	Littleton	**343Z**	80120	2000-2899	
	Littleton	**343W**	80123	4800-5199	
MAPLEWOOD CIR	*Longmont*	**11J**	80503	2400E-2499E	
MAPLEWOOD CIR E	*Arapahoe Co*	**347W**	80111	9500-9899	
	Arapahoe Co	**349X**	80016	17700-17899	
MAPLEWOOD CT E	*Centennial*	**344Z**	80121	1400-1599	
MAPLEWOOD DR	*Erie*	**102P**	80516	100-499	
MAPLEWOOD DR	*Highlands Ranch*	**375S**	80126	8600-8899	
MAPLEWOOD DR E	*Arapahoe Co*	**347X**	80111	10500-10999	
	Arapahoe Co	**348Z**	80016	15900-16099	
	Arapahoe Co	**349W**	80016	16800-17499	
	Arapahoe Co	**349X**	80016	17900-18499	
	Arapahoe Co	**812Z**	80102	44700-45599	
	Centennial	**344Y**	80121	300-599	
	Centennial	**345Z**	80121	4900-5299	
	Centennial	**348X**	80016	14800-15099	
MAPLEWOOD DR W	*Jefferson Co*	**342Z**	80123	5500-6399	
	Jefferson Co	**342W**	80123	8700-8999	
	Jefferson Co	**341Z**	80123	9000-9299	
	Jefferson Co	**341Y**	80127	10500-10599	
	Jefferson Co	**341X**	80127	11300-11499	
MAPLEWOOD LN	*Parker*	**410S**	80138	11500-11599	
MAPLEWOOD LN E	*Arapahoe Co*	**350T**	80015	22300-22799	
	Centennial	**349Z**	80016	20000-20199	
	Centennial	**350W**	80016	20500-20799	
MAPLEWOOD PL	*Centennial*	**345Z**	80121	4900-4999	
MAPLEWOOD PL E	*Arapahoe Co*	**347X**	80111	10700-11299	
	Arapahoe Co	**348Z**	80016	16100-16399	
	Arapahoe Co	**349Y**	80016	19100-19499	
	Arapahoe Co	**350Y**	80015	22400-22499	
	Arapahoe Co	**349W**	80016	None	
	Centennial	**345Y**	80121	4000-4099	
	Centennial	**345Z**	80121	5200-5299	
	Centennial	**346X**	80111	7000-7299	
	Centennial	**348W**	80111	13900-14099	
	Centennial	**348X**	80016	14800-14899	
	Centennial	**349Z**	80016	19600-20399	
	Centennial	**350W**	80016	20500-20799	
MAPLEWOOD PL E	*Aurora*	**351X**	80016	None	
MAPLEWOOD PL W	*Jefferson Co*	**342Z**	80123	5500-5699	
	Jefferson Co	**342Y**	80123	6100-6399	
	Jefferson Co	**341Z**	80123	9300-9599	
MAPLEWOOD WAY E	*Centennial*	**345Y**	80121	4200-4599	
MARATHON RD	*Boulder Co*	**70M**	80503	8800-8999	
MARAUDER DR	*Jefferson Co*	**822Q**	80433	9400-9799	
MARBLE CIR	*Golden*	**279Q**	80401	1-299	
MARBLE CT	*Boulder Co*	**130F**	80303	1000-1099	
MARBLE CT	*Broomfield*	**162P**	80020	1300-1399	
MARBLE CT	*Castle Rock*	**467M**	80108	2000-2199	
MARBLE LN	*Castle Rock*	**467M**	80108	6200-6699	
MARBLE LN	*Park Co*	**841S**	80421	1-199	
MARBLE LN	*Superior*	**160U**	80027	2700-3099	
MARBLE ST	*Broomfield*	**162W**	80020	300-599	
	Broomfield	**162S**	80020	600-999	
MARBLEHEAD PL	*Castle Rock*	**496F**	80109	4000-4299	
MARBLE MILL PL	*Frederick*	**726G**	80516	None	
MARCH CT	*Erie*	**132A**	80026	1900-1999	
MARCH DR	*Denver*	**258F**	80239	14500-14799	
	Denver	**259H**	80249	None	
MARCH PL	*Denver*	**258G**	80239	15300-15499	
MARCHANT ST	*Black Hawk*	**780D**	80422	100-199	
MARCLIFF RD	*Jefferson Co*	**823S**	80433	10700-11099	
MARCOTT ST	*Parker*	**409J**	80134	10700-10799	
MARCUS LN	*Castle Pines North*	**436F**	80108	1-99	
MARFAK DR	*El Paso Co*	**908N**	80132	19400-19499	
MARFELL CT	*Erie*	**102T**	80516	2000-2099	
MARFELL ST	*Erie*	**102T**	80516	800-999	
MARGARET DR	*Elbert Co*	**851K**	80107	40000-40399	
MARGE CT	*Elbert Co*	**851E**	80138	2000-2299	
MARGE LN	*Jefferson Co*	**336X**	80439	30100-30299	
MARGIE LN N	*Douglas Co*	**496J**	80109	200-599	
MARGUERITE PKWY S	*Aurora*	**348G**	80014	4000-4299	
MARIA CIR	*Broomfield*	**163T**	80020	12400-12599	
MARIA ST	*Westminster*	**223K**	80030	7800-7999	
MARIAH TRAIL	*El Paso Co*	**909R**	80908	19100-19999	
MARIBOU CT	*Highlands Ranch*	**376X**	80130	9100-9299	
MARICOPA RD	*Jefferson Co*	**338J**	80454	23000-23299	
MARIE LN	*Jefferson Co*	**336X**	80439	30200-30499	
MARIE RD	*Jefferson Co*	**842A**	80470	33700-33999	
MARIGOLD CT	*Greenwood Village*	**345U**	80121	5500-5599	
MARIGOLD CT	*Highlands Ranch*	**404L**	80126	10400-10499	
MARIGOLD CT	*Lafayette*	**131R**	80026	1300-1399	
MARIGOLD DR	*Adams Co*	**224E**	80221	1-1599	
MARIGOLD DR	*Lafayette*	**131R**	80026	1400-1499	
MARIGOLD LN	*Littleton*	**343S**	80123	4400-4499	
MARILYNN JEAN DR	*Arvada*	**252B**	80004	7600-7699	
MARIN CT	*Lone Tree*	**406G**	80124	7600-7699	
MARIN DR	*Greenwood Village*	**346U**	80111	None	
MARINA DR E	*Aurora*	**318W**	80014	13100-14499	
MARINE ST	*Boulder*	**127C**	80302	400-1299	
	Boulder	**127D**	80302	1400-1899	
	Boulder	**128B**	80303	2800-3799	
MARINER DR	*Longmont*	**10R**	80503	2200-2299	
MARINER LN	*Longmont*	**10R**	80503	3200-3299	
MARION	*Platteville*	**708B**	80651	None	
MARION AVE	*Platteville*	**708C**	80651	300-699	
MARION CIR	*Adams Co*	**224M**	80229	7900-7999	
MARION CIR S	*Arapahoe Co*	**374R**	80122	7900-8199	
	Arapahoe Co	**374D**	80122	6700E-6899E	
	Denver	**314V**	80210	2700-2799	
MARION CT	*Adams Co*	**224M**	80229	7900-7999	
MARION CT S	*Arapahoe Co*	**374R**	80122	7900-8199	
MARION DR	*Adams Co*	**254D**	80216	5800-5999	
MARION DR	*Clear Creek Co*	**801R**	80439	1-299	
MARION DR	*Thornton*	**164M**	80241	13400-13599	
MARION PKWY S	*Denver*	**284Z**	80209	100-699	
MARION PL S	*Centennial*	**344Z**	80121	6300-6499	
MARION ST	*Adams Co*	**254H**	80216	5400-5599	
	Denver	**284M**	80218	100-1999	
	Denver	**284D**	80205	2000-2799	
	Denver	**254Z**	80205	2800-3799	
	Denver	**254M**	80216	4601-4799	O
	Northglenn	**194R**	80233	10400-10599	
	Northglenn	**194H**	80233	11200-11399	
	Northglenn	**194D**	80233	11400-11699	
MARION ST	*Park Co*	**820Y**	80421	1-599	
MARION ST	*Thornton*	**194V**	80229	9900-9999	
	Thornton	**194R**	80229	10100-10399	
	Thornton	**164R**	80241	13000-13099	
	Thornton	**164R**	80241	13300-13399	
	Thornton	**164M**	80241	13400-13499	
	Thornton	**134M**	80602	16400-16599	
MARION ST S	*Arapahoe Co*	**374D**	80121	6400-6699	
	Arapahoe Co	**374M**	80122	7300-7499	
	Denver	**314R**	80210	1300-2699	
	Englewood	**314Z**	80113	2900-3599	
MARION WAY	*Northglenn*	**194R**	80233	10400-10599	
	Thornton	**194V**	80229	1300-9699	
MARION WAY S	*Arapahoe Co*	**374R**	80122	8200-8299	
	Centennial	**344Z**	80121	6100-6299	
MARIPOSA AVE	*Boulder*	**127M**	80302	1200-1599	
	Boulder	**128J**	80302	1600-2299	
MARIPOSA CT	*Adams Co*	**134W**	80020	14800-14899	
	Westminster	**164S**	80234	12400-12499	
	Westminster	**164N**	80234	13300-13399	
	Westminster	**164A**	80020	14600-14799	
MARIPOSA DR	*Adams Co*	**224J**	80221	1200-1499	
	Jefferson Co	**368V**	80465	8200-8699	
MARIPOSA RD	*Douglas Co*	**527W**	80104	4200-4799	
MARIPOSA RD	*Jefferson Co*	**336M**	80439	27800-28299	
MARIPOSA ST	*Adams Co*	**224S**	80221	6800-6999	
	Adams Co	**224N**	80221	7100-7299	
	Adams Co	**134S**	80020	None	
	Adams Co	**224J**	80221	None	
	Denver	**284S**	80223	100-299	
	Denver	**284N**	80204	600-1499	
	Denver	**254S**	80211	3300-3999	
	Denver	**254N**	80211	4200-4399	
	Federal Heights	**224E**	80260	8400-8499	
	Thornton	**224A**	80260	8600-8799	
	Westminster	**164W**	80234	12000-12199	
	Westminster	**164N**	80234	13200-13399	
	Westminster	**164E**	80020	None	
MARIPOSA ST S	*Denver*	**314E**	80223	1100-1499	
	Englewood	**344A**	80110	3900-3999	
	Englewood	**344J**	80110	4600-4799	
MARIPOSA WAY	*Denver*	**254N**	80211	4400-4599	
MARIPOSA WAY S	*Denver*	**314A**	80223	700-799	
MARKET ST	*Denver*	**284B**	80202	1400-1999	
	Denver	**284B**	80205	2000-2299	
MARKET ST	*Douglas Co*	**408D**	80134	None	
MARKET ST	*Keenesburg*	**732A**	80643	7000-7499	
MARKET ST	*Morrison*	**309Z**	80465	100-199	
MARK'S DR	*Jefferson Co*	**822X**	80433	11000-11499	
MARKS LN	*Park Co*	**840D**	80421	1-199	
MARLBOROUGH DR S	*Parker*	**410S**	80138	11400-11499	
MARLIN CT	*Elbert Co*	**851W**	80107	36600-36899	
MARLIN DR	*Longmont*	**10R**	80503	3100-3199	
MARLIN WAY	*Douglas Co*	**867P**	80109	2000-2799	
MARLOWE AVE W	*Jefferson Co*	**341K**	80127	10200-11599	
	Jefferson Co	**341J**	80465	11600-11999	
	Jefferson Co	**340M**	80465	12800-13399	
	Jefferson Co	**340L**	80465	13500-13999	
MARLOWE DR W	*Jefferson Co*	**341L**	80127	10600-10799	
	Jefferson Co	**341J**	80465	11700-11899	
MARLOWE PL W	*Jefferson Co*	**341L**	80127	10100-10799	
	Jefferson Co	**341K**	80465	11600-11899	
MARMOT CT	*Longmont*	**12X**	80501	900-1099	
MARMOT DR	*Elbert Co*	**911B**	80106	21000-21799	
MARMOT LN	*Jefferson Co*	**306K**	80439	1600-1699	
MARMOT PT	*Lafayette*	**131Z**	80026	300-399	
MARMOT RIDGE CIR	*Douglas Co*	**432Q**	80125	9500-9899	
MARMOT RIDGE PL	*Douglas Co*	**432R**	80125	7200-7399	
MAROON	*Thornton*	**193V**	80260	None	
MAROON CIR	*Broomfield*	**163J**	80020	4400-4599	
MAROON CIR S	*Douglas Co*	**407B**	80112	9500-9799	
MAROON PEAK	*Jefferson Co*	**371K**	80127	7700-7799	
MAROON PEAK DR	*Superior*	**160Y**	80027	800-999	
MAROON PEAK PL	*Douglas Co*	**436U**	80108	6100-6199	
MARQUETTE DR W	*Denver*	**342D**	80235	5700-5899	
MARQUIS CT	*Dacono*	**727J**	80514	400-599	
MARRY AVE	*Weld Co*	**728X**	80621	1600-1999	
MARS CT	*Highlands Ranch*	**376U**	80124	500-599	
MARSHALL CIR	*Arvada*	**222L**	80003	7900-8099	

M

STREET NAME	CITY or COUNTY	MAP GRID	ZIP CODE	BLOCK RANGE	O/E
MARSHALL CIR S	Lakewood	312L	80232	1800-1899	
MARSHALL CT	Arvada	222L	80003	8000-8099	
	Arvada	222G	80003	8200-8499	
	Arvada	252G	80002	None	
MARSHALL CT	Erie	102P	80516	2300-2499	
MARSHALL CT	Lakewood	282Q	80226	500-599	
	Westminster	222Q	80003	7200-7299	
	Westminster	222C	80031	8800-9099	
	Westminster	192G	80020	11300-11399	
	Westminster	192C	80020	11500-11599	
	Wheat Ridge	252Y	80214	2900-2999	
MARSHALL CT S	Jefferson Co	342Y	80123	6100-6299	
	Jefferson Co	372C	80123	6500-6699	
	Jefferson Co	372R	80128	7600-7899	
	Jefferson Co	372Q	80128	7900-8299	
	Lakewood	312G	80232	1200-1399	
	Lakewood	312L	80232	1600-1699	
	Lakewood	342U	80123	5700-5799	
MARSHALL DR	Boulder	159C	80303	5600-7299	
	Boulder Co	743R	80305	5200-5599	
MARSHALL DR S	Jefferson Co	342Y	80123	6000-6099	
MARSHALL LN	Jefferson Co	336Q	80439	28900-29099	
MARSHALL PL	Longmont	42A	80501	1-199	
MARSHALL PL	Westminster	192Y	80031	9100-9199	
MARSHALL RD	Boulder Co	743R	80305	700-5599	
MARSHALL RD	Douglas Co	887H	80118	7100-7399	
MARSHALL RD	Superior	160F	80027	300-7599	
MARSHALL ST	Arvada	252L	80002	5000-5699	
	Arvada	252C	80003	6000-6199	
	Arvada	222Y	80003	6400-6799	
	Arvada	222U	80003	6800-7199	
	Arvada	222Q	80003	7400-7599	
	Arvada	222L	80003	7600-7999	
MARSHALL ST	Boulder	127G	80302	1200-1399	
MARSHALL ST	Edgewater	282C	80214	2000-2599	
	Lakewood	282U	80226	1-299	
	Lakewood	282L	80214	1000-1399	
	Westminster	192G	80020	11000-11499	
	Westminster	192C	80020	11500-11599	
	Wheat Ridge	282C	80214	2600-2799	
	Wheat Ridge	252Y	80033	3200-3499	
	Wheat Ridge	252U	80033	3500-4399	
	Wheat Ridge	252Q	80033	4400-4799	
	Wheat Ridge	252L	80033	4800-4999	
MARSHALL ST S	Denver	312U	80227	2700-2799	
	Denver	312Y	80227	3200-3299	
	Denver	342U	80123	5500-5699	
	Denver	342Q	80123	6300-6499	
	Jefferson Co	372C	80128	6700-6899	
	Jefferson Co	372G	80128	6900-7299	
	Jefferson Co	372L	80128	7700-7899	
	Jefferson Co	372Q	80128	7900-8299	
	Lakewood	282U	80226	1-99	
	Lakewood	282Y	80226	300-699	
	Lakewood	312C	80226	700-1099	
	Lakewood	312G	80232	1100-1599	
MARSHALL WAY	Westminster	192U	80021	9700-9899	
MARSHALL WAY S	Denver	342C	80235	3600-3699	
MARSH HAWK CIR	Castle Rock	497A	80109	1600-1799	
MARSH HAWK LN	Jefferson Co	370B	80127	1-99	
MARSHMERRY LN	Jefferson Co	367A	80439	6500-6899	
MARSTON PL W	Sheridan	343C	80110	3000-3099	
MARSTON TRAIL	Golden	279N	80401	800-899	
MARTI CIR	Longmont	42M	80501	1901-1999	O
MARTIN DR	Boulder	128K	80305	200-3799	
	Boulder	128P	80305	3800-4599	
MARTIN DR	Clear Creek Co	304Q	80439	1-199	
MARTIN LN	Cherry Hills Village	344D	80113	1-99	
MARTIN LN	Jefferson Co	365N	80433	8300-8999	
MARTIN LN N	Douglas Co	496J	80109	200-599	
MARTIN RD	Jefferson Co	842A	80470	33700-33999	
MARTIN RD	Longmont	12W	80501	900-1299	
MARTIN ST	Longmont	42A	80501	100-899	
	Longmont	12W	80501	1300-1499	
	Longmont	42J	80501	None	
MARTIN ST	Weld Co	729R	80603	3000-4399	
MARTIN ST S	Longmont	42E	80501	1-199	
	Longmont	42N	80501	None	
MARTINDALE DR	Denver	314U	80210	600-699	
MARTINEZ PL	Longmont	12N	80501	1-99	
MARTINGALE DR	Parker	408M	80134	16100-16799	
MARTINGALE LN	Parker	410W	80138	21200-21399	
MARTINGALE RD	El Paso Co	908U	80132	17500-18399	
MARTINIQUE AVE	Boulder	98K	80301	3100-3799	
MARTIN LUTHER KING BLVD	Denver	254Z	80205	1200-1799	
	Denver	255X	80205	1800-3999	
	Denver	255Y	80207	4000-5599	
	Denver	256W	80207	5600-7299	
	Denver	256X	80207	7300-7699	
	Denver	257W	80238	7700-10099	
MARTZ RD	Castle Rock	496A	80109	None	
MAR VISTA PL	Denver	286X	80224	6500-6599	
MARY AVE	Weld Co	729A	80621	1600-16599	
MARY CT	Castle Pines North	436U	80108	6700-6799	
MARY DR	Jefferson Co	822Y	80433	29100-30499	
MARY LN	Boulder	97H	80304	None	
MARY LN	Jefferson Co	822Y	80433	30300-30499	
MARY BETH RD	Clear Creek Co	801R	80439	1-699	
MARY CLARKE PL	Douglas Co	410M	80138	9000-9199	
MARYLAND AVE W	Jefferson Co	311F	80232	10900-10999	
	Lakewood	312F	80232	7300-7399	
MARYLAND DR W	Lakewood	311H	80232	9500-10199	
	Lakewood	311F	80228	12000-12299	
	Lakewood	311E	80228	12400-12499	
MARYLAND PL W	Lakewood	311H	80232	9100-9399	
	Lakewood	311E	80228	12500-12599	
MARYS LN	Park Co	840D	80421	1-299	
MARY'S TRAIL	Jefferson Co	822Z	80433	11300-11399	
MASEARO LN	Erie	103N	80516	None	
MASEY ST	Adams Co	224S	80221	7000-7299	
MASHIE CIR	Castle Rock	496C	80109	None	
MASON CIR	Adams Co	223F	80031	8300-8599	
MASON ST	Erie	103S	80516	None	
MASONVILLE DR	Parker	409J	80134	11600-11699	
MASSEY CIR W	Jefferson Co	372S	80128	8000-8099	
MASSEY DR W	Jefferson Co	372S	80128	7600-8399	
MASSIVE RD	Thornton	194S	80260	None	
MASSIVE PEAK CIR	Douglas Co	436U	80108	6100-6199	

STREET NAME	CITY or COUNTY	MAP GRID	ZIP CODE	BLOCK RANGE	O/E
MASSIVE PEAK LOOP	Douglas Co	436U	80108	6100-6199	
MAST RD	Boulder Co	99G	80301	4400-4499	
MASTERS CT	Castle Rock	497X	80104	2900-2999	
MASTERS CT	Superior	160Q	80027	1500-1699	
MASTERS DR	Castle Rock	497X	80104	200-299	
MASTERS LN	Castle Rock	497X	80104	2800-2899	
MASTERS CLUB CIR	Castle Rock	497X	80104	2800-2999	
MASTERS POINT DR	Castle Rock	497X	80104	3000-3299	
MASTHEAD WAY	El Paso Co	908T	80132	1300-1499	
MATCHLESS ST	Louisville	130R	80027	200-399	
MATHER CIR	Brighton	138T	80601	100-199	
MATHER ST	Brighton	138T	80601	200-799	
	Brighton	138R	80601	2500-2699	
MATHEWS AVE	Weld Co	729X	80621	2000-2999	
MATHEWS CIR	Erie	102U	80516	500-799	
MATHEWS WAY	Erie	102U	80516	None	
MATSUNO ST	Brighton	139K	80601	None	
MATT DILLON CIR	Elbert Co	891X	80106	None	
MATTERHORN DR	Jefferson Co	338E	80454	23700-24399	
MATTERHORN RD	Jefferson Co	365N	80439	7700-7799	
MATTHEW LN S	Highlands Ranch	406E	80130	10000-10099	
MATTIVE PL	Brighton	138V	80601	2200-2299	
MAUFF CT	Jefferson Co	822Y	80433	30400-30499	
MAUFF WAY	Jefferson Co	822Y	80433	12000-12099	
MAVERICK CT	Castle Rock	467U	80104	3800-3999	
MAVERICK WAY	El Paso Co	908V	80132	400-18499	
MAXIMUS DR	Highlands Ranch	376U	80124	1-9099	
MAXINE CT	Jefferson Co	823V	80465	10400-10499	
MAXINE LN W	Douglas Co	496J	80109	1600-2099	
MAXWELL AVE	Boulder	97Y	80304	200-1199	
MAXWELL DR	Jefferson Co	823V	80465	19600-20399	
MAXWELL PL	Denver	258E	80239	13100-16399	
	Denver	258H	80239	None	
	Denver	260E	80249	None	
MAXWELL ST	Erie	103N	80516	None	
MAXWELL HILL RD S	Jefferson Co	824Y	80127	11500-12799	
MAY CT	Jefferson Co	337W	80439	5900-6099	
MAYA PL	Boulder Co	98P	80301	2800-2899	
MAYBERRY DR	Highlands Ranch	404A	80129	None	
MAY CHERRY	Jefferson Co	370Q	80127	1-99	
MAYEDA CT	Brighton	139K	80601	None	
MAYEDA ST	Brighton	139K	80601	None	
MAYFAIR ST	Douglas Co	407D	80112	9700-9899	
MAYFAIR WAY	Douglas Co	407D	80112	12800-12899	
MAYFIELD CIR	Longmont	41P	80501	1400-1499	
MAYFIELD CT	Douglas Co	439R	80134	7100-7199	
MAYFIELD LN	Longmont	41T	80501	1500-1599	
MAY LONG CT	Jefferson Co	842F	80470	13600-13899	
MAYWOOD CT N	Adams Co	750R	80603	14400-14799	
MAZZINI ST	Erie	103N	80516	400-599	
McAFEE CIR	Erie	103P	80516	100-299	
McAFEE CT	Erie	103P	80516	600-799	
McARTHUR DR W	Douglas Co	406P	80124	1-1499	
McARTHUR RANCH RD	Douglas Co	406J	80124	1700-5899	
	Highlands Ranch	405L	80130	None	
McCALL DR	Boulder Co	704F	80503	6500-6799	
McCALL PL	Longmont	12N	80501	1900-2099	
McCART RANCH CIR	Elbert Co	871Q	80107	5200-5999	
McCASLIN BLVD	Louisville	130X	80027	1-599	
	Superior	160X	80027	None	
McCELLA CT	Broomfield	163T	80020	12400-12599	
	Westminster	223K	80030	7800-7899	
McCLELLAN RD	Parker	408R	80134	10800-10998	E
McCLURE AVE	Firestone	727B	80504	None	
McCLURE CT	Erie	102U	80516	600-799	
McCLURE DR	Erie	131D	80026	None	
McCLURE DR	Longmont	12Y	80501	1300-1399	
McCLURE LN	Douglas Co	466L	80108	5000-5099	
McCLURE WAY	Erie	102U	80516	None	
McCONNELL CT	Lyons	703C	80540	None	
McCONNELL DR	Lyons	703C	80540	None	
McCOY PL	Adams Co	223B	80031	8900-8999	
McCRACKEN LN	Castle Rock	497U	80104	None	
McCRUMB DR	Northglenn	194D	80233	11800-11999	
McCUNE RD	El Paso Co	911X	80106	12100-14399	
McDATA PKWY	Broomfield	191J	80021	1-99	
McDONALD CT	Erie	102Q	80516	100-299	
McDONNELL ST N	Arapahoe Co	795Y	80103	100-199	
McDONNELL ST S	Arapahoe Co	795Y	80103	200-599	
McDOUGAL RD	Park Co	820Y	80421	1-399	
McDOUGAL ST	Adams Co	225A	80229	1900-8699	
McDUFFEE CT	Denver	254X	80216	2200-2299	
McELWAIN BLVD	Adams Co	225E	80229	2000-8599	
	Adams Co	224D	80229	8600-8799	
McFARLAND DR	Denver	254R	80216	None	
McFARLANE DR	Jefferson Co	823P	80433	9400-9499	
McGILL CT E	Douglas Co	440V	80134	9300-9499	
McGREGOR CIR	Erie	102L	80516	100-1499	
McINTIRE ST	Boulder	128H	80303	800-999	
McINTOSH AVE	Broomfield	162Z	80020	900-1499	
McINTOSH DR	Longmont	10V	80503	2900-3099	
McINTYRE CIR	Jefferson Co	280S	80401	1-199	
McINTYRE CT	Arvada	220X	80403	6200-6299	
	Arvada	220W	80007	6400-6599	
	Arvada	220S	80007	7100-7199	
	Jefferson Co	280S	80401	1-99	
	Jefferson Co	220J	80007	7600-7899	
	Jefferson Co	250A	80403	1-299	
McINTYRE PKWY	Arvada	220X	80403	6000-6398	E
McINTYRE ST	Arvada	220W	80007	None	
	Golden	280N	80401	400-599	
	Jefferson Co	280J	80401	600-1099	
	Jefferson Co	250W	80401	3200-4199	
	Jefferson Co	250J	80403	4200-5999	
	Jefferson Co	220N	80007	7200-7399	
McINTYRE ST S	Lakewood	310N	80228	2200-2699	
	Lakewood	310X	80228	3300-3399	
McINTYRE WAY	Arvada	220X	80403	6200-6399	
McINTYRE WAY S	Jefferson Co	280S	80401	1-199	
	Jefferson Co	280W	80401	200-299	
McIVER CIR	Jefferson Co	823N	80433	25700-26199	
McKAY RD	Adams Co	196S	80640	None	
McKAY LANDING PKWY	Broomfield	163G	80020	2400-2698	E
McKAY PARK CIR	Broomfield	163C	80020	14000-14098	E
McKAY PARK DR	Broomfield	163G	80020	None	
McKEEVER ARENA RD	Jefferson Co	823Y	80433	None	
McKENZIE CT	Broomfield	163T	80020	12500-12599	
McKINLEY AVE	Fort Lupton	728L	80621	100-1199	

STREET NAME	CITY or COUNTY	MAP GRID	ZIP CODE	BLOCK RANGE	O/E
McKINLEY AVE	Louisville	130V	80027	600-999	
	Louisville	130M	80027	2300-2499	
McKINLEY AVE S	Fort Lupton	728L	80621	100-999	
McKINLEY CT	Louisville	131W	80027	300-399	
McKINLEY DR	Bennett	793J	80102	100-299	
McKINLEY DR	Boulder	128D	80303	4700-4899	
McKINLEY PL	Louisville	131N	80027	1400-1499	
McKINLEY PARK LN	Louisville	130V	80027	200-399	
McKINNEY RD	Jefferson Co	824T	80127	9900-10399	
McKISSIC AVE	Frederick	727F	80530	7901-7999	O
McLEAN CT	Castle Rock	466W	80109	None	
McMURDO GULCH CT	Douglas Co	469G	80134	6400-6499	
McSHANE CT E	Douglas Co	440V	80134	9300-9499	
McSHANE DR	El Paso Co	908S	80132	2700-2899	
McSHANE PL	Monument	908W	80132	100-499	
McSORLEY LN	Boulder Co	129F	80303	5900-5999	
MEACHUM WAY	Erie	102U	80516	1500-1699	
MEAD CT	Louisville	131W	80027	600-699	
MEAD CT	Mead	706D	80504	14400-14499	
MEAD DR	Boulder Co	100Z	80301	2000-2299	
MEAD ST	Louisville	131W	80027	700-799	
MEAD ST	Mead	706H	80504	14000-14399	
MEAD WAY N	Douglas Co	403B	80125	12200-12499	
MEADE CIR	Westminster	193T	80031	9700-9899	
MEADE CT	Adams Co	223X	80003	6500-6599	
MEADE CT	Adams Co	223B	80031	None	
MEADE CT	Broomfield	163T	80020	12500-12599	
	Westminster	193T	80031	9600-9699	
	Westminster	193P	80031	10000-10299	
	Westminster	193K	80031	10900-11099	
	Westminster	193F	80031	11000-11099	
	Westminster	193B	80031	None	
MEADE LN	Cherry Hills Village	345E	80113	1-199	
MEADE LOOP	Westminster	193P	80031	10300-10399	
MEADE ST	Adams Co	253F	80221	5200-5499	
	Adams Co	223B	80031	None	
	Broomfield	163T	80020	12600-12799	
	Denver	283T	80219	1-399	
	Denver	283K	80204	400-1999	
	Denver	283B	80211	2000-2699	
	Denver	253X	80211	2700-4099	
	Denver	253P	80211	4400-4799	
	Denver	253K	80221	4800-5199	
	Westminster	223P	80030	7200-7299	
	Westminster	223K	80030	7600-7899	
	Westminster	223K	80030	7900-7999	
	Westminster	223K	80031	8000-8199	
	Westminster	193X	80031	9100-9499	
	Westminster	193T	80031	9500-9699	
	Westminster	193B	80031	None	
MEADE ST S	Denver	283T	80219	1-699	
	Denver	313B	80219	900-1099	
	Denver	313K	80219	1300-2699	
	Denver	313T	80236	2700-3099	
	Denver	343P	80123	4700-5099	
	Littleton	343P	80123	5100-5299	
MEADE WAY	Westminster	223P	80030	7500-7599	
	Westminster	193K	80031	10900-10999	
MEADOW AVE	Boulder	97R	80304	1200-1399	
	Boulder	98N	80304	1900-2599	
MEADOW AVE	Broomfield	163U	80020	3100-3399	
MEADOW CT	Boulder Co	100E	80301	7300-7399	
MEADOW CT	Longmont	11R	80501	2100-2299	
MEADOW CT	Louisville	130U	80027	1000-1099	
MEADOW CT S	Boulder Co	100E	80301	7300-7399	
MEADOW DR	Elizabeth	871F	80107	300-399	
MEADOW DR	Jefferson Co	338X	80465	5800-6099	
	Jefferson Co	823W	80433	11700-11899	
	Jefferson Co	336H	80439	27800-28799	
MEADOW DR	Longmont	11R	80501	1900-2099	
MEADOW DR	Park Co	841D	80470	1-299	
	Park Co	841J	80421	300-899	
	Park Co	841R	80421	900-2399	
MEADOW DR S	Boulder Co	100E	80301	4300-4599	
MEADOW DR W	Jefferson Co	372S	80128	7600-8399	
MEADOW LN	Boulder Co	70G	80503	7200-7299	
MEADOW LN	Brighton	139M	80601	None	
MEADOW LN	Cherry Hills Village	345F	80113	1-99	
MEADOW LN	Clear Creek Co	304Y	80439	1-199	
MEADOW LN	Elbert Co	871J	80107	33300-33499	
MEADOW LN	Jefferson Co	335R	80439	31700-31899	
	Jefferson Co	366D	80439	None	
MEADOW LN	Longmont	12N	80501	1800-1899	
MEADOW LN	Palmer Lake	908S	80133	600-799	
MEADOW LN	Park Co	840C	80421	1-299	
MEADOW LN	Weld Co	729R	80603	3000-3999	
MEADOW LN E	Douglas Co	467E	80108	800-999	
MEADOW PL	Boulder	97R	80304	None	
MEADOW ST	Longmont	12W	80501	1100-1299	
	Longmont	12N	80501	1700-1899	
	Longmont	12J	80501	2100-2499	
MEADOW WAY	Gilpin Co	761E	80403	1-299	
MEADOWBRIAR LN	Highlands Ranch	405L	80126	10000-10299	
MEADOWBRIDGE WAY	Parker	409Y	80134	12400-12699	
MEADOWBROOK CIR	Elbert Co	830Z	80138	43100-43399	
MEADOWBROOK CIR	Littleton	374F	80120	1-99	
MEADOWBROOK CT	Broomfield	162M	80020	13700-13799	
MEADOWBROOK DR	Adams Co	223M	80221	2100-2799	
MEADOWBROOK DR	Boulder	128L	80303	600-699	
MEADOWBROOK DR	Broomfield	162M	80020	13800-13999	
	Jefferson Co	340T	80465	5800-6199	
MEADOWBROOK LN	Douglas Co	866B	80135	6300-7199	
MEADOWBROOK LN	El Paso Co	908U	80132	300-399	
MEADOWBROOK LN S	Jefferson Co	335K	80439	4200-4399	
MEADOWBROOK PL	Dacono	726V	80514	None	
MEADOWBROOK PL	Littleton	374F	80120	1-99	
MEADOWBROOK RD	Littleton	374E	80120	1-99	
MEADOWBROOK RD W	Littleton	374E	80120	1500-1599	
MEADOW CREEK CT	Highlands Ranch	375T	80126	3500-3599	
MEADOW CREEK DR	Highlands Ranch	375T	80126	8500-8799	
MEADOW CREEK PL	Highlands Ranch	375T	80126	3300-3599	
MEADOW CREEK RD	Lakewood	282Q	80214	600-1099	
MEADOW CREEK WAY					
	Highlands Ranch	375T	80126	3400-3499	
MEADOWCROSS LN	Boulder Co	98D	80301	4700-4899	
MEADOWDALE CT	Boulder Co	70F	80503	8100-8199	
MEADOWDALE DR	Boulder Co	70K	80503	7200-7399	
MEADOWDALE SQUARE	Boulder Co	70K	80503	8000-8199	

M

STREET NAME	CITY or COUNTY	MAP GRID	ZIP CODE	BLOCK RANGE	O/E
MEADOWGATE LN	Douglas Co	409D	80138	7100-7299	
MEADOW GLEN DR	Boulder	129E	80303	700-1099	
MEADOW GLEN LN	Douglas Co	867N	80135	3400-3499	
MEADOW GREEN CIR	Douglas Co	470Z	80116	2100-2399	
MEADOW HILL CIR	Lone Tree	406D	80124	8900-9099	
MEADOW HILL LN	Elbert Co	871M	80107	33300-33599	
MEADOWLAKE DR	Gilpin Co	761F	80403	1-1099	
MEADOW LAKE RD	Boulder Co	70P	80503	7300-8199	
MEADOW LAKE WAY	El Paso Co	908T	80132	1200-1499	
MEADOWLAND CT	Boulder Co	741M	80466	1-199	
MEADOWLARK AVE	Fort Lupton	729E	80621	None	
MEADOWLARK CIR	Highlands Ranch	374V	80126	8600-8799	
MEADOWLARK CIR	Lochbuie	140F	80603	1-99	
MEADOWLARK COVE	Lafayette	132P	80026	800-899	
MEADOWLARK CT	Elbert Co	851F	80138	3300-3599	
MEADOWLARK DR	Boulder Co	129C	80303	1200-1499	
MEADOWLARK DR	Clear Creek Co	304P	80439	1-99	
MEADOW LARK DR	Elbert Co	891U	80106	4500-4999	
MEADOWLARK DR	Elbert Co	871G	80107	33700-33999	
MEADOWLARK DR	Jefferson Co	307A	80401	27800-27999	
	Jefferson Co	306D	80401	28000-28299	
	Jefferson Co	276Z	80401	None	
MEADOWLARK DR	Lafayette	132K	80026	700-799	
MEADOWLARK DR	Lakewood	282N	80226	300-8799	
MEADOWLARK DR	Weld Co	706P	80504	2100-2199	
MEADOW LARK DR S	Castle Rock	466P	80109	4700-5299	
MEADOWLARK LN	Adams Co	168D	80601	14100-14599	
MEADOWLARK LN	Arapahoe Co	373A	80123	1-99	
MEADOWLARK LN	Golden	248V	80403	1500-1599	
MEADOWLARK LN	Jefferson Co	370A	80127	1-99	
MEADOWLARK LN	Lochbuie	140G	80603	600-699	
MEADOWLARK PL	Fort Lupton	729E	80621	None	
MEADOW LARK PL S	Castle Rock	466P	80109	5800-6099	
MEADOW LARK RD	Weld Co	729Q	80621	4000-4599	
MEADOWLEAF LN	Highlands Ranch	404K	80129	None	
MEADOWLOOK WAY	Boulder Co	97F	80304	1-599	
MEADOW MOUNTAIN DR	Broomfield	163E	80020	4800-5199	E
MEADOW MOUNTAIN RD	Jefferson Co	305F	80439	32300-34099	
MEADOW MOUNTAIN TRAIL	Lafayette	131E	80026	2700-2799	
MEADOW MOUNTAIN LN	Jefferson Co	305G	80439	32400-32699	
MEADOWOOD LN	Douglas Co	866G	80135	6200-6699	
MEADOWOOD LN	Parker	409Z	80138	11700-12099	
MEADOWOOD RD	Jefferson Co	336F	80439	None	
MEADOWPINE DR	El Paso Co	910N	80908	7000-7499	
MEADOW RIDGE LN	Douglas Co	407G	80134	11700-11799	
MEADOWRIDGE LN	Douglas Co	867E	80135	None	
MEADOW RIDGE LN	Jefferson Co	842F	80470	32300-32699	
MEADOW RIDGE PT	Douglas Co	407L	80134	10200-10299	
MEADOWROSE DR	Jefferson Co	308E	80401	1400-1799	
MEADOWROSE LN	Castle Pines North	436K	80108	800-999	
MEADOW ROSE LN	Jefferson Co	370Q	80127	1-99	
MEADOW RUE RD	Jefferson Co	336M	80439	28200-28499	
MEADOW RUN	Golden	248V	80403	800-1099	
MEADOW RUN DR E	Douglas Co	441P	80134	10000-10599	
MEADOWS BLVD	Castle Rock	466T	80109	1-3499	
MEADOWS DR N	Castle Rock	466Q	80109	3300-4399	
	Castle Rock	466U	80109	None	
	Castle Rock	466V	80109	None	
MEADOWS DR W	Jefferson Co	371F	80127	10000-11599	
MEADOWS LN	Castle Rock	497D	80104	2300-2399	
MEADOWS PKWY	Castle Rock	467S	80109	1-2499	
MEADOWSIDE DR	Clear Creek Co	335J	80439	1-199	
MEADOWSIDE WAY	Clear Creek Co	801V	80439	None	
MEADOW STATION CIR	Elbert Co	830Y	80138	300-999	
MEADOW STATION RD	Elbert Co	830Y	80138	1-299	
MEADOW SWEET LN	Erie	102P	80516	2000-2299	
MEADOWSWEET RD	Jefferson Co	280M	80401	1200-1399	
MEADOW TRAIL	Douglas Co	870K	80116	1200-1599	
MEADOW TRAIL	Jefferson Co	822Z	80433	28000-28299	
MEADOWVALE CIR	Highlands Ranch	405Q	80130	1000-11099	
MEADOW VALE RD	Weld Co	706P	80504	1700-2399	
MEADOW VIEW	Douglas Co	470A	80134	7200-7499	
MEADOW VIEW DR	Clear Creek Co	781Z	80439	1-1399	
MEADOW VIEW DR	Jefferson Co	307W	80439	27700-27899	
MEADOWVIEW LN	Greenwood Village	344R	80121	1-99	
MEADOW VIEW PKWY	Erie	102R	80516	100-499	
MEADOW VIEW RD	Jefferson Co	307X	80439	3100-3399	
	Jefferson Co	368F	80465	22000-22799	
MEADOWVIEW ST	Frederick	706Y	80504	None	
MEADOW VISTA CIR E	Parker	408U	80134	None	
MEADOW VISTA DR	Jefferson Co	275X	80439	300-599	
MEADOW WOODS ST N	Adams Co	750M	80603	14400-14599	
MEANDER AVE	Jefferson Co	843Y	80470	17700-17899	
MEANDER WAY S	Parker	410X	80138	12100-12199	
MEDALLION RD	Douglas Co	527Q	80104	3300-3699	
MEDEA WAY S	Denver	315B	80209	800-899	
MEDFORD CT	Castle Rock	498R	80104	6100-6199	
MEDFORD ST	Longmont	12P	80501	2100-2299	
MEDFORD WAY	Weld Co	707T	80504	None	
MEDICAL CENTER DR	Brighton	139X	80601	None	
MEDICAL CENTER DR	Park Co	841P	80421	None	
MEDINAH DR	Jefferson Co	306S	80439	2600-2699	
MEEKER CT	Louisville	160C	80027	300-399	
MEEKER DR	Longmont	12S	80501	1400-1499	
MEEKER PL	Longmont	42A	80501	300-399	
MEEKER ST	Longmont	42A	80501	600-899	
	Longmont	12W	80501	900-999	
MEEKER WAY	Broomfield	133N	80020	16000-16199	
MEGAN CT	Douglas Co	847E	80108	501-599	O
MEGAN CT	Longmont	42B	80501	700-899	
MEILLY ST	Lyons	703B	80540	None	
MELANIE CIR	Elbert Co	851V	80107	None	
MELANIE ANN CT	El Paso Co	908P	80132	20200-20299	
MELBORNE CT	Douglas Co	378Y	80134	9200-9299	
MELBOURNE CIR S	Highlands Ranch	405G	80130	9900-9999	
MELBOURNE PL	Highlands Ranch	405H	80130	9900-9999	
MELBOURNE WAY E	Highlands Ranch	405G	80130	4500-4599	
MELINDA LN	El Paso Co	908T	80132	1000-1199	
MELISSA LN	Boulder Co	100T	80301	3000-3099	
MELLER ST	Erie	102U	80516	1-999	
MELODY CIR	Northglenn	194T	80260	600-698	E
MELODY DR	Northglenn	194T	80260	200-799	
	Northglenn	194P	80260	9700-10399	
	Northglenn	194P	80234	10400-11199	
	Northglenn	194F	80234	11300-11499	
	Northglenn	194B	80234	11600-11799	
	Westminster	164X	80234	12000-12199	
MELODY LN	Platteville	708C	80651	100-599	

STREET NAME	CITY or COUNTY	MAP GRID	ZIP CODE	BLOCK RANGE	O/E
MELODY LN E	Castle Rock	498M	80104	5600-5799	
MELODY LN N	Douglas Co	379Z	80138	13000-13199	
MELODY WAY E	Castle Rock	498M	80104	5600-5799	
MELROSE DR	Wheat Ridge	252T	80033	7900-8099	
MELTING SHADOWS WAY	Elbert Co	851T	80107	37400-37499	
MELTING SNOW WAY	Castle Rock	467W	80109	None	
	Castle Rock	466Z	80109	None	
MELVINA HILL RD	Boulder Co	722S	80302	1-1599	
MEMMEN DR	Castle Rock	497M	80104	1-299	
MEMORIAL PARK WAY	Jefferson Co	842H	80433	28500-28799	
MEMORY LN	Longmont	12T	80501	700-799	
MEMPHIS CT	Commerce City	198M	80022	10700-10799	
MEMPHIS CT S	Arapahoe Co	348Z	80016	6100-6199	
	Centennial	348R	80015	5100-5299	
MEMPHIS DR S	Aurora	288V	80012	None	
MEMPHIS ST	Aurora	288R	80011	700-899	
	Aurora	288M	80011	1000-1299	
	Aurora	288H	80011	1800-1899	
	Commerce City	198V	80022	9700-9999	
	Commerce City	198R	80022	9900-9999	
	Commerce City	198M	80022	10501-10599	O
	Commerce City	198D	80022	11700-11899	
	Denver	258H	80239	5200-5599	
MEMPHIS ST S	Arapahoe Co	378M	80016	None	
	Aurora	318D	80017	1000-1099	
	Aurora	318H	80017	1100-1899	
	Aurora	318M	80013	2100-2199	
	Aurora	318R	80013	2200-2299	
	Aurora	318V	80013	2800-2899	
	Aurora	348M	80014	4000-4299	
	Aurora	348M	80015	4300-4899	
MEMPHIS WAY S	Arapahoe Co	378R	80112	8100-8199	
	Aurora	288Z	80017	300-599	
	Aurora	318D	80017	700-999	
	Aurora	318R	80013	2400-2699	
	Aurora	318Z	80013	3500-3599	
	Aurora	348H	80014	4100-4199	
	Centennial	348R	80015	None	
MENTHA DR	Castle Rock	469E	80108	6600-7099	
MEPHAM CT	El Paso Co	908P	80132	700-899	
MERCANTILE AVE	Castle Rock	466V	80109	None	
MERCATOR AVE	Lafayette	131L	80026	100-499	
MERCER CIR E	Aurora	348D	80013	15900-16299	
MERCER DR E	Aurora	349A	80013	16700-16799	
	Aurora	349B	80013	17100-17199	
	Aurora	349C	80013	18900-18999	
MERCER PL	Denver	346C	80237	7300-7699	
MERCER PL E	Aurora	348C	80013	15700-15899	
	Aurora	350B	80018	21700-22199	
	Aurora	350C	80018	22300-22399	
MERCHANT PL	Douglas Co	469B	80134	6000-6099	
MERCURY CIR	Highlands Ranch	376X	80124	700-999	
MERCURY DR	Highlands Ranch	376Y	80124	13000-13299	
MERCURY DR	Lafayette	131R	80026	900-1299	
MEREDITH CT	Lone Tree	406C	80124	9200-9399	
MEREDITH WAY	Boulder	128D	80303	4800-4999	
MERIDETH LN	Longmont	11V	80501	1-199	
MERIDIAN BLVD S	Douglas Co	407C	80112	9200-9899	
MERIDIAN RD	El Paso Co	911T	80106	17400-20499	
MERIDIAN LAKE DR	Weld Co	706M	80504	None	
MERIDIAN VILLAGE PKWY					
	Douglas Co	408K	80134	None	
MERIMBULA ST S	Highlands Ranch	405H	80130	9600-9899	
MERION LN	Jefferson Co	306T	80439	30100-30299	
MERION PL	Broomfield	162Q	80020	1100-1299	
MERL PL	Longmont	11Q	80501	1300-1399	
MERLIN DR	Lafayette	132P	80026	500-1299	
MERRIAM DR S	Jefferson Co	336T	80439	5800-5999	
MERRIMAN PL	Longmont	42C	80501	1100-1199	
MERRINGTON CT	El Paso Co	908V	80132	1200-1299	
MERRITT DR	Boulder	128H	80303	1100-5199	
MERRY LN	Boulder Co	129X	80303	700-799	
MERRYHILL CT	El Paso Co	908Z	80132	17700-17799	
MERRY MEN CIR	El Paso Co	908U	80132	19000-19199	
MERRY REST WAY	Castle Rock	466U	80109	None	
MERRYVALE CT	Douglas Co	441E	80138	9500-9699	
MERRYVALE TRAIL	Douglas Co	441A	80138	7700-8799	
MESA CIR	Lafayette	131L	80026	100-199	
MESA CT	Broomfield	162P	80020	800-999	
MESA CT	Golden	248R	80403	1200-1299	
MESA CT	Louisville	130Y	80027	100-199	
MESA CT S	Superior	160L	80027	1200-1399	
MESA DR	Boulder	98W	80304	1900-2299	
	Boulder Co	129T	80303	6000-6099	
MESA DR	Clear Creek Co	801V	80439	1-799	
MESA DR	Golden	248V	80403	500-599	
MESA DR	Jefferson Co	337S	80439	26800-27499	
MESA DR N	Douglas Co	467B	80108	4600-5799	
MESA ST	Brighton	139P	80601	100-399	
MESA ST	Jamestown	722A	80455	None	
MESA MEADOWS CT	Castle Rock	466X	80109	4000-4199	
MESA OAK	Jefferson Co	370L	80127	1-99	
MESA PARK PL	Thornton	195R	80229	None	
MESA POINT PL	Louisville	130Q	80027	1700-1799	
MESA RIDGE LN	Douglas Co	467B	80108	1300-1799	
MESA RUN W	Douglas Co	432N	80125	11100-11299	
MESA TOP CT	Boulder	69Y	80301	5400-5599	
MESA VERDE	Weld Co	706N	80504	3300-3399	
MESA VERDE LN	Parker	410S	80138	11200-11399	
MESA VERDE PL	Parker	410S	80138	11300-11399	
MESA VERDE RD	El Paso Co	907V	80132	None	
MESA VERDE ST	Golden	279U	80401	100-299	
MESA VERDE WAY	Parker	410S	80138	11200-11399	
MESA VIEW RD S	Douglas Co	888Z	80118	11700-12999	
MESA VIEW WAY	Golden	248U	80403	300-499	
MESQUITE ROW	Lone Tree	376Z	80124	8700-8899	
METEOR PL	Douglas Co	467E	80108	400-499	
	Douglas Co	436T	80108	1000-1099	
METROPOLITAN DR	Longmont	12U	80501	1600-1699	
METZLER DR	Castle Rock	467Q	80108	100-399	
METZLER WAY	Castle Rock	467D	80108	4901-4999	O
MEXICO AVE E	Arapahoe Co	317J	80247	9200-9499	
	Arapahoe Co	812C	80102	43200-45699	
	Aurora	317J	80247	9700-10099	
	Aurora	317L	80112	10700-13099	
	Aurora	318M	80017	15300-16899	
	Aurora	319J	80017	16800-17499	

Continued on next column

STREET NAME	CITY or COUNTY	MAP GRID	ZIP CODE	BLOCK RANGE	O/E
MEXICO AVE E (Cont'd)	Denver	314L	80210	1-1699	
	Denver	315J	80210	1700-1799	
	Denver	315K	80210	2500-3999	
	Denver	315L	80222	4000-5599	
	Denver	316J	80224	5600-7099	
	Denver	316L	80231	7900-7999	
MEXICO AVE W	Denver	314K	80223	1-299	
	Denver	314J	80223	1600-1999	
	Denver	313M	80223	2000-2399	
	Denver	313M	80219	2400-3299	
	Denver	313K	80219	3400-5199	
	Lakewood	312M	80232	5200-6599	
	Lakewood	312J	80232	8000-8999	
	Lakewood	311M	80232	9000-9499	
	Lakewood	311J	80228	12000-12399	
	Lakewood	310L	80228	13700-13799	
MEXICO DR E	Arapahoe Co	316M	80231	8800-8999	
	Aurora	317L	80112	11401-11599	O
	Aurora	318L	80012	14900-15299	
	Aurora	319K	80017	17700-17999	
	Aurora	319L	80017	18700-18999	
MEXICO DR W	Jefferson Co	311K	80232	10900-11299	
	Lakewood	312F	80232	6800-7599	
MEXICO PL E	Aurora	319K	80017	18200-18399	
MEXICO PL W	Lakewood	312L	80232	6600-6799	
	Lakewood	312K	80232	7600-7999	
	Lakewood	311K	80228	12000-12099	
	Lakewood	311J	80228	12200-12399	
	Lakewood	310G	80228	13800-13899	
MEYER DR	Jefferson Co	823P	80433	9600-9799	
MEYERS CT	Castle Rock	498L	80104	4400-4599	
MEYERWOOD CIR	Highlands Ranch	404J	80129	1200-1799	
MEYERWOOD CT	Highlands Ranch	404J	80129	10400-10499	
MEYERWOOD LN	Highlands Ranch	404J	80129	1200-1599	
MIAMI WAY	Boulder	128T	80305	900-1099	
MIBO CT	Boulder Co	70K	80503	6900-6999	
MICA CT	Superior	160U	80027	3000-3099	
MICA RD	Gilpin Co	761E	80403	1-399	
MICA WAY	Douglas Co	408L	80134	10200-10399	
MICA WAY	Jefferson Co	368V	80465	8300-8499	
MICA WAY	Park Co	820Y	80421	1-199	
MICA MINE GULCH RD	Jefferson Co	369Y	80127	8700-9399	
MICA MOUNTAIN RD	Jefferson Co	782H	80403	4900-5199	
MICHAEL GATES DR	Elbert Co	830M	80138	1700-1799	
MICHENER WAY E	Highlands Ranch	404M	80126	1000-1299	
MICHIGAN AVE N	Lafayette	132J	80026	100-599	
MICHIGAN AVE S	Lafayette	132J	80026	100-499	
MICHIGAN CT S	Littleton	343P	80123	5000-5099	
MICHIGAN WAY S	Denver	313K	80219	1500-1999	
MICHIGAN CREEK WAY	Parker	439B	80134	18200-18299	
MIDDLE RD	Cherry Hills Village	345C	80113	1-99	
MIDDLEBURY DR	Highlands Ranch	405P	80126	2700-2899	
MIDDLEBURY WAY	Highlands Ranch	405P	80126	10700-10799	
MIDDLE CREST RD	Boulder Co	703X	80302	8300-8399	
MIDDLEFIELD RD S	Columbine Valley	343X	80123	5900-6299	
MIDDLE FORK RD	Boulder Co	703X	80302	1-8699	
MIDDLE GLEN WAY	Palmer Lake	907Q	80133	None	
MIDDLEHAM PL	Castle Pines North	436Q	80108	7200-7299	
MIDDLETON AVE	Castle Rock	498R	80104	6100-6399	
MIDDLETON RD	Jefferson Co	336X	80439	30400-30899	
MIDLAND PL	Brighton	138M	80601	1900-2199	
MIDLAND ST	Brighton	138K	80601	500-1099	
	Brighton	138L	80601	1100-1599	
	Brighton	139L	80601	None	
MIDNIGHT ST	Lochbuie	140A	80603	None	
MIDSUMMER LN	Elbert Co	832X	80107	43300-43899	
MIDWAY BLVD E	Broomfield	163S	80020	900-1199	
MIDWAY BLVD W	Broomfield	162T	80020	100-1999	
	Broomfield	161V	80020	2000-2899	
MIDWAY BLVD W	Broomfield	161K	80020	None	
MIDWAY DR	Douglas Co	373X	80125	8000-8199	
MIDWAY DR	Gilpin Co	761E	80403	1-199	
MIKA PL	Castle Rock	497Q	80104	1200-1299	
MIKELSON BLVD	Castle Rock	498Q	80104	None	
MILAN AVE W	Sheridan	343C	80236	3000-3399	
	Sheridan	343C	80110	3400-3599	
MILAN CIR E	Aurora	349A	80013	16900-17199	
	Aurora	349C	80013	19100-19799	
MILAN DR E	Aurora	348C	80013	15300-15499	
MILAN PL E	Arapahoe Co	350A	80013	20400-20599	
	Aurora	349B	80013	17800-18199	
	Aurora	349C	80013	18800-18899	
	Aurora	350B	80018	22100-22199	
	Denver	346B	80237	6500-6599	
MILAN PL W	Denver	342D	80235	5500-5599	
	Jefferson Co	341C	80235	10600-10699	
MILANO LN	Longmont	40Q	80503	4000-4099	
MILBURY ST	Castle Rock	498R	80104	1300-1498	E
MILDRED DR	Northglenn	194M	80233	10800-10999	
MILDRED LN	Jefferson Co	337W	80439	27300-27499	
MILE CREEK CT S	Parker	439H	80134	12600-12699	
MILE HIGH STADIUM CIR	Denver	283H	80204	1601-1899	O
MILE HIGH STADIUM WEST CIR					
	Denver	283G	80204	None	
MILES DR	Lone Tree	406C	80124	9200-9399	
MILESTONE DR	Castle Rock	467T	80104	4600-4699	
MILESTONE LN	Castle Rock	467T	80104	None	
MILFORD LN	Parker	410Q	80138	None	
MILITARY TRAIL	Douglas Co	469C	80134	5300-5499	
MILKCAP PL	Brighton	140J	80601	None	
MILKY WAY	Thornton	224F	80260	600-799	
	Thornton	224A	80260	1100-1599	
MILL ST	Black Hawk	781A	80422	None	
MILL ST	Jamestown	722A	80455	None	
MILLBRIDGE AVE	Castle Rock	498R	80104	6000-6399	
	Castle Rock	498R	80104	6400-6498	E
MILLBRIDGE CT	Castle Rock	498R	80104	5900-6099	
MILLBROOK CIR	Castle Rock	497E	80109	500-999	
MILLBROOK CT	Castle Rock	497E	80109	1400-1599	
MILLBROOK CT N	Aurora	291P	80018	100-299	
MILLBROOK CT S	Aurora	351X	80016	None	
MILLBROOK ST N	Aurora	291P	80018	100-599	
MILLBROOK ST S	Aurora	381F	80016	7300-7499	
MILLBROOK ST S	Aurora	291T	80018	None	
MILLBROOK WAY S	Arapahoe Co	381P	80016	7900-8099	
	Aurora	351X	80016	6300-6599	
	Aurora	381F	80016	7100-7399	
MILL CREEK CT	Highlands Ranch	375W	80126	9200-9499	

M

STREET NAME	CITY or COUNTY	MAP GRID	ZIP CODE	BLOCK RANGE	O/E
MILLER AVE	Brighton	138S	80601	1-899	
MILLER AVE N	Lafayette	132J	80026	100-198	E
MILLER AVE S	Lafayette	132J	80026	100-899	
MILLER BLVD	Castle Rock	498N	80104	1900-2299	
MILLER CIR	Arvada	221G	80005	8000-8099	
MILLER CT	Arvada	221Q	80005	7500-7699	
	Arvada	221G	80005	8100-8399	
MILLER CT	Frederick	726D	80504	7600-7699	
	Lakewood	281Q	80215	600-999	
	Lakewood	281G	80215	2000-2399	
	Westminster	191L	80021	10700-10799	
	Wheat Ridge	251U	80033	3500-4099	
MILLER CT E	Castle Rock	497L	80104	300-399	
MILLER CT S	Jefferson Co	341C	80235	3600-3899	
	Jefferson Co	341L	80127	4500-4799	
	Jefferson Co	341Q	80127	4900-5099	
	Jefferson Co	341U	80127	5700-5899	
	Jefferson Co	371G	80127	6900-7099	
	Jefferson Co	371L	80127	7300-7499	
	Jefferson Co	371Q	80127	8400-8499	
	Jefferson Co	371U	80127	8500-8599	
	Jefferson Co	341Y	80127	None	
	Lakewood	311C	80226	700-899	
	Lakewood	311Q	80227	2200-2499	
MILLER DR	Dacono	727J	80516	100-199	
MILLER DR	Frederick	726D	80504	7300-7899	
MILLER DR	Longmont	41T	80501	1900-2199	
MILLER DR S	Lakewood	311U	80227	2600-2699	
MILLER LN	Jefferson Co	308U	80453	21600-22099	
MILLER PL	Frederick	726D	80504	7800-7899	
MILLER PL	Golden	248Z	80403	1100-1199	
MILLER RD	Douglas Co	410R	80138	None	
MILLER ST	Arvada	251G	80033	5400-5498	E
	Arvada	251C	80004	5800-6199	
	Arvada	221U	80004	6400-6899	
	Arvada	221Q	80005	7200-7499	
	Arvada	221L	80005	8000-8099	
	Arvada	221G	80005	8300-8599	
MILLER ST	Keenesburg	732A	80643	None	
MILLER ST	Lakewood	281Q	80215	800-899	
	Lakewood	281L	80215	900-1499	
	Lakewood	281G	80215	1500-2099	
	Lakewood	281C	80215	2100-2599	
	Westminster	191Q	80021	10000-10099	
	Wheat Ridge	251Y	80033	3200-3499	
	Wheat Ridge	251U	80033	3500-4199	
MILLER ST S	Jefferson Co	341Q	80127	5100-5899	
	Jefferson Co	341Y	80127	6200-6399	
	Jefferson Co	371C	80127	6300-6499	
	Jefferson Co	371G	80127	6800-6899	
	Jefferson Co	371G	80127	6900-7399	
	Lakewood	281Y	80226	300-599	
	Lakewood	311C	80226	600-1099	
	Lakewood	311L	80227	1900-1999	
MILLER WAY S	Jefferson Co	341L	80127	4900-5099	
	Jefferson Co	371U	80127	8500-8599	
	Jefferson Co	341Y	80127	None	
	Lakewood	311C	80226	900-1099	
MILLER/CALEY LN	Arapahoe Co	373E	80128	None	
MILLET CIR	Brighton	139G	80601	None	
MILL HOLLOW RD	Jefferson Co	824U	80127	10800-11099	
MILLIKEN AVE	Jefferson Co	823U	80433	10800-11499	
MILLIKEN CT	Boulder	128G	80303	4200-4299	
MILLIKEN ST	Parker	409N	80134	10700-10899	
MILLIONAIRE DR	Boulder Co	742B	80302	1-799	
MILLROCK TERRACE	Douglas Co	408G	80134	9900-9999	
MILLS ST	Lafayette	131G	80026	None	
MILLSTONE CT S	Highlands Ranch	406B	80130	9600-9799	
MILLSTONE PL E	Highlands Ranch	406F	80130	6500-6799	
MILLSTONE ST E	Highlands Ranch	406B	80130	6500-6799	
MILL VALLEY PL	Parker	410Y	80138	None	
MILL VALLEY ST	Parker	410U	80138	None	
MILL VILLAGE BLVD	Longmont	42G	80501	200-399	
MILL VISTA RD	Douglas Co	373U	80129	None	
MILLWAGON TRAIL	Castle Rock	466X	80109	4200-4499	
MILNE WAY	Boulder	99W	80301	None	
MILNER CT	Longmont	11W	80503	1201-1299	O
MILNER LN	Longmont	11W	80503	1200-1299	
MILO CIR	Lafayette	131R	80026	900-1299	
MILTON LN	Jefferson Co	306W	80439	31200-31399	
MILTON ST	Palmer Lake	907Q	80133	None	
MILWAUKE ST	Thornton	165P	80241	13100-13199	
MILWAUKEE CIR	Thornton	195B	80233	11600-11699	
MILWAUKEE CIR S	Denver	315T	80210	2900-3099	
MILWAUKEE CT	Northglenn	195K	80233	10600-10799	
	Thornton	195T	80229	9500-9599	
	Thornton	195T	80229	9700-9799	
	Thornton	195F	80233	11500-11599	
	Thornton	165X	80241	12300-12399	
	Thornton	165T	80241	12800-12999	
	Thornton	165P	80241	13300-13599	
	Thornton	165K	80602	13700-13799	
MILWAUKEE CT S	Centennial	375K	80122	7400-7499	
MILWAUKEE PL	Thornton	195A	80233	11600-11699	
	Thornton	165P	80241	13000-13099	
	Denver	285K	80206	100-1699	
	Denver	285B	80205	2600-2699	
	Denver	255X	80205	2700-3799	
	Denver	255P	80216	4000-5199	
	Northglenn	195K	80233	10500-10899	
	Thornton	195T	80229	9800-9999	
	Thornton	195N	80229	10000-10199	
	Thornton	195F	80233	11500-11699	
	Thornton	165K	80602	13600-13699	
	Thornton	165K	80602	13800-13899	
	Thornton	165F	80602	13900-13999	
	Thornton	165F	80602	None	
MILWAUKEE ST S	Centennial	375P	80122	8100-8199	
	Denver	285X	80209	200-299	
	Denver	315B	80209	700-899	
	Denver	315F	80210	1100-2799	
	Denver	315X	80210	3000-3299	
MILWAUKEE WAY S	Centennial	345X	80121	5900-6099	
	Centennial	375K	80122	7300-7499	
	Denver	315B	80209	900-1099	
MIMAS PL	Highlands Ranch	376X	80124	400-499	
MIMOSA ST	Douglas Co	409X	80134	None	
MINE LN	Boulder Co	722L	80302	1-499	
MINEOLA CT	Boulder	129N	80303	1-199	
MINER ST	Idaho Springs	780Q	80452	100-2399	
MINERAL AVE E	Arapahoe Co	374R	80122	1400-1699	
	Arapahoe Co	378L	80112	None	
	Centennial	375N	80122	1700-2199	
	Centennial	375Q	80122	3600-3999	
	Centennial	376K	80112	6500-7299	
	Centennial	376M	80112	8900-9299	
	Centennial	377J	80112	9300-9699	
	Littleton	374Q	80122	1-799	
MINERAL AVE W	Littleton	374N	80120	1-2099	
	Littleton	373L	80120	2100-3199	
	Littleton	373K	80128	3200-5299	
MINERAL CIR E	Centennial	375R	80122	4800-5599	
	Centennial	376R	80112	8400-8799	
	Centennial	376M	80112	9000-9199	
MINERAL CT E	Littleton	374Q	80122	400-499	
MINERAL CT W	Littleton	374K	80120	500-599	
MINERAL DR E	Arapahoe Co	380N	80016	21000-21299	
	Aurora	381L	80016	26700-27099	
	Aurora	380R	80016	None	
	Centennial	376N	80112	6000-6499	
	Centennial	376Q	80112	7300-8899	
MINERAL DR W	Littleton	373J	80128	4600-4999	
MINERAL LN	Jefferson Co	842N	80470	33800-34499	
MINERAL LN E	Centennial	375R	80122	5200-5599	
MINERAL PL E	Arapahoe Co	374R	80122	1400-1599	
	Aurora	380R	80016	23500-23799	
	Aurora	380Q	80016	None	
	Centennial	375Q	80122	3500-3899	
	Centennial	376N	80122	5500-5599	
	Centennial	376N	80112	5600-6599	
	Centennial	376Q	80112	7500-7699	
	Centennial	376R	80112	8800-8899	
	Centennial	379N	80016	16900-17699	
MINERAL PL W	Littleton	374K	80120	1100-1199	
MINERAL RD	Boulder Co	69R	80503	7100-7399	
	Boulder Co	70T	80503	7400-9099	
	Boulder Co	71N	80503	9100-9499	
	Boulder Co	71Q	80504	9500-10999	
	Boulder Co	72P	80504	11100-12699	
MINERS CT	Highlands Ranch	375X	80126	3500-3599	
MINERS DR	Highlands Ranch	375Y	80126	8800-8999	
MINER'S DR	Lafayette	132N	80026	100-1398	E
MINERS PL	Highlands Ranch	375Y	80126	8800-9099	
MINERS ST	Highlands Ranch	375Y	80126	8800-8999	
MINERS ALLEY	Golden	279A	80401	1100-1299	
MINERS CANDLE CT	Castle Rock	466X	80109	3900-3999	
MINERS CANDLE DR	Castle Rock	466X	80109	3900-4299	
MINERS CANDLE PL	Castle Rock	466X	80109	3800-4299	
MINERS CANDLE WAY	Gilpin Co	741Y	80403	100-199	
MINERS PEAK CIR	Frederick	726G	80516	None	
MINGLEWOOD TRAIL	El Paso Co	908Y	80132	17500-18099	
MINING WAY	Monument	908X	80132	None	
MINING CAMP TRAIL	Douglas Co	469B	80134	5100-5399	
MINITURN AVE	Broomfield	162L	80020	1-199	
MINNESOTA DR E	Denver	316E	80224	5600-6399	
MINNOW CIR E	Aurora	380V	80138	None	
MINNOW DR E	Aurora	380V	80138	None	
MINNOW PL E	Aurora	380V	80138	None	
MINOR ST	Central City	780D	80427	400-499	
MINOR ST	Idaho Springs	780Q	80452	None	
MINORS MESA RD	Black Hawk	780D	80422	None	
MINOS CT	Lafayette	131U	80026	1600-1699	
MINOT PL	Longmont	12P	80501	500-599	
MINOTAUR CIR	Lafayette	131R	80026	800-1299	
MINOTAUR DR	Lafayette	131R	80026	None	
MINSHALL DR	Boulder Co	99S	80301	None	
MINSTREL CT	Castle Rock	466Z	80109	None	
MINTER LN	Douglas Co	496J	80109	1700-1899	
MINWOK ST	Kiowa	872M	80117	800-899	
MIRA DEL SOL CT	Castle Rock	467V	80104	4400-4799	
MIRAGE DR	Douglas Co	466H	80108	4500-4599	
MIRAGE DR	Jefferson Co	843A	80433	26600-26799	
MIRAMONTE BLVD	Broomfield	162P	80020	100-999	
	Broomfield	161R	80020	None	
MIRAMONTE CT	Broomfield	162P	80020	1300-1399	
MIRAMONTE ST	Broomfield	162P	80020	1100-1299	
MIRAMONTE LAKE CIR	Weld Co	707J	80504	None	
MIRCOS ST	Erie	103S	80516	800-1199	
MIRIAM LN	Douglas Co	469C	80134	5000-5199	
MIRROR LAKE WAY	Broomfield	163N	80020	13200-13299	
MISSION LN	Jefferson Co	305R	80439	31800-32199	
MISSION PKWY S	Aurora	348C	80013	3600-4199	
MISSION RD	Lochbuie	729Y	80603	None	
MISSION WAY	Broomfield	163E	80020	14300-14399	
MISSISSIPPI AVE E	Arapahoe Co	316D	80247	7800-9298	E
	Arapahoe Co	812B	80102	41900-42499	
	Arapahoe Co	813B	80102	48900-49799	
	Arapahoe Co	813C	80102	50500-52099	
	Aurora	317A	80247	9300-9398	E
	Aurora	317A	80247	9400-9699	
	Aurora	317B	80247	9700-10498	E
	Aurora	317C	80012	10500-13299	
	Aurora	318C	80012	13300-15299	
	Aurora	318C	80017	15300-16899	
	Aurora	319A	80017	16900-19299	
	Aurora	320D	80018	22700-24199	
	Aurora	321A	80018	24200-24899	
	Denver	314C	80210	1-1199	
	Denver	314D	80210	1600-1699	
	Denver	315B	80210	1700-3999	
	Denver	315C	80246	4400-4599	
	Denver	315D	80246	4600-4998	E
	Denver	315D	80246	5000-5399	
	Denver	316B	80224	6100-7299	
	Denver	316D	80247	7801-9299	O
	Denver	317A	80247	9301-9399	O
	Denver	317B	80247	9701-10499	O
	Glendale	315C	80246	4000-4399	
	Glendale	315D	80246	4601-4999	O
	Watkins	811B	80137	34500-36099	
MISSISSIPPI AVE W	Denver	314A	80223	1-1999	
	Denver	313D	80223	2000-2499	
	Denver	313A	80219	2500-5199	
	Lakewood	312B	80226	5200-8999	
	Lakewood	311C	80226	9000-10499	
	Lakewood	311E	80226	11400-11599	
	Lakewood	311E	80228	11600-12699	
	Lakewood	310D	80228	12700-12899	
MISSISSIPPI CIR E	Aurora	320D	80018	None	
MISSISSIPPI CT W	Lakewood	310D	80228	13000-13699	
MISSISSIPPI DR E	Arapahoe Co	316G	80231	7500-7598	E
MISSISSIPPI PL E	Aurora	318B	80012	14100-14299	
	Aurora	319B	80017	17800-17899	
	Aurora	320D	80018	None	
MISSISSIPPI PL W	Lakewood	312G	80232	6100-6699	
	Lakewood	312E	80232	8600-8699	
MISSISSIPPI WAY W	Lakewood	312G	80232	6400-6699	
MISSOULA TRAIL	Castle Rock	468M	80108	5500-6099	
MISSOURI AVE	Longmont	41Q	80501	600-1499	
MISSOURI AVE E	Arapahoe Co	316D	80247	9100-9299	
	Arapahoe Co	317A	80247	9301-9499	O
	Denver	315D	80246	4800-5299	
MISSOURI GULCH RD	Gilpin Co	760G	80403	2500-4799	
MISSOURI PEAK PL	Douglas Co	436U	80108	6100-6199	
MISTLETOE RD	Jefferson Co	277V	80401	1-299	
MISTY CT	Broomfield	163P	80020	None	
MISTY RD	Jefferson Co	763S	80403	27600-27699	
MISTY ST	Broomfield	163P	80020	13300-13399	
MISTY WAY	Boulder Co	69K	80503	6100-6299	
MISTY ACRES BLVD	El Paso Co	908P	80132	None	
MISTY MORNING DR	El Paso Co	908Q	80132	19200-19599	
MISTY VALLEY LN	Jefferson Co	367V	80433	8600-8799	
MITCHELL AVE	Monument	908W	80132	1-699	
MITCHELL CIR	Denver	259R	80249	19800-20099	
MITCHELL CT	Boulder Co	11E	80503	9400-9499	
MITCHELL DR	Denver	259R	80249	19400-19599	
MITCHELL LN	Boulder	98Q	80301	3300-3499	
MITCHELL PL	Denver	258P	80239	15000-15199	
	Denver	259Q	80249	18700-19199	
	Denver	259R	80249	19800-20599	
	Denver	259E	80249	None	
MITCHELL PL E	Denver	260N	80249	20200-21099	
MITCHELL RD E	Arapahoe Co	792U	80102	42500-45799	
	Arapahoe Co	793S	80102	45800-47299	
MITCHELL ST	Castle Rock	498M	80104	None	
	Castle Rock	499J	80104	None	
MITZE DR	Adams Co	224E	80221	8100-8399	
MITZE WAY	Adams Co	224E	80221	8200-8399	
MIWOK TRAIL	Jefferson Co	335Z	80439	31700-31999	
MOBILE CIR S	Aurora	348H	80014	4100-4299	
MOBILE CT S	Centennial	348V	80016	5900-5999	
MOBILE PL S	Aurora	288Z	80017	None	
MOBILE ST	Adams Co	168D	80601	14400-14599	
MOBILE ST	Arapahoe Co	378H	80016	None	
	Aurora	288R	80011	700-899	
	Aurora	288M	80011	1000-1399	
	Commerce City	198V	80022	9700-9999	
	Commerce City	198D	80022	11700-11999	
MOBILE ST	Elizabeth	871E	80107	300-899	
MOBILE ST	Longmont	41H	80501	1-99	
MOBILE ST S	Arapahoe Co	348Z	80016	6000-6199	
	Aurora	318D	80017	700-1099	
	Aurora	318H	80017	1500-1899	
	Aurora	318M	80013	1900-1999	
	Aurora	318R	80013	2400-2499	
	Aurora	318V	80013	2700-2899	
	Centennial	348V	80015	5500-5899	
MOBILE WAY	Commerce City	198M	80022	10400-10499	
MOBILE WAY S	Arapahoe Co	378R	80112	8100-8199	
	Aurora	318R	80013	2100-2299	
	Aurora	318R	80013	2600-2699	
	Aurora	318V	80013	2900-3199	
	Aurora	348D	80014	3600-3799	
	Aurora	348M	80015	4500-4799	
MOCKINGBIRD CT	Highlands Ranch	404F	80129	400-499	
MOCKINGBIRD LN	Brighton	137V	80601	700-899	
MOCKINGBIRD LN	Cherry Hills Village	344H	80113	1-99	
MOCKINGBIRD LN	Highlands Ranch	404F	80129	10000-10199	
MOCKINGBIRD LN	Longmont	40U	80503	None	
MOCKINGBIRD ST	Brighton	137V	80601	600-1199	
MOCKINGBIRD TRAIL	Park Co	841Z	80421	1-2099	
MODEL T RD	Boulder Co	722V	80302	1-199	
MODENA LN	Boulder Co	69F	80503	6300-6499	
MODOC LN	Jefferson Co	365D	80439	6500-6599	
MODRED ST	Lafayette	132P	80026	900-1199	
MOFFAT CT	Douglas Co	436X	80108	800-899	
MOFFAT PL W	Adams Co	253H	80221	2200-2399	
MOFFAT RD	Jefferson Co	337J	80439	27600-27799	
MOFFAT ST	Erie	103J	80516	300-599	
	Erie	102M	80516	600-699	
MOFFIT CT	Boulder	97Q	80304	3700-3799	
MOHAWK CIR	Superior	160E	80027	100-299	
MOHAWK CT	Douglas Co	886M	80118	7600-7699	
MOHAWK DR	Boulder	128L	80303	100-699	
	Boulder	128G	80303	700-999	
MOHAWK DR	Douglas Co	846X	80135	3000-3198	E
MOHAWK DR	Douglas Co	887J	80118	4000-4399	
MOHAWK RD S	Littleton	343P	80123	5300-5499	
MOHAWK ST S	Jefferson Co	842E	80470	13100-13499	
MOHAWK WAY	El Paso Co	909S	80132	2500-2699	
MOHAWK TRAIL	Jefferson Co	842E	80470	34800-35199	
	Park Co	842E	80470	1-99	
MOLAS CT	Douglas Co	887G	80118	7500-7699	
MOLINA PL	Parker	409J	80134	16900-16999	
MOLINE CT	Adams Co	167Y	80640	11900-11999	
MOLINE CT	Aurora	287U	80010	200-299	
	Commerce City	197C	80640	11600-11699	
MOLINE CT S	Arapahoe Co	347Y	80111	6100-6199	
	Aurora	317L	80112	1700-1799	
	Aurora	317Q	80014	2200-2299	
	Aurora	317U	80014	2700-2799	
MOLINE PL	Adams Co	167Y	80640	11900-11999	
MOLINE PL S	Aurora	317U	80014	2900-2999	
MOLINE ST	Adams Co	167Y	80640	11800-12199	
	Adams Co	137L	80602	None	
	Aurora	287U	80010	1-99	
	Aurora	287G	80010	200-2599	
	Aurora	257U	80010	3300-3599	
	Commerce City	197C	80640	11400-12199	
	Commerce City	197G	80601	None	
	Denver	257L	80239	4700-5099	
MOLINE ST S	Aurora	287Y	80012	1-699	
	Aurora	317G	80112	700-1799	
	Aurora	317Q	80014	2100-2198	E

M

STREET NAME	CITY or COUNTY	MAP GRID	ZIP CODE	BLOCK RANGE	O/E
MOLINE WAY S	Arapahoe Co	347Y	80111	5900-6199	
	Arapahoe Co	377F	80112	None	
	Aurora	317L	80014	1900-2099	
	Aurora	317Q	80014	2400-2499	
MOLLY AVE E	Parker	439G	80134	19000-19299	
MOLLY CT S	Parker	439G	80134	12900-12999	
MOLLY DR	Jefferson Co	843E	80433	12300-25999	
	Jefferson Co	842D	80433	26000-27599	
MOLLY LN	Broomfield	163G	80020	3200-3298	E
	Broomfield	163C	80020	3300-3398	E
MONA CT	Adams Co	224L	80221	7800-7999	
MONACO CIR S	Arapahoe Co	316S	80222	3100-3199	
	Centennial	376P	80112	8000-8199	
	Centennial	376K	80112	7600E-7799E	
	Centennial	376K	80112	7600W-7699W	
MONACO CT	Thornton	166W	80602	12000-12099	
	Thornton	166J	80602	None	
MONACO CT S	Centennial	346X	80111	6300-6399	
	Centennial	376K	80112	7800-8299	
MONACO DR	Thornton	166X	80602	12000-12299	
MONACO PKWY	Denver	286K	80220	1-1999	
	Denver	286A	80207	2000-2799	
	Denver	256W	80207	2800-3999	
MONACO PKWY S	Denver	286X	80224	1-699	
	Denver	316P	80224	700-2099	
	Denver	316P	80222	2100-3499	
	Denver	346B	80237	3500-4199	
MONACO ST	Adams Co	226N	80022	7400-7799	
	Adams Co	196W	80640	9000-9699	
	Adams Co	136S	80602	15200-16099	
	Commerce City	256J	80022	4800-4999	
	Commerce City	256E	80022	5300-6099	
	Commerce City	226W	80022	6200-7399	
	Commerce City	226J	80022	7800-7999	
	Denver	256N	80216	4200-4699	
	Thornton	166W	80602	12000-12099	
	Thornton	166S	80602	12600-12799	
	Thornton	166J	80602	None	
MONACO ST S	Arapahoe Co	316T	80222	3101-3399	O
	Centennial	376P	80112	7400-8199	
	Centennial	376E	80112	7300E-7499E	
	Denver	316T	80222	2100-3299	
	Denver	316T	80222	3300-3398	E
	Denver	316X	80222	3400-3499	
	Denver	346K	80237	4300-5099	
	Douglas Co	406P	80124	10700-10799	
	Greenwood Village	346T	80111	5100-5899	
MONACO WAY	Commerce City	226W	80022	6500-6699	
	Thornton	166X	80602	6600-6699	
	Thornton	166N	80602	12900-13099	
MONACO WAY S	Centennial	346X	80111	5900-6299	
	Centennial	376K	80112	7500-7699	
MONAGHAN RD	Adams Co	770Y	80019	None	
MONARCH AVE	Longmont	12Y	80501	1200-1399	
MONARCH BLVD	Castle Pines North	436G	80108	7100-12499	
	Douglas Co	406S	80108	None	
MONARCH CIR	Elbert Co	830G	80138	47900-47999	
MONARCH CT	Broomfield	163Q	80020	12900-12999	
MONARCH CT	Jefferson Co	306K	80439	30400-30599	
MONARCH CT	Longmont	12Y	80501	1300-1399	
MONARCH CT	Louisville	130M	80027	100-199	
MONARCH DR	Boulder	98V	80301	None	
MONARCH DR	Elbert Co	831J	80138	46900-46999	
MONARCH DR	Firestone	706V	80504	4700-5899	
MONARCH DR	Longmont	12U	80501	1200-1599	
MONARCH PL	Elbert Co	831N	80138	3200-3399	
MONARCH RD	Boulder Co	69P	80503	5500-7399	
	Boulder Co	70N	80503	7400-7899	
	Boulder Co	71Q	80504	10300-10699	
MONARCH RD	Douglas Co	887M	80118	7800-8099	
MONARCH ST	Adams Co	792M	80102	None	
MONARCH ST	Frederick	726L	80516	3701-3799	O
MONARCH ST	Louisville	130M	80027	100-399	
MONARCH WAY	Superior	160Q	80027	900-1099	
MONARCH PARK CT	Boulder Co	70P	80503	6400-6599	
MONARCH PARK PL	Boulder Co	70N	80503	6200-6399	
MONARCH PARK PL	Boulder Co	70N	80503	6400-6499	
MONARCH TRAIL	Broomfield	162L	80020	200-299	
MONARES LN	Erie	103P	80516	100-399	
MONCRIEFF PL E	Aurora	258T	80011	13800-15299	
MONCRIEFF PL W	Denver	253X	80211	3300-3599	
	Denver	253W	80212	4400-5199	
MONICA LN	Jefferson Co	367L	80439	700-7399	
MONIHAN RD N	Aurora	790L	80137	2600-5599	
MONMOUTH AVE	Firestone	727B	80504	None	
MONMOUTH AVE W	Denver	343P	80123	None	
	Englewood	343P	80110	3000-3599	
	Littleton	343P	80123	3600-4099	
MONMOUTH PL E	Aurora	348L	80015	15300-15799	
	Centennial	349Q	80015	19400-19599	
	Denver	346M	80237	8500-8799	
MONROE CIR	Adams Co	225F	80229	8300-8399	
	Thornton	165P	80241	13400-13499	
MONROE CT	Adams Co	225F	80229	8500-8599	
MONROE CT	Louisville	130Z	80027	200-299	
MONROE CT	Thornton	165P	80241	13100-13199	
MONROE CT S	Centennial	375L	80122	7300-7499	
MONROE DR	Boulder	128G	80303	1000-4399	
MONROE DR	Jefferson Co	336X	80439	29900-30599	
MONROE DR	Thornton	195T	80229	9900-9999	
	Thornton	165X	80241	12200-12399	
	Thornton	165P	80241	13000-13099	
	Thornton	165T	80241	None	
MONROE DR S	Centennial	345Y	80121	6100-6299	
MONROE LN S	Cherry Hills Village	345G	80113	4300-4699	
MONROE PL	Louisville	130R	80027	1400-1499	
MONROE PL	Thornton	165Y	80241	12200-12299	
MONROE ST	Adams Co	794P	80136	1800-1999	
	Commerce City	225X	80022	6400-6599	
	Denver	285K	80206	1-1699	
	Denver	285B	80205	2600-2699	
	Denver	255X	80205	2700-3099	
	Denver	255T	80205	3300-3899	
	Denver	255P	80216	4100-4298	E
	Denver	255K	80216	4900-4998	E
	Denver	255F	80216	5100-5399	
	Thornton	225B	80229	8800-9099	

Continued on next column

STREET NAME	CITY or COUNTY	MAP GRID	ZIP CODE	BLOCK RANGE	O/E
MONROE ST (Cont'd)	Thornton	195Y	80229	9100-9199	
	Thornton	195T	80229	9800-9899	
	Thornton	195P	80229	10100-10199	
	Thornton	195B	80233	11500-11999	
	Thornton	165T	80241	12800-12899	
	Thornton	165K	80241	13400-13599	
	Thornton	165K	80602	13600-13799	
	Thornton	165F	80602	13800-13999	
	Thornton	165F	80602	None	
MONROE ST S	Cherry Hills Village	315Y	80113	None	
	Denver	285U	80209	1-399	
	Denver	315B	80209	900-1099	
	Denver	315Q	80210	1100-3299	
MONROE WAY	Adams Co	225F	80229	8400-8499	
MONROE WAY	Superior	160Q	80027	900-1099	
MONROE WAY	Thornton	195B	80233	11500-11999	
	Thornton	165P	80241	13200-13399	
MONROE WAY S	Centennial	375P	80122	7700-8199	
	Denver	285X	80209	600-699	
MONTAINVIEW AVE	Fort Lupton	728H	80621	900-1199	
MONTANA AVE	Palmer Lake	907Q	80133	None	
MONTANA AVE W	Lakewood	310M	80228	12800-13899	
MONTANA CIR E	Aurora	318K	80012	14100-14499	
MONTANA DR E	Aurora	319L	80017	18800-18999	
MONTANA DR W	Lakewood	310M	80228	12700-13099	
MONTANA PL E	Aurora	317L	80012	11600-12099	
	Aurora	318M	80017	16100-16199	
	Aurora	319K	80017	17700-18299	
	Aurora	319L	80017	18900-18999	
	Aurora	320M	80018	None	
	Denver	315K	80210	3300-3899	
	Denver	315L	80222	4300-4799	
	Denver	316K	80224	6900-7099	
MONTANA PL W	Jefferson Co	311K	80232	10900-11199	
	Lakewood	311M	80232	1700-1799	
	Lakewood	312L	80232	6600-6699	
	Lakewood	310M	80228	13200-13899	
MONTANE DR	Idaho Springs	780V	80452	1-299	
	Jefferson Co	308J	80401	1500E-2299E	
MONTANE DR	Jefferson Co	307L	80401	23900W-25499W	
MONTANO CT	Castle Pines North	436B	80108	12300-12399	
MONTANO PL	Castle Pines North	436A	80108	6400-6499	
MONTANO WAY	Castle Pines North	436A	80108	12300-12399	
MONT BLANC DR	Jefferson Co	338E	80454	23600-23999	
MONTCLAIR CT E	Highlands Ranch	405B	80126	2900-2999	
MONTCLAIR DR S	Highlands Ranch	405B	80126	9600-9699	
MONTCLAIR LN	Boulder	98L	80301	3900-3999	
MONTCLAIR PL	Denver	286K	80220	7000-7099	
MONTCOMBRE DR	El Paso Co	908R	80132	None	
MONTE WAY	Northglenn	194D	80233	None	
MONTEREY CIR	Northglenn	194P	80260	10200-10399	
MONTEREY CT	Broomfield	162P	80020	1400-1599	
MONTEREY DR	Broomfield	162P	80020	1300-1499	
MONTEREY LN	Jefferson Co	306T	80439	29800-29999	
MONTEREY PL	Boulder Co	98K	80301	3700-3899	
MONTEREY PL	Highlands Ranch	376W	80130	6200-6399	
MONTERRA CT	Castle Rock	497Q	80104	None	
MONTESSORI WAY	Boulder Co	99K	80301	None	
MONTE VISTA AVE	Boulder Co	70L	80503	8600-8699	
MONTE VISTA CT	Fort Lupton	728L	80621	400-499	
MONTE VISTA RD	Jefferson Co	278Y	80401	300-699	
MONTE VISTA ST	Brighton	139P	80601	300-399	
MONTEZUMA ST	Brighton	139P	80601	100-399	
MONTGOMERY AVE W	Jefferson Co	341Q	80127	10000-10799	
MONTGOMERY CIR	Longmont	12R	80501	1700-1799	
MONTGOMERY CIR	Weld Co	706P	80504	11600-11799	
MONTGOMERY CT S	Superior	160L	80027	1200-1299	
MONTGOMERY DR	Erie	103P	80516	1-499	
MONTICELLO AVE W	Jefferson Co	372Q	80128	6200-6499	
MONTICELLO PL W	Jefferson Co	371R	80128	9100-9199	
MONTROSE WAY S	Highlands Ranch	404D	80126	9200-9399	
MONTVALE CIR	Highlands Ranch	405Q	80126	10700-10899	
MONTVALE DR	Highlands Ranch	405Q	80126	4900-5099	
MONTVEW BLVD	Aurora	288C	80011	15300-15799	
MONTVIEW BLVD E	Aurora	286H	80010	8900-9298	E
	Aurora	287F	80010	9300-12099	
	Aurora	287H	80010	12100-13399	
	Aurora	288F	80011	14200-15299	
	Aurora	289F	80011	18500-19499	
	Denver	285G	80207	4000-5499	
	Denver	286G	80207	5500-6999	
	Denver	286G	80220	7000-8899	
MONTVIEW DR E	Aurora	289H	80011	19500-19999	
MONTVIEW LN W	Douglas Co	403R	80125	7000-7299	
MONUMENT CIR	Castle Rock	498H	80104	1400-1499	
MONUMENT DR	Castle Rock	498D	80104	1200-5999	
MONUMENT DR	Highlands Ranch	374X	80129	700-799	
MONUMENT HILL RD	El Paso Co	908S	80132	18700-20499	
MONUMENT LAKE RD	El Paso Co	908S	80132	100-599	
MOON CIR	Thornton	225A	80229	9000-9099	
MOON CT E	Thornton	195W	80229	9000-9199	
MOON DR	Park Co	841R	80421	1-99	
MOON DANCE LN	Gilpin Co	761E	80403	1-299	
MOONDARRA CIR	Elbert Co	872E	80117	None	
MOONDUST PL	Castle Rock	496B	80109	None	
MOONEY PL	Erie	133E	80516	100-2899	
MOONFIRE WAY	Castle Rock	466Z	80109	None	
MOONLIGHT DR	Jefferson Co	370W	80127	9200-9499	
MOONLIGHT DR	Longmont	12V	80501	None	
MOONLIGHT WAY	Douglas Co	469A	80134	5100-5499	
MOONLIGHT WAY	Palmer Lake	907U	80133	None	
MOONSHADOW LN	Jefferson Co	307X	80439	3100-3199	
MOONSHINE RIDGE TRAIL					
	Douglas Co	850N	80134	4600-4999	
MOONSTONE CT	Longmont	41U	80504	None	
MOONSTONE LN	Castle Rock	467M	80108	1600-1799	
MOORE CIR	Arvada	221Y	80004	6300-6399	
	Westminster	191L	80021	10700-10799	
MOORE CIR S	Lakewood	311L	80232	1700-1899	
MOORE CT	Arvada	221Q	80005	7500-7699	
	Arvada	221G	80005	8300-8599	
	Westminster	191Q	80021	10100-10499	
	Westminster	191L	80021	10600-10699	
	Wheat Ridge	251Y	80033	3200-3699	
	Wheat Ridge	251Q	80033	4400-4499	
MOORE CT S	Jefferson Co	371G	80127	7100-7399	
	Jefferson Co	371L	80127	7400-7499	
	Lakewood	311C	80226	700-799	
	Lakewood	311L	80232	1700-1899	
	Lakewood	311L	80227	2000-2099	
MOORE DR	Castle Rock	497M	80104	1-199	
MOORE DR S	Lakewood	311U	80227	2600-2699	
MOORE RD	Douglas Co	846B	80125	7500-9099	
	Douglas Co	403Y	80125	9100-9999	
MOORE ST	Arvada	251C	80004	6000-6199	
	Arvada	221U	80004	6500-6999	
	Arvada	221L	80005	7700-8199	
	Arvada	221G	80005	8200-8599	
	Lakewood	281Q	80215	600-799	
	Lakewood	281L	80215	1200-1299	
	Lakewood	281G	80215	1700-2099	
	Lakewood	281C	80215	2500-2599	
MOORE ST	Park Co	820Y	80421	1-599	
	Westminster	191Q	80021	10000-10499	
	Westminster	191L	80021	10600-10799	
	Wheat Ridge	251Y	80033	3200-3499	
	Wheat Ridge	251U	80033	3500-4099	
	Wheat Ridge	251Q	80033	4200-4399	
MOORE ST S	Jefferson Co	341C	80235	3600-3899	
	Jefferson Co	341L	80127	4700-4899	
	Jefferson Co	341U	80127	5500-5899	
	Jefferson Co	371C	80127	6400-6799	
	Jefferson Co	371L	80127	7300-7499	
	Jefferson Co	371U	80127	8400-8599	
	Jefferson Co	341Y	80127	None	
	Lakewood	281Y	80226	300-499	
	Lakewood	311C	80226	700-899	
	Lakewood	311Q	80227	2100-2299	
MOORE WAY	Westminster	191L	80021	10700-10799	
MOOREDALE RD	Park Co	840U	80421	None	
MOORHEAD AVE	Boulder	128K	80305	2700-4999	
MOORHEAD CIR E	Boulder	128V	80305	700-1099	
MOORHEAD CIR W	Boulder	128U	80305	700-4899	
MOORING RD	Boulder Co	41Y	80504	10300-10699	
MOORSIDE DR	Parker	409J	80134	17000-17199	
MOORWOOD PT	El Paso Co	908T	80132	1700-1799	
MOOSE CIR	Douglas Co	870E	80116	1-399	
MOOSE ST	Frederick	727B	80530	None	
MOOSE CREEK CT S	Parker	439C	80134	12500-12599	
MOOSE CREEK PL S	Parker	439C	80134	12500-12599	
MORAINE DR E	Aurora	381M	80016	27600-27899	
MORAINE PL E	Aurora	381J	80016	None	
	Aurora	381J	80016	None	
MORENGO ST	Lochbuie	729Y	80603	None	
MORGAN AVE	Keenesburg	732A	80643	None	
MORGAN DR	Boulder	128H	80303	700-999	
MORGAN PL	Douglas Co	466B	80108	100-199	
MORGAN RD	El Paso Co	910Y	80908	9100-9699	
MORGAN RD	Longmont	42B	80501	400-499	
MORGAN WAY	Frederick	707W	80504	None	
MORGAN TRAIL	Elbert Co	870D	80107	34400-35199	
MORMON DR	Jefferson Co	843F	80433	23800-23999	
MORNINGBIRD LN	Castle Rock	467W	80109	None	
MORNING DEW CT	Highlands Ranch	404L	80126	10500-10599	
MORNING DEW PL	Highlands Ranch	404L	80126	1-299	
MORNING DOVE DR	Longmont	12Y	80501	900-1099	
MORNING GLORY CT S					
	Highlands Ranch	405D	80130	9500-9599	
MORNING GLORY DR	Boulder	127L	80302	None	
MORNING GLORY DR	Castle Rock	466Q	80109	3500-3999	
MORNING GLORY LN	Littleton	343T	80123	5300-5899	
MORNING GLORY LN S					
	Highlands Ranch	405D	80130	9300-9499	
MORNING GLORY PL E					
	Highlands Ranch	405D	80130	5000-5399	
MORNING GLORY WAY S					
	Highlands Ranch	405D	80130	9300-9499	
MORNING HARVEST DR	Frederick	726D	80504	None	
MORNING ROSE DR	Jefferson Co	308E	80401	23300-23499	
MORNINGSIDE DR	Jefferson Co	823R	80465	9900-10099	
MORNINGSIDE DR	Longmont	12Y	80501	1400-1499	
MORNINGSIDE DR	Wheat Ridge	251Y	80215	1-99	
MORNINGSIDE PKWY	Frederick	726C	80530	3600-4099	
	Frederick	706Z	80530	None	
MORNINGSIDE WAY	Douglas Co	470D	80134	5000-5199	
MORNINGSIDE PARK DR	Boulder	97X	80304	200-299	
MORNING SKY PL	Elbert Co	890G	80107	300-899	
MORNING SONG CT	Castle Rock	466X	80109	3300-3499	
MORNING STAR CIR	Gilpin Co	761E	80403	1-699	
MORNING STAR CT	Elbert Co	851X	80107	4000-4499	
	Elbert Co	832W	80107	43900-44999	
MORNING STAR DR	Douglas Co	466H	80108	4200-4299	
MORNING STAR DR	Jefferson Co	336A	80439	31300-31499	
MORNING STAR LN	Lafayette	131F	80026	200-499	
MORNING STAR PL E	Douglas Co	440V	80134	9100-9299	
MORNING STAR WAY	Douglas Co	466H	80108	300-399	
MORNINGVIEW DR	Castle Rock	466C	80109	None	
	Castle Rock	496B	80109	None	
MORNINGVIEW LN	Castle Rock	496C	80109	1300-1799	
MORRAINE AVE W	Jefferson Co	372M	80128	5800-6299	
	Jefferson Co	372J	80128	8100-8299	
	Jefferson Co	371M	80127	9700-9799	
MORRAINE DR W	Jefferson Co	372J	80128	7800-8599	
MORRAINE PL W	Jefferson Co	372L	80128	6300-6699	
	Jefferson Co	371L	80127	9900-9999	
MORRIS AVE	Jefferson Co	823N	80433	25000-26499	
MORRIS AVE	Weld Co	729A	80621	15000-15999	
MORRIS CT	Aurora	257Z	80011	None	
MORRIS CT	Erie	132A	80026	1800-1899	
MORRIS DR	Erie	132A	80026	None	
MORRISON AVE	Jefferson Co	842V	80470	28300-28499	
MORRISON CT	Superior	160R	80027	1700-1799	
MORRISON DR	Adams Co	223V	80221	6800-6999	
MORRISON DR	Frederick	727B	80530	None	
MORRISON RD	Denver	283L	80204	1400-1499	
	Denver	283X	80219	3400-4299	
	Denver	313A	80219	4200-5199	
	Lakewood	312N	80227	7600-8999	
	Lakewood	311S	80227	9000-11599	
	Lakewood	311S	80228	11600-13499	
	Lakewood	310X	80228	13500-16099	
MORROW PT	El Paso Co	910W	80908	6100-6199	
MOSELLE CT	Federal Heights	193Z	80260	None	
MOSELLE ST	Federal Heights	193Z	80260	2000-2099	
MOSEY CIR E	Parker	410X	80138	None	
MOSIER CIR	Jefferson Co	823P	80433	24900-25699	

M

STREET NAME	CITY or COUNTY	MAP GRID	ZIP CODE	BLOCK RANGE	O/E
MOSIER PL W	Denver	314B	80223	1700-1899	
	Denver	313H	80223	2400-2499	
	Denver	313H	80219	2500-2699	
	Denver	313F	80219	3900-3999	
MOSIER ST	Jefferson Co	823P	80433	24900-25899	
MOSKO CT	Adams Co	223U	80221	3400-3499	
MOSQUITO CREEK RD	Gilpin Co	760X	80452	None	
MOSS CIR	Arvada	220W	80007	6400-6599	
MOSS CT	Arvada	220W	80007	6600-6699	
	Arvada	220S	80007	7000-7199	
	Jefferson Co	250A	80403	None	
MOSS ST	Golden	280S	80401	300-399	
	Jefferson Co	280N	80401	600-899	
	Jefferson Co	280J	80401	900-1399	
MOSS WAY	Jefferson Co	280S	80401	1-199	
MOSSBERG CT	Elbert Co	851W	80107	36600-36899	
MOSS ROCK PL	Boulder	97R	80304	1400-1599	
MOSS ROCK PL	Gilpin Co	741Z	80403	1-199	
MOSS ROCK RD	El Paso Co	910Q	80908	8500-8899	
MOSS ROCK RD	Jefferson Co	276Z	80401	28200-28799	
MOSS ROCK RD	Park Co	841J	80421	1-299	
MOSSROCK RUN	Douglas Co	432X	80125	10400-10699	
MOSS ROSE CIR S	Highlands Ranch	403D	80129	9600-9799	
MOSSY ROCK DR	Highlands Ranch	375U	80126	3800-3899	
MOSSY ROCK LN	Jefferson Co	336D	80439	3800-3999	
MOTHER MOUNTAIN WAY	Gilpin Co	761C	80403	1-199	
MOTSENBOCKER RD	Parker	439F	80134	8000-8999	
MOTSENBOCKER RD N	Douglas Co	409X	80134	9000-10999	
	Parker	409N	80134	11000-11399	
MOTSENBOCKER WAY	Parker	409J	80134	17000-17099	
MOULTON CT	Castle Rock	498V	80104	None	
MOUNTAIN DR	Longmont	40N	80503	None	
MOUNTAIN LN	Douglas Co	867N	80135	3600-3799	
MOUNTAIN RD W	Sheridan	343F	80110	3300-3599	
MOUNTAIN ALDER	Jefferson Co	370P	80127	1-99	
MOUNTAIN ASH	Jefferson Co	370Q	80127	1-99	
MOUNTAIN ASTER PL	Gilpin Co	761C	80403	1-99	
MOUNTAIN BASE RD	Gilpin Co	761L	80403	None	
MOUNTAIN BIRCH	Jefferson Co	370F	80127	1-99	
MOUNTAIN BLUEBIRD WAY	Jefferson Co	370A	80127	16100-16199	
MOUNTAIN BROOK DR	Jefferson Co	843A	80433	27400-27599	
MOUNTAIN BRUSH CIR	Highlands Ranch	376X	80130	6900-7199	
MOUNTAIN BRUSH CT	Highlands Ranch	376X	80130	9100-9299	
MOUNTAIN BRUSH LN	Highlands Ranch	376X	80130	7200-7299	
MOUNTAIN BRUSH PL	Highlands Ranch	376X	80130	9100-9199	
MOUNTAIN BRUSH ST S	Highlands Ranch	406B	80130	9200-9399	
MOUNTAIN BRUSH PEAK S	Highlands Ranch	406B	80130	9200-9299	
MOUNTAIN BRUSH TRAIL	Highlands Ranch	376X	80130	9200-9299	
MOUNTAIN CEDAR LN	Jefferson Co	370K	80127	1-99	
MOUNTAIN CHICKADEE RD	Highlands Ranch	374U	80126	300-699	
MOUNTAIN CLOUD CIR	Highlands Ranch	374Y	80126	100-399	
MOUNTIAN DAISY CT W	Highlands Ranch	404A	80129	1800-1899	
MOUNTIAN DAISY WAY S	Highlands Ranch	404A	80129	9600-9699	
MOUNTAIN GOLD RUN	Broomfield	133W	80026	4800-4899	
MOUNTAIN HIGH CT	Jefferson Co	370J	80127	1-99	
MOUNTAIN HOUSE RD	Gilpin Co	761P	80403	100-599	
MOUNTAIN IRIS DR	Erie	133D	80516	None	
MOUNTAINJOY LN	Gilpin Co	760H	80403	1-199	
MOUNTAIN LAUREL CIR	Highlands Ranch	375W	80126	1800-1999	
MOUNTAIN LAUREL DR	Jefferson Co	370F	80127	1-99	
MOUNTAIN LAUREL PL	Boulder	97Q	80304	3700-3799	
MOUNTAIN LAUREL WAY	Highlands Ranch	375W	80126	8900-9099	
MOUNTAIN LAUREL TRAIL	Highlands Ranch	375W	80126	None	
MOUNTAIN MAHOGANY	Jefferson Co	370F	80127	1-99	
MOUNTAIN MAN DR	Parker	409L	80134	18700-19199	
MOUNTAIN MANOR CT N	Douglas Co	440T	80134	6400-6499	
MOUNTAIN MAPLE AVE W	Highlands Ranch	404J	80129	1500-1599	
	Highlands Ranch	403M	80129	1600-2199	
MOUNTAIN MAPLE CT S	Highlands Ranch	403H	80129	10100-10199	
MOUNTAIN MAPLE DR S	Highlands Ranch	403M	80129	10100-10299	
MOUNTAIN MAPLE LN S	Highlands Ranch	403H	80129	10100-10199	
MOUNTAIN MEADOWS DR	Gilpin Co	761E	80403	1-1099	
MOUNTAIN MEADOWS RD	Boulder Co	722W	80302	1-1599	
MOUNTAIN MEADOWS TRAIL	Castle Rock	466N	80109	4900-5199	
MOUNTAIN MOSS CT	Jefferson Co	337Q	80439	25500-25599	
MOUNTAIN OAK	Jefferson Co	370Q	80127	1-99	
MOUNTAIN PARK DR	Jefferson Co	337U	80439	24600-25099	
MOUNTAIN PARK DR N	Jefferson Co	337U	80439	24700-25099	
MOUNTAIN PARK RD	Jefferson Co	337N	80439	26700-28099	
MOUNTAIN PINE DR	Jefferson Co	370Q	80127	1-99	
MOUNTAIN PINES RD	Boulder Co	722W	80302	1-1599	
MOUNTAIN RANCH RD	Douglas Co	907G	80118	1500-14099	
MOUNTAIN RANCH RD	Jefferson Co	365Z	80433	9100-9199	
MOUNTAIN RIDGE PL	Boulder Co	703T	80302	9500-9699	
MOUNTAIN RIDGE RD	Boulder Co	703T	80302	9100-9699	
MOUNTAIN ROSE LN	Gilpin Co	761C	80403	1-99	
MOUNTAIN SAGE DR	Highlands Ranch	375W	80126	1800-2299	
MOUNTAIN SAGE PL	Highlands Ranch	375W	80126	1800-1899	
MOUNTAIN SAGE RUN	Highlands Ranch	375W	80126	1800-1899	
MOUNTAIN SAGE TERRACE	Highlands Ranch	375W	80126	2200-2299	
MOUNTAIN SHADOWS BLVD	Firestone	707N	80504	None	
MOUNTAIN SHADOWS CT	Castle Rock	497C	80104	1-199	
MOUNTAIN SHADOWS DR	Wheat Ridge	251W	80215	3000-3199	
MOUNTAIN SHADOWS LN	Castle Rock	497C	80104	1-99	
MOUNTAINSIDE TRAIL	Jefferson Co	336A	80439	3700-3999	
MOUNTAIN SKY DR	Castle Rock	528A	80104	None	
MOUNTAIN SPIRIT WAY	Jefferson Co	338P	80454	22200-22899	
MOUNTAIN UTES TRAIL	Gilpin Co	761N	80403	None	
MOUNTAIN VIEW	Lyons	703C	80540	None	
MOUNTAIN VIEW	Monument	908W	80132	100-299	
MOUNTAIN VIEW AVE	Douglas Co	470S	80116	2600-2899	
MOUNTAINVIEW AVE	Federal Heights	223D	80260	None	
MOUNTAIN VIEW AVE	Longmont	11Y	80501	100-2799	
	Longmont	10Z	80503	2800-3899	
MOUNTAIN VIEW AVE E	Longmont	12X	80501	1-699	
	Longmont	12Y	80501	None	
MOUNTAIN VIEW BLVD	Erie	133C	80516	None	
MOUNTAIN VIEW CIR	Broomfield	133U	80020	None	
MOUNTAINVIEW CT	Frederick	706Y	80504	None	
MOUNTAIN VIEW CT	Longmont	10Y	80503	3600-3699	
MOUNTAIN VIEW CT	Louisville	130Y	80027	100-199	
MOUNTAIN VIEW DR	Broomfield	726Y	80516	1700-1999	
MOUNTAIN VIEW DR	Castle Rock	497C	80104	900-999	
MOUNTAIN VIEW DR	Clear Creek Co	801A	80452	1-699	
MOUNTAIN VIEW DR	Frederick	727F	80530	7700-7898	E
MOUNTAIN VIEW DR	Mead	706C	80542	101-199	O
MOUNTAIN VIEW DR N	Douglas Co	440T	80134	6300-6499	
MOUNTAIN VIEW LN	Boulder Co	130H	80303	None	
MOUNTAIN VIEW LN	Douglas Co	403N	80125	8500-8999	
MOUNTAIN VIEW RD	Boulder	127C	80302	400-599	
MOUNTAIN VIEW RD	Douglas Co	867N	80135	1800-2099	
MOUNTAIN VIEW RD	Gilpin Co	760G	80403	1-799	
MOUNTAINVIEW RD	Greenwood Village	346T	80111	1-99	
MOUNTAIN VIEW RD	Jefferson Co	277P	80401	25900-26199	
	Jefferson Co	822Z	80433	28500-28799	
MOUNTAIN VIEW RD S	Douglas Co	496W	80109	500-1599	
MOUNTAIN VIEW ST	Weld Co	726K	80516	1700-1999	
MOUNTAIN VIEW MEADOW CIR	Elbert Co	831K	80138	3900-3998	E
MOUNTAIN VISTA LN	Jefferson Co	336R	80439	None	
MOUNTAIN VISTA LN W	Castle Rock	466T	80109	4300-4499	
MOUNTAIN WILLOW DR	Jefferson Co	370K	80127	1-99	
MT ANTERO WAY	Parker	410K	80138	10700-10899	
MT AUDUBON PL	Boulder Co	69Z	80503	5500-5699	
MT AUDUBON ST	Frederick	707W	80504	5000-5299	
MT BAILEY DR	Park Co	841T	80421	1-599	
MT BELFORD DR	Brighton	139R	80601	None	
MT BIERSTADT ST	Brighton	139R	80601	None	
MT BROSS ST	Brighton	139V	80601	None	
MT BROSS WAY	Parker	410K	80138	10700-10899	
MT CAMERON DR	Brighton	139R	80601	None	
MT COLUMBIA PL	Parker	410P	80138	10500-10599	
MT ELBERT CT	Parker	410P	80138	10700-10799	
MT ELBERT PL	Parker	410K	80138	21600-21899	
MT ELBERT ST	Brighton	139Q	80601	None	
MT EOLUS ST	Brighton	139Q	80601	None	
MT EVANS BLVD	Park Co	841D	80470	1-2799	
MOUNT EVANS CT	Louisville	130U	80027	800-899	
MOUNT EVANS DR	Longmont	12S	80501	1300-1699	
MT EVANS LN S	Jefferson Co	305Q	80453	2500-2699	
MT EVANS PL	Boulder Co	70W	80503	5200-5599	
MT EVANS RD	Jefferson Co	277P	80401	400-699	
MT EVANS ST	Brighton	139U	80601	None	
MOUNT EVANS ST	Longmont	42A	80501	500-899	
MT EVANS VISTA RD	Jefferson Co	278Y	80401	400-699	
MT FALCON RD	Jefferson Co	338G	80454	21000-21899	
MT HARVARD ST	Brighton	139Q	80601	None	
MT HERMAN RD	El Paso Co	908Z	80132	2700-3799	
MT HOLY CROSS	Jefferson Co	371E	80127	7100-7399	
MT LINCOLN ST	Brighton	139Q	80601	None	
MT LINDSEY ST	Brighton	139Q	80601	None	
MT LOGAN DR	Park Co	840D	80421	None	
MT MAPLE RD	Jefferson Co	277V	80401	24000-24399	
MT MARCY	Jefferson Co	371L	80127	7500-7699	
MT MASSIVE DR	Brighton	139R	80601	None	
MOUNT MASSIVE WAY	Longmont	12N	80501	100-199	
MT MEEKER RD	Boulder Co	69Z	80301	5400-7099	
	Boulder Co	69Z	80503	7100-7399	
	Boulder Co	70W	80503	7400-7499	
MT NAVAJO ST	Frederick	707W	80504	None	
MT OSAGE ST	Frederick	707W	80504	5001-5099	O
MT OWEN	Jefferson Co	371L	80127	7500-7599	
MT OXFORD ST	Brighton	139Q	80601	None	
MT PAWNEE AVE	Frederick	707W	80504	5000-5198	E
MT POWELL	Jefferson Co	371E	80127	12100-12199	
MT PRINCETON ST	Brighton	139U	80601	None	
MT PYRAMID CT	Douglas Co	407F	80112	9700-9899	
MT ROSE WAY	Jefferson Co	308B	80401	900-999	
MOUNT ROYAL DR	Castle Rock	497X	80104	2200-3399	
MOUNT SANITAS AVE	Longmont	40N	80503	None	
MOUNTSFIELD DR	Jefferson Co	278U	80401	21500-21999	
MT SHAVANO ST	Brighton	139Q	80601	None	
MT SHERMAN RD	Boulder Co	69Z	80503	7100-7399	
	Boulder Co	70W	80503	7400-7499	
MT SHERMAN ST	Brighton	139Q	80601	None	
MOUNTSHIRE CIR	Highlands Ranch	405P	80126	10700-10899	
MOUNT SNEFFELS PL	Douglas Co	436Z	80108	6200-6299	
MT SNEFFELS ST	Brighton	139U	80601	None	
MOUNT SNEFFELS ST	Longmont	12N	80501	1800-2099	
MT SNOWMASS LN	Parker	410P	80138	21700-21899	
MT SOPRIS PKWY	Superior	160Y	80027	None	
MT VALENTINE DR	Jefferson Co	305C	80439	32600-32699	
MT VERNON AVE	Morrison	309Z	80465	200-399	
MT VERNON CIR	Jefferson Co	278X	80401	300-499	
MT VERNON RD	Jefferson Co	279R	80401	16400-17199	
	Jefferson Co	277V	80401	24200-25099	
MT VERNON COUNTRY CLUB RD S	Jefferson Co	277T	80401	1-199	
MOUNTVIEW DR	Elbert Co	850V	80107	1100-1499	
MT WILSON	Jefferson Co	842N	80470	None	
MT WILSON ST	Brighton	139Q	80601	None	
MT ZION DR	Golden	279E	80401	1800-1999	
	Golden	278H	80401	2000-2199	
MT ZIRKEL	Jefferson Co	371L	80127	7500-7699	
MOURNING DOVE CT	Frederick	706Y	80504	3300-3399	
MOURNING DOVE LN	Golden	279N	80401	700-799	
MOURNING DOVE LN	Highlands Ranch	374V	80126	8700-8799	
MOURNING DOVE LN	Jefferson Co	370A	80127	1-99	
MOUSE EAR	Jefferson Co	782A	80403	34700-34799	
MOVEEN HEIGHTS	El Paso Co	908T	80132	1600-1699	
MOWBRAY CT	Jefferson Co	307X	80439	26300-26499	
MOWRY PL	Westminster	193Y	80031	3100-3299	
	Westminster	193X	80031	3300-3599	
MUELLER DR	Highlands Ranch	404F	80129	700-799	
MUIRFIELD CIR	Broomfield	163F	80020	13800-13899	
MUIRFIELD CIR	Louisville	160G	80027	400-599	
MUIR FIELD CT	Boulder	69Z	80301	5300-5399	
MUIRFIELD CT	Broomfield	163F	80020	13800-13899	
MUIRFIELD CT	Louisville	160G	80027	400-499	
MUIRFIELD LN	Jefferson Co	305M	80439	1600-1799	
MUIRFIELD LOOP	Elbert Co	851C	80107	41000-41999	
MUIRFIELD PT	Broomfield	163K	80020	13800-13899	
MULBERRY CIR	Broomfield	192C	80020	300-399	
MULBERRY CT	Boulder	99E	80301	4500-4599	
MULBERRY LN W	Highlands Ranch	404E	80129	1000-1499	
MULBERRY PL W	Denver	283M	80204	2000-2399	
MULBERRY ST S	Highlands Ranch	404E	80129	9700-9799	
MULBERRY ST W	Louisville	130Y	80027	500-899	
MULBERRY WAY S	Highlands Ranch	404E	80129	9800-9899	
MULE DEER	Clear Creek Co	780E	80452	None	
MULE DEER PL	Douglas Co	432M	80125	7600-7999	
MULE DEER TRAIL	Jefferson Co	370B	80127	1-99	
MULLENS LN	Erie	103N	80516	None	
MULLIGAN DR	Mead	706D	80504	4000-4499	
MULLIGAN PL	Castle Rock	497Q	80104	1400-1599	
MULLIGAN LAKE DR	Mead	706C	80542	200-299	
MUMFORD AVE	Longmont	11M	80501	300-499	
MUMFORD PL	Longmont	12J	80501	1-99	
MUNOZ CT	Erie	102Q	80516	500-599	
MUNSTEAD PL	Douglas Co	408C	80134	None	
MURIEL DR	Northglenn	194G	80233	100-799	
	Northglenn	194H	80233	800-1599	
	Thornton	195G	80233	4000-4299	
MURIEL PL	Thornton	195G	80233	11000-11099	
MURPHY RD	Clear Creek Co	801V	80439	1-199	
MURPHY GULCH RD	Jefferson Co	369Z	80127	8700-9399	
MURRAY DR	Northglenn	194M	80233	10600-11199	
MURRAY PL	Northglenn	194H	80233	None	
MURRAY ST	Boulder Co	70J	80503	100-599	
MUSCADINE CT N	Aurora	291P	80018	100-599	
MUSCADINE CT S	Aurora	351X	80016	6200-6299	
	Aurora	381B	80016	6600-6699	
	Aurora	381F	80016	7300-7399	
MUSCOGEE VALLEY TRAIL	Monument	908W	80132	17200-17299	
MUSIC LN	Jefferson Co	306M	80439	27800-27899	
MUSK OX DR S	Arapahoe Co	812A	80102	1200-1299	
MUSKRAT RD	Gilpin Co	761S	80403	1-899	
MUSTANG AVE	Weld Co	729U	80603	None	
MUSTANG CIR	Douglas Co	846P	80135	4200-4899	
MUSTANG DR	Frederick	707W	80504	None	
MUSTANG DR	Mead	706G	80542	None	
MUSTANG RD E	Douglas Co	850T	80116	11200-11699	
MUSTANG WAY	El Paso Co	908Y	80132	300-399	
MUSTANG WAY	Jefferson Co	370Z	80127	13000-13199	
MUSTANG RUN PL	Castle Rock	496B	80109	None	
MUSTANG TRAIL	Elbert Co	870H	80107	34500-34999	
MUZZEL LOADER WAY	El Paso Co	908Y	80132	17400-17599	
MY RD	Jefferson Co	337B	80439	None	
MYERS GULCH RD	Jefferson Co	337C	80439	3300-4299	
MYRICK WAY	Douglas Co	825Z	80125	None	
MYRNA CT	Jefferson Co	842A	80470	33500-33899	
MYRNA PL	Thornton	194Z	80229	9100-9399	
MYRTLE PL W	Denver	283M	80204	1900-2399	
MYRTLE ST	Brighton	138Q	80601	1100-1699	
MYRTLEWOOD CT	Highlands Ranch	404C	80126	600-799	
MYRTLEWOOD LN	Lakewood	280D	80215	2100-2199	
MYSTIC CT	Douglas Co	410Z	80138	9400-9498	E
MYSTIC CT	Jefferson Co	306U	80439	29500-29599	
N					
NADM DR	Jefferson Co	762E	80403	33500-33899	
NAGEL DR	Thornton	194Z	80229	9100-9499	
NAIAD ST	Northglenn	194J	80234	800-1399	
NAKOTA DR	Jefferson Co	308B	80401	22400-22499	
NALL AVE	Lochbuie	729Z	80603	None	
NAMBE RD	Jefferson Co	338F	80454	4000-4499	
NAMBE TRAIL	Lone Tree	376Z	80124	9100-9199	
NAMPEYO RD	Jefferson Co	338J	80454	22800-23499	
NANCY AVE	Weld Co	729A	80621	15000-15999	
NANCY'S DR	Jefferson Co	822Y	80433	11400-11499	
NANCY'S LN	Jefferson Co	822Y	80433	12900-30199	
NANTUCKET CT W	Littleton	373R	80120	2000-2099	
NAPA DR E	Aurora	348D	80013	16700-16899	
	Aurora	349C	80013	18700-19199	
NAPA PL E	Aurora	348F	80014	14300-14399	
	Aurora	348D	80013	16600-16699	
	Denver	346C	80237	7600-7799	
	Denver	346H	80237	8500-8599	
NAPLES CT S	Aurora	318M	80013	1900-1999	
NAPLES LN	Longmont	40Q	80503	1500-1799	
NAPLES ST	Aurora	288M	80011	800-899	
NAPLES ST	Firestone	727B	80504	None	
NAPLES ST S	Aurora	318H	80017	1500-1899	
NAPLES WAY	Aurora	288R	80011	600-699	
NAPLES WAY S	Aurora	318D	80017	800-1099	
	Aurora	318R	80013	2100-2599	
	Aurora	348H	80014	4100-4299	
NARCISSUS WAY S	Denver	346B	80237	3600-4199	
NARIA DR E	Parker	439A	80134	None	
NARROWLEAF PL E	Aurora	380V	80138	None	
NARROW PINE LN	Parker	440A	80134	20400-20599	
NARROW PINE PKWY E	Parker	409Z	80134	None	
NASAU AVE E	Englewood	344C	80110	1-799	
NASAU AVE W	Englewood	344B	80110	1-1399	
NASHUA CIR N	Douglas Co	469D	80134	5200-5399	
NASHVILLE ST	Adams Co	751F	80642	None	
NASSAU AVE E	Arapahoe Co	350B	80013	None	
	Aurora	348C	80014	15100-15299	
	Denver	346C	80237	7600-7799	
	Denver	346H	80237	8500-8699	
	Denver	346D	80237	8900-9299	
	Englewood	344C	80113	1-799	
NASSAU AVE W	Jefferson Co	341G	80235	10301-10399	O
NASSAU CIR	Cherry Hills Village	345D	80113	5200E-5499E	
	Cherry Hills Village	345H	80113	3900W-5199W	
NASSAU CT	Highlands Ranch	376W	80130	6200-6499	

M

N

STREET NAME	CITY or COUNTY	MAP GRID	ZIP CODE	BLOCK RANGE	O/E
NASSAU DR E	Aurora	348C	80013	15300-15599	
	Aurora	348D	80013	15900-16299	
	Aurora	349F	80013	17900-18099	
	Aurora	349B	80013	18200-18399	
	Aurora	349C	80013	19100-19599	
NASSAU PL	Boulder	98L	80301	4000-4699	
NASSAU PL E	Arapahoe Co	350F	80013	None	
	Aurora	349A	80013	17100-17199	
	Aurora	349F	80013	17700-17899	
	Aurora	350B	80018	21800-21899	
	Aurora	350C	80018	22300-22399	
	Cherry Hills Village	346E	80111	5700-5799	
NASSAU WAY W	Englewood	344F	80110	600-799	
NATALIA LN	Mead	706M	80504	None	
NATCHES CT S	Sheridan	314W	80110	3500-3599	
	Sheridan	344E	80110	3600-4599	
NATE CIR	Parker	439C	80134	12300-12499	
NATE DR	Parker	439C	80134	12300-12799	
NATES RD	Westminster	193W	80031	None	
NATIONAL PL	Longmont	11V	80501	300-399	
NATIONAL WESTERN DR	Denver	254M	80216	4600-5199	
NATIVE DANCER TRAIL	Jefferson Co	366R	80439	7500-8199	
NATSHI RD	Jefferson Co	338P	80454	22100-22999	
NATURAL SPRING RD	Jefferson Co	842J	80470	None	
NATURE WALK TRAIL	Parker	379W	80134	17300-17599	
NAUTILUS CT	Lafayette	131Q	80026	1100-1199	
NAUTILUS CT N	Boulder	99C	80301	4800-4999	
NAUTILUS CT S	Boulder	99F	80301	4600-4799	
NAUTILUS DR	Boulder	99F	80301	6300-6599	
NAUTIQUE CIR	Douglas Co	889X	80118	4100-7199	
NAVAJO CIR	Westminster	194E	80234	None	
NAVAJO CT	Adams Co	226B	80022	None	
NAVAJO CT	Weld Co	707U	80504	9900-9999	
NAVAJO CT	Westminster	164S	80234	12400-12499	
NAVAJO PL	Boulder	128Q	80303	4500-4599	
NAVAJO RD	Jefferson Co	337M	80439	22100-24399	
NAVAJO ST	Adams Co	224S	80221	6800-6999	
	Adams Co	224N	80221	7200-7299	
	Adams Co	224J	80221	7600-7799	
	Adams Co	224E	80221	8200-8399	
	Adams Co	134W	80020	15200-15599	
	Denver	284N	80223	300-399	
	Denver	284N	80204	700-1099	
	Denver	254S	80211	3200-4599	
NAVAJO ST	Kiowa	872M	80117	200-499	
NAVAJO ST	Northglenn	194E	80234	11100-11199	
	Westminster	194E	80234	11200-11299	
	Westminster	194A	80234	11500-11599	
	Westminster	164J	80234	13500-13599	
	Westminster	164E	80020	None	
NAVAJO ST S	Denver	284W	80223	100-699	
	Denver	314A	80223	700-799	
	Denver	314E	80223	1100-1499	
	Denver	314J	80223	1900-2099	
	Denver	314N	80223	2300-2399	
	Englewood	344J	80110	4100-4599	
NAVAJO TRAIL	Clear Creek Co	365N	80439	1-199	
NAVAJO TRAIL	Jefferson Co	822Z	80433	11600-11899	
NAVAJO TRAIL	Lafayette	131G	80026	2000-2099	
NAVAJO TRAIL	Nederland	740L	80466	None	
NAVAJO TRAIL	Park Co	842E	80470	1-199	
NAVARRO DR E	Aurora	348D	80013	16600-16899	
	Aurora	349C	80013	19400-19499	
	Aurora	350C	80018	22300-22399	
NAVARRO PL E	Aurora	348F	80014	14500-14899	
	Aurora	348H	80014	15800-15899	
	Aurora	349E	80013	17100-17299	
	Aurora	349D	80013	19600-19799	
	Aurora	350B	80018	22200-22299	
	Denver	346C	80237	7600-7799	
NAVY HILL RD S	Jefferson Co	843N	80470	15700-15899	
NEAL RD	Park Co	820V	80421	1-699	
NEAL ST	Park Co	820V	80421	1-299	
NEBO RD	Boulder Co	723B	80302	3100-3699	
NEBRASKA DR	Denver	315H	80246	5300-5599	
NEBRASKA WAY	Boulder Co	72E	80504	7200-7399	
NEBRASKA WAY	Denver	316E	80224	5600-5699	
NEBRINA PL	Boulder	98P	80301	2800-2899	
NEBULA WAY	Castle Rock	467G	80108	None	
NEEDLE GRASS CT	Parker	378R	80134	8300-8399	
NEEDLELEAF CIR	Elbert Co	830Q	80138	46000-46399	
NEEDLES CT	Parker	410P	80138	11000-11099	
NEEDLES DR	El Paso Co	909X	80908	3300-3799	
NEEDLES LN	Parker	410P	80138	21500-21599	
NEEDLES TRAIL	Jefferson Co	366L	80439	28800-29099	
NEHER LN	Boulder	97R	80304	1-2199	
NEIGHBORS PKWY	Firestone	707S	80504	None	
NEIL PL	Denver	255Y	80205	3600-3699	
NEIL ST	Thornton	224B	80260	8800-8899	
NEISH ST	Park Co	820Y	80421	1-699	
NELL ST	Lochbuie	140A	80603	None	
NELLIE WAY	Lochbuie	729Z	80603	None	
NELLIES WAY	Douglas Co	528N	80104	3100-3299	
NELSON AVE	Jefferson Co	823N	80433	26000-26499	
	Jefferson Co	842E	80470	34000-34699	
NELSON AVE	Keenesburg	732A	80643	None	
NELSON CIR S	Jefferson Co	341C	80235	3500-3599	
NELSON CT	Arvada	251C	80004	5800-5999	
	Arvada	221G	80005	8400-8599	
	Lakewood	251Y	80215	3000-3199	
	Westminster	191P	80021	10300-10399	
	Westminster	191Q	80021	10400-10499	
NELSON CT S	Jefferson Co	311U	80227	2600-2799	
	Jefferson Co	341C	80235	3800-3899	
	Jefferson Co	341Q	80127	4900-5099	
	Jefferson Co	371G	80127	7100-7199	
	Jefferson Co	371U	80127	8500-8599	
	Lakewood	311Y	80227	3300-3399	
NELSON DR	Arvada	221G	80005	8400-8499	
NELSON DR	Broomfield	163E	80020	4200-4799	
	Lakewood	251Y	80215	3000-3099	
NELSON PL	Lakewood	281C	80215	2200-2299	
NELSON RD	Boulder Co	703T	80503	2700-5499	
	Boulder Co	704S	80503	5500-7199	
	Boulder Co	40K	80503	7500-9099	
	Boulder Co	41J	80503	9101-9299	O
	Boulder Co	41K	80501	9500-9899	
NELSON RD	Longmont	41K	80501	1400-1899	
	Longmont	41J	80503	2700-2799	
NELSON RD	Ward	720M	80481	None	
NELSON ST	Weld Co	729V	80603	17000-17999	
NELSON ST	Arvada	251C	80004	6000-6199	
	Arvada	221Y	80004	6200-6399	
	Arvada	221U	80004	6500-7199	
	Arvada	221L	80005	7600-7899	
	Lakewood	281L	80215	800-1499	
	Lakewood	281G	80215	1700-2099	
	Lakewood	281C	80215	2500-2599	
	Westminster	191P	80021	10000-10199	
	Westminster	191Q	80021	10200-10499	
	Westminster	191L	80021	10600-10699	
	Wheat Ridge	251Y	80033	3200-3799	
	Wheat Ridge	251U	80033	3800-4099	
	Wheat Ridge	251G	80033	4700-4799	
NELSON ST	Erie	103S	80516	None	
NELSON ST S	Arapahoe Co	795Y	80103	200-399	
	Jefferson Co	311U	80227	2800-2999	
	Jefferson Co	341G	80235	3900-4299	
	Jefferson Co	341L	80127	4700-5399	
	Jefferson Co	341U	80127	5800-5899	
	Jefferson Co	371G	80127	7100-7399	
	Jefferson Co	371U	80127	8400-8499	
	Lakewood	281Y	80226	300-699	
	Lakewood	311C	80226	700-899	
	Lakewood	311Q	80227	2100-2299	
	Lakewood	311Y	80227	3300-3399	
NELSON WAY S	Jefferson Co	341C	80235	3500-3799	
	Jefferson Co	371C	80127	6400-6499	
	Jefferson Co	341Y	80127	None	
	Lakewood	311C	80226	800-999	
NELSON PARK DR	Longmont	40M	80503	600-899	
NELSON PARK LN	Longmont	40M	80503	600-899	
NEMRICK PL	Castle Rock	497F	80109	1400-1599	
NEON WAY	Castle Rock	467F	80108	None	
NEON FOREST CIR	Longmont	41U	80504	700-799	
NEOTA WAY	El Paso Co	910X	80908	7300-7499	
NEPAL CT S	Arapahoe Co	350A	80013	None	
	Aurora	320W	80013	None	
	Centennial	350N	80015	5400-5499	
	Centennial	350T	80015	5700-5799	
	Centennial	350S	80015	5900-5999	
NEPAL ST	Denver	260J	80249	None	
	Denver	260E	80249	None	
NEPAL ST N	Arapahoe Co	290J	80018	800-1099	
	Denver	260N	80249	4100-4699	
NEPAL ST S	Arapahoe Co	350A	80013	None	
	Arapahoe Co	350J	80015	None	
	Centennial	350S	80015	5800-5899	
NEPAL WAY S	Aurora	320S	80013	None	
	Centennial	350N	80015	5100-5399	
	Centennial	350S	80015	5600-5899	
NEPTUNE CT	Highlands Ranch	376U	80124	300-499	
NEPTUNE DR	Lafayette	131R	80026	1100-1199	
NEPTUNITE WAY	Castle Rock	467G	80108	None	
NERHEIM RD	Gilpin Co	760H	80403	1-99	
NERO RD	Gilpin Co	761N	80403	1-299	
NESTING CRANE LN	Weld Co	706E	80504	500-599	
NETHERLAND CIR S	Centennial	350T	80015	5800-6099	
	Centennial	350W	80016	6100-6399	
NETHERLAND CT	Denver	260E	80249	None	
NETHERLAND CT S	Centennial	350P	80015	5400-5499	
NETHERLAND ST	Denver	260J	80249	4900-5599	
NETHERLAND ST N	Denver	260N	80249	4000-4399	
NETHERLAND ST S	Arapahoe Co	350B	80013	None	
	Arapahoe Co	350J	80015	None	
	Centennial	350S	80015	5500-5799	
NETHERLAND WAY S	Arapahoe Co	350K	80015	None	
	Aurora	380F	80016	6800-7099	
	Centennial	350N	80015	5100-5399	
	Centennial	350W	80016	6100-6499	
NETWORK PKWY	Broomfield	161X	80021	None	
NEU TOWNE CIR S	Parker	409S	80134	None	
NEU TOWNE PKWY E	Parker	409S	80134	None	
NEVA RD	Boulder Co	723C	80503	3100-3299	
	Boulder Co	70F	80503	7900-8299	
NEVADA AVE E	Aurora	287Z	80012	12100-13099	
	Aurora	288W	80012	13100-13699	
NEVADA AVE W	Lakewood	281Z	80226	None	
NEVADA CIR E	Aurora	287Y	80012	11900-11999	
	Aurora	287Z	80012	12800-12899	
NEVADA CIR S	Littleton	373M	80120	7500-7599	
NEVADA DR S	Littleton	373M	80120	7700-7799	
NEVADA DR W	Lakewood	281W	80228	12000-12199	
NEVADA PL E	Aurora	287Z	80012	12100-12399	
	Aurora	288W	80012	13600-13699	
	Denver	286X	80224	6500-6699	
NEVADA PL W	Denver	284W	80223	1200-1599	
	Denver	283W	80219	3100-5199	
	Lakewood	282Y	80226	6000-6899	
	Lakewood	282W	80226	8200-8399	
	Lakewood	311A	80228	12100-12599	
NEVADA ST	Central City	780C	80427	1-1299	
NEVADA ST S	Littleton	343V	80120	5400-5999	
NEVADAVILLE RD	Clear Creek Co	780C	80403	1200-2999	
NEVILLE LN	Jefferson Co	306D	80401	800-899	
NEVIS ST	Boulder	98K	80301	4000-4199	
NEWARK CIR S	Aurora	287Y	80012	200-299	
NEWARK CT	Aurora	287Q	80010	500-599	
	Commerce City	197G	80640	11200-11299	
NEWARK CT S	Aurora	287Y	80012	600-799	
	Aurora	317L	80112	1700-1799	
	Aurora	317U	80014	2600-2799	
NEWARK LN	Adams Co	137Q	80602	None	
NEWARK PL S	Aurora	317U	80014	2800-2999	
NEWARK ST	Adams Co	137L	80602	None	
NEWARK ST	Aurora	287U	80011	1-99	
	Aurora	287U	80010	200-599	
	Aurora	287L	80010	700-1299	
	Aurora	287C	80010	1600-2499	
NEWARK ST	Commerce City	197G	80640	11300-11399	
	Commerce City	197G	80601	None	
	Commerce City	197Q	80640	None	
NEWARK ST S	Arapahoe Co	347U	80111	5600-5699	
NEWARK WAY S	Arapahoe Co	347Y	80111	6100-6199	
	Aurora	287Y	80012	400-499	
	Aurora	317C	80112	900-1099	
	Aurora	317L	80014	1900-2299	
NEWBERN CIR S	Arapahoe Co	381K	80016	7800-8099	
	Aurora	351Y	80016	6400-6599	
NEWBERN CT S	Aurora	381B	80016	7000-7099	
	Aurora	381F	80016	7100-7199	
	Aurora	291T	80018	None	
NEWBERN ST	Castle Rock	498M	80104	None	
NEWBERN ST S	Aurora	381C	80016	6600-6699	
NEWBERN WAY N	Aurora	291Q	80018	None	
NEWBERN WAY S	Aurora	321P	80018	1900-2699	
	Aurora	351X	80016	6100-6399	
	Aurora	291T	80018	None	
	Aurora	351Y	80016	None	
NEWBERRY CIR W	Lakewood	342F	80235	7800-7899	
NEWBERRY CT S	Denver	316P	80224	2400-2499	
NEWBURY CT	Highlands Ranch	405P	80126	2800-3099	
NEWBY PL	Longmont	12J	80501	1-99	
NEWCASTLE CT N	Aurora	291U	80018	None	
NEWCASTLE CT S	Arapahoe Co	381P	80016	8000-8099	
	Aurora	321Q	80018	2300-2499	
	Aurora	291T	80018	None	
NEWCASLTE DR S	Highlands Ranch	405D	80130	9600-9799	
NEWCASTLE WAY N	Aurora	291Q	80018	None	
NEWCASTLE WAY S	Aurora	351X	80016	6301-6399	O
	Aurora	291U	80018	None	
	Aurora	291Y	80018	None	
NEWCOMBE CT	Arvada	251C	80004	5800-6099	
	Arvada	221Y	80004	6400-6499	
	Westminster	191P	80021	10200-10399	
NEWCOMBE CT S	Jefferson Co	341L	80127	4800-5099	
	Jefferson Co	371U	80127	8500-8599	
	Jefferson Co	371G	80127	None	
	Lakewood	311Y	80227	3300-3399	
NEWCOMBE DR	Lakewood	281G	80215	1900-1999	
NEWCOMBE ST	Arvada	251C	80004	6000-6199	
	Arvada	221Y	80004	6400-6499	
	Arvada	221U	80004	6600-7099	
	Arvada	221F	80005	8400-8599	
	Lakewood	281L	80215	800-999	
	Lakewood	281G	80215	2000-2099	
	Lakewood	281C	80215	2500-2599	
	Westminster	191P	80021	10300-10399	
	Westminster	191Q	80021	10400-10499	
	Westminster	191L	80021	10600-10699	
	Wheat Ridge	251Q	80033	4200-4399	
	Wheat Ridge	251G	80033	None	
NEWCOMBE ST S	Jefferson Co	311Q	80227	2400-2799	
	Jefferson Co	341U	80127	5500-5599	
	Jefferson Co	371G	80127	7000-7199	
	Jefferson Co	371U	80127	8400-8499	
	Lakewood	281Y	80226	300-499	
	Lakewood	311Y	80227	3200-3399	
NEWCOMBE WAY	Lakewood	281C	80215	2200-2499	
	Westminster	191L	80021	10600-10699	
NEWCOMBE WAY S	Jefferson Co	311T	80227	2800-3099	
	Jefferson Co	341C	80235	3600-3699	
	Jefferson Co	371U	80127	8400-8599	
	Lakewood	311C	80226	800-899	
NEWGATE CT	El Paso Co	908R	80132	800-899	
NEWHALL DR E	Highlands Ranch	406B	80130	7000-7199	
NEW HAVEN CT	Boulder	98K	80301	4000-4099	
NEWLAND CIR	Arvada	222L	80003	7900-7999	
	Arvada	222G	80003	8200-8299	
NEWLAND CIR S	Jefferson Co	342Y	80123	6500-6699	
NEWLAND CT	Arvada	222L	80003	8000-8099	
	Arvada	222G	80003	8200-8299	
	Arvada	222C	80003	8400-8599	
NEWLAND CT	Boulder Co	129G	80303	700-799	
NEWLAND CT	Lakewood	282U	80226	1-99	
	Lakewood	282G	80214	1800-1999	
	Westminster	192U	80021	9600-9899	
	Wheat Ridge	252Y	80214	2800-2899	
NEWLAND CT S	Denver	342Q	80123	5400-5499	
	Jefferson Co	372C	80123	6200-6699	
	Jefferson Co	372G	80128	6900-7099	
	Jefferson Co	372Q	80128	7900-8499	
	Jefferson Co	372U	80128	8400-8499	
	Lakewood	282U	80226	1-99	
	Lakewood	312C	80226	1000-1099	
	Lakewood	312G	80232	1200-1399	
	Lakewood	312Y	80227	3400-3499	
	Lakewood	342U	80123	5700-5799	
NEWLAND DR	Arvada	222G	80003	8400-8499	
NEWLAND PL S	Lakewood	312G	80232	1100-1199	
NEWLAND ST	Arvada	252G	80002	5300-5499	
	Arvada	252C	80003	6000-6199	
	Arvada	222Y	80003	6200-6899	
	Arvada	222U	80003	6800-7199	
	Arvada	222Q	80003	7400-7599	
	Arvada	222L	80003	7600-7799	
	Edgewater	282G	80214	2000-2399	
	Edgewater	282C	80214	2400-2599	
	Lakewood	282U	80226	1-599	
	Lakewood	282L	80214	1200-1499	
	Westminster	192G	80020	10800-11399	
	Westminster	192C	80020	11500-11599	
	Wheat Ridge	282C	80214	2600-2799	
	Wheat Ridge	252Y	80214	2800-3199	
	Wheat Ridge	252U	80033	3200-4399	
	Wheat Ridge	252Q	80033	4400-4799	
NEWLAND ST S	Denver	312U	80227	2700-3099	
	Denver	312Y	80227	3200-3299	
	Denver	342C	80235	3500-3699	
	Jefferson Co	342U	80123	5900-5999	
	Jefferson Co	372G	80128	6900-7499	
	Jefferson Co	372L	80128	7500-7899	
	Jefferson Co	372U	80128	8300-8399	
	Lakewood	282U	80226	1-299	
	Lakewood	282Y	80226	300-699	
	Lakewood	312C	80226	900-1099	
	Lakewood	312G	80232	1100-1699	
	Lakewood	312L	80232	1700-1899	
	Lakewood	342U	80123	5700-5799	
NEWLAND WAY	Arvada	252G	80002	5500-5699	
NEWLAND WAY S	Jefferson Co	372C	80123	6500-6699	

N

STREET NAME	CITY or COUNTY	MAP GRID	ZIP CODE	BLOCK RANGE	O/E
NEWLIN CT	Douglas Co	408M	80134	10500-10599	
NEWLIN GULCH BLVD	Parker	408U	80134	None	
	Parker	408Y	80134	None	
NEWLIN GULCH RD	Douglas Co	408Y	80134	9000-10499	
NEW LONDON RD	El Paso Co	908Y	80132	17600-17999	
NEW LONDON WAY	El Paso Co	908Y	80132	400-499	
NEWMAN AVE	Gilpin Co	760G	80403	100-298	E
NEWMAN CIR	Longmont	42B	80501	400-499	
NEWMAN DR	Elbert Co	850L	80138	800-999	
NEWMAN ST	Arvada	221U	80004	6600-7199	
	Arvada	221L	80005	7600-8099	
	Wheat Ridge	251U	80033	3800-4099	
NEW MARKET CT	Parker	409Y	80134	19700-19899	
NEWMARKET ST	Ward	720M	80481	None	
NEW MEMPHIS CT	Castle Rock	467N	80108	800-899	
NEW MEXICO AVE W	Lakewood	311J	80228	12200-12399	
NEW MEXICO PL W	Jefferson Co	311K	80232	11400-11999	
	Lakewood	311K	80228	12000-12099	
NEWPORT CIR	Castle Rock	497X	80104	2700-3199	
NEWPORT CIR	Thornton	166K	80602	None	
NEWPORT CIR S	Greenwood Village	346P	80111	5400-5499	
NEWPORT CT	Adams Co	136K	80602	16600-16699	
	Thornton	166X	80602	12300-12399	
NEWPORT CT S	Centennial	346X	80111	6300-6499	
	Centennial	376F	80112	7100-7199	
	Centennial	376K	80112	7500-7699	
	Centennial	376P	80112	8000-8299	
NEWPORT DR	Thornton	166X	80602	12000-12299	
NEWPORT LN	Boulder	97L	80304	3800-3999	
NEWPORT LN	Elbert Co	850R	80107	38700-38899	
NEWPORT LN S	Highlands Ranch	406B	80130	9300-9399	
NEWPORT ST	Adams Co	226K	80022	7700-7999	
	Commerce City	256K	80022	4800-4999	
	Commerce City	256F	80022	5200-5599	
	Commerce City	256B	80022	5800-5999	
	Commerce City	226X	80022	6400-6699	
	Commerce City	226T	80022	6900-7199	
	Commerce City	226P	80022	7400-7499	
	Denver	286T	80220	100-499	
	Denver	286K	80220	600-1999	
	Denver	286B	80207	2000-2799	
	Denver	256X	80207	2800-3999	
NEWPORT ST	Thornton	136T	80602	15200-15299	
	Thornton	136T	80602	15400-15599	
	Thornton	166K	80602	None	
	Thornton	166P	80602	None	
NEWPORT ST	Thornton	196B	80233	None	
	Thornton	196E	80233	None	
NEWPORT ST S	Arapahoe Co	316K	80224	1900-1999	
	Centennial	346X	80111	6000-6299	
	Centennial	376F	80112	7000-7099	
	Denver	286X	80224	600-699	
	Denver	316F	80224	1300-1499	
	Denver	316K	80224	1800-1899	
	Denver	316P	80224	2400-2699	
	Denver	316X	80224	2800-3399	
	Denver	346P	80237	4800-5099	
	Greenwood Village	346K	80111	5300-5399	
	Greenwood Village	346T	80111	5500-5699	
NEWPORT WAY	Thornton	166P	80602	None	
NEWPORT WAY S	Centennial	376F	80112	7100-7499	
	Centennial	376P	80112	8100-8299	
	Denver	286X	80224	300-499	
	Denver	316K	80224	1700-1799	
	Denver	346B	80237	3600-4199	
NEWTON CT	Adams Co	223X	80003	6200-6399	
	Adams Co	223T	80003	6600-6699	
	Broomfield	163K	80020	13400-13599	
	Westminster	193T	80031	9900-9999	
	Westminster	193P	80031	10000-10299	
NEWTON DR	Westminster	193B	80031	None	
NEWTON LOOP	Westminster	193P	80031	None	
NEWTON PL	Westminster	193B	80031	11600-11699	
NEWTON ST	Adams Co	253F	80221	5200-5499	
	Adams Co	223X	80003	6400-6599	
	Adams Co	223B	80031	None	
	Broomfield	163T	80020	12400-12599	
	Denver	283T	80219	1-399	
	Denver	283K	80204	400-1999	
	Denver	283B	80211	2000-2599	
	Denver	253X	80211	2900-4099	
	Denver	253P	80211	4400-4799	
	Denver	253K	80221	4800-5199	
	Westminster	223T	80030	7100-7199	
	Westminster	223P	80030	7200-7599	
	Westminster	223K	80030	7600-7999	
	Westminster	223F	80031	8100-8199	
	Westminster	193X	80031	9000-9499	
	Westminster	193T	80031	9500-9799	
	Westminster	193B	80031	11600-11999	
NEWTON ST S	Denver	283T	80219	1-699	
	Denver	313F	80219	700-1699	
	Denver	313P	80219	1800-2699	
	Denver	313X	80236	2700-3299	
	Denver	343K	80236	3300-4699	
	Littleton	343K	80123	5000-5299	
NEWTON WAY	Broomfield	163T	80020	12500-12599	
	Westminster	223P	80030	7400-7499	
NEWTON WAY S	Denver	313T	80236	2700-2799	
NEW YORK PL	Denver	287X	80231	10100-10299	
NEZ PERCE TRAIL	Castle Rock	466U	80109	None	
NIAGARA CIR S	Centennial	376F	80112	7100-7299	
NIAGARA CT	Thornton	166X	80602	12100-12299	
NIAGARA CT S	Centennial	346X	80111	6000-6099	
	Centennial	346X	80111	6100-6299	
	Centennial	376B	80111	6400-6599	
	Centennial	376B	80112	6700-6999	
	Centennial	376F	80112	7000-7199	
	Centennial	376K	80112	7500-7699	
	Centennial	376P	80112	8100-8299	
	Greenwood Village	346P	80111	5400-5499	
NIAGARA ST	Adams Co	226K	80022	7400-7999	
	Adams Co	136J	80602	16500-16599	
	Commerce City	256K	80022	4900-4999	
	Commerce City	256F	80022	5300-5799	
	Commerce City	256B	80022	6000-6199	
	Commerce City	226T	80022	6400-7199	

Continued on next column

STREET NAME	CITY or COUNTY	MAP GRID	ZIP CODE	BLOCK RANGE	O/E
NIAGARA ST (Cont'd)	Denver	286T	80220	100-499	
	Denver	286K	80220	600-1999	
	Denver	286B	80207	2000-2799	
	Denver	256X	80207	2800-3999	
	Denver	346K	80237	None	
NIAGARA ST	Douglas Co	406P	80124	10000-10799	
NIAGARA ST	Thornton	166X	80602	12000-12299	
	Thornton	196B	80233	None	
NIAGARA ST	Thornton	136S	80602	15200-15399	
NIAGARA ST	Thornton	136S	80602	15400-15499	
NIAGARA ST	Thornton	166P	80602	None	
	Thornton	196E	80233	None	
	Thornton	166K	80602	None	
NIAGARA ST S	Arapahoe Co	316K	80224	1900-1998	E
	Centennial	346T	80111	5900-5999	
	Centennial	376P	80112	8100-8299	
	Denver	286X	80224	300-599	
	Denver	316B	80224	800-1099	
	Denver	316F	80224	1300-1499	
	Denver	316K	80224	1901-1999	O
	Denver	316T	80224	2600-2699	
	Denver	316X	80224	3200-3299	
NIAGARA WAY	Broomfield	133L	80020	16700-16799	
NIAGARA WAY	Thornton	166P	80602	None	
NIAGARA WAY S	Centennial	346X	80111	6100-6299	
	Centennial	376K	80112	7600-8099	
	Denver	316K	80224	1700-1899	
	Denver	316T	80224	2900-3099	
	Denver	316X	80224	3300-3399	
	Denver	346B	80237	3700-4199	
NIAKWA RD	Jefferson Co	366A	80439	30700-31599	
NIBLICK CT	Boulder Co	723G	80503	3900-3999	
NIBLICK DR	Boulder Co	723G	80503	3900-4299	
NIBLICK LN	Columbine Valley	343Y	80123	1-99	
NICHOLL ST	Boulder	98S	80304	2200E-2299E	
NICHOLS AVE E	Arapahoe Co	374Q	80122	800-1099	
	Arapahoe Co	374R	80122	1300-1399	
	Arapahoe Co	374R	80122	1600-1799	
	Arapahoe Co	378R	80112	15900-16099	
	Centennial	375N	80122	1600-1799	
	Centennial	375Q	80122	3600-3799	
	Centennial	376N	80112	6000-6099	
	Centennial	376P	80112	6900-6999	
	Centennial	376R	80112	8500-9099	
NICHOLS AVE W	Jefferson Co	372N	80128	7700-8399	
	Jefferson Co	372N	80128	8800-8899	
NICHOLS CIR E	Arapahoe Co	374R	80122	1400-1599	
	Centennial	375N	80122	2400-3099	
NICHOLS CT E	Centennial	376R	80112	8800-8899	
	Littleton	374Q	80122	500-599	
NICHOLS DR E	Arapahoe Co	374R	80122	1400-1599	
	Centennial	375N	80122	1900-2299	
	Centennial	375R	80122	5100-5399	
NICHOLS DR W	Jefferson Co	372N	80128	8700-9199	
	Jefferson Co	371R	80128	9300-9599	
NICHOLS LN E	Centennial	375N	80122	1600-1699	
	Centennial	375R	80122	5100-5199	
	Centennial	376N	80112	5600-6199	
NICHOLS PKWY E	Arapahoe Co	380N	80016	21000-21399	
NICHOLS PL E	Arapahoe Co	374Q	80122	800-899	
	Arapahoe Co	378R	80112	15900-16099	
	Arapahoe Co	380P	80016	21300-21399	
	Aurora	381Q	80016	26600-26699	
	Aurora	380P	80016	None	
	Centennial	375N	80122	1800-2399	
	Centennial	375R	80122	5000-5499	
	Centennial	376N	80112	5900-6199	
	Centennial	376P	80112	6900-7499	
	Centennial	376R	80112	8800-8999	
	Centennial	379N	80016	16900-17699	
NICHOLS PL W	Jefferson Co	372Q	80128	6900-7099	
	Jefferson Co	372P	80128	7300-7599	
	Jefferson Co	371R	80128	9200-9699	
NICHOLS WAY	Jefferson Co	822Y	80433	11400-11799	
NICK & VERA RD	Mead	707B	80542	None	
NICKEL CT	Broomfield	162N	80020	1300-1399	
NICKEL ST	Broomfield	162W	80020	1-399	
	Broomfield	162S	80020	600-999	
NICKLAUS CT	Boulder Co	723G	80503	4400-4698	E
NICKOLAS AVE S	Highlands Ranch	406E	80130	10100-10299	
NIELSEN LN S	Denver	315U	80210	3400-3899	
NIGHTFIRE CIR	Douglas Co	527P	80104	1200-1299	
NIGHTHAWK CIR	Broomfield	133W	80026	4500-4699	
NIGHTHAWK CIR	Louisville	130U	80027	700-799	
NIGHTHAWK LN	Jefferson Co	783A	80403	5400-5899	
NIGHTHAWK PKWY	Brighton	139R	80601	5000-5299	
NIGHTHAWK PASS RD	Jefferson Co	782G	80403	4800-5699	
NIGHTHAWK VIEW TRAIL	Jefferson Co	782C	80403	29200-29899	
NIGHT HERON DR	Parker	408V	80134	11100-11899	
NIGHT HERON DR S	Parker	408V	80134	None	
NIGHTHORSE CT	Douglas Co	469F	80108	None	
NIGHTINGALE CT	Longmont	12P	80501	1900-1999	
NIGHTINGALE WAY	Highlands Ranch	375Y	80126	8800-8899	
NIGHT SKY CT	Douglas Co	436T	80108	1000-1099	
NIGHT SKY LN	Lafayette	131F	80026	2101-2199	O
NIGHT SONG WAY	Castle Rock	466Y	80109	None	
NIGHT WIND CIR	Douglas Co	527K	80104	1000-1099	
NIKAU CT	Boulder Co	70J	80503	7400-7599	
NIKAU DR	Boulder Co	70K	80503	7400-7999	
NILE CIR	Arvada	220W	80007	6400-6599	
	Jefferson Co	220J	80007	7800-7899	
	Jefferson Co	250A	80403	None	
NILE CT	Arvada	220W	80007	6400-6499	
	Arvada	220S	80007	6600-6699	
	Jefferson Co	280S	80401	1-99	
	Jefferson Co	280N	80401	800-899	
	Jefferson Co	220J	80007	7900-7999	
NILE CT S	Aurora	317L	80012	1500-1899	
	Aurora	317Q	80014	2200-2299	
NILE ST	Arvada	220N	80007	7200-7299	
	Aurora	287Q	80010	400-999	
	Jefferson Co	280N	80401	700-799	
	Jefferson Co	280J	80401	900-1499	
	Jefferson Co	250E	80403	5300-5399	
	Jefferson Co	220N	80007	7301-7399	O
	Jefferson Co	220J	80007	7600-7899	
NILE ST S	Aurora	287Y	80012	300-499	
NILE WAY	Arvada	220S	80007	6900-7099	

STREET NAME	CITY or COUNTY	MAP GRID	ZIP CODE	BLOCK RANGE	O/E
NILE WAY S	Aurora	317C	80012	700-1099	
NIMBUS RD	Boulder Co	723C	80503	3500-4099	
	Boulder Co	69H	80503	6700-7399	
	Boulder Co	70E	80503	7401-7699	O
NINEBARK LN	Longmont	40Q	80503	900-999	
NINEBARK WAY	Parker	378V	80134	16600-16699	
NINTH AVE	Hudson	730L	80642	None	
NISSAKI RD	Jefferson Co	338P	80454	5200-5399	
NISSEN CT	Broomfield	162Q	80020	1300-1399	
NISSEN PL	Broomfield	162Q	80020	1300-1399	
NIVER AVE	Northglenn	194T	80260	500-799	
	Northglenn	194S	80260	800-1199	
NIVER CT	Adams Co	224H	80229	1300-1399	
NIWOT PL	Parker	409J	80134	17200-17299	
NIWOT RD	Boulder Co	723H	80503	4400-5499	
	Boulder Co	69K	80503	5500-7399	
	Boulder Co	70K	80503	7400-9099	
	Boulder Co	71K	80503	9100-9499	
	Boulder Co	71K	80504	9500-10699	
	Boulder Co	72K	80504	11400-12699	
NIWOT ST	Ward	720M	80481	None	
NIWOT HILLS DR	Boulder Co	70M	80503	None	
NIWOT MEADOW FARM RD					
	Boulder Co	70G	80503	8300-8599	
NIWOT RIDGE LN	Lafayette	131G	80026	701-801	O
NIWOT SQUARE DR	Boulder Co	70J	80503	6700-6999	
NIWOT TRAIL	Broomfield	163P	80020	13200-13399	
NIXON CT S	Jefferson Co	342Y	80123	5900-5999	
NOAH AVE	Jefferson Co	823N	80433	25600-26099	
NOB WAY	Jefferson Co	762C	80403	11700-11899	
NOBEL CT	Boulder	98U	80301	3000-3299	
NOB HILL RD	Jefferson Co	306C	80401	900-1099	
NOB HILL TRAIL	Douglas Co	870F	80116	300-999	
NOBLE CT	Arvada	220S	80007	6600-6999	
	Arvada	220W	80007	None	
	Jefferson Co	280N	80401	800-899	
	Jefferson Co	220J	80007	7900-7999	
	Jefferson Co	250A	80403	None	
NOBLE DR	Elbert Co	830L	80138	600-899	
NOBLE PL E	Arapahoe Co	374D	80121	1400-1799	
	Centennial	375A	80121	1700-2299	
NOBLE ST	Arvada	220W	80403	6200-6299	
	Arvada	220W	80007	None	
	Jefferson Co	280J	80401	1000-1199	
	Jefferson Co	250E	80403	5600-5699	
	Jefferson Co	220J	80007	7600-7799	
NOBLES RD	Centennial	375B	80122	3400-3999	
NODDLE MOUNTAIN	Jefferson Co	371Q	80127	10400-10599	
NOE RD	Douglas Co	908A	80118	1-399	
	Douglas Co	907D	80118	400-1199	
NOE RD E	Douglas Co	888X	80118	1400-1799	
NOEL AVE	Longmont	41R	80501	400-599	
NOGALES CT	Boulder Co	98P	80301	2900-2999	
NOKA TRAIL S	Jefferson Co	842G	80470	12800-13699	
NOKOMIS TRAIL	Clear Creek Co	304R	80439	1-199	
NOLA DR	Adams Co	224E	80221	8100-8299	
NOLAN RD	Lyons	703C	80540	None	
NOLAN ST	Arvada	252G	80002	5300-5499	
	Arvada	252C	80003	5800-5899	
NOLAND CT	Lyons	703C	80540	None	
NOMA CIR	Lafayette	131Q	80026	1400-1499	
NOME CT	Longmont	12S	80501	1-99	
NOME CT S	Arapahoe Co	347Y	80111	6100-6199	
	Aurora	317L	80112	1800-1899	
	Aurora	317Q	80014	2200-2299	
	Centennial	377C	80111	6300-6699	
	Denver	347Y	80111	6200-6299	
NOME ST	Adams Co	137L	80602	None	
NOME ST	Aurora	287U	80010	200-599	
	Aurora	287Q	80010	800-999	
	Aurora	287L	80010	1101-1299	O
	Aurora	287C	80010	1500-2599	
	Aurora	257Y	80010	3000-3299	
	Commerce City	197G	80640	11200-11399	
	Commerce City	197C	80640	None	
	Commerce City	197G	80601	None	
	Denver	257U	80239	3700-3999	
	Denver	257L	80239	4700-5099	
NOME ST S	Arapahoe Co	347U	80111	5600-5799	
	Arapahoe Co	347Y	80111	5900-6099	
	Aurora	287U	80012	1-399	
	Aurora	287Y	80012	500-699	
	Aurora	317C	80112	700-1199	
	Aurora	317L	80014	1900-2099	
	Aurora	317Q	80014	2400-2699	
NOME WAY	Aurora	287U	80011	1-99	
NOME WAY S	Aurora	287Y	80012	400-499	
	Aurora	317L	80112	1700-1799	
NONAHAM LN	Erie	102D	80516	1200-1399	
NORDLAND TRAIL	Castle Rock	466T	80109	None	
NORFOLK CT	Commerce City	198M	80022	10400-10499	
NORFOLK CT S	Aurora	318H	80017	1400-1499	
	Foxfield	378D	80016	6800-6899	
NORFOLK PL	Castle Pines North	436L	80108	7300-7499	
NORFOLK ST	Aurora	288R	80011	100-499	
	Aurora	288M	80011	900-1499	
	Commerce City	198V	80022	9600-9999	
	Commerce City	198R	80022	10100-10299	
	Commerce City	198M	80022	10600-10799	
NORFOLK ST	Erie	133D	80516	2200-2399	
NORFOLK ST S	Arapahoe Co	378R	80112	8100-8199	
	Arapahoe Co	378M	80016	None	
	Aurora	318D	80017	700-1199	
	Aurora	318H	80017	1300-1899	
	Aurora	318R	80013	2100-2299	
	Aurora	318R	80013	2400-2699	
	Aurora	318V	80013	3000-3199	
	Aurora	348M	80015	4700-4799	
	Foxfield	378H	80016	6800-7099	
NORFOLK WAY	Aurora	288R	80011	600-799	
NORFOLK WAY S	Arapahoe Co	378R	80112	8100-8299	
	Aurora	318Z	80013	3100-3499	
	Aurora	348D	80014	3500-3799	
	Aurora	348M	80015	4500-4699	
	Aurora	288Z	80017	None	
	Centennial	348R	80015	None	
NORMAN CT S	Denver	316T	80224	2600-2699	
	Denver	316T	80224	3000-3099	

STREET NAME	CITY or COUNTY	MAP GRID	ZIP CODE	BLOCK RANGE	O/E
NORMAN LN	Jefferson Co	367M	80439	24500-24699	
NORMANDY CIR	Arapahoe Co	373E	80128	7100-7199	
NORMANDY PKWY	Arapahoe Co	373E	80128	4600-4899	
NORMANDY RD	Clear Creek Co	801Y	80439	1-599	
NORMANDY RD	Jefferson Co	280M	80401	1300-1499	
NORMANS ST	Golden	249S	80403	100-299	
NORSE ST	Arvada	220W	80007	6400-6498	E
	Golden	280S	80401	200-299	
	Jefferson Co	250E	80403	5300-5399	
NORTH AVE	Denver Federal Center	281P	80225	None	
NORTH DR	Jefferson Co	368P	80465	8200-8299	
NORTH ST	Boulder	97Y	80304	600-1199	
	Boulder	97Y	80304	1200-1699	
NORTH ST	Lafayette	132K	80026	None	
NORTHAMPTON CT E	Highlands Ranch	404D	80126	1000-1099	
NORTHAVEN CIR E	Thornton	165Y	80241	12000-12199	
NORTH BEASLY RD	Weld Co	706P	80504	11700-11899	
NORTHBROOK AVE	Castle Rock	498Q	80104	4800-5099	
NORTHBROOK DR	Boulder	98J	80304	3800-3899	
NORTHBROOK PL	Boulder	98K	80304	2700-2799	
NORTH COUNTY RD	Gilpin Co	740Z	80403	2-1698	E
NORTHCREST DR	Highlands Ranch	374V	80126	1200-1599	
NORTHEAST DR	Clear Creek Co	780U	80452	600-1199	
NORTHERN AVE	Brighton	138Q	80601	1100-1299	
NORTHERN WAY	Superior	160Q	80027	800-1099	
NORTHERN PINE AVE	Parker	440A	80134	20400-20699	
	Denver	256L	80238	7900-9599	
NORTHFIELD CT	Boulder Co	100E	80301	4500-4599	
NORTHFIELD DR	Highlands Ranch	374X	80129	None	
NORTHFIELD LN	Lafayette	101X	80026	1500-1598	E
NORTH FOLK CT	Boulder	69Y	80301	5400-5599	
NORTHGATE DR	Douglas Co	409A	80134	16800-16899	
NORTHGLENN DR	Northglenn	194L	80233	100-11299	
NORTHLANDS PL	Broomfield	134F	80516	None	
NORTHMOOR DR	Broomfield	162R	80020	1100-1199	
NORTHOUT ST	Elbert Co	831E	80138	None	
NORTHPARK AVE	Westminster	193P	80031	3000-3699	
NORTH PARK DR	Lafayette	131B	80026	1300-2699	
NORTHPARK DR	Westminster	193P	80031	3300-3599	
	Westminster	193P	80031	10200-10399	
NORTH RANCH RD	Jefferson Co	370B	80127	1-99	
NORTH RIDGE CT	Boulder	97M	80304	1300-1399	
NORTHRIDGE CT	Erie	103E	80516	1000-1099	
NORTHRIDGE CT	Jefferson Co	307F	80401	800-1399	
NORTHRIDGE DR	Erie	103A	80516	1000-1499	
NORTHRIDGE DR E	Highlands Ranch	374V	80126	1500-1699	
NORTHRIDGE RD	Highlands Ranch	374U	80126	200-1399	
NORTH RIDGE ST	Adams Co	750M	80603	None	
NORTH RIM	Weld Co	706N	80504	3200-3399	
NORTHRUP AVE	Fort Lupton	728H	80621	900-999	
NORTHRUP DR	Erie	102M	80516	100-299	
	Erie	102M	80516	None	
NORTH SHORE DR	Longmont	10R	80503	2100-2399	
NORTHSTAR CT	Boulder	97Q	80304	500-799	
NORTHSTAR DR	Thornton	224B	80260	8600-8799	
NORTHSTAR LN	Jefferson Co	306U	80439	29200-29399	
NORTHSTAR RIDGE LN	Douglas Co	440V	80134	6200-6299	
NORTH TRAIL CIR	Jefferson Co	844L	80127	13800-14199	
NORTHVIEW DR	Erie	103A	80516	1000-1399	
NORTHVIEW DR	Jefferson Co	336C	80439	29100-29199	
NORTHVIEW PL	Castle Rock	528A	80104	None	
NORTHWAY DR	Jefferson Co	338Y	80465	6300-6399	
NORTHWEST CT	Park Co	821Z	80470	11800-11899	
NORTHWESTERN RD	Longmont	10U	80503	1300-1699	
NORTHWOOD CT	Douglas Co	436Q	80108	900-1199	
NORTHWOOD DR	Jefferson Co	337U	80439	5500-5999	
NORTHWOOD LN	Douglas Co	436P	80108	1000-1199	
NORTHWOOD GLEN CT	Douglas Co	440V	80134	9000-9099	
NORTHWOOD GLEN DR	Douglas Co	440V	80134	6200-6299	
NORTON AVE	Jefferson Co	823U	80433	10800-11999	
NORTON DR	Gilpin Co	761S	80403	200-899	
NORTON ST	Boulder	128N	80305	300-399	
NORWICH CT	Castle Pines North	436Q	80108	700-799	
NORWICH ST	Adams Co	223F	80031	8400-8499	
	Adams Co	223B	80031	8500-8999	
NORWICH WAY	Adams Co	223F	80031	4000-4999	
NORWOOD AVE	Boulder	97R	80304	1100-1899	
	Boulder	98J	80304	1900-2599	
NORWOOD CT	Boulder	98J	80304	3800-3899	
NORWOOD DR	Highlands Ranch	373X	80125	3600-3999	
NORWOOD DR	Thornton	194W	80260	None	
NOTABON CT	Lafayette	131E	80026	3100-3198	E
NOTCH MOUNTAIN	Jefferson Co	371P	80127	7800-7899	
NOTTINGHAM CT	Boulder	98N	80304	3500-3599	
NOTTINGHAM DR	Douglas Co	407M	80134	10100-10399	
NOTTINGHAM ST	Lafayette	131M	80026	1100-1199	
NOTTING HILL GATE	Boulder Co	99F	80301	6200-6299	
NOTTS CT	Lone Tree	406D	80124	9300-9399	
NOVA AVE E	Littleton	374Q	80122	500-799	
NOVA AVE W	Jefferson Co	371M	80128	9300-9499	
	Jefferson Co	371M	80127	9700-9799	
NOVA CIR	Park Co	842E	80470	1-99	
NOVA CIR E	Aurora	381R	80016	27200-27299	
NOVA DR	Park Co	841D	80470	1-299	
NOVA DR W	Jefferson Co	372L	80128	6200-6599	
	Jefferson Co	372L	80128	6800-7099	
NOVA LN	Park Co	842A	80470	1-199	
NOVA PL	Castle Rock	467G	80108	None	
NOVA PL E	Aurora	381Q	80016	26600-26699	
	Aurora	381R	80016	27400-27599	
	Aurora	380Q	80016	None	
NOVA PL W	Jefferson Co	372K	80128	7700-7799	
	Jefferson Co	371M	80128	9300-9399	
	Jefferson Co	371L	80127	9900-9999	
NOVA RD	Jefferson Co	842E	80470	33100-33999	
	Park Co	841D	80470	1-3799	
NOVICK CT	Castle Rock	497E	80109	600-799	
NUCLA CT	Commerce City	198M	80022	10600-10699	
NUCLA CT S	Centennial	348V	80015	5400-5799	
NUCLA DR	Commerce City	198V	80022	None	
NUCLA ST	Adams Co	198D	80022	11200-11599	
	Aurora	288M	80011	700-1499	
	Commerce City	198V	80022	9600-9999	
	Commerce City	198M	80022	10400-10799	
	Commerce City	198R	80022	None	

STREET NAME	CITY or COUNTY	MAP GRID	ZIP CODE	BLOCK RANGE	O/E
NUCLA ST S	Arapahoe Co	378H	80016	None	
	Aurora	318D	80017	1000-1099	
	Aurora	318H	80017	1400-1899	
	Aurora	318V	80013	3000-3299	
	Aurora	318Z	80013	3500-3599	
	Aurora	348D	80013	3800-3999	
	Aurora	348H	80015	4500-4599	
	Aurora	348H	80014	None	
	Centennial	348R	80015	5500-5599	
NUCLA WAY	Aurora	288R	80011	500-699	
NUCLA WAY S	Aurora	318M	80013	2000-2099	
	Aurora	319N	80013	2100-2199	
	Aurora	318Z	80013	3300-3499	
	Aurora	348D	80013	4000-4099	
	Aurora	348H	80014	4100-4299	
	Aurora	348M	80015	4800-4899	
NUEVA VISTA DR	Adams Co	224H	80229	1300-1799	
	Adams Co	225E	80229	1800-2099	
	Adams Co	224H	80229	8300-8399	
NUGGET CT	Boulder	97R	80304	1600-1699	
NUGGET CT	Douglas Co	846D	80125	8300-8499	
NUGGET DR	Boulder Co	722G	80302	1-299	
NUGGET HILL RD	Boulder Co	722K	80455	100-799	
NUMA PL	Parker	409N	80134	17000-17099	
NURSERY RD	El Paso Co	908Z	80132	None	
NUTHATCH CIR	Douglas Co	440W	80134	7400-7699	
NUTHATCH RD	Clear Creek Co	801R	80439	1-299	
NUTHATCH RD	Douglas Co	470A	80134	5400-5599	
NUTHATCH WAY	Douglas Co	440W	80134	7600-7699	
NUTMEG PL	Castle Rock	496B	80109	None	
NUTMEG ST S	Arapahoe Co	792W	80102	300-1099	
	Arapahoe Co	812A	80102	1500-1799	
NYLAND WAY	Lafayette	130L	80027	None	

O

STREET NAME	CITY or COUNTY	MAP GRID	ZIP CODE	BLOCK RANGE	O/E
OAK AVE	Adams Co	794P	80136	56000-56899	
OAK AVE	Boulder	97M	80304	1500-1899	
OAK CIR	Boulder	97M	80304	1400-1499	
OAK CIR	Dacono	727S	80514	None	
OAK CIR	Westminster	191P	80021	10000-10099	
OAK CIR N	Broomfield	161R	80020	3000-3199	
OAK CIR S	Broomfield	161R	80020	1100-1199	
OAK CIR S	Jefferson Co	371B	80127	6500-6699	
OAK CT	Arvada	251G	80033	5500-5699	
	Arvada	251F	80033	None	
OAK CT	Boulder	97M	80304	1300-1399	
OAK CT	Douglas Co	848A	80108	8400-8499	
OAK CT	Elbert Co	871G	80107	34500-34799	
OAK CT	Westminster	191P	80021	10000-10099	
OAK CT S	Jefferson Co	311Y	80227	3100-3499	
	Jefferson Co	341K	80127	4600-5099	
	Jefferson Co	371C	80127	6400-6599	
	Jefferson Co	371G	80127	7000-7099	
	Jefferson Co	371K	80127	7100-7399	
	Jefferson Co	371U	80127	8400-8499	
OAK CT S	Longmont	41R	80501	1200-1399	
OAK CT W	Louisville	130Q	80027	800-899	
OAK DR	Lakewood	281B	80215	2600-2699	
OAK LN	Broomfield	162Y	80020	300-399	
OAK LN	Elbert Co	850U	80107	37500-37699	
OAK PL	Thornton	224D	80229	900-1599	
	Thornton	225A	80229	2000-2299	
OAK ST	Arvada	251F	80033	5400-5498	E
	Arvada	251B	80004	5800-6099	
	Arvada	221X	80004	6300-7199	
	Arvada	221K	80005	7500-8099	
	Arvada	221F	80005	8400-8599	
	Arvada	251K	80033	None	
	Denver	283A	80212	2400-2599	
	Federal Heights	193U	80260	None	
OAK ST	Fort Lupton	728H	80621	1700-1899	
OAK ST	Frederick	727F	80530	401-499	O
OAK ST	Lakewood	281L	80215	600-1499	
	Lakewood	281G	80215	1700-1999	
	Lakewood	251Y	80215	2800-3199	
OAK ST	Longmont	41V	80501	None	
OAK ST	Westminster	191P	80021	10000-10499	
	Westminster	191K	80021	10500-10799	
	Wheat Ridge	281C	80215	2600-2899	
	Wheat Ridge	251X	80033	3200-3499	
	Wheat Ridge	251T	80033	3600-4199	
	Wheat Ridge	251Q	80033	4200-4399	
	Wheat Ridge	251P	80033	4600-4799	
OAK ST E	Lafayette	132E	80026	300-599	
OAK ST S	Jefferson Co	311U	80227	2700-2899	
	Jefferson Co	341C	80235	3600-3999	
	Jefferson Co	341Q	80127	5100-5499	
	Jefferson Co	341Y	80127	5600-6199	
	Jefferson Co	371U	80127	8400-8599	
	Lakewood	281Y	80226	300-499	
	Lakewood	311L	80232	1800-1899	
	Lakewood	311L	80227	1900-2099	
OAK ST W	Lafayette	131H	80026	300-699	
OAK WAY	Arvada	221T	80004	6800-6999	
	Arvada	221F	80005	8400-8599	
OAK WAY	Clear Creek Co	801R	80439	1-99	
OAK WAY	Douglas Co	866K	80135	7800-7899	
OAK WAY S	Jefferson Co	311T	80227	2900-3099	
	Jefferson Co	341P	80127	5100-5499	
	Jefferson Co	341X	80127	5900-6399	
	Jefferson Co	371T	80127	8500-8699	
OAK BLUFF TRAIL S	Parker	408A	80134	None	
OAK BRIAR WAY	Castle Pines North	436G	80108	8100-8299	
OAKBROOK LN	Parker	409V	80138	20400-20599	
OAK BRUSH LOOP	El Paso Co	912W	80831	16600-17999	
OAKBRUSH WAY	Lone Tree	406C	80124	9300-9499	
OAK CREEK CT S	Parker	439C	80134	12600-12699	
OAK CREEK DR	Greenwood Village	345S	80121	1800-1999	
OAK CREEK LN	Greenwood Village	345S	80121	5700-5899	
OAK CREEK PL E	Parker	439C	80134	19000-19099	
OAK CREEK WAY E	Parker	439C	80134	18900-19199	
OAKCREST CIR	Castle Rock	498N	80104	1800-1898	E
	Castle Rock	498N	80104	1900-2199	
OAKDALE DR	Palmer Lake	907Q	80133	None	
OAKDALE PL	Boulder	97L	80304	1000-1199	
OAKDALE RD	Parker	410Q	80138	None	
OAKDALE TERRACE	Palmer Lake	907Q	80133	None	

STREET NAME	CITY or COUNTY	MAP GRID	ZIP CODE	BLOCK RANGE	O/E
OAKES MILL CT	Castle Rock	466X	80109	4300-4499	
OAKES MILL PL	Castle Rock	466X	80109	3200-3599	
OAKGROVE CT	Douglas Co	468Y	80108	4100-4199	
OAK GROVE ST	Lochbuie	729Y	80603	None	
OAKGROVE WAY	Douglas Co	468Y	80108	4200-4299	
OAK HILL CIR S	Arapahoe Co	381Q	80016	8000-8099	
	Aurora	381G	80016	7000-7299	
	Aurora	351X	80016	None	
OAK HILL CT S	Arapahoe Co	381Q	80016	7900-7999	
	Aurora	381G	80016	7100-7199	
	Aurora	291U	80018	None	
	Aurora	351Y	80016	None	
	Aurora	830B	80016	None	
OAK HILL ST	Denver	770T	80249	9400-9498	E
OAK HILL ST S	Aurora	381C	80016	None	
OAK HILL WAY	Commerce City	197G	80601	None	
OAK HILL WAY S	Aurora	351Y	80016	6100-6199	
	Aurora	381G	80016	6900-7399	
	Aurora	291U	80018	None	
OAK HILLS DR	El Paso Co	908T	80132	800-999	
OAK HILLS DR W	Douglas Co	436H	80108	1-599	
OAK HILLS LN	Douglas Co	848A	80108	400-699	
OAK HOLLOW DR	Jefferson Co	339R	80465	16500-16599	
OAKHURST DR	Broomfield	162Q	80020	1100-1299	
OAKLAND CIR S	Aurora	317Q	80014	2400-2499	
	Aurora	317U	80014	2700E-2899E	
OAKLAND CT	Adams Co	137Q	80602	None	
OAKLAND CT	Aurora	287U	80012	100-199	
	Aurora	287Q	80010	500-599	
OAKLAND CT S	Aurora	317C	80012	900-999	
	Aurora	317G	80012	1600-1699	
	Aurora	317U	80014	2800-2899	
OAKLAND DR	Commerce City	197G	80640	11200-11799	
	Commerce City	197G	80601	None	
OAKLAND PL S	Aurora	317U	80014	2800-2899	
OAKLAND ST	Adams Co	167Y	80640	11800-12399	
	Aurora	287U	80012	1-99	
	Aurora	287U	80010	200-499	
	Aurora	287Q	80010	600-999	
	Aurora	287C	80010	1600-2499	
	Aurora	257Y	80010	3000-3299	
	Commerce City	197C	80640	11500-11799	
	Commerce City	197G	80640	None	
	Commerce City	768B	80601	None	
	Denver	257L	80239	4700-5099	
OAKLAND ST S	Aurora	287Y	80012	600-699	
	Aurora	317G	80112	700-1899	
	Aurora	317Q	80014	1900-2199	
	Aurora	317U	80014	2500-2699	
	Aurora	317U	80014	2901-2999	O
OAKLAND WAY S	Aurora	317Q	80014	1900-2299	
	Aurora	317G	80112	None	
OAKLEAF CIR	Boulder	97M	80304	1200-1499	
OAK LEAF CT S	Highlands Ranch	403L	80129	10200-10299	
OAK LEAF LN	Greenwood Village	345S	80121	5700-5899	
OAK LEAF PL W	Highlands Ranch	403L	80129	3200-3499	
OAKLEAF ST S	Arapahoe Co	832E	80137	7400-8299	
OAK LEAF WAY S	Highlands Ranch	403G	80129	10000-10099	
OAKLEY CT	Castle Rock	498R	80104	6100-6199	
OAKLEY LN	Erie	102D	80516	1300-1399	
OAK MEADOWS BLVD	Firestone	707N	80504	None	
	Firestone	707P	80504	None	
OAKMONT LN	Jefferson Co	370Q	80127	1-99	
OAKMOOR CIR	Douglas Co	408M	80134	10500-10599	
OAKMOOR CT	Douglas Co	408M	80134	10600-10699	
OAKMOOR LN	Douglas Co	408M	80134	10500-10699	
OAKMOOR PL	Douglas Co	408M	80134	16300-16699	
OAK RIDGE DR	Castle Rock	497M	80104	1-99	
OAK RIDGE LN	Longmont	11T	80501	1600-1699	
OAK RIDGE RD	Douglas Co	867N	80135	2300-2599	
OAKSHIRE AVE	Highlands Ranch	405P	80126	10800-10999	
OAKSHIRE CT	Highlands Ranch	405P	80126	2900-2999	
OAK SPRINGS TRAIL	Douglas Co	890S	80116	10000-10099	
OAK TREE CT	Boulder	69Z	80301	5300-5399	
OAK TREE CT	Lone Tree	406H	80124	10000-10099	
OAK VALLEY RD	Douglas Co	866B	80135	400-1499	
OAKVIEW PL	Castle Pines North	436L	80108	7700-7799	
OAK VIEW TRAIL	Jefferson Co	369V	80127	16800-16999	
OAK VISTA CT	Castle Rock	498A	80104	2200-2699	
OAK VISTA LN	Castle Rock	498A	80104	2600-2899	
OAKWELL CT	Douglas Co	408H	80134	16400-16499	
OAKWOOD AVE E	Centennial	344Z	80121	800-1099	
OAKWOOD CT	Castle Rock	497G	80104	900-999	
OAKWOOD CT E	Centennial	344Z	80121	800-999	
OAKWOOD DR	Castle Rock	497G	80104	400-999	
OAKWOOD DR	El Paso Co	908T	80132	1600-1699	
OAKWOOD DR	Longmont	40L	80503	3600-3999	
OAKWOOD DR	Westminster	223E	80031	3900-4599	
OAKWOOD DR E	Arapahoe Co	348Z	80016	16100-16399	
OAKWOOD LN E	Arapahoe Co	349X	80016	17700-17899	
OAKWOOD LN W	Douglas Co	436H	80108	300-699	
OAK WOOD PL	Boulder	97L	80304	300-499	
OAKWOOD PL E	Arapahoe Co	349X	80016	17700-17799	
	Arapahoe Co	349X	80016	18100-18199	
OAKWOOD ST	Adams Co	223B	80031	8300-8999	
OAKWOOD ST	Elbert Co	851C	80107	42000-42999	
OARD CT	Longmont	42F	80501	700-799	
OASIS DR	Castle Rock	469K	80108	7100-7899	
OBAN CT	Lone Tree	406L	80124	7800-7899	
OBERLIN DR E	Aurora	349G	80013	19000-19199	
	Aurora	350G	80018	22300-22399	
OBERLIN DR W	Denver	342H	80235	5200-5399	
OBERLIN PL E	Aurora	348F	80014	14500-14699	
	Aurora	348G	80014	15400-15699	
	Aurora	349E	80013	17200-17299	
	Aurora	349G	80013	18600-18999	
	Aurora	349H	80013	19900-19999	
	Aurora	350F	80018	21800-21999	
	Aurora	350G	80018	22200-22299	
	Denver	346G	80237	8000-8099	
OBERLIN PL W	Denver	343E	80236	4600-4699	
OBERON RD	Arvada	221V	80004	6300-6899	
	Arvada	252A	80004	7800-8399	
	Arvada	222W	80004	8400-8899	
	Arvada	221V	80004	9000-9499	
OBERSTRASSE RD	Jefferson Co	337W	80439	6000-6299	
O'BRIEN ST	Park Co	820Y	80421	1-199	

STREET NAME	CITY or COUNTY	MAP GRID	ZIP CODE	BLOCK RANGE	O/E
O'BRIEN WAY	Adams Co	168U	80603	12400-12599	
O'BRIEN WAY	Douglas Co	496Y	80109	1200-1599	
OBSERVATORY PL	Gilpin Co	760D	80403	1-199	
OBSIDIAN LN	Castle Rock	467G	80108	None	
OCASO DR	Castle Pines North	436B	80108	6500-6699	
OCEANSIDE LN	El Paso Co	908U	80132	18600-18799	
OCELOT TRAIL	Jefferson Co	367E	80439	6900-7099	
OCHRE CIR	Castle Rock	466U	80109	None	
OCHRE DR	Castle Rock	496B	80109	4000-4099	
O'CONNOR RD	Boulder Co	130N	80303	7600-7799	
OCTILLO ST	Brighton	139P	80601	100-399	
OCTOBER PL	Castle Rock	497U	80104	100-299	
ODELL DR	Erie	102W	80516	2600-2899	
ODELL PL	Boulder	69Y	80301	6400-6599	
ODERO CIR E	Centennial	375R	80122	5000-5499	
ODESSA CIR S	Arapahoe Co	350B	80013	None	
	Centennial	350T	80015	5900-6099	
	Centennial	380F	80016	7100-7499	
ODESSA CT	Arapahoe Co	350K	80015	None	
ODESSA ST	Denver	260E	80249	5200-5499	
	Denver	260E	80249	None	
	Denver	260J	80249	None	
ODESSA ST N	Arapahoe Co	290J	80018	800-1099	
	Denver	260S	80249	3800-4199	
	Denver	260N	80249	4600-4799	
ODESSA ST S	Arapahoe Co	350B	80013	None	
	Arapahoe Co	350J	80015	None	
	Aurora	380F	80016	None	
	Centennial	350T	80015	5600-5799	
ODESSA WAY	Aurora	260S	80011	3500-3599	
ODYSSEY CT	Castle Rock	496B	80109	None	
ODYSSEY CT	Lafayette	131R	80026	1100-1199	
OEHLMANN AVE	Jefferson Co	823U	80433	10600-11199	
OEHLMANN PARK RD	Jefferson Co	823Y	80433	22000-23699	
OGALALLA TRAIL	Elbert Co	870V	80107	30400-30499	
OGALLALA RD	Boulder Co	40Z	80503	8700-9199	
	Boulder Co	41W	80503	9200-9499	
OGDEN CIR	Northglenn	194M	80233	700-999	
OGDEN CIR S	Littleton	374R	80122	8200-8299	
OGDEN CT	Adams Co	224M	80229	7800-7999	
	Thornton	194V	80229	None	
OGDEN CT S	Arapahoe Co	374H	80122	6900-6999	
	Arapahoe Co	374R	80122	7800-7899	
	Centennial	344V	80121	5900-5999	
OGDEN DR	Northglenn	194H	80233	11200-11299	
OGDEN ST	Adams Co	254D	80216	5800-5899	
	Adams Co	224M	80229	8000-8099	
	Adams Co	224H	80229	8200-8399	
	Adams Co	224D	80229	8500-8699	
	Denver	284V	80218	1-99	
	Denver	284H	80218	200-1999	
	Denver	284D	80205	2000-2599	
	Northglenn	194R	80233	10400-10799	
	Northglenn	194H	80233	11000-11199	
	Northglenn	194D	80233	11400-11699	
	Thornton	194Z	80229	9000-9199	
	Thornton	194V	80229	None	
OGDEN ST S	Arapahoe Co	374D	80121	6500-6699	
	Arapahoe Co	374R	80122	8100-8199	
	Cherry Hills Village	344D	80110	3700-3899	
	Cherry Hills Village	344M	80113	4600-4799	
	Denver	284Z	80209	1-699	
	Denver	314D	80209	700-1099	
	Denver	314M	80210	1100-2499	
	Englewood	314Z	80113	2700-3599	
OGDEN WAY S	Arapahoe Co	374H	80122	7300-7499	
	Arapahoe Co	374M	80122	7500-7899	
O'HAYRE CT	Lakewood	251X	80215	3000-3199	
OHIO AVE E	Arapahoe Co	320D	80018	23600-24099	
	Aurora	317D	80012	11900-13299	
	Aurora	318C	80012	14700-15299	
	Aurora	289X	80017	18000-18199	
	Denver	314C	80209	1-1199	
	Denver	314D	80209	1600-1699	
	Denver	315A	80209	1700-2399	
	Denver	316A	80224	6100-6499	
	Denver	317A	80247	9700-10099	
	Glendale	315C	80246	4000-4399	
OHIO AVE W	Denver	314A	80223	1200-1999	
	Denver	313D	80223	2000-2499	
	Denver	313B	80219	2500-5199	
	Lakewood	312D	80226	5200-5999	
	Lakewood	312C	80226	6000-6799	
	Lakewood	312B	80226	7200-7899	
	Lakewood	311D	80226	9500-9799	
	Lakewood	310D	80228	12900-13599	
	Lakewood	310C	80228	13600-14099	
OHIO CIR E	Aurora	319B	80017	17500-17799	
OHIO CIR W	Lakewood	311A	80228	12300-12399	
OHIO DR E	Aurora	319A	80017	17000-17899	
	Denver	316B	80224	6900-7199	
OHIO DR W	Lakewood	311D	80226	9500-9799	
	Lakewood	311B	80226	11100-11299	
	Lakewood	311A	80228	12100-12299	
	Lakewood	310D	80228	13400-13499	
	Lakewood	310C	80228	13600-13799	
OHIO PL E	Aurora	317B	80012	11000-11299	
	Aurora	318D	80017	16300-16399	
	Aurora	289W	80017	16900-17099	
	Aurora	317B	80247	None	
OHIO PL W	Lakewood	312A	80226	8400-8999	
	Lakewood	311D	80226	9500-9599	
	Lakewood	311B	80226	11000-11199	
	Lakewood	311A	80228	11900-12299	
OHIO WAY	Denver	315B	80209	2900-3299	
OH-KAY RD	Jefferson Co	338F	80454	None	
OHLSON RIDGE CT	Elbert Co	850C	80138	600-999	
OHM WAY	Denver	315B	80209	3000-3199	
OIL WELL RD	Fort Lupton	729J	80621	None	
OKEE TRAIL	Jefferson Co	842G	80470	30100-30299	
OLATHE CIR S	Aurora	348D	80014	3700-3899	
	Centennial	349N	80015	5000-5199	
	Centennial	348R	80015	5200-5399	
OLATHE CT S	Arapahoe Co	378R	80112	8200-8299	
	Aurora	348H	80014	4000-4099	
	Centennial	348V	80015	5700-5799	
OLATHE LN S	Centennial	348V	80015	5500-5699	

STREET NAME	CITY or COUNTY	MAP GRID	ZIP CODE	BLOCK RANGE	O/E
OLATHE ST	Aurora	288R	80011	500-599	
	Aurora	288M	80011	800-1299	
	Commerce City	198V	80022	9600-9999	
	Commerce City	198R	80022	10100-10299	
	Commerce City	198M	80022	10400-10699	
OLATHE ST S	Arapahoe Co	349W	80016	6001-6499	O
	Aurora	318D	80017	1000-1099	
	Aurora	318M	80017	1600-1899	
	Aurora	318M	80013	1900-2099	
	Aurora	319J	80013	2100-2199	
	Aurora	348D	80014	3700-3899	
	Aurora	349J	80015	4700-4799	
	Centennial	348V	80015	5700-5799	
	Centennial	349W	80016	6100-6499	
	Centennial	379A	80016	6400-6699	
OLATHE WAY	Aurora	288R	80011	600-699	
	Commerce City	198M	80022	10400-10499	
	Commerce City	198R	80022	None	
OLATHE WAY S	Aurora	318H	80017	1200-1499	
	Aurora	318R	80013	2500-2699	
	Aurora	319W	80013	2800-3499	
	Aurora	348D	80014	3500-3699	
	Aurora	348H	80014	4100-4199	
	Aurora	349J	80015	4700-4799	
	Centennial	348V	80015	5400-5799	
OLD ANTLERS WAY	El Paso Co	908P	80132	1100-1799	
OLDBOROUGH HEIGHTS DR	El Paso Co	909W	80132	16800-16999	
OLD BROMPTON RD	Boulder Co	99F	80301	6000-6299	
OLD CEDAR COVE	El Paso Co	908P	80132	None	
OLD CHEROKEE TRAIL	El Paso Co	909X	80132	17200-17599	
OLD COAL MINE AVE	Jefferson Co	371C	80123	9600-9999	
OLD CORRAL RD	Park Co	841K	80421	1-699	
OLD DENVER RD	Monument	908W	80132	16000-18299	
OLD DIVIDE TRAIL	Douglas Co	469C	80134	6200-6599	
OLD DORY HILL RD	Gilpin Co	761S	80403	1-499	
OLDE HAPPY CANYON RD	Castle Pines North	436K	80108	1400-1499	
OLDE STAGE RD	Boulder Co	723J	80302	5000-7399	
OLD FARM RD	Littleton	373J	80128	7100-7299	
OLDFIELD ST	Castle Rock	498R	80104	1000-1298	E
	Castle Rock	498R	80104	1300-1399	
OLD FORGE DR	Castle Pines North	436K	80108	1-99	
OLD FORT LN	El Paso Co	908P	80132	19300-19499	
OLD FORTY E	Arapahoe Co	795Y	80103	None	
OLD GATE RD	Douglas Co	527T	80104	3800-4599	
OLD GULCH RD	Jefferson Co	337E	80439	26700-27199	
OLD HAMMER CIR S	Aurora	321Q	80018	2300-2699	
OLD HAMMER CT	Aurora	321Q	80018	2100-2299	
OLD HAMMER CT S	Aurora	381C	80016	6700-6799	
OLD HAMMER LN S	Arapahoe Co	381Q	80016	8100-8299	
OLD HAMMER WAY S	Aurora	351Y	80016	6200-6499	
OLD HUGHESVILLE RD	Gilpin Co	760Z	80403	1-399	
OLD HWY 52	Weld Co	726K	80516	1500-1798	E
OLD LARAMIE TRAIL	Lafayette	132S	80026	100-199	
OLD LITTLE BEAR CREEK	Clear Creek Co	780Z	80452	1-5799	
OLD LOGGING RD	Gilpin Co	741Z	80403	1-499	
OLD MILL RD	Jefferson Co	365W	80433	8700-9299	
OLD MILL TRAIL	Boulder Co	100E	80301	7300-7499	
OLD OX TRAIL	Jefferson Co	276W	80401	31400-31599	
OLD PAINT CT	El Paso Co	912U	80831	18000-18199	
OLD POST CIR	Boulder Co	100A	80301	4800-4899	
OLD POST CT	Boulder Co	99H	80301	4700-4799	
OLD POST RD	Boulder Co	99H	80301	4500-7499	
OLD POST OFFICE RD	Boulder Co	721Z	80302	1-399	
OLD QUARRY RD	Jefferson Co	280C	80401	2200-2299	
OLD RANCH TRAIL	Douglas Co	432T	80125	6500-6999	
OLD ST VRAIN RD	Boulder Co	703F	80540	1-799	
OLD SAWMILL RD	Park Co	840D	80421	1-999	
OLD SCHOOLHOUSE RD	Douglas Co	469C	80134	5000-5199	
OLD SEQUOIA CT	Douglas Co	869D	80116	1400-1599	
OLD SQUAW PASS RD	Clear Creek Co	304G	80439	1-2599	
OLD STAGE AVE	Castle Rock	469J	80108	None	
OLD STAGE RD	Clear Creek Co	780A	80452	500-599	
OLD STAGE COACH RD	Jefferson Co	842V	80470	15800-16099	
OLD STAGECOACH RD	Park Co	840U	80421	None	
OLD STAGE COACH TRAIL	Gilpin Co	740Z	80474	None	
OLD STONE DR	Highlands Ranch	374U	80126	400-799	
OLD TALE RD	Boulder Co	129B	80303	1100-1599	
OLD TERRITORIAL RD	Douglas Co	887H	80118	None	
OLD TOM MORRIS CIR	Highlands Ranch	374W	80129	8900-9099	
OLD TOM MORRIS RD S	Aurora	320H	80018	None	
	Aurora	320M	80018	None	
OLD TOWNSITE RD	Boulder Co	741D	80302	1-1999	
OLD US HWY 285	Jefferson Co	368Y	80465	None	
OLD US HWY 285	Park Co	841P	80421	1-199	
OLD VICTORY RD	Adams Co	793K	80102	2700-52099	
OLD WADSWORTH BLVD	Jefferson Co	192A	80021	None	
OLD WESTBURY CT	Boulder	98L	80301	4000-4099	
OLD WHISKEY RD	Boulder Co	742C	80466	100-1199	
OLD WINDMILL WAY	Castle Rock	466T	80109	4300-4399	
OLD Y RD	Jefferson Co	278T	80401	1-499	
OLEANDER CT S	Denver	316X	80224	3400-3499	
OLIN CT	Erie	102U	80516	900-999	
OLIVE CIR S	Centennial	376K	80112	7600-7699	
OLIVE CT	Adams Co	136P	80602	None	
OLIVE CT	Erie	133C	80516	None	
OLIVE CT	Greenwood Village	345V	80121	5100-5199	
OLIVE CT S	Centennial	376B	80111	6600-6699	
	Centennial	376K	80112	7900-7999	
OLIVE DR	Thornton	194X	80260	None	
OLIVE LN	Platteville	708C	80651	200-699	
OLIVE RD S	Jefferson Co	336Q	80439	4900-5399	
OLIVE ST	Adams Co	136K	80602	16400-16699	
	Adams Co	136P	80602	None	
	Commerce City	256K	80022	4800-4999	
	Commerce City	256B	80022	5600-6099	
	Commerce City	226T	80022	6200-7299	
	Commerce City	226K	80022	7700-7999	
	Denver	286T	80220	200-499	
	Denver	286K	80220	600-1999	
	Denver	286B	80207	2000-2799	
	Denver	256X	80207	2800-3999	
OLIVE ST	Thornton	136T	80602	15200-15299	
	Thornton	136T	80602	15499-15499	
	Thornton	166P	80602	None	
	Thornton	196B	80233	None	

STREET NAME	CITY or COUNTY	MAP GRID	ZIP CODE	BLOCK RANGE	O/E
OLIVE ST S	Centennial	346X	80111	6300-6399	
	Centennial	376F	80112	7000-7099	
	Denver	286T	80230	100-299	
	Denver	316K	80224	1800-1999	
	Denver	316P	80224	2200-2399	
	Denver	346B	80237	3900-4199	
	Denver	346F	80237	4200-4299	
	Greenwood Village	346P	80111	5400-5499	
OLIVE WAY	Adams Co	136K	80602	16200-16299	
	Thornton	166P	80602	None	
OLIVE WAY S	Centennial	376F	80112	6800-7299	
	Denver	286X	80224	300-599	
OLMSTED DR	Denver	257H	80239	12200-12399	
	Denver	258F	80239	14300-15099	
OLMSTED PL	Denver	257H	80239	12900-13099	
	Denver	258E	80239	13100-13299	
	Denver	258H	80239	15500-15799	
OLSON PL	Boulder	128B	80303	2800-2899	
OLYMPIA AVE	Longmont	12K	80501	300-899	
	Longmont	12L	80501	1100-2399	
OLYMPIA CIR	Castle Rock	497R	80104	None	
OLYMPIA CIR	Jefferson Co	306T	80439	2700-3099	
OLYMPIA CT	Broomfield	163G	80020	None	
OLYMPIA LN	Jefferson Co	306T	80439	2800-2999	
OLYMPIAN CIR	Lafayette	131R	80026	1300-1399	
OLYMPIC CT	Douglas Co	886C	80118	6100-6199	
OLYMPIC WAY	Jefferson Co	337K	80439	4600-4699	
OLYMPUS CIR	Highlands Ranch	376V	80124	1-399	
OLYMPUS DR	Highlands Ranch	376V	80124	None	
OLYMPUS DR	Jefferson Co	367C	80439	6400-7099	
OMAHA AVE	Parker	410S	80138	20700-21099	
	Parker	410P	80138	21400-21899	
OMAHA LN	Parker	410P	80138	10800-10999	
OMAHA PL	Boulder	129J	80303	5400-5499	
OMAHA ST S	Jefferson Co	842E	80470	13100-13499	
OMAN RD S	Castle Rock	497M	80104	200-499	
OMEGA CIR	Highlands Ranch	376U	80124	13300-13899	
OMEGA LN	Highlands Ranch	376U	80124	600-799	
ON A HILL RD	Gilpin Co	761J	80403	1-99	
O'NEAL CIR NW	Boulder	98T	80301	3200-3299	
O'NEAL CIR SW	Boulder	98T	80301	3200-3299	
O'NEAL PKWY	Boulder	98T	80301	3000-3199	
	Boulder	98T	80301	3300-3399	
ONEIDA CIR S	Centennial	376F	80112	7000-7199	
ONEIDA CT	Adams Co	136N	80602	16100-16199	
ONEIDA CT	Denver	286T	80220	100-299	
ONEIDA CT S	Centennial	346X	80111	6300-6399	
	Centennial	376B	80111	6500-6699	
	Centennial	376K	80112	7600-7699	
	Centennial	376P	80112	8000-8099	
ONEIDA DR	Commerce City	226P	80022	7100-7399	
ONEIDA PL	Denver	286K	80220	1100-1198	E
ONEIDA ST	Adams Co	226K	80022	7600-7999	
	Adams Co	136K	80602	16000-16599	
ONEIDA ST	Boulder	129J	80303	200-499	
ONEIDA ST	Commerce City	256K	80022	4900-4999	
	Commerce City	256F	80022	5200-5299	
	Commerce City	256B	80022	5800-6099	
	Commerce City	226X	80022	6100-6399	
	Commerce City	226T	80022	6600-6799	
	Commerce City	226P	80022	7200-7599	
	Denver	286K	80220	100-1999	
	Denver	286B	80207	2000-2799	
	Denver	256X	80207	2800-3999	
	Denver	256P	80216	4000-4399	
	Douglas Co	406T	80124	10100-10599	
ONEIDA ST	Thornton	136T	80602	15200-15399	
	Thornton	136T	80602	15400-15499	
	Thornton	166P	80602	None	
	Thornton	196B	80233	None	
ONEIDA ST S	Arapahoe Co	316K	80224	1901-1999	O
	Centennial	376B	80112	None	
	Denver	286T	80230	100-299	
	Denver	316F	80224	700-1599	
	Denver	316K	80224	1600-1899	
	Denver	316K	80224	1900-1998	E
	Denver	316P	80224	2000-2699	
	Denver	316T	80224	2900-3099	
	Denver	346B	80237	3900-4199	
ONEIDA WAY	Thornton	136T	80602	15200-15299	
ONEIDA WAY S	Centennial	346X	80111	6100-6299	
	Centennial	376K	80112	7600-7899	
	Denver	286X	80224	300-699	
	Denver	316B	80224	700-799	
	Denver	316X	80224	3200-3499	
	Denver	346B	80237	3500-3799	
	Greenwood Village	346P	80111	5400-5499	
ONTARIO AVE W	Jefferson Co	372D	80128	5200-5699	
	Jefferson Co	372A	80128	8800-8999	
	Jefferson Co	371C	80127	10500-10899	
ONTARIO CIR W	Jefferson Co	372D	80128	6700-6799	
ONTARIO CT	Boulder	129N	80303	1-99	
ONTARIO DR E	Aurora	380B	80016	21800-22499	
	Aurora	380C	80016	22900-23099	
	Aurora	381A	80016	24500-24899	
ONTARIO DR W	Jefferson Co	371D	80128	9100-9599	
ONTARIO PL	Boulder	129N	80303	5400-5699	
ONTARIO PL E	Aurora	381A	80016	24200-24299	
	Aurora	381A	80016	24600-24799	
	Aurora	381C	80016	26500-26599	
	Aurora	381D	80016	27000-27299	
	Aurora	380D	80016	None	
ONTARIO PL W	Jefferson Co	372B	80128	7600-8099	
	Jefferson Co	371C	80127	10500-10899	
	Jefferson Co	371D	80128	None	
ONTARIO WAY S	Jefferson Co	371B	80127	10900-11599	
ONYX CIR	Longmont	41U	80504	None	
ONYX ST	Douglas Co	408C	80134	None	
ONYX WAY	Longmont	41U	80504	None	
ONYX WAY	Superior	160X	80027	300-399	
OPAL CT	Castle Rock	527C	80104	4200-4399	
OPAL LN	Superior	160T	80027	3200-3399	
OPAL ST	Broomfield	162N	80020	1000-1199	
	Broomfield	162S	80020	None	
OPAL WAY	Broomfield	162S	80020	700-899	
OPAL WAY	Superior	160X	80027	400-499	
OPAL HILL DR	Douglas Co	409E	80134	17000-17399	
OPEN SKY WAY	Castle Rock	466Y	80109	None	

O

STREET NAME	CITY or COUNTY	MAP GRID	ZIP CODE	BLOCK RANGE	O/E
OPHIR AVE	Broomfield	162L	80020	1-199	
OPPORTUNITY DR	Castle Rock	496B	80109	None	
ORANGE CT	Boulder	97L	80304	3800-3999	
	Denver	286P	80220	400-599	
ORANGE DR	Boulder	97H	80304	None	
ORANGE LN	Boulder	97Q	80304	3700-3799	
ORANGE PL	Boulder	97Q	80304	1000-1199	
ORANGEWOOD DR	Thornton	194S	80260	9600-10099	
ORCHARD AVE	Boulder	97M	80304	1400-1899	
ORCHARD AVE	Frederick	727E	80516	None	
ORCHARD CT	Arvada	220W	80007	6500-6699	
	Arvada	220S	80007	6900-6999	
	Arvada	220W	80007	None	
ORCHARD CT	Boulder	97L	80304	3900-3999	
ORCHARD CT	Jefferson Co	250J	80403	5000-5099	
	Jefferson Co	250E	80403	5400-5599	
ORCHARD CT	Louisville	160C	80027	700-799	
ORCHARD CT	Westminster	223P	80030	7300-7499	
ORCHARD DR	Adams Co	224E	80221	1600-8199	
	Adams Co	223M	80221	8200-8299	
	Jefferson Co	280M	80401	1400-1599	
ORCHARD DR	Louisville	160C	80027	400-799	
ORCHARD DR E	Aurora	351T	80016	26101-26199	O
ORCHARD DR E	Centennial	346S	80111	6200-6399	
	Greenwood Village	346S	80111	5600-6199	
	Greenwood Village	347S	80111	9400-9699	
ORCHARD LN	Centennial	345W	80121	2300-2399	
	Greenwood Village	344U	80121	1-99	
ORCHARD LN E	Centennial	345U	80121	4300-4399	
ORCHARD PL E	Arapahoe Co	347T	80111	10500-10899	
	Arapahoe Co	347U	80111	11400-11499	
	Arapahoe Co	349T	80016	18000-18099	
	Arapahoe Co	350S	80016	20400-20499	
	Arapahoe Co	350U	80015	22800-23299	
	Centennial	345U	80121	4200-4299	
	Centennial	346T	80111	6600-6699	
	Centennial	348U	80016	15400-15599	
	Centennial	348V	80016	16200-16499	
ORCHARD RD	Jefferson Co	280M	80401	1200-1399	
ORCHARD RD E	Arapahoe Co	347T	80111	10500-11799	
	Arapahoe Co	349T	80015	18500-20099	
	Arapahoe Co	350U	80015	23200-23299	
	Arapahoe Co	812Z	80102	45700-46499	
	Arapahoe Co	813W	80102	47300-48899	
	Aurora	350V	80016	None	
	Aurora	351S	80016	None	
	Centennial	344Z	80121	1-1599	
	Centennial	345T	80121	1600-4199	
	Centennial	345V	80121	4200-5599	
	Centennial	348V	80014	15300-16599	
	Centennial	349T	80015	16800-20099	
	Greenwood Village	346T	80111	6000-9699	
	Greenwood Village	347T	80111	9300-10499	
ORCHARD ST	Arvada	220S	80007	7000-7199	
	Golden	280S	80401	100-599	
	Jefferson Co	280J	80401	900-1499	
	Jefferson Co	250J	80403	5200-5399	
ORCHARD WAY	Louisville	160C	80027	400-599	
ORCHARD CREEK CIR N	Boulder	99E	80301	5700-5899	
ORCHARD CREEK CIR S	Boulder	99E	80301	5700-5899	
ORCHARD CREEK LN	Boulder	99E	80301	5700-5899	
ORCHARD GRASS LN	Parker	378V	80134	16200-16399	
ORCHID AVE	Adams Co	792M	80102	None	
ORCHID CT	Lafayette	131R	80026	1400-1499	
ORD DR	Boulder Co	130K	80303	300-699	
ORE CART WAY	El Paso Co	908Y	80132	500-599	
OREGON AVE W	Lakewood	312L	80232	6500-6799	
OREGON CIR E	Aurora	317G	80112	11900-12099	
OREGON CT W	Lakewood	310H	80228	13400-13499	
OREGON DR E	Aurora	317H	80112	12100-12899	
	Aurora	318K	80012	14500-15099	
	Aurora	319L	80017	18700-18999	
OREGON DR W	Jefferson Co	311K	80232	11000-11399	
	Lakewood	312K	80232	6800-7599	
	Lakewood	310M	80228	12900-12999	
OREGON PL E	Arapahoe Co	316H	80231	8400-8599	
	Aurora	319E	80017	17500-17599	
	Aurora	319F	80017	17900-18399	
	Aurora	321E	80018	24000-24099	
	Denver	316J	80224	6100-6299	
OREGON PL W	Denver	313J	80219	4800-5199	
	Jefferson Co	311K	80232	10900-11199	
	Lakewood	311M	80232	9300-9399	
	Lakewood	311M	80232	9500-9999	
	Lakewood	311L	80232	10100-10199	
ORIOLE CIR	Brighton	137Z	80601	1000-1099	
ORIOLE COVE	Lafayette	132P	80026	800-899	
ORIOLE CT	Elbert Co	871G	80107	33700-33999	
ORIOLE DR	Lafayette	132K	80026	700-799	
ORIOLE LN	Boulder Co	69L	80503	7000-7299	
ORIOLE ST	Federal Heights	193U	80260	2800-2999	
ORION CIR	Jefferson Co	250E	80403	5500-5699	
ORION CT	Arvada	220W	80007	6400-6699	
	Arvada	220S	80007	6700-6999	
	Arvada	220W	80007	None	
ORION CT	Boulder	97Q	80304	3800-3899	
ORION CT	Jefferson Co	250E	80403	5600-5699	
	Jefferson Co	250A	80403	None	
ORION CT	Longmont	42C	80501	None	
ORION DR	Lafayette	131M	80026	700-899	
ORION LN	Arvada	220S	80007	7000-7099	
ORION PL	Arvada	220W	80007	6400-6499	
ORION PL	Longmont	42C	80501	None	
ORION ST	Golden	280S	80401	100-399	
	Jefferson Co	280N	80401	800-899	
	Jefferson Co	280J	80401	900-1199	
	Jefferson Co	220N	80007	7200-7399	
	Jefferson Co	220J	80007	7600-7799	
ORION WAY	Arvada	220W	80007	6400-6499	
	Castle Rock	467G	80108	None	
	Jefferson Co	220J	80007	7900-7999	
ORLANDO WAY	Jefferson Co	221F	80005	8000-8199	
ORLEANS CIR	Adams Co	170X	80022	11500-21699	
ORLEANS CT	Denver	260P	80249	4200-4399	
	Denver	260K	80249	None	
ORLEANS CT N	Denver	260S	80249	3800-3899	
	Denver	260N	80249	4000-4199	
ORLEANS CT S	Arapahoe Co	350B	80013	None	
ORLEANS ST	Denver	260N	80249	4200-4299	
	Denver	260K	80249	4800-5599	
	Federal Heights	223D	80260	9000-9099	
	Federal Heights	193Z	80260	9100-9199	
ORLEANS ST N	Denver	260S	80249	3800-4199	
	Denver	260P	80249	4500-4799	
ORLEANS ST S	Arapahoe Co	350B	80013	None	
	Centennial	350T	80015	5700-5799	
ORLEANS WAY S	Centennial	350T	80015	5800-5899	
ORMAN DR	Boulder	128G	80303	800-899	
OROFINO CT	Douglas Co	466G	80108	4400-4499	
OROFINO DR	Douglas Co	466G	80108	300-699	
OROFINO PL	Douglas Co	466G	80108	4400-4499	
ORTEGA DR	Erie	103S	80516	None	
OSAGE	Jefferson Co	370L	80127	1-99	
OSAGE CIR	Westminster	194E	80234	None	
OSAGE CT	Elbert Co	850Z	80107	1000-1199	
OSAGE CT	Westminster	164J	80020	13800-13899	
	Westminster	164A	80020	14600-14799	
OSAGE DR	Boulder	128Q	80303	4400-4999	
OSAGE PL	Douglas Co	886M	80118	5500-5599	
OSAGE RD	Douglas Co	886G	80118	7200-7699	
OSAGE RD	Jefferson Co	338U	80454	21300-21999	
OSAGE ST	Adams Co	224S	80221	6800-6999	
	Adams Co	224J	80221	7600-7799	
	Adams Co	134S	80020	None	
	Denver	284N	80223	300-399	
	Denver	284N	80204	400-799	
	Denver	284J	80204	1000-1499	
	Denver	254S	80211	3200-4399	
	Denver	254J	80221	4800-5199	
	Northglenn	194E	80234	11100-11199	
	Thornton	224A	80260	8700-8799	
	Westminster	164W	80234	12000-12099	
	Westminster	164N	80234	13200-13399	
	Westminster	164J	80234	13400-13599	
	Westminster	164E	80020	None	
OSAGE ST S	Denver	314A	80223	700-1499	
	Denver	314J	80223	1900-2099	
	Englewood	344J	80110	4500-4599	
OSAGE WAY	Adams Co	224E	80221	8300-8399	
OSAGE WAY	Douglas Co	886M	80118	5500-5699	
OSCEOLA AVE	Denver	343F	80236	None	
OSCEOLA CT	Adams Co	223T	80003	6600-6699	
	Westminster	193P	80031	10200-10299	
	Westminster	193F	80031	11100-11199	
OSCEOLA DR	Westminster	193K	80031	10500-10799	
OSCEOLA LOOP	Westminster	193K	80031	10600-10699	
OSCEOLA ST	Adams Co	253F	80212	5200-5499	
	Adams Co	223X	80003	6400-6599	
	Broomfield	163T	80020	12600-12699	
	Denver	283T	80219	1-399	
	Denver	283P	80204	400-999	
	Denver	283K	80204	1200-1699	
	Denver	283B	80212	2000-2699	
	Denver	253P	80212	2700-5199	
	Jefferson Co	842E	80470	34500-34799	
	Westminster	223P	80030	7200-7599	
	Westminster	223K	80030	7600-7899	
	Westminster	223K	80031	8000-8099	
	Westminster	193X	80031	9000-9599	
	Westminster	193T	80031	9600-9699	
	Westminster	193B	80031	11600-11999	
OSCEOLA ST S	Denver	283T	80219	1-699	
	Denver	313B	80219	700-1499	
	Denver	313P	80219	2100-2699	
	Denver	313X	80236	2800-3299	
	Littleton	343K	80123	5000-5199	
OSCEOLA WAY	Adams Co	223X	80003	6200-6399	
OSCEOLA WAY S	Denver	313F	80219	1500-1599	
	Denver	313K	80219	2000-2099	
	Denver	313T	80236	2700-2799	
OSLO GROVE	El Paso Co	910P	80908	19600-19889	
OSPREY CIR	Frederick	726D	80504	4800-4899	
OSPREY CIR	Thornton	165N	80241	1-99	
OSPREY CT	Louisville	130V	80027	800-899	
OSPREY CT	Parker	408R	80134	10900-10999	
OSPREY CT E	Highlands Ranch	406F	80130	6800-6899	
OSPREY DR	Broomfield	133W	80026	None	
OSPREY LN	Jefferson Co	366G	80439	6800-6899	
OSPREY LN	Lyons	703C	80540	None	
OSPREY ST	Brighton	137Z	80601	1201-1299	O
OSTIA CIR	Lafayette	131Q	80026	1700-1799	
OSWEGO CT	Aurora	287Q	80010	300-499	
OSWEGO CT S	Aurora	287Y	80012	600-699	
	Aurora	317C	80112	700-899	
	Aurora	317G	80112	1300-1599	
	Aurora	317U	80014	2800-2899	
OSWEGO ST	Aurora	287U	80010	200-499	
	Aurora	287Q	80010	800-899	
	Aurora	287G	80010	1300-2499	
	Commerce City	197G	80640	11200-11799	
	Commerce City	197G	80601	None	
	Denver	257G	80239	5300-5499	
OSWEGO ST	Douglas Co	407G	80134	9900-10299	
OSWEGO ST	Douglas Co	407C	80112	11700-11899	
OSWEGO ST	Greenwood Village	347Y	80111	None	
OSWEGO ST S	Aurora	287Y	80012	600-699	
	Aurora	317L	80112	1600-1899	
	Aurora	317Q	80014	2200-2699	
	Greenwood Village	347Y	80111	6100-6199	
OSWEGO WAY S	Aurora	317L	80014	1900-2299	
	Aurora	317G	80112	None	
OTERO AVE E	Arapahoe Co	374R	80122	900-1099	
	Arapahoe Co	374R	80122	1600-1799	
	Arapahoe Co	378R	80112	16100-16499	
	Arapahoe Co	378P	80112	None	
	Centennial	375P	80122	2300-3399	
	Centennial	375Q	80122	4000-4099	
	Centennial	376N	80112	5600-6499	
	Centennial	376P	80112	6800-7299	
	Centennial	377N	80112	9500-9699	
OTERO AVE W	Jefferson Co	372P	80128	7200-7599	
	Jefferson Co	372N	80128	8100-8299	
OTERO CIR E	Centennial	375N	80122	1700-2399	
	Centennial	375P	80122	2900-3299	
	Centennial	376R	80112	8200-8799	
OTERO CT E	Littleton	374Q	80122	500-599	
OTERO DR E	Arapahoe Co	381Q	80016	25900-26499	
	Aurora	380R	80016	23400-23799	
	Centennial	375R	80122	5200-5499	
	Centennial	376N	80112	5900-6299	
OTERO LN E	Arapahoe Co	374R	80122	1500-1699	
	Centennial	375N	80122	1900-2099	
	Centennial	376R	80112	8400-8499	
OTERO PKWY E	Arapahoe Co	380N	80016	21000-21399	
OTERO PL	Centennial	375N	80122	None	
OTERO PL E	Arapahoe Co	374R	80122	1100-1199	
	Arapahoe Co	378R	80112	16000-16499	
	Arapahoe Co	380P	80016	21500-21699	
	Aurora	381R	80016	26900-26999	
	Aurora	381R	80016	27200-27499	
	Aurora	380P	80016	None	
	Centennial	375P	80122	2600-3199	
	Centennial	375R	80122	5200-5299	
	Centennial	376N	80112	6100-6499	
	Centennial	376R	80112	8300-8999	
OTERO PL W	Jefferson Co	372Q	80128	6900-7099	
	Jefferson Co	372P	80128	7300-7499	
OTIS CIR	Arvada	222L	80003	7900-7999	
	Westminster	192L	80020	10800-10899	
OTIS CT	Arvada	252G	80002	5500-5599	
	Arvada	222Y	80003	6600-6699	
	Arvada	222U	80003	6800-7199	
	Arvada	222G	80003	8200-8299	
	Edgewater	282C	80214	2400-2599	
	Lakewood	282U	80226	200-299	
	Westminster	222Q	80003	7200-7399	
	Westminster	192U	80021	9800-9899	
	Wheat Ridge	252Y	80214	2800-2999	
OTIS CT S	Denver	342Q	80123	5400-5499	
	Jefferson Co	342U	80123	5900-5999	
	Jefferson Co	372Q	80128	7900-8499	
	Lakewood	312C	80226	1000-1099	
	Lakewood	312G	80232	1200-1299	
	Lakewood	312L	80232	1700-1799	
	Lakewood	312Y	80227	3400-3499	
OTIS DR	Arvada	222C	80003	8300-8499	
OTIS DR	Longmont	12U	80501	None	
	Westminster	192U	80021	9600-9899	
OTIS PL S	Lakewood	312G	80232	1100-1199	
OTIS ST	Arvada	252G	80002	5300-5499	
	Arvada	252C	80003	6000-6199	
	Arvada	222U	80003	6200-7199	
	Arvada	222Q	80003	7400-7599	
	Edgewater	282G	80214	2000-2199	
	Edgewater	282C	80214	2400-2599	
	Lakewood	282Q	80226	300-499	
	Lakewood	282L	80214	1200-1499	
	Westminster	192Y	80031	9400-9599	
	Westminster	192U	80021	9800-9999	
	Westminster	192G	80020	10900-11399	
	Westminster	192C	80020	11500-11599	
	Wheat Ridge	252Y	80033	2900-3199	
	Wheat Ridge	252Y	80033	3200-3499	
	Wheat Ridge	252U	80033	3500-4399	
	Wheat Ridge	252Q	80033	4600-4799	
OTIS ST S	Denver	312U	80227	2700-2999	
	Denver	342U	80123	5500-5699	
	Jefferson Co	372U	80128	8300-8499	
	Lakewood	282Y	80226	300-699	
	Lakewood	312C	80226	700-999	
	Lakewood	312G	80232	1100-1599	
OTIS WAY S	Jefferson Co	372C	80123	6500-6699	
OTOE ST S	Jefferson Co	842E	80470	13100-13499	
OTOWI RD	Jefferson Co	338J	80454	23100-23999	
OTTAWA AVE E	Aurora	381A	80016	24200-24599	
OTTAWA AVE S	Aurora	830A	80016	24200-24599	
OTTAWA AVE W	Arapahoe Co	373E	80128	4900-5199	
	Jefferson Co	372G	80128	5200-5499	
	Jefferson Co	372D	80128	6600-6799	
	Jefferson Co	372C	80128	6800-6999	
	Jefferson Co	372A	80128	8700-8999	
	Jefferson Co	371G	80127	10200-10799	
OTTAWA CIR E	Aurora	380B	80016	21400-21599	
	Aurora	380B	80016	22100-22399	
OTTAWA CT	Douglas Co	886G	80118	5900-5999	
OTTAWA CT E	Aurora	380C	80016	None	
OTTAWA DR E	Aurora	380C	80016	22100-22499	
	Aurora	381B	80016	24000-25599	
	Aurora	381D	80016	27000-27399	
	Aurora	380C	80016	None	
OTTAWA DR W	Jefferson Co	372F	80128	7700-7799	
OTTAWA PL	Boulder	128R	80303	4400-4799	
OTTAWA PL	Douglas Co	886G	80118	None	
OTTAWA PL E	Aurora	380C	80016	22700-22899	
	Aurora	381A	80016	24200-24299	
	Aurora	381A	80016	25000-25099	
	Aurora	381C	80016	26800-27099	
	Aurora	380D	80016	None	
	Aurora	381B	80016	None	
OTTAWA PL W	Jefferson Co	372C	80128	6600-6999	
	Jefferson Co	372B	80128	7000-7899	
	Jefferson Co	371G	80127	10200-10299	
OTTAWA WAY E	Aurora	380D	80016	None	
OTTAWA TRAIL	Jefferson Co	366A	80439	31100-31199	
OTTER CT	Lafayette	131Z	80026	2500-2599	
OTTER WAY	Douglas Co	867J	80135	400-599	
OURAY AVE	Broomfield	162L	80020	200-599	
OURAY CIR S	Aurora	319E	80017	1500-1599	
	Aurora	319W	80013	3500-3699	
OURAY CT	Commerce City	198M	80022	10600-10699	
OURAY CT S	Arapahoe Co	349W	80016	6200-6299	
	Aurora	319J	80017	1700-1899	
	Aurora	348H	80014	4100-4199	
	Centennial	349N	80015	5100-5199	
	Centennial	349S	80015	5700-5799	
OURAY DR	Boulder Co	723D	80503	7800-8299	
	Boulder Co	703Z	80503	8300-8599	
OURAY RD	Clear Creek Co	365N	80439	1-399	
OURAY RD	Jefferson Co	842Q	80470	15300-16499	
	Jefferson Co	842V	80470	16400E-16698E	E
	Jefferson Co	842V	80470	16200W-16699W	
OURAY ST	Aurora	288M	80011	800-1299	
	Aurora	258V	80011	3300-3398	E

O

STREET NAME	CITY or COUNTY	MAP GRID	ZIP CODE	BLOCK RANGE	O/E
OURAY ST	Boulder	98P	80301	None	
	Commerce City	198V	80022	9600-9799	
	Commerce City	198R	80022	10100-10299	
	Commerce City	198M	80022	10400-10599	
	Commerce City	768H	80022	10400-10599	
	Commerce City	198H	80022	10600-10899	
	Commerce City	769A	80022	None	
	Commerce City	769E	80022	None	
OURAY ST S	Arapahoe Co	349W	80016	6000-6499	
	Arapahoe Co	379A	80016	6500-6699	
	Aurora	318D	80017	700-1099	
	Aurora	319J	80013	1900-2199	
	Aurora	319N	80013	2500-2599	
	Aurora	319S	80013	3000-3199	
	Aurora	349A	80013	3500-3699	
	Aurora	349J	80015	4700-4799	
	Centennial	349N	80015	5100-5199	
	Centennial	349S	80015	5500-5699	
OURAY WAY	Aurora	288R	80011	600-699	
OURAY WAY S	Arapahoe Co	349W	80016	6100-6499	
	Arapahoe Co	379A	80016	6500-6699	
	Aurora	319N	80013	2500-2599	
	Aurora	319W	80013	2700-3499	
	Aurora	349A	80013	3700-3899	
	Aurora	349E	80013	4100-4199	
	Aurora	349J	80015	4500-4799	
OUTBACK CIR	Elbert Co	871H	80117	6600-6699	
OUTBACK CT	Boulder	69Y	80301	5600-5699	
OUTBACK TRAIL	Clear Creek Co	781T	80439	None	
OUTER MARKER RD	Douglas Co	848J	80108	1100-1899	
OUTLOOK TRAIL	Broomfield	162F	80020	2200-2699	
OUTPOST LN	Clear Creek Co	781U	80439	None	
OUTRIDER RD	Douglas Co	432F	80125	8200-8399	
OUTRIDER WAY	El Paso Co	908P	80132	1500-1699	
OUTRIGGER CT	Boulder Co	99G	80301	6400-6499	
OUZEL CT	Parker	408R	80134	11000-11099	
OVERBROOK DR	Boulder Co	70L	80503	7000-7199	
OVERHILL RD	Jefferson Co	280M	80401	1300-1499	
OVERLAND CT	Lafayette	131K	80026	100-199	
OVERLAND DR	Brighton	138M	80601	2000-2199	
OVERLAND LOOP	Elbert Co	871G	80107	34000-34199	
OVERLAND ST	Lochbuie	140A	80603	None	
OVERLAND TRAIL	Brighton	139F	80603	15000-15399	
OVERLAND TRAIL	Elbert Co	832T	80107	44500-44999	
OVERLOOK DR	Boulder	128N	80305	300-399	
OVERLOOK DR	Broomfield	162N	80020	2300-2799	
OVERLOOK DR	Elbert Co	850U	80107	1-299	
OVERLOOK DR	Gilpin Co	740Y	80403	None	
OVERLOOK DR	Jefferson Co	762B	80403	11500-11699	
	Jefferson Co	337J	80439	27300-27499	
OVERLOOK DR	Lafayette	132U	80026	1300-1598	E
OVERLOOK DR	Park Co	841P	80421	1-599	
OVERLOOK LN	Boulder Co	722L	80302	1-499	
OVERLOOK LN	Park Co	841Q	80421	1-99	
	Park Co	841R	80421	1-99	
OVERLOOK RD	Castle Rock	497L	80104	200-299	
OVERLOOK ST	Park Co	820V	80421	1-199	
OVERLOOK WAY S	Littleton	373J	80128	7500-7699	
OVERLOOK TRAIL	Jefferson Co	336A	80439	3400-3799	
OVERTON DR	Castle Rock	497E	80109	1700-1999	
OVERTON ST	Adams Co	750M	80603	15100-15198	E
OVERVIEW DR	Castle Rock	497U	80104	1900-1999	
OVIDA PL	Douglas Co	466H	80108	300-399	
OWENS AVE	Keenesburg	732A	80643	None	
OWENS CIR	Westminster	191P	80021	10300-10499	
OWENS CIR S	Arapahoe Co	795Y	80103	500-599	
OWENS CT	Arvada	221X	80004	6500-6599	
	Arvada	221N	80005	7600-7699	
	Arvada	221K	80005	7800-7899	
	Arvada	221F	80005	8000-8599	
	Lakewood	281F	80215	1900-1999	
	Lakewood	251X	80215	2900-3199	
	Westminster	191K	80021	10700-10799	
OWENS CT S	Jefferson Co	311F	80232	1100-1199	
	Jefferson Co	311X	80227	3200-3499	
	Jefferson Co	341K	80127	4900-4999	
	Jefferson Co	341P	80127	5400-5498	E
	Jefferson Co	341X	80127	5900-6299	
	Jefferson Co	371B	80127	6500-6599	
	Jefferson Co	371K	80127	7300-7399	
	Lakewood	311B	80226	700-1099	
	Lakewood	311K	80227	2000-2199	
OWENS DR	Westminster	191P	80021	10000-10199	
OWENS LN S	Jefferson Co	311T	80227	None	
OWENS ST	Arvada	251B	80004	5800-6199	
	Arvada	221X	80004	6400-6499	
	Arvada	221T	80004	6800-7099	
	Arvada	221N	80005	7600-7699	
	Arvada	221K	80005	7800-7899	
	Arvada	251F	80033	None	
	Lakewood	281F	80215	1500-1699	
	Westminster	191P	80021	10000-10499	
	Westminster	191K	80021	10600-10699	
	Westminster	191L	80021	10700-10799	
	Wheat Ridge	251T	80033	3500-3799	
	Wheat Ridge	251P	80033	4200-4399	
OWENS ST S	Arapahoe Co	795Y	80103	100-599	
	Jefferson Co	311F	80232	1100-1499	
	Jefferson Co	311K	80232	1500-1999	
	Jefferson Co	341P	80127	4900-5399	
	Jefferson Co	371B	80127	6500-6699	
	Jefferson Co	371F	80127	6800-7199	
	Jefferson Co	371X	80127	8700-8899	
	Lakewood	281X	80226	300-499	
	Lakewood	311F	80226	1000-1099	
	Lakewood	311K	80232	None	
OWENS WAY	Jefferson Co	221F	80005	8000-8199	
OWENS WAY S	Jefferson Co	341K	80127	4700-4899	
	Jefferson Co	371F	80127	7000-7099	
OWL CT	Louisville	130U	80027	700-799	
OWL DR	Gilpin Co	740Y	80403	None	
OWL DR	Louisville	130Y	80027	300-799	
	Louisville	130U	80027	800-899	
OWL LN	Boulder Co	101E	80301	9400-9499	
OWL LN	Douglas Co	469C	80134	None	
OWL LAKE DR	Firestone	707X	80504	6500-9799	
OWL ROOST CT	Douglas Co	470B	80134	8200-8499	
OX PL	Douglas Co	469C	80134	None	

STREET NAME	CITY or COUNTY	MAP GRID	ZIP CODE	BLOCK RANGE	O/E
OXBOW CT	Douglas Co	527R	80104	2300-2399	
OXBOW DR	Brighton	139L	80601	None	
OXBOW DR	Douglas Co	528N	80104	2500-2599	
OXBOW RD S	Jefferson Co	306X	80439	2900-3099	
OXBRIDGE RD	El Paso Co	908Z	80132	17000-17599	
OXEN RD E	Douglas Co	441G	80138	11000-11499	
OXFORD AVE E	Arapahoe Co	350E	80013	21000-21099	
	Arapahoe Co	350E	80013	None	
	Aurora	348G	80013	15400-15599	
	Cherry Hills Village	345H	80113	4600-5599	
	Denver	346F	80237	7000-7699	
	Denver	346G	80237	7700-7799	
	Englewood	344G	80113	1-799	
OXFORD AVE W	Denver	343F	80236	2700-4199	
	Englewood	344E	80110	1-1599	
	Sheridan	344E	80110	1600-2199	
	Sheridan	343H	80110	1700-2699	
OXFORD CIR W	Lakewood	342F	80235	7800-7899	
OXFORD DR	Castle Pines North	436Q	80108	7000-7399	
OXFORD DR E	Aurora	348H	80014	16000-16299	
	Aurora	349E	80013	16700-16899	
	Aurora	349F	80013	17900-18199	
	Aurora	349G	80013	19000-19799	
	Aurora	350G	80018	22300-22399	
	Denver	346H	80237	8000-9299	
OXFORD DR W	Lakewood	342F	80235	7600-7799	
OXFORD LN	Superior	160R	80027	1900-2099	
OXFORD LN E	Cherry Hills Village	344H	80113	900-1599	
OXFORD PL	Broomfield	133L	80020	3001-3099	O
OXFORD PL E	Arapahoe Co	350E	80013	20600-20699	
	Aurora	348F	80014	13900-13999	
	Aurora	349F	80013	17700-17899	
	Aurora	350B	80018	21800-21999	
	Aurora	350G	80018	22200-22299	
	Cherry Hills Village	345G	80110	4400-4699	
OXFORD PL W	Englewood	344E	80110	1000-1199	
	Lakewood	342F	80235	7700-7799	
OXFORD RD	Boulder Co	723D	80503	4100-5499	
	Boulder Co	69B	80503	5500-6699	
	Boulder Co	70B	80503	7900-8299	
	Boulder Co	71B	80504	9500-10999	
	Boulder Co	72A	80504	11000-12699	
OXFORD WAY	Elbert Co	850R	80107	1-1499	
OXFORD PEAK CT	Douglas Co	436V	80108	6200-6299	
OXFORD PEAK LN	Douglas Co	436V	80108	6200-6299	
OXFORD PEAK PL	Douglas Co	436U	80108	6200-6299	
OX TRAIL	Douglas Co	469C	80134	5000-5099	
OX YOKE LN	Park Co	841F	80421	1-499	
OX YOKE WAY	El Paso Co	908Y	80132	200-299	

P

STREET NAME	CITY or COUNTY	MAP GRID	ZIP CODE	BLOCK RANGE	O/E
PACE ST	Longmont	42B	80501	400-499	
	Longmont	12T	80501	900-2499	
PACIFIC AVE	Fort Lupton	728M	80621	100-899	
PACIFIC AVE W	Lakewood	311N	80228	12800-12899	
	Lakewood	310L	80228	13700-14099	
PACIFIC CIR E	Aurora	317M	80014	12400-12899	
PACIFIC CIR W	Lakewood	312M	80227	5700-6199	
PACIFIC CT	Fort Lupton	728H	80621	900-1399	
PACIFIC CT W	Lakewood	311K	80227	11100-11199	
PACIFIC DR E	Aurora	317M	80014	12700-12899	
	Aurora	318M	80013	16600-16899	
	Aurora	319M	80013	19300-19799	
PACIFIC PL	Fort Lupton	728H	80621	900-1099	
PACIFIC PL E	Arapahoe Co	316L	80231	8200-8299	
	Aurora	317L	80014	11700-11799	
	Aurora	318K	80014	14500-14799	
	Aurora	318L	80014	14800-14999	
	Aurora	318L	80013	15500-15599	
	Aurora	319J	80013	16800-17199	
	Aurora	319K	80013	17900-18099	
	Aurora	317J	80247	None	
	Aurora	321J	80018	None	
	Aurora	321J	80018	None	
	Denver	315M	80222	4800-5599	
PACIFIC PL W	Denver	314J	80223	1600-1999	
	Denver	313M	80223	2100-2199	
	Lakewood	312M	80227	5700-5799	
	Lakewood	312J	80227	8500-8599	
PACIFIC WAY	Fort Lupton	728H	80621	1000-1299	
PACKER LN	Boulder	98V	80301	None	
PACKSADDLE TRAIL	Clear Creek Co	781U	80439	None	
PACTOLUS LAKE RD	Gilpin Co	741X	80403	1-999	
PADDOCK ST	Elbert Co	871J	80107	900-1799	
PADDOCK ST	Elizabeth	871E	80107	200-899	
PADEN ST	Fort Lupton	728L	80621	500-699	
PAGE ST	Palmer Lake	907Q	80133	None	
PAGENTRY PL	El Paso Co	908V	80132	18700-19199	
PAGOSA CIR S	Aurora	349E	80015	4400-4799	
	Aurora	349J	80015	4800-4899	
PAGOSA CT	Commerce City	769A	80022	None	
PAGOSA CT S	Aurora	319E	80017	1600-1699	
PAGOSA CT S	Aurora	319N	80013	2500-2699	
	Aurora	349E	80015	4100-4199	
	Centennial	349S	80015	5500-5699	
	Centennial	379J	80016	7600-7699	
PAGOSA ST	Aurora	289E	80011	1900-1999	
	Aurora	259W	80011	3100-3198	E
	Aurora	289A	80011	None	
	Commerce City	769A	80022	10401-10499	O
	Commerce City	769E	80022	None	
PAGOSA ST S	Aurora	319E	80017	1400-1599	
	Aurora	319J	80013	1900-2099	
	Aurora	319N	80013	2400-3299	
	Aurora	349A	80013	3900-3999	
	Aurora	349E	80013	4100-4199	
	Aurora	349J	80015	5000-5099	
	Centennial	349N	80015	5100-5199	
PAGOSA WAY	Aurora	289E	80011	1600-1899	
PAGOSA WAY S	Aurora	319J	80017	1700-1899	
	Aurora	319N	80013	2100-2699	
	Aurora	319W	80013	3300-3499	
	Aurora	349J	80015	4400-4899	
	Centennial	349N	80015	5200-5399	
	Centennial	349S	80015	5700-5899	
PAINE AVE S	Lakewood	342F	80235	7700-7899	
PAINT PL	Douglas Co	432F	80125	10500-10599	

STREET NAME	CITY or COUNTY	MAP GRID	ZIP CODE	BLOCK RANGE	O/E
PAINT BRUSH CIR	Jefferson Co	336C	80439	29300-29499	
PAINTBRUSH CT	Douglas Co	887F	80118	None	
PAINT BRUSH CT S	Littleton	343S	80123	5800-5899	
PAINT BRUSH DR	Gilpin Co	760H	80403	2-98	E
PAINT BRUSH DR	Jefferson Co	336B	80439	29500-29999	
PAINT BRUSH LN	El Paso Co	908Q	80132	600-699	
PAINTBRUSH LN	Elbert Co	831J	80138	None	
PAINTBRUSH LN	Lafayette	131F	80026	2500-2599	
PAINT BRUSH TRAIL	Boulder Co	99H	80301	7100-7399	
PAINTED CANYON CIR S					
	Highlands Ranch	403C	80129	9300-9599	
PAINTED CANYON PL W					
	Highlands Ranch	403C	80129	2800-2899	
PAINTED CANYON WAY W					
	Highlands Ranch	403C	80129	2800-2899	
PAINTED HILLS ST	Parker	410V	80138	23400-23599	
PAINTED SKY ST S	Highlands Ranch	374U	80126	8400-8499	
PAINTER DR	El Paso Co	908N	80132	None	
PAINT HORSE CIR	Elbert Co	891X	80106	3500-3599	
PAINTHORSE DR	Castle Rock	466T	80109	None	
PAINT PONY CIR	Castle Rock	498B	80108	None	
PAINT PONY CT	Castle Rock	498A	80108	None	
PAIUTE AVE	Boulder Co	70M	80503	6700-6999	
PAIUTE CT	Boulder Co	70R	80503	6600-6699	
PAIUTE RD	Clear Creek Co	365S	80439	2-198	E
PAIUTE RD	Clear Creek Co	821H	80439	200-799	
	Jefferson Co	365N	80439	34700-34899	
PALAMINO LN	Boulder Co	722L	80302	1-799	
PALAMINO ST	Weld Co	729V	80603	17600-17999	
PALAMINO TRAIL	Elbert Co	871E	80107	2200-2599	
PALE ANEMONE ST	Parker	409W	80134	None	
PALEO WAY	El Paso Co	910X	80908	7300-7999	
PALERMO PL	Longmont	40P	80503	4401-4499	O
PALEY ST	Northglenn	194J	80234	10500-10599	
PALI CT	Boulder Co	99H	80301	None	
PALI WAY	Boulder Co	99H	80301	4300-4599	
PALISADE CT S	Highlands Ranch	406B	80130	9300-9499	
PALISADE CT S	Louisville	160C	80027	800-999	
PALISADE DR	Boulder	98P	80301	None	
PALISADE DR E	Highlands Ranch	406B	80130	7000-7299	
PALISADE PKWY	Broomfield	134F	80516	None	
PALLADIO CT	Douglas Co	845B	80125	8000-8299	
PALMER AVE	Bennett	793J	80102	100-799	
PALMER CT	Boulder Co	723H	80503	4500-4699	
PALMER DR	Castle Rock	498H	80104	5600-5899	
PALMER LN	Erie	102Q	80516	1500-1799	
PALMER LN	Northglenn	194T	80260	9800-9899	
PALMER ST	Adams Co	793L	80102	None	
PALMER DIVIDE AVE	Douglas Co	908J	80118	1-5499	
PALMER DIVIDE AVE E	Douglas Co	910J	80118	8300-11299	
	El Paso Co	909L	80118	1300-6099	
PALMER DIVIDE RD	El Paso Co	907R	80118	1-1299	
PALMER RIDGE DR	Douglas Co	850N	80134	3500-4999	
PALMETTO CT	Castle Rock	469J	80108	6600-6799	
PALM TREE CIR	Thornton	194S	80260	None	
PALMYRA WAY	Broomfield	163M	80020	None	
PALO PKWY	Boulder Co	98P	80301	2800-3299	
PALOMA AVE	Brighton	139R	80601	1-299	
PALOMA ST	Brighton	139R	80601	5000-5199	
PALOMINO DR	Jefferson Co	306X	80439	30000-30499	
PALOMINO DR N	Douglas Co	407W	80108	9000-9599	
PALOMINO PKWY	Highlands Ranch	376T	80130	6700-6799	
PALOMINO RD	Jefferson Co	306X	80439	3200-3299	
PALOMINO WAY	Frederick	707W	80504	None	
PALOMINO PARK LN					
	Highlands Ranch	376W	80130	None	
PALO VERDE CIR S	Jefferson Co	336F	80439	3900-3999	
PALO VERDE RD S	Jefferson Co	336F	80439	3800-4099	
PALO VERDE ST	Thornton	195X	80229	9200-9399	
PAMPAS CT	Boulder	98J	80304	2500-2599	
PAN CT	Lafayette	131R	80026	600-899	
PANAMA DR E	Centennial	344Z	80121	1-1799	
	Centennial	345W	80121	1800-2199	
PANDORA CT	Lafayette	131U	80026	1100-1199	
PANDORA ST	Jefferson Co	339G	80465	4001-4099	O
PANORAM CIR	Weld Co	727J	80514	None	
PANORAMA AVE	Boulder	98W	80304	2300-2599	
PANORAMA AVE	Firestone	707X	80504	None	
PANORAMA CIR	Longmont	41B	80501	800-899	
	Longmont	41B	80501	901-1999	O
PANORAMA CIR E	Centennial	377J	80112	9300-9699	
PANORAMA CT	Boulder Co	130W	80303	700-799	
PANORAMA CT	Douglas Co	410J	80138	11200-11499	
PANORAMA DR	Elbert Co	850U	80107	200-899	
PANORAMA DR	Jefferson Co	278Q	80401	800-21899	
	Jefferson Co	278U	80401	21902-22098	E
PANORAMA DR	Park Co	841M	80421	1-299	
PANORAMA DR E	Centennial	376M	80112	8900-9299	
PANORAMA LN E	Arapahoe Co	316K	80224	6700-6899	
PANORAMA PT	Lafayette	132U	80026	None	
PANORAMA DR	Boulder Co	130W	80303	7200-7599	
PANTHER BUTTE	Douglas Co	406W	80124	5900-5999	
PANTHER HOLLOWS	Douglas Co	406J	80124	5900-5999	
PAOLI WAY	Parker	409N	80134	17300-17399	
PAONIA	Jefferson Co	370K	80127	1-99	
PAONIA CT	Castle Rock	497A	80109	1600-1799	
PAPAGO RD	Jefferson Co	338F	80454	22500-22599	
PAPERFLOWER DR	Douglas Co	410V	80138	9500-9999	
PAPOOSE AVE	Adams Co	226B	80022	None	
PAPOOSE WAY	Clear Creek Co	304H	80439	1-99	
PAR CIR	Columbine Valley	343X	80123	1-99	
PAR RD	Broomfield	162R	80020	1100-1199	
PARADISE AVE	Elbert Co	851Z	80107	None	
PARADISE CIR	Elbert Co	851Z	80107	36400-36499	
PARADISE CIR	Jefferson Co	278U	80401	21900-22099	
PARADISE LN	Boulder Co	161E	80020	9200-9599	
PARADISE RD	Jefferson Co	278T	80401	1-399	
PARADISE VALLEY PKWY	Gilpin Co	760U	80403	1-99	
PARADISO CT	Douglas Co	432E	80125	8000-8199	
PARAGON DR	Boulder Co	130N	80303	100-1099	
PARAGON PL	Jefferson Co	307H	80401	24300-24499	
PARAGON WAY	Douglas Co	466H	80108	300-399	
PARAMOUNT CT	Louisville	130M	80027	2300-2399	
PARAMOUNT PKWY	Wheat Ridge	281C	80215	1-99	
PARAMOUNT PL	Longmont	11U	80501	1400-1499	
PARDEE ST	Douglas Co	439B	80134	None	
PARENT ST	Weld Co	726J	80516	None	

O
P

STREET NAME	CITY or COUNTY	MAP GRID	ZIP CODE	BLOCK RANGE	O/E
PARFET CT	Arvada	251B	80004	5800-6199	
	Arvada	221T	80004	7000-7099	
	Arvada	221K	80005	7600-7699	
	Arvada	221F	80005	8400-8499	
	Lakewood	281B	80215	2600-2699	
	Westminster	191K	80021	10500-10599	
PARFET CT S	Jefferson Co	311F	80232	1100-1699	
	Jefferson Co	311K	80232	1700-1899	
	Jefferson Co	311X	80227	3400-3499	
	Jefferson Co	341K	80127	4500-4999	
	Jefferson Co	371F	80127	7100-7199	
	Jefferson Co	371K	80127	7300-7499	
	Jefferson Co	371P	80127	8400-8499	
	Lakewood	311B	80226	1000-1099	
	Lakewood	311P	80227	2100-2199	
PARFET DR	Lakewood	251X	80215	2800-3099	
PARFET DR S	Lakewood	311K	80227	1900-2199	
PARFET LN S	Jefferson Co	341P	80127	5300-5399	
PARFET ST	Arvada	251B	80004	5800-6199	
	Arvada	221X	80004	6300-6499	
	Arvada	221T	80004	6800-7099	
	Arvada	221K	80005	7700-7999	
	Arvada	251F	80003	None	
	Lakewood	281P	80215	600-899	
	Lakewood	281K	80215	900-999	
	Lakewood	281B	80215	2500-2599	
	Westminster	191K	80021	10600-10799	
	Wheat Ridge	251T	80033	3200-4099	
	Wheat Ridge	251P	80033	4200-4799	
	Wheat Ridge	251K	80033	4800-5199	
PARFET ST S	Jefferson Co	341K	80127	4700-4899	
	Jefferson Co	341T	80127	5600-6299	
	Jefferson Co	371B	80127	6400-6499	
	Jefferson Co	371F	80127	7000-7299	
	Lakewood	281X	80226	200-599	
	Lakewood	311B	80226	600-699	
PARFET WAY	Arvada	221K	80005	8000-8099	
PARFET WAY S	Jefferson Co	341K	80127	4900-4999	
	Jefferson Co	341P	80127	5100-5299	
	Jefferson Co	371B	80127	6400-6499	
	Lakewood	311B	80226	900-999	
PARFET ESTATES DR	Golden	279E	80401	1700-1999	
PARIS CIR	Aurora	287U	80012	100-199	
PARIS CIR	Elbert Co	850D	80138	1300-1499	
PARIS CT	Commerce City	197C	80640	11400-11499	
PARIS CT S	Arapahoe Co	347U	80111	5800-5899	
	Aurora	317C	80112	900-1098	E
	Aurora	317G	80112	1300-1599	
	Aurora	317L	80112	1800-1899	
	Aurora	317U	80014	2800-2899	
PARIS PL	Greenwood Village	347U	80111	None	
PARIS PL S	Aurora	317U	80014	2700-2799	
PARIS ST	Arapahoe Co	347U	80111	5800-5899	
	Aurora	287L	80010	900-999	
	Aurora	287G	80010	1600-1999	
	Aurora	287C	80010	2300-2499	
	Aurora	287L	80010	None	
	Aurora	287U	80012	None	
	Commerce City	197Q	80603	10400-10599	
	Commerce City	197G	80640	11200-11799	
	Commerce City	197C	80640	11800-11899	
	Denver	257U	80239	3700-3899	
	Denver	257L	80239	4600-5099	
	Greenwood Village	347Y	80111	None	
PARIS ST S	Aurora	287Y	80012	600-699	
	Aurora	317U	80014	2800-2998	E
	Centennial	377C	80111	6500-6699	
	Greenwood Village	347Y	80111	6100-6199	
PARIS WAY	Adams Co	137L	80602	None	
PARIS WAY S	Aurora	317L	80014	2000-2199	
PARK AVE	Denver	284B	80205	100W-1499W	
	Denver	254X	80205	1500W-1599W	
	Denver	254X	80216	1601W-1699W	O
PARK AVE	Fort Lupton	728L	80621	100-1099	
PARK AVE	Jefferson Co	823U	80433	22500-22699	
	Jefferson Co	842V	80470	28200-28999	
PARK AVE	Palmer Lake	907Q	80133	None	
PARK AVE S	Fort Lupton	728L	80621	100-799	
PARK AVE S	Morrison	309Z	80465	100-299	
PARK BLVD	Lochbuie	729Z	80603	100-599	
	Lochbuie	729Z	80603	None	
PARK CIR	Boulder Co	100E	80301	7300-7499	
PARK CIR	Jefferson Co	278X	80401	200-399	
PARK CT	Boulder Co	100E	80301	4300-4399	
PARK CT	Castle Rock	497B	80109	300-399	
PARK CT S	Arapahoe Co	795Y	80103	None	
PARK DR	Brighton	139K	80601	None	
PARK DR	Castle Rock	497R	80104	100-199	
PARK DR	Clear Creek Co	335J	80439	1-299	
PARK DR	Lyons	703B	80540	None	
PARK DR	Park Co	841Q	80421	1-199	
PARK DR E	Douglas Co	469V	80116	6900-7199	
	Douglas Co	470S	80116	7200-7899	
PARK DR S	El Paso Co	908T	80132	700-1399	
PARK LN	Boulder	127G	80302	800-899	
PARK LN	Elbert Co	871F	80107	4000-4699	
PARK LN	Jefferson Co	368B	80465	22300-22399	
PARK LN	Lafayette	131B	80026	2500-2599	
PARK LN	Lakewood	282P	80214	600-799	
PARK LN	Littleton	373H	80120	2400-2499	
PARK LN	Longmont	41L	80501	700-899	
PARK PL	Boulder Co	100E	80301	7300-7499	
PARK PL	Broomfield	162Q	80020	1300-1399	
PARK PL	Denver	285A	80205	2000-2099	
PARK PL	Greenwood Village	346V	80111	1-99	
PARK PL W	Denver	283U	80219	2700-2999	
	Denver	283S	80219	4900-5199	
PARK RD	Park Co	820Z	80421	1-399	
PARK ST	Broomfield	162W	80020	1-99	
PARK ST	Castle Rock	497B	80109	700-1899	
PARK ST	Golden	248V	80403	700-799	
PARK ST	Jefferson Co	336Z	80439	5900-6099	
PARK ST	Lafayette	132P	80026	1600-1699	
PARK ST	Lyons	703B	80540	None	
PARK ST	Palmer Lake	907Q	80133	None	
PARK ST S	Arapahoe Co	795Y	80103	100-399	
PARK WAY	Park Co	820Y	80421	1-199	
PARK-60	Park Co	840B	80421	1-299	
PARK 64	Park Co	840Z	80421	1-199	
PARK 68	Park Co	841X	80421	1-299	
PARK 72	Park Co	841U	80421	1-5699	
PARK CENTRE DR	Westminster	163Z	80234	None	
PARK CLIFF LN	Castle Pines North	436P	80108	800-999	
PARK COVE DR	Broomfield	163G	80020	None	
PARK COVE WAY	Broomfield	163G	80020	None	
PARK CRESCENT DR E	Aurora	381E	80016	24900-25499	
PARK CRESCENT PL E	Aurora	381E	80016	24500-24899	
PARKDALE CIR N	Erie	103X	80516	None	
PARKDALE CIR S	Erie	103X	80516	None	
PARKDALE CT	Erie	133B	80516	None	
PARK EAST RD	Aurora	287Q	80010	11600-11999	
PARKER AVE	Jefferson Co	842E	80470	12500-13099	
PARKER CT S	Aurora	317T	80014	2900-2998	E
PARKER DR	Longmont	11L	80501	900-1399	
	Parker	409L	80134	9100-12599	
PARKER RD E	Douglas Co	410M	80138	8400-9399	
	Douglas Co	411K	80138	9400-11999	
PARKER RD S	Arapahoe Co	316C	80231	1000-1098	E
	Arapahoe Co	316H	80231	1200-1899	
	Arapahoe Co	317J	80231	1900-2099	
	Arapahoe Co	317N	80231	2101-2299	O
	Arapahoe Co	378D	80016	7100-7499	
	Aurora	317N	80231	2100-2298	E
	Aurora	317P	80231	2300-2498	E
	Aurora	317P	80014	2500-3299	
	Aurora	348J	80014	3500-4299	
	Aurora	348J	80015	4300-5899	
	Aurora	378D	80016	6200-7099	
	Centennial	348J	80016	5900-6199	
	Centennial	379J	80016	7500-8299	
	Denver	316C	80231	1001-1099	O
	Denver	316C	80231	1100-1199	
	Douglas Co	469V	80116	6900-7899	
	Douglas Co	439M	80134	None	
	Douglas Co	469V	80134	None	
	Parker	379T	80134	8300-9399	
	Parker	439M	80134	12300-13099	
PARKER RD W	Douglas Co	408K	80134	3000-5999	
	Lone Tree	408E	80124	6000-6199	
PARKER HILLS CT E	Douglas Co	409M	80138	7000-7299	
PARKERHOUSE RD	Parker	379W	80134	None	
PARKER SQUARE DR E	Parker	409U	80138	19500-19799	
PARKER VISTA CIR	Parker	410N	80138	10800-20799	
PARKER VISTA CT	Parker	410N	80138	20700-20799	
PARKER VISTA LN	Parker	410N	80138	10800-10899	
PARKER VISTA PL	Parker	410N	80138	10900-10999	
PARKER VISTA RD	Parker	410N	80138	10800-20799	
PARKER VISTA ST E	Parker	410N	80138	10900-10999	
PARKER VISTA WAY	Parker	410N	80138	10900-10999	
PARK GLENN WAY	Parker	409L	80134	10100-19399	
	Parker	409G	80134	None	
PARKHILL AVE W	Jefferson Co	342W	80123	8400-9099	
	Jefferson Co	341Z	80123	9100-9399	
	Jefferson Co	341Y	80127	10600-10799	
	Lakewood	342W	80123	8300-8399	
	Littleton	344X	80120	300-599	
	Littleton	344W	80120	1200-1999	
	Littleton	343Z	80120	2000-2399	
PARKHILL DR W	Jefferson Co	341Y	80127	10600-10699	
	Jefferson Co	341X	80127	11300-11599	
PARKHILL PL W	Jefferson Co	341Y	80127	10600-10699	
	Jefferson Co	341W	80127	12100-12199	
PARKINGTON LN	Highlands Ranch	405L	80126	None	
PARK LAKE DR	Boulder Co	100Z	80301	1600-2999	
PARKLAND RD	Lone Tree	376V	80124	None	
PARKLAND ST	Broomfield	192E	80021	7800-11399	
PARKLANE DR	Parker	410N	80138	20700-20799	
PARK LANE DR E	Aurora	257Z	80011	12200-12999	
PARK LANE RD	Boulder Co	70W	80503	5800-7499	
PARK MEADOWS BLVD	Lone Tree	407E	80124	None	
PARK MEADOWS DR	Lone Tree	376U	80124	7300-9199	
	Lone Tree	407A	80124	9200-10499	
	Lone Tree	377W	80124	None	
PARK MEADOWS CENTER DR					
	Lone Tree	377S	80124	8300-8799	
PARK MOUNTAIN	Jefferson Co	371Q	80127	8000-8099	
PARK N RIDE RD	Frederick	726H	80516	None	
PARK PLACE DR	Brighton	138V	80601	None	
PARK POINT DR	Jefferson Co	277Y	80401	400-699	
PARK RANGE RD	Jefferson Co	371K	80127	10800-11599	
PARKRIDGE AVE	Boulder Co	11L	80504	10500-10699	
PARK RIDGE LN	Douglas Co	867N	80135	2100-2299	
PARK RIDGE RD	Douglas Co	867N	80135	3300-4499	
PARK SADDLE CT	Boulder	69Y	80301	5700-5799	
PARKSIDE DR	Douglas Co	408M	80134	15900-16599	
PARKSIDE DR N	Longmont	41R	80501	200-598	E
PARKSIDE DR S	Longmont	41R	80501	301-599	O
PARKSIDE PKWY	Federal Heights	223C	80260	None	
PARKSIDE CIR	Lafayette	132P	80026	1600-1699	
PARKSIDE DR	Commerce City	769E	80022	None	
	Commerce City	198H	80022	None	
	Commerce City	769E	80022	16900S-17299S	
PARKSIDE CENTER DR	Broomfield	133K	80020	3300-3599	
PARK TERRACE AVE E					
	Greenwood Village	346U	80111	8300-8699	
PARK TRAIL DR	Monument	908W	80132	700-17299	
PARK VIEW	Castle Rock	497C	80104	800-999	
PARKVIEW	Park Co	841S	80421	200-399	
PARKVIEW AVE	Jefferson Co	278Q	80401	100-799	
PARKVIEW AVE E	Aurora	291P	80018	None	
PARKVIEW CIR E	Centennial	375C	80121	4400-4499	
PARK VIEW CT	Castle Rock	497C	80104	1000-1099	
PARKVIEW CT	Golden	248Z	80403	500-599	
PARKVIEW CT	Park Co	841S	80421	1-199	
PARKVIEW DR	Aurora	288N	80011	12900-13699	
PARKVIEW DR	Jefferson Co	307A	80401	27300-27599	
PARKVIEW DR	Longmont	41T	80504	2100-2399	
PARKVIEW DR E	Aurora	287R	80011	12200-12899	
PARKVIEW PL	Broomfield	163L	80020	13600-13699	
PARK VIEW PL	Castle Rock	497G	80104	800-999	
PARKVIEW PL E	Aurora	291P	80018	25700-25999	
PARKVIEW ST	Brighton	139T	80601	15200-15499	
PARKVIEW ST	Louisville	131W	80027	800-1098	E
PARKVIEW MOUNTAIN	Jefferson Co	371K	80127	7500-7599	
PARK VILLAGE DR	Jefferson Co	336F	80439	29800-29899	
PARK VISTA DR	Northglenn	194E	80234	11100-11199	
PARKWAY DR	Boulder	128H	80303	900-999	
PARKWAY DR	Cherry Hills Village	315Y	80113	1-99	
PARKWAY DR	Commerce City	255D	80022	6000-6199	
PARKWAY DR E	Lone Tree	376Q	80124	7400-8399	
PARKWOOD LN	Castle Pines North	436P	80108	7100-7199	
PARLIAMENT CT S	Parker	410N	80138	20800-20899	
PARLIAMENT PL E	Parker	410N	80138	20800-20899	
PARLIAMENT WAY E	Parker	410N	80138	11200-11299	
PARMALEE GULCH RD	Jefferson Co	338K	80454	4400-5599	
PARMENTER AVE	Jefferson Co	823V	80433	10900-11099	
PARRAMATTA PL S	Highlands Ranch	405D	80130	9500-9699	
PARSON'S AVE	Castle Rock	498Q	80104	900-1399	
PARSONS RD	Jefferson Co	823S	80433	27200-27499	
PARSON'S WAY	Castle Rock	498Q	80104	4800-5099	
PARTHENON CT	Lafayette	131R	80026	600-899	
PARTRIDGE CIR	Golden	249S	80403	600-899	
PARTRIDGE LN	Jefferson Co	370B	80127	1-99	
PARTRIDGE ST	Highlands Ranch	375U	80126	8700-8899	
PASADENA WAY	Broomfield	163E	80020	4700-5199	
PASCHAL DR	Boulder Co	131K	80027	9800-9899	
PASEO WAY S	Denver	313K	80219	1800-2099	
PASEO DEL PRADO	Boulder Co	98P	80301	3600-3999	
PASQUE CT	Douglas Co	887F	80118	7000-7099	
PASQUE DR	Longmont	12X	80501	900-999	
PASQUE FLOWER LN	Gilpin Co	761C	80403	100-199	
PASS DR N	Brighton	139M	80601	None	
PASS ME BY RD	Arapahoe Co	794R	80136	1100-1499	
PASTURE GATE CIR	Elbert Co	851T	80107	3700-3799	
PASTURE WALK	Elbert Co	871B	80107	35000-35799	
PAT CREEK RD	Clear Creek Co	304A	80439	1-99	
PATE AVE W	Douglas Co	846C	80125	5800-5899	
PATHER TRACE	Douglas Co	406J	80124	10400-10499	
PATRICIA DR	Adams Co	224L	80229	7800-7999	
PATRICIA RD	Gilpin Co	740Z	80474	None	
PATRICK ST	Weld Co	729B	80621	7000-7999	
PATRICK TRAIL	Elbert Co	832J	80107	7100-8499	
PATSBURG CT S	Aurora	351Y	80016	6300-6499	
PATSBURG ST	Denver	770T	80249	None	
PATSBURG ST S	Aurora	381C	80016	6600-6699	
PATTERSON CIR	Douglas Co	870N	80116	10800-11099	
PATTERSON CT	Northglenn	194K	80234	10800-10999	
PATTERSON PL W	Jefferson Co	341T	80127	10300-11499	
	Littleton	343T	80123	3400-3599	
PATTON CIR	Boulder	128D	80303	1500-1599	
PATTON CT S	Denver	283X	80219	500-699	
	Denver	313F	80219	700-2699	
	Denver	313X	80236	2700-3299	
PATTON DR	Boulder	128D	80303	1400-1599	
PATTON ST	Broomfield	163T	80020	12600-12699	
PATTON WAY S	Denver	313X	80236	3300-3499	
PATTY DR	Clear Creek Co	801R	80439	1-799	
PATTY LN	Douglas Co	409W	80134	9000-9499	
PAUL RD	Clear Creek Co	801R	80439	1-399	
PAULA CIR	Monument	908X	80132	1200-1399	
PAULA DR	Gilpin Co	760G	80403	200-298	E
PAULETTE AVE S	Jefferson Co	842B	80470	12500-12799	
PAUL'S DR	Jefferson Co	822Y	80433	11100-11499	
PAUL'S LN	Jefferson Co	822Y	80433	11400-11499	
PAULS LN	Park Co	840D	80421	1-299	
PAVER WAY	El Paso Co	908Y	80132	17400-17499	
PAVILIONS PL	Brighton	138N	80601	200-399	
PAVILLION DR	Parker	409Q	80134	None	
PAWNEE CT	Elbert Co	850Z	80107	36600-36799	
PAWNEE DR	Boulder	128R	80303	1-499	
PAWNEE LN	Boulder Co	70L	80503	8300-8499	
PAWNEE LN	Broomfield	163J	80020	4501-4599	O
PAWNEE PKWY	Elbert Co	850Z	80107	1000-1999	
PAWNEE PL	Boulder	128R	80303	4600-4699	
PAWNEE PT	Lafayette	131G	80026	2000-2099	
PAWNEE RD	Douglas Co	886L	80118	8400-8799	
PAWNEE RD	Jefferson Co	338E	80454	22800-23399	
PAWNEE RD E	Douglas Co	440U	80134	8400-8799	
PAWNEE ST	Arapahoe Co	794T	80136	600-1099	
PAWNEE ST	Kiowa	872M	80117	300-599	
PAWNEE WAY	Boulder Co	70L	80503	6900-6999	
PAWNEE TRAIL	Clear Creek Co	821H	80439	1-199	
PAWNEE TRAIL E	Douglas Co	467F	80108	800-1299	
PAWNEE VALLEY TRAIL	Monument	908W	80132	16900-17099	
PAW-PAW AVE	Thornton	194S	80260	None	
PAW PRINT WAY	Castle Rock	466W	80109	None	
PAXTON CT	Parker	409J	80134	10500-10599	
PAYNE AVE W	Jefferson Co	372T	80128	6900-7599	
PAYNE CT	Aurora	289E	80011	1900-1999	
PAYNE CT	Erie	102W	80516	2500-2699	
PAYNE WAY	Aurora	289E	80011	1700-1899	
PAYNE GULCH RD	Park Co	840Z	80421	None	
PEABODY ST	Castle Rock	499J	80104	None	
PEACAN CT	Longmont	41V	80501	None	
PEACAN ST	Longmont	41V	80501	None	
PEACE ST	Frederick	727G	80530	None	
PEACE CHANCE TRAIL	Jefferson Co	366M	80439	7500-7999	
PEACEFUL WAY	Jefferson Co	842E	80470	13300-14499	
PEACEFUL HILLS RD	Jefferson Co	368F	80465	6800-7099	
PEACEFUL HILLS WAY	Jefferson Co	368F	80465	6900-7099	
PEACEFUL PINES RD	El Paso Co	909S	80132	18500-18699	
PEACEFUL PINES RD	El Paso Co	909S	80132	None	
PEACEFUL POND WAY	El Paso Co	908Q	80132	200-399	
PEACH CT	Boulder	97H	80304	None	
	Boulder Co	98F	80301	4300-4499	
PEACH CT	Brighton	138U	80601	1500-1599	
PEACH CT	Erie	133C	80516	None	
PEACH CT	Louisville	160C	80027	700-799	
PEACH DR	Thornton	194W	80260	None	
PEACH LN	Jefferson Co	336B	80439	None	
PEACH PL	Erie	133C	80516	None	
PEACH WAY	Boulder Co	98K	80301	4200-4499	
PEACH WAY S	Denver	346B	80237	3600-4099	
PEACHTREE CIR	Castle Rock	497T	80104	1-99	
PEACOCK DR	Highlands Ranch	376Y	80124	13000-13499	
PEACOCK ST	Federal Heights	193V	80260	9700-9799	
PEAK AVE	Boulder	98Z	80301	5200-5299	
PEAK AVE	Longmont	706N	80504	2900-2999	
PEAK DR	Jefferson Co	843B	80433	23900-24199	
PEAK LN	Weld Co	726K	80516	1600-1799	
PEAKS ST	Lochbuie	140A	80603	None	
PEAK TO PEAK HWY	Boulder Co	740D	80466	22600-39999	
	Boulder Co	720M	80481	None	
	Boulder Co	720Y	80466	None	
	Boulder Co	721A	80481	None	

P

STREET NAME	CITY or COUNTY	MAP GRID	ZIP CODE	BLOCK RANGE	O/E
PEAK VIEW	Nederland	740R	80466	None	
PEAKVIEW AVE	Firestone	707X	80504	None	
PEAKVIEW AVE E	Arapahoe Co	378A	80111	13200-13499	
	Arapahoe Co	379A	80016	16800-16899	
	Arapahoe Co	379B	80016	17600-18199	
	Centennial	375B	80121	2700-2999	
	Centennial	375D	80121	4400-5099	
	Centennial	375D	80121	5401-5599	O
	Centennial	376A	80111	6200-6299	
	Centennial	376D	80111	7300-8699	
	Centennial	377A	80111	9700-10499	
	Centennial	377C	80111	10900-12399	
	Centennial	377D	80111	12800-12899	
	Centennial	378C	80016	15500-15699	
	Centennial	379A	80016	16700-16799	
	Centennial	378B	80111	None	
	Greenwood Village	376D	80111	8900-9299	
	Greenwood Village	377A	80111	9300-9699	
PEAKVIEW AVE W	Jefferson Co	372B	80123	7200-7699	
PEAKVIEW BLVD	El Paso Co	908S	80132	2900-3799	
	El Paso Co	907V	80132	None	
PEAKVIEW CIR	Boulder Co	722H	80302	1000-1399	
PEAK VIEW CIR	Castle Rock	467Q	80108	None	
PEAKVIEW CIR E	Centennial	375B	80121	2700-3099	
PEAKVIEW CIR W	Littleton	374B	80120	800-1099	
PEAKVIEW CT E	Centennial	379D	80016	19900-20099	
PEAKVIEW CT W	Littleton	343Z	80120	2400-2499	
	Littleton	373D	80120	None	
PEAK VIEW DR	Gilpin Co	761S	80403	1-199	
PEAKVIEW DR E	Aurora	350X	80016	21900-22299	
	Aurora	351Y	80016	26300-26799	
PEAKVIEW DR S	Aurora	380C	80016	22300-22599	
PEAK VIEW DR S	Douglas Co	496X	80109	200-1899	
PEAKVIEW DR W	Jefferson Co	342X	80123	7700-7999	
	Jefferson Co	372A	80123	8000-8999	
	Jefferson Co	371D	80123	9600-9799	
	Jefferson Co	371C	80127	10600-10799	
	Littleton	374A	80120	100-1999	
PEAKVIEW PL	Elbert Co	850C	80138	2-398	E
PEAKVIEW PL E	Arapahoe Co	379A	80016	16800-16899	
	Arapahoe Co	379B	80016	17600-18199	
	Arapahoe Co	349X	80016	18200-18299	
	Arapahoe Co	350W	80016	20700-20799	
	Aurora	381C	80016	25800-26099	
	Centennial	A	80121	5200-5299	
	Centennial	376A	80111	6100-6299	
	Centennial	346X	80111	6600-6699	
	Centennial	376B	80111	6700-7199	
PEAKVIEW PL S	Aurora	380C	80016	22500-22699	
PEAKVIEW PL W	Jefferson Co	371C	80127	10400-10599	
	Jefferson Co	372D	80123	None	
PEAKVIEW RD	Boulder Co	722H	80302	1-1099	
PEAKVIEW ST	Weld Co	726Q	80516	4400-4999	
PEAK VISTA CT	Castle Rock	498E	80104	2200-2299	
PEAR CT	Louisville	160C	80027	700-799	
PEARL CIR	Douglas Co	408D	80134	9500-9599	
PEARL CIR	Northglenn	194G	80233	10900-11099	
	Thornton	164L	80241	13200-13399	
PEARL CT	Northglenn	194L	80233	10800-10899	
PEARL PKWY	Boulder	98Z	80301	3300-5499	
PEARL ST	Adams Co	254G	80216	5500-5599	
	Adams Co	224L	80229	7700-8299	
PEARL ST	Boulder	127C	80302	1-1099	
	Boulder	97Z	80302	1100-2099	
	Boulder	98W	80302	2100-2799	
	Boulder	98Y	80301	2800-5299	
PEARL ST	Denver	284L	80203	1-1999	
	Denver	254Q	80216	4400-4899	
PEARL ST	Douglas Co	408D	80134	9500-9599	
PEARL ST	Northglenn	194Q	80233	10400-10599	
	Northglenn	194L	80233	10800-11199	
	Northglenn	194G	80233	11400-11599	
	Northglenn	194C	80233	11600-11699	
	Thornton	224D	80229	8400-9099	
	Thornton	194Y	80229	9100-9299	
	Thornton	194Z	80229	9600-9999	
	Thornton	164Q	80241	13200-13399	
PEARL ST S	Arapahoe Co	344Q	80121	5100-5199	
	Arapahoe Co	374C	80121	6500-6699	
	Centennial	344U	80121	5700-5799	
	Centennial	344Y	80121	5900-6099	
	Denver	284Y	80209	1-699	
	Denver	314C	80209	700-1099	
	Denver	314L	80210	1100-2299	
	Denver	314U	80210	2500-2699	
PEARL ST S	Elizabeth	871E	80107	200-999	
PEARL ST S	Englewood	314U	80110	2700-2799	
	Englewood	314Y	80113	3000-3599	
	Englewood	344C	80110	3600-3699	
	Englewood	344G	80110	3900-4799	
PEARL WAY	Northglenn	194G	80233	10900-11099	
PEARL EAST CIR	Boulder	98Y	80301	4700-4999	
PEARL HOWLETT RD	Weld Co	706P	80504	2000-2798	E
PEARLWOOD CIR	Highlands Ranch	405K	80126	10500-10699	
PEARSON RANCH LOOP	Elbert Co	850C	80138	42000-43399	
PEAVINE WAY	Douglas Co	887B	80118	2200-2499	
PEBBLE CT	Boulder Co	70F	80503	7300-7399	
PEBBLE RD	Boulder Co	70F	80503	7800-8099	
PEBBLE BEACH CT	Columbine Valley	343Y	80123	None	
PEBBLE BEACH CT	Jefferson Co	306P	80439	2200-2299	
PEBBLE BEACH DR	Boulder Co	723G	80503	3900-4399	
PEBBLE BEACH DR	Jefferson Co	306P	80439	2400-2599	
	Jefferson Co	306T	80439	2600-2999	
PEBBLE BEACH LN	Jefferson Co	306U	80439	2700-2899	
PEBBLE BEACH LN	Lone Tree	374Y	80124	9800-9899	
PEBBLE BEACH WAY	El Paso Co	908T	80132	18800-19199	
PEBBLE BROOK LN	Parker	410T	80138	22000-22499	
PEBBLE CREEK CT	El Paso Co	908Z	80132	800-899	
PEBBLE CREEK WAY	Highlands Ranch	375U	80126	8300-8499	
PEBBLEWOOD CT	Douglas Co	408G	80134	15500-15599	
PECAN DR	Federal Heights	193Z	80260	None	
PECAN LN	Thornton	193Z	80260	None	
PECK DR	Longmont	40K	80503	600-698	E
PECOS CT	Westminster	164J	80234	13400-13499	
PECOS ST	Adams Co	254E	80221	5200-6199	
	Adams Co	224S	80221	6200-7599	
	Adams Co	224J	80221	7600-8999	
	Adams Co	134W	80020	14800-15199	
	Adams Co	134S	80020	15400-15699	
	Denver	284J	80204	1200-1299	
	Denver	254S	80211	3100-4799	
	Denver	254J	80221	4800-5199	
	Northglenn	194S	80260	10000-10399	
	Northglenn	194J	80234	10700-10799	
	Thornton	194S	80260	9200-9999	
	Westminster	194E	80234	11200-11999	
	Westminster	164W	80234	12000-12399	
	Westminster	164S	80234	12601-12799	O
	Westminster	164N	80234	13000-13399	
	Westminster	164J	80234	13400-13599	
	Westminster	164A	80020	14500-14899	
	Westminster	164E	80020	None	
PECOS ST S	Denver	284W	80223	100-699	
	Denver	314A	80223	700-899	
	Denver	314E	80223	1100-1399	
	Denver	314J	80223	1900-2099	
	Denver	314N	80223	2400-2498	E
PECOS WAY	Adams Co	224E	80221	1600-8299	
	Adams Co	254E	80221	5301-5399	O
PECOS WAY S	Denver	314A	80223	900-999	
PECOS TRAIL	Castle Rock	466T	80109	None	
PEERLESS ST	Louisville	130R	80027	300-399	
PEERY DR	Golden	249S	80403	500-599	
PEERY PKWY	Golden	249W	80403	300-599	
PEGASUS DR	Highlands Ranch	376V	80124	1-199	
PEGASUS PL	Lafayette	131R	80026	1000-1099	
PEGGY LN	Jefferson Co	307Y	80439	25700-29999	
	Jefferson Co	336T	80439	30000-30399	
PELICAN AVE	Brighton	140N	80601	None	
PELICAN SHORES CT	Weld Co	707J	80504	5701-5899	O
PELICAN SHORES DR	Weld Co	707J	80504	5701-5899	O
PELON DR	Northglenn	194T	80260	9400-9699	
PEMBERLY AVE	Highlands Ranch	405N	80126	2801-2899	O
PEMBERTON RD	Greenwood Village	344V	80121	5400-5599	
PEMBROKE CT	Castle Pines North	436L	80108	7400-7499	
PEMBROKE GARDENS	Boulder Co	99F	80301	4400-4499	
PEMBROOK ST S	Castle Rock	498L	80104	1-299	
PENA BLVD	Denver	769W	80249	7500-9199	
	Denver	259N	80249	None	
	Denver	769W	80239	None	
PENDIO CT	Highlands Ranch	405B	80126	9400-9599	
PENDLETON AVE	Longmont	42B	80501	700-999	
PENDLETON DR S	Highlands Ranch	404C	80126	9400-9699	
PENHURST CIR	Longmont	12P	80501	600-699	
PENHURST PL E	Highlands Ranch	405E	80126	2500-2599	
PENINSULA CIR	Castle Rock	497Q	80104	1300-1799	
PENINSULA DR	Littleton	374N	80120	7900-8099	
PENINSULA DR S	Littleton	374N	80120	8100-8399	
PENNINGTON LN	Highlands Ranch	404L	80126	10200-10299	
PENNINGTON ST	Highlands Ranch	404L	80126	10300-10399	
PENNOCK WAY	Longmont	11K	80501	2400-2499	
PENNSYLVANIA AVE	Boulder	127G	80302	600-699	
	Boulder	127H	80302	900-1399	
	Boulder	128F	80303	2800-3099	
	Boulder	128H	80303	4800-5399	
	Boulder	129E	80303	5500-5698	E
PENNSYLVANIA CIR	Thornton	164Q	80241	13100-13199	
PENNSYLVANIA CT	Adams Co	224L	80229	None	
PENNSYLVANIA CT S	Littleton	374Q	80122	7900-8299	
PENNSYLVANIA DR	Thornton	194U	80229	9800-9999	
PENNSYLVANIA DR S	Littleton	374L	80122	7500-7699	
	Littleton	374Q	80122	7900-7999	
PENNSYLVANIA PL	Boulder	129E	80303	5600-5699	
PENNSYLVANIA ST	Adams Co	254G	80216	5500-5599	
	Adams Co	224L	80229	7800-8299	
	Denver	284U	80203	1-299	
	Denver	284L	80203	400-1999	
	Denver	254Q	80216	4400-4799	
	Northglenn	194Q	80233	10400-10599	
	Northglenn	194C	80233	11600-11799	
	Thornton	194Y	80229	9100-9399	
	Thornton	164Y	80241	12000-12299	
	Thornton	164Q	80241	13000-13399	
PENNSYLVANIA ST S	Arapahoe Co	344Q	80121	5100-5299	
	Arapahoe Co	374C	80121	6600-6699	
	Arapahoe Co	374G	80122	6700-7299	
	Centennial	344U	80121	5700-5799	
	Centennial	344Y	80121	5900-6399	
	Denver	284Y	80209	1-699	
	Denver	314C	80209	700-1099	
	Denver	314L	80210	1100-2199	
	Denver	314U	80210	2500-2699	
	Englewood	314Y	80113	2700-3599	
	Englewood	344C	80110	3600-3699	
	Englewood	344G	80110	3900-4999	
	Littleton	374Q	80122	7800-8099	
PENNSYLVANIA WAY	Adams Co	224G	80229	8100-8299	
PENNWOOD AVE E	Arapahoe Co	350L	80015	None	
PENNWOOD CIR	Englewood	344Q	80113	400-599	
PENNWOOD CIR E	Arapahoe Co	350K	80015	None	
PENNWOOD PL E	Aurora	348K	80015	14600-14899	
	Aurora	348Q	80015	15300-15399	
PENNY RD	Jefferson Co	822Y	80433	11400-11799	
PENRITH BLVD	Adams Co	792M	80102	None	
PENRITH RD	Adams Co	772V	80102	None	
	Adams Co	792H	80102	None	
	Bennett	792R	80102	None	
PENRITH RD N	Adams Co	752M	80102	None	
	Adams Co	752Z	80102	None	
PENROSE BLVD	Frederick	727F	80530	None	
PENROSE CT S	Arapahoe Co	374G	80121	6600-6799	
	Arapahoe Co	374G	80122	6800-7299	
	Littleton	374L	80122	7500-7799	
PENROSE PL	Boulder	98P	80301	3300-3399	
PENROSE PL E	Highlands Ranch	374Z	80126	1200-1299	
PENSACOLA DR	Denver	258F	80239	14300-14499	
	Denver	258G	80239	15700-15799	
PENSACOLA PL	Denver	257H	80239	12900-13099	
	Denver	258E	80239	13100-13199	
	Denver	258F	80239	14800-15099	
	Denver	258G	80239	15400-15599	
PENSIVE CT	Parker	410Q	80138	22000-22199	
PENSTEMON	Jefferson Co	370K	80127	1-99	
PENSTEMON WAY	Castle Rock	466X	80109	2800-2999	
PENWOOD DR E	Arapahoe Co	350J	80015	None	
PEORIA CIR S	Arapahoe Co	377M	80112	7300-7699	
	Aurora	287Y	80012	300-399	
PEORIA CT S	Aurora	317G	80112	1300-1499	
	Aurora	317Y	80014	3100-3199	
PEORIA PKWY	Commerce City	197L	80603	None	
PEORIA ST	Adams Co	167Y	80640	10400-12399	
	Aurora	287U	80011	1-399	
	Aurora	287M	80011	600-1499	
	Aurora	287G	80010	1501-2499	O
	Aurora	257Y	80011	2600-3699	
	Brighton	197G	80640	10400-11998	E
	Commerce City	197Q	80022	9600-10399	
	Commerce City	197G	80640	10401-11999	O
	Denver	257U	80239	3700-5599	
	Douglas Co	407D	80112	9200-9899	
	Douglas Co	407H	80134	9900-10099	
PEORIA ST S	Arapahoe Co	377M	80112	7300-7999	
	Aurora	287U	80012	1-699	
	Aurora	317G	80112	700-1899	
	Aurora	317L	80014	1900-3199	
	Centennial	377G	80111	6500-6699	
	Centennial	377G	80112	6700-7399	
PEORIA ST S	Douglas Co	377V	80112	7400-9199	
PEORIA ST S	Greenwood Village	347Q	80111	5100-6499	
PEORIA WAY	Denver	257U	80239	3900-3999	
PEPPERTREE CT	Boulder Co	70J	80503	6800-6899	
PEPPERTREE DR	Boulder Co	70J	80503	6800-6999	
PEPPERTREE LN	Boulder Co	70J	80503	6800-6999	
PEPPERWOOD LN S	Highlands Ranch	404D	80126	9200-9399	
PEPPLER DR	Longmont	12J	80501	None	
PERCIVAL	Lafayette	132P	80026	None	
PEREGRINE	Jefferson Co	370B	80127	1-99	
PEREGRINE CIR	Broomfield	162L	80020	100-399	
PEREGRINE CIR	Longmont	42D	80501	None	
PEREGRINE CT	Broomfield	162L	80020	1600-1899	
PEREGRINE CT	Lafayette	101X	80026	1700-1799	
PEREGRINE DR	Parker	408R	80134	16100-16299	
PEREGRINE LN	Broomfield	162L	80020	1700-1899	
PEREGRINE LN	Lyons	703C	80540	None	
PEREGRINE RD	Dacono	727N	80514	None	
PEREGRINE WAY E	Highlands Ranch	406F	80130	6900-6999	
PERFIDY PL	Park Co	841S	80421	None	
PERIDOT CT	Castle Rock	467H	80108	1500-1799	
PERIDOT LN	Castle Rock	467H	80108	1600-1899	
PERIWINKLE	Jefferson Co	370F	80127	1-99	
PERIWINKLE CT	Douglas Co	408L	80134	15300-15399	
PERIWINKLE DR	Boulder	97M	80304	1200-1499	
PERIWINKLE PL	Longmont	40L	80503	4000-4099	
PERKINS ST	Denver	254U	80216	None	
PERRY CIR S	Littleton	343K	80123	5100-5199	
PERRY CT	Adams Co	223X	80003	6600-6699	
	Westminster	193K	80031	3600-3999	
	Westminster	193T	80031	9900-9999	
	Westminster	193K	80031	11000-11099	
PERRY CT S	Littleton	343P	80123	5200-5299	
PERRY DR	Westminster	193K	80031	None	
PERRY LN	Dacono	727J	80516	100-199	
PERRY PKWY	Greenwood Village	345R	80121	4200-5099	
PERRY PL	Westminster	223K	80030	7700-7799	
PERRY ST	Adams Co	253F	80212	5200-5499	
	Adams Co	223X	80003	6100-6599	
	Broomfield	163X	80020	12000-12299	
	Broomfield	163T	80020	12400-12599	
PERRY ST	Castle Rock	497L	80104	1-799	
PERRY ST	Denver	283T	80219	1-399	
	Denver	283K	80204	400-1699	
	Denver	283B	80212	2000-2699	
	Denver	253P	80212	2700-5199	
PERRY ST	Erie	103J	80516	100-299	
PERRY ST	Westminster	193X	80031	9000-9599	
	Westminster	193T	80031	9600-9699	
	Westminster	193N	80031	10300-10399	
	Westminster	193B	80031	11600-11999	
PERRY ST S	Castle Rock	497Q	80104	1-1799	
PERRY ST S	Denver	283T	80219	1-699	
	Denver	313F	80219	900-1699	
	Denver	313T	80219	2300-2699	
	Denver	313T	80236	2700-2899	
	Denver	343K	80123	4700-4999	
	Littleton	343P	80123	5000-5499	
PERRY WAY	Westminster	193T	80031	9700-9799	
PERRY WAY S	Denver	313K	80219	1800-2099	
	Denver	313T	80236	2900-2999	
	Denver	343K	80236	3000-4699	
PERRY PARK AVE	Douglas Co	887R	80118	1-1599	O
	Douglas Co	887R	80118	1600-2699	
	Larkspur	887R	80118	2-1598	E
PERRY PARK BLVD	Douglas Co	866Y	80135	1000-2999	
	Douglas Co	886C	80135	3000-6099	
	Douglas Co	886G	80118	6100-7999	
	Douglas Co	887A	80118	None	
PERRY PARK RD	Douglas Co	907C	80118	12600-13899	
	Douglas Co	907C	80133	14000-15999	
	Douglas Co	867J	80135	1N-1999N	
	Douglas Co	867S	80135	1S-5499S	
PERRYTOWN ST	Adams Co	751L	80642	15200-15399	
PERSERVERENCE TRAIL	Jefferson Co	763W	80403	26700-26899	
PERSIMMON DR	Boulder	97H	80304	None	
PERSIMMON LN	Castle Rock	496A	80109	None	
PERSON DR	El Paso Co	912X	80831	16000-17799	
PERTH CIR N	Denver	260N	80249	4200-4499	
PERTH CT	Denver	260K	80249	4900-5199	
	Denver	260F	80249	None	
	Denver	260F	80249	None	
PERTH PL	Highlands Ranch	405D	80130	None	
PERTH PL S	Centennial	350T	80015	5700-5899	
PERTH ST	Denver	260F	80249	5200-5499	
	Denver	260K	80249	None	
PERTH ST N	Arapahoe Co	290J	80018	800-1099	
	Aurora	260X	80011	None	
	Denver	260S	80249	3800-4199	
	Denver	260P	80249	4500-4799	

P

STREET NAME	CITY or COUNTY	MAP GRID	ZIP CODE	BLOCK RANGE	O/E
PERTH ST S	Arapahoe Co	350B	80013	None	
	Arapahoe Co	350K	80015	None	
	Aurora	380B	80016	6800-6999	
	Aurora	380F	80016	7000-7199	
	Centennial	350T	80015	5900-6099	
PERTH WAY S	Aurora	380F	80016	7200-7299	
	Centennial	350P	80015	5400-5499	
PERU CREEK AVE	Parker	439B	80134	18200-18299	
PETERSBURG CT	Parker	409Z	80134	19700-19899	
PETERSON CT	Denver	254J	80221	4800-4899	
PETERSON PL	Longmont	11K	80501	1500-1599	
PETERSON RD	Adams Co	772W	80102	None	
	Adams Co	792K	80102	None	
PETERSON RD	Douglas Co	846M	80135	5300-7499	
PETERSON RD N	Arapahoe Co	792T	80102	200-1499	
PETERSON WAY S	Denver	314A	80223	700-899	
PETITE AVE	Palmer Lake	907Q	80133	None	
	Palmer Lake	907U	80133	None	
PETRAS ST	Erie	103S	80516	900-1199	
PETTERSON	Adams Co	772A	80102	None	
PETTERSON RD	Adams Co	752N	80642	13600-16799	
	Adams Co	752E	80643	None	
PETUNIA PL	Castle Rock	469E	80108	6600-6999	
PETURSDALE CT	Boulder Co	99M	80301	7100-7399	
PEWTER LN	Monument	908W	80132	100-199	
PEYTON DR	Parker	409P	80134	17600-17699	
PEYTON HWY	El Paso Co	912V	80831	16000-20499	
PFEIFER CIR	Elbert Co	851V	80107	None	
PHANTOM CREEK TRAIL	Park Co	840C	80421	1-199	
PHEASANT AVE	Brighton	139R	80601	1-99	O
PHEASANT CIR	Lafayette	132W	80026	400-599	
PHEASANT CIR	Weld Co	729Q	80621	17200-17299	
PHEASANT CT	Parker	408R	80134	11000-11099	
PHEASANT DR	Longmont	11N	80503	2500-2799	
PHEASANT LN	Boulder Co	99S	80301	None	
PHEASANT LN	Jefferson Co	370B	80127	1-99	
PHEASANT ST	Federal Heights	193V	80260	2400-2499	
PHEASANT HILL CIR	Elbert Co	851E	80138	None	
PHEASANT RUN	Douglas Co	432N	80125	10800-10899	
PHEASANT RUN	Elbert Co	851U	80107	37000-37799	
PHEASANT RUN	Louisville	130R	80027	100-499	
PHEASANT RUN PKWY E	Aurora	348G	80015	14900-16999	
PHELPS ST	Castle Rock	497L	80104	200-299	
PHILIPPI WAY	Boulder Co	704N	80503	10200-10399	
PHILLIPS AVE E	Arapahoe Co	374R	80122	1300-1899	
	Centennial	375P	80122	3500-3699	
	Centennial	376N	80112	5900-6699	
	Centennial	376Q	80112	8000-8199	
	Centennial	376R	80112	8600-8699	
	Centennial	377N	80112	9500-9699	
	Littleton	374Q	80122	500-1299	
PHILLIPS AVE W	Jefferson Co	372P	80128	7000-7299	
	Jefferson Co	372N	80128	7700-8399	
	Jefferson Co	371R	80128	9200-9499	
PHILLIPS CIR E	Centennial	375N	80122	1700-2399	
	Centennial	375Q	80122	3500-3999	
	Centennial	376Q	80112	7500N-7999N	
	Centennial	376Q	80112	7500S-8199S	
PHILLIPS CT	Erie	102Q	80516	1700-1799	
PHILLIPS CT E	Littleton	374Q	80122	500-599	
PHILLIPS DR	Northglenn	194D	80233	700-1899	
	Northglenn	195A	80233	1900-2299	
PHILLIPS DR E	Arapahoe Co	378R	80112	16100-16499	
	Centennial	375N	80122	1900-1999	
	Centennial	375P	80122	2900-3299	
	Littleton	374R	80122	1100-1299	
	Littleton	374Q	80122	500N-799N	
PHILLIPS DR W	Jefferson Co	371R	80128	8800-9199	
PHILLIPS LN E	Arapahoe Co	374Q	80122	900-999	
	Arapahoe Co	378R	80112	16200-16999	
	Centennial	375N	80122	2000-2199	
PHILLIPS PL E	Arapahoe Co	378R	80112	16400-16699	
PHILLIPS PL E	Arapahoe Co	381Q	80016	26000-26399	
	Aurora	380R	80016	23300-23899	
	Aurora	381Q	80016	26600-26799	
	Aurora	380P	80016	None	
	Centennial	375N	80122	2000-2199	
	Centennial	375Q	80122	4100-4699	
	Centennial	376N	80112	6200-6399	
	Centennial	376P	80112	6500-6599	
	Centennial	376Q	80112	8200-8399	
	Centennial	376R	80112	8600-8999	
	Littleton	374R	80122	100-1299	
PHILLIPS RD	Boulder Co	101B	80026	9500-10199	
PHILLIPS RD W	Boulder Co	100H	80301	8700-9099	
	Boulder Co	101E	80301	9100-9499	
PHILLIPS PEAK W	Highlands Ranch	404F	80129	200-299	
PHIPPS CT E	Highlands Ranch	404H	80126	1100-1199	
PHIPPS PL E	Highlands Ranch	404H	80126	1000-1199	
PHOEBE GROVE	El Paso Co	910P	80908	20000-20499	
PHOEBES DR	Jefferson Co	822U	80433	11000-11099	
PHOENIX CT	Thornton	194Z	80229	1400-1699	
PHOTINIA	Jefferson Co	370K	80127	1-99	
PHYLLIS WHEATLEY WAY	Gilpin Co	741X	80403	None	
PIANO MEADOWS DR	Jefferson Co	843C	80433	12800-13099	
PICADILLY CT S	Arapahoe Co	350P	80015	5200-5499	
	Arapahoe Co	350K	80015	None	
	Aurora	320X	80013	3500-3599	
PICADILLY RD	Adams Co	769C	80022	11200-11799	
	Adams Co	170K	80022	11800-13599	
	Adams Co	170K	80603	13600-14799	
	Adams Co	140X	80603	14800-15499	
PICADILLY RD N	Adams Co	769Y	80019	None	
	Aurora	290P	80018	1-1499	
	Aurora	290B	80019	1700-2699	
	Aurora	260P	80019	2700-5599	
PICADILLY RD S	Arapahoe Co	290P	80017	300-699	
	Aurora	290P	80018	1-299	
	Aurora	350B	80018	3500-4299	
	Arapahoe Co	350F	80015	None	
	Aurora	380B	80016	6900-7099	
	Centennial	350S	80015	5500-5799	
	Centennial	350X	80016	6100-6499	
PICARDY PL	Lafayette	132A	80026	300-399	
PICCOLO DR E	Aurora	380V	80138	23200-23599	
PICCOLO PL E	Aurora	380V	80138	23600-23699	
PICKET LN	Longmont	12T	80501	700-799	
PICKETT CT	Erie	102W	80516	1600-1699	
PICKETWIRE WAY	Castle Rock	468Y	80104	None	
PICKLE POINT	Gilpin Co	760U	80403	1-399	
PICKLING RD	Brighton	140K	80601	None	
PICUTIS RD	Jefferson Co	338F	80454	4200-4799	
PIE CORNER	Palmer Lake	907Q	80133	None	
PIEDMONT AVE	Boulder Co	129F	80303	1000-1299	
PIEDMONT CT S	Highlands Ranch	405J	80126	10100-10199	
PIEDMONT DR	Cherry Hills Village	346J	80111	5600-5999	
PIEDMONT DR E	Aurora	349J	80015	16900-16999	
PIEDMONT DR S	Highlands Ranch	405J	80126	10100-10299	
PIEDRA CT	Boulder Co	98K	80301	4100-4199	
PIEDRA PL	Boulder Co	98K	80301	4100-4299	
PIEDRA RIVER RD	Weld Co	706M	80504	None	
PIERCE AVE	Platteville	708C	80651	300-499	
PIERCE AVE S	Louisville	161B	80027	400-799	
PIERCE CT	Arvada	252G	80002	5500-5599	
	Arvada	222G	80003	8200-8299	
PIERCE CT S	Jefferson Co	372C	80123	6300-6499	
	Jefferson Co	372G	80128	6900-7299	
	Jefferson Co	372L	80128	7300-7499	
PIERCE DR	Arvada	222C	80003	8700-8799	
PIERCE ST	Arvada	252G	80002	5200-5499	
	Arvada	252C	80003	5800-6199	
	Arvada	222U	80003	6200-7999	
	Arvada	252L	80002	None	
PIERCE ST	Erie	103J	80516	1-799	
PIERCE ST	Lakewood	282U	80226	1-599	
	Lakewood	282L	80214	1000-2799	
	Westminster	222C	80031	8800-9099	
	Westminster	192Y	80021	9100-9499	
	Westminster	192U	80021	9500-9899	
	Wheat Ridge	252Y	80214	2800-3199	
	Wheat Ridge	252U	80033	3200-4799	
PIERCE ST S	Denver	312U	80227	2700-2999	
	Denver	342G	80235	3500-4299	
	Denver	342G	80123	4300-4399	
	Denver	342U	80123	None	
	Jefferson Co	342Y	80123	5900-6299	
	Jefferson Co	372L	80123	6400-6699	
	Jefferson Co	372L	80128	6700-8299	
	Lakewood	282U	80226	1-199	
	Lakewood	282Y	80226	200-699	
	Lakewood	312L	80226	700-1099	
	Lakewood	312L	80232	1100-1899	
	Lakewood	312Y	80227	3000-3499	
PIERCE WAY	Arvada	222U	80003	6700-6799	
	Arvada	222C	80003	8700-8799	
PIERCE WAY S	Jefferson Co	372L	80128	7500-7999	
	Jefferson Co	372U	80128	8300-8399	
PIERRE ST	Boulder	97C	80304	4900-4999	
	Boulder	97C	80304	4901-4999	O
PIERSON CIR	Westminster	191K	80021	10500-10599	
PIERSON CT	Arvada	251B	80004	6000-6199	
	Arvada	221X	80004	6200-6799	
	Arvada	221K	80005	8000-8299	
	Arvada	221G	80005	8400-8499	
	Wheat Ridge	251T	80033	3800-3899	
PIERSON CT S	Jefferson Co	311F	80232	1100-1599	
	Jefferson Co	311K	80232	1800-1899	
	Jefferson Co	341K	80127	4700-4899	
	Jefferson Co	341P	80127	5300-5399	
	Jefferson Co	341X	80127	5900-6399	
	Jefferson Co	371B	80127	6500-6599	
	Jefferson Co	371K	80127	7300-7399	
	Lakewood	311B	80226	900-999	
PIERSON ST	Arvada	251B	80004	5800-6199	
	Arvada	221X	80004	6200-6599	
	Arvada	221T	80004	6900-7099	
	Arvada	221K	80005	7600-7799	
	Lakewood	281F	80215	1500-1699	
	Lakewood	281B	80215	2500-2599	
	Westminster	191K	80021	10600-10799	
	Wheat Ridge	251X	80033	3200-3499	
	Wheat Ridge	251T	80033	3800-3999	
	Wheat Ridge	251P	80033	4200-4399	
PIERSON ST S	Jefferson Co	311F	80232	1400-1699	
	Jefferson Co	311K	80232	1700-1799	
	Jefferson Co	341W	80127	5600-6499	
	Jefferson Co	371F	80127	7100-7399	
	Lakewood	281X	80226	300-499	
	Lakewood	311K	80227	1900-1999	
PIERSON WAY	Arvada	221K	80005	7800-7999	
	Lakewood	251X	80215	2800-2999	
PIERSON WAY S	Jefferson Co	341K	80127	4700-4899	
	Jefferson Co	341P	80127	5100-5399	
	Jefferson Co	371B	80127	6400-6599	
	Lakewood	311B	80226	900-999	
PIERSON MOUNTAIN AVE	Longmont	40S	80503	5500-5799	
PIGGOTT RD	Adams Co	794E	80136	1500-8199	
PIGGOTT RD N	Arapahoe Co	794S	80136	1-999	
PIGGOTT RD S	Arapahoe Co	794W	80136	1-599	
PIKA PT	Lafayette	131Z	80026	300-399	
PIKA RD	Boulder Co	742R	80302	1-1699	
PIKE CIR	Arvada	220W	80007	None	
PIKE CT	Arvada	220W	80007	6500-6599	
	Arvada	220S	80007	6900-7099	
	Arvada	220W	80007	None	
PIKE CT	Douglas Co	886G	80118	6500-6899	
PIKE DR N	Douglas Co	886G	80118	6600-6799	
PIKE DR S	Douglas Co	886G	80118	5000-7099	
PIKE PL	Douglas Co	886G	80118	6800-6899	
PIKE RD	Boulder Co	704X	80503	6500-7199	
	Boulder Co	40S	80503	7300-7499	
	Boulder Co	42U	80501	None	
PIKE RD	Longmont	41T	80501	1800-2099	
	Longmont	40U	80503	3800-3898	E
PIKE ST	Arvada	220W	80007	None	
PIKE ST	Bennett	793J	80102	None	
PIKE ST	Golden	280S	80401	100-499	
	Jefferson Co	280N	80401	700-799	
	Jefferson Co	280J	80401	1100-1499	
	Jefferson Co	250E	80403	5400-5699	
PIKE ST	Northglenn	194L	80233	100-499	
PIKES PEAK CT	Denver	346H	80237	None	
PIKES PEAK CT	Louisville	130T	80027	800-899	
PIKES PEAK CT E	Parker	409R	80138	19700-19799	
PIKES PEAK DR	Federal Heights	194W	80260	None	
PIKES PEAK DR S	Parker	409Q	80138	10900-11299	
PIKES PEAK LN	Louisville	130T	80027	900-999	
PIKES PEAK PL	Longmont	12S	80501	200-398	E
PIKES PEAK RD	Elbert Co	831N	80138	3000-45699	
PIKES PEAK RD	Thornton	193V	80260	None	
PIKES PEAK ST	Weld Co	726K	80516	1700-1999	
PIKES PEAK WAY	Douglas Co	440D	80138	9200-9499	
PIKEVIEW CT	Lakewood	282B	80214	7400-7499	
PIKE VIEW DR	Jefferson Co	822Y	80433	30800-31599	
PIKEVIEW LN	Parker	410J	80138	10700-10799	
PIKEVIEW ST	Lakewood	281M	80215	1000-1299	
PIKE VIEW WAY	El Paso Co	907V	80132	18500-18699	
PIKE VIEW FARM CIR	Elbert Co	870Y	80107	None	
PILGRIM'S PL E	Parker	409Q	80138	19500-19599	
PIMA CT	Boulder	128R	80303	1-99	
PIMA CT	Douglas Co	886L	80118	5900-5999	
PIMA RD	Jefferson Co	337H	80439	4300-4399	
PIMA TRAIL	Park Co	842E	80470	1-299	
PIMLICO AVE W	Denver	343L	80110	3300-3599	
PIMLICO CT	Boulder Co	130F	80303	800-899	
PIMLICO DR W	Englewood	343L	80110	3000-3299	
PIMLICO PL E	Aurora	348K	80015	14300-14399	
PINAL RD	Golden	279E	80401	1800-1999	
PINDAR CIR	Lafayette	131Q	80026	1700-1799	
PINE CIR	Gilpin Co	761S	80403	1-99	
PINE CT	Elbert Co	871G	80107	34200-34599	
PINE CT	Greenwood Village	346S	80121	5500-5599	
PINE CT	Longmont	41R	80501	None	
PINE CT W	Louisville	130T	80027	1200-1298	E
PINE DR	Clear Creek Co	801A	80452	1-499	
PINE DR	Gilpin Co	761E	80403	1-499	
PINE DR	Jefferson Co	367E	80439	26900-27099	
	Jefferson Co	336H	80439	27600-28899	
PINE DR	Parker	409V	80138	10700-12999	
	Parker	409Z	80134	11400-11899	
PINE DR E	Park Co	841J	80421	1-199	
PINE DR N	Park Co	841J	80421	1-1199	
PINE DR S	Park Co	841J	80421	1-1699	
PINE LN	Clear Creek Co	304G	80439	1-99	
PINE LN	Jefferson Co	842D	80433	12100-12199	
	Jefferson Co	338X	80465	22600-22899	
PINE LN	Parker	409A	80134	16900-17599	
PINE LN E	Douglas Co	409C	80138	6500-6699	
PINE PL	Broomfield	192C	80020	1-99	
PINE RD	Boulder Co	742X	80403	1-299	
PINE RD	Jefferson Co	278S	80401	1-399	
	Jefferson Co	336Q	80439	29000-29199	
PINE RD S	Jefferson Co	278S	80401	1-99	
	Jefferson Co	336L	80439	4600-4999	
	Jefferson Co	336Q	80439	5000-5399	
PINE ST	Arapahoe Co	795Y	80103	100-199	
	Arapahoe Co	373P	80128	None	
PINE ST	Boulder	97Z	80302	400-1899	
	Boulder	98W	80302	1900-2799	
PINE ST	Boulder Co	721R	80302	None	
PINE ST	Broomfield	192C	80020	100-199	
PINE ST	Central City	780C	80427	200-299	
PINE ST	Elizabeth	871F	80107	100-799	
PINE ST	Erie	133C	80516	None	
PINE ST	Federal Heights	193U	80260	2400-2999	
PINE ST	Frederick	727B	80530	401-599	O
PINE ST	Jamestown	722A	80455	None	
PINE ST	Jefferson Co	842V	80470	28200-28499	
PINE ST	Keenesburg	732A	80643	None	
PINE ST	Longmont	41R	80501	None	
PINE ST	Louisville	131S	80027	101-1199	O
	Louisville	130U	80027	None	
PINE ST	Nederland	740Q	80466	None	
PINE ST E	Nederland	740R	80466	None	
PINE ST S	Arapahoe Co	795Y	80103	None	
PINE ST W	Louisville	130V	80027	100-699	
PINE WAY	Broomfield	192C	80020	100-199	
PINE WAY	Elbert Co	891Y	80106	22000-22999	
PINE BARK TRAIL	Douglas Co	432T	80125	None	
PINE BASIN PL	Parker	439D	80134	None	
PINE BLUFF LN	Highlands Ranch	375S	80126	2500-2599	
PINE BLUFFS WAY	Parker	439D	80134	None	
PINE BRANCH WAY	Parker	439D	80134	None	
PINE BROOK RD	Boulder Co	97E	80304	1-1099	
	Boulder Co	722R	80304	None	
PINEBROOK ST S	Highlands Ranch	406B	80130	9500-9699	
PINE CLIFF (PVT) RD	Douglas Co	866G	80135	13000-14999	
PINECLIFF TRAIL	Nederland	740R	80466	None	
PINE CONE AVE	Firestone	707X	80504	None	
PINE CONE CT	Boulder Co	70M	80503	7100-7199	
PINE CONE LN	Boulder Co	70M	80503	8800-8899	
PINE CONE LN	Jefferson Co	306X	80439	30500-30799	
PINECONE LN E	Douglas Co	441P	80134	10500-10699	
PINE CONE RD N	Douglas Co	410C	80138	12300-12899	
PINECONE ST	Golden	279Q	80401	1-299	
PINE COUNTRY LN	Jefferson Co	843G	80433	13300-13999	
PINECREST AVE	Highlands Ranch	373S	80125	None	
PINE CREST CIR	Castle Rock	867Q	80109	None	
	Castle Rock	867R	80109	None	
PINECREST CIR	Park Co	841N	80421	1-299	
PINE CREST CT	Elbert Co	892H	80117	26600-26799	
	Elbert Co	872J	80117	32300-32499	
PINE CREST DR	Elbert Co	872J	80117	7200-7799	
PINE CREST DR	Jefferson Co	306F	80439	29000-30399	
PINECREST RD	Jefferson Co	278P	80401	22700-23099	
PINECREST WAY	Palmer Lake	907Q	80133	None	
PINECREST MOUNTAIN RD					
	Jefferson Co	336B	80439	None	
PINE DALE CT	Highlands Ranch	375Y	80126	3900-3999	
PINEDALE ST	Boulder	98P	80301	None	
PINEDALE RANCH CIR	Jefferson Co	306K	80439	1400-1799	
PINE DROP AVE E	Parker	408U	80134	None	
PINE DROP LN	Jefferson Co	307R	80401	2100-2199	
PINEFIELD CIR	Elbert Co	851E	80138	41200-41499	
PINEFIELD LN	Castle Pines North	436P	80108	900-1099	
PINE FOREST LN	Douglas Co	470A	80134	7100-7599	
PINE GLADE DR	Gilpin Co	761F	80403	400-799	
PINE GLADE RD	Boulder Co	741Q	80466	1-399	
PINE GROVE LN	Parker	410S	80138	11500-11699	
PINE GROVE TRAIL	Jefferson Co	822R	80433	27600-27999	
PINEHILL CT	El Paso Co	910S	80908	19200-19399	
PINE HILL ST	Parker	410V	80138	11500-11799	
PINE HILL WAY	Parker	410V	80138	11500-11599	
PINE HILLS PL	Elbert Co	870G	80107	33500-33599	

P

STREET NAME	CITY or COUNTY	MAP GRID	ZIP CODE	BLOCK RANGE	O/E
PINE HILLS WAY	Douglas Co	432Q	80125	7000-7399	
PINE HOLLOW	Park Co	841S	80421	1-899	
PINE HOLLOW DR N	Douglas Co	440T	80134	6000-6399	
PINEHURST CIR	Broomfield	163G	80020	None	
PINEHURST CIR	El Paso Co	909X	80908	3200-3699	
PINEHURST CIR N	Elbert Co	851C	80107	None	
PINEHURST CIR S	Elbert Co	851C	80107	None	
PINEHURST CIR W	Denver	342H	80235	3900-3999	
PINEHURST CT	Bennett	813B	80102	900-1199	
PINEHURST CT	Boulder	69Z	80301	5300-5399	
PINEHURST CT	Louisville	160D	80027	700-899	
PINEHURST DR	Boulder	69Z	80301	5200-5399	
PINEHURST DR	Douglas Co	886C	80118	6100-6198	E
PINEHURST DR	El Paso Co	908U	80132	200-299	
PINEHURST DR	Jefferson Co	306S	80439	2600-2899	
PINELANDS DR	Frederick	707W	80504	None	
PINE LANE AVE	Douglas Co	409C	80138	6200-6999	
PINE MEADOW AVE	Elbert Co	851E	80138	3400-3799	
PINE MEADOW CIR	Elbert Co	851E	80138	41300-41399	
PINE MEADOWS DR	Elbert Co	872V	80117	11200-11298	E
PINE MOR RD	Douglas Co	869D	80116	1500-1699	
PINE NEEDLE LN	Louisville	130U	80027	700-799	
PINE NEEDLE RD	Boulder Co	97K	80304	1-399	
PINE NEEDLE WAY	Castle Rock	497T	80104	300-399	
PINERIDGE AVE W	Littleton	343Z	80120	2000-2199	
PINE RIDGE CIR	Elbert Co	871G	80107	5000-6399	
PINERIDGE CT	Castle Pines North	436K	80108	1300-1399	
PINE RIDGE DR	Elbert Co	871B	80107	5000-6399	
PINE RIDGE DR	Jefferson Co	248L	80403	5000-5099	
PINERIDGE LN	Castle Pines North	436K	80108	1400-1499	
PINERIDGE PL	Castle Pines North	436K	80108	1400-1499	
PINE RIDGE RD	Clear Creek Co	781Z	80439	1-199	
PINE RIDGE RD	Douglas Co	470S	80116	7400-7899	
PINE RIDGE RD	Golden	248R	80403	4300-5299	
PINE RIDGE RD	Jefferson Co	248G	80403	5300-5599	
	Jefferson Co	762A	80403	34800-34999	
PINE RIDGE ST	Elbert Co	871J	80107	32500-33499	
PINE RIDGE ST	Elizabeth	871J	80107	300-899	
PINERIDGE WAY	Castle Pines North	436K	80108	7400-7499	
PINERIDGE TERRACE	Castle Pines North	436P	80108	7500-7699	
PINERIDGE TRAIL	Castle Pines North	436K	80108	7500-7599	
PINE RIVER TRAIL	Douglas Co	466M	80108	5100-5199	
PINERY PKWY N	Douglas Co	440N	80134	6900-7999	
	Douglas Co	439V	80134	8000-8999	
PINERY PKWY S	Douglas Co	469D	80134	6900-7599	
	Douglas Co	470B	80134	8300-9099	
PINE SHADOW DR	El Paso Co	909Q	80908	20300-20499	
PINE SLOPE RD	Idaho Springs	780U	80452	400-799	
PINE SONG TRAIL	Jefferson Co	277Q	80401	300-599	
PINES TRAIL N	Elbert Co	830L	80138	100-699	
PINE TOP ST	Parker	410Z	80138	11900-12199	
PINE TRAIL	Jefferson Co	822Z	80433	28300-28799	
PINE TRAIL	Park Co	841U	80421	1-299	
PINE TREE CIR	Park Co	841S	80421	1-299	
PINE TREE LN	Boulder Co	722V	80304	1-599	
PINE TREE LN	Jefferson Co	306N	80439	2300-2499	
PINETREE RD	Castle Rock	497M	80104	1-99	
PINEVALE LN	Douglas Co	870K	80116	11000-11299	
PINE VALLEY CT	Boulder	70W	80301	5300-5399	
PINE VALLEY DR	Douglas Co	870E	80116	9700-11799	
PINE VALLEY DR	Jefferson Co	307W	80439	27200-27799	
PINE VALLEY RD	Jefferson Co	842J	80470	12500-29999	
PINEVEW ST	Palmer Lake	907Q	80133	None	
PINE VIEW CIR S	Douglas Co	907G	80133	14300-14699	
PINE VIEW DR	Elbert Co	872N	80117	32000-32499	
PINEVIEW DR W	Douglas Co	403R	80125	7000-7399	
PINEVIEW LN	Boulder Co	722H	80302	1-199	
PINE VIEW PL	Jefferson Co	308E	80401	1400-1499	
PINE VIEW RD	Golden	248R	80403	1200-1499	
PINE VIEW RD S	Douglas Co	907G	80133	14300-14699	
PINE VISTA PL	El Paso Co	908T	80908	18100-18299	
PINE VISTA TRAIL N	Douglas Co	410D	80138	12200-12499	
PINEWALK WAY	Highlands Ranch	405R	80130	10700-10799	
PINEWICKET WAY	Elbert Co	830U	80138	600-1299	
PINEWOOD AVE E	Arapahoe Co	347W	80111	9700-10499	
	Centennial	344Z	80121	800-1199	
PINEWOOD CIR	Lafayette	131Z	80026	400-499	
PINEWOOD CIR E	Centennial	345V	80121	4700-4799	
PINEWOOD CT	Longmont	12U	80501	1400-1599	
PINEWOOD CT N	Douglas Co	436D	80108	8600-8799	
PINEWOOD DR	Clear Creek Co	304S	80439	1-199	
PINEWOOD DR	Douglas Co	439V	80134	6400-6699	
PINEWOOD DR	Jefferson Co	366F	80439	7100-7199	
PINEWOOD DR E	Arapahoe Co	349Y	80016	18900-19199	
	Arapahoe Co	349Z	80016	19300-19799	
	Aurora	351X	80016	None	
PINEWOOD DR E	Douglas Co	411P	80138	10000-10999	
PINEWOOD DR N	Douglas Co	436H	80108	8100-8599	
PINEWOOD LOOP	El Paso Co	908U	80132	1-299	
PINEWOOD PL E	Aurora	351X	80016	None	
	Centennial	345V	80121	4700-4799	
PINE WOOD RD	Douglas Co	867N	80135	1800-2299	
PINEY CT	El Paso Co	910Y	80908	17300-17399	
PINEY CREEK CIR S	Centennial	379C	80016	6400-6699	
PINEY CREEK RD E	Douglas Co	410C	80138	8300-9499	
PINEY HILL RD	Parker	439D	80134	12100-12299	
PINEY LAKE RD N	Douglas Co	411B	80138	12000-12599	
	Douglas Co	381Y	80138	12600-13999	
PINEY PEAK	Jefferson Co	371E	80127	7300-7399	
PINEY POINT ST S	Highlands Ranch	374U	80126	8400-8499	
PINEY RIDGE RD	Jefferson Co	307Y	80439	3000-3299	
PINEY RIVER RD	Broomfield	163E	80020	14100-14299	
PINION DR	Boulder Co	703W	80302	8400-8499	
PINK PHLOX DR	Parker	409S	80134	None	
PINNACLE CT	Broomfield	133K	80020	None	
PINNACLE CT	Lafayette	132X	80026	None	
PINNACLE ST	Longmont	706N	80504	None	
PIN OAK CIR	Douglas Co	870E	80116	100-299	
PIN OAK DR	Jefferson Co	370L	80127	1-99	
PINON CIR	Erie	133D	80516	2100-2199	
PINON CIR	Gilpin Co	760U	80403	1-699	
PINON CIR	Thornton	194S	80260	None	
PINON CT	Longmont	12X	80501	900-999	
PINON CT S	Denver	314Q	80210	2200-2299	
PINON DR	Boulder	128L	80303	3800-4199	
PINON DR	Elbert Co	871G	80107	4600-6099	
PINON DR	Erie	133D	80516	2000-2199	
PINON DR S	Jefferson Co	307W	80439	3100-3299	
PINON LN	Elbert Co	850U	80107	900-1099	
PINON PL	Broomfield	192C	80020	1-99	
PINON PL	Erie	133C	80516	2001-2099	O
PINON RD	Jefferson Co	822Z	80433	11900-11999	
PINON RD	Park Co	841J	80421	1-299	
	Park Co	841T	80421	300-499	
PINON ST	Broomfield	192C	80020	100-199	
PINON ST	Longmont	41V	80501	None	
PINON WAY	Boulder Co	741U	80466	1-299	
PINON PARK RD	El Paso Co	912T	80831	17800-19399	
PINTAIL AVE	Brighton	138S	80601	800-899	
PINTAIL AVE	Platteville	708G	80651	None	
PINTAIL CIR	Boulder Co	129F	80303	1100-1299	
PINTAIL CT	Boulder Co	129F	80303	1100-1199	
PINTAIL CT	Douglas Co	432L	80125	7500-7599	
PINTAIL CT	Jefferson Co	339R	80465	5200-5299	
PINTAIL DR	Longmont	41S	80504	2000-2299	
PINTAIL PL	Douglas Co	432L	80125	7400-7599	
PINTAIL WAY	Frederick	707W	80504	5700-5899	
	Platteville	708G	80651	None	
PINTO CT	Elbert Co	870H	80107	34000-34199	
PINTO DR	Boulder Co	722R	80302	1-199	
PINTO DR	Jefferson Co	842H	80433	28400-28799	
PINTO LN	Park Co	841Q	80421	1-199	
PINTO ST	Frederick	707W	80504	None	
PINTO ST	Golden	279Q	80401	100-299	
PINTO ST	Weld Co	729V	80603	17500-17799	
PINTO WAY	El Paso Co	909W	80132	17800-17899	
PINTO WAY	Park Co	841Q	80421	1-199	
PINTO TRAIL	Elbert Co	871E	80107	1800-2499	
PINY PT	Jefferson Co	365J	80439	34200-34599	
PINYON CIR	Lochbuie	140C	80603	600-699	
PINYON DR	Bow Mar	343N	80123	4800-5199	
PINYON DR	Castle Rock	497H	80104	1300-1399	
PINYON DR	Northglenn	194F	80234	11000-11199	
PINYON ST	Frederick	727F	80530	200-499	
PINYON WAY	Louisville	130U	80027	700-799	
PINYON JAY RD	Douglas Co	470B	80134	5100-5499	
PINYON PINE LN	Jefferson Co	370Q	80127	1-99	
PINYON PINE RD	Jefferson Co	370Q	80127	1-99	
PINYON TRAIL	Lone Tree	406C	80124	9300-9599	
PIONEER CIR	Thornton	195Q	80229	None	
PIONEER DR E	Douglas Co	440H	80138	9100-9499	
PIONEER PL	Brighton	139Q	80601	None	
PIONEER PL	Thornton	195R	80229	None	
PIONEER RD	Boulder Co	99E	80301	5500-5699	
PIONEER RD	Gilpin Co	761M	80403	100-599	
PIONEER WAY	Brighton	139G	80603	1-399	O
	Brighton	139C	80603	None	
PIONEER CROSSING	El Paso Co	909Y	80908	17000-17799	
PIONEER TRAIL	Jefferson Co	844F	80127	13400-13499	
PIONEER TRAIL N	Douglas Co	441F	80138	8200-8999	
PIPELINE DR	Clear Creek Co	801A	80452	1-199	
PIPER DR	Erie	133F	80516	100-299	
	Erie	133E	80516	2900S-3099S	
PIPER ST	Superior	160R	80027	1900-1999	
PIPIT RD	Boulder Co	42Q	80501	None	
PIRLOT PL	Lone Tree	406L	80124	7400-7599	
PISA CT	Longmont	40Q	80503	None	
PISCES CT	Highlands Ranch	376U	80124	13600-13699	
PISGAH LAKE RD	Clear Creek Co	780A	80452	1-1199	
PITCH PL	El Paso Co	909T	80908	3500-3599	
PITCHFORD PL	Douglas Co	378Z	80134	16000-16199	
PITCHFORK CT	Parker	408Z	80134	11800-11899	
PITKIN AVE S	Superior	160Q	80027	800-1899	
PITKIN CIR S	Aurora	319E	80017	1400-1699	
	Aurora	319J	80017	1700-1899	
	Aurora	319N	80013	2200-2299	
	Aurora	349A	80013	3500-3899	
PITKIN CT	Commerce City	769E	80022	None	
PITKIN CT S	Arapahoe Co	349S	80016	5900-5999	
	Aurora	319A	80017	900-999	
	Aurora	319E	80017	1400-1499	
	Aurora	349A	80013	3500-3599	
	Aurora	349A	80013	3700-3799	
	Aurora	349J	80015	4700-4899	
	Centennial	349N	80015	5300-5399	
	Centennial	379J	80016	7400-7799	
PITKIN DR	Boulder	128G	80303	4600-4699	
PITKIN LN S	Jefferson Co	842N	80470	15400-15699	
PITKIN PL S	Aurora	319J	80013	1900-2099	
PITKIN ST	Aurora	289J	80011	1000-1499	
	Aurora	289E	80011	1500-1999	
	Commerce City	769A	80022	None	
	Commerce City	769A	80022	None	
	Commerce City	769E	80022	None	
PITKIN ST S	Aurora	319A	80017	900-1099	
	Aurora	319E	80017	1600-1699	
	Aurora	319J	80017	1700-1899	
	Aurora	319J	80013	2000-2099	
	Aurora	319S	80013	2700-3199	
	Aurora	349E	80013	4200-4299	
	Aurora	349E	80015	4300-4799	
	Aurora	349E	80015	4400-4499	
	Centennial	349S	80015	5100-5599	
	Foxfield	379A	80016	6700-6899	
	Foxfield	379J	80016	7400-7499	
PITKIN WAY	Castle Rock	498Q	80104	500-899	
PITKIN WAY	Commerce City	769E	80022	None	
PITKIN WAY S	Aurora	319E	80017	1400-1499	
	Aurora	319N	80013	2100-2699	
	Aurora	319S	80013	3000-3099	
	Aurora	349A	80013	3900-4099	
	Aurora	349J	80015	4700-4899	
PITTS PL	Gilpin Co	741X	80403	1-199	
PIUTE DR	Jefferson Co	842E	80470	13100-13399	
PIUTE DR W	Douglas Co	846T	80135	7000-7499	
PIUTE ROW E	Douglas Co	440U	80134	8500-8699	
PIUTE TRAIL S	Jefferson Co	842E	80470	13000-13399	
PIXIE PARK RD	El Paso Co	907U	80132	18200-18599	
PLACER CIR	Elbert Co	871J	80107	33100-33399	
PLACER PL	Longmont	12W	80501	1-199	
PLACER ST	Idaho Springs	780Q	80452	1700-1899	
PLACER ST S	Douglas Co	870P	80116	2000-2499	
PLACID DR	Boulder Co	100Z	80301	2100-2299	
PLACID DR	Jefferson Co	305H	80439	1300-1399	
PLAINS CIR	Dacono	727J	80514	None	
PLAINS PKWY S	Aurora	350B	80018	3800-4299	
PLAINS ST	Dacono	727J	80514	None	
PLAINS EDGE CT	El Paso Co	912Z	80831	17800-17899	
PLAINS VIEW RD	Boulder Co	722W	80302	1-199	
PLAINVIEW RD	Jefferson Co	763G	80403	10000-11599	
PLANET PL	Thornton	224F	80260	500-699	
	Thornton	224B	80260	700-799	
PLANTATION CIR	Elbert Co	851C	80107	None	
PLANTER LN	Platteville	708B	80651	500-699	
PLASTER CIR	Broomfield	163L	80020	13600-13799	
PLASTER PT	Broomfield	163L	80020	13600-13799	
PLATA	Thornton	193V	80260	None	
PLATA ST	Weld Co	140E	80603	None	
PLATEAU CIR	Jefferson Co	368C	80465	21700-21999	
PLATEAU DR	Cherry Hills Village	346J	80111	6200-6499	
PLATEAU DR	Thornton	195Q	80229	None	
PLATEAU DR S	Aurora	349K	80015	17400-17499	
PLATEAU LN	Broomfield	133K	80020	None	
PLATEAU LN	Jefferson Co	368G	80465	6800-6999	
PLATEAU PKWY	Golden	249W	80403	100-599	
PLATEAU RD	Boulder Co	703X	80302	2700-3099	
	Boulder Co	703X	80503	3100-3999	
	Boulder Co	704W	80503	5900-6299	
	Boulder Co	40S	80503	7400-8999	
	Boulder Co	41T	80504	9500-10499	
	Boulder Co	41U	80504	10500-10699	
PLATINUM CT	Superior	160U	80027	2700-2799	
PLATT LN	Palmer Lake	907U	80133	None	
PLATTE AVE	Douglas Co	847N	80135	3700-5699	
PLATTE AVE E	Greenwood Village	345T	80121	3300-3399	
PLATTE DR	Fort Lupton	728H	80621	900-1199	
PLATTE DR E	Aurora	350V	80016	None	
PLATTE PL E	Aurora	351S	80016	None	
PLATTE ST	Denver	254W	80202	1500-1899	
PLATTE CANYON DR S	Arapahoe Co	373J	80128	7100-7399	
PLATTE CANYON RD S	Arapahoe Co	373B	80128	6900-7099	
	Arapahoe Co	373B	80128	7600-7899	
	Columbine Valley	343X	80123	5900-6399	
	Columbine Valley	373B	80123	6400-6899	
	Littleton	373B	80128	7100-7599	
	Jefferson Co	372R	80128	7900-8199	
PLATTE RIVER BLVD	Brighton	138S	80601	700-798	E
PLATTE RIVER DR	Weld Co	706M	80504	None	
PLATTE RIVER DR S	Denver	284X	80223	401-499	O
	Denver	314F	80223	700-3099	
	Englewood	314S	80110	2700-3499	
	Sheridan	313Z	80110	3501-3599	O
PLATTE RIVER PKWY S	Littleton	373L	80120	7300-7399	
PLATTE RIVER RD	Jefferson Co	844Y	80441	None	
PLATTE RIVER RD S	Douglas Co	845J	80127	2200-2699	
PLATTE RIVER RD S	Jefferson Co	432E	80127	None	
PLATTE RIVER RD SW	Jefferson Co	843Y	80433	15500-17799	
PLATTE RIVER RD W	Jefferson Co	844P	80127	15400-19899	
PLATTEVIEW DR S	Littleton	373J	80128	7500-7699	
PLAYERS CLUB DR	Castle Rock	497U	80104	100-399	
PLAZA AVE E	Aurora	350Z	80016	23900-23999	
PLAZA CT	Lafayette	131Q	80026	1300-1399	
PLAZA DR	Highlands Ranch	374W	80129	1-499	
	Highlands Ranch	373V	80129	None	
PLAZA DR	Louisville	131P	80027	1700-1999	
PLAZA DR E	Parker	409L	80134	17800-19399	
PLEASANT AVE E	Arapahoe Co	795Y	80103	300-799	
PLEASANT AVE W	Lakewood	281J	80401	11600-11999	
PLEASANT LN	Jefferson Co	275W	80439	34100-34799	
PLEASANT ST	Boulder	127G	80302	400-1299	
PLEASANT HILL RD	Weld Co	706P	80504	11700-11799	
PLEASANT PARK RD	Jefferson Co	823S	80433	20100-26699	
PLEASANT RIDGE RD	Boulder Co	98G	80301	3800-4699	
PLEASANT VALLEY CIR	Elbert Co	851C	80107	4500-4599	
PLEASANT VIEW DR	Castle Rock	468R	80108	3400-3899	
	Castle Rock	469J	80108	3900-4099	
PLEASANT VIEW DR	Douglas Co	468R	80108	3000-3399	
PLEASANT VIEW DR	Frederick	727F	80530	600-699	
PLEASANT VIEW ST	Castle Rock	497C	80104	900-999	
PLEASANT VIEW RIDGE	Weld Co	706K	80504	None	
PLESS DR	Brighton	139T	80601	15200-15599	
PLETTNER LN	Jefferson Co	336M	80439	4600-4699	
PLOVER CIR	Parker	408R	80134	11100-11399	
PLOVER CT	Parker	408R	80134	16200-16299	
PLOWMAN DR	El Paso Co	908P	80132	None	
PLOWMAN PL	El Paso Co	908P	80132	1600-1699	
PLOWSHARE LN	Platteville	708B	80651	100-199	
PLOWSHER WAY	Jefferson Co	368L	80465	7300-7399	
PLUM AVE	Douglas Co	847N	80135	5000-7999	
PLUM AVE	Lochbuie	140C	80603	800-1199	
PLUM CIR W	Louisville	130Q	80027	900-1899	
PLUM CT	Boulder	98E	80304	None	
	Boulder Co	98F	80301	4200-4299	
PLUM CT	Brighton	138U	80601	1500-1599	
PLUM CT	Erie	133F	80516	None	
PLUM CT	Greenwood Village	345V	80121	4200-4299	
PLUM PL	Denver	315V	80222	4800-4999	
PLUMB PL	Erie	102P	80516	2300-2399	
PLUM CREEK BLVD	Castle Rock	527B	80104	None	
PLUM CREEK BLVD S	Castle Rock	497Y	80104	901-2899	O
PLUM CREEK PKWY	Castle Rock	497K	80104	1-1599	
PLUM CREEK PL	Highlands Ranch	374U	80126	100-199	
PLUM CREEK RD	Douglas Co	888N	80118	None	
PLUM CREEK MEADOWS	Douglas Co	866Z	80135	4700-5399	
PLUM VALLEY LN	Highlands Ranch	374S	80129	1700-1799	
PLUTO CT	Highlands Ranch	376U	80124	400-499	
PLUTUS DR	Gilpin Co	761J	80403	1-299	
PLYMOUTH AVE W	Jefferson Co	372E	80128	8600-9099	
	Jefferson Co	371H	80128	9100-9199	
PLYMOUTH CIR E	Aurora	380C	80016	22300-22499	
	Aurora	381B	80016	25000-25299	
PLYMOUTH CT	Douglas Co	407H	80134	10100-10199	
PLYMOUTH DR E	Aurora	830A	80016	None	
PLYMOUTH DR W	Arapahoe Co	373E	80128	5100-5199	
	Jefferson Co	372H	80128	5100-6399	
	Jefferson Co	371G	80127	10200-10299	
PLYMOUTH PL E	Aurora	380C	80016	22300-22399	
	Aurora	381H	80016	26900-27099	
PLYMOUTH PL W	Jefferson Co	372F	80128	7600-8199	
	Jefferson Co	372E	80128	8200-8299	
	Jefferson Co	371F	80127	10900-10999	
POCHARD ST	Highlands Ranch	375Z	80126	8700-8899	
POCO AVE	Palmer Lake	907U	80133	None	

P

STREET NAME	CITY or COUNTY	MAP GRID	ZIP CODE	BLOCK RANGE	O/E
POCO PL	Jefferson Co	337E	80439	4200-4299	
POCO CALLE	Jefferson Co	278U	80401	100-299	
POINTER WAY	Highlands Ranch	375U	80126	3600-3699	
POINTE VIEW DR	Boulder Co	703L	80503	11600-11799	
POINT OF PINES DR	Boulder Co	97B	80302	2300-2399	
POLAR LN N	Douglas Co	825V	80125	10600-10999	
POLARIS PL	Thornton	224B	80260	200-799	
POLK AVE	Louisville	130Y	80027	100-299	
	Louisville	130Q	80027	1800-1899	
POLK AVE W	Jefferson Co	342X	80123	6800-7799	
POLK CT	Aurora	289E	80011	1900-1999	
POLK CT	Louisville	130Q	80027	1700-1799	
POLK DR E	Aurora	350Y	80016	22400-22499	
POLK DR W	Jefferson Co	317D	80123	9000-9299	
	Jefferson Co	341Z	80123	9700-9899	
	Jefferson Co	341X	80127	10800-11099	
	Jefferson Co	341Y	80127	None	
POLK PL E	Aurora	351X	80016	None	
POLK PL W	Jefferson Co	372C	80123	6600-7099	
	Jefferson Co	342W	80123	8000-8299	
	Jefferson Co	341Z	80123	9700-9899	
	Jefferson Co	341X	80127	11000-11099	
	Jefferson Co	341Y	80127	None	
POLLY AVE S	Jefferson Co	842A	80470	12800-12999	
POLLY DR S	Jefferson Co	842E	80470	12300-13499	
POLO CIR	Elbert Co	851N	80107	2800-2899	
POLO DR	Longmont	12T	80501	1700-1799	
POLO PL	Broomfield	162D	80020	12400-12799	
POLO WAY	Longmont	12T	80501	1700-1799	
POLO CLUB CIR	Denver	285X	80209	1-99	
POLO CLUB CT	Douglas Co	825V	80125	9500-9799	
POLO CLUB DR	Columbine Valley	373E	80123	4200-4499	
POLO CLUB DR	Denver	285X	80209	1-99	
POLO CLUB LN	Denver	285W	80209	1-99	
POLO CLUB RD	Denver	285X	80209	1-99	
POLO FIELD LN	Denver	285X	80209	1-99	
POLO PONY CIR	Douglas Co	869M	80116	1600-1699	
POLO RIDGE DR	Littleton	373K	80128	6900-7699	
POLO RUN DR	Elbert Co	851S	80107	37100-37499	
POMEGRANATE LN	Jefferson Co	307H	80401	1200-1399	
POMMEL CT	Parker	408M	80134	10600-10799	
POMMEL LN	Clear Creek Co	781U	80439	None	
POMO WAY	Nederland	740Q	80466	None	
POMONA DR	Arvada	222M	80003	5700-5999	
	Arvada	222G	80003	6800-7399	
	Arvada	222E	80005	7700-8399	
POMONA NORTH DR	Arvada	222F	80003	7400-7499	
POMONA SOUTH DR	Arvada	222F	80003	None	
POMPEY WAY	Northglenn	194J	80234	10400-10599	
PONCA PL	Boulder	128M	80303	300-399	
PONCA RD	Jefferson Co	842E	80470	34100-34499	
PONCHA CT	Douglas Co	887L	80118	1900-1999	
PONCHA DR	Douglas Co	887G	80118	7500-7899	
PONCHA PASS	Jefferson Co	371L	80127	10300-10399	
PONCHO CT	Douglas Co	887H	80118	7300-7399	
PONCHO RD	Douglas Co	887H	80118	600-899	
POND DR N	Brighton	138L	80601	1000-1099	
POND RD	Cherry Hills Village	346E	80110	1-99	
PONDEROSA AVE	Parker	379S	80134	17500-17699	
PONDEROSA CIR	Golden	279U	80401	100-299	
PONDEROSA CIR	Longmont	12X	80501	1000-1099	
PONDEROSA CIR E	Douglas Co	379V	80138	7000-7499	
	Douglas Co	380S	80138	7500-7999	
PONDEROSA CT	Boulder Co	98K	80301	4200-4299	
PONDEROSA CT	Fort Lupton	728M	80621	1600-1699	
PONDEROSA CT	Jefferson Co	365H	80439	7100-7199	
PONDEROSA CT	Louisville	130U	80027	600-799	
PONDEROSA CT E	Douglas Co	441S	80134	9800-9899	
PONDEROSA DR	Boulder Co	130P	80303	100-599	
PONDEROSA DR	Clear Creek Co	781Z	80439	1-1599	
PONDEROSA DR	Douglas Co	409D	80138	6400-8599	
	Douglas Co	440Y	80134	None	
	Parker	409F	80134	18700-18899	
PONDEROSA DR	Federal Heights	193Z	80260	None	
	Federal Heights	194W	80260	None	
PONDEROSA DR	Jefferson Co	336C	80439	3700-4099	
	Jefferson Co	842H	80433	13500-13999	
PONDEROSA DR	Nederland	740R	80466	None	
PONDEROSA DR	Lochbuie	140F	80603	None	
PONDEROSA DR E	Douglas Co	410B	80138	7500-8599	
PONDEROSA LN	Douglas Co	850X	80116	11000-11999	
	Elbert Co	850U	80107	1-999	
PONDEROSA LN	Jefferson Co	336C	80439	3700-3999	
PONDEROSA LN E	Douglas Co	410F	80138	7600-8699	
PONDEROSA PL	Broomfield	192C	80020	1-99	
PONDEROSA PL	Clear Creek Co	781V	80439	1-299	
PONDEROSA PL	Erie	133D	80516	None	
PONDEROSA PL	Fort Lupton	728M	80621	200-399	
PONDEROSA RD	Douglas Co	850X	80116	2000-3499	
PONDEROSA ST	Broomfield	192D	80020	100-199	
PONDEROSA ST	Castle Rock	498M	80104	1-399	
PONDEROSA WAY	Boulder Co	741U	80466	1-499	
PONDEROSA WAY	Clear Creek Co	801R	80439	1-399	
PONDEROSA WAY	Jefferson Co	365M	80439	31600-32099	
PONDEROSA WAY N	Douglas Co	440V	80134	5900-6499	
PONDEROSA TRAIL	Aurora	350Y	80016	6400S-6599S	
PONDEROSA TRAIL	Douglas Co	845Q	80125	4600-4899	
PONDLILLY DR E	Parker	409E	80134	17000-17599	
PONDS CIR W	Arapahoe Co	343W	80123	4100-4699	
	Jefferson Co	343W	80123	None	
PONDS DR W	Arapahoe Co	343W	80123	4400-4699	
	Jefferson Co	343W	80123	None	
PONDS WAY S	Arapahoe Co	343W	80123	6100-6399	
	Jefferson Co	343W	80123	None	
PONDS VIEW DR W	Arapahoe Co	343W	80123	4000-4699	
PONDS VIEW PL W	Arapahoe Co	343X	80123	4200-4299	
	Jefferson Co	343X	80123	None	
POND VIEW PL	El Paso Co	909Y	80908	17500-17899	
PONDVIEW PL	Jefferson Co	308A	80401	23500-23799	
PONTIAC CT	Adams Co	136P	80602	16000-16099	
	Adams Co	136K	80602	None	
PONTIAC CT	Thornton	136T	80602	15300-15399	
PONTIAC CT S	Centennial	346X	80111	6300-6499	
	Centennial	376B	80111	6500-6699	
	Centennial	376F	80112	6800-6999	
	Centennial	376K	80112	7700-7899	
PONTIAC DR	Thornton	136T	80602	15400-15499	
PONTIAC LOOP	El Paso Co	908U	80132	1-299	
PONTIAC ST	Adams Co	226K	80022	7600-8099	
	Adams Co	226F	80022	8300-8399	
	Commerce City	256K	80022	4800-4999	
	Commerce City	226X	80022	6200-6599	
	Commerce City	226T	80022	6700-7199	
	Commerce City	226F	80022	8100-8299	
	Denver	286T	80220	100-499	
	Denver	286K	80220	600-1899	
	Denver	286B	80207	2100-2799	
	Denver	256X	80207	2800-3999	
PONTIAC ST	Thornton	136T	80602	15200-15399	
	Thornton	136T	80602	15500-15599	
	Thornton	196B	80233	None	
PONTIAC ST S	Centennial	346X	80111	6200-6299	
	Centennial	376B	80112	6700-6999	
	Centennial	376F	80112	None	
	Denver	286T	80230	100-299	
	Denver	286X	80224	600-699	
	Denver	316K	80224	1700-1999	
	Denver	316P	80224	2300-2399	
	Denver	316T	80224	2900-3399	
PONTIAC WAY S	Arapahoe Co	316K	80224	1800-2099	
	Centennial	376F	80112	7200-7499	
	Centennial	376P	80112	7900-7999	
	Denver	286X	80224	300-699	
	Denver	316K	80224	1800-1899	
	Denver	346B	80237	3600-3699	
PONTLEY CT	El Paso Co	909N	80132	None	
PONY CART PL	Douglas Co	432F	80125	10500-10599	
PONY EXPRESS CT	Douglas Co	890X	80116	11100-11399	
PONY EXPRESS CT	Elbert Co	832W	80107	44000-44099	
PONY EXPRESS DR	Parker	409K	80134	18400-18699	
PONY EXPRESS LN	Douglas Co	890T	80116	11200-11299	
PONY EXPRESS RD	Douglas Co	890T	80116	11700-11899	
	Douglas Co	910C	80116	None	
POORMAN RD	Boulder Co	722Z	80302	1-1399	
POPE CT	Erie	102T	80516	700-899	
POPE DR	Erie	102T	80516	700-999	
POPE RD	Douglas Co	410Q	80138	None	
POPLAR AVE	Boulder	97L	80304	500-1199	
	Boulder	97M	80304	1900-2199	
POPLAR CIR	Brighton	138S	80601	400-599	
POPLAR CIR	Thornton	136T	80602	15500-15599	
POPLAR CIR S	Centennial	376P	80112	8100-8199	
POPLAR CT	Adams Co	136K	80602	16600-16799	
POPLAR CT	Commerce City	226T	80022	7000-7099	
POPLAR CT S	Centennial	346X	80111	6300-6399	
	Centennial	376B	80111	6500-6599	
	Centennial	376F	80112	7100-7199	
	Centennial	376K	80112	7500-7799	
POPLAR DR	Thornton	193V	80260	None	
POPLAR LN	Boulder	97M	80304	1900-1999	
POPLAR LN S	Centennial	376F	80112	7100-7199	
POPLAR PL	Boulder	97L	80304	900-999	
POPLAR PL	Commerce City	226X	80022	6100-6199	
POPLAR PL E	Greenwood Village	344V	80121	1300-1399	
POPLAR ST	Adams Co	226K	80022	7700-7999	
	Adams Co	136K	80602	16000-16299	
	Commerce City	256B	80022	5800-5999	
	Commerce City	226X	80022	6200-6599	
	Commerce City	226P	80022	7000-7199	
	Denver	286K	80220	100-1799	
	Denver	286B	80207	2100-2799	
	Denver	256X	80207	2800-3199	
	Denver	256T	80207	3300-3999	
POPLAR ST	Elizabeth	871F	80107	100-199	
POPLAR ST	Lochbuie	140G	80603	100-799	
POPLAR ST	Thornton	136T	80602	15200-15399	
POPLAR ST S	Centennial	346X	80111	6100-6299	
	Centennial	376K	80112	7700-7799	
	Denver	286T	80230	100-299	
	Denver	286X	80224	300-699	
	Denver	316B	80224	700-799	
	Denver	316F	80224	1300-1399	
	Denver	316K	80224	1700-1999	
	Denver	316P	80224	2200-2299	
	Denver	316X	80224	3400-3499	
	Denver	346B	80237	3500-3899	
	Denver	346F	80237	4100-4199	
POPLAR WAY	Broomfield	161Q	80020	1200-1299	
POPLAR WAY S	Arapahoe Co	316K	80224	None	
	Centennial	376F	80112	6900-7199	
	Centennial	376P	80112	7700-8299	
	Centennial	376K	80112	7700E-7799E	
	Denver	286X	80224	300-699	
	Denver	346F	80237	4000-4199	
POPLAR WAY S	Highlands Ranch	376T	80130	8500-8599	
POPLAR GROVE CT	Castle Rock	466X	80109	2600-2799	
POPPY CT	Arvada	220S	80007	6700-6999	
	Arvada	220W	80007	None	
	Jefferson Co	250E	80403	5500-5699	
POPPY CT	Lafayette	101X	80026	1700-1799	
POPPY CT S	Highlands Ranch	404F	80129	9800-9899	
POPPY DR	Brighton	138U	80601	400-899	
POPPY PL W	Highlands Ranch	404F	80129	600-799	
POPPY ST	Arvada	220W	80007	6400-6599	
	Golden	280S	80401	100-399	
	Jefferson Co	280N	80401	700-799	
	Jefferson Co	220N	80007	7400-7499	
POPPY WAY	Broomfield	162S	80020	600-699	
POPPY WAY	Golden	250A	80403	5700-5799	
	Jefferson Co	220N	80007	7200-7399	
POPPYWOOD CT E	Highlands Ranch	404G	80126	700-799	
POPPYWOOD DR E	Highlands Ranch	404G	80126	700-899	
PORCUPINE LN	Jefferson Co	370B	80127	1-99	
PORCUPINE PT	Douglas Co	470C	80134	8400-8599	
PORCUPINE TRAIL	Elbert Co	891Y	80106	4400-4699	
PORTAL RD E	Gilpin Co	740Y	80403	None	
PORTER WAY	Commerce City	226X	80022	6100-6599	
PORTICO LN	Boulder Co	40S	80503	None	
PORTICO PL	Boulder Co	40S	80503	None	
PORTLAND AVE W	Jefferson Co	372G	80128	6300-7299	
	Jefferson Co	372F	80128	7500-8399	
	Jefferson Co	372E	80128	8800-9199	
PORTLAND DR W	Arapahoe Co	373E	80128	5000-5199	
	Jefferson Co	372H	80128	5200-5999	
PORTLAND PL	Boulder	97Y	80304	900-1299	
PORTLAND PL E	Aurora	380C	80016	22400-22499	
	Aurora	380F	80016	None	
PORTLAND PL W	Jefferson Co	372G	80128	6300-6899	
PORTLAND RD	El Paso Co	908Y	80132	500-699	
PORTLAND WAY E	Aurora	380D	80016	23300-23699	
PORTMEIRION CT	Castle Rock	527B	80104	4300-4399	
PORTMEIRION LN	Castle Rock	527B	80104	100-499	
PORTOFINO DR	Longmont	40Q	80503	None	
PORTSIDE CT	Lafayette	131K	80026	500-699	
PORTSIDE WAY	Boulder Co	99G	80301	4600-4699	
POSSE RD E	Douglas Co	467F	80108	900-1099	
POST BOY RD	Boulder Co	722W	80302	1-299	
POST OAK CIR	Douglas Co	870E	80116	300-499	
POSTON PKWY	Highlands Ranch	405P	80126	2500-3999	
POSTON WAY	Boulder	100A	80301	7300-7399	
POSY LN	Jefferson Co	336Q	80439	29000-29399	
POTATO GULCH	Gilpin Co	760H	80403	None	
POTATO PATCH CIR	Clear Creek Co	801V	80439	1-599	
POTENTILLA CT	Douglas Co	470A	80134	5400-5499	
POTENTILLA ST	Brighton	139R	80601	None	
POTOMAC CIR	Aurora	288S	80011	300-399	
	Aurora	288J	80011	800-999	
POTOMAC CIR E	Aurora	288W	80012	400-499	
POTOMAC CT S	Aurora	318A	80012	900-999	
	Centennial	378A	80111	None	
POTOMAC ST	Adams Co	168J	80601	13600-14499	
	Aurora	288N	80011	1-1499	
	Aurora	288A	80011	1700-2099	
POTOMAC ST	Brighton	198A	80601	11600-11899	
	Brighton	168W	80601	11900-12499	
	Commerce City	198J	80022	9600-10298	E
	Commerce City	198J	80603	10700-11599	
POTOMAC ST S	Arapahoe Co	348W	80111	6200-6299	
	Arapahoe Co	378A	80111	6300-6699	
	Arapahoe Co	378J	80112	None	
	Aurora	288W	80012	1-599	
	Aurora	318J	80012	1200-1899	
	Centennial	378E	80112	6700-7699	
POTOMAC WAY	Aurora	288S	80011	300-399	
	Denver	258E	80239	5500-5599	
POTOMAC WAY S	Aurora	318A	80012	600-1099	
	Centennial	348W	80111	6100-6299	
POTOSI PL	Broomfield	133L	80020	2700-2999	
POTTER CT	Denver	254X	80216	2300-2399	
POTTS CT	Erie	103S	80516	None	
POUDRE CT	Lone Tree	406G	80124	10000-10099	
POUNDSTON DR E	Aurora	348P	80015	None	
POUNDSTON PL E	Aurora	348Q	80015	None	
POUNDSTONE PL	Greenwood Village	347N	80111	9300-9699	
POWDERHORN DR	El Paso Co	908Z	80132	300-799	
POWDERHORN DR	Lone Tree	406G	80124	7300-7599	
POWDERHORN LN	Boulder	128W	80305	2300-2499	
POWDERHORN PL	Longmont	12W	80501	1-99	
POWDER HORN ST N					
	Buckley Air Force Base	289T	80017	None	
POWDER HORN ST S					
	Buckley Air Force Base	289T	80017	None	
POWDERHORN TRAIL	Broomfield	162K	80020	200-299	
POWDER RIVER DR	Lafayette	132T	80026	None	
POWDER RUN DR	Central City	780C	80427	None	
POWELL RD N	Douglas Co	440V	80134	5800-6399	
POWELL ST	Erie	102W	80516	1600-1899	
POWER AVE E	Greenwood Village	346T	80111	5600-7299	
POWERS AVE E	Arapahoe Co	347U	80111	11500-11799	
	Arapahoe Co	350T	80015	22000-22199	
	Aurora	351S	80016	None	
	Centennial	348V	80015	16300-16499	
	Centennial	350S	80015	21000-21499	
	Greenwood Village	347S	80111	9700-10299	
	Littleton	344U	80121	1-699	
POWERS AVE W	Jefferson Co	341U	80127	10100-10399	
	Jefferson Co	341T	80127	10800-11899	
	Littleton	344T	80120	1-2599	
	Littleton	343T	80123	3400-3599	
POWERS CIR E	Centennial	348V	80015	16000-16199	
	Centennial	350S	80015	20700-21299	
	Centennial	350T	80015	21500N-21699N	
POWERS CIR W	Jefferson Co	341V	80123	9500-9899	
	Littleton	344T	80120	100-199	
	Littleton	343U	80123	3300-3399	
POWERS CT E	Arapahoe Co	347T	80111	10900-10999	
	Arapahoe Co	347U	80111	11000-11099	
POWERS DR E	Arapahoe Co	347T	80111	10600-10999	
	Arapahoe Co	349U	80015	18600-18999	
	Aurora	350R	80016	None	
	Centennial	348U	80015	15400-15799	
	Centennial	349S	80015	17400-17599	
	Centennial	349T	80015	17700-17899	
	Centennial	350T	80015	21800-21999	
	Greenwood Village	347S	80111	9600-9699	
POWERS DR W	Jefferson Co	341V	80123	9400-9599	
	Littleton	344T	80120	800-899	
POWERS LN E	Centennial	349V	80015	20300-20499	
	Centennial	350T	80015	21500-21599	
POWERS PL E	Arapahoe Co	349U	80015	18700-19699	
	Arapahoe Co	350U	80015	22200-22599	
	Centennial	348U	80015	15600-15799	
	Centennial	348V	80015	16400-16699	
	Centennial	349S	80015	17600-17699	
	Centennial	349T	80015	18100-18499	
	Centennial	349V	80015	20200-20499	
	Centennial	350S	80015	21100-21199	
	Centennial	350T	80015	21200-21299	
	Greenwood Village	347S	80111	9500-9699	
	Greenwood Village	347T	80111	10400-10499	
POWERS PL W	Jefferson Co	341V	80123	8800-8899	
	Jefferson Co	341T	80127	10800-11499	
	Littleton	344T	80120	200-399	
	Littleton	343T	80123	3400-3599	
POWERS ST	Erie	103N	80516	500-599	
POWHATAN TRAIL	Jefferson Co	843B	80433	12100-12299	
POWHATON RD	Adams Co	770X	80019	None	
	Aurora	790K	80019	1900-2599	
POWHATON RD N	Aurora	291Q	80018	1-1499	
	Aurora	291C	80019	1500-1899	
POWHATON RD S	Arapahoe Co	351L	80016	4300-5899	
	Aurora	291U	80018	1-699	
	Aurora	321Q	80018	1-2099	
	Aurora	351T	80016	None	
	Aurora	381C	80016	None	
	Aurora	381L	80016	None	

P

STREET NAME	CITY or COUNTY	MAP GRID	ZIP CODE	BLOCK RANGE	O/E
POWHATON ST	Denver	770T	80249	None	
POWHATTAN RD	Adams Co	750K	80603	13700-16799	
	Adams Co	750X	80022	None	
POZE BLVD	Thornton	195W	80229	2500-9199	
	Thornton	195X	80229	2600-2999	
	Thornton	224D	80229	8800-8899	
	Thornton	225A	80229	8900-8999	
PRADERA PKWY	Douglas Co	439W	80134	5200-5299	
	Douglas Co	848M	80134	None	
PRADO DR	Boulder Co	743U	80303	4200-4699	
PRAGUE DR	Elbert Co	850C	80138	41800-41999	
PRAIRIE AVE	Boulder	98X	80301	3200-3299	
PRAIRIE AVE	Lochbuie	140F	80603	500-799	
PRAIRIE CIR	Elbert Co	871H	80107	34000-34099	
PRAIRIE CIR	Frederick	727A	80516	None	
PRAIRIE CIR	Lone Tree	376Y	80124	7800-7899	
PRAIRIE DR	Brighton	139L	80601	None	
PRAIRIE LN	Castle Rock	467Y	80104	2400-2599	
PRAIRIE LN	Jefferson Co	366D	80439	6300-6499	
PRAIRIE LOOP	Elbert Co	871H	80107	34100-34199	
PRAIRIE PKWY	Commerce City	226Y	80216	None	
PRAIRIE PL	Broomfield	133Y	80020	15000-15199	
PRAIRIE ST	Palmer Lake	907Q	80133	None	
PRAIRIE WAY	Louisville	131Y	80027	1700-1999	
PRAIRIE CENTER PKWY	Brighton	169E	80601	2100-2299	
	Brighton	139X	80601	None	
PRAIRIE CLOVER	Jefferson Co	370F	80127	1-99	
PRAIRIE CLOVER WAY	Parker	378V	80134	8300-8499	
PRAIRIE DOG WAY	Jefferson Co	367S	80439	27100-27299	
PRAIRIE DUNES CT	Jefferson Co	305M	80439	31600-31699	
PRAIRIE FALCON CT S	Highlands Ranch	406F	80130	9900-9999	
PRAIRIE FALCON LN	Broomfield	162Q	80020	1500-1699	
PRAIRIE FALCON LN	Jefferson Co	370B	80127	1-99	
PRAIRIE FALCON LN S	Highlands Ranch	406F	80130	9800-9999	
PRAIRIE FALCON PKWY	Brighton	140N	80601	None	
PRAIRIE FARM CIR	Parker	408V	80134	16300-16399	
PRAIRIE FARM CT	Parker	408V	80134	11800-11899	
PRAIRIE FARM DR	Commerce City	769J	80022	None	
PRAIRIE FIRE CIR	Longmont	40L	80503	4100-4299	
PRAIRIE FLOWER PL	Parker	408V	80134	16500-16599	
PRAIRIE GOAT AVE E	Parker	408Z	80134	None	
PRAIRIE GOAT LN E	Parker	409W	80134	None	
PRAIRIE HARVEST CT	Parker	408V	80134	11800-11899	
PRAIRIE HAWK DR	Castle Rock	497B	80109	1-1999	
	Castle Rock	467S	80109	2000-3899	
See.. LIGGETT RD					
PRAIRIE HAWK DR	Longmont	12Y	80501	900-1099	
PRAIRIE HIGH RD	Castle Rock	467W	80109	None	
PRAIRIE KNOLL DR	Boulder Co	10M	80503	8800-8999	
PRAIRIE LAKE TRAIL	Douglas Co	440W	80134	7600-7799	
PRAIRIELAND LN	Parker	409J	80134	None	
PRAIRIE MEADOW CIR	Douglas Co	407L	80134	10100-10299	
PRAIRIE OWL RD	Elbert Co	850H	80138	1500-2099	
PRAIRIE RED CT	Adams Co	751J	80603	None	
PRAIRIE RIDGE CT	Lafayette	131A	80026	2700-2799	
PRAIRIE RIDGE DR	Lafayette	131A	80026	None	
PRAIRIE RIDGE RD	Highlands Ranch	374U	80126	1-899	
PRAIRIE ROSE CIR	Castle Rock	466X	80109	None	
PRAIRIE RUN	Douglas Co	432N	80125	10900-10999	
PRAIRIE SKY LN	Broomfield	163A	80020	14500-14699	
PRAIRIE SONG PL	Longmont	42C	80501	1500-1599	
PRAIRIESTAR CT	Douglas Co	440Q	80134	7100-7399	
PRAIRIE TRAIL DR	Douglas Co	378T	80112	8501-8599	
PRAIRIE VIEW DR S	Highlands Ranch	405A	80126	9100-9499	
PRAIRIEVILLE CT	Parker	408V	80134	11800-11899	
PRAIRIE VISTA DR	Castle Rock	466U	80109	3200-3499	
PRAIRIE WIND AVE E	Parker	408Z	80134	None	
PRAIRIE WIND LN E	Parker	409A	80134	None	
PRATT PKWY S	Longmont	41Q	80501	1-1899	
PRATT PL	Adams Co	223B	80031	8600-8699	
PRATT PL	Longmont	41L	80501	1-99	
PRATT ST	Adams Co	223E	80031	8400-8499	
PRATT ST	Longmont	41G	80501	100-899	
	Longmont	11Y	80501	900-1199	
	Longmont	11U	80501	1400-1599	
	Longmont	11Q	80501	2100-2499	
PRATT WAY	Longmont	41Q	80501	1400-1599	
PREAKNESS DR	Douglas Co	439T	80134	None	
PREBLE CREEK PKWY	Broomfield	133M	80020	None	
PREBLE'S PL	Broomfield	163E	80020	4900-4999	
PREMIER PL	Boulder	98J	80304	2400-2599	
PRENTICE AVE E	Arapahoe Co	347P	80111	10400-10499	
	Arapahoe Co	350Q	80015	22500-22899	
	Centennial	348R	80015	16400-16799	
	Centennial	349N	80015	17000-17099	
	Centennial	349Q	80015	18900-19499	
	Centennial	349R	80015	19800-19899	
	Greenwood Village	346P	80111	6500-7299	
	Greenwood Village	346Q	80111	7900-8999	
	Greenwood Village	346R	80111	None	
PRENTICE AVE W	Denver	342R	80123	6000-6099	
	Jefferson Co	342N	80123	8500-9099	
	Jefferson Co	341R	80123	9100-9699	
	Lakewood	342Q	80123	6200-6799	
	Littleton	344N	80120	400-1999	
	Littleton	343Q	80123	3000-3199	
PRENTICE CIR E	Centennial	348R	80015	16300-16899	
	Centennial	349N	80015	17300-17699	
	Centennial	349Q	80015	19000-19199	
	Greenwood Village	347N	80111	9600-9699	
PRENTICE CIR W	Denver	342R	80123	5400-5599	
PRENTICE CT W	Denver	342R	80123	5400-5499	
PRENTICE DR E	Centennial	348Q	80015	15400-15799	
	Centennial	349N	80015	16900-17299	
	Centennial	349P	80015	17600-17999	
	Centennial	349Q	80015	18700-18899	
PRENTICE DR W	Jefferson Co	341P	80127	11100-11799	
	Jefferson Co	341N	80127	12400-12799	
PRENTICE LN E	Centennial	348Q	80015	15400-15899	
	Centennial	348R	80015	16100-16699	
	Centennial	349Q	80015	19300-19399	
	Centennial	349R	80015	19800-20299	
	Centennial	350N	80015	21200-21399	
PRENTICE PL	Greenwood Village	345R	80121	4300-4499	
PRENTICE PL E	Arapahoe Co	347P	80111	10300-10499	
	Arapahoe Co	350P	80015	22000-22099	
	Centennial	348R	80015	16100-16299	
	Centennial	349P	80015	17900-17999	
	Centennial	349Q	80015	18600-19399	
	Centennial	349N	80015	19600-19799	
	Centennial	349R	80015	19800-20199	
	Centennial	350P	80015	21300-21399	
	Greenwood Village	346N	80111	5500-5999	
PRENTICE PL W	Denver	342Q	80123	6200-6599	
	Jefferson Co	341P	80127	10800-11799	
	Jefferson Co	341N	80127	12200-12599	
	Littleton	344P	80120	800-899	
PRESCOTT AVE E	Castle Rock	498H	80104	5200-5699	
PRESCOTT CT S	Littleton	374J	80120	7600-7699	
PRESCOTT ST S	Littleton	344N	80120	5200-5399	
	Littleton	344S	80120	5600-5899	
	Littleton	344W	80120	6100-6499	
	Littleton	374E	80120	6800-6999	
	Littleton	374J	80120	7500-7899	
PRESCOTT WAY S	Littleton	374A	80120	6600-6699	
PRESERVATION TRAIL	Douglas Co	440L	80134	7100-8799	
PRESERVE CIR	Jefferson Co	307G	80401	1100-1399	
PRESERVE CT	Greenwood Village	345R	80121	4900-4999	
PRESERVE DR	Greenwood Village	345R	80121	5300-5599	
PRESERVE LN	Douglas Co	847T	80109	2800-2899	
PRESERVE LN	Greenwood Village	345R	80121	4900-4999	
PRESERVE PKWY	Greenwood Village	345U	80121	4000N-5599N	
PRESSLER ST	Jefferson Co	823N	80433	26000-26399	
PRESTON CT	Douglas Co	436Q	80108	900-999	
PRESTON DR	Longmont	12T	80501	1700-1799	
PRESTON WAY	Douglas Co	436Q	80108	None	
PRESTWICK CT	Castle Rock	497X	80104	100-199	
PRESTWICK CT	Longmont	12Q	80501	2000-2099	
PRESTWICK LN	Jefferson Co	306T	80439	2500-2599	
PRESTWICK PL	Lone Tree	406H	80124	None	
PRESTWICK WAY W	Castle Rock	497X	80104	100-699	
PRESTWICK TRAIL	Lone Tree	406H	80124	10100-10299	
PRETICE PL E	Arapahoe Co	350Q	80015	22700-22799	
PREY RIDGE WAY	El Paso Co	908V	80132	None	
PRICE AVE	Greenwood Village	345P	80121	5500-5599	
PRICE RD	Longmont	41G	80501	200-299	
	Longmont	41L	80501	None	
PRICE ST	Park Co	820Y	80421	1-199	
PRICKLEY PEAR CIR	Parker	379X	80134	8800-8999	
PRICKLEY PEAR CT	Parker	379X	80134	8900-8999	
PRIMA LN	Jefferson Co	306K	80439	1700-1899	
PRIMOS RD	Boulder Co	741B	80302	1-1299	
PRIMROSE CIR	Brighton	168C	80601	None	
PRIMROSE CT	Brighton	168C	80601	None	
PRIMROSE CT	Broomfield	163T	80020	3900-3999	
PRIMROSE CT	Longmont	42F	80501	100-299	
PRIMROSE DR	Boulder	127L	80302	None	
PRIMROSE DR	Douglas Co	887G	80118	2000-2299	
PRIMROSE LN	Adams Co	253G	80221	5300-5499	
PRIMROSE LN	Boulder Co	70Q	80503	6500-6599	
PRIMROSE LN	Castle Rock	466Q	80109	3500-3899	
PRIMROSE LN	Erie	133C	80516	None	
PRIMROSE LN	Jefferson Co	823S	80433	None	
PRIMROSE LN	Lafayette	131R	80026	1000-1099	
PRIMROSE PL	Erie	133C	80516	None	
PRIMROSE ST	Palmer Lake	907Q	80133	None	
PRINCE CIR	Broomfield	163Q	80020	3000-12999	
PRINCE CIR	Erie	102W	80516	2800-2999	
PRINCE CIR S	Littleton	373D	80120	6800-6999	
PRINCE CT	Broomfield	163Q	80020	12900-12999	
PRINCE CT S	Littleton	343R	80123	4900-4999	
PRINCE ST	Longmont	41H	80501	1-99	
PRINCE ST S	Littleton	343M	80123	5000-5299	
	Littleton	343R	80120	5300-6499	
	Littleton	373D	80120	6500-7599	
PRINCE WAY S	Littleton	373D	80120	6800-6999	
PRINCE CREEK DR	Parker	439F	80134	12600-12799	
PRINCESS CIR N	Broomfield	163Q	80020	2900-3499	
PRINCESS CIR S	Broomfield	163U	80020	3000-12999	
PRINCESS CT	Broomfield	163T	80020	3400-3499	
PRINCESS DR	Longmont	11U	80501	1700-1899	
PRINCETON AVE E	Arapahoe Co	350E	80013	20500-20599	
	Aurora	348G	80014	15400-16099	
	Cherry Hills Village	345H	80113	4700-5299	
	Cherry Hills Village	346E	80111	5700-6299	
	Denver	346B	80237	7100-8499	
	Denver	346H	80237	8000-8599	
	Englewood	344G	80113	1-799	
PRINCETON AVE W	Denver	343E	80236	4600-5099	
	Denver	342G	80235	6700-7199	
	Englewood	344F	80110	1-699	
PRINCETON CIR	Longmont	10V	80503	1-99	
PRINCETON CIR E	Aurora	348H	80014	16200-16299	
	Aurora	350F	80018	22000-22199	
	Cherry Hills Village	346E	80111	5900-6199	
PRINCETON CIR S	Highlands Ranch	406B	80130	9300-9599	
PRINCETON CIR W	Denver	343F	80236	3400-3899	
PRINCETON CT	Longmont	10Z	80503	1000-1299	
PRINCETON CT	Louisville	130Y	80027	900-999	
PRINCETON DR	Longmont	10Z	80503	1000-1299	
PRINCETON DR E	Aurora	349E	80013	16900-17299	
	Aurora	349G	80013	18800-19699	
	Aurora	350F	80018	21900-22499	
PRINCETON DR W	Denver	342H	80235	5200-5699	
	Jefferson Co	340G	80465	13500-13699	
PRINCETON LN E	Arapahoe Co	350E	80013	20700-20799	
PRINCETON LN S	Highlands Ranch	406A	80130	9300-9499	
PRINCETON PL	Lafayette	131F	80026	600-699	
PRINCETON PL E	Arapahoe Co	350E	80013	20500-20899	
	Aurora	348F	80014	13900-13999	
	Aurora	348G	80014	15100-15299	
	Aurora	348G	80014	15700-16099	
	Aurora	348H	80014	16500-16599	
	Aurora	349F	80013	17700-17899	
	Aurora	349G	80013	19400-19999	
PRINCETON PL W	Denver	342G	80235	6700-6799	
	Englewood	344E	80110	1000-1299	
	Sheridan	343G	80110	4200-4299	
PRINCETON ST	Adams Co	223E	80031	8400-8499	
	Adams Co	223A	80031	8600-8999	
PRINCETON ST	Highlands Ranch	376W	80130	9300-9499	
PRINSEPIA ST	Parker	439F	80134	None	
PRIVATE DR	Park Co	842J	80470	200-399	
PRIVATE RD 7	Elbert Co	870M	80107	32000-32499	
PRIVATE RD 17	Elbert Co	851P	80107	38600-39599	
PRIVATE RD 19	Elbert Co	831L	80138	39100-39299	
	Elbert Co	851P	80107	39300-39599	
PRIVATE RD 23	Elbert Co	911H	80106	19300-19499	
PRIVATE RD 23	Elbert Co	871U	80107	30000-31999	
PRIVATE RD 27	Elbert Co	851Z	80107	36000-36499	
PRIVATE RD 29	Elbert Co	872J	80107	33000-33099	
PRIVATE RD 35	Elbert Co	872B	80117	34900-35699	
PRIVATE RD 39	Elbert Co	892Y	80106	22000-22999	
	Elbert Co	892L	80106	25000-25999	
	Elbert Co	832L	80107	43300-47999	
PRIVATE RD 43	Elbert Co	872V	80117	30100-30199	
PRIVATE RD 104	Elbert Co	890M	80116	1401-1499	O
PRIVATE RD 112	Elbert Co	890C	80107	900-999	
PRIVATE RD 124	Elbert Co	871U	80107	5500-5599	
PRIVATE RD 124.5	Elbert Co	872V	80117	10400-10999	
PRIVATE RD 126	Elbert Co	871U	80107	5500-5599	
PRIVATE RD 130	Elbert Co	870R	80107	1400-1799	
PRIVATE RD 132	Elbert Co	872J	80107	None	
PRIVATE RD 139	Elbert Co	832X	80107	None	
PRIVATE RD 144	Elbert Co	872B	80117	8000-8499	
PRIVATE RD 160	Elbert Co	851L	80107	4300-4399	
PRIVATE RD 162	Elbert Co	851L	80107	4300-4599	
PRIVATE RD 188	Elbert Co	831K	80138	4100-4699	
PRIVATE RD 192	Elbert Co	832L	80107	5000-5199	
	Elbert Co	831K	80138	9400-9599	
PROCTOR CT S	Superior	160Q	80027	1500-1599	
PROFESSIONAL LN	Longmont	41V	80501	1501-1599	O
PROGRESS AVE E	Arapahoe Co	347P	80111	10400-10999	
	Arapahoe Co	350Q	80015	22500-22899	
	Centennial	349N	80015	16900-17299	
	Centennial	349P	80015	18100-18499	
	Centennial	349Q	80015	18600-19299	
	Centennial	349R	80015	20100-20299	
	Centennial	350N	80015	20800-21399	
	Centennial	348Q	80015	None	
	Greenwood Village	346P	80111	6500-7199	
PROGRESS AVE W	Denver	342R	80123	6001-6099	O
	Jefferson Co	341Q	80123	9100-9999	
	Jefferson Co	341P	80127	10100-12699	
	Littleton	344P	80120	400-599	
	Littleton	343Q	80123	3000-3099	
PROGRESS CIR E	Arapahoe Co	350R	80016	23300-24099	
	Centennial	348Q	80015	15400-15799	
	Centennial	349Q	80015	19500-20099	
	Centennial	349N	80015	16900N-17299N	
	Greenwood Village	346P	80111	6500-6599	
	Greenwood Village	347N	80111	9700-9899	
	Greenwood Village	347N	80111	9800N-9999N	
PROGRESS CIR W	Lakewood	342P	80123	8000-8299	
PROGRESS CT	Greenwood Village	345R	80121	4900-4999	
PROGRESS CT E	Arapahoe Co	348P	80015	13900-14199	
PROGRESS DR E	Aurora	351N	80016	None	
	Centennial	348Q	80015	15400-15499	
	Centennial	349N	80015	17400-17699	
	Centennial	349Q	80015	18500-18799	
	Centennial	348R	80015	None	
PROGRESS DR W	Jefferson Co	342N	80123	8500-8999	
PROGRESS LN E	Centennial	349Q	80015	18900-19099	
	Centennial	349R	80015	19800-19899	
	Douglas Co	409G	80134	6200-6299	
PROGRESS LN W	Littleton	344P	80120	400-599	
PROGRESS PL E	Aurora	348Q	80015	15200-15299	
	Centennial	348R	80015	16100-16199	
	Centennial	349N	80015	17300-17399	
	Centennial	349P	80015	17900-18099	
	Centennial	349Q	80015	18600-18899	
	Centennial	349R	80015	19900-20299	
	Centennial	350P	80015	21300-21399	
	Greenwood Village	346P	80111	7500-7599	
	Greenwood Village	347N	80111	9500-9699	
PROGRESS PL W	Jefferson Co	342N	80123	8500-9099	
	Jefferson Co	341R	80123	9100-9199	
	Jefferson Co	341Q	80123	9800-9999	
	Jefferson Co	341P	80127	10800-11599	
PROGRESS ST W	Littleton	344N	80120	1600-1799	
PROGRESS WAY E	Arapahoe Co	348P	80015	13700-14199	
PROGRESS WAY S	Parker	409G	80134	10200-10399	
PROMENADE PL	Greenwood Village	346Q	80111	None	
PROMENADE PL S	Highlands Ranch	404H	80126	9600-9699	
PROMENADE NORTH DR	Westminster	192L	80020	5900-6899	
PROMENADE SOUTH DR	Westminster	192L	80020	5900-6499	
PROMINENCE	Elbert Co	870M	80107	None	
PROMONTORY CIR	Elbert Co	870L	80107	900-998	E
PROMONTORY CT	Boulder	97K	80304	3800-3999	
PROMONTORY DR	Douglas Co	867Q	80109	1700-1999	
PROMONTORY LOOP	Broomfield	133L	80020	None	
PROMONTORY WAY	El Paso Co	908P	80132	20000-20099	
PRONGHORN AVE	Elbert Co	851L	80107	5000-39999	
PRONGHORN CIR	Elbert Co	831S	80138	2000-2999	
	Elbert Co	870R	80107	2400-2599	
PRONGHORN PL	Douglas Co	870S	80116	10600-10699	
PRONGHORN ST	Broomfield	163T	80020	12600-12698	E
PROSPECT AVE	Palmer Lake	907R	80133	None	
PROSPECT AVE E	Aurora	350Z	80016	23900-24299	
PROSPECT DR	Douglas Co	466H	80108	300-4799	
PROSPECT RD	Boulder Co	704W	80503	5500-6499	
	Boulder Co	41V	80504	10700-11099	
	Boulder Co	42T	80504	11100-11499	
PROSPECT ST	Bow Mar	343J	80123	4400-4699	
	Bow Mar	343J	80123	4700-4899	
PROSPECT ST	Lyons	703B	80540	None	
PROSPECTOR DR	El Paso Co	912Z	80831	17100-17499	
PROSPECTOR WAY	Douglas Co	439V	80134	None	
PROSPECTORS WAY	Park Co	820Y	80421	1-199	
PROSS DR	Jefferson Co	823N	80433	9500-9699	
PROSSER ST	Central City	780C	80427	1-199	
PROUTY DR	Jefferson Co	306E	80439	1300-1599	
PROVIDENCE DR	Douglas Co	466H	80108	300-599	
PROVOST RD S	Arapahoe Co	813U	80136	4300-5099	
PTARMIGAN	Jefferson Co	370A	80127	1-99	
PTARMIGAN CIR	Boulder Co	69Z	80301	5400-5599	
PTARMIGAN CT	Lafayette	132A	80026	1200-1299	
PTARMIGAN DR	Broomfield	162M	80020	13800-13898	E

P

STREET NAME	CITY or COUNTY	MAP GRID	ZIP CODE	BLOCK RANGE	O/E
PTARMIGAN DR	Longmont	12Y	80501	1100-1299	
PTARMIGAN LN	Broomfield	162M	80020	5300-5399	
PTARMIGAN ST	Golden	249S	80403	300-399	
PTARMIGAN TRAIL	Lone Tree	406C	80124	9200-9399	
PTARMIGAN TRAIL	Park Co	841Z	80421	1-399	
PUBLIC RD N	Lafayette	132N	80026	100-299	
PUBLIC RD S	Lafayette	132J	80026	100-1499	
PUEBLO CT	Palmer Lake	907U	80133	None	
PUEBLO CT	Thornton	194Z	80229	1500-1699	
PUEBLO PL	Boulder	129J	80303	5400-5499	
PUEBLO RD	Palmer Lake	907U	80133	None	
PUEBLO ALTA WAY	Castle Rock	469J	80108	None	
PUFFIN CT	Highlands Ranch	375Y	80126	9000-9099	
PUMA WALK	Boulder Co	722T	80302	1-499	
PUMA DR	Boulder Co	742R	80302	1-299	
PUMA DR	Elbert Co	891Y	80106	4500-4999	
PUMA PT	Douglas Co	406N	80124	6100-6199	
PUMA BLUFF	Douglas Co	406N	80124	6101-6299	O
PUMA CHASE	Douglas Co	406N	80124	6000-6099	
PUMA CLIFF	Douglas Co	406N	80124	10900-11099	
PUMA CREST	Jefferson Co	365F	80439	33500-33599	
PUMA RIDGE	Douglas Co	406N	80124	6000-6099	
PUMA RUN	Douglas Co	406P	80124	10900-11099	
PUMA SANDS	Douglas Co	406N	80124	6100-6199	
PUMA TRAIL	Douglas Co	406N	80125	6900-7299	
PURCEL ST	Brighton	139S	80601	2900-2998	E
PURCELL PL	Brighton	138V	80601	2400-2499	
PURDUE AVE	Firestone	707X	80504	None	
PURDUE AVE S	Lakewood	342F	80235	7900-7999	
PURDUE AVE W	Jefferson Co	340G	80465	13400-13799	
PURDUE CIR E	Aurora	349G	80013	19300-19699	
PURDUE CT	Longmont	10Z	80503	1-99	
PURDUE DR	Longmont	11W	80503	1000-1099	
	Longmont	10Z	80503	1100-1299	
PURDUE DR E	Aurora	348G	80014	15600-15899	
PURDUE DR W	Jefferson Co	340H	80465	13400-13499	
PURDUE PL E	Arapahoe Co	349H	80018	20200-20299	
	Aurora	350F	80018	4200-4299	
	Aurora	348F	80014	14500-14699	
	Aurora	348H	80014	16500-16599	
	Aurora	349E	80013	17200-17299	
	Aurora	349B	80013	17700-17999	
	Aurora	349G	80013	19400-19799	
	Aurora	349H	80013	19900-19999	
PURGATOIRE PEAK	Jefferson Co	371Q	80127	10400-10499	
PURGATORY LN	Jefferson Co	306F	80439	1300-1399	
PURITAN LN	Frederick	726G	80516	3100-3399	
PURITAN WAY	Frederick	726L	80516	3700-3799	
PURPLE ASH	Jefferson Co	370F	80127	1-99	
PURPLE MUSTARD CT	Brighton	139M	80601	None	
PURPLE MUSTARD ST	Brighton	140J	80601	None	
PURPLE PLUM	Jefferson Co	370K	80127	1-99	
PURPLE SAGE LOOP	Castle Rock	467U	80104	900-1299	
PURSER CT	El Paso Co	908V	80132	19000-19099	
PUSSY WILLOW CT	Boulder	99E	80301	4500-4599	
PUTNAM ST	Highlands Ranch	405F	80126	None	
PUTNEY CURL	Thornton	195N	80229	10300-10399	
PUTTER CT	Boulder Co	723G	80503	6600-6699	
PUTTER PL	Castle Rock	497U	80104	1400-1599	
PYRAMID CIR	Broomfield	163J	80020	4600-4899	
PYRAMID CT	Superior	160Y	80027	3900-3999	
PYRAMID RD	Thornton	193V	80260	None	
PYRAMID PEAK	Jefferson Co	371P	80127	11000-11099	
PYRITE CT	Castle Rock	467H	80108	7300-7499	
PYRITE RD	Gilpin Co	761E	80403	1-199	
PYRITE WAY	Boulder Co	703F	80540	1-699	
PYRITE WAY	Castle Rock	467H	80108	7400-7599	
PYROLA CIR	Douglas Co	887F	80118	7000-7099	
Q					
QUAIL CIR	Boulder	97L	80304	300-599	
QUAIL CIR	Brighton	138W	80601	900-1099	
QUAIL CIR	Louisville	130R	80027	1900-2099	
QUAIL CIR S	Jefferson Co	371K	80127	7400-7499	
QUAIL COVE	Lafayette	132P	80026	800-899	
QUAIL CT	Arvada	251F	80033	5500-5599	
	Arvada	251B	80004	6000-6199	
QUAIL CT	Frederick	706Z	80504	4800-4899	
QUAIL CT	Golden	248Z	80403	1400-1599	
QUAIL CT	Lakewood	281F	80215	1900-1999	
QUAIL CT	Louisville	130R	80027	1800-1999	
QUAIL CT	Parker	408R	80134	11000-11099	
QUAIL CT	Westminster	191P	80021	10200-10299	
	Westminster	191K	80021	10500-10699	
	Wheat Ridge	251T	80033	3800-3899	
QUAIL CT S	Jefferson Co	311F	80232	1400-1499	
	Jefferson Co	341F	80127	4300-4399	
	Jefferson Co	341P	80127	5300-5399	
	Jefferson Co	371B	80127	6600-6699	
	Jefferson Co	371F	80127	7200-7399	
	Jefferson Co	371P	80127	8400-8499	
QUAIL DR	Elbert Co	850Z	80107	37100-37299	
QUAIL DR	Lafayette	132K	80026	700-799	
QUAIL DR	Lakewood	281B	80215	2000-2299	
QUAIL LN	Castle Rock	497D	80104	1500-1799	
QUAIL LN S	Jefferson Co	371B	80127	6700-6799	
QUAIL PL	Highlands Ranch	374V	80126	800-1099	
QUAIL RD	Boulder Co	40M	80503	8700-8999	
	Boulder Co	42N	80501	10700-11899	
	Longmont	41R	80501	301-399	O
QUAIL ST	Arvada	251F	80033	5500-5599	
	Arvada	251B	80004	5800-6199	
	Arvada	221X	80004	6200-6499	
	Arvada	221T	80004	6600-7199	
	Arvada	221T	80005	7200-7499	
	Arvada	221K	80005	7600-7999	
	Lakewood	281K	80215	600-1499	
	Lakewood	281F	80215	1500-1999	
	Lakewood	281B	80215	2500-2799	
	Lakewood	251X	80215	2800-3199	
	Westminster	191P	80021	10200-10399	
	Westminster	191K	80021	10500-10799	
	Wheat Ridge	251X	80033	3200-3499	
	Wheat Ridge	251T	80033	3600-3799	
	Wheat Ridge	251P	80033	4600-4699	
	Wheat Ridge	251K	80033	5200-5399	
QUAIL ST S	Jefferson Co	311F	80232	1100-1599	
	Jefferson Co	311K	80232	1700-1899	
	Jefferson Co	341K	80127	4400-4699	
	Jefferson Co	341T	80127	5400-5899	
	Jefferson Co	341X	80127	6200-6399	
	Lakewood	281X	80226	300-699	
QUAIL WAY	Westminster	191P	80021	10200-10299	
QUAIL WAY S	Jefferson Co	341F	80127	4300-4399	
	Jefferson Co	341K	80127	4800-4899	
	Jefferson Co	341P	80127	5300-5499	
	Jefferson Co	341X	80127	5900-6299	
	Jefferson Co	371B	80127	6600-6799	
	Jefferson Co	371K	80127	7400-7499	
	Lakewood	311B	80226	700-1099	
QUAIL CREEK DR	Broomfield	163G	80020	2400-2699	
QUAIL CREEK DR	Parker	410P	80138	10600-10899	
QUAIL CREEK LN	Boulder Co	99G	80301	4600-4799	
QUAIL HOLLOW CT	Boulder	99D	80301	5200-5299	
QUAIL RIDGE CIR	Elbert Co	851E	80138	3300-3499	
QUAIL RIDGE CIR	Highlands Ranch	374Y	80126	200-499	
QUAIL RIDGE CT	Jefferson Co	340S	80465	16400-16499	
QUAIL RIDGE DR	Broomfield	162M	80020	13800-14099	
QUAIL RIDGE DR	Parker	410K	80138	10700-10899	
QUAIL RUN CIR	Elbert Co	871D	80117	6800-6899	
QUAIL RUN CT	Parker	410Q	80138	10900-10999	
QUAIL RUN DR	Parker	410Q	80138	22300-22499	
QUAIL RUN LN	Parker	410Q	80138	10900-22499	
QUAIL RUN RD	Adams Co	751L	80642	None	
	Adams Co	751X	80642	None	
	Adams Co	771U	80642	None	
	Arapahoe Co	791U	80137	900-1499	
QUAIL RUN RD S	Watkins	811C	80137	1100-1799	
QUAIL RUN WAY	Parker	410Q	80138	22300-22399	
QUAKER CIR	Golden	280N	80401	None	
QUAKER CT	Arvada	219Z	80007	6400-6599	
	Jefferson Co	249M	80403	None	
	Jefferson Co	280S	80401	None	
QUAKER LN	Golden	249M	80403	4800-4999	
QUAKER LN	Jefferson Co	842D	80433	12100-12399	
QUAKER ST	Arvada	220X	80403	6200-6399	
	Arvada	220S	80007	6400-7199	
QUAKER ST	Golden	280S	80401	100-199	
	Jefferson Co	280J	80401	900-1599	
	Jefferson Co	250J	80403	5000-5199	
	Jefferson Co	250E	80403	5300-5699	
	Jefferson Co	220S	80007	7200-8199	
QUAKER WAY	Golden	280S	80401	100-299	
QUAKIE WAY	Park Co	841T	80421	1-999	
QUAKING ASPEN LN	Douglas Co	907F	80118	13100-13999	
QUALLA CT	Boulder	128R	80303	1-99	
QUALLA DR	Boulder	128R	80303	4600-4999	
QUAM DR	Northglenn	194D	80233	11700-11999	
QUANDARY LOOP	Broomfield	133N	80020	15800-16199	
QUANDARY PEAK	Jefferson Co	842P	80421	None	
QUANDARY PEAK ST	Brighton	139Q	80601	None	
QUANDRY RD	Thornton	193V	80260	None	
QUANDRY PEAK DR	Castle Rock	867R	80109	None	
QUANTOCK CT S	Aurora	381C	80016	6500-6599	
	Aurora	381L	80016	None	
QUANTOCK WAY S	Aurora	381C	80016	6600-6899	
	Aurora	381L	80016	None	
QUANTUM ST S	Denver	286T	80230	1-199	O
QUARI CT	Aurora	287M	80011	800-999	
	Aurora	287H	80010	None	
QUARI ST	Aurora	287V	80011	200-299	
	Aurora	287M	80011	800-1399	
	Aurora	257Z	80011	3100-3198	E
	Denver	257M	80239	4900-4999	
	Denver	257G	80239	5300-5599	
QUARI ST S	Aurora	287Z	80012	600-699	
QUARI WAY	Aurora	287H	80010	1700-1798	E
QUARLES AVE W	Jefferson Co	371G	80127	10500-10799	
QUARLES DR W	Arapahoe Co	373E	80128	4900-5199	
	Jefferson Co	372H	80128	5800-5999	
	Jefferson Co	372E	80128	None	
QUARLES PL W	Jefferson Co	371H	80128	9200-9499	
	Jefferson Co	372E	80128	None	
QUARRY CT	Boulder	69Y	80301	5600-5699	
QUARRY RD	Douglas Co	406Q	80124	600-999	
QUARRY WAY	Douglas Co	408M	80134	None	
QUARRY WAY	Monument	908X	80132	17400-17699	
QUARRY HILL DR	Douglas Co	408G	80134	15500-16399	
QUARRY HILL PL	Douglas Co	408G	80134	10000-10199	
QUARRY MOUNTAIN	Jefferson Co	371E	80127	7300-7399	
QUARTAR CIR S	Centennial	350T	80015	5700-5899	
QUARTAR CT S	Centennial	350T	80015	5600-5799	
QUARTER CIRCLE LN	Jefferson Co	275T	80439	300-599	
QUARTERHORSE LN	El Paso Co	910U	80908	18000-18299	
QUARTER HORSE RD	Jefferson Co	335D	80439	31200-31599	
	Jefferson Co	336A	80439	31600-32099	
QUARTER HORSE TRAIL					
	Castle Rock	467U	80104	700-1099	
QUARTERLAND ST	Adams Co	794J	80136	None	
QUARTO AVE W	Jefferson Co	372F	80128	7500-8399	
	Jefferson Co	372E	80128	8600-9099	
	Jefferson Co	371H	80128	9100-9199	
QUARTO CIR W	Jefferson Co	372E	80128	8700-8899	
QUARTO CT W	Jefferson Co	371G	80127	10500-10599	
QUARTO DR W	Jefferson Co	372E	80128	7700-8299	
	Jefferson Co	371G	80127	10600-10699	
QUARTO PL E	Aurora	380F	80016	22000-22199	
	Aurora	381E	80016	24600-24799	
	Aurora	381F	80016	25400-25499	
	Aurora	381G	80016	26800-26999	
	Aurora	830A	80016	None	
QUARTO PL W	Jefferson Co	372G	80128	6800-6999	
	Jefferson Co	371H	80128	8900-9199	
QUARTZ CIR	Arvada	219Z	80007	6400-6599	
QUARTZ CIR	Park Co	820Y	80421	1-699	
QUARTZ CT	Longmont	12X	80501	900-999	
QUARTZ DR	Broomfield	162N	80020	None	
QUARTZ LOOP	Arvada	249D	80403	6100-6299	
QUARTZ RD	Gilpin Co	761E	80403	1-399	
QUARTZ ST	Castle Rock	496B	80109	1700-2499	
QUARTZ ST	Golden	279M	80401	1000-1499	
	Jefferson Co	219R	80007	7200-7799	
	Lochbuie	729Z	80603	None	
QUARTZ WAY	Arvada	219V	80007	6700-6799	
	Boulder Co	703F	80540	1-699	
	Broomfield	162S	80020	600-699	
	Superior	160U	80027	2800-2899	
QUARTZ HILL RD	Gilpin Co	780G	80403	None	
QUARTZ MOUNTAIN DR	Douglas Co	887L	80118	1000-2399	
QUARTZ SPUR	Jefferson Co	844A	80433	12300-12499	
QUARTZ TRAIL	Jefferson Co	368V	80465	8400-8499	
QUARTZVILLE E	Elbert Co	870L	80107	12200-12299	
QUATAR CIR S	Arapahoe Co	350P	80015	5200-5499	
	Aurora	380P	80016	None	
QUATAR CT S	Arapahoe Co	350P	80015	5400-5499	
	Aurora	380K	80016	None	
QUATAR ST S	Aurora	350B	80018	3800-4199	
	Aurora	380F	80016	7100-7199	
	Centennial	350T	80015	5500-5599	
QUATAR WAY E	Aurora	380K	80016	None	
QUATAR WAY S	Arapahoe Co	350T	80015	None	
	Aurora	320X	80013	3500-3599	
	Aurora	350B	80018	3600-3899	
QUAY CIR	Arvada	222U	80003	7100-7199	
QUAY CT	Arvada	252G	80002	5500-5599	
	Arvada	222U	80003	6600-7099	
	Arvada	222G	80003	8200-8299	
	Arvada	252C	80003	None	
QUAY CT S	Jefferson Co	372C	80123	6300-6499	
	Jefferson Co	372L	80128	7300-7699	
	Jefferson Co	372Q	80128	8000-8199	
	Jefferson Co	372U	80128	8300-8399	
QUAY DR	Arvada	222G	80003	8200-8599	
QUAY DR S	Lakewood	312L	80232	1500-1799	
QUAY LOOP	Westminster	192T	80021	9700-9799	
QUAY ST	Arvada	252G	80002	5200-5499	
	Arvada	222Y	80003	6200-6399	
	Arvada	222U	80003	6600-7199	
	Arvada	222Q	80003	7400-7799	
QUAY ST	Broomfield	192C	80020	11600-11999	
QUAY ST	Lakewood	282U	80226	1-399	
	Lakewood	282G	80214	1600-1699	
	Lakewood	282C	80214	2500-2599	
	Lakewood	282C	80214	2600-2799	
	Westminster	192Y	80021	9300-9399	
	Wheat Ridge	252Y	80033	2800-3499	
	Wheat Ridge	252U	80033	3500-4199	
	Wheat Ridge	252Q	80033	4200-4799	
QUAY ST S	Denver	342U	80123	None	
	Jefferson Co	372U	80128	8300-8499	
	Lakewood	282U	80226	1-199	
	Lakewood	282Y	80226	400-499	
	Lakewood	312L	80232	1800-1899	
	Lakewood	312Y	80227	3400-3499	
QUAY WAY	Westminster	192T	80021	9800-9999	
QUAY WAY S	Denver	312U	80227	2700-2999	
QUAY WAY S	Jefferson Co	372Q	80128	8200-8299	
QUEBEC AVE	Longmont	41R	80501	300-599	
	Longmont	41Q	80501	600-899	
QUEBEC CT S	Centennial	376F	80112	7100-7399	
QUEBEC PKWY	Commerce City	226T	80022	None	
QUEBEC ST	Adams Co	256B	80022	5600-6098	E
	Adams Co	226P	80022	6200-7798	E
	Adams Co	226F	80022	7800-8299	
	Commerce City	256B	80022	5001-6099	O
	Commerce City	226P	80022	6201-7799	O
	Commerce City	226F	80022	8300-8599	
	Denver	286T	80230	1-99	
	Denver	286K	80230	100-698	E
	Denver	286K	80220	101-1099	O
	Denver	286F	80220	1100-1999	
	Denver	286B	80207	2000-2799	
	Denver	256X	80207	2800-3999	
	Denver	256P	80216	4000-4999	
	Denver	256G	80022	5000-5598	E
	Thornton	166X	80602	11900-14799	
	Thornton	136T	80602	14800-16799	
QUEBEC ST S	Arapahoe Co	316P	80231	2100-2498	E
	Centennial	376F	80111	6400-6699	
	Centennial	376F	80112	6700-8299	
	Denver	286T	80230	1-299	
	Denver	286X	80247	300-699	
	Denver	316B	80247	700-999	
	Denver	316K	80231	1900-2098	E
	Denver	316P	80231	2401-2799	O
	Denver	316T	80231	2900-2998	E
	Denver	346B	80237	3500-4199	
	Denver	346F	80237	4300-5099	
	Greenwood Village	346P	80111	5100-6299	
	Highlands Ranch	406J	80130	9200-10299	
	Highlands Ranch	406J	80124	10300-11099	
	Highlands Ranch	376X	80130	None	
QUEBEC WAY S	Arapahoe Co	316B	80231	1001-1399	O
	Arapahoe Co	316M	80231	1800-2099	
	Denver	286T	80230	2-98	E
	Denver	316B	80231	1000-1398	E
	Denver	316G	80231	1400-1799	
QUEEN CIR	Arvada	221T	80004	6900-6999	
	Arvada	221P	80005	7400-7599	
QUEEN CIR S	Lakewood	281X	80226	300-499	
QUEEN CT	Arvada	251B	80004	6000-6199	
QUEEN CT	Broomfield	163U	80020	3100-3399	
QUEEN CT	Wheat Ridge	251P	80033	4600-4699	
QUEEN CT S	Jefferson Co	311F	80232	1500-1599	
	Jefferson Co	341F	80127	4300-4399	
	Jefferson Co	341P	80127	5300-5399	
	Jefferson Co	371B	80127	6400-6799	
QUEEN DR S	Lakewood	311K	80227	1900-1999	
QUEEN LN S	Jefferson Co	371B	80127	6800-6899	
QUEEN RD S	Jefferson Co	371B	80127	6700-6799	
QUEEN ST	Arvada	251B	80004	5800-6199	
	Arvada	221T	80004	6600-7199	
	Arvada	221P	80005	7200-7699	
	Arvada	221F	80005	8000-8599	
	Lakewood	281B	80215	2500-2599	
	Westminster	191K	80021	10500-10799	
QUEEN ST S	Jefferson Co	311F	80232	1500-1699	
	Jefferson Co	341K	80127	4400-4999	
	Jefferson Co	341T	80127	5500-5899	
	Lakewood	281X	80226	300-499	
	Lakewood	311P	80227	2200-2299	

P Q

STREET NAME	CITY or COUNTY	MAP GRID	ZIP CODE	BLOCK RANGE	O/E
QUEEN WAY S	Jefferson Co	311K	80232	1700-1899	
	Jefferson Co	341T	80127	5300-5499	
	Jefferson Co	341X	80127	6000-6099	
	Jefferson Co	371B	80127	6100-6799	
	Lakewood	311B	80226	700-999	
QUEENS DR	Longmont	11Q	80501	1700-1899	
QUEENSBURG CT S	Aurora	351Y	80016	6300-6399	
	Aurora	381C	80016	6500-6599	
QUEENSBURG WAY S	Aurora	381L	80016	None	
QUEENSCLIFFE CT S	Highlands Ranch	405D	80130	9500-9599	
QUEENSCLIFFE DR S	Highlands Ranch	405D	80130	9500-9799	
QUEENS CRESCENT WAY	El Paso Co	909N	80132	None	
QUEENSMERE DR	El Paso Co	908Z	80132	17800-18099	
QUEENSVIEW ST	Adams Co	750H	80603	None	
QUEMOY CIR S	Arapahoe Co	350T	80015	5500-5599	
	Aurora	380B	80016	6600-6699	
	Aurora	380P	80016	None	
	Centennial	350T	80015	5700-5899	
QUEMOY CT S	Aurora	350B	80018	3800-3999	
	Aurora	350F	80018	4200-4299	
	Aurora	350X	80016	6200-6299	
	Aurora	380B	80016	None	
	Centennial	350T	80015	5600-5699	
QUEMOY ST S	Aurora	380F	80016	7100-7199	
	Aurora	380K	80016	None	
QUEMOY WAY S	Aurora	350B	80018	3600-4599	
	Aurora	380B	80016	6400-6599	
	Aurora	380P	80016	None	
	Centennial	350T	80015	5700-5799	
QUENCY ST	Adams Co	769G	80022	None	
QUENCY WAY	Adams Co	769C	80022	None	
QUENTIN ST	Aurora	287R	80011	300-599	
	Aurora	287M	80011	800-1399	
	Aurora	287H	80010	1600-1999	
	Aurora	257Z	80011	3100-3599	
	Denver	257V	80239	3700-3899	
	Denver	257H	80239	4800-5499	
QUENTIN ST S	Aurora	287Z	80012	600-699	
	Aurora	317D	80112	1100-1198	E
	Centennial	377H	80112	6800-7099	
QUENTIN WAY S	Aurora	317R	80014	2100-2299	
QUICK FOX CT	Castle Rock	466Z	80109	None	
QUICK FOX CT	Elbert Co	871B	80107	35300-35399	
QUICKSILVER AVE N	Castle Rock	498M	80104	1-199	
QUICKSILVER AVE S	Castle Rock	498M	80104	1-299	
QUICKSILVER RD	Boulder Co	42L	80501	11900-12699	
QUICKSILVER RD	Frederick	726G	80516	3300-3399	
QUIETO CT	Denver	254N	80211	4400-4599	
QUIETO CT S	Denver	314E	80223	1300-1699	
QUIETO WAY S	Denver	314A	80223	800-899	
	Denver	314E	80223	1200-1299	
QUIET RETREAT CT	Boulder Co	71J	80503	7000-7199	
QUIGLEY CIR	Firestone	707T	80504	6800-6999	
QUIGLEY DR W	Denver	343F	80236	3800-3999	
QUIGLEY ST	Adams Co	223E	80031	8300-8499	
	Adams Co	223A	80031	8600-8999	
QUILL LN	Elbert Co	871H	80107	33500-33699	
QUINCE AVE	Boulder	97L	80304	800-1899	
QUINCE CIR	Boulder	97L	80304	600-799	
QUINCE CIR	Thornton	136T	80602	None	
QUINCE CIR S	Centennial	376F	80112	7000-7099	
	Centennial	376P	80112	8000-8099	
QUINCE CT	Boulder Co	98K	80301	4200-4299	
QUINCE CT	Thornton	166P	80602	13000-13099	
	Thornton	136X	80602	None	
	Thornton	166X	80602	None	
QUINCE CT S	Centennial	376G	80112	7300-7399	
	Centennial	376L	80112	7600-7699	
QUINCE DR	Thornton	194X	80260	None	
QUINCE ST	Adams Co	166T	80602	12400-12899	
	Commerce City	226K	80022	7800-7999	
	Commerce City	226B	80640	None	
	Commerce City	226F	80022	None	
	Denver	286U	80230	1-99	
	Denver	286P	80230	301-399	O
	Denver	286P	80230	600-799	
	Denver	286K	80220	1100-1999	
	Denver	286B	80207	2000-2299	
	Thornton	136T	80602	None	
	Thornton	166X	80602	None	
QUINCE ST S	Arapahoe Co	316G	80231	1200-1298	E
	Arapahoe Co	316G	80247	None	
	Centennial	376G	80112	6800-7599	
	Denver	286U	80230	100-199	
	Denver	316B	80247	900-998	E
	Denver	316K	80231	1900-1999	
	Denver	316T	80231	2700-2799	
	Denver	346B	80237	3700-3899	
	Denver	346G	80237	4000-4199	
QUINCE WAY	Thornton	136X	80602	None	
QUINCE WAY S	Arapahoe Co	316G	80231	1100-1299	
	Centennial	376P	80112	7900-8099	
	Denver	316U	80231	3000-3099	
QUINCEY AVE	Firestone	707T	80504	6700-6999	
QUINCY AVE E	Arapahoe Co	810N	80137	28201-31299	O
	Arapahoe Co	811P	80137	31300-36999	
	Arapahoe Co	813P	80136	52100-53699	
	Arapahoe Co	812P	80102	None	
	Arapahoe Co	813P	80102	None	
	Aurora	348G	80015	13700-16799	
	Aurora	349G	80015	16800-21699	
	Aurora	350F	80015	21700-23299	
	Aurora	350H	80016	23300-23999	
	Aurora	351E	80016	24000-28199	
	Cherry Hills Village	344H	80113	800-1699	
	Cherry Hills Village	345G	80110	1700-4299	
	Denver	346F	80237	7000-7999	
	Denver	346H	80237	8000-8399	
	Englewood	344H	80113	1-799	
QUINCY AVE W	Denver	343E	80236	3700-4899	
	Denver	342G	80235	5200-6999	
	Englewood	344F	80110	1-1599	
	Jefferson Co	342E	80123	7900-8999	
	Jefferson Co	341H	80123	9000-9999	
	Jefferson Co	341F	80235	10000-11599	
	Jefferson Co	341E	80465	11600-12699	
QUINCY AVE W (Cont'd)	Jefferson Co	340L	80465	12700-14799	
	Lakewood	342E	80123	7000-7899	
	Sheridan	343G	80110	3000-3299	
	Sheridan	343G	80236	3300-3599	
QUINCY DR E	Arapahoe Co	350E	80015	None	
QUINCY DR W	Lakewood	342F	80235	7700-7899	
QUINCY LN E	Aurora	348G	80015	15600-15699	
QUINCY PL E	Arapahoe Co	350E	80015	None	
	Aurora	348G	80015	15500-15599	
	Aurora	349G	80015	18700-18899	
	Centennial	349H	80015	19600-19899	
QUINCY PL W	Jefferson Co	341F	80127	11201-11399	O
	Jefferson Co	341F	80465	11600-11799	
	Jefferson Co	341E	80465	12000-12099	
QUINCY ST W	Sheridan	344E	80110	1700-2099	
QUINLIN CT N	Douglas Co	440X	80134	5500-5699	
QUINN AVE W	Littleton	373H	80120	2400-2499	
QUINN CIR E	Aurora	348F	80015	14000-14299	
QUINN DR W	Jefferson Co	341E	80465	12200-12499	
QUINN PL E	Aurora	348G	80015	15500-15599	
	Aurora	349G	80015	18700-19099	
QUINN PL W	Denver	343F	80236	3800-4499	
QUINN ST	Boulder	128F	80303	900-999	
QUINTANA LN	Erie	103X	80516	None	
QUINTERO CIR S	Aurora	349A	80013	3700-3899	
	Aurora	349J	80015	4700-5099	
	Centennial	349S	80015	5600-5899	
	Foxfield	379E	80016	7300-7499	
QUINTERO CT S	Arapahoe Co	349S	80016	5900-5999	
	Aurora	319A	80017	900-999	
	Aurora	349E	80013	4200-4299	
	Aurora	349J	80015	4700-4799	
	Centennial	349N	80015	5200-5399	
	Centennial	379J	80016	7600-7699	
QUINTERO ST	Aurora	289E	80011	1600-1999	
	Commerce City	769E	80022	10000-10499	
	Commerce City	769A	80022	None	
	Commerce City	769A	80022	None	
QUINTERO ST S	Aurora	319A	80017	1000-1099	
	Aurora	319J	80013	1900-2299	
	Aurora	319S	80013	2700-3199	
	Aurora	319W	80013	3200-3399	
	Aurora	349A	80013	3500-3799	
	Aurora	349J	80015	4500-4899	
	Centennial	349N	80015	5100-5199	
	Centennial	349N	80015	5300-5399	
	Foxfield	379E	80016	7100-7299	
QUINTERO WAY S	Aurora	289W	80017	300-599	
	Aurora	319E	80017	1300-1399	
	Aurora	319E	80017	1600-1699	
	Aurora	319J	80017	1700-1899	
	Aurora	319N	80013	2500-2699	
	Aurora	319S	80013	3000-3099	
	Aurora	349A	80013	3900-4099	
	Aurora	349E	80013	4200-4299	
	Centennial	349N	80015	5400-5599	
QUITMAN CT	Adams Co	223X	80003	6600-6699	
	Broomfield	163X	80020	None	
QUITMAN LN	Westminster	193B	80031	11900-11998	E
QUITMAN PL	Westminster	193B	80031	None	
QUITMAN ST	Adams Co	253F	80212	5200-5399	
	Adams Co	223X	80003	6100-6599	
	Denver	283T	80219	1-399	
	Denver	283P	80204	400-1099	
	Denver	283K	80204	1200-1599	
	Denver	283B	80212	2000-2699	
	Denver	253P	80212	2700-5199	
	Westminster	223P	80030	7500-7599	
	Westminster	223K	80030	7600-7999	
	Westminster	193X	80031	9200-9399	
	Westminster	193B	80031	None	
QUITMAN ST S	Denver	283T	80219	1-699	
	Denver	313F	80219	700-2099	
	Denver	313T	80219	2300-2699	
	Denver	313T	80236	2700-3199	
	Denver	343K	80236	3200-4699	
QUITMAN WAY	Westminster	223P	80030	7400-7499	
	Westminster	193T	80031	9700-9799	
QUITMAN WAY S	Denver	313P	80219	2200-2299	
QUITO PL	Douglas Co	466D	80108	300-399	
QUIVAS CIR	Westminster	194A	80234	11600-11699	
QUIVAS DR N	Westminster	164N	80234	None	
QUIVAS LOOP	Westminster	194E	80234	11200-11299	
QUIVAS RD	Douglas Co	886M	80118	8300-8499	
QUIVAS ST	Adams Co	254E	80221	5200-5399	
	Adams Co	254E	80221	5500-5599	
	Adams Co	224N	80221	7000-7399	
	Adams Co	224J	80221	7400-7799	
	Adams Co	134W	80020	14800-14899	
	Adams Co	134S	80020	15200-15599	
	Broomfield	164J	80020	13600-13799	
	Denver	284N	80223	300-399	
	Denver	284N	80204	400-599	
	Denver	284J	80204	1100-1299	
	Denver	254S	80211	3200-4799	
	Denver	254J	80221	4800-4899	
	Northglenn	194J	80234	10400-10699	
	Thornton	194N	80260	10000-10399	
	Westminster	164N	80234	13100-13399	
	Westminster	164P	80234	13400-13599	
QUIVAS ST S	Denver	284W	80223	500-699	
	Denver	314E	80223	700-1699	
	Sheridan	314W	80110	3200-3499	
QUIVAS WAY	Adams Co	224J	80221	7800-7999	
	Adams Co	224E	80221	8300-8399	
	Westminster	193H	80234	11300-11399	
	Westminster	194A	80234	11400-11699	
QUIVER CT	Lafayette	132P	80026	1700-1799	
QUIVIRA DR	Adams Co	224H	80229	1200-8399	
R					
RABBIT DR	Lakewood	281J	80401	12200-12399	
RABBIT BRUSH WAY	Parker	378V	80134	8400-8599	
RABBIT EARS PASS	Jefferson Co	371E	80127	12100-12199	
RABBIT MOUNTAIN RD	Boulder Co	704B	80503	6400-7199	
	Boulder Co	10E	80503	7300-7599	
RABBIT MOUNTAIN RD	Broomfield	163J	80020	3700-4799	
	Broomfield	163P	80020	None	
RABBIT RUN DR	Golden	279J	80401	800-899	
RACCOON CIR	Clear Creek Co	304H	80439	1-299	
RACCOON CT	Lafayette	132W	80026	2600-2699	
RACE CIR S	Centennial	375A	80121	6500E-6699E	
RACE CT	Adams Co	165J	80602	13600-13799	
	Denver	255J	80216	5100-5199	
	Thornton	164R	80241	13000-13099	
	Thornton	135J	80602	None	
RACE CT S	Centennial	345W	80121	6300-6499	
	Centennial	375N	80122	7900-7999	
	Greenwood Village	345N	80121	5300-5499	
RACE ST	Adams Co	225S	80229	6700-6899	
	Adams Co	225N	80229	7300-7499	
	Adams Co	225E	80229	8200-8399	
	Denver	285S	80206	100-1999	
	Denver	285A	80205	2000-2699	
	Denver	255W	80205	2700-3999	
	Denver	255N	80216	4300-5199	
	Northglenn	165W	80233	12000-12299	
	Thornton	225A	80229	8800-8999	
	Thornton	195W	80229	9100-9399	
	Thornton	195S	80229	9600-9999	
	Thornton	165N	80241	13300-13499	
	Thornton	135W	80602	14900-14999	
	Thornton	135J	80602	16400-16499	
	Thornton	165A	80602	None	
RACE ST S	Centennial	375E	80122	6700-7099	
	Centennial	375J	80122	7500-7899	
	Denver	285W	80209	300-699	
	Denver	315A	80209	700-1099	
	Denver	315E	80210	1100-1599	
	Denver	315S	80210	2000-3099	
	Englewood	315W	80113	3100-3499	
	Greenwood Village	345N	80121	5100-5399	
	Greenwood Village	345S	80121	5900-5999	
RACE WAY	Thornton	195S	80229	9600-9699	
RACE WAY S	Centennial	375N	80122	8000-8099	
RACER ST	Adams Co	792M	80102	None	
RACHAEL PL	Castle Pines North	436C	80108	500-599	
RACINE CIR	Commerce City	197M	80022	None	
RACINE CIR S	Aurora	317H	80112	1500-1599	
	Centennial	347Z	80111	6200-6599	
RACINE CT	Brighton	197H	80640	11300-11399	
	Brighton	167Z	80640	11800-11999	
	Commerce City	197M	80022	None	
RACINE ST	Adams Co	167V	80640	12400-12599	
RACINE ST	Aurora	287R	80011	400-599	
	Aurora	287M	80011	800-1399	
	Aurora	287H	80010	1700-1798	E
	Aurora	257Z	80011	3100-3199	
	Commerce City	197M	80022	None	
	Denver	257H	80239	5500-5599	
RACINE ST S	Aurora	287Z	80012	300-398	E
	Aurora	287Z	80012	600-699	
	Aurora	317V	80014	2900-2998	E
RACINE WAY	Aurora	287H	80010	1600-1799	
	Commerce City	197M	80022	None	
RACINE WAY S	Aurora	317D	80112	1100-1198	E
	Aurora	317R	80014	2100-2499	
RACOON CIR	Clear Creek Co	304H	80439	1-299	
RACOON LN	Douglas Co	850T	80116	3200-3399	
RACOON PL	Douglas Co	432R	80125	9500-9599	
RACQUET CT	Boulder	129E	80303	5500-5599	
RACQUET LN	Boulder	129E	80303	700-5599	
RADBOURNE CT	El Paso Co	908Z	80132	17700-17899	
RADCLIFF AVE	Cherry Hills Village	346E	80111	6300-6499	
RADCLIFF AVE E	Arapahoe Co	350E	80015	None	
	Cherry Hills Village	344H	80113	800-1199	
	Denver	346H	80237	8300-8899	
	Englewood	344H	80113	1-799	
	Greenwood Village	346H	80111	8900-9199	
RADCLIFF AVE W	Denver	343F	80236	3600-5099	
	Englewood	344F	80110	1-799	
	Englewood	344E	80110	1100-1599	
	Jefferson Co	341E	80465	11600-12799	
	Lakewood	342F	80123	7000-7599	
	Sheridan	344E	80110	1800-2199	
	Sheridan	343G	80110	3000-3299	
RADCLIFF CIR E	Aurora	348F	80015	14000-14299	
RADCLIFF DR E	Arapahoe Co	350E	80015	None	
	Aurora	348F	80015	13900-14599	
	Aurora	348G	80015	14900-15299	
RADCLIFF DR W	Jefferson Co	341F	80127	11200-11499	
	Sheridan	343G	80110	3000-3299	
RADCLIFF PKWY E	Arapahoe Co	350K	80015	None	
RADCLIFF PL E	Aurora	348F	80015	13800-14899	
	Aurora	348G	80015	15300-15599	
	Aurora	348H	80015	15900-16499	
	Aurora	349F	80015	18500-18699	
	Aurora	349G	80015	18700-18799	
	Centennial	349H	80015	19700-19999	
	Greenwood Village	346H	80111	9100-9199	
RADCLIFFE DR W	Jefferson Co	341H	80123	8900-9199	
RADCLIFFE PL	Longmont	10U	80503	1600-1699	
RADCLIFFE PL W	Jefferson Co	342E	80123	8500-8999	
	Jefferson Co	341H	80123	None	
RAFFERTY GARDENS W	Littleton	344P	80120	1-399	
RAFTER RD	Douglas Co	469V	80116	7000-7299	
	Douglas Co	470S	80116	7300-7899	
RAIN ST	Lochbuie	140A	80603	None	
RAINBOW AVE	Adams Co	225E	80229	8400-8799	
RAINBOW CIR	Elbert Co	890G	80107	26900-27699	
RAINBOW DR	Adams Co	225A	80229	2200-2599	
RAINBOW LN	Broomfield	163J	80020	4300-4599	
RAINBOW PL	Douglas Co	846U	80135	4000-4199	
RAINBOW WAY	Boulder Co	129G	80303	900-1099	
RAINBOW CREEK RD	Douglas Co	846U	80135	4000-7599	
RAINBOW CREST DR	Jefferson Co	276X	80401	1-199	
RAINBOW HILL RD	Jefferson Co	276X	80401	28800-30799	
RAINBOW TRAIL S	Jefferson Co	276X	80401	None	
RAIN DANCE TRAIL	Douglas Co	432T	80125	5800-6299	
RAINDROP LN	Jefferson Co	307H	80401	1300-1399	
RAINDROP WAY	Castle Rock	496G	80109	1000-1599	
RAINLEAF CT	Elbert Co	871B	80107	35500-35699	
RAINLILLY LN	Boulder	97L	80304	800-999	
RAINRIBBON RD	Highlands Ranch	404Q	80126	10700-10999	

STREET NAME	CITY or COUNTY	MAP GRID	ZIP CODE	BLOCK RANGE	O/E
RAINTREE CIR	Douglas Co	848M	80108	4800-4899	
	Douglas Co	439W	80108	4900-5299	
RAINTREE CT	Louisville	130Y	80027	700-799	
RAINTREE CT E	Louisville	131W	80027	100-499	
RAINTREE DR	Douglas Co	469A	80134	5200-5299	
	Douglas Co	468D	80134	5500-5699	
RAINTREE LN	Dacono	727S	80514	None	
RAINTREE LN S	Louisville	131W	80027	100-199	
RALEIGH CIR	Castle Rock	498R	80104	5600-6199	
RALEIGH CT	Adams Co	223X	80003	6600-6699	
	Westminster	193X	80031	9300-9399	
	Westminster	193K	80031	11000-11099	
RALEIGH PL	Westminster	223J	80030	7800-7999	
	Westminster	193A	80031	None	
RALEIGH ST	Adams Co	253F	80212	5200-5399	
	Adams Co	223X	80003	6100-6599	
	Broomfield	163K	80020	13600-13799	
	Denver	283T	80219	1-399	
	Denver	283P	80204	400-1099	
	Denver	283K	80204	1200-1599	
	Denver	283B	80212	2000-2699	
	Denver	253P	80212	2700-5199	
	Westminster	223T	80030	6900-7199	
	Westminster	223N	80030	7400-7799	
	Westminster	223J	80030	7800-7999	
	Westminster	223E	80031	8000-8199	
	Westminster	193X	80031	9000-9399	
	Westminster	193P	80031	9700-10099	
RALEIGH ST S	Denver	283X	80219	1-699	
	Denver	313F	80219	700-2099	
	Denver	313T	80219	2200-2699	
	Denver	313S	80236	2700-3499	
	Denver	343K	80236	3500-4699	
RALEIGH PEAK RD	Jefferson Co	843Z	80470	17400-17799	
	Jefferson Co	844X	80441	None	
RALPH CT	Adams Co	224F	80221	800-899	
RALPH LN	Adams Co	224F	80221	8100-8399	
RALSTON CT	Frederick	727G	80530	7900-7999	
RALSTON RD	Arvada	252G	80002	6400-8799	
	Arvada	252A	80002	8800-8999	
	Arvada	251C	80004	9600-11199	
	Arvada	221Y	80004	None	
RALSTON ST	Boulder	97C	80304	None	
RALSTON ST	Frederick	727F	80530	6100-6399	
RALSTON CREEK LN	Gilpin Co	761U	80403	400-2099	
RALSTON CREEK RD	Jefferson Co	762S	80403	10500-10799	
RAMBLE LN	Parker	410X	80138	None	
RAMBLEWOOD CT	Castle Rock	497D	80104	1900-2199	
RAMBLING OAK PL	Douglas Co	470D	80134	9000-9099	
RAMBLIN ROSE RD	El Paso Co	909R	80908	5300-5899	
RAMIREZ CIR	Erie	103N	80516	None	
RAMONA AVE W	Douglas Co	825V	80125	9000-9499	
RAMONA RD	Boulder Co	742W	80403	1-199	
RAMPART CT	Douglas Co	432L	80125	10000-10199	
RAMPART DR	Jefferson Co	843F	80433	13300-13899	
RAMPART LN	Jefferson Co	843E	80433	25700-25899	
RAMPART LN N	Douglas Co	825V	80125	10500-10999	
RAMPART RD	Elbert Co	831T	80138	45200-45899	
RAMPART ST	Federal Heights	223D	80260	9000-9099	
	Federal Heights	193Z	80260	9100-9199	
RAMPART WAY	Denver	286U	80230	100-599	
RAMPART WAY	Douglas Co	432L	80125	7600-7899	
RAMPART RANGE RD	Douglas Co	432L	80125	6200-9999	
	Douglas Co	886S	80135	None	
	Douglas Co	906K	80118	None	
	Douglas Co	906K	80135	None	
	El Paso Co	906K	80863	None	
RAMPART RANGE RD	Jefferson Co	371L	80127	7700-7999	
RAMPART RANGE RD	Teller Co	906K	80863	None	
RAMPART RANGE RD N	Douglas Co	825Z	80125	9000-9999	
RAMPART STATION DR	Parker	409V	80134	None	
RAMSGATE CT E	Highlands Ranch	405A	80126	2500-2599	
RAMSHEAD CT S	Highlands Ranch	406F	80130	9900-9999	
RAMSHORN DR	Douglas Co	466B	80108	100-3199	
RAMS HORN RUN	Broomfield	133L	80020	None	
RANCH CIR	Thornton	195Q	80229	None	
RANCH DR	Mead	706G	80542	None	
RANCH DR	Westminster	193H	80234	2100-2399	
RANCH LN	Jefferson Co	368C	80465	6700-6799	
RANCH PL	Westminster	193H	80234	11200-11299	
RANCH RD	Boulder Co	721C	80481	1-799	
RANCH RD	Castle Rock	527B	80104	None	
RANCH RD	Clear Creek Co	335J	80439	1-499	
RANCH RD	Elbert Co	850M	80138	40500-40999	
RANCH RD	Thornton	195Q	80229	None	
RANCH RD N	Jefferson Co	340X	80127	6300-6999	
RANCH RD S	Highlands Ranch	404D	80126	9900-9999	
RANCH RD W	Jefferson Co	369Q	80465	1-99	
RANCH WAY	Park Co	841Q	80421	1-399	
RANCH ELSIE DR	Jefferson Co	762C	80403	30800-31199	
RANCH ELSIE RD	Jefferson Co	762B	80403	11100-11799	
RANCH ELSIE RD W	Jefferson Co	762B	80403	11600-11999	
RANCHERO DR	Monument	908W	80132	2100-2399	
RANCHERO RD	Jefferson Co	305A	80439	33800-34799	
RANCHETTES RD	Park Co	841Q	80421	1-299	
RANCH GATE CT	Douglas Co	527R	80104	3600-3799	
RANCH GATE TRAIL	Douglas Co	527R	80104	2000-2199	
RANCH HAND LN	Douglas Co	527R	80104	3700-3799	
RANCH HAND RD	El Paso Co	912X	80831	17500-18799	
RANCHO CT	Jefferson Co	843A	80433	12600-27699	
RANCHO ST	Lochbuie	729Y	80603	None	
RANCHO MONTECITO DR	Douglas Co	411S	80138	10100-10399	
RANCH RESERVE LN	Westminster	193G	80234	2600-2999	
RANCH RESERVE PKWY	Westminster	193C	80234	2500-11499	
RANCH RESERVE RIDGE	Westminster	193G	80234	2300-2699	
RANCH RIVER CIR	Highlands Ranch	375X	80126	9000-9199	
RANCH TRAIL W	Jefferson Co	369K	80465	1-99	
RAND CT	Jefferson Co	842C	80433	30400-30599	
RAND RD	Jefferson Co	842C	80433	30400-30699	
RAND WAY	Superior	160Q	80027	100-1299	
RANDALL RIDGE RD	Gilpin Co	761C	80403	1-399	
RANDOLPH AVE	Castle Rock	498R	80104	5800-6099	
RANDOLPH PL	Denver	257H	80239	12200-13099	
	Denver	258E	80239	13100-15099	
	Denver	258H	80239	None	
	Denver	259H	80249	None	
	Denver	259H	80249	None	
	Denver	260E	80249	None	

STREET NAME	CITY or COUNTY	MAP GRID	ZIP CODE	BLOCK RANGE	O/E
RANDOM CT	Boulder Co	102J	80026	11000-11299	
RANDOM RD	Cherry Hills Village	345F	80113	1-99	
RANDOM RD	Park Co	841Q	80421	1-399	
RANDOM WAY	Boulder Co	102J	80026	11100-11399	
RANDOM VALLEY CIR	Douglas Co	850P	80134	11000-11499	
RANDY DR	Douglas Co	409W	80134	5300-5699	
	Douglas Co	409W	80134	None	
RANGE CIR	Mead	706G	80542	None	
RANGE RD	Boulder Co	741Q	80466	1-399	
RANGE ST	Boulder	128D	80301	1600-1899	
RANGER RD N	Douglas Co	381W	80138	13000-13299	
RANGEVIEW CIR	Wheat Ridge	251Y	80215	1-99	
RANGEVIEW CT	Gilpin Co	761W	80403	1-599	
RANGEVIEW DR	Gilpin Co	761S	80403	200-1299	
RANGE VIEW DR	Jefferson Co	823R	80465	19900-20699	
RANGEVIEW DR	Littleton	373H	80120	100-499	
	Littleton	374E	80120	400-899	
RANGEVIEW DR	Park Co	841M	80421	1-299	
RANGEVIEW DR	Wheat Ridge	251Y	80215	1-99	
RANGEVIEW LN	Douglas Co	825Z	80125	9200-9399	
RANGEVIEW LN	Longmont	11X	80501	901-999	O
RANGEVIEW PL	Thornton	195R	80229	None	
RANGEVIEW PL	Wheat Ridge	251Y	80215	1-99	
RANGE VIEW RD	El Paso Co	907V	80132	3500-3899	
RANGEVIEW ST	Firestone	707S	80504	None	
RANGEVIEW TRAIL	Jefferson Co	277P	80401	300-699	
RANNOCH DR	Longmont	12Q	80501	1800-1999	
RAPHAEL LN	Douglas Co	432E	80125	7100-8399	
RAPP LN	Northglenn	194S	80260	9800-9899	
RAPP ST	Littleton	343V	80120	5700-5899	
RAPTOR POINT RD	Gilpin Co	781H	80403	1-399	
RARITAN CIR S	Englewood	314S	80110	2600-2699	
RARITAN CT	Denver	254N	80211	4500-4599	
	Westminster	163R	80234	13100-13399	
RARITAN PL	Boulder	129J	80303	5400-5499	
	Adams Co	254E	80221	5200-5398	E
RARITAN ST	Adams Co	223R	80221	7000-7299	
	Adams Co	224J	80221	7400-8099	
	Adams Co	133Z	80020	14900-14999	
	Denver	284W	80223	2-98	E
	Denver	254S	80211	4100-4599	
	Denver	254J	80221	4800-5099	
	Westminster	193H	80234	11200-11299	
	Westminster	163M	80234	13100-13599	
RARITAN ST S	Denver	284W	80223	1-699	
	Denver	314E	80223	700-2099	
	Englewood	314S	80110	2100-2899	
RARITAN WAY	Adams Co	253H	80221	5300-5599	
	Adams Co	254E	80221	5300-5599	
	Denver	284N	80223	300-399	
	Denver	284N	80204	400-599	
	Thornton	193R	80260	10000-10099	
	Westminster	163M	80234	13400-13599	
RASBERRY DR	Clear Creek Co	801A	80452	1-199	
RASPBERRY MOUNTAIN	Jefferson Co	371Q	80127	10500-10799	
RASPBERRY CT	Frederick	706Z	80504	None	
RASPBERRY DR	Frederick	706Z	80504	None	
	Frederick	726D	80504	None	
RASPBERRY RUN	Douglas Co	432S	80125	6800-6899	
RATHBONE CIR	El Paso Co	908R	80132	19600-19699	
RATTLESNAKE DR	Lone Tree	406F	80124	7300-7599	
RAVEN CT	Boulder Co	130F	80303	7800-7899	
RAVEN CT	Castle Pines North	436L	80108	7400-7499	
RAVEN DR	Clear Creek Co	780P	80452	1-399	
RAVEN DR	Park Co	841V	80421	1-599	
RAVEN ST	Firestone	707S	80504	None	
RAVEN CREST RD	Jefferson Co	339N	80465	19700-19999	
RAVEN GULCH RD	Jefferson Co	339N	80465	5200-19999	
RAVENHILL CIR E	Highlands Ranch	405B	80126	2600-3099	
RAVENNA PL	Longmont	40U	80503	None	
RAVEN RUN	Broomfield	133W	80026	4700-4899	
RAVEN RUN	Douglas Co	845Q	80125	10500-10599	
RAVENSWOOD CT	Highlands Ranch	405L	80130	4200-4399	
RAVENSWOOD CT	Park Co	841N	80421	1-299	
RAVENSWOOD LN	Highlands Ranch	405L	80130	10200-10499	
RAVENSWOOD RD	Cherry Hills Village	345B	80113	1-99	
RAVENSWOOD WAY	Highlands Ranch	405L	80130	10300-10499	
RAVENWOOD LN	Lafayette	131F	80026	2500-2699	
RAVENWOOD RD	Boulder Co	129G	80303	900-1299	
RAVINE CT	Lochbuie	140F	80603	1-99	O
RAVINE PL	Lochbuie	140F	80603	100-199	
RAVINE WAY	Lochbuie	140F	80603	None	
RAWHIDE CIR	Castle Rock	467Y	80104	3600-3999	
RAWHIDE CIR	Elbert Co	870H	80107	1000-1399	
RAWHIDE CT	Boulder Co	723K	80302	5000-6099	
RAWHIDE CT	Elbert Co	871W	80107	29100-29999	
RAWHIDE DR	Elbert Co	871W	80107	2100-2699	
RAWLINS WAY	Lafayette	132P	80026	None	
RAY DR	Douglas Co	908L	80118	15000-15999	
RAYBURN ST	Adams Co	750H	80603	None	
RAYMER LN	Superior	160M	80027	1000-1199	
REA AVE	Jefferson Co	823N	80433	25700-26499	
READING CT S	Denver	316U	80231	2700-2999	
READING WAY S	Denver	346G	80237	4000-4199	
REASONER DR	Adams Co	168U	80603	15700-15799	
RECREATION DR	Douglas Co	409E	80134	None	
RED ASH LN	Boulder Co	159D	80303	1100-1499	
RED BARN RD	El Paso Co	912T	80831	17000-17199	
RED BIRCH	Jefferson Co	370Q	80127	1-99	
RED BIRD CT	Castle Rock	468X	80104	None	
REDBIRD ST	Longmont	41R	80501	1200-1299	
RED BIRD WAY	Frederick	726F	80516	None	
RED BIRD TRAIL	Castle Rock	468X	80104	None	
RED BRUSH PL	Parker	408R	80134	16500-16599	
REDBUD	Brighton	139M	80601	None	
REDBUD ST	Brighton	139M	80601	None	
RED BUSH TRAIL	Highlands Ranch	375W	80126	8800-8899	
RED CANYON DR	Highlands Ranch	376T	80130	6100-6299	
RED CEDAR	Jefferson Co	370Q	80127	1-99	
RED CEDAR CIR	Elbert Co	830L	80138	400-499	
RED CEDAR DR	Highlands Ranch	405L	80130	None	
REDCEDAR ST	Frederick	727F	80530	None	
RED CLIFF CIR	Jefferson Co	339R	80465	16500-16799	
RED CLIFF WAY	Castle Rock	497E	80109	1400-1499	
RED CLOUD DR	Jefferson Co	843B	80433	24600-25699	
RED CLOUD RD	Longmont	12N	80501	1700-2099	
RED CLOUD ST	Thornton	193V	80260	None	
RED CLOUD WAY	Broomfield	133N	80020	15900-15999	

STREET NAME	CITY or COUNTY	MAP GRID	ZIP CODE	BLOCK RANGE	O/E
RED CLOUD WAY	Jefferson Co	823X	80433	12000-12099	
RED CLOUD PEAK	Jefferson Co	371P	80127	11400-11499	
RED CLOUD RIDGE	Elbert Co	892Z	80106	21100-21199	
RED CLOUD TRAIL	Douglas Co	890W	80118	None	
RED CLOVER CT	Parker	378V	80134	8600-8699	
RED CLOVER LN	El Paso Co	908U	80132	18200-18299	
RED CLOVER WAY	Brighton	138Y	80601	1500-1599	
REDCONE PL	Highlands Ranch	405M	80130	None	
REDCONE WAY	Highlands Ranch	405M	80130	None	
RED CROSS WAY	Denver	286Q	80230	None	
REDCUFF DR	Broomfield	133L	80020	2600-2699	
RED CURRANT PL	Douglas Co	411W	80138	None	
RED DEER CT	Jefferson Co	340N	80465	16200-16299	
RED DEER DR	Boulder Co	100W	80301	7300-7499	
RED DEER RD	Douglas Co	870E	80116	1-799	
RED DEER TRAIL	Broomfield	163J	80020	3600-13399	
RED DEER TRAIL	Lafayette	131E	80026	3000-3199	
REDDINGTON ST	Erie	103A	80516	None	
RED ELDER ST S	Parker	439F	80134	None	
RED FALCON WAY	Longmont	42D	80501	None	
RED FEATHER PT	Lafayette	131G	80026	2000-2099	
RED FERN CT	Douglas Co	432X	80125	5600-5699	
REDFERN PL	Longmont	41P	80501	1600-1699	
RED FERN RUN	Douglas Co	845Q	80125	5500-5699	
REDFIELD CIR	Longmont	12P	80501	2100-2199	
RED FOREST RD	El Paso Co	907Y	80132	4300-4799	
RED FOX CIR	Elbert Co	851E	80138	40800-40899	
RED FOX CT	Douglas Co	432L	80125	7500-7599	
RED FOX DR	Jefferson Co	367N	80439	7500-7999	
RED FOX LN	Greenwood Village	346N	80111	1-99	
RED FOX LN	Jefferson Co	370F	80127	1-99	
RED FOX LN E	Centennial	349R	80015	19900-20299	
RED FOX PL E	Highlands Ranch	374V	80126	1600-1899	
RED FOX WAY	Douglas Co	432L	80125	7300-7499	
RED FOX TRAIL	Boulder Co	99G	80301	4500-4699	
RED GULCH RD	Boulder Co	703F	80540	1-499	
REDHAVEN WAY	Highlands Ranch	405P	80126	2900-3299	
RED HAWK CT	Frederick	706Y	80504	3400-3499	
RED HAWK DR	Castle Rock	466V	80109	1900-1999	
	Castle Rock	497A	80109	1900-1999	
	Castle Rock	467W	80109	None	
RED HAWK LN	Frederick	706Y	80504	3400-3499	
REDHAWK LN	Jefferson Co	308C	80401	22100-22199	
RED HAWK PKWY	Brighton	139R	80601	5200-5399	
RED HAWK PL	Broomfield	133V	80020	None	
RED HAWK RIDGE DR	Castle Rock	496D	80109	2100-2199	
REDHAWK RUN	Cherry Hills Village	345B	80113	1-99	
RED HILL CIR	Boulder Co	723E	80302	6700-6799	
RED HILL RD	Boulder Co	723E	80302	6000-6799	
REDHILL RD	Douglas Co	887M	80118	7900-8099	
RED LANE ST	Adams Co	750D	80603	None	
RED LEAF CT	Longmont	42N	80501	None	
RED LILY PL	Clear Creek Co	335J	80439	1-399	
RED LOCUST	Jefferson Co	370Q	80127	1-99	
RED LODGE DR	Jefferson Co	306E	80439	1200-1399	
RED MAPLE CIR	Elbert Co	851E	80138	2100-2299	
RED MAPLE DR	Jefferson Co	370L	80127	1-99	
RED MESA CT	Douglas Co	432P	80125	7100-7299	
RED MESA DR	Douglas Co	432K	80125	7000-7199	
RED MESA RD	Jefferson Co	825N	80125	9800-10099	
RED MICA WAY	Monument	908X	80132	1200-1499	
REDMOND DR	Longmont	40K	80503	4200-4499	
RED MONTEREY CT	Parker	439D	80134	12200-12299	
RED MOON RD	Jefferson Co	306G	80401	1000-1099	
RED MOUNTAIN	Jefferson Co	371Q	80127	8000-8099	
RED MOUNTAIN DR	Longmont	12Y	80501	1200-1699	
RED OAK CT	Erie	102P	80516	1-199	
RED OAK DR	Longmont	12T	80501	900-1199	
RED OAK WAY	Douglas Co	470A	80134	5000-5299	
RED OAKES CT E	Highlands Ranch	404C	80126	1-99	
RED OAKES DR S	Highlands Ranch	404G	80126	9500-9799	
RED OAKES LN S	Highlands Ranch	404C	80126	9600-9699	
RED OAKES PL S	Highlands Ranch	404G	80126	9600-9799	
RED PASS CT	Douglas Co	466H	80108	5200-5299	
RED PASS LN	Douglas Co	466H	80108	600-699	
RED PASS WAY	Douglas Co	466H	80108	5200-5299	
RED PEAK DR	Castle Rock	497F	80109	1400-1499	
RED POPPY CT	Douglas Co	410Z	80138	9100-9299	
RED POPPY DR	Brighton	168C	80601	1701-1799	O
RED POPPY WAY	Brighton	168C	80601	1400-1599	
RED ROCK CIR	Douglas Co	886M	80118	7600-7999	
RED ROCK CT	Douglas Co	886M	80118	8100-8299	
RED ROCK DR	Douglas Co	887J	80118	4000-4499	
	Douglas Co	886M	80118	4500-5799	
RED ROCK LN	Broomfield	133K	80020	None	
RED ROCK PL	Douglas Co	886M	80118	8100-8299	
RED ROCK RANCH DR	El Paso Co	907U	80132	4400-4699	
RED ROCKS DR	El Paso Co	907Y	80132	17900-18299	
RED ROCKS VISTA DR	Morrison	339C	80465	100-599	
RED ROCKS VISTA LN	Morrison	339C	80465	100-299	
RED ROCKS BUSINESS DR	Lakewood	310N	80228	2000-2699	
	Morrison	310W	80228	100-199	
RED ROCKS PARK RD	Jefferson Co	309U	80401	2500-2899	
RED ROSA CIR S	Parker	439B	80134	None	
RED SKY DR S	Parker	408Z	80134	None	
REDSTONE DR	Broomfield	162L	80020	500-699	
REDSTONE LN	Boulder	128X	80305	3000-3299	
REDSTONE RD	Boulder	743Q	80305	3100-3399	
REDSTONE ST	Highlands Ranch	374V	80126	8500-8699	
REDSTONE RIDGE RD	El Paso Co	907U	80133	4500-4699	
RED SUMAC PL	Douglas Co	411W	80138	None	
REDTAIL CT	Longmont	12U	80501	1500-1599	
REDTAIL DR	Broomfield	162L	80020	None	
RED TAIL DR	Highlands Ranch	375X	80126	1-99	
REDTAIL RD	Gilpin Co	781H	80403	1-199	
RED TAIL RD	Jefferson Co	824X	80127	11800-11899	
RED TAIL RIDGE RD	Clear Creek Co	780E	80452	1000-1099	
RED TAIL TRAIL	Clear Creek Co	304H	80439	1-499	
REDTOP CT	Longmont	40V	80503	1800-1999	
RED TOP RANCH PL E	Douglas Co	439H	80134	20000-20999	
RED TREE PL	Castle Rock	497Y	80104	3200-3399	
REDVALE RD	Highlands Ranch	405P	80126	10600-10699	
REDWING AVE	Highlands Ranch	375U	80126	8700-8999	
RED WING CT	Mead	706C	80542	100-199	
REDWING LN	Broomfield	162Q	80020	1400-1799	
REDWING PL	Boulder Co	69L	80503	6400-7199	
RED WOLF LN	Jefferson Co	339R	80465	17100-17399	
REDWOOD AVE	Boulder	97M	80304	1200-1899	

STREET NAME	CITY or COUNTY	MAP GRID	ZIP CODE	BLOCK RANGE	O/E
REDWOOD AVE	Lafayette	132S	80026	2200-2399	
REDWOOD CIR	Broomfield	192C	80020	200-299	
REDWOOD CT	Boulder Co	98K	80301	4200-4299	
REDWOOD CT	Longmont	11J	80503	2400-2499	
REDWOOD CT E	Highlands Ranch	404G	80126	700-899	
REDWOOD DR	Bow Mar	343N	80123	4800-5199	
REDWOOD PL	Boulder Co	98K	80301	4200-4299	
REDWOOD ST	Thornton	193V	80260	None	
REED CIR	Arvada	222U	80003	7100-7199	
REED CT	Arvada	252G	80002	5400-5599	
	Arvada	222X	80003	6200-6399	
	Arvada	222Y	80003	6400-6599	
	Arvada	222X	80003	6600-6699	
	Arvada	222T	80003	7000-7099	
	Arvada	222P	80003	7100-7199	
	Arvada	222F	80003	8200-8299	
	Broomfield	192C	80020	11600-11699	
	Lakewood	282U	80226	1-99	
	Lakewood	282L	80214	800-999	
	Westminster	192Y	80021	9400-9499	
REED CT S	Jefferson Co	342Y	80123	6300-6399	
	Jefferson Co	372G	80128	6900-7399	
	Jefferson Co	372L	80128	7400-7699	
	Lakewood	282U	80226	1-199	
	Lakewood	282Y	80226	200-499	
	Lakewood	312C	80226	600-899	
	Lakewood	312L	80232	1800-1899	
	Lakewood	312Y	80227	3000-3299	
REED DR	Lakewood	282C	80214	2100-2299	
REED PL	Longmont	42A	80501	1-199	
REED RD	Platteville	708C	80651	100-399	
REED ST	Arvada	252K	80002	5100-5199	
	Arvada	252F	80002	5200-5399	
	Arvada	252G	80002	5400-5499	
	Arvada	252C	80002	5700-5799	
	Arvada	222Y	80003	6200-6399	
	Arvada	222T	80003	6600-6799	
	Arvada	222U	80003	7000-7099	
	Arvada	222Q	80003	7400-7899	
	Broomfield	162Y	80020	11900-11999	
	Jefferson Co	192K	80021	10400-10499	
	Lakewood	282U	80226	1-399	
	Lakewood	282Q	80214	600-899	
	Lakewood	282L	80214	900-1499	
	Lakewood	282G	80214	1500-1999	
	Lakewood	282C	80214	2400-2599	
	Westminster	192T	80021	9800-9999	
	Westminster	192Q	80021	10300-10399	
	Wheat Ridge	282C	80214	2600-2699	
	Wheat Ridge	252Y	80033	2700-3199	
	Wheat Ridge	252U	80033	3300-4199	
	Wheat Ridge	252Q	80033	4200-4799	
REED ST S	Denver	312U	80227	2700-3099	
	Jefferson Co	372Q	80128	8200-8299	
	Jefferson Co	372T	80128	8300-8599	
	Lakewood	282U	80226	1-199	
	Lakewood	282Y	80226	400-599	
	Lakewood	312G	80226	900-1099	
	Lakewood	312G	80232	1100-1499	
	Lakewood	312L	80232	1800-1899	
	Lakewood	312Y	80227	3400-3499	
	Lakewood	342G	80123	4300-4499	
REED WAY	Arvada	252C	80003	None	
	Broomfield	192F	80020	None	
	Westminster	192X	80021	9300-9399	
REED WAY S	Jefferson Co	372C	80123	6300-6699	
	Jefferson Co	372Q	80128	8200-8299	
	Lakewood	342P	80123	5300-5399	
	Lakewood	342U	80123	5800-5899	
REED RANCH RD	Boulder Co	723J	80302	1-1999	
REES CT	Longmont	42A	80501	700-899	
REESE CT	Erie	102U	80516	None	
REFLECTION DR	Weld Co	726E	80516	7101-7299	O
REGAL CT	Louisville	130R	80027	1700-1899	
REGAL PL	Louisville	130R	80027	200-298	E
REGAL ST	Louisville	130R	80027	100-299	
REGATTA LN	El Paso Co	908T	80132	1300-1499	
REGENCY CT S	Parker	410S	80138	11400-11499	
REGENCY PL S	Parker	410S	80138	11400-11499	
REGENCY WAY E	Parker	410S	80138	20500-20599	
REGENT DR	Boulder	128E	80302	None	
REGINA LN	Northglenn	194M	80233	1100-1499	
REGIS BLVD	Denver	253K	80221	3000-3599	
REGIS DR	Boulder	128P	80305	2600-3099	
REGIS RD	Adams Co	253G	80221	5200-5299	
REGULUS DR	Highlands Ranch	376X	80124	13100-13299	
REID TRAIL	Castle Rock	467Q	80108	None	
REINDEER CIR	Douglas Co	870J	80116	10300-10599	
RELIANCE CIR	Superior	160R	80027	1600-1999	
RELIANCE CT	Erie	103X	80516	None	
RELIANCE CT	Superior	160R	80027	1600-1799	
RELIANCE DR	Erie	103X	80516	None	
RELIANCE PL	Erie	103X	80516	None	
RELIC ROCK TERRACE	Douglas Co	408H	80134	10600-16099	
REMINGTON AVE	Firestone	707S	80504	None	
REMINGTON AVE W	Jefferson Co	371Q	80127	10000-11399	
REMINGTON DR	Hudson	730Q	80642	None	
REMINGTON DR W	Jefferson Co	371U	80127	10300-10499	
REMINGTON PL	Douglas Co	466D	80108	300-599	
REMINGTON PL S	Jefferson Co	371V	80128	8900-9999	
REMINGTON PL W	Jefferson Co	372U	80128	6800-6899	
REMINGTON RD	El Paso Co	910Y	80908	16500-17499	
REMMICK RIDGE RD	Douglas Co	850P	80134	10400-10999	
REMMINGTON RD	Elbert Co	851W	80107	2000-2899	
REMUDA CT	Boulder Co	723K	80302	None	
REMUDA LN	Lafayette	132W	80026	200-299	
REMUDA PL	Erie	133B	80516	None	
REMUDA TRAIL	Elbert Co	871T	80107	32000-32599	
RENAISSANCE DR	Longmont	40Q	80503	1300-1699	
RENAUD RD	Park Co	820Z	80421	1-399	
RENAUD ST	Jefferson Co	823N	80433	9800-10099	
RENDEZVOUS CIR	Elbert Co	851H	80107	40000-40999	
RENDEZVOUS DR	Lafayette	131E	80026	300-498	E
RENDEZVOUS DR S	Lafayette	131J	80027	100-299	
RENO DR	Arvada	252G	80002	6700-7099	
	Arvada	252F	80002	7600-8199	
	Arvada	252E	80002	8200-8399	
RENOIR DR	Highlands Ranch	375Z	80126	9000-9099	
RENSHAW ST	Adams Co	794J	80136	None	
RENSSELAER DR	Arvada	221Y	80004	9600-9999	
REPPLIER ST	Boulder	97V	80304	3100-3199	
RESERVE AVE	Lochbuie	729Z	80603	400-599	
RESERVE DR	Boulder Co	129F	80303	6000-6399	
RESERVE DR	Longmont	12U	80501	1200-1399	
RESERVE PL	Broomfield	163F	80020	None	
RESERVE RD	Jefferson Co	842J	80470	None	
RESERVOIR RD	Black Hawk	780D	80422	1-299	
RESERVOIR RD	Castle Rock	497H	80104	1600-1899	
RESERVOIR RD S	Aurora	349G	80013	3800-4299	
	Aurora	349G	80015	4300-4499	
	Centennial	349G	80015	4500-4699	
RESERVOIR DAM RD E	Aurora	351Q	80016	None	
RESORT DR S	Jefferson Co	843E	80433	13200-26999	
RESORT CREEK RD	Jefferson Co	843N	80433	20900-25999	
RETREAT WAY	Douglas Co	847P	80109	4300-4399	
REUNION DR	Commerce City	769E	80022	None	
REUNION PKWY	Commerce City	769E	80022	10000-10399	
REUNION PKWY N	Commerce City	769E	80022	10600-10699	
REVERE CT	Aurora	257Z	80011	12500-12599	
	Aurora	287H	80010	None	
	Commerce City	197M	80022	None	
REVERE PKWY S	Centennial	377D	80111	6300-6699	
	Centennial	377H	80112	6700-7399	
REVERE ST	Aurora	287R	80011	400-599	
	Aurora	287M	80011	700-1399	
	Aurora	257Z	80011	3100-3299	
	Commerce City	197R	80022	None	
	Denver	257V	80239	3700-3899	
	Denver	257H	80239	5500-5599	
REVERE ST S	Aurora	287V	80012	200-299	
	Aurora	287Z	80012	300-399	
	Aurora	317V	80014	2900-2999	
	Aurora	317D	80112	None	
	Aurora	317R	80014	None	
REVERE WAY S	Aurora	317R	80014	2400-2499	
REX LN	Jefferson Co	365Z	80433	8900-9099	
REX ST	Louisville	131W	80027	800-1099	
REYNOLDS AVE	Platteville	708C	80651	300-799	
REYNOLDS DR	Douglas Co	846G	80135	7100-7499	
REYNOLDS ST	Fort Lupton	728L	80621	300-699	
RG 1 RD	Gilpin Co	780F	80403	1-99	
RG 2 RD	Gilpin Co	780G	80403	1600-1999	
	Gilpin Co	780L	80403	None	
RG 3 RD	Gilpin Co	780M	80403	None	
RG 4 RD	Gilpin Co	780M	80403	None	
RHODONITE CT	Castle Rock	467H	80108	1700-1999	
RHODUS ST	Jefferson Co	823N	80433	9700-9899	
RHYOLITE WAY	Douglas Co	469C	80134	5300-5499	
RIALTO DR	Douglas Co	469B	80134	5000-5199	
RIATA CT	Boulder Co	723K	80302	None	
RICARA DR	Boulder	128R	80303	4600-4999	
RICE AVE	Longmont	11P	80501	1800-1999	
RICE AVE W	Jefferson Co	342E	80123	8400-8999	
	Jefferson Co	341H	80123	9000-9199	
RICE CIR E	Aurora	349E	80015	16600-17499	
RICE DR E	Aurora	349G	80015	19100-19299	
RICE PL E	Aurora	348E	80015	13700-13799	
	Aurora	348H	80015	15900-16499	
	Aurora	349G	80015	19200-19299	
RICE PL W	Denver	343E	80236	4100-4899	
	Jefferson Co	342E	80123	8400-8699	
	Jefferson Co	341F	80127	11200-11299	
	Jefferson Co	341E	80465	12000-12199	
RICE ST E	Aurora	348G	80015	15500-15599	
RICHARD CT	Elbert Co	851A	80138	2200-2299	
RICHARD RD	Adams Co	225A	80229	8500-8799	
RICHARD ST	Erie	102D	80516	None	
RICHARD ST	Weld Co	729B	80621	7000-7999	
RICHARD ALLEN CT	Denver	255Y	80205	2900-3199	
RICHARD'S CIR	Elbert Co	891G	80107	27000-27599	
RICHARD'S CT	Elbert Co	891G	80107	5000-5999	
RICHARDS CT	Erie	102D	80516	1100-1299	
RICHARDSON RD	Castle Rock	497M	80104	1-99	
RICHFIELD CIR S	Aurora	319W	80013	3500-3699	
	Aurora	349J	80015	4800-5099	
RICHFIELD CT	Castle Rock	498R	80104	6100-6199	
RICHFIELD CT S	Arapahoe Co	349S	80016	5900-5999	
	Arapahoe Co	349W	80016	6100-6199	
	Aurora	319E	80017	None	
	Centennial	349N	80015	5300-5399	
RICHFIELD ST	Aurora	289J	80011	1000-1399	
	Commerce City	769E	80022	10000-10799	
	Commerce City	769A	80022	None	
RICHFIELD ST E	Centennial	349N	80015	5100-5299	
RICHFIELD ST S	Arapahoe Co	349W	80016	6000-6099	
	Arapahoe Co	349W	80016	6300-6399	
	Arapahoe Co	379A	80016	6400-6599	
	Aurora	289W	80017	600-899	
	Aurora	319E	80017	1600-1699	
	Aurora	319J	80013	2000-2099	
	Aurora	319N	80013	2500-2799	
	Aurora	319S	80013	2800-2999	
	Aurora	319W	80013	3100-3299	
	Aurora	349A	80013	3500-4299	
	Aurora	349J	80015	4500-4599	
	Foxfield	379E	80016	6700-7599	
RICHFIELD WAY	Commerce City	769E	80022	None	
RICHFIELD WAY S	Aurora	319A	80017	900-1099	
	Aurora	319E	80017	1400-1599	
	Aurora	319J	80017	1700-1799	
	Aurora	319N	80013	2100-2199	
	Aurora	319S	80013	2800-2899	
	Aurora	319W	80013	3300-3499	
	Aurora	319W	80013	3500-3599	
	Aurora	349E	80013	3900-4299	
RICHFIELD WAY W	Centennial	349N	80015	5400-5599	
RICHLAWN DR	Douglas Co	439P	80134	5700-5999	
RICHLAWN LN	Douglas Co	439P	80134	5700-5799	
RICHLAWN PKWY	Douglas Co	439P	80134	7000-7299	
RICHMOND	Thornton	194W	80260	None	
	Thornton	224A	80260	None	
RICHMOND CT	Jefferson Co	843A	80433	12400-12499	
RICHMOND DR	Thornton	224A	80260	None	
RICHMOND ST	Black Hawk	780D	80422	100-499	
RICHMOND HILL CT	Douglas Co	466G	80108	5200-5399	
RICHMOND HILL RD	Jefferson Co	843A	80433	16200-28799	
	Jefferson Co	842D	80433	28800-29199	
RICHTHOFEN CIR	Aurora	288K	80011	13700-13899	
RICHTHOFEN CIR E	Aurora	288J	80011	13700-13899	
RICHTHOFEN PL	Aurora	286M	80010	8900-9299	
	Denver	286K	80220	6500-7499	
	Denver	286M	80220	8400-8899	
RICKI DR	Elbert Co	850D	80138	40900-42999	
RIDDLEWOOD CT W	Highlands Ranch	404E	80129	9800-9899	
RIDDLEWOOD LN	Highlands Ranch	404E	80129	800-1299	
RIDDLEWOOD RD W	Highlands Ranch	404E	80129	900-1299	
RIDER CREEK CT	Longmont	42B	80501	700-799	
RIDER RIDGE DR	Longmont	42B	80501	500-799	
RIDER RIDGE PL	Longmont	42B	80501	700-799	
RIDER RIDGE RD	Longmont	42B	80501	601-699	O
RIDGE AVE	Longmont	41R	80501	400-599	
RIDGE CIR	Broomfield	162N	80020	2300-2399	
RIDGE CIR	Park Co	821U	80421	1-199	
RIDGE CT	Littleton	343Z	80120	2400-2599	
RIDGE DR	Boulder Co	97F	80304	1-99	
RIDGE DR	Broomfield	162N	80020	2000-2499	
	Broomfield	161R	80020	2500-2899	
RIDGE DR	Dacono	727J	80514	None	
RIDGE DR W	Lafayette	131G	80026	None	
RIDGE LN	Boulder Co	71F	80504	None	
RIDGE LN	Park Co	840D	80421	1-199	
RIDGE PKWY	Broomfield	190C	80021	11600-11899	
RIDGE PL	Louisville	160C	80027	None	
RIDGE RD	Arvada	252E	80002	8000-8899	
	Arvada	251H	80002	8900-10199	
	Arvada	251K	80033	10200-10399	
	Arvada	251K	80033	11200-11599	
RIDGE RD	Boulder Co	130P	80303	1-299	
RIDGE RD	Boulder Co	740M	80466	1-499	
RIDGE RD	Boulder Co	721C	80481	100-1199	
	Boulder Co	741J	80466	500-4499	
RIDGE RD	Clear Creek Co	801U	80439	1-499	
	Clear Creek Co	335J	80439	500-599	
RIDGE RD	Douglas Co	468N	80108	None	
RIDGE RD	Golden	249S	80403	400-699	
	Golden	248V	80403	700-3099	
	Jefferson Co	336D	80439	3700-3999	
	Jefferson Co	249U	80403	4000-4099	
	Jefferson Co	762B	80403	11600-12099	
RIDGE RD	Park Co	821U	80421	1-699	
RIDGE RD	Wheat Ridge	251K	80033	10400-11199	
	Wheat Ridge	251K	80033	11600-11899	
RIDGE RD N	Castle Rock	498F	80104	1-999	
RIDGE RD N	Park Co	841J	80421	1-599	
RIDGE RD S	Douglas Co	498K	80104	1-2099	
	Douglas Co	528C	80104	2100-3199	
RIDGE RD S	Jefferson Co	843C	80433	11800-12499	
	Jefferson Co	844A	80433	12500-13099	
RIDGE RD S	Park Co	841T	80421	1-2299	
RIDGE RD W	Littleton	374A	80120	1-1999	
RIDGE WAY	Gilpin Co	761F	80403	1-199	
RIDGE WAY	Jefferson Co	277U	80401	24900-25999	
RIDGECREST CIR	Highlands Ranch	404J	80129	10500-10699	
RIDGE CREST LN	Jefferson Co	368L	80465	7400-7499	
RIDGECREST WAY	Highlands Ranch	404J	80129	1700-1899	
RIDGEFIELD LN	Highlands Ranch	405F	80126	10000-10099	
RIDGEGATE CIR	Lone Tree	406M	80124	None	
	Lone Tree	407J	80124	None	
RIDGEGATE PKWY	Lone Tree	407E	80124	10000-10199	
RIDGEGLEN WAY E	Highlands Ranch	374Y	80126	400-1299	
RIDGELINE BLVD	Highlands Ranch	404B	80129	9200-9599	
RIDGELINE BLVD S	Highlands Ranch	374X	80129	8700-9299	
RIDGEMONT CIR	Highlands Ranch	404L	80126	500-899	
RIDGEMONT PL	Highlands Ranch	404L	80126	600-799	
RIDGE OAK DR	Castle Rock	498P	80104	1000-1299	
RIDGE PLAZA DR	Douglas Co	466C	80108	2100-2699	
RIDGE POINT DR	Douglas Co	436D	80108	8700-8899	
RIDGE POINT WAY	Douglas Co	436D	80108	8800-8999	
RIDGE POINTE LN	Parker	410P	80138	10800-10899	
RIDGESIDE DR	Jefferson Co	307C	80401	500-799	
RIDGE TEE DR	Jefferson Co	340S	80465	15800-16099	
RIDGE TERRACE	Elbert Co	890R	80116	1400-1499	
RIDGE TOP RD	Jefferson Co	367L	80439	25300-25599	
RIDGE TRAIL	Bow Mar	342M	80123	5200-5599	
RIDGE TRAIL	Jefferson Co	823N	80433	26900-27399	
RIDGE TRAIL CIR E	Aurora	350X	80016	21900-22099	
RIDGE TRAIL CT	Castle Rock	497H	80104	1500-1799	
RIDGE TRAIL DR	Castle Rock	497H	80104	1300-1399	
RIDGE TRAIL DR E	Aurora	350X	80016	22000-22699	
RIDGE TRAIL LN	Castle Rock	497D	80104	None	
RIDGEVIEW	Elbert Co	870M	80107	None	
RIDGEVIEW AVE	Broomfield	162P	80020	400-1099	
RIDGEVIEW CIR	Broomfield	162P	80020	1100-1199	
RIDGEVIEW CIR	Douglas Co	866B	80135	7000-7199	
RIDGEVIEW CIR	El Paso Co	908P	80132	1500-1699	
RIDGEVIEW CT	Parker	410S	80138	11500-11699	
RIDGEVIEW DR	Erie	133H	80516	3100-3198	E
RIDGEVIEW DR	Jefferson Co	368D	80465	6400-6899	
RIDGEVIEW DR	Longmont	41U	80504	1900-2099	
RIDGEVIEW DR	Louisville	160C	80027	500-1099	
	Louisville	130Q	80027	1500-1599	
RIDGEVIEW DR S	Littleton	373H	80120	7200-7399	
RIDGEVIEW LN	Boulder Co	722M	80302	1-999	
RIDGEVIEW LN	Parker	410S	80138	11600-11899	
	Parker	410W	80138	11900-12099	
RIDGEVIEW WAY	Longmont	41T	80504	2000-2299	
RIDGE VILLAGE DR	Jefferson Co	336F	80439	4100-4199	
RIDGEWAY CIR N	Douglas Co	440P	80134	6700-6899	
	Douglas Co	441T	80134	None	
RIDGEWAY ST	Boulder	98P	80301	None	
RIDGE WOOD CT	Castle Rock	466T	80109	4500-4599	
RIDGEWOOD WAY	Elbert Co	892D	80117	11500-11599	
RIDGLEA WAY	Boulder Co	129G	80303	900-1299	
RIDING HOOD CT	Castle Rock	467W	80109	None	
RIFLE CT	Boulder Co	723K	80302	None	
RIFLE CT	Broomfield	162G	80020	None	
RIFLE CT S	Arapahoe Co	379A	80016	6500-6599	
	Aurora	319A	80017	800-999	
	Aurora	349A	80013	3900-4099	
	Aurora	349J	80015	4900-4999	
	Centennial	349N	80015	5300-5399	
	Centennial	349S	80015	5600-5699	
RIFLE ST	Aurora	289A	80011	2200-2499	

R

STREET NAME	CITY or COUNTY	MAP GRID	ZIP CODE	BLOCK RANGE	O/E
RIFLE ST	Commerce City	769E	80022	None	
RIFLE ST S	Arapahoe Co	349W	80016	6100-6399	
	Aurora	319A	80017	900-999	
	Aurora	319E	80017	1100-1199	
	Aurora	319E	80017	1600-1699	
	Aurora	319J	80013	2000-2099	
	Aurora	319N	80013	2300-2899	
	Aurora	319W	80013	3100-3599	
	Centennial	349N	80015	5400-5599	
RIFLE WAY	Broomfield	162G	80020	400-599	
RIFLE WAY S	Arapahoe Co	379A	80016	6500-6599	
	Aurora	319A	80017	800-899	
	Aurora	319E	80017	1100-1199	
	Aurora	319N	80013	2100-2199	
	Aurora	349E	80013	4000-4199	
RIFLE TERRACE	El Paso Co	910Z	80908	9500-9699	
RIGEL DR	Highlands Ranch	376U	80124	13000-13499	
RIGGI PL	Commerce City	225U	80022	4400-4599	
RILEY CT	Longmont	40U	80503	None	
RILEY DR	Longmont	40U	80503	4000-4299	
RILEY PEAK RD	Jefferson Co	843F	80433	13200-13499	
RIM DR	Broomfield	162N	80020	2300-2699	
RIM RD	Boulder Co	721V	80302	1-599	
RIM OF THE WORLD DR	El Paso Co	908Q	80132	19200-19499	
RIMROCK AVE	Firestone	707S	80504	None	
RIMROCK CIR	Lafayette	131K	80026	2300-2399	
RIMROCK CT	Boulder	69Y	80301	5600-5799	
RIMROCK CT	Highlands Ranch	374Y	80126	9100-9199	
RIMROCK DR	Golden	279G	80401	17200-17999	
RIM ROCK RD	Park Co	841M	80421	1-1099	
RIM VIEW PL	Douglas Co	439X	80134	5500-5599	
RINCONADA RD	Jefferson Co	368F	80465	21800-21999	
RINGSBY CT	Denver	254U	80216	3301-3799	O
RINKER WAY	Broomfield	133M	80020	16600-16799	
RINN VALLEY DR	Frederick	706Y	80504	3200-3599	
RIO CT	Denver	284J	80204	1300-1499	
RIO GRANDE AVE	Douglas Co	847N	80135	4100-4599	
	Douglas Co	846Q	80135	4600-6599	
RIO GRANDE AVE S	Littleton	343V	80120	4900-5699	
RIO GRANDE BLVD	Denver	284S	80223	1-299	
RIO GRANDE DR	Castle Rock	497K	80104	1-99	
RIO GRANDE ST	Brighton	139P	80601	None	
RIO GRANDE ST	Palmer Lake	907R	80133	None	
RIO RANCHO WAY	Brighton	139S	80601	500-699	
RISING LN	Jefferson Co	276W	80401	31000-31099	
RISING MOON WAY	Castle Rock	466Z	80109	None	
RISING SUN AVE	Elbert Co	890H	80107	1000-1099	
RISING SUN DR	Castle Rock	468W	80108	None	
RISING SUN RD	Park Co	840C	80421	200-599	
RISKY DR	Jefferson Co	762Z	80403	27700-27799	
RISKY RD	Jefferson Co	762Z	80403	7300-7399	
RISSE CT	Erie	102P	80516	1-199	
RITA PL	Castle Pines North	436G	80108	400-599	
RITENNOUR CT	Lone Tree	376Z	80124	9200-9299	
RIVA RIDGE ST	Parker	410P	80138	10500-22499	
RIVA ROSE CT	Douglas Co	527K	80104	1200-1299	
RIVER DR	Denver	283D	80211	2500-2699	
RIVER DR	Park Co	841W	80421	None	
RIVER RD	Jefferson Co	843Y	80470	23500-24099	
RIVER RD	Longmont	41G	80501	None	
RIVER RD	Platteville	708C	80651	100-699	
RIVERA PL	Erie	103S	80516	None	
RIVERA ST	Broomfield	163T	80020	12500-12599	
RIVERBEND CT S	Superior	160L	80027	1200-1299	
RIVERBEND LN S	Superior	160M	80027	1600-1699	
RIVER BEND RD	Boulder	128D	80301	4800-4899	
RIVERBEND ST E	Superior	160L	80027	900-1599	
RIVERBEND WAY	Superior	160L	80027	None	
RIVERBROOK CIR	Highlands Ranch	405P	80126	10600-10799	
RIVERCHASE WAY	Parker	410Q	80138	22500-23199	
RIVERDALE AVE	Thornton	195V	80229	4800-5499	
RIVERDALE DR	Parker	410U	80138	11600-11799	
RIVERDALE LN	Thornton	195V	80229	5200-5499	
RIVERDALE RD	Adams Co	166Y	80602	11900-13299	
	Adams Co	167J	80602	13600-14799	
	Adams Co	137X	80602	14800-16099	
	Thornton	225C	80229	8600-9099	
	Thornton	195Y	80229	9100-10399	
	Thornton	195M	80233	10400-10899	
	Thornton	196E	80233	10900-11699	
	Thornton	196E	80640	11700-11899	
RIVERDALE WAY	Parker	410U	80138	22300-22399	
RIVERDALE WAY	Thornton	195V	80229	5300-5499	
RIVER GLEN CT	Broomfield	163G	80020	None	
RIVER GLEN LN	El Paso Co	908Q	80132	19600-19999	
RIVERHAVEN WAY	Jefferson Co	340N	80465	None	
RIVER OAKS LN	Commerce City	197G	80601	None	
RIVER POINT DR	Sheridan	344A	80110	None	
RIVER POINT DR S	Sheridan	344A	80110	None	
RIVER POINT PKWY	Sheridan	344A	80110	None	
RIVER RUN CIR	Commerce City	197C	80640	11400-11699	
RIVER RUN CT	Commerce City	197C	80640	11500-11599	
RIVER RUN PKWY	Commerce City	197B	80640	11200-11699	
RIVER RUN PL	Commerce City	197B	80640	11300-11399	
RIVERSIDE AVE	Boulder	97M	80304	1200-4199	
RIVERSIDE DR	Boulder	97M	80304	2000-2199	
RIVERSIDE DR	Idaho Springs	780R	80452	1700-2899	
RIVERSIDE LN	Boulder	98J	80304	2000-2199	
RIVERSTONE CIR	Commerce City	197G	80601	None	
RIVERSTONE DR	Douglas Co	409E	80134	10100-10299	
RIVERTON RD	Lafayette	132N	80026	None	
RIVERVIEW CT	Longmont	42H	80501	200-399	
RIVERVIEW DR	Broomfield	163G	80020	None	
RIVERVIEW DR S	Jefferson Co	305U	80453	2600-2799	
RIVERVIEW PKWY W	Highlands Ranch	373S	80125	8300-8499	
RIVERWALK CIR W	Littleton	343Q	80123	2600-2899	
RIVER WALK LN	Longmont	41T	80504	2000-2199	
RIVERWOOD WAY	Castle Rock	466Z	80109	None	
RIVERWOOD WAY S	Aurora	381C	80016	6700-7099	
RIVIERA CIR S	Arapahoe Co	350P	80015	5200-5299	
RIVIERA CT	Columbine Valley	373B	80123	1-99	
RIVIERA CT N	Douglas Co	440V	80134	6200-6399	
RIVIERA CT S	Arapahoe Co	350P	80015	5100-5199	
	Aurora	350X	80016	6200-6299	
	Aurora	380B	80016	6700-6799	
	Aurora	380F	80016	None	
	Aurora	380Q	80016	None	
	Centennial	350T	80015	5800-5899	
RIVIERA LN S	Arapahoe Co	350P	80015	5300-5499	
RIVIERA PL	Longmont	41A	80501	2200-2299	
RIVIERA ST S	Arapahoe Co	350K	80015	None	
	Aurora	350F	80018	4000-4199	
	Aurora	380F	80016	6900-7199	
RIVIERA WAY S	Arapahoe Co	350K	80015	None	
	Aurora	380B	80016	6500-6599	
	Centennial	350T	80015	5400-5799	
RIVIERA HILLS DR	Greenwood Village	347N	80111	9300-9399	
RIVINGTON CT	Lone Tree	406M	80124	10400-10599	
ROAD 11A	Gilpin Co	761F	80403	None	
RD 56	Boulder	127J	80302	None	
RD 2915	Weld Co	139E	80603	None	
RD 2930	Weld Co	139E	80603	None	
RD 2940	Weld Co	139E	80603	None	
ROAD A S	Jefferson Co	337N	80439	4900-5299	
ROAD BH2	Gilpin Co	761E	80403	None	
	Gilpin Co	761J	80403	None	
ROAD CC6	Gilpin Co	780G	80403	None	
ROAD GR 5	Gilpin Co	761T	80403	None	
ROAD LC 13	Gilpin Co	761C	80403	None	
ROAD LC 18	Gilpin Co	741Y	80403	None	
RD MM61	Gilpin Co	761K	80403	None	
ROAD OF THE FOUR ROCKS					
	El Paso Co	908P	80132	19800-19899	
ROAD P-11	Park Co	820Y	80421	1-699	
ROAD P-61	Park Co	820X	80421	1-299	
ROAD P-62	Park Co	840B	80421	1-299	
ROAD P-67	Park Co	820Y	80421	1-199	
ROAD P-68	Park Co	820Y	80421	1-299	
ROAD P-69	Park Co	820Y	80421	1-999	
ROAD P-76	Park Co	820X	80421	None	
ROAD P 1184	Park Co	821Z	80470	None	
ROADRUNNER AVE	Firestone	707S	80504	None	
ROADRUNNER CT W					
	Highlands Ranch	404A	80129	1400-1499	
ROADRUNNER DR S	Highlands Ranch	374W	80129	9100-9299	
ROADRUNNER ST S	Highlands Ranch	374W	80129	9100-9299	
	Highlands Ranch	404A	80129	9300-9399	
ROADRUNNER WAY W					
	Highlands Ranch	404A	80129	1500-1599	
RD WV2	Boulder Co	742W	80403	None	
ROAMING DR	El Paso Co	909Q	80908	19700-20399	
ROAN CT	Boulder Co	723K	80302	None	
ROAN CT	Parker	408R	80134	16300-16399	
ROAN DR	Jefferson Co	306X	80439	29000-30099	
ROAN PL	Parker	408R	80134	16400-16499	
ROAN RD	Jefferson Co	306X	80439	3100-3199	
ROANOAK PL	Denver	343K	80236	4100-4399	
ROANOKE PL W	Jefferson Co	340H	80465	12800-13199	
ROARING FORK CIR	Broomfield	163E	80020	1400-14199	
ROARING FORK TRAIL	Boulder Co	99D	80301	6800-7099	
ROBB CIR	Arvada	221F	80005	8400-8499	
	Lakewood	251X	80215	2800-3199	
	Westminster	191K	80021	10500-10599	
ROBB CT	Arvada	221T	80004	6800-6899	
	Arvada	221N	80005	7400-7499	
	Arvada	221K	80005	7600-7699	
	Westminster	191P	80021	10300-10499	
ROBB CT S	Jefferson Co	311F	80232	1300-1599	
	Jefferson Co	341P	80127	5300-5399	
	Jefferson Co	371B	80127	6000-6799	
ROBB DR	Arvada	221N	80005	7200-7299	
	Westminster	191P	80021	10400-10599	
ROBB LN S	Jefferson Co	371B	80127	6600-6699	
ROBB PKWY	Arvada	221K	80005	8000-8099	
ROBB ST	Arvada	251B	80004	5800-6199	
	Arvada	221T	80004	6900-7099	
	Arvada	221N	80005	7300-7699	
	Lakewood	281F	80215	1500-2199	
	Lakewood	281B	80215	2400-2599	
	Westminster	191P	80021	10200-10299	
	Wheat Ridge	251T	80033	3800-3999	
	Wheat Ridge	251P	80033	4400-4799	
ROBB ST S	Jefferson Co	311K	80232	1600-1899	
	Jefferson Co	341K	80127	4400-4999	
	Jefferson Co	341T	80127	5600-5899	
	Jefferson Co	371B	80127	6600-6699	
	Jefferson Co	371F	80127	7000-7399	
ROBB WAY S	Jefferson Co	311K	80232	1500-1799	
	Jefferson Co	341K	80127	4900-4999	
	Jefferson Co	341P	80127	5300-5499	
	Jefferson Co	341X	80127	6000-6399	
	Jefferson Co	371B	80127	6400-6599	
	Lakewood	281X	80226	300-499	
	Lakewood	311B	80226	700-999	
	Lakewood	311K	80227	1900-1999	
	Lakewood	311P	80227	2000-2099	
ROBB LOU DR	Jefferson Co	842A	80470	33700-33899	
ROBERTDALE CT S	Aurora	381G	80016	6800-6999	
ROBERTDALE WAY S	Aurora	381G	80016	6600-7199	
ROBERTS AVE	Boulder Co	131K	80027	9600-9699	
ROBERTS DR	El Paso Co	908S	80132	2800-2899	
ROBERTS RD	Jefferson Co	842G	80470	31100-31299	
ROBERTS RD E	Arapahoe Co	813F	80102	48900-51299	
ROBERTSDALE CT S	Aurora	381M	80016	7800-7899	
	Aurora	351Y	80016	None	
ROBERTSDALE ST	Denver	770T	80249	None	
ROBIN COVE	Lafayette	132N	80026	800-899	
ROBIN CT	Boulder Co	99S	80301	None	
ROBIN CT	Douglas Co	432Q	80125	9600-9699	
ROBIN CT	Elbert Co	871F	80107	35500-36999	
ROBIN DR	Boulder Co	69G	80503	6300-6599	
ROBIN LN	Park Co	841Z	80421	1-99	
ROBIN RD E	Douglas Co	410J	80138	7500-7999	
ROBIN ST	Brighton	138K	80601	None	
ROBIN ST	Lafayette	131R	80026	800-899	
ROBIN WAY	Arapahoe Co	316S	80222	3000-3099	
ROBINCREST LN	Arapahoe Co	373A	80123	1-99	
ROBINDALE WAY	Castle Rock	496B	80109	None	
ROBINE LN	Adams Co	223L	80221	7800-7999	
ROBIN HOOD ST	Lafayette	132P	80026	1300-1799	
ROBINHOOD WAY	El Paso Co	908U	80132	19300-19399	
ROBINS DR	Denver	257H	80239	12900-13099	
	Denver	258E	80239	13100-13199	
	Denver	258F	80239	14400-15099	
	Denver	258H	80239	None	
	Denver	259H	80249	None	
ROBINSON PL	Boulder Co	99F	80301	4500-4599	
ROBINSON WAY	Arvada	252B	80003	7400-7599	
	Arvada	252B	80004	7600-8199	
ROBIN SONG CT	Castle Rock	466Z	80109	None	
ROBINSON HILL RD	Gilpin Co	781C	80403	1300-1799	
	Jefferson Co	782F	80403	30200-35299	
ROBINSON RANCH BLVD S					
	Douglas Co	439S	80134	12300-12599	
ROBINSON RANCH CT S	Douglas Co	439H	80134	12000-15899	
ROBINSON RANCH DR S	Douglas Co	439H	80134	12500-12899	
ROB ROY ST	Englewood	314W	80110	None	
ROCA PL	Douglas Co	466D	80108	300-399	
ROCHESTER CT	Castle Pines North	436Q	80108	7300-7399	
ROCK AVE	Jefferson Co	278T	80401	200-399	
ROCK CIR	Elbert Co	871W	80107	2900-2999	
ROCK LN	Castle Rock	497G	80104	1-99	
ROCK LN	Longmont	12L	80504	12300-12499	
ROCK PT	Broomfield	163K	80020	13600-13799	
ROCK RD	Park Co	840C	80421	200-699	
ROCK ST	Brighton	139S	80601	None	
ROCK ST	Castle Rock	497G	80104	1-99	
ROCKAWAY AVE	Castle Rock	498M	80104	1-299	
ROCKBRIDGE CIR	Highlands Ranch	373U	80129	2700-2999	
ROCKBRIDGE DR	Highlands Ranch	373Y	80129	2400-3299	
ROCKBRIDGE WAY	Highlands Ranch	373Z	80129	2500-2799	
ROCK BROOK BLVD	Douglas Co	409E	80134	None	
ROCK BROOK RD	El Paso Co	907V	80133	500-18999	
ROCK CANYON LN	Jefferson Co	339R	80465	5200-5399	
ROCK CANYON TRAIL	Castle Rock	498M	80104	None	
	Castle Rock	499J	80104	None	
ROCK CREEK CIR	Lafayette	132U	80026	1200-1299	
ROCK CREEK CIR	Superior	160U	80027	2801-2899	O
ROCK CREEK CT	Lafayette	132T	80026	1100-1199	
ROCK CREEK DR	Broomfield	161R	80020	3000-3399	
ROCK CREEK DR S	Castle Rock	466P	80109	5600-5999	
ROCK CREEK PKWY S	Superior	160L	80027	2300-2699	
ROCK CREEK RD	Jefferson Co	822W	80470	33000-34399	
ROCKCRESS WAY	Castle Pines North	436F	80108	1100-1199	
ROCKCRESS WAY	Jefferson Co	307R	80401	2100-2299	
ROCK CRYSTAL DR	Douglas Co	408H	80134	15900-16399	
ROCKDALE PL	Parker	410Y	80138	None	
ROCKDALE ST	Parker	410Y	80138	12000-12199	
ROCK DOVE LN S	Highlands Ranch	403G	80129	9700-9899	
ROCKGLEN CIR	El Paso Co	908P	80132	1400-1599	
ROCKHAMPTON CIR E					
	Highlands Ranch	405D	80130	5300-5499	
ROCKHAMPTON CT	El Paso Co	908R	80132	800-899	
ROCKHAMPTON WAY S					
	Highlands Ranch	405D	80130	9600-9699	
ROCKIES CT	Lafayette	101X	80026	1700-1799	
ROCKINGHORSE PKWY E	Aurora	380V	80138	23100-23499	
ROCK KNOLL DR	Clear Creek Co	304H	80439	1-199	
ROCK LAKE RD	Boulder Co	721C	80481	200-1299	
ROCKLAND DR W	Jefferson Co	371T	80127	10300-11199	
ROCKLAND PL W	Jefferson Co	372U	80128	6800-6899	
	Jefferson Co	371V	80128	9000-9199	
	Jefferson Co	371U	80127	10300-10399	
ROCKLAND RD	Jefferson Co	278W	80401	23600-23999	
	Jefferson Co	277Z	80401	24000-24399	
ROCKLEDGE COVE	Douglas Co	408H	80134	16700-16799	
ROCK LEDGE LN	El Paso Co	908U	80132	18400-18499	
ROCK LEDGE LN	Jefferson Co	340W	80465	6200-6299	
ROCKMONT CIR	Boulder	128W	80305	1400-1599	
ROCKMONT CT	Douglas Co	408G	80134	15500-15599	
ROCKMONT DR	Denver	254W	80202	3500-3599	
ROCKMONT LN	Douglas Co	408G	80134	15600-15699	
ROCK OAK CIR	Douglas Co	866B	80135	900-7199	
ROCK PIPIT CT	Highlands Ranch	375Z	80126	4700-4799	
ROCKPORT LN	Highlands Ranch	375Y	80126	9200-9299	
ROCK RIDGE RD	Jefferson Co	823Q	80465	23000-23299	
ROCK RIDGE RD	Palmer Lake	907U	80133	None	
ROCK RIDGE TRAIL S	Parker	408Y	80134	None	
ROCKROSE CT	Douglas Co	408G	80134	10000-10099	
ROCK ROSE CT	Louisville	130U	80027	800-899	
ROCKROSE DR	Jefferson Co	308J	80401	23600-23799	
ROCK SPUR LN	Jefferson Co	366F	80439	6900-6999	
ROCKSRAY CT	Longmont	11N	80503	2100-2199	
ROCK VALLEY ST	Parker	410V	80138	None	
ROCKVIEW CIR	Superior	160P	80027	1500-1799	
ROCKVIEW DR	Superior	160K	80027	200-299	
ROCKWAY PL	Boulder Co	130F	80303	700-899	
ROCK WILLOW LN E	Parker	408Z	80134	None	
ROCK WILLOW WAY S	Parker	408Y	80134	None	
ROCKWOOD TRAIL	Jefferson Co	368V	80465	20300-20399	
ROCK WREN	Douglas Co	432J	80125	11100-11299	
ROCKY CLIFF CIR	Elbert Co	870G	80107	400-499	
ROCKY CLIFF PL N	Douglas Co	870F	80116	1-399	
ROCKY CLIFF RD	Elbert Co	870G	80107	1-499	
ROCKY CLIFF TRAIL N	Douglas Co	870F	80116	1-499	
ROCKYFORD DR	Palmer Lake	907U	80133	None	
ROCKY MOUNTAIN DR	Castle Rock	466S	80109	4700-5199	
ROCKY MOUNTAIN DR	Lakewood	282F	80214	8000-8299	
ROCKY MOUNTAIN LN	Douglas Co	440D	80138	9000-9199	
ROCKY MOUNTAIN PL	Longmont	42B	80501	700-999	
ROCKY POINT LN	Douglas Co	907G	80118	31700-31999	
ROCKY POINT RD	Jefferson Co	340W	80465	16400-16599	
ROCKY RIDGE RD	Gilpin Co	741Y	80403	1-299	
ROCKY RIDGE RD	Jefferson Co	844E	80127	13500-13599	
ROCKY TOP AVE E	Aurora	380Z	80138	23200-23799	
ROCKY TOP PL E	Aurora	380Z	80138	None	
ROCKY TOP TRAIL	Jefferson Co	844E	80127	17700-18499	
ROCKY VIEW PL	Castle Rock	468U	80108	3600-3899	
ROCKY VIEW PT	Castle Rock	468Y	80108	4900-5099	
ROCKY VIEW RD	Castle Rock	498C	80108	1400-1999	
	Castle Rock	468U	80108	2000-2899	
RODEO CIR	Parker	409R	80138	11000-11499	
RODEO CIR W	Parker	409V	80138	None	
RODEO CT	Elbert Co	832T	80107	44000-44299	
RODEO CT	Longmont	40R	80503	1201-1299	O
RODEO DR	Boulder Co	72B	80504	7400-7799	
RODEO ST	Lochbuie	729Z	80603	1600-1799	
RODER GATE LN	Castle Pines North	436F	80108	1-99	
RODGER'S CIR	Platteville	708B	80651	700-899	
RODGER'S DR	Platteville	708B	80651	None	
RODRIGUEZ CT	Longmont	11Y	80501	1100-1199	
ROE CIR	Douglas Co	869H	80116	9400-9599	
ROGERS CIR	Arvada	249D	80403	6000-6099	

R

STREET NAME	CITY or COUNTY	MAP GRID	ZIP CODE	BLOCK RANGE	O/E
ROGERS CT	Arvada	249D	80403	6100-6199	
	Arvada	219Z	80007	6400-6499	
	Jefferson Co	279V	80401	1-99	
	Jefferson Co	279H	80401	1500-1599	
	Jefferson Co	249H	80403	5500-5599	
ROGERS RD	Boulder Co	40G	80503	8300-9099	
	Boulder Co	41E	80503	9100-9399	
ROGERS RD	Longmont	40G	80503	4000-4099	
ROGERS RD	Park Co	820Y	80421	1-199	
ROGERS RD E	Longmont	42F	80501	1-12599	
ROGERS ST	Arvada	219Z	80403	6300-6399	
	Golden	279M	80401	1000-1499	
	Jefferson Co	219R	80007	7200-7799	
ROGERS WAY S	Jefferson Co	279V	80401	1-199	
ROGGEN WAY E	Superior	160L	80027	900-1199	
ROLAND DR	Park Co	841L	80421	1-2399	
ROLFE CT	Wheat Ridge	251T	80033	3900-4099	
ROLLER COASTER RD	El Paso Co	909W	80132	17400-19799	
ROLLIE AVE	Fort Lupton	728M	80621	100-899	
ROLLING WAY	Parker	379W	80134	9100-9299	
ROLLING HILLS DR	Federal Heights	224A	80260	None	
ROLLING HILLS PL	Elbert Co	830L	80138	300-499	
ROLLING HILLS PL	Parker	408V	80134	16700-16799	
ROLLINS DR	Douglas Co	887L	80118	7500-7799	
ROMA CT	Longmont	40T	80503	1700-1799	
ROMAN NOSE DR	Jefferson Co	823X	80433	23800-24199	
ROMBLON WAY	Northglenn	193M	80234	10400-10599	
ROME AVE	Elbert Co	850C	80138	1-799	
ROME CIR S	Arapahoe Co	350P	80015	5300-5399	
ROME CT S	Aurora	380B	80016	6600-6699	
	Aurora	380Q	80016	None	
	Centennial	350T	80015	5800-5999	
	Arapahoe Co	350P	80015	5200-5599	
	Arapahoe Co	350T	80015	5600-5799	
	Aurora	350F	80018	4000-4199	
	Aurora	380B	80016	6600-6699	
	Aurora	380F	80016	6900-7299	
ROME WAY S	Arapahoe Co	350T	80015	5500-5599	
	Arapahoe Co	350K	80015	None	
	Aurora	350B	80018	3600-3899	
	Aurora	320K	80018	None	
ROMERO LN	Erie	103N	80516	None	
ROMER RANCH RD	Park Co	840C	80421	None	
ROMLEY CT	Parker	409S	80134	None	
ROMOCA LN	Palmer Lake	907U	80133	None	
RONALD LN	Northglenn	194J	80234	10400-10699	
RONNIE RD	Boulder Co	742W	80403	1-499	
ROON RD	Jefferson Co	306T	80439	3100-3199	
ROONEY RD S	Golden	279U	80401	200-399	
	Jefferson Co	309D	80401	700-799	
	Jefferson Co	309D	80401	1100-2099	
	Jefferson Co	309R	80228	None	
	Lakewood	309D	80401	800-1099	
	Lakewood	309R	80228	None	
	Morrison	310W	80465	3000-3099	
ROOSEVELT AVE	Bennett	793J	80102	None	
ROOSEVELT AVE	Louisville	131W	80027	100-599	
ROOSEVELT AVE	Thornton	195X	80229	2400-2899	
ROOSEVELT AVE N	Lafayette	132J	80026	100-198	E
ROOSEVELT AVE S	Lafayette	132J	80026	100-899	
ROOSEVELT DR	Palmer Lake	907U	80133	None	
ROOSEVELT LN	Douglas Co	407D	80112	12500-12999	
ROOSEVELT ST	Palmer Lake	907U	80133	None	
ROOSEVELT WAY	Aurora	289E	80011	1700-1799	
ROSALIE DR	Northglenn	194M	80233	10600-11099	
ROSALIE RD	Park Co	841Q	80421	1-1099	
ROSALIE TRAIL	Jefferson Co	277T	80401	26200-26399	
ROSATO CT	Highlands Ranch	405B	80126	9500-9599	
ROSATO DR	Highlands Ranch	405B	80126	3400-3499	
ROSE CT	Brighton	138U	80601	800-899	
ROSE CT	Louisville	131K	80027	None	
ROSE CT	Thornton	194Z	80229	9200-9499	
ROSE DR	Brighton	138U	80601	700-1399	
ROSE LN	Brighton	138V	80601	1700-1799	
ROSE LN	Commerce City	256A	80022	5800-6099	
ROSE PL	Centennial	376L	80112	None	
ROSE ST	Longmont	11X	80501	900-1099	
ROSE ST	Louisville	131W	80027	100-199	
ROSE ST	Palmer Lake	907R	80133	None	
ROSEANNA DR	Northglenn	194J	80234	1200-10999	
ROSEBAY CIR E	Parker	409A	80134	17000-17299	
ROSEBUD AVE	Jefferson Co	336Z	80439	28300-28399	
ROSEBUD PL	Douglas Co	378V	80134	8600-8799	
ROSE CLOVER	Jefferson Co	370F	80127	1-99	
ROSE CROWN AVE	Castle Rock	466Q	80109	None	
ROSE CROWN CT	Douglas Co	887F	80118	7200-7299	
ROSEDALE CT	Castle Rock	498R	80104	900-1099	
ROSEDALE ST	Castle Rock	498R	80104	1001-1299	O
	Castle Rock	498R	80104	1300-1699	
ROSE FINCH CIR W	Highlands Ranch	404F	80129	300-499	
ROSE HILL DR	Boulder	127G	80302	900-1099	
ROSEHILL LN	Lochbuie	729Z	80603	None	
ROSE HILL ST	Adams Co	794J	80136	None	
ROSE HIP LN	Clear Creek Co	304H	80439	1-199	
ROSELAND AVE	Boulder Co	11M	80504	10500-10599	
ROSEMARY CIR S	Centennial	376L	80112	7500-7699	
ROSEMARY CT	Castle Rock	497A	80109	1500-1699	
ROSEMARY CT	Thornton	166X	80602	None	
	Thornton	136X	80602	None	
ROSEMARY CT S	Centennial	376Q	80112	8000-8099	
ROSEMARY DR	Castle Rock	497A	80109	1200-1899	
ROSEMARY LN	Adams Co	253H	80221	2600-5399	
ROSEMARY ST	Commerce City	226G	80022	8000-8799	
	Denver	286U	80230	1-99	
	Denver	286L	80230	900-1099	
	Denver	286L	80220	1100-1999	
	Denver	286C	80207	2000-2299	
	Thornton	166Q	80602	12800-12999	
	Thornton	166K	80602	None	
	Thornton	166Y	80602	None	
ROSEMARY ST	Thornton	136X	80602	None	
ROSEMARY ST S	Arapahoe Co	316Q	80231	None	
	Denver	286U	80230	1-299	
	Denver	316L	80231	1600-1699	
	Denver	316U	80231	2900-3099	
ROSEMARY WAY	Denver	256Q	80238	None	
ROSEMARY WAY	Thornton	136X	80602	None	

STREET NAME	CITY or COUNTY	MAP GRID	ZIP CODE	BLOCK RANGE	O/E
ROSEMARY WAY S	Arapahoe Co	316C	80231	1101-1299	O
	Arapahoe Co	316Q	80231	None	
	Centennial	376L	80112	7600-7799	
	Denver	346C	80237	3700-4199	
ROSEMONT AVE	Lone Tree	406H	80124	9700-9899	
ROSE PETAL CT	Castle Rock	496D	80109	1800-2099	
ROSE PETAL LN	Castle Rock	497A	80109	1400-1799	
ROSE QUARTZ PL	Castle Rock	467L	80108	400-499	
ROSE RIDGE RD N	Douglas Co	381S	80138	13500-13899	
ROSE TUGGLE LN	Lone Tree	407J	80124	None	
ROSEWALK CIR W	Highlands Ranch	403G	80129	3600-3699	
ROSEWALK CT W	Highlands Ranch	403F	80129	3700-3799	
ROSEWALK DR S	Highlands Ranch	403G	80129	9800-9899	
ROSEWIND CIR	Douglas Co	527Y	80104	1200-1299	
ROSEWOOD AVE	Boulder	97G	80304	None	
	Boulder	97H	80304	None	
ROSEWOOD AVE	Firestone	707S	80504	None	
ROSEWOOD CIR S	Centennial	344Z	80121	6100-6199	
ROSEWOOD CT	Highlands Ranch	404C	80126	9300-9399	
ROSEWOOD CT	Parker	409M	80138	19600-19899	
ROSEWOOD DR	Centennial	344Z	80121	6100-6199	
ROSEWOOD DR	Lakewood	280H	80215	2000-2199	
ROSEWOOD WAY	El Paso Co	908T	80132	19100-19199	
ROSITA AVE	Palmer Lake	907U	80133	None	
ROSLYN AVE S	Denver	346C	80237	4000-4199	
ROSLYN CIR	Denver	286C	80207	2000-2099	
ROSLYN CIR S	Centennial	376C	80112	6800-6899	
ROSLYN CT	Denver	286L	80230	900-1099	
ROSLYN CT	Thornton	136U	80602	None	
ROSLYN CT S	Centennial	376L	80112	7600-7699	
ROSLYN ST	Commerce City	226K	80022	7800-7999	
	Commerce City	226F	80022	8400-8599	
	Denver	286U	80230	100-298	E
	Denver	286Q	80230	501-599	O
	Denver	286Q	80230	700-1098	E
	Denver	286L	80220	1100-1999	
ROSLYN ST	Denver	286C	80207	2200-2299	
	Denver	286C	80238	2600-2799	
	Denver	256Y	80207	2800-3599	
	Denver	256F	80238	5400-5598	E
	Thornton	166P	80602	12900-12999	
	Thornton	166K	80602	None	
	Thornton	136U	80602	None	
	Thornton	166X	80602	None	
ROSLYN ST S	Arapahoe Co	316U	80231	2500-2698	E
	Denver	286U	80230	1-299	
	Denver	316G	80231	1500-1599	
	Denver	316U	80231	2700-3099	
	Denver	346G	80237	4000-4199	
	Greenwood Village	346Q	80111	5300-5399	
ROSLYN WAY	Denver	256Y	80220	None	
	Thornton	136X	80602	None	
	Thornton	166X	80602	None	
ROSLYN WAY S	Centennial	376Q	80112	7900-7999	
ROSS CT	Westminster	191K	80021	10600-10799	
ROSS LN	Highlands Ranch	375W	80126	1700-1999	
ROSS PL	Westminster	191K	80021	10500-10599	
ROSS RD S	Jefferson Co	339W	80465	6200-6499	
ROSS ST	Westminster	191K	80021	10500-10799	
ROSSMAN LN	Erie	103N	80516	None	
ROSSMAN GULCH RD	Jefferson Co	368J	80465	7200-8299	
ROTHERWOOD CIR	Highlands Ranch	405M	80130	10200-10399	
ROTHROCK PL	Longmont	42E	80501	100-199	
ROUGH CT	Castle Rock	497A	80109	1800-1999	
ROUND HILL CIR	Elbert Co	851E	80138	41100-41199	
ROUND ROCK ST S	Highlands Ranch	374Y	80126	8900-8999	
ROUND TABLE DR	Lafayette	132P	80026	1-299	
ROUNDTOP LN	Douglas Co	848J	80108	800-1099	
ROUNDTREE AVE E					
	Greenwood Village	346V	80111	8700-8899	
ROUNDTREE CT	Boulder	98P	80304	3600-3699	
ROUNDTREE DR	Highlands Ranch	375X	80126	9100-9299	
ROUNDUP PL	Longmont	12K	80501	900-999	
ROUNDUP RD N	Douglas Co	411D	80138	12200-13099	
ROUNDUP RD N	Douglas Co	381Z	80138	None	
ROUTT CIR	Lakewood	251X	80215	2900-3099	
ROUTT CT	Arvada	251B	80004	5900-6199	
	Arvada	221K	80005	7600-7699	
	Arvada	221P	80005	None	
	Westminster	191K	80021	10700-10799	
ROUTT CT S	Jefferson Co	341K	80127	4700-4799	
	Jefferson Co	341P	80127	5100-5199	
	Lakewood	311B	80226	800-999	
	Lakewood	311K	80227	1900-1999	
	Lakewood	311P	80227	2000-2099	
	Lakewood	311K	80228	None	
ROUTT DR	Arvada	221N	80005	7200-7299	
ROUTT LN	Arvada	221N	80005	7400-7599	
	Westminster	191P	80021	10400-10599	
ROUTT ST	Arvada	251B	80004	5800-6199	
	Arvada	221T	80004	6700-7199	
	Arvada	221N	80005	7300-7399	
	Jefferson Co	221K	80005	8000-8199	
	Lakewood	281F	80215	1500-2299	
	Lakewood	281B	80215	2400-2599	
	Lakewood	251X	80215	3100-3199	
	Westminster	191P	80021	10000-10399	
	Westminster	191K	80021	10500-10799	
	Wheat Ridge	251X	80033	3200-3399	
	Wheat Ridge	251T	80033	3800-3999	
	Wheat Ridge	251P	80033	4500-4799	
ROUTT ST S	Jefferson Co	341K	80127	4400-4999	
	Jefferson Co	341T	80127	5500-5899	
	Jefferson Co	341X	80127	6000-6299	
	Jefferson Co	371B	80127	6300-6899	
ROUTT WAY	Westminster	191K	80021	10500-10799	
ROUTT WAY S	Jefferson Co	311F	80232	1100-1499	
	Jefferson Co	311K	80232	1600-1799	
	Jefferson Co	341P	80127	5300-5499	
	Jefferson Co	371B	80127	6700-6799	
	Lakewood	281X	80226	400-499	
	Lakewood	311B	80226	700-799	
ROWE PL	Frederick	706Z	80530	8400-8499	
ROWENA PL	Lafayette	131L	80026	100-199	
ROWENA ST	Thornton	194V	80229	1100-1999	
	Thornton	195S	80229	1500-1999	

STREET NAME	CITY or COUNTY	MAP GRID	ZIP CODE	BLOCK RANGE	O/E
ROWLAND AVE W	Arapahoe Co	373E	80128	4900-5199	
	Jefferson Co	372H	80128	5200-6299	
	Jefferson Co	372G	80128	6300-7199	
	Jefferson Co	371G	80127	10600-10799	
	Jefferson Co	371F	80127	11000-11199	
	Littleton	373H	80120	2400-2999	
ROWLAND CIR E	Aurora	380F	80016	21700-21799	
ROWLAND CIR W	Jefferson Co	372G	80128	6300-6799	
ROWLAND CT E	Aurora	380E	80016	None	
ROWLAND DR E	Aurora	380G	80016	22500-22899	
	Aurora	380F	80016	None	
ROWLAND DR W	Jefferson Co	371F	80127	11000-11099	
ROWLAND PL E	Aurora	380F	80016	21500-22199	
	Aurora	381E	80016	24700-24799	
ROWLAND PL W	Jefferson Co	372H	80128	5200-6399	
	Jefferson Co	372E	80128	8600-8899	
	Jefferson Co	371G	80127	10000-10599	
	Littleton	373G	80120	2800-2999	
ROWLEA	Commerce City	769E	80022	None	
ROWLOCK WAY	Douglas Co	408L	80134	10200-10399	
ROWORTH ST	Central City	780C	80427	200-499	
ROXANA POINT DR	Jefferson Co	307Y	80439	25600-25699	
ROXBOROUGH DR	Douglas Co	432T	80125	1-11299	
	Douglas Co	432J	80125	None	
ROXBOROUGH PARK RD	Douglas Co	846E	80125	6500-9099	
	Douglas Co	403S	80125	9000-11599	
	Douglas Co	432U	80125	None	
ROXBOROUGH PARK RD N					
	Douglas Co	825Z	80125	10000-11599	
ROXBURY AVE W	Jefferson Co	372G	80128	6800-7199	
	Jefferson Co	371G	80127	10100-11499	
ROXBURY CIR E	Aurora	381E	80016	24200-24499	
ROXBURY DR E	Aurora	380G	80016	None	
	Aurora	380H	80016	None	
ROXBURY DR W	Jefferson Co	372G	80128	6300-6799	
	Jefferson Co	372E	80128	8700-8899	
	Jefferson Co	371F	80127	11400-11499	
ROXBURY LN	Lochbuie	729Z	80603	None	
ROXBURY PL E	Aurora	380G	80016	22400-22499	
	Aurora	381E	80016	24500-24599	
	Aurora	381E	80016	24900-24999	
	Aurora	381F	80016	25000-25199	
	Aurora	381G	80016	26800-26999	
	Aurora	380H	80016	None	
ROXBURY PL W	Jefferson Co	372H	80128	5300-6399	
	Jefferson Co	372G	80128	6400-6699	
	Jefferson Co	371H	80128	9700-9899	
	Jefferson Co	371G	80127	10200-10299	
	Jefferson Co	371F	80127	11100-11499	
ROXWOOD LN	Boulder	129E	80303	800-1099	
ROYAL CT	Broomfield	163U	80020	12800-12899	
ROYAL CT	Park Co	820X	80421	1-299	
ROYAL DR	Park Co	820X	80421	1-899	
ROYAL ST	Federal Heights	223D	80260	9000-9099	
	Federal Heights	193Z	80260	9100-9199	
ROYAL ST	Longmont	41G	80501	1-99	
ROYAL ANN DR	Greenwood Village	346U	80111	1-99	
ROYAL ARCH WAY	Broomfield	163P	80020	13200-13299	
ROYAL ARCHERS LN	El Paso Co	908U	80132	19000-19099	
ROYAL CREST CT	El Paso Co	909W	80132	1300-1499	
ROYAL EAGLE LN S	Highlands Ranch	404K	80129	10000-10399	
ROYAL EAGLE RD	Highlands Ranch	404K	80129	None	
ROYAL EAGLE ST S	Highlands Ranch	404K	80129	10200-10399	
ROYAL MEADOWS AVE E	Parker	410V	80138	23900-24199	
ROYAL PINE ST	Brighton	139M	80601	None	
	Brighton	140N	80601	None	
ROYAL TROON	El Paso Co	908V	80132	19100-20099	
ROYAL TROON DR	Castle Rock	497R	80104	None	
ROYAL TROON LN	Castle Rock	497Q	80104	None	
ROYAL TROON LN	El Paso Co	909N	80132	19100-20099	
ROY CLARKE BLVD	Douglas Co	410M	80138	11100-11199	
ROY SMITH RD	Gilpin Co	780F	80403	500-999	
ROZENA DR	Boulder Co	704F	80503	7000-7199	
	Boulder Co	10N	80503	7300-7499	
RUBEY DR N	Golden	248V	80403	100-199	
RUBY AVE	Firestone	707S	80504	5100-5299	
RUBY LN N	Douglas Co	441Q	80138	6800-6999	
RUBY ST	Boulder Co	98J	80304	4400-4499	
RUBY WAY	Longmont	41U	80504	1300-1399	
RUBY WAY	Superior	160U	80027	3100-3199	
RUBY FOREST TRAIL	Jefferson Co	276W	80401	300-499	
RUBY HILL DR	Frederick	726G	80516	6300-6399	
RUBY RANCH PL E	Douglas Co	439S	80134	20000-20199	
RUBY RANCH RD	Jefferson Co	306A	80401	29600-31999	
RUBY TRUST CT	Douglas Co	466H	80108	600-699	
RUBY TRUST DR	Douglas Co	466M	80108	600-699	
RUBY TRUST WAY	Douglas Co	466M	80108	600-699	
RUCKER RD	Gilpin Co	741X	80403	1-199	
RUDD RD	Jefferson Co	366V	80439	8700-8999	
RUDI LN	Boulder Co	742W	80403	1-1299	
RUDI LN	Gilpin Co	742W	80403	1W-299W	
RUDIN CIR	Jefferson Co	306L	80439	29200-29299	
RUDOLPH RANCH RD	Gilpin Co	761K	80403	1-199	
RUE DE TRUST	Weld Co	103C	80516	1000-1999	
RUFOUS WAY	Lafayette	101X	80026	None	
RUGER CT	Elbert Co	851W	80107	36800-36999	
RUMBA WAY	Lochbuie	729Z	80603	500-599	
RUNNING BEAR TRAIL	Jefferson Co	842J	80470	None	
RUNNING BROOK LN	Elbert Co	871B	80107	35300-35699	
RUNNING BROOK RD	Elbert Co	851S	80107	2800-3999	
RUNNING BUFFALO RD	Douglas Co	870S	80116	9600-9899	
RUNNING CREEK LN	Parker	410S	80138	11500-11599	
RUNNING DEER DR	Castle Rock	466W	80109	3100-3899	
RUNNING DEER RD	Jefferson Co	823X	80433	23700-24399	
RUNNING FOX CIR	Elbert Co	851L	80107	5500-5598	E
RUNNING FOX WAY	Douglas Co	470A	80134	7700-7799	
RUSHMORE	Weld Co	706N	80504	3300-3399	
RUSHMORE ST	Elizabeth	871E	80107	100-499	
RUSSELL AVE	Jefferson Co	823N	80433	9500-9699	
RUSSELL BLVD	Thornton	194Y	80229	300-9099	
RUSSELL CIR	Frederick	727A	80504	5700-7499	
RUSSELL CT	Arvada	249D	80403	6100-6199	
	Arvada	219V	80007	7000-7199	
	Arvada	219R	80007	None	
	Jefferson Co	219R	80007	7200-7299	
RUSSELL CT S	Jefferson Co	279V	80401	1-99	
RUSSELL DR	Frederick	727E	80504	7100-7199	
RUSSELL LN	Arvada	249D	80403	6000-6099	

R

STREET NAME	CITY or COUNTY	MAP GRID	ZIP CODE	BLOCK RANGE	O/E
RUSSELL ST	Arvada	249D	80403	6000-6099	
	Golden	279R	80401	800-899	
	Golden	279M	80401	1400-1499	
	Jefferson Co	279M	80401	1100-1199	
RUSSELL WAY	Arvada	219Z	80007	6400-6499	
	Jefferson Co	219M	80007	None	
	Thornton	194Z	80229	9200-9699	
RUSSELL GULCH RD	Jefferson Co	307X	80439	1-3399	
RUSSELLVILLE RD	Douglas Co	869C	80116	1-999	
RUSSELLVILLE RD S	Douglas Co	870N	80116	1-4599	
	Douglas Co	890A	80116	4600-6999	
RUSSET LN	Highlands Ranch	375T	80126	8300-8499	
RUSSET SKY CT	Castle Rock	468W	80104	None	
RUSSET SKY TRAIL	Castle Rock	468W	80104	None	
RUSSIAN SAGE LN	Douglas Co	411S	80138	9600-9699	
RUSTIC AVE	Firestone	707S	80504	5401-5499	O
RUSTIC DR	Longmont	12V	80501	None	
RUSTIC DR E	Douglas Co	409M	80138	6500-6999	
RUSTIC KNOLLS DR	Boulder Co	99N	80301	5700-5899	
RUSTIC REDWOOD CT	Highlands Ranch	405K	80126	10200-10399	
RUSTIC REDWOOD LN	Highlands Ranch	405K	80126	10200-10299	
RUSTIC REDWOOD WAY	Highlands Ranch	405K	80126	10100-10299	
RUSTIC TRAIL	Boulder Co	99H	80301	4400-7299	
RUSTLER'S RD	Park Co	841A	80421	1-1099	
RUSTLERS RAVINE	Thornton	195Q	80229	None	
RUSTLER TRAIL	Douglas Co	469B	80134	5100-5399	
RUSTY DAWN CIR	Douglas Co	527N	80104	500-599	
RUTGERS CT	Westminster	193F	80031	11000-11099	
RUTGERS PL W	Denver	343F	80236	3800-4399	
RUTGERS RD	Longmont	10U	80503	3701-3899	O
RUTGERS ST	Adams Co	223A	80031	8300-8999	
RUTH DR	Thornton	194V	80229	1100-1499	
	Thornton	195S	80229	1500-1999	
RUTH RD	Broomfield	162P	80020	1-99	
RUTH WAY	Adams Co	223V	80221	6800-7299	
RUTHERFORD WAY E	Highlands Ranch	404M	80126	900-1199	
RUTLEDGE LN	Douglas Co	408K	80134	None	
RUTLEDGE ST	Douglas Co	408K	80134	None	
RUXTON CT	Parker	409J	80134	17500-17599	
RYANS LN S	Jefferson Co	305U	80453	2800-2899	
RYE CT	Boulder Co	70F	80503	8100-8199	
RYE GULCH RD	Jefferson Co	782H	80403	4900-5599	
S					
SABINO LN	Castle Rock	469K	80108	7400-8099	
SABINO WAY	Castle Rock	469K	80108	6300-6499	
SABLE AVE	Firestone	707T	80504	6000-6099	
SABLE BLVD	Adams Co	168X	80601	12000-14699	
	Adams Co	138X	80601	14700-15199	
	Aurora	288T	80011	1-599	
	Aurora	288K	80011	600-2799	
	Aurora	258T	80011	2800-3899	
	Commerce City	198P	80022	None	
SABLE BLVD S	Aurora	288T	80012	1-699	
	Aurora	318F	80012	700-1899	
	Aurora	318F	80014	1900-2399	
SABLE CIR S	Aurora	348B	80014	3900-4099	
SABLE CT	Douglas Co	887F	80118	6400-6599	
SABLE RD	Douglas Co	887F	80118	6500-7299	
SABLE ST	Denver	258N	80239	4300-4699	
	Denver	258K	80239	4900-5599	
SABLE WAY S	Aurora	318P	80014	2500-2699	
	Aurora	348B	80014	3900-4099	
SABLE RIDGE RD	Elbert Co	851U	80107	37400-37899	
SABLE RUN	Highlands Ranch	405G	80126	None	
SADDLE DR	Clear Creek Co	780E	80452	1-299	
SADDLE DR	Mead	706G	80542	13600-13799	
SADDLE DR N	Clear Creek Co	780E	80452	1-399	
SADDLE DR S	Clear Creek Co	780E	80452	1-299	
SADDLE LN	Park Co	841X	80421	1-399	
SADDLE RD S	Jefferson Co	336B	80439	3400-3699	
SADDLEBACK	Westminster	222A	80021	None	
SADDLEBACK AVE	Firestone	707T	80504	6100-6999	
SADDLEBACK CIR	Parker	410W	80138	20900-21199	
SADDLEBACK CT	Castle Rock	498A	80104	2400-2699	
SADDLE BACK CT	Fort Lupton	729J	80621	None	
SADDLEBACK CT	Parker	410W	80138	11800-11899	
SADDLEBACK DR	Castle Rock	497D	80104	1500-2199	
	Castle Rock	498A	80104	2200-2899	
SADDLEBACK DR	Clear Creek Co	781U	80439	1-1399	
SADDLEBACK RANCH PL E	Douglas Co	439S	80134	20300-20399	
SADDLE BLANKET LN	El Paso Co	912N	80831	19000-20199	
SADDLEBROOK CT	Parker	410P	80138	21800-21999	
SADDLEBROOK DR	Parker	410P	80138	21700-21899	
SADDLE CREEK TRAIL	Douglas Co	440W	80134	5600-5899	
	Douglas Co	439Z	80134	5900-6199	
SADDLE HORN DR	Elbert Co	832X	80107	43000-43899	
SADDLE HORN LN	Park Co	841A	80421	1-199	
SADDLEHORN LN S	Highlands Ranch	406F	80130	10000-10099	
SADDLEHORN TRAIL	El Paso Co	908U	80132	1-399	
SADDLE MOUNTAIN TRAIL	Jefferson Co	824Y	80127	11700-12199	
SADDLE RIDGE CT	El Paso Co	908Y	80132	17500-17699	
SADDLE RIDGE DR	Clear Creek Co	781U	80439	1-1699	
SADDLEROCK LN E	Aurora	380A	80016	21000-21299	
SADDLE ROCK TRAIL	Aurora	350X	80016	6200S-6399S	
SADDLESTRING RD	Park Co	840C	80421	1-799	
SADDLETREE CIR	Elbert Co	850C	80138	42500-42699	
SADDLEWOOD CIR	Highlands Ranch	374Y	80126	200-499	
SADDLEWOOD RD	El Paso Co	909W	80132	17100-18099	
SADDLEWOOD RD	Elbert Co	871B	80107	4000-4799	
SADELIA CT E	Douglas Co	441W	80134	9700-9799	
SAFFRON DR	Castle Rock	466V	80109	None	
SAGAR DR	Broomfield	163J	80020	13700-13898	E
SAGE AVE	Firestone	707T	80504	6100-6899	
SAGE CIR	Golden	278H	80401	1900-1999	
SAGE CIR	Highlands Ranch	374U	80126	500-699	
SAGE CIR	Jefferson Co	336B	80439	3700-3899	
SAGE CT	Boulder Co	100E	80301	4300-4399	
SAGE DR	Brighton	139P	80601	100-199	
SAGE DR	Golden	278H	80401	1900-1999	
SAGE LN E	Douglas Co	379U	80138	6600-6899	
SAGE PL	Longmont	12X	80501	700-799	
SAGE ST	Broomfield	162P	80020	900-1199	
SAGEBRUSH	Lochbuie	140F	80603	700-899	
SAGEBRUSH AVE	Elbert Co	831F	80138	None	
SAGEBRUSH CT	Boulder Co	100X	80301	7900-8099	
SAGE BRUSH CT	Broomfield	163J	80020	5000-5099	
SAGEBRUSH CT	Louisville	130U	80027	500-599	
SAGE BRUSH DR	Broomfield	162H	80020	4900-5199	
	Broomfield	163E	80020	5200-5499	
SAGEBRUSH DR	Douglas Co	410E	80138	7100-7499	
SAGEBRUSH DR	Louisville	130U	80027	600-699	
SAGEBRUSH ST	Brighton	139M	80601	None	
SAGEBRUSH ST	Elbert Co	831J	80138	2300-2399	
SAGEBRUSH ST	Golden	279Q	80401	1-199	
SAGEBRUSH WAY	Weld Co	729R	80603	18000-18299	
SAGE BRUSH TRAIL	Lone Tree	376Y	80124	9100-9299	
SAGEBRUSH WAY	Louisville	130V	80027	1000-1099	
SAGECREST ST	Highlands Ranch	405L	80126	10100-10399	
SAGER LN	Elbert Co	850D	80138	42600-42999	
SAGE SPARROW CIR W	Highlands Ranch	404F	80129	800-999	
SAGE SPARROW CT S	Highlands Ranch	404F	80129	10000-10099	
SAGE THRASHER RD	Douglas Co	470C	80134	5100-5499	
SAGE VALLEY RD	Boulder Co	703X	80503	8800-8999	
SAGEWOOD LN	Parker	410S	80138	11500-20499	
SAGRIMORE CIR	Lafayette	132P	80026	800-1699	
SAGUARO RIDGE RD N	Douglas Co	441G	80138	8000-8999	
SAILOR CT	Boulder Co	71C	80504	10300-10399	
SAINT ST	Frederick	727F	80530	6900-6998	E
ST ANDREWS CT	Douglas Co	886C	80118	6000-6199	
ST ANDREWS DR	Broomfield	162Q	80020	1400-1499	
ST ANDREWS DR	El Paso Co	908T	80132	18400-18899	
SAINT ANDREWS DR	Longmont	12T	80501	500-699	
ST ANDREWS LN	Jefferson Co	306S	80439	30800-30999	
ST ANDREWS LN	Louisville	160G	80027	500-799	
	Louisville	160D	80027	800-999	
SAINT ANNA	Boulder	98V	80301	None	
SAINT CLAIR AVE	Longmont	42A	80501	100-599	
ST CLAIR PL W	Adams Co	253E	80212	4400-4599	
ST CLAIRE AVE	Elbert Co	892N	80106	6800-6899	
ST CROIX ST	Boulder	98K	80301	4100-4199	
ST FRANCIS WAY	Denver	284E	80204	None	
ST FREDS PL	Clear Creek Co	304H	80439	1-99	
ST GILES CIR	El Paso Co	909N	80132	19500-19599	
SAINT IDA CIR	Lafayette	132J	80026	200-499	
ST JAMES ST	Central City	780C	80427	200-599	
ST JOHN ST	Erie	102D	80516	1100-1399	
ST JOHNS AVE	Boulder	98L	80301	3900-4699	
ST LUCIA ST	Boulder	98K	80301	4000-4199	
ST MORITZ DR	Jefferson Co	365P	80439	32400-32999	
ST MORITZ RD	Jefferson Co	365K	80439	7600-7799	
ST MORITZ WAY	El Paso Co	908Q	80132	400-599	
ST PAUL CIR	Thornton	195B	80233	11800-11999	
ST PAUL CT	Denver	255K	80216	4700-4799	
	Northglenn	195K	80233	10600-10699	
	Thornton	195X	80229	9400-9499	
	Thornton	195F	80233	11500-11599	
	Thornton	165X	80241	12300-12399	
	Thornton	165T	80241	12800-12999	
	Thornton	165P	80241	13100-13199	
ST PAUL DR	Thornton	195N	80229	10100-10199	
	Thornton	165P	80241	13100-13199	
	Denver	285P	80206	100-1699	
	Denver	285B	80205	2600-2699	
	Denver	255X	80205	2700-3799	
	Denver	255P	80216	4000-4499	
	Denver	255K	80216	4700-5199	
	Thornton	195T	80229	9500-9599	
	Thornton	195T	80229	9800-9899	
	Thornton	195N	80229	10000-10199	
	Thornton	195B	80233	11700-11999	
	Thornton	165K	80241	13300-13499	
	Thornton	165K	80602	13700-13899	
	Thornton	165F	80602	13900-13999	
	Thornton	135X	80602	15000-15199	
SAINT PAUL ST	Thornton	165F	80602	None	
ST PAUL ST S	Centennial	375F	80122	7100-7299	
	Denver	315B	80209	800-899	
	Denver	315F	80210	1100-3299	
ST PAUL WAY	Northglenn	195K	80233	10900-10999	
ST PAUL WAY S	Centennial	345X	80121	5900-6499	
	Centennial	375P	80122	8100-8299	
ST PETERSBURG ST	Boulder	98L	80301	3900-4099	
ST VINCENT PL	Boulder	98K	80301	3200-3899	
ST VRAIN DR	Frederick	727F	80530	None	
ST VRAIN DR S	Boulder Co	703B	80540	21600-32999	
ST VRAIN RD	Boulder Co	703R	80503	4300-5499	
	Boulder Co	704J	80503	5500-7199	
SAINT VRAIN RD	Boulder Co	10W	80503	7300-7499	
	Boulder Co	40C	80503	7500-8699	
	Boulder Co	42C	80501	11900-12699	
ST VRAIN RANCH BLVD	Firestone	707T	80504	6300-6999	
ST VRAIN RIVER RD	Weld Co	706M	80504	None	
SAKATA ST	Brighton	139K	80601	None	
SAL ST	Lafayette	132K	80026	700-799	
SALAZAR LN	Frederick	706Z	80504	None	
SALAZAR WAY	Frederick	706Z	80504	4001-4099	O
SALEM CIR S	Aurora	317H	80112	1500-1599	
	Aurora	317R	80014	2300-2399	
SALEM CT	Aurora	287V	80011	200-399	
	Aurora	287R	80011	500-599	
SALEM CT	Commerce City	197M	80022	None	
SALEM CT S	Aurora	287V	80012	200-299	
SALEM CT S	Highlands Ranch	406B	80130	9600-9699	
SALEM ST	Adams Co	167V	80640	12400-13599	
	Aurora	287V	80011	200-499	
	Aurora	287M	80011	700-1399	
	Aurora	257Z	80011	3100-3299	
	Brighton	197D	80640	11300-11999	
	Denver	257V	80239	3700-3999	
	Denver	257H	80239	5500-5599	
SALEM ST S	Aurora	287Z	80012	300-399	
	Aurora	317D	80112	900-1098	E
	Aurora	317R	80014	None	
SALEM WAY S	Aurora	317H	80112	1400-1499	
SALFORD LN S	Highlands Ranch	404G	80126	9600-9899	
SALIDA CIR S	Aurora	319J	80017	1700-1899	
SALIDA CT S	Arapahoe Co	349W	80016	6000-6099	
	Arapahoe Co	349W	80016	6100-6199	
	Aurora	319E	80017	1500-1599	
	Aurora	319S	80013	2800-2899	
	Aurora	349K	80015	4700-4999	
	Centennial	349N	80015	5300-5399	
	Centennial	379J	80016	7500-7599	
SALIDA ST	Aurora	289E	80011	1500-1899	
	Aurora	259S	80011	None	
	Aurora	259T	80011	None	
SALIDA ST	Commerce City	769E	80022	10000-10499	
SALIDA ST S	Aurora	319A	80017	900-1099	
	Aurora	319J	80013	2000-2099	
	Aurora	319N	80013	2500-2699	
	Aurora	319S	80013	2700-2799	
	Aurora	349J	80015	4500-4799	
	Centennial	349N	80015	5400-5599	
	Foxfield	379A	80016	6700-6999	
SALIDA WAY	Aurora	289J	80011	600-1399	
SALIDA WAY S	Aurora	319F	80017	1100-1699	
	Aurora	319N	80013	2200-2599	
	Aurora	319S	80013	2700-2799	
	Aurora	319W	80013	3200-3399	
	Aurora	349E	80013	4200-4399	
SALINA ST	Lafayette	131L	80026	100-299	
SALISBURY AVE	Platteville	708G	80651	300-499	
SALISBURY CT	Boulder Co	101Y	80026	2000-2199	
SALLY LN	Douglas Co	466N	80109	2200-2299	
SALTBUSH RIDGE RD E	Highlands Ranch	374Z	80126	1400-1599	
SALT LICK WAY	El Paso Co	908P	80132	19500-19799	
SALUGI RD	Jefferson Co	338P	80454	22300-22699	
SALVIA CT	Arvada	249D	80403	6100-6199	
	Arvada	219V	80007	6600-6799	
	Arvada	219M	80007	None	
	Jefferson Co	279H	80401	1500-1599	
	Jefferson Co	249H	80403	5500-5599	
	Jefferson Co	219R	80007	7200-7399	
SALVIA LN	Arvada	249D	80403	6000-6299	
SALVIA ST	Arvada	219Z	80403	6200-6299	
	Arvada	219V	80007	6900-7199	
	Golden	279R	80401	800-999	
	Golden	279M	80401	1400-1499	
	Golden	279H	80401	1600-1699	
	Golden	249R	80403	4100-6299	
SALVIA WAY	Arvada	249D	80403	6100-6199	
SAMANTHA PL	Weld Co	707J	80504	None	
SAMEDI RANCH RD	Jefferson Co	844B	80127	17000-17099	
SAMOS CIR	Lafayette	131Q	80026	1500-1899	
SAMPSON RD W	Jefferson Co	824U	80127	13800-16199	
SAMUEL DR	Adams Co	223R	80221	1700-7099	
	Adams Co	224S	80221	7100-7499	
SAMUEL PEAK E	Highlands Ranch	406E	80130	5500-5599	
SANBORN PL	Longmont	11Y	80501	1401-1499	O
SANBORNE ST	Castle Rock	499J	80104	600-699	
SANCHEZ CT	Platteville	708G	80651	1500-1599	
SANCTUARY CIR	Longmont	12T	80501	800-899	
SANCTUARY LN	Longmont	12T	80501	700-799	
SANCTUARY WAY	Douglas Co	847T	80109	4100-4299	
SANDALWOOD CT	Louisville	130U	80027	600-699	
SANDALWOOD PL	Highlands Ranch	404K	80129	100-298	E
SANDALWOOD WAY	Highlands Ranch	404L	80129	1-199	
SANDAU LN	Gilpin Co	761E	80403	1-299	
SANDBAR CIR	Louisville	130Y	80027	500-699	
SAND CHERRY	Jefferson Co	370P	80127	1-99	
SANDCHERRY PL	Longmont	40L	80503	4000-4099	
SAND CHERRY ST	Brighton	139M	80601	None	
SANDCHERRY WAY S	Highlands Ranch	404F	80129	9800-9999	
SAND CREEK	Jefferson Co	370Q	80127	1-99	
SAND CREEK DR N	Commerce City	256E	80022	None	
SAND CREEK DR S	Commerce City	255H	80022	None	
	Commerce City	256K	80022	None	
SAND CREEK RD E	Douglas Co	410D	80138	9100-9399	
SAND DOLLAR CIR	Longmont	10R	80503	2100-2199	
SAND DOLLAR CT	Longmont	10R	80503	2900-2999	
SAND DOLLAR DR	Longmont	10R	80503	2101-2199	O
SANDER RD	Gilpin Co	761D	80403	1-199	
SANDERLING WAY	Highlands Ranch	375Z	80126	8900-9099	
SANDERS CIR	Erie	102R	80516	200-399	
SANDERS RD	Jefferson Co	336W	80439	6200-6299	
SANDERSON AVE	Jefferson Co	823U	80433	22300-22599	
SAND HILL CT S	Highlands Ranch	405D	80126	9500-9599	
SAND HILL LN E	Highlands Ranch	405C	80126	4100-4199	
SAND HILL PL S	Highlands Ranch	405C	80126	None	
SAND HILL ST S	Highlands Ranch	405D	80126	9200-9299	
SAND HILL WAY S	Highlands Ranch	405C	80126	9300-9399	
SAND HILL TRAIL	Highlands Ranch	375Y	80126	9200-9299	
SAND HILL TRAIL S	Highlands Ranch	405C	80126	9200-9299	
SANDHURST DR	Castle Rock	498N	80104	1900-2299	
SANDIA CT	Jefferson Co	305H	80439	31500-31599	
SANDIA WAY	El Paso Co	910X	80908	7400-7599	
SANDIA TRAIL	Castle Rock	466T	80109	None	
SANDLER DR	Lafayette	132E	80026	100-399	
SAND LILY DR	Jefferson Co	307M	80401	1600-1799	
SAND LILY LN E	Douglas Co	850N	80134	9600-9699	
SANDOVAL ST	Brighton	139K	80601	None	
SANDOWN RD	Denver	256P	80216	6701-7299	O
SANDPEBBLE CT	Douglas Co	408G	80134	10000-10099	
SANDPIPER	Frederick	707W	80504	9000-9099	
SANDPIPER AVE E	Castle Rock	498L	80104	5200-5399	
SANDPIPER CIR	Thornton	165N	80241	1-99	
SANDPIPER DR	Lafayette	131K	80026	2300-2399	
SANDPIPER LN	Brighton	137Z	80601	1100-1499	
SANDPIPER PL	Longmont	10R	80503	2900-2999	
SANDPIPPER CIR	Boulder Co	99G	80301	4400-4499	
SANDPIPPER CT	Boulder Co	99G	80301	4400-4599	
SANDPOINT DR	Longmont	12P	80501	500-799	
SANDRA LN	Broomfield	162L	80020	1-99	
SANDRA PL	Broomfield	162L	80020	None	
SANDRA WAY	Arvada	251G	80002	5300-5399	
SANDREED CIR	Parker	378V	80134	8300-8499	
SANDROCK DR	Jefferson Co	337U	80439	5800-6199	
SANDROSE CT	Castle Rock	467L	80108	6300-6499	
SANDSTONE CIR	Frederick	726G	80516	None	
SANDSTONE CT	Boulder	128S	80305	1300-1399	
SANDSTONE CT	Frederick	706Y	80504	None	
SANDSTONE DR	Boulder Co	703F	80540	1-999	

STREET NAME	CITY or COUNTY	MAP GRID	ZIP CODE	BLOCK RANGE	O/E
SANDSTONE DR	El Paso Co	907U	80132	1-4899	
SANDSTONE DR	Jefferson Co	340W	80465	16000-16599	
SANDSTONE WAY	Superior	160U	80027	900-999	
SANDSTONE RUN	Douglas Co	432X	80125	10500-10599	
SAND TRAIL CT	El Paso Co	909P	80908	None	
SANDTRAP CIR	Broomfield	163F	80020	13800-13999	
SANDTRAP CT	Broomfield	163F	80020	13800-13899	
SANDTRAP LN	Broomfield	163F	80020	None	
SANDTRAP WAY	Jefferson Co	340S	80465	15700-15799	
SAND WEDGE WAY	Castle Rock	497U	80104	1500-1699	
SANDY CIR	Weld Co	726K	80516	1600-1699	
SANDY DR	Boulder Co	742B	80302	1-299	
SANDY LN	Jefferson Co	822P	80433	9200-9299	
SANDY CREEK LN	Parker	409V	80138	11500-11599	
SANDY HOLLOW TRAIL	Douglas Co	870F	80016	None	
SANDY LAKE RD	Cherry Hills Village	345B	80113	1-99	
SANDY RIDGE AVE	Firestone	707S	80504	4600-10199	
	Firestone	707S	80504	None	
SANDY RIDGE RD	Douglas Co	867S	80135	2700-2999	
SANDY RIDGE RD	Elbert Co	871S	80107	2000-3399	
SANFORD CIR	Cherry Hills Village	345D	80113	5200E-5399E	
	Cherry Hills Village	345D	80113	4900W-5199W	
SANGER AVE S	Jefferson Co	842A	80470	12400-12799	
SANGER DR	Jefferson Co	276U	80401	29200-29599	
SANGER WAY	Jefferson Co	368L	80465	7500-7599	
SANGRE DE CRISTO RD S					
	Jefferson Co	371Q	80127	7600-8499	
SANGUINE CIR	Castle Rock	466U	80109	None	
SANIBEL CT W	Littleton	374N	80120	1900-1999	
SAN ISABEL RD	Jefferson Co	338E	80454	23400-23899	
	Jefferson Co	337H	80439	23900-24399	
SAN JOAQUIN RIDGE	Jefferson Co	371K	80127	11200-11499	
SAN JUAN CIR W	Jefferson Co	371V	80128	9500-9599	
SAN JUAN CT	Parker	410K	80138	10700-10799	
SAN JUAN DR W	Jefferson Co	371V	80128	8900-9199	
SAN JUAN PL W	Jefferson Co	372U	80128	6801-6899	O
SAN JUAN RD	Jefferson Co	338Q	80454	21300-21599	
SAN JUAN WAY W	Jefferson Co	371U	80127	10000-10199	
SAN JUAN RANGE	Jefferson Co	371P	80127	7900-11599	
SAN LUIS	Douglas Co	407B	80112	None	
SAN LUIS PEAK	Jefferson Co	842P	80421	None	
SAN MARCO DR	Longmont	40Q	80503	None	
SAN MIGUEL CT	Castle Rock	469K	80108	6400-6599	
SAN SOUCI CT	Jefferson Co	336F	80439	4100-4299	
SANTA FE AVE	Monument	908W	80132	100-1299	
SANTA FE CIR S	Englewood	343M	80110	4600-4799	
SANTA FE CT	Brighton	139P	80601	None	
SANTA FE DR	Adams Co	224T	80221	6800-7299	
	Castle Rock	467N	80108	None	
	Denver	284P	80223	1-399	
	Denver	284P	80204	400-1399	
	Douglas Co	466L	80108	None	
SANTA FE DR	Longmont	12K	80501	2100-2399	
SANTA FE DR	Thornton	224B	80260	8600-8799	
	Westminster	194E	80234	11200-11299	
SANTA FE DR S	Denver	284X	80223	1-699	
	Denver	314P	80223	700-2699	
	Douglas Co	403L	80125	None	
	Douglas Co	404W	80125	None	
	Englewood	314T	80110	2701-3399	O
	Englewood	344E	80110	4300-4899	
	Littleton	343V	80120	4900-6399	
	Sheridan	314W	80110	3401-3599	O
	Sheridan	344E	80110	3600-4299	
SANTA FE ST	Northglenn	194N	80234	10400-10599	
	Northglenn	194J	80234	10700-10899	
	Westminster	164E	80020	None	
SANTA ANITA DR	Denver	343L	80110	3200-3299	
SANTA CLARA PL	Boulder	128M	80303	5100-5199	
SANTA CLARA RD	Jefferson Co	338U	80454	None	
SANTA FE DR	Lochbuie	729Y	80603	None	
SANTA FE MINE RD	Clear Creek Co	780L	80452	None	
SANTA FE MOUNTAIN DR					
	Clear Creek Co	781T	80439	1-2099	
SANTA FE TRAIL	Elbert Co	870U	80107	300-1699	
SANTANA DR	Castle Rock	498J	80104	1900-2199	
SANTERO WAY	Douglas Co	469F	80134	4800-4899	
SANTIAGO ST	Frederick	727F	80530	None	
SANTOLINA CT	Douglas Co	408M	80134	16600-16699	
SAPLING CT	Castle Rock	496D	80109	1700-1999	
SAPPHIRE DR	Castle Rock	467L	80108	400-1099	
SAPPHIRE LN	Longmont	41U	80504	1300-1399	
SAPPHIRE WAY	Superior	160Y	80027	900-1099	
SAPPHIRE POINTE BLVD					
	Castle Rock	467H	80108	6200-7399	
SARA GULCH CIR	Douglas Co	411W	80138	8300-9299	
	Douglas Co	410Z	80138	9300-9699	
SARA GULCH WAY	Douglas Co	411W	80138	None	
SARAH CT E	Highlands Ranch	404H	80126	1200-1299	
SARAH LN	Jefferson Co	822T	80433	31700-31799	
SARANAC WAY	Douglas Co	408M	80134	10300-10499	
SARATOGA AVE E	Arapahoe Co	350J	80015	None	
	Arapahoe Co	350K	80015	None	
	Centennial	349M	80015	19500-19599	
SARATOGA AVE W	Denver	343L	80110	3000-3399	
	Denver	343K	80123	3600-3899	
	Englewood	343L	80110	2900-2999	
	Jefferson Co	341K	80465	11600-11699	
	Jefferson Co	341J	80465	12000-12599	
SARATOGA CIR E	Aurora	349L	80015	18800-18999	
	Aurora	350M	80016	None	
SARATOGA CT	Boulder Co	130F	80303	900-999	
SARATOGA DR	Lafayette	132T	80026	None	
SARATOGA DR E	Arapahoe Co	350L	80015	None	
	Aurora	348J	80015	13800-13999	
SARATOGA DR W	Jefferson Co	341K	80127	11400-11499	
	Jefferson Co	340M	80465	13200-13499	
SARATOGA PL E	Arapahoe Co	350J	80015	None	
	Aurora	348J	80015	13900-13999	
	Aurora	348K	80015	14100-14399	
	Aurora	348L	80015	15300-15899	
	Aurora	349K	80015	18500-18699	
	Aurora	349L	80015	19000-19099	
	Aurora	350M	80016	23700-24099	
	Aurora	351J	80016	24600-24899	
	Denver	346M	80237	8500-8799	
SARATOGA PL S	Aurora	349K	80015	17400-17499	

STREET NAME	CITY or COUNTY	MAP GRID	ZIP CODE	BLOCK RANGE	O/E
SARATOGA PL W	Denver	341M	80123	9000-9999	
	Jefferson Co	341L	80127	10100-10299	
	Jefferson Co	341K	80127	10600-11599	
	Jefferson Co	341K	80465	11600-11699	
	Jefferson Co	340M	80465	12900-13199	
	Lakewood	342K	80123	7400-7499	
SARATOGA RD N	Douglas Co	470A	80134	5300-5399	
SARATOGA MINE DR	Douglas Co	436X	80108	200-299	
SARATOGA TRAIL	Frederick	726G	80516	2900-6599	
SARATOGA VIEW CT	Douglas Co	436X	80108	200-299	
SASKATOON LN S	Parker	439B	80134	None	
SASKATOON PL S	Parker	439B	80134	None	
SASKATOON WAY	Parker	439B	80134	None	
SASKATOON WAY S	Parker	439B	80134	None	
SASSAFRASS LN	Broomfield	162P	80020	900-1199	
SATISFACTION CIR	Longmont	41V	80504	600-798	E
SATSUMA PL	Castle Rock	497X	80104	100-199	
SATURN DR	Highlands Ranch	376X	80124	13000-13299	
SATURN PL	Highlands Ranch	376X	80124	300-399	
SAULSBURY CIR	Arvada	222P	80003	7100-7199	
	Westminster	192X	80021	9300-9399	
SAULSBURY CT	Arvada	252F	80002	5300-5599	
	Arvada	222X	80003	6400-6599	
	Arvada	222F	80003	8100-8299	
	Westminster	192X	80021	9400-9499	
	Wheat Ridge	252T	80033	3400-3499	
SAULSBURY CT S	Jefferson Co	342X	80123	6300-6399	
	Jefferson Co	372B	80123	6400-6599	
	Jefferson Co	372L	80128	7400-7799	
	Lakewood	312G	80232	1200-1299	
	Lakewood	312L	80232	1700-1899	
SAULSBURY ST	Arvada	252F	80002	5700-5799	
	Arvada	222X	80003	6200-6799	
	Arvada	222T	80003	6800-7199	
	Arvada	222P	80003	7400-7899	
	Broomfield	162X	80020	11900-11999	
	Lakewood	282U	80226	200-599	
	Lakewood	282Q	80214	800-899	
	Lakewood	282L	80214	900-1499	
	Lakewood	282C	80214	2400-2599	
	Wheat Ridge	252Y	80033	2900-3199	
	Wheat Ridge	252T	80033	3400-3499	
	Wheat Ridge	252P	80033	4400-4799	
SAULSBURY ST S	Denver	312U	80227	2700-3099	
	Jefferson Co	372B	80123	6300-6599	
	Jefferson Co	372F	80128	6800-6999	
	Jefferson Co	372Q	80128	7700-8099	
	Jefferson Co	372T	80128	8300-8599	
	Lakewood	282T	80226	100-199	
	Lakewood	282Y	80226	300-599	
	Lakewood	312B	80226	900-1099	
	Lakewood	312G	80232	1400-1499	
SAULSBURY WAY S	Jefferson Co	372P	80128	8200-8299	
	Lakewood	342P	80123	5300-5399	
SAUNTER CT S	Parker	410X	80138	None	
SAUNTER LN S	Parker	410W	80138	None	
	Parker	410X	80138	None	
SAURINI BLVD	Commerce City	225U	80022	4100-4499	
SAVAGE RD	Elbert Co	851W	80107	1900-2999	
SAVANNAH CT	Boulder	98L	80301	3900-4099	
SAVANNAH SPARROW CT S					
	Highlands Ranch	404E	80129	10000-10099	
SAVANNAH SPARROW DR W					
	Highlands Ranch	404E	80129	1100-1399	
SAVANNAH SPARROW WAY S					
	Highlands Ranch	404K	80129	10100-10199	
SAVORY CIR	Parker	408V	80134	15700-16199	
SAWATCH RANGE RD	Jefferson Co	371P	80127	7800-8299	
SAWDUST CT	Clear Creek Co	781U	80439	1-199	
SAWDUST LN	Brighton	140K	80601	None	
SAWDUST LOOP	Douglas Co	469F	80134	5500-5699	
SAWGRASS CT	Lone Tree	406L	80124	None	
SAWGRASS DR	Lone Tree	406L	80124	8100-8599	
SAWGRASS TRAIL	Castle Rock	466Q	80109	3500-3799	
SAW HORSE LN	Gilpin Co	761B	80403	1-299	
SAWMILL CT W	Castle Rock	466P	80109	4300-4399	
SAWMILL LN	Clear Creek Co	801A	80452	1-499	
SAWMILL RD	Boulder Co	720R	80302	None	
	Boulder Co	721S	80302	None	
SAWMILL RD	Clear Creek Co	801R	80439	1-299	
SAWMILL RD	El Paso Co	909Y	80908	17700-18099	
SAWMILL CREEK DR	Clear Creek Co	781T	80439	1-699	
SAWMILL GULCH RD	Jefferson Co	308Q	80453	2100-2199	
SAWTOOTH LN	Boulder Co	70L	80503	8200-8499	
SAWTOOTH PT	Lafayette	131G	80026	500-599	
SAXEBOURGH DR	Douglas Co	436M	80108	7600-7999	
SAXON PL	Douglas Co	466H	80108	400-499	
SAYBROOK ST S	Highlands Ranch	405G	80126	9700-9999	
SCARLET OAK CT	Castle Rock	466X	80109	3900-4199	
SCARLET THORN CIR	Jefferson Co	339Z	80465	6100-6199	
SCARSBROOK CT	El Paso Co	908Z	80132	1200-1299	
SCARSDALE CT	Lafayette	101X	80026	1800-1899	
SCARSDALE PL	Boulder	98L	80301	4300-4699	
SCENIC AVE	Firestone	707S	80504	5800-5999	
SCENIC CIR	Jefferson Co	368U	80465	21800-21999	
SCENIC CT	Firestone	707T	80504	6600-10199	
SCENIC CT	Golden	279F	80401	400-499	
SCENIC DR	Boulder Co	130F	80303	7800-7899	
SCENIC DR	Jefferson Co	368U	80465	8400-8499	
SCENIC PL	Longmont	11W	80503	2500-2599	
SCENIC RD	Gilpin Co	761J	80403	1-299	
SCENIC PARK DR	Parker	439D	80134	None	
SCENIC PINE DR	Douglas Co	470D	80134	8900-9199	
SCENIC VIEW CT	Boulder Co	129A	80303	5500-5599	
SCENIC VILLAGE DR	Jefferson Co	336F	80439	4200-4299	
SCHILLING AVE	El Paso Co	908W	80132	2700-3399	
SCHLAGEL ST	Boulder Co	40M	80503	9400-9799	
SCHNEIDER WAY	Arvada	222X	80004	6500-6599	
SCHOOL RD	Nederland	740L	80466	None	
SCHOOLEY RD	Park Co	820Y	80421	1-199	
SCHOOL HOUSE RD	Jefferson Co	762Z	80403	27600-27699	
SCHUMAKER RD	Adams Co	752K	80102	None	
	Adams Co	752X	80102	None	
	Adams Co	772P	80102	None	
	Adams Co	792K	80102	None	
SCHUMAKER RD N	Arapahoe Co	792T	80102	1-1499	
SCHUMAKER RD S	Arapahoe Co	792X	80102	1-799	
	Arapahoe Co	812B	80102	800-2699	

STREET NAME	CITY or COUNTY	MAP GRID	ZIP CODE	BLOCK RANGE	O/E
SCHUYLER GULCH RD	Jefferson Co	843S	80470	27100-27699	
SCHWEIGERT AVE	Jefferson Co	823U	80433	10800-11099	
SCORPIO DR	Highlands Ranch	376U	80124	600-699	
SCORPIOS CIR	Lafayette	131R	80026	1200-1299	
SCOTCH HEATHER	Jefferson Co	370L	80127	1-99	
SCOTCH PINE	Jefferson Co	370Q	80127	1-99	
SCOTCH PINE CIR	Elbert Co	830L	80138	100-299	
SCOTIA RD	Jefferson Co	306T	80439	2700-2899	
SCOTT AVE	Douglas Co	439Y	80134	5800-6799	
SCOTT BLVD	Castle Rock	467Y	80104	400-599	
SCOTT CIR E	Denver	260N	80249	20600-20899	
SCOTT CT	Longmont	11L	80501	2400-2499	
SCOTT DR	Adams Co	167D	80601	14400-14599	
SCOTT DR	Broomfield	162Q	80020	1N-99N	
SCOTT PL E	Denver	258P	80239	14700-14999	
	Denver	259Q	80249	19100-19399	
	Denver	259R	80249	19700-19899	
SCOTT PL W	Denver	254N	80211	1700-1899	
	Denver	253R	80211	1900-2699	
	Denver	253Q	80211	3000-3599	
SCOTT RD	Jefferson Co	823N	80433	10000-10199	
SCOTT ST	Jefferson Co	219M	80007	16400-16499	
SCOTTBURG CT S	Aurora	381Q	80016	7900-8099	
SCOTT CANYON LN	Castle Rock	497D	80104	1400-1599	
SCOTTISH PL	Castle Rock	497U	80104	None	
SCOTTSWOOD CT	Boulder Co	99F	80301	5900-6099	
SCOTTSWOOD DR	El Paso Co	908Z	80132	800-1399	
SCRANTON CT	Aurora	287R	80011	700-799	
	Denver	257M	80239	4800-5399	
SCRANTON ST	Aurora	287V	80011	200-499	
	Aurora	287M	80011	700-1399	
	Aurora	287H	80010	1900-2298	E
	Aurora	257Z	80011	3000-3299	
	Denver	257H	80239	4800-5599	
SCRANTON WAY	Commerce City	197M	80022	None	
SCRANTON WAY S	Aurora	317M	80014	2100-2499	
	Aurora	317V	80014	2900-2999	
SCRUB OAK CIR	Boulder	128S	80305	1200-1399	
SCRUB OAK CIR	El Paso Co	908Y	80132	300-499	
SCRUB OAK DR	Lone Tree	376Y	80124	9200-9399	
SCRUB OAK WAY	El Paso Co	908Y	80132	200-399	
SEABISQUIT TRAIL	Jefferson Co	366R	80439	28100-28299	
SEABROOK LN	Parker	410Q	80138	22100-22199	
SEABROOK LN S	Littleton	373R	80120	8200-8299	
SEASON CT S	Parker	440B	80138	12200-12299	
SEATTLE LN	Longmont	41R	80501	1-99	
SEAVER DR	Jefferson Co	762C	80403	29600-30199	
SEAWAY CT	Longmont	10R	80503	2100-2199	
SEBRING CT S	Denver	316U	80231	2800-2999	
	Denver	346C	80237	3700-3999	
SECOND AVE	Hudson	730L	80642	None	
SECOND ST	Palmer Lake	907U	80133	None	
SECOND CREEK PLAZA DR					
	Commerce City	769J	80022	None	
SECREST CIR	Arvada	219Z	80007	6600-6799	
SECREST CT	Arvada	219Z	80403	6100-6199	
	Arvada	219V	80007	6900-7199	
	Arvada	219M	80007	None	
	Golden	279M	80401	1500-1599	
	Jefferson Co	249H	80403	5400-5799	
	Jefferson Co	219R	80007	7200-7599	
SECREST DR	Arvada	252B	80003	5800-6099	
SECREST LN	Arvada	219Z	80403	6200-6299	
SECREST ST	Arvada	219Z	80403	6200-6399	
	Golden	279H	80401	1600-1699	
	Jefferson Co	279M	80401	900-1199	
SECREST WAY	Arvada	219Z	80403	6300-6399	
SECRETARIAT DR	Boulder Co	70N	80503	None	
SECURITY AVE W	Lakewood	281J	80215	11500-11599	
	Lakewood	281J	80401	11600-11999	
SECURITY DR E	Aurora	318B	80012	14200-14299	
SECURITY PL E	Aurora	288K	80011	14700-15099	
SECURITY WAY E	Aurora	288K	80011	14700-15199	
SEDALIA CIR	Commerce City	769E	80022	None	
SEDALIA CIR S	Aurora	319J	80017	1700-1899	
	Aurora	319P	80013	2300-2499	
SEDALIA CT S	Arapahoe Co	349T	80016	6000-6099	
	Arapahoe Co	379B	80016	6500-6599	
	Aurora	319S	80013	2800-2899	
	Centennial	349P	80015	5100-5199	
	Centennial	349N	80015	5300-5399	
SEDALIA ST	Commerce City	769E	80022	10000-10299	
	Commerce City	769E	80022	10400-10599	
	Commerce City	769E	80022	None	
	Commerce City	169W	80603	None	
SEDALIA ST S	Arapahoe Co	349W	80016	6100-6399	
	Arapahoe Co	349X	80016	6400-6599	
	Aurora	319E	80017	1500-1699	
	Aurora	319T	80013	2700-2799	
	Centennial	349N	80015	5400-5599	
	Centennial	379N	80016	7900-8099	
	Foxfield	379B	80016	6700-6899	
	Foxfield	379E	80016	6900-7399	
SEDALIA WAY	Aurora	289F	80011	1500-1599	
SEDALIA WAY S	Aurora	319W	80013	3100-3399	
	Aurora	349K	80015	4900-4999	
SEDGE WAY	Douglas Co	378V	80134	None	
SEDGE WAY	Lafayette	131H	80026	700-999	
SEDGE GRASS WAY	Highlands Ranch	404L	80129	10200-10399	
SEDGEMERE RD	El Paso Co	908R	80132	20100-20199	
SEDGEWICK CT	Parker	409J	80134	10600-10699	
SEDGEWICK WAY	Parker	409J	80134	10600-10699	
SEDONA CIR	Douglas Co	469F	80134	4700-5099	
SEDONA DR	Douglas Co	469E	80134	5100-5499	
SEDONA DR	Lochbuie	729Z	80603	None	
SEDONA LN	Dacono	726V	80514	None	
SEDWICK DR	Cherry Hills Village	345B	80113	1-99	
SEDWICK PL	Cherry Hills Village	345B	80113	1-99	
SEEFELD PL	Douglas Co	466G	80108	1-799	
SEGO LILY WAY	Gilpin Co	761C	80403	100-299	
SEIBERT CIR	Parker	409V	80138	11300-23099	
SEIBERT CT S	Superior	160Q	80027	1400-1599	
SEIDLER CT	Erie	102P	80516	1900-1999	
SEITZ RD	Jefferson Co	307X	80439	34600-34799	
SELAK ST	Black Hawk	780D	80422	200-299	
SELDOM SEEN RD	Gilpin Co	761Z	80403	500-699	
	Jefferson Co	782A	80403	500-699	
SELENITE CT	Castle Rock	467H	80108	2000-2199	

S

STREET NAME	CITY or COUNTY	MAP GRID	ZIP CODE	BLOCK RANGE	O/E
SELLERS DR	Castle Rock	**497R**	80104	None	
SELLERS CREEK RD	Douglas Co	**527R**	80104	None	
SELLMAN DR	Castle Rock	**466Y**	80109	None	
SELLY RD	Douglas Co	**440Y**	80134	8600-8899	
SELWORTHY CT	Lafayette	**131M**	80026	1100-1199	
SEMBRY CT S	Parker	**439E**	80134	None	
SEMBRY DR E	Parker	**439E**	80134	None	
SEMBRY LN S	Parker	**439E**	80134	None	
SEMINOLE CT	Douglas Co	**886G**	80118	None	
SEMINOLE DR	Boulder	**128M**	80303	100-399	
SEMINOLE DR	Douglas Co	**886G**	80118	7400-7899	
SEMINOLE PL	Douglas Co	**846T**	80135	3700-3999	
SEMINOLE RD	Denver	**284N**	80204	800-899	
SEMINOLE RD	Jefferson Co	**338R**	80454	5400-20999	
SEMINOLE TRAIL	Douglas Co	**886G**	80118	5700-5999	
SENATOR CT	Louisville	**130M**	80027	2300-2399	
SENATOR DR	Louisville	**130M**	80027	2400-2599	
SENDA ROCOSA ST	Boulder Co	**743R**	80303	1600-1999	
SENECA CIR	Lafayette	**131Q**	80026	1500-1599	
SENECA CT S	Denver	**314E**	80223	1300-1399	
SENECA PL	Boulder	**129J**	80303	5400-5499	
SENECA PL	Frederick	**726G**	80516	None	
SENECA WAY	El Paso Co	**908U**	80132	300-399	
SENECA WAY	Lochbuie	**729Z**	80603	500-599	
SENECA WAY S	Denver	**314E**	80223	1200-1299	
SENECIO CIR	Douglas Co	**887F**	80118	2100-2399	
SENECIO CT	Lafayette	**131H**	80026	800-999	
SENECIO DR	Douglas Co	**887F**	80118	1800-2199	
SENTER DR	Castle Rock	**497H**	80104	400-699	
SENTINAL ROCK TERRACE					
	Douglas Co	**887E**	80118	4400-4599	
SENTINEL DR	Boulder	**98U**	80301	3100-3399	
SENTINEL WAY	Clear Creek Co	**781Y**	80439	None	
SENTINEL ROCK LN	Boulder Co	**722L**	80302	1-299	
SEQUERRA ST	Broomfield	**162T**	80020	1100-1399	
SEQUOIA CT	Douglas Co	**408M**	80134	16400-16499	
SEQUOIA DR	Douglas Co	**408H**	80134	15900-16299	
SEQUOIA PL	Frederick	**707W**	80504	None	
SEQUOIA ST	Longmont	**41V**	80501	None	
SERAMONTE DR W	Highlands Ranch	**403G**	80129	3500-3899	
SERBING CT S	Denver	**346G**	80237	4000-4199	
SERENA AVE	Castle Pines North	**436B**	80108	6600-6999	
SERENA CT	Castle Pines North	**436B**	80108	12300-12499	
SERENA DR	Castle Pines North	**436B**	80108	6800-7499	
SERENADE RD	Douglas Co	**527U**	80104	3600-4299	
SERENDIPITY TRAIL	Jefferson Co	**275U**	80439	32800-33099	
SERENE CT	Erie	**103X**	80516	None	
SERENE DR	Erie	**103X**	80516	None	
SERENE VIEW WAY	Douglas Co	**470D**	80134	5000-5299	
SERENGETI CIR E	Douglas Co	**406K**	80124	6400-6599	
SERENGETI DR S	Douglas Co	**406J**	80124	10500-10599	
SERENGETI PL E	Douglas Co	**406K**	80124	6400-6499	
SERENITY CIR	Longmont	**12T**	80501	1400-1499	
SERENITY LN	Longmont	**12T**	80501	800-899	
SERENITY SPRINGS POINT					
	El Paso Co	**908P**	80132	None	
SERVICE DR	Golden	**250N**	80403	None	
SERVICE RD	Denver	**770T**	80249	None	
SERVICE RD	Jefferson Co	**823W**	80433	11500-11699	
	Jefferson Co	**822Z**	80433	11700-11799	
SERVICE RD	Lakewood	**312P**	80227	None	
SERVICE RD N	Mead	**707B**	80542	None	
SERVICE BERRY LN	Gilpin Co	**761J**	80403	1-199	
SETH PL	Castle Pines North	**436C**	80108	500-599	
SETON CT	Westminster	**193K**	80031	11000-11099	
SETON PL	Westminster	**193F**	80031	11100-11199	
SETON ST	Adams Co	**223A**	80031	8600-8999	
SETTING SUN AVE	Castle Rock	**466Z**	80109	None	
SETTLER WAY	Brighton	**139H**	80601	None	
SETTLERS DR	Jefferson Co	**368L**	80465	7300-8499	
SETTLERS DR N	Douglas Co	**409G**	80138	11400-11699	
SEVEN ARROWS TRAIL	Lone Tree	**376Y**	80124	9100-9199	
SEVEN HILLS DR	Boulder Co	**722Z**	80302	1-599	
SEVENTH AVE	Hudson	**730L**	80642	None	
SEVERANCE DR	Parker	**409J**	80134	10300-10399	
SEVERANCE LODGE RD	Gilpin Co	**760D**	80403	1-399	
SEVERN DR E	Denver	**286Q**	80230	7500-7899	
SEVERN LN	Douglas Co	**407H**	80134	10000-10299	
SEVERN PL	Denver	**286P**	80220	5500-7299	
SEVERN PL E	Aurora	**286R**	80230	8900-9299	
	Aurora	**288R**	80011	16000-16499	
	Denver	**285R**	80220	4800-5499	
	Denver	**286P**	80230	7300-7399	
	Denver	**286Q**	80230	7301-8899	O
SEVERN PL W	Denver	**283Q**	80204	2800-3299	
SEVILLE AVE	Castle Rock	**497Q**	80104	None	
SEVILLE DR	Castle Rock	**497Q**	80104	None	
SEVILLE PT	Castle Rock	**497Q**	80104	None	
SHADBURY LN	Douglas Co	**409X**	80134	None	
SHADECREST PL	Highlands Ranch	**405N**	80126	2500-2799	
SHADECREST PT	Highlands Ranch	**405N**	80126	10900-10999	
SHADE TREE LN	Douglas Co	**470D**	80134	2000-5399	
SHADOW CIR	Castle Rock	**466U**	80109	None	
SHADOW LN	Jefferson Co	**277U**	80401	1-299	
SHADOWBROOK CIR					
	Highlands Ranch	**405Q**	80130	10900-10999	
SHADOW BROOK DR	Jefferson Co	**822V**	80433	10400-10499	
SHADOW CANYON TRAIL	Broomfield	**163P**	80020	3600-13299	
SHADOWCLOUD CT	Highlands Ranch	**404Q**	80126	None	
SHADOW CREEK DR	Boulder	**128B**	80303	2800-2999	
SHADOW DANCE DR	Castle Rock	**466Y**	80109	None	
SHADOWGLEN CT S	Highlands Ranch	**404D**	80126	9200-9399	
SHADOW HILL CIR S	Douglas Co	**407A**	80124	None	
	Lone Tree	**407A**	80124	9300-9599	
SHADOW HILL CT S	Lone Tree	**407A**	80124	9900-9999	
SHADOW HILL DR S	Lone Tree	**407A**	80124	10000-10099	
SHADOW MOUNTAIN DR	El Paso Co	**908T**	80132	800-999	
SHADOW MOUNTAIN DR					
	Highlands Ranch	**374V**	80126	800-1399	
SHADOW MOUNTAIN DR	Jefferson Co	**822Q**	80433	10100-31599	
	Jefferson Co	**365Z**	80433	31600-32099	
SHADOW MOUNTAIN RANCH RD					
	Douglas Co	**908M**	80118	15100-15999	
SHADOWOOD CIR	El Paso Co	**908T**	80132	18900-19399	
SHADOWOOD DR	El Paso Co	**908T**	80132	18900-19399	
SHADOW RIDGE CT	Castle Rock	**466P**	80109	4700-4799	
SHADOW RIDGE RD	Castle Rock	**466P**	80109	4800-5099	
SHADOW ROCK	Douglas Co	**432P**	80125	10700-10799	

STREET NAME	CITY or COUNTY	MAP GRID	ZIP CODE	BLOCK RANGE	O/E
SHADOWSTONE DR	Highlands Ranch	**404K**	80129	700-999	
SHADOW WOOD CT	Adams Co	**751E**	80603	14200-14499	
	Adams Co	**751N**	80603	None	
SHADOW WOOD ST	Adams Co	**751J**	80603	15101-15199	O
SHADY LN	Highlands Ranch	**375T**	80126	2800-3099	
SHADY LN	Jefferson Co	**305U**	80453	None	
SHADY LN	Palmer Lake	**907Q**	80133	None	
SHADYCROFT DR	Littleton	**373M**	80120	300-399	
	Littleton	**374J**	80120	400-899	
SHADYCROFT LN	Littleton	**374E**	80120	400-899	
SHADY GLEN LN	El Paso Co	**908P**	80132	None	
SHADY GROVE CT S	Aurora	**381R**	80016	8200-8299	
SHADY GROVE ST	Denver	**770T**	80249	7100-7198	E
SHADY GROVE WAY	Aurora	**381G**	80016	None	
SHADY HOLLOW	Boulder	**98T**	80304	2900E-2999E	
	Boulder	**98S**	80304	2900W-2999W	
	Boulder Co	**741F**	80466	1-399	
SHADY KNOLL	El Paso Co	**912Y**	80831	18400-18499	
SHADY OAK LN	Castle Pines North	**436L**	80108	800-999	
SHADY PINE CT S	Parker	**409Z**	80134	None	
SHADY PINES DR	Jefferson Co	**823V**	80465	10600-10799	
SHADY RIDGE PKWY E	Parker	**409Z**	80134	None	
SHADY RIDGE RD E	Parker	**409Z**	80134	19900-20599	
SHAFFER DR	Jefferson Co	**371P**	80127	None	
SHAFFER LN S	Jefferson Co	**371J**	80127	7400-7499	
SHAFFER PKWY	Jefferson Co	**371J**	80127	7500-11899	
SHAHARA RD	El Paso Co	**909W**	80132	17000-17999	
SHALE CT	Superior	**160U**	80027	2900-2999	
SHALLOT CIR	Lafayette	**132T**	80026	700-1999	
SHALOM PARK CIR S	Aurora	**348Q**	80015	5100-5299	
SHAMROCK CIR	Frederick	**727F**	80530	6100-7999	
SHAMROCK DR	Superior	**160R**	80027	1800-2199	
SHANE VALLEY TRAIL	Castle Rock	**466X**	80109	3900-4099	
SHANGRI LA DR	Denver	**285U**	80246	4100-4299	
SHANNOCK AVE	Castle Rock	**499J**	80104	6600-6999	
SHANNON CIR	Elbert Co	**871H**	80117	6600-6699	
SHANNON DR	Arvada	**221Z**	80004	9600-9699	
SHANNON DR	Broomfield	**163G**	80020	3100-14199	
SHANNON RD	El Paso Co	**909T**	80908	18500-18799	
SHANNON TRAIL E	Highlands Ranch	**406J**	80130	6200-6799	
SHARILANE ST	Adams Co	**794F**	80136	3800-4099	
SHARI'S CT	Bennett	**793J**	80102	800-999	
SHARKSTOOTH PEAK	Jefferson Co	**371K**	80127	11400-11499	
SHARON LN	Arvada	**251H**	80002	8900-8999	
SHARON PKWY	Golden	**249W**	80403	400-499	
SHARPE CT	Longmont	**11X**	80501	1-99	
SHARPE PL	Longmont	**11Y**	80501	1300-1499	
SHARPS CT	Douglas Co	**867Q**	80109	1600-1699	
SHAR TRAIL	Douglas Co	**866Z**	80135	4900-5299	
SHASTA CIR	Littleton	**343S**	80123	5700-5999	
SHASTA CT	Kiowa	**872M**	80117	300-699	
SHASTA LN	Jefferson Co	**335Z**	80439	6100-6599	
SHAVANO CT	Jefferson Co	**305M**	80439	1400-1499	
SHAVANO DR	Broomfield	**133J**	80020	None	
SHAVANO PL N	Douglas Co	**440Z**	80134	5900-6099	
SHAVANO RD	Thornton	**194S**	80260	None	
SHAVANO ST	Longmont	**12S**	80501	1700-1899	
SHAVANO PEAK DR	Superior	**160U**	80027	900-999	
SHAVANO PEAK PL	Douglas Co	**436U**	80108	6200-6299	
SHAVANO PEAK WAY	Douglas Co	**436V**	80108	6200-6299	
SHAW BLVD	Adams Co	**223A**	80031	4000-4799	
	Westminster	**223F**	80031	3400-3999	
	Westminster	**164X**	80234	None	
SHAW CT	Parker	**409N**	80134	10800-10899	
SHAWNEE CT S	Aurora	**380B**	80016	6600-6699	
SHAWNEE LN	Jefferson Co	**306S**	80439	30800-31199	
SHAWNEE LN	Superior	**160E**	80027	300-399	
SHAWNEE PL	Boulder	**128M**	80303	4600-4799	
SHAWNEE RD	Jefferson Co	**338P**	80454	22000-22699	
SHAWNEE ST S	Arapahoe Co	**350P**	80015	5100-5399	
	Arapahoe Co	**350T**	80015	5600-5799	
	Aurora	**350F**	80018	3900-4199	
	Aurora	**380B**	80016	6600-6699	
	Aurora	**380K**	80016	None	
	Aurora	**380Q**	80016	None	
	Centennial	**350T**	80015	6000-6199	
SHAWNEE WAY S	Arapahoe Co	**350P**	80015	5100-5299	
	Arapahoe Co	**350P**	80015	5400-5499	
	Arapahoe Co	**350Q**	80015	None	
	Aurora	**380F**	80016	7000-7499	
	Aurora	**350C**	80018	None	
SHEA PL E	Highlands Ranch	**406E**	80130	6200-6599	
SHEA CENTER DR	Highlands Ranch	**374W**	80129	1700-1899	
SHEADER AVE	Lafayette	**132E**	80026	300-399	
SHEEPHORN MOUNTAIN	Jefferson Co	**371E**	80127	7200-7499	
SHEEP PATCH RD	Jefferson Co	**782H**	80403	4500-4799	
SHEFFIELD	Elbert Co	**870M**	80107	None	
SHEFIELD CT	Douglas Co	**850P**	80134	11000-11199	
SHEFFIELD CT E	Parker	**410N**	80138	20500-20599	
SHEFFIELD DR	Broomfield	**163T**	80020	3700-3899	
SHEFFIELD PL E	Parker	**410N**	80138	20800-20899	
SHELBY DR	Castle Rock	**498Q**	80104	4800-5299	
SHELDON AVE	Adams Co	**223V**	80030	2400-2499	
SHELDON AVE	Castle Rock	**499J**	80104	1-499	
	Westminster	**223V**	80030	2500-2699	
SHELDON DR	Adams Co	**224D**	80229	700-1599	
SHELDON ST	Jefferson Co	**307X**	80439	26200-26399	
SHELEY CT	Longmont	**41L**	80501	300-499	
SHELTON DR	Park Co	**820Z**	80421	1-2399	
SHELTON RD	Golden	**279J**	80401	800-899	
SHENANDOAH AVE	Firestone	**707T**	80504	5700-6499	
	Firestone	**707S**	80504	6100-6999	
	Frederick	**707W**	80504	4900-6499	
SHENANDOAH CT	Elbert Co	**832S**	80107	44300-44499	
SHENANDOAH DR	Elbert Co	**832W**	80107	7100-7899	
SHENANDOAH DR S	Elbert Co	**832W**	80107	7100-7899	
SHENANDOAH WAY	Lochbuie	**140F**	80603	100-799	
SHENANDOAH WAY S	Aurora	**348L**	80015	4700-5099	
SHENSTONE CT	Douglas Co	**408C**	80134	16000-16099	
SHENSTONE DR	Douglas Co	**408D**	80134	9400-9699	
SHENSTONE WAY	Douglas Co	**408D**	80134	9500-9699	
SHEPPERD AVE W	Littleton	**344T**	80120	200-1199	
	Littleton	**344S**	80120	1200-1799	
	Littleton	**343V**	80120	2000-2299	
SHERAMDI AVE	Boulder Co	**11J**	80503	12700-12999	
SHERATON PL	Brighton	**138Q**	80601	1-99	
SHERI LN E	Arapahoe Co	**347P**	80111	10200-10299	
SHERI LN W	Littleton	**344N**	80120	1600-1699	

STREET NAME	CITY or COUNTY	MAP GRID	ZIP CODE	BLOCK RANGE	O/E
SHERIDAN BLVD	Adams Co	**253E**	80002	5200-5798	E
	Arvada	**253A**	80003	5800-6199	
	Arvada	**222R**	80003	6200-6799	
	Broomfield	**162R**	80020	12000-13199	
	Denver	**283N**	80226	2-598	E
	Denver	**283N**	80214	600-998	E
	Denver	**283J**	80214	1000-1099	
	Denver	**283E**	80214	1100-2698	E
	Denver	**253W**	80214	2700-3198	E
	Denver	**253N**	80212	3200-4798	E
	Denver	**253J**	80212	4800-5199	
	Jefferson Co	**253E**	80002	5201-5799	O
	Lakeside	**253N**	80212	4401-4799	O
	Lakewood	**283N**	80226	1-599	O
	Lakewood	**283N**	80214	601-999	O
	Lakewood	**283E**	80214	1101-2699	O
	Mountain View	**253N**	80212	4101-4399	O
	Westminster	**222R**	80003	6800-9099	
	Westminster	**192R**	80031	9100-9799	
	Westminster	**192R**	80020	9800-11999	
	Wheat Ridge	**253W**	80214	2701-3199	O
	Wheat Ridge	**253S**	80212	3201-4099	O
SHERIDAN BLVD S	Arapahoe Co	**373A**	80123	6500-6799	
	Arapahoe Co	**373E**	80128	6800-7499	
	Denver	**283S**	80226	2-698	E
	Denver	**313A**	80226	700-1098	E
	Denver	**313E**	80232	1100-1898	E
	Denver	**313N**	80219	1900-2399	
	Denver	**313N**	80219	2400-2698	E
	Denver	**313S**	80227	2700-3499	
	Lakewood	**283S**	80226	1-699	O
	Lakewood	**313A**	80226	701-1099	O
	Lakewood	**313E**	80232	1101-1899	O
	Lakewood	**313N**	80227	2401-2699	O
SHERIDAN CT	Arvada	**222H**	80003	8100-8599	
SHERIDAN CT S	Jefferson Co	**372M**	80128	7100-7799	
	Lakewood	**312V**	80227	2600-2699	
SHERIDAN DR	Parker	**408R**	80134	16300-16499	
SHERIDAN LOOP S	Jefferson Co	**372D**	80123	None	
SHERIDAN PKWY	Broomfield	**133U**	80020	None	
	Broomfield	**133W**	80026	None	
	Broomfield	**163A**	80020	None	
SHERIDAN PKWY	Erie	**133H**	80516	None	
SHERIDAN WAY S	Jefferson Co	**342Z**	80123	5900-6099	
SHERIFFS COVE	El Paso Co	**908P**	80132	20100-20299	
SHERIFFS WAY	El Paso Co	**908Q**	80132	19400-19499	
SHERI-LYN PL	Boulder Co	**70L**	80503	None	
SHERILYNN CIR	Firestone	**727B**	80504	None	
SHERMAN CIR S	Littleton	**344U**	80121	5500-5599	
SHERMAN CT	Longmont	**41G**	80501	1-99	
SHERMAN DR	Longmont	**41L**	80501	1200-1399	
SHERMAN DR	Northglenn	**194G**	80233	11300-11399	
SHERMAN PL	Adams Co	**224L**	80221	7600-7799	
SHERMAN ST	Adams Co	**254G**	80216	5200-5399	
	Adams Co	**224G**	80221	7300-8299	
SHERMAN ST	Castle Pines North	**436L**	80108	600-799	
	Denver	**284L**	80203	1-1399	
	Denver	**284G**	80203	1500-1999	
	Denver	**254L**	80216	4200-5199	
SHERMAN ST	Longmont	**41G**	80501	200-299	
	Longmont	**41C**	80501	300-899	
	Longmont	**11Y**	80501	1100-1299	
	Longmont	**11Q**	80501	2100-2399	
	Longmont	**11L**	80501	2400-2499	
SHERMAN ST	Northglenn	**194Q**	80233	10400-10499	
	Northglenn	**194C**	80233	11600-11899	
	Thornton	**224G**	80260	8200-8299	
SHERMAN ST S	Arapahoe Co	**795Y**	80103	100-599	
	Arapahoe Co	**344Q**	80121	5100-5499	
	Arapahoe Co	**374C**	80121	6500-6699	
	Arapahoe Co	**374C**	80122	6700-6899	
	Arapahoe Co	**374G**	80122	7100-7299	
	Denver	**284Y**	80209	1-699	
	Denver	**314C**	80209	700-899	
	Denver	**314L**	80210	1100-2699	
	Englewood	**314Y**	80113	2700-3599	
	Englewood	**344G**	80110	3600-5099	
	Littleton	**344U**	80121	5500-5599	
SHERMAN ST S	Longmont	**41Q**	80501	600-1499	
SHERMAN WAY	Adams Co	**224L**	80221	7900-8099	
SHERMAN WAY	Broomfield	**133J**	80020	None	
SHERMAN WAY	Longmont	**11U**	80501	1600-1699	
SHERMAN WAY S	Centennial	**344U**	80121	5800-5899	
SHERRELWOOD CIR	Adams Co	**223M**	80221	1800-2099	
SHERRELWOOD DR	Adams Co	**224J**	80221	1600-1999	
	Adams Co	**223H**	80221	2000-2399	
SHERRELWOOD LN S					
	Highlands Ranch	**404D**	80126	9400-9599	
SHERRI MAR CT	Longmont	**11X**	80501	1100-1299	
SHERRI MAR PL	Longmont	**11X**	80501	2000-2099	
SHERRI MAR ST	Longmont	**11T**	80501	1400-1599	
	Longmont	**11P**	80501	2100-2499	
SHERWOOD CIR	Boulder	**98N**	80304	2600-2699	
SHERWOOD CT	Longmont	**12S**	80501	200-299	
SHERWOOD DR	Boulder Co	**741J**	80466	1-399	
SHERWOOD FOREST TRAIL					
	Elbert Co	**892H**	80117	26500-26699	
SHERWOOD GLEN N	El Paso Co	**908Q**	80132	1-199	
SHERWOOD GLEN S	El Paso Co	**908U**	80132	1-99	
SHERWOOD TRAIL	El Paso Co	**908R**	80132	19200-19499	
SHETLAND CT	Highlands Ranch	**376W**	80130	5400-5499	
SHETLAND DR	Frederick	**707W**	80504	None	
SHETLAND RD	Jefferson Co	**306Y**	80439	3100-3199	
SHETLAND ST	Weld Co	**729V**	80603	17500-17999	
SHETLAND WAY	El Paso Co	**909W**	80132	2400-2499	
SHETLAND TRAIL	Elbert Co	**871A**	80107	2300-2499	
SHILOH CIR	Jefferson Co	**843F**	80433	25300-25799	
SHILOH CT	Elbert Co	**832X**	80107	8300-8399	
SHILOH DR	Castle Rock	**498N**	80104	1900-2199	
SHILOH DR	Jefferson Co	**843F**	80433	13000-14199	
SHILOH LN	Jefferson Co	**843F**	80433	24700-24899	
SHILOH RD	Jefferson Co	**843F**	80433	13200-13799	
SHILOH PINES DR	El Paso Co	**908Z**	80132	17200-17799	
SHILOH POINT DR	Jefferson Co	**844D**	80127	12300-12699	
SHILOH RANCH DR	El Paso Co	**910T**	80908	18000-19999	
SHILOH RIDGE TRAIL	Jefferson Co	**843F**	80433	13900-14099	
SHIMLEY LN	Jefferson Co	**762A**	80403	11201-11299	O
SHIMLEY RD	Jefferson Co	**762A**	80403	11200-11599	

S

STREET NAME	CITY or COUNTY	MAP GRID	ZIP CODE	BLOCK RANGE	O/E
SHINGLE CREEK RD	Jefferson Co	308F	80401	22200-22799	
	Jefferson Co	308E	80401	23200-23699	
SHINING OAK CT	Jefferson Co	370P	80127	1-99	
SHINING OAK DR	Jefferson Co	370P	80127	1-99	
SHIRE CIR	Castle Rock	467Y	80104	3300-3599	
SHIRLEE CT	Platteville	708C	80651	500-599	
SHIRLEY PL W	Lakewood	312H	80232	5300-5399	
SHOAL CIR	Longmont	10V	80503	2800-2899	
SHOAL CREEK LN	Lone Tree	406D	80124	8800-8899	
SHOOTING STAR CIR	Elbert Co	891X	80106	None	
SHOOTING STAR CT	Boulder Co	71J	80503	None	
SHOOTING STAR DR	Jefferson Co	307M	80401	1400-24199	
SHOOTING STAR LN	Jefferson Co	308E	80401	23800-23999	
SHOOTING STAR WAY	Castle Rock	466N	80109	4500-4699	
SHOREHAM CIR	Douglas Co	436Q	80108	200-599	
SHOREHAM DR	Castle Pines North	436L	80108	7000-7499	
SHOREHAM PL	Castle Pines North	436R	80108	7300-7499	
SHORELINE DR	Weld Co	706U	80504	9801-9899	O
SHORE PINE	Jefferson Co	370Q	80127	1-99	
SHOREPINE CT	Douglas Co	408M	80134	10400-10499	
SHORT CT	Dacono	727J	80514	600-699	
SHORT CT	Louisville	130V	80027	1300-1399	
SHORT DR	Dacono	727J	80514	100-199	
SHORT PL	Louisville	130V	80027	200-299	
SHORT PL W	Denver	283Q	80204	2700-2999	
	Denver	283N	80204	4500-4699	
SHORT RD	Jefferson Co	844Y	80441	17100-17299	
SHORT ST	Castle Rock	497G	80104	None	
SHORT ST	Louisville	131S	80027	400-1199	
SHORT BEACH CT	Arapahoe Co	794R	80136	1200-1499	
SHORT DIRT RD	Gilpin Co	761U	80403	1-99	
SHORT GRASS CT	Castle Rock	497E	80109	1400-1599	
SHORT IRON CT	Castle Rock	496D	80109	None	
SHORTLINE DR	Fort Lupton	728H	80621	1000-1299	
SHORTRIDGE CT	Erie	102P	80516	2300-2499	
SHOSHONE CT	Boulder	128R	80303	100-199	
SHOSHONE DR	Douglas Co	886M	80118	4400-4799	
SHOSHONE DR	Frederick	707W	80504	11200-11399	
SHOSHONE PL	Douglas Co	886M	80118	7900-8099	
SHOSHONE RD	Jefferson Co	338E	80454	4100-4399	
SHOSHONE ST	Adams Co	254E	80221	5300-5699	
	Adams Co	223M	80221	7600-7899	
	Adams Co	223H	80221	8200-8399	
	Arapahoe Co	794T	80136	800-999	
	Denver	284J	80204	1200-1399	
	Denver	254S	80211	3200-4799	
	Denver	254J	80221	4800-5199	
SHOSHONE ST	Kiowa	872M	80117	None	
SHOSHONE ST	Westminster	163M	80234	13100-13599	
SHOSHONE ST S	Denver	284W	80223	500-699	
	Denver	314A	80223	700-899	
	Denver	314E	80223	1100-1899	
	Englewood	314S	80110	2700-2999	
	Sheridan	314W	80110	3300-3498	E
SHOSHONE WAY	Boulder Co	740L	80466	None	
SHOSHONE WAY	Thornton	193V	80260	10000-10099	
SHOSHONE WAY	Westminster	194A	80234	11600-11699	
SHOSHONE TRAIL	Elbert Co	850Z	80107	1300-1999	
SHOSHONE TRAIL	Lafayette	131E	80026	2700-3099	
SHOSHONE VALLEY TRAIL	Monument	908W	80132	2200-2399	
SHOSHONI WAY	Nederland	740L	80466	None	
SHOSHONI CAMP	Gilpin Co	740Z	80403	None	
SHOUP PL	Boulder	128H	80303	4700-4799	
SHRINE CIR	Douglas Co	887L	80118	7500-7699	
SHRINE RD	Douglas Co	887L	80118	7400-7699	
SHULL CT	Brighton	138T	80601	400-499	
SHUTTLEWORTH DR	Erie	102U	80516	800-999	
SIBRICA ST S	Parker	439F	80134	None	
SICILY CIR S	Arapahoe Co	350U	80015	5600-5699	
SICILY CT S	Arapahoe Co	350U	80015	5600-5699	
	Aurora	380C	80016	6800-6899	
	Aurora	380F	80016	None	
	Aurora	380Q	80016	None	
SICILY DR	Longmont	40P	80503	1500-1799	
SICILY ST S	Arapahoe Co	350Q	80015	5100-5599	
	Arapahoe Co	350U	80015	5600-5799	
	Arapahoe Co	350K	80015	None	
SICILY WAY S	Arapahoe Co	350Q	80015	5200-5599	
	Aurora	350Y	80016	6000-6399	
	Aurora	380K	80016	None	
SIDNEY CT S	Denver	316U	80231	2700-2999	
	Denver	346G	80237	4100-4199	
SIDNEY RD	Jefferson Co	762A	80403	11700E-11799E	
	Jefferson Co	762A	80403	33300W-33599W	
SIDON CIR	Lafayette	131Q	80026	1500-1599	
SIEGAL CT	Commerce City	225Z	80022	6400-6499	
SIENA WAY	Boulder Co	99D	80301	7200-7299	
SIENNA TERRACE	Douglas Co	408G	80134	15800-15999	
SIERRA AVE	Longmont	41R	80501	400-599	
SIERRA CIR	Douglas Co	409D	80138	12500-13099	
SIERRA CIR N	Douglas Co	379Z	80138	12500-13099	
SIERRA DR	Arvada	221M	80005	9300-9799	
SIERRA DR	Boulder	127M	80302	1400-1499	
SIERRA DR	Castle Rock	498J	80104	1300-1499	
SIERRA ST	Brighton	139P	80601	None	
SIERRA WAY	El Paso Co	908Z	80132	17400-17999	
SIERRA WAY	El Paso Co	907V	80132	None	
SIERRA TIMBER RD	Gilpin Co	761E	80403	100-399	
SIERRA VERDE CT	Castle Rock	467R	80104	2100-2199	
SIERRA VISTA RD	Weld Co	707T	80504	9300-9999	
SIESTA CIR	Clear Creek Co	801R	80439	1-199	
SIGNAL BUTTE DR	Douglas Co	432Q	80125	10000-10099	
SIGNAL CREEK BLVD	Thornton	165N	80241	2600-2699	
	Thornton	165P	80241	2700-3099	
SIGNAL CREEK DR	Thornton	165K	80241	2600-2899	
SIGNAL CREEK PL	Thornton	165K	80241	2700-2899	
SIGNAL RIDGE CIR	Elbert Co	850Q	80107	500-599	
SIGNAL RIDGE TRAIL	Elbert Co	850Q	80107	38100-38299	
SIGNAL ROCK RD	Boulder Co	742W	80403	1-299	
SIGNATURE CIR	Longmont	12U	80501	1100-1899	
SIGNATURE CT	Longmont	12U	80501	1800-1899	
SILBRICO WAY	Douglas Co	466H	80108	400-499	
SILENT HILLS DR S	Douglas Co	407A	80124	9500-9599	
	Lone Tree	407A	80124	9300-9499	
SILENT HILLS LN	Douglas Co	407A	80124	9500-9599	
SILENT HILLS PL E	Douglas Co	407A	80124	9500-9599	
SILHOUETTE WAY	El Paso Co	908Y	80132	500-599	
SILLASEN LN	Gilpin Co	741Z	80403	1-199	

STREET NAME	CITY or COUNTY	MAP GRID	ZIP CODE	BLOCK RANGE	O/E
SILO CT	Brighton	139L	80601	None	
SILO CT	Mead	706C	80542	100-199	
SILO LN	Westminster	222A	80021	None	
SILO RD N	Douglas Co	441F	80138	8000-8699	
SILVER AVE	Broomfield	163P	80020	3500-3599	
SILVER CT	Highlands Ranch	375X	80126	8900-8999	
SILVER PL	Superior	160U	80027	2700-2999	
SILVER RD	Boulder Co	740S	80466	None	
SILVER RD	Gilpin Co	761E	80403	1-199	
SILVERADO CIR	Frederick	726G	80516	3400-3499	
SILVERADO DR	Parker	379X	80134	None	
SILVER ASPEN	Jefferson Co	370Q	80127	1-99	
SILVERBERRY	Jefferson Co	370K	80127	1-99	
SILVERBERRY CIR S	Highlands Ranch	404F	80129	9600-9699	
SILVER BERRY CT	Lafayette	131M	80026	700-799	
SILVERBERRY LN	Jefferson Co	307D	80401	700-899	
SILVER BLUFF CT	Douglas Co	440W	80134	5600-5699	
SILVER BROOK DR	Parker	410P	80138	21700-21799	
SILVER CLIFF CT	Douglas Co	466H	80108	4500-4599	
SILVERCLIFF LN	Douglas Co	432G	80125	10000-10099	
SILVER CLOUD LN	Boulder Co	722L	80302	1-399	
SILVER CLOUD PL	Douglas Co	466H	80108	300-399	
SILVER CREEK CT S	Parker	439C	80134	12600-12699	
SILVERCREEK LN	Jefferson Co	306K	80439	1600-1799	
SILVER CREEK RD	Gilpin Co	760S	80403	100-199	
SILVERCREEK ST E					
	Buckley Air Force Base	290W	80017	None	
SILVER CREEK ST S	Parker	439C	80134	12500-12699	
SILVER CREEK TRAIL	Dacono	727J	80514	None	
SILVER DALE CT	Douglas Co	466H	80108	4500-4599	
SILVER DOLLAR CT	Castle Rock	467V	80104	1100-1299	
SILVER ELK LN	Jefferson Co	824R	80127	12900-12999	
SILVER FEATHER CIR	Broomfield	133W	80026	4900-15099	
	Broomfield	132Z	80026	5100-14999	
SILVER FEATHER WAY	Broomfield	133W	80026	5000-5099	
SILVER FIR CT	Jefferson Co	370K	80127	1-99	
SILVER FIR ST	Elbert Co	830Q	80138	46500-47099	
SILVER FOX CIR	Greenwood Village	345R	80121	1-99	
SILVER FOX CT	Greenwood Village	345R	80121	100-199	
SILVER FOX DR	Greenwood Village	345R	80121	1-199	
SILVER FOX LN	Jefferson Co	823Z	80433	11300-11999	
SILVER GARTER RD	Park Co	841A	80421	100-199	
SILVER GATE DR	Douglas Co	466H	80108	4500-4599	
SILVER GULCH RD	Black Hawk	781A	80403	None	
SILVERHEELS PL	Douglas Co	887L	80118	8100-8199	
SILVERHEELS RD	Douglas Co	887L	80118	1000-2199	
SILVER HILL CIR	Lone Tree	406D	80124	9500-9699	
SILVERHORN DR	Jefferson Co	367G	80439	6800-7399	
SILVERHORN LN	El Paso Co	908P	80132	19900-20499	
SILVERHORN LN	Jefferson Co	367F	80439	25700-25899	
SILVER LACE DR N	Castle Rock	466Q	80109	4700-5099	
SILVER LAKE AVE	Boulder	97G	80304	700-799	
SILVERLEAF AVE	Firestone	707S	80504	5700-5899	
	Firestone	706V	80504	6400-6999	
SILVER LEAF WAY	Douglas Co	466B	80108	100-199	
SILVERLEAF OAK	Jefferson Co	336A	80439	31100-31299	
SILVER MAPLE CIR S	Highlands Ranch	403H	80129	10000-10299	
SILVER MAPLE RD S	Highlands Ranch	403H	80129	9800-10199	
SILVER MAPLE ST	Highlands Ranch	403H	80129	9900-9999	
SILVER MAPLE WAY S					
	Highlands Ranch	403H	80129	9900-9999	
SILVER MEADOW CIR	Parker	410P	80138	21800-21899	
SILVER MEADOW LN	Parker	410P	80138	21700-21899	
SILVER MESA DR	Highlands Ranch	376S	80130	6400-6599	
SILVER MINES ST	Frederick	726G	80516	6400-6599	
SILVER MOUND	Jefferson Co	370F	80127	1-99	
SILVER MOUND LN	Parker	379S	80134	17100-17399	
SILVER NELL DR	El Paso Co	909Y	80908	None	
SILVER PEAK AVE	Dacono	726M	80514	None	
SILVER PINE DR	Castle Rock	467R	80108	4600-4999	
SILVER PLUME CIR	Boulder	128Y	80305	3800-3999	
SILVER PLUME LN	Boulder	128X	80305	3600-3999	
SILVER PLUME PL	Boulder	128X	80305	3500-3599	
SILVER PLUME ST S	Parker	439G	80134	12800-12899	
SILVER POINT DR	Boulder Co	740G	80466	900-1099	
SILVER RANCH RD	Jefferson Co	844A	80433	19100-20199	
SILVER ROCK LN	Jefferson Co	307J	80401	1200-1599	
SILVER SADDLE RD	El Paso Co	908Q	80132	200-799	
SILVER SAGE CT	Boulder Co	99D	80301	4800-4899	
SILVER SAGE WAY	El Paso Co	908U	80132	19200-19399	
SILVER SPRINGS BLVD	Jefferson Co	842J	80470	34400-34599	
SILVER SPRINGS RD	Park Co	841M	80421	1-399	
SILVER SPRUCE LN	Jefferson Co	336R	80439	4800-4999	
SILVER SPUR LN	Highlands Ranch	406B	80130	9500-9599	
SILVER STAR CT	Longmont	42B	80501	600-699	
SILVER SWAN PL	Castle Rock	496B	80109	None	
SILVERTHORNE DR	Frederick	726G	80516	3400-3799	
SILVERTHORN RUN	Douglas Co	432X	80125	5900-6099	
SILVERTIP LN	Jefferson Co	305F	80439	1200-1399	
SILVERTON DR	Broomfield	162L	80020	13600-13999	
SILVERTON ST	Boulder	98P	80301	None	
SILVERTOP CIR S	Parker	408Z	80134	None	
SILVERVALE LN	Jefferson Co	306L	80439	None	
SILVERWEED WAY	Lone Tree	376Y	80124	7700-7899	
SILVER WILLOW RD	Jefferson Co	278S	80401	100-299	
SILVER WING CT	Douglas Co	466H	80108	4500-4599	
SIMMONS CT	Erie	102Q	80516	400-499	
SIMMONS DR	Boulder Co	129F	80303	6000-6399	
SIMMONS DR	Douglas Co	908L	80118	2700-2899	
SIMMONS ST	Erie	102Q	80516	300-499	
SIMMONS WAY	Jefferson Co	763K	80403	24800-24999	
SIMMS CT	Arvada	221T	80004	6800-6899	
SIMMS CT	Arvada	221N	80005	7400-7599	
	Arvada	221E	80005	8200-8299	
	Wheat Ridge	251T	80033	3800-4099	
	Wheat Ridge	251P	80033	4500-4599	
SIMMS CT S	Jefferson Co	341K	80465	4500-4799	
	Jefferson Co	341X	80127	6000-6199	
SIMMS DR	Lakewood	251W	80215	2800-2999	
SIMMS PL	Lakewood	281B	80215	2100-2299	
	Wheat Ridge	251K	80033	5000-5199	
SIMMS ST	Arvada	251B	80004	5800-6199	
	Arvada	221T	80004	6200-7199	
	Arvada	221K	80005	7200-8499	
	Broomfield	191A	80021	11700-11999	
	Lakewood	281B	80401	600-1499	
	Lakewood	281B	80215	1500-2799	

Continued on next column

STREET NAME	CITY or COUNTY	MAP GRID	ZIP CODE	BLOCK RANGE	O/E
SIMMS ST (Cont'd)	Lakewood	251X	80215	2800-3199	
	Westminster	191P	80021	10000-11699	
	Wheat Ridge	251X	80033	3200-3499	
	Wheat Ridge	251T	80033	3500-4099	
	Wheat Ridge	251P	80033	4400-4799	
SIMMS ST S	Jefferson Co	311F	80232	1200-1499	
	Jefferson Co	341K	80465	4300-5099	
	Jefferson Co	341T	80127	5100-6499	
	Jefferson Co	371K	80127	6500-7499	
	Lakewood	281X	80228	300-599	
	Lakewood	311B	80228	600-999	
SIMMS WAY S	Jefferson Co	341P	80127	5200-5499	
	Jefferson Co	341T	80127	5500-5699	
	Jefferson Co	371B	80127	6500-6599	
	Jefferson Co	311T	80228	None	
SIMPSON RD	El Paso Co	908S	80132	None	
SIMPSON ST E	Lafayette	132J	80026	100-899	
SIMPSON ST W	Lafayette	132J	80026	100-499	
SINCLAIRE BLVD	Douglas Co	887B	80118	1600-1799	
SINGER DR	Park Co	820Z	80421	1-199	
SINGING HILLS CT	Boulder Co	100A	80301	7400-7499	
SINGING HILLS DR	Boulder Co	100A	80301	7400-7499	
SINGING HILLS RD	Elbert Co	850H	80138	1-1999	
	Elbert Co	851G	80138	2000-4999	
SINGING HILLS RD E	Douglas Co	411Q	80138	10500-11799	
SINGING RIVER RANCH RD					
	Clear Creek Co	801U	80439	100-1099	
SINGING SPRINGS LN	Jefferson Co	366H	80439	6700-7099	
SINGING WINDS ST	Parker	410Y	80138	None	
SINGLELEAF CT	Douglas Co	408M	80134	10600-10699	
SINGLETREE CT	Elbert Co	832X	80107	8300-8399	
SINGLETREE CT	Jefferson Co	339R	80465	16600-16799	
SINGLETREE CT	Mead	706C	80542	3700-3899	
SINGLETREE DR	Mead	706D	80542	15000-15499	
SINGLETREE LN	Brighton	139Q	80601	None	
SINGLETREE LN	Douglas Co	439Z	80134	5400-5999	
SINGLETREE LN	Erie	133B	80516	None	
SINTON RD	Clear Creek Co	304P	80439	900-2999	
SIOUX AVE	Adams Co	226F	80022	None	
SIOUX CT	Douglas Co	846U	80135	3800-3999	
SIOUX CT	Weld Co	707X	80504	7000-7199	
SIOUX DR	Boulder	128M	80303	4400-5199	
	Boulder	129J	80303	5400-5699	
SIOUX DR	Douglas Co	846U	80135	5500-5999	
SIOUX LN	Douglas Co	846U	80135	5600-5899	
SIOUX RD	Jefferson Co	338Q	80454	21600-21899	
SIOUX RD S	Jefferson Co	842U	80470	15700-15999	
SIOUX TRAIL	Clear Creek Co	365N	80439	1-399	
SIOUX TRAIL	Elbert Co	870D	80107	1000-1499	
SIOUX TRAIL	Jefferson Co	842E	80470	33900-34599	
SIOUX TRAIL	Thornton	195U	80229	None	
SIR GALAHAD DR	Lafayette	132P	80026	500-1299	
SIRUS DR	Highlands Ranch	376U	80124	9400-9499	
SISAL CT	Castle Rock	496B	80109	None	
SISKIN AVE	Brighton	139R	80601	100-199	
SISKIN AVE	Highlands Ranch	375U	80126	None	
SITTING BULL TRAIL	Jefferson Co	823W	80433	25800-25999	
SIX ST	Jefferson Co	189X	80007	None	
SIX BITS ST	Park Co	841A	80421	1-199	
SIXPENNY LN	El Paso Co	909S	80132	19100-19299	
SIX SHOOTER CT	Park Co	841K	80421	1-99	
SIX TREES LN	El Paso Co	908U	80132	18100-18199	
SKEEL ST	Brighton	138P	80601	1-1799	
	Brighton	138R	80601	2200-2699	
SKI HILL DR	Jefferson Co	307D	80401	24400-24999	
SKI MOUNTAIN DR	Jefferson Co	844F	80127	13500-13698	E
SKI TRAIL	Clear Creek Co	365N	80439	1-499	
	Jefferson Co	365E	80439	6500-7199	
SKOKIE LN	Jefferson Co	306S	80439	31100-31199	
SKUNK ALLEY	Jefferson Co	365F	80439	6900-7099	
SKY BEAR	Jefferson Co	306M	80401	None	
SKY CHURCH DR	Castle Rock	496C	80109	3400-3699	
SKY COVE DR	Broomfield	163H	80020	13900-13998	E
SKYDANCE DR	Highlands Ranch	404Q	80126	None	
SKYE LN	Highlands Ranch	376S	80130	1-99	
SKYE PL	Highlands Ranch	376S	80130	1-99	
SKYHAVEN DR	Federal Heights	194W	80260	None	
SKY HAWK CT	Castle Rock	466S	80109	3700-3899	
SKYHAWK WAY	Elbert Co	830U	80138	None	
SKYHILL DR	Jefferson Co	276X	80401	1-299	
SKYLAND DR	Boulder Co	70Q	80503	8500-8799	
SKYLANE DR	Erie	133F	80516	1-299	
SKYLARK CIR	Lafayette	132J	80026	200-399	
SKYLARK CT	Longmont	11N	80503	2000-2099	
SKYLARK DR	Lafayette	132J	80026	None	
SKYLARK ST	Highlands Ranch	375V	80126	8700-8799	
SKYLARK WAY	Boulder Co	130J	80303	200-399	
SKYLINE AVE	Frederick	727A	80516	None	
SKYLINE DR	Boulder Co	742W	80403	1-299	
SKYLINE DR	Clear Creek Co	780T	80452	1200-1499	
SKYLINE DR	Erie	133H	80516	None	
SKYLINE DR	Jefferson Co	762C	80403	30400-30999	
	Jefferson Co	762E	80403	33700-34299	
SKYLINE DR	Westminster	223Q	80030	2500-7499	
	Wheat Ridge	251Y	80215	1-99	
SKYLINE DR	Wheat Ridge	281C	80215	1-99	
SKYLINE DR S	Jefferson Co	335G	80439	3800-4099	
	Jefferson Co	337S	80439	5400-6499	
SKYLINE LN	Longmont	12T	80501	1500-1599	
SKYLINE ST	Frederick	727A	80516	None	
SKYLINE WAY	Frederick	727A	80516	None	
SKY MEADOW LN	Jefferson Co	278R	80401	20500-21199	
SKY RANCH RD	Aurora	259Z	80011	20100-20398	E
SKYREACH RD	Highlands Ranch	404L	80126	10400-10599	
SKYREACH WAY	Highlands Ranch	404L	80126	10400-10499	
SKY RIDGE AVE	Lone Tree	407E	80124	9100-9199	
	Lone Tree	406H	80124	None	
SKY ROCK WAY	Castle Rock	467W	80109	None	
SKYSAIL CT	Longmont	10M	80503	2400-2499	
SKY TRAIL DR	Bow Mar	343N	80123	5200-5299	
SKY TRAIL RD	Boulder Co	722L	80302	1-799	
SKYVIEW CT	Louisville	130Y	80027	100-199	
SKY VIEW DR	Boulder Co	741J	80466	1N-299N	
	Boulder Co	741J	80466	1S-399S	
SKY VIEW LN	Douglas Co	887C	80118	1700-1799	
SKY VU DR	Jefferson Co	762E	80403	33700-33898	E
SKYWALK ST	Douglas Co	409X	80134	None	
SKYWALKER PT	Lafayette	131E	80026	700-799	

S

STREET NAME	CITY or COUNTY	MAP GRID	ZIP CODE	BLOCK RANGE	O/E
SKYWARD WAY	Castle Rock	467W	80109	None	
SKYWAY CT	Boulder Co	130W	80303	None	
SKYWAY DR	Boulder Co	130W	80303	None	
SKYWAY DR	Weld Co	706P	80504	1500-1899	
SLASH PINE DR	El Paso Co	909Q	80908	4000-4399	
SLATE CT	Castle Rock	467H	80108	7300-7499	
SLATE CT	Superior	160U	80027	2700-2899	
SLATE WAY	El Paso Co	908X	80132	1000-1099	
SLAUGHTERHOUSE GULCH					
	Jamestown	722A	80455	None	
SLEEPING BEAR TRAIL	Douglas Co	432N	80125	7100-7499	
SLEEPING FOX CT	Douglas Co	867F	80109	300-399	
SLEEPING OWL PT	Lafayette	131K	80026	301-399	O
SLEEPY GRASS CT	Parker	379W	80134	8900-8999	
SLEEPY HOLLOW	Jefferson Co	308B	80401	900-1099	
SLEEPY HOLLOW DR	Park Co	841Q	80421	1-1299	
SLEEPY HOLLOW RD	El Paso Co	908Q	80132	19700-19799	
SLEEPYTIME DR	Boulder	99E	80301	4600-4799	
SLICK ROCK CT	Boulder	69Y	80301	5600-5799	
SLOAN LN	El Paso Co	908U	80132	18300-18499	
SLY FOX CIR	Elbert Co	871J	80107	2800-2999	
SLY FOX WAY	Douglas Co	867E	80135	100-499	
SMALL DR	Commerce City	226S	80022	6100-6299	
SMILEY DR	Boulder	128B	80303	None	
SMITH CIR	Erie	103P	80516	200-499	
SMITH CT	Longmont	11Q	80501	2300-2399	
SMITH DR	Longmont	11Q	80501	2200-2299	
SMITH DR E	Aurora	258X	80011	13700-14199	
SMITH RD	Aurora	257U	80010	11300-11398	E
	Aurora	257V	80011	None	
	Denver	256N	80216	5600-6298	E
	Denver	256T	80207	6500-9399	
	Denver	257T	80239	10200-11299	
SMITH RD	Douglas Co	910B	80118	11300-11599	
SMITH RD	Golden	278H	80401	1800-1899	
SMITH RD	Jefferson Co	842A	80470	33500-33899	
SMITH RD	Park Co	820Z	80421	1-599	
SMITH RD E	Aurora	258X	80011	13400-16899	
	Aurora	289B	80011	16900-20199	
	Aurora	290C	80011	20200-21699	
	Aurora	290C	80019	21700-24499	
	Aurora	291F	80018	24500-26599	
	Denver	255Q	80216	4800-5598	E
SMITH ST	Park Co	820Z	80421	1-299	
SMITH WAY	Aurora	290H	80019	None	
SMITH HILL RD	Gilpin Co	781F	80403	1-2699	
	Gilpin Co	761Y	80403	2700-4799	
SMOKEY PINE RD	Elbert Co	912L	80106	18200-18999	
SMOKEY ROCK RD	Park Co	840C	80421	1-399	
SMOKY HILL PKWY E	Aurora	381L	80016	25000-27299	
SMOKY HILL RD E	Arapahoe Co	350X	80016	23000-23999	
	Aurora	348F	80015	14000-16899	
	Aurora	350X	80016	21600-22999	
	Aurora	350X	80016	24000-24599	
	Aurora	381A	80016	24600-25999	
	Aurora	381L	80016	26000-26499	
	Centennial	349P	80015	16900-20599	
	Centennial	350X	80015	20600-20899	
	Centennial	350X	80016	20900-21599	
SMUGGLER CIR	Boulder	743Q	80305	3500-3599	
SMUGGLER PL	Boulder	128X	80305	3600-3799	
SMUGGLER WAY	Boulder	743Q	80305	3500-3799	
SMUGGLERS RD	El Paso Co	908Y	80132	17700-17999	
SMUGGLERS WAY	El Paso Co	908Y	80132	17900-17999	
SNAFFLE BIT CT	Douglas Co	432F	80125	8300-8499	
SNAP DRAGON CT	Superior	160Z	80027	1500-1599	
SNEAD CT	Boulder Co	723H	80503	6600-6799	
SNEFFELS CT	Broomfield	133J	80020	None	
SNEFFLES	Thornton	193V	80260	None	
SNOSHOE ST	Adams Co	133Z	80020	14800-14999	
SNOWBANK CT	Longmont	12X	80501	1200-1299	
SNOWBERRY AVE	Firestone	707S	80504	None	
SNOWBERRY CT	Boulder	97L	80304	4300-4399	
SNOWBERRY CT	Golden	248V	80403	400-499	
SNOWBERRY CT	Lafayette	131M	80026	700-799	
SNOWBERRY DR	Jefferson Co	308E	80401	1100-1399	
SNOWBERRY DR	Littleton	343S	80123	5700-5799	
SNOWBERRY LN	Boulder Co	70Q	80503	6300-6399	
SNOWBERRY LN	Broomfield	162P	80020	1200-1499	
SNOWBERRY LN	Castle Rock	497R	80104	1200-1299	
SNOWBERRY LN	Gilpin Co	761C	80403	1-99	
SNOWBERRY LN	Jefferson Co	337R	80439	4900-5199	
SNOWBERRY LN	Louisville	131K	80027	None	
SNOWBERRY PL	Littleton	343S	80123	5800-5999	
SNOWBERRY ST	Longmont	40Q	80503	700-999	
SNOWBERRY WAY	Parker	379S	80134	17600-17699	
SNOWBIRD AVE	Broomfield	163S	80020	4100-4399	
SNOWBIRD LN	Jefferson Co	306K	80439	30000-30799	
SNOWBIRD LN	Lafayette	131F	80026	700-899	
SNOWBIRD WAY	Douglas Co	378V	80134	8700-8899	
SNOWBIRD HILL WAY	Parker	410Y	80138	23100-23399	
SNOWBRUSH LN S	Highlands Ranch	374V	80126	8600-8699	
SNOWBUNTING CT	Highlands Ranch	375Y	80126	8800-8899	
SNOWCAP LN	Broomfield	133W	80026	4400-4499	
SNOW CLOUD TRAIL	Douglas Co	432N	80125	10800-10999	
SNOWCREEK CT	Parker	410S	80138	21300-21399	
SNOWCREEK LN	Jefferson Co	339R	80465	17000-17099	
SNOWCREEK LN	Parker	410S	80138	11600-11799	
SNOW CREST DR	Broomfield	133W	80026	14700-14999	
SNOWDROP RD	Jefferson Co	307X	80439	26200-26699	
SNOWFLAKE WAY	Douglas Co	439W	80134	5500-5599	
SNOW GOOSE ST	Brighton	139R	80601	5200-5298	E
SNOW LAKE CT	Arapahoe Co	791U	80137	900-1199	
SNOW LILY CT	Castle Pines North	436K	80108	1000-1099	
SNOW LILY LN	Castle Pines North	436K	80108	1100-1199	
SNOW LILY PL	Castle Pines North	436K	80108	7400-7499	
SNOWMASS CIR	Broomfield	162L	80020	2100-2199	
SNOWMASS CIR N	Superior	160X	80027	300-599	
SNOWMASS CIR S	Superior	160Y	80027	300-699	
SNOWMASS CT	Boulder	128S	80305	1400-1499	
SNOWMASS PL	Longmont	12W	80501	1-199	
SNOWMASS RD	Thornton	193V	80260	2100-2399	
SNOWMASS MOUNTAIN	Jefferson Co	371K	80127	7600-7699	
SNOW PEAK CT	Boulder Co	70H	80503	7100-7299	
SNOWSHOE CT	Parker	410W	80138	21100-21199	
SNOWSHOE DR	Parker	410W	80138	11800-11999	
SNOWSHOE LN	Parker	410W	80138	21200-21299	

STREET NAME	CITY or COUNTY	MAP GRID	ZIP CODE	BLOCK RANGE	O/E
SNOWSHOW RD	Jefferson Co	366A	80439	31100-31599	
	Jefferson Co	365D	80439	31600-31999	
	Jefferson Co	335Y	80439	32000-32899	
SNOWSHOE TRAIL	Jefferson Co	365F	80439	6700-6999	
SNOW VALLEY RD	Jefferson Co	367R	80439	24400-24599	
SNOW WATER RD	Park Co	840C	80421	1-399	
SNOW WILLOW CT	Castle Pines North	436F	80108	8200-8399	
SNOWWOOD DR	Monument	908W	80132	17000-17299	
SNOWY OWL DR	Broomfield	162L	80020	1400-1999	
SNOWY OWL LN	Jefferson Co	370B	80127	1-99	
	Parker	410W	80138	None	
SNOWY OWL PL	Highlands Ranch	374Y	80126	400-599	
SNOWY REACH CIR	Elbert Co	851T	80107	3800-3899	
SNOWY TRAIL	Jefferson Co	823V	80433	10500-10899	
SNYDER AVE	Jefferson Co	823P	80433	25200-26199	
SNYDER WAY	Superior	160L	80027	1100-1299	
SNYDER GULCH RD	Jefferson Co	305J	80439	1200-1599	
SNYDER MOUNTAIN RD					
	Clear Creek Co	304Y	80439	1-1399	
SOAPSTONE CT	Castle Rock	467G	80108	7300-7399	
SOAPSTONE WAY	Castle Rock	467G	80108	None	
SOAPWEED CIR	Douglas Co	470B	80134	5400-5499	
SOAR LN	Platteville	708B	80651	400-499	
SOARING EAGLE CT	Castle Rock	466S	80109	3500-3799	
SOARING EAGLE DR	Jefferson Co	306W	80439	31400-31499	
SOARING EAGLE LN	Castle Rock	466W	80109	3100-3599	
SOARING WING CT	El Paso Co	909Q	80908	19300-19599	
SOARING WING DR	El Paso Co	909R	80908	18800-20499	
SOBEY AVE W	Jefferson Co	372W	80128	7900-8399	
SODA CREEK DR	Jefferson Co	275V	80439	600-32899	
SODA CREEK DR S	Jefferson Co	305F	80439	600-32199	
SODA CREEK RD	Clear Creek Co	780U	80452	1-3199	
SODA CREEK RD	Jefferson Co	275U	80439	100-198	E
SODA CREEK RD S	Jefferson Co	275Z	80439	1-99	
	Jefferson Co	305D	80439	100-1199	
SODA CREEK TRAIL	Clear Creek Co	780Z	80452	1-499	
SODA LAKES RD	Jefferson Co	340A	80465	3500-3999	
SODALITE WAY	Castle Rock	467G	80108	None	
SOFTWIND PT	Castle Rock	498B	80108	None	
SOLANA DR	Adams Co	224H	80229	1200-8399	
SOLANA DR	Castle Pines North	436B	80108	6600-6999	
SOLANA PL	Castle Pines North	436B	80108	6900-6999	
SOLANO DR	Lochbuie	729Z	80603	400-599	
SOLANO PL	Castle Rock	469J	80108	None	
SOLAR DR N	Douglas Co	825V	80125	10500-10999	
SOLAR LN	Parker	409V	80134	11500-11599	
SOLITUDE CT	El Paso Co	908Z	80132	None	
SOLITUDE DR	Douglas Co	847S	80109	2200-3499	
	Castle Pines North	308B	80401	22800-22899	
SOLITUDE LN	Jefferson Co	306E	80439	1300-1499	
SOLSTICE WAY	Castle Rock	467H	80108	None	
SOMBERO DR	Bow Mar	342H	80123	5200-5499	
SOMERSET CT	Douglas Co	436Q	80108	7200-7299	
SOMERSET CT	Elbert Co	832X	80107	43300-43499	
SOMERSET DR	Boulder Co	70Q	80503	6200-6499	
SOMERSET DR	Broomfield	133K	80020	None	
SOMERSET DR	Golden	279P	80401	400-799	
SOMERSET ST	Lafayette	131M	80026	1100-1199	
SOMMERSET CIR	Greenwood Village	346U	80111	1-99	
SOMMERSET CIR	Longmont	12U	80501	1300-1399	
SONADO PL	Douglas Co	848M	80134	4500-4999	
SONATA BAY CT	Longmont	10R	80503	2900-2999	
SONGBIRD CIR	Boulder Co	129F	80303	6000-6299	
SONGBIRD CIR	Frederick	727F	80530	7800-7899	
SONGBIRD CT	Boulder Co	129F	80303	1300-1399	
SONGBIRD WAY	Douglas Co	470C	80134	5000-5499	
SONGBIRD HILLS PL	Parker	410Y	80138	23300-23499	
SONGBIRD HILLS ST	Parker	410Z	80138	11900-12199	
SONG SPARROW LN S					
	Highlands Ranch	404J	80129	10200-10299	
SONOMA CIR	Longmont	12P	80501	1000-1099	
SONOMA TRAIL E	Douglas Co	441F	80138	10100-10399	
SONORA DR	Broomfield	133K	80020	None	
SOPEKA POINTE DR	Frederick	726G	80516	None	
SOPHIE ST	Dacono	727J	80514	None	
SOPRIS CREEK DR N	Parker	439B	80134	None	
SOPRIS CREEK DR S	Parker	439B	80134	12600-12699	
SORENTO PL	Longmont	42A	80501	200-299	
SORI LN	Highlands Ranch	405B	80126	9200-9499	
SORREL CT	Longmont	12U	80501	1400-1499	
SORREL DR	Broomfield	163A	80020	14600-14799	
SORREL RD	Douglas Co	406V	80108	9400-9999	
SORREL ST	Lochbuie	140A	80603	None	
SORREL RUN	Broomfield	163A	80020	14600-14799	
SOURDOUGH DR	Jefferson Co	368M	80465	7200-7899	
SOUTH LN	Cherry Hills Village	344M	80113	1-99	
SOUTH PL	Louisville	130V	80027	300-399	
SOUTH ST	Boulder	98W	80302	2300-2399	
SOUTH ST	Castle Rock	497L	80104	200-1499	
SOUTH ST	Louisville	131S	80027	500-1199	
SOUTHARD ST	Erie	102W	80516	1700-1999	
SOUTH BOULDER RD E	Lafayette	131Q	80026	100-1399	
	Lafayette	132P	80026	11000-12199	
	Louisville	131P	80027	100-1699	
SOUTHBURY CT	Highlands Ranch	404J	80129	1000-1199	
SOUTHBURY PL	Highlands Ranch	404J	80129	1000-1199	
SOUTH END RD	Jefferson Co	307X	80439	26100-26499	
SOUTHERN ST	Brighton	139S	80601	2700-5199	
SOUTHERN ST E	Brighton	138U	80601	1300-2699	
SOUTHERN ST W	Brighton	138S	80601	1-599	
SOUTHERN CROSS LOOP	Elbert Co	872E	80117	None	
SOUTHERN HILLS CIR	Lone Tree	406D	80124	9400-9499	
SOUTHERN HILLS PL	Jefferson Co	305M	80439	31600-31699	
SOUTH FORK	Palmer Lake	907U	80133	None	
SOUTHHAVEN CIR	Highlands Ranch	405P	80126	10700-10799	
SOUTH JACKSON GAP WAY	Aurora	380M	80016	None	
SOUTHLANDS PKWY S	Aurora	350Z	80016	None	
	Aurora	351W	80016	None	
SOUTHLAWN CIR	Commerce City	769E	80022	10000-10399	
SOUTHLAWN PKWY E	Commerce City	769E	80022	None	
SOUTHMOOR CIR	Cherry Hills Village	346E	80111	5600-5799	
SOUTHMOOR DR	Denver	286S	80220	1-199	
SOUTHMOOR LN	Cherry Hills Village	346E	80111	5600-5999	
SOUTHPARK CIR S	Littleton	373Q	80120	8100-8299	
SOUTHPARK CT S	Littleton	373Q	80120	None	
SOUTHPARK DR	Littleton	374P	80120	100-499	
SOUTHPARK LN	Littleton	374N	80120	7900-8399	
SOUTHPARK RD	Highlands Ranch	374Y	80126	200-599	

STREET NAME	CITY or COUNTY	MAP GRID	ZIP CODE	BLOCK RANGE	O/E
SOUTHPARK WAY	Littleton	374N	80120	7900-8199	
SOUTHPARK PLAZA	Littleton	374P	80120	7900-8099	
SOUTHPARK TERRACE	Littleton	374P	80120	7900-8299	
SOUTH PEAK LN	Boulder Co	721Y	80302	1-299	
SOUTH PEAK RD	Boulder Co	721Z	80302	1-699	
SOUTH PEAK TRAIL	Boulder Co	721Y	80302	1-99	
SOUTHPOINTE DR	Lafayette	132W	80026	2600-2699	
SOUTHRIDGE CT	Jefferson Co	307K	80401	1300-1499	
SOUTHRIDGE LN S	Littleton	374A	80120	6700-6799	
SOUTHRIDGE PL	Longmont	41R	80501	300-399	
SOUTHRIDGE WAY S	Littleton	374A	80120	1-99	
SOUTHSHIRE RD	Highlands Ranch	405P	80126	2700-2899	
SOUTHSHORE PKWY E	Aurora	381C	80016	None	
SOUTHTECH DR E	Greenwood Village	376D	80111	8900-9299	
SOUTHVIEW DR	Jefferson Co	306W	80439	30700-30799	
SOUTHWIND CIR	Elbert Co	851C	80107	None	
SOUTHWIND CT	Jefferson Co	339R	80465	5400-5499	
SOUTHWOOD DR S	Centennial	344Z	80121	800-6499	
SOVEREIGN ST	Castle Rock	498M	80104	None	
SOVEREIGN ST E	Castle Rock	498M	80104	5400-5499	
SPANGLER DR	Northglenn	194N	80260	1100-1299	
SPANGLER PL	Longmont	12S	80501	None	
SPANISH OAKS WAY	Castle Rock	468X	80104	None	
SPANISH OAKS TRAIL	Castle Rock	468X	80108	None	
SPANISH PEAK E	Jefferson Co	371Q	80127	10500-10599	
SPANISH PEAK W	Jefferson Co	371Q	80127	7900-8099	
SPARROW AVE	Firestone	707S	80504	5800-5999	
	Firestone	707T	80504	6100-6499	
	Firestone	707S	80504	None	
SPARROW CT	Park Co	841U	80421	1-199	
SPARROW LN	Boulder Co	99S	80301	None	
SPARROW LN	Elbert Co	850U	80107	300-599	
SPARROW HAWK CT S					
	Highlands Ranch	404K	80129	10300-10399	
SPARROW HAWK DR	Longmont	12Y	80501	900-1099	
SPARROW HAWK DR W					
	Highlands Ranch	404K	80129	700-1099	
SPARROW HAWK WAY S					
	Highlands Ranch	404K	80129	10300-10399	
SPARROW POINT WAY	Jefferson Co	339Z	80465	16400-16899	
SPARTA DR	Lafayette	131L	80026	800-1299	
SPAULDING AVE W	Lafayette	132N	80026	100-699	
SPAULDING CIR	Superior	160R	80027	1800-1899	
SPAULDING ST E	Lafayette	132N	80026	100-799	
SPEARWOOD DR	Highlands Ranch	405K	80126	3000-3299	
SPECIALTY PL	Weld Co	706V	80504	4000-4199	
SPEER BLVD	Denver	284A	80204	600-2099	
SPEER BLVD E	Denver	284Q	80203	1-799	
	Denver	284V	80218	800-1199	
SPEER BLVD N	Denver	253Y	80211	2700-3299	
SPENCER ST	Longmont	11X	80501	900-1299	
	Longmont	11T	80501	1400-1599	
	Longmont	11P	80501	1700-2499	
SPERRY ST	Northglenn	193M	80234	10400-10799	
SPICA DR	Highlands Ranch	376Y	80124	13000-13299	
SPIKEGRASS CT	Castle Pines North	436F	80108	8100-8199	
SPINDRIFT DR	Longmont	10R	80503	2200-2499	
SPINE RD	Boulder	99K	80301	4200-5299	
	Boulder	69Y	80301	5300-5499	
	Boulder	99B	80301	6000-6499	
SPINNAKER CIR	Longmont	10M	80503	2200-2299	
SPINNAKER DR	Longmont	10M	80503	3100-3199	
SPINNAKER PL	Longmont	10M	80503	2900-2999	
SPINNAKER WAY	Boulder Co	71D	80504	7900-10699	
SPINNAKER TRAIL	El Paso Co	908T	80132	1200-1399	
SPINNING WHEEL DR	Brighton	139L	80601	None	
SPIRIT CT	Douglas Co	410Z	80138	9200-9298	E
SPIRIT HORSE TRAIL	Jefferson Co	762N	80403	8200-8599	
SPIRIT LAKE RD	Park Co	841C	80470	1-99	
SPIRITS LAKES RD	Gilpin Co	761N	80403	None	
SPIRIT VALLEY TRAIL (PVT)					
	Jefferson Co	842H	80433	13700-14099	
SPLENDOR DR	Castle Rock	466U	80109	None	
SPLIT ROCK RD S	Arapahoe Co	792X	80102	300-799	
	Arapahoe Co	812B	80102	800-1699	
SPOKE RD S	Douglas Co	380R	80138	13900-13999	
SPORTS BLVD	Denver	286U	80230	None	
SPORTS PARK CIR E	Aurora	289L	80011	None	
SPORTS PARK DR E	Aurora	289L	80011	18500-19199	
SPOTSWOOD CIR S	Littleton	343Z	80120	6300-6399	
SPOTSWOOD CT S	Littleton	374J	80120	7500-7699	
SPOTSWOOD PL	Boulder	98J	80304	2200-2499	
SPOTSWOOD ST S	Littleton	344S	80120	5600-5799	
	Littleton	344W	80120	5900-6499	
	Littleton	374E	80120	6700-6999	
SPOTTED DEER LN	Douglas Co	869H	80116	1-199	
SPOTTED FAWN RUN	Douglas Co	432U	80125	6300-8399	
SPOTTED HORSE TRAIL	Boulder Co	69Z	80301	5200-5399	
SPOTTED OWL AVE S					
	Highlands Ranch	404J	80129	10100-10299	
SPOTTED OWL CT S	Highlands Ranch	404J	80129	10200-10299	
SPOTTED OWL PL S	Highlands Ranch	404J	80129	10200-10299	
SPOTTED OWL WAY W					
	Highlands Ranch	404J	80129	1300-1499	
SPREAD EAGLE MOUNTAIN					
	Jefferson Co	371L	80127	9800-10399	
SPRING CIR	Park Co	841C	80470	1-299	
SPRING CT	Boulder Co	130S	80303	7100-7399	
SPRING DR	Boulder Co	130S	80303	500-7899	
SPRING DR	Jefferson Co	365X	80433	8800-8899	
	Jefferson Co	762J	80403	None	
SPRING DR	Northglenn	194D	80233	11700-11999	
SPRING DR	Park Co	841D	80470	1-499	
SPRING LN	Boulder Co	722M	80302	1-899	
SPRING PL	Broomfield	134F	80516	None	
SPRING PL	Elbert Co	831S	80138	2800-2899	
SPRING ST	Central City	780C	80427	100-299	
SPRING ST	Morrison	339D	80465	100-399	
SPRING ST	Nederland	740Q	80466	None	
SPRING ST	Palmer Lake	907Q	80133	None	
SPRING BEAUTY LN	Douglas Co	887G	80118	1900-2199	
SPRINGBRIAR DR	Castle Rock	466X	80109	3000-3599	
SPRING CREEK CIR	Boulder Co	70G	80503	7200-7299	
SPRING CREEK CT	Longmont	12Y	80501	1200-1299	
SPRING CREEK DR	Lafayette	131B	80026	1400-1498	E
	Lafayette	101X	80026	1500-1699	
SPRING CREEK PL	Boulder	98U	80301	3400-3699	
SPRING CREEK RD	Denver	346M	80237	None	

S

STREET NAME	CITY or COUNTY	MAP GRID	ZIP CODE	BLOCK RANGE	O/E
SPRING CREEK RD E	Douglas Co	411F	80138	10000-10999	
SPRING CREEK RD N	Douglas Co	410B	80138	12100-12799	
SPRING CREEK CROSSING	Lafayette	131B	80026	1500-1599	
SPRING CREEK PASS	Jefferson Co	371P	80127	8100-8199	
SPRING CREEK TRAIL	Boulder Co	70G	80503	8600-8899	
SPRINGDALE DR	Jefferson Co	842J	80470	34200-34499	
SPRINGDALE LN	Boulder	128F	80303	2800-2899	
SPRINGDALE PL	Longmont	12W	80501	1-99	
SPRINGER DR W	Highlands Ranch	374U	80129	1-199	
SPRINGFIELD CT	Parker	409N	80134	17200-17299	
SPRINGFIELD CT E	Parker	409N	80134	None	
SPRINGFLOWER DR	Jefferson Co	308B	80401	22400-22699	
SPRING GROVE AVE	Highlands Ranch	374Y	80126	400-599	
SPRING GULCH RD	Clear Creek Co	780T	80452	1-1799	
SPRING GULCH RD	Jefferson Co	369N	80465	19900-20099	
SPRING GULCH ST	Frederick	726G	80516	6300-6599	
SPRING HARBOR LN	Broomfield	163G	80020	None	
SPRING HARBOR WAY	Broomfield	163G	80020	None	
SPRING HILL AVE	Highlands Ranch	403H	80129	None	
SPRING HILL CT W	Highlands Ranch	403H	80129	2500-2599	
SPRINGHILL DR	Boulder Co	70K	80503	6800-6999	
SPRING HILL DR S	Highlands Ranch	403H	80129	9700-9999	
SPRING HILL LN S	Highlands Ranch	403H	80129	9700-9999	
SPRING HILL PKWY	Highlands Ranch	403H	80129	None	
SPRING HILL PL S	Highlands Ranch	403H	80129	9700-9999	
SPRING HILL ST S	Highlands Ranch	403H	80129	9700-9999	
SPRING HILL WAY	Highlands Ranch	403H	80129	None	
SPRING HILLPEAK W	Highlands Ranch	403G	80129	2800-2899	
SPRINGHOUSE CT	Brighton	139G	80601	None	
SPRING MEADOW CIR	Castle Rock	466U	80109	3200-4399	
SPRING MEADOW CT	Jefferson Co	367W	80439	9100-9199	
SPRINGMEADOW LN	Castle Rock	466Q	80109	4500-4699	
SPRING PARK DR	El Paso Co	908V	80132	1400-1599	
SPRING RANCH DR	Jefferson Co	307A	80401	300-1199	
SPRING RANCH LN	Jefferson Co	277W	80401	300-1199	
SPRING RIDGE TRAIL	Castle Rock	528F	80104	5300-5599	
SPRINGS COVE	Louisville	160D	80027	100-199	
SPRINGS DR	Louisville	160D	80027	200-299	
SPRINGS PL	Longmont	41T	80504	2100-2199	
SPRINGS RD	Jefferson Co	822Z	80433	11800-11899	
SPRINGVALE RD	Castle Rock	499J	80104	500-799	
SPRING VALLEY	Park Co	841S	80421	1-699	
SPRING VALLEY RD	Boulder	97P	80304	3700-3899	
SPRING VALLEY RD	El Paso Co	908S	80132	18700-19499	
SPRING VALLEY RD S	Douglas Co	889P	80116	7600-10499	
	Douglas Co	889P	80118	10500-12399	
	Douglas Co	909F	80118	12400-15999	
SPRING VALLEY TRAIL	Jefferson Co	336A	80439	3700-3999	
SPRING WATER CT S	Highlands Ranch	404E	80129	10100-10199	
SPRING WATER LN W	Highlands Ranch	404J	80129	1600-1899	
SPRING WATER PL W	Highlands Ranch	404J	80129	1500-1899	
SPRING WATER WAY W	Highlands Ranch	404J	80129	1500-1599	
SPRING WATER PEAK S	Highlands Ranch	404J	80129	10300-10399	
SPRINGWOOD CT N	Lafayette	132S	80026	2300-2399	
SPRINGWOOD CT S	Lafayette	132W	80026	2400-2499	
SPRUCE AVE	Adams Co	794P	80136	56000-56899	
SPRUCE AVE	Longmont	41F	80501	1200-1999	
SPRUCE AVE	Palmer Lake	907R	80133	None	
SPRUCE AVE E	Castle Rock	498M	80104	5200-5699	
SPRUCE CIR	Louisville	130U	80027	500-699	
SPRUCE CIR S	Centennial	376Q	80112	8000-8199	
SPRUCE CT	Boulder	127C	80302	200-299	
SPRUCE CT	Clear Creek Co	304U	80439	1-99	
SPRUCE CT	Denver	286L	80230	900-1099	
SPRUCE CT	Elbert Co	871G	80107	4800-4999	
SPRUCE CT	Erie	133G	80516	1900-1999	
SPRUCE CT	Frederick	727F	80530	800-899	
	Frederick	727A	80516	None	
SPRUCE CT	Parker	410J	80138	10300-10399	
SPRUCE CT	Thornton	136Y	80602	None	
SPRUCE CT S	Centennial	376L	80112	7700-7799	
	Centennial	376Q	80112	8100-8199	
SPRUCE DR	Jefferson Co	308F	80401	1200-1399	
	Jefferson Co	842H	80433	28000-28199	
	Jefferson Co	822Z	80433	28400-28799	
SPRUCE DR	Park Co	841K	80421	1-99	
SPRUCE DR	Weld Co	726K	80516	1700-1999	
SPRUCE DR E	Jefferson Co	842H	80433	13800-13899	
SPRUCE DR S	Centennial	376G	80112	6900E-7099E	
SPRUCE LN	Clear Creek Co	801A	80452	1-99	
SPRUCE LN	Jefferson Co	367A	80439	27200-27499	
	Jefferson Co	336G	80439	28900-29099	
SPRUCE LN	Louisville	130V	80027	300-499	
SPRUCE PL	Lochbuie	140C	80603	800-899	
SPRUCE PL	Thornton	166Q	80602	13000-13199	
SPRUCE RD	El Paso Co	907U	80132	18200-18499	
SPRUCE RD	Jefferson Co	277V	80401	1-499	
	Jefferson Co	306X	80439	29500-30299	
SPRUCE RD	Teller Co	906N	80863	None	
SPRUCE RD W	Douglas Co	907H	80133	700-1099	
SPRUCE ST	Arapahoe Co	373P	80128	None	
SPRUCE ST	Boulder	127C	80302	200-1099	
	Boulder	97Y	80302	1100-1899	
	Boulder	98W	80302	1900-2799	
	Broomfield	133U	80020	None	
	Broomfield	133X	80020	None	
SPRUCE ST	Central City	780C	80427	1-599	
SPRUCE ST	Denver	286U	80230	1-99	
	Denver	286Q	80230	200-299	
	Denver	286L	80230	900-1099	
	Denver	286L	80220	1200-1999	
	Denver	286C	80238	2400-2799	
	Denver	256Y	80238	2801-2899	O
SPRUCE ST	Elizabeth	871F	80107	100-299	
SPRUCE ST	Jamestown	722A	80455	None	
SPRUCE ST	Louisville	131S	80027	100-1299	
SPRUCE ST	Nederland	740Q	80466	None	
SPRUCE ST	Thornton	166Q	80602	12800-12999	
	Thornton	166L	80602	13300-13499	
	Thornton	166G	80602	None	
	Thornton	166U	80602	None	
	Thornton	166Y	80602	None	

STREET NAME	CITY or COUNTY	MAP GRID	ZIP CODE	BLOCK RANGE	O/E
SPRUCE ST S	Centennial	376C	80112	6700-6899	
	Centennial	376G	80112	7100-7499	
	Centennial	376L	80112	7700-7799	
	Denver	286U	80230	100-199	
	Denver	316G	80231	1500-1599	
	Denver	316L	80231	1801-1899	O
	Denver	346C	80237	3500-4199	
SPRUCE WAY	Boulder Co	741U	80466	1-499	
SPRUCE WAY	Denver	286C	80238	2300-2398	E
	Denver	256L	80238	None	
SPRUCE WAY	Gilpin Co	760U	80403	1-199	
SPRUCE WAY	Louisville	130V	80027	500-599	
SPRUCE WAY	Thornton	166L	80602	None	
SPRUCE WAY S	Denver	316U	80231	2900-3099	
SPRUCE CANYON CIR	Jefferson Co	762D	80403	11700-12099	
SPRUCE CANYON DR	Jefferson Co	762C	80403	29200-30399	
SPRUCE CREEK CIR	Douglas Co	907B	80118	13300-13399	
SPRUCEDALE AVE	Jefferson Co	337J	80439	None	
SPRUCEDALE DR	Jefferson Co	822R	80433	10000-10199	
SPRUCEDALE PKWY	Jefferson Co	366F	80439	6900-6999	
SPRUCE DELL CT	Castle Rock	466U	80109	3300-3499	
SPRUCE DELL DR	Castle Rock	466U	80109	3200-3399	
	Broomfield	133Y	80020	2400-2799	
SPRUCE MOUNTAIN S	Douglas Co	887V	80118	None	
SPRUCE MOUNTAIN RD	Douglas Co	907M	80133	14700-15999	
SPRUCE MOUNTAIN RD S	Douglas Co	888W	80118	11000-12499	
	Douglas Co	908A	80118	12500-14699	
SPRUCE POINT PL	Parker	409Z	80134	20100-20399	
SPRUCE TRAIL	Park Co	841U	80421	1-499	
SPRUCEWOOD CT	Lafayette	131V	80026	300-399	
SPRUCEWOOD DR	Douglas Co	866K	80135	7600-8199	
SPUR CT	Boulder Co	721C	80481	1-99	
SPUR CT	Golden	248R	80403	500-599	
SPUR LN E	Douglas Co	379V	80138	6900-6999	
SPUR PL	Elbert Co	892D	80117	11500-11599	
SPUR CROSS TRAIL	Douglas Co	469B	80134	5200-5599	
SPUR RANCH RD	El Paso Co	911V	80831	15700N-18199N	
SPUR RANCH RD N	El Paso Co	912W	80831	15700-18199	
SPYDERCO WAY	Golden	248R	80403	800-899	
SPYGLASS CIR	El Paso Co	908T	80132	18900-18999	
SPYGLASS CIR	Jefferson Co	306J	80439	1-1999	
SPYGLASS CIR	Louisville	160H	80027	800-899	
SPYGLASS CT	Douglas Co	886C	80118	6000-6099	
SPYGLASS DR	Broomfield	163E	80020	4701-5199	O
SPYGLASS DR	Columbine Valley	373B	80123	1-99	
SPY GLASS LN	Boulder Co	723G	80503	4000-4199	
SQUAW AVE	Adams Co	226B	80022	None	
SQUAW PASS RD	Jefferson Co	305K	80439	32100-34799	
SQUIRES CIR	Boulder	128U	80305	4400-4599	
SQUIRES CT	Longmont	11Q	80501	2300-2499	
SQUIRES ST	Longmont	11Q	80501	2100-2299	
SQUIRREL LN	Jefferson Co	842D	80433	28300-28799	
SQUIRREL CREEK CT	Weld Co	707J	80504	None	
SQUIRREL TAIL LN	Gilpin Co	761C	80403	1-199	
SQUIRREL TAIL PL	Parker	379T	80134	17700-17799	
STABLE CT	Brighton	139L	80601	None	
STABLE DR	Boulder Co	70L	80503	7100-7199	
STABLE LN	Douglas Co	432F	80125	10300-10599	
STABLE LN	Jefferson Co	306Y	80439	3200-3299	
STABLE LN	Mead	706G	80542	None	
STACY CT	Lafayette	131R	80026	500-599	
STACY DR	Adams Co	223H	80221	1900-8399	
	Federal Heights	223H	80260	8400-8499	
STACY PL	Douglas Co	432K	80125	None	
STADIUM DR	Boulder	128A	80302	None	
STAFFORD CIR	Castle Rock	497U	80104	500-799	
STAG LN	El Paso Co	908Q	80132	19400-19499	
STAGE DR	Fort Lupton	728H	80621	900-1299	
STAGECOACH AVE	Firestone	707T	80504	5800-6799	
	Firestone	707S	80504	None	
STAGECOACH BLVD	Clear Creek Co	801R	80439	1-1399	
STAGECOACH BLVD	Jefferson Co	306X	80439	28400-30599	
	Jefferson Co	305Y	80439	30600-34199	
	Jefferson Co	335A	80439	34200-34799	
STAGECOACH CIR	Elbert Co	870H	80107	1500-1699	
STAGECOACH DR	Lochbuie	140F	80603	600-999	
STAGE COACH DR	Mead	706G	80542	13800-13899	
STAGE COACH DR	Park Co	820Y	80421	1-599	
STAGECOACH DR E	Douglas Co	381Y	80138	11000-11999	
STAGECOACH LN	Jefferson Co	306X	80439	None	
STAGECOACH LN	Lochbuie	140F	80603	200-299	
STAGE COACH LN	Park Co	840D	80421	1-499	
STAGECOACH RD	Elbert Co	830U	80138	45000-45999	
STAGECOACH RD	Jefferson Co	823W	80433	26800-26999	
	Jefferson Co	822Z	80433	27000-27999	
STAGECOACH RD	Weld Co	706Q	80504	3500-3699	
STAGECOACH TRAIL	Elbert Co	850U	80107	1-499	
STAGE RUN	Parker	409Q	80134	18601-18699	O
STAGE RUN TRAIL	Elbert Co	870R	80107	400-1899	
STAGHORN DR	Longmont	40L	80503	3700-3899	
STAGHORN WAY	Douglas Co	870E	80116	1-399	
STALLION DR E	Douglas Co	381Y	80138	11000-11799	
STALLION DR S	Jefferson Co	822W	80470	11600-11999	
STALLION RD	Jefferson Co	822W	80470	None	
STALLION WAY	Mead	706G	80542	None	
STAMPEDE CIR	Elbert Co	870D	80107	34300-35999	
STAMPEDE CT	Castle Rock	467U	80104	1000-1099	
STAMPEDE CT	Elbert Co	832W	80107	43500-43699	
STAMPEDE DR	Castle Rock	467U	80104	3900-4199	
STAMPEDE DR	Lochbuie	140F	80603	600-699	
STAMPEDE PL	Lochbuie	140G	80603	100-199	
STAMPEDE WAY	Lochbuie	140G	80603	2-98	E
STANDING PINES RD	Jefferson Co	762K	80403	9700-9799	
STANFORD AVE	Boulder	128P	80305	2500-3599	
STANFORD AVE E	Aurora	348G	80015	15000-15099	
	Aurora	349G	80013	None	
	Centennial	349H	80015	19700-19899	
	Cherry Hills Village	344H	80113	800-1899	
	Cherry Hills Village	346E	80111	6300-6499	
	Englewood	344G	80113	1-799	
	Greenwood Village	346H	80111	9100-9199	
STANFORD AVE W	Arapahoe Co	344E	80110	1800-1999	
	Denver	343E	80236	4100-5199	
	Denver	342F	80123	7600-7899	
	Denver	342J	80123	8600-9099	
	Denver	341M	80123	9100-9999	

Continued on next column

STREET NAME	CITY or COUNTY	MAP GRID	ZIP CODE	BLOCK RANGE	O/E
STANFORD AVE W (Cont'd)					
	Englewood	344F	80110	1-1599	
	Englewood	343L	80110	3000-3299	
	Jefferson Co	341K	80127	11200-11299	
	Jefferson Co	341J	80465	12400-12699	
	Jefferson Co	340M	80465	12700-13799	
	Lakewood	342F	80123	7000-7399	
STANFORD CIR E	Aurora	348F	80015	13900-14099	
STANFORD CT	Boulder	128P	80305	3400-3499	
STANFORD DR E	Aurora	348G	80015	14900-15199	
	Aurora	349G	80015	18800-19299	
	Centennial	349M	80015	19700-19999	
	Cherry Hills Village	345K	80113	2600-3299	
	Cherry Hills Village	346E	80111	5600-5799	
STANFORD DR W	Englewood	344E	80110	800-1199	
	Englewood	343L	80110	3000-3099	
	Jefferson Co	341J	80465	11600-12599	
STANFORD LN	Longmont	10V	80503	1-99	
STANFORD LN W	Jefferson Co	341E	80465	11600-11799	
STANFORD PL E	Arapahoe Co	349M	80015	None	
	Aurora	348E	80015	13800-13899	
	Aurora	348F	80015	14500-14799	
	Aurora	348G	80015	15100-15299	
	Aurora	348H	80015	15700-16699	
	Aurora	349J	80015	16900-16999	
	Greenwood Village	346M	80111	9100-9199	
STANFORD PL W	Englewood	344E	80110	1000-1099	
	Jefferson Co	341K	80127	11100-11199	
	Jefferson Co	341E	80465	11600-11699	
STANFORD ST E	Aurora	349E	80015	16900-17299	
STANHOPE RD	Castle Rock	498M	80104	5700-5899	
STANLEY DR	Erie	102Q	80516	1600-1799	
STANLEY RD	Clear Creek Co	780P	80452	1-2399	
STANLEY PARK RD	Jefferson Co	337T	80439	24400-26799	
STANSBERRY CIR	Jefferson Co	823P	80433	25300-25799	
STANSBERRY ST	Jefferson Co	823N	80433	25600-26399	
STANTON DR	Jefferson Co	762E	80403	34400-34799	
STAPLETON DR	Jefferson Co	277S	80401	27400-27999	
	Jefferson Co	276V	80401	28000-28299	
STAPLETON DR E	Denver	255R	80216	5301N-5599N	O
	Denver	256N	80216	5601N-6799N	O
	Denver	255R	80216	4200S-5598S	E
	Denver	256N	80216	6100S-6898S	E
STAR AVE W	Jefferson Co	371V	80128	8800-8999	
STAR CIR W	Jefferson Co	372S	80128	8400-8699	
STAR DR W	Jefferson Co	372S	80128	8700-8799	
STAR LN	Boulder	98P	80301	None	
STAR LN	Park Co	841R	80421	1-199	
STARBOARD DR	Boulder Co	99G	80301	4500-4699	
STARBURST CIR	Douglas Co	527W	80104	100-299	
STAR CREEK DR	Broomfield	163G	80020	None	
STARDANCE CIR	Longmont	42C	80501	None	
STARDANCE WAY	Longmont	42C	80501	None	
STARDUST CIR	Douglas Co	527P	80104	1200-1299	
STARFIRE CIR	Douglas Co	527X	80104	4600-4799	
STARFIRE WAY	Jefferson Co	278U	80401	200-399	
STARFLOWER CT	Castle Rock	466Q	80109	5100-5199	
STARFLOWER RD	Castle Rock	466Q	80109	3400-4099	
STARGAZER DR	Broomfield	163A	80020	14500-14699	
STARGAZER LN E	Parker	408Z	80134	None	
STARGLOW CT	Highlands Ranch	404M	80126	10400-10498	E
STAR GRASS CIR	Highlands Ranch	374Y	80126	9100-9299	
STAR HILL CIR S	Lone Tree	377W	80124	9200-9299	
	Lone Tree	407A	80124	9300-9499	
STAR HILL LN E	Lone Tree	376Z	80124	9100-9299	
STAR HILL PT E	Lone Tree	406D	80124	9100-9199	
STAR HILL TRAIL E	Lone Tree	406D	80124	9100-9299	
	Lone Tree	407A	80124	9300-9399	
STARKEY CT	Erie	102U	80516	600-799	
STARLIGHT CT	Douglas Co	867N	80135	3800-3999	
STARLIGHT DR	Jefferson Co	368D	80465	6200-6999	
STARLIGHT RD	Jefferson Co	368C	80465	6500-6699	
STARLIGHT RD	Thornton	224B	80260	200-599	
STARLINE AVE	Lafayette	132E	80026	100-299	
STARLING CT	Boulder Co	69K	80503	6300-6399	
STARLING CT	Castle Rock	466X	80109	3000-3199	
STARLING LN	Elbert Co	850U	80107	700-1499	
STARLING PL	Broomfield	134F	80516	None	
STAR MARK CT	Broomfield	163G	80020	None	
STARMINE PL	Douglas Co	466D	80108	300-399	
STAR PEAK RD	Gilpin Co	761C	80403	100-299	
STAR RIDGE CIR	Elbert Co	870L	80107	33100-33299	
STAR RIDGE RD	Jefferson Co	308B	80401	1000-1099	
STARRY NIGHT LOOP	Castle Rock	496G	80109	3100-3999	
STARRY SKY WAY	Douglas Co	469A	80134	4900-5199	
STARSTONE LN	Castle Rock	527C	80104	None	
STARVIEW CIR	Palmer Lake	907Q	80133	None	
STAR VIEW DR	Broomfield	162H	80020	5800-5999	
STARVIEW DR	Jefferson Co	843F	80433	24700-24899	
STARWOOD DR	El Paso Co	908N	80132	19200-19599	
STARWOOD LN	Douglas Co	378V	80134	8700-8799	
STARWOOD LN	Jefferson Co	305G	80439	1200-1399	
STATE AVE E	Aurora	350Z	80016	6200-6299	
STATE ST	Fort Lupton	728M	80621	1000-1199	
STAZIO DR	Boulder	99T	80301	None	
STEAMBOAT AVE E					
	Buckley Air Force Base	289P	80011	None	
	Buckley Air Force Base	289U	80017	None	
	Buckley Air Force Base	289U	80011	None	
	Buckley Air Force Base	290S	80017	None	
STEAMBOAT CT	Jefferson Co	306K	80439	1500-1599	
STEARMAN CT	Erie	133A	80516	100-199	
STEARNS AVE	Boulder Co	129G	80303	900-6599	
STEAVENSON PL	Denver	255N	80216	2200-2499	
STEEL ST S	Greenwood Village	345P	80121	5100-5899	
STEELE AVE E	Douglas Co	890P	80116	11000-11999	
STEELE CIR S	Centennial	375F	80122	7300-7499	
STEELE CT	Thornton	165T	80241	12800-12999	
	Thornton	165P	80241	13000-13099	
STEELE CT S	Centennial	375P	80122	8200-8299	
STEELE DR	Thornton	195X	80229	9400-9499	
	Thornton	165P	80241	13000-13099	
STEELE ST	Adams Co	225F	80229	7800-8699	
	Adams Co	135K	80602	16400-16799	
	Denver	285P	80206	1-1699	
	Denver	285B	80205	2600-2699	
	Denver	255X	80205	2700-3999	
	Denver	255K	80216	4000-5399	

S

STREET NAME	CITY or COUNTY	MAP GRID	ZIP CODE	BLOCK RANGE	O/E
STEELE ST	Longmont	**11N**	80501	2100-2399	
STEELE ST	Northglenn	**195K**	80233	10500-10899	
	Northglenn	**195F**	80233	10900-10998	E
	Thornton	**195T**	80229	9600-9999	
	Thornton	**195N**	80229	10000-10399	
	Thornton	**195F**	80233	11200-11599	
	Thornton	**195B**	80233	11600-11899	
	Thornton	**165X**	80241	12000-12399	
	Thornton	**165K**	80602	13600-13799	
	Thornton	**225B**	80229	None	
STEELE ST S	Centennial	**345X**	80121	5900-6499	
	Centennial	**375B**	80121	6500-6699	
	Centennial	**375F**	80122	6700-7099	
	Centennial	**375K**	80122	7500-7799	
	Centennial	**375P**	80122	8000-8299	
	Denver	**285T**	80209	1-599	
	Denver	**315B**	80209	700-1099	
	Denver	**315F**	80210	1100-1899	
	Denver	**315T**	80210	2400-3299	
STEEPLE CT	Douglas Co	**439R**	80134	6900-6999	
STEEPLECHASE DR	Boulder Co	**704W**	80503	5500-5999	
STEEPLECHASE DR	Douglas Co	**870N**	80116	9500-10099	
STEEPLECHASE DR	El Paso Co	**912Y**	80831	17800-18799	
STEEPLECHASE RD	Douglas Co	**869Q**	80116	8400-9499	
STEEPLE ROCK DR	Frederick	**726G**	80516	2600-2899	
STEIN ST	Lafayette	**132E**	80026	900-1299	
STELLAR JAY WAY	Jefferson Co	**365J**	80439	None	
STELLARS JAY DR W					
	Highlands Ranch	**404K**	80129	300-599	
STELLARS JAY RD	Jefferson Co	**277U**	80401	25500-25999	
STENE DR W	Jefferson Co	**372T**	80128	7600-8399	
STENZEL DR	Jefferson Co	**822P**	80433	31500-32299	
STEPHEN PL S	Highlands Ranch	**406J**	80130	10100-10199	
STEPHENS RD	Boulder	**128S**	80305	2500-2899	
STEPPE DR	Longmont	**12N**	80501	None	
STEPPLER RD	El Paso Co	**909Z**	80908	16500-17799	
STERLING AVE	Cherry Hills Village	**344M**	80113	1-99	
STERLING AVE	Palmer Lake	**907U**	80133	None	
STERLING CIR	Boulder	**98V**	80301	3000E-3299E	
STERLING CT	Boulder	**98U**	80301	2900-2999	
STERLING CT	Frederick	**726G**	80516	2600-2699	
STERLING CT E	Highlands Ranch	**404H**	80126	1700-1799	
STERLING DR	Boulder	**98U**	80301	4700-4899	
	Boulder	**98V**	80301	4900-5399	
STERLING DR S	Highlands Ranch	**404H**	80126	9600-9899	
STERLING ST	Highlands Ranch	**404H**	80126	None	
STERLING HILL CT	Castle Rock	**498E**	80104	1300-1599	
STERLING HILLS PKWY	Aurora	**319Q**	80013	None	
STERNE BLVD E	Arapahoe Co	**374C**	80122	200-299	
STERNE CIR S	Littleton	**344W**	80120	6100-6199	
STERNE CT S	Littleton	**344W**	80120	6000-6099	
STERNE PKWY S	Littleton	**344W**	80120	6000-6299	
	Littleton	**374A**	80120	6300-6799	
STERNE PKWY W	Littleton	**374B**	80120	1-699	
	Littleton	**344W**	80120	6300-6399	
STETSON CT	Brighton	**139L**	80601	None	
STETSON CT N	Douglas Co	**440X**	80134	5700-5799	
STETSON PL W	Denver	**342F**	80123	6900-7399	
	Denver	**342J**	80123	8700-9099	
	Denver	**341M**	80123	9100-9899	
STETSON RD E	Douglas Co	**440X**	80134	8000-8199	
STEVEN LN	Jefferson Co	**822P**	80433	10000-10199	
STEVEN WAY	Jefferson Co	**822P**	80433	31700-32499	
STEVENS CIR	Erie	**131D**	80026	None	
STEVEN'S CIR	Platteville	**708B**	80651	400-599	
STEVENS CIR N	Erie	**132A**	80026	3000-3199	
STEVENS CIR S	Erie	**132A**	80026	3000-3199	
STEVENS CT	Douglas Co	**867P**	80109	2200-2299	
STEVENS ST	Central City	**780D**	80427	None	
STEWART AVE	Keenesburg	**732A**	80643	None	
STICKNEY ST	Lyons	**703B**	80540	None	
STILES DR S	Jefferson Co	**306B**	80439	700-999	
STILL GLEN DR	El Paso Co	**909Q**	80908	4300-19799	
STILL MEADOW PL	Castle Rock	**498H**	80104	None	
STILLWATER ST	Elbert Co	**850U**	80107	37400-37699	
STILLWATER WAY	Boulder Co	**131D**	80026	1800-1999	
STINKY GULCH RD	Nederland	**740R**	80466	None	
STIRRUP CT	Boulder Co	**704W**	80503	8400-8599	
STIRRUP LN	Boulder Co	**704W**	80503	8400-8599	
	Mead	**706G**	80542	None	
STIRRUP LN E	Douglas Co	**407W**	80108	500-598	E
STIRRUP WAY	Clear Creek Co	**781T**	80439	None	
STIRRUP TRAIL E	El Paso Co	**908U**	80132	1-499	
STIRRUP TRAIL W	El Paso Co	**908U**	80132	1-199	
STOCKHOLM WAY	Elbert Co	**850D**	80138	1200-1499	
STOCKHOLM GROVE	El Paso Co	**910P**	80908	7600-7799	
STOCKLEY AVE	Commerce City	**226S**	80022	6100-6199	
STOCKTON DR	Erie	**102R**	80516	1200-1499	
STOCKWELL ST	Castle Rock	**499J**	80104	None	
STOLL PL	Denver	**260J**	80249	None	
STOLL PL E	Denver	**257M**	80239	12100-12299	
STOLL PL W	Denver	**254J**	80221	1500-1899	
STONE CIR	Broomfield	**163K**	80020	13600-13799	
STONE DR	Castle Rock	**497M**	80104	None	
STONE PL	Boulder Co	**98K**	80301	4000-4199	
STONE ST	Morrison	**309Z**	80465	100-199	
STONEBRIAR DR	Douglas Co	**408H**	80134	15900-16599	
STONEBRIAR LN	Douglas Co	**408H**	80134	9700-9999	
STONEBRIDGE WAY	Jefferson Co	**340S**	80465	5600-5799	
STONEBRUSH DR	Highlands Ranch	**405L**	80126	None	
STONE CANYON DR	Lyons	**703C**	80540	None	
STONE CANYON RANCH RD					
	Douglas Co	**528T**	80104	3300-5299	
STONE CHIMNEY LN	Jefferson Co	**842E**	80470	13500-13999	
STONE CLIFF CIR	Gilpin Co	**742W**	80403	1-199	
STONECLIFF DR	Jefferson Co	**336G**	80439	25000-25099	
	Jefferson Co	**336F**	80439	30000-30099	
STONECREEK CT	Douglas Co	**408M**	80134	10600-10699	
STONE CREEK DR	Jefferson Co	**337X**	80439	None	
STONECREST PT	Highlands Ranch	**373Y**	80129	2700-2899	
STONECREST WAY	Highlands Ranch	**373Y**	80129	8900-9099	
STONECROP CIR	Castle Rock	**466P**	80109	5000-5099	
STONECROP CT	Castle Rock	**466Q**	80109	5000-5099	
STONECROP WAY	Jefferson Co	**308P**	80401	2100-2499	
STONECROP TRAIL	Jefferson Co	**842M**	80433	28000-28899	
STONEDALE DR	Castle Pines North	**436G**	80108	7800-7899	
STONEFELD PL	Douglas Co	**408D**	80134	16300-16599	
STONEFLOWER DR	Douglas Co	**408L**	80134	10300-10699	
STONEGATE BLVD	Douglas Co	**408D**	80134	None	
STONE GATE DR	Jefferson Co	**369B**	80465	18300-19399	
STONEGATE PKWY	Douglas Co	**408G**	80134	9500-16799	
STONEGLEN TRAIL	Lone Tree	**406G**	80124	9900-10299	
STONEGRASS PT	Broomfield	**163F**	80020	3900-3999	
STONEHAM AVE	Castle Rock	**498Q**	80104	4800-5099	
STONEHAM LN	Jefferson Co	**306K**	80439	1600-1699	
STONEHAM ST	Superior	**160L**	80027	1000-1599	
STONEHAVEN AVE	Broomfield	**162Z**	80020	900-1499	
STONEHAVEN CT	Highlands Ranch	**376W**	80130	1-99	
STONEHAVEN ST	Dacono	**727J**	80514	300-699	
STONEHAVEN ST CIR	Dacono	**727J**	80514	300-699	
STONEHENGE CIR	Boulder Co	**101Z**	80026	2000-2299	
STONEHENGE DR	Boulder Co	**131D**	80026	1700-1999	
STONEHENGE WAY	Parker	**410N**	80138	10900-11499	
STONE HILL CT	Castle Rock	**498E**	80104	1400-1599	
STONE HORSE RANCH RD	Elbert Co	**871Y**	80107	28200-28799	
STONE LEDGE DR	Douglas Co	**408H**	80134	16300-16499	
STONELEIGH TRAIL	El Paso Co	**909N**	80132	2001-2099	O
STONEMEADOW DR	Douglas Co	**408L**	80134	10500-10699	
STONEMONT CT	Castle Pines North	**436L**	80108	600-799	
STONEMONT DR	Castle Pines North	**436L**	80108	500-699	
STONE MOUNTAIN DR					
	Highlands Ranch	**404J**	80129	10400-10499	
STONEPOINT CIR	Elbert Co	**870Y**	80107	None	
STONE POST DR	Douglas Co	**468Y**	80108	4300-4399	
STONERIDGE TERRACE	Boulder Co	**703W**	80302	8300-8499	
STONERIDGE TERRACE	Douglas Co	**408G**	80134	10100-10199	
STONES PEAK DR	Longmont	**40N**	80503	None	
STONE TIMBER CT	Parker	**439D**	80134	12200-12299	
STONE VIEW RD	El Paso Co	**907Y**	80132	18000-18499	
STONEWALL LN	Lafayette	**131J**	80027	2500-2699	
STONEWALL PL	Boulder	**129E**	80303	5500-5599	
STONEWILLOW DR	Douglas Co	**408M**	80134	10300-10699	
STONEY DR	Boulder Co	**102K**	80026	3800-3999	
STONEYBROOK DR	Broomfield	**162H**	80020	5300-5799	
STONEYBROOKE ST	Parker	**410V**	80138	11600-11799	
STONEY CREEK WAY	Broomfield	**163A**	80020	14700-14799	
STONINGTON CT	Highlands Ranch	**405P**	80126	2800-2899	
STONINGTON ST	Highlands Ranch	**405P**	80126	10500-10799	
STONYBRIDGE CIR	Highlands Ranch	**375T**	80126	8300-8499	
STONY HILL RD	Boulder	**128W**	80305	1900-2299	
STORAGE TEK DR	Broomfield	**161K**	80020	None	
STORM CLOUD WAY	Castle Rock	**467U**	80104	3700-4199	
STORM CLOUD WAY	Jefferson Co	**306W**	80439	None	
STORM KING LN	Elbert Co	**831S**	80138	45000-45199	
STORM KING PEAK	Jefferson Co	**371P**	80127	8100-8199	
STORM MOUNTAIN	Jefferson Co	**371L**	80127	7500-7699	
STORM VIEW DR E	Parker	**408Y**	80134	None	
STORMY MOUNTAIN CT N	Douglas Co	**440U**	80134	6100-6299	
STOUT ST	Denver	**284F**	80204	1100-1399	
	Denver	**284F**	80202	1400-1999	
	Denver	**284C**	80205	2000-2699	
	Denver	**254Y**	80205	2700-3199	
STOWE CT	Jefferson Co	**306P**	80439	30100-30199	
STOWE ST E	Highlands Ranch	**404C**	80126	700-799	
STRAIGHT PATH LN	Douglas Co	**908H**	80118	700-799	
STRANSKY RD	Jefferson Co	**365K**	80439	33400-34799	
STRASBURG CT	Parker	**409Y**	80134	19700-19799	
STRASBURG RD	Adams Co	**794K**	80136	2000-14399	
STRASBURG RD N	Arapahoe Co	**794T**	80136	1-1499	
STRASBURG RD S	Arapahoe Co	**794X**	80136	1-799	
STRASBURG WAY	Parker	**409J**	80134	10400-10499	
STRATFORD CT E	Highlands Ranch	**405E**	80126	2000-2399	
STRATFORD LN	Longmont	**11S**	80503	1800-2699	
STRATFORD LN S	Highlands Ranch	**405E**	80126	9900-10099	
STRATFORD PL S	Highlands Ranch	**405E**	80126	9900-10099	
STRATFORD WAY E	Highlands Ranch	**405E**	80126	2300-2399	
STRATFORD LAKES DR	Westminster	**193G**	80031	11200-11499	
STRATH BLVD	Boulder Co	**69K**	80503	5900-7199	
STRATHFIELD CT	Highlands Ranch	**405G**	80126	4200-4299	
STRATHFIELD LN	Highlands Ranch	**405G**	80126	9900-10099	
STRATHMORE LN	Lafayette	**132N**	80026	400-499	
STRATHMORE ST	Louisville	**131N**	80027	1900-2099	
STRATTON AVE N	Castle Rock	**498G**	80104	1200-1499	
STRATTON CT	Jefferson Co	**306J**	80439	30700-30799	
STRAW CT	Brighton	**139L**	80601	None	
STRAWBERRY CIR	Boulder Co	**11J**	80503	None	
STRAWBERRY CT	Boulder Co	**70Q**	80503	6400-6499	
STRAWBERRY LN	Boulder Co	**70Q**	80503	8400-8599	
STRAWBERRY LN	Douglas Co	**848J**	80108	5500-5799	
STRAWBERRY LN	El Paso Co	**908T**	80132	19100-19199	
STRAWBERRY WAY	Boulder	**97H**	80304	None	
STRAWFLOWER	Jefferson Co	**370L**	80127	1-99	
STRAWFLOWER LN	Jefferson Co	**277U**	80401	1-99	
STREAMBED TRAIL	Douglas Co	**469F**	80134	4800-5399	
STREAMCREST DR	Boulder Co	**703X**	80302	8600-8799	
STROH PL	Longmont	**11X**	80501	1800-1899	
STROH RD	Parker	**439G**	80134	18500-20099	
STROH RD E	Douglas Co	**440E**	80134	7200-7999	
	Douglas Co	**440G**	80134	8700-9099	
STROH RANCH CT	Parker	**439H**	80134	12700-12999	
STROH RANCH DR	Parker	**439G**	80134	12900-13099	
STROH RANCH PL	Parker	**439H**	80134	12800-12899	
STROH RANCH WAY	Parker	**439H**	80134	12700-12999	
STROILWAY ST	Adams Co	**751A**	80603	None	
STROLL AVE E	Parker	**410X**	80138	21500-22199	
STROLL LN	Parker	**410X**	80138	None	
STRONG ST	Brighton	**138P**	80601	1-699	
	Brighton	**138Q**	80601	1100-1399	
STUART CIR	Westminster	**193K**	80031	10800-10899	
STUART CT	Arvada	**223W**	80003	6600-6699	
	Broomfield	**163K**	80020	13300-13599	
	Broomfield	**163X**	80020	None	
	Denver	**283B**	80212	2400-2499	
	Westminster	**193K**	80031	10800-10999	
	Westminster	**193J**	80031	11000-11099	
STUART CT S	Denver	**343K**	80123	5000-5099	
STUART PL	Westminster	**223J**	80030	7800-7999	
	Westminster	**223J**	80031	8000-8199	
	Westminster	**193A**	80031	None	
STUART ST	Adams Co	**253F**	80212	5200-5299	
	Adams Co	**223X**	80003	6100-6599	
	Broomfield	**163J**	80020	13600-13799	
	Denver	**283S**	80219	1-399	
	Denver	**283P**	80204	400-1099	
	Denver	**283K**	80204	1200-1699	
	Denver	**283B**	80212	2000-2699	
	Denver	**253P**	80212	2700-5199	
STUART ST	Longmont	**11X**	80501	1000-1099	
	Longmont	**11S**	80501	1300-1599	
	Longmont	**11P**	80501	2100-2399	
STUART ST	Westminster	**223S**	80030	7000-7199	
	Westminster	**223J**	80030	7500-7999	
	Westminster	**223E**	80031	8000-8199	
	Westminster	**193X**	80031	9000-9299	
	Westminster	**193J**	80031	10500-10699	
	Westminster	**193F**	80031	11000-11199	
STUART ST S	Denver	**283X**	80219	100-699	
	Denver	**313B**	80219	800-899	
	Denver	**313K**	80219	1300-2099	
	Denver	**313P**	80219	2200-2599	
	Denver	**313S**	80236	2700-3499	
STUART WAY S	Denver	**313F**	80219	1300-1399	
	Denver	**313T**	80219	2600-2699	
STUART WAY S	Parker	**439G**	80134	13000-13099	
STURBRIDGE DR	Highlands Ranch	**373Y**	80129	3200-3499	
STURBRIDGE PL	Highlands Ranch	**373Y**	80129	9000-9199	
STYVE RD	Jefferson Co	**842C**	80433	12200-12299	
SUDBURY RD	El Paso Co	**909Y**	80908	4000-4199	
SUDBURY ST	Castle Rock	**499J**	80104	400-599	
SUE CIR	Jefferson Co	**336U**	80439	29300-29599	
SUE RD	Jefferson Co	**336T**	80439	29200-30199	
SUE ST	Lafayette	**132K**	80026	700-799	
SUFFOLK AVE	Castle Rock	**498Q**	80104	5100-5599	
SUFFOLK CIR	Castle Rock	**498Q**	80104	5200-5499	
SUFFOLK LN	Douglas Co	**848E**	80108	200-499	
SUGAR CT	Boulder Co	**742A**	80302	1-199	
SUGARBEET PL	Brighton	**140K**	80601	None	
SUGARBIN CT	Longmont	**42G**	80501	200-399	
SUGARBOWL CT W	Castle Rock	**466Q**	80109	3100-3199	
SUGARBRUSH DR	El Paso Co	**908Q**	80132	200-299	
SUGARBRUSH DR	Jefferson Co	**306E**	80439	None	
SUGARFOOT ST	Castle Pines North	**436C**	80108	400-599	
SUGARHILL LN	Jefferson Co	**306E**	80439	31200-31399	
SUGARLOAF DR	Elbert Co	**831T**	80138	45200-45299	
SUGARLOAF RD	Boulder Co	**742B**	80302	1-1399	
	Boulder Co	**721Z**	80302	1400-1999	
	Boulder Co	**741B**	80302	2000-10999	
SUGARLOAF RD	Douglas Co	**887K**	80118	8100-8899	
SUGAR MAPLE CT	Castle Pines North	**436K**	80108	7400-7499	
SUGAR MILL AVE	Longmont	**42B**	80501	600-999	
SUGAR MILL PL	Longmont	**42B**	80501	500-599	
SUGAR MILL RD	Longmont	**42F**	80501	600-12399	
SUGARLOAF MOUNTAIN RD					
	Boulder Co	**721Z**	80302	1-799	
SUGAR PINE CIR	Elbert Co	**830Q**	80138	46300-46499	
SUGAR PINE TRAIL	Jefferson Co	**306T**	80439	2900-2999	
SUGAR PLUM WAY	Castle Rock	**497T**	80104	100-199	
SUGARSTONE CIR	Highlands Ranch	**376W**	80130	9100-9299	
SULFUR CT	Castle Rock	**467H**	80108	6800-7099	
SULFUR LN	Castle Rock	**467H**	80108	6900-7099	
SULKY LN	Jefferson Co	**306Y**	80439	3100-3199	
SULLIVAN DR	Jefferson Co	**365Y**	80433	32500-32699	
SULLIVAN ST	Park Co	**820Z**	80421	1-599	
SULLIVAN HUGHES E	Thornton	**165W**	80241	None	
SULLY WAY	Northglenn	**193M**	80234	10500-10799	
SULTON CT S	Highlands Ranch	**405A**	80126	9300-9399	
SUMAC	Boulder	**127L**	80302	None	
SUMAC AVE	Boulder	**97M**	80304	1200-1899	
	Boulder Co	**98J**	80304	2400-2599	
SUMAC AVE W	Denver	**342V**	80123	5700-5999	
	Denver	**342U**	80123	6100-6699	
SUMAC CT	Boulder	**98K**	80301	None	
SUMAC CT W	Louisville	**130Z**	80027	400-499	
SUMAC DR	Jefferson Co	**307H**	80401	24000-24199	
SUMAC LN	Littleton	**343T**	80123	4400-4599	
SUMAC PL	Longmont	**11X**	80501	1900-1999	
SUMAC ST	Longmont	**11X**	80501	900-1199	
	Longmont	**11T**	80501	1400-1499	
	Longmont	**11T**	80501	1700-1799	
	Longmont	**11P**	80501	2000-2199	
SUMAC RUN	Douglas Co	**845R**	80125	10000-10499	
SUMMER CIR	Elbert Co	**872J**	80117	7600-7699	
SUMMER DR	Highlands Ranch	**404D**	80126	800-899	
SUMMER RD S	Jefferson Co	**369A**	80465	6300-6599	
SUMMER ST	Morrison	**339D**	80465	100-299	
SUMMER BAY LN	Broomfield	**163H**	80020	14000-14099	
SUMMER DAY AVE	Castle Rock	**466U**	80109	None	
SUMMERFIELD CT	Erie	**102Q**	80516	100-299	
SUMMERFIELD DR	Castle Rock	**498N**	80104	1900-2299	
SUMMERGREEN LN	Jefferson Co	**277Y**	80401	25700-25899	
SUMMER HAWK DR	Longmont	**42D**	80501	500-899	
SUMMER HEAVEN DR	Gilpin Co	**761J**	80403	1-199	
SUMMERLIN DR	Longmont	**40U**	80503	2100-2199	
SUMMERLIN PL	Boulder Co	**40U**	80503	8500-8699	
SUMMER MIST CIR	Douglas Co	**527S**	80104	500-699	
SUMMER RIDGE WAY S	Castle Rock	**466T**	80109	5900-6199	
SUMMERSET AVE	Firestone	**707S**	80504	5800-5999	
	Firestone	**707T**	80504	6800-6999	
SUMMERSET CT	Parker	**409R**	80138	20000-20099	
SUMMERSET LN	Parker	**409M**	80138	19700-19999	
SUMMERSET WAY	Parker	**409R**	80138	10800-10899	
SUMMER STAR LN	Jefferson Co	**763W**	80403	6300-6799	
SUMMERTIME CT	El Paso Co	**907V**	80132	3600-3699	
SUMMER VIEW CIR	Elbert Co	**872J**	80117	None	
SUMMERVILLE CIR	Castle Rock	**496A**	80109	None	
SUMMERWIND LN	Douglas Co	**373U**	80129	None	
SUMMERWOOD DR	Jefferson Co	**308B**	80401	700-799	
SUMMERWOOD LN	Douglas Co	**436M**	80108	200-399	
SUMMIT BLVD	Broomfield	**161S**	80021	200-599	
SUMMIT BLVD	Cherry Hills Village	**344R**	80113	100-299	
SUMMIT CIR	Lafayette	**132A**	80026	200-299	
SUMMIT CIR	Superior	**160U**	80027	1200-1298	E
SUMMIT CIR N	Superior	**160U**	80027	None	
SUMMIT CIR S	Superior	**160U**	80027	None	
SUMMIT DR	Jefferson Co	**369N**	80465	8000-8299	
SUMMIT DR	Park Co	**841N**	80421	1-399	
SUMMIT DR W	Jefferson Co	**372C**	80123	6100-6399	
SUMMIT LN	Frederick	**726F**	80516	None	
SUMMIT LN	Jefferson Co	**336D**	80439	3700-3799	
SUMMIT LN S	Jefferson Co	**336C**	80439	None	
SUMMIT PL	Boulder Co	**101Z**	80026	1600-1999	
SUMMIT RD	Elbert Co	**831P**	80138	45300-45999	
SUMMIT RD	Jefferson Co	**336Q**	80439	29200-29499	
SUMMIT RD E	Douglas Co	**380Y**	80138	7500-9499	
SUMMIT ST	Douglas Co	**870P**	80116	1900-2299	

STREET NAME	CITY or COUNTY	MAP GRID	ZIP CODE	BLOCK RANGE	O/E
SUMMIT WAY	Park Co	820Y	80421	1-299	
SUMMIT WAY	Weld Co	726K	80516	5500-5599	
SUMMIT ASH	Jefferson Co	370Q	80127	1-99	
SUMMIT CEDAR DR	Jefferson Co	370Q	80127	1-99	
SUMMIT FOX AVE E	Parker	408Z	80134	None	
SUMMIT GROVE PKWY	Thornton	165P	80241	3100-3699	
	Thornton	165L	80241	3700-4199	
	Thornton	165Q	80241	4200-4699	
	Thornton	165R	80241	4700-5599	
	Thornton	165V	80241	5600-5699	
SUMMIT PEAK CT	Frederick	726G	80516	None	
SUMMIT RANCH DR	Jefferson Co	276Y	80401	28600-29199	
SUMMIT RANCH WAY	Jefferson Co	276Y	80401	1-99	
SUMMIT RIDGE CT	Douglas Co	411A	80138	9600-9699	
SUMMIT RIDGE PL	Douglas Co	411A	80138	9500-9799	
SUMMIT RIDGE RD	Douglas Co	411A	80138	12000-12699	
	Douglas Co	830J	80138	12700-12999	
SUMMIT TRAIL	Broomfield	162L	80020	200-299	
SUMMIT TRAIL SE	Jefferson Co	335K	80439	4500-4699	
SUMMIT TRAIL SW	Jefferson Co	335K	80439	4500-4699	
SUMMIT VIEW CIR	Elbert Co	850C	80138	1-299	
SUMMIT VIEW CT	Elbert Co	850C	80138	42600-42699	
SUMMITVIEW DR	Longmont	41T	80504	2000-2399	
SUMMIT VIEW PKWY	Highlands Ranch	405J	80126	2200-3399	
SUMMIT VIEW POINTE	Highlands Ranch	405J	80126	10100-10199	
SUMNER CIR S	Littleton	373L	80120	7400-7499	
SUMNER ST	Longmont	41B	80501	200-899	
	Longmont	11X	80501	1100-1399	
	Longmont	11T	80501	1500-1699	
	Longmont	11P	80501	1700-1999	
SUMNER ST S	Littleton	343Z	80120	5900-6199	
SUMPTER CT	Elbert Co	832X	80107	8300-8399	
SUN WAY	Park Co	841R	80421	1-399	
SUN WAY	Parker	409V	80134	11400-11599	
SUNBEAM AVE W	Douglas Co	825V	80125	9600-9899	
SUNBEAM TRAIL N	Douglas Co	440A	80134	8800-8899	
SUN BLAZE LOOP	Broomfield	163F	80020	14100-14199	
SUNBURST AVE	Firestone	707S	80504	5800-5899	
	Firestone	707T	80504	10400-10599	
	Firestone	707T	80504	None	
SUNBURST CT	Lafayette	131M	80026	1000-1099	
SUNBURST DR	El Paso Co	907V	80132	18000-18499	
SUNBURST DR	Jefferson Co	824U	80127	12800-14199	
SUNBURST LN	Jefferson Co	275Y	80439	32400-32599	
SUNBURST TRAIL N	Douglas Co	440E	80134	8200-8899	
SUNBURST VISTA	El Paso Co	908Q	80132	18000-18499	
SUNCHASE DR	Castle Rock	466T	80109	3500-3999	
SUN COUNTRY DR	Elbert Co	832T	80107	7100-45999	
SUN CREEK DR	Jefferson Co	306T	80439	None	
SUNCREST RD	Castle Rock	498A	80104	None	
SUN CREST RD	Palmer Lake	907U	80133	None	
SUNDANCE CIR	Dacono	727K	80514	500-3099	
SUNDANCE CIR	Nederland	740L	80466	None	
SUNDANCE DR	Longmont	12R	80501	1700-2099	
	Longmont	12L	80501	None	
SUNDANCE PKWY	Dacono	727K	80514	200-699	
SUNDANCE PL	Castle Pines North	436G	80108	500-699	
SUNDANCE PL	Longmont	12U	80501	1600-1699	
SUNDANCE MOUNTAIN	Jefferson Co	371Q	80127	10400-10799	
SUNDANCE SQUARE	Boulder Co	100A	80301	4900-4999	
SUNDANCE TRAIL	Douglas Co	845V	80125	9900-10099	
SUNDANCE TRAIL	Elbert Co	831P	80138	46400-46799	
SUNDANCE TRAIL E	Douglas Co	380X	80138	7700-7999	
SUNDEW ST E	Parker	409B	80134	17600-17799	
SUN DIAL PL	Boulder Co	69Z	80301	5200-5399	
	Highlands Ranch	404Q	80126	10600-10899	
SUNDIAL RIM RD	Highlands Ranch	404M	80126	None	
SUNDOWN CIR S	Littleton	374F	80120	7200-7299	
SUNDOWN DR	Castle Rock	498G	80104	800-1099	
SUNDOWN LN	Adams Co	224K	80221	400-8199	
SUNDOWN LN	Boulder	128B	80303	2800-2899	
SUNDOWN LN	Jefferson Co	305C	80439	500-699	
SUNDOWN LN	Nederland	740L	80466	None	
SUNDOWN TRAIL	Douglas Co	432T	80125	10800-10899	
SUNDOWN TRAIL	Elbert Co	832T	80107	44500-44999	
SUNDOWN TRAIL	Nederland	740L	80466	1-99	
SUNDOWN TRAIL N	Douglas Co	440E	80134	8000-8899	
SUNDROP LN	Brighton	168C	80601	None	
SUNDROP PL	Brighton	168D	80601	None	
SUNDROP WAY	Highlands Ranch	375W	80126	8800-8999	
SUNDROP TRAIL	Highlands Ranch	375W	80126	1900-2099	
SUNFLOWER CIR	Longmont	40R	80503	3600-3699	
SUNFLOWER DR	Brighton	140K	80601	None	
SUNFLOWER DR	Douglas Co	887B	80118	6100-6499	
SUN FLOWER DR	Gilpin Co	741Y	80403	1-499	
SUNFLOWER LN	Jefferson Co	370A	80127	16400-16499	
SUNFLOWER PL	Cherry Hills Village	315W	80113	1-99	
SUNFLOWER PL	Fort Lupton	729E	80621	None	
SUNFLOWER ST	Broomfield	163X	80020	12100-12299	
SUNFLOWER ST	Louisville	130T	80027	900-999	
SUNFLOWER ST S	Highlands Ranch	374U	80126	8400-8499	
SUNGOLD LN N	Castle Rock	466Q	80109	4800-5099	
SUNLAND ST	Louisville	130M	80027	2300-2399	
SUNLIGHT DR	Boulder Co	101G	80026	10400-10499	
SUNLIGHT DR	Longmont	12N	80501	1700-2199	
SUNLIGHT LN	Broomfield	163J	80020	4600-4799	
SUNLIGHT LN	Jefferson Co	822V	80433	10400-10499	
SUNLIGHT LN	Park Co	841M	80421	1-199	
SUNLIGHT LN	Thornton	224B	80260	None	
SUNLIGHT RD	Thornton	193V	80260	None	
SUNLIGHT WAY	El Paso Co	908Q	80132	19800-19999	
SUNLIGHT WAY	Superior	160Y	80027	800-899	
SUNLIGHT PEAK	Jefferson Co	371K	80127	8000-8099	
SUNLIT DR	Castle Rock	467W	80109	None	
SUN MEADOW ST S	Highlands Ranch	404E	80129	9600-9799	
SUNNINGDALE BLVD	Lone Tree	406C	80124	9800-9899	
SUNNY LN	Boulder Co	742W	80403	1-99	
SUNNY WAY	Boulder Co	130H	80026	800-999	
SUNNY FARM CIR	Elbert Co	851E	80138	41400-41499	
SUNNY MEADOWS CIR	Elbert Co	872E	80117	7500-7599	
SUNNY RIDGE LN	Park Co	841V	80421	1-299	
SUNNYSIDE CIR	Louisville	131N	80027	1900-1999	
SUNNYSIDE CT S	Highlands Ranch	374V	80126	8300-8399	
SUNNYSIDE LN	Boulder	128J	80302	400-699	
SUNNYSIDE LN	Longmont	42A	80501	300-499	
SUNNYSIDE PL S	Highlands Ranch	374V	80126	8300-8399	
SUNNYSIDE ST	Louisville	131N	80027	300-699	
SUNNYSIDE ST E	Highlands Ranch	374V	80126	1200-1499	
SUN PRAIRIE CT	Parker	410U	80138	11300-11399	
SUNRIDGE CIR	Broomfield	162N	80020	2000-2299	
SUN RIDGE CIR	Palmer Lake	907U	80133	None	
SUN RIDGE DR	Jefferson Co	307W	80439	None	
SUN RIDGE LN	Jefferson Co	307W	80439	3200-3299	
SUNRIDGE HOLLOW RD E	Douglas Co	440U	80134	8700-9199	
SUNRIDGE TERRACE CT	Castle Rock	466T	80109	4000-4099	
SUNRIDGE TERRACE DR	Castle Rock	466T	80109	3400-4899	
SUNRISE	Lochbuie	140F	80603	800-999	
SUNRISE AVE W	Douglas Co	825V	80125	9500-9699	
SUNRISE CIR	Frederick	726C	80530	3600-3699	
SUNRISE CT	Boulder	98J	80304	4100-4199	
SUNRISE CT	Frederick	726C	80530	8000-8099	
SUNRISE CT	Louisville	130M	80027	2500-2599	
SUNRISE DR	Cherry Hills Village	345A	80113	1-99	
SUNRISE DR	Douglas Co	866F	80135	None	
SUNRISE DR	Elbert Co	832X	80107	8200-8299	
SUNRISE DR	Jefferson Co	278X	80401	300-699	
	Jefferson Co	337Q	80439	5100-5299	
	Jefferson Co	368X	80465	22700-22799	
SUNRISE DR	Longmont	11L	80501	2200-2499	
SUNRISE LN	Boulder Co	722L	80302	1-799	
SUNRISE LN	Elbert Co	871H	80117	6600-6699	
SUNRISE LN	Gilpin Co	761J	80403	100-499	
SUNRISE LN	Jefferson Co	368X	80465	8200-9299	
	Jefferson Co	277U	80401	25500-25899	
SUNRISE LN	Weld Co	729R	80603	3500-5099	
SUNRISE PL	Frederick	726C	80530	8000-8099	
SUNRISE RANCH DR	Boulder Co	69F	80503	5900-6299	
SUNRISE TRAIL N	Douglas Co	440A	80134	7600-7899	
SUNROSE LN	Jefferson Co	308A	80401	23500-23899	
SUN SEDGE PL	Gilpin Co	761C	80403	100-199	
SUNSET AVE	Adams Co	794P	80136	56100-56399	
SUNSET AVE	Elbert Co	832S	80107	7100-7999	
SUNSET AVE W	Douglas Co	825V	80125	9600-9699	
SUNSET BLVD	Boulder	97Z	80304	1400-1899	
SUNSET CIR	Dacono	727K	80514	1000-1099	
SUNSET CIR	Elbert Co	871D	80117	6600-7199	
SUNSET CIR	Jefferson Co	306J	80439	1-1999	
SUNSET CIR	Longmont	41B	80501	1-99	
SUNSET CT	Castle Rock	497G	80104	900-999	
SUNSET CT	Hudson	730L	80642	None	
SUNSET CT E	Greenwood Village	344R	80121	900-999	
SUNSET DR	Bow Mar	342H	80123	5200-5599	
SUNSET DR	Brighton	138U	80601	300-399	
SUNSET DR	Broomfield	162P	80020	1100-1199	
SUNSET DR	Castle Rock	497G	80104	700-899	
SUNSET DR	Cherry Hills Village	345A	80113	1-99	
SUNSET DR	Clear Creek Co	335J	80439	1-99	
SUNSET DR	Elbert Co	832T	80107	44500-44599	
SUNSET DR	Erie	133F	80516	None	
SUNSET DR	Golden	279G	80401	300-3099	
SUNSET DR	Jefferson Co	278T	80401	22300-22599	
SUNSET DR	Lakewood	282N	80214	700-8199	
SUNSET DR	Littleton	373M	80120	2400-2499	
SUNSET DR	Longmont	11K	80501	2400-2599	
SUNSET DR	Louisville	131N	80027	500-1699	
SUNSET DR	Park Co	820U	80421	1-399	
SUNSET DR E	Douglas Co	441D	80138	11600-11799	
SUNSET LN	Boulder Co	71F	80504	None	
SUNSET LN	Dacono	727K	80514	200-399	
SUNSET LN	Douglas Co	866K	80135	1400-1499	
SUNSET LN	Greenwood Village	344Q	80121	1-99	
SUNSET LN	Jefferson Co	337Q	80439	25000-25599	
SUNSET LN	Weld Co	729R	80603	3000-17899	
SUNSET PL	Dacono	727S	80514	None	
SUNSET PL	Elbert Co	832T	80107	8000-8299	
SUNSET PL	Erie	133F	80516	None	
SUNSET PL	Longmont	41P	80501	1800-1899	
SUNSET RD	Cherry Hills Village	344M	80113	1-99	
SUNSET ST	Erie	133F	80516	None	
SUNSET ST	Longmont	41F	80501	100-899	
	Longmont	11X	80501	900-1299	
	Longmont	11T	80501	1300-1699	
SUNSET ST S	Longmont	41P	80501	1-1999	
	Longmont	41T	80504	None	
SUNSET WAY	Erie	133F	80516	None	
SUNSET WAY	Longmont	41K	80501	1900-2099	
SUNSET WAY S	Denver	313K	80219	1800-1899	
SUNSET HILL CIR	Lone Tree	407E	80124	9600-9999	
SUNSET HILL DR	Lone Tree	407E	80124	9500-9799	
SUNSET HILL PL	Lone Tree	407E	80124	9600-9699	
SUNSET RIDGE	Greenwood Village	344R	80121	900-1099	
SUNSET RIDGE CT S	Highlands Ranch	374Z	80126	8900-9099	
SUNSET RIDGE RD E	Highlands Ranch	374Z	80126	1400-1699	
SUNSET TRAIL	Jefferson Co	842G	80470	29000-31299	
	Jefferson Co	842G	80433	None	
SUNSET TRAIL E	Douglas Co	440A	80134	7400-7599	
SUNSET VIEW WAY	Elbert Co	830Q	80138	46300-46799	
SUNSHINE AVE	Boulder	97Y	80302	None	
SUNSHINE AVE	Longmont	12V	80501	None	
SUNSHINE CT	Thornton	193V	80260	None	
SUNSHINE DR	Dacono	726M	80514	None	
SUNSHINE DR N	Douglas Co	825V	80125	10500-10999	
SUNSHINE LN	Jefferson Co	275Y	80439	400-599	
SUNSHINE PKWY	Golden	249W	80403	300-699	
SUNSHINE PL	Broomfield	133N	80020	4800-4899	
SUNSHINE WAY	Brighton	139L	80601	None	
SUNSHINE CANYON DR	Boulder Co	97V	80302	1-9999	
	Boulder Co	722Q	80302	2000-9999	
SUNSHINE MEADOW PL	Douglas Co	470D	80134	9000-9299	
SUNSHINE PEAK	Jefferson Co	371K	80127	7600-7699	
SUNSHINE PEAK ST	Brighton	139M	80601	None	
SUNSHOWER PL	Highlands Ranch	404K	80129	10401-10599	O
SUNSTAR CT	El Paso Co	908V	80132	3500-3599	
SUNSTONE LN	Castle Rock	467Q	80108	5400-5599	
SUNUP CIR	Elbert Co	871W	80107	28500-28899	
SUN VALLEY CT	Castle Rock	498N	80104	2200-2299	
SUNVIEW CT	El Paso Co	907V	80132	3600-3899	
SUPAI RD	Jefferson Co	337H	80439	23700-24299	
SUPERIOR PLAZA WAY	Superior	160F	80027	100-199	
SURLYN CT	Castle Rock	497A	80109	1000-1099	
SURREY CT	Boulder Co	102J	80026	4000-4199	
SURREY DR	Jefferson Co	368R	80465	7400-8299	
	Jefferson Co	369J	80465	7400-7899	
	Jefferson Co	366Z	80439	8700-8999	
SURREY DR W	Jefferson Co	341L	80127	10100-10499	
SURREY PL W	Jefferson Co	341L	80127	10000-10199	
SURREY RD N	Douglas Co	406Z	80108	9200-9399	
	Douglas Co	407S	80108	9400-9699	
	Lone Tree	407S	80124	None	
SURREY RD W	Douglas Co	406Z	80108	1-499	
SURREY RIDGE RD	Boulder Co	722R	80302	1-299	
SURREY TRAIL	Douglas Co	432R	80125	6700-6999	
SURRY PL N	Douglas Co	440T	80134	6500-6699	
SURRY ST	Palmer Lake	907Q	80133	None	
SUSSEX CT	Boulder Co	70K	80503	7900-7999	
SUSSEX CT E	Parker	410S	80138	20800-20899	
SUSSEX ST	Lafayette	132T	80026	1700-1899	
SUTHERLAND CT	Highlands Ranch	376S	80130	1-99	
SUTTON AVE	Castle Rock	498L	80104	4700-4899	
SUTTON CIR	Lafayette	131M	80026	100-599	
SUTTON RD	Jefferson Co	823N	80433	25600-26599	
SWADLEY CIR	Arvada	221S	80004	7100-7199	
SWADLEY CT	Arvada	251B	80004	5800-5999	
	Arvada	221T	80004	6700-6999	
	Arvada	221S	80005	7000-7199	
	Arvada	221E	80005	8200-8599	
SWADLEY CT S	Jefferson Co	341F	80465	4300-4399	
SWADLEY CT S	Jefferson Co	341E	80465	4400-4599	
	Jefferson Co	341K	80465	4500-4699	
	Jefferson Co	341T	80127	5400-5699	
	Jefferson Co	371B	80127	6500-6599	
SWADLEY DR	Lakewood	251W	80215	11700-11799	
SWADLEY ST	Arvada	221X	80004	6500-6599	
	Arvada	221N	80005	7400-7599	
	Arvada	221E	80005	8200-8399	
	Lakewood	281F	80215	1500-1899	
	Lakewood	281B	80215	2500-2599	
	Wheat Ridge	251X	80033	3200-3399	
	Wheat Ridge	251T	80033	3700-3799	
	Wheat Ridge	251P	80033	4600-4799	
	Wheat Ridge	251K	80033	5000-5299	
SWADLEY ST S	Jefferson Co	341J	80465	4700-4899	
	Jefferson Co	311S	80228	None	
	Lakewood	281X	80228	300-599	
	Lakewood	311B	80228	600-999	
	Lakewood	311P	80228	1900-1999	
SWADLEY WAY S	Jefferson Co	341K	80465	4600-4699	
	Jefferson Co	341X	80127	5900-6499	
SWALE AVE	Parker	410T	80138	21600-21899	
SWALE DR	Parker	410T	80138	21800-21999	
SWALLOW CIR E	Aurora	380Z	80138	23500-23699	
SWALLOW CT	Boulder Co	129F	80303	1300-1399	
SWALLOW LN	Boulder Co	129F	80303	6300-6399	
	Boulder Co	99S	80301	None	
SWALLOW PL E	Aurora	380Z	80138	None	
SWAN AVE	Brighton	137Z	80601	1400-1499	
SWANDYKE CT	Douglas Co	436W	80108	800-899	
SWANDYKE DR	Douglas Co	436X	80108	800-899	
SWANSBORO CT	Highlands Ranch	375Z	80126	4500-4599	
SWANSBORO WAY	Highlands Ranch	375Y	80126	4300-4399	
SWANSEA DR	Douglas Co	407L	80134	11800-12599	
SWAPS LN	Jefferson Co	366Q	80439	7900-7999	
SWAPS TRAIL	Jefferson Co	366Q	80439	7700-8099	
SWARTHMORE AVE W	Jefferson Co	341E	80465	12000-12499	
SWARTHMORE DR W	Jefferson Co	342E	80123	8900-9099	
	Jefferson Co	341H	80123	None	
SWARTHMORE PL W	Jefferson Co	342E	80123	8400-8799	
	Jefferson Co	341F	80127	11200-11299	
SWEDE GULCH RD	Jefferson Co	307J	80401	700-899	
	Jefferson Co	306C	80401	900-2199	
SWEENEY PL	Longmont	11T	80501	1800-1999	
SWEET ALDER ST	Parker	409S	80134	None	
SWEETBRIAR TRAIL	Jefferson Co	307X	80439	26000-26499	
SWEETBRUSH DR	Douglas Co	408H	80134	16400-16599	
SWEET CLOVER PL	Fort Lupton	729E	80621	None	
SWEETCLOVER WAY	Douglas Co	378V	80134	8400-8599	
SWEET GRASS CT	Castle Rock	466Q	80109	5300-5499	
SWEETGRASS PKWY	Dacono	727S	80514	None	
SWEET ROCK CT	Douglas Co	409E	80134	10200-10299	
SWEET VALLEY CT	Longmont	42H	80501	200-399	
SWEETWATER CIR	Lafayette	131E	80026	2500-2599	
SWEETWATER CT	Boulder Co	99H	80301	6900-6999	
SWEET WATER RD	Lone Tree	376Y	80124	7800-8499	
SWEET WIND AVE	Castle Rock	466V	80109	None	
SWIFT CT	Park Co	841U	80421	1-199	
SWIFT CREEK CIR	Elbert Co	851K	80107	39600-39699	
SWIFT FOX PL E	Parker	408Z	80134	None	
SWIFT FOX WAY S	Parker	408Z	80134	None	
SWISS RD S	Jefferson Co	842Q	80470	15100-15399	
SWITCH GRASS CT	Castle Rock	497A	80109	1400-1499	
SWITCH GRASS DR	Castle Rock	497A	80109	900-1599	
SWITCH GRASS WAY	Castle Rock	497A	80109	2300-2499	
SWITZER LN	Northglenn	194X	80260	400-599	
	Thornton	194X	80260	600-799	
SWITZERLAND TRAIL	Boulder Co	740M	80466	1-399	
SWITZERLAND TRAIL	Boulder Co	721X	80302	300-12499	
SWITZERLAND TRAIL	Boulder Co	720Z	80466	900-999	
SWITZERLAND TRAIL	Ward	720L	80481	None	
SWITZER PARK LN	Parker	410S	80138	11400-11499	
SWITZER PARK PL	Parker	410S	80138	11400-11499	
SYCAMORE AVE	Boulder	129E	80303	800-1099	
SYCAMORE CIR	Louisville	130Z	80027	500-599	
SYCAMORE CIR	Superior	160E	80027	None	
SYCAMORE CT W	Louisville	130Z	80027	400-499	
SYCAMORE LN	Jefferson Co	370Q	80127	1-99	
SYCAMORE LN	Louisville	130Z	80027	100-399	
SYCAMORE LN N	Douglas Co	850X	80116	2200-2399	
SYCAMORE ST	Louisville	130Z	80027	500-599	
SYCAMORE ST S	Littleton	343V	80120	5500-5699	
	Littleton	343Z	80120	5900-6399	
	Littleton	373D	80120	6400-6999	
SYCAMORE ST W	Superior	160E	80027	500-598	E
SYDNEY AVE E	Highlands Ranch	405H	80130	5100-5299	
SYDNEY LN S	Highlands Ranch	405H	80130	9600-9899	
SYDNEY PL E	Highlands Ranch	406A	80130	5500-5599	
SYLVAN CT	Parker	410N	80138	11000-11099	
SYLVAN PL	Parker	410S	80138	11000-11199	
SYLVAN RD	Jefferson Co	762B	80403	31700-32499	
SYLVAN ST	Boulder Co	69J	80503	7000-7099	
SYLVESTOR CT	Highlands Ranch	404F	80129	9600-9699	
SYLVESTOR PL	Highlands Ranch	404F	80129	1-299	
SYLVESTOR RD	Highlands Ranch	404F	80129	9700-10099	

S

STREET NAME	CITY or COUNTY	MAP GRID	ZIP CODE	BLOCK RANGE	O/E
SYLVESTOR ST	Highlands Ranch	404G	80129	1-199	
SYLVESTOR WAY	Highlands Ranch	404F	80129	400-499	
SYLVESTOR TRAIL	Highlands Ranch	404F	80129	400-799	
SYLVIA DR	Northglenn	194D	80233	11800-11999	
SYLVIA LN	Weld Co	103B	80516	4600-4799	
SYMPHONY HEIGHTS	El Paso Co	908T	80132	1400-1599	
SYNDT RD S	Jefferson Co	336P	80439	5000-5099	
SYNTHES AVE	Monument	908W	80132	900-16699	
SYRACUSE WAY	Thornton	166L	80602	None	
SYRACUSE CT	Denver	256Y	80238	2800-2899	
	Denver	286L	80230	900-1099	
SYRACUSE CT S	Centennial	376G	80112	6900-7399	
	Centennial	376Q	80112	8200-8299	
SYRACUSE ST	Commerce City	226G	80022	8000-8599	
	Denver	286Q	80230	200-1099	
	Denver	286L	80220	1100-1999	
	Denver	286C	80207	2000-2299	
	Denver	286C	80238	2300-2799	
	Denver	256Y	80207	2800-3699	
	Thornton	166Q	80602	12800-12999	
	Thornton	166L	80602	None	
	Thornton	166U	80602	None	
	Thornton	166Y	80602	None	
SYRACUSE ST S	Centennial	376G	80112	7100-7399	
	Centennial	376Q	80112	8000-8199	
	Denver	286U	80230	1-299	
	Denver	316G	80231	1500-1699	
	Denver	346G	80237	4000-4199	
	Denver	346G	80237	4300-4399	
	Denver	346L	80237	4600-5099	
SYRACUSE WAY	Thornton	136Y	80602	None	
	Thornton	166U	80602	None	
SYRACUSE WAY S	Arapahoe Co	316Q	80231	2200-2699	
	Centennial	376C	80111	6600-6699	
	Denver	316V	80231	2800-3098	E
	Denver	346C	80237	3800-3999	
	Greenwood Village	346Y	80111	6000-7299	

T

STREET NAME	CITY or COUNTY	MAP GRID	ZIP CODE	BLOCK RANGE	O/E
TABLE DR	Golden	279B	80401	1900-2299	
TABLE BUTTE RD	El Paso Co	910U	80908	8500-8899	
TABLE HEIGHTS DR	Golden	279F	80401	2300-2499	
TABLE MESA CT	Boulder	128T	80305	2600-2799	
TABLE MESA DR	Boulder	128T	80305	1800-3799	
	Boulder	128Q	80305	3800-4999	
TABLE MOUNTAIN DR	Golden	250N	80403	4300-4799	
TABLE MOUNTAIN PKWY	Golden	250J	80403	15700-16699	
TABLE ROCK RD	El Paso Co	910U	80908	17500-18499	
TABLE TOP CT	Boulder	69Y	80301	5600-5799	
TABOR CIR	Arvada	221E	80005	8400-8499	
TABOR CT	Arvada	251E	80002	5600-5699	
	Arvada	221S	80004	6800-7099	
	Arvada	221E	80005	8200-8399	
	Jefferson Co	191J	80021	10500-10699	
	Wheat Ridge	251W	80033	3200-3299	
	Wheat Ridge	251S	80033	3600-3799	
TABOR CT N	Castle Rock	498H	80104	800-999	
TABOR CT S	Jefferson Co	341E	80465	4300-4399	
	Jefferson Co	341E	80465	4400-4499	
	Jefferson Co	341S	80127	5600-5699	
	Jefferson Co	341W	80127	6400-6499	
TABOR DR	Castle Rock	498H	80104	1500-5599	
TABOR DR	Lakewood	281E	80215	2000-2199	
	Lakewood	251W	80215	11800-11899	
TABOR PL	Lakewood	281B	80215	2100-2199	
TABOR PL E	Castle Rock	498H	80104	5800-5999	
TABOR ST	Arvada	251J	80002	5200-5499	
	Arvada	221W	80004	6500-6599	
	Arvada	221S	80004	6700-6799	
	Arvada	221N	80005	7200-7599	
TABOR ST	Elizabeth	871F	80107	100-899	
TABOR ST	Jefferson Co	251E	80002	5600-5799	
	Lakewood	281N	80401	700-999	
	Lakewood	281E	80215	1500-1699	
	Lakewood	281F	80215	1800-1999	
	Lakewood	281A	80215	2400-2699	
	Wheat Ridge	251N	80033	4100-4799	
	Wheat Ridge	251J	80033	4800-5199	
TABOR ST S	Jefferson Co	341J	80465	4700-4899	
	Jefferson Co	341T	80127	5400-5499	
	Jefferson Co	341W	80127	5900-6199	
	Jefferson Co	371A	80127	6400-6599	
TABOR WAY S	Jefferson Co	311N	80228	2300-2399	
	Jefferson Co	341J	80465	4600-4699	
	Jefferson Co	341N	80127	5100-5399	
TABRIZ PL	Boulder	98N	80304	2600-2699	
TACK DR	Douglas Co	409X	80134	None	
TACK ST	Frederick	707W	80504	None	
TACKER CT	Castle Rock	497H	80104	400-599	
TACOMA ST	Lochbuie	729Z	80603	None	
TAFT CIR	Arvada	221S	80004	6700-6899	
TAFT CT	Arvada	251E	80002	5600-5699	
	Arvada	251A	80004	5800-6199	
	Arvada	221S	80004	6800-7099	
	Arvada	221N	80005	7200-7599	
	Arvada	221J	80005	7600-7699	
	Jefferson Co	251J	80002	5200-5299	
	Lakewood	281A	80215	2500-2799	
TAFT CT	Louisville	130Y	80027	200-399	
	Louisville	130Q	80027	1500-1599	
TAFT CT	Wheat Ridge	251W	80033	3200-3299	
	Wheat Ridge	251S	80033	3600-3699	
TAFT CT S	Jefferson Co	341E	80465	4400-4499	
	Jefferson Co	341J	80465	4700-4799	
	Jefferson Co	341N	80127	5300-5499	
	Jefferson Co	341S	80127	None	
TAFT DR	Boulder	128A	80302	2500-2799	
TAFT DR	Lakewood	281E	80215	1900-1999	
TAFT LN S	Jefferson Co	341S	80127	None	
TAFT PL	Louisville	130Q	80027	1400-1499	
TAFT ST	Arvada	251E	80002	5600-5699	
	Arvada	251A	80004	5800-6099	
	Arvada	221W	80004	6500-6599	
	Arvada	221S	80004	7000-7099	
	Arvada	221N	80005	7400-7599	
	Arvada	221E	80005	8300-8599	
TAFT ST	Frederick	727F	80530	6200-6299	
TAFT ST	Lakewood	281E	80215	1500-1699	
	Lakewood	281A	80215	2600-2699	
TAFT ST S	Jefferson Co	341E	80465	4300-4399	
	Jefferson Co	341J	80465	4600-4999	
	Jefferson Co	341N	80127	5300-5499	
	Jefferson Co	341S	80127	5500-5699	
	Jefferson Co	341W	80127	5800-6099	
	Jefferson Co	341N	80235	None	
	Jefferson Co	341S	80127	None	
	Lakewood	281W	80228	100-299	
	Lakewood	281X	80228	300-599	
	Lakewood	311B	80228	600-999	
	Lakewood	311P	80228	1900-1999	
TAFT WAY S	Jefferson Co	341J	80465	4400-4599	
	Jefferson Co	341N	80127	5100-5499	
	Jefferson Co	341W	80127	5900-6399	
	Jefferson Co	341S	80127	None	
TAFT WAY W	Lakewood	281E	80215	1500-1599	
TAFT TERRACE S	Jefferson Co	341S	80127	None	
TAHOE CT	Boulder Co	100Z	80301	8800-8899	
TAHOE CT	Jefferson Co	306E	80439	31100-31199	
TAHOE LN	Boulder Co	100Z	80301	8900-9199	
TAILFEATHER WAY	Castle Rock	468X	80104	None	
TALAMORE CT	Broomfield	163K	80020	None	
TALAVERO PL	Douglas Co	469B	80134	5200-5399	
TALBOT DR	Boulder	128G	80303	4600-4699	
TALISMAN CT	Boulder	98Q	80301	3300-3399	
TALISMAN PL	Boulder	98U	80301	3700-3899	
TALKING ROCK HEIGHTS	El Paso Co	908P	80132	None	
TALLBERG LN	Jefferson Co	823T	80433	10400-10699	
TALLYHO CT	Boulder Co	99G	80301	4600-4799	
TALL FOREST LN	Parker	439D	80134	20200-20399	
TALL GRASS CIR	Lone Tree	406D	80124	9700-9799	
TALL GRASS PL	Lone Tree	406D	80124	8700-8799	
TALL HORSE TRAIL	Douglas Co	866R	80135	4600-5499	
TALLKID AVE E	Parker	410X	80138	21900-22098	E
TALLKID CT S	Parker	410X	80138	None	
TALLMAN CT	Parker	410S	80138	21200-21299	
TALLMAN DR	Parker	409V	80134	19900-20099	
	Parker	409V	80138	20400-20499	
	Parker	410S	80138	20500-21599	
TALLMAN LN	Longmont	11W	80501	2100-2299	
TALL PINE LN	Boulder Co	722L	80302	1-1999	
TALLPINE WAY	El Paso Co	908Y	80132	100-199	
TALL PINES LN	Jefferson Co	822R	80433	18000-28499	
TALL SPRUCE CIR	Brighton	140J	80601	None	
TALL SPRUCE ST	Brighton	140J	80601	5200-5599	
TALL TIMBER LN	El Paso Co	908V	80132	700-799	
TALL TIMBER LN	Park Co	820Y	80421	1-299	
TALL TIMBER LN E	Parker	848D	80134	None	
TALLYHO TRAIL	Boulder Co	99G	80301	4500-4699	
TALLYN'S REACH PKWY S	Aurora	381E	80016	6700-7299	
TALLYRAND CIR	Douglas Co	527T	80104	4300-4599	
TALON TRAIL	Jefferson Co	338G	80454	3900-3999	
TALON TRAIL	Parker	409M	80138	7300-7399	
TALQUESAL TRAIL	Douglas Co	870J	80116	None	
TALUS CIR	Gilpin Co	761B	80403	1-99	
TAMARAC CT	Douglas Co	470A	80134	7100-7299	
TAMARAC CT	Thornton	166G	80602	None	
	Thornton	136Y	80602	None	
TAMARAC CT S	Centennial	376L	80112	7000-7499	
	Denver	346C	80237	3900-3999	
TAMARAC DR	Jefferson Co	307K	80401	1400-1699	
TAMARAC DR S	Denver	316Y	80231	3100-3499	
	Denver	346C	80237	3500-4299	
TAMARAC LN	Cherry Hills Village	345G	80113	1-99	
TAMARAC LN	Erie	133C	80516	None	
TAMARAC PKWY S	Denver	346G	80237	4300-4499	
TAMARAC PL	Thornton	166Q	80602	13000-13099	
	Thornton	166L	80602	13400-13499	
TAMARAC ST	Commerce City	226C	80022	8700-8799	
	Denver	286U	80230	1-99	
	Denver	286L	80230	900-1099	
	Denver	286L	80220	1200-1899	
	Denver	286C	80238	2600-2799	
	Thornton	166Q	80602	13100-13299	
	Thornton	166L	80602	None	
	Thornton	166Y	80602	None	
TAMARAC ST S	Arapahoe Co	316G	80247	None	
	Centennial	376G	80112	7000-7499	
	Centennial	376Q	80112	8100-8299	
	Denver	286U	80230	1-299	
	Denver	316L	80231	1800-1899	
	Denver	316U	80231	2900-2999	
TAMARACK AVE	Boulder	97M	80304	1200-2299	
	Boulder	98J	80304	2300-2599	
TAMARACK CT	Boulder	98J	80304	4200-4299	
TAMARADE CT	Jefferson Co	370Q	80127	1-99	
TAMARADE DR	Jefferson Co	370P	80127	1-99	
TAMARASK CT	Douglas Co	886G	80118	5900-5999	
TAMARISK CT	Louisville	130U	80027	600-699	
TAMARISK LN	Jefferson Co	306N	80439	31300-31399	
TAMARISK ST W	Louisville	130U	80027	700-899	
TAMARRON CT	Parker	410R	80138	11100-11299	
TAMARRON DR	Parker	410R	80138	11100-11299	
TAMARRON PL	Parker	410R	80138	11100-11299	
TAMASOA WAY	Douglas Co	466H	80108	300-399	
TAMERLAIN CT	Highlands Ranch	375V	80126	None	
TAMMARON LN	Lafayette	131F	80026	2200-2298	E
TAMMY LN	Douglas Co	409W	80134	9200-9999	
TAMMYWOOD ST	Broomfield	163S	80020	12500-12599	
TAM O'SHANTER WAY	El Paso Co	908U	80132	200-699	
TANAFORAN DR W	Denver	343L	80110	3000-3399	
	Englewood	343L	80110	2900-2999	
TANAGER CIR	Longmont	42D	80501	700-899	
TANAGER CT	Louisville	130Y	80027	100-199	
TANAGER PL	Longmont	42C	80501	None	
TANAGER ST	Brighton	139V	80601	500-5198	E
TANAGER TRAIL	Broomfield	133W	80026	None	
TANAKA DR	Erie	102Q	80516	1500-1699	
TANBARK DR	Jefferson Co	370F	80127	1-99	
TANCRED ST	Northglenn	193M	80234	10400-10799	
TANFORAN AVE W	Jefferson Co	341J	80465	12000-12499	
	Jefferson Co	341K	80127	None	
TANFORAN CIR W	Jefferson Co	341K	80127	None	
TANFORAN DR E	Aurora	349K	80015	18200-18399	
TANFORAN DR W	Denver	342J	80123	8700-9099	
TANFORAN PL E	Aurora	349K	80015	18200-18699	
TANFORAN PL W	Jefferson Co	341L	80127	10300-10399	
	Jefferson Co	341K	80465	11700-11799	
TANGLE OAK DR	Castle Pines North	436M	80108	7500-7999	
TANGLEVINE DR	Castle Rock	466X	80109	None	
TANGLEWOOD CT	Boulder Co	100A	80301	4800-4899	
TANGLEWOOD RD	Douglas Co	850W	80116	9600-10599	
TANGLEWOOD RD E	Douglas Co	470Z	80116	1100-9599	
TANGLEWOOD ST S	Highlands Ranch	374U	80126	8400-8499	
TANGLEWOOD TRAIL	Boulder Co	100E	80301	4500-4899	
TANNER PEAK TRAIL	Brighton	139Q	80601	None	
TANOA CT	Castle Rock	467U	80104	4500-4599	
TANOA RD	Jefferson Co	306W	80439	30800-31499	
TANSEY LN	Jefferson Co	338P	80454	5000-5099	
TANSY DR E	Aurora	380Z	80138	None	
TANSY PL	Boulder	97H	80304	None	
TANTRA DR	Boulder	128Q	80305	500-4899	
TANTRA PARK CIR	Boulder	128U	80305	1000-1099	
TAOS RD	Jefferson Co	338Q	80454	5200-21999	
TAOS ST	Lochbuie	729Z	80603	1600-1899	
	Lochbuie	729Z	80603	None	
TAOS WAY S	Denver	313H	80223	1100-1199	
TAOS TRAIL	Elbert Co	832W	80107	43000-43999	
TAOS TRAIL	Lone Tree	376Z	80124	9100-9199	
TAPADERO CIR	Elbert Co	851H	80107	40600-40999	
TAPADERO CT	Castle Pines North	436B	80108	6500-6599	
TAPADERO PL	Castle Pines North	436B	80108	6500-6599	
TAPADERO RD	Park Co	841E	80421	1-1799	
TAPADERO WAY	Castle Pines North	436B	80108	12300-12599	
TAPE DR	Louisville	160M	80027	None	
	Louisville	161J	80027	None	
TAPPY TOORIE PL	Highlands Ranch	374W	80129	8900-8999	
TARCOOLA LN E	Highlands Ranch	405H	80130	4800-4999	
TARCOOLA PL S	Highlands Ranch	405H	80130	10000-10099	
TARGHEE LN	Jefferson Co	306Q	80439	29300-29599	
TARGHEE PT	Lafayette	131F	80026	2400-2499	
TARIE TRAIL	Elbert Co	851V	80107	None	
TARPAN PL	Castle Rock	467Y	80104	700-999	
TARRYALL WAY S	Douglas Co	870N	80116	2100-2499	
TATE AVE	Weld Co	729U	80621	2000-2999	
TATUM LN	Boulder	129E	80303	None	
TAUBER CT	Castle Pines North	436F	80108	1-99	
TAUBER DR	Castle Pines North	436G	80108	1-99	
TAURUS CIR	Lafayette	131L	80026	1200-1299	
TAVERN WAY	Castle Rock	497U	80104	None	
TAVERSHAW CIR	El Paso Co	909N	80132	20400-20499	
TAYLOR AVE	Firestone	707T	80504	10400-10599	
	Firestone	707T	80504	None	
TAYLOR AVE	Louisville	131X	80027	100-799	
	Louisville	131Y	80027	702-2098	E
TAYLOR AVE S	Louisville	161B	80027	400-699	
TAYLOR CIR	Douglas Co	887M	80118	7700-7899	
TAYLOR CT	Broomfield	163G	80020	None	
TAYLOR CT	Castle Rock	497M	80104	1-99	
TAYLOR DR	Gilpin Co	761C	80403	1-699	
TAYLOR DR	Jefferson Co	823N	80433	9600-9699	
TAYLOR LN	Erie	103X	80516	None	
TAYLOR ST	Frederick	727G	80530	6100-6399	
TAYLOR ST	Park Co	820Y	80421	1-399	
TAYLOR MOUNTAIN DR	Longmont	40P	80503	None	
TAYLOR MOUNTAIN RD	Douglas Co	887G	80118	1400-1799	
TAYLOR RENEE CIR	Elbert Co	871L	80107	None	
TAZA LN	Jefferson Co	842G	80470	13200-13399	
TEABERRY AVE	Castle Rock	498R	80104	5800-6099	
TEACUP RD N	Elbert Co	912K	80106	8400-8599	
TEACUP GROVE	El Paso Co	912P	80831	20200-20499	
TEAK PL	Castle Rock	497Q	80104	1000-1099	
TEAKWOOD CT	Highlands Ranch	374Y	80126	600-699	
TEAKWOOD LN	Thornton	193V	80260	None	
TEAL CIR	Longmont	41A	80503	600-799	
TEAL CT N	Boulder Co	129F	80303	1300-1399	
TEAL CT S	Boulder Co	129F	80303	1200-1299	
TEAL LN	Park Co	841V	80421	1-199	
TEAL ST	Northglenn	194L	80233	100-399	
TEAL CREEK CT	Broomfield	163J	80020	13700-13799	
TEAL CREEK DR	Broomfield	163E	80020	13800-13899	
TEAL RIDGE CT	Highlands Ranch	405C	80126	9600-9699	
TEAL TRAIL	Jefferson Co	366C	80439	6700-6899	
TECHNOLOGY CT	Broomfield	161Y	80021	300-399	
TECHNOLOGY DR	Broomfield	161Y	80021	100-199	
TECHNOLOGY DR	Golden	250N	80403	4600-4698	E
TECHNOLOGY PKWY	Weld Co	731J	80642	None	
TECHNOLOGY WAY	Denver	346L	80237	1-7799	
TECOMA CIR	Jefferson Co	370F	80127	1-99	
TECUMSEH TRAIL	Jefferson Co	823X	80433	11900-12299	
	Jefferson Co	843B	80433	12300-12699	
TEDDY LN	Douglas Co	377W	80124	9200-9399	
TEE LN	Castle Rock	497U	80104	1900-1999	
TEE BOX CT	Castle Rock	496D	80109	None	
TEJAS AVE	Jefferson Co	842E	80470	34100-34199	
TEJAS LN	Nederland	740L	80466	None	
TEJON CT	Adams Co	223H	80221	8100-8199	
	Westminster	163R	80234	13000-13099	
TEJON ST	Adams Co	253H	80221	5200-5699	
	Adams Co	223M	80221	7600-7899	
	Adams Co	223H	80221	8300-8399	
	Adams Co	163D	80020	14400-14799	
	Adams Co	133V	80020	14800-15599	
	Denver	283V	80223	1-299	
	Denver	283R	80204	800-1099	
	Denver	253V	80211	3000-4799	
	Denver	253M	80221	4800-5199	
TEJON ST	Federal Heights	223H	80260	8400-8599	
	Federal Heights	223D	80260	8800-9099	
	Federal Heights	193Z	80260	9100-9199	
	Westminster	163Z	80234	11800-12199	
	Westminster	163M	80234	13100-13599	
TEJON ST S	Denver	283Z	80223	1-699	
	Denver	313H	80223	700-2099	
	Englewood	313R	80110	2100-3099	
TEJON WAY	Federal Heights	223H	80260	8400-8599	
TEJON WAY	Thornton	193R	80260	10000-10099	
TELEEN AVE	Erie	102M	80516	1001-1199	O
TELEMARK DR	Jefferson Co	306P	80439	29600-29699	
TELLER CIR	Boulder	128H	80303	900-999	
TELLER CT	Arvada	222T	80003	6800-7099	
	Arvada	222F	80003	8200-8299	
	Lakewood	282B	80214	2500-2599	
	Westminster	192T	80021	9600-9899	

STREET NAME	CITY or COUNTY	MAP GRID	ZIP CODE	BLOCK RANGE	O/E
TELLER CT S	Jefferson Co	342X	80123	6300-6399	
	Jefferson Co	372B	80123	6400-6699	
	Jefferson Co	372F	80128	7100-7399	
	Jefferson Co	372K	80128	7500-7899	
	Lakewood	282Y	80226	500-599	
TELLER LN	Westminster	192T	80021	9700-9799	
TELLER ST	Arvada	252F	80002	5600-5799	
	Arvada	252C	80003	5800-5899	
	Arvada	222X	80003	6200-6699	
	Arvada	222P	80003	7200-7599	
	Arvada	222K	80003	7600-7799	
	Broomfield	192B	80020	11500-11999	
	Broomfield	192G	80020	None	
	Lakewood	282X	80226	1-399	
	Lakewood	282K	80214	800-1499	
	Lakewood	282F	80214	1500-2599	
	Westminster	222B	80021	8800-8899	
	Westminster	192X	80021	9200-9599	
	Wheat Ridge	282F	80214	2600-2799	
	Wheat Ridge	252X	80033	2800-3799	
	Wheat Ridge	252P	80033	4100-4799	
TELLER ST S	Denver	312T	80227	2700-3099	
	Jefferson Co	372K	80128	7400-7499	
	Lakewood	282X	80226	1-499	
	Lakewood	312B	80226	900-1099	
	Lakewood	312F	80232	1400-1499	
	Lakewood	312K	80232	1800-1899	
	Lakewood	342B	80235	3500-4099	
TELLER WAY S	Jefferson Co	372P	80128	8200-8299	
TELLER LAKE WAY	Broomfield	163P	80020	13200-13299	
TELLURIDE CIR	Boulder	128X	80305	1800-3799	
TELLURIDE CIR S	Arapahoe Co	349T	80016	5900-6099	
	Aurora	319X	80013	3500-3599	
TELLURIDE CT	Commerce City	769E	80022	None	
TELLURIDE CT	Douglas Co	432F	80125	10200-10299	
TELLURIDE CT S	Arapahoe Co	349X	80016	6200-6299	
	Aurora	319P	80013	2100-2299	
	Aurora	319T	80013	2700-2799	
	Aurora	349F	80013	3900-3999	
	Centennial	349P	80015	5300-5599	
	Centennial	349S	80015	5700-5799	
	Centennial	379K	80016	7500-7599	
	Foxfield	379F	80016	7400-7499	
TELLURIDE DR	Broomfield	162L	80020	13600-13999	
TELLURIDE LN	Boulder	128X	80305	1800-3899	
TELLURIDE LN	Jefferson Co	306F	80439	30000-30599	
TELLURIDE PL	Boulder	128X	80305	3800-3899	
TELLURIDE PL	Douglas Co	432L	80125	None	
TELLURIDE PL	Longmont	12W	80501	1-199	
TELLURIDE ST	Aurora	259W	80011	2900-3299	
	Commerce City	769E	80022	None	
	Commerce City	769A	80022	None	
	Commerce City	769N	80022	None	
	Commerce City	169X	80603	None	
TELLURIDE ST	Douglas Co	432F	80125	10000-10299	
	Frederick	726G	80516	None	
TELLURIDE ST	Weld Co	139S	80601	15200-16799	
TELLURIDE ST N	Aurora	289P	80011	600-1199	
	Buckley Air Force Base	289N	80011	None	
TELLURIDE ST S	Arapahoe Co	349X	80016	6100-6199	
	Arapahoe Co	349X	80016	6400-6499	
	Arapahoe Co	379B	80016	6500-6599	
	Aurora	319B	80017	900-999	
	Aurora	319E	80017	1200-1599	
	Aurora	319K	80017	1600-1999	
	Aurora	319K	80017	1800-1899	
	Aurora	319K	80013	2000-2099	
	Aurora	319P	80013	2100-2699	
	Aurora	319W	80013	3000-3499	
	Aurora	349P	80015	5000-5099	
	Centennial	349S	80015	5100-5899	
	Foxfield	379F	80016	6900-7099	
TELLURIDE WAY	Commerce City	769E	80022	10000-10399	
TELLURIDE WAY S	Aurora	319W	80013	3500-3599	
	Centennial	349P	80015	5300-5399	
	Centennial	349S	80015	5700-5799	
TEMPE CIR S	Centennial	380F	80016	7200-7399	
TEMPE CT S	Arapahoe Co	350U	80015	5700-5799	
	Aurora	350G	80018	4200-4299	
	Aurora	350Y	80016	6300-6399	
	Aurora	380C	80016	6700-6799	
TEMPE CT S	Aurora	380G	80016	7100-7399	
	Aurora	380G	80016	None	
	Aurora	380Q	80017	None	
TEMPE ST S	Arapahoe Co	350Q	80015	5100-5599	
	Arapahoe Co	350U	80015	5600-5699	
	Arapahoe Co	350K	80015	None	
	Aurora	380C	80016	6500-6799	
TEMPE WAY S	Arapahoe Co	350Y	80015	6100-6399	
	Aurora	350C	80018	None	
	Centennial	350U	80015	5900-6099	
TEMPEST RIDGE WAY E	Douglas Co	440T	80134	7000-8399	
TEMPLE AVE W	Denver	341M	80123	8900-9199	
	Jefferson Co	341K	80127	11400-11599	
TEMPLE DR	Denver	346M	80237	8500-8699	
TEMPLE DR E	Aurora	348K	80015	13900-14799	
	Aurora	348M	80015	16600-16799	
	Aurora	349J	80015	17400-17599	
	Aurora	349K	80015	17600-17699	
TEMPLE DR W	Jefferson Co	341J	80465	11600-12699	
	Jefferson Co	340M	80465	12700-12799	
TEMPLE LN W	Jefferson Co	341E	80465	11800-11899	
TEMPLE PL E	Aurora	348K	80015	14300-14399	
	Aurora	348K	80015	14500-14999	
	Aurora	348L	80015	15500-15799	
	Aurora	349J	80015	16900-16999	
TEMPLE PL W	Denver	343J	80236	3800-4799	
	Jefferson Co	341E	80465	11800-11899	
TEMPLIN LN N	Douglas Co	411P	80138	11600-11999	
TEMPTED WAYS DR	Longmont	41U	80504	800-1099	
TENACITY DR	Longmont	41U	80504	700-999	
TENBY CT	Douglas Co	436M	80108	7400-7499	
TENBY LN	Thornton	195N	80229	10300-10399	
TENBY WAY	Castle Pines North	436Q	80108	7100-7499	
TENDERFOOT AVE	Firestone	707P	80504	None	
	Firestone	707S	80504	None	
TENDERFOOT DR	Douglas Co	887L	80118	500-2499	
TENDERFOOT TRAIL N	Douglas Co	411B	80138	12000-12799	
TENINO AVE	Boulder	128M	80303	5200-5499	
TEN MILE PL	Douglas Co	466M	80108	5000-5199	
TENNESSEE DR E	Aurora	319A	80017	17000-17899	
TENNESSEE PL E	Aurora	319A	80017	17500-17899	
TENNESSEE AVE E	Aurora	317B	80012	10600-10698	E
	Aurora	317C	80012	11901-11999	O
	Aurora	318A	80012	13300-13499	
	Aurora	318B	80012	14100-14499	
	Aurora	318C	80017	15300-15499	
	Aurora	318D	80017	15800-16799	
	Aurora	319B	80017	17800-17899	
	Denver	314D	80209	400-1199	
	Denver	314D	80209	1600-1699	
	Denver	315A	80209	1700-2699	
	Denver	315B	80209	3200-3899	
	Denver	315C	80246	4400-4498	E
	Denver	315D	80246	4501-4599	O
	Denver	316A	80246	5400-5499	
	Denver	316A	80224	5600-6899	
	Glendale	315C	80246	4401-4499	O
	Glendale	315D	80246	4500-4598	E
TENNESSEE AVE W	Denver	314B	80223	500-999	
	Denver	314A	80223	1200-1999	
	Denver	313D	80223	2000-2499	
	Denver	313C	80219	2500-3699	
	Denver	313B	80219	3900-5099	
	Lakewood	312D	80226	6000-6099	
	Lakewood	312B	80226	6600-7599	
	Lakewood	312A	80226	8300-8399	
	Lakewood	311D	80226	8900-9599	
	Lakewood	311A	80228	12200-12299	
TENNESSEE CIR E	Aurora	317D	80012	12400-12599	
TENNESSEE CT W	Lakewood	311B	80226	11100-11299	
TENNESSEE DR E	Aurora	317D	80012	12000-12499	
	Aurora	318B	80012	14500-14899	
TENNESSEE DR W	Lakewood	311B	80226	11300-11599	
TENNESSEE PL E	Aurora	318C	80017	15800-15899	
	Aurora	318D	80017	16200-16299	
	Aurora	319B	80017	18400-18499	
TENNESSEE PL W	Lakewood	312A	80226	8500-8699	
	Lakewood	311A	80228	11400-12299	
	Lakewood	311A	80228	12400-12499	
TENNEY ST S	Arapahoe Co	795Y	80103	500-799	
TENNYSON CIR	Lafayette	132P	80026	None	
TENNYSON CT	Westminster	193P	80031	10000-10099	
	Westminster	193N	80031	10300-10399	
	Westminster	193J	80031	10800-10999	
TENNYSON LN	Douglas Co	409X	80134	None	
TENNYSON ST	Adams Co	253E	80212	5200-5499	
	Adams Co	253E	80003	5500-5799	
	Adams Co	253A	80003	5800-6198	E
	Arvada	253A	80003	5801-6199	O
	Arvada	223W	80003	6100-6699	
	Denver	283P	80219	300-399	
	Denver	283N	80204	400-1099	
	Denver	283J	80204	1200-1699	
	Denver	283A	80212	2600-2699	
	Denver	253S	80212	2700-5199	
	Westminster	223N	80030	7200-7399	
	Westminster	223E	80031	8000-8399	
	Westminster	193X	80031	9000-9299	
	Westminster	193J	80031	10800-10899	
TENNYSON ST N	Westminster	193A	80031	None	
TENNYSON ST S	Denver	313F	80219	900-2499	
TENNYSON WAY	Broomfield	163W	80020	None	
	Westminster	193J	80031	10700-10799	
	Westminster	193A	80031	11700-11899	
TENNYSON WAY S	Denver	313T	80219	2500-2699	
	Denver	313T	80236	2700-2799	
TEPEES WAY	Jefferson Co	306C	80401	28600-28699	
TERESA DR	Clear Creek Co	801V	80439	1-299	
TERESITA LN	Mead	706M	80504	None	
TERLAGO CREEK PL E	Parker	439C	80134	19100-19299	
TERN ST	Federal Heights	193V	80260	9700-9799	
TERRACE CIR	Boulder	97C	80304	None	
	Boulder	97C	80304	None	
TERRACE CT	Broomfield	163T	80020	None	
TERRACE DR	Highlands Ranch	375S	80126	1900-2499	
TERRACE DR	Longmont	12U	80501	1300-1398	E
TERRACE PL	Boulder Co	129R	80303	7200-7399	
TERRACE CLUB DR	Denver	313X	80236	None	
TERRARIDGE DR	Highlands Ranch	375S	80126	2100-2599	
TERRA VISTA ST	Brighton	139N	80601	100-399	
TERRAVITA WAY	Castle Rock	498B	80108	None	
TERRAWOOD DR E	Parker	408V	80134	None	
TERRITORIAL RD	Castle Rock	527A	80109	1600-1699	
TERRITORIAL ST	Douglas Co	469C	80134	5100-5399	
TERRITORY CIR	Elbert Co	850D	80138	1700-2299	
TERRITORY CT	Elbert Co	850D	80138	42800-42999	
TERRITORY WAY	Elbert Co	850D	80138	42400-42499	
TERRY CIR	Arvada	219V	80007	7100-7199	
TERRY CT	Arvada	249D	80403	6100-6199	
	Arvada	219V	80007	6600-7199	
	Arvada	219M	80007	None	
	Jefferson Co	219R	80007	7200-7599	
TERRY LN	Arvada	249D	80403	6000-6099	
TERRY ST	Arvada	219Z	80403	6200-6399	
	Arvada	219Z	80007	6400-6499	
	Jefferson Co	279M	80401	800-1199	
	Jefferson Co	219R	80007	7200-7299	
TERRY ST	Longmont	41H	80501	200-899	
	Longmont	11Z	80501	900-1099	
	Longmont	11V	80501	1300-1498	E
	Longmont	11V	80501	1700-2099	
TERRY ST S	Longmont	41M	80501	700-999	
	Longmont	41Q	80501	1200-1699	
TERRY WAY	Arvada	219Z	80403	6100-6299	
TERRYL AVE	Douglas Co	469C	80134	None	
TESLA CIR	Boulder	98V	80301	4900-4999	
TESLA CT	Boulder	98U	80301	4900-4999	
TESUQUE RD	Jefferson Co	338J	80454	23400-23799	
TETBURY CT	Douglas Co	436Q	80108	600-699	
TETON	Weld Co	706N	80504	3200-3399	
TETON AVE W	Jefferson Co	372S	80128	8500-8699	
TETON CIR W	Jefferson Co	372S	80128	8800-8999	
TETON CT	Lone Tree	406G	80124	10000-10099	
TETON DR	Frederick	707W	80504	3200-3399	
TETON PL W	Jefferson Co	371V	80128	8900-8999	
TEXAS AVE W	Jefferson Co	311F	80232	10900-11599	
	Lakewood	312E	80226	None	
TEXAS DR W	Lakewood	311H	80232	9200-9299	
	Lakewood	311E	80228	12000-12399	
TEXAS LN	Longmont	41R	80501	1-99	
TEXAS PL W	Lakewood	311G	80232	10100-10199	
	Lakewood	311E	80228	12500-12599	
TEXAS ST	Golden	248V	80403	600-699	
THAMES ST E	Highlands Ranch	404D	80126	800-1099	
THATCH CIR	Castle Rock	497A	80109	1100-1799	
THEA GULCH RD	Jefferson Co	783E	80403	25800-27599	
THE CORSO	Palmer Lake	907Q	80133	None	
THE COUNTRY CLUB LN	Jefferson Co	306P	80439	2600-2699	
THE GOLF CLUB PT	Jefferson Co	306P	80439	30400-30599	
THE LANE RD	Boulder Co	742X	80403	1-299	
THELMA AVE S	Jefferson Co	842A	80470	12700-12899	
THELMA DR S	Jefferson Co	842A	80470	12800-12899	
THERESA DR	Boulder Co	130K	80303	300-699	
THERMAL CIR	Elbert Co	890R	80116	1300-1499	
THE SCRAMBLE	Jefferson Co	843Y	80470	17600-17699	
THIMBLEBERRY LN	Jefferson Co	367A	80439	27100-27999	
	Jefferson Co	336C	80439	29200-29699	
THIMBLEBERRY WAY S	Parker	409B	80134	9500-9699	
THIRD AVE	Hudson	730L	80642	None	
THIRD ST	Palmer Lake	907U	80133	None	
THISTLE CT	Castle Rock	496A	80109	None	
THISTLE DR	Brighton	139M	80601	None	
THISTLE PL	Longmont	12X	80501	400-499	
THISTLEBROOK CIR	Highlands Ranch	405K	80126	3000-3499	
THISTLE RIDGE AVE	Firestone	707P	80504	None	
THISTLE RIDGE CIR	Highlands Ranch	375W	80126	1700-2399	
THISTLE RIDGE RD E	Highlands Ranch	374Z	80126	1500-1699	
THISTLESAGE CT	Castle Rock	466T	80109	4100-4399	
THISTLEWOOD CT	Elbert Co	871B	80107	35400-35599	
THOMAS AVE E	Arapahoe Co	795Y	80103	300-799	
THOMAS AVE W	Englewood	344J	80110	1400-1599	
THOMAS CT	Elbert Co	851E	80138	2100-2299	
THOMAS DR	Boulder	128L	80303	700-799	
THOMAS DR	Castle Rock	466V	80109	None	
THOMAS DR	Jefferson Co	822U	80433	10900-11199	
THOMASTON CIR	Douglas Co	407G	80134	11700-11899	
THOMPSON CT	Denver	255P	80216	4200-4799	
	Denver	255K	80216	5100-5398	E
THOMPSON DR	Jefferson Co	823N	80433	26100-26399	
THOMPSON PL	Palmer Lake	907Q	80133	None	
THOMPSON RD	El Paso Co	909Z	80908	16500-17999	
THOR AVE	Boulder Co	98D	80301	5200-5599	
THOR CT	Highlands Ranch	376U	80126	400-499	
THORN CIR	Gilpin Co	761K	80403	1-299	
THORN ST	Lochbuie	729Z	80603	None	
THORN APPLE CT	Castle Pines North	436C	80108	8700-8799	
THORN APPLE WAY	Douglas Co	436D	80108	300-499	
THORNBERRY ST	Frederick	706Z	80504	None	
THORNBIRD PL	Boulder	98S	80304	2600-2699	
THORNBURY PL W	Highlands Ranch	404E	80129	1000-1299	
THORNBURY WAY	Highlands Ranch	404E	80129	9800-9899	
THORNCREEK CIR	Thornton	164M	80241	13400-13599	
THORNCREEK CT	Thornton	164M	80241	900-1099	
THORNDIKE AVE	Castle Rock	498Q	80104	4800-5099	
THORNDYKE PL	Broomfield	163S	80020	4100-4399	
THORNGATE PL	Parker	410Y	80138	None	
THORNTON PKWY	Thornton	194Y	80229	1-699	
	Thornton	194V	80229	1300-1899	
	Thornton	195S	80229	1900-2399	
	Thornton	195T	80229	2400-3599	
THORNTON PKWY W	Thornton	194X	80260	1-799	
THORNWOOD CIR	Longmont	40L	80503	700-899	
THORNWOOD CT	Castle Rock	468X	80104	None	
THORNWOOD WAY	Longmont	40L	80503	700-799	
THORODIN DR	Gilpin Co	761M	80403	10200-10299	
THOROUGHBRED LN	El Paso Co	910U	80908	9300-9699	
THOROUGHBRED RUN					
	Columbine Valley	373F	80123	1-99	
	Columbine Valley	373F	80128	6900-6999	
	Littleton	373F	80128	7000-7099	
THREE PINES RANCH PL E					
	Douglas Co	439H	80134	20300-20499	
THREE SISTERS CIR	Jefferson Co	336N	80439	5300-5399	
THRESHING DR	Brighton	139L	80601	None	
THRILL PL E	Denver	255Z	80207	4800-5599	
THRUSH CT	Frederick	727A	80504	4800-4899	
THRUSH DR S	Douglas Co	410K	80138	11000-11399	
THUNDER RD	El Paso Co	910N	80908	19600E-20499E	
	El Paso Co	909R	80908	19300W-20599W	
THUNDERBIRD	Weld Co	706N	80504	11000-11199	
THUNDERBIRD CIR	Boulder	128R	80303	4800-4999	
THUNDERBIRD CIR E	Douglas Co	440U	80134	8600-8799	
THUNDERBIRD CT	Boulder	128M	80303	500E-599E	
THUNDERBIRD CT E	Douglas Co	440Y	80134	8700-8899	
THUNDERBIRD DR	Boulder	128M	80303	4900-4998	E
THUNDERBIRD LN	Jefferson Co	306S	80439	2400-2599	
THUNDERBIRD RD	Boulder	128R	80303	100-4999	
THUNDERBIRD RD	Douglas Co	886G	80118	6300-6599	
THUNDERBIRD RD E	Douglas Co	440Y	80134	8500-8999	
THUNDERBIRD TRAIL	El Paso Co	908U	80132	18500-18799	
THUNDERBOLT CIR	Elbert Co	830Q	80138	None	
THUNDERBOLT CIR	Jefferson Co	822R	80433	29200-29599	
THUNDER BUTTE RD	Castle Rock	469F	80109	1400-1499	
THUNDERCLOUD CT	Castle Rock	469J	80108	7000-7199	
THUNDERHEAD DR	Boulder Co	703W	80302	8300-9199	
THUNDERHILL AVE	Firestone	707P	80504	None	
THUNDERHILL RD	Elbert Co	851A	80138	41000-42799	
THUNDERHILL RD N	Douglas Co	440X	80134	5500-6099	
THUNDER HILL RD S	Elbert Co	851E	80138	None	
THUNDERHILLHEIGHTS E					
	Douglas Co	440X	80134	8400-8599	
THUNDER LAKE CIR	Lafayette	131E	80026	2900-3099	
THUNDER RIDGE RD	Boulder Co	741F	80466	1-299	
THUNDER RIDGE RD	Jefferson Co	843A	80433	26400-26699	
THUNDER RIDGE WAY					
	Highlands Ranch	375U	80126	8400-8499	
THUNDER RUN	Douglas Co	845R	80125	10000-10199	
TIBER RD	Gilpin Co	761J	80403	None	
TIBET CT S	Aurora	380C	80016	6600-6699	
TIBET ST S	Arapahoe Co	350Q	80015	5100-5599	
	Arapahoe Co	350U	80015	5900-6199	
	Arapahoe Co	350L	80015	None	
	Aurora	350Y	80016	6400-6499	

STREET NAME	CITY or COUNTY	MAP GRID	ZIP CODE	BLOCK RANGE	O/E
TIBET WAY S	Aurora	380G	80016	7000-7199	
	Aurora	350C	80018	None	
TIBURON CT	Lone Tree	406G	80124	9900-9999	
TICHY BLVD	Commerce City	226S	80022	5600-6099	
TIERRA ALTA DR	Castle Rock	467R	80104	4400-4799	
TIERRA RIDGE CT	Superior	160T	80027	None	
TIFFANY PL	Longmont	11Q	80501	900-1099	
TIFF GRASS CT	Castle Rock	497E	80109	1500-1699	
TIGER PT	Douglas Co	406K	80124	10500-10599	
TIGER BEND LN	Jefferson Co	339R	80465	5300-5599	
TIGER CHASE	Douglas Co	406K	80124	10500-10599	
TIGER GROTTO	Douglas Co	406K	80124	10500-10599	
TIGER PAW	Douglas Co	406K	80124	6600-6699	
TIGER RUN	Douglas Co	406K	80124	10400-10499	
TIGERS EYE	Douglas Co	406K	80124	10500-10599	
TIGER TOOTH	Douglas Co	406K	80124	6600-6799	
TIGER WALK	Douglas Co	406K	80124	6700-6899	
TILBURY AVE	Firestone	707P	80504	None	
TILBURY CT	Firestone	706V	80504	4500-4699	
TILBURY ST	Castle Rock	498M	80104	1-299	
TILDEN ST	Nederland	740Q	80466	None	
TILGHMAN RD	Boulder Co	721C	80481	1-199	
TILLY LN	Castle Pines North	436F	80108	1-99	
TIMARRON	Elbert Co	870L	80107	None	
TIMBER CT	Longmont	12X	80501	900-999	
TIMBER DR	Elbert Co	851U	80107	36900-37799	
TIMBER DR	Gilpin Co	761S	80403	1-499	
TIMBER LN	Boulder Co	97J	80304	1-1999	
	Boulder Co	722V	80304	2000-2099	
TIMBER LN	Clear Creek Co	304H	80439	1-199	
TIMBER LN	Elbert Co	851U	80107	5000-5199	
TIMBER LN N	Douglas Co	380W	80138	12700-12899	
TIMBER PL	Elbert Co	851U	80107	5100-5299	
TIMBER RD	Gilpin Co	761S	80403	1-299	
TIMBER CANYON DR	Castle Rock	467R	80108	None	
TIMBERCHASE	Highlands Ranch	405J	80126	2500-2699	
TIMBERCHASE POINTE TRAIL	Highlands Ranch	405J	80126	2600-3099	
TIMBER COVE ST	Adams Co	751E	80603	None	
TIMBERCREST DR	Castle Pines North	436P	80108	1000-1099	
TIMBERCREST LN	Castle Pines North	436P	80108	7100-7299	
TIMBERCREST WAY	Castle Pines North	436P	80108	7000-7199	
TIMBER FALLS TRAIL	Jefferson Co	824W	80433	19000-19099	
TIMBER HAWK CIR S	Highlands Ranch	405C	80126	9600-9699	
TIMBER HOLLOW LOOP	Castle Rock	466U	80109	4100-4399	
TIMBERLINE AVE	Firestone	706V	80504	4600-4799	
TIMBERLINE PL	Highlands Ranch	374Y	80126	400-599	
TIMBERLINE RD	Boulder Co	741J	80466	1-99	
TIMBERLINE RD	Highlands Ranch	406B	80130	6600-7299	
	Lone Tree	406B	80124	7300-8199	
TIMBER LINE TRAIL	Lafayette	131A	80026	None	
TIMBER RIDGE DR	Elbert Co	851Q	80107	5000-5499	
TIMBER RIDGE LN	Highlands Ranch	405Q	80130	10900-11099	
TIMBER RIDGE RD	Jefferson Co	365L	80439	32700-33299	
TIMBERS DR	Jefferson Co	367F	80439	6700-7199	
TIMBER SPRING LN	Parker	410Y	80138	None	
TIMBER SPRING PL	Parker	410Y	80138	None	
TIMBERTOP RD	Park Co	840C	80421	1-399	
TIMBER TRAIL	Boulder Co	722Z	80302	1-99	
TIMBER TRAIL	Clear Creek Co	801A	80452	1-299	
TIMBER TRAIL	Jefferson Co	823W	80433	27200-27699	
TIMBER TRAIL S	Douglas Co	907H	80133	14100-14499	
TIMBER TRAIL RD	Jefferson Co	365G	80439	7100-7399	
TIMBERVALE CT S	Highlands Ranch	404B	80129	9600-9699	
TIMBERVALE DR	Jefferson Co	336H	80439	4000-4299	
TIMBERVALE TRAIL W	Highlands Ranch	404F	80129	400-1399	
TIMBERWOLF LN E	Parker	408Z	80134	None	
TIMBERWOOD ST S	Highlands Ranch	374U	80126	8400-8499	
TIMELESS DR	Castle Rock	496F	80109	3800-3999	
TIMON CIR	Lafayette	131Q	80026	2000-2099	
TIMOTHY DR	Longmont	40M	80503	600-899	
TIMOTHY PL	Boulder Co	70G	80503	7200-7399	
TIMOTHY'S DR	Jefferson Co	822U	80433	10700-11099	
TIMOTHY'S TRAIL	Jefferson Co	822U	80433	31200-31399	
TIM TAM CIR	Parker	410P	80138	21400-21499	
TIM TAM WAY	Parker	410P	80138	10900-11099	
TIM TAM TRAIL	Jefferson Co	366Q	80439	7900-8399	
TIN CUP CIR	Boulder	128X	80305	2800-2999	
TINCUP CIR	Broomfield	162L	80020	13900-13999	
TIN CUP CT	Boulder	128X	80305	1900-1999	
TIN CUP CT	Parker	408R	80134	16600-16699	
TINCUP WAY	Douglas Co	870J	80116	1000-1199	
TINCUP TERRACE	Park Co	841A	80421	1-1299	
TIOGA TRAIL	Elbert Co	830U	80138	1-999	
TIPPERARY ST	Boulder Co	131A	80303	1200-1599	
TIPPLE LN	Gilpin Co	761E	80403	1-199	
TITAN AVE	Firestone	706V	80504	4700-10799	
TITAN CT	Aurora	288N	80011	400-499	
	Denver	257M	80239	4700-5399	
TITAN CT	Douglas Co	403V	80125	9500-9999	
TITAN CT S	Aurora	317H	80112	1500-1599	
TITAN PKWY	Douglas Co	403V	80125	None	
TITAN PL	Boulder Co	102J	80026	3900-3999	
TITAN PL	Douglas Co	466D	80108	300-399	
TITAN RD	Douglas Co	403S	80125	6900-10099	
TITAN RD W	Douglas Co	825Z	80125	9000-10099	
TITAN ST	Aurora	288N	80011	200-399	
TITAN WAY	Denver	257M	80239	4900-5099	
TITANITE CT	Castle Rock	467G	80108	None	
TITANITE LN	Castle Rock	467G	80108	None	
TITAN PARK CIR	Douglas Co	403V	80125	9500-9999	
TITUS CT S	Aurora	381M	80016	7900-7999	
TITUS ST	Denver	770T	80249	None	
TIVERTON AVE	Broomfield	164J	80020	1500-2099	
TOBOGGAN RD	Jefferson Co	842N	80470	15400-15599	
TOBOGGAN HILL RD	El Paso Co	908T	80132	18600-18799	
TODD DR	Douglas Co	409S	80134	5300-5499	
TOEDTLI DR	Boulder	128U	80305	700-1499	
TOLEDO CT S	Aurora	317H	80112	1600-1699	
	Aurora	317R	80014	2200-2299	
TOLEDO ST	Aurora	288N	80011	200-599	
	Aurora	288N	80011	600-999	
TOLEDO WAY S	Aurora	317R	80014	2500-2599	
TOLLAND CT	Douglas Co	467E	80108	500-599	
TOLLAND DR	Douglas Co	467E	80108	400-599	
TOLLER AVE W	Jefferson Co	372S	80128	8400-8999	
TOLLER DR W	Jefferson Co	371U	80127	10200-10999	

STREET NAME	CITY or COUNTY	MAP GRID	ZIP CODE	BLOCK RANGE	O/E
TOLLGATE DR	Boulder Co	703U	80503	9100-9399	
TOM CT	Highlands Ranch	406J	80130	5900-5999	
TOMAH RD	Douglas Co	867Y	80118	1-1799	
	Douglas Co	887A	80118	1800-3299	
TOMAHAWK AVE E	Arapahoe Co	794T	80136	55300-56699	
TOMAHAWK RD N	Douglas Co	411E	80138	9100-12599	
TOMAHAWK RD N	Douglas Co	381W	80138	12600-12999	
TOMAHAWK TRAIL	Jefferson Co	823X	80433	11600-11799	
TOMAHAWK TRAIL	Thornton	195U	80229	None	
TOM BAY CT S	Arapahoe Co	812T	80102	5200-5699	
TOM BAY PL S	Arapahoe Co	812T	80102	5200-5499	
TOM BAY RD N	Arapahoe Co	792T	80102	1-599	
TOM BAY RD S	Arapahoe Co	792X	80102	1-299	
	Arapahoe Co	812T	80102	4300-5899	
TOMBOY WAY	El Paso Co	908Y	80132	17900-17999	
TOMICHI DR E	Douglas Co	870J	80116	9800-11899	
TOMICHI DR S	Douglas Co	870K	80116	1100-1799	
TOM MIX CIR	Elbert Co	851F	80138	3600-3699	
TOM-TOM DR E	Douglas Co	411J	80138	9600-9999	
TONGUE RD	Jefferson Co	337H	80439	4300-4499	
TONKIN PL	Longmont	12L	80501	None	
TONTO CT	El Paso Co	912T	80831	18000-18099	
TONY PL	Longmont	11Q	80501	900-1099	
TOPANGA WAY	Lochbuie	729Z	80603	1700-1899	
TOPAZ CIR	Douglas Co	409E	80134	10200-10299	
TOPAZ CT	Longmont	41U	80504	1100-1199	
TOPAZ DR	Boulder Co	98J	80304	2000-2599	
TOPAZ ST	Golden	279Q	80401	1-99	
TOPAZ ST	Superior	160U	80027	700-1099	
TOPAZ VISTA PL	Castle Pines North	436A	80108	5900-6099	
TOPAZ VISTA WAY	Castle Pines North	436A	80108	12400-12599	
TOPEKA CT	Denver	257M	80239	4600-4799	
	Denver	257H	80239	5300-5499	
TOPEKA WAY	Castle Rock	497F	80109	500-1199	
TOP OF THE ROCK WAY	El Paso Co	908P	80132	1300-1499	
TOP O THE MOOR DR E	El Paso Co	908P	80132	19200-19999	
TOP O THE MOOR DR W	El Paso Co	908P	80132	19200-19999	
TOPPLER CT	Castle Pines North	436K	80108	1-99	
TOPPLER DR	Castle Pines North	436K	80108	1-99	
TOP T RANCH PL E	Douglas Co	439S	80134	20000-20999	
TORREY CT	Arvada	219Z	80007	6400-6599	
	Arvada	219R	80007	None	
TORREY LN	Arvada	219Z	80403	6200-6399	
TORREY ST	Arvada	219Z	80403	6200-6399	
	Arvada	219V	80007	6900-7199	
	Golden	279R	80401	800-899	
	Jefferson Co	279M	80401	900-1999	
	Jefferson Co	219R	80007	7200-7299	
TORREY WAY	Arvada	219Z	80403	6300-6399	
TORREY PINE CIR	Jefferson Co	305R	80439	31800-31999	
TORREY PINE DR	Jefferson Co	305R	80439	2100-2199	
TORREY PINES DR	Douglas Co	886C	80118	6000-6299	
TORREYS	Thornton	194S	80260	None	
TORREYS WAY	Broomfield	133N	80020	15900-16099	
TORREYS PEAK DR	Longmont	12W	80501	1300-1399	
TORREYS PEAK DR	Parker	410K	80138	10300-10399	
TORREYS PEAK DR N	Superior	160U	80027	2700-3399	
TORREYS PEAK DR S	Superior	160Y	80027	3800-3999	
TORREYS PEAK DR W	Superior	160T	80027	3000-3699	
TORREYS PEAK ST	Brighton	139M	80601	None	
TORRINGTON LN	Douglas Co	405P	80126	10600-10699	
TORY POINTE E	Highlands Ranch	406J	80130	5600-5699	
TOTARA PL	Boulder Co	70K	80503	6800-6999	
TOTEM RUN	Douglas Co	845Q	80125	10200-10399	
TOURMALINE CT	Douglas Co	408G	80134	9800-9899	
TOURMALINE LN	Jefferson Co	782D	80403	27800-28399	
TOURNAMENT CT	Jefferson Co	305R	80439	2000-2099	
TOURNAMENT DR	Douglas Co	466C	80108	2500-2599	
TOWER RD	Adams Co	169X	80022	12000-12799	
	Aurora	289F	80011	600-2499	
	Aurora	259T	80011	2800-3998	E
	Commerce City	769A	80022	8400-11799	
	Denver	259P	80249	4000-6099	
	Denver	769W	80249	7900-8399	
	Weld Co	139K	80601	16000-16799	
TOWER RD S	Arapahoe Co	349X	80016	5900-6299	
	Aurora	319F	80017	1100-1999	
	Aurora	319T	80013	2000-3499	
	Aurora	349B	80013	3500-3799	
	Centennial	349T	80015	5000-5899	
TOWER WAY S	Aurora	319T	80013	2800-2999	
	Aurora	349K	80015	4800-4899	
TOWERBRIDGE CIR	Highlands Ranch	405R	80130	None	
TOWERBRIDGE LN	Highlands Ranch	405R	80130	None	
TOWERBRIDGE RD	Highlands Ranch	405R	80130	None	
TOWER HILL CIR	Jefferson Co	277U	80401	1-399	
TOWHEE RD	Douglas Co	470B	80134	7800-8099	
TOWN CENTER DR	Highlands Ranch	374W	80129	1000-1099	
	Highlands Ranch	373Z	80129	None	
TOWN CENTER DR	Westminster	192K	80021	10400-10499	
TOWNE CT	El Paso Co	908T	80132	800-1399	
TOWNLEY CIR	Longmont	11U	80501	1000-1099	
TOWNSEND AVE	Firestone	707N	80504	4800-4999	
TOWNSEND DR E	Highlands Ranch	406B	80130	7000-7199	
TOWN SQUARE AVE E	Aurora	350Z	80016	23900-23999	
TOWNSVILLE CIR S	Highlands Ranch	405D	80130	9500-9899	
TRACERY CT	Douglas Co	408L	80134	10200-10399	
TRACEWOOD CIR	Highlands Ranch	405M	80130	10400-10599	
TRACEWOOD CT	Highlands Ranch	405M	80130	10300-10499	
TRACEWOOD DR	Highlands Ranch	405M	80130	10300-10499	
TRADE CENTRE AVE	Longmont	41N	80503	2400-2699	
TRADER ST	Keenesburg	732A	80643	None	
TRADITION PL	Lone Tree	406M	80124	10200-10299	
TRAIL CT	Parker	408Z	80134	11800-11899	
TRAILBLAZER WAY	Castle Rock	466Y	80109	None	
	Castle Rock	496C	80109	None	
TRAIL BOSS DR	Castle Rock	467U	80104	4400-4499	
TRAIL CREEK RD	Clear Creek Co	780N	80452	None	
TRAIL DUST RD	Gilpin Co	761U	80403	1-799	
TRAILHEAD RD	Monument	908S	80132	400-699	
TRAILHEAD RD E	Highlands Ranch	406A	80130	6000-6599	
TRAILMARK PKWY W	Littleton	825P	80127	9500-9699	
TRAILMASTER CIR S	Parker	409S	80134	None	
TRAILMASTER DR E	Parker	409S	80134	None	
TRAIL NORTH DR	Douglas Co	846A	80125	7500-7999	
TRAILRIDER PASS	Jefferson Co	371P	80127	10700-11099	
TRAILRIDERS DR	Douglas Co	432F	80125	10200-10299	
TRAIL RIDGE	Weld Co	706N	80504	3200-3399	

STREET NAME	CITY or COUNTY	MAP GRID	ZIP CODE	BLOCK RANGE	O/E
TRAIL RIDGE CIR	Louisville	130U	80027	None	
TRAIL RIDGE DR	Lafayette	131B	80026	2500E-2599E	
	Lafayette	131A	80026	2600W-2699W	
TRAIL RIDGE DR	Louisville	130U	80027	700-999	
TRAIL RIDGE RD	Longmont	12Y	80501	1200-1399	
TRAILS AVE	Broomfield	163P	80020	3100-3599	
TRAILS END	Douglas Co	470X	80116	2300-2399	
TRAILS END	Jefferson Co	823W	80433	11700-11799	
TRAILS END DR	Clear Creek Co	801A	80452	1-99	
TRAILSIDE CT	Castle Rock	466T	80109	4200-4299	
TRAILSIDE DR	Castle Rock	466T	80109	4500-4599	
TRAILSIDE LN	Castle Rock	466T	80109	4400-4499	
TRAILSIDE LOOP	Castle Rock	466T	80109	4400-4699	
TRAILSIDE RD	Jefferson Co	307D	80401	600-699	
TRAIL SKY CIR	Parker	408V	80134	16500-16799	
TRAIL SKY CT	Parker	409S	80134	11800-11899	
TRAIL SOUTH DR	Douglas Co	846B	80125	7500-8399	
TRAIL VIEW CIR	Parker	408Z	80134	16800-16899	
TRAIL VIEW LN	Parker	408V	80134	11800-11899	
TRAIL VIEW PL	Parker	408V	80134	16700-16799	
TRAILWAY AVE	Firestone	707P	80504	None	
TRAILWAY DR N	Douglas Co	441P	80134	6800-6999	
TRAILWAY DR S	Douglas Co	441T	80134	6500-6899	
TRAILWOOD LN	Jefferson Co	339R	80465	None	
TRAILWOOD WAY	Jefferson Co	842R	80470	14900-15099	
TRANQUILITY TRAIL	Castle Rock	466U	80109	None	
TRANSIT WAY	Broomfield	192A	80021	8100-8499	
TRANSITION TERRACE	Elbert Co	851J	80107	39400-39899	
TRAPPER CT	Douglas Co	469C	80134	6400-6599	
TRAPPER DR	Fort Lupton	728H	80621	900-1199	
TRAPPERS MOUNTAIN TRAIL	Jefferson Co	824Y	80127	11600-11899	
TRAPPER'S TRAIL AVE	Douglas Co	469C	80134	6300-6599	
TRAVER DR	Broomfield	133L	80020	3100-3499	
TRAVERTINE CT	Frederick	726G	80516	None	
TRAVERTINE PL	Douglas Co	408G	80134	10200-10299	
TRAVIS ST	Thornton	195X	80229	9200-9399	
	Thornton	195T	80229	9900-9999	
TRAVIS DRAW	Gilpin Co	760D	80403	1-199	
TRAVIS GULCH RD	Gilpin Co	760C	80403	1-1499	
TRAVOIS TRAIL S	Douglas Co	380S	80138	13000-13099	
TREE CIR	Monument	908W	80132	None	
TREE HAVEN ST	Adams Co	751E	80603	None	
TREE ROCK DR	El Paso Co	910U	80908	None	
TREETOP DR	Castle Rock	466Z	80109	None	
TREE TOP LN	Jefferson Co	308B	80401	22500-22599	
TREFOIL CIR	Brighton	168C	80601	None	
TREFOIL CT	Brighton	138Y	80601	1500-1599	
TREMOLITE CT	Castle Rock	467L	80108	None	
TREMOLITE DR	Castle Rock	467G	80108	None	
TREMOLITE LN	Castle Rock	467L	80108	None	
TREMONT PL	Denver	284F	80204	1200-1399	
	Denver	284F	80202	1400-1799	
	Denver	284C	80205	2100-2999	
TRENTON CIR S	Centennial	376G	80112	7000-7099	
TRENTON CT S	Centennial	376L	80112	7500-7799	
	Centennial	376Q	80112	8000-8099	
	Denver	316G	80231	1500-1699	
TRENTON DR S	Centennial	376G	80112	6900-7099	
	Centennial	376L	80112	7600-7699	
TRENTON PL	Thornton	166Q	80602	12900-13199	
TRENTON ST	Commerce City	256C	80216	None	
	Denver	286Q	80230	500-999	
	Denver	286L	80220	1200-1999	
	Denver	286C	80238	2601-2699	O
	Denver	256L	80238	None	
	Thornton	166Q	80602	12800-12899	
	Thornton	166G	80602	13400-13599	
	Thornton	166L	80602	None	
	Thornton	166U	80602	None	
TRENTON ST S	Centennial	376Q	80112	7800-7999	
	Denver	286U	80230	1-199	
	Denver	316C	80247	900-1099	
	Denver	316L	80231	1600-1899	
	Denver	316U	80231	2900-3099	
TRENTON WAY S	Arapahoe Co	316Q	80231	2100-2499	
	Centennial	376Q	80112	8100-8299	
TRESINE DR	Jefferson Co	336Z	80439	28000-28499	
TREVARTON DR	Boulder Co	704N	80503	6100-6399	
TREVOR CIR	Longmont	11P	80501	None	
TREVOR CT	Longmont	11T	80501	None	
TRIANGLE CT	Commerce City	197L	80603	None	
TRIANGLE DR	Douglas Co	846C	80125	8000-8199	
TRIBAL DR	Palmer Lake	907R	80133	None	
TRIBUTE	Elbert Co	870H	80107	None	
TRIBUTE PL	Castle Rock	466Y	80109	None	
TRINCHERA CREEK CT	Weld Co	707J	80504	None	
TRINCHERA PEAK	Jefferson Co	371Q	80127	8000-8199	
TRINCHERA TRAIL	Jefferson Co	337J	80439	None	
TRINIDAD LN	Palmer Lake	907U	80133	None	
TRINITY LOOP	Broomfield	133L	80020	2700-16699	
TRINITY MOUNTAIN RANCH RD	Gilpin Co	761F	80403	None	
TRIPLE CROWN DR	Douglas Co	409X	80134	None	
TRIPLE CROWN DR	Frederick	707W	80504	None	
TRIPLE CROWN ST	Douglas Co	409X	80134	None	
TRIPLE EAGLE TRAIL	Douglas Co	909E	80118	4401-4699	O
TRIPP DR	Golden	279P	80401	400-499	
TROJAN CT	Westminster	193E	80031	11000-11099	
TROON CIR	Broomfield	163K	80020	3700-4099	
TROON CT	Broomfield	163K	80020	13700-13799	
TROON CT	Douglas Co	886G	80118	6200-6399	
TROON CT	Louisville	160H	80027	300-399	
TROON VILLAGE DR	Lone Tree	406D	80124	9400-9599	
TROON VILLAGE PL	Lone Tree	406D	80124	8700-8799	
TROON VILLAGE WAY	Lone Tree	406D	80124	9400-9499	
TROPAE CIR S	Parker	439E	80134	None	
TROTTER CIR	El Paso Co	910Y	80908	9500-9699	
TROTTER LN	Lone Tree	406G	80124	7900-7999	
TROTWOOD WAY	Highlands Ranch	405P	80126	10800-10899	
TROUBLESOME RD	Jefferson Co	307W	80439	27200-28499	
TROUT CREEK CIR	Longmont	12Y	80501	1100-1299	
TROUT CREEK PL	Longmont	12Y	80501	1300-1399	
TROUTDALE PARK PL	Jefferson Co	336F	80439	29800-29999	
TROUTDALE RIDGE RD	Jefferson Co	336F	80439	29900-31099	
TROUTDALE SCENIC DR	Jefferson Co	336F	80439	29700-30799	
TROUTDALE VILLAGE DR	Jefferson Co	336F	80439	4200-4299	

STREET NAME	CITY or COUNTY	MAP GRID	ZIP CODE	BLOCK RANGE	O/E
TROXELL AVE	Longmont	40D	80503	2800-2999	
TROY CIR S	Aurora	287V	80012	200-299	
	Denver	347Z	80111	6200-6399	
TROY CT	Aurora	287R	80011	700-799	
TROY CT S	Aurora	317R	80014	2500-2699	
	Denver	347Z	80111	6200-6299	
TROY ST	Adams Co	167V	80640	12400-12599	
	Aurora	287R	80011	200-599	
	Aurora	287M	80011	700-1399	
	Aurora	257Z	80011	3100-3299	
	Commerce City	197M	80022	None	
	Denver	257V	80239	3700-3899	
	Denver	257M	80239	4800-5599	
TROY ST	Lafayette	132E	80026	900-999	
TROY ST S	Aurora	287Z	80012	300-599	
	Aurora	317H	80112	600-1799	
	Aurora	317R	80014	2300-2399	
TROY WAY	Commerce City	197M	80022	None	
TROY WAY S	Aurora	317M	80014	2100-2299	
TRUCKEE CIR	Commerce City	769E	80022	None	
TRUCKEE CT	Commerce City	769E	80022	None	
TRUCKEE CT S	Aurora	319X	80013	3100-3199	
TRUCKEE CT S	Aurora	349F	80013	3800-3999	
TRUCKEE CT S	Centennial	349P	80015	5300-5399	
	Centennial	349T	80015	5600-5799	
TRUCKEE ST	Commerce City	169X	80603	None	
TRUCKEE ST	Commerce City	769E	80022	None	
TRUCKEE ST	Commerce City	769J	80022	None	
TRUCKEE ST	Commerce City	769J	80022	None	
	Commerce City	769N	80022	None	
TRUCKEE ST S	Aurora	319B	80017	800-999	
	Aurora	319K	80013	1900-2099	
	Aurora	319P	80013	2100-2299	
	Aurora	319S	80013	2700-3099	
	Aurora	319X	80013	3000-3099	
	Aurora	349F	80013	3900-4299	
	Centennial	349P	80015	5100-5199	
	Centennial	349T	80015	5600-5799	
TRUCKEE ST S	Commerce City	769E	80022	None	
TRUCKEE WAY	Commerce City	169X	80603	None	
TRUCKEE WAY S	Aurora	319B	80017	1100-1199	
	Aurora	319K	80017	1800-1899	
	Aurora	319P	80013	2300-2599	
	Aurora	319X	80013	3200-3399	
	Aurora	349B	80013	3600-3899	
TRUDA DR	Northglenn	194D	80233	1000-1899	
	Northglenn	195A	80233	1900-2299	
TRUE MOUNTAIN DR	Douglas Co	908G	80118	14000-14999	
TRUE VISTA CIR	El Paso Co	908P	80132	18500-20399	
TRUFFLE RD	Gilpin Co	761C	80403	1-199	
TRUMAN AVE	Bennett	793J	80102	None	
TRUMAN AVE	Palmer Lake	907U	80133	None	
TRUMAN CT	Louisville	130Q	80027	1400-1499	
TRUMBULL LN	Monument	908W	80132	500-799	
TRUMPETERS CT	El Paso Co	908V	80132	800E-1199E	
	El Paso Co	908V	80132	700W-799W	
TRUMPETERS CT E	El Paso Co	909S	80132	None	
TRUSSVILLE ST	Commerce City	770B	80022	None	
TSCHAIKOVSKY DR	Gilpin Co	761J	80403	1-499	
TUCKER GULCH DR	Golden	248V	80403	1000-1099	
TUCKER GULCH WAY	Golden	248V	80403	900-1099	
TUCSON CIR S	Aurora	288S	80012	200-299	
	Aurora	317R	80014	2500-2599	
TUCSON CT	Longmont	12K	80501	2301-2399	O
TUCSON ST	Adams Co	167V	80640	12400-12699	
	Adams Co	137R	80601	16000-16799	
	Aurora	287R	80011	200-599	
	Aurora	288J	80011	700-1299	
	Aurora	257Z	80011	3100-3299	
	Commerce City	197M	80022	None	
	Denver	257M	80239	4800-4899	
	Denver	257H	80239	5300-5599	
TUCSON ST S	Aurora	317M	80112	1500-1799	
TUCSON WAY	Aurora	287H	80010	1900-1998	E
	Commerce City	197M	80022	None	
	Denver	257M	80239	5000-5399	
TUCSON WAY	Longmont	12P	80501	2200-2299	
TUCSON WAY S	Aurora	287Z	80012	300-399	
	Aurora	317R	80014	2200-2699	
	Centennial	378E	80112	6800-7499	
TUFTS AVE E	Aurora	348K	80015	14500-14899	
	Aurora	348L	80015	15700-15799	
	Aurora	349J	80015	17100-17399	
	Cherry Hills Village	344L	80113	800-1899	
	Cherry Hills Village	346E	80111	6300-6499	
	Denver	346L	80237	7800-8199	
	Englewood	344L	80113	1-799	
	Greenwood Village	346M	80111	8900-9199	
TUFTS AVE S	Aurora	348M	80015	16500-16799	
TUFTS AVE W	Denver	343J	80236	3800-4799	
	Denver	342J	80123	7800-9099	
	Denver	341M	80123	9300-9799	
	Englewood	344K	80110	1-1599	
	Englewood	343L	80110	3000-3599	
	Jefferson Co	341J	80465	12100-12499	
	Jefferson Co	340M	80465	12800-13199	
	Jefferson Co	340L	80465	13600-13999	
TUFTS CIR	Greenwood Village	346M	80111	9100-9199	
TUFTS CIR E	Centennial	349M	80015	19300-19599	
TUFTS CIR W	Denver	343J	80236	4600-4799	
TUFTS DR E	Arapahoe Co	349M	80015	None	
	Aurora	348K	80015	13900-14099	
	Centennial	349M	80015	19700-20099	
TUFTS DR W	Jefferson Co	341K	80127	10600-11199	
TUFTS LN W	Jefferson Co	341L	80127	10600-10699	
TUFTS PL E	Aurora	348K	80015	13900-14499	
	Aurora	348K	80015	14900-14999	
	Aurora	348L	80015	15000-15099	
	Aurora	349J	80015	16900-16999	
	Greenwood Village	346M	80111	9100-9199	
TUFTS PL W	Jefferson Co	341L	80127	10000-10699	
	Jefferson Co	341J	80465	11700-11899	
TULANE AVE W	Jefferson Co	341K	80127	10800-11199	
TULANE CT	Longmont	10V	80503	1-99	
TULANE DR W	Jefferson Co	341J	80465	11700-11899	
TULANE PL W	Jefferson Co	341K	80127	11500-11599	
	Jefferson Co	340M	80465	13600-13699	
TULANE ST	Federal Heights	193Z	80260	2000-2099	
TULARE CIR S	Denver	316Y	80231	3200-3399	
TULARE CT S	Denver	316Y	80231	3200-3399	
TULE LAKE DR	Littleton	343S	80123	4400-5199	
TULIP CT	Longmont	11T	80501	1500-1599	
TULIP ST	Longmont	11X	80501	900-1499	
	Longmont	11T	80501	1700-1799	
	Longmont	11P	80501	2000-2299	
	Longmont	11K	80501	2400-2499	
TULIP WAY	Longmont	11P	80501	2300-2399	
TULIP TREE PL	Castle Rock	467R	80108	1700-2099	
TULSA CT	Denver	257R	80239	4500-4899	
TULSA WAY	Denver	257H	80239	5100-5599	
TUMBLE BRUSH LN	Parker	408U	80134	None	
TUMBLE BRUSH ST S	Parker	408U	80134	None	
TUMBLE GRASS PL	Parker	378R	80134	8300-8399	
TUMBLEWEED CT	Adams Co	772F	80102	None	
TUMBLEWEED DR	Brighton	139L	80601	None	
TUMBLEWEED PL	Thornton	195R	80229	None	
TUMBLEWEED WAY	Parker	409R	80138	11100-11399	
TUMWATER LN	Boulder	98S	80304	2600-2699	
TUNDRA CIR	Erie	133D	80516	None	
TUNDRA PL	Longmont	12X	80501	700-799	
TUNGSTEN PL	Longmont	12X	80501	400-499	
TUNGSTEN RD	Boulder Co	740M	80466	None	
TUNNEL 19 RD	Boulder Co	742Y	80403	200-799	
TURF LN E	Douglas Co	436D	80108	100-399	
TURIN DR	Longmont	40P	80503	None	
TURKEY LN	Jefferson Co	338X	80465	22400-22499	
TURKEY LN	Park Co	841V	80421	1-199	
TURKEY CREEK RD	Jefferson Co	340J	80465	15000-16499	
	Jefferson Co	339M	80465	16500-17199	
TURKEY CREEK RD N	Jefferson Co	369E	80465	19200-20199	
	Jefferson Co	368E	80465	20200-25099	
	Jefferson Co	367E	80439	25100-27299	
TURKEY CREEK RD S	Jefferson Co	339W	80465	5800-6399	
	Jefferson Co	369K	80465	6200-9199	
	Jefferson Co	823R	80465	9200-10599	
TURKEY GULCH RD	Clear Creek Co	780N	80452	1-2099	
TURKEY ROCK RD	Douglas Co	432K	80125	7200-7499	
TURNAGAIN CT	Boulder Co	742D	80302	1-99	
TURNBERRY CIR	Louisville	160G	80027	1000-1099	
TURNBERRY CT	Broomfield	163F	80020	13900-14099	
TURNBERRY CT	Castle Rock	497R	80104	None	
TURNBERRY CT	Longmont	42N	80501	None	
TURNBERRY DR	Castle Rock	497R	80104	None	
TURNBERRY PKWY	Commerce City	197M	80022	None	
	Commerce City	198E	80022	None	
TURNBERRY PL	Castle Rock	497R	80104	None	
TURNBERRY PT	Broomfield	163F	80020	13900-13999	
TURNBURY CIR	Elbert Co	851C	80107	None	
TURNER BLVD	Weld Co	706R	80504	10700-10999	
TURNER CT	Castle Rock	498N	80104	2000-2099	
TURNER DR	Adams Co	224J	80221	7400-7799	
TURNING LEAF ST	Longmont	42N	80501	None	
TURNPIKE DR	Westminster	223K	80030	3000-3999	
	Westminster	223E	80031	8000-8399	
	Westminster	223A	80031	8400-8799	
TURNSTONE AVE	Castle Rock	498M	80104	6400-7099	
TURNSTONE PL	Castle Rock	498M	80104	5800-6299	
TURPIN WAY	Erie	103P	80516	600-899	
TURQUOISE CT	Douglas Co	409E	80134	10200-10299	
TURQUOISE DR	Longmont	41U	80504	1100-1199	
TURQUOISE ST	Parker	409J	80134	None	
TURQUOISE TERRACE PL					
	Castle Pines North	436A	80108	12400-12599	
TURQUOISE TERRACE ST					
	Castle Pines North	436A	80108	12300-12499	
TURRET WAY	Broomfield	133L	80020	16500-16699	
TURTLE MOUNTAIN	Jefferson Co	371L	80127	10400-10799	
TURTLE ROCK RD	Jefferson Co	336B	80439	None	
TURWESTON LN	Castle Pines North	436Q	80108	7000-7199	
TUSCANY CT	Highlands Ranch	375Z	80126	5100-5199	
TUSCANY CT	Longmont	40T	80503	1700-1799	
TUSCANY LN	Highlands Ranch	375Z	80126	8800-8999	
TUSCANY PL	Highlands Ranch	375Z	80126	5100-5199	
TUSCANY WAY	Highlands Ranch	375Z	80126	None	
TWENTY MILE RD	Douglas Co	409P	80134	10900-11599	
	Parker	409K	80134	10100-10899	
	Parker	379X	80134	None	
	Parker	409F	80134	None	
TWIGHLIGHT TERRACE DR	Park Co	840C	80421	1-399	
TWILIGHT AVE	Firestone	707P	80504	6100-6299	
	Firestone	707N	80504	None	
TWILIGHT CT	Longmont	12R	80501	1700-1799	
TWILIGHT DR	Longmont	12Q	80501	1600-1699	
TWILIGHT DR	Wheat Ridge	251Y	80215	1-10299	
TWILIGHT LN	Boulder Co	703G	80503	11900-12499	
TWILIGHT WAY	Douglas Co	469A	80134	5300-5499	
	Douglas Co	439W	80134	5500-5699	
TWILIGHT PEAK	Jefferson Co	371P	80127	11000-11099	
TWILIGHT RUN	Broomfield	134G	80516	None	
TWINBERRY ST E	Parker	409A	80134	17200-17399	
TWIN BUTTES PL	Elbert Co	831K	80138	3800-3999	
TWIN CUBS	Douglas Co	432N	80125	10900-10999	
TWIN ELK LN	Jefferson Co	824R	80127	13000-13299	
TWIN FLOWER	Jefferson Co	370F	80127	1-99	
TWINING ST	Brighton	140J	80601	None	
TWIN LAKES RD	Boulder Co	99G	80301	4800-6899	
TWIN OAKS DR	Douglas Co	496Y	80109	1000-1499	
TWIN OAKS RD	Douglas Co	496Y	80109	1-1399	
TWIN PEAKS CIR	Longmont	10Y	80503	1100-1299	
TWIN PINE AVE	Parker	409Z	80134	20300-20499	
TWIN PONDS TRAIL	Jefferson Co	368J	80465	22800-23099	
TWIN SISTERS DR	Longmont	12S	80501	1400-1699	
TWIN SPRUCE DR S	Jefferson Co	337T	80439	5400-5699	
TWIN SPRUCE RD	Jefferson Co	762F	80403	9500-11299	
TWIN THUMBS PASS	Jefferson Co	371P	80127	11100-11199	
TWISTED OAK DR	Castle Pines North	436F	80108	6600-6899	
TWISTED PINE CIR	Thornton	193Z	80260	None	
TWISTED PINE DR	El Paso Co	909Q	80908	19400-20399	
TWO BITS RD	Park Co	841A	80421	1-199	
TWO BROTHERS RD	Clear Creek Co	780K	80452	None	
TWO RIVERS CIR	Douglas Co	441J	80138	7600-7799	
TWYLBY RD	Douglas Co	908F	80118	2200-2399	
TYCOON AVE	Jefferson Co	339G	80465	17500-17999	
TYLER AVE	Longmont	11P	80501	1800-1999	
TYLER AVE	Louisville	130U	80027	300-499	
	Louisville	130R	80027	1700-1899	
TYLER AVE S	Louisville	130Z	80027	100-299	
TYLER DR	Arvada	221Y	80004	9600-9699	
TYLER DR S	Superior	160R	80027	2200-2298	E
TYLER PL	Erie	102D	80516	1200-1299	
TYLER RD	Boulder	97Z	80304	1900-1999	
TYNAN CT	Erie	102Q	80516	400-499	
TYNAN DR	Erie	102Q	80516	300-1999	
TYRRHENIAN CT	Longmont	12Q	80501	None	
TYRRHENIAN DR	Longmont	12L	80501	None	

U

STREET NAME	CITY or COUNTY	MAP GRID	ZIP CODE	BLOCK RANGE	O/E
UINTA CT	Thornton	166Q	80602	12900-12999	
	Thornton	136Y	80602	None	
UINTA CT S	Arapahoe Co	316G	80231	1300-1499	
	Centennial	376L	80112	7600-7699	
	Denver	316Y	80231	3300-3399	
UINTA PL	Douglas Co	887H	80118	1100-1199	
UINTA PL S	Centennial	376L	80112	7500-7599	
UINTA ST	Adams Co	226G	80022	8400-8799	
	Adams Co	166U	80602	12400-12799	
	Adams Co	166C	80602	14500-14799	
	Denver	286L	80220	1200-1999	
	Denver	286C	80238	2200-2899	
	Denver	256Z	80238	2900-2999	
	Denver	256Q	80238	None	
	Thornton	166Q	80602	13000-13399	
	Thornton	136Y	80602	None	
UINTA ST S	Centennial	376G	80112	6700-7199	
	Centennial	376L	80112	7700-7899	
	Denver	316U	80231	2700-2999	
UINTA WAY	Denver	286Q	80230	400-799	
UINTA WAY S	Arapahoe Co	316G	80231	1500-1899	
UKRAINE CIR S	Arapahoe Co	350Y	80015	5900-6099	
UKRAINE CT S	Arapahoe Co	350Y	80015	6300-6399	
	Aurora	380Q	80016	None	
UKRAINE ST S	Arapahoe Co	350Q	80015	5100-5399	
	Arapahoe Co	350U	80015	5900-6099	
	Aurora	380G	80016	7000-7399	
UKRAINE WAY S	Arapahoe Co	350Q	80015	5300-5399	
ULM ST S	Arapahoe Co	811G	80137	1500-3499	
ULSTER CIR	Greenwood Village	346U	80111	5700W-5799W	
ULSTER CIR	Thornton	136U	80602	None	
	Thornton	136Y	80602	None	
ULSTER CIR E	Greenwood Village	346V	80111	5700-5799	
ULSTER CIR S	Centennial	376C	80112	6800N-6999N	
ULSTER CT	Thornton	136Y	80602	None	
ULSTER CT S	Centennial	376G	80112	7300-7399	
	Centennial	376L	80112	7600-7699	
	Denver	316Y	80231	3300-3399	
ULSTER PL S	Centennial	376L	80112	7500-7599	
ULSTER ST	Adams Co	136Q	80602	None	
	Commerce City	226G	80022	8300-8799	
	Denver	286L	80220	1200-1999	
	Denver	286C	80238	2200-2499	
	Denver	256Y	80238	2500-2899	
	Denver	256U	80238	3900-4299	
	Denver	256Q	80238	None	
	Thornton	166L	80602	None	
ULSTER ST S	Arapahoe Co	316G	80231	1301-1499	O
	Centennial	376G	80112	7000-7399	
	Centennial	376Q	80112	7800-7899	
	Denver	286U	80230	1-299	
	Denver	316L	80231	1800-1899	
	Denver	316U	80231	2700-2999	
	Denver	346C	80237	3600-3799	
	Denver	346L	80237	4500-5099	
	Greenwood Village	346Q	80111	5100-5299	
	Denver	286Q	80230	500-799	
ULSTER WAY	Thornton	136Y	80602	None	
ULYSSES ST	Arvada	219V	80007	7000-7199	
	Arvada	219M	80007	None	
	Golden	279R	80401	600-1399	
	Golden	279H	80401	1400-1699	
	Jefferson Co	249M	80403	5200-5499	
ULYSSES WAY	Jefferson Co	249U	80403	4100-4399	
UMATILLA CT	Westminster	163R	80234	13100-13199	
UMATILLA DR	Gilpin Co	761B	80403	1-599	
UMATILLA ST	Adams Co	253H	80221	5400-5599	
	Adams Co	223M	80221	7600-7899	
	Adams Co	223H	80221	8100-8399	
	Adams Co	133Z	80020	14800-14999	
	Denver	283R	80204	700-799	
	Denver	283M	80204	1100-1499	
	Denver	253Z	80211	2700-3199	
	Denver	253R	80211	3800-4499	
	Denver	253M	80221	4800-5199	
	Federal Heights	223H	80260	8400-8499	
	Westminster	163R	80234	13100-13399	
UMATILLA ST S	Denver	313H	80223	1100-1799	
	Englewood	313V	80110	2900-3099	
	Sheridan	313Z	80110	3300-3499	
UMATILLA WAY	Thornton	193V	80260	10000-10099	
UMATILLA WAY S	Denver	313D	80223	700-899	
UMBER CIR	Arvada	219Y	80403	6300-6399	
	Arvada	219Y	80007	None	
UMBER CIR	Castle Rock	466Y	80109	None	
UMBER CT	Arvada	219U	80007	7000-7199	
	Arvada	219Q	80007	None	
	Jefferson Co	219C	80007	8900-8999	
UMBER ST	Arvada	249C	80403	6000-6199	
	Arvada	219Y	80403	6200-6299	
	Arvada	219U	80007	7000-7199	
UMBRIA LN	Longmont	40Q	80503	None	
UMPIRE CT	Adams Co	751E	80603	None	
UMPIRE ST	Adams Co	751E	80603	13700-15199	
UMPIRE ST	Adams Co	751N	80603	13700-15199	
UNBRIDLED AVE	Parker	410T	80138	21500-21899	
UNBRIDLED DR	Parker	410T	80138	21300-21499	
UNCOMPANGRE PEAK CT	Brighton	139M	80601	None	
UNDERGROVE CIR	Denver	770T	80249	None	
UNDERGROVE ST	Denver	770T	80249	7600-7898	E
UNDERPASS RD E	Arapahoe Co	793U	80102	48900-52099	
UNION AVE	Boulder	97L	80304	500-1199	
UNION AVE	Firestone	707P	80504	None	
UNION AVE	Morrison	339C	80465	200-17899	

STREET NAME	CITY or COUNTY	MAP GRID	ZIP CODE	BLOCK RANGE	O/E
UNION AVE E	Arapahoe Co	350J	80015	None	
	Aurora	348L	80015	15700-16099	
	Aurora	348M	80015	16200-16299	
	Aurora	349J	80015	16600-16799	
	Cherry Hills Village	346J	80121	5400-5599	
	Denver	346K	80237	6500-7699	
	Denver	346L	80237	7700-8299	
	Denver	346M	80237	8500-8799	
	Englewood	344L	80113	1-799	
	Greenwood Village	346M	80111	8900-9199	
UNION AVE W	Denver	343L	80110	3300-3599	
	Denver	343J	80236	3600-5199	
	Denver	342J	80123	8400-8799	
	Denver	341M	80123	9000-9799	
	Englewood	344K	80110	1-1199	
	Englewood	343M	80110	1800-3299	
UNION BLVD	Lakewood	281S	80228	1-599	
UNION BLVD S	Lakewood	281S	80228	1-599	
	Lakewood	311K	80228	600-1899	
UNION CIR	Arvada	221E	80005	8500-8599	
	Arvada	251E	80002	None	
UNION CIR E	Arapahoe Co	350J	80015	20400-20599	
	Arapahoe Co	350L	80015	None	
UNION CT	Arvada	221W	80004	6200-6399	
	Arvada	221S	80004	7100-7199	
	Arvada	221N	80005	7200-7299	
	Arvada	221J	80005	7500-7599	
	Arvada	221E	80005	8300-8499	
	Jefferson Co	251J	80002	5200-5299	
	Wheat Ridge	251S	80033	3600-3899	
UNION CT S	Jefferson Co	311N	80228	2300-2399	
	Jefferson Co	341E	80465	4400-4499	
	Jefferson Co	341J	80465	4700-4899	
	Jefferson Co	341N	80127	5400-5599	
	Jefferson Co	341S	80127	None	
	Lakewood	311K	80228	1700-1899	
UNION CT S	Superior	160L	80027	1400-1499	
UNION DR	Lakewood	281E	80215	1800-2199	
UNION DR E	Arapahoe Co	349M	80015	20100-20399	
	Arapahoe Co	350J	80015	None	
	Arapahoe Co	350K	80015	None	
	Aurora	349J	80015	17400-17599	
	Aurora	349K	80015	18200-18699	
	Aurora	349L	80015	18800-19099	
	Centennial	349M	80015	19600-19999	
UNION LN S	Jefferson Co	341S	80127	None	
UNION PL E	Arapahoe Co	350J	80015	None	
	Arapahoe Co	350L	80015	None	
	Aurora	349J	80015	17100-17499	
	Aurora	349L	80015	18700-18899	
UNION PL S	Lakewood	311K	80228	1900-1999	
UNION ST	Arvada	251A	80004	5800-6199	
	Arvada	221W	80004	6200-6699	
	Arvada	221S	80004	6700-7199	
	Arvada	221E	80005	None	
UNION ST	Firestone	706R	80504	None	
UNION ST	Jefferson Co	251E	80002	5600-5699	
	Lakewood	281N	80401	800-999	
	Lakewood	281J	80401	1000-1499	
	Lakewood	281E	80215	1700-1999	
	Wheat Ridge	251W	80215	2900-3199	
	Wheat Ridge	251W	80033	3200-3499	
UNION ST S	Jefferson Co	341E	80465	4300-4499	
	Jefferson Co	341J	80465	4500-4999	
	Jefferson Co	341N	80127	5100-5299	
	Jefferson Co	341W	80127	5900-5999	
	Jefferson Co	341S	80127	None	
UNION WAY	Arvada	251E	80002	5300-5399	
	Jefferson Co	191J	80021	10600-10699	
	Lakewood	281A	80215	2100-2199	
UNION WAY S	Jefferson Co	341N	80127	5300-5399	
	Jefferson Co	341S	80127	None	
UNION TERRACE S	Jefferson Co	341S	80127	None	
UNITA CT S	Denver	346C	80237	3700-3799	
UNITA ST S	Denver	346C	80237	3700-3999	
UNITA ST S	Denver	346G	80237	4000-4099	
UNITY CIR	Commerce City	769A	80022	None	
UNITY PKWY	Commerce City	769E	80022	None	
UNIVERSAL CT	Castle Rock	467G	80108	None	
UNIVERSITY AVE	Boulder	127C	80302	400-1599	
UNIVERSITY AVE	Longmont	10V	80503	2900-3199	
UNIVERSITY BLVD	Denver	285S	80206	1-599	
UNIVERSITY BLVD S	Arapahoe Co	315W	80110	3300-3498	E
	Centennial	345J	80121	6000-6499	
	Centennial	375E	80122	6500-8299	
	Cherry Hills Village	315W	80110	3500-3599	
	Cherry Hills Village	345J	80113	3600-5099	
	Denver	285W	80209	1-699	
	Denver	315A	80209	700-1099	
	Denver	315N	80210	1100-3099	
	Denver	315W	80210	3100-3298	E
	Englewood	315W	80110	3001-3499	O
	Greenwood Village	345J	80121	5100-6099	
	Highlands Ranch	405C	80126	9200-9599	
	Highlands Ranch	405C	80130	9600-9799	
	Highlands Ranch	375X	80126	None	
UNIVERSITY CIR	Longmont	10V	80503	1-99	
UNIVERSITY DR	Longmont	10V	80503	1-99	
UNIVERSITY LN	Greenwood Village	345N	80121	1-99	
UNIVERSITY WAY S	Centennial	375J	80122	7800-7899	
UNIVERSITY HEIGHTS AVE	Boulder	128E	80302	2400-2799	
UNO ST	Arvada	253A	80003	6000-6199	
UNO WAY S	Denver	313N	80219	2500-2599	
UNSER AVE W	Jefferson Co	371V	80128	9100-9999	
UNSER DR W	Jefferson Co	371Y	80128	None	
UPCHURCH WAY	El Paso Co	909N	80132	None	
UPHAM CIR	Arvada	222P	80003	7300-7399	
UPHAM CT	Arvada	222P	80003	7300-7699	
	Arvada	222F	80003	8100-8299	
	Lakewood	282K	80214	900-999	
	Westminster	192T	80021	9800-9899	
	Wheat Ridge	252X	80033	3000-3099	
UPHAM CT S	Jefferson Co	372F	80128	7200-7399	
	Jefferson Co	372K	80128	7700-7899	
	Lakewood	282T	80226	1-199	
	Lakewood	282X	80226	500-599	
	Lakewood	342K	80123	6600-6699	
UPHAM DR	Arvada	222T	80003	6600-6699	
	Westminster	192T	80021	9800-9899	
UPHAM ST	Arvada	252F	80002	5600-5799	
	Arvada	222X	80003	6300-6599	
	Arvada	222T	80003	6600-7099	
	Arvada	222P	80003	7200-7499	
	Arvada	222K	80003	7600-7799	
	Broomfield	192B	80020	11800-11999	
	Lakewood	282T	80226	1-399	
	Lakewood	282K	80214	900-1399	
	Lakewood	282F	80214	1600-2399	
	Lakewood	282B	80214	2400-2599	
	Wheat Ridge	282B	80214	2600-2699	
	Wheat Ridge	252X	80033	2700-3499	
	Wheat Ridge	252T	80033	3600-4399	
	Wheat Ridge	252P	80033	4400-4799	
UPHAM ST S	Denver	312T	80227	2700-3099	
	Jefferson Co	372B	80123	6600-6699	
	Jefferson Co	372F	80128	7200-7399	
	Jefferson Co	372K	80128	7400-7499	
	Jefferson Co	372P	80128	7700-8299	
	Lakewood	282X	80226	500-599	
	Lakewood	312B	80226	900-1099	
	Lakewood	312F	80232	1200-1399	
	Lakewood	312K	80232	1500-1899	
	Lakewood	312X	80227	3400-3499	
UPHAM WAY	Westminster	192X	80021	9200-9399	
UPHAM WAY S	Jefferson Co	372T	80128	8300-8599	
UPHILL ST	Lochbuie	140E	80603	None	
	Lochbuie	140A	80603	None	
UPLAND AVE	Boulder	97M	80304	1200-2299	
UPLAND DR	Douglas Co	378T	80112	8500-8598	E
UPLAND DR	Lochbuie	729Z	80603	None	
UPLAND ST	Lochbuie	729Z	80603	1700-1899	
UPLANDS SPUR	Lakewood	281B	80215	2200-2399	
UPPER APEX RD	Gilpin Co	760X	80403	None	
UPPER ASPEN LN	Park Co	821Z	80470	35300-35699	
UPPER BEAR CREEK RD					
	Clear Creek Co	335J	80439	1-199	
	Clear Creek Co	801T	80439	200-34799	
	Jefferson Co	335J	80439	4500-35099	
	Jefferson Co	336E	80439	None	
UPPER COLD SPRINGS GULCH RD					
	Jefferson Co	277W	80401	26900-27599	
UPPER ELK VALLEY RD					
	Clear Creek Co	781U	80439	400-499	
UPPER GILPIN RD	Gilpin Co	760H	80403	None	
	Gilpin Co	761E	80403	None	
UPPER GLEN WAY	Palmer Lake	907Q	80133	None	
UPPER HIGHLAND DR	Weld Co	706U	80504	10601-10699	O
UPPER LAKE GULCH RD E					
	Douglas Co	888J	80118	600-3399	
	Douglas Co	889E	80118	None	
	Douglas Co	889E	80104	None	
UPPER MOON GULCH RD	Gilpin Co	740Y	80403	None	
	Gilpin Co	760B	80452	None	
	Gilpin Co	760C	80403	None	
UPPER MOSS ROCK RD	Jefferson Co	276U	80401	28900-29299	
UPPER RANCH DR S	Jefferson Co	822W	80470	11500-35499	
UPPER RANCH RD	Jefferson Co	822W	80470	None	
UPPER RIDGE RD	Jefferson Co	843D	80433	12700-13199	
UPPER RIDGE RD	Weld Co	706U	80504	10600-10799	
UPPER TRAVIS GULCH RD					
	Gilpin Co	760C	80403	100-499	
UPPER TWIN CREEK RD					
	Douglas Co	889A	80104	5300-5799	
UPTON CT	Castle Rock	499P	80104	None	
UPTON CT	Denver	257M	80239	4900-5099	
UPTON ST	Northglenn	193M	80234	10600-10799	
UPTOWN AVE	Broomfield	192A	80021	7800-11799	
URA LN	Northglenn	194J	80234	1600-1999	
	Northglenn	193M	80234	2000-2199	
	Northglenn	193M	80234	10400-10599	
	Thornton	193R	80234	10000-10399	
URAVAN CT S	Arapahoe Co	349X	80016	6000-6099	
	Arapahoe Co	379B	80016	6500-6599	
	Aurora	319B	80017	1000-1099	
	Aurora	349K	80015	5000-5099	
	Centennial	349P	80015	5300-5399	
	Centennial	349P	80015	5400-5499	
	Centennial	349T	80015	5500-5599	
	Centennial	379K	80016	7600-7799	
	Foxfield	379F	80016	7100-7299	
URAVAN PL S	Centennial	349P	80015	5100-5199	
URAVAN ST	Aurora	289B	80011	2400-2699	
	Brighton	139T	80601	15200-15699	
	Commerce City	169X	80603	None	
	Commerce City	769E	80022	None	
	Commerce City	769J	80022	None	
	Commerce City	769N	80022	None	
URAVAN ST S	Aurora	319B	80017	800-1099	
	Aurora	319F	80017	1100-1699	
	Aurora	319K	80017	1800-1899	
	Aurora	319K	80013	2000-2299	
	Aurora	319S	80013	2700-3099	
	Aurora	349B	80013	3500-3899	
	Aurora	349F	80013	3900-4299	
	Centennial	349P	80015	5100-5199	
URAVAN WAY S	Aurora	319X	80013	3100-3499	
	Aurora	349B	80013	3700-3799	
URBAN CIR	Arvada	221S	80004	6700-6799	
URBAN CT	Arvada	251A	80004	5800-5899	
	Arvada	221W	80004	6200-6699	
	Arvada	221S	80004	6700-6799	
	Arvada	221N	80005	7500-7599	
	Arvada	221J	80005	7600-7699	
	Arvada	221E	80005	8300-8499	
	Arvada	221E	80005	None	
	Lakewood	281N	80401	600-799	
	Wheat Ridge	251S	80033	3500-3599	
URBAN CT S	Jefferson Co	311N	80228	2300-2399	
	Jefferson Co	341E	80465	4400-4499	
	Jefferson Co	341N	80465	4900-4999	
	Jefferson Co	341N	80127	5300-5399	
	Jefferson Co	371A	80127	6400-6499	
	Jefferson Co	341S	80127	None	
	Lakewood	311K	80228	1700-1899	
URBAN DR	Arvada	221N	80005	7200-7399	
	Lakewood	281E	80215	2000-2299	
URBAN DR S	Lakewood	311A	80228	700-799	
URBAN ST	Arvada	251A	80004	5800-6199	
	Arvada	221W	80004	6200-6699	
	Arvada	221S	80004	6800-7199	
	Arvada	221J	80005	7500-7599	
	Jefferson Co	191J	80021	10600-10799	
	Lakewood	281W	80228	100-199	
	Lakewood	281N	80228	400-599	
	Lakewood	281N	80401	700-1199	
	Lakewood	281J	80401	900-1399	
	Lakewood	281E	80215	1500-1799	
	Lakewood	281A	80215	2300-2599	
	Wheat Ridge	251S	80033	3500-3899	
	Wheat Ridge	251J	80033	None	
URBAN ST S	Jefferson Co	341S	80127	5500-5699	
	Jefferson Co	341W	80127	6100-6399	
	Lakewood	311J	80228	1900-1999	
URBAN WAY	Arvada	221S	80004	7000-7099	
	Arvada	221N	80005	7500-7599	
URBAN WAY S	Jefferson Co	341J	80465	4600-4799	
	Jefferson Co	341S	80127	None	
	Lakewood	311J	80228	1300-1899	
URSULA CIR S	Aurora	317V	80014	3000-3099	
URSULA CT	Aurora	287H	80010	2000-2198	E
URSULA CT S	Aurora	317M	80112	1500-1799	
	Aurora	317V	80014	2800-3099	
URSULA ST	Adams Co	167Z	80640	12200-12399	
	Aurora	288N	80011	200-599	
	Aurora	288J	80011	700-799	
	Aurora	287M	80011	900-1299	
	Aurora	288J	80011	1300-1499	
	Aurora	287H	80010	1500-2399	
	Aurora	287D	80010	2300-2398	E
	Aurora	258W	80011	3000-3299	
	Commerce City	197M	80022	10400-10598	E
	Commerce City	768C	80022	10400-10599	
	Denver	257M	80239	4900-5099	
URSULA ST S	Aurora	288S	80012	100-299	
	Aurora	317V	80014	2800-2898	E
URSULA WAY	Commerce City	768G	80022	None	
	Denver	257H	80239	4900-5299	
URSULA WAY S	Aurora	287Z	80012	300-399	
URUGUAY ST S	Lakewood	312F	80232	1200-1399	
US HWY 285 ACCESS RD S					
	Jefferson Co	842C	80433	12500-30099	
US HWY 285 FRONTAGE RD S					
	Jefferson Co	842B	80470	12600-12899	
	Jefferson Co	842F	80470	12900-13499	
UTAH AVE W	Lakewood	312K	80232	7300-7599	
	Lakewood	312J	80232	8500-8699	
	Lakewood	311M	80232	9200-9499	
	Lakewood	310M	80228	12800-13999	
UTAH CIR E	Aurora	318K	80012	13900-14099	
	Aurora	319L	80017	18700-18999	
UTAH CIR W	Lakewood	310M	80228	13200-13699	
UTAH CT	Golden	279H	80401	1600-1699	
UTAH CT	Thornton	225A	80229	8800-8999	
UTAH DR	Golden	279H	80401	1700-1799	
UTAH PL E	Aurora	317K	80112	10600-10699	
	Aurora	317L	80112	11300-12099	
	Aurora	318L	80012	14800-15199	
	Aurora	318L	80017	15800-15899	
	Aurora	318M	80017	16100-16299	
	Aurora	319K	80017	17600-18199	
	Aurora	319L	80017	19400-19699	
	Denver	315L	80222	4300-4799	
	Denver	315M	80222	5300-5599	
UTAH PL W	Jefferson Co	311K	80232	11200-11299	
	Lakewood	311M	80232	9200-9499	
UTAH ST	Golden	279G	80401	1400-1799	
UTAH WAY	Longmont	41U	80501	None	
UTE AVE	Kiowa	872M	80117	1-899	
UTE AVE W	Jefferson Co	372S	80128	8400-8899	
	Jefferson Co	371V	80128	9200-9999	
	Jefferson Co	371U	80127	10000-10999	
UTE CT	Adams Co	226B	80022	None	
UTE CT	Douglas Co	886G	80118	5800-5899	
UTE DR	Jefferson Co	763K	80403	8800-9599	
UTE DR W	Jefferson Co	372S	80128	8400-8799	
	Jefferson Co	371V	80128	9300-9599	
	Jefferson Co	371Y	80128	None	
UTE HWY	Boulder Co	10K	80503	7300-9299	
	Boulder Co	11J	80503	9300-9499	
	Boulder Co	11K	80504	9500-10899	
	Boulder Co	12J	80504	10900-12699	
UTE PL W	Jefferson Co	371Y	80128	None	
	Boulder Co	704F	80503	4000-7199	
UTE RD	Jefferson Co	338P	80454	5000-5299	
UTE RD	Jefferson Co	842U	80470	30300-30699	
UTE WAY	Lochbuie	729Z	80603	1600-1799	
UTE WAY	Nederland	740M	80466	None	
UTE CREEK DR	Longmont	12Q	80501	2000-2999	
UTE MOUNTAIN TRAIL	Castle Rock	466T	80109	None	
UTE TRAIL	Clear Creek Co	365N	80439	1-299	
UTICA AVE	Boulder	97L	80304	400-1199	
UTICA AVE	Firestone	707P	80504	None	
UTICA CIR	Boulder	97L	80304	900-1199	
UTICA CIR	Broomfield	163S	80020	12600-12799	
UTICA CIR	Westminster	193E	80031	None	
UTICA CT	Adams Co	253E	80212	None	
	Arvada	223W	80003	6300-6399	
UTICA CT	Boulder	97L	80304	500-599	
UTICA CT	Broomfield	163W	80020	12300-12399	
UTICA CT	Firestone	707P	80504	6100-6199	
UTICA CT	Westminster	193W	80031	9000-9299	
	Westminster	193J	80031	10900-10999	
	Westminster	193J	80031	11000-11099	
UTICA DR	Douglas Co	436X	80108	900-999	
UTICA DR S	Littleton	373J	80128	7500-7599	
UTICA PL	Broomfield	163W	80020	12200-12399	
UTICA ST	Adams Co	253E	80212	None	
	Arvada	253A	80003	6000-6199	
	Arvada	223W	80003	6300-6599	
	Broomfield	163W	80020	12200-12399	
	Broomfield	163S	80020	12400-12599	
	Denver	283S	80219	1-199	
	Denver	283N	80204	400-999	
	Denver	283J	80204	1200-1699	

Continued on next page

U

STREET NAME	CITY or COUNTY	MAP GRID	ZIP CODE	BLOCK RANGE	O/E
UTICA ST (Cont'd)	Denver	283A	80212	2600-2699	
	Denver	253W	80212	2700-2899	
	Denver	253S	80212	3200-4599	
	Denver	253J	80212	5000-5099	
UTICA ST	Ward	720M	80481	None	
UTICA ST	Westminster	223S	80030	6800-7199	
	Westminster	223N	80030	7200-7399	
	Westminster	223A	80031	8800-8899	
	Westminster	193W	80031	9000-9399	
	Westminster	193J	80031	10800-10899	
UTICA ST S	Denver	283S	80219	1-699	
	Denver	313A	80219	700-999	
	Denver	313J	80219	1100-2099	
	Denver	313N	80219	2300-2599	
	Denver	313S	80236	2700-3499	
	Denver	343E	80236	3500-4699	
	Littleton	373J	80128	7400-7499	
UTICA WAY	Westminster	193A	80031	11700-11899	
UTOPIA CT	Denver	257M	80239	4900-5099	
UTRILLO LN	Northglenn	193M	80234	10400-10699	
UVALDA CIR S	Aurora	287Z	80012	400-499	
UVALDA CT	Aurora	288E	80045	1700-1899	
UVALDA ST	Aurora	288N	80011	300-599	
	Aurora	288J	80011	700-1099	
	Aurora	258W	80011	3000-3299	
	Commerce City	197R	80022	10400-10499	
	Commerce City	198J	80022	None	
	Denver	258S	80239	3900-3999	
	Denver	258E	80239	5000-5599	
UVALDA ST S	Arapahoe Co	348W	80111	6400-6599	
	Aurora	287Z	80012	300-499	
	Aurora	317H	80112	1000-1799	

V

STREET NAME	CITY or COUNTY	MAP GRID	ZIP CODE	BLOCK RANGE	O/E
V CIR	Palmer Lake	907Q	80133	1-99	
VACQUERO CIR	Castle Pines North	436E	80108	6000-6399	
VACQUERO DR	Castle Pines North	436E	80108	6000-6399	
VAIL CIR	Douglas Co	887M	80118	7600-7699	
VAIL LN	Longmont	11W	80503	1200-1299	
VAIL PL	Jefferson Co	336M	80439	4800-4899	
VAIL ST	Buckley Air Force Base	319C	80017	None	
VAIL ST N	Buckley Air Force Base	289Y	80011	None	
VAIL ST S	Buckley Air Force Base	289Y	80011	None	
VAIL PASS	Boulder	98V	80301	None	
VAIL PASS	Jefferson Co	371E	80127	12000-12299	
VALDAI AVE	Lochbuie	140C	80603	701-799	O
VALDAI CIR S	Aurora	380G	80016	7200-7399	
VALDAI CT S	Arapahoe Co	350Y	80015	6200-6399	
	Aurora	380C	80016	None	
	Aurora	380Q	80016	None	
VALDAI ST	Lochbuie	140G	80603	100-599	
VALDAI ST S	Arapahoe Co	350Q	80015	5100-5399	
	Arapahoe Co	350U	80015	5400-5599	
	Aurora	380G	80016	7000-7099	
VALDAI WAY S	Arapahoe Co	350Q	80015	5300-5499	
	Arapahoe Co	350U	80015	5500-6099	
VALDERAMA CT	Douglas Co	466F	80108	700-799	
VALE DR	Denver	315D	80246	5200-5499	
	Denver	316A	80246	5500-5599	
VALE PL	Erie	133G	80516	None	
VALE ST	Palmer Lake	907Q	80133	2-198	E
VALE WAY	Erie	133G	80516	2300-2499	
VALENCIA CIR	Erie	103N	80516	None	
VALENCIA RD	Northglenn	193M	80234	10700-10799	
VALENTIA CT S	Denver	316Y	80231	3300-3399	
	Denver	346C	80237	3800-3899	
VALENTIA ST	Adams Co	226C	80022	8600-8699	
	Adams Co	166U	80602	12400-12699	
	Commerce City	226G	80022	8400-8599	
	Commerce City	256C	80216	None	
	Denver	286L	80220	1200-2199	
	Denver	286C	80238	2000-2799	
	Denver	256Y	80238	2800-2899	
	Thornton	166Q	80602	12800-12899	
	Thornton	136U	80602	None	
	Thornton	166L	80602	None	
VALENTIA ST S	Arapahoe Co	316D	80247	1200-1398	E
	Arapahoe Co	316Q	80231	1900-2299	
	Centennial	376G	80112	6900-7099	
	Centennial	376L	80112	7700-7999	
	Denver	316G	80247	1001-1099	O
	Denver	316U	80231	2800-3099	
	Denver	346G	80237	4000-4199	
VALENTIA WAY S	Centennial	376G	80112	7100-7399	
	Centennial	376L	80112	7800-7899	
	Greenwood Village	346Q	80111	5300-5599	
VALENTINE CT S	Lakewood	311J	80228	1600-1699	
VALENTINE LN	Longmont	11V	80501	1-199	
VALENTINE ST S	Lakewood	311J	80228	1700-1899	
VALENTINE WAY S	Lakewood	311E	80228	1100-1199	
	Lakewood	311J	80228	1400-1799	
VALERIAN CT	Douglas Co	887F	80118	7200-7299	
VALERIAN ST	Brighton	140J	80601	None	
VALHALLA DR	Boulder Co	98C	80301	4500-5399	
VALHALLA ST	Castle Rock	497C	80104	800-899	
VALKYRIE DR	Boulder Co	98C	80301	4800-5199	
VALLE DR	Fort Lupton	728L	80621	100-199	
VALLEJO CIR	Westminster	163R	80234	12800-13099	
VALLEJO CT	Westminster	163R	80234	13100-13299	
VALLEJO ST	Adams Co	253H	80221	5200-5899	
	Adams Co	223M	80221	7600-7999	
	Adams Co	223H	80221	8100-8399	
	Denver	283V	80223	100-399	
	Denver	283R	80204	700-999	
	Denver	253Z	80211	2700-4799	
	Denver	253M	80221	4800-5199	
	Westminster	193D	80234	11800-11899	
	Westminster	163M	80234	13500-13599	
VALLEJO ST S	Denver	283Z	80223	500-699	
	Denver	313D	80223	700-2099	
	Englewood	313R	80110	2100-2299	
	Englewood	313V	80110	2700-3099	
VALLEY AVE	Lochbuie	729Z	80603	200-399	
VALLEY CIR	Jefferson Co	368C	80465	6300-6799	
VALLEY DR	Castle Rock	498J	80104	400-498	E
	Castle Rock	498J	80104	501-599	O
	Castle Rock	498N	80104	None	

STREET NAME	CITY or COUNTY	MAP GRID	ZIP CODE	BLOCK RANGE	O/E
VALLEY DR	Frederick	727A	80516	None	
VALLEY DR	Jefferson Co	336C	80439	3600-3899	
	Jefferson Co	338X	80465	6100-6799	
VALLEY DR N	Mead	706H	80504	4000-4199	
VALLEY DR S	Castle Rock	498J	80104	2-198	E
	Castle Rock	498J	80104	200-299	
VALLEY DR S	Jefferson Co	368C	80465	6100-6899	
VALLEY DR S	Mead	706H	80504	3900-4199	
VALLEY HWY S	Centennial	377J	80112	7801-7899	O
	Denver	315R	80222	2100-2699	
	Douglas Co	377T	80112	7800-8599	
	Douglas Co	407B	80112	9300-9899	
VALLEY LN	Boulder Co	723E	80302	1-6499	
	Boulder Co	99S	80301	None	
VALLEY LN	Jefferson Co	338X	80465	6200-6499	
VALLEY PKWY	Jefferson Co	370K	80127	1-199	
VALLEY RD	Boulder Co	741J	80466	1-199	
VALLEY RD	Douglas Co	406U	80124	500-10699	
VALLEY RD	Jefferson Co	306F	80439	900-1199	
VALLEY RD	Jefferson Co	369N	80465	19300-19599	
VALLEY RD S	Jefferson Co	370V	80127	1-199	
VALLEY RD S	Palmer Lake	907Q	80133	1-299	
VALLEY WAY	Bennett	793Y	80102	400-499	
VALLEYBROOK CIR	Highlands Ranch	405Q	80130	10800-11199	
VALLEYBROOK CT	Highlands Ranch	405Q	80130	10700-10899	
VALLEYBROOK DR	Highlands Ranch	405Q	80130	4400-4699	
VALLEY CREEK RD	Jefferson Co	278W	80401	23100-23399	
VALLEYHEAD CT S	Aurora	381M	80016	7600-7699	
VALLEYHEAD WAY S	Aurora	381M	80016	7700-7999	
	Aurora	381R	80016	8000-8099	
VALLEY HI CT N	Douglas Co	379P	80138	13800-13999	
VALLEY HI DR E	Douglas Co	379T	80138	5500-5999	
VALLEY HI RD	Douglas Co	886C	80118	6000-6399	
VALLEY HIGH RD	Jefferson Co	368W	80465	22800-23399	
VALLEY OAK CT	Castle Rock	498S	80104	None	
VALLEY OAK RD	Castle Rock	498S	80104	None	
VALLEY PARK BLVD W	Douglas Co	887T	80118	2000-3599	
VALLEY PARK DR W	Douglas Co	887T	80118	2000-3299	
VALLEY VEW CT	Elbert Co	851M	80107	40500-41999	
VALLEY VIEW	Nederland	740R	80466	None	
VALLEYVIEW AVE E	Centennial	378A	80111	None	
VALLEYVIEW AVE W	Littleton	374B	80120	400-799	
VALLEY VIEW CT	Golden	248Y	80403	1500-1599	
VALLEY VIEW DR	Adams Co	223M	80221	2000-2199	
	Adams Co	223L	80221	2400-7999	
VALLEYVIEW DR	Boulder	97Y	80304	300-599	
VALLEY VIEW DR	Clear Creek Co	801A	80452	1-399	
VALLEY VIEW DR	Douglas Co	866J	80135	1200-1499	
VALLEY VIEW DR	Jefferson Co	335F	80439	33400-33699	
VALLEY VIEW DR	Lochbuie	729Z	80603	None	
VALLEY VIEW DR W	Douglas Co	907G	80133	1100-1399	
VALLEY VIEW LN	Clear Creek Co	304R	80439	1-299	
VALLEY VIEW LN	Park Co	841D	80470	1-299	
VALLEY VIEW RD	Jefferson Co	336Q	80439	28900-29499	
VALLEY VIEW RD	Park Co	840D	80421	1-299	
VALLEY VIEW RD N	Castle Rock	498F	80108	1500-1598	E
VALLEYVIEW ST S	Littleton	344X	80120	6000-6299	
VALLEY VIEW WAY	Boulder Co	97E	80304	1-199	
VALLEY VISTA AVE	Firestone	707P	80504	6000-6299	
VALLEY VISTA DR	Federal Heights	224A	80260	None	
VALLEY VISTA DR W	Douglas Co	496W	80109	1800-1999	
VALLEY VISTA LN	Boulder Co	722L	80302	1-299	
VALMONT RD	Boulder	98T	80304	2300-2799	
	Boulder	98T	80301	2800-5599	
	Boulder Co	99U	80301	5600-6999	
	Boulder Co	100S	80301	7000-9099	
	Boulder Co	101N	80301	9100-9499	
VALTEC CT	Boulder	129D	80301	7100-7299	
VALTEC LN	Boulder	129D	80301	1600-1999	
VAN BIBBER CT	Jefferson Co	249E	80403	None	
VAN BIBBER ST	Jefferson Co	249A	80403	None	
VAN BUREN CT	Louisville	130Z	80027	300-399	
VAN BUREN WAY	Aurora	289E	80011	1600-1999	
VANCE CT	Jefferson Co	192T	80021	9400-9599	
	Westminster	192X	80021	9200-9299	
VANCE CT S	Jefferson Co	372F	80128	7200-7299	
	Jefferson Co	372K	80128	7800-7899	
	Jefferson Co	372P	80128	7900-8099	
	Lakewood	282T	80226	1-199	
VANCE DR	Arvada	222K	80003	7600-8199	
VANCE ST	Arvada	252F	80002	5200-5599	
	Arvada	252B	80003	5800-5999	
	Arvada	222X	80003	6200-6399	
	Arvada	222T	80003	6800-6999	
	Arvada	222P	80003	7200-7599	
	Broomfield	192B	80020	11800-11999	
	Lakewood	282T	80226	100-199	
	Lakewood	282P	80226	300-599	
	Lakewood	282P	80214	700-899	
	Lakewood	282K	80214	1000-1499	
	Lakewood	282F	80214	1500-2099	
	Lakewood	282B	80214	2100-2499	
	Westminster	222B	80021	9000-9099	
	Westminster	192X	80021	9100-9199	
	Wheat Ridge	252X	80033	2700-3299	
	Wheat Ridge	252T	80033	3700-3799	
	Wheat Ridge	252P	80033	4400-4699	
VANCE ST S	Jefferson Co	372B	80123	6400-6699	
	Jefferson Co	372F	80128	7200-7399	
	Jefferson Co	372K	80128	7400-7499	
	Jefferson Co	372P	80128	7900-8099	
	Lakewood	282X	80226	200-699	
	Lakewood	312B	80226	700-1099	
	Lakewood	312F	80232	1200-1399	
	Lakewood	312X	80227	3200-3399	
	Lakewood	312X	80227	3400-3499	
	Lakewood	342B	80235	3500-3599	
	Lakewood	342B	80235	6400-6699	
VANCE WAY S	Denver	312T	80227	2700-2899	
VANCOUVER CT S	Lakewood	311E	80228	1400-1499	
	Lakewood	311J	80228	1700-1899	
VANCOUVER ST S	Lakewood	311J	80228	1700-1799	
VANCOUVER WAY S	Lakewood	311E	80228	1100-1199	
VANDERHOOF CT S	Arapahoe Co	813G	80136	1600-1899	
VANDERHOOF ST	Adams Co	793L	80102	None	
VANDEVENTOR DR W	Jefferson Co	371Z	80128	9100-9899	
VANDEVENTOR LN W	Jefferson Co	371Y	80128	None	
VANDRIVER ST	Denver	770T	80249	7600-7698	E

STREET NAME	CITY or COUNTY	MAP GRID	ZIP CODE	BLOCK RANGE	O/E
VAN DYKE WAY S	Lakewood	311J	80228	1400-1799	
VAN GORDON CT	Arvada	221W	80004	6500-6699	
	Arvada	221S	80004	7000-7099	
	Arvada	221E	80005	8500-8599	
	Lakewood	281N	80401	700-799	
VAN GORDON CT S	Jefferson Co	341J	80465	4600-4699	
	Jefferson Co	341S	80127	None	
	Lakewood	311A	80228	600-1299	
	Lakewood	311J	80228	1500-1899	
VAN GORDON DR	Lakewood	281A	80215	2600-2699	
VAN GORDON LN S	Jefferson Co	341S	80127	None	
VAN GORDON ST	Arvada	251A	80004	5800-6199	
	Arvada	221S	80004	6700-7199	
	Arvada	221E	80005	None	
	Lakewood	281S	80228	1-599	
	Lakewood	281N	80401	800-1299	
	Lakewood	281A	80215	2300-2599	
	Wheat Ridge	251N	80033	4300-4399	
	Wheat Ridge	251J	80033	4800-4999	
VAN GORDON ST S	Jefferson Co	341N	80465	4900-4999	
	Jefferson Co	341N	80127	5100-5199	
	Jefferson Co	341S	80127	5500-5599	
	Jefferson Co	341W	80127	5900-6099	
	Jefferson Co	341S	80127	None	
	Lakewood	281S	80228	1-199	
	Lakewood	311J	80228	1700-1999	
VAN GORDON WAY	Jefferson Co	191J	80021	10600-10699	
VAN GORDON WAY S	Jefferson Co	341E	80465	4300-4599	
	Jefferson Co	341S	80127	5500-5599	
	Jefferson Co	341W	80127	6100-6299	
	Jefferson Co	371A	80127	6300-6399	
	Jefferson Co	341S	80127	None	
VANGUARD DR	Adams Co	224E	80221	8100-8299	
VANTAGE	Elbert Co	870L	80107	None	
VANTAGE DR	Weld Co	730S	80642	3000-3299	
VAN VOORHIS WAY	Arvada	252B	80004	None	
VAQUERO DR	Boulder Co	130N	80303	1-299	
VARDA CIR	Douglas Co	466N	80109	3301-3399	O
VARESE LN	Northglenn	193M	80234	10400-10799	
VASEEN CT	Jefferson Co	842C	80433	12000-12199	
VASQUEZ BLVD	Commerce City	255G	80022	5300-5599	
	Denver	255K	80216	4700-5299	
VASQUEZ BLVD	Platteville	708C	80651	400-1299	
VASQUEZ ST	Golden	249W	80401	None	
VASSAR AVE E	Arapahoe Co	315R	80222	4800-5199	
	Arapahoe Co	316S	80222	5500-5599	
	Arapahoe Co	316V	80231	8900-9299	
	Aurora	318R	80013	16100-16499	
	Aurora	319N	80013	17100-17399	
	Aurora	319R	80013	19700-20099	
	Aurora	319R	80013	None	
	Denver	314Q	80210	1-799	
	Denver	314R	80210	1200-1699	
	Denver	315P	80210	1700-3699	
	Denver	315U	80222	4300-4699	
	Denver	316N	80222	6200-6399	
	Denver	316P	80224	6600-6999	
VASSAR AVE W	Denver	314P	80223	1-399	
	Denver	313N	80219	2400-5199	
	Englewood	313R	80110	2001-2399	O
	Jefferson Co	311S	80228	12700-12799	
	Lakewood	312P	80227	7100-7599	
	Lakewood	311V	80227	9600-9799	
VASSAR CIR	Boulder	128N	80305	1900-1999	
VASSAR CT	Longmont	10V	80503	1-99	
	Longmont	10Z	80503	1200-1299	
VASSAR DR	Boulder	128N	80305	1900-3099	
VASSAR DR E	Arapahoe Co	316Q	80231	7900-8199	
	Arapahoe Co	316U	80231	None	
	Aurora	317Q	80014	10800-11599	
	Aurora	317R	80014	12100-12999	
	Aurora	319Q	80013	18500-19699	
	Denver	317N	80231	9800-9898	E
VASSAR DR W	Jefferson Co	311U	80227	10500-10699	
	Lakewood	312S	80227	8300-8599	
	Lakewood	310T	80228	14600-14699	
VASSAR LN E	Arapahoe Co	315R	80222	4800-5099	
VASSAR PL E	Aurora	319P	80013	18100-18199	
	Aurora	321N	80018	None	
VASSAR PL W	Jefferson Co	311U	80227	10600-10699	
	Jefferson Co	310V	80228	13000-13099	
	Lakewood	311U	80227	10000-10099	
	Lakewood	310S	80228	16400-16699	
VASSAR WAY W	Lakewood	312V	80227	5800-6899	
	Lakewood	311U	80227	9800-9999	
VAUGHN CIR S	Aurora	317H	80112	1400-1599	
VAUGHN CT	Commerce City	197M	80022	10500-10599	
VAUGHN CT S	Arapahoe Co	378J	80112	7600-7699	
	Aurora	318J	80012	1600-1699	
VAUGHN PL S	Aurora	317V	80014	None	
VAUGHN ST	Aurora	288S	80011	200-699	
	Aurora	288J	80011	700-1299	
	Aurora	288J	80011	1300-1499	
	Aurora	258W	80011	3000-3299	
	Commerce City	197M	80022	10400-10599	
	Commerce City	198J	80022	None	
	Commerce City	768G	80022	None	
	Denver	258E	80239	5100-5599	
VAUGHN ST S	Arapahoe Co	378A	80111	13200-13499	
	Arapahoe Co	378A	80111	None	
	Aurora	318J	80012	1600-1699	
VAUGHN WAY	Aurora	288E	80045	1600-1699	
	Commerce City	198J	80022	10400-10699	
	Denver	258J	80239	5000-5099	
VAUGHN WAY S	Aurora	288W	80012	300-499	
	Aurora	317R	80014	1900-3199	
VELVET ASH	Jefferson Co	306W	80439	3300-3399	
VENABLE CREEK ST	Parker	439C	80134	None	
VENETO CT	Highlands Ranch	375X	80126	2900-3099	
VENICE AVE	Firestone	727B	80504	None	
VENICE LN	Longmont	40Q	80503	1400-1499	
VENICE ST	Longmont	11Y	80501	900-1499	
VENNEFORD RANCH RD					
	Highlands Ranch	375W	80126	8700-9999	
VENNEFORD RANCH RD S					
	Highlands Ranch	405A	80126	9200-9999	
VENTANA ST	Parker	439B	80134	12700-12999	

U V

STREET NAME	CITY or COUNTY	MAP GRID	ZIP CODE	BLOCK RANGE	O/E
VENTANA MESA CIR					
	Castle Pines North	436A	80108	12400-12599	
VENTANA MESA CT	Castle Pines North	436A	80108	12400-12499	
VENTURA CIR S	Aurora	319F	80017	1100-1299	
VENTURA CT	Weld Co	139K	80601	16400-16599	
VENTURA CT S	Arapahoe Co	349X	80016	6000-6099	
	Arapahoe Co	349X	80016	6100-6199	
	Arapahoe Co	379B	80016	6500-6599	
	Aurora	319B	80017	900-999	
	Aurora	349K	80015	5000-5099	
	Centennial	349P	80015	5300-5399	
	Centennial	349P	80015	5400-5499	
	Centennial	349T	80015	5600-5699	
	Centennial	379K	80016	7800-7899	
VENTURA DR	Commerce City	769J	80022	None	
	Commerce City	769N	80022	None	
VENTURA ST	Aurora	289P	80011	600-899	
	Commerce City	769E	80022	None	
	Commerce City	769E	80022	None	
	Commerce City	769E	80022	None	
	Commerce City	769J	80022	None	
	Commerce City	769N	80022	None	
	Commerce City	169X	80603	None	
VENTURA ST	Commerce City	769J	80022	None	
VENTURA ST S	Aurora	319B	80017	900-999	
	Aurora	319F	80017	1400-1599	
	Aurora	319K	80017	1800-1899	
	Aurora	319K	80013	2000-2299	
	Aurora	319T	80013	2700-3499	
	Aurora	349B	80013	3800-3899	
	Aurora	349K	80015	5000-5099	
VENTURA WAY S	Aurora	319B	80017	900-1099	
	Aurora	349B	80013	3500-3799	
	Centennial	349P	80015	5100-5299	
VENUS CT	Highlands Ranch	376U	80124	400-499	
VENUS RD	Gilpin Co	761J	80403	1-299	
VERA LN	Jefferson Co	366A	80439	6400-6599	
VERA MARIE LN	Gilpin Co	740Z	80474	None	
VERANO AVE	Palmer Lake	907Q	80133	None	
VERBENA CIR	Douglas Co	887F	80118	2600-2799	
VERBENA CIR S	Centennial	376H	80112	7000-7099	
VERBENA CT	Adams Co	136Y	80602	14700-14799	
	Frederick	726G	80516	None	
	Thornton	136U	80602	None	
VERBENA CT S	Denver	316Z	80231	3300-3399	
VERBENA DR	Douglas Co	887F	80118	2700-2899	
VERBENA ST	Adams Co	226C	80022	8600-8699	
	Adams Co	166U	80602	12400-12699	
	Adams Co	136Q	80602	16000-16299	
	Commerce City	226C	80022	8700-8799	
	Denver	286L	80220	1100-1999	
	Denver	256Q	80238	None	
	Denver	286C	80238	None	
	Thornton	166Q	80602	8100-12999	
	Thornton	136Y	80602	14900-14999	
VERBENA ST S	Denver	316Y	80237	3601-3699	O
	Denver	346H	80237	4100-4599	
VERBENA WAY S	Centennial	376H	80112	7100-7299	
	Denver	316U	80231	2900-2999	
VERDANT CIR	Longmont	12X	80501	400-499	
VERDI DR	Gilpin Co	761J	80403	1-399	
VERDIGRIS ST	Douglas Co	408G	80134	None	
VERDOS DR	Elbert Co	850U	80107	300-999	
VERMEJO PEAK	Jefferson Co	371Q	80127	8000-8099	
VERMILLION CT	Douglas Co	466L	80108	5000-5099	
VERMILLION DR	Douglas Co	466G	80108	500-5099	
VERMILLION DR W	Jefferson Co	341L	80127	10300-10599	
VERMILLION LN	Douglas Co	466G	80108	5000-5099	
VERMILLION RD	Boulder Co	10H	80503	8700-9299	
	Boulder Co	11E	80503	9300-9499	
	Boulder Co	11G	80504	9500-10899	
	Boulder Co	12G	80504	10900-12699	
VERMILLION WAY	Broomfield	133N	80020	15900-15999	
VERMILLION TRAIL	Boulder Co	12C	80504	13400-13699	
VERNA LN	Northglenn	194K	80234	10800-10999	
VERNIER CT	Lafayette	131L	80026	400-599	
VERNON DR	Golden	279B	80401	2100-2299	
VERNON LN	Superior	160Q	80027	1700-1899	
VERNON ST	Golden	279B	80401	None	
VERNON WAY	Parker	409N	80134	11300-11399	
VERONICA RD	Douglas Co	887B	80118	2200-2399	
VERSAILLES CT S	Aurora	350Y	80016	6400-6499	
	Aurora	380C	80016	6500-6599	
VERSAILLES PKWY S	Arapahoe Co	350U	80015	5400-6099	
VERSAILLES ST	Lochbuie	140G	80603	100-299	
VERSAILLES ST S	Arapahoe Co	350Q	80015	5100-5199	
	Arapahoe Co	350U	80015	5400-5999	
	Aurora	380G	80016	7000-7199	
VERSAILLES WAY S	Arapahoe Co	350Q	80015	5400-5499	
	Aurora	380G	80016	7100-7199	
	Aurora	380C	80016	None	
VESTA CIR	Lafayette	131Q	80026	1300-1399	
VESTAL LOOP	Broomfield	133K	80020	3400-3699	
VESTAL RD	Boulder Co	703D	80503	None	
VESUVIUS RD	Jefferson Co	367C	80439	6400-6599	
VETCH CIR	Lafayette	131H	80026	900-999	
VIA APPIA WAY	Louisville	130U	80027	500-999	
VIA CAPRI	Louisville	130R	80027	None	
VIA DE LOS PINONS	Castle Rock	467R	80104	1600-1999	
VIAGGIO WAY	Highlands Ranch	405B	80126	9100-9499	
VIALPANDO ST	Brighton	139K	80601	None	
VIA MARGARITA	Douglas Co	466N	80109	3200-3298	E
VIA ROMA	Louisville	130R	80027	None	
	Broomfield	161K	80020	13400-13699	
	Louisville	161K	80020	1600-2499	
VIA VERDE LN	El Paso Co	908Q	80132	19600-19799	
VICTOR DR	Weld Co	706P	80504	11600-11799	
VICTOR ST	Aurora	288S	80011	200-399	
	Aurora	288J	80011	700-1299	
	Aurora	288E	80011	1400-1499	
	Aurora	288E	80045	1600-1699	
	Aurora	288E	80010	1900-2098	E
	Aurora	288E	80045	2000-2298	E
	Aurora	258W	80011	3000-3199	
	Commerce City	198J	80022	10400-10599	
	Denver	258E	80239	5500-5599	
VICTOR ST	Douglas Co	847N	80135	5000-5599	
VICTOR ST S	Aurora	288W	80012	300-599	
	Aurora	318E	80012	1200-1399	
	Aurora	318E	80012	1600-1699	
	Aurora	318J	80014	2100-2199	
	Aurora	318N	80014	2400-2599	
	Aurora	317V	80014	2700-2799	
VICTOR WAY	Aurora	288E	80045	1600-1699	
	Denver	258J	80239	5000-5299	
VICTOR WAY S	Aurora	318A	80012	500-1099	
VICTORIA CT	Lafayette	131K	80026	700-799	
VICTORIA DR W	Jefferson Co	371Z	80128	9500-9899	
VICTORIA LN	Douglas Co	440Y	80134	8900-8999	
VICTORIA PL W	Jefferson Co	371Y	80128	None	
VICTORIA RD	Park Co	842A	80470	1-199	
VICTORIAN CIR	Parker	409R	80138	None	
	Parker	409Q	80138	None	
VICTORIAN DR	Parker	409R	80138	10700-10899	
VICTORIAN WAY	Parker	409R	80138	19800-19999	
VICTORY WAY	Commerce City	256C	80216	None	
VIENNA DR	Elbert Co	850G	80138	100-899	
VIEW CT	Mead	707B	80542	100-199	
VIEW DR	Golden	279P	80401	1-99	
VIEW ST	Douglas Co	846G	80125	7700-7899	
VIEWPOINT AVE	Firestone	707P	80504	6000-6199	
VIEWPOINT DR	Lakewood	281J	80401	12100-12399	
VIEW POINT RD	Boulder	128W	80305	1700-1899	
VIEWPOINT RD	Lakewood	281E	80215	1500-1799	
VIEWPOINT WAY	Boulder Co	101M	80026	3800-3999	
VIEWPOINTE	Elbert Co	870M	80107	None	
VIEWRIDGE CT	Bennett	793K	80102	1-199	
VIEWRIDGE DR	Bennett	793K	80102	None	
VIEW RIDGE DR	Elbert Co	850Y	80107	36400-36999	
VIEWRIDGE RD	Bennett	793K	80102	1100-1399	
VIGILANTE AVE	Park Co	841A	80421	1-2699	
	Park Co	840D	80421	None	
VIKI CIR	Elbert Co	830R	80138	None	
VIKING CT	Erie	133B	80516	200-299	
VIKING DR	Cherry Hills Village	344M	80113	1-99	
VILAS CT S	Superior	160R	80027	1500-1699	
VILLA DR	Douglas Co	848E	80108	400-699	
VILLAGE CIR	Commerce City	168Y	80603	None	
VILLAGE CIR	Douglas Co	432Q	80125	7300E-7999E	
	Douglas Co	432P	80125	7900W-8099W	
VILLAGE CIR	Jefferson Co	277U	80401	25100-25999	
VILLAGE CT	Columbine Valley	343X	80123	1-99	
VILLAGE DR	Columbine Valley	343X	80123	1-99	
VILLAGE DR	Fort Lupton	728H	80621	900-1299	
VILLAGE DR E	Brighton	139N	80601	None	
VILLAGE DR W	Brighton	139N	80601	None	
VILLAGE LN	Broomfield	134F	80516	None	
VILLAGE LN	Longmont	41A	80503	2301-2399	O
VILLAGE PKWY	Lakewood	281M	80215	9200-9399	
VILLAGE RD	Cherry Hills Village	345F	80113	1-99	
VILLAGE RD N	Douglas Co	440M	80134	6400-7999	
VILLAGE WAY S	Greenwood Village	345T	80121	5800-5899	
VILLAGE CENTER DR	Douglas Co	409E	80134	16800-16999	
VILLAGE CREEK PKWY	Douglas Co	409H	80138	None	
VILLAGE PINES CIR	Douglas Co	869D	80116	8900-8999	
VILLAGE RIDGE POINT	El Paso Co	908X	80132	None	
VILLAGE SQUARE	Erie	102H	80516	None	
VILLAGE SQUARE DR	Douglas Co	848E	80108	7000-7599	
VILLAGE SQUARE LN	Douglas Co	848E	80108	300-399	
VILLAGE SQUARE TERRACE					
	Douglas Co	848E	80108	7200-7298	E
VILLA GROVE	Monument	908X	80132	1201-1399	O
VILLANOVA CIR E	Aurora	319S	80013	16800-16899	
VILLANOVA CT	Longmont	10Z	80503	2700-2799	
VILLANOVA DR E	Aurora	317V	80014	12100-12999	
	Aurora	319R	80013	19600-19799	
	Aurora	321N	80018	None	
VILLANOVA PL E	Arapahoe Co	316P	80231	7300-7499	
	Aurora	318T	80014	14300-14399	
	Aurora	318R	80013	16200-16599	
	Aurora	319S	80013	17400-17699	
	Aurora	319R	80013	18900-20099	
	Aurora	319R	80013	None	
	Denver	316T	80224	6600-6999	
VILLARD CT N	Douglas Co	441W	80134	5800-6099	
VILLAS ST	Parker	409N	80134	11200-11299	
VILLASUR CT E	Douglas Co	441S	80134	9700-9799	
VINCA	Jefferson Co	370L	80127	1-99	
VINCA PL	Superior	160Z	80027	1400-1499	
VINCENNES CT S	Denver	346G	80237	3900-4199	
VINCENNES WAY S	Centennial	376Q	80112	7900-7999	
	Denver	316U	80231	2800-2899	
VINCA CT	Boulder	98J	80304	4200-4399	
VINDALOO DR	Castle Rock	466V	80109	None	
VINE CIR S	Centennial	375E	80122	7100E-7299E	
	Centennial	375E	80122	7100W-7199W	
VINE CT	Adams Co	225W	80229	6500-6599	
	Thornton	195S	80229	9800-9999	
	Thornton	195N	80229	10000-10199	
	Thornton	195N	80229	10200-10299	
	Thornton	164R	80241	13100-13199	
VINE CT S	Centennial	345W	80121	6300-6499	
	Centennial	375E	80122	7200-7299	
	Centennial	375N	80122	7900-7999	
	Englewood	315W	80113	3100-3199	
VINE PL	Adams Co	225E	80229	8300-8399	
VINE PL	Boulder	98J	80304	2400-2599	
VINE PL	Thornton	195T	80229	2500-2599	
VINE ST	Adams Co	225E	80229	8200-8399	
	Denver	285S	80206	100-399	
	Denver	285E	80206	600-1999	
	Denver	285A	80205	2000-2699	
	Denver	255W	80205	2700-3799	
	Denver	255N	80216	4300-4799	
VINE ST	Fort Lupton	728H	80621	1000-1199	
VINE ST	Jefferson Co	339G	80465	3900-4099	
VINE ST	Thornton	225A	80229	8900-8999	
	Thornton	195W	80229	9100-9399	
	Thornton	195S	80229	9500-9699	
	Thornton	195S	80229	9800-9999	
	Thornton	195N	80229	10000-10099	
	Thornton	165N	80241	12800-12999	
	Thornton	165J	80241	13400-13599	
	Thornton	135W	80602	14900-14999	
	Thornton	165A	80602	None	
VINE ST S	Centennial	375A	80121	6500-6699	
	Centennial	375E	80122	7100-7299	
	Centennial	375J	80122	7500-7899	
	Cherry Hills Village	345N	80110	4800-4999	
	Denver	285W	80209	300-699	
	Denver	315A	80209	700-1099	
	Denver	315E	80210	1100-1599	
	Denver	315S	80210	2100-3099	
	Englewood	315W	80113	3100-3199	
	Greenwood Village	345S	80121	5900-5999	
VINE WAY S	Centennial	375N	80122	8000-8099	
	Cherry Hills Village	345J	80113	4400-4699	
VINEGAROON WAY N	Douglas Co	441F	80138	8000-8599	
VINELAND DR	Parker	409N	80134	17000-17099	
VINE WOOD CT E	Highlands Ranch	404C	80126	500-599	
VINEWOOD ST	Littleton	343Z	80120	6000-6199	
VINEWOOD ST S	Littleton	343Y	80120	6001-6499	O
VINEYARD DR	Castle Rock	498N	80104	1900-2299	
VINEYARD PL	Boulder	98E	80304	2200-2499	
VINTAGE PL	Douglas Co	436T	80108	1000-1099	
VIOLA LN E	Parker	439E	80134	None	
VIOLA ST	Palmer Lake	907Q	80133	None	
VIOLA ST S	Parker	439E	80134	None	
VIOLET AVE	Boulder	97H	80304	900-2599	
VIOLET CT	Arvada	219Y	80403	6300-6399	
	Arvada	219L	80007	None	
	Arvada	219Q	80007	None	
VIOLET PL	Arvada	249C	80403	6000-6199	
VIOLET ST	Golden	279Q	80401	400-599	
	Golden	279G	80401	1600-1699	
VIOLET WAY	Arvada	219Y	80007	None	
	Arvada	249C	80403	None	
VIREO CT	Longmont	42C	80501	801-899	O
VIRGIL CT	Arvada	219L	80007	None	
	Arvada	219Q	80007	None	
VIRGIL CT	Jefferson Co	249C	80403	5800-5999	
VIRGIL ST	Arvada	249C	80403	6000-6299	
	Jefferson Co	249Y	80401	3200-3399	
VIRGIL WAY	Arvada	219Y	80007	None	
	Arvada	219Y	80403	None	
VIRGINIA AVE	Palmer Lake	907U	80133	None	
VIRGINIA AVE E	Aurora	287X	80012	10500-10899	
	Denver	284Y	80209	1-1699	
	Denver	285W	80209	1700-2399	
	Denver	285X	80209	3200-3699	
	Denver	286W	80224	5800-7299	
	Denver	287X	80231	10100-10499	
	Glendale	285Y	80246	4000-4999	
VIRGINIA AVE W	Denver	284W	80223	1100-1999	
	Denver	283Z	80223	2000-2499	
	Denver	283Y	80219	2500-3599	
	Denver	283X	80219	3800-5199	
	Denver	284X	80223	None	
	Lakewood	282Z	80226	5200-5999	
	Lakewood	282Y	80226	6100-6799	
	Lakewood	282X	80226	7000-7799	
	Lakewood	282W	80226	8100-8899	
	Lakewood	281Y	80226	10000-10699	
	Lakewood	281X	80226	10800-11599	
	Lakewood	281X	80228	11600-12099	
	Lakewood	281W	80228	12300-12499	
	Lakewood	280Z	80228	12500-12799	
VIRGINIA CIR W	Lakewood	281Z	80226	9200-9699	
VIRGINIA CT E	Aurora	287Z	80012	None	
VIRGINIA DR	Park Co	841S	80421	None	
VIRGINIA DR E	Aurora	287Y	80012	11200-12399	
VIRGINIA DR W	Lakewood	281Z	80226	9200-9799	
	Lakewood	281W	80228	12000-12099	
	Lakewood	280Y	80228	13000-14099	
VIRGINIA PL E	Arapahoe Co	794X	80136	56000-56799	
	Aurora	287Y	80012	11200-11299	
	Aurora	287Y	80012	11500-12499	
	Aurora	287Z	80012	12800-13099	
VIRGINIA PL W	Lakewood	282Y	80226	6900-7099	
	Lakewood	281Z	80226	9200-9299	
	Lakewood	281W	80228	12000-12099	
VIRGINIA ST	Golden	248R	80403	600-699	
VIRGINIA ST	Idaho Springs	780Q	80452	1-2399	
VIRGINIA CANYON RD	Clear Creek Co	780L	80452	None	
VIRGINIA CANYON RD	Gilpin Co	780F	80403	1-1199	
VIRGO CT	Highlands Ranch	376U	80124	13400-13499	
VIRGO DR	Highlands Ranch	376U	80124	13300-13599	
VIRIDIAN DR	Castle Rock	466V	80109	None	
VISCOUNT CT	El Paso Co	908Z	80132	17000-17099	
VISIONARY TRAIL	Jefferson Co	307D	80401	800-899	
VISTA AVE	Jefferson Co	278U	80401	400-499	
VISTA AVE	Lochbuie	729Z	80603	None	
VISTA BLVD	Lochbuie	729Z	80603	100-599	
VISTA CIR	Parker	410N	80138	20300-20399	
VISTA DR	Boulder	97V	80304	1900-3399	
VISTA DR	Castle Rock	497G	80104	400-599	
VISTA DR	Jefferson Co	335R	80439	31700-32099	
VISTA DR W	Douglas Co	887T	80118	2000-2599	
VISTA LN	Douglas Co	867N	80135	4100-4299	
VISTA LN	Jefferson Co	367A	80439	26800-26899	
	Lakewood	282P	80214	600-799	
VISTA LN	Louisville	130Y	80027	100-199	
VISTA LN	Park Co	841D	80470	1-199	
	Erie	102Z	80516	None	
VISTA PKWY	Erie	103X	80516	None	
	Erie	133B	80516	None	
VISTA RD	Cherry Hills Village	345F	80113	1-99	
VISTA RD	El Paso Co	907V	80132	None	
VISTA RD	Parker	410N	80138	10700-10899	
VISTA CANYON DR	Castle Rock	499J	80104	1-199	
VISTA CANYON LN	Castle Rock	498M	80104	None	
VISTA CANYON PL	Castle Rock	498M	80104	None	
VISTA CLARA LN	El Paso Co	908Q	80132	19800-19999	
VISTA CLIFF CIR	Castle Rock	499J	80104	100-499	
VISTA CLIFF CT	Castle Rock	499J	80104	300-499	
VISTA CLIFF LOOP	Castle Rock	499J	80104	6300-6499	
VISTA LODGE LOOP					
	Castle Pines North	436K	80108	6700-6899	
VISTANCIA CT	Douglas Co	439X	80134	5600-5799	
VISTANCIA DR	Douglas Co	439X	80134	5500-5799	
VISTA RIDGE	Elbert Co	851A	80138	41500-42999	
VISTA VIEW	Elbert Co	870M	80107	None	
VISTA VIEW DR	El Paso Co	907V	80132	18500-18699	

V

STREET NAME	CITY or COUNTY	MAP GRID	ZIP CODE	BLOCK RANGE	O/E
VISTA VIEW DR	Weld Co	**706P**	80504	1500-1899	
VISTA VIEW DR W	Jefferson Co	**371G**	80127	10300-10899	
VISTA VIEW RD	Douglas Co	**867N**	80135	2400-2599	
VITO TRAIL	Jefferson Co	**366M**	80439	7500-7599	
VIVIAN CIR	Arvada	**251E**	80002	5400-5499	
VIVIAN CIR	Boulder	**128H**	80303	1000-1099	
VIVIAN CT	Arvada	**251A**	80004	6000-6199	
	Arvada	**221S**	80004	7000-7199	
	Arvada	**221E**	80005	8500-8599	
	Lakewood	**281N**	80401	700-799	
	Wheat Ridge	**251W**	80033	3300-3799	
VIVIAN CT S	Jefferson Co	**341J**	80465	4600-4799	
	Jefferson Co	**341N**	80465	4900-5099	
	Jefferson Co	**341S**	80127	5500-5599	
	Jefferson Co	**341W**	80127	5900-5999	
	Lakewood	**311A**	80228	900-1099	
	Lakewood	**311J**	80228	1700-1799	
VIVIAN DR	Wheat Ridge	**251W**	80033	3200-3399	
VIVIAN ST	Arvada	**251J**	80002	5200-5399	
	Arvada	**251A**	80004	6000-6199	
	Arvada	**221W**	80004	6500-6699	
	Arvada	**221S**	80004	6700-6899	
	Arvada	**221E**	80005	8300-8399	
	Lakewood	**281N**	80401	700-899	
	Lakewood	**281J**	80401	900-1399	
	Lakewood	**281A**	80215	2400-2699	
VIVIAN ST	Longmont	**41B**	80501	100-899	
	Longmont	**11X**	80501	1100-1399	
	Longmont	**11T**	80501	1500-1699	
	Longmont	**11P**	80501	2100-2299	
VIVIAN ST	Wheat Ridge	**251W**	80215	2900-3199	
	Wheat Ridge	**251N**	80033	4200-4399	
VIVIAN ST S	Jefferson Co	**341E**	80465	4400-4499	
	Jefferson Co	**341J**	80465	4600-4899	
	Jefferson Co	**341N**	80127	5300-5499	
	Jefferson Co	**341W**	80127	5900-6299	
	Jefferson Co	**341S**	80127	None	
	Lakewood	**311E**	80228	800-1199	
	Lakewood	**311J**	80228	1900-1999	
VIVIAN ST S	Longmont	**41P**	80501	1400-1699	
VIVIAN WAY S	Jefferson Co	**341E**	80465	4300-4499	
	Jefferson Co	**341S**	80127	None	
	Lakewood	**311E**	80228	1400-1499	
VOILES DR	Brighton	**138U**	80601	400-699	
VOILES PL	Brighton	**138T**	80601	600-799	
VOILES ST	Brighton	**138T**	80601	400-1399	
VONA CT S	Superior	**160Q**	80027	1500-1599	
VONNIE CLAIRE RD	Jefferson Co	**762B**	80403	11700-11999	
VOORHEES RANCH WAY					
	Douglas Co	**466J**	80109	1400-1599	
VOSLER ST	Jefferson Co	**823N**	80433	25600-26799	
VRAIN CIR	Broomfield	**163S**	80020	12300-12599	
VRAIN CT	Adams Co	**253E**	80212	None	
	Westminster	**193W**	80031	9200-9299	
	Westminster	**193S**	80031	10000-10099	
	Westminster	**193N**	80031	10100-10199	
	Westminster	**193E**	80031	11000-11099	
VRAIN DR	Westminster	**193E**	80031	11200-11299	
VRAIN ST	Adams Co	**223A**	80031	8800-8999	
	Adams Co	**253E**	80212	None	
	Arvada	**253A**	80003	6000-6199	
	Arvada	**223W**	80003	6300-6599	
	Arvada	**223S**	80030	6800-6899	
	Broomfield	**163S**	80020	12500-12799	
	Denver	**283S**	80219	1-399	
	Denver	**283N**	80204	500-999	
	Denver	**283J**	80204	1200-1699	
	Denver	**283A**	80212	2400-2699	
	Denver	**253S**	80212	2700-4599	
	Denver	**253J**	80212	4900-5099	
	Westminster	**223S**	80030	7000-7199	
	Westminster	**223N**	80030	7200-7399	
	Westminster	**193W**	80031	9000-9199	
	Westminster	**193J**	80031	10800-10899	
	Westminster	**193E**	80031	11000-11199	
VRAIN ST S	Denver	**313A**	80219	700-999	
	Denver	**313J**	80219	1100-2099	
	Denver	**313N**	80219	2200-2599	
	Denver	**313S**	80236	2700-3499	
	Denver	**343E**	80236	3500-4699	
VRAIN WAY S	Denver	**313E**	80219	1300-1499	
VULCAN ST	Louisville	**130R**	80027	200-299	

W

STREET NAME	CITY or COUNTY	MAP GRID	ZIP CODE	BLOCK RANGE	O/E
WABASH AVE	Elbert Co	**892N**	80106	None	
WABASH CIR S	Denver	**316V**	80231	2800-2999	
	Denver	**316Z**	80231	3300-3399	
	Thornton	**136Q**	80602	None	
WABASH CT	Thornton	**166R**	80602	None	
WABASH CT S	Centennial	**376M**	80112	7800-8199	
	Denver	**316Z**	80231	3200-3399	
WABASH PL	Adams Co	**166U**	80602	None	
	Thornton	**136U**	80602	None	
WABASH ST	Denver	**286M**	80220	1100-1999	
	Denver	**256Z**	80238	2800-2899	
	Denver	**256Z**	80238	3300-3699	
	Denver	**256L**	80238	4500-4898	E
	Denver	**256R**	80238	None	
	Denver	**286D**	80238	None	
WABASH ST S	Arapahoe Co	**316R**	80231	2100-2599	
	Centennial	**376R**	80112	7900-7999	
	Denver	**316V**	80231	2900-2999	
	Denver	**346D**	80237	3700-3999	
	Denver	**346H**	80237	4000-4099	
	Denver	**346M**	80237	4600-5099	
WABASH WAY	Adams Co	**166C**	80602	14500-14599	
WABASH WAY S	Greenwood Village	**346Z**	80111	6100-6199	
WACO CT	Commerce City	**769E**	80022	None	
WACO CT S	Arapahoe Co	**379B**	80016	6500-6699	
	Aurora	**319K**	80017	1700-1899	
	Aurora	**319K**	80013	2100-2299	
	Aurora	**319P**	80013	2300-2499	
	Aurora	**319X**	80013	3000-3299	
	Aurora	**319X**	80013	None	
	Centennial	**349T**	80015	5500-5699	
WACO DR	Commerce City	**769J**	80022	None	

STREET NAME	CITY or COUNTY	MAP GRID	ZIP CODE	BLOCK RANGE	O/E
WACO ST	Adams Co	**169T**	80022	None	
	Commerce City	**769E**	80022	None	
	Commerce City	**769J**	80022	None	
	Commerce City	**769J**	80022	None	
	Commerce City	**769N**	80022	None	
WACO ST	Weld Co	**139F**	80601	None	
WACO ST N	Aurora	**289P**	80011	600-899	
WACO ST S	Arapahoe Co	**349T**	80016	5900-5999	
	Arapahoe Co	**349X**	80016	6300-6499	
	Aurora	**319B**	80017	1100-1199	
	Aurora	**319K**	80017	1700-1799	
	Aurora	**319K**	80013	2100-2299	
	Aurora	**319T**	80013	2800-3399	
	Aurora	**349B**	80013	3500-3899	
	Aurora	**349K**	80015	4900-4999	
	Centennial	**349P**	80015	5200-5499	
	Centennial	**379K**	80016	7500-7799	
	Foxfield	**379B**	80016	6700-7399	
WACO WAY S	Arapahoe Co	**379B**	80016	6500-6699	
	Aurora	**319B**	80017	900-1099	
	Aurora	**319T**	80013	2700-2899	
	Aurora	**349B**	80013	3500-3699	
WADE RD	Longmont	**40D**	80503	800-899	
WADSWORTH BLVD	Arvada	**252P**	80002	4900-5199	
	Arvada	**252F**	80002	5200-5599	
	Arvada	**252F**	80003	5800-6199	
	Arvada	**222P**	80003	6200-8799	
	Broomfield	**192B**	80020	11300-11599	
	Broomfield	**192B**	80020	11600-11999	
	Lakewood	**282X**	80226	1-599	
	Lakewood	**282P**	80214	600-2799	
	Westminster	**222P**	80021	8800-8999	
	Westminster	**192X**	80021	9200-10099	
	Westminster	**192K**	80021	10100-11299	
	Wheat Ridge	**252P**	80033	2800-4899	
WADSWORTH BLVD S	Denver	**342S**	80123	4300-4899	
	Denver	**342S**	80123	5400-5899	
	Jefferson Co	**372P**	80123	6400-6699	
	Jefferson Co	**372P**	80128	6700-9299	
	Jefferson Co	**825Y**	80127	9400-12299	
	Jefferson Co	**432A**	80127	None	
	Lakewood	**282X**	80226	1-699	
	Lakewood	**312F**	80226	700-1099	
	Lakewood	**312F**	80232	1100-1899	
	Lakewood	**312T**	80227	1900-3499	
	Lakewood	**342F**	80235	3500-4299	
	Lakewood	**342K**	80123	4800-5099	
	Lakewood	**342S**	80123	5100-5399	
	Lakewood	**342S**	80123	5900-6399	
WADSWORTH CIR	Longmont	**42A**	80501	200-399	
WADSWORTH CIR S	Lakewood	**312P**	80227	2601-2699	O
WADSWORTH CT	Longmont	**42E**	80501	300-399	
WADSWORTH CT S	Jefferson Co	**372F**	80128	6800-6999	
	Jefferson Co	**372K**	80128	7500-7599	
	Jefferson Co	**372T**	80128	8300-8999	
	Lakewood	**312T**	80227	2500-2599	
WADSWORTH PKWY	Broomfield	**192E**	80021	None	
	Jefferson Co	**192J**	80021	11300-11599	
	Westminster	**192J**	80021	9100-11299	
WADSWORTH WAY S	Denver	**342K**	80123	4300-5099	
WADSWORTH WAY S	Jefferson Co	**372K**	80128	7800-7899	
	Lakewood	**312T**	80227	2500-2699	
WADSWORTH BLVD SERVICE RD S					
	Lakewood	**312K**	80232	1500-1899	
WADSWORTH BY-PASS	Arvada	**252F**	80003	5200-6199	
	Arvada	**252F**	80003	6200-6599	
WAGNER CIR	Boulder Co	**722R**	80304	1-99	
WAGNER CT	Highlands Ranch	**375Y**	80126	8800-8899	
WAGNER DR	Adams Co	**223E**	80031	4100-4499	
	Adams Co	**223A**	80031	8400-8799	
WAGNER LN	Adams Co	**223A**	80031	8800-8899	
	Westminster	**193S**	80031	9900-9999	
WAGNER ST	Adams Co	**794P**	80136	1200-1899	
	Adams Co	**794K**	80136	2800-3899	
	Adams Co	**223A**	80031	8800-8999	
WAGON CT	Parker	**408R**	80134	16300-16399	
WAGON PL	Parker	**408R**	80134	16400-16499	
WAGON WAY	Mead	**706G**	80542	None	
WAGON BOX CIR	Highlands Ranch	**405M**	80130	None	
WAGON BOX PL	Highlands Ranch	**405M**	80130	None	
WAGON BOX WAY	Highlands Ranch	**405M**	80130	None	
WAGON TONGUE RD	Park Co	**841B**	80421	1-599	
WAGON TONGUE WAY	Jefferson Co	**368R**	80465	20700-20799	
WAGON TRAIL	Jefferson Co	**822Z**	80433	11700-11799	
WAGONTRAIL AVE E	Aurora	**351E**	80016	24100-24599	
	Aurora	**350H**	80016	None	
WAGON TRAIL CIR E	Aurora	**349K**	80015	17600-19199	
WAGON TRAIL CIR W	Denver	**341M**	80123	9300-9499	
WAGONTRAIL CT	Douglas Co	**469F**	80134	4800-4999	
WAGON TRAIL DR E	Aurora	**348K**	80015	14400-15099	
	Aurora	**348M**	80015	16200-16599	
	Centennial	**349M**	80015	19700-20099	
WAGON TRAIL DR W	Bow Mar	**343J**	80123	4500-5199	
	Denver	**343K**	80123	3600-4499	
	Denver	**341M**	80123	9000-9999	
WAGON TRAIL LN E	Centennial	**349M**	80015	20000-20099	
WAGON TRAIL PKWY E	Aurora	**349J**	80015	16900-17399	
WAGON TRAIL PL E	Aurora	**348K**	80015	14400-15099	
	Centennial	**349M**	80015	20000-20099	
WAGON TRAIL RD	Jefferson Co	**306B**	80439	900-999	
WAGON TRAIN CIR	Elbert Co	**870H**	80107	1200-1499	
WAGON WHEEL DR	Brighton	**139G**	80603	15100-15399	
WAGON WHEEL DR	Fort Lupton	**728M**	80621	200-1699	
WAGON WHEEL DR W	Douglas Co	**825V**	80125	9000-9499	
WAGON WHEEL RD	Jefferson Co	**368R**	80465	7900-8299	
WAGON WHEEL WAY E	Douglas Co	**380R**	80138	9000-9399	
WAGONWHEEL GAP RD	Boulder Co	**97A**	80302	1-1699	
WAGON WHEEL TRAIL	Castle Rock	**498G**	80104	300-5799	
WAGON WHEEL TRAIL	Elbert Co	**870G**	80107	34200-34799	
	Elbert Co	**870D**	80107	34800-35399	
WAGON WHEEL TRAIL	Gilpin Co	**761E**	80403	1-199	
WAITE DR	Boulder	**128H**	80303	800-1099	
WAKE ST	Frederick	**727F**	80530	None	
WAKEFIELD AVE	Castle Rock	**498L**	80104	4500-4699	
WAKONDA WAY	El Paso Co	**908N**	80132	2200-19499	
WALDEN AVE W	Jefferson Co	**371M**	80128	9200-9699	
	Jefferson Co	**371L**	80127	9800-9999	
WALDEN CIR	Boulder	**128R**	80305	600-699	

STREET NAME	CITY or COUNTY	MAP GRID	ZIP CODE	BLOCK RANGE	O/E
WALDEN CIR S	Centennial	**349P**	80015	5100-5299	
WALDEN CT	Longmont	**12U**	80501	1300-1399	
WALDEN CT E	Highlands Ranch	**404C**	80126	600-799	
WALDEN CT S	Arapahoe Co	**349X**	80016	6300-6399	
	Aurora	**319F**	80017	1600-1699	
	Aurora	**319T**	80013	2900-2999	
	Aurora	**319X**	80013	None	
	Centennial	**349P**	80015	5400-5499	
	Centennial	**349T**	80015	5800-5899	
WALDEN DR	Commerce City	**769J**	80022	None	
WALDEN DR W	Jefferson Co	**372K**	80128	7100-7399	
WALDEN LN	Cherry Hills Village	**345R**	80121	1-99	
WALDEN LN S	Arapahoe Co	**349X**	80016	6300-6399	
WALDEN PL W	Jefferson Co	**372K**	80128	6800-7299	
WALDEN ST	Adams Co	**169T**	80022	12500-12599	
	Aurora	**259X**	80011	2800-3199	
	Commerce City	**169X**	80603	None	
	Commerce City	**769E**	80022	None	
	Commerce City	**769J**	80022	None	
	Commerce City	**769N**	80022	None	
WALDEN ST	Commerce City	**769J**	80022	None	
WALDEN ST N	Aurora	**289P**	80011	600-799	
WALDEN ST S	Arapahoe Co	**349T**	80016	5900-6099	
	Arapahoe Co	**379B**	80016	6400-6699	
	Aurora	**319B**	80017	900-999	
	Aurora	**319K**	80013	2200-2299	
	Aurora	**319T**	80013	2800-2999	
	Aurora	**349B**	80013	3600-4099	
	Centennial	**349T**	80015	5600-5899	
	Centennial	**349P**	80015	5400-5499	
WALDEN WAY	El Paso Co	**909X**	80908	17400-17999	
WALDEN WAY S	Arapahoe Co	**349X**	80016	6200-6499	
	Aurora	**319B**	80017	800-1099	
	Aurora	**319K**	80017	1600-1899	
	Aurora	**319K**	80013	1900-2099	
	Aurora	**319T**	80013	2800-2999	
	Aurora	**349B**	80013	3700-3799	
WALDENWOOD DR	Highlands Ranch	**405H**	80130	4600-5099	
WALDENWOOD PL	Highlands Ranch	**405M**	80130	4700-4899	
WALDORF CT	Parker	**409S**	80134	None	
WALDORF PL	Idaho Springs	**780R**	80452	1-99	
WALKER AVE	Boulder Co	**70M**	80503	None	
	Longmont	**40G**	80503	None	
	See.. ROGERS RD				
WALKER AVE W	Jefferson Co	**372C**	80123	6800-7199	
	Jefferson Co	**371C**	80127	10000-10399	
WALKER CT	Boulder Co	**70R**	80503	6600-6799	
WALKER CT	El Paso Co	**908S**	80132	2600-2799	
	El Paso Co	**909Y**	80908	18000-18199	
WALKER DR	Boulder Co	**70M**	80503	6800-6999	
WALKER DR E	Aurora	**351Y**	80016	26400-26699	
WALKER DR W	Jefferson Co	**372B**	80123	7200-8199	
	Jefferson Co	**372A**	80123	8200-8299	
	Jefferson Co	**371B**	80127	10900-11199	
	Aurora	**348X**	80016	None	
WALKER PL W	Jefferson Co	**372B**	80123	7200-7399	
	Jefferson Co	**371D**	80123	9200-9999	
	Jefferson Co	**371C**	80127	10400-10799	
	Jefferson Co	**371A**	80127	12300-12499	
WALKER RD	Boulder Co	**70R**	80503	8800-9999	
WALKER RD	El Paso Co	**909Z**	80908	3000-6099	
	El Paso Co	**910T**	80908	6100-10599	
	El Paso Co	**911S**	80908	10600-12099	
WALKER RD N	Douglas Co	**469Y**	80116	2100-2599	
WALKER ST	Erie	**102W**	80516	1500-1799	
WALL ST	Idaho Springs	**780Q**	80452	1400-2399	
WALL ST	Palmer Lake	**907U**	80133	None	
WALLACE AVE	Jefferson Co	**823U**	80433	10900-11199	
WALLACE CT S	Arapahoe Co	**377R**	80112	8000-8299	
	Highlands Ranch	**404G**	80126	9800-9899	
WALLACE ST	Northglenn	**194K**	80234	100-399	
WALLENS PL	Gilpin Co	**761E**	80403	1-199	
WALNUT	Platteville	**708B**	80651	None	
WALNUT AVE	Palmer Lake	**907Q**	80133	None	
WALNUT CT	Longmont	**42N**	80501	None	
WALNUT DR	Brighton	**138Q**	80601	1500-1799	
WALNUT DR	Frederick	**727B**	80530	1-399	
WALNUT LN	Louisville	**130V**	80027	300-399	
WALNUT ST	Boulder	**127C**	80302	600-1599	
	Boulder	**98W**	80302	2200-2699	
	Boulder	**98X**	80301	3000-4799	
WALNUT ST	Brighton	**138P**	80601	300-1399	
WALNUT ST	Denver	**284E**	80204	500-1399	
	Denver	**254Y**	80205	2300-4099	
WALNUT ST	Frederick	**727F**	80530	600-698	E
WALNUT ST	Longmont	**41R**	80501	None	
	Louisville	**130V**	80027	200-399	
WALNUT ST	Louisville	**131S**	80027	400-1099	
WALNUT ST E	Elizabeth	**871F**	80107	100-699	
WALNUT ST W	Brighton	**138N**	80601	1-199	
WALNUT GROVE ST	Frederick	**726G**	80516	6200-6399	
WALNUT GROVE WAY	Frederick	**726G**	80516	3000-6299	
WALNUT HILL CT	Castle Rock	**497Q**	80104	None	
WALNUT HOLLOW LN	Boulder	**98W**	80302	1800-1899	
WALSH AVE	Parker	**409N**	80134	17000-17099	
WALSH DR E	Aurora	**318B**	80012	14600-15199	
	Aurora	**289W**	80017	16900-17299	
WALSH PL E	Aurora	**317C**	80012	11600-11699	
	Aurora	**318B**	80012	14500-14599	
	Aurora	**318C**	80012	15100-15199	
	Aurora	**318D**	80017	16100-16199	
	Aurora	**289W**	80017	16900-17299	
	Denver	**316B**	80224	6900-7199	
	Denver	**317A**	80247	9800-10099	
WALSH PL W	Denver	**313B**	80219	3000-4299	
WALTER DR	Jefferson Co	**842C**	80433	30800-30999	
WALTER WAY	Broomfield	**162Q**	80020	1-99	
WALTERS CIR	Jefferson Co	**823V**	80465	10400-10599	
WALTERS DR	Erie	**102P**	80516	2400-2499	
WAMBLEE TRAIL	Jefferson Co	**842M**	80433	13500-14499	
WAMBLEE VALLEY RD S	Jefferson Co	**842H**	80433	12100-13999	
WANDA LN	Northglenn	**194K**	80234	10700-10899	
WANDCREST DR S	Jefferson Co	**842N**	80470	13800-15799	
WANDERING WAY	Castle Rock	**467W**	80109	None	
WANDERLUST PL E	Parker	**410X**	80138	None	
WANDERLUST WAY S	Parker	**410X**	80138	12000-12199	
WANEKA PKWY	Lafayette	**132N**	80026	1-599	
WANEKA LAKE CT	Weld Co	**706M**	80504	None	

V
W

STREET NAME	CITY or COUNTY	MAP GRID	ZIP CODE	BLOCK RANGE	O/E
WANEKA LAKE TRAIL	Lafayette	131K	80026	1600-2499	
WANGARATTA CT S	Highlands Ranch	405D	80130	9500-9599	
WANGARATTA WAY E					
	Highlands Ranch	405D	80130	5200-5499	
WAPITI CT	Boulder Co	99H	80301	6900-6999	
WAPITI DR	Jefferson Co	367N	80439	26900-27199	
WAPITI PL	Boulder Co	721C	80481	100-199	
WAPITI TRAIL	Douglas Co	887G	80118	6400-6599	
WAPITI TRAIL	Jefferson Co	842G	80470	13000-13299	
WAR ADMIRAL TRAIL	Jefferson Co	366M	80439	27700-28299	
WARBLER CT	Douglas Co	470C	80134	5100-5199	
WARBLER CT	Louisville	130Y	80027	100-199	
WARBLER ST	Federal Heights	193V	80260	2400-2799	
WARBONNET TRAIL E	Douglas Co	380S	80138	7500-7999	
WARD CIR	Douglas Co	870A	80116	1200-1899	
WARD CT	Arvada	220H	80005	8500-8599	
	Lakewood	280V	80228	1-99	
	Lakewood	281S	80228	100-199	
	Lakewood	281E	80215	1800-1899	
	Wheat Ridge	251W	80215	2900-3199	
WARD CT S	Lakewood	311E	80228	1200-1499	
	Lakewood	311J	80228	1900-1999	
WARD DR	Lakewood	281A	80215	2300-2599	
WARD RD	Arvada	251E	80002	5200-5799	
	Arvada	251E	80004	5800-6199	
	Arvada	221W	80004	6200-7199	
	Arvada	221N	80005	7500-7599	
	Arvada	220M	80005	7600-8699	
	Arvada	221E	80005	8300-8699	
	Wheat Ridge	251W	80033	3200-3799	
	Wheat Ridge	251E	80033	4400-5199	
WARD ST	Gilpin Co	760G	80403	201-299	O
	Gilpin Co	760H	80403	None	
WARD ST	Jamestown	722A	80455	None	
WARD ST	Lakewood	281S	80228	100-199	
WARD ST	Park Co	820Y	80421	1-499	
WARD ST S	Jefferson Co	341N	80127	5100-5299	
	Jefferson Co	341S	80127	5900-5999	
	Jefferson Co	371A	80127	6000-6699	
	Lakewood	311E	80228	1400-1599	
WARD WAY	Jefferson Co	251E	80002	5600-5799	
WARD WAY S	Jefferson Co	341J	80465	4500-5099	
	Jefferson Co	341S	80127	5300-5599	
	Lakewood	311E	80228	1300-1499	
WARHAWK RD S	Jefferson Co	365V	80433	8300-9299	
	Jefferson Co	366S	80433	9300-9399	
	Jefferson Co	822Q	80433	9700-25099	
WARHAWK WAY S	Jefferson Co	366S	80433	8300-8499	
WARING LN	Greenwood Village	345P	80121	1-99	
WARMSTONE CT	Castle Rock	466Y	80109	None	
WARNER DR	Golden	279P	80401	700-799	
WARNER PL W	Denver	254K	80216	200-498	E
WARNE TRAIL CIR	Elbert Co	891C	80107	None	
WARREN AVE	Longmont	11X	80501	1400-1999	
WARREN AVE E	Arapahoe Co	316R	80231	8500-8899	
	Aurora	317N	80247	10000-10399	
	Aurora	317P	80014	10600-11499	
	Aurora	318P	80014	14500-14799	
	Aurora	318Q	80014	14800-14999	
	Aurora	318R	80013	16300-16399	
	Aurora	319K	80013	17800-18299	
	Denver	314Q	80210	1-1699	
	Denver	315N	80210	1700-1899	
	Denver	315P	80210	2300-3999	
	Denver	315Q	80222	4000-4699	
	Denver	315R	80222	4800-5499	
	Denver	316N	80222	5700-6299	
WARREN AVE W	Denver	314P	80223	1-699	
	Denver	314N	80223	900-1199	
	Denver	313R	80219	2400-2999	
	Denver	313N	80219	3300-5199	
	Denver	312R	80227	5200-5999	
	Englewood	314N	80110	1700-1999	
	Englewood	313R	80110	2000-2399	
	Lakewood	311Q	80227	10000-10599	
	Lakewood	311N	80228	12500-13099	
	Lakewood	310R	80228	13100-13699	
	Lakewood	310Q	80228	13900-13999	
	Lakewood	310P	80228	None	
WARREN CIR E	Arapahoe Co	316L	80231	7500-7699	
	Aurora	319L	80013	18900-19999	
WARREN CIR W	Lakewood	310R	80228	13100-13599	
	Lakewood	310Q	80228	14100-14199	
WARREN CT	Elbert Co	831S	80138	3200-3499	
WARREN CT	Jefferson Co	842B	80470	33100-33199	
WARREN CT	Longmont	11X	80501	900-999	
WARREN CT W	Lakewood	312R	80227	6000-6099	
WARREN DR	Adams Co	223V	80221	6800-7199	
WARREN DR E	Arapahoe Co	316L	80231	7300-7699	
	Aurora	317R	80014	12500-12698	E
	Aurora	319L	80013	18800-19099	
	Aurora	321N	80018	None	
	Denver	316P	80224	7000-7299	
WARREN DR W	Lakewood	312N	80227	8600-9199	
	Lakewood	311Q	80227	10000-10799	
	Lakewood	310L	80228	13700-13899	
	Lakewood	310P	80228	14000-14299	
	Lakewood	310P	80228	None	
WARREN LN W	Lakewood	312N	80227	8600-8699	
WARREN PL E	Aurora	317Q	80014	11301-11699	O
	Aurora	318P	80014	14100-14499	
	Aurora	318R	80013	16000-16399	
	Aurora	319L	80013	19400-19699	
	Aurora	321J	80018	None	
	Aurora	321J	80018	None	
WARREN PL W	Lakewood	312R	80227	6000-6099	
	Lakewood	310Q	80228	14200-14299	
WARREN RD	Gilpin Co	761E	80403	1-99	
WARREN RD	Jefferson Co	842A	80470	33300-33799	
WARRENS RD	Jefferson Co	762B	80403	31800-31999	
WARRINGTON CT	Douglas Co	409H	80138	11500-11699	
WARRIOR WAY	Lafayette	131Q	80026	1200-1299	
WARRIORS MARK DR	Douglas Co	869D	80116	9000-9199	
WARRIORS RUN	Douglas Co	432S	80125	6300-6599	
WARSAW DR	Elbert Co	850G	80138	1-399	
WARWICK PL	Castle Pines North	436R	80108	200-299	
WASACH DR	Longmont	12Q	80501	1800-1999	
WASACH PT	Lafayette	131A	80026	1300-1398	E

STREET NAME	CITY or COUNTY	MAP GRID	ZIP CODE	BLOCK RANGE	O/E
WASATCH ST S	Jefferson Co	842E	80470	13200-13299	
WASHBURN AVE	Erie	102D	80516	1200-1399	
WASHBURN AVE W	Lakewood	311U	80227	None	
WASHBURN CT	Erie	102D	80516	1100-1299	
WASHBURN PL W	Lakewood	311V	80227	9000-9099	
	Lakewood	311U	80227	10100-10199	
WASHBURN ST	Erie	102D	80516	1300-1499	
WASHBURN WAY W	Lakewood	311U	80227	10100-10199	
WASHINGTON AVE	Adams Co	169K	80603	None	
WASHINGTON AVE	Bennett	793J	80102	100-699	
WASHINGTON AVE	Golden	248V	80403	100-699	
	Golden	249W	80401	700-1099	
	Golden	279A	80401	1100-2199	
WASHINGTON AVE	Louisville	130Y	80027	100-298	E
	Louisville	130Q	80027	1400-1999	
WASHINGTON AVE	Platteville	708C	80651	300-399	
WASHINGTON CIR	Golden	279F	80401	2000-2099	
WASHINGTON CIR S	Arapahoe Co	374M	80122	7300-7499	
	Englewood	344Q	80113	600-699	
WASHINGTON CT	Adams Co	224L	80229	700-799	
WASHINGTON DR	Frederick	727F	80530	None	
WASHINGTON LN	Douglas Co	407H	80112	12500-12699	
WASHINGTON PL	Bennett	793J	80102	None	
WASHINGTON ST	Adams Co	254G	80216	5200-6199	
	Adams Co	224Q	80216	6200-6399	
	Adams Co	224Q	80229	6400-8299	
WASHINGTON ST	Boulder	97V	80304	2900-3199	
WASHINGTON ST	Denver	284Q	80203	1-1999	
	Denver	284C	80205	2000-2599	
	Denver	254L	80216	4300-5199	
WASHINGTON ST	Elizabeth	871F	80107	300-499	
WASHINGTON ST	Golden	248Z	80403	100-499	
WASHINGTON ST	Monument	908W	80132	1-599	
WASHINGTON ST	Northglenn	194Q	80233	10400-11999	
	Thornton	224G	80229	8300-8999	
	Thornton	194Y	80229	9000-10399	
	Thornton	164L	80241	12000-13599	
	Thornton	164C	80020	13600-14799	
	Thornton	134L	80020	14800-16799	
WASHINGTON ST S	Arapahoe Co	344Q	80121	5100-5399	
	Arapahoe Co	374G	80121	6500-6699	
	Arapahoe Co	374G	80122	6700-7199	
	Arapahoe Co	374M	80122	7300-7499	
	Centennial	344U	80121	5500-5699	
	Denver	284Y	80209	1-699	
	Denver	314C	80209	700-1099	
	Denver	314L	80210	1100-2199	
	Denver	314U	80210	2500-2599	
	Englewood	314Y	80113	2700-3599	
	Englewood	344G	80110	3900-5099	
WASHINGTON WAY	Northglenn	194Q	80233	10400-10599	
WASHINGTON WAY S	Arapahoe Co	374H	80122	7100-7299	
WASHINGTON CENTER PKWY					
	Thornton	164Z	80241	700-12099	
WATADA DR	Brighton	139S	80601	3400-3599	
WATADA ST	Brighton	139S	80601	3400-3499	
	Brighton	139K	80601	None	
WATER AVE W	Denver	313V	80219	2400-2799	
WATER DR E	Aurora	319Q	80013	None	
WATER PL E	Aurora	319Q	80013	None	
WATER ST	Denver	283D	80211	600-1099	
WATER ST	Golden	249W	80401	600-699	
WATER ST	Idaho Springs	780Q	80452	1400-1799	
WATERBURY RD	Boulder Co	11L	80504	12700-12999	
WATER CRESS CT	Longmont	41S	80504	2300-2499	
WATER FLUME WAY	Monument	908X	80132	17500-17699	
WATERFORD CT	Boulder Co	70L	80503	7100-7199	
WATERFORD CT S	Highlands Ranch	406B	80130	9300-9399	
WATERFORD WAY	Boulder Co	70L	80503	8500-8599	
WATERHOUSE CIR	Parker	379W	80134	8900-17399	
WATERMAN WAY	Frederick	726G	80516	None	
WATER MILL CT	Brighton	139M	80601	None	
WATER MILL DR	Brighton	139M	80601	None	
	Brighton	140J	80601	None	
WATERSIDE LN	Broomfield	163H	80020	None	
WATERSIDE TERRACE					
	Cherry Hills Village	345B	80113	1-99	
WATERSONG CIR	Longmont	41S	80504	2200-2399	
WATERSTONE DR	Boulder Co	98H	80301	5200-5499	
WATERTON RD W	Douglas Co	432F	80125	10900-11399	
WATKINS RD	Adams Co	791N	80137	1-1499	
	Adams Co	771S	80022	None	
	Adams Co	771S	80642	None	
	Aurora	771S	80022	None	
	Aurora	771S	80642	None	
WATKINS RD N	Adams Co	751S	80603	14300-15099	
	Adams Co	751S	80022	None	
WATKINS RD N	Watkins	791S	80137	1500-2099	
WATKINS RD S	Arapahoe Co	811E	80137	800-4299	
	Watkins	791W	80137	1-799	
WATONGA WAY	Boulder Co	130J	80303	7600-7699	
WATSON LN	Columbine Valley	343U	80123	100-899	
	Littleton	343U	80123	None	
WATSON GULCH RD S	Jefferson Co	824P	80127	9200-9799	
WAUCONDA CT	Douglas Co	886H	80118	6800-6999	
WAUCONDA DR	Douglas Co	886H	80118	6200-6999	
WAUCONDA WAY	Douglas Co	886H	80118	6400-6499	
WAVE WAY	Elbert Co	890R	80116	1300-1399	
WAVERLY WAY E	Highlands Ranch	405G	80126	4300-4499	
WAVERLY MOUNTAIN	Jefferson Co	371L	80127	7600-7999	
WAVERTON RANCH RD	Douglas Co	466N	80109	1400-1599	
WAVY OAK DR	El Paso Co	909Q	80908	3800-4599	
WAXBERRY WAY S	Denver	316Z	80231	3100-3199	
WAXWING AVE	Brighton	137Z	80601	1300-1399	
WAXWING CT	Boulder Co	69K	80503	6000-6399	
WAYNE'S WAY	Jefferson Co	308J	80401	23400-23799	
WAZEE ST	Denver	283H	80204	400-599	
	Denver	284E	80204	700-1399	
	Denver	284B	80202	1400-1999	
	Denver	254V	80216	3400-3799	
WEASEL WAY	Douglas Co	850T	80116	3000-3399	
WEASEL WAY	Gilpin Co	760V	80403	1-299	
WEASEL WAY	Jefferson Co	365F	80439	6800-6999	
WEATHERSFIELD CT	Highlands Ranch	404K	80129	10600-10699	
WEATHERSFIELD WAY					
	Highlands Ranch	404K	80129	10500-10599	
WEATHERSTONE CIR					
	Highlands Ranch	375W	80126	2100-2399	

STREET NAME	CITY or COUNTY	MAP GRID	ZIP CODE	BLOCK RANGE	O/E
WEATHERSTONE CT	Highlands Ranch	375W	80126	9100-9199	
WEATHERSTONE LN S					
	Highlands Ranch	405A	80126	9300-9399	
WEATHERSTONE WAY					
	Highlands Ranch	375W	80126	None	
WEATHER VANE ST	Longmont	42J	80501	None	
WEATHERVANE WAY E	Douglas Co	381S	80138	9900-10099	
WEAVER AVE E	Arapahoe Co	347W	80111	10000-10099	
	Arapahoe Co	349W	80016	17300-17499	
	Arapahoe Co	349X	80016	18100-18199	
	Arapahoe Co	350W	80016	20400-20699	
	Centennial	345X	80121	2600-3199	
	Centennial	345Y	80121	3800-3999	
	Centennial	375D	80121	5000-5099	
	Centennial	346W	80111	5200-6199	
	Centennial	376B	80111	7200-7299	
	Centennial	378C	80016	15500-15699	
	Centennial	349W	80016	16800-16899	
	Centennial	348W	80111	None	
	Greenwood Village	346X	80111	7200-7299	
WEAVER AVE W	Jefferson Co	372C	80123	6400-6799	
	Jefferson Co	372A	80123	8700-8799	
	Littleton	344W	80120	1200-1999	
	Littleton	343Z	80120	None	
WEAVER CIR	Castle Rock	499J	80104	7000-7799	
WEAVER CIR E	Arapahoe Co	347X	80111	10300-10499	
	Centennial	375D	80121	4600-4699	
	Centennial	376A	80111	5600-5999	
WEAVER CIR W	Littleton	344W	80120	1200-1299	
WEAVER CT	Centennial	375C	80121	None	
WEAVER DR E	Arapahoe Co	349W	80016	17300-17499	
	Arapahoe Co	349X	80016	18100-18199	
	Arapahoe Co	350W	80016	20500-20799	
	Aurora	350Y	80016	22400-22699	
	Centennial	375D	80121	5100-5399	
	Centennial	346W	80111	6200-6399	
WEAVER DR W	Jefferson Co	342Z	80123	5500-6499	
	Jefferson Co	371D	80123	9100-9599	
	Jefferson Co	341Y	80127	None	
WEAVER LN E	Arapahoe Co	349W	80016	16800-16899	
	Centennial	348W	80111	None	
WEAVER PL E	Arapahoe Co	374C	80121	1-99	
	Arapahoe Co	347W	80111	10100-10199	
	Arapahoe Co	347X	80111	10300-10399	
	Arapahoe Co	349W	80016	16800-16899	
	Arapahoe Co	349X	80016	17600-18299	
	Arapahoe Co	350W	80016	20800-20899	
	Aurora	351X	80016	None	
	Centennial	345X	80121	2700-3199	
	Centennial	345Y	80121	4100-4399	
	Centennial	375D	80121	4500-5199	
	Centennial	346W	80111	5600-5699	
	Centennial	346W	80111	6300-6499	
	Centennial	377D	80111	12400-12499	
	Centennial	350X	80016	21200-21399	
	Centennial	348W	80111	None	
	Centennial	348W	80111	None	
WEAVER PL W	Jefferson Co	372B	80123	7100-7399	
WEAVER RD	Boulder Co	722Y	80302	1-1399	
WEAVER PARK RD	Longmont	42F	80501	400-999	
WEBB AVE	Jefferson Co	823U	80433	10800-11099	
WEBBER CT	Erie	102Q	80516	400-499	
WEBSTER CT	Westminster	192X	80021	9200-9299	
WEBSTER CT S	Jefferson Co	372K	80128	7500-7899	
	Lakewood	342F	80123	4300-4399	
	Lakewood	342K	80123	4700-4999	
WEBSTER DR	Arvada	222B	80003	8400-8799	
WEBSTER ST	Arvada	252F	80002	5600-5799	
	Arvada	252B	80003	6000-6199	
	Arvada	222T	80003	6700-6999	
	Arvada	222P	80003	7300-7499	
	Arvada	222F	80003	8100-8399	
	Lakewood	282P	80226	500-599	
	Lakewood	282F	80214	1600-1799	
	Wheat Ridge	252X	80033	2900-3499	
	Wheat Ridge	252P	80033	4600-4699	
WEBSTER ST S	Denver	312T	80227	2700-3099	
	Jefferson Co	372B	80123	6500-6699	
	Jefferson Co	372F	80128	6700-7499	
	Jefferson Co	372P	80128	7900-7999	
	Lakewood	312B	80226	900-999	
WEBSTER WAY	Arvada	222K	80003	7600-7999	
	Jefferson Co	192T	80021	9400-9599	
	Westminster	192X	80021	None	
WEBSTER WAY S	Jefferson Co	372F	80128	6800-7899	
	Jefferson Co	372P	80128	7900-7999	
WEDGE CT	Boulder Co	723G	80503	3900-3999	
WEDGE WAY	Columbine Valley	373B	80123	1-99	
	Jefferson Co	340S	80465	15600-15799	
WEDGEWOOD AVE	Longmont	11S	80503	2300-2699	
WEDGEWOOD CT E	Highlands Ranch	404G	80126	700-799	
WEDGEWOOD DR S	Highlands Ranch	404G	80126	9700-9899	
WEDGWOOD RD	Gilpin Co	761B	80403	1-1899	
WEEDEN PL	Lone Tree	406K	80124	10300-10399	
WEEPING ROCK (PVT) DR					
	Jefferson Co	842R	80470	28800-28899	
WEEPING WILLOW CIR E					
	Highlands Ranch	405D	80130	5000-5299	
WEEPING WILLOW CT					
	Highlands Ranch	375Z	80126	None	
WEEPING WILLOW PL					
	Highlands Ranch	375Z	80126	None	
WEEPING WILLOW WAY					
	Highlands Ranch	375Z	80126	None	
WEIMAN CT	Commerce City	225V	80022	6900-6999	
WEIMER ST	Golden	279Q	80401	900-999	
WEIR DR S	Denver	283S	80219	100-299	
WEISSHORN CIR	Jefferson Co	842Q	80470	30100-30299	
WEISSHORN DR	Jefferson Co	338E	80454	23400-24099	
WELBY CIR	Thornton	195X	80229	9200-9299	
	Adams Co	225B	80229	8500-8799	
	Thornton	225B	80229	8800-9099	
	Thornton	195X	80229	9100-9499	
WELBY TERRACE	Thornton	195X	80229	None	
WELCH AVE	Jefferson Co	307X	80439	3400-3499	
	Jefferson Co	823V	80433	None	
WELCH CIR S	Lakewood	311E	80228	1100-1799	
	Lakewood	310M	80228	1800-1899	
	Lakewood	310R	80228	2000-2199	

W

STREET NAME	CITY or COUNTY	MAP GRID	ZIP CODE	BLOCK RANGE	O/E
WELCH CT	Arvada	221W	80004	6400-6699	
	Arvada	221S	80004	6700-7199	
	Jefferson Co	281J	80401	900-999	
	Lakewood	281N	80401	700-799	
WELCH CT	Lyons	703C	80540	None	
WELCH CT W	Lakewood	311E	80228	1400-1499	
WELCH DR	Brighton	139T	80601	None	
WELCH DR	Lyons	703C	80540	None	
WELCH ST	Arvada	251A	80004	6000-6099	
	Arvada	221W	80004	6400-6699	
	Lakewood	281J	80401	800-1399	
	Lakewood	281E	80215	1500-1599	
WELCH TRAIL	Elbert Co	870D	80107	35300-35499	
WELD ST	Lochbuie	140A	80603	None	
WELDONA LN S	Superior	160L	80027	1200-1399	
WELDONA WAY E	Superior	160M	80027	1300-1699	
WELFORD PL	Castle Pines North	436R	80108	6900-7199	
WELLINGTON AVE	Lafayette	131M	80026	100-599	
WELLINGTON CT S	Arapahoe Co	374D	80121	6600-6699	
WELLINGTON DR	Parker	409J	80134	17000-17099	
WELLINGTON PKWY	Arvada	252D	80003	5200-5799	
WELLINGTON PL	Douglas Co	436Q	80108	6700-6899	
WELLINGTON RD	Boulder	99F	80301	4400-4499	
	Boulder Co	99F	80301	4500-6099	
WELLINGTON ST	Northglenn	194K	80234	100-499	
WELLINGTON ST S	Arapahoe Co	374M	80122	7300-7499	
	Arapahoe Co	374M	80122	7600-7899	
WELLINGTON LAKE RD	Park Co	841W	80421	None	
WELLS PL W	Denver	283J	80204	4700-4799	
WELLS ST	Douglas Co	467K	80108	900-999	
WELLS ST	Erie	103J	80516	100-599	
WELLS FARGO CT	Park Co	840D	80421	1-99	
WELLSHIRE CIR	Broomfield	162Q	80020	1100-1199	
WELLSHIRE CT	Boulder Co	70K	80503	7900-7999	
WELSH CT	Louisville	130V	80027	800-899	
WELSH LN	Frederick	707W	80504	None	
WELSH PL	Boulder Co	98K	80301	4000-4099	
WELTON ST	Denver	284F	80204	1100-1399	
	Denver	284F	80202	1400-1999	
	Denver	284C	80205	2000-2899	
	Denver	254Y	80205	2900-3099	
WEMBLEY PL	Castle Pines North	436R	80108	7200-7299	
WENATCHEE CT S	Aurora	350Y	80016	6400-6599	
WENATCHEE ST	Lochbuie	140G	80603	1-299	
WENATCHEE ST S	Arapahoe Co	350Q	80015	5100-5299	
	Arapahoe Co	350U	80015	5500-5999	
WENATCHEE WAY S	Aurora	380G	80016	None	
WENTWORTH CT	Lone Tree	406D	80124	8700-8799	
WENZEL AVE	Lochbuie	729Z	80603	None	
WERNER LN	Jefferson Co	306P	80439	2000-2099	
WESCROFT AVE	Castle Rock	498M	80104	5900-6299	
WESLAKE DR	Broomfield	163Q	80020	12900-13599	
WESLEY AVE E	Arapahoe Co	316R	80231	None	
	Aurora	317Q	80014	10800-11899	
	Aurora	317R	80014	12400-12599	
	Aurora	318P	80014	14300-15299	
	Aurora	318R	80013	15900-16599	
	Aurora	319P	80013	17000-17399	
	Denver	314Q	80210	1-199	
	Denver	314R	80210	900-1699	
	Denver	315P	80210	1700-3999	
	Denver	315Q	80222	4000-4399	
	Denver	316N	80222	6300-6499	
	Denver	316P	80224	6800-7299	
WESLEY AVE W	Denver	314P	80223	1-799	
	Denver	314N	80223	900-1599	
	Denver	313Q	80219	2400-2999	
	Denver	313P	80219	3300-3599	
	Englewood	314N	80110	1700-1999	
	Englewood	313R	80110	2000-2399	
	Lakewood	311Q	80227	9400-9999	
	Lakewood	310Q	80228	13500-14199	
WESLEY CIR W	Lakewood	310Q	80228	14300-14399	
WESLEY CT W	Lakewood	311R	80227	9700-9999	
WESLEY DR E	Arapahoe Co	316R	80231	None	
	Aurora	319Q	80013	18700-20099	
WESLEY DR W	Lakewood	311R	80227	9200-9599	
	Lakewood	311Q	80227	10000-10399	
WESLEY PL E	Aurora	317P	80014	10800-11199	
	Aurora	317R	80014	12600-12699	
	Aurora	318P	80014	14300-14399	
	Aurora	319P	80013	17500-18399	
	Aurora	319R	80013	19700-19799	
	Aurora	321N	80018	None	
WESLEY PL S	Lakewood	311Q	80227	None	
WESLEY PL W	Jefferson Co	311N	80228	12600-12699	
	Lakewood	312N	80227	8500-8899	
	Lakewood	311Q	80227	10000-10399	
WESSEX CIR E	Highlands Ranch	404C	80126	300-399	
WEST DR	Golden	248Y	80403	200-299	
WEST LN	Park Co	841R	80421	1-199	
WEST ST	Golden	279U	80401	1-399	
	Jefferson Co	823N	80433	26100-26799	
WEST ST	Louisville	131W	80027	300-799	
WEST WAY	El Paso Co	908U	80132	300-18999	
WESTBROOK LN	Highlands Ranch	373Y	80129	3100-3499	
WESTBURY CIR S	Highlands Ranch	404A	80129	9700-9799	
WESTBURY CT S	Highlands Ranch	404E	80129	9800-9899	
WESTBURY WAY S	Highlands Ranch	404A	80129	9600-9899	
WESTCHESTER CIR	Douglas Co	436T	80108	900-999	
WESTCHESTER CIR	Elbert Co	851C	80107	None	
WESTCHESTER DR	Adams Co	223M	80221	2400-2699	
WESTCLIFF DR	Lafayette	131H	80026	700-799	
WESTCLIFF PKWY	Westminster	192P	80021	6000-7799	
WESTCLIFF PL	Highlands Ranch	405L	80126	10500-10599	
WESTCLIFF WAY	Highlands Ranch	405L	80126	10500-10599	
WESTERN AVE	Boulder	128D	80301	5300-5499	
WESTERN CT	Jefferson Co	336H	80439	28500-28699	
WESTERN DR	Jefferson Co	336G	80439	28700-28799	
WESTERN DR	Weld Co	730S	80642	3000-3299	
WESTERN LN	Jefferson Co	336G	80439	28900-29099	
WESTERN EVENING CT	Castle Rock	466P	80109	4700-4799	
WEST FORK WAY	Arapahoe Co	791U	80137	700-1299	
WESTGATE AVE	Highlands Ranch	405P	80126	2600-2899	
WESTGLOW LN E	Greenwood Village	344V	80121	800-999	
WESTHAMPTON CT	Broomfield	163F	80020	13900-13999	
WESTHAVEN PL	Highlands Ranch	405Q	80126	3300-3499	
WEST HILL CT	Fort Lupton	728L	80621	None	

STREET NAME	CITY or COUNTY	MAP GRID	ZIP CODE	BLOCK RANGE	O/E
WESTIN AVE	Lochbuie	729Z	80603	100-399	
WESTIN CIR	Erie	102U	80516	None	
WESTIN DR	Erie	102U	80516	1400-1698	E
WESTLAKE CT	Longmont	11N	80503	2600-2799	
WESTLAKE DR	Longmont	11N	80503	2100-2199	
WESTLAKE PL	Broomfield	163Q	80020	13000-13099	
WESTMEADOW RD	Jefferson Co	305A	80439	34700-34899	
WESTMINSTER BLVD	Westminster	192Z	80031	9400-9599	
	Westminster	192Q	80020	9600-10399	
	Westminster	192L	80020	10400-11199	
WESTMINSTER PL	Westminster	223P	80030	3300-3599	
WESTMOOR CIR	Westminster	191F	80021	10900-11599	
WESTMOOR DR	Westminster	191F	80021	10000-11699	
WESTON AVE E	Castle Rock	498R	80104	5300-5399	
WESTON RD	Douglas Co	887H	80118	600-799	
WESTON ST	Denver	254T	80216	3000-3099	
WESTON WAY	Broomfield	133L	80020	16500-16699	
WESTON PASS CIR	Brighton	140J	80601	None	
WESTOUT AVE	Elbert Co	831N	80138	2300-2399	
WESTRIDGE DR	Boulder Co	98D	80301	5200-5499	
WESTRIDGE RD	Jefferson Co	763P	80403	24700-25499	
WESTRIDGE KNOLLS AVE					
	Highlands Ranch	404A	80129	1700-1799	
WESTRIDGE KNOLLS LN					
	Highlands Ranch	404A	80129	9700-9799	
WESTRIDGE VILLAGE PKWY					
	Highlands Ranch	403L	80129	10200-10399	
WESTSIDE CIR	Douglas Co	432G	80125	8000-8299	
WESTSIDE CT	Douglas Co	432G	80125	10100-10299	
WESTSIDE ST	Douglas Co	432F	80125	10000-10199	
WESTVIEW AVE	Adams Co	794P	80136	56100-56499	
WESTVIEW AVE	Jefferson Co	278T	80401	22300-22598	E
WEST VIEW CIR	Dacono	727J	80514	100-199	
WESTVIEW CIR	Douglas Co	469C	80134	6100-6399	
WESTVIEW CT	Lafayette	131M	80026	1000-1099	
WESTVIEW CT	Longmont	42G	80501	300-499	
WESTVIEW DR	Boulder Co	129G	80303	800-1599	
WESTVIEW DR	Lakewood	282P	80214	7700-7999	
WESTVIEW DR	Monument	908W	80132	100-399	
WESTVIEW RD	Lone Tree	376R	80124	9000-9199	
WESTVIEW RD	Weld Co	72V	80516	1-199	
WESTVIEW ST S	Littleton	344X	80120	6000-6199	
WESTWARD DR	Lafayette	131B	80026	2200-2798	E
WESTWARD LN	Palmer Lake	908S	80133	700-799	
WESTWAY DR	Jefferson Co	368C	80465	21100-21299	
WESTWIND LN	Highlands Ranch	375S	80126	8700-8799	
WESTWOOD CT	Boulder	98S	80304	3100-3199	
WESTWOOD DR	Denver	285N	80206	400-499	
WESTWOOD PL	Erie	103N	80516	None	
WEST WOOD RD	Douglas Co	890K	80116	None	
WESTWOODS CIR	Arvada	219V	80007	6600-6899	
	Arvada	220W	80007	6600-6899	
WETHERILL CIR	Castle Pines North	436F	80108	8100-8399	
WETHERILL RD	El Paso Co	909S	80132	18500-18599	
WETHERSFIELD DR	El Paso Co	908U	80132	18600-18699	
WETLAND LOOP	Frederick	707W	80504	5700-5899	
WETLANDS DR	Frederick	707W	80504	5500-5599	
WETLANDS DR E	Frederick	707W	80504	5700-5899	
WETTERHORN RD	Thornton	193V	80260	None	
WETTERHORN WAY	Broomfield	133N	80020	15900-15999	
WETTERHORN WAY	Longmont	12N	80501	100-199	
WETTERHORN PEAK	Jefferson Co	842N	80470	None	
WEWATTA ST	Denver	284A	80204	600-1299	
	Denver	284A	80202	1401-1599	O
WEWOKA DR	Boulder Co	130K	80303	400-699	
WEXFORD RD	Boulder Co	131A	80303	9100-9299	
WEYBRIDGE ST	Highlands Ranch	405B	80126	None	
WHALE ROCK WAY	Jefferson Co	340S	80465	5800-5899	
WHALEY DR	Boulder Co	130U	80303	6000-6799	
WHARTON CT	Erie	132B	80026	2500-2599	
WHEAT AVE	Lafayette	131G	80026	None	
WHEAT BERRY CT	Erie	102P	80516	2000-2199	
WHEATBERRY DR	Brighton	140J	80601	None	
WHEAT BERRY DR	Erie	102P	80516	300-499	
WHEATFIELD DR	Longmont	42J	80501	None	
WHEATFIELD LN	Brighton	139L	80601	None	
WHEATFIELD LN	Parker	410P	80138	10700-10899	
WHEAT GRASS CIR	Parker	378V	80134	8300-8599	
WHEATLANDS PKWY E	Aurora	381A	80016	None	
WHEATLANDS PKWY S	Aurora	351X	80016	None	
WHEATRIDGE BLVD	Palmer Lake	907U	80133	None	
WHEELER CT S	Highlands Ranch	404D	80126	9200-9399	
WHEELING CIR S	Aurora	318E	80012	1400-1699	
WHEELING CT S	Arapahoe Co	378J	80112	7800-7899	
WHEELING DR	Commerce City	198J	80022	10700-10799	
WHEELING ST	Adams Co	168W	80601	12000-12199	
	Adams Co	168W	80640	12200-12399	
	Aurora	288J	80011	900-1299	
	Aurora	288E	80045	1500-2299	
	Aurora	288A	80011	2700-2799	
	Aurora	258W	80011	3000-3199	
	Commerce City	198J	80022	10400-10799	
	Denver	258S	80239	3700-3899	
	Denver	258E	80239	4900-5599	
WHEELING ST S	Arapahoe Co	378J	80112	7700-7799	
	Aurora	318A	80012	400-999	
	Aurora	318W	80014	3200-3399	
WHEELING WAY	Denver	258J	80239	5000-5099	
WHEELING WAY S	Aurora	288W	80012	300-499	
	Aurora	318J	80012	1200-1799	
	Aurora	318S	80014	2700-3199	
WHETSTONE CT	Elbert Co	871B	80107	35300-35399	
WHILES CT	Erie	102Q	80516	500-699	
WHIMBREL DR E	Highlands Ranch	375U	80126	4600-4799	
WHIMSICAL AVE	Lochbuie	729Z	80603	200-399	
WHIPPOORWILL DR	Lakewood	280M	80215	1500-1599	
WHIPPOORWILL PL	Castle Rock	466X	80109	None	
WHIPPOORWILL ST	Broomfield	163T	80020	12500-12599	
WHIRLAWAY AVE	Parker	410T	80138	21500-21899	
WHIRLAWAY LN	Boulder Co	70J	80503	None	
WHIRLAWAY TRAIL	Jefferson Co	366R	80439	27600-27899	
WHISKEY JAY HILL RD	Clear Creek Co	335J	80439	1-299	
WHISPER CT	Douglas Co	846D	80125	8500-8599	
WHISPER CANYON RD					
	Castle Pines North	436K	80108	12900-13199	
WHISPERING HOPE WAY	Gilpin Co	761B	80403	100-399	
WHISPERING OAK DR	Castle Rock	467Y	80104	600-1299	
WHISPERING PINE	Elbert Co	871B	80107	35600-35899	

STREET NAME	CITY or COUNTY	MAP GRID	ZIP CODE	BLOCK RANGE	O/E
WHISPERING PINES	Boulder Co	722K	80302	1-499	
WHISPERING PINES DR E	Douglas Co	381X	80138	10300-10999	
WHISPERING PINES TRAIL					
	Jefferson Co	842N	80470	34400-34799	
WHISPERING WOODS	Jefferson Co	308E	80401	23000-23099	
WHISPER WIND LN	Castle Rock	498H	80104	None	
WHISPERWOOD CT	Douglas Co	440F	80134	8200-8399	
WHISTLEPIG DR	Broomfield	162G	80020	None	
WHISTLEPIG LN	Broomfield	162G	80020	1700-1899	
WHISTLER DR	Longmont	12J	80501	2300-2399	
WHISTLER ST	Jefferson Co	306J	80439	31200-31299	
WHISTLING ELK DR	Jefferson Co	825N	80127	9800-10099	
WHITAKER CIR E	Aurora	349L	80015	18500-18899	
	Aurora	351J	80016	24400-24699	
WHITAKER CT E	Aurora	351J	80016	24400-24599	
WHITAKER DR	Englewood	344K	80110	900-1099	
WHITAKER DR E	Arapahoe Co	350J	80015	None	
	Aurora	348J	80015	13800-14099	
	Aurora	349J	80015	16900-17599	
	Aurora	350M	80016	23500-24499	
	Aurora	351J	80016	24500-24799	
WHITAKER PL E	Aurora	348K	80015	14100-14399	
	Aurora	349L	80015	19000-19199	
WHITBY CT	Castle Pines North	436R	80108	7100-7299	
WHITE CT	Castle Rock	498N	80104	1900-1999	
WHITE CT S	Jefferson Co	341L	80127	4600-4699	
WHITE LN	Erie	102D	80516	1000-1099	
WHITE LN S	Jefferson Co	341L	80127	4600-4699	
WHITE PL	Boulder	129E	80303	5400-5499	
WHITE WAY S	Jefferson Co	341L	80127	4500-4599	
WHITE ALBA LN	Parker	409S	80134	None	
WHITE ALDER	Jefferson Co	370Q	80127	1-99	
WHITE ANTELOPE DR	El Paso Co	910P	80908	8200-8699	
WHITE ASH CT	Parker	410W	80138	21300-21399	
WHITE ASH DR	Golden	248V	80403	100-499	
WHITE ASH LN	Parker	410S	80138	21100-21299	
WHITE ASH PL	Douglas Co	470A	80134	7400-7599	
WHITE BARK PINE	Jefferson Co	336A	80439	3300-3399	
WHITEBAY DR	Highlands Ranch	375Y	80126	3300-3999	
WHITE BEAR LN	Jefferson Co	822V	80433	28800-28899	
WHITE BIRCH	Jefferson Co	370Q	80127	1-99	
WHITECHAPEL ST	Castle Rock	498M	80104	5700-5899	
WHITECLIFF PL S	Highlands Ranch	403H	80129	9600-9799	
WHITE CLIFF WAY	El Paso Co	909N	80132	None	
WHITECLIFF WAY	Highlands Ranch	403D	80129	None	
WHITE CLOUD CT S	Highlands Ranch	374U	80126	8300-8399	
WHITE CLOUD DR E	Highlands Ranch	374U	80126	500-799	
WHITE CLOUD RD	Jefferson Co	843B	80433	12300-12399	
WHITE CLOUD ST S	Highlands Ranch	374U	80126	8300-8399	
WHITE DEER DR	Jefferson Co	825N	80127	12500-12699	
WHITE EAGLE RD	Jefferson Co	842L	80470	None	
WHITEFACE CT	Jefferson Co	306P	80439	30600-30699	
WHITE FAWN DR	El Paso Co	908T	80132	18200-19299	
WHITE FEATHER DR	Longmont	42D	80501	1700-1898	E
WHITE FIR CT	Jefferson Co	370K	80127	1-99	
WHITE FIR TERRACE	Castle Rock	467R	80108	None	
WHITEHALL DR	Cherry Hills Village	346J	80111	4700-4899	
WHITEHALL DR	Longmont	12U	80501	1100-1399	
	Longmont	12U	80501	1400-1699	
	Longmont	12T	80501	1700-1799	
WHITEHALL LN	Highlands Ranch	375Y	80126	4500-4799	
WHITEHAVEN CIR	Highlands Ranch	404L	80129	1-299	
WHITE HAWK DR	Parker	408R	80134	16100-16299	
WHITE HAWK RANCH RD	Boulder Co	130H	80303	1100-1499	
WHITE HORSE LN	Jefferson Co	366V	80439	8600-8699	
WHITE HOUSE TRAIL	Jefferson Co	337N	80439	4900-5199	
WHITEKIRK PL	Castle Rock	497U	80104	None	
WHITE MARBLE DR	Monument	908X	80132	17500-17799	
WHITEMARSH DR	El Paso Co	908U	80132	18700-18799	
WHITE OAK CT E	Lafayette	131A	80026	None	
WHITE OAK CT S	Highlands Ranch	403G	80129	10000-10099	
WHITE OAK CT W	Lafayette	131A	80026	None	
WHITE OAK DR	Jefferson Co	370Q	80127	1-99	
WHITE OAK LN W	Highlands Ranch	403G	80129	3000-3499	
WHITE OAK PL S	Highlands Ranch	403G	80129	10000-10099	
WHITE OAK ST W	Highlands Ranch	403G	80129	2700-3499	
WHITE OAK WAY S	Highlands Ranch	403G	80129	10100-10199	
WHITE OAK TRAIL W	Highlands Ranch	403G	80129	2900-3299	
WHITE PEAKS CT	Castle Rock	498A	80104	None	
WHITE PELICAN CIR	Thornton	165N	80241	1-99	
WHITE PELICAN WAY	Highlands Ranch	375Y	80126	9000-9199	
WHITE PINE CT	Parker	410S	80138	21300-21399	
WHITE PINE DR	Douglas Co	408M	80134	10400-10599	
WHITE PINE DR	Jefferson Co	370Q	80127	1-99	
WHITE PINE LN	El Paso Co	910U	80908	19100-19299	
WHITE PINE LN	Parker	410S	80138	21100-21299	
WHITE PINE PL	Jefferson Co	370L	80127	1-99	
WHITE RABBIT TRAIL	Jefferson Co	369V	80127	8500-8699	
WHITE RAVEN LN	Superior	160V	80027	None	
WHITE ROCK CIR	Boulder Co	99F	80301	4600-6099	
WHITESTONE DR	Douglas Co	408M	80134	16000-16299	
WHITETAIL CIR	Lafayette	131Z	80026	300-399	
	Lafayette	132W	80026	400-2999	
WHITETAIL CT	Mead	706C	80542	3700-3899	
WHITETAIL DR	Castle Rock	497H	80104	1300-1799	
WHITE TAIL DR N	Douglas Co	870E	80116	400-999	
WHITE TAIL DR S	Douglas Co	870E	80116	1-999	
WHITETAIL LN	Jefferson Co	825N	80127	9900-9999	
WHITE TAIL WAY	El Paso Co	908Y	80132	400-499	
WHITEWATER RD	Idaho Springs	781N	80452	None	
WHITEWING LN	Castle Rock	468X	80104	None	
WHITEWING WAY	Castle Rock	468X	80104	None	
WHITFORD DR	Highlands Ranch	405Q	80126	3400-3599	
WHITING WAY S	Denver	316U	80231	2900-2999	
	Denver	346H	80237	3900-3999	
WHITLOCK DR	Castle Rock	466U	80109	None	
WHITMAN DR	Jefferson Co	306W	80439	3000-3099	
WHITNEY CIR	Broomfield	163G	80020	None	
WHITNEY PL	Boulder	128U	80305	4200-4599	
WHITTAKER CIR	Elbert Co	870Q	80107	31900-31998	E
WHOOPING CRANE DR	Parker	408R	80134	None	
WHOOPING CRANE PL E	Parker	408R	80134	16100-16199	
WICKERDALE CT S	Highlands Ranch	406A	80130	9400-9499	
WICKERDALE LN E	Highlands Ranch	406A	80130	5400-5699	
WICKERDALE PL E	Highlands Ranch	406A	80130	5500-5599	
WICKLOW ST	Boulder Co	130H	80303	1200-1599	
WIDE ACRES RD	Jefferson Co	280M	80401	12700-13999	
WIDEFIELD LN	Douglas Co	403V	80125	10000-10199	

STREET NAME	CITY or COUNTY	MAP GRID	ZIP CODE	BLOCK RANGE	O/E
WIDGEON DR	Longmont	41A	80503	300-499	
WIDGEON LN	Longmont	41A	80503	300-399	
WIELER RD	Jefferson Co	306Q	80439	1800-2399	
WIER WAY	Arvada	219Y	80403	6200-6399	
WIETZ CT	Douglas Co	440L	80134	8400-8799	
WIGAN CT E	Highlands Ranch	405A	80126	2300-2399	
WIGEON PL E	Parker	408V	80134	16100-16199	
WIGGETT CT	Erie	102P	80516	100-199	
WIGGINS ST E	Superior	160L	80027	600-799	
WIGHAM ST	Thornton	195X	80229	9100-9499	
	Thornton	195T	80229	9900-9999	
WIKIUP DR	Adams Co	226B	80022	None	
WILCOX ST	Castle Rock	497L	80104	1-1099	
WILCOX ST S	Castle Rock	497L	80104	1-1199	
WILD ALFALFA PL	Parker	378V	80134	8300-8499	
WILD BASIN	Weld Co	706N	80504	11000-11199	
WILD BASIN WAY	Broomfield	163J	80020	13200-13499	
WILD BERRY CT	Douglas Co	440W	80134	5700-5799	
WILD BERRY RD	Jefferson Co	340W	80465	16200-16599	
WILD BERRY WAY	El Paso Co	908P	80132	1300-1399	
WILD BLOSSOM WAY	Castle Rock	498E	80104	None	
WILDCAT N	Douglas Co	432N	80125	7200-7299	
WILDCAT CT	Jefferson Co	339R	80465	5300-5399	
WILDCAT LN	Boulder Co	722V	80304	1-399	
WILDCAT ST S	Highlands Ranch	374U	80126	8400-8499	
WILDCAT RESERVE PKWY E					
	Highlands Ranch	404L	80126	1-1299	
	Highlands Ranch	405J	80126	1300-4699	
WILDCAT RESERVE PKWY W					
	Highlands Ranch	404J	80129	1-2399	
WILDCAT RIDGE	Douglas Co	406J	80124	None	
WILD CROCUS CIR	Douglas Co	850N	80134	9700-9899	
WILD DUCK LN	El Paso Co	908Y	80132	200-299	
WILD DUNES CT	Boulder	70W	80301	5300-5399	
WILDE AVE	Parker	379W	80134	17200-17599	
WILDE LN	Parker	379W	80134	9100-9299	
WILD ELK PL	Douglas Co	470D	80134	9200-9299	
WILDER CT N	Douglas Co	440V	80134	6100-6299	
WILDERMAN PL	Aurora	288E	80011	1700-1799	
WILDERNESS PL	Boulder	98U	80301	2800-2999	
WILDERNESS PL	Douglas Co	469E	80134	4800-4999	
WILDERNESS PT	Clear Creek Co	801R	80439	None	
WILDERNESS CORNERSTONE RD					
	Clear Creek Co	801R	80439	1-99	
WILDEWOOD CT	Nederland	740R	80466	None	
WILDEWOOD DR	Nederland	740R	80466	None	
WILDFIELD LN	Douglas Co	403V	80125	10000-11099	
WILDFIRE CIR	Douglas Co	527Q	80104	1700-1799	
WILDFIRE CT	El Paso Co	910N	80908	5900-6099	
WILDFIRE CT	Longmont	40R	80503	1200-1299	
WILDFLOWER CIR	Elbert Co	870H	80107	33700-33799	
WILDFLOWER CIR	Frederick	726C	80516	None	
WILDFLOWER CT	Boulder Co	741R	80466	1-99	
WILDFLOWER CT	Brighton	168C	80601	1500-1599	
WILDFLOWER CT	Dacono	727S	80514	None	
WILDFLOWER CT	Jefferson Co	336F	80439	4100-4399	
WILDFLOWER DR	Brighton	168C	80601	1100-1299	
WILDFLOWER DR	Longmont	42C	80501	None	
WILDFLOWER LN	Douglas Co	470Z	80116	9000-9199	
WILDFLOWER PL	Brighton	168C	80601	1500-1599	
WILDFLOWER PL	Dacono	727S	80514	None	
WILDFLOWER PL	Lone Tree	376Z	80124	8400-8499	
WILDFLOWER ST	Broomfield	163Q	80020	13300-13399	
WILDFLOWERS WAY N	Castle Rock	466Q	80109	4500-4999	
WILDFLOWER TRAIL	Elbert Co	851T	80107	None	
	Elbert Co	851U	80107	None	
WILD FLOWER TRAIL	Jefferson Co	337K	80439	26100-26999	
WILD FOX PL	Douglas Co	870F	80016	None	
WILD FOX PT	Douglas Co	870F	80016	None	
WILDGRASS PL	Dacono	726V	80514	None	
WILDGRASS PL	Douglas Co	848M	80134	4600-4699	
WILD GULCH CT	Douglas Co	410Z	80138	9401-9499	O
WILD HORSE CIR	Boulder Co	722V	80304	1-599	
WILD HORSE DR	El Paso Co	908P	80132	1000-1099	
WILDHORSE LN	Douglas Co	432F	80125	10500-10599	
WILD HORSE WAY	Frederick	707W	80504	None	
WILDHORSE PEAK	Jefferson Co	371P	80127	11100-11299	
WILD HORSE TRAIL	Elbert Co	851V	80107	6000-6499	
WILDHURST CIR	Highlands Ranch	405K	80126	10500-10699	
WILDING CT S	Denver	316Z	80231	3100-3199	
WILD IRIS RUN S	Highlands Ranch	374Z	80126	8800-9099	
WILDLIFE PL	Longmont	12V	80501	1700-1799	
WILDLIFE WAY	Douglas Co	825Z	80125	10000-10599	
WILD PLUM CIR	Jefferson Co	340W	80465	16200-16499	
WILD PLUM CT	Boulder	97P	80304	3700-3799	
WILD PLUM LN	Castle Rock	467Y	80104	None	
WILDRIDGE CIR	Lafayette	132E	80026	600-698	E
WILD RIDGE CT	Parker	410L	80138	10700-10799	
WILDRIDGE LN	Lafayette	132E	80026	500-699	
WILDROSE CIR	Elbert Co	851A	80107	3100-3499	
WILD ROSE CT	Golden	248Z	80403	1500-1599	
WILDROSE CT	Highlands Ranch	374V	80126	8700-8799	
WILDROSE CT	Longmont	40R	80503	1300-1399	
WILDROSE CT	Louisville	130U	80027	500-599	
WILD ROSE DR	Jefferson Co	336C	80439	28700-29499	
WILDROSE DR	Longmont	40V	80503	1400-1999	
WILD ROSE LN	Jefferson Co	367A	80439	6700-6899	
WILDROSE PL	Longmont	40V	80503	3600-3699	
WILDROSE WAY	Louisville	130U	80027	500-799	
WILDROSE TRAIL	Cherry Hills Village	345B	80113	1-99	
WILD RYE CT	Castle Rock	497A	80109	1600-1799	
WILDSTAR WAY	Castle Rock	498A	80104	None	
WILD TIGER LN	Boulder Co	722W	80302	1-99	
WILD TIGER RD	Boulder Co	722W	80302	1-299	
WILD TIMBER CT	Douglas Co	869D	80116	None	
WILD TIMBER DR	Douglas Co	869D	80116	None	
WILD TROUT TRAIL	Jefferson Co	844A	80127	12400-12599	
WILD TURKEY LN	Jefferson Co	370B	80127	1-99	
WILD TURKEY TRAIL	Boulder Co	722T	80302	1-799	
WILD TURKEY TRAIL	Jefferson Co	369B	80465	6300-6399	
WILDWOOD CIR	Boulder	128S	80305	1200-1299	
WILDWOOD CT	Boulder	128S	80305	1300-1399	
WILDWOOD LN	Boulder	128S	80305	1400-1599	
	Boulder Co	97E	80304	1-399	
WILDWOOD LN	Castle Rock	497D	80104	1300-1399	
WILDWOOD RD	Boulder	128S	80305	1100-1499	
WILDWOOD ST	Lochbuie	729Z	80603	1600-1899	
	Lochbuie	729Z	80603	None	

STREET NAME	CITY or COUNTY	MAP GRID	ZIP CODE	BLOCK RANGE	O/E
WILDWOOD WAY	El Paso Co	908P	80132	19300-19499	
WILDWOODS	Jefferson Co	336A	80439	31000-31099	
WILEY CIR	Adams Co	223E	80031	8500-8599	
WILEY CT S	Superior	160L	80027	900-999	
WILEY PL E	Parker	409J	80134	17000-17099	
WILEY ST	Dacono	727J	80514	None	
WILKERSON RD	Jefferson Co	823N	80433	25200-26399	
WILKERSON WAY	Longmont	12Y	80501	1300-1399	
WILKINS RD	Park Co	820Y	80421	1-299	
WILLA LN	Jefferson Co	367G	80439	6800-7299	
WILLAMETTE AVE E	Arapahoe Co	350N	80015	20500-20799	
WILLAMETTE LN E	Centennial	349R	80015	19900-20299	
WILLAMETTE LN E	Greenwood Village	345P	80121	2300-3799	
WILLAMETTE PL E	Centennial	350P	80015	21300-21399	
WILLAMS DR S	Greenwood Village	344R	80121	5100-5199	
WILLARD DR	Brighton	139C	80603	None	
WILLETS AVE	Jefferson Co	823U	80433	22500-22699	
WILLIAM PL	Longmont	40T	80503	None	
WILLIAM ST W	Superior	160F	80027	100-499	
WILLIAM BAILEY AVE	Frederick	727A	80504	None	
WILLIAM CODY DR	Jefferson Co	366Z	80439	8600-9299	
WILLIAMS AVE	Weld Co	727B	80530	100-299	
WILLIAMS CIR S	Arapahoe Co	374D	80121	6500E-6699E	
	Arapahoe Co	374D	80121	6600W-6699W	
	Centennial	375N	80122	8000-8099	
	Centennial	375A	80121	6500E-6699E	
	Greenwood Village	345N	80121	5100-5199	
WILLIAMS CT	Erie	132A	80026	1800-1899	
WILLIAMS CT	Thornton	194V	80229	9600-9699	
	Thornton	194V	80229	9800-9899	
	Thornton	135J	80602	None	
WILLIAMS CT S	Centennial	375N	80122	8000-8099	
WILLIAMS ST	Adams Co	135W	80602	14900-14999	
	Denver	285N	80218	300-799	
	Denver	285E	80218	1200-1999	
	Denver	285A	80205	2100-2699	
	Denver	255W	80205	2700-3999	
	Denver	255J	80216	4600-4799	
	Northglenn	195N	80233	10400-10599	
	Thornton	194V	80229	9900-9999	
	Thornton	165J	80241	13400-13499	
	Thornton	165A	80602	14400-14899	
	Thornton	135J	80602	16600-16699	
WILLIAMS ST S	Centennial	344Z	80121	6100-6199	
	Centennial	375A	80121	6300-6499	
	Centennial	375J	80122	7500-7699	
	Denver	285W	80209	200-699	
	Denver	315A	80209	700-1099	
	Denver	315N	80210	1700-3099	
	Englewood	315W	80113	3100-3299	
WILLIAMS WAY	Northglenn	194D	80233	11700-11999	
	Thornton	194R	80229	None	
WILLIAMS WAY S	Centennial	375N	80122	8000-8099	
WILLIAMS FORK TRAIL	Boulder Co	99C	80301	5100-5199	
WILLIAMSON DR E	Parker	409V	80138	20100-20199	
WILLIES LN	Gilpin Co	740Z	80474	None	
WILLIS WAY	Longmont	12V	80501	None	
WILLOBE WAY	Jefferson Co	308B	80401	800-899	
WILLODENE DR	Longmont	12S	80501	1500-1699	
WILLOW CIR	Denver	286R	80230	None	
WILLOW CIR S	Centennial	376M	80112	7500-7599	
	Denver	346D	80237	3700-3799	
WILLOW CT	Broomfield	192C	80020	100N-199N	
WILLOW CT	Castle Rock	498L	80104	5200-5399	
WILLOW CT	Lakewood	281E	80215	2000-2099	
WILLOW CT	Lochbuie	140G	80603	500-599	
WILLOW CT	Longmont	40R	80503	1000-1099	
WILLOW CT	Louisville	130Q	80027	500-599	
WILLOW CT S	Arapahoe Co	316M	80231	1600-1699	
	Centennial	376R	80112	7900-8099	
	Denver	316V	80231	2800-2899	
	Denver	316Z	80231	3200-3399	
WILLOW DR	Lochbuie	140G	80603	101-699	O
	Lochbuie	140F	80603	700-999	
WILLOW DR	Thornton	136V	80602	None	
	Thornton	194W	80260	None	
WILLOW DR S	Greenwood Village	346Z	80111	5900-6199	
WILLOW LN	Boulder Co	99F	80301	6200-6299	
	Boulder Co	70K	80503	8200-8299	
WILLOW LN	Gilpin Co	761F	80403	1-199	
WILLOW LN	Jefferson Co	280H	80401	12800-13399	
WILLOW LN	Lakewood	281A	80215	1700-12799	
WILLOW LN	Longmont	11J	80503	2400-2499	
WILLOW PL	Broomfield	192C	80020	100N-199N	
WILLOW PL	Lafayette	131M	80026	1000-1099	
WILLOW PL	Lochbuie	140G	80603	500-599	
WILLOW PL	Louisville	130T	80027	1000-1099	
WILLOW RD	Frederick	706Y	80504	3500-3599	
WILLOW ST	Adams Co	794E	80136	3900-4099	
WILLOW ST	Adams Co	136M	80602	16200-16299	
	Commerce City	226D	80022	8600-8799	
	Denver	286M	80220	1100-1999	
	Denver	256Z	80238	2800-2999	
	Denver	256Z	80238	3200-3699	
	Denver	256R	80238	None	
WILLOW ST	Keenesburg	732A	80643	None	
WILLOW ST	Longmont	41R	80501	None	
WILLOW ST	Louisville	130P	80027	None	
WILLOW ST	Thornton	136V	80602	None	
WILLOW ST N	Castle Rock	498M	80104	1-399	
WILLOW ST S	Arapahoe Co	316H	80247	1200-1399	
	Centennial	376H	80112	6700-7199	
	Centennial	376Q	80112	8100-8199	
	Denver	316V	80231	2900-3199	
	Denver	316Z	80231	3400-3499	
	Denver	346D	80237	3700-3799	
	Denver	346H	80237	4400-4499	
	Denver	346M	80237	4700-4799	
	Lone Tree	376R	80124	8300-8399	
WILLOW WAY	Adams Co	136Q	80602	16000-16099	
WILLOW WAY	Jefferson Co	280H	80401	1600-13099	
	Thornton	136Q	80602	None	
	Thornton	136U	80602	None	
WILLOW WAY S	Centennial	376M	80112	7500-7799	
	Denver	346H	80237	3800-4099	
	Greenwood Village	346V	80111	5900-5999	
WILLOW BEND CT	Boulder Co	100X	80301	8000-8199	
WILLOWBEND LN	Parker	409Z	80138	20200-20899	

STREET NAME	CITY or COUNTY	MAP GRID	ZIP CODE	BLOCK RANGE	O/E
WILLOWBRIDGE CT	Highlands Ranch	405K	80126	10300-10399	
WILLOWBRIDGE WAY					
	Highlands Ranch	405K	80126	10200-10299	
WILLOWBROOK AVE E	Parker	410V	80138	23900-24099	
WILLOWBROOK DR	Jefferson Co	340T	80465	5600-6299	
WILLOWBROOK DR	Longmont	12U	80501	1400-1599	
WILLOWBROOK LN	Jefferson Co	340T	80465	15100-15499	
WILLOWBROOK RD	Boulder	127G	80302	700-899	
WILLOW BROOM TRAIL	Douglas Co	432T	80125	6100-6699	
WILLOW CREEK CIR	Longmont	40R	80503	1000-1099	
WILLOW CREEK DR	Boulder Co	100X	80301	1600-2999	
WILLOW CREEK DR	Golden	279F	80401	2100-2399	
WILLOW CREEK DR	Longmont	40R	80503	3100-3299	
WILLOW CREEK RD	Clear Creek Co	801Y	80439	1-399	
WILLOW CREEK RD	Jefferson Co	823R	80465	9500-9599	
WILLOW CREEK RD E	Douglas Co	498U	80104	4000-5399	
	Douglas Co	499W	80104	5400-6299	
WILLOW CREEK ST S					
	Highlands Ranch	374U	80126	8400-8499	
WILLOW CREEK RUN	Weld Co	707J	80504	None	
WILLOWGLEN CT	Boulder Co	97X	80302	200-299	
WILLOWHERB LN	Jefferson Co	308E	80401	23700-23799	
WILLOWHERB ST	Brighton	140J	80601	None	
WILLOWICK CIR W	Highlands Ranch	404B	80129	100-399	
WILLOW LAKE DR	Douglas Co	499K	80104	1-899	
WILLOWLEAF DR	Jefferson Co	370K	80127	1-99	
WILLOWMORE CT	Highlands Ranch	376W	80130	6100-6199	
WILLOWNOOK RANCH TRAIL					
	Elbert Co	871W	80107	3200-4199	
WILLOW OAK	Jefferson Co	370Q	80127	1-99	
WILLOW OAK RD	Castle Rock	498N	80104	1300-1599	
WILLOW O THE WISP WAY	El Paso Co	908U	80132	18200-18499	
WILLOW PARK CT	Parker	410N	80138	10800-10899	
WILLOW PARK DR	Parker	410N	80138	10800-10899	
WILLOW PARK PL	Parker	410N	80138	21100-21199	
WILLOW PARK WAY	El Paso Co	908T	80132	1800-1899	
WILLOW REED CIR	Parker	409N	80134	10800E-10899E	
WILLOW REED CT	Parker	409N	80134	10700-10799	
WILLOW RUN CIR	Elbert Co	870L	80107	601-699	O
WILLOWRUN CT	Castle Rock	466X	80109	3400-3499	
WILLOWRUN DR	Castle Rock	466X	80109	2900-3399	
WILLOWRUN LN	Castle Rock	466X	80109	4200-4399	
WILLOW RUN PKWY	Broomfield	163U	80020	None	
WILLOWS PL	Parker	379S	80134	8400-8699	
WILLOW SPRINGS DR	Jefferson Co	340S	80465	5300-6299	
	Jefferson Co	370A	80127	6300-6499	
	Jefferson Co	339Z	80465	6500-6599	
WILLOW SPRINGS RD	Jefferson Co	339M	80465	4900-5299	
WILLOWSTONE PL	Douglas Co	408H	80134	9900-9999	
WILLOWSTONE ST	Douglas Co	408H	80134	16100-16299	
WILLOWWISP WAY	Highlands Ranch	404L	80126	10400-10599	
WILLOW WOOD CT	Broomfield	162H	80020	13900-14099	
WILLOW WOOD CT	Jefferson Co	340S	80465	16400-16499	
WILLOW WOOD DR	Jefferson Co	339V	80465	5400-5699	
WILMAR DR	Dacono	727M	80514	None	
WILMINGTON CT S	Highlands Ranch	406B	80130	9300-9399	
WILMOT AVE	Jefferson Co	250A	80403	None	
WILSON CIR	Erie	102Q	80516	1700-1999	
WILSON CIR	Parker	409V	80134	11500-11699	
WILSON CT	Boulder	97R	80304	1600-1699	
WILSON CT	Denver	255X	80205	3000-3099	
	Westminster	223P	80030	7300-7599	
WILSON DR	Broomfield	133N	80020	4600-4799	
WILSON PL	Louisville	130R	80027	1400-1499	
WILSON RD	Thornton	194S	80260	None	
WILSON ST	Lafayette	131H	80026	400-599	
WILSON ST W	Lafayette	131H	80026	None	
WILSON PEAK	Jefferson Co	842N	80470	None	
WILTSHIRE CT E	Highlands Ranch	406B	80130	7200-7299	
WILTSHIRE DR S	Highlands Ranch	406B	80130	9200-9499	
WILTSHIRE PL	Highlands Ranch	376X	80130	7200-7299	
WILTSHIRE PL E	Highlands Ranch	406B	80130	7200-7299	
WIMBLEDON CT S	Highlands Ranch	404H	80126	9700-9799	
WINCHESTER CIR	Boulder	69U	80301	6700-7099	
WINCHESTER RD	El Paso Co	910Y	80908	16500-17499	
WINCHESTER RD	Elbert Co	851W	80107	36000-36999	
WINCHESTER WAY N	Douglas Co	381S	80138	13100-13799	
WINDBREAK LN E	Parker	408Y	80134	None	
WINDCHANT CIR	Douglas Co	527P	80104	3700-3899	
WINDCREST ROW E	Douglas Co	440N	80134	7600-8099	
WIND DANCE CT	Castle Rock	466Z	80109	None	
WINDEMERE LN	Boulder Co	130P	80303	1-199	
WINDEMERE LN	Erie	133G	80516	None	
WINDER PL	Jefferson Co	763P	80403	24300-24399	
WINDERMERE CIR S	Littleton	344W	80120	6100-6199	
	Littleton	374J	80120	7700-7999	
WINDERMERE ST S	Englewood	344A	80110	3700-4099	
	Englewood	344E	80110	4300-4899	
	Littleton	344S	80120	4900-6499	
	Littleton	374A	80120	6500-7699	
	Littleton	374J	80120	7700-7899	
WINDERMERE WAY S	Littleton	344W	80120	6000-6299	
WINDFIELD AVE N	Douglas Co	440T	80134	6300-6799	
WINDFLOWER DR	Longmont	42C	80501	800-899	
WINDFLOWER LN	Highlands Ranch	405M	80130	None	
WINDFLOWER LN	Jefferson Co	822V	80433	28800-28999	
WINDFONT ROW E	Douglas Co	440T	80134	7700-7999	
WINDFORD ST E	Douglas Co	440S	80134	7400-7699	
WINDHAM	Douglas Co	440S	80134	6500-6599	
WINDHAVEN DR	Douglas Co	470C	80134	8300-9399	
WIND HOLLOW CT N	Douglas Co	440S	80134	6400-6599	
WINDING DR	Longmont	12J	80501	2400-2499	
WINDING HILL AVE E	Lone Tree	407A	80124	None	
WINDING HILLS RD	El Paso Co	908Q	80132	600-699	
WINDING MEADOW DR	Elbert Co	892H	80117	10400-11999	
WINDING MEADOW WAY	El Paso Co	908Y	80132	1-499	
WINDING RIVER CT	Broomfield	163H	80020	14000-14098	E
WINDING RIVER DR	Broomfield	163H	80020	2500-2598	E
WINDING TRAIL DR	Boulder	98N	80304	2600-3899	
WINDING TRAIL PL	Boulder	98N	80304	2600-2799	
WINDLAWN WAY E	Douglas Co	440S	80134	7300-7699	
WINDLER ST	Brighton	138L	80601	None	
WINDLOCH CIR N	Douglas Co	440T	80134	6500-6599	
WINDMILL CIR	Elbert Co	851S	80107	2200-2899	
WINDMILL DR	Brighton	139L	80601	None	
WINDMILL DR	Longmont	12J	80501	None	
WINDMILL PL	Highlands Ranch	374U	80126	700-899	
WINDMILL RD	Douglas Co	467E	80108	200-599	

STREET NAME	CITY or COUNTY	MAP GRID	ZIP CODE	BLOCK RANGE	O/E
WINDMONT AVE N	Douglas Co	440T	80134	6300-7099	
WINDOM DR	Jefferson Co	305M	80439	1500-1599	
WINDOM LN	Broomfield	163J	80020	13600-13899	
WINDOM LOOP	Broomfield	133L	80020	None	
WINDOM RD	Thornton	193V	80260	None	
WINDOM PEAK DR	Superior	160Y	80027	900-999	
WINDOM PEAK ST	Brighton	139M	80601	None	
WINDOM PEAK WAY	Douglas Co	436U	80108	6100-6199	
WINDOVER RD	Greenwood Village	344R	80121	1-99	
WINDOW ROCK LN	Jefferson Co	370A	80127	6600-6699	
WINDPOINT CIR N	Douglas Co	440N	80134	6700-6899	
WINDRIDGE CIR	Highlands Ranch	405P	80126	2800-3299	
WINDRIDGE CT	Highlands Ranch	405P	80126	10700-10799	
WINDRIVER TRAIL	Castle Rock	466T	80109	None	
WIND ROSE PL	Castle Rock	468X	80108	None	
WINDROW LN	Lafayette	131K	80027	2400-2499	
WINDROWER CT	Brighton	139L	80601	None	
WINDSONG CT	Jefferson Co	339R	80465	5400-5499	
WINDSONG TRAIL	Gilpin Co	761U	80403	100-299	
WINDSOR DR	Aurora	259U	80011	3401-3599	O
WINDSOR DR	Boulder Co	99D	80301	7300-7399	
WINDSOR DR S	Denver	283S	80219	100-299	
WINDSOR ST S	Arapahoe Co	373E	80128	7000-7099	
WINDSOR WAY	Greenwood Village	346U	80111	None	
WINDSOR WAY S	Highlands Ranch	404D	80126	9200-9399	
WINDVIEW CIR N	Douglas Co	440N	80134	6800-6899	
WINDWARD CIR	Elbert Co	870L	80107	400-499	
WINDWOOD CIR N	Douglas Co	440N	80134	7300-7399	
WIND WOOD WAY	Douglas Co	439R	80134	7100-8199	
WINDWOOD WAY E	Douglas Co	440P	80134	7100-8199	
WINDY CT	Arvada	219Q	80007	None	
WINDY CT	Jefferson Co	249C	80403	5900-5999	
WINDY PINE PL E	Parker	409Z	80134	None	
WINDY TRAIL LN S	Parker	410Y	80138	None	
WINFIELD CIR	Lakewood	280H	80215	1-99	
WINFIELD DR	Lakewood	281E	80215	1600-1999	
WINFIELD PL	Jefferson Co	280H	80401	13200-13399	
WINGED FOOT CT	Douglas Co	886G	80118	6400-6599	
WINGED FOOT WAY	Columbine Valley	373B	80123	1-99	
WINGER DR	Boulder Co	741L	80466	1-199	
WINGFOOT DR	Jefferson Co	306T	80439	30100-30499	
WINGLER PL	Brighton	138V	80601	2200-2299	
WING TIP CT	El Paso Co	909P	80908	18900-18999	
WING TIP RD	El Paso Co	909P	80908	18000-19999	
WINGTIP WAY	Castle Rock	468X	80108	None	
WINKS WAY	Gilpin Co	741X	80403	1-99	
WINNEBAGO DR	Douglas Co	846U	80135	2800-3699	
WINNEBAGO WAY	Douglas Co	846U	80135	6500-6899	
WINNIPEG CIR S	Aurora	380Q	80016	None	
WINNIPEG CT S	Aurora	380C	80016	6400-6599	
	Aurora	380Q	80016	None	
WINNIPEG ST S	Arapahoe Co	350U	80015	5400-6099	
WINONA CIR	Broomfield	163S	80020	12600-12799	
WINONA CT	Adams Co	223A	80031	8800-8999	
	Adams Co	253E	80212	None	
	Arvada	253A	80003	6000-6099	
	Arvada	223W	80003	6400-6599	
	Broomfield	163W	80020	12300-12399	
	Broomfield	163S	80020	12500-12699	
	Denver	283S	80219	1-299	
	Denver	283N	80204	400-1099	
	Denver	283J	80204	1200-1699	
	Denver	283A	80212	2400-2599	
	Denver	253S	80212	3700-4599	
	Westminster	223S	80030	7000-7199	
	Westminster	223N	80030	7200-7599	
	Westminster	193W	80031	9000-9299	
	Westminster	193N	80031	10300-10399	
	Westminster	193E	80031	11100-11299	
	Westminster	193A	80031	11600-11899	
WINONA CT S	Denver	283S	80219	1-99	
	Denver	313E	80219	1100-2099	
	Denver	313N	80219	2200-2699	
	Denver	313S	80236	2700-3499	
	Denver	343E	80236	3500-4599	
WINONA DR	Broomfield	163W	80020	12200-12399	
WINONA PL	Broomfield	163W	80020	4400-4699	
WINONA ST	Adams Co	253E	80212	None	
	Arvada	223W	80003	6300-6399	
	Arvada	223S	80030	6800-6899	
	Westminster	193S	80031	9900-9999	
WINONA WAY S	Denver	313E	80219	1400-1499	
WINROCK ST S	Highlands Ranch	374Y	80126	8900-8999	
WINROW CT	Highlands Ranch	375X	80126	9100-9199	
WINSLOW CIR	Longmont	42C	80501	1100-1299	
WINSLOW CT	Erie	102Q	80516	1500-1599	
WINSTON DR S	Jefferson Co	308F	80401	1300-1599	
	See.. S GRAPEVINE RD				
WINSTON ST S	Aurora	318U	80013	2900-3199	
	Aurora	318Y	80013	3200-3499	
WINTER WAY	Elbert Co	831N	80138	2600-2899	
WINTER WAY	Lone Tree	376Y	80124	None	
WINTER BERRY DR	Castle Pines North	436F	80108	8300-8599	
WINTER BERRY LN	Castle Pines North	436F	80108	7100-7499	
WINTER BERRY PL	Castle Pines North	436B	80108	None	
WINTER CRESS	Jefferson Co	370F	80127	1-99	
WINTERCRESS LN	Boulder	97H	80304	None	
WINTERFLOWER WAY	Douglas Co	408L	80134	10400-10699	
WINTERGATE CIR	Douglas Co	527P	80104	1100-1299	
WINTERGREEN DR	Parker	410Q	80138	11200-11299	
WINTERGREEN PKWY S	Parker	409A	80134	9500-9699	
WINTERGREEN WAY	Parker	410Q	80138	22100-22199	
WINTER HAWK CIR	Douglas Co	527J	80104	3500-3599	
WINTERLEAF CT	Douglas Co	408L	80134	15400-15499	
WINTER PARK AVE E					
	Buckley Air Force Base	289P	80011	None	
	Buckley Air Force Base	289Q	80011	None	
WINTER RIDGE CT	Castle Pines North	436F	80108	6800-6899	
WINTER RIDGE DR	Castle Pines North	436F	80108	7000-7399	
WINTER RIDGE LN	Castle Pines North	436F	80108	6900-7199	
WINTER RIDGE PL	Castle Pines North	436F	80108	6900-7099	
WINTERSONG WAY	Highlands Ranch	404Q	80126	10801-10999	O
WINTER SPRINGS PL E	Parker	410V	80138	23800-24099	
WINTERSWEET CT	Douglas Co	408M	80134	10500-10599	
WINTERSWEET PL	Douglas Co	408M	80134	10600-10699	
WINTERTHUR CIR S	Highlands Ranch	404F	80129	400-499	
WINTERTHUR CT S	Highlands Ranch	404F	80129	10000-10099	
WINTERTHUR WAY S	Highlands Ranch	404F	80129	100-599	
WINTER TRAIL S	Jefferson Co	843D	80433	12300-12399	
WINTERWHEAT LN	Brighton	140J	80601	None	
WINTHROP CIR	Castle Rock	499J	80104	6800-7199	
WINTHROP CT	Castle Rock	499J	80104	7100-7299	
WINTON PL	Douglas Co	467E	80108	400-499	
WINWOOD DR	Cherry Hills Village	344M	80113	1-99	
WISCONSIN AVE W	Jefferson Co	311F	80232	11100-11199	
	Lakewood	311H	80232	9000-9199	
WISCONSIN DR W	Lakewood	311E	80228	12000-12299	
WISE RD	Park Co	820Y	80421	1-499	
WISP LN	Park Co	841R	80421	1-199	
WISP CREEK DR	Park Co	841M	80421	1-1099	
	Park Co	841H	80470	None	
WISSLER RANCH RD	El Paso Co	909Q	80908	19900-20399	
WISTERA WAY	Broomfield	132Z	80026	14900-14999	
WISTERIA CT S	Denver	346D	80237	3800-3999	
WISTERIA DR	Erie	133H	80516	None	
WISTERIA LN	Douglas Co	887G	80118	2000-2099	
WISTERIA WAY	Lafayette	131F	80026	300-399	
WISTERIA WAY S	Denver	346H	80237	4000-4099	
WITNEY PL	Lone Tree	406L	80124	7800-8099	
WITTEMAN RD	Jefferson Co	842C	80433	30800-31199	
WITTEN CT	Parker	409J	80134	17300-17399	
WITTER GULCH RD	Clear Creek Co	335E	80439	1000-1599	
	Clear Creek Co	304X	80439	1600-4499	
	Clear Creek Co	801R	80439	None	
WOLCOTT CT S	Denver	313A	80219	700-799	
	Denver	313J	80219	1500-2199	
	Denver	343E	80236	4400-4499	
WOLCOTT LN	Adams Co	223A	80031	8800-8999	
WOLCOTT ST	Castle Rock	498R	80104	1100-1199	
WOLCOTT WAY S	Denver	313E	80219	1400-1499	
WOLF CT	Frederick	707W	80504	5300-5399	
WOLF CT	Monument	908S	80132	11800-18899	
WOLF RD	Gilpin Co	760V	80403	1-299	
WOLF RD	Park Co	820Z	80421	1-199	
WOLF ST	Frederick	707W	80504	5400-5499	
WOLF CREEK DR	Brighton	138V	80601	2400-2499	
WOLF CREEK DR	Longmont	12Y	80501	900-1099	
WOLF CREEK DR E	Arapahoe Co	794S	80136	600-1299	
WOLF CREEK RD	Adams Co	793H	80136	None	
WOLF CREEK RD N	Arapahoe Co	793Z	80136	None	
WOLF CREEK RD S	Arapahoe Co	793Z	80136	None	
	Arapahoe Co	813M	80136	None	
WOLF CREEK TRAIL	Broomfield	162L	80020	100-199	
WOLFDALE DR	Lone Tree	376Y	80124	9200-9399	
WOLFE CT S	Highlands Ranch	404A	80129	9400-9499	
WOLFE DR S	Highlands Ranch	404A	80129	9300-9499	
WOLFE PL S	Highlands Ranch	404A	80129	9300-9499	
WOLFE ST S	Highlands Ranch	404A	80129	9300-9499	
WOLFENSBERGER RD	Castle Rock	497F	80109	1-399	
WOLFENSBERGER RD W	Castle Rock	496M	80109	1-799	
WOLFENSBERGER RD W	Douglas Co	496P	80109	800-1999	
WOLFENSBERGER RD W	Douglas Co	867G	80109	2000-2599	
	Douglas Co	867G	80135	2600-3599	
WOLFF AVE S	Jefferson Co	823N	80433	9600-9899	
WOLFF CT	Broomfield	163W	80020	12200-12399	
	Broomfield	163S	80020	12700-12899	
	Westminster	223J	80030	7800-7999	
	Westminster	223A	80031	8600-8799	
	Westminster	193S	80031	9800-9899	
	Westminster	193N	80031	10100-10199	
	Westminster	193E	80031	11300-11399	
WOLFF CT S	Arapahoe Co	373A	80128	6700-6799	
	Littleton	343W	80123	5900-6399	
WOLFF DR	Broomfield	163W	80020	12200-12399	
WOLFF PL	Broomfield	163W	80020	12200-12299	
WOLFF ST	Adams Co	253E	80212	None	
	Arvada	253A	80003	6000-6199	
	Arvada	223W	80003	6200-6599	
	Broomfield	163S	80020	12500-12799	
	Denver	283N	80219	1-399	
	Denver	283N	80204	400-1099	
	Denver	283J	80204	1200-1699	
	Denver	283A	80212	2400-2699	
	Denver	253S	80212	2700-4599	
	Westminster	223S	80030	6900-7199	
	Westminster	223N	80030	7200-7599	
	Westminster	223J	80031	8000-8099	
	Westminster	193S	80031	9900-10099	
	Westminster	193N	80031	10100-10399	
	Westminster	193E	80031	11200-11399	
	Westminster	193A	80031	11500-11899	
WOLFF ST S	Denver	283S	80219	1-699	
	Denver	313A	80219	700-999	
	Denver	313J	80219	1100-2099	
	Denver	313N	80219	2200-2599	
	Denver	313S	80236	2700-3499	
	Denver	343E	80236	3500-4599	
	Littleton	373J	80128	7400-7599	
WOLFF WAY	Westminster	193J	80031	10600-10799	
	Westminster	193E	80031	11000-11199	
WOLFF WAY S	Denver	313N	80219	2600-2699	
WOLF POINT DR	Jefferson Co	339R	80465	5300-5399	
WOLF POINT TRAIL	Jefferson Co	339V	80465	5400-5499	
WOLFTONGUE RD	Boulder Co	741E	80466	1-299	
WOLF TOOTH PASS	Jefferson Co	371P	80127	11300-11499	
WOLHURST DR	Littleton	373P	80128	None	
WOLVERINE CT	Douglas Co	436T	80108	600-899	
WOLVERINE CT	Jefferson Co	824R	80127	12900-13199	
WOLVERINE LOOP	Broomfield	133K	80020	None	
WOLVERINE WAY	El Paso Co	908Y	80132	400-499	
WOLVERINE TRAIL	Jefferson Co	367P	80439	26200-26599	
WONDER DR	Castle Rock	499N	80109	None	
WONDER DR	Jefferson Co	823W	80433	11700-11899	
WONDERLAND HILL AVE	Boulder	97Q	80304	3700-4199	
WONDERLAND HILL CIR	Boulder	97Q	80304	3700-3799	
WONDER TRAIL	Boulder Co	742W	80403	1-299	
WONDERVIEW AVE	Jefferson Co	336Z	80439	28000-28199	
WONDERVIEW CT	Boulder Co	129B	80303	1400-6099	
WOOD CT	Longmont	40C	80503	900-999	
WOOD LN	Morrison	339C	80465	100-199	
WOOD RD	Clear Creek Co	801A	80452	100-199	
WOODARD CIR W	Lakewood	312P	80227	7700-7899	
WOODARD DR W	Lakewood	312P	80227	7600-8399	
	Lakewood	312J	80227	8400-8999	
	Lakewood	311M	80227	9000-9199	
WOODBINE CT	Douglas Co	432T	80125	6200-6399	
WOODBINE PL	Gilpin Co	741Y	80403	1-99	
WOODBOURNE HOLLOW RD					
	Boulder Co	99J	80301	5700-5899	
WOODBOURNE TERRACE					
	Castle Rock	497D	80104	1800-2099	
WOODBRIAR DR	Highlands Ranch	405P	80126	2800-3199	
WOODBROOK LN	Parker	410S	80138	20400-20499	
WOODBURY LN	Jefferson Co	306Q	80439	2300-2399	
WOODCHUCK WAY	Jefferson Co	365F	80439	6700-7099	
WOODCLIFF CT	Elbert Co	912L	80106	9500-9699	
WOODCREST CIR	Douglas Co	907H	80133	14300-14499	
WOOD DUCK AVE	Platteville	708G	80651	None	
WOOD DUCK CT	Frederick	707W	80504	5800-5899	
WOODFERN	Jefferson Co	370L	80127	1-99	
WOODFIELD DR	Monument	908W	80132	None	
WOODGLEN PL	Castle Pines North	436P	80108	7300-7399	
WOODGLENN BLVD	Thornton	195C	80233	3700-4399	
WOOD GROVE CT	Castle Pines North	436P	80108	7300-7399	
WOODHALL CT	Douglas Co	887H	80118	6800-6899	
WOODHAVEN CT	Longmont	42N	80501	None	
WOODHAVEN DR	Douglas Co	870A	80116	1100-1799	
WOODHAVEN DR	El Paso Co	909T	80908	17600-18599	
WOODHAVEN PL	El Paso Co	909T	80908	18000-18099	
WOODHAVEN RIDGE RD	Douglas Co	850N	80134	10200-10899	
WOODHOUSE LN	Castle Rock	496B	80109	None	
WOODHURST CIR	Highlands Ranch	405R	80130	None	
WOODLAND CIR E	Highlands Ranch	374X	80126	1-99	
WOODLAND CT	Boulder	128S	80305	1100-1199	
WOODLAND CT	Brighton	140J	80601	None	
WOODLAND CT E	Highlands Ranch	374Y	80126	100-199	
WOODLAND DR	Highlands Ranch	374Y	80126	9000-9299	
WOODLAND DR	Jefferson Co	305F	80439	32200-34399	
WOODLAND LN	Highlands Ranch	374X	80126	None	
WOODLAND LN	Jefferson Co	278T	80401	100-499	
	Jefferson Co	305F	80439	1100-1199	
WOODLANDS	Jefferson Co	336A	80439	3400-3499	
WOODLANDS BLVD	Castle Rock	497H	80104	1300-1599	
	Castle Rock	467U	80104	3500-4599	
WOODLANDS DR	Elbert Co	892H	80117	26800-26999	
WOODLAND TRAIL N	Douglas Co	410C	80138	12300-12999	
WOODLAWN DR	Boulder Co	11M	80504	12600-12799	
WOODLEY AVE	Douglas Co	846V	80135	4900-4999	
WOOD LILY DR	Jefferson Co	308E	80401	900-1099	
WOODMAN DR E	Parker	379X	80134	None	
WOODMAN WAY S	Parker	379X	80134	9000-9099	
WOODMONT WAY	Castle Pines North	436P	80108	1300-1399	
WOODMOOR DR	El Paso Co	908T	80132	500-1999	
WOODMOOR ACRES DR	Monument	908X	80132	None	
WOODMOOR WEST DR	Douglas Co	907C	80118	13500-13599	
WOODPECKER LN	Elbert Co	850V	80107	1900-2299	
WOODRIDGE CT	Jefferson Co	339R	80465	17000-17199	
WOODRIDGE RD	Douglas Co	870K	80116	500-899	
WOODROCK DR	Douglas Co	408M	80134	10500-10599	
WOODROSE CT S	Highlands Ranch	403L	80129	10100-10299	
WOODROSE LN S	Highlands Ranch	403L	80129	10100-10399	
WOODROSE PL W	Highlands Ranch	403M	80129	2500-2699	
WOODRUFF	Jefferson Co	370F	80127	1-99	
WOODRUFF ST	Weld Co	729B	80621	7000-7999	
WOODRUFF WAY	Douglas Co	408L	80134	15300-15499	
WOODS DR	Jefferson Co	336P	80439	29700-29999	
WOODS LN	Park Co	841W	80421	None	
WOODS RD	Douglas Co	867S	80135	3600-4299	
WOODSAGE LN	Castle Rock	468X	80104	None	
WOODSIDE CIR	Jefferson Co	842A	80470	1-99	
WOODSIDE DR	Jefferson Co	842E	80470	9400-12899	
	Jefferson Co	305C	80439	32400-32799	
WOODSIDE DR	Park Co	841D	80470	1-2299	
WOODSIDE LN	Parker	410W	80138	20900-21399	
WOODSIDE RD	Longmont	12U	80501	1000-1199	
WOODSMOKE LN	Jefferson Co	277T	80401	26100-26199	
WOODSON DR	Erie	102Q	80516	300-499	
WOOD SORREL	Jefferson Co	370L	80127	1-99	
WOOD SORREL DR	Littleton	343T	80123	5800-5999	
WOOD SORRELL RD	Douglas Co	887F	80118	None	
WOODSTOCK CT	Douglas Co	436M	80108	7700-7899	
WOODSTOCK LN	Douglas Co	436M	80108	200-399	
WOODSTOCK PL	Boulder	128S	80305	2500-2599	
WOODSTONE WAY	El Paso Co	908T	80132	1600-1699	
WOODWARD ST	Erie	102W	80516	1500-1799	
WOODWARD ST	Keenesburg	732A	80643	100-599	
WOODWARD ST	Weld Co	732B	80643	None	
WOODWORTH ST	Monument	908S	80132	300-599	
WOODY LN	Jefferson Co	249V	80403	None	
WOODY WAY S	Highlands Ranch	374V	80126	8400-8699	
WOODY CREEK	Jefferson Co	336A	80439	3400-3499	
WOODY CREEK RD N	Douglas Co	410A	80138	12100-12599	
WOOSTER AVE	Firestone	727B	80504	None	
WOOSTER DR	Firestone	727B	80504	None	
WORCHESTER CT	Aurora	288A	80011	None	
WORCHESTER CT S	Aurora	318N	80014	2400-2599	
WORCHESTER DR	Commerce City	198J	80022	10400-10699	
WORCHESTER ST	Aurora	288J	80011	1000-1299	
	Aurora	288J	80011	1300-1399	
	Aurora	288A	80045	2200-2299	
	Aurora	258W	80011	3000-3199	
	Commerce City	198J	80022	10500-10699	
	Denver	258J	80239	4900-5599	
WORCHESTER ST S	Aurora	318A	80012	600-799	
	Aurora	318J	80014	2000-2099	
WORCHESTER ST S	Centennial	348W	80111	None	
WORCHESTER WAY S	Aurora	288W	80012	400-499	
WORLEY DR	Adams Co	224N	80221	1000-7399	
WORTHINGTON CIR	Douglas Co	408J	80134	None	
WORTHINGTON PL	Douglas Co	408J	80134	None	
WRANGER CT	Highlands Ranch	375Y	80126	None	
WRANGLER RD	Thornton	195U	80229	None	
WRANGLER RD E	Douglas Co	467A	80108	400-599	
WRANGLER WAY	Mead	706G	80542	13600-13899	
WRANGLER TRAIL	Jefferson Co	844F	80127	16901-16999	O
WRAY CT	Parker	409J	80134	11500-11599	
WREN	Jefferson Co	370B	80127	1-99	
WREN CIR	Weld Co	729Q	80621	17100-17199	
WREN COVE	Lafayette	132N	80026	800-899	
WREN CT	Frederick	707W	80504	4800-4999	
WREN CT	Longmont	41R	80501	1200-1298	E
WREN ST	Federal Heights	193V	80260	9700-9799	
WRIGHT AVE	Boulder	98U	80301	3100-3299	
WRIGHT CIR	Boulder	98U	80301	3300-3399	

STREET NAME	CITY or COUNTY	MAP GRID	ZIP CODE	BLOCK RANGE	O/E
WRIGHT CT	Arvada	221S	80004	6700-7199	
	Jefferson Co	281J	80401	900-999	
	Lakewood	281S	80228	1-99	
	Lakewood	281E	80215	1501-1599	O
	Lakewood	251W	80215	2800-2899	
	Longmont	11Q	80501	2100-2199	
	Wheat Ridge	251W	80215	2900-3199	
	Wheat Ridge	251W	80033	3200-3299	
	Wheat Ridge	251S	80033	3800-3899	
WRIGHT CT	Erie	103N	80516	None	
WRIGHT CT S	Jefferson Co	341E	80465	4300-4499	
	Jefferson Co	341J	80465	4900-4999	
	Jefferson Co	341W	80127	5900-6099	
	Lakewood	281S	80228	1-99	
	Lakewood	311E	80228	1200-1299	
	Lakewood	311J	80228	1500-1599	
WRIGHT DR S	Jefferson Co	823N	80433	9500-9699	
WRIGHT ST	Arvada	251A	80004	6000-6299	
	Arvada	220Z	80004	6400-6499	
	Arvada	221S	80004	6700-6899	
	Arvada	220H	80005	8400-8499	
	Lakewood	281S	80228	200-599	
	Lakewood	281N	80401	700-799	
	Lakewood	281J	80401	1100-1299	
	Wheat Ridge	251W	80215	2900-3199	
	Wheat Ridge	251W	80033	3300-3899	
	Wheat Ridge	251N	80033	4200-4399	
WRIGHT ST S	Jefferson Co	341E	80465	4400-4499	
	Jefferson Co	341S	80127	5900-5999	
	Jefferson Co	371A	80127	6400-6599	
	Lakewood	280Z	80228	400-499	
	Lakewood	311E	80228	1100-2399	
WRIGHT WAY	Broomfield	163E	80020	14200-14399	
WRIGHT WAY S	Jefferson Co	341E	80465	4300-4499	
	Jefferson Co	341J	80465	4600-4899	
	Jefferson Co	311S	80228	None	
WYANDOT CIR	Thornton	193R	80260	10000-10199	
	Westminster	193D	80234	11800-11999	
WYANDOT CT	Westminster	163R	80234	13000-13099	
WYANDOT DR	Adams Co	223M	80221	2000-2299	
WYANDOT ST	Adams Co	253H	80221	5200-5899	
	Adams Co	223M	80221	7600-8099	
	Adams Co	223H	80221	8300-8399	
	Adams Co	133Z	80020	14800-14899	
	Denver	283V	80223	200-399	
	Denver	283R	80204	800-999	
	Denver	253Z	80211	2700-4799	
	Denver	253M	80221	4800-5099	
	Northglenn	193R	80234	10400-10599	
	Westminster	193H	80234	11200-11299	
	Westminster	163R	80234	13100-13199	
	Westminster	163M	80234	13500-13599	
WYANDOT ST S	Denver	313M	80223	1300-1899	
	Englewood	313V	80110	2900-3099	
WYANDOT WAY	Westminster	163R	80234	12901-12999	O
WYANDOT WAY S	Denver	313H	80223	1200-1299	
WYANODOTTE RD	Jefferson Co	338V	80454	20700-20999	
WYATT DR	Hudson	730Q	80642	None	
WYCO DR	Northglenn	195A	80233	11500-11799	
WYDEMERE CIR	Longmont	12Q	80501	1000-1099	
WYECLIFF CT S	Highlands Ranch	405F	80126	10000-10099	
WYECLIFF DR S	Highlands Ranch	405F	80126	9800-10099	
WYECLIFF LN E	Highlands Ranch	405F	80126	2900-3099	
WYECLIFF PL S	Highlands Ranch	405F	80126	9900-9999	
WYECLIFF WAY E	Highlands Ranch	405F	80126	2800-3099	
WYMAN WAY	Westminster	223S	80030	6800-6899	
WYNDHAM	Elbert Co	870M	80107	None	
WYNDHAM HILL PKWY	Frederick	726G	80516	2700-4099	
WYNDHAM PARK DR	Arvada	220Y	80004	6200-6399	
	Arvada	250D	80004	None	
WYNKOOP ST	Denver	284A	80202	1400-1999	
	Denver	254V	80216	3400-4599	
WYNSPIRE RD	Highlands Ranch	405Q	80126	10600-10799	
WYNSPIRE WAY	Highlands Ranch	405L	80126	10500-10799	
WYNTERBROOK DR	Highlands Ranch	405E	80126	2100-2599	
WYNWOOD CIR	Highlands Ranch	405L	80126	3800-3999	
WYNWOOD WAY	Highlands Ranch	405L	80126	10000-10199	
WYOMING CIR	Golden	248R	80403	400-599	
WYOMING CIR E	Aurora	317H	80112	12700-12899	
	Aurora	319E	80017	16800-16899	
	Aurora	321E	80018	24600-24799	
WYOMING DR E	Aurora	318G	80017	15400-15599	
	Aurora	318H	80017	16300-16599	
	Aurora	319E	80017	16900-17199	
	Aurora	319G	80017	19100-19199	
WYOMING PL E	Aurora	317E	80247	9900-10099	
	Aurora	317H	80112	12700-12899	
	Aurora	318E	80012	13300-13399	
	Aurora	318F	80012	14200-14499	
	Aurora	319F	80017	17800-18399	
	Aurora	319G	80017	19100-19199	
	Aurora	321E	80018	24600-24799	
	Aurora	319E	80017	None	
	Denver	315H	80222	4500-4799	
	Denver	316F	80224	6900-7199	
WYOMING PL W	Denver	313E	80219	4400-5199	
WYOMING ST	Golden	248R	80403	500-1499	

X

STREET NAME	CITY or COUNTY	MAP GRID	ZIP CODE	BLOCK RANGE	O/E
XANADU ST	Aurora	288J	80011	1000-1299	
	Aurora	288E	80045	1700-1899	
	Aurora	288A	80011	2500-2799	
	Aurora	258W	80011	3000-3199	
	Aurora	258S	80239	3700-3799	
	Commerce City	198J	80022	10500-10799	
	Denver	258J	80239	4900-5599	
XANADU ST S	Aurora	288W	80012	300-499	
	Aurora	318W	80014	3200-3299	
XANADU ST S	Centennial	348W	80111	None	
XANADU WAY S	Aurora	318S	80014	1900-2899	
	Centennial	348W	80111	None	
	Centennial	378A	80111	None	
XANTHIA CT	Denver	256V	80238	3300-3599	
	Denver	286D	80238	None	
	Thornton	166R	80602	12800-12899	
	Thornton	136V	80602	None	
XANTHIA CT S	Centennial	376M	80112	7500-7599	
	Centennial	376R	80112	7900-7999	
	Denver	316V	80231	2900-2999	
	Denver	316Z	80231	3300-3399	
XANTHIA PL S	Centennial	376D	80112	6700-6799	
	Centennial	376M	80112	7500-7599	
XANTHIA ST	Adams Co	226D	80022	8600-8699	
	Denver	286M	80220	1100-1999	
	Denver	256Z	80238	2800-2899	
	Denver	256V	80238	3300-3599	
	Denver	286D	80238	None	
XANTHIA ST S	Centennial	376H	80112	6800-7399	
	Denver	316V	80231	3000-3199	
	Denver	346D	80237	3800-3899	
	Denver	346H	80237	4400-4499	
	Denver	346M	80237	4700-4799	
XANTHIA WAY	Denver	286D	80238	None	
XANTHIA WAY	Thornton	136R	80602	None	
XANTHIA WAY S	Centennial	376H	80112	7200-7399	
XAPARY ST	Aurora	288J	80011	1200-1299	
XAPARY ST S	Aurora	288W	80012	300-399	
	Aurora	318N	80014	2200-2399	
XAPARY WAY	Denver	258E	80239	5500-5599	
XAPARY WAY S	Aurora	318N	80014	2100-2299	
XAVIER CIR	Arvada	223S	80030	6800-6899	
XAVIER CT	Arvada	223W	80003	6100-6599	
	Westminster	223J	80030	7700-7799	
	Westminster	193S	80031	9800-9899	
	Westminster	193N	80031	9900-10399	
	Westminster	193E	80031	11300-11399	
	Westminster	193A	80031	11700-11899	
XAVIER CT S	Littleton	343W	80123	6300-6399	
XAVIER DR	Lochbuie	729Z	80603	400-599	
XAVIER DR	Westminster	193E	80031	11200-11299	
XAVIER LN	Broomfield	163J	80020	13600-13699	
XAVIER ST	Adams Co	223A	80031	8800-8999	
	Adams Co	253E	80212	None	
	Arvada	223W	80003	6100-6599	
	Broomfield	163S	80020	12600-12799	
	Denver	283N	80219	1-399	
	Denver	283N	80204	400-599	
	Denver	283J	80204	1200-1699	
	Denver	283A	80212	2400-2699	
	Denver	253W	80212	2700-2899	
	Denver	253S	80212	3800-4599	
	Westminster	223S	80030	7000-7199	
	Westminster	223N	80030	7200-7599	
	Westminster	223J	80030	7800-7999	
	Westminster	193N	80031	10300-10399	
	Westminster	193W	80031	None	
XAVIER ST S	Denver	283W	80219	1-599	
	Denver	313A	80219	700-799	
	Denver	313N	80219	1100-2599	
	Denver	313S	80236	2700-2799	
	Denver	343J	80236	2800-4499	
XAVIER WAY	Westminster	223N	80030	7100-7199	
	Westminster	193A	80031	11600-11699	
XAVIER WAY S	Denver	343E	80236	4100-4199	
XENIA CIR S	Centennial	376H	80112	7100-7399	
XENIA CT	Adams Co	136M	80602	16200-16299	
	Thornton	136V	80602	None	
XENIA CT S	Arapahoe Co	316M	80231	1800-1999	
	Centennial	376M	80112	7500-7599	
	Centennial	376R	80112	7900-8299	
	Denver	316V	80231	3000-3099	
XENIA PL S	Centennial	376M	80112	7500-7599	
XENIA ST	Adams Co	226D	80022	8600-8699	
	Adams Co	226D	80022	8700-8798	E
	Adams Co	136Q	80602	16100-16199	
	Commerce City	226D	80022	8701-8799	O
	Denver	286M	80220	1100-1999	
	Denver	256Z	80238	2800-2899	
	Denver	256V	80238	3300-3499	
	Denver	286D	80238	None	
	Thornton	136Z	80602	14800-15299	
XENIA ST S	Arapahoe Co	316H	80247	1100-1399	
	Denver	316Z	80231	3000-3399	
	Denver	346D	80237	3700-3899	
	Denver	346H	80237	4400-4499	
	Denver	346M	80237	4700-5099	
XENIA WAY	Thornton	136V	80602	None	
XENIA WAY S	Arapahoe Co	316M	80231	1900-2099	
XENON CT	Arvada	220V	80004	7000-7199	
	Arvada	220H	80005	8200-8299	
	Jefferson Co	281J	80401	900-999	
	Jefferson Co	250D	80002	5600-5799	
	Lakewood	280H	80215	1900-1999	
XENON CT S	Jefferson Co	311S	80228	2500-2599	
	Jefferson Co	341E	80465	4300-4399	
	Jefferson Co	341J	80465	4900-4999	
	Jefferson Co	371A	80127	6400-6599	
	Lakewood	280Z	80228	500-799	
	Lakewood	310M	80228	1500-1599	
	Lakewood	311N	80228	2000-2099	
	Lakewood	311A	80228	None	
XENON DR	Arvada	220V	80004	6600-6799	
XENON LN	Castle Rock	467G	80108	None	
XENON ST	Arvada	251E	80002	5200-5399	
	Arvada	250D	80004	6000-6199	
	Arvada	220V	80004	6800-6899	
	Arvada	220H	80005	8200-8399	
	Jefferson Co	281J	80401	1000-1399	
	Lakewood	280V	80228	1-199	
	Lakewood	281N	80401	700-799	
	Lakewood	251W	80215	2800-2899	
	Wheat Ridge	251W	80215	2900-3199	
	Wheat Ridge	251N	80033	4100-4399	
XENON ST S	Jefferson Co	311N	80228	2500-2599	
	Jefferson Co	341E	80465	4300-4399	
	Jefferson Co	341N	80127	5300-5499	
	Jefferson Co	370D	80127	6400-6599	
	Lakewood	311J	80228	1900-2199	
XENON WAY	Castle Rock	467G	80108	None	
XENON WAY	Lakewood	251E	80002	5600-5799	
XENON WAY S	Jefferson Co	311S	80228	2400-2599	
	Jefferson Co	341J	80465	4600-4899	
XENOPHON CT	Jefferson Co	281J	80401	900-999	
XENOPHON CT S	Jefferson Co	340R	80127	5100-5299	
XENOPHON ST	Arvada	250D	80004	6000-6099	
	Jefferson Co	280M	80401	1000-1299	
	Lakewood	280R	80401	700-899	
XENOPHON ST S	Jefferson Co	311S	80228	2500-2599	
	Jefferson Co	341E	80465	4300-4499	
	Jefferson Co	340M	80465	4700-4899	
	Jefferson Co	370D	80127	6400-6599	
	Lakewood	311N	80228	2000-2299	
XENOPHON WAY S	Jefferson Co	340H	80465	4300-4499	
	Jefferson Co	340M	80465	4800-4999	
	Jefferson Co	340R	80127	5300-5499	
	Jefferson Co	340Z	80127	6000-6099	
XENOPHONE CT	Arvada	220H	80005	8200-8299	
XERIC CT S	Denver	316V	80231	3000-3199	
XERIC WAY S	Denver	346H	80237	4400-4499	
XYLON ST	Golden	279U	80401	None	

Y

STREET NAME	CITY or COUNTY	MAP GRID	ZIP CODE	BLOCK RANGE	O/E
YAKIMA CT	Lochbuie	140C	80603	500-799	
YAKIMA ST	Lochbuie	140G	80603	100-199	
YAKIMA ST S	Arapahoe Co	350U	80015	5500-5699	
	Arapahoe Co	350Y	80015	5900-6099	
YAKIMA WAY S	Arapahoe Co	350U	80015	5500-5799	
YALE AVE E	Arapahoe Co	316S	80222	5600-6199	
	Arapahoe Co	316U	80231	7501-8299	O
	Arapahoe Co	316U	80231	8300-8499	
	Arapahoe Co	810G	80137	26700-31299	
	Arapahoe Co	811E	80137	31300-32899	
	Aurora	317U	80014	10500-13199	
	Aurora	318L	80014	13200-15299	
	Aurora	318V	80013	15300-16899	
	Aurora	319S	80013	16800-17999	
	Aurora	321M	80018	None	
	Denver	314V	80210	1-1199	O
	Denver	314V	80210	1200-1699	
	Denver	315T	80210	1700-3199	
	Denver	315U	80222	3500-5499	
	Denver	316S	80222	5500-5599	
	Denver	316S	80222	6200-6499	
	Denver	316T	80224	6500-7299	
	Denver	316V	80231	8600-8898	E
	Denver	317S	80231	9900-10499	
	Englewood	314V	80113	2-1198	E
YALE AVE S	Lakewood	310R	80228	None	
YALE AVE W	Denver	314T	80223	1-499	O
	Denver	313P	80219	2400-5199	
	Denver	312U	80227	5200-6898	E
	Denver	312U	80227	6900-7599	
	Englewood	314T	80110	300-598	E
	Englewood	313V	80110	2000-2399	
	Lakewood	312U	80227	5201-6899	O
	Lakewood	312S	80227	7600-8999	
	Lakewood	311V	80227	9000-9999	
	Lakewood	310R	80228	13100-14799	
	Lakewood	310S	80228	15900-16399	
YALE CIR	Boulder	128T	80305	1000-1099	
YALE CIR E	Aurora	319Q	80013	None	
	Denver	315V	80222	5100-5299	
YALE CT	Louisville	130Y	80027	900-999	
YALE CT E	Aurora	317U	80014	11800-11999	
YALE DR	Longmont	10U	80503	3600-3799	
YALE DR E	Highlands Ranch	406A	80130	6200-6799	
YALE LN S	Highlands Ranch	406B	80130	9300-9499	
YALE PKWY E	Aurora	320R	80018	23300-23999	
	Aurora	321N	80018	24200-24899	
YALE PL E	Aurora	317U	80014	11400-11499	
	Aurora	318V	80013	16500-16599	
	Aurora	319T	80013	17800-17899	
	Aurora	319R	80013	None	
	Englewood	314U	80110	600-699	
YALE PL W	Jefferson Co	311S	80228	None	
	Lakewood	311U	80227	10100-10199	
	Lakewood	310R	80228	13100-13199	
	Lakewood	310U	80228	14300-14599	
YALE RD	Boulder	128P	80305	500-899	
	Boulder	128T	80305	900-1099	
	Boulder Co	159B	80303	None	
YALE ST	Palmer Lake	907R	80133	None	
YALE ST W	Englewood	314S	80110	1600-1999	
YALE WAY	Longmont	10U	80503	3700-3799	
YALE WAY E	Aurora	317U	80014	11400-11999	
YALE WAY E	Denver	315T	80210	3200-3499	
YAMPA CIR S	Centennial	349P	80015	5100-5299	
YAMPA CT	Boulder Co	99D	80301	7000-7099	
YAMPA CT	Commerce City	769J	80022	None	
YAMPA CT S	Arapahoe Co	349X	80016	6000-6199	
	Aurora	319F	80017	1300-1499	
	Aurora	319K	80013	2200-2299	
	Aurora	319T	80013	2900-2999	
	Aurora	319X	80013	3500-3699	
	Aurora	349K	80015	5000-5099	
	Centennial	349P	80015	5200-5299	
	Centennial	349T	80015	5500-5599	
	Foxfield	379F	80016	6900-7899	
YAMPA DR	Douglas Co	887H	80118	6700-6999	
YAMPA ST	Adams Co	169T	80022	12500-12599	
	Commerce City	769E	80022	None	
	Commerce City	769J	80022	None	
	Commerce City	769N	80022	None	
	Commerce City	169X	80603	None	
	Denver	769W	80239	None	
YAMPA ST S	Arapahoe Co	349X	80016	5900-6199	
	Aurora	289X	80017	900-999	
	Aurora	319B	80017	1000-1099	
	Aurora	349B	80013	3600-4099	
	Aurora	349K	80015	4700-4799	
	Aurora	319X	80013	None	
	Centennial	349P	80015	5100-5599	
	Centennial	349T	80015	5600-5899	
	Centennial	379K	80016	7500-7799	
	Foxfield	379F	80016	7000-7499	
YAMPA WAY	Weld Co	139K	80601	16400-16699	
YAMPA WAY S	Aurora	319F	80017	1300-1899	
	Aurora	319T	80013	2800-2999	
	Aurora	319X	80013	3500-3699	
	Aurora	349B	80013	3700-3799	
YAMPA RIVER RD	Weld Co	706M	80504	None	

STREET NAME	CITY or COUNTY	MAP GRID	ZIP CODE	BLOCK RANGE	O/E
YANK CIR S	Lakewood	**310R**	80228	2300-2499	
YANK CT	Arvada	**250D**	80004	6000-6199	
	Arvada	**220Z**	80004	6200-6499	
	Arvada	**220M**	80005	7800-7999	
	Arvada	**220H**	80005	8400-8699	
	Jefferson Co	**280H**	80401	1700-1999	
	Jefferson Co	**250M**	80002	5100-5299	
	Lakewood	**280V**	80228	100-299	
YANK CT S	Jefferson Co	**340R**	80465	4900-5099	
	Jefferson Co	**340R**	80127	5100-5299	
	Jefferson Co	**340V**	80127	5500-5699	
	Jefferson Co	**340Z**	80127	6000-6099	
	Lakewood	**310H**	80228	1200-1299	
	Lakewood	**310M**	80228	1700-1899	
	Lakewood	**311N**	80228	2200-2299	
	Lakewood	**310R**	80228	2400-2499	
YANK PL S	Lakewood	**310M**	80228	1800-1899	
YANK ST	Jefferson Co	**280M**	80401	1000-1499	
YANK ST S	Lakewood	**310R**	80228	2300-2399	
	Jefferson Co	**340M**	80465	4300-4999	
	Lakewood	**310H**	80228	1300-1499	
	Lakewood	**310H**	80228	1500-1599	
YANK WAY	Arvada	**220Z**	80004	6300-6699	
	Arvada	**220U**	80004	13700-13799	
	Jefferson Co	**250H**	80002	5200-5599	
YANK WAY S	Jefferson Co	**340M**	80465	4700-4899	
	Jefferson Co	**340V**	80127	5400-5499	
	Lakewood	**280V**	80228	1-299	
	Lakewood	**310M**	80228	1800-1899	
	Lakewood	**311N**	80228	2000-2299	
YANKAKEE DR	Douglas Co	**466H**	80108	600-5299	
YANKEE CT	Arvada	**219L**	80007	None	
YANKEE CREEK RD	Clear Creek Co	**801X**	80439	100-2099	
	Clear Creek Co	**821B**	80439	2100-2499	
YARMOUTH AVE	Boulder	**97H**	80304	1200-1999	
	Boulder Co	**98E**	80301	2000-2599	
YARNELL CT S	Denver	**316V**	80231	3000-3099	
YARNELL DR W	Douglas Co	**907G**	80133	900-1499	
YARROW CIR E	Superior	**160V**	80027	2900-3199	
YARROW CIR W	Superior	**160U**	80027	2900-3299	
YARROW CT	Arvada	**222F**	80005	8200-8499	
YARROW CT	Boulder	**128S**	80305	2500-2599	
YARROW CT	Jefferson Co	**192T**	80021	9800-9899	
	Wheat Ridge	**252X**	80033	3200-3399	
	Wheat Ridge	**252T**	80033	4100-4199	
YARROW CT S	Jefferson Co	**342X**	80123	6300-6399	
	Jefferson Co	**372F**	80128	7200-7299	
	Jefferson Co	**372P**	80128	7700-7799	
	Lakewood	**312K**	80232	1600-1699	
	Lakewood	**342F**	80235	4200-4299	
YARROW PL	Castle Pines North	**436C**	80108	400-499	
YARROW ST	Arvada	**252K**	80002	4900-5199	
	Arvada	**252F**	80002	5600-5799	
	Arvada	**252B**	80004	6000-6199	
	Arvada	**222X**	80004	6200-6499	
	Arvada	**222T**	80004	6700-6999	
	Arvada	**222F**	80005	8000-8499	
	Brighton	**140J**	80601	None	
	Jefferson Co	**192T**	80021	9900-10099	
	Lafayette	**131B**	80026	None	
	Lakewood	**282T**	80226	1-99	
	Lakewood	**282K**	80214	1200-1399	
	Lakewood	**282F**	80214	1500-2099	
	Lakewood	**282B**	80214	2200-2599	
	Westminster	**192X**	80021	9100-9199	
	Westminster	**192F**	80021	11000-11199	
	Wheat Ridge	**252X**	80033	3200-3399	
	Wheat Ridge	**252T**	80033	3900-4099	
	Wheat Ridge	**252P**	80033	4200-4599	
YARROW ST S	Jefferson Co	**372B**	80123	6300-6699	
	Jefferson Co	**372F**	80128	7000-7299	
	Jefferson Co	**372K**	80128	7500-7899	
	Jefferson Co	**372P**	80128	8000-8099	
	Jefferson Co	**372T**	80128	8300-8999	
	Jefferson Co	**342K**	80123	None	
	Lakewood	**282T**	80226	1-299	
	Lakewood	**282X**	80226	500-799	
	Lakewood	**312B**	80226	900-1099	
	Lakewood	**312F**	80232	1300-1499	
	Lakewood	**312P**	80227	2100-2199	
	Lakewood	**312T**	80227	2300-2699	
	Lakewood	**312X**	80227	3300-3499	
	Lakewood	**342F**	80235	4001-4099	O
YARROW WAY S	Jefferson Co	**372B**	80123	6500-6599	
	Jefferson Co	**372F**	80128	7200-7399	
	Lakewood	**312P**	80227	2300-2499	
YATES CIR	Broomfield	**163S**	80020	4800-12799	
YATES CT	Arvada	**223W**	80003	6100-6199	
	Broomfield	**163W**	80020	4700-12299	
	Westminster	**223S**	80030	7000-7099	
	Westminster	**193N**	80031	10300-10399	
YATES CT S	Arapahoe Co	**373A**	80128	6700-6899	
	Littleton	**343W**	80123	5900-6399	
YATES DR	Westminster	**223A**	80031	8700-8799	
	Westminster	**193J**	80031	10600-10799	
YATES PL	Broomfield	**163W**	80020	5100-5199	
YATES ST	Adams Co	**253E**	80212	None	
	Broomfield	**163S**	80020	12600-12799	
	Denver	**283S**	80219	1-399	
	Denver	**283N**	80204	400-999	
	Denver	**283J**	80204	1200-1699	
	Denver	**283A**	80212	2400-2699	
	Denver	**253S**	80212	2700-4599	
	Westminster	**223S**	80030	6900-7199	
	Westminster	**223N**	80030	7500-7599	
	Westminster	**223J**	80030	7700-7999	
	Westminster	**223A**	80031	8800-9099	
	Westminster	**193W**	80031	9100-9199	
	Westminster	**193S**	80031	9800-10099	
YATES ST S	Denver	**283W**	80219	1-599	
	Denver	**313E**	80219	700-1699	
	Denver	**313N**	80219	1800-2599	
	Denver	**313S**	80236	2700-3099	
	Denver	**343J**	80236	3100-4699	
YATES WAY	Westminster	**193A**	80031	11600-11699	
YATES WAY S	Denver	**283S**	80219	100-199	
	Denver	**313J**	80219	1600-1699	
	Denver	**343E**	80236	4100-4199	

STREET NAME	CITY or COUNTY	MAP GRID	ZIP CODE	BLOCK RANGE	O/E
YAUPON AVE	Boulder	**97H**	80304	1400-1799	
YEAGER DR	Longmont	**11U**	80501	1000-1099	
	Longmont	**11R**	80501	1700-2099	
YEAGER PL	Longmont	**11Q**	80501	900-1099	
YEGGE RD	Jefferson Co	**369W**	80465	9000-9299	
	Jefferson Co	**823R**	80465	9300-9699	
YELLOWBELLS CT	Douglas Co	**887G**	80118	7300-7499	
YELLOW DAISY DR	Parker	**409S**	80134	None	
YELLOW FIELD WAY	Erie	**102P**	80516	100-399	
YELLOW FLAX	Jefferson Co	**370K**	80127	1-99	
YELLOW GRANITE WAY	Monument	**908X**	80132	1300-1399	
YELLOW JACKET RD	Arapahoe Co	**795N**	80136	900-1499	
YELLOW LOCUST	Jefferson Co	**370Q**	80127	1-99	
YELLOW PINE AVE	Boulder	**97G**	80304	700-1199	
	Boulder	**97H**	80304	1700-1799	
YELLOW PINE DR	Park Co	**841T**	80421	1-1099	
YELLOW ROSE WAY	Parker	**379W**	80134	17100-17299	
YELLOWSTONE	Weld Co	**706N**	80504	11000-11199	
YELLOWSTONE CT S	Arapahoe Co	**350Y**	80016	6300-6399	
YELLOWSTONE ST	Bow Mar	**342M**	80123	5200-5399	
	Jefferson Co	**280D**	80401	2100-2299	
YELLOWSTONE WAY S	Arapahoe Co	**350Y**	80016	6300-6399	
YELLOW TAIL ST	Adams Co	**792M**	80102	None	
YELLOW WING CT	El Paso Co	**909P**	80908	19500-19599	
YERKES CT	Adams Co	**794K**	80136	2800-2999	
YEW CT	Longmont	**12X**	80501	900-999	
YEW LN	Park Co	**841T**	80421	1-299	
YOKE TRAIL	Jefferson Co	**368M**	80465	20500-20699	
YORK AVE E	Parker	**410Q**	80138	23000-23299	
YORK CT S	Centennial	**375N**	80122	8100-8199	
YORK PL	Thornton	**195N**	80229	10200-10299	
YORK ST	Adams Co	**255A**	80216	5600-5999	
	Adams Co	**225N**	80229	6400-7999	
	Adams Co	**225E**	80229	8300-8599	
	Adams Co	**165A**	80602	13900-14399	
	Adams Co	**135S**	80602	14800-16799	
	Commerce City	**255E**	80022	5400-5799	
	Denver	**285N**	80206	600-1999	
	Denver	**285A**	80205	2000-2699	
	Denver	**255W**	80205	2700-3999	
	Denver	**255J**	80216	4000-5299	
	Northglenn	**195E**	80233	10900-11099	
	Thornton	**225A**	80229	8800-8999	
	Thornton	**195W**	80229	9100-9399	
	Thornton	**195S**	80229	9600-9999	
	Thornton	**195N**	80229	10000-10399	
	Thornton	**195A**	80233	11200-11999	
	Thornton	**165W**	80241	12100-12199	
	Thornton	**165S**	80241	12500-13599	
	Thornton	**165A**	80602	13600-13899	
	Thornton	**165A**	80602	14400-14799	
YORK ST S	Denver	**285W**	80209	300-699	
	Denver	**315A**	80209	700-1099	
	Denver	**315E**	80210	1100-1599	
	Denver	**315J**	80210	1900-2099	
	Denver	**315S**	80210	2300-3099	
	Englewood	**315W**	80113	3100-3199	
YORK WAY	Northglenn	**195E**	80233	11000-11199	
	Thornton	**165N**	80241	13300-13499	
YORK GULCH RD	Clear Creek Co	**780E**	80403	1-3099	
YORKSHIRE DR	Castle Pines North	**436M**	80108	7400-7999	
YOSEMITE CIR	Denver	**286M**	80230	None	
YOSEMITE CIR S	Arapahoe Co	**316R**	80231	2200-2299	
	Greenwood Village	**376D**	80111	6500-6699	
YOSEMITE CT S	Centennial	**376D**	80112	6800-6899	
	Centennial	**376R**	80112	8200-8298	E
	Greenwood Village	**346H**	80111	4300-4599	
	Greenwood Village	**376D**	80111	6600-6699	
YOSEMITE ST	Adams Co	**226D**	80640	8800-8999	
	Adams Co	**196Z**	80640	9000-9199	
	Adams Co	**166R**	80602	13100-13599	
	Adams Co	**166H**	80602	13600-14099	
	Adams Co	**166D**	80602	14500-14799	
	Adams Co	**136V**	80602	14800-16799	
	Aurora	**286M**	80230	1000-1099	
	Aurora	**286M**	80220	1100-1998	E
	Denver	**286R**	80230	700-1099	
	Denver	**286M**	80220	1101-1999	O
	Denver	**286D**	80238	2500-2599	
	Denver	**256Z**	80238	2800-2899	
	Denver	**256V**	80238	3300-3599	
YOSEMITE ST S	Arapahoe Co	**316R**	80231	2100-2299	
	Centennial	**376H**	80112	6700-8299	
	Denver	**316Z**	80231	2700-3499	
	Denver	**346M**	80237	3500-5099	
	Greenwood Village	**346Z**	80111	5900-6399	
	Greenwood Village	**376D**	80111	6400-6699	
	Lone Tree	**406D**	80124	9200-10199	
	Lone Tree	**376H**	80124	None	
YOSEMITE WAY	Adams Co	**196M**	80640	None	
YOST CT	Denver	**258E**	80239	5500-5599	
YOST ST	Aurora	**288J**	80011	1100-1299	
YOST ST S	Aurora	**288S**	80012	1-99	
	Aurora	**288W**	80012	300-399	
YOUNG CIR	Douglas Co	**527W**	80104	300-699	
YOUNG CT	Denver	**283S**	80219	100-199	
YOUNG CT	Erie	**103S**	80516	400-499	
YOUNG DR	Adams Co	**168C**	80601	14500-14699	
YOUNGBERRY ST	Castle Rock	**498R**	80104	6100-6199	
YOUNGFIELD CIR	Arvada	**220Z**	80004	6600-6699	
YOUNGFIELD CIR S	Lakewood	**280Z**	80228	400-499	
YOUNGFIELD CT	Arvada	**220V**	80004	6600-6799	
	Jefferson Co	**280H**	80401	1700-1899	
	Jefferson Co	**250M**	80002	5100-5199	
YOUNGFIELD CT S	Jefferson Co	**340R**	80465	5000-5099	
	Jefferson Co	**340R**	80127	5100-5499	
	Jefferson Co	**370D**	80127	6400-6499	
	Jefferson Co	**340V**	80127	None	
	Lakewood	**310D**	80228	500-899	
	Lakewood	**310H**	80228	1300-1399	
	Lakewood	**310H**	80228	1400-1599	
	Lakewood	**310M**	80228	1700-1799	
	Lakewood	**310M**	80228	1800-1899	
	Lakewood	**311N**	80228	2200-2299	
YOUNGFIELD DR	Lakewood	**280V**	80228	200-299	
	Lakewood	**280M**	80215	1500-1599	
YOUNGFIELD PL S	Lakewood	**310M**	80228	1800-1899	

STREET NAME	CITY or COUNTY	MAP GRID	ZIP CODE	BLOCK RANGE	O/E
YOUNGFIELD ST	Arvada	**250D**	80004	6000-6099	
	Arvada	**220Z**	80004	6400-6499	
	Arvada	**220M**	80005	7700-8099	
	Jefferson Co	**280M**	80401	1000-1499	
	Jefferson Co	**250M**	80033	4900-4999	
	Jefferson Co	**250H**	80002	5600-5799	
	Jefferson Co	**220R**	80005	7200-7399	
	Jefferson Co	**220D**	80005	8600-8699	
	Lakewood	**280H**	80401	1500-2799	
	Wheat Ridge	**250V**	80401	2800-4399	
YOUNGFIELD ST S	Jefferson Co	**310V**	80228	2600-2699	
	Jefferson Co	**340M**	80465	4300-4899	
	Jefferson Co	**340V**	80127	5400-5799	
	Lakewood	**310H**	80228	1400-1499	
	Lakewood	**311N**	80228	1900-2299	
YOUNGFIELD WAY	Jefferson Co	**250H**	80002	5200-5599	
YOUNGFIELD WAY S	Jefferson Co	**311N**	80228	2300-2399	
	Jefferson Co	**340V**	80127	5500-5699	
YOUNGHEART WAY	Castle Rock	**466Z**	80109	None	
YOUNGIELD CT S	Jefferson Co	**310V**	80228	2600-2699	
YUBA ST	Aurora	**288E**	80011	1300-1499	
YUBA ST S	Aurora	**288S**	80012	1-99	
	Aurora	**288S**	80011	None	
YUBA WAY	Denver	**258E**	80239	5500-5599	
YUBBA ST	Aurora	**288J**	80011	1000-1299	
YUCCA W	Douglas Co	**432N**	80125	11100-11299	
YUCCA CT	Boulder Co	**100E**	80301	7300-7399	
YUCCA CT	Golden	**279E**	80401	1800-1999	
YUCCA CT	Longmont	**12X**	80501	900-999	
YUCCA DR	Jefferson Co	**306Y**	80439	3000-3099	
YUCCA LN	Douglas Co	**908H**	80118	4000-4199	
YUCCA RD	Douglas Co	**908H**	80118	14000-14499	
YUCCA ST	Brighton	**140J**	80601	None	
YUCCA WAY	Thornton	**195X**	80229	8900-9399	
YUCCA HILLS RD E	Castle Rock	**497N**	80109	1-899	
YUCCA TRAIL N	Douglas Co	**441R**	80138	6500-6999	
YUKON CIR	Westminster	**192F**	80020	None	
YUKON CT	Arvada	**252B**	80004	5900-5999	
	Arvada	**222X**	80004	6200-6399	
	Arvada	**222F**	80005	7700-7799	
	Arvada	**222K**	80005	8200-8299	
	Jefferson Co	**192T**	80021	9600-9799	
	Wheat Ridge	**252T**	80033	3700-3799	
	Wheat Ridge	**252P**	80033	4400-4599	
YUKON CT S	Jefferson Co	**342X**	80123	6300-6399	
	Jefferson Co	**372F**	80128	6900-7399	
	Jefferson Co	**372K**	80128	7500-7599	
	Lakewood	**312K**	80232	1600-1699	
	Lakewood	**312P**	80227	2300-2399	
	Lakewood	**312T**	80227	2600-2699	
YUKON ST	Arvada	**252F**	80002	5600-5799	
	Arvada	**252B**	80004	5900-5999	
	Arvada	**222X**	80004	6200-6399	
	Lakewood	**282T**	80226	1-199	
	Lakewood	**282P**	80226	400-599	
	Lakewood	**282K**	80214	1200-1399	
	Lakewood	**282F**	80214	1600-1999	
	Westminster	**222F**	80005	8600-8799	
	Westminster	**222B**	80021	8800-9099	
	Westminster	**192X**	80021	9400-9599	
	Westminster	**192K**	80021	10600-10999	
YUKON ST S	Denver	**342K**	80123	4800-4899	
	Jefferson Co	**372B**	80123	6400-6699	
	Jefferson Co	**372F**	80128	6700-7299	
	Jefferson Co	**372P**	80128	8000-8299	
	Jefferson Co	**372T**	80128	8300-8999	
	Lakewood	**282T**	80226	1-199	
	Lakewood	**312B**	80226	900-1099	
	Lakewood	**312F**	80232	1300-1399	
	Lakewood	**312K**	80232	1600-1699	
	Lakewood	**312P**	80227	2100-2199	
YUKON WAY	Jefferson Co	**192P**	80021	10400-10599	
YUKON WAY S	Jefferson Co	**372B**	80123	6500-6699	
	Jefferson Co	**372F**	80128	6800-6999	
	Jefferson Co	**372K**	80128	7700-7799	
	Jefferson Co	**372P**	80128	8000-8299	
	Lakewood	**312P**	80227	2100-2599	
	Lakewood	**342F**	80235	4100-4299	
YULE CIR	Jefferson Co	**336Z**	80439	27800-27899	
YULE CT	Arvada	**219Q**	80007	None	
YULLE RD	Adams Co	**793R**	80102	None	
YULLE RD N	Arapahoe Co	**793V**	80102	1-1299	
	Arapahoe Co	**793Q**	80102	1300-1499	
YULLE RD S	Arapahoe Co	**793Z**	80102	1-799	
	Arapahoe Co	**813D**	80102	800-1099	
YUMA CIR	Boulder	**129J**	80303	500-599	
YUMA CIR	Douglas Co	**886L**	80118	7900-8299	
YUMA CT	Douglas Co	**886M**	80118	5500-5599	
YUMA PL	Douglas Co	**886L**	80118	8200-8299	
YUMA ST	Denver	**283V**	80223	1-399	
	Denver	**283R**	80204	400-499	
	Denver	**283M**	80204	900-1199	
YUMA ST S	Denver	**283Z**	80223	1-299	
	Denver	**313M**	80223	1700-1899	
YUMA TRAIL	Clear Creek Co	**821H**	80439	1-99	
YUMA TRAIL	Douglas Co	**886L**	80118	5800-5899	
YUM YUM TREE LN	Park Co	**841T**	80421	1-399	

Z

STREET NAME	CITY or COUNTY	MAP GRID	ZIP CODE	BLOCK RANGE	O/E
ZACHARY CT	Longmont	**42B**	80501	700-899	
ZACHARY LN	Keenesburg	**732A**	80643	None	
ZAMIA AVE	Boulder	**97G**	80304	700-899	
	Boulder	**97H**	80304	None	
ZAMIA CT	Boulder	**97G**	80304	700-799	
ZANE LN	Elizabeth	**871E**	80107	200-499	
ZANE ST	Adams Co	**223M**	80221	7600-7699	
ZANE GRAY LOOP	Elbert Co	**851F**	80138	3500-3599	
ZANG CIR	Arvada	**220Z**	80004	6500-6699	
ZANG CT	Arvada	**250D**	80004	5800-5999	
	Arvada	**220Z**	80004	6300-6699	
	Lakewood	**280V**	80228	100-199	
ZANG CT S	Jefferson Co	**310R**	80228	2300-2399	
	Jefferson Co	**340M**	80465	4700-5099	
	Jefferson Co	**340V**	80127	5400-5499	
	Lakewood	**310H**	80228	1500-1599	
	Lakewood	**310M**	80228	1700-1899	
	Lakewood	**310R**	80228	2200-2299	

STREET NAME	CITY or COUNTY	MAP GRID	ZIP CODE	BLOCK RANGE	O/E
ZANG PL S	Lakewood	**310M**	80228	1800-1899	
ZANG ST	Arvada	**220Z**	80004	6400-6699	
	Arvada	**220M**	80005	7800-8099	
	Arvada	**220H**	80005	8100-8199	
	Broomfield	**161S**	80021	500-599	
ZANG ST	Jefferson Co	**280M**	80401	1000-1299	
	Jefferson Co	**280H**	80401	1800-1999	
	Jefferson Co	**280D**	80401	2100-2299	
	Jefferson Co	**250Z**	80401	3000-3199	
	Jefferson Co	**250M**	80002	5100-5199	
	Lakewood	**280R**	80228	200-599	
	Lakewood	**280R**	80401	700-799	
ZANG ST S	Jefferson Co	**340H**	80465	4300-4699	
	Jefferson Co	**340V**	80127	5400-5999	
	Lakewood	**310H**	80228	1400-1599	
	Lakewood	**310R**	80228	2500-2599	
ZANG WAY	Arvada	**250D**	80004	5800-6099	
	Jefferson Co	**250Z**	80401	2800-2899	
	Lakewood	**280V**	80228	100-199	
ZANG WAY S	Jefferson Co	**340M**	80465	4700-4899	
	Jefferson Co	**340R**	80127	5100-5199	
	Lakewood	**280V**	80228	100-199	
	Lakewood	**310M**	80228	1900-2199	
ZANTE CIR S	Arapahoe Co	**350U**	80015	5600-5899	
	Arapahoe Co	**350U**	80015	6000-6099	
ZANTE CT	Lochbuie	**140C**	80603	300-399	
ZANTE CT S	Aurora	**380Q**	80016	7700-7899	
	Aurora	**380U**	80138	8500-8698	E
ZANTE ST	Lochbuie	**140G**	80603	100-299	
ZANTE ST S	Aurora	**380U**	80138	8300-8699	
ZANTE WAY	Lochbuie	**140C**	80603	400-599	
ZANTE WAY S	Arapahoe Co	**350U**	80015	5600-6099	
ZA ZA LN	Clear Creek Co	**801Y**	80439	1-99	
ZEBULON CIR E	Douglas Co	**440V**	80134	9000-9099	
ZENITH AVE	Lafayette	**131L**	80026	100-599	
ZENO CIR S	Aurora	**319F**	80017	1200-1299	
	Aurora	**319X**	80013	3500-3599	
ZENO CT	Commerce City	**169X**	80603	None	
	Weld Co	**139F**	80601	17900-18499	
ZENO CT S	Arapahoe Co	**349T**	80016	5900-6199	
	Arapahoe Co	**349X**	80016	6400-6499	
	Arapahoe Co	**379B**	80016	6500-6599	
	Aurora	**319T**	80013	2900-2999	
	Aurora	**319X**	80013	None	
	Centennial	**349P**	80015	5200-5299	
	Centennial	**349T**	80015	5500-5599	
ZENO ST	Adams Co	**169T**	80022	None	
	Aurora	**289F**	80011	1300-1499	
	Commerce City	**169X**	80603	None	
ZENO ST	Brighton	**138G**	80601	None	
ZENO ST S	Aurora	**319F**	80017	1300-1499	
	Aurora	**319K**	80013	2100-2299	
	Aurora	**319P**	80013	2300-2599	
	Aurora	**349K**	80015	4700-4899	
	Centennial	**349P**	80015	5400-5499	
	Centennial	**379K**	80016	7800-7899	
ZENO WAY S	Aurora	**319B**	80017	900-1099	
	Aurora	**319F**	80017	1100-1299	
	Aurora	**319F**	80017	1300-1599	
	Aurora	**319K**	80017	1800-1899	
	Aurora	**319T**	80013	2800-2999	
	Aurora	**349B**	80013	3600-3699	
	Centennial	**349P**	80015	5200-5399	
ZENOBIA CIR	Arvada	**223S**	80030	6800-6899	
	Westminster	**193N**	80031	10100-10299	
ZENOBIA CT	Arvada	**223W**	80003	6100-6299	
	Westminster	**193N**	80031	4900-5099	
	Westminster	**223J**	80030	7700-7899	
	Westminster	**193N**	80031	10000-10099	
	Westminster	**193N**	80031	10300-10399	
	Westminster	**193A**	80031	11600-11699	
ZENOBIA CT S	Littleton	**343W**	80123	5900-6399	
ZENOBIA LOOP	Westminster	**193A**	80031	11700-11899	
ZENOBIA PL	Westminster	**223S**	80030	7000-7099	
ZENOBIA ST	Adams Co	**253E**	80212	None	
	Arvada	**223S**	80030	6800-6899	
	Denver	**283S**	80219	1-399	
	Denver	**283N**	80204	400-999	
	Denver	**283J**	80204	1200-1699	
	Denver	**283A**	80212	2400-2699	
	Denver	**253S**	80212	2700-4599	
	Westminster	**223S**	80030	7000-7199	
	Westminster	**223N**	80030	7500-7599	
	Westminster	**223J**	80030	7800-7999	
ZENOBIA ST S	Denver	**283W**	80219	1-299	
	Denver	**313E**	80219	1100-1699	
	Denver	**313N**	80219	1900-2599	
	Denver	**313S**	80236	2700-3099	
	Denver	**343E**	80236	3100-4699	
ZENOBIA WAY S	Denver	**313J**	80219	1600-1699	
ZEPHYR AVE	Jefferson Co	**278T**	80401	101-499	O
ZEPHYR CIR	Arvada	**222T**	80004	7000-7099	
ZEPHYR CT	Arvada	**222F**	80005	8400-8499	
ZEPHYR CT	Lochbuie	**729Z**	80603	200-299	
	Westminster	**222B**	80021	9000-9099	
	Westminster	**192K**	80021	10800-10999	
	Wheat Ridge	**252X**	80033	3200-3499	
ZEPHYR CT S	Jefferson Co	**342X**	80123	6300-6399	
	Jefferson Co	**372B**	80123	6400-6499	
	Jefferson Co	**372A**	80128	6800-6899	
	Jefferson Co	**372K**	80128	7400-7499	
	Lakewood	**312B**	80226	900-999	
	Lakewood	**312K**	80232	1300-1899	
	Lakewood	**312K**	80227	2000-2299	
	Lakewood	**312T**	80227	2500-2699	
	Lakewood	**342F**	80235	4000-4199	
ZEPHYR DR	Gilpin Co	**741X**	80403	None	
ZEPHYR DR	Jefferson Co	**192S**	80021	9700-9899	
ZEPHYR ST	Arvada	**252F**	80002	5600-5799	
	Arvada	**222X**	80004	6200-6499	
	Arvada	**222T**	80004	6700-6799	
	Arvada	**222F**	80005	8200-8499	
	Jefferson Co	**192N**	80021	10100-10499	
	Lakewood	**282T**	80226	1-499	
	Lakewood	**282K**	80214	1200-1499	
	Lakewood	**282F**	80214	1900-2099	
	Lakewood	**282B**	80214	2200-2599	

Continued on next column

STREET NAME	CITY or COUNTY	MAP GRID	ZIP CODE	BLOCK RANGE	O/E
ZEPHYR ST (Cont'd)	Lochbuie	**729Z**	80603	1700-1899	
	Westminster	**192E**	80021	10800-11199	
	Wheat Ridge	**252T**	80033	3900-4099	
	Wheat Ridge	**252P**	80033	4400-4599	
ZEPHYR ST S	Jefferson Co	**372E**	80128	6800-6899	
	Jefferson Co	**372P**	80128	8000-8199	
	Jefferson Co	**372T**	80128	8300-8999	
	Jefferson Co	**342K**	80123	None	
	Lakewood	**282T**	80226	1-299	
	Lakewood	**312F**	80232	1300-1499	
	Lakewood	**312P**	80227	2100-2499	
	Lakewood	**342F**	80235	4100-4299	
ZEPHYR WAY S	Jefferson Co	**372F**	80128	7200-7399	
	Lakewood	**312P**	80227	2300-2499	
ZETA ST	Golden	**279U**	80401	300-399	
ZEUS DR	Lafayette	**131U**	80026	1700-1799	
ZEUS PL	Highlands Ranch	**376Z**	80124	None	
ZEV LN	Jefferson Co	**366R**	80439	8200-8299	
ZIMMERMAN AVE	Frederick	**726G**	80516	None	
ZINGER ST	Boulder	**99E**	80301	4700-4799	
ZINNIA CIR	Lafayette	**131B**	80026	1400-1699	
ZINNIA CT	Arvada	**250D**	80004	5800-6099	
	Arvada	**220H**	80005	8400-8499	
	Jefferson Co	**280H**	80401	1700-1999	
	Jefferson Co	**250Z**	80401	3000-3299	
	Jefferson Co	**250M**	80002	5100-5399	
	Lakewood	**280V**	80228	1-99	
ZINNIA CT S	Jefferson Co	**310V**	80228	2600-2699	
	Jefferson Co	**340R**	80465	5000-5099	
	Jefferson Co	**340R**	80127	5200-5499	
	Lakewood	**310D**	80228	600-799	
	Lakewood	**310M**	80228	1800-1899	
ZINNIA ST	Arvada	**250D**	80004	6000-6199	
	Arvada	**220Z**	80004	6200-6399	
	Arvada	**220Z**	80004	6400-6599	
	Arvada	**220V**	80004	6600-6799	
	Arvada	**220M**	80005	7800-8099	
	Jefferson Co	**280M**	80401	900-1199	
	Jefferson Co	**280H**	80401	1700-1999	
	Jefferson Co	**280D**	80401	2100-2299	
	Jefferson Co	**250Z**	80401	3100-3199	
	Jefferson Co	**220D**	80005	8800-8899	
	Lakewood	**280R**	80401	700-799	
ZINNIA ST S	Jefferson Co	**340H**	80465	4300-4499	
	Jefferson Co	**340V**	80127	5500-5799	
	Jefferson Co	**310R**	80228	None	
	Lakewood	**310M**	80228	1800-1899	
ZINNIA WAY	Jefferson Co	**280D**	80401	2100-2299	
ZINNIA WAY S	Jefferson Co	**310R**	80228	2400-2599	
	Jefferson Co	**340M**	80465	4800-4899	
	Lakewood	**280V**	80228	1-299	
	Lakewood	**310M**	80228	1800-1899	
ZION	Weld Co	**706N**	80504	11000-11199	
ZION CT	Castle Rock	**496A**	80109	None	
ZION CT	Denver	**258E**	80239	5500-5599	
ZION ST	Aurora	**288S**	80011	200-599	
	Aurora	**288N**	80011	600-999	
	Aurora	**288B**	80011	2300-2799	
	Aurora	**258W**	80011	3000-3299	
ZIP LN	Park Co	**841V**	80421	1-99	
ZIRCON WAY	Superior	**160Y**	80027	500-599	
ZODIAC PL	Castle Rock	**496F**	80109	4000-4299	
ZODIAC ST	Golden	**279Q**	80401	1-99	
ZODO AVE	Erie	**103S**	80516	900-1199	
ZUGSPITZ RD	Jefferson Co	**337Y**	80439	25600-25799	
ZUNI DR	Westminster	**193M**	80234	10700-10799	
ZUNI PL	Douglas Co	**846U**	80135	3500-3699	
ZUNI RD	Jefferson Co	**337M**	80439	4900-4999	
ZUNI ST	Adams Co	**253H**	80221	5200-5899	
	Adams Co	**223V**	80221	6900-7199	
	Adams Co	**223M**	80221	7200-8399	
	Adams Co	**163D**	80020	14300-14799	
	Adams Co	**133Z**	80020	14800-15999	
	Broomfield	**163V**	80234	12400-12798	E
	Broomfield	**163V**	80020	12401-12799	O
	Broomfield	**163M**	80020	13600-14099	
	Denver	**288M**	80204	800-1499	
	Denver	**283D**	80211	2600-2699	
	Denver	**253V**	80211	2700-4799	
	Denver	**253M**	80221	4800-5199	
	Federal Heights	**193R**	80260	2401-10399	O
	Northglenn	**193R**	80234	10400-10599	
	Thornton	**193R**	80260	2400-10398	E
	Westminster	**223H**	80260	8400-8798	E
	Westminster	**223H**	80260	8401-8799	O
	Westminster	**193D**	80234	11700-11899	
	Westminster	**163Z**	80234	11900-12099	
	Westminster	**163R**	80234	12800-13599	
	Westminster	**163D**	80020	14100-14299	
ZUNI ST S	Denver	**283Z**	80223	1-699	
	Denver	**313M**	80223	700-2099	
	Denver	**313R**	80219	2101-2699	O
	Denver	**313V**	80236	2701-3099	O
	Englewood	**313V**	80110	2200-3098	E
	Englewood	**313Z**	80110	3100-3298	E
	Littleton	**343R**	80120	4900-5099	
	Sheridan	**313Z**	80110	3101-3299	O
	Sheridan	**313Z**	80110	3300-3499	
ZUNI TRAIL	Clear Creek Co	**365N**	80439	1-99	
ZURICH CIR S	Jefferson Co	**842Q**	80470	15100-15199	
ZURICH CT S	Denver	**313N**	80219	2200-2699	
	Denver	**313S**	80236	2700-3099	
ZURICH DR	Jefferson Co	**842Q**	80470	30200-30499	
ZURICH ST	Golden	**279Q**	80401	1-99	
ZWECK CT	Longmont	**40D**	80503	800-899	